no lasered 5/11

ENCYCLOPEDIA OF GLOBAL INDUSTRIES

FOURTH EDITION

ENCYCLOPEDIA OF GLOBAL INDUSTRIES

FOURTH EDITION

Grey House Publishing, Inc.
185 Millerton Road
Millerton, NY 12546
518.789.8700
FAX 518.789.0545
www.greyhouse.com
e-mail: books@greyhouse.com

Fourth edition published 2007

Publisher's Cataloging-In-Publication Data
(Prepared by The Donohue Group, Inc.)

Encyclopedia of global industries / prepared by the Gale editorial staff. -- 4th ed.

p. : ill ; cm.

Previous editions published: Detroit, Mich. : Gale Group.
Includes bibliographical references and index.
ISBN: 978-1-59237-243-0

1. Industries--Encyclopedias.

HD2324 .E528 2007
338/.003

TABLE OF CONTENTS

ALPHABETIC LIST OF INDUSTRIES

Introduction

Welcome to the fourth edition of the *Encyclopedia of Global Industries* and the first edition produced by Grey House Publishing under an exclusive license from The Gale Group. Previous editions were published by Gale, and this edition has also been prepared by the Gale editorial staff. This volume presents a thoroughly revised and expanded look at business sectors of global significance. It continues to serve as a key source for inquiries into industry sectors on a global scale. No other publication or electronic database offers the same level of international breadth and industry depth as the *Encyclopedia of Global Industries*.

The work includes 125 articles in 23 chapters. As in previous editions, it continues to offer thorough studies of some of the biggest and most frequently researched industry segments, including:

- Aircraft
- Biotechnology
- Computers
- Internet Services
- Motor Vehicles
- Pharmaceuticals
- Semiconductors
- Software
- Telecommunications

Specific articles in this edition include: **Agricultural Production**; **Credit and Debit Card Issues**; **Defense and Armaments**; **Information Retrieval Services**; **Toys and Sporting Goods**; and **Trucking and Courier Services**.

Content and Arrangement

All essays are focused and highly readable, and provide a wealth of relevant, current, factual data previously available only through a variety of diverse sources. Despite the varied subject matter in this volume, all essays include standard category topics, including:

- **Industry Snapshot**: Identifies issues covered in the article and highlights the industry's key facts.
- **Organization & Structure**: Covers logistical and structural aspects of the industry, including definitions of leading products and services, regulatory and legal matters, and the international make-up of the industry.
- **Background & Development**: Introduces treatment of the industry's origins and past trends, including important innovations and the individuals who made them.
- **Current Conditions**: Provides important recent trends and statistics, including those with implications for the future.
- **Research & Technology**: Discusses recent advances in technology that may signal emerging trends for the industry in the future.
- **Work Force**: Addresses demographics, compensation and issues of the labor force.
- **Industry Leaders**: Profiles major companies, including recent annual sales, historical notes, and specialties within the industry.
- **Major Countries in the Industry**: Provides country- or region-specific summaries of the industry.
- **Further Reading**: Lists sources for additional research, including specific books or articles that may be referenced in the entry, as well as works offering general industry information. This section includes both print sources and reputable Internet sites.

Indexes & Tables

The *Encyclopedia of Global Industries* includes three indexes:

- **SIC Index**: Provides a numerical listing of references based on four-digit Standard Industrial Classification (SIC) codes. The SIC codes may correspond fully or partially to the encyclopedia topics.
- **Geographic Index**: Provides an alphabetic listing of countries and regions cited in this edition and is subdivided by industry. The index includes cross-references for variant names.

- **General Index**: Provides an alphabetic listing of industries, companies, organizations, legislation, concepts, and prominent individuals referenced throughout the book. Specific encyclopedia topics are referenced with bold page numbers in the index, along with cross-references to common keywords and acronyms.

The publication also includes a **NAICS Conversion Table** - a numerical listing of five- and six-digit North American Industry Classification System (NAICS) codes. This includes codes of those industries that are associated in full or part with the entries in this encyclopedia.

A valuable resource, this fourth edition of the *Encyclopedia of Global Industries* continues to be the authoritative reference for studies of international industry.

AGRICULTURE

SIC 0100

NAICS 111

AGRICULTURAL PRODUCTION—CROPS

Crop production provides the bulk of human nourishment. Primary categories in the industry include grains, general field crops, vegetables, and fruits. The cultivation of plants underwater is discussed under the heading **Aquaculture**.

INDUSTRY SNAPSHOT

With new markets opening up worldwide as a result of global trade agreements, and with rising incomes in developing countries such as China and other parts of Asia, crop producers in the early 2000s gained greater access to world markets. The rapid growth of China's economy, for example, made that country the world's leading consumer of grain by 2005. Moreover, new technology for storing, transporting, and producing crops also enhanced the trade and production potential of agricultural businesses around the world. However, fluctuations in the Asian and world economies will continue to affect the long-term outlook for the grain, fruit, vegetable, and specialty agricultural markets. In addition, weather conditions and other events, such as the devastating tsunami that hit southern Asia in December 2004, could have unpredictable impacts. The tsunami, for example, washed away topsoil and contaminated cropland with salt water, damaging thousands of kilometers of agricultural land. Some 50,000 hectares of farmland in Sumatra and 5,500 hectares in Sri Lanka were severely damaged; in the Maldives, according to the United Nations Food and Agricultural Organization(FAO), about half of the country's field plots were destroyed. Though world impacts are not expected to be significant, local agriculture in these areas may take several years to recover.

The trend toward more efficient production of crops was expected to continue through the early 2000s. For example, in 1992 some 223.2 million hectares were devoted to wheat production with an output of 561.8 mmt, or a yield of 2.52 metric tons per hectare; by 2005, approximately 235.6 million hectares were anticipated to produce 653.8 mmt, or a yield of 2.77 metric tons per hectare, according to Economic Research Service (ERS) of the U.S. Department of Agriculture(USDA) projections. In effect, the area planted would grow by 5 only percent, while the yield, or amount produced, would grow by 16 percent.

The FAO reported in March 2002 that raisers of crops in the next three decades must find a way to grow more crops with less water, because by 2030 the world's water supply would be unable to meet projected crop irrigation demands. Irrigation use would have to increase by more than 80 percent by 2030 to satisfy projected global food demands.

One solution to global hunger that drew serious attention is to have the world's agricultural education community halt the spoilage of tons of fruit and produce wasted annually in countries where a large number of people with nutritional deficiencies live. In Pakistan, for example, agricultural analysts estimated up to 3 million tons of fruit and produce are wasted each year because of substandard harvesting and packing measures.

GRAINS

Falling output of grain in the early 2000s raised international concern. According to a U.N. Wire report from September 2003, the estimated world grain harvest in 2003—the fourth consecutive year of shortages—was 93 million tons short of demand, plunging world reserves to their lowest levels in 30 years. Drought and water shortages were blamed for much of the collapse, according to the USDA; the Earth Policy Institute blamed climate change. Shortages in 2001 and 2002 were particularly acute in China, the world's most populous country, and in a reversal of a more positive trend through the 1990s, China in 2004 became a net importer of wheat. Total grain harvests improved in 2004, reaching an estimated 1.85 billion metric tons; this favorable trend was expected to boost output to more than 2.0 billion metric tons in 2005.

Corn production throughout the world was forecast to total 700.6 mmt in 2005, more than 27 percent above 1992's level, as corn became the world's leading cash grain, according to the ERS. In contrast to wheat, most of the corn crop went to feeding animals; about 70 percent of 1998's corn crop was expected to be used as feed. Corn exports also were slated to rise, climbing to 90.7 mmt in 2005. Expanding agricultural economies in China, Argentina, and North African countries were expected to add to the demand because these countries would require more grain for feeding livestock. The United States dominated corn exports by a substantial margin: in 2004 the country's corn exports were estimated at 50.0 mmt. Other important exporters for 2004 included Argentina with 9.0 mmt, China with 8.0 mmt, and Brazil with 5.5 mmt.

Global output of wheat, the second leading grain in terms of production volume, was just below that of corn and once exceeded corn in total global production. Wheat production fluctuated slightly in the early 2000s but averaged almost 580 mmt a year. Though harvests reached only 566.96 mmt in 2003 and 552.83 mmt in 2004, production was expected to exceed 620.8 mmt in 2005. The leading wheat producers are the European Union, China, India, the United States, Russia, and Canada.

Rice ranked third globally in grain production in the early 2000s, at 389.2 mmt in 2004. Among the leading grains, rice production has grown at the steadiest pace. China, by far the leader, produced 35 percent of the world's rice, followed by India with 21 percent and Indonesia with 8 percent. Bangladesh and Vietnam are also significant producers. According to USDA projections, the global rice trade was expected to grow at a 2.4 percent average from 2004 through 2013, which represented 6 to 7 percent of all agricultural trade. In the early 2000s, rice in the United States was a US$1 billion industry, although it only amounted to about 2 percent of all production.

World soybean production rose from 189.2 mmt in 2003 to 206.4 mmt in 2004. Brazil and Argentina, which had steadily increased production from 1997 through the early 2000s, accounted for almost 45 percent of world soybean production in 2003. The United States remains the single largest producer, with 66.78 mmt in 2004 and a projected 85.4 mmt in 2005. Brazil ranks a close second, with a projected harvest of 644.5 mmt in 2005, followed by Argentina, with a projected crop of 39 mmt.

FRUIT

Bananas are the largest single fruit crop in the world, followed by grapes, oranges, and apples. Global banana production exceeded 70.6 mmt in 2004, while grape production topped 65.4 mmt and orange production reached 63 mmt. Global apple production, which rose through the 1990s, exceeded 59 mmt in 2000 and remained relatively steady through 2004. China produced 20.5 mmt in 2004, with harvests in the United States at 4.2 mmt and in Chile at 1.1 mmt. World pear production, which reached 17.9 mmt in 2004, was dominated almost exclusively by China, which raised 10.1 mmt. The European Union ranked second with 3.0 mmt.

HORTICULTURAL PRODUCTS

According to the ERS, the value of total horticultural exports worldwide in 2003 exceeded US$12.3 billion. The largest importer and exporter of horticultural products is the European Union, followed by the United States, with imports valued at US$21.9 billion and exports at US$12.3 billion of in 2003. Leading exporters were Netherlands, Spain, Mexico, the United States, and China, while leading importers were the United States, Germany, Britain, and Japan.

Among nations that dramatically increased production in the early 2000s was Vietnam. At the start of 2002, Vietnam's Ministry of Agriculture and Rural Development (MARD) predicted an end-of-year production of 11.4 million tons of fruit and vegetables with an export worth of US$440 million. Also in Asia, the government of Shandong Province in China dedicated considerable areas of land in order to become competitive in the production of green vegetables, according to *Asiainfo Daily China News.*

OILSEEDS

The ERS predicted that oilseed trade would expand quickly in the twenty-first century and that the United States, and to a lesser extent Argentina and Brazil, would continue to dominate oilseed trade through 2005. The United States accounted for 34 percent of the world crop in 2003 and supplied 40 percent of world exports. Brazil was the second largest producer, contributing 28 percent of global soybean production, followed by Argentina with 18 percent. China, the largest market for U.S. soybeans, imported US$2.9 billion in 2003. It was followed by the European Union, with imports totaling US$1.1 billion. Increased demand for peanuts in Eastern Europe, Asia, and the Middle East contributed to a 20 percent growth in world peanut trade between 1998 and 2004. China's peanut export in 2003 reached about 600,000 tons, according to the *People's Daily*—accounting for approximately 40 percent of global export volume. Other major exporters included the United States and Vietnam.

Of increasing concern for global oilseed producers was the possible negative effect of development projects. A natural gas pipeline from Bolivia to Brazil, completed in 2002, caused researchers to fear that natural wild peanut species native to the area could be wiped out. Scientists hoped that such species, many of which remain undiscovered, could help decrease the need for pesticides and also could prove resilient to drought and other adverse conditions. Because pipeline construction increased human settlement in remote regions, however, native peanut species might become extinct unless samples could be collected in the near future.

FIELD CROPS

Field crops of global importance include sugar, cotton, coffee, and tobacco. World production of sugar cane reached 1.3 billion metric tons in 2004. Brazil remained the leading producer, with a harvest of 411.0 mmt. Other leading sugar cane producers were India (244.8 mmt), Thailand (63.7 mmt), Mexico (45.1 mmt), and Cuba (24 mmt). Global production of sugar beets, which topped 237.8 mmt in 2004, was dominated by the European Union, with harvests of 125.7 mmt. Production in the United States reached 27 mmt.

After a slight slump in the late 1990s, worldwide cotton production increased in the early 2000s and by 2004 reached an all-time high of 116.7 million bales-substantially more than the predicted level of 103 million bales. USDA projections for 2005, however, indicated a 14-million-bale drop, the largest decline ever and the biggest percentage of decline since 1992/93. But world consumption of cotton was expected to rise by 3 percent. U.S. production reached 23 million bales in 2004.

After a dramatic jump in 1997, world coffee output declined significantly in the early 2000s. Production in 2003/04 reached about 105.3 million 60-kilogram bags, a drop of approximately 15 percent from 2002/03. Major producers were Brazil, Ivory Coast, Indonesia, Dominican Republic, India, Angola, and Vietnam.

The upward trend in tobacco production, which increased significantly through the early 1990s, was expected to continue although at a slower rate. According to a FAO report from 2004, world production in 2000 reached 6.137 mmt and was expected to grow to more than 7.1 mmt by 2010. Leading producers are China, India, Brazil, the United States, Turkey, Zimbabwe, and Mali.

ORGANIZATION AND STRUCTURE

The crop production industry encompasses small subsistence farmers, immense vertically integrated food conglomerates, and everything in between. Subsistence farmers generally operate small plots. Larger organizations typically operate larger fields, up to thousands of acres. Fields may be either owned or rented by the farm family or farming establishment.

The organizational levels within the farming community are geared toward moving raw ingredients from the farm to the end consumer. Sometimes this chain is short and direct: a farmer grows produce and his customer comes to the farm to make a purchase, or the farmer himself carts his produce to a local market. More often, however, many marketing and processing levels are involved. A frequently employed intermediate step can be farm sales to granaries, processors, or wholesalers.

Farm transactions can be arranged in several different ways. For example, the farmer may grow a crop, harvest it, and receive payment when it is delivered to market, or the farmer may make arrangements to sell his entire crop (or a predetermined percentage of it) at a specified price before he grows it.

Because a successful agricultural industry is essential for a successful political and social climate, many governments, especially those of the world's major crop producers, tended to carefully regulate this industry and offer price supports such as direct subsidies, low-interest loans, and guaranteed prices to ensure its strong performance. However, agreements such as the General Agreement on Tariffs and Trade (GATT) call for the reduction of such practices, making farmers around the world more self-reliant and market dependent. In the mid- to late 1990s, large agricultural producers such as the United States, the European Union, China, and Japan began implementing programs to eliminate and reduce many crop subsidies. Other countries such as New Zealand, Sweden, and Australia had privatized their agricultural industries in the 1980s and boasted of success in the 1990s.

By the early 2000s, only about a third of global agricultural land was used for crops. Yet world food production doubled in the last three decades of the twentieth century, largely because of increased yields rather than increased acreage. Though total food production kept pace with population growth, food shortages in many regions posed perennial problems. Consequently, the leading producers, including Australia, the European Union, Japan, and the United States, donated a portion of their output each year to help support these regions, especially Sub-Saharan Africa, Bangladesh, and India. Wheat has been and was expected to continue to be the primary grain that countries receive as food aid. In addition, various organizations throughout the world, including the United Nations Food and Agriculture Organization, research agricultural methods and crop hybrids that will increase productivity, shorten growing periods, and strengthen resistance to pests.

INTERNATIONAL TRADE AGREEMENTS AND ORGANIZATIONS

Current agreements that regulate international trade include the General Agreement on Tariffs and Trade (GATT) and the North American Free Trade Agreement (NAFTA). In its original form, GATT governed trade from 1948 to 1994, when a revised version that resulted from the 1986 to 1994 Uruguay Round discussions replaced it. According to GATT, participating countries may not introduce any new export subsidies, and U.S. and EU subsidies are subject to restrictions. The agreement called for the reduction and elimination of tariffs designed to protect domestic businesses from foreign competition. All participating countries agreed to cut back tariffs by 33 percent, and the United States, the European Union, Canada, and Japan decided to remove most of the tariffs inhibiting trade among these nations. GATT also established a formal organization to govern global trade policies, the World Trade Organization.

Implemented in 1994, NAFTA was expected to gradually eliminate trade barriers such as tariffs and trade restrictions between Canada, Mexico, and the United States. The United States and Canada negotiated their own trade accord, and each of them developed its own agreement with Mexico. The combination of these agreements made up NAFTA. It phased out tariffs on most agricultural products and established initial trade quotas to prevent price dumping while the agreement was being implemented. Most of the safeguard tariffs and quotas expired in 2004 and the rest were to be eliminated by 2005, creating virtually unrestricted trade among these countries.

Established in 1995, the World Trade Organization (WTO) oversaw trade among nations participating in the Uruguay Round. The organization's goals were to liberalize trade and ensure stable and fair trading conditions for participating members. Based in Geneva, Switzerland, the WTO allowed any country to challenge the trade policies of any other country before its tribunal, the Dispute Settlement Body. As of 2005 the WTO consisted of 148 members, including countries from all around the globe as well as the leading agricultural producers such as the United States, the European Union, Japan, Argentina, and Brazil.

One of the WTO's most urgent concerns through the early 2000s was the elimination of agricultural subsidies that protected farmers in wealthy countries, such as France and the United States, at the expense of farmers in developing countries. Analysts argued that such subsidies, estimated at some $300 billion annually, pushed down commodity prices, leading to overproduction and illegal dumping (the practice of selling goods to other countries at less than their cost of production). In 2004, the European Union—widely seen as implementing the biggest protections for its domestic agriculture—agreed to eliminate all its export subsidies. The United States that year agreed to cut its $19 billion in annual subsidies by 20 percent. These new agreements, scheduled to go into effect in 2006, are expected to contribute to more equitable global trading conditions.

The Asia Pacific Economic Cooperation (APEC) forum supervised and assisted economic development in this budding region. Formed in 1989, APEC encouraged growth in the region and sought to increase multilateral trade that benefited the region as well as the rest of the world.

BACKGROUND AND DEVELOPMENT

Some historians have equated the beginning of agriculture with the origins of civilization. Although they do not always agree on where crop cultivation originated, some possible places are China, India, the Middle East, South America, Sudan, and Southeast Asia. Some believe that agricultural techniques began in one place and from there spread throughout the world; others believe that agriculture rose independently in various locations.

GRAINS

One of the most important crop families in the worldwide economy is grain. Examples of grains are wheat, rice, millet, sorghum, quinoa, and maize (corn). Grain cultivation began in prehistoric times when early farmers, perhaps relying on their experience with nature, selected seeds from useful plants and attempted to control where and how they grew.

According to some accounts, the first grain to be domesticated was probably wheat. Wheat was important because of its unique gluten content, the protein that gives wheat-based dough its ability to rise. Rising occurs when carbon dioxide produced during yeast fermentation becomes trapped in the dough. Without wheat, there would be no leavened bread.

Another grain with a long history of cultivation is rice. Rice cultivation probably originated in Asia and was introduced to other areas from the Asian mainland. Cultivation of rice in the Philippines dates back to possibly 3000 or 4000 B.C. When rice was adopted by the indigenous peoples, it probably supplemented domestic root crops such as taro and sago. As it became more firmly established it gained esteem and became interwoven in the nation's culture.

In drought-susceptible regions of Africa, native crop production originally focused on millet and sorghum. One type of millet, commonly referred to as "pearl millet," was able to grow quickly in a short, rainy season. Sorghum was cultivated in tropical regions. When irrigation was possible, yields improved, which enabled farmers in drought-plagued areas to achieve self-sufficiency.

In the Andes mountains in South America the Incas cultivated, stored, and distributed grain harvests. Early grains included quinoa, kiwicha, and kaniwa. Quinoa, a versatile grain able to grow in rugged terrain and withstand extreme weather fluctuations, was one of the most popular. When conquering Spanish colonists sent local farmers to work in gold mines, the cultivation of indigenous plants diminished. Subsequently, indigenous agriculture was further eroded by the initiation of large-scale wheat imports by Peruvian government officials.

Maize was an important grain crop native to the American continent. The first maize was a tropical grass that may have originated in Mexico. Some historians place the origins of its domestication and cultivation in South America around 5000 B.C. Maize cultivation in North America began sometime in the first two centuries A.D. in the Southwest. Here it was adopted by an indigenous population that presumably had prior knowledge of agricultural techniques. By 800 A.D., maize was also under cultivation in the eastern part of North America.

Maize was unknown in Europe before the time of Columbus. Columbus was said to have discovered it in Cuba and carried seeds back on his voyage home. By the middle of the 1500s, maize was popular in southern Europe. In northern Europe, maize became more commonly used for livestock than for human consumption. From Europe, the grain was exported to the Philippines and Asia and was taken to Africa by Portuguese traders where it thrived, standing up well in drought conditions. Over-reliance on maize, however, led to vitamin deficiencies for some African populations.

CITRUS FRUIT

Pineapples are another type of plant originating in the New World and said to have been discovered by Columbus. Pineapples, thought to have been native to Brazil, spread throughout the tropical regions of the globe and were a common part of the diet in tropical South America during the fifteenth century. In the twentieth century an estimated 90 different varieties of pineapple were being grown. Major pineapple-producing areas were Hawaii, the Philippines, Malaysia, Australia, South Africa, Puerto Rico, Kenya, Mexico, Cuba, and Taiwan. One of the most common ways in which pineapple-producing nations marketed the fruit was as a canned product. Five countries—the United States, the United Kingdom, Germany, Canada, and Japan—imported approximately 70 percent of the world's canned pineapple production. During the 1970s and 1980s, tropical fruits grew increasingly popular for their use in juices, with trade quadrupling and sales reaching US$4 billion in one decade. Developing countries played an important role, with their production accounting for almost half of the total.

Citrus fruits (such as oranges, grapefruits, lemons, and limes) originated in Southeast Asia and in the East Indies. They were first introduced to Europeans during the twelfth century. Prior to the development of modern processing technology, citrus was sold in fresh form in limited areas. Primary regions involved in commercial citrus production were North and South America, the Mediterranean, Australia, and South Africa.

In the 1940s, the development of citrus concentrate brought changes to the citrus industry. Other developments were the ability to extend product storage life and improvements in transportation. Instead of being limited to a local market, growers were able to reach all corners of the world and overcome problems associated with their products' seasonality. Large-scale, modern commercial citrus producers generally grew fruit in orchards with what were called "composite" trees. Composite trees are trees with a rootstock that differed from their "scion," the upper portion of the plant that was grafted onto the rootstock. The rootstock was selected on the basis of its ability to thrive in specific conditions. Sought-after features included a natural resistance to plant diseases and pests and the ability to grow well in local soils. The scion was selected for the quality of its fruit.

Vegetables and Melons

Indigenous to South America, tomatoes were introduced to Europe in the 1500s. Because the English believed tomatoes were poisonous based on an early misclassification, they did not begin to cultivate them until the early 1800s. However, some southern European countries embraced tomatoes immediately, integrating them into their diet and treating them as a delicacy. Long before Europeans discovered the tomato, though, the Aztecs mixed them with chili peppers, making salsa. By the twentieth century, tomatoes had become one of the world's most popular vegetables, in both fresh and processed forms.

Potatoes also originated in the Americas, perhaps in Mexico, and spread south. Wild potatoes grew at least 13,000 years ago and have been cultivated for 9,000 to 10,000 years. During the sixteenth century, Spanish explorers took potatoes back to Europe. They were introduced again to the North American continent by British settlers via Bermuda in the seventeenth century. Potatoes were introduced to Japan and China during the seventeenth century and to New Zealand during the eighteenth century.

In Europe during the eighteenth and nineteenth centuries, potatoes were popular among the poor because they could be grown easily in small family plots and had very high nutritional value. With potatoes, an average farmer could feed about four times as many people per acre as could be done with wheat or rye. Potatoes also supplied high amounts of vitamin C. As a result, sailors took potatoes with them on long voyages to help prevent scurvy. However, overdependence on potatoes gave rise to potato famines, such as those of Ireland in the nineteenth century, when the potato crop was contaminated repeatedly by a blight.

Despite problems with outbreaks of blight, potatoes became a favored crop in many places around the globe. Numerous potato varieties were developed to thrive under various growing conditions. In addition to being popular and nutritious as a food item, potatoes were also put to work in several industrial applications. During the nineteenth century, potato starch derivatives were used to make syrup and sizing agents. Manufacturers also used potatoes in the production of paper, adhesives, and textiles. During World War II, the German military used potatoes to make an alcohol-based aircraft fuel, to light streetlights, and to power ground vehicles. Potatoes provided ingredients for cosmetics, pharmaceuticals, and even disposable diapers.

Field Crops

Field crops with global significance include sugarcane and sugar beets, both of which are used to produce sugar. The first of these two species to be cultivated was sugarcane, which grew in tropical and semitropical regions. Historians believe sugarcane was first cultivated in prehistoric Asia and exported to Europe perhaps as early as the fifth century A.D. Sugarcane was grown in Egypt's Nile River Valley in the eighth century and was introduced to Central and South America during the sixteenth century. Sugar beets originated in southern Europe, where cultivation began about 1800. There are many varieties of sugar beets, but *Beta vulgaris* is the most important commercially.

Current Conditions

In the early 2000s the future of farming in industrialized nations was becoming evident as production continued to expand while the number of farms continued to dramatically decrease. Also during this period the United States government, through the USDA, became sensitive to indications of global climate change and the need for future land ecosystem adjustments. Liberalized trade measures initiated in the 1980s and 1990s to make crop producers more market dependent also produced positive agriculture conditions through the early 2000s. Trade pacts such as the General Agreement on Tariffs and Trade (GATT) reduced trade barriers between many countries around the world, and governments began to privatize their agricultural industries, eliminating government price supports and planting restrictions.

Generally, the outlook for world agricultural production and trade looked positive with countries such as China and Vietnam becoming highly competitive in raising crops in addition to rice. As the U.S. dollar strengthened in 2002, the United States faced diminishing sales for crops such as wheat; international buyers sought lower prices from countries with less solid currencies. With the elimination of approximately $300 billion in annual farm subsidies in wealthy countries, expected to go into effect in 2006, overall conditions for agricultural trade are expected to remain favorable. The value of U.S agricultural exports, for example, which fell to only $49 billion in 1999, exceeded $62 billion in 2004 and was expected to reach $59 billion in 2005.

Grains

Used as both food and feed, corn (also known as maize) in the early 2000s moved slightly ahead of wheat as the leading grain in the world, according to the ERS of the USDA. Global corn production soared from a high of 580.6 million metric tons (mmt) in 1997 to 622.5 mmt in 2004, and was projected to reach 700.6 mmt in 2005. The United States by far remained the leading producer, with harvests of 256.9 mmt in 2004 and 299.9 mmt in 2005. In the United States, corn was the most popular feed grain and constituted more than 90 percent of feed grain value, according to the ERS. U.S. corn acreage, about 80 million acres in the late 1990s, was expected to increase gradually through 2013, according to the USDA, while U.S. exports were expected to rise faster than global trade.

Though the ERS predicted continued slow growth in world wheat production through 2005, devastating heat waves in 2003 decimated the harvest in Eastern Europe, resulting in the smallest crop in 30 years. The USDA projected that this crisis would contribute to a decline in U.S. wheat exports through 2007, followed by a modest recovery through 2013. Population and income increases and continued competition from Europe, Canada, Argentina, Australia, Russia, and Ukraine were expected to keep U.S. market share at about 23 percent. Leading wheat exporters in 2004 included the United States with 31.0 mmt, Canada with 16.0 mmt, and the European Union with 7.0 mmt, while the leading importers included Egypt with 6.3 mmt, Japan with 5.8 mmt, and Brazil with 5.6 mmt.

World rice production increased steadily since the early 1990s and was expected to reach 402 mmt in 2005, up from 389.2 mmt the previous year. Unlike most other grains, rice was used exclusively for human consumption. Even though world per capita consumption of rice was likely to continue falling through 2005, overall rice demand was anticipated to expand because of population growth. Major rice exporters for 2004 were Thailand with an estimated 8.0 mmt, Vietnam with 4.0 mmt, the United States with 3.0 mmt, and China with 2.24 mmt. Primary importers were Indonesia with 2.0 mmt, Nigeria with 1.23 mmt, Iraq with 1.1 mmt, and Iran with 1.0 mmt. In early 2005 the United States reached an agreement with the European Union, its top market for brown rice exports, to ensure market access for that crop, worth $33 million annually.

FRUIT

Global apple production in the early 2000s was dominated by China, which produced almost half of the world's total crop, and the United States. According to the FAO, world apple production reached a record high of 57.9 million tons in 2001, but declined the following year to 55.8 million tons. By 2004, however, global production surpassed 2001 levels to reach 59 million tons. China's crop in 2004 reached 20.5 million tons, while apple production in the United States, where harvests had declined in the early 2000s, rose to 4.2 million tons. Production also increased slightly in the European Union, exceeding 12.2 million tons. Though apple crops among South America's top producers, including Chile and Argentina, were expected to drive an increase in that sector's production to 4.4 million tons, levels fell short of that estimate, reaching only 3.2 million tons in 2002 and 3.5 million tons by 2004.

World production of canned peaches, which dropped to 858,000 tons in 2003 after a devastating crop failure in Greece, was forecast to return to normal levels in 2005, reaching 1.1 million tons. Exports were expected to exceed 568,000 tons. Greece remained the leading exporter, followed by the United States, Spain, Italy, South Africa, Argentina, Chile, and Australia. Other major exporters were the United States, Spain, Italy, South Africa, Argentina, Chile, and Australia.

Citrus Fruit. Citrus fruits, which include oranges, tangerines, grapefruit, and lemons, were the leading global fruit category by value. Oranges accounted for more than half of all citrus production. According to USDA statistics, world citrus production in 2004 increased almost 12 percent from the previous year, reaching 73.3 million tons. Brazil and the United States, the two leading producers, with Mexico accounted for almost all of the increase.

Brazil, the leading orange grower, produced 18.2 million tons in 2004, an increase of almost 23 percent from 2002. Orange yields also rose in the United States to an estimated 12.3 million tons, an increase of almost 17 percent from the previous year and a 79 percent share of the country's total citrus crop. U.S. citrus exports reached about 1.1 million tons in 2003, including 665,000 tons or oranges; 335,000 tons of grapefruit; 100,000 tons of lemons; and 15,000 tons of tangerines. Growth of about 2.3 percent annually was predicted for U.S. exports of fresh oranges through 2011, with the import market expected to grow annually by 3.1 percent during that same period. In China, citrus production rose slightly from 13.9 million tons in 2003 to 14.4 million tons in 2004. Total citrus production in Spain reached a record high in 2004 of almost 6.1 million tons, an increase of 6 percent from the previous year. The orange crop reached 2.9 3 million tons, tangerines 2.1 million tons, and lemons and limes exceeded 1 million tons; approximate increases respectively of 4 percent, 3 percent, and 30 percent from the previous year.

VEGETABLES AND MELONS

Vegetables and melons are grown throughout the world. Some of the leading crops are carrots, tomatoes, potatoes, and onions. The worldwide carrot harvest in 2004 totaled 23.6 mmt. Major producers included China, the United States, and Russia. World tomato production in 2002 totaled more than 108.5 mmt, a 10 percent increase since 1985, and grew to 115.9 mmt in 2004. World production of potatoes grew from 318.2 mmt in 2003 to 328.8 mmt in 2004. The leading producer, China, accounted for more than 20 percent of the global potato crop in 2002, and remains the leading grower. Potato production in China reached 75.0 mmt in 2004. The United States grew 20.4 mmt in 2004, while Canadian production reached 5.0 mmt. Largely because of increased imports from Canada, the U.S. trade balance in potatoes and potato products went into deficit in 2003 for the first time ever. U.S. exports that year were valued at US$646 million, while imports reached $US682 million. Total onion production reached approximately 53.5 mmt in 2004, with China, India, the United States, Turkey, and Pakistan the leading producers. World cantaloupe and melon production reached 27.3 mmt in 2004; China, Turkey, and the United States were the leading growers. Total production of watermelon, the leading U.S. melon crop, exceeded 92 mmt in 2004.

OILSEEDS

The biggest disappointment for the United States in the early 2000s was the plunging markets for certain oilseeds including peanuts, caused in part by record production levels in 2000 and 2001. World soybean production in 2004 reached 206.4 mmt, with the United States, Brazil, Argentina, and China the primary growers. In the United States, record soybean production in 2004 and 2005, along with decreased global demand, led to the largest soybean stock levels since 1985. The value of US soybean exports in 2005 was expected to reach US$6.1 billion.

Global production of cottonseed, the second-leading oilseed crop, reached 35.56 mmt in 2004 and was projected to increase to 44 mmt in 2005. Rapeseed production was just behind, at a projected 43.6 mmt. Worldwide peanut production in 2005 was expected to reach 34.4 mmt, with 90 percent of the crop coming from developing countries, particularly in Asia and Africa. Sunflower seed harvests fell from 26.5 mmt in 2004 to a projected 25.35 mmt in 2005. Palm kernel production grew from 7.6 mmt in 2003 to a projected 8.5 mmt in 2005, while copra remained relatively unchanged from 5.33 mmt in 2004 to 5.48 mmt in 2005.

Field Crops

Global consumption of sugar was expected to exceed production in 2005 by an estimated 831,000 tons; the second consecutive year that demand outstripped production. According to FAO projections, harvests in Latin America were expected to increase by about 1.7 percent, led by Brazil. Asian output was projected to grow by only about 1 percent, with severe droughts in China resulting in a 5.8 percent drop in production. Sugar production in the European Union was forecast at 42.6 million tons for 2005, up 2.3 percent from the previous year. Adverse weather conditions in the United States, however, contributed to a projected harvest of only 8 million tons, a decrease of 30,000 tons from the previous year.

World cotton production grew from 94.9 million bales in 2004 to 116.7 million bales in 2005, an increase of 23 percent. U.S. production expanded above the world average, rising 26 percent from 18.2 million bales in 2004 to more than 23 million bales in 2005. Exports, however, rose only marginally during this period, by 0.6 percent. U.S. exports fell by 5.5 percent, largely because of reduced shipments to China.

A relatively poor coffee harvest in Brazil in 2003 contributed to a decrease in world exports by about 5.0 million bags from the previous year. Brazil, the top exporter, saw total exports of only about 24.5 million bags in 2004, down from 4.9 million bags the previous year. Production also fell in Ivory Coast, Indonesia, Dominican Republic, India, and Angola but Vietnam saw a production increase of 1.1 million bags. Stocks in coffee producing countries declined by about 24 percent in 2004 in order to maintain the revised level of trade. World consumption, on the other hand, was projected to rise by less than 1 percent. Smaller crops in Brazil and other major producing countries, coupled with continued demand for high quality beans, resulted in dramatically higher prices in 2004. Arabica coffee futures were expected to average US$1 per pound in 2005, a 30 percent increase over prices in 2004.

In early 2005, the United States announced that it would rejoin the 2001 International Coffee Agreement. The United States is the largest consumer of coffee, with imports representing 24 percent of the global market. World exports of coffee reached 7.33 million bags in early 2005, a 13 percent increase from the previous year. Brazil was the largest exporter, followed by Vietnam and Colombia.

Though world tobacco production dropped substantially in the mid-1990s, global production grew steadily later in the decade and, according to a UN report, was expected to increase through 2010, fueled largely by greater demand in developing countries. Demand in developed countries, however, was slowly declining and was expected to reach about 2.05 mmt tons in 2010—10 percent less than consumption in those regions for 1998. Consumption in developing countries, however, was expected to grow to 5.09 mmt by 2010. China's share in the world tobacco market was projected to remain about 37 percent. Developing countries were expected to increase production in response to increased demand.

Research and Technology

Crop production research is conducted in several areas aimed at improving yield, or the amount of harvest taken per unit of cultivated land. Some scientists have worked to develop plant varieties more suited to diverse growing conditions or varieties that are naturally resistant to pests and diseases.

The process of hybridization; cross-fertilizing two different plant species in an attempt to blend the best features of both, is commonly used to produce crops with improved yields. For example, the practice of cross breeding maize varieties enabled U.S. producers to experience a six-fold increase in maize yield. Other successes in plant genetic engineering led to a reduction in the length of the rice growing season. Worldwide rice production time fell from an average of 180 days to 110 days. As a result, some regions were able to produce three rice crops annually. Some researchers estimated that, with further refinements, rice production could be increased by an additional 60 percent.

Maize and rice were not the only crops subjected to intense research efforts. Some scientists worked with potatoes, researching more efficient cultivation methods. Potatoes were not planted from traditional seeds, as were many other principal crops, but from seed potatoes. Seed potatoes were bulky and heavy. Their use created storage problems and also created the potential for transmitting insects and diseases from one crop to the next. True potato seeds (TPS) were minuscule seeds produced by potatoes that needed to be grown in a nursery before they could be planted in the field. According to some researchers, if technological problems related to the use of TPS could be overcome, potato production could be made more economical.

Plant diseases were another major concern to researchers. One of the most notorious diseases was potato blight. During the nineteenth century a naturalist, the Rev. M. J. Berkeley, discovered that the blight on the potato was not the result of disease but rather its cause. The origin of the fungus responsible for blight, however, was not discovered until the middle of the twentieth century. Although chemicals were developed to keep blight at bay, they were expensive and not universally available. Subsistence farmers in developing nations, for example, typically did not have access to them.

To help combat potato blight, researchers sought to develop potatoes that were naturally resistant to blight. One potato researcher, Dr. John S. Neiderhauser, winner of the 1990 World Food Prize, worked under the auspices of the International Potato Center in Lima, Peru. Neiderhauser's studies examined the wild Andean potato gene pool in an attempt to discover the genetic key to blight resistance. Neiderhauser's work with potatoes was credited with resulting in a four- to six-fold harvest increase over four decades in some developing countries including Mexico, Pakistan, India, Turkey, and Bangladesh.

By the early 2000s, genetic research had led to new strands of genetically-modified (GM) food crops. Unlike traditional crossbred species, however, GM crops contain genes from entirely different organisms—a plant, for example, might contain genetic material from an animal or a bacterium. Advocates of GM agriculture maintain that such crops can be tailored to resist pests or withstand climate extremes. But critics maintain that GM foods have not been proven safe. By 2003, according to a *Guardian* article, GM crops were grown by at least 6 million farmers in 16 countries, including the United States, Argentina, Canada, and China. The major GM crops were soybeans, corn, cotton, and rapeseed. Use of GM crops remained controversial, however, and resistance from some regions, including Britain and Europe, could affect world trade in the early 2000s. In 2004, the United Nations released a report stating that, to date, GM crops were safe and that their use could help farmers in poor regions.

In addition to working to improve crop yields, researchers were also developing better ways to farm without causing damage to the environment. No-till crop methods have been developed to help protect important topsoil from erosion. According to some estimates, no-till farming reduced erosion by up to 98 percent. Critics claimed, however, that no-till procedures caused other types of environmental damage because they required more chemicals, such as herbicides and pesticides. Proponents of no-till methods pointed out that newly designed pesticides killed targeted species by disrupting reproduction cycles without causing harm to other species.

MAJOR COUNTRIES IN THE INDUSTRY

CHINA

China is a leading producer in many categories of crop farming. Because of economic liberalization first implemented in the 1980s, China grew into a dominant crop producer in the 1990s. In the late 1980s when political changes led to decentralized agriculture, farmers were given the opportunity to develop small farms (ranging in size from one-half acre to three acres) instead of working solely on communal farms. In 2001 China not only led the world in apple production, but its estimated 1.5 billion bushels were more than the next seven competing countries or regions combined. In 1997 China led the world in wheat production (121 mmt), rice production (195 mmt), cotton production (4.2 mmt), tangerine production (6.07 mmt), and tobacco production (3.1 mmt). China also ranked as the world's second-largest corn producer, with harvests totaling more than 105 mmt, behind only the United States, which produced 236.5 mmt.

But in spite of China's enormous production, it has often failed to meet its domestic demand. In 1996, for instance, China produced 109 mmt of wheat, but the country required 114 mmt for domestic consumption, forcing the country to import 4 mmt. Grain production fell significantly in the late 1990s and early 2000s, and in 2003 China was forced to import more wheat than it exported to meet domestic demand. China faced the same problem with its other leading crops, either breaking even or importing heavily to satisfy demand. The ERS predicted that China would become a net importer of corn in 2007.

In 2005 the Chinese government announced that it would spend 5.5 billion yuan (about US$66 million) to subsidize agriculture in hopes of boosting grain production and increasing farmers' incomes. The country's wheat crop, which had faltered in the early 2000s, had already risen by 9 percent in 2004 to 469 million tons, and the country hoped to strengthen this upward trend in production.

UNITED STATES

The value of combined U.S. agricultural exports, after reaching a record of nearly US$60 billion in fiscal year 1996, fell to $49.1 billion in 1999. But exports recovered steadily in the early 2000s, reaching US$62.3 billion in 2004. The following year, however, due to global oversupply, lower prices, and increased competition, the value of US agricultural exports fell slightly to a projected US$59 billion. Steady economic growth and expanded international trade, however, are expected to boost both export volume and prices for U.S. agricultural goods, with the value of U.S. exports expected to reach US$78.6 billion in 2014. Western hemisphere countries continued to be the major markets for US agricultural goods. Canada led as the primary export destination, with an estimated US$10.2 billion of US agricultural goods delivered there in 2005. The next biggest market was Mexico, with about US$8.5 billion, followed by Japan, the European Union, and China. The United States also remained a major consumer of agricultural imports. The value of total agricultural imports in 2005, projected at US$58 billion, nearly matched the value of exports that year, and is projected to increase to US$76 billion by 2014.

In a significant development, global grain shortages overseas worked to the advantage of the United States in the early 2000s, as exports of grain neared the record highs of 1996. In 2004, however, wheat exports fell to about 900 million bushels. The USDA projected slow growth of wheat exports after 2007, with U.S. market share remaining relatively steady at around 23 percent.

The United States remained the world leader in corn production, with exports reaching a projected 48 mmt in 2005. The value of US corn exports, however, which reached US$5.8 billion in 2004, fell sharply in 2005 due to lower shipments and intense competition from Argentina. The total value of corn exports that year was projected at only US$4.7 billion. The United States was also the world's leading wheat exporter and the leading producer and exporter of soybeans.

Although Brazil overtook the United States in commercial orange production in the late 1980s, the United States remained a major producer with a harvest nearing 12.3 mmt in 2004. Devastating hurricanes in Florida in late 2004, however, led to a decline in U.S. citrus production of an estimated 23 percent for 2005. Florida's orange crop was expected to drop by about 27 percent, and its grapefruit harvest by 63 percent. Slight increases in production were projected in California and Texas.

The United States was also a major sugar producer. Although some sugarcane was grown in regions around the Gulf of Mexico and Hawaii, most of the nation's sugar came from sugar beets. In 2003, the United States ranked fifth behind Brazil, India, the European Union, and China in sugar production, with 7.4 mmt. Top producing sugar beet states were California, Idaho, Minnesota, Colorado, Washington, North Dakota, Nebraska, and Michigan. In addition, the United States was among the leading producers of several other crops, including tobacco and apples. In 2002, the United States ranked third in global cantaloupe production and fourth in watermelon production.

THE EUROPEAN UNION

The European Union constituted another major producer and trader of a number of crops, including sugar, wheat, corn, apples, and pears. In 2003 the European Union ranked third in global sugar production, with 18.3 mmt, and third in wheat exports. The European Union was also among the top producers of apples and peaches. In 2004 the European Union admitted 10 new member nations, which brought its total membership to 25 countries. This expansion increased the number of farmers in the European Union by almost 70 percent. Funding of 5.8 billion euros was planned after expansion to assist these farmers to modernize equipment, develop environmentally friendly farming practices, and improve marketing strategies. In 2004 the European Union was the world's largest food importer and the largest market for agricultural products from developing countries.

INDIA

Although India usually trailed agricultural leaders such as the United States and China, it nonetheless constituted one of the world's major crop producers. In 2001 it ranked seventh among apple-producing nations, and in 2003 it ranked second in both sugar production, with 19.45 mmt, and rice production, with 89.0 mmt. India also ranked among the world leaders in tobacco production.

BRAZIL

In South America, one of the leading crop-producing nations was Brazil, where sugarcane and coffee were major crops. By 2003 Brazil led the world in sugar production, with 22.7 mmt. It was also the leading grower of coffee, with production estimated at 32.0 million bags for 2004. After increasing its soybean acreage in the early 2000s, Brazil gained greater access to the soybean and soybean meal export market. Its share of this market was expected to grow from 35 percent in the early 2000s to 45 percent by 2014.

In the early 1970s, the Brazilian government had subsidized farming and offered guaranteed assistance in land development. According to one estimate, half the cost of land in Brazil was associated with clearing the land. As a result, Brazilian farming efforts increased dramatically as crop lands were carved out of forests. Government officials encouraged farmers to focus on growing crops for export. One favorite was soybeans and throughout the 1990s Brazil ranked as the number two soybean producer and exporter, trailing only the United States.

Brazil also held a secure position as the world's major producer of citrus products, primarily oranges. Brazil's orange crop for 2005 was expected to reach 18.4 mmt, a 23 percent increase from the previous year. Favorable weather conditions, in addition to improved crop management, contributed to robust yields.

FURTHER READING

American Farm Bureau. Available from www.fb.com.

Brown, Lester A. "Record Temperatures Shrinking World Grain Harvest." *AgWord Wide,* 27 August 2003. Available from www.agriculture.com.

"China Becomes Largest Exporter of Peanuts." *People's Daily,* 2004. Available from English.peopledaily.com.cn/.

"GM Crops.rdquo; *Guardian,* 3 June 2003. Available from www.guardian.co.uk/.

Illovo Sugar. *Sugar Statistics, World of Sugar,* 2004. Available from www.illovo.co.za/.

"Interim Trade Triumph Short on Hard Details." *New York Times* (2 August 2004).

"Modified Crops Help Farmers, UN Says." *Boston Globe* (18 May 2004).

"Scientists Fear Irreparable Loss of Peanut Crop Biodiversity for World Food Supply." *Future Harvest,* 17 December 2004. Available from www.futureharvest.org/.

Smith, Nathan. "2002 Peanut Situation and Outlook." *The University of Georgia College of Agriculture and Environmental Sciences Cooperative Extension Service* (29 January 2002).

Soy Stats, 2004. Available from www.soystats.com/.

"Two to Three Million Tons Fruits and Vegetables Going to Waste." *The Pakistan Newswire* (12 March 2002).

United Nations Food and Agricultural Organization. *After the Tsunami.* 2005. Available from www.fao.org

———. *Agricultural Data: FAOSTAT, 1997-2005.* Available from www.fao.org.

———. *Higher World Tobacco Use Expected by 2010,* 8 January 2004. Available from www.fao.org/.

———. *Sugar Outlook,* December 2002. Available from www.fao.org/.

U.S. Department of Agriculture. Economic Research Service. *International Baseline Projections to 2013,* 2004. Available from www.usda.gov.

U.S. Department of Agriculture. Economic Research Service. *China's New Farm Subsidies.* 2005. Available from www.usda.gov.

———. Foreign Agricultural Service. *Coffee Updates,* 2004. Available from www.fas.usda.gov.

———. *Cotton: World Markets and Trade,* February 2005. Available from www.fas.usda.gov.

———. *Grain: World Markets and Trade,* February 2005. Available from www.fas.usda.gov.

———. *Oilseeds: World Markets and Trade,* February 2005. Available from www.fas.usda.gov.

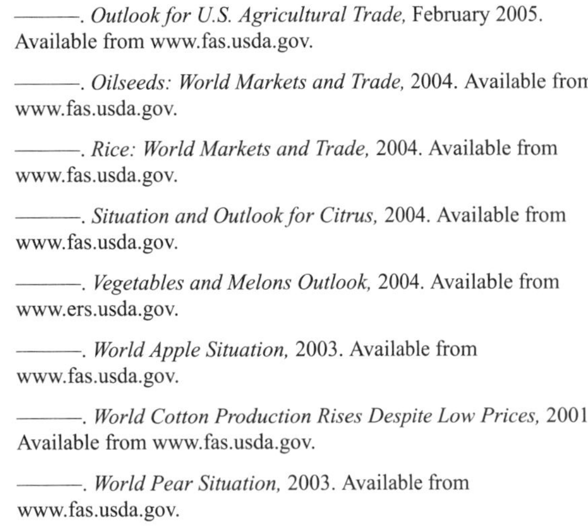

———. *Outlook for U.S. Agricultural Trade,* February 2005. Available from www.fas.usda.gov.

———. *Oilseeds: World Markets and Trade,* 2004. Available from www.fas.usda.gov.

———. *Rice: World Markets and Trade,* 2004. Available from www.fas.usda.gov.

———. *Situation and Outlook for Citrus,* 2004. Available from www.fas.usda.gov.

———. *Vegetables and Melons Outlook,* 2004. Available from www.ers.usda.gov.

———. *World Apple Situation,* 2003. Available from www.fas.usda.gov.

———. *World Cotton Production Rises Despite Low Prices,* 2001. Available from www.fas.usda.gov.

———. *World Pear Situation,* 2003. Available from www.fas.usda.gov.

———. *World Trade in Fresh Vegetables,* 2003. Available from www.fas.usda.gov.

U.S. Exports: FAPRI 2000 World Agricultural Outlook. Washington, DC, 2002. Available from www.fapri.org/.

"Vietnam to Produce 11.4 Million Tons of Vegetables in 2002." *InfoProd* (13 February 2002).

Weekly Outlook: Soybean Prices, University of Illinois College of Agricultural, Consumer, and Environmental Sciences, 24 February 2004. Available from web.aces.uiuc.edu/news/.

"World Grain Harvest Short of Demand Four Consecutive Years." *U.N. Wire,* 17 September 2003. Available from www.unwire.org/.

SIC 0200

NAICS 112

AGRICULTURAL PRODUCTION—LIVESTOCK

The livestock agriculture industry includes commercial farms, ranches, dairies, hatcheries, and other facilities that raise or tend animals to supply the world's food markets. Specific categories include dairy and beef cattle, goats, hogs, poultry, and sheep. (See also **Agricultural Production—Crops**).

INDUSTRY SNAPSHOT

While overall food demand is considered relatively fixed on a per capita basis, purchasing power may determine which foods and quantities are consumed. As a result, the health of the livestock industry often mirrors that of the general economy: in periods of expansion, livestock production increases, and in recessions the industry stagnates. The Economic Research Service(ERS)of the U.S. Department of Agriculture(USDA)anticipated moderate world growth rates in gross domestic product, averaging 3 percent through 2005. The continued liberalization of global trade would also spur further growth in both production and cross-border trade.

An overall rise in meat production through the 1990s was fueled mainly by increased economic growth and demand. In 1997 the global meat supply, the largest market for livestock agriculture, was valued at US$500 billion. The overall rise in meat production was mostly attributed to activity in the United States, the European Union, and China. In 1997 global production of meat advanced to approximately 220 million metric tons (mmt). The leading meats; beef, veal, pork, poultry, lamb, mutton, and goat climbed to 190 million metric tons, up from about 155 mmt in 1992, according to the Foreign Agricultural Service (FAS) of the USDA. After a sharp fall in 2001, global production of meat climbed back to 247 mmt in 2002 and reached 257.5 mmt in 2004, according to United Nations Food and Agricultural Organization(FAO)statistics. More than 60 percent of the gains in the global meat market in the early 2000s came from increased demand in developing countries. Despite this overall increase in production, the World Bank noted that meat production must increase by 64 percent by 2020 to meet the needs of the world's swelling population.

Leading livestock-producing nations were China, the United States, the European Union (EU), Australia, New Zealand, Brazil, and Canada. These countries had high-technology meat industries and sophisticated regulatory agencies. Each was also a major exporter of packaged meat, carcasses, and live animals. Second-tier producers, including Uruguay, Venezuela, Thailand, India, and some African countries, also had well-developed meat and poultry industries.

Pork continued to hold its place as the world's most popular meat based on carcass weight produced, accounting for almost 40 percent of global meat production. In 2002 pork production was listed by the FAO at 95.3 mmt; by 2004 it had reached 100.3 mmt. Poultry supplanted beef in the late 1990s as the second most popular meat, with 78.2 mmt produced in 2004. Beef production, which tapered off in 1997, totaled 58.7 mmt in 2004, while lamb, mutton, and goat meat reached 12.1 mmt.

BEEF CATTLE

The United States was the world's largest producer and the second-largest exporter of beef, according to the USDA's ERS. In 2004 the FAO reported U.S. beef production at 11.2 mmt and amounts for Brazil, the second-largest producer, at 7.7 mmt. Total exports of beef, according to USDA statistics, were projected at 6.2 mmt in 2004, with Brazil dominating the market with 1.6 mmt of exports in 2005. Australia's beef exports were forecast at 1.3 mmt, while U.S. exports were expected to reach only 272,000 tons-a 35 percent increase from 2004 but significantly lower than historical levels, due largely to bans on U.S. beef because of concerns about BSE contamination. Strong world demand, as well as favorable economic conditions, helped boost Argentina's beef exports to an expected 25-year high in 2005. New Zealand exports of beef rose to a record 413,000 tons in 2004, fueled by high demand from key Asian markets, particularly Korea.

Australia's sheep producers reaped the benefits of U.S. restrictions on imports of Australian beef, following a World Trade Organization ruling. Australia shipped an estimated

72,000 mmt of mutton to the U.S, in 2002, up from 67,000 mmt in 2001, according to the USDA.

DAIRY PRODUCTS

Worldwide milk production reached 613 mmt in 2003 and remained almost unchanged in 2004. The European Union (EU) led in global milk production with an estimated 146 mmt, followed by India, which dramatically increased milk production from about 70 mmt in 1997 to 90.4 mmt in 2004. The United States, which slipped behind India in the late 1990s, was ranked third in 2004 with an estimated 77.5 mmt. The Russian Federation, with 31.1 mmt, came fourth. The EU also dominated cheese production, with 5.55 mmt in 2003. Australia, with an output of 3.68 mmt, came second. The Organisation for Economic Co-operation and Development(OECD)reported that demand for dairy imports, particularly in Asia, was likely to remain strong through 2005.

In 2000 a major global dairy products story was the whopping price hike in nonfat dry milk (NDM) by 41 percent in non-U.S. international markets, bringing the price in line with U.S. prices for nonfat dry milk. This price increase saw a corresponding drop in demand by about 40 percent. U.S. exports of NDM fell from 142 metric tons in 2000 to only 96 metric tons in 2001, but by 2004 rose to approximately 200 metric tons. U.S. sales of NDM in 2005 were projected to reach 150 metric tons.

POULTRY

In the mid- to late 1990s, poultry was the fastest growing segment of the global meat industry. In 2000, world poultry meat production (including broiler chicken, duck, goose, turkey, and other poultry) reached 69.2 mmt; by 2004, the amount had grown to 78.2 mmt. The leading producers, which included the United States, China, the EU, and Brazil, contributed 65 percent of global production. Chicken remained the most popular poultry meat, accounting for about 85 percent of world production. In 2004 the United States was the leading producer of chicken meat, with 15.5 mmt, and turkey meat, with 2.4 mmt. China, on the other hand, dominated global production of duck meat (2.1 mmt) and goose meat (1.9 mmt).

In 2002 some international markets had grown distrustful of U.S. chicken, claiming that growers' use of hormones and growth-inducing drugs posed long-term adverse health effects for humans. The first country to issue a ban on U.S. chicken was Russia, and U.S. President George W. Bush listed his determination to overthrow the ban as a major agenda item. Though Russian authorities in 2004 indicated that an agreement about poultry imports might occur in the near future, strict Russian quotas on poultry imports remained in effect. In 2003 and 2004 poultry markets were shaken further when avian influenza (bird flu) broke out in many parts of Asia. The FAO estimated that trade bans on poultry in 2004 could result in losses of up to US$10 billion.

EGGS

Egg sales were buoyed by a 1997 study that held that egg consumption does not pose certain health risks previously attributed. Earlier studies had linked high intake of dietary cholesterol (which is abundant in eggs) with high levels of blood cholesterol, which in turn is related to increased risks for heart disease and other health problems. However, late 1990s research suggested that moderate cholesterol intake does not lead to substantially higher levels of blood cholesterol. Health concerns over egg consumption hindered the growth of the egg industry since the 1980s, especially in the United States and Europe. Per capita in 2001, Japanese consumers ate the most eggs, at 348 per person annually. Next in per capita consumption came China (270 eggs per person), the United States (252), Malaysia (246), and Singapore (230). The world average per capita egg consumption was 144 eggs.

HOGS

In 2005 pork remained the most popular meat in the world, with global production forecast by the USDA at 91.6 mmt. China and the EU were the primary producers, with China's output expected to reach 47.5 mmt and the EU's to reach 21.1 mmt. China also led in world consumption of pork, at about 47.1 mmt in 2005; on a per capita basis, however, Europe consumed more pork than did any other region. World pork exports, according to USDA projections, were expected to reach a record 4.2 mmt in 2005. The European Union, with 25 member nations by 2005, continued to lead in world pork exports, followed by Canada, the United States, Brazil, and China.

ORGANIZATION AND STRUCTURE

INTERNATIONAL TRADE AGREEMENTS AND ORGANIZATIONS

General Agreement on Tariffs and Trade. The General Agreement on Tariffs and Trade (GATT) was the key trade agreement governing international trade of livestock-related commodities. An older version of GATT was in place from 1948 until 1994, when a revision resulting from the 1986 to 1994 Uruguay Round discussions was adopted. Under the new agreement, participating countries could not introduce any new export subsidies, and U.S. and EU subsidies were subject to restrictions. GATT called for the reduction and elimination of tariffs designed to impede and to control foreign competition in favor of domestic businesses. All participating countries agreed to cut back tariffs by 33 percent, and the United States, the EU, Canada, and Japan decided to remove most of the tariffs inhibiting trade among themselves. GATT also established a formal organization for the implementation of systematic global trade policies, the World Trade Organization.

North American Free Trade Agreement. Taking effect in 1994, the North American Free Trade Agreement (NAFTA) gradually removed trade barriers such as tariffs and trade restrictions among the North American countries; Canada, Mexico, and the United States, enabling freer trade between these nations by 2004. The United States and Canada, which already had established a more limited free trade agreement in 1989, renegotiated their own trade accord and each of them developed its own agreement with Mexico. The combination of these agreements constituted NAFTA. It eliminated tariffs on most agricultural products and established initial trade quotas to protect individual countries from over-importing while the agreement was being implemented.

Most of the safeguard tariffs and quotas expired in 2004, and the rest would be eliminated by 2005, creating virtually unrestricted trade among these countries.

World Trade Organization. The World Trade Organization (WTO) was established in 1995 to govern trade between nations participating in the Uruguay Round. The organization's objective was to liberalize trade and ensure stable and fair trading conditions for participating members. Based in Geneva, Switzerland, the WTO allowed any country to challenge the trade policies of any other country before its tribunal. In 2005 the WTO consisted of 148 members, including countries from all around the globe as well as leading agricultural producers such as the United States, the EU, Japan, Hong Kong, Argentina, and Brazil.

Asia-Pacific Economic Cooperation. Headquartered in Singapore, the Asia-Pacific Economic Cooperation (APEC) oversaw and assisted economic development in the Pacific region. Formed in 1989, APEC promoted economic growth in the region and sought to stimulate multilateral trade within and outside the region. With 17 members, the group included Australia, Brunei, Canada, Chile, China, Indonesia, Japan, Malaysia, Mexico, New Zealand, Papua New Guinea, the Philippines, Singapore, South Korea, Taiwan, Thailand, and the United States.

MARKET SEGMENTS

Beef Cattle. The beef cattle industry thrives in countries with large areas of pasture such as the United States, Argentina, Brazil, China, and New Zealand. While as little as one acre of land may be required to support a cow and her calf for one year in areas of abundant rainfall or irrigation, desert ranches may need as many as 600 to 700 acres to support the same cow and calf.

Production of cattle, from birth to slaughter, takes from 18 months to 2 years. During the first 6 to 8 months, beef cows nurse their calves on a farm or ranch. At weaning time, calves in most countries move on to graze on grassland until they are ready to be slaughtered. However, in the United States the vast majority of older yearling calves are confined in feedlots and fattened (or "finished") on a high-energy diet of grain. While the United States produced the vast majority of feedlot beef, some foreign producers used feedlots to produce the highly marbled (fatty) beef prized by many consumers, particularly those in Japan and the United States. For example, New Zealand opened its first commercial grain feedlot in 1991 to supply highly marbled beef to Japan. Meat from grass-fed cattle is considerably leaner than feedlot beef and is increasingly in demand because of health-conscious eating trends.

The number of cattle raised and prices at which they are sold varies widely from year to year. In 1996, the world cattle inventory was 1.044 billion head, up slightly from the year earlier; by early 2002 that number remained almost unchanged, according to Spectrum Commodities. Inventories declined significantly in the former USSR, however, dropping to about 50 percent of levels in 1992. At the same time, inventories in China rose to more than 150 million head. Ultimately, most cattle are sold as beef.

In 2005, the United States led the world in beef production and remained a leading exporter. Brazil, the second-largest producer, was the primary exporter in 2005, although it produced more hamburger than choice beef sections. Choice imported beef can cost as little as half the cost of domestically produced beef. U.S. imports of range-fed Latin American beef, used almost exclusively for hamburger, are even less expensive.

Exports represent a minority of world beef production. Most beef is consumed in the nation where it is produced, though changes were underway as a result of the new GATT treaty. Certain beef-producing countries were already dependent on exports; for example, New Zealand and Australia respectively exported 81 and 63 percent of their 1997 beef outputs.

Dairy Farms. Since milk must be continually refrigerated while it is processed and sent to retail outlets, dairy farms have tended to operate locally or regionally in most countries. While international trade in milk is limited, products made from milk, such as cheese, are widely exported. Milk production is more efficient in cooler climates, such as northern Europe and the northern United States. Milk consumption is largely a regional phenomenon, as a large share of the world's adult population is unable digest it.

Poultry. The sharp increase in chicken consumption since the 1960s was based mainly on the lower production and consumer costs of poultry compared with other meats. The world's poultry producers were able to drive down production costs by improving feed efficiency. Consumers also purchased more chicken because of its nutritional profile. Poultry producers in many countries evolved into large, vertically integrated production/processing/marketing companies. Broiler chicks were typically bought by the growing farm in bulk and then housed and sold together to help break any potential disease cycles. In the United States, nearly all producers were vertically integrated.

While more than 50 countries were significant poultry producers, the top 12 accounted for 80 percent of world output. World poultry production is divided into three major segments: broiler chicken, turkey, and other poultry. Broilers account for around 68 percent of the world market. Turkeys account for 8.5 percent and other poultry for 24.5 percent.

Eggs. Some farms still produce eggs from "free range" chickens that are allowed to roam outside, but the majority of eggs are produced in vast factory farms where hens are kept in wire-floored cages. In the United States and other industrialized countries, technology plays a large role in egg production. Hens are bred carefully to maximize egg-producing characteristics such as early maturity, efficient use of feed, and production of white eggs. The modern laying house automates most of the production process with mechanized feeders, sanitizers, egg collectors, and temperature and light controls. The size of the egg-production flock can grow to 100,000 and even to 1 million hens. While most eggs are sold fresh in the shell, a growing percentage are pasteurized and sold in liquid, frozen, or dried forms. In 2003, there were about 278 million laying hens in the United States.

Hogs. Pork production has traditionally been highly segmented, with different farms and firms performing the separate functions of raising hogs, slaughtering, processing, and retailing. However, the world pork industry followed in the footsteps of the chicken industry by consolidating functions and vertically integrating them in a small number of large firms. Hog farming also became more "industrialized," with a large number of hogs fed and housed in confinement rather than being free to roam outside. In order to manage these high-volume hog farms, producers used sophisticated genetic breeding programs, nutrition science, and computerized record-keeping systems. Ownership of high-volume hog farms, particularly by large agricultural companies, was controversial in areas of the United States, such as Iowa, where small family farms continued to operate.

CURRENT CONDITIONS

Through the early 2000s global markets for meat were affected by several factors. Economic gains and increased meat consumption in the developing world spurred demand, yet prices for U.S. meat shrank while the availability of livestock raised in competing markets continued to increase. In addition, health concerns affected trade. In 2001 global meat markets plummeted to their lowest level in 13 years after the discovery of bovine spongiform encephalopathy (BSE, or mad cow disease) in European beef. Though markets recovered the following year, an FAO report indicated that disease outbreaks in 2004 affected approximately one-third of global meat exports and threatened to affect US$10 billion in world trade. According to the USDA, total exports of meat and poultry in 2005 are expected to reach a record 17.6 million tons, a 5.4 percent increase from the previous year.

The ERS forecast that beef production would rise by an average of 1.5 percent annually through 2005 and that world per capita beef consumption also would increase as China became the fastest growing beef consumer. In contrast, the ERS forecast called for a deceleration of growth in global pork production and consumption to about 2.8 percent per year through 2005, as greater environmental restrictions and robust competition from poultry impeded the pork segment's continued expansion. Increasing demand in developing economies such as China, Russia, and Mexico was expected to offset declining demand in developed economies such as the EU, the United States, and Japan. Finally, bolstered by lower production costs relative to other meats and by economic growth around the world, poultry production and consumption were expected to continue rising through 2005. However, the weakening of Japan's economy early in 2002 and the growing concern about avian influenza could dampen growth.

BEEF

Great Britain (and potentially all beef producers) faced a beef production crisis in 1986 that escalated in late 1995 and continued to plague the industry in 2002. Researchers discovered that cows fed with animal parts could develop BSE. The European Union banned beef from Britain, and the British Agricultural Ministry ordered the slaughter of millions of British beef cattle, which cost the country US$10 billion. Scientists believed that consumption of diseased beef could lead to the development of a new deadly strain of Creutzfeldt-Jacob disease (CJD) in humans. Consequently, the European Union persuaded Britain to cease use of animal parts in livestock feed. By March 2002, more than 180,000 bovines had been slaughtered after contracting the disease or being exposed to it, according to the medical journal *Post Graduate Medicine*. Japan had one confirmed case of a carcass infected with mad cow disease. In 2003 the disease surfaced in Canada and in the United States, which confirmed one case. This incident resulted in a ban that threatened that country's US$3.6 billion export business in beef and veal and restriction of exports to Japan and Mexico. Though Mexico reopened its borders to U.S. beef in March, 2004, the Japanese ban remained in effect through 2005. In October, 2004, Japan and the United States agreed to a trade framework that would reopen trade in beef beginning in 2006.

In the early 2000s, heightened demand in Russia and Brazil were expected to be a catalyst for industry growth, but demand and production would taper off in the United States and the European Union, according to the USDA. Moreover, rising income around the world would lead to greater global per capita consumption of beef, especially in rapidly growing economies such as China. The USDA also expected demand for imported beef to remain brisk in areas with limited agricultural resources and less efficient agricultural methods such as the Pacific Rim and Russia. However, when domestic production increased enough to satisfy domestic demand, reliance on imported beef would slacken in these emerging markets. Most of the major beef exporters—Australia, Argentina, and the United States—were predicted to increase their output through 2005, but the European Union's exports were forecast to recede.

DAIRY PRODUCTS

In 2004, world demand for dairy products exceeded exportable supplies, leading to significantly higher prices. USDA forecasts placed U.S. milk production at about 78.9 million tons for 2005 — a rise of 2 percent from the previous year — while production in the EU was expected to increase by only 0.6 percent to 131.1 million tons. Output in Australia was forecast to reach 10.5 million tons, and New Zealand milk production, which grew 4.5 percent in 2004, was expected to increase another 2.5 percent to 15.4 million tons. After steady growth in the late 1990s and early 2000s of about 5 to 6 percent annually, world exports of cheese were expected to increase by only about 1 percent in 2005. Increased domestic consumption in EU countries contributed slower growth of exports. World production of butter grew from 5.7 mmt in 2000 to a projected 6.9 mmt in 2005. Exports were expected to grow by 2.1 percent, with India increasing its sales to about 10,000 tons.

While dairy herd numbers were expected to diminish slightly from 2000 to 2015, according to ERS projections, output per cow was expected to increase dramatically after 2006 when bovine growth hormone again became readily available.

POULTRY

The poultry segment enjoyed significant growth in the 1990s and early 2000s. In 2004 it was the second most popular meat in the world, trailing only pork and representing the fastest growing segment in the worldwide meat industry. In 2004, total production of poultry meat reached 78.2 mmt.

The majority of the poultry produced through the late 1990s and early 2000s was broiler meat; world broiler production in 1997 was estimated to be 37 mmt. Broiler exports, while still a minority of the total output, grew significantly in the mid- to late 1990s. The United States led broiler exports, with 2.1 mmt in 1997, up sharply from 518,000 metric tons in 1990. Hong Kong and China followed, exporting 625,000 and 500,000 metric tons, respectively. Broiler meat exports fell worldwide in 2004 but were expected to rise to 6.2 mmt in 2005.

In 2002 the two biggest producers of poultry, the United States and China, received a rude awakening. Russia temporarily halted U.S. imports of chicken, alarmed by fears about chemicals used to help growth. Then China found its own poultry exports stopped by the European Union, and again the suspect was a chemical; specifically the antibiotic chloramphenicol, which some Chinese growers employed to thwart bacterial infections and cause fast growing of meat birds.

Outbreaks of avian influenza (bird flu) in 2003 and 2003 further affected global trade. Because of concerns that this type of flu could infect humans and lead to a devastating pandemic, infected birds were destroyed and export bans were imposed on affected countries. Asia was hardest hit, with more than 100 million birds destroyed in 9 countries. Canada and the United States also reported cases of bird flu. According to the FAO, countries affected with bird flu accounted for 4 mmt (50 percent) of poultry export products. China's poultry exports in 2004 were expected to decline by about 20 percent in response to bird flu concerns, with imports falling by 25 percent. To meet import demands for poultry, nontraditional exporters including Malaysia, the Phillippines, and Brazil increased their output and sales.

In 2004, Brazil surpassed the United States as the worlds leading exporter of broiler meats, and market conditions in 2005 pointed to further growth of 10 percent for Brazilian exports. Concerns about avian influenza, which closed Asian markets to U.S. and Canadian exports, worked to Brazil's advantage, as did competitive pricing, favorable exchange rates, and aggressive marketing strategies such as an increase of value-added poultry meat. In addition, production costs in Brazil continued to be the lowest in the world among all major broiler meat producers.

Broiler meat output in the United States, which was the world's leading producer in the late 1990s and early 2000s, was forecast at 16 mmt for 2005, up 3 percent from the previous year. Exports for 2005 were expected to increase by 6 percent. After recovering from avian influenza outbreaks in 2003 and 2004, China increased its broiler meat production in 2005 to an estimated 10 mmt. With significantly increased shipments to Japan, China's total broiler exports were expected to reach 300,000 tons in 2005— an increase of 20 percent from the previous year. China has requested approval to export cooked poultry meat to the United States, which would allow it to further expand its market share.

China's share of the industry was even more sizable when Hong Kong was considered. Hong Kong, which returned to Chinese rule in 1997, produced less broiler meat than other leading exporters, such as Brazil and China, but exported a greater percentage of its overall production. However, four deaths in Hong Kong attributed to the H5N1 variety of strain A influenza transmitted by domestic poultry led to the slaughter and disposal of 1.2 million of the country's chicken flock in 1997. The ramifications of this disaster was expected to cripple the territory's production and exportation for some time. Hong Kong's Agriculture and Fisheries Department planned to compensate producers for their losses.

Broiler exports from the European Union, which by 2005 included 25 member nations, were expected to reach almost 8 mmt, an increase of less than 1 percent from the previous year. Russia's broiler production fell rapidly after 1993 when the country's output reached 540,000 metric tons. In 1997 Russia produced only 290,000 metric tons, a 46 percent drop, but improvements in the country's old, inefficient production facilities in the late 1990s began to reverse this trend. By 2004, Russia was expected to produce 640,000 tons of broilers, with production growing by 13 percent in 2005. The decrease in poultry production made Russia and other former Soviet Union countries major importers of chicken.

Argentina's broiler meat production and exports were expected to reach record highs in 2005, with production at 990,000 tons and exports reaching 90,000 tons. Heavy investment in plant upgrades, as well as overall economic recovery from the 2002 financial crisis, helped the country nearly double its broiler exports between 2002 and 2004. Major export markets include China, Chile, Saudi Arabia, and South Africa.

EGGS

World egg production grew from 50.1 mmt in 1997 to a projected 62.7 mmt in 2004. According to the International Egg Commission, world output of eggs could reach almost 90 mmt by 2030. China remained the primary producer of eggs, with 28.4 mmt in 2004, an increase of almost 160 percent from 1991 levels. The United States, ranked second in production, produced 73.18 billion table eggs in 2002, of which 48.1 million were exported at a value of US$30.5 million. Production increased marginally in 2003, when the country produced a total of 73.93 billion table eggs. Other major egg producers were Japan, Russia, India, and Brazil. FAO forecasts published by the International Egg Commission projected rapid growth in egg production in developing countries, accounting for an estimated 77 percent of global production by 2030.

HOGS

Global pork production rose from 83 mmt in 1997 to 100.3 mmt in 2004. China's surging demand remained the stimulus behind most of the increase. In 1997 China produced 37.1 mmt, and in 2004 the country's output topped 47.7 mmt. In contrast, in 2002 the United States had an excess of pork production early in the year, as higher hog birth rates and lower costs of beef drove the market for pig meat to low levels that even creative marketing could not overcome. But because of export restrictions on poultry and beef, following outbreaks of avian influenza and BSE in 2003 and 2004, demand for pork rose significantly in 2004.

Though U.S. pork production declined slightly in the late 1990s, the country remained the world's leading exporter. In fact, 2004 marked the fourteenth consecutive year of record breaking sales by volume for U.S. pork products. According to the U.S. Meat Export Federation, the value of U.S. pork exports in 2004 exceeded US$2 billion. Pork exports by volume were more than 900,000 mmt. Though Mexico was the biggest market for U.S. pork in terms of tonnage (329,7670), exports to Japan had the highest value (US$893.7 million).

MAJOR COUNTRIES IN THE INDUSTRY

UNITED STATES

With its large and highly efficient agricultural economy, the United States has long been a leader of the global livestock industry. As in other major countries, the U.S. livestock sector maintained a complex relationship with the government, characterized by extensive regulation, heavy subsidies, price support programs, and other programs affecting the price, production, and exportation of livestock products. However, there was a trend toward decreased levels of government involvement in the U.S. livestock business because of the Federal Agriculture Improvement and Reform Act of 1996, which included policies geared toward making U.S. farmers more market dependent. Similarly, recent trade agreements such as GATT and NAFTA were slowly opening the United States and other international markets to more competition by eliminating farm subsidies, price supports, and trade restrictions.

The USDA projected total U.S. meat exports to rise 6.4 percent in 2005, up to 3.5 million tons, though market share was expected to remain unchanged at 20 percent. Pork exports were forecast at a record 959,000 tons, representing about 23 percent of the world market. Beef and veal exports, however, dropped in 2004 and 2005 as a result of continued concern about BSE. U.S. broiler meat and turkey exports for 2005 were expected to reach almost 2.3 million tons, constituting 34 percent of the world market.

U.S. Beef. While the United States was the largest producer of beef products in the world through the 1990s and early 2000s, it ranked only fourth in total number of beef animals. That was due to the high efficiency of U.S. producers in obtaining the maximum amount of meat possible per animal. In 1997 the United States produced 11.5 mmt of beef from about 101 million head of cattle; cattle inventory declined further in the early 2000s, reaching about 96.1 million head in 2003.

Though U.S. beef exports increased steadily through the 1990s, reaching a record volume of 2.57 billion pounds in 2003, export restrictions imposed after the discovery in late 2003 of a BSE-infected cow from Oregon prompted to a devastating decline. Every country except Canada banned U.S. beef in 2004, resulting in plummeting sales. Though Mexico resumed imports of U.S. beef later that year, important Asian markets such as Japan remained closed. Negotiations in late 2004 established a time frame for the United States to resume beef sales to Japan in 2006.

Dairy Farms. The U.S. milk-per-cow average has increased over the years largely because of the controversial hormone bovine somatotropin (BST), which makes cows produce more milk. This trend was likely to further decrease the U.S. herd, as fewer cows were needed to produce larger quantities of milk. Under the Dairy Export Incentive program, cheese exports rose by 10 percent in 1997 to 32.5 metric tons. The United States also exported large amounts of butter, dried milk, evaporated and condensed milk, and ice cream to countries such as Canada, Mexico, Japan, Korea, and China. The value of U.S. dairy exports, which reached US$982 million in 2003, was forecast to rise to US$1.17 billion in 2004 and US$1.3 billion in 2005. California produces the most milk by state; in 2001, California cows gave 33.1 billion pounds of milk, a fifth of U.S. milk output.

Poultry. The United States led the world in production of broiler meat from chicken and turkeys. According to the National Turkey Federation, turkey production grew by more than 300 percent since 1970, due to increased demand. By 2002, U.S. consumption of turkey was 17.7 pounds per person, an increase of 113 percent since 1970; consumers in Asian countries such as Japan, Hong Kong, and Singapore also fueled demand. U.S. turkey exports for 2002 reached 438.5 million pounds. The value of turkey exports, though, rose only slightly in the early 2000s, from US$2.6 billion in 1994 to US$2.7 billion in 2003.

Hogs. Although the United States had many small, independent pork producers throughout its history, its pork industry became more vertically integrated and concentrated in large company operations in the mid- to late 1990s. Similar to the development of the broiler chicken industry, many pork companies controlled all phases of the production process, from birth to grocery store sales. These changes allowed pork producers to buy feed in larger quantities and spread costs over more hogs, thereby creating a more efficient pork production process. The country posted production of 7.7 mmt of pork in 1997, with volume rising to 8.75 by 1999. Production fell slightly in 2000 and 2001, climbing back to about 8.71 in 2002 and rising to 9.3 mmt in 2004. Since U.S. per capita pork consumption, about 51.4 pounds in 2003, was low relative to countries such as Poland (84.3 pounds), the Czech Republic, France, Denmark, Spain, and Hong Kong, the United States exported a large portion of its pork. Key markets for U.S. pork were China and other Pacific Rim countries, while Canada, Mexico, and Denmark constituted the country's primary export competitors.

In March 2002, U.S. hog farmers continued their struggle as declining demand, shrinking prices, and steadily rising hog births (8 percent increase in 2001) combined to drive prices lower. Readily available supplies of chicken, increasingly popular with buyers, led to a number of farm closings nationwide in 2001. About 1,000 of Indiana's 64,000 farms shut down in 2001; many of them were pork-producing operations, according to Purdue University Agricultural Service.

EUROPEAN UNION

In 2004 the European Union admitted 10 new member nations, bringing the total to 25. This expansion led to many expected gains in the agricultural and livestock sectors.

Beef and Veal. The European Union, which ranked as the second-largest producer of beef and veal in the late 1990s and early 2000s, dropped behind Brazil in 2004, producing 8 mmt. France and Germany were leading producers, with 1.59 and 1.2 mmt, respectively. The EU typically consumed substantially less beef per capita than the other leading beef producers such as the United States, Argentina, and Brazil; in 1997 EU per capita consumption stood at 19.5 kilograms. In 2001 and 2002, fears over mad cow disease seriously compromised the British exportation of beef and led to increased pork production.

Poultry. The European Union was one of the leading poultry producers and exporters. Although the EU lagged far behind the United States and China in production in the mid- to late 1990s, it was the third-largest producer of poultry meat with 10.7 mmt in 2004. The expansion of the European Union from 15 member states to 25 member states in 2004 contributed to substantial gains for the EU poultry industry, which the USDA predicted would grow by 3 percent in 2005. Exports of broiler meat increased 8 percent between 2003 and 2004, despite high competition from Brazil.

Hogs. Also a major pork producer, trailing only China in overall production, the European Union produced about 21.5 mmt of pork meat in 2004. Chief pork production areas in 2004 included Germany with 4.3 mmt, Spain with 3.3 mmt, France, with 2.2 mmt, and Poland with 2.1 mmt. With an average of 46.6 kilograms per person in 1997, the EU consumed more pork per capita than did any other region and produced enough pork to satisfy domestic demand; consumption began a downward trend in the early 2000s, however, and is expected to decline slightly more in 2005.

CHINA

China had a long history of subsistence agriculture that fed its massive population. Protein sources were rare and used mainly as a supplement to a steady diet of rice. Much of Chinese livestock production was in "backyard" or household production systems. However, China's dramatic economic liberalization in the 1980s set the stage for a fast-growing agricultural economy and with it a growing focus on centralized production systems. After this change, China emerged as one of the world's primary livestock and meat producers; by 2005 it led the world in production of pork, sheep, duck, and goose meat.

Beef. Between 1993 and 1998, China's beef cattle herd expanded by 40 million head to 147 million and its production more than doubled, climbing to 5.8 mmt in 1998, according to FAS estimates. In 2004 China continued to rank as one of the world's biggest producers of beef, raising 6.2 mmt of beef and veal. Relatively low domestic consumption led China to export a significant portion of its output in the 1990s, but with beef consumption rising sharply in the early 2000s China's export volume dropped proportionally, accounting for only about 1 percent of total production in 2001.

Poultry. China's poultry production also expanded dramatically since the early 1990s, and China became one of the dominant global producers, behind only the United States. Despite outbreaks of avian influenza in 2004, which caused both production and consumption to fall temporarily, China's total production of broiler meat that year reached about the same levels as in 2003. In 2004 China instituted stricter measures to ensure sanitary conditions and safe processing for broiler meat. According to FAO figures, China produced 13.6 mmt of poultry in 2004, most of which was from ducks and geese.

Hogs. China was the world's top pork producer throughout the 1990s and expanded its lead considerably in the mid- to late 1990s through the early 2000s. Though small farms still accounted for most swine production, larger commercial operations, which can raise animals more efficiently, have expanded in recent years. According to the USDA, this trend is expected to continue in 2005.

ARGENTINA

In 2001, Argentina's beef industry was hurt significantly by an outbreak of bovine foot and mouth disease. After the country's herds were declared officially disease-free in 2003, Argentina saw exports of US$323 million in the first half of the year. Even though Argentina's production tapered off in the 1990s and early 2000s, the country remained an important low-cost producer and exporter of beef. In 1997 a resumption of exports to the United States, which had banned Argentine beef for almost seven decades, boosted Argentina's position as a leading beef producer and exporter. Disease-free status also made Argentina a formidable competitor for markets in Australia, North America, and Asia. Argentine beef production in 1997 dipped slightly to 2.5 million tons, while exports were estimated at 430,000 metric tons. In 2004 production was estimated at 2.7 mmt, with exports expected to reach 420,000 metric tons.

NEW ZEALAND

In the early 2000s, meat exports accounted for 15 percent of New Zealand's total exports. New Zealand exported 90 percent of its lamb, giving it a 53 percent share in that global market. In addition, New Zealand was also a major cattle producer, with an output of 610,000 metric tons of beef in 1997 and 700,000 metric tons in 2004. The nation tended about 47.3 million sheep and 8.9 million cattle as of 1997, while its human population numbered only about 3.6 million. In 2002 New Zealand was the fourth-largest beef exporting nation, with 321.7 million kg of frozen meat and 20.4 million kg of fresh meat. New Zealand gained greater access to the U.S. market as the result of GATT. New Zealand's livestock and meat industry, the nation's largest employer, was highly dependent on exports. One major export region for New Zealand was the Middle East, which consumed large quantities of lamb. According to *Meat & Poultry*, New Zealand was the world's largest supplier of Halal slaughtered sheep meat, which was processed in accordance with Islamic religious requirements.

BRAZIL

Brazil raised its beef production in the early 2000s to become competitive with the United States as one of the world's main producers. In 2004 Brazil was the second-largest producer and the largest exporter of beef, with sales 40 percent higher by volume than in 2003. According to USDA estimates, Brazil's beef production was expected to near 8.5 mmt in 2005, up about 6 percent from the previous year. Brazil was also a significant producer and exporter of pork, with a projected output of almost 2.7 mmt in 2005. In 2004 Brazilian pork exports grew 3 percent in volume but 41 percent in value. Despite a Russian ban on imports of Brazilian meat during much of 2004, Russia remained the primary destination for Brazilian pork products.

FURTHER READING

Baxter, Tom. "Trade Fight Unhealthy for Poultry Producers." *Atlanta Journal and Constitution,* 10 March 2002.

Becker, Elizabeth. "Mexico Lifts Ban on Many U.S. Beef Products." *New York Times,* 5 March 2004.

Bilgili, S. F. "Sarge." *Poultry Products and Processing in the International Marketplace,* 2001. Auburn University. Available from www.fass.org/.

"Bird-Flu Fears Lead Hong Kong to Slaughter 1.2 Million Chickens." *Wall Street Journal,* 29 December 1997.

"Brazil's Increased Pork Production Threatens U.S. Domestic Crop Markets." *Minnesota Issue Watch,* October 2001. Available from www.mnplan.state.mn.us/.

"Commodity News." *Bloomberg News,* 27 March 2002.

Dorgan, Michael. "Food Safety Is Growing Problem in China, Say Consumers, Experts." *Knight Ridder/Tribune News Service,* 15 March 2002.

Egg Industry Fact Sheet, June 2003. Available from www.aeb.org/.

"Egg Prices May Fall with Oversupply." *The Nation,* 11 March 2002.

Egg Statistics. United Egg producers, 2004. Available from http://www.unitedegg.org.

Estrada, Richard T. "Prices of Food Expected to Rise This Year." *Modesto Bee,* 27 March 2002.

———. "Finding the Milky Way." *Modesto Bee,* 23 March 2002.

McCoy, David. "Pigmeat Production Forecast." *Belfast News Letter,* 16 February, 2002.

National Turkey Federation. *Turkey Statistics,* 2002. Available from www.eatturkey.com/.

"New Zealand Beefs Up Exports." *Meat & Livestock Australia,* January 2005. Available from http://www.mla.com.au/.

New Zealand Meat Exports. 2003. Available from www.marketnewzealand.com.

Reuters. "Food and mouth won't affect Argentina beef status," 9 September 2003. Available from www.agriculture.com/.

Tucci, Louis A. and James J. Tucker III. "The General Agreement on Tariffs and Trade (GATT): Implications for Consumer Products Marketing." *Journal of Consumer Marketing* (Winter 1996): 35.

United Nations Food and Agricultural Organization. *Food Outlook: Meat,* May 2002. Available from www.fao.org/.

———. "Animal Disease Outbreaks Hit Global Meat Exports," 4 March 2004. Available from www.fao.org/.

U.S. Department of Agriculture Economic Research Service. *Agricultural Baseline Projections.* February 2004. Available from www.ers.usda.gov/.

———. *Livestock, Dairy, and Poultry Outlook,* 17 February 2004. Available from ers.usda.gov.

U.S. Department of Agriculture Foreign Agricultural Service. *Brazil: Livestock and Products, Semi-Annual Report, 2005.* (31 January 2005). Available from www.fas.usda.gov.

———. *China: Poultry and Products Semi-Annual 2005.* February 2005. Available from www.fas.usda.gov.

———. *EU-25: Poultry and Products Semi-Annual 2005.* 31 Januayr 2005. Available from www.fas.usda.gov.

———. *Dairy: World Markets and Trade.* December 2004. Available from www.fas.usda.gov/.

———. *International Meat Review.* February 2003. Available from www.ams.usda.gov/.

———. *Livestock and Poultry: World Markets and Trade.* October 2004. Available from www.fas.usda.gov/.

"Where's the Meat?: Pork." *American Farm Bureau Information.* December 4, 2001. Available from www.fb.com.

"World Agriculture Supply and Demand Estimates." *Bloomberg News,* 8 March 2002.

"World Growth at Less than 2 Percent per Year." *International Egg Commission Newsletter,* April 2003. Available from www.internationalegg.com/.

"U.S. Pork Industry Exports More than $2 Billion for First Time." U.S. Meat Export Federation, 14 January 14, 2005. Available from http://www.usmef.org/.

SIC 0182, 0273

NAICS 111411, 112511

AQUACULTURE

Unlike fisheries, which capture wild fish from open waters, the global aquaculture industry cultivates plants and animals in freshwater and saltwater under a controlled environment in which producers can regulate reproduction, feeding, and climate.

INDUSTRY SNAPSHOT

Aquaculture began in ancient China, Rome, and Egypt. Since the 1970s modern aquaculture as an industry flourished throughout the world, particularly in inland nations. According to the United Nations Food and Agriculture Organization (FAO), world aquacultural production has grown by an average of 8.9 percent annually since 1970, more than any other animal-food producing sectors. In the mid-2000s, the aquaculture industry enjoyed substantial global output increases, in part due to increasing dependence on fish by residents of China and also in large part because fishery waters in many parts of the world reached the limits of exploitation. Long-term predictions by the FAO pointed to the aquaculture industry as a significant economic player in world markets as an employer and producer of revenue. Most of the overall increase in world fishery production through 2010, the FAO said, would come from the rapid growth of aquaculture.

The raising of aquatic plants such as seaweed and animals such as fish and crustacea, particularly shrimp, continued to be dominated by Asian enterprises, but aggressive development of aquaculture production by other areas, and China's marketing strategy to raise more higher-value fish (reducing the higher tonnage of lower-value fish) slightly reduced that continent's share of the world market. Asia continued to dominate world aquaculture, with China the dominant country by far. In 2006 China' total aquaculture production reached 52.5 million metric tons (mmt).

In spite of its rising importance in world markets, the aquaculture industry found itself coming under intense fire and scrutiny as environmental groups demanded stricter controls to protect wild fish species that could be lost due to intermingling with similar aquaculture species. In particular, the industry was being asked to demonstrate accountability as it increasingly cultivated genetically altered fish-food species with an extra gene, which greatly increased the length and size of fish in shorter and shorter time periods. Environmentalists stressed the need for fish producers to produce sterile, single-sex fish used for consumption purposes only. Such polyploid aquatic animals have more chromosome sets than sexually normal fish, making them unable to produce and thereby saving their energy for growing meatier. In addition, scientific research published in 2004 found significantly higher levels of dioxins, PCBs, and other environmental carcinogens in farm-raised salmon than were found in captured fish, leading some specialists to recommend limiting intake of contaminated fish. Others, though, believed the risk was overstated.

Nonetheless, a number of experts at the Kyoto Conference predicted in their formal presentations that aquaculture production would increase significantly in spite of protests by some commercial fisheries and environmentalists. In the year 2010, industry experts predicted, aquaculture production might harvest 47 tons of fish and seaweed, with about 33 million tons of fish and crustacea intended for food use.

ORGANIZATION AND STRUCTURE

PRODUCTION TYPES AND METHODS

Aquaculture serves six primary functions: food, bait, aquarium stock, fee-fishing stock, biological supply, and lake stock. Food aquaculture was by far the leading form and included the fresh-water, brackish-water, and marine-water production of species such as catfish, shrimp, bass, trout, salmon, and tilapia. Characterized by many small operations, bait aquaculture raised minnows, suckers, goldfish, and crayfish for use as fishing bait. Limited mostly to warmer climates, aquarium aquaculture produced fresh-water and marine fish, such as guppies, gouramis, cichlids, clown fish, trigger fish, and goldfish, and plants used for aquariums. Featuring small, well-stocked ponds, fee-fishing aquaculture operations offered facilities primarily to sport fishers who paid to catch fish such as trout and catfish from stocked ponds or reservoirs. Some fee-fishing organizations functioned like hunting clubs, allowing members to fish freely with a membership, while others charged daily or hourly rates. Biological supply houses raised a host of aquatic organisms such as turtles, mollusks, and shrimp for research and educational purposes. Finally, lake-stocking aquaculture raised fish to replenish city and county lakes, and these operations produced bass, trout, walleye, and blue fish.

When raising fish and growing aquatic plants, producers must monitor the water quality constantly to ensure a successful harvest. Producers pay special attention to the water's temperature, since fish are cold blooded and their body temperatures conform to their environment. Different species of fish require different temperatures of water, yielding the classification of fish as cold water (which thrive in 48- to 60-degree water); cool water (which thrive in 55- to 75-degree water); and warm water (which thrive in 70- to 85-degree water). Other concerns are the water's alkaline (or acid) pH, ammonia contamination, and dissolved oxygen levels as well as its mineral content and other chemical characteristics such as chlorine if tap water is introduced. Suffocation of fish due to overcrowding or poor aeration, bacterial and parasitical infections, and diseases related to high quantities of fish excrement are problems that lead to unintended fish mortality and cause critics of the industry to call for reforms to institute more humane fish farming methods.

Producers use four general kinds of facilities for aquaculture: ponds, cages, raceways, and recirculating systems. Ponds include existing small bodies of water infused with aquaculture fish and plants as well as ponds specially designed for aquaculture. These can range in size from a quarter of an acre to over 20 acres. To take advantage of existing bodies of water, producers also use cages to raise fish. The cages contain the fish but allow water to pass through; they come in rectangular, square, and round varieties ranging from four to eight feet in width and height. Raceways function largely as facilities for raising trout, and producers position them on slightly sloped areas of land, allowing the water to run down the raceways. Water recirculating systems usually are indoor vats set up in a similar way to aquariums with a filtration and circulation system.

Industry analysts also distinguish between freshwater and marine aquaculture. In the mid-1990s, freshwater production dominated the industry, accounting for over 65 percent of the world's total aquaculture harvest in 1995. However, some observers expected marine aquaculture—or mariculture—to continue to expand in subsequent years, as it did in the late 1990s, especially because 40 percent of the leading seafood species were caught faster than they could reproduce, according to the National Marine Fisheries Service. Although a number of countries farm fish along their coasts, maricultural technology allowed producers to cultivate fish further out in the ocean. Mariculturists placed large cages in the ocean and filled them with young fish and food. They then waited for the fish to mature and then harvested them. Leading species of fish for mariculture included red drum, red snapper, striped bass, and mahi mahi.

TRADE ORGANIZATIONS

The World Aquaculture Society (WAS) advanced aquaculturists education and the development of new techniques to make aquaculture a sustainable and profitable enterprise worldwide. With chapters in Japan, Southeast Asia, the United States, and Latin America, WAS provided technical information, research, and a forum for the enhancement of aquaculture. In addition, WAS worked with governments and industries to promote the ongoing success of aquaculture through legislation, agreements, and alliances.

Europe had its own support organization, the European Aquaculture Society (EAS). Founded in 1976, EAS members worked to improve aquaculture research, farming, education, promotion, and processing. EAS was based in

Belgium and facilitated contact and information exchange between aquaculturists around the world.

In the United States, the National Aquaculture Association was the main aquaculture organization that looked out for the interests of members and served as an information source and ethical voice for environmental responsibility. In addition, other support organizations for aquaculture professionals in the United States tended to be active at the state level such as the California Aquaculture Association or the Wisconsin Aquaculture Association. Other U.S. organizations tended to be grouped by specific fish species such as the U.S. Trout Farmers Association.

BACKGROUND AND DEVELOPMENT

Some historians cite ancient manuscripts as proof that a form of freshwater aquaculture, the raising of carp, first was practiced in China between 3100 and 4000 thousand years ago. In addition, a primitive form of mariculture in China dates back about 2000 years. China's reliance on aquaculture increased over the centuries so that in the twentieth century, China raised more fish than it caught via conventional means. Elsewhere in Asia, such as in India, Japan, and Indonesia, aquaculture expanded as well, becoming a significant source of food fish. These regions raised common carp in ponds. The ancient Romans also practiced a limited form of aquaculture in oyster raising in ponds for gourmet appetites. Many European nations began practicing aquaculture in the Middle Ages and expanded the practice to include the scientific study of spawning, habitat, and feeding. In 1833, German aquaculturists developed methods for artificial fertilization of trout eggs and the raising of these fish under ideal conditions.

Aquaculture grew into a vital component of developing economies where low-cost seafood could be raised and harvested efficiently to help feed populations. Moreover, these countries began to rely on the proceeds of high-value seafood such as shrimp and prawns, which they could export for high profit.

The United States did not practice aquaculture until the mid- to late nineteenth century, when brood fish and fingerlings were first cultivated in small-scale operations. However, after the 1960s the United States began to raise fish other than trout and bait. Early U.S. endeavors were plagued by inexperienced aquaculturists, inadequate ponds, fish illnesses, and insufficient technology, which prevented expansion into other kinds of fish production. Starting in the late 1950s, catfish became a favorite of U.S. producers, especially in the South. Proof of aquaculture's twentieth-century origins in the United States is the fact that catfish production area increased from only 400 acres in 1960, to 161,000 acres by 1991, and 185,700 acres at the start of 2002, according to the United States Department of Agriculture (USDA). The leading U.S. catfish producers were Mississippi, Alabama, Arkansas, and Louisiana.

Aquaculture was one of the most rapidly growing sectors of food production at the beginning of the twenty-first century, and through the 1990s and early 2000s the aquaculture output grew steadily. From 1990 to 1995 the total food output nearly doubled from 12.41 mmt to 20.94 mmt. Continued growth was expected through 2010, with the FAO estimating outputs by that year of between 27 and 39 million tons. While global capture fishing rates remained relatively stable after 1995, aquaculture fishing increased. In 2002, world aquaculture production (including plants) totaled 51.4 million tons, an increased of 6.1 percent from 2000. In 1995 the world's aquaculture output including seafood, aquatic plants, and ornamental fish climbed to US$44.7 billion in value. In 1999, that figure rose to US$53.6 billion, and by 2002 it had grown to US$60 billion, 2.9 percent higher than in 2000. China was the leader in aquaculture production.

Trade regulations affected the aquaculture industry at the beginning of the twenty-first century. In 2004, according to an *Agence France* report, the International Trade Commission ruled that shrimp from Vietnam and other developing countries was being dumped in the United States, clearing the way for the U.S. Department of Commerce to impose tariffs later that year. U.S. shrimp farmers claimed that dumping by foreign competitors caused the value of U.S.-harvested shrimp to drop from US$1.25 billion in 2000 to only US$559 million in 2002.

With the appropriate technology, certain kinds of aquaculture can be practiced in any climate, and producers can raise fish in regions that cannot sustain crops. Leading aquaculture producers were developing countries with limited or over-exploited natural resources and large populations such as China, India, and Bangladesh. Because these countries obtained significant portions of their seafood from aquaculture, the natural fish supply in these areas was able to regenerate. At the same time, however, the environmental impact of aquaculture in these regions has raised increasing concern. Shrimp farming, for example, has resulted in the destruction of more than 50 percent of the world's mangrove forests; an ecosystem that offers natural protection from storms. When a devastating tsunami hit south Asia in December 2004, thousands of lives were lost and extensive tracts of cropland were destroyed. The impact would have been far less, according to a report on Indiatogether.org, if not for the negative impact of the shrimp farming industry.

As the world's population continued to increase and the global natural fish supply decreased due to over-exploitation, aquaculture constituted one method available to food producers to avoid shortages or depletion of certain popular species. The issue had some urgency, as a *Wall Street Journal* report highlighted, because fertility rates combined with agricultural production levels could lead to heightened world starvation by 2025.

However, the increasing availability of low-cost grain coupled with aquaculture expansion could help avert this worst-case scenario. Governments and institutions battling world hunger are hoping the twenty-first century will see more traditionally impoverished countries become producers of food protein with steadily increasing home-based aquaculture. One notable holdout was the continent of Africa, which had yet to begin large-scale aquaculture practices, although many of its nations had the coastline or inland waters essential to developing an aquaculture industry as, for example, India had done. The U.S. AID committed assistance to help Tanzania, an African nation whose government expressed strong interest in adding aquaculture to its agricultural practices.

CURRENT CONDITIONS

The aquaculture industry saw tremendous growth from the mid-twentieth century to the early twenty-first century. By 2004, almost 60 million tons of product resulted from aquaculture worldwide, with a U.S. value of US$70.3 billion. Almost 70 percent of that total came from China, whereas about 22 percent originated from other Asia-Pacific countries. Other regions contributed also, with the least coming from Sub-Saharan Africa, though the region had natural potential, including the fact that tilapia was native to the continent.

Whereas wild catch in the oceans had dominated the world fisheries industry for decades, aquaculture was expected to increase worldwide throughout the mid- to late 2000s, according to the USDA. Reasons for this growth were a growing demand for seafood and the over-fishing of oceans. The most common fish grown in aquaculture environments worldwide as of 2007 were carp, oysters, clams, mussels, salmon, shrimp, and tilapia.

MAJOR COUNTRIES IN THE INDUSTRY

CHINA

China was the world leader in aquaculture production. In 2006 China produced 52.5 mmt of aquaculture products, continuing a trend of yearly increases. The increase in production is attributed to the country's rapid economic growth, rising disposable incomes, and greater consumption of aquatic products. According to the 11th Five-Year Plan for Fishery Development (2006-2010) released by China's Ministry of Agriculture, total aquatic production is expected to increase by more than 3 percent annually to reach 60 mmt by 2010.

China's government paid little attention to aquaculture until the mid-1990s, emphasizing grain production. In the mid-1990s it began to implement measures to increase aquaculture production and stability by offering marketing and infrastructure support as well as tax exemptions for new aquaculturists.

China's aquaculture industry consisted of two key sectors: producers who cultivate inexpensive products for the local market, and companies and joint ventures that produce high-value products for the country's higher income consumers. Aquaculture production in the late 1990s increasingly began harvesting higher-value fish and shellfish. By the early 2000s China had introduced more than 30 high-value species for freshwater cultivation.

In 1995, China devoted 4.6 million hectares of water to inland aquaculture and 653,500 hectares to marine aquaculture. By 2005, the total aquaculture area in China was 7.5 million hectares, including 5.85 million hectares of inland areas. There were 9,128 aquatic processing facilities in 2005, 383 more than the previous year. China's primary inland products were common carp, cyprinus, grass carp, bighead carp, silver carp, mud carp, and gold carp. Marine aquaculture in China centered primarily on shrimp, oysters, clams, seaweed, scallops, mussels, and other shellfish.

China's aquaculture industry faced several challenges in the mid-2000s, including an increase in the rate of aquatic diseases, low technical innovation by the industry, and water utilization inefficiency. Despite these issues, the aquaculture industry in China was expected to continue to grow, especially in regard to exports. Aquatic exports, the largest category in all agriculture exports in China, reached US$7.2 billion in 2005. The largest importer of Chinese aquaculture products was Japan, followed by the United States.

INDIA

India remained a leading aquaculture producer, with an output of 2.1 mmt (excluding aquatic plants) in 2002. Though carp, a freshwater species, accounted for 80 percent of cultivated fish in 1999, intensive shrimp farming grew in importance since the late 1990s. By the early 2000s, according to the FAO, shrimp farming in India employed about 200,000 people and generated about 1.6 percent of the value of India's export economy.

Although India's aquaculture industry achieved great success in the earlier part of the decade, it underwent intense government scrutiny of widespread misuse of chemicals, other environmental degradation, and wholesale fish losses. The future of the country's aquaculture industry depended on whether the government could convert the country's fish farms into a sustainable enterprise. Both the public and the private sectors initiated programs to exploit brackish-water aquaculture, especially in shrimp production.

INDONESIA

Indonesia's produced 5.11 million tons of fish and seafood products in 2003, up 5.2 percent from the previous year. Freshwater aquaculture was dominated by carp, catfish, tilapia, and others. A major concern for the near future was the lack of fry (hatchlings) for stocking freshwater areas. It might be necessary to increase investment in hatcheries to protect species from depletion.

JAPAN

Although Japan was fourth in the world for aquaculture products in the early 2000s, by 2007 production had fallen to 5.72 mmt and was expected to continue a downward trend. While other leading aquaculture producers concentrated primarily on freshwater production, in Japan, where inland waters were narrow, mariculture dominated. However, total inland water fishing and culture decreased by 10,000 metric tons, or 9.6 percent, in 2005. Some of the reasons for the decrease in aquaculture production in Japan were economic; other factors included the trend of young people to move away from agricultural areas to urban areas. In 2006 most male workers in the fishery industry were over 60 years old. Major mariculture products included seaweeds, oysters, scallops, yellowtail, and seabream. Inland fisheries primarily produced eels, carp, trout, and ayu sweetfish.

THAILAND

Aquaculture in Thailand quadrupled from the 1980s through the 1990s, and placed the country as the fifth-largest aquaculture producer in 2001 when its output of aquaculture fish reached 742,000 tons. In 2002, however, fish output declined to 644,890 tons, placing Thailand in sixth place behind Bangladesh. The Thai government launched several programs to promote pond aquaculture in rural areas and to increase environmentally sound methods of shrimp production. Thailand remained the largest supplier of shrimp to the United States, with a value averaging about US$2.5 billion in 2003.

VIETNAM

Vietnam made aquaculture a dominant industry, posting a mere 167,899 tons in 1992, compared to 518,500 tons by 2002. Inland waters, including the productive Mekong River, were intensively cultivated. About 75 percent of Vietnam's aquaculture production in the late 1990s came from various types of carp, with the remainder from catfish. By the mid-2000s, Vietnam was also a major supplier of shrimp. The expansion of brackish-water culture, which began in the 1990s, was expected to continue.

CHILE

Chile, with aquacultural production (excluding plants) totaling only 86,442 tons in 1993, increased its output dramatically through the late 1990s. Production leaped from 391,587 tons in 2000 to 566,096 tons in 2001. The main fishery exports in the mid-2000s were salmon and trout, valued at US$1.72 billion in 2005. More than 74 percent of the salmon exported went to Japan, Brazil, and the United States.

THE UNITED STATES

The United States dropped from its fifth-place ranking in aquaculture production in 1995 to tenth in the world in 2001; it remained in this position in 2002, with a harvest of 497,346 tons of fish and 47,183 tons of plants. The United States produced via aquaculture large amounts of several fish species, including catfish, trout, tilapia, crawfish, and ornamental fish. One reason for the decline was that the U.S. government and environmentalists spread awareness about the need for more environmentally friendly management methods. Though cultivated fish production in 2001 increased slightly from the previous year, reaching a total of 460.998 mmt, this amount remained below the 1999 harvest of 478,679 mmt. Despite relatively flat production, the value of U.S. aquaculture products increased from US$45 million in 1974 to more than US$978 million by 1998. The U.S. Department of Commerce's Aquaculture Policy for the early 2000s included initiatives that would significantly boost production and value of aquacultural production.

According to the Department of Agriculture, consumption of seafood in the United States will increase from its 2006 rate of 12 billion pounds of fish a year to 16.4 billion pounds by 2025. It is estimated that 50 percent of the U.S. seafood supply will come from aquaculture by 2020. In the mid-2000s, about 70 percent of the seafood consumed in the United States was imported, and at least 40 percent of that total was farm-raised.

The leading and most successful aquacultural product in the United States is catfish. Between 1990 and 1996, catfish production rose by over 30 percent. By 2005, the United States produced 638.4 million pounds of catfish worth US$449.9 million. Leading U.S. aquaculture states were Mississippi, Alabama, Arkansas, and Louisiana.

According to the USDA, 59.7 million pounds of trout were sold valued at US$62.6 million in 2005. The value of U.S. trout exports, which had reached US$1.2 million in 1999, fell to only US$1.5 million in 2000. Lower sales to Canada and Japan accounted for much of this decline. Although sales climbed dramatically in 2003, the following year, dramatically reduced shipments to Japan again lowered the total value of U.S. trout sales, which reached only US$2 million. Idaho, with approximately 75 percent of production, led the country, followed by North Carolina and California.

The United States consumed nearly 100 million pounds of tilapia per year, but the country itself only produced about 15 to 20 million pounds; hence, the United States imported large quantities of tilapia from countries such as Taiwan and Costa Rica. Nonetheless, tilapia constituted one of the country's leading aquaculture products.

Crawfish production fell in the 1990s after reaching 71 million pounds in 1990. In 1996 production reached only 44.4 million pounds, down 20 percent from 1995, yet it was more than twice as much as the wild harvest, according to the USDA. After reaching 49 million pounds in 1997, crawfish production plummeted to 17 million pounds in 2000. Yet the product's value, at US$28 million, remained unchanged from the previous year, when production reached 43 million pounds. Louisiana was by far the leading crawfish producing state. In 2003 the value of its farm-raised crawfish reached approximately US$47 million.

The United States also excelled in ornamental fish production. While production levels remained relatively flat through the 1990s and early 2000s, value increased dramatically. The National Marine Fisheries Service estimated that the value of U.S. miscellaneous fish (including ornamentals) rose from US$75 million in 1995 to US$141 million in 2000. Production levels, which reached 23 million pounds in 1997, rose slightly to 26 million pounds in 2000. Ornamental fish alone, according to an Aquafeed industry report, accounted for U.S. exports worth US$5.1 million in the first half of 2004, a 16 percent increase from the same period in 2003. Canada is the largest market for U.S. ornamental fish exports.

FURTHER READING

Agence France Presse, 18 February 2004. Available from www.enaca.org/.

Canadian Ministry of Agriculture and Agri-Food. *Development Plan for Aquaculture Market Study-China, 2003.* Available from http://atn-riae.agr.ca/.

Jain, Shubhanyu. "Promise of Plenty: MPEDA Steps Up Effort to Put India on the Global Seafood Map." *Seafood Business,* March 2007.

"Shrimp Media Monitoring, 2004." Network of Aquacultural Centres in Asia-Pacific. Available from www.enaca.org.

"Tsunami, Mangroves, and Market Economy." *Indiatogehter.org.* (January 2005); http://indiatogether.org.

U.S. Census Bureau. "U.S. Private Aquaculture: Trout and Catfish Production and Value: 1998 to 2005." 20 March 2007. Available from www.census.gov.

U.S. Department of Agriculture. *Fishery Country Profile: The United States of America,* February, 2003. Available from www.fao.org/.

———. *Value of U.S. Exports of Trout, by Country, 1999-2004.* Available from http://ffas.usda.gov.

U.S. Department of Agriculture, Foreign Agricultural Service. "Chile Fishery Products Annual, 2006." *GAIN Report,* 22 September 2006. Available from http://fas.usda.gov.

———. "China Fishery Products Annual, 2006." *GAIN Report,* 31 December 2006. Available from http://fas.usda.gov.

———. "Indonesia Product Brief, Fish and Seafood, 2005." *GAIN Report,* 19 May 2005. Available from http://fas.usda.gov.

———. "Japan Fishery Products Annual Report 2006" *GAIN Report,* 4 October 2006. Available from http://fas.usda.gov.

———. "State of World Aquaculture." 2 April 2007. Available from http://fas.usda.gov.

———. "U.S. Seafood Imports Continue To Soar." *International Trade Report,* 8 July 2005. Avaiable from http://fas.usda.gov.

"U.S. Seafood Consumption Losing Share to Meat; Growth Has to Come from Imports," *Aquafeed,* 8 October 2004. Available from www.aquafeed.com.

"Soy and Aquaculture." *Southwest Farm Press,* 12 March 2007.

Vannuccini, Stefania. *Overview of Fish Production, Utilization, Consumption, and Trade,* May 2003. Available from www.fao.org/.

Wright, James. "Task Force Calls for Responsible Aquaculture." *Seafood Business,* February 2007.

SIC 0910

NAICS 1141

FISHING, COMMERCIAL

This industry includes commercial harvesters of finfish, shellfish, and miscellaneous marine products from open waters, as opposed to aquaculture, which harvests fish from captive waters. For discussion of fish production from controlled habitats see **Aquaculture**.

INDUSTRY SNAPSHOT

Global fishery production between 1950 and 2004 increased from an estimated 20 million metric tons (mmt) to 90.0 mmt, with a record high of 95.6 mmt in 2000, according to Food and Agriculture Organization (FAO) of the United Nations statistics. During this period, the number of participants in the industry also grew rapidly. As a result, more fishermen were attempting to catch fewer fish as fish stocks declined. Consequently, commercial fishing experienced accelerated competition from aquaculture fish farming because of greater control over fish production and because of strained natural resources. By the mid-2000s, major fishing countries such as China, Peru, and Chile were posting declines in total catches, while less developed fishing industries, such as those in Morocco and South Africa, saw significant increases in production.

Two ocean regions play the largest roles in the commercial fishing industry. The world's three most productive areas, according to statistics compiled by the FAO, were the Pacific Northwest, the Pacific Southeast, and the Atlantic Northeast. These areas have large continental shelves with the ability to support substantial stocks of important fish species. After 1971, the Pacific Northwest was the most productive region for commercial fishing. The amount of fish caught in this region in 2000, according to FAO statistics, was 23 mmt, double the amount harvested there in the 1970s. The North Atlantic region and Pacific Southeast were also major fishing sites. In addition to their topography, the social conditions in the bordering coastal nations contributed to the development of robust fishing industries in the Northwest Pacific and North Atlantic. Japan, the Russian Federation, China, and South Korea were in close proximity to the Northwest Pacific. Norway, Denmark, Iceland, Canada, and the United States bound the North Atlantic. Other major fishing regions were located in the Southeast Pacific, West Central Pacific, and inland Asia.

As a result of years of unrestrained fishing, the number of fish available began to shrink drastically in the 1990s as fisheries caught fish faster than they could reproduce. In particular, the number of ground fish (including black cod, ocean perch, lingcod, and dover sole) plummeted in the 1990s. Furthermore, the FAO reported that companies had overfished two-thirds of the world's most popular marine species, including lobster, prawns, cod, and snapper. In response, national governments and the international community developed policies to make the industry sustainable. In order to meet the international demand for seafood, many of the leading seafood-producing countries started to promote aquaculture with government subsidies. Asia, the leading aquaculture region, achieved considerable success with the transition from catching to raising fish. Other countries, such as the United States, France, Peru, Chile, and Canada, also increased their aquaculture industries in response to dwindling wild fish stocks.

FAO studies concluded that the outlook for the global commercial fishing industry depended on the remedial measures taken to improve overfished regions. If fisheries could manage their production in a sustainable manner that allowed species to reproduce faster than they are caught, then the fishing industry was expected to have a chance to produce 105 million metric tons by 2010. However, if the global industry failed to improve fishing conditions worldwide, then the industry's output might drop to 80 million metric tons. Therefore, the commercial fishing industry could only expect slight growth at best through 2010, as aquaculture would most likely play a greater role in the world's overall fish output. In the twenty-first century, according to the FAO, it would be increasingly important to pay attention to the replacement of inadequate fleets, particularly in artisan waters, where post-harvest losses could total 20 to 50 percent of the annual catch. The fleets were expected to provide equipment to retard spoilage and to keep the catch fresh until brought to shore for processing and consumption.

While it was clear that some 30 percent of all popular food fishes in the sea were threatened and that at least some would never recover, the industry was expected to rebound as wasted catches were eliminated and stricter management controls were enforced by the seafood industry. "The demise of the fish industry has been proclaimed more than once, but in all likelihood, in 50 years our grandchildren will still be making a living from the sea and feeding an increasingly hungry world," according to the *National Fisherman*. However, should the industry tarry too long and allow the seas to be overfished by the unscrupulous, "the ocean's bounteous fisheries may become a distant memory," cautioned *Business Week*.

ORGANIZATION AND STRUCTURE

Traditionally, fishing was practiced by independent fishermen, often operating family-owned boats and fishing in the waters where their ancestors had fished. These fishermen operated under the control of fishing associations, local authorities, national governments, and regional treaties. When the industry became mechanized, larger corporate-owned vessels sailed to more distant waters. As a result, commercial fisheries came under the supervision of conventions, which existed by treaty, governing specific areas of the seas. One of the first conventions to be created was the Inter-American Tropical Tuna Commission (IATCC), established by treaty, in 1949, for the purpose of studying tuna and tuna-like species in the eastern Pacific. The commission's first task was to make recommendations regarding efficient use of the Pacific's tuna resources.

The North Atlantic Fisheries Organization (NAFO), established in 1979, was given the task of governing fishing in the international waters of the northwest Atlantic. Contracting parties to the NAFO treaty included Bulgaria, Canada, Cuba, Denmark (in respect of the Faroe Islands and Greenland), Estonia, the European Community, Iceland, Latvia, Lithuania, Norway, Poland, Romania, the Russian Federation, and South Korea. One of NAFO's responsibilities was to protect overfished species—such as cod and flatfish—from exploitation. To preserve sustainable fish stocks, NAFO established and allocated catch quotas.

The South Pacific Forum Fisheries Agency (FFA), also established in 1979, was created to help increase cooperation among those fishing in the South Pacific, primarily for tuna. The FFA Convention comprised 16 independent member nations: Australia, the Cook Islands, the Federated States of Micronesia, Fiji, Kiribati, the Marshall Islands, Nauru, New Zealand, Niue, Palau, Papua New Guinea, the Solomon Islands, Tonga, Tuvalu, Vanuatu, and Western Samoa. The FFA provided its members with help in establishing fisheries policies, developing a system of licensing, and monitoring the activities of distant water fleets.

The Northeast Atlantic Fisheries Commission (NEAFC) was established in 1982. Its origins, however, extend to 1946 when the Convention for the Regulation of Meshes of Fishing Nets and the Size Limits of Fish was established. NEAFC membership included Cuba, Denmark (in respect of the Faroe Islands and Greenland), the European Community, Iceland, Norway, Poland, and Russia. The commission's responsibilities included conservation and ensuring optimum utilization of fishery resources within its jurisdiction, which included parts of the Atlantic and Arctic Oceans and the Baltic and Mediterranean Seas. Specific regulations governed types of permitted fishing gear, mesh sizes, fish size limits, area closures, fishing seasons, and catch quotas. Non-member nations operating within its territory included Belize, the Cayman Islands, Honduras, Panama, Sierra Leone, St. Vincent and the Grenadines, the United States, and Venezuela.

The European Community (subsequently known as the European Union) instituted its Common Fisheries Policy (CFP) in 1983. CFP ruled governed access to fishing grounds, set catch limits, restricted time spent at sea, determined the number and type of vessels authorized to fish in certain areas, established the type of fishing gear able to be used, set minimum sizes, and created incentives to reduce by-catch losses. In January 1995, a licensing policy was created requiring that all boats operating in EC waters be licensed.

The Pacific Salmon Commission (PSC), formed as a result of the Pacific Salmon Treaty between the United States and Canada, was signed in 1985. PSC was created to provide recommendations and advice regarding catches of migratory salmon in western U.S. and Canadian waters. The commissioners represented the interests of commercial fishermen as well as the interests of tribal governments and recreational fishermen.

Many other organizations operate to monitor fishery activities. For example, the International Baltic Sea Fishery Commission, with eight contracting parties—Estonia, the European Community (subsequently known as the European Union), Finland, Latvia, Lithuania, Poland, the Russian Federation, and Sweden—governed operations in the Baltic Sea. The Commission for the Conservation of Antarctic Marine Living Resources was initiated in 1982. It served to develop policies for the protection of marine life in Antarctica's waters. The North Atlantic Salmon Conservation Organization was established in the early 1980s to protect wild salmon. The Ocean Fisheries Commission monitored the activities of distant water fleets in the western Indian Ocean. Members included Seychelles, Comoros Islands, Madagascar, and Mauritius.

In 1995, some 28 countries signed the Straddling Fish Stocks and Highly Migratory Fish Stocks Agreement. For years, countries battled over rights to fish that are born in one country's exclusive economic zones (EEZ) but migrate to another country's EEZ, where they are captured. Popular species such as tuna, marlin, swordfish, sailfish, and frigate mackerel are all highly migratory fish. The agreement established a set of obligations to replace the previous policy that allowed fishers to catch fish if they were found in their own EEZ—a first-come first-serve policy. Participants also hoped that the accord would reduce by-catch (the unintentional taking of animals in addition to the targeted species), discards, and pollution as well as promote fishery management based on scientific research. In addition, the agreement required its signatories to refrain from using any method, or taking any action, that had the possibility of destroying a stock's sustainability, until scientific evidence confidently supported its use.

In 2002, the Interim (now, International) Scientific Committee for Tuna and Tuna-Like Species in the North Pacific Ocean met in Japan to discuss ways to assure the sustainability of species such as the tuna and swordfish. The committee was made up of Japan, the United States, South Korea, Russia, and Taiwan. Absent from the meetings were China, Canada, and Mexico.

In 2002, *Nature* challenged FAO figures that reported the world's catch was increasing by 700 million pounds annually. Its findings stated that the number of fish available for harvesting had decreased by about 800 million pounds annually. The news was indeed somber for the 54 million people employed in the fisheries industry, as well as for the industry itself which might find worldwide collapse in twenty to thirty years. The report also meant disturbing news for the world, since a collapse of the fisheries industry would mean massive world hunger unless aquaculture industries could step up production far above 2002 totals. It was believed the only way to correct the depletion would be to severely limit the harvesting of fish, an action that might cause world catch totals drop drastically by 2010, said fisheries expert Joshua S. Reichert.

BACKGROUND AND DEVELOPMENT

Although fishing is one of the most ancient professions known to mankind, the modern fishing era began in the fifteenth century. The discovery of the Grand Banks, attributed to John Cabot in 1497, led to the development of the cod industry in Labrador-Newfoundland (Canada) and in New England area (of the subsequently named United States). During the seventeenth century, Atlantic fishery operations expanded to include additional species such as herring, mackerel, and capelin. In the eighteenth century, fishermen first observed a relationship between fish stocks in the North Atlantic and climactic variations. As the century closed, North Atlantic catch totals approached 140,000 tons. A century later, approximately 600,000 tons of fish were harvested from the North Atlantic.

Following World War II, the fishing industry experienced rapid growth. Mechanization and motorization led to increased yields and enabled fishermen to travel to distant waters. As demand for fishery products increased, fishermen looked for ways to improve productivity. Steam trawlers and purse seines—two types of fishing gear that later dominated the industry—were refined. Trawlers operate by pulling a catching device through the water near the bottom to scoop up fish. Purse seines are nets deployed around fish schools, that can be closed in a manner similar to a drawstring purse, and are retrieved using hydraulic power.

Purse seine fishing enabled catch rates per vessel to double. As a result, during the late 1950s and early 1960s, many bait-boats were converted to purse seine vessels. Purse seines proved to be an economical means of providing large volumes of fish for massive canning operations. Purse seining also caused problems, however, because some types of dolphins swam near yellowfin tuna. When purse seiners set nets around tunas and dolphins, dolphin injuries and drowning escalated. Although purse seines were efficient in catching large quantities of fish, they yielded catches of insufficient quality to meet the demands of fresh markets—such as Japan's sashimi market. To produce better quality fish, longlines were developed. Longlines employed hooked lines of vast lengths that were deployed and retrieved in waters where target fish populations were known to exist.

Other innovations leading to expansion within the fishing industry included the development of refrigeration equipment, factory freezer trawlers, and fish-finding equipment. Fish-finding equipment, using sonar and radar, enabled fishermen to accurately locate fish. The first fish finder was developed by British fisherman Ronald Balls, in 1933. Balls discovered that he could detect fish above the ocean floor using echo-sounding equipment. During the early 1950s, Norwegian whalers were the first fishing vessels to use the technology successfully. They were followed by Iceland's herring seiners, who used the equipment to locate schools of fish that could not be sighted from the surface. Catches increased dramatically. According to a NAFO estimate, annual fish catches in the Northwest Atlantic reached 1 million tons during the 1950s. The 1968 catch was judged to be 4.5 million tons.

In the United States sensitive fish-finding equipment able to detect even individual fish was developed. Although early units were cumbersome and ill suited for use in a marine environment, by the 1970s they had become easier to use and more popular. As the computer age dawned, color displays enabled fishermen to locate school edges more precisely, and the need for recording paper was eliminated. Further refinements led to miniaturization, improved function, and reduced prices.

During the late 1960s and early 1970s, growing public concern about marine mammals, such as Canadian harp seals, whales, and dolphins, led to the passage of the Marine Mammal Protection Act in the United States in 1972. The act's goal was to reduce injury and mortality among marine mammals by commercial fishing operators. A ban on the importation of commercial fish and fish products, taken by means that did not meet U.S. standards, was among its provisions.

The ban led to a change in global fish distribution. Prior to its imposition, about 85 percent of the yellowfin tuna harvested from the Eastern Pacific was sold to the United States. By the early 1990s, the amount had dropped to about 10 percent. Following imposed embargoes, fishermen were forced to develop other markets. These included increased consumption by Latin American countries (Mexican consumption underwent a fivefold increase) and a growth in exports to other nations. As exports to other nations increased, surpluses developed, which depressed prices for Eastern Pacific fisheries products.

As Eastern Pacific fishing declined, fishing increased in the Indian Ocean. Seychelles, an island nation north of Mauritius in the Western Indian Ocean, gained independence from the United Kingdom in 1976 and expanded its exclusive economic zone (EEZ) to 200 miles in 1978. During the early 1980s French tuna fishermen discovered rich tuna resources in the area. To accommodate foreign fishing fleets, the Seychelles government built the necessary infrastructure to provide marine support facilities to purse seiners and longliners from France, Spain, and the Soviet Union. The area within 60 miles of shore, however, was held exclusively for Seychelles fishermen.

Another change in global fishing patterns occurred during the 1970s. Negotiations to draft a new treaty regarding the international law of the sea began in 1973 and created a movement among coastal nations to adopt 200-nautical mile exclusive economic zones(EEZs). EEZs afforded coastal countries an opportunity to protect valuable fishing grounds and regulate the operations of distant water fleets. One important exception to the widespread movement to adopt 200-mile EEZs occurred in the Mediterranean Sea where such an action would have led to disputes as a result of overlapping zones. Malta, Morocco, and Egypt each instituted exclusive 25-mile zones; other countries adopted zones varying from 6 to 35 miles. The abundant waters of the Mediterranean Sea, with 46,000 kilometers of coastline and a total area of 2.5 million square kilometers, yielded nearly 100 different commercial species of fish and shellfish.

In the Pacific, climatic changes associated with El Niño (an ocean current with cyclical deviations) led to changes in South American fisheries operations. Peruvian anchovy stocks collapsed in 1971 and 1972 and did not begin expanding again until 1977. El Niño again negatively impacted eastern Pacific fisheries during 1982 and 1983, and the problem of reduced fish populations was compounded by high fuel prices. Fishermen responded by diversifying their catch among several species. Because other species responded differently to ocean conditions, catches of small pelagic species became more stable. In 1970, Peruvian anchovies had represented 60 percent of the small pelagic harvest. In 1985 the largest single species taken was the South American sardine. It represented only 27 percent of global small pelagic catch.

While climatic conditions impacted some fisheries, over-exploitation began taking its toll on others. As important fish stocks became depleted, international tensions mounted. The issue of fishing rights was one of the concerns that led to the 1982 war between the United Kingdom and Argentina in the Falkland Islands. Fishing commissions began instituting policies to protect fish populations. In 1983, the European Community identified a restricted region, called the Shetland Box, off the northern coast of Scotland. Because the Shetland Box was known to be an important breeding ground, officials limited access to fishing in the area. In another region, the Norway Pout Box, part of the North Sea, was closed to industrial fishing vessels.

Regulators faced complex challenges in their efforts to make decisions aimed at protecting fish populations. Incomplete knowledge made it difficult to assess fish stocks accurately. Without reliable information about the numbers of fish available, however, projections to determine allowable catch quotas were uncertain. The task was further compounded by the necessity of getting governments to agree. As a result, some catch ceilings were set inappropriately. In addition to problems associated with overfishing, some fisheries experienced degradation as a result of pollution. Runoff from industrial and agricultural lands resulted in contamination of fisheries products by chemicals and pesticides. Areas suffering the greatest impact were located in estuaries and freshwater.

The 1980s also saw a reduction in the dominance of traditional fishing nations. At the beginning of the decade, fleets of developed countries were responsible for 53 percent of the global catch. By 1986, developing nations landed 52 percent of the total worldwide harvest.

According to an estimate made by the United Nation's Food and Agriculture Organization (FAO), 1986 saw a fishery harvest of almost 90 million metric tons, including fish, shellfish, and other aquatic products. The figure represented a 5 percent increase over 1985 and a 25 percent increase since the beginning of the decade. Most of the increase was attributed to the expanding participation of developing nations, particularly those in Asia and Latin America.

The largest single species taken in 1986 was Alaska pollock, representing 7 percent of the global catch. Other major species included Peruvian anchovy (6 percent), Japanese sardine and South American sardine (at 5 percent), and capelin, Atlantic cod, Chilean jack mackerel, Chub mackerel, and Atlantic herring (each representing 2 percent). Between 1983 and 1989 the estimated number of overexploited fishery stocks increased from twenty-three to fifty-one.

During the early 1990s, the tuna catch in South Pacific waters represented approximately 40 percent of the worldwide annual tuna harvest. Fleets operating in the area were predominately from Japan, the United States, Taiwan, South Korea, and the Philippines. Because of different fish habits, South Pacific tuna does not associate with dolphin in the same way Eastern Pacific yellow fin tuna does. As a result, dolphin mortality was not a major issue for harvesters in the South Pacific. Eastern Pacific tuna, however, continued to represent about 25 percent of the global yellowfin tuna catch. Yielding to pressure from groups concerned with the safety of marine mammals, ten nations agreed to participate in an international program to reduce dolphin mortality associated with tuna fishing, without turning to harvest methods that would potentially jeopardize other species such as sharks or sea turtles.

Annual global trade in fish and fish products (including aquaculture) reached US$58.2 billion in 2002, a 5 percent increase from 2002 and a 45 percent increase since 1992. Fish exports, according to the FAO, were an important source of foreign currency for many countries, especially developing nations; in some countries, earnings from fish sales accounted for as much as half of total export revenues. In the early 2000s, developing countries had begun to shift the focus of their fishing trade away from exports of raw material (usually destined to be processed in developed countries) and toward higher-value live fish or value-added products.

The world's commercial fisheries pinpointed the collective goal of finding ways to guarantee a protracted supply of fish and shellfish as food resources. According to the FAO, the overall world fish catch including crustaceans and mollusks was estimated at 90.3 million metric tons (mmt) in 2003, down slightly from 93.2 mmt the previous year. A decrease in production among some major fishmeal-producing regions accounted for this decline. Despite the smaller overall catch, however, bigger aquaculture harvests brought the total production of edible fish in 2003 to about 103 mmt, which the FAO determined was enough to meet the average per capita demand. Of the 2003 world capture totals, 81.3 mmt came from ocean waters and 9 mmt came from inland waters.

The most fertile marine fishing grounds in the mid-2000s remained the Northwest and Southeast Pacific Oceans. Total catches however, showed a decline since 2000. Eastern Central and Southwest Atlantic catches also decreased substantially, but production increased in the tropical Pacific and Indian Oceans—a trend that the FAO predicted would continue. Catches in the Northeast Atlantic and Mediterranean remained similar to production from previous years, while catches in the Northwest Atlantic and the Northeast Pacific increased.

The health of the fishing industry is directly related to the abundance of fish in the earth's waters. During the late 1980s and mid-1990s many important fish stocks were threatened by overfishing. World production in 2000 led the FAO to conclude that about half of marine fish resources were at the very limit of a sustainable yield, about one quarter of all ocean waters were dangerously depleted, and about another quarter could yield additional annual catches. The FAO's 2004 report on the State of World Fisheries and Aquaculture described an even more dire picture, stating that "the global potential for marine capture fisheries has been reached, and more rigorous plans are needed to rebuild depleted stocks and prevent the decline of those being exploited at or close to their maximum potential". To counter threats of overfishing, governments around the world began to impose restrictions and quotas to help preserve global fish stocks. Scientists also began trying to learn more about El Niño's Southern Oscillation effects, causing temperature changes in the world's waters that resulted in greatly diminished catches for the fisheries.

CURRENT CONDITIONS

China, the leading producer since 1992, continued to dominate production in 2004, with a catch of 16.8 million tons of fish from marine and fresh waters. Peru was second with 9.6 million tons, followed by the United States (4.95 mmt), Chile (4.93 mmt), Indonesia (4.81 mmt), Japan (4.40 mmt), and India (3.6 mmt).

In 2007, the U.S. Congress passed the Magnuson-Stevens Fishery Conservation and Management Act, which is intended to reduce overfishing and increase limited access privilege programs. The law was a follow-up to the 1996 Sustainable Fisheries Act, which was intended to prevent overfishing, rebuild stocks of depleted fish, protect habitat, reduce amounts of bycatch (fish unintentionally caught with a regular harvest and then discarded), and improve research and monitoring. According to a report from the National Marine Fisheries Service, by 2003 biomass of many species of groundfish—including Georges Bank haddock, Georges Bank yellowtail flounder, and Georges Bank and Gulf of Maine cod—had begun to increase. Yellowtail flounder spawning stock size, for example, increased from just over 2,000 mt in 1994 to 39,000 mt in 2001. In 2003, the NOAA Fisheries reported that the Gulf of Maine/northern Georges Bank silver hake was declared officially restored. It also reported that between 1997 and 2002, overfishing was corrected 26 times and stocks had been rebuilt above biomass thresholds 20 times, though the reverse occurred in 27 cases. The number of stocks that were overfished increased from 81 in 2001 to 86 in 2002, and the number of stocks not overfished decreased from 163 to 150. Fishing mortality thresholds were unknown, however, for 695 stocks.

In addition to gaining some control over the fishing industry in the United States, the Magnuson-Stevens Act included provisions for monitoring other nations's fishing activities. According to the National Sea Grant Law Center, " The Secretary may undertake activities to promote improved monitoring and compliance for high seas fisheries or fisheries governed by international fishery management agreements by several means, including sharing information on harvesting and processing capacity and illegal, unreported, and unregulated (IUU) fishing activities with relevant law enforcement organizations." Proponents were hopeful that the act would improve the situation. Said Bill Hogarth, director of NOAA Fisheries, overfishing " jeopardizes both its [the fish stocks'] biological future and the future of those who depend on it for their livelihood. "

In addition, the FAO predicted that population growth and higher incomes would cause demand for fish and fish products to expand by almost 50 million tons by 2015. Though this amount is high, it indicates annual growth of 2.1 percent compared to 3.1 percent during the last two decades of the twentieth century. Growth in fish production, however, is expected to decline from 2.1 percent annually between 2001 and 2010 to 1.6 percent annually between 2010 and 2015. Furthermore, all of the growth in total fish production will come from aquaculture. Capture fishing rates are expected to stagnate.

RESEARCH AND TECHNOLOGY

To meet the challenges of the twenty-first century, several fisheries research programs were aimed at more accurately assessing fish stocks and determining how many fish could be harvested without further endangering fish populations. Because the job of setting and enforcing catch quotas was impeded by a lack of firm, reliable data, some analysts hoped that better information would lead to improved fisheries management and more efficient use of sea resources.

One such program, the Fisheries and Aquaculture Research Program (FAR), was established in 1987 by members of the European Community. Its original purpose was to investigate fisheries management, fishing techniques, industry products, and aquaculture (raising sea animals in a farming environment). Although initiated as a five-year program, many individual FAR projects continued beyond the expiration of the original funding commitment.

Advances in fishing technology sometimes seemed to conflict with the goals of fisheries management researchers. While some researchers looked for ways to protect fish populations, others developed equipment to help fishermen catch greater quantities of fish. Examples included temperature-probing equipment, night vision apparatuses, and on-board computers. Not all new gear was aimed at increasing catch sizes however. Improvements in technology also included tools designed to help eliminate problems associated with by-catch. One device was created to let finfish escape capture by shrimp boats, another, a time-release float mechanism, served to help retrieve lost crab pots and reduce unintentional crab mortality. Another device sounds an alarm to steer marine mammals away from gill nets and cod traps.

WORKFORCE

Although commercial fishing was not necessarily a major national employer in the world's leading fishing nations, it was often a vital part of the economy in coastal regions where fishing provided both direct and indirect employment. According to one estimate, for every job at sea four to five were needed on shore in boat yards, fish processing plants, packaging operations, equipment manufacturers, and other industry suppliers.

Commercial fishing jobs also can include a strong element of danger. In the United States, fishers face the greatest risk of any workers in any occupation, according to National Institutes of Health statistics. Every two years, 120 of 100,000 fishers are killed. It is interesting to note that almost 25 percent of these fishing fatalities occurred on the Alaskan seas. Indeed, the fatality rate for commercial fishers in Alaska, according to the Centers for Disease Control and Prevention, was 28 times the U.S. average for workplace deaths.

Furthermore, in many countries, modernization, new technology, and depleted fish stocks were displacing traditional workers. According to one estimate, artisan fisheries required a workforce 20 times as large as modern industrial fisheries. Compounding the problems associated with worker displacement was the fact that in many areas where fishing was a traditional employer, relatively few alternate sources of employment existed. In some places, large foreign fleets had done little to employ people from the local population. As a result, some countries, such as the Pacific Island nations, initiated regulations requiring distant water fleets to hire a quota of local workers in order to maintain fishing rights within the EEZ.

INDUSTRY LEADERS

The industry was affected in the early 2000s when environmental groups seized hold of United Nations admissions that China, and possibly other Asian nations, had tremendously overestimated annual catches. This led activists and governments alike to demand universal limits on catches to assist badly depleted fish stocks in many parts of the world. Boycotts on purchasing fish from Chile in 2002 could spread to other parts of the world's fishing waters. International attention also was focused on overfishing in waters visited by Japanese fishing interests. Several Japanese companies moved away from fish caught by fleets of ships to aquaculture, and this clearly was also a trend in Korea and Thailand. Canada continued to keep a presence in the industry in spite of the collapsed cod catches. Norway, New Zealand, and Iceland also kept a determined presence and were alert for changes in fishing regulations, as the world's governments attempted to reconcile devastating estimates of the true numbers for the oceans' commercial fishes.

FISHERIES PRODUCTS INTERNATIONAL

Fisheries Products International (FPIL) is a St. John's, Newfoundland fishing-fleet giant. In February of 2002 it attempted to consolidate its position as an even larger industry giant by taking over Canada's other giant fleet, Clearwater Fine Foods of Bedford, Nova Scotia. The estimated US$321 million takeover was bitterly fought by the Canadian government, which clearly did not want Canadian Fisheries Products International to have such an overwhelming market share of US$630 million revenue, and Clearwater survived the bid.

In the early 2000s Fishery Products International made substantial investments in new equipment to enhance its groundfish operations. It added a US$15 million groundfish freezer and trawler that year, and, according to a Canada News Wire report, expected to invest more than US$20 million to modernize its processing plants. The company's revenues reached US$752.9 million in 2006.

THAI UNION FROZEN PRODUCTS

Makers of the famous Chicken of the Sea brand, Thai Union Frozen Products, posted slight profits, even in the face of declining world tuna populations and the falling sales of Heinz's Starkist tuna line, that forced the manufacturer to close U.S. canning facilities in 2002. In 2003 the company's sales reached 40.3 billion baht (approximately US$1.05 billion). Largely due to reduction in tariffs on U.S. imports of Thai shrimp, the company expected to see revenues and profits increase.

MAJOR COUNTRIES IN THE INDUSTRY

CHINA

In almost every aspect Asia dominated the commercial fishing industry. According to FAO figures for 2003, 85 percent of the world's fishing and aquaculture workers lived in Asia, with almost a third of the world total living in China. The fishing industry in China, the region's top producer, remained state owned. China's production in 1992 reached 8.3 mmt but soared dramatically through the 1990s. In 1999 the country claimed a record high catch of 17.2 mmt. Amounts have decreased slightly since then, reaching 16.9 mmt in 2000 and 16.8 mmt in 2004. China's aquaculture production, by contrast, has increased; fish landings and aquaculture together gave the country an estimated 27.7 kg of fish protein per capita in 2003.

PERU

Peru has ranked second in total captured fish production since 1992. In 2004, the country's total catch reached 9.6 million metric tons—a substantial decrease from its production in 2000, when dramatic recovery of stocks of Peruvian anchoveta boosted the total global catch by more than 2 million tons above normal levels. Most of Peru's catch was small pelagic fishes such as sardines, anchovies, and mackerel; indeed, variations on anchoveta stocks are one of the most significant influences on the country's total production levels. In 1987, the Peruvian government instituted the Fisheries Reactivation Fund with the goal of rebuilding and modernizing its fishing fleet. The government also created a state-owned fishing fleet and entered into joint venture agreements with other countries operating fishing vessels in Peruvian waters.

UNITED STATES

In 2001, the U.S. commercial fishing industry moved ahead of Japan to become the third major producer, reporting a harvest of 4.9 mmt, slightly up from 4.7 mmt in 2000. Production rose again in 2002, when the total U.S. catch was reported at 4.9 mmt. By 2004, that figure was 4.95. In 2003, U.S. edible fish imports were valued at US$11.1 billion, an increase of US$974.2 million from the previous year. Shrimp imports, valued at US$3.8 billion, comprised 34 percent of total edible fish imports. Other major imports included salmon and tuna. U.S. edible fish exports in 2003 totaled US$3.1 billion, a slight increase from US$3.0 billion in 2002.

In March 2004, the U.S. government banned commercial fishing for swordfish in the Pacific Ocean between the U.S. West Coast and Hawaii. This action was taken to protect endangered sea turtles, which are caught by longline hooks used for swordfish. The U.S. industry, however, accounted for only about 5 percent of swordfishing in the area. Other bans occurred around the nation; for instance, the Gulf of Mexico Fishery Management Council initiated an individual fishing quota (IFQ) for red snapper in 2006 and was considering a grouper IFQ.

Continued concern about mercury levels in some species of fish, including tuna, appeared to impact U.S. consumption levels in the mid-2000s. Statistics from 2004 suggested a significant decline in canned tuna consumption, though some analysts disputed this trend. At the same time, other news reports in 2004 touted the health benefits of eating fish, including evidence that one meal of tuna per week can slow the narrowing of arteries in postmenopausal women. The FDA in 2004 approved the use of omega-3 health claims in the labeling of food products containing these fatty acids (plentiful in such fish as salmon and tuna), a development that the fishing industry hoped would boost consumer confidence and demand.

CHILE

Like Peru, the bulk of the Chilean fishery catch was anchovies, sardines, and mackerels. The country caught 4.93 mmt in 2004, up from 4.3 mmt in 2000 and significantly more than its disastrous harvest of only 3.2 mmt in 1998. As with Peru, the fate of Chile's commercial fishing industry remained uncertain because of years of overfishing its resources. To retain its role as a major seafood exporter, Chile has begun to invest in aquaculture.

INDONESIA

In 2004, FAO ranked Indonesia the fourth-largest producer of captured fish with 4.81 mmt. The fishing industry in Indonesia was also predominantly traditional with many non-powered vessels such as dug-outs and plank-built boats. However, the fleet also contained mechanized purse seines and modern long-lining vessels that were introduced during the late 1960s and early 1970s. Purse seines were popular for catching Indian mackerel, and long-lining was used predominantly for tuna in the eastern part of Indonesia, in the Indian Ocean, and Banda Sea. The waters off Indonesian shores supported a wide variety of fish habitats including continental shelves and deep-sea waters. The nation's jurisdiction spanned 2.8 million square kilometers of internal waters, 300,000 square kilometers of territorial waters, and an EEZ comprising 2.7 million square kilometers. Indonesian fishermen landed 45 species of commercial fishes (including chub mackerel, sardine, scad, anchovy, skipjack tuna, and needle fish), 8 types of crustaceans, and 8 kinds of mollusks.

JAPAN

Although Japan led the industry in the late 1980s, it fell behind China, as well as Peru and Chile, in the 1990s and by 2001 ranked fifth in total capture production. In 2004, Japan reported a catch of 4.4 mmt, well behind its 1994 banner year total of 12 mmt. Japan remained the world's leading market for sashimi-grade tuna. Imports of tuna suitable for sashimi totaled 60,489 tons in 2003.

Japan's fishing industry remained privately owned and an efficient provider of food and jobs. Prior to the late 1970s, Japanese fishermen relied heavily on distant water catches. When foreign governments implemented 200-mile EEZs, Japan was forced to plan a new strategy for its fishing operations, and the nation's focus turned more toward its own offshore and coastal areas. During the mid-1980s sardines taken from waters in the Sea of Japan and in the Pacific off the eastern coast of Hokkaido and the northern coast of Honshu represented the biggest increase in Japanese catch statistics. Changing industry conditions, however, continued to impact the profitability of Japanese fishing operations. When the Commonwealth of Independent States (CIS) restricted access to its waters and instituted a salmon-fishing ban in 1992, one projection anticipated a 40 percent reduction in Hokkaido's fleet.

INDIA

India's fishing industry saw significant growth in the early twenty-first century. Total capture figures rose to 4.8 mmt in 2004 from 3.9 in 1999.

FURTHER READING

"Announcement of Legislative Development, March 2007." National Sea Grant Law Center, 3 April 2007. Available from www.observernet.org/.

Chea, Terence. "Feds Ban U.S. Commercial Swordfishing in Much of Pacific to Save Turtles," Associated Press, 12 March 2004. Available from www.enn.com.

Childers, Hoyt. "The 3 Keys to IFQs: Allocation, Allocation and Allocation." *National Fisherman,* April 2007.

"Fishery Products International Invests in New Groundfish Vessel." Newswire Canada, July 2003. Available from www.newswire.ca.

Fishery Products International Annual Report, 2004. Available from www.fpil.com.

"FPI Limited Announces 2006 Annual Financial Results." 9 March 2007. Available from www.fpil.com.

Hogarth, Bill. "Meeting New Magnuson-Stevens Challenges." *National Fisherman,* March 2007.

Moore, Kirk. "With Cuts in Fishing Time and Quotas, Fluke Alternatives Could Enter Market." *National Fisherman,* August 2006.

National Institute for Occupational Health and Safety. "Commercial Fishing in Alaska." Available from www.cdc.gov.

National Marine Fisheries Service, National Oceanic and Atmosphere Administration. *Imports & Exports of Fisher Products: Annual Summary, 2003.* Available from www.st.nmfs.gov.

———. *Implementing the Sustainable Fisheries Act: Achievements from 1996 to the Present.* June 2003. Available from www.nmfs.noaa.gov.

Thai Union Group Company Information. Available from www.thaiuniongroup.com.

Tuna Market Report. June 2004 and December 2004. Globefish. Available from www.globefish.org.

United Nations Food and Agricultural Organization, Fisheries Department. *Projection of World Fishery Production in 2010.* Available from www.fao.org.

———. *The State of World Fishers and Aquaculture 2004.* Available from www.fao.org.

———. *Yearbook of Fishery Statistics, 2004.* Available from http://ftp.fao.org/.

SIC 0800

NAICS 113

FORESTRY

Forestry organizations operate timber tracts, tree farms, forest nurseries, and related activities such as reforestation services and the gathering of gums, barks, balsam needles, maple sap, Spanish moss, and other forest products. For discussion of logging and wood production, see also the article entitled **Logging.**

INDUSTRY SNAPSHOT

Forestry is the science of developing and managing woodlands and the water resources that sustain them. The purpose of forestry is to develop fuelwood (for fuel), sawlogs (for lumber), and pulpwood (for paper production) that can be extracted through logging. The production of fuelwood, sawlogs, and pulpwood grew steadily between 1960 and 2000, rising from 62 billion cubic feet in 1960 to 84 billion cubic feet in 1980, and 110 billion cubic feet in 1995. Global population growth increased demand for wood by 77 million cubic meters per year in the early 2000s. By 2005, production was expected to reach 122 billion cubic feet. About half the wood harvested each year is used for fuel.

Since forestry directly affects the environmental quality of every nation and involves the use of enormous amounts of public and private land, it is a focus of intense public debate in many countries. In most nations, the forest industry—which cuts timber—is also responsible for regenerating and maintaining the land. While intense worldwide debate continued over the extent and location of timber harvests, the forest industries of most major industrial nations have, for the most part, become more responsible and careful in their management of forest resources.

In some developing nations, overcutting of land to create farmland, ranchland, or fuel continued to degrade the environment. While Southeast Asian nations producing tropical timber moved to check overcutting through regulation, taxation, and export bans, overcutting was said to continue despite safeguards. The loss of tropical rain forests in South America is a major example of this problem. Another problem was the massive damage done in Indonesia from 1997 through 2002, when fires—some deliberately set—ravaged lands where timber had been cut or where forests were being cleared for agriculture. The burnings were supposed to help prepare or clear the land for agricultural purposes, but once the fires were out of control, they created intense smog and haze that affected the entire region for months. Monetary damages from the fires and the haze they caused were estimated at US$4.4 billion in a study from the Economy and Environment Program for South East Asia (EEPSEA) and the World Wildlife Fund (WWF).

Likewise, forest fires burned out of control in Mexico in May and June 1998. While these forest fires were attributed to extremely dry weather caused by the El Nino phenomenon, Mexican authorities were criticized for being unprepared for the disaster. The fires wiped out vast sections of Mexico's forestland, and the damage included the holdings of forest products companies. Fires have also been problematic in Chile. In 1999, fires flamed out of control to destroy 242,000 acres of forest. In 2002, some 93 fires in Chile threatened both forest preserves and cash-crop forests. In 2003, the Russian Federation lost 23.7 million hectares of forested land to fires; Australia, France, and Portugal also weathered significant fire losses that year. The biggest fire threat, however, is in sub-Saharan Africa, where the Food and Agriculture Organization of the United Nations (FAO) estimated that approximately 170 million hectares of forests are burned each year (about 10 percent of this, the FAO said, was necessary for woodland renewal). The costs associated with forest fires, which consume about 350 million hectares—the size of India—worldwide each year, are estimated by the FAO at several billion dollars annually.

While forests exist in every nation on earth, the scientific management of forests tended to be concentrated in countries that produce large volumes of forest products although these countries did not necessarily have the most total forest area. For example, Finland and Sweden were leaders in forestry management and produced very high volumes of forest products yet did not rank among the top ten countries in terms of total forest area. Leading areas in terms of total forest cover were the Commonwealth of Independent States (former Soviet Union), North America, Scandinavia, continental Europe, Southeast Asia, New Zealand, and Latin America. In Latin America several companies established highly productive plantation forests (artificially planted forests intended for harvest at a specific time), particularly in Brazil and Chile.

Forest policies around the world differed based on each country's political history. In the United States, the federal and state governments own and manage substantial shares of forestland— especially in the West—but private corporations and individuals also own large woodland tracts, particularly in the South. In former communist countries, where forests were owned by the state, emerging market economies privatized forestry to varying degrees. Mixed ownership of woodlands, like that of the United States, is found throughout most of Asia, Western Europe, and South America. In Japan, most forests—a precious commodity in such a densely populated country—are state owned. In many African countries, tribal ownership is prevalent, a practice that can make modern forestry management difficult.

Although there are thousands of tree, plant, and shrub varieties growing in the world's forests, foresters cultivate a relatively small number of tree species. Most forestry activities focus on two broad varieties of trees: coniferous and nonconiferous (broadleaf). Coniferous trees, known as softwoods, include pines, spruces, firs and hemlocks while nonconiferous trees are hardwoods that include oaks, maples, and beeches. Forested areas around the world also contain a large variety of woody shrubs and grasses (such as bamboo). In 2005 about 41 percent of the annual world harvest of wood was comprised of softwood species. Plantation forests accounted for only 4.7 percent of forestry acreage worldwide.

Forests regenerate naturally through seeding or sprouts that grow from the roots of cut trees or artificially by planting seedlings. Hardwood trees are usually allowed to regenerate naturally. Most softwoods do not sprout from the roots of cut trees and are most often replanted after harvest. In the early 2000s, according to USDA statistics, about 2.6 million acres of trees were planted annually in the United States;roughly 1.8 billion trees. The forest industry planed 45 percent of this total, and the national forest system planted 6 percent. Other government and industries accounted for another 7 percent, with the remainder planted by noncommercial owners. Replanting by forest products companies and other groups created a net growth in the amount of forested land in most major countries. In Western Europe, for example, there was 30 percent more forested land in the mid-1990s than there was 50 years prior. From the early 1970s to the mid-1990s, the total acreage of trees growing in the United States increased by 20 percent.

Conflicting Demands

The global forestry industry has often struggled under the pressure of two conflicting demands: (1) the world's growing population demands more lumber, paper, and other wood products; and (2) the environmental goal of permanently preserving a larger share of the world's forests from commercial development.

Environmental groups, for example, argue that further use of wood resources will damage the environment. The timber industry contends that if timber production were reduced significantly worldwide, the use of more damaging wood substitute materials would likely increase. According to some sources, these substitute materials have substantially higher negative environmental impacts than tree harvesting and planting, an infinitely renewable process. For example, metals, cements, and other substitute materials would require environmentally damaging mining or quarrying activities. Also, the processing of most substitute products would require far more energy than is needed to create wood products.

Organization and Structure

Major commercial forestry operations are concentrated in the forest product producing countries—mainly the United States, the Commonwealth of Independent States, and tree-rich countries with small populations such as Sweden, Finland, and Canada. However, nontraditional forestry operations are growing fast in countries such as Brazil, Chile, and New Zealand. Also, Southeast Asian nations, such as Malaysia and Indonesia, having rapidly depleted their stands of virgin timber, are now establishing large plantations to supply the many pulp and paper operations being built there.

Forestry operations are driven by the global demand for lumber and wood fiber, which is increasing at a rate parallel to or slightly greater than the increase in world population. In societies in which most of the population exists at a subsistence level, forestry management is based on the demands for firewood and cleared, arable land. In fact, more trees are used for firewood around the world than any other single use. In more industrialized countries, forestry focuses on growing trees to make building materials, paper, and other manufactured products.

Considerable tension remains between the world's desire for forest products and the demand for the permanent preservation of natural forests. Between 1960 and 1985, the amount of protected land worldwide grew from 100 million hectares (247 million acres) to 400 million hectares (988 million acres). In the United States, much of the battle over preservation focused on "old growth" timber, mostly in the Pacific Northwest. Old growth is the final stage in a forest's natural cycle of growth and renewal. It is characterized by large, old trees of varying heights and large, dead trees. Old growth timber is favored by sawmills since its extremely large trees produce exceptional timber products. There are 13.2 million acres of old growth in the United States, mostly in the Pacific Northwest. Over half—eight million acres—is already preserved in national parks and preserves. Pressure is mounting to remove even more old growth timber from harvesting.

According to the Finnish Forest Research Institute about 27 percent of the world's 3.4 billion hectares of land area is covered with forests that have "closed" upper canopies. These closed forests consist of broadleaf and coniferous trees. "Open forests," (also called savannas), usually contain woody shrubs and grasses and are usually found in tropical climates. Coniferous forests are usually found in cooler, drier areas, and broadleaf forests are more prevalent in warmer, moist regions. Tropical forests, such as those found in Southeast Asia, consist almost exclusively of broadleaf, hardwood species. Mixed broadleaf and coniferous forests are found near the boundaries between these two climatic areas, such as in the southern United States. About 42 percent of the world's forests are located in developed countries. The former Soviet Union contains 22 percent of overall forest area.

Coniferous forests are heavily concentrated in the Northern Hemisphere. In fact, 85 percent of all coniferous forests are found in North America and the Commonwealth of Independent States (CIS). Coniferous trees are generally favored for making lumber and pulp for paper products and tend to be intensively cultivated. Hardwood trees, while used to make furniture and paper pulp, tend to be less valuable than softwood.

In the 1970s and 1980s, several countries in the Southern Hemisphere took advantage of their superior tree-growing climate to expand production of several marketable tree species. For example, companies in Brazil established vast eucalyptus (a hardwood) plantations for use in making market pulp, which was then shipped to papermaking operations around the world. Likewise, Chile and New Zealand established large plantations of radiata pine (a softwood), which can be used to make lumber as well as pulp. In the 1990s, these plantations were turning Brazil and Chile, in particular, into formidable competitors in the global forest products industry. According to the World Forest Institute, South American ranked fourth in the industry by 1998. The institute projected that Chile's wood fiber production would double by 2020 and that Argentina and Uruguay would become significant players early in the twenty-first century. Despite the growth of plantation forestry, plantations accounted for less than 5 percent of productive world forests in 2005.

Most modern forestry efforts are guided by the concept of multiple use: using the world's forests simultaneously for harvesting trees, grazing animals, protecting watersheds and wildlife habitats, and providing recreation. This means that foresters must create multiple use plans for vast forested areas in order to balance competing interests. For example, timber production may have the highest priority in less populated rural forests but densely populated urban and suburban areas (or popular travel destinations) will place a higher priority on recreation. In some areas, the multiple-use concept has been replaced by the "ecosystem management" concept, in which forests are managed to reduce all traces of modern human activities. In ecosystem management, harvesting is typically reduced substantially to achieve a desired condition, typically that of the forest before human settlement.

One of the most controversial topics in global politics has been "sustainable development." This is the concept that human industry must be organized in such a way as to be able to sustain itself indefinitely without damaging the earth. The sustained yield concept is very important in forestry management where, according to this theory, a forest is managed in such a way that modest timber crops may be harvested indefinitely. Thus, foresters must precisely calculate net annual growth rates, including total forest growth minus harvesting and losses due to fire, insects, and disease. Sustainable yield focuses on optimal rotation, which is the age at which a crop of trees can be successfully harvested and used (this is different from the familiar concept of crop rotation in field crop agriculture).

Rotation varies widely by species and climate. Trees in subtropical areas which have a year-round growing season and a rich environment grow the fastest. For example, eucalyptus trees in tropical areas can be harvested for pulpwood in just seven years, while pine in the same area takes slightly longer. In the 1990s, advances in genetic research made those short rotations even shorter. In northern Europe and North America, however, the rotation for softwood for wood pulp can be as long as 50 years, though rotation for southern U.S. pine can be as short as 20 to 25 years. Softwood trees used for lumber need between 50 and 100 years of growth in northern climates, while hardwood trees can require as much as 200 years of growth before being used for sawlogs. But due to genetic research by major forest products companies, universities, and government agencies, growth rates in many species are dramatically increasing which was expected to allow northern foresters to compete more effectively with their counterparts in the Southern Hemisphere.

SILVICULTURE

The term "silviculture" describes the forestry science concerned with how trees are reproduced, planted, and then protected and thinned as they grow to maturity. Silviculture can include natural regeneration of a cut stand from seed trees left standing after others are harvested or planting of seedlings on land that has been clearcut. Most silviculture by forest products companies focuses on the planting of seedlings, which allows foresters to alter and improve the genetic composition of trees. Many forest products companies have, through genetic manipulation, produced "super trees" that grow faster, resist insect damage, have fewer knots, and thus make forestland more productive.

Softwood seedlings are grown in vast seed orchards before they are planted, either mechanically or by hand, in newly cut lands. Competing weeds and grasses are sometimes removed to help the trees grow faster. In the late 1990s and early 2000s, many companies increased the use of small doses of herbicides to control weeds that can retard seedling growth.

Wildlife management is also an important part of forestry. Every major change in a forest; such as wildfire, hurricanes, or harvesting, benefits some wildlife species and harms others. Critics of industrial forestry charge that creation of large tracts of artificially planted trees, often of the same species, inhibits biodiversity. Industrial foresters counter that while some species may be hurt by this approach, others thrive. Industrial forests may support as diverse a group of wildlife as forests that are allowed to grow, mature, and decline naturally.

BACKGROUND AND DEVELOPMENT

It is believed that early humans used wood for fuel at least 750,000 years ago. It is not clear exactly when humans began to cultivate trees, but they have been grown from seeds or cuttings since biblical times. The Romans imported seedlings from elsewhere in the Mediterranean area and Germany. They planted large groves of trees such as those in Lebanon and Carthage and regulated the cutting and use of wood resources. However, when the Roman Empire fell, its forests were overcut and overgrazed. Fires destroyed many forested areas. When forests were overcut, the land was degraded by soil erosion and the subsequent silting of streams and harbors. Many of the forests became unusable scrubland.

In medieval Europe, forestry was the domain of feudal landowners who regulated forests to preserve hunting grounds. They allowed peasants to gather fuel and timber. It is believed that the systematic management of forests began in the German states during the sixteenth century. Under the German system, each forest property was divided into sections for harvesting and regeneration on a regular rotation so as to ensure a sustainable timber yield.

Silviculture is believed to have begun in the 1500s in England, where landowners were urged to produce artificial tree plantations. By the 1990s, virtually all of Britain's woodlands consisted of planted woodlands. While other countries maintained more of their natural forests, most forested areas in the heavily populated Northern Hemisphere had been cut by man at some time, leaving a very small amount of virgin forests. Formal education in forestry apparently began in the nineteenth century when Germany, France, and England founded private forestry schools. German foresters were particularly skilled and were highly sought after in many other countries.

The twentieth century saw the steady growth of national forest laws and policies that protected woodlands and regulated the increased use of forest resources to satisfy the rapidly multiplying demand for timber and paper products. In the 1930s, countries in North America and Europe began repairing the extensive damage done by the relatively unregulated deforestation of the industrial revolution. Beginning in the 1940s, vast land reclamation was undertaken in the Mediterranean region, including Greece, Israel, Italy, Spain, and North Africa. These efforts were needed to save soil cover and protect watersheds. Some countries are fighting a losing battle in forestry. For example, in China, where forests once extended over 30 percent of the land, centuries of overcutting, grazing, and fires reduced forests to 7 percent of total land area.

CURRENT CONDITIONS

Despite the strain on wood supply that occurred in the mid-1990s as a result of logging bans in several countries, some experts were optimistic about the future of world forestry. They anticipated that after 2010, when many current plantations in the Southern Hemisphere would be ready for harvesting, wood supply might be plentiful. While there may be severe shortages in wood coming from the world's forests in the 2000s, supply should eventually catch up with demand. Some experts also felt that with prudent management, faster growth cycles, and a political solution to the debate over forest preservation, North America would likely be able to support increased harvests and should return to forestry self-sufficiency in the future.

Other observers, however, predict that higher demand and restrictions on supply were likely to cause serious disturbances in the global timber supply system early in the twenty-first century, as supply was cut in some areas, such as North America, and increased in others, such as South America. Rapidly growing demand from China, for example, which imported 1.5 billion cubic feet of timber in 2003 and was poised to become the world's largest consumer of wood by 2010, could pose a significant threat to world supply, according to WWF statistics published by CNN. While domestic consumption has increased, China has been unable to meet demand because of logging bans that went into effect in parts of the country after devastating floods in 1998. The WWF called for China to improve its forest management to boost production, and to enforce regulations to hinder imports of illegally harvested logs. China's rapidly growing demand for paper and packaging products(it was the world's largest consumer in the early 2000s)was expected to lead to significant changes in that country's forestry industry. To meet domestic demand for pulpwood China planned to develop 12.5 million acres of plantation forests to produce fast-growing trees suitable for use in pulp and paper manufacture. This plan suggested that China, which had traditionally made paper from mostly non-wood fibers, would switch to wood-based paper production.

As traditional supply sources are restricted and underused or newly developed resources are brought into the supply cycle, governments and forest products companies will need to make additional investments in global infrastructure, land/timber management, and environmental protection. All of these factors are expected to drive up global costs for logs and pulpwood, according to some observers. In addition, wood product usage tends to go up considerably in times of economic plenty.

As with other industries in the twenty-first century, the forestry industry was expected to experience increasing numbers of consolidations similar to the takeover of U.S.-based Willamette by Weyerhaeuser Co. in January 2002. Following pressure put on Willamette stockholders and employees by Weyerhaeuser Co., Willamette Industries Inc. yielded and agreed to be taken over for a cash payment of and assumption of debt service amounting to more than US$7 million. Weyerhaeuser chairman and chief executive officer Steven Rogel was a former Willamette employee, and his takeover bid was resented by some in Willamette's top management. In 2002 he told a University of Washington business class that consolidations had become the natural order of things in the cutthroat competition among forestry companies in the twenty-first century. The takeover and economic conditions in 2001 dropped earnings to about 50 percent of 2000 earnings, but by March 2001, Weyerhaeuser announced that its shares had jumped $1.19 to US$64, an 18 percent increase that brought stock value to near-2000 levels. Frank Waung, senior economist at Societe Generale told a reporter from *The News Tribune* in 2002 that Weyerhaeuser seemed to be poised for full recovery as the economy rebounded and the demand for boxes increased. The pickup of Willamette put Weyerhaeuser Co. into the number-two slot in size among U.S. companies.

DEFORESTATION THREATS

While forest cover is gradually increasing in most parts of the Northern Hemisphere, the Southern Hemisphere continues to experience brisk deforestation. Between 1981 and 1990, over 15 million hectares of tropical rain forests were cut and/or burned out of a total forest area in the tropics of just under 2 billion hectares. A similar rate of destruction continued well into the 2000s. The destruction of the rain forest is a complex economic story and is largely separate from the establishment of tree plantations in the same area. Contrary to popular belief, most tree plantations in the Southern Hemisphere are on land that has already been cleared and used for agriculture.

The major causes of tropical deforestation appear to be poverty, inappropriate development, weak political institutions, monopolistic land ownership, low agricultural productivity, and rapidly expanding populations. Close to half of the rain forest area lost each year is cleared by landless farmers who then move on to new tracts in following years. Land clearing for permanent agriculture is the second leading cause of deforestation, followed by the cutting of wood for heating and cooking. Another frequent use of cut wood by smugglers is in the form of plywood, which is easily loaded on ships for sale to unscrupulous merchants.

Much of the rain forest debate has focused on Brazil, which has the world's largest reserves of rain forest. One of the conflicts over the rain forest is between rubber tappers, who extract rubber from rubber trees without killing them, and ranchers and farmers who clearcut rain forest for pasture or cropland. In the early 1970s, the Brazilian government wanted to open rain forest areas for development. With the assistance of the World Bank, the government built roads and helped people buy land in the rain forests. Rubber tappers and nut gatherers, who traditionally worked this land, were removed. Some of the rubber tappers organized opposition groups. Farmers and ranchers reacted with violent, and sometimes murderous, confrontations. In the 1990s, however, the Brazilian government moved to further slow the destruction of rain forests, though results have been mixed. By the early 2000s, Brazil had increased its area of certified forests to slightly more than 1 million hectares.

Southeast Asian nations also aggressively cut their huge forest reserves from the 1970s to the 2000s. Much of the output went to Japan, which, with its extremely limited forest resources and affluent population, had a seemingly insatiable demand for tropical hardwood. In the 1980s Malaysia cut more tropical trees than any country except Indonesia and Brazil. The rate of forest clearance in Asia tripled from 1960 to the mid-1990s. Some countries in Southeast Asia have already felled the vast majority of their trees without replanting them. While forests occupied 60 percent of the Philippines in 1950, just 10 percent remained forested in 1994; by 2005 this figure had fallen to about 7 percent. The situation was also urgent in Africa, home of the world's second-largest rain forest, which stretches across 500 million acres and 10 countries in the Congo River basin. By 2005, it was estimated that illegal logging and poaching in this region contributed to the loss of 3.7 million acres of forest land each year. In 2005, seven Central African countries signed a treaty aimed to preserve the remaining tracts of forest; in particular, nations agreed to streamline and enforce logging regulations. It remained doubtful, however, that the treaty would prove effective in the face of entrenched government corruption among the signatories.

In addition, attempts by Indonesia to change its forestry strategies in the 1990s apparently had been defeated in the 2000s. The Indonesian military government under President Suharto in the mid-1990s had required companies that acquired the right to cut trees on state land to replant areas that they cut, but lawlessness and corruption won out following Suharto's ousting in 1998. In part because of corruption that allowed local province leaders to give permits to crooked loggers without restrictions, the forests of Tanjung Putting and Kalimantan were likely to disappear in the first decade of the twenty-first century. In large part, the blame for the depletion of forests and the resultant floods that have devastated parts of Indonesia can be shared by Malaysia, China, and Japan, which have allowed shiploads of illegal shipments with impunity. Indonesia's exported wood products, valued at US$6.5 billion in 2002, are shipped in the form of plywood, sawmill-quality timber, pulp and wood products such as furniture. As world pressure on the Indonesians increased in the 2000s, exports diminished slightly to a projected US$4 billion. Yet analysts contend that illegal logging continues almost unchecked. Indeed, according to the environmental organization Rainforest Information Centre, as much as 90 percent of all industrial wood extraction in Indonesia in 2004 was illegal. While just under 7 million cubic meters was harvested legally under government quota, some 80 million cubic meters was cut that year for illegal export as plywood, pulp, and sawmill timber.

For years, some environmental advocates argued that forestry practices, particularly in Indonesia, remained unsustainable. For example, the EEPSEA/WWF study of the 1997 forest fires in Indonesia found that the fires were promoted by several "poorly designed policies" including:

- a program to drain and convert one million hectares of peat forest to rice cultivation;
- confusing land ownership laws that encouraged people to clear land as a way of staking a claim to that land;
- weak enforcement of laws to regulate the use of fire for land clearing;
- policies that keep the prices of wood to processing mills low; and
- short-term leases of forest land to timber companies which leave them with little incentive to manage forest sustainability.

The EPPSEA/WWF study found that direct damages from the fires (not including the haze that blanketed the region) topped US$3 billion, including US$493 million in timber losses; US$470 million in foregone agricultural production; US$1.8 billion in ecological services provided by forests (such as food and medicine, water supply, and erosion control); and US$272 million for the contribution to global warming.

As a result of such problems, in the mid- to late-1990s international pressure was growing for tropical timber producers to certify whether logs were produced using sustainable forestry methods. While producers initially resisted this demand, without certification they faced the prospect of losing sales in Europe and the United States—top markets for high-value wood products. Both Indonesia and Malaysia began certification procedures in the early 2000s.

While reforestation is widely considered a laudable goal, not all reforestation projects are free of controversy. For example, the Environmental Defense Fund (EDF), a U.S. environmental group, attacked the World Bank's funding of a project to grow eucalyptus trees in India in the early 1990s. The eucalyptus tree, according to EDF, crowds out other vegetation, uses too much water, and is used exclusively for industrial purposes. According to the EDF, much of the eucalyptus crop in India was not being used for firewood and its cultivation was displacing subsistence farmers.

EFFECT OF RECYCLING ON FORESTRY

In the mid-1990s, Europe experienced a boom in paper recycling as the result of restrictive packaging laws. One of the reasons given for increasing paper recycling in Europe and elsewhere was to reduce the consumption of virgin fiber made from wood pulp. Ironically, however, increased recycling in Europe may have a negative effect on forest health, according to a report by the Food and Agriculture Organization of the United Nations (FAO). As recycling rates in Europe increased in the 1990s to meet stringent regulations, industries consumed increasing amounts of wastepaper and the demand and price for small diameter pulpwood decreased. In some areas, prices paid for small diameter trees dropped below the cost of harvesting them. This was one of the reasons that European forest landowners reduced their management of existing timber stands in the 1990s. Instead of thinning (cutting) small diameter trees, these trees were allowed to continue growing.

While this may seem to be a good thing, an unmanaged forest eventually produces a diminished value of forest products. According to foresters, a well-managed forest—one that is periodically thinned—will produce a larger volume of higher value forest products than an unmanaged forest. Stands that grow too thick may become "stagnant" with small-sized, low-quality trees competing for diminished nutrition and sunlight. Undesirable species of trees may also begin growing. A crowded forest is also more susceptible to fire, insects, and disease. As of the early 2000s, whether the poor market for pulpwood would lead to permanent changes in forestry in Europe was not established.

EFFECTS OF CUTBACKS

Severe cutbacks on harvests in the U.S. Pacific Northwest begun in the early 1990s appeared to have become more or less permanent, the effects of these cutbacks became clearer. Logging restrictions reduced the annual harvest of trees from federal land in the northwestern United States in the late 1990s to less than 20 percent of levels in the 1980s. Also, additional restrictions in British Columbia further curtailed timber cutting.

The growing shortfall in North American softwood supplies was expected to be made up by increased harvesting in other major wood producing regions, particularly in Western and Eastern Europe, the Nordic countries, and the Southern Hemisphere. While Japan has the potential for increased cutting, it was not expected to produce more softwood due to high operating costs, the structure of forest ownership, and high labor costs.

The shortfall in North American softwood production was further exacerbated by increased competition from softwood plantations in Chile, New Zealand, and Australia. To address this issue, Canada implemented its Forest 2020 initiative, which aimed to increase yields in Canadian forests through genetic improvements of tree stocks and through the introduction of fast-growth plantations.

While harvesting restrictions in the U.S. Pacific Northwest were intended to reduce the damage associated with tree harvesting, Roger Sedjo, a fellow with the research group Resources for the Future, argued that such timber bans will simply relocate damage by stimulating increases in timber harvests in other parts of the world. Many of these alternative areas are difficult to replant or renew, which means that more environmental damage will be done on a global basis, not less. For example, if timber cutting shifts to old growth forests in South America, environmental damage could be severe. Also, the Russian Federation, with its vast timber holdings, is a likely candidate for future development. Russia's unforgiving climate makes timber regeneration difficult in many eastern Russian forests. Shipping of cut trees is also problematic due to outdated equipment such as skidders and the challenges of geography in areas of Siberia where roads do not exist or are of poor quality.

RESEARCH AND TECHNOLOGY

The primary purpose of research in forestry is to produce hybrid trees that grow faster, are more resistant to disease, and produce better lumber. This science is called "high-yield forestry" and is particularly important in cooler climates, where trees grow much more slowly than in warmer areas.

Amid pressures to preserve more land, faster growing trees would allow the forestry industry to reduce the amount of forestland it needs to produce the same amount of wood. This would neutralize one of the arguments against using trees to make lumber and paper. However, developing more "super trees" will require major investments in plant biology and other high-tech genetic research. This area in particular will require more extensive networking between forestry companies, research institutions, and government agencies.

Another area of forestry research is carbon dioxide uptake. Excess carbon dioxide in the atmosphere, which contributes to global warming, is caused largely by the burning of fossil fuels. Young, growing trees consume large amounts of carbon dioxide and produce large amounts of oxygen. (As trees mature, this cycle is eventually reversed.) Planting billions of young trees may help fight global warming by capturing carbon dioxide.

Another major research area in forestry is in the relatively new topic of biodiversity. This was one of the most publicized topics to emerge from the 1992 United Nations Conference on Environment and Development (The Earth Summit) held in Rio de Janeiro. Since then, there has been much discussion and research concerning the benefits of maintaining the maximum amount of biological diversity through preserving more of the world's forests.

A study of tropical forests (which contain 50 to 90 percent of the world's species)found that if deforestation continues at rates equal to those reached in the early 1990s, between 17 percent and 35 percent of the world's rain forests would be destroyed by 2040. If this occurs, between 7,300 and 27,000 plant and animal species (out of 10 million known varieties in the mid-1990s) would become extinct each year. In 2002, a special United Nations task force was launched to attempt to address the problem of threatened species due to deforestation of trees.

Much of research on biodiversity has focused on Southeast Asia. In August 1994, the governments of Indonesia, Japan, and the United States signed the Indonesian Biodiversity Conservation Program (IBCP), with the goal of studying, managing, and conserving Indonesia's rich biological resources. This type of cooperative effort is critical to maintain biodiversity.

MAJOR COUNTRIES IN THE INDUSTRY

RUSSIA

In Russia, journalists have joked that money may not grow on trees, but the forestry industry could represent about US$100 billion annually if the government spearheaded attempts to modernize the industry, noted a 2002 white paper written by the Union of Forestry Industrialists and Exporters. Russia in 2002 represented 2.3 percent of the world's timber and paper products, a small amount since it boasts the largest forest reserves of any country on earth—about 23 percent of the total. Russia's forestry industry plunged into in crisis after the Communist regime was overturned in the early 1990s; under chaotic economic conditions, Russian timber exports declined. But beginning in 1999 the industry saw a significant upward trend, with increased private investment in forestry infrastructure. As a result, the Russian forestry industry took steps toward more efficient and transparent corporate management. Once forestry began to recover, however, competition among private investors in the sector led to several power scrambles between 2000 and 2004, which prevented the industry from achieving the higher production levels and profits that had been the goal of reform.

Despite these challenges, some analysts saw significant opportunities for improvement in Russia's forestry sector in the early 2000s. Government investment and tax concessions, which have been periodically discussed, could boost output in many regions; the influx of cash from overseas investors, too, is expected to contribute to significant growth. There are vast areas of native forest in eastern Russia and the terrain is relatively flat, making logging easier. Also, being in a very cold climate, Russian forests contain considerably less biodiversity than tropical forests, so damage to wildlife habitat is less controversial. Yet, according to 2002 statistics published by *The Russia Journal,* Russia cuts only 15 percent of the 700 million cubic meters it could harvest annually.

Other aspects of Russia's eastern forests suggest that increased logging may cause serious environmental problems. Russia's eastern forests have a relatively low volume of timber per acre, meaning that very large areas would have to be logged in order to produce acceptable timber volume. In addition, it is difficult to regenerate timber in many eastern Russian forests, particularly in the colder regions in the north. This could raise the costs of forestry and perhaps tempt logging operations not to replant harvested forest areas. Lands that do not have an adequate forest cover for long periods of time can suffer severe environmental damage.

CANADA

Canada has over 260 million hectares of forests in eight major forest zones from the Atlantic to Pacific Oceans. That represents about 50 percent of its total land area. Canada contains 10 percent of the world's forests and accounts for about 18 percent of the world's forest products exports. Canada's exports of lumber slipped in the 1990s in total value, in part because of U.S. reluctance to allow additional shipments of lumber exports in the country. The U.S. timber industry has argued that Canada's production and pricing unfairly subsidize Canadian logging, since most of the country's timber is cut from government-owned land and is sold below market value. Pressure from U.S. timber companies resulted in stiff tariffs on Canadian lumber, which in 2004 stood at 27 percent but were to 17.18 percent in early 2005. Canada has strenuously rejected U.S. claims of subsidies, and has sought adjudication of the matter through a NAFTA trade dispute panel.

Each year, about one million hectares—or 0.5 percent of Canada's productive forest land—is harvested, a level that may be permanently sustained. Canada's vast forest resources have been a key element of its economy for hundreds of years. As of the early 2000s, forest products were Canada's largest source of export income; they accounted for 20 percent of world trade in manufactured forest products in 2003. Forests support Canada's largest manufacturing industry, which exports pulp, paper, paperboard, and wood products to more than 100 countries.

In Canada, 51 million hectares of forests have been removed from harvesting, an area equivalent to half the forest area of the European Union. In Canada's "heritage forests," 27 million hectares have been removed, and in its "protection forests," 24 million hectares have been removed. Another 193 million hectares are open forests with no commercial activity. Of the 209 million hectares classified as commercial, productive forests, 112 million hectares were as of 2004 managed for timber production.

Of Canada's forestland, 80 percent was owned by the provincial governments, 11 percent by the national government, and 9 percent by private landowners. Forestry operations were inextricably tied to changes in government policy. Canada's high level of government ownership was a contrast to 40 percent public ownership in the United States and 28 percent in Sweden. In the 1990s, provincial governments in Canada responded to pressure from environmental groups by restricting logging on a greater percentage of public land. In British Columbia (BC), for example, the provincial government proposed banning logging on about 12 percent of BC forestland, up from about 8 percent. Environmental groups would like to increase that percentage further.

As timber restrictions reduce available timber in Canada, there have been calls for more intensive cultivation of forests that remain open to logging. This would involve bringing middle-aged timber stands into production sooner by using precommercial and commercial thinning and fertilization.

In the 1990s and 2000s, Canadian forest managers began adopting "ecosystem-based planning," an approach that attempts to balance the natural processes of forest ecosystems with sustainable economic benefits and includes the objectives of biodiversity conservation. In 1995 Canada adopted national certification standards for sustainable forest management, developed under the oversight of the Canadian Standards Association. Canadian forest managers were adopting new, lower-impact harvesting technologies and strategies that speed regeneration. Where appropriate, clearcutting was replaced by other harvesting methods, such as selective cutting and the use of "seed trees."

UNITED STATES

Despite holding just 4 percent of the world's forestland, the United States is the world's leader in the production of wood and paper. Many U.S. forests are intensively managed for wood production. Despite its enormous appetite for wood, as of 2004 the United States still had 70 percent of the forests that stood in 1600.

In the United States about 67 percent of all forest lands, about the equivalent of 488 million acres (393 million acres suitable for wood industry use) are owned by private companies, individual states, Indian tribes, or individuals, according to the National Coalition for Sustaining America's Non-Federal Forests, an activist group. According to the University of Georgia Forest Department research, about 7 million private owners own 288 million acres of timberlands in the United States that do not engage directly in harvesting of trees for industry purposes. The remaining lands are under the jurisdiction of the federal government. The coalition was formed with the intent of protecting U.S. forests outside direct government control against losses due to building sprawl, industry cutting, and tree diseases. The coalition listed its intention of addressing present and future forest challenges identified by the National Research Council in a 1998 investigation of the state of the nation's forest areas. The ultimate goal was to assure future generations that all non-federal lands would be subject to proper stewardship practices or that accountability for violations would be assessed.

In the United States, as of 2004, 247 million acres are reserved from harvest by law or are slow-growing woodlands unsuitable for timber production. Another 490 million acres are called timberlands—forests that can produce more than 20 cubic feet of wood per acre annually. Between 1952 and 1992, the amount of hardwoods growing in the United States increased 82 percent, from 184.1 million cubic feet to 335.7 million cubic feet, while the amount of softwoods increased 4 percent, from 431.8 million cubic feet to 449.9 million cubic feet.

With many forest products companies and government agencies sponsoring research into forestry practices, the United States is clearly a leader in world forestry. In the 1990s, as environmental demands grew, U.S. foresters began to examine the concept of sustainable forestry. In 1994 the forest products industry—through its trade group, the American Forest and Paper Association (AF&PA)—announced the Sustainable Forestry Initiative (SFI). This initiative binds member companies of the AF&PA to a set of forest principles and detailed guidelines that require companies to reforest harvested land promptly; provide for wildlife habitat; minimize the visual impact of harvesting; improve water quality and ecosystem diversity; and protect forestland of special ecological significance. The SFI requires detailed reporting of forest management practices by member companies, and the information is then released in annual reports to the public on the progress made toward achieving sustainable forestry. Under SFI, AF&PA members are committed to reforest their forestland within two years of final harvest by planting or direct seeding or within five years using planned natural regeneration.

Another matter of critical importance is the protection of forested lands from wildfires. In 2003, after catastrophic fires destroyed more than 1.8 million acres of forests in the western part of the country, President George W. Bush signed the Healthy Forests Initiative, which funded measures to thin dense undergrowth in public forests and thereby reduce the risk. According to a White House press release, more than 2.24 million acres of overgrown forests were thinned in 2002, and 2.57 million acres were slated for thinning in 2003. In 2006, according to a USDA report, the initiative was expected to reduce fire hazards and insect infestation on almost 4.3 million additional acres.

In 2005 the undisputed leader of the world forest industry was International Paper, which controlled more than 8 million acres of forests in the United States and 1.5 million acres in Brazil. Harder economic times and a general economic slowdown after the terrorist attacks of September 11, 2001 cut profits for the giant, but it continued to show profit margins nonetheless. With operations in almost 40 countries worldwide, IP employed about 83,000 people in 2003 and posted total sales in 2004 of US$25.5 billion.

Weyerhaeuser Company, with forest holdings of 6.4 million acres in the United States and 30 million acres of leased forests in Canada, remained one of the largest U.S. forest products producers. The company reported total 2004 sales of US$22.6 billion, and employed more than 53,000 people.

FURTHER READING

"As Weyerhaeuser profit falls, so does CEO's pay," *Seattle Times,* 7 March, 2002.

Canadian Department of Foreign Affairs and International Trade. *Building Momentum: Sustainable Development in Canada.* 1997.

Embassy of Brazil, London, England. "Certified Forests," 2002. Available from www.brazil.org.uk.

"Chile Fires." *EFE News Service,* 25 February 2002.

Clements, Barbara. "Consolidation Is Par for Course in Timber Industry, Weyerhaeuser CEO Says." *The News Tribune,* 21 February 2002.

"Congo Basin Nations Pledge to Save Forest." MSNBC (7 February 2005). Available from http://msnbc.msn.com/.

Crouching Fiber, Paper Dragon: China and the Global Paper Market. Metafore, 2004. Available from http://www.metafore.org/.

Finnish Forest Research Institute. *World Forest Statistics,* 1995. Available from www.for.gov.bc.ca/.

"Indonesia's Forests in Crisis." Rainforest Information Centre, January 2004. Available from www.rainforestinfo.org.au/.

International Paper Company Profile. International Paper, 2005. Available from www.ipaper.com.

Office of the White House, Washington, DC. *President Bush Promotes Healthy Forests in Arizona,* August 2003. Available from www.whitehouse.gov/.

Reforestation: Growing Tomorrow's Forests Today. Washington, DC: American Forest & Paper Association, 1998.

Sandul, Irina and Claire Bigg. "Russian Forestry Still a Thieves' Market." *The Russia Journal,* 7 March 2004. Available from www.therussiajournal.com.

Sedjo, Roger A., "Ecosystem Management: An Uncharted Path for Public Forests." *Resources for the Future* (fall 1995): 10.

ldquo;Timber Industry 2000-2004." *Kommersant,* 10 March 2005. Available from http://www.kommersant.com/.

United Nations, Food and Agriculture Organization. "Fires Are Increasingly Damaging the World's Forests,"" 9 September 2003. Available from fao.org/.

U.S. Department of Agriculture. "Bush Administration Proposes Increased Funding for FY 2006 to Maintain and Restore Forest and Rangeland Health," 3 February 2005. Available from www.usda.gov/.

———. "Tree Planting Statistics for the United States," 2003. Available from www.forestry.about.com/.

World Forest Institute. *South America: Overview,* 2003. Available from www.worldforestry.org.

Virgin, Bill. "Weyerhaeuser Finally Wins; Willamette Gives In". *Seattle Post Intelligencer,* 22 January 2002.

CHEMICALS

SIC 2891

NAICS 325520

ADHESIVES AND SEALANTS

Adhesive and sealant makers produce such diverse bonding compounds as caulking, glues, epoxies, rubber cements, and related products for household and commercial use.

INDUSTRY SNAPSHOT

The adhesives and sealants industry was increasingly competitive during the mid-2000s. *Chemical Week,* an industry magazine, placed the 2003 world market for adhesives and sealants at US$18.5 billion with a market growth of 3 percent over 2002 despite an economic recession affecting North American, Japanese and Western European markets. A study done by the Freedonia Group projected global demand of these products to rise 4.2 percent per year to 16.6 million metric tons by 2004. Projections for the industrialized market through the year 2006 were 4 to 5 percent, slightly above Gross Domestic Product (GDP) and additional demand of 845,000 metric tons, with emerging markets forecast at 4 to 7 percent growth per year. Plagued by high raw materials and energy costs, in addition to still uncertain auto and construction markets, companies in the industry were adapting products and expanding product lines to serve new market trends.

While adhesive prices rose substantially in 2003 and 2004, the cost of raw materials had, in many cases, increased even more, offsetting revenue gains. This was one of the factors prompting expectations that mergers and acquisitions (M&A) were set to increase rapidly. According to ChemQuest Group Inc., the top companies in the industry command less than half of the market worldwide.

In 2003 and early 2004, sales of adhesives and sealants had increased in North America, Latin America, Europe, and Asia. According to ChemQuest, North America and Western Europe held a 54 percent market share of the global adhesives industry in 2001. The fastest growing non-pressure-sensitive adhesive markets in North America in 2001 were auto interior, electronic, and film lamination, while the fastest growing markets in Western Europe were furniture manufacturing, auto exterior, and film lamination. In contrast, developing countries such as India and China were growing at three times the U.S. rate in the mid-2000s. The Americas accounted for 36 percent of market share in this sector, followed by Europe at 34 percent, the Asia-Pacific region with 27 percent, and the rest of the world making up the remaining 3 percent. Excluding Japan, Asia had 61 percent of the market total in developing regions for 2003. Asia and Latin America, which had 23 percent of the market for developing countries in 2003, promised to provide continuing sales growth for makers of adhesives and sealants.

In the U.S., forecasted figures for 2006 gave non-rigid bonding adhesives a commanding 23 percent share of the market. Packaging adhesives were close behind with 22 percent, followed by construction with 17 percent. The remaining percentages were expected to be distributed among all other adhesive segments, according to *Market Share Reporter.*

ORGANIZATION AND STRUCTURE

Makers of adhesives and sealants have historically located their production facilities at sites that combined three factors: ready availability of raw materials, customers' production facilities nearby, and a skilled workforce. For this reason, both the largest producers and consumers of adhesives and sealants are located in the most heavily industrialized countries of the world, notably Western Europe, the United States, and Japan.

The market is centered around several industries that use large amounts of adhesives and sealants: automobiles, housing, aircraft, and packaging. The United Nations' commodity export statistics on several categories of natural and man-made adhesives reported US$6.5 billion in exports in 1991. With the exception of Europe, where a lingering recession led to continued sluggish sales through the mid-1990s, the market overall grew steadily toward the year 2000.

By 1995, almost all of the major consumers of adhesives and sealants showed signs of recovery from the recession of the early part of the decade. Most producers of sealants and adhesives, particularly those not heavily tied to Europe's markets, experienced a very healthy 1994. Europeans and makers of bulk chemicals experienced overcapacity and subsequent low prices that hurt some companies and helped others.

Car sales boomed in the mid-1990s in the United States, as recovery from the recession of the early 1990s released pent-up demand and low interest rates gave consumers the ability to buy. U.S. auto sales in 1994 were 15.4 million units, and analysts projected 16.1 million units to be sold in America in 1995, with the trend rising. Globally, auto sales were expected to move upward as improved economies in Latin America, the North American Free Trade Agreement (NAFTA), and growth in Southeast Asia boosted demand in those areas. Volkswagen AG of Germany, France's Peugeot-Citroën, and U.S.-based Chrysler Corporation and General Motors set up joint ventures in China to take advantage of lower labor costs and the expectation of rising demand in Asia for vehicles.

In construction, new housing starts in the United States shot up in the early 1990s as mortgage rates fell drastically during the recession. Buyers took advantage of the lowest mortgage rates since World War II, as well as considerable recession-driven price drops in major housing markets such as Los Angeles and Washington, D.C. The largest builders of commercial and industrial projects saw their markets also recover and were predicting continued steady growth as long as interest rates remained low. Adhesive and sealant makers noted a strong pickup in the do-it-yourself market by the mid-1990s, and sales of existing homes bore that out. Both Europe and North America saw a recession-driven growth in the do-it-yourself markets as homeowners repaired or upgraded existing dwellings.

The headquarters of leading manufacturers of military and civilian aircraft are located in the United States, Europe, and the Commonwealth of Independent States. Components are made in many countries, mainly in the United States and Europe, but also in Canada, Asia, and Latin America. The military market, which had dropped since 1991, was extremely poor in the early and mid-1990s, with tens of thousands of workers in the United States alone being laid off and major companies disappearing in acquisition deals. Demand for commercial aircraft rose after mid-decade, with flights increasing as the recession lessened. Asia, with its large population, was expected to grow at the most rapid rate, prompting U.S.-based Boeing and McDonnell Douglas to export some assembly work to China in attempts to gain market share there.

Forest products companies in North America and Europe were greatly affected by environmental laws that prompted large scale recycling, particularly of newsprint and consumer packaging. By the mid-1990s, pulp and lumber prices were still high, causing wood producers to increase their use of adhesives to turn more of the sawdust and short pieces into usable building products. Packaging companies, in turn, turned to newer specialty adhesives to help them keep profit margins up by offering niche or custom-made packaging.

Makers of household and office appliances, including computers, continued to see sales rise through the mid-1990s in North America. Improving economies and opening markets in developing nations sent major consumer goods manufacturers overseas in search of new markets by the turn of the century. Consumer goods makers like Avon, Gillette, Procter & Gamble, Duracell, and Colgate in the United States, Belgium's Alcatel Bell Telephone Manufacturing, and Japan's Matsushita Electronics Corporation, Hitachi TV Company, and Sanyo Electric, all entered the mainland Chinese market, and several companies established joint ventures. Adhesive maker H.B. Fuller Company of Minneapolis (U.S.) also opened for business in China in 1986 and by 1992 began to show a profit selling to packaging and consumer goods firms there. Unilever, a joint Netherlands/United Kingdom-owned company, announced plans in 1993 to open a manufacturing subsidiary in Korea to make Ablestik brand adhesives for electronics manufacturers in Asia. Unilever later sold its adhesives business to Imperial Chemical Industries.

BACKGROUND AND DEVELOPMENT

Adhesives and sealants have been used by many civilizations worldwide for thousands of years. Egyptians glued caskets shut in 3000 B.C. using animal byproducts; the Romans used albumin from dried blood; and casein, a milk protein, was used by the ancient Chinese and Mediterranean peoples. The first glue factory was built in 1690 in the Netherlands.

Adhesive substances have been and still are made from animal byproducts, including hide, bones, and blood; from vegetables such as soybeans, cassava, corn and potatoes; from tree resins; and from fish. Anti-gelling agents are added during manufacturing to keep the glue from solidifying in the tube or can.

Synthetic resins, developed in the 1920s and first manufactured cheaply in the 1930s, changed many adhesive-dependent industries with their strength and durability. They are especially suitable for high stress applications, such as aircraft and automobiles, but one of the industry's key markets is the more mundane world of envelopes, cellophane tape, and packaging. Hot melt adhesives were invented to temporarily tack labels on canned food. Hot varnish emulsified in a casein solution was designed to resist water and allowed combatants in World War II to dump supplies into the South Pacific and float them ashore. Self-adhesive labels, consisting of a sandwich of paper, a release coating, an adhesive, and a paper liner, fit the needs of the computer age. U.S.-based Minnesota Mining and Manufacturing Co. (3M) had a strongly favorable response from the market when it introduced Post-its, small adhesive-backed memo slips of paper made up into pads that could be pulled off and stuck on again.

Adhesives are also a critical ingredient in plywood and other manufactured construction components. These gained increasing use worldwide as a growing global population and a dwindling supply of forest products created demand for construction materials that wasted less of each tree and polluted less.

Leaders in the industry have been successful because they have had access to raw materials, chemistry know-how that was transferable to the related field of adhesives and sealants, and proximity to manufacturers needing the end product. Six of the eight countries leading in the production of adhesives and sealants had both oil production or refining capabilities and significant automobile and/or aircraft production facilities to buy the adhesives. Finland and Switzerland are adjacent to other European countries, such as France, Germany, Italy, Russia, and Sweden, that manufacture cars and aircraft.

The rise of synthetics meant an increasing dependence on oil, and the industry needed a reliable flow of petroleum at a reasonable price for the factories. The Oil Producing and Exporting Countries' (OPEC) oil embargo of the 1970s drove oil prices much higher, but more stable prices in the early 1990s contributed to a glut of product, pushing oil prices so low that oil industry profits suffered.

Fears of fluctuating oil prices began a move by the industry in the 1970s to develop non-petroleum based synthetics. The cyanoacrylates ("super glues") became popular, as did the two-part emulsion polymer isocyanate adhesives patented in Japan during that decade.

Another development of the 1970s that greatly affected the industry was an increasing awareness of the effects of man-made chemicals on the environment. Adhesives and sealants came under close scrutiny as possible contributors to "indoor pollution." Buildings constructed to be energy-efficient were sealed tightly from outside air, and particle board, paneling, window sealants, wallpaper paste, carpet and flooring adhesives, as well as fumes given off by adhesives, paints, and plastics in the appliances, furniture, and computers, came under suspicion as sources of possible toxicity. Criticism also came because petroleum-based adhesives required petroleum-based solvents to manufacture and remove, and concern arose over the effects of solvents on air and water quality. State and national governments acted to control the use, manufacture, application, and disposal of adhesives and sealants, and manufacturers moved to change formulations whenever possible to water-based, rather than petroleum-based products.

Current Conditions

By 2004 the world adhesives and sealants market had reached US$18.5 billion. While the industry had consolidated in the late 1990s and early 2000s, it remained fragmented with many small and mid-sized firms.

Due to weakening demand in various markets and high raw material costs, many companies in the industry set forth new business initiatives that included cost cutting, consolidation, global expansion, and product diversification. While the industry had looked to both the auto and construction markets for the majority of its sales in the past, new uses for adhesives continued to positively affect the North American and Western European markets. For example, demand for new adhesives applications in the medical industry, including use in transdermal drug patches, assembled disposable syringes, and tissue bonding and skin repair, forced major industry leaders including Henkel to spend heavily in research and development in order to take advantage of growth potential. In early 2002 Henkel, through its Loctite subsidiary, had tissue-bonding adhesives up for FDA approval. The products already had been cleared in Europe.

According to industry executives, portions of the medical adhesives market were growing by as much as 30 percent per year. The industry also continued to capture market share from mechanical fasteners. Sales growth in the electronics adhesives market was at 6 percent per year, up from the 2 to 4 percent adhesives average. The industry also was expected to benefit from changing demand in the construction industry, with more than an average of 4 percent annual growth expected through 2009. This would be caused by a shift to engineered wood that requires specialty adhesives, as well as the explosive growth of the market in China.

The industry's performance typically varied with both demand for its products and the cost of its raw materials. During 2003 the price of raw materials—from 20 to 80 percent— and energy costs were high, putting pressure on profit margins. As demand increased in new markets for new products, merger and acquisition activity continued in the 2000s, but at a slower pace. Companies eyed acquisitions as a way to diversify product lines and expand into higher-margin product offerings, such as those in the medical industry.

Research and Technology

One of the most compelling research areas in the adhesives industry has been developing new product formulations that meet environmental standards set by the European Union or the U.S. Environmental Protection Agency (EPA). In Europe the adhesives and sealants industry was the second-largest consumer of solvents, and consequently has been greatly affected by volatile organic compound (VOC) directives. Such environmental initiatives as the 1997 Kyoto Protocol on Climate Change and the impending renewal of U.S. clean water legislation ensure that environmental issues will continue to press the industry toward lower solvent usage and more emission controls.

Thus, the biggest innovations as the industry entered the twenty-first century were expected to be product adaptations that would meet higher environmental standards and help present the consumer with a product perceived as more environmentally friendly, perhaps using less packaging, fewer toxic adhesives, or no propellants. Companies were reducing solvents and VOCs to avoid polluting air and water and reducing the ozone content of the atmosphere. In Europe, Germany's "Green Dot" environmental laws (so named because companies in compliance are allowed to display a green dot in advertisements and on packages) have impacted nearly every country in the European Union, because companies exporting to Germany were affected as well as those German firms selling domestically. The laws limit packaging of consumer products, mandate packaging recycling, and will eventually require the recycling of automobiles. Green Dot laws were expected to spread throughout the European Union and perhaps to the United States. Therefore, companies such as Apple Computer and Dow Chemical Co. began to meet Europe's standards and to develop plans for the eventuality of Green Dot laws in the United States.

After manufacturers recover the research and development costs involved in creating products that can replace solvent-based adhesives, the directives may actually improve profits. Water-based adhesives and those with a high solids percentage are more expensive and more profitable; new product lines give manufacturers another venue for continual upgrades that customers are likely to buy. Firms still specializing in solvent-based adhesives for applications requiring them may pick up jobs, product lines, or competitors abandoning that market.

By the mid-1990s, solvents were no longer used in consumer adhesives, and overall their use in Europe's adhesive and sealant manufacturing would decline from 160,000 metric tons in 1994 to 100,000 by the year 2000. Solvent-based adhesives accounted for less than 10 percent of Henkel's adhesives sales, according to *Chemical Week,* which annually publishes a special section on the global adhesive and sealant industry.

In the United States, solvent use also continued to decline and hot melts and water-based products claimed larger market shares. By 1995, waterborne adhesives had a 61.7 percent share of the U.S. market, hot melts a 20.7 percent share, and solvents a 9.8 percent stake. Industry observers cited by *Chemical Week* felt that application limitations on the customer end would keep those proportions at roughly the same level for the foreseeable future.

Among new technologies entering the market in the 1990s were those that improved the safety of manufacturing and using adhesives. Microwavable hot melts introduced by U.S.-based Loctite could replace hot glue guns, and National Starch's new ethylene vinyl acetate-based hot melt was processed at lower temperatures and therefore was less risky to handle. TOTAL and Elf Atochem introduced heat resistant adhesives, while TOTAL's U.S. subsidiary, Bostik, developed a caprolactam-free polyamide powder for the automotive market.

Many companies responded to environmental pressures. National Starch was developing dispersible, vinyl-based, hot-melt adhesives for paper packaging makers that used recycled feedstock in hopes of alleviating gummed machinery and thereby increasing the recyclability of paper products. 3M introduced a water-based neoprene contact cement. H.B. Fuller developed a new water-based adhesive and a resin-based starch additive that would make adhesives waterproof, increasing the rigidity of cardboard shipping containers and thus cutting down on spoilage and waste. In the United States, a 1994 settlement between Sherwin-Williams Company and the state of California, fining the company US$1 million for violating limits on toluene, was expected to result in reformulation of some of the company's products and very likely those of competitors. By the mid-2000s, the majority of research and development in the industry was in modifying already existing products to meet new demands.

INDUSTRY LEADERS

HENKEL KGAA

With estimated 2001 adhesive sales of US$2.6 billion, the chemical conglomerate Henkel led the German adhesive industry and was the world's largest adhesive manufacturer with operations in over 60 countries. In 1999 its market share was 14 percent, more than double that of its closest competitor. In 1997 it acquired U.S.-based Loctite Corporation, one of the United States' top five adhesives companies, and mid-sized Canada Adhesives Ltd. During the same year Henkel made a pair of smaller acquisitions in the United States and initiated joint ventures in India with The Anand Group, a Delhi-based automotive contractor, and Chembond Chemicals Ltd., a metal chemicals firm in Bombay. The Indian ventures were mainly to serve the adhesive and chemical needs of that nation's automotive industry.

Upon entering the new millennium, Henkel continued to make small purchases to diversify its product line and also consolidated by divesting under-performing businesses. As part of this strategy the company sold Cognis, its specialty chemicals business, and revamped its adhesives business under the Henkel Technologies Division. Company-wide sales rose 17 percent to US$11.8 billion in 2003. Henkel expected to secure future growth by focusing on reducing raw material costs, developing new products, and focusing on its international operations.

ATOFINA

Atofina, the chemicals subsidiary of the French petrochemical giant Total SA, formerly TotalFina Elf, was created in the 2000 merger of TotalFina and Elf Aquitaine. Its subsidiary, Bostik Findley Inc., was established when Bostik and Ato Findley were merged together during TotalFina's purchase of Elf Aquitaine. During the late 1990s, Elf Atochem had begun an adhesives buying spree to enhance its international portfolio. It acquired adhesives operations from two leading companies, Findley Adhesives of the United States and Laporte PLC of the United Kingdom. Both were integrated into AtoFindley.

Through Bostik Findley, Atofina held the number two slot in the adhesives industry. The company continued its acquisition strategy into 2000, purchasing both the Durabond brand commercial floor coverings and the installation products business of DAP Products. Company-wide sales were US$22.4 billion in 2003. Bostik Findley manufactures adhesives used in the automotive, aerospace, construction, packaging, non-woven, and textiles industries.

H.B. FULLER COMPANY

During 2000, 92 percent of Fuller's sales stemmed from its adhesives, sealants, and coatings business, and company-wide sales reached US$1.4 billion in 2004. The firm's products are used by the automotive, converting, engineered systems, footwear, graphic arts, non-woven/hygienic, packaging, polymer, tobacco, window, and woodworking industries. Fuller operates in over 36 countries in North America, Latin America, Europe, and the Asia/Pacific region. During 2001 the company reorganized into global business units and shut down approximately 20 percent of its worldwide capacity in order to cut costs. Fuller also continued to diversify its product line and focus on new technology.

IMPERIAL CHEMICAL INDUSTRIES PLC

Through its 1996 purchase of the major U.S. adhesive maker National Starch and Chemical, U.K.-based Imperial (ICI) vaulted into a leadership status within the adhesive industry. One of the world's largest paint manufacturers, ICI had total 2004 sales of about US$10.73 billion. National Starch, its primary adhesives holding, generated US$3.3 billion in 2003 sales and employed 9,670. In addition to non-adhesive products, National produces a wide range of adhesives for important industry segments including non-wovens, food packaging, paper converting, wood, building components, automotive, pressure sensitive products, and medical. Nearly 40 percent of company sales were derived from its adhesive business. North American operations accounted for nearly half of National's total sales.

MINNESOTA MINING AND MANUFACTURING COMPANY (3M)

3M ranks prominently in the United States' adhesive industry, as well as internationally. In early 2000 the company produced about US$350 million worth of adhesives annually, much of which was used in its own production of various tapes and labels. By 2004, 3M had sales reaching more than US$20 billion. In the late 1990s and into the new millennium, the company retreated from some of its electronic media forays to focus on its core businesses: consumer/industrial products such as tape and Post-it notes, and medical supplies such as polymer wound sealants.

ROHM AND HAAS COMPANY

Rohm and Haas significantly increased its presence in the global adhesives and sealants industry with the purchase of Morton International. In 2004, total company sales were US$7.3 billion. The company established manufacturing plants in Brazil and Bombay in 2001 and also made two purchases to strengthen its position in the automotive and cold-seal adhesives markets. Rohm and Haas is focusing on product development related to food packaging, hot-melt technologies used in industrial lamination, and energy-cured adhesives.

MAJOR COUNTRIES IN THE INDUSTRY

ASIA/PACIFIC

A 2001 world adhesives study published by the Freedonia Group reported that the annual growth rate for adhesive sales in the Asia/Pacific region more than doubled that of North America and Western Europe during the 1990s. In early 2000, China, Japan, and Korea were the largest adhesives and sealants markets in the Asia/Pacific region. According to DPNA International, the three countries were responsible for the manufacture of nearly 80 percent of all adhesives in the region. During 2000 China's adhesive sales grew between 6 and 8 percent over 1999 and were projected to grow by 8 percent through 2005. China produced nearly 15 percent of all adhesives manufactured in the region. Because of its strong growth rates, the Chinese market is expected to remain lucrative for adhesive manufactures.

Adhesive sales in Japan were forecast to grow by 4 or 5 percent through 2006. DPNA attributed the slow growth in Japan to a maturing industry and high production costs. In Korea the gross domestic product (GDP) began to rise to 4.0 percent in 2000, up from -5.8 percent in 1997. DPNA, along with market research firm PG Phillips & Associates Inc., reported that annual adhesives sales growth in Korea was 4.5 percent, just above the country's GDP. South Korea produced 9.1 percent of the region's adhesives and was expected to grow by 4.0 percent annually through 2004.

EUROPE

A 2000 ChemQuest Group report predicted that the European adhesives industry would grow to 2,248 million metric tons in 2003, up from 2,148 million metric tons in 1998. Europe's adhesive industry was also expected to grow by just under 3 percent per year through 2009. Germany was the region's largest market in 1999 sales, followed by France, the United Kingdom, Italy, and Spain. The largest market segment in the Western Europe adhesive market based on 1999 sales was paper/board, followed by building and construction, assembly operations, consumer and do-it-yourself, woodworking, and transportation. As prospects for future growth remained steady for Western Europe, the region's development of environmentally friendly adhesive technology was considered to be a step above U.S. efforts, which positioned the region to take advantage of future opportunities in this sector.

THE UNITED STATES

With the largest national adhesives industry in the world, the U.S. adhesives and sealants market was projected to grow to US$13.5 billion by 2003. ChemQuest estimated that the adhesives industry would grow to 6.82 billion dry pounds in 2004 in the U.S. with an average annual growth rate of 3.9 percent per year, exceeding the GDP through 2010. According to the International Trade Commission, the United States imported US$114 million in adhesives and sealants for consumption during 2003. That year, the industry exported US$387 million worth of products. Using figures from the *2000 Rauch Guide to the U.S. Adhesives and Sealants Industry, Adhesives & Sealants Industry* magazine reported that general purpose adhesives and sealants secured 54 percent of U.S. sales; engineering adhesives and films, 14 percent; binders, 12 percent; hot melts, 10 percent; and pressure sensitives, 10 percent.

The United States also had eight major end-use markets including packaging, industrial assembly, transportation, wood and related products, and on-site construction. The *Rauch Guide* reported that in the U.S. market, there were approximately 45 different chemical types of adhesives and sealants. Phenolics, the leader, accounted for 14 percent of sales, polyolefins represented 11 percent, followed by polyurethanes, silicone rubber, and starches and dextrin. The *Rauch Guide* also stated that consumption in the United States varied by whether the product was an adhesive or sealant. Phenolics, polyolefins, starch and dextrin, polyvinyl acetate, and acrylics were the leading adhesives in the market, while silicones, thermoset polyurethanes, bitumens and polyesters were the largest in sealants. According to the *Rauch Guide,* there were nearly 800 suppliers in the industry, but only 19 with U.S. sales of at least US$100 million. This segment however, represented just 43 percent of the domestic total.

FURTHER READING

"The Adhesive and Sealant Market in the Americas." *Adhesives & Sealants Industry,* November 2004.

"Adhesives Growth to Stretch in Developing Regions." *Chemical Week,* 7 January 2004.

"Big Surprise: Industry Sales Rise Despite Mounting Price Pressures." *Chemical Week,* 15 September 2004.

Draper, Deborah J., ed. *Business Rankings Annual.* Detroit: Thomson Gale, 2004.

"The Global Adhesive and Sealant Market." *Adhesives & Sealants Industry,* October 2004.

"H.B. Fuller to Cut Capacity and Restructure." *Chemical Market Reporter,* 21 January 2002.

"Henkel Creates Line for Supermarkets." *Marketing,* 5 February 2004.

"Henkel Extends its Grip on the Adhesives Industry." *ASI Magazine,* 31 July 2001.

"Hoover's Company Capsules." 2005. Available from http://www.hoovers.com.

Hume, Claudia. "Adhesives and Sealants." *Chemical Week,* 21 March 2001.

"International Trade Statistics." 2003. Available from http://www.wto.org.

Lazich, Robert S., ed. *Market Share Reporter.* Detroit: Thomson Gale, 2004.

"New Raw Materials: The Key to Industry Growth." *Adhesives & Sealants Industry,* April 2005.

Schmitt, Bill. "Adhesives and Sealants: Business on the Mend." *Chemical Week,* 10 April 2002.

———. "Margins on a Slippery Slope." *Chemical Week,* 2 April 2003.

Schwartz, Jody. "Asia/Pacific." *Adhesives Age,* March 2000.

"Sticking to Growth Markets." *Chemical Week,* 7 April 2004.

"Study: European Adhesives Industry Will Grow." *Adhesives Age,* February 2000.

"U.S. Adhesives and Sealants Market to Reach US$13.5 Billion in 2003." *ASI Magazine,* 27 September 2000.

Williams, Tom. "Foreign Markets." *Coatings World,* June 2001.

SIC 8731

NAICS 541710

BIOTECHNOLOGY

Biotechnology firms harness living organisms and biological components at the molecular, subcellular, and cellular levels to create marketable products. Such products include bacterial and viral vaccines; serums, plasmas, and various microbiological substances; and genetically engineered plants and animals. The industry also encompasses firms that perform related research services, such as genetic coding and forensic testing. Biotechnology is closely aligned with the pharmaceutical segment within the broader chemical industry. More information about the broader drug industry is provided under the heading **Pharmaceuticals**.

INDUSTRY SNAPSHOT

After enduring difficult times during the early 2000s, when industry players struggled to keep research initiatives alive despite falling investment levels, the biotechnology industry is showing signs of improvement. According to research by Ernst & Young (E&Y) the global revenues of public companies in the biotech field were US$41.4 billion, net losses were US$12.5 billion, and the industry employed 194,000 people. Although biotechnology industries were emerging in countries like China, Singapore, Russia, Japan, and India, the United States continues to lead the global biotech industry on a single-country basis. In 2002, the total number of global players was more than 4,300, with 1,466 of these in the U.S., 1,878 in Europe, 601 in the Asia/Pacific region and 417 in Canada. U.S. industry revenues were US$39.2 billion in 2003, according to the Biotechnology Industry Organization (BIO), an association of companies, educational institutions, and state biotechnology centers. Industry analysts at E&Y predicted the U.S. industry would achieve profitability for the very first time in 2008.

Europe continues to be the second leading biotechnology market. According to the BioIndustry Association (BIA) of the United Kingdom, at the end of 2003, the European biotech industry employed 82,400 people and was generating more than US$21 billion in annual revenues. The United Kingdom accounted for US$9.4 billion in revenue, followed closely by Denmark (US$8.8 billion), then Germany (US$5.7 billion), France (US$3.6 billion) and Ireland (US$1.8 billion). However, some industry analysts were concerned that the European industry was in jeopardy of losing its luster as competition increased from emerging countries. Continued investment and the development of breakthrough biotechnology products were key to the region's survival.

Biotech's emergence has been controversial. As the industry introduces new break-throughs such as cloning, stem cell research, and genetically modified foods, various social and political entities have responded with boycotts and bans, and in some extreme cases, violence. The Unites States is the world's largest producer and promoter of genetically modified crops, but most countries have been hesitant to accept even test fields of the products, with Thailand a notable exception. Despite the concerns of activists, many other countries were expected to follow, as large countries search for ways to more efficiently feed their populations and others try to compete for trade dollars.

Biotechnology-related debates continue to occur in other areas. For example, The British Broadcasting Corporation (BBC) reported that top British scientists were backing an international campaign to stop the U.S. in its attempts to have the United Nations impose a global ban on any form of human cloning. The United Kingdom is one of a number of nations that supports the use of cloning and stem cell research for all but reproductive purposes. With the industry continuing to suggest the numerous cures potentially available through continued research, the debate should continue to take on interesting dimensions outside of the purely economic ones.

As private industry, at the urging and, in some cases, the financial support of the government, moved away from traditional projects to put laboratories to work combating germ warfare with new vaccines, the industry's public profile changed dramatically for the better, particularly in the United States. In 2002, the National Institutes of Health (NIH) appropriated more than US$1.7 billionfor research to respond to bioterrorism. "This is the largest increase in NIH (funding)—much larger than the war on cancer a few years ago," James Meegan, program officer for the division of microbiology and infectious diseases and the National Institute of Allergy and Infectious Disease, a division of the NIH, informed the Toronto Star.

Organization and Structure

Although still in the early stages of its development, the biotechnology industry continues to globalize. In 2003, the United States alone was home to 1,473 companies with 198,300 employees, according to BIO. This was an increase from 1,466 companies with 194,600 employees in 2002.

A significant share of breakthrough biotech products originate in the United States. According to BIO, some 250 million people globally have benefited from the 117 biotechnology prescription drugs and vaccines that earned U.S. Food and Drug Administration (FDA) approval. Of those 117 drugs, three-quarters gained FDA approval between 1996 and 2002.

A relatively advanced biotech sector also exists in Europe. By 2002 1,878 companies were active in Europe, the bulk of which were headquartered in the United Kingdom, Germany, and France. In other areas of the world, the number of biotechnology firms continues to grow as governments provide the funding necessary for their establishment. By 2002, 601 firms were doing research in in the Asia/Pacific region and 417 in Canada—a significant presence considering the country's population size.

Generally, biotech companies start out with an idea for a promising new technology, such as a cure for acquired immune deficiency syndrome (AIDS) or a better method of testing DNA. The risk of failure is high, but success leads to potentially huge profits, status for the developing company and researchers, and important benefits to society. A company that is developing a treatment for arthritis, for example, commonly spends its first two to four years identifying the biology of the disease and the potential therapeutic impact of a compound. It may spend another one to two years isolating a compound and figuring out how to get the substance to specific points in the human body. Then another year or two is often spent designing a system to manufacture, modify, and purify the compound on a commercial scale. By that time, the company may have been laboring and investing for three to eight years with virtually no product sales. By 2005, there were more than 370 clinical trials in progress for vaccines and drugs connected with more than 200 human diseases including Alzheimer's, multiple sclerosis, and AIDS, according to BIO.

Biotech companies, which often begin with a few individuals, are typically funded using seed money contributed by venture capitalists. At some point in the first few years, if early research and development efforts are encouraging, additional capital may be contributed by private investors. If a firm can come up with what appears to be a promising new product, a well-heeled partner will inevitably step in. That partner is usually a large drug company that can support the start-up biotech firm with hefty research expenses, as well as testing, government approval, and production. In return for its support, the drug company may receive compensation in the form of marketing and distribution rights to the new product. Some companies garner additional funds by going public with their stocks.

An increasing number of companies are obtaining government support for their research, particularly in Asia. Governments are seeing the potential social, economic, and political benefits that could be received if their countries hold the secrets to particularly useful biotechnological processes.

Background and Development

Broadly defined, biotechnology has been applied commercially since at least 7000 B.C., when people began using fermentation to produce drinks, food, and fuel. A sort of "second generation" biotechnology, which involved processes not completely understood by researchers of the time, emerged in the first half of the twentieth century. Scientists of that period began using microbiology and biochemistry to process waste and to produce pharmaceuticals, chemicals, fuels, and food. In the 1930s humans began using beef insulin, a protein, to treat diabetes. But that protein was one of only a few that humans were able to exploit until decades later because researchers were limited by their ability to extract a single protein from the hundreds of proteins that might be manufactured by a group of cells.

The pivotal breakthrough that opened the door to the realm of modern biotechnology occurred in 1953, when British scientists James Watson and Francis Crick discovered the structure of DNA. That understanding led to a realization of the process by which proteins are produced by cells, and then to the creation of the biotechnology industry. DNA research reached another milestone in 1973. In that year, U.S. scientists Stanley Cohen and Herbert Boyer succeeded in snipping an individual piece of DNA out of an African clawed toad. They were able to splice the snippet into a common bacterium, where it resumed functioning with the foreign gene; the process of recombinant DNA was born. For their efforts, Cohen and Boyer received a Nobel Prize. The chief benefit of the breakthrough was that scientists discovered how to genetically alter microorganisms and then, through fermentation, produce large quantities of proteins that occurred naturally only in small quantities. These proteins can be designed and manipulated for specific purposes.

A series of biotech advances followed the 1973 achievement. In 1975 the first monoclonal antibodies were produced. Monoclonal antibodies are essentially cloned cells that can be used to attack foreign toxins, viruses, and cancer cells. In 1976, the first working synthetic gene was developed; in 1977 important methods for reading DNA sequences were discovered. Within a year of the latter discovery, the first identification of the high-level structure of a virus, and the first production of recombinant human insulin was achieved. The first human growth hormone was synthesized in 1979, and in 1980 biologists succeeded in transplanting the gene for human insulin into a bacterium. By the early 1980s scientists were learning to transfer a number of newfound genes into bacteria to create large amounts of disease-fighting proteins. In 1981 scientists created the first Chimera, a creature carrying a gene placed there by humans rather than nature. That experiment, which involved a mouse, demonstrated how biotechnology could be used by humans to influence the genetic makeup of living creatures. It also showed how animals could be used to test biotech treatments designed for humans, following the precedent used in conventional medical experiments.

Although researchers in the United Kingdom, and later Europe, contributed to the biotechnology revolution during the 1960s and 1970s, scientists in the United States assumed an early and dominant lead in the emerging science. All of the significant early biotech start-ups were U.S. firms: Cetus (1971), Genentech (1976), Genex (1977), Biogen (1978), Centocor (1979), and Amgen (1980). These and a few other companies were able to capitalize on the belief of many investors that biotechnology was going to heavily impact many areas of industry, medicine, food, energy, and agriculture. Although some of those companies made significant contributions to the burgeoning field of biotech, it was not until the 1980s that the industry boomed. The growth was largely the result of a U.S. Supreme Court ruling that genetically engineered bacteria could be patented. For many, that ruling suggested the possibility of massive financial rewards for biotech innovators.

During the early and mid-1980s, the biotech industry surged as new companies started and technology rapidly advanced. At the start of the 1980s only 40 different genes had been identified. Throughout the decade, new genes were identified regularly and more than 4,000 had been distinguished by the 1990s. Such discoveries sparked enthusiasm about the potential to develop new treatments and cures for diseases, to develop improved plants and foods, and to create a range of industrial products that could, for example, clean up oil spills or produce substitutes for petroleum-based fuels. Although industry receipts were negligible early in the 1980s, the number of biotech start-ups was impressive. The United States led the world with about 50 new start-up companies in 1980. That figure rose to roughly 100 new start-ups annually throughout much of the decade.

For reasons related primarily to politics and the attitude of the British financial community, the United Kingdom ceded its early lead in biotechnology to the United States. It did, however, follow the U.S. industry's lead and became the second major global player during the 1980s. The first British biotech start-up, Celltech, was founded in 1980 as a combined effort between academic, government, and private-sector players. Similar start-ups that followed included Cambridge Life Sciences, Agricultural Genetics Co., British Biotechnology, and Delta. France and Germany followed with various government-supported biotech ventures. French start-ups included Transgene, Genetica, and G3. West Germany's interest in biotechnology was evidenced in the 1970s by the creation of federally funded agencies, and Germany entered the industry relatively early compared to other continental European countries. By the late 1980s, Germany was rivaling the U.K. in its biotech investments.

At first Japan lacked the basic skills needed to participate in the biotechnology industry in the early 1980s. During that decade, though, the Japanese government partnered with private industry to develop expertise in such technologies as recombinant DNA and mass culturing of cells. Japan's biotech ventures were conducted through large companies rather than through entrepreneurial concerns. Although it produced few biotech innovations, Japan invested heavily and successfully converted some important technologies, initially developed elsewhere, into marketable products.

The biotech industry surge of the mid-1980s was largely a corollary of financial markets. Investors, excited by the possibility of huge returns from cancer-curing wonder drugs and other biotech products, invested massive sums of money in promising biotech start-ups. Some of the cash floated to Europe, but most of it was infused in cutting-edge U.S. concerns. A combination of factors quashed the flow of capital beginning in 1987, and many observers believed that the industry was reaping its just reward for promising too much. Following a three-year lull, however, investor enthusiasm returned and the industry enjoyed explosive growth. Much of the rally was sparked by the successes of a few star players—most notably Amgen, of the United States, which introduced a successful drug designed to battle anemia. Funding from all sources into the U.S. biotech industry exploded from about US$1.2 billion in 1990 to US$4.4 billion in 1991. Subsequently, the number of industry competitors in the United States and Europe surged to more than 1,500 by 1993, and the stock prices of publicly traded firms gained nearly threefold on average.

By 1993 the biotech industry was beginning to live up to its promise of being able to provide life-enhancing, genetically engineered breakthroughs. A handful of companies, almost all of which were in the United States, succeeded in getting several important products approved for sale. Amgen, with huge sales and profits in 1993 and 1994, was the biggest winner. Another success story was Biogen, which was pushing an Alpha interferon for hepatitis and cancer as well as a hepatitis B vaccine. Likewise, biotech pioneer Chiron was marketing an anticancer agent and a treatment for multiple sclerosis, and Genentech was selling a human growth hormone and a treatment for cystic fibrosis.

Despite a few encouraging success stories, some investors grew disillusioned with biotech. Indeed, after years of hefty capital investments in research and development, many had become impatient waiting for returns. Inflaming their frustration were a number of big failures that consumed millions of dollars with little or no return. One of many examples of biotech failures can be seen in an attempt made by Synergen, a U.S. firm, to create an antisepsis drug called Antril. Sepsis is an infection that floods the bloodstream of cancer and burn victims. It affects hundreds of thousands of people annually and often results in death. Armed with US$300 million in capital, Synergen built manufacturing plants and hired a sales force during the early 1990s, despite lackluster test results for Antril. The company eventually stopped developing the drug, but only after losing US$165 million.

In December 2001, federal regulators turned thumbs down on the cancer drug Erbitux developed by ImClone Systems. By the end of January 2002, the price of the company's stock was about one-quarter of what it had been before the drug failed to pass muster.

Economic failures like Erbitux or Synergen's sepsis project highlighted structural problems that plagued the biotech industry in the mid-1990s. Too much money was chasing technology that simply was not working. Wary investors tightened their purse strings, suggesting a possible industry shakeout that would eliminate companies that were not producing results. Doubts were most obviously evidenced by plunging biotech stock prices. Part of the problem in the eyes of some observers was that the industry was too fragmented. In the United States as well as in parts of Europe, several companies were often competing to produce the same products. One result was that research and development efforts were overlapping, resulting in overall inefficiency. These and other dynamics indicated that the biotech sector could be entering a period of consolidation.

The net effect of industry turbulence in the mid-1990s was that the investment community effectively shifted new capital away from small, entrepreneurial start-ups with unproven technology to more established competitors with greater chances of success. Shifting financial dynamics had numerous effects on the capital-intensive industry. Among these was an increase in collaboration. Smaller firms, generally faced with diminished access to funds in comparison to the early 1990s, were increasingly seeking joint ventures with large pharmaceutical firms, big brokerage houses, and other biotech firms with complimentary technologies or operations.

Regardless of the state of the global biotech industry in the mid-1990s, the long-term outlook for the sector was good to excellent by the 2000s—if objections from certain U.S. legislators could be deflected. In the 1990s, new products entered the market, pivotal technologies advanced, and sales of approved drugs and vaccines rose rapidly. By 1995, about 1,800 biotech firms were operating in Europe and North America, with nearly 1,300 in the United States. In addition, a growing number of large pharmaceutical companies were becoming more active in biotech. In the United States, which continued to account for the majority of industry revenues and product introductions, biotech sales surged from US$2.7 billion in 1989 to US$7.7 billion in 1994. Although aggregate industry losses increased from US$2.1 billion to about US$4.1 billion annually during the period, both employment and research spending were up significantly.

Validating positive projections for the global biotech industry in 1995 were a number of successful biotech drugs that were already being sold or were in the process of being approved for sale. Effective cures or treatments were being marketed for afflictions ranging from hemophilia and heart disease to genital warts and kidney cancer. Some of the more important biotech breakthroughs included Betaseron, a treatment for multiple sclerosis; Pulmozyme, a treatment for cystic fibrosis and possibly bronchitis; and a number of experimental compounds to treat AIDS.

In the mid-1990s, U.S. firm Calgene Corp. introduced a controversial genetically altered tomato that could ripen on the vine and remain fresh for two weeks after picking. In addition, biotech processes had been developed to allow forensic pathologists to prosecute or clear criminals based on minute samples of body materials. However, infamous court cases such as that of O.J. Simpson, in which the defendant was acquitted despite purported DNA evidence from hair and fibers linking him to the crime, highlighted the tenuous status of such technology in courtrooms. Nonetheless, a number of cases in which prisoners or defendants were freed as a result of DNA testing indicated that such testing would become increasingly visible during the twenty-first century.

Forensic and agricultural biotech advances were noteworthy, but the industry continued to focus on the development of drugs and gene therapy techniques in the mid-1990s. Although relatively few drugs had been produced by the biotech industry, the few success stories merited praise. For example, four of the top-selling drugs worldwide in 1994 were biotech drugs—an impressive proportion considering the size of the established pharmaceutical industry. Furthermore, a few biotech experiments suggested a promising future for the field of gene therapy. In 1994, researchers in Philadelphia corrected a cholesterol disorder in a woman by injecting her with genetically engineered copies of genes that she lacked. Two girls with a genetic defect disabling their immune systems were restored to health in a similar manner.

By 1995 the biotechnology industry had already consumed more than US$25 billion in capital, most of which was invested in research and development. Biotech companies in the United States alone were raising additional capital at a rate of about US$5 billion annually in 1995, and biotech ranked number one worldwide in expenditures as a percentage of total revenues and total costs. After years of R&D, biotech pioneers in the mid-1990s had failed to produce the cancer cures and wonder foods that many investors and industry participants had hoped for. Nevertheless, research efforts were beginning to bear fruit and a number of new development ventures suggested that breakthroughs would eventually be achieved. By 1995 biotech drugs were already helping cystic fibrosis patients breathe more easily, reducing the number of heart attack-related deaths by eliminating blood clots, and diminishing the threat of hepatitis with new vaccines and blood-screening tools.

AIDS was a key focus of research in the biotech industry in the mid-1990s. A cure for AIDS was still not in sight, and the chance of finding one was 1 in 10,000, according to one estimate. The disease had succeeded in quickly becoming resistant to all of the potential cures that had been tested, but a number of new therapies had been developed that were helping to mitigate its effects. Furthermore, a variety of government, private sector, and academic groups were teaming up to attack the AIDS virus. In 1993, 15 U.S. and European pharmaceutical companies joined together to share information, drug supplies, and technologies in an effort to speed up trials of different drug therapies. Some of the most important AIDS-related breakthroughs involved the means of testing for the virus. For example, one product tested for AIDS without the use of a blood sample.

In addition to advances related to disease and human genetics, biotech research was producing breakthroughs in other segments of the industry. For example, the market for DNA testing equipment was exploding in 1995 as a result of new test kits that allowed multiple DNA tests to be conducted using one small sample of body tissue or fluid. Similar test kits were being marketed to cattle breeders, who used them to identify desired genetic traits in cattle. Potential markets for the bio-testing equipment were unlimited. The kits could be used to identify the sex of small animals at an early age, for example, or to determine the exact origin of a piece of lumber that may have been cut from a government-protected forest.

Other futuristic breakthroughs being investigated in the mid-1990s were those related to aging. Many researchers believed that biotechnology could be used to slow the aging process and significantly extend the human life span. Scientists at Washington University had already achieved surprising results in helping to identify a gene, known as Bcl-2, that served to prevent the death of cells. Researchers deleted the gene from laboratory mice, causing the creatures to age extremely rapidly. Similarly, biotech researchers were making gradual gains in the field of nerve regeneration, and companies were working to develop nerve growth substances that could eliminate senility. Such substances may one day be able to treat paralysis and mental disorders.

In the late 1990s through the early 2000s, important new technological breakthroughs, new drugs, and significant increases in global biotech participation occurred. In 1997, Roslin Institute researchers in Scotland announced that a sheep named Dolly was the first mammal to be cloned with material taken from another. That development sparked widespread international debate about the moral and ethical aspects of genetic engineering, particularly of human beings. Most countries agreed that cloning of human beings was not an acceptable or desirable event, and several nations signed a ban to that effect. By April 2002 the industry's biggest battlefield seemed to be in the U.S. Senate, as lobbyists for BIO fought against the Brownback bill (S. 1899), which banned not only the cloning of human beings, but also might lead to criminal charges against scientists who cross certain boundaries of genetic research.

Europe and Asia recognized the importance of biotechnology to their health and future economic prosperity. Europe witnessed a 50 percent increase in the number of small biotech firms. Although Asia still trailed the United States and Europe in biotech development, several countries, notably Japan and China, made significant gains. Japan was developing its own pharmaceutical industry and had introduced several products to treat infections and to detect diseases such as AIDS. Japanese researchers were also active in genetic engineering and had succeeded in cloning a cow. China's biotech focus was largely on bioagriculture, although its pharmaceutical industry was growing. China produced several genetically engineered crops such as tomatoes, wheat, and rice with the expectation that they would be more disease-resistant, have a longer shelf life, and be more nutritious. The Chinese pharmaceutical industry was comprised of roughly 35 firms including joint ventures, and those figures were expected to increase. Collaboration and consolidation among biotech and large pharmaceutical firms continued to characterize the U.S. industry.

Government drug approval time spans were shrinking, so that new products appeared on the market sooner. On average, the U.S. FDA took 18 months to review and approve new drugs (a minimum of six months were required by law) in comparison to about 12 months in the European Union. Significantly, according to an annual industry report by Ernst & Young International, Europe was the leading region for new medicine introductions, in terms of both originating companies and market arrivals, at mid-decade, but findings from the FDA itself claimed a faster turnaround closer to 15 months. Priority drugs, notably for cancer, AIDS, and other viruses, usually receive much faster approval, according to FDA figures. Numerous new drugs were introduced for the treatment of AIDS, cancer, Parkinson's, heart disease, and other conditions, and the rate of new drug treatments was continuing to rise rapidly. Most analysts agreed that the global biotechnology sector had finally emerged as a key economic player despite industry fluctuations. The long-range outlook for the industry going into the twenty-first century was largely upbeat.

Other promising research in 2002 was in the area of immunization against anthrax, anticipating additional worst-case scenarios similar to the deaths caused by anthrax-infected envelopes sent through the United States mail following the 11 September 2001 terrorist attacks. According to the *Toronto Star*, St. Louis University's Department of Molecular Microbiology and Immunology was developing a vaccine with a scaled-down, modified touch of adenovirus that provides immunity, thwarting the advancing of the often fatal disease. In addition, the NIH has funded research into a vaccine that could similarly stop terrorist-induced hoof-and-mouth disease. One irony of the bioterrorism scare of the early 2000s is that it has mobilized university, government, and private sector researchers into a single fighting unit that could lead to important discoveries about ways to immunize humans and animals against deadly diseases.

Biotechnology endured difficult times during the early 2000s. As capital investment levels declined, industry players struggled to keep their research and development initiatives alive with existing funds. Citing figures from *BioWorld*, the Biotechnology Industry Organization (BIO) noted that while industry funding was US$38 billion in 2000, levels fell to US$15.1 billion in 2001 and US$10.5 billion in 2002. By 2003, conditions were improving as investors returned to the biotechnology market. BIO indicated that funding levels began to increase in 2003, reaching US$16.9 billion. In addition some companies benefited from increased funding related to IPOs, as well as mergers and acquisitions.

Current Conditions

According to a study by consulting firm E&Y, there are three main issues facing the biotechnology industry.

First, there are too many players in an industry that has been in a loss position profit wise. With the increasing difficulty many firms are experiencing in raising necessary research funding, mergers and acquisitions (M&A) are increasing, particularly for firms in similar areas of business where operational savings may be encountered through amalgamation. Companies with fundraising problems, but that choose not to seek M&A options, have found themselves facing bankruptcy. One high-profile example of this involved Scotland's PPL Therapeutics, the company made famous when it was part of the group that successfully cloned the first adult mammal, Dolly the sheep, in 1996. By 2004, the company's bid to sell its shares to management had led to its bankruptcy.

Second, the industry is starting to mature. As a result, companies that once tried to be involved in diverse activities are seeing the benefits of specialization. Again for funding reasons, many companies are forming alliances with firms doing research in similar areas whereby each becomes responsible for a part of the research process of a particular problem under study. According to Jon Hess and Ello Evangelista writing in *Contract Pharma* magazine, alliances between large pharmaceutical companies and smaller biotechnology firms are becoming more common. Almost one-third of new pharmaceutical products are developed as a result of such alliances. One alliance that has proven successful is that between CuraGen Corporation and Bayer Pharmaceuticals who are working toward treatments for diabetes and obesity. In 2001, Bayer announced that it would spend up to US$1.5 billion to use CuraGen's gene hunting technology. What was unique about this deal was that due to the amount of money CuraGen was able to previously receive from investors interested in its human genome research, it was able to enter into an alliance that will include a share of the profits from any drugs developed.

The third issue facing the biotechnology industry involves the continued globalization of the market. Companies have been trying to expand their markets in order to increase their competitiveness and, perhaps more importantly, increase their investor base. Many public firms are listing on global stock exchanges. The globalization of the industry is also being helped along by an increase in government support. For example, in March 2005, the United Kingdom announced a huge increase in funding for scientific research, with a large portion of the budget going to the growing area of stem-cell research. Poorer countries are also having their successes. For example, Cuba's creation of a vaccine for meningitis B has led to a biotech sector that has proven internationally successful.

RESEARCH AND TECHNOLOGY

On the research and development front, U.S. companies spent US$17.9 billion on research and development in 2003, according to the BIO. This was a decrease from US$20.5 billion the previous year. A number of important new biotechnology developments occurred during 1990s and 2000s. These can be broadly categorized into three areas:

- chemistry-based technologies
- genetic engineering technologics
- tissue engineering and biological products

CHEMISTRY-BASED TECHNOLOGIES

Several important advances in drug development occurred during the mid-1990s. One of these was a new screening technique called combinatorial chemistry. The process involved use of advanced robotics and synthesis techniques to develop new drug compounds. The technique essentially created new compound "libraries." Researchers then analyzed combinations displaying potential therapeutic benefits. One advantage of combinatorial chemistry was the significantly increased volume of compounds that could be initially screened. Traditional screening methods often took months or even years. The greater volume of compounds tested also resulted in a higher number of potentially beneficial compounds being identified and further analyzed. Many large pharmaceutical companies recognized the importance of combinatorial chemistry techniques. In early 1998, biotech leader Chiron Corporation and the pharmaceutical giant Pharmacia & Upjohn formed a strategic partnership to identify molecule inhibitors of the hepatitis C virus. The partnership would use Chiron's strengths in combinatorial chemistry, virology, high throughput assay development, and protein expression along with Pharmacia & Upjohn's expertise in biology, medicinal chemistry, and knowledge of pre-clinical procedures. The two corporations would share worldwide marketing rights.

Rational drug design was another important new chemistry-based technique. The process involved creation of a three-dimensional molecular image of a given protein in order to identify the location of its key functional sites. Once those sites are identified, new compounds could be designed that would bind to them. As with combinatorial chemistry techniques, rational drug design significantly reduced screening time and increased both the volume and accuracy of identifying potentially beneficial compounds. Agouron Pharmaceuticals and Vertex Pharmaceuticals were among the leading developers of rational drug design and both had used the technique to develop HIV protease inhibitor drugs.

A third chemistry-based technique, high-throughput screening (HTS), also used rapid automation of tests to identify possible compounds that would interact with certain proteins. As with the other chemistry-based techniques, millions of various compounds could be screened rapidly.

Signal transduction was the fourth important chemistry-based technique. It involved deciphering the means by which cells communicated within the human body. Researchers hoped to use that information to manipulate cell activity in relation to disease.

GENETIC ENGINEERING TECHNOLOGIES

During the 1990s, several revolutionary advances in the broad field of genetic engineering occurred. These included the launch of a massive U.S. federal project to identify the entire human genome; the appearance of the first cloned mammal; the emergence of xenotransplantation and transgenics; gene therapy; and use of genetic engineering in forensics, criminal identification, paternity cases, anthropology, and wildlife management.

Human Genome Project. In addition to efforts in the private sector, there were large government-backed ventures to map the human genome underway in both the United States and Great Britain. Most notable was the Human Genome Project, an international effort spearheaded by the U.S. Department of Energy in participation with various academic institutions. Funded by the United States' National Institutes of Health and the Department of Energy, the project was launched in 1990 with the goal of identifying the approximately 100,000 genes that make up the human genome. By mid-1994, molecular descriptions of about 45,000 genes had been successfully developed and the project was working aggressively to record and determine the function of the entire genome. Identifying the genes would enable scientists to develop new therapies and techniques to prevent and treat disease. Researchers completed their work ahead of schedule in the year 2003. A related effort was underway by Institute for Genomic Research, a nonprofit center working to ensure that gene research becomes available to the entire scientific community.

Cloning. The 1996 birth of the first cloned mammal, a sheep named Dolly, astounded the world. Dr. Ian Wilmut, an embryologist at the Roslin Institute in Scotland, cloned Dolly from a cell taken from the udder of an adult sheep; Dolly was born on July 5, 1996, but Dolly's birth was not announced until seven months later. After being mated with a Welsh mountain ram, Dolly gave birth to a lamb in April of 1998. Dolly's cloning set off a maelstrom of worldwide reactions and concerns over the possible eventual cloning of human beings and the moral and ethical considerations of such revolutionary technology. Responding to public opinion, U.S. President Clinton established the National Bioethics Advisory Commission (NBAC) to offer recommendations on the moral, ethical, religious, legal, and regulatory aspects of cloning. In June 1997, the NBAC produced a report stating that cloning human beings would be "morally unacceptable" based on ethical and safety considerations. The NBAC also encouraged the president to continue, at least for the next three to five years, the ban on using federal funds for human cloning. In early 1998, the U.S. Food and Drug Administration (FDA) stated its position as regulator of human cloning activities and announced that cloning human beings without its approval would be a federal offense. Around the same time, approximately 20 European countries signed a human cloning ban, although the door remained open for other areas of cloning research that might lead to key medical benefits. In March 2005, the United Nations General Assembly voted to approve a non-binding statement urging its members to adopt a total ban on all forms of cloning. Many nations abstained from voting or voted against the ban, citing that there was no consensus among UN members as to whether or not the use of stem-cells in research was valid or if it constituted the destruction of human life.

Xenotransplanting and Transgenics. Xenotransplanting involves the transplantation of animal organs, tissues, and cells into human beings. Transgenics involves implanting human genes into an animal in order to produce animals with therapeutic properties. Animals most commonly used in these two techniques include pigs, cows, goats, and sheep. One company, Diacrin, Inc., transplanted porcine cells into the brains of 23 patients suffering from Parkinson's. The company reported positive results from the procedures. Diacrin also used the technique for patients suffering from Huntington's, Alzheimer's, focal epilepsy, and other neurological conditions. Diacrin entered into a US$50 million joint venture agreement with Genzyme Corporation's Tissue Repair Division in late 1996. The venture was for the development of NeuroCell, Diacrin's porcine cell transplantation technology to treat Parkinson's and Huntington's. As of May 1998, the project was completing Phase I clinical trials, the first step toward U.S. regulatory approval. Genzyme Transgenics Corporation, a spin-off of Genzyme Corporation, was one of only three corporations in the world that developed transgenic animals. PPL, Ltd., which derived from the Roslin Institute, the facility that cloned Dolly, and a Dutch biotech firm called Pharming BV, were the other two. Genzyme Transgenics created transgenic cows and goats that produced beneficial enzymes and proteins in their milk. These products could be used to treat various human diseases and could be purified into medicines. Genzyme Transgenics' first drug, an anti-coagulant called Antithrombin III, was designed for the treatment of coronary artery bypass grafting surgery, and was to undergo Phase II clinical testing by the middle of 1998. In April 1998, researchers at the University of Colorado Health Sciences Center, the University of Massachusetts, and Advanced Cell Technologies announced their successful treatment of Parkinson's in rats by using fetal brains cells obtained from cloned cows.

Gene Therapy. Gene therapy techniques involve using recombinant DNA to correct hereditary disorders such as cystic fibrosis and muscular dystrophy. One of the key difficulties in gene therapy is that a treated cell often adds random parts of DNA so that it is impossible to determine what resulting chromosomes will look like. In other words, scientists have had difficulty making the gene therapy technique "stick" so that the treated gene could accomplish its mission. In May 1998, Japanese researchers announced their construction of an artificial chromosome, about one-tenth the size of a human chromosome, which they believed might fix the problem. Also in May 1998, two companies, Matrigen, Inc., and Prizm Pharmaceuticals, announced their merger into a new company called Selective Genetics, Inc. The new corporation could deliver genes, with a high level of accuracy, into specific cells in order to repair or regenerate cell tissues. The resulting merger created the first gene therapy company specializing in tissue repair and regeneration. In 2005, several advancements in gene therapy were announced, including gene therapy's use against colon cancer (The University of Hong Kong)and ADA deficiency (London's Great Ormand Street Hospital), an immunity deficiency whose victims are often referred to as "bubble babies."

DNA Identification. Every living organism has its own unique DNA which is made up of two interwoven strands that contain chemicals. The chemicals form genes that determine the unique makeup of each organism. DNA typing uses a variety of tissue (e.g., hair strands, skin, bodily fluids) and mixes it with enzymes that essentially "read" and "cut" the DNA wherever a specified combination is found. The resulting cut genetic pieces make up the DNA pattern and form each individual organism's own unique genetic fingerprint. DNA typing has enabled forensics scientists to more easily identify bodily remains, as in the recent DNA typing of the suspected remains of Czar Nicholas Romanov II of Russia and his family. DNA samples from living descendants, such as Prince Philip of the United Kingdom, were compared to DNA samples from the remains. DNA typing of suspected criminal perpetrators was also an increasingly common procedure, although its universal credibility has yet to be established in the courts, where it is sometimes seen as being open to deliberate or inadvertent contamination that yields a particular result. If properly employed, it would substantially increase the accuracy of criminal convictions and could exonerate falsely accused individuals. Many U.S. states passed laws requiring criminals to be DNA typed and their information entered into a statewide DNA database. DNA typing was also increasingly used to determine paternity by comparing DNA samples from the mother, child, and alleged father. The mother and child's matching combinations are identified and then eliminated; the remaining combination is then tested against that of the alleged father to determine whether there is a match. DNA typing is also increasingly used in anthropology to determine a variety of information about fossil remains, past historical periods, and other types of antiquities such as the Dead Sea Scrolls. With the number of endangered species continuing to rise, DNA typing has been an important technique for preserving species and also for identifying species that may be used illegally.

Tissue Engineering and Biological Products

Tissue engineering, also known as regenerative medicine, was one of the emerging biotechnologies during the mid- to late 1990s. According to a study by Brown University, by the end of 2002, more than 2,600 people in 89 firms located in 15 countries were researching tissue engineering. However, the number involved in the field had been on the decline since 2000, with many researchers moving into the similar field of stem-cell research. Despite FDA approvals for a variety of procedures, including allowing the use of a patient's own cartilage cells for later re-injection back into damaged sites, and growing new skin from cells taken from the foreskins of newborns to be used for burn victims and patients requiring plastic surgery, the field had yet to produce a profitable product by 2004.

Biological and Chemical Warfare

Concerns about the use of biological and chemical (CB) warfare agents increased substantially following the 1991 Gulf War. The international marketing consulting firm Frost & Sullivan reported that United States' CB defense spending would amount to more than US$250 million in 1998. The United States led worldwide R&D expenditures for CB defense and detection, and spending was expected to rise throughout the following decade. Frost & Sullivan's report, *World Markets for Chemical and Biological Warfare Agent Detection,* outlined the global participants and challenges surrounding CB detection and defense, and estimated a 12 percent increase in demand for CB detectors between 1998 and 2005. The report also noted that U.S. and European CB defense programs to acquire protective clothing and destroy suspected underground CB weapons sites were already underway. In March 1998, Novavax, Inc., a biopharmaceutical drug delivery company, announced that it had subcontracted with the University of Michigan to test several microbicides it had developed. The microbicides were designed to inactivate viruses, bacterial spores (e.g., anthrax), and bacteria, on contact by disrupting the invading organisms' membranes. Topical creams and environmental and nasal sprays were among some of the formulations being tested. In 2001 anthrax-related illnesses and deaths claimed some victims when they were exposed to the spores in pieces of mail sent by persons unknown that used the U.S. postal service. Other pieces of mail tainted with anthrax spores were intercepted by detection equipment.

The biotech industry continued to play a key role in protecting the world from the threat of biological terrorist attacks in the mid 2000s. On July 21, 2004, U.S. President George W. Bush signed Project BioShield into law. According to the White House, the new initiative "provides new tools to improve medical countermeasures protecting Americans against a chemical, biological, radiological, or nuclear (CBRN) attack." It is "a comprehensive effort overseen jointly by Secretary [of Health and Human Services Tommy] Thompson and Secretary [of Homeland Security Tom] Ridge, and involving other Federal agencies as appropriate, to develop and make available modern, effective drugs and vaccines to protect against attack by CBRN weapons."

A related area within the realm of biological products was chemical and biological warfare (CB) agents. Toward the end of the decade, concerns over terrorists' use and manufacture of biological and chemical warfare agents had led many countries to decry such tactics and to step up national and international security measures. The deaths of postal workers and a mail recipient from anthrax in late 2001 led to widespread public fears and massive media coverage.

BIO President Carl B. Feldbaum dubbed biotechnology "a critical first step toward the development of the drugs and vaccines needed to protect our nation's citizens and military personnel against biological or chemical weapons attacks." Feldbaum stressed that liability protection and the development of a procurement system would help to ensure participation in Project BioShield by the greatest number of industry players.

Industry Leaders

Amgen. In an April 2002 feature on the biotechnology industry, *Forbes* magazine informed readers that if they had purchased Amgen stock in 1983, they "would now be sitting on a 182-fold gain." In 2005, Amgen continued as the biotech industry's unrivaled leader. Three Amgen drugs—Epogen, Neupogen, and Procrit—topped the list of the world's ten leading drugs based on 1996 worldwide sales. Combined worldwide sales for the three drugs were nearly US$3.2 billion. By 2003, Epogen and Aranesp were responsible for half of Amgen's sales. The company was started in 1980 by George Rathman. Rathman was working for U.S. research giant Abbott Laboratories at the time and had become intrigued by recombinant DNA technology. Abbott offered to fund 52 percent of his venture, but Rathman turned them down because he believed that his company would need to be free from corporate influence to achieve its goals. The company started with funding from venture capitalists before going public in 1983. Its research focus was on a chicken growth hormone designed to reduce feeding costs. Additional public offerings brought enough cash into Amgen's coffers to fund intense research and development efforts throughout the 1980s.

Amgen's main research and development efforts have focused on several areas: inflammation, metabolic disease and osteoporosis, oncology, hematology (the study of blood cell formation and differentiation) nephrology, and neurology. The drugs Epogen and Neupogen were developed as part of Amgen's focus on hematopoiesis. Amgen's rapid growth during the late 1980s was largely the result of its market introduction of Epogen, with 1996 worldwide sales of nearly US$2 billion. Epogen was approved by the FDA to treat anemia associated with chronic renal failure. Sales jumped to US$150 million in 1991, and the value of the company's stock exploded to US$3 billion, up from a value of just US$19 million in 1981. Soon thereafter, Amgen received FDA approval of Neupogen, a drug that stimulates the production of a specific white blood cell and can be used to treat cancer-related anemia. Following that product introduction, Amgen's sales shot up to US$1.5 billion in 1993, about US$383 million of which was netted as income. Neupogen followed closely behind Epogen with 1996 worldwide sales of roughly US$1 billion.

By 2004, the company had 24 programs in human clinical trials, and approximately 40 programs in development.

In 2004, Amgen's sales were nearly US$20.6 billion, an increase of almost US$7 billion since 2001. The company employed 13,000 people in its U.S. based research facilities, as well as in manufacturing plants around the world.

Genentech. Another global biotech leader, Genentech markets and develops products based on human genetic information. Its latest drug, Avastin, is used in the treatment of colon cancer. Sales rose to almost US$4 billion in 2004, an increase of over 42 percent.

Genentech is headquartered in San Francisco and had more than 7,600 employees in 2004. Founded in 1976 by Robert A. Swanson and Herbert Boyer, Genentech focuses on three main areas: oncology, cardiovascular conditions, and endocrinology. Genentech was the first company to splice a human gene into a bacterial cell to manufacture a usable protein. The company manufactures and markets a number of products in the United States, several of which are for the treatment of human growth deficiencies (e.g., Protropin, Nutropin, Nutropin AQ). Other products include Activase, a treatment for acute myocardial infarction (heart attack); Actimmune, for the treatment of infections from chronic granulomatosis (a deficiency of the immune system); Pulmozyme, a treatment for cystic fibrosis; and Rituxan, for the treatment of non-Hodgkin's lymphoma.

In 1995 Roche Holdings Ltd., of Basel, Switzerland, became Genentech's majority stockholder, and owned about 56 percent of the company by 2004. The agreement enabled Genentech to receive royalties from sales of its products in Canada, and on sales of Pulmozyme in Europe. The company also receives royalties on sales of its other products through various licensees in the United States and Canada. It also receives royalties on five products which originated from Genentech research and are marketed worldwide by other companies. In 1992 Genentech opened the US$85 million Founders Research Center, the world's largest biotechnology research facility, which was dedicated to the company's two founding researchers.

Chiron. Chiron Corporation, founded in 1981, has business units for blood testing, vaccines, and biopharmaceuticals which focus on infectious diseases and cancer. The company generated revenues of more than US$1.7 billion in 2004, up 81.6 percent from 2002 revenues, but a significant slowdown to 2.4% over 2003 sales. By the end of 2004, the company employed approximately 5,400 workers in 18 countries on five continents. In addition to research centers in Emeryville, California; Seattle, Washington; and Siena, Italy; the company had manufacturing operations in the United States, the United Kingdom, Germany, Italy, the Netherlands, and India. Of note is Chiron's distinction as the first company to market a drug in the United States to treat multiple sclerosis. The drug, Betaseron, reduces the frequency and severity of attacks caused by some forms of the disease.

Chiron is the world leader in blood testing systems for screening by blood banks. In 2004, the company was the fifth-largest developer of vaccines in the world, including a vaccine against meningococcal C disease. Its growth in this area has primarily been the result of global acquisitions. Chiron also develops a range of therapeutic products for cancer and infectious and pulmonary disease. In 2004, the company filed for marketing approval for two additional products: Pulminiq, an inhalation solution for use by patients receiving lung transplants, and Cubicin for skin and soft tissue infections. With one of the broadest and deepest product lines in the biotechnology industry, Chiron maintained ongoing collaborations with more than 500 research institutions and commercial organizations. Its most significant partnership was with the Swiss company Novartis (formed by a merger of Ciba Geigy Ltd. and Sandoz), with a focus on combinatorial chemistry.

Genzyme. Based in Cambridge, Massachusetts, Genzyme was founded in the early 1980s by a group of entrepreneurs with enzyme expertise. The company began by developing and manufacturing diagnostic products. Thus, unlike many other biotech start-ups, it had an early source of revenue. The company focuses its research efforts in the areas of genetic diseases, disorders of the immune system, cardiovascular disease and oncology. At the end of 2004, the company acquired Ilex Oncology, bringing with it two FDA-approved cancer treatment drugs. In 2004, the company had revenues of more than US$2.2 billion, employing approximately 7,000 people in 30 countries.

In April 2002, Genzyme saw its stock value rebound and rise from US$2.31 to US$42.98 as its drug Renagel appeared to have life-saving benefits to prevent heart disease deaths in patients on dialysis. The *Boston Globe* said in 2002 that Renagel "could be the next billion-dollar drug." By 2004, the company was focused on developing treatments for rare genetic disorders. In addition, it acquired ILEX Oncology that year. Despite increases in revenues, the company experience several years of losses, before achieving a net gain in 2004.

Biogen Idec Inc. November 2003 saw the merger of two of the world's leading biotech firms: Biogen Inc. and IDEC Pharmaceuticals Corp. to form Biogen Idec Inc. The merger was yet another sign of the maturation of the industry, and the need for companies to strengthen their investor base, while decreasing their expenditures through the amalgamation of services. This new company concentrates on treatments for inflammatory and autoimmune conditions, as well as various forms of cancer. Based in Cambridge, Massachusetts, the company also has offices in Canada, Australia, Japan, and throughout Europe, employing approximately 4,000 people worldwide. In 2003, the company recorded sales of US$2.21 billion, a staggering 225 percent increase over the previous year's sales. Although this increase was matched with a relatively small net income figure of US$44 million, it was a significant improvement of the previous year's net loss of US$875.1 million.

IDEC Pharmaceuticals was established in 1985 in San Francisco. During its early years, the company developed "anti-idiotype" monoclonal antibodies, which it described as "a patient-specific, customized approach to treating non-Hodgkin?s lymphoma." By 1991, the company went public and was traded on the NASDAQ. IDEC's breakthrough cancer drug Rituxan, used to treat non-Hodgkin's lymphoma, was approved by the FDA in 1997.

Biogen was formed in 1978 when a group of biologists, all leading researchers in the emerging field of genetic engineering, convened in Geneva. Two of the biologists received Nobel Prizes for their discoveries. The discoveries led the way to products based on the alpha interferon gene and hepatitis B antigens.

In early 2005, the company voluntarily suspended sales of its multiple sclerosis drug, Tysabri, after the death of a patient from a rare disease. The company immediately saw a 44 percent decline in the price of its shares, with the announcement having a negative affect on the industry as a whole.

MAJOR COUNTRIES IN THE INDUSTRY

Canada. According to a study by Ernst & Young (2002), on a per-country basis, Canada ranks second to the U.S. in terms of the number of companies doing business in the biotechnology industry. In fact, when compared with the size of its economy, Canada leads the world with 0.65 companies per $billion in GDP, while the U.S. has about 0.15 companies and Europe has 0.2. A 2004 study by KPMG showed that, in terms of clinical trial costs, the country had a 22.4 percent cost advantage over the U.S., which ranked eighth in the study. In 2001, the human health sector accounted for 52 percent of the biotech firms, followed by 17 percent for the agricultural biotech sector. Approximately, 12,000 people are employed in the industry, with the vast majority working in companies of fewer than 50 employees.

Many Canadian firms have strong alliances with American and other global companies, particularly for marketing and distribution. For example, in 2003 cardio-vascular drug company, Cardiome signed a US$68 million co-development and marketing agreement with the U.S. subsidiary of Japanese pharmaceutical company Fujisawa. 2004 saw a similar agreement between Canada's Xenon Pharmaceuticals Inc. and Switzerland's Novartis AG. However, Dr. Stelios Papadopoulos, Vice Chairman of SG Cowen investment bank has stated that Canada has too many small companies while potential investors are looking for companies with strong management and well developed development pipelines.

Prominent discoveries attributed to Canadian organizations include the completion of the first publicly available draft sequence for the coronavirus, important for the development of diagnostic tests for Severe Acute Respiratory Syndrome (SARS).

Europe. In 2002, Europe was home to 1,878 biotech companies in all, ahead of the 1,466 in the United States. However, the region did not benefit from the same market vibrancy found in the United States. In *Europe Agri,* E&Y Life Science partner Bruce Gellatly explained that in Europe, the biotech industry was challenged by a difficult funding and investment climate in 2004.

As Europe faced these and other challenges, including competition from an emerging biotech industry in Asia, some industry analysts were uncertain if the region would remain a viable player in the future. For example, in *Chemical Market Reporter,* E&Y UK Health Sciences leader William Powlett Smith said: "There is a real risk that in five to 10 years there may be virtually no biotech industry in Europe of any significance if there is not a scaling-up in the size of European biotech companies. Without an increasing number of larger companies, Europe will succumb to stronger companies from outside the region. This possible loss of control over European biotechnology is obviously a doomsday scenario. There are some exciting areas of bioscience in Europe, so the commercial potential is there. It is a question of whether it gains its fair share of the revenues from its own innovations."

United Kingdom. Despite Europe's challenging climate, the United Kingdom remained a biotech leader in this market area. According to The BioIndustry Association (BIA) of Britain, as of 2005, Britain accounted for 27 percent of Europe's entrepreneurial (private) companies and 93 percent of the continent's publicly traded companies. More than 40,000 people worked in the industry in 2005, experiencing a 20 percent growth rate each year. By this time, six of Europe's ten leading biotech companies were British. The United Kingdom was home to some 300 biotech companies, comprising a US$13 billion market. In addition to private funding, the British government announced in March 2005 that it would spend approximately US$1.87 billion on biotechnology research by the year 2008.

Between 1975 and 1994 the United Kingdom contributed 14 percent of globally significant drugs. That development put the United Kingdom in second place behind the United States in terms of important drug development, and made it a leader in the European biotech sector. Its strength in comparison to other European nations was derived partly from its early lead in biotech research and development. Beginning with the development of a smallpox vaccine in 1796, the United Kingdom can boast a long tradition of biotech-related innovations. In addition to the 1953 discovery of the structure of DNA, British scientists made subsequent breakthrough discoveries, such as interferon findings (1957), the structure of insulin (1958), monoclonal antibodies (1975), and the cloning of the first adult mammal, Dolly the Sheep, in 1996. According to Linda Nordling in *The Guardian,* the United Kingdom has failed itself by not being the ones to bring its own discoveries to market. For example, despite developing magnetic resonance imaging (MRI), it was the Americans who marketed the product.

A major factor giving the U.K. biotech industry an advantage over other European nations was access to venture capital. About half of all European biotech venture capital in the early 1990s was invested in the United Kingdom. In 1993, for example, venture capital investments in British biotechnology were about two times greater than those in Germany, which placed second in Europe in the amount of biotech venture capital funding. Biotech players in most countries outside the United States were forced to rely much more heavily on largely inaccessible public equity markets and government grants. To that end, the U.K. biotech community got a finance-related boost in 1993 when it convinced the London Stock Exchange to allow young biotech companies to be listed without having to prove profitability. By 2003, U.K. firms were attracting approximately US$157 million in venture capital funding. In 2004, a new company, PowerMed, was formed after receiving more than US$35 million in venture capital funding. The company will develop DNA vaccines.

Although funding is available, there is still a shortage in the U.K. As a result, many firms look to mergers and acquisitions to find the necessary money to continue their research. 2003 and 2004 brought an increase in M&A activities in the U.K., with the biggest deal in the U.K. industry's history occurring when Belgium's UCB Pharma purchased CellTech Group for US$2.8 billion.

Germany. In 2002 the chief executive office of Pfizer, Inc. lamented Germany's declining position of leadership in the technology industry. "The medicine chest of the world used to be Germany," said Dr. Hank McKinnell. "Now, it's New York, New Jersey and Connecticut."

By mid-2004, *Biopharm International* reported that the German government was actively helping the country become a more prominent player in the biotech industry. It sought to accomplish this by eliminating bureaucratic roadblocks and helping to quiet fears regarding the use of genetically engineered crops, which had caused setbacks in the United Kingdom. In addition, the German government also matched private funds in order to expedite biotech growth.

Germany became active in the biotech industry with the 1974 creation of the Bundesministerium für Forschung und Technologie, a government effort aimed at promoting biotechnology. Most of the country's biotech research and development is carried out through large pharmaceutical companies and through government-backed projects and consortiums. Major biotech powers in Germany include pharmaceutical giants Hoechst, Bayer, and BASF. Smaller companies are often created as specialty research arms of larger companies or with the help of venture capital from the United States and other countries.

According to a May 2004 report by E&Y, by 2003, Germany had 350 biotechnology firms, employing 11,535 people, a continuing fall from 2001 levels of 365 companies employing 14,408. However, despite these decreases the number of products that had reached the preclinical to approval phase, known as the pipeline, increased by 14 percent over 2002 levels, a figure matched by a 4 percent increase in venture capital funding.

Several problems exist for the German biotech sector. First, there is a large number of small companies which lack the monetary backing or number of emloyees needed for long-term existence. Second, because many of these firms only focus on the development of one product, they do not have a fall-back position should this product fail, nor do they have other products to provide ongoing funding for research and development activities in other areas. Third, despite slight increases in venture capital funding, this well may be running dry. According to E&Y, only one-quarter had funds to last them more than twelve months.

Denmark. By the end of 2003, Denmark was fast approaching the United Kingdom in terms of the percentage of biotech revenues it was contributing to the European market ($US8.8 billion from Denmark versus US$9.4 billion from the U.K.). The region is often grouped with other Scandinavian countries for statistics as well as marketing purposes, with many biotech organizations encompassing all of the countries in the region. Denmark is the top-performing country in terms of obtaining drug approvals and U.S. patents.

France. Historic French expertise in the biosciences, highlighted by the legacy of Louis Pasteur, waned in the 1980s and early 1990s. Like Germany, France's biotechnology industry is dominated by large pharmaceutical firms, particularly Rhône-Poulenc Rorer, Roussel-Uclaf, and Sanofi. A 2004 report by France Biotech, the French biotechnology industry association, states that the years 2003 and 2004 were notable for their significant drops in funding which in turn led to stagnation in jobs and company investments. Young companies are thought not to be taking the steps necessary to protect their innovations.

Asia. Although the Asian biotechnology sector had lagged behind the United States and Europe, by the late 1990s most Asian countries had come to recognize the importance of the field to their future economic prosperity. In 2002, 601 companies were engaged in biotechnology research. Japan leads Asia's biotech industry, but China, South Korea, the Philippines, and Indonesia are also very active in the sector.

Japan. By 2002, Japan's biotech industry was estimated to be worth approximately US$13.4 billion and was expected to reach US$230 billion by 2010, according to the *JETRO Japan Biotechnology Market Report (2004).*

Despite its leadership position, Japan's biotech industry started late, as Japanese chemical companies followed the U.S. lead. Because Japan's financial markets generally do not benefit high-risk start-up companies, large companies became the major participants in the industry. About 250 large Japanese companies have become involved in biotech. Those organizations typically differ significantly from many U.S. and European biotechnology companies. Japanese companies engaged in biotech have tended to emphasize bringing innovations developed elsewhere to market. For example, a Japanese company may obtain a license from a U.S. firm to manufacture a biotech drug that the U.S. company developed and patented.

Throughout the 1980s the Japanese government teamed up with major companies to try to build a formidable biotech industry. They invested at home in research and development of proprietary drugs and products, and also invested heavily in the comparatively advanced U.S. biotech industry. They purchased significant shares in some U.S. biotech companies in an effort to gain access to their research. In the late 1980s, many U.S. observers feared that Japan was going to overcome North America's lead and soon dominate the global biotech industry. By the early 1990s, however, Japan's biotechnology sector had failed to introduce even one significant product. Indeed, of the few Japanese biotech successes by the mid-1990s, most were companies that manufactured drugs licensed to them by U.S. companies like Amgen and Genentech.

Pharmaceuticals remained the dominant area of the Japanese biotech sector with several large firms investing heavily in new drug development. One firm used pieces of human chromosomes in mice to develop antibodies against infections. In 1997 Japanese researchers successfully cloned a cow. The use of microbes as "factories" in which to produce human growth hormones, proteins, and antibiotics was also on the rise among Japanese biotech firms. In other Asian countries, microbes were being used in a number of innovative ways such as to clean up man-made messes like oil spills and sewage, and to reduce landfill waste.

China. Ever mindful of its population and scarcity of arable land, China was one of Asia's more aggressive countries in developing and using biotechnology. Chinese researchers focused primarily on bioagriculture and sought to develop more nutritional and disease-resistant crops. They succeeded in producing a number of genetically altered crops such as peppers, rice, potatoes, wheat, and others. China was also working hard at developing pharmaceuticals. Some of the larger Chinese firms had successfully produced anti-cancer and hepatitis products. According to research by Datamonitor,China's biotechnology market was worth US$5.1 billion in 2003 and had been experiencing growth rates of greater than 20 percent each year since 1993.

Despite their overall support of biotechnology, many people in Asian countries continue to debate the wisdom of genetic engineering. Observers question the possible effects of transgenic animals and plants on the environment and also wonder about the future of biodiversity. Regarding cloning, most Asian governments agree that replicating human beings is not acceptable. Nevertheless, some western biotech industry players were concerned about the directions in which China might travel with research initiatives. For example, some thought that philosophical differences might lead China to pursue the cloning of human embryos. Even though China banned reproductive cloning in 1998, there was skepticism about whether or not regulations would be enforced.

The Economist reported in 2002 that, according to one researcher at the Peking University Stem Cell Research Centre, "if Chinese scientists want to collaborate with foreign research groups, publish in international journals or attract overseas investment, they have to abide by international rules. Practicality, if not morality, will help to keep most scientists in line with international notions of acceptable biological research." In the late 1990s and early 2000s, Asian nations attempted to remove barriers hindering biotechnology industry dominance. For example, university professors now are permitted to work in private enterprise, where formerly it was not government permitted.

United States. By 2005, the United States still retained its dominant lead in the biotechnology industry. According to a 2004 study conducted by the Santa Monica, California-based Milken Institute, the city of San Diego was home to the leading U.S. biotechnology hub, ahead of Boston and San Francisco. In its 14 June 2004 issue, the *San Diego Business Journal* revealed that the city's biotech industry directly or indirectly accounted for US$5.8 billion in income, as well as 55,600 jobs. However, the publication indicated that, aside from three large biotech companies (Genentech Inc., Chiron Corp., and Applied Biosystems), San Diego's biotech cluster was home to many smaller firms that depended heavily on venture capital. Moving forward, it was critical for the city to produce FDA-approved drugs in order to maintain interest among investors.

In 2004, a number of states were offering incentives to attract biotech companies. States such as Massachusetts, California, Maryland, New Jersey, and Pennsylvania offered a variety of grants, investments, and tax credits to support the formation, or ensure the continued growth of, their respective biotech industries.

Between 1975 and 1994, the United States had developed 45 percent of the world's most important drugs; the next largest drug developer was the United Kingdom, which contributed 14 percent. These new treatments targeted respiratory conditions, AIDS, Parkinson's, heart disease, stroke, hypertension, cancer, and non-Hodgkin's lymphoma. The United States led its overseas counterparts in major research efforts such as a biotech cure for AIDS and identification of the human genome.

The United States assumed an early lead in the global biotech industry partly because of its entrepreneurial environment, but also because of factors such as efficient capital markets, and strength in technologies related to biotechnology. The United States produced a number of biotech start-ups and technological breakthroughs during the 1970s and early 1980s. Throughout the mid-1980s, the U.S. biotech industry thrived. Even during the industry downturn of the late 1980s, investment and research efforts continued to increase. By the end of the decade, 1,275 U.S. biotech companies employed 140,000 workers and generated annual sales of US$13 billion, although net revenues exceeded US$17 billion when non-product income was included. Despite rising sales, the industry continued to post net losses to a tune of US$4 billion per year, due in large part to the US$9 billion, or half of all revenues, invested annually in R&D.

Only during the 1990s did the U.S. industry build up most of its sales. Industry sales surged from about US$3 billion in 1990 to US$6 billion in 1992 to nearly US$8 billion in 1994. The number of start-ups that were not producing revenue, combined with U.S. biotech losses of about US$4 billion in 1994, caused many analysts to predict an industry shakeout and a consolidation of research and development operations during the late 1990s. Financial markets supported those predictions by shifting funds from start-ups to more established companies. In June 1994, a study showed that about half of all U.S. biotech companies did not have enough cash to last for two years. By 1995 the number of biotech companies had increased to about 1,300, and total industry employment swelled to more than 100,000. By 1996 industry sales were nearly US$11 billion. The accounting firm E&Y tabulated 1996 industry revenues, derived from a combination of product sales and payments from research partnerships, at US$14.6 billion. By 1997 the number of firms declined from 1,287 to 1,274, supporting predictions of consolidation, but it was hardly a shakeout. The five largest biotech firms accounted for roughly one-third of total industry revenues. R&D spending, including nonprofit research, had increased dramatically from US$2 billion in 1980 to a projected US$20.6 billion in 1998. During the late 1990s, increased R&D spending and more streamlined drug approval processes were rapidly increasing the rate at which new treatments appeared on the market. Although most of the industry was still made up of small and medium-sized companies, many of which still struggled with financial constraints, analysts predicted solid long-term industry growth. The United States' aging population was a key factor. Between 1996 and 2010, it was estimated that the over-65 segment of the population would grow by 16 percent. The 45 to 65 segment of the population was expected to grow by 46 percent. Given those projections, a larger senior population would benefit from therapies developed by the biotech industry.

Financial turbulence in the U.S. biotech industry opened the door for several European competitors to boost their involvement in the industry in the mid-1990s. Many U.S. biotech companies, hungry for capital, had turned to large, cash-rich European pharmaceutical companies as development partners. The arrangement worked well for the European companies, many of which were lagging far behind their technologically superior U.S. counterparts. They also benefited from the unrivaled ability of U.S. companies to transfer biotechnology from academe to the private sector. At the same time, U.S. firms benefited from their European partners' familiarity with regulatory approval processes on the continent. In fact, many U.S. firms were seeking and gaining approval for their biotech products through less restrictive European regulatory bodies, rather than through the comparatively strict U.S. Food and Drug Administration. Biotechnology research investment in the United States has grown tenfold since 1990, twice as fast as in Japan and Europe.

FURTHER READING

"2004 French Biotechnology Industry Report." France Biotech. Paris, France. December 2004. Available from http://www.bioindustry.org.

Aoki, Naomi. "Genzyme Pins Hopes on Dialysis Drug." *Boston Globe,* 10 April 2002.

"Banking on Biotech." *Fortune,* 9 June 2003.

BioIndustry Association. *BIA Media Guide.* London, England, 2004. Available from http://www.bioindustry.org.

"Biotech Matures as Industry Shifts to Product-Driven Market." *Chemical Market Reporter,* 2 August 2004.

Biotechnology Industry Organization. *Biotechnology Industry Facts.* Washington, D.C., 2004. Available from http://www.bio.org.

———. "Project BioShield Is Important Step Forward in Securing the National Defense." Washington, D.C., 19 May 2004. Available from http://www.bio.org.

———. *Welcome to the Gateway to Biotechnology.* Washington, D.C., 2002. Available from http://www.bio.org.

"Biotech's Yin and Yang; Chinese Biotechnology." *The Economist,* 14 December 2002.

"Britons Attack US Cloning Ban Bid," 29, August 2004. Available from http://news.bbc.co.uk.

"Brownback Bill Would Criminalize Medical Research," 2005. Available from http://www.bio.org.

Cohen, Judy Radler. "Cash-rich Biogen Creates Corporate Development Post." *Mergers and Acquisitions Report,* 8 April 2002.

Denneler, Barry. "States Respond to an Industry in Demand: The Explosion of the Biotech Industry During the Past Decade has Forced States to Begin Tailoring Packages to Attract, Retain Companies." *Expansion Management,* May 2004.

Ernst & Young International, Ltd. *European Biotech,* 2005. Available from http://www.eyi.com.

Ernst & Young LLP. *Biotech Industry Report,* 2005. Available from http://www.eyi.com.

European Federation of Pharmaceutical Industries and Associations. Available from http://www.efpia.org, 2002.

Government of Canada. *Follow the Leaders: Celebrating Canada's Biotechnology Innovators,* June 2003. Available from http://investincanada.com.

Gwynne, Peter and Gary Heebner. "Drug Discovery and Biotechnology Trends—Advances In Europe: Joining the Revolution." *Science,* 19 September 2003.

"Japan's Biotech Business Market to Top US$202 Billion by 2010." *Japanese Biotechnology & Medical Technology,* April 2001.

Jarvis, Lisa. "Biotech Sector Enjoyed a Modest Recovery in 2003." *Chemical Market Reporter,* 15 March 2004.

Kilpatrick, Robert Lee. "Global Biopartnering: A Personal Perspective: Biotechnology Players are Emerging in Countries that Historically Have Not Been Substantially Active in This Industry." *Biopharm International,* May 2004.

Langreth, Robert, and Zina Moukheiber. "Make Money In Biotech." *Forbes,* 15 April, 2002.

"Life Sciences: EU Biotech Industry Lags Behind America." *Europe Agri,* 11 June 2004.

Lysaght, Michael and A.L. Hazelhurst. "Tissue Engineering: the End of the Beginning." *Tissue Eng.,* 2004 Jan-Feb.

McCord, Mark. "Asia Heads Toward Use of GMO Foods Despite Activist Protests." *Manila Times,* 28 August 2004.

Milmo, Sean. "Hobbled By Financing, European Biotech Lags Behind the US: Confronted By Skeptical Capital Markets and Unsympathetic Legislation, Most European Biotech Companies Are Small and Struggling to Survive." *Chemical Market Reporter,* 7 June 2004.

Newton, Alastair. "Europe's Biotechnology Hub: The United Kingdom." *Biopharm International,* November 2003.

Nordling, Linda. " Show Me the Money." *The Guardian,* 15 March 2005.

O'Connell, Brian. "Have Biopharm Business, Will Travel: The Global Market for Biopharmaceuticals Points to a Healthy Future for Industry." *Biopharm International,* May 2004.

"Pfizer Leader Calls for a New Relationship Between Pharmaceutical Innovation and Europe Governments." *PR Newswire European,* 11 February 2002.

Pharmaceutical Research and Manufacturers of America. Available from http://www.pharma.org, 2002.

Reynolds, James. "Scots Scientists Set for Funding Bonanza; *The Scotsman,* 8 March 2005.

Rooss, Ursula. "Germany's Biotech Sector in Danger of Running Out of Cash." *Biotechnology, Medical & Life Sciences,* 14 May 2004. Available from http://www.britischebotschaft.de

Ross, Rachel. "Biotech Called to Duty in the U.S. War on Terrorism." *Toronto Star,* 13 June 2002.

Sapienza, Alice M. and Diana Stork. 2001. *Leading Biotechnology Alliances: Right From the Start,*U.S.: Wiley.

"U.S. Concerned over Possible Bioterrorist Foot and Mouth Disease Threat." *Agence France Presse,* 12 June 2002.

Van Arnum, Patricia. "U.S. Biotechnology Industry: On the Rebound: Analysts Expect Overall Profitability by 2008." *Chemical Market Reporter,* 7 June 2004.

Webb, Marion. "Biotech Execs Encouraged by New Study: Report Ranks S.D. as Top U.S. Hub Ahead of Boston and S.F." *San Diego Business Journal,* 14 June 2004.

SIC 2870

NAICS 3253

CHEMICALS, AGRICULTURAL

The agricultural chemicals industry manufactures the world's basic nitrogen and phosphate fertilizers, mixed fertilizers, pesticides, and related chemicals for agriculture. For coverage of other types of chemicals, see also **Chemicals, Industrial Inorganic** and **Chemicals, Industrial Organic**.

INDUSTRY SNAPSHOT

The agricultural chemical industry is the smallest of all the chemical industries, and includes production of both pesticides and fertilizers. By the mid-2000s, the pesticide market was in decline. In addition, according to the Food and Agriculture Organization of the United Nations (FAO), estimates on fertilizer usage over the next three decades are substantially lower than estimates made in the 1990s. Lowered estimates in large part have to do with more efficient apportioning of fertilizers due to computer projections and because of more efficient use of available fertilizers, according to the FAO study. In addition, the health benefits of non-chemical, organically grown products have led to a reduction in both pesticide and fertilizer usage. Fertilizer use, estimated to be about 138 million metric tons (mmt) in 2005, could rise as high as 199 mmt in 2030, or decline as low as 167 mmt, according to the study's authors. As of 2003, agricultural chemicals made up 10 percent of the US$1.79 trillion global chemicals market.

In the mid-2000s, the top companies in the industry were Syngenta and Bayer, followed by DuPont, Dow, BASF, Agrium, Monsanto, and others. While some of the top agricultural chemical manufacturers had spun off or sold their chemical operations by the early 2000s, others opted to concentrate on the briskly expanding market for biotechnology. The biotechnology industry, in part, strives to develop crops that are hardy and resistant with and without the aid of fertilizers, pesticides, and fungicides. Industry observers foresee greater interaction between genetically engineered crops and farm chemicals with the growing application of integrated pest management approaches to agriculture. (See also **Biotechnology**.)

The fate of genetically modified (GM) crops was yet to be decided by the mid-2000s. For example, industry leader Monsanto, which was restructured in late 2003 in order to concentrate more on promoting the widespread use of GM crops, pulled the plug in 2004 on plans for GM wheat. While the company cited bottom-line issues, opponents of genetically engineered food claimed the industry was dying because it was unwanted and unneeded. Particularly outside the United States, GM crops have been slow to gain acceptance. In addition, a 2003 report based on USDA data found that in contrast to claims that GM crops required reduced pesticides, actual pesticide use had increased by 23,000 tons over the previous six years.

ORGANIZATION AND STRUCTURE

The agricultural chemical industry produces chemicals for four principal end uses: pesticides, herbicides, fungicides, and fertilizers. Pesticides, which usually are organic chemicals, kill or discourage insects and other animal life that attack crops. Herbicides attack weeds that compete with crops for the nutrients in the soil, while fungicides kill fungus or prevent it from growing. Fertilizers replenish lost nutrients in the soil in order to make it more productive and raise crop yield.

Pesticides are manufactured in concentrated form and need to be mixed with adjuvants (inert ingredients designed to make pesticides more effective, such as attractants and extenders) before use. Certain manufacturers specialize in this mixing process, called formulation, to prepare a pesticide for the end user, who may be a farmer or home gardener. Adjuvant manufacturers supply their products to formulators and distributors, which prepare the product and market it to consumers.

Fertilizers include usable forms of three elements that all plants need to grow: nitrogen, phosphate, and potassium. The primary ingredient of most nitrogenous fertilizers is anhydrous ammonia, which may be reacted with nitric acid to produce ammonium nitrate. While it is an excellent fertilizer, ammonium nitrate is also highly combustible. Approximately 70 percent of the cost involved in producing ammonia covers the price of natural gas, one of its basic ingredients. Therefore, producers in countries with inexpensive access to natural gas, such as the Commonwealth of Independent States (an alliance of former Soviet republics), Canada, and Mexico, have a significant advantage over those in areas with high natural gas prices, such as Europe. Once the world's leading nitrogenous fertilizer, ammonium nitrate has lost market share to urea, which has a higher nitrogen content and is easier and safer to handle and store.

Nitrogenous fertilizers accounted for about half of all fertilizer production in the 1990s, with phosphorous and potassium each holding a quarter of the market. As the fertilizer industry evolves, fertilizers become increasingly concentrated. Not surprisingly, all three types of fertilizers are often mixed in combination products. Manufacturers label such products with three numbers separated by hyphens, such as 15-10-5, which represent the mixture's percentages of nitrogen, phosphorus oxide, and potassium oxide, respectively.

Farmers usually test the chemical makeup of their soil before applying any kind of fertilizer. Government or privately operated laboratories test the soil and recommend a custom combination of fertilizers to suit its needs. Most fertilizers come in solid form to be spread on the ground, but some are liquids made for injection into the soil under pressure.

Environmental factors are extremely important in the manufacture, shipping, distribution, and use of pesticides. Increasingly strict environmental laws have contributed to the sluggish growth of the pesticide industry, and products have been subjected to stringent tests that measure their toxicity. According to the U.S. Department of Commerce, research and development (R&D) costs for just one new type of pesticide in the 1990s could top US$50 million, compared to about US$6 million in the 1970s. From the mid-1990s through the early 2000s, pesticide manufacturers spent as much as 10 percent of their sales revenue on R&D. Pesticide products, subjected to rigorous tests by governmental agencies, took as long as five years to complete. The total R&D process can take as long as 10 years from "test tube to field," and only one in 20,000 substances tested is eventually produced on a commercial basis.

Governmental and private watchdogs in industrialized countries were on the lookout for damage done to the environment through pesticides and other pollutants. Pesticides impact the environment through accidental spills during transport; by leaching into the water supply; by affecting the growth of microorganisms in soil; and by being ingested by wild animals, causing death and deformity.

Industrialized countries have been concerned with indiscriminate use of pesticides and other agricultural chemicals in developing countries anxious to increase their level of food production. The spread of global trade means that a developing country's liberal use of pesticides on food crops could easily affect consumers living in another country. Consequently, developed countries have been searching for ways to diplomatically encourage developing countries to apply first-world policies to pesticide and herbicide use. Developed countries have also been forced to question their own policies of exporting to the third world pesticides that are banned in their own countries.

In the mid-1990s, the European Union was developing its own standards for environmental testing, which included tracking the efficacy of pesticides. Intolerance for careless use of herbicides and pesticides is increasing worldwide. In Denmark, for instance, the Danish Environmental Protection Agency routinely sent employees into the fields to see if farmers were properly using atrazine, a pesticide intended to protect corn crops. Offenders were sternly warned the first time, but officials were known to levy fines on perennial offenders.

On the other hand, spokespersons for agribusiness argue that the use of pesticides has to be balanced against their benefits. Pesticide manufacturers have been developing products that let farmers manage their soil more conservatively, resulting in less erosion as well as higher productivity. One significant advance is the introduction of pre-emergence herbicides, which attack weeds and invasive plants as they germinate. Still, the search for new products that are tough on weeds and bugs but kind to crops continues. Several trends expected to develop at the turn of the twenty-first century include the use of natural predators (bugs eating other bugs); products expressly developed to kill insects and plants that threaten only one or two crops; efforts to stay ahead of insects' ability to develop a tolerance for pesticides; substances that are effective at lower dosages; and packages that household users can more easily handle and store safely.

Patents are vital to the success of agricultural chemical producers in that one of the primary ways companies can earn profits is by developing a unique, successful product. However, when products once produced by a single company become generically available, their sales decline, leading to lower profits.

The permeability of national borders resulted in several intercompany and intercontinental alliances among major pesticide producers. For example, Hoechst Schering AgrEvo, a partnership between two German companies, Hoechst AG and Schering AC, headed up a North American venture (Hoechst Nor-Am AgrEvo).

Much of the world—100 countries including the United States, Asia, and European nations such as Spain, Japan, Italy, and Greece—is battling a problem exacerbated, not caused by, fertilizers: desertification. Overgrazing, diverting of water supplies, and unwise farming practices have led to vast areas of land drying up throughout the world. The 2002 United Nations Secretariat of the Convention to Combat Desertification in Bonn told participating delegates that as the lands dry up, "chemical residues from fertilizers and pesticides [will] further degrade the land," according to the *International Herald Tribune*.

BACKGROUND AND DEVELOPMENT

The desire for the biggest, highest-quality crop with the least amount of interference from insects and weeds has been a goal since early man first furrowed the ground to plant seeds. In order to grow properly, plants need carbon dioxide, water, and sunlight, as well as a very specific diet of other substances to develop according to their genetic program. Most plants also need a dose or two of magnesium, sulfur, calcium, potassium, phosphorus, and nitrogen. Moreover, some crops need trace elements such as chlorine, copper, and zinc. Heavily hybridized cash crops can quickly deplete soil of its natural balance of nitrogen, phosphorus, and potassium, leaving plants hungry for these elements.

Until manufactured fertilizers became commonly available, farmers would rotate crops that depleted the soil's stock of nutrients with crops that added elements back into the soil. Some organic farmers continue to manage crops in this manner. For example, alfalfa, clover, and legumes draw nitrogen from the air and release it back into the soil. At the end of the growing season, they are plowed back into the soil to enrich it for the next cycle. Manure, consisting of the excrement and soiled straw bedding of farm animals, was still used globally in the late 1990s. Though it is usually in plentiful supply (each year, farm animals in the United States alone produce more than one billion tons), manure is not necessarily the best fertilizer for a particular field or crop.

John Bennett Lawes, a British Victorian, dedicated his life to fertilizers and plant nutrition and thus has been considered to be the father of the fertilizer industry. Lawes experimented with different combinations of phosphoric acid, lime, bone dust, and other substances. Another pioneer was German Justus von Liebig. He outlined the importance of nitrogen in plant growth and developed a theory about plant growth and nutrition.

Widespread use of manufactured fertilizers came about indirectly as a result of the defense industry's buildup during World War II. Factories built to draw nitrogen from the air to use for explosives were easily converted after the war to make nitrogenous fertilizers. Because of the rapid adoption of commercial fertilizers, Western Europe became self-sufficient in terms of crop production, thus preserving European rural life.

In the 1940s, organic phosphates, including Malathion and Parathion, were briefly popular. Spraying pesticides from small, low-flying airplanes dramatically increased the efficiency of their application. Instead of taking hours to spread chemicals by hand on the ground, planes could dust 1,000 acres in just a few minutes. There are, however, no permanently effective pesticides to this date. Plants and insects alike adapt their tolerance for the chemicals in just a few generations; consequently, scientists must constantly monitor the effectiveness of the pesticides and develop new formulas.

Several innovations served to improve conditions in the industry. In 1944, 2/4-dichlorophenoxyacetic acid, a substance that selectively kills only broad-leafed plants, was commercially introduced. It turned out to be the first in a steady stream of more than 100 commercial herbicides introduced on the market in the subsequent 50 years.

Scientists also developed several chemicals to help farmers control the size of crops and the period when plants could grow, which allowed farmers to better time crops for market. By using certain hormones, fruit could even be kept from rotting before it was picked.

Although the global farm chemical industry experienced robust sales in 1996 and 1997, prospects for 1998 were more subdued. Increased production of corn, soybeans, and wheat spurred on growth in the farm chemical industry since producers required more chemicals to treat the greater amount of land farmed. Moreover, analysts predict that Asia's population growth will drive agricultural chemical sales in the future.

In 1996 and 1997, several of the world's largest agrochemical firms divested themselves of their general and specialty chemical divisions to focus on life science products. Two of the world's leading producers, Ciba-Geigy and Monsanto, both liquidated their chemical concerns during this period. In 1996 Ciba merged its life science division with drug maker Sandoz, Ltd., to form Novartis, while Monsanto completed its restructuring in 1997, giving up its chemical arm to make a concentrated foray into the budding life science business (and in 1998 merged with pharmaceutical maker American Home Products Corporation). Similarly, Hoechst, the parent company of AgrEvo, announced that it would sell off its chemical operations by 2000, and top-ten farm chemical producer Rhône-Poulenc increased its commitment to the pharmaceutical industry by spinning off its chemical and fiber operations to form Rhodia in 1998. This restructuring marked the movement of the agricultural chemical industry away from the mainstream chemical industry and its stronger alignment with the biotechnology and the food and nutrition industries, as companies began to focus on producing genetically enhanced crops in addition to conventional agrochemicals.

However, other leading farm chemical producers such as Bayer, DuPont, and BASF have reasoned that general chemical and biotechnology operations are complementary. Company executives have noted that such diversification balances the risks involved in both industries and allows them to benefit from advances in both fields.

Current Conditions

Since the 1990s, pesticide and fertilizer manufacturers have faced flat or declining demand in many of the world's key markets, although increased crop production in the United States and Europe was expected to cushion pesticide sales, and increased demand from developing countries, particularly in Asia, was expected to bolster the market for fertilizers. In 2002 the U.S. Department of Labor attributed some decline of pesticides to the use of computers that help farmers and agribusinesses determine which specific areas of the farm to treat with chemicals, rather than simply covering a whole farm, as was formerly prevalent. In addition, some industrialized countries have been seeking ways to minimize dependence on commercial fertilizers. A small but influential trend toward organic agriculture has raised consumers' awareness of the chemicals used to produce food.

In 2002 the United Nations Environment Program (UNEP) estimated that synthetic pesticides such as fungicides, herbicides, and insecticides had annual sales revenue of up to US$30 billion. Nonetheless, the UNEP cautions that improper application of such pesticides can and does have adverse effects on farmers' health, the environment, domestic animals, and food consumers.

Developing East Asian countries, such as China, Indonesia, India, Vietnam, Cambodia, Pakistan, Thailand, and Malaysia, have remained major growth markets for fertilizers. In 2003, the Asia-Pacific region's agricultural chemicals market reached US$291.26 billion and was expected to control 51.9 percent of the global market by 2008. These areas were expected to use more than 11 million metric tons (mmt) by 2005. Because agriculture in these areas is a major economic sector—for example, nearly two-thirds of Thailand's labor force is engaged in agriculture—and its structure follows the traditional family farm model, crop quality is crucial. In 2001 and 2002, South Korea shipped huge quantities of crop fertilizer to North Korea in an attempt to relieve massive food shortages, a move hailed by many world leaders as a small, important step toward reconciliation.

The use of fertilizers and pesticides, particularly in China and India, is increasing at a faster rate than the world average due to government subsidies for fertilizer purchases. These two nations are perceived as very important to the international fertilizer market. Governments in the Middle East, China, and India subsidize fertilizer use, which partly explains the steady increase in demand in these regions. These policies are likely to remain, as most Asian countries have been under pressure to increase production from their arable land due to exploding population growth. In like manner, some governments in Africa distributed fertilizers and seeds to small rural farmers, the result being that some small success was claimed in 2002 at fighting hunger locally through the production of crops such as soybeans.

Shipments of fertilizers to Europe, on the other hand, continued to slow as heavy annual rains, particularly in 2002, affected agricultural regions. In 2002 countries such as Spain, Portugal, Greece, and Italy began fighting against the adverse effects of chemical residues on lands already ruined by unwise farming practices that cause desertification. In the United States, the amount of acreage exempted from crop production had a significant impact on the demand for fertilizer. As in Europe, the Food and Agriculture Organization of the United Nations (FAO) expected overall consumption of fertilizers to remain flat with only slight increases. Latin America, on the other hand, was forecast to be a strong export region later in the first decade of the twenty-first century. The European agricultural chemicals market was worth US$107.85 billion in 2003, a slight increase in growth over the previous year. France, the largest market in this sector in Europe, reached a value of US$12.9 billion, up 1.2 percent over the previous year, but this was not expected to be the general trend over the next five years. The leading markets for agricultural chemicals through 2010 were projected to be Asia and South America, which have rapidly expanding economies and agricultural sectors.

Research and Technology

Agricultural researchers began emphasizing integrated pest management (IPM) in the mid to late 1990s. According to the American Crop Protection Association, integrated pest management (IPM) includes four major kinds of technology: biological (natural pest controls), cultural (crop rotation, cultivation, and pest monitoring), chemical (pesticides and insect growth regulators), and genetic (genetically engineered crops). Researchers continued to search for the most successful combinations of these crop protection methods. Following the IPM approach, researchers must consistently develop farm chemicals to meet the needs of the biological, cultural, and genetic methods.

A larger portion of the research in the latter part of the decade focused on chiral chemistry. Chiral chemistry studies molecules with two structural forms that are mirror images of each other, just as the left hand is the mirror image of the right hand. These molecules often have similar chemical and physical properties but different biological properties, which in the pharmaceutical and farm chemical industries can produce different results. The importance of chiral chemistry to the farm chemical industry is that it can determine which molecular structures benefit crops the most, since one structure could be more effective than another.

In the mid-1990s, Responsible Agricultural Product Information and Distribution (RAPID) developed PowerAg, a computer network for the dissemination of information pertaining to farm chemicals and for the electronic distribution of farm chemicals. In 1997 more than 30 of the world's producers subscribed to PowerAg. The network allowed manufacturers to stay informed about safety and environmental regulations. Further, PowerAg offered a venue for electronic commerce, letting producers reduce their inventories, which include about US$1.5 billion worth of unsold products each year. Users can also track orders and shipments with PowerAg.

Institutionalized composting was another endeavor that the industrialized agricultural economies flirted with in the mid-1990s. One method of efficiently delivering fertilizer used during this time is the use of biodegradable tapes placed at the plant's roots. Earthworms have also been used to replenish nutrient-stripped soil; as the worms eat through waste, they produce castings rich in nitrogen, phosphorous, and potassium. The French firm Sovadec developed a method called the Naturba Process, which separates recyclables from organic waste and then sterilizes the resultant waste to be sold as a fertilizer called "vermicompost."

In 2004, a model was introduced that was able to predict the effect of pesticides on animals. Researched for a quarter of a century, it was hoped the model would help crop growers assess the effect of such chemicals on the ecosystem ahead of time, because it could take factors such as climate into account in conjunction with animal physiology and behavior.

Industry Leaders

Syngenta

The world's biggest fertilizer company, Syngenta, was formed by combining the former companies Novartis and AstraZeneca. One of the biggest challenges for the company in the early 2000s was to meet demands from environmental action groups, most notably Greenpeace, that the company clean up massive quantities of chemical residues left by the companies Syngenta purchased. In January 2002, for example, Syngenta agreed to clean up a site near Katmandu, Nepal, although a spokesperson for the company stated that his company could not be held responsible for practices of another company two decades ago. The problems were those of Sandoz AG and Ciba-Geigy, two companies absorbed by Novartis, which itself was acquired by the firm known today as Syngenta.

In 2004, this global leader in chemicals had sales totaling US$7.27 billion, which represented a one-year sales growth of 10.5 percent, and a net income of some US$460 million. The number of employees in 2004 totaled nearly 19,500.

Novartis AG, a Swiss firm, had 2000 sales approaching US$41 billion, with a net income of some US$8 billion. The company employed some 68,000 people in 2000. Novartis resulted from the merger of agrochemical leader Ciba-Geigy and prescription drugmaker Sandoz in 1996. Novartis produced a wide variety of pharmaceuticals and medical and nutrition supplies, but it also played a key role in the agricultural chemical industry. One of the world's most potent and controversial pesticides, DDT, was invented by a Geigy scientist. Ciba-Geigy was formed in 1970 by a merger of two prominent Swiss chemical companies. Geigy SA is the older of the two, with elements of the company dating back to 1758. Ciba, Ltd. was founded in the 1850s and became the largest chemical company in Switzerland by 1900. Ciba-Geigy has subsidiaries in Argentina, Australia, Austria, Belgium, Brazil, Canada, Chile, Colombia, Denmark, France, Italy, Japan, Korea, Lebanon, the Netherlands, Portugal, Spain, Sweden, the United Kingdom, and the United States.

The group formerly known as Zeneca Agrochemicals was part of the Zeneca Group that produced drugs for cardiovascular and cancer treatments, as well as herbicides, insecticides, and fungicides. In 1996 the company's revenues totaled US$9.1 billion, and farm chemicals accounted for 11 percent of its overall US$2.7 billion in sales. In 2004, Syngenta announced plans to purchase a majority stake in corn and soybean seed company Advanta from AstraZeneca. Along with the purchase of genetically modified corn technology from Bayer, the acquisition of Advanta was expected to put Syngenta at the forefront of the corn and soybeans market by 2005.

Bayer

Bayer AG, along with BASF and Hoechst, is heir to the German chemical cartel IG Farben. Originally founded in the late 1890s to produce synthetic dye, its 1996 sales totaled US$33.5 billion, 6 percent or US$2.2 billion of which came from agrochemicals. The company is also involved in the production of pharmaceuticals, dyes, polyurethane, organic and inorganic chemicals, and synthetic rubber. As one the world's leading chemical producers, Bayer consists of 350 companies in 150 countries. In 2004, Bayer had sales of approximately US$40.3 billion. The company employed 113,825 people. In 2002 Bayer acquired the agrochemicals giant Aventis CropScience, itself formed by a merger of France's Rhône-Poulenc and Germany's Hoechst, making Bayer the second largest company in the industry. In 2003, Bayer had 20 percent of the worldwide market, and was expecting to knock Syngenta out of the number one position by 2006. In 2004, France's ministry of agriculture banned Bayer's corn insecticide Gaucho, due to its potentially harmful effect on bees. The ban potentially could last for two years.

In 1982 Rhône-Poulenc was taken over by the French government. Just 11 years later, after suffering massive losses, it was re-privatized and by the mid-1990s the farm chemical powerhouse had more than 200 production plants and research labs around the world. In 1996 Rhône-Poulenc's sales totaled US$16.5 billion, with agrochemicals accounting for a 13 percent share, or US$2.2 billion. In addition to agrochemicals, Rhône-Poulenc is involved in pharmaceuticals, specialty chemicals, and plastics. In the agrochemical sector, the company produces herbicides, insecticides, seed protection, and genetic formulations. Rhône-Poulenc has subsidiaries in Australia, Austria, Belgium, Cameroon, Canada, Germany, Greece, Guatemala, Indonesia, Italy, the Ivory Coast, Japan, Madagascar, Mexico, Morocco, the Netherlands, Portugal, Senegal, Spain, and Switzerland.

Hoechst AG of Germany had 1996 sales of US$33 billion, 7 percent of which was derived from agricultural chemicals. The company focuses on pharmaceuticals, but its AgrEvo division produces herbicides and insecticides as well as other chemicals used to keep crops and animals healthy. Hoechst began in 1863 by producing dye in Frankfurt and is the largest of three chemical companies formed in 1952 after the German chemical cartel IG Farben was disbanded under the Allied postwar occupation. In 1987 Hoechst acquired Celanese Corp., one of the leading chemical producers in the United States. Hoechst has been criticized by environmentalists because of the company's production of chlorofluorocarbons (CFCs) but has since planned to produce an alternative called R134a. It also has begun to recycle and reduce solid waste and wastewater in its plastics facilities. In 1997 Hoechst announced it would restructure the company to focus on pharmaceuticals and agricultural chemicals.

Monsanto

Monsanto Company, the creator of Roundup, the top herbicide worldwide, and NutraSweet, withdrew from the chemical business in late 1997 to concentrate on life science products, including genetically engineered seeds and crops such as cotton and soybeans, as well as agricultural chemicals. To prepare itself for its new role, Monsanto began acquiring and forming alliances with life science operations between 1996 and 1997. Some of these companies included Calgene (a plant biotechnology leader), Asgrow Agronomics (a corn and soybean seed leader), Holden's Foundation Seeds Inc. (the world's largest foundation seed company), and DeKalb Genetics (the second largest U.S. seed company). In 1998 it agreed to merge with American Home Products Corp. In 1997 Monsanto posted sales of US$7.5 billion, and farm chemicals contributed US$2.9 billion or 38 percent to this total. Founded in 1901, Monsanto has conducted business in 130 countries. In the early 2000s, while involved in other agriculture-related businesses other than pesticides, the company did considerable business in Latin America and was estimating losses caused by the devaluation of the peso in Argentina. In 2004, Monsanto had sales of approximately US$5.45 billion and employed some 12,600 people. In April of 2002, Monsanto formed an agreement with DuPont and its subsidiary Pioneer Hi-Bred International to advance agricultural technologies for all three.

DU PONT

In the mid-1990s, E.I. du Pont de Nemours and Company was the largest chemical company in the world with 1996 revenues of about US$44 billion. Agricultural chemicals accounted for about US$2.5 billion of that total. Founded in 1802, the company began as a partnership in gunpowder and explosives. Du Pont grew from a family business to a multinational conglomerate through the acquisition of companies and the diversification of product lines. In addition to agricultural herbicides and insecticides, Du Pont is involved in producing various chemicals, plastics, petroleum products, fibers, and medical products, among others. Sales in 2004 were approximately US$27.34 billion, of which US$4.5 billion was from the company's Agriculture & Nutrition division. Du Pont employed about 60,000 people in 2004. In April of 2002, DuPont and its subsidiary Pioneer Hi-Bred International formed an agreement with Monsanto to advance agricultural technologies for all three.

DOW AGROSCIENCES

Dow Chemical Company, for which Dow Agrosciences is a division, took in nearly US$20 billion in sales in 1996 from its line of more than 2,000 products, half of which are basic chemicals. In addition to producing agricultural products, the company manufactures plastics, consumer products, and pharmaceuticals. Begun in 1890 by Herbert Dow to extract bromine from brine, the company came up with the revolutionary idea of using an electric current to separate bromides from brine. Dow eventually discovered chlorine bleach and pioneered the production of metal magnesium, used to manufacture automobiles after World War I. To produce agricultural chemicals, the company formed DowElanco, a joint venture with Eli Lilly, in 1989. DowElanco posted revenues of nearly US$2 billion in 1996, representing 10 percent of the parent company's sales. Dow AgroSciences was formed in 1997 after Dow Chemical bought out Eli Lilly & Company's 40 percent interest for US$1.2 billion. In 2004, Dow AgroSciences' annual sales topped US$3.36 billion, and the company employed approximately 5,500 people.

BASF

In 2000 the German chemical manufacturer BASF became the third largest fertilizer manufacturer in the world following acquisition of American Cyanamid. In 2004, total sales from all divisions reached approximately US$51.57 billion. Since the company's founding in 1865, Badische Analin und Soda Fabrik AG (now known as BASF) has been a major influence in the world chemical industry. BASF was also one of the three German chemical companies to make up the cartel IG Farben. Best known in the United States for its video and audiocassettes, the company is involved in the production of plastics, chemicals, oil and gas, dyes, and finishing products. In March of 2002, BASF insisted that it had no plans to sell off its 17 percent interest in Kali und Salz, the potash and fertilizer division. BASF admitted in 2002 that the company's plastics division had suffered in the generally stagnant economy of Europe, incurring a loss of US$412 million during the fourth quarter of 2001.

BASF acquired American Cyanamid Corp. from American Home Products Corp. in 2000 for US$3.8 billion. Founded in 1907, American Cyanamid developed the first synthetic fertilizer for North American farmers. The company grew to have a significant presence in 145 countries around the world and was acquired by American Home Products Corp., a pharmaceutical and health care company. In 1996 the parent company reported sales of US$14.0 billion, and American Cyanamid accounted for 13 percent of these revenues with US$1.9 billion.

AGRIUM

With about 8 percent of its annual US$2.5 billion revenues tied up in fertilizer shipments to Argentina, in the spring of 2002 Agrium was attempting to ascertain its exact losses following the extreme devaluation of the peso in that country, according to *Chemical Week*. Argentina once produced crops with little or no chemical fertilizers, but Canada-based Agrium saw huge potential in Argentina in the early 1990s as pesticide sales in 1992 tripled from 1991 levels of US$286 million. Agrium was part of a corporate team that built a US$600 million urea fertilizer plant in the early 1990s. Agrium, the Calgary, Canada chemical giant, achieved part of its great size in 1996 when it merged with Viridian Inc., for US$887.4 million, creating one of the biggest fertilizer corporations in the world.

Agrium also was a global leader for nitrogen. As of 2001, Agrium had 14 plants in North America and Argentina, producing mainly nitrogen products, but also phosphate, potash, sulfate and micronutrients used mostly in fertilizers. Additionally, the company had some 225 fertilizer retail stores in the United States alone, and an additional 20 in Argentina. Approximately 55 percent of the company's total sales came from the wholesale market. In 2004, total sales were nearly US$2.84 billion, up 13.6 percent from the previous year, and the company employed 4,667 people.

MAJOR REGIONS IN THE INDUSTRY

NORTH AMERICA

The United States began importing an increasing proportion of its potash fertilizers, importing a total of 10.4 mmt in 1996. However, nitrogen exports increased by 6.5 percent to 5.1 million metric tons (mmt). The United States used 53.5 million tons of fertilizer in 1999, according to the FAO, and is second to China in nitrogen production. It produces as much as 20 mmt of ammonia, much of which is used as a fertilizer product. The United States also is a large potash producer, getting much of its potash from Canada and other nations.

Canada retained its status as a leading producer of potash, selling about 60 percent of its production to the United States. In 1996, Canada's production level grew, allowing the country to post record exports. Domestic fertilizer consumption also expanded in 1996. In 1999, Canada's fertilizer industry added US$1.6 million in domestic imports and exported US$2.0 billion worth of product.

The early 2000s were a particularly hard time for the agricultural chemicals business, and in 2002 analysts said zero growth was expected for some time to come unless a blockbuster pesticide can be developed to lift business revenues.

The United States and Canada accounted for 29 percent of the world's farm chemical market, with sales of US$8.98 billion in 1996. In the United States, total consumption of fertilizers and plant nutrients increased from 24,877 tons in 1960 to 52,319 tons in 1994. Pesticide production was US$6.81 billion in 1993, according to the American Crop Protection Association, and pesticide consumption totaled US$6.35 billion. Fertilizer production in the country totaled US$318.7 million in 1994. However, in the mid-1990s, the use of nitrogenous fertilizers and potash declined by 4 percent and use of phosphates declined by 2 percent. The leading U.S. farm chemicals have traditionally been herbicides, which represented 65 percent of the country's market in 1996, followed by insecticides with 23 percent, and fungicides with 7 percent. The U.S. market was valued at US$20.2 billion in 2002. A surge in the chemicals market in general occurred in 2004, with an 8.8 percent increase in the volume of agricultural chemicals in particular. Growth was then expected to slow to 1.3 percent in 2005, and .8 percent in 2006 in that market.

EUROPE

Fertilizer consumption fell by 1.0 percent in Western Europe in 1996 to 17.7 mmt, reversing the previous year's advances. Fertilizer exports edged up that year by 3.5 percent to 10 mmt and imports slowed to 12.4 mmt. Although production in this region rose by 2.0 percent to 17.6 mmt, imports still represented 70 percent of Western Europe's fertilizer consumption.

In Eastern Europe, fertilizer consumption continued its slow recovery, climbing by one percent to 3.3 mmt. As the leading fertilizer user, Poland helped the regional increase, consuming 1.5 mmt in 1996, 6 percent above 1995 levels. Even though Bulgaria's use plummeted by 43 percent, other countries such as Hungary, Slovakia, and the Czech Republic experienced moderate increases, which offset Bulgaria's drop in use. Exports in the region grew the most. In 1996 they jumped 19 percent to 3.1 mmt, and overall fertilizer production rose by 14 percent to 5.3 mmt.

In the 15 countries that make up the former Soviet Union (FSU), fertilizer consumption has fallen since 1990. In 1996 it dropped to 4.4 mmt. The FSU accounted for 3.4 percent of the world's fertilizer use in 1996, in contrast to 17 percent in 1990 before its political dismantling. Inflation, poor distribution networks, and loss of subsidies have stifled fertilizer use in these nations. However, exports from FSU countries enjoyed considerable success in 1996, growing by 20 percent to 11.8 mmt. The Russian Federation and the Ukraine led in fertilizer production and exportation.

Western Europe ranked second largest in crop protection chemical sales in 1996, representing 26 percent of the global market. In 1996 farm chemical sales rose 3 percent to US$8.2 billion in Europe. However, pesticide use in Europe declined 6 to 10 percent in the early 1990s and was not expected to increase before 2000. Fertilizer consumption also has been dropping during this time and is predicted to continue doing so at a rate of about two percent per year throughout the decade. This trend has been brought about in part through the new Common Agricultural Policy (CAP) of the European Union. In 2001, the industry came under scrutiny following an explosion of a fertilizer plant at Toulouse, France, causing destruction and loss of life inside and outside the factory.

Despite the overall decline in the industry in this region from 1999 through 2002, in 2003, the European fertilizers and agricultural chemicals market rose by .9 percent to reach a volume of 22.41 billion metric tones (bmt) and was valued at US$107.85 billion. The leading sector by volume in 2003 was nitrogenous fertilizers, accounting for 60 percent of the market's volume at 13.46 bmt, followed by the phosphate fertilizers sector which accounted for 24.4 percent of the market's value at 4.02 bmt. It is projected that by 2008, the European market will have a value of US$105.34 billion, a decrease of 2.3 percent from 2003, and will account for 17.6 percent of the global market value.

ASIA

While Indonesia has been using increasingly larger amounts of fertilizers, higher prices for chemical fertilizers, urbanization, and decreasing agricultural growth in the 1990s and early 2000s led to lower fertilizer consumption in India, once the biggest consumer of chemical fertilizers. A governmental decision to decontrol fertilizers in 1992 led to the escalating prices for phosphatic and potassic fertilizers that caused shipments to drop, according to a 2002 report by *India Business Insight.*

In 1996 Asia made up the third largest market for agricultural chemicals, purchasing 22 percent of the global sales. In South Asia, most countries experienced growth in fertilizer use. India faced reduced subsidies in 1996 of phosphate and potash fertilizers, and therefore consumption of these kinds dropped off. On the other hand, nitrogen fertilizer remained subsidized, and its use increased. Pakistan, the second largest consumer, expanded its use of fertilizers, especially potash, because of strong wheat and cotton prices.

Developed Asian countries such as Japan and South Korea consumed 2.6 mmt of fertilizer in 1996; however, Japan's agricultural labor problems led to a 4 percent drop in the production and consumption of fertilizer, while imports increased by 4 percent. Exports from the region stood at only 700,000 metric tons, about 70 percent of which came from Korea.

Oceania reported a 3 percent rise in fertilizer consumption in 1996. In this case, 2.4 mmt of it was the result of an 11 percent increase in nitrogen fertilizer use in Australia. New Zealand's fertilizer use edged up by one percent to 700,000 metric tons, while its production held at 300,000 metric tons. The region's imports climbed dramatically, by about 14 percent.

From 1999 through 2003 the compound annual growth rate in market volume was one percent. By 2003, the Asia-Pacific fertilizers and agricultural market had a total value of US$291.26 billion, up 2.2 percent from the previous year. Nitrogenous fertilizers are the top source of revenue in the region, making up 61.9 percent of the market's value. It is forecast that by 2008, the Asia-Pacific region will account for 51.9 percent of the global market in this sector, an increase of 1.2 percent since 2003.

SOUTH AMERICA

South America held 12 percent of the world pesticide market in 1996, with Brazil accounting for 40 percent of that amount. Argentina and Colombia are also major players in the industry, with the smaller countries in the region relying mostly on imports. In 1996 agricultural chemical sales climbed 13 percent to US$3.8 billion. Although the rate of fertilizer consumption in Latin America is lower than the world average, the industry outlook is optimistic for the region, particularly in Brazil, as many economic problems of the 1980s have been resolved. Adding to the positive forecast is the fact that many South American countries have abundant supplies of resources, such as phosphate rock and sulfur, to utilize in the future. Moreover, increasing privatization in the region is expected to boost industry competitiveness both within South America and internationally. In early 2002, large fertilizer interests worldwide were still assessing their exact losses following the devaluation of the peso in Argentina.

Stagnant and fragile economies in Latin America caused a 20 percent drop in shipments of fertilizer to this region in 2001 as compared to 2000. In 1996, Latin America consumed 8.7 mmt of fertilizer, down more than 5 percent from 1995. South America accounted for almost 75 percent of the 8.7 mmt total, and Brazil and Mexico accounted for 60 percent of the total. Yet Brazil's use of fertilizer slipped in 1996 because of credit problems and Mexico's use dropped due to the devaluation of the peso, which drove prices up.

FURTHER READING

"Asia-Pacific—Fertilizers & Agricultural Chemicals." *Datamonitor Industry Market Research,* 1 November 2004.

"Bayer CropScience Intends to Overtake Syngenta." *Chemical Week,* 10 September 2003.

"Business Communications Company, Inc.," 2002. Available from http://www.bccresearch.com .

"The Canadian Fertilizer Institute," 2002. Available from http://www.ca/fertfacts .

Clapp, Stephen. "Monsanto Wheat Decision Raises Questions about Future Products." *Pesticide & Toxic Chemical News,* 17 May 2004.

Draper, Deborah J., ed. *Business Rankings Annual.* Detroit: Thomson Gale, 2004.

"Europe—Fertilizers & Agricultural Chemicals." *Datamonitor Industry Market Research,* 1 November 2004.

"Fertilizers and Pesticides in France, Germany, UK, US." *Euromonitor,* August 2004. Available from http://www.majormarketprofiles.com .

"Fertilizer Growth Lower in 1990s." *India Business Insight,* 26 March 2002.

Food and Agriculture Organization of the United Nations. *Current World Fertilizer Situation and Outlook,* 2002. Available from http://www.fao.org.

"France—Fertilizers & Agricultural Chemicals." *Datamonitor Industry Market Research,* 1 November 2004.

"Global—Chemicals." *Datamonitor Industry Market Research,* 1 November 2004.

Guiro, Angela. "EU Clears BASF's Acquisition of Cyanamid." *Bloomberg News,* 5 December 2001.

"Hoover's Company Capsules." 2005. Available from http://www.hoovers.com .

"International Trade Statistics." 2003. Available from http://www.wto.org .

James, Barry. "World Loses Ground to Deserts." *International Herald Tribune,* 4 April 2002.

Koprowski, Gene J. "Model Predicts Impact of Pesticides on Ecosystem." *Pesticide & Toxic Chemical News,* 9 February 2004.

Pfenniger, Chantal. "Syngenta to Help Clean Up Pesticides." *Bloomberg News,* 16 January 2002.

———. "Syngenta 2001 Earnings Little Changed." *Bloomberg News,* 28 February 2002.

Scott, Alex. "Bayer's Gaucho Insecticide Suspended in France." *Chemical Week,* 26 May 2004.

Sissell, Kara. "Argentine Uncertainties Hurt Agrium, Monsanto, and Eastman." *Chemical Week,* 13 February 2002.

"Strong Growth May Moderate in 2005." *Chemical Week,* 15 December 2004.

"Syngenta Says Lumax Is a U.S. Success." *Chemical Week,* 13 August 2003.

Walsh, Kerri. "Syngenta and Private Equity Firm Buy Advanta Seeds." *Chemical Week,* 19 May 2004.

Warrington, Hannah, and Rudy Ruitenberg. "BASF Sees Difficult 2002." *Chemical Week,* 14 March 2002.

Winder, Robert. "A Growing Debate." *Chemistry and Industry,* 19 January 2004.

"Zimbabwe; Rural Farmers Make Inroads into Soybean Production." *Africa News,* 9 April 2002.

SIC 2810

NAICS 325

CHEMICALS, INDUSTRIAL INORGANIC

The industrial inorganic chemical industry extracts and processes from inanimate material of the earth's crust a variety of chemicals and gases, often known as basic chemicals. Examples of industry products include alkalies, carbon dioxide, chlorine, nitrogen, numerous pigments, and a wide array of other chemicals for industrial use. For more information about the organic chemical industry, see also **Chemicals, Industrial Organic.**

INDUSTRY SNAPSHOT

Inorganic chemicals account for approximately one-quarter of total global chemical sales (not including allied products, such as plastic), which were hovering around US$1.94 trillion per year in 2003. The industrial inorganic chemical industry consists of four segments: alkalies and chlorine (or chloralkalies); industrial gases; pigments; and miscellaneous inorganic chemicals, which make up the bulk of industry output. Organic chemicals, which are derived from materials that contain carbon, make up most of the remainder of the industry. Because most leading companies and countries in the industry produce both organic and inorganic chemicals, both categories are closely intertwined statistically. Most inorganic (or basic) chemicals are building-block materials used to manufacture other compounds and products. Therefore, industry performance is closely tied to the health of the global economy.

A global economic slowdown in the early 2000s forced many chemical firms to restructure operations. Turbulent economies also brought on a wave of merger and acquisition activity. In 2001 the U.S. chemicals industry as a whole experienced its worst year since the early 1980s. The American Chemistry Council attributed the downswing to the faltering U.S. economy, rising energy costs, a strong U.S. dollar, overcapacity, weakening demand related to the consolidating manufacturing industry, and falling prices.

By the mid-2000s, competition was rising from emerging economies, particularly China. The American Chemistry Council predicted that by 2006 global chemical sales would reach US$382 billion.

Organization and Structure

Key Segments

Chloralkalies. Examples of alkalies and chlorine are chlorine, sodium hydroxide (caustic soda), sodium bicarbonate, sodium chlorate, and various potassium compounds. Chlorine and caustic soda are major chloralkalies. They both are created through the electrolysis of salt brine. Chlorine is used in the manufacture of numerous products: to make paper (a controversial application because of its environmental impact); for water and sewage treatment; as a fuel additive; and in a multiplicity of other applications. Other major chemicals in the chloralkalies group include soda ash and sodium chlorate. Soda ash is primarily consumed in the production of glass, other chemicals, and detergents and soaps. Sodium chlorate can be used as a cleaner substitute for chlorine in many applications, particularly paper manufacturing. The United States is the largest global producer of chloralkalies, partly because of its dominance of the natural soda ash market. The U.S. annual capacity of soda ash is 13.1 million metric tons.

Industrial Gases. Industrial gases include the major gases nitrogen, oxygen, hydrogen, carbon dioxide, and argon. They also encompass more than 100 specialty gases (such as krypton and xenon) which are used in medicine, electronics, aerospace, and other industries. Nitrogen, the largest gas product by volume, is used in the production of other chemicals because of its inert "blanketing" qualities. It is also utilized in applications ranging from metal manufacturing to food processing. Oxygen is also employed in a variety of applications, particularly chemical and glass manufacturing and medical care. Carbon dioxide is commonly used for refrigeration and freezing, and to carbonate beverages. Hydrogen is used in oil refining and ammonia production, among other applications. Gases are often sold in compressed liquid or solid form and then stored in cylinders or transported via pipelines.

The industrial gas sector differs from most other chemical segments in that it is dominated by four companies: Praxair Inc. (U.S.), Air Products and Chemicals, Inc. (U.S.), L'Air Liquide (France), and BOC Group PLC (United Kingdom). Each of those manufacturers controls a major portion of the global market for industrial gas. Both L'Air Liquide and Praxair controlled 18 percent of the worldwide industrial gas market, which was estimated at US$34.5 billion in 2001 by J.R. Campbell & Associates. BOC had a 14 percent market share, while Air Products secured an 11 percent share.

Inorganic Pigments. Inorganic pigments are used primarily to make paints and coatings. This category includes metallic oxides, metal powder suspensions, earth colors, and lead chromates. The largest selling pigment is titanium dioxide, which is consumed mostly by producers of paints and dyes, paper coatings and fillers, plastics, and rubber. According to the U.S. Geological Survey, worldwide titanium dioxide capacity was 4.3 million metric tons per year. During 2000, complex inorganic pigments that could provide diverse characteristics such as lightfastness and chemical resistance were growing in popularity. However, growth in heavy metal inorganic pigments was faltering due to environmental concerns. Major producers of pigments are Du Pont (U.S.) and Imperial Chemical Industries PLC (United Kingdom).

Other Inorganics. Miscellaneous inorganic chemicals, which constitute the bulk of industry sales, include basic building-block chemicals used to make a plethora of other chemicals, compounds, and products. The most common industrial inorganic chemical by far is sulfuric acid, with the United States producing almost 40 billion kg each year. Most sulfuric acid is used to produce fertilizer, but it is also used in numerous other applications ranging from oil refining to paper production. The U.S. Geological Survey estimated that nearly 75 percent of sulfuric acid used in 1999 was for phosphate fertilizer. Sulfuric acid is commonly consumed on the site at which it is produced. An oil company, for example, may produce the chemical for use on site to refine oil.

Another major inorganic is sulfur, most of which is used to make sulfuric acid. Major sulfur-producing countries include Poland, the United States, the former Soviet Union, and Canada. The United States is the world's largest consumer and producer of sulfur. Phosphoric acid is another important industrial inorganic. Most of it is used to make fertilizer, but it is also utilized in the manufacture of animal feed, food processing, and for other industrial uses. Other important inorganics include ammonia (and ammonia nitrate and sulfate), nitric acid, and hydrochloric acid.

Production Dynamics

The industrial inorganic chemicals industry differs from the organic chemical industry in that it is more mature. Most inorganic chemicals have existed commercially for several decades, and basic production techniques have changed little. Thus, market growth closely parallels expansion of the major industrial sectors that consume the base inorganics: the paper, construction, packaging, transportation, healthcare, paint and inks, and fertilizer industries. Overall, industry growth generally mimics overall economic health with the exception of a few segments including specialty gases. This industry looks for growth in the developing Asian and Latin American countries, where industrialization fuels demand for inorganics.

Because the industry is mature, particularly in industrial countries, most of its products are produced on a very high-volume, commodity basis. As a result, the industry is exceptionally consolidated with just a few producers in each geographic region dominating specific segments. Furthermore, it is characterized by low profit margins and emphasis on containing production costs. The most successful producers are those that can minimize labor and energy costs, obtain access to relatively low-cost raw materials, and minimize distribution costs (by locating near their primary customers, for example).

Because low production costs are crucial, a major industry issue since the 1970s, and particularly in the 1990s and beyond, has been environmental regulation. The inorganic chemical industry is one of the most polluting of all manufacturing businesses. To reduce detrimental impacts, all of the industrialized nations have implemented strict environmental controls that limit output and disposal of pollutants and by-products. Adherence to these regulations costs the industry billions of dollars annually and forced many companies out of business by the mid-1990s. Indeed, a corollary of increased production costs associated with environmental laws has been reduced competitiveness of companies in industrialized nations in relation to those in developing nations with less burdensome restrictions.

BACKGROUND AND DEVELOPMENT

Inorganic chemistry has its roots in the metallurgical and medical arts of ancient societies. The early Chinese and Egyptians were aware of simple alloys such as metallic salts and mineral products, as well as chemical processes related to glassmaking, enameling, dyeing, and painting. It was not until the eighteenth century, though, that rapid advances in the inorganic chemical sciences took place. In 1751 Sweden's G. Brandt isolated cobalt, a pivotal new discovery. Subsequent breakthroughs during the eighteenth century included British scientist Henry Cavendish's identification of hydrogen, his discovery of water's chemical composition, and his synthesis of nitric acid from moist air.

Despite the enormous influence of scientists before and during his time, Nicolas Leblanc of France is most often credited with giving birth to the chemical industry. Leblanc differed from his peers and predecessors in that he was determined to find commercial applications for chemical processes. Near the start of the nineteenth century, Leblanc achieved his goal when he made sodium carbonate (soda ash) out of salt. He is recognized as being the first person to deliberately convert one or more chemicals into other chemical products for economic purposes. Leblanc's goal remains the chief aim of the chemical industry today—to produce new and better chemical products more economically.

While Leblanc's discovery was neglected in France, it became extremely important in England in the soap and textile industries. As British alkali producers advanced the inorganic chemical industry during the 1800s, they lay the foundation for the modern inorganics business. Boosting industry success were important scientific breakthroughs of the late nineteenth century including the formulation of the periodic law in 1869 by Russia's Mendeleyev, and the discovery of the electron in 1897 by England's Sir Joseph J. Thompson. Of equal consequence were two developments early in the twentieth century in Germany: the articulation of the quantum theory by Max Weber in 1900, and the development of quantum mechanics in the early 1920s by Werner Heisenberg and Erwin Schrodinger.

During the first half of the twentieth century, both World War I and World War II caused massive demand for inorganic chemicals that were needed to feed the war machines. Although those wars spotlighted the importance of the inorganic chemical industry, they also were the source of the industry's decline in stature in relation to the organic chemical industry. Indeed, because of a shortage of raw materials during the wars, the chemical industry shifted its focus to the production of synthetic materials that could be created using organic chemicals.

Despite the emphasis on organic chemistry following World War II, the demand for inorganic chemicals continued to swell in the mid-1900s, particularly in the United States. The industry in the United States benefited from strong national economic and population growth and access to inexpensive raw materials. It also profited by supplying war-torn economies in Europe and Japan with inorganics. By the 1950s the United States was supplying and consuming the majority of global industry output in most industry segments.

By the 1960s, the inorganic chemical industry had largely achieved technological maturity. Most of the known inorganics were being produced commercially. The only technological barriers that remained were related primarily to increasing the efficiency of extraction and processing. Furthermore, the massive U.S. inorganic chemical market was reaching maturity, meaning that demand growth in that key market was waning. As a result, demand and profit growth in the inorganics industry became closely linked with the health of the global economy, which was indicative of demand for inorganics by other industries (e.g., steel and textiles). In addition, the business became more consolidated and increasingly focused on cutting production costs.

During the 1970s and 1980s the inorganics industry continued to grow more competitive. The United States managed to keep its global market share at about 25 percent, but both Western Europe and Japan ceded markets to emerging economies. South America and the Pacific Rim, for example, boosted their share of both demand and supply. China's inorganic industry made gains during the 1980s and early 1990s as a result of a flourishing domestic industrial sector and improvements in its transportation infrastructure.

The inorganic chemical market emerged as a truly global industry in the 1990s and it experienced cyclical performances related to worldwide economies as a result. In 1996 manufacturers saw declining demand in most industrial chemical sectors, including inorganics, but in 1997 sales picked up and key producing countries in North America and Europe reported modest increases in total production and exports. However, East Asia faced economic problems including currency devaluations, and skyrocketing debt in 1997 and 1998 thwarted domestic inorganic chemical production as well as trade. These Asian countries, on the other hand, began to show improvement by the early 2000s.

During the 1990s chemical manufacturers looked to the increased liberalization of international markets through trade agreements such as the General Agreement on Tariffs and Trade (GATT) and the North American Free Trade Agreement (NAFTA) to spur new growth, especially in developed economies. These agreements made it easier for established inorganic manufacturers from the United States and Europe to export their products to new markets, and also enabled developing countries to ship their chemicals to major industrial countries where they had the potential for pronounced price advantages over the domestically produced chemicals.

Following a mid-1990s trend, manufacturers in the chemical industry began merging and specializing in the late 1990s. This changed the look of companies from previous decades, when highly diversified chemical producers reigned and single companies manufactured agricultural chemicals, pharmaceuticals, organic chemicals, inorganic chemicals, and more. In the mid-1990s, firms in the agricultural chemical sector aligned with the life science industry and began divesting other concerns. Similarly, organic and inorganic chemical manufacturers began to concentrate on their core businesses and smaller operations merged with larger ones.

CURRENT CONDITIONS

General Trends. Indeed, merger and acquisition activity was a prominent trend throughout the chemicals industry in the late 1990s and beyond. During 1999 the global industry experienced US$38 billion in such activity. In 2000 that number dropped to US$33 billion and rose again in 2001 to US$37 billion. In 2001, 55 percent of all businesses acquired were European, 19 percent were based in the United States, and 26 percent were from Asia and the rest of the world. European buyers made the majority of purchases (48 percent), while the United States accounted for 30 percent. Prospects for future merger and acquisition activity in Europe remained strong due to the country's restructuring efforts.

A driving force behind this activity was the trend toward consolidation that had started in the 1990s. Highly dependent upon energy, the industry was exposed to high energy costs in 2000. Chemical manufacturers also were subject to continued government regulation and falling demand. Modest growth was projected for the basic chemicals industry, due in part to its maturity. According to the Federal Reserve Board, production levels in the United States had only changed by 0.1 percent from 1990 to 2000. However, from 1999 to 2000 production levels increased by 3.8 percent.

Another trend in the chemicals industry was the increased use of the Internet as a sales venue. According to the American Chemistry Council, chemicals sales by way of electronic data interchange (EDI) reached US$7.2 billion in 2000, 1.6 percent of total chemical sales. The Council predicted that by 2006, 17 percent of total global chemical sales would take place electronically and reach US$382 billion. U.S. Internet sales of industrial chemicals were expected to reach US$54.1 billion by 2006.

As globalization of business accelerated in the early 2000s, chemical companies in the United States faced intense competition from manufacturers in emerging economies, where quality control had greatly improved while production costs remained low. According to a *Business Week* report, 70 U.S. chemical plants shut down in 2004, and the industry planned at least 40 additional closures in 2005. At the same time, 120 major plants were under construction around the world; 50 of these were sited in China, while only one of these was located in the United States.

Chloralkalies. The chloralkali segment struggled in the early 1990s due to an international recession, but manufacturers experienced renewed growth by the mid-1990s because of increased demand for chlorine by vinyl producers. During the 1990s chlorine manufacturers also faced mounting resistance from environmental organizations (who called for a complete ban on chlorine production), as well as declining demand from paper manufacturers who switched to alternative methods of bleaching. (See also **Paper Mills**).

According to the Consulting Resources Corporation, an international management consulting firm, growth in the chlorine, caustic soda, and soda ash markets was expected to remain fairly stagnant. The company predicted that in the United States, with the world's largest supply of soda ash, production rates would increase by just 1.4 percent per year, from 39.7 million tons in 2002 to 42.5 million tons by 2007, and to 45.7 million tons in 2012. This segment of the industry is subject to maturing demand and is highly affected by fluctuating global economies. Exports of soda ash were 3.9 million tons in 2000, of which 44 percent went to Asian countries.

Industrial Gases. The industrial gases segment continued to grow moderately in the early 2000s, with worldwide sales of US$34.5 billion in 2001. This segment historically has performed well during industry downturns, and many companies with gas operations reported stronger earnings than their chemical counterparts. As with other segments of the chemical industry, competition became brisker as companies began to merge. Despite the merger trend, during 2001 the acquisition of BOC by L'Air Liquide and Air Products was thwarted by antitrust laws, along with Linde's planned purchase of Messer Greisheim.

Growth in industrial gases was expected to continue due in part to new growth opportunities in the hydrogen, electronics, healthcare, and food markets. The growing use of noncryogenic production technology also bode well for industrial gas firms. Two types of noncryogenic production, membrane separation and pressure swing absorption, used less energy than the traditional cryogenic air separation process, in which air was cooled and pressurized until it took liquid form. The improvements could produce gas at nearly half of the cost of regular cryogenic procedures. Noncryogenic production technology thus created new application opportunities in the industrial gases industry that previously had been too expensive. As for hydrogen, new cleaner fuels regulations have prompted petroleum refiners in North America and Europe to use more hydrogen, stimulating demand from outside suppliers. Analysts expect hydrogen demand to grow by more than 10 percent annually through 2008.

Inorganic Pigments. The U.S. color pigment segment, including organic, inorganic, and specialty pigments, was expected to grow by 5 percent per year to US$3.6 billion in 2007. London-based Information Research claimed that demand in Western Europe for pigments, extenders, and fillers for coatings would grow at 2.5 percent per year through 2006, while demand for titanium dioxide would grow at 2.8 percent per year. While organic pigments held the strongest growth potential, heavy metal inorganic pigments were expected to experience slower growth due to their unfriendly environmental characteristics. However, according to the Freedonia Group Inc., the complex inorganic pigments market, producing pigments with better lightfastness, chemical resistance, and various performance characteristics, held promising growth opportunities.

Other Inorganics. Industrialized nations' market share of most other inorganic chemicals was projected to decline as developing nations became larger players in the chemical industry. Several factors contributed to increased inorganic production by emerging economies during the new millennium. Perhaps the greatest advantage that manufacturers in developing nations have over established producers is proximity to growing industrial sectors, which drastically reduces important distribution costs. However, companies in less industrialized countries also benefit from inexpensive labor and cost advantages stemming from looser environmental regulations.

Environmental Regulation. The two chemical-producing regions most affected by environmental regulations since the 1970s have been North America and Western Europe. Chemical producers in those two regions are by far the largest contributors to global pollution. Regulatory measures enacted in the United States, where the chemical industry and the primary metal industry release the largest amounts of chemical waste, are typical of the enormous hurdles that inorganic chemical producers in most industrialized nations have had to overcome at the expense of billions of dollars annually.

Dominant legislation in the United States includes the sweeping federal Clean Air Act, the Toxic Substances Control Act, the Clean Water Act, the Superfund, the Resource Conservation and Recovery Act, and the Occupational Safety and Health Act. Most of these initiatives were enacted during the 1970s and 1980s and have been amended to include new restrictions. In essence, they serve to reduce pollutants released into the air, water, ground, and human body. They also establish measures to fund the cleaning of existing waste sites and to take care of future problems caused by the chemical industry.

In addition to the major core of environmental laws, U.S. producers are subject to many supplementary regulations including the Chemical Divisions and Trafficking Act; the Pollution Prevention Act; the Safe Drinking Water Act; the Food and Drug Cosmetic Act; and the Federal Insecticide, Fungicide, and Rodenticide Act of 1972. When combined with complementary state legislation, such a regulatory environment poses a disadvantage for companies attempting to compete with manufacturers in less regulated developing regions, a reality that has prompted many European, Japanese, and U.S. producers to set up operations in countries with less restrictive environmental laws.

The Environmental Protection Agency released a Toxic Release Inventory (TRI) in 2001 stating that the chemical industry reduced certain toxic chemical emissions by as much as 56 percent from 1988 to 1999. The American Chemistry Council claimed that the cost of complying with the TRI was approximately US$600 million in 2000.

Research and Technology

The industrial inorganic chemicals industry is characterized by a very low level of product research and development (R&D). However, many companies conduct and fund research related to the environment, most of which is aimed at developing cleaner production facilities and processes and minimizing the environmental impact of wastes. Most capital investment in the industry is oriented toward improving production and distribution processes. Such initiatives include factory automation, and information systems designed to reduce labor and energy costs and improve customer service. According to the American Chemistry Council, the total U.S. chemicals industry spends more than US$22 billion annually in research and development.

In South Africa, the Chemical and Allied Industries' Association developed a questionnaire to guide interviews with key groups on their concerns about chemical hazards and their suggestions for improvements. Groups considered for the pilot study included government representatives, organizations, and customers.

In Brazil, another pilot study utilized the Internet. ABIQUIM, the Brazilian chemical association, and the University of Brazilia developed a Web-based questionnaire with subjects covering availability of data. Target subjects included chemicals, education, and training courses on handling processes, and successful technology applications. The questionnaire was sent to more than 600 chemical companies, 200 government agencies, and departments of 12 major universities in Brazil with related interests. Results will help outline an action plan under auspices of the National Commission on Chemicals Safety.

Workforce

International employment figures for inorganic chemical production are inexact because not all countries separate inorganic from organic chemical manufacturing for statistical purposes. In the United States approximately 98,000 people were employed in inorganic chemical production in 2000. These workers earned between US$13.91 per hour to US$29.97 per hour depending on the job. According to the U.S. Department of Labor, employment in the chemicals industry is expected to decline by 17 percent from 2002 to 2012. For more information on chemical industry workforces, see also **Chemicals, Industrial Organic** later in this chapter.

Approximately three-fifths of the industry is employed in production, installation, maintenance, and repair. Just over one-fifth work in management, business, finance, and administration. The industry is characterized by a high degree of automation; it employs a relatively large number of skilled production workers in relation to less mature industries. As a result wages tend to be higher on average than other manufacturing industries. Furthermore, labor unions, particularly in Europe and the United States, are established within the industry and tend to boost wages and benefits.

Characterized by generally high wages and comparatively good working conditions, the inorganic chemical industry workforce has declined steadily since the 1970s and 1980s. Regardless of large increases in output, rampant automation and downsizing have reversed industry employment growth in industrialized nations. The downsizing effect was particularly pronounced in the early and mid-1990s, when European inorganics producers moved toward the practices that U.S. manufacturers had initiated in the early 1980s. The only employment gains were found in emerging countries, where wages are much lower and inorganics producers can afford to be much less automated. Overall, the inorganic chemicals industry was projected to lose nearly 16,000 jobs by 2010.

INDUSTRY LEADERS

As with workforce statistics, the value of inorganic chemical sales and profits is diluted by manufacturers' crossover activities, such as organic chemical and plastics production. All of the industry leaders described above are active in both the inorganic and organic chemical industries, and most are active in other businesses as well. With the exception of the industrial gas segment, the inorganic industry leaders are profiled in greater detail under the heading **Chemicals, Industrial Organic**.

L'Air Liquide SA. L'Air Liquide is the world's largest manufacturer of industrial gases. The French producer generated revenues of US$10.5 billion in 2003, about 88 percent of which were attributable to gas sales. L'Air Liquide was founded in 1902 by Georges Claude, a pioneer of acetylene technology by age 26. Claude enjoyed success with his company throughout the early 1900s. After World War II, though, he was convicted of helping the Nazis to develop a "flying bomb" and was jailed until 1950.

L'Air Liquide continued to prosper during the mid-1900s, despite the absence of its founder. In the 1960s and 1970s the company expanded in the United States and grew through mergers and acquisitions. Its global expansion into Japan, Australia, and numerous other overseas markets during the 1980s complemented its virtual lock on the French gas market and its strength in the United States.

In the early 2000s L'Air Liquide controlled about 18 percent of the global industrial gas market, had more than 130 subsidiaries in 65 countries, and employed a workforce of 31,900. In 2004 Air Liquide's parent company acquired esser Griesheim's North American, German, and U.K. business for more than US$3 billion. Air Liquide America supplies industrial gases to companies in the automotive, chemicals, food and beverage, and healthcare industries. Capabilities exist to ship its products in cylinders or by pipelines, or manufacture it on site. In June 2004 Air Liquide America announced it had signed an exclusive 15-year carrier gas supply agreement for a new 300 mm semiconductor manufacturing facility to be constructed in Richardson, Texas, according to *Asia Intelligence Wire.*.

BOC Group PLC. One of the top three gas producers in the world is BOC Group PLC, which also manufactures specialty gases and vacuum pumps for the microchip industry, and supplies food and clothing for Marks and Spencer stores found in the United Kingdom. BOC was founded in 1885 by two French brothers, Arthur and Leon Quentin Brin. The company originally was named Brin's Oxygen Company but became the British Oxygen Company (BOC) in 1906. BOC prospered during the early twentieth century by pioneering advances in various gases. It continued to expand during the mid-1900s and started to diversify its operations in the 1960s. It expanded globally through mergers and acquisitions during the 1970s and 1980s and became particularly active in the healthcare and graphite markets. It later sold its healthcare interest, through the Afrox unit, to focus more on its gas business. Industrial gases remained a key revenue source going into the new millennium, accounting for as much as 90 percent. Through BOC Edwards, it also makes high-purity gases used for industrial metals and other products. BOC's Gist unit managed supply-chain and logistics for UK retailer Marks and Spencer, among others.

In 2004 BOC registered about US$8.3 billion in sales, the majority of which came from chemical industry operations. In June 2004 *Asia Intelligence Wire* reported that a new air separation unit would be built by Eastern Industrial Gases (EIG), a joint venture between BOC and Air Liquide. This expansion follows the signing of a 15-year contract for the supply of oxygen from EIG to Siam Asahi Technoglass. The new plant also will supply oxygen and nitrogen to other industrial customers. The *Asia Intelligence Wire* also reported that BOC had acquired a 30 percent stake in Compania de Nitrogeno de Cantarell SA de Mexico, a nitrogen company, from Duke Energy Corp. SinoCast stated that Shanghai Petrochemical Company Limited, a Sinopec Corp. subsidiary, and BOC signed a letter of intent to build a joint venture. It would ensure the supply of industrial gases in Jinsahn District. Rumors spread about a possible merger between BOC and Linde. *Europe Intelligence Wire* claimed that a Goldman Sachs broker said: "The geographical complementarity between BOC and Linde is excellent—it is probably the best combination of any of the five major global industrial gas companies."

In 2005 BOC announced a US$50 million deal to supply hydrogen to Chevron and Holly Corporation's refineries in Utah. The hydrogen will be used in the production of cleaner-burning fuels. When the new plant in Salt Lake City begins operations in 2006, it will, together with the company's two Ohio plants, bring BOC's total hydrogen output in the United States to 175 million standard cubic feet per day.

Linde AG. Linde AG of Germany is divided into three units: Gas and Engineering, Material Handling, and Refrigeration. The company is a leading producer of industrial and medical gases. It also has an engineering unit that builds process plants for companies in the petrochemical, pharmaceutical, and gas manufacturing industries. Its material handling division is among the world's top makers of forklifts. Linde manufactures warehouse equipment, engines, transmission systems, and hydraulic control devices. Plans were announced to sell the refrigeration equipment and cooling systems units to Carrier for US$400 million. In July 2004 Linde announced plans to acquire German respiratory homecare specialist Crio Medizintechnik, according to *Europe Intelligence Wire*. Linde reported 2003 revenues of US$11.2 billion.

MAJOR COUNTRIES IN THE INDUSTRY

Europe. With sales worth 580 billion euros (about US$700 billion) in 2004, the European Union was the largest chemical producing area in the world, ahead of Asia and the United States. It was also the largest exporter and importer of chemicals, controlling more than 50 percent of the global market. Germany remained the leading producer, followed by France, Italy, and the United Kingdom. Among former eastern-bloc countries that joined the European Union in 2004, Poland was the largest chemicals producer. Despite its market dominance, Europe saw its exports fall in 2004, due primarily to competition from the weak dollar. Analysts expected this trend to continue at least through 2005, though production was expected to increase by about 2.6 percent.

Germany. Germany, the second largest chemical-producing country in the world, suffered from a weak economy during the early 2000s and experienced relatively sluggish growth compared to other E.U. producers. The improved global economy in 2004, however, contributed to a 3.5 percent sales increase over 2003 figures. Production also increased, with output of inorganic base chemicals growing by 8 percent. Faced with rising costs for raw materials, however, the industry raised prices by about 1 percent in 2004, and industry analysts expected further price increases in 2005.

France. France's chemistry industry was ranked fifth in the world as of 2005, and accounted for about 20 percent of the chemical industry in the European Union. It has been called "the cradle of modern chemistry," and has earned praise for major scientific and industrial development in this field. In 2000 France's exports to the United States increased by 27 percent. In Central and Eastern Europe they rose by 21 percent, and Asian growth eclipsed 20 percent. Of France's 130 major chemical companies, 43 produce inorganic chemicals, a segment that employed about 7,000 workers in 2004.

Increasing costs for raw materials contributed to production declines in the French chemical industry in the early 2000s, and the strong euro against the weak dollar resulted in smaller export profit margins through 2003. Still, France exported US$58.8 billion of chemicals in 2003. Because exports are more important than domestic sales to the French chemicals industry, manufacturers were worried about proposed new regulations to tighten environmental safeguards, which could go into effect in January 2006. The cost of compliance, analysts feared, could adversely affect sales to major markets such as the United States.

Growth in France's chemical industry in 2004 was led by consumer products such as soaps, perfumes, and household cleaning products. This sector was projected to grow by about 4 percent in 2005. Inorganics were expected to grow by 2.4 percent.

Emerging Nations. By 2000, one-third of global chemicals sales came from regions outside of the United States, Canada, Western Europe, and Japan. According to the American Chemistry Council, long-term industry growth rates from 1999 to 2010 for the major chemical regions in percent per year were: China and East Asia, 7.5 percent; other Asia/Pacific countries, 6.25 percent; Mideast, 5.5 percent; other Latin American countries, 5.25 percent; Mexico, 4.75 percent; Africa, 3.75 percent; Central and Eastern Europe, 3.5 percent; United States, 3.25 percent; Canada, 3.25 percent; Western Europe, 2.75 percent; Japan, 2.0 percent.

Mexico's National Chemical Industry Association reported that the country's chemical industry registered a US$6.0 billion trade deficit in 2001. Exports fell by approximately 3 percent over 2000 figures to 5.1 million metric tons. Chemical production fell, especially in the industrial inorganics sector, due to the weakening economy in the United States. India's chemical industry, including the agrochemical, petrochemical, and pharmaceutical segments, reached US$28 billion in 2004 accounted for about 12.5 percent of the country's total industrial output. It exports several categories of inorganic and organic chemicals to the United States, the United Kingdom, and Taiwan. The Indian Chemical Manufacturers Association predicted that chemical demand in the country would grow at approximately 11 percent per year through 2010. In Peru, the basic chemicals industry grew by 3 percent. Mining investments in the country created increased demand for basic chemicals while imports of inorganic chemicals were expected to increase by 5 percent during 2001.

Analysts at the 2002 Asia Plastics and Chemical Industry Meeting (APCIM) in Singapore claimed that the Asia/Pacific region would offer the most promising growth prospects for the industry during the first decade of the 2000s. These analysts also claimed that the region accounted for nearly one-third of global chemical consumption and that it would soon account for nearly half. The APCIM projected that the Asian industry would grow from US$260.0 billion in 2000 to US$1.0 trillion by 2010, and that Asia would account for approximately 40 percent of the US$2.6 trillion global chemical output by 2010.

United States. The U.S. chemical industry, worth US$460 billion in 2003, is the largest producer and consumer of inorganic chemicals in the world. It supplied approximately 25 percent of global chemical output in 2003. That year, U.S. total exports of chemicals exceeded US$91 billion, according to the American Chemistry Council, making chemicals the largest exporting sector in the country. Approximately 9,125 corporations made up the U.S. chemicals industry at the beginning of the 2000s, of which about 1,725 produced and marketed industrial inorganic chemicals.

Basic inorganic chemical production rose by 3.8 percent in 2000. However, in 2001 the U.S. chemical industry experienced its worst year overall since the early 1980s. Inorganic chemicals felt the brunt of high energy costs, overcapacity, and weakening demand. Production levels for aluminum sulfate fell by 10.6 percent from 1999 to 2000; ammonia fell 4.5 percent; ammonium sulfate fell 0.3 percent; chlorine fell 1.0 percent; nitric acid fell 1.7 percent; phosphoric acid fell 5.9 percent; sodium hydroxide fell 8.2 percent; sodium sulfate fell 19.2 percent; and sulfuric acid fell 2.5 percent. Production levels rose for titanium dioxide, sodium chlorate, hydrochloric acid, and ammonium nitrate.

Production increased in all segments of the U.S. chemicals industry in 2004 by an average of 5.3 percent. Output of basic inorganics grew by only 0.2 percent, but paints, coatings, and adhesives grew by 5.4 percent. Helped by the relative weakness of the dollar, exports rose significantly in late 2004, and analysts predicted export growth of about 13 percent in 2005. Rising costs for raw materials contributed to price increases that raised the value of U.S. chemical shipments by an average of 7.6 percent. Production growth was expected to moderate in 2005, reaching about 3.4 percent.

Employment in the U.S. chemicals industry has fallen consistently since 1998, when it reached 982,500 workers. This figure was 907,900 in 2003 and dropped further to 891,000 in 2004. Even so, labor productivity rose by about 5.1 percent in 2005. The trend toward more efficient production and lower overall employment was expected to continue, with the U.S. Department of Labor projecting an employment decline in the industry of about 17 percent from 2002 to 2012.

In emerging economies, inorganics producers continued to compete for shares of the U.S. import market in the early 2000s, particularly in the case of commodity inorganics because they could effectively undercut the prices of U.S. domestic output. As a result, many U.S. producers have shifted their focus to specialty organic chemicals that, unlike most inorganics, are not considered commodities. These specialties are harder to produce, require more sophisticated technology, and thus garner higher prices and wider profit margins than commodity chemicals. However, the United States was expected to benefit, at least in the short term, from proliferating demand for inorganics in emerging regions.

Further Reading

Arndt, Michael. "No Longer the Lab of the World: U.S. Chemical Plants Are Closing in Droves as Production Heads Abroad." *Business Week,* 2 May 2005.

"BOC Signs Contracts to Supply Hydrogen to Chevron and Holly Oil Refineries." *Business Wire,* 23 June 2005.

The Business of Chemistry: Essential to Our Quality of Life and the U.S. Economy. American Chemistry Council, 2005. Available from http://http://www.accnewsmedia.com.

Career Guide to Industries: Chemical Manufacturing. U.S. Department of Labor Bureau of Labor Statistics, 27 February 2004. Available from http://www.bls.gov.

Chang, Joseph. "Global Chemistry Industry Completes $37 Billion in Transactions in 2001." *Chemical Market Reporter,* 25 February 2002.

"Chloralkali's Delicate Balance: Strong Worldwide Demand for PVC Is Driving Increased Chlorine Production." *Chemical Marketing Reporter,* 16 September 1996.

Denton, Timothy. "Reaching New Shades with High Performance Pigments." *Chemical Market Reporter,* 3 November 1997.

"Facts and Figures for the Chemical Industry." *Chemical and Engineering News,* 25 June 2001.

Freeburn, Christopher T. "Helium Suppliers Step In as Uncle Sam Step Out." *Chemical Week,* 19 November 1997.

"Global E-Sales Take Off." *Chemical Business Newsbase,* 22 May 2001.

Hunter, David. "Industrial Gases: Getting a Lift from Recovery." *Chemical Week,* 18 February 2004.

"Industry Could Be Nearing Trough of Current Down Cycle." *Chemical Market Reporter,* 21 January 2002.

Johnson, Dexter. "Electronic Chemicals To Face Competition as Market Matures." *Chemical Market Reporter,* 17 November 1997.

———. "Industrial Gas Industry Is Driven by Economic, Environmental Forces." *Chemcial Market Reporter,* 22 September 1997.

———. "Industrial Gases Move on Site." *Chemical Market Reporter,* 28 April 1997.

Layman, Patricia L. "Strong Exports of 1997 To Slow and Grow To Moderate in '98." *Chemical & Engineering News,* 15 December 1997.

"Outlook for Pigments Demand Brightens Up." *Chemical Week,* 15 October 2003.

Peaff, George. "Mexico's Economy, Chemical Trade Still Robust." *Chemical & Engineering News,* 15 December 1997.

Storck, William J. "U.S. Chemical Industry To See Modest Growth Next Year as Economy Cools." *Chemical & Engineering News,* 15 December 1997.

"Summary of Pilot Studies," 2002. Available from http://www.icca-at-wssd.org.

Tremblay, Jean-Francois. "Regional Economic Crisis, Capacity Additions Will Hurt Profits." *Chemical & Engineering News,* 15 December 1997.

Warren, Robert. "An Unsettled Japan: A Combination of Blossoming Asian Markets and Drooping Japanese Economy Is Forcing the Pace of Japan's Chemical Trade Evolution." *Chemical Market Reporter,* 19 February 1996.

Westervelt, Robert, and Ian Young. "Global Economic Slowdown Prompts More Profit Warnings." *Chemical Week,* 4 July 2001.

"World Chemical Outlook." *Chemical & Engineering News,* 10 January 2005. Available from http://www.pubs.acs.org.

SIC 2860
NAICS 325

CHEMICALS, INDUSTRIAL ORGANIC

The organic chemical industry manufactures a large number of compounds for commercial and industrial uses. Important industry products include non-cyclic organic chemicals and their metallic salts; solvents; polyhydric alcohols and fatty acids; synthetic perfumes and flavoring materials; rubber processing chemicals; plasticizers; synthetic tanning agents; chemical warfare gases; cyclic crudes; dyes and organic pigments; and natural gum and wood chemicals.

Many industry firms also produce inorganic chemicals. For more detailed coverage of these businesses, see **Chemicals, Industrial Inorganic**.

INDUSTRY SNAPSHOT

Organic chemistry emerged during the middle and late nineteenth century, largely as a result of the efforts of French, English, and German scientists. Not until the early twentieth century, though, were organic chemicals manufactured on a commercial scale. A shortage of natural materials during World War II prompted intense research and development efforts related to synthetic materials, particularly in the United States.

By the mid-1900s, the United States had assumed a commanding lead in the global organic chemical industry. Its dominance was challenged during the late 1900s as Western Europe and Japan vied for world market share. By the mid-2000s, global output was expected to rise by more than 30 percent, but most of the increase was projected to be in Asia, largely due to China's exploding market. In fact, while consumers worldwide were expected to double in number by 2015, the number of chemical consumers in China was predicted to grow tenfold.

Organic chemicals represent a significant segment of the global chemical industry, which reached US$1.79 trillion in 2003. For the fourth quarter of 2003 alone, worldwide revenues hit nearly US$1.6 billion. International trade accounted for a large portion of revenues: for 2003, 30 percent of all global chemical sales were international sales. The U.S. exported US$20.5 billion in organic chemicals. The chemical industry was especially robust in 2004, with volumes, prices, profits, and chemical stock prices all increasing despite high raw material and the rapidly rising cost of oil. The industry was expected to continue this trend in 2005.

ORGANIZATION AND STRUCTURE

Chemical industry products are divided into organic and inorganic substances. Chemical companies make goods that fall into one or both categories. Inorganic chemicals, which are derived from the inanimate material of the earth's crust, include compounds such as sulfuric acid, sulfur, phosphoric acid, and hydrogen peroxide. Organic chemicals are mostly derived from substances that contain carbon, such as petroleum, coal, and natural gas. Petroleum-based chemicals, or petrochemicals, account for the large majority of organics industry shipments in the United States. For example, petrochemicals including ethylene and propylene were the largest organic chemicals in terms of volume. In 2000, production of ethylene was 55.4 billion pounds while propylene accounted for 31.8 billion pounds.

The organic chemical industry serves one primary purpose: to take a relatively few fundamental raw chemicals that contain carbon and combine and transform them into new substances with desirable physical properties. Using carbon as a basic building block, chemists are able to unite other elements such as nitrogen, hydrogen, oxygen, sulfur, and chlorine to generate a multitude of different compounds. Furthermore, each resultant compound can be manipulated, with heat or additives, for example, to produce an infinite variety of characteristics and grades. Organics play an indispensable role in modern society. They are essential ingredients to plastics, synthetic fibers, rubber, adhesives, inks, dyes, explosives, and fertilizers, and provide vital support for the health, food, transportation, and communication industries.

The organic chemicals business is separated into three major segments: wood and gum chemicals; intermediates and pigments; and miscellaneous organics, which encompass the large majority of global output. Wood and gum chemicals represent the smallest sector of the industry. Such products are distilled from both softwoods and hardwoods and include natural dyes, fuels, tar and pitch, rosin, lacquers, solvents, alcohol, and oils. They are often sold in pure form, but may also be altered or used as additives to produce products ranging from wood treatments and paints to roof shingles and flame retardants.

Intermediate chemicals are distinguished from other organics by their closed-ring molecular structure, which allows them to combine with other chemicals to create a nearly infinite variety of intermediate compounds. The three primary "aromatic" chemicals manufactured by this sector are benzene, xylene, and toluene. They are used to create a multiplicity of intermediates. For example, benzene may be combined with sulfuric acid or other substances to make plastic resins, epoxy, rubber, nylon, and detergents. Xylene is often mixed with other chemicals to create gasoline additives, solvents, polyester fibers, plastic bottles and coatings, and high-tech engineering resins. Toluene is commonly used in the production of textiles, drugs, inks, adhesives, and photographic film. Toluene is also utilized in the manufacture of benzene. Organic dyes and pigments classified in this segment are usually obtained from petroleum through lengthy chemical processes. They are used to color food, clothing, and other goods.

The organic chemical industry also produces thousands of miscellaneous chemicals and resultant compounds that comprise the bulk of industry output. The most common category of organics is aliphatics, or olefins, which are straight-chain hydrocarbons. They can be made using either petroleum or (usually) natural gas, and turned into marketable products such as ethylene, propylene, and butadiene—the basic ingredients for most organic chemicals and synthetic materials. Ethylene, the largest industry product by volume, is used in the production of plastic, rubber, fibers, detergents, solvents, and anesthetics. Olefin is often used in the production of packaging, foam, gasoline, and fibers. Butadiene is most commonly consumed by manufacturers of synthetic rubber and nylon. Synthetic methanol and methanol derivatives also comprise a significant portion of miscellaneous organic chemical industry output. For example, methyl tert-butyl ether (MBTE), a gasoline oxygenate, is among the most common methanol derivatives.

International Standards and Organizations

In an effort to unify the global chemical industry, regional and international standards and organizations have been established. Chief among them is the International Union of Pure and Applied Chemistry (IUPAC), and the International Organization for Standardization (ISO). IUPAC was formed in 1919, relatively early in the development of modern chemistry, as a means of creating international standards for chemically related symbols, atomic weights, and nomenclature. It is a nonprofit organization composed of representative National Adhering Organizations (NAOs) in member countries, Associate National Adhering Organizations (ANAOs), and regional and international groups and consortiums like the European Federation of Chemical Engineering. In 2002, IUPAC had 45 NAOs, 16 ANAOs, and nearly 1,000 chemists from around the globe who volunteered for its 37 commissions.

IUPAC has four primary goals: to promote international cooperation among chemists; to study issues of global importance, such as regulations and standards; to coordinate the efforts of other international chemical groups; and to advance chemistry in all aspects on an international scale. It achieves its goals through various ongoing programs and initiatives such as CHEMRAWN, a series of international conferences. Its seven main divisions include physical and biophysical chemistry; inorganic chemistry; organic and bio-molecular chemistry; macromolecular chemistry; analytical chemistry; chemistry and the environment; and chemistry and human health. In the early 2000s IUPAC focused its attention on issues related to sustaining chemical production given the harmful environmental effects inherent to the chemical manufacturing process.

Unlike IUPAC, the International Organization for Standardization (ISO) is a multi-industry initiative that has been adopted in several international areas of business, including the chemical industry. The ISO adopted a set of standards designed to assure quality and standardization in product development and production for use in business-to-business contracts. For example, it establishes specific quality requirements for chemicals that must be met by registered members. Similarly, the ISO requires that chemical producers document processes to ensure that, even if all facility personnel were replaced, the company would continue to produce the exact same quality and grade of material.

Companies that demonstrate adherence to the standards may become certified by the ISO. Thus, customers that demand high-quality chemicals often prefer to deal with companies that are certified, or "licensed to compete," by the ISO. The cost of ISO registration is high, but it had become commonplace and nearly a necessity for competitors in the chemical industry by the new millennium. In 2001 the ISO had 143 national standards bodies, some 2,885 technical bodies, and more than 13,500 international standards and standards-type documents. The ISO claimed that in 2001 there were approximately 12 technical ISO-related meetings on each working day somewhere in the world.

Background and Development

Chemicals have been produced for commercial use since ancient times. Ancient Egyptian and Chinese civilizations were the first to develop chemical processes related to dyeing, leather tanning, and glass making. It was not until the mid-1800s, after the presence of carbon in all organic chemicals was discovered, that the organic chemical industry began to develop.

Englishman William Henry Perkin, known as the father of the organic chemical industry, was the first chemist to synthesize an organic chemical for commercial use. Working in his father's house in 1856, the 18-year-old inventor accidentally created a synthetic dye using a piece of coal tar. Although he received knighthood for his efforts, it wasn't until 1865 that the chemical structure of Perkin's dye was understood. In that year, German Friedreich von Kekule announced his breakthrough theory of the benzene ring. Building on Kekule's theory, chemists were able to build millions of new organic chemicals during the nineteenth and early twentieth centuries, many of which displaced natural materials and dyes. Chemists learned to synthesize petroleum and natural gas to create petrochemicals on a commercial scale in the early twentieth century.

The organic chemical industry was originally centered in both England and France. German chemists assumed a leading role in the industry in the early twentieth century, in part because of intense research efforts during World War I. During that period a huge demand arose for gasoline, rubber products, textiles, detergents, and plastics that could be created with petrochemicals. Germany assumed a dominant industry position with the formation of the government-supported IG Farben conglomerate, which it created in 1925 through the combination of three large chemical companies.

It was during World War II that the organic chemical industry vaulted to international prominence. During the war, a shortage of natural and man-made materials resulted in massive industry expansion. For instance, production of synthetic rubber in the United States bolted from 72,000 tons in 1939 to more than 800,000 tons in 1945.

Japan and the United States joined their European counterparts during the early 1940s as leaders in the development and production of organic chemicals and related products. After the conclusion of the war, however, the U.S. organic chemical industry was the only one left largely intact. IG Farben was dismantled by the Allies, while the facilities of other countries had been battered by the conflict. As a result, U.S. chemical sales ballooned after World War II, as international customers looked to the United States to supply their chemical needs. The United States also benefited from strong domestic population growth and technological advances in other industrial sectors. By the 1950s, U.S. organic chemical manufacturers supplied and consumed well over half of global production.

To supply surging global demand, the U.S. organic chemical industry grew at a faster rate than any other U.S. industrial sector during the mid-1900s, with the exception of the automobile industry. The explosion of automobile production in industrialized nations during the 1950s, 1960s, and 1970s created a massive demand for chemicals utilized in the production of rubber, paint, and gasoline. Likewise, commercial and residential construction booms generated huge needs for paneling, roofing, insulation, carpet, draperies, upholstery, varnishes, and other chemical-based building materials. Defense and consumer products markets soared also.

The United States' share of the global market began to slip during the 1960s and 1970s, as war-torn European economies regained their strength. During the 1980s, both European and U.S. manufacturers ceded some markets to the Japanese organic chemical industry, which maintained an aggressive assault on global organic markets that began in the 1970s. In addition, manufacturers in emerging countries such as South Korea and Mexico began to vie for market share. At the same time, several other factors impacted the international industry. High petroleum prices during the early 1980s pummeled overall industry profits, while manufacturers in industrialized nations were hampered by a wave of costly environmental legislation that reduced their ability to compete against producers in less-regulated emerging nations. Finally, new technologies, particularly those related to automation and information systems, increased the efficiency of the industry.

These varied influences resulted in a major power shift in the international chemical industry during the 1980s. While Western Europe, Japan, and the United States all enjoyed demand, revenue, and profitability gains during the decade, especially the latter 1980s, their share of the global market slipped because of increased competition from emerging nations. For instance, while U.S. chemical sales ballooned nearly 100 percent between the early 1980s and early 1990s, the U.S. share of the global chemical export market slipped from about 17 percent to 15 percent. Even the vaunted Japanese organic chemical industry lost market share during the early 1990s. Perhaps the greatest success story in the global chemical industry during the 1980s was China, which led the world in percentage of GDP represented by chemical sales and in chemical industry growth rate among the leading 10 chemical-producing countries. China's chemical industry was slumped by the global slowdown of the early 1990s, but its long term potential was seen by some industry observers as phenomenal, particularly in the inorganic and commodity chemicals markets.

The winners in the new economic world order were manufacturers in emerging regions, particularly in the Pacific Rim. Those companies found that they could produce low-tech, commodity-like organics much less expensively than could their counterparts in more industrialized nations. Labor costs were much lower than those in industrialized nations, while emerging economies were also unencumbered by environmental laws that were costing competitors in the United States, Europe, and Japan billions of dollars every year. Such factors enabled developing countries to double their combined share of the global export market for all chemicals and allied products from 7 percent in 1980 to nearly 14 percent in the early 1990s.

With countries such as China and India competing in the world organic chemical market, traditional leaders including the United States lost shares of the market in the late 1990s. With low-price dyes, China and India garnered significant exports throughout the 1990s in this segment of the industry. Environmental concerns and labor costs drove manufacturers in Europe and the United States to move production to Asia, in particular to China, Taiwan, and India. In the dye segment, this trend was the most pronounced, since these countries also have strong textile and apparel industries that rely on dyes.

In the mid- to late 1990s, manufacturers in the chemical industry began to merge and specialize. Although diversified chemical producers thrived in previous decades, manufacturing agricultural chemicals, pharmaceuticals, organic chemicals, inorganic chemicals, and more, they began repositioning themselves during this period. The agricultural chemical sector aligned itself with the life science (pharmaceutical) industry and began divesting itself of other concerns. Similarly, organic and inorganic chemical manufacturers started to concentrate on their core businesses, and smaller operations merged with larger ones. Global merger and acquisition activity continued into the new millennium, including Dow Chemical's US$9 billion merger with Union Carbide.

Organic chemical trade increased throughout the 1990s and beyond as established developers tapped emerging chemical markets and as industry newcomers from China, India, and South Korea began exporting large quantities of organic chemicals. The weakening U.S. economy actually benefited several foreign chemical industries. The United States' import levels in organic chemicals rose significantly between 1998 and 2001 due to the weakening economy and a strong U.S. dollar. U.S. products also began to lose their competitive edge during this time, making the region a lucrative export destination for foreign chemical manufacturers. In 1998, U.S. organic chemical imports were US$18.3 billion. By 2001 that number had climbed to more than US$30 billion.

CURRENT CONDITIONS

Worldwide, the overall chemical industry records some US$1.8 trillion in yearly sales. In what was deemed a turnaround year for the industry, global production rose more than 6.3 percent in 2004. That year, the U.S. accounted for US$506.5 billion in chemical shipments. In 2001, U.S. exports of organic chemicals were estimated at US$16.5 billion, a fall from US$17.9 billion registered in 2000. By 2003, the numbers were back up to US$20.5 billion, out of US$94.2 billion for the overall chemical industry. Japan exported US$51.3 billion, of which US$13.5 billion were organic chemicals.

In 2001, the chemical industry in the U.S. experienced its worst year since the early 1980s. Large players in the industry, including the European Union (EU), felt the pressure of weakening economies. Production growth in the EU was 4.6 percent in 2000, but was estimated at -1.1 percent in 2001. Export growth also slowed in 2001 to 4.3 percent, just half of what it was in 2000. The European Chemical Industry Council (CEFIC) reported in December 2001 that the industry was having "rough times," and stated that petrochemicals and polymers, part of the segment that constitutes 57 percent of the EU's entire chemical industry, were declining.

In the United States, chemical shipments were valued at US$506.5 billion in 2004, an increase of more than 10.6 percent from the previous year. In Canada, the total increased to some US$35 billion. The European Union chemical output grew 2.4 percent in 2004. Research and development (R&D) spending was down industrywide.

Though the United States, European Union, and Japan have traditionally supplied the majority of the world's organic chemicals, including petrochemicals, other countries continued to emerge as significant manufacturers. Countries in Asia, South America, Africa, and the Middle East had strong petrochemical capacities in the new millennium and analysts predicted that these emerging regions would gradually take market shares away from the developed leaders. China in particular was seeing explosive growth in demand for chemical products. In 2003, production of methanol in China rose nearly 42 percent over 2002 and was expected to continue to increase both demand and production well into the late 2000s.

RESEARCH AND TECHNOLOGY

The organic chemical industry invests a large portion of its revenues in R&D in comparison to most other industries. The U.S. chemical industry spent more than US$31 billion on R&D in 2001, and overall the industry accounted for nearly 11 percent of all industrial R&D spending in the United States. In addition, the United States typically spends more than twice as much money on R&D as Japan and more than four times as much as Germany, which is the third largest organic chemical producing nation. R&D spending related to organic chemicals was slowing in the new millennium along with capital spending. As economies in major industry sectors remained unstable, chemical analysts predicted that future growth in R&D spending would remain unremarkable.

Japan made the greatest strides related to R&D spending during the 1980s, while R&D chemical spending by Germany and other Western European competitors languished. Japan's emphasis on R&D during this period was reflected by the number of U.S. chemical patents it received (the United States is the principal source of patents in the global chemical industry). Of the 29,433 chemical patents issued by the U.S. Patent & Trademark Office (PTO) in 1995, U.S. chemical manufacturers accounted for 52 percent, Japanese manufacturers for 21 percent, and German manufacturers for 8 percent. However, U.S., Japanese, Italian, and Dutch companies received fewer patents than in 1994. Taiwan and South Korea represented the fastest growing chemical patent recipients, advancing by 33 percent and 44 percent from 1994 to 1995, respectively.

In the 2000s, investment in research and technology increasingly focused on the design and production of high-profit chemicals. Automation and information systems that increased productivity and met stringent environmental regulations continued to be emphasized, but companies also tried to develop new molecular structures and compounds that would allow them to create new markets and sustain a technological edge over their competitors. Areas of emphasis included advanced chemicals used to make new pharmaceuticals, better fuel additives, high-performance resins and fibers, and environmentally friendly chemicals.

WORKFORCE

Despite a turnaround in business conditions in the industry in the mid-2000s, cost-cutting, downsizing and outsourcing in the U.S. chemicals industry forced employment levels down. According to the U.S. Department of Labor, the chemicals industry employed about 889,900 workers in 2004, down from 899,100 the previous year and from 1.0 million workers in 2001. Job reduction in the industry was expected to continue in the mid-2000s.

Global employment figures for this industry are scant because countries divide their chemical and allied product groups differently. For example, the delineation between organic chemical operations and biosciences (a category that includes pharmaceuticals and certain intermediates) has become increasingly blurred. Moreover, many companies produce both organic and inorganic chemicals, compounds, and related products, and they do so in several different countries. In the United States, which supplied about 27 percent of industry output in the early 2000s, approximately 120,000 people were engaged in activities specifically attributable to the organics industry. However, more than six times that number were engaged in all chemical and chemical-related industries.

About two-thirds of organic chemical industry workers in industrialized nations are production workers. The other third are engaged in management, administration, and research and development. Organic chemical manufacturers are major employers of highly educated workers such as scientists and researchers, raising the average wages in the industry above those of most other manufacturing sectors. High wages also are a result of the strength of industry labor unions in Europe and the United States, and the widespread use of skilled laborers. In 2002, wages in the United States ranged from US$26 per hour for a chemical engineer to more than US$18 per hour for a machine setter.

Although the industry employs large numbers of workers at generally high wages, the chemical industry employment per pound of output, a key measure of productivity, plummeted in the mid-1990s. While production volume rose, many producers reduced their labor and management forces through restructuring, increasing automation, and moving production facilities to lower-wage labor markets. By the new millennium, employment in this industry was faltering because of these factors along with increased consolidation through merger and acquisition activity.

INDUSTRY LEADERS

All of the leading international chemical producers by sales volume are located in Japan, the United States, and Western Europe. All are diversified chemical and chemical products manufacturers engaged in making both inorganic and organic chemicals and related goods. As with workforce statistics, the value of industry sales statistics is diluted by the lack of separation of inorganic and organic chemical manufacturing activities, and by sales potentially attributable to related industries like plastics, drugs, and bioscience.

BASF AG

BASF AG operated as the world's largest chemical manufacturer in 2004, with more than US$51.5 billion in sales. BASF, formed in the early 1860s, became a major supplier of dyes and fibers, and was integrated into the mammoth IG Farben cartel that dominated the global industry during the 1930s. After the dissolution of IG Farben, BASF emerged as a leader in the international production of mineral oil, natural gas, plastics, fibers, and intermediates. BASF has aggressively pursued U.S. markets in recent years, although it continues to secure nearly 60 percent of sales from its European operations. In the new millennium, the firm switched its emphasis from pharmaceuticals to its core chemical operations.

DOW CHEMICAL

The Dow Chemical Company is the second largest global chemical concern and the largest in the United States. Dow was founded in 1890 as Canton Chemical. The company initiated its legacy of industry innovation by using electric current to separate bromides from brine to distill other chemicals. It made other breakthroughs in rubber, plastic, and pharmaceutical manufacturing during the first half of the twentieth century, and profited handsomely from overseas operations, which accounted for more than half of its sales by the mid-1900s. After stumbling in the early 1980s, Dow reorganized, cut its workforce, and began to switch its focus to high-margin chemicals and products. The company generated revenues of more than US$40 billion from its operations in 2004.

DU PONT

U.S.-based E.I. Du Pont de Nemours and Company ranked third in the global chemical industry with sales of US$27.3 billion in 2004. With operations in more than 70 countries, Du Pont was the largest chemical firm in the United States. Founded in 1802 by French immigrant and explosives expert Eleuthere Irenee Du Pont, the company dominated the U.S. explosives market by the early 1900s. Its experiments with nitroglycerin led it into other chemical-related businesses, particularly synthetic fiber production.

Du Pont's landmark invention of nylon in 1930 helped establish modern polymer-related industries. Explosive growth and continued product breakthroughs thrust Du Pont to the forefront of the chemical industry by the middle of the twentieth century. In the mid-1990s, Du Pont shifted its emphasis from commodity products to specialty high-tech chemicals and compounds. At the start of the new millennium, the firm restructured its operations and formed six business units consisting of coatings, crop protection chemicals and genetically modified seeds, electronic materials, polymers and resins, safety and security materials, and textiles and interiors.

EXXONMOBIL CHEMICAL COMPANY

Operating as the chemical subsidiary of Exxon Mobil, ExxonMobil Chemical was one of the largest chemical companies based on 2004 sales of US$27.7 billion. The company is active in petrochemicals manufacturing—a segment in which it ranks either number one or number two worldwide, depending on the specific chemical—polypropylene films, fuel additives, synthetic lubricant base stocks, and various other product manufacturing.

BAYER

Bayer Group, with 2004 sales of US$40.3 billion, was founded in the 1860s, became a world leader in dyestuffs, and pioneered the pharmaceutical industry early in the twentieth century. Bayer's development of aspirin around 1900 and anti-bacterial drugs in the 1920s ensured continued growth. After the breakup of IG Farben, Bayer offered new insecticides, drugs, fibers, and plastics. It expanded globally during the 1960s, 1970s, and 1980s, with a particular emphasis on U.S. markets. By 2000, Bayer had more than 350 operating companies in Europe, the Far East, and North America. In 2004, Bayer agreed to pay a US$66 million fine for price-fixing certain chemicals from 1995 to 2001. In 2003, the company announced that its chemical division, Lanxess, would be spun off in 2005. Lanxess had 2003 sales of US$4.27 billion.

MAJOR COUNTRIES IN THE INDUSTRY

JAPAN AND ASIA/PACIFIC

Japan's chemical industry suffered in the early 2000s, as its region entered its fourth recession in 10 years. Japanese production of most organic chemicals fell from 2000 to 2001, including butadiene, ethylene, phenol, and styrene. Overall, the petrochemical sector was hit the hardest. By 2003, however, Japan's economy began to rebound. The Asian Development Bank estimated that Japan's gross domestic product grew 4 percent in 2004, outpacing estimates of 1.8 percent forecast earlier that year. Although China was increasingly viewed as the biggest growth market in Asia, Japan's economy remains five times larger than China's, so this modest growth in the Japanese economy is of equal impact. Despite a downtrend for many chemicals, ethylene and benzene grew 2.9 and 2.8 percent in 2004, respectively.

There was also an uptrend in the chemical industries in other Asia/Pacific regions—including China, Taiwan, India, and South Korea. The Asian Development Bank estimates that China's gross domestic product increased by 9.3 percent during 2004, exceeding previous estimates of 7.9 percent earlier in the year. During 2001 it entered the World Trade Organization in order to strengthen its industrial industries. With import tariffs on chemicals anticipated to fall as a result of its new membership, China appeared to be well positioned to benefit as the world's largest importer of polyolefins.

Taiwan's economy was on the upswing in the mid-2000s, with estimated GDP widely exceeding forecasts in 2004. The chemical industry in India was expected to grow at a clip of nearly 11 percent per year through 2010, according to the Indian Chemical Manufacturers Association. Even as the industry suffered from high energy costs, India's strong economy and growing demand were boding well for the nation's chemicals industry. In the midst of a strong economy, South Korea saw a major portion of its chemicals industry experience gains in 2004, including the organics segment, which reported an increase in production from .2 to 6.7 percent, with the exception of propylene, which fell 2.3 percent.

Germany

During the early 2000s, Germany's chemical industry faltered due to the weak U.S. economy as well as a downturn in its domestic economy. Even though the country's export share fell throughout the 1990s, it remained tied with the United States as a leading global exporter of chemicals. Germany's reliance on exports to the United States, as well as its manufacturing operations there, left the country's chemical industry exposed to the U.S. downswing. Production in Germany was falling in 2001, and industry sales were stagnant. Due to an improved global and national economy, however, German chemical industry sales rose 3.5 percent in 2004. Output in 2004 was expected to increase 2 to 2.5 percent. The market was expected to increase 5 percent into the late 2000s.

France

Despite the fact that most of the European Union experienced a slowdown in the chemical industry in the early 2000s, the French chemical industry, the world's fourth largest, experienced growth in 2000 and 2001. Accounting for nearly 20 percent of the chemical industry in the European Union, France's chemical sales grew by 4.6 percent in 2000 and were expected to grow by nearly 11 percent into 2008. The country's exports to the United States increased by 27 percent in 2000; in Central and Eastern Europe by 21 percent; and in Asia by 20 percent. In 2004, France had growth in all chemicals of 3.2 percent and was predicted to rise to 4 percent in 2005. Organic chemicals were expected to climb 3.6 percent that year.

The United States

The United States leads the global organic chemical industry. It accounts for 27 percent of global chemical and allied product sales, and its share of organic chemical sales is significant. In 2004, the country exported about US$25 billion worth of product, up from US$16 billion in 2001, and it imported US$35.0 billion. The organic chemical trade deficit stood at US$10.4 billion, down from nearly US$13.6 billion in 2001 as the global and national economy improved. Overall, the industry had one of its biggest growth years in the last five years, with shipments of chemicals valued at US$506.5 billion in 2004, up 10.6 percent over the previous year. The U.S. also had a competitive advantage during the mid-2000s, in that it was less affected by the rapidly climbing oil prices as most U.S. petrochemicals use natural gas feedstocks.

It was predicted that U.S. chemical production would increase approximately 3.4 percent in 2005 and that prices would rise 4.5 percent, down from a 7.6 percent increase in prices in 2004. Chemical shipments were expected to rise nearly 6 percent in 2005, to US$535.5 billion.

Much like the early 2000s, U.S. organics manufacturers had suffered setbacks during the late 1970s and early 1980s for reasons that ranged from increased foreign competition and high oil prices to environmental regulations. Industry competitiveness improved significantly during the 1980s and domestic manufacturers were aided by both price and demand growth late in the decade. Although profitability improved, foreign competition continued to dilute global market share. A worldwide economic slowdown in the early 1990s posed serious setbacks for most manufacturers. Compounding U.S. organic industry woes in the early 1990s was excess production capacity, the result of expansion during the late 1980s and early 1990s. Oversupply still depressed organic prices entering the new millennium, thus eliminating profit growth. Despite its diminished dominance of global markets, the U.S. organic chemical industry was the largest, most advanced, and most competitive in the world in 2000. Its strength reflected a number of key advantages, including access to raw materials, an extremely advanced research and technology infrastructure, and unparalleled marketing expertise. Nevertheless, U.S. producers expect to continue facing stiff competition in commodity chemicals markets well into the mid-2000s, particularly from emerging Pacific Rim nations.

Latin America

After years of political and economic uncertainty, the Latin American region began a rebound in the petrochemical industry in 2003 due to a greatly improved economy and high profits in this sector. The gross national product in Argentina grew 7 percent in 2004 and was expected to grow 4 percent in 2005. Brazil's and Mexico's GDPs both grew 4 percent in 2004. Chile saw a 4.9 percent rise in GDP in 2004. Venezuela enjoyed a 12.1 percent GDP increase in 2004, which was expected to taper off to 3.5 percent in 2005. Latin America had also gotten a boost in the sector due to large petrochemical projects in the region.

Output was largely up throughout the region. In Argentina, benzene production rose from 149,000 metric tons in 2003 to 158,000 metric tons in 2004; in Brazil from 904 thousand metric tons to 929 thousand metric tons; in Mexico from 112,000 metric tons to 121,000 metric tons; and in Venezuela from 13,000 metric tons to 18,000 metric tons. Ethylene production also has similar increases in the region.

Further Reading

"2004 Year in Review" *Chemical & Engineering News,* 20 December 2004.

"Bayer Pleads Guilty to Price Fixing." *Chemical Week,* 19 July 2004.

Chang, Joseph. "Global Chemistry Industry Completes $37 Billion in Transactions in 2001." *Chemical Market Reporter,* 25 February 2002.

"Facts and Figures for the Chemical Industry." *Chemical & Engineering News,* 5 July 2004.

"Facts and Figures for the Chemical Industry." *Chemical & Engineering News,* 7 July 2003.

"Facts and Figures for the Chemical Industry." *Chemical & Engineering News,* 25 June 2001.

Franz, Neil. "Economic Woes Hurt Investment in R&D." *Chemical Week,* 5 December 2001.

"A Global Voice for the Chemical Industry." International Council of Chemical Associations, 2004. Available from http://www.icca-chem.org.

"International Trade Statistics." 2003. Available from http://www.wto.org.

Office of Industrial Technology. "Industry Profile." U.S. Energy Information Administration, 30 January 2004. Available from http://www.oit.doe.gov.

"Strong Growth May Moderate in 2005." *Chemical Week,* 15 December 2004.

Winder, Robert. "Look to the Long Term." *Chemistry and Industry,* 5 January 2004.

"World Chemical Outlook." *Chemical & Engineering News,* 10 January 2005.

SIC 2833

NAICS 325411

MEDICINAL AND BOTANICAL PRODUCTS

Closely tied to the pharmaceutical industry, medicinal and botanical processors create saleable forms of organic and inorganic chemicals as well as botanical drugs and herbs.

INDUSTRY SNAPSHOT

Throughout the history of civilization, cultures have relied on the curative and preventive qualities of medicinal and botanical products. With little more than word-of-mouth testimony, traditional folk-concoctions and blends of herbal remedies reportedly cured the sick, perpetuated the aura of optimal health, and supposedly released thousands from the clutches of fatalistic demons. But as tales of these self-medicated, miraculous cures fueled communal fireside chatter, they also prompted rigorous scientific investigations to pinpoint the mysterious therapeutic values of herbal medicine. These vigorous investigations elevated the status of medicinal and botanical products from being of interest to a relatively narrow counterculture, to an industry that produced plant-derived prescription drugs valued at US$17 billion annually during the 2000s. Not surprisingly, approximately one-quarter of drugs prescribed in the United States contained at least one compound derived from plants. The National Nutritional Foods Association estimated that 100 million people in the United States—more than one-third of the entire population—used herbal dietary supplements regularly.

Some observers estimate that two-thirds of the world's population uses medicinal botanicals as a primary source of health care. The Medical Association of South Africa reports that 80 percent of black South Africans rely on herbal healers. The Nepal Department of Drug Administration has 495 traditional herbal remedies on file, and 566 modern drugs. In Canada, surveys show that 57 percent of the population has used alternative therapies and 25 percent would trust an herbal remedy more than a medical prescription. In addition, representatives of the Centre for Scientific Research into Plant Medicine (CSRPM), located at Mampong in Ghana, West Africa, has touted the economic benefits of plant derived medicines in Ghana, which is home to an estimated 10 percent of available medicinal plants—potentially worth up to US$1.7 billion annually.

According to the World Health Organization, the global market for traditional medicines in the early 2000s exceeded US$60 billion and was growing fast. Spending on traditional medicines in the United States reached US$17 billion, and sales in the United Kingdom totaled US$230 million. The U.S. market expected robust growth through the mid-2000s, driven by the aging baby boomers segment. In addition to comprising the largest segment of the population, baby boomers also were comfortable with plant-derived pharmaceuticals. The majority of the medicinal plants harvested for the multi-billion dollar industry were harvested from the wild in the early and mid-2000s, causing significant concern about species extinction.

ORGANIZATION AND STRUCTURE

Historically, most medicinal botanicals were drawn from ordinary wild plants that proved adaptable to cultivation outside their natural environment. Void of any fanfare, tribal healers, communal caretakers, herbal doctors, and other folk healers came to possess the knowledge of plant identification, location, and appropriate application. The fanfare emerged only after pharmaceutical companies validated the therapeutic values of herbal medicines and their ensuing profits. Until the 1950s, almost all pharmaceutical research relied on vascular plants as sources for medicines. Soon after the discovery of sulfa drugs, antibiotics such as penicillin, and synthetic drugs, interest in medicinal plants declined. Pharmaceutical companies placed their hopes for miraculous cures in the accumulation of huge databases of synthetic chemicals; however, the synthetics panacea never pivoted the drug market. Consequently, pharmaceutical companies once again returned, foraging the world for new and expanded sources of herbal medicine.

Newer methods of medicinal plant screening reflected several methodology refinements. During the 1960s, a standard screening assay to determine the potential of drugs for medicinal application consisted of injecting test material into a rodent and assessing subsequent reactions. Modern bioassay, occasionally automated, produced more precise, less time-consuming, feedback. Tiny amounts of material could be screened rapidly against an array of up to 60 distinct human tumor cell lines. Other assays determined the ability of an extract to influence the activity of a single enzyme involved in the biochemical interactions that underlie a disease. Once an extract displayed significant activity in a bioassay, investigators returned to the source site to collect bulk samples (normally 50 to 100 kilograms) of the original plant.

Organizationally, the medicinal and botanical industry in the mid-1990s consisted of a growing number of multi-sized companies involved in the research and manufacturing of medicinal and botanical chemicals. The industry also consisted of ethnobotanists, mostly from emergent countries, who identified botanical medicinal sources. The industry investigated plant and herbal medicines frequently identified by consumers under the heading of alternative medicine, folk medicine, homeopathy, chiropractic, naturopathy, and sometimes even supernatural healing. According to the World Health Organization (WHO), medicinal plants are important because they serve as sources of direct therapeutic agents; function as a raw material base for the elaboration of more complex semi-synthetic chemical compounds; provide chemical structures usable as models for new synthetic compounds; and can be used as taxonomic markers for the discovery of new compounds.

Pharmaceutical raw materials include crude drugs such as botanical, animal, or other biological products, inorganic elements and compounds, and organic compounds. A source substance designated "official" indicates that the material has been the subject of a monograph in a pharmacopoeia or national formulary, that specifies the minimum acceptable degree of chemical purity. The term "crude drug" applies to plant or animal organs, and whole organisms or exudations, either in fresh or dried state, ground or not ground, that derive from cultivated or wild sources.

Production methods differ for inorganic and organic compounds. Organic compounds used as pharmaceuticals are either extracted from natural sources or prepared by chemical synthesis. In contrast to inorganic and organic materials, uncovering the therapeutics of crude drugs requires an extensive harvesting process. After identification of potential therapeutic value, a cleaning process removes direct and undesired plant components. Next, in order to activate the plant's therapeutic ingredients, plants are cured via sweating or drying for a period of up to a year. Either procedure halts the weakening effect of chemical reactions and also reduces the weight and bulk of plants.

Despite the demonstrated therapeutic advantages of medicinal products, companies encounter several obstacles in the mass production of medicinal botanicals. One of the earlier problems of mass production related to determining a uniform measurement of dosage. To solve this problem, researchers assumed that only a certain part of the crude drug, known as "the active principle," had the ability to act on the body. The active principle was identified and standardized so that definite quantities could be converted to powders, tablets, capsules, and other medicinal vehicles. This knowledge also enabled physicians to prescribe precise drug quantities and to be knowledgeable about the anticipated effects.

Another key problem for the industry stemmed from the difficulty of obtaining financially worthwhile patent property in botanical products. In 1994, the United States granted five patents related to plant medicinal products. Without patent protection, opportunities for clinical trials and funding are practically impossible. In response, drug companies sometimes perform clinical trials in countries in which there are fewer testing restrictions. Pharmaceutical firms also test drugs abroad because they fear involvement with herbals might adversely affect regulatory approval of their conventional drugs. In some instances plants aren't patentable, but their extracting processes are. Procedures to determine efficacy of botanical products sold in the United States included clinical trials and safety testing for each constituent. According to drug industry figures, the total package of FDA licensing procedures carried a US$300 million price tag in the mid-1990s. On the other hand, segments external to the drug companies discounted the US$300 million clinical trial label as an inflated cost, perpetuated by the drug industry's attempts to justify an unrealistic cost of doing business. Detection of modest but valuable benefits in botanical medicines requires random clinical trials conducted with 30,000 to 50,000 respondents at a cost of around US$231 million, according to some experts.

Europe's much simpler regulatory system for botanical medicines recognizes plant extracts as a whole unit, thereby eliminating testing requirements of each individual component. Considerations of costs and other circumstances prompted some researchers to suggest that historical evidence of reasonable effectiveness should be acceptable as U.S. marketing criteria. For instance, standards for Germany's marketing criteria blended historical/traditional use with modern scientific information.

Another problem in the search for botanical medicines involved the gradual disappearance of ethnobotanists—local healers, tribal medicine men, shaman, and other nontraditional caretakers. Because tropical areas of the world were the most fertile grounds for medicinal plants and herbs, ethnobotanists have served as the primary sources for identifying therapeutic plants. Botanists have estimated that only 10 percent (or less) of the more than 250,000 flowering plant species in the world have been surveyed for pharmacological activity. Unfortunately, as aging ethnobotanists and local healers faded from an increasingly urbanized world, so faded plant-healing expertise. Few apprentices remained to perpetuate healing practices.

Some family legacies were notable exceptions offering a remedy for carrying on traditions. Michael Tierra, a well-known herbalist and author, taught his daughter. Shasta Tierra also worked with herbalist Christopher Hobbs and acupuncturist Miriam Lee. She practiced traditional Chinese medicine in her San Jose, California clinic. The father and daughter were frequently featured on Web sites with their online articles.

In 2004, the American Botanical Council (ABC) launched its first training and certification program. Offered via its website, the "ABC Herbal Information Course" is based on the *ABC Clinical Guide to Herbs.* Topics include history, regulation, trends, science, and insights about 29 commonly-used herbs. After herb retailers and health practitioners are certified, they have complimentary access to one-page monographs for each herb discussed during the course.

BACKGROUND AND DEVELOPMENT

The first verifiable hint of the use of plants as medicine came from ancient Chinese, Hindu, and Mediterranean civilizations. Around 2735 B.C. the Chinese emperor Shen Nung wrote an herbal (a book about herbs or plants) describing the antifever capabilities of a substance known as Ch'ang Shang (later proven to contain antimalarial alkaloids). Later in Europe, the Greek physician Galen (around 130 A.D.) was reported to have included hyoscyamus, opium, squill, and viper toxin, among other drugs, in his apothecary shop.

There are many examples of crude plant and herbal remedies that have become basic home medications. Common treatments for constipation in ancient Egypt included senna pods and castor oil, along with caraway and peppermint to relieve indigestion. Up until 1900, when the much simpler compound benzococaine was introduced, cocaine had an essential use as the only available potent local anesthetic. Neither the Chinese nor the Central American Indians could explain the curative effects of fermented soybean curd for skin infections or fungi treatments on wounds, until Louis Pasteur's fermentation study led to the discovery of penicillin. Today penicillin and numerous other antibiotics, derived from fermenting mold, represent a major branch of the drug industry.

Industry Regulatory Standards. In the early 1990s, the promulgation of several pieces of legislation heightened drug safety and consumer awareness in utilization of all drugs. The U.S. Dietary Supplement Health and Education Act of 1994 purportedly facilitated integration of plant medicine in U.S. health care, by mandating labels specifying the structure and function of various products. Presumably, this expanded knowledge base was expected to increase sales, and provide incentives for additional research funding and scientific validation of quality control for these products. This legislation was also intended to facilitate the marketing of dietary supplements, herbs, and botanicals by the drug companies. After drug safety and efficacy claims were validated, the new legislation permitted marketing opportunities without preclearance, provided the product claims conveyed to the public its intrinsic values. While the U.S. Food and Drug Administration (FDA) refrained from clarification or regulations regarding this new legislation, the FDA still maintained that randomized, controlled testing reflected the best and most credible source of evidence for the efficacy of most therapies. International guidelines for herbal medicine assessment adhered to criteria established by the WHO.

Notably significant in the business objectives of some botanical organizations was the attention to environmental and humanitarian aspects of the industry. As searches for medicinal and botanical industry products intensified, so did concern regarding tropical forests being stripped of flora. Tropical plants from indigent countries comprised a primary source of botanical raw materials. These raw materials engendered profits for drug companies, while plant-producing countries derived few, if any, benefits for their productivity or their knowledge. One example is Eli Lilly's research with extracts from Madagascar's wild rosy periwinkle plant. Research led to production of vincristine and vinblastine, drugs that drastically reduced the mortality of childhood leukemia and produced a 19-80 percent remission rate in Hodgkin's disease patients. Since the 1960 discovery, these drugs earned the company roughly US$100 million annually while Madagascar earned nothing. Such practices were not limited to Lilly. For more than 20 years, U.S. pharmaceutical drugs derived from naturally occurring compounds accounted for sales estimated at US$20 billion, with minimal benefits for the producing countries.

By the mid-1990s, host countries for botanical production were demanding more for their intellectual and biological contributions. The rationale was that indigenous people maintained intellectual property rights by virtue of possessing a wealth of esoteric knowledge about local plants. Conservationists argued that the wisdom of local inhabitants should be accorded an economic value. Scientists, on the other hand, maintained that their work—discovering the usefulness of medicinal compounds in plants—had to be protected. Perhaps the most notable efforts to promote intellectual rights emerged from the 1992 Convention on Biological Diversity (the Rio Convention). Despite opposition from pharmaceutical companies, representatives from 167 nations persisted in recommending that less developed countries receive intellectual property rights, for pharmacologically useful chemicals, derived from their biological resources. Notwithstanding the ambiguities surrounding the issue of intellectual patents, the convention accentuated the conservation responsibilities of drug companies.

At least two U.S. drug companies, Merck & Co. Inc. and Shaman Pharmaceutical, took the lead in establishing a more equitable distribution of profits. These companies contracted with Latin American nations to gain access to virgin biological raw materials, in exchange for a share in the profits from resulting products. Shaman further pledged to pass up endangered plants and committed to furnishing royalties from drug revenues to both the local government and the native communities from which the plants were harvested. Merck agreed to pay US$1 million over a two-year period directly to Costa Rica's National Institute of Biodiversity for collecting plants, insects, and microbes, as well as royalties for any pharmaceutical discoveries. In the mid-1990s, the U.S. National Institutes of Health (NIH) announced a five-year, US$12.5 million program to spur conservation as well as bioprospecting in Central America, South America, and Africa. Through alliances with organizations such as Conservation International, local persons identifying medicinal plants would be eligible for patent and joint patent rights.

Recent intergovernmental and corporate efforts may not be sweeping enough to stem the disappearance of both the land that produces these raw materials and the indigenous healers who know how to exploit them. According to the World Resources Institute, roughly 17 million hectares of rain forest are lost to deforestation annually. Loss of rain forest led to a loss of potential new drugs. In the mid-1990s, an investigator from the U.S. Environmental Protection Agency speculated that, given rates of extinction and the probability of 5 in 10,000 that any plant would be the source of a marketable drug, the foregone value of lost drug products in 1992 alone was US$150 million. Also noteworthy was the burden placed on a plant species after its medicinal efficacy was discovered. Conservationists worried that the pacific yew tree, an exclusive source for the cancer-fighting agent taxol, would be eradicated in order to extract the compound. To obviate concerns over the yew, Bristol-Myers Squibb, the sole purveyor of the drug, developed alternative taxol sources. The dwindling group of traditional shamans, healers, and teachers exacerbated the extinction of rain-forest plant species. Recognizing the potential cultural loss, groups such as the Association of Traditional Healers organized to train young people in the traditional use of plants, in an effort to pass on generations of accumulated medicinal knowledge.

Similar to intellectual biodiversity rights, rainforest property rights also remained ill defined and less enforced, primarily because these areas were held collectively or designated as government-owned reserves. Drug company participants defended their practice of foraging tropical forests by reiterating that open access rainforest policies did not preclude anyone from searching for natural samples in developing countries. Void of enforceable property rights, rain forests did indeed operate as open access territory.

Asia Intelligence Wire shared insights about options before the Agreement on Trade-Related Aspects of Intellectual Property Rights (TRIPS) takes effect in 2005. Until then, intellectual property law in India protects only the means of producing drugs without covering the medication. Consequentially, Indian AIDS drug manufacturers can use unpatented production processes and offer drugs at lower prices. In India, the government has been concerned about the quantity of health care for its large population. In 1998, the government released its intention to promote a new awareness strategy "to popularize various alternative systems of medicine" like Ayurveda, Unani, Shiddha, homeopathy, yoga, and naturopathy. Thinking that its rural constituents have difficulty seeing a traditional Western physician, the goal is to expand health care for all.

In the late 1990s several mainstream manufacturers were bought or subsidized as investments by leading pharmaceutical manufacturers, such as Boehringer, Boots, and Ciba-Geigy. Eli Lilly & Co., a major California-based drug company, made a US$4 million equity investment in Shaman Pharmaceutical. The agreement included a four-year collaborative effort in developing drugs that worked against fungal disease. Shaman Pharmaceutical, a company less than five years old, wanted to combine drug development with an effort to preserve rainforest flora. The company sent teams of botanists and physicians to Latin America, Africa, and Asia, to search for plants that worked against viruses, fungi, and diabetes, or that had sedative or analgesic properties. Once therapeutic benefits were identified, a cadre of local people was hired to gather plants for commercial production. Of the 200 plants that passed preliminary stages, more than half showed activity against a targeted malady (as compared with less than 1 percent for mass screening). During a 16-month period, Shaman discovered an antiviral drug for childhood flu and brought it to the FDA for testing in humans. Shaman investigators also turned up an antiviral agent that works against drug-resistant herpes infections.

In 2004 *New Scientist* reported that two-thirds of the 50,000 medicinal plants in use in the early 2000s were harvested from the wild, causing increased concern about species extinction. Plantlife International found that 11 of 16 herbal remedy companies in the United Kingdom, including The Body Shop, obtained all the plants they sell from the wild. Ethnobotanists and activists called for companies using these plants to invest in cultivation to ensure adequate future supplies. Among the plants in danger of being overharvested was the African cherry (Prunus Africana), valued for its bark which is used in Europe as a treatment for enlarged prostate. Traditionally, less than half of a tree's bark would be taken, allowing the tree to survive. But sudden high demand led to indiscriminate stripping and destruction of entire forests. As a result, exports of dried bark plummeted 50 percent between 1997 and 2000, and the main exporter, Plantecam, was forced to close its processing facility in Cameroon.

With the exception of a few plant-derived agents, herbal products were marketed in the late twentieth century as food additives, dietary supplements, or vitamins. Although consumers, including many physicians, used herbal products for a range of physical disorders, the lack of evidential documentation on the effectiveness in alleviating or treating diseases represented a global concern. Governments found it especially difficult to control mail-order businesses that offered consumers little supervision of herbal medicine intake.

As reported by the deputy director-general, the production of an ethnobotany of Ghana is a work in progress. It will feature approximately 600 plants with pictures and recipes of the products for the disease they treat. This project was initiated in 1996 by the Organization of African Unity and the Science and Technology Research Committee.

Chinese herbal medicine, rooted in a folk pharmacopoeia of over 5,273 separate plants, offered a global potential for numerous botanical based remedies. Before the Chinese Cultural Revolution ended in 1976, the mysteries of Chinese medicine remained isolated from the world. In the latter decades of the twentieth century, China's guarded tolerance for capitalism resulted in aggressive promotion of herbal medicines worth more than US$1 billion.

In the mid-1990s most clinical studies in China were still conducted in hospitals. The hub of lab research was at the Chinese University of Hong Kong where, since the early 1980s, Western-trained scientists engaged in research to authenticate the chemical fingerprints of thousands of herbs. But lack of clinical testing was not the only factor that hampered the development of a world market for Chinese herbal products. While probing complex herbal mixtures containing hundreds of active compounds, scientists often found that isolated ingredients contained less potency than crude mixtures, thus precluding the consistent replication required for patenting. Undaunted by disappointments, Chinese entrepreneurs continued to invest US$140 million to upgrade herb factories and diagnostic equipment.

CURRENT CONDITIONS

In 2000, the medicinal, supplement, and botanical industry was valued at US$12 billion, with the related alternative medicine industry at large valued at US$34 billion. The Lonza Biotech firm estimates the market for biopharmaceuticals will reach US$50 billion by 2005. The World Health Organization had a larger estimate, putting the world's revenues for alternative medicines at US$70 billion in 2002. According to World Wildlife Federation data reported by *New Scientist*, the North American and European market for herbal remedies grew by approximately 20 percent annually from 1994 to 2004, and was worth at least US$19.34 billion.

Regional Trends. Established pharmaceutical giants found themselves facing drastically reduced market share as a number of them see patents expiring by 2005. The situation has placed immense responsibility on company researchers to replace the lost patent drugs with new discoveries in medicine that provide equivalent moneys.

In the future, significant long-term opportunities for this sector are expected to come from bulk analgesics, antibiotics, and digestives. However, FDA objections to claims made by some manufacturers for the benefits of their products have proliferated in the 2000s, leading to equally bitter attacks on the FDA by some members of the industry. In all likelihood, protests for and against the industry will continue to be rancorous.

For the U.S. industry, other positive factors were improvements in the FDA's review procedure and improvements in the submissions for approval. However, according to Alan Holmer of the Pharmaceutical Research & Manufacturers Association, the roughly US$800 million expense required to get a new medicine approved by the FDA and to market has put the price of drugs out of reach of some consumers, including those who could benefit from them the most. The US$800 million figure, however, was been attacked in 2002 as highly inflated by consumer advocates such as Michael Davis of Cleveland State University.

In many areas, tribal folklore medicine transcended local boundaries. No longer were herbal apothecaries selling age-old remedies and secrets in unmarked bottles. In their stead came modern, high-class retail establishments, catering to average consumers and targeting wealthier clients who could afford to pay up to US$19,000 for a rare, wild, Chinese ginseng root. At the other extreme, Wal-Mart Stores Inc. does a brisk business with its Nutrition Centers, offering a large assortment of value-priced therapeutic food supplements.

Entering the industry in the 2000s was not easy for entrepreneurs, partially because of the predominance of large-scale pharmaceutical companies with money and resources to survive the challenges of high start-up costs. However, in an effort to overcome entry barriers, many of these large companies were able to engage in a variety of collaborative efforts with nonprofit botanical organizations and smaller drug companies. Monsanto Company, for instance, contracted with the Missouri Botanical Garden to supply several thousand plants from the United States and various tropical countries. Merck & Co. Inc. entered into an arrangement with the New York Botanical Garden's Institute of Economic Botany and received plants from around the world for testing. Bionics, a small start-up British company, utilized a science broker approach and negotiated contracts to supply Glaxo and SmithKline Beecham with samples and chemical extracts from tropical plants. Often, enterprising companies narrowed their search for new drugs by combing tomes of traditional pharmacopoeia for identification of relatively nontoxic medicines. Similar approaches worked for Chemex Pharmaceutical of New Jersey, which won FDA approval in the 1990s to market Actinex (a drug derived from the creosote bush) as a treatment for precancerous skin lesions.

Despite the dominance of major pharmaceutical corporations, smaller start-up companies still saw opportunities in the market. MediMush, a Danish company founded in 2002, emerged in 2005 as a supplier of medicinal mushroom ingredients for the pharmaceutical and supplements industries. Mushrooms contain compounds used in treating cancer, and are also widely used to enhance immune system function. According to company literature, MediMush has derived the world's first oral form of pure lentinan, a polysaccharide, from shiitake mushrooms. MediMush estimated that the global market for shiitake-based products was worth at least 400 million euros (about US$481.6 million).

In 2002 *China Business* magazine announced that exports of traditional Chinese medicine (TCM) products declined 2.3 percent, with at least some of that loss due to aggressive medicinal herb growing in other countries. Nonetheless, exports in the first 11 months of 2001 still earned a respectable US$478 million, though the total for the same period in 2000 was US$467 million. The magazine noted that "Eastern coastal provinces and municipalities along the western Sichuan and Gansu Provinces accounted for 81.7 percent of the exports."

In April 2004, a new E.U. regulation was adopted requiring suppliers of herbal medicines to obtain the EU Good Manufacturing Product (GMP) certificate, a measure intended to ensure quality. China supplied US$108.3 million in traditional medicines to the European market, worth US10 billion annually, in 2004. As a result of the new regulation, exports dropped significantly. The value of traditional medicine shipments from Shanghai to Europe fell 60 percent in May and more than 30 percent in June. While industry leaders in China acknowledged the initial negative impact of the regulation, they hoped that exports would grow over the long term since, as Liu Zhanglin of the China Chamber of Commerce of Medicines & Health products Importers & Exporters told *China Daily,* the regulation "for the first time grants TCM legal status as medicines" and would thus open new European markets. According to *Asia Intelligence Wire,* many medical experts conducted decades of research and have now concluded that traditional Chinese medicines have few side effects and are cheaper than most Western medicines.

In 2002, the *Financial Times of London* reported on exciting research into AIDS pharmaceuticals with a promising medicine known to the ancients as ayurveda. Although India's share of the export market was only 0.2 percent in 2002, it is expected to become a leading exporter before 2010. In June 2004, African church leaders stated their commitment to "The 3 by 5 Initiative" calling for treatment of 3 million individuals with HIV/AIDS by 2005. Some 200 Protestant church leaders from 39 African countries showed support at the All Africa Conference of Churches (AACC) held in Nairobi, Kenya. AACC President Right Reverend Nyansanko Ni-Nku said approximately 40 percent of African health delivery facilities were owned by churches.

RESEARCH AND TECHNOLOGY

In the mid-1990s, scientists began tapping the medical potential of the marine environment. In the early 1990s nearly 2,000 compounds of marine origin were studied for possible use as antimicrobial, antiviral, or antitumor agents. Antibacterial and antiviral properties were identified in certain invertebrate species, such as sponges. Of the thousands of others investigated by the National Cancer Institute, about 4 percent demonstrated some antitumor effect. One marine compound under clinical trial at the time was Didemnin-B, isolated from the tunicate (sea squirt). Didemnin-B demonstrated properties as a potent killer of melanomas, as well as a measure of antiviral activity. The search for effective natural marine medicine aligned with the expertise described in traditional Asian pharmacopoeias. Asian folk cures were derived from dried seaweed, ground mollusk shells, and the vertebrae and livers of various species of fish. These folk medicines purportedly allayed diseases and a host of illnesses such as high blood pressure, impotence, insomnia, and others. Although some remained unverifiable, a seaweed known as the Corsican weed contained an alpha-kainic acid that kills nerve endings and was reputed to be effective for intestinal worms. At least 37 compounds with sodium-channel blocking properties, proven effective for cardiovascular illness, were isolated from sea anemones and other marine life. The most notable of these discoveries were fish oils that contained eicosapentaenoic acid and docohexaenoic acid. These compounds proved to work well in the prevention of atherosclerotic heart disease. The oils of cold-water fish not only proved effective in reducing cholesterol and triglycerides, but also were beneficial for people with rheumatoid arthritis and diabetes.

Another promising development in the early 2000s was growing interest in plant sterols, a market worth US$75 million in Europe in 2003. Sterols, which are derived from soybeans and other plants and can lower cholesterol, are not sold directly to consumers, but are added to foods that can then be marketed as beneficial to health. These are known in Europe as functional foods, and in the United States as nutraceuticals. In the early 2000s, regulatory agencies expanded the range of foods approved for sterol as an ingredient. As a result, sterol suppliers expected significant growth in this segment. Sterols were one of the best-performing products for leading producer Cognis, which enjoyed 8.9 percent growth in its Nutrition and Health unit in 2004. Rival supplier Raisio reported that sales of its Benecol sterol esters increased 66 percent in 2004. Rising demand from obesity-treatment and weight-loss markets is likely to spur further growth for sterol manufacturers.

In 2005, Canada became the first country to approve Sativex, a pain medication derived from cannabis (marijuana). Sativex, which targets nerve pain associated with MS, was created by GW Pharmaceuticals. In 2003, GW sold marketing rights to Bayer. In addition to a signature fee in the deal, GW will receive a share of Sativex revenues as well as additional fees up to 25 million pounds (US$43.8 million) when the drug is approved in the United Kingdom.

INDUSTRY LEADERS

Merck & Co. Inc. Merck & Co. Inc. traces its beginnings to Freidrich Jacob Merck's 1688 purchase of an apothecary in Germany. Heinrich Emmanuel Merck began manufacturing drugs in 1827—his first product was morphine. By the time he died in 1855, Merck products were used worldwide. The 24-year-old grandson of Heinrich Merck traveled to the United States and established his own business venture. In 1989, a plant site was acquired in Rahway, New Jersey—today the same location houses the corporate headquarters of Merck & Co. Inc. and four of its divisions. Merck operates 16 manufacturing plants and has established subsidiaries in Australia, Europe, South America, Africa, and the Middle East. It is the largest drug manufacturer in the United States and employs 63,000 people. Merck is tied with Glaxo Wellcome, Plc. as the world leader in prescription drugs. Along with drugs for cardiovascular health and pain management, Merck also produces vaccines for hepatitis A and B plus chickenpox.

In 2002, Merck Chairman and CEO Raymond V. Gilmartin was on the hot seat, as several key drug patents expired without equivalent new drugs being found to capture shareholder excitement, reported *Business Week*. Nonetheless, the company's total 2003 revenue was US$22.5 billion, an increase of nearly 57 percent from the previous year.

In May 2004, the company signed an agreement with DHL, an air express delivery leader, to work jointly on expanding access to critically needed HIV medicines throughout sub-Saharan Africa. June 2004 marked the announcement of plans for Merck to expand cooperation with Dutch pharmaceutical company H Lundbeck A/S regarding joint development and distribution of the sleep disorder compound gaboxadol. After working together in the United States, the companies will expand efforts to Japan according to *Europe Intelligence Wire.* In June 2004, *Asia Intelligence Wire* reported that Merck announced its collaboration with Vertex Pharmaceuticals to produce a compound for cancer treatment. Merck will coordinate worldwide clinical development and commercialization of VX-680 and pay Vertex product royalties on sales. Yet another collaboration announced in June 2004 called for Merck to work with Alnylam Pharmaceuticals to jointly develop gene-suppression therapies for eye diseases. Terms involved a multiyear deal with potential to net Alnylam a total of US$19.5 million, according to *Dow Jones Business News.*

In September 2004, Merck pulled its best-selling painkiller, Vioxx, off the market after a study indicated that it could double the risk of heart attack or stroke. Lawsuits were brought against the company alleging that patients had died after long-term Vioxx use. On the day that congressional investigations revealed that Merck officials had downplayed Vioxx's health risks, Merck CEO Raymond Gilmartin resigned. The controversy cost the company billions in sales and legal fees; indeed, total sales in 2004 reached only

US$22.9 billion. Nevertheless, Merck continued with cutting-edge research in 2005, including a possible vaccine for sudden acute respiratory syndrome (SARS) and a cervical cancer vaccine.

GlaxoSmithKline Plc. Glaxo began in the late nineteenth century, in New Zealand, as an independent company importing and exporting goods that ranged from whalebone to patent medicines. Moving to London, the company began to produce baby food products and expanded into Indian and South American markets. During the 1930s and 1940s, Glaxo expanded into the production of pharmaceuticals and quickly grew through acquisition and consolidation in the following decade. The anti-ulcer medication Zantac was launched simultaneously in several European markets in the late 1970s, and by 1984 the medication captured 25 percent of the new prescription market. In 2000 the company merged with SmithKline Beecham. Total sales in 2001 for the renamed GlaxoSmithKline Plc. were US$25 billion. In 2003, sales were US$38.2 billion, an increase of nearly 12 percent from the previous year. Revenue growth slowed considerably in 2004, however, when sales reached only US$39 billion. In June 2004, Glaxo entered into an agreement with Thembalmi Pharmaceuticals. Thembalmi is a joint venture between Adcock Ingram and Ranbax, the Indian pharmaceutical giant. The agreement involved a voluntary license for Thembalmi to make generic copies of patented medicines, according to *Africa News Services*.

The company's subsidiary, GlaxoSmithKline Biologicals s.a., develops vaccines for diseases such as hepatitis, influenza, rubella, and typhoid fever. It works with the World Health Organization (WHO) to improve access to medicines in underveloped regions.

Bristol-Myers Squibb. In addition to being one of the most profitable pharmaceutical manufacturers in the world, Bristol-Myers Squibb is also recognized worldwide as a major producer and distributor of consumer products such as toothpaste and drain opener. Two former fraternity brothers, who invested US$5,000 each in the failing New York-based Clinton Pharmaceutical Company, founded Bristol-Myers in 1887. Selling medical preparations by horse and buggy to local doctors and dentists, the company began making profits in the early 1900s, by sales of such products as Sal Hepatica, a laxative mineral salt, and Ipana toothpaste, the first such product to contain a disinfectant.

During both World Wars, the company was heavily involved in the production of pharmaceuticals such as penicillin and other antibiotics. Through acquisitions, such as Clairol and Mead Johnson, Bristol-Myers continued to grow throughout the decades. In the 1970s, the company was the first pharmaceutical firm to invest in anticancer drugs—a move that awarded them more than US$200 million in sales. Achieving success with its Excedrin and Bufferin brands, Bristol-Myers furthered its piece of the analgesic market through a joint agreement with Upjohn (now Pharmacia & Upjohn) that enabled it to introduce a new nonprescription pain reliever called Nuprin. Despite several tampering incidents, the company continued to grow as a manufacturer of prescription pharmaceuticals, moving into the area of acquired immune deficiency syndrome (AIDS) research. Merging with Squibb Corporation (which was founded in 1858 in the United States), Bristol-Myers Squibb posted sales of US$10.2 billion in 1997, with 40 percent coming from non-U.S. markets. In 2004 the company posted total sales of US$19.3 billion.

In May 2004, during the period when U.S. Secretary of Health and Human Services Tommy Thompson commented on the need for increased treatment options for people with HIV/AIDS in developing countries, Bristol-Myers Squibb linked with two other companies. Through partnership with Gilead Sciences and Merck, plans were announced to develop fixed-dose combination of three HIV medicines. The World Health Organization applauded new government support expediting the process to review fixed-dose combination medicines and co-packaging of existing therapies for the treatment of HIV/AIDS in developing countries.

In 2005 Bristol-Myers Squibb announced plans to sell its consumer products divisions in the United States and Canada. Also that year, the company sold Swiss firm Novartis the rights to produce and market a range of over-the-counter brands worth US$258 million in annual sales. Current therapeutic categories for the company include oncology, cardiovascular and metabolic disorders, infectious diseases, HIV/AIDS, and psychiatric disorders.

Sanofi-Aventis. Sanofi-Aventis, the third-largest pharmaceutical company, was formed in 2004 when French drugmaker Sanofi-Synthélabo merged with another French giant, Aventis. The newly-formed Sanofi-Aventis, which employs more than 96,000 people worldwide and posted sales of US$20.3 billion in 2004, conducts research and development in cardiovascular disease, thrombosis, neurological disease, oncology, metabolic disorders, internal medicine, and vaccines. Among its major products are Copaxone, a treatment for MS; Lantus, an insulin injection; and Taxotere, a cancer treatment.

Aventis had been created from a merger of Hoechst and Rhône-Poulenc, two companies bothered by threats of lawsuits for miscellaneous reasons. Rhône-Poulenc began in the nineteenth century, and its early history has been known for a series of mergers and diversity. Started by a pharmacist named Etienne Poulenc, eventually uniting with the Société Chimiques des Usines du Rhône, a manufacturer of dyestuffs and raw materials for perfumes, the company had a strong commitment to research and development. Involved in agricultural and industrial chemicals, in addition to pharmaceuticals, the company was privatized in the early 1990s. By 1994 the public owned about half of the company; a group of banks, employees, and the state owned the remainder. In the late 1990s, the company was subject to a series of lawsuits, and settled with Baxter, Bayer, and Green Cross, its share of a US$670 million legal settlement over blood products that infected hemophiliacs with HIV.

Hoechst sales came from dyestuffs in the nineteenth and early twentieth centuries. Much later, the company gained control of the entire diuretic market, and was a leader in oral medication for diabetics by the 1970s. Fueled by the increased production of antibiotics, serum, and steroids, Hoechst's pharmaceutical sales managed to grow at a rate of 13 percent a year during this decade. Continuing its program of overseas expansion that began in the 1960s, Hoechst built a US$100 million plant in the United States, and soon secured a large portion of the U.S. drug market (23 percent of its sales came from North America in 1993). In the early 1990s, the company was subject to freak chemical spills that caused it to jettison its chlorofluorocarbon (CFC) business in 1993. In 1997, the company stopped making Seldane, which had come under attack, and replaced it with the popular product Allegra.

Aventis received a major blow in 2002 when the FDA refused to endorse Picovir as a cure for the common cold. Authorities decided that Aventis failed to demonstrate a clinical benefit that would outweigh possible side effects from the drug.

FURTHER READING

"African Heads of Churches Summit Commit to '3 by 5.'" 2005. Available from http://www.who.int.

"The American Botanical Council," 2005. Available from http://www.herbalgram.org.

"American Botanical Council Launches First Online Training and Certification Course for Herb Retailers and Health Practitioners," 2005. Available from http://www.herbalgram.org.

Barrett, Amy. "Why Merck's Spin-Off Is No Cure." *Bloomberg News,* 31 January 2002.

"Bitter Medicine: Pills, Profit and the Public Health." *ABC News,* 29 May 2002.

Bleecher, Michele Bitoun. "Gold in Goldenseal: Healing Herbs Have Become a Cash Crop." *Hospitals & Health Networks,* 20 October 1997.

Datta, Mrinalini. "Aventis Pharma Expects Sales to Grow about 13 Percent This Year." *China Business,* 18 January 2002.

Edwards, Rob. "No Remedy In Sight for Herbal Ransack." *New Scientist,* 10 January 2004.

"Environment and Health Sector," 2005. Available from http://www.csir.org.gh.

"E.U. Regulation Affects TCM Exports." *China Daily,* 7 August 2004. Available from http://http://www.china.org.cn.

Fernandez, Edna. "Ancient Cures in a Global Market." *Financial Times,* 30 April 2002.

"Ghana; Nation Can Reap From Medicinal Plants." *Africa News,* 8 March 2002.

ldquo;Hoover's Company Capsules," 2005. Available from http://www.hoovers.com.

Krauskopf, Lewis. "Cure for Its (Merck) Blahs?" *The Record (Bergen County, NJ),* 30 January 2002.

Neimark, Jill. "On the Frontlines of Alternative Medicine." *Psychology Today,* January 1997.

Olson, Nigel. "Canada Becomes Sativex Country." *Cannabis Culture,* 19 April 2005. Available from http://www.medicalmarihuana.ca.

"Patent Pitfalls Unsettle Top Drug Makers." *The Business,* 30 January 2002.

Patton, Dominique. "Cognis Ramps Up Plant Sterol Capacity." *Nutra Ingredients,* 11 July 2004. Available from http://www.nutraingredients.com.

Stein, Lisa. "More Fallout from the Vioxx Mess." *U.S. News & Word Report,* 16 May 2005.

"Swiss Pharmaceuticals Firm Acquires Key U.S. Drugs Portfolio." Asia Intelligence Wire, 16 July 2005. Available from http://http://www.hoovers.com.

Tierra, Shasta. "Increase Vitality and Productivity with Some Simple Food Tips," 2005. http://www.planetherbs.com.

"A Time of Ferment for Biopharmaceutical Contract Manufacturing." *Chemical market Reporter,* 23 March 2001.

Wechsler, Jill. "More Changes and Challenges at FDA." *Pharmaceutical Executive,* February 1998.

"WHO Statement on US Proposal for Rapid Review of Fixed Combinations," 2005. Available from http://www.who.int.

SIC 2851

NAICS 325510

PAINTS AND COATINGS

The global paint industry produces paints and coatings for architectural (known in Europe as decorative), marine, packaging, transportation equipment, and many additional end uses. Industry products also include varnishes, lacquers, enamels, and shellac, as well as chemical paint removers and brush cleaners. Makers of pigments alone are discussed in **Chemicals, Industrial Inorganic** and **Chemicals, Industrial Organic** based on the specific pigment's chemical composition.

INDUSTRY SNAPSHOT

The paint industry has been a relatively small but rapidly growing segment of the broader chemical industry. Environmental pressures and regulations have been some of the biggest challenges faced by the industry. Skyrocketing prices of basic raw materials have also been a perennial concern, although by the late 1990s prices had stabilized somewhat. To counter increasing prices, paint manufacturers and suppliers worked together to formulate improved paints to justify price premiums. A simultaneous challenge for the industry was to incorporate the use of environmentally friendly materials and abide by the regulations and pressures on volatile organic compounds (VOCs) and hazardous air pollutants (HAPs). Coatings in general were moving away from being solvent-based toward being water-based as of the mid-2000s.

Following the worldwide slump of manufacturing industries during the end of the 1990s and the beginning of the 2000s, the paints and coatings industry showed overall improvement by 2005, particularly in the architectural/decorative coatings segment, which grew 11 percent in value for U.S. manufacturers. Special purpose coatings declined slightly. While the product OEM (original equipment manufacturer) coatings segment improved worldwide, due in part to increased manufacturing in Asia and South America, the U.S. segment declined 13 percent in value.

Measured by consumption, North America and Asia are the world's largest paint markets, each consuming about 29 percent of world production. These regions are trailed by Western Europe at 22 percent, and other regions consume the remaining 19 percent. China showed the biggest growth in annual consumption from 1997 to 2002, with a 6.4 percent rise.

In 2004, the top ten paint and coatings manufacturers worldwide, as ranked by *Coatings World,* were Akzo Nobel Coatings NV, PPG Industries Inc., ICI Paints, Henkel, Sherwin-Williams Company, DuPont Coatings & BASF Coatings AG, Valspar Corp., RPM, and SigmaKalon Group BV. The top ten manufacturers in the United States were Akzo Nobel Coatings Inc., Sherwin-Williams Company, PPG Industries Inc., DuPont Coatings & Color Technologies, ICI Paints North America, BASF Coatings AG, Valspar Corp., RPM Inc., Sigma-Kalon Group BV, and Nippon Paint.

ORGANIZATION AND STRUCTURE

Paints and coatings fall into three broad categories: architectural paints, original equipment manufacturer (OEM) paints, and special purpose coatings. Specialized paints such as skid-resistant paint, heat-reflective paints, heat-absorbent paints, phosphorescent paints, fluorescent coatings, electrically conductive/non-conductive paints, and temperature sensitive paints were used for a variety of purposes, especially in industry.

ARCHITECTURAL PAINTS

These paints are used for decorating and protecting homes, apartments, farm buildings, office buildings, and other commercial structures. Architectural paints include both solvent and water-based paints for interior and exterior surfaces. In industrial economies, such as those of Japan and Western Europe, architectural coatings are considered a mature market, with long-term growth projected at about 1 to 2 percent per year.

ORIGINAL EQUIPMENT MANUFACTURER (OEM) PAINTS

OEM coatings, also known as industrial or product finishes, are mostly used to protect and decorate durable and industrial goods. This group of paints is typically sold by paint companies to various equipment manufacturers who apply the paints to their particular products, such as automobiles, trucks, aircraft, railroad equipment, home appliances, office machines, furnaces, and air-conditioning equipment.

Many of the latest paint technologies were developed for the OEM segment, where there was a growing focus on increasing the efficiency of application methods and reducing volatile solvents content to meet strict environmental regulations. A major challenge facing manufacturers of OEM coatings was the increased use of plastics in automobiles and other durable goods. The need for OEMs to match the paint finish of steel body panels with plastic body panels that are painted separately was yet to be satisfied.

SPECIAL PURPOSE COATINGS

This category includes paint products generally used for maintenance work and as coatings for the transportation aftermarket. They are designed for special applications and for withstanding unusual environmental conditions. Special purpose coatings are used widely in high specialty applications. These products include anti-corrosive paints, traffic and marine paints, weather resistant paints, spray paints in aerosol containers, and chemical resistant paints.

BACKGROUND AND DEVELOPMENT

DEVELOPMENT OF PAINT MATERIALS

Some of the earliest examples of painting occurred thousands of years ago, when Paleolithic artists devised elaborate cave paintings in blacks, yellows, reds, and whites at Lascaux, France. These early paints came from such substances as charcoal, iron oxide, clay, and calcite. Paints in the modern sense came into being when the early artists discovered that colors could be applied much better when the pigments were mixed with binders such as egg whites, beeswax, gum arabic, and pitches and balsams from trees. Some of the main ingredients used in paints were pigments, binders, volatile solvents and additives.

Pigments are materials that impart color and opacity to a paint film. White lead was the most important pigment used in paint from the end of the seventeenth century until early in the twentieth century, when titanium dioxide was introduced. Other pigments became popular in the mid-nineteenth century and led to the formation of multi-pigment paints.

Binder is the portion of the paint that holds the other ingredients together and serves to form the solid film of paint. Around the sixth century A.D., oils obtained from vegetable seeds and nuts began to be used as paint binders. Alkyd resins began to be used as paint binders around 1927. The excellent properties and great versatility of alkyd resins made their discovery and development one of the most important in modern paint technology. Numerous other resins and polymers were developed for highly specialized industrial and maintenance uses.

Volatile solvents or thinners are used in paints to facilitate their application. Turpentine was the first recorded thinner used in paint. Used by ancient Egyptians, it was the most widely used paint thinner until the middle of the twentieth century when it was largely displaced by cheaper petroleum-based solvents, first used in the 1860s. With the increased use of latex paints and other water-borne coatings, water was also widely used as a solvent.

Additives are used in paints and coatings to perform specific functions not accomplished by the three major ingredients. Additives facilitate the performance of a variety of special functions, such as drying or hardening of paints, dispersing of pigment, preventing uneven color patterns, preventing pigment from settling, and resisting mildew growth on surfaces.

ORIGINS OF THE INDUSTRY

A rudimentary chemical industry is said to have begun in the early seventeenth century with the production of wood tar, used as pitch for the bottom of ships, and potash, used for making soap. The spread of industrialization outside of Europe and the United States and the First and Second World Wars acted as catalysts for the chemical industry.

Industrial growth in the United States increased civilian demand for chemicals, especially those used in bleaching and dyeing textiles. In 1867, D.R. Averill, an Ohioan, patented ready-to-use paint. It was not until the 1880s that quality ready-mixed paints were produced. During both World Wars, paint and varnish were vital to the U.S. military effort for protection and camouflage of equipment and personnel. The unique needs of the military compelled the development of specialized paints and coatings.

Time-tested technologies and processes are utilized for the production of conventional paints. Mixing of primary materials followed by blending, testing, and filling operations compose the production process. Unlike many basic and intermediate chemicals, paints and coatings are sold under a brand name. Research and development and technological advances occur quite rapidly in a consumer environment and this has been the case in the paints and coatings industry.

The maturity of the paint business and increased technology requirements resulted in an extended period of industry consolidation. The growing burden of complying with government regulation, intense industry competition, and low profit margins contributed to a large number of mergers and acquisitions.

ENVIRONMENTAL CHALLENGES

Overcapacity and merger mania were not the only problems chemical companies confronted during the 1970s and 1980s. The industry faced an increase of government regulation and a growing environmental movement that saw chemical manufacturers as the prime villains. Many disasters that occurred within the chemical industry contributed to the increasing environmental restrictions, including the Union Carbide disaster causing the tragedy in Bhopal, India; revelations about the horrible disease caused by mercury contamination of the residents of the village of Minamata in Japan by a chemical company called Chisso; the 1976 explosion at an Italian chemical plant that released a dioxin-contaminated cloud over the town of Seveso; and growing evidence that freon, used by Du Pont in aerosol cans, was contributing to the destruction of the ozone layer.

These environmental concerns prompted the U.S. Congress to enact a series of laws regulating the chemical industry as a whole. The paint coatings industry was directly affected by these laws, as it was an integral part of the chemical manufacturing sector. The Environmental Protection Agency (EPA) was created to regulate the introduction, generation, transportation, treatment, and disposal of hazardous waste, and the Occupational Safety and Health Administration (OSHA) was created to monitor the workplace. In 1970 the Australian Government Paint Committee (GPC) was set up, in its present form, as an "onus of proof" scheme. It approved products for use by state and federal government departments and bodies.

Regulation of the industry accelerated dramatically during the environmentally conscious 1970s and 1980s when federal clean air regulations were adopted to encourage the production of less polluting and less toxic paints. Other regulations that came into being include the Federal Insecticide, Fungicide and Rodenticide Act of 1972; the Toxic Substances Control Act of 1976; and the Comprehensive Environmental Response Compensation and Liability Act of 1980. This last law established a Superfund program for cleaning up toxic waste sites, and the estimated bill for chemical manufacturers ran up to tens of billions of dollars. Since the Resource Conservation and Recovery Act (RCRA) had already classified paint wastes as hazardous materials, virtually all paint manufacturers found themselves subject to fee collection under Superfund.

The 1986 Emergency Planning and Community Right-to-Know Act led to the creation of the Toxic Release Inventory (TRI), a database containing releases of toxic substances into the environment by manufacturing companies. The TRI showed that the manufacturers were pouring several billion pounds of toxins into the environment each year. Chemical producers at the top of the list began to take steps to reduce their reported toxic releases.

LEAD

Once a primary component of paint, lead ranked as one of the top environmental threats to children's health in the 1990s. The effects of lead, which was also used in gasoline, ceramic finishes, plumbing and many other products, were discovered in the 1930s. White lead pigments were essentially eliminated from architectural paints in the 1940s, but it was not until 1977 that the use of lead-based paints was outlawed in the United States. Government and medical reports published in the late 1980s and early 1990s revealed evidence that lead poisoning could occur with much lower doses than was previously thought. The lead problem therefore turned out to be more pervasive than earlier believed. One of the most significant outcomes was that in 1993, all paint manufacturers in California were assessed special fees under the state's Childhood Lead Poisoning Act of 1991. According to *Forbes* and the Alliance to End Childhood Lead Poisoning, by the late twentieth century the previous decade had seen just one single death from lead poisoning due to a child's eating of the substance—thanks to greater public awareness.

In the twenty-first century, *Forbes* predicted that paint manufacturers would likely find themselves in courtroom hot seats as firms such as Ness, Motley, Loadholt, Richardson & Poole follow through with civil suits against the paint and pigment industry for once relying so heavily on lead. Sherwin Williams' lead attorney denounced the suits and the Rhode Island attorney general for going ahead with one against the company, noted *Forbes.* Others have pointed out that thirty years ago, lead also was present in certain containers and in lead-based gasoline.

VOLATILE ORGANIC COMPOUNDS (VOCs)

As paint dries, the organic solvents in the paint evaporate, thus releasing VOCs into the atmosphere. VOCs react with sunlight to contribute to smog. The U.S. Clean Air Act was introduced in 1977, which required that states regulate geographic areas that failed to meet air quality standards. There was growing pressure to reduce emissions of VOCs from the use of paints and the consumption of solvents, especially in the original equipment and industrial applications. The paint industry is a major user of hydrocarbon solvents, accounting for about 25 percent of the demand.

RECYCLING

As a result of strict regulations and concern for the environment, recycling—an ongoing trend of the 1980s and 1990s—also extended to the paint industry. Laidlaw Environmental Services of Canada was one of the pioneers in recycling old paint. It began running its US$3 million plant in Mississauga, Ontario in 1992, then the sole automated paint recycling facility globally. Major Paint, a company in Torrance, California, introduced Cycle II, the first recycled paint in the United States, which was composed of 50 percent post-consumer and post-industrial latex waste. It sold at half the cost of new paint—even the paint containers were recycled. In one instance, Rasmussen Paint of Beaverton, Oregon switched to the use of recycled materials in all of its bulk paint containers.

GLOBAL TRADE

In the early 2000s, more than US$18 billion worth of paints and coatings was traded among nations each year. Exports are dominated by a few leading countries. and the top five exporters supplied more than half of the world's exports. The leading world exporters included Germany (with about 20 percent of world export market share); the United States (11 percent); the United Kingdom (9 percent); Japan (7 percent); and the Netherlands (7 percent). On the other hand, import markets are considerably more fragmented. France, Germany, and the United States each account for about 7 percent of world imports, followed by the United Kingdom (5 percent), Italy (5 percent), and Canada (4 percent). In contrast to export market concentration, the top ten importers purchased just over 50 percent of all paint imports, whereas the top ten exporters controlled more than three-quarters of the market.

CURRENT CONDITIONS

The world's paint markets underwent a reversal of sorts in the 1990s, in that some of the fastest-growing markets early in the decade had slowed by the late 1990s and early 2000s. In addition, some of the slowest had picked up speed, a trend that continued into the mid-2000s. Since 1995, demand growth has revived to about 3 percent annually, a pattern that was expected to continue through 2000, but sputtered with a souring economy in 2001. A growth rate of two to three percent was expected again by 2003 as the global economy proceeded back on track. However, the growth was not expected to come for U.S. manufacturers, who saw much of the industry moved to cheaper offshore facilities, particularly in the product OEM sector. In fact, according to *Paints & Coatings Industry,* 2002 marked the first time in 70 years that chemical imports in general had a higher value than exports. In the mid-2000s, Asia and South America were the world's most important growth markets.

The top ten companies in the industry worldwide all had increased sales in 2004, and the majority of the top U.S. companies had increased sales. Almost rampant in the industry by the mid-2000s were declarations by global companies that employee layoffs and other cost-cutting measures were a certainty as all of them pushed to return to profitability again. For example, according to *Paintings & Coatings Industry News,* Akzo Nobel, the world's giant in coatings production, promised to significantly scale back its global employee base in the areas of both chemicals and coatings.

RESEARCH AND TECHNOLOGY

ENVIRONMENTAL REGULATION

A high proportion of R&D in the paints and coatings industry has been directed toward creating environmentally friendly products designed to comply with current or anticipated government regulations. Funds that might otherwise have been poured into technological innovations aimed at performance improvement have been diverted.

The U.S. EPA proposed reductions in volatile organic compounds (VOCs) in architectural coatings and industrial maintenance coatings that would be implemented in a three-step process beginning in 1996. Using 1990 as the base year, the first phase required a 25 percent reduction in VOC content by 1996, rising to 35 percent in the year 2000, and 45 percent by 2003. According to the U.S. National Paints and Coatings Association, a trade group, the VOC limits would affect 65 percent of the industry's volumes. The U.S. EPA also established a national program to train and accredit individuals and firms engaged in lead-based activities in September 1994.

The 1990 Clean Air Act (CAA), designed to eliminate VOCs, ozone depleters, and other hazardous air pollutants (HAPs), put limits on many organic solvents. In spite of search attempts for greener solvents, solvent sales have declined steadily since 1990, according to *Chemical Week* magazine. It was predicted that solvent sales would drop from 1993 to 1996 because of environmental regulations on chlorofluorocarbons (CFCs) and high-VOC solvents. It also was predicted that the market would recover slightly from 1996 to 2000, with increased demand for unregulated solvents. Odor regulations were another constituent of the Clean Air Act; paints and coatings producers were forced to reduce odor emissions by fall 1995. Since odors could not be classified as easily as VOCs, some confusion continued to exist about the impact of odor regulations.

NEW PRODUCTS AND PROCESSES

By the early 1990s, many companies were coming to the conclusion that toxic reduction was not only a political and social necessity, but that it also made economic sense in terms of improved efficiency. The result was reduced solvent consumption, lowering the industry's unit growth rate, especially in the original equipment and special purpose paint categories.

Traditional paints contain low solids content—that is, they have a high share of potentially hazardous chemical liquids that can evaporate into the air—and are based on environmentally harmful chemical solvents. Although their high use of solvents makes them the most environmentally damaging, in 1995, 40 percent of the world's paint still came from this class. While the industry is moving away from low-solids, solvent-based paints, they still represented about 30 percent of the market in 1999. More substantial reductions were expected in the early 2000s, when consumption was forecast to fall to 15 percent of all paints by 2005, and to 7 percent by 2010.

High-solids coatings, in which solids account for more than 60 percent of the paint by weight, are an example of the industry's efforts to reduce solvents. Water-borne coatings, where the solvent is primarily water, dominate the architectural coatings segment. Use of high-solids coatings that use solvents other than water is expected to decline entering the twenty-first century.

Powder coatings, which contain epoxy, polyester and polyurethane resins, are replacing conventional solvent paints and other surface treatments such as porcelain. Powder coatings are sprayed on dry and are then electrically bonded to a surface. Since powder coatings contain no solvents, they comply with environmental standards. Major markets for powder coatings included metal finishing, 53 percent; appliances, 21 percent; automobile applications, 15 percent; lawn and garden, 8 percent; and architectural products, 8 percent. While powders accounted for just 8 percent of the world paint market in 1995, they were expected to reach 12 percent by 2000 and top 20 percent by 2010.

While the initial cost of equipment and materials necessary to convert from solvent paint manufacturing to powder coating production is high, factors such as increased material utilization, reduced energy and labor costs, and the elimination of solvent emissions that occur with the use of liquid coatings can more than offset the initial investment.

Radiation curing, which is the smallest of the alternative processes, involves the use of ultraviolet light or an electronic beam to harden a reactive liquid into a solid. Coatings are the largest market for radiation curing, at about 70 percent, and are used on plastics paper, wood, and metals, as well as for such electronic applications as optical fibers and printed circuit boards. Radiation curing claimed just 3.5 percent of the global coatings market in 1995, and its share was expected to rise slowly to 7.5 percent by 2010.

Technological Advancements

An article in *Japan Chemical Week* stated that the Japanese paint industry has increased its technological innovations to produce value-added products to cope with the economy. Nippon Paint and Kansai Paint developed transparent powdered paints for cars and competed to develop solvent-free powdered paints. The companies also accelerated unleaded electrodeposition paint technology as an answer to a U.S. ban on lead content in paint. Japanese paint manufacturers collaborated with companies in Turkey and China to produce electrodeposition auto coatings and bicycle-use coatings, with sales that were expected to double.

Magna Paints of Cape Town, South Africa, introduced a new fireproof paint, which can delay the spread of fire for at least an hour. The paint was made of ingredients that react at only 200 degrees Celsius. New or reformulated materials for paints and coatings exhibited at a New Orleans Coating Technology show in October 1994 substantiated that 1994 was a breakthrough year for compliant technology, especially waterborne systems.

Industry Leaders

Akzo Nobel N.V.

The number one company worldwide, Akzo Nobel is based in Arnheim, the Netherlands. Akzo Nobel traces its roots back to a German rayons and coatings producer founded in 1899. The German company merged in 1929, creating Algemene Kunstzijde-Unie (AKU). In 1967 two Dutch companies merged to form Koninkijke Zout Organon (KZO) and in 1969 KZO merged with AKU, and Akzo was born. In the 1970s Akzo's main business was fibers. When Aarnout Loudon became chairman in 1982, Akzo's reliance on fibers was reduced; and in 1985, Akzo sold its largest U.S. fiber business to BASF. In the 1980s, the company began a major restructuring and reorganizing operation, centralizing management, reducing its workforce, and streamlining R&D.

In 1993, Akzo sold its paper and pulp business to Nobel Industries and got it back a few months later when it agreed to acquire Nobel from a Swedish government-owned holding company. In 1994 the merger was completed, creating Akzo Nobel. This merger created the world's second largest paint manufacturer. Since the merger, Akzo Nobel has concentrated on streamlining its operations, including eliminating duplicate positions. Akzo produced chemical products, man-made fibers, coatings, and health care products. International operations grew to include more than 60 countries.

Akzo Nobel's 1998 purchase of Courtaulds, which had been the world's eighth largest paintmaker, securely placed it at the industry's forefront in terms of sales volume, a position for which it had long jockeyed with ICI to attain. Based on Akzo Nobel's 1997 paint sales of US$4.13 billion, the acquisition would add another US$1.2 billion in annual sales from Courtaulds, bringing Akzo Nobel's annual paint sales to more than US$5.3 billion. The company as a whole took in US$11.87 billion in 1997 revenues. While widely diversified in the coatings sector, in the late 1990s Akzo's main product lines included architectural/decorative paints, industrial coatings, and car refinishes. The Courtaulds line brought a variety of transportation equipment coatings to the mix, such as those for ships, airplanes, and motor vehicles, among other products. While, as with ICI, architectural paints form Akzo's largest sales segment, that category accounts for a substantially lower proportion of sales at Akzo Nobel. Architectural paints occupied less than 40 percent of Akzo's paint volume after the Courtaulds acquisition.

In 2001, with costs for oils and other base materials escalating, Akzo Nobel saw itself reflecting a drop in other areas of the economy when its second quarter profits dropped 6 percent to US$217 million, in spite of rising sales, according to *Bloomberg News*. In 2004, sales went up to US$17.18 billion, a 4.7 percent increase over 2003, but profits rose 53.1 percent, for a net income of US$1.15 billion. The company employed 60,350 people.

PPG INDUSTRIES INC.

PPG Industries, based in Pittsburgh, Pennsylvania, is the world's second-largest coatings manufacturer. Pittsburgh Plate Glass (PPG) was founded in Creighton, Pennsylvania, in 1883 by John Ford and John Pitcairn. PPG became the first commercially successful U.S. plate glass factory. In 1924 PPG revolutionized the glass production process and in the 1930s and 1940s successfully promoted structural glass for use in the commercial construction industry. PPG was listed on the New York Stock Exchange in 1945, started producing fiberglass in 1952, and in 1968 it had adopted its present name, PPG Industries Inc.

PPG's second most profitable segment (behind its relatively small chemicals division) was coatings and resins, which generated about 43 percent of the company's operating profits as of 1997. Operating margins in PPG's coatings business hovered in the 18 to 19 percent range during the late 1990s. PPG has 72 major plants in the United States, Canada, Germany, Italy, Mexico, the Netherlands, Spain, Taiwan, and the United Kingdom. Its brands include Monarch, Lucite, and Olympic.

Since the mid-1990s, paints and resins have emerged as PPG's largest product segment, surpassing glass and fiberglass to contribute 55 percent of total revenues as of 2003. PPG Industries found itself contemplating layoffs and strategy changes in 2001 as fourth quarter income declined from the same period one year earlier to US$83 million. For the year 2001, net income was US$387 million, a major downslide from 2000 net revenues of US$620 million, according to *Paint Coatings Industry News*. By 2004, sales were US$9.51 billion and the company employed 31,800 people.

THE SHERWIN-WILLIAMS COMPANY

The Sherwin-Williams Company was born in 1870, when Henry South bought out paint materials distributor Truman Dunham and joined with Edward Williams and A.T. Osborne in Cleveland, Ohio. Sherwin-Williams began making paints in 1871 and in 1877 patented a reclosable can. In 1880 the company introduced an improved liquid paint, making Sherwin-Williams' brand the industry leader. In 1874 Sherwin-Williams introduced a special paint for carriages, beginning the concept of special-purpose paint. By 1900 Sherwin-Williams had introduced special-purpose paints for floors, roofs, barns, metal bridges, railroad cars, and automobiles. A dealership was established in Massachusetts in 1891, the forerunner of company-operated retail stores. In 1895 the "Cover the Earth" trademark was obtained. In response to wartime restrictions, Sherwin-Williams developed a new paint—fast-drying and water-reducible—called Kem-Tone, and the forerunner of the paint roller, the Roller-Koater.

In the 1960s the company continued to make acquisitions, and in spite of doubling sales, rising expenses kept earnings flat. In 1972 the company expanded its stores to include other decorating items. However, by 1977 the company lost US$8.2 million and suspended dividends for the first time since 1885. John Breen joined the company as CEO in 1979. He reinstated dividends, restructured management positions, closed inefficient plants, concentrated company store products on paints and wallpaper, and purchased Dutch Boy in 1980. Acquisitions in 1990 included the Krylon and Illinois Bronze aerosol operations from Borden, and DeSoto's architectural coatings business. In 1991 Sherwin-Williams purchased the Cuprinol brand of coatings and two coatings business units from Cook Paint and Varnish. In 2003 the company acquired Accurate Dispersions, and the following year the company acquired Duron.

The world's third largest paint-maker in terms of both sales and volume, Sherwin-Williams is the United States' largest paint manufacturer, principally through its market leadership in architectural paints. It controls an estimated 25 percent of the U.S. paint market. The company is divided into two segments. The paint stores segment distributes architectural coatings, industrial maintenance products and finishes, and related items. The coatings segment consists of six divisions: coatings, consumer brands, automotive, transportation services, specialty, and international. Sherwin-Williams is also the leading maker of private-label paints, selling products to Sears, Roebuck and Co., Wal-Mart Stores Inc., and other retailers.

In 2004 Sherwin-Williams registered total sales of US$6.11 billion, of which about 40 percent came from its manufactured shipments and about 60 percent through its 2,700 retail outlets. Architectural paints generate some 60 percent of Sherwin-Williams' sales.

In the 2000s, as Sherwin Williams becomes one of a number of major paint-makers likely to face lengthy and costly lawsuits over its one-time use of lead in paint, Morgan Stanley downgraded Sherwin-Williams' worth in spite of billions of dollars in annual sales, according to *Forbes*.

IMPERIAL CHEMICAL INDUSTRIES PLC

ICI was created in 1926 through the merger of four British chemical companies: Nobel Industries Ltd.; Brunner, Mond and Company Ltd.; United Alkali Company Ltd.; and British Dyestuff Corporation Ltd. The most famed of these companies was Nobel Industries, which was created as the British arm of Alfred Nobel's explosives empire. In 1929, ICI and Du Pont signed a patents and process agreement, sharing research information. ICI, as Britain's representative in the chemical industry, plunged into research. ICI's skilled chemists, engineers, and managers created 87 new products between 1933 and 1935 in its Dyestuffs Group Laboratory. Soon after the end of World War II, the ICI-Du Pont alliance crumbled in 1952. Faced with new competition, ICI added operations in Germany, the United Kingdom, and the United States in the 1960s. In spite of this, profits declined, and in 1980 ICI posted losses and cut its dividends for the first time.

Under the leadership of John Harvey-Jones in 1982, ICI was reorganized and shifted production from bulk chemicals such as soda and chlorine to high margin specialty chemicals, or "effect chemicals," such as pharmaceuticals and pesticides. Harvey-Jones purchased 100 companies from 1982 until his retirement in 1987. Some of ICI's major purchases were Glidden Paints in 1986 and Stauffer Chemicals in 1987, of which it sold all but the agricultural chemicals operations. The acquisition of Glidden was one of ICI's most important paint transactions and contributed to the company's rapid emergence as a paint industry leader. The wisdom of this purchase, however, was questioned in the 2000s after ICI became entangled in Glidden's lead paint suit and its stock dropped 5 percent, according to *Forbes*.

Throughout the 1990s, ICI maintained the rapid pace of its acquisition and divestiture activities. Its overall strategy was to move from a commodity chemical manufacturer to a specialty chemical business. In the mid-1990s it sold its bioscience holdings to the Zeneca Group. By 1998, an estimated 38 percent of its revenues came from its specialty chemical line, which had been recently expanded with the purchase of a Unilever chemical division. In 1997 ICI also sold off its polyester and titanium dioxide (a key paint ingredient) business to Du Pont and spun off its majority position in ICI Australia (renamed Orica) in a public offering. It also sold its explosives business that year. Already in 1998 ICI was looking for buyers for segments of the Unilever acquisition that did not meet ICI's objectives. As of 1998, paints and coatings were considered solidly inside of ICI's business strategy.

Among the company's highly internationalized businesses, ICI's paint holdings in India were a particular priority because that nation's market was growing by 10 or more percent annually in the mid to late 1990s. ICI owns ICI India Ltd., a US$200 million operation (to which paints contribute 43 percent) that held about 14 percent of India's architectural paint market in 1997. In the mid to late 1990s, paint production at ICI India, the country's third largest decorative paint manufacturer, was growing at a frenetic 27 percent annually as it gained market share, although growth was expected to taper off at the end of the decade. Another facet of ICI's Indian market penetration was a failed attempt to acquire a sizable stake in the country's leading supplier, Asian Paints Ltd. The move was blocked by Indian regulators.

In 2004, company revenue was US$10.73 billion. More than 91 percent of ICI's coatings volume was dedicated to architectural paints, with the remaining 9 percent devoted to metal container and industrial coatings.

E.I. du Pont de Nemours and Company

E.I. du Pont de Nemours and Company began as a family owned gunpowder and explosives partnership in 1802. The plant grew to be the largest of its kind and within several decades added dynamite, nitroglycerine, and guncotton. The outbreak of World War I generated about US$89 million in business and the company diversified into paints, plastics, and dyes. Some of Du Pont's most significant inventions include neoprene synthetic rubber (1931), Lucite (1937), and nylon and Teflon (1938). This chemical giant makes a variety of products classified into six principal segments: life sciences; chemicals—pigments, paints, and refrigerants; fibers—Stainmaster Plus and Lycra; polymers—polyester resins, Teflon, and packaging; petroleum—Conoco (acquired in 1981); and diversified business such as agricultural and medical products and electronics. The company placed considerable emphasis on its life science business in the late 1990s. Du Pont, which is headquartered in Wilmington, Delaware, along with its subsidiaries, conducts business in some 70 countries worldwide. Its corporate sales were US$27.34 billion in 2004, but coatings accounted for only a small portion of that figure. The Coatings & Color Technologies Group was the world leader in coatings for the automotive market in 2003. Nearly half of Du Pont's sales come from outside the United States.

BASF

BASF is the world's largest chemical manufacturer and the sixth largest paints and coatings manufacturer. The German conglomerate has six sectors: oil and gas, chemicals, agricultural products, plastics and fibers, dyestuffs and finishing products, and consumer products. Founded in Mannheim, Germany in 1861, BASF was originally known as Badische, Anilin, and Soda Fabrik. A pioneer of coal tar dyes, in 1897 BASF successfully developed a synthetic indigo. BASF's synthetic dyes started replacing more expensive, inconvenient organic dyes. BASF, which had been largely dependent on sales of basic chemicals, expanded globally and diversified into related businesses mainly by way of acquiring chemicals, pigments, and paint and ink companies. In 1990 BASF became the first outsider to purchase a major chemical company in Eastern Europe. In the late 1990s it moved to refocus and restructure its coatings business by creating BASF Coatings AG, a new European unit to centralize its various paint businesses.

Total 2004 sales from all BASF businesses exceeded US$51 billion, but paints and coatings accounted for approximately 7 percent of this sum. Producing about 1.14 million metric tons of paints and coatings annually, in 1997 BASF obtained US$2.19 billion from its coatings operations, which form the largest segment of its Colorants & Finishing Products division.

SigmaKalon Group

Europe' second largest decorative coatings manufacturer, SigmaKalon Group BV reported 2003 sales of US$2.13 billion. Based in the Netherlands, SigmaKalon was owned by TOTAL SA until that year, when it was sold to Bain Capital, a private investment firm. The company derived three-fourths of its sales from decorative paints, with the remainder spread out among industrial, marine, and protective coatings. In 2003, the company acquired the largest paint manufacturer of Czech/Slovak, Primalex Brasy.

The Valspar Corporation

Valspar was the world's eighth largest paint-maker by volume in 2003. The company was incorporated in Delaware in 1934. In the 1960s, 1970s, and 1980s, the company acquired a number of paints, glass, and plastics firms. Valspar, with its principal offices in Minneapolis, Minnesota, conducts operations at 21 locations. It manufactures and distributes a full line of latex acrylic and oil-based paints and varnishes marketed primarily under the names Valspar, Minnesota, Colony, BPS, Magicolor, Enterprise, and Masury. Other coatings businesses include product finishes for machinery, vehicles, composition board, wiring and containers, coil applications, metal equipment, leisure products, and other specialty items. The company also manufactures marine coatings, resins for use in paint and coating manufacturing, and color tinting systems. Paint sales in 1997 amounted to US$1.05 billion. In the latter half of the 1990s, the company produced about 440,000 metric tons of paint per year, giving it an estimated two percent share of the world market.

In 2000 Valspar purchased Lilly Industries for US$975 million. This increased Valspar's annual sales from US$1.4 billion to about US$2.0 billion. By 2004, the company reported US$2.44 billion in revenues, with about 75 percent of sales attributed to the United States.

NIPPON PAINT CO. LTD.

Established in 1881, Nippon Paint is Japan' oldest and largest paint company. It was headquartered in Osaka, Japan. With divisions in architectural, automotive, and industrial coatings, as well as powder coating and chemical segments, the company reported sales of US$1.88 billion in 2004. In the United States, its subsidiary was Nippon Paint America (NPA), which manufactured both powder and automotive coatings.

KANSAI PAINT CO. LTD.

Kansai Paint was established in Japan in May 1918. Headquartered in Osaka, Japan, Kansai manufactures synthetic resin paint, odorless interior use paint, tin-free anti-fouling paint and other coatings for automobiles and trains. Kansai's largest paint segment by sales is automotive coatings, which claim more than 40 percent of its annual paint sales. The company's other product groups include architectural paints (28 percent), metal coatings (18 percent), and marine/structural paints (12 percent).

In 2004 Kansai reported sales of US$1.7 billion, up 2.6 percent from the previous year. Within Japan alone, Kansai is bigger than rival Nippon, but Nippon had the lion's share of the international market. Kansai was pursuing a variety of international ventures, notably in China, Southeast Asia, and the United States, to fuel its growth. In 2001 the company launched a 51 percent joint venture with an Indonesia company for the making of automobile paints.

MAJOR COUNTRIES IN THE INDUSTRY

ASIA

In 2002 Asia consumed about 29 percent of the world's paint. China exceeded Japan as the biggest national consumer in Asia, accounting for nearly 30 percent of Asia's paint demand due to persistent economic woes in Japan that hurt the paint industry in the 2000s. The financial crisis that began to sweep the region in 1997 also temporarily diminished demand in some parts of Asia as construction projects were placed on hold and consumer spending on manufactured goods stagnated or declined.

Nonetheless, several Asian countries present outstanding market conditions for paint- makers, and the region as a whole suffers from a capacity shortage that makes it dependent, at least in the short term, on imported paints. The region was estimated to need 200,000 metric tons of new paint production each year through the early 2000s. As local and multinational paint firms expanded their production facilities in Asia, many nations became more self-sufficient in paint production in the early 2000s. However, in certain places, notably China, local production continued to fall short on quality as well, forcing manufacturers to source high-performance coatings from abroad even when locally produced coatings were available. Thus, at the same time that the region's paint capacity expands, local manufacturers are likely to move toward newer, more sophisticated kinds of coatings that currently are formulated mostly by major Japanese, European, and U.S. chemical and paint conglomerates.

By 2002, although some problems remained, more and more companies expressed confidence in China. For example, Connecticut-based Arch Chemicals Inc., noting China's annual furniture exports of nearly US$3 billion each year, has increased coatings business operations in such areas as sales and support, according to *Paintings & Coatings Industry News*.

India has proven to be an exceptionally strong paint market in the region, though a slightly volatile one, and it continues to expand its domestic paint manufacturing base. India's per capita consumption of paint trails that of other developing nations in Asia. Whereas in the late 1990s Thailand consumed 1.2 kg per person annually and the Philippines consumed 6 kg per capita, India's much larger population purchased only 0.5 kg per capita. The country's largest producer is Asian Paints Ltd., which controls about 45 percent of India's organized architectural paint market— representing 70 percent of the nation's paints and coatings market—and has a strong presence in industrial coatings as well. Asian Paints has a net market share of 36 percent in India for all types of coatings and possesses that country's most extensive paint distribution network. From 1996 to 2000, Asian Paints embarked on an expansion plan that would add 80,000 metric tons of capacity to its plants. Goodlass Nerolac and ICI India Ltd. are the subcontinent's second and third largest paint companies, respectively.

EUROPE

In 2004, demand for paint in Western Europe totaled approximately 6.43 million tons and was expected to rise about one percent annually to 6.81 million tons by 2009. Western Europe continued to show low growth in the high-volume decorative paints sector, modest growth in industrial coating, and high growth in the architectural paints sector.

In the mid to late 1990s, Europe was a comparatively lackluster paint market, and the German BASF conglomerate showed significant net sales drops by the 2000s. Late decade annual growth estimates for the region ranged from 1.5 to 2.5 percent, while such segments as conventional automotive refinishing paints actually experienced volume declines in 1996 and 1997. Other segments were virtually flat in 1997, with the notable exceptions of aerospace coatings and the environmentally friendly powder and radiation-cured coatings. In a number of cases, European production levels as of 1998 were at or below levels achieved in the late 1980s. Contributing to Europe's slack volume demand have been a number of environmental laws that called for reductions in the amount of paint used in certain applications as a means of curtailing release of harmful toxins. The same laws, however, are fueling crossover sales of powder coatings and other less polluting formulations in place of conventional coatings. Such attention to Europe's powder coatings—seen earlier in the decade as a promising high-margin specialty business—has unleashed fierce competition and price slippage to commodity levels, undermining the profitability of that segment. As a result, in Europe powder coatings have achieved twice the penetration rate than they have in the United States.

THE UNITED STATES

The US$19 billion U.S. paint industry under-performed in the general economy, as measured by gross domestic product, in the early and mid-2000s. Annual growth was in the range of two to three percent and actually dropped between 1997 and 2002 with economic faltering that occurred in related industries. As in other markets, though, certain U.S. segments have been considerably stronger than the market as a whole, particularly powder coatings, which have enjoyed annual increases of nearly 10 percent. Architectural paints make up about 48 percent of the U.S. market by volume, but only 38 percent in terms of value. This segment was valued at US$7.6 billion in 2003, and was projected to reach US$9.0 billion by 2008. A significant trend in architectural paints has been the rise of powerful mass merchandisers, such as The Home Depot Inc. and Wal-Mart Stores Inc., which have altered the pricing and marketing equations for U.S. paints. These stores demand low prices from manufacturers and wield the threat of dumping a paint brand if a coatings maker fails to meet their criteria. Such was the case with Sherwin-Williams' Dutch Boy paint, which Home Depot dropped from its 670 outlets in 1997; ICI's Glidden brand was chosen as a replacement.

FURTHER READING

"2004 Top Companies Report." *Coatings World,* July 2004.

"Architectural Coatings Continue to Grow." *Paint & Coatings Industry,* 1 July 2004.

Bourguignon, Edward. "PCI 50." *Paint & Coatings Industry,* 1 July 2004.

Brezinski, Darlene. "2003 Bottom Line Improves." *Paint & Coatings Industry,* 1 July 2004.

D'Amico, Esther. "On an Expedition." *Chemical Week,* 26 November 2003.

Draper, Deborah J., ed. *Business Rankings Annual.* Detroit: Thomson Gale, 2004.

Freedman, Michael. "Turning Lead Into Gold." *Forbes,* 14 May 2001.

"Home Sales Drive Profits." *Chemical Week,* 20 October 2004.

"Hoover's Company Capsules," 2005. Available from http://www.hoovers.com.

Hume, Claudia, et al. "Paints and Coatings," *Chemical Week,* 18 October 2000.

Hunter, David. "Getting Creative with Additives." *Chemical Week,* 24 December 2003.

"International Trade Statistics." 2003. Available from http://www.wto.org.

Lazich, Robert S., ed. *Market Share Reporter.* Detroit: Thomson Gale, 2004.

"Mixing and Matching." *Paint & Coatings Industry,* 1 July 2004.

"Paints & Coatings." *Chemical & Engineering News,* 3 November 2003.

"Paints and Coatings in France, Germany, UK, US." *Euromonitor,* August 2004. Available from http://www.majormarketprofiles.com.

Proctor, David. "Challenges Ahead for the Chemical Industry and Its Suppliers." *Paint & Coatings Industry,* 1 July 2004.

Ruitenberg, Rudy. "Akzo-Nobel Second-Quarter Net Seen Falling 6.2 Percent." *Bloomberg News,* 23 July 2001.

———. "ICI First-Quarter Profit Seen Falling." *Bloomberg News,* 2 May 2001.

U.S. Department of the Census. *Economic Census 2002,* 2005. Available from http://www.census.gov.

Walsh, Kerri. "Signs of Improvement After a Mixed Quarter." *Chemical Week,* 13 August 2003.

Warrington, Hannah. "BASF Probably Had Fourth-Quarter Loss" *Bloomberg News,* 7 March 2002.

"Western European Paint Demand to Hit 6.81 Million Tons by 2009." *Coatings World,* January 2005.

"World Paints and Coatings Demand to Reach 28.8 Million Tons in 2007." *Industrial Paint & Powder,* June 2004.

SIC 2834

NAICS 325412

PHARMACEUTICALS

Pharmaceutical manufacturers produce a diverse range of preparations for human and veterinary treatment. The majority of these firms' products are produced in final form for consumption, such as ampoules, tablets, capsules, vials, ointments, medicinal powders, solutions, and suspensions. Industry output consists of two important lines. Pharmaceutical preparations promoted primarily to the dental, medical, or veterinary professions are called "ethical" drugs, also known as prescription drugs. Those sold openly to the public are commonly described as "over-the-counter" (OTC) drugs. Industry firms may also produce therapies derived from genetic engineering or related biotechnology processes.

INDUSTRY SNAPSHOT

The pharmaceutical industry is one of the world's most dynamic and lucrative in terms of sales volume. Despite rising pressure from government agencies and employers to lower drug prices, worldwide pharmaceutical spending increased 11 percent in 2003. That year, spending totaled approximately US$500 billion, according to IMS Health. Of this total, US$230 billion was attributed to the United States and Canada. By 2008, according to Business Communications Company, the world market for pharmaceuticals will reach US$900 billion.

Mergers and product turnover continue to refashion the companies and products that lead the industry, but all of the top companies have historical ties to the industry often dating 50 years or longer. Because there are numerous specialties within the industry—numerous forms of cancer, AIDS, hypertension, cholesterol, and neurological drugs to name a few—many of the leading producers may at first only compete with one or two others on a product-by-product basis. This pattern derives in part from the enormous research costs usually involved with producing a new drug, a reality that has led many drug makers to specialize in a few therapeutic fields.

A source of continuing vigilance within the industry is the expiration of brand-name patents. While laws vary by country, in most world markets a new drug may be patented—that is, produced exclusively by its originator or firms authorized by the patent holder—for a fixed term. After the term expires, which is sometimes as long as 17 years, the compound is open to generic competition, and thus market forces usually bring prices down substantially from the levels obtained during the founding company's monopoly.

In early 2004, IMS reported that while the overall pharmaceutical market was expected to experience single digit growth in 2004, generic drug sales would increase 20 percent, reaching US$34.8 billion. The research firm indicated that branded drugs would face noteworthy competition from generics through at least 2010. However, certain factors limit generics' ability to capture market share. Large patent holders can manufacture their own generics, force legal actions to protect intellectual property, or simply pay competitors to delay market launch of generics. A 2000 investigation by the U.S. Federal Trade Commission found Abbott Laboratories paying a generic drugmaker US$4.5 million per month to delay a generic product. Occasionally, generic drugs reach the market only to find patent holders with new drugs ready to supplant their predecessors, rendering generics out-of-date before gaining market presence. However, with health care costs rising near double digit percentages, U.S. lawmakers were considering reducing patent protection times, among other remedies, to allow greater competition by generics.

Another key issue for the industry is controlling the cost and duration of research and development (R&D). A rising share of company sales—more than 18 percent in the United States in 2002—are funneled into R&D, and development times have been on the upswing as well. The U.S. industry, the world's largest, averages 10 years to bring a new drug to the market. As a result, a number of major firms engage in resource-sharing schemes such as joint ventures with other companies or undertake internal restructuring to arrive at a more cost-efficient workflow. Pharmaceutical consultants also push companies toward better data management. Successful manufacturers can feed back point-of-sale data to optimize current production, thus reducing inventory.

A trend continuing in the mid-2000s has been the increasing percentage of marketing targeted directly to consumers. Following a softening of the U.S. Food and Drug Administration's (FDA) stance on the issue, for example, drug makers spent an estimated US$2.27 billion in 2000 on direct to consumer advertising, up 41 percent from 1999. According to a study by Harvard University and MIT, a 10 percent increase in direct-to-consumer advertising resulted in a 1 percent increase in sales.

Organization and Structure

The global pharmaceutical market continues to consolidate. Notwithstanding high profile mergers and acquisitions by Pfizer, Glaxo, and Aventis, the single largest pharmaceutical company in 2001 accounted for only about 8 percent of the world's total market value by sales. As companies merged, they often shook off the "pharmaceutical" label for a more encompassing one—"life sciences". Many are chemical companies with separate divisions producing a wide range of products, from pharmaceuticals to agricultural chemicals.

Pharmaceutical preparations are commonly divided into two categories: ethical and over-the-counter (OTC). Worldwide, most ethical drugs are paid for by governments or consumers (patients) indirectly through third-party payers like health insurance companies.

Ethical Drugs. The top six classes of prescription drugs were: central nervous system and sense organs; cardiovascular; digestive and genitourinary; neoplasms, endocrine and metabolic diseases; parasitic and infectious diseases; and respiratory.

These classes of finished-form drugs commanded the highest profit margins (30 percent of sales was commonplace), but also demanded high research and development and marketing expenses—15 percent and 24 percent of sales, respectively. Pharmaceutical firms used two primary methods to maximize the profit potential of their discoveries: marketing and patenting.

Specialized marketing techniques unique to the pharmaceutical industry evolved in the twentieth century. Since doctors usually made the purchase decision for the customer or patient, and (in most countries) ethical drugs could not be advertised to the general public, most pharmaceutical marketing was directed at general practitioners. Branding was a primary method of product differentiation. Knowledgeable sales forces made regular calls on doctors in an effort to sway their prescribing decisions. Most pharmaceutical firms also employed advertising in medical journals, direct mail, conference sponsorships, and promotional giveaways. In 2000, pharmaceutical companies spent US$15.7 billion on promotion of ethical drugs, over half the amount they spend on research and development, with an increasing share of the U.S. marketing budget going to direct-to-consumer pushes.

A recent trend in pharmaceutical marketing is the rise of online drug stores and mail order pharmaceuticals. According to the pharmaceutical market research firm IMS Health, prescription drug orders to U.S. mail order pharmacies rose 27 percent to US$13.6 billion for the year ending in June 2000. The total market, including traditional retail pharmacies, rose 17 percent to US$82 billion. The typical mix of name brand to generic sales in those pharmacies is 59 percent to 41 percent, respectively. Mail order drug stores, however, typically fill name-brand prescriptions 72 percent of the time—a significant difference for maintaining or increasing brand market share. With health care costs rising dramatically in the United States at the end of the twentieth century, the FDA is also monitoring the rise of offshore online pharmacies, which offer pharmaceuticals at low prices, sometimes without a doctor's approval. The FDA bans such practices, but is unable to handle enforcement effectively due to the sheer volume of sites and the ephemeral nature of the World Wide Web.

Patenting was one of the most important aspects of the pharmaceutical industry. Most patents fell under two categories: product patents, which covered a given chemical substance, and process patents, which protected the manufacturing technique used. Until the mid 1950s, most countries found process patents sufficient to protect pharmaceutical preparations. But since circumventing these copyrights was relatively easy, many countries, including most of Europe and the United States, switched to product patents.

Although nominal patent life—the span of time from patent issue to expiration—exceeded 15 years in all countries that granted patents, effective patent protection began to grow shorter in the 1970s due in part to the often lengthy government approval process. The proliferation of so-called "me too" and derivative drugs shortened pharmaceutical companies' "pay back" period even further. By the early 1990s, all but 10 percent of patented drugs had a direct competitor, and some had more than one.

The 1962 Thalidomide scare precipitated more stringent global drug safety and approval standards. The United States had required federal inspection of new compounds since the beginning of the twentieth century and had toughened those controls with the formation of the FDA in the late 1930s. However, it was not until the 1960s that governments in industrialized nations began imposing the stringent pre-market approval systems that sometimes met with criticism during the 1990s. A German drug company had introduced Thalidomide as a "safe" sleeping pill in the 1950s. In the early 1960s, an American drug company began testing the drug with a view to licensing it for sale in the United States. FDA tests observed that, when taken during a particular period of pregnancy, the drug caused severe birth defects. Although the drug never made it to market in the United States, the implications spurred more rigorous approval requirements, including clinical tests, in the United States and Europe. For better or worse, some industry observers have linked stronger pre-market regulations to the much-reduced flow of new drugs since 1960. The FDA also tightened controls in light of a number of drugs pulled from the market from 1997 to 2000. Approval times in 2000 rose to an average of 17 months, up from 12.6 months in 1999. Longer approval times shorten the effective patent protection of new compounds.

Out-of-patent or generic drugs gained considerable clout in the 1980s and remained strong into the 2000s. Also known as multi-source drugs, generics were ethical drugs that had lost their patent protection. These compounds were then manufactured by smaller manufacturers and sold by prescription under a new brand name, usually at a lower cost. Intense price competition (30 percent to 70 percent below patented versions) and low profit margins characterized this segment of the pharmaceutical industry. Generic producers tended to limit their operations to domestic and regional markets. Nonetheless, in the United States, generics accounted for 47 percent of prescriptions written in 1999, up from 35 percent in 1992. By 2004, this rose to 56 percent, according to IMS Health figures cited by *USA Today.* Prices for prescription generics in the United States increased by 3.7 percent in 2003 and another 1.7 percent in 2004, reaching an average of US$28.71 per prescription-well below the name-brand average of US$95.86.

Furthermore, approximately US$12 billion worth of name-brand medications were scheduled to go generic in 2005. At the same time, intense competition from overseas manufacturers of generics, particularly in India, will likely pressure U.S. companies to keep prices down.

The proliferation of government funded health care programs, especially in Europe but to a lesser degree in the United States, helped promote the generic segment of pharmaceutical preparations. "Positive" and "negative" lists published by governments enumerated the prescription drugs that would or would not be reimbursed by social security programs, thereby exerting influence on doctors' prescribing practices. Managed care corporations produced formularies, lists of acceptable drugs for their members, which accounted for market comparisons on price, and published efficacy studies of the drug and physicians' recommendations. These subtle methods of market control were used in most of Western Europe and to a limited extent in the United States, but not in Japan. As recently as the early 1990s some industry observers prognosticated a massive shift toward generic drugs—to as much as 50 percent of the world market by 1995. By the late 1990s it was evident that such a change would take longer, although the trend was decidedly toward generics.

In the early 1990s, many leading pharmaceutical producers began manufacturing their own "after-patent" versions of popular drugs by either affiliating with, acquiring, or forming their own generic firms in order to stop the profit-margin squeeze. Although billions of dollars worth of patent drugs were slated to go generic by the turn of the century, some analysts speculated that the big pharmaceutical companies could retain their hegemony by introducing their own generic versions before the patents expired. Some of the largest "cash cows" slated to lose patent protection beginning in 2001 included Losec/Prilosec, Prozac, Zocor, Claritin, and Glucophage-each earning over US$1 billion in the United States in 2000.

Over-the-Counter Drugs. Over-the-counter (OTC) or non-prescription drugs were sold directly to consumers without a prescription. In general, these preparations had high advertising and low research expenditures, and few were genuinely new products.

While OTC drugs made a relatively small contribution to industry-wide sales and profits in the 1990s, they had the potential to increase faster than forecasted as consumers increasingly turned to self-diagnosis (i.e., at home pregnancy and cholesterol-testing kits) and self-medication. Prescription to OTC transfers also accelerated in the early 1990s. The British government, for example, converted 15 drugs from prescription to OTC status in 1993, whereas it had only made 11 such transfers in the previous decade. Consumption of OTC drugs were forecasted to grow fastest in developing nations, but would also remain strong in Europe and North America, as governments there transferred more prescription drugs to OTC status in order to shift costs to patients.

BACKGROUND AND DEVELOPMENT

Although some sources trace the pharmaceutical industry back only half a century, pharmaceutical practice evolved slowly over thousands of years of practical use of herbs, minerals, and other compounds. The word pharmacy derives from the Greek term "pharmakon," used by Homer in the *Odyssey* to describe a drug or charm. The discoveries of opium and hemlock have also been traced to ancient Greece. In spite of the spread of pharmaceutical knowledge throughout the Roman Empire, that civilization's decline and the onset of the Middle Ages suppressed pharmacological progress in the Western world. While Asian and Middle Eastern medical knowledge continued to develop during the ensuing 12 centuries, little of that information made its way to the West. The Renaissance revived pharmaceutical discovery beginning in the late fifteenth century. The discovery of the "New World" brought new plant-based medicaments, such as belladonna, ipecacuanha, Jesuit's bark, and cocoa. The sixteenth century witnessed the publication of the world's first pharmacopoeia, or guide to the preparation of known drugs and medicinal chemicals, in Germany. Pharmaceutical practices were professionalized with the 1617 establishment of the Society of Apothecaries in London. Some of the modern industry's largest companies grew from modest beginnings as small apothecaries, preparing treatments one dose at a time.

The modern pharmaceutical industry can be traced to the isolation and development of several potent medicinal compounds that could be mass-produced in the nineteenth century. The first of these were the alkaloids, which were derived from plant sources. Many of the powerful drugs in this group, including morphine, strychnine, quinine, nicotine, and cocaine, were still in use in the late twentieth century. The isolation of these compounds allowed for accurate dosing and testing of purity. Discernment of these drugs' chemical structure encouraged efforts at laboratory synthesis, and those experiments often yielded valuable related compounds. For example, in 1856, while trying to make quinine from aniline, William Perkins created the first artificial dye, aniline purple.

Germany, already the focal point of the chemical industry, became a pharmaceutical center as well. Researchers at chemical companies like Agfa, Bayer AG, and Hoechst AG formulated or isolated drugs from the by-products of their established businesses. Antipyretics (fever reducers) and analgesics (pain relievers) were distilled from coal tar, for example. The most familiar and enduring of these products, aspirin (acetylsalicylic acid), was discovered by Charles Gerhardt in 1853, but was not exploited until 1899 when Germany's Bayer recognized its therapeutic qualities. Hoechst sponsored Paul Erlich's ground breaking discoveries in drug delivery and action at the turn of the twentieth century. Most notable was his isolation of Salvarsan, one of the first disease specific medicines, for the treatment of syphilis. Through investment in such fundamental research (as well as some questionable business practices), German chemical/pharmaceutical companies dominated the industry until World War I, when hostilities obliged many nations to establish their own manufacturers and research programs.

Independent research also contributed to the advancement of the pharmaceutical industry. Frenchman Louis Pasteur's conception of the germ theory of disease, combined with Briton Joseph Lister's application of that hypothesis in the use of antiseptics, has been called a "signpost to the modern pharmaceutical industry."

By the early twentieth century, patents were a familiar method used by European companies to protect their discoveries. Although the pace of drug development slowed in the first three decades of the twentieth century, the accidental rediscovery of sulphamides and their therapeutic qualities spurred increased research on the part of pharmaceutical companies, especially in America, where original research had previously been limited.

The pharmaceutical industry followed a somewhat unique pattern of internationalization. Although some pharmaceutical companies began exporting before the turn of the twentieth century, most relied on licensing and marketing agreements as well as joint ventures to gain an international presence before World War II. Since many governments impeded the import of finished drugs with complicated testing and packaging requirements, pharmaceutical companies infiltrated foreign markets through the creation of affiliates. U.S. drug makers led the postwar overseas push through the establishment of subsidiaries. These companies could import the active ingredients from the overseas parent and then convert them into finished products under the laws of the new country.

World War II also marked the beginning of a period of intense competition to develop, patent, manufacture, and market new drugs. Many industry leaders—including Bayer and Hoechst in Germany; Roche Holding Ltd. and Ciba-Geigy AG in Switzerland; Pfizer Inc., Eli Lilly & Co., Merck & Co., Inc., and Abbott Laboratories in the United States; and Glaxo Holdings PLC, SmithKline Beecham, and Wellcome plc in the United Kingdom—were well established by this time. Fuelled by intensified research during the war, major pharmaceutical discoveries came in rapid succession. For example, methods for mass production of penicillin were discovered. Streptomycin, which was used in the treatment of tuberculosis, was brought to light in 1943. The first broad spectrum antibiotic, chloramphenicol, was discovered in 1947. Tetracyclines, corticosteroids, oral contraceptives, antihistamines,antidepressants, diuretics, semi-synthetic penicillins, and hundreds more were patented in the late 1940s and early 1950s. These developments transformed the pharmaceutical industry from a commodity chemicals business (in which pharmacists compounded the actual doses) into a field that relied on heavy investments in research and marketing to achieve the patents and brand names that drove sales. The 1960s and 1970s saw the advent of anticancer drugs, along with a nascent autoimmune therapy market.

CURRENT CONDITIONS

Worldwide pharmaceutical spending increased 9 percent in 2004, reaching nearly US$500 billion according to data from the research firm IMS Health. Of this total, nearly half was attributed to the United States and Canada. By 2008 the global pharmaceutical market is projected to exceed US$900 billion.

As the over-65 segment of the world's population continued to grow in the twenty-first century, pharmaceutical companies stood to benefit from a related rise in chronic health conditions such as heart disease and diabetes. However, a number of roadblocks threatened industry profitability. In addition to an increase in the use of generic drugs, supported by expiring name-brand patents, fewer new drugs were being approved in the United States.

In early 2004, IMS reported that while the overall pharmaceutical market was expected to experience single digit growth in 2004, generic drug sales would increase 20 percent, reaching US$34.8 billion. The research firm indicated that branded drugs would face noteworthy competition from generics into the late 2000s.

Perhaps the most significant industry challenge during the mid-2000s was rising pressure from governments to lower drug prices. As Ceci Connolly wrote in the March 16, 2004, issue of *The Washington Post,* "pharmaceutical companies are facing rising anger over what many American consumers view as greed. Over the objections of the Food and Drug Administration, a few governors and mayors have begun helping constituents purchase medications from Canada, where the price can be 30 percent to 70 percent less than in the United States because of Canadian government price controls. A growing bipartisan coalition in Congress supports changing the law to make drug importation legal."

Pressure from the United States government was likely to increase during the late 2000s, following a drug benefit program for Medicare participants enacted in late 2003. In the April 5, 2004 issue of *B to B,* Richard T. Evans, a senior analyst with the New York firm of Sanford C. Bernstein & Co., indicated that when the Medicare drug program became effective in 2006, the government's portion of overall drug purchases would rise from 16 percent in 2004 to 45 percent.

Amid these conditions, a debate began between drug makers and consumers over obtaining drugs from other countries, namely Canada, where government price controls kept costs lower in comparison to the United States—sometimes as much as 60 percent. As states like California pursued legislation that would allow lower-cost pharmaceuticals to be imported into the United States, industry players argued that the practice was not safe, since quality and safety measures could not be assured. Furthermore, they charged that re-importation jeopardized research and development in the United States. Manufacturers reacted by changing the names of certain drugs in Canada, thereby creating confusion in pharmacies, and stepping up political action. In fact, some consumer groups were critical of the industry's contributions to political campaigns, charging them with "greasing' legislatures in an effort to preserve profits. The situation was further complicated in 2005 when Canada, citing the danger of potential domestic shortages, announced that it was drafting legislation that would limit bulk exports of essential drugs to the United States. By 2005, Canadian online pharmacies was exporting more than US$800 million worth of drugs annually to the United States.

During the mid-2000s, corporate mergers and acquisition activity continued at a strong pace. During the first half of 2004, Thomson Financial reported that mergers and acquisitions increased more than 43 percent from 2003, reaching US$896 billion. This high level of activity was bolstered by deals within the European pharmaceutical industry, as well as activity in Asia.

As pharmaceutical companies pursued mergers as one way to cut costs, some industry insiders were concerned about the strategy's implications. At a time when the development of new drugs was quite low, a number of observers argued that mergers only hurt the research and development process. This was because mergers often created distractions among workers as companies joined operations and concern about layoffs increased among staff.

Despite these concerns, research and development continued at a strong pace heading into the mid-2000s. In 2004, Pharmaceutical Research and Manufacturers of America estimated that R&D spending increased approximately US$1 billion in 2003, reaching US$33.2 billion. That year, 86 drugs were granted FDA approval, including 21 new molecular entitles and 14 biologics. The association revealed that, among global pharmaceutical manufacturers, R&D spending was 40 percent higher in the United States than in Europe. This marked a departure from the previous decade, when European R&D spending was 50 percent higher than in the United States.

RESEARCH AND TECHNOLOGY

Because of its profound reliance on new product introductions, the pharmaceutical industry spends more than any other industry on R&D activities. An average of 20 percent of sales was earmarked for R&D budgets in 2000. According to Pharmaceutical Research and Manufacturers of America, R&D in the year 2000 topped US$25.7 billion, up from US$24 billion in 1999. Many of the mergers and acquisitions seen in the 1990s stem in large part from rising R&D bills and a commensurate lack of blockbuster drugs on the market. Those unable to keep their development pipeline full are usually the first to seek mergers. Research comes at a steep price, however. Only one in 5,000 compounds discovered actually reaches the market. Pressures from other companies, FDA approvals, and demographic trends are a few pieces of the tricky drug discovery and delivery puzzle.

Although some industry representatives blamed the high cost of regulatory approval, which could consume up to two-thirds of an R&D budget, the increasing complexity of the industry's methods and goals also contributed to rising R&D expenses. In the 1980s, pharmaceuticals embraced genetic engineering and biotechnology as new methods of unraveling the causes and treatments of such complicated diseases as cancer and AIDS, which account for a major share of ongoing research efforts. Genomics or gene-based research is expected to drive up the drug discovery rate. Decisions Resources, Inc, a healthcare consultancy in Waltham, Massachusetts, estimates that genomics research will account for 20 percent of new central nervous system drugs in 2000. That number was expected to double by 2005. One-quarter of cardiovascular drugs will have roots in genomic research by 2000, and cancer drugs could expect to reach 50 percent by 2005. According to a report published in *The Scientist,* biotech drugs accounted for about 7 percent of the pharmaceutical market in 2002 and were expected to comprise 12 percent by 2006. As of 2005, some 700 new genomic drugs were being tested, of which 200 were in late-stage trials.

In 2005, about half of the estimated 170 companies making biotech drugs were located in the United States, where manufacturing costs were high. With demand for biotech drugs expected to exceed production capacity by as much as 400 percent in 2005, analysts predicted that firms would look to overseas manufacturing facilities to boost output while containing costs.

The Promise of Proteomics?. A new field of research building on genomics data, called proteomics, is the study of proteins and their functions. Once considered an unimaginably complex undertaking, the recent mapping of the Human Genome has given breath to the possibility of understanding all known proteins and their functions through a thorough number crunching of their genes. Although some leading scientists discount the hype around a field whose very term was coined in 1994, investors since mid-2000 have infused over US$700 million into proteomics companies, genomic companies, and pharmaceutical firms with proteomics divisions. The sheer vastness of describing a "proteome" involves data many times more voluminous than the human genome. Yet small research initiatives have begun delving into small slices of the pie. Myriad Genetics, a genetics research firm in Salt Lake City, has identified 115,000 proteins derived from 157 different human tissues. With partners Oracle and Hitachi, the focus on data intensive work is not lost on most in the field. With most large pharmaceutical companies already investing in proteomics divisions, their potential to catalog and perhaps engineer proteins targeted toward specific tissues is not lost on drugmakers.

Race-Based Medicines. A new and controversial step in health care was taken in 2005 when the FDA approved the first medication intended for a particular racial group, BiDil. The drug, made by NitroMed of Lexington, Massachusetts, was shown to reduce heart failure deaths among African Americans by 43 percent, and was cleared for marketing to that target group. While geneticists expressed concern that the FDA was using "race as a crude shortcut for genetic typing," as *New York Times* writer Stephanie Saul reported, many African American political and scientific organizations welcomed the use of BiDil, which could significantly improve the odds for the 750,000 black Americans who suffer from heart failure. Financial analysts, furthermore, predicted that the drug might also be found to benefit other groups as well, and projected sales of between US$500 million and US$1 billion by 2010.

Industry Leaders

Pfizer, Inc. With US$52.5 billion in 2004 revenues, Pfizer was the world's largest research-based drug enterprise. The company's acquisition of Warner-Lambert in 1999 moved the company into a major presence in the pharmaceutical industry. Pfizer was founded in 1849 by cousins Charles Pfizer and Charles Erhart. Its first major product, santonin, was a treatment for parasites. Early in its history, the company was responsible for the mass production of citric acid, made from fermented sugar rather than expensive imported limes and lemons. It was also responsible for the successful mass production of penicillin, discovered earlier by Dr. Alexander Fleming. Its discovery of Tetracyn (tetracycline) in 1954, the first broad spectrum synthetic antibiotic, heralded the beginning of the pharmaceutical fight against bacterial infection.

Pfizer's products include Lipitor, a cholesterol-lowering drug; Viagra, which treats erectile dysfunction; Zithromax, an antibiotic; Celebrex, a treatment for arthritis, developed by Pharmacia and co-promoted by Pfizer; Norvasc, an anti-hypertensive; Zoloft, an anti-depressant; and Diflucan, an anti-fungal. In 2004, Pfizer was fined US$430 million when its Warner-Lambert division was charged with encouraging doctors to promote off-label use of the epilepsy drug Neurontin. David Franklin, a former employee who exposed the wrongdoing, was awarded more than US$26 million, according to the *CBS Evening News with Dan Rather.*

In 2005 Pfizer announced plans to acquire Vicuron Pharmaceuticals, Inc., a firm that develops anti-infective medications. Among Vicuron's potentially profitable medications were Andulafungin, a treatment for fungal infections; and Dalbavancin, a treatment for complicated skin and soft tissue infections.

GlaxoSmithKline. Glaxo Wellcome's merger in 1999 with SmithKline Beecham to become Glaxo SmithKline followed similar pharmaceutical merger and acquisition fever in the late 1990s. By 2003, the company was the world's second-leading pharmaceutical enterprise. Its US$38.2 billion in total sales represented an increase of nearly 12 percent from 2002. Net income that year was US$8 billion, an increase of more than 26 percent from 2002. Sales grew by only 2.1 percent in 2004, however, reaching US$39 billion.

Based in the United Kingdom, Glaxo's overseas sales accounted for nearly 90 percent of the company's revenues in the early 1990s, and the United States continues to be its largest market. Although the company's anti-ulcer drug Zantac ranked as the world's top seller in the early 1990s, the company suffered predictable revenue losses when Zantac lost its patent in several major markets during 1997, and prices were halved.

The top three therapeutic areas for Glaxo SmithKline were treatments for respiratory, viral infection, and central nervous system disorders. Flagship products included Serevent, Ventolin, Flixotide/Flovent, and Becotide/Beclovent, all for the treatment of respiratory diseases. Combivir, Epivir, anti-HIV drug, and Zovirax are leading antiviral products. SmithKline Beecham introduced the broad spectrum antibiotic Augmentin and its anti-depressant Seroxat/Paxil, to the Glaxo line. Avandia, a treatment for Type II diabetes, was introduced in 1999.

Through the 1990s and early 2000s, Glaxo continued extensive research and development of AIDS medications. With Vertex Pharmaceuticals, Inc., a biotech firm based in Cambridge, Masssachusetts, Glaxo developed two orally active HIV protease inhibitors and in 2005 received FDA fast track approval to study and develop a third.

In 2005, Glaxo entered a dual licensing agreement with Adherex Technologies, of Durham, North Carolina. The terms allow Adherex to take over clinical development from Eniluracil, a Glaxo drug that improves effectiveness of oncology medications. Glaxo will retain rights to buy back the drug during the development. At the same time, Glaxo negotiated rights to license Adherex's tumor-fighting drug, ADH-1. The dual-licensing deal was reported to be worth as much as US$200 million, plus royalties.

Glaxo was established as an offshoot of Joseph Nathan's New Zealand-based import-export business in 1873 to produce baby food, especially powdered milk sold under the Glaxo brand. Son Alec Nathan established the firm's marketing focus in Great Britain in the early twentieth century with the memorable slogan "Builds Bonnie Babies." The company expanded internationally after World War I, around the same time that it got into vitamin production. Glaxo entered the pharmaceutical market in 1927 with the launch of a liquid vitamin D concentrate, Ostelin. Acquisitions diversified the firm into veterinary medicine, medical instruments, and drug distribution in the post World War II era. Glaxo grew quickly in the 1980s on sales of its blockbuster anti-ulcer drug Zantac, and claimed 5 of the top 50 prescription drugs in the early 1990s.

Sanofi-Aventis. One of the newest giants in the industry was formed in 1999 as Aventis, following the merger of Rhone-Poulenc and Hoescht's pharmaceutical, agricultural, and veterinary businesses. In 2004, Sanofi-Synthelabo acquired Aventis, forming Sanofi-Aventis, Europe's largest pharmaceutical company and the world's third-largest.

Based in France, Sanofi-Aventis saw 2004 sales of US$20.3 billion, more than double the previous year's sales. Top sellers for Sanofi-Aventis have included its antihistamine, Allegra, and its anti-thrombotic, Lovenox/Clexane, each of which reaped over US$1 billion in sales in 2000. Other key products include Taxotere, an anticancer agent; Amaryl, for type II diabetes; Arava, for the treatment of rheumatoid arthritis; and the thrombosis drug Plavix.

Rhone-Poulenc was formed through the 1928 merger of two chemical firms, the Établissement Poulenc-Frères and the Société Chimiques des Usines du Rhône. Over-diversification and over-dependence on France's protective tariffs led to decline in the 1970s. Rhône-Poulenc was nationalized in 1982 by the French government after the company had endured a decade of decline. A government appointed chairman, Loïk Le Floch-Prigent, reorganized the firm with an emphasis on pharmaceuticals and returned it to profitability for the first time in four years by the end of 1983. From 1986 to 1992, Rhône-Poulenc spent more than US$7 billion on acquisitions and sold at least 80 subsidiaries, thereby doubling sales from about US$7.5 billion to US$15.4 billion. The US$3.3 billion purchase of the U.S.-based Rorer Group Inc. ranked among the world's biggest transactions and sealed the conglomerate's position among leading pharmaceutical companies. By 1992, over 75 percent of the firm's business was outside France. In the late 1990s, the parent company moved to concentrate on its life sciences (including pharmaceuticals) business, spinning off its specialty chemicals operations as a new publicly quoted division named Rhodia. However, in the short term, Rhône-Poulenc's pharmaceutical division was delivering disappointing returns in the late 1990s. This fueled speculation that a merger or similar transformation would be necessary.

Hoechst was founded in 1863 to synthesize chemical dyes. The company was a pivotal force in the early pharmaceutical industry, supporting the development of Novocain and Salvarsan among other compounds. After the turn of the century, Hoechst also developed Adrenaline and Insulin. Hoechst was an affiliate of IG Farben, the German chemical industry cartel formed early in the twentieth century. Although IG Farben was disintegrated after the war, Hoechst continued to dominate the world's chemical industry until the 1980s. The company's pharmaceutical business grew rapidly in the 1960s and 1970s on strengths in diuretics, diabetic medicaments, antibiotics, and steroids.

Novartis AG. Novartis, a leading pharmaceutical and consumer health company, had sales of US$28.2 billion in 2004. Novartis supplied a broad range of products covering many disease areas. Key products included Exelon, a novel treatment for Alzheimer's disease; Diovan and Cibacen/Lotrel, anti-hypertensives; and Zometa and Gleevec, two anti-cancer drugs, which received FDA approval in late 2001. It also markets the controversial ADHD drug Ritalin.

Headquartered in Basel, Switzerland, Novartis was formed in 1996 with the merger of two diversified chemical businesses, Ciba-Geigy and Sandoz, which had in fact previously been joined during the first half of the century.

Sandoz was founded as Kern and Sandoz in 1886 by Dr. Alfred Kern and Edouard Sandoz to manufacture the synthetic dyes that Kern, a leading chemist of his era, patented. In spite of early setbacks, the company expanded rapidly and was taken public in 1895 after the departure of the founders. In spite of Switzerland's isolation during World War I, the reorganized Sandoz and Company expanded quickly in the early decades of the twentieth century. Sandoz's pharmaceuticals division came to the fore in the post-World War II era, when ergotamine-based drugs Methergin (which inhibited postpartum hemorrhage), Gynergen (for the treatment of migraine headaches), and Delysid (or LSD, a hallucinogen) were developed. Acquisitions and organic expansion encouraged dramatic growth in the 1960s and 1970s. The firm's 1994 acquisition of Gerber Products Co., the U.S. baby-food stalwart, fortified its standing in the nutrition market.

Ciba-Geigy's predecessor was founded to sell spices, natural dyes, and other organic products by Johann Geigy in 1758. The Geigy family's aggregate knowledge of dyestuffs came in handy in the mid-nineteenth century when synthetic dyes came to form the foundation of the modern pharmaceutical industry. Geigy joined Ciba, Switzerland's top chemical firm, and Sandoz in the inter-war period. Geigy and Ciba operated as competing companies during the 1950s and 1960s, expanding geographically and diversifying into agricultural chemicals. The two "re-merged" in 1970 when intensifying global competition warranted the move. In the late 1980s and early 1990s, Ciba-Geigy invested in alternative research methods like biotechnology and genetic engineering. By 1995, the entire former cartel was reunited when Ciba-Geigy merged with Sandoz to create Novartis AG.

The year 2000 saw the spin-off of Novartis' agribusiness division to Zeneca to form a new company, Sygenta AG. In 2005, Novartis announced plans to acquire rights to Bristol-Myers-Squibb Company's over-the-counter portfolio, which includes the pain reliever Excedrin. The US$600 million deal further strengthened Novartis's position in the U.S. over-the-counter market.

Merck & Co., Inc. With US$22.9 billion in total 2004 revenues, Merck & Co., Inc. was among the top leaders in the world pharmaceutical industry. Merck initiated the 1990s trend toward purchasing drug distributors with its 1993 acquisition of Medco Containment Services Inc. for US$6.6 billion; by 1999, its Merck-Medco managed care program was contributing over US$15 billion in annual sales. Merck's three leading product areas include cholesterol, hypertension/heart failure, and osteoporosis. Its blockbuster anti-arthritis drug, Vioxx, tapped a market of aging baby boomers, but led the company intro controversy in 2004 after a study indicated that it could double the risk of heart attack or stroke. Lawsuits were brought against the company alleging that patients had died after long-term Vioxx use, and Congress demanded an investigation. On the day in September 2004 when hearings revealed that Merck officials had downplayed Vioxx's health risks, Merck CEO Raymond Gilmartin resigned. Merck pulled Vioxx, which had been its best-selling painkiller, off the market, and the controversy cost the company billions in sales and legal fees.

Merck's leading cholesterol drugs included Mevacor and Zocor. U.S. patent protection on these drugs expired in 2001 and 2005. The company's second largest product category in 1999 was hypertension/heart failure drugs, including Vasotec, Cozaar, and Hyzaar. A third area, osteoporosis, features Fosamax. These three categories of pharmaceuticals account for well over half of its drug sales. Cancidas, an anti-fungal was new in mid 2001, and pipeline drugs include Invanz, an injectable antibiotic, and Etoricoxib, an anti-arthritic. During the early 2000s, approximately 14 percent of Merck's earnings came from foreign sales.

Merck traces its history across the Atlantic Ocean to Germany, where Freidrich Jacob Merck established an apothecary in 1668. A descendant, Heinrich Emmanuel Merck, started manufacturing drugs (including morphine, codeine, and cocaine) in 1827. Around the turn of the century, he sent his grandson, George, to the United States to set up operations there. The two companies were separated during World War I, when George Merck temporarily relinquished much of his firm's stock to the U.S. government in an effort to combat anti-German sentiment in that country. After the war, the government returned corporate control to Merck, but the German and U.S. firms retained their separate entities. His successor and son, George W. Merck, established the company's reputation for innovative research. Some of the company's major discoveries included vitamin B12, cortisone, and streptomycin. Merck merged with another U.S. firm, Sharp and Dohme, Incorporated, in 1953 to beef up marketing and distribution. Those capabilities, combined with efficient production and continuing research, catapulted Merck to the top of the drug world in the late 1980s, where it remained in the 2000s.

In May 2004, the company signed an agreement with DHL, an air express delivery leader, to work together to improve access to critically needed HIV medicines throughout sub-Saharan Africa. Also that year, Merck announced plans to expand its cooperation with Dutch pharmaceutical company H Lundbeck A/S regarding joint development and distribution of the sleep disorder compound gaboxadol, and to collaborate with Vertex Pharmaceuticals to produce a compound for cancer treatment. Merck will coordinate worldwide clinical development and marketing of VX-680 and pay Vertex product royalties on sales. In yet another collaboration, announced in June 2004, Merck planned to work with Alnylam Pharmaceuticals to jointly develop gene-suppression therapies for eye diseases. Terms involved a multiyear deal with potential to net Alnylam a total of US$19.5 million, according to *Dow Jones Business News.* Among Merck's products under development in 2005 were a possible vaccine for sudden acute respiratory syndrome (SARS) and a cervical cancer vaccine.

Johnson & Johnson. With total 2004 sales of US$47.3 billion, Johnson & Johnson remained one of the world's leading pharmaceutical companies. Johnson & Johnson produces consumer health care products as well as medical devices and diagnostics, but pharmaceuticals is its largest segment. In 1999 the company acquired Centocor, Inc., a leader in monoclonal antibody, vascular, and immunology research. By 2002, some 38 percent of the company's earnings came from foreign sales.

Johnson & Johnson's history dates to 1885 when brothers Robert Wood Johnson, James Wood, and Edward Mead Johnson founded a startup company in New Brunswick, New Jersey selling antiseptic surgical dressings. In 1891 they produced their first sterile product for surgeons. 1921 saw the introduction of Band-Aid bandages. With the spin-off of Ethicon in 1941, a separate business was created for surgical sutures and related products and equipment. In 1959 it purchased McNeil Laboratories, followed in 1961 by Belgium-based Janssen Pharmaceutical. Many companies followed in the 1980s, and by its hundredth anniversary, Johnson & Johnson was a well-established leader in healthcare supplies, equipment, and pharmaceuticals. Today Johnson & Johnson is comprised of 190 companies worldwide and markets health care products in more than 175 countries. Its brand names are well recognized—Tylenol, Aveeno, Mylanta, Motrin, and others. Its creation of a stanol ester designed to help control cholesterol levels is incorporated into various products under the brand name Benecol—an unusual foray into the foodstuffs market. Johnson & Johnson announced plans in 2005 to buy Guidant, a leading producer of cardiac care devices, for about US$25 billion.

In 2005, the Senate Finance Committee began investigating the company's alleged use of educational grants in the 1990s to fund a medical text promoting use of Propulsid, a heartburn medication, in pediatric patients despite evidence suggesting it was unsafe. The company pulled Propulsid from the market in 2000 after reports linked 80 deaths and 341 injuries to the product; in 2004, Johnson & Johnson paid US$900 million to settle lawsuits that claimed the drug caused 300 deaths and 16,000 injuries.

Bristol-Myers Squibb. With US$19.3 billion in total revenue for 2004, Bristol-Myers Squibb is a diversified company with interests in medical devices and household products as well as pharmaceutical preparations. Its early 1990s cash cow had been Capoten, a hypertension drug, but when it went generic, sales tapered off substantially. The late 1990s saw the rise of Pravachol, a cholesterol treatment, as well as its oncological products. Its anticancer agent Taxol was approved by the FDA in 1999 as a treatment for non-small lung cancer in combination with other pharmaceutical agents in patients where surgery and radiation therapy are not advisable. Other top anticancer names include Paraplatin, an anticancer agent specifically indicated in combination with other treatments for ovarian cancer; and Ifex, a treatment for testicular cancer. Other offerings include Vanlev, an anti-hypertensive, which differs from other anti-hypertensives by lowering both systolic and diastolic blood pressure. Glucophage/Glucovance is a successful treatment for Type 2 diabetes. The Gluco-family held 39 percent of the market share as of late 2001, more than triple that the nearest competitor.

Bristol-Myers Squibb also marketed a host of well-known OTC remedies such as Excedrin and Bufferin, and other consumer and medical products. The company garnered positive press in the late 1990s by being the first to gain FDA approval to market its OTC product Excedrin as an anti-migraine. But with prescription medications comprising the bulk of its sales in the early 2000s, the company decided in 2005 to sell its U.S. and Canadian consumer products operations. Novartis planned to purchase rights to its over-the-counter portfolio, which included the popular painkiller Excedrin, for US$600 million.

Bristol-Myers Squibb was formed in 1989, when Bristol-Myers acquired Squibb for US$12.7 billion. The older of the two companies, Squibb, was founded in New York City in 1858 by Edward Squibb. In the early years, the firm focused on the production of pure ether and chloroform. William Bristol and John Myers launched their firm in 1887 and initially named it for its hometown, Clinton, New Jersey. While Bristol-Myers (renamed in 1900) was an acquirer for much of its history, Squibb was often the object of acquisition. After the merger, the company shed many of its consumer products to concentrate on pharmaceuticals. Its primary therapeutic areas included anticancer and high blood pressure drugs. In the late 1980s, the company's Oncogen subsidiary began testing DDI, an AIDS treatment. When the drug won FDA approval in 1991, it was released under the brand name VIDEX.

Roche Group. With about US$27.6 billion in 2004 sales, Switzerland's Roche Holding Ltd. was another leader among the world's pharmaceutical firms. Some of the firm's total sales include revenues from diagnostic tests, including those used for DNA testing.

Roche was founded in 1894 by Fritz Hoffmann-La Roche to standardize production of pharmaceutical compounds. The founding family retained a controlling interest into the early 1990s. Roche had operations on four continents by the early 1910s and began synthesizing vitamins during the inter-war period. In anticipation of World War II, Roche split off its overseas operations under a holding company, Sapac. Roche created its most successful drug, Valium, in 1963. Valium, called "the world's first blockbuster prescription drug" in a 1994 *Forbes* article, dominated global pharmaceutical sales until 1981. During the 1970s, Roche was condemned for price fixing and for an industrial accident at one of its Italian plants. Problems continued in the 1980s when Valium went off patent, and Roche's annual sales were halved as a result. The Roche Group was formed in 1989 to reunite Sapac and F. Hoffman-La Roche. In the early 1990s, the firm concentrated on acquisition and R&D as its keys to growth. Top sellers for Roche in 2004 included Rocephin, an antibiotic; the anti-influenza drug Tamiflu; the obesity drug Xenical; and Roaccutan/Accutane, an anti-acne drug.

AstraZeneca plc. The April 1999 merger of Astra AB and Zeneca Group plc created AstraZeneca, a pharmaceutical and agricultural chemical products company. Total sales in 2004 were US$221.4 billion.

Astra was founded in 1913 in Sweden by Adolf Rising, Hans von Euler, and Knut Sjöberg. Its marketing of Xylocaine (lidocaine) in the late 1940s was one of its first worldwide breakthroughs. But its marketing of Neurosedyn, better known as thalidomide, under license from German-based Chemie-Grünenthal, nearly brought the company and its image to ruin in the 1960s.

Zeneca's history began in name in 1993 with the divestiture of the pharmaceuticals, agro and specialty chemicals divisions of UK-based Imperial Chemical Industries. ICI's history began in the dyes and dyestuffs industries of the late 1850s.

AstraZeneca's top seller during the mid-2000s was Nexium, an anti-gastric. Its other offerings included drugs for cancer and cardiac care. In 2005 the company announced a partnership with Avanir, US, to license and research cardiovascular drugs. AstraZeneca agreed to pay Avanir an initial US$10 million, with as much as US$330 million in possible additional fees pending successful development of the drugs.

MAJOR COUNTRIES IN THE INDUSTRY

United States. The United States remained the world's top producer and consumer of pharmaceutical preparations, as well as the fastest-growing pharmaceutical market, with sales totaling US$216 billion in 2003. Despite all of the challenges facing the pharmaceutical industry, analysts expected that the U.S. drug market would maintain its leadership position well into the 2000s. Standard & Poor's projected that the U.S. market would grow at a compound annual rate of 10 percent from 2002 to 2007. The United Kingdom was expected to experience growth of 7 percent, followed by Germany (5 percent), France (4 percent), and Japan (2 percent).

According to U.S. Census Bureau data released in September 2004, U.S. pharmaceutical industry shipments were valued at nearly US$114 billion in 2002, up from US$100.3 billion in 2001 and US$88.7 billion in 2000. In 2002, the U.S. industry consisted of 723 companies. These firms operated a total of 901 establishments, 465 of which had 20 employees or more. California had the greatest number of establishments with 136, followed by New Jersey with 99, and New York with 98.

The August 2004 *IMS National Sales Perspectives* revealed that, as of mid-2004, chain stores accounted for more than 36 percent of U.S. pharmaceutical sales (US$82.2 billion), followed by independent stores (14.4 percent, US$32.7 billion), mail service (13.8 percent, US$31.2 billion), non-federated hospitals (10.5 percent, US$24 billion), clinics (9.2 percent, US$20 billion), food stores (8.8 percent, US$20 billion), long-term care facilities (3.5 percent, US$8 billion), federal facilities (1.6 percent, US$3.5 billion), home health care (1 percent, US$2.2 billion), HMOs (0.7 percent, US$1.6 billion), and miscellaneous (0.4 percent, US$0.9 billion).

Health care reform topped the industry's list of concerns for the U.S. market starting in the 1990s, when government and popular criticism of high drug prices and profits sparked a call for controls. Although the Clinton administration's health care reform plan failed to pass in 1994, some industry observers noted that other market forces, including managed care providers—which serviced nearly half of the country's prescription drug customers—would bring about their own brand of price controls. Their effect began to be felt in the early 1990s when year-to-year prescription drug price increases slowed from 9.6 percent to 3.3 percent. Indeed, by 1996 the rate of U.S. pharmaceutical price inflation was slightly lower than that for the general economy. According to 1998 U.S. Department of Commerce figures, U.S. consumers spent an average of 64 cents a day on prescription drugs compared with 92 cents a day on electricity and US$1.05 a day on car repairs. Legislation on health care reform continued into the mid-2000s under the administration of George W. Bush.

Since 1995 the United States has maintained a rising trade deficit in pharmaceuticals after years of trade surpluses. In 1997 U.S. exports were estimated at US$9.6 billion, while imports led at US$12.8 billion; this created a trade deficit of US$352 million. By 2004, U.S. exports of pharmaceutical products exceeded US$19.5 billion, and imports were valued at US$31.3 billion, leading to a trade imbalance of US$11.8 billion.

Europe. Accounting for approximately 25 percent of worldwide pharmaceutical sales in 2003, Europe is the second largest market for pharmaceuticals. The rollout of the new European currency, the Euro, in January of 2002, was seen as the beginning of quasinational Europe's competition with the United States. The harmonization of drug approval processes in member countries is performed under the European Medicines Evaluation Agency based in London.

Global mergers and acquisitions were occurring at a strong pace during the mid-2000s. Much of this activity was attributed to European firms. For example, the 2004 merger of French drug companies Sanofi and Aventis resulted in Europe's largest pharmaceutical enterprise and the world's third largest. The rise in market share for European pharmaceutical firms bodes well for continued competition in that market.

Japan. Holding about 12 percent of the world market in 2002, Japan ranked just behind Europe. As was the case with Europe, Japan accounted for a significant share of global mergers and acquisitions during the mid-2000s. One example was the US$7.2 billion merger of Yamanouchi Pharmaceutical Co. and Fujisawa Pharmaceutical Co.

Japan's insular market was unique among the global leaders. Not one Japanese firm had made it into the industry's top 10 by the turn of the century. The growth of the Japanese pharmaceutical industry was based on a practice known as *bungyo,* wherein physicians prescribed and dispensed drugs and were reimbursed by the Japanese Ministry of Health, Labor, and Welfare. Japanese pharmaceutical manufacturers commonly sold their products to doctors at a lower price than the reimbursement rate, thereby encouraging overall sales. By the late 1980s, Japan led the world in per capita drug consumption. Protectionist laws allowed the country's pharmaceutical firms to license foreign companies' preparations for domestic sale with little competition until the mid 1970s.

This provinciality came with a strategic cost, however. Japanese manufacturers lagged behind their American and European competitors in R&D. Growth topped 23 percent in 1998, higher than the 17 percent rate of U.S. firms. Sales in Japan are only expected to increase 1.5 percent from 2000 to 2005, according to IMS Health.

Japan's Pharmaceutical Affairs Law, which went into effect in April 2005, removed restrictions that had limited outsourcing in drug manufacturing. The new law, requested by the pharmaceutical industry, creates a marketing authorization system similar to European and U.S. models, and allows companies to outsource up to 100 percent of manufacturing. The measure, which should enable pharmaceutical firms to reduce costs, is expected to improve the industry's competitiveness.

China. Legislation enacted in 2001, which standardized pharmaceutical drug procurement and distribution in China, was an effort to counteract a rise in drug counterfeiting and purchasing corruption. China, whose pharmaceutical market suffered under government decentralization of drug and medical device regulation, anticipates the law will provide greater open market competition. Data reported in the *People's Daily* showed that China's total pharmaceutical output reached US$54.4 billion in 2004. Even so, market share for the country's entire industry, comprised of more than 6,000 domestic companies, equaled that of only one top company, GlaxoSmithKline.

China, along with the rest of Asia, Africa, and Australia, comprises only 8 percent of the worldwide pharmaceutical market. However, China's pharmaceutical industry was poised for growth heading into the mid-2000s, as the nation's economy boomed. By 2004, 20 of the leading 25 global pharmaceutical firms had established Chinese joint ventures, according to *Chemical Market Reporter.* As it became more modern and sophisticated, the industry was experiencing a flurry of consolidation and acquisition activity. This spurred Chinese citizens who had previously left the country, in pursuit of western education and employment, to return to China.

FURTHER READING

Adiga, Aravind, et al. "Where to Look for Growth." *Money,* September 2001.

Beach, Marilyn. "China Opens Drug Market by Revising Pharmaceutical Law." *Lancet 257(9260),* 24 March 2001.

Boswell, Clay. "Rolling Out the Strategies of the Chemical Dot-Coms." *Chemical Market Reporter 257(16),* 17 April 2000.

Brichacek, Andra and L.J. Sellers. "Flexing Their Budgets: Big Pharma Spend Trends." *Pharmaceutical Executive,* September 2001.

"Can Pfizer Keep It Up? Drug Giants Battle for Warner-Lambert." *Institutional Investor 34(1),* January 2000.

"Chinese Officials Stress IPR Protection in Pharmaceutical Sector." *People's Daily,* 20 July 2005. Available from http://http://english.people.com.cn.

"Chinese Pharma in Midst of Major Consolidation." *Chemical Market Reporter,* 29 March 2004.

Cohen, Jon. "The Proteomics Payoff." *Technology Review 104(8),* October 2001.

Connolly, Ceci. "2003 Drug Spending Up Despite Pressure to Cut Costs." *The Washington Post,* 16 March 2004.

"Durham-based Biotech Signs Deal with GlaxoSmithKline," *Herald-Sun* (Durham, NC), 17 July 2005.

The European Agency for the Evaluation of Medicinal Products (EMEA), 2005. Available from http://www.eudra.org.

"Fine Chemicals: Running at Full Throttle." *Chemical Week 162(7),* 16 February 2000.

Freidman, Katherine. "IMS Health Reports 27 Percent Rise in U.S. Mail Order Pharmaceutical Sales." *IMS Health Press Release, London,* 16 August 2000.

Gundling, Richard L. "Discount Prescription Card Offers Medicare Benficiaries Temporary Relief." *Healthcare Financial Management,* September 2001.

Impact of Direct-to-Consumer Advertising on Prescription Drug Spending. The Henry J. Kaiser Family Foundation, June 2003. Available from http://www.kff.org.

"Pharmaceutical Products" Officee of Trade and Industry Information, Manufacturing and Services, International Trade Administration, U.S. Department of Commerce, 2005. Available from http://tse.export/gov.

Krauss, Clifford. "Canada Is Drafting Regulations to Curb Bulk Drug Exports to U.S." *New York Times,* 30 June 2005.

Lipson, David. "A Five-Year Forecast: Clear Seas Ahead." *Pharmaceutical Executive,* October 2001.

Lowenbach, Janet. "New Outsourcing Law Readies Japanese Companies for Global Pharmaceutical Markets." OutsourcingAsia.com, Mach 2004. Available from http://www.outsourcing-asia.com.

McCook, Alison. "Manufacturing On a Grand Scale: As More Biotech Drugs Make It to Market, the Question Becomes 'Can They Be Made More Cheaply?'" *The Scientist,* 14 February 2005.

Milmo, Sean. "SKB and Glaxo Merger Creates a Powerhouse." *Chemical Market Reporter 257(4),* 24 January 2000.

Mirasol, Feliza. "IMS Reviews Pharma Growth and Outlines Future Trends." *Chemical Market Reporter 257(13),* 27 March 2000.

Nemes, Judith. "Industry Outlook: Medicare Drug Benefit, Election Hot Spots in '04." *B to B,* 5 April 2004.

Novak, Viveca. "The Assault on Generics." *Time 155(21),* 22 May 2000.

"Pharma R&D Stats Released." *R&D,* March 2004.

Pharmaceutical Research and Manufacturers of America. *Annual Report.* 2003-2004.

Pondel, Evan. "Pharmaceutical Firms Rush to Push Risks of Buying Drugs Abroad." *Daily News (Los Angeles),* 6 June 2004.

Rather, Dan, and Jim Axelrod. "Pfizer Fined Millions." *CBS Evening News with Dan Rather,* 13 May 2004.

"Report Shows Corporate Mergers, Acquisitions Picking Up in Global Market." *Kyodo News International (Japan),* 21 July 2004.

Saul, Stephanie. "FDA Approves a Heart Drug for African-Americans." *New York Times,* 24 June 2005.

Saul, Stephanie. "Senators Ask Drug Giant to Explain Grants to Doctors." *New York Times,* 6 July 2005.

Schmidt, Julie. "Generic Drug Prices Hold Steady." *USA Today,* 26 June 2005.

Siegel, Robert. "Analysis: Continuing Mergers in the Pharmaceutical Industry Cause Problems for Research and Development of New Drugs." *All Things Considered (NPR),* 3 May 2004.

Standard & Poor's Industry Surveys. New York: Standard & Poor's, 26 June 2003.

"Strong Growth for Generic Drugs." *Chemical Week,* 17 March 2004.

U.S. Census Bureau. "Pharmaceutical Preparation Manufacturing: 2002." *2002 Economic Census.* Washington, D.C.: September 2004. Available from http://www.census.gov.

World Pharmaceutical Markets, Business Communications Company, Inc., Norwalk, CT, March 2004.

SIC 2841

NAICS 325611

SOAPS AND DETERGENTS

Industry manufacturers formulate personal and laundry soaps, synthetic organic detergents, inorganic alkaline detergents, and related compounds. The soap category includes granulated, liquid, cake, flaked, and chip soap; textile soap; scouring and washing compounds; and dishwashing compounds and presoaks. Manufacturers of shampoos and shaving preparations are discussed separately under **Toiletries and Cosmetics**.

INDUSTRY SNAPSHOT

Following a trend begun in the late 1990s, during the mid-2000s the global soap and detergent industry faced tight competition in established markets and had shifted its focus to Asia, Eastern Europe, and Latin America for new growth. Amid a late 1990s economic downturn in several Asian markets—and a slowdown in Latin America—multinational soap makers found themselves squeezed for new markets. Faltering economies in these regions, along with a slowdown in the United States, and fierce competition, these tough market conditions forced soap and detergent companies to develop new products while controlling costs and price. Many firms also looked to acquisitions or joint ventures to solidify their global position in the industry.

Among the established markets such as Western Europe, Japan, Canada, and the United States, soap and detergent producers competed largely on price and their ability to satisfy changing consumer preferences, which varied from region to region. For example, liquid detergent sales continued to be stronger than powder sales in the United States, where washing machines were manufactured to work well with liquid detergents. However, demand in Europe for concentrated powder tablets continued to grow, especially in the United Kingdom. New products were often developed to appeal to a specific consumer region. A water-soluble capsule containing concentrated liquid detergent was launched in Europe by both Unilever and Proctor & Gamble— but was not marketed in North America.

Laundry detergents form the largest component of the industry in terms of sales value, accounting for as much as 50 percent of industry revenues in the United States and approximately 40 percent in Europe. In the United States alone, laundry detergent sales reached US$3.3 billion in 2004. Liquid detergents accounted for most sales by far, exceeding US$2.4 billion while powders accounted for only US$850 million. Worldwide, the laundry detergent market was worth about $35.8 billion in 2005, according to Euromonitor (Chicago). Western Europe accounted for 29 percent of this total, followed by Asia/Pacific (25%), North America (18%), and Latin America (7%). Africa/Mideast and Australia accounted for only 5 percent and 1 percent of the market, respectively.

Although bar soap remained the most popular cleansing product among U.S. residents, with penetration into approximately 75 percent of the nation's homes, sales in that category were declining as consumers turned to newer forms of cleansers such as shower gels, body washes, and liquid soap. According to Research and Markets (Dublin), the U.S. market for soap and bath/shower products was worth about $1.6 billion in 2006, with bar soap accounting for just under half of those sales. Although bar soap remained the largest segment, more growth was seen in the other segments.

ORGANIZATION AND STRUCTURE

The soaps and detergents industry is dominated by a handful of major multinational players originating in Europe and the United States. Although some are just regional powerhouses, a few leading firms are thoroughly internationalized and hold significant, and sometimes dominant, market positions in numerous countries. In most nations a second tier of companies usually operates on the national level and often produces for the low-price (or even generic brand) market.

Top-tier companies have found it necessary to compete in diverse global markets in order to sustain the growth rates and profits their shareholders seek. Often their home markets, such as Western Europe, are relatively saturated and afford few opportunities for growth. In a small number of cases, companies have pursued growth through acquisitions—sometimes simply at the product level rather than the company level—in order to better their stance in a particular product category or regional market. More often, however, leading soap and detergent manufacturers have battled one another for shares of these finite markets through discounting and product innovation, or have entered emerging markets where use of competitive products may be minimal.

Companies also keep track of distribution channels. Procter & Gamble (P&G) took the lead in developing a policy of everyday low pricing, reducing the traditional coupon and trade promotion discounts that retailers had long known. Such an arrangement encourages sales, especially to consumers who do not use coupons and who make purchase decisions based on in-store price comparisons. Although angry retailers initially reduced support for affected P&G brands, because the lower prices were believed to also cut into the retailers' profit, product sales increased by about 4 percent in 1993; subsequently, about 90 percent of the firm's brands were similarly priced.

The soap and detergent industry is under pressure to reduce production costs due to rising competition from private label, or store brand, products. Though private labels continued to make inroads in the late 1990s, in most leading economies they still accounted for a relatively small share of the market.

Additionally, manufacturers deal with fluctuating costs for necessary raw materials, such as ethylene- and benzene-based ingredients. Europe, in particular, suffered from overcapacity for basic materials production, which depressed prices in that category. (Some soap and detergent makers produce raw materials as well, and thus can be hurt by low prices.) Other ingredients, notably phosphates, face environmental controversies, and some countries either have banned phosphate-based detergents or regulated their use.

BACKGROUND AND DEVELOPMENT

Traced back to ancient Rome, soap has been an integral part of human civilization. While the first soaps, made from wood ashes and animal fat, were used for medical purposes, by the second century A.D. soap was used to clean. During the Middle Ages, soap was still homemade but had developed into use for personal and laundry cleaning. In the late eighteenth century, soap evolved from a homemade product into a full-fledged industry, propelled by Nicholas LeBlanc's discovery of a method to manufacture soda ash from brine. However, it was not until the nineteenth century that cake soap went from being a luxury to a common-use item.

In 1806 William Colgate founded a company to make soap, starch, and candles. By 1906 the firm was producing 160 different types of soaps. In 1876 Fritz Henkel formed Henkel & Cie in Aachen, Germany, to manufacture a universal detergent. Just two years later, he launched "Henkel's Bleaching Soda." As early as the 1880s, Henkel was making water glass—a detergent ingredient. Henkel's "Persil" (a brand name later used by Unilever) eliminated the need to rub or bleach clothes, and was brought to market in 1907.

William and James Lever presented the first packaged, branded laundry soap, Sunlight, in 1895. Initially serving Britain, Lever Brothers, the predecessor of today's Unilever, was marketing soaps in the United States, South Africa, and Australia less than 20 years later. Another industry milestone occurred in 1898 when J.B. Johnson launched Palmolive soap, which used palm and olive oils.

The worldwide soaps and detergents industry grew rapidly in the twentieth century. However, as with many other areas of life, it was forever changed during World War II when natural ingredients for soap became rare. Synthetic detergents were developed as substitutes for all soaps except those used for personal bathing. By the 1950s detergents surpassed the use of soaps in laundering and dishwashing. While the majority of the manufacturers sold their products in traditional markets, companies such as Amway Corp. revolutionized the industry when distributors sold products in-home rather than via traditional retail methods.

Heading into the 2000s, consumers throughout the world were demanding more than mere cleansing properties from soap products. Bath and shower products, worth US$20.5 billion in 2003, continued to meld with those traditionally found in the skin care category as people looked for soaps that exfoliated, moisturized, and toned their skin. In addition, a growing number of people looked for soaps that offered certain emotional benefits, namely relaxation. For example, a number of specially scented soaps offered so-called aromatherapy to bathers, or a "spa at home" experience. Some industry observers correlated the popularity of these products to rising levels of stress.

The Proctor & Gamble Company (P&G) and Unilever continued to hold a leading market share in the detergents sector. According to data from Chicago-based research firm Information Resources Inc., in 2003 U.S. laundry detergent sales totaled US$3.2 billion, US$2.4 billion of which was liquid detergent and US$869 million of which was powder. P&G's detergent sales were approximately US$2 billion, accounting for nearly 62 percent of all detergent sales. Unilever's sales totaled US$465 million, representing 14.5 percent of all sales. Together, the two companies controlled a sizable share of the broad personal care and household cleaning products industry. With sales growth tepid in many established markets, though, detergent companies sought product enhancements, such as new fragrances, that would strengthen the performance of leading brands. In 2005 Procter & Gamble introduced Tide with a Touch of Downy, which combined detergent with fabric softener. Company executives described this move as the biggest initiative since the introduction of Tide with Bleach in 1980.

Bar soap remained the most popular cleansing product among U.S. residents in 2003, with penetration into approximately 75 percent of the nation's homes. In its March 22, 2004 issue, *MMR* cited data from Information Resources Inc., a Chicago-based research firm, placing sales of bar soap at US$857.5 million for the 12 months ended January 25, 2004. Of this total, nondeodorant soaps accounted for nearly 57 percent of sales, with the remaining 43 percent attributed to deodorant soaps. In the nondeodorant category, there were a number of clear brand leaders. These included Dove, with sales of US$219.4 million, Caress (US$50.5 million), Ivory (US$40.3 million), and Olay (US$33.7 million). Together, these four soaps accounted for nearly 71 percent of all nondeodorant bar soap sales.

As competitors tried to chip away at the leaders' shares during the early 2000s, the industry experienced an increase in merger and acquisition activity. In October of 2003, P&G announced that it would acquire the European detergent business unit of Colgate-Palmolive. Two years before, in 2001, Church & Dwight Co. Inc. purchased USA Detergents, increasing its U.S. laundry detergent market share to 9 percent and securing its position as the third-largest supplier in the United States.

The biggest merger of 2004 was Henkel KGaA's US$2.9 billion acquisition of Dial, which had put itself up for sale due to low earnings and increased competition. Henkel had previously established a joint venture with The Dial Corp. in 1999 to gain access to the U.S. market, but the deal was terminated in early 2001. Despite this, other joint ventures continued between the two companies, including one to market detergent tablets in the United States and one devoted to dry cleaning. The Dial acquisition contributed to a 20.8 percent increase in sales third-quarter sales for Henkel. In addition to its relationship with Dial, in 2000 Henkel had purchased the Mexican heavy-duty detergents business of Colgate-Palmolive and also acquired a majority interest in Pemos, a soap and detergent manufacturer based in Russia.

One leading trend in personal soaps during the 2000s was the use of gels or body washes in place of conventional bar soap. These products have been especially successful in Japan and the United States. Manufacturers also prefer them because they allow more flexible formulations than do solid bars. According to Euromonitor data reported in *Global Cosmetic Industry,* worldwide sales of liquid soaps, body washes, and shower gels grew by 15 percent in value in 2003. By contrast, sales of bar soap fell by 4 percent. A related development has been the adoption of antibacterial soaps, which are marketed as convenient and effective preventives against tactile germ transmission. U.S.-based Dial Corp. is a major producer in this category. Compounds with similar properties have been offered in the dishwashing segment of the market.

Instant foaming hand soaps, which were introduced in 2001, were another important product development during the 2000s. In its February 2003 issue, *Soap & Cosmetics* reported that foaming hand soaps had been introduced throughout the world by a number of industry leaders. Dial was among the first companies to introduce a foaming product, with its Dial Complete antibacterial foaming hand wash. Other product introductions included Colgate-Palmolive's Softsoap Foam Works, as well as products from Bath & Body Works. In addition to a foaming hand soap, Johnson & Johnson also unveiled a foaming hair detangler product for children. Foaming hand soaps also experienced adoption in other world markets, especially in Europe. In addition to the introduction of Carex Gentle Foaming Handwash by the United Kingdom's Cussons, Italy's Manetti & Roberts began introducing foaming hand soap products to the European market.

Going beyond the consumer sector, foaming hand soaps have made institutional inroads as well. In addition to adoption in restaurant, conference center, and shopping store bathrooms, foaming hand soap was being used by the airline industry. For example, Celeste Industries Corp., which supplies a number of international airlines, began offering its clients mechanical foamers for use in restroom cabins.

Current Conditions

Challenges for the soap and detergent industry in the latter mid-2000s included high energy, freight, and raw material costs. Although raising prices helped some producers offset costs, according to a report in *Chemical Week,* it was not enough. As a result, some companies turned to alternative energy and raw material sources. For example, Proctor & Gamble signed a US$1.8 billion contract with an Indonesia olechemical plant in 2006. (Oleochemicals are ingredients derived from the fats and oils of plants.) According to the firm, the plant will produce more than 200,000 tons a year of fatty alcohols, fatty acids, and glycerine, which will be used as raw materials in its shampoo and laundry detergents. Proctor & Gamble also had a joint venture with an olechemical plant in Malaysia planned. According to Colin A. Houston Associates, in 2007 expanded olechemical units in Indonesia, Malaysia, Thailand, the Philippines, China, and India would produce an additional 960,000 tons/year of detergent-grade long-chain alcohol products.

Many suppliers were focusing on innovation to increase their profit margins. According to David Del Guercio of U.S.-based Goldschmidt, watching consumer trends could help manufacturers of detergent and soaps create new products that were in demand. Said Del Guercio, "In addition to laundry detergents with bleach, we are seeing versions with fabric softener, for cold wash, for dark color wash, and with multiple fragrances and additives to enhance freshness." Mild detergents for people with sensitive skin were also in increased demand. On the other hand, fragrance was one of the fastest-growing sectors of the detergent market. According to the Freedonia Group, demand for detergent fragrances will increase about 9 percent to $265 million by 2009. Producers were also churning out more sophisticated fragrances, such as Seaside Escape and Sunshine Clean (from Henkel's Purex line).

Another trend in the mid-2000s in the detergent market was the increased demand for biodegradable surfactants. The growth in this market was especially strong in Europe, where the European Union's Detergent Directive was enacted in 2005. The initiative requires that all detergent and cleaning products be biodegradable and derived from renewable resources.

Research and Technology

Increased environmental concerns have led this industry to be constantly involved in research and technology, including the development of concentrated formulas and refillable containers. Leading environmentalists have called for an end to the pollution-causing detergent foam residues that coat the globe's waters. The problem is that while soap molecules break down, the molecules in synthetic detergents are too complicated to allow for similar breakdown. Manufacturers resolved this environmental issue by changing the structure of the hydrocarbon properties in soap ingredients.

Since the early 1950s, detergents containing phosphates have been causing water pollution. That problem was eased as manufacturers found biodegradable substitutes for detergent ingredients that were not harmful and allowed the phosphates to be more easily broken down and absorbed. In hard water, which contains major amounts of dissolved mineral salts, the molecules in the water can respond to the salts and form the notorious gray tub ring.

In the early 1990s Procter & Gamble introduced N-methyl glucosamide in its liquid detergents. This sugar-based surfactant is similar to the alkyl polygylcosides (APG) introduced by Henkel KGaA in 1992. The P&G product "is being marketed based on its biodegradability and claims of mildness," according to Robert Westervelt in *Chemical Week.* In 1994 P&G brought to market its reformulated Tide with Carezyme.

Specific formulations to ensure that soap and detergents manufacturers' needs are met are underway. The U.S. surfactant industry grew almost 5 percent in 1994. However, petrochemical and oleochemical raw material costs grew in the second half of 1994. There is movement in the surfactant industry to use multifunctional raw materials to minimize chemical content. Specific and directed applications, such as hotel, restaurant, or a manufacturing facility's laundry, present separate and unique cleaning problems. This means that ingredient suppliers must work closely with industry customers.

Surfactant manufacturers developed several new products in the early 2000s to meet environmental and consumer concerns. Biosil Technologies, based in New Jersey, pioneered innovations in the use of silicone in surfactant systems. Its Biosil Basics Cocosil, as described by Nancy Jeffries in *Global Cosmetic Industry,* is "an amphoteric surfactant that is complexed with a silicone to yield a highly effective mild surfactant with softening and conditioning properties." Another surfactant company, Cognis, introduced Plantapon[R]LC 7 as well as a biodegradable surfactant from corn which is useful in dishwashing detergents. Uniqema Americas has developed Avanel[R]150 CG, a mild surfactant suitable for facial washes for sensitive skin and acne. According to Jeffries, these new formulations will continue to offer the soap and detergent industry materials that "will target specific areas and specialized surfactants [that] will not only work to clean, but will protect, rebuild and even moisturize with a highly edited and diversely sourced ensemble of ingredients and system orchestration."

The next major laundry detergent innovation will likely be fueled by the adoption of new, energy-efficient washing machines. Such machines will use less water and electricity and will have lower water temperatures than their predecessors. However, they will require different detergent formulations that can function in reduced water and different machine cycles. In the low-water, low-temperature environment, detergents must be more soluble since they need to dissolve more easily, because both decreased temperature and less water reduce the rate at which detergent is dissolved. Current detergents would tend to leave residues or particles if used in such a process.

The introduction of foaming hand soaps in the early 2000s, according to an article by Martin Kleinman in the February 2003 issue of *Soap & Cosmetics,* was made possible by the development of new mechanical foam dispensers, which release soap with one touch. "These are proven, precision-engineered, high-performance engines that provide instant, perfect foam without the use of chemical propellants," explained Kleinman. "They allow a precise mixture of liquid and air with a single stroke of a smooth-action button. Their sophisticated valve technology ensures reliability and ease-of-use. The consumer gets soft, creamy foam from just one stroke of the pump. With state-of-the-art units now available, even shaking the product before use does not affect the quality of the foam. The foam is instant, easy to spread, easy to rinse and seems to wash better.

"An additional advantage to product developers and consumers alike is that these premium pumps can be fully filled and emptied completely, thanks to the design of the dip tube," continued Kleinman. "Further, product manufacturers can select from an appealing range of custom colors and container shapes, including square, triangular, domed, oval or flat."

INDUSTRY LEADERS

UNILEVER

One of the top-ranked companies in the soaps and detergents industry is Unilever, which has two headquarters: Unilever PLC, in London; and Unilever NV, based in Rotterdam. With US$54.4 billion in 2006 sales, the company and its affiliates were market leaders in many categories throughout Europe, North America, and parts of the Pacific Rim. In 2003, the European market generated 42.6 percent of Unilever's sales, followed by North America (22.9 percent), Asia/Pacific (16.5 percent), Latin America (10 percent), and the Africa/Middle East/Turkey region (7.6 percent).

During the 1990s, Unilever was plagued by competitive blunders, such as the Persil debacle in Europe, and loss of market share to Procter & Gamble and other competitors. The Persil incident involved negative advertising by P&G that uncovered that Unilever's Persil detergent actually damaged fabrics. The embarrassing episode caused Unilever to reformulate its product, but it never recovered the lost market share. In the 1990s critics also charged that the company remained bloated and inefficient, prompting a number of restructuring initiatives.

These conditions led the company to implement its Path to Growth program, which involved reducing the number of brands to 400—down from 1,600—through a series of over 50 divestitures. It also created two major business segments, food and nonfood products. During 2003, the company's brand reduction strategy was well underway, and its Home and Personal Care division, which includes such leading brands as Lifebuoy and Dove, accounted for nearly 43 percent of sales. Although growth in the laundry detergent category was flat that year, a number of the company's soap brands experienced double-digit growth. Dove, in particular, was a standout, achieving a remarkable growth rate of 21 percent.

Yet by 2005 Unilever was forced to admit that its expectations for Path to Growth had not been met. Faced with tough market conditions, particularly in Europe, total sales for the company in 2004 grew by only 0.4 percent, with top brands growing by only 0.9 percent. Nevertheless, Unilever's personal care segment performed relatively well in 2004, making the company the global leader in skin cleansers through brands such as Dove and Lifebuoy. On the other hand, detergents saw declining revenues, due primarily to lower prices. Despite gains for detergents in developing markets, declines in Europe and North America contributed to an overall decrease in market share for this segment. After Unilever's overall poor performance in 2004, the company announced a major corporate reorganization. One result was its sale in 2005 of its cosmetics unit to Coty for approximately US$800 million.

Unilever was founded in 1895 by William Hesketh Lever and his brother, James. Under the Lever Brothers name, they manufactured Sunlight, the first packaged and branded laundry soap and sold initially in Britain. A decade and a half later, the company was marketing its soap in the United States, South Africa, and Australia. Between 1906 and 1915 Lever acquired soap companies in Australia, Britain, and South Africa. The company also entered the plantation and trading company business to fill its requirements for vegetable oil, an ingredient in soap. Lever also expanded, dominating the U.S. market until 1946 when P&G introduced Tide, the first synthetic detergent. In Europe, however, Lever enjoyed a resurgence and found markets green for new detergents, personal care products, and margarine. Along with the company's home and personal care products, it stands as a leading food concern in the global diversified foods industry.

THE PROCTER & GAMBLE COMPANY

Procter & Gamble (P&G), the leading U.S. manufacturer of household products, is responsible for a variety of soaps and detergents, including Ivory and Tide. The Cincinnati-based company was founded in 1837 by William Procter, a candle maker, and James Gamble, a soap maker. In 1879 they produced Ivory, touted as the "floating soap." This represented one of the first direct-to-the-consumer advertising campaigns. Procter & Gamble was also responsible for the development of radio and television soap operas. In fact, Tide detergent was first introduced on a radio soap opera in 1947. P&G was a family-headed company until 1930, when William Deupree was named president and later chairman. He helped steer the company to its position as the biggest producer of packaged consumer goods in the United States.

Procter & Gamble is a highly savvy competitor in all of its markets, a trait that has helped it maneuver market position away from established players when it enters new markets. P&G introduced Bold laundry detergent in Japan during August 2002, which captured almost 10 percent of the market and helped the company corner nearly 30 percent of the Japanese detergent market overall. P&G has also stepped up its presence in China. The company speculated that its sales in developing markets could reach US$70 billion by the early 2010s, equaling its sales in Western Europe and North America.

In 2006 P&G registered total sales of more than US$68.2 billion, up 20.2 percent from the previous year. In 2005 the firm purchased Gillette, the world leader in shaving supplies, in the company's biggest deal ever. Number of employees rose 25.5 percent in 2006 to 138,000 workers.

Henkel KGaA

Serving more than 125 countries in 2004, Henkel is headquartered in Düsseldorf, Germany. The company's European operations account for nearly 70 percent of sales. Fritz Henkel formed Henkel & Cie. in 1876 in Aachen. Two years later he launched "Henkel's Bleaching Soda," credited as one of Germany's first brand name products. As early as the 1880s, Henkel was making water glass, a detergent ingredient.

By the 1920s Henkel was using newly introduced phosphates in its cleaning products. Henkel purchased Deutsche Hydrier-werke and Bohme Fettchemie. The latter had introduced a revolutionary synthetic detergent. Although most of Henkel's foreign holdings were lost during World War II, the company continued producing homemade soap. From the 1950s through the 1960s, Henkel was embroiled in a four-way battle with Colgate-Palmolive, P&G, and Unilever for market share on its home turf. While Henkel earned the number two position on some occasions, by 1968 it had rebuffed the triad and had a firm hold on 50 percent of Germany's soap and detergent business. Henkel entered the U.S. market in 1960 when it acquired Standard Chemicals. The company earned a patent on a phosphate substitute and in 1971 acquired the chemical business division of General Mills Corp. Subsequent acquisitions included Nopco, a specialty chemical business; Ford Motor Co.'s Parker Chemical division; a metal surface pretreatment operation; and Emery, a leading oleochemicals manufacturer.

Henkel'slargest national market is its home country, Germany, which is Europe's largest. While it holds a commanding position throughout much of the European market, Henkel was noticeably absent from the U.S. market until 2004, when it purchased the Dial Co. The company attributed much of the 28.9 percent growth in its laundry and home care sector in 2004 to the performance of its Dial and Clorox products. Henkel posted total sales of US$14.1 billion in 2006 and employed 52,565 people.

Kao

Kao Corporation is Japan's leading producer of soaps and detergents. Like Henkel it is primarily a regional player. As behemoths like Unilever and P&G have focused on Asia, including Japan, Kao has seen its market share shrink at home and has faced stiffer competition in neighboring countries. Kao participates in the U.S. soap market chiefly through its Andrew Jergens Company subsidiary. In 2006, Kao posted revenues of US$8.2 billion. Its main brands included laundry detergent Attack and dishwashing detergent Family Power Gel. As a result of increased competition, Kao was focused on increasing brand loyalty and strengthening its core products in the new millennium. An attempt to bolster its presence in the Japanese beauty segment by acquiring Kanebo ended in February 2004. Kao also participates in other industries such as specialty chemicals, edible oils, and blank recording media.

Dial

With one of the United States' best selling bar soaps, Dial Corporation has emerged far from its roots. In 1914 Carl Eric Wickman used a passenger car to transport miners between the mines and a saloon. He expanded his transportation services and began working under the label of Northland Transportation in 1925. In 1928 his company added on the Great Northern Railroad and continued to add transit lines. In 1930 Northland transportation changed its name to Greyhound and moved its headquarters to Chicago. In 1970 Greyhound acquired Armour & Co. for US$355 million. Not only did Greyhound pick up Armour's meat products, it also acquired Dial, a leading U.S. deodorant soap.

Dial's 2004 sales reached US$1.3 billion, 4.9 percent above sales in 2003. During the early 2000s, the company's Dial brand and other soap products had a 20 percent market share in the U.S. soap industry. Its namesake Dial brand held status as America's leading antibacterial soap, with sales of some 1 million bars each day. In addition, Dial Corp.'s Purex laundry detergent was the nation's second-best-selling detergent brand. Dial became a subsidiary of Germany's Henkel KGaA in March 2004.

Colgate-Palmolive Company

The world leader in toothpaste and oral care products, Colgate-Palmolive also produces bar soaps, liquid soaps, and dishwashing and laundry detergents, as well as pet nutrition. Top brands include Irish Spring, Softsoap, Ajax, and Palmolive. Founded by William Colgate in 1806, Colgate & Company began as a manufacturer of chemical soaps and perfumes. One of its first products was Cashmere Bouquet, a perfumed bar soap, introduced in 1872. A year later the company introduced its first toothpaste; Colgate eventually discontinued its perfume operations. A rival company, B.J. Johnson Soap, introduced Palmolive Soap in 1898. The product, made from palm and olive oils instead of animal fats, was such a marketing success that the manufacturer changed its name to Palmolive. After merging with Kansas-based Peet Brothers, Palmolive became Palmolive-Peet. In 1928, a merger with Colgate resulted in the Colgate-Palmolive-Peet Company, later renamed Colgate-Palmolive.

To compete with rival P&G during the early years of television, Colgate-Palmolive sponsored afternoon soap operas, and was the sole sponsor of the program *The Doctors.* Among Colgate's popular early brands was Octagon, a laundry and all-purpose cleaning soap. In 1991, Colgate acquired Murphy Oil Soap, the top-selling wood cleaning product in the United States. By the early 2000s, Colgate operated in more than 200 countries and derived more than 70 percent of sales from international operations.

In 2005 the company finalized plans to sell its North American laundry detergent brands, including Fab, Cold Power, Dynamo, ABC, Arctic Power, and Fresh Start, to Phoenix Brands. Colgate posted total sales of US$12.2 billion in 2006 with 35,800 employees.

MAJOR COUNTRIES IN THE INDUSTRY

UNITED STATES

In 2004 the United States exported US$7.7 billion worth of soaps, cleaners, and toilet preparations; imports were valued at US$5.3 billion. Soap accounted for US$342.2 million in exports and US$427.1 in imports. Exports of detergents and cleaning agents reached US$1.6 billion, while imports were valued at US$608.3 million.

The U.S. market leader remained Procter & Gamble, maker of the top-selling detergent in both liquid and powder categories, Tide. Combined U.S. sales for Tide reached about US$1.2 billion in 2006. Unilever, Dial Corporation, Church & Dwight, and Colgate-Palmolive Co. were the other major companies in the detergent segment. Regarding the sale of soap, in 2006 the United States saw deodorant bar soap sales decline 10.8 percent, whereas nondeodorant bar soap sales increased 2.6 percent. However, sales of liquid hand soap saw even greater growth of about 7.4 percent to US$260.1 million, and other liquid soaps increased 9 percent to about US$569 million. Irish Spring was the top-selling deodorant bar soap in the United States, garnering US$45.7 million in sales in 2006, followed most closely by Dial (US$44.2 million) and Lever 2000 (US$43.5 million). Along with private labels sold by stores like Wal-Mart, soaps and detergents are sold through distribution outlets including U.S.-based Amway, which markets soaps as well as a wide range of unrelated wares via in-home sales presentations.

JAPAN

According to the March 25, 2003 issue of *Cosmetics & Toiletries & Household Products Marketing News in Japan*, figures from Japan's Ministry of Economy, Trade, and Industry revealed that sales volume within the Japanese soap and detergent industry was Yen 469.5 billion in 2002, an increase of 4 percent from the previous year. Of this total, solid bath soaps, liquid hand soaps, and other soaps totaled 12 percent of all sales. Synthetic detergents, including liquid and powder laundry soaps, represented about 55 percent of all sales. The remainder was attributed to fabric softeners, bleaches, acid/alkaline cleansers, and powder/liquid cleansers. According to the Japan Soap and Detergent Association, demand for special-care detergents, such as products for delicate or dry-clean-only fabrics, was growing significantly in the early 2000s.

The Japanese market in the 1990s and into the 2000s was stable but not rapidly growing, owing to persistent recessive conditions in Japan's economy. Despite inroads made by P&G, Kao still controlled a majority share of the Japanese detergent market. It was joined by Tokyo-based Lion Corporation. During 2001 the United States imported US$12.2 million in soaps and detergents from Japan, an increase of 0.7 percent over 2000.

EUROPE

In its February 2003 issue, *Soap Perfumery & Cosmetics* reported that, on average, 64 percent of the population of the Big 5 European countries use shower gel each week, making it Europe's leading washing product. This especially was the case in Germany. Citing data from Taylor Nelson Sofres, the publication indicated that shower gel had a market penetration of 63.8 percent in late 2002, followed by bar soap (52.3 percent), liquid soap (32.1 percent), bath liquids (21.6 percent), bath foam (17.1 percent), washes and scrubs (10.7 percent), all-over shampoo (7.2 percent), and body washes (2.2 percent). In 2002, Euromonitor reported that the bath and shower market was worth US$4.4 billion in both Western Europe and the United States, followed by the United Kingdom (US$846 million), Germany (US$733 million), Italy (US$713 million), France (US$613 million), and Spain (US$254 million). By 2003, Western Europe accounted for 28 percent of global sales of bath and shower products, overtaking Asia-Pacific as the top regional market.

Among Europe's largest players are Procter & Gamble, Unilever, Henkel, and Beiersdorf, Cussons, and Sara Lee, although in the United Kingdom, especially, private/store labels have generated a rising share of industry sales. While Western Europe has traditionally provided a more reliable base of customers, Eastern Europe offered a higher growth potential for leading companies in the new millennium. Household laundry products account for the majority of industry sales in Europe, followed by industrial and institutional products, hard surface household cleaners, domestic maintenance products, dishwashing household products, soaps, and domestic bleach products.

According to a Euromonitor report cited by *HAPPI Magazine,* most growth in the European market through 2008 will come from laundry aids, such as stain pretreatments, which are forecast to grow by more than 40 percent in value. By contrast, detergents themselves are expected to grow by about 4 percent during this period.

FURTHER READING

"Bar Soap Retains Broad Appeal." *MMR,* 22 March 2004.

Branna, Tom. "Suppliers Make Many Moves to Keep Innovations Rolling." *Household & Personal Products Industry,* March 2007.

Graff, Gordon. "Buyers at Detergent Makers Leverage Natural Ingredients to Reduce Costs." *Purchasing,* 1 March 2007.

Guzman, Doris De. "Detergents Get Healthy." *ICIS Chemical Business Americas,* 22 January 2007.

"High Hopes for Soaps." *Global Cosmetic Industry,* January 2005.

"Hoover's Company Capsules." Hoover's, Inc, 2007. Available from http://www.hoovers.com.

Jeffries, Nancy. "It All Comes Out in the Wash: Surfactants for Personal Care and Household Cleansers as Well as Detergents Add a Touch of Softness to Effective Cleaning Thanks to High-Tech Ingredients." *Global Cosmetic Industry,* January 2005.

———. "Wake Up and Wash: Soaps, Whether of the Household Variety or Those Intended for Personal Care, Do More Than Cleanse." *Global Cosmetic Industry,* December 2003.

Kleinman, Martin. "New Life in the Handsoap Market: A New Generation of Products Drives Re-invigoration of US$960 Billion Industry." *Soap & Cosmetics,* February 2003.

International Association for Soaps, Detergents, and Maintenance Products (AISE). "Market and Economic Data," 15 April 2007. Available from www.aise-net.org.

"Laundry Daze." *HAPPI Magazine,* January 2005. Available from www.happi.com.

MacDonald, Veronica. "Soap and Detergents: Going the World Over to Clean." *Chemical Week,* 26 January 2005.

———. "Soaps and Detergents: Shedding Extra Costs." *Chemical Week,* 1 February 2006.

"Making Waves: Manufactures are Focusing on Emotional Benefits of Ingredients to Drive Growth in the Bath and Shower Sector. SPC Reports. (Bath & Shower: Market Report)." *Soap Perfumery & Cosmetics,* February 2003.

Molaro, Regina. "Soap Specialties: Specialty Soaps Use Scent and Color to Enhance the Bath Experience. (Specialty Soaps)." *Soap & Cosmetics,* February 2003.

"Nondeodorant Bar Soap." *MMR,* 22 March 2004.

Prior, Molly. "Dove Spreads Its Wings into New Categories." *Drug Store News,* 21 June 2004.

"Sales of Soap & Detergents in 2002 (January-December)." *Cosmetics & Toiletries & Household Products Marketing News in Japan*, 25 March 2003.

"Soap Suppliers Make It New." *MMR,* 18 September 2006.

Sustaining Growth. 2003 Annual Report. Cincinnati, Ohio: The Procter & Gamble Co. 2003. Available from www.pg.com.

"The 46th Clean Survey: The Truth About Doing the Laundry" *Japan Soap and Detergent Association News,* September 2004. Available from www.jsda.org.

Unilever Annual Review 2004. Unilever plc, 2005. Available from www.unilever.com.

U.S. National Trade Data, 2004. Office of Trade and Industry Information, Manufacturing and Services, International Trade Administration, U.S. Department of Commerce, 2005. Available from http://tse.export.gov.

Walsh, Kerri. "Soaps and Detergents: Crossing the Atlantic to Find New Customers." *Chemical Week,* 28 January 2004.

SIC 2844

NAICS 325620

TOILETRIES AND COSMETICS

The toiletries industry manufactures the world's perfumes, cosmetics, shampoos, and related personal toilet preparations. Coverage of general soap and detergent manufacturing may be found under the heading **Soaps and Detergents.**.

INDUSTRY SNAPSHOT

The cosmetics and toiletries industry experienced difficult times during the early 2000s. Overall profits and growth stagnated in January 2001, and dropped even more after the September 2001 acts of terrorism in the United States. This followed regular, if unspectacular, profits for many companies through the end of 2000. Kline & Co. reported that the U.S. cosmetics and toiletries industry grew by less than 2 percent in 2003, the third consecutive year of single-digit growth. Mature markets and saturation from competing lines were major factors that contributed to flat sales. Conditions improved slightly in 2004, however, with global sales approaching US$150 billion, an increase of more than 4 percent.

Global Cosmetic Industry blamed price cutting at megastores such as Wal-Mart for the decrease in large profit margins that many department stores and other outlets typically enjoyed. In addition, sales in such stores have blurred the once definitive line between producers of luxury care products and those typically bought by ordinary consumers.

In a separate industry analysis, published in the June 2004 issue of *Global Cosmetic Industry,* Euromonitor data placed the global retail market for cosmetics and toiletries at US$201.5 billion in 2003, up 4.8 percent from the previous year. At US$62.9 billion (31.2 percent), Western Europe held the largest market share, followed by North America (24.6 percent), Asia Pacific (23 percent), Latin America (9.3 percent), Eastern Europe (6.2 percent), Africa/Middle East (4.4 percent), and Australasia (1 percent). The greatest growth in 2004 was attributed to growing markets such as Argentina, Brazil, Russia, and China.

Of the 11 categories tracked by Euromonitor, the top five accounted for more than 75 percent of global sales. At US$42.5 billion, hair care was by far the leading category, with 21.1 percent of sales, followed by skin care (19.1 percent), color cosmetics (13.9 percent), fragrances (11.1 percent), and bath/shower products (10.3 percent). Worldwide sales of perfume rose almost 9 percent in 2004, reaching US$25.2 billion. Increased interest in luxury brands helped drive this growth, according to Euromonitor.

As the industry headed into the late-2000s, better times seemed to be on the horizon, according to the observations of several industry leaders. Growth in anti-aging products was expected as the baby-boomer generation headed into its senior years, while new interest in grooming products for men suggested significant potential in that relatively untapped segment.

ORGANIZATION AND STRUCTURE

The structure of the toiletries industry is complicated by the vertical integration of many of its firms. Multinational companies from various countries are active in the market. These large multinational firms are engaged in every aspect of the production process, from the cultivation of the plants and flora used in fragrances through the final production stages. The major cosmetics companies traditionally originated as either marketing companies or research companies, yet modern corporations generally operate in both areas.

These major companies may have several brands in the market at one time. For instance, L'Oréal, the French giant, sells Lancôme brand cosmetics and fragrances in department stores, and at the same time markets L'Oréal beauty supplies in mass outlets, next to the shelf with its other brand names such as Belle Colour haircolor.

Department store sales of cosmetics stayed relatively stagnant in the late 1990s, but mass brands such as Revlon, Cover Girl, and Maybelline sold very well, harvesting double digit growth. Fragrance sales, however, run much the opposite, with department store sales higher than those at mass retail outlets. Department stores find that bringing new fragrances to the market reaps sales, but mass stores contend that tried and true scents do better on their shelves. Existing perfumes, such as Jovan for Women and Vanilla Fields, performed distinctly better in the United States than the retail launches of Coty's Raw Vanilla or Revlon's Cherish. In Great Britain, 43 percent of cosmetics and toiletries sales are at mass-market counters such as Boots, where high-end brands declined. The balance of Europe is similar, with drug stores and mass-market retailers accounting for much of cosmetic and toiletry sales. While high-end companies have traditionally avoided placing their products in mass retail outlets, some U.S. companies have begun to tap this potentially lucrative distribution channel. In 2004, for example, Estée Lauder announced an agreement to become the exclusive beauty products supplier for Kohl's stores, a discount chain with about 600 stores in the United States. Lauder will create three new brands for Kohl's, and will retain ownership of these brands.

The toiletries industry is affected by the continued threat of government regulation and intervention, consumer concern over animal rights, and environmental concerns. However, these issues are not new— they have affected the industry for more than 100 years. The first law concerning colorings in food and other goods was enacted in Germany in 1887. It remained in effect for 90 years, until a new German cosmetics law superseded it in 1977. In 1936 the second law came when the U.S. Pure Food and Drug Act was passed. What were then called "coal tar" colors were not permitted to be used in cosmetics; today they are known as colorants or synthetic organic dyestuffs. In 1952 the German Research Association published a list of approved food colorings and pigments that had proven safety records.

In the late 1960s, several fragrance suppliers united to form the Research Institute for Fragrance Materials (RIFM). Their mission was to test independently fragrances for safety. RIFM tested approximately 1,400 materials and restricted or prohibited the use of about 100. The International Fragrance Association (IFRA), representing 100 manufacturers in 15 countries, also works to conduct these types of tests independently and impartially and issues recommendations for use, as well as restrictions, through its "Code of Practice."

Consumer outcry against the use of animals in cosmetics research has led to numerous changes in the industry. One particular test that came under attack was Lethal Dosage50 or LD50, which involved the force-feeding of animals with cosmetics until half of the animals died. On 23 December 1980, Revlon announced that it was setting up a research project with the Rockefeller University of New York to find an alternative to the Draize Testa test in which albino rabbits' eyes where injected with shampoos to test for irritation, often resulting in blindness.

Companies continue to search for alternatives to animal testing. A January 1995 article in *Self* magazine reported that 40 percent of U.S. cosmetics makers had begun to test cosmetics on artificial skin rather than lab animals. In this process, cells from discarded human foreskins are cultured on a nylon mesh to form a living laboratory skin for testing.

Concern about aerosols and fluorocarbons emerged in the mid-1960s. The ozone depletion theory suggests that release of fluorocarbons into the air lowers the ozone level in the atmosphere—the layer that protects the earth against the heat of the sun. The U.S. government ordered that fluorocarbons no longer be used after 1978. Other product ingredients also continue to cause concern, such as a new group of skin care ingredients that emerged on the marketplace in the early 1990s called alpha hydroxy acids (AHAs). In 1997, AHA-product sales approached US$1 billion. The substances include malic acid (from apples), citric acid (from citrus fruit), tartaric acid (wine), lactic acid (sour milk), and glycolic acid (sugar cane). Studies indicated that AHAs can effectively treat dry skin, cleanse pores, improve skin tone and texture, reduce skin discoloration and age spots, and protect against damage from harsh substances. However, the U.S. FDA received over 100 reports of blistering, bleeding, rashes, and stinging from such products.

Senator Edward Kennedy, in a September 1997 press release regarding the FDA reform bill, quoted a GAO study that found that "cosmetics are being marketed in the United States which may pose a serious hazard to the public." The study reported 125 potentially carcinogenic substances used in cosmetics. In December 2001, according to the *San Francisco Chronicle,* the FDA reported that companies would need to provide warning labels if they proceeded to manufacture certain popular dandruff control products with higher levels of coal tar. U.S. and U.K. warnings to consumers and hairdressers were released in 2001 that said there were studies suggesting a link between certain permanent hair dyes and bladder cancer. In 2002, a new federal Child-Resistant Closure Rule came into existence that affected toiletries such as baby oil containing 10 percent or more hydrocarbons by weight with a viscosity of less than 100 Saybolt Universal Seconds (SUS) at 100 degrees F., according to *Global Cosmetic Industry.* The high-hydrocarbon content was associated with a number of infant deaths and thousands of emergency room visits, according to FDA spokespersons.

Not as widely publicized, the long-term consequences of diethanolamine (DEA) and its derivatives (used in products from lotion to bubble bath), potentially carcinogenic substances, may be the final straw that propels the FDA into cosmetic and toiletry regulation. The European Union in 1996 took strong action to limit the use of DEA in products within its jurisdiction, but the FDA, which in 1997 employed just two people to specifically regulate cosmetic labeling and packaging, had taken no specific measures, despite encouragement from the Cancer Prevention Coalition. The domestic cosmetics and toiletry industry has been responding to urging from the Cosmetics and Fragrance Association to ban the use of the ingredient.

Though the U.S. Food and Drug Administration does not require testing of cosmetics, the organizatioin notified manufacturers in 2005 that it would start enforcing its requirement that product labels must include the statement "Warning—the safety of this product has not been determined." The step was necessary, authorities argued, because many cosmetic and toiletry products contained ingredients that had not been determined to be safe. This move, according to a London *Times* report, "could be highly damaging to the beauty sector, an industry that depends heavily on promoting images of health and wellbeing."

On the research and development front in 2003, a number of industry leaders were focusing on the link between the body's immune system and the skin, as well as how factors such as the sun and stress affected the skin. Along these lines, Clinique consulted with immunologists and university researchers to stay on top of the latest advancements. More specifically, the company was seeking to develop a skin care product that provided skin protection against both ultraviolet light and the impact of everyday living. This also was an area of interest to other cosmetic companies, including Estee Lauder.

As the mid-2000s approached, another hot research topic focused on skin and hair properties of different racial and ethnic groups. In its November 3, 2003 issue, *MMR* explained that the L'Oréal Institute for Ethnic Hair and Skin Research had recently hosted its Second International Symposium on Ethnic Hair and Skin. With the subtitle "New Directions in Research," the gathering involved 200 clinicians, dermatologists, and scientists from 11 nations. These experts presented individual research findings related to the construction of artificial skin for different racial and ethic groups. One of the major objectives was to determine why different skin types react differently to environmental and other conditions. Related information was discussed for different hair types.

BACKGROUND AND DEVELOPMENT

The use of cosmetics predates recorded history. Beauty secrets and lore have been handed down throughout the ages. Cleopatra is said to have bathed in donkey milk. She painted her eyebrows and lashes black, her eyelids dark blue-black and green. Catherine de Medici used white lead to whiten her skin during the Renaissance (and also, it is reported, to poison her enemies). Egyptians commonly used henna on their hair and nails, white lead on their faces, and black kohl around their eyes. Roman women made use of mud packs (made from crocodile dung) to beautify their complexions.

These early "natural" products eventually gave way to manufactured toiletry items. During the nineteenth century, with an increase in industrialization and growing worldwide economic participation, cosmetics and pharmaceutical companies began to emerge. Colleges and other institutions specializing in pharmacology helped to fuel developments that would lead to industry growth and diversification. By the beginning of the twentieth century, the cosmetics industry was firmly established. While the companies that would dominate after World War II had not yet appeared on the scene, certain conglomerates that would later purchase these industry leaders were already firmly entrenched in the industry.

The cosmetics industry is truly an international one. One of the oldest cosmetics firms in the world is Yardley, a company that was first formed in 1670 when its namesake paid King Charles I a large sum of money for a soap concession in London. In the 1960s Yardley was able to cash in on the "London look," popularized by Jean Shrimpton. In Japan, Tokyo-based Shiseido controls about 30 percent of the cosmetics sales in that country. France has long been considered the home of fragrance and, while many French fragrance houses are owned by larger conglomerates today, French-named fragrances still hold allure for consumers.

For nearly 60 years beginning in the early 1900s, the cosmetics industry was dominated by three major players: Elizabeth Arden, Helena Rubinstein, and Charles Revson. Born Florence Nightingale Graham in Ontario, Canada, in 1878, Elizabeth Arden went to New York in 1908 when she was almost 30. Her first job there was as a treatment girl with Eleanor Adair, a leader in the cosmetics world at the time, who specialized in "Grecian preparations." Later Graham set up her own establishment and, in 1910 with a loan from a cousin, began what was to become the Elizabeth Arden empire. During World War I, Arden began to develop some new ideas in cosmetics, most notably her "whipped face cream," developed in conjunction with A. Fabian Swanson, a chemist at the company of Stillwell and Gladding. The war years were notable for another reason. Arden was faced with competitor Helena Rubinstein, the Polish dynamo who would from then forward be her fiercest rival. Although the two women claimed never to have met, they had a major impact on each other's lives and on the development of the cosmetics industry.

Rubinstein started her beauty empire in 1902 with a small salon in Melbourne, Australia, where she sold face cream reportedly obtained from a Dr. Lykusky in Poland. In 1908, leaving the Melbourne salon in the hands of two sisters, Rubinstein returned to Europe where she established the Maison de Beauté Velaze, renamed the Maison de Beauté Helena Rubinstein in 1912. With her greatest success ahead of her, Rubinstein sailed to the United States in 1914 and opened a salon in New York.

Arden's range of products was much larger than Rubinstein's however, and between 1915 and 1920 Elizabeth Arden was the biggest cosmetics firm in the world. Rubinstein, in the meantime, concentrated her efforts on salons. She was noted for being the first to put color into foundation and face powder; to realize that not all skins were the same; and to use silk in her makeup.

Rubinstein and Arden ruled the cosmetics world during the 1920s. In 1928, Rubinstein sold two-thirds of her business to Lehman Brothers, and what followed was a slowdown for the company—Lehman Brothers were not cosmetologists, and the business suffered. From Paris, where she had relocated to run the overseas business that she still controlled, Rubinstein began to buy stock back and eventually obtained a controlling interest less than a year after selling to Lehman Brothers.

While Rubinstein and Arden established a stronghold on the East Coast of the United States, the Max Factor company began to establish its own position on the West Coast in the late 1920s, with a direct tie to the movie industry. Max Factor was born in Russia in 1877 and had been a wigmaker as a young boy. With his wife and three children, Factor left Russia in 1904 and went to St. Louis, where he opened a makeup, perfume, and hair-products shop with a partner. His partner soon left the firm with most of its profits; fortunately, Factor was able to find money to open another shop. In 1908 he moved his family to Los Angeles, establishing the first Max Factor studio in the Pantages Theater.

Initially concentrating on the formulation and testing of theatrical makeup, Factor became renowned in the film industry. He was known for the revolutionary concept of "color harmony," the selection of makeup to harmonize with the hair, eyes, and skin color of the women who used it. In 1927 "Color Harmony Make-up" was introduced to the general marketplace (having previously been used only by actresses).

While Max Factor had little impact on Rubinstein and Arden, in 1931 the women were faced with a true rival—Charles Revson. Working at Elka, a New Jersey firm that produced nail enamel, Revson became enamored with the concept of opaque nail varnish. Choosing to leave Elka, he set up Revson Brothers in New York where he continued to sell Elka nail varnish. When Elka declined to allow Revson to expand his territory he looked for new opportunities and joined forces with Charles Lachman, who owned Dresden Brothers in New York, a company that made nail polish and sold them to other companies who retailed them under their own brand names. Joining forces with Revson, the two formed Revlon Nail Enamel. Although Lachman continued to control a large percentage of the business, he was not an active partner (based in large part on Revson's urging).

During the Depression in the 1930s, Revson concentrated on hair and beauty salons. By 1941 he was selling to 100,000 salons and controlled a virtual monopoly with his nail products. In 1940 he added lipstick to his line. It was not until 1962, though, when Revlon introduced its first skin cream that the company was first viewed as a competitor by Rubinstein and Arden.

Surprisingly, the Depression did not have a destructive impact on the cosmetics industry. In fact, many new companies were launched, including Almay Cosmetics (1931), Clairol (1932), Wella Corporation (1935), and Germaine Monteil (1936). Revlon, too, began its dominion in the 1930s, a decade that also saw growing government interest in the cosmetics industry. Concerned with both product safety and unfair trade practices, the U.S. Federal Trade Commission (FTC) eventually decided to investigate the industry. A board of standards for cosmetics advertising had been established by the American Medical Association (AMA), resulting from a concern about untrue medical claims being made. As a result of the Wheeler-Lee Amendment to the Pure Food and Drug Act, the cosmetics industry was placed under the control of the U.S. Food and Drug Administration (FDA). The year 1937 consequently saw a rash of lawsuits initiated by the FTC and FDA against many well-established companies including Chanel, Helena Rubinstein, Yardley, and Bristol-Myers.

Until the late 1930s, the major cosmetics manufacturers sold their wares through salons or department stores; then Avon emerged on the cosmetic scene. It was the successor to the California Perfume Company, an establishment that had started trading in the nineteenth century. Its owner, David H. McConnell, started by selling bibles, along with small samples of perfume. The success of the door-to-door bible sales business seemed to be bolstered by the perfume McConnell gave away. This success led to the idea of a door-to-door cosmetics company. The structure of McConnell's company, particularly its unique distribution, meant that the other cosmetics companies of the time did not view it as a direct competitor. Avon was restricted from selling its existing products in retail stores in the United States by FTC regulations that preclude a company from selling simultaneously through door-to-door channels and in retail stores.

Estee Lauder was established in 1946 and soon became a bitter competitor for Charles Revson; their competition continued throughout the next several decades. In 1948, Saks Fifth Avenue began to sell the Lauder line of All-Purpose Cream, Cleaning Oil, Crème Pack, and Skin Lotion. Unlike other early members of the cosmetics industry, Lauder did not use salons to boost its sales. Lauder is credited with introducing the "gift-with-purchase" concept, a technique so effective that it was quickly copied.

The beginning of an interest in cosmetics for men developed during the early postwar period and Lauder introduced one of the most successful aftershaves ever in 1965—Aramis. In 1968, Lauder introduced Clinique, the first full allergy-tested fragrance-free line of cosmetics.

The 1960s saw a change in the cosmetics industry, an aging of sorts, perhaps brought on by the loss of some of the industry's early pioneers. Rubinstein died in 1965 at the age of 93; Elizabeth Arden died a year later at 88. Large public companies controlled the industry, with small firms—if they survived— being bought by larger conglomerates. Companies such as Revlon, Max Factor, and Arden controlled most sales outlets.

Europe remained the leader in the perfume world for many years, due to centuries of expertise in the development of such fragrances as L'Origin, which was introduced by Coty in 1909 and Chanel No. 5, which was introduced in 1921. However, even the most stalwart European companies were no match for their more aggressive U.S. counterparts. Avon entered the British market in 1959 and within two years was the biggest seller in the United Kingdom. Avon is also one of the few independent companies still in operation today. The multinationals rule the industry, and the decades since the merger mania of the 1960s and 1970s have seen major changes in the structure of the toiletries industry.

CURRENT CONDITIONS

The cosmetics and toiletries industry experienced difficult times during the early 2000s. In its report *Cosmetics and Toiletries USA,* Kline & Co. revealed that by the end of 2003, the industry had recorded "low single-digit growth" for three straight years, according to *Chemical Market Reporter.* The report also indicated that cosmetics and toiletries sales were declining at a gradual, steady pace. As evidence, the industry's growth rate totaled 3 percent in 2003, compared to average annual growth of approximately 5 percent during the late 1990s.

Kline & Co. reported year-over-year declines in more than 50 percent of the 34 product categories included in *Cosmetics and Toiletries USA.* On the positive side, in 2003 facial treatments grew at four times the industry average, skin care products for men increased by almost 15 percent, and sales of eye makeup climbed 10 percent. However, categories that had not experienced a decline for several decades—including products for sun care and hair coloring—experienced falling sales that year.

Yet as the industry headed into the mid-2000s, better times seemed to be on the horizon. *WWD* interviewed executives from many of the industry's leading firms in 2003, including Estee Lauder Cos., the Luxury Products Division of L'Oréal USA, Chanel Inc., Unilever Cosmetics International, Avon Products Inc., P&G Cosmetics, and Elizabeth Arden. In all, these leaders were optimistic about conditions in 2004. As *WWD* summarized, "After dealing with SARS, the U.S./Iraq conflict and rough weather in the first half of 2003, vendors said in July that they were beginning to see a glimmer of hope for the second half of this year—which has been borne out over the past several months by many of the major players. Even the year's most challenging category—fragrance—seems, in many vendors' eyes, to be stabilizing its downslide."

Heading into the mid-2000s, the cosmetics and toiletries industry was becoming more global than ever before, as industry leaders continued to capitalize on developing international markets. Indeed, in 2004 Argentina, Brazil, Russia, and China were the fastest growing markets for cosmetics, with sales in Argentina alone growing by 17 percent compared to 2003. China's cosmetics market grew by 12.5 percent in 2004, while India's increased by 7.7 percent. Together, China and India accounted for US$10 billion in sales in 2004. The leading category in terms of growth was skin care, followed by hair care. Sales of skin care products in Asia reached about US$17.5 billion in 2004, led by Japan.

Because each consumer market had its own unique preferences and needs, a one-size-fits-all approach was not the key to success for industry players. For example, in less developed nations like India, leading manufacturers were challenged to penetrate distant rural areas where residents were consuming products like hair oil, bar soap, and even lipsticks in growing numbers. In more developed regions like Western Europe, demand was especially strong in the upper tier of the mass-market product category. In fact, growth within this segment was eroding market share from some lower-level premium products. In France, this trend was evident within the skin care products category.

The so-called "metrosexual" male was of increasing importance to manufacturers of cosmetics and toiletries. By 2004, young males were more image conscious than ever before. Skincare and facial products were rising in popularity among many men, prompting companies like Lancôme to offer a line of 10 male skincare products that addressed everything from anti-aging and stubble issues to fatigue.

Celebrity endorsements appeared to be an increasingly profitable trend for perfume companies in the early 2000s. Estée Lauder launched fragrances by Sean Combs and Beyoncé, while Elizabeth Arden marketed perfume by Britney Spears. Coty enjoyed tremendous success with its first J-Lo fragrance, introduced in 2002. Sales in its first six months alone reached US$47 million. The following year Coty signed with Celine Dion, whose Celine Dion Parfums rose to ninth-place in women's fragrances in 2003 with sales of US$11.7 million. Coty also tapped into the emerging men's market, signing with English soccer superstar David Beckham and his wife Victoria in 2005 to launch a fragrance for men. It will be marketed in Europe and North America.

On the more extreme end of developments, the United Kingdom's KoS offered more cosmetic products, including gels that concealed blemishes, eye creams, and moisturizers that tanned and toned the skin. In 2003, KoS was considering lip gloss, nail polish, and a body scrub for men as well. These products all would be marketed in a masculine way, in order to maximize their acceptance. As Kos founder Will King said in the July 17, 2003, issue of *Marketing Week,* "Men now know they can beautify without being a 'sissy.' Male cosmetics is the last area to be cracked and the potential is huge—it is totally virgin territory."

The concept of wellness was of continued importance to consumers during the mid-2000s. As Claire Briney explained in the June 2004 issue of *Global Cosmetic Industry,* "In developed markets, the concept of wellness, more proactive than simply health, has become increasingly pervasive, penetrating almost every aspect of life, from food and drink to cosmetics and toiletries. Previously considered the preserve of alternative lifestyles, practices such as aromatherapy have become part of the mainstream through health food and mood-influencing air fresheners and bath additives. The generalized nature of the wellness trend is evident in the fact that retailers have aligned their beauty lines with non-beauty products, positioning health products such as vitamins in close proximity to cosmetics. Moreover, manufacturers have moved into supplying complete wellness systems, expanding beyond cosmetics and toiletries to 'beauty' products that enhance health from the inside."

With this in mind, it is no surprise that the Freedonia Group Inc. expected cosmetic and toiletry chemical demand would reach US$6.8 billion by 2005, according to *Cosmetics International.* Freedonia indicated that plant-based additives and ingredients with the ability to offer protection from the likes of pollutants and other environmental elements would fuel much of this demand.

In mid-2004, *Global Cosmetic Industry* reported that cosmeceuticals, especially products with anti-aging properties, remained popular as consumers continued to demand more from cosmetic products. This served to elevate the importance of research and development within the industry, prompting even mass-market manufacturers to put a premium on research and development initiatives.

INDUSTRY LEADERS

L'Oréal SA. In 2004, L'Oréal continued its reign as the global cosmetics queen with sales of US$19.8 billion, a rise of 12.6 percent from 2003. The company continues to reap success from sharp marketing in the hair salon and general-consumer drugstore outlets. Drugstore products include Vichy Laboratoires and La Roche-Posay skin upkeep varieties. The company was founded by controversial French chemist Eugene Schueller who promoted what he termed the first safe commercial hair dye, the French Harmless Dye Co., later named L'Oréal. L'Oréal originally found the United States to be a tough market, but has become the leading cosmetics company in the world.

Based in France, L'Oréal is a publicly quoted company with about 52,000 employees. The majority of its stock is held by the Choudon family, direct descendants of the French chemist who originally founded the company. Liliane Bettencourt, daughter of the company's founder, and her family are the primary stockholders. Food company Nestlé also is a major L'Oréal stockholder. The company has a long history of international business. Its products were first used in the United States by the Ogilvie sisters, who worked with Elizabeth Arden before World War I. The company now sells product across Europe, Asia, Canada, and the United States.

By 2004, roughly 50 percent of L'Oréal's sales came from outside of Europe, which prompted the company to buy up brands in those markets. It acquired the major Chinese brand Yue-Sai in 2004, and announced plans in 2005 to buy SkinCeuticals of Dallas, Texas.

Elizabeth Arden Inc. Elizabeth Arden, a Canadian entrepreneur who sold her own beauty creams at her New York City salon, launched her first perfume in 1935. By 1966, when Arden died, her company consisted of 17 Elizabeth Arden corporations and 40 salons, and was grossing about US$60 million annually. Unilever later bought the Elizabeth Arden brands. In 2001 these were purchased by French Fragrances, which took the Elizabeth Arden name. The company reported sales of US$222.8 million in 2004.

Revlon. Revlon, known by its Almay, Ultima II, and Mitchum lines, sells to large masses of consumers in 175 countries. Controlled by Chairman Ron Perelman, who owns a 60 percent interest, the company was founded in 1932 by Charles Revson and his brother Joseph as a nail polish company. U.S.-based Revlon went public in 1996 and in 2004 had 6,400 employees. In 2001, Revlon lured Jack Stahl from Coca-Cola Co. to become the new president and chief operating officer of the manufacturing giant producing Revlon and Almay cosmetics, as well as the Flex brand of shampoo. In 2002, Revlon reported that it was particularly hard-hit in the competitive lipstick end of cosmetics, reporting an 11 percent sales plunge in lipstick sales. The company had been struggling with its image since 2000 when it ceased its association with supermodel Cindy Crawford. In 2002, it also changed ad agencies, signing with Deutsch Inc. in an effort to reverse its downward spiral, and announcing plans to target African-American and Hispanic consumers. After six years of disappointing sales, Revlon reported a profitable fourth quarter in 2004, its first in six years, with net earnings of US$46 million. Total sales in 2004 reached US$1.29 billion.

Unilever. Unilever is composed of two companies—the British Unilever PLC and the Dutch Unilever NV— of roughly equal size. The companies report consolidated financial results and have identical boards of directors. The roots of the company trace back to the Lever Brothers soap business in Great Britain and the leading margarine producer in Holland. While the company has gone head to head with its fiercest competitor, Procter & Gamble, in the United States, the company has made some substantial U.S. acquisitions and promises to become a major force in the market. The company sells products across the world, from Africa to Latin America, as well as established northern hemisphere markets. Unilever markets such popular brands as Q-tips, Vaseline, and Lipton; as well as Faberge, Helene Curtis, and Calvin Klein cosmetics. After several years of downturns in sales and earnings, in 2002 Unilever reported an upturn in part because of lower media advertising costs which were cut following the general slowdown in ad sales after the September 11, 2001 terrorism acts. In 2004, Unilever posted sales of US$54.4 billion. In 2003, the European market generated 42.6 percent of Unilever's sales, followed by North America (22.9 percent), Asia/Pacific (16.5 percent), Latin America (10 percent), and the Africa/Middle East/Turkey region (7.6 percent). In 2005 plans were underway for the sale of the company's Unilever Cosmetics International unit to Coty for approximately US$800 million.

Procter & Gamble. Procter & Gamble (P&G) is a highly savvy competitor in the toiletries and cosmetics industry. In 2004 P&G registered total sales exceeding US$51.4 billion. Procter & Gamble is a leading producer of personal and home care products, including such brands as Bain de Soleil, Camay, Cover Girl, Max Factor, Oil of Olay, and Vidal Sassoon. Major acquisitions in the early 2000s included Clairol (2001) and Wella (2003). The company's planned 2005 takeover of Gillette, the world leader in shaving products, promised to be the most significant in P&G's history. The deal cost about US$57 billion in stock.

The company was formed in 1837 when candle maker William Procter and soap maker James Gamble merged their two small businesses. Their company had become one of the largest in Cincinnati just 20 years later. Under William Deupree, who became president of the company in 1930, the company grew to become the largest seller of packaged consumer goods in the United States. In 1985 CEO John Smale led a movement to improve existing products and introduce new ones after the company realized its first profit decline in 33 years. Since 1989 the company has increased new product introductions by 30 percent and has produced more than 2,300 brand varieties. P&G established a foothold in Eastern Europe in 1990 by positioning sales managers in such countries as Hungary and Poland. Moving into the beauty products arena, P&G purchased Noxell, the company that makes Cover Girl and Noxema products. In 1991 the company spent more than US$1 billion to purchase Revlon's Max Factor line and its German operation, Betrix.

Avon Products, Inc. Avon is the world leader in direct sales of cosmetics and beauty products, with total sales in 2004 of US$7.7 billion. In addition to direct sales, the company offers products online and through catalogs, mall kiosks, and a day spa. Avon has about 4.9 million independent sales representatives, and hopes to expand this number in coming years to appeal to a younger demographic. The company reports more than a billion customer transactions each year, with more than US$3 billion in representative earnings annually.

Avon traces its origins to 1886, when David H. McConnell started the California Perfume Company, which included an office that operated out of one room in New York City. By 1906, the company had grown to include 10,000 direct sales representatives. That number almost tripled by 1928, when the company offered its first products with the Avon brand. In 1939, California Perfume changed its name to Avon Products, Inc. and established itself as a respected manufacturer of skin care products. With North American sales increasing, Avon branched out into various overseas markets starting in the early 1950s.

In 1990, the company successfully fought off takeover bids from several competitors, pledging to renew its focus on core brands. At the same time, it stepped up overseas expansion in developing markets such as eastern Europe and Asia. By 1997, annual sales exceeded US$5 billion. Avon launched a range of skin care products for men in 2004, available by catalog.

Coty Inc. A subsidiary of German corporation Benckiser GmbH since 1996, Coty is the world's top producer of mass-market perfumes for men and women. The company makes both moderately priced fragrances and colognes, sold in mass retail stores, and higher-end brands offered in department stores. Coty scored a success with its celebrity lines by Jennifer Lopez and Celine Dion, first introduced in 2002. Glow by JLO posted sales of more than US$80 million in its first year, and a second fragrance, Still Jennifer Lopez, was introduced in 2003. Coty's other brands include Calgon bath products as well as foot care and suncare products. In 2005 the company posted net sales of US$2.1 billion. Fragrances and toiletries accounted for 72 percent of sales, with color cosmetics contributing 23 percent and skincare and suncare items contributing 5 percent.

Coty purchased the Marc Jacobs and Kenneth Cole fragrance lines in 2003, and went on to sign with German designer Jette Joop in 2005. Also in the works that year were celebrity fragrances from Sarah Jessica Parker and Baby Phat.

FURTHER READING

Allen, Margaret. *Selling Dreams: Inside the Beauty Business.* New York: Simon and Schuster, 1981.

Ambrosini, Dana. "Cincinnati-Based Procter & Gamble to Cut Jobs." *Connecticut Post,* 7 March, 2002.

Born, Pete, et. al. "Beauty Hoping for a Kinder 2004." *WWD,* 12 December 2003.

Briney, Claire. "State of the Industry: Cosmetics and Toiletries Trends are Taking On a Global Character." *Global Cosmetic Industry,* June 2004.

"Bristol-Myers Squibb: Earnings For 4Q, Full-Year Announced." *Biotech Week,* 20 February, 2002.

Buss, Dale. "Changing the Face of Private Labels." *Brand Home,* 10 May 2004. Available from http://www.brandchannel.com.

Cardona, Mercedes M. "Gain at Unilever." *Advertising Age,* 18 February, 2002.

"Celebrity Fragrances: What Price, Fame?" *Cosmetics Design,* 26 May 2005. Available from http://www.cosmeticsdesign.com.

Conry, Tom. *Consumer's Guide to Cosmetics.* Garden City, NY: Anchor Press/Doubleday, 1980.

Deen, Mark. "L'Oréal 2001 Sales Rise 8.4 Percent." *Bloomberg News,* 23 January, 2002.

D'Innocenzio, Anne. "Revlon Fights Red Ink with Corporate Makeover." *The Deseret (Utah) News,* 23 February, 2002.

———. "Elizabeth Arden, Inc. Provides Update On Fourth Quarter Activities and Guidance for Fiscal 2003." *Business Wire,* 31 January, 2002.

Finn, Kristin. "Clinique Explores Skin Immunity." *WWD,* 14 November 2003.

"Few Bright Spots Emerge in Lackluster Year for Cosmetics and Toiletries Industry," Kline & Company, 6 May 2004. Available from http://http://www.klinegroup.com.

"Fourth-Quarter Loss Narrows at Revlon." *Bloomberg News,* 26 February, 2002.

"French Perfume and Cosmetics Sectors Unaffected by Economic Downturn." *La Tribune,* 6 February, 2002.

Kay, Jane, "Dandruff Shampoo Must Carry Coal-tar Warning." *San Francisco Chronicle,* 21 December, 2001.

Koser, Glenn. "An In-Depth Review of the 2001 Personal-Care Market." *Global Cosmetic Industry,*December 2001. Available at http://www.cosmeticindex.com

"Global Report: Fine Fragrance." *Global Cosmetic Industry,* June 2005. Available from http://www.globalcosmetic.com.

"Kline Study Pegs Global Cosmetics and Toiletries Market at Nearly $150 Billion." Kline & Company, 6 July 2005. Available from http://www.klinegroup.com.

"L'Oréal Sees Further consolidation in Cosmetics Industry; *AFX European Focus,* 21 February, 2002.

Mateev, Iordan. "High-end Cosmetics Take a Down Market Route." *Cosmetics Design,* 20 August 2004. Available from http://www.cosmeticsdesign.com.

Mortished, Carl. "Cosmetics Firms Fear Crackdown on Safety of Products." *Times* (London, England), 22 March 2005. Available from http://business.timesonline.co.uk.

"News Watch: Report: Cosmetics, Toiletries Grow Slowly." *Supermarket News,* 17 May 2004.

"Research Yields New Insights." *MMR,* 3 November 2003.

"The Demand for Cosmetic and Toiletry Chemicals in the US will Increase by More Than 5% Per Year to $6.8bn in 2008 according to Research Company The Freedonia Group Inc." *Cosmetics International,* 26 March 2004.

"Making a Case for 'Masculine' Vanity: Male Grooming is One of the Fastest Growing Sectors of the Cosmetics Industry, with More Companies Launching Skincare Products for Men, and Some Going As Far As to Launch Cosmetic Products." *Marketing Week,* 17 July 2003.

"US C&T Growth Drops in 2003." *Chemical Market Reporter,* 17 May 2004.

COMPUTER HARDWARE AND SERVICES

SIC 3571

NAICS 334111

COMPUTERS

The industry produces digital computers that may be in such configurations as mainframe computers, super computers, and personal computers. This diverse class of machines shares these common abilities:

- they store the processing programs and data necessary to execute programs
- they can be freely programmed in accordance user requirements
- they perform arithmetical computations specified by the user
- they execute—without human intervention—a processing program requiring them to modify execution by logical decision during a processing run

INDUSTRY SNAPSHOT

Three mature world markets—Japan, the United States, and Europe—accounted for the majority of global production and sales of computers and related products during the early 2000s. Between 2003 and 2005, the worldwide computer market grew 11.3 percent annually, and during the first quarter of 2005 alone, growth was 10.3 percent.

In the mid-2000s, Dell remained the worldwide market leader, with 18 percent of sales. HP commanded 16 percent, IBM garnered 7 percent, and Fujitsu had 4 percent. In the United States, Dell led with 33 percent of the market, followed by HP with 19 percent, Gateway and IBM with 6 percent each, and Apple with 4 percent. Prices were shrinking, largely due to market maturity and technological advances driving parts costs down. Two new companies entered the top ten ranks, as reported by Gartner: Aver Corp. and Lenovo Group Ltd.

The trend toward digital technology was set to explode in the mid- to late 2000s with digital convergence, whereby technologies from different tech industries were merging. According to *Business Week,* the tech industries were poised for a "Big Bang" as the computer, consumer electronics, and communications industries merged technologies and products, forming new alliances and partnerships as well as new competitors.

ORGANIZATION AND STRUCTURE

PRODUCT STRUCTURE

The electronic computer industry can be divided into three categories: supercomputers, mainframes, and personal computers. Each category is distinguished roughly by the speed with which a computer can process instructions and data.

Supercomputers. Supercomputers are the most powerful class of computers with extremely high bandwidth to provide users with the greatest possible capability for complex uses by scientists, security experts, mapping professionals, theorists, and economics experts. Medical researchers use them to conduct research in cell studies and other uses that may save lives and prevent or reverse disease. A variety of professionals benefit from conducting theoretical and applied research enhanced with digital imaging. In the 1980s, the manufacturer Cray built powerful supercomputers and to this day has an enviable reputation for building complex, high-end supercomputers favored by many scientists and engineers. During the 2000s, supercomputers were used for weather forecasting and in engineering research related to aerospace, automobiles, and nuclear science. In 2005, IBM was near completing its latest supercomputer, the Blue Gene/L. Housed at the Department of Energys Lawrence Livermore National Laboratory, the Blue Gene/L ran at 135.3 trillion floating-point operations per second (TFLOPS) in March 2005. Engineers at the laboratory expected the machine to achieve 270 TFLOPS that summer, as reported in *Popular Science,* five times as fast at its nearest competitor. About 50 times smaller in size than previous supercomputers, the Blue Gene/L was used for nuclear weapon simulations as well as biochemical applications. Collectively, 2005 supercomputers were about 1,000 times faster than their 1995 predecessors.

Mainframes. Mainframe computers are used to process high-volume general business applications where increased performance is required. These are large and powerful machines, albeit with less bandwidth capacity than a supercomputer, that can hook up with other computers or terminals to allow dozens or even hundreds of employees to work at low security risk stations. The term in the early days of computers referred to the "main frame" or "central processor unit" of a so-called batch computer.

Personal Computers. A personal computer (PC) is a system with imbedded processing capabilities that primarily is intended for a single user. All are based on the microprocessor—manufacturers use technology to put an entire central processing unit or "CPU" on one silicon chip. Businesses rely on personal computers for a variety of functions, including word document creating, accounting, desktop publishing, and for running spreadsheet and database management applications. Microsoft typically sells all these functions in a single software package that many computer hardware sellers either install on the machine or sell to customers with the PC.

Personal computers first appeared in the late 1970s. One of the first and most popular personal computers was the Apple II, introduced in 1977 by Apple Computer. In the next four years, new models and competing operating systems seemed to appear daily and some disappeared overnight. Then, in 1981 IBM became competitive with a personal computer, quickly dubbed a *PC*. The IBM PC sold well, and attracted so-called IBM "compatible" machines or "clones" by makers such as Kaypro. Kaypro and others eventually went into rummage sale lots, but Apple Computer remained, and many so-called "Mac Addicts" attached loyalty to the brand which by 2002 relied on a popular operating system called the MAC OS X.

In the twenty-first century, one's personal computer is either a "Mac" or a PC that is a distant, cousin of that first IBM PC. As distinctions fade, the newer, more powerful, video card-enhanced personal computers in the workplace and classroom have replaced what used to be slightly higher-end models called "workstations." Today, off the shelf or with an upgrade, Macs and PCs are used for work and recreational uses such as playing video games with startling real graphics, downloading music (leading to cries of copyright infringement from the music industry), and providing space to load information and entertainment on DVDs and CDs.

MARKET STRUCTURE

The United States and Japan were the largest supercomputer manufacturers with the largest markets. Japan—although the second-largest global market—purchased most of its supercomputers from domestic sources, primarily from industry leaders NEC, Fujitsu, and Hitachi. Foreign suppliers had difficulty making advances in Japan's supercomputer market for three primary reasons: Japan's government greatly supported its domestic industry; Japanese industry's own tendency to purchase from domestic manufacturers; and Japanese industry's investment in Japanese-manufactured proprietary equipment and software. Almost all foreign imports to Japan came from the United States, which accounted for 25 percent of Japan's computer hardware sales, approximately US$40 billion.

Due to the rise and development of client/server technology in the late 1980s and 1990s, mainframe sales decreased sharply. For example, U.S. mainframe sales were about US$12.4 billion in 1992 and fell to US$11.3 billion in 1993. However, the demand for mammoth repositories of information generated by the Internet has created renewed interest in mainframe systems. Industry leader IBM still held 80 percent of that market, and mainframe revenues were growing. Sales of IBM's zSeries mainframes were up 14.9 percent from 2003 to 2004. IBM was being challenged by Japanese leaders Hitachi and Amdahl (recently acquired by another major player, Fujitsu). U.S. leader Dell also claimed US$312 million of the mainframe market in 1997 and showed itself increasingly competitive in the 2000s.

In 1997 the midrange systems market was showing renewed growth, especially in foreign markets. As the economy strengthened and the role of midrange systems in client/server technology grew, sales began to increase. According to a report in *VARBusiness*, midrange systems were slated to become the hottest market in computing during the late 1990s. Major players in the industry included IBM and Hewlett-Packard. IBM was still the leader in midrange systems, and during the mid-2000s focused on making its platform competitive with other systems, such as Linux, and with other companies in terms of operational and development cost. Hewlett-Packard was a strong competitor, partnering with Intel to facilitate its growth in the market and using its economic clout to merge with Compaq for wider capabilities and marketing clout.

Worldwide revenues for the server market grew 6.2 percent in 2004, and the market was valued at more than $49 billion. Between IBM and Hewlett-Packard, the two companies accounted for 60 percent of sales. In terms of revenue, IBM remained the market leader, but HP shipped more servers. Total number of units shipped grew 19.3 percent in 2004. IDC reported a declined in the mid-range and high-end server sectors, but other servers were realizing steady market growth, including Unix, Windows, and Blade servers. Linux servers remained the highest growth segment of the market, worth $1.3 billion in the fourth quarter of 2004.

Regulation. Environmental concerns also played a major role in the electronic computer industry. In 1993 a collaborative report—*A Workstation Life Cycle Environment Study*—produced by several government agencies urged U.S. manufacturers to become more environmentally conscious. The study pushed manufacturers to better recycle products and parts and reduce pollution created by manufacturing. In the same year, then-President Bill Clinton issued an executive order directing U.S. agencies to purchase only computers that adhered to the Environmental Protection Agency's (EPA) Energy Star program. This program called for each part of a computer system, including some peripherals (such as printers) to enter into a standby mode when not in use, thus reducing energy consumption. The EPA predicted that the Energy Star program requirements could reduce carbon-dioxide emissions enough to forestall the need for 10 coal-burning power plants. Many U.S. computer manufacturers followed the guidelines of the broader program as well and started to recycle processor boards, power supplies, and batteries.

BACKGROUND AND DEVELOPMENT

The computer was born several centuries ago out of a need to speed and aid computation. Though certainly not a computer by modern standards, the first such tool was a simple tabulation machine called the abacus, which originated in the Middle East. The first tabulation machine to have significant global impact was the mechanical calculator created by French mathematician Blaise Pascal in 1642. Built from a long wooden box and a combination of wheels and gears, numbers were entered into Pascal's calculator via six wheels located on the front of the machine, and the answers were displayed in windows above each wheel.

In the mid-nineteenth century, English mathematician Charles Babbage drafted designs for two calculating devices, the difference engine (1820s) and the analytical engine (1840s)—neither were ever built. His designs for the analytical engine were enhancements based on the difference engine, which depicted the primary components of the modern electronic computer, such as programs being stored on punch cards.

This idea was more fully developed later in the nineteenth century by Herman Hallerith, an American who created a machine that would sort and count cards based on the pattern of holes punched into them. Hallerith's machine was first used in the 1890 U.S. Census to aid in statistical analysis. Though the reading device certainly improved, Hallerith cards were still used for inputting program instructions into computers well into the late 1970s and early 1980s. In 1896 Hallerith started a company called the Tabulation Machine Company. This company was one of three companies that later became International Business Machines Corporation (better known as IBM).

In the 1940s Howard Aiken developed what was considered the first electronic computer. Instead of using Hallerith cards, his machine used rolls of paper with instructions punched into them. Because it required extensive rewiring for each program entered into the computer, its design was limiting and time-consuming. The first general-purpose computer was completed in 1946 and was used by the military. Although the electronic numerical integrator and calculator (ENIAC) still needed partial rewiring like its predecessor, it had far greater processing speed. Later in the same decade, created from the concepts of Hungarian-American mathematician John von Neumann, a computer was built that had the ability to internally store instructions, thus reducing many of the problems found with Aiken's computer and the ENIAC.

In 1951 the U.S. Bureau of the Census purchased the first UNIVAC I. Created by J. Presper Eckert and John Mauchly, UNIVAC I was the first computer to be made commercially available. The two men later formed Remington Rand, one of IBM's first rival companies. As advances were made in the 1950s—such as the development of transistors, which replaced vacuum tubes used in earlier computers—the electronic computer finally became a truly viable and useful business tool. Further advancements that increased processing speed and memory were made in the 1960s and 1970s with the creation of the integrated circuit, which combined many transistors into a single compact unit; and the invention of the microprocessor, a further advancement of the integrated circuit. Both of these advancements continued to reduce both the size and cost of electronic computers, making them increasingly more common in business, government, and education.

By the 1980s supercomputers, mainframe systems, and minicomputers had already filtrated the world market. Where there were only about 100 computers worldwide in the early 1950s, there were millions in use by the 1980s. It was a lucrative market. Mainframe and minicomputer manufacturers earned high profit margins, some as high as 90 percent on a sale. These systems were proprietary in design—often only the manufacturer of a system provided the hardware, maintenance, and even the software needed for it. Once a company selected a system, it was very difficult and expensive to change to a system made by another manufacturer. However, with the advent of the personal computer and quicker, more powerful microprocessors, this trend changed.

Personal computers were low-cost, non-proprietary, and did not offer the high profit margins that mainframe and minicomputers did. When personal computers first became available, some computer manufacturers viewed them as low-profit, low-power machines with low market potential, and essentially ignored them. However, when linked together in a network, a group of personal computers could provide an inexpensive means of handling tasks previously performed by more powerful computers. This was especially true as personal computer technology increased in the 1980s and 1990s, and the lines that divided the various computer types became increasingly blurred. By the mid-1990s home PCs and even hand-held video games would have the graphics capabilities similar to the supercomputers of a decade before. No longer could personal computers be ignored.

A volatile global economy and increasing competition marked the global computer market. Another factor influencing the industry was the market's continuing movement away from large, expensive, nonstandardized (closed or proprietary) mainframes to smaller, cheaper, standardized (open) computer systems. Since these smaller systems garnered a much lower profit margin than mainframes, revenues were greatly reduced and a higher quantity of sales became more important. In addition, government pressures caused computer manufacturers to make products more environmentally friendly, and to create equipment and develop production methods that use less energy and emit less radiation and other harmful pollutants.

In the booming 1990s, it seemed the growth rate in the computer industry would always be 20 percent annually or more. Analysts predicted that the industry would continue to grow in the new millennium, but in 2002 they lowered some of these expectations for annual growth. Competition would continue to increase as manufacturers found new ways to produce computers more cheaply and efficiently through automation. Also, to improve sales volume and decrease costs, companies reduced prices to the consumer, decreased the workforce, and shared research and development costs with other companies. For example, Microsoft and Intel were working together on development of a Net PC, and were probably spurred on by Oracle's developments of a "thin client," or NC (network computer). As such alliances increased, more mergers between computer manufacturers were expected to take place, such as the one that took place between NEC's PC operations (except China and Japan) and Packard Bell, forming a new venture named Packard Bell-NEC. Similarly, Compaq acquired Digital Equipment Corporation in 1998.

The impact of network computing was also being felt in the computer industry, especially the PC segment. Most growth in the PC market was expected to result from the rapidly increasing use of all networks—local area networks, wide area networks, Intranets, and the Internet. Growth was especially strong in areas such as France and Japan, once resistant to network technology. In tandem with the spread of client/server technology and networking as business tools, the market for PC servers was growing at a rate of 23 percent each year during the 1990s. Manufacturers were building servers with enough power to compete with (and replace) workstations.

The global market for personal computers in 1997 was US$67 billion—still strong, but a slowdown from its 30 percent growth rate in past years. The number of PC shipments worldwide increased 16.5 percent, from 17.4 million to 20.2 million units. After the slowdown in 2001 and 2002, growth was expected to return in late 2002 for PCs, and in 2003 for business-purpose computers. The market for portable computers—handhelds, notebooks, and laptops—was expected to grow at a higher rate than desktop PCs.

In the late 1990s, another challenge to the computer industry was becoming readily apparent to businesses and computer manufacturers all over the globe—systems that stored dates as only two digits, registering 1998 as "98," were destined to read the year 2000 as "00" or 1900. For businesses and agencies of all kinds, the year 2000 seemed to spell disaster, but thanks to precautionary measures worldwide, the so-called "Y2K bug" was far less problematic than some computer viruses being circulated by unscrupulous or revenge-seeking computer users.

In March 2002 computer company executives once again were regaining confidence, and major companies such as IBM, Oracle, and Macintosh began putting on trade shows in San Francisco again after a period of complete stagnation in 2001. No one announced that the crisis was over, but many analysts were confident that the technology sales crisis of 2001 had been met head-on.

CURRENT CONDITIONS

According to *Market Share Reporter*, the commercial market in 2003 had the highest share of PC shipments in the United States, with 33 percent. In contrast, the consumer market had 18 percent of the total. The business sector was expected to continue as the largest consumer into 2007. According to *Euromonitor*, the business sector would have US$26.1 billion of the total US$50.3 billion market. A number of Media Center PCs were introduced in 2004 from HP, Microsoft, and Gateway. The digital revolution was set to explode in a wave of new products in the mid-2000s, as the computer, electronic, and communications industries combined technologies.

Following several years of double-digit growth through 2005, Gartner Inc. reported that global shipment of PCs would slow, rising about 5.7 percent annually between 2006 and 2008. More than 60 percent of that projected growth was expected to come from emerging markets. According to IDC, the replacement market for desktop computers was particularly strong, with demand highest in the Americas and Europe. Latin America, in particular, continued to grow by more than 20 percent per year. A Gartner study found that in addition to the growing use of digital features in computers, the replacement market was going to drive sales in the mid-2000s, with 120 million PCs set for replacement in 2005. IDC expected total PC shipments to reach 199.2 million units in 2005 (up 11.4 percent) and 217 million units (up 9 percent) by 2006, reported in June 2005.

IBM dominated the supercomputer market, manufacturing half of the world's top 500 supercomputers, as reported in "Top 500 Supercomputer Rankings." Five of the top ten machines on the list were based on IBM's Blue Gene/L supercomputer. As reported in *eWeek* in June 2005, HP's share dropped, and the company held 26 percent of the market, with 131 of the top supercomputers, down from 34 percent six months before. Silicon Graphics held 5 percent of the market with 24 supercomputers on the top 500 list, with Dell and Cray Inc. slightly behind. China's rise in the global marketplace was also evident. When it entered the top 500 list in 2002, Chinese companies only had three supercomputers on the list, compared to 19 in 2005, just behind Japan, with 23. In May 2005, Japan announced plans to build a machine capable of handing 1 quadrillion calculations a second by 2010.

RESEARCH AND TECHNOLOGY

Research and development plays a major role in the electronic computer industry, where some product cycles are measured in months and the power of the personal computers has doubled every 12 to 18 months. To help combat escalating expenses, some manufacturers have sought alliances with other companies to share in the high cost of research.

One of the major areas of PC research was the rapid spread of analog to digital conversion in the electronics market. As a result, once separate industries were both in cooperation and in competition. Computers, telecommunications, consumer electronics, entertainment, publishing, and television companies all had a stake in digital technology, and all were devoting research and development resources in that direction. Digital technology affected PC technology by spurring the rapid growth of multimedia, which put video on computers. And it was digital technology that allowed manufactures to begin development of hybrid PCs/televisions. Also, computer manufacturers were engaged in efforts to expand communication bandwidth, an area of strong interest to entertainment and information content providers. The U.S. Federal Communications Commission was keeping a close eye on electronics and computer manufacturers and broadcasters, and issued standards for new digital televisions with specifications for the new technology.

WORKFORCE

All three mature markets—the United States, Japan, and Europe—maintained or slightly increased their workforce from 1996 to 1997. Following a period where companies were laying off employees to reduce costs, industry employers hoping to hire skilled personnel were finding a shortage of qualified workers in the late 1990s. As a result of the downsizing trend of the mid-1990s and again in 2001, companies were not seeing much loyalty from computer industry employees, safe in the knowledge that they could easily find work elsewhere. While computer engineers were competing for a limited number of jobs earlier in the decade, employment in the area was expected to improve significantly through 2010, according to U.S. Department of Labor findings in 2002. Reasons for the rise in employment potential included a rebounding U.S. economy and computer systems with needs that were increasingly interconnected. Computer engineers were responsible for not only designing hardware systems, but also for integrating software into established systems as new technologies were adopted.

In its April 2004 monthly jobs report, the U.S. Department of Labor reported continued upturn in employment for computer professionals. Computer and electronic product manufacturing realized an increase of 2,600 jobs in the United states, totaling more than 1.3 million. The management and technical services sector added 3,400 jobs the same month.

INDUSTRY LEADERS

IBM (International Business Machines Corporation). Charles Flint created Calculating-Tabulating-Recording (CTR) in 1910 by merging his two companies, International Time Recording Co. and Computing Scale Company, with a third company called Tabulation Machine Company, which was started by Herman Hallerith. In 1914 Flint hired Thomas Watson as general manager of CTR. Watson later became president and created a powerful business sales force that became known for its superior customer service. Under his leadership the company quickly expanded in both in sales and size, moving into Europe, Asia, and Latin America. In 1924 CTR came to be known as International Business Machines, focusing on large tabulation machines. By 1949 it had operations in 58 countries. IBM World Trade Corporation was created that same year, which enjoyed the same dominance in foreign markets as it did in the United States.

U.S. giant International Business Machines Corporation was the world's largest producer of electronic computers in 1997 with $78.5 billion in sales. However, IBM was not alone at the top anymore. Compaq later surpassed IBM in PC sales, and Hitachi closed in on the mainframe market. Due to its size, some experts believe, IBM was not able to react to the ever-changing computer market fast enough—its sales dropped, and IBM lost billions of dollars in profits between 1985 and the early 1990s.

In response to these problems, IBM began major restructuring efforts. To make it easier for multinational companies to conduct business with IBM and break down barriers between countries, a plan to have one contract and one discount cover them wherever they did business was implemented. In addition, efforts to unify its global operations shifted power from managers who oversaw the operations of an entire country to 14 managers of industry sectors. IBM's efforts seemed to be working, and in the first quarter of 1998 the company performed above analysts' projections. Hardware revenue for that period was down, but the loss was attributed to IBM's lower PC prices in response to PC price wars.

On March 1, 2002, IBM began what it hoped would become a return to greatness under its newest chief executive, longtime IBM chieftain Samuel J. Palmisano. Palmisano was personally involved during the company's humiliating time period in 2000-2001 when its technology was mocked as inferior by upstart rivals and its ability to deliver machines in a reasonable time period—once its crowning hallmark—had become embarrassingly problematic, according to *Business Week*. Palmisano's first job was to stop the bleeding. In January 2002 IBM's once revered stock plunged more than US$5 in a single day. Promising to update the company and to build, for the first time, an Internet presence for sales, IBM shareholders were watching hopefully, albeit understandably with nervousness, to see if the new CEO could turn the company around. Palmisano also faced the challenge of increasing software sales, which crept along at a 3 percent growth rate even as some rivals achieved up to 30 percent growth rates, according to *Business Week*.

Palmisano and IBM shifted the company's focus during the early to mid-2000s, focusing more on global IT services, including application management and e-business hosting. By 2004, IBM was ranked first in IT services in the world. IBM reported $96.5 billion in 2004 revenues from all divisions, 8 percent growth over the previous year. Of that, global services revenue was $46.2 billion, software revenue was $15.1 billion, and hardware revenue was $31.2 billion, 10 percent more than in 2003. The company's net income rose to $8.4 billion, an 11.2 percent jump over 2003 levels. IBM employed 319,273 people by the end of 2004, and was the world's leading computer hardware company.

Hitachi. In 1910 Namihei Odaira created Hitachi in the Japanese city of the same name and produced electric motors. The company began manufacturing transistors in the mid-1950s and integrated circuits in the 1960s. In 1974 it created an IBM-plug-compatible computer and sold them worldwide through such companies as National Semiconductor, Olivetti, and BASF. In 1991 Hitachi began selling IBM notebook PCs under its own name in Japan, and in 1993 sold its first eight-processor mainframe computer. Hitachi was one of the leading semiconductor producers in the world and Japan's largest electrical machinery manufacturer. It was the second-largest company in the industry with US$68.7 billion in revenues and the industry's largest employer with 330,152 workers.

Hitachi was the world's second-largest dynamic random access mechanization (DRAM) chip producer and built many of IBM's mainframe systems. However, its reliance on the mainframe industry made it extremely vulnerable to changing consumer needs and it thus suffered losses. In response, Hitachi began to make advances with its 4 MB DRAM, which would be needed in the growing multimedia computer market, and entered into a joint venture with Mitsubishi Corp. to create flash-memory chips. In 1998 Hitachi released what it claims was "the world's fastest 3.5-inch hard disk drive, the DK3E1T-91 series, with the speed of 12,030-rpm." Also in 1998 the company introduced its first disk drive incorporating giant magneto-resistive (GMR) head technology. With an areal density of 3.9 Gigabits (Gb) per square inch, the new DK228A-65 notebook drive provided a storage capacity of 6.48 Gb. This development further positioned Hitachi as a leader in the rapidly growing computer storage industry, and in the words of *Business Week*, allowed the company to "eat IBM's lunch." In 2002 Hitachi positioned itself to become the true leader in new handheld technology, putting together a model with remarkable power for business, game, and personal usage. For 2005 the company reported US$84.2 billion in revenue, a 3.4 percent increase over 2004.

Hewlett-Packard. Hewlett-Packard, a U.S. company, was the fourth-largest computer manufacturer in 1997 with US$42.9 billion in sales. It was the sixth-largest employer in the industry with 121,900 employees worldwide. The company has operations in 17 countries worldwide, including France, Mexico, Germany, and Japan. Of 1997 sales, 45 percent were generated inside the United States, 33 percent in Europe, and the remaining sales in other countries. Eighty-three percent of Hewlett-Packard's revenues were generated by sales of computers and computer services and support, making it the second-largest company (behind IBM) in terms of sales generated by computer operations.

In May 2002 HP's shareholders and management purchased Compaq Computer Corp. for US$18.69 billion in HP stock, the largest merger in the industry's history. The merger gave HP's sagging sales a tremendous boost, even as IBM was regrouping under a new CEO and big Japanese competitors Hitachi and Toshiba were reeling with reports that the yen had still lower to drop before that nation returned to prosperity. The combined company reported 2003 revenues of US$73.1 billion, one-year growth of 29 percent. In 2004, Hewlett-Packard earned $79.9 billion in revenues, up 9.4 percent from 2003. The company employed more than 150,000 people.

William Hewlett and David Packard officially created Hewlett-Packard (HP) in 1939, although they worked together earlier to create eight oscillators for Walt Disney Studios. In 1966, HP created its first computer for internal use, never intending to enter the computer market. However, two years later it created the first desktop calculator capable of performing scientific calculations, and by 1974 committed itself to moving into the computer industry with the HP3000. The HP-85, Hewlett-Packard's first personal computer, was released in 1985. Reaction to it was poor because it was not compatible with IBM's designs. This caused HP not only to create IBM-compatible PCs, but to move toward making all its computers, at least in part, cross-compatible. To better position itself for the global market, it increased cooperative efforts, and in the late 1980s HP entered into trade agreements with companies such as Hitachi, Canon USA Inc., and Sony.

Compaq was started in 1982 by three former Texas Instruments engineers, including Joseph "Rod" Canion. By 1983, the company went public and earned more than US$100 million. In 1991 Eckhard Pfeiffer replaced Canion as CEO. Compaq made its mark as a maker of PC "clones," selling desktop PCs with standard computer components from Microsoft and Intel, among others. The company took this model and used it to venture into the corporate market, building servers that hold mammoth amounts of data and are stealing business from microcomputers and mainframes. In January of 1998 Compaq was named "Company of the Year" by *Forbes* magazine, citing its swift growth, great returns, and great strategic leadership by Eckhard Pfeiffer. In 1998 Compaq also approved a deal to buy Digital Equipment Corporation for US$9.6 billion. Under the deal, Digital became a subsidiary of Compaq, and the merger proved disastrous, significantly hurting shareholder confidence after losses mounted into the 2000s.

Although relatively new to the industry, Compaq had its best year as the world's largest PC maker in 1998. With US$24.6 billion in sales, Compaq ranked seventh in terms of gross revenues among the overall industry's top 10 companies. In 2002, Compaq claimed more than 13 percent of the global PC market, surpassing first-ranked IBM. Even so, PCs accounted for only half of Compaq's sales—other products include servers, disk drives, modems, workstations, monitors, and printers. Compaq employed 37,004 people, making it the eighth-largest employer in the industry, and large numbers of layoffs and early retirements were expected following the HP purchase.

Toshiba. Toshiba is a major manufacturer of portable computers. The company was created in 1939 by the merger of Hakunetsu-sha and Company and Tanaka Seizo-sho (Tanaka Engineering Works), both Japanese electrical equipment manufacturers. In 1924 Hakunetsu-sha created Japan's first cathode ray tube and began creating computers in 1954. In 1985 it was the first company to manufacture one-megabit memory chips, and it began shipping laptop computers the following year. Toshiba had US$44 billion in sales in 1997 and was the world's fourth-largest computer manufacturer. It was the fourth-largest employer in the industry, employing 186,000 workers. Toshiba was the world's largest memory chip producer, a major supplier of color flat-screen displays used for many portable computers, and the third-largest maker of liquid screen displays. Its willingness and success in creating joint ventures with companies such as IBM and Apple made it one of the industry's strongest companies, despite the Japanese recession and an ever-increasing competitive worldwide market. However, Toshiba was losing market share in the notebook market, dropping from 30 percent of the market in 1996 to 20 percent in early 1998. The loss was attributed to stiff competition from IBM and Compaq in price and technology.

In March 2002, with sales stagnant and the Japanese economy experiencing serious hurt, Toshiba executives could wait no longer. According to *Electronic Buyers News*, Toshiba was in the process of shutting down a quarter of its

98 domestic plants and was cutting its Japanese workforce 12 percent to improve cash flow. By 2004 Toshiba's revenues were US$52.8 billion, an 11 percent increase over 2003, and net income was up 77 percent to US$273 million.

Dell. Dell Inc. was new to the list of industry leaders in 1998, but along with Compaq was one of the fastest growing computer companies in the industry. By 2004, Dell was the world's leading direct sales computer company, with no store overhead of its own, and the largest PC maker in the world. The company reported 2005 revenues US$49.2 billion, 18 percent growth from 2004. Dell employed more than 55,000 people. Of the top ten PC makers worldwide, Dell was the only one that remained consistently profitable during the early to mid-2000s. In 2004, Dell retained 16.4 percent of the global PC market, up from 14.9 percent in 2003, as reported by Gartner Japan. Sales were attributed largely to strong growth in Europe and Japan, as reported in *eWeek.*

A May 1998 *Fortune* article titled "Michael Dell Rocks" claimed that Dell's CEO "has transformed his industry and enriched thousands of shareholders. Dell stock is up 29,600 percent this decade. And now the company looks stronger than ever." In 1997 Dell earned US$12.3 billion in revenue, up from US$7.75 billion in 1996. From 1995 to 1998, the company grew by an average of 53 percent annually. And according to the same article in *Fortune*, Dell is growing at twice the rate of any of its competitors, such as Gateway, Compaq, and IBM. Dell's stock rose from its initial public offering price of US$8.50 in 1988 to US$69.25 in mid-1998, which explained how the company "enriched" its shareholders. Dell's success, found after some hard learning experiences, was built on its direct made-to-order PC sales and its success using the Internet as a sales medium. Not limited to PCs, Dell also markets servers, CD-ROMs, modems, network hardware, disk drives, and other peripheral equipment. The company still has room for growth, however. It only claimed 6 percent of the global PC market in 1998, behind Compaq and IBM, and generated 70 percent of its sales inside the United States.

Michael Dell founded "PCs Limited" from his dorm room at the University of Texas in 1984. He began buying excess computers from local retailers, enhancing them, and reselling them directly to consumers at low prices. It took him under a year to begin earning sales of US$50,000 per month, and Dell soon decided to devote all of his time to the company. In 1988 he changed the company's name to Dell Computer Corp. and took the company public. Dell's company employed more than 10,000 people worldwide in 1998. In 2001, with an aggressive TV and print marketing campaign, Dell kept its sales of PCs at a respectable level even as other rivals saw their share of the market fall or collapse.

NEC. Japan's Nippon Electric Company (NEC), was created in 1898 as a joint venture between Western Electric of the United States and a group of Japanese investors. While it began as an importer of telephone equipment, it soon became a manufacturer and supplier. After struggling through an earthquake in 1923 and World War II, NEC entered into the computer industry in 1954. By 1986 NEC had become Japan's second-largest computer company, and was one of the largest manufacturers of semiconductors in the 1990s. In 1997 it had US$39.9 billion in sales, making it the world's fifth-largest computer company. In Japan, NEC ranked first in sales of personal computers, holding 40 percent of Japan's domestic market and deriving 80 percent of its revenue there. By 2005 the company had US$45.29 billion in revenue, a slight decline from 2004, but net income rose 60 percent to $633 million. NEC's IT Solutions Business, which included systems integration, hardware, and software, was responsible for generating 44 percent of the company's revenue. NEC competed with Fujitsu for the number one spot in Japan.

Fujitsu. Fujitsu, a Japanese company, was the world's sixth-largest computer manufacturer in 1997 with US$36.37 billion in revenue. Counting 167,000 employees, it was the industry's fourth-largest employer and was Japan's second-largest computer manufacturer. By 2004, the company rivaled NEC for Japan's number one spot, having reported US$45.1 billion in revenue for 2004, more than 17 percent more than in 2003. It also provided stiff competition to Hitachi as the world's second-largest mainframe provider. Company developments during 1998 included a joint venture with Computer Associates International Inc. to build Internet business systems for client/server systems. Fujitsu had operations in more than 400 areas around the globe, including Australia, the United States, Mexico, France, Colombia, Indonesia, and Zimbabwe, among others. Fujitsu also entered the groupware market in the late 1990s with its Teamware, and was already gaining market share in Japan, where Lotus Notes and Microsoft currently dominate.

In 1935 Fuji Electric Co. Ltd. created Fujitsu to build telephone equipment. In 1954 it entered the data processing arena by developing Japan's first computer, which was called the FACOM 100. To ensure the success of its new computer industry, Japan's Ministry of International Trade and Industry (MITI) put up trade barriers. In addition, Japan sponsored the development of new computers through a public utility created in the 1950s called National Telephone and Telegraph, which essentially created a guaranteed market for Japanese-made computers. In the 1960s, MITI helped fund and direct Fujitsu's creation of mainframe systems. Despite these efforts, however, Fujitsu computers were still technologically far behind those of IBM. In 1972 Fujitsu invested money into the Amdahl Corporation, which was owned by the primary creator of IBM's extremely successful 360 series computers. In 1997 they bought the remaining 55 percent of Amdahl to complete its full acquisition. This investment gave Fujitsu the technological knowledge it needed and put Fujitsu on a more level ground with IBM. It shipped its first supercomputer in 1982, and by 1994 was the second-largest maker of supercomputers. In 2002, as sales in all areas of the company slowed along with Japan's larger economic crisis, Fujitsu reduced its labor force by more than 25,000 workers.

Sun Microsystems. Sun Microsystems was founded in 1982 by four young entrepreneurs, and has since grown into a *Fortune* 500 company with operations in more than 150 countries. Sun's first product was a high-performance Unix-based system computer. In 1997 it also developed what was claimed to be one of the most powerful single-system servers. Taking another direction, in the late 1990s the company revolutionized the Internet software industry by developing the Java programming language.

Based in Palo Alto, California, Sun Microsystems was a leading manufacturer of network computing systems and Unix-based workstations. In 1997 Sun earned US$8.6 billion in revenue and employed 21,500 people, making it the world's tenth-largest company and employer in the industry. Sun generated about half its sales outside the United States, and demonstrated consistent 15 to 20 percent growth during the late 1990s. Sun's goal in 1998 was to transform itself into "an enterprise computing firm focused on global network computing." By 2004 the company was reporting US$11.2 billion in revenue, employing 36,000 people.

Apple Computer Inc. In 2002 executives at Apple had stopped reminiscing about the good old days when Mac market share steadily climbed. Instead, the company resisted the slump in PC sales with strong orders for G-4 laptops and the new Imac flat screen models. These models featured the company's newest addition to the world of operating systems, OS X. Derived from the tried-and-true Unix program, the suddenly hot new OS X, complete with splashy graphics, was introduced with more bells than bugs, and more flash than flaws. In 2002 the company's guru Stephen Jobs announced that 40 percent of those entering the growing nationwide chain of Apple Mac stores say they are customers new to the Mac product line. During the fourth quarter of 2004, Apple shipped 836,000 Macintosh units (a 6 percent increase) and more than 2 million iPods (a 500 percent increase). Retail store revenues grew 95 percent from 2003 to 2004. Apple posted 33.4 percent growth in 2004, with US$8.27 billion in revenue.

Gateway. A strong surge in sales in the 1990s catapulted Gateway into fourth place among personal computer sellers; however, the company staggered due to consumer disinterest and the general economic slowdown in 2001. Gateway stocks fell to US$4.24 one month after the September 11, 2001, terrorist attacks, putting the stock back to 1995 prices. In less than a year, Gateway lost its enviable 15 percent of the PC market, as it found itself with less than 9 percent at the start of 2002. Much of Gateway's misfortune became rival Dell's good fortune as the rival muscled away Gateway's market share, according to nonprofit research company IDC. Unlike Dell, which has no store overhead, Gateway found itself at a disadvantage as it pondered closing stores that had been so recognizable with its trademark black and white logo. Gateway also found itself confusing buyers in 2001, changing its selling mission regarding low-end buyers in mid-year. By 2004 Gateway closed all of its stores and moved to selling products only through other retailers and directly over the phone and the Internet. The company acquired eMachines that year. In 2004 revenues were US$3.6 billion.

MAJOR REGIONS IN THE INDUSTRY

United States. The United States was the world's leader in the computer industry. In contrast to other major markets, the U.S. market was only forecast to grow 3.5 percent into 2007, according to *Euromonitor,* due to market maturity and saturation. Consumer demand was expected to remain solid in the United States, with portable PCs generating the largest amount of demand. In June 2005 Current Analysis, a research firm, announced that for the first time in history, notebook computers outsold desktops, accounting for 53 percent of the total PC market, an increase of 46 percent. The change was expected to accompany growth in telecommuting and wireless network access. Also facilitating sales were declines in laptop prices (17 percent) compared to declined in desktop pricing (4 percent). Desktop growth was expected to show low growth, if any, in the United States.

In 2002, trying to help the beleaguered computer industry, the U.S. federal government bowed to computer industry pleas and relaxed restrictions on computer exports, letting the industry sell computer exports to China, Russia, India, Pakistan, and others which have 190,000 Mtops, or millions of theoretical operations per second—more than double previously allowable Mtops, according to *Electronic Engineering Times*. The move gave some nations with security limitations the ability to import far more powerful computers than previously allowed by the U.S. government.

Europe. The European market was hit hard during the first half of the 1990s by a weak economy. During the early 1990s, three of Europe's top computer manufacturers—Siemens Nixdorf, Olivetti, and Groupe Bull—each lost at least 12 percent in revenues from the previous year. Further, European computer manufacturers had a more difficult time competing in the global market because they lacked the research and development funding and strength found in their counterparts from the United States, and to a smaller degree, Japan. Without innovating new technologies, American and Japanese computer manufacturers continued to gain strength and dominance in the European market. As reported in a 1997 *Fortune* article, the outlook for European technology did not improve during the late 1990s.

In 2002 analysts revealed that a soft economy and fallout from the September 11 terrorist attacks created havoc with the growth of the computer industry in Germany. As evidence, 2001 PC sales plunged 7.3 percent from 2000, reaching US$6.42 million. Besides Germany, the European nations of Britain, France, Italy, and the Netherlands also had disastrous 2001 PC sales. As of early 2005, consumer demand gave the European market a boost, and laptop sales climbed almost 16 percent in January 2005. Most European nations saw double-digit growth, mainly in France, Spain, and Sweden. The Spanish PC market realized 24.7 percent growth during the first quarter of 2001, with the desktop market growing at almost the same rate as laptops in the country. Only Germany saw declines in sales, falling by one percent. Following a similar trend in the United States, laptop sales were expected to overtake desktop sales within the year. As reported by Tony Glover, long-term growth in Europe looked solid during the mid-2000s, due to mobile adoption, replacement of aging systems, and better market penetration. Into 2007, the U.K. market was expected to grow 47 percent, the German market was expected to grow 28 percent, and the French market was expected to grow 17 percent, according to *Euromonitor.*

Asia. In 2002 a depressed Japanese economy and a soft market for personal computers saw the nation's computer manufacturers in nail-biting mode. Previously, during the late 1990s Japan saw renewed growth in hardware purchasing, particularly in the networking area. Part of the reason for this surge in growth was the Japanese government's goal to achieve a "Fiber-to-the-Home" network. This network would connect all government offices, businesses, homes, and institutions by the year 2010. PC servers, workstations, and peripheral and networking interface systems were expected to be the best products for manufacturers hoping to market to Japan. During the 2000s, consumer demand was expected to boost growth in Japan, but slowing commercial growth was expected to limit growth overall.

Outside of Japan, the Asia-Pacific region realized growth lower than was expected in the late 1990s, according to International Data Corp. This slowdown was attributed to weakened currencies in Asia, high interest rates, and slowdowns in economic growth. Regions hardest hit included Thailand, Singapore, Malaysia, Indonesia, and the Philippines. Some countries in the region did experience substantial growth, however, such as China, Taiwan, and India. China realized more than 50 percent growth in the PC market from 1996 to 1997, according to the Ministry of Electronics Industry. *Euromonitor* reported that China saw more than 15 percent growth in 2002, and was forecast to grow another 86 percent into 2007. South Korea was also expected to see growth into 2007, with 40 percent increases projected.

One of the fastest growing markets in Asia during the late 1990s was Taiwan. According to *Business Week*, "As neighboring economies falter, this humming entrepreneurial dynamo is the envy of Asia." The country encourages the start-up of new industries, in contrast to countries such as Japan and China, which rely on established large corporations to support their economies.

India, while still counted as one of Asia-Pacific's hottest growth areas, was experiencing difficulty in its domestic hardware industry. Reasons for difficulty included increasing competition from multinational companies, which created price wars and stunted growth for domestic companies. Additionally, lower import duties and devalued currency were narrowing profit margins for domestic companies. India was still counted as an area with enormous potential, however. The area had remarkably low technology penetration, leaving much room for growth.

Latin America. Another region identified with high-growth potential was Latin America. Notebook PC shipments for the third quarter of 1997 were 935,000, and the regional PC market grew 32 percent from 1996 to 1997. Leading countries in the area were Venezuela (53 percent growth) and Chile (49 percent growth), while Argentina and Colombia were also making substantial progress. The collapse of the Argentine economy in 2001 and slow sales in other Latin American nations contributed to the general ill health of the computer industry in the early 2000s. Compaq was credited by *Business Wire* with 22.9 percent of computer shipments to this region in 2001. IBM, which provided higher-end machines, came away with the lion's share (40 percent) of 2001 revenue from computer sales. Dell lost some money in 2001, but began to make its presence known in the region. As of 2005, Latin America was the fastest growing region in the global computer market.

FURTHER READING

"3 of Top 10 PC Makers to Exit Market by 2007: Gartner." *Japan Computer Industry Scan,* 13 December 2004.

Baker, Stephen, and Heather Green. "Big Bang!" *Business Week,* 21 June 2004.

Burt, Jeffrey. "Big Iron Is Back" *eWeek,* 11 October 2004.

"Computer Shipments Rise in Q1." *Purchasing,* 19 May 2005. Available from http://www.purchasing.com.

"Current Analysis Reveals That Laptops Outsell Desktops in the US for the First Time." *Worldwide Computer Products News,* 6 June 2005.

"Desktop Personal Computers in Australia, China, France, Germany, Japan, South Korea, UK, US." *Euromonitor,* August 2004. Available from http://www.majormarketprofiles.com.

Glover, Tony. "Users Switch to Laptops." *MicroScope,* 4 April 2005.

"Hoover's Company Capsules," 2004. Available from http://www.hoovers.com.

"HP Launched Media Center PC in China." *PC World,* April 2004.

Lazich, Robert S., ed. *Market Share Reporter.* Detroit: Thomson Gale, 2004.

Leopold, George. "U.S. Relaxes Export Restrictions on PCs, MPUs." *Electronic Engineering Times,* 7 January 2002.

Menn, Joseph. "Gateway Stock Drops After Strategy Swing." *Los Angeles Times,* 1 March 2002.

"Microsoft Extends the Media Center PC." *PC Magazine,* 9 January 2004.

"PC Outlook Is Still Strong, According to IDC: Portable Adoption and Growth in Emerging Markets Remain Key Drivers." IDC, 16 June 2005. Available from http://www.idc.com.

"PC Recovery Continues, Fueled by Strong Performance in Europe and Moderate Enterprise Demand, According to IDC." IDC, 15 July 2004. Available from http://www.idc.com.

"Personal Computer Prices Industrywide Fell By 9 Percent During the First Three Quarters of 2003." *Purchasing,* 3 June 2004.

"Replacement Purchases Will Drive PC Industry." *Fairfield County Business Journal,* 31 May 2004.

Salkever, Alex. "Finally, a Chance for Apple to Flourish; Steve Jobs Certainly Has the Needed Pieces. The Key Question: Will its Hot Products and a Major Retail Effort Boost Market Share?" *Business Week,* 23 January 2002.

"Servers." *Information Age,* 10 March 2005.

"Strong PC Growth Seen in 2004." *Client Server News,* 1 March 2004.

Taylor, Josh. "Gateway Crashes the Living Room." *PC World,* April 2004.

Tompkins, Joshua. "Monster Mainframes Battle for Bragging Rights." *Popular Science,* June 2005.

"Top 500 Supercomputer Rankings Show IBM Surge." *eWeek,* 22 June 2005.

U.S. Department of Labor, Bureau of Labor Statistics. "Computer and Electronic Product Manufacturing," 23 July 2004. Available from http://www.bls.gov.

SIC 7374

NAICS 518210

DATA PROCESSING SERVICES

Data processing firms provide diverse computer-related services primarily to other businesses. Specialties within the industry include:

- Data entry
- Database management
- Text or graphics digitization
- Payroll processing
- Credit card transaction processing
- Medical claims billing
- Computer time leasing
- Off-site data management facilities

Certain firms in the industry also perform computer systems design, hardware consulting, contract maintenance, on-site management, and integration services. For discussion of these activities, see **Computer Services**.

INDUSTRY SNAPSHOT

A key beneficiary of the global trend toward outsourcing non-core business functions, the data processing industry obtained double-digit sales growth in leading markets throughout much of the 1990s, and continued to grow well into the new millennium. According to the Bureau of Labor Statistics, the computer and data processing industry was the fastest growing industry in the U.S. economy, with employment projected to increase 86 percent between 2000 and 2010. During 2000, the information technology outsourcing market, a loose measure of data processing receipts, was nearly 20 percent of all outsourcing expenditures in the United States. According to International Data Corp., total global outsourcing spending was projected to reach US$151 billion by 2010.

Long-term prospects for the data processing industry worldwide remain strong. Trends supporting industry growth include a continued swing toward outsourcing for cost savings and, in some countries, a shortage of technologically savvy workers available to firms outside the information technology industries. The Outsourcing Institute reported that, outsourcing related to e-commerce functions continued to be the fastest growing sector, with an annual growth rate of about 18 percent. The institute also claimed that demand for such support would continue to increase. By 2004, the institute reported that while the original intent of outsourcing was to save money, the reasons have ballooned to include the desire for access to the best providers in the industry, but on an as-needed basis.

By 2004, the outlook for data processing services was strong, as the outsourcing of IT services in general began an upswing. The Bureau of Labor Statistics reported more than 286,000 U.S. employees in the industry in 2003, the vast majority of whom worked in computer or administrative support positions.

ORGANIZATION AND STRUCTURE

Data processing companies perform services such as credit card authorization and billing, data entry, medical claims processing, payroll processing, and off-site data center management. Data processing services generally use their own facilities and proprietary software to process their customers' data. Many of the big data processing services tend to specialize. Historically, the largest segments of the industry by revenue were data center management, payroll processing, and credit card transaction processing, but with the proliferation of the Internet and the growing popularity of e-commerce, new sectors in the data processing services industry have become popular including online database management and Web site hosting and management.

Although many industry firms work with multi-year contracts, data processing services are often delivered on either a timesharing or a transaction basis. A timesharing service vendor usually sells customers a portion of time on a large computer. Timesharing is valuable to companies that need access to computing power that they could not otherwise afford. Companies also use timesharing services to handle part of their data processing needs in cases where their in-house facilities cannot accommodate the additional capacity, or when they are upgrading or building their own in-house computing systems.

Firms that provide transaction processing services assume responsibility for a company's high-volume office functions, such as payroll processing. Transaction providers base their rates on the number of transactions processed, rather than on the time it takes to process them (as with timesharing). One disadvantage for establishments that provide this kind of service is that transaction processing is sensitive to shifts in the economy. If a company offers payroll services, for instance, it may find that during a recession a client that trims its workforce needs fewer payroll checks processed.

Many companies turned to outsourcing in the late 1990s because of their increased need to consolidate operations, control costs, and make more efficient use of existing resources. Outsourcing continued to experience substantial growth into the early 2000s. Outsourcing has a particular appeal to companies that often spend hundreds of millions of dollars a year on data processing. Because computers generally account for between 3 to 5 percent of a company's operating budget, using an outsourcing vendor can lower costs significantly. The vendor is able to offer computerization on a large scale and can consolidate its data centers. The vendor will typically charge a fixed (or at least predictable) annual amount, and this gives the customer better control over costs.

The United States continues to command the greatest share of the world's data processing business. This is true in part because U.S. companies have been quicker to outsource various data management tasks, notably payroll management and credit card transaction processing, to independent services that specialize in the various kinds of data handling.

The United States also has been quick to adapt to changing technologies brought on by the increased use of the Internet. Major industry participants in the United States, several of which lead the world in certain service categories, have also aggressively courted business worldwide and are market leaders within other countries, particularly in Canada and Europe. In addition to the leading companies that primarily sell computer services, the global market also is served by major hardware companies such as IBM, which have found that offering contract data management services can help cushion their profits during volatile periods in the hardware business.

Legal and Trade Issues. The U.S. government has placed a high priority on removing the barriers to cross-border trade and investment. Information service companies have benefited from implementation of both the North American Free Trade Agreement (NAFTA), and expansion of the General Agreement on Tariffs and Trade (GATT) to include services under the General Agreement on Trade in Services (GATS). Because its companies are so central to the world industry, the United States accrues a significant trade surplus in computer service revenues each year.

Provisions regulating telecommunications and intellectual property protection are important to the data processing industry. One of the greatest challenges facing the industry is the need to develop methods to protect personal privacy, security, and intellectual property. Industry firms process highly sensitive information for consumers and businesses—including paychecks, credit card transactions, and medical information—and thus data security is of paramount importance. As a larger portion of transactions began to take place either on the Internet or through company intranets, the need for security grew as data became susceptible to theft, credit card fraud, and computer viruses.

The International Chamber of Commerce (ICC) started to focus on security-related issues surrounding electronic commerce. The ICC created the Commission on Telecommunications and Information Technologies to develop policies on information security. The ICC also created the Electronic Commerce Project (ECP). The ECP consisted of experts from various other ICC commissions including Banking Technique and Practice, Telecommunications and Information Technologies, Financial Services and Insurance, Transport, and International Commercial Practice, and was created to promote safe and secure e-business transactions. In 2001, the project was divided into three major areas including the General Usage for Internationally Digitally Ensured Commerce (GUIDEC), the Electronic Trade Practices Working Group, and E-terms service. GUIDEC, a set of international rules, definitions, and guidelines for the use of electronic authentication techniques, was considered to be one of the first sets of global regulations for electronic commerce.

BACKGROUND AND DEVELOPMENT

Many of the world's leading data processing service companies began as early computer designers and manufacturers. Control Data Corporation (now known as Ceridian Corporation) was established in 1957 by a dozen former Sperry Rand engineers. Co-founder Seymour Cray, an American electronics engineer who designed early supercomputers, is regarded as one of the world's brightest and most influential computer designers.

The Second World War had a significant impact on the development of data processing companies because it hastened the conversion from office tabulating equipment to data processing. The computer industry grew after the conclusion of World War II, and a large number of companies formed that were devoted to data processing. The majority of these new companies specialized in the areas of payroll processing and banking.

A large portion of the companies in the computer and data processing and preparation service industry have strong historical ties to financial services. Some leading companies in the field grew out of the check and payroll processing area. Others like Control Data Corporation and TRW developed out of the defense industry, the military, and the scientific community.

One of the first major examples of outsourcing took place in 1989 when Eastman Kodak signed a 10-year contract with IBM. For the first time, outsourcing was seen as a viable alternative to in-house information systems. Other large companies followed suit, and by the late 1990s outsourcing, at least on a limited scale, was considered a norm in the United States and was a growing trend elsewhere in the world. By the early years of the 2000s, outsourcing was one of the fastest growing segments in the computer and data processing services industry.

In addition, companies increasingly utilized processing companies for "front office" functions. Up until the mid-1990s data processing services were used primarily for clerical, high-volume tasks like payroll processing, health care claims processing, and other general accounting and record keeping duties. Some organizations, however, began to take advantage of low-priced, higher performance computer technology to improve in areas such as customer service, fund transfers, materials replacement, or inventory requisition. As the Internet became a popular forum for business applications in the late 1990s and early 2000s, most companies looked to data processing firms for their expertise in handling complex data processing systems.

The global computer outsourcing industry as a whole grew by as much as 13 percent annually in the latter half of the 1990s, according to published figures from International Data Corporation (IDC). Outsource-related spending reached US$99 billion in 1998 and was expected to grow to more than US$151 billion by 2003. In 1998, processing services including payroll, claims, and credit card processing were responsible for nearly 60 percent (US$59.5 billion) of global outsource spending.

CURRENT CONDITIONS

Revenue from data processing and related services is expected to continue to increase as new methods of data processing are introduced. The increasing need of companies to integrate multi-vendor systems is one reason for this growth. Corporations and other end users purchase hardware and software from multiple vendors. This means that organizations can build more cost-effective computer-based information systems. The complexity of designing and maintaining integrated systems has grown, and computer service firms help organizations with this. Specifically, data processing providers' staff provide the expertise to process the requirements, and work with other computer consultants to design the system.

Several factors led to the increased use of outsourcing in the data processing services industry, including globalization, privatization, deregulation, and technological advancement. The United States continues to dominate the industry, but the information systems and processing services segments in other countries were expected to experience steady growth. IDC estimated that in some countries, growth rates were reaching nearly 27 percent per year. IDC also believed that the Asia/Pacific region would increase its spending on outsourcing by 15 percent per year.

In the mid-2000s, business continued to rise for this industry segment. Fueled by increasing activity in bank and merchant accounts, and coupled with the stabilizing economy and favorable business climate, the industry was growing steadily. By 2004, the health care industry had become a major market for processing accounts. The use of patient information cards, similar to credit and debit cards, but without payment functions, was on the horizon. In California, for example, insurance provider Spot Check offered medical cards with magnetic stripes. This card design allowed the patient to swipe it and give medical providers instant access to patient information such as insurance, doctor, and referrals.

Research and Technology

Consumer demand for electronic data continued to grow during the mid-2000s. Stimulants to growth in the industry included the expansion of e-commerce and a flood of new services related to developments in computer technology. Such services included computer mapping, computerized airline ticketing, electronic toll processing, Web site design, and online database management.

Data warehousing, the organization and assembly of data created from day-to-day business operations, became increasingly popular during the late 1990s. Companies that needed an efficient method of analyzing business transactions often turned to computer and data processing firms to manage the flood of data brought on by new technological advancements. This was extremely important for companies with online marketplaces. Having data placed in a warehouse allowed the company to retrieve important demographic and sales information that was beneficial to business and marketing plans. The need for data warehousing was expected to continue to grow as both brick and mortar companies and dot-com firms utilized advanced data management technology to analyze information, make business forecasts, and control inventory.

Workforce

The Bureau of Labor Statistics reported that the computer and data processing services industry was the fastest growing industry in the economy in the new millennium. This industry was expected to account for 36.6 percent by 2006. Industry employment was expected to increase by 86.0 percent between 2000 and 2010.

Employees typically work in an office environment, telecommute, or work at a client's office. The majority of the workforce falls within the 25-34 age group, while the second largest group is 35-44 years of age. The largest occupational group in the industry is comprised of computer analysts, computer engineers, and computer programmers. The level of education needed for employment in this industry varies with each job and ranges from a high school diploma to a college degree, as well as specialized training.

Industry Leaders

Electronic Data Systems Corp. The leading data processing company in the United States is Electronic Data Systems (EDS), which for more than 40 years has provided claims processing for the U.S. federal and state Medicaid and Medicare programs. In addition, the company is the primary provider of data processing services for General Motors. In 2004 EDS posted sales of US$20.7 billion and employed 117,000 people. Forty-three percent of sales stemmed from international operations. EDS also provides services related to systems integration, network and systems operations, data center management, application development, outsourcing, and management consulting. In 2005, EDS announced a joint venture company with Towers Perrin called ExellerateHRO (85 percent owned by EDS), which combined EDS' payroll and related human resource outsourcing business with the pension, health and welfare administration service business of Towers Perrin.

EDS was founded in 1962 by H. Ross Perot, a disgruntled IBM salesman. After presenting IBM executives with his idea of providing companies with electronic data processing management services, only to be turned down, Perot decided to do it himself. It took Perot five months to find his first customer, but when he did he found himself pioneering the long-term, fixed-price contract. At the time, service companies usually offered 60- to 90-day contracts. EDS contracts were written for a five-year period.

In the 1960s the company became involved in Medicare and Medicaid claims processing, insurance company data processing, and data management for banks. EDS eventually established itself as the number one service provider in all three of these market segments. Acquired by General Motors Corporation in 1984, EDS was later spun off as an independent company in 1996. Although EDS had long been highly diversified, services to General Motors still accounted for 9.5 percent of EDS's revenues in 2004, although this figure had been steadily falling.

In May 2007, EDS announced it was selected by the U.S. General Services Administration to provide end-to-end satellite communications services to all federal government agencies under the Satellite Services-II contract. Related services enable agencies to obtain satellite communications bandwidth plus experience many diverse applications. Those applications include distance learning, streaming video, Telemedicine, broadcast satellite service plus engineering and maintenance support services.

Another May 2007 announcement spotlighted EDS' purchase of a 74.9 percent stake in the IT arm of KarstadtQuelle, Itellium Systems & Services GmbH. The agreement called for EDS to handle running, development and maintenance of KarstadtQuelle's applications for eight years. Estimated value for the contract was US$1 billion.

Affiliated Computer Services, Inc. Dallas, Texas-based Affiliated Computer Services (ACS) is a leading supplier of business process and information technology outsourcing, with local and state governments providing about 59 percent of its revenues in 2004. In the government sector, ACS provides focus on transaction processing and program management services such as child support payment processing, electronic toll collection, welfare and community services, and traffic violations processing. For commercial customers, in addition to systems integration and information technology outsourcing services, the company provides data processing services in the areas of healthcare claims processing and financial information processing. Total revenues in 2004 were US$4.1 billion. The company sold its federal business to Lockheed Martin Corporation in 2004. In 2005 the company reported having 52,000 employees. By 2006, business process outsourcing accounted for 75 percent of sales. Revenues were reported as being US$5.4 billion.

In April 2007, ACS announced that the Colorado Department of Health Care Policy and Financing awarded a three-year contact to continue operating the state's Medicaid Management Information System. ACS had operated the system since 1996. The contract calls for ACS to process more than 25 million claims annually. Additional services include providing systems development and maintenance, pharmacy benefits management, decision support services, fraud and abuse detection and recovery, claims processing, call center and program policy support plus third-party recovery.

Another April 2007 announcement reflected that ACS had completed the acquisition of certain Albion Inc. company assets. Albion was a company specializing in integrated eligibility software solutions. The acquisition enhanced capabilities of ACS in the health and human services area.

Computer Sciences Corporation. With 2005 revenues of US$14.1 billion, Computer Sciences (CSC) is a diversified computer services contractor to industry and governments worldwide. That year, 40 percent of company revenues stemmed from sources outside the United States, while 33 percent came from contracts with the U.S. federal government and 27 percent from U.S. commercial firms. Known for its strong position in the information technology services sector, the company provides outsourcing, management consulting, network design, and systems integration. CSC was ranked as the global market leader in insurance business process outsourcing (BPO). The company had 200 BPO customers and 20 BPO centers around the world in 2005.

By 2007, CSC reported having 77,000 employees. It had revenue of US$14.7 billion in 2006. CSC announced its plans to acquire Covansys for US$34 per share in an all-cash transaction. The transaction was valued at approximately US$1.3 billion. It was considered as an important move toward achieving the CSC strategic goal of increasing shareholder value and growing more business. The acquisition nearly doubled the size of CSC's workforce in India to approximately 14,000 employees. Both Convasys and CSC's operations in India were listed among the top 10 places to work for IT professionals in India.

First Data Corp. Posting US$10.1 billion in revenues during 2004, First Data Corp. originated as American Express Information Services Corp. in 1982; the name was changed to First Data Corp. in 1992. In 1995 it merged with competitor First Financial Management Corp., which also held the Western Union chain of money transfer outlets. In the same year First Data purchased Card Establishment Services, a major merchant credit card processing operation formerly held by Citicorp, making it the largest credit card transaction processor in the United States, a position it continued to hold in the early 2000s.

First Data's payment services business accounted for nearly 40 percent of sales prior to a restructuring announced in 2006. The company spun off Western Union plus related Orlandi Valuta and Vigo Remittance units. First Data provides check verification through Telecheck and ATM network operation through NYCE. In 2004, First Data further expanded when it acquired Cashcard Australia Limited. During 2005 the company had 33,000 employees. Kohlberg Kravis Roberts agreed to buy First Data.

First Data agreed to use Vivotech, a contactless payments company responsible for developing Near Field Communication hardware, products. Those products include Near Field Communication terminals, wallets and over-the-air provisioning systems for mobile commerce.

Automatic Data Processing Inc. Operating as the world's largest payroll and tax filing processor, Automatic Data Processing (ADP) generated 2004 sales of US$7.4 billion. ADP's employer services unit, which accounted for two-thirds of its sales, handled nearly 470,000 business accounts. By 2007, ADP reported more than US$7 billion in revenues and 570,000 clients worldwide.

In addition to its payroll processing, ADP has a wide array of other data processing and related services, including brokerage services, inventory and data services for the auto and truck dealer industry, and accounting and insurance estimates for insurers. The company made nearly two dozen acquisitions from 1998 through early 2002 as part of its strategy to build its small business and Internet-related services.

ADP was founded in 1949 by Henry Taub as Automatic Payrolls, a payroll preparation service. During the 1950s the company continued selling its payroll services to new clients. The company changed its name to Automatic Data Processing in 1961 and went public. The following year ADP bought its first computer and began offering back-office services to brokerage houses, beginning the automation of the company's manual accounting systems.

The 1970s marked an especially fertile time of growth for ADP. The company bought more than 30 companies engaged in data and payroll processing, shareholder services, computer networks, inventory control, or automated banking in the United States, Canada, and Germany. In 1971 revenues reached US$50 million. ADP has recorded per share earnings growth for 40 consecutive years.

In April 2007, ADP made the welcome announcement that it was hiring for its Northwest El Paso, Texas facility. There were more than 200 part- and full-time positions available. A hiring fair was held to facilitate filling positions.

In May 2007, Visa USA announced a five-year agreement with ADP Employer Services to offer Visa-branded cards to its clients. The Visa ADP Total Pay card was issued by several Visa member financial institutions. Visa Payroll cards are accepted at the same outlets that accept Visa debit cards.

Capgemini. France's Capgemini, became one of the world's top computer service outsourcing firms, and the largest in Europe, when it merged with Ernst & Young Consulting in 2000. In 2005, Capgemini, previously known as Cap Gemini Ernst & Young, employed more than 61,000 and had revenues of about US$8.2 billion. It had operations in more than 30 countries. The firm provides management consulting, systems design and management, and professional services to customers in Europe, North America, and the Asia/Pacific region. The company provided business process outsourcing services to many companies, including Canada's Hydro One (human resource and finance functions) and Australia's BlueScope Steel (accounting and human resources services).

According to Kable research, Capgemini rose from seventh to fourth place in rankings of the top suppliers to public ICT market. Analysts acknowledged that Capgemini had experienced its first full year delivering a huge HMRC Aspire contract. It was among the leading service providers who had increased their influence at the expense of smaller generalists. Kable stressed that recent achievements did not guarantee ongoing success.

Ceridian Corp. Ceridian had 2006 sales of approximately US$1.6 billion. About three-quarters of its revenues came from the human resource solutions segment accounting for approximately 70 percent of the company's sales. In 2005, Ceridian reported having 9,433 employees.

The company sold off its defense electronics business to General Dynamics in order to concentrate on information services. Previously known as Control Data Corp., Ceridian sold some operations, closed others, and spun off its computer business as Control Data Systems in order to overcome substantial losses suffered in the 1980s. It also spun off Arbitron, its demographics research service, which was not considered part of data processing. Under its current structure, Ceridian has two main units: Human Resource Services and Comdata. Along with its payroll and tax processing business, the firm also provides benefits administration, human resource information systems, and training to clients in the United States, Canada, and the United Kingdom. Ceridian's Comdata operations were fortified by the firm's 1998 acquisition of a US$28 million per year service offered by competitor First Data Corp. In exchange, Ceridian sold Comdata's US$130 million gaming services business to First Data, a move lauded by analysts as signaling Ceridian's commitment to the data processing business. Through this segment, the company provides fuel cards, licenses, cash advances, vehicle escorts, and trucking industry-related services.

During the late 1990s, a growing share of Ceridian's data processing revenue came from foreign acquisitions. In 1998 it purchased the payroll processing units of two leading Canadian banks, Toronto-Dominion Bank and Canadian Imperial Bank of Commerce, valued at about US$77 million in annual receipts. The move made Ceridian the leading payroll-outsourcing firm in Canada. In the new millennium, Ceridian planned to diversify its product line by adding Internet-based services and also continued to look for key acquisitions.

In 2006, Ceridian experienced a challenge from its major investor. William Ackman, principal for Pershing Square Capital Management, ordered Ceridian to spin off its Comdata payment card business. The order was reportedly based on lagging sales and profits for the human resources division. Ackman felt spinning off Comdata would allow Ceridian to focus more on building the troubled division. Ceridian CEO Kathy Marinello instead announced that the company was planning a strategic review to determine the best option. In response, Pershing proposed an alternative slate of directors to challenge company's nominees.

In April 2007, Ceridian admitted its responsibility for the leaking of confidential data to the Internet. Innovative Interactive, a New York advertising firm, unfortunately had confidential data released about its 150 employees to a Web site. The data included names, addresses, Social Security numbers, salary information and checking account data. Ceridian claimed the information ended up on the Web site of a former employee who took the data by accident upon departing from the company in March 2006.

In May 2007, Ceridian announced that its Comdata subsidiary's card was being accepted at the Ambassador Bridge. That bridge was one of the international crossing points between U.S. and Canada. Drivers could swipe a Comdata Card in order to pay their tolls.

Another May 2007 announcement came after accusations that Comdata Executive Vice President Gary Krow had held unauthorized meetings with Pershing and revealed confidential information to third parties. Consequentially, Krow was fired. Pershing's Founder Ackman claimed that Krow revealed contents of letters criticizing the performance of former CEO Ronald Turner. Pershing had planned to use those critiques in its campaign to remove company directors. CEO Marinello shared a five-point plan that may include offshoring jobs and consolidating facilities.

MAJOR COUNTRIES IN THE INDUSTRY

In 2004, there were more than U.S. 30,000 companies providing data processing and preparation, according to Zapdata. Of this number, only 40 had more than 1,000 employees. But while the United States dominates the world data processing and preparation market, its foreign competitors are starting to gain market share. Most of the large U.S. data processing services providers have successful operations overseas.

A factor pointing toward growth in the Asia/Pacific data processing services industry is the increasing expansion of the information systems outsourcing market in that region. The region is expected to increase spending by 15 percent per year during the early 2000s. As more companies in various countries begin to utilize personal computers and the Internet, demand in the data processing services industry is expected to rise.

In the past, Japan possessed a comparatively underdeveloped data processing industry. This primarily was due to obstacles in Japanese trade legislation and the structure of the Japanese economy. Japanese companies were cautious about investing in multimedia and information delivery. They also had fewer resources to invest than they did before the prolonged recession of the 1990s, and directed much of the available capital into maintaining manufacturing competitiveness. The country did appear to be making headway in the industry in the new millennium. Japanese information technology providers began acquiring firms, both local and foreign, to beef up product lines and created international subsidiaries to provide data processing services.

FURTHER READING

"ACS Awarded USD67m Contract by State of Colorado." *Telecomworldwire,* 27 April 2007.

"ACS Completes Acquisition of Assets of Albion." *Telecomworldwire,* 27 April 2007.

"Brave EDS Move Could Backfire." *Computer Weekly,* 13 January 2004.

"Business Week in Review." 28 April 2007. Available from http:/www.startribunecom.

"Capgemini and HP Gain Ground in Public Sector Marketplace." *Kablenet,* 2 May 2007.

"Comdata Card Now Accepted at Ambassador Bridge." *PR Newswire,* 9 May 2007.

"CSC to Acquire Convansys for $34.00 Per Share Acquisition Increases CSC's India Delivery Capabilities, Accelerates Development of Strategic Offshore Offerings." *PR Newswire,* 25 April 2007.

"Dissident Shareholder: Ceridian Firing Completes "Corporate House Cleaning." 14 May 2007. Available from http://www.twincities.com

"EDS Selected by GSA for Satellite Communications Services Contract for Federal Agencies." *Canada Newswire English,* 4 May 2007.

Friedlander, David. "Why Outsource Desktop Management?" *Computer Weekly,* 21 February 2002.

"Hoover's Company Capsules." 2007. Available from http://www.hoovers.com.

"Industry Report: Data Processing and Preparation (7374)." Dun & Bradstreet, accessed June 30, 2005. Available from http://www.zapdata.com.

Kuykendall, Lavonne. "Volume on the Rise for Top Processors." *American Banker,* 22 July 2004.

"The New Workplace: Outsourcing in Japan." The Outsourcing Institute, 2001.

Park, Andrew. "Can the Buddy System Boost EDS?" *Business Week Online,* 14 January 2004.

Peterson, Susan E. "Ceridian Sees Strong Earnings." *Star Tribune,* 1 May 2007.

"The Processing Industry Views Health Care as a Major Market." *Cardline,* 9 January 2004.

Rosato, Donna. "ADP: Here's a Company That Will Benefit from the Economic Rebound—and Doesn't Have to Worry About Rising Interest Rates." *Money,* 1 June 2004.

Ryan, Vince. "First Data Invests in Mobile Commerce Outfit." 3 May 2007. Available from http://www.banknet360.com.

U.S. Census Bureau. *Service Annual Survey.* Washington, 2004. Available from http://www.census.gov.

Wels-Maug, Cornelia. "EDS Buys a Majority Stake in Itellium Systems & Services." *Telecoms and Software News,* 9 May 2007. Available from http://www.ovum.com.

SIC 7371, 7373, 7378

NAICS 541511, 541512, 811212

INFORMATION TECHNOLOGY SERVICES

The information technology (IT) services industry provides the following services on a contract or fee basis:

- computer programming services
- custom computer software design and analysis
- modifications of custom software
- training software end users and systems administrators
- integrated systems design
- computer maintenance and repair, including hardware and peripheral installations, upgrades, replacements, and troubleshooting
- hardware and software consulting

Additional IT services include computer services outsourcing, disaster recovery, and overall facilities management, which involves on-site management of a customer's computer systems and networks, including computer maintenance and repair. Service firms that provide off-site data processing services are covered separately under **Data Processing Services** and developers of mass-produced software are discussed in detail under **Packaged Software**. Certain industry participants provide consulting services unrelated to information technology; these activities are included under **Management Consulting Services**.

INDUSTRY SNAPSHOT

The information technology services market realized exceptional growth in the late 1990s. IT services represented US$350 billion worldwide in programming, systems integration, consulting, outsourcing, education and training, and maintenance services revenues in 1998 alone. By 2004, this value had increased to US$607.8 billion, according to Gartner. The world leader in the IT service sector continued to be IBM, accounting for 7.6 percent of the total sales worldwide.

Following the economic downturn of the early 2000s, which lasted into 2003, the IT services industry suffered through declining revenues and mass job insecurity. By 2004, industry consolidation was the norm; *InternetWeek* reported 57 mergers and acquisitions in the first half of the year alone. The overall outlook for outsourcing was positive, with more growth expected in management services. As of the mid-2000s, 59 percent of the market, remained with U.S. companies.

ORGANIZATION AND STRUCTURE

IT services constitute one of the largest, relatively unregulated, and most rapidly changing industries dealing with high technology. As a result, the rigid organization and structure of the early days, when mainframe computer manufacturers dominated the industry, has disintegrated into many different webs of mergers, alliances, and commercial relationships among manufacturers, independent service companies, and customers. The constancy for companies large and small, for manufacturers, retailers, and independent service companies, has been more competition for IT services and increasing demands for service and reliability from customers. Though IT service providers prefer to sign lucrative, comprehensive contracts as sole service providers for their clients, most companies still use multiple vendors to meet IT service needs rather than rely on all-inclusive contracts.

New technology, competition in the industry, and growing demands from customers have led to blurred distinctions among programming, maintenance, and outsourcing services. Large mainframe manufacturers continued to rely on services for a large part of their revenues. IBM created a separate division, IBM Global Services, that provides customers with network services (for all products, IBM or not). The company offers a product called ServicePacs, providing maintenance, disaster recovery, and other services for small and midsize businesses. IBM's ServicePacs were offered through resale channels. IBM added two more service-oriented products in 1998—ServiceSuite, for midsize companies, and ServiceSelect, sold directly to IBM's largest customers. IBM also devised a partnership with J.D. Edwards to offer its outsourced energy resource planning services to IBM customers.

Meanwhile, other computer manufacturers concentrated on acquisition to bolster service offerings. Computer Associates (CA) offered clients total "end-to-end" product and service solutions. Wang Laboratories Inc. made an agreement to acquire Olivetti SpA's computer services business. Compaq acquired Digital Equipment Corporation (DEC)—some believe primarily because of DEC's services offerings. Other large companies, such as Hewlett-Packard, not only offered IT services to their customers but then outsourced those services to smaller service companies specializing in a particular area of expertise, such as help desk support or maintenance and repair. Customers calling the support numbers were not always aware that they were talking to a separate service provider.

Computer manufacturers are not the only companies heavily involved in IT services. In partnership with Microsoft, Oracle, and Sun Microsystems, the consulting firm Ernst & Young offered an Advanced Development Center and Accelerated Solutions Environment, places where clients could come to the company to plot strategy and acquire resources from software solutions to mainframe hardware. Xerox acquired a systems integration company to support document-management systems sales and a software vendor to support new application management/outsourcing services to be launched in summer of 1998. And Big Six accounting firm Price Waterhouse entered into a merger with Coopers & Lybrand in July of 1998. PriceWaterhouseCoopers, the result, was the largest IT services firm in the world, generating more than US$13 billion in annual revenue and employing more than 160,000 people. PriceWaterhouseCoopers does business in more than 160 countries.

In response to the changing market, countries around the globe participated in the adoption of an Information Technology Agreement, which in 2000 eliminated tariffs on many information and communication technology products, such as hardware, software, electronic components, and digital photocopiers. It was anticipated that countries participating in the World Trade Organization agreement would realize job growth in almost every industry by accelerating technological development, lowering production costs, and increasing productivity. Twenty-eight countries signed the initial agreement at the Singapore Ministerial in 1996, representing almost 85 percent of the information technology trade. By the beginning of 2001, the Information Technology Agreement had 40 participants that made up about 93 percent of the global information technology industry. A few holdouts were eventually expected to sign the Information Technology Agreement.

In the United States, the IT industry was served by the Information Technology Association of America. With 500 domestic members and partners in 49 countries, the ITAA provided information and services to the industry as well as help in strategic planning and policy.

BACKGROUND AND DEVELOPMENT

Computers revolutionized the workplace and made a dramatic impact on world markets for many goods and services. None of that impact would have been possible, of course, without the programming that instructs computers what to do and how to do it. In recent years, a growing number of companies have come to rely on customized services to make computers perform specified functions and talk to other systems within the same organization. Changes in technology and market conditions dramatically altered the technology services industry. These include the rise in popularity of desktop computers and client/server systems; the increasing demand for new, better, and cheaper technology from the business community; advances in packaged software; and the rise of Internet technology. The more computers do for the workplace, the more the workplace demands of computers—a key driver of the information technology services market.

In the late 1980s, networking became a more important part of computer programming services, particularly as more local area networks (LANs) became connected to other LANs, mainframes, and minicomputers. Programmers were increasingly asked to customize network operating systems, workstation operating systems, and network shells (the software that determines whether user commands are processed by individual workstations or by the network). One of the challenges of network programming is to follow the open system interconnection reference model, developed by the International Organization for Standardization (ISO) to develop standard network protocols.

With the world economic recovery in the early and mid-1990s, the computer services industry emerged, reflecting the new popularity of personal computers, laptops, and notebooks and the rise of client-server systems. As prices dropped and competition sharpened, manufacturers were forced to embrace open systems, producing machines that could work in conjunction with other manufacturers' hardware. Sometimes customized services were offered as part of a package. However, it became more common for manufacturers to purchase equipment at the most reasonable cost and then contract independent services firms to make sure all the components worked together and customize the software for specific user needs. As a result, businesses were more likely to buy system components from different manufacturers and shop around among various software manufacturers to meet their needs. In this new era of open architecture, the computer industry has created demand for more flexibility and all-around technical competence from computer service professionals. Thus, workers who can work on many different types of systems and machines are the most highly sought.

Heightened competition among hardware manufacturers not only led to lower prices for computing power but also led to better service, from longer warranty protection to promises of improved technical support, including help desks and on-site repair. More and more, particularly among large clients, contracts required repair and maintenance firms to do more than simply keep machines running. They also were asked to develop, integrate, maintain, and inventory hardware. For many major computer manufacturers, repair and maintenance and other post-sale services to customers, all lumped under the general heading of "aftercare," amounted to up to 50 percent of annual revenues. Many companies have moved to outsourcing, where they contract with a third party, which may or may not be the hardware supplier, to provide maintenance and service. In some cases, the third party brings in its own people and takes over an existing contract.

IT service professionals were being asked to integrate software into the workplace and to improve interfaces and applications to make them more efficient and intuitive to end users. Most corporations outside the computer industry don't want to become technology companies and their executives don't want to become technology experts in order to obtain the systems and software that would make their businesses run better. Rather, they want technology—particularly information systems and computer networks—to make the organization operate more smoothly and efficiently and to help the people who work for the company, including the executives, do a better job. They want system-wide planning that not only allows workers to perform business functions, but also track how the system is being used and how it could be used more efficiently. Third-party independent service providers are able to handle the computer needs of more than one client, thus spreading technical overhead costs among a number of clients. This economy of scale helps computer purchasers hold down maintenance and repair costs to less than 10 percent of the purchase price of the equipment. Many computer consumers arrange for maintenance and service from computer manufacturers, either as a package or as part of separate aftercare contracts. Increasingly, however, the trend among computer purchasers has been to shop around for maintenance and repair service contracts—not only from the manufacturers, but also from other manufacturers and the growing number of independent IT service providers.

Competition among service providers has led to some innovative packaging and marketing of IT services, including service contracts that bundle system development, programming, and maintenance with a variety of other services. One concept that has grown in popularity is the "turn-key" system, under which a corporation contracts with the service providers for a ready-to-operate computer system including all the hardware, software, training, maintenance, and repair support services necessary. The companies that offer outsourcing for computer maintenance and repair have spread the message that they can do as much or more—and at lower cost—than in-house technicians.

The international market helped a number of smaller U.S. computer software programming services grow. However, companies in the industry include not only the smaller firms concentrating on specific services, but also computer giants that have branched out into these services. A number of major companies reconfigured themselves in the 1990s to put a new emphasis on professional computer services. NCR Corp., for example, created two service-oriented divisions, one of which concentrated on consulting and systems integration with a focus on helping customers move into open systems and develop system-wide architectures. The U.S. giants IBM and Digital Equipment Corporation (later part of Compaq), two of the world's largest suppliers of networked computer systems, software, and services, both placed new emphasis on professional services as an important part of company reorganizations.

Enterprise resource planning (ERP) software is a growing area of customized programming for corporate customers. ERP software is customized to help companies manage complete business, manufacturing, and communication functions, all within one system. Leaders in the development of ERP software included SAP AG, Oracle, Baan, and PeopleSoft. In 1997 Oracle released Oracle Applications, a suite of 30 software modules for financial and supply-chain management, manufacturing, project management, human resources, and sales and marketing, customized for each customer according to its industry. According to a *Fortune* article, ERP software helps corporate technology professionals automate manufacturing processes, organize accountants' books, streamline departments (like human resources), and many other functions. Companies that offer ERP design and implementation solutions are among the fastest growing in the IT industry. ERP has become so important in business because it takes care of all detail work for the client, including everything from product planning to interactions with suppliers and tracking orders. ERP software is an e-commerce solution that keeps businesses from having to juggle all their components and avoid the risk of crucial details falling through the cracks.

In the 1990s, one of the hottest sectors of the IT industry was the upgrading of systems to accommodate the year 2000. In the late 1990s, companies hired outside vendors to develop strategies and implement system-wide fixes. The problem stemmed from practices in the 1960s and 1970s when memory was costly and programmers saved a good deal by storing dates in systems and software as only the last two digits; for example, 1975 was represented as 75. However, when the date changed to the year 2000, computers across the globe would read 2000 as 1900, potentially causing crippling system failures throughout the world. The problem affected hardware, software, networks, legacy systems, and any machines that relied on a central processing unit with embedded clocks or dates. And since companies worldwide were facing the same deadline, they all were competing for the same resources to fix the problem—namely, programmers (to isolate the problems and fix old code) and testing personnel. IT service providers were cashing in on the problem, offering comprehensive year 2000 solutions that helped companies identify and repair systems that weren't year 2000 compliant.

Likewise, in the late 1990s and early 2000s, another major conversion that put corporate resources in need of information technology services was the adoption of the euro (the standard European currency unit) as the new currency of the European Union. Twelve participating European Union countries (a few EU members opted out of the initial monetary union) began using the euro on January 1, 2002, when their national currencies became denominations of the euro rather than separately traded currencies. The twelve included Austria, Belgium, France, Germany, Italy, Portugal, Spain, Luxembourg, Finland, Ireland, Greece, and the Netherlands.

Other national currencies were eliminated in 2002. Such conversion requirements cost software developers up to US$300 billion. Banks and retailers needed software and system upgrades, but the conversion also extended to manufacturers and almost all other sectors of not only the European economies, but also those of companies and countries that did business with unified Europe. This major system change afforded IT services companies additional opportunity to offer comprehensive solution packages to companies doing business in Europe.

Although IT service revenues tend to slump when the global economy falters, the industry continued to see tremendous earnings growth during the late 1990s and, to a lesser extent, in the early 2000s. In part, this growth has been the result of a shortage in IT professionals, the sales of high-profit service contracts, and the growing demand for such services. After the economic downturn and terrorist attacks of 2001, IT services took a nosedive along with many other industry segments. However, by 2002 there was increasing demand from transportation and governmental entities.During this time period, billing rates rose far higher than the actual cost of labor.

CURRENT CONDITIONS

In the early to mid-2000s, one of the most notable trends in IT was that the drive in technology was being fueled by consumer demand. Traditionally, technological advances were developed and offered by the companies themselves. This created the demand for those products and services, which often were incompatible with competing offerings. However, in the more technologically advanced and aware world of the new century, consumers knew what they wanted and companies were scrambling to offer products and services to meet those desires.

Security issues continued to dominate the industry's projects. Financial companies in particular were looking at ways to improve security of their data, while retailers had similar concerns, particularly as web-based purchase activity was on the rise, but consumer confidence in the safety of the systems was on the decline.

By late 2003 and early 2004, a more stable economy and market growth in the U.S. supported demand for IT services across industry lines, particularly on a contract basis. Even so, many companies had already moved or were in the process of moving jobs offshore, making the immediate future somewhat uncertain for the labor force. Some industry analysts were concerned about the movement of white collar jobs, following the mass movement of blue collar employment. According to the ITAA, although the obvious negative effect on domestic employment was clear, the offshore movement will still help the economy as a whole due to inherent cost savings. The association took a firm stand against the offshore movement of government sector outsourcing, however. Overall, it was projected that the IT industry would demand more than 500,000 new skilled workers by 2008, with more than half of the positions would be based offshore.

Gartner had estimated the value of the IT services industry to be US$607.8 billion in 2004, up 6.7 percent from 2003 figures. The world leader in the industry continued to be IBM, which held 7.6 percent of the market. EDS held a 3.4 percent market share, while Fujitsu held 2.8 percent, and Hewlett-Packard, Accenture and CSC each held 2.3 percent.

In 2005, Gartner was predicting that IT outsourcing would grow globally from a level of about US$20 billion in 2004 to about US$50 billion by 2007. However, increasing wage costs coupled with increasing competition could mean tighter margins for IT service companies. Further, with the financial services industry being one of the largest users of IT services (spending 8.7 percent of their revenue on IT, according to Gartner), this sector was also expected to grow as it tried to compete in a world of increased consolidation and tighter regulations. India continued to expand its outsourcing capabilities, although China could catch up to it in the next few years due to its rapid economic growth in all industries.

RESEARCH AND TECHNOLOGY

Research in the IT services area during the late 1990s and early 2000s was focused on the issues facing companies as they approached the new millennium. These issues included the year 2000, the change in European currency, the rise of client/server and integrated systems, increased use of enterprise resource planning systems, and the integration of the Internet into complex business systems. Disaster planning also became an important part of the area of facilities management. When a computer system suffers a massive crash, either from an internal problem or because of an outside force, such as natural disaster or criminal attack, repair and maintenance personnel are often called in to recover data and restore the system.

Following the September 11, 2001, terrorist attacks, as well as numerous break-ins into supposedly secure corporate and educational sites (including the *New York Times* and Purdue University), information technology services companies increased their resolve to perfect encryption to lock out hacker assaults on client systems. In 2005, security issues and customized software development continued to be a leading component of IT service company offerings.

Companies offering programming services also dealt with the rapid expansion of new technologies. Some of those presenting special challenges for programmers include the rapid spread of analog to digital conversion in the electronics market and artificial intelligence (AI), including "smart" software and natural language processing. Smart software has many applications, but the most important are the large programs (financed by large corporations) that administer computer networks. Typically, these networks are too vast and complicated for human management, and production has become highly automated. Some examples include the Internet, urban traffic systems, waste control systems, aerospace production, and many other forms of manufacturing. All involve computer networks that communicate with, instruct, and monitor each other. Smart software can not only make sure things work smoothly within a system, it also can identify and resolve problems and system "bugs" before managers realize a potential problem is there.

WORKFORCE

The IT services industry has been hampered by a shortage of professionals, and this shortage was expected to heighten. Globally, Gartner research was predicting in 2005 that the number of IT staff would decline by 15 percent by 2010. The U.S. Department of Labor predicted a greater than 35 percent industry job growth through 2010. Other factors, such as integration of Internet applications, development of e-commerce, and the design and implementation of enterprise resource planning systems, all point toward increased demand for skilled professionals such as programmers and project managers. According to Karen Carrillo in *InformationWeek*, the top 10 most sought after IT skills were experience in project management, business management, ERM/ERP, infrastructure, architecture, the C++ programming language, data warehousing, Oracle programming, team-based work, and Unix programming. By 2003, job prospects and salaries were both on the upswing, but the hours were longer than they had been in the past.

In some respects, the shortage of programmers in the United States has created opportunities for workers from emerging countries, notably India, Pakistan, Indonesia, and China. Many engineers from Taiwan, China, Pakistan, India, and other nations in Southeast Asia have earned advanced degrees from U.S. colleges and universities. These engineers often work in Silicon Valley or for high-tech firms elsewhere in the United States. A number eventually return to their home markets or find work in other countries.

Whether in-house or on contract, computer programming services remain a significant part—typically one-third or more—of the average information systems budget for corporations. Other IT services accounted for another 20 percent. Personnel costs were expected to remain high because so many companies wanted specific applications, from customized customer support to management of inventory. Typically, the biggest outlays for custom programming services are for maintaining and upgrading older applications. Spending on encryption services, ERP systems, and rising salaries have seriously impacted corporate training budgets, and companies have not been able to offer as much training and tuition reimbursement as they have in the past.

INDUSTRY LEADERS

International Business Machines Corporation (IBM). Charles Flint created Calculating-Tabulating-Recording (CTR) in 1910 by merging two companies, International Time Recording Company and Computing Scale Company, with Tabulation Machine Company, which had been started by Herman Hallerith. In 1914 Thomas Watson was hired by Flint as general manager of CTR and later became president. Watson created a powerful business sales force that became known for superior customer service and devoted most of the company's resources to the tabulator division. Under his leadership, it quickly expanded in sales and size, moving into Europe, Asia, and Latin America. In 1924 CTR was renamed International Business Machines and focused on large tabulations machines. By 1949 IBM had operations in 58 countries and had created IBM World Trade Corporation, which enjoyed the same dominance in foreign markets as it did in the United States.

International Business Machines Corp. continued to be the world's largest provider of information technology services as well as computer products in 2004 with US$96.3 billion in revenues. IBM employed more than 369,000 people worldwide that year. IBM Global Services, which accounted for about 48 percent of revenues in 2004, was one of the company's fastest growing divisions, in part because IBM capitalized on its experience as the world's largest computer manufacturer. Before its services division was created, IBM support focused solely on IBM products. However, in 1995 it formed IBM Global Services by restructuring capabilities that had previously been managed by separate groups into an integrated global office. Global Services contained five units, including Integrated Systems Solutions Corp. (ISSC), IBM Global Network, Availability Services, the Consulting

Group, and Education and Training. Since its inception, IBM's service area has made profitable outsourcing deals with companies such as Rubbermaid, Kodak, and McDonnell Douglas. In 2005, IBM was continuing to look for growth through acquisitions in companies providing key software and services, as well as those in emerging growth countries, such as China, Russia, India, and Brazil.

Electronic Data Systems Corp (EDS). Electronic Data Systems, better known as EDS, was the founder of the information technology outsourcing industry, and in 2005 continued to be the largest IT services provider in the United States. Employing 117,000 who worked in 60 countries in 2004, EDS earned revenues of more than US$20.7 billion that year. One of the largest government contractors in the U.S., in the month of June 2005 alone, EDS, as the nation's largest supplier of Medicaid IT services, earned federal contracts of US$102 million as well as a US$48 million contract to provide services to Massachusetts' Medicaid program. The company also owns management consultant giant, A.T. Kearney.

EDS was founded in 1962 by H. Ross Perot. He started the company with US$1,000 and an idea for a company that provided "information services," with a focus on improving clients' business. EDS helps companies to meet business needs in the areas of systems and technology services, business process management, management consulting, electronic markets, and EDS' CoSourcing Service. The systems and technology area offered services such as systems development, systems integration, systems management and desktop services, and year 2000 conversion. Another area of high growth for EDS was its webmasters area. The company was awarded its first major contract in 1969 by Blue Shield of California. Subsequent major accounts included the U.S. Navy and Xerox, for whom EDS provides most of its information technology needs. By 1973 EDS revenues reached US$100 million. In 1984 General Motors purchased EDS, but EDS was spun off from GM in 1996. Services to GM still accounted for 30 percent of EDS revenues in 1997. Efforts to further global expansion included the 1990 acquisition of SD-Scicon, a U.K. computer services company, and the 1995 acquisition of A.T. Kearney, a global management consulting firm. EDS was the one of the largest IT services provider in the industry, with earnings of US$21.5 billion in 1997, approximately one-third of which was generated by outsourcing services for computer systems and networks. The company employed 110,000 people worldwide, making it the industry's fourth-largest employer. The boost in the IT industry was expected to translate into great rewards for EDS in 1997 and 1998. In 1997 EDS was estimated to generate more than US$15 billion in new service contracts, almost double the amount booked in 1996 (US$8.4 billion). In 2001 EDS listed revenues of US$21.5 billion, an indicator of company health. However, in early 2002 EDS saw its stock plunge more than 6 percent due to management problems, according to the *American Banker.* EDS signed service contracts in the spring of 2002 worth around US$1 billion, a sign of customer support for EDS services. By 2003, company revenues of US$21.5 billion and 132,000 employees made EDS one of the largest companies in the industry.

Fujitsu Limited. The world's third-largest IT services provider and the largest such provider in Japan, Tokyo-based Fujitsu earned revenues of about US$44 billion in 2004 of which about 44 percent could be attributed to its software and services division. About 70 percent of these revenues came from Japan, while 13.3 percent were from Europe, 9.8 percent from Australasia, and 6.7 percent from North America. The company is also a large supplier of computer hardware. With its foundings going back to 1935 as a manufacturing subsidiary of Fuji Electric, the company began producing computers in the 1960s.

Hewlett-Packard Company (HP). By 2005, Hewlett-Packard (HP) was active in 178 countries serving 1 billion customers. It was ranked number 11 on the *Fortune*500 listing that year. In 2004, the company employed 151,000 people, of which about 65,000 worked in its services division. Although predominantly a hardware and software provider, HP's services division works with its other departments as well as local systems integrators to provide IT solutions to its customers. Most of its services were for outsourcing. Approximately 17 percent of the company's total revenues of US$79.9 billion in 2004 were attributed to its services division.

William Hewlett and David Packard officially created Hewlett-Packard (HP) in 1939, although they worked together earlier to create eight oscillators for Walt Disney Studios. In 1966, HP created its first computer for internal use, never intending to enter the computer market. However, two years later it created the first desktop calculator capable of performing scientific calculations, and by 1974 committed itself to moving into the computer industry with the HP3000. The HP-85, Hewlett-Packard's first personal computer, was released in 1985. Reaction to it was poor because it was not compatible with IBM's designs. This caused HP not only to create IBM-compatible PCs, but to move toward making all its computers, at least in part, cross-compatible. To better position itself for the global market, it increased cooperative efforts, and in the late 1980s HP entered into trade agreements with companies such as Hitachi, Canon USA Inc., and Sony.

Hewlett-Packard's 2002 year began with a lawsuit filed by Walter Hewlett against the HP Board and management team, which it called spurious. In May 2002 HP's shareholders and management purchased Compaq Computer Corp. for US US$18.69 billion dollars in HP stock.

Computer Sciences Corporation (CSC). Providing IT management consulting and planning, as well as systems integration and outsourcing, Computer Sciences Corporation (CSC) earned revenues of US$16 billion for the fiscal year ended March 2005 and employed about 90,000 people.

CSC was founded in 1959 by Fletcher Jones of North American Aviation and Roy Nutt of United Aircraft. It began as a small firm concentrating on services to government agencies and grew to become the United States' third-largest commercial outsourcing company by acquiring large IT management contracts as the federal government cut spending by reducing in-house programming services. William Hoover of the California Institute of Technology later joined the company, and it was under his direction that CSC truly became a systems integration firm. Federal contracts still accounted for 30 percent of the company's business as of 1997. European operations accounted for 20 percent, almost two-thirds of the company's international commercial business (32 percent of 1997 revenues). Based in California, the company has made numerous acquisitions and has opened subsidiaries around the world. CSC also used acquisition as a means of diversifying its service offerings, and in recent years acquired a financial IT services firm, Continuum Company, and a health-care consulting firm, American Practice Management. The company was sought as a target for acquisition in 1998, when Computer Associates made an unsuccessful hostile takeover bid.

Accenture. Once the consultancy arm of the former Arthur Andersen group, Accenture split from its parent (prior to the accounting scandal that envelope Arthur Andersen) as a result of conflicts with its consultants over pay. In 2000, an international arbitrator granted the consulting group independence. Today, little company information can be found to link Accenture to its former parent. A global management consulting, technology services and outsourcing company, Accenture operates more than 100 offices in 48 countries and has more than 100,000 employees. Revenues for 2004 were US$13.67 billion, with about 52 percent coming from the EMEA region, 41 percent from North America, and 7 percent from the Asia/Pacific region.

Capgemini. As Europe's leading IT services provider, Paris-based Capgemini provides IT consulting focusing on systems architecture, integration and infrastructure. It addition, the company offers an outsourcing service, often managing all of a client's IT resources. In 2005 Capgemini had 59,000 employees in 30 countries. The company has grown through a series of acquisitions, including: Sesa in France in 1987; Hoskyns in the U.K. and United Research in the U.S., both in 1990; Mac Group of the U.S. in 1991; Volmac in the Netherlands and Programator in Scandinavia both in 1992; Gruber Titze in 1993; and Bossard in 1997 in Europe. But its largest acquisition came with the purchase of Ernst & Young Consulting in 2000. For a while the company was known as Cap Gemini Ernst & Young. Revenues in 2004 were approximately US$7.6 billion, of which more than 76 percent came from Europe, 22 percent from North America, and the remainder from the Asia/Pacific region.

Atos Origin S.A. Another Paris-based company, Atos Origins, provides its clients with consulting, operations management, and systems integration services. Employing more than 46,000 people in 2005, the company was operating in 50 countries, although it was predominant in Europe. Grown out of the merger of two France-based IT services companies—Axime and Sligos— in 1997, the group aquired KPMG Consulting in the United Kingdom and the Netherlands in 2002. It became one of the leading global IT services companies with its 2004 purchase of Sema Group from Schlumberger. This added 21,000 employees to its count. Revenues for Atos Origin exceeded US$7 billion in 2004.

Getronics. In 1999 the Dutch information technology company Getronics acquired Wang Global for US$1.8 billion. In March of 2002, the company reported its worst financial statement in 17 years and cut its workers by 6 percent. The company reported losses of about US$920 million in 2001. By 2003, sales were back up to US$3.4 billion, and the company reported a profit of about US$309 million.

Wang was started in 1951 by An Wang in Boston, Massachusetts. Wang's first success was built on its minicomputers and word processors, but the business topped out in the mid-1980s. The company endured years of losses and restructuring, but came back after filing for bankruptcy in 1992. Wang's new-found success was based on its offering of services to other companies and its strategy to build up those offerings by acquiring existing service companies. Examples include Wang's 1995 purchase of Groupe Bull's U.S. systems integration services and its 1996 purchase of Dataserv Computer Maintenance and I-NET, a client/server, network, and desktop management services provider.

In 1997 U.S. industry leader Wang earned US$1.26 billion in revenues and employed 9,300 people. In order to increase its services business, Wang agreed to acquire the computer-services segment (Olsy) of Italian Olivetti SpA in 1998 for approximately US$391 million. The acquisition would almost triple Wang's revenues and expand its operations to Europe and Asia. Wang hoped to be able to compete more evenly with giants such as IBM and EDS. The company announced its name would be changing to Wang Global in March 1998. Since 1993, Wang has been focusing on hardware and software consulting and installation services—only about US$200 million of its revenues were generated by the company's hardware (minicomputer) sales. Services provided include design and installation of systems and warranty, help desk, maintenance, and software support.

MAJOR COUNTRIES IN THE INDUSTRY

The United States. The United States has been a dominant force in the IT services industry, with the computer consulting services market being valued at almost US$249 billion in 2003 by Euromonitor. Of this value, about half is attributed to the provision of systems integration services. While most of the largest global players are U.S.-based, the domestic industry still remained highly fragmented, with the top five companies (IBM, Fujitsu, Hewlett-Packard, EDS, and Computer Sciences Corp.) only accounting for about 18 percent of the total market. Growth in the industry between 2003 and 2004 was expected to reach more than 29 percent.

The United States also has been an attractive market for companies from other countries, particularly those from emerging economies. A number of computer programming services companies from countries such as Pakistan and India, for example, have gained a foothold in the United States as subcontractors for larger firms with multinational contracts.

Japan. By 2003, the IT business in Japan was worth US$2.4 billion, but growth over the following five years was expected to exceed 30 percent. Most of the industry' growth in this area could be attributed to one sector: Enterprise Resource Planning (ERP), accounting for almost 67 percent of the market according to Euromonitor. ERP systems usually are involved in handling such business activities as manufacturing, logistics, distribution, inventory, shipping, invoicing and accounting. There was little competition in the market, and not much room for the smaller players; the three leading players (Oracle, SAP, and Fujitsu) had control of almost 95 percent of the market.

While several Japanese companies participate in the IT services industry, most of their business has been confined to the Japanese market, particularly to major corporate and industrial customers within Japan. Forays into the international market have been, for the most part, on behalf of corporate and industrial clients for whom they have worked locally. Similarly, major European companies offering computer programming services find most clients within the European Union. For both Japanese and European companies, however, that is expected to change, and those firms are expected to begin competing more openly with the U.S. firms that have been leading the way in international expansion. Japan has also moved to improve its global profile in software development and programming, largely through a giant research center in Tochigi, north of Tokyo. According to preliminary plans published by the Japan Personal Computer Software Association, the center will be open to cooperation with U.S. and other foreign software companies.

India. Valued at about US$12.7 billion in 2004, India has one of the most vibrant IT services industries in Asia. Many global companies have shifted their IT services to India, where costs can be kept lower due to lower wages in the country.

China. With its stunning economic growth in all sectors, it is no surprise that in China the IT services industry is growing at similarly unprecedented rates. Between 2003 and 2008, the market was expected to grow from a value of almost US$6.6 billion to almost US$20.6 billion—a growth of over 200 percent. Most of the firms in the industry were foreign, with IBM holding an 11 percent market share in 2003, according to *Euromonitor.* Altogether the top four firms (IBM, Accenture, Hewlett Packard, and Digital China) held almost 32 percent of the market. The provision of network services primarily to financial service companies is expected to be remain the largest sector in the industry in China.

The United Kingdom. More than half of the U.K.'s market value of almost US$46 billion in 2003 was attributed to outsourcing. Euromonitor reported that although fragmented, the industry was undergoing a trend of consolidation. This could be seen through the market strength of Paris-based Atos Origins, the leader in the country. It had grown through a series of acquisitions, including the acquisition of the IT services segment of Schlumberger during 2004. Other prominent players in the U.K. market include IBM, EDS, Accenture, and Capgemini.

Australia. Another country experiencing excellent industry growth was Australia. In 2003, the market was valued at almost US$7.8 billion, but was expected to grow by more than 60 percent over the next five years. Outsourcing and processing accounted for about 40 percent of the market, areas that were expected to grow share by another 5 percent by 2008.

FURTHER READING

"2005 Trends: Analysts Predict Modest Growth IT Budgets To Hide Some Major Shifts Below Surface." *Syntelligence*, Vol.5, No. 1. Available from http://www.syntelinc.com.

Bickerton, Ian. "Getronics Positive Despite Its Worst Year on Record." *Financial Times (London),* 6 March 2002.

Bills, Steve. "EDS Follows Two Downgrades With $1B Package of Deals." *American Banker,* 1 April 2002.

Bray, Hiawatha. "Now Comes the Harp Part." *Boston Globe,* 1 April 2002.

Chabrow, Eric. "Slow Traffic in Tech IPOs." *InternetWeek,* 13 July 2004.

Day, Ron. "Oracle Shares Fall." *Bloomberg News,* 15 March 2002.

Einhorn, Bruce. "Taiwan's Info-Tech Triumphs." *Business Week Online,* 15 June 2004.

"Feel Good Factor." *Information Age (London),* 10 June 2004.

"Gartner predicts that by 2010, the number of IT staff in the profession will shrink by 15 percent (press release)." 24 May 2005. Available from http://www.gartner.com.

"Global IT Services Revenue Grows 6.2 Percent." *Weboptimiser,* 23 June 2004. Available from http://www.weboptimiser.com.

Hoffman, Thomas. "Demand for IT Contractors Rising Slowly." *Computerworld,* 5 April 2004.

"Hoover's Company Capsules." 2004. Available from http://www.hoovers.com.

Horvitz, Paul. "IBM Wins $1 Billion, 10-Year Invensys Services Contract." *Bloomberg News,* 22 March 2002.

Humer, Caroline. "American Express and IBM Sign $6.4 Billion Deal." *Toronto Star,* 26 February 2002.

"Inside the Debate Over Outsourcing Information Technology Service Jobs." *Manufacturing & Technology News,* 17 October 2003.

"IT Pay Still Flat, but Beginning to Recover." *Report on Salary Surveys,* May 2004.

Keefe, Bob. "HP Moves to Oust Dissident Director." *Atlanta Journal and Constitution,* 2 April 2002.

"Major Market Profiles (short profiles): Computer Consulting Services in Australia, China, France, Germany, Japan, South Korea, UK, and USA." *Euromonitor,* October 2004. Available from http://www.euromonitor.com.

Moschella, David. "Users Are Taking the Lead in IT." *Computerworld,* 31 May 2004.

"Survey Finds IT Services Business May Be Brightening," 4 November 2002. Available from http://www.itaa.org.

Thibodeau, Patrick. "More IT Jobs to Go Offshore, Controversial ITAA Report Says." *Computerworld,* 5 April 2004.

Zarley, Craig. "IBM Dazzles Wall Street with Numbers." *ComputerWire,* 15 November 2001.

Construction Materials and Services

SIC 2950

NAICS 32412

ASPHALT PAVING AND ROOFING MATERIALS

This industry group encompasses firms that manufacture asphalt and tar paving mixtures, paving blocks made of asphalt, and various compositions of asphalt or tar with other materials. Using asphalt and tar, industry companies also produce, usually from purchased materials, rolls, shingles, and coatings for roofing. For coverage of concrete paving and building materials, see **Concrete, Gypsum, and Plaster Products.**

Industry Snapshot

The fragmented asphalt paving and roofing materials industry comprises a diverse collection of corporations worldwide. Well over 300,000 people were directly employed by the U.S. asphalt industry in the mid-2000s. More than one billion tons of asphalt are produced worldwide every year, of which a substantial portion comes from diversified global corporations loosely associated with the construction and oil industries. Asphalt companies compete with concrete producers for pavement materials market share, though many of the leading asphalt makers sell concrete as well. As of 2004, roughly 96 percent of roads in the United States alone were surfaced with asphalt. The U.S. industry accounted for US$20 billion of the worldwide industry, with 500 million tons of asphalt produced each year.

Environmentalism, particularly regarding the recycling of asphalt products, the most recycled American product in 2004, continues to play a major role in the industry. Recycled asphalt pavement, which has won increasing favor in the United States and Europe, can often constitute up to 35 percent of an asphalt mix, saving taxpayers an estimated US$300 million annually. As environmental concerns have increasingly become an issue of pressing global concern and publicity, a new competitive arena has opened for companies to produce recyclable goods and practice efficient production methods. Environmentalism has also given rise to interest in cool roof systems that reduce roof temperatures in warm climates in an effort to lower energy costs and usage.

Organization and Structure

In the United States, more than half of the asphalt produced is used in highway and street pavement. An estimated 25 percent is sold commercially for use in private parking lots, driveways, and sidewalks, while the remainder is used for roofing materials and other applications. Most asphalt producers supply road materials and general road construction as well, and are often subsidiaries of larger diversified corporations. Asphalt paving companies not only compete with each other, but also often vie with concrete producers for contracts. While concrete's primary use in the field of road construction is for new roads, the battle for new construction was about evenly split in the late 1990s. With a 90 percent share, asphalt clearly dominated in terms of resurfacing projects. Similarly, asphalt roofing materials compete with wood, stone, and ceramic tile.

Traditionally, government agencies have dictated how pavement is to be constructed, including specification of the asphalt mix design. The late 1990s, however, witnessed a gradual transformation of this system, whereby road construction contractors have consolidated and initiated the design of asphalt pavement that utilizes the industry's advancing technology to tailor mix designs for particular geographic and logistic variables.

Several organizations, including the National Asphalt Pavement Association (NAPA) in the United States and the European Asphalt Pavement Association (EAPA), help to organize and oversee the industry, most prominently in the field of road construction but also in the research, development, and production of asphalt paving materials.

Background and Development

The use of asphalt, a brownish-black hydrocarbon, dates back at least 5,000 years to the time when Mesopotamian cultures began mining naturally occurring bitumen. The Dead Sea was an ancient source of bitumen. Lumps of the substance often washed up on its shores, giving rise to the Dead Sea's original name, Lake Asphaltites. West Asian societies not only utilized bitumen as a sealant for reservoirs, but also exported it to Egypt, where it was used in that kingdom's famous mummification process. Asphalt further functioned as mortar and caulk and in paving, waterproofing, and paints. Trinidad's Pitch Lake, discovered by Sir Walter Raleigh, became the first large commercial source of bitumen. The first modern asphalt pavement was laid in Paris in 1854 using a natural rock bitumen from Switzerland. Within two decades, this type of road surfacing had spread to Great Britain, Germany, Switzerland, and the United States.

Asphalt shingles also date back to ancient times. These roofing materials, which are made of a paper-like core of felted organic fibers soaked with asphalt, are now described as organic-based asphalt shingles. The paper core of these roofing materials has since been replaced with recycled newspaper and sawmill scraps. Fiberglass-based asphalt shingles were developed in the United States in the 1950s. Their durability, low maintenance, and fire-resistance have made them the primary asphalt roofing product. Often referred to as a built-up roofing system, asphalt shingles dominated the roofing market from their inception in the mid-nineteenth century until the late 1980s.

The invention of the automobile lent a sense of urgency to previously haphazard road-building efforts. It soon became evident, both in Europe and the United States, which would become the top producers and consumers of asphalt, that the task would require the efforts of all levels of government as well as industrialists. The sheer volume of roads needed to traverse the United States propelled many advances in large scale (but not necessarily high quality) paving. This was especially true during the construction of the interstate highway system in the 1950s.

The development of the petroleum industry in the eighteenth, nineteenth, and twentieth centuries encouraged the gradual replacement of natural bitumen with asphalt refined from heavy oils and propelled corresponding shifts in the centers of production. Although sources of bitumen and asphalt are widely distributed around the world, deposits of heavy oil and tar sand are concentrated in the Western Hemisphere, especially in Venezuela, which claims half of the world's heavy oil, and Canada, which is endowed with a whopping 75 percent of global tar sand reserves.

U.S. manufacturers distinguish bitumen, the naturally occurring form of the substance, from asphalt distilled from heavy petroleum as a waste product of the oil refining process. Europeans, on the other hand, characterize both forms as bitumen. When applied in the paving industry, the term usually refers to asphalt combined with an aggregate of sand or gravel. Within that category, the end product may range from light road pavement to heavy, high-viscosity industrial asphalt.

Other important modern uses of asphalt include canal and reservoir linings, dam facings, and other harbor and sea works. These applications commonly use a thin, sprayed membrane of asphalt. Asphalt is also used in floor tile, soundproofing, and other building materials. Petroleum industry research, especially in the United States after World War II, contributed to the development of new products for the asphalt roofing industry, including rolled and membranous coverings.

After rising slowly and erratically in the 1980s, global asphalt production declined rapidly in the 1990s. By the late 1990s, however, production was high again. In Europe, production has remained steady since the early 1990s.

Because of Europe's monetary unification in 1999, and the necessity of efficient international trade and transportation assuming increasing importance, the harmonization of European asphalt production and application standards has emerged as a pressing issue among European asphalt producers. And, as U.S. road contractors strive for more durable and cost-efficient asphalt pavement, they are looking to Europe, whose roads are internationally recognized as the model of durability, for production innovation. As a result of these factors, combined with the high proportion of worldwide asphalt production by the United States and Europe, the industry is likely to see increased international cooperation and uniformity of production methods and technology in the twenty-first century.

Current Conditions

Several important environmental issues are catalyzing change within the asphalt industry. Some U.S. states have responded to environmental pressures to reduce emissions from asphalt plants by requiring enclosed facilities for asphalt production. Some industry observers speculate that this move signals the possibility of additional environmental legislation affecting the industry, in particular regarding respiratory exposure to plant workers. In the mid-2000s, the industry was studying ways to reduce production temperatures by 100 degrees Fahrenheit, which would not only reduce fumes, but also reduce energy consumption.

The technology behind cool roofs is being developed and implemented to reduce energy usage. The California Energy Commission (CEC), for example, led a campaign in 2001 to educate consumers about the technology and its cost and energy-saving benefits. Because this technology prevents the roof from becoming as hot as traditional roofs, less energy is required to keep the house or building cool in the summer. Other advantages of cool roofs include exceptional waterproofing and increased comfort within the buildings using these systems. Campaigns, such as the one sponsored by the CEC, inform consumers that the technology is significant and can decrease utility bills. In California, incentives were offered in 2001 to encourage people to try the cool roof technology. The Sacramento Municipal Utility District offered rebates directly to consumers, and the Tree Foundation offered rebates to contractors.

Still another important environmental concern in this industry is recycling. An enormous amount of asphalt is recycled every year, saving waste disposal resources and cutting costs for contractors and, in turn, buyers. The estimated savings due to the use of recycled asphalt were US$300 million annually in the United States alone. Surprisingly, asphalt was the most recycled product in the United States in the mid-2000s. Interest in recycling tends to rise and fall with oil prices because the industries are so closely related. When oil prices start to rise, interest in recycled asphalt also rises.

Another major change in the asphalt production industry has derived from emerging computer technology and an increasing awareness of specific weather and traffic effects on asphalt roads. As control over design specification moves into the hands of the contractors and developers, a methodological shift in the production approach has occurred. Whereas asphalt production has in the past relied on an empirical, "recipe-based" mix design specification, innovations have allowed for the widespread and rapidly proliferating use of performance-based specifications, whereby producers apply a volumetric mix design tailored to the specific needs of individual roads and regions.

RESEARCH AND TECHNOLOGY

Ever-increasing traffic demands and fluctuating petroleum stocks have forced asphalt producers to begin to examine the chemical composition of asphalt and work to obtain predictable results. In the late 1980s, the chemical composition of asphalt (about 90 percent carbon and hydrogen and 10 percent sulfur, nitrogen, oxygen, and trace metals) was finally pinpointed, allowing for a wealth of innovations and programs aimed at improving the quality of roads and the efficiency of asphalt production techniques.

Many of these initiatives originated in Europe, which is considered the leader in paving research. One of Europe's most celebrated innovations, stone matrix asphalt (SMA), was developed in Germany and Sweden in the 1960s. This material, which incorporates coarser, larger aggregates to form a "stone skeleton" within the asphalt binder, was created to withstand heavy European truck traffic. The product has proven more durable than conventional asphalt and is gaining favor in North American markets.

Although cold-mix asphalt, also known as asphalt emulsion concrete, has been in existence since the 1940s, it has recently been refined by Swedish engineers. The product's advantages over traditional hot-mix asphalt include lower energy costs and no unpleasant odor. True to its name, asphalt emulsion concrete uses emulsified asphalt, meaning that the asphalt binder is suspended in water to promote viscosity, instead of using heat to induce flexibility.

The U.S. government followed Europe's lead by establishing the Strategic Highway Research Program (SHRP) in 1987. The US$150 million initiative developed Superpave, a computer analysis system that can produce a set of volumetric asphalt mix design specifications for a given geographic area and traffic level. It was hoped that given the new knowledge of asphalt's composition, pavements could be made to last longer and perform better. And, as of the late 1990s, that hope was a reality, as states that had implemented and monitored these new developments reported that they had saved hundreds of millions of dollars on the rehabilitation and reconstruction of roads. In 2000 this computer technology was applied to recycling asphalt; as a result, computers were designed to manage the mix of discarded asphalt with hot rocks and gravel.

Recycling asphalt, especially asphalt used in road surfaces, has captured the attention of many in the industry. The development and application of efficient, smoke-free manufacturing equipment for processing reclaimed asphalt pavement started in the late 1970s and has won increasing favor in recent years. In fact, asphalt pavement is the most recycled material in the United States, far outpacing other recyclables. Every year, an average of 73 million tons of asphalt is recycled, which amounts to almost double the volume of paper, glass, and plastic combined. This recycled asphalt is used in both paving and roofing. In the roofing industry, recycled asphalt void of ozone-depleting chemicals, called a "green" roof system, is popular among environmentally conscious professionals who hire contractors to construct residential or commercial buildings.

The use of rubberized asphalt is a hotly debated issue in the industry. The product was developed in the late 1960s in the United States. It incorporates bits of scrap rubber in the asphalt mix and has been embraced by environmentalists and tire industry representatives, who think it is the answer to their tire disposal problems. Proponents of rubberized asphalt maintain that the material is safer, more durable, and more cost-effective than standard asphalt. But opponents of the process said that augmenting asphalt with "waste material" such as scrap tires only renders it unrecyclable, thereby postponing its eventual arrival in the landfill. Still, asphalt rubber advocates, and some quiescent asphalt industry observers, asserted that expansion of their product's use is "inevitable."

Other pavement industry trends include limiting traffic noise and introducing quality assurance programs and performance guarantees in the form of warranties. Issues in the asphalt roofing industry include recycling, appearance, durability, low-odor asphalt, and cool roof technology. Many new shingles are made to resemble wood or slate or to give a more three-dimensional look. Laminated, or heavyweight, shingles have been developed to be more durable. Single-ply, or modified bitumen, roofing has been gaining popularity and market share, especially in commercial applications. Cool roof technology controls the temperatures that roofs can reach in the heat of the summer. A traditional roof can reach 170 degrees Fahrenheit on a 90-degree day, but a cool roof is likely to stay at 100 degrees. The idea behind this technology is relatively simple and is most easily understood by noting the difference between a black surface in the sun and a white one. Cool roofs are white, thereby increasing the solar reflectivity.

WORKFORCE

Technology works both for and against the asphalt paving and roofing workforce. While it enables a contractor to offer more, and better, options to a prospective client, it also requires that contractors stay abreast of the latest developments. Contractors must stay current on mixing improvements, environmental concerns, and computerization. Indirectly, technology in general has made it more difficult for contractors to find good workers. In the twenty-first century, young people are computer savvy and thus have skills they can use in office jobs. This is a challenge for contractors, who need young workers willing to put in long hours of hard work outside. As a result, contractors spend more time recruiting and training than they did in the past.

INDUSTRY LEADERS

ASPHALT PAVEMENT

Europe. Lafarge SA, one of Europe's largest building materials groups, made substantial movement into markets throughout Europe, North and Latin America, and the Pacific Rim in the 1990s. With the acquisition of the United Kingdom company Blue Circle Industries, Lafarge became the world's largest cement manufacturer. One of North America's largest suppliers of building materials, Lafarge's total sales for 2004 reached more than US$19.5 billion, 40 percent of which was from the Western Europe market.

Skanska AB, a Swedish company, had net sales of almost US$18.34 billion in 2004. During the 1990s, the company reorganized into regional units to accommodate its rapid international expansion (especially into Europe and North America). As of 2005, Skanska had subsidiaries in more than 60 countries and employed 53,803 people.

The United States. Ashland Paving and Construction, or APAC, Inc., a subsidiary of the giant U.S. oil company Ashland, Inc., is the largest producer of hot-mix asphalt in the United States, as well as the largest U.S. asphalt and concrete paving contractor, generating more than US$2.4 billion in 2003 revenue. Vulcan Materials Company, which produces aggregates, asphalt, and ready-mix concrete, saw its Construction Materials division account for roughly 70 percent of the corporation's US$2.5 billion in net sales for 2000.

ASPHALT ROOFING

Among asphalt roofing materials producers, CertainTeed Corp. of the United States is a major player and is highly regarded in the industry. It is a subsidiary of Saint-Gobain, a major French industrial company. CertainTeed reported US$2.3 billion in sales in 2003. In 2002, CertainTeed owned 50 plants in North America. Diversified fiberglass manufacturer and designer Owens Corning, which is also the leading U.S. manufacturer of industrial asphalt (used primarily in commercial roofing), earned almost US$5 billion in total sales in 2003. Emco, a Canadian corporation, reported 2003 revenues of US$857 million, a portion of which was derived from its Building Products Group.

MAJOR COUNTRIES IN THE INDUSTRY

The United States, with approximately 500 million tons of hot-mix asphalt produced in 2003, easily dominated the industry. The European Union followed, with 301.3 million tons, which represents the output of Germany (55 million), France (38.7 million), Italy (42.4 million), the United Kingdom (27.8 million), and Spain (30 million). Europe remains a major center of asphalt and road construction innovation and design. Japan is also a leading manufacturer, with 63.7 million tons produced in 2003.

FURTHER READING

"Asphalt in Figures." *European Asphalt Pavement Association Website,* 2005. Available from http://www.eapa.org.

"Asphalt Industry." *Beyond Roads Web Site,* 2005. Available from http://www.beyondroads.com.

"Built-up Roofing." *Building Design and Construction,* September 2000.

Cervarich, Margaret Blain. "Cooled and Ready to Serve." *Roads & Bridges,* September 2003.

Hoke, Kathy. "Well Traveled Road." *Business First-Columbus,* 10 November 2000.

"Hoover's Company Capsules," 2005. Available from http://www.hoovers.com.

"International Trade Statistics," 2005. Available from http://www.wto.org.

Lamb, Celia. "Chill Out the Roof, Get Cash." *Sacramento Business Journal,* 6 April 2001.

Moore, Walt. "Paving 2000: Trends, Techniques, and Machines." *Construction Equipment,* February 2000.

———. "Paving's Mega-Trends and Other Hot Topics." *Construction Equipment,* February 2001.

"National Center for Asphalt Technology." *Auburn University Web Site,* 2004. Available from http://www.eng.auburn.edu/center/ncat.

Patterson, John. "Understanding All the Talk Behind Cool Roofs." *Los Angeles Business Journal,* 3 December 2001.

"What Is the New Asphalt?" *Asphalt Pavement Alliance Web Site,* 2003. Available from http://www.asphaltalliance.com.

SIC 1622

NAICS 237310

BRIDGE, TUNNEL, AND ELEVATED HIGHWAY CONSTRUCTION

This industry includes general contractors who build bridges, viaducts, elevated highways, and tunnels for pedestrians, vehicles, and trains (excluding subways).

INDUSTRY SNAPSHOT

The market for bridge, tunnel, and elevated highway construction has become increasingly globalized since the 1980s. The dominant players in the industry—companies from North America, Western Europe, and Japan—have looked beyond these mature markets to seek out the opportunities for growth that are available in developing economies. However, funding for infrastructure construction projects such as bridges, tunnels, and elevated highways is quite dependent upon the economic health of a country, so economic weakness within these developing economies can cause the monetary resources in these markets to dry up or can shift resources away from infrastructure construction.

Even in mature and stable economies, infrastructure funding can be difficult to come by. Funding comes largely from public coffers, and many other concerns compete for these resources. Additionally, since the 1990s governments have been under pressure to balance their budgets, which emphasizes the finite nature of spending levels for infrastructure.

While developing economies need additional infrastructure in order to sustain their growth, the United States is increasingly faced with the need to repair or replace existing bridges, tunnels, and elevated highways that are aged and deteriorating or inadequate to carry the current volume of traffic. With such needs and demands for these infrastructure projects, countered by the limited nature of public funding, modest growth is expected for the industry worldwide. Though Asia's late 1990s economic crisis produced a chilling effect on heavy construction on much of that continent in the early 2000s, a significant exception was China, where astronomical development spurred the planning and execution of several monumental civil engineering projects.

ORGANIZATION AND STRUCTURE

As with general contractors in other construction sectors, companies involved in bridge, tunnel, and elevated highway construction bid on potential projects or "jobs" based on estimates of overhead costs, desired profit margin, and estimated time necessary to complete the job. Winning bidders are responsible for managing the construction project, although they may subcontract some or all of the project to other companies. Consequently, in some instances the winning bidders may be companies that are known primarily as engineering firms rather than conventional construction contractors. (See also **Engineering Services.**)

Contracts to assume responsibility for construction of a bridge or tunnel (or most other types of construction) can take different forms. In cost-reimbursement contracts, builders are paid for reasonable costs incurred during the life of the project. Fixed-price contracts, on the other hand, require contractors to absorb cost overruns themselves. By the early 2000s, incentive-based contracts that reward builders for timeliness and quality of construction had become increasingly commonplace.

According to a report in the *U.S. Industry & Trade Outlook,* across the construction industry in general, U.S. companies that win jobs overseas tend to use local labor through their foreign affiliates to carry out the work. Hence, U.S. construction firms generally export only their management and engineering skills, not their actual construction services.

Government budgets for new construction or renovation of existing structures are of great importance to the industry's vitality, as government contracts from around the world account for the vast majority of industry revenue. Government involvement in the construction process varies from country to country. In the United States, for instance, federal or state agencies are often involved in the execution of projects, as well as the funding. In less developed countries, such as those in Africa, parts of Asia, or Eastern Europe, funding sources often include the World Bank and regional development banks.

BACKGROUND AND DEVELOPMENT

Historic advances in this industry's development have resulted in some of the world's most notable architectural achievements. Led by European and U.S. builders who capitalized on the development of steel and other technological advances, bridge and tunnel construction has been characterized over the years by continuous improvement in design and execution. By building on the work of previous generations of architects, engineers, and builders, industry participants continue to devise ways to improve engineering and construction methods, as well as construction materials.

The early nineteenth century featured the introduction of several revolutionary bridge designs. In 1822 construction of the world's first iron railroad bridge was completed. It was followed three years later by the opening of the world's first wire suspension bridge in France. The first bridge of that type in the United States was opened in 1842 near Philadelphia, Pennsylvania. That bridge—25 feet wide and 358 feet long, with five wire cables on either side—cost US$35,000 to build. In 1845 the first wire cable suspension aqueduct bridge was opened over the Allegheny River at Pittsburgh, Pennsylvania. In 1849 the B&O Railroad bridge, which crossed the Ohio River and spanned 1,000 feet, became the world's longest bridge. By 1855 trains were able to cross a wire cable bridge that spanned Niagara Gorge between Canada and the United States.

Engineering and construction innovations continued through the latter part of the nineteenth century. The Brooklyn Bridge, the world's first steel-wire suspension bridge, opened in 1883 in New York City. Tunnel designs improved during this period as well. A railroad line completed in 1867 extended from Austria to Italy and included more than 20 tunnels to negotiate passage through the forbidding Brenner Pass. In the latter part of the nineteenth century much of the construction in the tunnel and bridge building industry centered on movable bridges that could accommodate river navigation. Numerous vertical-lift and swing-span bridges were built during the 1890s, which also featured the introduction of reinforced concrete bridges.

The industry continued to grow as the twentieth century began, although U.S. builders, long among the world leaders in bridge and tunnel construction, saw their fortunes sag immediately after the conclusion of World War I as labor strife and other problems diminished new business. Meanwhile, in Europe it was necessary to rebuild after the war but some European economies could not afford new construction given the high inflation and various social problems of this period.

The Detroit-Windsor Tunnel opened in 1930. The tunnel, which runs under the Detroit River and connects the United States and Canada, was built of prefabricated tubes floated over a trench and laid out in sections like pipeline. The celebrated Golden Gate Bridge, a 4,200-foot bridge that spans San Francisco Bay (the world's longest suspension bridge at the time), was completed a few years later. Halfway around the world in Sydney, Australia a new structure, the Harbour Bridge, assumed the title of the world's longest arch bridge when it opened in 1932.

But while bridge and tunnel construction accelerated around the world in the 1930s and 1940s, the industry's greatest growth was in the United States. Buoyed by the establishment of the Works Progress Administration (WPA) in 1935, industry contractors took advantage of the New Deal's economic environment, characterized by federal programs to stimulate economic growth, to secure building contracts across the United States. The surge in construction resulted in the creation of 78,000 bridges and more than 650,000 miles of public roads. The victory of the Allied forces in World War II further strengthened the bridge, tunnel, and elevated highway construction industry in the United States. *ENR* noted that by the end of 1945, it had "identified a backlog of US$28 billion in proposed projects and half of those were already in the blueprint stage. Bridge construction rose by 220 percent in 1945." The postwar era also saw the introduction of the interstate highway system in the United States, which provided steady growth for the industry.

The industry outside the United States continued to grow as well, and the 1950s and 1960s were marked by new engineering marvels such as the Oosterscheldebrug Causeway in the Netherlands (1965), the Tagus River Bridge in Portugal (1966), and the Zdakov Bridge in Czechoslovakia (1967). In 1975 the Great Uhuru Railway was opened in Africa. This 1,160-mile rail line featured 300 bridges and 23 tunnels.

In the United States, meanwhile, the bridge and tunnel industry felt the effects of economic conditions that rocked the entire construction industry in 1970. Inflation had increased the cost of doing business; labor costs were particularly high. The *ENR* Construction Cost Index rose by 10.8 percent at this time.

In the 1980s bridge and elevated highway construction took on increased importance in the United States. Construction of bridges and elevated highways accounted for more than 72 percent of public work in 1987, an increase of almost 10 percent over 1982. Tunnel construction, however, fell during that time, from almost 17 percent of total construction in 1982 to less than 10 percent by 1987. While the drop in tunnel building during this period dragged the figures down somewhat, U.S. participants in the industry registered a significant increase in total revenues. In 1982 a total value of US$2.82 billion was attributed to bridge, tunnel, and elevated highway construction in the United States. By 1987 the value of new construction in these areas had exploded to US$4.48 billion.

A new funding mechanism for U.S. construction projects was set up by Congress in 1995: state infrastructure banks (SIBs). These banks were to grant loans and other forms of credit to fund local transportation projects facing fiscal uncertainty. However, SIBs were not immediately created in all states. *ITS World* reported that the U.S. Department of Transportation estimated that about US$1.6 billion in projects had been financed by SIBs by the beginning of fiscal year 1998.

In the early 2000s, the transportation infrastructure in the United States had begun to age and deteriorate, and in some cases the structures could not meet the needs and demands of usage. Bridges and other infrastructure aged rapidly due to increasing traffic and speeds and heavier vehicles. A 2003 national inventory of U.S. bridges estimated some 22.3 percent of the country's 286,195 interstate and state bridges had become structurally or functionally obsolete. Hence, there was an increased need to spend transportation dollars on repairing or replacing existing bridges, tunnels, and elevated highways (which might serve to divert a certain level of spending from the construction of new projects). According to *New Steel,* "federal government spending to build and maintain U.S. highways and bridges reaches about US$20 billion per year."

Two replacement projects of note link the cities of Port Huron, Michigan, and Sarnia, Ontario. A second Blue Water Bridge spanning the St. Clair River was completed in 1997, and, when repairs were completed on the original Blue Water Bridge, each bridge began to carry one-way traffic at this busy and often backed-up border crossing. According to *American City & County,* the original bridge, built in the 1930s, had exceeded its traffic load capacity and was in need of structural renovation. Also, a new 1.1-mile rail tunnel below the St. Clair River was completed in 1995 at a cost of US$160 million. It replaced a leaking tunnel that had been built in 1890; the old tunnel had cost US$2.7 million to build. The new tunnel cuts travel time across (or rather, under) the river, as trains are able to travel at 60 mph, as opposed to 15 mph in the old tunnel, according to the *Flint Journal.* Furthermore, the new tunnel could accommodate double-decker and triple-decker vehicles. Previously, these vehicles were dismantled, loaded on barges, and ferried across the river, a process which took twelve hours. The *Flint Journal* reported that, "General Motors officials have said that the new tunnel will save the company about a day's time hauling its new cars and trucks to Chicago from Oshawa, Ontario."

In 1994 transportation service began through the Channel Tunnel, or Chunnel, that runs beneath the English Channel and connects Great Britain to France. The Channel Tunnel was the second longest rail tunnel in the world, and the section that runs under the water (24 miles) is the longest undersea tunnel. The cost of this monumental 31-mile-long achievement exceeded US$17 billion.

Another noteworthy project was the Confederation Bridge, which connects the two Canadian provinces of New Brunswick and Prince Edward Island. This bridge, completed in 1997, spans 12,880 meters—about eight miles—and is among the longest in the world. In 1998, Japan opened the Akashi Kaikyo Bridge, which connects the islands of Honshu and Shikoku and is the longest suspension bridge in the world. The bridge, which took ten years to complete and cost about US$3.6 billion, involved more than 100 contractors. Japan is also home to the Seikan Tunnel, the longest (34-mile) railway tunnel in the world.

The biggest and most complex highway project in American history began in 1991 in Boston, Massachusetts, and was completed in 2004. The "Big Dig," as the project was called, replaced the city's antiquated Central Artery, an elevated six-lane highway, with a larger underground expressway. It also extended Interstate 90 (the Massachusetts Turnpike) through downtown Boston to Logan Airport. The project included four major highway interchanges; a two-bridge, 14-lane crossing of the Charles River, including the widest cable-stayed bridge in the world; a tunnel under Boston harbor; and a seven-building tunnel ventilation system. At its peak, the Big Dig employed about 4,000 construction workers. Originally funded at US$2.5 billion, US$14.6 billion had been spent on the project by 2006.

The economic growth, urbanization, and industrialization of developing economies requires the development of major infrastructure projects, including bridges, tunnels, and elevated highways. In the late 1990s the countries with the most promising growth prospects were in East Asia and the Pacific Rim, specifically China, South Korea, Malaysia, Vietnam, the Philippines, Indonesia, and Thailand. However, after slowdowns in some places during 1996, the region's severe economic crisis in 1997 began to negatively impact infrastructure construction in several countries. South Korea, Indonesia, and Thailand were hit particularly hard by the crisis and were being pressured by the international financial community to reform their economic, financial, and business practices. Similarly, fiscal tightening by Japan's government coincided with a downturn in the Japanese economy that left the region's largest economy—and the world's second-largest—in what appeared to be early stages of recession in 1997 and 1998. As a result, government-funded construction projects were scaled back, causing lean times for the construction industry. Major companies in Japan looked increasingly to overseas projects in order to remain profitable. In 2001, Japan agreed to fund an extensive portable steel bridge project in Bangladesh. In 1994, the country had conducted a basic design study for the bridges, and two years later purchased the materials for 74 bridges to be constructed. In 1999, Japan began repairing another 80 Bangladesh bridges. Although the project was extensive, the bridge shortage remained, particularly in rural areas.

Twenty-First Century Developments

Despite some contraction for the market in Asia, demand for new infrastructure surged in China. In 2001 the country launched 48 railway, highway, tunnel, and bridge projects with combined contractual foreign funding of US$470 million. A cross-country highway linking Shanghai with the Kazakhstan city of Horgos, under construction in 2004, was expected to include the world's longest tunnel. Another major project was the Dong Hai Bridge, linking Shanghai's new port with Yangshan Island. Completed in late 2005, it is the longest oversea bridge in the world. Halcrow and NRS were among foreign contractors involved with the project, most of which was designed and built by Chinese construction companies. T. Y. Lin International, an American engineering firm, designed two other major bridges in China and was joint contractor for construction of the Shibanpe Yangtze River Bridge, completed in 2006.

More bridge and tunnel projects in China were being awarded exclusively to domestic contractors. One such project was the Chaotianmen Bridge across the Yangtze River in Chongquing. The two-level bridge, begun in 2004 and scheduled for completion in 2008, will carry both light rail and six lanes of highway. China Harbour Engineering, the country's largest bridge building firm, is constructing the US$360 million project, which will be the longest arch bridge. Another project announced in 2005 was the Sutong Bridge, a cable-stayed bridge over the Yangtze River estuary at Nantong. With a central span of 1,088 meters, the Sutong Bridge would become the world's longest cable-stayed bridge. Total investment in the project, which was being built entirely by Chinese companies, was estimated at about US$725.77 million, and completion was expected in 2009.

Additional projects being planned or under construction in the mid-2000s were the Yichang-Wanzhou Railway, a US$2.1 billion project covering 378 kilometers and including 183 bridges and 114 tunnels, and the US$396 million Xiamen East tunnel, China's first undersea tunnel, due to be completed in 2010.

One of the few major infrastructure projects in Europe in the early 2000s was the Dublin Port Tunnel, completed in 2006. Japan's Nishimatsu Construction Company, Britain's Mowlem & Company, and Ireland's Irishenco Construction were all awarded contracts for the project. The Millau Viaduct Bridge in France, which connects the major highway between Paris and Barcelona, Spain, was built with private funds. It opened in 2005. A single-span suspension bridge across the Strait of Messina, which would link Sicily with mainland Italy, was being planned in 2005. The 3.3 kilometer bridge would become the longest single-span bridge in the world and was expected to cost 6 billion euros. Construction began in late 2005 and was expected to be completed in 2011.

Greater potential for growth remained in Russia, the former Soviet republics, Eastern Europe, and South America—particularly in Brazil and Argentina. A Slovenian highway project that was to span the country from east to west and that includes several tunnels was funded by the European Bank for Reconstruction and Development as well as a gas tax. Russia's plan to improve transit in its relatively isolated far eastern regions, largely to facilitate cheaper shipment for raw materials such as coal, resulted in several major highway programs. In 2001, seven bridges were constructed in Sakhalin alone; numerous projects throughout eastern Siberia were planned through 2012. In Mexico, a major highway maintenance and restructuring plan financed by the World Bank began in the late 1990s and was extended well into the 2000s. Upgrades of some 100 bridges will be included in the project. Venezuela's Economic Recovery Plan opened public works projects to foreign investors and builders.

Current Conditions

In the United States, funding for transportation construction, including bridges, tunnels, and elevated highways, was continued with passage of the Transportation Equity Act for the 21st Century (TEA-21) in 1998 and extended to 2003. The Safe, Accountable, Flexible, Efficient Transportation Equity Act: A Legacy for Users (SAFETEA-LU) was enacted in 2005 as a replacement of the TEA-21. It authorizes a federal program for highways, highway safety, and transit for the five-year period 2005-2009. The Federal Highway Administration, addressing the ongoing problem of the nation's deteriorating transportation infrastructure, reported that 593,885 state and highway system bridges were deficient as of December 2004, estimating that it would cost US$50 billion to correct the problem.

The value of new highway and bridge construction increased by 16 percent to $76 billion in 2006 in the United States. This was the largest increase since 1984, and analysts believed activity would stay elevated for a time due to the passage of the SAFETEA-LU. According to Kenneth Simonson, chief economist of the Associated General Contractors of America, "A lot of projects had either been deferred or had continued at prior-year levels; SAFETEA-LU ended that uncertainty about when the funding would come through." The SAFETEA-LU provides 38 percent more funding for transportation construction than the TEA-21.

RESEARCH AND TECHNOLOGY

The bridge, tunnel, and elevated highway construction sector has historically advanced in accordance with innovations and new developments in design, construction, and engineering. The industry continues to rely on these improvements—whether in the areas of construction materials, construction equipment, or engineering design—as it seeks ways to produce safer, more cost-effective, and (in some cases) more spectacular results.

In Japan, for example, three companies—Tokyo Electric Power Company, Taisei Corporation, and Ishikawajima-Harima Heavy Industries Company—joined forces to develop the world's first tunnel boring machine with the capability of turning 90 degree angles. The machine works, according to *ENR,* by using two shields. The smaller of the shields is located in a spherical housing at the front of the larger shield. The larger shield can tunnel either horizontally or vertically to the planned corner, whereupon the sphere at its front pivots and sends the smaller shield off in the desired direction. Such innovations provide the industry with continued vitality.

In the realm of bridge construction, builders around the world continually explore the feasibility of new techniques and methods. The DRC Consultants engineering firm, for example, designed widely instituted refinements in cable-stayed and segmental box girder bridge construction in the 1980s. An article published in *Civil Engineering* remarked, however, that innovative designs and construction methodologies are not always pursued with the same zeal in different regions of the world. In Europe, for example, supply-side engineering—in which designers and owners work closely together—has enabled firms to take a lead in innovative construction, whereas the United States lagged in this area, although by the mid-1990s it had begun to take steps in that direction.

Advances in the quality of materials also played a role in the steady development of the industry. Gall-Tough stainless steel, for example, has been used for bridge parts such as link hinge pins. Gall-Tough—an austenitic stainless alloy that is high in silicon and manganese content and is nitrogen-strengthened—possesses superior self-mated galling and metal-to-metal wear resistance. *Machine Design* noted that the alloy shows higher strength and high-temperature oxidation resistance compared to other stainless steel alloys with similar corrosion resistance. With a galling threshold rated 15 times higher than standard stainless steel, the alloy also has a high stress resistance, though it sacrifices a small amount of the corrosion resistance that other materials offer.

While steel remains a popular material for bridge and tunnel construction, industry researchers have also looked to other suitable materials such as aluminum and plastics where practical. In addition, alternatives to traditional welded-wire highway concrete reinforcements include fiber-reinforced concrete that uses acrylic, carbon, nylon, and polyethylene materials. Carbon steel plates and glass-fiber reinforced concrete have also been introduced in highway and bridge construction.

Several factors must be considered when choosing materials for bridge construction: cost, weight, life span, and reparability. The American Iron and Steel Institute (AISI) claimed in *New Steel* that, despite the dominance of concrete in the bridge market, "steel-supported bridges last longer, are easier to build and repair, and weigh less than bridges supported only by concrete. . . . If the concrete bridge deteriorates, it normally needs to be replaced altogether." The AISI stated further that, according to a study conducted by the Organization for Economic Cooperation and Development, steel bridges can last twice as long as concrete bridges without needing major repairs—50 years for steel as opposed to 25 years for concrete. Concrete bridges have been favored in the United States largely because they tend to be the cheapest, a trend some observers view as short sighted.

The U.S. government has set up a program to spur the development of new types of steel for highway bridges. The goal is to lower the cost of bridge building. One result has been the development of "a low-carbon 70W steel processed via hot rolling reheat quench and tempering," according to *American Metal Market,* which will allow the elimination of one step of the fabricating process, thus reducing construction costs. This high-performance steel was expected to be used to construct a bridge in Tennessee and should reduce construction costs by 16 percent. This particular steel was developed jointly by three steel companies—U.S. Steel, Bethlehem, and Lukens—along with the U.S. Navy and the Federal Highway Administration.

The National Science Foundation funds numerous research projects that aim to find new materials with which to construct bridges. One of the expected outcomes is to find a material that lasts longer than steel or concrete. In the early 2000s work was being done by both Lockheed Martin Corporation and the University of California at San Diego's Frieder Seible to develop bridges made of glass fibers. Building bridges with this lightweight material was expected to be quicker and less expensive than materials used at that time. Bridge maintenance with such a material would also be less costly.

In the latter part of the 1990s, high performance concrete (HPC) was put to the test, and by 2204, only six states had not used HPC in bridge specifications. HPC uses precast, high-strength concrete than conventional mixes. Because higher temperatures are required in the casting process, the concrete becomes stronger during casting. However, because the casts retain heat for longer periods, strength testing cannot occur for at least 56 days, compared to 28 days with traditional concrete products.

In 2001, the U.K. Highways Agency began to study the use of plastic as a building material. The plastic would be used in fiber-reinforced polymers (FRP) on bridge decks. According to *Presswire*, FRP has the potential to provide a cost-effective alternative to conventional steel and concrete, as well as being strong, lightweight, and resistant to moisture and de-icing salts.

Other advances in the bridge building industry focus on worker safety and environmental protection. Steps taken to ensure worker safety during the construction of Canada's Confederation Bridge included doing 85 percent of the actual construction work on land using a 150-acre facility, providing food and heat at offshore work sites in case workers were stranded due to inclement weather or rough seas, and monitoring the whereabouts of offshore workers using electronic ID cards. In addition, the precautions taken to protect the environment and wildlife around the construction site earned this bridge project an environmental achievement award from the Canadian Construction Association.

Industry Leaders

Early in the twenty-first century, U.S. companies dominated the bridge and tunnel construction industry. One of the largest U.S. companies in this industry in 2004 was Flatiron Construction Corp., the U.S. arm of Dutch company Royal BAM. Originally founded in 1947, Flatiron was bought by Hollandsche Beton Groep in the 1990s. When BAM acquired HBG, it formed HBG Constructors, but changed the company's name back to Flatiron in 2004. Flatiron Construction, which includes Flatiron Constructors and FCI Constructors, completed several major bridge and tunnel projects in the United States in the early 2000s, including the Ted Williams Tunnel in Boston and the Carquinez Suspension Bridge in California. As of 2005, the company's projects included the San Francisco-Oakland Bay Bridge, valued at US$1.06 billion, and the Cooper River Bridge in South Carolina, valued at US$531 million.

Bechtel Group, Inc. In the early 2000s the largest civil engineering company in the world, the Bechtel Group, was based in San Francisco, California and employed about 40,000 people in 66 countries. Though the company specialized in construction of petrochemical plants, it also worked on several major bridge and tunnel projects, including the Chunnel and the Big Dig. Sales reached US$18.1 billion in 2005.

Peter Kiewit Sons', Inc. Another leading U.S. company was Omaha-based Peter Kiewit Sons'. The employee-owned firm had completed projects in 35 states, Canada, and Puerto Rico. Government contracts accounted for more than 75 percent of its jobs, and about 50 percent of its sales came from transportation contracts, including bridges, railroads, and mass transit systems as well as highways. Sales in 2005 reached US$4.14 billion, a 23.7 percent increase from the previous year, with 14,500 employees.

Besix. Belgium-based Besix, which constructed such projects as the Piet Hein tunnel in Amsterdam, saw earnings slip in the early 2000s but has turned increasingly to international projects to regain profitability. In the mid-2000s it was engaged in major operations in Eastern Europe, the Middle East, Asia, and Africa. The company completed the Sheikh Khalifa Causeway Bridge in Bahrain and the Wadi Muddi Gillay tunnel in the UAR, among other projects. Sales for the company totaled US$522 million in 2005.

Balfour Beatty plc. Balfour Beatty plc, based in London, provided engineering, construction, and project management services and worked on several major projects, including the Chunnel. The company is also responsible for repair and maintenance of more than 60 percent of London's busy subway system. In 2004 Balfour reported sales of US$6.6 billion in 2005 with about 27,600 employees. The company acquired rival Birse Group in 2006.

Major Countries in the Industry

Companies from the United States, Western Europe, and Japan dominate the international market for bridge, tunnel, and elevated highway construction. While the United States has long held the preeminent position in this industry, Japan established a strong presence in the area of long-span bridge engineering. *ENR* noted that Japan recovered from a slow start in the construction of major suspension bridges—its first suspension bridges with spans over 500 meters were built more than 50 years after similar bridges had been constructed in Europe and North America—to take the lead in this segment of the industry.

Further Reading

Alcantara, Jaclyn. "Focus on Transportation." *Electrical Construction & Maintenance,* 1 December2006.

American Road and Transportation Builders Association. *Transportation Construction Market Intelligence Reports.* Avaiable from www.artba.com.

"Big Dig Facts." Available from www.bigdig.com.

"Bridge over Yangtze River Starting Construction." *China Daily,* 29 December 2004. Available from http://www.chinadaily.com.cn.

"China to Speed up Building Second Silk Road." *China View,* 15 April 2004. Available from news.xinhuanet.com.

"Companies Battle to Rebuild Iraq." CNN News, 14 January 2004. Available from cnn.worldnews.

"Congress Advances TEA-21 Renewal Prior to Easter Recess." *Transfer,* 25 March 2005. Available from http://www.transact.org.

"Hainan Mulls Bridge/Tunnel Link to Mainland." Xinhua News Agency, 3 February 2005. Available from www.china.org.cn.

"Hoover's Company Capsules." *Hoover's Online,* 2007. Available from www.hoovers.com.

Hulse, Carl. "The President's Budget Proposal: Transportation; Senate Presses Confrontation on Costly Transportation Bill." *New York Times*, 3 February 2004.

Monthly U.S. Transportation Construction Market Report, 22 March 2007. Available from artba.org.

"New Port to Benefit from Cross-Sea Link." *Bridge Design and Engineering,* 26 August 2003. Available from www.bridgeweb.com.

"N.J. Team Builds Bridges with Recycled Plastic." *Waste News,* 12 May 2003.

Sigmund, Pete. "Road, Bridge Work to Sustain Industry in '07." *Construction Equipment Guide,* 11 December 2006.

Sleight, Chris. "Messina Plans Outlined." *KHL News,* 10 August 2004. Available from http://www.klh.com.

Triandafilou, Louis N. "HPC Bridge Response Favorable." *The Concrete Producer,* October 2004.

U.S. Department of Transportation, Federal Highway Administration. *Bridge Inventory,* December 2004. Available from http://www.fhwa.dot.gov.

"Channel Tunnel." *Wikipedia,* 4 April 2007. Available from http://en.wikipedia.org.

SIC 3241

NAICS 327310

CEMENT, HYDRAULIC

The global cement industry manufactures various types of hydraulic cement, including portland, the most common form, as well as natural, masonry, and pozzolana cements.

INDUSTRY SNAPSHOT

Cement's highly cyclical demand is dependent on the world's construction markets. Where there are many new projects, the cement industry thrives. The regional economic recoveries, and in some places, the economic booms of the early and mid-1990s stimulated worldwide production growth spurts as high as 6.35 percent. By 2003, yearly world production stood at nearly 1.9 billion metric tons, up from almost 1.8 billion metric tons in 2002 and approximately 1.5 billion metric tons during the late 1990s.

Fueling much of this growth was the briskly expanding Asian economies led by China, by far the world's largest cement producer and consumer. In the mid-1990s, the region found itself short of cement supply, and numerous firms within the region and around the world moved quickly to meet the excess demand. Growth was restrained by the 1997 financial crisis, however, as numerous companies, governments in the region scaled back construction projects, and as Asian cement manufacturers grappled with debt and cash flow problems. Heading into the mid-2000s, China's economy was booming. By 2004, the nation was responsible for 43 percent of cement consumption worldwide, a number that was expected to reach 52 percent by 2020.

While the industry includes a number of sizable multinational companies, most cement production still occurs relatively close to its intended consumers because the logistics of handling cement over long distances are cost prohibitive for many manufacturers. Nonetheless, innovative firms such as Cemex have helped stimulate a thriving regional trade, particularly in Asia and Central and South America.

ORGANIZATION AND STRUCTURE

Cement makers grind controlled mixtures of minerals, most often limestone and clay, in either a wet or dry environment to produce a powder. The powder is then heated in a kiln until it chemically changes into clinker pellets, which in turn are reground into a fine powder with additional minerals such as gypsum. This finished powder, the actual cement, may be mixed with water and sand or gravel, known as aggregate, to produce concrete. Various nations and trade associations prescribe minimum standards for cement composition and strength. Two widely recognized international standards for the industry are the American Society for Testing and Materials C150 specification and the British Standard Institution 12 specification; both specifications are revised periodically.

Portland cement, named after the British island of Portland and attributed to Englishman Joseph Aspdin, who obtained a patent for it in 1824, comprises by far the largest segment of the hydraulic cement market. It is the key ingredient in the concrete used in the construction of highways, dams, airports, sewage facilities, power plants, office buildings, and other structures. Although some concrete structures have stood a century or more, those made from portland cement paste are vulnerable to acids, sulfates, and some other salts. Portland cement is usually made from limestone or chalk and from clay or shale. Tetracalcium aluminoferrite contributes to its characteristic gray color. If a white cement is desired, use of tetracalcium aluminoferrite is kept down to about 1 percent.

Concrete can be mixed near the construction site or mixed at a central plant and transported by special agitator trucks, provided the operation can be completed within about 90 minutes. Transported concrete is known as ready-mixed.

While a number of international companies staked out greater control of some market segments entering the mid-1990s, the cement industry remained largely decentralized and competitive. Markets historically tended to be localized because of high transportation costs and the need for on-time delivery to construction sites. Because it is heavy and moisture-sensitive, cement requires special handling in transit as well. Thus, cement companies often own their own principal raw material quarries and locate their manufacturing plants at those sites to minimize material handling. Since clay and limestone are relatively abundant in many regions of the world, local production is usually feasible.

Cement production is a capital-intensive enterprise. The process requires continuous operations and utilizes a heating process that takes 4.4 million British thermal units (Btu) of heat to make one ton of cement. Facility shutdowns can be very expensive. Clinker and cement can be stored, but inventory maintenance can also be expensive. Moreover, cement production is a volume-sensitive industry in which any drop in sales has a disproportionately severe effect on profits. Because cement producers sell their product primarily to the construction industry, they are frequently buffeted by unpredictable, seasonal, and cyclical economic conditions felt by contractors.

CURRENT CONDITIONS

The United States is among the world's largest cement manufacturers. However, it ranks far below developing nations. Citing data from OneStone Consulting Group, *World*

Cement's World Review 2004 revealed that the North American region ranked fourth in cement production during 2003, at 105 million tons. By comparison, China produced 765 million tons, followed by Western Europe (including Turkey) with 236 million tons, and the Far East/Oceania region (excluding China, India, and Japan) with 215 million tons. In all, world production totaled nearly 1.9 billion tons in 2003.

On the consumption side, *World Review 2004* estimated that that developing countries consumed nearly 75 percent of cement in 2003, based on estimates from J.P. Morgan. Of the total cement produced worldwide that year, China accounted for 973.8 million tons, followed by Western Europe (226.2 million tons), North America (115.2 million tons), and Latin America (92.7 million tons).

While U.S. cement exports are negligible (totaling US$58.8 million in 2002), the United States is a sizable importer, with a total of US$940 million in 2002. Leading sources of U.S. imports include Canada, Spain, Mexico, and Venezuela. In general, most U.S. imports come from foreign facilities of companies also operating in the United States.

China constitutes the world's largest cement maker, producing about 41 percent of world supply annually. By the mid-2000s, many of the nation's more than 500 cement and concrete additive producers were merging or forging alliances. In its *World Review 2004* report, *World Cement* indicated that China produced 765 million metric tons of cement in 2003, up 8.5 percent from the previous year. In addition, China was responsible for 43 percent of cement consumption worldwide, a number that was expected to top 50 percent by 2020.

By 2004, China's economy was booming. Following growth of 9.1 percent in 2003, Chinese Vice-Premier Zeng Peiyan revealed that the Chinese economy would achieve a growth rate of more than 10 percent in the first half of the year. This prompted the government to restrain credit and investment in fixed assets, amid concerns that the economy was "overheating," according to *The Australian.*

China exports a small share of its production to other nations, mostly elsewhere in Asia. However, Chinese exports have been at a disadvantage because the nation traditionally has not met international standards for strength and durability. Bringing cement up to standards is a priority for Chinese producers, who were focusing on research and development during the early and mid-2000s in order to bolster the country's export position.

In the April 2004 issue of *The Concrete Producer,* the Portland Cement Association (PCA) was optimistic for the portland cement sector heading into the mid and late 2000s. Edward Sullivan, the PCA's chief economist, said: "The overall outlook for cement consumption is very positive for 2005 through 2007, with 2004 a transition year." Sullivan estimated that nonresidential construction would surpass the residential sector as a growth leader in mid-2004, saying that "softer second-half residential construction activity is expected to be offset by marginally higher nonresidential and public spending activity." In fact, Sullivan estimated that nonresidential construction would surpass the residential sector as a growth leader in mid-2004.

In the PCA's annual spring forecast, Sullivan estimated that in 2004, portland cement consumption would increase 1.9 percent from 2003, reaching 109.5 million tons, according to *Cement Americas.* In 2005, this number was expected to reach 111.8 million tons. Portland cement consumption is expected to increase 2 to 3 percent annually between 2005 and 2007, reaching 115.1 million tons by 2008.

During the first half of 2004, the United States experienced a cement shortage. Twenty-three states were affected, and shortages were especially pronounced along the East Coast and in Florida. A number of factors contributed to this situation. Among them were strong residential construction levels supported by low interest rates and an uncharacteristically active winter construction season. These factors prevented the replenishment of cement inventories that normally occurs during the off-season. Hindering imports was the booming Chinese economy, which was tapping much of the demand for bulk shipping and leading to increased shipping costs. In June of 2004, the PCA indicated that supply would likely improve during the second half of 2004, as interest rates began to rise, thereby slowing the construction market and reducing cement consumption. Shortages, however, were still prevalent in the first half of 2005, as prices surged an estimated 15 to 20 percent from the previous year. Price increases were due to domestic demand from increased building and greatly increased shipping costs to import supplies. More cement imported from Mexico, which was much cheaper, was one solution. Concrete prices stood at about $90 a metric ton in 2005, up from $75 in 2004, and demand was 120 million tons in the U.S.

RESEARCH AND TECHNOLOGY

Cement production entails mixing ingredients in a long, rotating kiln, then gradually heating the blend to a temperature of about 1500 degrees centigrade by burning coal, oil, or other fuels. Consequently, high oil prices in the 1970s prompted cement producers to devise ways to reduce fuel consumption. One way was to convert plants to the so-called dry process manufacturing, wherein water is added to the mix after blending instead of before. The wet process (in which water is added before blending) requires much more fuel. First developed in Europe, the dry process added to the European producers' competitive advantage. Cement producers also cut energy costs by investing in either heating equipment that burned waste and solid fuels instead of oil and gas, or equipment that utilized fuel more efficiently.

Typically 100 to 150 meters long and 3 to 5 meters in diameter, cement kilns are capable of processing large volumes of materials. By the 1990s cement producers responded to the need to reduce energy costs and to provide cost-effective solutions to waste and environmental problems by putting cement kilns to work as waste disposal systems. The cement industry serves as a model for using tonnage materials facilities to recover or dispose of waste streams produced by others. Pressures from environmental organizations continued to push cement manufacturers to improve processes into the mid-2000s. Efforts are underway to establish uniform emissions standards and procedures for enforcing such standards. Many companies (especially the largest ones) are voluntarily taking steps to be environmentally responsible. Other areas of concern are handling of by-products and seeking alternatives to fossil fuels.

Producers can process and utilize waste from the cement-making process in three ways. First, they may substitute a by-product from another industrial operation for one or more of the original ingredients in the feedstream as long as the composition and performance of the cement product is unimpaired. Some say this process at times can yield better product. Among the by-products that manufacturers successfully use are spent sand from metal foundries, blast furnace slag (which supplies iron that cement requires and contains lime and silica in the ideal ratio), and gypsum (a required ingredient of cement) resulting from the "scrubbing" operation used to clean the stack-gas emissions from power plants and other industrial facilities, including cement plants.

Second, cement producers have also fueled their kilns with the combustible by-products of other industrial operations. These fuels include waste oils, organic sludges, and spent solvents such as carbon tetrachloride, trichloroethane, and toluene left over from the manufacture of paint and other chemicals. Cement companies often obtain waste fuel at no cost and may actually receive payment for disposing of potentially toxic materials. When a material to be burned is classified as hazardous waste, though, the cement maker must keep careful records to document that all the hazardous materials are indeed destroyed.

Finally, cement producers can incorporate some waste materials into cement without impairing the quality of the product. Kilns' high temperatures can destroy certain toxic wastes by breaking them into benign elements and compounds that may be harmlessly encapsulated in the cement. Lubricating oil waste and sludge from steelmaking plants are two such materials. Within the United States, researchers explored ways in which the country's scrap tire dumps could be used. The U.S. scrap-tire stockpile increases by 275 million annually, so the supply is vast. Researchers have thus tested grinding them into powder and combining the powder with cement for roadways. In 1994 fatigue tests were underway on "rubcrete" (a cement containing up to 10 percent ground rubber); tests already showed that using rubcrete caused only minor changes in a pavement's durability and resistance to inclement weather.

Manufacturers in the United States were slow to pursue the potential use of cement kilns to recycle and dispose of other materials because energy was plentiful and cheap and solid wastes could be readily disposed. That was not the case in Japan or Western Europe. Countries there implemented extensive energy-saving and waste-recycling measures in their cement industries. Japan became a leader in incorporating various solid wastes, including steelmaking slag and coal-plant tailing, into feedstreams for cement kilns. The government also encouraged use of waste tires as a fuel for cement kilns. In 1992 Mitsubishi Materials burned more than 23,000 tons of tires at its cement plants.

The concrete made from cement underwent revolutionary formulation changes between 1980 and 1995. In the 1960s, high-strength concrete withstood a force of 5,800 pounds per square inch (psi). Thirty years later, high-performance concrete (HPC) produced strengths of 15,000 to 20,000 psi. HPC contains admixtures known as superplasticizers that help to drastically lower the ratio of water to cement, while maintaining enough workability to form a structure. HPC is favored for use in tall buildings, bridges, offshore structures, pavements, and other applications. Due mainly to transportation costs, however, ready-mixed HPC is available only in major metropolitan markets. Another concrete innovation is reinforced cement composites. These composites contain steel, carbon, polypropylene, glass, or fibers and provide better strength-to-weight ratios and energy absorption capacity than conventional concrete.

In 2003 the Strategic Development Council (SDC) released a research report entitled *Roadmap 2030: The U.S. Concrete Industry Technology Roadmap,* produced in cooperation with the U.S. Department of Energy (DOE). The report was a detailed follow-up to the SDC's report, *Vision 2030,* which was published in 2001. According to *The Concrete Producer,* in addition to reducing a 15-year lag between research and the development of actual technologies, the report identified four research areas as being a high priority for the industry. These included concrete production, delivery, and placement; constituent materials; design and structural systems; and repair and rehabilitation.

The DOE conducts industry research at the Oak Ridge (Tenn.) National Laboratory via the Concrete and Containment Technology Program. *The Concrete Producer* indicated that future research goals include a 500 percent increase in concrete recycling; a 60 percent reduction in jobsite material rejection; and a 20 percent reduction in power demand at cement plants. Another goal is to have structural concrete used to produce 50 percent of all new homes.

WORKFORCE

In 2001, the hydraulic cement industry in the United States employed 17,220 people. Of these employees, the majority (12,733) were production workers who earned an average hourly wage of US$20.69, or US$43,041 per year.

In 2001, there were 159 cement manufacturing firms in the United States with a total annual payroll of more than US$877 million. There were 37 firms with four or fewer employees and a total annual payroll of US$3.6 million; 29 with between five and nine employees and a total annual payroll of US$6.7 million; 24 firms with between 10 and 19 employees and a total annual payroll of US$12.7 million; 31 firms with between 20 and 99 employees and a total annual payroll of US$27.2 million; 20 firms with between 100 and 499 employees and a total annual payroll of US$104.8 million; and 119 firms with 500 employees or more and a total annual payroll of US$722.5 million.

INDUSTRY LEADERS

Lafarge SA. Lafarge originated in 1831 when Auguste Pavin de Lafarge, a French noble, established a small lime kiln. There was nothing unique about the company's quarry, but the Lafarge family showed an ability to find markets for lime, which enjoyed an expanding range of industrial uses. In the 1840s Lafarge sold its product in far-flung regions, including the Mediterranean Basin. The company won a contract in 1864 to supply 110,000 tons of hydraulic lime for concrete blocks to form the jetties of the Suez Canal. During the nineteenth century, the company sought growth through acquisitions and established an organization able to supply markets in such far-flung world centers as New York City, Rio de Janeiro, and Saigon. The company's sales of cement products rose to 800,000 tons annually at the outbreak of World War I, making it the world's largest lime producer.

Lafarge Coppée's expansion in the early part of the twentieth century depended on its technical expertise in developing new cement products, for the invention of portland cement made hydraulic lime virtually obsolete. The stock market crash of 1929 contributed to an economic swamp wherein one-third of all workers in the French cement trade were laid off before 1936. During that period Lafarge obtained a number of failing competitors. World War II also created doldrums, but Lafarge emerged by 1959 to take the lead in the French cement industry with 3.2 million tons of cement produced annually.

In 1956 Lafarge entered Canada and in 1970 it merged with Canada Cement to form Canada Cement Lafarge. Canada Cement perfected the shift from cement production on the construction site to ready-mix concrete mixed at a central site and then transported to delivery points by bulk carriers. Lafarge gained prominence in the North American industry in 1981 when it merged Canada Cement Lafarge with Dallas-based General Portland to create a new subsidiary called Lafarge Corporation. By the 1990s Lafarge Corporation was the United States' second-largest cement maker. In 1989 Lafarge acquired Cementia of Switzerland and Asland of Spain and became the world's second-largest cement producer.

Renamed Lafarge SA in 1995, the company continued to pursue growth globally in the late 1990s largely through acquisitions. It moved swiftly into eastern European markets to glean sales from those nations' economic transitions and has continued to accumulate holdings in North and South America. In 1997 Lafarge succeeded in a hostile takeover bid for U.K. roofing tile maker and aggregate processor Redland PLC; the deal was the largest ever in the European building materials sector.

Lafarge's 2001 acquisition of Blue Circle Industries made it the world's largest cement maker. In addition, Lafarge SA holds a controlling interest in Lafarge North America Inc., one of the top cement makers in the United States. As of mid-2004, the company's Cement Division operated 117 cement factories and 24 grinding mills in 43 countries. In 2004, Lafarge's worldwide operations generated more than US$19.5 billion on the strength of 77,075 employees, including nearly 36,000 in its Cement Division. Approximately half of the company's total revenue comes from cement production.

Holcim. Formerly known as Holderbank, Holcim is one of the world's largest manufacturers of cement. It began its global expansion campaign in the early 1950s by buying a small Brazilian company and since then has selectively acquired numerous companies worldwide. Holcim avoided Asian countries where local companies were strong and concentrated instead on markets in Australia and New Zealand. The company entered the U.S. market by making several acquisitions, including Ideal Basic Industries, in the late 1980s. The assets of U.S. acquisitions were merged into Holnam Inc., the largest U.S. cement company.

Holcim's cement empire includes operations in more than 70 nations, with the bulk of its holdings in the Americas and Europe and a growing presence in Asia. During 2003, the company achieved increases in all of its global operating regions. The acquisition of a cement plant in Spain; the consolidation of operation in the Philippines; improved efficiency; and strong performance in Latin America, Asia Pacific, and Africa Middle East were all factors that allowed the company improve its net income—despite a generally weak economic climate.

In 2003, Holcim's revenues totaled US$10.1 billion. The company's net income increased more than 51 percent from 2002, reaching US$552.2 million. In all, the company employed 48,220 workers worldwide.

Cemex, S.A. de C.V. Cemex was the third largest cement maker in the world as of 2004, behind Holcim and Lafarge. Its previous acquisition of Southdown, the second largest cement maker in the United States, was billed as important to the company's future. Cemex, founded in 1906, has in many ways set the industry leaders' pace by focusing largely on amassing market share in the world's rapidly growing economies and by leading in technological and logistical innovations. Its 1992 acquisition of two Spanish cement makers, Valenciana and Sanson, vaulted Cemex into the arena with such world players as Holcim and Lafarge. The Spanish venture enabled Cemex to skirt U.S. antidumping duties by exporting to the United States from Spain, which was not subject to the duties.

By 2004, Cemex had cement concerns in more than 30 countries. North America accounted for more than half of the company's sales in 2004, led by Mexico (36.7 percent) and the United States (24 percent). Other leading markets included Spain (16.7 percent) and the Central America/Caribbean region (7.8 percent).

Cemex is possibly the industry's most technologically advanced, in terms of both manufacturing plant and management infrastructure. It operates some of the world's most efficient and up-to-date cement facilities and supports production with an extensive information system for monitoring operations worldwide. Cemex also has developed viable and profitable export channels to countries where it holds no plants, notably in Asia, where it acquired its first local stake in 1997. Via Cemex Asia Holdings, the company has a 23.5 percent stake in PT Semen Gresik, Indonesia's top cement maker. Such diversification has helped insulate the Cemex parent company from regional slowdowns, although some analysts still consider Cemex to have considerable exposure to local market downswings.

In 2004, Cemex achieved revenues of nearly US$8.15 billion. Its net income totaled US$1.3 million, an increase of 107.6 percent from 2003. Cement accounted for about 75 percent of the company's revenues.

Taiheiyo Cement Corporation. Taiheiyo, Japan's leading cement company, is the result of the 1998 merger of Chichibu-Nihon and Onoda Cement Ltd. Chichibu-Nihon's emergence as a world leader largely occurred in the short span of the early to mid-1990s and is testimony to the high degree of consolidation and occasional instability in Japan's cement industry. Chichibu had been Japan's leading producer since it was formed in a 1994 merger with Onoda Cement Ltd. By 1997 it commanded more than 21 percent of the Japanese market share, some four percentage points higher than its next-closest rival did. Propelling it to the world scene was its 1997 agreement to merge with third-largest Nihon Cement Co., which itself had been Japan's leading cement maker until Chichibu and another rival displaced it. The merger was approved in 1998, and the two companies arrived at a new name, Taiheiyo. Within months of its announcement, the proposed Chichibu-Nihon transaction triggered another merger of cement operations between two smaller competitors, Mitsubishi Materials Corp. and Ube Industries Ltd.

Taiheiyo's revenues totaled more than US$8.3 billion in 2004, at which time the company commanded a 30 percent share of the Japanese market. Taiheiyo also produces ready-mix concrete and construction materials, which complement the company's real estate holdings. The company's interests are largely concentrated in Asia. A full 85 percent of Taiheiyo's products go to the Japanese market.

FURTHER READING

"Cement Prices Continue to Fuel Surge in Construction Costs." *Knight-Ridder Tribune Business News,* 24 June 2005.

"Chapter I: Introduction." *Chinese Markets for Cement Additives.* Asia Market Information & Development Co., December 2003.

"China Predicts 10pc Growth." *The Australian,* 7 July 2004.

"Economist Gives Bullish Outlook." *The Concrete Producer,* April 2004.

"Forecast 2004." *Cement Americas,* 1 January 2004.

"Global Review of Operations." Nuevo Leon, Mexico: CEMEX, S.A. de C.V. 23 July 2004. Available from http://www.cemex.com/ar2003/eng/ma_gr.asp.

Hoover's Company Capsules. Hoover's Inc., 2005. Available from http://www.hoovers.com.

International Trade Administration (ITA). *Industry Sector Data: Cement Manufacturing.* 22 July 2004. Available from http://www.ita.doc.gov/td/industry/otea/industry_sector/tables_naics/327310.htm.

Klemens, Tom. "Questions, Answers, and Applications: High-Tech Research Is Yielding Concrete Results." *The Concrete Producer.* August 2003.

"No Cement Shortage in Alaska." *Knight-Ridder Tribune Business News,* 23 June 2005.

Owers, Paul. "Builders Ask for Help in Cement Shortage." *Palm Beach Post,* 30 June 2004.

"PCA Forecasts Modest Gains Despite Mixed Outlook." *Cement Americas,* 1 May 2004.

"Prospects for Cement Shortage Relief Emerging." Skokie, Ill.: Portland Cement Association. 10 June 2004. Available from http://www.cement.org.

"Results for 2003: Holcim Improves Efficiency and Reports Significantly Higher Group Net Income Despite Weak Dollar." St. Gallen, Switzerland: Holcim Ltd. 9 March 2004. Available from http://www.holcim.com.

U.S. Census Bureau. *Annual Survey of Manufactures.* January 2003. Available from http://www.census.gov.

———. *Statistics of U.S. Businesses: 2001: Cement Manufacturing.* Statistics of U.S. Businesses, 23 July 2004. Available from http://www.census.gov.

"World Review 2004." *World Cement,* July 2004. Available from http://www.palladian-publications.com/Cement/WC_regional_review_july04.htm.

SIC 3270

NAICS 327

CONCRETE, GYPSUM, AND PLASTER PRODUCTS

Companies in this industry process and manufacture materials mostly for use in construction. The five major subsets are

- concrete blocks and bricks
- general concrete products
- ready-mixed concrete
- lime
- gypsum products

Production of cement, a key ingredient in concrete, is discussed in greater detail under the heading **Cement, Hydraulic.**

INDUSTRY SNAPSHOT

The world's volatile building materials markets follow the trends set by the broader construction industry. In the late 1990s and early 2000s, the steel industry started losing revenue to the concrete industry when engineers and contractors more often chose concrete for their infrastructure needs. In the commercial and residential markets, new building construction and renovation drive global demand for the various concrete, lime, and gypsum products. Manufacturers of these products, like manufacturers of most building materials, are realizing the benefits of offering buyers more choices. In both the commercial and residential markets, buyers are looking for customized options. By 2004, innovations like self-consolidating concrete (SCC) allowed builders to make more elaborate concrete shapes by using forms and molds that were more elaborate than those used with traditional concrete.

China's economy was experiencing explosive growth in the mid-2000s. As China's economy boomed, the nation's demand for construction-related materials caused shortages in other world markets—including the United States. Material shortages occurred for concrete, as well as gypsum products like drywall. While this shortage was partially attributed to a squeeze on available container ships, which slowed import activity worldwide, a considerable share of the shortage stemmed from the massive amount of construction materials China was consuming. By 2004 and into 2005, these factors caused all U.S. states, except Alaska, to experience shortages of the cement needed to make concrete. Shortages were especially pronounced along the East Coast and in Florida, where the residential construction market was booming. Coupled with the prospect of rising interest rates, some observers expected a slowdown in Chinese demand for construction materials. These factors had the potential to correct the industry's material shortages later in the mid-2000s.

Owing to convention and prohibitive transportation costs, international trade in most kinds of building materials remains quite small compared to the value of production. Nonetheless, in such places as the United Kingdom and the United States, imports account for a growing share of consumption, and this trend is expected to accelerate.

Environmental concerns affect the building materials industry more every year. Pressure from advocacy groups and legislators, along with the emerging technologies that result from that pressure, are making environmentally safe materials more available and affordable. In the gypsum industry especially, strides are being made to utilize recycled materials.

ORGANIZATION AND STRUCTURE

The industry's output, which constitutes a significant share of the world's nonwood, nonmetal building materials, comprises a number of diverse product categories. Most industry participants specialize in a few of these categories rather than producing the entire breadth of industry goods. A number of major companies operate in multiple stages of their products' supply chains, however, such as quarrying stone, processing it into cement, and then adding self-supplied aggregate (sand or gravel) to create concrete—the finished product—for customers. In this sense, some of the industry's largest firms are more vertically integrated than horizontally. Still, many building materials manufacturers obtain all of their raw materials from other firms.

While technological innovations in these building materials occur regularly, most are considered low-profit commodities best suited for mass production. Some technological entry barriers exist, however, for participation in world class materials production. Certain material processing equipment requires significant capital investment, and hence cost precludes smaller firms from participating in those segments of the industry.

Concrete. In essence, concrete is a mixture of powder cement, water, and coarse or fine aggregate (gravel or sand, respectively). Its production is thus wholly dependent on the production of cement, which means that many of the leading cement companies (see **Cement, Hydraulic**) also produce concrete. Other concrete companies source their raw materials from unaffiliated manufacturers and perform their own mixing.

Concrete is used in diverse applications that cross virtually all subsets of the construction industry—some construction firms even manufacture their own. Leading uses include roads, bridges, airports, and buildings. To meet these end needs, concrete products may be delivered to customers as ready-mixed concrete to be poured on site or as preformed structures to be installed. Because of its widespread use in public structures such as roads, the concrete segment is more dependent on government public works spending than are other parts of the industry. Still, private construction demands a major share of the world's concrete as well.

Lime. The mineral by-product lime derives from quarried limestone, dolomite, and similar stones. Manufactured lime has numerous uses outside of construction, especially applications in the chemical and steel industries. In construction, lime is used to make mortar and plaster. Such construction uses account for a relatively small share of the world's lime production.

Gypsum. As with lime, gypsum comes from processed minerals. Unlike lime, however, the vast majority of gypsum is used for construction purposes, primarily in the fabrication of wallboard (also known as drywall or plasterboard). Over the course of the twentieth century, wallboard supplanted plaster in industrial countries to become the key material in residential walls, with a strong presence in nonresidential buildings as well. In addition, gypsum is sometimes used in plaster and other building materials. Gypsum plasters are, in actuality, a type of cement that is used widely in construction materials such as wallboard, slabs, flooring, and decorative moldings. These are made of a combination of gypsum and a dehydrated form of gypsum known as anhydrite. In addition, other chemicals can be added for properties needed in particular applications. For example, sulfate salts are added to some construction plasters to speed up the setting of the compound.

More so than in other building materials segments, gypsum product manufacturing is dominated by a handful of major producers that hold large shares of the market. In the late 1990s, for example, the largest U.S. wallboard maker controlled nearly a third of the U.S. market.

BACKGROUND AND DEVELOPMENT

The raw materials from which building products are derived have been with humanity throughout the ages. Ancient Egypt first used gypsum as a building material 5,000 years ago. After heating, crushing, and remixing it with water, it was used as plaster on walls. Ancient cultures also combined these materials to make forms of cements and other types of plasters that could be used in conjunction with other common construction materials. The pyramids in Egypt, for example, were constructed of gypsum. Raw materials were plentiful and inexpensive and the products based on these minerals proved to have natural fire retardant properties.

The concrete block industry began in earnest in England in the mid-nineteenth century when bricklayer Joseph Aspdin created and patented Portland cement. Concrete block was prized as a construction material for its durability and price as well as its safety, compared to typical construction materials of that age, namely wood. Today, the primary use of cement and concrete products is by the construction industry.

Gypsum—also known in its purest form as the material alabaster—was initially sold as a fertilizer. In the late nineteenth century, changes in the composition of gypsum plasters, or plasters of paris, placed it in a position to compete with lime plasters.

One of the changes in the building materials industry was the invention of a gypsum material used primarily in the covering of framed structures as walls. It is known today by various names: drywall, plasterboard, wallboard, and by the trade name Sheetrock. Wallboard was invented in the United States in 1890 by Augustine Sackett and first marketed in 1894. The product is made from a layer of gypsum placed between two pieces of paper. The material has been utilized in construction because it is both fireproof and an excellent insulating material. In 1901, the U.S. Gypsum Company purchased the machine invented by Sackett as well as the proprietary information on its production and continued to make improvements. It was not until 1917 that production of the material was perfected. Army barracks used in World War I were among the first structures to use wallboard rather than fiberboard.

In the early 1900s, changes in transportation made a significant impact on these types of industries, such as the advent of trucks that could both deliver and mix concrete on site. In addition, more concrete and concrete products were needed in order to make easier travel possible.

In the 1920s, a price war in the United States wallboard industry drove prices down and a smaller company, CertainTeed Corporation, into compliance with the product guidelines and price controls set forth by U.S. Gypsum. Because U.S. Gypsum had patented the process of manufacturing wallboard, it was able to control the price under its licensing agreement with other manufacturing firms, including CertainTeed. One factor that allowed U.S. Gypsum to dominate the industry was its large size and the fact that the company was vertically integrated, a strategy that allowed it to control product costs from mining of the gypsum to shipping and even sales. It was also this position that caused problems decades later for the company. In 1940, the U.S. Justice Department charged wallboard manufacturers, including U.S. Gypsum, with price fixing as a result of cross-licensing. The decision put an end to price controls as well as the ability of U.S. Gypsum to license the patent to other wallboard manufacturers. The company was charged with price fixing again in 1973. However, this time, justice was not as lenient. The company settled for US$28 million and faced criminal indictment. The case was finally settled in 1980.

In Europe and the United States, the presence of several large, dominant producers in certain building materials segments—wallboard, in particular— meant relative stability throughout the 1990s for capacity. In fact, U.S. wallboard capacity utilization in the late 1990s was at extraordinarily strong levels, hovering in the 90 to 93 percent range from 1994 to 1998—and U.S. Gypsum was at 99 percent capacity in late 1997.

The reverse of this situation was in Japan and Southeast Asia in part as a result of the late 1990s financial crisis. Southeast Asia had been building up capacity to meet its own rapid expansion needs as well as to serve as an export base. The harsh fiscal climate stifled demand and battered some of the region's producers, who were struck with three potential setbacks: capacity for anticipated new demand that never materialized; declines in established demand; and internal debt, including any debt incurred to build new capacity and financial distress because of the currency and market declines. Consequently, at least for the short term, Southeast Asia's building materials companies grappled with overcapacity and falling prices in the late 1990s. Other parts of Asia, such as China and India, remained comparatively healthy.

Because industry products tend to be large, heavy, and relatively inexpensive, in most regions no substantial international trade has been realized (and when it has, it is usually between adjacent countries). More often, companies have entered foreign markets through establishment or acquisition of foreign affiliates that produce materials in the target country. However, building materials trade began to rise in the 1990s, and nonwood materials were among the fastest growing trade segments.

As Americans enjoyed a healthy economy in the late 1990s, they had the means to customize new buildings, both residential and commercial. After a slump, the economy began to rally again toward the end of 2001, and consumers were still interested in customized features for their building projects. While the concrete and gypsum industry is less affected than decorative industries by the desire for customization, the effect is worth mentioning. In 2001, The Bomanite Corporation (which specializes in concrete paving and flooring), for example, offered a wide variety of colored (100 patterns and 25 colors), textured, and imprinted concrete paving choices. Also in 2001, a psychiatric hospital in Pembroke Pines, Florida, was renovated using a high-impact wallboard that is new to the industry. It installs easily, can be repaired easily, is fire-resistant, features a less institutional look, and is highly resistant to penetration. This is important because it creates a better atmosphere while minimizing the risk of escape. This facility serves as an illustration that all wallboard is not the same and that the expanding array of options available enables builders to make customized choices.

Current Conditions

The industry's conditions are ever changing due to fluctuations in construction markets and internal industry dynamics alike. The industry passes through cyclical capacity and pricing conditions that factor into a given participant's sales and profits. When building materials manufacturers perceive an expanding market, many respond by investing in new plants to accommodate higher production levels. Once this new capacity is achieved, especially when several manufacturers expand simultaneously, it can create excess supply, which tends to induce price cuts. Lower prices, in turn, mean lost revenue and tighter profit margins. In highly competitive markets, manufacturers may introduce price cuts to lure market share from competitors, but this practice can reduce industry profitability in general when other firms respond in kind, and may not yield any market share to the initiating firm. Industry analysts therefore evaluate building materials companies in part by their discipline to expand capacity judiciously and to maintain sustainable pricing.

By 2004, China's economy was experiencing explosive growth. Chinese Vice-Premier Zeng Peiyan revealed that the Chinese economy would achieve a growth rate of more than 10 percent in the first half of 2004, following growth of 9.1 percent in 2003. According to *The Australian,* these conditions caused the government to restrain investment in fixed assets, as well as credit, amidst concerns that the economy was "overheating."

As China's economy boomed, the nation's demand for construction-related materials caused shortages in other world markets—including the United States. In addition to concrete, gypsum products like drywall, and steel, shortages of roofing materials and lumber also developed. Part of this shortage stemmed from a squeeze on available container ships, which slowed import activity worldwide. However, much of the shortage stemmed from the massive amount of materials China was consuming. For example, when construction of a 1.6 mile hydroelectric dam on China's Yangtze River called for the relocation of 1.5 million people, the Chinese government began building new cities for them to live in, requiring enormous supplies of concrete and steel.

Forty-nine U.S. states experienced a shortage of the cement needed to make concrete in early 2005. However, shortages were especially pronounced along the East Coast and in Florida. In June 2004, Florida's *Ocala Star-Banner* reported that while the United States imported 13 percent of its concrete from Asia and Europe, Florida was more susceptible to global shortages because the state's booming residential construction industry relied on imports to satisfy nearly 50 percent of concrete demand.

In addition to China's demand for building material, other factors contributing to the shortage of building products included strong residential construction levels fueled by low interest rates, as well as an uncharacteristically active winter construction season. In mid-2004, some industry observers noted that China expected to scale back its consumption of materials. Coupled with the prospect of rising interest rates, these conditions would likely correct the material shortages of 2004.

In 2003, *Cement Americas* reported on the results of a study conducted by economists with the U.S. Department of Labor, Bureau of Labor Statistics. According to the study, prices for gypsum and cement increased by 17.4 percent and 15.4 percent, respectively, over the five-year period from 1996 to 2001.

RESEARCH AND TECHNOLOGY

When terrorists attacked the World Trade Center in New York City on September 11, 2001, people watched as the skyscrapers collapsed. As a result, many building material manufacturers asked themselves how they could improve the quality of their products. Researchers are working to create products that are sturdier, more durable, or more flexible. They are also focused on examining the ways in which their products fail (as they ultimately will, one way or another) so that they can take control of the ways they will break down, respond to destructive forces, or deteriorate.

Research began to address how materials could be improved and how those products' ultimate dilapidation could be controlled. Following the attacks, attention turned to the work of researchers such as the team at North Carolina State University who sought to create a high-performance, fiber-reinforced concrete (HPFRC) system that would improve the way buildings and other structures made with concrete react to destructive forces. This system capitalizes on the flexibility of mats constructed of recycled stainless steel fibers; these mats are then infused with concrete for application. Researchers note that this technology is not limited to new buildings because the mats can be fitted around existing supporting elements such as beams and columns or used to create new supporting structures by using the mats as tubular forms that can be filled with concrete.

Changing technology has made mining, refining, and manufacturing construction materials much easier. Bodies such as the American Society for Testing and Materials monitored minimum standards for concrete materials. The European Committee for Standardization planned to design criteria for building materials in the European Union. As the technology changed, so too did the criteria for the composition of these construction products. Industry was compelled to keep pace with these changes to remain competitive in the marketplace.

Continual and sometimes dramatic changes in science and engineering produced positive changes in the industry. The advent of automation meant that computers could be adapted to measure raw materials in the production of concrete as well as assist in packaging and transportation.

The rise of synthetic materials meant new developments in the manufacture and use of construction materials. There are plastic cements that have been developed for use as a construction binding material. Epoxy, polyester, and other resins have been used as well in conjunction with cement structures for joints as well as in the repair and protection of concrete.

The use of carbon as a conducting agent in concrete also opens up new possibilities. The introduction of special carbon fibers into concrete is being tested for use in heating buildings and paved surfaces, detecting earthquakes, and building submarines. The conductivity could make heating buildings more efficient, provide a safe lightning rod on the side of a building, and melt snow or ice on driveways and runways. Concrete containing these carbon fibers undergoes reduced conductivity when heavy pressure is applied. This is what makes the concrete act as a sensor as well as a building material. Possible applications of the sensory ability include weighing moving vehicles, providing electromagnetic shielding for security and privacy, and detecting earthquakes.

Many people are surprised at the possibility of using concrete to make submarines, but researchers are working to create just such a formula. A concrete submarine would have two important advantages over traditional steel vessels. First, it could go deeper into the ocean because concrete can withstand more pressure than steel; and second, it would be less detectable by sonar. Researchers continue to work toward a formula for bendable concrete, which would be valuable to the construction industry and the automotive and aircraft industries. A contributor to *The Economist* commented, "Unlikely as it may seem, concrete could be the wonder material of the future."

In Europe, increasingly tighter standards for emissions released into air and water were expected to particularly impact the precast concrete industry. Also limits placed on mining activities were anticipated to result in supply problems for related industries in the late 1990s. As a result, research into the recycling of waste concrete was starting to allay supply problems.

However, not all of the production processes for these materials produced environmental problems. Some private industries, in partnership with government entities, are searching for new methods to responsibly manufacture materials as well as incorporate recycled goods into products. In eastern Germany, for example, wallboard factories were planned in six cities to convert some of the gypsum produced through desulphurization of brown coal power stations. Officials at Veag, the utility involved in the project, estimated that one power plant alone could produce 1 million tons per year of gypsum. The plasterboard factory at that site can only utilize 250,000 tons per year; the balance would be stored. Processing would continue well after the closure of the coal-burning power plants.

In the United States, USG has implemented a plan similar to the program in Germany and has begun drawing gypsum from coal-fueled power station smokestacks. In accordance with environmental regulations, utility companies using coal for fuel must scrub out their smokestacks to prevent pollutants from creating acid rain. The gypsum-rich chemical sludge that is scrubbed out of the smokestacks is a combination of smoke by-products and materials sprayed into the smokestacks to reduce air pollution. USG's decision to buy gypsum from utility companies benefits both parties; the utility company now makes money instead of spending it to have the waste taken to a landfill, and USG gets gypsum that is purer than what is mined out of the ground. In 2001, USG also introduced its Fiberock Brand Underlayment Aqua-Tough, an underlayment (sub-flooring) made completely of recycled gypsum and cellulose. Besides being environmentally sound, this product provides a moisture-resistant layer that is designed for indoor or outdoor use beneath virtually any type of flooring. Breakthroughs like this offer consumers the option to choose recycled materials without sacrificing function. The company benefits from extending the life of its product and also from presenting itself to the public as a company that takes steps toward preserving the environment. Other environmental initiatives by USG include using recycled newspapers and boxes to make ceiling panels and using steel mill slag to make ceiling tiles.

Canadian government officials and the private sector have also been working together to support and create the building of environmentally sound buildings with recycled materials. For example, in one demonstration project, colored chips of recycled glass were added to terrazzo floors; and drywall in the construction used the maximum available recycled materials. Another innovation may come from Dr. Bill Price of the University of Houston. His work toward creating transparent concrete was making progress in 2001, when he succeeded in creating partial transparency.

In 2003, the Strategic Development Council (SDC) released a research report entitled *Roadmap 2030: The U.S. Concrete Industry Technology Roadmap,* produced in cooperation with the U.S. Department of Energy (DOE). The report was a detailed follow-up to the SDC's report, *Vision 2030,* which was published in 2001. According to *The Concrete Producer,* in addition to reducing a 15-year lag between research and the development of actual technologies, the report identified four research areas as being a high priority for the industry. These included concrete production, delivery, and placement; constituent materials; design and structural systems; and repair and rehabilitation.

The DOE conducts industry research at the Oak Ridge (Tenn.) National Laboratory via the Concrete and Containment Technology Program. *The Concrete Producer* indicated that future research goals include a 500 percent increase in concrete recycling; a 60 percent reduction in jobsite material rejection; and a 20 percent reduction in power demand at cement plants. Another goal is to have structural concrete used to produce 50 percent of all new homes.

In January of 2004, *The Concrete Producer* reported that Texas EMC Products—a joint venture between the Dutch enterprise EMC Cement BV and the United States' Few Ready Mix Concrete Co.—was preparing to introduce an energetically modified cement (EMC) called CemPozz. Concrete producers could use the EMC as a 60 percent substitute for Portland Cement when mixing concrete. The EMC consisted of modified fly ash—a coal combustion byproduct—that produced a stronger concrete mixture at a lower cost. In addition, production required less energy, thereby benefiting the environment.

The patented process for producing EMC was developed in the early 1990s by Dr. Vladimir Ronin, a researcher at the Lulea University of Technology in Sweden. According to *Concrete Producer*: "CemPozz improves concrete's chemistry. Portland cement reacts with water to produce ordinary concrete. That chemical process, called hydration, forms two cementing compounds in the concrete—calcium silicate hydrate and calcium hydroxide.

"The calcium silicate hydrate gives concrete its strength and dimensional stability. The calcium hydroxide, which makes up about 25 percent of ordinary concrete, is relatively weak and porous. As a continuing part of the hydration process, CemPozz consumes the calcium hydroxide, turning it into additional hardened concrete. This results in a denser, less permeable, and more durable concrete."

Industry Leaders

USG. A division of the USG Corporation, U.S. Gypsum is the world's largest manufacturer of gypsum wallboard. Its main products are various wallboards, and its Sheetrock brand is the top-seller in the world. The company was formed in the late 1800s and early 1900s from a union of 35 gypsum manufacturers in the United States. At the time, the firm controlled half of the gypsum products market in the country. The company also had substantial assets in the production of lime products as well as other construction materials. The aftershocks of legal actions against the firm in the 1970s and 1980s, which ranged from antitrust matters to various claims from asbestos contaminated products, meant the company had to retrench fiscally. Although by 1998 USG was seen as a healthy and more disciplined company, its parent company filed Chapter 11 in 2001 to restructure in light of the significant financial implications of mounting asbestos claims. USG's chairman, president, and CEO, William Foote, explains in *Walls and Ceilings*, "The filing is not about restructuring our company's operating units or dealing with a liquidity crisis. Rather, the Chapter 11 process was our only alternative to prevent the value drain that has been occurring as U. S. Gypsum was forced to pay for the asbestos costs of other companies that have already filed Chapter 11." USG's parent company's 2004 sales totaled more than US$4.5 billion. During the early 2000s, approximately 60 percent of the company's revenues came from sales of gypsum products in North America.

BPB Industries. With some 40 percent of Europe's wallboard market and 9 percent of the North American market, U.K.-based BPB is a major player in the European market with a growing presence in North America and other parts of the world. Wallboard is a crucial product line for BPB, as it represented 64 percent of sales in 2004, up from 48 percent in 2001. BPB's plasterboard volume growth increased 30 percent 2003 and 11 percent in 2004. In 2004, revenues totaled US$3.9 billion. The company also produces paper and packing goods, which integrate well with its wallboard production.

Tarmac Ltd. One of the leaders in the U.K. construction materials trade only entered into the brick, tile, and assorted concrete products market in the 1980s. Tarmac Ltd. was founded on the creation of road material made from a combination of tar and slag; the company's name is still sometimes used as a generic reference to driving surfaces. Though primarily vested in interests in quarrying and sales of road-building materials as well as civil engineering, the company began positioning itself for growth in the brick and concrete markets in 1971. In the 1980s Tarmac began expanding into the global marketplace, and the purchase of The Hoveringham Group cemented Tarmac PLC's entry into the brick, tile, and assorted concrete products market as well as international commerce. The purchase, combined with subsequent purchases, gave Tarmac substantial holdings in quarrying and concrete production in the United States. In the late 1990s it was, by a narrow margin, the United Kingdom's second-largest producer of ready-mix concrete. The company registered 2001 sales of US$1.7 billion. Individual sales figures were not available in 2004, by which time the company was a subsidiary of Anglo American.

Lafarge SA. France's Lafarge is one of the world's top building materials conglomerates. It has market-leading shares in several product categories and in several countries, but its international presence spans most parts of the world. Lafarge is the world's second-largest cement maker, but it also produces ready-mix concrete, aggregates, gypsum wallboard and other gypsum products, roofing tiles, and a variety of other building materials. In 1997 Lafarge transacted the largest acquisition ever in the European building materials industry when it bought out the United Kingdom's Redland PLC in a US$3.6 billion hostile takeover. Redland was a diversified aggregates, concrete, and roofing materials firm with a stronger market presence in the United Kingdom than Lafarge. The takeover was expected to have repercussions in the U.K. industry, particularly in the ready-mix concrete segment, and possibly lead to further consolidation. In 2001, Lafarge acquired Blue Circle Industries, propelling it to status as the world's leading cement producer. Lafarge had 2004 sales of US$19.5 billion, up 13.9 percent from the previous year. In 2004, cement accounted for approximately half of the company's sales.

FURTHER READING

Brown, Michael. "National Gypsum's Hi-Impact[R] Brand Wallboard Supports State Hospital's Plan for Conventional Interiors that Resists Penetration." *Walls & Ceilings,* November 2001.

"Building Materials Industry." *Value Line Investment Survey,* 2005.

"Cement Prices Continue to Fuel Surge in Construction Costs." *Knight-Ridder Tribune Business News,* 24 June 2005.

"Cement Shortages Threaten Construction Market." *Pit & Quarry,* June 2004.

Drake, Bob. "Could New Concrete System Have Prevented World Trade Center Buildings from Collapsing?" *Pit & Quarry,* October 2001.

"High-Tech Concrete." *The Economist,* 24 July 1999.

Hoover's Company Capsules. Hoover's Inc., 2005. Available from http://www.hoovers.com.

"How to See Through Walls." *The Economist,* 22 September 2001.

Klemens, Tom. "Another Mix Option: Portland Cement Substitute Yields Economic, Environmental, and Durability Benefits." *The Concrete Producer,* January 2004.

———. "Questions, Answers, and Applications: High-Tech Research Is Yielding Concrete Results." *The Concrete Producer,* August 2003.

"Maybe It's Not so Hard Being Eco-friendly." *Business Week,* 16 April 2001.

"No Cement Shortage in Alaska." *Knight-Ridder Tribune Business News,* 23 June 2005.

Stanfield, Frank. "Collision of Global, Local Growth Poses Problem for Ocala, Fla.-Area Builders." *Ocala Star Banner (FL),* 24 June 2004.

Sullivan, C.C. "For Liquid Stone, A Virtual Chisel: New Concrete Mixes Revive Classical Ornament." *Architecture,* August 2004.

"Survey: Cement, Gypsum are Price Increase Leaders." *Cement Americas,* 1 January 2003.

"USG Files Chapter 11 to Manage Asbestos Costs and Liability." *Walls & Ceilings,* August 2001.

"USG Introduces Environmentally Friendly Underlayment." *Floor Covering Installer,* July-August 2001.

SIC 1540
NAICS 2362

CONSTRUCTION, NONRESIDENTIAL BUILDING

Nonresidential construction firms build, alter, remodel, repair, and renovate a wide range of commercial, industrial, and public buildings, including industrial buildings, warehouses, office buildings, churches and synagogues, hospitals, museums, schools, restaurants and shopping centers, and stadiums. See also **Construction, Residential Building** and **Engineering Services.**

INDUSTRY SNAPSHOT

The global construction industry is closely tied to general business and economic conditions. Certain segments of the nonresidential building construction industry proved healthier than others amid the fluctuating economic trends of the early 2000s. While office building construction was plagued by oversupply in the early 1990s, economic conditions improved later in the decade. Despite problems like corporate downsizing, temporary work forces, and inventory reduction, the strong economy facilitated a rapid decline in office vacancies in the United States. The economic situation was particularly beneficial for smaller office building construction in smaller cities around the world as many corporations began to decentralize their operations and moved divisional offices closer to manufacturing and distribution centers. Some corporations in search of lower costs abandoned large cities completely. This trend created an upturn in demand for new office buildings in some medium-sized cities in the southeastern United States. Furthermore, the industry, especially in the United States and parts of Western Europe, saw a shift in demographics in office building construction, as many businesses moved away from their traditional urban settings into suburbs and outlying areas.

The nonresidential building segment of the construction industry is aided by the fact that institutional building, like governmental buildings and schools, tends to remain relatively stable. Additionally, even in mature construction markets like the United States, new facilities, or at least upgrades to older facilities, are quite often needed to replace or refurbish aging schools, hospitals, and other publicly funded structures. In the case of schools, quite often increasing enrollment can bolster construction needs.

The rapid expansion of the Asian economies in most business sectors enabled construction companies worldwide to tap into this market. When companies established themselves in the Asia-Pacific region, construction contractors would then build the new facilities. Gains in the Asian market made it possible for international contractors to offset the more modest gains in the mature markets of Europe and North America, as well as regions with comparatively low demand such as Latin America, the Middle East, and Africa. Asia (excluding Japan) was expected by most industry analysts to remain the leading region for new construction in the world early in the twenty-first century; areas such as Latin America and Eastern Europe were also predicted to grow, albeit somewhat more slowly.

ORGANIZATION AND STRUCTURE

International construction companies and the design firms that work closely with them are among the most independent of corporations. While international manufacturing corporations may diversify their products and services, builders tend to remain focused on construction. One division may specialize in high-rise office buildings while another will concentrate on petrochemical plants.

Most international construction companies and design firms manage their businesses independently of their respective governments. However, this does not mean that they are not regulated. Companies must build to local or national building codes and follow local or national environmental standards. They are usually monitored for safety on the work site by government departments and their own safety directors. In the United States the Occupational Safety and Health Administration (OSHA) regularly issues and monitors rules that govern various aspects of the nonresidential building industry. In early 1995, for example, OSHA issued a safety regulation that mandated that all construction employees wear harnesses if working near the edge of a building. The harnesses, which are secured to the building, are designed to prevent the wearers from falling more than a few feet.

In the early 2000s many of the largest construction firms were private companies, such as Bechtel Group Inc. and Parsons Corporation. Some companies were owned and headed primarily by their founding families. While many corporations hired for their higher management positions "business"people who often had little practical knowledge of the company, construction companies and engineering design firms were more typically headed by builders and engineers. Many in key positions in the industry began working in the field as project managers and subsequently learned how to run the business by working their way up.

BACKGROUND AND DEVELOPMENT

After reaching peak levels in 1998, due to strong economies in both North America and Europe, the nonresidential construction market began to decline in 2000 as a result of weakening economic trends. Companies in Europe, the United States, and Japan in particular saw significant reductions in new contracts, particularly for domestic projects. This downward trend, however, had begun to improve by 2004, when worldwide spending on construction, fueled in large part by surging demand in China and India, reached US$3.9 trillion. In the early 2000s, about 65 percent of the construction industry's business was in the form of new construction, while the remainder was derived from alterations, maintenance, and repair. While the United States remained a world leader in the nonresidential construction industry, about 80 percent of the world's construction activity took place outside U.S. borders.

Demand for office building construction increased when the dot-com boom of the late 1990s fueled numerous start-ups and expansion among existing businesses. However, in 2000 the growth in the office building market slowed considerably when the dot-com firms began disappearing and many technology firms began scaling back operations to weather the downturn. In fact, U.S. office building construction declined 22 percent in 2001, more than any other nonresidential construction sector. In comparison, the U.S. nonresidential building industry as a whole fell only 4 percent, from US$173.1 billion in 2000 to US$165.8 billion in 2001. According to *U.S. Construction Trends,* a report released by construction industry research firm F. W. Dodge, "After a very strong 2000, the demand for office space was dampened by the dot-com correction, as a substantial amount of sublease space was put back on the market. The decline for office construction was especially pronounced in those cities that benefited from the high-tech boom, such as Washington D.C., Seattle, San Jose, and Dallas." More favorable economic conditions after 2004, however, began to reverse this downward trend. According to McGraw-Hill Construction, office building construction in January 2005 rose 11 percent nationwide (adjusted annual rate).

In the early 2000s oil refinery and chemical plant construction around the world remained one of the fundamental cornerstones of the industry. Industry observers noted that, with China and other Asian countries such as Vietnam becoming more receptive to outside influence, the market for petrochemical plants was expected to remain steady early in the twenty-first century. U.S. companies particularly had the advantage in this market with decades of international experience building oil refineries. The rapid growth in global trade has also increased the need for projects such as port facilities and airports, especially in developing countries.

Construction of manufacturing plants has traditionally remained relatively steady over the years. Manufacturing plants, according to conventional wisdom, always need to be expanded, upgraded, rebuilt, and built in new locations. In fact, most of the construction activity in this industry segment is done to increase capacity, which was expected to continue as companies expand globally and need greater capacity— with the caveat that cyclically many manufacturing industries reach stages of over-capacity that spell lean times for construction firms. The manufacturing plant construction attracts a wide range of international expertise. However, the construction of huge manufacturing plants in the United States such as those that assemble automobiles and trucks was never again expected to rival the pace of construction achieved earlier in the twentieth century. Factories built at the end of the twentieth century were expected to last well into the next century, although renovation work on these facilities was likely to be done. In the United States, however, manufacturing over the last several decades of the twentieth century slowly declined as the country's economy became increasingly based on service industries. At the same time, the shifting of manufacturing jobs to developing countries, particularly in Asia, opened opportunities there for substantial growth in construction. In China, for example, construction investment—much of it for new factories—was projected to grow at about 7.9 percent through 2012. Even higher growth of 9.2 percent was projected for India.

One key to any developing country's efforts to build its own industrial base is access to electric power. While the construction of new electric generation plants in the United States slowed through the 1980s and 1990s, the world's hunger for power was expected to grow. China alone announced that it intended to double its electric power generating capacity over a five-year span. Doing that required the help of scores of international companies.

Although periodically threatened by tight budgets in the deficit-conscious 1990s, the construction of governmental and educational buildings was likely to remain one of the foundations of the nonresidential construction industry. Besides demographic trends that necessitated new school construction, the need to upgrade schools for Internet capabilities was a major challenge in the late 1990s and early 2000s. This factor, combined with growing importance of school vouchers and other school choice programs, led to US$32.8 billion in school construction alone in the United States in 1996. As state and local governments began to approve the construction of new schools and the refurbishment of existing institutions, school construction soared to record levels in both 2000 and 2001. During the same period, the construction of transportation terminals grew 25 percent; courthouses and jails, 5 percent; and churches, 1 percent. The need for new or upgraded hospitals and related healthcare facilities, such as nursing homes, contributed to a 10 percent increase in construction in 2001; this growth trend was expected to continue through the 2000s as the U.S. population ages. In early 2005, the value of public construction of schools reached about US$64.6 billion and construction of public healthcare facilities was approximately US$6.6 billion.

Hotel and recreational facility construction benefits much from a healthy economy, as economic prosperity fosters more business and leisure travel. In addition, this industry segment has been boosted by the proliferation of gambling casinos, which are often integrated with hotels. When the economy weakens, however, construction dollars for these types of projects tend to evaporate more quickly than for other market sectors. In 2001, amusement-related projects, such as movie theaters, fell 14 percent in the United States. However, store and shopping center construction, which declined by only 9 percent, found the impact of the recessionary conditions offset a bit by those retail chains working to expand their reach despite a sluggish economy. As economic conditions improved through 2004 and 2005, investment flowed back into the hotel and recreation sector. Between December 2004 and January 2005, hotel construction grew by 34 percent, while building in the amusement sector increased by 75 percent.

The challenges facing the engineers, architects, and constructors who design and build these buildings, industrial plants, and manufacturing facilities are daunting. As the nonresidential construction markets in industrialized countries continued to mature and competition in those areas continued to intensify, many analysts recommended that industry players look to developing countries for new growth.

Current Conditions

The commercial construction industry was healthy in the mid-2000s, especially in the United States. Nonresidential construction starts accounted for US$209 billion in 2006. Of this amount, about 47 percent was in commercial and industrial buildings and 51 percent was in institutional buildings (e.g., education and health care). The fastest growing type of construction was in the hotel market, which increased by about 50 percent in 2006. Construction of education buildings was also on the rise, following a decline that began in 2002. In 2001 education construction saw a record high of 273 million square feet, after which the industry slumped due to the economic recession of the early 2000s. In 2004 construction of education buildings dropped 23 percent to 209 million square feet. The trend reversed, however, in 2005, and the industry showed an increase of 5 percent. In 2006, education square footage grew another 4 percent to 227 million square feet. Construction spending for malls, shopping centers, and large discount stores was also growing, and in December 2006 was almost 50 percent higher than it was at the same time in 2005. Office and manufacturing construction were also on the rise.

The increase in nonresidential construction in the United States also had a positive impact on the job market in the industry. According to Ken Simonson, chief economist for the Associated General Contractors of America (AGC), during 2006, nonresidential builders boosted employment by 160,000, or 5 percent. Wages for these workers also rose, netting an increase of 4.5 percent in 2006, as compared to 4.0 for all private industry production workers.

Research and Technology

The building construction industry has not been as motivated to develop new materials as other industries because steel and concrete are proven raw materials with well-known building properties. However, construction companies are expected to research new building materials as these become available due in part because of concerns about the ability of manufactured structures to withstand the tremendous force unleashed by periodic natural disasters. The major technical challenge is to find ways to construct earthquake-proof buildings. Even after years of research on how seismic forces affect buildings, some factors are still unknown. In Kobe, Japan, engineers were astonished to find that apartment buildings built on soft fill dredged up from the ocean floor survived the quake while carefully designed office buildings built on the mainland sometimes "pancaked" their center floors. The terrorist attacks on the New York City World Trade Center on September 11, 2001, further underscored the need to continue researching methods for constructing buildings, particularly large ones, able to withstand various kinds of disasters.

A growing trend in the early 2000s was "green engineering," which aimed at minimizing the negative environmental effects of construction projects. Green buildings are often constructed using recycled or renewable materials and use energy-efficient technologies to reduce heating and cooling costs. The headquarters for Genzyme Corp., a global biotechnology company based in Cambridge, Massachusetts, is considered a model of green construction. The building uses no electricity for heating or cooling and is expected to use 33 percent less water and 40 percent less electricity than a conventional building of the same size. The building uses mirrors to bring natural light into office spaces, recycles rainwater, and relies on a computerized climate management system to maintain optimal interior conditions by automatically raising or lowering window blinds and louvers. While the US$140 million Genzyme building, which opened in late 2003 and accommodates 900 employees, cost about 16 percent more than a conventional building would, the company expected to realize significant savings in utilities costs. In addition, company officials said that the building's amenities would attract high-caliber employees. Though green technologies are more expensive than conventional construction, it is possible, according to the *Boston Globe,* to erect environmentally friendly buildings for as little as 2 percent above conventional costs. Furthermore, energy savings over the lifetime of the building could average 20 percent.

Interest in green building has skyrocketed in the United States since the late 1990s. In 2000, Seattle became the first metropolis in the nation to officially adopt a citywide sustainable building policy. Other cities soon followed, including Chicago, which in 2004 announced that all new public construction in the city would be certified by the U.S. Green Building Council. In 2003, products and services for green buildings across the nation reached about US$5.8 billion, up about 33 percent from 2002. Sustainable construction is also a major goal of the European Union, where many green building practices were pioneered. A partnership between the European Union and China, launched in 2003, aims to improve the environmental efficiency of major construction projects in China through the early 2000s, including the Beijing Olympic Village under construction for the 2008 summer games.

The design-build process, in which one firm contracts to design and build an entire project from scratch, began to take on increased significance in the late 1990s. By 2000, these projects accounted for roughly 25 percent of all nonresidential construction projects, up from about 6 percent in the late 1980s. The advantages of this type of contract include the single point of responsibility for the project, which lessens the risk and potential litigation expenses; faster project completion, as designs are implemented with a specific and familiar building technique in mind; and diminished administrative burden. However, some industry analysts have noted that such projects could pose potential problems in the face of increased globalization. Specifically, as international consortiums collaborate on projects, the design-build process may suffer from a lack of international design and building specifications and regulations.

Workforce

The vast majority of construction companies are relatively small businesses, with fewer than ten employees, although some of the largest companies employ as many as 95,000 people worldwide. The United States—with more than 7.0 million wage and salary workers and 1.9 million self-employed workers (including small residential homebuilders) in 2004—boasted one of the largest construction labor forces in the world yet was still plagued by chronic labor shortages. Analysts forecast that by 2010 the industry would face as many as 2.4 million unfilled jobs for skilled and unskilled positions. Indeed, according to a *New York Times* article, Francis X. McArdle, managing director of the General Contractors Association of New York, predicted that, in response to acute demand, many workers would be pressed to work six- or seven-day weeks. Pay scales, however, would remain relatively high, reflecting the fact that construction workers are increasingly required to work with new technologies, including highly specialized equipment that incorporates computerized systems. In 2004, average wages for construction workers in the United States were about US$19.23 per hour. According to the U.S. Bureau of Labor Statistics, the number of construction jobs was expected to grow roughly 11 percent by the year 2014. Furthermore, "Employment in nonresidential construction is expected to grow a little faster because industrial construction activity is expected to be stronger as replacement of many industrial plants has been delayed for years, and a large number of structures will have to be replaced or remodeled." Also impacting this sector, according to the Bureau, will be the growth in demand for nursing home and drug treatment facilities, as well as increased school enrollment.

Japan employed roughly 6 million construction workers in the late 1990s, but the industry saw a continued decrease in employment from 1998 through 2002, with an overall loss of 220,000 jobs after 1993. Japanese government figures suggested that this trend would continue. European construction employees in the late 1990s numbered more than 10 million, but a stagnant industry from the late 1990s through 2003 threatened significant job losses. Figures are harder to estimate in growing regions like Asia (excluding Japan), which continued to rely to a large degree on international firms for its construction needs.

INDUSTRY LEADERS

VINCI

France-based VINCI was as of the mid-2000s one of the largest construction companies in the world with approximately 133,500 employees and operations spanning more than 100 countries. The company has completed many extremely tall buildings, including a 700,000 square meter residential and commercial complex in Kuala Lumpur, Malaysia. Company sales grew 17.6 percent in 2003 after the firm's acquisition of GTM Enterpose Ltd., which operated in over 90 countries and maintained a payroll of 67,000 employees, 33,872 in building and civil engineering. The company posted revenues of US$25.5 billion in 2006.

KONINKLIJKE BAM GROEP NV

When Koninklijke BAM Groep (also known as Royal BAM) bought the giant Hollandsche Beton Groep (HBG) in 2002, the company became one of Europe's leading construction and engineering firms. While BAM's civil engineering divisions operated worldwide, its construction and property division remained in the Netherlands, Belgium, Britain, and Germany. In 2006, the company increased its residential construction activity when it bought the developer AM for more than US$1 billion. Sales for 2005 totaled US$8.79 billion, and the firm employed 27,190 workers.

KAJIMA CORPORATION

Kajima Corporation, based in Tokyo, was a leader in construction of skyscrapers in Japan and made major contributions to earthquake-proof building technologies. One of Japan's oldest and largest construction companies, Kajima was founded in 1840. In 2006 it listed total sales of US$15.09 billion and had 9,234 employees. Despite its primarily domestic focus, the firm maintained subsidiaries in North America, Europe, and in other Asian countries; as the Japanese construction market cooled in the early 2000s the company expanded its overseas operations and branched out into related services, such as environmental management.

BOUYGUES SA

Bouygues SA, founded in 1952 and headquartered in Cedex, France, employed 115,441 workers in 2006. Besides construction (its core business), Bouygues engages in engineering, telecommunications, media, public utilities, and other activities. In the mid-2000s the company owned 90 percent of the stock in Bouygues Telecom (France's third largest mobile phone carrier) and around 40 percent of TF1 (the number-one TV channel in France). Total revenues were US$31.9 in 2006, although only a portion of this came from the construction branch. Although it has grown increasingly diversified, the firm remains one of the largest construction companies in Europe and maintains 40 subsidiaries and affiliates in 80 countries.

BECHTEL GROUP, INC.

Based in San Francisco, California, the Bechtel Group was the largest construction company in the United States in 2007. Sales exceeded US$18.1 billion in 2005, and the firm had 40,000 employees. In 2003 it received contracts to reconstruct damaged infrastructure in post-war Iraq. As of November 2004, the company had completed renovations and repairs of 1,200 schools, 10 fire stations, and 52 health clinics, in addition to other infrastructure projects.

KELLOGG BROWN & ROOT, INC.

Founded in 1919, Brown and Root Inc. began operating as a subsidiary of Halliburton in 1962. In 1996, it split into three entities, one of which was named Brown and Root Engineering and Construction (BREC). When Halliburton acquired Dresser Industries in 1998, BREC was merged with Dresser's MW Kellogg division to form Kellogg Brown & Root, Inc., a global engineering and construction firm, which builds petrochemical facilities and power plants, hotels, office buildings, shopping centers, hospitals, universities, correctional facilities, and other public buildings. The firm operated as a wholly owned subsidiary of KBR and reported sales of US$363.6 million in 2006.

MAJOR COUNTRIES IN THE INDUSTRY

UNITED STATES

In the United States the value of nonresidential building construction fell from US$173.1 billion in 2000 to US$165.8 billion in 2001, and private spending for nonresidential construction fell by 15.9 percent in 2002. Office, retail, and hotel construction, which saw growth over 12 percent annually from 1993 to 2000, declined by 4.2 percent in 2001 and dropped by as much as 30 percent in 2002. Many leading U.S. nonresidential construction firms began looking to expand into emerging markets like Asia and Latin America. Most firms sought established businesses with which to partner in an effort to avoid some of the cultural barriers inherent in establishing a new business overseas. The decline in the industry ended in 2005, and by 2006, it had recovered as predicted. Hotel construction was one of the strongest markets. Overall the value of U.S. construction starts (excluding residential projects) totaled $26.5 billion in January 2007, up 28.7 percent from January 2006.

EUROPE

The construction market in Europe is characterized as very mature and offers little prospect for dramatic growth in the twenty-first century. Economic recession contributed to a flat performance for the industry through the early 2000s. Analysts forecast renewed but modest growth. Most new construction, though, is expected to occur in markets where significant economic reconstruction is taking place, including Ireland, Portugal, and Poland. Construction in Western Europe is projected to grow at about 3.9 percent annually through 2012, slightly below the projected world average of 4.8 percent.

In Germany, historically the largest construction industry in Europe, the economic recession of 2001-02 hit construction companies hard. One of the country's leading firms, Philipp Holzmann AG, went bankrupt in 2002 after struggling with mounting debts since 1999. Industry analysts expected a further slump, including the loss of approximately 90,000 jobs in 2004 but predicted that the industry would recover.

Britain's construction industry in the early 2000s was the third-largest in Europe and the fifth-largest in the world, employing approximately 2 million people. Publicly funded projects such as hospitals, infrastructure, and housing accounted for most of Britain's domestic construction; international projects, however, especially in South and East Asia, accounted for a substantial part of earnings. Britain's construction industry was dominated by small companies, but analysts predicted a greater degree of consolidation in the early 2000s.

ASIA

Through the 1970s, 1980s, and 1990s, Japan's enormous construction industry faced criticism, especially from U.S. firms, that the market remained closed to foreign contractors. In 1994, yielding to demands for increased access, the Japanese government initiated its Action Plan on Reform of the Bidding and Contracting Procedures for Public Works. Many international contractors responded, mostly from the United States, South Korea, China, and France. U.S. contractors accounted for an overwhelming US$190 million of the total US$230 million in foreign contracts in the market in 1997. However, this total only reflected a small fraction of Japan's construction market. Like the United States and Europe, Japan was viewed as a shrinking market with growing competition early in the twenty-first century. Indicative of these difficult conditions was the performance of four of Japan's largest general contractors in fiscal 2001: Shimizu Corp. and Obayashi Corp. posted losses, while Taisei Corp. and Kajima Corp. struggled to remain profitable. Though the decline in construction investment continued through 2003, the industry remained one of Japan's primary employers, with a labor force of almost 6 million workers.

The hottest region of the world for nonresidential construction in the early 2000s was Asia (excluding Japan); China, which was the second-largest construction market in the world in 2005, accounted for the majority of new construction projects in the region. The largest construction firm in the nation, China State Construction, held only 2 percent of the Chinese construction market in 2000. In addition, the largest of the 500,000 firms engaged in some form of construction there only accounted for 10 percent of the industry. Analysts predicted strong demand for nonresidential construction in China through the 2010s. Among China's major projects in the early 2000s was the Olympic Village in Beijing, scheduled for completion for the 2008 summer Olympics. India and South Korea were also expected to emerge as a major player in the global industry in the twenty-first century.

The devastating tsunami that hit southern Asia in December 2004 drove demand for much new building in the affected regions. Analysts predicted that construction needs would be substantial.

AFRICA

Africa continued to be a difficult market for international contractors to penetrate in great numbers, primarily due to the lack of business investment in the continent. The top 225 contractors conducted US$10.3 billion in business in the region in 1996. Africa's acute need for infrastructure, however, pointed to significant opportunities in the construction sector, which grew at an average of 4 percent per year on the continent after 1995. This performance varied considerably, however, from country to country, with underdeveloped nations such as Mozambique seeing growth of up to 14 percent, while more stable and well-developed countries such as Tanzania enjoyed growth of about 5 percent. Improvements in industry management also contributed to a positive outlook for the early 2000s. In Senegal, which instituted reforms that required open bidding on government contracts, construction costs in the late 1990s were cut by 40 percent. At the same time, these reforms led to the creation of 3,000 permanent construction jobs.

Growth in the tourism and manufacturing sectors was also expected to contribute to construction demand. In 1999, some 665 construction projects for tourist accommodations were built in Egypt alone. South Africa invested US$144 million in the expansion of the Johannesburg International

Airport. According to *African Business,* at least 50 percent of all fixed capital investments in most African countries came from the construction sector alone, making it likely to remain one of the continent's strongest engines of economic growth through the early 2000s. Nevertheless, the region's need for foreign investment to fund large-scale building projects remained critical. In 2005, British prime minister Tony Blair announced a massive aid plan for Africa, including debt relief and increased trade to foster development. As the region increases its participation in the global economy through the 2000s, demand will rise for new manufacturing plants, office complexes, health care facilities, schools, and other nonresidential buildings.

In 2007 construction of the King Shaka International Airport began in South Africa. The larger airport, with an estimated price tag of US$353 million, will replace the Durban International Airport and will be completed by 2010, in time for the FIFA World Cup, which South Africa will host.

LATIN AMERICA

In 1996, the top 225 international contractors in Latin America signed US$8.1 billion in construction business, continuing the steady incline of construction industry growth there during the 1990s. Many international contractors were optimistic about Latin America, however, as the economies of several nations in the region, including Colombia, Chile, Mexico, and Argentina, were expanding. By the end of the 1990s, yearly investment for infrastructure development in Latin America reached 40 billion, more than twice the amount allocated in 1995. In the early 2000s, Argentina announced a US$30 billion public works and housing project that was expected to give a much-needed boost to the construction sector. Venezuela implemented an Economic Recovery Plan that would allow foreign contractors to participate in several public works construction projects, including airports and hospitals. Industry observers expected Latin America to be a growth market well into the century.

FURTHER READING

Baker, Kermit. "Nonresidential Construction Poised for Solid Gains in 2005." *AIArchitect,* January 2005. Available from www.aia.org.

"Commercial Building Starts Soar." *Midwest Contractor,* 26 March 2007.

"Construction." European Commission. Available from europa.eu.int.

"Construction & Materials in Latin America." Latin Sector Watch. March 2005. Available from www.latin-sectors.com.

Construction Specifications Institute. "Construction Industry Statistics," 2003. Available from www.csinet.org.

"Forecasts & Trends," McGraw-Hill Construction, 28 February 2005. Available from http://cotest.construction.com.

"Hoover's Company Capsules." *Hoover's Online,* 2007. Available from www.hoovers.com.

"International Airport." *International Construction,* September 2006.

Japanese Ministry of Public Management, Home Affairs, Posts and Telecommunications. *Statistical Handbook of Japan.* Available from www.stat.go.jp.

Kennedy, Kim. "Education Construction Turns Upward." *Engineering News Record,* 9 April 2007.

Haughey, Jim. "U.S. Construction Starts: Show Strength Early in 2006." *Business Credit,* June 2006.

"Lodging, Hospitals Fuel Nonres Growth." *Construction Equipment,* 1 January 2007.

"New Study Forecasts Improving Outlook for Global Construction Industry." Global Insight Inc., 9 June 2003. Available from www.globalinsight.com.

"Nonresidential Construction Growth Continues In '07." *Building Design & Construction,* 1 December 2006.

"Nonresidential Construction Jobs Grow." *Construction Bulletin,* 5 March 2007.

Palmer, Thomas C., Jr. "Building Green: Many More Developers Building Green." *Boston Globe,* 6 September 2004, p. D1.

"Profile: Japan's Construction Industry." *AsiaPulse News,* 14 October 2003.

"Turning Point for German Construction Industry Expected in 2005." *Europe Intelligence Wire,* 4 November 2003.

UK Trade and Investment Bureau. *Sector Profile: Construction.* Available from www.uktradeinvest.gov.uk.

U.S. Department of Labor, Bureau of Labor Statistics. *Career Guide to Industries* 2005. Available from www.bls.gov.

"U.S. Real Estate and Construction Industry Overview, 2005" 2006. Available from www.plunkettresearch.com.

VINCI 2004 Financial Statements. March 2005. Available from www.vinci.com.

SIC 1520

NAICS 2631

CONSTRUCTION, RESIDENTIAL BUILDING

Contractors in this segment of the world's construction industry create new residential structures, including single- and multifamily dwellings, as well as additions, alterations, remodeling, and repairs to residential buildings. For details on other aspects of the construction trades, see also **Construction, Nonresidential Building** and **Engineering Services.**

INDUSTRY SNAPSHOT

While most residential buildings—whether for single families or multiple families—are constructed by local, domestic, small-scale operations, an estimated one-fifth of all construction worldwide is performed by large-scale companies. The international residential construction industry is dominated by well-funded U.S., European, and Pacific Rim (particularly Japanese) companies.

The early 2000s' decline in the Japanese and other Asian economies hit their domestic construction markets hard. The most telling sign of the financial times was the dramatic reduction in the amount of money Japan spent on construction. While the industry was strong in the early 1990s, by 2002 the number of new building contracts had significantly declined—largely because of concerns about high vacancy rates. Analysts projected that investments in Japan's domestic construction industry would continue to decline. Nevertheless, employment in the construction industry and the number of new small construction companies entering the tough market rose due to the fact that the government spent US$550 billion on public works in the mid-1990s. The economy continued to suffer in subsequent years, however, because of this and other deficit spending.

By the mid-2000s the Asian housing market had started to bounce back; housing starts in Japan increased in 2006. China and India also showed growth.

In the United States, the already slowing economy took a downturn after September 11, 2001. Many feared that this trend would take a catastrophic toll on the construction industry, since people in uncertain times generally stop looking to buy or build new homes, preferring the security of their existing housing. That the country witnessed widespread lay-offs seemed to ensure that housing projects would drop significantly. To the surprise of most industry analysts, however, residential construction proved quite resilient. In 2006, private housing starts in the United States totaled about 1.46 million units, after reaching the highest number since 1978 the year before (1.71 million). This growth, spurred by extremely low interest rates and an improving economy, reversed expectations of a market decline. According to figures reported by *Mortgage News*, the housing market—including spending from mortgage refinancing—contributed 33.8 percent of U.S. economic growth in 2003. In 2005 there were 1.6 new housing starts, but the market slumped as expected in 2006.

Global Insight Inc. forecast that surging demand in India and China would drive global construction growth at about 5 percent through 2012. Construction in India was expected to grow at about 9.2 percent, with China close behind at about 7.9 percent. Though demand for industrial and commercial construction would initiate this growth, an influx of workers to new employment sites would stimulate demand for more residential construction. In the United States, the construction industry was expected to grow more moderately, at about 4.8 percent, while the European industry was expected to see growth of about 3.9 percent.

Organization and Structure

Residential construction includes single-family houses, multifamily dwellings, and apartment buildings. The industry is highly fragmented: the United States and Japan combined hold approximately 1 million construction-related firms. The business also tends to be highly cyclical, reflective of changing demographic and economic factors like interest rates, property values, and the financial climate.

Residential builders are regulated in a variety of ways. Laws governing the habitats of wildlife (such as the Endangered Species Act in the United States) can impact builders, while regulations delineating criteria for energy efficiency, access for disabled persons, worker safety, and public safety also have to be taken into account. At the beginning of the new millennium there was little concern in the industry regarding antitrust violations because none of the domestic leaders accounted for a large segment of the market activity. Although 2001 saw two notable acquisitions (Pulte bought Del Webb Corporation for US$1.8 billion, and Lennar Corporation bought U.S. Home Corporation for US$1.2 billion), there was still ample room for growth by individual companies.

In Germany building plans for homes must conform to German industrial standards prescribing dimensions for stairways and other parts of a home. In some densely populated cities in Asia and elsewhere, however, evasion of building codes seemed almost a way of life, as owners and tenants thwarted safety plans through illegal subdivisions of apartments, obstruction of evacuation routes, and poor building maintenance.

Construction of housing, however, is a vitally important issue to virtually all countries, so most nations also support their residential construction industry through government programs and agencies. Many countries have institutions with responsibilities not unlike those of the Federal Housing Administration (FHA) in the United States. The FHA seeks to stimulate the residential home building industry by making houses more affordable through low-interest mortgages. Indeed, knowledgeable governments are aware that construction of all types accounts for increasing portions of the economic activity of developing countries.

Companies hoping to enter lucrative foreign markets typically boost their reputation and experience in three ways: by working first on public works projects, by building the overseas projects of domestic clients (particularly among Japanese companies), and by entering into joint ventures.

Background and Development

The earliest known houses date back to 9000 B.C., although there is earlier evidence for more crude forms of shelter. Constructed of mud and reeds, these structures featured circular stone bases and conical roofs. The use of reeds as a building material ultimately led to the discovery of structural elements such as the frame, the column, the arch, and the vault. Baked mud bricks allowed greater flexibility in house design and enabled the first rectangular houses to be built in the Jordan valley around 7000 B.C. This design endured as the dominant shape for Western houses. Five thousand years later, more sophisticated dwellings featured second stories and balconies, elements designed to address the demands of urban life. The Romans introduced apartment buildings as a means of accommodating many people in a limited space; the earliest apartments were limited to five stories or less by decree and had no kitchen or bathroom facilities. These early structures demonstrated an awareness of the trade-offs between efficiency and customization.

While the principles of modularity and standardization reached their peak perhaps in the post-World War II houses of the suburban United States, the need to rebuild Europe and East Asia after that war helped turn construction into the international industry it was in the early 2000s. U.S. contractors controlled 90 percent of the global construction market by 1956. Soon, however, western European firms were able to offer similar quality at competitive prices. Japanese contractors needed to import technology, but when they did, their lower wages and increasing productivity made them keenly competitive, first domestically and then in neighboring countries. Some of the first substantial international joint venture projects for the Japanese construction industry arose from work done for the United States in Okinawa at the beginning of the Korean War. Japan eventually emerged as a significant player in the world marketplace, successfully competing with U.S. and European firms for the abundant Middle Eastern petroleum facility contracts of the 1970s despite language and geographical disadvantages. South Korea later used low bids and other practices to maneuver its way to a position of international relevance as well. Turkey, Mexico, India, and China were poised to follow on the strength of inexpensive, productive workforces.

After a period of growth in the mid- to late 1990s, the residential construction industry began slowing toward the end of the 1990s and into the 2000s. This trend worsened considerably after the terrorist attacks on the World Trade Center and the Pentagon on September 11, 2001. Still, the industry remained in relatively good health, and by 2003 analysts were projecting moderate global growth through 2012. Worldwide, spending on construction (including housing and other projects) reached US$3.9 trillion in 2004, according to Global Insight Inc., and residential construction grew by a projected 6.6 percent. In 2004, the US$882 billion-a-year American construction industry accounted for almost 8 percent of the U.S. gross domestic product. The largest segment of this industry was in private sector residential construction, which generated more than US$453 billion worldwide in 2002.

CURRENT CONDITIONS

Despite the general economic slowdown at the beginning of the new millennium, the U.S. residential construction industry was on the rise. In 2003, U.S. Department of Housing and Urban Development figures showed that housing starts and project completions that year reached near-record levels. More than 1.78 million permits were taken out, and construction began on 1.848 million new housing units. Much of this growth was attributed to very low mortgage rates. A surge of new housing starts in the United States in early 2005 again boosted construction more than expected. According to the U.S. Commerce Department, a record number of starts of single-family dwellings contributed to the highest level of total housing starts since 1984. In January 2005, construction began on 2.159 million new housing units (adjusted annual rate). Single-family starts reached 1.76 million-the highest on record. Construction of multifamily housing rose to 399,000 units. Numbers rose again in February 2005, when single-family housing starts reached a record high of 1.77 million.

The year 2006 saw 1.6 million new housing starts, down 14.8 percent from 2005. According to Bernard Markstein of the National Association of Home Builders (NAHB), the downturn could be attributed to a rise in housing prices. Said Markstein, "All of a sudden, people stepped back and said, Wait, I can't afford this anymore, so there was an oversupply. Then, when builders saw demand dropping off, they said, Wait a second, I can't afford to keep building like this. Prices had just moved too high." The forecasting arm of NAHB, however, predicted the market would rebound.

Demographic factors influence the housing market to a great extent. Young families have traditionally been the primary buyers of new housing, and the number of newly formed families has risen significantly since the late 1980s. During the 1990s, about 12.5 million new households were started in the United States as members of "Generation X" reached adulthood. Demographers predicted that in the 2000s, in large part because of high rates of immigration, new households will number between 13.4 and 15.4 million. Another significant factor in the growing demand for new construction is the aging of U.S. housing stock. According to the *Wall Street Journal,* the average U.S. house is about 33 years old; about 25.8 million houses are more than 50 years old. As these dwellings wear out, many are torn down and replaced with new construction. One estimate suggested that about 7.4 million obsolete homes (about 740,00 per year) were demolished between 1985 and 1995. The U.S. Census Bureau cites a lower estimate of about 450,000 per year removed from the housing stock between 2005 and 2013.

Increased wealth in the 2000s has also contributed to vigorous growth in the U.S. home construction industry. Sales of second homes, for example, have increased dramatically as Baby Boomer families with the financial means seek vacation homes or investment properties. Analysts estimated that between 5 percent and 15 percent of the 2.82 million second homes sold in the United States in 2004 were newly constructed buildings.

Typically in times of extended growth within the construction industry, increased demand leads to higher prices for building materials. Fortunately for contractors, however, the rapidly expanding international market and intense global competition have helped keep material prices in check; they remained relatively flat in the early 2000s. Near-record numbers of new housing starts in the United States in 2004 and 2005, however, contributed to shortages of some basic supplies, including brick, concrete (used primarily for basements), vinyl siding, and roof shingles.

One of the major trends in the residential construction industry, especially in the United States but also in western Europe, was the shift of construction activity from major urban centers to suburban and outlying areas. As businesses moved their offices out of big cities into the more serene suburban surroundings, people followed, exacerbating a move that began en masse with the proliferation of the automobile earlier in the twentieth century. In the United States, which continued to maintain a healthy amount of open space especially in its Midwestern and Southwestern regions, this trend was expected to increase rapidly in the short term. At the same time, however, analysts also predicted a renewal of interest in urban housing, especially for new developments modeled on an "urban village" concept. Impatience with long commutes was cited as a significant factor influencing this trend. In response to growing concerns about suburban sprawl, states and municipalities changed zoning laws and created incentives for builders to site new housing near urban centers. Cambridge, Massachusetts, was one city that promoted new housing in densely built areas. Between 2004 and 2005, five major development projects were scheduled to begin in one neighborhood alone, adding a total of 4,500 new homes to a densely built section of the city. This was the largest number of new homes built in Cambridge since World War II. New York City has also seen record levels of new housing. In 2001 the city spent $US174 million on construction of new homes; in 2004 that amount rose to US$575 million.

Demand for urban lofts, townhouses, and condominiums has driven new construction and renovation projects in inner cities of the United States and western Europe. The typical buyer of an urban loft is a young, single professional who wants to be close to work and nightlife by living very close to, or right in, the heart of a major city. Cities that have seen this trend include Atlanta, San Francisco, San Diego, Austin, Denver (where a hospital slated for demolition was saved to be renovated into lofts), and London. Industry experts observe that buyers are often willing to sacrifice square footage for features such as hardwood or concrete floors or granite countertops. Buyers' willingness to accept smaller units benefits builders because they are able to offer more lofts per building. New urban housing has also attracted "empty nesters," who find that the suburban homes in which they raised their families are too large for them once their children have grown up and moved away.

RESEARCH AND TECHNOLOGY

Most countries have been increasing the standardization of their building specifications. With globalization of the industry a reality, however, the issue of international standards is one that many industry analysts say needs to be addressed in the 2000s. Some important issues include building codes, which can dramatically affect costs of building (and hence, the affordability of housing) and safety regulations. In the United States, a major safety concern is the long-term health effects of mold. In 2001 the National Association of Home Builders received numerous inquiries from contractors and buyers about mold; in fact this topic was the top-ranked subject of phone calls they received. This surge of interest in the topic forced builders to seek solutions to the problems of mold and to be proactive in addressing them.

Environmental concerns continued to impact new building projects and restorations. Not only was there an increasing desire on the part of buyers to live in environmentally friendly homes, but legislation was playing a greater role in dictating construction standards. These joint pressures kept researchers busy seeking solutions to real and potential environmental problems.

All residential building contractors—from the smallest operator to the largest international conglomerate—take note of technical innovations in construction. Industry analysts expect that increasing numbers of future homes will feature solar power and accommodations designed to meet the needs of older people, a population segment that grows each year.

In the late 1990s and early 2000s, the desire for customized houses was balanced with the need to reduce costs through standardization and universalization of mass-produced modular elements. The support/infill concept, first developed in the Netherlands and later in Japan, epitomized this approach. This process allows customization decisions to be made later in the construction process, facilitating input from homeowners and allowing property managers to match market conditions more accurately.

Nontraditional materials were used with increasing frequency in the late 1990s and early 2000s. Soaring wood prices made cold-formed steel, which offers relatively stable prices but that has not traditionally played a major role in the residential construction industry, an attractive alternative. Observers note that the transformation need not be dramatic; specifications and standards used for wood-frame building can be modified for steel-frame building without completely overhauling the guidelines. In addition, plastics manufacturers demonstrated that their recyclable products could be used as an energy-efficient alternative for roofing, window, siding, plumbing, and foundation construction, while fiber-cement proved a durable and efficient moisture-resistant material for siding and roofing in humid climates. Other structural materials were researched or improved, including engineered* wood, laminated fiberboard, foam-core materials, and high-strength concrete.

The National Association of Home Builders reported an increase in demand for "green" buildings, which are energy-efficient in design and construction. Green buildings are often built using as many recycled and environmentally friendly materials as possible. Environmental conditions within and around houses—"green" or otherwise—receive the careful scrutiny of some architects. Environmentally conscious designs typically strive to maximize the positive effects of sunlight and good ventilation in a dwelling while minimizing energy costs through heavy insulation and the careful design of windows. The building materials themselves, as well as appliances, are also examined for possible toxic ingredients or emissions. In 2001, a study cited by the City of Seattle's Department of Planning and Development indicated that 96 percent of homebuyers would be willing to pay extra for "green" construction. Some 80 percent stated that they would not want old-growth lumber used in their homes, and more than 60 percent indicated a preference for sustainable harvested lumber.

Home buyers in the United States were becoming more technologically savvy in the early 2000s. It was common in upscale homes for an entertainment room to include cinema-style seats and a projection television system for viewing television and movies. These rooms are built to resemble movie theaters, complete with state-of-the-art sound and video systems. The growing demand for technology at home also feeds the market for "smart" housing. In these homes, owners can control lighting, security systems, heating and air conditioning, lawn watering, and appliances with a keyboard or remote control.

Another trend that demonstrates the ways in which people hope to get more out of their homes is the emergence of health-related housing features. In *The Futurist*, Battelle, a nonprofit technology research center, projected significant advances in the following areas by 2010: air quality, water quality, home power generators, and home security.

Earthquake and vibration control are other areas of enduring interest to building contractors. In Japan, which was victimized by the Kobe earthquake in the mid-1990s, visionaries sought to pioneer new horizons for the industry. Japan's heavily populated urban centers also contributed to that country's research efforts. In order to meet the housing needs of the world's increasing population, Japan's Ministry of Construction proposed the "hyper building" concept: structures 1,000 meters tall designed to last 1,000 years. Such buildings would fill their million square feet of space with both residences and offices. In the United States, contractors witnessed an increase in demand for "safe rooms" in residences. Such a room is reinforced with steel, has no windows, is centrally located in the floor plan, stores emergency provisions, and has a back-up power supply. The purpose of these rooms is to provide refuge in the event of an earthquake or other natural disaster.

WORKFORCE

Construction is one of the most labor-intensive industries in the world. In the United States alone, 7 million wage and salary earners and about 1.9 million self-employed people worked in construction in 2004. These numbers were expected to grow, with analysts predicting about 7.7 million wage-earners in construction by 2012. Construction is also a relatively high-paying industry in the United States, where wages increased faster than the average for other industries overall. In 2004 U.S. workers earned an average of US$19.23 per hour. In Germany construction workers make almost US$20 per hour. In Italy unskilled laborers make US$13.68 per hour, and skilled laborers make US$15 per hour. In Japan a bricklayer earns US$150.76 in an eight-hour day, a carpenter makes US$161.28 per day, and a plumber makes US$137.81 per day. Other nations like Korea and Thailand do not provide such wages.

While compensation to employees in the construction industry was relatively high in the United States and other advanced economies, shortages of labor—particularly skilled labor—persisted, especially in developed countries. Health insurance coverage also added dramatically to labor costs, as did worker's compensation insurance in an industry that can be quite dangerous. In 2002, the U.S. construction industry had 1,121 work-related fatalities—more than any other industry; about 38,000 injuries were reported among workers in residential construction. Though construction work accounted for 20 percent of all work-related deaths, the industry ranked far below mining, agriculture, forestry, and trucking in the percentage of its total workforce (12.2) who were fatally injured on the job.

Labor shortages and discrepancies in wages have encouraged some contractors to import workers. In some areas labor contractors pay illegal aliens much less than the going rate. Public outcry about hiring illegal aliens stems from two main objections: first, this practice takes jobs from legal workers, and second, illegal aliens are paid in cash and therefore pay no income tax on their earnings.

In the mid-2000s there were legal initiatives in place to address the labor shortage. Programs were available that offer training to individuals with few job prospects. These provide them with the skills necessary to enter a trade, while addressing the labor shortage in the industry. One such program is the Home Builders Institute's Project CRAFT (Community Restitution and Apprenticeship Focused Training), which trains juvenile offenders. This training provides a means of rehabilitation for those who want it, and their entry into the job market addresses labor issues in the housing industry.

INDUSTRY LEADERS

SHIMIZU CORPORATION

Shimizu Corporation of Tokyo has consistently won the industry's informal "triple crown"—work completed, new orders received, and profit. The company, which originated in the nineteenth century, was incorporated as Shimizu Gumi in 1915. It is involved in a wide range of engineering and construction projects, including both commercial and residential buildings. By the late 1990s it had become established as a global competitor with 15,300 employees, but by 2004, that number had dropped to 11,680. Of these, some 2,500 were licensed architects and 1,800 were licensed civil engineers. In 2005 Shimizu reported total sales of US$13.8 billion. Despite an average decline of 8 percent in the Japanese construction industry in 2003, Shimizu was able to keep its decline to 1.3 percent. With fewer contracts for extensive new domestic projects coming in, the company planned to increase its share of projects that involve remodeling existing buildings.

In the mid-2000s, Shimizu completed major residential and nonresidential projects in Japan. Its chief overseas projects, however—including buildings in China, Indonesia, the United States—were industrial and commercial buildings. Major projects have included the Tokyo Dome Hotel and the Paske Bridge in Laos.

Like its competitors, the company supports a variety of research interests. Shimizu was a proponent of support/infill projects. It also developed a computer-aided design system (operable in either Japanese or English) that allowed architects to cut design time 40 percent on some projects. Elaborate intelligent building systems that offer special amenities such as programmable aroma control (including lemon, nutmeg, and peppermint) were another specialty.

TAISEI CORP.

Taisei Corp. originated in the construction company Okuragumi Shokai, which was founded by Kibachiro Okura in 1873. Okura was a businessman, not a builder. He started a trading company, a leather and shoe factory, a brewery, a hotel, and many other enterprises. Okuragumi Shokai completed Japan's first railway station and became known as Taisei in 1946, after its shares were distributed to employees. Taisei's core business was construction, especially residential housing, but it was also highly active in civil engineering and real estate development. Based in Tokyo, Taisei maintained offices in the United States, Peru, England, Saudi Arabia, Turkey, and West Africa. The company was especially active in South and East Asia, where it had offices in China, Vietnam, Cambodia, India, Kuala Lumpur, Singapore, Myanmar, Thailand, Indonesia, Korea, India, and Pakistan. Though it remained one of Japan's top four construction companies, Taisei was forced to downsize some of its operations in the early 2000s because of difficult market conditions in Japan. By 2004 it had reduced its workforce to about 9,700 employees. Total sales in 2005 exceeded US$15.8 billion.

OBAYASHI CORPORATION

Obayashi Corporation (formerly Ohbayashi) was founded by Yoshigoro Obayashi in 1892. The company's largest early projects were associated with the development of Osaka Harbor. In 1918 two of its engineers were sent to the United States to be trained by the Fluor Corporation in advanced construction techniques. After completing a Cambodian agricultural center—its first project outside Japan—the company revisited the United States in the 1960s to build a variety of civil works and residential projects. Obayashi also established itself as a builder of tunnels and dams; it constructed the world's largest suspension bridge over the Akashi Straits in Japan. The highly diversified company, which employed 13,377 people in 2004, also had interests in real estate, finance, and furniture manufacturing. Though 95 percent of its revenue came from construction operations in 2003, Obayashi expanded its operations into environmental services in response to the slowdown of Japan's construction industry in the early 2000s. In 2005, the company posted total sales of US$13.0 billion.

KUMAGAI GUMI CO. LTD.

Kumagai Gumi Co. Ltd. was incorporated in 1938. Santoro Kumagai, the company's founder, began his construction career as a stonemason, crafting religious monuments and performing work for the expanding railway system. The company eventually became known for its ability to handle risky projects. It created additional markets through its build-own-transfer strategy, a means of privatizing the development of public works projects. Like its peers, the company has been active on a variety of civil engineering projects such as dams, tunnels, and highways. Kumagai also built a major Buddhist temple and a unique 3,300-unit housing project in Japan. The company has been particularly successful in Hong Kong and has landed substantial residential contracts in China. With 5,987 employees Kumagai's sales in 2005 totaled US$3.0 billion.

Since the 1990s, however, when Japan's real estate market dramatically weakened, Kumagai has experienced financial difficulties. In the early 2000s, the company negotiated an unprecedented debt waiver—about 430 billion yen was forgiven by bank creditors—in order to stay afloat. It also abandoned its announced merger with Tobishima Corporation, scheduled for early 2005.

D.R. HORTON, INC.

In fiscal 2005, D.R. Horton sold more than 51,000 homes in the United States. Most of its buildings are single-family homes aimed at first-time buyers, but it also constructs luxury-level dwellings. Horton, which bought Hawaii-based contractor Schuler Homes in 2001, has operations in 25 states across the country. In 2006, total sales exceeded US$15.0 billion with almost 9,000 employees.

PULTE HOMES INC.

In 2006, Pulte Homes was one of the top four home builders (by number of units) in the United States. Pulte greatly expanded its business when it bought retirement community builder Del Webb in 2001, making the new company the largest residential construction firm in the country at that time. Pulte offers single-family homes, duplexes, townhomes, and condominiums at prices ranging from US$62,000 to more than US$3 million. An American company, Pulte sells most of its residences in the western and eastern parts of the country, and also markets homes in Mexico and Argentina. In 2006 Pulte employed 13,400 people and earned revenues of US$14.27 billion.

LENNAR

Lennar is one of the largest residential construction companies in the United States. In the early 2000s, it built more than 36,000 homes each year, including units in retirement communities, and also offers financial services associated with buying a home. In 2004 the company employed about 11,700 people and saw total sales of US$10.5 billion.

CENTEX CORPORATION

Centex Corporation, among the largest construction companies in the United States, has made its Centrex Homes business one of the country's top residential builders. Centrex Homes, which operates in the United States and Britain, built about 49,000 homes in 2005. Centex Corporation, which is also involved with commercial contracting, mortgage banking, and commercial real estate, employed 13,867 people in 2006 and earned total revenues of US$16.26 billion.

OTHER LEADERS

In the mid-2000s, other leading contractors involved in residential construction were also based in Asia. Sekisui House Ltd., which designs and erects prefabricated homes, employed around 15,000 workers. In 2006 the company generated more than US$13.25 billion. Other major companies included Daiwa House Industry Co. Ltd., which in 2006 employed 12,725 and had sales of US$13.0 billion, primarily from residential construction but also from hotels, resorts, and home improvement stores; Fujita Corporation, a Tokyo-based leader in urban redevelopment with 2006 sales of US$2.97 billion; Mitsui Fudosan, with approximately 13,000 employees in Asia, the Americas, Europe, and the Middle East and revenues exceeding US$10.43 billion in 2004; and Toda Corporation, an urban development specialist with revenues of US$4.56 billion in 2006.

MAJOR COUNTRIES IN THE INDUSTRY

JAPAN

Japan has historically been a leader in the global construction market. After years of dominating the world construction marketplace, Japan finally opened its markets to foreign contractors in the late 1980s under intense political pressure from the United States. The South Koreans proved most adept at penetrating this market initially, usually through joint ventures. Nevertheless, Japanese contractors experienced their biggest boom since the early 1970s, earning ¥750 billion (US$6 billion) a year on overseas contracts alone. An economic downturn in the late 1990s, however, took its toll on the Japanese construction industry. Government spending for public sector projects fell off, and as a result, new contracts among the country's top building companies declined by an average of 8.8 percent between 2001 and 2002. According to *AsiaPulse News,* some 5,863 Japanese construction companies went bankrupt in 2002—the third consecutive year in which more than 5,000 such companies failed. According to Japanese government figures, total investment in construction dropped 35.9 percent from 1992 to 2003. In 2004 the market rebounded somewhat; housing contracts were up 7 percent from the previous year.

In response to such market challenges, several top construction firms restructured, scaled back their labor force, or expanded into related services such as waste management. Another strategy was to focus on large urban renewal projects built around new technologies such as access to broadband communications. As a result, major construction firms weathered Japan's economic downturn relatively well. In 2003 the construction sector accounted for about 10.7 percent of the country's gross domestic product and employed about 10 percent of the Japanese workforce. By 2003, the picture had improved slightly for residential construction. That year, building started on 1.17 million new homes—the first increase in four years.

The top Japanese construction firms tend to be quite large compared to their counterparts in the United States, with extensive research and development investment. Japanese contractors have experienced greater success in the United States than U.S. firms have enjoyed in Japan. U.S. companies have battled to counter the perception in Japan that Americans are competitive in management and design but weak in the "dangerous and dirty" business of actual construction.

RUSSIA

Russia is another major region in the global residential construction industry. However, the vast demand for housing has been hampered by shortages of materials, infrastructure problems, and lack of accessible financing. Although cooperative housing was a priority, it accounted for only a fraction of new building space commissioned.

Between 1930 and the breakup of the Soviet Union, Soviet engineers gained enough experience at home to export it to the world market. Although proven Soviet technologies were usually supplied, at times new designs were also offered. Like their Japanese counterparts, the Soviets often used a turnkey strategy, subcontracting project management to Finnish and Austrian companies and basic construction to local companies in the client country. Even during the cold war, however, the Soviets turned to Western companies to supply technology and equipment for more complex ventures.

Housing remained in relatively short supply in Russia in the early 2000s, and the government announced plans to increase residential units from 36 million in 2004 to 80 million by 2010. Shortage of housing in Moscow and St. Petersburg fueled residential construction growth of about 7.2 percent between 2003 and 2004. Yet the price of new housing built between 2000 and 2004 more than doubled, contributing to a slowdown in sales. To remain competitive with Western companies and to meet demand for new housing, Russian construction firms have expanded holdings so that they control companies that produce building materials, thus reducing costs. They have also added real estate financing to their services.

UNITED STATES

In the United States, low interest rates and relatively poor returns on other investments boosted the market for residential real estate in the early 2000s. An increase in sales of second homes, for either vacation or investment purposes, contributed to high demand for residential construction. In 2005, some 2.159 million houses were started across the country. Single-family housing starts totaled about 1.76 million units. While domestic contracts were essential to residential contractors in the United States, U.S. contractors and their foreign subsidiaries also had a substantial share of international construction contracts.

Unlike Japan, the U.S. construction industry has a relatively high number of self-employed workers. In 2002, the country had about 792,000 construction companies, of which 237,000 were building contractors. The vast majority of these firms were small operations employing fewer than 10 workers. According to the U.S. Bureau of Labor Statistics, about 80 percent of construction workers in the United States are employed by companies of this size. However, industry analysts, such as Carl E. Reichardt of Banc of America Securities, predicted that there would be more domestic mergers in the future of the industry. He estimated that there were 80,000 home builders in the United States and that the top twenty captured 30 percent of the business. These numbers are important because they indicate that the industry still has plenty of opportunity for consolidation before running into antitrust issues.

CHINA

China experienced a boom in construction in the 1980s and 1990s, much to the benefit of developers in Hong Kong. The Chinese government sought to control this development—and accompanying inflation—by cutting down demand for materials and transportation. Thousands of projects, including some residential blocks, were suspended by the government in 1988 and 1989. This action cost hundreds of thousands of construction workers their jobs. The residential housing sector, however, was largely spared from these cutbacks because of the severe shortage of housing.

The building boom in China also put a strain on the country's energy resources. Coal rationing resulted in many partially heated buildings. While such rationing conserved resources somewhat, it also undercut the energy-efficient designs of the buildings and boilers.

China's 28,000 construction companies have built millions of homes each year for the past 20 years. Demand for housing remained particularly high in cities, where populations skyrocketed due to an influx of workers from rural areas. According to *China Daily,* the number of homes sold in many Chinese cities exceeded the amount being built, and prices soared as a result. By 2003, the average urban Chinese resident spent 16.7 percent of his or her salary on housing, compared to 13.65 percent in the United States. Some analysts warned that greater government regulation would be necessary to curb prices and prevent a future glut in new home construction.

Europe

Europe's housing construction industry varies by country. The relatively low percentage of home ownership in Germany, for example, can be attributed in part to German culture. Families in that country commonly buy only one house in a lifetime; as a result, homes are often of elaborate construction and thus quite expensive. In Italy children tend to live in their parents' homes well into adulthood. In addition, industry analysts have noted that, for the sake of the European Monetary Union (EMU), some fiscal measures will have to be applied that will negatively affect the residential construction industry in the long run but that are not expected to have a lasting effect. Overall, Europe's construction market is characterized as very mature, making substantial growth unlikely. High real estate costs (which often account for 50 percent of residential housing costs) and construction expenses, however, have slowed any improvement in the situation. An economic slowdown in the early 2000s contributed to a flat performance for the European construction industry in 2003. According to Global Insight Inc., however, Europe was expected to see construction growth averaging about 3.9 percent through 2012.

Further Reading

"2007 Construction Activity Expected to Wane. " *Bulk Transporter,* 26 March 2007.

Barnett, Megan. "Is It Boom Or Bust?" *U.S. News & World Report,* 5 September 2005.

Clark, Kim. "Construction," *U.S. News & World Report,* 21 March 2005.

Construction Specifications Institute. *Construction Industry Statistics, 2003.*. Available from www.csinet.org.

Diesenhouse, Susan. "East Cambridge, Boomtown to Be." *Boston Globe,* 19 September 2004.

"Emerging Trends in Real Estate 2005." *Buildings,* January 2005.

"The Expert 400: Construction." *Gateway to Russia,* 2 December 2004. Available from http://www.gateway2russia.com.

Ford, Constance Mitchell. "What's Behind Hot Home Building Pace?" *Wall Street Journal,* 21 March 2005, p. 2.

Heavens, Alan J. "Builders' Blues," *Philadelphia Inquirer,* 27 March 2005.

"Hoover's Company Capsules." *Hoover's Online,* 2007. Available from www.hoovers.com.

"Housing Construction Reaches 21-Year High." *New York Times,* 17 February 2005.

"Housing: Where The Market Is Really Headed." *Business Week,* 10 July 2006.

"Housing: Will Surging Supply Pop The Bubble?" *Business Week,* 6 February 2006.

International Trade Administration, U.S. Department of Commerce. *Building Projects and Construction.* 3 April 2007. Available from www.ita.dot.gov.

Japanese Ministry of Internal Affairs and Communications, Statistics Bureau. *Japan Statistical Yearbook,* 2006. Available from www.stat.go.jp/English.

"Kumagai Gumi, Tobishima Scrap Planned Merger." *Japan Times,* 16 November 2004.

"Major Trends Affecting the Real Estate & Construction Industry." Plunkett Research, 2004. Available from www.plunkettresearch.com.

"New Study Forecasts Improving Outlook for Global Construction Industry." Global Insight Inc., 9 June 2003. Available from www.globalinsight.com.

Nicholson, Jonathan. "U.S. Housing Starts Post Unexpected Rise in December." *Mortgage News,* 21 January 2004. Available from www.homebundmortgage.com.

"Overseas Investors Eye China's Housing Market." *AsiaPulse News,* 25 August 2003.

"Profile—Japan's Construction Industry." *AsiaPulse News,* 14 October 2003.

Sigmund, Pete. "Road, Bridge Work to Sustain Industry in '07." *Construction Equipment Guide,* 11 December 2006.

Sleight, Chris. "Construction Europe." *KHL News*, 10 August 2004. Available from http://www.khl.com.

Strong Market Expected to Remain for Near Future." *TTJ: The Timber Industry Magazine,* 17 February 2007.

"Taylor Wimpey: Europe's Largest House Builder." *Construction Europe,* 26 March 2007.

Tulacz, Gary J. "World Construction Spending Nears $4 Trillion for 2004." *enr.com,*, January 3-10, 2005. Available from http://www.enr.com.

U.S. Department of the Census. *New Privately Owned Housing Units Authorized Unadjusted Units for Regions, Divisions, and States,* February 2005. Available from www.census.gov/.

U.S. Department of Housing and Urban Development, Office of Policy Development and Research. *U.S. Housing Market Conditions Summary,* February 2004. Available from www.huduser.org.

U.S. Department of Labor, Bureau of Labor Statistics. *Career Guide to Industries.* 20 December 2005. Available from www.bls.gov.

———. *Fatal Occupational Injuries and Employment by Industry,* 2004. Available from www.bls.gov.

U.S. Housing Market Conditions, Fourth Quarter 2006. February 2007. Available from www.huduser.org.

"U.S. Real Estate and Construction Industry Overview, 2005" 2006. Available from www.plunkettresearch.com.

Yin Zhongli and Guo Jianbo, "House Market Needs Regulation." *China Daily,* 1 April 2005. Available from http://www.chinadaily.com.cn/English.

SIC 2411

NAICS 113310

LOGGING

The world's logging industry cuts timber to produce rough, round, or hewn wood for use as building materials, fuel, paper, and numerous other purposes. The logging industry is closely allied with forest management. For more extensive treatment of this topic, see **Forestry.**

INDUSTRY SNAPSHOT

In the early twenty-first century, industrial logging was taking place in virtually every major forested region in the world, including both temperate and tropical regions. Logging includes the harvesting of both coniferous trees, such as pine and spruce—called softwood—and deciduous trees, such as eucalyptus, maple and oak—called hardwood. The United States led the world in total removals of industrial roundwood from forestland, with annual harvests of hardwood and softwood timber reaching 467 million cubic meters in 2003. This amount, however, showed a decrease from the 500 million cubic meters harvested in 2000. According to the U.S. Department of Agriculture Forest Service, approximately 88 million cubic meters of lumber and 25 million cubic meters of structural panel product were produced in 2002.

Industrial wood in the rough consists of four elements: sawlogs, used to make lumber; veneer logs; pulpwood, used to make pulp for papermaking and wood-based panels; and other industrial wood. Removals of industrial wood in the rough from Western Europe, Eastern Europe, and the Nordic countries combined reached 434.5 million cubic meters in 2000. Removals of industrial roundwood totaled 399.1 million cubic meters in 2001, rising to 413.6 million cubic meters in 2002 and 488.3 million cubic meters in 2003. The Asia-Pacific region showed removals of 107.1 million cubic meters in 2000, due primarily to production declines in Asia. In 2003, developing nations in Asia harvested some 206 million cubic meters of industrial roundwood. Removals from the former Soviet Union rose steadily in the late 1990s and 2000s. About 95 million cubic meters were harvested in 1998, and some 143.6 million in 1999, an increase of more than 50 percent. Removals rose 10 percent in 2000, to 158.1 million cubic meters. Removals in 2001 were 164.7 million cubic meters, and in 2002 were 174.2 million cubic meters.

Some experts predict a global shortage of wood production in the twenty-first century, particularly in softwoods. Total global production of industrial roundwood (industrial wood in the rough plus fuelwood, which is burned for heat and cooking) from softwoods was 935 million cubic meters in 1992. By 2010, softwood demand was expected to reach 1.14 billion cubic meters, a net increase of 10 percent over the period.

Most projections for softwood roundwood supply do not come close to matching anticipated demand. For example, annual softwood roundwood supply from the U.S. Pacific Northwest was expected to drop by 60 million cubic meters between 1992 and 2010, with an additional 10 million cubic meter decline from British Columbia. Government-imposed harvesting restrictions on public land in these regions are causing the declines. Over the same period, supply increases were expected from Eastern Europe (85 million cubic meters); fast-growing plantations in several countries (65 million cubic meters); Scandinavia and Western Europe (20 million cubic meters); and the U.S. South and the rest of Canada (10 million cubic meters). After factoring in the declines from other regions, these production increases should produce a net increase in softwood supply of 110 million cubic meters by 2010, leaving softwood-derived roundwood supply 95 million cubic meters short of the anticipated demand.

However, worldwide economy, and particularly the North American economy, experienced a slowdown in the early years of the 2000s. Forest products markets reached record highs in 2000, but declined in 2001. Further, roundwood was in oversupply in Europe throughout 2000, following severe windstorms, which felled some 200 million cubic meters of timber. Wind-throw damages in Estonia in July 2001 drew attention to the fact that storm damage poses a permanent risk for roundwood markets and that practices may need to be modified to mitigate future storm damage.

The hardwood situation was not as critical as softwood, but hardwood supply was likewise expected to lag demand. World production of industrial hardwood roundwood was 440 million cubic meters in 1992. North America produced and consumed 36.6 and 38.3 million cubic meters respectively of sawn hardwood in 2000. By 2010, hardwood demand was expected to reach 550 million cubic meters, an increase of 110 million cubic meters. Under a realistic market forecast, several regions might produce hardwood roundwood increases totaling 55 million cubic meters annually by 2010. Fast-growing hardwood plantations were likely to contribute another 50 million cubic meters. However, hardwood production in Malaysia and Indonesia was expected to drop 45 million cubic meters by 2010, producing a net hardwood roundwood supply gain for the global market of just 60 million cubic meters, which would theoretically create a supply deficit of 50 million cubic meters by 2010.

The economic performance of the Asia-Pacific region was considered a critical factor in the industry's supply/demand outlook. The region was a net importer of fiber, and as the pulp and paper industry developed in countries such as Indonesia and Malaysia, such imports grew. Japan alone accounted for two-thirds of the world's total imports of woodchips by 2003.

China was a rapidly expanding market in the early twenty-first century, with retail lumber sales up by more than 10 percent in 2001. Total imports of roundwood in 2002 reached 16 million cubic meters, eleven times the amount imported in 1997. China imported 5.4 million cubic meters of sawnwood in 2002, up 33.5 percent from the previous year, and also imported 22 million cubic meters of roundwood. Fueled by rising incomes and substantial investments in the housing sector, China's market for wood products is expected to continue growing at comparable levels through the early 2000s. By 2010, China's demand for timber was expected to rise to 200 million cubic meters, of which half probably would be imported.

One of the major issues in world logging was the continuing depression of the Russian forest products industry. Harvesting of logs dropped dramatically as a result of the economic contraction in the Russian Federation and other former Soviet states. Environmental problems, organizational problems, lack of funds for infrastructure investments, and social and management problems all contributed to disappointing results. In Russia, total removals of wood in the rough were just 66.5 million cubic meters in 1996, far below levels in the 1980s. Despite these difficulties, Russia remained a major exporter of raw logs through the early 2000s. Exports were 20.9 million cubic meters in 1998 and rose to 28.2 million the following year. Industrial wood exports reached 32 million cubic meters in 2000, 32.8 million in 2001, and 37.4 million in 2002. Though analysts predicted a gloomy future for the Russian logging industry into the early 2000s, Russian removal rates exploded in 1999, growing by 50 percent in one year. Harvests in Ukraine and Belarus also increased, bringing the total removals for the Commonwealth of Independent States (including Russia) from 109.7 million cubic meters in 1998 to more than 191.9 million cubic meters in 2002. During this period, Russia began to expand its exports to Pacific Rim nations. By 2005, its timber exports to China had increased about 31 times in volume, from 0.53 million cubic meters in 1996 to 17.02 million cubic meters in 2004. The average increase was more than 50 percent annually. In 2004, Russia exported 10.16 million cubic meters of sawn softwood, 10.2 million cubic meters of softwood logs, and 25.5 million metric tons of pulpwood; exports for 2005 were projected at 11.60 million cubic meters of sawn softwood, 8.1 million cubic meters of softwood logs, and 25.6 million metric tons of pulpwood.

Several major controversies have engulfed the world logging industry. Disputes were truly global, including protests over the cutting of tropical timber in the Pacific Rim; federal court bans on harvesting from government-owned timberland in the northwest United States; boycotts of wood, pulp, and paper products from British Columbia; and protests over the cutting of forests in Chile. Throughout the early to mid-2000s, controversy continued, as did ongoing litigation in the courts of individual countries.

Problems surfaced in the relatively new logging areas of the Pacific Rim and Latin America. Most of the growing stock in tropical hardwood forests either has low productive potential or is commercially inaccessible. Over-cutting of native Asia-Pacific forests without proper reforestation has greatly reduced the timber available for harvest. Also, environmental pressures to limit harvesting in Latin American tropical forests have been effective in reducing harvest levels there as well.

ORGANIZATION AND STRUCTURE

Companies of various sizes were involved in the logging industry. Large, integrated forest products firms, such as Georgia-Pacific in the United States and Stora in Europe, own large private timberland tracts and hold cutting rights on government forests, while small independent logging crews do much of the cutting for major companies. Large forest products companies often send their logs to company-owned sawmills, but small one-unit sawmills still survive in some countries. In less developed nations, thousands of individuals cut timber for use as firewood.

Most industrial logging is carried out according to complicated management plans established by the owners of the land. Owners of forests could be national, state, or provincial governments, forest product companies, or private landowners. Regulation of harvesting yields and methods vary widely from country to country, though in the early 2000s it was generally accepted that replanting and management of cut stands was vital to sustainable forestry. A substantial share of logging is carried out by large forest products companies, although in the by the early 2000s many contracted more of the actual logging out to small, independent companies or to individual contractors. For example, most logging of pulpwood in the southeast United States—formerly done by pulp and paper companies—was being subcontracted.

Individual forest management plans determine the yearly yield and the method of removing timber from forested land. Harvesting methods included clear-cutting all trees from large areas or selective cutting of individual trees or groups of trees. Much of the controversy over industrial forestry focused on the practice of clear-cutting. Loggers argued that it was, by far, the most efficient means of harvesting timber and was environmentally sustainable. Selective cutting, they claimed, was too expensive in some areas and would not necessarily lead to optimal growing conditions for new trees since the remaining large trees screened out much of the light that new trees needed to survive and grow. Environmental groups, however, lobbied heavily against clear-cutting. They alleged that clear-cutting and reforestation damaged an area's ecosystem and its biodiversity.

As of the mid-2000s, clear-cutting had not been banned in major forest-producing countries. Still, logging companies began to use more selective cutting. They were also more careful in their selection of sites for clear-cutting, leaving "buffer zones" around rivers and lakes to prevent soil runoff, avoiding cutting near roads and scenic areas, and using sophisticated computer models to select cuts that caused the least aesthetic and environmental disruption.

INTERNATIONAL TIMBER TRADE

In the late 1990s and early 2000s, there was significant international trade in logs, though trading volume varied considerably in response to changing economic conditions. Europe exported 9.29 million cubic meters of softwood and hardwood logs (used for making lumber) in 1996 and imported 17.5 million cubic meters, while the United States exported 12.5 million cubic meters and imported 3.4 million cubic meters. There was also substantial international trade in pulpwood (used for making paper and some wood products). Europe exported 14.7 million cubic meters of pulpwood in 1996 while importing 28.8 million cubic meters. According to statistics from the European Commission, the market for pulpwood in Europe peaked in late 2000, but production and consumption had risen substantially by 2004. The United States, on the other hand, saw significant declines in production and exports of pulpwood and pulp products. Production of pulpwood was 193 million cubic meters in 2001, a 5.4 decrease from the previous year; production declined a further 1.4 percent in 2002 to reach 191 million cubic meters. Exports of paper and pulpwood products, which fell by 8 percent in 2001, increased by 0.5 percent in 2002. According to the U.S. Department of Agriculture Forest Service, the pulpwood market in the early 2000s was hit with its steepest declines since the 1970s. By 2002, industry earnings were down by approximately 50 percent of their levels in 2000.

The Asia-Pacific region, once a major exporter of logs, saw its export volume collapse in the mid-1990s. Asia-Pacific exports of tropical timber plunged from 21.3 million cubic meters in 1992 to just 9.4 million cubic meters in 1996, 8.5 million cubic meters in 1997, and 7.9 million cubic meters in 1998. Exports grew only tepidly at best through the early 2000s, reaching 8.6 million cubic meters in 2003. Africa exported a substantial amount of tropical logs through the late 1990s. Exports of industrial roundwood topped 5.3 million cubic meters in 1996 and 6 million cubic meters in 2000. Shipments fell to 4.2 million cubic meters in 2003. Almost all of Africa's timber comes from sub-Saharan countries.

Another factor affecting the international tropical timber trade was the rapid economic growth in many Southeast Asian countries. This expansion produced an intense boom in residential, office, and industrial building construction. The net result of this activity was that more timber stayed in the country of origin. As a result, traditional importers of tropical timber began moving to other sources. For example, Japan, the world's largest importer of tropical logs, replaced much of its import volume from the Pacific Rim with tropical supplies from Latin America and Africa. Japan also began substituting temperate, coniferous timber for applications that had traditionally used tropical wood, such as concrete forming.

North America, with its vast forestland, has long been a major producer, user, and exporter of logs. For many years, logging, lumber, and paper production were the dominant industries in areas such as the Pacific Northwest and British Columbia. However, growing demand for timber and environmental restrictions changed that situation. In the United States, controversy developed regarding the shipment of U.S. logs overseas. U.S. logging in the Pacific Northwest was cut dramatically in the 1990s, mainly due to environmental restrictions, and exports of U.S. roundwood fell sharply as well.

The Harvesting Process

Actual harvesting of logs consists of several processes, including felling (cutting), bucking (cross-cutting into logs), limbing, debarking, skidding (removing the logs from the cut site), and transporting logs to various industries. Felling is done by large machines, such as feller/bunchers, or manually, by large chain saws. Larger trees destined for the sawmill to be made into lumber are usually cut by chain saw. Smaller pulpwood trees that are used to make wood pulp are typically cut mechanically with devices such as the combine harvester, which shears trees off at the base. Another device, the feller/buncher, cuts and holds a group of trees together, then deposits the load onto a log truck.

Where possible, logs are loaded directly onto large log trucks. When necessary, logs are skidded to another site by tractors and steel cables or, in some countries, by animals. In rare cases, logs are removed with helicopters. After World War II, logging gradually became more mechanized, but areas existed where limited yields or difficult topography made the use of machinery too expensive or problematic. In these cases, human and animal labor were still used.

Background and Development

Wood and logging have played a crucial role in the evolution of human civilization. Wood has been used for everything from providing heat, building carts, and sailing vessels to creating housing, windmills, mineshafts, and countless other applications. Plato once wrote that all arts and crafts are derived from mining and forestry. Pioneer societies in many places of the world depended almost entirely on wood.

Civilizations have also tended to misuse wood resources, overcutting or burning large forest tracts and causing severe environmental consequences. The industrial revolution worsened deforestation in Europe and North America, and between 1800 and 1920, many of those regions' great forests were completely cleared. However, the 1930s and 1940s saw the dawn of modern forestry and logging methods, which had been accompanied by extensive reforestation in many countries. In general, total forest cover was maintained or increased since World War II in North America, Europe, and other major logging countries. However, deforestation continued to be a problem in less developed regions, such as Africa, South America, and Southeast Asia.

The global logging industry follows the boom and bust cycle of its principal customers, the lumber industry and the pulp and paper industry. Typically, as the housing market recovers after a recession, demand for lumber jumps and logging increases. The same is true of pulp and paper, where a more robust economy means increased demand for paper; in turn, that leads to the construction of large pulp and paper mills and the need for more pulpwood.

In the 1990s, however, this equation was altered by increased environmental restrictions on logging and the production of more recycled paper. Bans on logging in the Pacific Northwest and slowdowns in cutting in British Columbia, for example, depressed the logging industries there, put many loggers out of work, and drove prices up for finished lumber. A corresponding increase in the amount of recycled paper used in North America and Europe in the 1990s further depressed demand for pulpwood and made lasting structural changes in the way the logging industry operated in those regions. Also, the financial crisis in the Asia-Pacific region, which began in 1996 and intensified rapidly in 1997, reduced demand for imported logs and lumber, particularly from Canada. Poor economic conditions in Japan in the late 1990s led to decreased housing starts, and, consequently, reduced imports of Canadian lumber.

Canada's timber industry was hurt further in August 2001, when the U.S. Commerce Department, acting on a complaint by a group of U.S. lumber producers that claimed Canadian rivals were subsidized, imposed a 19.3 percent duty on Canadian softwood imports. In December 2003, however, the United States and Canada announced an agreement that eliminated the new tariff, which, according to CBC News, had cost the industry thousands of jobs and losses of as much as US$1.5 billion. The agreement, however, imposed limits on the amount of softwood that Canada could export duty-free to the United States. CBC News reported that this condition required Canada to reduce its share of the U.S. market from 33 percent to 31.5 percent. Canada brought the issue before NAFTA, which in 2004 rejected the U.S. argument that subsidized Canadian lumber imports were damaging the U.S. industry. Appealing this ruling, the United States set import duties on most softwood lumber from Canada at 21.2 percent. In early 2005, Canada proposed a negotiated settlement, offering to impose an export tax on softwood that would be reduced or eliminated as the country changed its method of harvesting from government land.

The effect of new environmental policies on logging volume is illustrated by changes taking place in North America, due, among other things, to changes in forest practices to conserve biodiversity and to ensure a sustainable timber supply over the long term. In Canada, three British Columbia government programs reduced roundwood removals in the mid- to late 1990s: the 1995 Forest Practices Code, the Timber Supply Review, and the Protected Areas Strategy. Other reasons cited for the changes included overcutting in British Columbia's forests from 1960 to 1990, lack of intensive reforestation during that period, environmental pressures, and public demand for more parks and recreational lands. British Columbia forestry experts estimated that the Forest Practices Code would restrict the annual allowable cut in the province by 6 percent immediately and possibly by as much as 20 percent in the long term, reducing harvesting from 74 million cubic meters in 1996 to about 60 million cubic meters in 2000. In 2002, the province announced changes to the code to improve its administration.

In the United States, U.S. Forest Service timber sales dropped sharply from 1986 onward, as court decisions in favor of protecting the habitat of endangered species such as the northern spotted owl essentially ended logging on vast areas of federal land in the Pacific Northwest. For example, in 1986 the Forest Service sold about 50 million cubic meters of timber (which was cut by private companies), but by 1996 the volume was down roughly 70 percent to about 15 million cubic meters. In early 1997, warm, wet weather further reduced harvesting operations in the Pacific Northwest. New forestry guidelines stopped logging since the forest floor was wet and would be damaged by heavy motorized logging equipment.

Reduced harvest levels in the Pacific Northwest began when federal judges ruled in favor of environmental groups that had sued the U.S. Forest Service under the Endangered Species Act. The judges ruled that the Forest Service had to stop logging on vast areas of federal land until the agency drew up approved plans to protect the endangered spotted owl. The Clinton administration imposed a settlement in 1993-1994 that allowed some logging, though at only 15 to 25 percent of historic levels. The subject of lawsuits by both environmental groups and logging interests, the Clinton plan withstood several court challenges. However, the almost complete cutoff in harvesting of large, old-growth trees, used mostly for lumber, caused a massive closure of sawmills and extensive job losses.

However, in 2001 and 2002, the Bush administration unveiled plans to relax the stricter policies of the previous decade. According to a 2001 article in the *National Journal,* Bush promised he would put the national forests "back to work" by approving more logging. Upon taking office, Bush filled key positions with pro-logging advocates who asserted that more timber sales would help prevent devastating and dangerous forest fires like the western U.S. wildfires of 2000. The National Forest Service reported in 2001 some 50 million acres of federal forest lands were at high risk for fires.

In February 2002, Bush announced a plan which would place control of federal forest lands under local private management. Called the "charter forest," the U.S. Forest Service lands would be withdrawn from the Forest Service's control, and a "local trust entity" would be put in place to reduce management bottlenecks and costs. According to a *Primedia* article, environmental groups had long complained the Forest Service focused too heavily on timber sales and oil leasing, rather than environmental preservation. Criticism became more heated after President Bush took office and froze a Clinton-era rule banning new roads needed for logging, drilling, and mining in one-third of all national forests.

Restrictions on logging in the northwestern United States appeared to be a boon for logging in the pine forests of the southeastern United States. Unlike the Northwest, most of forestland in the southeastern United States was not in federal hands. Nearly 60 percent of southeastern U.S. forests were owned privately, compared to 30 percent of northwestern forests. However, environmental restrictions and wildlife preservation issues affected even these private landholdings. Overproduction in the southern states, as well as oversupply of Canadian imports, resulted in depressed prices for timber in southern states in the early 2000s. According to a report from Mississippi State University, the value of Mississippi's timber harvest fell by 17.4 percent in 2001—a trend that worsened after the terrorist attacks of 9/11. In 2002, the decline was 3.6 percent. By 2003, however, conditions had begun to improve. The value of timber production in Mississippi that year fell by less than one percent, due largely to increased housing starts.

The cutting and use of tropical timber in Asia and Latin America was also restricted for environmental reasons. Despite the growing importance of these regions in the pulp and paper industry, over-harvesting in the 1980s, restrictions on logging, and other factors combined to reduce the production of tropical forest products in the 1990s. For example, the total production of logs from these three regions was 139 million cubic meters in 1992, but by 1996 that total had dropped to 127 million cubic meters. The downward trend was caused by massive drops in the Pacific Rim, where log production dropped from 104 million cubic meters in 1992 to just 86 million cubic meters in 1996.

Production in Latin America increased from 28 million cubic meters in 1992 to 32 million cubic meters, and African production increased from 8 million cubic meters to 9.2 million cubic meters in the same period. While African production is low on a global scale, it is notable that several nations of south central Africa derive a major share of their GDP from forest products, making the industry key to their national economies.

Some public and private groups developed certification programs that would identify timber produced in an environmentally responsible manner. Producers of tropical timber responded by moving away from cutting stands of virgin timber toward the concept of sustainable forest management, including the planting and harvesting of tree plantations using other tree species. To save endangered types of tropical timber, users of timber also replaced their use of tropical hardwood with temperate coniferous and nonconiferous species in many applications.

REMOVAL RATES

Despite these restrictions, global production of wood continued to grow in the early 2000s. Economic conditions, however, produced the peaks and valleys typically associated with this industry. For example, weak demand for lumber and wood pulp caused removals of roundwood to decrease by 3.2 percent in Europe from 1995 to 1996. Further, roundwood was in over-supply through 2000 and 2001, after devastating December 1999 windstorms felled enough lumber to account for nearly half the average annual production in most of Europe. Yet, roundwood removal was up to 443.5 million cubic meters in 2001, from 391 million cubic meters in 2000. Removals fell to 399 million cubic meters in 2001 but rose to 413.6 million cubic meters in 2002. Removals were expected to grow through 2004 at between 1.5 and 2 percent, but consumption was expected to increase by 4.1 percent annually.

In the Russian Federation, the decline of the forest industry continued in the mid-1990s. Softwood roundwood removals fell by 18.5 percent to 69.4 million cubic meters in 1996, reaching only 50 percent of levels in 1992. Hardwood removals also fell by 18.3 percent to 25.7 million cubic meters. Improvement occurred in 1998, however, when combined roundwood removals rose to 95 million cubic meters. The following year, total removals rose to 143.6 million cubic meters. Levels increased steadily through the early 2000s, reaching 158 million cubic meters in 2000 and 164.7 million cubic meters in 2001. Total roundwood removals for the Russian Federation reached 174.2 million cubic meters in 2002. According to the U.N. Economic Commission for Europe, forest products markets in Europe were expected to grow in 2004 and 2005, with volumes in Russia and former Eastern bloc nations approaching the levels they had reached prior to their economic transition in the early 1990s.

In the United States, roundwood removals wavered in the last half of the 1990s. As housing starts grew in the last few years of the twentieth century, the industry realized a slightly higher demand, and roundwood removals increased from 485.8 million cubic meters in 1997 to 500.1 million in 2000. Though removals dipped again the following year, totaling only 471 million cubic meters, the decline reversed in 2002, when removals reached 477.8 million cubic meters. Removals were steadier in Canada, which harvested 188.8 million cubic meters of roundwood in 1997, 176.9 million in 1998, 193.7 million in 1999, and 200 million in 2000. Levels remained at about 200 million cubic meters in 2001 and 2002, and grew by about 7.6 percent from 2003 to 2004. According to analysis from the *Journal of Forestry,* the projected annual U.S. harvest of all species will rise 23 percent, about 4.2 billion cubic feet, from 1996 to 2050, with softwood harvests increasing by 3 billion cubic feet.

European pulpwood production (separate from log production, which is used for lumber) experienced a steep drop in 1996. After recovering over the next two years, the market reached a peak in late 2000. A significant increase in pulp production and consumption was expected in 2004, with slower growth in 2005. However, the United States experienced a substantial drop in pulpwood production, which by 2001 reached only 193 million cubic meters. This sharp decline was attributed to the increasing use of recycled paper as a fiber source.

TRADE AGREEMENTS

International trade in forest products has been affected by legislation that came into effect in the first half of the 1990s. These agreements included the Uruguay Round of the General Agreement on Tariffs and Trade (GATT), the European Union, and the North American Free Trade Agreement (NAFTA). Under GATT, tariffs on wood and paper products were expected to decrease more slowly than on other industrial products. For example, Japan offered to cut its base rate tariffs by 50 percent during a five-year period. The intent was to reduce tariffs on about 60 percent of Japanese wood and wood products by a margin of 2.6 to 10 percent. European countries offered to reduce tariffs by 44 percent, but with a long phase-in period. Major wood products exporters, such as the United States and Canada, wanted complete and rapid elimination of tariffs.

China's entry into the World Trade Organization, which by 2004 included 147 countries, was expected to boost world timber exports to meet increased demand in China's housing and furniture sectors. In 2001, China imported about 77 million metric tons of timber and timber products. From 2003 to 2004, the value of China's forest products market grew 24.8 percent, reaching US$32.3 billion. Exports were valued at US$16 billion, up 34 percent from the previous year, and imports were valued at US$16.34 billion, up 17.2 percent. Plywood exports increased by more than 110 percent in volume and 152 percent in value. The production of solid composite floor material is a significant segment of China's timber products industry. By 2004, China was manufacturing about 30 percent of world demand for solid composite floors, which totaled about 25 million square meters that year. All of this production went to supply domestic demand. Growth in this segment averaged about 40 percent annually between 2001 and 2004.

As international trade increased, concerns about illegal logging also grew. In 2003, the U.S. Department of State launched President Bush's Initiative against Illegal Logging to provide assistance to countries that were fighting the sale and export of illegally harvested timber. The Department of State cited World Bank figures estimating that illegal logging costs developing countries as much as US$10 to US$15 billion per year. Illegal logging has also been linked to environmental degradation. In late 2004, more than 1,000 people in the Philippines were killed by flash floods that sparked massive landslides on slopes where forests had been cut illegally. Illegal logging in the African rainforest is threatening the habitat of gorillas and chimpanzees.

CLIMATE CHANGE

The impact of global warming trends may bring significant changes to the international logging industry in the 2000s. Warmer temperatures could weaken forests in temperate zones, which in 2002 accounted for about 77 percent of industrial timber production. Subtropical areas, however, where softwood trees can grow twice as fast as in temperate regions, could greatly expand production. According to an Ohio State University repoArt, one analyst predicted that tropical timber plantations would increase by about 675,000 acres annually during the next 50 to 100 years. At the same time, softwood species in North America and Europe would migrate into northern hardwood forests and some hardwood species there would die out. This shift could bode ill for the northern timber industry, as lumber from this deadfall would flood the market and depress prices.

CURRENT CONDITIONS

In the hardwood market, logs from North America and Europe accounted for a large share of total world production in the latter mid-2000s. The United States produced approximately 61 million cubic meters of hardwood logs, 62 million meters of sawn softwood, and 27.8 million meters of sawn hardwood in 2005. China was the largest export market for North American hardwood, placing orders valued at US$328 million in 2006, an increase of 38 percent over the previous year. Europe was an important contributor to the worldwide logging industry, accounting for more than half of total exports, according to the United Nations Food and Agricultural Organization (FAO). The United Kingdom was seeing a decline in the industry, however, with the number of hardwood mills falling from 26 in 2001 to 18 in 2005. The number of softwood U.K. mills stood at 155 in 2005, according to the U.K. Forestry Commission. Relatedly, growth in Eastern Europe was expected to be greater than that in Western Europe through 2020. Total forest area in Europe was also expected to increase about 5 percent annually through 2020, and increased demand for renewable energy was predicted to drive growth in the industry.

INDUSTRY LEADERS

Leading logging and wood products companies also tended to be integrated forest products companies: they produced pulp, paper, and packaging as well as wood products and lumber. The United States was by far the world leader in logging; therefore, U.S. companies tended to be the largest forest and wood products companies.

In the mid-2000s, International Paper Company was the world's largest forest products company. Although in the early 2000s it owned 6.3 million acres of forested land in the United States, as well as 1.2 million in Brazil and smaller tracts in New Zealand and Russia, by 2007 it had sold much of its forested land, retaining about 500,000 acres in the United States and harvesting rights for about 1 million acres in Brazil and Russia. In 2006 the company posted total sales of US$21.9 billion, with paper and packaging accounting for about two-thirds of sales. That year the company employed 68,700 people. Second behind International Paper was Georgia-Pacific Corporation, which was the world's largest producer of tissue products. Its major brands include Brawny, Quilted Northern, and Dixie. Sales in 2004 exceeded US$19.6 billion. Weyerhaueser Company, which owned 6.4 million acres of timberland in the United States and leased about 30 million acres in Canada, was also licensed to harvest timber in Australia, New Zealand, France, and Ireland. In 2000, the company bought Canadian giant MacMillan Bloedel. In 2006, Weyerhaueser's total sales topped US$21.8 billion with 49,900 employees. Boise Cascade Holdings produces building materials and paper and reported sales of US$5.9 billion in 2006 with 10,155 employees.

Swedish-based Stora Enso Oyj, which was formed when Stora merged with Finnish pulp and paper company Enso Oy in 1998, paid US$4.8 billion for U.S.-based Consolidated Papers Inc. two years later. By 2000 it was the world's leading producer of paper and paperboard. Stora saw sales of US$15.7 billion in 2006. Svenska Cellulosa Aktiebolaget SCA of Sweden, which acquired a majority stake in Papierwerke Waldhof-Aschaffenburg AG of Germany (PWA) in the 1990s, also had extensive forest products operations. It owned 5 million acres of forested land in Sweden and had operations in Africa, North and South America, Asia, Australia, and Europe. In 2004 the company realized US$13.6 billion in sales.

MAJOR COUNTRIES IN THE INDUSTRY

The nontropical logging industry is dominated by the United States, the European Union, and Canada. At the start of the twenty-first century, the United States was, by far, the leading logging country in the world. It maintained a relatively steady removal rate in the late 1980s and early 1990s until the advent of bans on timber cut removals. Total U.S. production of coniferous and nonconiferous wood in the rough in 1996 amounted to 414 million cubic meters. European production in the same year was 262 million cubic meters. In 2000, production had jumped to 500 million cubic meters in the United Sates and 434.5 million cubic meters in Europe. In 2003, Europe removed 488.3 million cubic meters of industrial roundwood, while the United States produced about 405 million cubic meters.

Coniferous softwood accounted for the majority of U.S. removals of wood in the rough, 289.6 million cubic meters in 2002, but the United States also produced a very large amount of nonconiferous hardwood wood in the rough, 188 million cubic meters in 2002. Softwood, the more valuable of the two, is used to make lumber for housing construction, wood pulp, and other applications. In 2004, some 680 U.S. sawmills produced 27 million cubic meters of hardwood, compared to 33 million cubic meters produced by 1,000 sawmills in 1997. Because of improved efficiency, however, sawmill turnover increased from about US$4.4 billion in 1997 to US$6.5 billion in 2004.

The southern United States, with its warm winters, flat land, and easy access to timberlands, is an easier place to log than the northwest. Southern trees also grow faster than northern trees, improving the forest yield. With almost no old-growth timber, the south experienced much less environmental controversy than the northwest.

Strong demand for pine products in 2003, which was tied to growth in residential construction, contributed to a stabilization of the timber industry in southern states. According to a report from Mississippi State University, the value of timber from southern states fell by 17 percent in 2001, and by 3.6 percent in 2002. By 2003, however, this decline had slowed to less than 1 percent. The U.S. timber industry also benefited from U.S. government purchases in 2003 of softwood panels and lumber for reconstruction after the war in Iraq. With U.S. housing starts surging in 2004 and 2005, consumption of sawn hardwood increased, and in 2006 was expected to continue its upward trend, although somewhat more slowly than in the early 2000s.

FURTHER READING

Ali, Amina, et al. "Softwood Lumber Dispute." CBC News, 8 December 2003. Available from http://www.cbc.ca/news.

"ANU Forestry Market Report," March 2004. Available from http://sres.anu.edu.au.

Brack, Duncan. "Illegal Logging." Chatham House, March 2005. Available from http://www.illegal-logging.info.

"Canada Offers Wood Deal." *New York Times,* 10 March 2005.

"China's Annual Timber Demand to Reach 200 Million Cubic Meters by 2010." Xinhua, 3 November 2003. Available from http://forests.org.

"China Wood Products Prices." *Global Wood,* 16-30 April 2005. Available from http://www.globalwood.org.

Hoover's Company Capsules. Hoover's Inc., 2007. Available from www.hoovers.com.

ldquo;Market Report: Winds of Change?" *Forestry & British Timber,* 2 April 2007.

Mississippi State University Office of Agricultural Communications. "State's Timber Industry Remains Steady in 2003." Report by Linda Breazeale, 18 December 2003. Available from http://msucares.com.

"New Developments in Logging." *E & P Magazine,* 20 August 2006.

Pfahlert, Patrick. "Lumber Market Opportunities." *Sinomedia,* 14 July 2003. Available from www.sinomedia.net.

Simon, Bernard. "U.S. Will Impose 29 Percent Tariff on Canada Building Lumber." *New York Times,* 23 March 2003.

"Traders Are Braced for Another Difficult Year." *TTJ: The Timber Industry Magazine,* 17 March 2007.

UNECE Trade and Timber Division. "Forest Products Statistics." *Timber Bulletin,* February 2007.

United Nations, Food, and Agricultural Organization. "European Forest Sector Outlook Study." 2005. Available from www.unece.org.

———. "Forest Products Annual Market Review 2005-2006." 15 April 2007. Available from www.unece.org.

———. "Forest Products Statistics 2001-2005." Available from www.unece.org.

"U.S. Appeals NAFTA Ruling Against Tariffs on Canadian Lumber." *New York Times,* 25 November 2004.

U.S. Department of Agriculture. Forest Service. *U.S. Forest Products Annual Market Review and Prospects, 2001-2005.* Report by James L. Howard. Available from www.fpl.fs.fed.us.

U.S. Department of State. "The President's Initiative Against Illegal Logging," 28 July 2003. Available from www.state.gov.

Warnook, Matt. "Environmental Agency Takes Action Against Timber Smuggling." *Wood & Wood Products,* September 2006.

ELECTRICAL AND ELECTRONIC EQUIPMENT

SIC 3630
NAICS 3352

APPLIANCES, HOUSEHOLD

The world's appliance manufacturers output an extensive range of consumer household devices. These include electric and non-electric cooking equipment such as stoves, ranges, and ovens (including microwaves); refrigerators and freezers; laundry equipment (such as washing machines, dryers, and ironers); electric housewares for heating (such as electric space heaters, electrically heated bed coverings, and portable humidifiers and dehumidifiers); electric fans; vacuum cleaners; water heaters; dishwashers; food waste disposal units; and sewing machines.

INDUSTRY SNAPSHOT

From 2004 to 2007, global demand for major household appliances is projected to enjoy annual increases of nearly 4 percent, according to estimates from the Freedonia Group. This growth is expected to propel demand to 367 million units. Although China had become the largest global supplier of so-called "white goods" by 2004, the world appliances market includes production by numerous nations all over the world and consumption by virtually every country. A unique aspect of this industry is that it offers something to almost every consumer, regardless of lifestyle or income. Within individual segments of the market are many choices and price ranges, making products accessible to almost anyone. The leading segments of the industry are refrigerators, stoves and ranges, washing machines, ovens, and dryers.

Because of maturing markets in the United States and western Europe, appliance manufacturers in these regions chose two avenues to expand sales: developing innovative products with time-and energy-saving features to lure new customers in existing markets, and tapping new markets. The emphasis on energy efficiency is a major consideration for American buyers, so features designed to save utility costs and/or help preserve the environment are popular. As economies in Asia, South America, and eastern Europe expanded, manufacturers strove to capitalize on these areas' increasing disposable incomes and rising standards of living by developing export markets there and by forming joint alliances with manufacturers in these regions.

Waves of consolidation have characterized the U.S. industry, and a similar trend appeared later in Europe. U.S. consolidations left the country with only four major producers: Whirlpool, General Electric, Maytag, and Goodman Holding Company (Amana). In Europe, Electrolux and Bosch-Siemens started to acquire smaller manufacturers in an effort to achieve this kind of dominance and market positioning. Manufacturers in Asia, where appliance production has burgeoned, and elsewhere, are forecast to consolidate or close down operations because of the faltering economy.

ORGANIZATION AND STRUCTURE

Unlike industries with high fixed costs, appliance firms' costs are more variable because they are somewhat vulnerable to price changes in raw materials and parts. Company profits are enhanced by lower borrowing costs, market conditions that tolerate higher prices, and strong sales of high-end merchandise. Higher prices are not easily passed along to customers, especially since industry competition has increased significantly. One result of this heightened competitiveness has been an upsurge in industry consolidation.

Premium appliance models generally carry higher profit margins for industry manufacturers. Conversely, lower-end models have smaller profit margins. Washers, dryers, and refrigerators tend to be more profitable to appliance manufacturers than dishwashers and cooking equipment. The average life span of a major appliance is 10 to 15 years.

According to the Association of Home Appliance Manufacturers (AHAM), demand for household appliances varies from year to year depending on a number of economic and social factors: replacement demand, original purchase demand, saturation levels, state of the economy, and specific product demand.

APPLIANCE REPLACEMENT

Replacement demand for a particular type of appliance depends on that appliance's average life span and, to a lesser extent, the rate of technological innovation that distinguishes new models from old. In some countries, replacement demand is a large percentage of total demand for household appliances. Home remodeling activity also influences replacement demand, for changes in a home's layout can often prompt consumers to upgrade from older models to newer ones for the sake of aesthetics and convenience.

Replacement demand tends to be stronger when real appliance prices remain constant over time, only rising at the general rate of inflation. As the costs of acquiring a new machine stay relatively constant, the desire to repair instead of replace the appliance typically decreases. The availability of affordable new appliances thus prompts greater replacement demand when the need to repair arises.

ORIGINAL APPLIANCE MARKET

In addition to replacement demand, new residential home construction is an important factor in the demand for household appliances. A typical new home can account for up to six different major units: dishwasher, refrigerator, oven, washer, dryer, and range.

SATURATION LEVELS

Within each product category, saturation is defined as the presence of at least one unit of that particular appliance per household. In markets like the United States, saturation levels are high, resulting in lower levels of first-time home appliance purchases. In growing economies, such as in Asia and South America, saturation levels are comparatively low, and their markets present greater opportunities to companies seeking to increase their market share.

STATE OF THE ECONOMY

Appliance sales trends usually mirror national economic growth trends. When an economy is in early recovery, the household appliance industry is one of the first to show signs of improvement. This reflects the crucial role of consumer discretionary income in fueling appliance purchases.

SPECIFIC PRODUCT DEMAND

Each type of appliance is affected differently by the cycles of the economy. For instance, range sales depend largely on housing starts because comparatively few are bought during the life of the home. Dishwashers, meanwhile, have shorter life spans and possess the lowest saturation levels. Refrigerators have a medium life expectancy and are less dependent on housing starts.

BACKGROUND AND DEVELOPMENT

The modern-day appliance industry traces its beginnings back to 1878 when Thomas Edison invented the light bulb. The Edison Electric Light Company became General Electric in 1892. Edison left the company in 1894 to go into mining, but the company went on to develop electric elevators, toasters, electric ranges, electric motors, various appliances, and light bulbs.

In 1908 W. H. Hoover formed the Electric Suction Sweeper Company to make vacuum cleaners after he saw his wife's cousin, J. Murray Spangler, demonstrate a homemade version of a crude vacuum cleaner that he created to help in his janitorial work. Spangler made the vacuum cleaner out of a fan motor, a broom handle, a soap box, and a pillowcase that collected dirt. Hoover was in the saddlery business at the time, which was being overtaken by the auto industry, but he was wise enough to see that such a product would meet the needs of everyone who cleaned. The vacuum was first sold in hardware stores, but its popularity surged after salesmen turned to home demonstrations. After World War I, the company went back to selling vacuums through dealers because of a change in consumer preferences.

During the course of the twentieth century, appliances such as refrigerators, stoves, freezers, dishwashers, clothes dryers, and microwave ovens became staples of households in industrialized nations. In the latter half of the twentieth century, the entry of more women into the workforce also led to an increase in the demand for household appliances that saved time in doing everyday chores—a huge factor in the popularity of the microwave oven.

In the United States, the domestic household appliance industry went through a period of rapid consolidation in the 1980s. Maytag Corp. bought Magic Chef and JennAir to round out its product line at differing price levels and to increase its overall sales. Whirlpool did the same in the 1980s, adding the KitchenAid and Roper names to its product line. These mergers helped U.S. firms compete internationally, while giving foreign firms the chance to enter into joint ventures and partnerships with U.S. firms.

In North America and Europe, the home appliance market began to stagnate toward the end of the 1990s, after experiencing record sales in 1994 and 1995. Nonetheless, even with slight growth, U.S. appliance manufacturers reported record shipments in 1997. Because appliance ownership in these mature markets was already widespread, demand in the late 1990s was modest. Still, home appliance stores recorded total revenues of more than US$12 billion in 2000, a 7.1 percent increase over 1999.

During the late 1990s, higher growth was to be found in Asia and South America, which were much less saturated. Although many Asian economies suffered from currency depreciation and debt in 1997 and 1998, appliance sales still grew because of the low number of appliances per household. In particular, China's prodigious population drove the industry, while revenues grew limp in industrialized countries.

ENVIRONMENTAL ISSUES

A U.S. statute called the National Appliance Energy Conservation Act of 1987 directed the U.S. Department of Energy to raise the environmental compliance standards for several types of appliances to meet tougher environmental goals. New energy efficiency standards were written for all types of appliances to encourage the use of more efficient motors, auxiliary water heaters, lower wash temperatures, reduced water usage, better insulation of components, and heat controlled shutoffs.

While energy efficiency was a concern for industry participants, chlorofluorocarbon (CFC) reduction became the leading issue for the appliance industry. CFCs, which had been used in freezers and refrigerators as coolants since the

1940s, provoked intense scrutiny because they were thought to damage the protective ozone layer of the Earth's atmosphere. Under the Montreal Protocol of 1987, CFC production must end by the year 2000. In early 1992 scientific studies were released that described findings of higher levels of CFCs than expected in the North American stratosphere. These findings encouraged the United States to commit to halting CFC production by 1996.

The U.S. industry was relatively slow to convert to non-CFC coolants, however, compared to European household appliance manufacturers, which have been selling refrigerators and freezers without CFC coolants since the mid-1980s. In 1993 these new appliances were priced roughly 7 percent higher than appliances that contained CFCs. HFC-134a, a nonflammable agent, is the leading replacement for CFCs. It requires compressors to be redesigned for maximum efficiency.

The worldwide appliance industry is also being encouraged by governments to increase the recycling of old appliances. In the United States, congressional bills were introduced in 1992 that set measures for the recycling and packaging of major appliances. Mandates of the legislation covered recycling rates, the number of reuses of packaging, and the percentage of recycled content. Many in the industry contended that the new rules were not attainable. Analysts expected this struggle to balance the needs of the industry and the environment to continue in the twenty-first century.

Trends and Features

Features that provide convenience and simplicity of use have garnered much of the attention in the 1980s and 1990s, as opposed to radically new breakthrough products, which have been slow to develop. Convenience features that proved successful included easy-to-clean induction cooking units, quieter dishwashers, greater appliance capacity, improved energy efficiency, and more appealing cosmetic appearances. Toward the close of the twentieth century, however, industry and consumer home shows revealed new products and future prospects to the public. Computer technology opened up new possibilities, and dramatic breakthroughs were already in application by the 2000s.

Appliance manufacturers have also placed renewed emphasis on increasing speed in delivery of products. Historically, most retailers held large inventories of appliances to ensure that they were able to meet customer demand when the market for household appliances was strong. However, this was expensive and conflicted with retailers' interests in keeping overheads down. Retailers increasingly partnered with manufacturers to help them with the carrying costs of warehousing products. This trend triggered a surge in the use of appliance showrooms, where customers could place an order for an appliance and the product was shipped directly from the manufacturer to the customer the next day. Appliance manufacturers in the mid-1980s first developed this quick delivery system with parts suppliers to help cut the carrying costs of parts inventories.

Current Conditions

The appliances industry emerged from the early 2000s recession ahead of many other industry sectors. By 2003, positive conditions were supported by improved consumer confidence levels, as well as low interest rates and strong housing starts. According to estimates from The Freedonia Group, a Cleveland, Ohio-based consultancy, global demand for major household appliances is projected to increase at an annual rate of nearly 4 percent from 2004 to 2007. This growth is expected to propel overall demand to 367 million units.

Citing figures from Delano Data Insights, in November 2003 *Appliance Manufacturer* revealed that automatic washer shipments were expected to increase 4.3 percent from 2003 to 2004, reaching nearly 8.3 million units. During the same period, dryer shipments were expected to increase 4.1 percent, reaching 7.4 million units. Freezer shipments were forecast to rise 4.5 percent, exceeding 2.6 million units. Finally, shipments of gas ranges were marked to rise 3.1 percent, growing to 3.4 million units.

Although the major appliance manufacturers began to globalize in the 1990s, some of their products remained unique relative to the needs of the target markets. Because of cultural differences, manufacturers cannot always ship the same product to North America, South America, Europe, and Asia. Instead companies have to develop appliances suited to individual market demands. Hence, in many cases the globalization of the industry meant consolidating the materials, component development, technology, and manufacturing to create technology and a basic manufacturing process common to all appliances.

Trade agreements such as the General Agreement on Tariffs and Trade (GATT) and the North American Free Trade Agreement (NAFTA) made international trade increasingly accessible by removing tariffs and duties. By the early 2000s, these trade accords had made progress toward reducing barriers that previously hindered trade between the United States, the members of the European Union, Japan, South Korea, and developing economies around the world.

The United States

U.S. consumers enjoy state-of-the-art household appliances at relatively low prices because of intense competition brought about by both domestic and foreign firms. About 50 percent of the domestic market in many appliance categories is made up of imports. At the same time, many major U.S. appliance manufacturers have global presences too. Overall, however, the United States consistently imports more than it exports. In 2002 the value of America's household appliance imports was more than triple the value of exports: imports were valued at US$10.8 billion, while exports totaled US$2.9 billion. In the larger classification of electrical equipment, appliances, and components, U.S. exports totaled nearly US$23.3 billion in 2003. This included exports of US$6.2 billion to Mexico, followed by Canada (US$6 billion), Japan (US$1 billion), the United Kingdom (US$912.1 million), and Germany (US$788.8 million). Total U.S. imports in this broader category were almost US$42.6 billion in 2003. Led by China (US$11.9 billion), other leading nations included Mexico (US$11 billion), Canada (US$3.5 billion), Japan (US$3.2 billion), and Germany (US$2.8 billion).

EUROPE

Increasing market share in Europe is a difficult task for U.S. and Asian firms because the various cultural differences, languages, and even electrical standards in the region present significant challenges for any offshore company. Firms producing for Europe face the marketing challenge of trying to reach the most people in a way that is both economical and effective. Appliance manufacturers also must adapt to European demand for smaller and more efficient appliances.

ASIA

If Asia's population of 2.6 billion were to achieve the same market penetration as that of the United States, Asian demand for refrigerators alone would top 70 million units per year, according to analysis published by *Appliance Manufacturer.* Similarly, if other appliances rose to this level, production and sales would escalate rapidly. By mid-2004, China was in the midst of an economic boom and had become the largest global supplier of so-called "white goods." This followed industry analyst predictions that China's world market share would rise from 8 percent in 2002 to 30 percent by 2005, according to *Modern Plastics.* Indeed, China's exports were expected to reach levels of US$10 billion by 2005.

Three Japanese conglomerates—Matsushita, Toshiba, and Hitachi—have historically controlled much of the Southeast Asian market, with pricing power and distribution channel barriers that are hard to penetrate. Analysts expect these manufacturers to lead a wave of consolidations in the twenty-first century, similar to those in the United States and Europe, as local markets mature and exports increase.

RESEARCH AND TECHNOLOGY

Technology for household appliances focused on three primary objectives. First is the development of more energy-efficient and environmentally safe appliances; second is the development of "smart" appliances; and third is the development of better materials that are more lightweight, durable, and clean.

With pressure from environmental and governmental organizations and agencies, appliance manufacturers have been designing more efficient appliances that use less energy and fewer natural resources. Global demand for household appliances totals about a half billion units, which is good for the industry but potentially dangerous for the environment. Not only do appliances consume energy but also they must eventually be discarded. Researchers are studying both challenges, striving to reduce the amount of energy required to operate them and seeking safer, more recyclable materials.

An example of efforts to conserve energy is Maytag's Neptune washing machine. In conjunction with the U.S. Department of Energy, Maytag developed a front-loading horizontal axis washer that uses only 23 gallons of water per load, in contrast to 40 to 46 gallons used by conventional top-loading vertical axis washers. The Neptune also features an automatic water-level meter, which determines how much water is needed for each load. This feature prevents water from being wasted when users fail to set the water-level control for different size loads. U.S. consumer research indicates that almost 50 percent of all households do not change the water level, no matter what the size of the load, according to *Appliance Manufacturer.*

"Smart" appliances are unique in that they perform certain tasks automatically to streamline users' tasks. The key to smart appliances is that they are networked and connected, either to the Internet or to a central computer system. In an article for *Chain Store Executive with Shopping Center Age,* author Suzanne Barry Osborn remarks, "They aren't just appliances any more—they are infopliances." Economically, industry leaders hope that the more technologically advanced the appliances become, the more often people will replace them. To illustrate this point, consider the computer industry in which emerging technology creates constant motion in the buy cycle. Further, offering appliances that network to manufacturer software products creates an additional revenue stream for the manufacturers. Just as users of the Palm Pilot personalize them by buying various types of software to meet their needs, so might users of Internet-connected household appliances purchase software to make their appliances meet their specific needs.

The kitchen is the room that gets the most attention from researchers working on smart appliances. After all, it is the room in which the most appliances are used. Whirlpool already offers a refrigerator that maintains an Internet connection with an online grocer, so that the user only has to punch some keys on the door to order groceries. There are also refrigerators that generate shopping lists when users scan bar codes of empty containers. Kitchen appliances are also available that can store favorite recipes. One interactive product being developed will supply recipes based on search criteria and subscribe to designated cooking magazines so that it can upload new recipes. It will even make wine suggestions.

Technology is under development that will create self-sufficient refrigerators and pantries. Armed with sensors, they will be able to detect when an item needs to be restocked. Then they will shop for it online, arrange for its delivery, and pay. In the future, a person could start dinner cooking in the oven from work by using e-mail or some other type of remote control device. Research on innovative materials is also projected as an important means of progress in future kitchens. Smart materials with sensors open up new possibilities. For example, consumers could have a tea kettle that changes color when the water reaches the desired temperature.

The laundry room is another area of appliance research. Whirlpool has introduced a washing machine that downloads its own instructions for stain removal. In fact, the user can e-mail the washing machine, so that the download is complete when he or she is ready to do laundry. This machine is designed to save time and money for the consumer in the long run.

Improved materials can be used in appliances in any room of the house. Dramatic advances in home appliance efficiency and ease of use have been made possible by the tough, lightweight, and corrosion-resistant properties of modern plastics. According to *Appliance Manufacturer,* the household appliance industry has increased its use of plastics from less than one percent of material content in the early 1960s to approximately 25 percent by weight, and more than 60 percent by volume, in the mid-1990s. Some analysts claim that without the high strength to weight ratio, corrosive resistance, and ease of fabrication properties of plastic, household appliances would cost about 25 percent more and consume 30 percent more energy, while losing 20 percent of storage space. Additionally, some analysts have reported that if plastic had not been introduced, corrosion would reduce the product life of clothes washers and dishwashers by about 50 percent.

The environmental aspect is relevant in materials development, and the need to recycle used plastics is still a daunting task. By 2007 refrigerator disposal alone is projected to yield approximately 125 million pounds of polyurethane foam and more than 200 million pounds of other plastics.

In a move away from secrecy and corporate protectionism, many household appliance manufacturers are sharing some of their research and development (R&D) efforts in this area. U.S. firms have joined with major universities, consulting firms, and major research firms to help them gain a more global perspective on all aspects of their industry. Utility-sponsored organizations, such as the Electric Power Research Institute and the Gas Research Institute, have assisted in efforts by U.S. firms to speed up the product development process as well. Accelerated production schedules increasingly demand input and contributions from sources outside company walls. By utilizing other sources of R&D knowledge, appliance manufacturers have also opened themselves up to other financing sources—often utility industry groups—for new products that never existed before. Research laboratories and universities can also be a great source of pooled resources.

According to the December 2003 issue of *Appliance Manufacturer,* the development of innovative, cutting edge appliance features continued during the early 2000s, despite a sluggish economy. For example, Italy's Merloni marketed Ariston Smart Tag appliances that were capable of reading embedded radio frequency identification (RFID) tags on clothing and food packaging. This capability enabled refrigerators to warn consumers when certain food products were about to expire. Whirlpool marketed a washer and dryer pair capable of communicating about specific wash loads, enabling the dryer to prepare for the next load and adjust its settings accordingly. Other developments included talking appliances from Electrolux.

Although research and development have long been important in developed markets like Europe and the United States, by mid-2004 they were also a growing concern in emerging economies like China. In its July 2004 issue, *Appliance Manufacturer* revealed that factors such as energy conservation, performance, and quality were quickly becoming more important to Chinese consumers than price. In fact, through a survey conducted by its Institute of Market Economy, the Development Research Centre of the State Council found that 85 percent of Chinese consumers ranked high performance and quality as being more important than cost in 2004.

INDUSTRY LEADERS

AB Electrolux was the world's largest household appliance manufacturer in 2005, and was known for its refrigerators, freezers, dishwashers, and washing machines. More than 55 million Electrolux products were sold in 150 countries every year. The company courted the South American market, where Whirlpool has a stronghold, in an effort to expand its international scope. Electrolux bought a 6 percent stake in Refrigeracao Parana SA, Brazil's second largest manufacturer of household appliances. The company also owned a subsidiary in Argentina that it used to distribute its household appliances under the Electrolux, Zanussi, and Frigidaire brand names. The company posted sales of more than US$18.2 billion in 2004, an increase of almost 6 percent from the previous year. Of total revenues, Sweden earned 3.6 percent, the rest of Europe earned 44 percent, North America earned 38.9 percent, and the rest of the world generated the remaining 13.5 percent of sales. Outside of Europe and North America, the company's largest international markets were in Brazil, India, China, and Australia. Consumer durables (mainly major appliances) accounted for 76 percent of Electrolux sales in 2004.

Whirlpool Corporation is the world's second largest manufacturer and marketer of major home appliances and is the United States' largest. Headquartered in Benton Harbor, Michigan, the company manufactures in 13 countries and markets products in more than 170 countries. Worldwide revenues climbed to US$10 billion in 2000, and reached US$13.22 billion by 2004, at which time the company employed 68,125 people. Major brand names include Whirlpool, Sears, KitchenAid, Roper, Estate, Laden, Bauknecht, Inglis, and Kenmore. The company is also involved in a number of joint ventures. In the mid-1990s it retained a 47 percent interest in Philips Electronics N.V., a leading European appliance maker. Whirlpool is also involved with companies in Brazil, Canada, Mexico, India, Argentina, and Taiwan. About $8.3 billion of the company's sales came from North America in 2004, $3.1 billion from Europe, $1.7 billion from Latin America, and $382 million from Asia. As of 2005, close to 68,000 people were employed by Whirlpool.

The diversified manufacturing firm Matsushita Electric Industrial Co. Ltd. has 380 operating units throughout the world. Based in Osaka, Japan, Matsushita is one of the world's top companies in audio/video equipment, home appliances, communication and industrial equipment, and electronic component manufacturing and is the second largest consumer electronics producer. In 2001 the company posted US$61 billion in total sales. By 2004, sales reached nearly US$81.4 billion, the majority of which were attributed to the Asian market.

MAJOR COUNTRIES IN THE INDUSTRY

While the United States remains a key market for household appliance manufacturers, it is not considered a high growth area for the industry. Still, it is a crucial player in the global industry because of the billions of dollars spent on imports.

By 2004, foreign competitors such as BSH, Haier, LG, and Samsung were making stronger inroads in the United States, pressuring traditional domestic leaders. For example, in 2002 China's Haier established a US$40 million manufacturing facility in Camden, South Carolina to produce refrigerators, with a goal of cornering 10 percent of the U.S. full-size refrigerator market by 2005. This strategy was unprecedented among Chinese appliance firms. According to *Fortune,* although labor costs were cheaper in China, it was expensive to ship large appliances like refrigerators from Asia to the United States. In addition, Haier preferred to manufacture its products directly within local market areas. Therefore, it installed Chinese management and hired American workers to produce its products domestically, further benefiting from a "Made in the U.S.A." label. Haier began expanding internationally after achieving a leading market share in China. In 2002 alone, the company held 26 percent of China's washing machine market and 29 percent of its refrigerator market, according to *Fortune.*

In decades past, the introduction of new products stimulated demand for industry products. Consumers in leading economies in the 1960s wanted dishwashers and dryers. During the 1970s and 1980s, households sought out microwave ovens. In the 1990s, however, such new product introductions slowed. Variations on existing products (such as a washing machine that cleans clothes with sonic technology instead of using water or a dryer that uses microwaves instead of conventional electric or gas heat to dry clothes) were unveiled, but these prototypes failed to attract a large following. With the emergence of computer technology in household appliances, however, consumers are intrigued by the potential new products and features for the future.

Most household appliance markets in the United States are fully mature. This has put pressure on companies to try and cut costs in the face of flat pricing environments. Often, price increases that can be passed along to consumers are just high enough to cover the increases in costs. Market share growth has in some cases been achieved solely through price competition.

FURTHER READING

Beatty, Gerry. "Major Appliance Biz Reflects (Not Always Happily) On Record Year." *HFN The Weekly Newspaper for the Home Furnishing Network,* 5 January 2004.

———. "White-Goods Shipments in '04 Could Be Major Success Story." *HFN The Weekly Newspaper for the Home Furnishing Network,* 15 December 2003.

BizStats. *Retail Sales Comparison-Calendar Years 2000 & 1999.* 13 January 2001. Available from http://www.bizstats.com/.

"China to Focus On R&D." *Appliance Manufacturer,* July 2004.

"China's Consumer Goods Manufacturers Mounting a U.S. Assault." *The Kiplinger Letter,* 14 March 2003.

"Forecasts." *Appliance Manufacturer,* November 2003.

"Hoover's Company Capsules." Hoover's, Inc., 2004. Available from http://www.hoovers.com.

International Trade Commission, Office of Trade and Economic Analysis. *U.S. Industry Sector Data.* 17 August 2004. Available from http://http://www.ita.doc.gov/td/industry/otea/industry_sector/tables_naics.htm.

Jancsurak, Joe. "Innovations Strong During Weak Economy." *Appliance Manufacturer,* December 2003.

Koucky, Sherri. "Keeping It Green: Take a Look at How Appliance Manufacturers Are Addressing Environmental, Energy, and Performance Issues." *Machine Design,* 13 December 2001, 56-60.

Moore, Stephen. "China Seeks to Expand Exports." *Modern Plastics,* May 2002.

Osborn, Suzanne Barry. "The TechnoHome." *Chain Store Executive with Shopping Center Age,* February 2001: 24.

Remich, Norman C., Jr. "Gunning for Global Gains: World Smarts Coupled with New-Product Initiatives Are Needed to Put a Plus Sign Next to Each Industry Segment for 1998." *Appliance Manufacturer* January 1998, 73.

Sprague, Jonathan. "China's Manufacturing Beachhead: No Foreign Brand Has Ever Made It Big in the U.S. Major-Appliance Market. But China's Top White-Goods Maker Is Determined to Change That." *Fortune,* 28 October 2002.

"World Majors." *Appliance Manufacturer,* March 2004.

SIC 3651

NAICS 334310

AUDIO AND VIDEO EQUIPMENT, HOUSEHOLD

The global household audio and video equipment industry manufactures a diverse number of electronic entertainment devices, including television sets; radio receivers (including automotive); compact disc (CD) and other digital disc players and recorders; tape players and recorders; amplifiers and speakers; phonographs; and videocassette players and recorders

For discussion of makers of electronic components for such products, rather than the finished goods, see also **Electronic Components**.

INDUSTRY SNAPSHOT

Audio/video equipment is a strong industry worldwide that grows with developing technology. With maturing markets in the United States, Europe, and Japan, digital and other high tech products provided the highest growth rate in the 2000s. Some of these products included high definition televisions (HDTV), digital televisions (DTV), digital versatile disc players (DVD), mini-disc (MD) players, and digital video recorders (DVRs). Producers also targeted the emerging economies of Eastern Europe, Southeast Asia, and South America with basic model audio and video equipment. Areas of opportunity for mature markets were also available within the automotive industry.

The Consumer Electronics Association (CEA), predicted the total value of consumer electronics shipped would grow approximately 4 percent in 2005, earning just under $100 billion in worldwide revenue for the industry. 2004 sales of consumer electronics in the United States exceeded US$113 billion, and were slated to top an industry record US$125.7 billion in 2005, a 10.7 percent growth over 2004. Digital products were expected to generate 70 percent of that revenue, according to Gary Shapiro, president of the CEA. Sales of DTV products reached US$10.7 billion in 2004, 78 percent higher than 2003. The CEA projected sales of more than 47 million DTV units by 2007, up from 7.3 million in 2004. LCD television sales were expected to account for more than $3 billion in 2005, compared to $2 million in 2004, largely due to price decreases.

CEA "Home Technology Study" estimated that 35,000 firms were installing home theaters. Furthermore, its "Home Theater Opportunities Study" claimed there was a multi-tiered market with several types of consumers desiring to spend money on equipment and services.

ORGANIZATION AND STRUCTURE

GOVERNMENT POLICY AND REGULATION

National governments have played a key role in the industry's development. The Japanese audio and video equipment industry was aided throughout the post-World War II years by the Japanese Ministry of International Trade and Industry (MITI). MITI provided subsidized loans to favored producers in the industry and facilitated research and development. MITI's activities were part of a broader strategy of the Japanese government that sought to protect its domestic market from imports and penetrate foreign markets by offering quality products at low prices.

In the United States, two government agencies—the International Trade Administration (ITA) and the U.S. International Trade Commission (ITC)—are responsible for monitoring trade practices of foreign firms. The ITC identifies foreign firms that sell products in the United States below market value, known as dumping. The ITC also determines whether U.S. industries have suffered material injury when the agency finds that dumping has taken place. Upon a finding of material injury, the ITA issues an antidumping order, which is enforced by the U.S. Customs Service.

INDUSTRY ASSOCIATIONS

Japan's leading trade group, which includes as members all of the industry's leading companies, is the Tokyo-based Electronic Industries Association of Japan. Asian manufacturers are served by the Asia Electronics Union, established in 1968 and headquartered in Tokyo. The union publishes the English language bimonthly *Journal of AEU* and facilitates cooperation among its members in the areas of research, applications, and manufacturing techniques. Many Chinese producers of audio and video equipment are members of the China Audio Industry Association, the China Radio and T.V. Equipment Industry Association, or the China Electronics Chamber of Commerce. These three organizations were all established in the 1980s, a reflection of the relative newness of the consumer electronics industry in China. The U.S. industry is served by the Consumer Electronics Manufacturers Association of the Electronic Industries Association, established in 1924 and headquartered in Washington, D.C. Association publications include the *Electronic Market Data Book* and the *U.S. Consumer Electronics Industry Today.*

BACKGROUND AND DEVELOPMENT

The household audio and video equipment industry originated in the late nineteenth century. Thomas Edison's development of the phonograph in 1877 and Guglielmo Marconi's use of wireless transmissions in 1895 were major innovations. Another important early innovation was Lee DeForest's vacuum tube, developed in 1906, which allowed electronic signals to be amplified.

The 1920s were important years of research and commercialization for the industry. Developments included the first commercial radio broadcast in 1922; the Western Electric Company's patents for electrical sound recording and the placement in radios of loudspeakers instead of headphones in 1924; the introduction of the alternating current (AC) radio in 1926; Philo Farnsworth's television patents and the introduction of automobile radios in 1927; and the first U.S. experimental television station permits issued by the government in 1928.

The industry enjoyed rapid growth in the 1920s and 1930s. During that period more than 100 million radios were sold in the United States. The Federal Communications Commission (FCC) was established in the United States in 1934 to regulate broadcasting. The FCC authorized FM radio and television broadcasting in 1941, but these developments were forestalled by the country's entry into World War II. By the end of World War II, there were nine commercial television stations, 46 commercial FM stations, and 943 AM stations in the United States.

The late 1940s saw the industry return to its prewar patterns of rapid growth and innovation. In 1947 the first magnetic tape recorders were marketed, and Bell Telephone Laboratories demonstrated the first transistor. The transistor marked the birth of solid-state electronic components, commercialized in 1954 with the mass-marketing of the first "pocket radio." Home audio hobbyists who put together their own systems revealed that the capacity for fidelity of sound reproducing equipment far exceeded the fidelity of existing recordings. This led to the introduction of 45 rpm records and 33 rpm long-playing records in 1948. These records were the first mass produced "hi-fi" recordings. Other important developments in these years included color television broadcasting in 1954, videotape recording for television stations in 1956, and stereophonic audio systems in 1958.

Sales of color televisions surged during the mid-1960s. The first solid state color televisions were marketed in 1967. By the mid-1970s, solid state color sets dominated the market. The first color videocassette recorders for household use were marketed in 1975, and sales increased rapidly after the early 1980s. The 1980s saw the introduction and rapid diffusion of digital technologies in household audio and video equipment. The industry developed compact disc and accommodating audio systems—first mass-marketed in 1983—that quickly supplanted phonograph systems.

JAPAN'S EMERGENCE

One of the most important developments in the industry after World War II was the dramatic competitive success of Japanese producers, which progressively unseated U.S. manufacturers as the world's leading audio/video equipment producers. The foundations of Japan's ascendance were established in the immediate post-World War II years. The Japanese government's Ministry of International Trade and Industry (MITI) favored a handful of firms in the audio and video equipment industry, creating a powerful cartel. MITI's policy was to grant large low-interest loans to favored firms and deny credit to other firms. The Fair Trade Commission of Japan (FTCJ) argued that the consumer electronics cartel violated Japan's Antimonopoly Law of 1947. In a 1957 decision, the FTCJ ruled that Japanese firms had conspired to set prices. The FTCJ also stated in a 1970 decision that Japanese producers of consumer electronics were in violation of the Antimonopoly Law. In spite of these findings, however, the cartel continued to operate.

At the same time, foreign producers had great difficulty establishing a viable presence in the Japanese market. The domestic dominance of Japanese firms resulted in part from the common practice of granting exclusive retail dealerships. Retailers were given large rebates by affiliated manufacturers if they agreed to sell only that manufacturer's products. By the mid-1960s two-thirds of consumer electronics retailers in Japan were exclusive dealerships, and this share increased by the mid-1980s. Japanese producers of audio and video equipment also controlled the home market by purchasing wholesalers. By the 1970s, Japanese firms had acquired majority stakes in nearly all consumer electronic wholesale businesses in Japan.

Japan's trade policies helped buffer its audio/video equipment industry against foreign competition. The Foreign Exchange and Foreign Trade Control Law banned imports of a number of products, while the Law Concerning Foreign Investment prohibited foreign firms from establishing more than 10 wholly controlled facilities in Japan. Both of these laws were overturned in 1967. Until 1968, however, tariff rates on televisions were between 20 and 30 percent, which was reduced to 4 percent by 1973. Government regulations also required that all imports be paid for within four months of import.

MITI's control of foreign exchange enabled it to impose quantitative restrictions on imports. In the early 1960s, the Zenith Corporation of the United States attempted to market its televisions in Japan through a Japanese wholesaler. A letter from the wholesaler to Zenith stated, however, that owing to the popularity of Zenith televisions, MITI would not allocate the foreign exchange required.

The Japanese government also facilitated research and development in the industry. In recent years, for instance, the government assessed a US$10 tax on every color television sold. The money was earmarked for research on high-definition television.

However, nongovernmental factors also contributed to the success of the Japanese audio and video equipment industry. In many cases, Japanese manufacturers were more efficient and more innovative than international counterparts, and this made their products more enticing to consumers in terms of both pricing and features.

TRADE DISPUTE

U.S. producers argued that Japanese firms conspired to restrain competition among themselves, selling products at below market value to penetrate the U.S. market. In 1970 the National Union Electric Corporation of the United States filed suit under the Sherman Antitrust Act on behalf of U.S. producers Motorola Inc. and Sears, Roebuck and Co. The Zenith Radio Corporation joined the suit in 1974. The Japanese firms named in the suit were Hitachi Ltd., Matsushita Electric Industrial Company Ltd., the Toshiba Corporation, the Sony Corporation, the Mitsubishi Electric Corporation, Sanyo Electric Company Ltd., and the Sharp Corporation, all of which still rank as leading world companies. The case came before the U.S. Supreme Court in 1984 and became known as *Matsushita et al. v. Zenith Radio et al.* In a controversial 1986 ruling, the Supreme Court held that the Japanese firms had acted legally, affirming the position of the Reagan administration.

The U.S. International Trade Administration (ITA) continued to find evidence of price dumping by Japanese firms into the 1990s, however. Price dumping was measured by a "dumping margin," the difference between the home market price and export price expressed as a percentage of the export price. The ITA found that in 1991, the average dumping margin for Japanese televisions was 35 percent. The average dumping margin for all Japanese goods imported into the United States between 1980 and 1989 was estimated at 44 percent.

Events in the 1980s helped to solidify Japanese producers' gains and U.S. firms' marginalization. Japan's production expanded three times faster than U.S. production during the decade, and European output rose almost twice as fast. The U.S. hold on the market dropped from 44 percent in 1980 to 11 percent by decade's end. Not surprisingly, the U.S. trade deficit with Japan in consumer electronics stood at more than US$10 billion in 1990. However, the decline of U.S. consumer electronics firms could also be traced to factors within U.S. borders. The production of color televisions in the United States was hindered by the country's lag in integrated circuit technology. In the face of falling prices, U.S. producers responded with a short-run approach, cutting investment and increasing volume rather than emphasizing quality and productivity, the approach taken by their Japanese counterparts.

Japanese firms pursued similar strategies of market penetration in Europe. Some Japanese manufacturers turned to direct foreign investment in Europe as a means of circumventing import restrictions. Sony was the first Japanese consumer electronics firm to establish production facilities in the United States and in Europe. After Sony opened its television production plant in the United Kingdom in 1968, several other Japanese firms followed suit. Many of the televisions produced in the United Kingdom were shipped to other European countries. From 1979 to 1981, the Japanese share of the West German television market more than doubled. In the 1980s, Japanese penetration into the European market also was facilitated by the expiration of patents protecting broadcasting technologies. These patents were held by the German firm AEG-Telefunken and applied to all western European countries except for France.

The production of consumer electronics in the newly industrializing countries of East Asia increased rapidly during the 1980s and 1990s, especially in South Korea, China, Singapore, Hong Kong, Malaysia, and Taiwan. Much of this production resulted from the foreign investment of European, U.S., and especially Japanese firms, who were attracted by the substantially lower wages paid to skilled workers in these countries. By the early 1980s, however, both South Korea and Taiwan had large, locally owned television production plants. Much of the production of consumer electronics in these countries was exported to other nations. These overseas sales further contributed to the highly competitive nature of the world market for audio and video equipment.

In 1994 the North American Free Trade Agreement (NAFTA) was implemented. The purposes of this agreement were to stimulate trade among the United States, Mexico, and Canada; to create jobs; to increase wages in Mexico; to improve environmental policies on the continent; and to generate goodwill among the nations. Among the effects of NAFTA is the growth of Mexico's television exports.

Current Conditions

By the mid-2000s, rapid growth caused DVD player sales to outpace VCR sales. Jim Barry, a spokesperson for the Consumer Electronics Association (CEA), told the Associated Press that the rapid acceptance of DVD players resembled the quick acceptance of black-and-white television sets by Americans after World War II. By the mid-2000s, more than half of U.S. households contained a DVD player, buoyed by Wal-Mart's bargain-basement price of less than US$30 in 2003, a mere three percent of the DVD player's original price.

In 2003, DVD rental revenues topped VHS rentals for the first time, as reported by the Video Software Dealers Association. Spending by consumers on all video rentals was $8.06 billion in 2004, off just 0.4 percent from 2003. DVD rental revenue, however, rose 39.2 percent to $5.73 billion, about 70 percent of the total rental market. VHS rentals slid to $2.33 billion.

Growth in consumer electronics was also powered by the transition to digital products in mature markets. A 2005 CEA study showed the analog to digital transition was influencing purchasing decisions as high-definition and flat-panel televisions gained market share, as did digital video recorders and DVD players. Portable MP3 players in particular performed well above expectations, doubling in the number of units shipped and tripling in revenue during 2004, as reported in *Business Wire.*

According to *Euromonitor,* the U.S. market for audio products was projected to increase 5.5 percent by 2008, and the market for video products was projected to increase 37.9 percent. By comparison, the French market for audio products was projected to increase 9 percent by 2008, and the market for video products was projected to increase 199 percent, largely due to DVD players. The German market for audio products was projected to increase 24 percent by 2008, with a 74 percent decrease expected for video products, largely due to market saturation. In the United Kingdom, audio products were expected to enjoy a market increase of 46 percent by 2008, with a 16 percent decline anticipated for video products.

Research and Technology

HDTV offers the picture quality of a 35-millimeter photograph combined with the sound quality of a compact disc player. In contrast to conventional analog television with its 525 horizontal lines, HDTV (high definition television) has 1,080 horizontal lines, providing much keener images and detail. One of the factors hindering the sales of HDTV was standardization. The Advanced Television Advisory Committee of the United States' Federal Communications Commission (FCC) fought for an HDTV standard but gave up the fight in 1997 and let private industry decide. Led by Dolby Laboratories and Zenith Electronics, the U.S. industry developed a standard incompatible with that of Europe. Consequently, U.S. and European manufacturers, with their different technologies, competed vigorously to win as many foreign customers as possible. In mid-1998, commercial U.S. television companies planned to begin broadcasting HDTV shows, and manufacturers anticipated full-scale HDTV set deliveries.

Wide-screen television was introduced into the United States in 1993 by a European manufacturer who marketed it under the name Pro Scan. The advantage of wide-screen television is that its width-to-height ratio of 16 to 9 was much closer to that of 35-millimeter movies than the standard set with its 4 to 3 width-to-height ratio. Wide-screen televisions are not high-definition, but are designed to be adaptable to HDTV. With the increased viewing of feature films on television—in large part a result of the popularity of pay television (see also **Cable and Other Pay-Television Services**), VCRs, and DVD players—the growth prospects of wide-screen television appear promising. One alternative to wide-screen television is the so-called letterboxing of broadcasts and videos. In this practice, the top and bottom parts of conventional sets are blocked out to accommodate 35-millimeter films. Films that are letterboxed, however, make use of only 60 percent of the conventional television's screen height.

As the Internet generation approached adulthood, the television industry was investigating the unique desires of this market. According to Consumer Electronic Association (CEA) research, members of Generation Y (children of the Baby Boomers, born between 1979 and 1994) were expected to find interest in accessing information about programming while watching. Examples include getting more information about a product, reviewing athletic statistics, or scanning movie reviews. There was interest expected in combining Internet features with television viewing, so users could check e-mail, shop online, or "surf" the Internet while watching television.

Another important development for the industry was the home theater, which integrates large screen televisions with high quality audio systems. These products provided a significant boost to high-end producers of speakers and audio components. In 2002 Zenith introduced a 52-inch rear projection HDTV intended primarily for consumers with home theaters, thus responding to the market for wide-screen HDTVs with rear projection technology. To enthusiasts, this type of product represents the best of all worlds. The growth of the home theater market also led to several joint ventures between large furniture companies and producers of household audio and video equipment. LCD and plasma televisions were increasing in popularity as well. Technology advanced quickly during the early to mid-2000s, and price declines made the technology more affordable to consumers worldwide.

Statistics indicate that the majority of households with televisions also have VCRs. Unfortunately, the majority of VCR owners are unable to program their units and reap the full advantages of the device. This led to developments such as voice-activated programming that were designed to simplify programming procedures. Eight Japanese and two European VCR manufacturers developed a world standard for digital VCRs in an effort to avoid the incompatibility problems caused by the dual VHS and Beta videocassette formats. Digital VCRs were largely designed for use with high-definition television. The Zenith Electronics Corporation of the United States and Goldstar Ltd. of South Korea co-developed a digital VCR that used standard Super-VHS videocassettes and could record and play back in both HDTV and standard television formats.

Another answer to the difficulties of recording missed or concurrent programs is digital video recorder (DVR) technology. DVRs allow viewers to record any show on any channel at any time, without loading videotapes into the machine or programming it to record. Viewers simply set up the system to record whatever shows they choose, and every day the system records the appropriate program. This is convenient for new episodes and for episodes in syndication. The system also has the capability of matching viewer preferences with other shows not selected, in essence recommending new shows the viewer might enjoy. Another feature viewers enjoy about DVR technology is that it gives them the power to pause a show being watched without losing any of the show. Watching television then has the convenience of watching traditional videotapes that can be stopped, paused, rewound, and played at the touch of a button. The leader and originator of this technology is TiVo, whose customer satisfaction is so high that 97 percent recommend the system to friends. In 2002 the service was available through three different receivers. In January of the same year, TiVo introduced the TiVo Series 2 DVR, which offers greater recording capacity, lower cost, and entertainment features such as digital music, broadband video on demand, and video games.

In the late 1990s, DVD emerged as the successor to existing CD audio, CD-ROM, and laser videodisc formats. Pioneering manufacturers Matsushita, Sony, and others hailed it as the next revolutionary consumer electronics product. Robust sales of DVD players were anticipated because they hoped the format would eventually replace the VCR. With a 4.7 gigabyte capacity, DVDs can store an entire movie in stereo on a five-inch disk that allows speedy random access to any portion of the recording, as with the audio CD player, compared to videotape's slower sequential access. Furthermore, manufacturers designed their DVD players to be backwards compatible— that is, to recognize older formats such as the audio CD and the CD-ROM. In the mid-2000s, sales of DVD players exceeded sales of VCRs.

Important innovations in audio formats include digital audiotape recorders (DATs), digital compact cassettes (DCCs), and minidiscs (MDs). These formats offer the same sound quality of conventional CDs, but also provide buyers with the additional ability to record. DCCs have the same copy-protection mechanism of the earlier developed DATs, but their standard cassette format enables the use of analog cassettes. While sales of DCC and MD audio equipment were slow in the early 1990s, proponents of the new technology accurately contended that it would become more popular as prices dropped and larger numbers of titles were made available on the formats.

By the mid-2000s, the development and inclusion of plastic computer chips in most electronic devices was becoming a reality. Not only is plastic cheaper than traditional glass or silicon chips, it is more durable. According to the independent research firm Gartner, plastic chips eventually will be produced with polymer inks, by any press or printer. When this occurs, specialized semiconductor manufacturing will not be needed, making plastic chip technology more available to a variety of companies and for a variety of applications. Some industry players projected the market for plastic chip technology will eventually reach a value of US$300 billion or more.

INDUSTRY LEADERS

HITACHI LTD.

Hitachi was established in 1910 and incorporated in 1920. The firm, headquartered in Tokyo, is one of the world's leading producers of electrical and electronic equipment and boasts a diversified global network. Hitachi Ltd.'s 2006 revenues were $80.5 billion. The company employed more than 327,000 people worldwide as of 2007.

In March 2007, Hitachi stated its plans to close a parts factory in Guadalajara, Mexico and cut 4,500 jobs resulting in an estimated savings of US$300 million during five years. Related moves were part of restructuring measures focused at turning around the company's hard-disc drive business. That part of the business, acquired from IBM in 2002, had been consistently in the red. Hitachi planned to shift production to developing countries in Asia by focusing on manufacturing hard-disc drives at its factory in Shenzhen, China. The company also planned to phase out production in Odawara, Japan by the fourth quarter of 2007.

TOSHIBA CORP.

Headquartered in Tokyo, the Toshiba Corp. has entered into cooperative arrangements with the General Electric

Company of the United States, Siemens AG, and Olivetti of Italy. Toshiba's sales totaled US$54 billion in the fiscal year 2006. The company had 172,000 employees. Electronic devices were responsible for $12.2 billion in 2005, or 21 percent. Sales within Japan accounted for $46.8 billion, or 64 percent of revenue.

In January 2007, Toshiba announced its plans to appeal a European Union fine for price-fixing. Fines were issued against five European and five Japanese companies for fixing prices on switchgears used by power utilities. Toshiba protested claiming it had "not engaged in illegal activity."

Toshiba also announced it had established a software research and development center geared toward digital consumer products in Vietnam. Toshiba Software Development Co. was established as a wholly owned subsidiary located in Hanoi. It was scheduled to begin its full operations in June 2007. Initial staff of about 20 was expected to grow to around 300 by fiscal year 2010. Toshiba already had software development bases in both China and India.

Toshiba America Consumer Products announced its plans to launch marketing initiatives to support the company's HD DVD and REGZA brands. Soprano's TV show star Michael Imperioli will appear in HD DVD print as and REGZA and HD DVD TV commercials. Toshiba's REGZA premium LCD TV line offered eight different screen sizes. A major objective of the campaign was to share the "REGZA difference." The other HD DVD campaign would spotlight key player attributes.

SONY CORP.

Tokyo-based Sony wields one of the most powerful brand names in the industry. In 2005, televisions, VCRs, stereos, and other consumer electronics accounted for more than two-thirds of the company's revenues, which totaled US$63.5 billion in 2006. Sony reported having 158,500 employees. More than 80 percent of its 225 designers were based in Japan.

Sony was listed among the world's 25 most innovative companies in *BusinessWeek*'s third annual special report. The company ranked 10th moving up from 13th in previous listing due in part to the development of software for use in online game consoles. Boston Consulting Group consulted nearly 2,500 executives worldwide to vote for the companies worthy of listing.

Sony announced its plans to introduce its first HD radio products in July 2007. The hot product summer launch would allow Sony to join the growing group of companies striving to make the next-generation of radio technology a standard feature in audio products. HD Radio in the form of digital radio broadcasting that allows radio stations to deliver extra music content on a maximum of four side channels that link to technology already in use. In excess of 1,200 radio stations had adopted the technology.

According to *Business Week,* Sony's U.S. chiefs were becoming more confidant in their ability to reject products created in Japan that wouldn't work for their market. They rejected a Walkman that was considered to be too small to be a worthy alternative for Apple's iPod. Some Sony principles worked out of a design center in Santa Monica, California. Furthermore, products designed or improved in the U.S. were believed to be having a positive impact on Sony's sales.

MITSUBISHI ELECTRIC CORP.

Headquartered in Tokyo, Mitsubishi was established in 1921 from the electrical machinery division of Mitsubishi Shipbuilding's Kobe shipyard. Mitsubishi's diverse output includes televisions and VCRs, as well as satellites, cellular phones, fax machines, semiconductors, medical equipment, and security equipment. Electronic devices were responsible for 4.3 percent of Mitsubishi revenue in 2004, and home appliances for 22.8 percent. Mitsubishi Electric Corporation's sales totaled US$31.9 billion in 2004, a one-year increase of just over 5 percent, and the company employed almost 99,000 workers.

SANYO ELECTRIC COMPANY LTD.

Sanyo was established in 1947 and is headquartered in Osaka, Japan. Revenues for 2006 were US$21.9 billion. The company employed about 106,389 people.

In March 2007, Sanyo announced a major change in its leadership ranks. Executive Officer Seiichiro Sano was set to replace Toshimasa Iue as president putting an end to the founding family's leadership of Sanyo's management. It was the first time a member of the founding family would not hold either the chairman or president position. The announcement followed Sanyo Chairwoman Tomoyo Nonaka's resignation. The resignation was in response to conflict about whether to launch a through investigation into an accounting scandal at the group.

SHARP CORP.

Also headquartered in Osaka, Sharp originated in 1912. In the early 2000s, consumer audio/visual products accounted for 20 percent of total revenues. Sharp has a significant presence in international markets; the Asian market represented 70 percent of Sharp's sales in 2001. In 2004 Sharp experienced a 28 percent increase in sales, to US$21.4 billion, and employed 46,000 people.

PIONEER ELECTRONIC CORP.

Pioneer was established in 1947 in Tokyo as a successor to a loudspeaker manufacturing company. Unlike some of its more diversified competitors, the firm produces household audio and video equipment almost exclusively. Pioneer's innovations in laser optical hardware and software in the 1980s made the firm a leader in consumer and industrial audiovisual equipment. In 2004 the company posted sales of US$6.6 billion, an increase of 11 percent, and had 34,000 employees.

MATSUSHITA ELECTRIC INDUSTRIAL COMPANY LTD.

Matsushita was founded in 1918 and is headquartered in Osaka, Japan. Matsushita is a top maker of consumer electronics. The firm produces products under the brand names of Panasonic, Technics, Quasar, and National. Its principal operating subsidiary in this industry is the Matsushita Communication Industrial Company Ltd., which was established in 1958 and is headquartered in Yokohama, Japan. In the mid-1990s Matsushita began manufacturing many of its products abroad to take advantage of lower labor costs elsewhere. In 2005 the company posted sales of US$81.4 billion, an increase of 13.2 percent.

In April 2007, Matsushita announced that it had started manufacturing liquid crystal display TVs in Malaysia in order to meet a growing demand in the region. The company's local subsidiary, Panasonic AVC Networks Kuala Lumpur Malaysia Sdn. Bhd., said it officially started producing the Viera series LCD TVs at its plant in Shah Alam which was located near Kuala Lumpur. Panasonic AVC Managing Director Akihiko Hayase claimed that global demand for LCD TVs had reached 51 million sets and was expected to rise to 100 million sets by 2010.

Another April 2007 announcement revealed that Matsushita and CMS Magnetics Corp. reached a settlement in a lawsuit the first company had filed against the second one related to its use of patented technologies regarding DVD discs. Matsushita will receive patent royalty from CMC to pay for damages and use of proprietary technologies.

Business Week Online discussed Matsushita's practice of using the same basic technology platform of microprocessors and software in Panasonic TVs, DVD recorders and navigation systems. Director of Platform Development Satoru Fujikawa was reportedly responsible for the plan to design consumer electronics capable of connecting with each other.

MAJOR COUNTRIES IN THE INDUSTRY

The U.S. Bureau of Labor Statistics projected declines in all 32 occupations in the industry between 1992 and 2005. Most of these occupations were projected to suffer double-digit declines, with 13 of the 32 occupations projected to have declines of 30 percent or greater. However, trade liberalizations of the mid-1990s—brought about by the North American Free Trade Agreement (NAFTA) and the Uruguay Round of the General Agreement on Tariffs and Trade (GATT)—were expected to stimulate growth of the industry in general. In 2003, the United States imported $5.2 billion of household audio and video equipment, increasing $5.2 billion over a five-year period. U.S. exports declined $485 million over the same period to a low of $5.2 billion in 2003.

Japan was the world's leading producer and exporter of household audio and video equipment throughout the 1990s. However, its dominance was challenged during the 1980s and 1990s by rapidly expanding production in South Korea, China, Singapore, Hong Kong, Malaysia, and Taiwan. Nevertheless, Japan remained a major exporter of audio and video equipment. Companies used strategic partnerships to strengthen their positions in the face of increased competition worldwide. As of early 2005, Hitachi and Matsushita had agreed to cooperate in the plasma display business; Sharp Corporation agreed to buy Fujitsu's LCD business and related patents; and Sony has signed a cross-licensing pact with South Korea's Samsung Electronics Co. covering a range of digital technologies.

Japan's leading export position eroded in a number of key respects. With greater competition from other Asian countries such as South Korea, Singapore, China, and Malaysia, Japan's stronghold on world exports diminished. Therefore, control of the audio and video equipment market in the 1990s became more evenly distributed among Asian countries with developing economies. However, the successful production of household audio and video equipment in these Asian countries resulted in part from investment by Japanese firms, many of which had extensive overseas operations.

Mexico, backed by Japanese and U.S. manufacturers seeking a lower-wage labor market, emerged as a leading force in the industry. Mexico became the top exporter of televisions in 1994 and retained this position through 2001. Because of its participation in NAFTA and its proximity to the United States, the leading market for audio/video products, Mexico became an advantageous place to manufacture televisions. Most of Mexican production, however, was based on investment by Japanese, South Korean, and U.S. firms. In this sense, Mexican production of audio/video equipment was an extension of trade between the United States and Asia.

FURTHER READING

Alpeyev, Pavel. "Hitachi to Cut 11% of Disk Jobs; Action will Also Shutter Factories in Japan and Mexico." *International Herald Tribune,* 23 March 2007.

Archer, Bob. "CE Pro Consumers, Manufacturers Increase Focus on Good-Looking Products." 11 May 2007. Available from http://www.cepro.com.

"Audio Products in France, Germany, UK, US." *Euromonitor,* August 2004. Available from http://www.majormarketprofiles.com.

"Average Selling Price of Tech Products Continues to Decline: Plasma TV Prices Dip Below $2,500 According to Latest Results from NPD CD Price Watch." *Business Wire,* 29 November 2004.

BizStats. *Retail Sales Comparison—Calendar Years 2000 & 1999,* 13 January 2001. Available from http://www.bizstats.com.

"CEA: Sales of Consumers Electronics Set to Surge." *Wireless News,* 7 January 2004.

Consumer Electronics Association. "2004 Sales of Consumer Electronics to Set New Record, Surpassing $100 Billion Mark, Says CEA," 5 January 2004.

———. "After Record-Breaking First Quarter, April Sales Continue the DTV Climb." Consumer Electronics Association, 16 June 2004.

"DVD Rental Revenue Tops VHS for 1st Time." *Hollywood Reporter,* 21 March 2003.

Edwards, Cliff and Kenji Hall. "Remade in the USA; Sony's Comeback May Ride on Its Yankee Know-How." *Business Week,* 7 May 2007.

"Fierce Global Competition in the Flat Panel Television Market is Leading Major Japanese Electronics Makers to Seek Partners for Advanced Technologies and Lower Costs." *Asia Africa Intelligence Wire,* 7 February 2005.

"ECA Index Goes Back Up in April, Continuing Its Seesaw Ride in 2005." *Business Wire,* 10 May 2005.

Green, Heather. "Consumer Electronics: Free-Falling Prices and Rocketing Sales." *Business Week,* 12 January 2004.

Hall, Kenji. "Matsushita's Platform for Success; An Engineer's Vision of Using the Same Microprocessors and Software to Power a Slew of Panasonic Devices is Transforming the Japanese Electronics Giant." *Business Week Online,* 29 March 2007.

"Hoover's Company Capsules." 2007. Available from http://www.hoovers.com.

"Household Penetration of CE Products Soars in 2005; Ownership Improved in Every Category of Survey." *Business Wire,* 17 May 2005.

Lazich, Robert S., ed. *Market Share Reporter.* Detroit: Thomson Gale, 2004.

Magiera, Marcy. "Rental Finishes Flat." *Video Business,* 3 January 2005.

"Matsushita Begins Production of LCD TVs in Mallaysia." *Kyodo News International,* 5 April 2007.

"Matsushita, Taiwan Optical Maker Settle Patent Violation Suit." *Kyodo News International,* 2 April 2007.

Nordwall, Eric. "Sony to Introduce HD Radio Devices." *USA Today,* 29 May 2007.

"Pioneer Hires AIS for Digital Needs." *Marketing,* 28 February 2007.

Port, Otis. "Just Two Words: Plastic Chips." *Business Week,* 10 May 2004.

"Research and Markets Assesses Plasma TV Market." *Wireless News,* 1 May 2005.

Sanchanta, Mariko. "Hitachi Shuts Mexican Plant Amid Revamp of Hard-Disc Unit." *The Financial Times,* 23 March 2007.

"Sanyo Approves Iue's Resignation, to Have Sano as New President." *Kyodo News International,* 29 March 2007.

Sowinski, Laura L. and Jeremy N. Smith. "World Trade 100 Annual Trade Review." *World Trade,* October 2004.

"Technology: Sales of DVD Players Booming." *The Nando Times,* 13 January 2001. Available from http://www.nando.net.

"TiVo Introduces TiVo Series2—Next-Generation Digital Video Recorder; Low Cost Platform Offers More Recording Capacity and Enables New Entertainment Services Starting at $299." *PR Newswire,* 8 January 2002.

"Toshiba to Appeal EU Cartel Fine; Other May Follow Suit." *AsiaPulse News,* 25 January 2007.

"Toshiba's New Marketing Campaign to Feature Soprano's Star Michael Imperioli." *Wireless News,* 7 May 2007.

"Toshiba Sets Up Vietnamese R&D Center for Embedded Software." *AsiaPulse News,* 9 May 2007.

"TV, VCRs and Camcorders in France, Germany, UK, US." *Euromonitor,* August 2004. Available from http://www.majormarketprofiles.com.

"US - Consumer Electronics sales to Grow by 11% in '05." *The Americas Intelligence Wire,* 6 January 2005.

SIC 3640
NAICS 3351

ELECTRIC LIGHTING AND WIRING EQUIPMENT

Lighting and wiring equipment manufacturers supply such myriad electrical goods as light bulbs, lighting fixtures, electrical outlets, switches, fuses, and similar devices, and hardware for commercial and residential electrical service.

INDUSTRY SNAPSHOT

The electric lighting and wiring equipment industry incorporates a wide variety of products and companies. It includes among its major players some of the largest diversified corporations in the world, and mergers and acquisitions are common. The various facets of this broad field constitute a multibillion-dollar industry. Due to the global nature of the industry, most manufacturers were able to stay competitive. Whenever one nation's economy suffers, thereby impacting sales, there are numerous customers in other parts of the world to counterbalance the lost revenue.

A highly competitive industry, lighting and wiring equipment manufacturers move quickly to meet changing environmental and economic demands. Few revolutionary technological breakthroughs have occurred in recent years and, as a result, most companies' research and development (R&D) efforts were focused on increasing the energy efficiency of lighting fixtures and related electrical devices to accommodate the demand for environmentally sound, efficient products. Still, lighting and wiring manufacturers continue to seek new markets, which has led them to address specialized needs such as highway, emergency, entertainment venue, and landscape lighting.

Closely tied to construction and renovation activity, growth in the lighting and wiring categories depends largely on general economic health and projections, and thus the climate for building, in each country. While the incandescent bulb is still the mainstay all over the world, manufacturers are increasing offerings to the construction industry. In times of economic bounty, there is more demand for specialized and customized products.

The U.S. lighting industry was steadily increasing in the mid-2000s— after a downturn during the recession of the early part of the century— largely due to new construction and the growing remodeling and renovation market sectors. In 2003, the lighting industry was up 5 percent, to more than US$5 billion. In the United States, lighting products were expected to account for around 30 percent of electrical distribution sales in 2005, reaching $26 billion. Worldwide, the market was valued at about US$12 billion in 2003 according to an analyst from Strategies Unlimited. Globally, the lighting market was expected to grow about 6.2 percent annually through 2008, according to a December 2004 report by the Freedonia Group. In the mid-2000s, China was the largest exporter to, and one of the largest importers from, the U.S. market. By 2004, China's market accounted for more than 80 percent of all U.S. lamp and lighting imports. Lamp imports, which totaled US$166 million in 2001 and US$409 million in 2002, increased another 8 percent in 2003.

ORGANIZATION AND STRUCTURE

Most of the leaders in production and sales of electric lighting and wiring equipment are divisions of major, diversified international corporations. Maximizing the potential financial impact of increased international trade through agreements such as the North American Free Trade Agreement (NAFTA) has proven to be a major springboard for many of these and smaller corporations. Increasingly, companies, especially in the United States, manufactured products overseas where labor is significantly cheaper, and imported them back into other markets for sale, a trend that caused imports to surge in the 1990s.

While lighting is an essential aspect of life in industrialized countries, production levels of the lighting industry are linked to the notoriously cyclical construction industry. During periods when relatively few houses and office buildings are erected, fewer lighting fixtures are sold. Conversely, when the construction industry is booming, sales of lighting fixtures are also strong. The 1980s saw a period of unparalleled real estate construction worldwide, with the downtowns and peripheries of large cities undergoing extensive expansion and refurbishment. In the early 1990s, construction inevitably slowed before a mild upturn in the mid-1990s. A decade later, construction would be back on the rise.

Production and sales of wiring were largely dependent on nonresidential building, of which there was substantial growth in the mid-1990s. However, fluctuations in that segment were far more dramatic and commonplace than for residential construction, to which the lighting industry was closely linked. Non-current-carrying wiring devices, in particular, derived the vast majority of applications from nonresidential construction.

Environmental concerns continued to play a major role in the industry. Because most countries spend a substantial amount of electricity on lighting (close to one-quarter in the United States), the industry has seen pressure from the outside and from internal competition to develop more energy-efficient products. In 1997, the U.S. Environmental Protection Agency (EPA) initiated a voluntary Energy Star program, which encouraged manufacturers of electric lighting equipment to produce lighting that emits less carbon dioxide, sulfur oxide, and nitrogen oxide while simultaneously realizing cost-saving benefits.

BACKGROUND AND DEVELOPMENT

ELECTRIC LIGHTING

The first electric light was invented in 1860 by English physicist Joseph W. Swan. He created a vacuum inside a glass bulb that allowed a small piece of carbonized paper to burn for a short time. However, it was difficult to maintain the perfect vacuum pressure required for steady, consistent burning. Nevertheless, Swan's work paved the way for Thomas Alva Edison, a young New Jersey scientist, to invent the electric light in 1879. In that year, both inventors developed a way to manufacture reliable electric light bulbs by putting the filament inside the bulb, pumping out the air, and then sealing it up. Early successes relied on platinum wires to conduct the electricity into the bulb, but subsequent experiments revealed that copper-plated nickel alloy was also suitable. That alloy is the material used in today's light bulbs.

Edison worked on electric lights for nearly his entire adult life. He was determined to develop a lamp in which the filament became incandescent— that is, glowing white light resulting from the heat of the electric current going through it. Subsequently, he spent thousands of dollars and devoted most of his time to experimenting with different combinations of metals and gases that would result in a long-lasting incandescence. On 21 October 1879, Edison's work paid off when he was able to get a piece of burnt cotton thread in a glass vacuum bulb to burn for more than 40 hours. The cotton was eventually replaced by charred bamboo, which in turn was replaced by tungsten, a metal that was not discovered until 1910. Additional refinements included spraying hydrofluoric acid inside the bulb to create a frosting that diffused the light and reduced glare, and filling the bulb's vacuum with a bit of argon or nitrogen to prolong the life of the tungsten filament. Not incidentally, Edison also developed an entire system of electric generation and distribution. Such a system, of course, needed to be installed in every city and town to deliver electric light to residences and businesses, and for public use.

Neon lights were invented in the late nineteenth century when scientists realized that electricity applied to both ends of a glass tube filled with neon gas would start to glow bright red. Mercury vapor used in the same way glows blue; helium, golden; and mercury in a yellow-tinted tube, green. Several gases combined yielded white. This technology was immediately adopted for advertising and signs.

In the 1930s, fluorescent lights were invented by coating the inside of a glass tube with a substance that reacted with mercury gas to glow white a hundred times more brightly than it would have without the coating. Subsequent developments, such as high-pressure gas lamps, were adapted for street lighting.

WIRING

Ancient civilizations probably made wire for jewelry and decorative purposes by rolling gold and other metals into narrow strips. The process of making perfectly round wire in long strings by pulling metal through a tiny die by hand took root in Europe in the Middle Ages. By 1270 in France and 1465 in England, wire was a commodity that was manufactured in large quantities for domestic use and export.

Such early precursors set the stage for electrical uses, which required electrically conductive yet concealed wire to carry electrical service into homes and businesses and within devices powered by electricity. Wire was crucial to various manufacturing and telecommunications industries, so its quality was constantly monitored. The basic process of making wire has changed little since the 1940s. Wire is made by heating a bar of metal to about 2,200 degrees Fahrenheit and rolling it into a thin rod. Very thin wire is made by a drawing block, powered by an electric motor, that pulls the rod through a die; the narrower the hole, the thinner the wire. The finest wires are drawn through numerous dies, each 5 to 20 percent narrower than the last. In between drawings the metal is briefly heated to keep it pliable. This process rapidly erodes the dies, which must be constantly replaced.

Wire is essential to the production of heating elements in household and commercial appliances, electric motors and generators, light bulbs, screens, vehicles, and stringed instruments. Wire made of copper and aluminum, which has low resistance to electricity, is required by the telecommunications industry. To prevent the loss or misconduction of electricity, those wires usually are coated with plastic, rubber, or waxy cotton fibers. Most current-conducting wire is made of a nickel and chromium alloy.

Current Conditions

The electric lighting and wiring equipment industry has seen steady growth since the 1990s. Competing manufacturers continue to produce high quality, reliable, everyday lighting and bulbs, but they also look to more niche markets to build customer bases. Specialized lighting for buildings such as laboratories, performance halls, restaurants, and twenty-four hour facilities is being improved constantly. Manufacturers are asking customers for input about these venues, and the results are mutually beneficial. In the public sector, improved highway lighting makes travel safer and reduces utility costs, and innovations in emergency lighting help to ensure safety in times of crisis. Considerable attention and research funding also have gone into improving automotive lighting. Residential housing is another area in which manufacturers are offering more choices for indoor and outdoor lighting, such as patio sconces and landscaping lights.

As of late 2004, the top five global lighting technologies were compact fluorescent, linear fluorescent, halogen, high-intensity discharge, and light-emitting diodes. Whether lighting solutions were needed to reduce energy costs, cover a large area, highlight a display, or deliver high brightness, each technology required a unique solution.

While the traditional incandescent light is still the bulb of choice, with 15 billion sold annually, the halogen bulb is slowly gaining in popularity. Although halogen bulbs are often undesirable because they generate more heat than their incandescent counterparts, researchers hope to offer low-heat-producing halogen bulbs in the future. According to a Freedonia Group study, high-intensity-discharge (HID) and fluorescent lamps also were expected to see growth into 2007, largely due to increasing demand for energy-efficient products. In addition, industry analysts expected energy-efficient and long lasting light-emitting diodes (LEDs) to grow in use as production costs declined. According to *EDN,* by 2007 LED costs would drop 75 percent, bringing LEDs in line with fluorescents. As reported in *Harvard Business Review,* Sandia National Laboratories predicted that solid-state lighting could decrease global electricity consumption by 10 percent during 2005. The article stated that LEDs can "light an entire rural village with less energy than that used by a single conventional 100-watt lightbulb."

As environmentalism moves to the forefront of global concerns, the electric lighting and wiring equipment industry has scrambled to meet rising consumer demand for energy-efficient products. Customers from the residential, commercial, and public sectors are becoming more aware of how costly energy consumption is becoming, both financially and environmentally. Manufacturers in the electric lighting and wiring industry are responding to these emerging realities with educational programs and new energy-efficient products. The variety of these products continues to increase, boosting sales in what is perhaps the most competitive and quickly changing realm of the industry. In the 2000s came the expectation by some industry analysts that companies offering products that can be retrofitted to accommodate existing structures will be good sellers.

Research and Technology

In the United States, a substantial fraction of all electricity generated is used for lighting. The search for efficiency is ongoing. Manufacturers are always looking for better ways to make longer-lasting, cooler lights. Producers of electrical lighting and wiring work closely with power generators to develop, market, and encourage consumer use of energy-saving devices. The benefit of such a strategy is reduced, or at least stagnant, use of electrical power for lighting.

In 1991, the U.S. Environmental Protection Agency introduced "Green Lights," a voluntary program to encourage U.S. companies to install energy-efficient lighting. The goal was to cut electrical use for lighting in half, saving about US$18.6 billion annually, with a drop in pollutants put out by power plants. To supplement this program and further its ends, the EPA established its "Energy Star" program. Still going strong as of the mid-2000s, the Energy Star program honors numerous organizations, companies, and schools every year for "outstanding contributions to reducing greenhouse gas emissions through energy efficiency." By 2005, in fact, more than 7,000 organizations had become Energy Star partners. The combination of these efforts with increased consumer concern and demand for efficient products has spurred producers of electric lighting to invest heavily in the research and development of such products.

Due to its efficiency, variety of design and color, lighting quality, longevity, and low cost, fluorescent lighting accounts for the majority of electric lighting installations worldwide. Fluorescent lamps, especially in combination with electronic ballasts—which even out the flow of current—are quickly becoming a virtual standard in new construction. Ballasts offer an appealing set of advantages to the building or renovation of residential or commercial buildings. Ballasts can interface with automation systems, reduce eyestrain and fatigue, be programmed enabling users to control the amount and direction of light, and reduce utility costs. They are also safer for the environment than fluorescent lighting, which is common in commercial buildings. There were more than 7 billion fluorescent lamps in use in 2001, most of which provided workplace lighting.

Lamp manufacturers continue to experiment with new materials and concepts. The xenon-discharge lamp, for instance, produces the artificial light considered most like sunlight. Light-emitting diodes (LEDs) remain popular because they can be used in very small devices, do not use much power, and are long lasting. As LEDs increased in brightness and came down in price, LED technology continued to displace incandescent bulbs. Internationally, about 500 million lamps are discarded each year according to the International Association of Lighting Management companies. Specialty lamps have been developed for television, industrial applications, photography, moviemaking, and other uses.

The dramatic increase in home Internet connections, along with the trend toward home offices, led to home wiring upgrades, which have generated a great deal of new business for manufacturers of non-current-carrying wiring devices. It also has led to an increased demand for lighting that is better for the eyes, which is a selling point for ballasts. Some companies addressed the computer-using public's desire for devices to enhance the use of computers. Philips, for example, introduced a product in 2000 that allows computer users to designate an area of the screen for high-resolution imaging. This enables them to watch streaming video or participate in Web conferencing and perform simple tasks such as document composition simultaneously.

The category of related electrical components has seen the introduction of the ground fault circuit interrupter (GFCI). These devices shut off current to an outlet or an entire house as soon as they detect moisture. The U.S. National Electrical Code now requires GFCIs in new construction and renovation, which virtually guarantees steady demand for the product.

Improvements to existing products generally are well received by buyers. GE's Reveal line of bulbs are sold in supermarkets and discount stores for the average consumer's use, but they offer the advantage of casting vivid light that is less yellow than other bulbs. In answer to environmental concerns, GE also released its Ecolux XL T8 fluorescent lamps, which contain less mercury, thereby limiting potential spill-outs in landfills. These same lamps also are designed to be up to 50 percent more energy efficient. In 2001, a company called Allied Lighting Systems worked with the California Department of Transportation to create better lighting for highway signs. The product that resulted from this collaboration produces the same amount of light but costs significantly less to operate and lasts four times longer than previously used products.

INDUSTRY LEADERS

ROYAL PHILIPS ELECTRONICS N.V.

The largest manufacturer of light bulbs and related products in the world, Philips emerged from the World War II rubble of Europe's manufacturing base as one of the leading innovators of the industry. The company concentrated almost solely on consumer electronics and related products, shunning heavy industrial products such as engines. Philips was formed in 1891, only 12 years after Edison invented the incandescent light bulb. Gerard Philips, a Dutch engineer, was fortunate to have a father with money to invest and a younger brother, Anton, with a flair for management. By the 1920s, Philips was making inroads in neighboring countries and the United States. Philips was an early competitor with GE in fine-tuning the incandescent light bulb with variations on filaments, inert gases, and other innovations.

After World War II, Philips rebuilt its Dutch plants and moved into manufacturing transistors, integrated circuits, television, and appliances. It was one of the first companies to introduce VCRs, audiocassette systems, and compact disc players. In the 1980s, Philips bought the lighting operations of the U.S. firm Westinghouse. It also offered wiring solutions through its Phillips-MECO division. Phillipsrsquo; 2004 sales were US$38 billion, compared to $36.4 billion in 2003. Sales were highest in Europe and Africa, which accounted for US$16.7 billion, followed by the Asia Pacific, which had sales of US$10 billion in 2004. North American revenues were $9.36 billion, followed by Latin America, which provided Phillips with $1.9 billion in sales. However, the market in China offered great opportunity for Phillips, which expected sales in China to top $10 billion in 2005. Phillipsrsquo; sales in the lighting sector accounted for US$5.68 billion, or 13.1 percent of overall sales. Philips employed more than 161,000 people as of early 2005.

GENERAL ELECTRIC COMPANY

Another company that has dominated the light manufacturing industry is General Electric (GE). Based in Fairfield, Connecticut, GE is a direct descendent of Edison Electric Light Company, formed in 1879 by Thomas Edison. Business magnates of the day immediately recognized the value of Edison's inventions and capital flowed in to finance expansion of the fledgling company.

In 1892, financial mogul J.P. Morgan took over Edison General Electric and combined it with other firms to form General Electric. True to form, Morgan immediately came up with a high-profile scheme to demonstrate to the world the benefits of electricity: an elevated electrical train at the Chicago World's Fair in 1893. GE also created the first-ever corporate research facility, which developed the tungsten filament still used in light bulbs. The X-ray was another of the lab's early triumphs. Developed in 1913, it was the forerunner of GE's entrance into medical diagnostic equipment.

To accelerate demand for its power plants, GE inventors introduced a steady stream of electric household appliances to an eager public. Toasters and irons were first introduced in 1905, followed by electric stoves, waffle irons, refrigerators, vacuum cleaners, and washing machines in the next decade. By the 1920s, GE's influence was so widespread that the U.S. government used antitrust legislation to force the company to divest itself of its power generating businesses. Subsequently, GE also was forced to make public its patent for light bulbs. In the 1980s, GE added entertainment and consumer credit services. Still, it continued to be an innovator in lighting, inventing a small but sturdy bulb for auto manufacturers that enabled them to redesign headlights. In 1989, the company bought Tungsram, a Hungarian lighting manufacturer; and in 1991, it added the light bulb business of the European firm Thorn EMI.

GE's total revenues for 2004 were US$152.4 billion according to GE's annual report. International revenues were $71.8 billion, or 47 percent of total earnings. GE's lighting solutions were offered through its Consumer & Industrial division, which was a $13 billion business employing 75,000 employees in 2005.

SIEMENS AG

Siemens of Munich, Germany, is a major European player in the manufacturing of lighting equipment. Founded in 1847 when hobby scientist Werner Siemens became fascinated with telegraphy, the small company got its first big break when it was hired to set up a telegraph system between Frankfurt and Berlin. Other government contracts soon followed and Siemens became a specialist in laying intercontinental cables and inter-oceanic cables, including cables from London to India.

When news of Edison's incandescent bulb reached Siemens, he immediately got a license to manufacture the bulbs. In the 1920s, Siemens added traffic lights to its repertoire and formed a European light bulb consortium with two other German companies, AEG and Auer.

Like its counterparts in the United States and the Netherlands, Siemens branched into manufacturing a variety of medical, industrial, computer, and telecommunications products after World War II. In 1993, Siemens acquired the Sylvania lamp company from GTE and merged it with Osram, Siemens' lighting manufacturing division. Total revenues for Siemens AG in 2004 were US$93.4 billion; Osram sales in 2004 were more than $5.3 billion.

HITACHI LTD.

Tokyo-based Hitachi Ltd. is one of the world's largest producers of various types of wire. Namihei Odaira, an engineer and dedicated tinkerer, formed Hitachi in 1920. In the 1930s, Hitachi became Japan's first manufacturer of light bulbs and vacuum tubes. The company lost many plants during World War II and nearly failed. However, it re-emerged during the reconstruction period of the 1950s. Hitachi regained its prominence in household appliances and electronics and was engaged in joint partnerships with several major U.S. firms, including GE, RCA, and IBM. Total revenue for fiscal year 2004 was US$84.36 billion, an increase of 5 percent over 2003. Hitachi's High Functional Materials & Components sector, which included wiring products, earned more than US$14 billion. Overseas revenues increased 10 percent to US$53.7 billion, with Japan remaining the company's primary revenue source at US$30.6 billion. The rest of Asia provided US$13.1 billion in revenue, North America US$8.4 billion, Europe US$6.6 billion, and other areas of the world US$2.4 billion.

COOPER INDUSTRIES

Another important player in the production of wire, lighting, and related products is Cooper Industries, based in Houston, Texas. In 1997 the company announced that it would sell its Automotive Products division to focus on its Electrical Products and Tools and Hardware divisions. The Electrical Products division, which makes fuses, electric wires and cables, and security lighting, contributed US$3.7 billion to the companyrsquo;s total US$4.46 billion in 2004 revenues, 9.9 percent more than Cooper earned in 2003. Cooper Lighting was responsible for 27 percent of annual revenues, Cooper Wiring Devices for 6 percent, and Cooper Menvier for 6 percent. Cooper Menvier was the companyrsquo;s overseas anchor for global market expansion, helping Cooper Industries branch into markets in Eastern Europe and the Middle East.

FURTHER READING

Costlow, Terry. "LED Outlook Brightens: More Applications Are Switching to Solid-State Lighting." *Design News,* 18 April 2005.

"Energy-Efficient Lighting and LightQuick [TM] Service Provide New Opportunities." *EC&M Electrical Constructions & Maintenance,* July 2001.

Funk, Dale. "Lamp Demand to Reach $5 Billion by 2007." *Electrical Wholesaling,* 1 April 2004.

"'Green' Economics in Relamping." *EC&M Electrical Constructions & Maintenance,* April 2000.

"Hoover's Company Capsules." 2004. Available from http://www.hoovers.com.

"The Lighting Report." *HFN,* 7 June 2004.

"Lowes, Pardee Homes, 3M Among 50 to Win Recognition for Energy Efficiency, Greenhouse Gas Reductions." *EPA National News,* 11 March 2005.

Meyer, Nancy. "A Brighter Perspective." *HFN,* 7 June 2004.

———. "A Matter of Increasing Imports." *HFN,* 7 June 2004.

"Philips China Expects Over $10 Billion in Sales by 2005." *Emerging Markets Economy,* 10 September 2004.

Ribarich, Tom. "The Top Five Global Lighting Technologies." *Power Electronics Technology,* October 2004. Available from http://www.powerelectronics.com.

Salzhauer, Amy. "The Light Fantastic." *Harvard Business Review,* 1 October 2004.

"A Solid Future for Lighting." *The Economist (US),* 5 October 2002.

Strassberg, Dan. "LEDs Glow in Anticipation." *EDN,* 8 January 2004.

"Waking Up Lighting Sales." *Electrical Wholesaling,* March 2005. Available from http://www.ewweb.com.

Zion, Lee. "Caltrans Sees the Light for Its Freeway Signs." *San Diego Business Journal,* 20 August 2001.

SIC 3670

NAICS 3344

ELECTRONIC COMPONENTS

The global electronic components industry fabricates an extensive array of electronic devices used in the manufacture of finished electronic products. Examples of industry output include:

- printed circuit boards
- electron tubes
- electronic capacitors
- electronic resistors

- electronic connectors
- electronic transformers
- electronic coils
- electronic inductors

Finished electronic goods, such as audio and video gear, are discussed in separate articles, as are semiconductors. See also **Audio and Video Equipment, Computers, Semiconductors,** and **Telecommunications Equipment.**

INDUSTRY SNAPSHOT

Electronic component manufacturing is characterized by intense competition among companies as well as countries. Most electronic components, which are the unassembled or partially assembled parts used in virtually any electronic device, are traded as commodities with slim profit margins for their makers.

Three chief divisions of industry output exist: printed circuit boards (PCBs), electron tubes, and passive components. By far the most ubiquitous and remunerative are PCBs and passive components; by value passive components—a catch-all term that encompasses many distinct products—is the largest category. A finished electronic end product, such as a television, generally contains components from all categories, including numerous kinds of passive components. In the mid-2000s, the increased use of electronic devices, particularly digital electronics such as digital versatile disc (DVD) players, mobile phones, high-speed devices, and flat-screen televisions, fueled a dramatic upswing in demand for connectors, resistors, switches, and other passive components, and an accompanying upswing in materials prices.

While the industry has important contenders in many parts of the world, Asian countries, notably China and its territories, Japan, Malaysia, and South Korea, have been perennially strong and efficient producers of low-cost and often high-quality components. However, in the mid-2000s the U.S. industry was the largest electronics components market and Japan remained the second largest. With the backing of U.S. and European producers, nations such as Mexico and Ireland also emerged as important production centers for electronic components.

ORGANIZATION AND STRUCTURE

The electronic components industry is made up of original equipment manufacturers (OEMs), such as IBM and Hewlett-Packard, and contract manufacturers, with electronic distributors also playing a key role. When OEMs produced electronic components, it was typically for use in their own products, an arrangement known as captive production, and they did not derive any direct revenue from the components themselves. In the past, contract manufacturing operations began as printed circuit board assemblers. In the late 1990s, however, OEMs such as IBM and Hewlett-Packard were increasingly turning to contract manufacturers to manufacture either subsystems or complete electronic products. Thus, brand-name manufacturers might not be involved in the physical manufacturing of products bearing their names. Contract manufacturers specialized in manufacturing and did not invest heavily in brand development, advertising, sales, distribution, or customer support. U.S. contract manufacturing revenues topped US$190 billion in 2004, up 20.1 percent from 2003. Worldwide revenues from contract electronic manufacturing were expected to reach $164.4 billion by 2008, and ODM sales forecasts predicted a rise of 21.2 percent to $134 billion by 2008 as reported by iSuppli in April 2005.

Distributors of electronic components also were jumping into the fray. As profit margins on component sales shrank, distributors attempted to drive profits through higher volume sales. These distributor-contractor manufacturers typically had three major advantages over those that were strictly contract manufacturers: (1) the distributorship provided a ready source of capital, hard to come by for many contract-only firms; (2) the distributorship's established supply channels provided an abundant supply of components, which many smaller contract manufacturers lacked; and (3) the distributorship provided an existing customer base. According to *Electronic News,* the largest components distributors in the world were Great Neck, New York-based Avnet Inc., with US$10.24 billion in 2004 revenues, and Arrow Electronics of San Jose, California, with US$10.6 billion in 2004 revenues.

BACKGROUND AND DEVELOPMENT

Electron tubes in the form of gas-discharge tubes were invented in the late nineteenth century and vacuum tubes were developed a short while later. The cathode ray tube, used in televisions, was invented in 1897 by Karl Ferdinand Braun at the University of Strasbourg in France. In terms of picture quality and price, the tube is still much better than liquid crystal displays, according to Steve Bush in *Electronics Weekly.*

In the 1920s, the first widespread use of these tubes began in radios; vacuum tubes were later crucial to the development of television and early computers. In the 1940s and 1950s, solid-state technology—in which a signal passes through a solid instead of a vacuum—represented a substantial advance in technology. The 1960s, however, saw the invention of integrated circuits, which could do much of the same work as the comparatively bulky transistor. Solid-state technology lends itself to complex, low-power circuitry, such as that found in consumer radios. However, electron tubes remained useful in applications that required higher powers and frequencies because they are smaller, lighter, cheaper, and more reliable. Vacuum tube transmitters still do quite well against solid-state technology, particularly in commercial applications for television, radio, and microwave ovens.

The global electronic components industry in the mid-1990s experienced modest growth. OEMs began to outsource more functions to contract equipment manufacturers (CEMs), a move that allowed OEMs to lower cost, reduce time to market, and gain access to the latest technologies. Some companies added capacity to meet growing demand, while others divested unprofitable business lines to increase profits. Since many electronic component manufacturers did business on a worldwide basis, the Asian financial crisis of the mid-1990s affected the entire industry; in addition, electronic component production in Japan declined from ¥9.57 trillion in 1996 to ¥9.45 trillion in 1998.

Advances in technology boosted component demand in the late 1990s. For example, new computer microprocessors required higher density interconnect packaging, and the increased use of ethernet switches for local area networks (LANs) required more passive and active fiber-optic components. Other growth stimulants were the new ultra-thin notebook computer design, which required new types of connectors, and the rise of high-speed digital signals that required new interconnect methods. Also important to the industry was a dramatic increase in the use of cellular phones.

Capacitors and resistors experienced solid growth in the late 1990s. Along with soaring cellular telephone sales, analysts credited the increased use of electronics in automobiles and new developments in computer technology for the upswing. However, of concern to many capacitor and resistor manufacturers was the rising price of palladium, a base metal used in many component parts. Many capacitor and resistor firms also found themselves struggling to keep up with surging demand in 2000.

One of the more significant trends in the electronic components manufacturing industry in the late 1990s was the outsourcing of production. In other words, OEMs hired other manufacturers who specialized in manufacturing to complete subsystems or even entire products, often more inexpensively than the OEMs could do it themselves. This "virtual manufacturing" allowed the original equipment maker to control costs and concentrate on core competencies. The largest customer of contract manufactured products was the computer hardware industry, followed by the communications and medical equipment industries.

After eight years of steady growth, the connectors sector of the electronic components industry saw sales fall dramatically. After growing 7.1 percent in the first quarter of 2001, global connector sales fell 17.7 percent in the second quarter, 29.2 percent in the third quarter, and 28.3 percent in fourth quarter. In North America, connector sales fell from US$13.3 billion in 2000 to US$9.6 billion in 2001. Sales in Europe dropped from US$8.1 billion to US$7.2 billion. Japanese connector sales tumbled from US$5.1 billion to US$3.7 billion, while Asia-Pacific sales slipped from US$3.5 billion to US$3.2 billion. According to Ronald Bishop in a January 2002 *Electronic News* article, an industry-led recession was to blame for falling sales: "First, the failure of the dot-com business model caused numerous bankruptcies and had a ripple effect throughout the telecommunications/data communications market. Demand for routers and other Internet-related equipment dried up. This caused a decline in demand for system support equipment such and servers and storage equipment." Other factors included an overall slowing of the U.S. economy, which eventually made its way to both Europe and Asia, and the World Trade Center attacks in September.

In 2001, Korea displaced Japan as the world's leading producer of liquid crystal displays (LCDs). Korean LCD manufacturers, led by Samsung Electronics Inc. and L.G. Philips LCD Co., secured a 41.5 percent share of the global LCD market, compared to the 39.5 percent share held by Japanese firms. As stated by Jack Robertson in *Electronics Business News*, "The victors are not celebrating much, however. A huge production ramp-up in the last year in Korea and Taiwan has sent LCD panel prices into a tailspin." In fact, falling prices undercut profitability for most major LCD suppliers that year.

CURRENT CONDITIONS

Early in the twenty-first century, the LCD market was faced with competition from developments such as the flat plasma display unveiled by Matsushita; the organic display developed by Kodak, which could process images 100 times faster than LCD or plasma screens while using considerably less energy; and CRT arrays, a less expensive alternative to plasma. But by 2004, major manufacturers were putting US$10 billion into building 10 inch or more large capacity LCDs for flat-screen televisions. According to the independent research company Display Search, worldwide sales of large LCD panels reached almost 98 million units in 2003, with demand continuing to increase.

Sales of LCD panels were expected to grow during the mid-2000s by around 40 percent, generated worldwide revenues of $53 billion in 2005. iSuppli forecast the increases would continue through 2008, reaching $82 billion. The flat screen market was the fastest growing segment of the industry and showed growth rates near 50 percent. Industry growth was attributed to falling prices resulting from oversupply, and capital spending on LCD manufacturing was expected to decline, as reporting in *CMR* in April 2005.

The global connectors market experienced a modest recovery in 2002. According to the research firm Bishop & Associates, by 2003 the connector market was back up to an estimated US$25 billion, fueled largely by soaring demand for high-speed computer and other communication technologies. The market continued to shift during the mid-2000s, as prices stabilized and demand from all industries grew. Growth of 13.2 percent was expected in 2004, with the most growth coming from China, 28.6 percent. As reported in *Purchasing,*, Bishop reported that China accounted for 10 percent of global connector demand, and expected that to double by 2007. The United States market actually dropped by 1 percent, and companies were expanding operations to China and Malaysia to take advantage of the market. 2005 was expected to provide the industry with its first year of significant growth, as new products and designs helped grow the market.

As with most sectors of the electronic components industry, capacitor and resistor sales dropped significantly in the early 2000s. As a result, the firms that had been scrambling to increase capacity suddenly found themselves burdened with excess inventory. Industry analysts forecasted a turnaround for the industry, basing predictions on anticipated growth in cell phone sales and increased U.S. defense spending, likely sparking demand for various communication devices, as well as on growth from the computer and digital electronic sectors. Studies from iSuppli Corp., for example, predicted an increase in the resistor market from US$848 million in 2003 to US$1 billion in 2006. This played out with growing demand from various market segments helping to stabilize prices during 2004. Price declined slowed, and market research from Frost & Sullivan predicted the global capacitor market would realize double-digit growth through 2006.

INDUSTRY LEADERS

Capacitors and Resistors. The world's largest passive electronics suppliers in the world, including capacitors and resistors, in 2005 were Murata Manufacturing Co. Ltd., headquartered in Kyoto, Japan; EPCOS of Munich, Germany; and Vishay Intertechnology Inc., based in Malvern, Pennsylvania. Other notable companies were AVX Corp. of Myrtle Beach, South Carolina; TDK Corp. of Tokyo, Japan; Kyocera Corp. of Kyoto, Japan; and Rohm Co. Ltd., also of Kyoto, Japan.

Connectors. In 2005 the world's largest connector manufacturers were Tyco Electronics, of Middletown, Pennsylvania, and Molex Inc., of Lisle, Illinois. Other notable companies were Amphenol Corp. of Wallingford, Connecticut, and Kyocera Corp. of Kyoto, Japan, as well as Delphi Connection Systems, FCI, and Yazaki. Consolidation was a major trend among the largest connector firms in the late 1990s. For example, Tyco International acquired AMP Inc., which had been the global leader in connector production in the mid-1990s, as well as the OEM arm of Thomas and Betts. In addition, Molex acquired the interconnect operations of Axsys Technologies Inc. Of the world's estimated 1,245 connector makers, the largest 100 firms accounted for 80.5 percent of the North American market, 88.8 percent of the European market, and 94.5 percent of the Japanese market. The leading markets for connectors continued to be computers and peripherals, followed by telecommunications, automotive, and industrial.

Liquid Crystal Displays (LCDs). In 2005, the largest manufacturers of LCDs, the leading alternative to cathode-ray tube displays, were Merck KGaA of Germany and Samsung Electronics Inc. and L.G. Philips LCD Co., both based in Korea. Merck KGaA held around two-thirds of the global LCD market, as reported by Ivan Lerner in *CMR*. The company expected strong demand for LCD in relation to flat-screen televisions. Merck's LCD sales rose 33 percent in 2004. Other industry leaders, all based in Japan, included Sharp Corp.; Seiko Epson Corp.; Display Technologies Inc., a joint venture involving Japan's Toshiba Corp. and IBM; NEC Corp.; and Hitachi, Ltd.

MAJOR COUNTRIES IN THE INDUSTRY

ASIA

In the Asia-Pacific region, connector sales slipped from US$3.5 billion to US$3.2 billion. Excluding Japan, Asia was expected to be the highest growth market for connectors during the mid-2000s, but remained the fourth largest in the global market during the mid-2000s. Bishop & Associates reported that connector sales there rose 13.8 percent to $3.3 billion in 2003.

Japan. In Japan electronic component production in 1997 rose about 7.6 percent, to ¥10.3 trillion (about US$82 billion). Excluding semiconductors and similar devices, the value was ¥5.5 trillion (US$44 billion). Japan's passive component production in 1996 was worth ¥1.09 trillion, a figure that includes ¥216.1 billion in resistors, ¥518.5 billion in capacitors, ¥231.6 billion in transformers, and ¥82.4 billion in crystal oscillators. Production of LCDs was expected to expand because of higher shipments of notebook PCs, and during the 2000s due to demand for flat-screen televisions. The electronics component industry in Japan grew from US$45.5 billion in 1999 to US$52.3 billion in 2000, due to increased global demand. Japan was the third largest market in connector sales, totaling $4.91 billion in 2003 and showing one-year growth of 14.2 percent.

NORTH AMERICA

In North America, connector sales fell from US$13.27 billion in 2000 to US$9.6 billion in 2001, then down to $8.24 billion in 2003. This was due to a slowdown in the telecommunications and data communications industry, which weakened demand. Recessionary economic conditions and the September 11 terrorist attacks also were blamed for the slowdown. Although capacitor and resistor sales also dropped significantly in 2001, they were expected to rebound in 2002 as well, as increased U.S. defense spending fueled demand for various communication devices.

United States. In 1996 the value of capacitor shipments decreased 8.7 percent, from US$1.63 billion in 1995; resistors fell 4.9 percent, to US$906.5 million; coils and transformers decreased 3.1 percent, to US$1.37 billion; electronic connector shipments were valued at US$4.19 billion, down 1.5 percent from 1995; and other electronic components rose 0.6 percent to US$35.38 billion. Although U.S. electronic component manufacturers lost market share to foreign rivals in the mid-1990s, they began to reverse that trend later in the decade. Electronic component production in the United States grew roughly 30 percent in 1999 and 70 percent in 2000.

Canada. According to Statistics Canada, the total value of Canada's electronic parts and components manufacturing in 1996 totaled C$5.27 billion, up 8.8 percent from C$4.93 billion in 1995. These figures include semiconductor shipments. In 1999, Canada imported US$11.8 billion in electronic components from the United States, accounting for 48 percent of worldwide component imports to Canada. Additionally, Canadian exports to the United States reached US$3.2 billion.

EUROPEAN UNION

The eight-member countries of the European Electronic Components Manufacturers Association (EECA) reported electronic component (including semiconductors) sales in 1997 of ECU35.28 billion (about US$38 billion), up 4.4 percent from 1996's ECU33.78 billion. Europe remained the second largest connector region of the global market in 2003, totaling $7.24 billion in 2003 and reporting an increase of $16.8 percent.

One emerging European stronghold in the electronic components industry was Ireland, where more than 300 electronics companies employed more than 30,000 workers. According to the U.S. Department of State, the move by global technology leaders like Apple Computer, Dell Computer, and Gateway Inc. into Ireland in the late 1990s fostered the growth of the electronic components industry there. As a result, by 2000, the components market in Ireland was worth US$2.45 billion, more than half of which was produced locally. The recessionary economic conditions and reduced technology spending that plagued the North American market had also reached Europe by late 2000. As a result, connector sales in Europe dropped from US$8.07 billion in 2000 to US$7.22 billion in 2001.

FURTHER READING

Bishop, Ronald. "Connectors Stuck in the Doldrums; Industry Working Its Way Through the Downturn." *Electronic News,* 1 January 2002.

Chin, Spencer. "Capacitor Prices Continue to Fall As OEMs Pressure Suppliers." *EBN,* 23 June 2003.

———. "November Component Orders Reach Two-Year High." *EBN,* 15 December 2003.

"Connector Industry to Grow Slightly." *Purchasing,* 18 September 2003.

Electronic Business Today, 19 February 2001. Available from http://www.e-insite.net/ebmag.

Elliott, Heidi. "Mirror, mirror: Distributors Expect 2002 to Be Exact Reverse of 2001." *Electronic News,* 1 January 2002.

"EMS, ODM Sales to Reach $300B by 2008." *Circuits Assembly,* April 2005.

European Electronic Component Manufacturers Association. *Market Situation Report.* Brussels, 2001. Available from http://www.eeca.org.

Fleck, Ken. "2002 Will See a Slow Rebound." *Electronic News,* 14 January 2002.

Haughey, Jim. "The China Migration Slows." *Electronic Business,* March 2004.

"Hoover's Company Capsules." 2004. Available from http://www.hoovers.com.

"LCD Spending to Rise in 2004." *The Mobile Internet,* February 2004.

Lerner, Ivan. "LCDs: Heading for Overcapacity?" *CMR,* 25 April - 1 May 2005.

Levine, Bernard. "Passive Makers: Goodbye 2001—and Good Riddance." *Electronic News,* 1 January 2002.

McKeefry, Hailey L. "Capacitors and Resistors." *Electronics Business News,* 19 September 2000. Available from http://www.ebnews.com.

Ojo, Bolaji. "Electronics Sector Sees Revenue Growth in 2003 Amid Tight Capex." *ESM,* 10 December 2002.

Robertson, Jack. "Korea's LCD Makers Assume Lead in Shaky Display Market." *Electronics Business News,* 1 October 2001. Available from http://www.ebnews.com.

Roos, Gina. "Leadtimes Extend, Prices Stabilize for Connectors." *Purchasing,* 20 May 2004.

———. "Recovery Builds for Resistors, Capacitors." *Purchasing,* 17 August 2004.

———. "Rising Materials Costs May Drive Resistor Prices Up." *Purchasing,* 15 April 2004.

———. "Speed Drives Connector Makers' Growth." *Electronics Business News,* 12 February 2001. Available from http://www.ebnews.com.

Sakelson, Roy. "Living in an (Electronic) Materials World." *CircuiTree,* April 2004.

"Sizing Up the LCD Shortage." *Electronic Business,* April 2004.

U.S. Department of State. *Country Commercial Guides.* Washington: GPO, 2001.

Wilson, Ron. "Downturn Could Revamp High-Tech Arena." *EE Times,* 3 October 2002.

The World's Top 100 Electronic Connectors Manufacturers. Bishop and Associates, Inc., July 2001. Available from http://www.bishopinc.com.

SIC 3621

NAICS 335312

MOTORS AND GENERATORS

The motors and generators industry manufactures electric motors and power generators for a diverse range of industrial applications, mostly as components for other manufacturers' finished products. Industry output includes motors and generators for trains, buses, and trucks.

INDUSTRY SNAPSHOT

Electric motors and generators provide much of the power for the world's industrial production. Typically, manufacturers purchase motors and generators for use in a wide range of products. The most widespread use of motors has been for integration into consumer and industrial appliances, including heating and air-conditioning systems, refrigerators, and cleaning equipment such as vacuum cleaners.

Household appliances were projected to be one of the fastest growing markets for motors into 2005. According to *Appliance Manufacturer,* volume was projected to exceed 61 million units in 2005, a significant increase from 19 million units in 2000. Especially in the United States, the automotive industry is another important market for manufacturers of motors, generators, and related parts. Automobile manufacturers use motors as components for accessories such as air conditioners and windshield wipers.

In late 2003, the U.S. Census Bureau reported that industry shipments were valued at US$8.0 billion. Fractional horsepower motors accounted for US$3.0 billion, followed by integral horsepower motors (US$1.3 billion), prime mover generator sets (US$2.0 billion), and electric motor generator sets (nearly US$929 million). According to the Freedonia Group, explosive growth is projected in the newer fuel cell sector, which is set to reach US$1.1 billion by 2008 and US$4.6 billion by 2013.

The motor and generator manufacturing industry was one of the key industries of the so-called second industrial revolution of the late nineteenth century. The pioneering and dominant countries for most of the industry's history have been the United States and Germany. In the post-World War II years, Japan joined these countries, becoming a leading producer and exporter. Most of the industry's largest firms were based in these three countries, and rank among the world's largest multinational companies.

Like many manufacturing industries, motor and generator production has been affected by environmental concerns. Specific issues facing this industry include energy efficiency, noise pollution, and the effects discarded motors have on the environment once they occupy landfills.

ORGANIZATION AND STRUCTURE

Standards of compatibility in the United States for the motors and generators industry were developed under the sponsorship of the National Electrical Manufacturers Association (NEMA). NEMA is a member of the American National Standards Institute (ANSI) Committee on Electrical Rotating Machinery. The committee serves as a forum to hear the views of motor and generator manufacturers, users of these products, and other concerned parties. Upon establishing a consensus, ANSI publishes national standards. Other organizations in the United States have also developed standards for safety and performance. These organizations include the Institute of Electrical and Electronics Engineers (IEEE), Underwriters Laboratories Inc., the American Gear Manufacturers Association, the Edison Electric Institute, and the Hydraulic Institute.

European manufacturers of motors and generators produce goods to the standards of the International Electrotechnical Commission (IEC). These different production standards were argued by the U.S. Department of Commerce to work to the advantage of European and other foreign manufacturers. The department based this argument on the larger size of the U.S. market, a situation that allegedly makes it more cost effective for foreign producers to tailor specific product lines.

The major competitors with U.S. firms in the domestic market in the 1990s were large internationally oriented firms, including the Toshiba Corporation, the Mitsubishi Electric Corporation, and Hitachi, Ltd. of Japan; Siemens AG of Germany; and Asea Brown Boveri AG of Switzerland.

International trade for the leading producers of electric motors and generators is marked by strong patterns of regional specialization. For Germany, the most important export market was the rest of Europe; for Japan, most exports went to Asia and North America; for the United States, the most important export markets were North American Free Trade Agreement (NAFTA) partners Canada and Mexico.

European manufacturers in the industry were served by the European Committee of Manufacturers of Electrical Machines and Power Electronics (CEMEP). The committee was founded in 1960 and is headquartered in Paris. It seeks to represent members regarding standards, policies, and legislation affecting the industry.

BACKGROUND AND DEVELOPMENT

Electric motors convert electricity into rotary mechanical energy, while generators do just the opposite. Technological advances have thus allowed the same machine to serve as both an electric motor and generator, with energy flowing in either direction. Generators have historically been most widely used in centralized power production facilities, although they are also used to generate electrical power in automobiles, ships, trains, and aircraft. The use of electric motors is more decentralized, ranging from home appliances to heavy industrial applications. Motors and generators are designated as either permanent magnet or electromagnetic, and typed as either alternating or direct current.

The electrical motors and generators industry originated in the 1880s, when firms arose in the United States to commercialize the inventions of Thomas Edison, Elihu Thomson, and George Westinghouse. The industry was one of the few in which the key inventors successfully commercialized their inventions and launched companies that became industry leaders. Compared with most manufacturing industries, these firms required greater numbers of technically trained employees. These employees were necessary not only for designing and producing commercially viable electrical machines, but also for marketing, installing, and maintaining them. Producers of electrical machinery also made large investments in research and development.

As a result of the great expense of manufacturing electrical machinery, producers found it necessary to establish substantial lines of credit to buyers. The largest German firms established banks to facilitate sales of their machinery. Buyers also purchased electrical equipment with their own stocks and bonds, leading some producers of electrical machinery to establish holding companies. Firms in the industry thus became vertically integrated across a wide range of activities early in the sector's development.

In these early years, the Thomson-Houston company established the industry's most sophisticated domestic and international marketing organization. Thomson-Houston merged with Edison General Electric in 1892 to form the General Electric Company. The merger was facilitated by the firms' complementary product lines; Thomson-Houston was strong in arc lighting and alternating current, while Edison's strength lay in incandescent lamp lighting and direct current. In 1896 General Electric and Westinghouse formed a patent pool, a move that accelerated their dominance of the U.S. market.

General Electric and Westinghouse then entered into cooperative arrangements with the two large German producers in the industry, Siemens and Halske and Allgemeine Elektricitäts Gesellschaft (AEG). The four firms dominated the world market for electrical machinery by the early 1900s, a state of affairs that continued uninterrupted for several decades. The power of these companies was based not only on sales but also on direct investment. For example, in England, two-thirds of electrical equipment manufactured in the mid-1910s was produced by subsidiaries of General Electric, Westinghouse, and Siemens. In terms of electrical machinery exports, Germany was the most successful of these countries prior to World War I. German companies were responsible for three times more exports than the United States and two-and-one-half times more than England. In the 1920s, General Electric purchased large shares of Siemens and AEG. Siemens and General Electric remained among the world's largest producers of electrical motors and generators into the 1990s.

One of the growth strategies of these firms was diversification into related products, including household appliances. Diversification into household appliances provided a direct outlet for parts (such as small electric motors) produced in increasing quantities by these firms. At the same time, appliances contributed to the growing demand for electrical power, which these firms also supplied via other equipment. In his book *Scale and Scope,* Alfred Chandler Jr. described General Electric's rapid diversification as follows: "The number of GE's product lines rose from 10 in 1900 to 30 in 1910, to 85 in 1920, to 193 in 1930, and to 281 in 1940. By World War I, GE had developed one of the most diversified product lines of any industrial enterprise in the world. Nearly all these products were related to its electrical equipment base."

The fortunes of U.S. producers of motors and generators took a substantial turn for the worse after the mid-1970s. From 1972 to 1985, there was very little growth in real output and the industry was plagued with excess capacity. As measured by after-tax return on sales, profitability declined over these years. It was also during these years that the United States changed from a net exporter to a net importer of electric motors and generators. For example, in 1976, exports accounted for 17 percent of industry shipments in the United States, while imports accounted for 7 percent of domestic use. By 1986 exports accounted for only 10 percent of shipments, but imports accounted for 18 percent of domestic use. In an effort to improve international competitiveness, leading U.S. producers looked to produce goods in regions that featured lower labor costs. They built plants in Canada, Mexico, Brazil, and Singapore and entered into joint ventures in Taiwan, South Korea, and other countries.

World industry output increased from the early 1980s to the early 1990s. A highly cyclical industry, sales of motors and generators slumped as a result of the economic recession of the early 1990s, but recovered steadily. It was not until the 1990s that conditions for U.S. producers of motors and generators improved. This resulted in large part from generally improved business conditions in the United States, long the world's largest market for motors and generators.

The value of shipments in the U.S. motors and generators industry was US$12 billion in 2000, down 2 percent from 1999. Projections for the future are optimistic, however, and continued long-term growth is expected based on the demand for high-efficiency motors resulting from environmental and energy considerations. The sluggish economy of 2000 and 2001, made worse by the terrorist attacks on the United States on September 11, 2001, took a toll on the motor and generator industry, as it did on most industries. As the economy began to rally in 2002, however, rising consumer confidence helped many industries regain hope.

Current Conditions

A major worldwide trend in the motor and generator industry was the push for smaller, lighter, and more energy-efficient products. The rapid development of energy-efficient technologies triggered new demand. In *Air Conditioning, Heating, & Refrigeration,* the National Electrical Manufacturers Association stated that electric motors require ten to twenty-five times the amount of the purchase price in annual electricity costs. This demonstrated how important any degree of improved efficiency can be. New developments in the area of energy efficiency were among the most important for manufacturers in terms of maintaining profitability and market position.

Because of sporadic energy shortages and energy prices that were prone to unexpected spikes, many industrial facilities were seeking ways to generate power on-site. While meeting the extensive energy needs of such facilities is possible with diesel-fired generators, interested companies found regulatory obstacles, particularly with regard to air quality, to be prohibitive. In addition, increased consumer concern and demand for environmentally friendly products pushed research and development efforts in that direction to the point where a company's future success or failure in the motor and generator market was largely dependent upon it. Researchers were challenged by demands to create energy-efficient motors that were also affordable and durable. Electronic components and software represented areas of broadening research. For example, Ford Motor Company was working with the Environmental Protection Agency (EPA) on a Clean Diesel Combustion program, hoping to offer low-emission diesel engines. The first phase of the program was complete in 2005.

One major trend in the motors segment was the development of hybrid engines that draw power from both gasoline and an electrical battery. Similarly, researchers were working toward creating reliable fuel cells for vehicles. Fuel cells draw energy directly from fuel sources without requiring the combustion system of traditional automobile engines. In a fuel cell, energy comes from the chemical process of combining fuel with an oxidizer. Because fuel cells derive power from a renewable source, natural resources are preserved. In addition, the absence of combustion means fumes are not released into the air. Economically, fuel cells had the potential to substantially reduce dependence on foreign oil. As of 2005, automobile manufacturers Ford, Chevrolet, and Lexus offered trucks with hybrid engines.

The fuel cell market was expected to grow rapidly. While estimates of total sales in 2000 were US$218 million, projected sales for 2013 were US$4.6 billion. Some 2,800 systems were produced in 2003, and by early 2004 there were 7,000 systems in operation. *Fuel Cell Technology News* reported that the European Union had slated nearly US$3.5 billion for such projects into 2015. Major universities across the globe such as the California Institute of Technology, the University of Tokyo, and Technical University of Denmark made fuel cell technology application the focus of their research, as did industry leader Toshiba. According to a Freedonia Group study, the largest market for fuel cells in 2004 was electric power generation. By 2008, 50 percent of fuel cell demand was slated to come from grid support, cogeneration, and remote power supplies.

According to a Frost & Sullivan study, however, the large generator set market, for on-site power generation, was not dead yet. In 2002, the market was valued at US$1.4 billion. By 2011, the market was projected to grow to US$1.9 billion.

RESEARCH AND TECHNOLOGY

From development in the late nineteenth century through the 1970s, the basic technology of electric motors and generators changed little. However, since the 1980s, significant advances have been seen in the development of new high-efficiency motors, miniature motors, insulating materials for electric motors' wire windings, and the use of superconducting materials.

Hybrid motors were receiving more attention and were gaining acceptance as a viable strategy for the future. Hybrid engines draw on two types of energy, usually gasoline and electrical batteries. In 2001, Ford Motor Company announced its agreement with the Environmental Protection Agency to develop a hybrid engine using pressurized liquid in place of batteries. Ford maintained that this type of vehicle would be superior to those using electrical batteries because the tanks holding the pressurized liquid are much lighter than batteries. Ford expected to have a functioning prototype of its hybrid by 2010.

The potential of fuel cells as energy for vehicles was being explored by researchers. In early 2002, for example, the U. S. Department of Energy announced that it would work with three auto manufacturers to produce viable hydrogen generators to supply fuel cell vehicles. Fuel cells in the automotive industry had the potential to benefit automobile and parts (including motors) manufacturers, government organizations such as the Environmental Protection Agency, consumers, and the environment. However, the applications of fuel cells go beyond the automotive industry. The National Aeronautics and Space Administration (NASA) was working to realize the potential of fuel cells for use in satellites, aircraft, space stations, and planetary bases in zero-gravity and micro-gravity environments. The Army National Automotive Center hoped to utilize fuel cells for auxiliary power aboard military battlefield vehicles.

High-efficiency motors were an important area of development for the industry. The development of high-efficiency motors was significant not only for the user's operating costs, but also for the energy requirements of the economy at large.

In the late 1980s, researchers discovered superconductive ceramic-like materials that were cheaper and more practical than previously known superconductive materials. Research was launched to investigate the use of these superconductive materials to construct electromagnets of unprecedented power. Some engineers estimated that these superconductive materials, which transmit electricity without resistance, could enable the production of electric motors one-half the size of, lighter than, and more efficient than conventional motors for a given level of horsepower. The general consensus within the industry was to make high-horsepower electric motors using high-temperature superconducting technology (HTS) ready for commercial use by 2000. Although the industry did not meet this goal, it seems to be within reach. In later years, two groups of engineers, one from the Siemens Research Center at Erlangen, Germany, and the other from Rockwell Automation in South Carolina, introduced motors with high-temperature superconducting technology. This brought the industry closer to the commercial use of this technology.

Toshiba Corp. of Japan announced its development of the world's smallest electromagnetic motor in 1992. It was considered too small and insufficiently powerful to have any commercial applications, but in 2001 Scottish engineer Rod MacGregor announced his matchstick-sized electric motor. Called the Nanomuscle, this motor had potential applications in computers, consumer electronics, office equipment, telecommunications equipment, movable automobile parts, and medical equipment. MacGregor claimed that this motor was five times more efficient than its existing counterparts. The toy company Hasbro planned to use the Nanomuscle in toy products released for the 2002 Christmas season. By 2004, Nanomuscle Inc. had offices in North America, Europe, and Asia. In 2001, Pennsylvania state engineers introduced an ultrasonic motor that is the size of a grain of rice. Its intended application is breaking down kidney stones.

Products such as General Electric's Power in a Box power generators offer energy efficiency and self-contained power. In 2001, two of these units were slotted to go to a resort in California. Installation was scheduled for 2002. Expected to operate at 80 percent efficiency, these generators were intended to drastically reduce the resort's electricity costs. The generators met strict emission guidelines, making them especially environmentally friendly.

INDUSTRY LEADERS

TOSHIBA CORPORATION

Tokyo-based Toshiba Corp. was one of the world's largest producers of electric machinery and electronic equipment. In addition to motors and generators, the firm is a top maker of portable computers and producer of computer peripherals, medical equipment, industrial machinery, home appliances, and semiconductors. Top executives are concerned about the possibility of being too diversified, however, and plans are being made to streamline operations by cutting less profitable product lines and reducing the workforce. The 2004 sales total was US$52.8 billion. The firm had entered into cooperative arrangements with other key producers in the industry, including Siemens AG of Germany and the General Electric Co. of the United States.

MITSUBISHI ELECTRIC CORPORATION

Mitsubishi Electric Corp. is also headquartered in Tokyo. The firm was established in 1921 from the electrical machinery division of Mitsubishi Shipbuilding's Kobe shipyard. Of the US$32.6 billion in revenues the company generated in 2001, information systems accounted for 22.6 percent, electric systems for 22.0 percent, home appliances for 17.7 percent, electronic devices for 17.2 percent, and automation equipment and other industrial products for 16.0 percent, with miscellaneous product lines comprising the balance. In 2004, revenues totaled US$31.9 billion, up more than 5 percent from 2003. In addition to motors and generators, Mitsubishi produces electronics, telecommunications products, industrial machinery, automotive electronics, and consumer appliances. The firm had an expansive worldwide network, with operations in more than 35 countries, and employed 98,000 people.

HITACHI LTD.

Hitachi was established in 1934 and is headquartered in Osaka, Japan. Its product lines include mainframes; semiconductors; elevators and escalators; industrial equipment; cable, audio and video equipment; and consumer appliances. To stay competitive in the fast-paced technology market, Hitachi is focusing on developing its Internet-related and information technology products, which accounted for about one-third of total revenue. The firm has 1,000 subsidiaries and related companies worldwide. By 2004, Hitachi reported US$81.4 billion in sales, an increase of more than 35 percent in one year.

MEIDENSHA CORPORATION

The Meidensha Corporation was established in 1897 and is headquartered in Tokyo. Meidensha's products fall into three categories: Powertronics (utility plant construction and generators); Mechatronics (factory automation machinery); and Electronics (including information technology and communications products). Its primary customers come from the utility, construction, and transportation industries. In 2004, Meidensha's revenues reached US$1.7 billion with net income of $22.1 million.

FANUC LTD.

Fanuc Ltd. was established in 1956 and is headquartered in Yamanashi, Japan. A diversified manufacturer of factory automation and various industrial motors, Fanuc is the world leader (with more than 50 percent of the international market) in production of computer numerical controls (CNCs), which are used on machinery. Fanuc is also known for its excellent robotics, a product line that accounts for about 45 percent of the company's annual sales. The firm has subsidiaries in the United States, Japan, and Europe, and was partly owned by Fujitsu. Revenue in fiscal year 2004 totaled US$2.5 billion, 40.2 percent more than in 2003.

SIEMENS AG

Siemens AG, headquartered in Munich, is one of Germany's largest industrial firms, employing 460,000 people in more than 190 countries. The firm produces a wide array of electrical and electronics-related equipment and maintains a highly diversified range of manufacturing interests. Siemens rapidly expanded its overseas operations throughout the 1990s, with particular growth in China. Total revenue from all divisions in 2004 reached US$93.4 billion, and net income rose 48.6 percent to $4.2 billion. Siemens AG had 430,000 employees as of 2004.

MABUCHI MOTOR CO. LTD.

The Chiba, Japan-based Mabuchi Motor Co. Ltd. was established in 1954. Compared with most other industry leaders, Mabuchi was a relatively specialized producer of electric motors. In 2004, sales reached US$963.6 million. Small electric motors accounted for 46 percent of the firm's revenues in 2000, and motor parts accounted for 23 percent of revenues. Sales within Asia comprise 77 percent of total revenue.

ABB

ABB Ltd. of Zurich, Switzerland, was jointly owned by ABB AG of Switzerland and ABB AB of Sweden. These companies are participants in utilities, process industries, manufacturing, and oil and gas. Total 2004 revenues were US$18.1 billion. While the firm had been moving heavily into the Asian-Pacific region, its core business area was Europe.

GENERAL ELECTRIC COMPANY

The General Electric Co. of Fairfield, Connecticut is by far the largest U.S. company in the industry in terms of both sales and employment. A highly diversified company, GE produces household appliances, lighting, electric distribution and control equipment, generators, engines, turbines, nuclear reactors, medical equipment, and plastics. The 1990s witnessed substantial sales growth at GE. Sales increased from US$70.0 billion in 1995 to more than $151.3 billion in 2004, up almost 14 percent, with net sales of almost $16.6 billion. GE employed 307,000 people worldwide. According to Euromonitor, GE captures the largest share of the U.S. market for motors and generators, with 25 percent.

EMERSON ELECTRIC COMPANY

The Emerson Electric Company of St. Louis, Missouri, is another major U.S. producer in the industry. Emerson operates 380 facilities globally. Emerson's sales in 2004 totaled US$15.6 billion with net income of $1.2 billion. The firm has greatly expanded its foreign operations. Sales abroad accounted for 40 percent of Emerson's 2000 revenues.

MCDERMOTT INTERNATIONAL INC.

McDermott International Inc., based in New Orleans, Louisiana, is a major U.S. player in the industry, with 24,600 employees. McDermott's sales totaled US$1.8 billion in 2000 and US$1.9 billion in 2004, a substantial decline from 1997, when sales were US$3.15 billion. As of 2004, McDermott International had 12,500 employees.

Other major industry players included Yaskawa Electric Corporation. Headquartered in Kitakyushu, Japan, the company produced mechanical-electronic products, including industrial robots, servomotors, generators, automated factory production systems, electrical industrial equipment, and motion controllers. In 2004 Yaskawa earned $283.4 million in sales and employed 450 people. Baldor Electric Company, based in Fort Smith, Arkansas, designed, manufactured, and marketed electric drives, motors, and generators for industry. In 2005, Baldor ran fifteen plants in the United States and one in Bristol, England. During 2004, sales went up more than 15 percent to $648.2 million, and the company's net incomes rose 35.1 percent.

MAJOR COUNTRIES IN THE INDUSTRY

The leading countries in the motors and generators industry throughout the 1990s were the United States, Japan, and Germany. The United States and Germany have been dominant countries in the industry since its origins in the late nineteenth century, while France, Italy, the United Kingdom, and Spain have long been important secondary countries.

According to *Euromonitor,* the U.S. market was valued at US$8.3 billion in 2003, and was projected to increase 13.2 percent between 2004 and 2008, reaching US$10.1 billion by 2008. Fractional horsepower motors were the largest segment, with more than 35 percent of the market. Germany's market was valued at more than US$2.2 billion in 2002, and was forecast to reach US$2.3 billion in 2007. Multi-phase AC motors were the largest segment, and the biggest end user was the commercial appliance sector.

Fractional horsepower motors continued to be an important product for the U.S. industry, worth $3.1 billion. The United States imported US$5.5 billion and exported US$3.2 billion in 2003, although the value of imports was half of the value of domestic products sold in the domestic market, as reported by the Office of Trade and Industry Information in 2005.

FURTHER READING

Allan, Roger. "MEMS: A New Power Source for Portables." *Electronic Design,* 17 March 2005.

Dolan, Kerry A. "Emissions-Free Investing." *Forbes,* 22 December 2003.

"Hoover's Company Capsules." 2004. Available from http://www.hoovers.com.

"Industry News: Looking Back, Looking Forward." *Fuel Cell Technology News,* January 2004.

"International Trade Statistics." 2003. Available from http://www.wto.org.

Johnson, Mark, ed. "FYI." *ABRN,* April 2005. Available from http://www.abrn.com.

Kaporech, Thomas. "Driving the Future." *Appliance Manufacturer,* September 2001.

"Large Generator Set Market on Comeback Trail." *Pipeline & Gas Journal,* April 2004.

Lazich, Robert S., ed. *Market Share Reporter.* Detroit: Thomson Gale, 2004.

"Market Projections: UPS & Fuel Cells." *Plant Engineering,* September 2001.

Mazurkiewicz, Greg. "Premium Motor Program Gains Wide-Ranging Support." *Air Conditioning, Heating, & Refrigeration News,* 1 October 2001.

"Mini Motors Crush Kidney Stones." *Design Engineering,* December 2001.

"Motors and Generators." *Current Industrial Reports.* Washington: U.S. Department of Commerce, 2002.

"Motors and Generators in France, Germany, UK, US." *Euromonitor,* August 2004. Available from http://www.majormarketprofiles.com.

Mraz, Stephen J. "Superconducting Research Spawns Superefficient Motor." *Machine Design,* 27 September 2001.

Randerson, James. "A Generator You Can Take on the Subway." *New Scientist,* 20 September 2003.

"Shape Memory Motor." *Design Engineering,* December 2001.

"Superconductor Start-Up." *Global Design News,* October 2001.

U.S. Census Bureau. "Motors and Generators," 12 January 2001. Available from http://www.census.gov.

"U.S. Fuel Cell Demand." *Batteries International,* April 2004.

SIC 3861

NAICS 333315

PHOTOGRAPHIC EQUIPMENT AND SUPPLIES

Manufacturers of photographic equipment and supplies provide the world's cameras, film, developing and enlarging equipment, photographic chemicals and papers, and related supplies. Industry output includes both still and motion cameras, but not video cameras, which are discussed in a separate article, **Audio and Video Equipment.**

INDUSTRY SNAPSHOT

The photographic equipment and supplies industry's products include five general categories:

- still picture equipment
- motion picture equipment
- photocopying and microfilming equipment
- sensitized photographic film, plates, paper, and cloth
- prepared photographic chemicals

In established markets, growth in the photographic goods industry was generally fueled by the introduction of new products using innovative technology, particularly digital cameras and One Time Use (OTU) disposable cameras. By 2003, digital cameras outsold traditional cameras. As a result, the overall film sector began to weaken, although certain types of consumers were returning to a demand for film prints, this time for prints of digital images. In addition, major industry players began to scale back their Advanced Photo System (APS) camera activities in favor of digital cameras, sales of which were expected to grow 13 percent in 2005 to 20.5 million according to the Photo Marketing Association International (PMAI). The fastest growing sector was digital cameras with four or more megapixels. Consequently, major companies in the industry began to focus less on combating digital technology and more on developing products for the organization and storage of digital images. Industry analysts expected the digital market to level in the coming years, as the sector hit saturation.

In 2004, OTU cameras peaked at 218 million units. That number was expected to remain flat in 2005. Film sales declined to 438 million units in 2004, down 157 million, and further decline to 315 million was anticipated in 2005. 35mm film still had the majority, with 66 percent, while APS trailed with 6 percent. Prints made from digital images increased a whopping 71 percent over 2003 levels. Traditional camera sales remained in decline, with analog camera sales dropping 45 percent and 35mm cameras sales dropping 43 percent in 2004. Despite the continuing decrease in film sales, the market was not dead, and approximately 532 million rolls of film were expected to sell in 2005.

Organization and Structure

The majority of the photographic equipment industry's products were considered leisure or nonessential goods, and thus industry sales to a degree were sensitive to reduced consumer spending during times of economic stagnation or recession. The broad range of photographic products offered, however, partially insulated the industry from fluctuations in consumer demand. Because it provided an essential service in most business and government offices, photocopying equipment sales were relatively independent of consumer spending levels. In the mid- to late 1990s, photocopying equipment accounted for roughly one-third of industry sales, and high-end photocopiers were one of the industry's most lucrative products.

The industry has grown increasingly globalized. Leading photographic equipment companies had worldwide research and development, manufacturing, marketing, and servicing divisions. Industry leaders operated through a global web of affiliates and subsidiaries that served as business offices and "transplants" (foreign manufacturing sites), providing access to both regional or national consumer markets and to local labor pools. Among international leaders, the industry was characterized by a complex and shifting network of affiliation and cooperation, on the one hand, and competition and rivalry, on the other.

The international circulation of industry products stood to benefit from the economic globalization reflected by political treaties such as the mid-1990s General Agreement on Tariffs and Trade (GATT) and the North American Free Trade Agreement (NAFTA). National and local governments, moreover, provided various forms of economic incentives to encourage industry firms to continue or establish operations and facilities within their areas of jurisdiction. In 1993, the regional government of Castilla y Leon in Spain arranged a Pta850 million guaranteed loan through the Argentaria state bank to assist Valca, a local manufacturer of photographic equipment that faced severe financial difficulties. In 1994, the French government granted financial aid for Toshiba to expand its photocopier and toner plant near Dieppe.

National and international courts had historically monitored trade, monopoly, and patent issues within the industry. For example, the Eastman Kodak Company was fined US$873 million for infringement of copyrights held by the Polaroid Corporation, and Honeywell won a US$96 million judgment against the Minolta Camera Company for copyright infringements involving autofocus cameras. Further, the European Court of Justice upheld a complaint by European companies against unfair trade practices by Japanese photocopying equipment manufacturers, including Minolta. With the ratification of GATT, the United Nations established the World Trade Organization (WTO) in 1995 to govern global trade and trade policies. Shortly after its inception, the WTO began hearing complaints from the United States and Europe alleging that Japan's film market was unfairly restrictive. In 1998, however, the WTO found in favor of Japan.

Background and Development

The development of the photographic equipment and supply industry resulted from research and technology from around the world. The precursor of the modern camera was the closet-sized "camera obscura" developed by tenth-century Islamic scientists. In the sixteenth century, the Italian scientist Giambattista della Porta published his research on fitting the camera obscura with a lens to strengthen or enlarge the image projected. In 1727, the German professor Johann Heinrich Schulze took an important step forward by capturing the image produced by a camera obscura in permanent form by discovering that silver salts darkened when exposed to sunlight. As early as 1816, the French amateur inventor Joseph Nicephore Niepce, building on his interest in lithography, obtained an image of Paris on paper treated with silver chloride. By 1827, Niepce had achieved the first permanent photographic image taken from nature, a view of his country estate. Niepce termed his discovery "heliography" (Greek for "sun writing").

In 1826, the French scene-painter Louis Jacques Mande Daguerre, hoping to exploit photographic images in the creation of theatrical backdrops, began corresponding with Niepce about heliography. Working with copper plates coated with silver iodine, Daguerre discovered that a latent image, exposed for the relatively short span of 30 minutes, could be developed by exposing it to mercury vapor. Ignoring the role played by Niepce, Daguerre marketed this discovery as the "daguerreotype," which proved to be a commercial sensation.

During this same period, the English scientist William Henry Fox Talbot, attempting to capture a permanent photographic image on paper, created an early form of negatives (in which black and white tones are reversed). Talbot's photograph of Lacock Abbey, Wiltshire, dating to 1835, is considered the first successful photograph derived from a negative image to be taken from nature. Talbot subsequently developed a portable camera consisting of a wooden box fitted with a lens and partially lined with treated paper. By 1841, Talbot had perfected his discovery and patented it under the name of "talbotype." However, it was not until the early 1850s, when the English sculptor and inventor Frederick Scott Archer promoted the use of glass plates treated with collodion, that the daguerreotype was superseded as the most popular form of photography.

The U.S. inventor George Eastman was responsible for the mass-merchandising of photography and amateur manual cameras. Experimenting in his mother's kitchen, Eastman was able to coat glass photographic plates with a gelatin emulsion containing silver chloride. The emulsion, once solidified, left a light-sensitive "dry plate" that was 60 times more sensitive than plates based on the collodion process, thereby freeing the camera from the tripod. In 1881, Eastman founded the Eastman Dry Plate Company, through which he rapidly introduced dry plates and several other advances in photography. The paper and gelatin photographic film that Eastman patented in 1884, packaged in a small cassette, enabled a significant reduction of camera size. Five years later, Eastman marketed a celluloid film that was much tougher than his original paper and gelatin version. Adopting the international trade name "Kodak" in 1888, Eastman successfully marketed innovative folding, hand, and pocket cameras that made photography accessible to even the casual amateur.

In the late 1850s, Scottish physicist James Clerk Maxwell developed what became the standard method of color photography: the additive three-color process. Employing this process, the U.S. inventor Frederic Eugene Ives first made color photography practical for professional photographers with his 1893 Photochromoscope camera. French inventors Auguste and Louis Lumiere, in addition to developing cinematography, introduced the first method of color photography accessible to amateurs: the autochrome method. In 1912, German scientist Hans Fischer made a further breakthrough by proposing that color photography could be achieved chemically, rather than optically, through oxidation of chemicals in a multi-layered film. By mid-century, George Eastman—in collaboration with others—had developed the color film marketed as Kodachrome.

In 1947, Dr. Edwin Herbert Land, founder of the Polaroid Corporation, introduced the first "instant" film and camera. In 1959, the Haloid Company (soon to be renamed the Xerox Corporation), introduced the first successful commercial photocopier, the 914 model.

During the 1980s and 1990s, Japan, the United States, and Germany led the world in production of photographic equipment and supplies, accounting for 80 percent of the global market. Japan and the United States held the largest share, while Germany remained a distant third. Japan led in exports of photographic equipment and supplies, with a 36 percent market share for equipment and a 24 percent market share supplies in 1995. The United States controlled 9.0 percent of the equipment export market and 13.9 percent of the supply export market. According to preliminary United Nations estimates, total industry trade in 1996 reached about US$30 billion, about even with 1995, but up from US$24 billion in 1994.

International trade policies on photographic equipment and supplies came under increased scrutiny during the 1990s as the United States and the European Union both argued that Japan unfairly shielded its photographic equipment and supply market from outside competition. Spearheaded by Kodak, the United States and the EU took their complaint before the World Trade Organization (WTO) in 1996. Although the United States expected the WTO to agree with Kodak's allegations, the WTO ruled in January of 1998 that the Japanese government did not restrict film imports, specifically from Kodak. The United States announced in February of that year that it would not appeal the decision.

CURRENT CONDITIONS

The development of the digital camera proved a major turning point in the global photographic equipment and supplies industry. At first, industry analysts speculated as to how the camera, with its limited ability to produce high quality photographs, would fare. Technological advances that increased resolution, as well as declining prices, transformed the digital camera from a personal computer accessory to a full-fledged rival to the standard 35-millimeter camera. Nearly one-third of U.S. households owned digital cameras in 2003, the first year ever that traditional film cameras were outsold, and by the close of 2004 that percentage was expected to reach 42 percent. According to predictions by research firm NUA, the global digital camera market would be worth US$9 billion by 2006, and nearly two-thirds of all cameras sold by then would be digital.

As digital camera sales began to outpace 35 mm camera sales early in the twenty-first century, new players entered the photographic equipment and supplies industry. Traditional players like Eastman Kodak found themselves having to compete with the likes of Sony Corp. In fact, in 2001 Sony held a 25 percent share of the global digital camera market, compared to the 14 percent held by Kodak. A handful of major camera makers in Japan, including Konica Corp., Olympus Optical Co., and Minolta Co., all shuttered their APS camera operations. In addition, Nikon Corp. and Asahi Optical Co. both downsized APS activities to pour resources instead into digital technology. Conversely, despite the shrinking APS market, both Fuji and Canon, two of the world's largest APS camera makers, announced their intent to launch new APS products during 2002.

Along with undercutting sales of APS cameras, the growth in the digital camera market also began to impact the film sector, which traditionally boasted high profit margins and provided consistent business for industry leaders like Eastman Kodak and Fuji. Because digital technology allowed for the storage of photographs on either a hard drive or disk, film was simply unnecessary for digital camera users. Those wishing to print photographs—only 10 to 15 percent of all digital camera users in 2001—had a wide range of high-quality paper options from which to choose. According to the PMAI, however, the outlook for prints was positive in the mid-2000s. Women and young families—the typical users of traditional film cameras—were shifting to the digital market, and were more likely to want actual prints of digital images. PMA predicted that long before the decade's end, total prints produced would return to 2000 levels.

By 2004 one-time-use disposable cameras (OTU) was the fastest growing film processing sector. In contrast to other sectors, which were declining, the OTU sector commanded more than 22 percent of film processing, a 3 percent increase over 2003 levels.

While Japan proved to be the largest digital camera market in 2001, many analysts expected China to claim that title by 2005. In response to such predictions, both Kodak and Fuji began pursuing plans to manufacture their digital cameras in China via transplant operations. Kodak teamed up with Seagull, a Chinese camera maker, to jointly manufacture digital cameras in Shanghai, while Fuji forged a similar joint venture in Suzhou. The Chinese photocopier industry was also expected to grow rapidly—at least 10 percent annually during the early 2000s. As a result, Ricoh Co., Fuji Xerox Co., and Canon established photocopier plants there.

Research and Technology

Research and development (R&D) was the lifeblood of the photographic equipment and supply industry. For example, in 1997 the Eastman Kodak Company invested US$1.04 billion (7.0 percent) of US$14.5 billion in net sales toward R&D, the Fuji Photo Film Company invested about US$600 million (5.6 percent) of its US$10.6 billion in sales, and Xerox invested about US$1 billion (5.0 percent) of its US$18.1 billion in sales.

In the 1990s, the most significant technological innovation within the photographic equipment and supplies industry was the advent of electronic imaging, a technology that uses semiconductor sensors instead of film to record images and display them on television screens or computer monitors. Electronic imaging threatened to radically affect the sales of photographic equipment and supplies because the technology did not employ film, paper, or conventional photographic chemicals to produce an image. By the mid-1990s, the Eastman Kodak Company alone spent over US$1 billion in the development of this technology.

In the early 1990s, technological developments in the photocopier market included Ricoh Company's creation of a photocopying machine that turned the pages of a book as it was being photocopied and one that translated documents from English to Japanese in the process of reproducing them. In addition, Mita Industrial Company announced a five-year joint venture with the University of Tokyo to develop photocopying machines that were self-repairing. Industry leaders, in addition, responded to the need to install sophisticated anti-counterfeiting technology in color photocopiers.

A broader technological trend within the industry was the modification of design, manufacturing, packaging, and waste disposal processes to create environmentally sound products. In 1988 the Polaroid Corporation set up a Toxic Waste and Use Reduction program that achieved company-wide waste reductions of 6 percent annually. In 1990 Canon Inc. began refurbishing used photocopying equipment as a form of recycling. In the early 1990s, various industry leaders achieved significant reductions in photocopier ozone emissions and discontinued the use of chlorofluorocarbons (CFCs) in their manufacturing processes. During this same period, the Konica Corporation developed a minilab system using tablet form photo-chemicals, thereby halving levels of chemical effluent. In 1993, the Ricoh Company developed a "peel off" toner system such that photocopying paper could be reused, for which Ricoh UK Products Ltd. received the inaugural Queen's Award for Environmental Achievement. In 1994, German photographic companies and the recycling organization Vereinigung für Werstoffrecycling set up a recycling system comprised of 800 sites to collect used retail packaging.

During the mid-1990s, photographic equipment and supply manufacturers also rolled out Advanced Photo System (APS) cameras and film. Although earlier attempts to supplant the 35mm format, such as Kodak's disk camera, failed, manufacturers hoped the convenience and power of this camera would catch on. Using silver halide technology, APS cameras and film made it easier to take pictures and to develop them—that is, according to manufacturers, they offered the power of a 35mm camera with the simplicity of a point-and-shoot camera. In addition, APS technology was supposed to yield higher-quality pictures because magnetic codes on the film automatically adjusted the camera settings for factors such as lighting. In a joint effort, Kodak, Canon, Nikon, Fuji, and Minolta developed the APS format and introduced the product in the form of disposable cameras initially to test the market. Although touted by manufacturers, retailers reported mixed responses to the product in 1997. Nonetheless, analysts predicted that APS would remain on the market for some time and that sales would rise, accounting for about 20 percent of all camera purchases and 7 percent of all film sales. What these analysts failed to foresee, however, was the impact of digital technology on traditional 35mm cameras.

With the growing penetration of personal computers and the global popularity of the Internet, camera manufacturers in the late-1990s launched digital cameras, which stored images on computerized camera device's disk or hard drive memory and attached to a computer so that images could be downloaded for manipulation and printing. Digital cameras produced higher-quality images than most scanned photographs and allowed users to quickly take a photograph and place it in a report, Web page, or e-mail message. By the end of 2000, companies like Nikon and Olympus were selling digital cameras with a resolution of 2 million pixels for roughly US$500. Such cameras were able to compete with standard 35mm cameras because they were capable of producing high-quality 4x6 photographs. By 2004, 38 percent of digital cameras sold had resolution of 3-3.9 megapixels, 27 percent were 4-4.9 megapixel cameras, and another 28 percent of buyers purchased cameras with even greater resolution. In 2004 the average price per megapixel, as reported by the PMAI, was $82, compared to $119 only one year earlier.

In 2006, FotoNation launched its FotoNation Face Tracker for cameraphones. The innovative approach identifies and locks onto human faces in a preview image plus follows them as they move around and makes automatic adjustments. Face Tracker was also made available for digital cameras.

Vimcro, a fabless semiconductor company that designed advanced mixed-signal multimedia products and solutions, offered another 2006 innovative technology application. The company announced that its PC camera processor VCO326 received Windows Hardware Quality Lab (WHQL) certification for Windows Vista by Microsoft. This distinction addressed the need for next generation PC camera to be compatible with standard driver within Windows Vista OS.

Workforce

In the early to mid-2000s, the international photographic equipment and supplies workforce continued to decline. Kodak further streamlined its workforce and shut down offices and facilities in Brazil, Canada, Germany, Japan, and Spain, among other locations. The company reduced its workforce by 9,600 positions in 2004. Xerox eliminated about 10,000 jobs in the 1990s, including 200 jobs from a Canadian plant and 478 jobs from its sales subsidiary in France. In 2004, the firm trimmed another 4.9 percent from its ranks. Even though some companies, including Ricoh and Canon, added to their workforce during the late 1990s and early 2000s, most positions were for other operations such as manufacturing computer printers.

Industry Leaders

Kodak. The largest producer of photographic film in the world, which in 2003 accounted for 70 percent of sales, Eastman Kodak also produced photographic paper, cameras, motion picture films, microfilm paper, and X-ray film. Worldwide net sales totaled US$13.5 billion in 2004, up 5 percent from 2003. Sales related to digital and film imaging totaled more than $9 billion, $5.3 million of which were generated outside the United States. International sales accounted for more than half of annual revenues. In 2006, sales totaled U.S.$13.3 billion.

The Eastman Kodak Company was established in 1881 by George Eastman in Rochester, New York. The historic leader of the photographic equipment and supplies industry, Eastman Kodak in the early 1990s controlled 75 percent of the U.S. market and 50 percent of the international market for photographic film and paper. Later in the decade, Kodak began targeting new sectors of the population such as children, the elderly, and childless adults, as well as forming alliances with stores to offer Kodak film exclusively.

Due to increased competition on the domestic front from rivals like Fuji in the late 1990s, Kodak strove to expand its sales by tapping the potentially largest market in the world: China. Although per capita film use in China was just a half roll of film per year, Kodak planned to stimulated Chinese consumption by opening manufacturing plants there and accelerating marketing. In 1998 Kodak acquired three unprofitable Chinese manufacturers of photographic supplies and began modernizing them. By 2001, the firm had also launched more than 6,000 Kodak franchises in China, which proved to be the second largest consumer film and paper market for Kodak by then.

Despite Kodak's success in China, sales continued to decline throughout the late 1990s and into the 2000s. Along with increased competition, the firm faced a shrinking film market. According to Goldman, Sachs and Co., global film use declined 5 percent in 2001, mainly due to the growing popularity of digital cameras. Although Kodak had added digital cameras to its product line by then, its 14 percent share of the global digital camera market lagged well behind the 25 percent share held by Sony. Compounding the problem was the fact that digital cameras were simply a much less profitable business than film. The firm's EasyShare digital camera, launched in April of 2001, proved to be a best seller throughout the year and boosted Kodak's market share in that sector considerably. In order to stay competitive, Kodak was putting more and more money into digital equipment and technologies in the mid-2000s, with an accompanying reduction in workforce. The company had 54,800 employees worldwide in 2004, compared to 62,300 the year before.

In a 2005 advertorial, Kodak discussed an industry dilemma. Retailers who had invested in digital minilabs for their full-service photofinishing business were being faced with an expensive choice. They needed to decide whether to extend leases while hoping customers would start making more traditional prints again or explore more economical options. The recommendation Kodak made was to consider its "Kodak Picture Maker". Its primary benefits were considered to be an increase in return on investment and improved customer experience. The advertorial also claimed that households using traditional film capture approximately 240 images each year and make an average of 340 prints from them. Digital camera users shot more photos capturing an average of 400 images annually but chose to print a lot less.

In 2007, Kodak celebrated the second straight year of being recognized by an international panel of design experts. The new Kodak Easyshare V1003 digital camera earned a 2007 red dot Award for product design. This model features digital stabilization, a 2.5-inch LCD screen and a high ISO 1600 mode for shooting in low-light conditions. Experts evaluated 2,548 innovative products produced by companies from 43 countries. The red dot Award is one of the most highly regarded forms of recognition in Europe. There it is considered to be a "seal of quality for sophisticated and innovative design."

Another 2007 announcement reflected the fact six newspaper printers opted for Kodak thermal digital solutions. They ordered 11 thermal CTP devices along with digital plates. The transition was described as "painless" but was destined to result in sharper reproduction of photographs. As an added bonus, Kodak Service and Support backed the sale of Kodak products. This team includes more than 3,000 professionals in 120 countries. Kodak was named the Best Support Organization at the 2006 International Business Awards.

Still another 2007 announcement acknowledged that Rohm and Haas Company and Kodak entered into an agreement for the aforementioned companies to acquire Kodak's Light Management Films business. This agreement includes rights to patents and trademarks, know-how, trade secrets, the business's portfolio of current and future products plus a license to additional intellectual property. Kodak developed a family of light management films used in a variety of applications. Initially it was used for the flat panel industry.

In April 2007, Kodak introduced an industry-first service for Kodak Gallery Premier members. The Kodak Picture Protection plan applied to all digital photos stored on the Kodak Gallery. It also protected prints and other gift items stored purchased through the Kodak Gallery. If they are destroyed, members will receive a credit up to US$500 to recreate these items through the Kodak gallery. Kodak Gallery Premier members pay an annual subscription fee of US$24.99 for the basic fee.

Fuji. The top photographic film and paper manufacturer in Japan, Fuji was nearly neck and neck with Kodak in the global race in the mid-2000s. Of Fuji's US$24.1 billion in revenues earned during 2004, 31.9 percent were driven by the company's Imaging Solutions area, including film digital cameras, photofinishing equipment, paper, chemicals, and photofinishing services. The company had a presence in the Americas, Asia, Europe, and Australia, but the majority (52.2 percent) of Fuji's sales came from the Japanese market in 2004. The company reported revenues of US$22.6 billion in 2006 with a one year net income growth of 59.9 percent.

The Fuji Photo Film Company was established in 1934 by Mokichi Morita in Tokyo. The company's photographic products included photographic films and papers, motion picture films, still and instant cameras, camcorders, and photocopiers. In contrast to the company's steady growth in the early 1990s, sales remained stagnant in the late 1990s and fell 16 percent in 2001 to US$11.5 billion. In the late 1990s, Fuji remained Japan's leading film producer and controlled 70 percent of the country's general photo supply market. Worldwide, Fuji had a 37 percent market share. By 2001, the firm had secured a 30 percent share of the film market in China, compared to the 50 percent share held by Kodak. Fuji employed more than 75,000 people in 2005.

Xerox. The Xerox Corporation—the pioneer in photocopying—was established in 1906 as the Haloid Company and adopted its present name in 1961. As of 2004, corporate headquarters were in Stamford, Connecticut. Xerox's photographic products included plain paper and color photocopying equipment. Xerox's total revenues stood at US$15.7 billion in 2004. Equipment sales rose slightly from 2003.

Xerox's international workforce fell from 99,000 in 1991 to 58,100 in 2004; throughout the years, the firm struggled to overcome sluggish sales and high costs. In the early 2000s, Xerox continued to develop and market digital color copiers and integrated copier and communications hardware, as well as printers, scanners, and software. International operations accounted for roughly 45 percent of annual revenues.

Canon. Canon Inc. was established in 1937 in Tokyo and laid the foundations for its role as a global exporter by selling "Kwanon" cameras to post-World War II U.S. occupation forces. The company's photographic products included single-lens reflex (SLR) cameras; compact cameras; camcorders; and full-color, office, and personal photocopiers. By the late 1990s, Canon led the world in camera and copier sales. Canon posted sales of US$33.3 billion in 2004. Printers and other peripheral devices for PCs brought in approximately 40 percent of revenues, while copiers secured 30 percent. Cameras garnered less than 13 percent of sales. Efforts to increase its presence in Asia resulted in Canon securing a 25.1 percent share of the digital camera market in Malaysia by the end of 2001. That year, less than one-third of sales were attributed to domestic clients. By 2007, Canon had grown to become the top patent holder in technology, ranking third overall in the U.S., with global revenues of U.S.$34.9 billion.

In March 2007, the Canon Medical Services division of Canon U.S.A. demonstrated its total digital imaging and workflow management solutions at the International Vision Expo East Show in New York City. The solutions included Eye Q Prime Imaging Systems. The system's software linked retinal images from the Canon Non-Mydriatric camera with measurement devices such as the tonometer and auto-ref keratometer. This process enhanced opportunities for quicker diagnosis by collecting patient data in one database that was easy to utilize.

In April 2007, Canon U.S.A. made several hardware and software announcements about new solutions designed to enhance the digital printing workflow experience for corporate users, print service providers and production printers. Canon also introduced its new imagePRESS C7000VP digital press and related imagePRESS workflow solutions at AIIM on Demand in Boston.

Ricoh. The Ricoh Company, Ltd. was established in 1936 as Riken Sensitized Paper Company in Tokyo. Ricoh's photographic products included cameras, video cameras, and photocopying equipment. The company's revenues were almost US$16.9 billion in 2004. As of the mid-2000s, the company boasted more than 400 subsidiaries around the world and ranked among the world's leading copier, fax machine, and camera manufacturers. Ricoh Corporation, Lanier Worldwide and Savin were listed among the company's U.S.-based subsidiaries. To boost sales, the firm began to focus on laser printers and other networked imaging products early in the twenty-first century.

For the third consecutive year, Ricoh was listed among the Corporate Knights Inc. of Canada's "Global 100". The selection was made after evaluating the sustainability of more than 1,800 major corporations in all business sectors based on research and analysis data provided by Innovest Strategic Value Advisors of the United States. Among the world's leading corporations, Ricoh's aggressive environmental policy, plus its long-term vision extending to 2050, was highly regarded by others.

Agfa-Gevaert NV. Agfa-Gevaert NV was established in 1964 with the merger of the Belgian partnership Agfa-Gevaert N.V. and the German partnership Agfa-Gevaert AG. It had been a wholly owned subsidiary of Bayer AG since 1981, but Bayer sold it off in 2002. As of 2000 the firm's headquarters were in Mortsel, Belgium. Its photographic products included photographic film, paper, chemicals, and machinery; photo-laboratory and minilab equipment; and photocopiers. The company's sales rose slowly in the 1990s, reaching US$4.9 billion in 2000, up from US$4.0 billion in 1991. By 2004, sales were US$5.13 billion. More than 80 percent of Agfa's sales came from exports.

Polaroid. The Polaroid Corporation was established in 1937 by Edwin Herbert Land and, as of 2004, has its headquarters in Waltham, Massachusetts. Polaroid's photographic products included hand-held instant cameras; instant cameras under license by Minolta; amateur and professional photographic films; and film holders, film recorders, and photocopiers. Polaroid led the industry in instant image photographic equipment and supplies, which accounted for nearly 75 percent of sales. Due to waning demand for instant cameras and film, Polaroid's sales sagged in the late 1990s, eventually falling to US$752.7 million in 2003, compared to US$2.1 billion in 1997. In April 2005, Petters Group Worldwide acquired Polaroid for US$426 million.

MAJOR COUNTRIES IN THE INDUSTRY

As of the mid-2000s, the United States and Japan dominated the international photographic equipment and supplies industry. The U.S. photographic equipment market grew 11.2 percent to US$8.9 billion in 2003; the nation's five largest companies accounted for 75 percent of the market that year. The digital camera sector proved to be the most successful. This sector surged 645 percent in value between 1996 and 2000, and was expected to reach a value of US$7.2 billion by 2008, which would represent half of the photographic market. To maintain market share in this intensely competitive market, manufacturers have continued to pour money into marketing endeavors, as well as research and development efforts designed to yield innovative product developments. *Euromonitor International* predicted that the U.S. photographic equipment industry would grow 35.7 percent to US$17.1 billion by 2005. This growth will likely be fueled by growing digital camera sales.

In 2000, U.S. imports of photographic/imaging products declined by 3.6 percent to US$7.62 billion, while exports grew 15.3 percent to $4.86 billion, according to the Photo Marketing Association. Japan led the world in photographic equipment and supply exports with 36.6 percent and 24.0 percent shares, respectively, as of 1995. In 1996, Japan's equipment exports totaled US$4.48 billion and its supply exports were at US$4.02 billion. As the world's leading camera producer, Japan focused on digital and compact models in the late 1990s and early 2000s.

China was expected to replace Japan as the largest digital camera market in the world by 2005. The country also was considered one of the most promising new markets for photocopiers, as well as other photographic equipment and supplies. Thanks to the Internet, Polaroid fans found a gathering place. Lu, a freelance commercial photographer, uses a digital camera for work and ;ldquo;pola;rdquo; for leisure time. The Polaroid, or ldquo;pola" has become sort of a cult favorite. Lu started a related online forum in China with two others. It has grown to in excess of 2,500 registered members from all over China. In addition to sharing experiences, members living in the same city shoot Polaroid photos around a theme. Even considering modern alternatives, Lu praised Polaroids for having "unique color, which we call the attitude of the 'pola'.

Digital cameras dominated some European markets. For example, in 2003 the total German market was valued at US$2 billion, with digital cameras accounting for 40 percent. In the United Kingdom, however, film was the largest market sector, accounting for 80 percent of sales.

FURTHER READING

"About PMA." Photo Marketing Association International, 2004. Available from .http://www.pma.org .

Armstrong, Larry. "Digital Cameras Are Coming Into Focus." *Business Week,* 4 December 2000. Available from .http://www.businessweek.com.

"Camera Makers Eye Local Market." *Alestron,* 12 July 2001.

"Canon Digital Cameras Take Top Spot in Malaysia." *The Malaysian National News Agency,* 22 December 2001.

"Canon U.S.A. Showcases Its imagePRESS C7000VP and Digital Printing Workflow Solutions at 2007 AIIM On Demand in Boston." *Business Wire,* 17 April 2007.

"Canon U.S.A. Showcases Total Imaging and Workflow Management Systems for the Opthalmic World at Vision Expo East." *Business Wire,* 23 March 2007.

"Canon to Build Large Photocopier Plant in China." *Alestron,* 6 June 2001.

Clifford, Mark. "China: Coping With Its New Power." *Business Week,* 16 April 2001. Available from .http://www.businessweek.com.

"Digital Camera Growth 'Exponential.'" *Africa News Service,* 11 May 2004.

Draper, Deborah J., ed. *Business Rankings Annual.* Detroit: Thomson Gale, 2004.

Eastman Kodak Company Annual Report 2004. Eastman Kodak, 2005. Available from http://www.kodak.com.

"Fact Sheet." Fuji Photo Film Co., Ltd., 2005.

"FotoNation Announces Face Tracker for Better Cameraphone Pictures." *Digital Imaging Digest,* June 2006.

Fujifilm 2004. Fuji Photo Film Co., Ltd., 2005. Available from http://www.kodak.com.

"Hoover's Company Capsules." 2007. Available from http://www.hoovers.com.

"Japan's Camera Makers Exiting APS Camera Business." *AsiaPulse News,* 18 January 2002.

"Kodak Announces First-of-its Kind Picture Protection Plan to Replace Treasured Pictures." 16 April 2007. Available from http://biz.yahoo.com.

"Kodak Earns International Design Award for Kodak Easyshare V1003 Digital Camera." Available from http://www.kodak.com.

Lazich, Robert S., ed. *Market Share Reporter.* Detroit: Thomson Gale, 2004.

Minji, Yao. "The Magic of Polaroid - a Vanishing Image." *Shanghai Daily,* 3 April 2007.

"Photo Industry 2005 Review and Forecast." Photo Marketing Association International, 2005. Available from http://www.pma.org.

"Photographic Equipment in France, Germany, UK, US." *Euromonitor,* 2004. Available from http://www.majormarketprofiles.com.

"PMA Launches Digital Outreach." *Association Management,* February 2004.

"PMA Processing Survey Through April 2004." *Photo Marketing Association International,* 12 July 2004.

"The Print Predicament." *Photo Marketing Magazine,* July 2005.

"Ricoh Was Listed Again in 2007 in the '2007 Global 100 Most Sustainable Corporations in the World' for Three Consecutive Years." 14 February 2007. Available from http://www.ricoh.com.

"Rohm and Haas Company Agrees to Acquire Kodak's Light Management Films Business." 18 April 2007. Available fromhttp:/biz.yahoocom.

"Show Report." *PC Magazine,* 17 March 2003.

"Six Newspaper Printers Migrate to Kodak Thermal Digital Solutions to Meet Quality and Deadline Demands in Competitive Market.

Tarnowski, Joseph. "The Hybrid Theory." *Progressive Grocer,* 1 May 2004.

"Vimcro Launches PC Camera Multimedia Solution Certified for Windows Vista." *Wireless News,* 8 November 2006.

SIC 3674

NAICS 334413

SEMICONDUCTORS

The semiconductor industry consists of manufacturers of semiconductors and related solid-state devices. Industry products include semiconductor diodes and stacks (for example, rectifiers, integrated microcircuits, transistors, solar cells, and light-sensing and emitting semiconductor devices). Semiconductors are used in the manufacture of electronic goods that range from television sets and toys to computers and missiles. High-speed computer processor chips and computer memory chips rank among higher profile industry products. The manufacture of products that integrate semiconductors and the manufacture of machines used to produce semiconductors are not categorized as part of the semiconductor industry itself.

INDUSTRY SNAPSHOT

The semiconductor industry has traditionally been characterized by swift change, hefty capital investments, and high risk. It is highly consolidated, with just a handful of companies in a few countries supplying the majority of industry output. According to the Semiconductor Industry Association (SIA) 2006 Annual Report, the industry employed nearly 234,000 people in the United States. With an excess of US$43 billion in exports for 2005, the seminiconductor industry was the leading U.S. exporter. More than 75 percent of U.S. chip industry sales, however, occurred outside the United States.

High technological requirements, massive capital investments related to research and production facilities, and entrenched market leaders generally discourage new entrants to the industry. However, leaps in technology in recent years made by the industry's market leaders opened the door to new manufacturers who specialized in commodity products and helped to satisfy increased customer demand.

On average, the semiconductor industry has enjoyed a growth rate of 17 percent per annum since 1959. In 1990, global sales hit a then record US$50.5 billion. Five years later, sales had tripled to US$144.4 billion, and in 2000 sales reached US$204.0 billion. By 2004, after the sharp economic downturn in the early years of the decade, global sales topped $200 billion for the first time since 2000. As reported in *CMR,* semiconductor sales for 2004 were US$227.246 billion. Of that total, 13 percent was earned by industry leader Intel. World semiconductor shipments were expected to continue rising into the late 2000s, as the rapid expansion of the telecommunications industry continued to create more demand for semiconductors, used in devices for networking and wireless communications. The rapid increase in the use of digital technologies and the world's appetite for electronic devices assured that robust growth would continue to characterize the industry.

In 2004, the semiconductor market was strongest in the Asia Pacific region. Japan retained its position as the global leader with a market value of $8.2 billion, followed by Taiwan with $7.7 billion, and North America, with $5.81 billion. Coming up close were Korea with $4.61 billion and China with $2.68 billion.

By 2005, according to Standard & Poor's *Semiconductor Industry Survey,* the top 10 largest semiconductor companies mainly featured established, dominant industry leaders. They were Intel, Samsung, Texas Instrument, Toshiba, STMicroelectronics, Infineon, Renesas, TSMC, Freescale and NXP.

According to World Semiconductor Trade Statistics, growth of 8.6 and 12.1 percent was expected for 2007 and 8 respectively. Asia-Pacific was expected to be the largest regional market. The forecast anticipated a consistent, positive growth peaking in 2008. Although the semiconductor market did not show a pronounced cyclical pattern, it did reflect that some product groups maintained cycles similar to historical patterns.

ORGANIZATION AND STRUCTURE

Semiconductor devices effectively act as the brains of the mechanisms that they control and coordinate. In essence, a semiconductor is a material that conducts electricity at room temperatures better than an insulator. When treated or "doped," a semiconductor (e.g., silicon) can be made to act as an insulator under some conditions and a conductor under others. Besides managing global communication, financial, and information systems, semiconductors are found in automobiles, planes, tractors, toys, consumer electronics, medical equipment, and other goods. The single largest market for semiconductors is the computer industry, which uses the chips primarily in the construction of personal computers and workstations. Other markets for semiconductors include both the rapidly growing consumer electronics industry and the automotive industry.

Categories of semiconductor devices utilized in analysis of the global semiconductor market include metal oxide semiconductor (MOS) memory (including DRAM), MOS micro (microprocessors and digital signal processors), MOS logic, analog products, and discretes (devices that perform a single function affecting the flow of electrical current).

The MOS memory market declined in the mid-2000s, depressed in part by lowered prices for DRAM memory chips and the uncertainty in the Asian economy. However, during the 2000s, memory sales recovered, thanks to the booming wireless market and demand for flash devices used in consumer electronics applications. The DRAM market grew 61 percent during 2004, earning $26.8 billion.

BACKGROUND AND DEVELOPMENT

The United States' Bell Laboratories invented the solid state transistor, the first semiconductor device, in 1948. The device was an improvement over conventional vacuum tube mechanisms because it had no filament to burn, consumed less power, and was dramatically smaller. Further, transistor operation was dependent on the characteristics of the solid material rather than heat. In 1956 Bell Laboratory scientists William Shockley, John Bardeen, and Walter H. Brattain were awarded a Nobel Prize for their 1948 invention. That same year, Shockley left the company to form his own concern, Fairchild Semiconductor. Fairchild Semiconductor and Texas Instruments, also of the United States, simultaneously unveiled the integrated circuit (IC) in 1958, a pivotal breakthrough that effectively combined the functions of several discrete devices into a single silicon wafer. Robert N. Noyce, the head of Fairchild during the development of the IC, left the company in 1968 to form an enterprise called Intel, which introduced the memory integrated circuit in 1971. That and other developments spawned a massive rise in consumption of semiconductors during the 1970s.

In addition to huge technological advances, declining prices boosted semiconductor use during the 1970s. Industry employment reflected this increased semiconductor usage and surged from about 100,000 in the early 1970s to about a quarter million by 1980. Despite a cyclical downturn in 1975, global semiconductor production grew at a rate of about 30 percent annually between 1976 and 1980. Although the United States still supplied nearly 70 percent of all semiconductors and had a near lock on the high tech, high margin segments, other countries were entering the marketplace. Most notably, Japan invested heavily in semiconductor technology and controlled 25 percent of the world market by the early 1980s.

The industry experienced a major production shift during the 1980s. Japan, buoyed by a government/industry consortium, targeted the quickly growing DRAM market. It flooded the United States with inexpensive integrated circuits (ICs) and managed quickly to gain market share. By blocking semiconductor imports and taking advantage of low export barriers into the United States, Japan succeeded in capturing 38 percent of the world IC market by 1990, even while chip production in Europe and other Asian nations increased. Meanwhile, U.S. IC market share dropped from 67 percent in 1980 to just 29 percent. Frustrated U.S. producers succeeded in securing a trade pact between the Japanese and U.S. governments requiring Japan to boost semiconductor imports. Japan failed to meet the terms by 1991, and a diluted version of the original agreement was negotiated.

Regardless of which countries produced the devices, semiconductor sales mushroomed during the 1980s, and prices for commodity-like chips plummeted as competition proliferated and new manufacturing techniques were introduced. That price drop contributed to a rise in the number of applications for semiconductors in industries such as personal computers, telecommunications, consumer electronics, and automobiles. Sales also were boosted by ongoing advancements that vastly increased the power, reduced the size, and increased the flexibility of semiconductors and the devices into which they were incorporated. Consequently, annual worldwide semiconductor industry sales shot up from about US$20 billion in the early 1980s to nearly US$60 billion by the early 1990s.

In 1998 and 1999, the semiconductor industry had three major challenges: weak pricing and too much inventory, recession in the Asian economy, and the changing personal computer market. The oversupply was due to the industry's attempts to keep up with rapid growth in the personal computer market during the mid-1990s. Manufacturing was expanded to accommodate the demand at the time, but when demand slowed, the large facilities were still producing goods. The Asian economy affects the American economy because the two are interdependent in so many ways, and so the reduction in revenues from Asian buyers was a hit to the semiconductor industry. Finally, consumers are responsive to the influx of low-priced computers that offer many of the same abilities and performance features of higher-priced models.

CURRENT CONDITIONS

According to the SIA, the industry was valued at US$166 billion worldwide in 2003. The United States accounted for US$80 billion of this total, of which nearly three-fourths was attributed to international sales.

According to *Euromonitor,* the market in China was seeing explosive growth and was expected to increase 141 percent by 2007. By comparison, the U.S. market was expected to grow 65 percent, followed by France (39 percent), Japan (22 percent), the United Kingdom (19 percent), and Germany (9 percent). Integrated circuits were the biggest producer worldwide, with sales of US$184.6 billion projected for 2005, according to World Semiconductor Trade Statistics. The consumer semiconductor market was expected to double between 2004 and 2009, rising from $14 billion to almost $30 billion during over the five-year period, as reported in *Electronics News* in May 2005.

Given the explosive growth of technology in the mid-2000s, growth in the semiconductor industry seemed assured. Gartner Dataquest forecast a more than 20 percent growth in 2004, spread among a variety of diverse applications, from mobile phones to PCs to flat screen televisions. Suppliers that focused on memory chips showed the best growth in 2004, ranging from 29 to 58 percent, and outperforming growth in other industry areas.

RESEARCH AND TECHNOLOGY

The semiconductor industry was distinguished from many other growth industries by its extreme emphasis on technology, an emphasis that served as a major entry barrier to potential competitors. Companies that concentrated on proprietary technology had to risk massive capital investments to drive the research and development (R&D) machines that generate new semiconductor designs. Likewise, entities and nations that concentrated on the production or commodity side of the industry needed to invest heavily to develop sophisticated, complex manufacturing operations.

The race between Intel, Digital, and IBM to achieve gigahertz microprocessor unit (MPU) speeds dominated semiconductor technology news in the late 1990s. Intel, the leader in commercial production of microprocessor units (MPUs), coupled announcements of higher-speed processors with price cuts that made existing chips even more attractive to consumers. The Intel Pentium II processor was based on advanced fabrication technology that created circuits just 0.25 microns in width, the equivalent of packing 400 lines of circuitry into the size of a human hair. Although smaller companies, notably Cyrix Corporation and Advanced Micro Devices (AMD), possessed an increased market share as the new century approached, it remained difficult for them to mass produce chips of comparable power.

Gallium arsenide (GaAs) emerged in the mid to late 1990s as a profitable technology, although it had been proffered as early as the 1980s as a synthetic alternative to silicon. GaAs proponents cite its advantages of high speed, superior temperature tolerance and low power requirements. In addition, GaAs can emit light, making it useful in fiber optical communications systems. Because it is brittle and difficult to process, however, GaAs was slow to emerge as a viable technology. In the early 1990s, only 50 percent of the chips produced per batch were usable, compared to 70 percent or more for most silicon chips. As a result, GaAs chips typically cost five times more to produce than similar silicon circuits.

In 2003, U.S. companies invested US$14 billion in semiconductor research and development. Further, more than 30 percent of total revenues were invested in the future in some way, such as in research or education. This suggests a commitment on the part of industry leaders to stay competitive and build a strong foundation for the future of the industry. Industry leaders of other countries were also investing heavily in R&D. In 2004, *Solid State Technology* reported that South Korea would invest US$830 million into R&D over five years.

Trends in the industry include a push to make chips and transistors smaller, experimentation with new materials such as copper, and the emergence of new consumer goods such as chip cards. Chip cards can be used as debit or credit cards and to place calls at pay phones. This popularity comes from convenience and security. As new applications are developed for chip cards, industry analysts expect numbers and popularity to grow among increasingly technologically savvy consumers.

WORKFORCE

During the late 1990s and early 2000s, the number of firms and employees in the semiconductor industry increased. In 1998 the industry was comprised of 750 firms and 204,610 employees. However, by 2001 the number of firms had risen to 866 and the number of employees was 243,893. By 2003, according to the SIA, there were 226,000 workers in the U.S. industry. According to the SIA' 2006 Annual Report, the industry employed nearly 234,000 people in the United States.

Trade organizations (such as SIA) and alliances have made safety a priority in the semiconductor industry, and as a result, it is among America's safest industries for workers. According to the U.S. Bureau of Labor Statistics, the semiconductor industry had one of the lowest rates of work-related injuries and illnesses in 1999, with only 2.2 cases per 100 full-time employees. By working with the Environmental Protection Agency, manufacturers have reduced the emissions to which workers are exposed, while at the same time taking steps toward protecting the environment.

INDUSTRY LEADERS

INTEL CORPORATION

Intel was ranked as the number one semiconductor manufacturer worldwide in 2006 with sales of US$35, 382 billion. It continued its reign as the world's dominant producer of microprocessor chips and arguably the best known one, too. Dell and Hewlett-Packard were on the company's roster listed among its largest clients together representing 35 percent of sales. As of 2005, Intel reported having 99,900 employees.

Founded in 1968 by Robert N. Noyce, Gordon E. Moore, and Andrew S. Grove, Intel unveiled the first memory integrated circuit (IC) in 1971. The company also pioneered metal oxide semiconductor technology. In the 1970s and early 1980s, Intel was recognized as a major supplier of memory chips for mainframe and minicomputers, and it became the top producer of microcomputer integrated circuits (ICs) in the mid-1980s.

Development of a series of advanced microcomputer chips helped Intel make its mark during the late 1980s and early 1990s. From 1981 onward, Intel processors drove IBM and IBM-compatible PCs. Intel is known for its computer flash-memory chips, microcontrollers, networking products, and videoconferencing systems, but it probably is most closely associated with the processor technology that has so many PCs stamped with "Intel Inside." R&D efforts in this arena culminated in Intel's introduction of the Pentium—and later Pentium II and Pentium III—processors, very high-performance microprocessors that incorporated reduced instruction set computer (RISC) technologies. Intel's sales and profits boomed during the 1990s, as shipments of the new Pentium chips increased. As of the mid-2000s, the majority of PCs contained Intel processors. In 2004, the company reported US$34.2 billion in revenue, an increase of almost 14 percent more than 2003. Revenues were earned largely in the Asia Pacific region, where the company earned $4.4 billion or 46 percent of sales. Remaining revenues were earned in the Americas ($2.04 billion or 21 percent), Europe ($2.2 billion or 24 percent), and in Japan ($853 million or 9 percent). Intel's workforce numbered 85,000 people in 2004.

As smaller firms, such as Cyrix and AMD, increased penetration of the market, Intel's expansion policies became more aggressive. Intel's spending on R&D during 2004 totaled close to $4.8 billion, but with competitors' research and development departments contending for the equivalent of a processor "blue riband" award for high speed, Intel ceased to rely exclusively on the market growth provided by its own outstanding technology and turned to acquisition to strengthen its market presence.

In May 2007, three industry visionaries announced that they had entered into an agreement to create a new semiconductor company. Intel, STMicroelectronics, and Francisco Partners were planning to utilize key assets of companies with combined annual revenue of US$3.6 billion. Targeted focus for the new company was set to be supplying flash memory solutions for a variety of consumer and industrial devices. Those products included cell phones, MP3 players, digital cameras, and computers. The new company will unite the established companies' efforts for key research and development, manufacturing, sales, and marketing. In addition to serving its customers, company goals include accelerating the move to future non-volatile memory technologies.

SAMSUNG ELECTRONICS

South Korea's Samsung Electronics, part of the Samsung Group, was the fastest growing company in the semiconductor top 10 in the early 1990s, due largely to its aggressive manufacture of commodity-like DRAM (dynamic random access memory) chips. It jumped to the number-two position among industry leaders when ranked by semiconductor sales. Supported by the Korean national government, Samsung invested heavily in the development of semiconductor manufacturing technology during the middle and late 1980s. By 1997 Samsung was shipping more than US$6 billion worth of semiconductors. However, because of the softening of the DRAM market, this figure actually was 7 percent less than the previous year's sales. Samsung was the number one manufacturer of DRAM, SRAM (static random access memory), and flash memory worldwide in 2003. That year, total sales reached US$54.3 billion. Fully two-thirds of Samsung's sales were from exports. 2004 semiconductor sales for Samsung Electronics were $15.8 billion, compared to $10.4 billion in 2003. By 2006, its parent company sales and net income, for which Samsung Electronics was a major contributor, were US$63.4 billion snf US$8.5 billion respectively. Samsung Electronics was a recognized leading producer of digital TVs, memory chips, cell phones, and TFT-LCDs.

TEXAS INSTRUMENTS

Texas Instruments (TI) is among the world's oldest and largest manufacturers of semiconductors. In 2000, semiconductors represented fully 90 percent of its sales, or $10.9 billion in 2004 and 4.5 percent of the global market. With total revenues of US$12.6 billion in 2004, the company achieved a 31 percent increase in excess of 2003 levels. By 2006, sales were nearly US$14.3 billion. Analog chips accounted for about 40 percent of the company's ales in 2006. TI easily earned its ranking as the world's leading supplier of analog chips. In spite of its dominance, TI Chief Executive Richard Templeton discussed plans with *BusinessWeek* for increasing analog chip market share. Of TI's total sales, 75 percent originate outside the United States. TI produces a variety of other technological products, too. The world leader in digital signal processors (DSPs), more than 50 percent of wireless phones worldwide contain Texas Instruments DSPs. These digital signal processors, which convert sound and light into digital signals, are used in a variety of programmable products, such as VCRs. Activity in this arena and explorations into digital light processor (DLP) technology did not supplant TI's earlier focus on chip production. The memory chip market, rendered unstable by heavy chip production on the part of Pacific Rim corporations, still was attractive to TI, which protected itself through a variety of joint ventures that relied on business partners to remarket TI licensed technology.

INFINEON TECHNOLOGIES AG

Infineon Technologies AG, based in Germany, was Europe's top chip maker and moved up to fourth place in 2004 with semiconductor sales of US$9.18 billion and 4 percent of the global market. The company's revenues increased nearly 25 percent from 2003, the largest portion of which were derived from memory chips. In 2006, Infineon had sales of US$7.9 billion with approximately 42,000 employees.

RENESAS TECHNOLOGY CORP.

Renasas Technology is an industry leader based in Toyko. It achieved consolidated revenue of 983 billion JPY for fiscal year 2006 ending in March 2007. Renasas has a global network of manufacturing, design and sales operations in approximately 20 countries with about 26,500 employees worldwide. The company was formed by a merger of Hitachi and Mitsubishi's non-DRAM chip assets into a new entity, which ranks as one of the world's top chip makers.

STMICROELECTRONICS

STMicroelectronics is the Switzerland-based global leader in developing and delivering semiconductor solutions across a spectrum of microelectronics applications. It provides a distinctive compination of silicon and system expertise, manufacturing strength, Intellectual Property portfolio and strategic partners placing the company at the forefront of System-on-Chip technology and its products help enable convergence markets. In 2006, STMicroelectronics' net revenues were US$9.85 billion with net earnings of US$782 million.

STMicroelectronics launched a strategy to focus on electronics companies in Japan and China in order to grow the proportion of revenues derived from domestic manufacturers in both countries. In 2006, the company's Japanese revenues grew by 31 percent. In 2007, STMicroelectronics ranked third in the Chinese semniconductor market (excluding microprocessors and D-Ram memory) with about 40 percent of sales coming from local manufacturers. STMicroelectronics planned to operate plants in five cities across China. By May 2007, the company employed 4,000 people in Greater China.

TOSHIBA

Holding 3.9 percent of global market, Toshiba also manufactured a variety of other products. From computers, cell phones, and X-ray machines to elevators, electric tubes, and railway transportation systems, the company's diverse offerings crossed industry lines. In 2004, Toshiba reported US$52.8 billion in revenues, a 12 percent increase over 2003. $8.5 billion was attributed to semiconductor sales. The company employed 166,000 people.

NEC CORPORATION

NEC dropped to ninth place, with 2.9 percent of the world semiconductor market in 2005. The company stayed in the top ten and remained a leader in the manufacture of computers, peripheral equipment, and network solutions. Founded in 1899, NEC gained an international presence during the early 2000s, with 20 percent of its sales coming from outside Japan in 2001. With increased global use of all aspects of technology, NEC exported a large variety of computers. In the 1980s NEC partnered with Honeywell Information Systems and Groupe Bull of France to enhance penetration of the mainframe market. By 1997, attention was back on the desktop, and the company held a 49 percent stake in Packard Bell NEC Inc., the third largest U.S. PC manufacturer. Smaller, more limited applications of high technology and, in particular, semiconductor use, were not overlooked. Worldwide, NEC products included any number of electronic products, from cellular phones to highly sophisticated digital switching systems. During the 1980s NEC achieved respected status in the semiconductor industry by efficiently producing vast quantities of DRAM chips, a pursuit that in the 1990s became far less valuable with the entry of Samsung and other companies into the memory chip race. NEC's strong ASIC and microprocessor sales have helped insulate it from the steep declines in DRAM prices. In 2007, the company stated it had 25 subsidiaries worldwide including NEC Electronics America and NEC Electronics (Europe) GmbH.

In May 2007, NEC Electronics announced the availability of system LSI chips. Those chips were capable of enabling reception of global TV broadcasts on personal computers. TV broadcasts in America, Europe, and Japan were rapidly migrating from analog to digital formats. The new chips expanded previously existing feature sets. They allowed PC OEMs to provide many flexible, state-of-the-art TV tuner solutions to customers, regardless of format.

PHILIPS SEMICONDUCTORS

Philips Semiconductors, based in the Netherlands, was another of the world's largest suppliers of semiconductors. The company had 2.5 percent of the world market and $5.69 billion in semiconductor revenue in 2004. As reported on the company's Web site, Philips Semiconductors ran 20 manufacturing facilities and delivered products to clients in 60 countries. Manufacturing facilities were located in the United States, the Asia/Pacific, and Europe. More than 35,000 people were employed by Philips in 2005.

FOUNDRIES

During the mid-2000s, foundries thrived as outsourcing of chip production increased. According to market research company IC Insights, revenues for semiconductor foundries grew 45 percent to $16.7 billion in 2004. New to the list of top semiconductor companies as rated by *Electronic Business* was TSMC, a semiconductor foundry based in Taiwan. TSMC was the leading foundry with 2005 revenues of $8.2 billion. Other strong foundries included UMC of Taiwan and SMIC of China. Foundries showed strong growth from 2001 and remained strong through 2005.

MAJOR COUNTRIES IN THE INDUSTRY

As recently as 1990, the semiconductor industry consisted of just two countries: the United States and Japan. By the end of the century, the European market had grown to the point that companies from two European nations occupied positions in the top 10 of worldwide semiconductor producers. As of the mid-2000s, Japan had widened its lead as leader of the semiconductor capital equipment market, with a value of $8.28 billion, as reported in *Solid State Technology* in May 2004. But Taiwan was closing in on the global market, valued at $7.76 billion, followed by North America with $5.81 billion, Korea with $4.61 billion, Europe with $3.44 billion, and China with $2.68 billion. The rest of the world accounted for $4.49 billion of the global market valued at $37.08 billion. Korea and China saw the largest growth in the industry, increasing market share by 45 percent and 132 percent respectively from 2003 to 2004.

In the face of industry globalization, the World Semiconductor Council (WSC) was formed in 1996 to enhance mutual understanding, address market access matters, promote cooperative industry activities, and to expand international cooperation in the semiconductor sector, facilitating the healthy growth of the industry into the twenty-first century.

The council was conceived during bilateral semiconductor trade negotiations between the United States and Japan, which together once held a near-exclusive grip on the industry, but the organization's scope was expanded to address the growing globalization of the industry. The WSC included the Semiconductor Industry Association (SIA), the Electronic Industries Association of Japan (EIAJ), the European Electronic Component Manufacturers Association (EECA), the Korea Semiconductor Industry Association (KSIA) and, as of 1998, the Taiwan Semiconductor Industry Association (TSIA).

FURTHER READING

"2001 Worst Year Ever for Chips, Says Research Firm Gartner." *Silicon Valley/San Jose Business Journal,* 21 December 2001.

"Asian Equipment Markets Flex Muscles in 2004." *Solid State Technology,* May 2005.

Beucke, Dan and Arik Hesseldahl. "Taking the Pulse at Texas Instruments; CEO Templeton Discusses the Company's Desire to Capture Even More of the Analog Chip Market and Hints at Future Involvement in Advanced Medical Devices." *Business Week OnLine,* 16 May 2007.

"Consumer Semi Market Set to Double, IDS Predicts." *Electronics News,* 2 May 2005.

Draper, Deborah J., ed. *Business Rankings Annual.* Detroit: Thomson Gale, 2004.

"Foundries Thrive as More Chips Are Outsourced." *Purchasing,* 19 May 2005. Available from http://www.purchasing.com.

Harris InfoSource International. *Semiconductor,* 13 January 2001. Available from http://www.harrisinfo.com.

"Hoover's Company Capsules." 2007. Available from http://www.hoovers.com.

Intel. "Intel, STMicroelectronics and Francisco Partners Establish a New Leader in Flash Memory." 22 May 2007. Available from http://www.intel.com.

Lazich, Robert S., ed. *Market Share Reporter.* Detroit: Thomson Gale, 2004.

Lerner, Ivan. "Consumers Driving Semiconductors." *CMR,* 18-24 April 2005.

"Low-Cost Semiconductors." *R & D,* May 2004.

"Memory Chip Makers Posted Double-Digit Growth in '04." *Purchasing,* 19 May 2005.

Mello, Adrian. "The Top Semiconductor Companies." *Electronic Business,* May 2005.

NEC Electronics. "NEC Electronics Announces System LSI Chips That Enable Reception of Global Television Broadcasts on Personal Computers." 21 May 2007. Available from http://www.necel.com.

"New Spin on Electronic Devices." *Nanoparticle News,* June 2004.

Ohr, Stephan and Brian Fuller. "As It Seeks to Widen Margins CEO Says Strong Growth of 31 Percent in 2004 Laid to Analog, DSP." *Electronic Engineering Times,* 16 May 2005.

Samsung. "IBM, Chartered, Samsung, Infineon and Freescale Expand Technology Agreements." 23 May 2007. Available from http://www.samsung.com.

"Semi-Conductors and Related Devices in China, France, Germany, Japan, UK, US." *Euromonitor,* August 2004. Available from http://www.majormarketprofiles.com.

Semiconductor Industry Association. *Annual Report.* 2006. Available from http://www.sia-online.org.

———. *Industry Facts and Figures.* 2004. Available from http://www.sia-online.org.

"Semiconductor Market Forecast." *World Semiconductor Trade Statistics,* 28 October 2003.

"South Korea Plans to Invest Approximately $830 Million Over the Next Five Years in Semiconductor Research and Development." *Solid State Technology,* February 2004.

Starnes, Tom. "Rich Processor Variety Adds Up to 18 Percent Growth in 2004." *Electronic Design,* 12 January 2004.

Taylor, Paul. "STMicro Looks to Japan, China for Growth." *The Financial Times,* 14 May 2007.

"The Tech Dragon Stumbles; China's Upstarts Are Finding Life in the Big Leagues Tougher Than They Reckoned." *Business Week,* 14 May 2007.

U.S. Business Reporter. *Industry Report: Semiconductor Industry,* 13 January 2001. Available from http://www.activemedia-guide.com.

World Semiconductor Trade Statistics. *WSTS Semiconductor Market Forecast Autumn 2006,* 31 October 2006. Available from http://www.wsts.org.

SIC 3873

NAICS 334518

WATCHES AND CLOCKS

The global watch and clock industry comprises the manufacture of clocks, watches, watchcases, and clock and watch parts.

INDUSTRY SNAPSHOT

In 2004 the Federation of the Swiss Watch Industry (FHS) estimated the number of timepieces produced worldwide at around 1.2 billion, down slightly from 2003. The world's largest consumers of clock and watch materials were Hong Kong, the United States, Japan, Switzerland, and China. These countries, as reported by the FHS, accounted for more than 70 percent of global trade.

World clock production has steadily decreased since 1997, when an estimated 440 million units were produced, according to figures published by JCWA. However, the market was beginning to pick back up in the mid-2000s, albeit slowly, due to the changed purpose and use of household clocks. By 2003, production was at 360 million units, a 13 percent increase over 2002 totals. According to *HFN,* because most households have clocks in many locations, such as the microwave and VCR, clockmakers were challenged to create new demand for clocks as decorative items, including such technologies as sound chips.

ORGANIZATION AND STRUCTURE

The international watch industry produces three major types of watches: quartz analog, digital, and mechanical. Quartz analog watches represent the world's leading segment in the industry, accounting for the majority of the watches produced throughout the world. In the 1980s Switzerland's Swatch watch helped spark worldwide interest in inexpensive fashion quartz analog watches at a time when digital and mechanical movement watches overshadowed them. Consequently, the quartz analog watch became the industry leader even in the most prosperous developed countries, and producers of high-end mechanical watches such as Rolex started offering quartz analog watches.

Digital watches, which dramatically changed the dynamics of the watch industry in the 1970s, remained popular in the mid- to late 1990s but trailed quartz analog watches considerably in terms of sales. This market segment remained a steady one in the 1980s, registering modest annual upturns in production. However, because of the surge in production of, and demand for, quartz analog models, the digital watch annual market share dropped from about 50 percent in 1982 to less than 25 percent in the mid-1990s.

Production of mechanical-movement watches rebounded in the mid-1990s, after suffering declines because of competition from quartz and digital watches. While annual unit production has hovered around 100-135 million since the 1980s—when digital and quartz analog models swiped significant market share—mechanical-movement watches experienced renewed growth in the latter half of the 1990s. Swiss companies, long the industry leaders in the production of expensive watches, exported about 25.1 million watches in 2004 worth US$7.9 billion. A Federation of the Swiss Watch Industry report argued that the surge in exports indicated the recovery of the timepiece once thought obsolete. Industry analysts expect the high-end watch market will remain a viable one in the future.

BACKGROUND AND DEVELOPMENT

The clock first emerged as a marketable product in the sixteenth century, though weight-driven clocks had already been in existence for several centuries. In the sixteenth century, however, the popularity of timepieces increased with the introduction of watches in Germany and France. Primarily regarded as ornamental jewelry at the time, watches slowly took on greater functional importance.

Clock manufacturers dominated the industry for years, however. Though most models were expensive, heavy, and delicate, they were also regarded as significant investments and important family heirlooms. The Industrial Revolution spurred the development of less cumbersome clocks and the growth of watch manufacturing. By the latter part of the nineteenth century, pocket watches, first produced in quantity by the American Waltham Watch Co., were popular possessions, and Switzerland had become established as a renowned center of watch and clock craftsmanship. The world's leading watch and clock maker in the 1990s was founded during this period as well. In 1881 K. Hattori & Co.—the company that eventually became Seiko Corporation—was established in Tokyo as an importer of clocks. By the early 1900s, the company was manufacturing wall and table clocks, pocket watches, and alarm clocks.

In 1918 the Shokosha Watch Research Laboratory, the precursor to Citizen Watch Co., was established in Japan. The organization manufactured its first pocket watch six years later and gradually emerged as one of Seiko's chief competitors. These two companies, as well as a few other Japanese manufacturers, battled for control of the Asian market. With the onset of World War II, however, they made no inroads into other markets until well after the conclusion of the war.

Industry giant Timex Enterprises, Inc., was founded in the United States in 1941 by two Norwegian refugees, who had fled their own country after the German invasion in 1940. They purchased the nearly bankrupt Waterbury Clock Co. in Connecticut and instituted a highly mechanized assembly process. The Timex watch became known as a dependable product, and the company quickly expanded despite its negligible presence in jewelry stores. Instead, Timex sold their watches through consumer outlets such as drugstores; by the 1960s the company had established a distribution network of 250,000 outlets and posted sales over US$70 million.

By the late 1960s Timex was dominant in the U.S. market, though international competitors such as Seiko and Citizen sought to expand their international sales. Switzerland, however, continued to reign as the world's watch production leader based on its control of the luxury watch market. The Soviet Union had become a significant presence in the industry as well via exports of low-cost, low-quality products to developing countries.

In 1967 the electronic quartz wristwatch was announced by the Swiss Horological Electronic Center; a number of Swiss firms had pooled together millions of dollars in research money to develop the watch. Yet it was Seiko—still known at the time as K. Hattori—that marketed the first quartz wall clock and watch. Japanese watch manufacturers proved more proficient at adapting to the popularity of the quartz watches and the new digital technology that swept through the industry in the 1970s. Both Seiko and Citizen tallied huge gains in the vital U.S. market during this period, and Japan slipped past Switzerland as the industry leader in unit production. Embattled Swiss manufacturers and U.S. companies such as Timex belatedly turned their attention to the new technologies that were proving so profitable for their competitors in Japan and Hong Kong.

Inexpensive brands proliferated around the world in the 1980s, and Japan became entrenched as the world's leading manufacturer of watches. By 1989 worldwide watch production reached approximately 690 million units; industry leader Seiko Corporation produced about 109 million of those units itself, in addition to another 32 million clocks.

In the mid- to late 1990s, mid-grade and high-end clock and watch sales benefited from rising disposable incomes in countries such as Japan, the United States, Germany, Italy, France, and the United Kingdom. On the other hand, low-price clocks and watches have benefited from income growth around the world and from fashion trends. These trends spurred new growth because of increased interest in watches that complement clothing, accounting for expanding sales of inexpensive fashionable watches such as those by Swatch. Consumers began buying more than one watch in order to have timepieces to complement both formal and casual attire.

During the late 1990s and the turn of the century, Hong Kong, Japan, and Germany traded places as the leading exporter of finished watches, with France making a surge in 2000, as reported by FHS. In 1998 Hong Kong controlled 9.1 percent of the export market based on value, followed by Japan with 6.5 percent, and Germany with 3.8 percent. In 1999 these three countries shared nearly identical percentages: 4.9 percent for Japan, 4.6 percent for Hong Kong, and 4.5 percent for Germany. In 2000 Germany claimed 5.1 percent with Japan and France sharing 3.3 percent each. Hong Kong's share of the global watch export market fell to 1.8 percent, behind the United Kingdom, which captured 2.5 percent of the export market.

Also in the late 1990s, clock and watchmakers experienced a period of acquisition and consolidation with the rise of multinational conglomerates such as Swatch Group and LVMH. Throughout the mid- to late 1990s and into the twenty-first century, the watch industry remained highly competitive, with manufacturers and retailers launching major television and print campaigns to promote products. Companies such as Swatch Group also began opening chic "mono-brand" stores to showcase popular brands. Consumer demand for luxury watches was especially high in the late 1990s, which benefited many Swiss manufacturers who specialize in that market. Michael Balfour reported in the *Financial Times* that at the Swatch Group alone sales for luxury watches increased 30 percent in 2000.

In 2000 the world produced approximately 1.5 billion finished watches and movements worth close to US$12 billion, according to figures published by the Federation of the Swiss Watch Industry (FHS). The Japan Clock and Watch Association (JCWA) estimated that nearly 1.3 billion watches were produced worldwide in 2000. JCWA breaks down world watch production by type as follows: 908 million analog quartz watches (71 percent), 340 million digital quartz watches (27 percent), and 22 million mechanical watches (2 percent).

Of the total watch and components produced, finished watches accounted for 700 million units in 2000, according to FHS. The vast majority of finished watches, approximately 80 percent, were produced in China or Hong Kong. However, Switzerland, the leader in high-end luxury watches, led the industry based on sales, controlling over half the market with revenues of approximately US$6.3 billion.

CURRENT CONDITIONS

In Japan, which the JCWA estimated produced more than half the world's watches and movements in 2000, consumers showed a strong interest in expensive foreign watches and cell phones. In a March 2001 article in *Jewelers' Circular Keystone*, William George Shuster explained that many young Japanese consumers prefer small cell phones—with their date/time display functions—over traditional wristwatches. "A few Japanese watchmakers," Shuster wrote, "worry that something similar could develop in Europe or the United States (which has 97 million cell phone users vs. Japan's 50 million), though most still think the markets are too dissimilar for that to happen." Nevertheless, watches produced at the turn of the twenty-first century offered more high-tech features, such as built-in pagers and computer-download capabilities. Another emerging trend was the development of new marketing strategies in response to the increased popularity of Internet retailing, particularly online auctions.

The luxury watch market segment, focused on units priced at US$10,000 or more, continued to grow into the mid-2000s. As *Brandweek* observed, this largely was because the estimated US$65 billion luxury goods market is relatively recession-proof. Tom Kuczynski reported in *National Jeweler* that fine watch sales in the United States generated about $3.8 billion in retail sales in 2004. While revenues were up, however, dollars earned were attributed to the number of consumers purchasing pricier merchandise. The number of watches sold fell by 4 percent.

In 2004 the Swiss watch industry produced 25.1 million units with a value of 10.2 billion Swiss francs (almost $US 8 billion). Exports of mechanical watches rose 12.7 percent in 2004, compared to .7 percent for electronic watches. Most of the Swiss market's products were exported, with more than 99 percent going to Asia and Oceania, Europe, and the Americas. The United States was the largest consumer, with 16.9 percent of Swiss exports valued at 1.87 billion Swiss francs (US$1.45 billion). Hong Kong was the fastest growing market for Swiss exports, with a 2004 increase of 15.6 percent.

RESEARCH AND TECHNOLOGY

The watch and clock industry has been transformed several times during its history by technological advances. Timepieces that operated using electricity, quartz crystal vibrations, and atomic or molecular oscillations (atomic clock) all changed the manner of production of clocks and watches to some degree. Digital technology dramatically altered the fortunes of many watch manufacturers during the 1970s and 1980s.

As the watch manufacturing industry entered the twenty-first century, significant research advances continued to have an impact. Timex's Indiglo brand, which features an electroluminescent light powered by the watch's battery, proved vital to the company's efforts to recover from market losses of past years. In 1993 the Indiglo brand accounted for 40 percent of all units sold by the company. Timex believed that illumination would become a standard feature of watches just like water resistance, though some of Timex's competitors dispute this contention.

Proposals for more radical innovations, including watches with computing or communications functions, pagers, small electronic personal organizers, and similar devices, gained popularity in the late 1990s. However, industry observers cautioned that in the mid-1990s prototype watches equipped with such communication capabilities were cumbersome units that couldn't be worn comfortably. Such devices, in fact, may interest companies outside the watch industry more than they appeal to traditional watch companies. Telecommunications giants such as AT&T were active participants in this area of research in the mid-1990s.

In the late 1990s, companies also rolled out voice-controlled clocks and watches, such as Voice Clock, that allow users to change the time and activate and deactivate the alarm simply by uttering a command. Watchmakers also experimented with radio-controlled watches that could be programmed via radio signals to change when entering different time zones.

During the 2000s, innovations included "eco-drive" watches, which ran by converting light into electrical energy using a rechargeable battery. Innovations in clocks included "wave clocks" or atomic clocks, which adjusted anywhere in a given geographical area based on electric waves that set the time automatically.

INDUSTRY LEADERS

Citizen Watch Co., Ltd. Japan's Citizen Watch Co. was the world's leading watch and clock manufacturer in 2003. While Citizen has branched out into several manufacturing areas over the years, most notably electronics, it remains primarily known for its watch business. Founded in 1918 and incorporated in 1930, the company sold its products only in

Asia prior to World War II. It was battered by the economic devastation in postwar Japan but eventually returned to its former stature. By the late 1950s, it had resumed exporting watches to China, and in 1960 the company entered the American market, distributing watches manufactured by another firm, Bulova. By 1965 Citizen and K. Hattori & Co. (later known as Seiko) together accounted for approximately 80 percent of total watch production in Japan. Citizen's success at the time was due in part to its knack for developing new products, such as shock-resistant and water-resistant watches.

In 1968 Citizen opened its first international subsidiary—Citizen de Mexico. During the 1970s Citizen diversified into several other business areas, though the watch-manufacturing arena remained its primary concern. Convinced that it would be unable to overtake K. Hattori as Japan's leading watch producer without a significant American product, Citizen introduced its own watches in the mid-1970s. Both its quartz analog and digital product lines proved tremendously successful, and Citizen posted significant increases in market share in the late 1970s. During the 1980s and 1990s, the international watch industry grew increasingly crowded, but Citizen was able to maintain a sizable presence. Citizen was a leader in developing light-powered wristwatches and in 1995 introduced the Eco-Drive line that uses solar cell and thermal power technologies. In 1999 Citizen began producing Aspec watches made of a highly durable stainless steel and titanium composite. Citizen also uses the Internet to allow consumers to design their own watches and reported approximately 40,000 orders were generated through this channel in the late 1990s and early 2000s.

In fiscal 2004, Citizen posted annual sales of US$3.5 billion, a 27.6 percent increase over 2003. Watches and clocks accounted for almost 34 percent of sales in 2004. Sales of wristwatches and clocks showed a 4.4 percent decline from 2003. Sales did increase in one market segment, however, that of radio-controlled watches, both in Japan and overseas. Citizen, a component of the Nikkei 25 Stock Average, employed approximately 17,987 people as of 2004, with watch, movement, and clock production concentrated in Japan. Additional production facilities operate in Hong Kong, China, and Korea, with some assembly work done in Germany.

The Swatch Group Ltd. The Swatch Group (formerly Société Suisse de Microélectronique & d'Horlogerie, SMH) was the world's second leading producer of watches in 2003. The Swatch Group's roots date back to two major Swiss watchmakers of the 1930s: Allgemeine Schweizerische Uhrenindustrie AG (ASUAG) and Société Suisse pour l'Industrie Horlogère SA (SSIH). Fierce competition from Japanese watchmakers in the 1970s and early 1980s nearly forced both ASUAG and SSIH out of business. Hayek Engineering, led by Nicolas G. Hayek, conducted a study and recommended the merger of ASUAG and SSIH and the creation of a new low-cost, technologically advanced watch to target a youthful, brand-conscious market. In 1983 ASUAG and SSIH merged, creating SMH, with Hayek as CEO.

In 1998 SMH changed its name to the Swatch Group to reflect the strength of its Swatch brand. Following the Swiss watch industry trend of the late 1990s of acquisitions and consolidations forming large watch conglomerates, Swatch is composed of the following brands representing the full range of price and market segments: Blancpain, Endura, FlikFlak, Lanco, Longines, Omega, Rado, and Swatch, among others. The company's 2004 revenues were US$3.5 billion, a 13.6 percent growth over 2003. The watch division accounts for about 70 percent of the Swatch Group's sales.

SMH captured a significant segment of the Asian market in the 1980s. Armed with the wildly popular Swatch brand—a thin plastic watch comprised of about only 50 parts—SMH dramatically increased its production capacity in the early 1990s and maintained this level throughout the decade. In 1997 SMH controlled 22 to 25 percent of the global market, according to the company's own figures.

Ultrathin watches featuring accurate timekeeping, innovative technology, and a sense of youthful individualism have been a hallmark of the Swatch brand. In 1979 a subsidiary of ASUAG launched the Kaliber 999, a gold watch just 0.98mm high, considerably thinner than the latest Japanese model that stood 2.5mm high. The Kaliber 99 eventually led to the development of the 3.9mm-high plastic Swatch watch, which could be easily mass-produced and offered a variety of colors. Throughout the remainder of the 1980s the marketing of the Swatch watch became increasingly personalized, as unisex watches became gender-specific, and traditional model number names were replaced by phrases such as "Don't be too late" and "Black Magic."

In 1991 Swatch integrated a pager into the Swatch the Beep wristwatch. In 1994 SMH introduced the Swatch Irony line of shockproof, water-resistant, and thicker watches made of steel and later of aluminum. The Swatch Access, which provides access to ski resorts around the world using microchip technology and a small antenna, debuted in 1995. Also in 1995, the light-powered Swatch Solar first appeared. Other popular models include the Swatch Chrono and the Swatch Beat, which feature Internet timekeeping. The Swatch Group has been named the official timekeeper for the Olympics through 2010.

Employing nearly 21,000 employees worldwide, Swatch is headquartered in Switzerland with plants in Europe, the United States, the Virgin Islands, and Asia Pacific. Swatch also operates about 500 retail outlets. In addition to finished watches, Swatch produces watch movements and components, as well as advanced technology components for the telecommunications, electronic, and automotive industries.

Seiko Corporation. The world's leading producer of watches and clocks in the mid-1990s, Seiko, controlled by the Hattori family of Japan, fell behind the Swatch Group in the late 1990s. Watch brands under the Seiko umbrella include Pulsar, Lorus, Lassale, Alba, and Seiko. Founded in 1881, the company first produced wall clocks, the most popular timepiece of the period. In 1893 the company's manufacturing plant was moved to Taihei-cho, Tokyo. In the early 1900s, the company initiated its first export venture while also introducing its first wristwatch models.

In 1917 K. Hattori & Co., Ltd., became a public company. An earthquake destroyed its manufacturing facility in

1923, but the company persevered and eventually regained its former stature. By 1936 K. Hattori marketed 2.06 million of Japan's total clock and watch production of 3.54 million units. World War II interrupted the business, as the company's facilities were converted to produce military items. During the mid-1950s, however, the company resumed its position as a leader in the Japanese market. It also turned its attention to the lucrative U.S. market for the first time. In the late 1960s, K. Hattori offered the world's first quartz watch and quartz wall clock, and in 1973 it unveiled a digital watch with a liquid-crystal display. Over the next several years, the firm diversified, marketing a variety of new products under new brand names. The company name was changed to Seiko Corporation in 1990.

In the 1990s Seiko manufactured a wide array of products, including batteries, personal computers, ophthalmic frames and lenses, jewelry, contact lenses, semiconductors, and printers. Watch sales, however, continued to lead its product line, accounting for 57 percent of Seiko's sales. The company sold its goods in more than 100 countries in the late 1990s and held approximately 30 percent of the medium- and high-quality watch market in the United States.

In 2001 Seiko Corp. became a holding company, and Seiko's watch business was spun off as a wholly owned subsidiary, Seiko Watch Corp. Seiko Watch handles design and marketing, and other Seiko subsidiaries, Seiko Epson Corp. and Seiko Instruments, Inc., are responsible for watch and movements production. Seiko Corp.'s sales for fiscal years 2005 were US$1.9 billion, a loss of 3.1 percent over 2004. Approximately 70 percent of sales come from watches and clocks. Tsutomu Mitome, former president and CEO of Seiko Corp. of America, was named the president of Seiko Watch.

Timex Enterprises, Inc. Founded in 1854, Timex is the biggest watch manufacturer in the United States. Timex, which had long been known as a manufacturer that provided reliable, if unexciting, watch models at affordable prices, appeared to have recovered in the early 1990s from earlier marketing miscalculations. Slow to react to new digital technology in the 1970s, Timex saw its share of the U.S. consumer market drop. This deterioration was exacerbated by the drop in digital watch prices during the 1970s. By 1976 the price of a digital model was competitive with that of mechanical models—Timex's primary product. Timex continued to lose market share. Front-office turmoil and questionable marketing strategies also hurt the company. In the 1980s and 1990s, however, Timex turned to new brands and designs in an effort to shake its staid image. Its popular Ironman Triathlon digital sports watch, introduced in 1986, quickly became a bestseller. In 1992 Timex debuted the Indiglo night-light watch face, which would appear on more than 75 percent of Timex watches manufactured in the 1990s. In the mid- and late 1990s, Timex introduced high-tech watches that featured computer-download and pager technology, such as the Beepwear wrist pager.

Timex estimates it controls about a third of the U.S. watch market, according to William George Shuster of *Jewelers' Circular Keystone*. Annual sales for the privately owned Timex, which employs 7,500 people, were estimated at US$800 million in 2003. Timex, the only U.S. watchmaker with production facilities in the United States, announced in June of 2001 the closing of its last domestic plant in Little Rock, Arkansas.

MAJOR COUNTRIES IN THE INDUSTRY

Switzerland. After years of solid growth in the mid 1980s and early 1990s, the Swiss watch industry experienced a brief stagnant period in the mid-1990s. However, the late 1990s and early twenty-first century were a period of tremendous success for the Swiss watch industry. Switzerland produced 25.1 million finished watches valued at about US$7.9 billion in 2004, an increase of 2.1 percent over 2003. This was the first year of growth in the number of units sold in ten years, as reported by the FHS. Growth of the Swiss watch industry had been based on increased value, not production volume. The number of finished watches produced has steadily dropped since 1998, going from about 34 million in 1998 to 31 million in 2000, with a further reduction in volume through the early 2000s. In its 2000 annual report, the FHS explained that the record performance of 2000 was due to "sustained demand in major markets, a weak Swiss franc against the dollar, and the 'millennium' effect, difficult to quantify but real none the less."

Switzerland, which exports about 95 percent of its watch output, dominates the world in exports of finished watches and has steadily increased its share into the twenty-first century. In 1998 Swiss manufacturers accounted for 74 percent of value of exports of finished watches, which increased to 80 percent in 1999 and 84 percent in 2000, according to FHS. In 2000 Swiss exports exceeded 10 billion Swiss francs for the first time (about US$6 billion), and by 2004 the export market was up to 11.11 billion Swiss francs (about US$8.63 billion). Switzerland exported approximately 34 percent of its watches to Europe in 2004. Asia and Oceania accounted for 44 percent of Swiss exports, North and South America combined accounted for 21 percent, and Africa for 1 percent.

Historically regarded as the world's leading producer of luxury watches and clocks, the high quality of Swiss products enabled Swiss watchmakers to charge premium prices. As a result, the average 2000 export price of a Swiss watch was US$187, which the FHS estimated to be more than twice the average export price of watches from other countries. The quartz analog watch accounted for the largest segment of Swiss production, both in terms of volume and value in 1997 through 2000, as reported by the FHS. During this same time period, the total annual value of complicated mechanical watches—often prized as collector's pieces—accounted for an average of 47 percent of total Swiss production, while worldwide production volume hovered at a mere 8 to 9 percent. Quartz digital watches have consistently made up a minor portion of overall Swiss watch production. 25.9 million total units were produced in 2003, of which 22.8 million were quartz analog.

China. China, including Hong Kong, is the most important player in the industry based on volume. With the return of Hong Kong to Chinese rule in 1997, China became the global watch powerhouse, producing about 80 percent of the world's finished watches. China also exports a large portion of its output as the world's largest unit exporter. Dependent on quartz analog models, China shipped more than a quarter of its total watch and clock exports to the United States. In addition, China constitutes the largest import market for clocks and watches. Imports to Hong Kong alone were valued at US$4.6 billion in 2004, and China's imports were valued at US$1.1 billion.

Writing in *American Time*, Norma Buchanan reported that Hong Kong's 460 watch companies exported a total of US$5.6 billion in watches and clocks in 2000. Figures for the first half of 2001 showed exports down 4 percent, with exports to the United States—Hong Kong's leading export destination—down 7 percent, mainly due to the U.S. economic slowdown. In 2004, Hong Kong's watch exports were back on the rise, increasing 9 percent to $5.9 billion. China's export market was valued at $2.1 billion. Roughly 25 percent of Hong Kong's exports go to the United States.

Japan. Japan ranked third in the industry in terms of clock and watch exports. Led by Citizen and Seiko, Japan produced an estimated 731 million finished watches and movements in 2000, valued at about US$1.9 billion (216.7 billion yen), according to the Japanese Clock and Watch Association (JCWA). This total, which is almost entirely exported, represented approximately 58 percent of total world output of finished watches and movements, as estimated by JCWA. Total Japanese exports for 2004 were valued at US$1 billion, down 4 percent from 2003. Asia and North America represented the largest export destinations by volume.

In *Jewelers' Circular Keystone*, William George Shuster reported that Japan's leading watchmakers saw sales and profits in their watches and clocks divisions decrease in the late 1990s. This occurred as a surplus of watches, and especially movements, resulting from several years of sustained high production volumes worldwide, increased competition from Swiss and Far East producers and as Japan's recession decreased regional sales.

Germany. Germany ranks among the world's largest producers, importers, and exporters. Though Germany led the world in clock production in the early 1990s, China and other countries with low-cost labor surpassed it by the mid-1990s. Michael Balfour of the *Financial Times* reported that sales of German watches, clocks, and clock movements amounted to approximately US$265 million in 2000. Several prominent German watchmakers were acquired by the watch and luxury goods conglomerates. Most notably, the Richemont Group acquired A. Lange & Sohne, and the Swatch Group acquired Glashutter Uhrenbetrieb. Another leading German brand, Junghans, marked its 140th year of business in 2001.

FURTHER READING

Balfour, Michael. "Expansion into the Global Marketplace is the Watchword: Germany." *Financial Times,* 24 March 2001.

Bernard, Sharyn. "A Hands-On Decision." *HFN,* 16 February 2004.

———. "The Good Times Roll on in the Luxury Sector: In Spite of Continuing Brand Consolidation and the Declining Numbers of Leading Watch Companies, Family-Controlled Groups Are Flourishing." *Financial Times,* 25 March 2000.

Buchanan, Norma. "The Elimination Game: Even Before the Calamity of Sept. 11 Put the U.S. in an Economic Tailspin, Many Hong Kong Watch Companies Were Duking it Out in a Fight to Survive." *American Time,* December 2001.

Citizen Watch Co. *Overview of the Year Ended March 31, 2005,* 2005. Available from http://www.citizen.co.jp.

Federation of the Swiss Watch Industry. *Swiss Watch and Microtechnology Industry: A Profile,* 5 July 2000. Available from http://www.fhs.ch.

———. *Swiss Watchmaking Exports January-June 2001: Five Billion in Six Months,* 6 August 2001. Available from http://www.fhs.ch.

———. *The Swiss Watch Industry Today,* 5 July 2004. Available from http://www.fhs.ch.

———. *The Swiss and World Watchmaking Industry in 2004.* 2005. Available from http://www.fhs.ch.

Green, Barbara. "Swiss Watch Exports Fall, but Less Than Expected." *National Jeweler,* 1 May 2004.

"Hoover's Company Capsules." 2004. Available from http://www.hoovers.com.

Japan Clock and Watch Association. *The Japanese Watch and Clock Industry in 2000: An Outlook on its Global Operation,* 2000. Available from http://www.jcwa.or.jp.

———. *The Japanese Watch and Clock Industry in 2003: An Outlook on its Global Operation,* 2003. Available from http://www.jcwa.or.jp.

Japan External Trade Organization. "Timepieces." *Marketing Guidebook for Major Imported Products,* 2000. Available from http://www.jetro.go.jp.

Karimzadeh, Marc. "Focusing on Best Facets." *WWD,* 3 December 2001.

Lazich, Robert S., ed. *Market Share Reporter.* Detroit: Thomson Gale, 2004.

Murphy, Robert. "Swiss Watch Sales See Significant Gains." *WWD,* 22 March 2004.

O'Loughlin, Sandra. "Good Timing." *Brandweek,* 8 September 2003.

Shaw, Kerry. "LVMH Sales Dropped 5% in October." *New York Times on the Web,* 12 November 2001. Available from http://www.nytimes.com.

———. "SCA's Mitome Will Head New Seiko Watch Corp." *Jewelers' Circular Keystone.* 23 March 2001.

———. "Swatch Group's Profits Fall 9.8%, Despite Rise in Sales, Earnings." *Jewelers' Circular Keystone.* 1 November 2001.

———. "Swiss Watch Exports Down 4.4 Percent in 2003." *Jewelers' Circular Keystone.* April 2004.

———. "Timex Ends 56 Years of Watchmaking in the U.S." *Jewelers' Circular Keystone,* 22 June 2001.

———. "'Value' and 'Style': The New Watchwords of Japan's Watchmakers." *Jewelers' Circular Keystone,* 1 March 2001.

ENTERTAINMENT AND RECREATION

SIC 7996

NAICS 713110

AMUSEMENT PARKS

Amusement parks operate a variety of entertainment attractions on one premises. Popular features include mechanical rides, electronic and conventional games, stage shows, refreshment stands, and picnic grounds. The industry includes such venues as theme parks, water parks, kiddie parks, and similar recreational facilities.

INDUSTRY SNAPSHOT

Worldwide, attendance at theme parks was escalating, bringing worldwide revenues to more than US$20 billion, with a whopping 25 percent growth projected into 2008. A new Disney theme park was scheduled to open in Hong Kong in September 2005, and most parks continued to try to outdo each other with the development of new rides that technology was permitting to be higher and faster. U.S. theme parks boasted revenues of approximately US$10.8 billion for 2004, with an estimated 328 million visitors in attendance, according to the International Association of Amusement Parks & Attractions (IAAPA).

This growth was despite concerns in 2003—affecting the very dynamics of the amusement industry—about the U.S.-led war with Iraq and potential terrorist attacks. According to a 2002 *USA Today* poll, 10 percent of Americans rated amusement parks and sporting events as the most likely target for a terrorist attack, behind nuclear plants (14 percent), all places (15 percent), and large city downtowns (19 percent). By comparison, Americans were less concerned about terrorist attacks at airports (7 percent), reservoirs (7 percent), national monuments (6 percent), military installations (5 percent), and bridges/tunnels (5 percent).

In 2004, 328 million people around the world visited amusement parks. According to PricewaterhouseCoopers (PWC), visitors spent approximately US$20 billion and that amount was expected to grow to US$24.7 billion by 2008. International Association of Amusement Parks and Attractions Vice President of Communication Services Beth Robertson expected the amount to be even more because 100 new attractions opened or had been announced in 2005. Robertson acknowledged, however, that the energy crisis and currency rates would have an impact on actual results.

PWC also stated, as fewer people traveled from afar to visit so-called destination theme parks, such venues attempted to attract more local and regional visitors. This trend had a negative impact on per capita spending. Another trend saw local and regional parks trying to attract more overnight visitors, which had the effect of increasing per capita spending for those venues. In the mid-2000s, the trend was away from roller coasters toward more family-oriented entertainment and enhanced amenities.

The practice of marketing amusement parks to religious groups was becoming more wide-spread. Great America estimated that 2,700 people came for its Sikh Youth Day. Although there were a lot of event planning details involved in carrying off these types of targeted events, it was believed to be well worth the effort. A national trend was gaining momentum for amusement parks to place on their calendar Praise Days, Muslim Unity Days, Jewish Heritage Days and other faith-linked celebrations. They ranged from times where group members might be invited in while the park handled business as usual or days with special activities planned and food ordered just for them. Some parks considered the practice to be an outgrowth of JoyFest events featuring a lineup of Christian acts.

ORGANIZATION AND STRUCTURE

Amusement parks and their thrill rides were regulated in 42 of 50 states by 2005. However, according to Saferparks, a non-profit organization that follows safety issues in the amusement park industry, in the United States only 37 states were required to report ride-related injuries as of 2004. Of these, about half limited their reporting requirements to deaths or the most serious injuries. Alabama, Arizona, Kansas, Mississippi, Montana, Nevada, North Dakota, South Dakota, Tennessee, Utah, and Wyoming did not regulate amusement park rides at all.

Of the states that do require amusement parks to report safety data, Saferparks reports that this information is often difficult for consumers to obtain. Some states, such as Pennsylvania, prohibit the public from accessing such information. In other states, reporting requirements are not applied across the board. For example, in Florida—home to such leading destinations as Universal Studios and Disney World—those parks employing more than 1,000 people were exempt from reporting requirements, even in the case of accident-related deaths. State investigators were not allowed to inspect rides or investigate accidents at such leading parks.

A CNN article in August of 2001 indicated that between 1993 and 2000 there was a 57 percent rise in the number of injuries reported on fixed-site rides However, the IAAPA argues that amusement park and attraction rides are among the safest recreation available to the public, based on industry data. The U.S. Consumer Product Safety Commission estimated there were about 3,800 injuries involving amusement rides at amusement parks with fixed sites in 2002. Of those, 76 (0.2 percent) were serious enough to require hospitalization, and there are an average of two fatalities per year. Based on both government and independent data, the IAAPA placed the risk of serious injury on a fixed amusement ride at 1 in 20 million, and the risk of being fatally injured at 1 in 760 million.

Amusement park safety was a global concern as of the mid-2000s. By 2004, the European Union (EU) was in the process of developing a uniform amusement safety standard. According to the IAAPA, the EU was pursuing this "so that all rides located throughout its member countries will be built and maintained to the same exacting specifications. Once this process is complete, the code is expected to be designated as a universal standard which can be adopted by any nation in the world." In addition to the EU's efforts, the American Society for Testing and Materials (ASTM) amusement ride standard was expanded during the 2000s, with international input, and made available globally.

BACKGROUND AND DEVELOPMENT

The amusement park industry's roots date to medieval Europe. In approximately 1133 A.D., the monk Rahere, a former jester in the court of Henry I, held the first trade fair beginning on August 25, the day after Bartholomew's day, and continuing for 10 days. For 500 years, traders from all over the world came to Bartholomew Fair to display and sell their wares. While designed for commercial purposes, the public came for strolling entertainers, the food, and the atmosphere. During the Elizabethan period, the fair slowly became an amusement with jugglers, puppet shows, freak shows, and dancers among other performers. The last Bartholomew Fair was held in 1855, with unruly mobs, petty thieves, and unsavory characters.

In the late seventeenth and eighteenth centuries, pleasure gardens began to appear attached to taverns and inns on the outskirts of European cities. The pleasure gardens featured live entertainment, dancing, fireworks and even primitive amusement rides. By the late eighteenth century, the gardens featured fireworks, tightrope walkers and fees for admission. Political unrest in the eighteenth century forced many of these attractions to close. In the United States, by the late nineteenth century, electric trolley companies began building amusement parks at the end of the trolley line as a way to encourage patronage on the weekends when there were few riders. These facilities consisted of picnic areas, restaurants, dance halls, and a sprinkling of amusement rides. The parks quickly became successful and sprang up across the United States.

The golden era of amusement parks began with the 1893 World's Fair Columbian Exposition held in Chicago. There, the Ferris wheel and the midway were introduced to the world, with a selection of rides and concessions. The midway was a huge success and dictated the design of amusement parks for the next six decades. In 1894, Paul Boynton opened his Water Chutes attraction on Chicago's South Side; the success of that attraction persuaded him to open a similar facility at the Coney Island resort in New York in 1895. Over the next three decades, Coney Island became the center of the industry, which grew tremendously as hundreds of new amusement parks opened around the world.

By 1919 there were more than 1,500 amusement parks in operation in the United States. A decade later, the country entered the Great Depression, and by 1935 the economic downturn had exacted a terrible toll on the fledgling industry. Only 400 parks survived, and they struggled to break even. The ones that did faced a new struggle, World War II, when many parks closed and others held off adding new attractions because of rationing.

After World War II, the amusement park industry enjoyed record attendance and revenues. A new concept, Kiddieland, was born to take advantage of the postwar baby boom and introduced a new generation to the fun that could be had at amusement parks. However, as the 1950s arrived, television, desegregation, urban decay, and suburban growth all took their toll on urban amusement parks.

By 1955 a new concept in amusement parks had begun at Disneyland in Anaheim, California, but many did not think Disneyland would survive without a midway. In place of the midway, Disneyland Park had five themed areas, which allowed guests to travel to different lands and different times: Main Street U.S.A., Adventureland, Frontierland, Fantasyland, and Tomorrowland. Within six months, more than 1 million visitors had been to Disneyland, followed by 4 million more visitors in 1956. The 50 millionth visitor passed through the turnstiles in July 1965. One of the primary attractions of the park, as Judith Adams observed in her book, *The American Amusement Park Industry: A History of Technology and Thrills,* is that it allows the visitor to be immersed in historical environments and fantasy worlds instead of observing them on TV. The Disneyland formula reflected the public's desire for both entertainment and escape.

Disneyland's success spawned a series of imitators. It was not until 1961, when Six Flags Over Texas opened, that another theme park would succeed. The 35-acre Six Flags park had six themed areas, each representing a flag that had waved over Texas, including Spain, France, Mexico, the Republic of Texas, the Confederacy, and the United States. Unlike Disneyland, however, thrill rides were liberally sprinkled throughout each theme area. The Six Flags backers started a corporate park chain, Six Flags Inc., and built two new parks, Six Flags Over Georgia, near Atlanta, and Six Flags Over Mid-America, near St. Louis, Missouri. Unlike

Disneyland, which required separate coupons for each attraction, admission to these parks allowed access to all the rides and attractions located there. Other theme parks were built across the United States in the 1970s and began spreading around the world in the 1980s. The amusement park remained an international favorite through the 1990s.

In 2005, the world's oldest operating amusement park was Bakken, north of Copenhagen, Denmark, which opened in 1583. Next was the Prater in Vienna, Austria, which opened in 1766. It was followed by the Blackgang Chine Cliff Top Theme Park in Ventnor, United Kingdom, which began operating in 1842, and the Tivoli, also in Copenhagen, which opened in 1843. The oldest operating amusement park in the United States, which also was among the oldest amusement parks in the world, was Lake Compounce Amusement Park in Bristol, Connecticut, which began operating in 1846. The only other U.S. park on the National Amusement Park Historical Association's list of the world's 10 oldest parks was Cedar Point in Sandusky, Ohio, which began operating in 1870.

There are several classic amusement park rides that had all but disappeared by the late 1990s. The most familiar of these are the carousel and the roller coaster. The carousel, also known as the merry-go-round, is a ride with seats most often in the form of horses that revolves around a fixed center. The roller coaster is an elevated railway constructed with curves and inclines upon which cars roll. The world's oldest operating roller coaster began operating in 1912 at Luna Park, in Melbourne, Australia. The world's oldest existing roller coaster, the Leap-the-Dips coaster at Lakemont Park in Altoona, Pennsylvania, was built in 1902; in the late 1990s, efforts were begun to restore the ride and place it back into operation.

Other classic amusement park rides include: Auto Race, in which small electric cars travel along a wooden track; Caterpillar, similar to today's Himalaya Rides in which a train goes in a circle along an undulating track; Circle Swing, in which passengers ride in circles in gondolas suspended by cables from a structure overhead; Fly-O-Plane, in which passengers ride in airplane-shaped cars and try to flip the cars over; Flying Coaster, three-person cars that travel in a circle along a track; Flying Scooter, in which two-seater cars are suspended from a center arm with wings in the front of each car controlling the ride's motion; Fun House, a walk-through attraction with obstacles like revolving barrels; Noah's Arc, a walkthrough attraction similar to the famous boat; Old Mills, also called the Tunnel of Love, in which boats travel down dimly lit passageways; Racing Derby, a high-speed carousel simulating a horse race; Tumble Bug, where riders sit in circular cars moving over an undulating track; Venetian Swing, with riders in passenger boats suspended from a large A-frame; and The Whip, in which cars travel along an oval-shaped course with a whipping effect.

As amusement parks added attractions in the late 1990s, ticket prices crept inexorably upward, as they had since the late 1950s. As Tim O'Brien wrote in *Amusement Business*, each time prices were raised, park officials thought they were as high as they could go. But as the popularity of the parks picked up steam in the 1970s and 1980s, all the parks raised their rates to previously unthinkable levels.

In the late 1990s, industry consolidation began to occur, as operators such as Premier Parks gobbled up smaller parks and family-run operations. As a result, theme parks became hot commodities, and acquisition prices for theme park properties rose to record levels. Late 1997 and early 1998 saw the largest deals to that time. The largest acquisition was the US$1.9 billion paid for the Six Flags Theme Parks chain by Premier Parks, a publicly owned theme park operator based in Oklahoma City, Oklahoma. Premier bought the chain from Time Warner and Boston Ventures, an investment firm. In late 1997, Cedar Fair L.P. made what was then the largest park deal in U.S. history, paying US$250 million for Knott's Berry Farm in Buena Park, California, which was eleventh on the list of North American parks ranked by attendance in 1997. By January of 2002, Cedar Fair owned and operated six amusement parks and five water parks, and they announced that the combined attendance for their 2001 season was a record 11.9 million people.

In August of 2001, theme and amusement park operators were concerned with the drops in attendance at many parks. Cedar Fair suffered a 4.5 percent drop in revenues compared to the prior year. Revenues at Disney were reported as stagnant, primarily because of falling attendance. Attendance at Universal Studios and other theme parks in California and Florida had also declined. Kathy Styponias, the senior entertainment analyst for Prudential Services, described this as the "dichotomy with the amusement park industry" in an interview with Edwin McDowell of the *New York Times*. This refers to the vulnerability of parks whose visitors come from at least 150 miles or more to visit. The terrorist attacks on September 11, 2001 hit the already lagging amusement and theme park industry hard, as people became hesitant to travel. Bruce Orwall of the *Wall Street Journal* reported in an article in early 2002 that Disney had been hit especially hard by the terrorist attacks, which resulted in a significant plunge in their attendance rates and caused Disney to cut 4,000 jobs in early 2001.

In its December 22, 2003 issue, *Amusement Business* reported that North America's leading 50 amusement parks suffered a 1.6 percent decline at the gate, as attendance fell nearly 2.8 million from 2002—the second consecutive year that attendance declined. Other sectors of the entertainment and recreation industry also suffered in 2003. For example, at 11.4 million attendees, the leading 15 U.S. water parks saw their numbers fall 26,066 from 2002 levels. The top 50 fairs suffered a decrease in visitors as well. At 43.2 million, attendance declined 1.6 percent from 2002. Carnivals at the tope 50 fairs also experienced a decline, with attendance falling from 38.1 million in 2002 to 37.4 million.

Difficult times were not specific to North America. Severe Acute Respiratory Syndrome (SARS) affected the industry in Asia, although the impact was minimal. In Europe, the U.S.-led war with Iraq, hot weather, and economic factors contributed to a slight decline in attendance. Gate totals for the region's leading 10 parks fell to 40.2 million visitors in 2003, down from 41 million visitors the previous year.

CURRENT CONDITIONS

In 2004, the world's amusement parks earned about US$20 billion in revenues according to research done by PricewaterhouseCoopers. Growth is expected to be more than 25 percent in the period up to 2008. The situation was looking good for the industry that had suffered difficult times during the early 2000s, due to an economic recession, high unemployment, and a drop in consumer travel amidst concerns over terrorism. According to the International Association of Amusement Parks & Attractions (IAAPA), in 2003 attendance at U.S. amusement parks and attractions was 322 million, down from 2002 levels of 324 million. That year, revenues totaled $10.2 billion, up from $9.9 billion in 2002 and $9.6 billion in 2001.

The ten leading parks around the world, based on attendance during 2004 and as reported by *Forbes*, were: Magic Kingdom at Walt Disney World (Florida) with 15.17 million visitors, Disneyland (California) with 13.36 million, Tokyo Disneyland with 13.2 million, Tokyo Disney Sea with 12.2 million, Disneyland Paris with 10.2 million, Universal Studios (Japan) with 9.9 million, Epcot at Walt Disney World with 9.4 million, Disney-MGM Studios also at Walt Disney World with 8.26 million, Lotte World (Seoul, South Korea) with 8 million, and Disney's Animal Kingdom at Disney World with 7.82 million.

As fewer amusement park properties become available due to consolidation in the U.S. industry, operators must work harder to attract and retain attendees by adding new rides, new shows, and new experiences. These additions also are needed to keep visitors coming back to the parks. During the early 2000s, such additions had several broad themes. They added interactivity, allowing the audience to react and participate and riders to control factors such as speed and height; high-tech gadgets, such as motion simulators, holograms, lasers, and virtual reality; education, such as vacations built around cooking or horticulture; and animals, as almost every theme park operator now has some type of animal attraction.

Although new attractions are important to industry players, by the mid-2000s amusement parks were not investing as heavily in magnificent roller coasters. Instead, they were focusing more on family-oriented rides and amenities like air-conditioned restrooms and better food. In its January 5, 2004, issue, *Amusement Business* reported that only 12 of the nearly 50 roller coasters announced across the globe could not be categorized as family-oriented rides. Commenting on the movement away from super rides, IAAPA Chairman John Collins said: "The coasters were the remedy for a great deal of the ills of the industry a decade ago. People wanted coasters, parks obliged, and the people came. Now, the masses of people don't necessarily want more coasters, but many operators keep throwing them out there and wonder why their gales don't increase."

In 2005, PricewaterhouseCoopers was predicting that improved economic conditions in the U.S. as well as a weakening dollar would be a benefit to parks as they would encourage tourism. A new park in Hong Kong in 2005 and two others in Japan and South Korea (2008 openings) were also thought to be positive for the future earnings of the industry.

INDUSTRY LEADERS

Walt Disney Company. In 2006, the world's largest theme park operator continued to be the Walt Disney Company. Although the company's media holdings generated the largest share of its total revenues, followed by its studio entertainment segment, parks and resorts earned the company US$9.93 billion of its total earnings for 2006. The company owned Walt Disney World Resort in Florida and Disneyland Park in California. It had a 51 percent interest in Disneyland Resort Paris and a 43 percent interest in Hong Kong Disneyland. In addition, Walt Disney earned royalties on Tokyo Disneyland Resort that saw an increase in attendance from April to September 2006 of 3.3 percent from the previous year to 12,044,000. According to Oriental Land Company, the operator of Tokyo Disneyland and Tokyo DisneySea, that increase reflected the first rise on the first six-month basis for three years. Walt Disney World Resort is North America's most visited tourist attraction and it features four theme parks. Those acclaimed parks were the Magic Kingdom, Disney-MGM Studios, Epcot and Animal Kingdom. The resort also featured hotels, water parks and golf courses. Walt Disney also acknowledged its connection to the residential community founded in 1994 known as Celebration, Florida.

Euro Disney was a sore spot for the Walt Disney Co. in mid-2004. Although Disneyland Paris and Disney Studios Park rated as the Europe's leading tourist destinations, poor earnings and financial woes prompted a second restructuring that year, following an initial restructuring in the mid-1990s. Euro Disney was initially established as an independent enterprise, in which the Walt Disney Company had an ownership stake. However, new accounting rules forced the parent company to consolidate Euro Disney into its corporate structure in 2004, which was expected to impact Walt Disney in a number of ways, including stock investment and the provision of credit.

Disney Imagineer Stephen Silvestri was confronted with a creative challenge for the "Year of a Million Dreams" 15-month campaign. The company vowed to give away more than one million prizes. One popular prize was the opportunity to spend a night in Cinderella's castle. That Magic Kingdom icon did not have a Royal Suite when the campaign was launched so one had to be created for it. Silvestri and his team researched 17th-century royal French life and tried to create artwork and furnishings representative of that time period. Modern complimentary items such as shampoos and lotions were packaged in French glassware. To maintain an overall look appropriate for the Cinderella story-linked experience, technology such as a large TV was hidden from view and creatively stored for the lucky family to discover during their visit. The design evolved into a 650-square foot suite with a bedchamber, bathroom and parlor. The elevator was inspired by Cinderella's carriage. Two sets of three parlor windows revealed views of Fantasyland and Liberty Square.

As part of its 15th anniversary Disneyland Resort Paris promotion, Mickey and Minnie Mouse were scheduled to make announcements. A jazz band was also booked to entertain customers waiting to board Waterloo and Ashford Internationals.

Six Flags Inc. Six Flags was the second-largest theme park operator in the United States in 2006. It was formerly known as Premier Parks, an Oklahoma City company, that began acquiring parks aggressively in 1996. Premier catapulted into the number-two position from the number-seven slot with its acquisition of the Six Flags Theme Parks chain in early 1998. Approximately 28 million visitors traveled to the company's 27 North American parks in 2006, providing the company with revenue of US$945.7 billion. More than half of the company's sales are attributable to gate receipts, with the remainder coming from merchandise and food. Most of the company's parks operate under the Six Flags name. These include Six Flags Great America, Six Flags Over Texas, and Six Flags Magic Mountain. Most Six Flags parks feature water slides, thrill rides, and other forms of family-oriented entertainment. Six Flags enhanced its popularity by licensing Warner Bros. characters such as the Looney Tunes, Batman and Superman.

According to Six Flags, it is "the world's largest regional theme park company" in the world. However, its strongest presence is in the United States, where the company operated 15 of the nation's largest theme parks. In fact, 98 percent of the U.S. population lived within an eight-hour drive of a Six Flags location during the mid-2000s. In April 2004, Six Flags completed the sale of its European Division, which included locations in Belgium, France, and Germany, for approximately US$200 million. Six Flags' European operations formerly contributed about 20 percent of total revenue. Following the sale, Six Flags continued to operate international parks in Canada, Mexico, and Spain. In addition, the company also sold Six Flags Worlds of Adventure in Ohio for about US$145 million.

Due to a controversial Halloween 2006 promotion, Six Flags and the People for Ethical Treatment of Animals (PETA) had a confrontation. The promotion was "A Cockroach is Your Ticket to the Front of the Line" and called for visitors to eat a live Madagascar hissing cockroach. Their reward would be unlimited line-jumping privileges for the park's scariest rides. PETA was outraged that a corporation with animal theme parks would have this type of promotion. Six Flags official spokesperson Debbie Evans responded that "Cockroaches are insects. They are considered a delicacy in many parts of the world. They are a great source of protein." Some Six Flag parks offered the promotion stunt opportunity for one weekend while others made it available every weekend in October.

In 2007, Six Flags Great Adventure unveiled its "Wiggles World" theme area It was designed allow young visitors to experience the setting of these popular children's entertainers. Their recognition was high among two to six year olds. They have sold more than 22 million DVDs and videos plus more than five million albums worldwide. The Wiggles' popular TV show had been broadcast on Disney Channel's Playhouse Disney since 2002.

Anheuser-Busch Companies Inc. The world's largest brewer of beer was also in the theme park business. Its Busch Entertainment Corporation (BEC) subsidiary operated nine theme parks in five states. Those attractions included Busch Gardens' theme parks called Busch Gardens Tampa and Busch Gardens Williamsburg in Florida and Virginia respectively. In 2005, they earned revenues of about US$924 million for the parent company. BEC owned three SeaWorld parks in California, Florida and Texas. The Florida location was also the home of Discovery Cove where visitors could swim with dolphins and other marine life. The roster of other BEC attractions included Florida' Adventure Island and Virginia's Water Country USA.

Busch Gardens showed off its high-tech savvy with the launch of "BG Blast" billed as an "online community for teens by teens". It features music download opportunities, commentary from teens across the country and Busch Gardens promotions. There will also be teen hosts and chances for fans to serve as hosts.

A special partnership resulted in Sesame Street-themed attractions and characters appearing at Busch Gardens' park Planned attractions included rides, special effects theatre and live character shows. Sesame Street characters visiting the parks included Big Bird, Elmo and the Count.

Universal. Operating three theme parks in the U.S. and one in Japan, Universal Parks and Resorts, a subsidiary of Universal Studios, earned approximately US$893 million in 2004. Part of Vivendi Universal until 2004, the theme parks were sold along with Vivendi"s other entertainment assets to NBC, a subsidiary of General Electric.

Universal followed Walt Disney World and SeaWorld in its move to drop trans-fat additives from food sold at its parks. It took a long process to do so. That process included changing hundreds of recipes in ways to ensure they were more healthy but remained tasty.

The Tussauds Group. Marie Tussaud started her famous waxworks museum in London in 1835 after 33 years of touring Britain with a collection she inherited from wax modeler, Phillippe Curtius. After opening several other museums and attractions over the years, the company was purchased by Pearson plc, the owner of the Chessington Zoo in England. In 1987, the zoo was remodeled into a theme park, starting the company's ventures into this market segment. In 1990, it acquired Alton Towers, another theme park. Tussauds was acquired by Charterhouse Development Capital in 1998, and went on to manage and operate the London Eye, the world's tallest observation wheel. By 2005, in addition to other entertainment holdings, Tussauds was operating four theme parks in the United Kingdom. The company's total 2004 revenues exceeded US$300 million.

In 2007, Tussauds was sold to Blackstone as part of the U.S. private-equity group's attempt to create a European challenger for Disney. The deal meant Tussauds would become part of the Blackstone-controlled theme park operator Merlin Entertainments. Merlin already owned Alton Towers, Legoland, London Dungeon, the Sea Life aquarium chain and many other European attractions.

MAJOR COUNTRIES IN THE INDUSTRY

United States. Valued by the IAAPA at US$10.8 billion in 2004, the theme park industry in the United States remained highly consolidated. The top five companies in the industry accounted for 97.5 percent of the total market according to Euromonitor. The industry leaders operating in the U.S. were Walt Disney Company, Anheuser-Busch Companies, Six Flags Inc., Vivendi Universal (now NBC Vivendi), and Cedar Fair LP. The market was expected to grow by 14 percent into 2008.

Multi-generational destination parks were becoming innovative competitors for U.S. amusement parks. These parks offered diverse play experiences and outdoor physical fitness opportunities for groups ranging from toddlers to senior citizens. They might feature play structures for young children, skate ramps for teens and wellness paths for active adults/seniors. The parks were becoming popular attractions for residents in local communities as well as tourists reportedly traveling hundreds of miles.

Japan. In 2004, about 11 percent of visitors to Japan's various and numerous tourist attractions chose to visit a theme park. About 31 percent of the money spent on tourist attractions added to theme park revenues. However, new parks in nearby countries were posing a threat competitively. In 2006, Tokyo Disney Resort saw an increase in attendance but Universal Studios Japan experienced a decrease in its attendance figures.

United Kingdom. In 2003, the U.K.'s amusement parks had almost 50 million visitors. And when most Brits think amusement, they think Blackpool. Packed along 12 miles of seaside promenade, Blackpool in England offers visitors wax museums, amusement rides, and numerous other leisure activities. The country's biggest tourist attraction was Blackpool Pleasure Beach, founded in Blackpool in 1896. In 2004, this theme park hosted 6.2 million visitors and held about 14 percent of the total market. Other industry leaders included Tussauds Group Ltd. and Lego.

France. Theme parks in France had 35.4 million visitors in 2003, with Disneyland Paris accounting for 37 percent. Other industry leaders included Grevin et Compagnie SA (which was operating Parc Astérix north of Paris), Futuroscope and Nausicaa. Euromonitor expected the industry growth of more than 23 percent between 2003 and 2005.

Asia. Heading into the mid-2000s Asia was experiencing the strongest growth within the amusement park industry, in terms of both visitors and parks. In fact, a 2003 report from Economics Research Associates indicated that North America's share of the global theme park industry would fall from 43 percent in 1990 to 32 percent in 2005. That year, Asia was expected to surpass the relatively mature North American market with a share of 35 percent. Europe was expected to hold 25 percent of the market, with the remainder attributed to other nations. At 8 percent, Asia was forecast to have the strongest annual growth rate of any country between 2005 and 2010. China, in particular, was poised for explosive growth, as the nation prepared to host the 2008 Olympics in Beijing. A PWC Global Entertainment and Media Outlook report predicted the attraction and amusement industry in Asia will grow faster than in any other region of the world. Asia was projected to generate average annual revenue increases of 5.7 percent for a total of US$8.1 billion in revenues by 2009. Improved global economy plus moderization and development of new rides were key contributing factors.

FURTHER READING

"Amusement Industry Expects Strong 2004 Season." Alexandria, Va.: International Association of Amusement Parks and Attractions. 21 May 2004. Available from http://http://www.iaapa.org.

"Attendance at Tokyo Disney Resort Rises for 1st Time in 3 Years." *Jiji,* 2 October 2006.

Banay, Sophia. "World"s Most Fun Amusement Parks 2005." *Forbes,* 2005. Available from http://www.forbes.com.

Benz, Matthew. "Survey Shows Parks Shifting Strategies (PWC Projects 3.4 Percent Growth Rate)." *Amusement Business,* 16 June 2003.

"Blackstone Pays Pounds 1bn to Take Over Tussauds." *The Independent,* 6 March 2007.

Bogues, Austin. "A Kid-Friendly Addition: Big Bird and the Sesame Street Crew Are Coming to Several Amusement Parks to Entertain Children." *Daily Press,* 2 September 2006.

Boyd, Christopher. "Universal Shoves Trans Fat Off Plate: Disney and SeaWorld Have Already Announced Efforts to Shift Toward Healthful Menus." *Orlando Sentinel,* 21 December 2006.

"Economic Forecast Bright for Asian Attractions and Amusement Industry, Leading Experts Say." 23 May 2006. Available from http://iaapa.org.

"Fear of Terror Attacks Highest for Downtowns." *USA Today,* 13 March 2003.

"For Your Information." Oklahoma City, Okla.: Six Flags Inc. 21 July 2004. Available from http://www.sixflags.com.

Hoover Online. *Company Profiles,* 2007. Available from http://www.hoovers.com.

Johannes, Amy. "Pity the Roaches: Six Flags Dare Bugs PETA." *Promo,* 29 September 2006.

"Launchpad: Disney Takes Over Eurostar." *Travel Trade Gazette UK & Ireland.* 23 March 2007.

Mooradian, Don. "Industry Rides Out Rough '03." *Amusement Business,* 22 December 2003.

"Multi-generational Destination Parks Promote Fun and Fitness Among All Ages and Abilities." *Government Product News,* January 2007.

Nakamoto, Michiyo. "Sega Plans Vietnam Venture." *London Financial Times,* 2 September 1997.

National Amusement Park Historical Association. *History of Amusement Parks.* Alexandria, VA: NAPHA, 1997. Available from http://www.napha.org.

———. *Operating Classic Amusement Park Rides.* Mount Prospect, IL: NAPHA, 1997. Available from http://www.npha.org.

———. *World's Oldest Operating Amusement Parks.* Mount Prospect, IL: NAPHA, 1997. Available from http://www.npha.org.

Norris, Floyd. "Disney Gives Details of Plan to Aid European Parks." *The New York Times,* 1 July 2004.

O'Brien, Tim. "Admission Prices Continue to Rise." *Amusement Business,* 4 May 1998.

———. "Big Ticket Projects Scarce in 2004: Parks Focus on Family Rides, Amenities." *Amusement Business,* 5 January 2004.

———. "Parks Report Predicts Steady Growth: Asia Set to Lead the Pack." *Amusement Business,* 10 November 2003.

Powers, Scott. "Details Fall Into Place at Disney: Designers Create a Suite Where Some Lucky Winners Stay as Part of the Year of a Million Dreams Campaign." *Orlando Sentinel,* 14 November 2006.

Reklaitis, Victor. "Busch Gardens Aims at Teenagers: a Web site Will Feature Comments, Music Downloads and Promotions for the Theme Park." 4 October 2006.

"Report: Injuries Rising at Amusement Parks." *CNN,* 24 August 2001. Available from http://www.cnn.com.

"Safety in the Amusement Industry: Serious Business Around the World." Alexandria, Va.: International Association of Amusement Parks and Attractions. 19 July 2004. Available from http://www.iaapa.org.

"Six Flags Closes Previously Announced Sales of European Division and Six Flags Worlds of Adventure." Oklahoma City, Okla.: Six Flags Inc., 13 April 2004. Available from http://www.sixflags.com.

Sloan, Gene. "Are Amusement Park Mishaps Up or Down?" *USA Today,* 29 October 2001. Available from http://www.usatoday.com.

State Regulation Governing Amusement Rides. Safer Parks, 20 July 2004. Available from http://www.saferparks.org.

"Theme Parks in Germany (US, UK, and France)." *Euromonitor,* October 2004. Available from http://www.euromonitor.com.

"Top 10 Amusement/Theme Park Chains Worldwide." *Amusement Business,* 22 December 2003.

Townsend, Tim. "Theme Parks Predict a Summer of Thrills, Few Chills—Industry Relies on Role as Affordable Vacation Option as Economy Slows." *Wall Street Journal,* 11 April 2001. Available from http://www.townsendstories.com.

Traiman, Steve. "ERA Research Eyes Park Biz in 2005." *Amusement Business,* 10 May 2004.

"Travel and Tourism in Japan: Executive Summary." *Euromonitor,* March 2005. Available from http://www.euromonitor.com.

"U.S. Amusement/Theme Parks & Attractions Industry—Attendance & Revenues." Alexandria, Va.: International Association of Amusement Parks and Attractions. 19 July 2004. Available from http://www.iaapa.org.

"Video: Six Flags Great Adventure Unveils Wiggles World Based Off the Most Popular Children's Entertainers in the World, "The Wiggles", April 2 Six Flags Wild Safari Debuts the Exploration Station - a New, Interactive Adventure." *PR Newswire,* 3 April 2007.

Vo, Kim. "Marketing Fun to the Faithful: Amusement Parks, Teams Court Religious Groups. *San Jose Mercury News,* 6 August 2006.

Zoltak, James. "Industry Execs Foresee Strong Business in '04: The Year Ahead." *Amusement Business,* 5 January 2004.

SIC 7993, 7999

NAICS 713120, 713990

GAMING AND GAMBLING ESTABLISHMENTS

Gambling organizations, which may include governments as well as for-profit companies, provide various means for betting or wagering money based on a chance of a winning outcome, usually in the form of a game. The most common gambling venues are lotteries, casinos, and the Internet. Certain industry firms also operate hotels and restaurants; see also the industry profiles entitled **Hotels and Lodging** and **Restaurants**.

INDUSTRY SNAPSHOT

The gambling industry includes government-run operations, such as state and national lotteries, as well as private operations such as casinos. The gambling industry continued to receive greater acceptance around the world, with most countries that had already legalized gambling permitting more operations, and with many other countries considering its legalization in order to remain competitive. In 2004, the United Kingdom remained the leading country in betting, with revenues channeled through bookmakers and permitted—while taxed and overseen—by the British government. The year 2005 was bringing major changes to the regulations governing U.K. gambling. The U.S. remained the main source of gambling dollars, particularly in the growing online gambling segment.

In the 1990s and 2000s, casinos around the world started to shift to theme-oriented gaming houses. In part, this was an effort to attract families—a move anti-gambling activists deplore out of fears that children may become gamblers later in life. Companies such as Harrah's, Mirage, Sun International, and Circus Circus led in operating theme casinos throughout the world, combining gambling with other forms of entertainment. The theme format also helped differentiate one casino from another, because most were located in gambling districts and offered otherwise similar services. In addition, more casinos relied on slot machines for their revenues, because gamblers like their easy-to-use, low-wager format. By 2004, leading manufacturers of slot machines were reporting record earnings, benefiting from both so-called cashless machines, which were rapidly replacing traditional coin-operated slots, and from relaxed laws and increased machine placement in a handful of locations.

ORGANIZATION AND STRUCTURE

The gambling industry comprises five main categories: parimutuel betting at race tracks, off-track betting, bingo/keno, government lotteries, and casino gambling—all of which involve chance or have odds of winning. Parimutuel betting refers to a pool of bets for racing (mostly horse or dog) where bettors on the first three winners share the prize money, minus a cut for the racing operation. Parimutuels incurred income slippage in the late 1990s and 2000s because of competition from casinos and the Internet. Off-track betting is wager by bettors who do not attend the race, but place bets through a booking agency instead. In bingo and keno, players cover the numbers on their playing cards, trying to cover five in a row and win prize money if they succeed. Government lotteries in their various kinds, including daily and weekly drawings, award monetary prizes for ticket holders who match a certain amount of numbers correctly, or otherwise purchase tickets that have the potential to result in winning, as in so-called instant lotteries. Casino gambling includes live games of chance, such as blackjack, poker, craps, and roulette, as well as machine-based betting, such as slot machines. Casino gambling accounts for the greatest share of revenues in most countries where it is legal. Casino games also give players the greatest odds of winning, while lotteries usually have the lowest odds.

Some casinos have changed drastically since their inception, moving from purely gaming houses to theme and fantasy parks and trying to cater to the family crowd. Casinos also may offer services such as child care or video arcades. Casino gambling districts and resorts are often combined with 24-hour shopping malls and visual attractions, like talking statues, erupting volcanoes, and mock ocean battles between pirate ships. Slot machines have been an increasingly popular addition to casinos. At one point, casinos devoted only around 30 percent of their space to slot machines, but by the mid- to late 1990s they began to devote as much as 90 percent of their space to these money makers.

Although some businesses and political leaders view the gambling industry as an economic panacea, or at least as an economic benefactor, industry observers and religious organizations offer a far more grim account of the industry and its effects on economies and societies. Gambling advocates often portray casinos and other gambling operations as economic stimulants that create jobs and pump more money into local and national economies. However, opponents point out that the jobs created are primarily low-skill, low-paying positions, such as money counters and janitors. Further, detractors claim that simply building casinos in declining and blighted cities has failed to revitalize them, and competition among casinos usually erodes their profits, according to the *Economist.*

In addition, casinos, unlike other forms of gambling such as lotteries, require peripheral services that cities usually incur, including additional law enforcement and street cleaning expenses. Moreover, some critics argue that casinos also cause a variety of social problems, such as gambling addiction, mismanagement of personal finance, and deterioration of families, creating the need for additional social services such as counseling. The cost of a casino, in terms of the problems associated with one, brings a community nearly twice the expense compared to its benefits, claims Earl L. Grinols, a University of Illinois economist who estimates the annual U.S. national loss to be US$27.5 billion.

Numerous religions forbid gambling, including Hinduism, Buddhism, Islam, and some Christian denominations. Under Islamic law, gamblers must donate their winnings to the poor, and evidence given by gamblers is not acceptable in an Islamic court. However, betting on horse racing has generally been an exception to this prohibition. Texts of Hinduism, such as the *Rig Veda*, ban and warn against gambling and several other sacred texts refer to it as a vice. Gamblers also cannot serve as legal witnesses under Hindu law. Buddhism views gambling as a worldly distraction that leads believers astray. Finally, Protestant denominations, as well as Mormons and Jehovah's Witnesses, also oppose gambling, considering it a sinful recreation with harmful social and economic consequences. Other churches, such as the Catholic Church, have long supported bingo and gaming wheels at church functions, such as lawn fetes.

In 2005, gambling remained highly regulated in most countries in which it was legal, with participating governments earning large amounts of money from the industry. However, online gambling, which easily crosses borders was proving more difficult to regulate. In the United States, providing online gaming remained illegal, however the government was not taking action against foreign-based companies doing such business with Americans.

BACKGROUND AND DEVELOPMENT

Cultures throughout the ages have gambled through lotteries and other games of chance, and ancient texts and artifacts from many cultures all over the world refer to gambling and games of chance. For example, the ancient Romans gambled for entertainment, and medieval Europeans instituted gambling as a recreation for festivals. Gambling in China dates back about 4,000 years, and excavations at Ur, Crete, India, and Egypt (2000-1000 B.C.) showed signs of gambling in these cultures, because dice and gambling boards were found. Later in Europe, feudal rulers and merchants relied on gambling for revenues. During the sixteenth century, European governments became particularly interested in gambling for income, and many began to require licensing from the crown and established government monopolies over the industry. England, for example, would issue licenses for gambling operations in England and the country's colonies, and the government operated its own lotteries from 1709 until 1826, when it was banned.

In the eighteenth century, European aristocracy enjoyed gambling in the resorts of Europe, although European governments officially opposed gambling, and some countries outlawed it. With the rise of the middle-income merchant class, Europe began to establish permanent gambling venues throughout the continent, including Baden-Baden and Wiesbaden, Germany, and Baden, Austria. Moreover, the Casino de Monte Carlo became a model for casinos throughout Europe, which continued to spread through the nineteenth century.

The U.S. gambling and casino industry grew out of the westward migration of pioneers, who shunned the puritanical ways of some of the eastern cities and states. With few other forms of entertainment available, many of these U.S. settlers chose gambling as a key leisure activity. Between 1800 an 1840, towns along the Mississippi River became ports for the riverboats transporting goods and people. The riverboats also became moving gambling parlors. Further west, in the mining camps and small towns, public, organized systems of gambling were evolving. Most of the gambling involved card games, such as Monte and Poker, but some wheel games existed.

As emerging U.S. cities in the Midwest, South, and West grew wealthier and more sophisticated, they sought acceptance from the East. In order to gain acceptance, they tried alleviating their problems, including gambling, since the East largely prohibited it. Many of these cities, therefore, outlawed gambling and arrested gamblers.

As U.S. cities began banning gambling in the mid-nineteenth century, Europe continued to embrace it. This especially was true of casino gambling, which was considered a more elegant form of gambling. Casino gambling differed from other forms, because it used large tables and machinery, such as roulette wheels. Esteemed vacation resorts and health spas, such as Baden-Baden and Bad Homburg, Germany, along with Nice, Cannes, and Monte Carlo on the French Riviera, soon offered casino gambling.

François Blanc, a former casino manager in Bad Homburg jailed for stock fraud, moved to Monaco in 1863 where he built and ran a casino—despite resistance and protestations from Prince Charles II. Blanc successfully transformed Monaco into a wealthy gambling resort, and is considered the founder of the modern casino. Later, Las Vegas casinos adopted his management theories and rules for customer relations.

Although interest and acceptance of casino gambling games, such as baccarat and roulette, grew rapidly in Europe, these games faced heightened resistance in the United States because of national scandals in the late nineteenth century affecting the country's lotteries and horse races. By 1910 the government outlawed most forms of gambling in the United States.

U.S. betting on horse races became legal again in the 1930s, but was subject to strict state laws and regulations. During the U.S. Prohibition, speakeasies were venues for various forms of illegal gambling, such as crap pits, poker and blackjack tables, and slot machines. In the 1940s and 1950s, Las Vegas became the country's gambling capital, using its gambling resorts to attract tourists. In 1946, Benjamin "Bugsy" Siegel, a notorious gangster, decided to bypass California's prohibition of gambling by opening a luxury hotel and casino (the Flamingo), in Las Vegas. Siegel's casino ushered in the highly influential trend, which the industry followed through the late 1990s, of large flamboyant hotel and casino operations. The Flamingo also offered free lodging and meals to keep gamblers playing as long as possible. Nevada monopolized the U.S. industry until 1976, when New Jersey opened up casinos in Atlantic City.

Although the gambling industry experienced exceptional growth in the early to mid-1990s, it began to slow down in the late 1990s, notably in the United States. Analysts attributed the industry's lower growth rates to less government involvement in the late 1990s, in contrast to a plethora of casino initiatives around the world early in the decade, when many economies worldwide underwent recessions. For example, after the U.S. industry's revenues rose by more than 10 percent annually throughout the first half of the decade, they grew by only 5 percent in 1997. The United Kingdom continued to lead the world in gambling revenues with US$65 billion in 1997, followed by the United States with US$49 billion. However, the United States possessed the largest casino industry, whereas much of the United Kingdom's gambling revenues came from its National Lottery. In 2002, casino interests were exploring the feasibility of opening casinos, similar to those in Nevada, in the United Kingdom. In 2002 the United Kingdom prohibited bookmakers from gambling on the national lottery, although bookmakers did accept bets on the Irish national lottery.

The global industry benefited from the rise of slot machine casinos and the addition of slot machines to other casinos in the 1990s. Slot machines contributed significantly to the industry's growth in the mid- to late 1990s, accounting for the majority of casino revenues in countries such as the United States and France. In addition, because they are easy to use, slot machines appeal to neophyte gamblers and gamblers with limited budgets, since gamblers typically wager with small-denomination coins.

As a result of the high demand, casinos around the world began to change their formats to emphasize slot machines and some even began to move away from posh theme-oriented casinos. In fact, many successful casinos of the late 1990s featured only slot machines. Furthermore, slot machine manufacturers began to enhance their products, making them more interactive and visually stimulating. Nevertheless, grand theme casinos continued to fare well and gambling companies continued to launch more of them in recent years.

Casinos also began to market their services to families in the mid- to late 1990s. They added family-oriented themes to their gaming houses, such as circus, carnival, ancient Egypt, and lost treasure themes, and started to provide other services to make casinos a viable option for family outings. These services included offering childcare for adults who wanted to gamble, as well as providing alternative activities for older children. The themes, furthermore, aided casino operators in distinguishing their gaming houses from those of other operators as competition increased.

Although analysts believed Asia had a strong market for gambling, many Asian countries still resisted gambling and casinos in the late 1990s. China, for example, remained adamant in its ban on gambling, even though investors built the resort town Sanya, on Hainan Island, where they wanted to entice visitors with gambling amenities. Japan officially opposed gambling as well, but the country did allow gambling to accompany pachinko, a popular game of chance that is roughly a cross between a slot machine and a pinball machine. Even Hong Kong, where annual bets totaled US$90 million in 1996 for horse racing, faced gambling restrictions when it returned to Chinese rule in 1997. In 2002, Hong Kong officials were considering legislation to tax Internet gambling profits and to safeguard Hong Kong's horse racing enterprises. However, many Asians traveled to Australia and Macau, where gambling was legal.

CURRENT CONDITIONS

According to a 2004 Gallup study, approximately two-thirds of the U.S. adult population gambled in the previous year. Lotteries were the most popular choice, followed by casinos. While sports betting was the leading choice in the United Kingdom, it had grown more and more unpopular each year since 1989 in the United States.

In 2005, many countries were making the move to legalize gambling, and those that had already done so were imposing new regulations to allow for online gambling and providing licenses to new entities in the industry. The United Kingdom continued to be home to the two largest companies in the industry, betting companies Ladbrokes and William Hill. China's Macau region was readying itself to surpass Las

Vegas in terms of revenues generated. Worldwide, gambling in 2004 was estimated to be worth in excess of US$243 billion in 2004.

By 2004, casinos were legal in 20 states, although Las Vegas and Atlantic City were still the market leaders. American Indian casinos in particular were growing exponentially, both in terms of location and in terms of the number of machines and tables per location. The largest centers of Indian casino locations were on opposite coasts, in California and New York.

Critics continued to attack the success of casinos as a means of revitalizing declining city centers, especially in the United States where some of the most ambitious programs were launched. Unlike Las Vegas, most other cities that allowed gambling failed to draw visitors for extended stays. Instead, customers largely patronized only the casinos in these cities, including Atlantic City, not the restaurants, hotels, and other businesses. Moreover, according to the *Economist*, the money earned tends not to be additional money, but to be a share of the money that would have been spent on other industries in the area, as businesses discovered in Gary, Indiana. However, along with the nation's economic upswing, the gaming industry was a rising star again. Las Vegas held the honor of being the most popular tourist spot in the country.

The global online gaming industry was growing rapidly by 2005. Having been established in the 1990s, this sector of the industry had not yet begun to be fully developed. Research by Christiansen Capital Advisors estimated that about US$8.2 billion was generated by online gaming in 2004, and predicted the value would rise to almost US$25 billion by 2010. About 50 percent of the online market is estimated to come from the United States, which was considered to be the result of the high degree of Internet use in the country as well as its level of discretionary income. However, as such income levels improve in other parts of the world, growth rates in Europe and Asia were expected to exceed those in the U.S. by 2009. Although online gambling remained illegal in many countries, including the U.S., players appeared willing to participate.

RESEARCH AND TECHNOLOGY

The growth of Internet use and the development of effective online security systems, from 1995 through the 2000s, prompted casino operators to establish online gambling sites. Although this part of the industry only began to take off in the late 1990s, analyst Sebastian Sinclair predicted that income by the end of 2002 could be as high as US$3 billion in worldwide revenues, according to

USA Today. Internet gambling sites allow users to bet on sports events, participate in lotteries, and play virtual versions of casino games. Most of the online gambling operations are based in the Caribbean, where licenses are easy to acquire.

Online gambling operations have come under considerable attack because existing laws on gambling do not cover the specifics of the Internet in any straightforward way. U.S. law, for example, prohibits placing bets via interstate telephone lines; however, this law does not include waging across international boundaries, such as those that exist on the Internet where gambling houses from all over the world can set up online casinos and lotteries. Consequently, U.S. senators began introducing bills that would ban online gambling and punish gamblers, although very few convictions were recorded in the early 2000s. Major casinos expressed mixed opinions; while some supported online gambling, others resisted, fearing it would reduce their profits. In 2002, Nevada gambling regulators rejected requests by the casino industry for Internet gambling approval.

Moreover, the United States started to prosecute offshore gambling operations that allowed U.S. citizens to place bets, in violation of U.S. federal law in 1998. Despite the antagonism to online gambling, analysts believe this portion of the industry will continue to grow with or without government support. On the other hand, Australia and the United Kingdom supported online gambling and promised to help regulate it, making it inevitable that the United States will follow suit.

In the late 1990s, gambling equipment manufacturers also introduced slot machines with new technology. These slot machines included new features, such as more accurate calculation software and a nudge option, which allows players another chance at a jackpot. Equipment makers believe these features make slot machines more fun to play, and casino owners like them because of their power to draw both novice and returning customers.

In the late 1990s, Wells Fargo & Co. and Mr. Payroll Corp. developed a new kind of automatic teller machine (ATM) for casinos that recognizes the face of the user. The ATM, called Quest, dispenses cash and tickets without the use of an ATM card and is designed to expedite ATM use, allowing customers to quickly cash checks, receive cash advances, and withdraw money. The face-recognition technology is the same as that used in security systems of the Pentagon and other high-security places.

By 2005, gaming was being highly influenced by several new distribution channels. Online gambling was growing globally, particularly as the number of people with high-speed Internet access continued to grow. Interactive television and wireless telephone applications were also allowing for gaming to be done using those mediums.

INDUSTRY LEADERS

Hilton Group PLC (Ladbrokes). Hilton Group of the United Kingdom owns the rights to the Hilton hotel brand name around the world, with the exception of the United States. Ladbrokes is the company's betting and gaming division, and in 2005, it continued to be the world's biggest bookmaker. It was operating more than 2,300 betting shops in the United Kingdom, Ireland, and Belgium, as well as operating telephone betting and e-gaming sites available around the world in more than 13 languages. Through its various services, one could bet on horses, greyhounds, soccer, and other sports, and play poker and casino games. Gaming laws in the U.K. required that participants register as members 24 hours in advance of playing. Ladbrokes' telephone betting system claimed 125 million active members at the end of 2004, while e-gaming held an active membership base of 390 million people. With a worldwide employee count of more than 12,800, Ladbrokes earned revenues in 2004 approaching US$18 billion and had profits of more than US$480 million. The growth of online betting continued to increase each year. Prior to the Euro 2004 and the summer Olympics, the company invested millions of pounds into reworking the site architecture.

William Hill PLC. Founded in 1934, William Hill was the second-largest off-track betting organization in the United Kingdom in 2005. Processing an average of 859,000 betting slips each day from its more than 1,600 betting shops, telephone betting systems and e-gaming site, the company was accepting bets on more than 25 sports as well as offering casino-style games. In 2004, the company had revenues of more than US$14.5 billion and employed more than 10,700 people. In May 2005, William Hill announced plans to acquire Stanley Leisure for $880 million, which will make it the United Kingdom's biggest bookmakers and allow the company to enter Northern Ireland and the Republic of Ireland where it previously did not have any betting shops.

Stanley Leisure PLC. In addition to owning more than 600 betting shops, Stanley Leisure was the U.K.'s largest operator of casinos with 41 casinos across the country. The company began in 1958 when it operated two betting shops in Belfast. The company moved into the English market in the 1970s growing through the acquisition of other betting shops and casinos. In 1979, Stanley Leisure moved its head office to Liverpool. Revenues for the year 2004 were about US$2.9 billion, during which time it employed almost 7,000 people.

MGM MIRAGE. MGM MIRAGE operates some of the most famous casino-resorts in the United States including the Las Vegas-based Bellagio, MGM Grand, The Mirage, Luxor, Excalibur, Circus Circus, and New York-New York. In total, the company had 24 operations in 2005 in Nevada, Michigan, Mississippi, and New Jersey, all of which had a total of almost 25,000 slot machines and over 1,000 gaming tables. These properties also offered customers a choice from almost 27,000 rooms and suites for accommodation. In 2004, MGM MIRAGE reported revenues of US$4.24 billion of which about 75 percent came from its Las Vegas based properties. More than US$2.22 billion was earned directly from gaming in the casinos, while the remainder was non-casino revenue consisting of money earned from room accommodation, food, entertainment, and retail services. In 2002 MGM Mirage was the most active casino in the United States in terms of exploring profitable possibilities on the Internet, and by 2004 it acquired the Mandalay Resort Group for US$4.8 billion. In 2005, the company was working on the development of another 4,000-room casino-resort in Las Vegas and the MGM Grand Detroit hotel-casino complex. In addition, it had formed strategic alliances with several U.K. companies in anticipation of gambling reforms there, and had also established a joint-venture agreement to build a hotel-casino resort in Macau.

Harrah's Entertainment Inc. In 2005, United States-based Harrah's Entertainment Inc. owned or managed more than 40 casinos in the United States, Australia, and New Zealand, mainly under the brands of Harrah's, Caesars, Bally's and Horseshoe. In the United States, Harrah's owned casinos in thirteen states, including Nevada, Arizona, Illinois, Indiana, Mississippi, Louisiana, Missouri, New Jersey, North Carolina, and Washington. Harrah's also published annual surveys on the gambling and casino industry. One of the comeback business stories for Harrah's was its New Orleans casino, long a troubled franchise. Harrah's Entertainment Inc. had done well financially with out-of-the-mainstream sites in Council Bluffs, Iowa, and Maricopa, Arizona. By 2004, combined sales from its operations were US$4.55 billion of which US$4.08 billion came directly from casino operations. In 2005, the company acquired Caesars Entertainment, formerly Park Place Entertainment, in a more than US$9 billion dollar deal.

Sociedade de Jogos de Macau. Casino tycoon Stanley Ho enjoyed a monopoly on gambling on the island nation of Macau until a few years after the Portuguese colony was handed back to Chinese rule. In 2002, the government allowed others into the market. However, Ho's license was extended for 20 years. His 12 casinos earned revenues of US$3.7 billion in 2003.

The Rank Group PLC. In 2004, gaming operations earned London-based The Rank Group more than US$1.6 billion in revenue. About 31 percent of its revenues came from its 120 bingo clubs operating under the Mecca Bingo name. With 4.6 million members in 2005, the company was second in bingo gaming to Gala Group. A further 21 percent of Rank's gaming revenues came from its Grovenor Casinos business which operated 36 casinos under both the Grovenor and Hard Rock brands. The casino business had 1.2 million members. About 47 percent of the company's gaming revenues came from its Blue Square division, which operated Internet and telephone betting services. The remainder of the gaming revenue was derived from 35,000 amusement machines operating in various venues. However, the company sold its machine segment in 2004. In addition to gaming services, Rank also owns the Hard Rock Cafe brand and provides a range of manufacturing, distribution, and related services for the motion picture and media industries.

Trump Entertainment Resorts Inc. Trump Entertainment Resorts (formerly Trump Hotels & Casino Resorts Inc.) filed for Chapter 11 bankruptcy protection in November 2004 after accumulating US$1.8 billion in debt. The company reorganized, reduced its debt and reissued its stock, emerging from bankruptcy protection in May 2005. This was the third time the company had been through bankruptcy, failing to turn a profit in ten years. Chairman Donald Trump's share was reduced from about 53 percent to about 29 percent after the reorganization. The company owns Trump Plaza Hotel and Casino, Trump's Marina, Trump Indiana Casino, and Trump Taj Mahal in Atlantic City, New Jersey. In 2004, revenues were US$1.5 billion of which about US$1.25 billion was from gaming. Net losses were US$37.3 million.

Mashantucket Pequot Gaming Enterprises, Inc. (Foxwoods). Of the casinos run by Native American tribes in the United States, the largest is the Foxwoods Resort and Casino, operated by the Mashantucket Pequot tribe in Connecticut, who were considered the wealthiest tribe in the U.S. In fact, in 2005, Foxwoods was the largest casino resort in the world. Mashantucket Pequot Gaming Enterprises, Inc., the tribe's corporate entity, owns the casino, which is estimated to garner sales of roughly US$1 billion each year. By 2005, the tribe owned six casinos, three hotels, and 25 restaurants in Connecticut.

Gala Group Limited. In the United Kingdom, Gala means bingo. In 2005, the company was operating 166 bingo clubs across the country, which were accommodating 33 million admissions each year. In addition to bingo, the company was also operating 32 casinos in the U.K., the Isle of Man and Gibraltar, as well as 93,000 gambling machines in multiple locations. Players must become members, and Gala boasted more than 5 million bingo members and 1.2 million casino members in 2004. Between 1998 and 2000, the company grew significantly through acquisitions, including Ritz Clubs (17 bingo clubs), Jarglen Clubs (10 bingo clubs), Riva Clubs (27 bingo clubs), and 27 Labrokes casinos from the Hilton Group. Revenues for the company during 2004 were almost US$960 million. The company sold its high-end casino, Maxim's, located in London in early 2005.

PartyGaming Plc. Online gambling was growing rapidly. As a means to provide gambling globally and with most countries lacking any regulation for this sector of the industry, people from countries where gambling was illegal could participate. PartyGaming was operating the world's most successful online poker operation. Founded in 1997 by Ruth Parasol, an operator of pornographic chat lines and web sites, the firm is based in Gibraltar, a British overseas self-governing territory and a tax haven. The company began its PartyPoker.com web site in 2001. In 2004, the company had revenues of about US$600 million.

MAJOR COUNTRIES IN THE INDUSTRY

United Kingdom. The United Kingdom has the largest market for gambling in terms of annual revenues, with a strong national lottery. From 2002 to 2003, the amount staked on gambling totaled approximately US$113 billion, according to the Gaming Board for Great Britain. By March 2004, there were 131 casinos open in the country with 24 in London alone, the largest number held by a capital city anywhere in the world. Industry casino staff totaled about 13,000 and they handled about 11.9 million visits to casinos. At the same time, there were about 695 commercial bingo clubs, with about 18,500 employed to handle this sector's 3 million members. An additional 22,000 people found employment handling the 250,000 gaming machines operating at a variety of sites and establishments. Ticket sales for lottery sales were about US$225 million, which resulted in revenues of approximately US$115 million for various causes.

The United Kingdom's industry had suffered from inconsistent and out-of-date laws and regulations covering gambling. However, in April 2005, a new gambling act was established. As part of the act, a Gambling Commission, which was to be independent of the government, was to be set up beginning in the autumn of 2005. It will have the power to license gambling operators, while local authorities will license individual establishments. Under the new regulations, casinos can stay open 24 hours per day, there will not be a membership requirement, advertising will be allowed, age checks would be compulsory for gambling web sites operating from the U.K., and it would become a criminal offence to encourage or cause a child to gamble.

United States. According to a 2003 survey conducted by Harrah's, 53.4 million Americans over the age of 21 had gambled at a casino. That was 26 percent of the adult population who made an average of 5.8 trips to a casino. The American Gaming Association reported that gross gambling revenues reached US$72.87 billion in the United States in 2003, making the U.S. industry the world's second largest. Commercial casinos accounted for about 30 percent of the industry's revenues, while lotteries took 27 percent, casinos on Native American reservations 23 percent, parimutuels 5 percent, charitable games and bingo 3 percent, and card rooms and legal bookmaking took the remaining percent. The United States houses some of the biggest gambling and casino cities in the world with Las Vegas and Atlantic City.

Las Vegas controlled the largest share of the U.S. industry, accounting for 26 percent of the industry's revenues in 2003. Atlantic City ranked second with 15 percent of the revenues. Atlantic City's revenues grew at a faster rate than those of Las Vegas in the mid- to late 1990s, as the city vied with Las Vegas to be the country's leading gambling city. By 2003, Atlantic City hotels were maxing occupancy rates, with other establishments being planned and built. But as of the mid-2000s, Las Vegas was still on top. It had moved away from the lackluster family-oriented entertainment of roller coasters and amusement parks, and back to its once-again wildly successful gambling and casino roots. In addition to the steady stream of people relocating to the area, the city was the nation's biggest tourist draw in 2003, with a reported US$32.8 billion in revenue, $6.1 billion of which was related to the gaming industry that year.

France. Napoleon laid the foundation for the gambling industry in France in 1806, when he established state-controlled lotteries to raise tax revenues. Although France's casinos once emphasized elegant gambling facilities with upscale gaming, dining, and lodging services, in the late 1990s France began to model establishments on the style of Las Vegas casinos, catering to its largest customer segment: middle-age suburban wives spending about US$16 a day on slot machines. Casinos are allowed to be set up in towns on the sea, and in 2004 there were about 182 such operations. In 2003, gaming was valued at about US$21 million in France.

There were two major players in the industry. Groupe Partouche SA held about 27 percent of the market through its operations of about 45 casinos in France. The company also had casinos in Switzerland, Morocco, Belgium, Spain, and Tunisia. In 2004, Partouche had revenues of about US$550 million. The other leader in the industry in France was SHCD, a company created in 2004 through the merger of casino assets held by Barriere-Deseigne family, Accor Casinos, and Colony Capital of the U.S. After the merger, the group operated 37 casinos and had gross revenues of approximately US$1.1 billion.

Online gambling was very popular with the French. Nielsen/NetRatings announced that in February 2005, 22 percent of those who were online spent more than one hour gambling. That was estimated to be about three times the amount of time than that being spent by Britains. Interestingly, the laws in France only allowed for state-managed, land-based gambling. But in 2005, there were indications that France was going to legalize online gambling.

Canada. Canada's gambling industry also ranks among the world's leaders, as a multi-billion dollar industry that serves 45 million visitors a year. In 2005, a team of researchers working for the Law Commission of Canada valued the industry at about US$11 billion. About 59 percent of the country's population earning less than about US$16,600 dollars per year gambled in 2001, while of those earning more than about US66,000, 77 percent gambled. In 2001, it was estimated that the average household spent almost $215 per month on government lotteries alone.

In 2002, Statistics Canada figures showed that about 42,000 people were employed in the industry across the country, with 55 percent being women. To compare, non-gambling businesses averaged 46 percent women.

South Africa. South Africa embraced the gambling industry in the mid-1990s, although the country allowed gambling under apartheid in the reservations for black South Africans. Casino operator Sun International built Sun City in Bophuthatswana during this period, and owned 17 casinos in South Africa before gambling was legalized throughout the country. The country's mid-1990s legislation paved the way for the licensing of 40 new casinos and a national lottery. Even though the majority of the country's citizens possessed very little disposable income, the South African government figured its rising number of tourists would patronize its casinos. For the year ended March 2005, gross gambling revenue for the country was approximately US$1.5 billion, with casinos accounting for 83.8 percent, betting a further 15.6 percent, and bingo and other forms the remaining 0.6 percent.

China. Macau, the former Portuguese colony returned to Chinese rule in 1999, has developed a vibrant gaming industry. Revenues in the country's 17 casinos were valued at US$5 billion, making it almost equal to Las Vegas. Industry analysts projected that it would surpass Las Vegas in 2005. In 2002, the 40 year monopoly held by Sociedade de Turismo e Diversoes (STDM) was ended by the government, and three new gaming licenses were granted to Sociedade de Jogos de Macau (SJM), Galaxy Casino, and Wynn Resorts. SJM is the newly formed subsidiary of STDM that holds the new 18 year gaming concession. In 2004, plans were announced for a joint venture casino held equally between SJM and MGM MIRAGE. Gambling remained illegal on mainland China, although it was a significant part of the culture. Most gamblers in Macau came from the mainland.

Macau' success in the industry has prompted other Asian countries to follow into the gaming business. Singapore reversed its ban on casinos and gave permission for the building of two casino resorts. These were expected to be in place by 2009. The Philippines, Malaysia, South Korea, and Cambodia were also operating casinos, making the total value of the Asian market about US$20 billion. Japan and Thailand were expected to enter the industry by 2010.

FURTHER READING

Berns, Dave. "Numbers Confirm 2001 Was Poor Year for State's Casinos." *Las Vegas Review-Journal,* 13 February 2002.

"Bet and Board in the New South Africa." *Economist,* 5 August 1995, 43.

Brumback, Nancy. "Here She Is, Atlantic City." *Restaurant Business,* 1 October 2003.

Brumley Bryan. "Venetian Reveals Option to Back Out of Macau." *The Associated Press,* 13 March 2001.

"Conference Analysis." *High Yield Report,* 24 May 2004.

DeFoe, Jeannine. "Harrah's Shares Rise." *The Bloomberg News,* 8 March 2002.

———. "MGM Mirage Ventures into Internet" *Bloomberg News,* 13 February 2001.

Eckl-Dorna, Wilfried. "A Jackpot or a Risky Bet?" *Fortune,* 26 July 2004.

"The French Out Bet the British in Online Gambling." *Casino City Times*, 20 April 2005. Available from http://www.casinocitytimes.com.

"Gambling: An Update." *The Daily*, 22 April 2003. Available from http://www.statcan.ca.

Gambling Cultures: Studies in History and Interpretation. New York: Routledge, 1996.

"Gambling Law Changes on the Way." *SAPA (South African Press Association),* 18 April 2002.

"Gaming Revenue." *American Gaming Association,* 2004. Available from http://www.americangaming.org.

"Harrah's Survey '04 Election Year Edition: Profile of the American Casino Gambler." 2004. Available from http://www.harrahs.com.

"Hoover's Company Capsules." 2005. Available from http://www.hoovers.com.

"Internet Gambling Estimates." 2004. Christiansen Capital Advisors, April 2005. Available from http://www.cca-i.com.

"Ladbrokes to Launch Fantasy Footie Website." *Precision Marketing,* 18 June 2004.

Lazich, Robert S., ed. *Market Share Reporter.* Detroit: Thomson Gale, 2004.

"Maintain a Poker Face as You Read This Item." *Adweek,* 19 April 2004.

Montlake, Simon. "Asia Lays Bet on Casino Gambling." *BBC News*, 20 April 2005. Available from http://news.bbc.co.uk.

"National Gambling Statistics: National Gambling Board, 2004/2005 Fiscal Year." 2005. Available from http://www.ngb.org.za.

Nguyen, Chris T. "Casinos Display Golden Touch." *Monterey County Herald,* 7 July 2004.

O'Leary, Christopher. "US Company News." *High Yield Report,* 19 July 2004.

Palmeri, Christopher, and Laura Cohn. "Ready to Bet Big on Britain." *Business Week,* 23 February 2004.

"Park Place Move Awaited." *Leisure Report,* November 2003.

"Report of the Gaming Board for Great Britain 2003-04." 25 June 2004. Available from http://www.gbgb.org.uk.

Rosenthal, Franz. *Gambling in Islam.* Leiden: Brill, 1975.

Savvass, Antony. "Ladbrokes Gears Up for e-Bet Spree." *Computer Weekly,* 25 May 2004.

Stein, Joel. "The Strip Is Back!" *Time,* 26 March 2004.

Stovall, Sam. "Lady Luck Smiles on Investors." *Business Week Online,* 23 June 2004.

"Update on the Macau Gaming Industry and the Opportunities for U.S. Companies to Supply Gaming-related Equipment and Services." 1 March 2005. Available from http://www.strategis.ic.gc.ca.

"Vegas-Style Gambling Here." *Birmingham Post,* 27 March 2002.

"William Hill PLC." *AB UK,* June 2004.

Wong, Gillian. "Asia's Casino Business to Take Off Following Singapore Liberalization." 22 June 2005. Available from http://www.goldsea.com.

SIC 7011

NAICS 721110

HOTELS AND OTHER LODGING PLACES

The hotel industry provides short-term lodging and related amenities to business and recreational travelers. Common formats include hotels, motels, and vacation resorts that integrate lodging with recreation. Many industry firms also host conferences and events.

INDUSTRY SNAPSHOT

The international lodging industry is a vital part of the travel and tourism trade and is one of the largest economic forces in the world. Accounting for 11 percent of the world's economic output and more than 250 million jobs, the hotel industry is the third-largest foreign currency earner.

The industry is dominated by hotel chains, especially in the United States and Europe, although Asia saw a supply increase of 10 percent in 2003, the largest rise worldwide. Most of the world's largest hotel chains are based in the United States. Attempting to expand their customer base, hotel chains, led by Holiday Inn, turned to segmentation. This approach involved offering various types of lodging facilities based on size, service and space. Another trend was the adoption of computer technology. Although the hotel industry once failed to fully comprehend the benefits of computerized operations, in recent years hotel companies have turned to technology to standardize operations, communicate among properties and the home office, and create more efficient and cost-effective operations. Centralized reservation systems have become critical to any large lodging chain.

According to a 2004 MKG Consulting survey, the world's top-ten hotel groups handle three-quarters of the global hotel market, which totaled approximately 4.6 million rooms. About 70 percent of these hotels are located in Europe and North America, according to the International Hotel Association.

The hotel industry continues to rely on both business and leisure travelers. Since the 1980s business travel has been the leading money-maker for hotels, providing nearly two-thirds of all sales. The robust business segment of the industry also gave rise to extended-stay hotels in the late 1990s that specifically targeted business travelers. Nonetheless, leisure travel increased during this period as well. In part, this shift resulted from changing demographics, especially in the United States, and from rising disposable incomes around the world as part of the global economic recovery.

Each year, the hotel industry has increased its marketing dollars for campaigns to attract more business and leisure travelers. A PKF Hospitality Research study reported that there was an additional 6.1 percent in marketing spending in 2004. Yet, travelers still left their destinations dissatisfied with the level of service received and their overall experience. It was a challenge for hospitality companies to get beyond creative campaigns and amazing promises to actually provide the quality of service that would generate return visits and positive word of mouth.

Hotel Interactive pointed out that, from a management perspective, resort hotels were a unique form of lodging. Their multiple offerings, such as several restaurants and shops, made them more complex to operate than typical hotels. They were also frequently located in remote locations. Consequentially, there were frequently challenges for managers to overcome. Those potential challenges included supply deliveries, utilities, transportation and weather. According to a PKF Hospitality Research study, room revenues at 53.7 percent comprised just over half of the total revenues at a sample size of 199 resorts averaging 366 rooms in 2005.

Lodging Econometrics announced the compilation and publication of the first ever comprehensive "Lodging Development Pipeline" with forecast for new hotel openings through 2009 and beyond for every country in Europe. The resource reported that there were 513 construction projects being actively pursued by developers including 93,669 rooms in the 40 countries throughout Europe. Approximately 59 percent of the total or 302 projects having 52,580 rooms, were already under construction. Another 74 projects with 13,380 rooms were scheduled to start construction in the next 12 months. An additional 137 projects with 26,989 rooms were in various stages of early planning.

According to TravelCLICK;rsquo;s 2006 fourth quarter and consolidated full-year eTRAK results, the hotel industry maintains steady growth while consumers continue to shop for their hotels online and book electronically. The Internet was believed to have accounted for 38.3 percent of 2006 brand hotel bookings. That estimate reflected a 20.2 percent growth rate compared to 2005.

ORGANIZATION AND STRUCTURE

The major types of hotels found throughout the world are full-service, economy, resort, all-suites, conference centers, and convention hotels. A full-service hotel generally provides a wide variety of facilities and amenities, such as food and beverage outlets, meeting rooms and recreational activities. These types of hotels can be further classified as basic, upscale, or luxury. A basic property offers minimal expected services. Upscale hotels, such as the facilities operated by Hilton Hotels Corp. or ITT Sheraton Corp., have additional services and higher quality facilities, while luxury hotels, such as the Four Seasons and Ritz-Carlton, offer top-of-the-line service for a premium price.

Economy properties, such as Days Inn and La Quinta, provide comfortable rooms at low rates, but lack additional services. This type of hotel can be divided into two general groups: limited service and hard budget. Limited service hotels offer little or no food and beverage service and have marginal meeting facilities. Meanwhile, hard budget hotels, such as industry leader Motel 6, provide spartan accommodations at inexpensive prices.

Although relatively new, all-suite facilities have continued to report high occupancy rates. With 20 percent more space than a conventional hotel room, a suite is separated into a living area and a bedroom. These hotels have targeted both business travelers and weekend vacationers. A second type of all-suite property is the growing category of extended- and long-stay properties. Catering to guests who stay five days or longer, the extended-stay suite provides a full kitchen. Many properties offer a fitness center, executive work area, and grocery shopping services as well. Resort hotels provide recreational facilities and entertainment and many are located in close proximity to established vacation spots.

Conference centers and convention hotels are often used by companies for specialized training classes. A conference center may offer a complete package of guest accommodations, meals, full-service meeting rooms and staff. Some conference centers are operated by major corporations, while others are part of universities or operated by private companies. Convention hotels serve large groups such as trade shows and corporate annual meetings. These properties provide facilities and services geared to meet the specialized needs of large groups. These hotels typically have hundreds of guest rooms and a substantial amount of flexible meeting space.

The hotel industry—especially in the United States—has experienced substantial structural changes as a result of hotel segmentation and the consolidation of companies. As the industry tries to anticipate customer needs—whether the customer is a business traveler or budget-minded vacationer—hoteliers have divided lodging facilities along the line of price, service and space. With U.S. companies leading international expansion, the usage of segmentation has spread to areas outside North America.

Lodging companies have found that segmentation has added to their growth. Since hoteliers have had little control over increasing demand, they instead have expanded their customer base by providing all levels of lodging managed by one parent company. Segmentation also has allowed companies to leverage corporate resources such as management experience, access to capital markets and back-office operations.

Participation in the Industry. Participation in the lodging industry has taken various forms. Companies may choose to own, manage, or franchise properties, and some combine all three. Franchising has been one of the most common ways for companies to expand internationally. Using a franchise agreement, the local hotel owner pays an initial fee and monthly royalty fees in exchange for the use of the chain name, logo, reservation system, and national advertising campaign. Franchised hotels can be found in nearly every country. Franchising has allowed companies to maintain their basic brand images while offering lodging services that fit the specific needs and desires of the local company.

Strategic alliances in the hospitality industry are a type of joint venture intended for a specific geographic region. For example, when Radisson Hotels International became interested in moving into international markets, the company allied itself with Moevenpick in Switzerland and Germany and opened a series of Moevenpick-Radisson hotels. In a strategic alliance, each partner brings its strongest assets to the venture. Usually, the U.S. partner will offer an internationally recognized brand name, a technologically advanced reservation system, and management expertise. The local partner contributes an understanding of local operations and labor, and authority to negotiate contracts with government suppliers.

International Investment in the United States. International hotel owners and operators have expanded into the United States through direct investment in well-known U.S. hotels. This investment and acquisition strategy is used because the U.S. lodging industry is an extremely competitive market already full of well-established and commonly known brand-name hotels. Given this level of development, a substantial investment would be necessary for a new company to successfully enter the U.S. market with a new product line. One example of such foreign investment was the 1990 acquisition of Motel 6 by the French firm Accor SA.

BACKGROUND AND DEVELOPMENT

Until the development of commerce and the standardization of a compact medium of financial exchange, the hotel remained a scant one-room inn, nothing more than an extra room sold to an infrequent traveler. However, by the present era the advent of money suddenly expanded the trading radius of the ancient world and brought about significant growth of travel.

The Industrial Revolution (1760) spurred the creation of the English inn. Located along coach trails, inns provided modest accommodations and food for stagecoach passengers. As roadways were built into the countryside, the famed English cottage was established. The first U.S. hotels were similar to their English counterparts and could be found on stagecoach trails and in seaport towns. These included inns of approved London style and were residences, some with additions built on. At their best, they were like an average well-kept home, but not much bigger.

As the United States expanded westward, the railroad created new population centers and new hotels, grand in size and service. When stock companies began to finance hotel construction, the industry moved from a small-time operation to big business, similar to the development of the railroads and industrial plants.

The first of the large-scale hotels built by a stock company was the City Hotel of New York, which was established in 1794. Compared to a colonial inn, this 73-room facility was enormous. During the years prior to the Civil War, American hotels were built in established cities and boom towns. Some of these facilities were both elegant and expensive. Those who could not afford such extravagance were left to rooming houses, but scores of people were drawn to these first-class establishments. Some even took up residence in these facilities. Public areas of hotels—such as the lobby and the bar room—became popular social settings and meeting places. The hotel also was host to numerous balls and banquets and became a focal point for political and business activities.

The 1920s brought a boom in hotel construction in the United States. With occupancy rates reaching 85 percent in 1920, companies expanded properties and constructed hundreds of new and larger facilities. The industry came to a screeching halt with the onset of the Great Depression. In the 1930s nearly 80 percent of all hotel companies were forced into foreclosure or receivership. With all travel stymied, the average hotel occupancy rate hovered at 50 percent. While it forced many hoteliers out of business, the Depression gave some lucky buyers new properties at rock-bottom prices. It was during this time that the future industry giants ITT Sheraton Corp. and Hilton Hotels Corp. first purchased many of their hotels.

The onset of the Second World War revived the U.S. hotel industry as the national occupancy rate soared to nearly 90 percent. Although most cities needed additional lodging facilities, few were built because financing, materials, and labor were diverted to the war effort.

The motel, or motor-hotel, developed as a direct result of the explosive growth of the auto industry and the expansion of highway systems following the war. The first motels were simple, single-story structures, usually with 20 rooms or less. Located on inexpensive land on the edge of town, motels usually were managed by resident owners and had few paid employees.

During the 1950s, the motel business was still in its infancy and had few industry standards. Lacking brand identity, patrons had no guide to judge the quality, comfort, and price of motels. Travelers often examined the accommodations prior to payment (a custom still practiced in Europe). But the motel market changed dramatically at the hands of Tennessee resident Kemmon Wilson.

Wilson, already a successful Memphis home builder, became irritated with the inconsistent quality and fluctuating prices of lodging accommodations during the course of a family vacation. Wilson decided that with the growing love of the automobile and the open road, the American family needed and would welcome inexpensive, efficient motels. By the time he returned from his vacation, Wilson had calculated the minimum size of a hotel room and called a friend who was a draftsman to work the dimensions into a hotel. The first Holiday Inn—named after a Bing Crosby feature film of the same name—was thus built in Memphis in August 1952. It included a restaurant, a gift shop, and a swimming pool. In addition, each room was equipped with an air conditioner and a television. When Wilson wanted to expand his operations, he first approached his fellow home builders. When only three decided to join him in the hotel business, Wilson turned to franchising his product. The facilities were an instant hit and in five years Holiday Inn became a public company.

Accor founders Gerard Pelisson and Paul Dubrule had similar ideas in France. In 1967, they decided to build moderately priced American-style hotels along the highway. The first to break into this market in Europe, Pelisson and Dubrule met with immediate success, and by 1973 they formed Sphere SA, a holding company for a new hotel chain called Ibis. Accor was also the first to tap into the European hotel market of budget-conscious consumers.

Since the 1950s the hotel industry, led by the United States, had experienced cycles of growth and decline, and each upturn has brought a new type of hotel into the market. The budget motel arrived in the late 1960s and flourished during the boom of the early 1970s. These properties offered accommodations at prices substantially lower than the established rates of existing full-service motels. Companies also began to expand their chains through franchising during this time, following the example first set by Holiday Inn.

The combination of readily available financing and aggressive companies selling franchises led to an influx of hotels managed by inexperienced owners and situated in poor locations. Combined with inflation, rising construction costs and interest rates, and the energy crisis, the hotel industry fell again in the late 1970s until all-suite hotels arrived in the 1980s with new construction.

In the late 1990s, the industry's assets, principally in the form of land, buildings, and furnishings, amounted to around US$170 trillion. Until the economy slowdown in 2000-2001 and the September 11 attacks, the global industry's sales in the mid- to late 1990s indicated its full recovery from the recession that hampered the world market in the early 1990s during the Iraq crisis. During mid- to late 1990s, occupancy levels and revenues reached record highs throughout the world, particularly in Europe and the United States.

After the global recession in the early 1990s, many countries recovered in the mid-1990s and continued to prosper going into the late 1990s. The economic turnaround, the emergence of new markets, and the balancing of hotel supply and demand all played a decisive role in the industry's success in the mid- to late 1990s. During this period, hotels around the world reported record revenues and occupancy rates. The United States, for example, saw its hotel industry revenues grow by 4 percent from 1995 to 1996, reaching a record US$75.4 billion, according to the American Hotel and Motel Association. Further, occupancy levels soared in Europe with London reporting more than 85 percent, Rome 83 percent, Zurich 79 percent, Amsterdam 78 percent, and Edinburgh 76 percent. Simultaneously, the Middle East experienced the most significant increase in visitor arrivals worldwide. With ongoing peace talks between countries in the region, a number of new hotels cropped up, especially in Jordan, where the price of hotel rooms rose by 11.5 percent in 1996.

The hotel industry consolidated in the mid- to late 1990s. In the first half of 1997 alone, the United States reported mergers and acquisitions worth US$4.1 billion, twice as much as reported in the first half of 1996. Marriott International made one of the largest acquisitions, purchasing Renaissance Hotel and its holdings such as Renaissance and Ramada International for US$1 billion. Extended Stay America also bought Studio Plus hotels for US$290 million.

Large hotel chains, especially those in the United States, began seeking new markets in the late 1990s as their domestic markets verged on saturation. Companies such as Sheraton relied on their brand names to fuel their international expansions, setting up hotels in large cities and branching out into smaller cities after successfully establishing themselves. Smaller operations opted to place their hotels in strategic locations after careful planning to ensure sufficient demand. In the late 1990s, the top five international emerging hotel markets included Chile, Cuba, India, Poland, and Saudi Arabia, according to *Hotel & Motel Management*.

In Asia, Japan's domestic hotel operations continued to lose the struggle against foreign-owned chains such as Park Hyatt Tokyo, Westin Tokyo, and Four Seasons Hotel Tokyo. Both domestic and international customers prefer these hotels to Japan's domestic hotels, according to a *Nikkei Weekly* report. Additional hoteliers, including Ritz-Carlton Hotel, planned to tap into Japan's market in the late 1990s and early 2000s.

Though luxury hotels led the industry in Asia in the 1980s, moderate-priced hotels forged ahead of them in the 1990s. Heightened travel between Asian countries by middle-income travelers sparked demand for these hotels, according to *Lodging Hospitality*. Despite the success of mid-priced hotels, luxury hotels flourished in Indonesia and the Philippines by combining social and business functions with lodging services.

China's hoteliers, however, concentrated on expanding their business accommodations by developing business suites. South Korea's hotel industry confronted serious challenges in the late 1990s. The country's devalued currency, which reduced domestic purchasing power, coupled impeded investment and new hotel construction, even though the country has a paucity of hotel rooms. Korea has only 118 hotel rooms per 10,000 tourist arrivals, in contrast to the United States, which boasts of 683 rooms per 10,000 arrivals. Nonetheless, South Korea experienced increased growth in its tourist traffic, which circulated about US$5.6 billion through the country's economy.

Throughout Asia, hotels witnessed the improvement of infrastructure, the growth of new business opportunities, and the possibility of international expansion. Nonetheless, because some markets neared saturation points and faced labor problems, the trade journal *Hotels* predicted accelerated consolidation would take place in these areas. However, the number of resorts and conference centers in Asia was forecast to grow from the late 1990s through 2010.

The health of the international hotel industry continues to depend largely on the strength and stability of national economies, as the number of travelers, whether business or pleasure, increases with economic growth and prosperity, as well as a perception that travel is safe. In 2001, deflated by a recession that had started the previous year, the industry was hit with the slowdown in bookings attributed to terrorist attacks of September 11, 2001, leading to a significant stoppage in the worldwide building of new hotels, according to the *Financial Times*. The attacks were blamed for the loss of up to 500,000 jobs worldwide, some of which were regained as bookings for some hotels began to return to normal demand levels, according to industry analyst Plasencia Group Inc. Significantly, the slowest chains to recover have been the luxury hotels such as Four Seasons and the resorts run by Club Med. Industry analyst firm PwC expected a 59.4 percent hotel occupancy rate in the United States in December 2002, compared to 60.3 percent in 2001 and 63.7 per cent in 2000.

Hotel industry sales grew to approximately US$295 billion in 1999, a significant increase from 1996 figures of US$250 billion. The world hotel industry recorded a strong growth rate in the late 1990s through 2000 as well. However, terrorist attacks on September 11, 2001, coupled with an existing downturn in U.S. travel because of recessionary economic conditions, left the industry reeling and undercut normal profits. The hardest hit U.S. cities were Boston, Seattle, and San Francisco, the latter of which saw its room occupancy rates drop 24 percent in one year, according to the *Financial Times*.

CURRENT CONDITIONS

Quick to rebound was New York City, where room occupancy rates returned to 69 percent as of December 2001, compared to 77 percent in December 2000, according to the *Financial Times*. However, various acts of terrorism around the globe continued to cause the industry to hold its collective breath, since a single incident such as the World Trade Center bombings by plane has indeed had a corrosive effect on tourism. As of February 2002, Smith Travel Research, the industry's data tracking company, reported that U.S. hotel occupancy rates were 45.4 percent, down from 48.3 percent the previous year.

After three bad years, beginning with the 2000 economic downturn and solidified by the 2001 terrorist attacks, the hotel industry was set for an upswing in 2004 and 2005. Around the world, occupancy rates increased. According to Deloitte Touche Tohmatsu, increases for the year ended January 2005 were 6.9 percent in the Asia/Pacific region, 10.5 percent in Central and South America, 6.7 percent in the Middle East and Africa, 3.5 percent in North America, and 3.2 percent in Europe. Revenues per available room were also up significantly: 19.1 percent in Asia/Pacific, 25.8 percent in Central and South America, 29.4 percent in the Middle East and Africa, 8 percent in North America, and 11.6 percent in Europe. Several cities around the world showed signs of a remarkable upswing. Beijing, recovering from the effect of the SARS virus, had an increase in occupany exceeding 33 percent. Hong Kong and Singapore also showed increases of more than 18 percent. However, areas in Asia affected by the tsunami of December 2004 were seeing few tourists by June 2005.

The extended-stay segment of the industry continued expanding to meet the needs of the influx of business travelers. Extended-stay hotels cater to businesses by offering rates and amenities targeted to meet corporate budgets and needs. According to *Market Share Reporter,* the extended-stay segment of the market was projected to rise to 294,361 rooms in 2007 from 2002's count of 229,852.

RESEARCH AND TECHNOLOGY

With a growing global market and increased customer needs, communication between individual hotels, the corporate office, travel agencies, and airlines became necessary. The computer remains one of the most important operational tools in the hotel industry, improving both efficiencies and guest services. Most hotels have automated front-office functions such as reservations, and many have considered adding applications like yield management (maximizing occupancy or revenues at any given time) and integrating their point-of-sale and restaurant computer systems. In addition, hotels have begun using the Internet to market their services and to allow customers to make reservations and obtain information.

Technological growth has been especially evident in the area of reservation systems, the backbone of any international lodging operation. The development of worldwide central reservations systems (CRS) has created a global network in which a guest can make a reservation for a hotel room from anywhere in the world. In addition, such a system can be used for targeted marketing and yield management, the science of last-room availability. Hotels can instantly access guests' history and preferences to efficiently accommodate them. The key to success, however, has been to link hotel systems with airline systems. Because of this connection, some industry observers contend that independent properties without access to a global reservations system will be seriously threatened by chain operators.

Technological advances have also been used to increase security at hotel facilities around the world. Of all the new security devices available, the card key locking system has become the most commonly used product in all segments of the hotel industry. Continued advances in card technology have led to the creation of the smart card, a credit card with a computer chip that contains information such as a traveler's personal data, medical history, and credit card numbers. Proponents argue that at some point in the future these cards may be used for transactions with a wide range of institutions associated with the travel industry, including airlines, hotels, and car rental agencies. Although relatively new, the smart card has already been used in Europe. Other security methodologies under examination by the hotel industry center around biometrics, the technology of recognizing a person by some physical characteristic, such as a fingerprint. This type of security device already has been used in some controlled areas of hotels, especially in casinos, but remains quite expensive to implement.

Launched in 2003, Marriott's ldquo;At Your Service" system was designed to keep track of a guest's preferences, from room service food to the type of in-room amenities to room location. As of late spring 2004, the service only worked within stays at the same property, but Marriott planned to have such guest preference information accessible by the staff at any Marriott location.

WORKFORCE

The hotel industry ranks among the world's largest employers, accounting for 11 million jobs worldwide or 5 percent of the world's travel and tourism workforce. North and South America represent about 40 percent of these workers, with 4 million. In Europe the figure has jumped as high as 1 in 10 tourism jobs. Industry employment was expected to nearly triple from 1990 to 2005, according to the Brussels-based World Travel and Tourism Council, an outlook that makes travel and tourism and the affiliated hotel industry among the most promising of international job markets.

When the question was "How Long is the Road?" there were some interesting answers about the journey from bellboy to general manager. The question was posed and answers analyzed by 4hoteliers.com. Data reflected insights gained from 60 people working in numerous countries with distinctive backgrounds. It takes only 14.75 years on average in North America for the shortest length of time. At the other spectrum end Asia had an average of 16.5 years. The area of specialization had an impact on how fast employees moved from entry level to executive suite. It took the shortest time (14.8 years) for people who started as management trainees. The second shortest time (15.3 years) category was people who came through the rooms division. Survey findings reflected that a clear majority at 40 percent of general managers started their careers in the food and beverage division. Throughout the world, general managers tended to earn respect. They frequently moved on to other important roles such as CEOs and COOs.

According to Bill Marriott, immigration laws could have a tremendous impact on hotel jobs. If laws were passed to deport illegal immigrants, there would be problems finding people to replace them. Marriott predicted that inflation would result from related efforts.

Some analysts have predicted future jobs in the hotel industry will be concentrated in low-level service areas since management has continued to remain lean. Opportunities for employment in the hotel industry in Europe remained more promising than in the United States and some other regions. Because of a relatively small number of people in the 16-to-24-year-old bracket, traditionally a leading source of entry-level service workers, the United States faced a shortage of hotel employees during the late 1990s. "We've tapped virtually all the available resources," John Gay of the American Hotel & Lodging Association admitted to *RCI Timeshare Business* magazine. "The only answer is foreign workers." According to the Hotel & Restaurant Employees International Union, about 18 percent of some 17.7 million employees working in the United States in 2001 were foreign nationals in the hospitality industry, many of whom were hired through broker services abroad that assist with travel, proper documentation, and other necessary paperwork.

INDUSTRY LEADERS

InterContinental Hotels Group PLC (formerly Six Continents, formerly Bass Hotels & Resorts). The world's largest hotel company with approximately 556,000 rooms,

Intercontinental Hotels is also the most global, operating in almost 100 countries. Intercontinental is the owner of such well-known brands as Holiday Inn, Crowne Plaza Hotels & Resorts, and Intercontinental running more than 3,600 leased, managed, owned and franchised properties. About 1,500 limited-service locations operate as part of the Holiday Inn Express brand. In 2005, the company reported revenues of US$3.29 billion, and employed 21,986 people.

In 2007, building on its distinction as the "Official Hotel of Major League Baseball", Holiday Inn announced confirming National Baseball Hall of Famer Cal Ripken, Jr. to participate in the brand's successful "Look Again" integrated marketing campaign. A Scarborough Research national study found that more than six in ten Holiday Inn guests or approximately 13.5 million guests are self-identified Major League Baseball fans. In addition, those fans who go to games comprised approximately one quarter or 24 percent of Holiday Inn guests and accounted for more traffic to the chain's hotels than attendees of any other sport. Ripken joins the roster of professional athletes, including NASCAR drivers Jeff Burton and Scott Wimmer, championing the Holiday Inn brand. The "Look Again" campaign takes a humorous look at life on the road for today's business travelers. The primary target of the campaign is what has been identified as the "modern everyday hero", a blended attitudinal segment that spans Generation X and Baby Boomers.

The launching of IHG Agency Awards was another exciting 2007 InterContinental Hotels Group announcement The purpose of this new awards program was to recognize teams and individuals who provided the hotel industry with the highest levels of value, innovation and support throughout the past year. Award categories included Agency Account Manager/Director of the Year, Conference and Incentive Agency of the Year, Agency Booking Team of the Year and overall Agency of the Year. Winners' prizes included a brand new Vauxhall car and a luxury bread at the InterContinental Carlton Cannes. Holiday Inn had maintained a two-year sponsorship of the Vauxhall's VX Racing Team in the British Touring Car Championship.

Tracing its roots back to an English brewery company started in 1777 that purchased a small chain of hotels in 1987, the company's real growth in the industry came with its purchase of Holiday Inn International in 1988 and the remainder of the North American business in 1990. During the late 1990s through 2002, its Holiday Inn chain was the single largest hotel brand in the world. With Holiday Inn Worldwide headquarters based in Atlanta, Georgia, approximately 83 percent of the company's hotels were located in the United States. The Holiday Inn chain began with the creation of a single hotel in 1952.Crown Plaza hotels were launched in 1994, aimed at an upscale market. Mid-scale hotels were sold off in 1997, but the company maintained its brands through franchising agreements. Pan Am Airlines founded Intercontinental Hotels in 1946. The hotel chain acquired the company in 1998. South Pacific Hotels was acquired in 2000, strengthening the firm's position in Southeast Asia. That same year, the company sold off its brewery business to focus on the hospitality trade, changing the name of Bass Hotels & Resorts (BHR) to Six Continents Hotels in 2001 to reflect the corporation's growing worldwide presence. The company continued to expand globally: In 2001 it acquired the U.K. chain Posthouse and the Intercontinental Hotel in Hong Kong. Further brands were added in the mid 2000s: Candlewood Suites and Staybridge Suites, extended-stay hotels mostly in the U.S., and Hotel Indigo.

Cendant Corporation (formerly Hospitality Franchise Systems Inc.). A giant in the real estate brokerage business through its ownership of the Century 21 and Coldwell Banker brands, as well as being the world's largest car renter with its Avis and Budget brands, Cendant was also the second largest hotel franchisor by the end of 2004. It had 520,860 rooms across 6,396 properties. In addition, the company had the lion's share of timeshare condominiums.

Revenues for the entire company were US$19.79 billion in 2004, of which 15 percent was related to the company's hospitality services division. About 2 percent of total revenue was from the lodging franchise business, with Cendant operating eight brands in this sector: Wingate Inn (138 properties; 12,934 rooms); Ramada (1,005 properties; 119,991 rooms); Howard Johnson (466; 44,923); AmeriHost (107; 7,451); Days Inn (1,872; 153,701); Travelodge (527; 40,476); Super 8 Motel (2,076; 125,844); and Knights Inn (205; 15,540). In 2004, the company issued master franchises in China and Russia.

From the timeshare sector was 3 percent of Cendant's total revenues in 2004. The company's One Resort Condominiums International subsidiary provided more than 3 million subscribers with access to more than 3,900 resorts in 100 countries. In 2004, 10 timeshare resorts were added in China. Vacation rental properties accounted for a further 1 percent of revenues. Providing global marketing services to approximately 42,000 independent owners of villas, cottages, bungalows, apartments and caravans in vacation parks, this business sector was active in 22 countries.

Hilton Hotels. With one of the most recognizable names in the hotel industry, Hilton Hotels Corporation operates primarily in the United States, where its Waldorf Astoria Hotel in New York is world famous. United Kingdom-based Hilton Group plc owns the rights to the Hilton name outside of the U.S. The two companies operate under a strategic alliance whereby they share sales and marketing functions, loyalty programs, and a central reservation system. In 2004, the U.S.-based group posted revenues of US$3.68 billion and employed 70,000 people, while the U.K.-based group reported revenues of approximately US$5 billion from its hotel division.

Together, the two companies provided customers with a choice of 2,800 hotels and 490,000 rooms in 80 countries in 2006, operating under the Hilton, Hampton Inn, Homewood Suites, and Scandic brands. The U.S.-based group was also operating Hilton Grand Vacation Club, a vacation ownership business. Other affiliated brands included Doubletree and Embassy Suites Hotels. The companies had a team of about 150,000 members worldwide. In October 2004, terrorists bombed the Taba Hilton in Egypt near the Israeli border killing 31 members of the staff and guests.

The company's Conrad brand was named in honor of its founder, Conrad N. Hilton. In 2006, that brand included 19 world-class luxury hotels or resorts. They operated in the U.S., England, Ireland, Belgium, Egypt, Turkey, Indonesia,

Hong Kong, Singapore, Thailand, Australia and Uruguay. Plans for new Conrad Hotels, both in major U.S. cities and resort destinations around the world, are in various stages of development.

In January 2006, Hilton announced plans to introduce a new luxury hotel line called "The Waldorf-Astoria Collection". The collection was launched with its world-renowned hotel and three world-class luxury resorts that will be newly managed by Hilton. Those three properties were Grand Wailea Resort Hotel & Spa on the island of Maui in Hawaii, Arizona Biltmore Resort and Spa in Phoenix and La Quinta Resort & in California. Criteria for the exclusive designation will include architectural significance, unique decorative items and original artwork, historic or landmark status and a reputation for product and service excellence.

In September 2006, Hilton announced it had become "founding corporate partner" of the Hispanic Hotel Owners Association (HHOA). Hilton received the exclusive sponsorship designation by providing initial funds required for the association's formation and preliminary development. The formation of HHOA was a direct result of Hilton's minority franchise development outreach "Hospitality 101" seminar. This seminar was piloted by Hilton and has become a "best practice" in minority franchise development outreach across the industry. It focuses on teaching minority entrepreneurs on the basics of hotel development. In addition to HHOA, Hilton enthusiastically continues to support the National Black Hotel Owners and Developers and the Asian American Hotel Owners Association.

Marriott International Inc. What started in 1927 as a root beer stand in Washington D.C. turned into a chain of 2,800 lodging properties across the U.S. and 67 other countries by 2007. By year-end 2006, it had approximately 151,000 employees. Marriott thrived by operating utilizing many different brands, several of which incorporate the Marriott name in them. However, one of its most famous brand names stands alone—The Ritz-Carlton, with luxury hotels and resorts around the world. In October 1993 Marriott Corp. was divided into two companies: Host Marriott Corporation, which owns real estate and operates airport concessions; and Marriott International, the lodging business. By 2004, Marriott's had about 255,000 rooms, with revenues of more than US$10 billion. In 2004, Marriott controlled 17 percent of all branded full-service hotel rooms in the United States. In fiscal year 2006, Marriott International reported sales from continuing operations of US$12.2 billion.

While other hoteliers have moved into the gaming industry, Maryland and Washington, D.C.-based Marriott has focused on continued segmentation and international expansion. Its product line includes Marriott, JW Marriott, The Ritz-Carlton, Renaissance, Residence Inn, Courtyard, TownePlace Suites, Fairfield Inn, SpringHill Suites, Bulgari, Ramada International Marriott Ownership Resorts (vacation time-sharing), and Marriott Golf, which operates golf facilities. By converting existing properties and developing new hotels, Marriott's international expansion has included the establishment of full-service properties in the Pacific Rim, Europe, Latin America, and the Caribbean.

Marriott International is also a 2006 U.S. Environmental Protection Agency Energy Star Partner. Further evidence of environmental consciousness was found in its long-term strategic plans. In March 2007, the company reported being on tract to reduce its greenhouse gas emissions by nearly one-fifth during the ten-year period from 2000 to 2010. This industry leading effort is part of a comprehensive effort to reduce Marriott's environmental footprint and save energy costs. In April 2007 all of its 2, 800 hotels helped to celebrate Environmental Awareness Month. The company planned to launch a pilot program at 30 hotels to measure, standardize and expand recycling company wide. It was estimated that more than 96 percent of Marriott hotels around the world actively recycle. Each hotel in the Marriott system has a designated energy and environmental ambassador who helps the property maintain standards and finds new ways to improve the environment.

According to *DiversityInc* magazine, for the fourth consecutive year, Marriott was ranked among the "Top 50 Companies for Diversity" as the highest in the lodging industry. Marriott also placed number four in the "Top 10 Companies for People with Disabilities" category. A total of 317 companies completed the survey. Additional noteworthy recognition in 2007 included several special distinctions for the company. They included being named as one of the "Top 10 Companies for Executive Women" by the National Association for Female Executives, "Top 50 Corporations for Supplier Diversity" by *Hispanic Trends* magazine and "Top 50 Places to Work" for African-American women by *Essence* magazine.

Accor. Paris-based Accor SA is the largest European hotel operator and among the top five in the world. Accor has a presence in nearly every international hotel market, operating 4,000 hotels with more than 475,000 rooms in 100 countries by 2007. The company owns hotels in all price ranges, but the majority of its holdings include moderate and low-price hotels. Brand names include: Novotel, Sofitel, Mercure, Ibis, Red Roof Inn, Motel Six, Motel Formula 1, Suitehotel and Etap Hotel. Accor employed 160,000 workers in 2007.

Accor offers valued services to corporate clients and public institutions. An estimated 21 million people in 35 countries benefit from Accor Services products including meal and food vouchers, people care plus incentive and loyalty programs.

Opening its first Novotel hotel in Lisse, France in 1967, Accor was soon one of the first lodging companies to have segmented service. Although Accor owned about 50 percent of its hotels in the late 1990s in order to maintain tight control on its operations, by 2005 it owned 21 percent of its properties, franchised or managed another 37 percent, and leased space at the remaining 42 percent. In June 2005, the company added its 4,000 hotel with the addition of a Novotel in Madrid, Spain.

In keeping with its global development strategy aiming at opening 200,000 new hotel rooms by 2010, of which 60 percent will be in emerging markets, Accor signed into partnerships that promote major expansion in India. This expansion plan covered the full spectrum of India's hotel market. It included budget Formule 1 hotels, economy Ibis hotels, mid-market Novotel hotels and upper-upscale Sofitel properties. In addition, Accor is discussing opportunities with leading Indian business groups for a variety of developments including the launch of the Mercure brand in India. Accor is already present in India through its Services business. Accor Services is a global leader in the field of employee benefit, incentive and loyalty programs. It opened its Indian subsidiary in 1997 and introduced two of its major products: Ticket Restaurant meal vouchers and Ticket Compliments gift vouchers used by more than 180,000 Indian company employees.

Club Meditérranée SA is most commonly known to many as Club Med. This French company pioneered the all-inclusive resort, featuring deluxe accommodations and a full schedule of sports, entertainment, and activities for guests. The club gained a reputation among North Americans as a young singles resort, but by 2002 analysts said the old formula of games and communal meals at high prices was a turnoff to vacationers. As a result, the company vowed to make significant changes in approach and in marketing. Nearly 60 percent of its visitors came from Europe. The company has tried to enlarge its markets to include couples, families with children, and business meeting attendees. After two years of losses, Club Med reported sales of about US$1.9 billion for 2004. That year, Accor became the company's primary shareholder, jumping out of its main corporate concerns to expand in the leisure/pleasure hotel market. In 2005, sales were again reported as being about US$1.9 billion.

MAJOR COUNTRIES IN THE INDUSTRY

United States. The United States remains the hotel industry's international giant, routinely posting the highest amount of international tourism revenue. Tourism was the country's third-largest industry, behind automotive and food stores. However, although valued at US$70.4 billion by Euromonitor in 2003, growth in the hotel industry had been flat, posting only a 0.5 percent increase over the previous year. Pre-tax profits for the industry were US$12.8 billion according to research done by Smith Travel Research. To compare, in 1999, the industry had pulled in US$22.0 billion in pretax profits, according to the American Hotel & Motel Association (AH&MA). But in 2003, the industry was still feeling the effects caused by September 11th terrorist attacks. The small hotel sector (fewer than 75 rooms) did grow by more than 10 percent between 2002 and 2003. By 2008, the entire spectrum of hotel sizes was expected to grow by 21 percent, but almost three quarters of the revenue was to come from the small hotel sector.

Leading destinations in the United States included Florida, Southern California, and New York. Top American markets for hotel expansion in recent years have included Las Vegas, Nevada; Orlando, Florida; and San Antonio, Texas. Hotel developers also have watched the surge in legalized gambling in the United States with great interest, a development that could benefit the hotel industry tremendously. In the early 2000s, the average room rate stood at US$85.00, a fairly hefty increase from 1996 when the average room rate was US$69.66, according to Smith Travel Research. However, by 2004, this had declined to US$82.52. Of the total number of U.S. hotel guests, vacationers account for 23 percent, business travelers for 30 percent, conference and meeting attendees for 26 percent, and other travelers for the remaining 20 percent.

Hotels in New Orleans struggled to rebuild after the devastating impact of Hurricane Katrina. Some of the damage they incurred included shattered windows and flooding. Many of the hotels, however, reopened by year-end 2005. Hotel supply continues to increase due to completion of renovations of damaged rooms. Many of the demand generators lagged behind such as completion of renovations on tourist attractions. Thus far, the tourist crowds and major conventions had not returned to New Orleans.

France. Hotel industry giant Accor makes its home base in France, but small, independent hotels account for about 50 percent of the market's value. Here the hotel and lodging industry was valued by Euromonitor at about US$17.6 billion in 2003, and was expected to rapidly increase by more than 17 percent. After Accor, three other companies hold small, but significant market shares: Best Western International, Intercontinental Hotels, and Group Taittinger. In 2005, Paris was vying to be the host city for the Olympic Games in 2012, viewed to potentially benefit many hoteliers in the city.

Morgan Stanley, the Wall Street firm that owns in excess of 80 hotels worldwide, announced plans to purchase two hotels in France in 2007. One hotel was identified as the Hilton Charles de Gaulle near Paris. Morgan Stanley sought to benefit from increased travel to Europe and hotel companies's efforts to sell properties but continue to profit from managing them.

United Kingdom. As in France, the small hotel dominated the U.K. market in 2003. More than 80 percent of the hotel and lodging market's value of US$10.6 billion was attributed by Euromonitor to hotels of 50 rooms or less. In 2005, there were about 22,000 hotels and guesthouses registered, plus an additional 16,000 bed and breakfast establishments. Of the large players in the market, Granada plc was the largest, capturing a 9 percent marketshare. Other leaders included Whitbread, Thistle Hotels, and Hilton Group. The U.K. industry, like others, was greatly affected by the events of September 11th. However, by 2004, occupancy rates had increased to levels last seen in the late 1990s.

China. In 1978, China was the 48th ranked nation in the world for tourism. Its doors had been closed to most foreigners for so long, that when the government did make it easier to enter the country, it took some time for the tourists to come. But come they did. In 2002, China was the fifth-ranked tourist destination, playing host to 33 million visitors. A short time later, according to Deloitte Touche Tohmatsu, in the first eight months of 2004, 71 million overseas visitors came to China. Many foreign hoteliers have added China to their expansion plans. At the end of 2004, Intercontinental Group had 44 hotels in greater China, plus additional 53 management agreements, signed and under negotiation. As of March 2005, Accor had more than 5,550 rooms in 20 hotels, providing employment for almost 8,300 people.

FURTHER READING

"Accor Takes a Major Step in its Expansion in India." 27 November 2006. Available from http://www.accor.com.

"Accor to Help Reposition Club Med." *Hotels,* July 2004.

Adams, Bruce. "On the Rise." *Hotel & Motel Management,* 3 May 2004.

"All New Orleans Needs Are Travelers." 5 March 2007. Available from http://www.4hoteliers.com

Brudney, David M. "Mood of Hotel Investors and Operators is Euphoric." 24 April 2007. Available from http://4hoteliers.com.

Burgess, Robert. "Cendant CEO Silverman Tries to Reassure Investors." *Bloomberg News,* February 6, 2002.

"Cal Ripken, Jr. Teams Up With Holiday Inn." 29 March 2007. Available from http://www.ihgplc.com.

Carpenter, Candace. "Accor's Flaxman on Outlook for Hotels After Sept. 11 Attacks." *Bloomberg News,* 13 December 2001.

Doland, Angela. "Club Med Paradise Troubled After Rough Year." *Chattanooga Times/Chattanooga Free Press,* 22 January 2002.

Draper, Deborah J., ed. *Business Rankings Annual.* Detroit: Thomson Gale, 2004.

Deloitte Touche Tohmatsu and Smith Travel Research. "Global Lodging Review." 2 March 2005, Vol. 2, Issue 6. Available from http://hotelbenchmark.com.

"First Ever Development Pipeline and Three Year Hotel European Openings Reveals Robust Development Through Decade's End." *Hotel Interactive,* 5 March 2007. Available from http://www.hotelinteractive.com.

Fitch, Stephane. "Soft Pillows and Sharp Elbows." *Forbes,* 10 May 2004.

"HHC Extends World's Greatest Hotel Name to Create Luxury Brand Line." 17 January 2006. Available from http://phx.corporate-ir.net.

"Hilton Hotels Corporation Becomes Founding Corporate Partner of Hispanic Hotel Owners Association (HHOA)." 22 September. Available from http://phx.corporate-ir.net.

"Hoover's Company Capsules." 2006. Available from http://www.hoovers.com.

"Hotels in France, Germany, UK, US." *Euromonitor,* October 2004. Available from http://www.majormarketprofiles.com.

"Hotels: Rebranding for Bass. Name-change to Six Continents Hotels." *Bangkok Post,* 16 August 2001. Available from http://www.bangkokpost.net.

"IHG Launches Travel Agency Awards." 3 April 2007. Available from http://www.ihgplc.com.

Lazich, Robert S., ed. *Market Share Reporter.* Detroit: Thomson Gale, 2004.

Mandelbaum, Robert. "Resort Hotels - Wanted: Eaters, Golfers, and Shoppers." *Hotel Interactive,* 26 June 2006. Available from http://hotelinteractive.com.

"Marriott International Reports," *PR Newswire,* 13 February 2002.

"Marriott on Track to Reduce Greenhouse Gases by 1 Million Tons Over 10 Years - 2000 to 2010." 22 March 2007. Available from http://marriott.com.

"Marriott Ranks Highest in Lodging Industry for Diversity." 21March 2007. Available from http://www.marriott.com

McArthur, Stacey. "The New Workforce." *RCI Timeshare Business,* November/December 2001.

"Ranking of Hotel Groups 2004." *Hotel Online,* 2004. Available from http://www.hotel-online.com.

Sullivan, Aline. "Falling Occupancy Rates Fail to Halt the Rise in Hotel Stocks." *Financial Times London,* 7 February 2002.

Veller, Tatiana. "Bellboy to General Manager - How Long is the Road?" 27 April 2007. Available from http:www.4hoteliers.com

Wang, Terry. "Beyond the Wall: China Reveals Its Hidden Tourism Potential." *Executive Report,* January 2005. Available from http://www.deloitte.com.

Weinstein, Jeff. "April 2004 Market Performance." *Hotels,* July 2004.

———. "Radical Thinking?" *Hotels,* July 2004.

"Worldwide Online Bookings Up 8 Percent" *TravelCLICK,* 20 April 2007.

Young, Fara. "Perfecting the 180." *Hotel Interactive,* 10 March 2006. Available from http://www.hotelinteractive.com.

Yu, Hui-yong. "Morgan Stanley Plans to Buy 10 European Hilton, Person Says." 26 April 2007. http:www.bloomberg.com.

SIC 7812, 7822

NAICS 512110, 512120

MOTION PICTURE PRODUCTION AND DISTRIBUTION

In what is commonly known as the movie industry, global firms record, publish, and disseminate motion pictures primarily to theaters and broadcasters. In addition, a strong secondary market exists in which films, after movie showings (or bypassing theaters in some cases) are transferred to videotape or DVDs and sold or rented directly to consumers. The movie industry also produces movies exclusively for television viewing. See also **Video Tape Rental and Retail.**

INDUSTRY SNAPSHOT

In the movie industry, globalization is the name of the game. In mid-2004, for example, *The New York Times* revealed that international ticket sales represented about 60 percent of worldwide box office receipts, up from 40 percent in 2002. In 2003, member companies of the Motion Picture Association of America (MPAA) reported total global revenues of US$41.2 billion, with 40 percent coming from international sales. As the industry became more international, casting actors with international appeal became more important to success at the box office.

In the early 2000s, economic conditions swung in favor of the motion picture industries of many industrialized countries such as the United States, France, Germany, the United Kingdom, and Japan. In most cases, particularly as much of the world found itself in a recession in 2001 and in a mood for cheaper, close-to-home entertainment after the September 11 acts of terrorism, box-office receipts and attendance rose during this period to new highs in some cases, and several countries released record breaking blockbusters.

Following record box office totals in the early 2000s, the U.S. motion picture industry continued to fare well heading into the mid-2000s. In 2003, box office receipts totaled US$9.5 billion, down less than 1 percent from 2002 and the second-highest level in industry history. Theater admissions were down 4 percent in 2003, to about 1.6 billion. Nevertheless, this was still impressive considering the competition movie theaters faced from the likes of video games, television, VCRs, DVD players, the Internet, cable television, and satellite TV.

By the mid-2000s, DVDs represented a growing revenue pool for moviemakers. Citing data from Adams Media Research, *The Economist* indicated that DVD rentals and sales made up some 40 percent of movie studio revenues by 2003, up from 1 percent in 1997. In the United States alone, consumers spent US$22.5 billion on videocassettes and DVDs combined in 2003. Some analysts argued that relying on DVD sales made the industry more vulnerable to the growing problem of piracy, which had wreaked havoc on the music industry. In mid-2004, the MPAA reported that the motion picture industry lost US$3.5 billion because of piracy.

BACKGROUND AND DEVELOPMENT

The U.S. film industry began in 1889 when Thomas Edison invented the kinetoscope, a primitive version of the movie projector. In 1896, Edison showed the world's first movie in New York with his Vitascope projection device. Technological advances in the 1920s synchronized a movie's sound with its picture, enhancing the cinema experience and opening the door to many new possibilities. Hollywood, California, soon became the world's capital of movie production and the home of the blockbuster, the kind of film in which large amounts of money are invested in production and marketing in the hope of reaping huge profits. In 1915, D.W. Griffith produced *Birth of a Nation* with US$110,000. That 158-minute U.S. Civil War epic reaped over US$50 million at the box office. Griffith also helped put Hollywood on the map by spending the winter of 1910 in Los Angeles with his cast and crew.

While France and Italy all but owned the world's movie market before World War I, after the war Hollywood emerged as the industry powerhouse, a position it held for the rest of the century. Hollywood was full of business-smart immigrants who were bent on making a mark in their new homeland. Adolph Zukor merged his own production company into his new acquisition of Paramount Pictures in early 1910. Carl Laemmle started Universal Film, and William Fox created Twentieth Century-Fox in 1912. Marcus Loew purchased Metro Pictures, which was owned by Louis Mayer, and merged the two companies with Goldwin Pictures to create Metro-Goldwyn-Mayer. The four Warner Brothers started filmmaking in 1912. These companies dominated films by 1919, much to the consternation of Charles Chaplin, Mary Pickford, Douglas Fairbanks, and David Griffith, who founded the sixth major studio, United Artists. All these firms competed fiercely against each other during the 1930s. The 1940s were even better times for the industry, with military propaganda and home-front melodramas to produce before and during World War II, and the upbeat post-war U.S. mood to portray after the war. However, the creation of television in the 1950s shook Hollywood for about 15 years, until movie makers assumed a meaningful role in producing television shows. Soon, the blockbuster production movie created a new era of US$10 million movie advertising budgets that helped to draw world audiences.

In the mid- to late 1990s, the movie industries of countries around the world began to privatize and become more market dependent—instead of government dependent—allowing them to compete more effectively with the U.S. industry. The growth of international demand for movies was supported by the worldwide expansion of large multi-screen theaters (multiplexes) that allow theaters to screen many movies at once.

From 1997 to 2002, U.S. movies such as *Pearl Harbor* and many other films earned more abroad than at home, partially because of weakened cinema industries around the world and partially because of better release schedules in other countries than in the United States. For example, in 2002 when studios released the three action-adventure movies *Collateral Damage, Hart's War,*, and *John Q* around the same time in the United States, these movies were forced to compete head to head for the U.S. audience. However, international distributors have more control of their release dates and can phase them to leave several weeks between each launch, allowing audiences in those countries to develop an appetite for a certain genre again.

CURRENT CONDITIONS

Although many entertainment sources vied for consumer attention by the mid-2000s, home theaters in general and DVDs in particular provided apt competition for traditional movie theatres. As DVD player prices fell below the US$30 mark for some units and the number of available titles continued to explode, the number of DVD-equipped households continued to rise. By the end of 2004, more than 70 million U.S. households and 171 households internationally had a DVD. In China, about 42 million households had DVDs. Citing data from Adams Media Research, *The Economist* revealed that DVD rentals and sales made up some 40 percent of movie studio revenues by 2003, up from 1 percent in 1997. In the United States alone, consumers spent US$22.5 billion on videocassettes and DVDs combined in 2003. In its 2004 annual report, Time Warner reported that the largest driver behind its growth in the filmed entertainment segment was the sale of DVDs from its library of film titles.

Just as DVDs represented lucrative profits for moviemakers, some industry analysts warned that reliance on DVDs made the industry more vulnerable to the growing problem of piracy, which had decimated profits in the music industry. By the mid-2000s, the proliferation of DVD recorders made it easier and faster than ever to pirate copies of movies. This problem was especially prevalent in Asia, where illegal copies of popular movies—made with video recorders in theaters or from advance preview releases—were available on street corners and high-class hotels alike for less than US$1. The rising number of broadband Internet connections also made illegal movie downloads easier for computer users.

According to MPAA figures, by 2004 piracy cost the motion picture some US$3.5 billion worldwide. In the March 29, 2004 issue of *Amusement Business,* Warner Brothers Pictures International Distribution President Veronika Kwan-Rubinek explained that in 2003, losses from piracy totaled US$275 million in Russia, followed by US$120 million in the United Kingdom, and US$100 million in Germany. Although there were no easy answers to the growing problem of piracy, the industry was responding with educational outreach to promote the criminal aspect of piracy, as well as digital rights management technology.

The movie industry's globalization continued into the mid-2000s. By mid-2004, international ticket sales represented about 60 percent of worldwide box office receipts, up from 40 percent in 2002. In 2003, the MPAA's member companies reported total global revenues of US$41.2 billion, with US$16.6 billion coming from international sales.

As some blockbuster films, including those in the *Lord of the Rings* and *Harry Potter* series, doubled their U.S. box office returns with strong international showings, actors with international appeal became more important. In the July 5, 2004 issue of *The New York Times,* Stephen Moore, president of international film and home entertainment at Twentieth Century Fox, said that "Hiring international talent is a movie-making law." In this environment, international actors who formerly played supporting or villainous roles in American films suddenly were elevated to star status. One example was the casting of Japanese actor Ken Watanabe in 2003's *The Last Samurai.*

RESEARCH AND TECHNOLOGY

Computers and digital technology revolutionized filmmaking in the 1990s. Audiences often see a movie to view stylized visual effects and digitized images. Computer technology has cut expenses from movie production. The digital studio business is growing at a rate of 25 to 30 percent per year. Some unions of carpenters, decorators, and electricians fear they are at risk of losing their jobs, for large scenes can now be synthesized into a computer and images of live action by actors can be created, according to the U.S. Department of Labor. Because a top actor can demand upwards of 18 percent of a movie's gross box office receipts, some studios are working on developing virtual actors. This process is the same one used to create a digitized running dinosaur in the film *Jurassic Park.* Some industry analysts say that between 2005 and 2010, extensive use of computer-derived human images will become viable, replacing the need for studios to hire costly, sometimes hard-to-obtain people to serve as movie extras, for example.

U.S. companies such as Silicon Graphics, IBM, Microsoft, and Autodesk, and Canadian firms Soft-Image and Discreet Logic are leading firms in this new area. Special effects firm Industrial Light and Magic employed 400 digital specialists, and Sony's firm Imageworks, founded in the early 1990s, employed 100 digital artists. Disney has also been a leader in this technology for years with its world-class animation division. Other specialists include Boss Film Studios and Digital Domain. In mid-1994, Twentieth Century-Fox announced it was spending US$100 million to start a computerized animation studio in Arizona. California's Silicon Valley's high-tech computer firms have joined forces with Hollywood to create this new technique to filmmaking, earning the Santa Monica area the title *Silwood.* Further, movie producers began to rely on high-bandwidth connections to facilitate filmmaking in the late 1990s. Although the investment remained considerable at this time because movie studios require high-speed connections to transmit images, some studios started to use this technology to increase communication and efficiency.

While film remains important in motion picture production, digital technology and computer-generated imaging is the wave of the future, according to the U.S. Department of Labor. Editing changes that would cost costly scene setups can be done quite inexpensively with digital manipulation. Scene location can be digitally altered instantly should a director find a script locale unsatisfactory. Even actors can be created digitally. Some of the greatest experimentation in this area is being done by independent filmmakers, the savings in total production costs helping to make these small companies occasionally quite competitive with mega-studios, according to the U.S. Department of Labor.

In the future, digital technology will also transform distribution, bringing film into theaters via satellite or fiber optic cable, noted the U.S. Department of Labor. As of now, many new theaters are constructed with the ability to receive distributed films through use of the new technology. Major studios and independent companies alike welcome such advances as a means to cut distribution costs.

INDUSTRY LEADERS

Time Warner Inc. A 1989 merger between Time Inc. and Warner Communications resulted in the world's largest publishing and entertainment company, at which time film entertainment accounted for 25 percent of the company's revenues.

Warner Brothers was founded in the 1920s by four brothers (Harry, Albert, Jack, and Sam Warner) and produced the first talking feature film, *The Jazz Singer,* in 1927. One of Hollywood's largest movie studios, Warner is known for such classics as *Casablanca* and *Rebel Without a Cause.* Following a decline in the 1950s and 1960s, the studio was acquired by Kinney National Service Corporation and renamed Warner Communications in 1971. The 1980s saw an earnings decline and a takeover attempt by Rupert Murdoch, but the company rebounded to become one of the most stable studios in the movie industry. In 1989, Time Inc. merged with Warner Communications to form Time Warner Inc. In 1991, the company sold a 12.5 percent interest in its cable television, cable programming, and film operations to two Japanese companies. The same year, Time Warner entered into a long-range agreement with the Dutch-owned Regency International Pictures, the French pay-TV company Canal Plus, and the German production and distribution firm Scriba & Deyhle. The three companies agreed to provide Time Warner with US$600 million to produce at least 20 movies for international distribution. Later, Time Warner increased its control of the entertainment world by acquiring Turner Broadcasting in the mid-1990s, which owned New Line Cinema.

In 2000, Time Warner merged with AOL creating an industry giant with US$160 billion in its wallet. Nevertheless, while total profits of the combined venture disappointed shareholders and media predictors as AOL advertising sales sagged, AOL Time Warner did achieve instant financial success as a maker of blockbuster movies. The powerful Internet presence of America Online boosted Warner Bros. and its affiliate New Line Cinema to number-one box office respectability over the previous champ, Walt Disney, in 2001. With 10 films in the number one box office position right after opening, the studio gobbled up more than a fifth (22 percent) of all movie studio profits for 2001. Leading the charge for the studio were the *Harry Potter and the Sorcerer's Stone* and *The Lord of the Rings: The Fellowship of the Ring,* productions which continued to amass tremendous profits in 2002 as tickets went on sale at international theaters.

By 2004, AOL Time Warner had changed its name to Time Warner Inc., with America Online Inc. operating as a separate subsidiary. That year, its Warner Bros. Pictures segment released 22 motion pictures, including *Harry Potter and the Prisoner of Azkaban* and *Million Dollar Baby* which won the year's Academy Award for Best Picture. The segment distributed films to 125 countries, and released internationally 18 English-language films and 23 local-language films that it had acquired or produced. New Line, a producer and distributor of "independent" films, released 14 movies during 2004. The segment also continued to receive significant revenue from its video distribution, with *The Lord of the Rings: The Return of the King* being particularly profitable in this format. Warner Home Video Inc. distributes the vast library of film products from the company's other subsidiaries. At the end of 2004, the library contained more than 6,600 motion picture titles, 40,000 television titles, and 14,000 animation titles. Time Warner's filmed entertainment segment produced US$11.85 billion in revenues in 2004 (26 percent of the total company revenue). The company attributed the largest drivers of its revenue growth to the sale of DVDs.

Walt Disney Company. Brought to life in 1923 when Walt Disney and his brother Roy started a film studio in Hollywood, the Walt Disney Company established the reputation as the preeminent producer of animated films in the world. Walt Disney Company has diversified into a number of other business areas over the years, including theme parks and hotels, cable television, publishing, and merchandising. While the Walt Disney Company has enjoyed a long and generally successful life, the company's film business did suffer through a difficult period in the 1970s. Disney films went from producing over 50 percent of company revenues in 1971 to only 20 percent in 1979. In 1980, the company's leadership changed and in 1984 the Bass family of Texas bought a controlling interest in the company. Michael Eisner, formerly of Paramount, was installed as the company's new CEO. Together with Frank Wells, a former Warner Brothers executive, Eisner is credited with Disney's reemergence as a major presence in the film industry during the 1980s. In 1993, Disney acquired Miramax, a privately held independent producer. Miramax, which was founded in 1980, was a top producer of movies made outside the traditional Hollywood studio system. In late 1994, Disney announced the creation of a new subsidiary under Miramax to promote French films in the United States. Buena Vista Pictures Distribution, Disney's releasing company, is the country's largest film studio subsidiary. In addition, Disney also owns Touchstone Pictures, a prominent U.S. movie distributor.

By February 2002 Disney had lost both its undisputed title of number-one studio (held since 1995) and also its primary reputation as a maker of animation films. Some commentators reasoned that Disney's executives dabbled in many areas traditionally outside the studio's traditional strength, floundering in the process as expected blockbusters, such as *Pearl Harbor,* performed well below ticket sale expectations. As a result, in the opening months of 2002, Disney saw its stock fall to US$23.90, a collapse of 26 percent from the same period of 2001. During the crisis, Walt Disney Studios Chairman Peter Schneider bailed out, and in mid-February 2002 was replaced by Richard Cook, a one-time Disneyland amusement park employeewhose main job was to help the company regain its number-one status. In particular, Cook's job was to assemble a first-rate animation film of *Fantasia* quality, since in recent years only the 1999 *Tarzan* animated film had attracted both revenues and critical acclaim. Snatching the lead from Disney in the area of animation was Dreamworks SKG, which not only acquired creative acclaim with its edgy *Shrek*, but also garnered US$267 million in box office ticket receipts and moved rapidly in 2002 to put the sequel, *Shrek 2* onscreen.

In 1991, Disney entered into a feature film agreement with computer animations studio, Pixar. Owned 51 percent by the co-founder and CEO of Apple Computers, Steve Jobs, Pixar went on to produce six full-length animated films all released by Walt Disney. These films included: *Toy Story* (1995), *A Bug's Life* (1998), *Toy Story 2* (1999), *Monsters Inc.* (2000), *Finding Nemo* (2003), and *The Incredibles* (2004). All of the movies did extremely well both domestically and internationally, with several beating box office records held at the time of their release. In all, Pixar had received 15 Academy Awards for its films. The final film under the Pixar/Disney agreement is expected to be released in 2006, after which Pixar's relationship with Disney for any new titles will end.

In 2004, the Studio Entertainment segment of Walt Disney Company contributed US$8.71 billion of the company's total revenues of US$30.75 billion. This segment's revenue represented a 19 percent increase over the previous year. However, revenues from worldwide theatrical film distribution were down US$215 million, with movies such as *Arthur, The Alamo*, and the animated feature *Home on the Range* failing to pull strong box-office numbers. The gain in overall revenues came from higher DVD sales, with such DVD releases as *Pirates of the Caribbean* and *Finding Nemo*.

As of September 30, 2004, the Company had released 832 full length live action features—primarily color—69 full length animated color features, approximately 540 cartoon shorts and 53 live action shorts under the Walt Disney Pictures, Touchstone Pictures, Hollywood Pictures, Miramax and Dimension banners. During 2005, Disney was expecting to distribute 37 feature films.

In July 2005, Disney announced that it had reached an agreement with the founders of Miramax, Bob and Harvey Weinstein. The filmmakers were going to leave the company in September 2005, with Disney retaining the Miramax name and the Weinsteins taking the Dimension name. The Weinsteins had been responsible for such films as *Pulp Fiction* (1994), *Chicago* (2002), and *The Aviator* (2004), with the subsidiary garnering 53 Academy Awards, including three for best picture.

Viacom Inc. With its ownership of Paramount, one of the original major motion picture film studios, Viacom was one of the world's leading film producers and distributors in 2005. It owned a library of more than 1,100 titles, including the highest grossing movie of all time, *Titanic*, as well as *Forrest Gump*, and the franchises for *Star Trek*, *The Godfather*, and *Indiana Jones*. In 2004, 18 percent of Viacom's revenues of US$25.26 billion came from its Entertainment division, of which its motion picture production and distribution business was a part. This division also included publisher Simon & Schuster, Paramount theme parks, Famous Players movie theaters, and Famous music which was involved in music publishing. That year, Paramount released 16 movies, including *Collateral* with Tom Cruise. In addition, the company earned revenue through DVD sales and through license fees for television usage of films in its library. Revenue from feature film exploitation earned the company US$2.21 billion.

Viacom was formed in 1970 by the Canadian Broadcasting Corporation (CBC) after the Federal Communications Commission (FCC) ruled that networks could not own cable systems and television stations in the same market. After a hostile takeover attempt by Carl Icahn in 1986, and a six-month bidding war with movie theater chain Sumner Redstone's National Amusements, Redstone purchased 83 percent of Viacom for US$3.4 billion. In 1994, under Redstone's guidance, Viacom won its bid to purchase Paramount, a much larger company, for an estimated US$10 billion. This occurred only after a fierce battle with TV Shopping Network, a hostile bidder. While the price Viacom paid for Paramount was high, Viacom was heartened by the company's success in the summer of 1994, when it pulled in a company record US$413 million in box office receipts.

In 1994, Viacom also completed an acquisition of Blockbuster Entertainment Corporation, an international home video and music retailer. In the late 1990s, Blockbuster Entertainment reigned as the king of the video rental industry in the United States, with about 25 percent of the domestic market. Blockbuster operated more than 5,300 video stores in the United States and throughout the world. Nonetheless, Viacom considered selling Blockbuster in the late 1990s, fearing the decline of the video rental industry. Viacom's sales rose by 9 percent to US$13.2 billion in 1997 and Paramount ranked third with a 13 percent market share in 1996. By 2002, Viacom once again was bolstered by a revitalized Blockbuster, and the publishing, video, and entertainment conglomerate announced 2001 revenues of US$23.2 billion, a 16 percent increase.

In 2005, Viacom was expecting to release 15 feature films. In addition, in June 2005, the company announced plans to spin off its holdings into two separate, publicly traded companies: a new Viacom (of which the company's film production and distribution will be a part) and CBS Corporation.

The News Corporation Limited. One of the world's most extensive media empires, News Corporation has holdings on four continents and in all of the major English-speaking communications centers. The Australian company was founded in 1923 by Sir Keith Murdoch, and was taken over by his son Rupert in 1952 when the elder Murdoch died. The younger Murdoch expanded the existing newspaper properties into magazines, radio, and television. In 1985, News Corporation made a move into the motion picture industry with the purchase of the Twentieth Century Fox film company for US$575 million. Twentieth Century Fox had formed as the result of a 1935 merger between Fox Film Corporation, an independent producer, and Twentieth Century Pictures.

The company's Fox Filmed Entertainment business was one of the world's largest distributors and producers of motion pictures in 2004 under its Twentieth Century Fox, Fox 2000, Fox Searchlight Pictures, and Twentieth Century Fox Animation subsidiaries. That year, the company produced and/or distributed such films as *Master and Commander* and *The Day After Tomorrow*. That year, filmed entertainment accounted for about US$5.4 billion of the company's total revenues of approximateyly US$22 billion.

Sony Corporation. Founded in 1946, Sony has long been recognized as a leader in consumer electronics, but did not move into entertainment until the 1970s when it sparked the mass market for home video through the introduction of the Betamax videocassette recorder. Sony later purchased Tri-Star Pictures and Columbia Pictures Entertainment Inc., acquisitions that served notice to the rest of the film entertainment industry that a significant new competitor had emerged. Columbia Pictures was founded in the 1920s as a small independent film producer. Columbia was known as the first outfit to film movie scenes out of sequence to reduce production costs, and was also the first studio to move into television production. In 1982, Coca-Cola Co. purchased Columbia Pictures and later combined it with Tri-Star Pictures to form Columbia Pictures Entertainment (Tri-Star Pictures was founded in 1982 as a joint venture between Columbia Pictures, Home Box Office, and CBS). Sony purchased Tri-Star and Columbia Pictures in 1989 and acquired the Guber-Peters Entertainment Company as part of the transaction. Sony earned US$50.7 billion in 1997 from its various businesses (the majority outside the movie industry) and its movie studios held an 11 percent market share in 1996.

For the fiscal year ended March 2005, the company's Sony Pictures Entertainment (SPE) subsidiary earned the company about 10.7 percent of its total revenue of approximately US$66.6 billion. SPE had operations in 67 countries.

During 2006, the company expected to distribute 51 films under the banners of Columbia, TriStar, Sony Pictures, and Revolution Studios.

Metro Goldwyn Mayer Inc: In April 2005, a consortium of investors, including Sony Corporation of America, purchased Metro Goldwyn Mayer, keeping the company privately held. As part of the deal, Sony Pictures Entertainment was to take on the distribution of MGM's library of 4,000 films and 10,400 television episodes. It is also expected that MGM will co-finance the production of films with SPE.

With 2004 sales of US$1.72 billion, MGM remained an important industry player. However, the company was not without its challenges. It reported a net loss of US$29.2 million that year, which followed on a 2003 loss of US$161.8 million. MGM hits in the early 2000s included *Hannibal* and *Legally Blond*. The venerable studio also had a film library of studio hits, such as the James Bond sequels, over its long history.

NBC Universal Inc. NBC Universal was created in 2004 through the combination of NBC and Vivendi Universal Entertainment, the entertainment assets of media and telecommunications giant, Vivendi Universal. The new company was 80 percent owned by General Electric and 20 percent by Vivendi Universal. Sales that year were approximately $US13 billion, with the company releasing such films as *The Bourne Supremacy* and *Ray* through its Universal Studios company. The company also earns revenues from its catalog of more than 4,000 titles.

Vivendi CEO Jean-Marie Messier spearheaded a 2000 merger with Seagram that combined a media empire with a movie and TV studio, recording studio, and theme park empire. According to *USA Today*, Vivendi purchased Seagram for US$34 billion, or US$77.35 per share. Upon completion of the deal, the French-run Vivendi Universal assumed the status of a major player in Hollywood. By the end of the 2001, Vivendi Universal produced ledger sheets showing a 9 percent gain in revenues by the company as a string of movie hits offset some faltering in its music division, according to *Financial Times*. Vivendi Universal posted 2001 profits of US$25.3 billion 2001 as its Universal Studios division produced audience pleasers such as *Jurassic Park 3* and *The Mummy Returns*. By 2003, Vivendi Universal had sold its movie studio, as well as its theme parks and TV interests, to NBC as it sought to pay down debt. Vivendi continued to concentrate on telecommunications, and on its Universal Music division.

Universal Studios began as Music Corporation of America or MCA. MCA was founded in 1924 as an entertainment booking company. In addition to representing bands, the company began to buy up talent agencies and individual entertainer contracts. In the 1950s, MCA moved into the area of television production, which in turn, provided jobs for MCA's clients. By the late 1950s, MCA derived revenues from over 45 percent of all network evening programs. The 1970s and early 1980s brought the company into the bright lights of the major motion picture arena with its success of Jaws and The Deer Hunter. The late 1980s, however, were bringing fewer successes, and the company began to lower production costs. Under the foreign ownership of Matsushita Electric Industrial Co., entertainment profits only amounted to a 2.7 percent five-year average in 1994. In 1995, Seagram Co. acquired 80 percent of MCA and later changed its name to Universal Studios, which had a strong year in 1995 with Apollo 13 and Casper. Despite its lack of blockbusters in 1996, the company still controlled 8 percent of the market.

MAJOR COUNTRIES IN THE INDUSTRY

United States. Following record box office totals in the early 2000s, the U.S. motion picture industry continued to fare well heading into the mid-2000s. In 2003, box office receipts totaled US$9.5 billion, down less than 1 percent from 2002 and the second-highest level in industry history. The top five companies in the U.S.—Sony, Walt Disney, Time Warner, General Electric, and The News Corporation held about 64 percent of the market in 2003. That year, 495 films were produced in the U.S., up from 467 the year before according to Euromonitor.

Although 2003 theater admissions were down 4 percent from 2002, an admission tally of almost 1.6 billion was still very impressive. In a March 23, 2004 news release, Motion Picture Association of America (MPAA) CEO Jack Valenti remarked: "Remember, in order to find any range of admissions that compared to 2003, you have to go back 48 years, to 1955, before television and cable." After leading the MPAA for 38 years, Valenti retired in July 2004. Two months later, he was succeeded by former Kansas Congressman and Secretary of Agriculture Dan Glickman.

Indeed, 2003's admission totals were quite remarkable considering the heightened competition that movie theaters faced for viewer attention. In the same news release, Valenti noted that, in addition to an explosive video game market, during the mid-2000s theaters competed with television sets in 108 million homes, VCRs in 98 million homes, and DVD players in 47 million homes. The number of households with computers numbered 67 million, followed by Internet connections (62 million), cable television (74 million), and satellite TV (20 million).

Because of the success of newly merged companies such as AOL Time Warner and Vivendi Universal, Hollywood was in the midst of "golden age" of prosperity during the early 2000s, similar to the 1930s and 1940s. However, it faced the alarming reality that increasing numbers of people were turning to video games and other forms of home entertainment over the cinema. Most of these companies were seeing increases in the sale of DVDs from their library of films as a result.

A major employer, the motion picture production and distribution industry oversaw about 287,000 wage and salary jobs in U.S. studios by 2000. According to the U.S. Labor Department, jobs included directing, scriptwriting, casting, acting, editing, film processing, motion picture and videotape reproduction, and equipment and wardrobe rental. Other businesses such as catering, security, and hairdressing also provided vital services to studios.

India. Indian feature films often have several qualities in common: they are usually about three hours long, they are musical with the actors lip-synching and dancing at various points in the movie, and they often are stylized remakes of Hollywood films. With the country having many languages, the film is regionalized by language. Mumbai (formerly Bombay) is the largest region, and has become known as Bollywood due to the large number of movies made there. Indian films were becoming more popular in Western countries. In 2004, the English-language films *Bride and Prejudice* and *Vanity Fair* were popular around the world.

In 2004, the industry was valued at about US$1.3 billion, and the country continued to be the world's largest producer of films, turning out about 1,000 each year. However, the industry is noted for the amount of criminal activity involved in it. According to *Business Week*, loan sharks and gangsters bankroll more than half of the country's movies with 40 percent interest rates, because banks consider lending money for movies too risky. In the late 1990s, the industry faced widespread corruption as angry gangsters began killing movie industry affiliates. Much of India's more than US$1 billion film industry rakes in profits that are never registered due to various illegalities such as usury. Films are produced for far less expense in India compared to Hollywood. A movie with a US$2 million budget would be considered a high-budget film.

The film industry in India dates back to 1896 when a pioneering cinematography company from France called the Lumière Brothers' Chinematographe filmed six silent films. Prior to the nineteenth century, the first films made by an Indian filmmaker, Harishchandra Sakharam Bhatvadekar, were two short, entertaining documentaries on wrestling and monkeys. Not until 1913 did a full-length silent movie made entirely in India appear in theaters; this was *King Harishchandra* created by filmmaker Dhundiraj Govind Phalke. Eighteen years later, the Imperial Film Company of India released a full-length feature with sound called *Alam Ara*.

Hong Kong. In the 1980s, Hong Kong was third in the world in terms of film exports, producing about 300 films per year. However, in 2004, 64 movies were made locally. The industry was greatly affected by the availability of inexpensive, pirated copies of DVDs and videos, an issue affecting both local and popular foreign films. According to PricewaterhouseCoopers, up to 98 percent of films in mainland China were pirated copies. Further adding to local woes was the fact that despite sovereignty being turned over to China in 1997, by 2003, films made in Hong Kong were still considered "foreign" and were therefore subject to restrictions in terms of the number allowed to enter the mainland.

France. Based on ticket revenues, France boasted one of Europe's most productive film industries in the early 2000s. With government subsidies making profits almost inevitable, and government-imposed regulations to keep films from Hollywood overshadowing national films, France was second in the world with 184 million tickets sold. *Amelie,* a Miramax film directed by Jean-Pierre Jeunet, was France's leading artistic success and box office moneymaker, selling 8 million tickets. The sequel *La Verité si je mens? 2* (*Would I Lie to You? 2*), was nearly as successful with 7.8 million tickets.

The French industry began to make a stand against Hollywood domination in the late 1990s, churning out 150 movies in the first 10 months of 1996. In 2001, Hollywood movies accounted for only about half of all movie receipts, in part because the blockbuster films *Lord of the Rings* and *Harry Potter and the Sorcerer's Stone* were released at Christmas, meaning they would be audited for 2002 gate receipts. Therefore, in 2001 *Shrek* was Hollywood's top money earner in France with 3.9 million tickets sold. Many U.S. films, including *Cast Away* with Tom Hanks and *A.I* by Steven Spielberg, played to universally empty theaters in France.

To lead the country's renaissance, the Commission Nationale du Film formed in 1996, promoting French films and filming in France by movie makers from other countries. French studios upgraded their equipment throughout the 1990s to attract more outside movie producers, especially U.S. moviemakers. France also continued building multiplex theaters during this period, erecting 233 new screens in 1996 alone.

In the country's film production industry, valued at about US$1.4 billion in 2003, about 73 percent were entirely French-produced films. Leading industry players included Gaumont, TF1, Canal+ and Pathé. According to Euromonitor, entirely French produced films are expected to account for the majority of the French market in the period leading up to 2008.

Germany. Like other countries around the world, Germany saw a spate of multiplex theaters go up in the mid- to late 1990s, which fueled some of the industry's sales. Analysts were concerned that without more restraint, multiplex theaters could flood the market and undercut the industry's growth. Nevertheless, Germany's movie ticket sales showed a boost of 15 percent from 2000 to 2001, grossing US$109 million as of October 2001. In 2003, Germany theaters faced a number of difficulties, including sour economic conditions and rising competition from DVDs. That year, box office figures fell11.5 percent to US$1.1 billion, according to *Variety*. Germany's 1,831 theaters, with 4,868 screens, reported 149 million admissions in 2003.

According to Euromonitor, more than 100 films were produced or co-produced by German film production companies in 2003. The market leader in the country was X-Filme Creative Pool which produced the film *Good Bye Lenin*.

Japan. Though Japan's motion picture industry suffered from declining theater attendance in the early 1990s, the industry's fortune changed in 1997, when attendance shot up 17.7 percent to 140.7 million moviegoers. Japan's *Princess Mononoke* was the big blockbuster that led the industry's comeback as the best selling movie in the country's history, garnering US$142 million at the box office. In addition, multiplex theaters contributed to the resurgence of the industry as did the economic prosperity of the country. Japan had 1,884 screens in the late 1990s and over 2,825 by 2004. In 1997 box-office sales totaled US$1.41 billion. In 2004, that figure had escalated to about US$2 billion. About 60 percent of the leading movies were foreign, although the number-one film at the box office that year was a Japanese animated film titled *Howl's Moving Castle*, followed by the U.S. film, *The Last Samurai*.

Although movies from the United States had long been popular in Japan, a new trend was the increase in movies from South Korea. In 2004, 29 films were released from that country, although they did not dominate in terms of box office receipts.

Mexico. Approximately 400 million people around the world speak Spanish, making Spanish-speaking nations the largest single-language market in the world, offering great potential to international firms. Mexico is considered the only Latin American country with a true film industry, albeit one just emerging in 2000. Mexico's film industry hoped to revive its previous "golden age" of the 1940s and 1950s, when it produced 15 percent of the world market for movies, many of them slapstick comedies. After World War II, the country released many big-screen romantic classics until the nationalization of the film and television industry in 1975. In the early 1990s, Mexico's recession stifled its film industry. In two years, the country produced only 29 movies during this period. However, as Mexico's economy recovered, its movie industry began to perk up as well. Ticket sales began to increase by the late 1990s. Theatergoers in Mexico City, for example, bought 46.8 million tickets in 1999 compared to just 28 million in 1995. While only eight movies were made in 1998, around 25 were filmed by Mexican filmmakers in 2000. Two of the top ticket sellers in recent years by Mexican filmmakers were the 1999 production of the comedic *Sexo, Pudor y Lagrimas* (*Sex, Shame, and Tears*) and the earthy 2002 film *Amores Perros*(*Love's a Bitch*), winner of the Critics' Week first prize at Cannes 2000.

Spain. The cinema remained as popular in Spain in 2002 as it had been in the late 1990s. Spain makes up one of Europe's largest markets for movies, and it seems to have weathered the national increase in the price of tickets in 2001, despite having once had nearly the lowest ticket prices worldwide. After experiencing financing problems in the previous decade, the native Spanish film industry was surprisingly strong in 2001 as *The Others* secured revenues of US$24 million, and the comedy *Torrente 2* brought in US$21 million. Increased sales of around 140 million tickets led to an estimated 10 percent increase in 2001 box office profits. Another boost to the Spanish film industry in 2001 was the fact that local audiences provided a much more lukewarm reception to Hollywood films than they did in the late 1990s.

By 2003, Spain continued to have some of the lowest ticket prices in Europe. However, the country's movie market was cooling off. According to *Variety*, admissions fell from a record 146.8 million in 2001 to 140.7 million in 2002 and 137.5 million in 2003. Explosive growth in the number of movie screens, which skyrocketed 137 percent from 1993 to 2003, also had slowed by 2003 as the market reached a saturation point. In 2003, the country had 1,194 theaters with 4,253 screens. Some 458 movie releases, led by *Mortadelo & Filemon: The Big Adventure*, resulted in total box office sales of about US$770 million that year.

Canada. In 1996, the combined revenues of Canada's film and television production industries totaled US$2.7 billion. The Canadian government plays an instrumental role in the country's movie industry, helping by awarding grants and tax incentives to film investors to advance the industry. Sheila Copps, Canadian Heritage Minister, promised to change Canadian film policy to help increase the number of Canadian movies shown on Canadian screens. However, even though Canada has been able to produce a good number of movies per year, few Canadians actually watch them. In the late 1990s, about 3 percent of the country's total screen time was devoted to Canadian movies. In 2001, with an upswing in the building of megaplex theaters in Canada, Statistics Canada reported that the nation's movie attendance was its highest per capita in decades. However, smaller theaters were closing in large numbers as their quality of screen, sound, and ambiance failed to match the attraction of the giant theater complexes. In contrast to declining movie profits from the mid-1990s until 1999, in 2001 the movie industry announced all-time record profits of US$8.4 million and all-time high ticket sales of US$1.49 billion, according to *Film Journal* magazine. In 2003, *Variety* reported that Canada's 529 movie releases resulted in sales of US$714 million.

Britain. In 2003, film production in the United Kingdom was valued at approximately US$2 billion by Euromonitor, with Time Warner having the largest market share at 30 percent. Although dominated by U.S.-based industry giants, 109 films were produced in the U.K. or had a U.K. financial involvement in 2003. Theatre admission in 2003 was 167.3 million, down slightly from 2002 levels of 176 million. British feature films released that year earned about US$14.5 million, while co-productions with other countries had box office grosses of more than US$234 million. The most successful co-production that year was the film *Love Actually*. The British moving-going public viewed some 422 movie releases, including the leading *Lord of the Rings: Return of the King*, which grossed more than US$105 million in the U.K. The industry's strong performance in 2003 followed a period of general prosperity during the early 2000s. For example, Britain's box office sales for 2001 were estimated at around 152 million tickets, easily besting the 143 million gate receipts collected in 2000.

Curiously, many of the most successful films in Britain during the early 2000s were either based in England or were about English subjects, yet they were Hollywood financed and produced. One popular film in England, *Captain Corelli's Mandolin* with Nicholas Cage, fared poorly in the U.S. market. Predictably, U.S. smash hits based in England, such as *Lord of the Rings, Harry Potter and the Sorcerer's Stone*, and *Bridget Jones's Diary* were successes overseas as well. *Potter* earned US$63 million and *Bridget Jones's Diary*, considerably cheaper to film, raked in just under that total at US$61 million.

British studios have been particularly attractive to international film producers because of their lower costs. Historical dramas with authentic backdrops were in demand, as well as English-speaking actors and film crews. The British are well known for their quality stage constructors and technicians, and are developing a reputation for their special effects work. In 1992, the British Film Commission used its state-financed resources to attract foreign investment. The Conservative government pledged to provide over US$130 million of national lottery money and put it into the production and distribution of British films from 1995 to 2000. In the late 1990s, the government began to restructure the industry to make it stable and ensure its success with the Film Policy Review by Department of Culture, Media, and Sport.

Italy. Once as receptive to Hollywood films as Germany, in 2001 Italian filmmakers had hopes that the earnings of Italian pictures signified a more receptive local market for Italian films. Among the highest audience-drawing films of 2001 were Aldo, Giovanni & Giacomo's *Ask Me If I'm Happy* and Gabriele Muccino's *The Last Kiss.* Nonetheless, U.S. films such as the successful *Bridget Jones* still dwarfed Italian films overall, albeit not as noticeably as in the past. Hollywood movies earned 60 percent of all Italian revenues, and Italian films had an 18 percent slice of the pie.

By 2003, multiplex theaters represented only one-third of Italy's cinema screens, according to *Variety.* Although this was low in comparison to other European countries, Italy's multiplexes brought in half of the country's movie sales. Italy's 2,298 theaters had 3,628 screens in 2003. That year, 109.3 million admissions, supported by top film *Harry Potter and the Chamber of Secrets,* produced box office sales of US$766.5 million.

Egypt. In 1923, Egypt started producing silent films, and patterned its first large production facility, Studio Misr, after Hollywood in 1935. In the 1940s and 1950s, Egypt's film industry was known as *Hollywood on the Nile,* when it produced more than 100 films per year. However, by 1994 the number of films Cairo produced dropped drastically to 22. The outlook for the 1990s was not expected to improve, for the combination of heavy taxes, censorship, satellite dishes, and video piracy were all responsible for this industry's decline. There were approximately 36 fees and taxes placed on the industry, with assessments going to everyone from the Minister of Finance to the Police Benevolent Society. The state's censor office placed all films through a synopsis, final script, and release approval, often resulting in substantial revision of the original script. The Ministry of Tourism often charges high fees for the use of the great ancient sites like the Great Pyramids for use as backdrops. However, efforts to revive the country's cinema arose in the late 1990s. In 2001, U.S. movies earned US$2.7 million, roughly consistent with earnings of US$2.9 million in 1998, the highest profits ever recorded in Egypt.

FURTHER READING

Andrews, Nigel. "Bullets over Bollywood." *Financial Times,* 22 November 1997, WFT1.

Bentsen, Cheryl. "Don't Call It Bollywood." *CIO,* 1 December 2000. Available from http://www.cio.com.

Brown, Amanda. "What has happened to the once prolific Hollywood of the East?" *Asian Broadcaster,* April 2003. Available from http://www.pwchk.com.

Chipman, Kim. "Disney Studio Promotes Cook to Head Its Namesake Film Studio." *Bloomberg News*, 15 February 2002.

"(Canada's) Cinemas Paying for Overcapacity." *The Record (Kitchener-Waterloo)*, 2 February 2002.

"Dan Glickman to Succeed Jack Valenti as Head of MPAA; Valenti Resigns After 38-Year Tenure." Los Angeles: Motion Picture Association of America Inc., 1 July 2004. Available from http://www.mpaa.org.

Dawtrey, Adam. "United Kingdom: Blighty Distribs Feeling New 'Passion' for Indie Pics." *Variety,* 10 May 2004.

De Pablos, Emiliano. "Spain: Dire TV Situation Forces Distribs to Renegotiate Pic Pacts." *Variety,* 10 May 2004.

———. "Spain: Screen Slowdown Hits B.O." *Variety,* 21 June 2004.

"Film Industry in Hong Kong." May 2005. Available from http://www.info.gov.hk.

Fineman, Josh. "New Line's 'John Q' May Top Four Other Films." *Bloomberg News*, 15 February 2002.

Gross, Neil, et al. "The Entertainment Glut." *Business Week,* 16 February 1998.

Groves, Don. "Mideast Finds Film Oasis." *Daily Variety,* 21 November 2001.

Hasden, Don. "A Sign of America's Changing Tastes." *Chattanooga Times/Chattanooga Free Press,* 11 February 2002.

———. "International Actors a Passport to Profitability." *The New York Times,* 5 July 2004.

"Homegrown Pix Gain in Europe." *Variety,* 6 January 2002.

"Jack Valenti Announces Resignation After 38 Years as Head of MPAA/MPA." Los Angeles: Motion Picture Association of America Inc., 1 July 2004. Available from http://www.mpaa.org.

James, Alison. "France: Territory Overheats Under Release Overload, as Ancillary Markets Cool Off." *Variety,* 10 May 2004.

"Japanese Film Industry." *Japan Economic Monthly*, May 2005. Available from http://www.jetro.com.

Kelly, Brendan. "Canada: Quebec Pics Still on a Winning Streak, While DVD and TV Improve." *Variety,* 10 May 2004.

Kilday, Gregg. "International Film Piracy Hot Topic at ShoWest." *Amusement Business,* 29 March 2004.

Kingsley, Simon. "Germany: Teutonic B.O. Hit by Economy and Piracy." *Variety,* 21 June 2004.

Kingsley, Simon, and Ed Meza. "Germany: Smaller Distribs See Opportunity in Wake of Big 2003 Losses." *Variety,* 10 May 2004.

"Major Market Profiles: Film Production in USA (Germany, UK, and France)." *Euromonitor,* October 2004. Available from http://www.euromonitor.com.

"MGM Reports Record Earnings." *Agence France Presse,* 6 February 2002.

"Reversal of Fortune: The Need to Forge a New Strategy for Canadian Productions." Canadian Film and Television Production Association, February 2005. Available from http://www.cftpa.ca.

"Romancing the Disc; The Movie Business." *The Economist,* 7 February 2004.

Schwarzacher, Lukas. "Japan: Losses and Consolidation Spur Local Pic Focus." *Variety,* 10 May 2004.

"Valenti Reports 2003 Box Office as Second Highest in History at ShoWest." Los Angeles: Motion Picture Association of America Inc., 23 March 2004. Available from http://www.mpaa.org.

Vivarelli, Nick. "Italy: Lack of Screens Curbs Exhibits." *Variety,* 21 June 2004.

Vivienne, Walt, and David Lieberman. "Vivendi Confirms Seagram Purchase: French Firm Now Powerful Player in Entertainment." *USA Today,* 20 June 2000.

Watling, John D. "Amores Perros Spearheads New Age of Mexican Cinema." *Business Mexico,* 1 August 2000.

Waxman, Sharon. "I Love You, Now Go Away; Egypt's Relationship With the West Is a Case Study In Contradictions." *The Washington Post,* 17 December 2001.

SIC 7941

NAICS 711211

SPORTS CLUBS AND PROMOTERS

Firms in the industry operate professional athletic teams and clubs around the globe. Examples of sports clubs discussed in this article include franchises for soccer (known in many parts of the world as football), basketball, baseball, American football, hockey, and rugby. The sports industry also encompasses sporting event promoters and players' agents.

INDUSTRY SNAPSHOT

At the close of World War II, increasingly sophisticated means of public communication drew together a sports audience that, theretofore, had been loyal but difficult to address as a unit. Even as television introduced a huge audience to the visual impact and drama of sports, franchise owners, athletes, and promoters were quick to view resulting fan accessibility as an extremely lucrative source of revenue. Suddenly, sport became not just business, but big business. The fact that the U.S. sports business was intertwined with virtually every aspect of the economy—from media and apparel to food and advertising—added to its explosion, but it also added to the industry overhead.

In some eyes, sport itself mutated into a means to an end, a component of an entertainment package—important, but only part of a total entertainment offering capable of bringing in fans and generating revenue. As the dollars handled in the name of sport increased, players' unions, first attempted some 100 years before, became an entity to be reckoned with. The business of sport spawned sophisticated player/player, agent/owner negotiations; gave rise to a huge emphasis on venue, such asstadium construction; and introduced potential franchise owners to a whole new concept of high-stakes profit and loss, as well as wheeling and dealing. This, in turn, changed the games themselves, as the attempt to bring in more and more fans to a given event inspired a need to appeal to the general public, not just sports aficionados.

ORGANIZATION AND STRUCTURE

The sports industry includes a wide range of establishments that are involved in one aspect or another of the presentation of sporting events. Team owners may be individuals or companies that own sports clubs (although in the United States the National Football League (NFL) forbade outright corporate ownership). Promoters include global entities (for example, the Federation Internationale de Football Association or the International Olympic Committee), and regional or national sports organizations, commercial promoters, and organized groups of players.

Whereas in years past athletes approached or were approached by sports clubs directly, by 1990 most professional athletes were represented by agents or managers who negotiated on their behalf with clubs, sponsors, and event-promoters. The establishment or ongoing maintenance of sports franchises involved similar negotiation with advertisers/sponsors, broadcasters, host cities, and merchandisers. Each of these participating camps proceeded to forge the best possible economic deal for itself, and, inevitably, less-than-altruistic goals created conflict. Negotiations between agents for athletes and teams were often contentious, reflecting the desire of both sides to secure as much of the money as possible flowing in from ticket sales, television rights, advertising, and merchandising rights. Conflict often escalated to arbitration, and occasionally litigation. In some sports, wholesale player strikes occurred, adding the intangible monetary losses associated with fan dissatisfaction to the more obvious tally for legal advice and lost revenues. In the U.S., a baseball players' strike from 1994 to 1995 had an outright cost to team owners of more than US$1 billion, and the fallout from fan dissatisfaction remained in evidence throughout the remainder of the century.

World Competitive Dynamics. The competitive structure of the late twentieth century sports industry varied by region and country. While the sports leagues in the United States commonly practiced some sort of revenue-sharing philosophy, professional leagues in Europe, South America, and elsewhere often conveyed a survival-of-the-fittest mentality.

In the United States, revenue sharing within organized sports leagues allowed small-market teams to compete, on equal or nearly equal footing, with wealthy teams that were located in major metropolitan areas. In accordance with this philosophy, each league established a company to sell merchandising rights, and profits from this merchandising were shared equally among league members, regardless of individual team contribution to total sales. This approach extended significantly to include the very lucrative national television rights without which many smaller teams would disappear into oblivion. Even so, the disparities in local television and stadium revenues disadvantaged certain smaller-market teams, who had less money to spend and, thus, less voice in league-wide negotiations. This was particularly evident when affluent organizations signed players to large-sum contracts. The escalating salary benchmarks placed huge pressure on the smaller and middle-market teams. The revenue-sharing philosophy lessened the discrepancy between have and have-not clubs, and in fact did much to ameliorate a situation that otherwise could have resulted in several franchises going out of business.

Elsewhere in the world, the situation was dramatically different. In many nations, the cost of fielding competitive teams with star players was entirely beyond the capacity of some clubs. Without revenue-sharing mechanisms, richer teams secured the lion's share of high-priced talent—increasing the value of their ticket sales and television rights—while poorer teams stumbled toward financial ruin.

Lacking the sheer bulk associated with the U.S. sports industry, international sports organizations were forced into increased reliance on outside entities to remain viable. Private investment initially had been seen as a disadvantage. In the early 1990s, critics claimed that too many teams, in nearly all sports, "lived off" wealthy owners or their companies. But doing so increasingly became sheer necessity. In Spain, where soccer was a national obsession in the early 1990s, only one or two clubs were capable of showing sizable profits. The situation was similar in France, where Olympique Marseille, the champion club, operated in 1991 at a loss of more than US$3 million, and lesser clubs lost division placement solely because of their debts. In Brazil, heavy private investment was necessary to ensure funding to sign acceptable players. Inevitably, by the late 1990s, the "Americanization" of global sports had begun. In 2002 the Florentina professional soccer team was struggling to find enough cash to operate another season, and the collapse of the Argentine economy threatened the existence of all but the wealthiest of soccer teams. And, even these teams pondered selling their best players for operating capital paid in dollars, not devalued Argentine pesos.

Soccer led the way in the increased commercialization of sports originating outside the United States. In Europe, broad deregulation of the television industry opened up competition for television broadcast rights, and spin-off monies resulted in player salary increases. The German Soccer Association experimented with the notion of pay-per-view events in 1996, and in South America Pepsi Cola bought heavily into the Argentine Soccer Federation. All these and similar events combined to pattern international soccer more and more like the heavily marketed, heavily endorsed U.S. sports industry. At the same time, rugby, although dependent on amateur talent, went through many of the trials and tribulations of its professional cousin. In Wales, where rugby was coming off of a century of being viewed as much as a religion as national sport, it still took aggressive marketing and outside investment to save a struggling national team from oblivion. Where rugged men still stained from work in the mines used to be the only persons allowed on the playing field, suddenly female mascots waved new logos, and small children paraded the Welsh dragon for TV cameras. British Gas joined such high profile investors as Schweppes, South Wales Electricity, Heineken, and Volkswagen, in sponsorship of the game, and the Welsh Rugby Union relaxed its emphasis on amateurism to allow top players to be compensated financially.

Background and Development

During the 1960s and early 1970s, professional and amateur sports, while popular for the most part, were not financial juggernauts. Television contracts for broadcast rights to a sporting event were modest and relatively few. Instead, the sports industry relied almost exclusively on ticket sales. While the dependence on tickets gradually lessened, they remain a significant source of revenue for the sports industry, fueled in the late 1990s by the sale of enclosed private boxes and corporate suites.

Steady public enthusiasm for sporting events, combined with the technology of television, increased the profile of the industry. Other companies with products and services to sell gradually recognized that sporting events offered significant advertising possibilities, and sponsorship of sports events, including advertising in sports broadcasts, became increasingly commonplace. Certain industries that were prevented by law or by convention from advertising on television, and in certain other media (e.g., tobacco and liquor producers) saw athletic event sponsorship as a method of circumventing these regulations and advertising their products. The most obvious circumvention occurred when a restricted-advertising vendor, such as a tobacco company, sponsored large signs bearing its brand names inside stadiums, courts, or arenas, and these ads could then be seen adorning the walls during television coverage of the game.

Sponsorship eventually became standard practice for many companies, and extended to sponsorship of individual players, items of clothing, tarpaulins, lists of statistics, leagues, events or series of events, sports news broadcasts, and entire ballparks. In 1998 it was not unusual to hear a play-by-play broadcaster with a comment similar to, "That home run places [player name] on the [company name] all-time list of home run hitters." Machinery and equipment frequently in public view bore multiple advertising logos. Signage in 1998 ballparks and arenas flourished in a way it had not done since a time 60 years earlier, when poster boards were used as the sole vehicle for sports advertising. Indeed, many ballparks and stadiums now bore the name of corporate sponsors, causing some newspapers to threaten to leave out the corporate name, and causing fans to grumble about the greed of the sponsors in erasing the traditional names of the stadiums they had come to love.

The post-war advent of television evolved quickly into a force capable of driving the entire sports market. Although professional sports had existed throughout recorded history, television spread multiple sports to broader audiences than ever before, even extending across national and cultural borders. Basketball, relatively unknown in France, blossomed when French television began to pick up U.S. games. Soccer, long outside the mainstream of U.S. sports, was common on American playgrounds in 1998. While sports of all sorts initially functioned as a boon to a fledgling television industry, it was not long until the relationship reversed itself. By the 1960s the purveyors of various sporting events came to realize that advertising dollars, associated with an expanding viewer audience, could be channeled as easily into direct support of sports franchises.

As a result of the infusion of television dollars, the cash value of sports franchises exploded. Particularly in the United States, where owners were quickest to utilize the new source of revenue, franchise values grew exponentially. In 1983, US$43 million was a record price for a baseball team. In 1993, it was US$173 million. Three years later, in 1996, the New York Yankees were valued at US$241 million. In 1988 an NBA expansion team cost US$32.5 million; in 1994 it cost US$125 million. In 1996, the NFL's Dallas Cowboys carried a price tag of US$320 million. The Boston Red Sox went to a consortium of bidders in 2002 who made a US$700 million offer—more than double the previous highest price ever paid for a baseball club, that of US$323 million for the Cleveland Indians in 2000.

Individual team values rose worldwide throughout the 1990s and into the 2000s, despite a drop in team profits. In the United States, where such things were regularly documented, it was apparent that as team revenues increased, cost of player salaries increased even faster. The effective impact on operating income was to reduce it by as much as 35 percent for the average team. In spite of this, the actual value of each franchise increased at a pace that matched the revenue stream.

Escalating player salaries and increased overall operating costs may have placed a huge burden on the sports industry in the final years of the century, but they did little to dampen the enthusiasm of potential investors. As major corporations began to endorse professional sports organizations worldwide, the phenomenon of corporate and private investment approached a zenith in the United States.

Television. Television remained a huge source of income for members of the sports industry, but some networks such as Fox Sports have been financially staggered by losses as advertising revenues and viewer numbers were far lower than anticipated in 2000s. In 2002, the News Corporation elected to write off its football, baseball, and NASCAR TV contracts as bad investments, and some analysts were predicting future TV contracts would be declining or staying roughly equal for some time, not escalating.

Although early attempts at satellite broadcasting met with degrees of failure, 1990s satellite proponents pointed to new technology—direct broadcast satellites (DBS)—that ushered in an age of better, smaller, and less-expensive satellite dishes. Fans willing to pay for a dish chose from a much wider array of sports programming than would otherwise have been available. Satellite television leaders such as DirecTV and BSkyB featured heavy doses of sporting events and actively pursued a variety of sports contracts, and thus represented a further windfall for professional sports, both in terms of increased exposure and in the realization of further direct television revenue. Sports and leagues with a smaller fan base than other major professional sports were expected to enjoy a proportionally greater shot in the arm from satellite TV arrangements, but the potential for conflict with more conventional broadcasting arrangements caused some observers to reserve opinion regarding the long term impact.

Merchandising and Sponsorship. The single aspect of late twentieth century and early twenty-first century sports that most obviously differed from prior decades was the exponential increment in sports marketing and merchandising. When Nike announced a US$18 million unilateral marketing agreement with the Dallas Cowboys in 1995, revenue-sharing defenders were appeased by a subsequent agreement for US$200 million made with the NFL as a whole. The Nike logo, seen everywhere in the 1990s, appeared to symbolize the proliferation of similar licensing and marketing agreements. In the five-year period between 1988 and 1993, spending by U.S. and Canadian corporations to sponsor sporting events of all kinds increased at a 15 percent annualized clip, reaching US$2.4 billion dollars in that time. Simultaneously, league-licensed merchandise sales soared. NBA-licensed goods, which had garnered less than US$200 million in retail sales in 1986, pulled in nearly US$3 billion in 1993. In 1973, Rich Products spent US$1.5 million for a 25-year license to place its name on the Buffalo Bills' new stadium. A little over 20 years later, it cost MCI US$4.4 million a year (US$44 million over a ten-year span) to have naming rights for a new Washington, D.C., arena.

The revenue potential of merchandising contracts can be illustrated by the experience of the Portland Trail Blazers (NBA), which earned US$2.2 million in the 1994-1995 season, through the sale of suites, signage, parking, and concessions. The following year, the team moved into a new arena, which offered a greater opportunity to exploit the same revenue sources, with these "venue revenues" promptly increasing to US$15.2 million for the season. After winning the Super Bowl in 2002, the New England Patriots were able to finagle millions in merchandising deals because they had astutely lined up media properties under their own control with an Internet Web site, merchandise shops, TV and radio shows, and a print medium, according to the *Providence Journal-Bulletin*.

Along with everything else, the price of tickets to sporting events continued to rise in the 1990s and 2000s. Fans found the cost of tickets, parking, food, and souvenirs for the average family increasingly prohibitive, and it can be argued that many sports venues priced themselves out of the reach of the common consumer, forcing club dependency on corporations and the moneyed elite. In 2002, the St. Louis Rams charged an average ticket price of US$53.52, and that only placed the team tenth among all National Football League teams for average ticket prices.

With such large amounts of revenue streaming into league coffers around the world, team owners' relations with athletes and their agents were tested. This was particularly true in the United States, where both National Hockey League and Major League Baseball seasons were disrupted by work stoppages in the mid-1990s and even umpires have gone on strike for higher pay. Fan anger at these events was particularly pronounced during the baseball strike, which was marked by unusually insensitive player and owner attitudes. The profound fan disgust for players and owners alike, combined with rising ticket costs, produced significant variations in game attendance in subsequent seasons, and continued to impact franchise operation in the twenty-first century.

Salary Cap. In the United States, where team payrolls jumped tremendously in the mid- to late 1990s, owners of the four major leagues turned to the salary cap as a substitute for self-restraint. The NBA had successfully utilized the cap as part of its effort to revitalize the league when it was losing money. Players and agents fought the institution of any such cap, while other observers argued that the cap was not reliable. Some teams spent as much or more time and money circumventing the cap than they did trying to fit their payrolls into it. Similarly, after the first full season of the NFL's salary cap, one observer described it as a disaster, creating "a refugee class of unwanted, highly paid veteran talent." Although many talked about the cap's elimination, as part of the scheduled 1999 contract talks, proponents of the limit argued that it remained necessary. The difficulty in measuring the overall impact of a salary cap increased the level of debate. While other sports regarded basketball's salary cap as a contributor to the success of the NBA, that success occurred at a time that all-star players such as Larry Bird, Michael Jordan, Magic Johnson, and Isiah Thomas flourished. In 2002, the Denver Nuggets, with a losing record, guaranteed years of future struggling by trading their high scorers, Nick Van Exel and Raef LaFrentz. It was all in an effort to get rid of about US$100 million in contracts to hire cheaper, arguably inferior, players and to trim a fatty salaried roster, according to general manager Kiki Vandeweghe.

The Importance of Stadiums. In 2002, jaws of fans dropped when the city of Jacksonville and boosters offered its professional football team, the Jaguars, some cosmetic improvements to Alltel Stadium worth US$33 million, to be completed by 2005. Construction of new playing venues came to be regarded by many professional sports clubs as an absolute precursor to successful operation. However, legions of investigative reporters have blasted owners for holding cities at gunpoint with edicts to either build them a new stadium or see the team find a greener locale. Modern stadiums were touted as a panacea that would restore flagging attendance, entice reluctant athletes to sign contracts, and even revitalize entire metropolitan downtown areas. With all the hyperbole, one thing stood out as fact: new stadium construction, with its emphasis on luxury boxes (which sold for upwards of US$100,000 a season), entertainment centers, and club-controlled parking, dramatically boosted so-called "venue revenue," at least in the short term. Even the construction period itself was utilized as a fundraiser. Naming rights, signage, and various services were sold to the highest bidder. But amid the frenzy of stadium construction that occupied the United States and other parts of the world in the late 1990s and early 2000s, several issues remained open to question. Specifically, these included the best way to fund stadium construction; how to control construction costs; how long the impact of a new venue would last in a given market; and finally, how much was lost as ballparks, integral to the history of the sport they served, were met by the wrecking ball.

The prophecy that new stadiums were essential to profitability became self-fulfilling, when franchises attempted to raise revenue dollars in old stadiums by the same methods used in newer edifices. In judging the economic viability of various franchises, many senior sports executives insisted that stadium revenue was essential. Analysts recommended that teams should expect to receive at least 50 percent of revenues from stadium concessions, 100 percent of stadium advertising revenue, and 50 percent of parking revenues. Add to this the enormous ticket revenue attached to the sale of luxury boxes and suites, and the significance of total stadium revenues became even more apparent.

In some cases, the surge in new stadium construction had a significant effect on an entire sport. For example, the NHL, with clubs in both Canada and the United States, credited its success at drawing fans, at least in part, to the opening of nine new arenas within a three-year time span. Major league baseball, in the throes of rampant stadium construction in the late 1990s, obviously hoped that new ballparks would offset the negativism spawned by the player and umpire strikes earlier in the decade. Minor league teams in multiple sports invariably prefaced their initial marketing efforts with liberal attention to whatever park, stadium, or arena construction was being undertaken for their franchise.

Unfortunately, the golden geese that were stadiums did not hatch spontaneously from eggs. Professional sports clubs rarely attempted to finance construction or substantial renovation of stadiums out of their own pockets. Instead, they generally took one of two approaches. Some targeted private placement funding, a process that normally demanded substantial owner investment, relatively high interest charges, the presale of luxury suites and skyboxes, and even the licensing of the right to buy suite tickets, in order to bring in the necessary amount of money. Interestingly, as a result of the combined corporate oversight, implied by private placement funding, stadiums built in this way often were completed closer to original budget estimates than were other stadiums.

The other approach was to seek taxpayer dollars from local or state governments, an approach that teams often underlined by wielding the threat of departure from the host city. The emotional blackmail represented by the specter of a beloved team's possible departure to greener pastures led many cities to sink large amounts of money into the renovation of old facilities or the wholesale construction of new ones. Some of these cities hoped, conservatively, to receive a return on the public investment in terms of new tax revenues or spin-off economic activity. Others blithely expected new sports arenas to revitalize dying city centers. Whatever the rationale, the phenomenon of full or partial public funding for stadiums grew steadily in the last decades of the century. In 2002 for example, the St. Louis Cardinals baseball team was angling for a stadium that opponents argued could cost US$1 billion over 30 years, and this at a time when many public improvement projects lacked funding.

In part because of the unpopularity of providing public funding for the benefit of the millionaire owners of sports franchises, various governments became increasingly creative in identifying public revenue sources. Taxes on hotels, restaurants, and rental cars were more palatable because their burden was less likely to be borne by local citizenry. Similarly, taxes on gaming, cigarettes, and liquor (so-called "sin" taxes) arguably were voluntary. In most cases, would-be stadium builders did not rely on a single source of revenue, but on a combination of sources.

Control of actual stadium construction costs had both a practical and political aspect. When construction estimates repeatedly proved unreliable, fundraising became more difficult. Over and again, labor problems and unforeseen construction issues played havoc with target dollars. Some analysts blamed the tendency of new stadium builders to seek out water (lakes, rivers, and so forth) as a setting, invoking drainage problems and similar challenges. Equally often, removal of existing antique infrastructure in urban locations, or simple land acquisition costs, proved to be a complicating factor, as bidders and landholders vied with each other to profit from the new economic activity. Banks asked to underwrite owner contributions balked at implied risks. In Detroit, the Tigers baseball franchise owner Mike Ilitch was unable to entice local banks to bet on his solvency, and was forced to turn to Japanese interests to complete the franchise's portion of funding for anticipated stadium construction. In 2001, the

Florida Marlins baseball team was stunned when its request for a stadium, or long-term tax break, was nixed, potentially leading to the team's liquidation during the 2000s.

Corollary to rising cost estimates was the fear that revenue increments might not be indefinite. Baltimore's Oriole Park at Camden Yards, possibly premier among new baseball stadiums, continued to draw heavily in the years following its construction. New Comiskey Park in Chicago, on the other hand, had lesser impact. While the differential may have derived from stadium design and overall community demographics, other factors were likely at work. Small businesses driven out of downtown areas by new stadium construction contradicted the theory that new parks could automatically be equated with revitalized city centers. Cities beset by cost overruns watched in vain for returns on initial investments. In Cleveland, a group-loan program made loans of US$28 million to projects related to stadium construction. In spite of sellouts at Jacobs Field, businessmen expected to write off the US$28 million as a loss.

Finally, the need to turn to new stadiums begged the issue of the disposition of the old structures, many of which held history that was precious in the eyes of serious fans. Usually the wrecking ball was the only answer, but fan resistance could be high. In Detroit, fans turned out in droves to circle their old ballpark in highly publicized "hugs." The impact on construction decisions was nil, but many of those same fans were expressing overall dissatisfaction with the direction of the sport.

Although statistics to document the fact are less available for scattered worldwide sites, it is important to realize that the necessity of new stadiums to the sports industry did not end at the borders of the United States, nor did public involvement in their construction. Taxpayers worldwide were involved in the construction of sports venues. In communities throughout Europe, arena-operating costs could and were sometimes subsidized.

Insurance Costs. A maverick added expense for sports franchise owners was a dramatic upturn in premiums necessary to insure athletes, who had been hired at exorbitant salaries. Because athletes were paid the full amount of their contracts, even if they were injured or otherwise lost their skill to play, insurance underwriters became uneasy about long-term contracts, and insurance company unease was reflected in higher premiums. The insurance issue worsened in the 2000s, as the Baltimore Orioles filed a US$27 million total disability claim, when Albert Belle left the team with career-ending hip damage in 2001.

CURRENT CONDITIONS

Television remained a major player in the industry during the mid-2000s, despite wildly inflated rates for television rights and lowered ratings for most sports. Football, the industry's cash cow at US$77 million per team, was a notable exception. In fact, the sport benefited from a US$2 billion DirecTV satellite deal finalized by the NFL. In 2003, nearly 16 million households watched each televised game. Baseball's bottom line revenue also stood to skyrocket by an estimated US$500 million due to televised games if the major leagues agreed to sport product logos from corporate sponsors on player uniforms.

As of 2004, the top 50 highest paid athletes in the world had a combined income of US$1.1 billion, 40 percent of which was from product endorsements. In contrast to earlier times, three-fourths of these athletes played team sports as opposed to individual sports. Despite the appearance of a football player in the number three spot, football salary caps served to keep player compensation in line with the overall revenue of the teams. At the top of the list was golfer Tiger Woods, followed by race car driver Michael Schumaker, football player Peyton Manning, basketball player Michael Jordan, basketball player Shaquille O'Neal, basketball player Kevin Garnett, tennis player Andre Agassi, soccer player David Beckham, baseball player Alex Rodriguez, and basketball player Kobe Bryant.

In North America in 2004, *Forbes* reported that the National Football League had $5.3 billion in revenues, as compared to US$4.3 billion for Major League Baseball, US$2.9 billion for the National Basketball Association, and US$2.2 billion for the National Hockey League. In Europe, the top 25 soccer teams earned a combined total of US$4.2 billion in revenues.

On the horizon in the United States was a bill, introduced in Congress in 2004, which stood to benefit franchise owners. Originally intended to manage a dispute with the European Union (EU) over trade, the bill had many other items tacked on, including one that would allow owners to write off the total values of their franchises over the course of fifteen years. Franchise values, which were approximately $41 billion, stood to gain US$2 billion in value when the bill passed. The bill was expected to become a law before the end of the year.

INDUSTRY LEADERS

The professional sports franchises of the United States dominated the international sports industry. Global broadcasts of U.S. sporting events have combined with the marketing and merchandising savvy of promoters to lend the National Hockey League (NHL), Major League Baseball (MLB), National Football League (NFL), and National Basketball Association (NBA) to created business valued in the mega millions. However, the number-one ranked team in terms of both value and fan base was the United Kingdom's soccer franchise, Manchester United.

Baseball. The top five franchises in Major League Baseball in 2004 were the New York Yankees (valued at US$950 million), the Boston Red Sox (US$563 million), the New York Mets (US$505 million), the Los Angeles Dodgers (US$424 million), and the Seattle Mariners (US$415 million).

New York Yankees Partnership: The most winning team in American history, the New York Yankees has established a brand reputation that is internationally famous. With 2004 earnings of about US$315 million, this privately held company was owned by George Steinbrenner and partners. Steinbrenner also owned the New Jersey Nets and 60 percent of the Yankee Entertainment & Sports television channel.

The highest paid baseball player in the world in 2004 was Alex Rodriguez of the Yankees who earned US$26.2 million. His ten-year US$252 million contract was the highest in the sport's history.

Yamiuri Giants: In Japan, baseball remained the country"s favorite sport, with the Yamiuri Giants the oldest and most popular team. Formed in 1934 by the Yamiuri Newspapers, this Tokyo-based team has been the home of many national sports heros, including Oh Sadaharu whose record surpassed that of the U.S."s Babe Ruth and Hank Aaron.

Football. The top five franchises in the National Football League in 2004, ranked by value according to the 2005 *Forbes* list of NFL valuations, were: the Washington Redskins (US$1.1 billion), Dallas Cowboys (US$923 million), Houston Texans (US$905 million), New England Patriots (US$861 million), and the Philadelphia Eagles (US$833 million). The average team value increased 17 percent from 2003 totals, to US$733 million. The eight top teams in the league own their own stadiums, allowing them to earn sponsorship and advertising revenue. Twenty stadiums exclusively for the use of NFL teams were built or completely redone in the decade between 1993 and 2003.

Washington Football Inc.: Founded in Boston in 1932 and moved to Washington in 1937, the Washington Redskins was the richest sports franchise in the United States, breaking the US$1 billion value mark. The privately held company had earnings of US$245 million in 2004.

Basketball. The top five franchises in the National Basketball Association in 2004, ranked by value, were the Los Angeles Lakers (valued at US$510 million), New York Knicks (US$494 million), Dallas Mavericks (US$374 million), Houston Rockets (US$369 million), and the Chicago Bulls (US$368 million). As in other sports, the leaders own their venues and earn significant revenue from sponsorships and advertising.

The Los Angeles Lakers Inc.: In 2004, The Los Angeles Lakers earned revenues of US$170 million (matching that of the New York Knicks. Begun in Minneapolis in 1947, the Lakers franchise moved to Los Angeles in 1960. Kobe Bryant, the tenth highest paid athlete in the world, was playing for the Lakers in 2004 when his earnings were US$26.1 million.

Soccer. On a worldwide basis, the most popular sport remained soccer. Although not popular on a professional basis in the United States, it was the country's fastest growing sport. The number-one ranked team by value of any type of sport in the world was the soccer team, Manchester United from the United Kingdom which was valued in 2004 by *Forbes* at US$1.25 billion. On the top ten on the *Forbes* list of the richest soccer teams were also: Real Madrid of Spain (US$920 million), AC Milan of Italy (US$893 million), Juventus of Italy (US$837 million), Bayern Munich of Germany (US$627 million), Arsenal of the United Kingdom (US$613 million), Internazionale of Italy (US$608 million), Chelsea of the U.K. (US$449 million), Liverpool of the U.K. (US$441 million), and Newcastle United of the U.K. (US$391 million).

Manchester United PLC: The most popular team in the world in terms of fan base remained Manchester United of the United Kingdom. With a global fan base of 75 million people, the company has been able to establish strong commercial partnerships with several major companies, including Nike and telecommunications company Vodafone. A four-year deal with Vodafone beginning in 2003 was worth more than US$60 million. In the first year of its 13-year contract with Nike, "Man U" added more than US$6 million to its revenue figures. In addition, the company launched soccer schools in Disneyland Paris and in Hong Kong, taking advantage of the strong fan base in those two areas. The company even has a licensed partner who opened two One United Cafes in mainland China. In 2004, revenues for the company approached US$300 million, which it earned through not only ticket sales, but through its ownership of retail outlets, hotels, and catering services, as well as sponsorship deals and partnerships with finance-related companies that offer its customers credit cards, mortgages, loans, and car insurance. In 2005, American businessman, Malcolm Glazer, obtained control of 98 percent of the company, over the protests of fans who feared Glazer's use of debt for the takeover would mean increased ticket prices for them.

Once a member of the Manchester United Team, but a member of Madrid Real in 2005, David Beckham was arguably the sport's most famous player around the world. He was on the verge of obtaining far-reaching name recognition in the U.S. with his appearance on the cover of *Vanity Fair*, and through his association with the popular movie, *Bend it Like Beckham*. In 2004, Beckham earned about US$32 million and earned the most from endorsements of any player in the sport. He was ranked eighth on the *Forbes* 2005 list of the highest paid athletes.

Ice Hockey. In the 2004-2005 season, the 30 rinks of the National Hockey League in North America were empty. The players had been locked out by the owners. *Forbes* reported that overall, 17 teams had lost money the previous season, with the total loss for the league being US$96 million. The league was demanding a salary pay cap per team of US$31 million, down from US$41 million the previous year, but the players refused it.

The top five hockey teams in terms of value in 2004 were the New York Rangers (valued at US$282 million), Toronto Maple Leafs (US$280 million), Philadelphia Flyers (US$264 million), Dallas Stars (US$259 million), and Detroit Red Wings (US$248 million).

Promoters and Agents. Although the relative maturity of the U.S. sports industry essentially compelled leading promoters and agents to be located in the United States, this aspect of the game has strong entries worldwide.

IMG (formerly International Management Group), a Cleveland-based marketing and management company for athletes, as well as performing artists, writers, fashion models, and broadcasters, was founded by Mark McCormack in the early 1960s when he took on golfer Arnold Palmer as a client. With 2,200 employees around the globe, the company's estimated revenues in 2003 were US$1.2 billion. In 2005, the company managed the number-one ranked athlete in terms of earnings in the world, Tiger Woods, who *Forbes* had listed as earning US$80.3 million in 2004.

SFX Sports Group Inc. counted tennis players Andre Agassi and Andy Roddick and golf professional Greg Norman among its clients in 2005. The company was the management representative for more than 500 professional athletes through its 10 offices in the United States and branches in Europe and Australia. In 2004, the company was opening offices in Buenos Aires and Moscow, and had formed an alliance with Globo Media Group to explore the opportunities in India. The company was a subsidiary of Clear Channel Entertainment, a producer and promoter of live entertainment.

The Interpublic Group of Companies operates a sports and entertainment group that includes 10 subsidiaries. One of these subsidiaries, Octagon employed more than 1,000 people in 60 offices around the world. It represented such athletes as tennis star Anna Kournikova. In 2003, revenues for the sports and entertainment segment of Interpublic were US$428 million.

MAJOR COUNTRIES IN THE INDUSTRY

The interest in global sports is made no more apparent that when the Olympic games are on. Although designed to promote amateur sport, the Games are big business. In 2000, of the 3.9 billion people who had access to a television around the world, 3.7 billion could tune in to watch the Games in Sydney. The broadcasting rights were valued at US$1.32 billion. Winning a gold medal can mean millions of dollars in endorsements for American athletes, and the dollar figures have been increasing for athletes in other countries as markets open.

While no other country approached U.S. dominance in terms of the total revenue generated by sports, professional leagues in Japan, Canada, and many areas of Europe and South America brought in huge amounts of money as well. In the mid-2000s, the rate at which the international sports industry expanded (in terms of the number of sports and leagues that were established with each passing year) showed no sign of slackening. Commercialization, the use of each game venue for as much profit as possible, had its appeal the world over—even as television continued to carry a great variety of sports to an increasingly broader audience.

Some export of sports, from areas strongest in the industry, was to be expected. Games first established in Canada and the United States became popular around the world, spawning fledgling professional leagues as their appeal spread. Professional baseball and basketball leagues were commonplace in many countries by the late 1990s. While the quality of play wasn't at the level regularly available to North American fans, it was apparent that the worldwide talent pool was improving. In fact, in the late 1990s and 2000s, Japanese baseball teams were supplying their U.S. counterparts with outstanding players, and the Seattle Mariners' Ichiro Suzuki was the Most Valuable Player in 2001. Also, in 2002 the San Francisco Giants signed top-rated Japanese star, Tsuyoshi Shinjo, even though he was already 30 years old. Even the game of American football, once eschewed in other countries, caught on outside the United States, if only for its value as a curiosity, as U.S. teams made world tours to play exhibition games. More significantly in 1998 the NFL Europe League, which evolved from the NFL-sponsored World League of American Football, fielded professional teams in Holland, Scotland, Germany, Spain, and Great Britain.

The interchange and expansion of professional sports was not limited to North American export. The Federation Internationale de Football Association took soccer's World Cup tournament to the United States in 1994, in an effort not only to turn a profit, but also to stir American interest in a sport that already was wildly popular worldwide. By 1998 the viability of soccer in the United States was well established. Multiple major and minor professional leagues were publicized and decently attended, and the success of amateur soccer in schools and on playgrounds offered ongoing promise to the professional version of the game. Soccer also achieved popularity in Africa.

In Japan, the Japanese soccer league, the "J-League," was the nation's first professional sports league to be run as an independent business, and was a tremendous success. This league took advantage of unexploited regional loyalty by naming teams after cities rather than businesses, as was the standard practice for other Japanese sports. By the end of the league's first season, more than 4.0 million Japanese had been to a professional soccer game. In the following year, attendance climbed to 5.5 million, and almost all games were selling out within two days of tickets becoming available. Not to be outdone, Japanese baseball became more and more part of a global enterprise. While professional baseball in Japan, like baseball in the United States, endured considerable loss of appeal when faced by the popularity of soccer in the late 1990s, there were signs suggesting an eventual resurgence. As athletes began to resist the harsh discipline and poor playing conditions long associated with Japanese baseball, player dissatisfaction actually brought a more colorful style of play to the Japanese game. Even if the most rebellious of its players found themselves exported to the United States, conservative cultural traditions had begun to give way by the late 1990s and early 2000s. The implied vigor in a game that was updating its principles and actively competing for business with other sports brightened the future of Japanese baseball.

Baseball and soccer were the most "American" in style and marketing, and had the overall grip on fans of worldwide sport, but narrower venues also felt the influence of the driving industry that twentieth century sport had become. In England and Wales, amateur rugby lost fans, lost money, and lost appeal, and then embraced dramatically renewed popularity as it was managed increasingly like a professional sport. This manipulation of fan attitude through skillful marketing illustrated both the lucrative potential of professional sports, and the tradeoffs and sacrifice of tradition. This was the new reality of aggressive marketing of games to non-fans, and the treatment of the sport as part of a larger entertainment package.

FURTHER READING

Aznoff, Dan. "Baseball Star Coverage Harder to Come By." *National Underwriter,* 29 October 2001.

"The Best-Paid Athletes." *Forbes Online,* 24 June 2004. Available from http://www.forbes.com.

"The Business of Basketball." *Forbes Online,* 6 February 2004. Available from http://www.forbes.com.

Curran, Tom E. "Patriots Hit the Jackpot on Field and in the Wallet." *Providence Journal-Bulletin (Providence, RI),* 26 February 2002.

Dukcevich, Davide. "The Business of Baseball." *Forbes Online,* 23 April 2003. Available from http://www.forbes.com.

Ferzoco, George. "A Suspicion of Bribery (Canadian Soccer Association)." *Maclean's,* 17 August 1987.

Ganey, Terry. "Few Speak Against Ballpark." *St. Louis Post-Dispatch,* 7 March 2002.

Jessell, Harry A. "Sports on the Rocks." *Broadcasting & Cable,* 3 November 2003.

Lapper, Richard. "Playing for Survival." *Financial Times (London),* 19 January 2002.

Lowery, Tom. "The NFL Machine." *Business Week* 27 January 2003.

Ozanian, Michael K. "Football Feifdoms." *Forbes,* 3 September 2004. Available from http://www.forbes.com.

Ozanian, Michael K. "Ice Capades." *Forbes,* 29 November 2004. Available from http://www.forbes.com.

"The Richest Soccer Teams." *Forbes Online,* 24 March 2004. Available from http://www.forbes.com.

Ringolsby, Tracy. "Players Association All in Favor of Some Kinds of Revenue Gaps." *Chicago Sun-Times,* 17 February 2002.

Ryan, Thomas J. "Major Leagues Debate Corporate Logos on Uniforms." *Sporting Goods Business,* May 2004.

Sandomir, Richard. "The Media Business." *The New York Times,* 14 December 2002.

Sharkey, Peter. "Italian Crisis Spells Cash Warning." *The Evening Standard (London),* 14 January 2002.

Thomas, Jim. "Rams Are Raising the Price of Tickets." *St. Louis Post-Dispatch,* 20 February 2002.

Vaillancourt, Meg, et al. "Red Sox Sale." *The Boston Globe,* 21 December 2001.

Wilson, Duff. "Bill Would Raise Franchise Value of Sports Teams." *New York Times,* 2 August 2004.

SIC 3940

NAICS 33992, 33993

TOYS AND SPORTING GOODS

Manufacturers in this industry produce toys, dolls and doll clothing, stuffed toys, children's vehicles (except bicycles—see SIC 3751), games (except electronic game cartridges—7372), and sporting and athletic equipment. Excluded from this discussion is athletic apparel (SIC 2300), athletic footwear (3021), small arms (3484) and small arms ammunition (3482).

INDUSTRY SNAPSHOT

According to the ICTI, in 2003 sales of traditional toys around the world was US$59.4 billion. While the toy market always had an international flavor—the creations of German toy makers delighted U.S. children in the nineteenth century—by the 1990s the industry had become truly global. This continued to be the case as the industry entered the mid-2000s. Giant toy makers, such as the United States' Mattel Inc., Denmark's Lego, and Japan's Nintendo, generated much—if not most—of their revenue overseas. Indeed, parents in Moscow sometimes gave up a month's wages so their daughters could own Mattel's Barbie, the most popular doll in the world and a US$1.5 billion annual revenue producer worldwide.

Like the toy business, the sporting goods manufacturing segment is also global in nature. Speaking at the World Sports Forum in Lausanne, Switzerland, in 2002, Margaret Mager (President of Research at Goldman Sachs) and Andre Gorgemans (Secretary General of the World Federation of Sporting Goods Industry) indicated that the world sports market was worth US$92 billion, with the United States accounting for 50 percent of sales and the European Union taking a further 38 percent. However, these markets were maturing and the U.S in particular was showing a decline in interest for sports. New growth was expected to come from Asia and other developing markets in the mid-2000s. Around the world, several brand names dominate the industry, with Nike, Reebok and adidas-Salomon providing one-fifth of the market. Sporting goods manufacturers have also come under criticism for several issues, with the most predominant involving the use of child labor.

Common to both industries is the fact that the majority of manufacturing facilities are located in China, although these are primarily third-party manufacturers doing contract work for companies from other countries. By 2005, according to the International Council of Toy Industries (ICTI), 75 percent of the world's toys were being produced in China.

In 2005, the toy industry continued to face the concerns of consumers, workers, environmental groups and human rights organizations. These concerns covered a number of issues, including the use of PVC and chemicals in toy manufacturing, packaging and electronic waste, the effects of electromagnetic interference, working conditions in factories, the use of child labor, and sales and marketing practices aimed at children. From a business-to-business perspective, the industry itself faced the ongoing problem of toy counterfeiting.

ORGANIZATION AND STRUCTURE

TOYS

While the largest market for toys continues to be the United States, by far the largest source for toys is China. According to the *China Plastics and Rubber Journal*, China's more than 6,000 toy manufacturers were producing 70 percent of the world's toys in 2004. However, approximately two-thirds of the toys produced use designs and raw materials supplied by other countries, and a large share of the revenues come from contract manufacturing for large toy companies and license holders.

Four large companies dominate the global toy manufacturing scene: Mattel, LEGO, Bandai, and Hasbro, with Bandai and Mattel having a marketing alliance. However, on the whole, the industry is very fragmented and more regionally based rather than globally based. In addition, many toys are produced on behalf of license holders, including Disney, Warner Brothers, and McDonalds.

According to business researchers from INSEAD, about 95 percent of toys are sold via retail outlets. Few manufacturers sell directly to the final consumer. However, by 2005 there were an increasing number of partnerships between manufacturers and fast-food chains, cinemas, and direct-sellers, including Avon. In addition to traditional retailers, an increasing number of sales were being made through new Internet-based companies.

Since the early 1980s, U.S. law has enforced standards for small parts, breakability, paint, and other points of safety in children's toys. The standards have been effective in reducing deaths and injury, but children under three, playing with the toys of their older siblings, still posed a major safety problem. According to the Consumer Product Safety Commission (CSPC), 143,000 children were treated each year in hospital emergency rooms because of toy-related injuries.

Although manufacturers are regulated by the governments of the companies in which they operate, the toy industry has faced growing concerns from consumers, labor and human rights groups, environmentalists, and trade associations for increased global regulations. The International Council of Toy Industries (ICTI), based in New York, is made up of toy associations from Australia, Austria, Brazil, Canada, China, Chinese Taipei, Denmark, France, Germany, Hong Kong, Hungary, Italy, Japan, Mexico, Russia, Spain, Sweden, the United Kingdom and the United States. Among other objectives, the ICTI promotes ethical and safe working practices, establishes toy safety standards, and attempts to reduce or eliminate trade barriers. According to the code of business practice of the ICTI, member companies and their suppliers must not use forced or underage labor and must provide a safe working environment. In 2004, the council established a committee to draft a voluntary code for advertising aimed at children. This code was expected to follow guidelines set by the U.S.-based Better Business Bureau.

SPORTING GOODS

The sporting goods segment includes a wide scope of businesses and products, and there are numerous participants. A few large companies might dominate a specific sector, however. For example, Calway is the world's leading supplier of metal golf clubs. Nike and adidas-Salomon are among the most recognizable names in the world, but they are predominantly footwear and apparel manufacturers. However, their acquisitions into the sports equipment field and the licensing of their brand on many related products have made them industry leaders in the equipment arena, too.

BACKGROUND AND DEVELOPMENT

TOYS

The first toy was probably made around the time the first child was born. The children of ancient Egypt played with balls, tops, and pull-along animals, and kites were developed in China around 200 B.C. Germany, however, was generally considered the pioneer in toy making as an industry. By the end of the eighteenth century, one German toy firm, Bestelmeier of Nuremberg, was issuing a catalog with more than 1,200 entries. At the beginning of the twentieth century, toy making was one of Germany's most important industries, and one-fourth of the toys produced there were exported to the United States.

Because of the reliance on European toy makers, the industry in the United States developed slowly. But U.S. toy makers received a strong boost at the start of World War I, when shipments from Germany were cut off. Imports from Germany rose after the war, but the U.S. Congress installed high tariffs on imported goods, thereby protecting U.S. manufacturers. By 1939, some 95 percent of all American toys were manufactured domestically, compared with 50 percent in 1914. The toy industry in the United Kingdom followed relatively the same pattern as the United States—initially a heavy reliance on Germany, and then strong growth in the first decades of the twentieth century. In its infancy, the toy industry in Japan gained a reputation for shoddy workmanship, since inexpensive labor allowed it to flood European markets with cheap toys. As in many other industries, however, Japan gained a reputation for fine products.

In the postwar period, toys dealing with the United States' Wild West were popular in both Europe and North America, and construction toys, pioneered by the Danish firm Lego, also captured kids' imaginations. Television also contributed to the spread of toy culture, fueling the mass merchandising of toys that were considered requisites in mainstream households. Two of the most successful toys in history were Barbie and G.I. Joe, introduced, respectively, in 1959 by Mattel and in 1964 by Hasbro, bringing both companies to the forefront of the industry. By 2002, Hasbro had decided to put more marketing attempts into these perennial favorites and family games such as Monopoly eschewing the sometimes lucrative but often boom-or-bust toy fads that led to some rocky economic times for the company.

By the mid-1990s, the world's two largest markets, the United States and Japan, showed signs of maturity, while Southeast Asia had the fastest growth. The video game craze, which had come to Europe later than to the United States, shored up European markets. In the United States, sales of so-called traditional toys (which excludes video games) rose only 1.6 percent in 1993, but video game volume jumped 18 percent. The traditional toy market did get a boost in 1994 from the popular Mighty Morphin Power Rangers, even though some parents thought both the toys and the TV show on which they were based were too violent. Concerns about violence in U.S. society and its causes also forced Toys "R" Us and other retailers to stop selling several realistic-looking toy guns. However, in 2002, the TIA had gathered research from university professors denying a link between violence and such toys. The debate promised to continue or even step up well into the 2000s.

Gendered Toys. Throughout much of the history of toys, a significant gender gap has existed in toy offerings. While boys in the 1990s could look forward to action figures, radio-controlled cars, boats, planes, sports toys, and construction sets, girls' playthings were, at least ostensibly, often limited to dolls and their accessories. Critics said that the industry had not worked hard at offering imaginative toys for girls, and that its marketing remained geared to the Barbie mentality. Industry executives, however, tended to blame societal norms and a conservative streak in many mothers, who in the United States purchased 75 percent of all toys. They cited statistics that showed parents were more generous with sons than daughters when it came to spending money on toys. They also noted that girls tended to mature faster than boys; they generally started asking for items such as clothes and music CDs as gifts rather than toys during their preteen years.

In Japan, however, the industry found a non-doll toy that appealed to girls: the electronic organizer. The petite digital assistants featured not only appointment calendars and phone directories, but also fortune-telling and computer-animated virtual pets. The primary market for the digital assistants was girls in the fourth and fifth grades.

U.S. Trends. The hard times following September 11, 2001 terrorist acts in the United States took a relatively small toll on the toy industry, but did soften sales enough during the holiday season to result in belt tightening measures nationwide. In 2002, Toys "R" Us shut 64 stores and eliminated 1,900 jobs. In 2001, Zany Brainy and FAO Schwarz were in dire financial straits; particularly Zany Brainy, which suffered after a merger with top rival Noodle Kidoodle when no top toy sellers emerged to draw buyers into stores. In 2001, highflying competitor The Right Start acquired Zany Brainy and FAO Schwarz, creating a single company called FAO Inc., featuring three divisions under The Right Start, Zany Brainy ,and FAO Schwarz. However, by 2003 FAO Inc. had filed for bankruptcy and closed stores in its Zany Brainy division amidst a cut-throat industry climate. In addition, in early 2004 KB Toys had plans to close a third of its stores in the wake of its bankruptcy filing.

A great deal of consolidation took place among toy makers in the 1980s and 1990s. For example, Mattel purchased Fisher-Price and Hot Wheels, and the more broadly based Hasbro owned Playskool, Kenner, Milton Bradley, and Parker Brothers. Nevertheless, smaller companies were still able to succeed in the business, provided they could come up with a product that sold well. Cash requirements for start-up were relatively low, since manufacturing could be contracted out. Foreign-made products dominated many sectors; for example, they represented the vast majority of the dolls and stuffed toys segment in the 1990s. Large U.S. toymakers not only produced overseas, but also vigorously expanded their marketing efforts abroad. For example, in 1993 Mattel decided to set up an independent sales and marketing organization in Scandinavia to boost growth; formerly, it had distributed its products through Swedish toy maker Brio.

The U.S. toy industry typically relies as much on instinct and gut feeling as market research, although statements by executives from Hasbro and other executives noted there would be renewed marketing on tried-and-true family toys and less emphasis on mere fads that could end up unsold in warehouses. Each year, some 5,000 to 6,000 new toys are introduced, but only 20 percent or so remain on store shelves by the following Christmas. A few dolls have perennial appeal, such as G.I. Joe, which was introduced in the early 1960s. Some 30 years later, about 250 million G.I. Joe figures had been sold, along with 115 million vehicles. Industry analysts credited successful brand extensions, such as melding G.I. Joe with Street Fighter II video game characters, for the brand's longevity.

Educational Toys. While educational toys once accounted for only about 20 percent of the overall U.S. toy market, they began gaining popularity. Part of that strength came from computer-based toys, with names such as Little Smart Alphabet Desk and Talking Whiz Kid Genius. Toy makers and retailers liked educational toys, since their profit margins tended to be 50 percent compared with about 30 percent for conventional items. However, labeling a toy as "educational" can reduce its appeal to children who have learned to view "educational" toys as being less enjoyable as conventional ones. Thus, marketing campaigns for educational toys were sometimes conducted through parenting magazines rather than through Saturday morning cartoons. Curiously, in Japan, which is perceived as being more educationally rigorous than the United States, educational toys only took from 7 percent to 10 percent of the market in the early 1990s, a share that steadily increased in subsequent years.

Multi-ethnic Offerings. In the early 1990s, the number and quality of dolls that reflected the ethnic diversity of Americans increased significantly. According to one manufacturer, black and Hispanic consumers represented about one-sixth of total toy purchases in 1991, and many were eager to give their children dolls that projected a positive self-image. Because African American, Hispanic, and Asian children were projected to represent 41 percent of all U.S. children in 2010, versus 32 percent in 1994, manufacturers were developing dolls with more realistic features, such as authentic-looking hair, and making them with better materials; they also made dolls modeled on black historical figures. The big toy companies increased their advertising budgets for black versions of best-selling dolls such as Barbie and Thumbelina, and were able to boost their sales significantly. In the 2000s, one of the success stories were Baby June dolls with Asian features created by entrepreneur Selina Yoon.

Japan. In 1992, in what some observers saw as a watershed event for both Japanese society and the toy industry, Mattel decided to market in Tokyo the same Barbie doll it sold in Chicago. The earlier Barbie dolls sold in Japan had a decidedly innocent, school-girlish look that supposedly was more in tune with local tastes. However, they made little headway against the Jennie and Licca dolls made by Takara, which held 90 percent of the segment. Mattel decided that with Japanese pop idols becoming more adventurous and even risque, the Ferrari-driving, hipper Barbie adored by Western children was ready for Japanese markets.

By far the largest player in the Asian market was Japan, which represented about 85 percent of the continent's total 1992 volume. It was also the second-largest toy market in the world, which attracted the attention of foreign toy makers and marketers. In the 1990s, Toys "R" Us opened several stores in Japan. The company's stunning variety and low prices had begun to change the buying habits of the Japanese consumer, which in turn affected the Japanese toy industry. The convoluted distribution system and the close relationships between manufacturers and retailers began to break down, and Japanese toy makers could not afford to ignore the buying muscle of Toys "R" Us, which reduced its costs by going around wholesalers and purchasing directly from the manufacturer. The country's large department stores, as well as the big toy chains such as Chiyoda's Hello Mac and Marutomi's Ban Ban, responded by offering sharp discounts on toys, even during the Christmas season.

An industry fact of life is that new toys eventually become old. For many years, Pokemon toys were best sellers for Japan's Tomy Co., but that market collapsed in time for Christmas 2001, forcing Tomy to pay a dividend only half that of the 2000 dividend. The news was welcomed by other Japanese toymakers such as Takara Co. and Bandai Co. that moved in relentlessly to secure market share in 2002. In 2001, various robots were the toys of choice for youngsters in Japan, Europe, and the United States.

Europe. Germany, France, the United Kingdom, and Italy accounted for about 70 percent of the overall European market in 1992, while all of Eastern Europe represented less than 7 percent. In general, European firms continued to make traditional toys as opposed to the "fashion" toys that required high outlays for publicity and had short economic lives. The vast majority of European toy companies—some 80 to 90 percent—were small concerns that employed fewer than 20 people on a full-time basis. European output was highly fragmented, spread out over a vast number of products. With the exception of the Danish manufacturer Lego, Europe had produced no multinationals on the order of the United States' Mattel or Japan's Nintendo. Firms also tended to be concentrated within certain regions: Bavaria and Baden-Wurtemberg in Germany, Lombardy in Italy, Jura and Rhone-Alpes (Ain) in France, and Barcelona and Alicante provinces in Spain. Each country also tended to specialize in a certain product line: plastic toys, model trains, and paper toys in Germany; dolls and board games in Italy; die-cast and mechanical toys, board games, and stuffed toys in France; and metal and plastic miniatures, as well as table and board games, in the United Kingdom.

The emergence of international retailer Toys "R" Us accelerated a trend toward consolidation in the European toy industry. With Toys "R" Us taking a greater share of the retail market, for instance, the purchasing decision fell into fewer hands. In addition, the company often dealt with the more professional, international manufacturers that may not have previously been major factors in local markets. Toys "R" Us also contributed to an increase in overall demand. When the company tried to open its first store in Germany, it was greeted with a partial boycott by German toy manufacturers who ridiculed the idea of a toy superstore. Toys "R" Us persisted and it became Germany's largest toy retailer in 1991. The company has been given credit for reviving the German toy market, which was largely stagnant during the 1980s. Similarly, Toys "R" Us took 15 percent of the U.K. market within two years of opening its first store there, but the country's total toy sales still grew 7 percent in 1991.

The news from Europe for Toys "R" Us was less than encouraging in the 2000s as the giant U.S. chain decided it had overexpanded in international locales such as Germany and the U.K. The result was a decision in 2002 to slice some of its nearly 500 international stores that were experiencing losses, which resulted in plans to close at least two dozen stores by 2003.

Sporting Goods

The history of any sport was intimately related to the history of its equipment. For example, the first golf balls were made from wood, but in the early seventeenth century balls made out of boiled feathers were introduced, which could be hit further. In the nineteenth century, gutta-percha balls—made from the evaporated milky juice of various trees—were much cheaper to produce, and thus made golf more affordable and hence more appealing. The first balls made from rubber came in the twentieth century. The impact of these balls, which were easier to hit and gave the player a sense of power, was revolutionary, drawing whole new classes of players, including women, into the game.

Such technological advances have often helped propel the sporting goods industry. Its expansion in the twentieth century was also due to the rise in leisure time, the increase of professionalization of sports, and the influence of television. Sports such as American football became so integral to the fabric of U.S. culture that it was hard to believe that they were once the sole preserve of prep school boys at elite colleges. There was also a general trend of sports moving from West to East: golf, baseball, and soccer became as popular in Japan as in any Western country, if not more so.

Although the sports manufacturing industry is home to numerous small players, some segments have historically been dominated by a few companies. For example, Prince and Wilson held 70 percent of the U.S. tennis racquet market in the mid-1990s, and the share of the top six tennis racquet manufacturers together was 98 percent. The top firms in the industry as a whole were often parts of conglomerates that engaged in a variety of business activities. Wilson Sporting Goods, for example, which offered a broad range of sporting goods equipment, was owned by the Amer Group, a Finnish company that also made paper envelopes and textbooks, among other products.

After a decade of strong growth, the U.S. sports equipment industry slowed in the early 1990s because of the recession and, for some sports, the wrong weather. Toward the end of 1992, however, as the economy began to pick up, the sector's sales rebounded. In 1993, manufacturers' shipments rose about 4 percent, nearly the same increase as in 1992. European and Japanese demand for sporting goods in the early 1990s continued to be held down by the weakness in those economies.

Performance among the industry's numerous segments varies significantly as a sport's popularity waxes or wanes depending on demographics, economics, marketing skill, and simple fads. For example, during the 1990s in-line skating remained a standout performer as skate sales in the

United States rose from US$53 million in 1990 to US$243 million in 1993. In-line skating also appeared to have good prospects in Europe. Revenue from tennis goods, on the other hand, was notably down in the United States with sales of racquets dropping from US$170 million in 1983 to US$111 million 10 years later. Industry observers attributed the problem to declines in the number of baby boomers at peak tennis-playing age (tennis was primarily played by those under 25); shifting tastes (some said tennis's image was too highbrow); and poor marketing by the industry. Still, in world markets much depended on the quality of the stars: tennis sales took off in France in the mid-1980s because of the popularity of Yannick Noah. By the early 1990s, the French passion for tennis had cooled, only to be rekindled in Germany on the strength of stars Boris Becker and Steffi Graf.

The golf segment has done well because of technologically improved products and new adherents among an older population. Demand for golf clubs helped to sustain the Japanese sporting goods industry during the recession, although much of the increased demand was for U.S. products such as those by Callaway. Fitness equipment was another sector where changing demographics had improved performance: U.S. sales grew at a compound annual rate of 14 percent between 1988 and 1993. Changing health fashions boosted popularity of some products while others faded.

Europe. Demand for sporting goods grew in Europe throughout the 1980s, albeit at different rates for different countries, as general economic prosperity and increased emphasis on fitness combined to boost sales. The economic slowdown of the early 1990s, however, cooled the growth in these markets. Skiing was the favorite sport in Alpine regions, such as Northern Italy and Switzerland, while in the United Kingdom golf was the largest market, with sales of approximately US$115 million a year. The European sporting goods industry was characterized by numerous small- to medium-sized companies, but as in the toy industry there was a move toward consolidation.

Asia. Because of changing lifestyles and government efforts to alleviate persistent trade surpluses, the Japanese population began working less and playing more in the early 1990s. Japanese consumers were therefore devoting more time to pursuing traditional sports, such as golf, as well as relatively new ones, including soccer. Japan's first professional soccer league, the J League, was a huge marketing success story—one analyst estimated that it generated US$4.8 billion in economic activity in 1993, its first year. While most of that activity was not due to sales of soccer balls alone, the long-term trend of more free time was expected to increase sporting goods volume. In China, what is perhaps emblematic of the tremendous upsurge in sporting goods sales and popularity has been the founding of The Highsun Sport City in Guangzhou. The privately-owned Highsun Enterprises Group is like an entire U.S. mall with floor space amounting to 7,000 square meters and shops dedicated to both Chinese products and international best sellers such as Andi, YY-Yonex, Dunlop, adidas, Nike, K-Swiss, Umbro, Kappa, and Fila.

Latin America. The restoration of democracy to many Latin American governments was accompanied by better economic conditions, giving consumers more spending power. Moreover, the trend toward freer trade was also a significant factor, as Argentina, Brazil, and Chile sharply reduced trade barriers to overseas goods. While Latin Americans were always passionate about soccer, they also started to take up typically American sports such as basketball and in-line skating, where U.S. companies held an edge. They were also eager to join health clubs, which helped increase fitness equipment sales. For producers of fishing equipment, Brazil represented by far the largest market, with roughly 20 percent of the population—some 30 million people—taking part. Nonetheless, the general economic slowdown in the early 2000s had not led to signs of a financial comeback in South America by 2002. For example, Fila, the Italian sportswear maker, attributed part of its poor sales performance overall in 2001 to slumping South American sales. The posted loss for the fourth quarter was US$46.8 million and the annual loss was US$144.8 million, according to company figures.

CURRENT CONDITIONS

TOYS

The world market for traditional toys (exluding video games) in 2003 was US$59.4 billion, according to the ICTI. Of that total, the United States held 41 percent of the market, Europe had a 30 percent market share, Asia and Oceania had 29 percent, while Africa held only 1 percent. According to a report from The NPD Group Inc., a Port Washington, New York-based research firm, toy industry sales in 2004 in the United States totaled US$20.1 billion, down 3 percent from 2003 figures, which themselves were down 2.9 percent over 2002 levels. However, there was growth in the categories of electronic learning toys. The sale of action figures and building sets continued to decline, but these declines were slowing. Much of the decline was attributed to the closure of many toy retailers and increase competition for other product categories, including consumer electronics and video games.

Although by the mid-2000s a few companies dominated the toy manufacturing industry, most toys were still being manufactured by small, regionally based companies, with the vast majority being made in China, Hong Kong and Taiwan. According to the *China Plastics and Rubber Journal*, in 2004, 50 percent of the toys sold in the United States and Europe were made in China. As the toy industry continued to outsource manufacturing to China, this often had grave consequences for U.S. towns that depended on toy production. In 2004, the town of Bryan, Ohio, was still feeling the effects of a decision by Ohio Art Co. to shift the production of its famous Etch-A-Sketch to Shenzhen, China, several years before. In addition to job loss, the move also hurt the city's already suffering tax base, which had been impacted by a declining U.S. manufacturing sector. A similar move occurred at Chicago-based Radio Flyer Inc. in April 2004. The 87-year-old firm announced a decision to shed half of its 90-person workforce and transfer the manufacture of its metal wagons to China, where its scooters and tricycles were already being made.

In 2005, several trends were greatly impacting the toy manufacturing industry. Consolidation among retailers was having an immense effect on where manufacturers could sell their products and the profit margins they could receive. For example, in the United States, Wal-Mart and Target stores were accounting for an increasing share of the retail toy market, 25 percent and 12 percent respectively in 2004, and decreasing the profit margins of manufacturers as these retailers engaged in pricing wars. In March 2005, the second largest U.S. toy retailer, Toys "R" Us (with a 16 percent share of the market in 2004) was privatized by an investment group. This was cause for some concern among manufacturers as historically, Toys "R" Us carried a much broader range of toys than other outlets and was continuously willing to market new types of toys.

As a result of this increasing retail consolidation, a second trend continued to affect the industry. Toy manufacturers continued to look for alternative distribution sources for their toys in 2004. Partnerships with other types of retailers, including food outlets and drug retailers, were frequently being sought out. Many manufacturers had even begun partnering with home furnishing stores, sports stadiums and home improvement outlets.

According to the U.S.-based Toy Industry Association Inc., age compression and its associated "Kids Getting Older Younger" theory (KGOY) has altered the marketing patterns of toy makers. Children are becoming more technologically sophisticated each year, increasing their use of non-traditional toys, such as electronic toys and games, and at an increasingly younger age. Associated with this is a shortened life-cycle for products, as technological advances are fueled by the need to remain competitive and vie for the attention of the young consumer.

Sales of toys introduced prior to 1990 represented a mere 3 percent of sales in 2003, according to The NPD Group. However, this apparently was changing as nostalgic toys began to make a comeback. For example, in 2003 NPD figures showed toy sales related to *The Hulk* movie were US$156 million, followed by Care Bears (US$136 million), Disney Princess (US$81 million), Strawberry Shortcake (US$60 million), Ninja Turtles (US$58 million), Polly Pocket (US$56 million), Transformers (US$50 million), and My Scene Barbie (US$43 million). According to the Toy Industry Association, in the middle of the decade, the Smurfs were expected to make a comeback.

SPORTING GOODS

Like the toy industry, the majority of the manufacturing of sports equipment (about 65 percent) is done in China, however the primary marketplace is the United States. Globally, the sports manufacturing industry is heavily dependent on trade, with approximately one-third of the world market involving the international flow of goods. Typically, low cost items are produced in the Far East, where lower wages offer a pricing advantage. Higher value goods are produced primarily in developed countries and Taiwan.

The sporting goods market in the United States has grown every year since 1985, until an economic slowdown and events of September 11, 2001 led to losses in many sectors. Because disposable income, especially in the U.S., was expected to continue growing as well by 2003, the outlook for the sporting goods industry remained healthy. In addition, unlike what had been traditional with past generations, as Americans aged their participation in recreational activities did not wane. Instead, overall sports participation increased. However, this trend also marked a reduction in the market for high-impact, strenuous activities, and a marked increase in activities such as golf and exercise using low-impact equipment with built-in monitors. Many exercise machines were sold through "infomercials" broadcast on the ultimate non-exercise recreational equipment, the television.

In its *2004 SGMA International State of the Industry Report,* the Sporting Goods Manufacturers Association reported that U.S. manufacturers shipped US$49.8 billion worth of merchandise in 2003, down 0.5 percent from 2002. A slight increase of 1.3 percent was expected in 2004, as consumers continued to buy sale items and the industry was hindered by lower average sales prices, as well as a glut of retail capacity. Summarizing the sporting goods retail climate as the industry headed into the mid-2000s, the SGMA said: "The excess of sporting goods retail space continues to plague the industry. The excess results in severe price competition, mergers and acquisitions, and a threat of bankruptcy for many companies."

Amid these conditions, the industry experienced a high level of consolidation in 2003. Noteworthy examples include the merger of retailers The Sports Authority and Gart Sports, and the purchase of Worth Inc. by Rawlings. In addition, Spalding sold its Top-Flite and Hogan golf lines to Callaway, as well as its team sports division to Russell Athletic. Other examples include Technica's purchase of Rollerblade, and Brunswick Corp.'s acquisition of Navman NZ Ltd. and Land 'N' Sea.

The SGMA also noted that manufacturers were shifting or outsourcing production to nations where production costs were lower. In addition, leading retailers were increasing their private label brands, which further pressured brand name sporting goods retailers. Combined with declining levels of team sports production, which various industry players were trying to counteract with promotional campaigns, these conditions all combined to create a challenging environment as the industry headed into the second half of the 2000s.

RESEARCH AND TECHNOLOGY

The rapid introduction of computer technology by retailers allowed many of the largest stores to reduce inventories, as they received goods "just-in-time" to make the sale. While this greatly reduced inventory costs, it had one major drawback in the toy sector: when a toy became an instant hit, the retailer had no backup stock and often could not satisfy demand. Moreover, the store might not be able to get more products from the manufacturer, which needed a three-month lead time or longer to make the goods. This proved a boon to toy collectors, who made a business out of predicting which products would become discontinued or unavailable, and hence more valuable as collectibles.

Research and development (R&D) played a vital role in the sporting goods market. Consumers were often driven to purchase new equipment because of the real or perceived advantages of products incorporating new technology. While the relative sales strength of golfing equipment over fishing gear reflected several factors, undoubtedly new technology was an important element. The introduction of oversized woods was a boon for makers such as Callaway, while technological advances in fishing gear were fairly few.

Additionally, innovative entrepreneurs sometimes created substantially new sports through their products. In the mid-1970s, NordicTrack ushered in a new generation of exercise equipment with its cross-country ski systems based on a mechanical flywheel. In the mid-1990s, however, as its patents ran out and competing flywheel designs became available, NordicTrack looked toward an electronic flywheel design to protect its markets and give sales a boost. According to some observers, the new design would help the user regulate resistance force and so-called snow conditions more easily.

The traditional wooden tennis racket stayed pretty much the same until the 1960s, when manufacturers began to redesign it in an effort to improve performance and ease of play. The introduction of durable metal and fiber-reinforced-composite rackets was followed by oversized and wide-bodied models. More recently, manufacturers introduced finely balanced rackets with shock- and vibration-dampening handles and new string bed patterns for greater accuracy. One manufacturer, Inova Inc., used computer software to design a racquet called the Handler, which was said to eradicate tennis elbow.

Perhaps the most famous example in recent times of a sport created through new technology was the development of in-line skating by Scott Olson. According to the story, Olson was a 19-year-old goaltender with a minor-league hockey team in 1980 when he found a pair of roller skates with the wheels arranged in a single row. Olson tried them out, and while they felt clumsy, they gave him the sense of skating on ice. Olson located the manufacturer, who had stopped making the line, and bought up the existing stocks; eventually, he began putting blades on good skate boots, and sold them out of his house. In 1983, he bought up the existing patents and started the company that eventually became Rollerblade, now a generic term for in-line skates. Designers have continued to improve the skates Olson first developed. The number one cause of skating-related injuries was the inability of skaters to slow down. In 1994, Rollerblade introduced active braking technology (ABT) to reduce these injuries. The new design used a built-in brake lever and ankle cuff to engage the break pad when a skater's breaking foot was extended. Rollerblade, which had lost much market share to upstart competitors producing cheaper skates, was hoping that new technology would restore luster to its product line.

INDUSTRY LEADERS

TOYS

Mattel, Inc. Founded in 1945 out of a garage workshop in Southern California, Mattel is the world's largest toy maker, a position it has held off and on since the end of the 1960s. The company achieved sales of US$5.1 billion in 2004, employing 25,000 people in 42 countries, and selling its products in more than 150 countries.

Dollhouse furniture was Mattel's first toy offering, with its most famous product, the Barbie doll, being immediately successful upon its introduction in 1959. The following year, Mattel began selling Chatty Cathy, the first talking doll, which was another hit. The company went public that year, and continued to enjoy strong results and popular products throughout the 1960s. It aggressively diversified with worldwide acquisitions. However, the early 1970s brought hard times and disrepute. The company's chief financial officer was caught recording cancelled orders as sales; eventually Mattel reported a big loss and the U.S. Securities and Exchange Commission stepped in to investigate. While the company recovered in the late 1970s, the 1980s was another period of poor performance. Many of Mattel's acquisitions proved unprofitable, and a slump in video game sales drove it out of that sector. In 1984 the company teetered on the verge of bankruptcy.

A new president, John Amerman, began turning the company around in 1987. He closed 40 percent of the company's operating capacity and slashed headquarters staff. Perhaps most importantly, he focused on the company's core products, including the Barbie doll. The Barbie line was expanded to 90 different dolls and some 250 kinds of accessories. Between 1987 and 1992, sales of Barbie products more than doubled to over US$1 billion. Three brands accounted for half of Mattel sales: Barbie products, toys and other items based on licensed Disney characters, and die-cast cars sold under the name Hot Wheels. Mattel also continued to acquire companies—in 1994 it bought Kransco, maker of Frisbees and Hula Hoops.

Amerman, who had been head of the overseas division, continued to strengthen the company's international operations. For example, the company bought the major New York-based toymaker for infants, Fisher-Price, in 1993 with the conviction that it could expand the company's strong product line overseas, where Fisher-Price had relatively few sales. By 2004, the international market accounted for 42 percent of Mattel's sales. The company's main manufacturing facilities are located in China, Indonesia, Thailand, Malaysia and Mexico, but it also makes use of many third-party manufacturers in the United States, Europe, Mexico, Asia and Australia.

In 1998, Mattel made a disastrous purchase with its buyout for US$3.8 billion of The Learning Company, unloading it two years later to the Gores Technology Group. Then in 2001 the company suffered further problems as Kmart store closings resulted in a glut of Mattel products. Still the world's largest toy company in 2004, Mattel was seeking to reduce its dependence on the likes of Toys 'R' Us, Target and Wal-Mart which accounted for a total of about 46 percent of its sales by engaging in direct-to-consumer sales through its own catalog and via Internet sales.

Hasbro, Inc. The company famous for G.I. Joe, Play Doh and Tonka, as well as producer of some of the world's most recognizable board games such as Scrabble and Monopoly, Hasbro was ranked as the second largest toy manufacturer in the world in 2005. Although the company had 2004 sales of almost US$3 billion, it employed significantly fewer employees than its lead rival, Mattel, having 6,000 workers at Hasbro. This was largely because Hasbro only maintained two of its own manufacturing plants, one in Massachusetts and one in Ireland, with the the remainder being supplied by third-party manufacturers around the world.

This toy company traces its origins to a small textile business begun by the American Hassenfeld brothers in 1923. Using cloth leftovers, the company began by making pencil-box covers. It then extended that business to pencils, school supplies, and ultimately toys. In 1952, the company introduced Mr. Potato Head, the first toy to be advertised on TV, which still generated high-margin sales in the 1990s. In 1954, Hasbro became an important licensee for Disney characters. By 1960, Hasbro was one of the largest toy companies in the United States. In 1964, the company released the action figure G.I. Joe, an immediate hit that soon represented two-thirds of the company's sales.

Hasbro went public in 1968, although most of the stock remained in the hands of the Hassenfeld family. The 1970s were an unhappy decade for Hasbro. Ill-conceived product introductions, discontinuance of G.I. Joe in 1975 (partly induced by higher plastic costs), and family squabbling hurt profitability. In the 1980s, however, the company fought back. It reintroduced G.I. Joe in 1982, and two years later its highly popular Transformer line came on the market. It also began to acquire other toy companies, taking over Milton Bradley in 1984, Coleco Industries in 1989, and Tonka in 1991, including the Kenner and Parker Brothers lines. Hasbro also purchased Galoob, once ranked number three among U.S. toy makers with its popular Micro Machines, licensed vehicles and Star Wars film trilogy tie-ins, and Pound Puppies.

In 1994, Hasbro vied with Mattel for the title of the United States' biggest toy company. Hasbro was the more diversified—none of its toys or games represented more than 5 percent of sales. It expanded into Asia with the purchase of Nomura Toys, a Japanese toy manufacturer, and Palmyra, a Southeast Asian toy distribution firm. Both companies were expected to become distribution channels for Hasbro's push into Asia. Hasbro also began to sell electronic versions of some of its most popular games, including Monopoly. By 1998, Hasbro ranked number two among U.S. toy manufacturers, behind its long-time rival Mattel, which had unsuccessfully attempted to buy Hasbro in 1996.

Bandai Co. Ltd. The world's third-largest toy manufacturer, Japan 's Bandai, is most famous for its Digimon toys, Tamagotchi virtual pets and Mighty Mophin Power Rangers line. However, Bandai is more diversified than the other two top toy makers, with business lines that also include apparel, animated film production, candy and video games.

Founded in 1950, Bandai began by producing celluloid toys, metallic cars and rubber swimming rings. The U.S. arm of the company was established in 1978, with most global expansion occurring in the 1980s. In 1993, the Power Rangers series of action toys were a huge hit in the United States, with the virtual pet, Tamagotchi following closely on its heels in 1996. The Tamagotchi was so successful by 1997, that the company was unable to keep up with demand and had to issue a public apology to consumers.

By 2004, the company's sales had reached almost US$2.5 billion, an increase of almost 22 percent over 2003 revenue levels, with an employee count of 923.

The LEGO Group. Lego is the maker of Lego System bricks, a construction toy that in the early 1990s could be found in 80 percent of households with children in Europe and 70 percent in the United States. The company traces its origins to the decision of Ole Kirk Christiansen in 1932 to extend his carpentry business by making a line of hand-carved, wooden toys. He created the name "Lego" from a contraction of two Danish words, *leg godt*, meaning "play well." The Lego System dates from 1954, when the company decided to design a toy that would be enjoyable for either gender, span a wide age range, include a large number of components, and have compatible pieces that could be added on to parts already purchased. After several years of trying to come up with the right product that fit these criteria, in 1958 the company created the now-famous Lego brick, with studs on top and tubes underneath. The child could place the bricks together in any configuration; indeed, three eight-studded bricks could be combined in 1,060 ways.

The toy was an immediate success, and the company's facilities in the village of Billund, Denmark, were flooded with orders from around Europe. By 1960 the company had stopped making all other toys to concentrate exclusively on the small plastic bricks. In the United States, the toy was initially licensed in 1961 to the Samsonite Corporation, which thought the plastic toy would mesh well with its plastic and retailing businesses. It did well with the toy, but it never recreated the success Lego enjoyed in Europe, and in 1973 it gave up its license. Lego immediately established an American sales company and, through heavy advertising and promotion, increased volume ten times within two years. By 1994, Lego held the leading position in the toy construction market in the United States and continued to hold it in 2005. The company's headquarters remains in Billund, Denmark.

During the 1990s the firm introduced new lines geared to different themes—e.g., town, space, castle, pirates, etc.—each brick remained compatible with the components of all other product lines. In addition to toys, Lego has four theme parks in Denmark, California, England and Germany. In 2004, Lego total sales declined to approximately US$1.36 billion, a drop of 6 percent, and brought with them the worst pre-tax loss in the company's history. As a result of its losses, this privately owned company decided to sell off its non-core lines, including its theme parks, and to decrease its 8,000 strong workforce across 30 countries.

SPORTING GOODS

adidas-Salomon AG. Second in the world in terms of sales of athletic footwear, German-based adidas entered the sports equipment market with its merger with Salomon, the French golf and ski equipment manufacturer. The new company became a leader in high-tech sports equipment. The company is also noted for producing such brands as Maxfli and TaylorMade golf equipment, Mavic cycle components, and Cliche skateboard equipment. By the end of 2004, the company employed 17,000 people and had sales of approximately US$8.4 billion, of which 19 percent was equipment sales.

Amer Sports Corporation. Finnish company Amer Sports is one of the world's leading sports equipment manufacturers, but is perhaps most famous for its Wilson-branded volleyball staring opposite Tom Hanks in the movie *Cast Away*. By 2005, it had become of one the top two suppliers in all its selected sports areas, including racquet sports, golf, team sports, winter sports, sports instruments and fitness. In addition to its Wilson brand, Amer also has the internationally recognized Atomic, Suunto, and Precor brands. By the end of 2004, the company employed 4,066 people, and had sales of approximately US$1.37 billion.

K2 Inc. K2 Inc. provides a diversified range of sports products covering fishing, watersports activities, baseball, softball, alpine skiing, snowboarding, in-line skating and mountain biking. During 2003 and 2004, K2 went on an acquisition spree, acquiring, among others, Rawlings, the leading supplier of equipment for U.S. major league baseball teams in 2003. The vast majority of the company's products are manufactured in China. In 2004, its sales reached US$1.2 billion.

Brunswick Corp. Brunswick is a leading U.S.-based manufacturer of recreation and leisure products. Founded in 1845 to make billiard tables, it is now the world leader in its product categories of pleasure boats, marine engines, fitness equipment, bowling equipment and billiards tables. Sporting goods represented about 19 percent of the firm's 2004 sales of US$5.23 billion, with marine engines and pleasure boats accounting for the remainder.

Nike. The world's leading seller of athletic footwear and apparel, Nike is also a leading supplier of sports equipment, including Bauer/Nike branded hockey equipment. Of the company's US$12.25 billion in sales in 2004, about US$751 million came from the worldwide sale of sports equipment.

Callaway Golf Company. Callaway's Big Bertha line made it the largest maker of metal golf woods in the world. During the early 1990s, the company grew astonishingly fast, with revenues doubling and net income tripling each year. In the 2000s Calloway and IBM teamed up to create a means for serious golfers to record swing characteristics to improve individual scores. By 2003, the company was the leading player in the golf market. That year, it acquired the Ben Hogan, Strata, and Top-Flite golf brands from Spalding Holdings, which declared bankruptcy. Callaway's sales were US$935 million in 2004, an increase over 2003 and 2002 levels. However, its gross profits continued to show decline.

Russell Corporation. Founded in 1902 as a producer of sporting apparel, Russell Corporation was still continuing that tradition in 2005, but was also famous for its sports equipment brands, most notably Spalding, which is a leading producer and marketer of basketballs, footballs, volleyballs and soccer balls under the Spalding brand name and softballs under the Dudley brand. In 2004, Russell recorded sales of almost US$1.3 billion, with just under half of this coming from equipment sales.

Mizuno. Japan's largest sporting goods manufacturer was founded in 1906. The company's 2004 sales reached US$1.33 billion, with approximately 80 percent of that going to the Japanese marketplace. However, the company was showing increases in its non-domestic sales in 2004, with more than 5 percent going to the U.S. market, and 10 percent going to the European market.

MAJOR COUNTRIES IN THE INDUSTRY

TOYS

By far, the country with the greatest number of toy manufacturers in 2005 was China, accounting for 75 percent of the world toy production. However, approximately two-thirds of the toys produced used designs and raw materials supplied by other countries, and a large share of the revenues come from contract manufacturing for large toy companies and license holders. The world's biggest marketplace continued to be the United States, followed by Europe and Asia.

According to the U.S. Census Bureau's International Trade Administration, total exports of toys, games, and dolls from the United States were US$835 million in 2002, down from US$867 million in 2001 and US$1 billion in 2000. During the early 2000s, some analysts predicted that the strongest export growth regions in coming years would be developing regions and countries such as Latin America, the former Soviet states, India, and China. There has been concern among U.S. manufacturers that China, which has been commonly accused of not enforcing foreign intellectual property rights, would allow products to be copied without permission, and this could limit U.S. exports to that country, even though its economy is growing rapidly.

SPORTING GOODS

Once again, in 2005 China was the leader in the manufacture of sports equipment, accounting for about 65 percent of all goods produced. However the primary marketplace was the United States. The industry depends heavily on trade, with about one-third of the world market involving the international flow of goods. Typically, low cost items are produced in the Far East, where lower wages offer a pricing advantage. Higher value goods are produced primarily in developed countries and Taiwan. For products such as baseballs or fishing equipment, labor is the key factor in production, and so these products are more likely to be produced in less developed countries where labor costs are lower. Often U.S. manufacturers contract to have such labor-intensive goods produced abroad. One example of an internationally based operation is the titanium golf club; Russian suppliers, who used to sell titanium for use in military aircraft, now sell the metal to manufacturers of high-priced golf equipment.

In 2003, the Sporting Goods Manufacturers Association (SGMA) reported that U.S. exports were valued at US$1.84 billion. According to SGMA International Director of Market Intelligence Sebastian DiCasoli, this followed a decline of 7.2 percent in 2002, and was attributed to a rosier economic climate in much of Europe and Canada. In addition, another factor was a U.S. dollar that was weak against the

Euro, yen, and Canadian dollar. The largest export increase was in tennis racquets (176.7 percent), while the largest decrease was in basketballs (51.6 percent). The SGMA further reported that total sporting goods imports totaled US$9.38 billion in 2003, up 4.1 percent from the previous year. Sports equipment was a leading category, at US$4.13 billion, an increase of 8.2 percent from 2002. Leading exporters of sports equipment to the United States in 2003 were Mainland China (56 percent), Taiwan (9.3 percent), Canada (4.8 percent), Mexico (4.2 percent), and South Korea (2.5 percent).

FURTHER READING

Coleman-Lochner, Lauren. "Diversity in Toys," *Indianapolis Star,* 13 March 2002.

———. "Toys "R" Us Plans Cutbacks," *The Record (New Jersey),* 29 January 2002.

Cummins, H.J. "A '90s baby boom," *Star Tribune (Minneapolis, MN),* 22 May 2001.

Elkin, Toby. "PlayGloom," *Advertising Age,* 4 February 2002.

Fasig, Lisa B. "Coming of Age—It's a Brand New Game for Hasbro," *The Providence Journal-Bulletin,* 17 February 2002.

"Fila Fourth-Quarter Loss Widens as Sales Decline; *Bloomberg News,* 28 February 2002.

Fraser, Antonia. *A History of Toys.* New York: Delacorte Press, 1966.

Fun Facts. Port Washington, N.Y.: The NPD Group, Inc., 2004. Available from http://www.npd.com.

Gill, Ronnie. "Robots Lead March of Season's Toys," *Newsday (New York, NY),* 9 December 2001.

Hallett, Vicky, and Marc Silver. "Toyland Tuneup." *U.S. News & World Report,* 23 February 2004.

Hoovers Inc. *Hoover's Company Capsules.* Austin, TX: Hoover's Inc., 2004. Available from http://www.hoovers.com.

International Council of Toy Industries. *The traditional toy market in the world in 2003 (without video games).* Available from http://www.toy-icti.org/resources/wtf&f_2003/.

"Japan's Tomy Expects Group Loss on Waning Pokemon Sales," *Asia Pulse,* 6 February 2002.

Kahn, Joseph. "An Ohio Town Is Hard Hit as Leading Industry Moves to China." *The New York Times.* 7 December 2003.

Kepos, Paula, ed. *International Directory of Company Histories.* Detroit: St. James Press, 2005.

Kiley, Erin. "Parents Moving to Box Stores, Internet for Toys." *Business Record (Des Moines),* 1 March 2004.

"Overseas Adventure for U.S. Toys." *Business Week,* 3 November 2002.

Peers, Alexandra. "Barbie Boom Going Bust," *Forbes,* 30 January 2002.

Sporting Goods Manufacturers Association. *Today's Sporting Goods Industry: The 2004 Report.* Orlando, Fla., 11 January 2004. Available from http://www.sgma.com.

———. *U.S. Sporting Goods Exports Resume Growth.* North Palm Beach, Fla., 20 February 2004. Available from http://www.sgma.com.

———. *U.S. Sporting Goods Imports Continue Growth.* North Palm Beach, Fla., 8 March 2004. Available from http://www.sgma.com.

Toy Industry Association Inc. Annual Report, *2004 A Year In Review: The Growth, Challenges & Opportunities of the Toy Industry.* Available from http://www.toy-tia.org.

"Toy Industry Upbeat on 2001." *Consumer Electronics,* 11 February 2002.

"Toy Trends are Cited by ShopKo." *MMR,* 17 November 2003.

Toy Manufacturers of America. "Industry Statistics." *Toy Manufacturers of America Home Page.* Available from http://www.toy-tma.com.

U.S. Department of Commerce. *Annual Survey of Manufactures.* Washington, 2005.

"Wagon Maker to Close Chicago Plant." *The New York Times,* 1 April 2004.

World Federation of the Sporting Goods Industry. *Newsletters,* 2004. Available from www.wfsgi.org

World Federation of the Sporting Goods Industry. *Official International Handbook 2003,* Available from www.wfsgi.org.

SIC 7841

NAICS 532230

VIDEO TAPE RENTAL AND RETAIL

The global video industry includes outlets that rent and sell video tapes, DVDs (digital video discs), and related items to the general public. See also **Motion Picture Production and Distribution**.

INDUSTRY SNAPSHOT

The global video rental industry looked as if its best performance days were behind it by 2005. Although revenue figures for home video entertainment were on the rise and sales of DVDs had been growing far more rapidly than the declines in VHS sales, rental revenues were continuing to fall. Piracy issues, competition from video-on-demand, and the trend of consumers to buy DVDs and then trade them in, were all having a strong affect on the industry.

Beginning in 1999 with the creation of Internet-based Netflix, the video rental and retail industry joined the ranks of other industries finding success with e-commerce. By 2005, Netflix boasted 40 million DVDs and 3 million subscribers. Other upstart companies such as California-based QwikFliks hoped to cash in on the enormous and growing online DVD rental business, as did Video Island and other companies in the United Kingdom. Even brick-and-mortar players, including international behemoth Blockbuster, jumped into the world of online DVD rentals; Blockbuster launched its offering in 2004, first to the U.K. market and then to the U.S. market. Discount giant Wal-Mart also was a player in this niche, and in 2003 it surpassed Blockbuster for the first time in terms of video sales. Due to reduced overhead fees, such operations could keep a far greater selection of titles than a traditional store could even dream about.

ORGANIZATION AND STRUCTURE

Operations that rent and sell videos and DVDs largely include two groups: exclusive video rental shops or video specialty shops (VSS) such as Blockbuster Video and Hollywood Video and video rental departments of supermarkets and general retailers such as Target and Wal-Mart Stores Inc. Supermarkets have found the video business to be especially lucrative as a convenience offering to shoppers who would otherwise need to stop at a separate store to obtain videos. However, given the increasingly competitive market, some supermarkets and general retailers have turned to video rental chains to run their video rental services. First-run movies usually come to video about six months after their initial releases or after a six-month window, whereas they come to pay-per-view service after another one-to-three-month window and to cable movie channels after an additional three-to-five-month window. Video rental operations usually pay between US$50 and US$80 for each first-run video cassette for rental use and between US$10 and US$15 for sell-through use.

In addition to offering videos and DVDs, rental and retail shops also may provide video games and CD-ROMs for rent. Many national VSS chains have diversified in this manner, and competitive in-store services have followed this pattern in order to keep up. Larger VSS chains may rent VCRs and/or DVD players as well. Besides their rental items, these outlets also often sell a host of concessions such as candy, microwave popcorn, and soda, as well as new and used video cassettes. In addition, many in-store video outlets also sell new and used video cassettes.

Depending on the laws and rating systems of various countries, VSS chains and in-store shops may cater to specific crowds. In the United States, some VSS operations court the adult crowd by providing an X-rated section, although many larger companies such as Blockbuster and Hollywood Entertainment have averted potential problems by eliminating adult sections or not introducing them in the first place. Small, independent U.S. video shops often concentrate on or exclusively offer art and foreign films. Furthermore, a number of in-store shops only target the family crowd, not wanting to offend the sensibilities of shoppers who might object to R-rated fare. However, in countries such as Germany, video specialty stores offer the whole gamut of movies from pornography to children's movies.

A number of movie video distributors provide videos to rental and retail stores. While many stores rely on several distributors, some video operations began to consolidate their accounts in the late 1990s. For example, U.S.-based Kroger Co. announced in 1997 that it would pare its distributors down to just one and began taking bids to see which distributor would win its contract. In addition, Blockbuster bypassed distributors altogether and began to buy directly from movie studios in 1996.

In 2000, the studios and major video chains adopted what is known as the rental revenue-sharing business model. The goal was to get customers to move from VHS to DVD. Prior to the agreement, video stores were paying an average of US$40 per video to purchase videos which they could then rent out to recoup their costs. Under the new agreement, the major chains were given the movies on a consignment basis, with the two sharing any rental revenue received. The studios received 60 percent of the revenues, and the video chains received the remaining 40 percent. Eventually, the used videos were sold for between US$5 and US$15 and the revenues split evenly between studio and chain. Once consumers started accepting DVD over VHS, the studios began to decrease the number of videos entered into the revenue-sharing scheme, and began to offer discounts to wholesalers and retailers to encourage consumers to purchase DVDs.

In 2002, however, independent video retailers filed lawsuits against Blockbuster and other video giants claiming that the revenue-sharing model used by Blockbuster and the major studios constituted unfair competition, a charge Blockbuster's attorneys denied. Undeniably, however, Blockbuster's ability to purchase huge quantities of new releases gave the chain a leverage few rivals could compete with since a tape that costs Blockbuster US$10 could cost a rival six times that amount because of Blockbuster's agreements to share revenues with studios. In addition to the bankruptcies of numerous small stores, a small number of national chains have gone bankrupt or have seen their demise predicted by industry analysts.

The Video Software Dealers Association (VSDA) serves the U.S. video rental industry. With headquarters in Encino, California, the VSDA promotes home video rental through conventions, newsletters, education, and industry reports. The VSDA also provides members with screening videos and retailing handbooks to help them market new releases and remain competitive. The VSDA's accomplishments include lobbying for and helping bring about the adoption of state and federal antipiracy laws, as well as the maintenance of competitive pay-per-view windows. The International Video Federation (IVF) serves the European industry, providing support for video rental and retail operations and statistics on the industry.

Outside of the United States, the video industry operates in an environment that includes some similarities to the U.S. system, as well as some important and impactful differences. Similar is the fact that movies are released using a sequential distribution plan for economies of scale. However, in some countries and trading blocs, home video retailers are required to obtain a license to purchase then rent videos. Studios often charge home video retailers more for a video that is to be used for rental purposes then they do for one that is going to be sold to the consumer. This two-tiered pricing has increased the competition faced by video rental stores in such markets as the United Kingdom, Ireland, Spain, and Italy, who must compete with mass merchandisers.

BACKGROUND AND DEVELOPMENT

The video cassette recorder (VCR) appeared on the market in 1975, as the first step in the development of the video rental and retail industry. New entertainment services also emerged around this time including cable television that fueled the popularity and usefulness of the VCR, because the VCR allowed users to tape TV movies and television shows. Shortly after the introduction of the VCR, movie studios released video cassettes of classic movies to add to their revenues. The advent of the VCR/videotape movie combination presented consumers with more entertainment options. They no longer had to rely on the schedules of movie theaters or premium cable channels to see movies. Instead, they could see them any time they wanted by purchasing movies on video cassette, known in the trade as sell-through videos. However, sell-through videos carry a financial burden because few consumers can afford to pay US$10 to US$25 for each movie they want to see.

In 1977, George Atkinson of Los Angeles bought 50 VHS and 50 Betamax movies, and placed an advertisement in a local paper saying that they could be rented for US$10 per day. He established a rental store, but was soon facing threats of a lawsuit by the film production industry. However, U.S. copyright law allowed for the rental of videos, so soon Mr. Atkinson had 600 franchised stores in operation. He passed away in 2005 with the claim to the moniker "the inventor of video rental." Video rental and retail shops emerged to serve people who wanted the convenience of home video without the expense of purchasing sell-through video cassettes, in addition to those consumers willing to purchase their own copies. Video rental grew quickly, since, after an initial US$150 to US$500 investment for a VCR, people could rent a cassette for a lower price than an individual ordinarily would pay for movie theater admission. Video rental especially filled the family entertainment niche where consumers needed tickets for the entire family, which cost a total of US$20 to US$30, in contrast to a US$3 expenditure to rent a video. By 1985, the U.S. industry alone took in revenues of US$3.5 billion, which grew to US$9.8 billion by 1990, according to the Video Software Dealers Association.

A new laser disc format called the digital video disc (DVD) emerged in the late 1990s as an increasingly popular replacement for the video cassette: DVDs can store between 4.5 and 17.0 gigabytes of data, which translates to between 135 and 540 minutes of playing time. Besides offering a higher capacity and better audio and video qualities, DVDs also have interactive capabilities, allowing users to witness multiple angle shots of a single scene, to read sets of multiple subtitles, and to move to favorite parts of movies by pressing a button. DVD player prices started at about US$500 in the mid-1990s.

Depending on the maturity of the industries, and on domestic economic conditions, the video rental and retail industries of various countries and regions experienced different results in the late 1990s. After a period of strong growth through 1994, video rental and sell-through revenues dropped in 1995 in the United States, the industry's largest and most mature market, but began rebounding strongly in 1998. Following the 1995 drop in revenue, the U.S. industry became alarmed and took extra measures to increase its revenue. The following year, sales rose to US$16.0 billion and climbed 3 percent to US$16.6 billion in 1997. Research by the Video Store group found that consumers spent US$2.6 billion on both VHS and DVD videos during the first quarter of 2002 alone, a significant increase of nearly 7 percent from the US$2.4 billion spent during the same quarter in 2001. Movie distributors tried to shorten windows to increase revenues from video sales in the late 1990s, especially for movies that performed below expectation at the box office.

Asia's economic crisis of the late 1990s affected its video rental and retail industry as consumers became less willing to spend money on non-essential items. Because of the region's growing inflation and unemployment, consumers in countries such as South Korea, Indonesia, and Thailand drastically cut their video rentals and purchases in late 1997 through mid-1998. For example, Thailand reported a 30 percent drop in video sales in mid-1998. Nonetheless, Japan's industry remained the bright spot in Asia as video rentals increased in the late 1990s because of hit movies such as *Princess Mononoke*, *Independence Day*, and *Lost World*.

The European Union's video industry posted moderate growth in the mid- to late 1990s as strong growth in some countries compensated for stagnation and declines in others. While video purchases rose in the European Union, rentals continued to fall, so that purchases surpassed rentals as the industry's leading source of revenues in the mid-1990s. The EU bought an average of approximately 220 million videos in the mid-1990s, valued at about US$3.7 billion. The EU's total market was worth an estimated US$6.4 billion in 1996, when video rentals accounted for only US$2.7 billion. The EU's VCR penetration stood at about 64 percent during this period and 27,000 video rental and 56,000 retail stores operated in EU countries.

With a drop in sales in 1995 and the emergence of competitive alternatives to video rentals and sales, video rental and retail stores began seeking ways of maintaining and increasing their customer traffic. Supermarkets with video shops have tried to offer "dinner and movie" specials to keep their video departments thriving, according Dan Alaimo in *Supermarket News*. Stores have provided promotions giving customers movie rental discounts with the purchase of deli items and prepared entrees. With such promotional campaigns underway, some video stores considered large-scale alliances with restaurants. Blockbuster launched a promotional campaign with Planters Nuts, and Hollywood Entertainment teamed up with Domino's Pizza to offer free movies with pizza purchases.

Other modes of home entertainment continue to compete with the video rental industry. Alternative forms of home entertainment such as digital television, pay-per-view, and direct-broadcast satellite remained a challenging force for video stores in the late 1990s. Although these alternatives provided some advantages over video rental—including higher resolution for digital television and some greater conveniences such as not having to return videos for pay-per-view and direct broadcast movies—video industry proponents point out that they also cost substantially more and sacrifice features such as being able to pause and rewind movies. Furthermore, these alternatives have a much more limited selection than video stores. Nonetheless, an A.C. Nielson survey conducted in the United States indicated that only 35.8 percent of the participants with direct satellite systems rented a video during the three-month sampling period, even though 95 percent of them owned a VCR. Moreover, 73 percent of the participants reported that they rented fewer videos after installing direct satellite systems.

Inadequate international copyright protection is a perennial problem plaguing the industry. Pirated video cassettes make up a large part of some markets in Latin America, and piracy also undercuts the video rental industries in East Asia, the Middle East, and Eastern Europe (though the practice, of course, also occurs in the United States and Western Europe). Piracy in China is officially banned by the government, but fines are low for video counterfeiters and the financial rewards have been worth the risk for the unscrupulous. Such copyright infractions have strained relationships between video producers and distributors and government agencies of various countries. In the late 1990s, the video industry continued to lose a large amount of revenues to piracy. For example, the U.S. industry annually lost about US$250 million to worldwide video piracy, according to the Motion Picture Association of America (MPAA), and Europe lost about US$275 million, according to Federation Against Copyright Theft (FACT). Consequently, agencies and associations such as the MPAA, the VSDA, and FACT increased their efforts to combat and prevent video piracy.

At the end of 2001, the video and DVD rental industry found itself among the few industries to substantially benefit, particularly in the United States, from the terrorist attacks in New York. In late 2001, more families opted for entertainment they could enjoy at home, according to some industry observers, and revenues for the industry surged. Also helping to bolster sales was a weak North American economy, which prompted consumers to look for less expensive entertainment options.

Lower DVD prices have coincided with increased sales and market competition for customers. To respond to customer demand, many video stores have emptied their old tape sections to offer new movie releases and popular classics on DVD. Blockbuster, for example, replaced approximately 25 percent of all tapes with DVD discs in 2001, enticing customers to make the changeover with US$99 offers for DVD players and even free DVD players to those who purchased a US$199 DVD rental card.

CURRENT CONDITIONS

According to *The Hollywood Reporter*, the video rental and retail industry in the United States boasted almost US$26 billion in revenue for 2004, $16 billion of which was for DVDs. By the end of 2004, more than 70 million U.S. households, 42 million Chinese households, and 171 households in other countries had DVDs. Citing data from Adams Media Research, *The Economist* revealed that DVD rentals and sales made up some 40 percent of movie studio revenues by 2003, up from 1 percent in 1997. In its 2004 annual report, Time Warner reported that the largest driver behind its growth in the filmed entertainment segment was the sale of DVDs from its library of film titles. The industry move to DVD allowed Internet companies such as Netflix to thrive; because DVDs are smaller and more lightweight than video cassettes, they were comparatively more affordable to mail. Waiting time was becoming increasingly less of an issue as well. By 2005, Netflix had 35 distribution centers handling its 40 million DVDs, allowing for 24-hour delivery in most markets. Seeing the competition's success, Blockbuster entered the online market in 2004 in both its U.S. and U.K. markets.

Sales and rentals of VHS-format movies continued their downward spiral, dropping by 50 percent in 2004. However, the overall increase in revenues for the sales and rental market of all video formats was not only due to the acceptance of the DVD format, but of the desire for consumers to own movies in this format. The rental market, when analyzed independently of sales, was actually on the decline. Adams Media Research had found that rentals of both DVD and VHS had dropped by 11 percent from US$9.8 billion in 2003 to about US$8.8 billion in 2004. Industry analysts were projecting that as other options become more widely used, the rental market will decline 4 to 5 percent annually. A possible monkey wrench in the phenomenal growth of both traditional and online stores could prove to be the growing popularity and availability of video-on-demand (VOD), a service that allows viewers to choose movies from home to view instantly. According to PricewaterhouseCoopers, the VOD market will encompass 20 million households by 2007. However, the VSDA projected that the VOD market would not be a major factor until 2008, when revenues were expected to hit US$2.5 billion.

According to *The Hollywood Reporter*, the trading of DVDs was also expected to aid in the decline of the rental market. Consumers were buying DVDs and then trading them in for cash or credit. The advantage to store owners was the ability to resell DVDs without having to share the profit with film studios. This trend took off in 2004, with estimates on the value of this type of selling being about US$1 billion.

Netflix initiated the strategy of not charging its customers late fees. For a flat fee, consumers could keep a video as long as desired. The other major video chains followed suit, reducing or eliminating late fees. However, such fees had accounted for as much as 10 percent of the fees earned by studios and about 15 percent of revenues earned by Blockbuster. Several studios responded to these trends by discounting the price of its DVDs to both wholesalers and retailers. As a result, the cost of buying a new DVD dropped to between US$10 and US$17 dollars, with many selling for less than US$5 in bargain bins. This pricing strategy served to further encourage the number of DVDs purchased rather than rented. Discounters, such as Wal-Mart and Target, began to outpace the video chain giants in terms of sales of DVDs. In addition, the studios were more aggressively promoting video-on-demand. Where once video renters received movies first after box-office release, the playing field was expected to become more even, with cable television companies being offered the chance to be the first to show movies after their box-office runs.

But this buying trend was also showingsigns of a decline. In 2004, the average number of DVDs purchased per year per household dropped from 10 in 2003 to eight. High-definition DVDs were expected to be launched in 2005, a move many were hoping would help to revitalize the industry. Franchised films made the most money for the industry in 2004. *Shrek 2* led the video rental and sales market, with about US$458 million in revenue of which about US$44 million was from rentals. *The Lord of the Rings* trilogy also earned significant money for the industry, with sales and rentals of US$415 million.

According to Kagan Research, although the home video market is expected to grow to a value of US$33.8 billion by 2009, the amount of revenues from rentals is expected to continue to decline, reaching US$6.3 million in 2009. With this trend will come the continued consolidation of the industry. A July 2005 report in *The Hollywood Reporter* even commented on the struggle facing the Video Software Dealers Association, as the number of independent rental stores declines.

RESEARCH AND TECHNOLOGY

To track industry performance and consumer habits, the VSDA introduced VidTrac to the U.S. industry in January of 1996. The point-of-sale service collects data from a large sample of video rental operations throughout the country. More than 4,500 stores participate in VidTrac with nine of the most successful rental chains among them. The VSDA tabulates and circulates the data each week, offering statistics and projections for the video rental community. The tabulations are made available on the VSDA Web site. In 2002, *Variety* charged that the statistics may be off by 20 to 40 percent and demanded more accurate figures.

Internet rental pioneer Netflix developed software to offer recommendations for other movies based on past rental activity. This ability offers the best of both worlds, because customers received a personalized service that also had the advantage of being automated.

In 2005, two technologies were expected to have great influence on the video industry. The first was the introduction of high-definition DVDs. This new system will provide consumers with surround sound and three-dimensional-like pictures. With the ability to hold six-times more data than conventional DVDs, studios will not have to spend so much time compressing data to fit, and will be able to add more marketing-related information. Consumers will be required to buy new players in order to take advantage of this new viewing format.

The second technology affecting the industry is the availability of video-on-demand (VOD). In 2003, according to the VSDA, about 12.5 million U.S. households already had access to VOD, with 25 percent having access to the Internet through high-speed broadband. With VOD, consumers can access movies and television programs when they want via their cable, satellite or Internet service.

INDUSTRY LEADERS

Blockbuster Inc. Headquartered in Fort Lauderdale, Florida, Blockbuster Entertainment Group led the global video rental and retail industry in 2005, after beginning operations with a single store in 1985. After watching its revenues fall a whopping 20 percent in 1997, Blockbuster devised a strategy of providing good service and value to the greatest number of customers. Stripping from shelves the games and little-rented titles to make room for more copies of blockbuster movie releases, Blockbuster immediately won accolades for improved customer service and the availability of desirable hit titles. A subsidiary of Viacom Inc. from 1994, Blockbuster divested in 2004 to become an independently trade public company. At the end of 2004, Blockbuster had more than 9,100 stores in 25 countries, and revenues of US$6.1 billion. Revenues from outside of the United States made up 30.5 percent of all sales. The company was a franchisor of its stores, with 1,095 franchised operations in the U.S. and 734 in other countries. To compete with the success of Internet-based video rental companies, Blockbuster launched its own online subscriptions service in May 2004 in the United Kingdom and in August 2004 in the United States.

Movie Gallery Inc. Movie Gallery grew its video chain in the United States by concentrating on rural and secondary markets. In early 2005, the company had about 2,500 retail stores located in small towns and suburban areas of cities. Revenues for 2004 were US$791 million.

In January 2005, the company acquired Hollywood Entertainment. Based in Wilsonville, Oregon, Hollywood Entertainment Corp. grew quickly in the mid-1990s to become the second-largest U.S. national video rental chain. Hollywood Video claimed in 2002 that it was opening one new store every day. From a single store in 1988, Hollywood operated 1,006 stores in the U.S., eschewing the international competition that Blockbuster had embraced. Hollywood Entertainment was begun by husband-and-wife entrepreneurs Mark and Holly Wattles and expanded through a series of acquisitions. The firm's profits in the early 2000s were hurt by its previous US$90 million purchase of online video merchant Reel.com, an acquisition widely criticized as extravagant. Eventually, Amazon.com took over the site, but Hollywood continued to provide content. The company had US$1.78 billion in sales in 2004.

Movie Gallery also acquired St. Paul, Minnesota-based Video Update in 2002. Video Update had unexpectedly declared bankruptcy in 2000. The chain continued to do business in January 2002, despite cutting loose some 110 stores to streamline operations. That year, Video Update came under fierce criticism for its payment of huge salaries to its top executives, even as the company demanded Chapter 11 protections. In 2000, the chain had swelled to 586 units after purchasing the Moovies Inc. chain of stores.

Netflix Inc. The early 2000s saw a rise in e-commerce, and the video rental industry was no exception. Begun in 1999, Netflix offered access to thousands of DVD titles available for rental. By 2002, Netflix had emerged as the reigning king of online DVD rentals. For one fee (between US$9.99 and US$17.99 monthly in 2005), customers could go online to rent a pre-specified number of movies and keep them as long as they pleased, with no late fees. The DVDs arrive via the U.S. post office and are returned the same way, postage paid. In January 2002, Netflix boasted that it had 500,000 subscribers, and by the 2005 that number had swelled to more than 3 million. Subscription numbers were continuing to grow, and the company projected it would reach a count of 5.0 million by 2006. Netflix reported 2004 revenues of US$506.2 million, an increase of more than 200 percent over 2003 levels.

Tsutaya. The largest franchised video rental chain in Japan, Tsutaya began operations in 1983. By 2005, the company operated more than 1,155 stores and had more than 18 million members in Japan. The company held a 31.5 percent market share in Japan in 2003. The company is part of Culture Convenience Club Co. Ltd. which had revenues of approximately US$1.7 billion in 2004.

MAJOR COUNTRIES IN THE INDUSTRY

United States. The United States led the world in revenues from video tape rentals and sales and housed the world's top video rental chains, such as Blockbuster and Hollywood Video, owned by Movie Gallery. The VSDA reported that these three video store chains held 50 percent of the U.S. market for rentals in 2003. The number of video stores had been on the decline since 1990's high of 31,000; by 2003 there were 24,300 video rental specialty stores. Most of this decline has been attributed to consolidation and the rise of the video mega-shops. However, in 2003, about half of all stores were still single-store operations, and an additional 4,100 other retailers (mainly pharmacies and supermarkets) were also renting videos. Blockbuster was surpassed in terms of video sales for the first time in 2003; Sam's Clubs had more in revenues from this source than did Blockbuster.

U.S. video rental operations have achieved their success in part because of the 90 percent VCR penetration into U.S. households and 53 percent DVD penetration in 2003. However, DVD sales and rentals were dominating the market. Of the US$22.2 million spent on video sales and rentals in 2003, 16 million was spent on DVDs—a 40 percent increase over 2002 levels. Video sales and rentals was also contributing significantly to the bottom lines of the major film studios in the U.S., with home video accounting for about 60 percent of all revenues received from filmed entertainment.

United Kingdom. In the mid- to late 1990s, the United Kingdom led Europe in revenues from video rentals and purchases, and while there was a slight dip in 2000 and 2001, annual revenues jumped here in 2002 thanks to strong interest in DVD format videos and the release of the Harry Potter video. With videos priced at US$16.75 apiece in the United Kingdom, video sales make up about 63 percent of the U.K. industry's revenues. Since VCR penetration remains on par with the United States, the U.K. industry accounts for about one-third of the European Union's video rentals and sales. In December 2001, following the September 11 terrorist attack in the United States, the UK's largest home-based store franchise, HMV Media, reported a return to strong video sales and rentals. In a January 2004 report, the British Video Association estimated that video retail market in all formats was up 29.7 percent from 2003 to around 199 million units. While VHS sales dropped by 19 percent to 60 million, DVD sales increased 75 percent, making up for any decline.

Germany. Europe's second largest video rental and retail market is Germany, which has about 6,000 video stores. Germany's video rental industry slumped in the late 1990s, experiencing its slowest year in 1997 since 1993. Because of stagnation in German consumers' disposable incomes, the country recorded an 11 percent drop in video rentals in 1997. The industry's total revenues for rentals and purchases fell to US$878 million that year. In 2001, Germany continued to experience a continuation of its recession, according to *Fortune International* magazine, but nonetheless video store sales and rentals were US$1.04 billion, a 22 percent gain over 2000.

Japan. In the late 1990s through 2002, many Japanese citizens, especially those who worked in service industry-related jobs, suffered through hard economic times. Until 2001, video and DVD rental stores reported the same downturn in the industry that was seen in the United States during the late 1990s. However, the downturn ended in 2001 in Japan as customers in increasing numbers began staying at home and turning to movie rentals, which typically cost one-third to one-quarter the price of a US$20 cinema seat ticket. Japan's industry also grew during this period, led by *Princess Mononoke*, the country's most popular video rental of all time, which had been released in 1997. The leading Japanese video store is Tsutaya, a franchise operation owned by the Culture Convenience Club Company; Tsutaya also owns stores in Thailand.

FURTHER READING

"About Us." *Netflix, Inc. Website,* 2004. Available from http://www.netflix.com.

Amdur, Meredith. "Vid Biz to Stop Skid?" *Daily Variety,* 20 February 2004.

Andrews, Sam. "The Year in Video 2001." *Billboard,* 12 January 2002.

Behar, Richard. "Bejing's Phony War on Fakes." *Fortune,* 30 October 2000.

Desjardins, Doug. "Blockbuster Looks Ahead After Viacom Spinoff." *DSN Retailing Today,* 19 July 2004.

———. "Hollywood Video Looks to Chart a Private Course." *DSN Retailing Today,* 19 April 2004.

Draper, Deborah J., ed. *Business Rankings Annual.* Detroit: Thomson Gale, 2004.

"DVD Boosts Germany's Video Industry to Record Highs." *Deutsche Presse-Agentur,* 3 March 2002.

"DVD Player Sales Take Off." *Reuters,* January 2002.

Ford, Rosemary. "Are the Big Chains Stomping Out the Little Guy?" *The Eagle-Tribune (Lawrence, MA),* 22 April 2001.

Frankle, Daniel. " Video City Re-emerges with New Stores, Focus." *Video Business,* 18 March 2002.

"Future Bleak for Video Rental Market." *Europe Intelligence Wire,* 23 July 2004.

Harvey, Fiona. "The Smash Hit." *New Media Age,* 26 February 2004.

"Helen Mirren Calls on Public to Reject Piracy as Video Sales Grow by 30 Per Cent." British Video Association (news), 7 January 2004. Available from http://www.bva.org.uk.

"Hoover's Company Capsules." 2004. Available from http://www.hoovers.com.

Huffstutter, P.J. "Yahoo's Search for Profits Leads to Pornography." *Los Angeles Times,* 11 April 2001.

Kapner, Fred. "HMV Media Puts U.S, Jitters Aside." *Financial Times (London),* 8 December 2001.

Lazich, Robert S., ed. *Market Share Reporter.* Detroit: Thomson Gale, 2004.

McCartney, Jim. "A Dream Unravels: Video Update." *St. Paul Pioneer Press,* 25 February 2001.

Mullaney, Timothy J., and Tom Lowry. "Netflix: Moving Into Slo-Mo?" *Business Week,* 2 August 2004.

Muller, Henry. "Shadows Over Germany Globalization and a Business Downturn are Forcing Europe's Biggest Economy to Reinvent Itself." *Fortune International,* 23 July 2001.

Ranii, David. "Blockbuster: Like Gangbusters." *The News & Observer (Raleigh, NC),* 27 December 2001.

"Record-Breaking First Quarter DVD Rental Revenue Surpasses Entire Year 2000." *PR Newswire,* 23 April 2002.

Sporich, Brett. "2004 home video wrap." *The Hollywood Reporter,* 19 January 2002. Available from http://www.hollywoodreporter.com.

Sporich, Brett. "Research: DVD Rentals Spin Faster." *The Hollywood Reporter,* 24 April 2002.

"Tiny QwikFliks Seeks to Carve Out Piece of Netflix's DVD Action." *Los Angeles Business Journal,* 5 April 2004.

Twist, Jo. "What high-definition will do to DVDs." BBC News, 31 January 2005. Available from http://ww.bbc.co.uk.

Video Software Dealers Association. "2004 Annual Report on the Home Entertainment Industry," 2004. Available from http://www.vsda.org.

"Video Software Dealers Association." *DSN Retailing Today,* 21 July 2003.

"Video Store Trade Association Mourns Passing of 'Inventor' of Video Rental." Video Software Dealers Association (Press Release), 7 March 2005. Available from http://www.idealnk.org.

"Yahoo! Reports Fourth Quarter, Year End 2001 Financial Results." *Business Wire,* 16 January 2002.

FINANCE, INSURANCE, AND REAL ESTATE

SIC 6000, 6100, 6300, 6400

NAICS 5221, 5222, 524

BANKING AND INSURANCE

Banks and insurance companies constitute a major component of the broader global financial industry. The banking segment comprises commercial banks, savings banks, international banks, credit unions, mortgage bankers, loan brokers, and trust companies. Insurance encompasses life, casualty, property, surety, pension funds, and health policy brokerages and agents. Certain banks derive all or a significant share of their revenues from credit card accounts. For more details specific to this business, see also **Credit and Debit Card Issuers**.

INDUSTRY SNAPSHOT

The finance and insurance industries experienced growing deregulation, globalization, and consolidation into the mid 2000s. As countries throughout the world—including industrial leaders such as Japan, the United States, Germany, and France—liberalized their finance systems, banks and insurance brokers pursued foreign markets and began to integrate their services. In addition, banks and insurers continued consolidating in order to achieve cost-effective economies of scale and scope, as well as to increase their product offerings to customers. Rankings of the world's largest financial service firms were repeatedly reshuffled as mergers created new industry giants; there were many companies that ended 2004 with total assets valued over US$1 trillion. In total, the banking industry's top 1000 banks had total assets of US$52.39 trillion in 2004.

ORGANIZATION AND STRUCTURE

BANK STRUCTURE

Commercial banks are usually classified in three categories: unit, branch, and group. Some nations are characterized by only one type, but most nations have all three. Unit banking exists when a single-office institution provides banking services. Historically, this was the most common form of banking in the United States. The presence of unit banking is often a result of tradition, law, vested interests, and the ability of this type of organization to meet the demands of local banking customers. When communities are homogeneous and small businesses and farming are dominant, unit banking works well. Unit banking becomes less practical as a nation becomes increasingly industrialized, culturally diverse, and geographically enlarged. This is especially evident as large geographical areas become economically interdependent. In industrial societies, populations are highly mobile and place increasing importance on the convenience that multiple bank locations provide. The need for larger institutions is even stronger among businesses, which engage in transactions on a national or even international scale and thus require complex services to support such activities as issuing stock, acquiring other businesses, or financing a new business venture. As a result, branch banking has become the norm in the world's major economies.

Branch banking exists when a single banking firm conducts operations at multiple sites. Branches are wholly owned and usually controlled by one headquarters. The level of service may vary between branches of the same bank, as some small satellite offices may not offer the full line of services available at major branches or headquarters.

One of banking's essential functions is facilitating the transfer of funds. As the use of checks, credit cards, debit cards, electronic transfers, and other non-currency payment media accelerates among the world's populations, this function is increasingly important.

Banks' second major function is to serve as a financial depository for customers' liquid assets. This service provides an efficient and highly secure means of storing wealth for accumulation or future use. Banks generally hold a fixed proportion of their customers' aggregate deposits in reserve in order to have funds available on demand. The remainder of deposited funds are channeled into various operations of the bank, notably as credit to other customers.

Extending to customers different types of credit, including diverse loans and credit accounts,;is what traditionally makes banking lucrative. By charging the borrower interest fees in excess of what they pay back to the depositor, banks earn revenue by serving as the intermediary. Bank lending is very important to all nations' economies because it enables communities to finance agricultural, commercial, and industrial activities. This type of credit-infused growth is called indirect or "roundabout" production. Direct production refers to consumer goods secured by the direct application of labor to land or natural wealth. Most countries regulate their banking systemsexclusively on the national level. The United States, however, regulates its banking system on both the national and regional levels.

Commercial banks also serve a variety of functions specific to business transactions. They can issue commercial letters of credit, sometimes called lines of credit, which are written statements guaranteeing that a bank will loan a customer a specified range of money. Banks issue letters of credit when a seller is unwilling to release his or her products and wait for payment to arrive in the mail. A letter of credit makes a loose financial arrangement more binding and businesslike. When a bank issues a letter of credit, both the buyer and seller are protected. The credit of the bank is substituted for the credit of the buyer, an arrangement designed to reassure the seller. A great deal of international trade is financed in this manner. Such financing of foreign trade and travel by commercial banks contributes to a freer flow of commerce among nations. As foreign trade and travel increase throughout the world, so too do the services of international commercial banks.

Commercial banks also provide trust services to customers worldwide. Individuals who have accumulated estates, even of moderate size, provide for the distribution of assets prior to death by writing wills and securing bank trust departments to act as executors. In many cases, bank trust departments are responsible for investing and caring for the funds within an estate. They also distribute the proceeds as established by trust agreements.

The oldest service provided by commercial banks is the safekeeping of valuables. Banks have vaults that are nearly impossible for non-authorized people to enter and that have established records of safety. In most cases, the protection of valuables falls into two areas or departments within a bank: safe deposit boxes and safekeeping. Customers can rent safe deposit boxes from banks. Under such an arrangement, customers have control of their own valuables at all times. The bank simply provides the vault, the box, and the other facilities necessary for a proper safe deposit box. Most important, however, the bank controls access to the vault and guarantees that the customer who rented the box is the only one permitted access. Customers use their safe deposit boxes for securities, deeds, insurance policies, and other items of value.

Safekeeping differs from safe deposit box services because the bank assumes custody of the valuables and acts as an agent for the customer, often a corporation. Items accepted for safekeeping differ considerably, but the service usually cares for securities such as stocks and bonds. In most commercial banking situations, the department is concerned with holding securities that a customer has pledged as collateral for a loan or turned over to a trust department as part of an estate.

Commercial bank trust departments provide many additional services to corporations. In some cases they administer pension and profit-sharing plans for companies. They also serve as trustees in connection with bond uses and as transfer agents and registrars for corporations. In some cases, commercial bank trust departments administer sinking funds and perform other duties associated with the issuance and redemption of stocks and bonds.

Throughout the late twentieth and early twenty-first centuries, commercial banks have engaged in brokerage services, buying and selling securities for customers. This diversification has encouraged banks to form joint ventures with full-service brokerages to provide complete advisement and investment services. In many countries, the authority of commercial banks to provide brokerage services is prohibited. Governments justify this prohibition on the belief that excessive bank credit based on speculation can lead to bank failures and economic disarray. Although international banking authorities are less successful in controlling banking stability because of the lack of well-defined jurisdictions from one nation to another, national authorities within many large industrial countries have introduced elaborate controls on banking practices. These controls are designed to prevent banks from failing and to safeguard the country's financial system if they do.

In the United States, the *Glass-Steagall Act* of 1933 formally separated banking from securities and prevented banks from establishing securities affiliates. However, by the late 1990s this separation was eroding quickly. *The Gramm-Leach-Bliley Act* of 1999 officially repealed Glass-Steagall, leaving U.S. banks free to diversify into new arenas such as securities and insurance. *The Interstate Banking and Branching Efficiency Act* of 1994 opened up new commercial bank growth opportunities and created incentives for them to merge. The Japanese banking industry underwent similar deregulation in the late 1990s. Consequently, the merger and acquisition of financial services surged in both the United States and Japan at the turn of the twenty-first century. Unlike the United States and Japan, Europe has a long history of offering many services under one company, and banks there continued in the early 2000s to combine banking, insurance, and securities operations.

Insurance Structure. With increased competition from banks, all sectors of the insurance segment have changed the way they operate and the kinds of policies they offer. Nonetheless, in their most basic form, insurance companies collect payments or premiums from policyholders; invest the premiums; return some of the investment to policyholders through dividends, annuities, or policy payments; and provide reimbursement for qualifying events, such as death, disability, loss of property, or medical treatment, depending on the type of insurance. Insurers obtain their money for investment from policy reserves, liability for unearned premiums and deposited funds, and separate account liabilities. Policy reserves make up the money companies put away for paying future policy payments.

For insurers to profit, they must accurately strike a balance between the money kept in loss reserves for paying policy claims and the money invested. If a company reserves too much money for losses, it will lose potential investment growth and may have to raise its rates in order to be profitable. However, if a company reserves too little for losses, it will look more profitable, but run the risk of being tight on funds should it suddenly have to pay an unexpected number of claims. To achieve this accurate balance, companies must estimate the value of future claims as precisely as possible, which entails considering variables such as real economic growth, inflation, and interest rates, as well as the likelihood of claims arising at a particular time.

Two kinds of ownership exist in the insurance segment: companies owned by stockholders, known as stock insurance, and companies owned by policyholders, known as mutual insurance. For stock insurance, companies issue stock as shares of their ownership. Mutual insurance companies use capital called "policyholders' surplus." The property and casualty sector of the industry bears the risk of future losses, sharing these costs with policyholders. Major property/casualty policies include home-owners', auto, theft, and other kinds of insurance, as well as workers' compensation.

The life insurance sector has evolved from making payment only when policyholders die to offering a wide selection of policies for finance, taxes, retirement, and estates. Life insurance products include whole life, universal life, variable life, term life, group life, and annuity policies.

- Whole life policies provide a payment at death and require a savings plan throughout the life of the policy.
- Universal life policies offer a term life policy as well as a savings feature with interest rates similar to those of money market accounts; policyholders determine the premium, the death benefit, and the savings amount.
- Variable life policies came about as a response to high interest rates offered by certificates of deposit and mutual funds and include a death benefit as well as a more full-scale investment component that allows policyholders to choose stocks, bonds, or money market investments.
- Term life insurance allows policyholders to obtain insurance for a set number of years, such as five or 10, and the coverage ends even if the policyholder survives the term; term life does not include an investment component and is the most affordable kind.
- Group life insurance covers people under a group program and provides policyholders with renewable one-year term policies.
- Annuities are insurance contracts that make numerous payments to the policyholder; payments may begin either immediately or at a future date.

Background and Development

In the West, the modern banking industry formed in northern Italy, where it began in conjunction with long-distance trade in the fourteenth century. Because the Catholic Church prohibited usury, which at the time was considered any lending of money for interest, the primary activities of these banks included exchanging and transferring money, rather than holding deposits and lending money. These early banks consisted of pawnbroker-like operations that provided small loans to farmers and artisans, as well as operations that sent papal taxes from various regions in Christian Europe to Rome.

As commercial trade spread throughout Europe, trade centers adopted these banking techniques. In the fifteenth century, Lyons, France, replaced Geneva, Switzerland, as the leading financial nexus, and Bruges, Belgium, lost its key trade position to Antwerp, Belgium. Bankers in Antwerp developed bank endorsement and discounting in the sixteenth century, facilitating negotiating and transferring of money. When these bankers moved to Amsterdam, Holland, the state established the Amsterdamsche Wisselbank, a public deposit and clearing bank that proved highly successful. As a result of its innovative banks, Amsterdam remained a powerful financial center through the early part of the eighteenth century.

Public banks opened along European trade routes during the medieval period and gradually took on more characteristics associated with the contemporary bank. Over time the prohibition against usury waned and banks began lending, which became one of their key activities by the eighteenth century as they provided loans for governments. Furthermore, banks offered services to the public such as savings accounts, loans on collateral, and check-like paper documents and credit receipts. In the eighteenth century, banks such as the Neapolitan Public Bank and Sweden's Bank of Stockholm introduced paper money.

In the United States, the Continental Congress established the first chartered bank in North America. Based in Philadelphia, the bank supported the credit of the budding country and issued paper money that could be converted into gold and silver. The bank fared well, and other banks quickly followed its example. By the beginning of the nineteenth century, more than 30 commercial banks operated in the country, including the First Bank of the United States.

Banks began to play a decisive role in the Japanese economy around 1882 when the country founded the Bank of Japan as its central bank. From its inception through the early 1970s, the Bank of Japan helped Japanese industries grow by supporting city banks, regional banks, and other operations that lent money to industries. Though the Bank of Japan continued to provide growth money to industries, it took on the additional responsibility of maintaining the yen's stability in 1973 when inflation soared.

The mid-1990s ushered in a new trend in the commercial banking industry: the merging of banks and insurance brokers, creating diversified companies to offer banking, securities, and insurance services. Although banks have merged and acquired one another for decades, Europe pioneered the way for more-diversified acquisitions as Deutsche Bank bought 10 percent of the insurer Allianz and Credit Lyonnais through it subsidiary Union des Assurances Federales and also through Allianz. This meld of banks and insurers is sometimes referred to as "bancassurance." In 1998, in anticipation of industry deregulation that would allow banks to offer insurance services, Citicorp, a leading U.S. bank, announced plans to merge with insurance giant, Travelers Group Inc., creating the first such integrated service in the United States. Reforms of the financial services industry in Japan also led to companies offering a wider array of services, blurring the lines between banks and insurance brokers.

Traditional consolidation in the banking industry continued as well. For example, U.S.-based Chase Manhattan Corp. acquired Chemical Banking Corp. in 1996. In Japan, two of the country's largest banks—Mitsubishi Bank Ltd., and Bank of Tokyo Ltd.—also merged in 1996, becoming the world's largest financial institution at the time, with assets of more than US$700 billion and annual revenues of US$46.4 billion.

Expansion into international markets became more feasible in the late 1990s due to the increased deregulation that took place on a global scale. At the end of the Uruguay Round of Multilateral Trade Negotiations, which resulted in the 1994 General Agreement on Tariffs and Trade (GATT), financial services negotiations had remained incomplete. Participating countries made commitments to open their markets to outside nations, but felt that the negotiations were not satisfactory. The 1994 agreement allowed reciprocity-based exemptions for most-favored-nation treatment wherein countries could offer trade benefits to whatever countries they chose. In 1995, the World Trade Organization (WTO) sponsored another round of talks, producing the Interim Agreement of 1995. For the Interim Agreement, 29 members of the WTO intensified their commitments, while three members opted for most-favored-nation reciprocity. Discussions resumed in 1997, and 102 WTO members pledged to make their financial services markets more accessible by March 1999. The new commitments reduced or eliminated restrictions on foreign ownership of local financial operations and on expansion of existing operations. Moreover, the agreement offered all signing members the same trade benefits available to any other country, eliminating most-favored-nation treatment. WTO members account for 95 percent of the world's financial services market.

For the 29 members of the Organization for Economic Cooperation Development (OECD), which account for 95 percent of the global insurance market, insurance providers posted premiums worth US$2.05 trillion in 1995, up 9 percent from 1994. Life and non-life insurance each represented about 50 percent of the total premiums. The United States led the world with US$758 billion, or 37 percent of the market, followed by the European Union with US$635 billion, or 31 percent, and Japan with US$471 billion, or 23.3 percent, according to the OECD. The U.S. market spent US$1,167 per capita on property and casualty insurance in 1996, followed by Japan with US$714 per capita and Western Europe with US$621 per capita. In contrast, China's premium per capita stood at only US$3. However, emerging markets reported the highest growth rates in the 1990s, as Eastern Europe, South America, and Southeast Asia increased their demand for insurance. The *National Underwriter Property & Casualty-Risk & Benefits Management* forecast that these markets would account for 50 percent of the world's insurance sales by 2025.

The financial services industry of the late 1990s was characterized by increasing globalization and diversification as banks expanded both their geographic reach and their selection of services (to include categories such as annuities, mutual funds, insurance, and capital market products). In the U.S. market alone, between 1997 and 2001, securities firms participated in more than 400 mergers and acquisitions, the average value of which reached US$2.5 billion in 2000, according to *Business Week*. One of the most noteworthy deals, completed in the late 1990s, was the merger of Travelers Group and Citicorp to form Citigroup, the second-largest financial services firm at the time. In its quest to further diversify its services, in 2000 Citigroup paid US$30.8 billion for Associates First Capital Corp., the leading consumer lender in the United States. To extend its global reach, Citigroup strengthened its position in South America the following year when it paid US$12.82 billion for Grupo Financiero Banamex, one of Mexico's leading banks.

Like Travelers Group and Citicorp, many firms within the United States first took advantage of deregulation on a domestic level. In early 2001, Chase Manhattan and investment banker J.P. Morgan merged in a US$36.5 billion deal that created J.P. Morgan Chase. Meanwhile, banks and insurance providers in Europe also began capitalizing on U.S. deregulation as they found it easier to move into the U.S. market. For example, Credit Suisse, one of Switzerland's largest banks, added two U.S.-based brokerage firms (Donaldson, Lufkin, and Jenrette and First Boston) to its holdings. Another Swiss bank, UBS AG, acquired Paine Webber. ING Group, a leading Dutch insurer, acquired the financial services operations of Aetna Inc., as well as ReliaStar Financial.

Germany's Deutsche Bank, the world's largest bank in terms of assets in 1999, found itself dethroned in 2000 after the Industrial Bank of Japan, Fuji Bank, and Dai-Ichi Kangyo Bank joined forces to create Mizuho, then the world's largest bank, with assets of US$1.2 trillion. Deutsche Bank, with assets of US$874.7 billion, was also surpassed that year by Citigroup, which boasted assets of US$902.2 billion. In 2000 the world's 1,000 largest banks secured US$317 billion in profits, a slight increase over 1999 profits of US$310 billion. Profits for the top 25 banks reached US$118.1 billion; the United States and the European Union accounted for roughly 74 percent of this total, as Japanese banks continued to struggle with non-performing loans.

Consolidation in Japan continued in 2001 with a flurry of activity that included the merger of Sakura Bank and Sumitomo Bank to form Sumitomo Mitsui Banking Corp.; the joining of Bank of Tokyo-Mitsubishi, Nippon Trust Bank, and Mitsubishi Trust to create Mitsubishi Tokyo Financial Group Inc.; and the combining of Sanwa Bank, Tokai Bank, and Toyo Trust and Banking Co. into UFJ Holdings Inc. When the dust had settled, the number of banks in Japan had fallen to nine, compared to twenty in 1996. According to *AsiaPulse News*, the consolidation was part of an effort by the Japanese banking industry to improve profitability by streamlining operations. Saddled with massive nonperforming loans, Japan's major banks are more hard-pressed than ever to cut costs. As part of such measures, banks are stepping up efforts to slash the number of their branches. In fiscal 2000, Sumitomo Mitsui closed 75 branches, while UFJ shuttered 13 units and planned to shut down more than 100 additional offices and lay off 5,280 workers by the end of 2005. In total, Japanese banks had plans to reduce their combined workforce by roughly 25,000 employees by then.

Although weakening economies in both the United States and Europe helped to slow the pace of consolidation by the end of 2001, major deals continued to materialize. American International Group Inc. paid US$23 billion for American General Corp., creating the largest insurance deal in industry history to that point. Also, Germany's leading insurer, Allianz AG, acquired the 80 percent of Dresdner Bank that it did not already own.

In June 2003, the United States Agency for International Development announced it would provide assistance of $10 million for the next four years for the development of the Indian insurance sector. Bearing Point was awarded the contract to implement this program of technical assistance with the Insurance Regulatory and Development Authority (IRDA). This U.S. assistance was expected to help the IRDA build its institutional capacity in the areas of solvency and market conduct supervision, promote an enabling policy, regulatory and institutional environment for the development of the health insurance system, develop key professions associated with the insurance sector, and also develop comprehensive databases on insurance.

Although small compared to many other countries, China"s insurance industry experienced rapid growth in 2003. Life premiums came in at US$36 billion, up 32 percent from one year earlier. Property premiums increased to US$10.4 billion. According to the China Insurance Regulatory Commission, the severe acute respiratory syndrome (SARS) outbreak mildly disrupted insurance sales in some regions of China. However, it "served to catalyze a surge in demand for insurance coverage."

Karl-Heinz Goedeckemeyer, a Frankfurt, Germany-based independent financial analyst, concluded that consolidation in the international sector would continue. He acknowledged that size was becoming increasingly important as a strategic factor. There was expected to still be room for banks targeting specific customers, products, or regions.

CURRENT CONDITIONS

In 2004, the world's top 1000 banks had aggregate pre-tax profits of US$417.4 billion dollars, up a massive 65 percent over 2003 levels according to *The Banker.* This profit growth was attributed to improved economic conditions, led by the U.S. and followed by Japan and most of the European Union. However, Germany's banks showed a net aggregate loss of US$306 million as its economy was slower to recover. Total industry-wide assets grew more than 19 percent, reaching US$52.39 trillion.

Although improved, the world's major economies showed relatively slow growth during 2004, while the economies of developing countries were showing very strong growth. While this growth was a positive for those in the financial services industry, some countries were also showing record-levels of debt and bankruptcies. In 2004, in the United States and the United Kingdom, personal bankruptcies remained at historically high levels and consumer debt levels were also very high. As a result, banks were looking for ways to manage their credit risks, including using a third party to insure them against defaults.

While consolidation through mergers and acquisitions slowed during 2002, since then such consolidations have been increasing. Deloitte Touche Tohmatsu credits this increase with the need for banks to add to their product offerings for customers as well as to broaden their coverage in international markets. In 2005, UFJ Holdings of Japan was set to create the world's largest bank when it merged with Mitsubishi Tokyo. In 2004, Bank of America added 6 million customers when it acquired FleetBoston Financial, the same year the Bank of Scotland acquired Charter One Financial of the United States, and Spain's Santander Central Hispano purchased Abbey National of the United Kingdom. The world's largest banks began to more-actively pursue interests in Asia; CitiGroup purchased KorAm, while HSBC took an interest in a Chinese bank.

Deloitte's research also showed that banks were having to deal with growing dissatisfaction among their customers. In the U.S., banks were retaining an average of only 50 percent of their customers. Many banks had begun to realize they had lost a valuable form of marketing when they pushed their customers out of the branches and into the ATMs, and were looking at ways to bring customers back to the branch in their efforts to directly market other services to them. Also affecting customer perceptions was the fact that many banks had transferred some of their services to lower-cost providers in other countries. Some that had moved call centers were experiencing problems with customer service, while others who had transferred technology out of country were having to concern themselves with data integrity and security.

The financial service industry has also come under increasing regulatory pressure, with the cost of compliance bearing down heavily on many companies. The *Basel II Capital Accord* required banks to have set aside enough capital to cover any risks. The *Sarbanes-Oxley Act* in the U.S. puts the burden on CEOs and directors to certify that their control systems are adequate. In addition, the International Accounting Standards Board, based in London, set new standards adopted by many European banks in 2005.

The insurance industry has also been hit hard with regulatory issues. Marsh & McLelland and AON were under investigation for "bid-rigging". These brokers were accused of getting insurance providers to submit deliberately high bids in order to give consumers the idea that they were getting competitive quotes. These high-bidders would then be "given" the next customer. Some companies were also coming under scrutiny for providing loss mitigation insurance products to clients, who then transferred losses off their balance sheets.

Mother Nature took her toll on the insurance industry too in 2004, making it the most costly year on record for the insurance business. That year, four hurricanes hit the Florida coast, bringing with them the most-significant single catastrophic event in U.S. history, with an estimated US$21 billion in insured losses. This was considerably more than the estimates being made as a result of the tsunami that hit 10 countries and killed more than 200,000 people in south Asia at the end of 2004. Unlike Florida, in this region much of the loss of life and property was uninsured, and as a result industry estimates were stating that the cost to insurers would be only US$5 billion to US$10 billion.

In terms of mergers and acquisitions, very little occurred in the insurance industry in 2004. The most notable consolidation took place in 2003 when Travelers and St. Paul merged. However, experts at Ernst & Young were predicting that consolidations were ripe to continue, as the industry was too fragmented.

RESEARCH AND TECHNOLOGY

Banks have employed massive computers and other sophisticated forms of technology to speed the check-clearing process, reduce personnel and expenses, and improve the accuracy of record keeping. A single computer often handles the work that many employees once did manually, requiring little paperwork since most tasks are accomplished electronically. As a result, world economists predicted that commercial banking was headed toward a "checkless banking society" in which the electronic transfer of funds would eliminate the need for bank checks and all the work they entail. In the late 1980s and early 1990s, members of the banking community began to experiment with a system that uses debit cards somewhat similar to credit cards. Use of a debit card in financial transactions, such as purchases, activates computers in banks worldwide and automatically transfers funds from the purchaser's account to the seller's account. Automatic teller machines (ATMs) are forerunners of this debit system. Subsequently installed in most banks and many retail establishments throughout the world, ATMs allowed customers to withdraw cash, make deposits and loan payments, and transfer funds between depositors' savings and checking accounts without having to set foot in a banking institution.

Throughout the international banking community, banks scrambled to take advantage of customers' needs for new import/export products and services, most notably services for mid-sized corporations. In the early 2000s, mid-sized companies were looking to commercial banks for solutions to their global business challenges. Banks could help companies structure their financing; arrange for shipping, handling, and insurance; track the movement of goods; and provide data on sales and receivables.

This effort is evidence of the move toward "one-stop shopping" in the banking industry. The concept that one bank should be able to meet all of a company's international financial services needs was as of 2004 relatively new. Many banks had found that by packaging international services under one umbrella, they could offer a competitive, value-added product. For example, the French banking giant Credit Lyonnais provided a range of services to foreign companies doing business in France, including financing, site location, aid in locating suitable joint-venture partners, and legal and tax advice. The bank also offered the full complement of standard cash-management and corporate banking services.

In the early 2000s, the concept of the corporate bank gained favor among large companies. A corporate bank differs from a commercial bank in that it confines its activities within a single multinational company and never involves the public. Many corporate banks are the primary holding companies for major corporations. Such a setup is ideal for the global economy as trade barriers fall and national financial markets open to monetary transfers, borrowing, and investment. The corporate bank's functions include conducting intercompany banking, handling financial transactions, and managing corporate liabilities within the financial community.

TECHNOLOGY IN COMMERCIAL BANKING

Many experts believed that future success in global banking was predicated on an understanding of the business advantages possible through new technology. Throughout the international community, there was a growing demand for immediate information, and most banks have instituted programs that provide online access to cash-management and trade-related services. However, international banks still had far to go in the area of integrated information and services. For example, customers could gather information in a basic foreign exchange/cash-management package that allowed them to access accounts and make transfers and payments in various currencies. By contrast, trade packages allowed customers to open letters of credit, make collections, and manage open accounts. Banks in the early 2000s developed the technology to combine the two types of packages. Once this was accomplished, banks would be able to manage international trade and treasury under a single system. The result was expected to be improved efficiency for the banks and greater convenience for the customers.

Despite its shortcomings, many local and regional banks used available technology to enter the global market. They succeeded by establishing direct links to correspondent banks in other countries and rounding out the international trade services they could offer customers. By doing so, small banks were able to compete service to service with the major money centers around the world. This type of competition was possible because the cost of technology drops each year, a trend that allowed much smaller competitors to gain access to these systems. Technology enabled small banks to compete in the once-inaccessible world of international banking.

Another boost for many regional banks was the emergence of new global markets at the end of the twentieth century. Banks in the southeastern United States, for example, benefited from increased growth and trade within South American and Central America and the Caribbean Basin. Likewise, U.S. banks along the borders with Canada and Mexico had geared up for increased trade with those countries due to the implementation of the North American Free Trade Agreement (NAFTA).

In the buyer's market of the early 2000s, many analysts believed that the most successful banks in the future would be those that were most sensitive to their corporate customers' international needs. For most banks, this meant developing a good international correspondent network, top-notch technology, attentiveness to customer requests, and flexibility in adjusting quickly to a rapidly changing global marketplace.

Banks around the world had by this time implemented online banking services, allowing customers to conduct banking activities via the Internet at any time. Internet transactions allowed banks to provide more cost- and time-efficient services to more customers, since online transactions typically involved less time and expense than their traditional counterparts. The Internet let customers apply for loans, find account information, transfer funds, and make payments from a personal computer.

In addition, digital technology allowed for a new kind of currency: electronic money. Rather than instilling value in paper and coins, developers created ways of storing value in a digital format represented by a string of numbers. Electronic money permits users to easily trace their transactions and spending, since computers would automatically balance accounts and provide instantaneous financial statements and reports. Furthermore, electronic money is replaceable if lost because its owner can simply cancel the digits representing the money lost and replace them with new digits.

INDUSTRY LEADERS

BANKING AND FINANCING

Citigroup. Taking first place on the *Fortune* list of the 2000 largest global companies in 2005 was Citigroup of the U.S. However, CitiGroup continued to compete with Mizuho of Japan for the title of the world's largest financial services enterprise on other listings, depending on what criteria were used to establish the lists. With more than 200 million customer accounts in 2005, this diversified financial services company was operating in more than 100 countries, offering customers banking, insurance, lending, investment services, asset management, and credit cards. Truly global, the company employed almost as many people outside of its home base in the U.S. as it did domestically; at the end of 2004, 148,000 people were employed in the U.S., while 146,000 were employed internationally. The group had assets of US$1.48 trillion, total deposits of US$562 billion, and net income of more than US$17 billion.

The outcome of the 1998 Citicorp/Travelers Group merger, Citigroup forged a new level of vertical integration in the U.S. industry. The Travelers Group included the investment bank and bond trader Salomon Brothers in addition to the Smith Barney brokerage firm. The Travelers Group also owned the consumer loan provider Commercial Credit and the mutual fund broker Primerica Financial Services. In May 2004, Citigroup announced plans to set up a life insurance joint venture in China. Through the Beijing and Shanghai branches of the U.S. Citibank, a new personal foreign exchange deposit product market-lined account was launched as the first such product from Citibank since it began offering related services in China on March 25, 2004. The product required a minimal investment of US$25,000. In 2005, Citigroup sold Traveler's Life & Annuity, including almost all of its international insurance business, to MetLife.

Mizuho Holdings Inc. Mizuho Holdings was created in September 2000 with the merger of Industrial Bank of Japan, Fuji Bank, and Dai-Ichi Kangyo Bank. With assets of US$1.3 trillion, it was the second-largest financial services provider in the world in 2004. Mizuho held US$733.5 billion in deposits and had net income of almost US$3.9 billion. In 2002 Mizuho divided operations into Mizuho Bank—a consumer bank—and Mizuho Corporate Bank. After the merger, Mizuho reduced its number of domestic branches from 560 to 444, and its overseas branches from 49 to 41. Planned cost-cutting measures included eliminating more than 7,300 jobs by 2006. In May 2004 Mizuho announced plans to reorganize its wholesale operations to better meet customer needs. Plans included consolidating 26 wholesale banking departments into 16 with each focusing on a particular industrial sector such as electrical machinery, automobiles and general contractors. Another May 2004 announcement revealed Mizuho Trust and Banking Co. planned to have the industry's first foray into handling intellectual property rights in trust by overseeing the software copyright owned by a Nippon Life Insurance Co. subsidiary.

Crédit Agricole Groupe. With its acquisition of Crédit Lyonnaise in 2003, Crédit Agricole joined the ranks of the giant of banking. France's largest bank, the organization was made up of 2,629 local banks serving 21 million customers in 2004. In addition, it operated in 66 countries. Its total assets in 2003 were US$1.09 trillion, with net income of more than US$3 billion.

JPMorgan Chase. A new JPMorgan Chase was created in July 2004 when the company (the second largest bank in the U.S. in terms of assets) merged with Bank One Corporation (the sixth largest bank in the U.S.). The company had assets of US$1.1 trillion at the end of 2004, and provided investment banking, financial services for consumers and businesses, financial transaction processing, asset and wealth management, and private equity in more than 50 countries.

HSBC Group. Named after its founding member, The Hongkong and Shanghai Banking Corporation Limited, HSBC was initially created in 1865 to finance the growing amount of trade between China and Europe at the time. By 2005, HSBC was based in London, and was one of the world's largest banking and financial services providers. The organization had almost 10,000 offices in 77 countries in Europe, the Asia/Pacific region, the Americas, Africa, and the Middle East.

Royal Bank of Scotland Group plc. With a history going back to 1727, the Royal Bank of Scotland (RBS) has grown through a series of big-name acquisitions. In 1988, it entered the U.S. market with the acquisition of Citizens Bank of Rhode Island. In 2000, RBS acquired NatWest which was then the biggest takeover in British history. The year 2004 saw further expansion in the U.S. with the acquisition of Mellon Bank and Charter One. RBS also has a strong place in the motor insurance industry, having created Direct Line in 1985. The company's insurance segment became the second-largest provider in the U.K. upon its acquisition of Churchill. RBS ended 2004 with total assets of US$1.06 trillion and net income of about US$8.7 billion.

Bank of America. In 2005, the U.S.'s third-largest bank had more branches across more states than any other bank. In addition to its 5,889 banking centers, the company also had offices in 35 other countries covering Asia, Europe and the Americas. Bank of America was also the leading issuer of debit cards in the U.S. with nearly 17 million cards issued, and the leading online bank with about 12 million active online customers and 6 million bill-payment customers. At the end of 2004, the bank had assets of US$1.11 trillion, with total deposits of US$618.6 billion, and net income of US$14.1 billion, making it the world's fifth most-profitable company.

In 2004, the company acquired FleetBoston Financial, adding 6 million customers.

Deutsche Bank. Once the world's largest bank, Deutsche Bank found itself in third place after global consolidation in the late 1990s and early 2000s created a host of new industry behemoths. However, by 2004 it was ranked sixth in terms of assets. That year the company's total assets amounted to approximately US$1.1 trillion, deposits were US$413.6 billion, and net income was US$3.1 billion. The firm employed 65,400 workers in 74 countries. Deutsche Bank operated two divisions: Private Clients and Asset Management, and Corporate and Investment Banking. A planned merger with domestic competitor Dresdner Bank fell through in 2000, prompting a management shakeup. Sluggish retail banking operations resulted in a series of cost-cutting measures, including the elimination of jobs in the early 2000s; employment fell from 98,000 in 2000 to 65,400 by 2004. In early 2005, the company was coming under criticism for its plans to reduce its domestic workforce by a further 6,400 people. The company's domestic retail banking unit was suffering from low returns which it attributed to competition from non-profit financial institutions.

Mitsubishi Tokyo Financial Group Inc. With 2001 sales of US$20.4 billion, Mitsubishi Tokyo Financial Group was another of the world's largest banks. It was created in April of 2001 when Mitsubishi Trust and Banking and Nippon Trust merged with Bank of Tokyo-Mitsubishi, the leader in the global finance and insurance industry in 1996. Combined services included commercial, investment, foreign exchange, investment management, load production, real estate management, retail, securities banking services, and specialized trust services. The group served more than 40 countries. In the United States, it owned approximately two-thirds of UnionBanCal, the parent company of United Bank of California. The group reported having 57,500 employees in 2003.

BNP Paribas. France's BNP Paribas is one of the largest banks in Europe and also has a large international presence in Asia and the United States. The company deals in corporate and investment banking, retail banking, and asset management, with a global presence in 85 countries. Total assets for BNP Paribas reached US$1.13 trillion in 2004, with customer deposits of approximately US$411 billion, and net income of US$5.8 billion. The company operates BancWest (Bank of the West and First Hawaiian Bank) in the Western United States, Banque Internationale pour le Commerce et l'Industrie (BICI) in French-speaking Africa, as well as having operations in Morocco, Tunisia, Algeria, Madagascar, the Comoro Islands, the Middle East, and the Near East.

INSURANCE

American International Group, Inc. (AIG). AIG is the world's leading insurance company and one of the top financial services providers, operating in more than 130 countries. The company offers property/casualty insurance, life insurance, retirement services, and asset management. In 2004, the group came under investigation by the Securities and Exchange Commission for allegedly helping a client hide underperforming loans. The company was then accused of failing to adequately inform its investors about the probes by the SEC and the Justice Department. AIG paid a SEC-imposed fine of US$10 million without admitting any guilt. In 2003, AIG reported net income of US$9.3 billion, and had delayed filing its annual report for 2004 pending a reevaluation of its financials.

Allianz AG. Allianz, based in Munich, Germany, was founded in 1890 as a personal accident, fire and transport insurance provider. By 2005, the company had 60 million customers in more than 70 countries and was providing property and casualty insurance, life and health insurance, and asset management and banking services. Most of the company's income was being earned outside of Germany. Allianz posted revenues of more than US$121 billion in 2004, with profits of US$8.6 billion in the same year. In July 2001, after acquiring the 80 percent of German bank Dresdner it did not already own, Allianz moved into the number four spot among the world's largest financial services firms. The firm also holds a stake in Deutsche Bank.

ING Groep N.V. Formed in 1991 from the merger of Nationale-Nederlanden and NMB Postbank Groep, Internationale Nederlanden Group was soon to change its name to ING. The company grew through acquisitions, the first major one occurring in 1995 when it acquired Barings Bank, making ING a well-known name worldwide almost overnight. Other acquisitions followed. In 1997 it acquired the Belgian Bank Brussels Lambert, U.S. insurer Equitable of Iowa and U.S. investment bank Furman Selz. In 1999 it acquired German merchant bank, BHF-Bank. Its acquisitions of ReliaStar and Aetna Financial increased its U.S. presence two-fold and made the company the largest insurer in South America and the second-largest insurer in the Asia/Pacific region. By 2005, ING was obtaining 22 percent of its profits from each of its American and European insurance segments, 10 percent from its Asian insurance segment, 25 percent from wholesale banking, 15 percent from retail banking, and 6 percent from direct retail banker ING Direct. ING had total assets of approximately US$1.08 trillion in 2004 and net income of US$7.5 billion.

Nippon Life Insurance Company. One of the world's largest insurance companies and the largest in Japan, Nippon Life Insurance Company experienced difficulty during the early 2000s when it saw its sales and profits plunge. By 2004, the company had been actively changing its management, and had seen an increase in its core operating profit. However, it was still experiencing declines in its income from insurance and reinsurance premiums. Nippon Life offered life insurance and annuities, and, thanks to Japan's deregulation of the industry, it also provided property and casualty insurance as well as financial planning services. With more than 20 branches spread throughout North America, Europe, and the Pacific Rim, Nippon was an international insurance provider. Its major focus for overseas activities was providing coverage to Japanese companies and citizens abroad. In March 2004 Nippon announced expansion of its alliance with Marsh & McLennan Companies, which was involved in risk and asset management worldwide. It would roughly double its investment in Marsh & McLennan to US$217 million. Since its sales in Japan dropped, Nippon planned to expand its presence in other Asian countries, where it hoped to drastically increase its global market share. The company also planned to raise the reserves that it had set aside against a rise in the mortality rate plus other internal reserves by around 380 billion yen to more than 1.3 trillion yen for fiscal year 2003.

AXA. Based in Paris, France, AXA offered the whole gamut of insurance products, including life insurance, property and casualty insurance, and reinsurance, as well as financial services and real estate investment. Its operations were diverse geographically with major operations in Western Europe, North America and the Asia/Pacific region. International subsidiaries included AXA Financial, previously known as the Equitable Companies, which owned Alliance Capital Management. In May 2004, AXA Financial announced that stockholders of The MONY Group voted to approve a US$1.5 million merger with the company. The merger was viewed as an opportunity to add scale to the company. Founded in 1816 as Mutuelles Unies, AXA acquired the Drouot group in 1982 and became France's largest insurance company. The company changed its name to AXA in 1984. In 2004 AXA earned appro[AP1]ximately US$90 billion in revenues of which 65 percent came from its life insurance segment, 25 percent from property and casualty, 5 percent from international insurance, 4 percent from asset management, and 1 percent from other financial services.

Major Countries in the Industry

Japan

In 2005, Japan was preparing to be the home of the world's largest bank; Mitsubishi was set to purchase Japan's fourth-largest bank, UFJ Holdings. The combined company would have assets of US$1.8 trillion. Analysts at Deloitte Touche Tohmatsu believed that this was setting the stage for further consolidations in the banking industry. By 2003, Euromonitor had valued the commercial banking sector in Japan at US$7.6 trillion, with four banks dominating the industry: Mizuho Banks, Mitsui Sumitomo Bank, Tokyo Mitsubishi Group, and UFJ.

Banks in Japan had become much more cautious about lending in 1998 in an attempt to avoid risky loans, and the government proposed a US$250 billion bailout to rescue the banking industry. At the time, Japanese banks ranked among the world's least profitable, even reporting a net loss in 1996. However, operating profits outweighed bad debts by 1997, leaving the country's city banks (Bank of Tokyo-Mitsubishi, Fuji, Dai-Ichi Kangyo, Daiwa, and others) with marginal profits. In addition, Japan's trust banks (Mitsui, Mitsubishi, Sumitomo, Yasuda, Nippon, Toyo, and Chuo) posted combined net profits of US$23.8 billion, according to *Banker*. By 1998 the worst of the industry's troubles appeared over; however, nonperforming loans continued to pose problems in the early 2000s.

Japan began deregulating its banking and insurance system in March 1998. Japan's Ministry of Finance reduced its role in the overall administration of the finance and insurance industry via this deregulation program, known as "the Big Bang," which permitted holding companies to operate in Japan and allowed banks to offer investment and insurance products; the legislation was also designed to introduce greater investor protection.

Asia Pulse Businesswire reported that Japan's major banking groups and regional lenders recorded a remarkable rebound of market capitalization in fiscal 2003. Many regional banks, however, were lagging behind in their recoveries.

United States

The United States represented another of the world's leading countries in the banking and insurance industry and was home to the world's most profitable banking and insurance companies. The commercial banking industry was valued by Euromonitor to be worth US$6.5 trillion, with the five largest players (Citigroup, Bank of America, JPMorgan Chase, Wells Fargo, and Wachovia) accounting for about 55 percent of the market. The retail banking market was valued at about US$1.24 trillion, with the market being highly fragmented. In this sector, the top five players (the same as the previous listing, but with Bank One replacing Wachovia) accounted for only about 35 percent of the market, with the rest going to a large number of small, regional banks. Both sectors were expected to grow by more than 10 percent by 2008. However, U.S. banks were facing a serious problem retaining customers; research by Deloitte Touche Tohmatsu showed that only 26 percent of customers would recommend their bank to someone else.

The life insurance industry in the U.S. was valued at US$128.6 billion in 2008, while property insurance was valued at US$324.5 billion, and healthcare insurance was at US$65.5 billion. Growth in all sectors was expected to approach or exceed 10 percent by 2008. Property insurance remained concentrated among the top five companies: State Farm, Allstate, American International, Nationwide, and St. Paul Travelers, with automobile insurance being the largest part of the market. In the life insurance sector, 88.1 percent of the market was covered by Prudential, Metropolitan, New York Life, Northwestern Mutual, and John Hancock Financial. However, the healthcare market remained highly fragmented, with the largest companies (CIGNA, UnitedHealth, Kaiser, AFLAC, and Aetna) taking less than 36 percent.

With significant mergers in the mid-1990s, the United States gained a greater global presence, following the trends of banks and insurance brokers in Japan and Europe. The repeal of the *Glass-Steagall Act* in 1999 allowed U.S. banks to grow even larger and resulted in the creation of such behemoths as Citigroup and JPMorgan Chase.

Germany

With commercial banking valued at US$3.97 trillion and retail banking valued at US$4.05 trillion, Germany provided Europe with its largest banking community. Deutsche Postbank, spun off from Deutsche Post in 2004, was the market leader in both segments. However, Deutsche Bank was the leading banking group, with a strong international presence. Dresdner Bank and Commerzbank were also significant players in the industry.

In the mid-1990s, German banks established a large, new bond market, making it a strong source of international investment. They also developed a significant global presence by acquiring U.S. and U.K. investment firms. In 1996, 3,551 banks operated in Germany, giving it the world's densest bank concentration. However, to become more competitive, German banks consolidated. Between 1990 and 1996, large banks absorbed more than 1,000 small banks.

Like other banking/financial systems around the world, Germany's also underwent restructuring in the late 1990s and early 2000s. Two of Germany's larger banks, Bayerische Hypo-Bank and Bayerische Vereinsbank, announced they would merge in 1997. At the same time, Deutsche Bank bought a 5.2 percent share of Bayerische Vereinsbank. Allianz, the country's leading insurance company, owned 22 percent of both Bayerische Vereinsbank and Germany's second-largest bank, Dresdner Bank. In 2001 Allianz acquired Dresdner Bank, creating a new German powerhouse.

In pursuit of new clients, German banks also turned to Eastern Europe, particularly Poland, the Czech Republic, and Hungary. German banks launched operations in Slovakia, Slovenia, and the Baltic states as well. Deutsche Bank established its presence in Eastern Europe by opening its own branches there, while Commerzbank opted to acquire local banks in the region. Though German banks began by offering standard commercial services in the region, they added investment banking services once they had established a strong customer base.

While in 2003 80 percent of Germany's health care premiums value of US$106 billion came from the statutory health system, the market for other forms of insurance was wide open to private companies. Allianz remained a worldwide leader and a leader domestically in both the life and property insurance lines.

UNITED KINGDOM

The United Kingdom not only represented one of the world's largest finance and insurance markets, but also one of the most profitable. U.K. banks recovered from losses suffered from failed lending ventures, posting enormous profits in the mid-1990s. The five leading U.K. banks at the time (Abbey National, Barclays, Lloyds, TSB, Midland, and NatWest) generated a combined US$13.1 billion in profits in 1996. The banks turned to consumer-oriented business to achieve their turnaround, focusing on savings accounts, credit cards, and car loans, which compensated for the dwindling profit margins of corporate banking services. Banks in the United Kingdom also began to convert themselves from mutually owned operations to stockholder-owned diversified financial services. In 2000, the Bank of Scotland aquired NatWest. Leading U.K. bank, HSBC Holdings, paid US$63 million for an 8 percent stake in Bank of Shanghai in 2002, becoming the first foreign commercial bank to own a portion of a bank in mainland China in more than half a century. According to *Europe*, the purchase was the result of China's entrance into the World Trade Organization. The acquisition "is expected to lead to more alliances between overseas banks and insurers in the run-up to full liberalization of the country's financial services in 2006." Domestically, commercial banking was valued by *Euromonitor* at about US$624 billion, while retail banking was valued at about US$2.7 trillion. Barclays held the highest share of both markets, with greater than 18 percent of each.

FRANCE

France also ranked among the leading nations in the industry. Top bank BNP Paribas and leading insurer AXA were both located there, and both were major global players outside of the domestic market. In 2003, commercial banking was valued at US$2.5 trillion, while retail banking was worth US$2.3 trillion. Domestically, Crédit Agricole was the market leader in the retail sector, while BNP Paribas was the leader on the commercial side.

French banks and insurers followed the international trend of consolidation. Insurance giants AXA and UAP merged, becoming AXA-UAP, one of the top financial service providers in the world. AXA-UAP eventually changed its name back to AXA, and in 2003, AXA remained the market leader in all insurance sectors. The country also faced restructuring after some of its banks experienced losses early in France's deregulation process. Some banks, such as Credit Foncier de France and Suez, experienced great losses when they rushed into the property market right before it crashed. Moreover, France's state-owned Credit Lyonnais continued to flounder in the mid-1990s, reporting US$17 worth of bad loans after verging on bankruptcy in the early 1990s due to overly ambitious expansion. Loan fraud also contributed to the bank's woes. Restructuring unfolded slowly, however, and critics blamed the government's heavy-handed management for the delays. Consequently, bank profits in France slumped, deriving mostly from international markets, according to *Euromoney*. The French government appointed a commission to find remedies for some of the industry's problems.

By 2000 most of the country's banks, including Credit Lyonnais, had been privatized. However, scandal continued to pervade the French banking industry. In 2001 Credit Lyonnais remained under investigation for its dealings with Executive Life, a U.S.-based insurer that the French bank had helped rescue from collapse in the early 1990s.

FURTHER READING

"2005 Global Banking Industry Outlook." Deloitte Touche Tohmatsu, January 2005. Available from http://www.deloitte.com.

"AXA Financial Announces That MONY Stockholders Approve $1.5 Billion Merger," 18 May 2004. Available from http://www.axaonline.com.

Baker-Self, Terry; Beata Ghavimi; and Matthew Dickie.. "Top 1000 World Banks." *Banker*, 2 July 2004. Available from http://www.thebanker.com.

Barnard, Bruce. "HSBC, the London-Based International Bank, Paid $63 Million for 8 Percent of the Bank of Shanghai." *Europe*, February 2002.

"Briefing—Asia Insurance—May 19, 2004." *Asia Pulse Businesswire,* 19 May 2004.

"Business in Asia Today—March 26, 2004." *PR Newswire,* 26 March 2004.

"Citibank Launches New Personal Forex Product in China." *Asia Pulse Businesswire,* 20 May 2004.

"Citigroup Plans Life Insurance JV in China." *Asia Intelligence Wire,* 20 May 2004.

Cooper, Louise. "Deutsche Bank Faces Critics at Home." *BBC News,* 17 March 2005. Available from http://www.bbc.co.uk.

"The Fortune Global 500." *Fortune,* 2005. Available from http://www.pathfinder.com.

"Industry Outlook 2001: Banking and Securities." *Business Week,* 8 January 2001. Available from http://www.businessweek.com.

"Insurance Market Outlook." Deloitte Touche Tohmatsu, February 2005. Available from http://www.deloitte.com.

"Japan's Mizuho Corporate Bank to Revamp Wholesale Operations" *Asia Pulse Businesswire,* 20 May 2004.

"Major Market Profiles." Euromonitor, October 2004. Available from http://www.euromonitor.com.

"Nippon Life, 2 Other Insurers to Boost FY03 Internal Reserves." *Asia Pulse Businesswire,* 14 May 2004.

Nishio, Natsuo. "Japan Sector Outlook: Most Banks to Report Profit Recovery." *Dow Jones Newswires,* 17 May 2004.

"Profile: Japan's Banking Industry." *AsiaPulse News,* 16 May 2001.

"Profile: Japan's Banking Industry." *Asia Pulse Businesswire,* 13 May 2004.

"Pushing Limits in Europe." *Investment Dealers' Digest,* 7 January 2002.

Simms, James. "Japan FSA Issues Operations Improvement Order to Deutsche Bank." *Dow Jones Business News,* 20 May 2004.

"The State of the Industry 2005." *CrossCurrents*, Winter 2005. Available from http://www.ey.com.

Teichova, Alice, Ginette Kurgan-van Hentenryk, and Dieter Ziegler. *Banking, Trade, and Industry: Europe, America, and Asia from the Thirteenth to the Twentieth Centuries.* Cambridge, UK: Cambridge University Press, 1997.

"U.S. Economic Slowdown Drives Merger Rumors." *Banker,* July 2001.

SIC 6221

NAICS 523130

COMMODITY AND FUTURES TRADING

Commodity trading firms buy and sell commodity contracts on either a spot or future basis for themselves or on behalf of others. They are members, or are associated with members, of recognized commodity exchanges. This discussion also includes a review of commodity exchanges.

INDUSTRY SNAPSHOT

In 1972, 18 million futures and options contracts were traded worldwide. At the start of 2005, this volume had reached 1.5 billion contracts, according to figures compiled by the Futures Industry Association (FIA), the industry's trade association. Fueling the phenomenal growth of the futures industry in the early 2000s was the surge in interest rate and equity index trading activity. Financial trading as a whole grew 75.3 percent in 2001, with equity index trading up 117.9 percent and interest rate trading up 44 percent. Non-financial trading, however, dropped 4.5 percent, due to lagging agricultural commodity and non-precious metal trading.

Although still used interchangeably, the once commonly used term "commodity trading" was replaced by "futures trading" when contracts were developed on foreign currencies and government securities, not just on tangible or storable products. The terminology "futures trading" became more widely used after 1981 when the Chicago Mercantile Exchange (CME) introduced trading in Eurodollar futures, the first such market that called for settlement in cash rather than by delivery of the underlying physical commodity. CME is the largest futures exchange in the United States.

Futures and options on futures are classified by category. Categories include interest rate, equity indices, agricultural commodities, energy products, foreign currency/index, precious metals, non-precious metals, and other. Commodities and futures are known as "derivative instruments," because they are dependent upon underlying cash markets for their identities. They serve two economic functions: transferring risk—or hedging—and price discovery. The U.S. Commodity Futures Trading Commission (CFTC) defines hedging as "taking a position in the futures market opposite to a position held in the cash market to minimize the risk of financial loss from an adverse price change." Price discovery is simply the market's free negotiation of prices based on supply and demand.

In 2005 the Korean Stock Exchange (KSE) was the largest global futures and options exchange, in terms of volume. Eurex was in second place, followed by CME, Chicago Board of Trade (CBOT), and London International Financial Futures Exchange (LIFFE). Many of the largest exchanges began considering demutualization (converting to for-profit status) in the early 2000s, as a means of increasing efficiency and cutting costs.

ORGANIZATION AND STRUCTURE

Futures exchanges, industry members, and federal regulators share responsibility and work together to protect the interests of all futures market participants.

U.S. REGULATORS

The Commodity Futures Trading Commission (CFTC), which is based in Washington, D.C. and has offices in Chicago, Kansas City, Los Angeles, Minneapolis, and New York City, is the U.S. federal agency responsible for the regulation of the U.S. futures markets. Created in 1974 by an act of Congress, the CFTC has a threefold mission: to ensure fair practice and honest dealing in futures trading; to permit accurate price discovery; and to provide for efficient hedging through competitive, manipulation-free markets. The president of the United States, with the advice and consent of the U.S. Senate, appoints commissioners to fill vacancies on the five-person commission; each commissioner serves a staggered, five-year term.

The CFTC had a budget of US$89.9 million in 2004 and approximately 500 employees to oversee 13 commodity exchanges in the United States.

In 1998 the CFTC approved rules designed to facilitate the merger of the Coffee, Sugar & Cocoa Exchange with the U.S. Cotton Exchange into a new entity controlled by a holding company, to be called the Board of Trade of the City of New York. The merger was scheduled to be complete by mid-2004.

The National Futures Association (NFA) is the industry-wide, self-regulatory organization for the futures industry. Authorized by an act of Congress in 1982, NFA became the answer to a proposed futures transaction tax. Rather than institute the tax, Congress decided that an industry-funded, self-regulatory organization would serve as an effective, efficient, and equitable way to share the regulatory costs between the futures industry and public participants.

NFA has four main areas of responsibility: registration, compliance, arbitration, and education. NFA has accepted the responsibility for screening and registering firms and individuals who conduct business in the futures industry, including futures commission merchants (FCMs), commodity pool operators (CPOs), commodity trading advisors (CTAs), introducing brokers (IBs) (individuals previously known as agents of FCMs), associated persons (APs) (individuals associated with a firm, such as firm principals and sales personnel), and floor brokers and floor traders. NFA developed an arbitration program for the resolution of customer disputes between NFA members. NFA also monitors the financial and sales practices of its members. In 1998 NFA employed 257 full-time and 10 part-time employees and had a total budget of US$29.78 million. NFA is completely self-financed; its funds are derived from membership dues and fees as well as from assessments paid by NFA members and futures market users.

Another key organization in the futures industry, the FIA, based in Washington, D.C., is the industry's trade association, with representatives from all segments of the marketplace, including the largest brokerage firms, and domestic and international futures exchanges, banks, law and accounting firms, insurance companies, pension and mutual funds, and other market users.

INTERNATIONAL REGULATORS

Other countries use regulatory bodies to monitor the industry as well. In Australia the principal regulatory agency is the Australian Securities Commission, based in Sydney. Brazil's leading regulatory body is Comissao de Valores Mobiliarios (Brazilian Security Exchange Commission), while Canada maintains the Office of the Superintendent of Financial Institutions. In Europe, which is heavily involved in commodity trading, the primary regulatory agencies are as follows: for France, the Commission des Operations de Bourse and the Conseil du Marché à Terme; for Germany, the Bundesaufsichtsamt für das Kreditwesen; for Spain, the Comision Nacional del Mercado de Valores; and in the United Kingdom, the Department of Trade and Industry (DTI) and the Securities and Investments Board. Leading Pacific Rim regulatory agencies include the Securities and Futures Commission of Hong Kong; the Ministry of Finance and the Ministry of International Trade and Industry (MITI) in Japan; the Commodities Trading Commission in Malaysia; and the Monetary Authority of Singapore.

In July 1997, the CFTC established the Office of International Affairs to help the commission respond quickly to market crises that have global implications. On 31 October 1997, regulators from 16 countries issued an agreement on certain basic principles of regulation in futures and options markets, covering contract design, market surveillance, and information sharing. CFTC chair Brooksey Born testified on 31 March 1998 before the U.S. Senate Appropriations Committee Subcommittee on Agriculture, Rural Development and Related Agencies, that those principles would help protect U.S. markets from events occurring in foreign markets and would assist in leveling the international regulatory playing field for markets and commodities professions.

THE NATURE OF COMMODITY TRADING

Prices are not set by futures exchanges. Rather, futures exchanges are free markets where the forces that influence prices (including, but not limited to, supply and demand figures, currency exchange rates, inflation rates, and weather) are brought together in an open auction atmosphere. As the marketplace assimilates the new information that becomes available throughout the trading day, the fair market value or price as agreed upon by buyers and sellers is discovered.

The open-outcry auction market, which was first used in the nineteenth century, continued to be used in the early 2000s because it was considered by many to be the most-efficient method of assimilating new market information as quickly as possible and translating that information into a fair market price. Offers are made to buy or sell by open, competitive outcry so that any exchange member in the pit or ring can accept that offer. Agreed-upon prices are recorded and disseminated virtually instantaneously via state-of-the-art telecommunications equipment to market participants and interested observers worldwide. Although electronic platforms had supplanted open-outcry at most leading European exchanges by the early 2000s, open-outcry remained the main trading method at U.S. exchanges.

Floor brokers and floor traders in the pit or ring communicate in two ways: open outcry and standardized hand signals to confirm their verbal communications. The position of a trader's or broker's hand informs another trader or broker whether he is buying or selling: when the palm of a trader's or broker's hand faces himself, he is indicating that he "wants," or intends to buy; when the palm of a trader's or broker's hand is positioned outward, he is indicating that he "does not want," or intends to sell. When the trader or broker holds his arm and the fingers of his hand in a horizontal position, he is indicating the price at which he wants to buy or sell. These hand signals also are used to communicate the quantity or number of contracts that the trader or broker wants to buy or sell. Once a trade has been made, the price is posted immediately and is said to constitute "the market" until such time, which may be as soon as the next second, as another trade is made at the same or different price.

BACKGROUND AND DEVELOPMENT

The history of modern futures trading dates back to the early nineteenth century. As the City of Chicago's importance as a grain market grew, so did problems with supply and demand, transportation, and storage. The natural outgrowth was a centralized marketplace where buyers and sellers could meet to "exchange commodities," the forerunner to the commodities exchange.

CBOT was formed in 1848 by 82 merchants. This centralized marketplace used "cash forward contracts" that allowed buyers and sellers of agricultural commodities to specify delivery of a particular commodity at a predetermined price and date. However, one problem that became evident with these "cash forward contracts" was the lack of standardization, particularly as it related to quantity and delivery time. In 1865 the CBOT formalized grain trading by developing "standardized agreements," which became known as "futures contracts." The only non-standardized aspect, or variable, was the price, which was discovered through an auction-like or open-outcry system on the trading floor of this organized commodities exchange.

This standardization attracted two groups of market participants: producers/users of the commodity and speculators. Those who actually produced or used the commodity sought to hedge or protect themselves and their crops from uncertain price movements. Speculators, on the other hand, bought or sold contracts based on their perception of where the price might be in the future. If they looked for prices to rise, they would buy; if they were correct and the market rallied, they would sell and take their profit. Likewise, if they predicted lower prices in the future, they would sell; if they were correct and the market moved lower, they would buy back at this lower price and take their profit. In *Speculating in Futures,* the CBOT defined hedgers as individuals who use futures markets to protect their cash position against the risk of unfavorable or adverse price movement. The role of the speculator is to provide risk capital, while their goal is to profit by accurately forecasting future price movement.

Futures trading grew in popularity during the late nineteenth century and early twentieth century. But it was not until the early 1970s, following the introduction of the first financial futures and interest rates futures contracts that were designed to meet the demands of a changing world economy, that the practice registered truly huge gains. The world economy at the time was characterized by frequent changes in interest rates, sharp increases in government debt, and heightened financial interdependence among the nations of the world.

In the foreword to the book *Leo Melamed on the Markets,* Milton Friedman wrote that as long as the Bretton Woods system of fixed exchange rates was in effect, there was little need for a public futures market because exchange rates traded in narrow ranges, which limited market interest. Under the Bretton Woods Agreement, which took effect in 1946, countries within the International Monetary Fund (IMF) agreed that their currencies would have fixed parities in terms of both gold and dollars. However, that all changed on 15 August 1971, when the Bretton Woods system ended.

John J. Merrick Jr. noted in *Financial Futures Markets: Structure, Pricing & Practice* that the CME is credited with pioneering the first financial futures when the exchange's International Monetary Market (IMM) division introduced trading on 16 May 1972 in several foreign currency futures contracts, including the British pound sterling, the Canadian dollar, the West German mark, the Italian lira, the Japanese yen, the Mexican peso, and the Swiss franc. Since this introductory date, futures trading in the Italian lira was delisted and futures trading was added in both the French franc and the Dutch guilder.

The CBOT entered the financial futures and interest rate futures arena in October 1975 by introducing futures trading in Government National Mortgage Association certificates. In addition to the traditional hedgers and speculators who were expected to trade in this market, growth of this category has been attributed, in part, to the new breed of market participants such as banks, bond dealers, insurance companies, and pension funds who had been absent prior to this period.

The 1980s brought the introduction of stock index futures; leading the way was the Kansas City Board of Trade, which introduced trading in 1982 in the Value Line Stock Index. Soon after, the New York Futures Exchange and the CME introduced futures trading in the New York Stock Exchange Composite Index and the Standard & Poor's 500 stock index, respectively. Also in 1982, the CFTC designated the first contract markets for options on futures contracts. Unlike the underlying futures contract, an option gives the buyer the right, but not the obligation, to buy or sell a specified quantity of a commodity at a specific price within a certain time period, regardless of the commodity's market price.

The 1980s also saw substantial growth in financial futures contracts on non-U.S. futures exchanges, led by the London International Financial Futures Exchange in the United Kingdom, the Marché à Terme International de France in Paris, the Singapore International Monetary Exchange in Singapore, and the Tokyo Stock Exchange in Japan.

Another factor that contributed to the growth of this industry and others has been the increasing popularity of "managed account programs" or "managed account trading," in which an investor gives full trading authority to a professional money manager who has the time and expertise required to monitor several futures markets simultaneously. According to statistics provided by the CFTC in the *Vision and Strategies for the Future* strategic plan, the amount of money under management in U.S.-registered commodity pools increased to almost US$26 billion by the end of 1996, compared with approximately US$675 million in 1980.

On 30 April 1987, CBOT became the first domestic exchange to offer "night trading," which provides businesses around the world a vehicle for price discovery and hedging when the Chicago markets traditionally are not open. Creation of the night trading sessions was designed to help the CBOT regain its competitive edge as the largest and leading futures exchange worldwide. In September 1987 the CME entered into a long-range agreement with Reuters Holdings PLC to create an after-hours, global electronic automated transaction system for trading of futures and options on futures, which would become known as GLOBEX. After 18 months of intense negotiations, the CBOT decided to join the CME in GLOBEX because it had become clear that it would be cost prohibitive for the industry to maintain two after-hours systems. GLOBEX began operation on 25 June 1992.

On 24 June 1993, the New York Mercantile Exchange unveiled NYMEX ACCESS, its electronic trading system. Developed in cooperation with AT&T, NYMEX ACCESS was designed to permit "screen-based" trading in the exchange's energy contracts and platinum during nontraditional, non-pit trading hours.

On 15 April 1994, the CBOT announced that it had decided to withdraw from the GLOBEX joint venture. Instead, the exchange proceeded with PROJECT A, an alternative vehicle for listing CBOT financial futures and options on futures during off hours, or what is defined as "non-pit trading hours." PROJECT A would enable both CBOT members as well as public customers access to these CBOT financial contracts.

In 1997 the CFTC implemented new "fast-track" processing procedures to help speed approval of new contracts. In June the CFTC approved streamlined procedures for allocation of customer orders that are bunched for execution by Commodity Trading Advisors (CTAs). This provided relief to Futures Commission Merchants (FCMs) regarding the capital treatment of short options positions. The CFTC also streamlined many of its reporting and disclosure requirements, moved to allow FCMs to deliver confirmations and account statements solely by electronic media, and authorized CTAs and commodity pool operations (CPOs) to file their disclosure documents with the commission electronically.

Also that year, the CFTC approved 51 applications for new futures and options contracts, including contracts based on inflation-indexed debt instruments issued by the U.S. Treasury. On 20 March 1998, Chicago's two futures exchanges agreed to combine their clearing operations with the aim of providing industry standards, reducing costs and increasing efficiencies, as well as helping to ensure the ability of the exchanges to compete in a rapidly changing marketplace.

On 9 April 1998, the CFTC announced a pilot program designed to allow trading of agricultural trade options, which are off-exchange options offered to a commercial producer or commodity user. Trade options on many agricultural commodities had not been allowed for more than six decades, but the CFTC reviewed its ban because of the growing necessity in the agricultural community for risk management tools. The pilot program requires entities that solicit and offer the options to register with the CFTC as agricultural trade option merchants (ATOMs). The pilot program continued operating in the early 2000s.

SCANDALS AND MARKET IMPROPRIETIES

While the commodity trading industry was thriving entering the mid-1990s, the industry had not enjoyed a wholly unblemished record in last part of the twentieth century.

On 26 May 1976, the New York Mercantile Exchange declared a default in its May Maine potato contract. Potato futures are no longer listed for trading at the NYMEX. On 23 November 1977, the CFTC declared a market emergency in the December coffee "C" contract on the New York Coffee, Sugar & Cocoa Exchange. The contract remained active, though. And on 16 March 1979, the CFTC prohibited further trading in the March wheat contract at the CBOT. The futures contract was still traded.

The year 1979 proved to be a particularly tumultuous year. According to Jerome F. Smith and Barbara Kelly Smith in *What's Behind The New Boom in Silver and How to Maximize Your Profits,* any individual who kept up on current events in 1979 could hardly have missed the "Hunt silver bubble." The Hunts allegedly "pyramided" their silver holdings—purchasing additional quantities during a bull (rising) market—using the paper profits from the price gain as collateral for future purchases. This practice contributed to a dramatic rise in the price of silver. In 1973 the price was US$3 per ounce, while it reached US$6 per ounce in early 1979; by year-end 1979, the price of silver had leaped to a high of US$35 per ounce. A month later, the price topped the US$50 level. Then the market took a nosedive, losing in excess of 30 percent of its value in one week. The fall continued through the end of March, when the price stabilized at US$10.80 per ounce; however, by that point, the price of the precious metal had dropped 78.5 percent from its peak. The Hunts were unable to meet a US$100 million margin call.

Another factor in the rapid decline of silver prices, the Smiths noted, was an unprecedented ruling by CBOT and the Commodity Exchange (COMEX). Both exchanges refused to accept any new buy orders in the silver futures markets; only those buy orders already in the brokers' hands could be executed if and when the market hit those prices, and the only way for that to happen would be for prices to fall to lower levels. The marketplaces continued to accept new sell orders.

An investigation into the rapid rise and decline of silver prices by the CFTC, the Federal Reserve Board, and the Securities and Exchange Commission (SEC) did not reprimand the exchanges for their intervention. The CFTC concluded, however, that Nelson Bunker Hunt, William Herbert Hunt, and other individuals and firms had attempted to manipulate silver prices in 1979 and 1980.

In 1988 and 1989, the U.S. Attorney's Office and the Federal Bureau of Investigation launched a full-scale investigation into trading practices on Chicago's two largest futures exchanges, CBOT and CME. The investigation was allegedly triggered by customer complaints of alleged abuses in trading practices, wrote John J. Merrick, Jr. in *Financial Futures Markets: Structure, Pricing & Practice*. The exchanges were charged with several transgressions, including the following:

- prearranged trading, defined by the CFTC as trading between brokers in accordance with an expressed or implied agreement or understanding;
- accommodation trading, defined by the CFTC as noncompetitive trading entered into by a trader, usually to assist another with illegal trades;
- frontrunning, which the CFTC defined as taking a futures or option position based upon non-public infor-

mation regarding an impending transaction by another person in the same or related future or option;

- bucketing, defined by the CFTC as directly or indirectly taking the opposite side of a customer's order into the broker's own account or into an account in which the broker has an interest, without open and competitive execution of the order on an exchange;
- wash trading, the practice of entering into, or purporting to enter into, transactions to give the appearance that purchases and sales have been made, without resulting in a change in the trader's market position;
- curb trading—also known as kerb trading—the practice of trading by telephone or other means that takes place after the official market has closed;
- cuffing, which Merrick defined as "delaying the filling of customer orders to benefit another member."

As the investigation unfolded, specific traders were indicted, trials took place, and some guilty verdicts were returned. The exchanges pledged to do a better job of self-regulation in the future.

In 1995, one of Great Britain's most revered merchant banks, the 233-year-old Barings PLC, collapsed in dramatic fashion over the weekend of February 24 through 26. The bank's collapse was allegedly caused by a 28-year-old employee who made unauthorized purchases of futures on the Nikkei stock average listed on the Singapore International Monetary Exchange (SIMEX), and Nikkei 225 futures listed on the Osaka Securities Exchange (OSE), betting that the Japanese stock market would rise. Rather than taking a loss when the market fell, he increased his positions in the hopes that future profits would more than offset the early losses. The result was a loss of US$1 billion, a figure greater than the bank's assets. The Bank of England tried to organize a bailout, but other U.K. banks could not be convinced to recapitalize because no one knew the full extent of the losses. The Dutch financial firm ING Group won approval on 6 March 1995 from London's High Court to take over Barings for a symbolic one pound, equivalent to about US$1.65. The firm agreed to continue to use the Barings name.

In the summer of 1996, the venerable Sumitomo Corporation of Japan announced it had lost at least US$1.8 billion due to the alleged unauthorized trading in copper and copper derivatives on the London Metal Exchange (LME) by Yasuo Hamanaka, the Tokyo-based company's former chief trader. Following Sumitomo's announcement, the copper market immediately went into a 25-percent free-fall; when the dust settled, copper prices had ultimately plunged from US$2,800 per metric ton to US$1,860 per metric ton before settling out at US$2,045 a ton. Ultimately, closing out Sumitomo's positions cost another US$800,000, and the company's losses from Hamanaka's trades totaled a staggering US$2.6 billion. Sumitomo also agreed to pay a US$150 million fine.

Hamanaka was known as "Mr. Five Percent" by other copper traders because Sumitomo traded roughly 500,000 metric tons of copper annually, representing 5 percent of total world demand of about 10 million metric tons. Mr. Hamanaka was alleged to have manipulated the price of copper in 1995 and 1996 by buying up dominant amounts of copper futures on the London Metals Exchange, as well as acquiring a dominant position in the physical supply of copper stock. This caused an artificial spike in copper prices, including prices on the U.S. cash and futures markets. With prices high, the Sumitomo trader then allegedly liquidated the company's large portfolio of futures contracts and LME warrants.

On 19 February 1997, says Tsukasa Furukawa, in a dispatch from Tokyo for American Metals Markets Online, the international news service of the American metals market, Hamanaka pleaded guilty to fraud and forgery charges. The former copper trader was ultimately sentenced by a Tokyo court to eight years in prison for defrauding Sumitomo's subsidiary in Hong Kong of US$770 million by ordering remittances on fake transactions and forging the signatures of his superiors on funds transfer authorizations.

Tokyo General, a firm primarily engaged in trading commodity futures, was accused of mismanaging customer funds. *Futures Industry Magazine* reported that the firm failed to meet a margin payment due to the Tokyo Commodity Exchange on 7 January 2004 and forced the exchange to shut down the firm's trading activities and liquidate its positions. The final government investigation report has not been turned in but it appears that customer funds were mingled with the firm's capital then spent on investments by the company's owner and former chairman, Katsumi Iida. Some industry analysts believed the company's collapse resulted in a move toward stricter segregation of customer funds, more frequent inspections, and tougher capital gains requirements. Government officials, exchange representatives, and industry groups united to update and amend the Commodity Exchange Act and hoped to have legislation take effect in April 2005.

Demutualization—the process of converting to for-profit status, which quite often includes completing an initial public offering—was the largest item on the agenda of commodity and futures exchange operations in the late 1990s. In April 1999, LIFFE made the decision to demutualize after increased competition from fully electronic competitors began to whittle away its market share. The conversion to for-profit status proved highly beneficial, as LIFFE was able to streamline operations and cut costs over the next two years. Euronext, itself a merger of stock and futures exchanges in France, Belgium, and Holland, acquired LIFFE in 2001. Some analysts predicted that LIFFE/Euronext would surpass CME as the second-largest futures exchange in the world in 2002.

In Asia, the Hong Kong Futures Exchange completed its demutualization, as well as a merger with the Hong Kong Stock Exchange, in the late 1990s. The futures exchange in Singapore also merged with the stock exchange there, creating SGX in 1999; the newly merged entity completed its initial public offering the following year.

In the United States, both CBOT and CME began preparing themselves for initial public offerings by reducing expenses and laying off employees. After reporting losses for two consecutive years, CBOT and CME both returned to profitability in 2001. While this was due in large part to the unstable U.S. financial market, which prompted increased investment in futures and options, the cost cutting measures undertaken by both exchanges were also instrumental in the turnaround. In November 2000, CME took two key steps toward demutualization by offering shares to its members and then shifting to a holding company structure. Consolidation appeared likely throughout the remainder of the decade, according to some analysts, as exchanges like CME and CBOT would be looking for ways to continue cutting costs and boosting profitability once their public offerings were conducted.

Increased use of technology was another issue facing commodity and security exchange operations in the late 1990s. Both CBOT and the CME began pushing for new computerized trading systems, hoping to move away from the open-outcry style of trading, with the goal of increasing order entry speed and reducing trading costs through automation, wrote Greg Burns in the *Chicago Tribune*. In January 1998, CBOT completely shut down its evening trading session and replaced it with the PROJECT A computerized trading system, hoping to move closer to the goal of an entirely paperless trading floor. In August 2000, CBOT replaced PROJECT A with the a/c/e (Alliance/CBOT/Eurex) electronic trading system. Despite the new technology, the open-outcry system remained the primary trading method for CBOT traders. CME used the Globex2 electronic trading system, which accounted for roughly 20 percent of CME's total trading volume in 2001; as with CBOT, traditional open-outcry procedures continued to account for most CME transactions. While systems like GLOBEX and PROJECT A were once incompatible, forcing traders to use separate terminals for each exchange, cross-platform compatibility had largely been achieved by the early 2000s. In May 2004, CME reported that volume on GLOBEX averaged a monthly record of 1.6 million contracts per day in April 2004, up 62 percent compared to the same period in 2003.

The impetus for increased use of technology was competition from non-U.S. exchanges, particularly the success of Germany's Deutsche Terminboerse, known as DTB, an all-electronic exchange. In 1997, DTB's volume increased 47.8 percent, although a percentage of that growth was attributed to DTB's merger with the Swiss Stock Exchange to form Eurex. Other moves toward electronic trading also took place in the late 1990s. The Sydney Futures Exchange closed its open-outcry trading floor, France's Marché à Terme International de France launched electronic trading, and LIFFE began allowing all-day electronic trading alongside its traditional open-outcry trading system. By 2000 Eurex had moved into the number one spot among futures exchanges, with 289 million contracts trading hands. According to Jim Kharouf in *Futures Industry*, "the exchange's growth has highlighted one of the biggest advantages of electronic trading—its members do not need to be physically present in a single location. Eurex has created network hubs in market centers in other parts of the world to link its members to the exchange through dedicated lines." *Futures Industry* said, in the first quarter of 2004, Eurex's volume increased 9.3 percent to 289.6 million after setting a new monthly volume record in March. Eurex's EuroBund topped the list of futures contracts with volume over 62.1 million, although trading in the product declined 5.7 percent over the first quarter of 2003.

Debates over the deregulation of the U.S. futures market had been a key industry issue throughout the 1990s, and it remained a topic of debate into the 2000s. In 1998 the CFTC began considering whether to allow block trades, similar to block trades on the stock market, on the futures exchanges. Allowing block trades would simplify business and cut costs for big brokerage firms and institutional money managers, but floor brokers did not like the proposal because they would miss the chance to bid on a piece of those large transactions occurring on the exchange floors. The CFTC raised the issue in order to address the concerns of big investors and to make futures more vibrant when compared to the fast-growing over-the-counter derivatives market. In early 2000 the CFTC granted permission to the Cantor Exchange, a joint venture between the New York Board of Trade and eSpeed, for block trading of U.S. Treasury Futures.

Another regulatory issue centered on single stock futures, which were not traded in the United States as of early 2002. The global market for single stock futures, which are contracts for shares in a single company, grew from 2.2 million contracts in 2000 to 13.4 million the following year. Ten different exchanges offered single stock futures contracts during that time period, and all were located outside the United States. Proponents of deregulation believed U.S. exchanges should be granted access to this booming market.

Futures Industry reported that the Mexican Derivatives Exchange gained 15.6 percent, up US$6.1 million to a total of US$45.2 million in the first quarter. The 28-Day Interbank Equilibrium Interest Rate was up 25.4 percent to US$44.3 million contracts.

CURRENT CONDITIONS

In 2004, the volume of global futures and options trading contracts was approximately 8.9 billion, according to *Futures Industry*. Of this total, 3.5 billion transactions were for futures, up 16.3 percent over 2003 levels, while the remaining 5.4 billion transactions for options trading had shown an increase of 4.6 percent over 2003 levels. Trading in foreign currencies showed the greatest increase in volume that year; 105.4 million transactions took place representing an increase of an impressive 35.4 percent over the previous period.

By the start of 2005, U.S. exchanges were providing the industry's best results. In the first two months of the year, volumes in the U.S. increased by almost 19 percent, reaching 514.1 million contracts, with the most growth being seen in the equity, foreign currency and energy markets. The Chicago Mercantile Exchange was the fastest-growing exchange in terms of volume at the start of 2005, reaching 147.5 million contracts in the January and February. However, exchanges outside of the U.S. were not doing as well. In fact, volumes were down in the first two months of 2005 over the same period in 2004, with the overall decline of 2 percent being the result of a 4.4 percent decline in options trading. However, even this statistic is somewhat misleading as most of it could be attributed to continuing poor trading numbers at the Korea Exchange. The Eurex and Australian exchanges shown gains during the period.

While trading in agricultural commodities was on the rise in the U.S. in 2005, non-U.S. totals were down 19.7 percent. China's declines in soybean and rubber trading were the primary reasons for the overall decline globally. However, several commodities were doing well; the Tokyo Grain Exchange had become the leading coffee exchange, and at the New York Board of Trade, sugar trading volumes increase by 47 percent. Metals trading was down in almost all exchanges, with non-precious metalsshowing a 12.6 percent decline in contracts and precious metals trading at 28.4 percent lower volumes.

In May 2004, CME announced that combined open interest in CME and CBOT contracts—both managed by CME Clearing House—had surpassed the 50 million contract mark for the first time. CME also reported it moved approximately US$1.5 billion per day in settlement payments in the first quarter of 2004 and managed $38.1 billion in collateral deposits in March 2004. At that time, that was the busiest trading month in the exchange's history. April 2004 was its second consecutive month of record activity as average daily volume totaled 3.3 million contracts per day, up 44.4 percent compared to the previous year.

WORKFORCE

Futures industry participants include futures brokerage firms, which are known as futures commission merchants (FCMs). FCMs are individuals, associations, partnerships, corporations, and trusts that solicit or accept orders for the purchase or sale of any commodity for future delivery, subject to the rules of an exchange; an FCM also accepts payment from or extends credit to those whose orders are accepted. At year-end 1997, 233 FCMs were registered with the NFA, down nearly 41 percent from the 393 FCMs registered in 1980, according to figures NFA provided the CFTC, and reported in *Vision and Strategies for the Future: Facing the Challenges of 1997 through 2002*.

Other 1997 year-end registrations furnished by NFA included 1,583 introducing brokers (IBs); 2,606 commodity trading advisors (CTAs); 1,351 commodity pool operators (CPOs); 9,299 floor brokers (FBs); 1,331 floor traders (FTs); and 45,950 associated persons (Aps).

The CFTC defines IBs as any individual, other than an AP, who engages in soliciting or accepting orders for the purchase or sale of any commodity for future delivery on any exchange who does not accept money, securities, or property to margin, guarantee, or otherwise secure any trades or contracts. A CTA is an individual or firm that is compensated for issuing analyses or reports concerning futures and/or options on futures, including the advisability of trading in such futures or options on futures. A CPO is an individual or firm that solicits or accepts funds, securities, or property in order to trade futures and/or options on futures. An AP is an individual who associates with an FCM, IB, CTA, CPO, or leverage transaction merchant as a partner, officer, employee, consultant, or agent. A floor trader—often called a local—is a member of a futures exchange who trades for himself in the trading pit or ring. A floor broker is an individual who executes orders in the pit or ring for purchase or sale of a commodity for future delivery.

INDUSTRY LEADERS

In January 2005, The Korea Stock Exchange (KSE) was the leading derivatives trader in the world, handling more than 328 million transactions that month. In 2001, the KSE had moved from fourth place to first place among the world's largest futures and options exchanges. KSE's volume grew 300 percent from 213.49 million contracts traded to 854.7 million that year. In 2003, the KSE handled a total of 2.84 billion options contracts and a further 62 million futures contracts.

In the number two spot, at 1.07 billion contracts traded during 2004, was Eurex. Like other exchanges, Eurex had shown tremendous growth in trading; in the year 2000, less than 365 million contracts were traded. Eurox held the lead in the futures and options market for euro-dominated derivative instruments. Created in 1998, Eurex evolved from the merger of DTB (Deutsche Terminbörse) and SOFFEX (Swiss Options and Financial Futures Exchange). The company is operated jointly by Deutsche Börse AG and SWX Swiss Exchange. An electronic trading platform, traders were connected to the system from more than 700 locations around the world. In February 2004, Eurex US was started, an all-electronic futures and options exchange.

The Chicago Mercantile Exchange (CME) continued to be the largest U.S. futures exchange. Founded in 1898 as the Chicago Butter and Egg Board, the CME emerged in 1919, primarily trading agricultural products in an open outcry system. This system was still being used in 2005, but was enhanced through its linkage to an electronic trading platform. The first financial futures were created by the CME in 1972, and by 2004 it was the world's largest regulated foreign currency exchange trading 51 million contracts.

LIFFE (Holdings) plc—the London International Financial Futures and Options Exchange, was the world's fourth largest exchange in 2005. It was bought by Euronext in 2002, which had been formed by the merger of the Amsterdam, Brussels and Paris exchanges in 2000. Initially set up as a financial futures and options exchange, LIFFE's 1996 merger with the London Commodity Exchange added trading in such commodities as cocoa, coffee, white sugar, feed wheat, corn, milling wheat, and rapeseed. Potato futures are also traded. In 2005, Euronext was working to bring all of its trading venues under a single platform. The derivatives business of Euronext and LIFFE were combined to create Euronext.Liffe, trading under one electronic platform. In 2003, the Brussels and Paris markets were added.

The Chicago Board of Trade (legally CBOT Holdings Inc.) was founded in 1848, then trading agricultural commodities, such as corn, wheat and oats. Non-storable agricultural products were added followed soon after by gold and silver. In April 2005, CBOT converted from a non-profit corporation into a for-profit one. In 2005, the company traded both electronically and through open auctions in five categories: interest rate products, agricultural products, stock market indices, metals and energy products.

BROKERS

Refco Group Ltd. LLC. New York City based Refco Group is one of the world's leading providers of execution and clearing services for derivatives trade on exchanges, as well as one of the world's largest independent derivative brokers. The company brokers futures trading as well as cash market products in 14 countries. In 2005, Refco employed approximately 2,400 people, who managed the accounts of more than 200,000 global customers. During 2004, Refco provided the largest volume of customer transactions to the Chicago Mercantile Exchange, the largest derivatives exchange in the United States. That year, the company processed 461 million derivatives contracts. Revenues from principal transactions, commissions and brokerage fees, interest, and asset management and advisory fees was US$1.87 billion in 2004. In June 2005, Refco announced that it was set to acquire the global brokerage operations of Chicago based Cargill Investor Services.

ICAP plc. The world's largest interdealer broker, ICAP handles more than US$1 trillion of transaction volume each day, about half of which is done electronically. The company deals with over-the-counter derivatives, fixed-income securities, money market products, energy, credit and equity derivatives, and foreign exchange. Based in London, ICAP was formed in 1999 from the merger of Garban and Intercapital plc. In 2004, the company's revenue figures exceeded US$1.46 billion.

MAJOR COUNTRIES IN THE INDUSTRY

As of 2000, 85 international futures exchanges were in operation. Japan operated 11; the United States operated 8 (the country had 13 by 2005); the United Kingdom operated 4; Spain and Canada each operated 3; and Germany, Holland, and Italy all operated 2. China, which at one time boasted 40 exchanges, was left with only 3 in the early 2000s.

International Derivatives Week and the International Derivatives Conference, sponsored by the FIA and the Futures and Options Association was scheduled for London during June 2004. In anticipation, *Futures Industry* interviewed U.K. chairman of Calyon SA and chairman of the Futures and Options Association plus chair of the World Bank's International Task Force for Commodities Roy Leighton. Leighton pointed out distinctions between the U.S. and "European scene" "Firstly, OTC is much more developed and derivatives have been more embedded in other forms of financing in Europe than it seems to me they are in the U.S.," said Leighton. He claimed recent growth was due in large part to the demand for agricultural products to feed Asia and China. Leighton also discussed the Financial Services Action Plan (FSAP) "designed to create an integrated European market in financial services." After European elections of 2004, the subsequent two years would be spent implementing FSAP in member states. It focused on more than 40 directives addressing capital regulation, anti-money laundering, market abuse, and other issues.

During the first half of 2004, Asian derivatives exchanges accounted for 37 percent of the world's trading volume, according to *Futures Industry*. The region was expected to become home to the majority of trading, with equity trading the most dominant. More commodity products were being introduced to the trading exchanges as the desire for more efficient pricing grew. Although cross-border trading in Asia remained low in 2005, it was expected to grow. Holding back the region from more rapid development is a fear of speculation caused by the crisis of the late 1990s. At that time, the Chinese government had severely curtailed futures trading in the wake of a trading scandal that rocked the nation's financial industry. Despite this fact, China was considered by some industry experts to be a key growth market for futures trading due to its entrance into the World Trade Organization in the early 2000s. By 2004, China was continuing to experience rapid commodity trading growth. Also holding back development is the lack of a telecommunications and technology structure that can support trading on the same scale as in European and North American markets. The exception to all this was Korea, home of the world's largest futures and options exchange.

The first commodities exchange was created in Japan in the eighteenth century. However, a failure to modernize and make improvements in compliance and monitoring areas kept many global players out of the Japanese market. Japan's largest futures exchange, The Tokyo Commodity Exchange (Tocom), began to make changes in 2004, creating a clearing house and working with software engineers to provide electronic access to its products. The year 2004 also saw the demise of one of the country's largest futures brokers, Tokyo General, after the government claimed it had fraudulent business practices.

FURTHER READING

Acworth, Will. "A New Day for Kofex" *Futures Industry,* May/June 2004. Available from http://www.futuresindustry.org.

Acworth, Will and Mary Ann Burns. "The European Scene" *Futures Industry,* May/June 2004. Available from http://www.futuresindustry.org.

Burgert, Philip and Tsukasa Furukawa. "Sumitomo Copper Crisis Deals Aftershocks; Company Says It's Standing Behind Obligations in the $1.8 Billion Scandal." *American Metals Market Online,* 17 June 1996. Available from http://www.amm.com.

———. "Off the Charts: Futures Volume Soars to Record Highs." *Futures Industry,* January/February 2002. Available from http://www.futuresindustry.org.

"CME Clearing House More Than Doubles Cleared Volume in Less Than One Year," 11 May 2004. Available from http://www.cme.com.

Crawford, William B. Jr. "Barings Fiasco A 'Colossal Failure of Internal Controls.'" *Chicago Tribune,* 28 February 1995.

———. "Exchange Tax Sought." *Chicago Tribune,* 7 February 1995.

———. "U.S. Brokers Get Good News Even as Barings' Loss Builds." *Chicago Tribune,* 7 March 1995.

DeGrandis, Megan. "First Quarter 2004 Volume Report" *Futures Industry,* May/June 2004. Available from http://www.futuresindustry.org.

"Eurodollars on GLOBEX Increase 10 Fold to Nearly 390,000 Contracts per Day; Eurodollar Options Up 53 Percent vs. April 2003, 3 May 2004. Available from http://www.cme.com.

"Exchange Also Confirms the Re-Election of Other Officers and Special Advisors," 28 April 2004. Available from http://www.cme.com.

Fulsher, Mitch. "Japan: The big bang, finally." *Futures Industry*, May/June 2005. Available from http://www.futuresindustry.org.

Furukawa, Tsukasa. "Feud Looms as Hamanaka Trial Starts; Lawyer Plans Critique of Sumitomo." *American Metals Market Online,* 19 February 1997. Available from http://www.amm.com.

Futures: The Magazine of Commodities & Options 1992 Reference Guide, 99-100.

"Global Futures and Options Volume Rose 8.9% in 2004." Futures Industry Association: Press release, 31 March 2005. Available from http://www.futuresindustry.org.

Gorham, Michael; Susan Thomas and Ajay Shah. "India: The Crouching Tiger." *Futures Industry*, May/June 2005. Available from http://www.futuresindustry.org.

Grede, Frederick. " Unlimited Opportunities in Asia's Emerging Derivatives Markets." *Outlook 05*, 2005. Available from http://www.futuresindustry.org.

Kharouf, Jim. "Trading Engines Evolve to Meet Trader Demands." *Futures Industry,* August/September 2001. Available from http://www.futuresindustry.org.

Kojima, Eiichi. "Clearing the Deck: The Tokyo General Default." *Futures Industry,* May/June 2004. Available from http://www.futuresindustry.org.

McGregor, Megan. "Trading Volume: U.S. Exchanges Lead the Pack in First Two Months 0f 2005." *Futures Industry*, May/June 2005. Available from http://www.futuresindustry.org.

Melamed, Leo. *Leo Melamed on the Markets.* New York: John Wiley & Sons Inc., 1993.

"Merc, CBOT and FIA Reach Common Clearing Agreement." Futures Industry Association, 20 March 1998. Available from http://www.fiafii.org.

Merrick, John J. Jr. *Financial Futures Markets: Structure, Pricing & Practice.* New York: Harper & Row, 1990.

Pendley, Kevin. "Going Corporate: The Outlook for U.S. Futures Exchanges." *Futures Industry,* January/February 2002. Available from http://www.futuresindustry.org.

Smith, Jerome F. and Barbara Kelly Smith. *What's Behind the New Boom in Silver and How to Maximize Your Profits.* San Jose, Costa Rica: Griffin Publishing Co., 1983, 9-13.

Speculating in Futures. Chicago Board of Trade, 1990.

U.S. Commodity Futures Trading Commission. "Vision and Strategies for the Future: Facing the Challenges of 1997 through 2002." CFTC Strategic Plan, Washington, DC, September 1997. Available from http://www.cftc.gov.

Waller, Tracy. *World Futures & Options Volume Nears Two Billion Mark.* Futures Industry Association. Washington, D.C., 22 January 1998. Available from http://www.fiafii.org.

"Washington: Commodity Futures Trading Commission." *Wall Street Letter,* 5 January 1998.

xue Quin, Wang; and Nick Ronalds. "China: The Rise and Fall of Chinese Futures, 1990-2005. *Futures Industry*, May/June 2005. Available from http://www.futuresindustry.org.

SIC 6099, 6153

NAICS 522320, 522220

CREDIT AND DEBIT CARD ISSUERS

Industry firms grant credit and debit accounts to businesses and individuals. Certain banks in this industry are also engaged in other aspects of commercial banking; for more information on these activities, see **Banking and Insurance**.

INDUSTRY SNAPSHOT

In the mid-2000s, Visa, MasterCard and American Express were the world's largest players in the financial card market, offering credit and debit cards to consumers around the world. Visa controlled 52 percent of the U.S. market, whereas MasterCard held about 28 percent, American Express held 14 percent, and Discover held 6 percent. Worldwide, purchases made with Visa and MasterCard credit cards ballooned to nearly US$2 trillion in the early part of the century.

The top three credit card issuers—Citigroup, MBNA, and Bank One (now part of JP Morgan Chase)—controlled about 43 percent of the U.S. general purpose card market by 2003. Of these issuers, Bank One had been dominating the market for co-branded and affinity cards, having made deals with Walt Disney, Yahoo! British Airways, Sony and Borders.

The use of debit cards by consumers continued to increase, with the leading five PIN-based network organizations reporting 592.2 million transactions in the U.S. in 2003, up almost 27 percent over 2002 levels.

Smart card technology continued to make inroads in most areas around the globe, with the one major hold out being the U.S. Most European countries have sought to conform to the international Europay/Visa/MasterCard (EVM) standard for chipped cards so that cards can be read internationally. Contactless cards that transmit radio signals are the latest technology being promoted in the smart card arena.

ORGANIZATION AND STRUCTURE

The credit card industry consists of credit card associations, such as Visa and MasterCard, which provide an international brand name that are owned by their member issuers, as well as credit card issuers, such as Citicorp and MBNA Corp. Some credit card companies, notably American Express, also issue their own cards. The industry includes four major kinds of issuers: banks, oil companies, retailers, and travel and entertainment companies. In terms of revenues, bankcards have led the industry since their introduction. Banks and other financial operations issue universal cards, which are valid at any participating business or institution. Retail and oil cards (sometimes referred to as charge cards), nevertheless, remained popular throughout the last half of the twentieth century. Retailers and oil companies traditionally provided cards that were only valid at affiliated stores or gas stations, but many of these cards were joint ventures with major credit card companies, namely Visa and MasterCard, and might be used anywhere. Like retail and oil cards, travel and entertainment cards were traditionally valid only at a limited number of places relating to travel and entertainment. Cards such as American Express, Diners Club, and Carte Blanche provide this kind of credit card.

LEGISLATION AND REGULATION

The credit card business became an industry in its own right in the 1960s by offering common services and sharing features. At this point, governments began to pass legislation to cover the credit card industry as issues of privacy and equal access to credit cards arose. A major legal event in the United States stemmed from the practice of credit card companies sending people unsolicited credit cards in an effort to increase their number of cardholders. The Federal Trade Commission placed a moratorium on these mailings in 1970 and President Nixon decided to prohibit the practice altogether. The problems resulted from the interception of credit cards by criminals who would run up large bills, which the intended recipients would receive. Although existing laws protected consumers from incurring these charges, consumers would have to go to court and attempt to prove their innocence, a process that entailed considerable time and money.

Some governments established a series of laws and regulations to protect consumers against possible card credit-related problems. The United States passed the Fair Credit Billing Act of 1972, which required credit card issuers to allow a 60-day period for consumers to make written complaints about their bills, a 15-day period for credit card issuers to acknowledge these complaints, and a 60-day period for credit card issuers to investigate, correct, and explain their bills after receiving complaints. Congress revised this act in 1975 and added that cardholders must receive their bills 14 days prior to the end of the billing period. Further legislation and rulings addressed other consumer complaints involving privacy. At issue were credit card companies' sharing of personal information with state and federal agencies, as well as the sale of cardholder mailing lists to other companies.

The largest and most persistent problem the industry faces, however, has been fraud. Early kinds of credit card fraud resulted from stolen or lost credit cards. Later, some criminals developed methods for actually producing fraudulent credit cards, while others obtained credit card numbers through mail fraud and used them to place telephone orders. Furthermore, some merchants perpetuated credit card fraud by charging consumers for merchandise that they did not purchase. In 1996, credit fraud bore a US$436 million price tag in the United States alone. Credit card companies, along with state and federal government, collaborated to prevent and contain the proliferation of credit card fraud. As a result, U.S. federal law imposes a ten-year prison sentence and US$10,000 fine for credit card fraud from US$1,000 to US$5,000. Japan, on the other hand, still had not passed comprehensive credit card legislation by mid-1998. In cases of credit card fraud in Japan, the cardholder is mainly responsible for covering the damages, according to *Asahi Evening News*. In late 2001, fraud prevention legislation known as the Identity Theft Prevention Act was drafted in the United States. The bill would mandate that U.S. credit card companies must eliminate a portion of each customer's account numbers on receipts.

Another legislative action related to the U.S. credit card industry took place in 2001. In the mid-1990s, the U.S. Department of Justice launched an investigation of some allegedly anti-competitive activities of MasterCard and Visa. The main issue—the practice of restricting banks that issued MasterCard or Visa from issuing rival cards such as American Express or Discover—eventually resulted in a formal lawsuit, filed by the Justice Department in 1998. More than three years later, in October of 2001, a U.S. district judge ruled that MasterCard and Visa could no longer prevent member banks from issuing other cards. Analysts speculated that such a ruling, which could produce major changes in the way banks and other credit card issuers conducted business with credit card associations, could allow firms like American Express and Discover to increase their market share. Both MasterCard and Visa planned to file an appeal by February of 2002.

SOURCES OF CREDIT CARD REVENUES

Unlike retail and gas credit cards, which earn the issuer money through both finance charges and increased sales, universal cards issued by banks and other financial operations strive to make a profit mainly by enticing cardholders to use their credit lines. Consequently, credit card issuers implemented a number of measures to increase their profits, including raising the fee they charged merchants (typically issuers receive 2 to 3 percent of a transaction). Issuers also marketed such products as insurance, sold their cardholder lists, sold advertising space on their payment envelopes, and modified their methods of calculating interest.

Because many state laws placed caps on interest rates under usury laws, credit card issuers could not increase their basic finance charges. Instead, they decided to change the way interest applied to the account. At first credit card issuers charged interest on a cardholder's balance minus any payment made, but later many banks adopted an average daily balance method, where they charged interest on a daily basis from the point a charge was made, unless the cardholder paid the balance in full by the due date.

Credit card issuers also started marketing other financial products along with their credit cards, including insurance and loans. In addition, they began offering cardholders cash advances on their credit cards through a participating bank or an automatic teller machine (ATM). For cash advances many credit card issuers automatically charge interest on a daily balance basis, whether paid in full by the due date or not. Since banks and other financial institutions provide only a limited number of services, they also market a host of wares from other companies such as tape recorders, watches, pens, cameras, radios, and collectibles, among other things. The credit card issuer then receives 15 percent commission on these sales. Credit card issuers use their remittance envelopes and statements to advertise these products.

Some credit card companies also charge annual fees to increase their revenues, especially from cardholders who do not use their revolving credit, although the industry has grown much more competitive with issuers offering credit cards with no annual fees to shore up their cardholder ranks. Such moves force other issuers to waive their annual fees to retain their cardholders. In the late 1990s, the typical annual fee stood at US$49. However, rates were falling as credit cards became more competitive and obtained revenues from other sources. By 2003, the average annual fee in the U.S. had dropped to US$35.67.

Finally, since most standard credit cards charge interest rates well above those of other forms of consumer credit (e.g., loans), banks can easily borrow money at a comparatively low interest rate to extend credit lines to their cardholders, who must repay their charges at the much higher interest rate if they use their revolving credit. The combination of these methods provides credit card issuers with a means of garnering significant revenues and profits relative to other financial products. In April 2005 in the U.S., the average annual percentage rate (APR) for platinum credit cards was 11.44 percent, with interest rates ranging from a low of 5.75 percent to a high of 19.8 percent.

BACKGROUND AND DEVELOPMENT

The credit card evolved from the social, political, and economic conditions of the United States after the Second World War, and the United States remained the major proponent of the industry through the late 1990s; credit card companies and their subsidiaries controlled the largest share of the world's market. However, consumer credit has existed for millennia, with early references dating back to about 1750 B.C. with the ancient Babylonian Code of Hammurabi, a set of laws established by the Babylonian ruler Hammurabi.

The modern credit card developed from the combination of a number of credit options already available for much of the twentieth century. In 1949, Alfred Bloomingdale, Frank McNamara, and Ralph Snyder, two U.S. businessmen and an attorney, conceived of the credit card—a universal credit line issued by a third party—over lunch in New York. Although stores and gas stations had issued credit lines exclusive to their services for years, this new conception offered consumers the ability to use their credit card wherever accepted, instead of only at a specific chain store or gas company. Bloomingdale, McNamara, and Snyder's company would serve as an intermediary between the credit grantors and the credit users. The three thought that their primary customers would be traveling salespeople charging their accommodations and meals while on the road. Hence, they named their card Diners Club. Because Diners Club did not charge a fee, many business travelers signed up immediately. Diners Club earned its money from charging merchants a 7 percent service fee.

In its first month of business, Diners Club handled US$2,000 worth of credit, yielding income of 7 percent, according to the monograph *The Credit Card Industry*. The company's business expanded quickly as McNamara and Snyder, the primary owners of the company, relied on a simple inexpensive marketing technique: printing leaflets and placing them in nearby offices. Instead of performing a credit check on its members, McNamara and Snyder would conduct an interview with them.

Even though Bloomingdale bankrolled the operation, McNamara and Snyder wanted to remain the company's primary owners; when the two requested additional funds from Bloomingdale he decided to launch his own operation on the West Coast where he lived. Bloomingdale's Dine and Sign took off quickly with US$150,000 in business in the first month. However, he ran out of capital and failed to secure sources of sufficient credit for himself. At this time, Diners Club's business had grown to about US$250,000 per month. Finally, the two companies agreed to merge and began operating nationwide, adopting the name Diners Club.

Because Diners Club required substantial credit and funds to operate, the three entrepreneurs had to develop an assortment of methods to stretch their funds as far as they could. For example, Bloomingdale invented a technique later known as "float," by which Diners Club would pay its New York bills with a Los Angeles account and its Los Angeles bills with its New York account, according to *The Credit Card Industry*. This method allowed the company access to its funds for a few additional days, since it would take several days for the checks to clear. Nevertheless, as check clearing procedures began to take less time, the value of this technique declined.

In addition, they coordinated the payments of their cardholders with their payment due dates for the businesses. Businesses allowed them 30 days to pay for all the charges that accumulated through the month and their cardholders would pay their charges at the end of the month. While the industry was in its infancy, almost all cardholders paid their bills on time, which prevented Diners Club from incurring additional finance problems.

But the emerging industry encountered a number of other difficulties. Due to the structure and arrangement of the industry during this period, Diners Club had to rely on the signatures of the receipts in order to determine who made the charges for billing purposes. The three owners soon discovered that the signatures were not only often difficult to decipher, but also the signature would vary from the cardholder's name, since people would lend the card to friends. At the time, the company imposed no credit limit and had a list of stolen or misused credit cards. The company hired private detectives, however, to investigate deadbeat cardholders and confiscate their cards.

McNamara finally concluded that the credit card industry held no potential beyond business travelers and restaurants and sold his share of the company to the other two. From 1952 to 1970, the company continued to turn a profit, securing credit at first from small banks and then larger ones. The company opened offices in most major U.S. cities by the late 1950s, and in 1951 it opened its first international office. In 1970, Continental Insurance Company acquired Diners Club.

Other credit card companies soon entered the business. In 1958, American Express and Carte Blanche joined the industry, introducing universal credit cards. These cards did not offer revolving credit, where cardholders had the option of making partial payment and rolling the rest of the debt over to the next month. Instead, they required complete payment at the end of each billing period. However, at the end of the 1950s and into the early 1960s, Bank of America and

Chase Manhattan jumped into the fray by offering revolving credit, and the demand for it grew rapidly. In the late 1960s, Diners Club started to descend from its position at the top of the credit card industry. With accelerated competition from American Express, BankAmericard, Carte Blanche, and MasterCharge, Diners Club's profits slipped from US$2.4 million in 1968 to US$900,000 in 1969, according to *The Credit Card Industry*. By 1980 Citibank had purchased Diners Club as well as Carte Blanche.

While expanding within the United States, credit card companies also began to grow internationally during the 1970s. The country's leading cards, BankAmericard and MasterCharge, competed in Europe and Asia, forming franchise agreements with businesses and banks in these regions. Initially, MasterCharge led the industry at home and abroad; however, BankAmericard soon caught up with and surpassed MasterCharge. By 1972 BankAmericard International had 6.2 million cardholders, affiliations with 15,000 banks, and agreements with 250,000 businesses. Nonetheless, its presence in Europe remained weak, except for its Barclay Card in the United Kingdom. MasterCharge excelled in Europe, where it held a majority to share until European negative sentiments towards the U.S. involvement in Vietnam abated.

MasterCharge signed an agreement with EuroCard, Europe's leading credit card, which had affiliates in the United Kingdom, Germany, France, and Sweden. EuroCard functioned like a debit card, automatically withdrawing charges from its cardholders' accounts and not offering revolving credit. By the mid-1970s, BankAmericard began to catch up and surpass MasterCharge, in part by changing its name to Visa, a word easily recognizable around the world that had an international feel. With the new name and identity, Visa successfully forged alliances with banks in leading credit card markets such as France, Spain, and Israel. Later, MasterCharge also adopted a more global sounding name, becoming MasterCard in 1980, and formed similar agreements with banks throughout the world.

Because of the popularity of credit cards, U.S. consumer debt rose as 52 million people in the United States carried at least two credit cards by 1978. Consumer debt continued to climb from the late 1960s to the late 1990s. In 1969, U.S. credit card debt stood at US$2.7 billion, and by 1994 U.S. credit card debt had risen to US$74 billion, adjusted for inflation.

Despite the growth of the industry, credit card companies had trouble achieving profits without economies of scale. In the 1980s credit card issuers began to take additional measures to boost profits. Banks and lenders realized their profits would rise as soon as consumers stopped paying off their entire balances. Therefore, credit cards issuers started to increase their cardholders' credit lines to encourage additional use—use that would make the monthly expenses so large that many would prefer to spread the costs over months or even years. In addition, they offered cards to people who would be considered risky in less economically prosperous times. This strategy bore considerable fruit for the industry, as credit cards became the most profitable form of bank debt by the mid-1980s. Rising interest rates in the 1980s and the retention of high rates in the 1990s allowed credit card issuers to continue earning large profits through the 1990s. Moreover, 90 percent of all bank revenues in the mid-1990s came from interest on revolving credit.

The credit card itself also evolved throughout the industry's history. It began as a charge-plate in the retail industry, a paper card in the gasoline industry, and a paper book in the universal credit card industry. Eventually, credit card issuers—banks, retailers, and gasoline companies—adopted the standard magnetically encoded plastic card. Furthermore, as credit card issuers sought more secure credit cards, cards with cardholder pictures were issued, and merchants began matching the signature on the card to the signature on the sales receipt.

By the mid-1990s, credit card purchases accounted for about 17 percent of all transactions, compared to 11 percent in the early 1980s. Credit cards moved beyond being only for emergency and occasional use, and became a frequent form of payment, just like cash or checks. Cardholders used their credit lines for day-to-day products, such as food, gas, and clothing in the late 1990s, instead of only for larger purchases, such as furniture and appliances. This trend resulted from a number of factors, including the proliferation of credit cards around the world, the greater acceptance of credit cards at businesses and institutions worldwide, added security measures by the industry, and the growth of shopping on the Internet. In 1997 the world's credit card purchases rose to over US$1.8 trillion.

To fuel continued growth, credit card companies used promotions such as low introductory interest rates, no annual fees, and low-rate balance transfers to win over new customers. Using the balance transfer option, cardholders could move their balance from a high interest rate card to a new, lower-rate one. In another promotion, credit card issuers instituted reward programs to encourage cardholder loyalty by offering discounts and free credit on a variety of products and services after reaching designated spending goals.

Because technology rendered credit bills far more accurate than before and because of busier lifestyles around the world, more people relied on credit cards to avoid miscalculations that can happen with cash and check transactions and to avoid making additional trips to the bank or an ATM for cash. In the European Union, credit card use increased by 18 percent per year in the late 1990s, with fastest expansion in Italy, the Netherlands, Switzerland, and Spain. The United Kingdom and France remained the European Union's overall leaders, accounting for about 30 percent of all credit card transactions, whereas Greece used credit cards the least of any EU country. Consumers in the European Union used credit cards about 23 times per year, in contrast to those in the United States, who used them about twice per week. Canadian consumers, on the other hand, tended to use credit cards the most, averaging four credit card transactions per week.

Visa remained the world's leading credit card association in the late 1990s, representing US$1.1 trillion in purchases worldwide in 1997, and controlling about 52 percent of the world market. Visa became the first credit card to report total purchases of more than US$1 trillion, in 1996. MasterCard held its position as the world's number two credit card with US$602 billion in purchases, representing 30 percent of the market, in 1997.

Credit card portfolio sales—the transfer of a credit card operation from one issuer to another—increased in the late 1990s. In 1997 portfolio sales rose to US$20.8 billion, up from US$7.1 billion in 1996. By mid-1998, several high-profile credit card portfolio sales were already underway, including Citicorp's acquisition of AT&T's credit card operations for US$14 billion. Altogether, 22 portfolio sales took place in 1997, up from 21 in 1996. The largest purchase was Fleet Financial Group's acquisition of Advanta Corp.'s credit card unit for US$10.5 billion.

Despite the growth of the industry worldwide, credit card issuers faced declining profits in the mid- to late 1990s. For example, profits slipped from 2.71 percent of total credit card revenues to 2.14 percent in 1996 in the United States. However, credit card operations remained more profitable than other banking services, which yielded a return of only 1.86 percent on assets. Nevertheless, credit card issuers started to look for ways to increase their profits and urged legislators to review their caps on interest rates and fees.

The rise of credit card use led to increased consumer debt around the world, especially in the United States. During the mid- to late 1990s, consumer debt escalated to record highs. Furthermore, the American Bankers Association reported that credit card delinquencies reached a new peak in 1996. As a result, bankruptcy became a widespread means for consumers to unload their growing debt in the United States, and the number of bankruptcies in the country soared. By early 1997, seriously delinquent credit card accounts amounted to US$4.07 billion, or 1.8 percent of all outstanding credit card debt in the United States.

Improved economic conditions in the late 1990s helped reduce the number of bankruptcies in the United States. As a result, credit card issuers saw loan profits grow for the first time in five years, from 17.4 percent in 1998 to 17.9 percent in 1999. The following year, profits grew again, reaching 18.4 percent. The percentage of credit card profits secured by late fees and other charges increased by 33 percent between 1995 and 1999, growing from 18 percent to 25 percent. In 2000, fees accounted for 28 percent of earnings. This was partially due to the lower interest rates credit card companies found themselves having to offer to remain competitive. To compensate for lower rates, credit card issuers began reducing or even eliminating grace periods and upping fees for late payments and for charges that exceeded credit limits. They also began peddling accessory services, such as minimum payment insurance, which guarantees the payment of a card holder's minimum balance in the event of a disability.

Consolidation levels increased in 2000 as larger companies continued to purchase credit card portfolios from smaller card issuers. For example, MBNA bought the US$5.6 billion credit card portfolio of First Union Corp. in 2000. Also that year, Citigroup purchased the US$47.38 billion portfolio of First Capital Corp. The total number of significant portfolio transactions in 2000 reached 36, compared to 21 in 1999 and 26 in 1998. The economic slowdown that had taken hold of North America by the early 2000s prompted large banks to slow their spending. As a result, the number of portfolio purchases fell to 25 in 2001. The largest deal of the year was Bank One Corp.'s purchase of the US$8 billion portfolio of Wachovia Corp. In 2002, Next Card Inc. began looking to sell its US$2 billion portfolio, and Providian Financial Corp. put roughly US$3 billion of its credit card assets up for sale.

In Asia, credit card usage growth averaged 30 percent annually in the late 1990s, although China's market of nearly 1 billion potential cardholders remained largely untapped. According to the *Financial Times*, China had less than 15 million cards in circulation in the mid-1990s. By 2003 the number of cards issued in China was expected to reach 200 million. Chinatrust, based in Taipei, became the first Taiwanese bank to enter the ranks of the world's 100 largest credit card issuers in 2001, after it issued 400 million cards and increased its domestic market share to 17.65 percent. According to *Korea Herald*, nearly 90 percent of the Asia-Pacific market for credit cards remains untapped.

Research and Markets, Europe's largest resource for market research, announced the addition of a new report called *Credit Opportunities in China* in May 2004. The report revealed that The People's Bank of China and China Banking Regulatory Commission approved American Express, Citibank, and HSBC to issue credit cards in China. MasterCard partnered with ABN Amro to issue cards in the country. MBNA opened a representative office in Shanghai. Morgan Stanley planned to launch the Discover Card in China.

The credit card market in South America was also forecast to continue expanding rapidly through the early 2000s. South America, led by Brazil and Argentina, represented about US$20 billion per year in credit card purchases in the late 1990s, and the region had 13 million cards in circulation, divided evenly between Visa and MasterCard. However, economic turmoil in Argentina in 2001 undermined the potential of this growth market.

CURRENT CONDITIONS

The world's three largest financial card companies—Visa, MasterCard and American Express— continue to advance the use of debit, credit and charge cards around the world. Countries once opposed to capitalism, such as China and Russia, were allowing foreign financial companies to enter the market and establish card systems. These three companies saw their credit and debit card transaction volumes reach US$4.5 trillion in 2003, an increase of 15.4 percent over 2002 levels according to CardForum.

The purchase of Bank One (the third-largest credit card issuer in the United States) by JP Morgan Chase in 2004 was big news for the industry. Bringing with it more than 51 million cardholders as well as its other bank assets, Bank One's position as the sixth-largest bank in the U.S. combined with JP Morgan Chase's position as the third-largest bank to create the second-largest bank.

Card companies continued to enjoy increasing earnings into 2003, with that year showing the highest profit margins for the industry since 1992. Revenues from cardholder penalties (such as late fees and overlimit fees) dropped slightly in 2003, a drop attributed to lower debt levels. However, these penalty charges earned card companies approximately US$7.7 billion.

Merchants had begun to balk at the costs of accepting financial cards as payment. In 2004, WalMart stopped accepting debit MasterCard stating that the card cost too much for WalMart and that it only accounted for 1 percent of its sales. After several months of negotiations, the card was restated. This decision had followed on the heels of a class-action lawsuit headed by WalMart over the use of debit cards. The major credit card companies had been requiring merchants to accept all of their cards, including debit cards as part of their policy. Visa and MasterCard were accused of artificially inflating transaction fees paid by retailers. Visa and MasterCard settled with WalMart and the approximately 5 million other retailers who had joined the class action, with the card companies agreeing to pay US$3.05 billion in cash over 10 years. In addition, they agreed to stop the requirement that retailers honor all of their cards and also agreed to make it easier to distinguish between credit and debit cards.

The U.S. continued to be the only major country not embracing smart card technology. Part of this reluctance was attributed to the fact that in the U.S. only 1 percent of the total card sales volume had been attributed to fraud. However, data is easier to obtain off a magnetic strip than it is from a smart card chip, so technology experts believe fraud will increase in the U.S. where criminals will have the greatest pool of cards with magnetic strips.

The use of pre-paid gift cards has taken off in North America. Deloitte Touche Tohmatsu was reporting that such cards had generated about US$45 billion in sales in 2003. Many of these cards are being issued directly by retailers, but general purpose card issues, such as Visa, MasterCard, American Express, and Discover, are also issuing gift cards that have the advantage of being accepted at a wide number of retailers.

RESEARCH AND TECHNOLOGY

The most prominent technological advancement affecting the credit card industry in the late 1990s was the introduction of the multipurpose smart card. In 1994 France created the smart card version of the credit/debit card, which features a computer microchip, instead of a magnetic strip, to store financial data, and can function as both a credit card and a debit card, among other things. The smart card can also serve as identification and prevent fraud and misuse with built in encryption that scrambles codes and renders the card virtually useless to criminals. In late 1997 France also began putting in place an entire smart card system for the country and planned to launch the system in 1998. France signed an agreement to convert the country's currency system to this electronic format. In early 1998 French transportation services such as trains, buses, and subways, as well as bars, restaurants, and stores located in transportation stations, accepted smart cards. The country launched the system to coincide with the 1998 World Cup tournament in Marseilles.

Smart cards are also known as ePurses, or electronic wallets, have been more readily accepted in some countries than others. Europeans were more likely to use a pre-paid debit card with smart card technology (which requires a PIN number) for purchases rather than paying by use of a credit card. In the United Kingdom, the London Transport Company has had much success with its Oyster Card, allowing customers to pay for bus and subway transport by purchasing prepaid tickets that are added to their card. They simply pass the Oyster card over a receiver at the gate to the subway, and they are allowed entry. London Transport is expanding the cards to allow them to be used for other small-change purchases. However, experience in Germany has shown that such cards need to be multi-functional and provide the user with a benefit for their use, such as a savings over the regular price of a good.

Worldwide standards for the smart card varied. Visa, MasterCard, and Europay developed a standard, and most European countries were actively promoting acceptance of this standardized technology in order to facility international usage of card. Other countries such as the United States trailed France's smart card technology by four to six years, according to the *ABA Banking Journal*. Smart cards made their debut in the United States in 1999 when American Express launched its Blue Card. Smart cards, however, failed to gain widespread acceptance in the United States by the early 2000s. This was despite attractive interest rates offered on new smart card releases by firms like Bank One and Providian Financial.

Other key developments in the late 1990s emerged in response to the rise of Internet-based commerce. To promote the use of credit cards as a means of online payment, Visa and MasterCard collaborated with Microsoft, IBM, and Netscape to develop a standard for secure online transactions called Secure Electronic Transaction (SET). SET verifies the parties participating in the transaction and provides digital certificates to credit card issuers, which transfer them to their cardholders. This security system also uses advanced encryption technology developed by the Massachusetts Institute of Technology, which establishes two unique "keys" for both cardholders and businesses, a public and a private one. The public one is published in an electronic directory, while the private one is kept secret. When sending a message, the public key encrypts the message, while the private key unscrambles it. This method prevents hackers from obtaining confidential information such as credit card numbers, because, even if they intercept the message, they cannot decode it without the proper private key.

In May 2004, *Asia Intelligence Wire* announced that MBF Cards (Malaysia) Sdn Bhd introduced the new MBF Cards EMV Chip credit card, which offered more embedded data than other similar chips in bank and credit cards. Company president Al Alagappan said the product was not new but offered a new way to make cards more safe and secure. E-purse card technology is expected to take off in South Korea, where consumers like to be among the first in the world to use the latest technology.

Security remained of high concern to consumers. In June 2005, computer hackers breached the system of credit card processing company CardSystems Solutions of Atlanta, Georgia. Approximately 200,000 records were stolen and the data of 40 million credit card accounts compromised, with all brands of credit cards being exposed. In 2003, a similar incident had occurred at Data Processors International of Nebraska, where the account numbers of 8 million credit cards were stolen. New encryption methods are always being tested in efforts to secure data. However, the U.S. has come under some criticism for its privacy and data protection laws which lag behind those of other developed countries. In Europe, for example, most countries have laws requiring people to specifically opt-in to allowing their data to be share or stored. However, in the U.S., the default most often requires the consumer to opt out. In addition, Europe has enacted laws making it illegal for companies to share most financial information. Again, this is not the case in most states in the U.S. In Sweden, security is taken very seriously; credit card use requires a photo identification and a signature match.

INDUSTRY LEADERS

CARD ASSOCIATIONS

Visa. By 2005, Visa International continued to be the world's leading credit card, and the largest processor of financial transactions. There were 1.3 billion Visa-branded cards in circulation around the world, with acceptance in more than 150 countries. As a credit card association, Visa does not issue credit cards itself. Instead, Visa is owned by more than 21,000 financial institutions worldwide that compete with each other to offer Visa products, such as credit and debit cards. Visa was reporting that it had generated more than US$3 trillion in card sales. About 34 percent of transactions are for cash, while 66 percent is for purchases on a worldwide basis, although regions such as Latin America and Europe use their cards for a larger percentage of cash advances than purchases. Visa members also participate in VisaNet payment system, which provides authorization, transaction processing, and settlement services for purchases from 24 million merchants worldwide. Visa provides its customers with debit cards, Internet payment systems, value-storing cards, and traveler's checks.

Visa began as BankAmericard, Bank of America's credit card operation, in 1958. Bank of America licensed its BankAmericard to other banks starting in the 1960s. In 1977, after achieving a strong national and international presence, the credit card's name changed to Visa. Besides credit cards, Visa offers traveler's checks, smart cards, corporate and business cards, and Internet commerce systems.

MasterCard International Inc. Although it has more member enterprises (23,000), and is accepted in more countries (210), MasterCard continued to be the number two credit card association based on cardholders. With 679.5 million Mastercard-branded cards worldwide in 2004, MasterCard reported transactions worth US$1.5. The MasterCard brand is one of the most widely recognized in the world, but the company also has the Maestro brand, an online, PIN-based debit card system used at ATMs. The company also operates the Cirrus ATM network and Mondex International chip-based smart card subsidiary.

The company's "MasterCard Working for Small Business" was a comprehensive global program providing small business with payment cards, online tools, and other resources that deliver financial control, data management, analysis and reporting plus rewards and benefits. In May 2004, the program released its *MasterCard Procurement Opportunities Guide: An Entrepreneur's Guide to Selling to Governments and Corporations* at the Small Business Association Conference 2004. At that conference, the company also released results of a *Small Business Economic and Spend Outlook Survey*, which found that small businesses view managing expenses and finances as the most pressing concerns for them. The survey polled U.S. businesses with annual revenue between US$100,000 and US$10,000,000. MasterCard sponsored the Cards Middle East conference in May 2004 in Dubai. The number of delegates and exhibitors doubled from 2003 with new card technology such as online prepayment terminals being hot attractions. Dubai Ports, Customs and Free Zone Corporation became the first government organization in the region to adopt the new MasterCard corporate purchasing card. The system's B2B transaction application replaced petty cash with a payment card monitored online and reconciled to Oracle Financials software. MasterCard's award-winning "Priceless" advertising campaign expanded the company's global reach and scope by being seen in 96 countries and heard in 47 languages. By 2003, its workforce had grown to 4,000 employees.

The private company began in 1966 when a group of bankers decided to enter the credit card business. They initially called the venture Interbank Card Association, which issued MasterCharge cards. Later, the association was renamed MasterCard along with its credit card. With a declining market share, MasterCard began lobbying for acceptance in new kinds of businesses such as bus depots and hospitals.

American Express Company. By 2005, American Express was a global financial, travel and network services company operating three segments: Travel Related Services (charge and credit cards, travelers' checks, and the world's largest travel agency), American Express Financial Advisors (with more than 12,000 advisors offering financial planning, brokerage services, mutual funds, insurance and other investment products), and American Express Bank (banking services to wealthy individuals, corporations and retail customers outside of the U.S.). American Express remained the world's third-leading credit card, well behind the big two. In 2003, the company reported revenues of US$23.9 billion from all sources.

In the late 1990s, American Express began to reorganize itself to focus on its credit card and travel operations; therefore, the company spun off its stockbroker arm, Lehman Brothers. Berkshire Hathaway owned about 10 percent share of American Express. Although the company originally did not provide revolving credit to its clients, the company launched a new credit card called Optima in the mid-1990s that offered a revolving credit line. Besides its credit cards, American Express led the world in traveler's checks and published such magazines as *Food & Wine* and *Travel & Leisure*. The company offered Internet online banking, mortgage, and brokerage services. Strategic plans included global expansion with nearly 80 percent of American Express's revenues are U.S.-generated. American Express was a leading captive center (offshore shared service) operator and opened a related customer service center in India. In May 2004, it was reported that Charles Schwab Corp's U.S. Trust and American Express Co's American Express Financial Advisors were being investigated for alleged breaches in trading regulations.

DiscoverFinancial Services Inc. Discover remained another large credit card issuer in the mid 2000s. A business unit of Morgan Stanley, the company was in the process of being spun off from its parent in 2005. Overall, the company's sales totaled US$5.5 billion in 2004.

Formerly part of the Sears, Roebuck and Co. financial services, Dean Witter, Discover became an independent company in 1993. Dean Witter launched the Discover card in the 1980s while part of Sears. In 1997 Dean Witter merged with Morgan Stanley to become Morgan Stanley Dean Witter. Discover has more than 50 million cardholders. the Discover/NOVUS Network was the largest proprietary credit card network in the United States with more than 4 million merchant and cash access locations. Like other major credit card companies, Discover offered prepaid stored value gift cards. Discover Financial Services and Grupo Financiero Banamex entered into an agreement expanding acceptance of the Discover Card in Mexico. Corporate Director of Consumer Banking of Banamex Augusto Excalante believed the agreement provided an important way for Banamex to continue supporting Mexican tourism.

Discover launched some distinctive advertising campaigns and promotional partnerships. The "It Pays to Discover" tag line was linked to TV ads highlighting unique rewards and industry innovations. Cashback Bonus award opportunities were featured spotlighting how participating card members accrue awards on every purchase and merchants willing to double amounts. Another series featured Discover 2GO Card, the first of its kind in the industry. Its unique, compact shape housed in a protective case easily attaches to a key chain, belt or money clip for maximum convenience. Discover partnerships include ESPN's College Day. Discover acquired naming rights to a shopping center located outside Atlanta. Discover Mills let Discover Card members take advantage of special promotions, events, and offers. In December 2002, Discover served as the worldwide presenting sponsor for a New Year's Eve New York Times Square Guinness World Record Setting Event featuring Anita Ward singing her disco hit "Ring My Bell" on the main stage. Ten Discover Card members were awarded "balance paid in full prizes" for the first time. In February 2003, Fraud Prevention Expert Frank Abagnale was retained as a company advisor/consultant. He was scheduled to appear at various national retail and merchant association conferences on behalf of Discover to lead workshops, seminars and sign copies of his books.

JCB International Co. Ltd. Established in 1961, JCB (Japan Credit Bureau) remained a leader in the Japanese credit card industry in 2005. The company had 51.6 million cardholders in 18 countries, with its cards accepted at 11.70 million merchants in 190 countries. Annual sales volumes had reached US$52 billion. JCB launched a consumer credit card in the U.S. in 1993.

CARD ISSUERS

Citigroup Inc. Citicorp, the world's leading issuer of credit cards, became the world's largest financial services firm in 1998 when it merged with the Travelers Group, becoming Citigroup. By 2005, Citigroup offered MasterCard, Visa and private label credit and charge cards, with 120 million accounts in North America (22.6 percent of the market) and 20.9 million cards in 42 other countries. The company also offers Diners Club cards to affluent individuals and corporations. Private label cards include those for Sears and Home Depot. Internationally, Citigroup was the first foreign bank to issue credit cards in Russia, and is the owner of the majority of Diners Club Europe. In 2003, the company earned a net income of US$3.59 billion from its card business.

MBNA. MBNA Corp. ranked as the world's second-largest credit card issuer. Because of its affinity card marketing agreements with more than 5,000 professional, recreational, charitable, and other groups and organizations, MBNA was the world's largest independent credit card lender. The company also offers home equity financing, insurance premium financing, and professional practice financing. By 2005, MBNAhad operations in the United States (where it held 13.1 percent of the market at the end of 2003), Canada, Ireland, Spain, Mexico, and the United Kingdom.

Founded in 1982, MBNA held 15 percent of the U.K. credit card market by 2003, and was the first U.S. company to issue credit cards in Ireland. The company reported 2004 net income of US$2.68 billion from all sources.

JP Morgan Chase. In 2004, JP Morgan Chase bought the third largest credit card issuer (and sixth largest bank at the time), Bank One. The resulting entity was the second-largest financial services firm in the U.S. In 2003, Bank One held 11.6 of the U.S. credit card market. At the end of 2004, JP Morgan Chase had 94 million cardholders, generating revenues of more than US$15 billion and resulting in operating income of US$1.68 billion. Customers charged more than US$282 billion worth of goods to its cards that year.

MAJOR COUNTRIES IN THE INDUSTRY

UNITED STATES

The United States continued to have the largest market for credit cards as well as the leading number of credit card issuers. In 2004, 144 million Americans had a general purpose credit card. Of this amount, about 40 percent paid off their bill each month, according to a joint study by *The New York Times* and *Frontline.* The average household in the U.S. held eight cards with a total credit card debt of US$7,500. By 2003, the U.S. market for credit and charge cards was valued by Euromonitor at US$1.56trillion. However, the majority of this value (91 percent) could be attributed to credit cards, representing an increase of more than 39 percent over 1999 values. Card issuers earned a pre-tax profit of about US$2.5 billion each month. That year, the top five credit card companies were: Visa International, American Express, Morgan Stanley Dean Witter, MasterCard International, and JCB, although Visa continued to hold the position of having the most dominant brand, capturing more than 43 percent of the market.

Despite the economic downturn that gripped the nation between 2000 and 2002, credit card spending grew in the U.S. This growth was attributed to consumers using their cards as a means for short-term loans through cash advances.

The financial card industry also saw an increase in the use of debit cards, with such card usage expected to overtake credit card usage during 2004. But not far behind in terms of consumer acceptance was the smart cards. With their anti-fraud devices, ability to store personal information, and wide acceptance by retailers, industry experts expected smart card technology to replace traditional credit and debit card usage.

The U.S. credit card industry grew by 12 percent in 1997. That same year, the country's consumer debt escalated substantially, in part because of the number of cardholders and the frequency of credit card use in the United States. In 1997 consumer debt from credit cards reached US$530 billion, up from US$265 billion in 1991. This trend resulted in record numbers of bankruptcy filings in the late 1990s. About 750,000 consumers filed for bankruptcy in 1985, compared to almost 1.4 million in 1996. The credit card industry, therefore, petitioned Congress to pass more stringent bankruptcy laws to make it more difficult for consumers to file. The House Judiciary Committee responded by approving a new bankruptcy bill in 1998; the bill called for a new formula based on income and cost of living factors to determine if debtors must repay some credit card debt, or if they may eliminate all debt through bankruptcy, according to *American Banker.* A bullish economy in 1999 did help the rate of bankruptcies to decline. However, the recessionary conditions that had taken hold of the United States by the end of 2000 prompted some analysts to predict a rise in bankruptcy levels in the early 2000s. The average credit card balance carried by U.S. households in 2001 equaled US$8,562.

A U.S. District Court ruling in October 2001 threatened to strip both Visa and MasterCard of their ability to prevent the banks which issued their credit cards from issuing those of rivals. American Express had seen its share of the world market drop to about 10 percent during the mid-1990s due to increased pressure from Visa to prevent affiliated banks around the world from offering American Express cards, even though many already offered MasterCard and Diners Club cards. Although the European Union rejected Visa's by-law to exclude American Express, and Visa dropped its contention in South America after American Express put the matter before the court, Visa and MasterCard did secure this privilege in other countries and in the United States.

In May 2004, Visa USA and MasterCard International asked the U.S. Supreme Court to reverse an appeals-court ruling allowing the card association's members to issue American Express and Discover cards.

United Kingdom

In the United Kingdom, many consumers in the London area have taken to using smart cards to replace the need to carry small change, travel passes, security cards and even house keys. Oyster cards have the largest number of smart card customers in the U.K. at 2.2 million by 2004, with the cards being used 3 million times per day for travel on Transport London services. However, the uses for the cards were being expanded to include the ability to make other small payments for newspapers, grocery items and parking. These uses are seen as providing a new revenue source for Transport London.

The credit and card charge market was valued at US$216 billion by 2003, an increase of 8.6 percent over 2002 levels according to Euromonitor. The U.K.'s big banks and building societies are the largest providers of credit cards, with Barclays Bank and the Bank of Scotland being the leaders in the industry. Using credit cards, consumers spent the most on travel, with this item accounting for about 15 percent of all charges.

When the EU adopted a single currency, the euro, in 1999, analysts expected credit card and payment card use to increase in the 11 member countries participating in the switch to a common currency (four EU members had opted out of the monetary union). Dual currencies—national currencies that would circulate but would be handled as denominations of the euro rather than independent currencies—would exist into the early 2000s. As a result, industry observers expected consumer confusion to foster the use of credit cards over hard currencies for making payments and general spending.

Europe Intelligence Wire reported that the Consumers' Association was cautiously in favor of risk-based pricing and remained concerned about consumers understanding the increasingly complex UK credit card market. Risk-based pricing was also criticized for undermining transparency and making it impossible for consumers to accurately compare rates.

France

By 2003, France's six leading credit and charge card companies were existing in very competitive surroundings: these six players accounted for about 72 percent of the market, with Société Général being the overall leader with almost 16 percent of the market. However, in France, according to Euromonitor, only 27 percent of purchases were made using a banking card, as the French preferred to use their cards only for making essential purchases.

Japan

In the early 2000s, Japan experienced a slowdown in its economy; incomes were on the decline and there were fewer jobs. Euromonitor reported a slowdown in consumer spending. However, of the spending that was occurring, more was being done using credit cards, resulting in an increase in their usage. Between 2000 and 2003, credit card usage increased by 41 percent, reaching a value of approximately US$231 billion. With credit card fraud still on the rise in Japan, customers have taken to smart card technology, with smart card usage increasing by 185 percent between 2000 and 2003.

In Asia, Japan led the credit card industry with about 220 million credit cards issued in the late 1990s. Nippon Shinpan was the country's largest card issuer with 24 million cardholders. Although non-bank credit card issuers offered revolving credit in Japan, few cardholders actually used it; only 3 to 4 percent of all credit card transactions in Japan involved revolving credit. While revolving credit was allowed under Japanese law, consumer credit reporting had not developed effectively in Japan, leading card issuers to shy away from encouraging revolving credit among customers whose reliability they could not gauge. From the 1970s, annual growth rates typically reflected number of cards issued and credit card financed expenditures approaching 30 percent. In the late 1990s, a move to improve Japan's credit reporting emerged, as issuers were attracted by the enhanced revenues associated with revolving credit. Nonetheless, as the Japanese economy flirted with recession between early 1997 and early 1998, credit card use in Japan fell precipitously. The Japanese Consumer Credit Industry Association reported that credit card purchases dropped to 7.8 percent in March 1998, down from 14.6 percent in April 1997. Further, the value of credit card purchases also declined between 4 to 11 percent during this period. In 2000 the Japanese credit card industry was worth an estimated US$29 billion.

SOUTH KOREA

In South Korea, LG Credit Card was one of its major issuers. In the late 1990s, credit card use continued to grow, although the country faced severe economic setbacks in the wake of the won's 1997 plunge in value. The country reported 35.7 million credit cards in circulation in late 1996, when annual credit card purchases totaled US$60.6 billion. However, the credit card industry might be one of few in South Korea to actually benefit from a harsh economic climate. Because of the country's deficit and currency devaluation, credit card usage was forecast to grow even more in 1997 and 1998. According to *Korea Herald*, the South Korean government's efforts to promote "credit card use as a weapon against the black economy" was successful, as credit card use in South Korea doubled in size every year between 1999 and 2002. As a result, the Korean market grew to be the second- largest credit card industry in the world. Jong-Heon Lee, of United Press International, revealed South Korea barely avoided financial turmoil after LG Credit Card Co. was pulled back from the brink of bankruptcy after creditors extended a massive rescue package.

In 2003, banks in South Korea were experiencing large declines in profits, the result of bad debts from credit cards and household charges. The most commonly used financial card is a deferred debit card, known locally as a "charge card," which are linked to personal bank accounts. In an effort to boost spending, the government altered regulations on credit cards, with consumers given tax breaks for spending. However, by 2003, 10 percent of South Koreans had large credit card debts, with the country's total credit card debt equal to 14 percent of the Gross Domestic Product. In response to the "crash" in credit cards, the government provided a bailout package for debtors, while credit card companies cut back significantly on the limits allowed for cash advances.

FURTHER READING

"A Borrower Be; Credit Cards in Japan." *Economist,* 21 April 2001.

"American Express—Pioneering Captive Centres (It is Widely Acknowledged as a Leading Captive Centre Operator)." *Asia Intelligence Wire,* 12 May 2004.

"American Express, Schwab Unit Face Scrutity." *Europe Intelligence Wire,* 20 May 2004.

"Bells Will be Ringing: Discover Card Attempts World's Largest Synchronized Bell Ringing in Times Square on New Year's Eve." Available from http://pressroom.discovercard.com.

"Card Industry Directory (Sample Pages)." 16th Edition, 2005. Available from http://www.cardforum.com.

"Cards Mideast, Big Success." *Asia Intelligence Wire,* 22 May 2004.

"Credit Card Confidential: The pressure is on for retailers to tighten security of credit card transactions." Deloitte Touche Tohmatsu, 2005. Available from http://www.Deloitte.com.

"(Credit Card) Quo Vadis—Korea's Credit Card Industry?" *The Korea Times.* Available from http://times.hankook.

D'Innocenzio, Anne. "U.S. Credit Card Issuers Plan Debut of Smart Card." *The Detroit News,* 2 January 2001. Available from http://www.detnews.com.

"The Discover 2GO Card, a Leading Innovation in the Credit Card Industry in 2002 Offers the Key to Convenience," 2 December 2002. Available from http://pressroom.discovercard.com.

"Discover Card Launches New Ad Campaign and More," 4 June 2002. Available from http://pressroom.discovercard.com.

"Discover Card Teams with Fraud Expert Frank Abagnale: Discover Merchants Get an Education on Fraud and Prevention and Protection," 20 February 2003. Available from http://pressroom.discovercard.com.

"Discover Financial Services Partners with Grupo Financial Banamex to Increase Merchant Acceptance in Mexico," 27 March 2003. Available from http://pressroom.discovercard.com.

"European Credit Card Market (The)—Europe—February 2004." *InfoShop Report.* Available from http://www.the-infoshop.com.

Fickenscher, Lisa. "Credit Card Profitability Growth in '99 1st in 5 Years." *American Banker* 10 January 2000.

"Country Reports: Financial cards in United States (United Kingdom, France, Japan, and South Korea)." Euromonitor International, April 2004. Available from http://www.euromonitor.com.

"Credit card, bank rates on the rise." *CNN/Money,* 27 April 2005. Available from http://www.money.cnn.com.

"Financial Services Foresight – Credit Wars." Deloitte Touche Tohmatsu, February 2005. Available from http://www.deloitte.com.

"Japan: Thieves Use Sophisticated Technology to Forge Credit Cards." *Asahi Evening News,* 8 May 1998.

"Korea: Asia's Most Exciting Credit Card Market." *Korea Herald,* 19 December 2001.

Kuykendall, Lavonne. "Card Companies Sell Euro's Convenience." *American Banker,* 9 January 2002.

———. "Repeat of Profit Spike May Not Be in Cards." *American Banker,* 15 January 2002.

Lee, W. A. "Card Portfolios Are Up As Small Firms Get Squeezed." *American Banker,* 5 October 2000.

———. "Credit Card Profitability Improved Again Last Year." *American Banker,* 9 January 2001.

"Major Market Profiles: Credit and Charge Cards in USA; UK; Germany; France." *Euromonitor,* June 2004. Available from http://www.deloitte.com.

Mandell, Lewis. *The Credit Card Industry.* Boston, MA: Twayne Publishers, 1990.

"MasterCard, Corporate Card First." *Asia Intelligence Wire,* 22 May 2004.

"MasterCard Delivers Critical Sales Insight to Small Businesses." *Business Wire,* 20 May 2004.

"MasterCard Survey Points to Small Business Optimism Regarding Spending and U.S. Economy." *Business Wire,* 20 May 2004.

"MBF Introduces EMV Chip Credit Card" *Asia Intelligence Wire,* 22 May 2004.

Medoff, James L. and Andrew Harless. *The Indebted Society.* New York: Little, Brown and Company, 1996.

"Pint of milk and top up my Oyster card please." Deloitte Touche Tohmatsu, 4 March 2004. Available from http://www.deloitte.com.

"Money: Beware Credit Cards That Play the Joker" *Europe Intelligence Wire,* 23 May 2004.

"Security challenge: The ePurse." Infineon Technologies AG, accessed June 2005. Available from http:// www.silicon-trust.com.

O'Sullivan, Orla. "Is Off-Line Debit about to Derail?: Some See the Sudden Acceleration in Check Card Use as a Boon, Others as Fraud Waiting to Happen." *ABA Banking Journal,* September 1997.

"Research and Markets: The Chinese Credit Card Market Analyzed." *M2 PressWIRE,* 18 May 2004.

McGeehan, Patrick. "Soaring Interest Compounds Credit Card Pain for Million." *New York Times*, 21 November 2005. Available from http://www.nytimes.com.

Shawkey, Bruce. "Credit Cards: The Shape of Things to Come." *Credit Union Executive,* January-February 1998.

"Visa/Mastercard Antitrust Settlement Affirmed by Second Circuit." *Class Action Reports,* 2005. Available from http://www.classactionreportslaw.com.

SIC 6500

NAICS 531

REAL ESTATE

The real estate industry encompasses a broad range of businesses involved in the development, transfer, and management of real property. Major segments include developers, property managers, and real estate agents and brokers. For discussion of new building construction, see also **Construction, Residential Building** and **Construction, Nonresidential Building.**

Industry Snapshot

Historically, real estate has been a cyclical industry in which property values often mirrored the fluctuations and conditions of national and global economies. The U.S. economy suffered a downturn in the early 2000s, and a similar lack of verve held back the real estate market in many other parts of the world, including Latin America and much of the European Union, hitting Germany particularly hard. Certain sectors of the industry performed well, however. In Europe, for example, retail-related real estate transactions flourished. In many respects, real estate continued to be the one bright spot in the U.S. economy, as historically low interest rates led to record home sales in 2002 and 2003. Investors were also lured to real estate in greater numbers, as the stock market continued to give unimpressive returns throughout the early 2000s. The appearance of Real Estate Investment Trusts (REITs) in many markets showed their appeal to investors who could now purchase this type of investment through public exchanges.

The commercial real estate industry became more of a global affair during the boom years of the late 1990s, and the interconnectedness of global capital markets has continued to strengthen. Commercial real estate suffered from falling rents and rising vacancy rates virtually worldwide during the early 2000s. Globalization, lowering of trade barriers, and the easier mobility of capital in the early 2000s also meant that more companies could compete directly for real estate assets. Increased competition tended to keep prices down. Globally, however, conditions in the real estate industry varied widely because of local conditions. But by 2005, countries were again seeing gains in the industry. China, with the world's fastest-growing economy was seeing a tightening of available real estate in many of its popular urban centers, particularly once it allowed foreign investment in many industries. Despite Germany's position as the slowest European country to recover from the economic downturn, the sheer size of its market continued to make it an attractive opportunity for many investors.

According to the National Association of Realtors, commercial real estate achieved a record of US$306.8 billion in 2006. That was up from US$276 billion in 2005. The association predicted that the market would level off in 2007. Furthermore, it stated vacancy rates would edge up and rent increases slow down as the market absorbed new space.

On the residential housing scene, real estate auctions were gaining in popularity as a preferred method for matching home buyers and sellers. The National Auctioneers Association claimed the auction industry as a whole grew by seven percent in 2006. As a result, auctions generated more than US$250 billion in sales. The most significant growth attributed to the real estate sector was where auction sales increased by 12 percent with more than US$17 billion in revenue for 2006.

Industry support experts known as "stagers" were having an impact on sales success stories. They were hired to come in and eliminate clutter plus add some distinctive touches in order to combat a sluggish real estate market. As a result, there were substantial gains for minimal investment and property sold faster.

Organization and Structure

Property available for individual or corporate ownership in free-market economies is valued primarily by two factors: the marketplace, which establishes demand, and location, which determines value. Typically, there is a high demand in large cities for office and residential space centrally located in prime work and commercial areas. However, the softening of the economy in the United States and much of the rest of the world in the early 2000s led to slackening demand for just such property, bringing rents and prices down.

Many factors influence demand: access to public transportation, highway, and rail networks or port facilities; income levels of inhabitants; property taxes; access to good schools; employment opportunities; and local economic incentives. While a property may be well located, it is still subject to fluctuations of local, national, and global economies. For example, when localities experience increased crime, non-responsive government, economic downturn, or civic mismanagement, then demand may abate, property values sink, and the local real estate industry may experience a corresponding downturn.

In markets where property is sold or leased by the government, corporations or individual investors work with government officials to effect the transaction. To serve foreign investors or corporations, development boards are established to work as liaisons with authorities. Several of the most aggressive direct investment agencies are the Netherlands Foreign Investment Agency, the Invest in Britain Bureau, and the Hong Kong Industrial Promotion Office. India, which had a growing economy in the early 2000s, does not permit direct foreign investment in real estate. If the Indian government were to change its regulations, India would be a potentially hot growth spot for real estate investment. China, also a growing economy, began to privatize some land ownership in the 2000s. Almost half the direct foreign investment in China in the early 2000s was in real estate.

As the world's economies grow increasingly interconnected through international trade, many governments view locations that offer logistical advantages as increasingly important. These advantages include road and rail networks and accessibility to seaports and airports. In the United States, many ports sold or leased port-owned property as office and industrial sites to raise funds to upgrade port facilities. Many airports and seaports designated free zones with complete facilities and warehouses through which goods could enter the country duty free for assemblage, packaging, and redistribution.

In the 2000s, security concerns added a whole new layer of complexity to the economics of real estate. The attacks on September 11, 2001, that destroyed the World Trade Center in New York brought a new awareness of vulnerability to the world's other impressive buildings. In the United States, the insurance industry redefined its risk coverage after the attacks on the World Trade Center and in most cases made coverage against terrorist acts a separate category, instead of including it under general risk. Coverage against terrorist attacks was generally not available or only at very high rates. This situation left open the possibility of uninsured buildings being destroyed, and lenders, i.e. banks, being left with no collateral. The issue of terrorism insurance needed to be resolved by the real estate, banking, and insurance industries and by legislatures. This existing issue did not, however, slow the building of skyscrapers in Asia. The world's tallest building, Taipei 101, was completed in 2003 in Taipei, Taiwan. Taipei 101 overtopped the Petronas Towers in Kuala Lampur, Malaysia, completed in 1998. Taipei 101 was not expected to hold the world's record for long, as the Shanghai World Financial Center in Shanghai, China, was expected to be completed in 2007. Work on new skyscrapers carried on in Asia, despite evidence that commercial office space was already in abundant supply.

The spread of technology was changing the face of real estate, both residential and commercial. Buyers and potential buyers in technology-rich nations such as the United States were able to conduct independent research and comparison easily from their own homes. There was a wealth of information available on the Internet, enabling buyers to research communities, school districts, building and property costs, taxes, and any other real estate consideration. Homebuyers could even look online to find houses for sale, most with photos and some with video technology that offers a virtual tour.

BACKGROUND AND DEVELOPMENT

Agrarian societies are believed to be the first group to establish property rights. Ancient Greece, and later the Roman Empire, set laws that confirmed this absolute right of ownership. However, with the decline of the Roman Empire and the advent of the Middle Ages, much of European society fell into a period of feudalism wherein a landlord oversaw and owned vast quantities of land. Individuals or "vassals" worked this land on his behalf, paying rent in the form of farm products and labor in exchange for protection. With some notable exceptions, Europe's feudal systems were largely abandoned in the thirteenth century.

The concept of absolute freedom and the rights of the common man did not begin to develop in Europe until the late eighteenth century. No doubt, these ideas were developed through colonial expansionism, which revealed to the Europeans vast amounts of land previously unknown to them.

Development of real estate soared during the late nineteenth and early twentieth centuries, particularly in England and the northeast United States. Multistoried facilities for mass production of automobiles, textile products, and consumer goods were constructed. In turn, these industrial and commercial centers spurred the growth of towns and cities in surrounding regions.

Modern industrial development took on a different focus after World War II. Rapid postwar population growth, coupled with general economic recovery and expansion, spurred the development of both residential and commercial properties in many countries.

In most free-market economies, the 1950s saw an era of entrepreneurship. Small companies spun off from larger corporations. Real estate developers seized such opportunities and, responding to the need to create more commercial and industrial facilities, began building on speculation.

A glut of vacancies resulted in the real estate downturn of the 1970s. Real estate values fell, and many small developers and brokers left the industry. Large local and national developers and brokerage firms bought out their smaller competition. But the 1980s gave rise to a period of renewed global economic growth. Residential communities and office and industrial parks on large tracts of land were planned, developed, sold, and leased. Many sprung up around single industries; for example, the suburban area east of San Francisco known as the "Silicon Valley" largely resulted from commercial and residential development. Amenities that went beyond landscaping became the norm. They included day care, on-site restaurants, health clubs, hotels, travel services, and even heliports. The idea was to attract tenants and create value. Given that this period was often dubbed the "golden era" of real estate, developers spared no expense when it came to interior and exterior design. Some even included valued collections of art, crafts, and sculptures. Many developers built on speculation using state-of-the-art technologies and building materials, even where markets were not established. Despite warnings that markets were becoming overbuilt, the boom continued.

In the United States the economic crisis of 1987, dubbed the "cash crunch," brought the real estate development frenzy to a jarring stop. A sudden tightening of money by the U.S. Federal Reserve and changes in bank loan policies made financing unavailable for projects, particularly speculative ones. With too much product on the market, lessees began to shop for cheaper rents. Perhaps in desperation to attract business in a depressed market, some lessors even offered designated free-rent terms encompassing months, sometimes years. Buyers demanded lower prices. Commercial and residential property values dropped, particularly in markets that experienced the highest increases during the 1980s. As more and more firms declared bankruptcy or merged, groups such as the National Association of Industrial and Office Parks (NAIOP) saw their membership drop from about 7,000 in the late 1980s to less than 3,000 in the early 1990s.

Global recession continued to have an impact on the real estate industry during the last decades of the twentieth century. A wave of consolidations, mergers, and bankruptcies resulted in fewer, but larger, companies in the industry. Brokerage firms merged and, to combat diminished sales, became more heavily involved in property management. Likewise, developers also pared back their staffs, often concentrating on property and asset management. For example, Trammel Crow Company, the United States' biggest commercial-property developer in the 1980s, lost billions in the depressed market but survived by switching its main business to property management. In 2001, revenues were up again, reaching US$35.4 million and topped $692 million in 2003. Another boon to the U.S. real estate industry came in 1992 through a repeal of the tax code of 1986. Real estate professionals were once again allowed to write off paper losses against other income. Many developers entered into joint ventures with outside sources of venture capital to develop property.

The real estate industry mirrored global economic conditions in the early 2000s in some sectors, particularly commercial property, with rising vacancy rates, falling rents, and lower demand than in the generally more prosperous years of the late 1990s. The industry remained flat in many places, as large corporations trimmed jobs and held down costs. But conditions were not uniform. Some areas of the world saw continued growth during the early 2000s, particularly in India and China. Their real estate markets were not necessarily in synch with other economic factors, yet the conditions in their real estate industries remained distinct from much of the rest of the world. And in the United States, the residential housing market was particularly strong. Investors wary of poor stock market returns also increasingly turned to the real estate sector. Though returns on investment in real estate were not particularly high in the early 2000s, the real estate market was nevertheless favored by investors for its perceived stability.

In the United States, the consumer housing market remained very strong in the early 2000s, despite the generally poor economy and the loss of some 2.5 million jobs between 2001 and mid-2004. Sales of existing homes set a record in 2002, with 5.6 million houses changing hands. This record was bested in 2003, when 6.1 million existing homes were sold. Mortgage rates in the early 2000s were at their lowest point in thirty years, setting extremely favorable conditions for buyers. The retail property market in the United States, comprising non-office commercial space such as stores and malls also did well in the early 2000s. In general, rents remained stable and vacancy rates rose only slowly. Institutional investors gravitated toward the retail real estate market because the sector was thought to hold up well against recession. Malls anchored with groceries were presumed to be particularly good investments, pushing their prices up. Some cities saw more investment in downtown areas, as private and public entities pushed for revival of neglected urban shopping areas.

The office property sector of the real estate industry suffered the most in the early 2000s. The overall office vacancy rate rose over the period, hitting 16.8 percent in 2003 in the United States. And that figure was expected to rise over the following year. Rents, particularly in downtown offices, fell over the same period. Though there were indications of a strengthening economy by mid-2004, industry analysts expected that it would take a while before the effects hit the commercial real estate industry. Without strong job growth, and with increasing export of jobs overseas, the U.S. office real estate sector was anticipated to remain vulnerable.

These conditions were repeated in many countries around the world. Recession dragged down the real estate sector in many parts of Europe. Germany, France, the Netherlands, and Portugal did worse than some of their neighbors. Spain, Greece, and Britain showed stronger economic results in the early 2000s. In the poorer performing countries, the real estate sector in general sank, while in countries that did better, numbers for the real estate industry typically were flat. In Asia, local economies were volatile in the early 2000s. The outbreak of Severe Acute Respiratory Syndrome (SARS) in 2003 stalled economic growth and caused uncertainty about the future. The real estate sector across the Asia Pacific region was flat across 2003. But Asian economies were expected to pick up over the subsequent few years. China and India were both considered to be on the brink of a large upsurge in their real estate markets.

Most Latin American economies grew only slowly in the early 2000s. Vacancy rates in Mexico City office spaces rose to as much as 25 percent by 2004. Rents rose, while some 3.5 million square feet of office space was under construction by 2004. Vacancy rates in most South American metropolises were similarly above 20 percent, as many cities were already oversupplied with offices.

International investment in real estate in Africa remained limited over the early 2000s. Most countries allowed only domestic or inter-African investment in real estate. Johannesburg was a leading African real estate market, especially because ongoing challenges, such as high crime and HIV/AIDS, made real estate seem like a safer investment than some other options.

CURRENT CONDITIONS

By 2005, the world of real estate was literally taking place globally. Borders were becoming more transparent in terms of the transactions taking place. PriceWaterhouse Coopers was reporting that capital flow into the real estate market in the U.S. was valued at US$79 billion in the first half of 2004, compared to US$113 billion in all of 2003. Real Estate Investment Trusts (REITs), which were started in the U.S. in the 1960s, had allowed for property assets to be traded on public exchanges. These proved so popular that their availability had spread throughout the world. In 2005, the Hong Kong Housing Authority was expected to launch the largest initial public offering (IPO) of an REIT to date in the world. Markets were continuing to open up, particularly in India and China whose economies were doing very well, and in Central and Eastern Europe.

In terms of real estate market size, the North American market was valued by Deloitte Touche Tohmatsu at US$1.6 trillion or 34 percent of the total market. Continental Europe held US$1.3 trillion or 27 percent, Southeast Asia held US$825 billion or 17 percent, Japan at US$600 billion or 13 percent, the United Kingdom held US$361 billion or 8 percent, South America at US$50 billion or 1 percent, and Australia at US$38 billion or 1 percent.

In terms of specific regional or city markets, coastal locations were still preferred in the U.S., with the Pacific region seeing the largest amount of growth. However, in terms of urban centers, Washington continued to have the highest investment and development prospects. London was considered the leading European city in terms of commercial space development, and the city that had best fought back against the economic downturns of the early 2000s.

The greatest growth in the U.S. was happening in the industrial, apartment and office sectors, whereas in Europe, most growth in the real estate industry was occurring in the retail sector. Shopping center transactions in continental Europe were valued at more than US$9 billion in 2004, reaching their highest-ever level. In addition, the United Kingdom alone had retail transactions of US$8.4 billion. Outside of the U.K., Poland was the leading center for shopping-center investments. In Asia, 2004 saw the retail market in China opened to foreign investment. As a result, cities such as Beijing were experiencing shrinking supplies of retail space.

RISMedia discussed the evolution of "a shifting paradigm" for real estate business models. Some of the new models included MLM, annuity, residual, auctioneering, flat-fee and no fee. Many brokers, however, were hanging on to traditional models. It typically took between five to 10 years for a new business model to establish a paradigm shift but the timeline was viewed now as becoming shorter.

WORKFORCE

Real estate brokers and agents earn their living chiefly through commissions paid for selling or leasing a property. According to the U.S. Bureau of Labor Statistics, as of May 2004 there were 40,050 real estate brokers in the United States (not including self-employed workers), earning a mean annual wage of US$77,850. In addition, there were 126,470 real estate sales agents earning a mean annual salary of US$47,950. Real estate brokers and agents spend much of their time researching markets, inspecting properties, and working with both sellers and buyers. They first work with the owner of a property for sale to establish sales prices or rental rates and enter into an agreement that delineates how to market the property and the time frame of their agreement. Then, real estate agents coordinate the process of signing a lease or a sales agreement with the buyer. However, some buyers are uncomfortable with the biases brokers may present toward their own sales listings. To address this concern, a trend toward "buyers' brokers" has developed. A buyer's broker is paid to protect the buyer's interests; rather than try to get the buyer to pay the highest amount possible (so the broker receives a higher commission). The broker tries to get the lowest price and best overall deal for the buyer and is paid a flat fee or a flat fee plus a percentage of the reduction in price of the house.

Brokers were making changes in their staff by hiring agents better equipped to handle the cyclical trends of the industry. In order to do this, some companies were searching for potential agents in other fields that require similar skills. Coldwell Banker Mid America had been successful in working with teachers and planned to target nurses next. Recruiting the right agents was considered to be challenging for mid-level managers. Approximately 80 percent of new agents did not last more than two years after obtaining their real estate license.

Land developers purchase real estate in its "raw" or undeveloped state. They may work with local authorities to purchase and assemble parcels of land. Next, they either further develop the land as a residential, commercial, or industrial project, or they sell these assembled parcels to developers whose goal is to sell them or lease them to the public at large. Financing schemes as well as approvals for development and marketing plans are usually complicated and require banks or private investors.

Property managers oversee the business of owning real estate property. In May 2004, there were 159,980 such managers, with an average salary of US$48,760. They market vacant space; negotiate lease agreements; collect rents; and pay mortgages, taxes, insurance premiums, and other costs related to real estate. They are likewise responsible for hiring individuals or maintenance firms to keep the property in top shape and often interact with tenants, making sure their needs are met.

INDUSTRY LEADERS

EQUITY OFFICE PROPERTIES TRUST

With total assets of approximately US$24.6 billion and operating revenues of almost US$3.2 billion, Equity Office Properties Trust remained the world's largest real estate investment trust at the end of 2004. The company, which owns, manages, leases, acquires, and develops office properties, controlled some 125.7 million square feet of office space in 698 properties over 18 U.S. states. Equity operated in Los Angeles, San Francisco, San Diego, and Washington, D.C. among other places. It acquired Beacon Properties in 1997. Equity Office Properties Trust was led by Sam "Grave Dancer" Zell, whose nickname comes from his practice of purchasing and renovating dilapidated properties. The company had an occupancy rate of 87.7 percent at the end of 2004, up over the 2003 level of 86.3 percent. During 2004, the organization disposed of almost all of its industrial properties.

THE LINK MANAGEMENT LTD.

At the start of 2005, The Hong Kong Housing Authority had delayed what had been described as the world's largest initial public offering (IPO) of an REIT. The Housing Authority was citing legal issues for the delay. The REIT will be formed from 2.85 million square feet of ground floor retail space in Hong Kong and 59,000 commercial parking spaces owned by the Housing Authority. The IPO was being valued at US$2.7 billion. With land scarce in Hong Kong, the REIT was expected to be very popular with investors.

PROLOGIS

As the largest REIT devoted to industrial distribution facilities, ProLogis owns, manages or was developing more than 1,990 facilities in 72 markets in the United States, Europe and Asia in 2005. Founded in 1993 as Security Capital Industrial Trust, the company changed its name in 1998 to reflect its growing global business. The company began its expansion in 1998, entering markets in the Netherlands and Mexico. In 2001, expansion continued into Asia with completed developments in Japan reaching a value of more than US$1 billion by 2004. That year, the company also made forays into China. ProLogis added 137 properties to its portfolio when it merged with Keystone Property Trust in 2004. In June 2005, the company announced plans to merge with Catellus Development, a leading U.S. property development company. In May 2007, ProLogis announced plans to develop a large distribution center in northeast Spain for a subsidiary of ARC International. Plans called for construction of the distribution center to feature sustainable design techniques to reduce its impact on the environment.

CB RICHARD ELLIS GROUP INC.

CB Richard Ellis was the world"s largest commercial real estate services firm at the end of 2004, with revenues of US$2.37 billion. With 17,000 employees, partners and affiliates working in more than 300 offices in 50 countries, the company completed 41,600 sales and lease assignments, managed 989 million square feet of institutional and corporate space, and handled almost 40,000 valuation and advisory projects. Begun as a small, San Francisco-based firm in 1906, CB Richard Ellis was a leading real estate firm in the western U.S. by the 1940s. By the 1970s, the company had expanded across the U.S., expanding globally in the 1990s. Known as CB Commercial until its acquisition of Richard Ellis of London in 1998, the company also acquired Hillier Parker May & Rowden, one of the U.K.'s leading property management companies. In 2003, CB Richard Ellis merged with competitor Insignia Financial Group, a dominant player in the New York market. San Francisco financier, Richard Blum, owned the controlling interest of the company.

In 2006, CB Richard Ellis gained a total of US$224.6 billion in combined leasing and investment sales globally. That figure was up 33 percent from its US$150.4 billion in 2005 and nearly US$100 billion higher than its 2004 volume of US$127.4 billion. Some of the growth reflects full-year volume for Trammell Crow Company that CB Richard Ellis acquired in December 2006. Consequentially, CB Richard Ellis retained the top spot on National Real Estate Investor's Annual Top Brokerage Survey for the fourth consecutive year. CB Richard Ellis reported revenues of nearly US$4,032 billion from its operations in nearly 35 countries.

Another major 2006 development involved CB Richard Ellis' representation of MetLife as the seller for "the largest commercial property sale in history" of Peter Cooper Village/Stuyvesant Town. That apartment complex was a 110-building complex located on the east side of Manhattan. It sold for US$5.4 billion to New York-based Tishman Speyer Properties and its partner Blackrock Realty.

In April 2007, CB Richard Ellis announced its acquisition of DGI Davis George. That acquisition was evidence of the company's strategic plan to strengthen its position in the UK industrial and logistics sector. It also advanced the company's goals to enhance its full-service capabilities.

WESTFIELD GROUP

Although the largest share of its holdings are in the United States, Sydney, Australia-based Westfield Group is the world's largest owner, manager, developer, and leaser of shopping malls. In 2005, the company had investment interests in 129 properties in the United States (68 properties), Australia (42), New Zealand (11) and the United Kingdom (8), providing a total of 111 million square feet of leasable space to 21,200 retail outlets. Founded in the 1950s, Westfield expanded into the U.S. in 1977. At the end of 2006, Westfield had revenues of more than US$5.3 billion. The company also manages real estate assets for others.

TRIZEC PROPERTIES INC.

In the development and management segment of the industry, TrizecHahn Corporation Ltd. of Canada ranked among the leaders in North America. TrizecHahn was formed in 1996 through the merger of Horsham Corporation and Trizec Corporation and became a major player as the owner, manager, and developer of retail and office properties. In 2002, the company reorganized. It became the publicly traded real estate investment trust (REIT) called Trizec Properties Inc., a Chicago-based company. Trizec Canada Inc. owns a 40 percent share of Trizec Properties. The company owns or manages 52 officer properties in North America, including a share of the Sears Tower in Chicago and full ownership of the infamous Watergate office building in Washington, D.C. Trizec Properties was the second-largest REIT in the U.S. market, with revenues of more than US$712 million in 2004.

CENDANT CORP.

Cendant Corporation is a world leader in the hotel and car rental industries. But, it is also the parent of the world's largest real estate brokerage franchise company in the world, Century 21, as well as the U.S.'s oldest real estate company, Coldwell Banker. Although its primary business is franchising, Century 21 had more than 6,600 independently owned and operated offices in over 30 countries. In 1996, Century 21 expanded its real estate empire by acquiring Coldwell Banker Corp., another franchisor, which retained its own identity after the acquisition. More than 3,500 offices operate under the Coldwell Banker brand, The company was very active in moving into the newly privatizing real estate industry in China.

MITSUI FUDOSAN CO., LTD.

Japan's leading real estate services provider, Mitsui Fudosan reported more than US$10.5 billion in 2004 revenues. The company leased more than 5 million square meters of office and retail space, and held more than 40,000 rental housing properties. In addition it offered brokerage services on almost 28,500 units, and provided property management services. Mitsui Fudosan Finance Co., Ltd. was a subsidiary of Tokyo-based Mitsui Real Estate Development Co., Ltd., which was a member of the Mitsui Group, a general trading company. Mitsui Real Estate was Japan's leading developer of office buildings, commercial properties, and housing. Capitalizing on Japan's land shortage, Mitsui specialized in high-rise complexes that make profitable use of premium space. Its Kasumigaseki Building in Toyko is cited as the country's first skyscraper. The company also owns hotels and offers real estate brokerage services. Mitsui Real Estate was founded in 1941 as the real estate division of Mitsui Gomei Kaisha, a central holding company of the Mitsui financial group. The company's steady growth continued throughout the 1970s, when it began international operations. By 1990, Mitsui Real Estate owned property in New York City, Honolulu, San Francisco, and Nepal as well as 88 subsidiaries. Its U.S. subsidiary, Mitsui Real Estate Sales USA, sold in excess of $1 billion worth of property in the United States between 2000 and 2003, much of it in California. The subsidiary was applauded for its acquisition and redevelopment of the renowned Halekulani Hotel in Waikiki, Hawaii.

MAJOR COUNTRIES IN THE INDUSTRY

THE UNITED STATES

The United States possesses one of the world's largest and most sophisticated real estate markets. In 2002, new home sales rose by 7.7 percent. The percentage of homeowners in the United States reached 68.6 percent by 2003, a record surpassing even the 1980s high of 65.8 percent. The U.S. Census Bureau predicted that through 2010 the number of households in the country would grow by 1.1 percent a year, or 1.15 million units, indicating strong demand for both residential and commercial properties over the following decade.

The record low in interest rates in the early 2000s led many more people into homeownership, making the apartment rental market suffer. Investors focused instead on retail properties, formerly a neglected category. Malls and commercial strips became popular investment items, particularly those anchored with a grocery store. U.S. retail property sales rose sharply in 2002, topping $10 billion nationwide.

The commercial real estate and property management market was valued at US$35.5 billion in 2003 by Euromonitor, with office real estate being the largest sector holding 42.5 percent. Most growth in the U.S. was occurring in the Pacific region, which accounted for almost 42 percent of the market. However, the market had many players taking part in it, with the leading four controlling less than 19 percent of the market. The four top players in 2003 were CB Richard Ellis, Trammell Crow, Lincoln Property, and Cushman & Wakefield, with CB Richard Ellis gaining on its lead position through its acquisition of Insignia Financial in 2003. Growth in commercial real estate is expected to be large up to 2008, with a rate of almost 35 percent being predicted.

Across the U.S., vacancy rates were on the decline over those of the early 2000s. By the beginning of 2005, rates in major downtown locations stood at 13.8 percent, while those in suburban locations had decline to 16.3 percent from their 17.1 percent level in 2004. The levels of construction of new office space remained low. CB Richard Ellis was also reporting that strong demands for shipping activities and a stabilizing manufacturing sector were the cause for low vacancy rates in the industrial sector of the real estate market. In the U.S., the national rate stood at 10.1 percent by early 2005.

According to Real Capital Analytics, investment sales throughout the U.S. were US$317 billion. That amount reflected a 15 percent increase beyond 2005 sales volume of US$270 billion.

Robert Trussell analyzed the trend for real estate developers to be featured as TV stars. Although the real estate market was down, there were many cable TV shows featuring people trying to achieve their goals while working in the industry. Such new programs included "Bought & Sold" that premiered on HGTV in May 2007. It tracked real estate agents in Essex County, New Jersey. Established programs included "Flip This House" in its third season on A&E. It showcased the efforts of real estate developers in three cities. The shows tended to have an educational focus sharing dos and dont's. The personalities frequently seemed larger than life and experienced dramatic developments. Trussell claimed "The real estate world is a magnet for these kinds of personalities. So there's no shortage of bold, in-your-face individuals who are at times likable and at other times not so likable."

A nationwide survey conducted by Housing Predictor.com revealed the Hottest 10 Buyers Markets in the U.S. were mainly located in the nation's southern half. The top spot was Albuquerque, New Mexico. It was projected to appreciate 9.1 percent by the end of 2007. Growth resulting in a population of almost a million people was attributed to substantial business growth including new movie studios and an airplane factory. Housing Predictor made its selections based on surveys conducted in 75 markets under construction from the more than 250 local housing markets forecast on the Web site. All selected markets represented growing local economies set to continue growing through 2008 and perhaps the following decade. Major changes in the national housing market were expected to occur based on changes in the composition of U.S. population.

China

China continued to be home to the world's fastest growing major economy in 2005. Foreign investors hurried to get on board. The real estate market was hot in Shanghai, which saw the building of several new skyscrapers. Prices for all categories of real estate, from residential to commercial, rose sharply in Shanghai in the early 2000s, leading to fears that speculators were fueling a pricing bubble that would soon burst. China's central government enacted rules to curb real estate speculation, including increasing the amount of required down payment. Shanghai's neighboring provinces, Jiangsu and Zhejiang, also saw a lot of new industrial development and foreign investment, and real estate there was expected to follow a similar upward pattern.

In 2004, there were about 25,000 real estate brokerage agencies in China, with a total employment of about 200,000 agents, however many did not hold the proper license. The property management sector was a huge employer, giving jobs to more than 2 million people in the country. Until 1999, the home resale market was almost non-existant in China; people stayed in their home. However, the government began to encourage the sale of old home in favor of new, bigger ones. Approximately 59 percent of Chinese in urban areas owned their homes in 2004, with the average household of two to four people having about 538 to 861 square feet of space. Most houses were being financed using personal savings, although the use of bank loans and government funding for financing was on the rise.

The luxury sector of the real estate industry saw particularly strong growth in China. Yet oversupply led some developers to simply abandon projects unfinished. The number of luxury apartments and villas grew by 35 percent over 2002. The Chinese government imposed a ban in 2003 on further sales of land for luxury housing.

In 2006, Chinese real estate developers invested US$251 billion in projects. In addition, the Chinese Academy of Social Sciences claimed input in residential housing projects was 1.9 percent higher than the figure in 2005. The related breakdown was as follows: 41.8 percent for developing ordinary residential housing projects, 3.6 percent for low-cost housing projects and 7.3 percent for upmarket apartments and villas.

China's Supreme People's Procuratorate focused its anti-graft campaign on officials taking bribes from real estate developers. Prosecuting departments investigated in excess of 9,000 cases of commercial corruption in 2006. One-third of those cases involved engineering projects and land sales. The campaign was expected to last until the end of 2007.

Europe

As they entered the twenty-first century, European countries tried to assert their national identity in an ever-increasing global market. Often, by grouping like-industries together in industrial and office parks, governments created a business synergy that helped establish national reputation in key, domestic industries.

A number of U.S. firms established operations in the European Union's increasingly unified markets. Many of these real estate firms engaged in myriad development projects such as major office complexes; retail (shopping) centers; and especially resort and recreational development including hotels, second homes, golf and ski resorts, retirement housing, and other recreational venues. In some cases, U.S. brokers and developers were sponsored by European corporations seeking to expand or develop real estate projects.

Typically, firms operating in the global real estate industry found European development a lengthy process because of more restrictive planning controls. Foreign-based development companies frequently engaged in joint ventures with other European developers, local governments, or corporate tenants. Most developers in Europe, however, were merchant builders that developed projects only after investors secured permission. U.S. firms were often sought for European projects; the experience in leasing, master planning, gaining approvals, and creating mixed-use developments these firms possessed made them comfortable working a project from ground zero, thereby building an added-value product.

Developing distribution patterns throughout the European Union (EU) to create a pan-European market changed land-use patterns across Europe. Signatories agreed to work in concert to create an EU marketplace that was conducive to economies of scale. Thus, member nations worked independently and jointly to enhance transportation networks and create centralized warehouses. Corporations consolidated their manufacturing operations (and sometimes physical plants) to serve new distribution systems.

Although most European economies remained sluggish through the early 2000s, industry analysts expected the European community to enjoy a rebounding economy in the latter part of the following decade. Falling rental markets were expected to stabilize in 2004 and after. Milan had particularly strong rental growth by 2003, and Moscow too had rising rents caused by high demand. France passed legislation allowing real estate investment trusts in 2003, and Germany and United Kingdom were expected to do the same. New job growth and low interest rates across Europe were also expected to help boost the real estate industry in the middle and late 2000s.

In the industrial sector, demand continued for space near major transportation lines. New construction increased in France, Italy, and Spain over the early 2000s but was almost nil in Germany and Belgium. The entrance of more Eastern European countries into the European Union in 2005 was expected to improve infrastructure. This development would in turn heat demand for good industrial property. Eastern Europe was considered a top growth area, while in other parts of Europe, growth in this sector was expected to be slight or stable.

Germany. Europe's largest economy, Germany, was one of the worst hit by the economic downturns in Europe, with the country coming slowly out of a mild recession that hit in 2003. That year, the commercial real estate and property management market was valued at about US$8.4 billion, with office space holding 55 percent of the market. The leading companies in the industry captured a larger share of the market; Bayerische Hypo- und Vereinsbank, Deutsche Sparkassen Leasing, and Viterra increased their combined market share to 38 percent in 2003, up from 31 percent in 2002, according to Euromonitor.

The United Kingdom. Of Europe's large economies, the U.K. had the most success at managing the economic turmoil of the early 2000s. Euromonitor had valued the commercial real estate and property management markets at about US$13.1 billion, with retail accounting for 50 percent of the market. PriceWaterhouse Coopers had acknowledged that retail was the top performing sector leading into 2005, but a weakening retail environment was expected to have an affect on this sector. The industry remained highly fragmented, with the top four players (Land Securities, MEPC plc, Slough Estates, and British Land Company plc) taking only a total of 22 percent of the income from this sector.

India. Many industry insiders considered India to be a land of emerging potential. *Little India* reported that international funds invested some US$2.5 billion in Indian real estate. Approximately 24 domestic funds had raised another US$3.5 billion for similar investments. Indian policy changes in 2005 offered encouragement for investors by allowing foreign investment of up to 100 percent in construction development projects with fast-track approvals. *Little India* claimed the major attraction was potential investment returns of 25 percent and more in Indian projects that might be hard to find in the U.S. and Western Europe.

Financial Express reported on a new tactic for staying ahead of the competition gaining popularity in India. Domestic real estate developers were outsourcing construction and design assignments to foreign companies through joint ventures. This so called "USP" would reportedly "bring in the latest technology and international expertise in design, construction, safety, speed and efficiency." It afforded excellent opportunities for domestic developers to establish meaningful partnerships with foreign engineering and infrastructure majors.

FURTHER READING

"2003 Real Estate Investment Survey." *National Real Estate Investor,* 1 September 2003.

Bureau of Economic Analysis. *Industry Accounts Data, 1994-2000,* 14 January 2001. Available from http://www.bea.doc.gov.

Burrell, Andrew. "European property markets overview." *Global Real Estate Now,* March 2005, Vol. 10., No. 1. Available from http://www.pwcglobal.com.

"Castles in the Sky." *Economist,* 24 January 2004.

CB Richard Ellis. "Global MarketView." January 2005. Available from http://www.cbre.com.

Chapman, Parke. "Hong Kong Prepares for Biggest REIT IPO." *National Real Estate Investor,* 1 January 2005. Available from http://www.nreionline.com.

Charlton, Mark. "Emerging Trends in Real Estate — Comparing the US with Europe." *Global Real Estate Now,* March 2005, Vol. 10., No. 1. Available from http://www.pwcglobal.com.

"China's Anti-Graft Body Targets Real Estate Corruption." 27 April 2007. Available from http://english.people.com.

"Chinese Real Estate Developers Pump US$251 bin into Projects." 3 May 2007. Available from http://www.antara.co.id.

Creamer, David E. "Terror's Economic Impact on Commercial Real Estate." *American Banker,* 5 April 2002.

Deloitte Touche Tohmatsu. "Breaking Out: A Sea Change in Real Estate Capital Markets." 2004. Available from http://www.deloitte.com.

Downs, Anthony. "Some Truths About U.S. Job Losses." *National Real Estate Investor,* 1 April 2004.

Duell, Jennifer D. "Withering of U.S. Dollar May Stall Global Real Estate Plans." *Commercial Property News,* 1 March 2004.

Ernst & Young. "Real Estate Market Outlook 2005." 2005. Available from http://www.ey.com.

"Existing Home Sales in 2003 Set Record." *Chain Store Age,* March 2004.

Grubb & Ellis. *2004 Global Real Estate Forecast.* Grubb & Ellis Management Services Inc., 2003.

Hooson, Ben. "Russian Real Estate: The New Frontier." *Euroweek,* 3 October 2003.

"Hottest 10 Buyers Real Estate Markets Announced." 3 May 2007. Available from http:www.webwire.com.

"Location, Location, Location." *Economist,* 31 May 2003.

"Major Market Profiles: Commercial Real Estate and Property Management in the US (UK, France, Germany)." *Euromonitor,* October 2004. Available from http://www.euromonitor.com.

Martin, Robert Scott. "Real Estate Finds Favor." *Research,* November 2002.

McDaniels, Iain. "A Critical Eye on Shanghai." *China Business Review,* January-February 2004.

"Optimism Comes to the Front for European Investors." *Real Estate Finance and Investment,* 17 November 2003.

PriceWaterhouseCoopers. *Korpacz Real Estate Investor Survey,* 14 May 2004. Available from http://www.pwcreval.com.

"ProLogis to Develop Distribution Center in Spain for ARC International — International Tableware Distributor Will Occupy 516,000 Feet in Zaragoza — New Warehouse Facility Will Feature Environmentally Advanced Design." *PR Newswire,* 3 May 2007.

"Property Giant Snaps Up Industrial Services Specialist." *Daily Post,* 25 April 2007.

"Real Estate Auction Wave Led by Pacific Auction Exchange." 3 May 2007. Available from http://home.businesswire.com.

"The Real Estate Industry, Through Volatile, Offers Riches to Those Who Know Where to Look." 2 May 2007. Available from http://knowledge.wharton.upenn.edu.

"Realogy Corporation Named to the Fortune 500 as the No. 1 Company in the Real Estate Industry." 19 April 2007. Available from http://www.realogy.com.

"Riding the Deal Wave to New Heights." *National Real Estate Investor,* 12 April 2007.

Reynolds, Jamie. "2004: 'Transition' Period in Real Estate." *Architecture,* December 2003.

Rolin, Pierre. "Global real estate trends for private investors." *Global Real Estate Now,* March 2005, Vol. 10., No. 1. Available from http://www.pwcglobal.com.

"Scaling the Peak." *Economist,* 17 April 2004.

Soni, Varun. "Outsourcing Construction, Realty Companies' New USP." 23 May 2007. Available from www.financialexpress.com.

Snell, Robert. "Stagers Help Put Best Face on Slow-Moving Homes." *Detroit News,* 29 May 2007.

Trussell, Robert. "Real Estate Without Work." *Detroit Free Press,* 13 May 2007.

U. S. Census Bureau. *New Residential Sales,* 26 April 2004. Available from http://www.census.gov.

"U.S. Investors Bullish on Indian Real Estate." *Little India,* April 2007.

"What the Real Estate Industry Fears Most." 4 May 2007. Available from http://www.rismedia.com.

Food, Beverages, and Tobacco

SIC 2082, 2084, 2085

NAICS 312120, 312130, 312140

ALCOHOLIC BEVERAGES

Three major segments constitute the global alcoholic beverage trade: breweries, which manufacture beers and ales; wineries, which produce wines and brandies; and distilleries, which produce various liquors and blended alcoholic drinks. For discussion of nonalcoholic beverages, see **Soft Drinks and Bottled Water.**

Industry Snapshot

Alcoholic beverages have long been a part of cultures throughout the world. They are important consumer products and are heavily advertised and marketed. There are literally tens of thousands of brands of alcoholic beverages. Global consumption of alcoholic beverages increased steadily through the late 1990s and early 2000s, reaching about 195 billion liters by 2003. Average per capita consumption was about 31 liters per year. By 2004, China had overtaken traditional leader the United States in terms of market volume. After China and the United States, the largest markets for alcoholic beverages were Germany, Russia, and Brazil. According to Zenith International, global consumption of alcoholic drinks was expected to reach about 210 billion liters in 2007.

Beer

Beer dominates the alcoholic beverage industry, with about 74 percent of volume in 2002. Production of beer throughout the world increased from 1.395 billion hectoliters (36.85 billion gallons) in 2000 to some 1.468 billion hectoliters (38.78 billion gallons) in 2003. In the early 2000s, there were 56 major beer markets in the world, and the average global per capita consumption of beer was 5.6 gallons. The country with the highest per capita consumption was the Czech Republic with 45.3 gallons. Next were Ireland, Germany, Slovenia, and Austria. Though the United States had traditionally been the largest beer market by volume, vigorous growth in China spurred both production and sales in that country, which became the world's top producer in 2002 and was the largest and most rapidly expanding market as of 2004.

Although Asia suffered economic downturns, beer consumption, in general, remained stable through the 1990s. The demand in Asia accelerated in the early 2000s, especially in China. The outlook in the early 2000s was positive as well for Latin America's beer market due to factors including fast population growth; increase in the beer-drinking age group; and weather conditions in the region conducive to drinking beer. Consumption in Eastern European countries, particularly Russia, also rose in the early 2000s, prompting major brewing companies to step up investment in those regions.

Wine

In 2002, wine comprised 13 percent by volume of the global alcoholic beverage market. Even though exports were the mainstays of wine markets in most countries, there was a growing trend in the international wine industry toward a more global, market-oriented strategy. Countries were recognizing the need to work with each other in solving problems in regard to the reduction of trade barriers in the wine market. Western Europe, with its long history of old-world wines, was no longer setting the standard in the wine trade. Branded varietals (grape types) from other parts of the world, including Australia and California, played a bigger role in the international wine market, even though they accounted for only 5 to 7 percent of global exports and were responsible for just one-seventh of the world's wine production.

In 2004, according to the U.S. Department of Agriculture (USDA), the countries with the largest vineyard acreage and highest levels of wine production in the world were Spain, France, and Italy. Europe accounted for more than 50 percent of global consumption. The top five countries in the world ranked by wine consumption were France, Italy, the United States, Germany, and Spain. Per capita wine consumption showed Luxembourg in first place, followed by France, Italy, Portugal, and Croatia; the United States ranked thirty-fourth. In 2000, wine sales in the United States totaled US$19 billion, compared to US$6.2 billion in 1980. In 2004, U.S. wine sales reached a record volume of 278 million cases; imports grew by 4.4 percent, totaling 72 million cases.

LIQUOR

Economic downturns in high-growth markets caused the global distilled spirits industry difficulty. To remedy this problem, large multinational organizations established premium brand groups that accounted for increased growth in international markets. They targeted other brands more narrowly, using a local or regional slant. In the early 2000s, white spirits made up approximately 42 percent of the market for branded distilled spirits. Local spirits accounted for 28 percent, and whiskey came in at 18 percent. Together, spirits made up 10 percent of the alcoholic beverages industry. China, Russia, and India were the largest spirits markets in 2002.

Branded beverages made up approximately 71 percent of U.S. distilled spirits exports in the early 2000s. Whiskey made up 59 percent; rum, 7 percent; and liquors and cordials, 3 percent. Vodka and gin were at the low end with 1.3 percent and 0.4 percent, respectively. The largest U.S. export market for whiskey was Japan. The biggest U.S. export markets for distilled spirits overall were Japan, Germany, and Australia.

ORGANIZATION AND STRUCTURE

BEER

Beer is made from a "mash" of fermented barley, malt, and rice or corn. It is naturally cloudy from sediment in the brews, but most commercial beers are clarified through filtration systems. U.S. brewers frequently use additives to stabilize foam and to maintain freshness, while European brewers use these additives less often. Almost all bottled and canned beer is pasteurized in the container to make sure that any remaining yeast does not continue to ferment. Draft beer, served from large kegs in taverns, bars, and other outlets, is not pasteurized and must be refrigerated to prevent spoilage.

In the early 2000s, lager, a pale, medium-hop-flavored beer, was the highest produced beer in the United States. It averaged 3.3 to 3.4 percent alcohol by weight and was highly carbonated. While Europe also produced many lagers, a higher percentage of European production was in heavier, dark beers. Stout, a very dark, almost syrup-like beer, was also popular in Europe, particularly in the United Kingdom and Ireland. Porter is a sweet malt brew with a high alcohol content of 6 to 7 percent. Malt liquor is beer made mostly from malt with a high level of fermentable sugars. Light beers have reduced calories and are made either by reducing the amount of grain or by adding an enzyme to reduce the starch content of the beer.

There are many different types of commercial beer, including pilsner, lager, ale, stout, light, malt liquor, dry, ice-brewed, bottled draft, and nonalcoholic. In the United States, the market was further segmented by price and quality, with beers being categorized as super premium, premium, and popular-priced. In the United States in 1999, light beer held a 40.1 percent share of the beer market, with premium accounting for a 25.9 share, and popular-priced accounting for the remainder, according to the 2002 *Market Share Reporter.*

Microbreweries and brewpubs in the United States had annual double-digit increases throughout most of the 1990s. By the early 2000s, craft beer was the country's fastest growing segment of the alcoholic beverage industry. According to a study by the *American Journal of Sociology,* the surging popularity of "craft brewing" was in part due to consumer reaction against established industrial brewers' lack of attention to new consumer preferences for more variety of flavor characteristics, color, freshness, foam, and other qualities of beer. In particular, 1997 was a banner year for the U.S. microbrewery industry. That year the number of American breweries surpassed those in Germany for the first time in at least two hundred years. Germany operated 1,234 breweries in 1997 compared to 1,273 in the United States, and by the middle of 1999 there were 1,414 American breweries, compared to just 43 in 1983. In 2004, the craft beer segment posted its second consecutive year of higher growth than imports.

However, at the end of the 1990s, a number of microbreweries experienced declines due to rapid over-expansion, although firms that tended to focus on regional sales saw better results. Acquisitions, mergers, and shutdowns were more common, but new microbrewery firms kept opening throughout the United States and continued to show significant growth. In 2002, the Association of Brewers reported 396 microbreweries, 46 regional specialty breweries, and 994 brewpubs in the United States.

WINE

Usually made from fermented grape juice, most wines are classified as red, white, or rose and also as dry, medium, or sweet. Wine categories include vintage wines, table wines, sparkling wines, and fortified wines.

Europe traditionally dominated the international wine business, though increasing competition from quality vineyards in Australia, California, and Chile altered this market. French wines are still considered world leaders in quality. Important French wine-growing regions include Bordeaux, Burgundy, Champagne, the Rhône valley, Alsace, the Midi, and Provence. German wine producers are known mainly for producing light, fruity white wines. The best German wines are said to be made from the Riesling grape in three areas: the Rhine River (Rheingau, Rheinhesse, and Rheinpfalz), the Nahe Valley, and the Mosel/Saar/Ruwer valleys.

Italy was the world's second leading wine producing nation (by volume) in 2003-04, just behind France. About two-thirds of Italian wines are classified as table wines. Its most popular wines come from the north: Barolo, Asti Spumante, and vermouth from Piedmont; Chianti from Tuscany; and Soave, Valpolicella, and Bardolino from Veneto. The sparkling, sweetish red Lambrusco comes from central Italy. While not considered a world leader in quality, Italian viticultural standards and vinification methods were said to be improving. Italy's quality seal is known as the Denominazione d'Origine Controllata (DOC).

Spain is known for its sherry, a fortified wine produced in the southern part of the country. Vineyards in northeast Spain produce Rioja, the country's leading table wine. There are a wide variety of Portuguese wines, from the popular light, slightly sparkling pink wines such as Mateus and

Lancers, to the "granddaddy" of fortified dessert wines, port. Madeira, an island owned by Portugal, produces dessert wines of the same name.

As of the early 2000s, over 90 percent of U.S. wine production came from California. Once considered an inferior wine-producing region, California became a world leader in the last half of the twentieth century. In the 1950s, a few fine California wines were recognized in the United States. By the 1980s, some California wines had gained worldwide recognition, albeit grudgingly. The number of premium California wineries exploded in the 1970s and 1980s, reaching more than 600 by the mid-1980s. In the early 2000s, California produced a large quantity of good commercial wines as well as some very high quality vintage wines. While French wines are usually named by the region, town, or vineyard where they are produced, California wines are most often named for the principal grape variety in the wine. A small amount of U.S. wine also comes from New York's Finger Lakes region, south of Lake Ontario.

The global wine industry consists of two parts: the high volume, heavily marketed commercial segment, which was in the early 2000s dominated by large, multinational conglomerates; and the lower volume, high-quality vintage wine business, which is dominated by small vintners with long histories. The high-quality wine trade has a rich culture, which includes exclusive trading houses, wine critics and writers, auctions of rare vintages, and high prices for individual wines. The commercial segment produces lower quality wines but in the 1970s and 1980s helped expand the appeal of wine to a wider global audience. In the mid-1990s, however, wine consumption stabilized or even fell in some established markets, leading many observers to consider the market mature in traditional areas, such as North American and Europe.

Liquor

The distilled spirits business includes two major groups: clear "white goods" such as gin, vodka, rum, and tequila; and "brown goods" (whiskey) such as bourbon, scotch, or straight whiskey. Younger drinkers tended to prefer lighter drinks, creating small increases in white goods sales in the early 1990s while sales of brown goods fell sharply. In the United States, consumption of distilled spirits rose 4.1 percent in 2004, the seventh consecutive year of growth. Bacardi Rum, Smirnoff Vodka, and Seagram's Gin—all white goods—were among the five top selling brands in the mid to late 1990s.

Whiskey is distilled from a fermented mash of grains. This mash may contain barley, oats, corn, wheat or rye. Straight whiskeys are made from at least 51 percent of a single grain and are aged in new, charred white oak barrels for at least two years. Light whiskeys are typically made from corn. Blended whiskey is a blend of straight and light whiskeys and may have as many as 50 ingredients. Bourbon whiskey must have at least 51 percent corn in the mash. This is almost exclusively a U.S. product and U.S. exports of Kentucky bourbon and its close relation, Tennessee whiskey, more than tripled from 1985 to 1990, to 11 million gallons.

Scotch whiskey is made from corn and barley and is processed in continuous stills. Distillers combine up to 40 true malt whiskeys with grain whiskeys to create the individual flavor of their brands. Scotch whiskey is sold in 190 countries and four of the top 10 spirits in the world were as of the early 2000s scotch whiskeys. In the early 2000s, the biggest exporter of spirits was the United Kingdom, with annual exports of 60 million cases—90 percent of which were scotch. (The world's largest spirits manufacturer, Diageo, created in 1997 following the merger of Guinness PLC and Grand Metropolitan PLC, is based in the United Kingdom.) Irish whiskey, a cousin to scotch, is made with barley dried in a closed kiln and is distilled three times, unlike all other whiskeys, which are distilled no more than twice.

The leading white goods are gin, rum, vodka, and tequila. Gin, made from a mixture of grains, is flavored with juniper berries and has a slightly bluish cast. It was first made in Holland in the seventeenth century and spread quickly throughout Europe. Gin is thought of as an English liquor and has been very popular there since the early eighteenth century. Since it was cheap and widely available, gin became known as "blue ruin" for those who overindulged. English-style gin is very dry compared with the Holland or Geneva gin, which is heavy-bodied, strongly flavored and has a malty taste.

Tequila is made from the fermented and distilled sap of agave plants. Tequila originated in Mexico, which remains a major producer. Tequila is double-distilled to increase potency and purity. While tequila has been thought of mostly as a party drink for young adults, some manufacturers are promoting premium tequilas made from 100 percent agave juice (cheaper brands contain as little as 51 percent agave). Premium brands include El Tosoro, distributed by Jim Beam, and Patron, distributed by Seagram. In the mid- to late 1990s, the largest tequila producer, Diageo's Jose Cuervo SA, stepped up marketing of its premium brand, Cuervo 1800.

Vodka is traditionally associated with Russia and Poland, where its production and use are widespread. Vodka is practically tasteless and is made from grain, sugar beets, potatoes, or other starchy foods. Vodka is widely traded in the world market, with major producers including the United States, Russia, Sweden, and Finland.

Other major segments in the alcoholic beverage market are the cordials and liqueur category and ready-to-drink cocktails. Originating in Europe, cordials and liqueurs are prepared by mixing spirits with flavorings. The cordial category includes schnapps, liqueurs, cremes, and brandies.

Background and Development

Beer

Beermaking has been part of society and commerce almost from the beginning of civilization. A Mesopotamian tablet from 7000 B.C. includes a recipe for beer, described as the "wine of the grain." The town of Pilsen (now in the Czech Republic) produced the first pilsner beer in 1292. Pilsner Urquell, a major brand, traces its roots back to that thirteenth century brew.

Germany, famous for its high quality brews, claims one of the world's oldest breweries—Brauerei Beck. Germany's first brewing guild was formed in Bremen in 1489, and Beck was founded four years later, in 1553. All German beers are still brewed to standards of what is called the world's first consumer protection act: the "Reinheitsgebot" purity law of 1516, which calls for the use of only water, barley, hops, and yeast in brewing beer.

WINE

Cultivation of grapes for winemaking began several thousand years ago. The ancient Egyptians made wine and the early Greeks exported it on a considerable scale. Vineyards were a major part of the Roman Empire's economy and were extended into France, Germany, and England. From about 1200, monasteries throughout Europe became centers for winemaking. During the nineteenth century, European vineyards were devastated by several diseases and pest infestations. The plant louse phylloxera was particularly debilitating, destroying European vines by attacking their roots. The European wine industry was saved by the grafting of European vine species onto immune U.S. rootstock.

Winemaking came to the United States along with the colonists. California's earliest vineyards were planted by Franciscan monks in 1769, and commercial wine operations began operating in the 1830s. The commercial era of wine production began in 1830 with the efforts of Frenchman Jean Louis Vignes from Bordeaux, France. His vineyard was located in what subsequently became downtown Los Angeles. The U.S. wine industry was devastated when Prohibition went into effect in 1921 but revived after its repeal in 1933.

TAXATION AND ABUSE

Alcoholic beverage industries in all countries deal with similar issues, including high taxation, growing regulation, legal challenges, and the specter of alcohol abuse. Taxation is a critical issue because governments around the world are partial to heavily taxing all forms of alcohol, both to raise revenue and discourage consumption. Taxes on alcoholic beverages are particularly effective, since high-volume consumers tend to buy the same amount of alcoholic beverages no matter how high the taxes. The Nordic countries have some of the highest taxes on alcohol in the world, partly to discourage high alcohol consumption rates. Many European countries also have high rates of taxation. The United States has historically had lower alcohol taxes than many other Western countries. However, U.S. taxes on alcoholic beverages were raised sharply in 1991. At that time, the federal excise tax on beer was doubled to US$18 per barrel, the equivalent of 16 cents to 32 cents per six-pack of 12-ounce bottles or cans.

Producers of alcoholic beverages have also come under fire in many countries over alcohol abuse, underage drinking, and drunk driving. Alcohol abuse has had devastating health and social consequences in almost every country. For example, between 40 and 50 percent of all traffic accidents in the United States are said to be alcohol related. Alcohol abuse also reduces productivity in the workplace and causes family stress. In the United States, the National Institute of Alcohol Abuse and Alcoholism estimated the entire cost of alcohol abuse at nearly US$140 billion annually.

Sentiment grew for harsher punishments for drunk drivers in the United States in the late 1990s. In March 1998, the U.S. Senate passed an amendment to federal highway legislation requiring states to toughen drunken driving laws. Senators voted 62 to 32 to pressure states to reduce the legal blood alcohol level to .08 percent from .10 in most states. Under the bill, states that did not adopt the legislation by 2001 would lose 5 percent of their federal highway construction money, with the annual loss increased to 10 percent the following year. The same measure would have applied to states that did not ban open alcohol containers from cars and trucks by 2002. In 22 states it was legal, as of 1998, for passengers to hold drinks, and in 5 states a person was allowed to drink while driving. However, the amendment was opposed by beer, wine, and liquor manufacturers as well as the American Beverage Institute, which represents restaurants and retailers that sell alcohol. Due to opposition to the measure in the House of Representatives, the amendment was deleted from the final highway bill, which passed in May 1998. However, some of these proposed changes later became law.

Alcoholism was reportedly rampant in the Commonwealth of Independent States (CIS) and Eastern Europe during the 1990s. During the communist era, widespread alcohol abuse was linked to the failing economic system and lack of personal freedom. However, even after the collapse of the communist system, alcoholism appeared to increase rather than decrease. In 1995, Poland's minister of health said that Poland's annual per capita consumption of alcohol was 11 liters of pure alcohol—nearly double the 1987 rates. In Western countries, per capita consumption of two liters of pure alcohol was considered high. Ironically, improving economic conditions in Poland were blamed for making alcohol more affordable.

In Russia and the Ukraine, alcoholism is also rampant. Per capita consumption in those countries soared from 4.4 liters in the mid-1960s to a staggering 15 liters 25 years later. A major public anti-alcohol campaign by former Soviet leader Mikhail Gorbachev in the late 1980s was a notable failure. In the late 1990s, the Russian government banned television advertising of liquor, but the rate of consumption continued to rise. Per capita annual consumption of neat spirits (a straight shot of any spirit taken in a single gulp without accompaniment) in Russia grew from 5.3 liters to 8.3 liters between 2000 and 2001, and by 2004, about 2.2 million Russians were reported to have alcohol-related problems. In Hungary, which also had an annual per capita consumption rate above 10 liters, it was estimated that 8.1 percent of all citizens are alcoholics.

In Western Europe, regulation and public pressure were successful in curbing some of the adverse effects of alcohol consumption. For example, extremely strict drunk driving laws in Norway and Sweden greatly reduced highway deaths caused by drunk drivers. In the United States, Mothers Against Drunk Drivers (MADD) was effective in lobbying for tougher state laws that punish drunk drivers.

CURRENT CONDITIONS

BEER

As of the early 2000s, the Czech Republic had the highest per capita beer consumption rate in the world, almost twice as much as the United States. The country produced 18 million hectoliters annually, with 1.5 million hectoliters exported. At the beginning of the twenty-first century, it was the sixth largest market for beer in Europe. However, Czech breweries suffered losses of approximately US$28 million at the end of the twentieth century mainly because of overcapacity. Poor management also plagued some companies. However, it was forecasted that the Czech beer industry would be increasingly competitive in the twenty-first century with the help of investment and management expertise from abroad.

According to the Beer Institute, the American beer industry grew steadily after 1996, with more than 3,500 brands on the market by 2002—twice the number in the early 1990s. Production reached about 6.2 billion gallons in 2003. However, domestic consumption grew more slowly, reaching only 0.7 percent in 2003. Analysts pointed to cool weather, the Iraq war, and increased sales of wine and spirits to explain this disappointing performance, and predicted improved growth in 2004. Beer firms in the United States continued to embrace the hot import sector and entered into agreements to become American distributors of international brands. Of the top 13 American malt beverage producers, six are either import firms or are U.S. affiliates of beer suppliers based outside the United States. Licensing agreements, direct exports, and foreign investment all played a role in the continuing trend of U.S. beer producers growing foreign markets. The American beer industry exported to almost one hundred countries in the world. In 2003, the most U.S. beer by gallons was exported to Mexico, followed by Hong Kong and Canada. U.S. beer exports to Japan, which ranked third in 2001, dropped by 33.8 percent between 2002 and 2003. Beer imports to the United States were led in 2003 by Mexico, Netherlands, Canada, and Ireland.

In 2001, the *German Embassy Newspaper Online* reported that the average German was drinking less beer, and the industry was suffering as a result. Per capita consumption, once 156 liters in the 1970s, fell to roughly 126 liters in 2001, a 20 percent decline; by 2003, consumption dropped to 120 liters. Overproduction plagued the 1,270 German breweries that produce more than 5,000 different brands. Beer suppliers were producing 30 percent more beer than demand required. Declining sales meant that small companies—which have historically dominated the industry—were finding it increasingly difficult to remain competitive. Between 2002 and 2003, Dutch brewer Heineken and Belgian company Interbrew took over 18 percent of German production, and analysts saw more mergers and closures in the near future. According to *Time Europe,* a Credit Suisse First Boston analyst predicted that a handful of global companies would control 70 percent of German production by 2010. Factors contributing to the decreasing rates of beer drinking include consumer preference for wine and soft drinks; the blood alcohol limit for drivers being lowered to 0.05 percent; young consumers associating beer with the older generation; and beer being seen as unhealthy. However, microbreweries offering beer mixed with various flavorings and fruit juices were seeing success with young beer drinkers.

Beer sales in Japan decreased after 1997, and with no signs of an economic recovery, the future looked dim for the country's beer industry. However, *The Economist* reported that Japan's low-malt beer (or *happoshu* in Japanese) was making strides as the only sector of the beer market showing growth. Production of low-malt beer in Japan started in the late 1990s. Brewers recognized that they could charge less for low-malt brews because the government taxed beer in accordance to its malt content. Prices for low-malt beer were two-thirds less than for regular beer; therefore, consumers looking for a bargain began stocking up. In 2000 low-malt beverages accounted for one-fifth of Japanese beer sales. Kirin continued to be the top selling beer brand in Japan, and it dominated the low-malt market as well. However, rival Asahi was catching up. In 1994, Asahi owned only one-fourth of the beer market, with half of all beer sales in Japan going to Kirin. That changed, however, with the worldwide success of Asahi's Super Dry brand, which became the third best- selling beer in the world. In 2000 Kirin held 38 percent of the beer market, with Asahi right behind it at 36 percent. Asahi's low-malt *Honnama* beer, released in February 2001, helped it to overtake Kirin as Japan's top beer maker in 2001. With sales of low-malt beer remaining brisk through the early 2000s, Asahi introduced another happoshu beer in 2005, with plans to ship three million cases in the first month alone.

The Latin American beer market continued to grow. In 2002, Venezuela topped the list with the highest per capita beer consumption in the region (an average of 21.8 gallons). By 2003, the two largest beer markets in the region were Brazil and Argentina, which enjoyed average annual growth of 5 percent. When AmBev, the Brazilian company that virtually controlled the Latin American beer market (with a 64 percent market share in Brazil, 77 percent in Argentina, 94 percent in Paraguay, and 99 percent in Uruguay and Bolivia), merged with Belgian company Interbrew in 2004, analysts predicted that the move would greatly improve exports for AmBev brands outside of Latin America.

WINE

France has long been the world leader in wine and remained number one in 2003 with sales of US$6.82 billion. But the volume of French wine exports, which account for about 25 percent of national production, dropped by almost 10 percent in 2003, according to the *Guardian.* Domestic sales also declined that year by about 5 percent. The change in domestic consumption was blamed on shifting demographics, as well as stricter enforcement of drunk-driving laws. Exports, however, were being devastated by market-savvy winemakers from such disparate places as California, Chile, and Australia, known as the "New World" producers. These vintners market heavily in North America, Northern Europe, and Asia, where consumption of wine, especially offerings under US$15, continued to rise. They discovered that the typical wine consumer wanted lighter, lower-priced wines instead of a heavy, expensive Bordeaux that needs time to mature. Of the ten biggest winemakers in the world in 2000, only one company—Castel Freres— was French, and it ranked fifth. The top spot went to U.S. E&J Gallo Winery, with sales that year of US$1.5 billion. In 2000, French wine exports fell in value to US$4.6 billion, a 5.4 percent drop. The country's U.S. market share decreased from 7 to 5 percent after 1998. By contrast, Australia saw its U.S. market share jump to 3 percent, with sales tripling since 1995.

In the early 2000s, increasing mergers and takeovers in the beverage industry also adversely affected the French wine market. In October 2000, Australia's Foster's Group purchased Napa Valley's Beringer Blass Wine Estates for US$1.9 billion. In February 2001, Australia's Southcorp purchased winemaker Rosemount for US$725 million. Among other factors, the deeper pockets of these newly merged firms bolstered their marketing efforts, making it difficult for smaller French vintners to compete. For example, Gallo's 2000 marketing budget in England was US$2.5 million, more than double the amount the entire Bordeaux region spent on advertising and promotions. The marketing tactics used by many New World vintners proved particularly savvy. Several California wineries are tourist destination places that boast such amenities as art galleries, cooking demonstrations, and lavish tasting rooms. By contrast, many French chateaux are not open to the public. Australia has used celebrities to attract attention to its brands. Foster's Beringer hooked up with Australian golfer Greg Norman to create Greg Norman Estates wines. In addition, actor Jackie Chan was a mascot for Lindemans in the Asian market.

French winemakers face other disadvantages as well. The weather in Burgundy and Bordeaux is unpredictable, which can lead to variations in vintages. However, the steady climates of wine production regions in the United States, Australia, and Chile make for regular harvesting and consistency in product. French wine labels display the geographic origin of the wine instead of the grape type (varietal). This factor makes French wines difficult to distinguish for the average wine consumer. In contrast, American and Australian wine labels boast brand names that are easy to remember and clearly indicate the varietal, whether, for example, it is Pinot Noir, Chardonnay, or Cabernet Sauvignon.

LIQUOR

According to *Beverage Industry*, the distilled spirits market continued to thrive at the beginning of the twenty-first century due to several trends, including new flavored spirits and high-end offerings. For instance, although Scotch sales were generally lower in 2000, the high-end single malt sector demonstrated a 7.6 percent rise in consumption. This lead gave way to a number of new single malt Scotch products, including the introduction of a 15-year-old Glenmorangle from Brown-Forman Beverages Worldwide. The Scotch market posted significant gains by 2004, when U.K. exports of malt whisky alone rose 15 percent, totaling more than 55 million bottles. U.K. exports of all Scotch whiskies reached 953 million bottles that year. The United States remained the most valuable export market for Scotch, while emerging markets in Brazil, Russia, Turkey, and especially China presented substantial opportunities for export growth in this segment.

The overall U.S. whiskey segment saw a decline, but that did not stop high-end bourbons from selling well. Handcrafted straight whiskies such as Evan Williams Single Barrel 1991 Vintage and Russell's Reserve from Wild Turkey became popular.

A number of high-end gins, new cognacs, premium Irish whiskies, and boutique tequilas all debuted in the United States, hoping to cash in on the upscale trend. Upscale vodkas were also in the mix. Import Stolichnaya saw an increase in sales by 11.3 percent. In 2001, Allied Domecq Spirits USA acquired the distribution and import rights for the vodka maker. France's Grey Goose high-end vodka saw sales increase by 175 percent in 2000. The company introduced an orange-flavored version called Grey Goose L'Orange. Smirnoff, the best selling vodka in the United States, also joined the trend with its Smirnoff Orange Twist and Raspberry Twist offerings.

INDUSTRY LEADERS

ANHEUSER-BUSCH

Located in St. Louis, Missouri, Anheuser-Busch was the largest brewer in the world and the biggest beer producer in the United States as of the early 2000s. The company produced more than 30 beer brands, including Budweiser, Busch, Bud Light, and Michelob. The company also produced the specialty brands ZiegenBock Amber, Red Wolf Lager, and the nonalcoholic brew, O'Doul's. In addition, Anheuser-Busch operated popular theme parks and water parks, including Busch Gardens and SeaWorld. Anheuser-Busch held a 50 percent interest in Mexico's Grupo Modelo. The firm's outlook in China, where it established local production of Budweiser and invested some US$1.2 billion in the early 2000s, was favorable. Main competitors included Miller Brewing, Adolph Coors, and Heineken. Total revenues in 2004 topped US$14.9 billion.

INBEV

When Belgian giant Interbrew acquired Companhia de Bebidas das Americas, a Brazilian company, in March 2004, it created the world's largest brewer by volume. The new company, InBev, controlled 14 percent of the global beer market. InBev also owned the Canadian company Labatt and the German company Brauerei Beck & Co. Its leading brands were Beck's, Bass, Stella Artois—the number seven international lager brand worldwide in 2000— Hoegaarden, Labatt Blue, Leffe, and Rolling Rock. U.S. sales of InBev's popular Bass Ale overtook sales in the United Kingdom. To gain regulatory approval for its 2000 acquisition of Bass Brewers, which was criticized by some rivals in the UK beer industry as anti-competitive, the company sold Carling, the United Kingdom's top standard lager, to brewer Coors. InBev posted total sales in 2004 of US$8.8 billion, up 20.7 percent from the previous year.

SABMILLER PLC

When South Africa Breweries (SAB) acquired Miller Brewing Company in July 2002, the new firm, renamed SABMiller, became one of the largest brewers in the world. SABMiller controlled 98 percent of the South African beer market in 2003; its Castle Lager brand was the continent's best seller. SABMiller produced other local brands as well, including Hansa Pilsener and Ohlssons. With operations in 40 countries, SABMiller was looking to expand in Europe. In 2003 it acquired Dojlidy Brewer in Poland, and was planning to expand its market in Russia as well. In 2004, the company employed more than 39,500 workers and reported revenues of US$11.3 billion.

HEINEKEN N.V.

Headquartered in The Netherlands, Heineken as of the early 2000s annually brewed 80 million hectoliters of beer. The company boasted operations in more than 110 breweries worldwide and sold beer in more than 170 countries. Heineken was Europe's number one brand and it was the number two imported beer in the United States. Corona, from Grupo Modelo, is number one. Other globally marketed brands included Murphy's (sold in more than 65 countries) and Amstel, Europe's number two brand. Heineken's other international brands were Asia's Tiger, Italy's Moretti, and Argentina's Quilmes. Heineken reported total sales of US$13.6 billion in 2003. Major competitors were Interbrew, Guinness/UDV, and Anheuser-Busch.

ASAHI BREWERIES LTD.

Asahi ranks as Japan's number one beer maker, with total beer sales slightly over those of rival Kirin, primarily due to the success of its Super Dry brand. In 2001, Asahi debuted its low malt offering, Asahi Honnama, which also helped the brewer retain its top spot. Asahi also had operations in Europe and America and boasted distribution and production arrangements with Miller Brewing, Molson, and Bass Brewers. Along with Kirin, major competition came from Sapporo Breweries and Suntory. Asahi, which also branched out into the food, pharmaceuticals, real estate, soft drinks, wine, and whiskey industries, posted total sales in 2004 of US$14 billion.

KIRIN BREWERY COMPANY, LIMITED

Located in Tokyo, Kirin had long been the market share leader in Japan, holding as much as 60 percent. By 2002, however, the company lost its lead to archrival Asahi Breweries. It realized a 14.7 percent sales growth from 2002 to 2003, reporting total sales of US$10.8 billion. Kirin's best known beers are Ichiban Shibori, Kirin Lager, and Kirin Tanrei, the top low malt beer in Japan. Distribution deals included one with Anheuser-Busch, and the company invested in the Lion Nathan brewery in Australia. Top competitors to Kirin, in addition to Asahi, were Sapporo Breweries and Suntory.

DIAGEO PLC

Diageo, the world's leading producer of alcoholic drinks, was formed in 1997 when brewing giant Guiness merged with Grand Metropolitan. The company continued to pursue aggressive growth, acquiring in 2000 spirits manufacturer Joseph E. Seagram & Sons, known for such popular brands as Crown Royal, Chivas Regal, and Glenlivet. By 2003, the London-based Diageo controlled 21 percent of the U.S. spirits market, and analysts predicted that its share could reach 25 percent before 2010. Through its Guiness/UDV unit, Diageo produced Guiness Stout, Harp Lager, and Kilkenny Irish beer. Diageo also produced Johnnie Walker Scotch, Tanqueray gin, and Smirnoff vodka. The company pushed hard to air liquor advertisements on U.S. television—a policy that has been taboo since 1946. In 2004, Diageo reported total sales of US$16.1 billion.

SCOTTISH & NEWCASTLE PLC

Founded in 1749, Scottish & Newcastle was the biggest beer producer in the United Kingdom and Europe. Its top brands included Courage, John Smith's, Kornenbourg, McEwan's, Newcastle, and Theakston's. It also produced licensed beers. In 1999, Scottish & Newcastle Retail acquired a chain of pubs, restaurants, and lodges that sold its brands. Most of these establishments were sold off by the end of 2001, placing the company in a highly favorable position as consolidation accelerated in Europe. In 2000, Scottish & Newcastle announced partnerships with two leading European beer companies, the French Group-Danone and Sociedade Central de Cervejas in Portugal. In 2002, Scottish & Newcastle acquired Finland's leading beverage company, Hartwell, which opened additional markets in Russia, Ukraine, Kazakhstan, Lithuania, Latvia, and Estonia. Further expansion occurred in 2004 when Scottish & Newcastle acquired a 19.5 percent interest in Chinese brewer Changqing Brewery Company. Along with Heineken, major competitors included Interbrew and Guinness/UDV. In 2004 Scottish & Newcastle posted sales of US$8.5 billion.

CARLSBERG A/S

Carlsberg Breweries, a 60 percent owned subsidiary of Denmark-based Carlsberg A/S, was the fifth largest beer producer by volume worldwide. The firm was Denmark's top brewer, but 90 percent of production was sold in some 150 countries. Brands included Carlsberg and Tuborg, as well as many regional beers. In 2001, Carlsberg and Orkla of Norway, which owned 40 percent of Carlsberg Breweries, brought together their beer operations and planned to expand further into Asia and Europe. Major competition for Carlsberg came from Heineken, Anheuser-Busch, and Scottish & Newcastle. In addition to its brewing operations, Carlsberg operated the Carlsberg Research Center, which included 80 beer-brewing laboratories. In 2004 the company bought out Swedish firm Orkla's 40 percent interest in Carlsberg Breweries and in Holsten-Brauerei, a German brewery. Carlsberg reported total sales in 2004 of US$6.5 billion.

SAPPORO HOLDINGS LTD.

Sapporo ranked third in Japan in both the beer and wine markets. Beer brands included the premium Yebisu, the Black Label flagship offering, and Brau, a low malt brew. Sapporo also had success with The Winter's Tale, the first limited run, seasonal brew in the Japanese beer market. The company also had a distribution agreement with Guinness to sell its beer in Japan. Wine holdings included the Ureshii and Uogashi brands as well as the Okayama and Katsunuma wineries. Other businesses included ownership of more than two hundred beer halls and eating establishments. Competition came from the top two beer producers in Japan, Asahi and Kirin, as well as from Suntory. In 2004, Sapporo posted sales of US$4.8 billion.

E. & J. GALLO WINERY

Gallo is one of the biggest wine producers worldwide. Along with making approximately 30 percent of the wine consumed in the United States, Gallo is also the country's top wine exporter. While the company has made much of its fortune on inexpensive brands such as Thunderbird, Carlo Rossi, and Gallo, it has also seen success in the premium wine market with its Gossamer Bay and Turning Leaf offerings. Owned by the Gallo family, the winery holds more than 3,000 acres in Sonoma County, California. The vintner also produces its own bottles and labels. Gallo is also an importer and seller of Ecco Domani, an Italian wine, and is a top brandy producer as well. Major competitors include Robert Mondavi, Beringer Blass, and Constellation Brands. Gallo enjoyed a 50 percent growth in sales in 2004, boosting revenues that year to an estimated US$3 billion.

MAJOR COUNTRIES IN THE INDUSTRY

THE UNITED STATES

Long the world's dominant beer industry, the United States slipped behind China in terms of production in 2002. The year 2003 saw the United States producing an estimated 6.2 billion gallons of beer, according to *Modern Brewery Age.* Exports went to more than one hundred countries worldwide. In 2001 ,Mexico imported the most beer by gallons from the United States. Hong Kong came second, followed by Canada and Japan. Microbreweries and craft breweries continued to enjoy particularly strong performances. The Association of Brewers reported growth in this segment of 3.4 percent in 2003 and 7 percent in 2004. Total annual retail sales for the U.S. craft beer industry in 2004 exceeded US$3.7 billion. Though beer remained the most popular alcoholic beverage in the United States in the early 2000s, growth in this market slowed substantially. As consumption of wine increased and as the spirits industry invested heavily in advertising, beer's share of U.S. alcoholic drinks sales fell 3 percent from 1995 to 2003. In response to tepid growth in domestic beer consumption, major brewers announced significant increases in promotions in 2003 and 2004.

In 2000, the United States was ranked as the fourth largest wine producer worldwide in terms of vineyard area, with 880,880 acres. Some analysts predicted that the country's wine exports, valued at US$548 million in 2001, could increase to US$914 million by 2005. Domestic consumption was also poised for growth. *Wine Spectator* reported the results of a study by Vinexpo, which indicated that by 2005, the average U.S. wine drinker would consume approximately three more bottles of wine annually on average than the person did in 2001. This adds up to about 17 bottles per year, compared to 14 bottles on average consumed in 2001. Not only has volume increased, but American consumers are buying more expensive wines as well. By the year ending in March, 2005, dollar sales of wines had risen 7 percent over the previous year. According to industry analyst Jon Fredrikson, the United States was poised to become the largest wine consuming country in the world by 2010, though it was not expected to rank among the leaders in per capita consumption.

CHINA

The fastest growing beer market in the world by 2004, China increased beer production by 25 percent annually through the 1990s. In 2002 it surpassed the United States in beer output, producing a total of 239 hectoliters. By 2004, beer production reached 29.1 million metric tons, a 15.2 percent increase from the previous year. As of 2004, China was the second largest global market for beer, with total sales rising by 85.99 percent since 1996. Significant potential existed for further growth through 2010, since per capita consumption—about 5 gallons per year—remained relatively low but was expected to rise with improving income levels. Analysts considered it likely that China's beer market would be the largest in the world by 2010. China's entry into the World Trade Organization spurred the country to improve quality and develop new products in the alcoholic beverage industry to attract overseas customers. In the Chinese alcoholic beverage industry, the beer sector was the strongest. According to *Global Sources,* by 2001 the country had approximately 530 breweries. Two-thirds of the segment was made up of small-scale enterprises with yearly output of below 50,000 tons each. The top two Chinese beer brands were Yanjing (headquartered in Beijing) and Tsingtao (hailing from Shandong). In 2000, Yanjing's total output was valued at US$550 million; Tsingtao was ahead with US$716 million. By 2002, China's fragmented market had attracted the interest of big international players like Anheuser-Busch, which that year increased its shares in Tsingtao from 4.5 to 27 percent. In 2004, Anheuser-Busch went on to acquire Harbin, one of the three most popular brands in China, for US$757 million. That same year, Scottish & Newcastle purchased a 19.5 percent interest in Chongqing Breweries. Analysts expected continued rapid consolidation in the sector through the remainder of the decade.

Chinese wine-making traditions go back more than two thousand years, and in 2001 China had approximately 300 makers of wine. Eighty percent of the country's wine output was from the Shandong, Beijing, Hebei, Anhui, Henan, and Tianjing areas. China has exported its wine to more than ten countries, including the United States, Japan, Germany, Belgium, Australia, Russia, Malaysia and Korea. One of the largest wine exporters has been Tonghua Grape Wine Stock Co. Ltd., which specializes in wine made from grapes grown in Jilin Province's Changbai Mountain. Wine output from China was expected to reach 500,000 tons by 2005. China's liquor market, however, experienced a decline at the end of the 1990s. In 2000, the country produced 5.02 million tons, 14 percent less than the previous year's output. Whiskey also rose in popularity in China, which imported only about US$1.9 million of Scotch in 1999 but more than US$47.8 million in 2004.

JAPAN

While Japan had a growing liquor market for much of the 1980s, consumption rates leveled off or declined in the 1990s as the Japanese economy went into recession. That recession continued throughout the 1990s, leading to decreased demand for liquor. One of the most popular liquors was bourbon, consumption of which grew at a 50 percent annual clip in the late 1980s before leveling off or declining in the early to mid-1990s. Most alcohol consumption in Japan has historically been on-premise, either in bars or restaurants. As on-premise consumption rates fell in the early to mid-1990s, however, beverage alcohol marketers began to promote at-home consumption. Another popular liquor was a traditional product, shochu. Consumption of this liquor, which has an alcohol content ranging from 36 to 25 percent compared with 40 percent for most spirits, grew steadily from 1995 to 2001 and remains on the rise. Once thought of as a drink for the working classes, shochu benefited from savvy packaging and marketing campaigns, and has emerged as a top choice for sophisticated drinkers in Japan's trendy nightclubs.

Japan was also a major beer market. Happoshu, a low malt beverage that has a similar taste and appearance to regular beer but is taxed at a lower rate, continued to outsell traditional beer in the first part of 2002. *Reuters Business* reported that shipments of traditional beer decreased by 14.7 percent in March of 2002 compared to figures in 2001. Beer shipments totaled 333,199 kilolitres, declining for the twenty-fourth month in a row, while happoshu shipments rose for the seventieth month in a row. However, a possible tax increase was expected to eliminate happoshu's advantage over traditional beer. The overall beer sector showed decreasing shipments, declining by 3.1 percent in March 2002 and by 8 percent in 2003. The sluggish beer market and stiff competition in the happoshu market resulted in only slight profit margins.

RUSSIA

Russians remained the world leaders in consumption of alcohol and in the beginning of the twenty-first century were consuming 16 quarts of pure alcohol annually. Despite the country's economic turmoil, Russia remained the world's largest vodka market into the twenty-first century. However, according to the *Christian Science Monitor,* sales of vodka decreased, and production was down 9 percent in 2000. In the same year production of alcohol was responsible for US$3.2 billion in revenue for Russia, more than 5 percent of the state's total income. In August 2000, Russia's president Vladimir Putin signed into law a new system of excise stamps to help the alcohol industry stem the tide of increased bootlegging, which has made up from 40 to 70 percent of the country's alcohol market. However, confusion over the new regulations resulted in the shutdown of a number of the country's legal vodka producers and, ironically, ensured a golden opportunity for the nation's bootleggers. In 2002, Russia re-instituted its government monopoly on the manufacture of leading vodka brands, including Stolichnaya and Moskovskaya. It also acted to restrict alcohol imports in order to create fair trading conditions.

Vodka remains the dominant alcoholic drink in Russia, accounting for about 70 percent of domestic sales. But new products began to play a larger role in the market. According to *World Food Moscow 2002,* Russian production of beer in 2000 increased by 20 percent over 1999 statistics, and by the end of 2001, the Russian beer market was worth approximately US$5 billion per year, with annual production at between 3.5 and 3.7 billion liters. Beer is appealing increasingly to the under-30 market, according to a BBC report, and showed prospects for vigorous growth through the early 2000s. Indeed, beer consumption grew by more than 10 percent annually between 1996 and 2001, and rose by 11.4 percent in 2002. Vodka's primacy among Russian alcoholic beverage consumers was also challenged by a new nonalcoholic beer called Baltika No. 0, which debuted in 2001. It advertised itself as a health-conscious alternative to vodka and became especially popular as Russians became more aware of the dangers of alcoholism. In 2000, there were 34,000 deaths from alcohol poisoning, an increase of 13.7 percent over figures in 1999. The mortality figure worsened in 2002, exceeding 40,000 that year. Analysts attributed 40 percent of these deaths to illegally manufactured spirits.

FURTHER READING

Anderlini, Jamil. "Beer Run on China." *Asia Times,* 22 March 2005.

"Asahhi To Release '3rd Category Beer' Wednesday." *Kyodo News,* 19 April 2005. Available from jttp://www.beverageworld.com.

Brandes, Richard. "Liquor Holds Its Breath as Economy Teeters." *Beverage Industry,* (May 2001): 12.

Brandes, Richard. "Stateways Identifies the Fastest-Growing Brands of Wines and Spirits in the Beverage Alcohol Industry." Adams Beverage Group, 2005. Available from http://www.beveragenet.net.

"Brewers Association Reports Craft Beer Production Grows 7 Percent." 2 February March 2005. Available from www.beertown.org.

"China's Beer Market: Still Room for Investment." *Food Production Daily,* 8 June 2004. Available from http://www.foodproductiondaily.com.

Chura, Hillary and Kate MacArthur. "Leveling the Playing Field: Diageo Bucks Convention, Markets Spirits Like Soda." *Advertising Age,* 13 October 2003.

Ciolett, Jeff. "A New Global Giant Is Born." *Beverage World,* 15 March 2004.

Cline, Harry. "U.S.Expected to be No.1 Wine Market." *Western Farm Press,* 12 February 2005. Available from http://westernfarmpress.com/.

"Convergence Starts to Show in Beer Markets." *Beverage Daily,* 12 January 2005. Available from http://www.beveragedaily.com.

Echikson, William. "Wine War." *BusinessWeek Online,* 3 September 2001. Available from www.businessweek.com.

Gaffney, Jacob. "U.S. Wine Consumption to Increase Into 2005, Report Shows." *Wine Spectator,* 5 February 2001. Available from www.winespectator.com.

"Global Beer: Consolidation Continues." *Beverage World,* 15 February 2004. Available from http://www.beverageworld.com.

"Japanese Beer Shipments Slump Again in March" *Reuters Business,* 10 April 2002. Available from biz.yahoo.com.

Henley, Jon. "France's Wine Industry in Decline." *Guardian,* 24 February 2004. Available from www.guardian.co.uk.

"Here's to Shochu." *Trends in Japan,* 24 September 2003. Available from http://www.web-japan.org.

"Malt Whiskey Exports Soar in Solid Year for Scotch." The Scotch Whiskey Association, 22 March 2005. Available from http://www.sctoch-whiskey.org.uk.

McGraw-Hill, Department of Commerce, and International Trade Administration. *U.S. Industry and Trade Outlook 2000.* New York: McGraw-Hill, 2000.

"Makers Shift to Nutritious, Low-Alcohol Drinks," 21 February 2002. Available from www.globalsources.com.

Nigro, Diana. "United States Ranks as the World's Fourth-Largest Wine Producer" *Wine Spectator,* 11 April 2002. Available from: www.winespectator.com.

Peterson, Scott. "In the Land of Vodka, A Boom in Alcohol-Free Beer." *The Christian Science Monitor,* 13 June 2001. Available from www.csmonitor.com.

Phillips, Kevin. "China's Beer Market Anything But Fragile." *Beverage Daily,* 6 April 2004. Available from http://www.beveragedaily.com.

"Proposed Transaction Between SAB and Phillip Morris Regarding Miller," 30 May 2002. Available from www.sab.co.za/index.asp.

"What's Tasteless but Very Expensive (Vodka)." *Wall Street Journal,* (2 April 1998): B1.

"Russia: Drunkenness a Killer as State Moves to Impose Spirit Monopoly." Channel One TV, Moscow, 3 May 2003. Available from http://www.cdi.org.

"Russian Vodka Faces Flood of Beer." BBC News, 20 June 2002. Available from news.bbc.co.uk.

"Two Percent a Year Growth for Alcoholic Drinks Worldwide." Zenith International, 2003. Available from www.zenithinternational.com.

U.S. Department of Agriculture, Foreign Agricultural Service. "2003 Wine Production Lowest in 10 Years." *Gain Report: European Union: Wine.* 11 October 2003. Available from www.fas.usda.gov.

U.S. Department of Commerce, Bureau of the Census. "U.S. Beer Exports," January 2003. Available from www.beerinstitute.org.

"Wine Prices Rebounding." *Wine Business Insider,* 18 April 2005. Available from http://www.winebusiness.com.

Wiseman, Paul and William M. Welch. "Senate Votes to Lower Drunken Driving Limit." *USA Today,* (5 March 1998): 11A.

"World Beer Production 2000-2003." *Modern Brewery Age,* 8 December 2003.

World Food Moscow 2002. Available from www.ite-exhibitions.com.

Zwick, Steve. "German Beer Goes Flat." *Time Europe,* 11 August 2003.

SIC 2043

NAICS 311230

CEREAL PRODUCTS

Cereal makers around the world manufacture hot and cold breakfast foods and related products from milling and processing various grains.

INDUSTRY SNAPSHOT

First formulated as a "health food" by Americans, ready-to-eat (RTE) cereals have grown into a multibillion-dollar global business. According to an AC Nielsen study, 95 percent of American households purchase ready-to-eat cereals. *Progressive Grocer* reported in 2007 that there are more than 250 types of breakfast cereals and U.S. consumers purchase almost 3 million packages annually.

Kellogg Company, a pioneer in the business, has historically led the industry and remained the number one U.S. breakfast cereal company in 2006 with 33.1 percent of the market and sales of US$1.89 billion. Close behind was General Mills, which garnered US$1.68 billion and held 26.6 percent of the market. Kraft Inc., which owns the Post and Nabisco labels, came in third with US$806.7 million, and Quaker fell to fifth place with US$374.9, behind private label brands, which in 2003 had held only 10 percent of the market. In 2006, private label brands slid into the number four spot with US$536.8 million in sales and a 12.9 percent market share. Other branded cereal manufacturers held smaller shares of the global market. Of the top five, only Kellogg and private label brands showed an increase in sales from the previous year, and even these were minimal.

However, after years of flat performance of ready-to-eat (RTE) cereals in the late 1990s and early 2000s (according to research firm Mintel International, sales of RTE cereals grew only 1 percent annually between 1998 and 2003, when the market was valued at about US$9 billion) sales finally started to pick up in the mid-2000s, due in part to the efforts of the industry to address Americans' increasing health concerns. With more products containing whole grain and less sugar, the industry was hoping to see a revival in the late 2000s.

Cereal products offer taste profiles that appeal to a wide variety of consumers of all ages in many different markets. Their convenience makes them a frequent choice in time-pressured households, a significant fact as the middle class grows in Asia and South America. RTE cereals also have a positive nutritional image, and some cereals can contribute to the type of low fat, high fiber diet recommended by medical authorities throughout the world. Global growth prospects for the RTE cereal market were further enhanced by the successful conclusion of the Uruguay Round of the General Agreement on Tariffs and Trade (GATT) and the signing of the North American Free Trade Agreement (NAFTA) in 1994. Growing political stability and economic development in major markets around the world have also helped the cereal industry.

For the most part, English-speaking countries are the high volume consumers of RTE cereals. For example, cereal consumption in non-English markets in the mid-1990s was about 25 percent of English-speaking markets. In the early 2000s, Middle Eastern markets were just emerging, with Saudi Arabians consuming over 5,000 metric tons annually, over half of which was supplied by U.S. cereal producers. Per capita consumption of RTE cereal in France was just 1.8 pounds in the mid-1990s, while per capita consumption in England was 13.3 pounds. This led Kellogg and other cereal manufacturers to invest heavily in raising consumption in continental Europe. With an educated population and modern grocery distribution system, the European market held significant growth potential as its citizens moved away from traditional breakfasts. Latin America also held promise. Mexico represented the world's third-largest breakfast cereal market in dollar terms in 2003. In Chile, where RTE cereals were one of the fastest growing grocery products, imports soared almost 50 percent from 1996 to 1998.

BACKGROUND AND DEVELOPMENT

RTE cereals were first developed in the United States in the late nineteenth century. These cereals—in the form of flakes, puffs, shreds, biscuits, and granules—were the first packaged convenience food, a category that exploded in popularity in the twentieth century.

RTE cereals were an outgrowth of the U.S. vegetarian/health foods movement of the nineteenth century. These cereals developed from a succession of new food products, which included graham crackers, invented in 1829 by Sylvester Graham; Granula (later Grape Nuts), developed by James Jackson of the Jackson Sanitarium; and Shredded Wheat, invented by Henry Perky in 1893.

Battle Creek, Michigan, was the center of the RTE cereal industry from the late 1800s throughout the twentieth century. The Eastern Health Reform Institute was founded in Battle Creek by the Seventh Day Adventist Church in 1866. The institute, later renamed the Battle Creek sanitarium, came under the leadership of John H. Kellogg in 1876. Kellogg, a physician, surgeon, and inventor, advocated the use of cereal grain foods that he had developed. Kellogg was joined at the sanitarium by his brother, W. K. Kellogg. A patient at the sanitarium, Charles W. Post, was inspired to found the Postum Cereal Company in Battle Creek in 1897. The company sold Postum, a hot cereal beverage, and Grape-Nuts cereal. The Postum Cereal Company became General Foods Corp. in 1929. General Foods by the early 2000s was part of Kraft Foods Inc., which continued to produce Post cereals. W. K. Kellogg left his brother John and the sanitarium in 1906 to form the Kellogg Company, also based in Battle Creek. The RTE cereal industry soon grew and helped create a burgeoning market for other packaged foods as well.

General Mills began as the Washburn Crosby Company, entering the RTE cereal market in the 1920s. Its Wheaties cereal was developed in 1924. Crispy Corn Kix joined the General Mills lineup in 1937, and Cheerioats (subsequently Cheerios) became the first RTE oat cereal in 1941. The Quaker Oats Company, another important cereal producer, was founded in 1873 as the North Star Oatmeal Mill in Cedar Rapids, Iowa. North Star reorganized with other companies to form the Quaker Oats Company in 1901.

During the 1940s, U.S. cereal makers improved their methods of puffing cereal products. During the first decade of the twentieth century, the puffing process was accomplished by shooting grains from cannons. Characteristically, the cereal industry incorporated this into advertising, with one cereal boasting that it was "shot from guns."

In the twentieth century, RTE cereals were introduced to other English-speaking countries, largely by the Kellogg Company. Domestic competitors developed in these new markets and made incremental progress in taking market share from Kellogg. However, they still had a long way to go. Kellogg had an early start in the world market by entering Canada in the 1910s, Australia in the 1920s, the United Kingdom in the 1930s, and South Africa in the 1940s. In the 1950s, Kellogg entered its first non-English speaking market, Mexico, as well as many other countries in the following three decades.

While RTE cereals began as health foods, in the 1950s the industry developed high-calorie, pre-sweetened cereals aimed at the children's market. Later developments included Total, a highly enriched vitamin cereal, which was developed in 1961. The RTE cereal business was subject to various nutritional fads in the 1980s and 1990s, as specific "healthy" ingredients became known, promoted, and then controversial. For example, the RTE cereal industry latched onto oat bran in the 1980s, which was touted as a way to reduce cholesterol. Products specifically labeled "oat bran" sold at a US$34.9 million rate in the United States in 1987, jumped to US$105.2 million in 1988, and peaked at US$328.2 million in 1989. Scientific studies then emerged challenging the ability of oat bran to lower cholesterol levels, leading to the demise of many oat bran products. However, a good number of the oat-based cereals introduced in this era survived. Also, research in the mid-1990s confirmed the positive health benefits of oat bran, which helped spur sales of oat-based products once again. As the RTE cereal market experienced flat or near-flat growth in the early 2000s, Kellogg and others increased promotion of more portable breakfasts, such as cereal bars and RTE cereal/milk combinations.

Heavy promotion was a characteristic of the RTE cereal industry since its beginning. Advertising, premiums, coupons, rebates, and buy-one-get-one-free deals were all used to promote RTE cereals. In fact, of the US$3.26 cost of a box of Honey Nut cereal in the mid-1990s, just 39 cents reflected the cost of the cereal; 97 cents went to its marketing and advertising.

At the beginning of the twenty-first century, the cereal market was characterized by pricing and marketing wars in the United States, sluggish growth in established markets such as North America and the United Kingdom, and strong sales growth in low per-capita consumption markets such as continental Europe.

In the spring of 1996, Kraft Foods initiated an industry price war when it instituted a 20 percent price cut in its Post brand cereal line. Post experienced a significant gain in volume through August 1996, when other industry players responded with similar price cuts. The price cuts seriously damaged the industry's profits in 1996, and only partial recovery in profits was achieved in 1997.

Ironically, despite the lower prices, volume did not increase markedly. As a result, total U.S. dollar sales of RTE cereals dropped to about US$7.2 billion in 1997, from as high as US$8.5 billion a year earlier, according to a report in the *Wall Street Journal.* The 2001 sales volume increased only slightly to US$7.4 billion. Even with cereal prices falling, consumers switched to lower-priced bagged cereals or more "portable" breakfast foods, such as cereal bars and bagels.

Minneapolis-based General Mills' move in 2000 to merge with cross-town rival Pillsbury allowed it to double international operations and move the new company to the third slot in North American food sales and fifth in worldwide food sales. A ten-year joint venture with Nestle to form Cereal Partners Worldwide (CPW) steadily increased its non-North American RTE market share through the 1990s—to a six percent growth in 2001—in a market still dominated by Kellogg. For its part, Kellogg had introduced several successful new line extensions, including Smart Start in early 1998 and runaway hit Special K Red Berries in 2000.

Chicago-based Quaker Oats in the late 1990s successfully introduced a line of low- priced bagged, rather than boxed, cereal. In 1997 the company enjoyed dramatic volume and share gains from the bagged cereal line. While most of the volume gains in the line were said to come from gaining new outlets for the product line and from new products in the line, growth also came from established products and accounts. The bagged cereal product line grew faster than the industry average through the late 1990s, but Quaker saw 2000 sales drop 5 percent, the first negative year since its 1997 introduction of bagged cereal. Quaker Oats was acquired late in 2001 by snack food giant Pepsico. Quaker's 2000 sales were US$5 billion, including US$690 million of Quaker's RTE cereal share. Its RTE sales were down 5 percent from 1999. Quaker held the top slot in the hot cereal market at US$515 million, which was a 6 percent increase. The acquisition also brought Pepsico the top-selling sports beverage brand worldwide, Gatorade, as well as a larger market share of Quaker's healthier snacks.

NUTRACEUTICALS

The development in the 1990s of "nutraceuticals," or foods that go beyond the "low-fat, low-sodium" profiles and are marketed as being able to prevent specific diseases, was a continuation of the industry's venture into providing healthier products. Some cereal products were ideally suited to this trend since grains, their primary ingredient, have been found to have several health-enhancing properties.

Kellogg maintained a functional foods division in order to develop and market new nutraceutical products. In early 1998 Kellogg expanded its Healthy Choice cereal line, licensed from ConAgra Inc., by converting two existing brands, Low-Fat Granola and Mueslix, to the Healthy Choice label. The move was said to be an attempt to conserve marketing dollars and rejuvenate the brands, which had seen sharp sales declines. Kellogg already had three Healthy Choice cereals and discontinued one of them, golden Multi-Grain Flakes, as part of the reorganization.

All major cereal producers took advantage of the U.S. Food and Drug Administration's (FDA) 1997 approval of limited health claims for oat bran. Quaker had enriched many of its products with a soluble, oat-based fat substitute, which, in addition to oatmeal's well-known ability to lower total cholesterol, replaced fat content. In early 1998, the FDA ruled that more breakfast cereals and dietary supplements could claim to reduce the risk of heart disease. Products containing soluble fiber from psyllium seed husks could claim to reduce heart disease risks, the FDA ruled, if they are consumed as part of a diet low in saturated fat and cholesterol. Kellogg's Bran Buds cereal contained soluble fiber from psyllium husks, which are cultivated mostly in India.

However, the Center for Science in the Public Interest (CSPI), a nutrition-focused consumer group, said the FDA's action simply encouraged a cereal marketing fad and failed to underscore the underlying dietary habits, such as eating fresh fruits and vegetables, that collectively produced the touted health benefits.

PRIVATE LABEL CHALLENGE

Private label products, also known as store brands, have long been a part of the RTE cereal market. They gained share in the early 1990s as many consumers in North America and Europe responded to a global recession by increasing their purchases of less costly cereal products.

The quality and packaging of private label RTE cereals improved markedly in the 1980s and early 1990s. As a result, private label cereals gained new appeal. In the United States, both the Malt-O-Meal Company and Kraft made high-quality RTE cereals under the brand name of major retailers. In Europe, and especially the United Kingdom, where private labels are known as stores' "own labels," the private label challenge was even more of a threat, as powerful retailers such as J. Sainsbury in the United Kingdom were successful in promoting and stocking their own brands.

While this trend was less prevalent in the United States, one U.S. chain, Save-A-Lot, a unit of the major Minneapolis-based food distributor Supervalu Inc., was successful in specializing in private label brands. While branded products continued to account for about 80 percent of supermarket sales in the United States, at Save-A-Lot, 85 percent of sales came from private label items.

Some major brand manufacturers began using legal weapons against private label products in the 1990s. In Europe, Irish grocery chain Dunnes Stores launched a private label brand, Crispy Rice Pops, in the fall of 1994. Kellogg sued Dunnes, charging an infringement of its registered trademarks, which include Pop!, Pop, and Pops. Kellogg was particularly sensitive about the Irish market since per-capita consumption there was three times higher than in continental Europe.

Not all the major brands were at war with private label products, however. In addition to making its own brands in Europe, CPW was quietly manufacturing private label products for major European supermarket chains.

Ultimately, the appeal of private label cereals was limited since it depended on the marketing and promotion activity of national brands to create an identity for the category. Also, improving economic conditions usually lessened private labels' appeal. In the mid to late 1990s, when they cut prices, major manufacturers reduced the price difference between their products and private label products.

CURRENT CONDITIONS

At the start of the twenty-first century, following trends in consumer health consciousness and widespread alarms over obesity, brands labeled "organic" and cereal brands containing healthier ingredients saw increasingly strong sales in the industry. Private label brands and organic brands saw the biggest growth, while traditional companies such as Kellogg and General Mills struggled to find ways to adapt to Americans' changing preferences. To capture a share of the organic sector, General Mills launched four new organic cereals through its Cascadian Farms brand. Kellogg entered the segment with its acquisition of Kashi in 2000 and subsequently introduced Kashi Apple Pie Pillows and Kashi Good Friends

Cinna-Raisin Crunch. In 2003, organic brands accounted for about US$55 million of the total RTE cereal market and the organic brand cereal market reached about US$250 million in sales.

Nature's Path, which marketed 60 kinds of breakfast cereal, was the leading organic brand, generating sales of about US$82.2 million in 2006. This figure showed a significant increase from 2001, when sales totaled only US$20 million. Two of its brands, Nature's Path and EnviroKidz, together were the top-selling USDA Organic-certified breakfast cereal in U.S. natural food supermarkets. In 2002 the company also added flaxseed to its Hemp Plus Granola. Flaxseed is another health ingredient found in RTE cereals and advertised as a good source of omega-3 fatty acids, which promotes cardiac health.

Alarming rates of obesity in children and adults, which increases the risks of heart disease, diabetes, cancer, and many other illnesses, raised concern throughout the world and impacted the industry. Diets high in simple carbohydrates, sugar, fat, and salt, including several breakfast cereal brands, were implicated in the trend toward excessive weight gain. A British consumer group in 2004 found that 9 out of 28 cereals marketed to children contained 40 percent sugar, and 18 brands were high in salt. To combat the rise in obesity, health officials and consumer advocates began pressuring food manufacturers to reduce calories in their products.

In response, several breakfast cereal companies announced changes to their children's brands. In 2004, Kellogg introduced versions of Frosted Flakes and Froot Loops containing one third less sugar. In 2005 the company introduced Tiger Power, a whole-grain kids' product, and Smart Start Healthy Heart, aimed at adults, touting it as "the only nationally distributed cereal with ingredients that can help lower blood pressure and cholesterol." General Mills cut the sugar content in Trix, Cinnamon Toast Crunch, and Cocoa Puffs by 75 percent. General Mills also announced that it would increase the whole grain content of selected children's brands.

Advertising of sugary foods to children, too, came under attack. In the United States, where 15 percent of children ages 6 to 19 and 10 percent of those ages 2 to 5 are obese, future legislation allowing broad regulation of advertising to children via television, the Internet, and other media was a distinct possibility. The food industry opposed government regulation and argued that companies should be allowed to regulate themselves. Kraft, for instance, "now only runs commercials featuring healthy foods such as sugar-free drinks . . . and whole-grain products," according to a *Boston Globe* report. At the same time, industry leaders touted cereal as a wise choice for weight and health conscious consumers. Kellogg introduced its "Kellogg's Special K 2-Week Challenge" diet, which claimed that participants could lose up to 6 pounds while following dietary guidelines that included meals with Special K. Kellogg also cited studies showing that "children who eat breakfast—and cereal in particular—have a lower body mass index (a measure of fatness). Cereal eaters also have lower fat and cholesterol intakes compared to people who don't eat cereal."

In France, public anti-obesity campaigns stressing the importance of eating a healthy breakfast contributed to substantial growth in sales of RTE cereals. According to *NutraIngredients.com,* the French market for healthy breakfast cereals grew by 20.4 percent from 2003 to 2004. Ironically, however, the greatest growth was in chocolate brands aimed at children, which rose by 35.7 percent. The market for all children's sugary brands grew by more than 50 percent.

DIVERSIFICATION

General Mills began a marketing trend in 2001 with CD-ROM giveaways in boxes of several of its most popular brands. Partnering with toymaker Hasbro and similar companies, the company experienced dramatic growth, in part because the games are full versions of well-known classics, not demos. Following Kellogg's success with its Special K Red Berries, General Mills launched two kinds of Berry Burst Cheerios—strawberry and "Triple Berry," which featured strawberries, blueberries, and raspberries.

In 2001, General Mills broke new promotional ground by opening its own retail store in the Mall of America in Minneapolis, Minnesota, which as of the early 2000s annually attracted 43 million international customers. The store provides play areas and gives customers the opportunity to see how cereals are manufactured. General Mills is hoping that the store will boost awareness of its brands and expand its customer base.

General Mills was not the only cereal producer seeking to grow and diversify. Following its 1999 acquisition of Worthington Foods Inc, a leading producer of meat alternatives, Kellogg acquired Illinois-based Keebler Foods in March 2001 for US$4.5 billion. The move strengthened Kellogg's position in the cookie and cracker market and provided a larger presence on U.S. supermarket shelves by inheriting Keebler's strong brand recognition.

In 2002 the company entered a global relationship with Disney, creating cereals tied to Disney movie releases such as *Finding Nemo, Lilo and Stitch,* and *The Incredibles.* Kellogg also boosted its health-conscious profile, announcing its Healthy Beginnings Health Check program in 2005, which provides consumers at participating stores with free health screening and information.

RESEARCH AND TECHNOLOGY

The beginning of the twenty-first century saw diminishing profits in the RTE cereal market. Furthermore, price cuts and the willingness of the public to buy generic private label brands led to a difficult road in new product introduction. Kellogg's 1998 introduction of its Ensemble line of cholesterol-fighting foods failed after only a year. Its Breakfast Mates cereal/milk combinations struggled early on. General Mills and Kellogg invested heavily in research and development. Eye-catching nuggets, quick-to-market seasonal products, and advances in packaging led to the goal of cereal brand identification.

CHARMED

In 1975 General Mills first changed the contents of its Lucky Charms cereal, long advertised with four kinds of solid-colored candied marshmallows called "marbits." The addition of "blue diamonds" led to a 31 percent increase in sales. Later additions of purple horseshoes and red balloons led to similar increases, which, according to General Mills' former chairman and chief executive Bruce Atwater, resulted in permanent gains in sales.

Food engineers tackled difficult technical manufacturing and production issues, such as producing swirled rather than solid-colored marbits. Such small-sized marbits could not be baked but must be extruded, or squeezed out, through small dies. Multiple colors must be co-extruded at the same rates to achieve the desired design effect, and small dots or faces are even more technically challenging, requiring changes in consistency and micro-precision flow rates.

The ability to change the cereal's composition frequently allowed General Mills to capitalize on current events, such as the Olympics; seasonal changes such as snowmen or mittens; and even Millennium Fever, when many manufacturers introduced number two shapes to go along with their O-shaped cereal. A new manufacturing process developed by J. Rettenmaier, which can create either high or low-absorbent food fibers, is expected to be useful in keeping breakfast cereals crisp after the addition of milk. In addition, because vitamins, minerals, and other nutraceutical substances can have unpalatable tastes and textures, the trend toward fortification of cereals has led manufacturers to explore new ways of enhancing flavor in such products.

WORKFORCE

According to U.S. Census Bureau statistics, about 13,447 people were employed in the breakfast cereal segment of the nation's grain-based foods industry in 2005. Average annual wages were US$48,861. With North American growth in RTE essentially flat from about 1996 to about 2004, employers were expected to keep layoffs to a minimum through attrition and retirement and anticipated growth in international markets.

INDUSTRY LEADERS

KELLOGG

Founded in 1906, the Kellogg Company has long been the world's market leader in ready-to-eat (RTE) cereals. Kellogg had total sales of almost US$11 billion in 2006, up 7.2 percent from the previous year. Though approximately 80 percent of sales came from RTE cereal in the late 1990s, by the mid-2000s the company was relying increasingly on its snack foods category to generate revenues. Kellogg's share of the U.S. breakfast cereal market fell to around 30 percent in 2000 but recovered the following year and reached about 33 percent in 2003, just ahead of General Mills. Kellogg produces an extensive line of grain-based convenience foods, including toaster pastries, frozen waffles, cereal bars, and bagels; and in 2001 it acquired Keebler Foods, a leading cookie and cracker producer. In 1997 the company opened the W. K. Kellogg Institute for Food and Nutrition Research (WKKI) in Battle Creek, Michigan. This facility brought together Kellogg research and development (R&D) people from 23 nations to generate products for launch in multiple markets.

Kellogg's international RTE cereal volume decreased in 1998 by 2 percent but rebounded in 1999 by 3 percent. Kellogg has seen strong growth in the Asia-Pacific region, particularly in Korea. Growth was also reported in Spain, Venezuela, and Latin America. In 2003, Kellogg saw net sales growth of 3 percent (adjusted for currency conversion) in Europe. The company reported a 1 percent gain in market share for RTE cereals in Britain and a 2.4 percent gain in France. As of 2004, Kellogg had manufacturing facilities in 19 countries and marketed to more than 180 countries worldwide.

Kellogg was the first U.S. company to venture into the international RTE cereal market when it began distributing its products in Canada in 1914. The first Kellogg plant in the United Kingdom opened in 1938, and Kellogg moved onto the European continent in the 1950s. In 1999 the company held 37 percent of the world's RTE cereal market (down from 42 percent in 1994 and 39 percent in 1997). That global share included 31 percent in North America, 40 percent in Europe, 43 percent in the Asia Pacific region, and 60 percent in Latin America. The value of RTE imports in 1998 reached US$5.4 million, with Kellogg and Quaker the primary importers. Kellogg owned the two leading global cereal brands: Kellogg's Corn Flakes and Kellogg's Frosted Flakes. In 1997 it opened a new plant in Thailand, streamlined its European cereal infrastructure, and purchased cereal businesses in Ecuador and Brazil.

GENERAL MILLS

As of 2004, General Mills was Kellogg's closest competitor. It took over the number one spot in the North American market from perennial rival Kellogg in 1999, capturing a 32 percent share of the cereal market compared with 31 percent for Kellogg. Though its market share held steady, however, General Mills slipped back to number two after Kellogg gained a 33 percent share in 2003. General Mills' consumer foods division included familiar brands such as Wheaties, Chex, Cheerios, Gold Medal Flour, Betty Crocker mixes, Hamburger Helper, and Yoplait and Columbo yogurts. General Mills' 2006 sales were US$11.6 billion, up 3.5 percent from 2005. July 2000 saw the acquisition of its cross-town rival Pillsbury for US$10 billion. Pillsbury's parent company, European giant Diageo, acquired one-third of General Mills. The deal made General Mills the third largest food company in the United States and the fifth largest worldwide, and brought a stronger international presence to the General Mills mix. The largest gains in the acquisition might prove to be distribution and supply chain efficiencies and new international markets for General Mills. This deal followed only three years after the General Mills acquisition of Ralcorp Holdings Inc., including Chex cereals and Chex Mix snacks.

KRAFT

Kraft Foods and Kraft Foods International, previously units of Philip Morris Companies but spun off in 2007, together comprise the second largest food company in the world and the largest in the United States. Post brands include Shredded Wheat, Grape Nuts, Honey Bunches of Oats, Blueberry Morning, Alpha-Bits, Waffle Crisp, and Great

Grains. In 2005 Kraft announced its "Post Healthy Classics 3-Step Plan," a weight-loss program featuring singer Naomi Judd. The company claimed that the program, which advocated daily servings of Post Grape Nuts, Raisin Bran, or Shredded Wheat, could help people lose an average of 10 pounds. Also that year, the company announced the debut of several products, including cereal, under the South Beach Diet brand, associated with the popular diet of the same name. Kraft markets its products in 155 countries, and total sales in 2006 equaled US$34.5 billion. Seven of Kraft's brands (Jacobs, Kraft, Milka, Nabisco, Oscar Mayer, Philadelphia, and Post) bring in annual revenues of US$1 billion; more than 50 other brands net US$100 million per year.

QUAKER

Quaker Oats Co., which merged with PepsiCo in 2001, was an early 2000s active player in several world RTE cereal markets. Its leading brand, Cap'n Crunch, was the top-selling pre-sweetened children's brand in the United States in 2004. Within the much smaller hot cereal segment, Quaker held over 60 percent of the U.S. market in 2001 and remained the leader in 2004. In addition to cereal products, Quaker Oats produced several other food products, including pasta (Pasta Roni), rice (Rice-A-Roni), and side dishes (Near East).

FURTHER READING

Adwan, Lyla. "Where Next for Cereals?" *Euromonitor,* 19 June 2003. Available from www.euromonitor.com.

Analysis: Cereal Makers Hoping to Sweeten Market with Healthy Options." *Marketing Week,* 6 July 2006.

"Breakfast Foods—Ready-to-Eat Cereal: Industry Overview." *Progressive Grocer,* 15 November 2006.

Cereal Bars Lead the Way to Healthy Sales." *Candy Business,* November-December 2006.

Food and Agricultural Organization. "Production of Cereals and Share in World," *Statistical Yearbook, 2004.* Available from www.fao.org.

General Mills Annual Report. Minneapolis, MN: General Mills, 2004.

"General Mills Revealed Plans to Promote the AD Council's Coalition for Healthy Children Message of Nutritional Balance, Portion Control and Physical Activity." *The Food Institute Report,* 12 February 2007.

Gregory, Helen. "They're Rising and Shining." *Grocer,* 20 January 2007.

"Health Driving French Cereal Market." *Nutraingredients.com,* 7 December 2004. Available from www.nutraingredients.com.

"Hoover's Company Capsules." *Hoover's Online,* 2007. Available from www.hoovers.com.

Howell, Debbie. "Sugary Cereals Sales go a Bit Soggy; Cereals Touting Nutrition are Earning Their Place on the Breakfast Table." *DNS Retailing Today,* 8 September 2003.

Howell, Debbie. "Wellness-marketed Cereals Fatten Profits; Ready-to-Eat Bars also Boost Bottom Line." *DNS Retailing Today,* 22 March 2004.

Kellogg Company Annual Report. Battle Creek, MI: 2004.

Kirsche, Michelle L. "Healthy Cereal Choices for Breakfast." *Drug Store News,* 25 October 2004.

Kraft Annual Report, 2004. Available from www.kraft.com.

Lempert, Phil. "Super Bowl: The New Snap, Crackle, and Pop of Product Diversity in the Cereal Aisle Seem to be Working." *Progressive Grocer,* 1 March 2007.

Mishra, Raja. "Push Grows to Limit Food Ads to Children." *Boston Globe,* 18 April 2005.

Pehanich, Mike. "Cereals Run Sweet and Healthy." *Prepared Foods,* March 2003.

"Ready-to-Eat Cereal." *Progressive Grocer,* 1 July 2006.

Reyes, Sonia "What Will Become of the Box?" *Brandweek,* 27 January 2003.

Roberts, William Jr. "A Soggy Cereal Market." *Prepared Foods,* August 2004.

Standaert, Michael. "Quaker Oats: Lumpy Road." Brandfeatures profile. Available from www.brandchannel.com.

"Success Mixed in Organic Cereal Segment." *DSN Retailing Today,* 24 February 2003.

The Asia-Pacific Bakery & Cereals Market to 2006. Datamonitor, 13 March 2003.

U.S. Census Bureau. 2002 Economic Census Industry Series Reports, Manufacturing. Available from www.census.gov.

Wade, Marcia A. "Double-Duty Dietary Fibers." *Prepared Foods,* 1 April 2005. Available from www.preparedfoods.com.

"Watchdog Names Worst 'Obesity' Cereals." *Times* (London, England), 31 March 2004. Available from www.timesonline.co.uk.

"Where Next for Cereals?" *Euromonitor,* 19 June 2003. Available from www.euromonitor.com.

White-Sax, Barbara. "Industry Seeks to Tie Cereal to Healthy Trends." *Drug Store News,* 5 March 2007.

SIC 2095

NAICS 311920

COFFEE, ROASTED

Firms in the world's coffee industry roast, grind, and package coffee beans for retail and commercial sale. Coffee producers may also manufacture specialty coffees and instant coffees in various forms. For additional details on the growing of coffee beans, see **Agricultural Production—Crops.**

INDUSTRY SNAPSHOT

Coffee is the second most widely traded commodity in the world. The global coffee industry enjoyed significant growth through the early 1990s, but in the early 2000s, oversupply and waning demand contributed to market conditions that, according to the *New York Times,* plunged the industry into the most serious crisis in its history.

At the onset of the twenty-first century, the total global coffee retail trade was valued at US$33 billion. Global exports, according to an *Observer* report, were US$10 to US$12 billion per year in the 1990s, and retail sales of coffee contributed some US$30 billion to the world economy. But by 2003, coffee consumption was growing much more slowly than production. In a report from the Foreign Agricultural Service of the United States Department of Agriculture, world coffee consumption for the 2000-2001 crop year (which varies by region, but starts in April, July, or October) was estimated at 111.1 million bags (one bag equals 60 kilograms). But while production grew by about 3 percent, reaching 115 million bags in 2002 and 119.44 million bags in 2003, demand grew by only about 1 percent. As of early 2003, according to the *New York Times,* green coffee prices were at their lowest point since the early 1970s, and, adjusted for inflation, real prices were the lowest in one hundred years. The value of world coffee exports plummeted to only US$4.8 billion. Small and medium-sized producers were the hardest hit; the economies of many coffee-exporting nations were all but destroyed. Taking advantage of extremely deflated prices, roasters and distributors were able to reap hefty profits, with retail sales of coffee worldwide rising to more than US$70 billion in 2002. Niche marketing to consumers of gourmet coffees also enabled large companies to increase prices while keeping costs low.

Prices of the industry's raw material, green coffee beans, are highly volatile and influence the industry's financial performance. In general, when green coffee prices are high, coffee growing is more profitable, and conversely when prices are low, coffee roasters profit. (Relatively few coffee enterprises in the world integrate growing and roasting operations.)

In the early 2000s, four multinational companies accounted for the bulk of coffee sales, but the industry was characterized by intense competition. The global in-home coffee market was controlled by Nestlé SA with 22 percent and Kraft Foods (formerly Philip Morris, which continued to retain part ownership) with 14 percent. Sara Lee Coffee & Tea Worldwide accounted for 6 percent, edging out Proctor and Gamble, which captured 5 percent. More than one third of market share was controlled not by a single, large company but by smaller, specialized coffee roasters.

ORGANIZATION AND STRUCTURE

COFFEE SPECIES

Two species of coffee historically have made up the vast majority of the world's commercial coffee: *Coffea arabica* and *Coffea robusta.* The output of the two main species is divided further by commercial classification due to varying processing methods, altitudes of growth, bean size, bean density, and age—all factors that impact flavor. The London-based International Coffee Organization categorizes the varieties as follows: Colombian milds, which made up 15 percent of the world's coffee production at the beginning of the 2000s; other milds (25 percent of world production); Brazilian and other arabicas (35 percent); and robustas (25 percent).

While arabica beans continued to command the largest market share through the 1990s and early 2000s, the demand for robusta beans increased following the introduction of commercially produced soluble—better known as instant—coffee. The robusta bean's ascendance was fueled by its higher yield of soluble extracts than arabicas during the processing for instant coffee; robustas are also considerably cheaper. According to Richard L. Lucier in *The International Political Economy of Coffee,* robustas rose from only 8 percent of world production in the late 1940s to nearly triple that in the 1970s. In the same period, soluble coffee's share of the world market went from almost zero to about 25 percent.

DEVELOPMENTS IN ROASTING EQUIPMENT

As the popularity of roasted coffee spread throughout the world, the methods of roasting beans changed. Europeans first roasted beans at home in their ovens. In the nineteenth century, equipment was developed that enabled people to roast larger quantities of coffee. The introduction of this equipment spurred the commercialization of coffee roasting.

Three main types of roasting equipment are used in commercial production. A batch roaster roasts beans in about 15 to 18 minutes, depending on the types of beans, by tumbling them in a drum that is blown with hot air. The beans are then cooled on a tray and mechanically stirred. Batch roasters can accommodate amounts ranging from less than a pound to more than 500 pounds of beans, and some batch roasters can run continuously. A fluid bed roaster roasts beans in 6 to 12 minutes. It operates much like a hot air popcorn popper, blowing air from the bottom of a stationary cylinder containing beans. Continuous roasters, first developed in the United States in 1940 by Jabez Burns, roast beans in about three minutes. Made of long cylinders with six-inch-wide compartments, continuous roasters turn like corkscrews. As the cylinder turns, the beans pass into different compartments that heat and then cool the beans. Continuous roasters can roast from 500 to 10,000 pounds of coffee per hour. Unlike other types of roasters, continuous roasters are most often monitored and controlled by computers.

ROASTING PROCESS

Despite the differences in roasting equipment, each process obtains similar results. When green coffee beans are roasted, a series of chemical changes alters their weight, appearance, and taste. The International Coffee Organization estimated that 1.19 pounds of green coffee beans go into a pound of roast coffee. Sugars, oils, proteins, and minerals develop and change within the beans as they are subjected to heat. Coffee beans absorb heat relatively uniformly, and during the last few minutes of a roast, the beans make a popping noise as they enlarge and unfold. The popping noise indicates that the production stage known as the development of the roast is taking place.

Because the changes in the beans occur quickly, the roastmaster (the person in charge of roasting the coffee beans) must keep a careful eye on the batch to achieve the desired flavor in the beans. The roastmaster's goal is to roast the coffee beans to a color consistent from the inside to the outside of the bean as well as throughout the batch. In large commercial operations, computers determine when to end the roast using photometric reflectance instruments that measure the color of the roast as it relates to the temperature of the beans. There are myriad degrees of roast, but they can be simplified into four categories: light, medium, dark, and very dark. Each variation has a distinct flavor.

BLENDED COFFEE

Blended coffee has long dominated the world roasted coffee market. Because different types of coffees contain varying amounts of taste, aroma, and body, coffee is often blended to create a unique product. Beans can be blended before they are roasted if they are of similar variety, but blending can also take place after the roasting process if the beans in question require different roasting criteria. Coffees are blended to suit different tastes. For example, in Japan mild coffees, such as those from Peru, are most popular, while in Germany, coffee drinkers are more likely to prefer full-bodied blends, such as those from Honduras.

Though large commercial roasters blend coffee beans to achieve a consistently flavored drink, specialty coffee roasters blend coffee beans to make uniquely flavored coffee. Some coffees are sold as varietals—coffee beans from a particular country of origin that have been roasted alone. But blended coffee has usually been marketed without mention of the types of coffee beans contained within the blend. Many coffee blends are sold by emphasizing company brand names, rather than coffee species or country of origin.

INSTANT COFFEE

Instant coffee is the extracted form of roasted, ground coffee. It is made by blending and roasting beans in the same way as regular coffee, although the end product is generally of a coarser quality. The ground coffee is then fed into industrial percolators, which have hot water pumped into them to make a concentrated coffee extract. The coffee's coarser grind keeps excessive pressures from developing in the percolator's hydraulic system.

Once the solubles have been extracted, they are dried into a powder by spray or freeze-drying. Though spray-drying was the most common form of drying instant coffee in the 1990s, freeze-drying, which became commercially sustainable in Europe and the United States in the 1960s, was associated with higher quality instant coffee because freeze-dried coffees retain more of their aroma. The dried powder that is the final product is packaged in glass jars or plug-closure metal containers with foil liners. Since the process of making instant coffee takes away some of the flavor and aroma of the coffee, instant coffee's aroma is often enhanced with collections from coffee grinders, percolator vents, or concentrated percolate.

Instant coffee sales are greatest in countries with little history of coffee drinking. In the United Kingdom, Japan, and Australia—predominantly tea-drinking countries—instant coffee accounts for a much higher percentage of total coffee consumption than in countries where regular coffee drinking had a long history. Even though instant coffee continued to be viewed as a product of lesser quality than regular ground-roasted coffee, instant coffee experienced gains in the 1990s due to consumer demand for convenience and the addition of specialty coffees to the instant coffee market in Europe.

DECAFFEINATED COFFEE

Decaffeinated coffee first became commercially available around 1900 in Europe. Most coffee is decaffeinated while it is green. In green form, arabica coffees contain about 1 percent caffeine by weight, while robusta coffees contain twice that amount. To decaffeinate coffee, green coffee beans are moistened, a step that moves the caffeine to the surface of the beans. Solvents are then used to wash the caffeine from the beans' surfaces. After the decaffeination process, the green beans are dried to their original moisture content before roasting.

Before the 1980s, man-made solvents removed caffeine from the beans. In the 1980s, however, natural solvents were made commercially available to remove the caffeine. Some natural solvents used for decaffeination include water, carbon dioxide, fats and oils, and ethyl acetate. Although caffeine has a slightly bitter taste, its removal from the coffee bean has little effect on the strength of the coffee's taste. A coffee's strength is dependent more on the degree of roast and the ratio of water to coffee in the brewing process.

PACKAGING

Packaging is of paramount importance to the roasted coffee industry because coffee is highly perishable. After coffee is roasted it begins to oxidize or grow stale. Roasted coffee first loses its aroma and then its flavorful oils and fats. In addition, roasted and ground coffee can quickly become contaminated through the absorption of other foods, flavors, or odors. Although specialty coffee is often sold in wax-lined paper bags with tin ties, most coffee retailers use airtight containers to package their coffee. Vacuum-packed metal cans were the most popular packing method until the late 1970s, according to the Specialty Coffee Association of America. By the 1990s, however, vacuum packages—called one-way valve bags—and brick packs had become popular as well.

One-way valve bags allow producers to package coffee immediately after it is roasted or ground. This ability is important because after coffee is roasted or ground, it releases carbon dioxide. As a result, roasters commonly had to let coffee sit for one to 30 hours, depending on the roast or grind, before packaging. The one-way valve bags are made of many layers of polyethylene and aluminum foil and include a valve that allows carbon dioxide to escape without letting oxygen enter. Other coffee packages include polyethylene or nylon film pouches that have been flushed with nitrogen, glass jars, and plastic-lined paper cartons.

MAJOR TRADE AGREEMENTS

Since the 1989 failure of the International Coffee Agreement (an agreement of the 72-nation International Coffee Organization cartel that set coffee prices since 1962), the roasted coffee industry has been subject to market forces. Without the support of the cartel, green coffee prices plunged more than 45 percent in 1989 and consuming countries built up a surplus of green coffee. As a result, the artificially high profit margins that had supported the coffee-producing nations shifted to benefit the coffee-roasting companies. Retail prices of coffee did not drop as precipitously as green coffee prices after the failure of the cartel but increased rapidly in 1994 in the wake of a frost that battered the all-important Brazilian coffee crop.

By the mid-1990s, coffee manufacturers' high profits were in jeopardy. The 1993 organization of 28 producing nations that formed into the Association of Coffee Producing

Countries (ACPC) devised a supply quota scheme to withhold about 20 percent of exportable coffee from the market in an attempt to raise coffee prices, and efforts continued toward negotiating a new International Coffee Agreement. By 1995, however, the United States had withdrawn from the negotiations, citing a preference for free trade of coffee.

When coffee was traded freely after the demise of the International Coffee Agreement, coffee prices fell and importing countries built up stocks of green coffee. When the producing countries retained some of their stocks, importing countries were forced to draw down their stocks. This strategy, however, did not result in higher prices for green coffee. Indeed, production continued to soar while demand lagged. By early 2002, green coffee prices (adjusted for inflation) reached their lowest level in one hundred years.

In 1994 a new version of the General Agreement on Tariffs and Trade (GATT) resulted from the Uruguay Round discussions of 1986 to 1994. Under the agreement, participating nations cannot introduce any new export subsidies, and U.S. and EU subsidies are subject to restrictions. GATT called for the reduction and elimination of tariffs designed to impede and to control foreign competition in favor of domestic businesses. All participating countries agreed to cut back tariffs by 33 percent, and the United States, the EU, Canada, and Japan decided to remove most of the tariffs inhibiting trade among themselves. GATT also established a formal organization for the implementation of systematic global trade policies, the World Trade Organization.

COFFEE CRISIS

By the early 2000s, the lifting of quotas had contributed to significant oversupply, especially of lower-quality robusta. Brazil, for example, doubled robusta production in the 1990s. At the same time, Vietnam increased robusta production from 84,000 tons in 1990 to 950,000 tons in 2000, making it the second largest producer in the world. To maintain profitability, some big roasters reconfigured their blends with larger amounts of cheaper robusta beans and smaller proportions of higher quality arabica beans. This step, according to Marcelo Vieira of Brazil's specialty coffee association, created an inferior product and contributed to further decline in demand. While a small number of producers with access to capital were able to grow and process higher quality blends for the expanding niche market of specialty coffees, most producers faced significant losses. From 1992 to 2002, coffee revenues in Colombia—the second leading coffee producer before being overtaken by Vietnam—dropped by 50 percent. According to the U.S. Agency for International Development (USAID), the situation—exacerbated by serious droughts in many parts of Latin America—led to coffee export losses of about US$1 billion in 2000 and 2001. Conditions were so alarming by 2003 that some analysts recommended radical measures. The charity organization Oxfam, for example, called for the destruction of 5 million bags of low quality coffee in warehouses, which it believed would boost market prices by 20 percent. Others believed that stimulating more demand was the most important response to diminishing sales.

The U.S. Agency for International Development (USAID) defines itself as an independent federal government agency that gives, with input from the State Department on foreign policy objectives, foreign assistance and humanitarian aid to countries recovering from disaster, trying to escape poverty, or attempting democratic reforms. In response to the alarming conditions that prevailed in 2003, USAID initiated two major programs in Central America and Colombia to assist the coffee industries there. The agency established an alliance with Green Mountain coffee to help small and medium-size producers to grow, process, and market high quality coffees for export. In 2002, USAID signed a Quality Coffee Agreement with Costa Rica, El Salvador, Guatemala, Honduras, Nicaragua, the Dominican Republic, and Panama that promoted similar goals. USAID has also instituted several programs in Africa to help improve coffee quality and provide access to markets. In 2003, the government of Tanzania passed new legislation allowing direct exports, which enabled coffee growers to begin selling directly to foreign buyers.

According to the International Coffee Organization (ICO), the supply imbalance began to improve by 2004, when total crop production fell to 112.67 million bags. Production of arabicas fell to an estimated 62.86 million bags, compared to 80.36 million bags the previous year. Robustas showed a smaller decline, falling from 39.08 million bags in 2003 to 38.52 million bags in 2004. Total exports in the first part of 2004 fell by about 9.7 percent from the corresponding period in 2003. The ICO expected further production cutbacks in 2005-2006, to an estimated total of 106 million bags. As a result of smaller harvests, opening stocks in exporting countries in 2004 were the lowest in more than 10 years. A further positive development was the announcement in 2005 that the United States would accede to the 2001 International Coffee Agreement and would rejoin the International Coffee Organization. With export volumes increasing in 2004 and 2005, ICO analysts were cautiously optimistic that the industry had begun to recover.

COFFEE ASSOCIATIONS

The International Coffee Organization (ICO) includes major exporters and importers around the world such as Brazil, Vietnam, Ecuador, and Colombia. Established in 1963, the ICO administers the International Coffee Agreement and coordinates diplomacy in world coffee trade. In addition, the ICO publishes information and statistics on the industry and leads campaigns to promote coffee consumption.

The Specialty Coffee Association of America (SCAA) serves specialty and gourmet coffee roasters as well as retailers, producers, exporters, importers, green coffee brokers, and manufacturers of coffee-related equipment and other products. The SCAA strives to advance the specialty coffee industry through the development and circulation of information that fosters coffee excellence within the trade.

FAIR TRADE-CERTIFIED BEANS

Beginning in the 1990s and continuing into the twenty-first century, coffee beans began to be certified in a new manner, based not on flavor or aroma, but on human rights and environmental concerns. Starting first in Europe and then moving to North America and Japan, a fair trade consumer movement led to the establishment of labeling coffee that passes certain criteria, namely that coffee importers pay at least US$1.26 per pound for green coffee. The fair trade certification program assists "marginalized" coffee growers—typically family-run farms, cooperatives, and plantation workers—by ensuring that they are paid fairly rather than allowing middlemen to absorb overly large shares of profits, leaving the producer at times with barely enough to cover production costs.

The Fairtrade Labeling Organizations International (FLO), established in 1997, was the umbrella organization that oversaw worldwide fair trade labeling programs for products such as coffee. Coffee retailers paid the FLO (or one of its regional affiliates) a licensing fee that allowed them to label their products with the fair trade seal. The consumer, who has been educated to look for this seal, is willing to pay a higher price for the coffee at a retail outlet, knowing that the coffee producer is being paid fairly and that in many cases the producer uses sustainable agricultural practices. In 2000, Starbucks, the leading gourmet coffee retailer in the United States, agreed to become the nation's first coffee retailer to sell fair-trade-certified beans in more than 2,000 of its outlets after activists and consumer groups threatened a large scale protest. Other companies in North America followed suit, including Sara Lee Coffee & Tea, Green Mountain Coffee Roasters, Tully's, Mountain View Coffee Co. in Canada, and many other regional and independent roasters and importers. According to TransFair USA, the U.S. member of FLO, Fair Trade coffee is also served in the European Parliament and in Toyota and Warner Brothers Europe's corporate headquarters. The *New York Times* reported in 2003 that, since 2000, approximately 140 coffee companies in the United States were offering fair-trade blends in some 10,000 outlets throughout the country. Sabrina Vigilante, marketing coordinator for the Rainforest Alliance, expected the niche for fair trade coffee to double in 2004.

BACKGROUND AND DEVELOPMENT

Coffee was used for myriad purposes and in many forms—from medicinal potions to food and wine—beginning as early as A.D. 800. *Caffea arabica* is believed to have been first cultivated in Ethiopia, where it grows wild, and first roasted in present-day Yemen on the Arabian Peninsula. By the late Middle Ages, coffee had become a staple beverage in the Mediterranean region's Islamic cultures, which eschewed alcoholic beverages, although alcoholic coffee drinks existed. Coffee was thus known in the period as "the wine of the Arabs."

During the seventeenth century, coffee consumption spread throughout Europe. As early as 1570, coffee was traded in Venice, and over the next 150 years its consumption gradually spread to most of continental Europe's urban and cultural centers. By the mid-eighteenth century, European colonists and merchants traded coffee in Africa (where both species were indigenous), North America, and South America. And Dutch colonists began cultivating coffee beans in what was later called Indonesia, notably on the island of Java, leading to another of coffee's nicknames. In the late eighteenth century, coffee gained popularity in British colonial North America as an alternative to tea when militant colonists rebelled against a British tea tax through boycotts and such incidents as the Boston Tea Party.

GOURMET COFFEES AND EMERGING MARKETS

Although consumption of regular coffee stagnated in the late 1980s and early 1990s, the trend toward increased consumption of gourmet coffee was a worldwide phenomenon. In the United States, sales of gourmet coffee quadrupled between 1986 and 1997, and by the latter part of the decade, gourmet coffee accounted for about 30 percent of market sales. The bulk of specialty coffee sales in the United States came through specialty coffee retail stores. Starbucks Coffee Co. and Caribou Coffee were two of the leading specialty coffee roasters/retailers in the United States in 1998, with a spate of smaller coffee roasters and cafes spread throughout the country.

INSTANT COFFEE

Instant coffee was developed in 1899 by a Japanese chemist and used by members of an Arctic expedition, according to C. F. Marshall's *The World Coffee Trade*. In the 1980s, instant coffee accounted for one fifth of the world coffee market. Instant coffee was the fastest growing segment of some roasted coffee markets.

Considered inferior by some continental European consumers, instant coffee nonetheless enjoyed healthy sales growth throughout Europe in the mid-1990s and gained ground in prime roast and ground coffee markets such as Germany, France, and Italy, where despite instant coffee's small market penetration, high coffee consumption rates translated into sizable sales volume for instant coffee. Furthermore, eastern European countries such as Poland and Russia represented increasingly important markets for instant coffee. Russia, for example, consumed more instant coffee than France and Germany combined in 1996. Instant coffee was also increasingly popular in China, where coffee sales have grown 90 percent between 1998 and 2003. Nestlé is the most popular brand, accounting for 46 percent of retail coffee sales in 2002.

PROFIT MARGINS

Profit margins for regular coffee sales at leading companies narrowed in the 1980s. Some analysts predicted that the belated entry of some of the largest coffee processing companies into the specialty coffee market would reverse this trend, for specialty coffee typically garnered higher margins. Nevertheless, after the collapse of the 1989 International Coffee Agreement, coffee roasters' profits remained tied to the fluctuating green coffee market. In 1995 the market experienced price hikes after frost devastated Brazil's coffee crop.

Europe's coffee roasters also faced shrinking profit margins in the mid-1990s as retailers slashed prices in new marketing schemes to increase their store-wide sales. Coffee price wars, most pronounced in Germany and France, led to retail prices that fell below the open market price paid by coffee companies. Small roasters and cafes were hit particularly hard.

THE ROLE OF THE INTERNATIONAL COFFEE ORGANIZATION

The International Coffee Organization (ICO) aggressively marketed coffee in China and Russia with its generic coffee promotions. In fact, the organization devoted its entire advertising fund of US$3.8 million to these two largely tea-drinking countries in 1997. As a result of promotions, coffee imports increased in Russia in the 1990s, rising from 1.08 million 60-pound bags in 1991 to 2.44 million bags in 1995. The ICO also subsidized marketing efforts in Japan to build up that country's coffee market.

CURRENT CONDITIONS

COFFEE CONSUMPTION

Over the last several decades of the twentieth century, coffee consumption trends varied greatly from country to country. Countries that import their coffee (as opposed to those that produce it domestically) consumed almost three-fourths of the world's coffee in 2000, and this pattern remained relatively unchanged through 2003. The United States remained the largest consumer of coffee, but growth in that country averaged only 0.26 percent between 1990 and 2002, which was far below levels of production. Consumption in developing countries, however, including Russia and China, increased by 4.05 percent annually, causing analysts to predict that these markets will demonstrate the best potential for growing coffee sales through the early 2000s. According to International Coffee Organization (ICO) estimates, world coffee consumption in 2004 totaled about 113.4 million bags.

In terms of per capita consumption, ICO statistics showed that Finland led the world in 2004, consuming 11.99 kilograms. Denmark came next with 9.46 kilograms, just ahead of Norway with 9.31 kilograms. Belgium/Luxembourg consumed 8.15 kilograms, Sweden consumed 8.06 kilograms, and Austria's consumption was 7.64 kilograms. Germany's per capita consumption was 7.01 kilograms. Per capita consumption in the United States was 4.62 kilograms, while it reached only 2.43 kilograms in the United Kingdom. U.S. consumers favored roast and ground coffees while those in the United Kingdom greatly preferred soluble (instant) coffee. Japanese per capita coffee consumption in 2001 was 3.36 kilograms.

Throughout the 1990s and into the twenty-first century, the popularity of high quality, specialty coffee continued to grow, especially in the mature markets of the United States and the European Union, which together consumed an estimated 64 percent of the world's coffee. The fastest growing markets in the roasted coffee industry, however, were countries relatively new to coffee drinking, such as the Eastern European countries of the Czech Republic, Hungary, Latvia, Lithuania, and Slovenia, where coffee consumption generally increased throughout the late 1990s and into the twenty-first century, according to the ICO. Consumption has also steadily increased in Australia, Puerto Rico, and Taiwan.

TYPES OF COFFEE DRINKERS

In a study of 95 markets and regions worldwide, Nestlé SA developed a profile of coffee drinkers as "Sophisticated," those who drink one or more cups daily; "Intermediary," those who drink somewhere between one cup per day to one cup per week; and "Starting," those who consume only one cup a week or less. The vast majority (57%) of people labeled themselves as starters, while sophisticated drinkers made up about 17 percent of the population. Yet, as expected, the sophisticated group consumed the majority of the world's coffee at 65 percent, while intermediate drinkers accounted for 29 percent.

GREEN COFFEE PRICES

Depressed in the early 1990s, green coffee prices rose substantially in the latter half of the decade, topping a 20-year high in 1997. However, after 1999, prices steadily dropped. The International Coffee Organization (ICO) reported the average annual per pound price for green coffee fell 47 percent from nearly US$0.86 cents in 1999 to just under US$0.46 cents in 2001. Though the price of arabica beans rose 85.6 percent between 2002 and 2004 to reach US$0.87 per pound, prices remained well below the record highs of the late 1990s. As *African Business* explained, world coffee production flourished in the 1990s due to exceptionally warm and dry climates in key coffee-growing regions, causing the world's coffee supplies to further increase, while consumption has remained essentially flat, particularly in the European Union and in the United States.

GOURMET COFFEE

Crain's Chicago Business reported that Kraft Food's coffee sales dropped almost 20 percent after 1996. A major reason was that many consumers prefer going out to a coffeehouse, café, or a restaurant for a gourmet cup of coffee. Much of the surge in interest in gourmet coffee was fueled by Starbucks, which opened up a new market in the United States. According to Crain's New York Business, sales in the United States for regular Columbian coffee stagnated while demand for Guatemalan Antigua, Kona, Mountain, and other premium coffees and blends flourished as consumers grew more sophisticated in their tastes. Premium and flavored coffees can be readily purchased at fast food chains and delis. The trend toward gourmet coffee and the increasingly consolidated coffee processing industry favored small, independent roasters. Such regional roasters often specialize in providing unique blends customized to local tastes along with a high level of customer service, and are adept at providing a constantly changing array of flavors that consumers seek.

SOLUBLE COFFEE

Soluble coffee, also known as instant coffee, continued to be popular in many regions of the world, especially in the Philippines and Chile, where nearly 100 percent of coffee consumption is of soluble coffee. Other countries where soluble coffee consumption accounts for more than 90 percent of total coffee consumption are China (97%), Korea (97%), South Africa (94%), Australia (93%), the United Kingdom (92%), Russia (92%), and Thailand (91%), according to data from Nestlé SA. Countries with the lowest percentage of instant coffee consumption are Italy (4%) and Sweden and Brazil (9% each). In the early 2000s, the world consumed approximately 196 billion cups of soluble coffee (as compared to 355 billion cups of roast and ground coffees). Nestlé dominated the soluble market, controlling 59 percent, followed by Philip Morris (subsequently Kraft Foods) with 13 percent, and Proctor and Gamble with 3 percent. According to Nestlé, world sales of soluble coffee rose by 35 percent between 1993 and 2003.

In Russia, more than 100 brands of Brazilian soluble coffee are sold, according to the *Tea & Coffee Trade Journal.* Brazil's soluble coffee exports totaled US$200 million in 2001, and the country continued to seek new markets for soluble coffee through the early 2000s. Under a new agreement with the European Union, the *Tea & Coffee Trade Journal* reported, starting in 2002, the EU would likely allow Brazilian imports to make up a quota of 87.4 percent of its total imports of instant coffee from around the world.

INDUSTRY LEADERS

NESTLÉ SA

Created from the 1905 merger of two competing condensed milk companies, Nestlé SA of Vevey, Switzerland, is the world's market leader in coffee production. Nestlé entered the coffee market in 1938 with Nescafé, its first non-dairy product, prompted by the Brazilian Coffee Institute, which asked if Nestlé could make "coffee cubes" to help Brazil deal with its large coffee surplus. Nestlé developed Nescafé, a soluble coffee powder. The company originally intended to produce Nescafé in Brazil, but the number of administrative barriers in that country convinced Nestlé to begin production in Switzerland instead. By 1991, Nescafé was sold in more than 100 countries.

Nestlé brought ground roast coffee to its product line when it bought the third largest U.S. coffee firm, Hills Brothers Inc. in 1985. By the start of the twenty-first century, Nestlé was a truly diverse and multinational company, with more than 500 factories operating in over 70 countries worldwide. It upgraded many of its facilities in the early 1990s as well. Nestlé SA became more productive as a result and expanded its presence in a number of countries. Developments of note at these facilities include the company's 1992 announcement that its French facility would not participate in the four-week holiday Europeans normally take in August. The company also opened a production facility in China in 1991. In 1999, Nestlé divested its Hills Brothers, MJB, and Chase & Sanborn roast and ground coffee brands in the United States to concentrate on promoting a new premium line of Nescafé products which were introduced on the West Coast.

Through the early 2000s Nestlé continued to dominate the world's instant coffee market. The company posted beverage (excluding water) revenues of CHF21.79 billion (about US$18.3 billion) in 2004, with soluble coffee accounting for CHF8.079 billion (US$6.78 billion) in sales. According to the company's own statistics, its sales of Nescafé alone rose 40 percent from 1993 to 2003. The company's chief markets are the United States, France, Germany, Brazil, the United Kingdom, Italy, and Japan. In 2004 Nestlé relaunched its Nescafé premium coffees throughout Europe, and also successfully relaunched Nescafé Cappuccino. The company claims that every second, 3,000 cups of its coffee are consumed. Nestlé's soluble coffee brands—its most popular coffee—include Nescafé, Taster's Choice, Ricoré, and Ricoffy; its roast and ground coffee brands are Nespresso, Bonka, Zogas, and Loumidis.

KRAFT FOODS INC.

Philip Morris, one of the world's largest cigarette manufacturers, spun off Kraft Foods, one of the world's largest coffee producers, in June, 2001, while retaining 84 percent ownership. Philip Morris first entered the coffee market when it purchased the world's largest coffee roaster, General Foods Corporation, in 1985.

Although General Foods had distributed Sanka brand coffee since 1927, it did not begin roasting coffee until 1928. That year, the company, known at the time as the Postum Company, acquired Maxwell House Coffee, a company that had started in 1892. The company continued to enlarge its coffee business, purchasing the Sanka Coffee Corporation in 1932; developing instant coffee for the U.S. Army in 1941; and acquiring French coffee-roaster Établessements Pierre Lemonnier SA in 1961.

When Philip Morris acquired Kraft Inc. in 1988, the cigarette maker merged Kraft with General Foods. This 1989 merger created the world's second largest food company, Kraft General Foods Inc. The two segments were later integrated further as Kraft Foods Inc. In 1990, Philip Morris bought Kraft Jacobs Suchard (KJS), a Swiss coffee and chocolate manufacturer and Europe's largest coffee roaster. KJS controlled 30 percent of Germany's large roasted coffee market. Since 1998, Kraft has marketed and sold Starbucks brand coffee to retail grocery stores in the United States under a licensing agreement with the coffee chain giant.

In 2000, Kraft Foods International experienced strong volume growth in emerging markets in Central and Eastern Europe, as well as in the mature markets of Sweden, Austria, Italy, and the United Kingdom. Volume in the Chinese market increased with the re-launch of Maxwell House coffee mix. The company held the top spot in the 2000 coffee market based on volume shares in France, Germany, and Sweden. Worldwide, Kraft Foods was the top brand in the roast and ground coffee market in 2000, controlling 15 percent of the market. In the total in-home coffee market, Kraft Foods captured 14 percent of the market, trailing Nestlé. In 2003, Kraft was the leading coffee company in seven European countries as well as South Korea.

Kraft posted net revenues in 2004 of more than US$32 billion. Its international beverage division sold approximately 94 billion cups of coffee annually, or about 257 million cups of coffee daily. As of 2004, Kraft Foods' coffee brands in the United States included General Foods International Coffees, Gevalia, Maxim, Maxwell House, Sanka, Starbucks (under a licensing agreement), and Yuban. Its international brands included Carte Noire, Gevalia, Grand' Mère, Kaffee HAG, Jacobs Krönung, Jacobs Milea, Jacobs Monarch, Jacques Vabre, Saimaza, Kenco, Maxwell House, and others.

SARA LEE/DE

Sara Lee/DE, formerly Sara Lee Coffee & Tea Worldwide and a business segment of Sara Lee, sells to both the retail and the foodservice sectors around the world. In 2000 the company completed the acquisition of the Chock Full o' Nuts coffee brand, which had annual sales of US$350 million. Sara Lee also purchased the Hills Brothers, MJB, and Chase & Sanborn roast and ground coffee brands from Nestlé USA Inc., a business that generated about US$280 million in annual revenues. The company holds the top position in coffee sales in Brazil and several European countries, and its Superior Coffee is the leader in the U.S. foodservice market. And thanks to its Hills Brothers acquisition, the company has the third best selling coffee in the U.S. retail sector. Sara Lee's European coffee brand is Douwe Egberts and its South American brands are Caboclo, Cafe do Ponto, and Pilao. Its SENSEO coffee pod system, sold throughout Europe and in the United States, brews single servings of frothy-style coffee. The company reported net beverage sales totaling US$3.1 billion in 2004.

THE PROCTER & GAMBLE COMPANY

The Procter & Gamble Company started in 1837 as a manufacturer of candles and soap. With the acquisition of Folger Coffee Company in the 1960s, Procter & Gamble applied its aggressive and extensive marketing and advertising strategies to its new brand and made it one of the world's most popular coffees. By 2002, Folgers had overtaken Maxwell House as the top U.S. coffee brand. According to the company's own statistics, Americans drink 85 million cups of Folgers coffee each day. Procter & Gamble posted total corporate sales of US$51.4 billion in 2004.

MAJOR COUNTRIES IN THE INDUSTRY

BRAZIL

For two centuries, Brazil has been the world's leading producer and exporter of coffee. As of the early 2000s, the country accounted for about a third of global coffee production each year. Exports in 2004-05 totaled 27.2 million 60-kilo bags, up from 24.8 million bags in the previous year. Hit by the overproduction crisis of the late 1990s and early 2000s, Brazil aggressively promoted domestic consumption, resulting in a doubling of the country's internal market. By the early 2000s, more than half of Brazil's coffee crop was consumed domestically. Brazil also took steps to boost consumption in foreign markets. To increase coffee usage in China, for example, the Brazilian Ministry of Agriculture in 2002 began a program establishing Chinese coffee chains based on the Starbucks model.

COLOMBIA

Traditionally the second largest coffee exporter, Colombia slipped to second place in the early 2000s behind Vietnam. In the mid-1970s, coffee comprised 50 percent of Columbia's legal export market; by the 1990s, this figure had plummeted to only 7 percent. With domestic consumption at only about half the world's per capita average, the Colombian coffee industry was particularly hard hit by the collapse of the export market. Starting in 2003, the industry launched several initiatives to increase coffee drinking in Columbia, in hopes of raising domestic consumption from 1.4 to 2.8 million bags per year. In 2004-05, Colombia exported 10.66 million bags of coffee, barely above the 10.63 million bags exported the previous year.

VIETNAM

A relative newcomer to the world coffee market, Vietnam dramatically boosted production through the 1990s and by the early 2000s had overtaken Colombia as the second ranked coffee exporting nation. In 2001, Vietnam's coffee output reached a record high of 900,000 tons. In response to oversupply problems, however, Vietnam cut production to only 700,000 tons by 2003. At the same time, it shifted production to higher-value Arabica beans. In 2003-04, Vietnam had overseas sales of 12.5 million bags; in 2004-05, the country increased exports to 14.4 million bags.

THE UNITED STATES

Although coffee consumption declined significantly in the United States from 3.1 cups per day in 1962 to 1.6 cups per day in 1996, coffee consumption rebounded to 3.3 cups per day in 2000 and the size of the cup increased over time so that it averaged nine ounces. According to *Nation's Restaurant News'* report of the National Coffee Association's (NCA) annual survey, coffee consumption hit an all-time high in the United States in 2000 when 79 percent of adults, or 161 million people, indicated that they drank coffee. Approximately 54 percent consumed coffee on a regular basis, while 25 percent were occasional drinkers. NCA also found that about 18 percent of coffee drinkers consumed gourmet coffee on a daily basis. *DSN Retailing Today* reported that in the United States, retail coffee sales reached US$18.5 billion in 2000. The U.S. market remained flat in 2003, however, with a slight decline in volume sales offset by an increase in coffee prices. In 2004, according to ICO figures, Americans consumed a per capita average of 4.62 kilograms of coffee.

THE UNITED KINGDOM

The UK coffee market is dominated by instant coffee, which accounted for nearly 90 percent of consumption in the early 2000s. Nestlé held a 57.9 percent market share in the instant coffee market in 1994. While ground coffee has traditionally been a very weak seller in the United Kingdom, the 1990s saw a strong increase in ground coffee sales. Between 1992 and 1996, ground coffee consumption rose by 53 percent. In 1997 the United Kingdom consumed US$154 million worth of ground coffee and US$1.2 billion worth of instant coffee, according to estimates by *Market Intelligence.*

At the onset of the twenty-first century, Britons consumed more coffee (generally soluble coffee) than tea outside the home with consumption at 0.5 kg of coffee per person annually, substantially less than many other European countries. Sweden, for example, consumes almost 9 kg per person each year, according to BBC News. And while the number of coffee bars is steadily increasing—there were eight times more coffee bars in Scotland alone in 2000 than in the mid-1990s—there is still considerable room for market penetration. The BBC News reported that in 2000, there was real estate space available for 1,500 coffee houses across the

United Kingdom, but with less than half of the sites in use, "it is felt there is a long way to go before the UK sees a coffee house on ever corner, like some continental countries."

JAPAN

Although coffee consumption was almost nonexistent in Japan as late as the 1950s, by 2000, the country became the third largest importer of coffee behind the United States and Germany. In 2004, imports reached 7.1 million bags of coffee, while per capita consumption totaled 3.36 kilograms. Japan's fondness for coffee arose out of increased "Westernization" of consumer trends, an overall increase in living standards, the popularity of instant (soluble) coffee, the increased accessibility of coffee makers for home use, and the emergence of chic coffee bars as places for young people to socialize. While consumption of coffee outside the home accounts for approximately 20 percent of consumption, in-home consumption is the largest and fastest growing coffee trend, with soluble coffee the leader in this segment. More than half of Japanese coffee consumption occurs in the home, and this was expected to rise as regular coffee sales increase. Another popular form of coffee in Japan is canned, ready-to-drink (RTD) coffee, both hot and cold, which makes up about one-third of the coffee market.

CHINA

Chinese interest in Western culture has increased interest in coffee drinking in that country, regarded by some analysts as a potential gold mine of untapped customers. As in many countries with a history of tea drinking, instant coffee was the most popular type of coffee sold in China. Since the mid-1980s, the coffee market in China has nearly doubled every two years, and analysts project that volume sales will grow by 70 percent between 2003 and 2008.

Though prospects for growth in China were appealing, coffee sales made up a minuscule portion of the country's total drinks market at the beginning of the 2000s. According to various estimates, mainland China consumed annually about 1,500 cups of tea per capita, but only 1.2 cups of coffee per capita. Consumption of roast ground coffee in China was so low that it was difficult to measure. Nestlé's Nescafé brand led the Chinese coffee market in the early 1990s, while Kraft's Maxwell House brand held second position in the market. Coffee shops, Internet cafes, and fast food restaurant account for most coffee sales. China's policies also have impeded the availability of coffee. The country established a 40 percent tariff for unroasted coffee imports and a 60 percent tariff for roasted coffee. Since China became a member of the World Trade Organization, many expected the market to further open.

FURTHER READING

Ahmed, Rafiq. "Tea Brings Little Cheer." *African Business.* (September 2000): 18-19.

."Big boxes discover perks of gourmet coffee sales." *DSN Retailing Today.* (23 July 2001): 19.

"Brazil to Establish Coffee Chain Stores in China." *Peoples Daily,* 5 July 2002. Available from http://www.china.org.cn.

"Coffee house market bubbling." BBC News, 1 September 2000. Available from http://news.bbc.co.uk/.

Ensor, James. "Eastern Europe—A Tough, But Strategic, Nut to Crack." *Grocer.* (16 November 1996): 52.

Flisi, Claudia. "Grounds for Optimism as Instant Coffee Sales Surge." *The European.* 16 May 1996, 25.

Flamm, Matthew. "Roaster Redux." *Crain's New York Business.* (9-15 April 2001): 17-18.

Gallun, Alby. "A Powerful Pantry of Brand Names." *Crain's Chicago Business.* (2 April 2001): 46.

Harris, Brian. "Coffee Market Perking Up, but Growers Still Smarting and Cautious." *Miama Herald,* 22 November 2004.

Hornblower, Margot. "Wake Up and Smell the Protest." *Time.* (17 April 2000): 58.

International Coffee Organization. "Coffee Market Report," March 2005. Available from www.ico.org.

———. "ICO Indicator Prices Monthly and Annual Averages 1999 to 2002," February 2002. Available from www.ico.org.

———. "Press Release: International Coffee Agreement, New Initiatives," 1 October 2001. Available from www.ico.org.

Kraft Foods, 2004 Annual Report. Available from www.kraft.com.

Luxner, Larry. "Brimming with Optimism." *Tea & Coffee Trade Journal.* (20 January 2002): 51-5.

Madeley, John. "Coffee Price Rise Is Just a Hill of Beans." *Observer,* 4 April 2004. Available from www.ico.org.

Nestlé SA. "Coffee at Nestlé: A Presentation by Olle B. Tegstam, Head of Coffee & Beverages Strategic Business Unit," 25 October 2001. Available from www.ir.Nestlé.com.

Nestlé SA, 2004 Annual Report. Available from www.Nestlé.com.

Philip Morris Companies Inc., 2004 Annual Report. Available from www.philipmorris.com.

Ruggless, Ron. "Better Latte than Ever: Coffee Players Perked Up Over Sales." *Nation's Restaurant News,* 12 February 2001.

Sara Lee/DE Annual Report, 2004. Available from http://www.saralee-de.com.

Smith, Tony. "Difficult Times for Coffee Industry as Demand Falls." *New York Times,* 25 November 2003.

Sorby, Kristina. "Coffee Market Trends." Background paper to "Toward More Sustainable Coffee." World Bank Agricultural Technology Note 30, June 2002. Available from lnweb18.worldbank.org.

U.S. Agency for International Development. "USAID's Response to the Global Coffee Crisis." Available from www.usaid.gov.

U.S. Department of Agriculture. Foreign Agricultural Service. "Coffee Update," December 2001. Available from www.fas.usda.gov.

———. *Tropical Products: World Markets and Trade,* June 2003. Available from www.fas.usda.gov.

SIC 2070
NAICS 311225

FATS AND OILS

Industry firms extract and process a variety of fats and oils, mostly for use in human foods and animal feed. Major production categories include cottonseed oils, soybean oils, other vegetable oils, animal fats and oils, and margarine, shortening, and related products. (Production of butter, however, is not included under this topic.)

INDUSTRY SNAPSHOT

In the mid-2000s, global supplies of fats and oils were sufficient to meet steadily increasing world demand. According to analysis of the Food and Agricultural Organization (FAO) of the United Nations, production of oil-bearing crops increased by 4 percent worldwide in 2005. World consumption of oilseeds rose steadily through the 1990s, reaching 347 million metric tons (mmt) in 2004. Of this total, about 288 million metric tons (mmt) were expected to be crushed for oil or oilmeal.

Growing demand in developing countries was expected to account for more than 60 percent of this increase. Soy and palm oil consumption was expected to increase the most, while use of sunflower seed oil was likely to decrease. Use of non-edible oils was also expected to rise, most notably for the production of biodiesel fuels.

Global trade in oilseeds and oilseed products experienced astronomical growth in the late twentieth century, due largely to expanded production of soybeans. Trade in oilseeds, cakes, and meals increased almost 900 percent from 1964 to 2004, while the global market for vegetable oils during the same period grew by a stunning 1,800 percent. While trade slowed in 2004, it picked up again in 2005. Most of the increase, according to the UN's Food and Agricultural Organization (FAO), could be attributed to palm oil, with trade in soybean and rapeseed oils also increasing. The market for sunflower seed and ground seed oils, however, diminished. Although the United States and the European Union have historically led world production, much of the industry's recent expansion came from developing markets in Asia. India, Indonesia, and Malaysia, in particular, are they expected to continue to lead worldwide market expansion, both in terms of production and consumption. By the late 1990s, Malaysia had already become the world's largest edible oil producer because of its prodigious output of palm oil. By 2005, the world's seven top exporters of oils and fats accounted for 82 percent of global import needs, and the FAO expected this concentration to continue.

Consumers worldwide continued to shift from high-cholesterol animal and marine oils to lower-cholesterol vegetable oils. While vegetable oil output increased 60 percent from 1970 to 1980, animal and marine oil production only grew by 9 percent and actually started to decline in the 1990s. In addition, consumers also began to bypass oils high in saturated fat, such as tropical oils, and choose those with low levels of saturated fat, like olive and canola oil. Consumers' desire to have low-fat and low-cholesterol alternatives for their diets was a major motivator in research efforts. Americans, in particular, wanted to reduce the fat in their diets without sacrificing taste or texture. Consumers also wanted to avoid eating trans fats, often used to cook French fries, chips, and other popular snack foods, and also used in the production of baked goods such as cookies and muffins. Manufacturers responded by announcing changes in their ingredient lists. Frito Lay, for example, announced in 2005 that it was the first U.S. company to completely eliminate trans fats from its major snack brands.

ORGANIZATION AND STRUCTURE

Most fat and oil products (over 60 percent) of this industry are produced and consumed domestically. Although many nonfood uses for fats and oils have been discovered, the vast majority (about 80 percent) of the industry's production in the mid-2000s was still for human or animal consumption. In the United States, for example, salad and cooking oils accounted for 50 percent of all vegetable oil production. Another 40 percent is used in baking or frying, and almost 10 percent is used to produce margarine. Notwithstanding the negative health connotations associated with consumption of fats and oils, these substances constitute one of the three primary nutrients. Also, because fats carry more than twice as much energy as the other two groups, proteins and carbohydrates, they have been characterized as "nature's storehouse of energy." (A gram of fat contains nine calories compared to four calories per gram in carbohydrates and proteins.) In many cultures, the consumption of rich fatty foods is considered a sign of affluence. Not surprisingly, per-capita consumption of edible fats and oils in developed countries outstripped that of developing nations by a three-to-one margin. In developing countries, according to the U.S. Department of Agriculture (USDA), for every 1 percent increase in income, consumers will spend an additional 0.55 percent on fats and an additional 0.40 percent on oils. By the early 2000s, per-capita consumption of edible fats and oils in both developed and developing countries was on the rise, growing from 22.7 kg and 7.2 kg respectively in 1980, to 28.4 kg and 14.6 kg respectively by 1996. The FAO projected that world consumption of oils and fats would grow by 2.8 percent annually in developing countries (compared to 1.8 percent growth in developed countries) through 2010. Developing countries were expected to capture 62 percent of the market during that period, up from a 60 percent share in 2004.

Industry output can be classified according to its sources (animal or vegetable), its products (mealcake, fat, or oil), and its uses (food or nonfood). Fat and oil meal cakes can be consumed as fodder by animals or used as fertilizer. In the mid-1990s, vegetable oil cakes and meals constituted about 37 percent of the world's total output for the fats and oils industry. Cottonseed oil, soybean oil, and vegetable oil mills produce oil for purposes other than human consumption such as animal feed. Oil from these mills only constitutes about 1.3 percent of the world's total fats and oils output. Other businesses produce animal and fish mealcake, greases, and fats. The mealcake can be used as fodder or in manufacturing but not as food for humans. Crude animal fats and vegetable oils are processed for human consumption by manufacturers and include shortenings, table oils, margarines, and other edible fats and oils. Production is subject to the vagaries of the seasons, the weather, and demand.

The markets for cottonseed oil, soybean oil, and vegetable oil mills are driven by the highly volatile demand for animal feed. Since livestock producers have a wide variety of feedstock from which to choose, they are very sensitive to price. By extension, demand for oil cakes and meals is also driven by the amount and variety of demand for meats. The primary factors driving demand for edible fats and oils are price, consumer health concerns, product innovation, and international trade regulations. Heavy outlays for advertising and promotion of the top branded edible fats and oils also characterize this industry segment. These concerns have influenced the evolution of large consumer products companies that have the financial wherewithal to compete effectively.

There are three basic steps in the production of fats and oils: growing, processing, and refining. Some companies only process and refine oil, while others are vertically integrated and perform all three tasks. Although most modern processors use solvents to remove oil from seeds, they are nonetheless referred to in the literature as "crushers," in reference to the historical pressing method. Refiners, who process vegetable oil or crude animal fats, use techniques such as bleaching, filtering, deodorizing, and/or hydrogenating to extract oil. Many companies in this industry group are subsidiaries or divisions of major consumer products conglomerates.

NONFOOD OILS

Cottonseed oil mills. This industry segment includes companies that manufacture cottonseed oil, cake, meal, and linters, or process purchased cottonseed oil into forms other than edible cooking oils. In 2004 global cottonseed cake output stood at 26.4 million metric tons (mmt). Production in the United States reached 1.8 mmt in 1994, but declined steadily through the late 1990s and early 2000s. In 2003, U.S. cottonseed crushings were 2.48 million short tons, a 6.1 percent decrease from the previous year's output.

Until the early nineteenth century, unplanted cottonseed was considered a health hazard because it contained the poisonous pigment gossypol. But after 1833, when the first successful cottonseed oil mill was launched, the southern United States soon became the industry's largest producer and consumer. Cottonseed was a leading product in the global fats and oils industry, but production fell steadily in the late twentieth century. In the early 1990s, rapeseed supplanted cottonseed as the second most produced oil cake in the world. Cottonseed cake constitutes the majority of this industry segment's production. It is usually used as a high-protein supplement to livestock and poultry feed. Virtually all crude cottonseed oil is refined into salad or cooking oil, but low grades of the substance are sometimes used in the manufacture of lubricants, paint, and soap. Linters—short cotton fibers extracted from cottonseeds before they are crushed—are used to make sterile absorbent cotton and in the manufacture of paper, film, explosives, plastics, and rayon.

Soybean oil mills. This portion of the industry includes manufacturers that produce soybean oil, cake, meal, and soybean protein isolates and concentrates or process purchased soybean oil into something other than edible cooking oils. Throughout most of the twentieth century, soybean meal and oil constituted the most important segment of the fats and oils industry. The soybean originated in Asia, where it was used for many centuries as a high-protein diet staple. It was developed commercially in the United States, where it was first planted in the early nineteenth century. The legume languished as a horticultural oddity until the introduction of three new Japanese varieties in the early twentieth century. The development of an oil-deodorizing process in the early 1930s and the rising demand for edible oil during World War II promoted the use of soybean oil in margarine, shortening, salad oil, mayonnaise, and other food products (however, such food uses are not considered part of this segment).

Soybean cake (crush) and meal are the main output of this industry segment. Global production of soybean meal grew from 116.48 million metric tons (mmt) in 2001 to a approximately 137 mmt in 2005. Soybean cake output rose from 146.91 mmt to 174.29 mmt during the same period. U.S. production of soy cake remained relatively stable through the early 2000s, reaching 44.63 mmt in 2001 and about 45 mmt in 2005. U.S. production of soybean meal, which reached 35.73 mmt in 2001 but fell to 32.95 mmt in 2004, grew to approximately 36 mmt in 2005. The oil cake is used primarily as an animal feed, but the development of isolated soy proteins has the potential to open up a vast consumer market as a high-protein supplement to the human diet. These products, which are essentially flavorless yet consist of 90 percent protein, can be used as dietary supplements or as replacements for dairy products and eggs. They are also used as emulsifiers and binders in meat products as well as meat and milk substitutes. The very small percentage of crude soybean oil that is not processed into food is used in chemical products, mainly in the resins and plastics industries.

Other vegetable oil mills. This industry segment comprises companies that manufacture vegetable oils, cake, and meal (with the exception of corn, cottonseed, and soybean) or process such vegetable oils into forms other than edible cooking oils. This industry segment produces the meals and inedible oils of sunflower seeds, peanuts (sometimes called "groundnuts"), linseeds, rapeseeds (canola), coconuts (or copra), and palm. World production of oil cake, according to FAO statistics, topped 250.1 mt in 2004. Oilseed cake and meal production in the United States fluctuated substantially in the 1990s, reaching 811.8 mmt in 1993 and falling to 160.1 mmt in 2000. Output for 2001 was projected at 260.9 mmt. Production of oilseed crush was projected at 48.7 mmt for 2005, with meal production expected to reach 37.6 mmt. Like soybeans and cottonseeds, the meals of these oilseeds are also used for livestock feed and fertilizer.

While the vast majority of these seeds' oils are refined for human consumption (see below), there are notable exceptions that fall into this industry category. Virtually all linseed oil, for example, is used in the production of resins, plastics, paint, and varnish. Rapeseed oil that contains high levels of erucic acid (a known carcinogen) is used in steel and iron production. Coconut, olive, and palm oils are used in the manufacture of soap, paint, varnish, and fatty acids.

Animal fats and oils. This industry segment includes companies that produce animal oils (including fish oil and other marine animal oils) and fish and animal meal, together with those rendering inedible stearin, grease, and tallow from animal fat, bones, and meat scraps. At just 3.93 mmt of global annual production, fish and animal meals constituted only about 7 percent of the world's total meal output. The primary products of this industry segment are high protein sources of feed for fisheries and livestock. Tallow (rendered cattle fat) is marketed as both an edible and inedible product. The inedible product is derived from inedible slaughterhouse and locker plant by-products, from fat trimmings collected from retail butchers and institutions, and from dead or condemned animals. It is used mostly in the production of animal feed, fatty acids, and soap.

Oils from fish and marine animals fall into three general categories: fish liver oils, fish body oils, and other marine animal oils. Cod liver oil is a well-known example of the first type of oil. Fish body oils, known in the industry as menhaden, are used in the production of paint, linoleum, leather, and other products. They are also used in the production of margarine in Europe and Canada. Fish meal, another by-product of fish processing, constitutes a small but growing proportion of the market for livestock feedstuffs.

EDIBLE OILS

Often referred to as edible fats and oils, this is the most important category in the fats and oils industry. It constitutes 98 percent of all fats and oils produced worldwide and 59 percent of the industry group as a whole. This category encompasses the refined products of edible fats and oils, namely, shortening, salad and cooking oils, and margarine. These products may be made from soybean oil, cottonseed oil, sunflower seed oil, peanut oil, rapeseed (canola) oil, coconut oil, palm oil, or olive oil, as well as animal and marine oils and fats. Some of the products are sold in bulk to food service institutions and food manufacturers, and some quantities are sold on the consumer market.

The manufacturing of shortening, cooking oils, and margarine requires full or partial hydrogenation of refined vegetable oil. This process helps prevent rancidity and converts some fats from liquid to semi-solid or solid forms for particular food uses. Although soybean oil is the most widely hydrogenated oil, cottonseed, corn, sunflower, and other oils or fats also undergo the process. Notwithstanding its widespread use, hydrogenation came under fire in the early 1990s when medical research linked use of hydrogenated oils (especially margarine) to increased incidence of heart attack.

Vegetable oils. Global production of vegetable oils and fats exceeded 100.5 mmt in 2004 and was projected to rise. Vegetable oils, including soybean, sunflower seed, peanut, cottonseed, rapeseed, and olive oils, constitute the most important segment of this category, contributing over half of the edible oil production in the mid-2000s. Soybean oil, which is used on its own and in combination with others to make a variety of products, continued to dominate this category. Production of edible soybean oil totaled 30 mmt in 2004, or more than one-fourth of all edible fats and oils. Growth of both production and consumption of soybean oil lagged the industry overall for the last third of the twentieth century. The net result of this trend was that soybean oil's contribution to total oil production declined from 35 percent in 1970 to 30 percent in 1985 and 21 percent in 1997. Other oils clearly made inroads into its share during this period.

Perhaps the most aggressive growth in the industry was enjoyed by **palm oil.** From the late 1980s to 1997, production increased 70 percent, accounting for 19 percent of the global output and catapulting the product to rank second only to soybean oil. By 2004, production exceeded 31 mmt, and further growth was expected. The primary force driving this rapid expansion was the burgeoning demand in the huge, and as yet largely untapped, markets of Asia. In addition, palm yields a high percentage of oil per hectare, roughly 10 times the yield of soybeans, and requires only low production and refining costs. Malaysia and Indonesia are the largest producers and exporters of palm oil.

Rapeseed (canola) oil, which grew at an average of 10.5 percent annually in the 19980s, was another challenger to soy oil's traditional dominance. The seed's low levels of saturated fats appealed to consumer health concerns, with consumption growing fastest in North America and northern Europe. Through the early 2000s, canola oil ranked third in global production of major vegetable oils, with outputs reaching a 16 mmt in 2005.

Sunflower seed oil was another high-potential commodity, especially popular in Europe. While its growth rate, at 4.7 percent per year in the 1980s and less than 1 percent in the 1990s, was far below that of canola and palm, sunflower seed oil was the fourth highest produced oil in the world in 2005, with a projected 8.78 mmt.

Olive oil enjoyed rising popularity in the early 2000s as well. Although production levels constituted only 2.5 percent of global edible fats and oils, they increased by over 50 percent to 2.5 mmt in 1997 alone as consumers around the world discovered its low levels of saturated fat and its unique flavor. By 2004, global production exceeded 3 mt for the first time in history. The vast majority came from the European Union, with an output of almost 2.5 mt. Spain produced about 1.4 mt, while Greece produced almost 370,000 tons.

Margarine. Many combinations of the edible animal and vegetable fats and oils discussed above are used to manufacture margarine (also known as oleomargarine), a key product of this industry. It was invented in 1869 by a French chemist named H. Mége-Mouriés, at the behest of Napoleon III. After initial resistance to the product—especially and predictably from dairy interests—margarine production expanded rapidly in Europe, North America, and eventually to most of the world. Consumer protection concerns prompted most countries to require that the fat content of margarine be at least 80 percent and that water not exceed 16 percent by weight. Rising health concerns about dietary fat gave rise to a growing array of low and no-fat "margarines" that were subsequently more correctly classified as "table spreads." U.S. production of margarine fell from 2.69 million pounds in 1991 to 2.39 million pounds in 2000. Domestic consumption also fell. In 1999, per capita consumption was 10.6 pounds; by 2003, this figure had fallen to 8.3 pounds.

Concerns about health problems related to *trans* fatty acids, which occur in partially hydrogenated fats such as margarine, may have contributed to this decline. Starting in 2006, food manufacturers were to be required by the U.S. Food and Drug Administration (FDA) to label *trans* fat content separately from other fat content on product nutrition labels. Manufacturers began to research and develop alternative types of margarines with reduced levels of trans fats, or with no trans fats at all. There was general consensus that the manufacture of low fat products would continue to grow, given consumer demand and cost savings (since the new products were expected to contain more water).

Shortening. Baking and frying fats (also called shortening) include both unmixed hydrogenated vegetable oils and compounds of hydrogenated vegetable oils with animal fats such as lard or tallow. In 2003, world production of margarine and shortening together totaled 13.1 mmt. That year, world exports of hydrogenated vegetable oils totaled 1.8 mmt.

BACKGROUND AND DEVELOPMENT

Fats and oils from animal and vegetable sources have been a primary source of energy for humans and animals since prehistoric times. Many ancient cultures also discovered nonfood uses for the substances, for example in lamps. The Egyptians used oils and greases as lubricants, and the Greeks made soap from tallow and oil. While the Chinese developed a three-step pressing process that highly resembled modern oilseed crushing, many civilizations used a simple mortar and pestle to extract oil from seeds and fruits. The availability of certain fats and oils has greatly influenced the development of regional food ways. For example, Asian soybeans are used in the production of tofu and soymilk, and olive oil is a staple of Mediterranean cuisine.

However, it was not until the late eighteenth and early nineteenth centuries that insight into the chemical composition of oilseeds—and the invention of the hydraulic press—led to the commercial production of fats and oils. Most of the early discoveries were made in Europe. In 1779, Swedish chemist C. W. Scheele isolated glycerol from olive oil, and Michel-Eugéne Chevreul of France expanded on that work in the early 1800s. Later that century, the development of the hydrogenation process—which transformed liquid oils into solids—was a cornerstone of the modern vegetable oil and shortening industry. The expansion of the chemical industry after World War I led to the discovery of many new applications for fats and fatty acids, which in turn bolstered the market for fats, oils, and oilseed meals.

World trade in oilseeds and their products grew to become an important segment of the global agricultural industry, comprising 10 percent of total agricultural trade by the 1970s. Vertical and horizontal integration through mergers and acquisitions, typical of many modern industries, have resulted in a highly globalized fats, oils, and oil cake market. Most of the leading companies have affiliates around the world and are often part of a larger consumer products company. Although the industry in general is highly automated and centralized, some segments (for example, olive oil) are characterized by small production facilities.

Global production of oil meal between 1992 and 1998 rose by about 21 percent to 156.2 mmt, according to the USDA's Economic Research Service (ERS). The ERS estimated that the worldwide output of edible oil reached 75.5 mmt in 1998, up 23 percent from 61.3 mmt in 1992. Cross-border trade of oil meal totaled an estimated 52.1 mmt in 1998, up from 42.4 mmt in 1992, according to the USDA's Economic Research Service (ERS). Meanwhile, the ERS estimated that international edible oil trade grew to 30.6 mmt in 1998, up from about 22 mmt in 1992.

Through the early 2000s, the oil meal segment continued expanding, reaching 175.7 mmt in 2005. Global oil meal trade also climbed. According to FAO statistics, global exports of oilseed cake and meals was more than US$23.4 billion in 2003, while trade in edible oils reached about US$3 billion. FAO analysts expected consumption of fats and oils to expand most rapidly in newly industrialized countries. Demand for oil meals was expected to grow steadily through the 2000s. Global consumption increased about 22 to 24 percent from 1992 to 1998 and was expected to continue to grow, according to the ERS.

World production of major oilseed crops, according to USDA figures, grew from 314.23 million metric tons (mmt) in 2001 to a projected 382.79 mmt in 2005. The largest crop by far was soybeans, at 219.23 mmt in 2005, followed by rapeseed (45.55 mmt), cottonseed (45.12 mmt), peanut (33.44 mmt), and palm kernel (8.74 mmt). Expansion was expected to accelerate. Most of this increase was expected to come from developing countries, especially in South America and Asia. Significant growth in oil production was also expected in China and India, where improvements in extraction facilities had increased output of oils.

In 2005, global oil cake (crush) production was broken down as follows: soybean cake, 174.29 mmt; rapeseed (canola) cake, 40.72 mmt; cottonseed cake, 32.46 mmt; sunflower seed cake, 21.73 mmt; groundnut (peanut) cake, 15.82 mmt; and palm kernel cake, 8.64 mmt. World production of soybean oil reached 32.09 mmt, just ahead of palm oil, at 31.13 mmt. However, combined palm oil production—including palm kernel oil output of 3.76 mmt—exceeded that of soybean oil. Rapeseed oil totaled 15.6 mmt, while ground nutoil was 5.03 mmt and cottonseed oil was 4.69 mmt.

Since 1980, palm oil production and consumption have increased dramatically to make this the world's second largest vegetable oil segment. In addition, palm oil was the most traded oil, reaching 22.68 mmt in 2001. Global exports of palm oil topped 20.8 mmt in 2003, while exports of palm kernel oil were 1.6 mmt. That year, the world exported more than 10 mmt of soybean oil.

Asia since the late 1990s has increased its own production capacities for fats and oils, necessitating fewer imports. By the early 2000s, however, substantial growth in Asian economies boosted both demand production. The FAO estimated that Southeast Asia would remain a primary importer of oilseed meals throughout the mid-2000s.

CURRENT CONDITIONS

One of the significant issues in the mid-2000s regarding fats and oils was health concerns. In response to these concerns, many restaurants in the United States became "trans-fat free," including Kentucky Fried Chicken, Wendy's, Ruby Tuesday, California Pizza Kitchen, and Taco Bell. McDonald's had vowed to replace its trans-fat cooking oils in 2002, but it was'nt until 2007 that it found a substitute that would retain the desired flavor and texture of their French fries. Some changes were taking place in Europe, also. European president of McDonald's Denis Hennequin stated that a new cooking oil (a mixture of rapeseed and sunflower) with lower trans-fat levels will be used in the McDonald's outlets beginning in 2008. According to *Oils & Fats International* despite the rally against trans-fats in the United States, many fast-food places that do continue to use trans-fat oils have not lost business. Trans-oils are so common in Americans's diets, in fact, that the average individual consumes 4.7 pounds a year. According to ERS data, Amercians' intake of fats and oils has increased 63 percent since 1970.

Despite the questionable health status of the actual products, the fats and oils industry remained healthy in the United States in the mid-2000s. According to the USDA, agricultural exports were expected to reach an all-time high in the later 2000s. Two-thirds of the increase was attributed to the grain and oilseed sectors. One of the trends responsible for the rise in oilseed exports was a slower production growth rate of oilseed in South America.

Another notable trend in the mid-2000s was the use of oils to produce biodiesel fuel. Biodiesel, an alternative fuel that is derived from fats and is biodegradable and nontoxic, can be used in standard diesel engines with little or no modification. Europe is the largest producer of biodiesel fuel, with an output in 2005 estimated at between 2.4 and 2.6 million tons. According to private sector estimates cited by the FAO, between 10 to 15 percent of EU vegetable oil production in 2005 was destined for biodiesel. *Energy Bulletin* reported that biodiesel processing consumed nearly 50 percent of EU rapeseed oil production in 2005; the ERS estimates this level at about 30 percent. Though biodiesel is seen as an affordable means of reducing world dependence on petroleum, it is not without its critics, who charge that it is unethical to use food products to run machines.

WORKFORCE

The majority of this manufacturing industry's employees are engaged in direct production. Others oversee finances, participate in management, and market the products. In general, the fats and oils industry is highly automated; labor costs for operations in the United States and Europe account for less than 20 percent of total costs. But in developing countries, where labor is far less expensive than technology, employment levels are higher. Vertical and horizontal integration throughout the global industry have also helped to raise productivity. These factors, combined with a modest growth rate in the industry overall, contributed to a generally shrinking rate of employment.

RESEARCH AND TECHNOLOGY

The fats and oils industry is research intensive. Most research and development expenditures focus on the development of new consumer products such as fat replacements. Biodiesel, an automotive fuel derived from vegetable oils and animal fats, had the potential to increase the nonfood aspect of animal and vegetable oil consumption. Most biodiesel progress was made in the United States, where a major processing plant was built in the 1990s. In 2003, the U.S. Department of Energy funded a joint research program with Cargill, a leading fats and oils company, to evolve technologies for developing chemicals and alternative fuels from oils. Environmental concerns also stimulated new waste-reducing initiatives, both in terms of production and packaging. In addition, fat and oil producers also researched ways of reducing the fat and cholesterol content of their edible oils in the mid to late 1990s in response to consumer demands, especially in the Europe Union and the United States. One notable product to reach the market was Procter & Gamble's Olestra, a controversial fat substitute introduced in the United States in 1996. The product, used initially in snack foods, is an engineered fat that cannot be digested like conventional fats and thus has no nutritional or caloric value. However, its passage through the digestive tract actually depletes certain beneficial substances such as vitamins, and consumption of Olestra can trigger digestive problems.

INDUSTRY LEADERS

UNILEVER

World leader Unilever, a British/Dutch conglomerate, was a major oilseed processor at the beginning of the twentieth century. In 1885, the company was founded in the United Kingdom by William Hesketh Lever to manufacture soap. It ventured into oilseed crushing in the early 1900s and began producing edible vegetable oils and margarines shortly thereafter. The company maintained its leading position in the industry and the food market in general through vertical integration, aggressive globalization (it had overseas operations as early as 1900), and many acquisitions. The company spent over US$5 billion on acquisitions in the late 1980s. In 1993, Unilever acquired olive oil manufacturer Bertolli from Italy's Fisvi for about US$90 million. The purchase added US$150 million in annual olive oil sales and 8.5 percent of that market to Unilever's existing 14 percent share. In the late 1990s, Unilever's oil products—margarine and olive oil—held some of the highest market shares in the industry worldwide. In 2000, Unilever became one of the world's top three food companies when it acquired Bestfoods (which included the brands Hellmann's and Skippy). As of the mid-2000s, Unilever owned the following brands, among others: Ben & Jerry's, Lipton, Bird's Eye, and Slim-Fast. The long-term goal, however, was to reduce the number of brands from 1,600 to about 400 in order to streamline the company and ensure efficiency and manageability. The company's overall sales totaled US$54.4 billion in 2006.

ARCHER DANIELS MIDLAND (ADM)

Activities of the Archer Daniels Midland Company (ADM) are concentrated in the United States, Europe, South

America, and, more recently, Asia. Founded in 1903, the firm earned a spot among top fat and oil producers by maintaining a focus on agriculture and investing in research, especially studies of textured soy protein. ADM manufactures oil from soybeans, sunflowers, canola, corn, and other oilseeds for home use and for further processing into margarine. As of 2004, two-thirds of Archer Daniels Midland's revenues came from oilseed products (especially soybean and peanut), including vegetable oils, animal feed, and emulsifiers. The company's overall sales exceeded US$36.5 billion in 2006, and it employed more than 25,000 people.

ConAgra

Another U.S. company, ConAgra, ranked among the world's largest manufacturer of oilseed products in the mid-2000s. ConAgra is also one of the largest food service manufacturers in the United States, providing poultry, French fries, and dough-based products for the food service industry. Some of its brands include Banquet, Chef Boyardee, Egg Beaters, Healthy Choice, Hunt's, Jiffy, Orville Redenbacher's, PAM, Slim Jim, and Van Camp's. With total sales of more than US$14.5 billion in 2004, agricultural processing was a minority segment of the conglomerate's activities, which focused on production of prepared foods by the mid-2000s. ConAgra generated US$11.5 billion in sales in 2006 and had 33,000 employees.

Bunge Limited

Founded in 1818, Bunge became the world's leading oilseed processing company in 2003 with its acquisition of Cereol. The largest player in South America since the 1990s, the company further expanded its capacity in 2004 with the acquisition of a major crushing facility in Ukraine. Its placement near key transport facilities was expected to boost sales in Asian markets. Bunge is also the world's top seller of bottled vegetable oils, as well as Europe's primary producer of soybean meal. Bunge recently entered into a partnership with DuPont to create Solae, a top producer of soy protein products. In 2006 Bunge reported total sales of more than US$26.2 billion and employed 23,495 workers.

Other Leaders

Other major producers include Toshoku (Japan); Cargill (United States); and Nisshin Oil Mills (Japan).

Major Countries in the Industry

The United States

The United States has historically led the global fats, oils, and oil cake industry, due primarily to its dominance in the largest oilseed category, soybeans. In 2003, the United States produced more than 40 percent of the world's total soybean crop and accounted for almost half of world soybean exports. Though production decreased in 2004, production in 2005 totaled 19.5 billion pounds. Other production that year included corn oil at 2.4 billion pounds, cottonseed oil at 983 million pounds, and peanut oil at 160 million pounds. The United States also ranked among the leading traders of fats and oils with total exports in 2001 of 5.8 mmt of oil meals (11 percent of world exports) and 1.5 mmt of edible oils (4.9 percent of world exports). In 2003, the United States led global production of oil cakes and meals with total output of 38.19 mmt. It also produced 9.5 mmt of vegetable oils and fats. Soybean cake (44.91 mmt) accounted for the vast majority of U.S. output in 2004. The country also produced 1.0 mmt of cottonseed cake.

China

Ranking second in production in 2003 and the world's major market for oils and oilseed products, China was expected to boost total oilseed production from about 50.8 mmt in 2004 to 58.5 mmt in 2005. Demand for vegetable oils and oilmeal increased dramatically in China in the late 1990s and early 2000s. Consumption of edible oils grew by an unprecedented 60 percent between 1999 and 2000, while consumption of oil meal rose by 40 percent. Production of total oilcakes and meals reached 28.5 mmt in 2003. Soybean cake output rose impressively from 18.9 mmt in 2001 to a projected 29 mmt in 2005, while soy oil production was expected to total 5.17 mmt. By 2004, China's consumption was thought to account for almost 20 percent of world usage in this market. In 2004, imports of soybeans were estimated 22 mmt (33% of world trade), and imports of vegetable oils were about 5 mmt (14% of world trade).

Brazil

Among several developing countries that emerged as competitors in the global oils and fats industry in the late 1980s and 1990s, Brazil dominated in 1998 with 18.4 mmt or 12 percent of total world oilmeal output. Production continued to climb, reaching 23.8 mmt in 2003 and making Brazil the third-ranking country in total oil cake and meal output. Of this total, soybean cake accounted for 22.45 mmt and soybean oil production was 5.5 mmt. In 2004, production of oil cakes and meal exceeded 40.5 mmt. Brazil's soybean exports skyrocketed 425.7 percent between 1996 and 2002, but its soymeal and oil exports fell by 5.2 percent. In 2003, its oilseed cake and meal exports totaled 13.6 mmt.

Argentina

Argentina, which ranked sixth worldwide in 1998, rose to fourth place in 2003 after expanding its soybean production by 132.3 percent. Argentina's output of oil cake and meal grew further from 20.7 mmt in 2003 to 27 mmt in 2004. Exports of oilseed cake and meal, which increased 117.1 percent from 1996 to 2002, exceeded 19.8 mmt in 2003. Argentina is also a major producer of sunflower seeds and oil.

The European Union

Tied with China for total production in the late 1990s, the European Union (EU) slipped to fifth place in 2003. Production of oil cakes and meals that year exceeded 19.8 mmt, and production of vegetable oils and fats reached 10.6 mmt.; FAO statistics place EU oil cake production for 2004 at 12.1 mmt. The EUrsquo;s fat and oil industry grew slowly in the mid to late 1990s as a result of its internal production quotas that limit the amount each country can produce. Nonetheless, the EU remained one of the leading producers of oil meal and edible oil, with prospects for significant growth after 2004, when former eastern-bloc countries became members. The entry of Poland, which joined the EU in May 2004, was expected to result in significant increases in rapeseed acreage and production. According to *FWN Financial News,* Poland's rapeseed harvest was expected to grow by about 40 percent in 2005, while rapeseed meal production would increase about 23 percent. Rapeseed was the dominant oilseed crop by far in Europe, with production in 2005 projected at 14.65 mmt, followed by sunflower seed (3.7 mmt). The European Union also remained the world's leading producer of olive oil.

INDIA

India's oil cake production surpassed 16.9 mmt in 2004, as the country ranked sixth in this segment. India also produced 6.01 mmt of edible oil in the same year. While India exported no edible oil, the country remained a major exporter of oil meal in the late 1990s with 4.1 mmt in 1998. In 2001, a variety of factors (the weakening rupee against the U.S. dollar, declining world oil meal prices, and bumper crops) resulted in a substantial increase (almost 39% over 2000 totals) in oil meal exports for India. This boon to exports was much needed after sharp declines between 1998 and 2000 that came from the weakening Asian economy during that time.

MALAYSIA

In the early 2000s, Malaysia remained by far the world's leading producer of palm kernel oil. The country accounted for more than 52.8 percent of world production and, with Indonesia, for approximately 90 percent of world trade. From 2002 to 2003, Malaysia's production of palm oil grew 12.1 percent, reaching 13.1 mmt, while production of crude palm kernel oil, a non-edible product, grew by 11.6 percent to reach 1.64 mmt. In 2005, palm oil output reached 14.75 mmt. The country's burgeoning demand for soap and detergent was expected to increase consumption of crude palm kernel oil by 10 to 15 percent in 2004. Exports also increased. Total exports of palm oil, palm kernel oil and cake, oleochemicals, and finished products grew by 14.2 percent in 2003, totaling 16.78 mmt. In 2005, Malaysia exported 12.9 mmt of palm oil alone.

FURTHER READING

Buckley, John. "Supply Hopes Pinned on Rebound in Soya." *Oils & Fats International,* September 2004.

"Bunge Moves East with Ukraine Venture." *Food Navigator Europe,* 18 March 2004. Available from www.foodnavigator.com.

Canadian Department of Agriculture and Agri-Food Canada. *Market Analysis: Overview: World Oilseed Sector and Canadian Marketing Opportunities,* 2 April 2004. Available from www.agr.gc.ca.

"Cargill Receives Matching Grant to Develop Products from Oilseeds." *Feedstuffs,* 24 November 2003.

"Cottonseed Meal Comes Full Circle." *Southeast Farm Press,* 13 March 2007.

Food and Agriculture Organization of the United Nations. *FAOSTAT.* Online database. 2 April 2007. Available from www.fao.org.

"Hoover's Company Capsules." *Hoover's Online,* 2007. Available from www.hoovers.com.

Lim, Serena. "Transforming the Food Industry." *Oil & Fats International,* 2 January 2007.

Low, Benjamin. "Biodiesel Boom Raises Ethical Issues." *Energy Bulletin,* 7 March 2005. Available from www.energybulletin.net.

McDonald's Set To Be Trans Fat-Free." *The Food Institute Report,* 5 February 2007.

Peksa, Vlad, and Eszter Dargo. "Outlook for Edibles Oils Market." *Oils & Fats International,* May 2006.

"Poland's Rapeseed Crop to Rise 40 Percent." *FWN Financial News,* 5 April 2004.

"Record Olive Oil Production." *Oils and Fats International,* January 2005. Available from www.oilsandfatsinternational.com.

"U.S. Food Consumption Up 16 Percent Since 1970." *Amber Waves,* November 2005.

U.S. Department of Agriculture. "Crop Projection Update," 8 April 2004. Available from www.usda.gov.

U.S. Department of Agriculture. *Oilseeds: World Markets and Trade,* April 2005. April 2004. Available from www.usda.gov.

———. Economic Research Service. *Oil Crops Outlook,* 11 April 2005. Available from www.ers.usda.gov.

———. *The Oils and Fats International File 2000–2007,* 7 March 2002. Available from www.marketfile.com/.

Frumkin, Paul. "Trans-Fat Future Revolves Around Alternative Oil Outlook." *Nation's Restaurant News,* 26 February 2007.

U.S. Department of the Census. *Fats and Oils: Oilseed Crushings: 2003.* December 2004. Available from www.census.gov.

"World Business News: U.S. Agricultural Exports Booming." *Farmers Guardian,* 16 March 2007.

SIC 2041

NAICS 311211

FLOUR AND OTHER GRAIN MILL PRODUCTS

Manufacturers in this industry mill flour or meal from various raw grains, excluding rice. The products of flour mills may be sold plain or in the form of prepared mixes or dough for specific purposes.

INDUSTRY SNAPSHOT

For the flour market (the primary end use of wheat), fluctuating wheat production imposes the most critical global ramifications. As of the mid-2000s, more than 60 percent of the world's wheat supply was converted to flour for making breads, biscuits, cakes, and other dough products. On a consumer level, flour and grain products constitute a substantial part of the world's staple diet, since they are basic ingredients of practically every meal consumed by the world's 6.2 billion people. Fluctuating wheat production statistics largely portend the amount of food consumption and, in many parts of the world, the availability of food supply. In the United States, some 944.8 million bushels of wheat were ground for flour in 2000, but this number dropped steadily through the early 2000s, reaching 865.1 million bushels in 2004. This was the smallest amount in years, and represented the lowest per capita consumption since 1989. However, in 2005 IBIS World predicted industry revenue would grow at around 2.7 percent annually through 2009.

A key factor affecting companies' survival in the flour industry is the ability to compete within the fluid conditions of wheat production and consumption. Companies must maintain the structural and financial stability to weather fluctuations in national currencies, weather-induced wheat shortages, and socioeconomic realities that figure so prominently in the industry. Many companies struggling to reinforce their market foothold attempt to expand their flour-based operations by acquiring new products or tapping new investment sources. Insufficient knowledge of consumer tastes and failure to take a long-term approach invariably lead to costly lessons for some companies, particularly those attempting to penetrate foreign flour markets.

ORGANIZATION AND STRUCTURE

The flow of wheat from field to table relies on a multitude of factors. The quality of a bountiful wheat crop ripe for the flour market industry depends on mild weather that lacks the extremes of cold or heat, rain or drought, wind, snow, or hail. Flour's various end uses derive from the milling process. In some parts of the world, even in the early 2000s, homemakers or local village millers still ground flour by crushing wheat between two stones or pounding wheat with a mortar and pestle. However, most modern mills employ sophisticated high-tech rollers, sifters, and purifiers for cleansing, grinding, separating, and blending wheat. Because individual flour mills normally grind only one wheat class prior to milling, several wheat varieties may be blended and tested. Hard wheats are primarily used for breads and rolls; soft wheats are used in sweet goods, crackers, and prepared mixes; while durum wheat is used in pasta noodles.

Two factors have largely determined flour utilization patterns: national food preferences and flour availability. Although wheat flour is the most popular, any grain can be converted to flour. Part of the universal appeal of wheat flour is that wheat cultivation adapts to a wide variety of climatic conditions. The global acceptance of wheat flour as a food staple resulted from its nutritional qualities. Wheat contains a unique protein called gluten. Mixed with water, gluten forms elastic dough capable of expanding several times its original volume during baking. The smaller amount of gluten protein contained in rye flour produces better dark rye breads, or if blended with wheat flour produces finer-textured light rye breads. Oat flour, the most nutritious flour, and oat meals are primarily used in breakfast food and granola-type products, while barley flour can be found in baby foods and malted milks. In some countries, large quantities of barley flour are used for bread making. Sorghum and millet flours are popular in India, Central America, and Ethiopia in the making of flat bread, tortillas, and pancakes. A small percentage of rice is converted to flour for use in baby foods and sauces. Buckwheat flour is often used in pancakes. Soybean technology has introduced soya flour and grits, which contain 50 percent protein and are adaptable to a variety of bakery products such as cereals, meat products, and soup mixes. Less appealing characteristics of soybean flour result from the multiplication of bacteria, especially during processing with steam and moisture. An excessively high bacterial count causes emission of off-odors and undesirable flavors. There has been continued research aimed to eliminate these adverse side effects.

All flour products must meet certain nutritional and cleanliness standards promulgated by various government agencies such as the U.S. Food and Drug Administration (FDA). The amount and type of additives, carbohydrates, protein, and other nutrients included in flour products derive from required nutritional and safety standards. By law, bread labeled "whole wheat" must be made from 100 percent whole wheat flour. U.S. legislation requiring truth-in-nutrition labeling mandates all food products to be labeled with a list of nutritional contents. The average composition of white flour includes 73.6 percent nitrogen-free extract and 13.5 percent water or other moisture. Millers can ill afford substandard products caused by too much or too little moisture, flour, or sugar, so most dough batches, under government controls, contain very small amounts of potassium bromate and other ingredients to enhance dough baking or other preservation qualities. Likewise the differences between bleached and unbleached flour also affect color and baking quality: bleached flour adds to baking quality and color values while unbleached flour performs better for cookies, pie crusts, and crackers. Despite numerous changes in flour composition and uses, the U.S. public's preference for white flour or bread remains undiminished—probably a carry-over from past eras when white bread symbolized a status befitting royalty.

Because grains are harvested close to the ground, sanitation factors largely determine the survival of flour mills. The Food and Drug Administration regulates sanitation controls for the United States' milling industry by defining levels for unavoidable, naturally occurring food defects considered non-hazardous to human health. High levels of flour bacteria are normally exterminated through numerous milling processes. It has been argued that the cleansing effectiveness of modern machinery not only removes all the bran and germ but also removes the part of the traditional bread flavor as well. On the other hand, some reports cite popular raw cookie dough as a contamination source because of the persistence of live microbes, apparently unaffected by milling heating or baking processes.

The primary structural change by the early 2000s was the worldwide shift of control over wheat and flour production and purchasing decisions from governmental agencies to private enterprises. In 1990, about 80 percent of these decisions where made by governments; in 1998, private millers and grain traders made 70 percent of such decisions. Latin America, in particular, underwent a very dramatic shift of this kind in just a few years. In most cases, privatization led to increased wheat consumption, quality-consciousness, and competition.

MAJOR USES OF FLOUR

In the mid-2000s the heaviest volume users were commercial bakers who used more than 72 percent of the U.S.

flour supply to make breads and cakes. Professional bakers buy flour by grades of refinement, while individual consumers purchase straight flour and convenience mixes. Typically, 100 pounds of wheat yield an average of 72 pounds of white flour, or depending on the variety, 100 pounds of wheat flour. Besides bread, flour is essential in the production of rolls and sweet goods (such as pastries, doughnuts, cakes, and cookies); tortillas, which account for one-fourth of the corn flour market, alongside corn chips and other snack foods; and pasta and noodles, for which the enrichment value ranks the highest of wheat flour-based products.

Perhaps the greatest impetus to guilt-free use of prepackaged foods was the 1920 introduction of biscuit mix, which promised a convenient, tasty product by following a few simple steps. As popularity of mixes increased, flour mills began producing large unit volume mixes, which expanded commercial bakers' application of mixes for all types of products such as doughnuts, pastries, pie shells, cakes, and different breads. After a while, the lustrous period of mixes plummeted because flour marketers believed consumers lacked the time and interest in traditional home baking. A Pillsbury official reiterated the potential of the flour mix market by reminding management that modern bakers are mostly mothers who crave convenience and easy-to-use products that are capable of producing homemade bread. The evidence was sufficiently convincing for Pillsbury to energize flour marketing and spark sales of bread machines and bread mixes by 1994. In the 1990s, 47 percent of volume baking mix users were homemakers with children aged 6 to 11.

BACKGROUND AND DEVELOPMENT

Perhaps more than any other food, wheat has survived consumer fickleness and food fads throughout the ages. In the 2000s, wheat continued to hold its 10,000-year-old status as the staff of life. Anthropologists have ascribed the cultivation and storing of wheat as a pivotal factor in stabilizing habitation patterns. This stability soon stimulated experimentation in expanding wheat as a food supply. Nomadic tribes discovered that using wheat as a food source increased their chances of survival. Archeological finds along the Nile River documented Egyptians applying various techniques of wheat harvesting and using the leavening process in bread making around 2600 B.C. The Romans improved the milling process and are acknowledged as the first people to make white bread. Bread became so important that it gained symbolic significance in some religions. As wheat and bread developed into more lucrative commodities, questions about the more unseemly aspects of bread consumption also arose. During the eighteenth century, for example, controversy erupted regarding the use of new versus old (aged) wheat preferred by French bakers. While the profit factors of new wheat appealed to traders, the public believed that new wheat caused diarrhea, pernicious gas, and possibly epidemic diseases. And according to twentieth-century investigations, contaminated bread—allegedly a cause of psychosis—contributed to witchcraft persecution, which was prevalent during the eighteenth century in Europe.

One of the oldest types of wheat known is bulgur wheat, and the earliest means used to separate the parts of the wheat kernel involved rubbing the grain between the hands. Other methods included having hoofed animals walk over grains that had been spread on hard ground, and winnowing, a process in which grains were tossed in the air so that the chaff would blow away (removing the individual grains from the rest of the plant was necessary before milling could take place).

Grain milling practices were developed to separate the kernel components and make flour. The first types of milling procedures involved the use of rubbing stones, mortar and pestles, or querns. Querns were devices made from two stacked, disk-shaped stones. Wheat grains were poured into the quern through a hole in the top stone. As the two stones turned against each other with a rotary motion, the abrasive movement separated the parts of the wheat kernels and ground the endosperm into flour. The flour was then discharged between the stones.

The first continuous system for milling wheat into flour was developed during the last part of the eighteenth century by an American, Oliver Evans. Evans' mill design used steam technology and employed conveyors and bucket elevators to move the grain through a multi-phase milling process. Further advances in milling technology occurred during the nineteenth century. In 1865, Edmund La Croix developed a middlings purifier that separated the granular endosperm from the bran so that it could be reground to produce a better grade of flour. During the 1870s, the first roller mills were constructed in the United States.

Roller mills possessed several advantages: they eliminated the need to dress millstones; they were able to produce flour through a more gradual extraction process, which enabled millers to yield a larger percentage of better grade flour; and the greater efficiency of these mills made the construction of larger mills more feasible.

During the middle of the twentieth century, fundamental changes occurred in the primary location of mills. Prior to the 1950s, the cost of shipping wheat and the cost of shipping flour were approximately equal, and mills were frequently built close to wheat fields. During the early 1960s, the cost of shipping grain decreased following the introduction of hopper rail cars. At the same time, costs surrounding sanitation requirements increased the price of shipping flour. As a result, mills were constructed closer to end markets rather than near the wheat fields.

Granular flour, a product made with particles of a uniform size with carefully controlled amounts of atomized moisture to reduce clumping, was introduced during the 1960s. Although granular flour was more expensive than regular flour, it offered several advantages: there was less dust, it was easier to pour, it did not require sifting, and it dispersed in cold liquids.

During the 1970s, sales of household flour declined as developed societies moved away from home baking and homemakers demonstrated a preference for the convenience and consistency of prepared mixes. In addition, many mixes were less expensive than individual ingredients. Baking from "scratch" ceased to be an activity of necessity and was relegated to hobby status. Demographic information revealed that households with higher incomes were more likely to use flour than lower income households. Declines in flour use by households were partially offset by increases of flour sales to commercial bakers. Also during this period, the flour and grain mill industry was adversely affected when a nutrition-conscious population denounced starchy breads and tantalizing sugar products. Others rejected the reduced quality of commercial bakery products because of overuse of additives.

Acquisition activity and globalization continued to transform the industry, particularly as such activity was concentrated in emerging markets in Asia, Eastern Europe, and South America. China's transition from an agrarian economy to an industrial one posed opportunities for major international corporations such as U.S.-based Cargill Inc. and Archer Daniels Midland to make substantial inroads into that country. Middle Eastern countries continued to modernize their milling operations, allowing for the region's growing global presence within the industry. Qatar's flour milling industry, for example, realized the effects of a healthy economy and improved technology and computer mechanization. As a consequence, grain-based food consumption in Qatar increased about 10 to 15 percent annually in the late 1990s.

In the 2000s, not all developing countries were greeting increased internationalization with open arms, however. Zambia, for instance, countered what it viewed as unfair foreign competition with a ban on flour imports in 2002. Indonesia, amid massive deregulation of its economy, maintained a flour consumption rate that was roughly a quarter that of the United States, which presented a significant market for potential growth to foreign corporations. But, as the market itself became privatized, the government implemented substantial tariffs on wheat flour to stave off foreign competition that could overpower domestic producers.

Such protective actions were not limited to developing nations. In the United States, the federal government took action against what it saw as harmfully high imports of wheat gluten.

Another issue of increasing prominence within the industry was health consciousness and quality control. Consumer demand for a nutritionally positive product dramatically altered the dynamics of the industry. As individual millers and companies assumed control of production and purchasing activities from governments, the focus shifted from the high quantity, low price demand that prevailed under governmental authority to the increased competition among industry players to offer consumers a high quality product at affordable prices. As a result, many companies invested substantial sums in research aimed at improving quality control. Grain quality includes an assessment of the physical characteristics of grain such as weight and moisture content, cleanliness and phytosanitary conditions (such as presence of weed seeds or pests), and an assessment of the intrinsic nutritional characteristics such as protein and gluten content. Reportedly less than a third of the world market demands these high wheat standards, but these markets include higher income groups that prefer protein, wholesome white bread, corn sweeteners, and tofu. Purchasing decisions may be affected by other factors, particularly price, but USDA studies found that grain importers most often base purchases on intrinsic characteristics. Purchases by state trading agencies in developing countries reportedly reflect less attention to quality and more to price. In the wake of world trade liberalizations such as the General Agreement on Tariffs and Trade (GATT), U.S. exporters may need to treat each market individually, dealing with importers' preferences almost on a retail basis.

CURRENT CONDITIONS

In 2006, world wheat flour exports reached 10.7 billion tons, making it the second biggest year on record. The all-time high was reached in 1997, when wheat flour exports totaled 11.6 billion tons. The European Union, traditionally the world's largest flour exporter, lost its number-one spot in 2006 to Turkey. The E.U. was responsible for 2 million tons, whereas Turkey exported 2.25 million tons. The question of export subsidies for E.U. wheat remained controversial. In January 2005, the European Commission announced that subsidies, which had been suspended for 18 months, would resume for 2 million tons of wheat exports.

Kazakhstan, a member of the Commonwealth of Independent States, emerged as a leader in flour exporting in 2006 with 1.3 million tons. Argentina was also a major player, exporting 700,00 tons in 2006. Other countries seeing gains in flour exports included Brazil, Bolivia, Nigeria, Chile, Pakistan, and China. The United States, which at one time competed with the E.U. as a flour export leader, exported only 300,000 tons in 2006.

While the top exporters remain fairly constant, the names of the major importers change frequently. From 1998 to 1999, the top importers were Libya (with more than 800,000 tons imported) and Yemen (importing slightly over 1 million tons). Again from 1999 to 2000, these countries were the top importers; Libya imported a little over 1 million tons, and Yemen imported 700,000 tons. At various times, major importers have included the former USSR, Algeria, and Egypt. In 2004, Libya again led in flour imports with an estimated 1.2 million tons. According to International Grains Council (IGC) statistics, Libya's flour imports accounted for 17 percent of total world trade in 2003 and about 13 percent in 2004. Demand in Indonesia also continued to grow, making it a major importer of flour in 2006.

One trend affecting domestic flour sales in the mid-2000s was the growing popularity of low-carbohydrate diets. Per capita consumption of flour in the United States decreased by 7 pounds per year between 2001 and 2003, due largely to the influence of low-carbohydrate diets. This trend particularly affected bread and pasta manufacturers. In response, companies were introducing low-carbohydrate versions of these products in which some portion of refined flour was replaced by a higher-protein ingredient, such as whole wheat flour, wheat germ, or soy protein.

The United States is recognized as having the most technologically advanced and most efficient grain handling industry. Since U.S. flour mills could not keep up with increased domestic demand through much of the late twentieth century, U.S. exports fell accordingly, declining 57 percent between 1970 and 2000. But after reaching record levels in 2000, domestic consumption began to decline. Flour consumption in the U.S. dropped by 2.6 percent in 2001 and 2 percent in 2002. Though demand grew by 0.4 percent in 2003, per capita usage fell by about one pound from the previous year. This trend continued through 2004, with per capita consumption falling to a 16-year low. According to the U.S. Department of Agriculture's Economic Research Service (ERS) estimates quoted in *Bakingbusiness.com,* "much of the consumption gain posted in the last half of the final decade of the 20th century has been wiped out by the reductions posted thus far in the 21st century."

RESEARCH AND TECHNOLOGY

In the mid-2000s, new flours and ingredients continued as research priorities for the flour and grain industry. Milo grain, a sturdy, nutritious variety of sorghum cultivated for about 30 percent less cost, was being studied as a wheat flour substitute for pancake mixes. The wet and dry milling process for milo offered tremendous potential as a top-quality wheat flour steeped in vitamins and minerals. Without the grittiness and bitter taste of whole grain, the palatability of milo grain products could possibly convert almost 40 percent of the population to whole grain products. By making whole grain flour more easily extruded, ConAgra planned to stimulate this virgin market with the introduction of ultra fine whole grain flour mixes in schools for making pizza crust, griddle mix, buttermilk muffins, and a host of other products. Genetic engineering and unconventional use of baker's yeast may possibly lead to wheat that produces a superior baking flour with more nutrients.

A United Nations report in 2004 blamed "alarming" deficits in IQs, productivity, and health across entire countries on the lack of simple nutrients such as folic acid, niacin, and iron. Folic acid, a natural component of wheat and whole wheat products that is mostly lost in the milling process, is an essential vitamin that aids metabolic processes and produces red blood cells. The United States has, since 1998, required that food companies must add folic acid to most enriched bread, corn meal, flour, pasta, and rice products. Since then, incidents of two major birth defects, spina bifida and anencephaly, have declined by at least 20 percent. Flour is also routinely enriched in other western countries, but nutrients are not added to flour in developing countries, where grain is most often processed in small mills. To prevent vitamin deficiencies, which contribute to mental impairment, birth defects, and other debilitating conditions, the United Nations has urged that developing countries increase their production of enriched foods such as flour.

Genetic selection and genetic engineering made up an area of concentration for researchers in the mid-2000s. It has been found that protein content and overall quality of corn meal and other products can be enhanced by these means. In addition, debranning techniques, by which bran layers are stripped from the endosperm and hydrated before the milling process, came into play in the late 1990s. This technique allows for greater, more accurate control of finished flour moisture, which in turn improves bread quality and baking quality. A process to separate gluten and starch from wheat flour using ethanol instead of water may reduce waste treatment costs associated with the conventional process.

NEW EQUIPMENT

Excessively high or low moisture content signals a problem for the flour industry. Moisture content affects insect growth if moisture is below 14 percent and mold accumulation if it is higher than 14.5 percent. Wheat arrives at the mill with different moisture levels; therefore, without manual adjustment of moisture, mills have difficulty maintaining flour finish moisture of 14 percent. A U.S. company, Maple Leaf Flour Mill, installed a precise moisture control microwave-type system, which caused milling efficiency to increase 0.5 percent. Moreover, daily production of 550 tons of flour was maintained with 4.75 tons less wheat per day, which saved the company US$104,000 annually. Upon installation of new sifters capable of sifting diverse materials six days a week, the machine eliminated down time with a perfect reliability record.

INDUSTRY LEADERS

ARCHER DANIELS MIDLAND COMPANY (ADM)

Started as the Archer-Daniels Linseed Company in 1903, the Archer Daniels Midland Company spent its first two decades purchasing oil processing companies in the Midwest United States. In 1930, the Commander-Larabee Company, a major flour miller, was purchased. By the company's fiftieth anniversary in 1952, Archer Daniels Midland was manufacturing over 200 standard products and had extended its operations overseas. ADM, whose grain milling division produces flour for bread, cakes, pasta, tortillas, and various ingredients for the baking industry, generated revenues of US$36.5 billion in 2006, with wheat and other milled products accounting for about 12 percent of the total. Approximately 33 percent of ADM's revenues come from outside the United States, and the company has food processing plants in Asia, Canada, Europe, South America, and the United States. ADM's reputation was tarnished in the early 2000s by a federal investigation and subsequent lawsuits stemming from price-fixing allegations relating to high-fructose corn syrup. In 2004 the company agreed to pay US$400 million in damages to Coca-Cola, Pepsi Cola, and other food manufacturers that had brought claims against ADM.

GENERAL MILLS, INC.

For more than 60 years, General Mills survived as an independent corporation by relying on its flour milling and breakfast cereals. Although incorporated in 1928, the company's origins date back to 1866, when Cadwallader Washburn opened a flour mill in Minnesota. His business, which soon became the Washburn Crosby Company, competed with local miller C. A. Pillsbury. In 1928, General Mills was formed, employing 5,800 workers and generating sales of US$123 million. Its strongest products at the time were Gold Medal Flour, Softasilk Cake Flour, and Wheaties, a then recently introduced ready-to-eat cereal. Also in 1928, Betty Crocker's name was introduced in connection with General Mills' consumer goods. Although the company through the years bought and sold such diverse entities as Eddie Bauer, Talbot's, and the Red Lobster and Olive Garden chains, in the late 1990s General Mills again focused on food products as evidenced by its decision in 2001 to double its size by purchasing Pillsbury from Diageo. General Mills also produces its own flour, which it sells to bakeries. In 2006, sales continued their steady climb to reach US$11.6 billion.

CARGILL INC.

The largest U.S. private corporation, Cargill Inc. is one of the largest grain and commodities players in the world and a longtime leader in the U.S. flour milling industry. William Wallace Cargill began his grain business in 1865 in Iowa. The business grew as it followed the expansion of the railroad in the period after the U.S. Civil War. During the Great Depression, Cargill invested heavily in the storage and transportation of grain, secure in the knowledge that a recovering economy would find Cargill reaping the benefits. By 1940, 60 percent of Cargill's business involved foreign markets. In 1955, the company opened a Swiss subsidiary to sell grain in Europe; and in the early 1960s, Cargill began its move into communist countries. In the 1990s, Cargill stepped up its foreign ventures, resuming trade with post-apartheid South Africa and expanding its Asian and Eastern European operations. Total revenues rose from US$59.8 billion in 2003 to US$75.2 billion in 2006.

CONAGRA FOODS, INC.

ConAgra maintains a strong presence in nearly all areas of the U.S. food processing industry. Conceived in 1919 when a collection of mills consolidated to form Consolidated Mills Inc., the company steadily diversified and grew to become a national food powerhouse. In 1971, Consolidated Mills changed its name to ConAgra Inc., and then it grew consistently through the 1990s, by which time it had diversified heavily within the food industry and expanded into a global outfit, with employees in 32 countries. ConAgra in the mid-2000s was one of the largest food service manufacturer in the United States, providing poultry, French fries, and dough-based products for the food service industry. In 2006, ConAgra's total revenues totaled US$11.5 billion. Only a small segment of this was attributed to agricultural processing, however, as the company's focus shifted to prepared foods in the late 1990s. ConAgra's top brands, such as Chef Boyardee, Banquet, Healthy Choice, and Van Camp's, generate approximately US$100 million in sales each year.

FURTHER READING

"Business Outlook: Flour Mill Product Manufacturing." *Food Magazine,* 24 February 2005.

China's Corn Output Reaches Record High." *Asia Pulse,* 14 March 2007.

Day, Sherri. "They Come to Praise the Carb, Not Bury It." *New York Times,* 4 February 2004.

"Hoover's Company Capsules." *Hoover's Online,* 2007. Available from www.hoovers.com.

"International Grains Council Says E.U. Flour Exports May Rise." *Bakingbusiness.com,* 14 March 2005. Available from www.bakingbusiness.com.

Manor, Robert. "ADM to Pay $400 Million in Price Fixing Case." *Chicago Tribune,* 23 June 2004. Available from http://prorev.com.

Ramachandran, Arjun. "Flour Mill Product Manufacturing." *Food Magazine,* 1 February 2006.

"Flour Power." *Chemistry and Industry,* 2 October 2006.

Shelke, Kantha. "Grain-based Foods Fight Back." *Ingredients,* 2 April 2004. Available from www.foodprocessing.com.

Schlachter, Barry. "Giving Bread a Boost: New Additives Are Touted as a Way to Help Lower Bad Cholesterol, Aid Health." *Fort Worth Star-Telegram,* 4 April 2007.

Sosland, Morton. "IGC Estimates 3 Percent Decline in World Flour Exports in 2003-03." *Baking Business,* 8 March 2004. Available from www.bakingbusiness.com.

"Opening Up New Markets for UK Wheat." *Farmers Guardian,* 20 March 2007.

———. "Sharp Fall Affirmed in Total, Per Capita Flour Use." *Bakingbusiness.com,* 30 March 2005. Available from http://www.bakingbusiness.com.

———. "Upturn in World Flour Exports as Kazakhstan Looms." *bakingbusiness.com,* 5 April 2007.

———. "U.S. Flour Usage Increases for First Time since 2000." *Baking Business,* 5 April 2004. Available from www.bakingbusiness.com.

U.S. Census Bureau. "Flour Milling Products: 2005."*Current Industrial Reports,* June 2006. Available from http://www.census.gov.

U.S. Department of Agriculture, Economic Research Service and Foreign Agricultural Service. *Outlook for U.S. Agricultural Trade, 2005.* Available from www.fas.usda.gov.

U.S. Department of Agriculture, Foreign Agricultural Service. *Turkey Grain and Feed Annual, 2005.* Available from www.fas.usda.gov.

———. *Grain: World Markets and Trade.* March 2007. Available from www.fas.usda.gov.

———. *World Wheat, Flour, and Products Trade,* 9 March 2007. Available from www.fas.usda.gov.

"U.S. Flour Use Down." *Bakery-Net Newsletter,* July 2003. Available from www.bakery-net.com.

SIC 2086

NAICS 312111

SOFT DRINKS AND BOTTLED WATER

Producers in this industry supply the world's sodas, bottled waters, and other prepared nonalcoholic beverages. See also **Alcoholic Beverages.**

INDUSTRY SNAPSHOT

The global soft drinks industry is almost exclusively a marketing phenomenon. The actual product is a comparatively simple blend of water, sweeteners, flavors, and other additives. The industry's genius lies in convincing billions of consumers to drink soft drinks instead of plain water or other beverages. Through its vast annual investments in advertising and marketing, the industry enjoyed some of the highest brand recognition in the world along with spectacular sales. In 2002, according to USDA's *Agricultural Outlook,* annual sales of carbonated soft drinks reached US$193 billion, with sales for fruit and vegetable drinks reaching approximately US$69 billion each. The overall trend through the early 2000s was expected to be an increase in product variety, improved infrastructure and packaging, and expanded markets—particularly in the developing world.

Global soft drinks consumption reached 327 billion liters in 2003, a 5.7 percent increase from the previous year, with the global soft drink industry being valued at US$393 billion in 2002. While soft drinks are enjoyed in virtually every nation on earth, most of the major markets—such as North America, Europe, and Japan—were considered mature, meaning that per-capita consumption was expected to rise slowly, if at all. For example, in Europe, only about 2.5 billion gallons of soft drinks are consumed annually, according to Britvic, a leading soft drinks manufacturer in the United Kingdom and Europe. As a result, throughout the 1990s and into the twenty-first century, soft drink manufacturers moved aggressively into developing but highly populated areas, such as the alliance of 11 former Soviet Republics that make up the Commonwealth of Independent States (CIS), Eastern Europe, China, and India. The industry was projected to grow at about 5 percent through the early 2000s, with the largest increase coming from Asia.

The global soft drinks industry in the early 2000s was dominated by the Coca-Cola Company and PepsiCo Inc. at an unprecedented level seen in international business. Coca-Cola in 2003 controlled about 25 percent of the global soft drinks market, and had a 43.3 percent share of the U.S. market in 2004. The company also held an enormous share of nearly every major international market; as of 2000 it held a 47 percent share of the global carbonated soft drinks (CSD) market. PepsiCo ranked second, with about 11 percent of the global market in 2002 and 32 percent of the U.S. market in 2004. Cadbury Schweppes, the third largest soft drink company, captured 8 percent of the global market in 2000 and 14.3 percent of the U.S. market in 2003. Cott Corporation, the world's largest producer of store-brand carbonated soft drinks (CSDs), claimed 2 percent of the global market and 4.7 percent of the U.S. market in 2003. And while most country's local brands captured a significant share of their markets, few of these could match the manufacturing, marketing, and distribution prowess of Coca-Cola and, in some markets, Pepsi (which does business in international markets as Pepsi-Cola International(PCI)).

Some industry analysts believe the traditional concept of equating soft drinks primarily with carbonated beverages, particularly colas, must be revised to reflect the growing popularity of other ready-to-drink (RTD) beverages, such as teas, coffees, herbal beverages, juices, and sports and energy drinks. When viewed in this broader sense, another group of soft drink competitors emerge, most notably Proctor & Gamble in the United States, France's Danone, Switzerland's Nestle Beverages, and England's Unilever. The latter company estimated its share of the total nonalcoholic ready-to-drink (RTD) beverage market in 2000 at about 19 percent. As of 2004, Coca-Cola-trademarked RTD beverages accounted for 1.3 billion of the 50 billion beverage servings of all kinds consumed around the world each day.

ORGANIZATION AND STRUCTURE

Soft drink manufacturing is remarkably similar worldwide. Soft drink companies manufacture and sell beverage syrups and bases to bottling operations, a growing proportion of which are owned by the soft drink manufacturers themselves. The bottling operations add sweeteners and carbonated water to produce the final product and distribute it, usually in specific territories assigned by the soft drink manufacturers.

Global soft drink manufacturers usually develop local bottling operations in the countries in which they operate. They license bottlers to sell their products or buy local bottlers outright. While they might import ingredients, bottling is done locally. By the early 2000s, PepsiCo and Coca-Cola had company-owned franchised bottling plants in more than 120 countries that produced their respective brands. Some soft drinks, including mineral waters such as Perrier, have distinctive qualities that cannot be reproduced in local markets and thus are exported in bottled form to foreign markets.

In the bottling operation, incoming water is cleaned and clarified. Carbon dioxide gas, which provides effervescence, is supplied to bottlers either in solid form (dry ice) or under pressure in liquid form. To create a finished product, the flavoring syrup is diluted with water, and then cooled, carbonated, and bottled. The bottling process is highly automated, as is the washing of returnable bottles.

In the United States and overseas, major soft drink manufacturers such as Coca-Cola and PepsiCo (PCI) have acquired many independent bottlers and consolidated them into single enterprises. Coca-Cola Enterprises (CCE), for example, was the world's largest soft drink bottler in 2003, accounting for approximately 62 percent of case volume in Coca-Cola trademark beverages. CCE's net operating revenues in 2003, according to Coca-Cola's annual report, reached approximately US$17.3 billion. Pepsi bottling operations accounted for 52 percent of Pepsi's soft drink products in the United States. The same trend was evident in the company's overseas market, particularly in Latin America, where PCI was active in integrating various bottling operations.

CULTURAL DIFFERENCES

Soft drink consumption varies widely by region and by culture. As a result, consumption does not necessarily coincide closely with population or economic development. For example, combined sales of Coca-Cola Co. products in Germany, Great Britain, Spain, Italy, France, and the Benelux countries (Belgium, Netherlands and Luxemborg)—some of the most highly developed economies in the world—were matched by sales in Mexico and Brazil, despite their developing economies

Soft drinks are available around the world in two forms: packaged and fountain service, where soft drinks are dispensed into cups. While packaged products account for the majority of soft drink volume in most countries, fountain sales grew faster in the early to mid-1990s as soft drink manufacturers aggressively sought additional outlets for their products. In the United States, Coca-Cola dominates the fountain business, with 65 percent of the market at the beginning of the 2000s, compared to 25 percent for Pepsi and 10 percent for Cadbury Schweppes.

PACKAGING AND VENDING

Most packaged soft drinks come in glass or plastic bottles and aluminum, steel, or plastic cans. While the majority of packaged soft drinks are sold in multi-packs in stores, a large proportion is sold from vending machines, which began in the early twentieth century as ice coolers. In the early 2000s, refrigerated vending machines dispensed soft drinks in cups, cans, or bottles.

The world-wide growth in vending continued in the early 2000s among nations with rising living standards and receding inflation levels. The high inflation rates in many countries were one of the main barriers to international vending because of the speed in which vending prices can become obsolete. However, as inflation came under control in most countries in the mid to late 1990s, vending operations took off.

IMPACT OF PRIVATE LABELS

While branded products are the heart of the soft drink industry, private label soft drink products (also referred to as "store brands" or "own labels"), sold exclusively by individual retailers such as supermarkets, garner a significant share of many of the world's markets. As supermarkets and general merchandisers have grown in size and influence around the world, they have become more aggressive in marketing their brands, including soft drinks.

Although consumers usually prefer advertised brands to private label products, they do look for bargains in their selections. During recessions, sales of private label soft drinks tend to rise. Major brands can respond by lowering their prices to compete with private labels, but at the cost of lower profits.

Still, private label products present strong competition for soft drink manufacturers. Most supermarkets, particularly those in Europe, carry an extensive array of private label products. Private label soft drink products were a hot trend in the mid-1990s, largely because of the spectacular success of Toronto, Canada-based Cott Corp. Cott adopted a strategy of offering top-notch quality for its private label products, mostly colas. Using syrup from Royal Crown Co., Cott packaged its private label brands in eye-catching packages and sold them for 25 percent less than Coke and Pepsi. More importantly, Cott developed close relationships with some of the most powerful food and general merchandise retailers in the world, such as J. Sainsbury (Great Britain) and Wal-Mart (United States). As a result, Cott gained prized shelf space in stores, often the premium eye-level positions.

In the United Kingdom, the J. Sainsbury chain introduced Sainsbury Classic Cola in April 1994, supplied by Cott, with spectacular results. The Classic brand accounted for 75 percent of Sainsbury cola sales just a few months later, dropping Pepsi's share of Sainsbury soft drink sales from 21 to 10 percent and Coke's share from 44 percent to 9 percent.

While branded products still accounted for about 80 percent of supermarket sales in the United States, at Save-A-Lot, a unit of Minneapolis-based food distributor Supervalu Inc., 85 percent of the chain's sales derived from private label items. The successful fast-growing chain, which specialized in private label brands, had opened more than 1,000 stores in 37 states by 2004. By the early 2000s, Save-A-Lot had produced a net profit margin of about 2 percent of sales, nearly double the supermarket industry average of just over 1.1 percent. In the soft drink category, the chain marketed Bubba Cola instead of Coke, and Dr. Pop as a replacement for Dr Pepper, as well as other brands

INTERNATIONAL CHALLENGES

One interesting aspect of the global soft drink industry is how various companies operate in war-torn or dangerous areas. The nearly universal demand for soft drinks requires companies to use creative strategies to supply customers under sometimes very difficult circumstances. For example, the soft drink bottler and distributor Postobon(known formally as Gaseosas Posada Tobon SA)thrived in Colombia even in the midst of a civil war in the late 1990s. With headquarters in Medellin, Colombia, Postobon had 33 bottling plants. It was able to operate in "hot" areas of the country by deftly handling charged situations involving two guerilla armies and local authorities. The frequent kidnapping of businessmen was another major problem in Colombia. To minimize this risk, the sites and timings of monthly Postobon meetings were frequently changed. And so as not to appear to be taking sides, managers never visited local army bases. If they did, the guerrillas would likely destroy the local bottling plants.

Postobon was competing effectively with the national Coca-Cola bottler, owned by Mexico's Panamerican Beverages Inc. (Panamaco). Postobon spent about US$100 million in 1996 and 1997 to distribute thousands of new coolers bearing the Postobon name around the country. Panamaco spent about the same amount to distribute its own coolers.

BACKGROUND AND DEVELOPMENT

The term soft drink was coined to distinguish flavored drinks from hard liquor. Soft drinks are nonalcoholic beverages, carbonated or uncarbonated, containing a natural or artificial sweetening agent, natural or artificial flavors, and other ingredients. Coffee, tea, milk, cocoa, and undiluted fruit and vegetable juices are not usually classified as soft drinks. Soft drinks were originally designed to substitute for liquor in an effort to reduce alcohol consumption.

Soft drinks first appeared in seventeenth-century Europe as a mixture of water and lemon juice sweetened with honey. In 1676, the Paris-based Compagnie de Limonadiers was founded and granted a monopoly by the French monarchy. Company vendors dispensed cups of lemonade from tank packs on their backs. The first carbonated beverages, again appearing in Europe, were inspired by the popularity of effervescent water from natural springs, which were widely thought to have medicinal value.

Joseph Priestley, called by some the father of the soft drinks industry, experimented with carbon dioxide gas from brewery fermenting vats. In 1772, he invented a small carbonating apparatus in London, which pumped carbon dioxide into water. At first, bottled waters were used medicinally.

Mineral salts and flavors were later added as the appeal of soft drinks spread.

In 1886, John Pemberton, an Atlanta, Georgia, pharmacist, invented Coca-Cola, the first cola drink. In the nineteenth century, soft drinks were only sold in outlets that could provide fountain service, but when bottling machinery was invented in the 1890s in the United States, soft drinks could be distributed to other retail outlets. By the beginning of the twentieth century sales of Coca-Cola were booming throughout the United States as a network of bottlers sprung up. This type of distribution system began to be used by other manufacturers and in other countries.

The consumption of soft drinks continued to expand worldwide throughout the twentieth century, as rising disposable incomes in industrialized countries allowed more consumers the luxury of drinking beverages other than water. During the 1960s, low-calorie soft drinks using artificial sweeteners first became popular with consumers concerned about the excess calories in sugar. These diet soft drinks were first sweetened with cyclamates (later banned after being deemed carcinogenic), then saccharine, and finally aspartame (NutraSweet), a more natural-tasting artificial sweetener. During this time, Gatorade, a sports soft drink designed to replace fluids lost during exercise, was developed at the University of Florida. It gained in popularity, attracting new competitors in the late 1980s and early 1990s. In the early 1990s, so-called New Age beverages, such as ready-to-drink teas and coffees, trendy fruit juice combinations, and flavored waters, became popular in the United States and soon spread to other countries.

While markets with high per capita consumption of soft drinks like that of the United States, Mexico, and Canada produced the highest sales volume for soft drink manufacturers, in the late 1990s manufacturers were working to develop franchises in low per capita consumption markets. Many of these markets, such as Eastern Europe, Russia, and China, were closed to competition for decades but invited expansion from soft drink manufacturers as their economies became liberalized. India and Vietnam were liberalizing their economies in the mid to late 1990s as well, and soft drink makers rushed in. South Africa, long closed to Western investment during the apartheid period, was reopened in the mid-1990s and attracted high profile soft drink investors.

With growing international trade and falling trade barriers, very few countries remained closed to the largest multinational beverage companies in the mid-1990s. For example, by the early 2000s, Coca-Cola did business in almost every country in the world.

CURRENT CONDITIONS

In 2002, the world produced over US$393 billion worth of soft drinks, according to figures from the USDA. The largest soft drink markets were the United States, Japan, Mexico, Germany, China, and Brazil. The United States also ranked first in per capita consumption—in 2003 Americans consumed an average of just over 52 carbonated soft drinks per year. The next leading consumer was Germany, with about 8 percent of the market by volume at the beginning of the 2000s. The largest market segment in 2001, according to USDA statistics, was carbonated beverages, with sales of US$193 billion. Fruit and vegetable drinks ranked second that year, with sales of about US$6.9 billion each. However, by 2004 bottled water overtook juices as the second largest market segment, with sales that year of US$9.2 billion.

The United States also controlled global soft drinks sales, with two U.S.-based companies, Coca-Cola and PepsiCo, dominating this increasingly concentrated industry. Coca-Cola, which posted total revenues of US$21.96 billion in 2004, controlled about 25 percent of the global soft drink industry, according to a USDA report. PepsiCo controlled about 11 percent, with worldwide beverage sales of US$7.6 billion in 2003. The third leading soft drinks manufacturer, Cadbury Schweppes, reported sales of $US12.9 billion (including snack foods) in 2004.

However, significant growth in the United States and other mature markets was not expected, especially in the carbonated soft drink (CSD) market. Global sales growth of CSDs reached only 0.8 percent in the United States in 2002, and analysts predicted that the strongest performances through the early 2000s would come from the industry's non-carbonated segment. The Asian and South American markets were expected to show the largest growth, outpacing North America, Europe, Africa, and Oceania (countries and territories in the Pacific Ocean). Mid-range growth was expected for the Middle East. Both PepsiCo and Coca-Cola expected a similar overall growth rate.

MOVING AWAY FROM TRADITIONAL COLAS

In the soft drinks industry, the consumer trend in the early 2000s was toward increasing health awareness, with declining demand for traditional colas. Although Coca-Cola and Pepsi-Cola remained the top carbonated sodas in 2004, each dropped in popularity between 1998 and the early 2000s, when consumers began demanding healthier beverages—or those perceived as healthier—such as diet colas, fortified fruit juices, bottled waters, sports and energy drinks, and iced teas. In a Beverage Digest/Maxwell's report, diet colas posted strong growth in 2000 in the United States: Diet Pepsi posted the biggest overall gain with a 4 percent volume growth and Diet Coke claimed the third spot in terms of volume growth at 2.5 percent.

Unlike the carbonated soft drink market, the non-carbonated beverage market—the fastest growing segment of the industry—was fragmented at the onset of the twenty-first century, with several key players and products vying for market share. The multinationals responded to growing popularity in this segment through acquisitions and new product launches. Coca-Cola acquired Nestea iced teas, Minute Maid fruit juices brands, and introduced Dasani bottled water. Likewise, through a combination of acquisitions, a merger with Quaker Oats Company, and new products, PepsiCo's brand portfolio in 2004 included Tropicana fruit juices, SoBe new age beverages, Gatorade sports drinks, Frappucino coffee drinks, Lipton iced teas, and Aquafina bottled water, along with its core group of colas.

Large multinational companies dominated large portions of nearly every segment of the non-carbonates market, which included sports and energy drinks, bottled water, and fruit juices and fruit drinks. However, in a few instances, such as the energy drinks market, other smaller companies led.

Sports drinks also developed into a major international soft drink category. Sports drinks are consumed to replenish fluids, minerals, and energy lost during exercise. Leatherhead Food RA reported that sport and energy drinks were valued at US$7.45 billion with a market volume of 5 billion liters in 2000. A press release from beverage industry analysts Canadean estimated a 6 percent average annual growth rate through 2005 for this segment, with global sales to exceed 10 billion liters by 2004. PepsiCo's Gatorade dominated the overall sports and energy drink market, producing nearly one third of the global volume, according to Canadean. However, in the energy drinks sector, Red Bull GmbH, a private Austrian company founded in 1987, controlled 60 to 70 percent of the global energy drinks market, which saw more than 30 new brands introduced in 2001.

Bottled water has long been a major category in certain parts of the world. Europeans, for example, drink bottled water instead of tap water. While slower to begin drinking bottled water than the Europeans, U.S. consumers took to bottled water in a big way in the late 1990s, including both bulk still water and so-called refreshment water beverages, which were usually carbonated. In the United States, bottled water sales grew significantly in the late 1990s to US$5.7 billion in 2000, and by 2004 it was the second top-selling beverage behind carbonated soft drinks in the United States, with sales worth almost US$9.2 billion. Canadean expected bottled water to take the top spot by 2010, citing that the U.S. market for bottled water was growing annually by 16 percent.

The top-selling bottled water company in 2004 was Nestle Waters North America, accounting for about 30 percent of sales. PepsiCo's Aquafina brand, the leading bottled water brand, captured 11.3 percent of the market while Coca-Cola's Dasani took a 10 percent share. Several innovations in the bottled water segment were introduced in the early 2000s, including new flavored waters and vitamin-enhanced products. Others focused on specific health claims. In 2004, for example, Eon Beverage Group, Inc. launched Eon, a "structured water", with claims that the product provided cellular absorption and improved the body's oxygenation. Zaqua!, a micro-structured water from Advanced H2O, boasted an adjusted pH level to help with digestion and with the elimination of waste products from the body.

In the mid-1980s, when Snapple Beverage Company introduced the first ready-to-drink (RTD) iced tea, the category began to grow dramatically. By 1994 there were 122 different tea labels in the United States alone, including offerings from Snapple, Coca-Cola, Nestlé Refreshments, Pepsi-Lipton, Tropicana Fruit Teas, and Celestial Seasonings (herbal teas). In 2001 the top-selling RTD tea in the United States was PepsiCo's Lipton Brisk, but by 2004, a relative newcomer, AriZona Iced Tea, had ousted Brisk to take the number one spot. With impressive sales growth of 45 percent that year and revenues of more than US$147 million, AriZona took 23.3 percent of the market compared to second place rival Snapple with 14.5 percent. Lipton Brisk ranked third, with 13.5 percent of the RTD tea market.

NATIONAL AND PRIVATE LABEL CHALLENGES

In 2000 private labels captured nearly 14 percent of carbonated soft drink (CSD) volume in the United States and approximately 7 percent of sales. By 2004, according to *Business Week,* the U.S. market for private label goods had stabilized at about 16 percent. Private labels also proved increasingly popular in Europe, where they accounted for 13 percent of volume in the soft drinks market in 1999, while national brands claimed 53 percent, compared to 34 percent for multinational brands. With European retailers devoting more shelf space to private labels, global brands suffered; their share of European bottled water sales, for example, declined from 53 percent in 1997 to only 40 percent in 2004. Nestle's sales of Perrier and Vittel in Europe fell by 8.4 percent between 2002 and 2004. Rapid growth of discount retailers such as Aldi Group in Germany and Leader Price in France, which almost exclusively stock private labels, is expected to drive further growth in private label soft drink sales.

Private labels also performed well in the bottled water market. With US$325 million in sales in 2004, private label bulk bottled water ranked second only to PepsiCo's Aquafina. "Consumers drink bottled water for its perceived purity and healthfulness," according to an industry analyst in a *Beverage Industry* feature, who observed that "Private label is reaping the benefits."

At the beginning of the 2000s, while the multinational soft drink companies were not as effective in selling universal, one-size-fits-all products in markets where consumers favored regional flavors and brand images, national brands surpassed the multinationals in growth. For example, in the Czech Republic, Poland, Romania, and Russia, national brands dominated the soft drink market with 75 to 80 percent, based on volume. In Eastern Europe, multinationals saw volume growth of about 25 percent between 1995 and 2000, while national brands grew by 33 percent. Non-carbonated drinks and bottled water were the primary products in this segment. National brands were more adept at forging partnerships with retail and supermarket chains. They could also produce beverages at a much lower cost, as much as 14 percent lower when compared to a multinational cola, as estimated by Canadean.

BOTTLING OPERATIONS

Coke's relationship with its bottlers both helped the company and hurt it. According to*Fortune,* many claimed Coke used its bottlers to make its own profits look better. During the mid-1980s and throughout the 1990s Coke began to spin off its bottling operations, which were typically capital-intensive, retaining ownership of less than 50 percent. In doing so, according to a *Wall Street Journal*article, Coke was able "to wipe capital-intensive assets and billions of dollars in debt off its books. But it also saddled its bottlers with huge debts." The system allowed Coke to raise the price of its concentrate, the syrup sold to the bottlers, who then add the water and packaging, even if the bottlers were unable to raise prices at the consumer level. Admittedly, Coke would subsidize the marketing efforts of the bottlers, but according this article, "this funding often didn't make up for the concentrate price increase."

Coke, responding to complaints from the bottlers, in 2001 made a commitment to alter how it calculated concentrate prices and advertising funds, at least with its largest bottler, Coca-Cola Enterprises Inc. (CCE). Of course the bottlers' struggle eventually negatively impacted Coke. According to the *Wall Street Journal*, Coke reported US$155 million in income from its bottlers in 1997, which fell dramatically to a US$280 million loss by 2000 (CCE reported sales of US$14.8 billion, with net income of US$233 million in 2000). Meanwhile Pepsi's largest bottler, Pepsi Bottling Group (PBG), posted revenues of nearly US$8 billion in 2000, with net income of US$229 million.

TWENTY-FIRST CENTURY CHALLENGES

By the early 2000s physicians had begun to recognize obesity as a significant public health threat throughout both the developed world and developing countries. Though many factors are involved in the development of obesity, one significant contributor is the consumption of high-calorie foods and drinks. It was expected that public health officials would increasingly target soft drinks in anti-obesity campaigns. Indeed, in its 2003 annual report, Coca-Cola listed obesity first among the key challenges facing the company in the early 2000s. Industry leaders planned to respond to this challenge by contributing to fitness campaigns and by continuing to offer a wide range of consumer choices, including diet soft drinks, juice-based drinks, and water. PepsiCo, for example, announced in 2004 its launch of Pepsi Edge, described in a company news release as a "full-flavored cola with 50 percent less sugar, carbohydrates, and calories than regular colas."

The quality and availability of water, the primary ingredient in soft drinks and bottled waters, was also expected to affect the industry as droughts, pollution, and climate change threatened global water supplies. According to Coca-Cola's 2003 annual report, this limited resource faces "unprecedented challenges from over-exploitation, increasing pollution, and poor management." In 2004, for example, Coca-Cola halted production at its Plachimada plant in India because of government pressure about the company's usage of scarce groundwater. India claimed that this usage, during a period without rain, contributed to the loss of needed farmland and depleted the region's water table.

INDUSTRY LEADERS

THE COCA-COLA COMPANY

The Coca-Cola Company has been a virtually unstoppable marketing machine for over 40 years. Not only is it the leading soft drink company in the world, it is also, according to a 2003 *Business Week* special report, the number one global brand. Coca-Cola's domination of the international market had its roots in World War II, when the company underwent a vast expansion to supply U.S. soldiers in Europe and Asia with soft drinks. By 2004, Coca-Cola grew to include over 400 brands manufactured and sold in 200 countries—or virtually every nation on earth.

Through the mid-1950s, the company sold one product, Coca-Cola, in one or two bottle styles. From then on, however, it became a marketing giant with product and packaging diversity. Coca-Cola introduced the Fanta line of soft drinks in 1960, which grew to become the fourth best-selling brand in the world. Sprite, launched in 1961, became a leading lemon-lime carbonate.

In 1963, Coca-Cola created the first successful diet soft drink, Tab. In 1982, the company launched Diet Coke, the first-ever extension of the Coca-Cola trademark. Although Diet Coke diminished Tab sales, it quickly became the most successful new soft drink entry in the twentieth century, becoming the world's best selling low-calorie soft drink—in just two years. Diet Coke was one of the first diet soft drinks to use the NutraSweet brand of aspartame, which eventually replaced saccharin in most bottled and canned diet soft drinks.

Even Coca-Cola's mistakes turned out well. On April 23, 1985, the company stunned soft drink consumers worldwide by changing the hallowed, secret Coke formula. While the new taste was widely preferred in blind taste tests, a huge consumer backlash forced Coca-Cola to bring back the original product within three months as Coca-Cola Classic, retaining the new version as Coke or Coke II. Sales of the combined brand hardly missed a beat.

In the late 1990s, the Coca-Cola Company continued to expand through acquisitions. For example, in 1996 Coca-Cola essentially bought out an unusual franchise agreement it had with a major competitor, Cadbury Schweppes. The two companies agreed to end their 10-year-old joint venture in the United Kingdom, called Coca-Cola and Schweppes Beverages Ltd. (CCSB). CCSB was created in 1986 as a franchisee to produce, distribute, and sell the two companies' brands in what was then considered an undeveloped market. The plan was for each company to take charge of marketing its own brands, while CCSB acted as a franchisee to produce, distribute, and sell them. However, in subsequent years, the partnership was strained as both firms put more focus on their own products.

In June 1996, Coca-Cola and Cadbury Schweppes agreed to sell their CCSB stakes to Coca-Cola Enterprises (CCE) Atlanta, Coke's major bottling partner worldwide. As a result, CCE, which was 44 percent owned by the Coca-Cola Company, became the key bottler in a strong market. Meanwhile, Coca-Cola regained control over much of the marketing of its brands, while Cadbury Schweppes took £620 million (about US$1 billion) away from the deal. Cadbury Schweppes intended to make acquisitions in the confectionery industry with the proceeds.

Coca-Cola continued its acquisition strategy in 1997 when it agreed in late December to purchase the Orangina brand from France's Pernod Ricard SA for FFr5 billion (US$840.5 million). The deal included all Orangina brands and four bottling and concentrate plants. The transaction gave Coca-Cola control of about 58 percent of the French soft drink market, up from about 50 percent. That large market share prompted some to speculate that the deal could be challenged by France's Competition Council.

The vital importance of the globalization of the soft drink industry is illustrated by examining Coca-Cola 's sales distribution. By 2003, more than 70 percent of Coca-Cola's sales came from global markets outside the United States. When developing new markets, Coke, like archrival Pepsi, usually created strong identities for their famous brands. However, in some countries a different approach was called for. For example, after being absent from the market in India for over 15 years, Coca-Cola purchased the Thums Up brand from an Indian bottler in 1993. Coca-Cola became India's biggest manufacturer of soft drinks, with 45 soft drink plants and 20 water plants in 2001, according to Business Line.

The history of Thums Up dates back to 1977, when Coca-Cola left India after a new government there ordered the company to reduce its stake in its Indian unit and reveal its secret formula. As a result, Coca-Cola bottlers were left without a product to sell. One bottler formulated Thums Up and packaged it in Coke bottles. After Coca-Cola returned to India in 1993 by buying Thums Up and other brands from the Parle Group, the company aggressively merchandised Coke brands, but resistance from bottlers and consumer indifference prompted the company to change course and put more advertising and marketing support behind Thums Up. With the combined strength of Coke brands, Thums Up and other products, Coca-Cola held about 52 percent of the Indian market as of 1999, compared to 46 percent for Pepsi.

In 1997, the Coca-Cola Company's long-time leader, CEO Roberto Goizueta, died. Goizueta, who took over leadership of the company in 1981, was credited with vastly improving the firm's profitability and global profile. Not surprisingly, the new chairman of Coca-Cola, M. Douglas Ivester, pledged no major shifts in the company's successful business strategy. However, in December 1999, Ivester abruptly quit amidst difficulties within the company and in the global marketplace. With the Asian market crisis and collapsing economies in Russia and Brazil and strong challenges by PepsiCo for market share, Coke's earnings fell two straight years under his tenure. Coca-Cola was also plagued with other problems. In the spring of 1999, 2,200 African American employees charged Coca-Cola with race discrimination, resulting in a US$192.5 million settlement in November 2000. In the summer of 1999, Belgian schoolchildren became sick after drinking Coke, which turned out to contain contaminated carbon dioxide. Then a fungicide was found in cans of Coke shipped from France. The contamination problems turned out to be relatively minor, although Ivester was faulted for not acting quickly to explain the situation and calm jittery European consumers. In November 1999, Coca-Cola announced a price increase of its concentrate (the syrup purchased by its bottlers), further adding to tensions between the company and its bottlers.

Douglas N. Daft assumed the task of solving the problems left by Ivester. Through internal restructuring, acquisitions, and strengthened partnerships, Daft hoped to turn Coca-Cola around, promising a 15 percent or better gain in earnings per share, as had occurred during Coca-Cola's peak period of global expansion during the 1980s, and predicting overall volume growth of 6 to 7 percent. In 2000, Coca-Cola cut roughly 20 percent of its 29,000 employees, removed or reassigned nearly 94 percent of its top management, and attempted to buy Quaker Oats, as reported by *Business Week*. However, Coca-Cola's board rejected the Quaker acquisition and Quaker—with its Gatorade brand, the top selling sports drink—later merged with PepsiCo.

In March 2001, the company announced a joint venture with Proctor & Gamble Co. to better position its Minute Maid juices only to call off the deal in September. However Coca-Cola did complete two key acquisitions in 2001: it purchased Mad River Traders (specialty iced teas, lemonades, and juice cocktails) and Odwalla Inc. (fruit and vegetable drinks, spring water, nutritional bars, and organic milk sold in health stores). The year 2001 also saw an expansion of the joint venture with Nestle S.A. originally created in 1991. The Coca-Cola and Nestle Refreshments (CCNR) venture was renamed Beverage Partners Worldwide (BPW). BPW, headquartered in Zurich, Switzerland, planned to operate in 40 countries, up from 24 countries under the initial CCNR venture. BPW was expected to compete against Unilever's Lipton brands in the much-coveted ready-to-drink (RTD) coffee and tea market.

Daft also oversaw changes on the advertising front. While predecessor Ivester discouraged movie deals, Daft invested $US150 million in 2001 to co-market Warner Brothers' blockbuster Harry Potter movie. Coca-Cola also made a "one-time" marketing investment of US$300 million in 2001. According to *Business Week,* Coca-Cola's bottlers felt the new ads did little to boost sales, which had declined in the United States since the mid-1990s. Since the mid-1990s, Coca-Cola's U.S. volume sales growth was 3.9 percent per year, while PepsiCo saw annual growth of 4.5 percent, according to *Business Week.* Yet despite near stagnant growth in the United States, Coca-Cola managed to continue its dominance of the U.S. market. A report by *Beverage Digest* showed Coca-Cola with a 44 percent market share in the United States in 2000, unchanged from the previous year. PepsiCo's market share was 31 percent, also unchanged from 1999. Coca-Cola sold five of the top ten carbonated soft drinks (CSDs) in the United States in 2000, with Coke Classic as the market leader. In 2000, Coke's unit case volume in the worldwide soft drinks market grew only 4 percent—much lower than Daft's projections, with a mere 1 percent growth in the North American market. In 2002, in hopes of boosting sales, Coca-Cola introduce Vanilla Coke, their first new flavor in 17 years, since introducing Cherry Coke in 1995.

In 2003, Coca-Cola extended Vanilla Coke and diet Vanilla Coke into more than 50 countries and also introduced various Sprite brand extension products in Belgium, Italy, Australia, and Hong Kong. In addition, it launched several new products in the United States, including the soft drinks Sprite Remix and Barq's Floatz. Other products were Minute Maid Premium Heart Wise, an orange juice containing cholesterol-lowering plant sterols; Minute Maid Limeade; and a milk-based product called Swerve. The company also launched a natural juice-flavored soft drink, Nativa, in Argentina and extended the Kuat line in Brazil. Dasani, Coca-Cola's bottled water brand, was introduced in Ghana and Kenya. Coca-Cola also bought several brands and trademarks in 2003, including Cosmos in the Philippines, Multivita in Poland, Neverfail Springwater in Australia, Chaudfontaine in Belgium, and Valpre in South Africa.

Coca-Cola also took steps in 2003 to streamline operations, eliminating 3,700 jobs. The following year, several new products were launched, including Zu, a ready-to-drink canned coffee with ginseng that debuted in Thailand, and

Aqua Shot, a flavored water with vitamins introduced in New Zealand. New flavors for existing brands also proliferated, including Sprite Icy Mint in China, Fanta Citrell in Germany, and Fanta Naranja Chamoy in Mexico. In 2005 the company introduced Coca-Cola Zero, a zero-calorie cola, in the United States. Coca-Cola reported total revenues in 2004 of US$21.96 billion, up 4.4 percent from 2003. Japan remained the company's most profitable market, while China represented the potential for highest future growth. As of the first quarter of 2005, Coca-Cola's sales in North America and Europe were relatively flat; by contrast, sales were up 28 percent in Africa, 12 percent in Latin America, and 8 percent in Asia.

PEPSICO INC.

Pepsi-Cola is the beverage division of PepsiCo Inc., which also owns Frito-Lay snacks and other businesses. Pepsi soft drinks, including Pepsi, Diet Pepsi, Slice, Mountain Dew, Mug Root Beer, and other products, held about 32 percent of the U.S. soft drink market as of 2004.

Pepsi-Cola was created in 1898 in New Bern, North Carolina, by druggist Caleb D. Bradham who claimed it cured dyspepsia (indigestion). The Pepsi-Cola Co. grew throughout the twentieth century and in 1963 acquired Frito-Lay, the largest U.S. snack foods company. The company changed its name to PepsiCo Inc. and later acquired restaurant chains, including Pizza Hut (1977), Taco Bell (1978), and Kentucky Fried Chicken (1986), later known as KFC. The restaurant holdings were divested in 1997 (see below).

By the late 1990s, Pepsi-Cola North America (PCNA), a division of PepsiCo, manufactured and sold soft drink concentrate to company-owned and independent bottlers operating facilities in the United States and Canada. The division also provided fountain beverage syrups to restaurants. Pepsi-Cola International (PCI), later renamed PepsiCo Beverages International (PBI), controlled the company's international soft drink operations. Through PCI, Pepsi-Cola products were sold in over 150 countries and territories and held about 18 percent of the international soft drink market. PCI owned the rights to produce and sell Seven-Up brands internationally, while U.S. Seven-Up operations were owned by Cadbury Schweppes.

Pepsi-Cola International (PCI), the second-largest international marketer of soft drinks, faced severe financial problems in the late 1990s. PCI lost US$846 million in 1996 and another US$50 million in 1997. However, PepsiCo vowed to challenge Coca-Cola overseas by having PCI concentrate in less developed markets rather than in those countries where Coca-Cola was entrenched, such as Venezuela. By the early 2000s, this strategy had paid off. Despite an economic slump in Latin America and a boycott of U.S. brands in the Middle East, PepsiCo Beverages International (PBI), as the division later became known, increased its volume by 5 percent from 2001 to 2002, with a revenue growth of 1 percent and an increase of operating profits of 23 percent. The strong numbers posted showed that PBI's attention to large emerging markets paid off. Volume growth in China, India, Turkey, and Russia remained at double digits in 2002.

PepsiCo dramatically changed its corporate structure in 1997 to more effectively compete in the soft drink business. In October, the company spun off its restaurant operations to shareholders as a new publicly traded company called Tricon Global Restaurants Inc. The idea was to make the new PepsiCo more attractive to investors since they would be able to see more clearly the results from the company's higher margin beverage and snack businesses after they were separated from the low margin restaurant business. However, 1997 profits at PepsiCo's beverage unit were squeezed by a combination of "cutthroat" soft-drink pricing, flat sales for the flagship Pepsi brand, and heavy investment in the beverage business. Pepsi executives characterized 1997 as extremely tough for Pepsi-Cola North America and a significant disappointment.

In the late 1990s, Pepsi was investing heavily in the fountain segment of the soft drink business, trying to attack Coca-Cola's dominance of that category. Coca-Cola's fountain business worldwide was three times that of Pepsi's. One of PepsiCo's strategies was to sue Coca-Cola in May 1998, charging that Coca-Cola was violating U.S. antitrust laws by attempting to "freeze" Pepsi out of the business of selling soft drinks in restaurants and movie theaters served by independent food distributors. The charges, denied by Coca-Cola, were that Coca-Cola threatened distributors with losing their Coke business if they supplied Pepsi. Coca-Cola countered that its contracts, which specified that Coke distributors not sell rival products, were not illegal. Some observers were puzzled by the suit, noting that Pepsi also had such exclusive contracts with its fountain customers.

In 1998, PepsiCo acquired Tropicana, which as of 2001 was the world's leading juice brand. Additionally, 1998 saw the launch of Pepsi One, a one-calorie cola designed for health-conscious men. In March 1999, PepsiCo spun off its Pepsi Bottling Group unit as PepsiCo began to focus on its soft drink products and its snack food operations. PepsiCo also unveiled its new "The Joy of Cola" advertising campaign, ending the reign of the "Generation Next" slogan. The following year, PepsiCo also resurrected its "Pepsi Challenge" campaign from the early 1980s. In 1999, Steven S. Reinemund was named president of PepsiCo. The Pepsi Center opened as the new home of the NBA Denver Nuggets and NHL Colorado Avalanche.

At the onset of the twenty-first century PepsiCo's core brands—Pepsi, Mountain Dew, and Slice—made up approximately 25 percent of its sales, with more than 60 percent of sales generated by the company's salty snacks division. Although still the number two soft drink maker in the world, PepsiCo made moves to significantly challenge Coca-Cola. In August 2001, PepsiCo purchased Quaker Oats for roughly US$14 billion to form the world's fifth largest food and beverage company. The move added the extremely popular Gatorade, an isotonic sports drink, to PepsiCo's beverage lineup.

PepsiCo has been lauded for successfully appealing to a younger audience with products beyond traditional colas. As a prime example, in 2001 it launched Code Red—a cherry-flavored version of the popular Mountain Dew—using a unique marketing approach. The brand was heavily advertised during the X Games, on the Mountain Dew web site, and 4,000 free bottles were sent out in advance of the product being available in stores. After its first eleven weeks of distribution, ACNielsen named it the fifth-largest-selling 20-ounce soft drink, as reported by Advertising Age. In 2004, PepsiCo launched Gatorade Endurance Hydration Formula, a sports drink tailored for the needs of high-endurance athletes, and Pepsi Edge, a full-flavored cola with half the sugar, carbohydrates, and calories than regular cola.

By 2001, PepsiCo had transformed itself and seemed on the verge of winning the cola war with archrival Coca-Cola, at least in terms of investor confidence. As explained in the April 2, 2001 issue of *Fortune,* "From 1997 to 1999, Pepsi gave itself a makeover—a very Coke-like makeover—by spinning off its fast-food restaurant business and some of its bottling operations. By the early 2000s Pepsi, like Coke, owned less than 50 percent of its bottlers, which means that this low-margin, capital-intensive business isn't consolidated in Pepsi's financials." Pepsi also shrewdly began expanding its offering of non-CSDs, a market that became the fastest selling at the turn of the century.

In 2003 PepsiCo combined its primary North American beverage brands into a new organization, PepsiCo Beverages North American (PBNA). In 2004 PepsiCo reported sales of US$29.2 billion (including snack foods), an 8.5 percent increase from the previous year. Net sales outside the United States accounted for about 34 percent of PepsiCo beverage sales. The company's largest foreign markets were Mexico, Great Britain, and Canada.

CADBURY SCHWEPPES

As of 2004, Cadbury Schweppes PLC was the number three global soft drink producer. The British soft drink and candy manufacturer acquired a large stable of soft drink companies and brands, including Dr Pepper/Seven-Up Companies Inc., which was purchased outright in late 1994. In addition to Dr Pepper and Seven-Up (United States only), Cadbury Schweppes soft drink brands, as of 2004, included Canada Dry, Hawaiian Punch, Mott's, Clamato, Schweppes, Orangina, Snapple, Nantucket Nectars, A&W, Oasis, Yoo-Hoo, Squirt, La Casera, TriNa, Spring Valley, and Wave.

Prior to the Cadbury purchase, the Dr Pepper Co. was a private company, having been made private in 1984 in a leveraged buyout. Dr Pepper later absorbed the U.S. operations of The Seven-Up Company. In August 1993, Cadbury Schweppes purchased 12.2 million Dr Pepper shares from Prudential for US$231.3 million, increasing its stake in Dr Pepper/Seven-Up to about 26 percent. At the time, industry analysts speculated that Cadbury could help Dr Pepper expand into international markets after a full buyout, a prediction that came true a little over a year later.

With the Dr Pepper buyout, Cadbury Schweppes cobbled together 17 percent of the U.S. market by combining its own 3.5-percent share with Dr Pepper/Seven-Up's 11.5 percent share and a 2 percent share from A&W Brands, which Cadbury had purchased earlier. Cadbury Schweppes controlled about half of the U.S. non-cola business and had a platform for further expansion in international markets.

In early 1998, Cadbury Schweppes bolstered the distribution of its soft drinks by purchasing, along with investment firm Carlyle Group LP, two Midwest U.S. bottlers for US$724 million. The two bottlers—Beverage America Inc. in Holland, Michigan, and Select Beverages Inc. in Darien, Illinois—were combined into a separate company called American Bottling Company. Cadbury's management was operating American Bottling even though its stake was only 40 percent. The deal was made to address Cadbury Schweppes' relative lack of strength in bottling in the United States compared with Coca-Cola and Pepsi. Plans called for the new bottling company to acquire smaller bottlers and eventually become a public company.

Cadbury acquired RC Cola in September 2000 as part of its $1.45 billion acquisition of the Snapple Beverage Group from Triarc. Then in 2001, Cadbury sold off its international RC Cola business to Cott Corp., keeping its RC Cola business in the United States, Mexico, Canada, and Puerto Rico, allowing the company to focus its efforts in North America, continental Europe, and Australia. Also, late in 2001, Cadbury acquired France's Pernod-Ricard's soft drinks business whose Orangina and Pampryl fruit juice brands are sold in continental Europe, North America, and Australia. In 2002, the company acquired Nantucket Nectars in the United States and Squirt in Mexico.

In 2003, Cadbury announced a business restructuring that included an amalgamation of its North American beverage businesses. Beverage sales, led by Dr. Pepper, rose 2 percent in 2004, and total sales for the company exceeded US$12.9 billion.

COTT CORP.

Riding its private label successes of the mid to late 1990s, Cott, once a small family business, increased its revenues from about US$65 million in 1991 to US$665 million in 1994 and more than US$1 billion in 1997. By 2003, according to figures from *Beverage Digest,* the company accounted for 4.7 percent of the global market. Cott's original "premium" private label product was President's Choice Cola, which was sold in Ontario's Loblaw supermarket chain. Cott captured 50 percent of all cola volume in Loblaw stores and 30 percent of cola volume throughout the province after expanding to nearly every supermarket chain in Ontario. Cott also supplies the Wal-Mart chain.

In 1991, Cott began purchasing Royal Crown (RC) concentrate from the RC Columbus, Georgia facility and using it in its private label colas. The high quality of the cola, along with improvements in packaging, not only helped Cott find success but also dramatically increased the image of private labels. As private label soft drink products caught on, they gobbled up large market shares at supermarkets in major markets in the mid-1990s, including 30 percent in Great Britain, 27 percent in Switzerland, 22 percent in Canada, 17 percent in France, and 9 percent in the United States.

However, by the late 1990s, Cott's star had fallen somewhat, and the company put itself up for sale in October 1997. According to a *Wall Street Journal* report, Cott was struggling with weak sales and earnings and reduced profit margins due to a protracted price war with branded soft drink companies in the mid to late 1990s. As a result, private-label bottlers such as Cott were forced to cut prices even more. Cott also tried to move into private label foods, but after disappointing results, it planned to sell the business. Cott also incurred a high debt load while building a bottling network in the United States. All of these factors hurt the company, although its market share in the United States continued to climb at the expense of smaller private label soft drink manufacturers. In early 1998, Cott took itself off the market, saying that the offers it received were not sufficient. At the same time, it was searching for a new CEO.

In mid-1998, Cott named Frank E. Weise president and CEO. Along with a new management team, Weise began a program of internal renovation with the goal of focusing the company on its core business, namely the premium private label business in Canada, the United States, and the United Kingdom. During the late 1990s and into the early 2000s, Cott took the first step in its restructuring process by divesting itself of non-soft drink interests, including its pet food subsidiary, frozen food division, and U.S. PET bottling operations. In 2000, Cott acquired Concord Beverage, a regional private label producer in the northeastern part of the United States, thereby strengthening its 56 percent market share of the private label carbonated soft drink industry in the United States. With the acquisition, Cott added A&P, Acme, Pathmark, and others to its customer base that already included Wal-Mart, Kmart, and Safeway.

In its most significant revitalization move, Cott purchased RC Cola's international business and its concentrate supply contracts from Cadbury Schweppes in 2001. The move gave Cott ownership of the formula used in its retailer brand colas as well as increased presence in 60 countries outside North America, including Israel and the Philippines. In 2001, Cott formed Northeast Retailer Brands (NRB) with independent bottler Polar Beverages of Massachusetts. NRB gave Cott additional leverage in the Northeast, where its sales had not matched those of other regions. In the meantime, Cott also looked internally to address quality, plant utilization, and customer service issues.

Cott initially posted losses in the late 1990s as its restructuring efforts took time to implement. But by the end of 2001, Cott—now the fourth largest soft drink company in the United States and the world's largest retailer brand soft drink supplier—reported eight consecutive quarters of profitable results. Sales rose steadily through the early 2000s, from US$990 million in 2000 to US$1.19 billion in 2002 and US$1.4 billion in 2003. Total sales grew by 16.1 percent in 2004 to exceed US$1.6 billion.

SNAPPLE

Snapple Beverage Corp., a smaller but influential company and one of the founders of the "New Age" beverage business, grew from US$13 million in 1988 sales to US$516 million in 1993. By 1994 Snapple produced 52 flavors of iced teas, fruit drinks, fruit juices, sports drinks, and carbonated sodas and seltzer. The company was one of the pioneers of the ready-to-drink (RTD) iced tea market, and its success spurred Coke to team up with Nestea and Pepsi with Lipton. In the early to mid-1990s, Snapple began to expand in international markets, including Canada, Mexico, and the Caribbean, as well as Europe and Japan. Coca-Cola created a whole new line, Fruitopia, to compete with Snapple. In early 1995, Snapple was acquired for US$1.7 billion by Quaker Oats, which already owned the Gatorade brand. However, Snapple sales and profits began to fall shortly after the acquisition, and distribution problems also hurt the brand. Plagued by huge losses, Quaker Oats sold the brand in 1997 to Triarc Beverage Group, owner of Mistic and Royal Crown, for just US$300 million. In 2000, Cadbury Schweppes purchased Triarc's Snapple Beverage Group for US$1.45 billion.

ARIZONA ICED TEA

Introduced in 1992, AriZona Iced Tea enjoyed amazing success competing against ready-to-drink (RTD) teas from established brands such as Lipton and Nestea. A small family-owned company founded in 1971, Ferolito, Vultaggio & Sons established itself as a distributor of beer products in New York City. By 1986, the company had introduced its first product, Midnight Dragon Malt Liquor. This was followed by Crazy Horse Malt Liquor, which in 1992 sold more than 1 million cases. In 1992, the company entered the RTD iced tea market with AriZona Iced Tea. As with Crazy Horse, the product was distinguished by innovative packaging; twenty-four-ounce single serve containers displayed the bright hues and graphics of southwestern culture. AriZona products went on to win many packaging design awards.

By the end of 1993, AriZona had sold more than 10 million cases and was selected as one of Fortune magazine's top products of the year. In 2002, Ferolito & Vultaggio signed with Celestial Seasonings and Allied Domecq to produce and market, respectively, Celestial Seasonings RTD teas and juices and Kalhua Iced Coffee. By 2004, the AriZona brand included 7 flavored teas, 7 juice drinks, 2 coladas, 4 flavored diet teas, a carbonated soft drink, and a line of Rx Herbal Tonics. By 2004, AriZona was the top-selling brand in the United States.

MAJOR COUNTRIES IN THE INDUSTRY

THE UNITED STATES

At the start of the twenty-first century, the U.S. soft drink industry was the largest in the world both in terms of sales and consumption. Yet growth remained relatively sluggish. Carbonated drink sales grew by only 0.7 percent in 2004, up by about 72.5 million cases from 2003. Per capita consumption, however, fell for the sixth consecutive year, reaching 53.7 gallons in 2004. Diet soft drinks accounted for most of the category's growth, as consumers sought healthier low-calorie drinks. In 2004, Coca-Cola controlled 43.3 percent of U.S. market, followed by PepsiCo with 32 percent. Dr. Pepper/Seven Up, the third largest branded soft drink company in the United States, saw 2.4 percent volume growth in 2004, increasing market share for the first time in several years, and saw Dr. Pepper overtake 7-Up as a top ten brand. Cott enjoyed a 17.5 percent volume increase.

The fastest growing category by volume in the United States was bottled water, which grew 8.6 percent in 2004, exceeding 6.8 billion gallons. Bottled water is now the second leading beverage among U.S. consumers, behind carbonated soft drinks. The U.S. bottled water market was valued at almost US$9.2 billion in 2004. The largest bottled water category was non-carbonated bottled water (6.4 billion gallons and 94.2 percent of volume in 2004). The leading U.S. bottled water company in 2004 was Nestle Waters North America (NWNA), with more than US$2.7 billion in wholesale revenues. PepsiCo's Aquafina was the second leading brand, with 11.3 percent of sales in 2004 and revenues reaching US$1 billion. Close behind was Coca-Cola's Dasani, which was expected to reach sales of US$1 billion in 2005. The market for flavored bottled water was expected to see rapid expansion in 2005 with the introduction of several new brands. According to *Beverage Marketing,* this segment should see sales of more than US$800 million by 2009.

Supermarkets were the biggest outlet for sales of soft drinks in the United States, accounting for 48 percent of total volume in 2000, followed by fountain/restaurant sales at 21 percent, convenience stores at 12 percent, vending at 11 percent, and mass merchandisers/club/drug stores at 8 percent.

While bottled water dominated sales of non-carbonated soft drinks, the outlook for fruit beverages also appeared favorable, particularly for shelf-stable juices. Single-serve products, which drove growth in this segment, saw several innovations in the early 2000s, including low calorie and low carbohydrate products and juice drinks enhanced with vitamins and other nutrients.

MEXICO

In the early 2000s, Mexico was the world's number two soft drink market. Mexico's more than 90 million people annually consumed an estimated 560 eight-ounce servings of soft drinks per capita, lagging just slightly behind U.S. levels. In 2001, according to a report by the Market Research Centre and the Canadian Trade Commissioner Service, sales of carbonated drinks in Mexico grew 5 percent to reach almost $15 billion. As with other North American markets, Mexico began to see significant growth in sales of juices and bottled water in 2002 and 2003. As of 2003, bottled water accounted for about 45 percent of nonalcoholic beverage sales in Mexico.

According to InfoLatina S.A. de C.V., as of 2001 there were about 43 soft drink companies in Mexico; however, 70 percent of sales came from eight of those companies, with Coke and Pepsi as the major players. As of 2001, Mexico's soft drinks market was dominated by Coca-Cola's approximately 70 to 75 percent market share, while PespsiCo controlled about 20 percent. Figures varied as both Coke and Pepsi battled fiercely for market share in a country where each franchise usually allowed one company to control a given geographical region. As a result, there was often the lack of competition that keeps prices in check and advertising became a crucial means of gaining market share.

According to its own figures, Coca-Cola employed more than 86,000 people in Mexico as of 2004. Operations included 15 bottlers, 78 bottling plants, and 465 supply centers. PepsiCo considered Mexico its second most important market outside the United States, so much so that in early 2002 PepsiCo announced its goal to invest more than $1.2 billion in Mexico by 2006, according to FWN Select. One key strategy was obtaining the contract to supply soft drinks to the country's largest cinema chain, Cinemex, which had previously been supplied by Coca-Cola. PepsiCo's Mexican sales accounted for over US$4 billion annually.

As of the early 2000s, PepsiCo's principal bottlers in Mexico were Grupo Embotelladoras Unidas, Grupo Embotellador Bret, and Pepsi-Gemex, S.A. de C.V., PepsiCo's second largest bottler outside of the United States. Fomento Economico Mexicano SA, or Femsa, owned Mexico's largest Coke franchise, located in Monterrey. In 2001, Arca became Coke's second largest bottler in Mexico as a result of the merger of Procor and Arma.

On January 1, 2002, the Mexican government approved a 20 percent tax on soft drink manufacturers who use fructose sweeteners in an effort to stimulate the domestic sugar industry. According to *Futures World News,* some soft drink producers had voluntarily switched to sugar-only formulas, while others, like Coca-Cola, did not expect the tax to cause a price increase or negatively impact sales.

THE MIDDLE EAST

Another active area was the Middle East, where shifting political trends changed the market. For example, the Coca-Cola Company for years was unable to do business in Saudi Arabia because of an Arab boycott stemming from Coke's operations in Israel. As a result, PCI (Pepsico) was able to build Saudi Arabia into its third largest foreign market in the mid-1990s, trailing only Mexico and Canada.

By March 1998, however, Coca-Cola claimed that it was outselling PepsiCo in the Middle East and North Africa, a claim that PepsiCo disputed. Coca-Cola's aggressive and expensive campaign there appeared to be working, and the company contended that its collective market share for the region was 38 percent compared with Pepsi's 36 percent. While Coca-Cola admitted that Pepsi was still the clear leader in Saudi Arabia and other Persian Gulf countries, it said its leadership in countries such as Israel and Egypt, combined with strong market share gains in other Arab countries, gave it regional supremacy. PepsiCo, however, claimed that its market share in the area was 46 percent, with Coke holding just 38 percent.

During the late 1990s, Coca-Cola made several key moves to increase its Middle East position. In 1998, Ramallah-based National Beverage Co. became the sole Palestinian Coca-Cola franchise; Coca-Cola planned to further invest in the bottling plant in 2000. In 1999, Coca-Cola opened a US$20 million bottling plant in Riyadh where it controlled 30 percent of the soft drinks market. In 2000, Coca-Cola relocated its Middle East and North Africa division from Britain to Bahrain to further strengthen its local presence and in keeping with the company's motto to "Think local, act local." At the time, Coca-Cola claimed a 45 percent market share in the region, which comprised 15 countries, with 55 plants.

With the outbreak of the Al-Aksa Intifada in the Palestinian Territories in the fall of 2000, Coca-Cola faced an increasingly difficult market in the Middle East and in the West Bank in particular. A boycott of American products sparked by the Intifada contributed to Coca-Cola's 7 percent growth loss in the Middle East and North Africa, according to the company's 2000 annual report.

FURTHER READING

All Change: Strategic Outlook for the Soft Drinks Industry in 2010, 7 February 2001. Available from www.industrysearch.com.au.

"Americans Dominate World of Soft Drinks." Leatherhead Food RA, September 2001. Available from www.foodlineweb.co.uk.

"The Big Brands Go Begging in Europe." *Business Week,* 21 March 2005. Available from www.businessweek.com.

Bolling, Chris. "Globalization of the Soft Drink Industry." *Agricultural Outlook,* Economic Research Service, United States Department of Agriculture, December, 2002. Available from www.ers.usda.gov/.

"Bottled Water Strengthens Position as No. 2 Beverage." *Beverage Marketing,* 25 April 2005. Available from http://www.beveragemarketing.com.

Cadbury Schweppes PLC, 2004 Annual Report, March 2001. Available from www.cadburyschweppes.com.

Chura, Hillary. "Pepsi-Cola's Code Red is white hot; Mountain Dew extension taps trends, flies off shelves." *Advertising Age,* 27 August 2001.

Coca-Cola Company, 2004 Annual Report. Available from www.coca-cola.com.

"Coke Halts Production at Indian Plant," 14 March 2004. Available from www.just-drinks.com/.

"Coke Winning Mexican Cola War: Analyst." InfoLatina S.A. de C.V., 26 June 2001.

Deogun, Nikhil and Jonathan Karp. "For Coke in India, Thums Up Is the Real Thing." *Wall Street Journal,* (29 April 1998): B1.

The Fruit Juice and Soft Drink Market in Mexico. Market Research Centre and the Canadian Trade Commissioner Service, July 2003. Available from http://atn-riae.agr.ca/.

"Global Soft Drinks Growing by 5 Percent a Year." *The Beverage Network,* November 2002. Available from www.bevnet.com.

Gutschi, Monica. "D. J. PepsiCo Reiterates to Invest $1.2B in Mexico Over 6 Years." *FWN Select,* 4 February 2002.

Heinzl, Mark and Nikhil Deogun. "Cott's Loses Sparkle Due to Price War, Chairman's Health." *Wall Street Journal,* (6 January 1998): B8.

"Increasing Soft Drink Sales Drive New Launches." *AP-Foodtechnology,* 23 July 2004. Available from www.foodtechnology.com.

Kevin, Kitty. "Water Log, 2004." *Beverage Industry,* 2004. Available from www.bevindustry.com.

"Local Players in a Multinational Landscape." Canadean press release, January 2001. Available from www.canadean.com.

Mallory, Maria. "Pop Goes the Pepsi Generation; A Struggling Pepsi-Cola Offers Cautionary Tale in Brand Stewardship." *U.S. News & World Report,* (16 June 1997): 48.

McKay, Betsy. "Coca-Cola: The Real Thing Can Be Hard to Measure." *Wall Street Journal Online,* 23 January 2002. Available from www.wsj.com.

McLean, Bethany. "Guess Who's Winning the Cola Wars?" *Fortune,* 2 April 2001.

"New Flavored Water Brands Flooding the Market." *Beverage Marketing,* 10 February 2005. Available from http://www.beveragemarketing.com.

"Pepsi Plans to Up Market Share in Mexico." InfoLatina S.A. de C.V., 3 September 2001.

PepsiCo Inc., 2004 Annual Report. Available from www.pepsico.com.

Phillips, Bob. "Fruit Beverages: Sweet Revenge." *Progressive Grocer,* 1 April 2005. Available from www.progressivegrocer.com.

Prince, Greg W. "Cott Corp. Acquires Concord, Expanding Private Label Lead." *Beverage World,* 15 November 2000.

———. "Steep to Conquer: Whether it's creating the best-selling tea or most successful beverage alliance, Pepsi and Lipton prove it's all about patience and good ingredients." *Beverage World,* 15 October 2001.

———. "Cott Dances with Bear: Private label leader teams with polar." *Beverage World,* 15 December 2001.

———. "Good Stuff: Private label's premium image is what has store brands maintaining their shelf space." *Beverage World,* 15 October 2001.

"Repairing the Coke Machine." *Business Week,* 19 March 2001.

"Shaking Up the Coke Bottle." *Business Week,* 3 December 2001.

"Soft Drinks: A Fluid Picture." TGI Global News, February 2004. Available from www.tgisurveys.com/.

"Soft Drink Facts." American Beverage Association, 2004. Available from www.ameribev.org.

"Soft Drink Markets in 174 Countries Worldwide Documented in Massive Five-Volume Report from Beverage Marketing Corporation." Beverage Marketing Corporation News Release, 15 June 2001. Available from www.beveragemarketing.com.

"Solid Growth Expected In Mexico's Soft Drink Market." InfoLatina S.A. de C.V., 24 August 2001

"Sports and Energy Sector to Remain High Value." Canadean press release, January 2002. Available from www.canadean.com.

Squires, Sally. "Soft Drinks, Hard Facts." *Washington Post,* 27 February 2001.

Steinriede, Kent. "Enrico Battles Back: Pepsi's International Efforts Will Focus on Developing Markets." *Beverage Industry,* (December 1996): 11.

Tarpley, Natasha A. "What Really Happened at Coke: Doug Ivester was a demon for information." *Fortune,* 10 January 2000.

Tarpley, Natasha A. "Crunch Time for Coke: His company is overflowing with trouble." *Fortune,* 19 July 1999.

Theodore, Sarah. "RTD Coffee, Tea Create a Buzz." *Beverage Industry,* 2004. Available from www.bevindustry.com.

"Top 10 U.S. CDC Companies and Brands for 2003." *Beverage Digest,* 5 March 2004. Available from www.beverage-digest.com/.

"The Top 10 Brands." *Business Week,* 2003. Available from www.businessweek.com/.

"U.S. Beverage Sales Threatened by Rising Water." Canadean press release, January 2002. Available from www.canadean.com.

"U.S. Soft Drink Sales Up Slightly in 2004." *Beverage Marketing,* 14 March 2005. Available from http://www.beveragemarketing.com.

Warner, Melanie. "Coke Finds Its Bright Spots in Faraway Places.rdquo; *New York Times,* 20 April 2005.

"Water, Water, Everywhere." *American Demographics,* 1 October 2001.

SIC 2100

NAICS 3122

TOBACCO PRODUCTS

The tobacco industry produces the world's cigarettes, cigars, smoking and chewing tobacco, snuff, and reconstituted tobacco. Certain industry firms are also involved in the industrial processing side of the business, which includes stemming and re-drying tobacco.

INDUSTRY SNAPSHOT

The tobacco products industry early in the twenty-first century was one of stunning contrasts. In many western countries consumption was falling, as it had done through the 1990s. The United States, for instance, was characterized by a particularly vocal and effective antismoking movement that helped bring down smoking rates and lobbied for increasing restrictions on smoking in public. Tobacco companies in the United States also faced a growing number of lawsuits brought on behalf of smokers and victims of second-hand smoke who had become seriously ill or died, as well as state and federal legislative proposals that threatened to further restrict the industry. For example, the Master Settlement Agreement, signed on November 16, 1998 by various state attorneys general and leading U.S. cigarette makers, included the stipulation that cigarette makers pay US$206 billion to U.S. states over a 25-year period to reimburse costs associated with treating illnesses related to smoking. Analysts predicted that the settlement would increase the cost of cigarettes and thus contribute to a decrease in cigarette smoking throughout the first decade of the twenty-first century. In fact, according to the U.S. Department of Agriculture, cigarette consumption in the United States fell by 7.5 percent between 1998 and 2000 as a result of increased prices, increased understanding of health risks, and bans on smoking in public places.

In Asia and Eastern Europe, however, cigarette sales increased as income levels rose (with U.S.-made cigarettes becoming very popular). In China, for example, it was estimated that per capita consumption rose 250 percent between the early 1970s and late 1990s. In total, global cigarette consumption, accounting for about 90 percent of all tobacco use, was fairly flat throughout the 1990s, tending to move upward at a rate of 1 percent or 2 percent a year. The divergent attitudes toward smoking between the East and the West had a profound impact on the major cigarette manufacturers. With markets in North America and Western Europe sluggish, the big multinational tobacco companies—Philip Morris, R.J. Reynolds, Japan Tobacco, and British American Tobacco (BAT) among them—aggressively pursued sales in emerging markets, such as Russia. Although a Russian economic downturn in 1998 allowed domestic brands to gain ground on more expensive imports, improved economic conditions there in 2000 boded well for the industry leaders, which by then were pursuing development of their own manufacturing facilities in Russia. A new excise tax on cigarettes, passed by the Russian Duma (parliament) in 2003, was not expected to diminish sales, which according to *Pravda* are worth about US$15 billion annually.

During the late 1990s, a growing number of people, especially in the United States, turned to products other than cigarettes, notably cigars and smokeless (chewing) tobacco. There was growing concern among public health officials at the possible misapprehension that cigars and smokeless tobacco were not health risks. Of concern as well was the rise in cigarette smoking among children and teenagers. Legislation emerged related to the targeting of teens in cigarette advertising, and several countries put in place laws that prevented tobacco companies from marketing their products to children under the age of 18.

Given the numerous uncertainties of the tobacco industry's future, few companies were eager to enter the business, thus limiting competition to current players. In addition, many industry leaders pursued consolidation aggressively in an effort to broaden international reach, a practice that reduced the number of large cigarette manufacturers further. At the beginning of the twenty-first century, Philip Morris, BAT, and Japan Tobacco accounted for 40 percent of the global tobacco industry. At the same time, however, the profit potential in cigarette manufacturing remained considerable. As famed investor Warren Buffett was quoted in *Barbarians at the Gate,* "I'll tell you why I like the cigarette business. It costs a penny to make. Sell it for a dollar. It's addictive and there's fantastic brand loyalty."

The World Health Organization has estimated that about one-third of the world population over the age of 15 smokes tobacco. In 2004 there were about 1.3 billion tobacco users. By 2025, this number was expected to rise to 1.7 billion. Tobacco is grown in at least 100 countries and international sales are estimated at over US$330 billion. The leading brand of cigarettes around the world is Philip Morris's Marlboro.

ORGANIZATION AND STRUCTURE

STEMMING AND RE-DRYING

In the United States and other countries, tobacco processors purchase tobacco leaf from farmers and prepare the plant for manufacture through stemming and re-drying. Three companies—Universal Corporation, Standard Commercial, and DIMON Inc.—control most of this business, and all have large operations in important tobacco growing regions of the world. DIMON is the result of a 1994 merger between Dibrell Brothers Inc. and Monk-Austin Inc., formerly rivals in this segment. The merger created the world's second largest leaf tobacco dealer behind Universal. In 2004, Universal remained the largest of the global leaf tobacco dealers, with sales of US$2.27 billion. Second-ranked DIMON, which posted sales of US$835.3 million in 2004, announced plans in 2005 to merge with Standard Commercial, which reported 2004 sales totalling US$780 million.

Large tobacco processors either purchase the farmers' tobacco at auction, a practice common in the United States, or buy tobacco directly from a farmer. In certain overseas markets where firms have contracted to buy a farmer's entire crop, such as in Zambia, the companies often provide financial and technical assistance to support the grower and ensure the tobacco's quality. In the United States, most processors' tobacco purchases at auction are made against specific orders from the major domestic and overseas cigarette producers. In many cases, the processors' relationships with cigarette producers extend over many years.

After purchase, tobacco is processed to meet the specific needs of the cigarette manufacturer, whose representatives are frequently at the processor's facilities to monitor the work on a company's particular order. At the factory, tobacco is reclassified according to grade; blended to meet customer requirements regarding color, body, and chemistry; and threshed to remove the stem from the leaf (although some tobacco is processed in whole leaf form). Processed tobacco is then again dried to remove excess moisture so it can be held in storage for long periods. The processors generally do not manufacture cigarettes or other consumer tobacco products.

ASIA

The tobacco industry in Asia has been dominated by national monopolies or near monopolies like the China National Tobacco Corporation, the Thailand Tobacco Monopoly, and the Korea Tobacco and Ginseng Corporation. China is the largest producer and consumer of cigarettes worldwide, manufacturing about 1.6 trillion cigarettes annually. In 1994, the Japanese government partially privatized its tobacco monopoly in a stock offering that received a notably poor reception from the investment community. Japan Tobacco International Inc. continued to control most of the market, although the share of imported cigarettes sold in the country rose after trade rules for the product were liberalized in 1985. By 2002, leading multinational firms had secured roughly 20 percent of the Japanese market, while Japan Tobacco maintained a 75 percent share. Tobacco production in India, the second largest country in terms of tobacco production and the third largest in terms of consumption, is regulated by the Tobacco Board, which sets output levels and manages unsold stocks.

EUROPE

The role of government in the tobacco industry tends to be more varied and less prominent in Western Europe. Italy and Portugal both feature state-owned tobacco monopolies that control the manufacture and retailing of tobacco products. The former monopolies of France and Spain, Seita and Tabacalera, respectively, were privatized in the late 1990s; the two companies eventually merged to form Altadis, one of the largest cigarette makers in the world and maker of the famous Gauloises brand. Tobacco companies are also privately owned in the United Kingdom, Germany, Belgium, Greece, and Ireland. In the United Kingdom, Imperial Tobacco is the top cigarette manufacturer; with second-ranking Gallaher Group, it controls about 80 percent of the industry there. Philip Morris, Reemtsma, and BAT are influential forces in the German market.

Even in countries with state-run monopolies, however, the big firms have gained substantial market share through licensing and export maneuvering. In France, for example, Philip Morris, Rothmans, and R.J. Reynolds secured 35 percent of the market before the state-run Seita was privatized. Philip Morris doubled its sales between 1984 and 1994 in Europe; its Marlboro brand became the industry leader—even though it often cost twice as much as products of the state monopolies.

The collapse of the Soviet Union and other communist regimes opened the markets of Eastern Europe to western firms. Smokers in the former Soviet bloc consumed about 700 billion cigarettes in 1993, about 40 percent more than the 500 billion units smoked in the United States. In Russia alone, according to *Pravda*, 50 percent of boys, 25 percent of girls, and 74 percent of young men were regular smokers, and sales of tobacco products reached US$15 billion each year. Recognizing this demand, western multinationals feverishly bought up production facilities in Russia and its former satellites. Philip Morris, for example, invested in Hungary, Lithuania, Russia, and Kazakhstan; its biggest investment was in Tabak, the former state tobacco monopoly of Czechoslovakia. Altogether, Philip Morris invested almost US$1 billion in the region, which was growing at more than 5 percent per year, between 1989 and 1993. By 2000, total foreign investment in the Russian tobacco industry had exceeded US$2 billion, making tobacco one of Russia's most successful industries. International firms held more than 65 percent of the cigarette production market there.

UNITED STATES

The tobacco products industry in the United States is entirely in private hands, although the government's price support program for tobacco did help stabilize leaf prices through the mid-1990s. Such price supports ended under a 1996 reform of U.S. farm subsidies. The top producers as of 2004 were Philip Morris USA, with almost 50 percent of the market; Reynolds American; and Carolina Grouprsquo;s Lorillard Tobacco. Large multinationals such as Philip Morris that have such a strong presence abroad have made the United States the world's biggest cigarette exporter. Exports reached a pinnacle of 250 billion cigarettes in 1996. By 2000, however, that number had fallen to roughly 150 billion, due to weakened demand, as well as the increasing numbers of transplant operations set up by U.S. manufacturers in other nations. Export volume continued to decline through the early 2000s, falling from 127.4 billion pieces in 2002 to 121.4 billion pieces in 2003. Exports declined more slowly in 2004, reaching 121 billion pieces. Until the late 1990s, the United States had also been the leading exporter of tobacco leaf. By 2000, however, Brazil had begun exporting larger leaf volumes.

LATIN AMERICA

The second largest market in the Western Hemisphere is Brazil, which produced 154 billion cigarettes in 1992. The industry was dominated by British American Tobacco (BAT), which carried about 83 percent of the market. An export tax levied by the Brazilian government in 1999 in an effort to prevent the importation of Brazilian cigarettes previously exported to Paraguay undercut production levels in 1999 to 144 billion. Production in 2000 was about 104 billion pieces. Though manufacturing increased to 106.6 billion pieces in 2002, levels fell to 96.7 billion pieces in 2003 and in 2004. The cigarette industry in Mexico, which is controlled by two manufacturers—PM Mexico, with 54.8 percent of the market, and Cigarrera La Moderna, with about 45 percent of the market—produced about 56.3 billion cigarettes in 2000. Both production and consumption of cigarettes in Mexico leveled off in the late 1990s due to price increases and growing health concerns. In 1995, for example, per capita cigarette consumption in Mexico was 856; the number dropped to 712 by 2000. Export volume, however, grew from 6.5 billion pieces to 10 billion pieces; the U.S. Department of Agriculture reported Mexican cigarette exports at 20 billion pieces per year from 2000 to 2004. In Argentina, where cigarette output reached approximately 40 billion units in 2000, Masalin Particulares, owned by Philip Morris, controlled 59.4 percent of the market in 2001. The remainder went to Nobleza Piccardo, a British American Tobacco (BAT) company. With domestic consumption declining from 1,976 cigarettes per capita in 1980 to 1,418 cigarettes per capita in 2000, Argentina's tobacco industry looked to international markets to remain profitable. Exports of cigarettes rose from 724 million in 1990 to 2.4 billion in 1995 and 2.5 billion by 2000. According to U.S.D.A. figures, exports held steady through 2004 at 2.4 billion pieces.

CANADA

The Canadian market is dominated by Imperial, RBH, and RJR-MacDonald, all of which are subsidiaries of large multinational tobacco companies. Imperial controlled 70.1 percent of the market in 2000 and 69.5 percent in 2001. Rothmans, Benson & Hedges, which held 35.5 percent of the Canadian market in 1980, saw its share decrease steadily through the 1990s. It ranked second as of 2001, with 16.4 percent of the market. Cigarette consumption was reduced by 31 percent between 1982 and 1991 in Canada because of major price hikes and increased awareness of the health risks associated with smoking. While cigarette exports rose rapidly in the early 1990s, most of the increase reflected tax avoidance schemes, and officials estimated that 80 percent of all foreign shipments found their way back to Canada. In 2001, domestic cigarette sales exceeded 42 billion pieces.

AFRICA

By the early 2000s, cigarette production had remained relatively low in Africa. South Africa was the biggest producer on the continent in 1990, with an output of 41 billion units. Consumption was also high, reaching about 34 percent of the adult population by 1995. The anti-apartheid government that came to power in 1993, however, launched aggressive anti-smoking measures that helped reduce the number of smokers by 20 percent by 1997. Because of economic sanctions against the apartheid government in the 1980s, the South African tobacco industry—dominated by Rothmans International, formed in 1995 with the merger of the Rembrandt and Richemont tobacco companies—faced little international competition until the early 1990s. British American Tobacco (BAT) manufactures its own brands in South Africa, and Philip Morris granted Rembrandt exclusive rights to manufacture Marlboros there. Africa also has two important leaf-producing countries, however—Zimbabwe and Zambia. Indeed, Zimbabwe was the world's third largest exporter by the early 2000s.

BACKGROUND AND DEVELOPMENT

In 1492, Rodrigo de Jerez, one of Columbus's crewmen, noted that the natives of Cuba ignited dried tobacco leaves and inhaled the smoke. De Jerez tried it himself and thus became Europe's first confirmed smoker. Back in Spain, however, his neighbors, terrified by the smoke that poured from his mouth, thought the devil had possessed him. He was imprisoned by the Inquisition.

Tobacco usage has often generated such controversy. King James I of seventeenth-century England despised smoking, wrote a "Counterblast to Tobacco" and beheaded Sir Walter Raleigh, the man who first imported tobacco to Europe. But King James was also the first in power to extract substantial revenue from tobacco import duties.

Paper-wrapped cigarettes were supposedly developed in the sixteenth century by the beggars of Seville, Spain, who rolled discarded cigar butts in scraps of paper. Factory production of cigarettes in quantity began in the nineteenth century. In 1881, a patent was issued for a cigarette-rolling machine capable of making 120,000 pieces a day. By 1900, there were over 160 brands available in the United States.

Despite the large number of brands, however, nine out of every ten cigarettes purchased in the United States was produced by the American Tobacco trust, run by the ruthless James Buchanan Duke. After decimating his competition in the United States, Duke turned to Britain in 1900 and prepared to invade that market with a price-slashing strategy that would, he hoped, enable him to dominate the market. Preparing for Duke's arrival, local producers banded together to form Imperial Tobacco. A battle ensued for the British market. After a year or so, Imperial announced it would counterattack by turning to the United States—the primary territory of American Tobacco—with its own brands. Duke decided to negotiate a settlement, which neatly carved up the global market. His company got the U.S. territory, while Imperial took Britain; and a new company, BAT Mfg. Ltd., was created to promote smoking and produce cigarettes in the rest of the world. The cartel lasted for a decade until 1911, when the U.S. Supreme Court broke up Duke's trust into a new "big four": American Tobacco, R.J. Reynolds, Lorillard, and Liggett & Meyers.

One legacy of the Duke trust and subsequent break-up is that a single brand may be produced by different multinationals in different countries. For example, British American Tobacco (BAT) owns Benson & Hedges in most markets, but in the United States, Philip Morris holds the trademark, and in Britain it belongs to American Brands' Gallaher subsidiary. Another example is Kent, which is owned by Lorillard in the United States but by BAT in other international markets.

In 1913, Richard J. Reynolds developed what came to be known as the American cigarette—a blend of flue-cured and burley tobacco mixed with a small amount of Turkish product. It became immediately popular in the United States. In the late 1920s, a machine was developed that combined several cigarette-making procedures into one process. The machine made the package, packed the cigarettes, and affixed the revenue stamps, thus decreasing the cost of cigarette packaging to less than 1 cent per 1,000 units.

Filter-tipped cigarettes were developed in Western Europe in the 1950s and began to gain popularity just as health considerations concerning smoking first came to light. Cigarette sales in the United States peaked in 1965 at 529 billion, an average of more than half a pack for every citizen over 18. Thereafter, as a consequence of the report of the U.S. Surgeon General on the dangers of smoking, consumption fell. In the 1970s, cigarette commercials were banned on radio and television in the United States, and legislation was passed that required that all cigarette packages and advertising include health warnings. U.S. consumption levels dropped fairly consistently throughout the 1980s, and recognition of the dangers to health that smoking presents spread throughout the world, most notably in Canada and Western Europe. In many countries, however, cigarette consumption rose during the 1980s and 1990s.

By the mid-1990s, along with the United States and Germany, China and Japan were the four leading nations in the global production of cigarettes. China continued to be the world's leading producer and consumer of tobacco products. India, despite its size, was only the fifth largest producer in the mid-1990s. However, in India the *bidi* (tobacco wrapped in a temburni leaf) was also extremely popular (leading to India's being ranked second in per capita tobacco consumption worldwide by the World Health Organization). The cigarette market in Asia, home to 60 percent of the world's population, continued to boom throughout the decade. While many Asian countries launched antismoking campaigns, and several, like China, banned tobacco advertising, the attitude toward cigarette smoking remained one of indulgence or even tacit approval. Indeed, a brand of cigarette remained a status indicator, with U.S. and other western brands regarded as the most prestigious. In Vietnam the cigarette of choice was BAT's 555; in Thailand it was Dunhill; and in China the Marlboro brand was favored. Many of the inroads made by western companies in the 1990s were attributable to market-opening measures instituted by Asian governments that lifted trade barriers to imports.

Cigarette smoking remained primarily a male pursuit in Asia in the 1990s. The World Health Organization issued in 1996 an estimate that in Southeast Asia 44 percent of men smoked versus only 4 percent of the women; in India, the figures were 40 percent versus 3 percent. This demographic breakdown contrasts to the fairly equal division by gender in many industrialized countries, such as New Zealand and the United States. Nevertheless, by the late 1990s young women in Asia were smoking in increasing numbers, although overall the percentage was below 10 percent.

As health concerns about smoking grew, consumption in Western Europe remained flat. In Eastern Europe, however, smokers were less aware of the health risks. As Michael Herron of the American Cancer Society told the *Los Angeles Times,* Russia was regarded as being more than three decades behind the United States in terms of social and medical awareness of smoking's risks. For major manufacturers, these markets presented new opportunities for sales and investment. In Eastern Europe, the prevalence of female smoking also was much higher than in other regions of the world. In the Russian Federation, for example, the World Health Organization estimated that 67 percent of men and 30 percent of women smoked.

In the United States, legislation was introduced in 1994 to allow federal recovery of Medicare and Medicaid costs associated with tobacco-related illnesses. This proposal copied state legislation with similar objectives. By 1998, courtroom and legislative battles were becoming daily fare for tobacco manufacturers in the United States. Juries awarded damages in the millions of dollars to survivors of smokers who had died of lung cancer, notably the Rose Cipollone (later overturned) and Milton Horowitz cases. Executives of the large cigarette companies were brought to testify before Congress about whether they had knowingly sold a hazardous drug, particularly targeting children and teenagers. The famous "Joe Camel" cartoon character, which antismoking advocates claimed was intended to draw children to smoking, vanished from advertisements for Camel cigarettes. At least 39 states filed lawsuits against tobacco companies, asking that damages be awarded and devoted to the healthcare costs caused by smoking. However, despite a prohibition on advertising tobacco on U.S. television, tobacco marketers successfully employed other media, including use of billboards, magazines, and large signs displayed at gas stations and convenience stores. All such practices provoked controversy with tobacco's detractors.

In 1998, the U.S. Congress carried on a heated debate about the "tobacco bill," sponsored by Arizona Senator John McCain, which proposed to raise cigarette prices by US$1.10 over a five-year period and impose a host of restrictions on the marketing of tobacco. A key component of the bill, which was at the center of the controversy, was whether there should be a cap of US$8 billion per year on damages awarded in lawsuits against tobacco companies. The companies claimed that even this amount could drive them to bankruptcy, while antismoking advocates such as C. Everett Koop (former U.S. surgeon general) and David Kessler (former head of the Food and Drug Administration) found it unacceptable that damage awards against the tobacco companies would be limited. It was estimated by the *Washington Post* that as of May 1998, tobacco companies had already spent US$25 million in advertising to defeat the tobacco bill. In June 1998, the legislation died in the Senate, owing, some observers claimed, to the tobacco lobby's pressure on senators.

Faced with this legal barrage, the once-solid front presented by the tobacco companies began to crumble—but only slightly. Liggett, which had been the defendant in the Cippolone suit, admitted that smoking can cause cancer (an argument still not publicly accepted by most other companies) and volunteered to release secret industry documents that showed tobacco companies had long been aware of the health risks of cigarettes and also had encouraged marketing to under-age smokers. In June 1998, these documents came back to haunt cigarette manufacturers, when Brown & Williamson was found guilty of conspiracy charges tied to the lung cancer death of a long-term smoker. The documents served as a strong factor in the award of the first punitive damages against a tobacco company.

Despite protracted legal wrangling in the 1990s, which eventually resulted in hundreds of billions of dollars paid to the U.S. Government in settlement, U.S. tobacco makers remained highly profitable during the decade. The industry was also heartened by several developments stemming from the mid-1990s. The boom in exports to Asia and Eastern Europe gave the industry a big lift, as did the initial defeat of proposals by the Clinton administration to levy heavy taxes on cigarettes. By the late 1990s, however, legal battles facing the U.S. tobacco manufacturers had escalated, and the percentage of adult smokers continued to drop; public opinion of the companies plummeted as records indicating their early awareness of health risks and their alleged targeting of underage smokers became public. Nevertheless, as of 1996, the Centers for Disease Control estimated that 47 million adults continued to smoke cigarettes, resulting in over 430,000 deaths per year and direct and indirect health costs of over US$100 billion. In light of the hostility they faced at home, U.S. companies began to increase their efforts to sell their products in developing nations.

Legal battles in the United States eventually resulted in the Master Settlement Agreement, signed on November 16, 1998, by the majority of U.S. states and the top U.S. cigarette makers. The agreement required cigarette manufacturers to pay US$206 billion to U.S. states over a 25-year period to offset treatment costs associated with smoking-related illnesses. In addition, the firms agreed to spend US$1.5 billion in a ten-year antismoking campaign, US$250 million on efforts to curb smoking by youths, and US$5.15 billion in a twelve-year program to compensate tobacco farmers for the reduced tobacco sales likely to result from the agreement. Between 1998 and 2000, cigarette consumption in the United States fell by 7.5 percent, according to the U.S. Department of Agriculture, and analysts pointed to a cigarette price increase of 45 cents per pack, which took effect when the Master Settlement agreement was passed, as a major cause.

U.S. cigarette smokers faced another price hike in January of 2000, when a federal excise tax was increased from 24 cents to 34 cents per pack. Although the tax was officially levied on manufacturers, most of the cost was eventually added to the retail price of cigarettes. The excise tax was increased by another 5 cents per pack in January of 2002. According to statistics released by the Centers for Disease Control, the average smoker paid US$250 in cigarette taxes in 2000; this figure was based on estimates that 22.7 percent of U.S. citizens over the age of 16 were smokers. According to the U.S. Department of Agriculture, U.S. tobacco usage, particularly cigarette smoking, was expected to continue to drop between one and 3 percent annually.

While cigarettes were being pummeled by the media and the medical establishment in the United States, the little-noticed cigar industry gained new aficionados and even a certain cachet. From 1989 to 1993, annual sales rose from 88 million to 109 million, an increase of almost 25 percent. About two thirds of cigars sold in the United States were imported. In recognition of the estimated 8 million cigar smokers in the United States, cigar clubs and cigar dinners and special events grew increasingly commonplace in the 1990s. Cuban cigars, illegal in the United States, nonetheless maintained their stature in the 1990s as well: up to 5 million were smuggled into the United States each year, at prices of up to US$30 each. By the late 1990s, however, some industry observers thought that the popularity of cigars had peaked.

The sales of smokeless tobacco, chiefly moist snuff, also rose in the United States during the 1990s, although cigarettes still accounted for 95 percent of tobacco product sales. Leading brands included Copenhagen and Skoal and were made by the United States Tobacco Company. Restrictions on smoking in public places helped the industry, which also benefited from effective advertising promotion.

Consolidation intensified in the tobacco industry throughout the late 1990s, allowing the largest players to grow even larger. In 1999, British American Tobacco (BAT), the world's second largest tobacco company, acquired 58 percent of Canadian tobacco giant Imasco (parent company of Imperial Tobacco of Canada). The C$10.7 billion deal marked one of the largest acquisitions in Canadian business history. That year, BAT also purchased Rothmans International, which held a 7.75 percent share of the U.K. market, from Compagnie Financiere Richemont AG in 1999. The deal allowed BAT to increase its global market share to 15.4 percent, gaining ground on rival Philip Morris, which held a 17 percent share. Also in the late 1990s, Japan Tobacco, the third largest tobacco manufacturer in the world, paid US$8 billion for the international operations of R.J. Reynolds, which were renamed JT International.

CURRENT CONDITIONS

Consolidation continued in the industry when in 2003, British American Tobacco acquired Ente Tabacchii Italiani, making BAT the number two player in Italy, the second largest tobacco market in the European Union. In 2002, Imperial Tobacco Group, the top-ranking cigarette manufacturer in Britain, purchased German tobacco company Reemtsma to become the world's fourth largest tobacco firm. In 2004, Reynolds merged with Brown & Williamson Tobacco to form Reynolds American Incorporated. Philip Morris expanded in 2005 with acquisitions of Indonesian cigarette manufacturer PT HM Sampoerna Tbk and Colombian cigarette company Coltabaco.

In addition to government regulation of cigarettes, the tobacco industry continued to face other regulatory challenges. In 2003, member states of the World Health Organization unanimously adopted the WHO Framework Convention on Tobacco Control, the world's first public health treaty. Aiming to reduce tobacco-related deaths worldwide, the treaty required countries to restrict tobacco advertising, sponsorship, and promotion; improve labeling of tobacco products; and enforce tighter laws against tobacco smuggling. It also addressed measures to protect consumers against second-hand smoke. WHO members also called for health professionals themselves to quit smoking. The treaty was signed by approximately 170 nations including the United States.

The European Union in 2002 voted to ban tobacco advertising in print media and on the internet, as well as at international sports venues. Set to go into effect in 2005, this regulation complemented an earlier ban on TV cigarette ads in the European Union. In addition, the European Union began talks in 2004 aimed at phasing out agricultural subsidies paid to tobacco farmers.

In Asia, where cigarette advertising on television and in magazines was banned, tobacco companies were able to make use of alternative outlets to convey their message. In China, tobacco companies sponsor sporting events, plaster their brand names on billboards and public transportation, and license their names to clothiers and shoe manufacturers. Philip Morris sells Western-style clothing, while R.J. Reynolds sponsors an annual tennis tournament in Beijing. Much of the advertising in Asia is directed at young women—beautiful models are pictured smoking in scenes of Western-style luxury. Some American companies play up their roots. In the Philippines, for example, Winston brand cigarettes are touted as "The Taste of the U.S.A."

Tobacco packaging is also an area that continues to face scrutiny from regulators. For example, the European Union passed legislation in February of 2001 requiring health warnings to cover 30 percent of the front and 40 percent of the back of all packs of cigarettes. Warnings were required to include graphic pictures of the negative health effects of smoking. In addition, labels were no longer allowed to include descriptions such as "light" or "mild."

RESEARCH AND TECHNOLOGY

Since people in many countries have become less tolerant of secondhand smoke, tobacco companies are eager to find ways to eliminate it or at least reduce its impact—thus the search for the "smokeless" cigarette, most notably by R.J. Reynolds. The company introduced its smokeless Premier brand in 1989, but the cigarette never made it out of test markets and wound up costing the firm as much as US$800 million. Test audiences complained about the tastelessness of the product as well as its foul smell.

That same year, Philip Morris introduced Next, a no-nicotine cigarette created through a high-pressure carbon dioxide process. But this product had higher levels of tar than many standard cigarettes and failed to attract consumers. It was withdrawn from the market. Five years later, Reynolds announced that it was testing a new and substantially different version of the smokeless cigarette, named Eclipse. Reynolds claimed that, by using a special charcoal tip, the cigarette did not burn tobacco at all. The company said that the new product eliminated most secondhand smoke and reduced the amount of tar and carcinogenic compounds inhaled by the smoker. A study by the Massachusetts Department of Public Health, however, concluded that Eclipse produced as many or even more toxins than two ultralight brands, and also produced higher levels of carbon monoxide. Reynolds also announced in 1994 the development of a new cigarette that the company said reduced the stale smell of smoke. The company claimed that the cigarette had smoother flavor, "with a proprietary paper technology that masks and changes the odor" of cigarette smoke.

In the late 1990s Philip Morris introduced its version of a smokeless cigarette, Accord. It included a US$40 kit containing a kazoo-shaped cigarette holder, a battery-operated lighter, and a carton of Accord cigarettes. The lighter contained a microchip that was activated when the user puffed on the cigarette in the holder. The process sent a burst of heat to the cigarette, giving the smoker one hit but producing no actual smoke. The company claimed that Accord produced 83 percent fewer toxins than regular cigarettes.

ADVANCES IN TOBACCO GROWING

The major tobacco companies became significantly involved in plant genetics and biotechnology. For many years the tobacco plant was the experimental plant of choice for researchers. Indeed, scientists probably know more about tobacco than any other plant in existence. *Nicotiana tobacum* became the scientific standard because it is easy to grow and easy to use to construct hybrids and crosses. In fact, the tobacco industry was successful in fighting plant diseases in large part because disease-resistant varieties of tobacco can be bred so easily.

Industry critics contend that the best known example of the industry's use of biotechnology was the development of Y-1—the high-nicotine tobacco plant FDA commissioner David Kessler cited in 1994 as an effort to manipulate nicotine levels and thereby further addict smokers. In 1998, the manufacturer of Y-1, DNA Plant Technology, pleaded guilty to illegally transporting this product to Brown & Williamson, leading to suspicion that the company had "spiked" its products with high nicotine levels. But researchers also believe that the tobacco plant can be genetically engineered to make products like anticancer agents, human vaccines, antibodies for therapeutic uses, enzymes that go into laundry detergents, and even food additives. Recently, tobacco companies have engaged in research to lower the content of nitrosamine, the most potent of the carginogens found in tobacco.

INDUSTRY LEADERS

PHILIP MORRIS

Philip Morris is a relative newcomer to the ranks of leading international cigarette producers. After the breakup of the American Tobacco trust in 1911, a few splinter companies not associated with any of the "big four" eventually came together under the name Philip Morris. But while the company was still a relatively small player in the early 1930s, by 1960 it was a major firm and ranked sixth among the tobacco companies. The Philip Morris International division, originally known as Philip Morris Overseas, was established in 1955.

In 1985, the company restructured, creating a holding company, Philip Morris Companies Inc., that became the parent company of Philip Morris Incorporated. Philip Morris Companies Inc. was renamed Altria Group Inc. in 2003. Philip Morris assumed its preeminent position in the 1990s on the strength of several business decisions made during the course of the 1960s and 1970s. The company was the first to anticipate the potential for overseas tobacco sales. In addition, the company's Marlboro Man advertising campaign became one of the most successful in the world. These factors played well off each other, and Marlboro became one of the industry's best-selling brands. Indeed, some cite Marlboro's popularity as the primary reason for the leading position of the United States in world cigarette exports in the mid-1990s.

As the health risks associated with smoking became more profound in the public's mind, the company sought diversification, most notably in the foods sector. It paid US$5.8 billion for General Foods in 1985 and US$12.9 billion for Kraft in 1988. Other company holdings include Miller

Brewing Co. and Kraft Jacobs Suchard, a Swiss maker of coffee and chocolate. By 1993, non-tobacco businesses made up more than half of Philip Morris's sales.

On April 2, 1993 or "Marlboro Friday", as it came to be known by industry followers, Philip Morris cut the price of its leading brand by 20 percent in order to regain market share that had been lost to discount brands and Reynolds' Camel line. While for many investors this move questioned the staying power of all consumer brand names, for Marlboro the price cut was a clear success. It soon regained eight points of market share, bringing it back to the 30 percent level.

In 1994 there was much discussion about a plan to segregate non-tobacco operations to protect shareholders from the negative impact of lawsuits and an unfavorable regulatory climate. The proposal was ultimately defeated, however. Disappointed institutional investors were wooed instead with a 20 percent increase in the dividend and a share buyback program. Some industry analysts noted that despite all the furor over the future of smoking, the fact remained that the tobacco business, especially the international segment, had proved far more profitable than food operations in the early 1990s.

As of 2003, Philip Morris continued to control almost half of the U.S. tobacco market and 17 percent of the global tobacco market, bolstered by the world-leading Marlboro brand. The company also continued to pursue acquisitions through the early 2000s, buying a 40 percent stake in Indonesian cigarette manufacturer PT HM Sampoerna Tbk for approximately US$5.2 billion in 2005. Also that year, Philip Morris paid US$299.6 million for a 96.65 percent share in Coltabaco, the largest cigarette manufacturer in Colombia. Altria, Philip Morris's parent company, reported that its tobacco segment had net domestic revenues of US$17.5 billion and net international sales of US$39.5 billion in 2004.

British American Tobacco PLC

According to the agreement between American Tobacco and Imperial Tobacco of Britain in 1902, British American Tobacco (BAT) was given full rein to produce and market cigarettes anywhere outside the United States and Britain. By the latter part of the twentieth century, some 80 percent of the company's assets were located outside Britain. Its products were sold in some 180 countries and duty-free markets, and it owned the leading brand in over 30 markets. The company continued as a prime player in major tobacco markets like Brazil and Germany, but its attempt to establish itself in the British market during the early 1980s proved unsuccessful. It owned the Brown & Williamson Company, the third largest U.S. tobacco firm. Under a settlement with the U.S. Federal Trade Commission at the end of 1994, it took over most of American Tobacco, the fourth largest tobacco company in the United States.

The takeover was a change in direction for BAT, which had spent much of the 1970s and 1980s diversifying beyond the tobacco industry. The company became a major player in insurance, retailing, and paper products during that period. After a hostile takeover bid from Sir James Goldsmith in 1989, however, the company sold or spun off all of its retail and paper operations. In 1990, after California insurance regulators blocked Goldsmith's attempt to force BAT, by then known as BAT Industries, to sell its Farmers Insurance subsidiary to Axa-Midi of France, Goldsmith called off the takeover. In the mid-1990s, BAT Industries carried on diversified activities, notably mortgage lending and insurance sales. Eventually, it spun off its tobacco interests as British American Tobacco PLC (BAT), which acquired Switzerland-based Rothmans International in 1999.

As of 2003, BAT held its ground as the world's second largest cigarette maker, behind Philip Morris, with a 15 percent share of the global market. The company sold 855 billion cigarettes and reported revenues in 2003 of US$43 billion. In 2004, BAT's former U.S. unit, Brown & Williamson, merged with J.R. Reynolds Tobacco.

Japan Tobacco Inc.

In the 1850s, British and American imports gave the Japanese their first exposure to cigarettes. In 1883, Iwatani, a trading company, began production of Tengu, Japan's first popular domestic brand. Murai Brothers initiated production of Sunrise cigarettes a few years later. The firm also imported Hero cigarettes from the United States. Like other governments, the Japanese authorities came to view cigarettes as a source of revenue, and Japan instituted taxes on the product in 1888. In 1898, a bureau was established within the Ministry of Finance to administer a government tobacco monopoly. In 1905, the government's salt monopoly was also brought under its jurisdiction.

When the Allies restructured the Japanese economy in 1949, they reorganized the bureau as the Japan Tobacco and Salt Public Corporation. While still wholly owned by the government, the company conducted its tobacco business on a commercial basis. In 1985 the company was restructured as Japan Tobacco International Inc., but the newly issued shares were still held entirely by the Japanese government.

In 1994, as part of a program to privatize government assets, the company was listed on the Tokyo Stock Exchange with the objective of selling one third of its equity to private investors. By most accounts, however, the move was a failure. The shares were poorly received by the investment community. Some critics charged that the government had mishandled the offering, while others noted the fundamental financial uncertainties surrounding the company. Tobacco sales had risen just 0.7 percent in 1993 and the long term picture was clouded by the shrinking adult population and increasing awareness of the health risks associated with consumption of their staple product. In addition, foreign competitors had penetrated the domestic market during the early 1990s (by 1994, foreign cigarettes had taken 18% of the market). Whatever profits the company was making appeared to come from cost-cutting, not new demand. Moreover, even with partial privatization, the company remained burdened by government-directed obligations such as the requirement that it buy 50 percent of its raw tobacco from Japanese farmers at three times the world price. The company's efforts at diversification—agribusiness, beverages, pharmaceuticals, real estate, and health-club operations—accounted for only 12 percent of revenue by the mid-1990s.

Remaining under majority control of the Japanese government, Japan Tobacco saw its domestic market share slip from 80 percent in the 1990s to just over 70 percent by 2003, due to increased competition from global rivals and to a decrease in domestic consumption from about 27 percent to about 24 percent of the adult population. The firm acquired the international operations of RJR Nabisco in 1999, gaining access to brands such as Camel, Winston, and Salem, sold through its newly named global unit, JT International. Total sales for Japan Tobacco, now the world's third largest tobacco company, surpasssed US$43.7 billion in 2004. Due to lose its license to sell Philip Morris's Marlboro brand in April 2005, Japan Tobacco continued to seek increased international sales in such promising markets as Russia (which was the fourth largest cigarette market in 2003) and in Turkey.

REYNOLDS AMERICAN INC.

The second largest U.S. tobacco company, R.J. Reynolds merged with third ranking Brown & Williamson in 2004 to create Reynolds American Inc. The new company included four operating subsidiaries: R.J. Reynolds Tobacco Company, Santa Fe Natural Tobacco Company, Inc., Lane Limited, and R.J. Reynolds Global Products. Reynolds American traces its origins to 1874, when Richard Joshua Reynolds began growing tobacco in Winston, North Carolina. In 1890, the J. R. Reynolds Company issued its first shares, but Reynolds still owned 90 percent of the firm. After manufacturing only chewing tobacco for 20 years, the company introduced its first smoking tobacco brand in 1895. Reynolds, who needed capital to expand his operations, reluctantly turned to industry czar James Buchanan Duke for help. By 1900, two-thirds of the company Reynolds had founded was in the hands of Duke, although Reynolds was allowed to keep much of his independence.

After the Supreme Court broke up Duke's tobacco trust in 1911, R.J. Reynolds became the smallest of the "big four" spin-offs. Within 12 years, however, the success of its Camel brand (the famous "I'd walk a mile for a Camel" campaign dates from 1919) and its innovative marketing techniques (like selling cigarettes by the carton) helped it surge past American Tobacco to become the industry's profit leader in the 1920s. In the 1950s, the company introduced its Winston and Salem brands, which made tremendous profits. This period, however, was also marked by the first critical attacks on the industry for the potential health risks of its products.

In the 1960s, the company diversified into food and other product areas, buying companies such as Chun King, Sea-Land Industries, and, in 1970, Aminoil; it later added Del Monte and Heublein. R.J. Reynolds' major non-tobacco purchase was Nabisco in 1985, which increased the company's revenues from non-tobacco business to 40 percent. At the same time, however, management sold off a number of its unrelated subsidiaries, including Aminoil.

In 1988 Reynolds became the focus of one of the great dramas of U.S. business history. F. Ross Johnson, Reynolds' president, proposed a massive leveraged buyout (that is, the company's assets would be used to collateralize the huge loans needed to buy the stock of shareholders) in which he and other company executives would become the principal owners. Some of Reynolds' directors did not like Johnson or his plan, and they opened the bidding to other proposals. After much suspense and intrigue, the eventual winner was Kohlberg Kravis Roberts & Co. (KKR), whose bid was actually lower than that made by Johnson's group.

KKR immediately began to cut costs and sell assets, including Del Monte and parts of Nabisco, to pay off the enormous debt. In 1991 the company once again went public, although KKR continued to hold the majority of shares. In the mid-1990s, the price cut that Philip Morris announced on Marlboro Friday trimmed Reynolds' share of the U.S. cigarette market. The company's cigarette business, though, continued to benefit from sharp increases in overseas exports and ownership of foreign subsidiaries.

In 1997, RJR Nabisco Holdings Corp., R.J. Reynolds' parent, had revenues of over US$17 billion, equally divided between its tobacco and food operations. RJR Nabisco spun off R.J. Reynolds in 1999. Earlier that year, RJR Nabisco had also sold its international tobacco operations to Japan Tobacco. In 2002, Reynolds acquired Santa Fe Natural Tobacco Co. for US$340 million.

The 2004 merger with Brown & Williamson added Kool and Lucky Strike to Reynolds American's major brands, which include Camel and Salem. According to a press release from British American Tobacco, which owns 42 percent of Reynolds American, Reynolds should expect annual sales of about US$8.4 billion. In 2004 the company posted sales of US$6.4 billion.

MAJOR COUNTRIES IN THE INDUSTRY

CHINA

In 2003, China had about 250 million smokers—representing one third of the world total, according to a CNN report. The country produced more than twice as many cigarettes as the world's next largest producer, the United States. By 2003, annual sales of cigarettes in China generated about US$16 billion. Cigarette consumption in China, according to U.S. Department of Agriculture figures, was 1.777 trillion pieces in 2004.

Tobacco was introduced in China as early as the seventeenth century and was often mixed with opium for pipe smoking. But it was James Duke and his cohorts at BAT who created the booming market for cigarettes early in the twentieth century. Duke's people proselytized smoking across China. The company blanketed thc country with advertising. In Ying-kvou, Manchuria, for instance, they put up 2,000 large paper placards and 200 large wooden and iron signboards. The resulting demand was supplied from four factories employing some 13,000 Chinese workers. Annual consumption grew from 1.2 billion cigarettes in 1902 to 25 billion in 1920. By that time, BAT was earning about one-third of its worldwide profits from China. While World War II ended the company's involvement in the country, the smoking habits they had induced became well entrenched in Chinese society.

China poured investment into its cigarette facilities throughout the 1980s and greatly expanded capacity. Production output advanced 2.8 percent in 1992 to 1.6 trillion units, following a similar rise in the prior year. These increases were held in check by a production cap instituted in 1991. Some 500 brands of cigarettes were produced by 147 factories and marketed regionally. The production facilities themselves were operated by semi-independent companies organized by province, but they all fell under the control of the state monopoly. Most Chinese cigarettes consisted of flue-cured tobacco, with the highest quality leaf coming from the Yunnan province in the south. In 1993, blended cigarettes represented less than 10 percent of production, but their popularity was rising.

China aggressively developed markets throughout Southeast Asia, Eastern Europe, and the Commonwealth of Independent States in the 1990s. At the same time, the Chinese cigarette market remained a difficult one for international competitors to infiltrate, although imports increased somewhat in the 1990s, a development that most observers attributed to the rising income of its citizens. Countries such as the United States continued to fight to bring down the barriers to foreign cigarettes, which had been exclusively sold in foreign currency shops. Only multinationals that had organized joint ventures with a domestic factory were allowed to produce in China. It was difficult, however, to determine true market share when the bulk of China's imports arrived via Hong Kong. Before Hong Kong's 1997 return to Chinese control, cigarettes exported to China often returned to Hong Kong through illegal channels to avoid Hong Kong's high taxes.

In anticipation of China's entrance into the World Trade Organization early in the twenty-first century, the State Tobacco Monopoly Administration and the China National Tobacco Corp. created the China Tobacco Import and Export Group in August of 2000. According to a January 2002 issue of *Tobacco Reporter,* the group was formed to "adapt to the trend of building transnational enterprise groups in the international tobacco circle, to beef up the strength of China's tobacco import and export and its competitiveness, and to improve the management of tobacco import and export." By 2002, the new group had forged alliances with Philip Morris, BAT, and Japan Tobacco. As of early 2004, however, it remained unclear to what extent China would open its tobacco market to international competition.

THE UNITED STATES

In the United States, four companies virtually control the cigarette market: Philip Morris; Reynolds American; Lorriland; and Liggett. Consumption fell as much as 2 percent annually in the 1990s, a downturn attributed to aggressive antismoking campaigns, increased awareness of smoking's dangers, higher prices, and increased taxes. In 1999 alone, U.S. cigarette consumption dropped 6.5 percent to 435 billion pieces. In addition, U.S. cigarette production fell from a high of 755 billion pieces in 1996 to 595 billion pieces in 2000. By 2003 the figures were even lower. According to the U.S. Department of Agriculture, U.S. cigarette consumption dropped by almost 100 billion pieces between 1993 and 2003, with a 4 percent fall in 2003. In 2004, U.S. consumption totaled 402 billion cigarettes. Per capita consumption among adults in 2003 averaged 1,903 pieces, while the rate for ages 16 through 18 was 1,833.

In 1997, the United States exported tobacco products valued at almost US$5 billion dollars to foreign nations. The ten leading destinations were Japan (US$1.6 billion), Belgium (US$1.1 billion), Russia (US$234 million), Saudi Arabia (US$206 million), Lebanon (US$179 million), South Korea (US$154 million), Turkey (US$137 million), Cyprus (US$127 million), Hong Kong (US$89 million), and Singapore (US$81 million). In turn, U.S. imports of tobacco products (excluding smuggled cigar products) totaled almost US$500 million in 1997. The top importers to the United States were the Dominican Republic (US$232 million), Honduras (US$76 million), Nicaragua (US$31 million), Canada (US$27 million), United Kingdom (US$16 million), Jamaica (US$12 million), Japan (US$11 million), Netherlands (US$11 million), and Spain (US$10.6 million). Though the United States remained the largest tobacco importer and exporter in the world, both volume and revenues of cigarette exports fell in the early 2000s. Volume dropped 5 percent in 2003, with export earnings valued at US$1.4 billion. The largest markets for U.S. cigarettes in 2003 were Japan, Saudi Arabia, Israel, Lebanon, Iran, and the European Union.

JAPAN

While Japan's domestic demand in the early 1990s was sluggish, exports of Japanese cigarettes rose during that period. Although cigarette consumption in Japan remained extremely high (more than half of adult men), tax hikes and economic turbulence did contribute to a 2.3 percent drop in consumption, to 324.5 billion cigarettes, in 2001. The U.S. Department of Agriculture estimated a further decline, to 278.885 billion cigarettes, in 2004. The leading producer within Japan in 2004 was Japan Tobacco, which held a 75 percent market share. The firm's Mild Seven brand, which is the second best selling cigarette in the world, held a 34 percent share of the domestic market.

GERMANY

In Germany, cigarette production in the early 1990s totaled 222 billion pieces a year. Official statistics put domestic sales at 153 billion cigarettes per annum, although industry followers noted that about 10 billion cigarettes were smuggled into the country each year. Some Germans also used "cigarette rolls," a specially designed device that enables the smoker to produce his own cigarette; this product was devised to skirt the high tax rates of packaged brands. Historically, some 75 percent of all German cigarette exports went to other EU member nations, but in the early 2000s, Germany developed export markets in Eastern Europe, the Commonwealth of Independent States (former Soviet Republics), and the Middle East.

Philip Morris dominated the German cigarette market with a 37 percent share in 2001. Reemtsma and BAT each controlled about 22 percent, while Japan Tobacco had gained a 3.6 percent share. Germany was one of the strongest cigarette markets in Western Europe through the mid-1990s, since roughly 30 percent of its adult citizens smoked. However, increased regulations and growing awareness of health concerns did result in a drop in sales from 145 billion cigarettes in 1999 to 139.6 billion cigarettes in 2000 and 127 billion cigarettes by 2004.

FURTHER READING

BAT Annual Report, 2004. Available from http://www.bat.com.

"China Mulls Cigarette Ad Ban." CNN News, 17 November 2003. Available from edition.cnn.com/2003/HEALTH.

Connolly, Ceci. "Tobacco Bill Faces Snags in House." *Washington Post,* 24 May 1998.

"EU Adopts Tobacco Ad Ban; BBC News World Edition, 2 December 2002. Available from http://news.bbc.co.uk.

"EU Eyes Ending Tobacco Subsidies." BBC News World Edition, 22 March 2004. Available from http://news.bbc.co.uk.

Fisher, Brandy. "Friends From Afar." *Tobacco Reporter,* January 2002. Available from www.tobaccoreporter.com.

———. "Powerhouse." *Tobacco Reporter,* January 2002. Available from www.tobaccoreporter.com.

Frankel, Glenn. "Big Tobacco's Global Reach." *Washington Post,* 18 November 1996.

———. "U.S. Aided Cigarette Firms In Conquests Across Asia." *Washington Post,* 17 November 1996.

Frankel, Glenn and Steven Mufson. "Vast China Market Key to Smoking Disputes." *Washington Post,* 20 November 1996.

Lewis, Jay. "A Firm Market." *Tobacco Reporter,* April 2001. Available from www.tobaccoreporter.com.

Parker-Pope, Tara. "'Safer' Cigarettes: A History." *Nova,* Public Broadcasting Service, 2 October 2001. Available from http://www.pubs.org/wgbh/nova.

Philip Morris International. Annual Report, 2004. Available from http://www.altria.com.

Reynolds American. Annual Report, 2004. Available from http://www.reynoldsamerican.com.

Ridgway, Laurence. "Merging in the Millennium." *World Tobacco,* January 2000.

Rupert, James and Glenn Frankel. "In Ex-Soviet Markets, U.S. Brands Took on Role of Capitalist Liberator." *Washington Post,* 19 November 1996.

"Russia is One of the Tobacco Most Smoking Countries." *Pravda,* 8 June 2001. Available from English.pravda.ru.

Schultz, Stacey. "Breathing Easy." *U.S. News & World Report,* 23 June 2003.

Shafey, Omar and Suzanne Dolwick and G. Emmanuel Guindon, eds. *Tobacco Control Country Profiles 2003.* American Cancer Society. Available from www.globalink.org/tccp.

Standard & Poor's Industry Surveys. New York: Standard & Poor's, annual.

Tobacco Institute of Japan. *Tabako Hambai Jisseki [Cigarette Sales].* Tokyo, 21 April 1997. Available from jin.jcic.or.jp..

Tobacco: World Markets and Trade. U.S. Department of Agriculture Foreign Agricultural Service, September 2004. Available from http://www.fas.usda.gov.

Tuinstra, Taco. "Saturation." *Tobacco Reporter,* October 2001. Available from www.tobaccoreporter.com.

U.S. Centers for Disease Control and Prevention. *Targeting Tobacco Use.* Atlanta, Georgia, 1998. Available from www.cdc.gov..

U.S. Department of Agriculture. Economic Research Service. "Tobacco Outlook-Summary," April 2004. Available from usda.mannlib.cornell.edu.

U.S. Department of Agriculture. *Trends in the Cigarette Industry After the Master Settlement Agreement,* October 2001. Available from www.ers.usda.gov.

U.S. Department of Commerce. *Annual Survey of Manufactures.* Washington, DC, annual.

World Health Organization. "An International Treaty for Tobacco Control," 12 August 2003. Available from www.who.int.

———. "The Tobacco Epidemic: A Global Public Health Emergency." *Tobacco Alert,* April 1996. Available from http://www.who.int.

FURNITURE

SIC 2510

NAICS 3371

FURNITURE, HOUSEHOLD

This industry's participants manufacture all types of furniture for household use. Their products range from all-wood furniture and cabinetry to upholstered pieces and mattresses. For coverage of office furniture, see **Furniture, Office.**

INDUSTRY SNAPSHOT

The production and sale of household furniture is a large, highly competitive business in which thousands of different companies worldwide participate. Once largely confined by national boundaries, household furniture has become a multibillion-dollar import and export business. Although dominated on all continents by a handful of growing corporations aiming at the mass market, the furniture market still has room for craftsmen and small companies. The majority of these small operations produce furniture within their native countries for two important reasons. First, they are unable to compete with the resources and distribution channels of larger companies. Second, they are better equipped to meet the needs of buyers looking for customized furniture and one-of-a-kind pieces, most of whom look to small, local operations to meet these needs. While industry dynamics make it unlikely that these small competitors will ever grow as large as the conglomerates, the furniture industry still invites growth for companies developing products that fill niche markets. The key is finding the correct blend of price, function, and appealing style, and supporting the product line with an efficient and extensive distribution system.

Household furniture, along with other home decor elements, is part of an industry that rises and falls with the state of the economy. As a general rule, manufacturers of household furnishings enjoy greater demand for their goods when employment and consumer confidence are high and interest rates are low. While there are exceptions (most notably retailers like Heilig-Meyers and Levitz Furniture, both of which filed for Chapter 11 bankruptcy restructuring during the economic boom of 2000), furniture manufacturers' success is closely related to the economy as a whole.

While many online retailers have made an impact on their industries, this is not the case with furniture. As of the mid-2000s, the presence of online retailers had had little effect on the industry, and consequently the failure of some high-profile online furniture retailers (such as living.com and furniture.com) did not weaken the industry. A new approach to selling furniture online was tested by both Ethan Allan and Pottery Barn. This approach, called "clicks and mortar," was proving to be a promising alternative to straight e-commerce. A clicks and mortar retailer is one that has both online ordering capabilities and traditional stores. More important than online retailers was the trend toward manufacturers entering the retail market directly. Rather than producing goods for wholesale to retailers, more manufacturers began introducing their products to consumers under new brand names.

Although all European countries host a domestic furniture industry, Germany, Italy, Belgium, Denmark, and Sweden possess the most competitive and the most highly developed industries. The vast majority of Europe's 65,000 furniture companies are small. Some countries such as Italy and Spain tend to specialize and customize their furniture, while others gravitate toward the mass market. This affects the number of companies operating in each country. For example, in the early 2000s, many of the 12,000 furniture makers in Spain tended to be artisans who made limited numbers of pieces to order for customers. Germany, in contrast, took a larger mass manufacturing approach, with fewer companies yet much higher production volumes.

Furniture manufacturing in the United States largely resembles the global industry in that it is made up of hundreds of small companies. As with most countries, furniture manufacturing is centered near the nation's wood supply—more than one-third of furniture manufacturers are located in North Carolina. While the industry in the 2000s supported hundreds of competitors, the top 25 U.S. manufacturers accounted for almost half of all furniture produced in the country. This was attributed to these manufacturers' domination of U.S. retail distribution channels.

Asia was a rapidly expanding manufacturing center, with dominant manufacturing countries such as China, Taiwan, Malaysia, and Indonesia, which led in worldwide furniture exports. Taiwan was one of the most successful producers both on the Asian continent and as an exporter to the West. By the early 2000s, China had become the largest furniture exporter in the world.

ORGANIZATION AND STRUCTURE

The home furniture industry is loosely structured. A company with a superior product can usually reach the market successfully, even if it has to bypass the traditional manufacturer-to-retail distribution chain dominated by the large conglomerates. Furniture companies in the United States can be part of conglomerates like Furniture Brands International, owner of Broyhill and Thomasville. They may also be large private companies like Klaussner or be one of the hundreds of smaller companies employing under 100 people.

European furniture manufacturers were usually much smaller with less sophisticated channels of distribution. Only a handful of European companies such as IKEA of Sweden and Natuzzi of Italy were considered international companies because of their success in exporting to the United States. As a consolidated European market emerged, the larger companies became more important because they were able to mass-produce popular pieces. At the outset of the twenty-first century, European customers enjoyed a wide variety of designs. Imports from the United States and Asia were relatively small, as European customers saw little need to buy foreign when the designs they liked were readily available to them from Continental manufacturers.

Most Asian manufacturers were even smaller than those found in Europe. For example, there were more than 12,000 manufacturers of wooden furniture in Japan. Almost 80 percent of these companies had fewer than 30 employees. Organized as handmade artisans, these companies were slow to produce pieces and were in danger of being replaced by imports from other Asian countries such as Taiwan. While individual Asian companies might be small, their collective economic power, when organized by their governments, was growing.

From about the mid-1990s, the liberalization of world trade, via such agreements as the North American Free Trade Agreement (NAFTA) and the General Agreement on Tariffs and Trade (GATT), contributed to rapid growth in the world furniture market. NAFTA phased out tariffs on most goods between Canada, Mexico, and the United States but established initial trade quotas to protect markets from price dumping while the agreement was being implemented. Most of the safeguard tariffs and quotas expired in 2004, with the remainder eliminated by 2005, creating virtually unrestricted trade between these countries. NAFTA appeared to have benefited Canada's furniture market; between 1992 and 2000, Canada's furniture exports increased by 405 percent. In 2003, Canada's total furniture exports, including residential, office, and institutional products, were worth US$6.9 billion. More than 90 percent of Canadian furniture exports went to the United States.

The 148-nation GATT, which reduces and eliminates tariffs that protect domestic industries, also affected the furniture trade. All participating countries, as members of the World Trade Organization, agreed to cut back tariffs by 33 percent, and the United States, the European Union, Canada, and Japan pledged to remove most of the tariffs inhibiting trade between them. China—already one of the top 10 furniture exporters in the mid-1990s— was able to greatly expand overseas furniture sales as it prepared for membership in the WTO, which it joined in 2001. In 2000, China's furniture exports exceeded US$3.5 billion, and the industry employed more than 3 million people.

BACKGROUND AND DEVELOPMENT

The technology of making household furniture was simple for generations—wood and other natural materials were pegged or nailed together to make objects on which people could sit, sleep, or eat. In the sixteenth and seventeenth centuries, artisans realized that hard wooden seats would feel better if they were covered with upholstery stuffed with animal hair or wool. By the twentieth century people began to think that furniture could do double duty—a couch could turn into a bed, and a chair could recline.

Automation of manufacturing had not been a tremendous force in the furniture industry. Robot-controlled saws were able to turn out wooden chair arms consistently; however, there was no machine that could tie a chair spring tighter or faster than a skilled person, robots did not have a fashion eye to check for the proper lineup of floral patterns on a sleeper sofa, and there was as yet no mechanical substitute for the beauty an artisan can add to a hand-inlaid table.

TWENTY-FIRST CENTURY TRENDS

In the early 2000s, the global furniture outlook was positive, especially with increasing demand for computer furniture at home, according to national trade associations and industry analysts. Previously, major furniture-producing countries such as the United States, Germany, France, and Italy experienced slightly falling revenues and production levels. Consumer demand for new styles resulted in a rise in imports from Asian manufacturers. These styles included rustic features, simple lines, carved wood, Asian embellishments, and mixed media, such as combining wood with marble or bamboo. Manufacturers in many of the leading countries enjoyed growth at the end of the 1990s, as economies flourished, disposable incomes rose, unemployment levels remained low, and international trade became easier. When these factors were adversely affected by the terrorist attacks on the United States on September 11, 2001, the household furniture industry, like most others, slowed. As the economy began to rally again, however, business analysts projected that most industries would benefit. In fact, the value of the U.S. furniture market increased 2.7 percent in 2002.

The furniture industry continued to be increasingly price-driven. Without established criteria of quality, retailers often marketed furniture solely on its price, giving rise to a proliferation of highly competitive discount furniture stores. Manufacturers' efforts to differentiate their products had failed thus far, strengthening the position of the price-competitive discount furniture brokers.

American demand for wood furniture changed the international dynamics of the industry by increasing imports. According to the International Trade Administration, wood household furniture in 2000 comprised 34 percent of total sales in the United States, a rise of 16 percent in eight years. This demand led to a substantial rise in imports of wood furniture, although upholstered furniture remained largely domestically produced. In 2002, according to *Asian Timber* magazine, the market value for wood furniture sold in the United States was US$11.3 billion, and half of this was for low-priced imports, primarily from Asia. As of 2005, about 54 percent of all wood furniture sold in the United States was imported; and nearly one-quarter of this came from China, which increased its exports of wood furniture 1,630 percent from 1995 to 2005. In fact, China rapidly became the top furniture exporter to the United States, with shipments of wood furniture in 2001 valued at US$1.9 billion. The second-ranking exporter of wood furniture to the United States was Canada, which sold goods in this category equivalent to US$1.37 billion in 2000.

Upholstered furniture was less impacted by the increase in importing because so much upholstered furniture was ordered with a degree of customization in fabric, style, accessories such as pillows, or any combination of these elements. Customization requires close contact with customers, which explains why this segment of the industry continued to be dominated by domestic manufacturers.

MAJOR CHALLENGES

Obtaining Raw Materials. There was growing concern that wood—the raw material in most home furniture—may become scarce within the first few decades of the twenty-first century as a result of the failure to renew trees cut from forests. Wood supply was rated almost as important as government regulations in a mid-1990s survey of the major concerns of the largest furniture companies' chief executive officers. The potential problem gained importance in the minds of executives. The report showed that 63 percent of those surveyed had come to think the issue was more important than in the previous year. With increasing pressure from environmentalists and consumers, the industry began to move toward use of certified wood, which is harvested from sustainably managed forests.

Government Regulations. Increasing concern about health problems associated with the industry's use of volatile organic compounds (VOCs) in its finishing processes led to government regulations in the United States. Furniture manufacturing uses a tremendous amount of chemicals, primarily solvents to clean the raw material, and a chemical finish to coat the furniture before final shipment to retailers. Upholstered furniture can also contain numerous VOCs, including formaldehyde. In 1995, the U.S. Environmental Protection Agency created the National Emission Standards for Hazardous Air Pollutants (NESHAP) to control emissions from the manufacture of wood furniture.

International Trade. Many traditional leaders in the furniture industry in the early 2000s faced increasing competition from Asia. China in particular captured significant market share. In 2004, it shipped more upholstered furniture (mostly leather) to the United States than did Italy, which had prior to that year dominated in this segment. China's world shipments of all types of wood furniture increased 1,630 percent from 1995 to 2005. During that same period, its exports of wood furniture to the United States grew by a stunning 7,418 percent. Vietnam, Malaysia, and Thailand also increased world exports of wood furniture by substantial amounts. The influx of furniture from China led U.S. manufacturers to push for anti-dumping policies. In 2004, the U.S. Department of Commerce imposed duties ranging from 10.92 percent to 198.08 percent on wood bedroom furniture imports from China, the largest U.S. anti-dumping action to date against that country. In 2005, the tariffs were reduced by about 2 percent. At the same time, Chinese companies began to outsource more of their production to cheaper suppliers such as Vietnam.

Bypassing Traditional Retailers. One of the most heated issues between furniture manufacturers and retailers was whether customers should be allowed to shop for their furniture directly from the manufacturer or through a wholesaler. Traditionally, furniture shoppers bought from their local furniture stores. As is common in retail trade, these stores set prices sometimes as much as 100 percent over the price they paid the manufacturer or distributor. In the late 1990s, some U.S. furniture manufacturers—particularly those based in North Carolina—opened their own discount operations. Shoppers in faraway states could go to their retailers, find furniture they liked, and copy down the name of the manufacturer and model number. They then would order the same furniture directly from the manufacturer, paying the manufacturer's price and the cost of shipping; customers realized a savings of hundreds of dollars off the cost of buying retail by shopping this way.

CURRENT CONDITIONS

The state of the industry in the United States and Canada was not particularly good in 2007, whereas China's industry statistics were on a what seemed to be a perpetual rise. In the United States, the housing boom of the early 2000s that had fueled furniture sales had ended, and imports from China had increased substantially, causing many furniture companies to shut down. According to a CEO of Robb and Stucky, "A huge shift from American furniture to imported Chinese furniture has caused prices to drop and thrown the whole industry into a state of flux." Other factors contributing to the downward trend in the furniture industry were the fact that people were spending more money on electronics such as big-screen televisions and less on furniture. The housing slowdown affected the industry because people spend six to eight times as much money on furniture in a year when they move, according to *The Tampa Tribune,* and people had stopped moving as much as they had earlier in the decade. These downtrends for retailers and manufacturers, however, were expected to be advantageous for the consumer, who saw drastic reductions in furniture prices as businesses attempted to compete.

Other than China, two other countries that were becoming influential in the industry in the later mid-2000s were Vietnam and Malaysia. Vietnam's furniture exports, though smaller in value than China's at US$3.7 billion in 2005, increased 171.4 percent that year, and furniture ranked fifth in overall export revenues for the nation, behind crude oil, footwear, garments, and seafood. The Vietnam government worked to increase foreign investment in the furniture industry, and as a result furniture outsourcing also increased. In Malysia, the value of furniture exports totaled US$1.97 in 2006. Rubberwood was the main source of materials for Malaysian furniture production, and experts were recommending an increase in hardware furniture production in order to remain competitive in the international market.

RESEARCH AND TECHNOLOGY

In the mid-2000s, wood was still the product of choice for tables and chairs; upholstered sofas were still the most popular; and plastic seating was just a fad that came and went quickly during the 1970s. Turn of the millennium innovations in home furniture were items designed for entertainment rooms. A few U.S. companies created easy chairs with built-in stereo speakers to enhance the "surround-sound" effect when the user is watching a video. Adjustable beds, once associated with the elderly market, received high-tech overhauls and were poised to appeal to a broader range of consumers.

Virtual reality—the most interesting technological advancement in buying home furniture—was mostly used as an arcade attraction for teenagers, but it presented a way people in the future might buy their furniture. As envisioned in 2004, buyers using virtual reality would be able to walk into a furniture store armed with the dimensions of their living room, a carpet swatch, and a paint chip so that the furniture store manager can match colors. Once a facsimile of the living room is entered into the computer, the customer may don a virtual reality helmet and step on a computer-controlled floor so he or she can experience "walking" around the living room with the new furniture in place.

WORKFORCE

While virtually every country in the world makes furniture, it is not a huge industry for employment. Neither are its positions typically well paid. In the United States, 491,200 people made their living in the furniture industry in 2002, of which 256,300 were employed in the household furniture segment. Between 2000 and 2004, however, woodworking factories in the United States, faced with increasing competition from Asian furniture manufacturers, lost 35,000 jobs. The average hourly wage for U.S. furniture workers was US$12.65, substantially below the manufacturing average of US$15.30. Manufacturing jobs were subject to decline as technology advances mechanized many of the mass production functions. In niche markets, however, artisans' skills, such as carpentry, specialty finishes, hand-painting, and inlaying wood, were less vulnerable to replacement by machinery.

The same was true for most of Europe, where roughly 90 percent of the continent's 65,000 furniture manufacturers had fewer than 20 employees. Only nine German companies had more than 1,000 employees each. The number of furniture manufacturers in each country had little to do with the number of people they employed. There were more than 12,000 furniture manufacturers in Spain and only 1,500 companies in Germany. However, Germany had a much larger industry, including a sizable export surplus, which it shipped to other European countries.

With regard to the Asian industry, Japan had more than 12,000 furniture manufacturers, around 80 percent of which had fewer than 30 employees. Indeed, more than half of Japan's 6,000 furniture manufacturers had three or fewer employees. Research reports on the Japanese furniture industry predicted that many of these small companies would disappear, as Japanese consumers succumbed to the lure of mass-produced furniture imported from Taiwan. In Asia, wages ranged from more than US$11 per hour in Japan to US$0.10 per hour in Vietnam.

INDUSTRY LEADERS

IKEA INTERNATIONAL A/S

IKEA International of Sweden was unusual in the global furniture industry in that it operated its own retail store chain. These stores were self-serve; the sales people did not follow prospects around from suite to suite. IKEA worked to produce and deliver quality furniture at affordable prices. It created its own designs, which were then manufactured by more than 1,300 suppliers in more than 50 countries. IKEA, which also sold its products by mail order and the Internet, operated more than 254 stores in 34 countries, and employed 104,000 people worldwide. In 2006 the company posted sales of US$22.1 billion.

LEGGETT AND PLATT INC.

Leggett and Platt Inc. led in production of bedding components such as box springs, mattress innersprings, and seating components. Based in Carthage, Missouri, Leggett and Platt also manufactured finished products, including recliners and beds with its Wallhugger and ADJUSTA-MAGIC brands. Over 70 percent of the company's sales derived from its finished products and parts for household and commercial furnishings; in 2006 Leggett and Platt, which had 33,000 employees worldwide, reported sales of US$5.5 billion.

FURNITURE BRANDS INTERNATIONAL, INC.

Furniture Brands International Inc., of St. Louis, Missouri, with its Broyhill Furniture Industries, Lane Co., and Thomasville Furniture Industries subsidiaries, became the leading U.S. residential furniture manufacturer in 2001 after the breakup of industry giants Masco Home Furnishings and Interco. Furniture Brands International produced wood and upholstered living room, bedroom, and dining room furniture. Its Broyhill subsidiary offered moderately priced domestic pieces, while Thomasville and Lane offered higher-end furnishings. In 2006 the company posted sales of more than US$2.4 billion and employed 15,150 workers.

LA-Z-BOY INCORPORATED

Founded in 1928, La-Z-Boy Chair Company of Monroe, Michigan, a U.S. manufacturer that operated its own retail stores, specialized in recliners. La-Z-Boy was the dominant manufacturer of upholstered furniture in the United States and continued to be the largest producer of recliners in the world. La-Z-Boy also offered wood furniture, and by acquiring smaller furniture makers, it came to be able to offer consumers high-end furnishings. The company's sales rose steadily in the 1990s, surpassing the US$1 billion mark in 1997 and reaching US$2.2 billion in 2001. Earnings for 2006 were US$1.9 billion. The company had about 13,000 employees.

ASHLEY FURNITURE INDUSTRIES, INC.

Founded in 1945, Ashley Furniture Industries was a leading U.S. manufacturer and exporter of home furniture. The company produced and sold upholstered, leather, and hardwood items as well as bedding. In addition to manufacturing, the company ran Ashley Furniture HomeStores, independently owned stores that carried Ashley products exclusively, in the United States, Canada, and overseas. Sales in 2005 reached approximately US$2.5 billion, representing a 27.5 percent increase from the previous year, and the company employed 13,400 people.

KLAUSSNER FURNITURE INDUSTRIES INC.

Klaussner Furniture Industries Inc. of Asheville, North Carolina, was one of the largest privately owned furniture companies in the world in the mid-2000s. Klaussner's core products included upholstered wood sofas, leather furniture, recliners, and occasional furniture. It operated 20 manufacturing facilities and sold its products in more than 60 countries. In addition to its Distinctions, Realistic, Realistic Motion, Klaussner, and Klaussitalia brands, the company licensed the Sealy and Dick Idol brands. In 2003 Klaussner posted sales of US$915 million.

NATUZZI S.P.A.

Natuzzi of Italy was one of the more successful exporters of high-quality leather furniture to the United States. In fact, it was the world's top maker of residential leather furniture and had a presence in 140 countries. Natuzzi operated 15 factories in Italy, with about 90 percent of production for export. Half of the company's sales, which in 2003 topped US$967 million, came from North and South America. In 2005, however, the company saw declining sales of its branded upholstered furniture, prompting a restructuring plan that included cutting about 1,320 jobs. Sales in 2005 totaled US$793.5 million, with 7,847 employees.

MAJOR COUNTRIES IN THE INDUSTRY

THE UNITED STATES

The U.S. household furniture market was worth approximately US$71.6 billion in 2003. The strongest demand for household furniture came from the metropolitan areas of New York City, Chicago, Los Angeles, and Washington, D.C. In 2002, upholstered furniture accounted for the largest portion of sales, 45.7 percent. Demand also grew for newer kinds of furniture, including entertainment furniture to house or store home theater components, stereo equipment, and other home electronic goods.

U.S. household furniture exports, which began to accelerate in the mid-1990s, were valued in excess of US$22 billion in 2000. Strengthened by NAFTA, Canada and Mexico became significant exporters to the United States with US$2.5 billion and US$645 million worth of furniture, respectively, in 2000. NAFTA countries were also the largest importers of U.S. furniture, with the biggest market, Canada, accounting for 49 percent of all U.S. furniture shipments in 2004. Mexico ranked second, followed by China. These figures changed quickly in 2005, when imports from China burgeoned.

CHINA

From the 1980s into the early 2000s, China rapidly expanded its wood furniture industry. By 2000 it had become one of the world's major producers, with a total turnover in 2002 of US$19.88 billion. About one-fourth of its output was sold overseas to major export markets such as the United States, the European Union, and Japan. The value of all Chinese furniture exports in 2002 rose 30 percent from the previous year, totaling US$5.42 billion; this figure increased in 2003 to US$7.33 billion. China led the world in furniture exports and was also the biggest exporter of furniture to the United States, which accounted for 52 percent of China's furniture shipments in 2004. U.S. imports of wooden bedroom furniture alone from China reached almost US$1.2 billion in 2003. By that year, according to some analysts, China manufactured 40 percent of all furniture sold in the United States.

In the mid-2000s, the furniture industry in China continued to grow. In 2005 the nation experienced a 27.4 percent increase in furniture sales over the previous year, churning out 333.9 million pieces, and sales of furniture in the first quarter of 2006 were 31.7 percent higher than they had been in the first quarter of 2005. The export value of furniture in China in 2005 reached US$13.7 billion, representing a growth rate of almost 33 percent.

China's growing economy also contributed to increased demand for furniture, and major international companies competed for a greater share of the Chinese market. Ethan Allen opened a store in Tianjin and partnered with Markor Furniture International, a leading Chinese manufacturer, to develop a chain of Ethan Allen retail stores throughout the country. IKEA also established a presence in China.

The overall furniture market in China was expected to remain promising, as rising incomes—averaging increases of 10 percent per year—stimulated increased demand for household furniture and other goods. China's hosting of the Olympic Games in 2008 was expected to give a significant boost to furniture sales.

JAPAN

In the 1990s and into the early 2000s, Japan produced around US$20 billion in household furniture annually. After recession struck the Japanese economy in 1991, the furniture industry remained unstable into the beginning of the twenty-first century, though by the early 2000s Japanese manufacturers hoped to start capturing a bigger share of the export market. In 2002, Japan imported about 377 billion yen worth of furniture, while exports were valued at only 53 billion yen, approximately US$450 million. Analysts pointed to the fact that Japanese furniture is designed for Japanese tastes. It is also relatively expensive. Most Japanese furniture is handmade by small furniture companies that stand little chance of significantly increasing capacity. Some major Japanese companies, however, began to focus on export markets, especially in the United States, Britain, China, South Korea, Australia, and countries in Southeast Asia.

EUROPEAN UNION

The European Union's furniture industry, valued by the European Commission at 82 billion euros, approximately US$99.6 billion, in 2004, produced about half of the world's furniture that year and employed approximately 1 million people. Germany, the largest furniture maker in the European Union, accounted for 27 percent of total production. Italy followed with 21.6 percent, while France and Italy accounted for 13.5 percent and 10.4 percent of production, respectively. World exports of EU furniture were valued at 10.2 billion euros (about US$12.7 billion) in 2002 and fell slightly to 9.6 billion euros (US$12.0 billion) in 2003. Imports grew steadily in value from 7.1 billion euros in 2000 (US$8.8 billion) to 8.2 billion euros (US$10.2 billion) in 2003. Germany faced some challenges in the early to mid-1990s, as it struggled to bring the former East German states into the fold of prosperity enjoyed by the states of former West Germany. By 1998, however, disposable income increased by 2.5 percent, leading to a 2.2 percent increase in domestic furniture consumption. In 2002, the German furniture market was worth about US$30.4 billion.

Italy was the second largest producer of furniture in the world in the early 2000s, with 35,000 companies employing about 230,000 people. Italy was also the leading furniture exporter, shipping about 45 percent of its total production, which accounted for 17 percent of the global market. Between 2002 and 2003, however, the Italian furniture industry saw production value decline by 4.1 percent, due mostly to a sharp decline in exports, which fell by 5.1 percent, while imports climbed by 8.5 percent. Italy's share of wood furniture exports to the United States fell from 16.6 percent in 2000 to only 11.9 percent in 2003. In 2004, for the first time, Italy lagged behind China in exports of leather upholstered furniture to the United States.

French furniture was made by about 773 companies in the early 2000s. More than 90 percent of these businesses employed fewer than 100 people, and about half of wood furniture companies employed fewer than 50. While most of its production stayed inside the country, France also imported more millions of dollars worth of furniture each year, notably from Italy. In 2003, declining domestic demand contributed to a 6.1 percent drop in the value of the French furniture market.

The vast majority of EU countries saw negative growth in their furniture markets in 2003, due largely to flat demand and a fall in exports to their traditional markets. Nevertheless, sales to countries outside the EU increased by 4 percent in value in 2003, though exports to the United States, which represented 25 percent of exports, declined by 4 percent in volume and 15 percent in value. Imports, however, rose substantially, led by China with a 45 percent volume increase.

CANADA

Canada's furniture industry grew significantly through the 1990s, with household furniture accounting for about 38.5 percent of production. In 2000, Canada was the world's fourth largest furniture exporter; by 2003, it had risen to second place, with exports of US$6.9 billion. Some 96 percent of its furniture exports in 2003 went to the United States; Canada also remained a leading importer of U.S. furniture. Furniture sales in Canada grew more than any other retail sector in 2003, rising 11.6 percent in 2002 and 6.5 percent in 2003.

By the latter mid-2000s, Canada was feeling the effects of increased imports. According to the Canadian Furniture Industry, in 2007 Canada saw an increase in both Chinese and American imports of home furnishings, whereas Canadian exports were on the decline. The Canadian Furniture Industry estimated the furniture industry was worth about US$5.2 billion that year. Joe Malko, president of Winnipeg-based Furniture West, told *Business Edge,* that the reason for the decline in the industry was the amount of imports coming from the United States and Asia. He said, "It's mainly from China, although other countries in Asia are becoming furniture manufacturers and exporting product as well. But China has been the giant." One of the ways by which Canadian furniture manufacturers were dealing with the situation was through the creation of the program Connections West. According to *Business Edge,* "the move will help the independent dealer work with the manufacturers to produce unique products with innovative designs that are appropriate for their markets."

FURTHER READING

"Advancing Technology Forcing Furniture Makers to Keep Pace." *HFN: The Weekly Newspaper for the Home Furnishing Network.* 22 December 2003.

"China Furniture Market Report, 2006-2007." *China Research,* December 2006.

"Employment and Wages in the American Furniture Industry," 2004. Available from www.globalwood.org.

"Exports Climb 10 Percent in 2004." *Furniture Today,* 7 April 2005. Available from www.furnituretoday.com.

"Home Furnishings." *Standard & Poor's Industry Surveys,* 2004.

"Hoover's Company Capsules." Hoover's, Inc, 2007. Available from http://www.hoovers.com.

Gunin, Joan. "Leather Sources Ready to Fire Global Shots." *Furniture Today,* 13 April 2005. Available from www.furnituretoday.com.

"In 2006, China's Furniture Industry Continued to Keep a Higher Growth Rate and the Export Value Amounted to USD 4.042 Billion in the First Quarter of 2006." *Business Wire,* 30 January 2007.

"Japanese Makers Have High Hopes for IFFT 2003," 20 April 2004. Available from www.cens.com.

"Made in Italy." Italian Ministry of Foreign Affairs. Available from www.esteri.it.

McLeod, Lashonda. "The Canadian Furniture Industry Presents Opportunities for U.S. Hardwoods." *AgExporter,* January 2004.

Normington, Mick. "N.C. Furniture Exports Up, China a Possible Target Market." *Business Journal,* 19 April 2004.

"Overview: EU Furniture Industry." European Union, 2006. Available from http://ec.europa.eu.

"Real Household Furniture Spending in U.S. Forecast to Grow by 23.8 Percent." *Furniture World,* 6 May 2005. Available from www.furninfo.com.

"Review—Far East: Thai Challenge." *Cabinet Maker,* 13 April 2007.

Sasso, Michael. "Housing Slump Hits Furniture Stores Hard." *The Tampa Tribune,* 4 April 2007.

Severs, Laura. " Furniture Industry Builds Creative Strategies: China's Market Growth Prompts Industry Rethink." *Business Edge,* 12 January 2007.

"The Residential Furniture Industry in Canada," 2004. Available from http://strategis.ic.gc.ca.

"UK Market for Upholstered Furniture." Global Wood, 27 September 2006. Available from www.globalwood.org.

U.S. Industry and Trade Outlook. New York: McGraw-Hill and U.S. Department of Commerce, 2000.

"U.S. to Slap Tariffs on Chinese Furniture." *China Daily,* 20 June 2004. Available from www.chinadaily.com.cn.

Foreign Agricultural Service/USDA Office of Global Analysis. *Wood Product Update,* March 2007. Available from www.fas.usda.gov/.

"Vietnam Now Malaysian Furniture Industry's Biggest Competitor." *Thanh Nien News,* 15 December 2006.

"Vietnam Rising in the Global Furniture Market." Business in Asia, 2006. Available from http://www.business-in-asia.com/.

Xu, Meiqi, et al. "China's Wood Furniture Industry." *Asian Timber,* September-October 2003.

"Zero Tariff Won't Harm Furniture Sector." *China Daily,* 19 November 2004. Available from www.chinadaily.com.cn.

SIC 2520

NAICS 3372

FURNITURE, OFFICE

This industry classification covers manufacturers of office furniture, including desks, conference tables, chairs, credenzas, bookcases, portable partitions, and other equipment used in both traditional office settings and the emerging home office environment.

INDUSTRY SNAPSHOT

Highly dependent upon a broad range of socioeconomic factors and general business practices, the global office furniture industry remained healthy in the mid-2000s. The industry was concentrated in the United States, which produces the majority of office furniture and also imports billions of dollars in office furniture every year. Changing dynamics in the workplace, as companies in all fields of business activity rearrange their organizational and operational structures, have resulted in new challenges in the industry. For example, many large corporations were forced to downsize in the sliding economy of 2000 and 2001, reducing demand for new furniture. However, small and mid-sized companies fared better and continued to buy office furniture. To keep costs down, though, more companies opted to purchase ready-to-assemble (RTA) or refurbished furniture. Although measuring the volume of refurbished furniture is difficult, the Business and Institutional Furniture Manufacturer's Association (BIFMA) cited estimates at 8 to 10 percent of new furniture sales. Increased sales of low-cost and RTA furniture affect distribution channels, as this type of furniture is sold through office superstores, discount stores, and warehouse clubs rather than through specialty office furniture stores.

Another key factor affecting the office furniture market is the price of steel, the primary raw material used in production of desks, office tables, cabinets, and chairs. After beginning to recover from a shaky market between 2000 and 2003, U.S. office furniture companies were faced with a sudden spike in steel prices in early 2004 that threatened newly reestablished profit margins. At the same time, increasing competition from lower-cost suppliers in developing countries was beginning to play a larger role in the market—a trend that analysts expected would continue through the first decade of the twenty-first century.

As the corporate world followed a trend toward cutting costs in the 1990s and early 2000s, offices were reorganized to adapt to the smaller spaces in which workers operate. Most notably, exclusive—and often divided—offices gave way to more communal cubicles. Furthermore, many companies altered their internal business dynamics. Rather than the hierarchical, individual-based productivity methods and office configurations that were the rule since the massive proliferation of white-collar jobs earlier in the twentieth century, companies fostered team-based, highly communicative business structures. As a result, the emphasis in the office furniture industry shift from elaborate and opulent design methods to efficient, "egalitarian" furniture that more readily reflects the need for active and frequent intercommunication in the workplace.

The massive proliferation and rapid development of office technology also had a dramatic effect on the office furniture industry. Companies within the industry had to adjust their design and manufacturing processes to efficiently accommodate new technology, while remaining abreast of rapidly emerging office technology. Overall, this shift resulted in an industry-wide focus on office furniture that is flexible and adjustable, so businesses can avoid having to purchase new furniture as technology is developed with different components and configurations. Furniture that allows the greatest degree of support and facility and that has reconfiguration and multipurpose capabilities is expected to continue as the dominant industry trend in the twenty-first century.

While the heaviest concentration of the office furniture industry's business is in the United States, nearly one-fourth of that in the state of Michigan, rapidly expanding markets all over the world are expected to broaden the industry significantly. Because small, domestic companies constitute the vast majority of industry participants, especially outside the United States, markets in Eastern Europe, Latin America, and the Pacific Rim region were expected to foster significant industry growth within those regions.

The U.S. office furniture industry saw record sales of US$13.3 billion in 2000, but the next four years were disappointing, as shaky economic conditions cooled demand. According to a report published in *Forbes,* office furniture shipments declined by 39.3 percent between late 2000 and late 2003. Sales reached about US$8.47 billion in 2003, a decline of 4.7 percent from the previous year. By 2004, however, signs were more favorable for the industry, with sales picking up 5.4 percent that year to reach US$8.93 billion. While much of the world's trade depends on imports and exports, office furniture tends to be manufactured and sold close to home.

ORGANIZATION AND STRUCTURE

While many industries are dominated by a handful of manufacturers, such is not the case in the global office furniture industry. Thousands of companies make office furniture, with varying degrees of specialization, and the general consensus within the industry in the mid-2000s was that any company able to deliver quality products had a healthy chance at profitability. In the United States, however, a handful of corporations manage to generate nearly half of the office furniture market. Still, while one company, Steelcase, posted sales doubling those of its largest competitor and amounting to more than a quarter of the U.S. market, there are few barriers to keep competitors from attacking its position in the marketplace. In both Europe and Asia, there are few large companies, though some of the largest American-based companies maintain a strong presence in these regions.

The largest companies sell their products through a network of representatives, wholesalers, and retailers. Depending on a company's size and distribution strategy, it may opt to bypass these middlemen and market its products directly to customers. Such cases, while not uncommon, constitute a relatively small share of the industry's distribution channels. In 1996, over 75 percent of office furniture sales were to dealers, while only 7 percent went directly to consumers.

The type of office furniture designs and the accompanying sales often vary depending on the country of origin. In the United States, there has always been a high priority placed on worker privacy. Company managers traditionally marked the occupation of an office (and its location) as an indication of seniority and authority. From the 1950s through the 1970s, authority was represented by an office in the corner of a building with windows and aesthetically pleasing and extravagant office furniture. The 1990s witnessed a rapid shift in this dynamic within the workplace. The downsizing of the office led to a new category of office furniture, called "systems furniture," which is usually comprised of a portable wall with electrical outlets, a desk surface, and a matching chair.

In Asia, portable walls are rare, as privacy is generally considered unnecessary to work performance. Desks and workers are arranged side by side in large open areas and supervisors frequently sit at elevated desks overseeing the workers. In Europe, this same custom of open space prevails with a similar emphasis on teamwork. Individual desks are often replaced with large, communal desks shared by teams of workers endeavoring to solve the same problem. The partitions so popular with office designers in the United States are rare. In some parts of Europe laws and employee contracts specify that employees must be able to look up from their work and see sunlight. Varying work customs such as these are part of the reason why office furniture is a regional industry that does not accommodate intercontinental exchange of products. Companies wanting to export must be absolutely sure they have a superior product, as thousands of domestic manufacturers are ready to meet any unfulfilled customer needs.

However, as markets expand globally, the industry has seen a push for international standardization of certain product specifications that will allow for simpler trade considerations. The International Organization for Standardization (ISO) instituted two new voluntary standards that began to influence the industry and were expected eventually to make way for increased international trade of office furniture. ISO 9000 standardizes quality assurance guidelines, while ISO 14000 regulates environmental aspects. These will most notably affect office furniture made from wood products. By 2005, most of the companies that adopted these standards were larger corporations, which are far more likely to engage in international trade.

BACKGROUND AND DEVELOPMENT

The office furniture industry as it exists in the mid-2000s is relatively new. Manufacturing of office furniture started in earnest in the early twentieth century when the service industry emerged—following the inventions of the telephone, electric power, and the typewriter—and more people began working at desks. White-collar and service jobs proliferated in the golden years of corporate growth between the world wars and in the 1950s. In those days, office furniture manufacturers selling through retailers delivered tens of millions of desks, tables, chairs, file cabinets, and book cases—everything to make the tasks of corporate employees easier. New sales were generated in large part due to the shift in the U.S. economy from a manufacturing to a service emphasis, a change that boosted the fortunes of the office furniture industry. When the information age dawned in the early 1980s, the massive influx of information processors into the workplace further expanded the office furniture industry.

The office furniture industry began to change in the late 1980s, when the *Fortune* 1000 businesses—the companies that had staffed up so dramatically during the previous 80 years—began to trim their labor forces in pursuit of lower operating costs. The effect on purchases of office furniture was devastating, as the elimination of employee positions caused a substantial decline in demand for new office furniture. The office furniture industry was hit hard by this first wave of mass corporate layoffs, which was followed by a related worldwide recession that slowed spending by corporations that were trying to maintain their employee ranks. By 1991, sales had actually declined by 8 percent compared to 1990, the first sales drop in two decades.

In the 1990s, the industry recovered steadily from the recession as the changing dynamics of the workplace, increased demand for facilitation of evolving office technology needs, and the growing trend toward home offices created challenging and competitive new areas in which the industry competes. A surge in start-up companies also increased demand. By 2000, U.S. sales of office furniture soared to a record US$13.3 billion.

In the early 2000s, an estimated 41 million Americans performed work to some degree in their homes. Increased computer efficiency and Internet availability allowed many people to engage in a diverse number of business-related activities in their homes, be it connection to a central office at which they were employed, the operation of a personal business enterprise, or the maintenance of a stock portfolio. Almost all of these home offices have desks, chairs, and filing cabinets—the same sort of equipment the office furniture industry supplies to the *Fortune* 1000. Instead of selling desks in bulk to a single corporate client, the industry sells an increasing number of desks to individuals. Office furniture for home offices is less industrial in look and feel, and people buying furniture for home offices look for designs that fit their homes and individual tastes. With this diversification of the industry's customer base has come a greater emphasis on competitiveness in the area of customer service practices.

The home office market has seen great penetration by the RTA segment of the office furniture industry. While old-style office furniture retailers delivered full-sized desks to the workplace, RTA manufacturers sell customers furniture in cardboard boxes. The customers follow the directions to build their own desks and bookcases. The desks may not be as attractive as the solid cherry executive model the corporate CEO has, but they are much less expensive.

In the first few years of the twenty-first century, the U.S. office furniture industry suffered setbacks as the economy took a pronounced downturn. Between 2000 and 2003, office furniture shipments fell by almost 40 percent. Total exports of non-wood office furniture, which had reached US$551 million in 2000, declined to only US$318 million in 2003. During this period, large corporations—which account for the majority of office furniture sales—cut back their spending. Facing sharp declines in profits, office furniture companies were forced to cut their workforces and scale back some product lines.

Not until 2004 did the situation begin to improve, as office construction showed signs of growth and economic recovery fueled demand for new furniture or replacements of worn items. Yet a sudden rise in the price of steel in early 2004 threatened this recovery. One steel manufacturer raised its prices to commercial customers by 8.5 percent, and the price of steel in some grades jumped more than 30 percent. As a result, major office furniture companies such as Steelcase, which had anticipated healthy profits for the first time in four years but then had to lower its forecasted first-quarter earnings, announced that they would raise prices on their products. This move led to concern that consumers would seek lower prices elsewhere. With steel prices remaining high into 2005, the availability and price of wood, which accounts for approximately 25 percent of production of office furniture, also continued to affect the industry. There was growing concern that forests worldwide were being depleted at a rate far outpacing their renewal, and environmental concerns stemming from this issue contributed to higher demand for products made from certified lumber—wood harvested from sustainably managed forests.

CURRENT CONDITIONS

The U.S. office furniture industry had recovered somewhat by 2005, when total market value of shipments reached US$10.0 billion, and 2006 saw another slight improvement to US$10.9 billion. These figures were still far from the record production of $13.3 billion seen in 2000, but experts predicted 7 to 8 percent annual increases in 2007 and 2008, slowing to a 4 to 5 percent growth rate thereafter. Twenty-seven percent of the office furniture sold in the United States in 2005 was wood. Systems furniture accounted for the largest share at 28.8 percent. Other items whose growth outpaced the overall office furniture industry included tables (up 31.2%), seating (up 12.7%), and desks (up 11.8%). Storage furniture was the fastest growing segment of the industry, having increased more than 50 percent between 1995 and 2005. Filing cabinets, on the other hand, grew by only 3.2 percent during that time, due in part to the transition from paper to electronic files. California remained the largest consumer of office furniture in the United States and was responsible for US$1.2 billion of the total market in 2005, followed by Texas (US$755 million), New York (US$635 million), and Florida (US$592 million). Together these four states accounted for more than 30 percent of the entire U.S. office furniture industry in 2005.

U.S. furniture export figures also improved in the latter mid-2000s. After experiencing steady drops from 2001 to 2004, the value of furniture exports increased to US$438 million in 2005, up from US$347 million in 2004, and rose again to US$492 million in 2006. A majority of office furniture exports went to Canada. Likewise, Canada provided about 45 percent of the United States' office furniture imports. China was the second largest importer of office furniture to the United States at that time, although by 2006 China had overtaken Canada's number-one spot. Other countries that exported large volumes of office furniture to the United States in 2006 included Taiwan and Mexico. U.S. imports of office furniture, totaling about US$2.5 billion in 2005, remained much higher than exports.

The upturn in the office furniture industry was not as pronounced in Europe, where factors that were affecting growth in the United States, such as white-collar employment, new office construction, and corporate profitability were not as prominent. Of the European markets, the United Kingdom showed the most positive trends.

Rapid economic growth in China remained a significant factor in the international office furniture market in the mid-2000s. Commercial booms in major Chinese cities resulted in strong demand for new or upgraded office spaces and furniture. With import tariffs eliminated at the beginning of 2005, analysts expected that China would substantially increase its consumption of office furniture from foreign suppliers, whose products are often considered superior to locally produced goods. At the same time, China was increasing its global exports of office furniture. By 2005, more U.S. office furniture came from China than any other country; shipments from China totaled US$1.05 billion in 2005 and almost $700 million in the first half of 2006 alone.

The retreat to more functional, less expensive systems in this mature product market resulted in the disappearance—by merger and acquisition—of many smaller companies that could no longer compete in some market niches due to the relatively small breadth of their product lines. Many of the larger corporations, on the other hand, acquired these smaller, more specialized companies in order to enter their market fields. Like many other industries, it is generally less expensive for larger companies to acquire smaller companies with existing products than it is for the larger companies to launch new product lines of their own.

At the same time, smaller companies offering unique or better-made products sustain a healthy profit. Small companies with the capital to carry out effective marketing and distribution strategies can still compete against the larger conglomerates. This is particularly true in the European and Asian markets where large companies are more rare than they are in the United States.

FLEXIBILITY

Quickly developing office technology has created demands for furniture that is designed with flexibility and durability to facilitate changing work configurations, varying computer systems, and use of other office equipment. Concurrently, the demand for lightweight design has modified production, as manufacturers engage in the assembly of adjustable, multi-level workstations.

FUNCTIONALITY

To further accommodate technological progress and the shift of office dynamics from an isolated, hierarchical structure to a more cooperative, team-based model, office furniture designers have shifted their focus. Primary consideration is now given to companies' specific organizational structure and interaction needs. The trend for businesses is toward functional, efficient, and inviting office atmospheres that foster productivity and cooperation, rather than extravagance. Ergonomics continues to be a concern for employees and employers, so comfort features and injury-prevention are popular selling points.

RESEARCH AND TECHNOLOGY

"Ergonomic" is a word and a value with which furniture manufacturers were barely familiar in 1990. Since then, all companies have tried to incorporate the concept into their designs and advertising. The word ergonomic has become a catchall phrase meaning furniture specifically designed for a person's physical well being. A primary concern of designers is the avoidance of contributing to repetitive strain injuries (RSI) that result from a worker's repetition of acts from the same position over a significant period of time. A common RSI among office workers is carpal tunnel syndrome. Furniture without the proper consideration given to ergonomic design can aggravate or help cause RSIs. Chairs reflecting these concerns should have the right amount of back support, encourage good posture, and not have too much padding in front, as blood circulation to the worker's legs may be cut off. Examples of ergonomic designs that account for this and other concerns include fold-down typing keyboard drawers in desks at the correct height so typists reach neither too high nor too low, adjustable desk portions of systems furniture to fit the height of different people, and furniture pieces that accommodate the disabled.

Although industry negotiations probably eliminated any long-term problems with regulations governing the use of chemicals in the workplace, many companies are continuing their own research on how to make furniture using fewer and safer chemicals. Their motivation is to reduce the cost of processing and reduce the danger to employees. In addition, BIFMA International has worked with regulatory bodies such as the U.S. Environmental Protection Agency (EPA) to coordinate efforts to maintain a clean-air environment in corporate and home offices. This would in turn reduce workmen's compensation claims and threats of employee lawsuits over dangerous workplaces.

Engineered wood has gained considerable favor among manufacturers and customers for its attractive look and its machinability. Companies worried about the long-term world supply of wood suitable for manufacturing, however, are constantly researching new materials. The systems furniture used in many office settings in the 1990s was often made of plastic or another composite. Even manufacturers long skilled in using wood were experimenting with substituting wood laminates that would make their products look like wood. Another material that made inroads in the office furniture market is vinyl. Vinyl's efficient and diverse design capabilities make it a favorable material for manufacturers striving to meet the market demand for ergonomic design and functionality. Furthermore, its flexible aesthetic capabilities allow it to resemble many different surfaces, including wood. Another option is the use of recycled materials. Steelcase and Herman Miller are among the companies that produce furniture using such materials.

WORKFORCE

The office furniture workforce is relatively small. Only a handful of companies have more than a thousand employees. In the United States, it is estimated that less than a half million people manufacture both office and household furniture.

Most European and Asian office furniture manufacturers are much smaller than these American corporations. The average German furniture company (both office and household furniture) has 125 employees. Only nine German furniture manufacturers have more than 1,000 employees. The employment figures in Asia are even smaller. Japan, the office furniture industry leader, has only a few companies employing more than a few hundred workers.

INDUSTRY LEADERS

STEELCASE

Steelcase of Grand Rapids, Michigan, remained the world's largest office furniture manufacturer, with sales exceeding US$2.8 billion in 2006, a 9.8 increase from the previous year. The company's brands include Leap, Pathways, and Turnstone. Steelcase distributes its products, which include all manner of office furniture, through more than 800 dealers in 120 countries. Steelcase is an innovator and global leader in the field of systems furniture and offers services such as workspace planning. The company employed 13,000 people in 2006.

HNI CORPORATION

Tied with Haworth as the number-two office furniture company in the United States, HNI manufactures desks and chairs, filing cabinets, shelving, modular systems, and similar products. Its subsidiaries include Allsteel, Gunlocke, Hearth & Home Technologies, Maxon Furniture, and Hearth & Home, which makes fireplaces. Sales in 2006 reached US$2.6 billion with 14,200 employees.

HAWORTH

Haworth, which made a name for itself when it invented prewired partitions for cubicles, continued to grow because of acquisitions that expanded its operations (which included distribution in 120 countries) and its product lines. Sales in 2006 reached US$1.4 billion. Among its brands were Berlin, if, PLACES, and X99. Haworth is privately held by the Haworth family and employs 7,500 people.

HERMAN MILLER INC.

With US$1.73 billion in 2006 sales and around 6,300 employees, Herman Miller of Zeeland, Michigan, was a leading U.S. manufacturer of office furniture. The company manufactures in the United States, the United Kingdom, and Japan and ships its products around the world to subsidiary sales companies. However, exports comprise a relatively small portion of total sales; over 80 percent of its sales in the early 2000s were in the United States. Like Steelcase, Herman Miller is one of the leading manufacturers of systems furniture. Herman Miller has developed a line of furniture especially for start-up companies; the furniture is marketed as affordable and reliable.

MAJOR COUNTRIES IN THE INDUSTRY

With an estimated one-third of world production, the United States dominated the global industry in office furniture manufacturing with shipments valued at about US$10.6 billion in 2004. Canada was the largest export market, accounting for about 50 percent of U.S. foreign sales. The value of U.S. office furniture exports to Canada reached US$224.4 billion in 2004, up from US$209.6 billion the previous year. Mexico ranked second, importing about US$41.8 billion of U.S. office furniture in 2003 and US$52.2 billion in 2004. The value of U.S. sales to Japan, however, plummeted in the early 2000s after reaching some US$37.9 billion in 1997. This figure fell to US$30.1 billion in 2000, US$20 billion in 2002, and US$15.6 billion in 2003.

The United States was also a major importer of office furniture, and during the 1990s, imports quadrupled. In 2000, the total value of U.S. imports was more than US$2 billion, an increase of about 18 percent; of this, about US$1.7 billion was for non-wood office furniture. Imports fell slightly in 2001 but rose in each of the next two years. In 2004, imports were valued at US$2.4 billion. Canada, the largest supplier, contributed about 45 percent of U.S. imports, down from about 60 percent in the late 1990s. China was the second leading supplier, followed by Taiwan, Mexico, and Italy. In 2005, China overtook the number-one position as top exporter of office furniture to the United States, followed by Taiwan, Canada, and Mexico.

European furniture production rose by 6.6 percent in 2000, and sales of office furniture in Europe rose by 6 percent. In 2001, the European furniture market was worth about 82 billion euros (US$98.9 billion). Office furniture, the third-leading category after upholstered and kitchen furniture, accounted for 11.7 percent. Germany, Italy, France, and the United Kingdom are the leading manufacturers of office furniture in Europe, and most of its output remains on the continent. Some of the trends shaping the American market are also shaping the European market, most notably the high demand for furniture that will accommodate changing technology in the workplace. European buyers are also concerned with flexibility and multifunctionality.

In Asia, thousands of small companies supply the needs of both domestic markets and regional trading partners along the Asian Pacific Rim. Japan accounts for the largest share of Asian manufacturers. Kokuyo Co. Ltd., the leading Japanese manufacturer of office furniture, office equipment and supplies, and information systems, generated revenues of US$2.58 billion in 2004.

FURTHER READING

Barile, Gina. "Profile of Quebec's Furniture Manufacturing Industry.". U.S. Commercial Services, 2006. Available from http://commercecan.ic.gc.ca/.

Berdon, Caroline. "On the Move: The Office Furniture Industry Is in a Much Better Place Than It Was Two Years Ago, But Growth Worldwide Is Uneven." *Office Products International,* February 2006.

Coleman, Katie. "Steelcase's Strategy for an Environmentally Sound, Profitable Business." *Wood & Wood Products,* February 2007.

Flaherty, Michael. "Steel Prices Pinching U.S. Office Furniture 2004." *Forbes,* 3 March 2004.

Furniture Design & Manufacturing, 2004.

Gold, Robert. "Outlook Improves for Office Furniture Industry." *Holland [Michigan] Sentinel*, 5 May 2004.

Hoover's Company Capsules. Hoover's Inc., 2007. Available from www.hoovers.com.

Koeing, Karen M. "Office Furniture Industry Takes Action." *Wood & Wood Products,* October 2006.

Miel, Rhoda. "Office Furniture Makers Cautiously Comfortable." *Plastics News,* 8 January 2007.

"Office Furniture Industry Performance and Projections." *Deseret News,* (Salt Lake City), 14 May 2006.

Phillips, Tom. "Sitting Pretty: All Rise Please for the Office Furniture Industry!" *Office Products International,* November 2006.

Scheiber, Noam. "Business: To Gauge a Recovery, Count the New Workstations." *New York Times,* 16 November 2003.

"Steelcase, Maker of Office Furniture, Will Cut 600 Jobs." *New York Times,* 29 March 2005.

"The Demand for Office Furniture in the United States." Global Wood, 1 November 2006. Available from www.globalwood.org.

"The U.S. Office Furniture Market." The Business and Institutional Manufacturers Association, 14 February 2007. Available from www.bifma.com/.

U.S. Department of Commerce, International Trade Administration. Office Furniture Export and Import Statistics, 1996-2005. Available from www.ita.doc.gov.

GLASS, PLASTICS, AND RUBBER PRODUCTS

SIC 3220
NAICS 3272

GLASS CONTAINERS AND GLASSWARE

This industry classification is divided into two principal groups: manufacturers who use techniques of blowing or pressing to shape glass into containers, and manufacturers who produce glass that is used for ornamental purposes. The use of glass for containers lends itself to a range of activities from commercial packaging and bottling to home canning. Glass containers may be cosmetic jars, fruit jars, jugs for packing, medicine bottles, wine bottles, milk bottles, vials, or water bottles. Ornamental glass includes art glassware, glass ashtrays, barware, bowls, candlesticks, centerpieces, glass chimneys for lamps, Christmas tree ornaments made from glass, glass and glass ceramic frying pans, glassware, goblets, glass lampshades, lantern globes, stemware, tableware, and vases.

INDUSTRY SNAPSHOT

During the early and mid-2000s, glass products experienced uneven demand, and at times delivered disappointing returns to their makers. Glass containers, which constitute the larger of the industry's two segments, face intense competition from both aluminum and plastics, especially polyethylene terephthalate (PET), a material commonly used for plastic drink containers. This is especially so in the food products and beverage sector, which accounts for the largest glass container production numbers in many markets. Nonetheless, glass retains marketing strength as an attractive material, and glass packaging is seen by many consumers as having a high-quality image. Glass enjoys numerous regional niche strongholds that make it still an attractive growth prospect for producers and investors willing to weather difficult times. Also, strides made by plastics in the container market could be counteracted by increasing concerns regarding toxic emissions and waste in the manufacturing and recycling of these materials, especially since glass manufacturing overall has a better environmental track record.

In its August 2002 issue, *Glass* revealed that glass containers accounted for 62 percent of all glass production worldwide, followed by flat glass at 26 percent. Within the larger glass industry, Europe had the world's largest market share (27 percent), followed by the United States (20 percent), and Japan (18 percent). In Europe, glass containers comprised 60 percent of the nation's glass industry. In early 2003, *Packaging Strategies* reported that the United States held 36 percent of the world market for glass containers in 2002, based on figures from the Glass Packaging Institute (GPI). In addition, the publication indicated that glass containers comprised more than half of all U.S. glass production.

In mature markets such as the United States and Western Europe, glass sales in certain categories have been flat or declining. Coupled with falling prices, these trends have made glass manufacture unprofitable for some companies and given rise to consolidation, particularly in Europe. However, most of the world's emerging economies are potentially strong growth markets for glass containers in the longer term. Within more mature markets, various niches, such as premium beverage bottles, and efficient, consolidated producers, will also continue to obtain favorable results.

In societies concerned about ecology, the stability of the glass industry is bolstered by the fact that glass never wears out, is 100 percent recyclable, and can be recycled forever. With the exception of recyclable aluminum beverage containers, no other packaging material has experienced as rapid a growth in recycling as glass. Recycling glass saves from 25 to 32 percent of the energy required to make glass. Most of today's bottles and jars contain at least 25 percent recycled glass, and the Texas Agricultural Extension Service reports that many plants have increased the amount of recycled glass, known as cullet, in their products to 40 percent or more.

ORGANIZATION AND STRUCTURE

Glass is part of the packaging market known as rigid packaging. Other rigid packaging materials include rigid metal, such as aluminum and tin-plated steel; plastic; and composite or multi-material containers. According to research compiled by First Boston Corporation, the rigid container market in 1960 was made up of 66.7 percent metal cans and 32.6 percent glass containers. By 1993, glass accounted for only 18 percent of the market, metal's share had fallen to 60 percent, and the plastic category had grown to 22 percent. Although the use of plastic gained favor in the 1970s, noticeably in the soft drinks market, glass remains a competitive packaging material because it is recyclable and contributes to marketing appeal.

To deal with the impact of plastic bottles and cans on the glass packaging industry, manufacturers have sought a variety of new packaging ideas. Although the standard wine bottle size is 750 milliliters, the industry designed a 500-milliliter bottle for special-occasion use. This allowed manufacturers to capitalize on the smaller bottle's appeal to consumers who consider the larger size wasteful. Long neck, commemorative, proprietary shape, and new-age market bottles are expected to shore up glass's share of the soft drink market and ultimately account for as much as 25 percent of all glass soft drink bottles. According to the Society of Glass and Ceramic Decoration, unusual glass packaging and decorating effects do much to advance various marketing efforts. Unique bottle design creates a demand among vendors who use glass packaging to enhance their product image, as well as among collectors who capitalize on the incremental value associated with limited edition bottles and containers.

As long ago as 1990, at the Conference on Glass Problems held at the Ohio State University, it was predicted that the need for glass would remain high due to the beer market, and that the soft drink market also would remain a solid one for glass—especially for those products sold in vending machines and convenience stores. In the face of pressure from plastic in food packaging and, to a lesser degree, in the soft drink market, the major opportunity for glass industry growth was seen in expansion of the glass container market. The corollary to this prediction was container manufacturers' need to improve productivity, quality, and the cost of the average glass container.

In 1997, emphasis was placed on the need to reduce contaminants in recycled glass. Contaminants causing most concern include aluminum caps, steel lids, lead bottle collars and light bulb filaments, ceramics, stones and dirt, plate or window glass, heat-resistant glass, and lead-based glass. Mixing of glass colors is discouraged, because most glass-container customers will not tolerate variances in glass color. Because specific colors of glass admit light to different degrees, container glass always is produced in one of three colors. Sixty-four percent of glass containers are flint (clear), 23 percent are amber, and the remaining 13 percent are green. In an attempt to improve the quality of recycled glass, the Glass Packaging Institute (GPI) launched "Glass Container Recycling: Today and Tomorrow," described as an outreach effort targeting public and private sector haulers, cullet processors, state agencies, and local recycling officials.

Background and Development

Glassmaking originated 5,000 years ago in the Middle East. To make glass, common sand, which contains silica, is mixed with ashes from trees (potash) or marine plants (soda). The mixture then is "fired," using intense heat (a minimum of 1,000 degrees Fahrenheit) until it melts. The resulting "molten blob" of glass can be blown, cut, and colored, according to how it is to be used. Glass was common in a number of ancient civilizations. Blown glasses and bottles have been used in Syria and Italy since the first century B.C.

In the seventeenth century, the technique of adding lead oxide to molten glass was discovered. In addition to making the crystal more brilliant and durable, the lead made the glass softer and easier to work. From the time the process was discovered, the beautiful products made of lead crystal have been regarded as a symbol of luxury.

The eighteenth century saw the expansion of both the glass and wine industries. As vintners proved they were learning how to make wine that aged, glassmakers discovered a new market: making bottles for long-term wine storage. Additionally, tabletop art was coming into vogue, and glassmakers began producing decorative glasses and decanters. Consumers in Georgian England (1714 to 1830) were adamant that a wine glass "be more than a mere receptacle for liquid." Pre-Georgian glasses are recognizable today by their simplicity and heaviness, but in 1746, a tax was levied on glass weight. Thus prompted, manufacturers began to produce lighter glassware with a more delicate form. Georgian wineglasses are characterized as having a foot, a stem, and a bowl that may be blown as a unit with the stem.

Following the Georgian era, the glass industry boomed, given a significant boost in 1780 when English glass houses set up shops in Ireland to take advantage of a newly established tax-free trading status in that country. Nineteenth-century developments furthering the industry's progress included the invention of the Mason jar in 1859 (enabling fruits and vegetables to be preserved) and the invention of the Owens automatic bottle machine in 1903 (leading to high-speed production of bottles and jars of uniform height, weight, and capacity). As a result of these innovations, labor-intensive glass blowing relinquished its place as the major method of glass production.

The processes of "press-and-blow" and "blow-and -blow" were discovered between 1850 and 1890. The blow-and-blow process employed an inverted blank mold in order to gain a larger opening to receive the charge of glass. In the same period, it was discovered that the finish of the bottle needed to be constructed first and that two molds, a neck ring and a tip, were required.

In recent years, the fact that glass fits so well into various recycling programs has brought new impetus to the glass container industry. Recycled glass, or cullet, is now a vital part of glass container manufacture. Cullet is combined with soda ash, limestone, and sand to create new glass.

Current Conditions

According to the U.S. Census Bureau, glass container production reached 248.5 million gross in 2002, up from 240.5 million gross in 2001. Of this total, glass beer bottles comprised the largest segment, at 52.9 percent. Food containers were the next largest category (19.8 percent), followed by general beverage bottles (8.9 percent), ready-to-drink alcoholic coolers and cocktail containers (5.8 percent), wine bottles (5.1 percent), other containers (4.4 percent), and liquor bottles (3.2 percent).

In 2003, the U.S. Census Bureau reported that total glass container production fell to 245.4 million gross. This downward trend continued through mid-2004, as production for the first six months of the year reached 123.7 million gross, compared to 126.5 million gross at the same time in 2003.

By early 2003, the U.S. glass container industry remained heavily consolidated. In its January 31, 2003 issue, *Packaging Strategies* revealed that Owens-Illinois controlled 44 percent of the nation's market, followed by Saint Gobain Containers (31 percent), and Consumers Packaging/Anchor (19 percent). The remaining industry players accounted for a mere 6 percent of the market. As further evidence of industry consolidation, by 2001 there were 54 manufacturing plants in the United States, compared to 121 in 1983.

Looking ahead to the late 2000s, glass container manufacturers looked to premium, "new age" beverages like natural juice drinks and teas to drive growth. Industry growth also depended on the continued popularity of so-called "malternatives"—pre-mixed flavored alcoholic beverages (FAB), such as Bacardi Silver, Smirnoff Ice, and Skyy Blue. *Packaging Strategies* reported that an estimated 8 percent of industry capacity was devoted to the FAB sector in 2003. However, rather than increase existing capacity to satisfy demand, many U.S. manufacturers looked to imports from foreign plants.

In August 2002, *Glass* reported that glass western European production reached 18.2 million tons in 2000 (the most recent data available), up from 15.3 million tons in 1990. Germany had the largest share of total production, with 23.4 percent, followed by France (20.1 percent), Italy (17.8 percent), Spain (10.8 percent), and the United Kingdom (9.4 percent).

GLASS VERSUS PLASTIC

During the early 2000s, polyethylene terephthalate (PET) containers continued to have a significant effect on the global glass container market. The leading glass container companies also established plastics packaging businesses. The many performance advantages of plastic packaging continue to undermine glass as the material of choice, especially in the food and beverage packaging sectors.

Based on data from the The Freedonia Group, in April 2004 *Beverage Industry* revealed that U.S. plastic container demand was expected to increase 4.9 percent annually from 2002 to 2007, rising from 53.8 billion units to 68.5 billion units. However, glass container demand was only expected to grow 1.1 percent during the same time period, rising from 27.2 billion units to 28.7 billion units. Glass containers for beer were expected to account for 75.7 percent of the glass beverage container market by 2007 (21.7 billion units). A variety of other containers were expected to comprise 28.7 percent of the market (4.9 billion units). Finally, wine bottles were expected to reach 2 billion units by 2007, accounting for about 7 percent of the market.

CeramicsIndustry.com, also reporting data from The Freedonia Group, indicated that in the early 2000s, baby food maker Gerber announced its plan to replace most of its glass jars with plastic. The company based its decision on market research that showed consumer preference levels of almost 70 percent for baby food in plastic containers. Miller Brewing Company, seeking to give consumers a flexible packaging choice, began marketing its Miller Lite, Miller Genuine Draft, and Icehouse brands in plastic bottles in March 2000. However, glass still stands tall as the material of choice for the packaging of beer. The Glass Packaging Institute expected beer bottle demand to increase 2 percent annually through 2005, reaching 220 billion units.

Many consumers in the developed world see glass containers as prestigious and associate the packaging with higher value. Therefore, companies will tend to use glass for new product introductions and for upscale products, such as specialty beers. However, research has shown that consumers in the developing world see aluminum packaging as being more attractive and of higher quality than glass.

Glass has a number of advantages over other packaging materials. Unlike plastic, glass containers are easy to sort (by color) for recycling and can be repeatedly recycled to make new containers. Using cullet makes for more efficient and cleaner production. Glass containers are reusable, retain carbonation for longer periods of time, and can be irradiated for use in sterilized applications. On the downside, glass containers have a risk of breakage; have higher weight and therefore higher shipping costs; often require an opener; and vary in how well they can be resealed.

LEGISLATION

Forced deposit laws lead the list of issues facing the glass packaging industry because glass surcharges—that is, bottle deposits—are thought to hurt sales and discourage packagers and retailers from using glass packaging. Advanced disposal fees (ADFs) offer another challenge. ADFs are applied to containers whose recycling rate is less than 50 percent. Since as recently as 1994 the glass industry's recycling rate was just 37 percent, imposition of ADFs has had its effect on industry development. Although in theory intended to encourage manufacturers to work more diligently to raise recycling rates, there has been an expressed concern that the fees are a detriment to sales, penalizing manufacturers despite their recycling efforts. ADFs enjoy international popularity, and, according to EcoRecycle Victoria (Australia), they tend to be low enough to minimize any impact on purchasing patterns. In the United States, Florida was the first state to impose an ADF, but then allowed it to lapse. California substituted a one cent ADF on packaged beverages as an alternative to container deposit legislation.

LABOR

It is estimated that labor accounts for 35 percent of total cost for glass, compared with 13 percent for plastic and 9 percent for cans. These relatively high labor costs are offset by the fact that direct materials only account for 28 percent of the cost for glass, compared with 60 percent for plastic and over 75 percent for aluminum.

Another issue facing the glass industry is revealed by an efficiency measure known as "percent pack." Only 85 to 90 percent of the raw materials melted to make glass convert to a marketable product; the remainder becomes recycled glass. It is unusual for an industry to put so much labor and energy into producing a product, only to discard 10 to 15 percent of it once it is manufactured. A need for quality control is implied by this degree of waste, and there is an increasing focus on efforts to monitor glass composition, glass temperatures, and the forming process, the ultimate goal being production of quality glass containers at least 95 percent of the time.

COST REDUCTION

Attempts to reduce glass production costs have led to what is termed "lightweighting," which allows for faster production of more glass containers, using less glass per container. A process known as "narrow-neck press-and-blow" has successfully trimmed glass weight by 10 to 15 percent versus the traditional blow-and-blow process. Other trends for reducing costs in the glass container industry include the usage of vision based and computer driven inspection systems for quality control; process control systems; just-in-time delivery to customers; and bulk palletization systems.

CONTROLLING OIL AND GREASE IN GLASS CONTAINER PLANTS

Many glass container plants are faced with the need to upgrade wastewater treatment technology. Research has shown that the majority of oil or grease found in the outflow or effluent from a glass manufacturing plant emanates from three sources: soluble oils used in glass shearing, forming machine lubrication oils, and condensate from compressed air systems. In addition to being a major source of oil or grease, the soluble oils used in glass shearing combine with forming machine oils to create additional pollutants.

One solution to the direct and indirect discharge of industrial wastewater is known as zero process water. Zero discharge can be attained through diligent control of water input into the cullet quench system, use of cullet quench water as batch wetting water, and/or installation of an evaporator for disposal of excess wastewater. The first approach, diligent control of water input, has been successful on a limited basis, most notably in smaller glass container plants. Difficulties tend to arise in larger, more complex plants. The second approach, use of cullet quench water as a batch wetting water, is considered to be viable, having been practiced successfully for approximately 15 years. The downside here, however, is that the amount of wastewater for disposal is limited to the amount of batch wetting water utilized, which often is less than the amount of wastewater available. The third approach, the installation of an evaporator, is considered to be the ideal means to control wastewater problems. However, as the operating cost for evaporation was approximately US$60 per thousand gallons, this solution may only be cost effective for small discharges.

Modification of existing systems may be the most economical remedy for plants with discharges that only slightly exceed regulatory standards. One modification calls for review of the design and operation of the cullet quench re-circulation system and oil separator. If not included in the original design and installation, inclusion of a cooling tower circuit within the cullet quench system is recommended. Cullet quench systems already installed need to be checked for biological growths that degrade the efficient removal of oil or grease and pose a potential health hazard from Legionnaire's disease.

RESEARCH AND TECHNOLOGY

By the mid-2000s, manufacturers were employing a variety of cutting-edge techniques to set glass containers apart from rival forms of packaging. These approaches included expensive acid etching to frost glass, the use of colors that are sprayed and baked onto glass, organic inks that enable manufacturers to spray labels directly onto glass containers, applied ceramic labeling, as well as embossed labels and plastic "shrink sleeves." Some of these techniques involved the use of computer-aided design (CAD) software, especially when it was necessary to design oddly-shaped bottles.

As writer Kate Bertrand summarized in the June 2004 issue of *Food & Drug Packaging,* because of "sophisticated decorating technologies and tools such as computer modeling, glass packaging is reinventing itself once again. For food and beverage packagers, the result will be packages that not only stand up to high-speed bottling and high-speed distribution but also catch the consumer's eye at the point of purchase."

RECYCLING

Prior to the 1980s, manufacturers made decisions regarding packaging preferences using two criteria: cost and consumer convenience. Environmental impact and recycling, two buzzwords of the 1990s, were not key considerations. Ironically, manufacturers discovered that one way to lower packaging costs was to reduce the materials required to produce the package, improving the industry's impact on the environment in the process. Reductions that lower manufacturing costs by as little as one-tenth of one cent can result in millions of dollars worth of savings. Over a 10-year period, the material weight of a 16-ounce glass bottle has been reduced by 30 percent. In the 1990s, glass containers were 44 percent lighter than those manufactured 20 years prior. This reduction in materials also meant that less packaging made its way to already-overcrowded landfills.

Every glass bottle and jar manufactured by the 1990s was 100 percent recyclable. According to the Washington, D.C.-based Glass Packaging Institute (GPI), glass recycling reduces the costs of landfill dumping and saves over a ton of natural resources for every ton of glass recycled. Similarly, use of 50 percent recycled glass can reduce mining waste by as much as 75 percent. Glass containers account for 1.6 percent of materials that end up in municipal solid waste systems. Overall, glass materials account for 5.5 percent of all solid waste, compared with 5.1 percent for aluminum, 4.8 percent for steel, 41 percent for plastic, and 43.6 percent for paper. According to the GPI, in 1998 Americans recycled about 13 million glass jars and bottles each day, and the average American was able to save six pounds of glass in one month. However, the Container Recyclying Institute reported in 2005 that U.S. consumers disposed of 131 billion plastic, glass and aluminum beverage containers in 2004 rather than recycling them, up from 127 billion in 2003 and 60 percent higher than 1990. Reasons cited were lack of incentive to recycle and lack of opportunity.

For glass manufacturers, recycling extends furnace life and reduces energy costs. Every one percent of cullet used results in a one-half of one percent drop in energy costs. Manufacturers use as much as 70 percent cullet in some glass mixtures.

CONSUMER PREFERENCES

Glass is popular among consumers for bottled water—known as the hydro segment of rigid packaging—but glass has many other consumer uses. In 1994 a qualitative research study was conducted by Glenn Bauer and Associates for Ogilvy, Adams, Rinehart and the Glass Packaging Institute (GPI). Titled "Consumer Attitudes Regarding Glass Packaging," this study was designed to help the GPI promote glass packaging by ascertaining consumer preferences toward glass, plastic, and metal packaging materials. The study demonstrated that recycling is a major concern for consumers and does influence their buying decisions. To glass's disadvantage, however, another noteworthy item was that consumers with young children indicated a preference for products that are packaged using unbreakable materials.

Study participants felt that factors such as price, brand name, and ingredients were more important than the material used to package the product. If all of these key factors were equal, only then would packaging material influence a purchase decision. Participants perceived both foods and beverages packaged in glass to be sanitary, fresh, pure, truer tasting, natural, and honest. They pointed out that the contents of glass packages are completely visible, that glass packages are resealable, and that glass is puncture and tamper resistant. They voiced a preference for buying pasta sauce and salsas in glass containers because glass enabled them to determine the "richness" and "chunkiness" of these particular foods. Similarly, they preferred to buy mushrooms in glass containers rather than cans that preclude visual examination of the product.

The study indicated an overall preference for purchasing single-serve size beverages in glass, with the possible exception of single-serve size bottled water. The safety and lightness associated with plastic made it the more practical choice for indoor/outdoor recreational use. Indeed, in the 1990s, major U.S. soft drink companies such as the Coca-Cola Company and PepsiCo, and their affiliated bottlers, moved away from glass in favor of plastic bottles. Elsewhere in the world, however, the same soft drink brands are still found in glass bottles. For example, according to a Donaldson, Lufkin & Jenrette Securities report, in Asia glass bottles occupy a 40 percent share of the soft drink market, considerably higher than the world average. In the U.S. consumer study, participants agreed they preferred beer in glass bottles to metal cans. A similar preference is found in Europe. Beer in plastic bottles was not even considered a viable choice. However, it is interesting to note that breweries began using plastic bottles during the early 2000s. Overall, plastic packaging evoked feelings of convenience, safety, and durability. The advantages of metal packaging included long shelf life and ease of storage. However, foods and beverages in metal packaging were considered to be low quality, processed, unresealable, and susceptible to contamination when the package was dented.

In March of 2004, *Packaging International* reported on research conducted by Glasspac, the promotional division of the British Glass Manufacturers' Confederation. Based on a survey of 1,000 consumers, Glasspac found that glass was the overwhelming choice for food and beverage packaging in the United Kingdom. More than 80 percent of respondents indicated that glass eclipsed plastic in terms of its attractiveness. In addition, 74 percent perceived glass as being more natural than other packaging. Finally, almost 70 percent indicated that glass conveyed an image of quality.

In the spring of 1998, the Society of Glass and Ceramic Decoration emphasized that glass packaging greatly enhanced a consumer's perception of a product. Non-commodity brands, including alcoholic beverages, iced teas, and sparkling waters, seeking a quality image can benefit from a glass container's appearance. Glassware manufacturers find that container decoration adds to a quality image and can be a crucial selling point for products packaged in glass. This emphasis on decoration and the flexibility of glass in that regard was echoed by the GPI in a Web page devoted to current trends in consumer habits. According to the GPI, visibility has surpassed labeling as a means to increase the consumer appeal of upscale foods and beverages: "From soup to spirits, marketers are matching glass with minimal labels to showcase premier products."

GLASS USE IN HAZARDOUS WASTE DISPOSAL

A US$1.3 billion U.S. Department of Energy plant was opened in South Carolina to test the feasibility of encasing radioactive material in glass. The initial plan was for the South Carolina facility to stabilize nuclear wastes by encasing them in "logs" of strong glass, which in turn are wrapped in steel cylinders that measure 10 feet high and two feet across. Each steel cylinder has the capacity to hold 165 gallons of waste. If experiments such as these prove successful, glass soon may play a significant role in the disposal of a variety of highly hazardous materials.

INDUSTRY LEADERS

OWENS-ILLINOIS, INC. (UNITED STATES)

Headquartered in Toledo, Ohio, Owens-Illinois is the biggest producer of glass containers in the United States. It is also the largest glass container manufacturer in North America, South America, China, Australia, and New Zealand, and one of the biggest in Europe. In 2004, the company's sales reached nearly US$6.15 billion. Its 28,700 employees serve general line distributors in the food, beverage, beer, drug, chemical, wine, and liquor industries, among others. Owens-Illinois also manufactures plastic containers such as prescription bottles and plastic closures. The firm's customers include Procter & Gamble, Anheuser-Busch, and Philip

Morris. Competition comes from Saint-Gobain, Consolidated Container, and Silgan.

COMPAGNIE DE SAINT-GOBAIN (FRANCE)

Saint-Gobain, a French company, operates in 45 countries. It is the European and worldwide leader in its three sectors: high performance materials, housing (approximately 50 percent of sales), and glass. Saint-Gobain produces 30 billion glass jars, bottles, and flasks annually and also supplied the glass for the Louvre pyramid. Sales in 2003 reached US$37.1 billion, up more than 17 percent from 2002. Major competition comes from CRH, Lafarge, and Owens Corning.

LANCASTER COLONY CORPORATION (UNITED STATES)

Lancaster is an eclectic company that makes a wide variety of products including salad dressings, potpourri, candles, and automotive accessories. Its offerings in the glass sector include floral containers marketed directly to the wholesale florist industry under the brand name Brody; glassware brands Indiana Glass and Colony; and industrial glass and lighting components made under the name Lancaster Glass. In 2004, sales fell slightly to US$1.09 billion while net income decreased nearly 29 percent to US$80 million. Based in Columbus, Ohio, the company employed 5,500 workers in 2004. Specialty foods was the company's largest and fastest growing business division.

GERRESHEIMER GLAS AG (GERMANY)

Although Gerresheimer's most important market is the pharmaceuticals industry, its various specialty systems continue to grow. Formerly a subsidiary of Owens-Illinois, the firm held roughly 35 percent of the German glass container market in the early 2000s and was bought by investment firm the Blackstone Group in 2004. In 2002, sales reached US$576.6 million, and the company employed 5,500 workers. New designs have bolstered sales of bottles for premium-brand products and liquors, and Gerresheimer further enhanced this segment of its operation by acquiring a 60 percent interest in the Belgian glass manufacturer Nouvelles Verreries de Momignies S.A., which produces high quality glass packaging for cosmetic products. In early 1997, Gerresheimer sought growth in international markets by acquiring the remaining 49 percent interest in its U.S.-based Kimble Glass Inc. joint venture with Owens-Illinois.

SHAMVIK GLASSTECH PVT. LTD. (INDIA)

In 1998, Shamvik Glasstech Pvt. Ltd. (SGPL) celebrated its 25th anniversary. Through emphasis on research and development, SPGL brought high-technology production methods to India's resident glass industry. As a result, the firm now employs the vast majority of the workers in India who operate the sophisticated independent/individual section (I.S.) machines used to create glass containers. A small but growing company, SGPL exports its technology as well as its glass products, serving the United States, the United Kingdom, Russia and the Ukraine, and a large number of developing countries. In 2004, SGPL indicated that it commanded 80 percent of the Indian market and employed 115 workers.

FURTHER READING

"Beer, 'Malternatives' Continue to Help Drive Glass Bottle Demand." *Packaging Strategies,* 31 January 2003.

Bertrand, Kate. "Glass Technologies Break the Mold: Glass Molding and Decorating Techniques Yield a Premium Look for Foods and Beverages." *Food & Drug Packaging,* June 2004.

Burrows, Stephen J. "European Glass Markets and the Minerals Supplier's Viewpoint: The EU Is the World's Largest Glass Market In Terms of Production and Consumption." *Food & Drug Packaging,* June 2004.

Business Rankings Annual. Farmington Hills, Michigan: Gale Group, 2004.

"Container Demand Grows, but Sizes Shrink." *Beverage Industry,* April 2004.

EcoRecycle. "EcoRecycle Reports: Waste Minimisation." Victoria, Australia: EcoRecycle, 1997. Available from http://www.ecorecycle.vic.gov.au.

"Glass Has Class, Say Consumers." *Packaging Today International,* March 2004.

GlassOnline. 2005. Available from http://www.glassonline.com.

"Hoover's Company Capsules." Austin, TX: Hoover's, Inc., 2005. Available from http://www.hoovers.com.

"Institute Wants to Reverse Container Trend." *Waste News,* 17 January 2005.

Lazich, Robert S., ed. *Market Share Reporter.* Farmington Hills, Michigan: Gale Group, 2004.

U.S. Census Bureau. "Glass Containers." *Current Industrial Reports.* August 2004. Available from http://www.census.gov.

———. "Glass Containers: 2002." *Current Industrial Reports.* May 2003. Available from http://www.census.gov.

SIC 2821

NAICS 325211

PLASTICS MATERIALS AND RESINS

Global plastics makers manufacture various synthetic resins and plastics that other industries process into sheets, rods, film, and other products. Related industries include plastic products, synthetic rubber, and man-made fibers.

INDUSTRY SNAPSHOT

Synthetic plastics were pioneered in Europe and the United States during the late nineteenth century and were produced commercially by the early 1900s. The industry expanded rapidly with the development of improved plastic materials. The United States assumed global industry dominance following World War II and continued to lead the production of plastics in the early 2000s. However, its share of the global market fell after the 1950s as manufacturers in both industrialized and developing nations boosted output. Plastics output is traditionally about equal to domestic consumption. Plastics and resins constituted a significant portion of the patents issued in the overall chemical industry.

World plastic production ballooned from 63.5 million metric tons in 1982 to more than 150 million in 1998. Although growth has been uneven across regions and years, the industry's long-term outlook remains decidedly positive, especially in emerging economies, as plastics are increasingly substituted for other materials in applications ranging from transportation and construction to packaging and consumer products. Japan, Western Europe, and the United States continued to lead output at the beginning of the 2000s, but low-cost producers of commodity plastics in developing regions amassed a rising share of world production by 2005, especially as economic growth accelerated in China.

One leading issue across national boundaries was environmental pollution, which sparked a wave of legislation and other initiatives to reduce toxic wastes resulting from plastics production as well as to control the amount of plastic consumed and disposed. These concerns motivated—and in some cases required—industry participants to recycle plastic and develop less toxic and biodegradable plastics. Among the primary targets was PVC, used extensively in the construction industry as well as in packaging. Though environmental campaigns resulted in several companies agreeing to eliminate PVCs from their products, U.S. output of PVCs actually increased in 2004 by 8.8 percent, reaching a total of 16 billion pounds.

Organization and Structure

Plastics are giant polymers—long-chain molecules that contain thousands of repeating molecular units. Although some plastics are made from natural materials such as wax or cellulose, most are synthesized from petrochemicals or other organic substances. Because synthesized materials can be manipulated into an infinite variety of grades and types, they are important alternatives to natural materials in numerous applications.

Products. Plastics manufacturing involves a three-step process: (1) synthesizing the polymer, usually from petrochemicals or coal-related processes (i.e., coal gasification); (2) compounding, which integrated additives; and (3) shaping, an activity not included in this industry classification. The physical properties of plastic can be altered at different stages of the production process, but the most versatile stage is during compounding. For example, additives, such as colorants, flame retardants, heat or light stabilizers, or lubricants may be added to the resin to achieve desired characteristics. The end result of the compounding process is resin, usually in the form of pellets, flakes, granules, powder, or liquid.

Plasticizers, the most common additives used to alter plastic resins, increase a resin's flexibility and are often used to make polyvinyl chloride (PVC) resins that can be utilized in construction products. Impact modifiers are additives that boosted a plastic's resistance to stress. Likewise, antioxidants retard the oxidation and breakdown of plastics, and heat-stabilizing additives help resins maintain their physical structure during processing. Light stabilizers filter out radiation that can cause a plastic to deteriorate as a result of exposure to sunlight and flame-retardants enable resins to resist combustion. Colorants are another major additive used in the compounding process. Aside from additives, fillers or reinforcement such as glass fibers, particulate materials, and hollow glass spheres can also be added during compounding. Another option is to combine polymers to create a polymer blend or alloy.

Thermoplastics and thermosets are the two main classes of plastics. Thermoplastics account for the bulk of industry output. They solidify by cooling and are repeatedly remelted to form new shapes. The major thermoplastic resins are: polyethylene (PE), used primarily to create packaging; PVC, commonly consumed in the manufacture of pipes, siding, gutters, windows, and other goods utilized in construction; polypropylene (PP), used to create fiber and filaments, molded consumer products, and packaging; and polystyrene, which is formed into disposable packaging, furniture finishings, and miscellaneous consumer products. Other thermoplastics segments include polyamide resins, styrene-butadiene, and some polyesters.

According to *U.S. Thermoplastic Elastomers,* news analysis from Frost & Sullivan revealed that this market generated revenues of US$1.29 billion in 2003, and is likely to reach US$1.72 billion in 2010.

Thermosets are a smaller, more mature, and less dynamic division of the plastics industry. In contrast to thermoplastics, thermosets harden by chemical reaction and cannot be melted and shaped after they are created. Typical thermosets include phenolics, which make adhesives, insulation, laminates, and other related goods; urea-formaldehyde resins, commonly used in the production of plywood and particle board; epoxies, often used as metal coatings in packaging and construction; and polyesters, used to create plastics reinforced with glass fiber and other materials.

Plastics resins span four major commercial divisions: commodity, intermediate, engineered, and advanced. Commodity resins, which represent the bulk of industry production, are low-tech plastics available in standardized formulas from many companies throughout the world. Intermediate resins are generally considered more advanced and somewhat specialized in comparison to commodity resins. Likewise, engineering resins exhibit more advanced performance characteristics and are produced on a smaller scale than commodity and intermediate resins. Finally, advanced resins are those most capable of withstanding impact and high heat, carrying loads, and resisting attacks by chemicals and solvents.

Competition and Markets. Partly because of technological requirements, the global plastics industry is dominated by major industrial powers. As a whole, North America, Japan, and Western Europe accounted for more than 80 percent of the industry output and around 60 percent of plastics use in the 1990s, though by 2005 growth in developing Asian markets's plastics industries outpaced that in North America and Europe. The output of plastics was roughly equal to domestic consumption in most nations, although industrialized countries tended to be net exporters. The United States, Japan, and Germany together consumed and produced slightly more than 50 percent of this output in the 1990s; the remainder of the market was widely distributed. Aside from technical expertise related to the production process, manufacturers in those countries benefited from immediate access to most of the companies that purchased and processed plastics and resins.

In general, commodity resins have been manufactured by large, integrated companies in industrialized regions, although a rising share of production occurs in emerging economies such as those of Southeast Asia. Intermediate, engineered, and advanced resins are more likely to be manufactured (and consumed) in developed nations, sometimes by smaller manufacturers with expertise in this niche. Industry profitability in each nation is closely linked with both global plastics prices and domestic economic performance; when other industries, such as construction and motor vehicles, are growing and consuming plastic products, prices and profits are usually high. Likewise, when demand slows, profits often plunge. Packaging is the largest market for plastics and resins, followed by building and construction products such as roofing materials and geotextiles. Other major markets include motor vehicles, electronic devices, furniture, housewares, and medical products.

Background and Development

Crude forms of natural plastic have been used since at least the 1740s. The first known use of plastic was in present-day Malaysia; it was later imitated by European and North American manufacturers in the mid-nineteenth century. Malayan natives were observed in 1843 molding a plastic made from gutta percha, or gum elastic, into knife handles and other articles. "Parkesine," the first synthetic plastic, was invented in 1862 by Alexander Parkes, an Englishman. John Hyatt, an American printer, recognized the important plasticizing effect in the Parkesine production process. He renamed the substance celluloid in 1870, giving birth to synthetic plastics applications. Despite its flammability, celluloid was used to make carriage and automobile windshields and motion picture film.

Dr. Leo Hendrik Baekland, a Belgian-American, invented the world's first moldable plastic material in 1909. Baekland's thermosetting phenolformaldehyde resin provided a tremendous impetus for other inventors, who began to develop molding techniques and add resins to paints and varnishes. Baekland's resin, later called "Bakelite," was also used in the electrical industry to make some of the first molded, synthetic plastic components. This led to a colorless resin, urea-formaldehyde, which was invented in 1918. Plastics research and development began to proliferate in the 1920s and 1930s.

German chemist Hermann Staudinger's polymer research spawned an outburst of scientific investigation that resulted in numerous breakthroughs. The Germans took the lead in the creation of many new thermosetting resins; however, researchers in the United States and several European nations made significant contributions in the area of plastic molding and extrusion machines and later in the advancement of thermoplastics. During World War II the plastics industry expanded explosively as warring nations scurried to develop new and better materials for war machines. Industry shipments continued to rise during the 1950s and 1960s, and the United States surpassed its war-torn European peers. As demand for all types of consumer, commercial, and institutional products soared, plastics producers scrambled to keep pace with expanding markets. The United States dominated, supplying well over 50 percent of global plastics output.

Pivotal breakthroughs in chemical technology and production techniques continued to open vast new markets during the 1970s and 1980s. Most importantly, producers in other industries began to realize the advantages of substituting plastics for more expensive, less versatile natural materials. A variety of factors, such as excess capacity and high petroleum costs, contributed to brief periods of slow production or stagnant profits in most regions. In general, however, industry participants in Europe, Japan, and the United States benefited from numerous influences. For example, new additives and plastic alloys contributed to demand growth by opening entirely new markets for resins.

As many segments of the industry matured and grew competitive, falling prices allowed plastics to penetrate a number of metal, glass, and wood markets. Automobile and truck manufacturers, seeking plastics' advantages of low cost and physical versatility, became a vital market for resins during the 1980s. Likewise, makers of electronic equipment, appliances, and other consumer products significantly increased their use of various resins in the same period. Packaging markets grew as well. Disposable items, such as microwavable food and beverage containers, gained in popularity. As evidence of that trend, the global portion of plastics-based packaging materials soared from 13.2 percent in 1985 to 36 percent in 1993.

Another important industry dynamic during the 1970s and 1980s was the entrance into the plastics industry of a number of developing nations, particularly in Latin America and the Pacific Rim. While developed nations still accounted for more than 80 percent of world output, plastics production in Africa and the Middle East skyrocketed to approximately 2 million metric tons (an increase of more than 400 percent) between 1982 and 1993. During the same period, Latin American plastic shipments jumped more than 100 percent to about 4.8 million tons. Although traditional plastics-producing nations surrendered a portion of the global market share, they still enjoyed solid gains. Plastic output in North America swelled nearly 70 percent, while output in Western Europe leapt 45 percent. Japan realized similar increases.

In the wake of the late 1990s Asian financial crisis, plastics manufacturers considered new locations for their expansions in 1997 and 1998. Some plastics manufacturers from Japan, Germany, and the United States turned to Mexico and elsewhere in Latin America for their new facilities. Mexico provided an appealing venue for plastics production, in part because of its low labor costs and participation in the North American Free Trade Agreement, which would make trade advantageous between Mexico and the United States and Canada.

Even though Europe, Japan, and North America already consume 60 percent of all polyethylene, their use will continue to grow as their share of the market declines. Analysts attribute the growth in demand to increased global reliance on convenience products including plastics films, containers, and bottles. In South America and Eastern Europe alone, use of plastic bottles made from polyethylene terephthalate (PET) resin—notably soft drink bottles—rose by approximately 20 percent annually in the late 1990s.

In the packaging market, plastics manufacturers began to capitalize on the growing bag-in-the-box trend. Throughout the world, especially in North America and Europe, producers of soft-drink syrup, milk, wine, oil, and other products for institutions responded favorably to the plastic bag stored inside a cardboard box for easily dispensed liquids.

World plastics and resins output continued to rise through the late 1990s and early 2000s. During this period plastic was the most widely used material in the world, making it the material with the most product volume. Although some industrialized nations suffered a profit downturn spurred by overcapacity earlier in the decade, profits started to rise by the middle of the decade. In the mid-1990s, the plastics industry took advantage of limited supply and robust demand and obtained strong prices for plastic products. Asia drove the market with its expanding use of plastics, and by the mid-2000s the region was a greater producer and exporter of plastics, reversing its role as an importer. Escalating demand in the Asian market, especially China, prompted substantial expansion of petrochemical output in the Middle East. According to a *Forbes* report, synthetic resin production in the region from 2010 to 2015 is likely to be 33 percent higher than output in 2004. According to *Asia Intelligence Wire,* BASF forecast global plastics demand to grow 5 percent per year until 2015, due to rising standards of living, especially in Asia.

In 2003 and 2004, the European plastics industry encouraged visitors to click visit its Aquaplastics Web site. For every click, an arrangement was made to donate US10 cents to help WaterAid deliver clean water and sanitation to people in Madagascar and Malawi.

In May 2004, the General Assembly of the Association of Plastics Manufacturers in Europe voted to change its statutes and officially establish a new pan-European plastics association to be named PlasticsEurope. It represents plastics raw materials manufacturers and handles issues that affect plastics in general, as well as product-specific issues through a series of work groups.

CURRENT CONDITIONS

The increased demand for plastics in China was having an effect on the industry in the mid-2000s. China's per capita consumption of plastics was around 48 pounds in 2006, compared to 11 pounds in India and 300 pounds in the United States, according to *Plastics News.* Overall demand for plastics in China grew 10 percent in 2006, and the huge rise in the use of recycled plastic was affecting the production of virgin resin. In 2006, 5.8 million tons of all kinds of recycled or scrap polymers were imported into China, according to David Jiang of Sinodata in Beijing. China's capacity for plastics production was also increasing. In 2006 this increase totaled 7.5 million tons a year, and the government's five-year plan set a goal of adding 10.5 million tons of capacity annually by 2010. The increase in capacity was reflected in the figures for China's exports of finished plastic goods, which grew from less than 4.4 billion pounds in 1995 to almost 19.8 billion pounds in 2006.

Another trend of the latter mid-2000s was the increase in demand for plastic packaging as opposed to paper. According to the Freedonia Group, growth in demand for plastic packaging will outpace that of paper packaging by a 10:1 margin through 2010. Demand for plastic packaging was predicted to increase 2.9 percent a year compared to a 0.3 percent annual increase in paper packaging demand. Freedonia cited the reasons for the growth in the demand for plastic packaging as cost and performance advantages over paper. Segments of the market that were expected to see the most rapid growth included soy and other nondairy beverages, pet food, frozen food, fruit beverages, and detergent.

Recycling continued to be a major issue facing the industry in the mid-2000s. As plastic consumption has expanded, so have efforts in developed nations to reduce related environmental hazards. Environmentalists hoped that the recycling of plastics would become more common in both developed and developing nations. Technology was not a barrier; rather, problems with collection (i.e., separation of plastic wastes by resin type and cleaning the plastics) and the comparatively low cost of making new resins hampered recycling growth. In the mid-1990s biodegradable plastics started to look like a viable alternative to recycling; however, they were not cost effective. Depending on the resin type, biodegradable plastics cost between 2 and 15 times more than conventional plastics.

In the United States, initiatives at the local, state, and federal levels succeeded in increasing recycling of common consumer plastics, such as those used to make milk jugs and soft drink bottles. According to the American Chemistry Council, in 2005 U.S. consumers recycled a record 2.1 billion pounds of plastic bottles, an increase of 187 million pounds from 2004. However, efforts were hindered by many problems, including the high cost of recycled resin. Legislation was bolder in several European nations. For example, Germany and other countries enacted ordinances requiring recycling of transport packaging, and some even required 100 percent. Nonetheless, recycled plastics could not compete with new plastics even by the latter part of the decade, forcing major plastics producers to jettison their recycling operations or otherwise exit the recycling side of the business. Still, other companies inaugurated new recycling businesses even as others withdrew.

WORKFORCE

In the mid-2000s, the United States employed about 638,000 people in the plastics product manufacturing industry, 60 percent of whom were production workers. The average hourly salary for production workers in the industry in the United States was US$11.53 an hour in 2004.

RESEARCH AND TECHNOLOGY

Producers of plastics and resins rely heavily on research and development (R&D) to create potential markets for their products and to increase market share. Aside from creating better resins and plastics, research expenditures have also been applied to the reduction of pollutants emitted during the production process, recyclability, and improvement of manufacturing productivity. The bulk of R&D expenditures at the beginning of the 2000s was shouldered by Japan, North America, and Western Europe, which rely on technology to compete not only with each other, but with low-cost producers in emerging regions. In general, Japan spent the largest share of its gross domestic product on R&D, followed by Germany, the United States, and several Western European countries.

The majority of R&D in the early to mid-2000s centered on the creation of better polymers, resins, and additives. Producers successfully developed plastics that were stronger, lighter, more durable, easier to process, and cheaper to manufacture. Most major producers in developed regions were pursuing breakthroughs in areas such as conductivity and increased tensile strength in hopes of developing plastics to replace metals and other costly materials for appliance and automotive manufacturing. Specialty plastics are also necessary for markets such as the medical industry and the military.

On the environmental front, low styrene emission products received a great deal of attention because they were able to limit volatile organic compound (VOC) emissions during production. New resins were introduced that could be used to manufacture products such as carpet padding and packaging foams that emitted little, if any, chlorofluorocarbons (CFCs). New biodegradable plastics, including weak-link and bacterial polymers, also offered growth opportunities. Although the production cost of most biodegradable plastics was prohibitive when they were first introduced, costs were expected to fall as technology was refined. In 1997, DuPont and Bayer launched biodegradable plastics that could be molded easily and formed into blister packs, waste bags, and other plastic products. But because plant-based plastics have poor heat resistance, they are poorly suited for molding into larger rigid shapes useful in other industries. In 2005, the Fujitsu and Toray companies announced a joint venture that had developed a new plant-based plastic that blends polyactic acid with a non-crystalline plastic to improve heat-resistance and moldability. According to a Toray Industries report, the new substance is the first environmentally friendly plastic suitable for large-size plastic housing for laptop computers. Additional uses were also being explored.

Researchers have also looked for more efficient methods of recycling plastics, since separating different types of plastic can take a considerable amount of time and precision. To address this challenge, improved plastic testers have been developed to simplify the process. Identification devices, called the Tribopen and the Portasort, provide recyclers with a means of sorting plastics efficiently. Tribopen determines the type of plastic by reading its static electricity and is designed for recycling companies that specialize in only a few kinds of plastic, while the Portasort uses infrared spectroscope to identify the kinds of plastic and can be used to determine a more diverse mix of plastics.

INDUSTRY LEADERS

BASF Aktiengesellschaft. German-based BASF AG is the world's largest chemical company, edging out other top companies such as DuPont and Bayer AG. Although BASF was incorporated in 1952, its history dates back to the early 1860s. The company was formerly part of the mammoth German cartel IG Farben, which dominated the world chemical industry during the 1930s (see also **Industrial Organic Chemicals.**) The company rebounded after the war to become one of the world's major plastics and chemical producers.

BASF reported total sales of US$69.4 billion in 2006, up from US$51.5 billion in 2004 and a 37.2 percent increase from 2005. Above-average growth in its plastics segment was a major factor in the company's strong performance. Other segments included consumer products, dyes, oil and gas, and chemicals. The European market accounts for 60 percent of BASF's revenues. In all, BASF has more than 150 major manufacturing facilities and does business worldwide. In 2006 the firm employed 80,954 people. The company sold its fiber unit in 2003 to focus on core chemical operations. In 2006 the company purchased the chemicals division of Engelhard, which it renamed BASF Catalysts.

In June 2004 *Asia Intelligence Wire* announced Nizhnekamskneftekhim, a Russian petrochemicals plant, talked with BASF about expanding cooperative efforts. Working committees will evaluate relevant projects including setting up production of acrylic dispersions for building materials at the Russian company. In the same news item, it was revealed that BASF is interested in North America because the petrochemicals sector in North America and Western Europe was exhibiting a downward trend. In mid-2004, BASF also announced a new license deal with Bayer to make polyether polyols using Bayer's Impact technology. The technology specifies a process for polyalkoxylation that uses double metal cynanide as catalyst. BASF planned to cut its ABS product line from 15,000 grades to 10 because the material "has increasingly developed from a specialty into a standard product," according to a new wire report.

Bayer AG. Top-ranked competitor to BASF, Bayer AG is best known for its aspirin, but the company's production includes a wide variety of chemical-based goods. Bayer, like BASF, was spun off from IG Farben after World War II. Bayer competed closely with BASF throughout the 1990s and posted revenues of US$32.4 billion in 2006 with 93,700 employees. The company's diverse portfolio includes basic and fine chemicals, plastic colorants and inorganic pigments, and specialty chemicals for the paper and textile industries. Among the other industries served by Bayer Chemicals are wood, metal, leather, paints, plastics, energy, and electronics. It maintains operations in 50 countries worldwide. In 2005, Bayer spun off its separate chemicals subgroup, completely converting the subgroup into a publicly traded company operating under the new name of Lanxess. In June 2004, *Asia Intelligence Wire* issued several reports about Bayer Chemicals' takeover of production for all the biocidal formulations based on thiabendazole and dibromodicyanobutane that it acquired from Ondeo Nalco at the end of 2002. Bayer invested some US$500,000 in the expansion of production facilities in Wellford, South Carolina, to service the global market. Another important acquisition included the US$20 billion purchase of pharmaceuticals giant Schering in 2006.

The Dow Chemical Company. The largest chemical company in the United States and the second-largest in the world, Dow Chemical is a leading manufacturer of engineering plastics, polyurethanes, and polyethylene resins for packaging, fibers, and films. The company includes six operating segments: Performance Plastics, Performance Chemicals, Agricultural Sciences, Plastics, Chemicals, and its smallest division, Hydrocarbons and Energy. In 2006, Dow had 165 manufacturing facilities in 37 countries, and employed almoast 43,000 people. Total sales in 2006 reached a record US$49.1 billion. Much of this growth was due to price increases, which grew by an average 24 percent in this segment between 2003 and 2004, while volume grew by an average of only 5 percent. Sales grew 32 percent for polyethylene, 34 percent for polypropylene, and 44 percent for polystyrene. In 2007 the company made more than 3,000 products.

Eastman Chemical Company. Eastman Chemical Company was separated in the 1980s from the Eastman Kodak Company, which traced its roots back to the late 1800s. Eastman Kodak was a pioneer in the global plastics industry and was credited with a number of innovations and improvements. In 2006, Eastman Chemical generated sales of about US$7.4 billion and employed a workforce of 12,000. The company manufactures a broad line of plastics materials for industrial customers specializing in high-performance plastics and related chemical products. The company's Peformance Polymers division is the world's largest manufacturer of polyethlene terephthalate (PET). PET is used in packaging for food and pharmaceutical products. In May 2004 the U.S. International Trade Commission ruled that there is a reasonable indication that the US domestic PET industry is being damaged by subsidized imports from Indonesia, India, Thailand, and Taiwan. The investigation was launched after complaints by DAK Americas, Nan Ya Plastics, Wellman, and Voridian. In 2006, Simon Moorhouse of Chemical Market Associates Inc. predicted in *Plastics News* that PET demand would grow faster than capacity through 2011. The journal estimated demand would grow an average of 7.2 percent annually, whereas capacity would increase only 4.5 percent per year.

MAJOR COUNTRIES IN THE INDUSTRY

United States. The United States was the leading producer of plastics materials and resins in the mid-2000s, and production and sales continued to grow. The economic slump after 2001 contributed to relatively flat volumes and sales through 2003, but according to data posted by the American Plastics Council, output of resins increased by 8.1 percent in 2004, reaching 115.1 billion pounds, while sales and captive use grew by 6.9 percent, the highest rate of growth since 1996. The United States accounted for more than 50 percent of global production and consumption following World War II, but its dominance waned as Western European and Japanese competitors gained a foothold during the mid- to late 1990s. The United States continues to trade as a net exporter. Among other advantages, producers in the United States benefit from extensive experience in the field, a strong technology base, and immediate access to the largest plastics market in the world.

In 2003, the U.S. plastics materials and resins market grew by 2.9 percent to reach almost US$53 billion. About 83.3 percent of value sales were attributed to thermoplastics (polyethylene and polypropylene products). Resin production grew 6.4 percent in 2004. In 2006, the U.S. plastic resins industry rebounded from the affects of the major hurricanes on the Gulf coast in 2005, registering a 3.1 percent increase from 2005. According to the American Chemistry Council, U.S. plastics and resin production reached 113.2 billion pounds in 2006, and total sales grew 2.2 percent to 113.0 billion pounds.

In 2004, the United States exported US$3.7 billion worth of polyethylenes and US$1.05 billion of amino resins, phenolics, and polyurethanes. Mexico was the primary destination for polyethylenes (US$936.9 million), followed by Canada, Belgium, and China. In 2006, U.S. exports of plastic resins increased 13.3 percent to a record $32.5 billion. Imports also increased in 2006, up 8.2 percent to $18.8 billion, another record.

Japan. At the beginning of the 2000s Japan ranked second in the industry with about 15 percent of global production. Most plastics in Japan, as in other industrialized nations, are produced as side businesses by large, diversified chemical and petroleum concerns. Japan enjoyed steady output gains during the 1980s as doméstic demand for plastics surged. Japan's broader recession in the 1990s was intensified for the plastics industry by proliferating competition from low-cost producers in South Korea, Taiwan, and China. Although production fell in the early 1990s, it rebounded in the mid-1990s. Increased domestic consumption and exports fueled the recovery. In the long term, Japanese producers sought to take advantage of increased regional demand for high-margin, high-performance resins and materials; some have also opted to transfer production of low-margin products to lower-wage economies.

Japan remains a major trading partner with the United States in the plastics materials and resins market. In 2004, Japan exported US$254.7 million of PVCs to the United States, making it the second-largest supplier behind Canada. Japan also ranked second in exports to the United States of polypropylenes and other olefins. Japan was the third-leading supplier of amino resins, phenolics, and polyurethanes, as well as polyamides.

Germany With approximately 10 percent of the global plastics market in the early 2000s, Germany was the industry's third-largest producer, with sales totaling US$58 billion in 2000. An industry pioneer, Germany continued to play a prominent technological role, investing heavily in research and development. Nevertheless, Germany's plastic materials and resins market shrank by 4.7 percent between 2002 and 2003, reaching an output of 13.9 million tons. Other technical plastics remained the largest market for plastics materials and resins, and industry analysts expected this sector to grow by about 1.9 percent through 2008. Other European countries were the primary market by far for Germany's plastic materials and resins sales, with Europe accounting for about 70 percent of exports and 80 percent of imports by volume. Euromonitor expected the German plastic materials and resins market to grow in volume by 6.3 percent by 2008.

The expansion of the construction industry in Germany was partly responsible for the upswing in the plastics industry in 2006 in Europe. Along with growth in France and a revitalized Eastern Europe, demand in Germany helped increase the plastics construction sector by approximately 2.8 percent in 2006. The overall plastics industry in Europe grew 3.9 percent that year, according to *Plastics News*.

FURTHER READING

American Chemistry Council. "ACC Released December 2006 Resin Production and Sales Stats." 28 February 2007. Available from www.americanchemistry.com.

———. "Plastic Bottle Recycling Reaches Record High of More Than 2 Billion Pounds Annually." 5 February 2007. Available from www.americanchemistry.com.

———. "U.S. Plastic Resins Industry Rebounds in 2006.". 5 April 2007. Available from www.americanchemistry.com.

Clayton, Mark. "Popular Plastic in Crosshairs." *Christian Science Monitor,* 17 March 2005.

Esposito, Frank. "Materials Briefs." *Plastics News,* 9 April 2007.

"Fujitsu and Toray Develop World's First Environmentally-Friendly Large-Size Plastic Housing for Notebook PCs." Toray Industries, Inc., 18 January 2005. Available from www.toray.com.

Higgs, Richard. "Europe's Processors Expect More Growth." *Plastics News,* 15 January 2007.

"Hoover's Company Capsules." Hoover's, Inc, 2007. Available from www.hoovers.com.

International Trade Association (ITA). *Trends Tables: Plastics Materials and Resins (SIC 2821).* U.S. Census Bureau, 2005. Available from www.tse.export.gov.

Martin, Mitchell. "The World Tilts Toward China." *Forbes,* 5 April 2004. Available from www.forbest.com.

Nina Ying Sun. "Foreign Firms Plan for Growth." *Plastics News,* 2 April 2007.

"Plastic Materials and Resins in Germany." *Euromonitor Reports,* 2004. Available from www.euronomitor.com.

"Plastic Materials and Resins in the USA." Euromonitor International, October 2004. Available from www.euromonitor.com.

Spaulding, Mark. "Plastics Demand Outpaces Paper 10:1." *Converting,* 1 February 2007.

"Thermoplastic Elastomers—Is It Still a Specialty Market?" 2005. Available from www.chemicals.frost.com.

"U.S. Plastic Resins Growth Surges in 2004." American Plastics Council, 10 March 2005. Available from www.apcnewsmedia.com.

SIC 3000

NAICS 326

RUBBER PRODUCTS, FABRICATED

Fabricated rubber products include a diverse assortment of goods made from both natural and synthetic rubber. Important product categories include rubber belts and hoses, rubberized fabrics, rubber gaskets and seals, rubber tubing, and mechanical rubber components.

Tires, which account for roughly 50 percent of the world's rubber output, are discussed separately under **Tires and Inner Tubes.**

INDUSTRY SNAPSHOT

The world tire and rubber market reached $53.3 billion in 2003, an increase of 3.6 percent from the previous year, and is forecast to climb 25.7 percent to reach $66.93 billion by 2008. According to the Rubber Manufacturers Association, in 2005 some 60 percent of all rubber produced was used for tires, with the remaining amount distributed among all other applications. Fabricated rubber products are often used as intermediaries for products in other industries: more than 80 percent of the industry's output is channeled into other products, including motor vehicle parts, sports equipment, and a wide variety of other applications. In the late 1990s synthetic rubber accounted for approximately 65 percent of all rubber production. About one-fourth of all synthetic rubber is used in the production of tires. In the mid-2000s, the world's top rubber manufacturers were Bridgestone, Michelin, and Goodyear. By that time, U.S. rubber plants were looking at ways to reduce emissions of cancer-causing 1,3-butadiene, among other air pollution toxicants.

By product type, world rubber consumption has changed little since the mid-1980s. The industry is now characterized as quite mature, with intense competition and enormous sales, but with relatively low profits. Immediately following the conclusion of World War II, the United States held more than 50 percent of the world's rubber market share. During the mid-twentieth century, Japan, Western Europe, and the Soviet Union joined the United States as leading producers of rubber goods. Since the 1980s, a chief industry trend has been increased production by emerging industrial powers in Latin America and Asia. Some industry analysts contend that long-term growth in rubber products shipments will mirror gains in global economic growth, with demand for non-tire applications increasing most quickly.

ORGANIZATION AND STRUCTURE

Rubber products are manufactured with both natural and synthetic materials. Natural rubber is a yellowish, elastic substance tapped from various tropical plants, particularly the renowned rubber tree. Synthetic rubber usually starts out as petroleum or coke (a distillate of coal) and is created through a process of polymerization whereby molecules are rearranged to resemble long chains. The resulting substance is a tacky, soft thermoplastic (a substance that can be re-melted and manipulated) that resembles natural rubber. Most synthetic rubber is produced in equatorial regions in Asia, Africa, and South America. Much of that output is shipped to developed nations for the manufacture of tires and other goods. Natural rubber is more commonly manufactured in the United States, Japan, Europe, and the Commonwealth of Independent States (CIS).

Natural rubber offers a narrow range of grades and characteristics in comparison to synthetic rubber, but it proffers superior attributes important to the manufacture of many products. Natural rubber is strong, sticky, resilient, fatigue-resistant, and has outstanding tensile strength. Those traits are necessary in products that require low heat build-up, tear resistance, and the ability to withstand repeated flexing. A common example of such an application is that of tire sidewalls. Natural rubber also is desirable as a latex for dipped rubber products such as condoms and surgical gloves. A chief disadvantage of natural rubber in comparison to synthetic rubber is poor resistance to oxygen, oil, and other natural elements.

The four primary stages of the manufacturing process for dry rubber goods are preparing the raw rubber, compounding, shaping, and vulcanizing. Compounding entails mixing rubber and chemicals to create different types and grades of rubber, and synthetic rubber and natural rubber are often combined during this stage of the manufacturing process. Rubber characteristics can be modified during this production step with additives and processing agents such as accelerators, antioxidants, flame retardants, and stabilizers. The goal is to produce rubber materials with the traits needed for specific applications. During the shaping and vulcanization processes, the rubber is formed and treated with heat and chemicals to contribute properties such as resilience and elasticity. The end product typically cannot be re-melted and formed.

Chief benefits of rubber products, as opposed to goods produced from other natural and man-made materials, include poor electrical conductivity; the ability to flex and regain an original shape; low production costs; and, particularly in the case of synthetic rubber, resistance to corrosion and breakdown caused by exposure to fluids and gases. Those characteristics have made rubber a desirable substance in demanding applications such as automobile tires and account for rubber's reputation as an ideal substitute for wood, ceramics, metals, and fibers. In addition to tires, the largest rubber production category, other major rubber product segments include vehicle parts such as hoses and belts; wire and cable covering; clothing and footwear; construction materials such as roofing products and geo-textiles; consumer items; and latex goods such as gloves and adhesives.

COMPETITIVE STRUCTURE

The rubber products industry is a mature one. New products play an important role, but producers compete largely on price. Factors such as high productivity, control of raw material resources, diverse markets, and economies of scale are thus crucial to a company's success or failure in the industry. The industry is highly consolidated and market leaders are entrenched. Many of them are integrated, with vast holdings of rubber plantations in developing nations. They are also heavily dependent on exports and invest extensively in foreign manufacturing operations. Major barriers to entry for new competitors, particularly in the tire segment, include massive start-up costs and technological expertise.

REGULATIONS

The rubber products industry is heavily impacted by both national and international regulations. In addition to tariff and trade restrictions that typify most commodity-like industries, environmental regulations were increasingly impacting producers in the 1990s. Rubber's longevity, combined with problems related to toxicity of manufacturing processes, have forced the industry to comply with pollution-related initiatives designed to blunt the impact of rubber manufacturing on the environment. Manufacturers have increasingly been forced to help find—and pay for—solutions. On the production side, proliferating national legislation in the mid-1990s in some countries sought to reduce toxic emissions of nitrosamines and other substances. Nitrosamines, a suspected human carcinogen, are released during the compounding, forming, and vulcanization process. Regulations designed to control emissions of such manufacturing by-products have in some cases resulted in higher manufacturing costs and reduced competitiveness of producers in developed regions.

BACKGROUND AND DEVELOPMENT

The rubber products industry dates back to at least the fifteenth century, when European explorers witnessed natives in the New World using latex to make bouncing balls, bottles, waterproof apparel, syringes, and other items. What was later called rubber first came to Europe in 1521, when Aztecs transported from Mexico played a game using a rubber ball in front of the Spanish royal court. In the early 1700s, rubber products made by Native Americans aroused the interest of the European scientific and professional community. In the 1750s, for example, Parisian architects discovered that rubbing the substance on pencil marks would erase them—hence the name "rubber." By the late eighteenth century and early nineteenth century, rubber was utilized in a number of applications.

One of the first manufacturers of rubber goods on record, a rubber band maker, was founded in 1803 near Paris. In 1811, J.N. Reithoffer opened another rubber goods factory in Vienna. During the mid-1830s, a recognizable rubber products industry emerged in Europe, North America, and a few other regions. The fledgling industry developed an international flavor as well. Rubber grown in the Amazon, for example, was made into rubber shoes in Brazil and then exported for sale in the northeastern United States.

Boosting industry growth during the period were several major technological advances. American Edward M. Chaffe invented a rubber milling and rolling machine in 1836. Nicknamed "The Monster," the machine weighed 30 tons. More importantly, American Charles Goodyear discovered the vulcanization process in 1839. That breakthrough eliminated many of rubber's drawbacks—most notably, susceptibility to temperature changes—and made the substance a desirable ingredient in the production of a broad new range of goods.

During the mid-nineteenth century, vulcanized rubber was used in industrializing nations to make toys, dipped products, clothing, and other goods. A pivotal event in the industry's development, though, was Germany's introduction in the 1880s of the automobile, which used rubber tires. During the early 1900s, mass automobile production was pioneered in the United States, spawning what would soon become a massive rubber tire industry. By the late 1930s, automobile tires were consuming the lion's share of global rubber output and the United States had assumed the global rubber products industry lead. Global production of rubber goods exploded during and after World War II, as reflected by a rise in rubber consumption from 1.25 million metric tons in 1940 to 2.59 million by 1950. By 1960 rubber goods manufacturers were devouring about 9 million metric tons of rubber annually.

Concurrent with and contributing to huge gains in rubber output during the mid-twentieth century was the introduction and popularization of synthetic rubber. Although scientists had made advances related to synthetic rubber, it was not until 1910 that Russian chemist S.V. Lebedev polymerized butadiene to produce the first commercially viable synthetic rubber. Germany and Russia were producing synthetic rubber commercially by the 1930s. Other nations joined them during World War II, as global output of synthetic rubber products lurched from about 10,000 tons in 1935 to more than one million tons by 1944. Synthetic rubber output even surpassed natural rubber production for a few years in the early 1940s due to the war. Nevertheless, superior natural rubber products continued to dominate the market through the 1950s and 1960s.

Major scientific advancements quickly boosted synthetic rubber's share of the market, however. German chemists Karl Ziegler and Giulio Natta discovered a polymerization process that created synthetic rubber virtually identical in molecular structure to natural rubber. In addition, new additives, processing, and molding techniques were pioneered. Synthetic rubber output ballooned during the 1960s from about 2 million metric tons in 1960 to roughly 6 million by the early 1960s. By the 1970s, rubber goods producers were consuming around 9 million metric tons of synthetic rubber annually, as well as about 4 million tons of natural rubber.

Industry growth was driven primarily by the global explosion of the car and truck industries. Between 1950 and 1980, annual worldwide tire production vaulted from 133 million to about 657 million. The evolution of synthetics allowed manufacturers in industrialized nations to displace equatorial countries as the leading suppliers of rubber.

Growth of the rubber goods industry slowed considerably in the mid-1970s for several reasons. Importantly, the huge postwar economic boom, highlighted by the growth of the automobile industry in North America and Europe, had come to an end. Other factors that squelched gains in rubber goods output included rising energy prices, which heightened the cost of synthetic rubber; a global trend toward smaller cars and, therefore, smaller tires; and the development of long-lasting radial tires that diminished the tire-replacement market. The mature industry registered only modest production gains during the 1980s. Total global rubber output increased from 12 to 13 million metric tons in 1980 to about 15 million by 1990. Much of the growth that did take place was the result of increased demand by rubber products manufacturers for natural rubber rather than synthetic rubber.

In addition to increased use of natural rubber in relation to synthetic rubber, another rubber products industry trend during the 1980s and 1990s was greater production of non-tire rubber goods. While consumption by rubber goods producers of both natural rubber and synthetic rubber for the manufacture of tires in the United States, Japan, and Germany rose 14 percent—to nearly 3 million metric tons—during that period, growth in the non-tire market was significantly higher. During the same period, rubber consumption for non-tire goods in those countries jumped more than 30 percent, to about 2.4 million tons. While tires still accounted for about 50 percent of industry output in the mid-1990s, that share was expected to fall. Major product segments driving non-tire industry expansion included automotive belts, hoses, gaskets, and moldings; adhesives, padding, belting, wire sheathing, and other industrial items; toys, door moldings, sporting equipment and other consumer goods; and construction products like roofing, sealants, and exterior moldings.

Current Conditions

While output of rubber products in developed nations slowed or stagnated, production in developing regions surged during the 1990s and continued in the 2000s. Bolstered by low production costs, loose regulatory environments, and access to growing markets, among other advantages, manufacturers in emerging industrial regions advanced greatly in comparison to their Western and Japanese peers. Areas realizing the greatest market share gains included South America and Asia, particularly the countries of Brazil, Mexico, China, and South Korea. Many industry analysts expect an even greater reshuffling among world producers as China takes on a more preeminent role in the world trade community. As developing nations vied for world rubber product market share, producers in developed nations scrambled to increase competitiveness and open new markets for rubber goods.

A potentially serious threat to the rubber products industry, and what has been characterized as an open secret within the industry, is the biological threat posed by a pest in the major Southeast Asia producers. The South China Sea-area plantations, which are the source for about 90 percent of the world's natural rubber, are the product of a genetic clone derived from plants in the Amazon more than 100 years ago. Unfortunately, a fungal pestilence that rendered cultivation of rubber in that region nearly impossible has found its way to Southeast Asia. While some industry insiders remain confident in the ability of synthetic rubber technology to make up for a decrease in natural rubber production, this potentially dramatic threat could have drastic consequences on a variety of industries. Many products, analysts note, have no potential substitute for natural rubber.

Advances in technology are looked upon as a vital area of development for rubber product manufacturers. Much of this technology, however, inherently limits the growth of sales volume. For instance, one of the primary concerns of manufacturers is greater durability of products, especially in the tire market. Because technological innovations are one of the prime selling points in this mature industry, the search for durability must be a major focus for producers who want to attract customers. For example, because tires generally do not perform properly after they are six years old, the feasibility of tire expiration dates was being considered. By early 2004, in fact, the National Highway Traffic Safety Administration was conducting multi-year studies on the correlation between tire durability and tire age, in order to determine if lab trials could accurately mimic tire aging and performance.

Another concern is the use of recycled rubber in new products. According to the Rubber Manufacturers Association, by the mid-2000s, about three-fourths of scrap tires were used annually for end use markets, of which the highest growing segment was civil engineering applications. The forecast was for annual growth in this area to increase exponentially, from 20 to 50 percent. Sales of industrial rubber products were forecast to grow 5 percent annually to more than $16 billion by 2008, according to a report published by the Freedonia Group.

RESEARCH AND TECHNOLOGY

The rubber products industry is heavily impacted by technological changes that contribute to the production of materials that are less expensive and feature desirable properties (such as moldability, strength, and flexibility). The greatest focus is given to the modification of existing polymers rather than on the development of new ones. The battle to utilize new technology to gain a competitive edge was particularly in evidence in the tire industry in the 1990s. Midway through the decade, manufacturers in that segment hoped to create tire products that would reduce rolling resistance, improve vehicle handling in harsh weather, and improve tire function after air loss. Significant advances had already been made in these and other performance areas since the late 1980s. By the mid-1990s, tire warranties had increased from 20,000 to 30,000 miles, on average, to as high as 80,000 miles. Other advances included models that reduced hydroplaning and non-pneumatic spare tires that were puncture-proof and weighed 20 percent less than conventional pneumatic mini-spares.

Consumers are becoming increasingly aware of the sheer volume of tires and other rubber products that must be disposed of every year. Not surprisingly, rubber manufacturers are feeling pressure from the public and environmental groups to address the need to dispose of used rubber responsibly. Researchers are tackling issues of recycling and long-term deterioration in hopes of curbing problems. As researchers learn more about different kinds of rubber and their production, they also are better able to protect employees from potentially carcinogenic emissions.

The product development process also accelerated during the early and mid-1990s through increased use of computer-aided design (CAD) systems. CAD allowed both tire and non-tire rubber products to be modeled and tested quickly by computer. Other notable areas of research in the 1990s related to reducing environmental hazards resulting from the production and disposal of rubber goods. In the early 1990s alone, new strategies for making use of old tires had resulted in a huge climb in the percentage of scrap tires reclaimed for other uses. In the United States, the largest tire-consuming nation in the world, that percentage jumped from less than 10 percent in 1990 to nearly 60 percent in 1996. New uses included paving materials, fuel, outdoor furniture, and artificial reefs.

Many rubber products manufacturers are looking to the chemistry field as a source of development, concentrating on the mixing process of their rubber supplies. Realizing that inefficiencies and missteps in this stage of the process can greatly exacerbate problems and add to costs later in the production process, manufacturers are working to perfect mix-design systems. One solution involves the increased reliability of temperature control within the mixer. Another innovation is a process called surface modification, in which scrap rubber reacts with gases, producing an irreversible chemical change, the result of which then bonds with other materials. This process is used primarily in the production of sealants.

In 2003, research in New Zealand found that scrap tires were a potential source of carbon for water treatment. When tires go through pyrolysis, activated carbon is produced, an element used to purify drinking water. If the use of this form of carbon is proven successful, such use of scrap tires would reduce the need to use up natural resources such as wood and coal in order to manufacture the carbon.

WORKFORCE

The rubber products industry workforce is primarily employed by large, multinational companies in developed nations. Partly because of the strong labor union presence, workers in the industry are well paid in comparison to most other industries. Workers in some European nations, particularly Germany, received higher salaries than their U.S. counterparts. The 1,229 American firms that manufacture fabricated rubber products, not including tires, employed about 90,093 people earning a total of $3.8 billion in 2002.

Most growth in the rubber products workforce in the 2000s was occurring in such emerging industrial powers as South Korea, China, and Brazil. While wages in those nations have improved somewhat in recent years, they remain quite low compared with those of traditional powers. Compensation in less developed rubber-producing regions—such as Malaysia, Indonesia, and Thailand—remained low as well. Wages for workers in those nations, which typically export most of their rubber and manufacture few products, ranged from about US$35 to US$150 per month. This state of affairs provided emerging nations with an important competitive advantage over companies in the United States, Japan, and Western Europe.

INDUSTRY LEADERS

BRIDGESTONE CORP.

Headquartered in Japan, Bridgestone is the world's largest tire manufacturer. In fact, tires account for fully 80 percent of the company's annual revenues, which totaled US$23.4 billion in 2004. The company was founded in 1931 as a general rubber products firm and became the leading Japanese tire producer during the mid-twentieth century. The company bolted to global leadership with the 1988 acquisition of Firestone, the U.S. tire leader. The company started out making rubber-soled footwear for Firestone's family clothing business. Tires were added in 1923 and, with Ford Motor Company as a major customer, Firestone became one of the big three tire makers in Akron, Ohio, which was dubbed the "Rubber Capital" of the world. The company opened factories in Indonesia, Singapore, and Thailand during the 1950s before expanding throughout the world in the 1960s, 1970s, and 1980s.

Bridgestone came under fire in 2001 when a widespread tire recall was initiated after the discovery that Ford Explorers were outfitted with faulty tires. Litigation mounted, and the fiasco ended Bridgestone's ninety-five-year relationship with Ford. By 2003 the company was back in control, and 2003 revenues rose more than 13 percent over 2002 levels. However, Bridgestone voluntarily recalled nearly 300,000 Steeltex tires in 2004 as a result of a class action lawsuit alleging design defects.

COMPAGNIE GENERALE DES ESTABLISSEMENTS MICHELIN

The world's second largest tire maker, Michelin makes 36,000 products, including tires for cars, aircraft, and motorcycles. Besides the Michelin brand, the company also owns BF Goodrich, Uniroyal, Kleber in Europe, and Warrior in China. The company operates seventeen plants in North America. Revenues in 2003 totaled US$19.3 billion.

GOODYEAR TIRE & RUBBER CO.

Goodyear Tire & Rubber Co. is the third largest tire manufacturer in the world. It is named after the inventor of the vulcanization process, and was founded in 1898 by Frank A. Sieberling. The company produces a wide range of rubber products, including belts, hoses, and other rubber products, for the transportation industry and for various industrial and consumer markets in addition to its core tire business. The company also sells Dunlop tires. Goodyear led the industry in international expansion before World War II and is credited with major innovations related to all-weather tires. It became the global tire industry leader during the mid-1990s, largely as a result of its strength in the expanding North American economy. Goodyear assumed significant debt in 1986 as part of an effort to avert takeover attempts by foreign suitors. Indeed, the merger and acquisition binge of the late 1980s made Goodyear and the Cooper Tire & Rubber Co. the only major domestically owned tire manufacturers in the United States by the early 1990s. Goodyear was aligned with Sumitomo Rubber Industries of Japan. The company generated sales of US$18.37 billion in 2004, up 21.5 percent from the previous year, and employed about 84,000 workers in 95 plants.

CONTINENTAL AG

Germany's Continental AG captured U.S. tire giant General Tire in 1987, dramatically expanding its scope. Continental's 2004 revenues totaled US$17.18 billion, of which the vast majority was derived from Europe. In addition to the Continental brand, the company sold Uniroyal and General tires.

MAJOR COUNTRIES IN THE INDUSTRY

THE UNITED STATES

The United States maintained its long-time position as the largest supplier of rubber products in the world throughout the 1990s and 2000s. The U.S. rubber goods industry was started in 1833 when the Roxbury India Rubber Company opened a rubber shoe factory in Connecticut. The nation assumed an early global lead when, in the early 1900s, it became the first nation to mass-produce automobiles. Although European nations challenged U.S. dominance during World War II, the United States emerged as the dominant global supplier of rubber products. The United States, in fact, supplied more than 50 percent of global rubber products demand in the late 1940s. Although the country continued to lead production, its share of the global market steadily declined to less than 25 percent by the 1990s. In 1990, manufacturing operations located in the United States accounted for 28 percent and 16 percent of international car tire and truck tire output, respectively.

In 2004, the United States produced more than 318 million tires with an expected increase of 6.1 million in 2005 to nearly 325 million tires. By 2010, tire production was forecast to reach 355 million. U.S. producers were churning out about US$21.3 billion worth of other rubber goods. There are more than 1,225 firms, more than a third of which are in the Midwest, manufacturing fabricated rubber products and another 139 making tires and inner tubes. Major trade areas include the NAFTA region (Mexico and Canada) and Western Europe. The fastest-growing trade region for U.S. rubber products manufacturers is Latin America. Although its leadership in the industry was acknowledged, U.S. global market share was difficult to precisely determine for several reasons. The United States commonly exports rubber goods that are subsequently imported back into the country on cars. Moreover, U.S. manufacturers were active in joint ventures and had investments in rubber companies throughout the world. Importantly, the 1980s and early 1990s were marked by heavy foreign investment that placed control of major North American producers in the hands of European and Japanese competitors.

RUSSIA

Russia is another major producer of rubber products. This country was an early leader in the production of synthetic rubber and related products, accounting for the bulk of world output during the early 1900s. Although it was eventually surpassed by the United States, the Soviet Union continued to boost production. During the 1980s, in fact, the Soviets increased synthetic rubber output from about 2.0 million metric tons to about 2.4 million metric tons, surpassing production in the United States. The rubber was used primarily to supply growing rubber products industries, many of which were military-related, throughout Russia and the Eastern Bloc. Total Soviet output of tires, for example, surged from 32.7 million in 1980 to about 51.4 million by 1990. Soviet output of synthetic rubber and related products plunged following the disintegration of the Soviet Union and the entire Eastern Bloc in 1991, however. In 2000, total tire production in Russia was more than 28.0 million units. Sales to individuals increased compared to 1999 figures, but commercial sales decreased, for a net increase in total sales of only 0.5 percent from 1999.

JAPAN

Japan achieved its position as a world leader in the rubber products industry by developing the biggest automobile industry in the world. Over half the rubber, by weight, in Japan was consumed by tire producers in the 1990s. As car production surged, Japanese tire output jumped from about 111 million units annually in 1980 to 150 million by 1990. Output of other vehicle-related products—gaskets, belts, and hoses—rose similarly. Japan displaced France in the early 1980s as the leading exporter of rubber goods. Growth of Japan's rubber goods sector slowed in the early 1990s, partly because of a domestic economic slowdown. Japanese producers also were plagued by increased competition from low-cost competitors in neighboring nations such as China and South Korea. To combat the threat, Japanese companies in the mid-1990s increasingly turned to investments and the establishment of links with companies in South Korea and Taiwan, among other areas. In 2002, Japan produced some 168 million tires and 41 million in the first quarter of 2003. Four of the top ten tire manufacturers in the world were based in Japan. They were Bridgestone (first), Sumitomo Rubber Industries (fifth), Yokohama Rubber Co. Ltd. (seventh), and Toyo Tire & Rubber Co. Ltd. (ninth). In addition, Bridgestone was the top producer of non-tire rubber products in the mid-2000s.

EUROPE

The other major players in the rubber industry are Germany and France, which both helped to pioneer the synthetic rubber and related goods industries during the early twentieth century. Synthetic rubber output in both countries was roughly equal throughout the middle of the century. West Germany, however, buoyed by its giant automobile industry, gained on France during the 1980s and 1990s. Both countries registered significant increases in rubber goods exports. German and French rubber products industries invested heavily in U.S. companies during the late 1980s. Although German and French rubber product manufacturers chafe under environmental and labor restrictions, both countries will likely retain leadership roles in the industry in the long term. Germany's growth, however, outpaced France's at the turn of the millennium. Germany's total output in 2002 was more than 69.3 million tires compared to France's 60.9 million.

EMERGING NATIONS

Among the fastest-growing national competitors in the mid-2000s were China, Brazil, South Korea, Indonesia, and Malaysia. Although these nations played relatively small roles in the rubber products industry during the mid-twentieth century, they benefited during the 1980s and early 1990s from strong domestic demand and hefty export gains. Low production costs and protected domestic markets were key advantages. Combined tire shipments in those three countries ballooned more than 90 percent between 1980 and 1990, to about 90 million units. Simultaneously, production of synthetic rubber rose to more than 1 million metric tons by the late 1990s. Indonesia's non-tire rubber industry grew significantly in the mid to late 1990s, specializing in rubber fabricated for sports shoes, latex gloves, hoses, belts, seals, and sports equipment. South Korea has become a major contender in the tire market since the late 1990s. Its production of 70 million units represented an increase of almost 7 percent over 1999. This volume, combined with the high growth rate, suggests that South Korea may not be considered merely an emerging market for long. China, which had tire output of 160 million in 2002, earned approximately $4 billion in the tire market in 2003, which amounted to about 5 percent of the world's total.

FURTHER READING

"About Us." Rubber Manufacturers Association. 2005. Available from http://www.rma.org.

"The American Synthetic Rubber Company Announced Last Week That It Will Be Installing a New Pollution Control Device." *Pesticide & Toxic Chemical News,* 24 May 2004.

"Bridgestone Recalls More Tires." *Claims,* April 2004.

"China is a Double-Edged Sword for Rubber Industry, Bryne Warns." *Rubber & Plastics News,* 4 April 2005.

Draper, Deborah J., ed. *Business Rankings Annual.* Detroit: Thomson Gale, 2004.

"European Car Sales Down Six Percent in November." *European Rubber Journal,* September 2003.

"Growth in Tire Shipments to Accelerate in 2004." Rubber Manufacturers Association. 19 April 2004. Available from http://www.rma.org.

"Global Tires & Rubber." *Datamonitor Industry Profile.* May 2004. Available from http://www.datamonitor.com.

Harris InfoSource. *Rubber and Plastics Products: Industry Breakdown, 1997-2001.* Harris InfoSource International, Inc., 2002.

Hoover's Company Capsules. 2005. Available from http://www.hoovers.com.

"International Trade Statistics." 2005. Available from http://www.wto.org.

Lazich, Robert S., ed. *Market Share Reporter.* Detroit: Thomson Gale, 2004.

"New York Enacts Scrap Tire Program." *US Newswire,* 15 May 2003.

"Predicted Growth of Tread Rubber Shipments to Continue." Rubber Manufacturers Association. 19 March 2004. Available from http://www.rma.org.

"Report Says Amount of Cancer-Causing Agents on the Rise in Louisville Air." *Respiratory Therapeutics Week,* 5 April 2004.

"Requested: A Use-By Date for Tires." *Consumer Reports,* January 2004.

"World Top 50: Non-Tire Rubber Products." *Rubber and Plastics News,* 9 July 2001. Available from http://www.rubbernews.com.

"Scrap Tire Clean Up and Market Development Efforts Improving." *US Newswire,* 5 December 2002.

"Tire Shipments Expected to Increase in 2005." *Rubber Manufacturers Association Website.* 29 April 2005. Available from http://www.rma.org.

SIC 3011

NAICS 326211

TIRES AND INNER TUBES

Known in British usage as "tyres," this industry's output includes tires and inner tubes for all types of vehicles, aircraft, bicycles, motorcycles, and farm equipment.

INDUSTRY SNAPSHOT

The global tires and rubber industry was valued at $53.3 billion in 2003. A mature industry, growth rates in most regions continued to be relatively small, with little possibility of a projected dramatic increase. Most large tire makers experienced a surge in sales in the mid-2000s due to the robust economies of North America, Europe, and Asia, and as the global economy improved from the beginning of the decade. Worldwide, demand was expected to rise about 25.7 percent by 2008 to reach a value of $66.9 billion.

In April 2004, the Rubber Manufacturers Association revealed that U.S. tire shipments increased 0.6 percent from 2002 to 2003, supported mainly by the replacement tire market. However, in 2004 the association expected shipment growth to reach 3.2 percent, fueled by general economic improvement and recovery within the commercial trucking industry. Tire shipments were expected to grow at an annualized rate of 2 percent into the late 2000s, rising from 310 million units in 2003 to 350 million through 2009.

Heading into the mid-2000s, the industry was dominated by a cosmopolitan array of seven multinational corporations—one headquartered in France, one in the United States, three in Japan, one in Germany, and one in Italy. Although the industry's top seven companies shared more than 73 percent of worldwide sales in 2002 (the top three alone accounted for nearly 56 percent), manufacturing of tires—a long-established commodity—is characterized by intense competition, most of which takes place in the realm of product development and innovation, though not always to the benefit of sales figures. A spate of mergers in the late 1980s and early 1990s presaged an intense examination of capacity, employment levels, and productivity. The top players in the global tire industry, as in the automobile industry to which it is closely allied, purchased or moved production facilities in order to reduce labor costs, take advantage of currency fluctuations, and circumvent trade limitations. Dominant concerns of these leaders included reduction of acquisition-related debt and overhead, retention and augmentation of market share, and recycling of waste tires.

Many industry observers have pointed to the strategic alliance between Goodyear and Sumitomo Rubber, which allowed Goodyear to make Dunlop tires in North America and Europe and Sumitomo to make Goodyear tires in Japan, as the precursor to another industry reshuffling mirroring, albeit on a smaller scale, the consolidation of the late 1980s. The second-tier firms—those falling just below the "Big Three" of Bridgestone, Michelin, and Goodyear in sales—are likely to get squeezed between their larger multinational competitors and the smaller regional and niche market firms. Some analysts believe that alliances with the Big Three will be necessary for survival in the twenty-first century.

Technological trends also promise to play a major role in the industry's future. From the late 1990s through the mid-2000s, companies worked to develop "run flat" tires, which continue to function for a specified period of time after being punctured. Overall, product development was geared toward longer-lasting tires, which inherently delimits future sales. But in this technology-driven market, durability was one of the premier selling points for customers, and thus companies attempting to maintain market share were required to invest heavily in this type of development. As of 2004, run flat tires were poised for strong growth during the remainder of the decade.

ORGANIZATION AND STRUCTURE

Tire sales are divided between the original equipment and replacement markets. Original equipment sales are made directly to auto manufacturers and comprise less than one third of the total market. Unit sales of replacement tires total over two-thirds of worldwide sales. During periods of economic growth, when new automobile sales typically surge, original equipment tire sales sometimes keep pace with sales of replacement tires. For example, global original equipment tire sales grew 4 percent in 2000, roughly the same rate as replacement tire sales growth that year, due to the highly favorable economic conditions that fueled record levels of automobile production.

The original equipment manufacturer (OEM) market offers both benefits and drawbacks. OEM sales can increase a tire maker's market share at a minimum advertising and distribution cost. Moreover, since car owners tend to replace original tires with the same brand, it follows that more OEM sales mean more replacement sales. Competition in this business segment is intense and automakers often use their buying power and marketplace clout to negotiate ever-lower margins on OEM sales.

The replacement market has proven more stable and profitable. Whether consumers purchase new cars or not, they need to replace worn tires. Tire makers also garner significantly higher profit margins on retail replacement sales. Ironically, the industry's development of longer-lasting radial tires has stunted this segment's growth. Some analysts predict that the private-label segment of this market is the key to future sales, but they caution that this shift may "cannibalize" premium brands or dilute their image.

BACKGROUND AND DEVELOPMENT

The history of the tire industry is intimately connected to the development of rubber, since virtually all tires were made from natural rubber until World War II. Early European explorers noted that indigenous peoples used the gum from certain trees for a variety of purposes, from constructing toy balls to waterproofing garments. Known initially as "caoutchouc," rubber earned its common name for its capacity to rub out pencil marks. In early nineteenth century Britain, Charles Macintosh and Thomas Hancock developed elementary processing techniques for the manufacture of rubberized rainwear that came to be known as "mackintoshes."

Rubber remained an unreliable substance, however. It was sticky and smelly, and subject to vast changes in consistency when temperatures changed. In 1839 the American inventor Charles Goodyear combined rubber, lead, and sulfur in the presence of extreme heat to create what he called "vulcanized" rubber. Although he himself did not benefit from the discovery, Goodyear's process formed the foundation of the global tire industry.

Most early tires were made of solid rubber. British engineer Robert William Thomson has been credited with the concept of a pneumatic, or air-filled, carriage tire, but his 1845 patent was not applied commercially for nearly half a century. Scottish veterinarian John Boyd Dunlop developed and patented pneumatic bicycle tires in 1888. His invention featured an inner canvas tube with a valve for inflation and an outer shell of vulcanized rubber, all mounted on a solid wooden rim. Detachable pneumatics were developed almost concurrently in Britain and France in the 1890s. In 1895 the Michelin brothers, André and Edouard, patented the world's first pneumatic auto tire. Virtually all the world's major tire producers were launched by the turn of the century. Although most early tires were designed for bicycles, the tire industry was soon intertwined with the automobile industry, which added a new and seemingly insatiable outlet in the early twentieth century.

Whereas rubber tree cultivation is limited strictly to equatorial regions with annual rainfall of 100 inches (2,500 millimeters) or more, global centers of natural rubber production are located in Southeast Asia (especially in nations on the South China Sea such as Malaysia) and West Africa (such as Liberia and Nigeria). Until the 1940s, all the world's rubber originated from these regions. Chemists and engineers struggled for decades to create a viable synthetic rubber and thereby reduce reliance on natural resources. The first synthetic rubber was developed in Germany during World War I. When Asian sources of rubber (which had supplied over 95 percent of U.S. tire manufacturers' needs) were cut off during World War II, American tire manufacturers hurriedly collaborated with government chemists to develop man-made alternatives. Although these butadiene/styrene combinations were expensive and largely abandoned at the war's end, experimentation continued. Low-temperature polymerization, or "redox" (for reduction and oxidation), produced a more uniform product and was perfected in Germany after the war.

After a sharp decline in the immediate postwar era, use of synthetic rubber equaled, then surpassed, natural rubber to become the preferred tire material. By the early 1990s, the two materials were used about equally in tire production. Although the development of synthetic rubber has reduced the industry's dependence on natural sources, it has tied manufacturers' fortunes to the petroleum industry.

Other innovations in tire production and design took place during the twentieth century as well. France's Michelin pioneered tubeless tires in 1930, treads in 1934, and low-profile tires in 1937. The company revolutionized the European (and later the world) tire industry with the 1946 patent of radial tire design. Before radials, tires were constructed with ply casings of fabric or steel cords arranged "on the bias" at 25 to 40-degree angles to the direction of travel, hence the name "bias ply." Michelin's design, launched in 1949 as the "X-tire," featured cords arranged perpendicular to the direction of travel. Considerably more durable than their predecessors, radials also handled better and helped lower fuel consumption. In spite of U.S. and British tire makers' reluctance to foot the expensive bill for conversion from bias to radial construction, by the late 1970s over 95 percent of all tires featured this superior structure.

The tire industry of the 1980s and 1990s was characterized by consolidation and competition. In 1985, fourteen companies shared three-fourths of the global market. After a series of mergers in the late 1980s, only six companies split that same 75 percent market share, and Goodyear, Michelin, and Bridgestone controlled over half of the industry. A confluence of forces spurred this globalization of the world tire market. In the late 1980s, as the world's leading tire makers registered record earnings, they sought ways to put the influx of cash to work. Acquiring companies sought increased penetration of original equipment markets, greater private brand business, more comprehensive product lines, and the benefits of global economies of scale. The marked devaluation of the U.S. dollar during this period, along with the weakness of some leading U.S. manufacturers, facilitated the revolution.

With European economic and monetary union imminent in the late 1990s, major players, like Germany's Continental, shifted their capacity and work force to less costly nations in Eastern Europe, in part because of the price advantages, but also out of recognition of the growth potential in that emerging region. While Japan, Western Europe, and North America remained the dominant regions in the global tire industry, producing a combined 75 percent of the world's car and truck tires, the largest growth regions in the late 1990s were the Asia-Pacific markets, where booming industry, increased proliferation of automobiles, and poorly maintained roads led to greater demand for tires. Overall, world tire sales reached 975 million units in 1997; 275 million in new tires and 700 million replacement tires.

Strong economies in Western Europe, Asia, and the United States boosted automobile production levels to record highs in 2000. As a result, worldwide tire production and sales also soared. Light vehicle tire sales grew 4 percent to more than one billion units, while commercial vehicle sales climbed to more than 100 million units. When economic conditions began to weaken in 2001, car production began to wane. As a result, light vehicles tire sales fell 2 percent and commercial vehicle tire sales dropped more than 10 percent.

Between 1995 and 2000, global replacement tire sales growth averaged roughly 4 percent. A massive tire recall by Bridgestone, related to accidents involving Ford Explorers fitted with Bridgestone tires, helped to offset the impact of the deteriorating economy in 2001 by fueling demand for replacement tires, particularly in North America. As a result, global replacement tire sales that year remained level with the previous year. The North American tire industry was among the hardest hit by the recession in 2001. Original equipment shipments fell from 321 million units to 303 million units, reflecting a nearly 6 percent decrease.

CURRENT CONDITIONS

In 2003, the Rubber Manufacturers Association (RMA) reported that U.S. tire shipments reached 310 million units that year, up 0.6 percent from the previous year. Although the original equipment sector experienced a decline of about 3 million units, a 5-million-unit hike in replacement tires supported overall shipment growth that year. After increasing 3.2 percent in 2004, due to economic improvement and commercial trucking growth, the RMA indicated that shipments would grow about 2 percent annually through 2009. In all, this would lead to estimated shipments of 350 million units in 2009.

China remained a key growth market for tire makers in the mid-2000s. This was consistent with previously established trends. For example, according to a February 2002 issue of *AsiaPulse News,* "Foreign tyre manufacturers are expanding their investments in China with the rapid expansion of the country's automobile market and rising demand for car tyres and high-performance tyres following China's entry into the World Trade Organization." For example, France-based Michelin and China's leading tire manufacturer, Shanghai Tire Co., created a joint tire production venture in Shanghai. Japan's Yokohama Rubber, which held a 3 percent share of the Chinese tire market, forged a joint tire production operation in Hangzhou with Hangzhou Rubber Group in January of 2002.

In December 2003, *European Rubber Journal* indicated that the global tire market increased 3.1 percent in 2002, with a significant share of the rise attributed to Chinese companies. According to the publication, much of this growth came at the expense of the world's "Big Three" tire producers. Of the world's leading 75 tire makers, 16 were Chinese concerns, with combined revenues of nearly US$3.3 billion. China's tire demand was expected to reach 40.5 million units by the mid-2000s and 108 million units by 2010, according to predictions by Yokohama Rubber.

RESEARCH AND TECHNOLOGY

Intense competition drove heavy investments in research and development in the early 1990s. New tire designs proved vital to higher profit margins and improved market share. Technological research and development targeted lightness, safety, comfort, fuel economy, and durability. In particular, companies have focused on developing wet weather tires and "run flat" tire technology.

Michelin continued to be a leader in product and process innovation. In 1991, the company launched the XH-4, a radial that offered 60 percent longer wear than most other tires on the market. The company introduced a new "green" tire in 1992. Its reduced rolling resistance promised up to 4 percent better fuel efficiency, and therefore less air pollution, than standard tires. That same year, the company helped promote tire recycling by paving a U.S. highway with "rubberized asphalt." In terms of process, Michelin's automated, secretive "C3M" process combined several stages of tire building and required only 10 percent of the floor space of existing plants, thereby holding the potential to dramatically reduce two of tire manufacturers' biggest costs: payroll and physical plant expenses. In response, Goodyear introduced its own production technology innovation in the form of its Integrated Manufacturing Precision Assembly Cellular Technology (IMPACT), which aims to diminish inventory levels and reduce cycle times.

After decades of experimentation, Bridgestone, Goodyear, and Michelin began to introduce "run-flat" tires, which allow drivers to continue driving at normal speeds after losing part or all of their air pressure. Run-flat tires make use of improved rubber mix-design technology that allows scrap rubber to react with gases to produce a chemical change, the result of which can bond with other materials and fill punctures in tires. Automobile manufacturers had eagerly awaited this innovation, which promised to do away with roadside tire changes and the ever-present heavy spare tire, thereby increasing fuel efficiency. However, the high cost of the air pressure sensors needed to make use of the new tire technology posed remained a deterrent, as did concerns over the heavy weight of run-flat tires, which compromised fuel efficiency.

In 1999, Goodyear began giving an air pressure sensor system free to anyone who purchased a set of Eagle Aquasteel run-flat tires. The following year, Michelin unveiled its PAX tire/wheel system, a more fuel efficient run-flat tire system. Eventually, Goodyear and Michelin created a joint venture to promote more widespread acceptance of run-flat tires. The two tire makers agreed to use Michelin's PAX system as its main product line. By 2003, run-flat tires were poised for growth after years of steady development. According to the April 2003 issue of *European Rubber Journal,* run-flat tire sales were expected to total about 2 million units that year, with a projected increase to 4 million units in 2004 and 6 million in 2005.

Closely related to run-flat tires were tire pressure monitoring systems, which notified drivers when tires lost air pressure. The same April 2003 *European Rubber Journal* article indicated that five years of research had led to the development of a number of direct and indirect pressure sensing systems. The former provided drivers with absolute pressure readings, while the latter used tire diameter measurements to determine if a loss in pressure was occurring. The article explained that while there was no consensus on which system was the best, manufacturers like Ford Motor Co. had received negative customer feedback regarding direct systems. Heading into the second half of the 2000s, U.S. government requirements—namely the National Highway Traffic Safety Administration's enforcement of the Transportation Recall Enhancement, Accountability, and Documentation

(TREAD) Act—were expected to spur U.S. growth in tire pressure management systems.

Growing concern over the adverse environmental impact of scrap tires pushed the issue of reuse (in retreads, for example), recycling, and ultimate disposal of tires to the forefront of the industry's environmental agenda. Proposed recycling uses included asphalt-based road coverings, footwear, and household items. In the early 2000s, Goodyear began reexamining the potential of urethane tires, which are fully recyclable, as well as not susceptible to flats or blowouts, because the tires use no air. Urethane had been tested by tire makers as early as the 1950s, but nothing commercially viable ever emerged.

WORKFORCE

Globalization and consolidation trends combined in the 1990s to herald both massive job cuts and radically changed labor-management relations. After the acquisition spree of the late 1980s, leading tire companies seeking economies of scale and increased productivity eliminated redundant plants and many of the workers in them. The Big Three of Michelin, Goodyear, and Bridgestone reduced their combined employment levels by an average of more than 10 percent from 1990 to 1993. Goodyear made the biggest cuts during that period, cutting its employment numbers by 12.4 percent. Employment in the industry overall hovered around 1986 levels. All the leaders embraced popular new management techniques emphasizing lean production, reliance on teams, and total quality management.

Adjusting to the leaner tire industry of the 1990s was particularly difficult for members of the U.S. United Rubber Workers (URW), who had used pattern bargaining to negotiate contracts with American tire companies since 1946. After Goodyear came to a relatively generous 1994 agreement with the group, the Rubber Workers expected their competitors with U.S. operations and subsidiaries to follow suit. Instead, other tire makers balked. Led by Michelin, which had studiously avoided organized labor before 1990, a number of manufacturers, including Sumitomo, Yokohama, Bridgestone, and Pirelli, objected to the union's demands. Some local unions made concessions, but 8 percent of the URW's membership went on strike. Early in 1995, Bridgestone hired 2,000 replacement workers. Some analysts hailed the end of pattern bargaining, noting that lower wage costs could allow manufacturers to increase capital and research budgets. Union supporters decried Bridgestone's decision, however.

Workforce reductions continued into the early 2000s as Goodyear trimmed nearly 10 percent of its staff in 2001. That year, Michelin revealed its intent to downsize its North American employment base by 7 percent. Some industry leaders, such as Tokyo-based Bridgestone Corp., continued to struggle into 2004. However, there were signs of brighter times on the road ahead as some industry leaders announced plans to expand operations. For example, by 2006, some 350 new jobs were expected to result from the establishment of a new U.S. factory by Japan's Toyo Tire & Rubber Co. Another 30 jobs would likely stem from expanded capacity at Cooper Tire & Rubber in Findlay, Ohio.

INDUSTRY LEADERS

In the early 2000s, seven multinational companies—Michelin, Bridgestone, Goodyear, Continental, Pirelli, Sumitomo, and Yokahama—accounted for almost 80 percent of the world's tire output. The top tier of companies consisted of the Big Three: Michelin, Bridgestone, and Goodyear. Together, these three companies produced approximately half of the world's tires.

BRIDGESTONE

Despite its status as the world's leading tire producer in 2000, sales at Tokyo, Japan-based Bridgestone Corporation fell 14.1 percent in 2000 to US$17.32 billion, and earnings dropped 82.1 percent to US$155 million that year. Blamed for the poor performance was the widely publicized recall of 6.5 million Firestone tires, many of which were used on Ford Explorers. Several accidents involving Explorer sport utility vehicles had revealed defects in the Firestone tires in 2000. The resulting recall cost Bridgestone roughly US$350 million and its long-standing partnership with Ford Motor Company. The firm also found itself targeted in several lawsuits initiated by parties who had been injured while driving on the tires. By 2004, Bridgestone's revenues totaled US$23.44 billion, and its earnings were US$1.11 million, an improvement of more than 34 percent from 2003. At this time, the company employed 113,699 workers, up 5 percent for the year.

Bridgestone founder Shojiro Ishibashi originally established his rubber company to manufacture footwear in 1931. During the years before World War II, Bridgestone's growth was based on the expansion of Japan's military and automotive sectors. The company expanded throughout Asia in the postwar era, then into Europe in the 1970s. Growth came primarily through acquisition in the 1980s. The most notable example of this was the 1988 purchase of Firestone Tire & Rubber Company. A period of wholesale restructuring and reinvestment followed, during which the Firestone operations suffered a loss. That retrenchment paid dividends in the late 1990s.

MICHELIN

France's Compagnie Générale des Établissements Michelin was the world's second-leading tire producer in 2003, with sales of US$19.3 billion, up from US$14.8 billion in 2000. In 2003, the company's earnings fell almost 35 percent, reaching nearly US$399 million. Michelin was also a leading producer of inner tubes. Although the majority of the company's sales were made in Europe and the Americas, Michelin spent much of the late 1990s working to increase its market share in Asia. As a result, sales in China grew 57 percent in 1999. With business in approximately 170 countries and about 76 manufacturing plants, Michelin maintained a payroll of 127,210 employees.

Originally founded in 1830 as a sugar manufacturer, Michelin soon diversified into rubber products. Production of pneumatic tires began after the Michelin brothers, André and Edouard, took charge of the company in the 1880s. The brothers established a tradition of innovation that was carried on by succeeding generations at the family-controlled company. Its most notable breakthrough was the radial tire, developed secretly during the German occupation of France during World War II. Michelin advanced from the second place rank among global tire manufacturers to number one in 1990 through its acquisition of the Uniroyal-Goodrich Tire Company in the United States. The company continued to be led by descendants of the Michelin family into the early 2000s.

GOODYEAR

The Goodyear Tire & Rubber Co. ranked third among the world's tire manufacturers in 2004, with US$18.37 billion in sales, up 21.5 percent from 2003. The firm recorded a US$203.6 million loss in 2001—its first annual loss in nine years—due to increasingly expensive raw materials, a weakening global economy, and unfavorable exchange rates. To cut costs, Goodyear pared down inventory, divested peripheral operations, and trimmed its workforce by 10,000 positions. Goodyear also raised replacement tire prices. The company recorded net income of US$114.8 million in 2004, at which time it employed 84,000 workers. Goodyear formed an alliance with Japan's Sumitomo Rubber Industries during the early 2000s, and plans to increase production levels in China threefold by 2007.

Frank A. Seiberling founded the company, named for the originator of vulcanized rubber, in 1898 to manufacture bicycle and carriage tires. The company began production of automobile tires in 1901 and grew quickly on the strength of contracts with the Ford Motor Company. Although it was not the world's first tire producer, it became the world's largest in 1916. Instead of acquiring its North American competitors in the late 1980s, Goodyear borrowed heavily to invest in a stock buy-back after a hostile takeover attempt in 1987. Goodyear relinquished its claim to the top spot in the international tire industry in 1990, but maintained its rank as one of only two publicly traded U.S. tire companies. A turnaround engineered by CEO Stanley Gault resulted in a massive expansion program geared toward recapturing Goodyear's status as the industry's first-ranked player. The company emphasized innovative new products, attacked the replacement market with new vigor, shored up distribution through mass retailers, and expanded into the emerging markets of Latin America and Asia. However, in the late 1990s, nearly two-thirds of the company's sales were still focused in North America.

CONTINENTAL

Ranked fourth among the world's tire manufacturers in 2004, with sales of US$17.18 billion, Germany's Continental AG was a premier company in the European market, generating a substantial share of its sales in the region. The company was formed in 1871 by a consortium of financiers and industrialists to manufacture a general line of rubber products, including fabrics, footwear, toys, and tires. The company became the first in Germany to produce pneumatic bicycle tires in the 1890s, and expanded into automotive tires by the turn of the century. Acquisitions within Germany helped promote Continental to the forefront of its home country's tire industry by 1929, but the company continued to lag behind its rivals in terms of international expansion. The German pre-war build-up helped boost Continental's operations, and the company participated in the development of synthetic rubber, but the postwar era brought stagnation and uncertainty. The vigorous expansion of the German car industry, however, brought equally rapid growth to Continental. A major acquisition spree begun in 1979 culminated in the 1987 purchase of General Tire, America's fifth largest tire producer, for US$650 million. Continental repulsed a takeover attempt by Italy's Pirelli in 1991, but speculation that the company was vulnerable to further unfriendly merger attempts continued in the early 1990s. However, the firm remained independent into the mid-2000s, at which time it employed 68,829 workers.

PIRELLI

Fifth-ranked Pirelli & C. SpA, based in Italy, generated sales of US$8.4 billion in 2003. Pirelli is one of the most diversified of the world leaders in tire manufacturing. Second to energy cables, tires constitute roughly 45 percent of sales.

The company was established by Giovanni Battista Pirelli in 1872 to manufacture a variety of rubber products. The company's product line eventually included bicycle and car tires. Pirelli gained a reputation as a producer of high-performance racing tires in the 1920s. The company expanded organically, establishing its own operations throughout Europe and beyond in the 1960s and 1970s. Acquisitions, including the 1988 purchase of the United States' Armstrong Tire Co., fueled growth during the 1980s. Ill-conceived battles for control of Firestone in the late 1980s and Continental in the early 1990s did not come to fruition. Some critics charged that these attempts only distracted management from concentrating on competition in the global market. Analysts estimated that the Continental attempt alone cost Pirelli US$300 million. Pirelli divested some extraneous businesses in the mid-1990s to concentrate on its core interests in cables and tires.

SUMITOMO

With revenues of US$16.17 billion in 2004, Japan's Sumitomo Rubber Industries, Ltd. ranked sixth among the world's tire producers. Tires account for roughly 71 percent of the firm's total revenues. Sumitomo also makes industrial products, marine products, and sports equipment.

The firm is an affiliate of the Sumitomo *keiretsu,* one of Japan's largest conglomerates. By the time Sumitomo Rubber was formed in 1917, its parent had already bought into Dunlop Japan, a subsidiary of Britain's Dunlop. In 1963, the Sumitomo group purchased a controlling interest in Dunlop Japan, combined it with its existing rubber interests, and renamed the venture Sumitomo Rubber Industries. Reasoning that its cheaper textile radials would maintain their market share, Dunlop had eschewed the European radial revolution of the 1960s, and the company had a difficult time catching up when it realized its mistake. Sumitomo used Dunlop as a stepping stone to greater global influence in the mid-1980s when it acquired a 98 percent interest in the latter's ailing European operations for US$240 million. The "white knight" merger and subsequent rationalization of both companies' operations helped each survive the cutthroat competition of the late 1980s and early 1990s. In 1999, Sumitomo sold the right to manufacture Dunlop tires in North America and Europe to Goodyear in exchange for the right to manufacture Goodyear tires in Japan.

YOKOHAMA

Another Japanese manufacturer, the Yokohama Rubber Co., Ltd., ranked seventh among world tire makers in 2004, with sales of more than US$3.8 billion. Tires accounted for roughly 70 percent of total revenues. Yokohama also makes aviation components and industrial rubber products. Employees total 13,264, and operations outside Japan span the remainder of Asia, Europe, and North America.

Established in 1917, Yokohama specialized in the manufacture of cord tires. Its reputation for innovation enabled it to become the supplier to top Japanese car manufacturers Nissan and Toyota. In the post-World War II era, the company expanded into aircraft tires, high-performance racing tires, truck and bus tires, and radials. Yokohama was relatively late to establish overseas operations: the company did not have a significant international presence until the late 1960s and early 1970s. The firm followed the global pattern of consolidation—albeit on a much smaller scale than the "Big Three"—when it joined Toyo Tyre and Rubber Co. and Continental in the cooperative construction of a radial truck and bus tire plant in the United States in 1988. The following year, Yokohama acquired Mohawk Rubber Co., Ltd., a U.S. tire manufacturer, for US$150 million and instituted a capital investment plan.

MAJOR COUNTRIES IN THE INDUSTRY

In the January 2003 issue of *European Rubber Journal,* University of Akron (Ohio) economics professor Dennis Byrne indicated that, as the mid-2000s approached, North America would increase its global share of tire production from 2000 levels of 31.2 percent. In 2003, North America held a 46.6 percent share of the global tire and rubber market. Annual growth of 1.8 percent was expected for total tire shipments in the U.S. through 2010.

Eastern Europe's share of the world market amounted to 15.2 percent in 2003. In June 2004, *European Rubber Journal* indicated that a pending tire disposal surcharge in France led to a surge in tire replacement sales during the early months of 2004. In all, Europe saw passenger tire sales rise 5.6 percent during the first quarter of the year (41.2 million units), while 4x4 tires increased 12.2 percent (1.4 million units), light truck tires rose 9.6 percent (3 million units), and heavy duty truck tires were up 7.3 percent (2.3 million units).

While the Japanese tire market was fairly stagnant in the late 1990s, it was also one of the world's most profitable over the years. The country was not spared from the effects of the global recession, however. Price sensitivity prevented retail increases into the mid-1990s. In the late 1990s, decline in Japanese auto production and an economic downturn negatively affected the country's tire industry. In 2004, Japan was home to four of the world's leading tire manufacturers, including the second-leading Bridgestone Corp., Sumitomo Rubber Industries Ltd., Yokohama Rubber Co. Ltd., and Toyo Tire & Rubber Co. Ltd. In 2003, the Asia-Pacific region as whole held about 34.5 percent of the worldwide rubber and tire market.

North America, Western Europe, and Japan have accounted for roughly 75 percent of world tire production in recent years. However, many analysts contend that the most promising markets for the international tire industry are the emerging markets in Asia and Latin America. Asia, which had a 34 percent world market share in 2003, was expected to increase its market share at an annual rate of 5 percent heading toward the late 2000s. China, which saw its global production increase from 55 million units to 61.5 million units between 1999 and 2000 alone, India, and Southeastern Asian countries are still considered to be in the developing stage. South America, despite a lack of large investments by major tire companies, nonetheless also shows significant growth potential.

FURTHER READING

Davis, Bruce. "China's Tyre Companies Start to Show: While Michelin Remains in Top Spot Among the World's Tyre Companies, Growth in China Is Starting to Have a Larger Impact Further Down Our Annual Ranking Of Top Tyre Makers Worldwide." *European Rubber Journal,* December 2003.

"ERJ Newsbriefs." *European Rubber Journal,* 1 April 2004.

"Foreign Businesses Eye China's Tire Industry." *AsiaPulse News,* 5 February 2002.

"Global Tires & Rubber." *Datamonitor Industry Profile.* May 2004. Available from http://www.datamonitor.com.

"Growth in Tire Shipments to Accelerate in 2004." Washington, D.C.: Rubber Manufacturers Association. 19 April 2004. Available from http://www.rma.org/newsroom/release.cfm?ID=117.

Hoover's Company Capsules. 2005. Available from http://www.hoovers.com.

"LMC Sees Sharp Downturn in Tire Sales." *Rubber World,* November 2001.

Raleigh, Patrick. "French Tyre Sales Surge, Rest of Europe Grows Too; A New Scrap-Tyre Surcharge in France Triggered a Short-Term Boom There, with Replacement Tyre Sales Up 11 Percent on the Year Prior to its Introduction." *European Rubber Journal,* 1 June 2004.

Shaw, David. "Runflat Technology Is Top Priority: Many Observers Predict Buoyant Future for Extended Mobility Tyres." *European Rubber Journal,* April 2003.

———. "UK Remains Good for Tyre Sales." *European Rubber Journal,* 1 April 2004.

"Tire Shipments Expected to Increase in 2005." *Rubber Manufacturers Association Website.* 29 April 2005. Available from http://www.rma.org.

"Top 75 Global Tyre Producers 2002-2003." *European Rubber Journal,* December 2003.

"Weak Economy Hurts 2001 Tire Shipments." *Rubber World,* September 2001, 16.

White, Liz. "China Has Most Growth Potential for Carbon Black." *European Rubber Journal,* January 2003.

INDUSTRIAL MACHINERY AND EQUIPMENT

SIC 3534

NAICS 333921

ELEVATORS AND MOVING STAIRWAYS

The vertical transportation industry includes the manufacturers of passenger and freight elevators, automobile lifts, dumbwaiters, and escalators. Elevators, as referenced here, are better known in Europe as "lifts" and are used to move passengers and equipment from level to level. They do not include farm elevators (primarily grain storage devices) or aerial work platforms (included under construction machinery and equipment).

INDUSTRY SNAPSHOT

According to *Buildings,* "elevators, escalators, and moving sidewalks are the building industry's equivalent to trains, planes, and automobiles." Although the industry experienced a brief expansion in the latter part of the twentieth century, the beginning of the twenty-first century brought the dual pressures of a downturn in construction and a simultaneous increase in the number of elevator manufacturers worldwide. Greater emphasis was placed on service companies. Large elevator manufacturers swallowed smaller corporations, making the industry increasingly global in nature. The industry subsequently consolidated into just a few major players by the mid-2000s. Otis Elevator Company, later part of United Technologies, founded the elevator industry and was first in the industry for decades. In fact, it wasn't until well into the 2000s that its leadership position was threatened by competitor Schindler Lifts. In 2005, other major worldwide players included Kone of Finland and ThyssenKrupp of Germany, as well as Mitsubishi and Hitachi of Japan.

The state of the elevator industry depends entirely on the health of the construction industry. Although service is an increasingly important aspect of the vertical transportation market, the manufacture of new elevators is dependent on the creation of the new buildings that require them. In the 2000s, the economic emergence of China and other Asian countries shifted the construction industry's focus from Europe and the United States to the rapidly growing construction markets in developing nations along the Pacific Rim. Developing technology included the implementation of multidirectional cabs, high-technology elevator-passenger interfaces, higher speed transportation, and optimal reliability, bringing with it an emphasis on greater environmental friendliness. According to the Freedonia Group, the U.S. market for elevators and escalators was expected to grow 6.5 percent annually through 2007, with most gains realized in residential construction and elevators or moving walkways for the disabled.

ORGANIZATION AND STRUCTURE

Once elevators were technologically able to service large buildings, two distinct categories of elevator construction emerged: electric elevators designed to be used exclusively in high-rise buildings and hydraulic elevators capable of accommodating low-rise buildings of five stories or less.

Hydraulic elevators are relatively slow with a maximum speed of 150 feet per minute (ft/min) or 46 meters per minute (m/min), which is not a disadvantage as long as a building has very few floors. Hydraulic elevators are seen as ideal for smaller buildings because they do not need overhead hoisting machinery. Generally, the elevator sits atop a piston that moves inside a cylinder that is sunk in the ground at a depth equal to the maximum height to which the elevator will rise. So-called hole-less hydraulic elevators rely on power that is transferred via a sliding plunger on the side of the elevator.

Electric elevators fall into one of two categories: gearless traction elevators and geared traction elevators. Gearless traction elevators are quite fast and regularly travel at 400 to 2000 ft/min (120 to 610 m/min). They are powered by large slow-speed motors and are generally installed in high-rise buildings with more than 10 stories. Geared traction elevators travel at a slower rate of speed—a maximum of 450 ft/min (140 m/min)—but can carry up to 30,000 pounds (13,500 kilograms) and have many industrial applications.

It is a given in the elevator industry that passengers often must wait for an elevator car to arrive. Escalators, on the other hand, offer a mode of vertical transportation that is continuously accessible. Depending on design, the "moving stairways" that make up escalators can transport up to 4,500 passengers per hour on a series of steps running in a continuous chain up an incline. Most escalators service floors separated by a 20-foot (6 meter) slope, although 100-foot (30 meter) escalators also are in use. All escalators are powered by alternating current electric motors and move at about 100 ft/min (30 m/min).

OTHER MODES OF VERTICAL TRANSPORTATION

A third, relatively small part of the vertical transportation industry is a dumbwaiter. Dumbwaiters are used exclusively as material-handling systems (they do not accommodate passengers) and are widely used for such applications as moving books between floors in libraries or transporting food and medical supplies in hospitals. Dumbwaiters are always operated from outside the system, never from inside a cab. Dumbwaiters are limited to nine square feet of platform area and must be of a height no more than four feet. Any system larger than this is classified as an elevator and is therefore subject to more stringent safety requirements.

REGULATORY AGENCIES

In the United States, the agency that regulates elevator and escalator safety, operation, and design is the American National Standards Institute (ANSI). ANSI is an organization of industrial and consumer groups and pertinent government personnel. Under their aegis, on-site safety inspections of elevators, dumbwaiters, and escalators are made by state and local inspectors.

BACKGROUND AND DEVELOPMENT

The elevator of the twenty-first century operates on many of the same basic principles first perfected by Elisha Graves Otis back in 1854. An elevator is basically either an open platform or a closed cab powered by a unit that moves it up and down an enclosed shaft through various combinations of pulleys, cables, counterweights, and gears.

While the concept of an elevator-like device able to move heavy loads vertically was investigated by the ancient Greeks (the Greek mathematician Archimedes invented a type of elevator in 230 B.C.), such apparatus of vertical transportation had limited application well into the Industrial Revolution because of seemingly unsolvable safety problems, especially the fact that there was no way known to stop a falling elevator. If the lifting cable or rope used in the operation of an elevator broke, the results were disastrous for the elevator, its passengers, and any freight on board. Demand, however, overrode safety concerns in certain situations. The advent of the Industrial Revolution saw elevator use increase in industrialized countries, especially in the United States and Great Britain. By the 1840s, patents had been granted for steam and hydraulic elevators. Still, the safety question cast a pall on elevators' general acceptance and thus stifled technological development. New buildings remained more or less "stunted," because the practical height of a building was inextricably tied to the ability to vertically move people and freight to the upper floors. Until this could be accomplished quickly and safely, the multi-story buildings and skyscrapers that are the hallmarks of modern urban architecture had to wait.

Vertical transportation embarked on its "golden age" in 1853 after Elisha G. Otis, a 43-year-old mechanic from Albany, New York, dramatically demonstrated an elevator safety device of his own invention. First unveiled at the Crystal Palace Exposition in New York City, the device had been constructed by Otis in a Yonkers, New York factory. Otis's safety innovation consisted of a pair of spring-loaded "dogs," which, if the elevator's lifting cable broke, would engage cogs mounted along the elevator shaft rails, thus halting the uncontrolled fall of the elevator. *Scientific American* called the device an "excellent" and "much admired" invention. Buoyed by the excited reception, Otis and his son began in earnest to manufacture "safety elevators." In 1857 Otis installed the first commercial passenger elevator in a department store in New York City. This steam-powered elevator rose through the building's five stories in just under one minute, carrying passengers effortlessly to the top floor and conveying the Otis Elevator Company with seemingly comparable ease to an undisputed position as leader of the vertical transportation industry.

Once Otis had shown the way, advances in elevator technology paralleled the increasing demand for higher buildings and skyscrapers. Elevators became faster, safer, and more capable of carrying heavier loads, and the steam elevators of the nineteenth century gave way to the electric and hydraulic elevators of the twentieth. Otis Elevator Company introduced the first escalator at the 1900 Paris Exposition, but development of this alternate approach to vertical travel did not begin in earnest until the 1920s. Prior to 1950, escalator use was generally restricted to stores and transportation terminals such as airports. After the middle of the century, however, they became increasingly popular features in schools, offices, public buildings, and other buildings where large numbers of people had to be moved among a relatively low number of floors.

In the 1980s the vertical transportation industry saw stability in Europe and a boom in Asia, but began to level off in the United States. The world market expanded in the latter part of the 1980s at a rate of roughly 15 percent a year, and by 1989 sales topped US$17 billion annually. This figure, however, included the influx of revenue sources based on maintenance and modernization, which by 1990 would account for 40 percent of industry revenue. In 1990, Otis, Schindler Holding Ltd., and Kone Corporation held approximately 50 percent of the market, in part through policies of expansion and acquisition.

In 1990 the United States was feeling the beginnings of a recession, and elevator sales dropped by 5 to 20 percent in certain domestic markets. In the five years immediately prior to the onset of the recession, the American market had already leveled off to an annual growth rate of about 2 percent. Dramatically higher growth in other market segments did much to offset this otherwise alarming trend. In Europe, the elevator market grew at a rate of about 10 percent a year, while portions of the expanding Asian market displayed growth rates as high as 40 percent. In consequence, many companies, including industry leader Otis, turned their attention to the more lucrative effort. To further compensate for the slowdown in the American market, savvy industry leaders were ready with modernization and service contracts to make up for the decline in new installations in the early 1990s.

By 1996, even allowing for the explosion of the Asian consumer market, annual worldwide demand for elevators and escalators dropped from 90,000 units in 1991 to 70,000 units—a fall of more than 22 percent. Although traditionally conservative, the elevator industry was suddenly forced into the same survival techniques used in more competitive industries as individual corporations cut costs and downsized. Smaller manufacturers and service groups were absorbed into larger corporations, which depended on increased research and development capabilities and greater global presence for survival.

By the end of the twentieth century, major elevator manufacturers, such as Otis Elevator Company and Schindler Elevator Corporation, had conducted extensive restructuring and implemented cost-cutting measures. Otis cut more than 1,000 jobs in 1998 in order to strengthen its financial position in the wake of the Asian economic crisis of the late 1990s. The European economy faced uncertainty as the Euro began its phase-in in 1999. Elevator companies and the building industry experienced significant slow-downs until the Euro began to stabilize late in 2001. Global companies (the European market accounted for more than 77 percent of Otis's sales in 2000) were impacted heavily by the fluctuation.

The recession of the early 1990s encouraged the elevator industry to concentrate on service contracts rather than new sales. In 1991 services accounted for just US$600 million of industry revenue. Four years later, in 1995, Kone gleaned more than 61 percent of its revenues from various service contracts and modernization efforts; and in 1997, Dover reported a similar 60 to 40 revenue split. Companies worldwide emphasized renovation and redesign of previously installed units, especially of control systems. In the United States, the passage of federal legislation aimed at making public and private facilities more accessible to persons with disabilities provided considerable impetus for the elevator industry to focus on service and modernization. Service became such an important segment of the industry that new equipment was often under-priced, and companies depended on profits generated by service contracts. By 1996 it was estimated that over the first 20 years in the life span of an average elevator, total maintenance costs would equal the original purchase price. The Japanese also embraced the concept of service as a lucrative adjunct to the elevator industry. In 1997 Hitachi introduced the high-technology Hitachi Elevator Remote and Intelligent Observation System (HERIOS), a remote maintenance system targeted particularly at providing optimal reliability, comfort, and security for elevator users, particularly the aged.

Expansion of operations through acquisition was an accepted means of coping with localized business slowdowns as early as the late 1980s and early 1990s. After the fall of the Berlin Wall in 1989, Eastern Europe presented a burgeoning market for business, including the elevator industry. Otis Elevator Company promptly used its European Transcontinental Operations subsidiary to acquire 60 percent of Berliner Aufzugs und Fahrtreppenbau, quickly establishing operations in East Germany. In 1993 Otis opened a joint venture with the Shcherbinka Lift Factory in Shcherbinka, Russia. The initial production goal for Otis's Russian venture was just 1,200 units annually, a tenth of the capacity of Otis' newly acquired Belarus facility. This goal was kept low in part because the lure of 260,000 grossly outdated units installed across Russia presented a huge potential market for service and modernization. With only Kone Corporation of Finland as a major competitor for this market (the approximately 5,000 Kone units installed in the Commonwealth of Independent States represented 99 percent of all Russian elevator imports), Otis continued to press forward.

In 1997 Otis looked toward the south and purchased more than 80 percent of Rade Koncar-Inzinjering Vertikalnog Transporta. This Croatian firm had offices in Croatia, Bosnia, and Macedonia, thus providing Otis with a grip on the Balkans, which were rebuilding after years of civil war. And, while Otis Elevator Company stood as the leading competitor in the emerging markets of Poland, Slovakia, Hungary, the Czech Republic, and the Ukraine, Schindler made overtures in the Middle East. In 1996 Schindler concluded negotiations to purchase a major interest in Nehustan, Israel's primary elevator company.

Even as high technology and acquisition alternately spurred and propped up the market in Europe and the United States, rapid economic changes in Asia brought construction upsurges that opened vast opportunities for newly successful elevator manufacturers. South Korea's focus on technology reached its elevator market, and Dongyang Elevator Company began in 1997 to tout "smart" elevators whose multifunctional capacities were reminiscent of some of the recent Schindler and Otis innovations. Hyundai Elevator Company turned to high speed as a niche, and LG Industrial Systems devoted an entire presentation room to its variety of elevator products.

In April 2000, Mitsubishi and Schindler entered into a cooperative agreement in which the two would supply each other with major components for elevators and escalators. Mitsubishi reported that the two companies negotiated for business cooperation on a global scale in an attempt to maintain the top positions in the world market and to expand further.

A major source for much-needed industry vitality came from various technological and design innovations, sparked both by the earnest effort of companies trying to remain competitive and by the zeal of emerging new firms. As late as 1987, U.S. Elevator was touting conservatism as the main reason it could pump profit into parent Cubic Corporation. Ten years later, giants such as Schindler and Kone depended on high technology displays and environmental friendliness to differentiate their businesses. In fiction, the voice-activated turbo lifts of Gene Roddenberry's *Star Trek* gave the more earthbound a sense of the possible future of the vertical transportation industry, and by the end of the twentieth century, multidirectional elevator passage became a reality. In 1996 Otis introduced Odyssey, whose "cabs" could carry passengers from their offices in 1000-foot office buildings to parking lots outside. Schindler Elevator Corporation, through its "Miconic," the previous year taught elevator passengers to communicate with an intelligent operating center and use keypads and displays to identify "assigned" elevators that would stop automatically at designated floors. In the late 1990s, Kone introduced the machine-room-less elevator, MonoSpace. The machine-room-less elevators boasted faster speeds and required less space, according to Kone.

Perhaps the most significant technological advances were born not from the elevator industry itself, but from the communications industry and the Internet, which enabled fast communication between elevator manufacturers and customers. In 1999, Otis launched its e-business strategy, which included online display, ordering, and customer service features. Thyssen developed its site in an effort to assist in communications, particularly relating to its 500,000 exclusive maintenance contracts.

Already braced for an American economic recession, United Technologies (Otis Elevator Company's parent company) announced Otis was recession-resistant after extensive restructuring and strong sales outside the United States. Early in 2002, elevator companies were reporting modest growth, despite the recession in the United States, as the Asian and European economies stabilized.

Although the service element of any industry tends to be recession-proof, renovation and modernization of existing machinery was ultimately regarded as a finite market. However, the service industry was a double-edged sword, as elevator service was increasingly provided by private companies specializing in service and not by the original manufacturer. This in turn led to increasing competition for the service fees and a downturn in some service revenues. In October 2004, Schindler Elevator announced an innovation in the service area called "Schindler FieldLink." This handheld device was the latest addition to the company's service programs, the Schindler Elevator Network for Service Excellence (SENSE). The FieldLink combined dispatching, parts ordering, manuals, troubleshooting, and cell phone capabilities into a single unit for service technicians to carry.

However lucrative modernization and service appeared to be, some industry analysts contended that the future still depended on new construction. In the mid-2000s, the National Association of Elevator Contractors pointed out that in addition to industry consolidation, changes in business models—including the emphasis on Internet business and e-commerce—made the industry small. To compete in the global society, a company had to be well known and well respected.

Indeed, globalization made for creative partnerships in the elevator industry. In December 2001, Kone of Finland and Toshiba of Japan entered into an agreement that provided for the exchange of shares and the extension of Toshiba's license to market Kone's MonoSpace machine-room-less elevators. Kone acquired a 20 percent share in Toshiba's Elevator and Building Systems Corporation, and Toshiba got a 5 percent shareholding in the Kone Corporation. Kone granted Toshiba exclusive rights to manufacture the MonoSpace in China, a rapidly growing elevator market.

Although a worldwide increase in demand was not predicted, Mitsubishi Electric estimated China's market would expand most rapidly. In 2001 Mitsubishi reported the demand for new elevator installations was 30,000. This was expected to increase to 50,000 by 2006, due to the strong demand for public infrastructure and housing, and by the special demand stemming from the Beijing Olympics.

CURRENT CONDITIONS

Enhancements and innovation in service and technology were important toward gaining a competitive edge during the mid-2000s. Of a global market approaching $40 billion, new sales accounted for 40 percent of revenues, with the remaining 60 percent coming from system maintenance and modernization. Industry leaders and smaller companies worked to gain market share in these areas. United Technologies Corp. (UTC) acquired security software systems maker Lenel Systems International Inc., as reported by Avital Hahn in *Investment Dealers' Digest.* By doing so, UTC hoped to adapt Lenel's traditional security systems and create central systems that monitor building entry, computer access, and elevator use through ID cards. Schindler's FieldLink system, the ability to monitor elevator systems remotely via the Internet, and other system innovations were used to help manufacturers gain and retain market share. All companies in the industry were moving toward quieter, more environmentally friendly equipment, and other industry leaders were following Kone's example and offering machine-room-less elevator systems, which required far less space.

Global market expansion continued to provide companies with sources of revenue growth. Almost half of new elevator sales were sold in the Asia-Pacific area, according to Kone Corporation. China and Russia were important areas in the elevator industry, with increasing opportunity for imports and new construction. Increasing imports meant increased competition among the industry's major manufacturers. In April 2005, Kone announced it was embarking on another joint venture with Toshiba Elevator and Building Systems Corporation (TELC) to build escalators in China. Kone planned to own 70 percent of the company, which would run both companies' existing manufacturing facilities in Kunshan and Shenyang. In the same month, Kone also announced a joint venture with Russian elevator company Karacharovo Mechanical Factory (KMZ). Together, Kone and KMZ hold more than a 35 percent market share of the new elevator market in Russia.

Industry leaders in Europe were facing challenges associated with the increased cost of raw materials such as oil and steel, rising labor prices in some markets, such as North America, and increased price competition. This was reflected by marginal revenue increases from 2003 to 2004. Industry leaders remained profitable, but did so because of innovation in service offerings, new technology, increased sales in new markets, or a combination of these factors, which helped to offset rising costs associated with labor and materials.

RESEARCH AND TECHNOLOGY

Leading industry players in the early 1990s relied on research and development in efforts to increase market share. Japanese elevator manufacturers concentrated on the development of faster elevators. Conversely, the focus of the Western world was on state-of-the art control systems.

Increasingly, Otis, Schindler, Kone, and other manufacturers moved away from the traditional electromechanical methods of running elevators and replaced them with microelectronic control systems and artificial intelligence capable of ensuring the most efficient and convenient use of installed elevator cars or cabs. In 1997 the environmentally friendly nature of this new technology was apparent, and Otis was selected as the elevator vendor supplying New York City's first "green" office tower, the Conde Nast building. Here, Otis was asked to install what would be the first U.S. example of high-speed elevators utilizing AC (alternating current) variable frequency drive systems. In this case, the importance of the chosen drive system was its low energy consumption and clean operation, not its speed.

Another innovation employed to make elevators more environmentally friendly was the use of soy-based hydraulic fluid in one of the United States' national symbols, the Statue of Liberty. Since November 2002, the Statue of Liberty's elevator has been running on this biodegradable fluid, which replaced petroleum-based mineral oil. Manufactured by Agri-Lube Inc. in Ohio, the soy-based oil was created by the ARS National Center for Agricultural Utilization Research in Peoria, Illinois, based on the National Park Service's request for "a hydraulic elevator fluid that would readily biodegrade in the environment, come from a renewable resource, be produced by an economical and nonpolluting process, and meet industrial safety and performance standards."

Japan's Mitsubishi held the certificate for the world's fastest passenger elevator, which reached speeds of 2,500 feet per minute. Installed in the 70-story Yokohama Landmark Tower, the elevator hurtled from the second floor to the sixty-ninth floor in 40 seconds. Hitachi Ltd. made similar claims about an elevator model of its own. This emphasis on speed was a calculated gamble on the part of the Japanese manufacturers, but they noted that elevators that broke speed records gained media attention and were strong selling points to the designers and owners of newer and higher buildings, who would use the speedy elevators to attract tenants.

Otis, Schindler, Kone, and other western elevator manufacturers resisted the elevator speed derby for numerous reasons. They reasoned that unless buildings increased considerably in size, there was little genuine need for faster elevators. Because of the time it takes an elevator to accelerate and decelerate, in most skyscrapers elevators reached maximum speed for a duration of only five seconds. Similarly, in nearly all cases, the extra time for a slower elevator to travel added only a few seconds to the trip from ground level to the upper stories of a building. When the elevator in question made numerous stops on the trip, the importance of speed decreased. The comparative example applied by engineers was that of a "bullet train" installed on a milk run, stopping for each town.

The high cost of super-speed elevators was another deterrent, at least from a Western perspective. The US$3 million to US$5 million price tag was approximately 20 percent higher than the price of comparable slower-speed units. The Japanese justified their strategy in constructing the pricey equipment by the fact that this ongoing research and development was a necessary investment in a future filled with 150-story buildings. This rationale did not appeal strongly enough to either Otis and Schindler to cause them to throw development energy into the direction of sheer speed.

To companies outside of Japan, elevator control systems were the key to future technology. The computer intelligence behind sophisticated "fuzzy logic" control systems took multiple factors into account in the course of elevator system operation. While traditional systems dispatched elevators according to which could reach a given floor most quickly, new high-tech elevator control systems examined multiple factors, not just speed and timing. Decisions were made based on real and perceived demand, the number of people in each car, passenger convenience and inconvenience, the number of times a waiting passenger depressed a button, and the relative proximity of the elevator to the desired floor. An ideal time spent waiting for an elevator was perceived to be about 20 seconds, although 30 seconds was considered an acceptable average. Developers believed that the longest a passenger should ever have to wait for an elevator under any circumstances was 90 seconds. With these relatively aggressive targets in mind, proponents of the new intelligent systems contended that "fuzzy logic" would reduce waiting time by up to 15 percent.

Another microelectronic control system under development was neural networking, a system wherein an elevator "learns from its mistakes." If, for instance, there was high demand for elevators at a certain time (such as lunch time or quitting time) on an upper floor, the elevator anticipated demand by recording usage patterns. The elevators subsequently "learned" to park themselves on the appropriate floors at the appropriate times instead of automatically awaiting calls at the lobby floor. Other technological innovations under development called for numerous elevator cars to circulate around a continuous shaft resembling a Ferris wheel. Research was also undertaken on linear motors that would propel elevators via a magnetic field, thus doing away with lift cables.

Otis led in researching elevator systems equipped with linear induction motors through its Nippon Otis Company, a Japanese joint venture. Unlike linear motors proposed for the future, the current units included lifting cables and needed special facilities for hydraulic pumps or a rooftop hoisting gear. The linear motor rode with the counterweights in back of the elevator cab and moved up and down the hoistway in opposition to the elevator. Elevators with linear induction motors had fewer moving parts than conventional elevators. Other benefits included lower construction, installation, and maintenance costs, and greater reliability. Because of code restrictions, linear motor elevators were not in operation in the United States in the 1990s. A growing market for this system was envisioned in Japan, however, because of different building codes and architectural preferences.

Otis and Schindler were not alone in the introduction of new technology to the industry. In early 1998 Kone announced a new drive system that eliminated the need for the familiar machine room that historically occupied the space above each elevator shaft. The new system used 40 percent less energy than hydraulic systems and was suitable for installation in newly constructed buildings or could be retrofitted into existing buildings. In response to an increase in building size, Hitachi also introduced an intelligent elevator supervisory-control system. In 1997 press releases, Hitachi representatives spoke of a "genetic algorithm" simulating "biological evolution," and using the resultant artificial intelligence to deploy elevators efficiently. That year, Hitachi extended its technology inwardly as well, announcing technical improvements in the design and production environments. Even the small producer Alimak brought a kind of innovation to the industry. Developed originally to meet the requirements of construction, the "rack and pinion" system perfected by Alimak found uses wherever simplicity and strength were desirable.

In 2004 ThyssenKrupp announced its ISIS elevator system, in development for three years. A machine-room-less elevator, ISIS saved an average of 60 square feet of space per elevator in buildings, because it was space-efficient and contained completely within the elevator shaft. In addition, the ISIS was quieter than other elevators, because it used DuPont Kevlar's synthetic rope instead of steel rope. By mid-2004, all leaders in the industry offered elevator solutions that did not require machine rooms.

INDUSTRY LEADERS

In the mid-2000s, the old guard manufacturers—Otis, Schindler, and Kone—were still on top, although they ceded market share to counterparts in Japan (notably Hitachi and Mitsubishi) and elsewhere. As the giants struggled for world market share at the turn of the century, the stubborn health of a variety of smaller international firms saw multiple small companies divide what was less than half the total market.

OTIS ELEVATOR COMPANY

The number one company in the industry, Otis Elevator Company is a wholly owned subsidiary of the United Technologies Corporation (UTC), and was responsible for generating 24 percent of UTC revenues and 33 percent of UTC operating profits. Otis held close to 28 percent of the world market for new elevator and escalator equipment in 2005. Many of Otis's elevator designs were particularly suited for high-speed passenger operations in high-rise buildings, and Otis elevators were installed in eleven of the world's twenty tallest buildings, according to an Otis Fact Sheet from March 2005. Otis was also involved in the maintenance and modernization of pre-existing vertical transportation systems and manufactured horizontal transportation systems such as moving sidewalks and shuttle systems. In 2005, Otis' global presence extended to manufacturing facilities in Europe and Asia as well as the Americas. In the mid-2000s, Otis boasted 60,000 employees, 51,000 outside the United States, and 1.7 million elevators and escalators in use worldwide. Company revenues in 2004 were US$9 billion, with foreign revenue accounting for 79 percent of that total.

One of the company's innovations for the mid-2000s was its NextStep escalator, a machine-room-less system built for commercial and public use. Otis advertised the system as environmentally friendly, as it does not require lubricant, and includes the added safety feature of the Guarded step, which removes the gap between moving risers and the escalator panels. By investing more than $115 million in engineering and research and development during 2004, Otis sought to keep its place as the industry leader.

Otis's parent company, United Technologies Corp., earned $37.4 billion in revenue during 2004 and employed 210,000 people. In early 2005, UTC purchased Lenel, a security software firm, with whom it planned to develop all-in-one systems that would monitor building, elevator, and network access and activity.

SCHINDLER HOLDING LTD.

Schindler Holding Ltd., the second largest company in the industry, began in 1874 in Lucerne, Switzerland, as a precision engineering firm. Solidly established as part of the Swiss economy a hundred years later, in the 1980s Schindler acquired several other firms involved in the vertical transportation industry. Many of these acquisitions were of relatively small operations, but in 1989 Schindler acquired the entire escalator and elevator business of the Westinghouse Electric Corporation the assets of Westinghouse's former Canadian operations. By the mid-2000s, Schindler had a market presence in more than 100 countries, with 250 locations in North America alone. Schindler overall reported operating revenues of US$6.9 billion, 6.9 percent more than reported in 2003. Sales in the elevator and escalator business rose 4.4 percent from 2003, reaching US$5.38 billion. The company realized a 12.8 percent increase in the number of unit orders for new installations during 2004. Schindler employed 39,443 people in 2004, and earned a net income of US$268.7 million.

KONE

The Kone Corporation was founded in Finland in 1920. In the 1980s it began to actively acquire smaller companies involved in the vertical transportation industry, and by 1998 Kone was firmly established on five separate continents: Europe, Asia, North and South America, and Africa, although Europe remained its biggest market. At the turn of the twenty-first century, Kone easily held its position as one of the three leading manufacturers of elevators worldwide. Offering an extensive variety of products and services, from planning and traffic analysis to post-installation maintenance, Kone elevators were in evidence in industrial and commercial buildings, as well as in office buildings, hotels, and hospitals. Kone held service contracts in 2004 for approximately 550,000 units. Major agreements in the mid-2000s included the company's joint ventures with China and Russia, as well as a contract to build 26 elevators reaching 97 floors for the new Trump Tower in Chicago.

Kone orders rose 10 percent in Europe (more strongly in eastern Europe), the Middle East, and Africa. In North America, order levels remained unchanged, as they were in the Asia Pacific. Kone reported 2004 net sales of US$5.7 billion; of this, sales of elevators and escalators were responsible for $3.7 billion, a 3 percent growth over 2003. Most 2004 sales revenue came from Europe, the Middle East, and Africa, where sales totaled $2.4 billion, followed by the Americas with $808 million and Asia Pacific with $468 million. Kone's net income rose by 8.5 percent, from $389 million in 2003 to $422 million in 2004. Kone expected improvement in revenue growth during 2005 through improved operations in the United States, restructuring, better management of major projects, and new plants in China and the Czech Republic, with streamlined processes leading toward increases in 2006 and beyond. Kone employed 33,000 people and operated 800 service centers in 40 countries in early 2005.

HITACHI, LTD.

Japan's Hitachi, Ltd. was formed in 1910. Over the years it became engaged in the manufacturing of a wide variety of consumer and industrial products, including power systems, electronic and communication devices, industrial machinery, and chemical products. The company's primary territory for elevator sales in the 1990s was Asia and the Pacific Rim. Underscoring this fact, in 1996 Hitachi established three joint venture companies in China's Canton province: Hitachi Elevator (Guangzhou) Co., Ltd.; Hitachi Escalator (Guangzhou) Co., Ltd.; and Guangzhou Guangri Elevator Co., Ltd. These three new ventures were in addition to Shanghai Yungtay Engineering Co., Ltd., which had been established in 1995; Beijing Hitachi Elevator Service Co., Ltd.; and Hainan Hitachi Elevator Co., Ltd. In 2000, Hitachi reorganized all elevator and escalator businesses, pulling them in under Hitachi Ltd.'s new Building Systems Group. The business was reorganized again, and elevator systems became part of Hitachi's Power & Industrial Systems division. Hitachi Ltd. reported 2003 revenues of $81.4 billion for the entire company. During the first nine months of the 2004 fiscal year, Hitachi earned $62 billion in revenue, $16.1 billion of which came from Power & Industrial Systems. Hitachi expected its domestic and Asian business to remain healthy, but due to cost of raw materials and declining market conditions, Hitachi expected global growth to slow.

MITSUBISHI ELECTRIC CORP.

Mitsubishi Electric Corp. was established in Japan in 1921. It manufactures a wide variety of electronic, heavy machinery, and industrial products. Its principal subsidiary in the elevator and escalator industry is Mitsubishi Elevator Co., based in Cypress, California. In the late 1990s, Mitsubishi's achievements included the world's fastest elevator, and perhaps the world's most graceful escalator. In 1997 Mitsubishi married escalators to the spiral staircase, resulting in spiral escalators capable of adding their curves to modern building design. The company reported 2004 revenue figures at US$30.4 billion, down 9 percent from 2003; however, like Hitachi, the figure included sales for the entire company. The company's Energy and Electric division, which included elevators as well as security systems and other electronics, accounted for 21.9 percent of Mitsubishi Electric's overall sales.

THYSSENKRUPP AG

In 1999, Germany's merger of Thyssen AG and Fried.Krupp AG Hoesch-Krupp created ThyssenKrupp. In the mid-2000s, the company was one of the world's largest steel producers. Thyssen's elevator segment reported income of US$480 million, up almost $19 million from 2003. ThyssenKrupp as a whole reported 2004 income of US$2.05 billion, almost a billion dollars more than in 2003. All business units in the elevator segment reported a profit in 2004, and the most significant increases were realized in Europc and Latin America. ThyssenKrupp attributed is growth in profits to ongoing strengthening of its service business. Profits in North America saw a slight decrease due to devaluation of the U.S. dollar and pricing.

FURTHER READING

"About NAEC." National Association of Elevator Contractors, 2004. Available from http://www.naec.org.

"Daily Update." *Elevator World,* 2004. Available from http://www.elevator-world.com.

Elevator World Source, October 2001. Available from http://www.elevator-world.com.

"Elevators and Escalators Take Center Stage at National Building Museum." *Buildings,* June 2003.

Hahn, Avital Louria. "M&A Transforms The World of Security." *Investment Dealers' Digest,* 4 April 2005.

Hill, Andrew. "UTC Record Run of Great Expectations Grinds to a Halt," 2000. Available from http://www.FT.com.

Hitachi Ltd. "Hitachi Announces Consolidated Financial Results for the Third Quarter of Fiscal 2004," 2 February 2005. Available from http://www.hitachi.com.

"Hoover's Company Capsules." 2004. Available from http://www.hoovers.com.

Kone. *Kone Company Profile,* 2001. Available from http://www.kone.com.

Kone. *Kone Interim Report: 1 January—31 December 2004, IFRS,* 28 January 2005. Available from http://www.kone.com.

"KONE Corporation to Establish Joint Venture in China." *Nordic Business Report,* 20 April 2005.

"KONE Corporation to Establish Joint Venture in Russia." *Nordic Business Report,* 19 April 2005.

Mitsubishi. *Investor Relations,* 2001. Available from http://www.mitsubishielectric.com.

Mitsubishi Electric. *Annual Report,* 2004. Available from http://www.mitsubishielectric.com.

Otis Elevator Co. *Company Milestones.* Farmington, CT: 2001. Available from http://www.otis.com.

Otis Elevator Co. *Otis Fact Sheet.* Farmington, CT: March 2005. Available from http://www.otis.com.

"Schindler Elevator Rolls Out FieldLink Service Handheld." *Wireless News,* 8 October 2004.

Schindler Holding Ltd. *Annual Report,* 2004. Available from http://www.schindler.com.

Schindler Holding Ltd. "Schindler: Sustantially Improved Results." 28 February 2005. Available from http://www.schindler.com.

"Statue of Liberty Goes Green with Soy." *Resource: Engineering&Technology for a Sustainable World,* December 2004.

ThyssenKrupp AG. *Annual Report,* 2004. Available from http://www.thyssenkrupp.com.

"ThyssenKrupp Introduces World's Most Technologically Advanced Elevator." *PR Newswire,* 17 February 2004.

"United Technologies Corporation: Company Profile." *Datamonitor,* 17 November 2004.

SIC 3510

NAICS 3336

ENGINES AND TURBINES

The turbine segment of this industry manufactures turbines powered by steam, hydraulic, gas, wind, and solar energy sources, along with complete steam, gas, and hydraulic turbine generator set units, commonly known as turbogenerators. In the engine segment, the industry includes companies that produce gasoline, diesel, semi-diesel, and other internal combustion engines (ICEs) for such uses as on-site power generation; powering construction equipment; marine applications; and many others. Aircraft and automotive engines are discussed elsewhere; see also **Aircraft Manufacturing** and **Motor Vehicle Parts and Accessories.**

INDUSTRY SNAPSHOT

The most important application of turbines, and to some degree diesel and other ICEs, is to produce electricity for power consumption. There are relatively few manufacturers of turbines and turbogenerators for this purpose worldwide because production requires large amounts of capital. As a result, leading firms in the industry—such as General Electric, Volvo, Siemens, and Caterpillar—are part of the world's largest multinational corporations, many of which are highly diversified across industry lines.

While other energy sources, particularly nuclear, were declining by the mid-2000s, so-called "green" turbines and engines powered by wind and solar energy were coming to the forefront. In 2003, the worldwide wind power industry was valued at approximately US$8 billion, and the solar power industry was valued at US$5 billion. In the United States, renewable energy sources were less than 10 percent of the industry, but were expected to grow throughout the decade.

ORGANIZATION AND STRUCTURE

Most turbines and turbogenerators are made to order, custom-designed to accommodate the specific requirements of a power plant. Equipment is produced in specialized factories that are generally erected and assembled at the power plant sites. While turbines have relatively few parts, their production tolerances—the allowable variations from their original production and assembly specifications—are exacting.

Trade Structure. One of the important distinctions between the United States and Japan and Europe is the decentralized nature of electricity production in the United States. In Japan and Europe, power equipment manufacturers, architects, construction firms, utilities managers, and governments typically develop projects on a partnership basis. The U.S. Department of Commerce has argued that, whatever its merits for the domestic operations of U.S. firms, this situation puts them at a decided disadvantage in penetrating the more mediated Japanese and European markets.

This arrangement is coordinated under the International Electrical Association (IEA), an export cartel formed in the 1920s by producers of power generation equipment. The U.S. Justice Department compelled U.S. producers to withdraw from the IEA in the 1930s. Japanese producers were admitted as special members of the IEA in the 1960s. Not surprisingly, the IEA comprises European and Japanese manufacturers of power generating equipment exclusively. The U.S. Department of Commerce contends that the IEA's system of price setting and market allocation has given European and Japanese producers a significant competitive advantage in the markets of the developed countries.

In an effort to improve their competitiveness, U.S. manufacturers have focused on increasing sales to developing countries and on entering into joint ventures with Japanese and European firms. At the same time, U.S. manufacturers have focused research and development efforts on:

- smaller plants
- combined-cycle gas and steam turbines
- pumped-storage hydroelectric systems
- high-temperature gas turbines, especially their materials and coatings, and
- cogeneration, which harnesses the excess heat or steam produced in industrial processes to make more energy available for consumption at a commercial or industrial site

Continuing deregulation of U.S. electric utilities in the early 2000s prompted U.S. producers to seek markets overseas, particularly in China and elsewhere in Asia. The European Union market was a difficult one for U.S. producers to penetrate because Europe's nationalized electric utilities most often favor European producers. However, deregulation of electricity markets in some EU countries could provide an opportunity for U.S. turbine producers to further develop small combined-cycle or cogeneration facilities. The best market prospects for U.S. producers in the early 2000s were in Germany, Italy, Spain, and the United Kingdom.

Turbine Trade Groups. Several large trade organizations serve the turbine industry. The International Gas Turbine Institute of the American Society of Mechanical Engineers is based in Atlanta, Georgia, and publishes the *Global Gas Turbine News.* The Paris-based International Conference on Large High Voltage Electric Systems was founded in 1921, has 5,300 members and 44 national groups, and publishes the bimonthly *Electra* in English and French. Other associations serving the industry include the European Commission of Manufacturers of Electrical Installation Equipment and the European Committee of Manufacturers of Electrical Machines and Power Electronics, both headquartered in Paris. The latter organization seeks to promote members' interests in accordance with trade agreements associated with the European Union.

Engine Trade Groups. The European Committee of Associations of Manufacturers of Internal Combustion Engines was founded in 1963 and is based in Zoetermeer, the Netherlands. The organization was established to represent the interests of European diesel engine producers in Europe's emerging collective market. The engine industry is also served by the International Council on Combustion Engines, founded in 1951 and based in Paris. The organization promotes the advancement of technical knowledge regarding internal combustion engines in various ways, including publishing a number of technical papers as part of its biennial *Congress Proceedings.*

BACKGROUND AND DEVELOPMENT

Turbines convert fluid motion into rotary motion, which is harnessed to perform a wide range of work—most notably the production of electricity. The principal types of turbines are defined by the energy source driving their blades. The most important in terms of market share are steam, water, and gas. Turbines generally consist of a number of blades or fins attached to a rotor so that the rotor spins as steam, water, or gas is forced past the blades or fins. Steam turbines may be powered by fossil fuels or nuclear energy. Water turbines are most widely used in hydroelectric dams. According to figures published by the U.S. Energy Information Administration (EIA), for all countries of the world in 1995, petroleum-based sources accounted for 61.8 percent of electricity produced, nuclear-fueled steam for 16.6 percent, and renewable sources (mostly hydroelectric) for 21.2 percent. By 2015, the EIA predicts that fossil fuels will expand to 67.8 percent of world electricity generation, while nuclear fuel will decline to 10.6 percent and renewables will remain largely unchanged at 21.5 percent. Natural gas will be the fastest-growing fossil fuel source for electrical power generation.

Rise of Steam and Gas Turbines. The majority of electrical power is produced by steam turbines from heat generated by fossil fuels or nuclear power. Steam turbines have the capacity to generate a large amount of electrical power in a small space—more than 1.3 million kilowatts from a single rotor. The first steam turbines that saw successful commercial application were developed by American William Avery in the 1830s. About 50 steam turbines of Avery's design were used in sawmills and cotton gins. Although as efficient as piston-driven steam engines in converting fuel to mechanical power, these early steam turbines gradually fell out of use due to their noise and frequent need for repair.

By the early twentieth century, generators driven by steam turbines were the most important producers of electricity in the world. Economies of scale were important in steam turbines, leading to increasingly larger units. By the 1940s, single-turbine units were capable of producing 100,000 kilowatts. Large steam turbines also were important as ship engines. The *Lusitania* (a British ship later made famous by its sinking during World War I) and its twin the *Mauritania,* launched in 1906, were driven by fossil-fueled steam turbines generating 68,000 horsepower. Nuclear-fueled military ships in the 1990s were also driven by steam turbines.

Though generally not classified as such, gas turbines are a form of internal combustion engine, with a turbine rather than a piston being driven by a controlled explosion. Gas turbines have an advantage over piston internal combustion engines in that they are able to create more power in less space. Gas turbines consist of a compressor, a combustion chamber, and the turbine itself. Industrial gas turbines are used to drive power generators, pumps, or propellers.

Gas turbines played an increasingly important role in generating power in medium-size plants and, in the early 2000s, in some of the world's largest new power plants. Since water for steam turbines requires several hours to heat, gas turbines provide a compact means to meet the demands of peak-hour production with low initial cost. Gas-fired plants accounted for only 8 percent of U.S. electricity capacity in the mid-1980s, but by the beginning of 2000 that figure had increased to nearly 22 percent. Gas turbine-generator manufacturers in the early 2000s included AEG-Kanis, Asea Brown Boveri, General Electric, Mitsubishi, Siemens, and Thomassen. (By 2000, one major turbine manufacturer, Westinghouse Electric Corporation, had been acquired by Germany's Siemens AG.)

The use of gas turbines for producing electrical power expanded with the development of gas/steam turbine-generators, also known as combined cycle or combined-heat-and-power (CHP) systems. These systems make use of the heat generated by gas turbines to provide heat for steam turbines with substantially greater efficiency than pure gas turbines. Combined cycle power is viable because exhaust gases from gas turbines are relatively clean and hot, ranging from 750 to 1,000 degrees Fahrenheit. Combined cycle power plants became increasingly viable following the oil crises of the 1970s and in the face of opposition to nuclear-fueled power production; this format had gained wider acceptance by 2000. Combined cycle plants are relatively environmentally friendly, emitting no ash and little air pollution.

By the year 2000, combined cycle power plants represented most of the market volume for power generation equipment in the United States. Gas turbine combined cycle plants had achieved 55 percent efficiency levels, with the prospects of reaching 60 percent thermal efficiency later in the early 2000s.

Steam Turbines. In terms of the number of steam turbines produced in 1990, the leading countries were Austria with 1,337, France with 823, the Commonwealth of Independent States (CIS) with 428, Germany with 426, and Japan with 406. In terms of share of world exports by U.S. dollar value, the leading countries in 1992 were Japan with 25.8 percent, Germany with 19.5 percent, the United States with 15.9 percent, England with 6.5 percent, and France/Monaco with 6.3 percent. Total value of world exports was US$2.1 billion in 1992. Among the Organization for Economic Cooperation and Development (OECD) countries, in 1999, the largest producers of nuclear-fueled steam electricity were the United States with 777,885 gigawatt hours, France with 394,244, Japan with 316,616, Germany with 170,004, and England with 96,281.

Hydraulic Turbines. Hydraulic turbine production in 1990 was led by France with 3,763, the Czech Republic with 112, Romania with 41, and Japan with 28. The CIS was also a significant producer in 1990 in terms of kilowatt capacity. Among OECD countries, in 1999 the largest producers of hydroelectricity were the United States with 318,619 gigawatt hours, Japan with 95,577, France with 77,082, Italy with 51,777, and Germany with 23,402.

Gas Turbines. Ranked by total world gas turbine exports, the leading countries in 1992 were the United States with 25.4 percent, Britain with 18.2 percent, Canada with 12.3 percent, Germany with 6.9 percent, and Japan with 6.8 percent. That year, the total value of world exports was US$3.5 billion.

Internal Combustion Engines. Among makers of non-automotive diesel engines as of 1991, the top countries were India with 1.6 million, Japan with 1.1 million, Germany with 228,132, and the United States with 184,245. In terms of the number of other nonautomotive internal combustion engines produced, the leading countries in 1992 were the United States with 18.2 million, Japan with 5.9 million, Romania with 110,000, Poland with 105,000, and Germany with 36,000.

Export market share for miscellaneous internal combustion engines in the early 1990s was divided among Japan with 19.5 percent, the United States with 16.7 percent, Germany with 16.4 percent, France/Monaco with 8.9 percent, and Britain with 7.3 percent. Total value of world exports was US$40 billion in 1992.

Water Turbines. Water turbines are essentially updated and more efficient versions of waterwheels, which were used for millennia. The first commercially successful water turbine design was developed by Frenchman Benoit Fourneyron (1802-1867) in the 1820s. More than 100 such turbines were eventually installed worldwide. These turbines were, however, costly to construct, physically unstable, and difficult to control for speed of rotation. They were eventually supplanted by the designs, developed in the 1830s, of American James Francis. Francis-type turbines remained one of the key turbine types used in contemporary applications. Water turbines were in widespread use by the mid-nineteenth century, primarily in powering saw and textile mills, though they were soon supplanted in these applications by steam engines.

The first use of water turbines to generate electricity on a commercial basis came in 1882, when a 12.5 kilowatt station in Wisconsin provided power to light two paper mills. The use of hydroelectric power grew rapidly thereafter, with the first 100,000-kilowatt installations built in the 1930s. From the 1940s to the early 1970s, a large number of small hydroelectric stations, most with less than 1,000 kilowatt capacity, were shut down due to their relatively high cost. Meanwhile, from the 1950s to the late 1980s, the production capacity of typical water turbine generators doubled, from 150,000 to 300,000 kilowatts, with the largest of modern units capable of producing 750,000 kilowatts.

The economic viability of hydroelectric production was determined not only by direct costs of energy production, but also by the costs of acquiring land and constructing reservoirs. The latter costs typically accounted for about half of the initial outlay for a project. In the Pacific Northwest and Rocky Mountain regions of the United States, hydroelectric power enjoyed a cost advantage over electricity produced by fossil fuels, partly because of the combined function of hydroelectric facilities, which also served to control floods and store water for municipal water systems and rural irrigation.

One key problem with water turbines was the inability to store large amounts of electricity. Another was that water turbines generally were much less efficient during off-peak production times, such as at night or on weekends. This problem was addressed by pumping water into a second higher-level reservoir during off hours for use during peak hours. This was accomplished by using reversible turbines, which served as pumps during off hours, and reversible generators, which served as electrical motors to drive turbines operating in reverse. In 2001, there were approximately 18,000 megawatts of this type of generating capacity, called "pumped storage" hydroelectric capacity, in the United States.

The vast majority of hydroelectric facilities are situated on rivers, but hydropower stations driven by tidal flows are also feasible along ocean coasts with high tides. A 240,000-kilowatt capacity plant with 24 water turbines operated on the Brittany coast in France, while the Commonwealth of Independent States built a similar plant on its eastern coast.

The largest producers of hydroelectric power are the United States, Russia, Brazil, and Canada. In Brazil, 92 percent of generating capacity was supplied by hydropower in 1997. In 2001, hydroelectric stations provided at least 10 percent of the electricity in the United States. However, the potential for increasing this share was limited, since about three-fourths of the potential capacity for hydroelectric production had been tapped in the contiguous United States. In fact, seven states—Washington, California, Oregon, New York, Tennessee, South Carolina, and Virginia—represented about 64 percent of all U.S. hydroelectric capacity in the late 1990s. Much untapped potential, however, remained in Alaska, northern Canada, the former Soviet Union, and parts of Africa, South America, and the Himalayan region. China also was aggressively developing its hydroelectric resources, but proposed hydroelectric stations in Malaysia and India were abandoned in the late 1990s because of protests by environmental groups. Canada projected a one-third increase in its hydroelectric capacity by 2020, with the lion's share expected to be added after 2010. Plans for large-scale hydro dams in Canada largely have been abandoned; future projects in Canada will be limited to 500 megawatts.

One major issue affecting hydroelectric power in the early 2000s in the United States was the expiration of operating licenses for many of the country's hydroelectric stations. According to the Federal Energy Regulatory Commission, more than 35 hydro operating licenses were scheduled to expire in the 1990s, while an additional 69 operating licenses were scheduled to expire in 2000 and 2001. The greatest amount of authorized generating capacity up for relicensing is expected to occur in 2007. All told, notes the Energy Information Administration, the expiring licenses between 1995 and 2010 account for more than 24 gigawatts of current generating capacity, or just about half of current non-federal hydro capacity.

A continuing issue for the hydroelectric industry in the United States is fish kills, particularly salmon and steelhead trout. These fish attempt to swim upstream, from the sea to the river, while spawning. However, when a hydroelectric station is along their path, the fish can get caught in the turbine blades. This is particularly problematic in the Pacific Northwest, in Washington's Columbia River Basin. Salmon and steelhead runs there declined from rates of 11-16 million fish a year in pre-Colonial times to 2 million or fewer fish in the late 1990s.

Wind Turbines. Wind-powered generators offer an increasingly viable alternative power source. Windpower often is cited as the fastest-growing form of renewable energy, enjoying a 28 percent increase in worldwide capacity in 2000. Single giant windmills capable of providing electricity to several thousand homes were operating as of 2001 in some areas of the United States.

With the 1996 bankruptcy of the U.S. manufacturer Kenetech, Denmark became the world's largest producer of wind turbines, accounting for 60 percent of the market, according to the Danish Wind Turbine Manufacturers Association. Denmark has a wind power capacity of 750 megawatts, or 5 percent of Denmark's electricity. Vestas of Denmark was the world's largest wind mill constructor, with a global market share of 21 percent. The combined sales of three Danish manufacturers accounted for at least half of the global wind-turbine market in 2001.

Since the mid-1980s, the cost of producing electricity with windmills has dropped more than fourfold, bringing windpower on a par with power produced using oil, coal, and natural gas. However, windmills had the disadvantages of being noisy and dangerous to birds. When properly situated, however, it is possible to mitigate these problems.

In 1992, the U.S. Department of Energy and the Electric Power Research Institute (EPRI) implemented a program to increase the commercial viability of windpower turbines by evaluating advanced turbines developed by U.S. electric companies. The first was a six-megawatt facility in Fort Davis, Texas, which used twelve 550-kilowatt wind turbines, while the second, with eleven 550-kilowatt turbines, began operating in Searsburg, Vermont, in 1997. Three 750-kilowatt wind turbines were installed in Algona, Texas, prior to 2000, while other wind turbine projects were on tap for Nebraska, Texas, Oklahoma, New York, Wisconsin and Alaska.

Market conditions in the United States and many industrialized nations moved from decent in the mid-1990s—limited in part by both overcapacity and by conservation and efficiency gains—to vibrant at the turn of the century. Demand in Asia, particularly China and India, offered significant growth opportunities. The power generation market, especially the gas turbine sector, enjoyed a growth pattern described as an "elongated bubble." Turbine shipments enjoyed a period of robust growth in the mid- to late 1990s, which continued through 2001, with North America constituting a hotbed for both gas turbines and internal combustion engines.

An anticipated return to the slow growth of earlier decades has not materialized. Still, industry experts doubted that growth could continue at the healthy pace of the period from 1995 to 2001. According to a Fredonia Group study, world turbine demand was expected to continue to increase through the early 2000s, thanks to strong demand for new and upgraded generating capacity in both developed and developing countries. Competition for these markets has been fierce; larger Western turbine manufacturers faced stiff competition from turbine producers in Eastern Europe, China, and Russia. Consequently, many producers heavily discounted prices of their older turbine technologies. From 1998 to 2001, the United States led a surge in turbine orders caused by capacity expansion and the upgrading of turbines necessary for combined cycle power plants. In addition, privatization and deregulation of electric power generating systems, along with the realities of power shortages and high electricity costs, ensured that U.S. orders of large turbine units will continue to increase, if perhaps somewhat more slowly than before.

The global picture for diesel, dual-fuel, and natural gas ICEs remained favorable, reflecting buyers' growing concerns about power quality and availability and the economic losses involved in power outages (most of these shipments constitute additions to diesel or other fuel-powered standby service). Additionally, concerns about energy shortages promoted purchases of diesel and natural gas engines for both standby and continuous service.

Relatively strong demand for turbines in the few years before 2000 prompted turbine producers around the world to rush turbines to the market before all potential problems were identified, according to a report from the *Wall Street Journal Europe.* New turbines from U.S.-based General Electric Co. and Europe's GEC-Alsthom had to be temporarily shut down because the bolts inside cracked. In addition, Siemens AG's new turbine, adapted from ring burner jet engine technology, experienced excessive vibrations, while Asea Brown Boveri's turbines had portions of their heatshields come loose during operation.

As of the late 1990s, 429 nuclear reactors were in operation globally, producing more than 345 billion watts (or gigawatts) of electricity. At that amount, nuclear power generated about 7 percent of the world's electricity. As of 2001, 30 nuclear reactors were under construction, most in developing and industrialized Asia. Combined, these were expected to produce an additional 22 gigawatts. However, the industry continued to be hindered by the safety and environmental problems of nuclear power plants, demonstrated most notably by the 1979 accident at the Three Mile Island plant in Middletown, Pennsylvania, and by the 1986 disaster at Chernobyl in the Ukraine, Soviet Union. In fact, there have been no new U.S. nuclear orders since 1977, and three reactors were closed down prematurely in the late 1990s, reducing the number of operating reactors in the United States to 104 as of 2001. Thus, nuclear never generated more than 20 percent of American electricity, whereas in 2001, France produced 78 percent of its electricity via fission reactors; Belgium, 62 percent; and Lithuania, 82 percent. These three were the world's leaders in domestic nuclear power generation.

According to the International Energy Agency, though France is a world leader in nuclear power, design flaws and public complaints about costs and unreliable service have nearly brought its construction of reactors to a halt. With the exception of two new reactors added in the late 1990s, no further French nuclear capacity has been announced. In Italy, all nuclear reactors were shut down, and authorities in Sweden debated over a timetable to do the same; the Swedish government eventually voted to retire two of the country's 12 operating units, one in 1998 and one in 2001. Construction of reactors was also halted in Germany, and Finland canceled plans for the construction of what would have been its only nuclear reactor.

Not surprisingly, opportunities for growth in the nuclear power industry in the late 1990s and beyond were limited to areas outside Western Europe and North America. At the end of 1996, 18 nuclear units were under construction in developing Asia. Countries in developing and industrialized Asia with operating nuclear plants at the turn of the century included China, Taiwan, India, Pakistan, and South Korea, with units scheduled to become operational in North Korea in 2020. In industrialized Asia, Japan's nuclear capacity was expected to increase by 11 units to a total of 12.5 gigawatts.

CURRENT CONDITIONS

By 2004, the gas turbine market was worth $67 billion and projected to increase 7 percent per year through 2007 to reach the $77 billion mark. The strong growth, however, could not equal the gains of the 1998 to 2001 period. In 2001, global gas turbine orders increased 55 percent in terms of capacity and 13 percent in terms of number of units. Specifically, capacity increased by 41,390 megawatts to 117,240 megawatts, and the number of units increased from 1,203 to 1,357. According to *Diesel and Gas Turbine Worldwide*, North America is still the most popular destination of these turbines, accounting for 67 percent of the total 1,357 units ordered. In the combined output ranges of 30 to 180 megawatts, North America received 76 percent of these turbines. South America saw an increase of 204 percent in large gas turbines to be located there, rising from 21 units in 2000 to 64 units in 2001. However, orders for Western Europe declined by nearly 32 percent.

As with turbines, orders for diesel, dual-fuel, and natural gas ICEs (also known as reciprocating engines) increased substantially in 2001, with units ordered up 68 percent to 10,795 and total output up 39 percent to 16,263 megawatts. Major growth continues in North America, with orders increasing 66 percent to 5,051 units. Western Europe's orders increased significantly as well, by 47 percent to 826 units. There also was a healthy increase of 111 percent in combined order activity throughout the Middle East, the Far East, and Central Asia. South America posted an astounding 126 percent increase in the number of orders—from 146 units to 330 units.

A number of nuclear reactors still in operation in the United States face possible shutdowns for technical and economic reasons. This early retirement trend is expected to continue to 2020, shaving off 25 percent of the generating capacity that existed at the turn of the twenty-first century. Other countries with more economical options for power generation also were expected to begin letting their nuclear capacity lapse, according to the Energy Information Administration. Experts forecast world nuclear generation capacity of 172 gigawatts in 2020, a more than 50 percent decline from a peak of 367 gigawatts. In Western Europe, only Turkey and France project increases in nuclear capacity by 2020; eight other European countries expect their total nuclear capacity to decrease because of reactor retirements.

As of the mid-2000s, wind and solar energy power generation was on the rise. In 2003, the worldwide wind power industry was valued at approximately US$8 billion and was expected to hit US$16 billion by 2007. GE Energy had 13 percent of the wind turbine market share worldwide in 2003. The solar power industry was valued at US$5 billion that year, of which the United States had US$700 million of the market share. As of that year, most of the solar energy power generation market came for photovoltaic panels.

As of 2004, wind power was the fastest growing segment in the energy generation industry, with annual 20 percent increases predicted through 2008. The world's main wind energy markets were, in order of estimated megawatt production, Germany, the United States, Denmark, Spain, India, the Netherlands, Italy, the United Kingdom, China, and Sweden. According to the European Wind Energy Association, wind capacity nearly doubled in 2001, with the largest percentage increases for Germany and Spain. Germany was the fastest-growing market for wind generation in Western Europe, while India was second to Germany in terms of capacity. Denmark, with 20 percent of its energy wind-generated in 2003, expected large gains in wind capacity by the early 2000s, as did the U.K. In addition, Greece could develop an estimated 100 megawatts of wind capacity in a few short years; before 2000, 13 wind farms had been constructed in the Greek Islands, with a combined capacity of 22 megawatts. In Italy, 120 megawatts of wind capacity were planned, as were 100 megawatts of wind capacity in Finland by 2005. GE acquired its wind turbine segment from Enron in 2002, and by the following year was the second largest company in wind power worldwide.

Solar energy markets also were beginning to see a surge in the 2000s. Industry leader GE, for example, acquired AstroPower Inc., the largest solar equipment company in the United Sates, in 2004 for US$15 million. Unlike wind power generation, however, solar technology has been a stagnant technology, with little advancement in more than 30 years, making it somewhat of a new technology with high cost and relatively low success. Photovoltaic panels, the leading product of solar energy conversion, were successful at converting only 15 percent of solar energy to useable power. In addition, installation of photovoltaic panels costs two to four times more than installation of a mid-sized wind turbine.

RESEARCH AND TECHNOLOGY

The industry has sought to implement cogeneration systems, which maximize the energy derived from a source fuel by harnessing both mechanical and thermal energy to serve various needs. The use of cogeneration systems grew rapidly in the last few decades of the twentieth century. Cogeneration is used in a number of applications outside traditional electric power utility plants, including paper production and oil refining. Paper mills use steam to cook and dry paper pulp. This steam is then captured by turbines that drive generators to fulfill the electrical requirements of the mill. Similarly, oil refineries used steam heat to break down crude oil into its refined components. Electrical power was then generated from the steam to drive refinery pumps. Cogeneration systems fueled by natural gas were particularly promising on both cost and environmental grounds.

The U.S. Office of Technology Assessment stated that gas turbine cogeneration systems used 25 percent less fuel energy than oil- or coal-fueled cogeneration systems and produced far less pollution. Natural gas also was widely available and low in cost compared to other fuels. The U.S. National Energy Technology Center (NETL) of the U.S. Department of Energy runs clean-energy research programs, including the Strategic Center for Natural Gas High Efficiency Engines and Turbines (HEET). A goal of the HEET program is to develop coal-fueled, ultra-high efficiency, zero emissions power modules for visionary, twenty-first century applications. HEET currently funds a Clean Energy System (CES) project that involves a zero-emission rocket engine used on NASA's space shuttles. Ongoing programs at CES in the early 2000s initially tested the gas generator at a 10 megawatt output level.

General Electric has demonstrated the feasibility of using biomass fuel—gas derived from wood chips and other organic material—to drive gas-turbine electric generating systems. Previously, natural gas, heating oil, and gasified coal were the only viable fuels for gas turbines. General Electric speculated that electricity generated from biomass fuel would be cost competitive with fossil fuels, since the expensive pollution-abatement equipment required in order to use the fossil fuels was not necessary. The firm acknowledged that gas-turbine power generation plants using biomass fuels would be small, in the 15-50 megawatt range. General Electric's research in biomass fuels was part of its overall effort to make gas turbines the predominant method of generating electricity.

Research and development in the production of diesel engines focused on minimizing noxious emissions and improving fuel efficiency, resulting in substantial improvements in the few decades before 2000. The U.K. firm Ricardo Consulting Engineers has experimented with the viability of recycling diesel engine exhaust (exhaust gas recirculation and catalytic cleaning had been more thoroughly developed for gasoline ICEs). In response to the U.S. Clean Air Act's diesel emission requirements, the Japanese firm Nippon Shokubai Co. Ltd. entered into a joint venture with the German firm Degussa AG to produce a catalyst that cleaned diesel exhaust.

In 1992, Volvo Truck of Sweden announced the development of the world's first turbocharger-supercharger diesel truck engine, which operated the supercharger up to 1,650 rpm and the turbocharger above 1,500 rpm. The hybrid design enabled the engine to produce low levels of pollutants at all engine speeds. Saab-Scania of Sweden introduced the first mass-produced turbo-supercharger diesel engine in 1994. That same year, Japan's Hino Motors Ltd. announced the development of a diesel engine with record fuel efficiency—up to 10 percent greater than the next most efficient diesel engines. Hino's engine featured graphite-containing cast-iron pistons and a redesigned turbocharger. In 1993, Hino introduced a diesel-electric hybrid engine, which used a multifunction electric generator-motor to reduce pollution.

Diesel emissions also could be slightly reduced by the use of vegetable oil fuels, such as those derived from rapeseed. The Federal Environment Office of Germany released a report in 1993 indicating that rapeseed oil fuel could reduce greenhouse gas emissions by 0.5 to 0.7 percent. Since the German government hoped to reduce emissions 25 percent by 2005, the office advocated research and development in new engine designs rather than in the use of biodiesel fuels. Nonetheless, the commercialization of biodiesel fuels in Europe was expected to continue.

The industry also continued to explore alternatives to ICEs, such as fuel cells, gas turbines, and electric motors. ICEs' thermal efficiency is poor—they use only 15 percent of the energy in a gallon of gasoline or diesel fuel. Diesel engines, it was hoped, would ultimately reach 45 percent thermal efficiency. Some industry observers, however, were skeptical that any viable alternatives would arise to replace ICEs on a large scale before the middle of the new century.

In the late 1990s, scientists were exploring the idea of using jet and rocket engines—specifically axial compression ram engines—for power generation, according to Becky Stevens in *Mechanical Engineering Power.* The engine was expected to produce operational efficiencies of 52 percent. The compact size of the engine would make it ideal for developing countries, or for applications in distributed generation, which often entails the siting of smaller power plants that are closer to population centers than more common central-station baseload generating facilities. The fuel in the axial compression ram engine burns cleaner than in a gas turbine, and the engine will burn natural gas, biogas, No. 2 diesel, and hydrogen, among other fuels. The engine has two main components: the ramjet engine and a synchronous generator that connects to the engines and locks it into a speed. Full production of the engines was expected to begin in 1999.

While wind power generation was still more expensive than non-renewable sources in the mid-2000s, new turbine designs were in development. The Wind Turbine Co. of Washington was continuing more than a decade of R&D on a two-blade downwind turbine, to replace the typical three-blade wind-facing turbine. If viable, the new turbines would shave 25 percent off the cost of construction, bringing the cost of wind technology into line with non-renewable sources. Another potential development in renewable energy was in cascading closed loop cycle (CCLC) technology. CCLC, which was on the way to being patented in 2004, allowed for generation of power from the waste heat produced by most industries. The San Antonio-based GCK Technology developed a Gorlov helical turbine in 2005, designed to provide inexhaustible energy from the flowing water of ocean and tidal currents, rivers, small dams, and hydro power dams and industrial plant discharges.

INDUSTRY LEADERS

General Electric. GE is the market leader in the design, manufacture, and servicing of turbines and generators—whether gas, steam, or hydroelectric. GE's gas turbines, for marine and industrial applications, stem from its highly successful jet engine programs. GE's Energy division, formerly the Power Systems (GEPS) division, based in Atlanta, Georgia, makes the turbines. One of GE's biggest divisions, it is ranked number one among engine/turbine manufacturers, with customers in 119 countries. GE Energy also provides nuclear fuels and services. GE's Italian manufacturing affiliate, Nuovo Pignone, produces turbines and related equipment. GE Energy ended 2001 with a total orders backlog of US$28.9 billion, up 15 percent over 2000. GEPS delivered as many as 86 heavy-duty gas turbines and 46 aero-derivative units per quarter in 2001. Its contractual services agreements were valued at US$24.6 billion that year, and GEPS also shipped its largest gas turbine ever and began installation of the first so-called "H" system, billed as the world's most energy-efficient combined-cycle system. In 2003, the company reported US$18.5 in revenue.

Siemens. Siemens AG, headquartered in Munich, is ranked second in the industry and is one of Germany's largest industrial concerns. Siemens, like GE, is a large and powerful multinational, with many divisions. Total 2004 revenue from all divisions was US$93.45 billion. Siemens acquired Westinghouse's fossil fuel power plant business in 1998, cementing its position as the market's number two supplier worldwide, with more than 90 percent of its orders outside Germany. By 2001, Siemens had merged its nuclear and hydroelectric power generation activities into two joint ventures, in which it held minority stakes. Both new companies were number one worldwide in power generation sales for nuclear and hydroelectric.

ABB. Third-ranked ABB Group, headquartered in Baden, Switzerland, is 50 percent-owned by the holding company ABB Brown Boveri Ltd. The other 50 percent of the ABB Group is held by the Sweden-based Asea AB. The ABB Group comprises 1,300 companies across the globe involved in the production of equipment for power generation, transmission, and distribution. The largest firm in the ABB Group is Asea Brown Boveri AG, based in Mannheim, Germany. An ABB company developed the first commercially successful gas turbine, which was used for oil refining. In the 1990s, the firm developed a gas turbine designed to compete directly with highly successful units produced by GE since 1989. However, in 2001 ABB divested its share of ABB Alstom Power to Alstom of France, finalizing the sale of its nuclear activities and completing its exit from the large-scale power generation field. The company launched a new business to focus on small-scale alternative energy solutions, including windpower, combined heat and power plants, microturbines, and fuel cells. ABB was a leading wind turbine generator supplier. More than 8,000 ABB generators, from a single unit to large windparks, operate worldwide. The company reported US$18.16 billion in 2004 revenue.

Mitsubishi. Mitsubishi Heavy Industries Ltd. (MHI), headquartered in Tokyo and ranked fourth in the turbines and engines industry, was established in 1917. Its power systems division is the gas and turbine maker of Mitsubishi, a highly diversified company that also produces autos, consumer electronics, planes, ships, farm machinery, and air-conditioning units. MHI reaped its share of the growing worldwide demand for gas turbines in the late 1990s and early 2000s. The company received orders for gas turbine combined cycle thermal power plants from Mexico, the United States, Azerbaijan, and Taiwan, and secured an order for a geothermal plant in Kenya. The total value of new orders for the power systems division in 2001 was US$5.9 billion. Total sales in 2004 reached nearly US$22.5 billion, all but 10 percent of which came from within Japan.

Volvo. Volvo AB, the largest industrial firm in Scandinavia and fifth-ranked in the industry, is headquartered in Göteborg, Sweden. In all of its commercial areas—marine and industrial power systems, construction equipment, trucks, buses, and aeronautics—its global presence is pronounced. Volvo Penta is the company division that produces its marine and industrial engines, with production facilities in the European Union, the United States, and Brazil. In the late 1990s, Volvo Penta's expanded product range, especially in new marine diesel engines, helped maintain strong sales. In 1997, marine and industrial engines accounted for 7.9 percent of Volvo AB's SEK 183.6 billion in sales. In 2001, Penta reported an increase in industrial engine orders of 50 percent. Penta's net sales that year totaled SEK 7.4 billion, and operating income reached a record SEK 658 million. Total 2004 revenues were US$31.8 billion.

Caterpillar. Based in Peoria, Illinois, Caterpillar Inc. is a legendary American company with total 2004 sales of US$30.25 billion. In the early 2000s, robust demand worldwide for electric power generation resulted in higher sales in North America, the Asia-Pacific region, and Europe, helping to offset Caterpillar's lower sales in South America. The firm's engines were used in semi-trailer trucks, locomotives, and construction machinery. In 1997, Caterpillar announced its intention to acquire Perkins Engines of the United Kingdom, a manufacturer of small and medium diesel engines, which posted sales of US$1.1 billion in 1996. The sale price was US$1.33 billion in cash. Caterpillar said the combination of the two companies created the world's largest full-line producer of reciprocating and turbine engines.

Isuzu. Established in 1937, Tokyo-based Isuzu Motors Ltd. produced cars, light trucks, trucks, and diesel engines, especially in cooperation with U.S.-based General Motors. Engine parts and components accounted for US$3.9 billion of the company's sales in 1997. In the late 1990s, Isuzu set up a new manufacturing base for its small diesel engines in Poland. In early 2001, Isuzu aimed to become the world's leading producer of diesel engines, with a production volume targeted at 1.8 million units by 2005. In July 2000, the joint venture between Isuzu and GM began production of diesel engines for GM full-size pickup trucks. The company reported 2004 revenues of US$13.5 billion.

Man. Headquartered in Munich, Germany, Man AG (also known as the Man Group) produced both turbines and diesel engines. With more than 77,000 employees across the globe, Man also produced commercial vehicles and components, printing presses, and other industrial equipment. The diesel engine subsidiary continues to profit from the shipbuilding market and from growth in power plants. In 2001, the company secured growth of 25 to 28 percent in its Diesel Engines division, having purchased the English manufacturer MBD Ltd. from Alstom in 2000. Turbo engine sales by Man's Industrial Equipment and Facilities division grew by 53 percent, due in part to Man's acquisition of Sulzer Turbomaschinen in 2001. The Industrial Equipment and Facilities division, as a whole, recorded growth of 3 to 5 percent. Due to the extremely high level of orders on hand at the beginning of 2001, Man Group's sales that year increased by 11 percent to Euro 16.2 billion. In 2004 total revenues were US$20.4 billion.

Kawasaki. Kawasaki Heavy Industries Ltd., headquartered in Kobe, Japan, was established in 1896 as a shipbuilder. Kawasaki focused on four fields of business: aircraft and jet engines; motorcycles and other general-purpose vehicles; rolling stock; and systems engineering/services, which covered power generation and distribution (i.e., industrial equipment including gas turbines, boilers, robots, medical equipment, and construction machinery). In 2001, while orders for industrial equipment, including turbines and engines, rose 16 percent to ¥412.9 billion, sales declined by 17.5 percent to ¥327.7 billion. Major orders included a cogeneration combined cycle power plant from Mexico and power generation equipment for Chubu Electric Power Co.'s Hekinan, Japan, thermal plant. In 2004 the company reported US$11.0 billion in sales.

Kubota. Like Kawasaki, Kubota Corporation, headquartered in Osaka, Japan, was established in the 1890s. The company is renowned for its machinery's agricultural applications. Kubota has grown to become an international leader in three product groups: internal combustion engines and machinery; industrial products and engineering; and building materials and housing. Sales in all three product areas were affected by the economic downturn in the Far East during the late 1990s and early 2000s, although sales in the industrial products and engineering sector proved to be the healthiest. By 2004 company revenues were US$8.8 billion. Kubota operates subsidiaries or affiliates in more than 130 countries.

Major Countries in the Industry

Global turbine production in the mid-2000s was led by the United States, followed by the United Kingdom, France, Germany, Denmark, Switzerland, Japan, and Italy. The import/export business in world turbines accounts for roughly 40 percent of global output in foreign trade per year. Although the largest producers are also the largest exporters, the large domestic demand for turbines in the United States resulted in the United Kingdom becoming the largest net exporters in turbine products. The U.K. trade surplus in turbines was $US2.7 billion in 2002; followed by Denmark with $US 1.8 billion, with mostly wind turbines; and the United States at $US1.6 billion. Other countries with positive trade balances of more than $US100 million in 2002 were Canada, Russia, Sweden, and Switzerland.

Further Reading

"Added Operational Flexibility Would Boost Combined-Cycle Profits." *Power Engineering,* September 2003.

"Energy Statistics of OECD Countries: 1998-1999." Washington: Organization for Economic Cooperation and Development, 2001.

"Engine Order Survey: Engine Orders Go Through the Roof." *Diesel & Gas Turbine Worldwide,* 2001. Available from http://www.dieselpub.com.

"Engine Suppliers Face Ownership Overhaul." *Flight International,* 19 July 2005.

Ernst, Steve. "New Design May Lower Costs to Run Wind Turbines." *Sacramento Business Journal,* 12 September 2003.

"Free Flowing." *International Water Power & Dam Construction,* May 2005.

"Global Wind Turbine Market to Grow Apace." *Modern Power Systems,* February 2003.

Hester, Edward D. "The Global Marketplace for Turbines." *The Freedonia Group,* July 2004.

"Hoover's Company Capsules." 2005. Available from http://www.hoovers.com.

Hydropower: Partnership with the Environment. Washington: U.S. Department of Energy Hydropower Program, June 2001.

"International Trade Statistics." 2004. Available from http://www.wto.org.

Perin, Monica. "New Electricity Technology Gathers Steam." *Houston Business Journal,* 30 April 2004.

Rubner, Justin. "GE Energy Entering Solar Biz." *Atlanta Business Chronicle,* 2 April 2004.

———. "GE Power Rides Wind Energy." *Atlanta Business Chronicle,* 7 November 2003.

Smith, Douglas J. "Gas Turbines Breaking Through the Barriers to Higher Reliability." *Power Engineering,* May 2003.

"Wind Power." *The Oil and Gas Journal,* 3 February 2003.

"Wind Turbines, Photovoltaics Winners in Distribution Market." *Energy User News,* May 2004.

SIC 3523

NAICS 333111

MACHINERY AND EQUIPMENT, AGRICULTURAL

The farm machinery industry manufactures a wide variety of products for planting, maintaining, and harvesting crops, as well as for performing other agricultural activities. Common kinds of farm equipment include tractors, combines, sprayers, planters, and harvesters.

Industry Snapshot

Despite difficulty in the early 2000s, the agricultural machinery and equipment industry rebounded during the middle part of the decade. U.S. sales of two-wheel drive tractors increased 7 percent from 2003 to 2004, and four-wheel drive tractor sales increased more than 100 percent. Self-propelled combines also surged in demand, with a 75 percent increase in sales from 2003 to 2004, followed by an 18.1 percent increase in sales from first quarter 2004 to 2005, as reported in the Association of Equipment Manufacturers' (AEM) March 2005 Flash Report. Both farm wheel tractors and self-propelled combines were projected to grow substantially into 2005. In its 2004 *State of the Ag Industry* report, the AEM found that the factors most influencing new equipment sales projections for 2006 were farm debt and credit availability, grain exports, and beef and hog prices.

Agricultural equipment sales also increased in developing markets. South Africa showed growth of 118 units, or 35.8 percent in tractor sales, according to the SA Agricultural Machinery Association. Combine harvester sales in June 2004 were almost double those of June 2003, rising from 15 units to 29, and baler sales showed a small increase (3 units) over the previous year as well. The Association expected tractor sales in South Africa would continue to increase. Indian tractor manufacturer Mahindra & Mahindra Ltd. (M&M) sold 15,066 tractors during the first quarter of 2004, compared to 10,049 for the same period a year earlier. The company has sold more than $100 million of equipment to the United States, and was working in late 2004 on a joint venture with Jiangling Tractor Company in China.

In the mid-2000s, several new innovations in agricultural machinery were joining the market. Tier III engines, tractor auto-steering capabilities, and site-specific GPS application equipment were just a few of the technologies to watch as of 2005. Such developments were aimed at improving the markets of industrialized economies. Agricultural machinery was a mature industry and primarily a replacement market, since sales depended mostly on replacement equipment and parts. The trend toward farm consolidation in developed countries hastened this transformation. Agricultural equipment manufacturers continued to discover new markets, particularly in developing countries such as Uruguay, Paraguay, Brazil, and Argentina. The United States exported $405.1 million of farm equipment to South America in 2004, an increase of 43 percent from 2003, according to the AEM. Exports to Australia/Oceania reached $673 million, a 64 percent increase.

ORGANIZATION AND STRUCTURE

PRODUCT SHARE

Although the agricultural machinery industry claims myriad products, the production of tractors and combines has accounted for the largest portion of the farm machinery and equipment market for many years. The scale of economy required to produce tractors and combines helped a few large multinational companies, referred to as full-line companies, dominate world markets. Nevertheless, more specialized products associated with the industry enabled many smaller companies to compete and profit as well.

The farm machinery industry serves large, medium, and small farms. Large farms prevail in the United States, Canada, Australia, Brazil, Argentina, and to an increasing extent in Europe. These operations require larger, more expensive machines and thus are capital intensive. The high cost of producing such machinery has effectively restricted participation in world markets to large multinational companies, many headquartered in the United States. Medium-sized farms, found mainly in Europe and supplied by European firms, diminished in number during the 1990s. During the 1980s, Japanese producers penetrated the medium-sized farm market and serviced the small-scale farm market in developed nations as well. Certain developing nations also produced machinery for small farms.

Differences in tractor size help describe how farms' needs vary according to the size of operations. According to the U.S. Department of Commerce, two-wheel drive tractors under 40 horsepower were built mostly in Japan, where farms are generally small. In the late 1990s, Japan's market for small tractors was 3.5 times the size of the market for small tractors in the United States. Two-wheel drive tractors between 40 and 100 horsepower were supplied by Japan and Europe. Europe's high share of medium-sized farms made European demand for such tractors three times that of the United States. Finally, two-wheel drive tractors with horsepower above 100 were mostly produced in the United States, where farms are typically large, though since the mid-1980s Japanese and European firms competed in this market as well.

DISTRIBUTION

Franchised dealers, who specialize mainly in one manufacturer's products, sell the majority of the world's farm machinery and equipment. Dealers may distribute more than one manufacturer's products if those products do not directly compete. Manufacturers generally support dealers by financing inventories, training staff, and advertising. Demand for farm machinery fluctuates seasonally, and farm machinery has a long life span. For example, tractors sold in the United States could last nineteen years. In the past, manufacturers were obliged to maintain large inventories of whole parts and replacement parts to meet supply demands with short notice. As the industry moved toward a build-to-order approach to manufacturing, however, dealers began consolidating inventories to sell to larger areas while servicing customers through closer satellite offices. The service end of this industry became increasingly important in the 1990s.

MAJOR TRADE AGREEMENTS

As the industry entered the twenty-first century, product standardization and international trade became paramount issues. Europe's economic unification spurred firms to seek cross-national standards that would allow them to compete throughout the common market. In addition, the General Agreement on Tariffs and Trade (GATT) signed in 1994 pledged a gradual reduction of trade barriers among participating countries, thereby leveling the competitive playing field for certain products in some markets. Among its other stipulations, the 1994 GATT eliminated farm machinery tariffs between the United States, the European Union, Japan, Canada, and other industrialized nations. The World Trade Organization (WTO), which was created on January 1, 1995, replaced the GATT as the formal institutional mechanism for regulating international commerce, but carried on GATT rules in expanded and revised form. As of April 2005, some 148 nations belonged to the WTO.

In addition, the North American Free Trade Agreement (NAFTA) promised to gradually eliminate tariffs and other trade barriers among the North American countries. Signed in 1994, NAFTA ultimately phased out tariffs on farm equipment. In its implementation, NAFTA initially established trade quotas to prevent price dumping and other disruptive trade practices. The majority of protective tariffs and quotas expired in 2004, with the rest eliminated by 2005.

BACKGROUND AND DEVELOPMENT

In most cases, working farmers were not responsible for the innovation and design of modern farm machinery. Most of the development of new farm equipment came from designs by various tradesmen, according to historian Reynold M. Wik in *Agricultural History.* Wik noted that some of the inventors of the plow, including John Deere, were blacksmiths, as were the inventors of the thresher, John and Hiram Pitt. One inventor of a reaper was a draftsman, and other inventors included machinists and practical engineers. Less surprising, Wik also found that most mechanical innovations came from the largest societies, with fewer contributions coming from inventors in less-developed regions.

One of the most significant innovations in modern farming was the gasoline-powered tractor. In the late nineteenth and early twentieth centuries, power for farm machines was transferred from steam traction engines to gasoline traction engines. John Froelich built one of the first machines with a gasoline traction engine in 1892. This machine became a forerunner to the John Deere tractor line. In 1907 C.W. Hart and C.H. Parr, two Iowans who had started the first tractor manufacturing business in 1906, coined the word tractor to refer to the gasoline traction engine.

Another important innovation in farm mechanization was the combine, a machine that harvests and threshes grain in one operation. Generally credited to Hiram Moore and J. Hascall of Kalamazoo, Michigan, the 1836 invention of the horse-drawn combine met with little demand until it was introduced to California's San Joaquin Valley in 1854. It took nearly 50 more years until other regions of the United States used the combine. According to Wik, the California valley's dry weather was particularly conducive to use of the first combines since the sun could cure the wheat, an impossibility in the damper grain-growing areas of the United States. After many improvements, including gasoline-powered engines, combines became one of the most important pieces of farm machinery in the world. Today combines harvest most of the commercially produced grain in the world.

The rate of farm mechanization varied greatly throughout the world. In general, the most industrialized nations possessed the highest levels of automation, although the developing world likewise had a long history in some types of agricultural mechanization. More than 3,000 years ago, the Chinese used cattle to ease the burden on human workers, and over 2,000 years ago, water power was first used in China and Mesopotamia, while wind power was used in the Mediterranean. These ancient innovations, however, did not spur farm mechanization in developing countries to the same extent as in the United States, Europe, and Japan.

Even in the United States, Europe, and Japan, however, many years separated the introduction and widespread use of some types of farm machinery. Reaper-binders, for example, were introduced in the United States in the mid-nineteenth century but did not become a substantial part of the European market for another 40 years or of the Japanese market for 100 years, according to Graham Donaldson, a contributor to the second International Conference on Agricultural Mechanization in Developing Countries. Donaldson concluded that farm size, nonagricultural demand for labor, and capital costs helped explain differing rates of farm mechanization.

Some observers posit that use of agricultural machinery is central to industrialization. A United Nations study entitled *Report of the Expert Group Meeting on Agricultural Machinery Industry in Developing Countries* found that the "agricultural machinery industry should have a very special place in a developing country since it diffuses technology throughout the countryside and involves a large sector of the working population in its activities." By the 1990s, many developing nations successfully initiated local production of farm machinery or entered into joint ventures with some of the industry's leading multinational firms. Farm equipment from Brazil, India, South Korea, Eastern Europe, Romania, and the Commonwealth of Independent States began reaching the United States and other export markets.

Since small farms were more prevalent in developing nations, the high cost of machinery impeded the sustained success of some initiatives within those countries. The United Nations publication, *Transnational Corporations in the Agricultural Machinery and Equipment Industry,* noted that the oligopolistic nature of the industry produced some global machinery-component standards that favored large-scale farming methods, to the disadvantage of small-scale farms. Consequently, new products specifically designed to be convenient and affordable to small-scale farmers unaided by government subsidies did not originate from large international manufacturers but from small, independent local manufacturers in developed and some developing countries.

The 1980s and early 1990s were marked by consolidations and acquisitions within the industry. The most significant changes in the industry occurred in the shuffling of the largest companies' stock. J.I. Case bought International Harvester, regained profitability, and was spun off by Tenneco Inc. Ford bought New Holland and then sold that stock to N.H. Geotech n.v., a Netherlands holding company owned by Fiat S.p.A. Deutz bought Allis Chalmers, and White merged with Avco New Idea. In 1994, AGCO acquired Massey Ferguson.

After a disastrous performance in the 1980s because of economic recessions and farm consolidations, the agricultural machinery industry came back in the mid-1990s with strong demand and healthy sales around the world. Major crop producers such as the United States, the European Union, and Canada continued to require new farm equipment. Further, South America became the fastest-growing market for agricultural equipment, with demand increasing by 15 percent in 1995.

In response to farmer demands in mature markets, the industry moved toward build-to-order equipment that fit farmers' specific needs during the 1990s. For example, French farms demanded environmentally friendly equipment that would increase productivity while reducing the emission of pollutants. This was happening in an industry once driven by the production of new technology that dealers convinced farmers they needed. However, due to economic difficulties in the 1980s, farmers became more cautious shoppers. Manufacturer and dealer inventories mounted and stalled by the 1990s. In order to avoid excess future inventories, manufacturers developed build-to-order systems and lean manufacturing plants modeled after the Japanese automobile industry.

Strong agricultural industries in the United States and the European Union, plus expanding markets in South America, helped fuel robust sales in the mid-1990s. Sales then dropped off toward the end of the decade. Trade liberalization agreements GATT and NAFTA were expected to further stimulate the industry and to allow established manufacturers greater access to other markets. In 1995 the United States, Germany, Italy, and the United Kingdom led the world in farm equipment exports, while imports were greatest in the United States, France, Canada, and Germany. Some significant acquisitions and sales within the industry shuffled the positions of the top producers in the mid-1990s, but industry dominance by large multinational corporations continued.

In the mid-1990s, many of the major farm machinery manufacturers planned to increase their presence abroad. For example, U.S. companies such as AGCO and Deere & Co. targeted South America and Europe as focal markets for the next century. These companies hoped to expand sales by acquiring producers and forming alliances with manufacturers in targeted countries. European producers turned to the United States and South America with similar tactics to achieve growth.

The *Financial Times* reported global sales of farm machinery totaling US$43.4 billion in 1996, more than twice 1991's US$21.3 billion. Western Europe continued to dominate the industry, led by Italy, Germany, France, and the United Kingdom, and posted sales of US$16.2 billion in 1996. North America ranked second with US$11.9 billion in revenues, followed by Eastern Europe with US$6.0 billion, Asia with US$5.0 billion, South and Central America with US$2.4 billion, Africa with US$800,000, and Oceania with US$1.1 billion.

By 1999, according to the Food and Agriculture Organization (FAO), low-income countries used just 11.0 percent of the world's agricultural tractors, with the least-developed countries using only 0.4 percent of the global count of farm tractors. In contrast, an estimated 18.0 percent of the world's farm tractors were used in the United States alone. Usage rates for harvesters and threshers were similar: just 0.3 percent in 1999 for the least-developed countries and 16.0 percent for the low-income countries—equivalent to the percentage used in the United States, 16.0 percent. Even more striking contrasts appeared in usage rates for milking machines worldwide (excluding counts for Mexico, Canada, and the United States and selected other countries): only 2.0 percent of milking machines tallied by FAO were used in the low-income countries while less than .02 percent were used in the least-developed countries. In contrast, Europe used nearly 78.0 percent of the milking machines counted. The difference between developed and developing nations in terms of mechanization in the agricultural sector was thus stark. Intra-regional differences also were pronounced.

In Africa, 527,621 farm tractors were in use in 1999, though only 160,795 of these were in sub-Saharan Africa. Similarly, of the 38,295 harvesters and threshers used in all of Africa that year, just 5,002 were in the sub-Saharan region. One example of an international initiative aimed at fostering development in this part of the world is the African Growth and Opportunity Act (AGOA), signed into law in the United States by President Bill Clinton in May 2000 as Title 1 of the U.S. Trade and Development Act of 2000. AGOA was designed to improve the trade climate between the United States and sub-Saharan African countries by reducing tariffs and rewarding African nations found to be practicing "good governance." In the year 2000, exports of agricultural machinery from the United States to sub-Saharan African countries were facilitated by AGOA and totaled US$68.5 million, contributing to the modernization of the agricultural infrastructure in this most-impoverished region of the world. By April 2005, 38 African countries were eligible to trade under AGOA.

Crop surpluses in wheat, corn, and soybeans led to significant drops in commodity prices and challenges for farmers in many developed countries, including reductions in the amount of funds available for purchasing agricultural machinery and equipment. The result was increased consolidation of farms into larger enterprises, the continued growth of multinational agribusinesses, and a trend toward the production and use of larger and more technologically advanced agricultural machines and equipment. In 1999, nearly 1.2 million agricultural tractors were sold for export around the world, with developed countries selling more than 1.0 million of these and developing countries exporting only about 145,000. According to *U.S. Industry and Trade Outlook 2000,* most farm machinery buyers were either leading food producers like Archer Daniels Midland or smaller providers of specialized crop production and maintenance services such as planting, fertilizing, and harvesting.

In the early 2000s, greater effort was directed toward encouraging the production and distribution in developing countries of a wider range of farm machinery and equipment suitable for small farmers as well as larger agricultural enterprises. A February 2000 United Nations Food and Agriculture Organization (FAO) report recommended greater public-private cooperation to promote and facilitate agricultural mechanization in the developing world. As L.J. Clarke, Chief of FAO's Agricultural Engineering Branch of the Agricultural Support Systems Division in Rome, noted in this report, for importers, distributors and small retail outlets to develop successful businesses, they need "a stable market in which to sell products, access to foreign exchange at undistorted rates, foreign contacts, removal of unfair competition from the state, access to business and marketing development assistance, access to credit for business and cash flow development." Clarke also observed that to produce farm machinery and equipment in developing countries, manufacturers must be able to purchase raw materials at stable prices on a regular basis and build and maintain relationships with international business allies.

Technological improvements in the marketing of agricultural machinery and equipment were also flourishing. In December 2001 two major farm machinery online traders—the United Kingdom's Farmec Limited, and The Ag Dealer, based in Canada and the northern United States—joined together to create one of the largest databases of farm machinery available for sale in the world. This initiative made the more than 800 Canadian and North American dealers registered in *The Ag Dealer* database dually accessible through Farmec. Farmec would thus be able to offer more than 28,000 machines advertised in *The Ag Dealer* to its European clientele directly through the Farmec Web site. Other online databases for specialized farm machinery and equipment were similarly attempting to capitalize on newly emerging electronic trading opportunities to increase sales around the world.

EMI's Flash Reports indicated that, in number of units sold, U.S. sales of under-40 HP, two-wheel drive tractors were strongest compared with all other categories of U.S. tractors. Totals increased 8.4 percent from January 2001 to January 2002, and were up again from June 2003 to June 2004. Retail sales of farm tractors in the United States increased by about 9.0 percent each year during 2000 and 2001. In January 2002, EMI forecast a decrease of 3.3 percent for U.S. farm tractor sales for the calendar year 2002. By mid-2004, the market had risen 8 percent over 2003 levels. Similarly, while U.S self-propelled combine sales increased 4.0 percent in 2000 and nearly 13.0 percent in 2001, sales of combines increased a whopping 75 percent between June 2003 and June 2004. And in 2003, global farm machinery and equipment sales exceeded $10 billion for the first time, according to *The 2004-2005 Outlook for the Farm Machinery and Equipment Market.*

Among other major agricultural machinery and equipment producers in the developed world, France was the European industry leader in the early 2000s. France's market for agricultural machinery in 2002 was US$4 billion, nearly a third of which came from tractor sales and another 30 percent from combine harvesters, with a decline forecast into 2007. The German market for agricultural machinery in 2002 was the next largest among the Europeans at US$3.2 billion, with growth forecast into 2007. In Germany, tractor sales accounted for 50 percent of the market. In the United Kingdom, agricultural machinery sales plummeted in the early 2000s.

CURRENT CONDITIONS

U.S. exports of agricultural machinery increased for the third straight year from $4.8 billion in 2003 to almost $5.7 billion in 2004. This increase of almost 19 percent was the result of growth in exports to all regions, according to the Association of Equipment Manufacturers (AEM), with the largest percentage increases reflected in exports to Australia (64 percent growth, to $673 million) and South America (43 percent growth, $401.5 million). As measured by dollar amount, Europe ($1.7 billion) and Canada ($1.6 billion) purchased the most agricultural machinery from the United States during 2004. Other regions importing U.S. farm equipment included Central America ($642 million), Asia ($486 million), and Africa, ($179 million).

The market abroad showed growth as well. The United Kingdom showed a 2.4 percent increase in agricultural tractor registrations from 2003 to 2004, according to the Agricultural Engineers' Association (AEA). It was the United Kingdom's highest new tractor registration number since 1997. Performance declined somewhat over the second half of the year, and a similar downturn was expected during early 2005.

According to the Association of Equipment Manufacturers' (AEM) *Annual Outlook for 2005 Farm Machinery Sales,* modest gains for most equipment types were expected during 2005. Two-wheel drive tractors were forecast to show a 1.4 percent gain in the United States, and a 6.2 percent gain in Canada, with four-wheel drive tractor sales expected to decline by the end of 2005 in both countries. Tractor growth was expected to be highest for those under 40 horsepower, while sales for tractors in the 40 to 100 horsepower range were expected to remain flat or decline. Self-propelled combine sales were expected to drop 2.9 percent in the United States and 6.6 percent in Canada. The strongest growth was projected for self-propelled sprayers, which were expected to gain 8.5 percent in Canada and 8.8 percent in the United States by 2006. The Canadian market for balers and mower conditioners was projected to increase during 2005, while the U.S. market for the same was expected to remain steady or decline. Both countries also expected a slight increase in purchasing of farm loaders during 2005.

Factors influencing the North American market for farm equipment in 2005 included modest increases in interest rates, cash receipts, and net farm income. Planted acreage in 2005 was expected to remain the same as in 2004. Equipment prices for new and used equipment increased from 2004 and remained a significant factor in the number of units sold. Of all sectors, the higher-horsepower (HP) machines were expected to sell at the most robust levels in the United States in the mid-2000s as U.S. farms continued to expand in size and shrink in number. The projected growth in sales through 2005 reflected a trend toward purchases of larger, more expensive machines rather than significant increases in numbers of machines purchased.

The farm machinery and equipment industry was expected to continue modest growth into 2006, reaching total revenues of $27.1 billion, according to Global Insight. Slight declines were expected following 2006, with expected revenues of $26.7 billion in $2007 and $25.5 billion in 2008. The broader global construction and farm machinery and heavy trucks sector was forecast to reach a collective value of $135.9 billion by 2008, a projected increase of 24.3 percent from 2003, according to a Datamonitor report.

INDUSTRY LEADERS

CATERPILLAR

While Caterpillar was one of the farm machinery industry's leaders in past years, the company divested itself of its tractor division and focused more on mining and construction. Caterpillar remains the industry leader in the global construction machinery and farm machinery and heavy trucks industry, controlling around 19.2 percent of the market, according to a May 2004 report published by Datamonitor.

DEERE AND COMPANY

Deere & Company was the global industry leader from 1963 until the November 1999 merger of Case Corp. with

New Holland N.V. In the years following the merger, CNH Global NV surpassed Deere and became the world leader in manufacturing agricultural tractors and combines. The two companies continued to vie for the industry leader position in the early to mid-2000s, and Deere & Company held the top spot in 2003 and 2004. Deere & Company was originally founded by John Deere in 1837 and for more than a century and a half led the world market with its trademark sales of green and yellow farm equipment. The company's original product was a self-scouring plow, built to turn over the tough soil of the Midwestern United States. Deere first began to manufacture overseas in 1956 when it acquired a controlling interest in the Mannheim, Germany-based Heinrich Lanz Company, a producer of farm machinery since 1859. In the mid-1990s, Deere began to profit from its restructuring efforts.

Employment, which peaked in the early 1980s at 68,000, was reduced to 34,400 by 1997, when the company produced goods in nine countries and sold farm machinery and equipment in 160 countries. In 2000, Deere experienced an average sales growth of just 3.3 percent but took 33.6 percent of the US$11.0 billion market for agricultural machinery in the United States. In its 2001 annual report, Deere noted that it had adapted to new farming practices aimed at controlling soil erosion and reducing production costs by designing and selling new forms of planters, drills, and tillage equipment. The company also developed a holistic approach to agricultural management that included advanced technology and global satellite positioning. By 2004, according to the company's annual report, Deere & Company reported $1.4 billion in net income. Net income from equipment operations was $1.09 billion, up from $305 million in 2003. Net equipment sales were up 32 percent to $17.67 billion, and at the end of 2004, Deere employed 46,465 people. Due to sales goals in Europe and expansion into foreign markets such as South America, India, and China, Deere & Co. expected continued growth during 2005 of around 5 percent.

CNH Global

CNH Global NV, formed by the merger of Case and New Holland, was the second-largest company in the U.S. farm machinery and equipment industry in 2004. More than two thirds of 2003 company sales were of farm equipment. CNH Global NV reported consolidated revenues of US$10.1 billion for 2003, an 8 percent increase over 2002. CNH was the market leader in Western Europe for agricultural equipment. By 2004, CNH Global NV reported net equipment sales of 11.5 billion, up 15 percent from $10.1 billion in 2003. Net sales increased 24 percent in the Americas, 2 percent in the rest of the world, and declined overall by 6 percent in Europe. The company's growth was fueled by better-than-expected growth in combine sales of 43 percent in North America, 17 percent in Western Europe, and 34 percent in the rest of the world. CNH Global NV expected worldwide unit sales to remain flat during 2005, with modest increases in the North American equipment market of about 5 percent. More than 25,000 people were employed by CNH Global NV in 2005.

The Case Corporation was founded as J.I. Case Threshing Machine Co. of Wisconsin in 1842, its original products being threshing machines. New Holland n.v. originated in 1895 as the New Holland Machine Company, a specialized farmstead engine maker. The first automatic hay baler, requiring only one operator instead of three, was one of New Holland's significant innovations before World War II. In 1947 New Holland became a division of the Sperry Corporation. After combining operations with part of Ford Motor Company, Ford New Holland Inc. was the world's third largest agricultural machinery manufacturer by 1987. New Holland n.v. was formed in 1991 when Ford sold its Ford New Holland Inc. stock to N.H. Geotech n.v., a Netherlands holding company owned by Fiat S.p.A. The intricacy of these mergers and acquisitions illustrates the degree to which multinational corporations set on capturing ever larger shares of the global market now dominate the industry.

AGCO Corporation

In 2003, AGCO Corp. was the third largest company in the U.S. agricultural machinery and equipment industry. Among the world's largest manufacturers and distributors of agricultural equipment, AGCO was headquartered in Duluth, Georgia, and sold 17 brand names in more than 140 countries. Massey Ferguson, reported by AGCO as the world's most widely sold brand of tractor, is one of AGCO's brands. By taking over Caterpillar's production and marketing of tractors in early 2002, AGCO was positioned to occupy an even larger share of the world tractor market. AGCO reported 2004 net sales of US$5.3 billion, a 51 percent increase over $3.5 billion in 2003. The company's plans for the late 2000s included focusing on global sales and increased the amount of spending for research and development by 20 percent.

Claas Gruppe

Germany's leading farm machinery manufacturer is Claas Gruppe, which also ranks among the top manufacturers worldwide. Founded in 1913 in Clarholz, Westphalia by brothers August and Franz Claas, Claas was a pioneering producer of agricultural machinery from its inception. Claas' achievements include the development of the European combine harvester in 1930, the manufacturing of the first pick-up baler in 1936, construction of the first self-propelled combine harvester in 1953, and contributions to the development of AGROCOM, a satellite-based agricultural information system. The company also launched a joint venture with Caterpillar to distribute its combine harvesters in North America. In 2004, Claas Gruppe earned $1.9 billion in net sales, a 28.9 percent increase over 2003. Of sales, 76.8 percent were earned in Germany, with the remainder due to exports. As of 2004, Claas Gruppe employed 8,134 people.

Kubota Corp.

One of the top Japanese manufacturers is Kubota Corp. Founded by Gonshiro Kubota in 1890 as a manufacturer of cast iron water pipe under the name Ohide Imono, the company first entered the agricultural machinery industry in 1922 as a producer of kerosene engines. By 1950 Kubota also produced horizontal diesel engines, and it made its first tractors a decade later. Four-wheel drive tractors followed in 1971. Kubota's strength is in lower horse-powered tractors that serve smaller farms. The company specializes in niche farm equipment markets, and the United States has been its largest overseas market. Kubota Tractor Corp. continued to enjoy success and opened new manufacturing facilities in the United States during 2004 and 2005. These included the company's fifth facility in Georgia, scheduled to open in Fall 2005. The new facility in Jackson County, Georgia was expected to employ 500 people when operations began. A subsidiary of Kubota, Kubota Tractor Corp. (KTC), formed in 1972, markets and distributes Kubota agricultural machinery in the United States. In 2004, the company's sales were US$8.8 billion.

FURTHER READING

"2004 Mid-Year State of the Ag Industry Outlook." *Association of Equipment Manufacturers,* 2004. Available from http://www.aem.org.

"AEM Releases Annual 'Outlook' for 2005 Farm Machinery Sales." *Association of Equipment Manufacturers,* 6 April 2005. Available from http://www.aem.org.

The Ag Dealer Magazine, 17 December 2001. Available from http://www.agdealer.com.

AGCO Corporation. "AGCO Reports Fourth Quarter and Year-End Results," 7 February 2002. Available from http://www.agcocorp.com.

"Agricultural Machinery in France, Germany, UK, US." *Euromonitor,* August 2004. Available from http://www.majormarketprofiles.com.

Bureau of Labor Statistics. "Covered Employment & Wages." Washington: U.S. Department of Labor Data, 2001. Available from http://data.bls.gov.

Clarke, L.J. "Strategies for Agricultural Mechanization Development: The Roles of the Private Sector and the Government." Rome, Italy: Food and Agriculture Organization, February 2000. Available from http://www.agen.tamu.edu.

Draper, Deborah J., ed. *Business Rankings Annual.* Detroit: Thomson Gale, 2004.

Equipment Manufacturers Institute. "Factors Influencing Future Sales 2002-2004." 2002. Available from http://www.emi.org.

"Exports of Farm Equipment Increase 19 Percent in 2004." *Association of Equipment Manufacturers,* 21 February 2005. Available from http://www.aem.org.

"Farm Machinery and Equipment Manufacturing." *U.S. Industry Quarterly Review: Machinery and Equipment.* Global Insight, December 2004.

"Farm Machinery Sales in 2003." *The Kiplinger Agriculture Letter,* 9 August 2002.

"Feed Sector Faces Further Rationalisation in Bid for Survival." *Dairy Farmer,* 11 March 2004.

Feldman, G. "U.S.-African Trade Profile." Office of Africa, U.S. Department of Commerce, and International Trade Administration, March 2001. Available from http://www.agoa.gov.

Food and Agriculture Organization, United Nations. *FAOSTAT Database,* 4 December 2001.

"From the Top." *Apply,* 1 May 2004.

Global Construction & Farm Machinery & Heavy Trucks: Industry Profile. Datamonitor, May 2004. Available from http://www.datamonitor.com.

———. "Industry U.S. Retail Sales Forecast Tractors & Combines." 2002. Available from http://www.emi.org.

———. "January 2002 Flash Report: U.S. Unit Retail Sales." 14 February 2002. Available from http://www.emi.org.

"International Trade Statistics." 2003. Available from http://www.wto.org.

Kubota Tractor Corporation. "Kubota Tractor Corporation: U.S. Operations Continue to Expand, New Products and Facilities Meet Demand for Kubota Equipment." February 2001. Available from http://www.kubota.com.

Lazich, Robert S., ed. *Market Share Reporter.* Detroit: Thomson Gale, 2004.

Machinery Outlook. "In This Issue." December 2001. Available from http://www.machineryoutlook.com.

Robertson, Don. "Sales of Heavy Agricultural Equipment Rockets." *Africa News Service,* 12 July 2004.

"South America." *Implement & Tractor,* July/August 2003.

"U.S. Ag Flash Report." *Association of Equipment Manufacturers,* 14 July 2004.

"Tractor Giant Agco Puts Faith in Innovation to Push Expansion." *Europe Intelligence Wire,* 7 March 2005.

U.S. Business Reporter. "Agriculture Industry Profile—Industry Analysis." 30 January 2002. Available from http://www.activemedia-guide.com.

Wiening, Mary R., ed. "Farm Machinery." *U.S. Industry & Trade Outlook 2000,* U.S. Department of Commerce/International Trade Administration. The McGraw-Hill Companies, 2000.

SIC 3560

NAICS 3332

MACHINERY AND EQUIPMENT, GENERAL INDUSTRIAL

The general industrial machinery and equipment industry comprises at least four major categories of products: 1) pumps for liquids; 2) fans, filters, and gas pumps; 3) mechanical handling and packaging equipment; and 4) ball and roller bearings. Lesser categories include speed changers, drives, and gears; industrial process furnaces and ovens; and mechanical power transmission equipment. Yet other segments include other types of parts and machines. For information on specialized industrial machinery, see **Machinery, Refrigeration and Service Industry.**

INDUSTRY SNAPSHOT

The products in this industry, and consequently the leaders in this industry, cover a broad range of machines and parts and are applied diversely. Therefore, the industry's fortunes are closely tied to the general health of world industrial production. Those fortunes equally provide an indicator of the level of a country's or region's industrial development. Mature industrialized countries—Germany, Japan, the United States, Italy, France, and the United Kingdom—continue to dominate world production and exports. Emerging countries such as South Korea, China, India, and Brazil have also become important producers and consumers of general industrial machinery and were forecast to fuel much of the industry's continued growth.

China, Taiwan, and India held the top three exporter positions for both pumps machinery and packing machinery in the mid-2000s. According to the Freedonia Group, bearings were expected to experience 4.5 percent annual growth in the United States into 2010, 6.4 percent annual growth in Canada and Mexico, 4.8 percent in Western Europe, and 7.8 percent in Asia and the Pacific Rim.

BACKGROUND AND DEVELOPMENT

The use of mass production technologies enabled U.S. manufacturers to master the world market for industrial machinery in the early twentieth century. In the years before World War I, leading U.S. producers rapidly expanded production and marketing facilities, establishing factories both domestically and abroad. In 1914 there were about 20 U.S. machinery firms operating two or more plants in Europe.

In *Scale and Scope,* Alfred Chandler Jr. described the situation of U.S. industrial machinery producers in this period. U.S. machinery producers dominated the European market, thanks to economies of scale and product-specific sales organizations in marketing and distribution. This was despite the fact that patents did not fully or even partially protect many of the machines. Few European companies could produce machines superior to those of the United States at similarly modest prices, as well as offer the necessary ancillary services of marketing, demonstration, installation, after-sales repair and service, and consumer credit. U.S. manufacturers of industrial machines continued to expand overseas facilities until the Great Depression.

As with many other U.S. industries in the early 1900s, in the non-electrical machinery and equipment industry there was a wave of mergers. These mergers were not so-called horizontal mergers—that is, involving a combination of directly competing firms. Rather, the mergers were based on the establishment of complementary product lines. Thus, the diversification strategies of U.S. firms had them staying within closely related product lines. The Ingersoll-Rand Company, for example, produced pumps, compressors, and engines—all of which were used for mining operations. Early in the twentieth century, Worthington Pump was the largest U.S. producer of pumps, making a wide range of steam and gasoline-pumping equipment, as well as compressors, generators, and meters. In the 1920s Worthington combined these products into systems for transferring water and heat, and later into cooling and air conditioning systems.

From the early twentieth century on, Germany rose to meet American dominance of the industry, becoming the leading European producer of industrial machinery. German producers of heavy industrial machinery were particularly competitive, with extensive international marketing operations and credit and repair services. They also were among the world's largest, with average employment ranging from 3,500 to 5,000 by World War I. Indeed, some German producers of industrial machinery employed more than 15,000 workers at this time.

German manufacturers grew primarily by investing retained earnings. Thus, they were less beholden to banks than German firms in the chemical, metal- making, and electrical machinery industries. Nor had they, like many firms in other industries, made extensive overseas investments before World War II. Thus, they suffered less the burden of reparations after the war. Given the nature of heavy industrial machinery and equipment, competition took place largely on the basis of performance and service, rather than price. As a consequence, the cartels notable in many other German industries did not play an important role in the industrial machinery industry.

German industrial machinery companies were generally more widely diversified across industry lines than U.S. counterparts. Maschinenbau-Anstalt Humboldt was established in the 1850s as a machine shop serving one of Germany's leading mining firms. From this starting point, the firm diversified into other material-handling machinery; locomotives and railroad cars; and air-moving and cooling machinery used in mines, breweries, and slaughterhouses. By World War I, Maschinenbau-Anstalt had diversified—by backwards integration—into the production of steel-making machinery and equipment. The firm claimed that this strategy reduced the manufacturing costs of any given product while still offering diversification.

The German firm Borsig provided another example of the broad diversification strategies of leading German producers of industrial machinery and equipment. Borsig began as one of Germany's pioneering locomotive producers. The firm then diversified into the production of steam engines and boilers; pumps and pump lines for oil production; and turbines, compressors, and cooling machinery. Allis-Chalmers of Milwaukee, Wisconsin was the only large U.S. producer of industrial machinery that was as widely diversified as the leading German firms. Allis-Chalmers had strong ties to Germany. Indeed, the merger by which it was created was financed by one of Germany's largest banks.

The leading German industrial machinery firms included Hannoversche Machinbau AG, Berliner Machinbau AG, Maschinenfabrik-Augsburg-Nuernberg, and Gebrueder Koerting AG. As distinct from U.S. and British counterparts, they were heavily involved in the production of locomotives. In Britain locomotives were produced by the major railroad companies. In the United States, they were produced by a handful of large, relatively specialized manufacturers.

The development of packaging machinery was closely tied to the rapid growth of branded, packaged products in the late nineteenth century. Packaging became more important and more mechanized, as both mass marketing and mass production, with their tendency to expand capacity, developed. Producers developed their own marketing operations, rather than relying on traditional wholesale merchants, and began to transform the economy.

Important innovations were made in the production and packaging of cigarettes and food products. Among the important innovations was James Duke's cigarette packaging machinery, developed as a response to the cigarette-making machines marketed in the 1880s. Grain processors took a similar route, leading to the establishment of companies like Quaker Oats Company, General Mills Inc., and Pillsbury

Company. As with the cigarette industry, the development of branded packages was in response to the dramatic increase of output made possible by the new rolling mills of the day. In both cases, packaging became an integral part of the production process. That is, the new firms took over the wholesalers' traditional task of subdividing bulk goods into quantities suitable for retail purchase. But, unlike wholesalers, these firms advertised and sold products across the entire United States rather than to certain regional or local markets.

Another important innovation in packaging machinery was the automatic canning line—first built in 1883. This innovation led to the formation of such U.S. food-packaging firms as Borden, Campbell Soup Company, Libby, McNeill and Libby, Del Monte, and Heinz Company, as well as the American Can Company and the Continental Can Company.

The British were generally unable to compete with U.S. and German producers with respect to industrial machinery in the twentieth century. However, the British had a great deal of success in the production of branded packaged products. The largest of the British producers in the industry was Lever Brothers,a soap company. The firm followed the example of U.S. producers and invested heavily overseas. By World War I, Lever Brothers had built plants in Australia, Canada, the United States, and Japan, as well as in seven European countries. The British also used mass-production packaging machinery for cigarettes and food products, although they were late in taking up automatic canning machinery—allowing U.S. canning firms to dominate. Also in contrast with the U.S. firms, British packaging firms generally remained family-owned and operated between the world wars, leaving them with fewer financial resources and less sophisticated structures of management. There also were relatively few mergers among packaging firms in Britain than in the United States, leaving British firms less diversified across product lines than U.S. counterparts.

PUMPS AND COMPRESSORS

Business in pumps and compressors was positive in the mid to late 1990s, with the global market growing about 5 percent annually. Gains in the emerging economies of Asia and South America fueled this growth, as did demand in North America, which also grew about 5 percent annually. Because of the use of compressors in higher-value applications and more mature markets, the global compressor market was expected to grow faster than the pump market. With prices rising in the mid to late 1990s for metal and other raw materials, pump prices rose slightly during this period. In 199,8 pump-for-liquids exports from the world's top 25 exporters totaled US$18.2 billion. As reported in *Purchasing,* demand for fluid-handling pumps was forecast to increase by almost 6 percent through 2008, according to a study by the Freedonia Group. Growth was primarily expected from undeveloped markets, such as China, where annual growth was projected to be as high as 10 percent per year for the next five years. This offset less than average gains expected from established markets such as the United States, Japan, and Western Europe.

BEARINGS

The demand for bearings was stronger than for pumps and compressors. The global market expanded by roughly 8 percent annually through 2000. Growth in Central and South America was the highest, followed by Asia and Africa. Growth in demand for bearings in North America was less, but still strong, at about 5 percent. However, by 1999, North American market growth had fallen to below 2 percent, thanks largely to Asian economic upheavals beginning in 1997. Many bearings suppliers suffered from a lack of demand from original equipment manufacturers supplying to Asia. This caused a chain reaction effect. With production down in many areas, manufacturing equipment was not used as much, and its parts, including the bearings, did not wear as quickly.

Still, by 1998, ball and roller bearing exports for the top 25 producing countries had risen to more than US$11.1 billion. To sustain their margins and market share, manufacturers worked on developing bearings created from plastics, ceramics, and composites, among other materials, in an attempt to make bearings ever lighter and more resistant to heat.

Tied to the uncertain automotive market, the North American market for bearings experienced a corresponding slump in the early 2000s. The U.S. market was expected to grow about 2 to 3 percent annually as of 2003. By comparison, the Freedonia Group forecast 6.5 percent growth for the global market into 2005. This would bring the worldwide bearings total to US$42 billion. The North American packaging machinery industry was expected to see a rise as well, particularly in the six markets that make up more than 80 percent of this segment: foods, beverages, personal care, durables, chemicals, and converters.

PACKAGING MACHINERY

The packaging industry benefited from increasing demand for packaging equipment in China, especially from China's food-packing industry. In the mid to late 1990s, the need for grain packaging equipment soared in the country, which helped drive production and trade in this segment. In 1998, global exports of mechanical handling equipment by the world's 25 top producing countries stood at US$27.7 billion. However, in the late 1990s, packaging equipment production fell in some leading countries such as the United States. Still, throughout the world, manufacturers continued to produce more efficient machinery, as packaging plants constantly sought greater productivity.

By 2003, U.S. shipments of packaging machinery climbed to $4.88 billion, according to *Packaging Digest.* The amount of machinery exported by the United States grew more significantly, increasing by 33.1 percent during 2003 to $952 million. The United States was the largest producer of packaging machinery, earning $4.9 billion in shipments during 2003, followed by Japan with $4.1 billion. Germany, Italy, and China all earned more than $1 billion in the industry as well. Shipments of new packaging machinery neared $5.5 billion in 2004, thanks in part to demand for variable speed drives in the North American market. The packaging machinery market in the United Kingdom was forecast to grow by about 9 percent between 2004 and 2008, according to *Packaging Magazine.* Global demand for packaging machinery was expected to rise 5 percent each year through 2008 to $31 billion, according to *Packaging Digest.* Most gains were expected in developing areas of Latin America and the Asia Pacific, where industrial output and consumption were on the rise.

MATERIAL HANDLING

Manufacturers were realizing increased volume in new business and expansion systems during 2004, as reported by the Material Handling Industry of America (MHIA). A study by the Freedonia Group suggested healthy increases in this segment's growth through 2008, increasing by 4.3 percent per year. Demand was attributed to technological innovations that led to greater efficiency, easier operations, and automation. Automated storage and retrieval systems were the largest category of automated equipment. The market for convention equipment, including trucks and lifts, was expected to reach $14.4 billion by 2008. Trucks and lifts remained the largest category of the material handling sector and also expected to see the largest gains.

CURRENT CONDITIONS

The global general industrial machinery and equipment trade expanded moderately into the 2000s. Taiwan, China, India, the United States, and Turkey led the industry in exports during 2004 and early 2005. The leading importers of industrial machinery at this time were India, China, Pakistan, Bangladesh, and the United Kingdom, as reported by the Bureau of Export Administration. A report published by Datamonitor in May 2004 projected the global market for industrial machinery would reach a value of $303.1 billion, a 17.3 percent growth from 2003 value of $258.5 billion. The largest segments of this category include elevators, pumps, and compressors. U.S. revenues attributed to industrial machinery during 2004 neared $40 billion, as reported by the U.S. Industry Quarterly Review. Global Insight forecast industry revenues would continue to rise through the end of 2008, reaching $50 billion.

International trade agreements such as the General Agreement on Tariffs and Trade (GATT) and the North American Free Trade Agreement (NAFTA) reduced or eliminated trade barriers. GATT, for example, brought about a 40 percent reduction of tariffs on industrial products, including machinery and equipment, imported by developed countries. GATT also fostered a 37 percent reduction in the volume of products imported from developed countries, according to the World Trade Organization (WTO). The agreement calls for the GATT tariff reductions to be fully implemented by 2005. NAFTA facilitated a similar gradual reduction of trade barriers in North America; this reduction of barriers was scheduled for full implementation in 2002. In 2004, India, Taiwan, China, the United States, and the United Kingdom were the top five exporters of packing machinery. That same year, China, India, Taiwan, Russia, and Italy were the top five exporters of pumps machinery.

In general, the need for companies to comply with expanding energy conservation policies and stricter conservation laws throughout the world led to a greater need for energy-efficient drives and speed changers. Because of the high costs of replacing malfunctioning drives and speed changers, more companies opted to have them rebuilt, creating a robust rebuilt market for these products. Customers were also concerned with energy conservation for industrial pumps, for which 85 percent of associated costs were attributed to energy consumption, according to *Purchasing.*

INDUSTRY LEADERS

INGERSOLL-RAND

Ingersoll-Rand Company, located in Woodcliff Lake, New Jersey, reported total 2003 sales of US$9.9 billion, a 10 percent growth over 2002 levels. The company comprises three main divisions: construction machinery and equipment, industrial machinery and equipment, and components such as bearings. The Industrial Solutions division handles the industrial machinery and equipment industry segment. Sales for the division were more than US$9.3 billion in 2004. The company's leading brands are Blaw-Knox, Bobcat, Club Car, Fafnir, Steelcraft, Thermo King, Torrington, and Worthington. About half of the company's manufacturing plants are located outside of the United States, and roughly 40 percent of its revenues are derived from exports.

SKF

Aktiebolegat SKF led the world in roller bearing production. The company produces a fifth or more of the world's roller bearings annually. Founded in 1907, the company includes three divisions: bearings and seals, tools, and special steels. Based in Göteborg, Sweden, SKF's bearing and seal division primarily serves the automotive and machinery industries. In the late 1990s, SKF had manufacturing plants at 80 locations in 20 countries. The company began to expand into new product areas with the acquisition of Russell T. Gilman Inc., one of the leading producers of spindles for machine tools in the United States. The company enjoyed the 5 percent growth in sales common in the industry during this time, with bearings typically accounting for 80 to 90 percent of total sales. In 2004 sales were up 18.7 percent to US$6.7 billion, and SKF's net income rose 59 percent from 2003 to reach $447.4 million in 2004.

EBARA

The Ebara Corporation was established in 1920 and is headquartered in Tokyo. The firm is one of the world's leading producers of industrial pumps, fans, and compressors, along with industrial systems that make use of these products. Pumps, fans, and compressors accounted for 34 percent of the company's total sales in the late 1990s. The company had six overseas subsidiaries, four in the United States and one each in Italy and the Netherlands. Although the company's exports have been small, Ebara planned to stake out other markets, especially in Asia. In 2004, Ebara's sales were US$4.8 billion, representing a one-year sales growth of 11 percent, and the firm employed 15,200 workers.

SUMITOMO

Sumitomo Heavy Industries Ltd. (SHI) was established by a merger in 1969 and is based in Tokyo. In the late 1990s, SHI's mass production machinery division remained its strongest, with steady sales and profit growth. That division accounted for about 70 percent of the company's profits during that period. At that time, Sumitomo had 14 overseas subsidiaries: five in the United States, three in Canada, two each in the United Kingdom and Germany, and one each in Mexico and Singapore. SHI's sales totaled US$4.5 billion in 2004, a 13.8 percent increase over 2003, and net income surged an incredible 586.3 percent to US$153.9 million. Sumitomo employed more than 11,000 people in 2004.

NSK

NSK Ltd. was established in 1916 and is headquartered in Tokyo. The firm is Japan's largest manufacturer of bearings. In 2003, bearings accounted for 65 percent of NSK's revenues. Automobile, aircraft, and train manufacturers use the company's bearings in their products. In the late 1990s, NSK had 17 plants in Japan and 20 overseas in Asia, Europe, and the Americas. NSK had net sales of US$4.9 billion in 2004, up from US$4.4 billion in 1997, and had 19,772 employees.

DAIKIN

Daikin Industries Ltd. was established in 1934 and is headquartered in Osaka, Japan. It is Japan's largest producer of air-conditioning, which comprises 80 percent of sales, and industrial refrigeration equipment. In the 1990s, the company had subsidiaries in Belgium, Australia, Singapore, Hong Kong, the United States, and Thailand. In 2004 Daikin's sales were US$5.9 billion, a one-year growth of 24 percent.

TOYOTA INDUSTRIES CORP.

The company that is perhaps Japan's best known, best-selling automaker is also a manufacturer of industrial machinery. Toyota's consolidated sales in 2004 were US$11 billion. Autos and auto parts accounted for 59.6 percent of those sales; industrial equipment, 30.8 percent; textile machinery—the company's original and sole product for years during the early twentieth century—4.3 percent; and other products, 5.6 percent.

MAJOR COUNTRIES IN THE INDUSTRY

OVERVIEW OF TOP PRODUCERS

Overall, Europe was responsible for 29 percent of world machinery production. The United States is the highest producer, making 36 percent of machinery products worldwide, and the world's leading revenue generator, earning 35.7 percent of the global market. Other key exporters in 2005 included Italy with 5 percent of export orders, the United Kingdom with 4 percent, South Korea with 4 percent, Australia with 3 percent, and Russia with 3 percent.

EXPORT SEGMENTS

For pumps and pumping equipment, the top five leading exporters in 2005 were China, with 29 percent of export orders; Taiwan, with 16 percent; India, with 15 percent; Italy, with 11 percent; and Russia, with 10 percent.

The top five exporting countries for compressors in 2005 were Taiwan, with 29 percent of exports; China, with 27 percent; India, with 24 percent; the United Kingdom with 15 percent; and South Korea with 4 percent.

In 2005, the top five exporters of packing machinery, also known as mechanical handling equipment, included India, at 28 percent of the export orders; Taiwan, with 19 percent; China, with 17 percent; the United Kingdom with 9 percent; and the United States at 9 percent.

FURTHER READING

"Aggregated Trade Statistics: International Trade Center, United Nations Conference on Trade and Development/World Trade Organization," February 2002. Available from http://www.intracen.org.

Annual Survey of Manufactures. Washington, D.C.: U.S. Census Bureau, February 2002. Available from http://www.census.gov.

Global Industrial Machinery Industry Profile. Datamonitor, May 2004. Available from http://www.datamonitor.com.

"Hoover's Company Capsules." 2004. Available from http://www.hoovers.com.

"International Trade Statistics." 2003. Available from http://www.wto.org.

"Machinery Demand Rising Worldwide." *Packaging Digest,* March 2005.

"Material Handling Equipment and Systems Demand to Reach $20.4 Billion by 2008." *Material Handling Management,* January 2005.

Murphy, Elena Epatko. "Mixed Automotive Demand Slows Recovery." *Purchasing,* 6 February 2003.

"New High-Tech Features Help Buyers Cut Total Costs." *Purchasing,* 21 October 2004.

"Packing Machinery Trade Statistics." Export Bureau, 24 July 2004. Available from http://www.exportbureau.com.

"PMMI Study Shows Strong Spending Trends for 2004." *Feedstuffs,* 7 June 2004.

"Pumps Machinery Trade Statistics." Export Bureau, 24 July 2004. Available from http://www.exportbureau.com.

Rasche, Michael J. "Floundering Global and Domestic Markets Frustrate U.S. Bearings Market." *Motor & Control News,* Market Research Report. February 2002. Available from http://www.motorcontrol.com.

"Machinery Global Industry Trade Statistics." Export Bureau, 27 April 2005. Available from http://www.exportbureau.com.

"UK Machinery Outlook." *Packaging Magazine,*, April 2004.

"U.S. Packaging Machinery Shipments Rise." *Packaging Digest,*, November 2004.

SIC 3580

NAICS 3334

MACHINERY, REFRIGERATION, AND SERVICE INDUSTRY

Refrigeration and service machinery manufacturing includes five major segments: vending machines; commercial laundry equipment; heating and cooling equipment; service station pumps and grease guns; and miscellaneous service machinery, such as floor-cleaning machines and commercial dishwashers and cooking equipment

INDUSTRY SNAPSHOT

After the down years of the early 2000s, the global service machine and refrigeration industry enjoyed generally strong growth worldwide. This uptick was fueled by the rapid emergence of several formerly underdeveloped economies into the technological and consumer economy mainstream, with China's seemingly insatiable product demand at the forefront. In 2003, the United States alone exported US$376 million in heating ventilation, air conditioning, and refrigeration (HVAC/R) equipment to China; and China exported 14.8 million units that same year. Sean Zhang reported in *Appliance* that industry experts expected 60 percent of China's 2005 air conditioner sales would be exported units. Total U.S. exports in that category during 2003 were just over $7.1 billion. By comparison, U.S. imports showed steady and significant growth over the five-year period from 1998, when U.S. imports were valued at $2.89 billion, to 2003, when imports were almost $5.3 billion. World demand for commercial refrigeration equipment was expected to grow through 2008 at about 5.8 percent per year, reaching $25.8 billion, according to researchers at The Freedonia Group.

Freedonia also reported that U.S. demand for heating ventilation and air conditioning (HVAC) equipment was expected to reach US$12 billion by 2007, fueled by increased construction and the growing replacement market. *Euromonitor* reported U.S. HVAC growth projections of 26 percent. In Europe, the market in France was expected to grow 10 percent, followed by 15 percent growth in both Germany and the United Kingdom. Refrigeration and freezing equipment were the largest sectors for Germany and the United Kingdom, and air conditioners were the largest segment in France and the United States. Environmental and cost reduction concerns led to a new generation of ever more efficient and sophisticated heating, refrigeration, laundry, and gas-pumping technologies.

The same study expects U.S. demand for vending machines to reach US$1.6 billion by 2006, of which beverage sales would account for US$690 million. Europe's large vending machine industry faced the challenge of converting machines from accepting various national currencies to accepting new Euro coins by 2002.

ORGANIZATION AND STRUCTURE

REFRIGERATION, AIR CONDITIONING, AND HEATING

The global heating ventilation, air conditioning and refrigeration (HVAC/R) equipment industry manufactured machines in several product categories in the early 2000s. The largest of these were self-contained, mechanically refrigerated, heat transfer equipment; unitary air conditioners; compressors and compressor units; commercial refrigerators and equipment; room air conditioners and dehumidifiers; and warm-air furnaces, humidifiers, and electric comfort heating equipment; as well as parts and accessories. Miscellaneous industry products included electric heat pumps, furnaces, refrigerated display cases, soda fountains, beer dispensers, and snowmaking machinery.

The HVAC/R industry has historically grown 2 to 3 percent a year. In the United States—one of the world's largest HVAC/R equipment markets—the motor vehicle and building construction industries were the primary end users of HVAC/R industry equipment. New home building was a primary factor in unitary air conditioner sales, which accounted for 50 percent of sector demand by 1999. Because of global agreements phasing out environmentally harmful coolants, the retrofit, or upgrade, of older heating and cooling systems was a significant end use for industry products by early 2000. As the result of these environmental policies, a new industry sector developing energy-efficient "green building" technology had emerged in the early twenty-first century. Common industrial uses of refrigeration equipment in 2000 included food distribution, storage and preparation, and, in the chemical industry, the manufacture of petrochemicals, liquefaction of gases, separation of chemicals, and process control. Heating systems, refrigeration equipment, and air conditioners, manufactured by industry firms, supply the world's office buildings, hospitals, schools, restaurants, supermarkets, hotels, and other nonresidential large-capacity environments that require climate control.

Unlike household air conditioners, commercial and industrial heating and ventilation systems are often customized to match the widely varying needs of each customer's building/installation—from warehouses or stores to high-rises and sports stadiums. Industry firms are motivated by the need to create the most efficient heating and cooling systems possible and to balance that goal with the need for "real-world" functionality. During the final decades of the twentieth century, industry revenues were directly affected by commercial construction activity, such as new office buildings or malls, environmental laws governing refrigerant use and recycling, and the willingness of customers to purchase new units rather than maintain old ones.

VENDING MACHINES

According to the National Automatic Merchandising Association (NAMA), vending sales rose from a US$2.5 billion industry in 1960 to a US$38.7 billion industry in 2000. By 2005, annual vending machine revenues were still hovering in that range. When first introduced to consumer markets, automated vending machines were relatively uncomplicated mechanical devices—product (mostly food items in prepackaged servings) was purchased when a coin was inserted in a slot. Later, these machines evolved into more complex electromechanical hybrids capable of dispensing an extremely diverse range of products and equipped to accomplish a financial transaction with paper bills, tokens, prepaid debit cards, and even credit cards. Although traditionally associated with simple coin-operated beverage, snack, newspaper, and cigarette machines, during the 1990s the vending machine industry's global marketing strategy addressed increased consumer leisure time for shopping and a dwindling interest in home cooking. In the early 2000s, economic uncertainty forced corporations to replace full scale food service operations with vending machines, as a labor scarcity made fully staffed facilities impractical. In the two largest vending machine markets, Japan and the United States, automatic merchandising machines comprised more than two-thirds of the vending machine manufacturing market by the late 1980s. In the early 2000s there were more than 5.5 million vending machines operating in Japan, one for every 20 people, totaling some US$56 billion in sales.

Traditionally, vending machines were fashioned from formed sheet metal and metal and plastic parts. Small electric motors and generators drove their product-dispensing mechanism and managed payment validation/acceptance (i.e., verifying the type of currency inserted based on such properties as weight, size, or magnetic qualities). In the late 1990s, the industry trend was toward electronic machines containing microprocessors and modems that were capable of keeping a machine's supplier updated on sales or notified of low product supplies. Such machines were expensive, however, and mechanical or simpler electronic vending machines were still common, particularly in the beverage sector. In 2001 technology allowing vending machine orders and payment via cell phone emerged, promising to reduce mechanical malfunctions of vending coin collection. By 2004, cash vending was emerging as the next big thing in vending machine sales. Reports on vending machine revenue predicted revenue from vending machines could increase to $70 million by the year 2010, according to *The Kiplinger Report.* This report claimed wireless-activated payments would "revolutionize vending," and that customers would be willing to spend more than $100 on cashless transactions. Customers who used debit or credit cards preferred these machines and were willing to spend more when using them. A pilot test in the United States at Regal Cinemas showed vending sales increased 139 percent over a one-year period, with credit or debit card transactions being responsible for more than 30 percent of total transactions, as reported in *Screen Digest.*

By far the most common industry practice was to sell vending machines directly to product manufacturers, such as soda beverage bottlers, or to third-party vending machine distributors who installed and maintained them. By 2001, some of the more active global vending machine manufacturers included Germany's NSM AG and CWS Deutschland GmbH; the United States' Cubic Corp., IMI Cornelius Inc., Rowe International Inc., and National Vendors; the United Kingdom's Enodis PLC; and Japan's Glory Ltd. and Sanden Corporation.

Commercial Laundry Equipment

The commercial laundry equipment manufacturing industry could be divided into three broad categories: commercial laundry equipment and laundry presses, dry-cleaning equipment and clothing presses, and miscellaneous commercial laundry equipment and parts. Within these product categories, however, a wide range of machines was manufactured: washers; ironers; laundry presses; drying tumblers; garment manufacturers' presses; extractors; feather cleaning and sterilizing machines; and equipment to clean, dry, and nap rugs. These generally were big machines, accommodating loads exceeding 22 pounds, and were used by a variety of institutional clients including hospitals, restaurants, hotels, government institutions (such as prisons), and of course commercial laundering businesses.

In the mid-1990s, it was not unusual for industry firms to turn out approximately 50,000 machines annually. Representative firms in the industry included Germany's Wanderer-Werke, MEIKO Maschinenbau GmbH and Co., and Alfred Kaercher; the United Kingdom's Dowding and Mills PLC; Mexico's Mexicana de Maquinaria; Japan's Fukui Machinery; and the United States' White Consolidated Industries, Whirlpool Corp., Bissell, Inc., Pellerin Milnor, and Staber Industries. In the sizable U.S. industry, the commercial laundry equipment business was estimated to be only one one-hundredth of the size of the U.S. residential laundry equipment business.

Measuring and Dispensing Pumps

The global measuring and dispensing pump industry primarily manufactures pumps for dispensing gasoline at filling stations. Such units usually have several pumps, capable of pumping ten gallons per minute or more, and are often computerized with digital readouts indicating the amount of gas pumped. Such machines usually offer consumers the ability to purchase fuel directly at the pump using a credit or debit card. Even as early as the late 1980s, computerized gasoline dispensing pumps in the United States—one of the world's largest exporters of measuring and dispensing pumps—constituted 42 percent of industry shipments. Other products of the industry include pump parts and attachments, non-computing and other measuring and dispensing pumps, miscellaneous measuring and dispensing pumps, lubricating oil pumps and barrel pumps, and grease guns.

The leading producers of liquid pumps in the 1990s were Germany, China, and the United States. Representative international firms in this industry segment, in the late 1990s, included the United States' Penn Process Technologies, Jesco Products, and Alfred Conhagen Inc.; Canada's Dresser Canada; Germany's Magdeburger Armaturen Maw; Japan's Tatsuno Corporation; and Mexico's Capacitores Componentes de Mexico. Additional participants engaged in the manufacture of measuring and dispensing pumps include Veeder Root Brasil Comercio e Industria (Brazil); Molson Companies, Tokheim, and Gasboy (Canada); Intent SA (Spain); Gilbarco (United States); Scheidt and Bachmann GmbH (Germany); and General Electric Company PLC and Enodis PLC (United Kingdom). Interestingly, all of these businesses also owned commercial laundry equipment firms in the United States—an increasingly commonplace industry trend in the measuring and dispensing pump industry.

MISCELLANEOUS SERVICE MACHINES INDUSTRY

The miscellaneous service machines industry was the second largest industry segment in the late 1990s and encompassed a wide variety of products. The first product group—commercial cooking and food-warming equipment—includes ovens, broilers, microwaves, deep-fat fryers, griddles, toasters, coffee urns, steam pressure cookers, and steam tables. The second group—commercial and industrial vacuum cleaners—includes both portable and central system vacuums and associated parts. And the third group—service industry machines and parts—includes such products as non-household water heaters; industrial and household water softeners; commercial and industrial floor and carpet cleaning equipment (including sanding, scrubbing, waxing, and polishing machines); commercial dishwashers; sewer pipe and drain cleaning equipment; high-pressure cleaning and blasting machinery; motor vehicle washing equipment; sewage treatment equipment; and trash and garbage compactors. End users of this segment's products ranged from sewer system construction companies, electrical repair shops, and government institutions to hotels, transportation and warehouse firms, and schools.

Industry sales are heavily dependent on the economic health of end users: restaurants and other food-preparation facilities, commercial cleaning firms, and certain consumer segments of the world economy. In the late 1990s, the wide range of firms participating in one of the industry's largest markets, the United States, indicated the sheer diversity of products included in this composite segment of the service machine industry. These included vacuum cleaner maker Hoover North America, water treatment supplier Culligan International, cooking equipment maker Frymaster Corp., and car wash equipment producer Hanna Car Wash International. Firms in Illinois, Ohio, and California dominated the U.S. industry.

A number of industry firms were exclusively engaged in the manufacture of such service machines in the late 1990s, including Brazil's Xerox Do Brasil; Canada's Bunn-O-Matic Corporation; Germany's Osorno Produktions für Autowaschtechnik; Japan's Chiyoda Manufacturing; and Mexico's Hermetik. Several other industry firms were diversified into other businesses, from sheet metal work to the manufacturing of precision instruments, but derived the lion's share of their sales from miscellaneous service industry machine manufacture. These include Canada's Garland Commercial Ranges, Japan's Japan Organo Company, and America's Amano Partners USA.

BACKGROUND AND DEVELOPMENT

VENDING MACHINES

Gum and penny candy vending machines were introduced on elevated train platforms in New York City in 1888, cigarette machines were first introduced in 1926, and the first soft drink machines began to appear in 1937. Long production shifts in factories during World War II greatly spurred the development of the vending machine industry, which responded to the need for a convenient dispenser of hot coffee by placing coffee vending machines on factory floors. After the war, the global reach of the vending machine industry was significantly extended when major U.S. beverage producers, like Coca-Cola and Pepsi, began to aggressively penetrate overseas markets. Because retail space in Japan is so limited, by the 1960s the vending machine had become a major factor in the growth of Japan's product distribution system. Microprocessor-controlled vending machines began to hit the market in 1992. By the late 1990s, vending machines were being used to sell such myriad goods as liquor, train tickets, toys, beef, fishing bait, power tools, business cards, women's clothing, and jewelry.

In the late 1990s, the world's largest vending machine markets were the United States, Japan, and Europe, and roughly 1,000 different types and models of vending machines were on the market. In 1995 the number of vending machines in operation in the United States climbed past 6.4 million, one for every 50 people, versus an estimated 5.5 million, 2.6 million for beverage alone, in Japan in 1997, one for every 23 people. Reflecting the greater importance traditionally placed on vending machines as a retail sales outlet in Japan, by 1997 the value of goods vended through Japanese vending machines had grown to US$55 billion, up 2 percent from 1996, versus US$28 billion in the United States in 1996. The European Union had about 5.0 million vending machines in operation, about one per every 75 people, in the late 1990s.

U.S. vending machines have historically been placed inside offices, factories, and public spaces, as private independent merchandising outlets. Conversely, Japanese vending machines—more than half of which sell beverages—are primarily located on public sidewalks and are often used as point-of-sale merchandizing outlets to evade Japan's high labor costs. By 2001, the food and beverage vending market in Japan offered excellent opportunities for international beverage machine manufacturers because of the Japanese consumer's openness to new food and beverage product mixes, merchandised through innovative vending technologies.

In the decade from 1987 to 1997, sales through vending machines in Japan almost doubled, and innovative uses for vending machines continued to be tried. By the 1990s, however, Japan's often quite elaborate vending machines were consuming almost 4 percent of all electricity consumed on the island nation, leading the government to mandate that the electricity consumption of canned beverage vending machines be reduced by 20 percent by 1997. When the Japanese vending equipment industry met this goal, a further 15 percent electricity reduction by 2002 was called for.

Between 1995 and 1998, the revenues of the roughly 105 U.S. automatic vending machine makers were estimated to have increased almost 10 percent, from US$940 million to US$1 billion. In 1999 worldwide industry sales rose to US$36 billion from US$34.8 billion in 1998, a gain of about 5 percent. By 2005, sales remained in that range, but were expected to more than double by 2010, largely due to cashless vending and new machines capable of accepting debit or credit cards. U.S. firms were among the world's leaders in implementing new high-tech vending machines that greatly improved the variety and quantity of goods vended, the serviceability of vending machines, and the accuracy of the vending operators' sales and inventory data. As early as 1993, the maturing international vending machine market had begun to become, in the words of one U.S. industry executive, "very hot." For the first time, many U.S. firms made a commitment to aggressively penetrate the world's growing vending machine markets. The growth of vending markets in some of the more urbanized regions in Middle Eastern countries, notably Saudi Arabia and Latin American countries such as Venezuela and Argentina, substantially surpassed growth in other international markets. Outside of Thailand, for example, vending machines existed hardly at all in Southeast Asia as late as 1998.

Roughly five million vending machines were in operation in the countries of the European Union in the late 1990s, with German machines, mostly for cigarettes, accounting for half the total. The sales of Germany's vending machine manufacturers and importers were US$305 million in 1996, and Germany's vending machines handled roughly US$9 billion in sales in 1997. Between 1996 and 1997, German vending equipment industry firms saw their revenues rise about 5 percent, with their business expected to grow by 9 to 12 percent per year through the remainder of the century.

Vending's traditional high-margin products, hot and cold cup beverages, remained strong in 1999. In the United Kingdom, vended beverage sales increased in the mid and late 1990s; canned cold drinks dominated, with dollar sales increasing 8.3 percent to US$15.7 billion, or 42.9 percent of total industry volume in 1999. Packaged confections and snacks held second place, with a 10.8 percent gain to US$7.2 billion.

Perhaps the biggest challenge facing European vending machine makers in the late 1990s was the European Monetary Union, which starting in 1999 was to begin phase-in of a common currency, the euro (also known as the European currency unit or ECU), in place of national currencies of participating countries. By 2002, national currencies were completely eliminated. The new currency was expected to strain vending machine manufacturers, who were estimated to spend upwards of 10 percent of their annual budgets to rebuild equipment to accommodate the euro. For example, European equipment firms reprogrammed the controllers and coin validators on all existing machines for the euro and then tested machines for reliability. Europe's vending machine operators, rather than the manufacturers, bore the brunt of the cost of retrofitting existing machines to the euro.

Laundry and Dishwashing Machinery

In the eighteenth century, laundering was already a viable small-business enterprise, typically operated by individuals and dependent on individual manual labor. The development of its auxiliary industry, the manufacture of laundering machinery, was made possible when the first patent for a clothes-washing device was awarded to Nathaniel Briggs in 1797. Over the next 50 years, more than 200 patents were granted for washing machines alone. The dry-cleaning process was invented between 1825 and 1845 when it was accidentally discovered that a volatile liquid, such as camphene, cleaned soiled clothes without the use of water. In 1863 Hamilton E. Smith patented a reciprocating washing device that reversed the motion of the revolving drum in the washing machine, turning the clothes over inside the drum and splashing them in soapy water. The first wooden-tub washing machine was introduced in 1900. A commercial laundry industry began to emerge as the development of washing and drying technology eventually evolved into electrical machines, and by 1924 the spin-dry washing machine was first introduced. The first electrically driven domestic dishwashers began to appear in Europe in 1929, and in the late 1970s the first computer-controlled washing machines, tumbling dryers, and "sensor-touch" dishwashers hit the market.

Firms in the United States, Asia, and Europe dominated the worldwide commercial laundry equipment industry in the late 1990s. Roughly 12 percent of all revenues for the U.S. commercial laundry equipment industry in 1996 were derived from exports.

In 1993 a European commission began awarding "Eco-Labels" to manufacturers of environmentally friendly laundry machines, reflecting the growing worldwide concern with energy savings and the impact of chemicals and detergents on the environment. Another factor that compelled many commercial laundry equipment makers to reevaluate their products was rooted in a European Union initiative that set safety standards for machinery sold throughout the common market. The new standards went into effect in 1995. To gain the "CE mark" of approval, firms were required to identify and reduce potential design/operational hazards in machines, as well as maintain technical construction files on each product built.

Industry activities in East Asia reflected that region's rapid growth as a center of service industry machine manufacture. South Korea's Daewoo Electronics Company invested heavily in the construction of washing machine plants in the mid-1990s and began exporting washing machines to Russia, while the South Korean firm LG Electronics exported 50,000 of its washing machines to Taiwan's Taistar in 1995. In 1994 Japan's Sanyo Electric announced plans to assemble and sell washing machines in mainland China.

Gas Pumps

The invention of the gas meter is credited to Samuel Clegg in 1815; however, the development of the gas pump in modern gas service stations had to wait for the development of the gasoline engine and the automobile. Following the worldwide adoption of the centrifugal pump by about 1850, John Tokheim, the founder of the U.S. Tokheim Corporation, invented the first underground gasoline tank in 1898. By 1906 gasoline measuring pumps specifically designed for the automobile were developed, followed later in the century by the first electrically operated pumps and computerized gas pumps with digital displays and automated payment features.

In 1998, the United States had one of the world's largest pump manufacturing industries with an estimated 70 companies generating revenues of US$1.33 billion. Close to 10 percent of U.S. industry shipments were exported in 1996. Other leading world exporters in this segment included Japan, Germany, Italy, and France.

In 2000 U.S. manufacturers pursued a domestic market consisting of roughly 200,000 service stations. Amoco's 3,000 service stations alone were estimated to require annual equipment purchases of US$12 million or more. Because of the dominance of the large gasoline and oil producers, like Amoco and Shell in the U.S. market, pump makers historically have tended to focus on large firms at the expense of small or independently run companies.

The world's less developed nations represented a major opportunity for industry firms in the late 1990s. China, for example, with five times the population of the United States, had only 5,500 service stations in the mid-1990s—less than 3 percent of the U.S. total. Large international measuring and dispensing pump makers continued to produce both sophisticated digital pumps for developed markets and simple non-computerized gas pumps for developing markets. In 1993 Tokheim Corporation, one of the world's largest international manufacturers of measuring and dispensing pumps, enjoyed increased sales in its Latin America and Asian markets, and in the same year it announced a US$72 million contract to supply pump equipment to Shell Europe and pursued a similar arrangement with Shell International.

Refrigeration, Air Conditioning, and Heating

Heating equipment manufacturing was already a mature industry in the 1700s. The first cast iron stove manufactured in the United States appeared in pre-Revolutionary colonies, and by 1744 Benjamin Franklin had invented a stove using movable ventilating doors to control temperature. Since then, the development of improved heating sources, insulating and construction materials, and temperature control have greatly improved the efficiency and sensitivity of equipment and made possible more innovative and productive commercial applications.

The knowledge that volatile liquids, such as ethyl ether, absorb heat when evaporated—the fundamental principle of modern refrigeration—was discovered by William Cullen in 1748, but it was not until 1918 that the refrigerator began to replace the icebox.

In 1902, Willis Carrier devised the first air conditioner, which was installed in a New York printing plant. Chlorofluorocarbons (CFCs), later found to be environmentally damaging, were first introduced by the industry in the 1930s as a substitute for the flammable coolants used in earlier air conditioners. In 1939 Carrier developed the first air conditioning system for high-rise buildings, and by the end of World War II the air conditioner was in widespread use. Since the 1980s, however, use of CFCs has been curtailed significantly in favor of more environmentally sound coolants.

In 1996 world exports of industrial heating and cooling equipment, based on United Nations figures, reached US$36.4 billion, an increase of less than one percent from the previous year and a slight decrease in inflation-controlled terms. The United States led this category with US$5.9 billion in exports, followed by Japan (US$5.4 billion), Germany (US$4.8 billion), Italy (US$4.8 billion), and France (US$2.6 billion). Leading importers that year included the United States (US$3.3 billion), Germany (US$2.4 billion), South Korea (US$2.2 billion), Canada (US$1.8 billion), France (US$1.8 billion), and China (US$1.7 billion).

The HVAC/R equipment industry is extremely cyclical in nature because demand for its products depends on the health of end-use industries that are themselves notorious for wild swings in demand. Auto sales, for example, tend to decline during periods of economic hardship when major purchases are delayed, and the building industry—subject to interest rates and periods of oversupply—is a significant source of market volatility. On the other hand, the industry benefited from a robust year in housing starts in 1998, with 1.54 million units purchased. Housing, industrial, and commercial construction in developing warm-weather countries, as well as Eastern Europe, drove demand in 1998; sales in Vietnam grew 18 percent each year; the Indian subcontinent 15 percent; Central Europe 10 percent; and Latin America nearly 8 percent. In the refrigeration sector, an aging population patronizing restaurants and an increasing demand for fresh and frozen food items shipped via refrigerated truck may boost sales.

Growth in world trade involving food products that require refrigeration also had a positive impact on equipment demand in the 1990s. In 1998 it was estimated that the heating, ventilation, and air conditioning equipment industry of the Pacific Rim countries was growing faster than the region's gross domestic product. As a newly prosperous global consumer class dined out more, restaurants multiplied, fueling the need for commercial refrigeration equipment. As office, store, and warehouse construction grew, so too did the need for bigger and more efficient heating, ventilation, and cooling machines. By 2002 industry analysts lauded industry growth due to widespread chain grocery "superstores" requiring extensive refrigeration cases. The world's heating and refrigeration industry was also increasingly intermeshed, with international joint ventures, acquisitions, and partnerships flourishing, particularly in Asia's emerging economies, such as China. Between 1987 and 1997, exports of U.S. heating, ventilation, and air conditioning equipment doubled, and international sales accounted for as much as 35 percent of revenues for many U.S. firms by the late 1990s.

The United Nations' Montreal Protocol of 1987 mandated the phase-out of the traditional industry refrigerant, chlorofluorocarbons (CFCs), in the 1990s, and many individual countries—such as the United States with its Clean Air Act Amendments—instituted their own restrictions. But factory and office building owners seemed to be in no hurry to meet the deadlines. Of the 80,000 centrifugal and screw chillers that used CFCs in the United States in 1992, roughly 76 percent still needed CFCs to operate in January 1997. In the United States alone there was an installed base of HVAC/R equipment valued at more than US$137 billion in the late 1990s. In addition, it was estimated that in 1993 one fifth of all U.S. heating systems were 20 years old or more and that 15 percent of all central cooling units were 10 or more years old. Moreover, in 1996 there were 130 million motor vehicle air conditioners and 5 million commercial refrigeration systems that still ran on CFCs. By 1998 about 20,000 CFC-based chillers had been converted or replaced in the United States. Clearly, at the turn of the twenty-first century, industry firms around the globe could look forward to a bountiful market supplying heating and cooling replacements and upgrades.

By 2000 the worldwide HVAC/R equipment industry was benefiting from a favorable global economy and the new technology brought about by international agreements to reduce the use of greenhouse gas coolants. Many industry firms were relying increasingly on international trade for profits, and the rapid rise of a global middle class in countries considered underdeveloped only a generation earlier—many in warm regions of the world—was opening up vast new markets for residential, commercial, and industrial air conditioning and cooling products. In addition, significant transportation costs and region-specific products were international trade factors driving companies to open plants worldwide and establish patterns of e-commerce.

In addition to keeping up with environmental mandates for equipment requiring less harmful refrigerants, other challenges faced by industry firms in 2000 included agreeing on a set of international performance standards for all heating, ventilation, and air conditioning products so international firms could reduce the number of machine types and specifications worldwide. In the United States, industry firms faced the effects of the increasing deregulation of the U.S. energy utilities industry with uncertainty.

In the U.S. HVAC/R equipment market, shipments of chillers doubled between 1987 and 1997, and in 1996 some 97 U.S. industry firms set a slew of all-time sales records: 5.25 million central heating units shipped in 1996; 5.36 million central air conditioners and air conditioner source pumps in 1997; and 14,239 reciprocating liquid chiller packages, which are used for comfort cooling in commercial, institutional, and government buildings, the same year.

CURRENT CONDITIONS

REFRIGERATION, AIR CONDITIONING, AND HEATING

According to a Freedonia Group study, HVAC demand was expected to rise more than 2 percent annually through 2007, reaching a value of US$12 billion. In addition to construction growth, the replacement market was expected to contribute to the growth of this sector. *Air Conditioning, Heating & Refrigeration News* reported a study from the Air-Conditioning and Refrigeration Institute that showed heat pump shipments had risen 11 percent from 2003 to 2004, and central air conditioners were up 6 percent over the same period. Reports from the Air-Conditioning and Refrigeration Institute were optimistic. Shipments of air source heat pumps and unitary air conditioners passed 7 million units for the first time in 2004, 9 percent more than in 2003. Furnace shipments were up 7 percent as well, with more than 3.5 million units of gas furnaces shipped. Canada's market in 2004 showed improvements for heater sales and residential furnaces, but registering declined for commercial and residential air conditioning shipments.

VENDING MACHINES

In 2002, U.S. colleges had the highest vending sales of any other market segment, and more hospitals were adding machines than any other market segment. Beverages accounted for the majority of sales, at 48 percent, followed by snacks with 22 percent. According to *The Kiplinger Report,* machine demand was expected to rise to $70 billion by 2010.

In the mid-2000s, the fastest-growing trend in vending was machines that only accept credit or debit cards, with sales authorized locally via wireless technology. Such a move was expected by industry leaders to reduce theft and vandalism, since there would be no cash in the machines at all. According to North County Vending, one of the largest vending companies in the United States with 16,000 machines in five Western states, in machines that had been retrofitted with card-only capabilities, vandalism and theft disappeared.

GASOLINE AND OIL PUMPS

By 2001, Tokheim Corporation claimed roughly one-third of the U.S. pump market and approximately one-sixth of the total world market, with subsidiaries in the Netherlands, Britain, Germany, South Africa, and Canada.

MISCELLANEOUS SERVICE MACHINES INDUSTRY

More than 1,000 firms competed in the U.S. miscellaneous service machines industry. In fact, more U.S. companies were active in this industry segment than in the U.S. vending, commercial laundry, gas pump, and HVAC/R equipment industries combined. Several diversified international producers of service machines were significant contributors to the industry, including Brazil's Xerox do Brasil, Germany's Schmalbach-Lubeca AG, Italy's Fonderie Sime, and Japan's Ebara Corporation.

RESEARCH AND TECHNOLOGY

REFRIGERATION, AIR CONDITIONING, AND HEATING

Technical advances in heating and refrigeration equipment in the late 1990s centered on improving the performance, quality, and efficiency of machines and developing technologies that used refrigerants that were not harmful to the environment and conformed to indoor air quality guidelines issued by urbanized countries. Such global consensus on protecting the environment led to more efficient refrigerant recycling and recovery components, and alternative, non-chlorine-based refrigerant technologies. The first widespread substitute refrigerant for CFC was hydrochlorofluorocarbon or HCFC. However, as a freon-type refrigerant, this was scheduled for phase-out by 2020. New alternatives were sought, from natural gas, steam, and low-pressure refrigerants, like Du Pont's SUVA 123, to ammonia, lithium bromide/water, and ammonia/water-based refrigerants. In the late 1990s, radically new heating and cooling systems were also unveiled. So-called ground-source or geothermal heat pumps (GSHP) exchange heat with the earth itself rather than the external air by using a loop of underground pipes, thus avoiding the greenhouse issue altogether. Another approach was to design fully closed or zero-emission chillers that, while using CFC-type refrigerants, allow none to escape into the atmosphere. At the current replacement rate, CFC chillers will not be eliminated in the United States until 2010, according to the American Refrigeration Institute.

By the late 1990s, the success of industry firms at improving the efficiency of heating and cooling products had been so great that engineers had to turn to the design of system controls to find areas for improvements. A new generation of electronic controls offers tighter tolerance ranges than ever before, ensuring greater efficiency by creating machines that run closer to their ideal performance set points. Other control innovations include self-contained diagnostic features that guide repair people to the malfunctioning part or run periodic self-checks and then alert repair people at remote locations via computer if a problem arises. Controls can notify the user when the machine needs to be cleaned or the air filter changed.

Other research thrusts by industry firms focused on reducing equipment noise levels in condensing units to conform to noise pollution regulations and adopting scroll compressor technology to replace traditional reciprocating methods in refrigeration condensers, improving energy efficiency. One innovative approach was a thermal energy storage (TES) system—a chiller that only operates at night when electricity rates are lowest. It then stores the cooling it generates in the form of ice, cold water, or other material. When cool air is required during the day, the system retrieves the cool energy it has stored the night before.

Industry firms in the 1990s also employed less complex designs for air conditioners, effectively reducing the number of parts and the amount of maintenance needed. Improved designs also included the adoption of double-wall construction in air conditioners, more advanced heat pumps, air conditioners with improved seasonal energy efficiency ratings (SEER), and heaters with enhanced heating season performance factors (HSPF). Industry product engineers were relying more and more on engineering software tools such as computer-aided design (CAD), which enabled them to design virtual components and systems on their computer monitors that were capable, to an increasingly accurate degree, of simulating the actual performance of a real product without the cost of manufacturing a prototype.

VENDING MACHINES

Despite the somewhat prosaic image of the vending machine, the very self-operating, or "robotic," nature of such equipment makes it a perfect target for creative technical innovation. Advances in technology, and the openness of the vended product firms to embrace innovative product merchandising approaches, continued to revolutionize the world's vending machine industry in the late 1990s. A growing range of products was dispensed by vending machines, from toys, plastic laminates for driver's licenses, cut flowers and picture frames, sandwiches, and greeting cards to pills (in hospitals), videocassettes and compact discs, cigars, frozen beef (in Japan), travel tickets, salads, and even beer and alcohol (in Canada and Asian countries).

The introduction of microprocessors and electronic controllers inside vending machines led to the development of features that improved marketability, such as elaborate multimedia displays and the capacity of some machines to perform a self-inventory of product supply or a self-diagnosis of mechanical functions. More and more machines could even transmit information about product supply and machine conditions to a computer at the vending service company via a modem contained within the machine, using either the Internet or proprietary electronic data interchange as the communication medium. Route service people of vending machine operating companies increasingly wore handheld computers that allowed them to visit only machines they knew to be low in product or in need of repair. The machines could also dump their highly detailed sales and self-diagnostic data into the service person's computer so it could be analyzed, graphed, and sent back at the office.

Vending service firms traditionally had to adjust thermostat controls in temperature-variable machines by hand, but self-adjusting vending machines were being designed in the mid and late 1990s that reacted to changes in their surroundings. Some machines were even programmed to stop selling products when temperatures reached a predetermined level. Other innovations rolled out by industry firms in the 1990s included vending machines equipped to process credit cards; machines that greeted potential buyers with computerized welcome and thank-you messages; driver's license validation features to prevent underage teens from buying tobacco or alcohol; machines that used laser scanning beams to accurately identify up to 4,000 different coin types; vandal-proof protection systems; and outsized vending machines capable of handling 36 separate columns of beverage cans or preparing 96 different beverage combinations.

COMMERCIAL LAUNDRY EQUIPMENT

In May 1994 the U.S. Department of Energy issued new energy efficiency standards for appliances, such as commercial washers and dryers, and planned to institute even more stringent standards by 1999. These guidelines compelled some industry firms to upgrade product lines to improve machine performance. Beginning in about 1991, innovations in the external design of commercial laundry machines, as well as in their internal functioning, began to result in substantial change. In 1993 Staber Industries of the United States began to market a top-loading, horizontal-axis washing machine similar in basic design to the washers commonly used in Europe. Because European top-loaders used less water and detergent, U.S. manufacturers hoped to capitalize on increasing concern for environmental issues to break through the U.S. attachment to front-loading vertical-axis machines. Innovations in washer technology included 18-pound wash load capacities; no clutch transmission or brake mechanisms; and improved washing processes that actively pumped detergent fluids into the laundry fibers, rather than relying passively on the motion of the clothes during the wash cycle.

GASOLINE PUMPS

In the late 1990s, worldwide research and development in the pump sector centered on modifications inspired by environmental concerns as well as technological advancements involving new payment, display, and automation features. The United States was a forerunner in the implementation of legislation aimed at reducing the amount of gasoline fumes released during vehicle fueling. Some states passed even more stringent laws, requiring industry firms to install vapor recovery features in fuel pump products that would be capable of recovering as much as 95 percent of escaping gas fumes.

Gas pumps with digital readouts and automatic card payment features became common in many developed economies in the late 1990s. Other innovations geared to urban markets included installing electronic sensors that shut a pump off when a gas tank reached capacity, or a customer drove off without removing the nozzle from the gas tank. New pump designs also offered more efficient electronic configurations that substantially reduced the amount of connections, boards, and cables used to construct and operate pumps.

MISCELLANEOUS SERVICE MACHINES

New developments in the miscellaneous service machine segment in the 1990s highlighted increasing energy efficiency, improving ease of use, and making products more environmentally sensitive. Improvements in design also enabled manufacturers to create products for more highly specific applications by incorporating sensors, automation, and computerized, or "smart," features. The results created greater functionality and productivity. Innovations developed by the industry were sometimes rooted in consumer applications, such as commercial scanning ovens that "read" coded cooking instructions and commercial kitchen appliances that reached higher temperatures in shorter periods of time. More traditional institutional end users also benefited from such advances as carbon dioxide steam cookers capable of cooking, pasteurizing, sterilizing, and cooling with a temperature accuracy of plus or minus 0.5 degrees and jet steam ovens that used high-intensity vertical air flow to evenly brown foods in high-yield food preparation environments.

WORKFORCE

REFRIGERATION, AIR CONDITIONING, AND HEATING

In the world's largest HVAC/R equipment industry, the United States, an estimated 208,250 employees, 75 percent of whom were on the production line earned an average of US$15.62 an hour in 2000, and the average establishment in the U.S. HVAC/R equipment industry employed 141 workers and paid its production workers about US$32,490 a year. Assemblers, fabricators, and miscellaneous hand workers constituted the largest single occupational category in this segment of the U.S. industry. The largest U.S. employers of refrigeration and heating equipment in 1996 were Carrier Corp. with 27,000 workers, American Standard with 38,000, and York International with 13,800.

Outside the United States, large industry employers included France's Unite Hermetique; the United Kingdom's York International Ltd. and Halma PLC; China's Chunlan Group Corp. and Baocheng General Electronics; Japan's Daikin Industries and Hitachi Air Conditioning Refrigeration Co.; and Germany's Wolf GmbH, Gebrueder Trox, and Viessmann GmbH.

VENDING MACHINES

Some of the industry firms with the largest number of employees in the late 1990s included Germany's Effem GmbH (1,375 workers); Japan's Glory Ltd. (1,800), Nippon Signal (1,939), and Sanden Corp. (2,608); and Holland's Philips Machinefabrieken Nederland (2,000). The largest U.S. vending equipment makers, IMI Cornelius and Rowe International, employed 1,500 and 1,200 employees, respectively, in 1997. Total employment in the U.S. vending machine industry in 1998 was estimated at 7,000 (73% were production workers) with average mid-1990s annual wages of US$20,000 for production workers.

COMMERCIAL LAUNDRY EQUIPMENT

Large international employers in the commercial laundry equipment segment of the industry in the late 1990s included China's Guangdong Jiangmen Washing Machine Factory (1,062 workers), India's HMP Engineers Ltd. (650), Hong Kong's Process Automation (Holdings) Ltd. (700), and Germany's Bosch-Siemens Hausgeraete GmbH (27,625).

In 1998 the United States was the world's largest commercial laundry equipment manufacturer, employing an estimated 5,000 workers. Firms in three states—Florida, Kentucky, and Louisiana—accounted for 45 percent of the segment's U.S. employment, and the typical U.S. establishment employed 67 workers with an average annual wage for production employees of US$22,174. The largest U.S. employers in this industry segment in 1996 were Pellerin Milnor (900 workers), Cissell Manufacturing (400), and Unimac Company (400).

SERVICE STATION PUMPS

In 1997, the largest employers in worldwide pump manufacturing were Japan's Kawamoto Pump Manufacturing, South Korea's Lee Chun Electric Manufacturing, Mexico's Capacitores Componentes de Mexico, and Switzerland's ABB Turbo Systems. In 1998 the U.S. industry in this segment, the world's largest, employed an estimated 6,400 workers, and a typical industry establishment employed 79 workers and paid production employees US$30,216 annually. The largest U.S. employers in this industry segment in 1996 were Graco Inc. (2,100 workers), Wayne (900), and Tokheim Corp. (1,900).

MISCELLANEOUS SERVICE MACHINES

In the late 1990s, many of the largest employers engaged in the manufacture of miscellaneous service industry machinery were U.S. firms. The segment employed some 44,200 workers in 1998, and in the mid-1990s a typical U.S. establishment employed 38 workers and paid production employees US$23,065 per year. The largest U.S. employers in this industry sector in 1996 were Welbilt Corp., Hoover North America, Ionics Inc., and Tennant Co. Major employers worldwide included two German firms, Kloeckner-Humboldt-Deautz and Schmalbach-Lubeca, the United Kingdom's Sapalux, Japan's Ebara Corporation, and Brazil's Xerox do Brasil.

INDUSTRY LEADERS

MATSUSHITA

Matsushita Electric Industrial Company's participation in the world service machines industry, particularly air conditioners, was rooted in its largest business division, communication and industrial equipment. Matsushita's combined sales in 2004 from its 380 companies were US$71.9 billion, a 16 percent increase over 2003. Through its world-leading consumer electronics products, Matsushita had been at the forefront of the high-tech home electronics revolution of the 1970s and 1980s, marketing video equipment, digital videodiscs, flat-panel televisions, personal digital assistants, miniature VCRs, and notebook computers. In 2002, its businesses included AVC networks, home appliances, industrial equipment, and components and devices.

To consolidate its market position and ensure corporate stability in its core industries, Matsushita invested heavily in refurbishing factories and vowed to raise its international sales from 45 to 50 percent of its total revenues, spearheaded by sales offices in Eastern Europe and Central and Southeast Asia. Nonetheless, Matsushita remained a highly diversified company in 2002, with major interests in electronic components, home appliances, audio equipment, batteries and kitchen appliances, and a wide range of other niches, from industrial robots and fax machines to pagers, copiers, and bicycles.

MITSUBISHI

In addition to its role as one of the world's largest air conditioning system manufacturers, Mitsubishi Heavy Industries, reporting US$22.4 billion in annual sales for 2004, was a significant multinational manufacturer of aircraft and industrial machinery and equipment. As one of Asia's largest multinationals, and part of Japan's Mitsubishi *keiretsu,* or conglomerate of affiliated companies, it was well positioned to exploit the rapidly growing industrial and infrastructure development occurring in countries like Malaysia, Thailand, and mainland China. Through its Mitsubishi Heavy Industries America division, it pursued aircraft development projects with Lockheed and Boeing, developed turbines with Westinghouse, and explored deals with equipment manufacturers Caterpillar and Briggs and Stratton. In the 1990s, Mitsubishi's international industrial and equipment operations included supplying press equipment to a newspaper publisher in the United States, establishing a tire plant in Iran, and pursuing energy plant construction projects in Algeria, Kuwait, and Syria. At the same time, Mitsubishi was also heavily involved in high-tech research and development in textiles, space technology, and superconductors.

Together, its machinery and construction divisions accounted for 40 percent of 2004 sales. In its air conditioner business, Mitsubishi expanded air conditioner production at its Asian plants and marketed a new line of ceiling-mounted air conditioners. In 1996 the company's machinery interests—through which it participated in the services industry machines market—accounted for 18 percent of its total sales. Like other Japanese companies (including Matsushita), Mitsubishi suffered from the protracted Japanese recession of the 1990s.

UNITED TECHNOLOGIES

The parent company of Carrier Corporation, the number one heating and air-conditioning company worldwide, United Technologies Corporation (UT), founded in 1934, reported US$36.7 billion in 2004 sales. UT was active in six other major industries in the late 1990s spread across 183 countries: aircraft engine manufacture, helicopters, elevators and escalators, heating and air conditioning systems, aerospace and industrial systems, and motor vehicles and car bodies. In an attempt to free itself from its dependency on defense contracts, UT began a policy of acquisitions and diversification in the 1980s that stressed the development of low-profile partnerships with foreign companies in such countries as Vietnam, Russia, and China. For example, Carrier successfully gained entry into a number of foreign markets by establishing joint ventures in which local companies maintained management control in exchange for a Carrier product platform that helped penetrate local air conditioner markets. In 1992 it bought a controlling interest in China's Tianjin Uni-Air Conditioning Co.

Between 1980 and 1990 Carrier expanded its European business by 800 percent, claiming 23 percent of the U.K. air conditioning market alone, and estimated its ventures in Thailand, Indonesia, and Malaysia would triple by the turn of the century. By the late 1990s, UT's Carrier division accounted for 24 percent of total sales and, in addition to air conditioners, operated in the building controls and larger refrigeration, heating, and ventilation industries. In 2003, Carrier's revenues were $9.2 billion, 60 percent of which was earned in the United States. Carrier employed almost 39,000 employees in 80 facilities around the world.

AMERICAN STANDARD

In 2004 American Standard listed sales of US$9.5 billion, an 11 percent increase over 2003. Trane, a subsidiary of American Standard, and the world's largest supplier of heating, ventilation, and air conditioning comfort systems for the building management industry, accounted for 60 percent of American's sales in the mid-1990s, about the time it unveiled a commercial air conditioner that did not use CFC coolants. American Standard/Trane also concentrated on enhancing its international presence in the Pacific Rim and Europe. Through its network of 89 manufacturing plants in 27 countries, Trane derived almost half its sales in 1995 from outside the United States. Its two primary service industry machinery business sectors were applied systems (custom-engineered air conditioners for commercial use) and unitary systems (factory-assembled central air conditioning systems).

MAJOR COUNTRIES IN THE INDUSTRY

In 2000 the United States, Japan, Germany, and Italy were the leading exporters of heating and cooling equipment worldwide. Other major exporters included France, the United Kingdom, Hong Kong, Denmark, Sweden, and the Netherlands. The United States, Germany, Hong Kong, and China were the leading importers. By the mid-2000s, China had joined the ranks of leading world exporters as well. The United States, a leader in the global industry, exported more than US$2.5 billion worth of refrigeration and heating equipment in 1996. Developing nations were expected to see the greatest opportunity as improved standards of living stimulate demand. Thanks to the burgeoning construction industry in China, the value of China's commercial air conditioner market was expected to come within US$2.4 billion by 2005, with demand in major cities growing 70 to 80 percent annually, as reported by Zhang in *Appliance.*

The United States

In the late 1990s, the United States ranked among the leading exporters of non-household refrigeration equipment and parts, heating and cooling equipment, air conditioning machinery, and pumps for gases worldwide. In 1999, more than 2,000 U.S. industry firms generated US$34.1 billion in revenues and employed some 179,000 workers. In sales, by far the largest product segment remained refrigeration and heating equipment, which accounted for 72 percent of industry shipments. According to *Euromonitor,* this market segment was expected to grow 26 percent to US$37 billion by 2007.

Japan

In the mid-1990s, Japan was the second largest exporter of heating and cooling equipment worldwide, accounting for 15 percent of all equipment exports. It ranked high in exports of gasoline pumps, air conditioning machinery, heating and cooling equipment, non-household refrigeration equipment, and refrigeration equipment parts. In the five-year period from 1988 to 1992, Japan's share of total global market exports for heating, refrigeration, and cooling equipment averaged 15 percent, but the country possessed much larger global market shares in two other industry sectors. Although gas pump exports were marked by flat performance in the early 1990s, Japan captured a consistent 22.5 percent market share. Air conditioner exports performed more spectacularly, rising from 23 percent in 1989 to almost 29 percent in 1992. During that period, its two most successful performers were Matsushita Electric and Mitsubishi Heavy Industries.

As in other industries, Japanese firms have served as the model for the adoption of quality control methods, benchmarking productivity improvements, and just-in-time inventory reduction and machinery techniques. International service industry machine manufacturers, from American Standard to Lennox Industries and United Technologies, have incorporated these methods into production processes. The economic drought that engulfed Japan after the 1989 meltdown of its stock market continued to hamper the country's economy—including its heating and refrigeration industry—in the late 1990s. By the mid-2000s, Japan was a mature market. Though it was expected to show below average gains through 2008, improvements over slower growth from 1998 to 2003 were expected.

Germany

Germany ranks among the top five exporters in heating and cooling equipment, service station pumps, air conditioning machinery, and non-household refrigeration equipment and parts. It has been the market leader in imports of non-household refrigeration equipment and parts. Despite a general decline in the German air conditioning market in the early 1990s, roughly 2,600 firms were still active in the industry in 1999 and accounted for DM11.5 billion. That year, sales of German air conditioning units began to rebound.

The disintegration of the Soviet bloc in the early 1990s offered enormous potential opportunities for German heating and refrigeration firms in Eastern Europe, as well as within the Russian Federation. Although monetary instability, changing tax laws, and a deeply uncertain business and political climate, made conducting business in Russia difficult, German heating and refrigeration manufacturers successfully sold large systems to Russian hotels, hospitals, and other buildings. The drag on Germany's economy, caused by its modernization investments in eastern Germany and its rigid and costly labor policies, stifled economic growth in the 1990s. The adoption of a single European Union currency, however, was expected to help further streamline international trade within the common market. Germany's heating and refrigeration industry was expected to benefit from these trends. According to *Euromonitor,* this market segment was expected to grow 15 percent by 2007.

Further Reading

"Cashless Machine Spurs Concessions Spend." *Screen Digest,* February 2005.

"Consumers 'In a Hurry' Ideal Market for USA Technologies' e-Port(R) Cashless Vending Solutions." *PR Newswire,* 2 March 2005.

Hall, John R. "What Does the Future Hold?" *Air Conditioning, Heating & Refrigeration News,* 3 May 2004.

"Hoover's Company Capsules." 2004. Available from http://www.hoovers.com.

"Industrial Air Conditioning, Refrigeration and Heating Machinery in France, Germany, UK, US." *Euromonitor,* August 2004. Available from http://www.majormarketprofiles.com.

"Leading Trade Publication Cites Cashless Vending as New Competitive Weapon; USA Technologies Recognized as Industry Leader." *PR Newswire,* 11 March 2004.

"MTI Reports That the Heat Treating Industry Generated Sales of $72.8m in September 2003." *Furnaces International,* January-February 2004.

"Occupational Outlook Handbook, 2002-2003." *US Department of Labor,* 2001.

Siegel, James J. "January A/C Shipments Rise 6 Percent." *Air Conditioning, Heating & Refrigeration News,* 15 March 2004.

———. "Study Predicts Rise in Equipment Demand." *Air Conditioning, Heating & Refrigeration News,* 15 March 2004.

"Study: Vending Machine Demand to Rise." *Beverage World,* 15 April 2004.

Sutton, William G. "Looking to the Future Through China's Eye." *Appliance Manufacturer,* June 2004.

Turpin, Joanna R. "Manufacturers Come Off Record Year." *Air Conditining, Heating & Refrigeration News,* 28 March 2005.

"U.S. Vending Machine Demand to Reach $1.6 Billion." *Candy Industry,* March 2003.

"Vending Machine Company Completes Installation of Card-Only Accepting Machines." *Cardline,* 11 July 2004.

"Vending Volume Up 20 Percent on Average." *Food Service Director,* 15 August 2002.

"World Commercial Refrigeration Demand to Grow Through 2008." *Appliance,* March 2005.

Zhang, Sean. "China Refrigeration 2004." *Appliance,* July 2004.

SIC 3579

NAICS 333313

OFFICE MACHINES

The global office machine industry supplies numerous devices used in office settings. Major product classes include word processing equipment (except computers), typewriters, adding machines and calculators, postage meters, envelope sealers and openers, other mail-handling machines, and simple mechanical devices such as staplers and paper cutters. Two important categories of office machines excluded from the following discussion are computers and photocopiers, which are treated separately under **Computers** and **Photographic Equipment and Supplies,** respectively.

INDUSTRY SNAPSHOT

Overall growth in the office machines industry remained stagnant into the mid-2000s, due primarily to the effect of technological developments outside the industry. Just as photocopying rapidly supplanted mimeograph duplicating, computers have largely supplanted typewriters and word processors due to increased demand in the business community for Internet and network connectivity. Furthermore, recent years have witnessed massive growth in the market for multifunction office machines, which typically contain facsimile, printing, photocopying, and scanning capabilities in one concise unit, which is then connected to the computer network. Such multifunctional equipment had the lion's share of the U.S. market, with 68 percent, a figure that was projected to reach 74 percent by 2007, according to *Euromonitor.* From the point of view of office machines manufacturers, however, technological transformations are only problematic if the manufacturer is unable to diversify into the newer products.

The quick migration to such newer technologies has been most pronounced in leading markets such as the United States and Japan, while other nations still rely more heavily on older forms of office machines. According to *Euromonitor,* France was projected to have 39 percent industry growth into 2007, while Germany was expected to have 9 percent growth and the United Kingdom was expected to have 5 percent growth. The Asia Pacific region was another area expected to realize growth. According to the World Trade Organization (WTO), office and telecom equipment accounted for one-third to two-thirds of total exports in 2004 for five Asian economies, contributing significantly to the area's success.

According to *Office Products International,* consolidation was key for industry players to remain competitive in the mid-2000s. The high rate of acquisition activity that has characterized the office machines industry for years continues to make the industry's boundaries relatively ambiguous. Manufacturers of office machines and related parts and accessories typically are highly diversified firms with operations in a variety of industries. In particular, electronics and computer manufacturers tend to be among the leading producers of office machines, especially word processors and typewriters, the most prominent products in the industry. In most cases, general office machines accounted for a small portion of such firms' revenues.

ORGANIZATION AND STRUCTURE

In spite of slow growth overall, markets for typewriters remain strong in some countries, including India, Indonesia, China, Brazil, and Germany. The major suppliers of office machines in these regions, as well as in more mature markets like Japan, the United States, and the European Union, are primarily large, highly diversified international corporations involved in everything from camera production to superconductor technology to personal pagers to business consulting. In addition to these industry giants, smaller, more specialized domestic firms maintain a healthy position in localized and niche markets. Most of the major players conduct the bulk of their business through large retail dealerships like Staples and Office Depot, though many supplement this business with outlet establishments and mail-order services. Due in large part to the flat or declining demand for typewriters and word processors, many industry players have focused attention on customer service operations, which have become one of the primary selling points in a market that has seen its research and development investments re-appropriated to rival industries like personal computers.

Two associations served the industry in Europe. The European Association of Manufacturers of Business Machines and Data Processing Equipment (EUROBIT) was established in 1974 in Frankfurt, Germany, and represented nearly all of the region's manufacturers of business machines. The European Federation of Importers of Business Equipment (FEIM), headquartered in DeMeern, the Netherlands, was established in 1965.

BACKGROUND AND DEVELOPMENT

The development of the typewriter was one of the most important and influential events in the office machines industry, as well as in the general business climate. The typewriter transformed the organization of offices in both public and private sectors, and was instrumental in adding to the number of office occupations, as well as the number of female secretaries, in the United States and Europe during the late nineteenth century. Moreover, typewriters played an important role in the development of other office machines. As typewriters facilitated the reorganization and systematization of the office climate and data records, typewriter manufacturers expanded operations to include data-processing equipment and other office appliances. Because research and development efforts were already geared toward office systems and needs, and because production methods were already in place to enable such diversification, these manufacturers used the massive profits derived from typewriter sales to manufacture this new equipment. In addition, these companies had already established a client base in the office products market and could easily offer new products to companies and individuals who took a liking to their typewriters.

During the late nineteenth century, there were approximately 20 significant typewriter-related innovations that preceded the commercialization of the typewriter in the 1870s. Most of these developments originated in the United States with the remainder in Europe. Working intensively between 1867 and 1873, Christopher Latham Sholes of Wisconsin developed the first commercially successful typewriter. Sholes' typewriter was manufactured by E. Remington and Sons of Ilion, New York, a producer of weaponry that had grown rapidly during the United States Civil War years. Seeking to diversify its production after the war, Remington sold several hundred typewriters during the first year of production, with prices ranging from US$25 to US$50.

A number of other firms began producing typewriters in the 1870s and 1880s, many of them with technical innovations. Most of the features associated with modern manual typewriters were available in the 1890s, including upper and lower case letters, a space bar, and "front-strike" technology, which enabled a typist to see what was being typed. The industry experienced rapid growth soon after its origins, and in 1886 a total of 50,000 typewriters were sold in the United States. In 1888, the Remington Standard Typewriter Company produced 18,000 typewriters and was still unable to keep up with demand.

A U.S. government survey estimated that there were 30 firms employing 1,735 workers in the U.S. typewriter industry during these early years. The rapid growth of the industry was predicated on manufacturers' development of a service and marketing apparatus to accommodate the complexity and relatively high cost (up to US$100 by 1890) of typewriters. The largest firms in the industry in 1905 were Remington (which became Remington Rand in the 1920s), Underwood, Royal, and L.C. Smith (which became Smith Corona in the 1920s).

In addition to typewriters, other important products for the industry were developed in the late nineteenth century. These included carbon paper for typewriters—patented in 1872—and mimeograph paper and machines, commercialized shortly thereafter by the A.B. Dick Company. Until the development of electrostatic copying by RCA in the 1950s and xerographic copying by the Xerox Corporation in the 1960s, carbon paper and mimeographs were the primary means of duplicating forms. Furthermore, the first commercial dictating machine was produced in 1888 by the Columbia Graphophone Company, which later evolved into the Dictaphone Corporation.

In the first half of the twentieth century, U.S. manufacturers dominated world trade—particularly in Asia and Latin America. The United States and Canada made up the world's largest market for office equipment, followed by Europe. Sales of office machines to Europe accounted for 30 to 45 percent of U.S. output. During these years of rapid growth, U.S. manufacturers established overseas distribution and production facilities. This growth was indicated by U.S. employment in the office machines industry, which by that time included the production of calculating machines and cash registers. In 1925, there were 69,000 employees in the United States. Employment subsequently rose to 78,000 in 1927 and 90,000 in 1930. Sales of leading manufacturers stagnated during the Great Depression, but rebounded dramatically upon the United States' entry into World War II. From 1940 to 1941, Remington Rand's sales increased from US$49 million to US$77 million, IBM's from US$46 million to US$63 million, Underwood's from US$26 million to US$37 million, Royal's from US$19 million to US$24 million, Smith Corona's from US$11 million to US$15 million, and Pitney Bowes' from US$4 million to US$6 million.

The development of the office machines industry followed a similar path in Europe, with smaller firms operating in Britain, Italy, France, and the Scandinavian countries. The country most like the United States in terms of firm size, research, and new product development was Germany. The largest German firm at the time was Brunsviga Machineworks, which was established in the late nineteenth century and developed a diversified product line and a sales and service network throughout Germany.

The growing market for typewriters and other office machines in the post-World War II years was in part the result of the rapidly growing service sector. Between 1920 and 1970, the share of service sector employees in the United States doubled from 30 percent to 60 percent. From 1940 to 1950, the number of clerical workers in the United States increased from 4.9 million to 7.2 million, and the number of factory workers producing office machines increased from 24,000 to 40,000. The growing use of the electric typewriter, with a typing stroke powered by an electrical motor, was an important change during these years. Though initially commercialized in the 1920s, the sales of electric typewriters did not take off until the postwar years, outstripping the sales of manual computers by the mid-1960s. IBM introduced its first electric typewriters in the 1930s and became one of the top sellers of typewriters after the war. Combined with its earlier developments in data processing equipment, IBM's entry into typewriter production facilitated its evolution into the world's largest producer of computers.

IBM divided its domestic and foreign operations by establishing the IBM World Trade Corporation in 1949. IBM World Trade established sales and production facilities in 58 countries in Europe, Asia, and Latin America, as well as its own research and development facilities in the United States. These specialized facilities enabled the firm to accommodate the requirements of individual foreign markets, including the development of machinery for Asian alphabets. In 1949, IBM World Trade's sales were only US$6.3 million. By 1956, sales had increased to US$158 million, compared to US$734 million for the domestic firm. In 1944, IBM developed the Mark I—a large electromechanical computer—in cooperation with Howard Aiken at Harvard University. IBM began production of computers for business in 1955. These so-called first generation computers were large, relying on vacuum tubes rather than solid-state electronics, and more on punched cards than on magnetic coding.

In 1948, Remington Rand was second only to IBM in terms of assets and employment and provided another example of the direct connection between the production of mechanical office machinery and the production of computers. Remington Rand evolved from being the first firm to produce typewriters on a commercial basis to becoming, after World War II and a name change to Sperry Rand, the first firm to produce computers on a commercial basis. Its breakthrough computer was the UNIVAC I, which was first used in 1951 by the U.S. Bureau of the Census. The UNIVAC I calculated on a purely electronic rather than electromechanical basis, and featured internally stored programs and extensive use of peripherals, including magnetic tape readers and high-speed printers. Sales of the UNIVAC I peaked in 1955. Olivetti of Italy was another large firm that made the transition from production of typewriters to production of computers and was the second largest firm in the industry in the early 1990s by volume of sales.

Network Ltd. pioneered the bilingual typewriter, introducing its Hindu-English typewriter in 1986, and went on to market five other types of bilingual electronic typewriters. Indonesia imported 191,457 typewriters in 1991—23 percent from Japan, 11 percent from Taiwan, and 7 percent from China. The Shanghai Electric Meter Factory of China entered into a joint venture with the NEC Corporation of Japan in 1992 to increase production of its advanced multilingual typewriter. Shanghai's typewriter noiselessly printed in seven languages and could also send facsimiles.

Word processors evolved from automatic typewriters, also called autotypists, which were developed in the mid-1930s. The autotypist made use of a punched paper tape to store information for form letters. The first true word processor was IBM's Magnetic Tape/Selectric Typewriter, produced in 1964. This version of the Selectric was a high-speed typewriter that made use of magnetic tape for storage and retrieval. By the early 1970s, minicomputers were being used for word processing while allowing greater flexibility and speed. One of the key changes in word processing equipment at that time was the use of visual displays. This was facilitated by the commercialization of the personal computer by Apple in the late 1970s and by IBM in the early 1980s. The development of the personal computer provided space for the rapid growth of word processing. At the same time, personal computer innovations were incorporated into more specialized typewriter-based personal word processors, which led to the development of hybrid units that combined features of typewriters and personal computers.

The value of world exports of office machines and office machinery parts and accessories decreased slightly in 1996, totaling US$95.8 billion compared to US$97.8 billion in 1995. The market for personal word processors grew at a rate of 21 percent per year in the early 1990s. World production of typewriters, on the other hand, declined from 7.7 million to 5.1 million units over the same years. In the mid-1990s, between 750,000 and 800,000 electronic typewriters were sold annually in the United States. This was down from a high of 1.4 million units sold annually between 1986 and 1988, reflecting the growing use of personal computers and personal word processors in place of typewriters of all kinds.

Japan, once the largest standalone word processor market, saw a significant decrease in the production of word processors. According to Teikoku Databank America, the integration of the standalone word processor's functionality with the personal computer is the main reason for this decline. In 2000, heavyweight home appliance manufacturers — including Fujitsu Ltd., Matsushita Electric Industrial Co. Ltd., and NEC Corporation — all eliminated the word processor from product offerings. South Korea further demonstrated the decline of the typewriter, as a number of the country's firms discontinued electronic typewriter lines; in the late 1990s, Samsung Electronics Company Ltd. was the only South Korean exporter of electronic typewriters.

CURRENT CONDITIONS

Datamonitor forecast that the market would increase an additional 38.4 percent by 2008, reaching $445 billion. The United States held 40.2 percent of the world market, the Asia Pacific held 23.6 percent, Europe held 20.1 percent, and the rest of the world comprised the remaining 16.1 percent of the global market. According to the Information Technology Industry Council, the number of typewriters shipped in the United States fell from 1,311 in 2000 to 1,195 in 2001. Still, in 2002 Americans purchased 434,000 word processors and electronic typewriters, according to the Consumer Electronics Association as reported in 2004 by *Technology Review.* Advantages of such obsolete equipment were cited in the article, such as a lack of viruses or corrupt disk drives, and the better performance of typewriters in envelope printing.

Pitney Bowes continued to be the leader in production of postage meters and mailing systems. The company went from manufacturing low-level technologies such as electronic meters in the 1970s to digital meters in the 1990s. In 2001 the company presented its sophisticated network architecture allowing two-way communication between users and postal facilities. Pitney Bowes Chairman and CEO Michael J. Critelli also noted that, in the wake of the Anthrax-tainted mail that surfaced in the United States in 2001, the use of metered mail could help companies easily identify the origin of a package or envelope. Firms could thereby teach employees how to distinguish a professional mailing from one that could be suspicious.

Other market concerns included the search by corporations for specialized markets upon which they can capitalize, such as the development of office machines specifically designed for the disabled, and the struggle to manufacture products whose production methods and functionality are deemed environmentally sound. In Europe, governmental bodies and industry regulatory boards continue work on the development of clear, concise standardization of product and legal guidelines to facilitate trade.

Japan's decreased demand for office machines impacted the growth of China's exports to that country. In 2006, there was only a reported 8.5 percent growth compared to 15.8 percent in 2005.

RESEARCH AND TECHNOLOGY

Since the early 1990s, an increasing number of office machine manufacturers have modified assembly and design systems to match new methods in production that coordinate relationships between product parts and their components during assembly. Whereas traditional production methods involved the independent production of parts that were subsequently assembled into an overall system designed around those separate parts, newer techniques call for system specifications that are laid out at the beginning of the process. These specifications are then implemented into the design and production of the various parts and components from the outset. This represents a veritable reversal in the production and design methods.

Electronic typewriters were first produced in 1978, when the Exxon Corporation introduced its QYX model. Electronic typewriters were distinct from electric typewriters in that mechanical elements—springs, belts, levers, and motors—were replaced with computer chips and circuit-board-mounted components. This enabled electronic typewriters to be less expensive in terms of both initial and maintenance costs. IBM and other manufacturers followed Exxon into the electronic typewriter market, and by the mid-1980s there were 25 electronic typewriter producers in the United States, Europe, and Japan.

Sales of electronic typewriters peaked in the mid-1980s but declined thereafter as personal computers made wider inroads into the market. As the computer industry has developed at astonishing rates, electronic typewriters have lost their footing in the competition for office systems. However, manufacturers of electronic typewriters continue to augment models with increased processing power, incorporating techniques from the computer industry as far as they can be implemented into the lower-technology platform of typewriters. Among the areas of improvement for electronic typewriters have been memory and display power.

Significant improvements have also been made in personal word processors. These units featured disk drives, large memories and displays, and built-in word processing programs. Some of the newest models had spreadsheet programs and others were DOS-compatible and could run commonly-used spreadsheet programs such as LOTUS 1-2-3. Most personal word processors made use of impact daisywheel printing, which limited font types and sizes. However, the most sophisticated units featured ink jet printing, enabling higher resolution and printing speed.

The classification of these products as electronic typewriters, personal word processors, or personal computers was ambiguous in some cases. This ambiguity was not merely academic, for it played a central role in a trade dispute between U.S. and foreign producers. In 1990, the U.S. Department of Commerce ruled in favor of Smith Corona of Connecticut against Panasonic, Canon, Sharp, and Brother of Japan, as well as Olivetti of Italy, when it held that typewriters with pop-up visual displays and disk drives were not personal computers. This distinction was important because typewriters were subject to price-dumping penalties whereas personal computers were not. Smith Corona sought to further its case by filing a complaint with the Department of Commerce arguing that typewriters with detached keyboards should also not be classified as personal computers.

Other office machine products have registered improvements and innovation as well. The standard time clock that allows an employee to "punch" a timecard when a work shift begins or ends is still in use in many industries. However, a number of sophisticated employee time tracking systems have also been developed as company needs have evolved into the twenty-first century. Some employ data collection terminals that use employee badges, along with time and attendance software. Others have replaced timecards with "hand punching," which uses biometric technology for error-free verification of an employee's identity. It is likely that the demand for sophisticated labor management solutions will increase. According to Kronos Incorporated, only one-third of firms in the United States employing more than one hundred workers have completely automated time and attendance processes.

Flexographic labeling machines have been developed that add a variety of features and options to businesses involved in extensive labeling. These machines are able to laminate, delaminate, color, and cut labels to the characteristics specified by the user. In addition, many are capable of producing self-adhesive labels.

INDUSTRY LEADERS

ACCO BRANDS CORP.

ACCO Brands has a strong heritage in the office machines' industry. It grew out of a partnership between rival industry leaders General Binding Corp. (GBC) and Fortune Brands. The company makes many popular products. They include Swingline staplers, Kensington computer accessories and Day-Timer personal organizers. ACCO products have been sold to office and computer products wholesalers, retailers, and mail order companies throughout the world. The product distribution reached out to more than 100 countries. The company reports annual revenues of US$2 billion.

GBC was a market leader in the production of laminating and binding business equipment. The company also made paper shredders, commercial laminators, and bulletin and marker boards. GBC, Ibico, Shredmaster, and Quartet are some of the company's brand names. The firm served customers via a global network of 16 manufacturing plants and more than 20 distribution centers in more than 115 countries. Sales for 2004 totaled US$712.3 million, $14.4 million or 2.1 percent more than the year before. Net sales were $191.2 million. Of 2004 revenue, approximately $85 million was attributed to shredder sales, which remained one of the fastest growing categories of office equipment. The increasing number of shredders sold was attributed to cautionary advice to consumers regarding identity theft, and competitors for shredder business included Fortune Brands and Fellowes Inc. In April 2005, GBC announced plans to merge with Fortune Brands' office products groups to form a new company, ACCO Brands Corp. General Binding would own 34 percent of the new company.

In May 2007, ACCO Brands Canada announced that it had enabled its Kensington computer products group to operate separately. The products had previously been sold as part of the ACCO family of products. Subsequent review resulted in the decision that Kensington was not an office products vendor.

BROTHER INDUSTRIES LTD.

Headquartered in Nagoya, Japan, and incorporated in 1934, Brother was the market leader in a variety of office machine products including typewriters, standalone word processors, and electronic labeling machines. Consolidated net sales for 2004 were US$4.2 billion, an 18 percent increase over 2003. The company employed more than 17,000 people worldwide.

Brother International Corporation, headquartered in Bridgewater, New Jersey, was founded in 1954. It produced portable electronic typewriters and personal word processors for the American market and also produced various business products, home appliances, and industrial products. Brother Industries faced revenue hits during 2005 in response to malfunctions with some of its printers, but sales were still up 2.2 percent due to strong demand in the European market.

In December 2006, Brother announced its plans to open a new sales facility in the city of Mumbai, India. Brother International (India) Pte. Ltd. was designated as the operational base for the company's sales activities in India. The market for Brother's flagship products was expected to increase along with the fast-growing population in India.

In March 2007, Brother received the first-ever patent granted under Accelerated Examination Program by the Department of Commerce's United States Patent and Trademark Office. The program was launched in August 2006. In September 2006, Brother applied for the patent. It related to ink cartridge technology for digital imaging products. Brother conducted searches that helped the patent process to move along. Based on its outstanding results, Brother planned to use the Accelerated Examination Program for important future inventions.

CASIO INC.

The United States subsidiary to the Japanese firm Casio Computer, Casio Inc. offers a variety of products including watches, handheld computers, digital cameras, and calculators. Casio Computer's sales for 2004 were US$5 billion, a 34 percent increase over 2002. The company reported revenues of US$4.9 billion in 2006. Casio sells to both the business and consumer markets.

KRONOS INC.

Founded in 1977, Kronos first was a manufacturer of traditional "time punch" time clock products. During the mid-2000s, Kronos produced data collection systems to manage automatically posted employee attendance data. The firm's ShopTrac system tracks labor hours and factory production. In 2004, Kronos posted sales of US$451 million, with a one-year sales growth of more than 13 percent. The company had 2,700 employees throughout the world.

In March 2007, Kronos agreed to U.S.$1.8 billion buyout of the company by private equity firms. The transaction was expected to close in the third quarter of 2007 after obtaining shareholder approval.

Kronos introduced a Strategic Sourcing Service to assist organizations with local sourcing dynamics. One impressive application case study featured Burgerville, a 39-restaurant chain in the U.S. Pacific Northwest. The Kronos' service identified locations with sourcing issues and drivers behind the recruitment challenges. It was applauded for helping to provide a steady stream of qualified applicants.

PITNEY BOWES INC.

Pitney Bowes was the world leader in the production of postage meters, with market share of approximately 60 percent worldwide and 80 percent in the United States, according to a 2004 report by Datamonitor. It also offered online postage services, shipping and weighing systems, and shipping management software. The firm's fax and copier division, Pitney Bowes Office Systems, is now a separate public company under the name Imagistics International. Sales grew 8.3 percent in 2004 to approximately US$4.9 billion. That year, the company's employment stood at more than 35,000. Pitney Bowes' top competitors include Neopost, Moore Corporation, and Francotyp-Postalia, as well as a host of national and local firms specializing in similar business areas. During the mid-2000s, Pitney Bowes focused on enhancing mail services to retain its competitive edge, offering all-in-one solutions that combined the utilities of software programs and paper handling. In 2007, the company reported revenues of US$5.8 billion and approximately 35,000 employees serving more than 2 million businesses through direct and dealer operations.

In May 2007, Pitney Bowes announced the latest releases of its CODE-1 Plus and Finalist address cleansing software received U.S. Postal Service CASS certification for the upcoming Cycle L requirements. Those requirements were scheduled for implementation on August 1, 2007. CASS solutions were components of Group 1 Software's Address Quality Hub platform designed to help mailers address the impact of upcoming postal rates plus CASS Cycle L requirements designed to reduce mail that was undeliverable as addressed.

Site managers from Pitney Bowes worked closely with clients to reevaluate their mailstream operations in anticipation of postal rate industry increases and changes in practices. They conducted webinars, such as "The Changing Postal Environment", to share money-saving insights. The company also launched a special Web site at http://www.pb.com featuring additional advice and downloadable reference materials.

Pitney Bowes prepared for a new CEO to take over the reigns on May 14, 2007 during its annual shareholders meeting. The company's CEO and Chairman Michael Critelli had assumed his preeminent leadership position to guide the company during a period of long-anticipated postal reform in the U.S. and Europe. Critelli had also served as co-chairman of the Mailing Industry Taskforce and advised Congress on postal reform. Murray Martin, who had joined Pitney Bowes after its acquisition of Dictaphone, was considered to be a very competent successor. Martin was credited with leading the company to move beyond just institutional customers and reach out to other areas touching mail such as the consumer market.

Pitney Bowes restated its commitment to growth strategies introduced several years ago. Those strategies were believed to be still suitable for the company's commitment to expansion in the fastest-growing segments of the global mailstream. They included growing company cash flow, increasing value for customers, improving operating efficiency, solidifying performance of core mailing business, expanding internationally and focusing on high-performance mailstream areas. Pitney Bowes' expansion in the software area was evident by its acquisition of MapInfo. That move allowed for an increased presence in location intelligence.

MAJOR COUNTRIES IN THE INDUSTRY

According to the World Trade Organization, the leading exporters of office machines and telecommunications equipment in 2003 were the European Union, China, the United States, Japan, and Hong Kong. The European Union had exports valued at $246.4 billion, with 26.4 percent of world market share. China's exports reached $117.9 billion, accounting for 12.6 percent, and the United States had exports worth $112.5 billion, with a 12.1 percent share. Japan had exports with a value of $90.1 billion, and a 9.7 percent share of the world market. Finally, Hong Kong showed domestic exports valued at US$1.5 billion, and re-exports valued at $70.8 billion. Share percentage statistics were not available for Hong Kong.

The top five leading importers of office machines and telecom equipment in 2003 were the European Union, the United States, China, Hong Kong, and Japan. The European Union's imports in 2003 were valued at $302.9 billion, 31.9 percent of the world market. The United States had imports with value of $180.5 billion, a 19 percent share. China imported $96.3 billion worth of office and telecom equipment, taking 10.1 percent, and Hong Kong claimed $77.4 billion in imports, retaining $6.6 billion. Share percentage statistics were not available for Hong Kong. Japan imported $54.5 billion and claimed 5.7 percent of the market in 2003.

FURTHER READING

"Brother Downgrades Profits Outlook." *Printing World,* 17 February 2005.

"Brother International Corp. Establishes Sales Facility in India." 20 December 2006. Available from http://www.brother.com.

"Brother Receives the First Patent Granted Under USPTO's Accelerated Examination Program." 16 March 2007. Available from http://www.brother.com.

Cullen, Scott. "Featured Product: Paper Shedders." *OfficeSolutions,* November to December 2006.

Del Nibletto, Paolo. "Kensington to Operate Independently." *IT Business,* 9 May 2007.

"Global Office Services & Supplies." *Datamonitor,* May 2004. Available from http://www.datamonitor.com.

"Hoover's Company Capsules." 2007. Available from http://www.hoovers.com.

"Office Equipment in France, Germany, UK, US." *Euromonitor,* August 2004. Available from http://www.majormarketprofiles.com.

Lazich, Robert S., ed. *Market Share Reporter.* Detroit: Thomson Gale, 2004.

Murphy, H. Lee. "Shredder Sales Jump." *Crain's Chicago Business,* 28 February 2005.

Scigliano, Eric. "Technologies That Refuse to Die." *Technology Review,* February 2004.

Troy, Mike. "After Several Years of Trying to Divest Its Office Products Groups, Fortune Brand Will Merge Its Office Products Business with the Operations of General Binding to Form a New Company Called Acco Brands Corp." *DSN Retailing Today,* 11 April 2005.

"World Trade Growth to Slow Down This Year." *Businessline,* 15 April 2005.

World Trade Organization. "International Trade Statistics." Geneva, Switzerland: 2003. Available from http://www.wto.org.

Yan, Dai. "China May Become Japan's Largest Trade Partner." 11 April 2007. Available from http://www.chinadaily.com.

INFORMATION MEDIA AND TELECOMMUNICATIONS

SIC 2731

NAICS 511130

BOOK PUBLISHING

The international book publishing industry includes publishers of mass-market, trade, academic, reference, electronic (e-book), and specialty books. For discussion of other print publishing trades, see also **Newspaper Publishing, Periodical Publishing,** and **Printing, Commercial.**

INDUSTRY SNAPSHOT

Global spending on books US$85.3 billion in 2000, and was expected to continue its growth of 4 percent annually to reach US$104.6 billion in 2005. The international book publishing industry faced significant challenges in the early 2000s. World demand for books, which had once topped US$80 billion, dropped significantly in 2002. Numerous factors in 2001 and 2002, most conspicuously the terrorist bombings of September 11, 2001, had thrown the industry into one of its worst downward spirals ever, threatening independent booksellers in particular and causing layoffs even among Amazon.com and the large independent chains. In response, some publishers, notably German giant Bertelsmann AG, owner of U.S.-based imprint Random House, engaged in unprecedented slashing of costs and employees in all sectors—including dictionaries and travel books, as well as high-ranking Ballantine imprint editors, executive editor Peter Borland, and nonfiction editor Jeremie-Ruby Strauss. The company's actions, and its unwillingness to provide the business press with exact information, led to fears that defensive strategies and cost slashing had replaced aggressive marketing as the new strategy for book industry survival in the 2000s.

In contrast to Random House, however, two other prestigious book publishers questioned the Bertelsmann budget and staff cuts, arguing that an aggressive but more positive strategy was needed in spite of two soft budget years. The two publishing houses that planned "business as usual" for the immediate future were the Penguin Putnam division of Pearson, the world's second largest book publisher; and the prestigious HarperCollins book division of News Corporation. Following the publication of the Penguin Putnam and HarperCollins strategies, a Bertelsmann-Random House spokesman told *Publishers Weekly* that he defended what appear to be the industry's most all-encompassing budget slashes in the face of hard economic accounting realities since 2000, in general, and September 11, in particular.

Though book sales began to improve slightly by late 2001, as consumers returned to the stores by Christmas, profits remained elusive for many industry players, as sales grew tepidly through 2003. Not until 2004 did the situation appear significantly brighter, as the global economy improved and book sales picked up in several major markets: weekly sales in the United Kingdom in May 2004, for example, rose 11.1 percent over revenues for the corresponding period in 2003. Guardedly optimistic that a leaner, better-managed book business might indeed rebound, industry members nonetheless admitted the need to contain rising production costs and attract a wider customer base in order to boost growth and profits.

With the worst of the slump apparently over in 2004, analysts Veronis Suhler Stevenson predicted that sales of consumer books in the United States would grow at about 1.9 percent through 2008. The United States led all nations in book shipments, with a value of US$19.53 billion in 2003, but the jarring side of that statistic is that only five conglomerates publish 80 percent of U.S. trade books, according to former Pantheon book executive Andri Schiffrin, author of *The Business of Books: How International Conglomerates Took Over Publishing and Changed the Way We Read.*

In the early 2000s, the increasingly interlinked world economy coupled with an increasingly educated and affluent global book-buying public suggested that—predictions of the death of the book as a medium notwithstanding—the international book publishing industry could look forward to steady, if unspectacular, growth in the remainder of the decade. The global adoption of U.S.-style intellectual property and copyright principles, the solidification of English as the lingua franca of world commerce, and the opportunities offered by new electronic formats (including the Internet) and distribution channels (such as online booksellers) gave the world's book publishers cause for some optimism. Major challenges, however, include:

- controlling enormous advances for new titles (which may be US$5-$10 million or more for sought-after writers and up to the US$8 million paid celebrity politician Hillary Clinton by Simon and Schuster in 2001);
- acquiring and protecting rights to foreign editions and fighting textbook piracy in Asia;
- rising book prices;
- escalating paper costs;
- managing excessively large print runs;
- rising return rates from booksellers; and
- escalating costs associated with development of electronic books

However, along with big expenses can come big profits if customers can be lured into stores by blockbuster books and celebrity writers such as John Grisham and Stephen King. As a result of 2001 releases of movies based on J.K. Rowling's *Harry Potter* books and the J.R.R. Tolkien's *The Lord of the Rings* series, stores did high global business with both authors, including boxed books sets by each author. Houghton Mifflin tallied sales of US$4.5 million for *The Lord of the Rings* in 2001, a tenfold sales increase over 2000 sales for that title. Even before the release of the sixth Potter book, *Harry Potter and the Half-Blood Prince,* in July 2005, Rowling's total sales had reached 250 million copies. Ever looking for prodigious receipts from tie-ins of best-selling books with hot-draw films, Viacom Inc. merged Simon & Schuster books with its film division in 2002, hoping for more cinema successes based on Simon & Schuster books such as *A Beautiful Mind,* by Sylvia Nasar.

ORGANIZATION AND STRUCTURE

The publishing industry deals in content development and marketing more so than in formatting the content on pages, which many times is done by independent typesetters or compositors, or in physical manufacturing of books, which may be outsourced to independent printers and binders. The book publishing process begins with an idea proposed either by a querying author (or a representing agent) or arising from the publisher itself. Once a concept is proposed, the publisher normally performs a market analysis to determine, for example, whether other books in the market cover the book's subject matter, and reshapes or rejects the book's concept accordingly. After it has been determined that the book's projected sales, minus anticipated production costs, can generate a profit for the publisher—and even sometimes when this is highly uncertain—a final decision is made to proceed with the project, and the development or acquisition of the book's content is secured through a cash advance to the author or some other form of book contract. As the author completes the actual writing or rewriting of the book—or responds to the editor's changes—the publisher's design and marketing staffs determine the book's type specifications, size, artwork, cover design, and marketing/distribution strategy. When the content of the book reaches its final form, the book is sent to a typesetter or is composed in-house. The typesetter may produce camera-ready copy (a high-resolution, formatted print copy of the entire book), film, or a digital file for the printer, who then creates plates of all the pages for use in a printing press. Plates also may be engraved by a specialty firm rather than the printer. After a book's pages come off the press, they are bound and the cover is attached. The finished books are usually shipped back to the publisher's warehouse for distribution.

International Publishing Structure. Some 10,000 book publishers in 180 countries constituted the international book publishing industry at the beginning of the 2000s. The products of this industry can be divided into five major categories: 1) trade books; 2) textbooks; 3) technical, scientific, and professional (TSP) books; 4) mass-market paperback books; and 5) all others.

In recent years, the largest segments of the world book industry were publishers of college textbooks (approximately 1,750 publishers worldwide); directories and reference books (1,600 publishers); children's books (1,500 publishers); juvenile and young adult books (1,400 publishers); scholarly books (1,300 publishers); and professional books (1,250 publishers). A substantial number of the world's book publishers also published hardcover general trade books (1,250 publishers) and paperback trade books (1,250). Other book categories widely represented internationally included secondary textbooks (approximately 775 publishers); foreign language and bilingual books (700 publishers); mass-market paperback books (700 publishers); belles lettres (or literary) books (700 publishers); and dictionaries and encyclopedias (625 publishers).

As the book industry became more global in the 1980s and 1990s, the issue of copyright—the legal protection accorded to an author for his or her intellectual product—grew in importance. The global book industry is governed by various conventions regulating the protection of book copyrights in the world market. The Universal Copyright Convention of 1952 requires that each signatory nation provide foreign works with the same copyright protection given to books published within its own borders. Similar copyright protection agreements observed by various countries worldwide include the Berne Convention of 1886 and the Buenos Aires Convention of 1910.

In the 1990s, an increasing number of book publishers began to focus on selling book rights to foreign producers rather than undertake the risks associated with selling their books directly in foreign markets. Indeed, the sale of book rights—a principal activity of the world's largest annual book fair in Frankfurt—became a more important source of publishers' revenues in some regions of the world than book sales (foreign rights alone for the United States' most popular novels can earn their authors US$10 million and more). In the mid-1990s the United States was the recipient of US$300-US$500 million in annual royalties from foreign publishers for the sale of rights and translations to U.S. works, a figure that some analysts expected could increase by 100 percent by the beginning of the 2000s. As the 1990s progressed, resolving "electronic rights" disputes, which arose when an author's material was used in new non-book formats, such as the Internet, also became an increasingly prominent issue. In 2001 the U.S. Supreme Court determined that publishers such as the *New York Times*must give royalties to freelance authors whose works were published in electronic databases without written permission in the form of a contract.

The factors affecting the characteristics of the world's book market are complex and varied—the number and budgets of public libraries, government support, political instability, birth rates, education, living standards, labor costs, cultural traditions, and the availability of leisure time are all factors influencing the book publishing industry's fortunes. The structure of the industry in every region of the world is based largely on these factors. What began as an attack on the United States on September 11, 2001 soon had a direct effect on book publishing throughout the world. In Germany, the 2001 Frankfurt Book Fair was poorly attended. In India, an already somewhat depressed economic climate declined further, especially in tourist books, which were a staple of success when travelers roamed the globe freely. Coffee table book sales also plummeted at India houses. Overall, Indian publishers hoped 2001 sales would only be about 10 percent lower than 2000's sales when all receipts were counted, and one saving grace was that textbook sales remained the sole booming area of trade, according to *Business Line*.

North America. While the United States book publishing industry is the world leader, Canada and Mexico are also significant book producers. The roughly 175 publishers in Canada's book industry employed about 5,830 workers in 1995 (a 3 percent decline from 1990) and generated 1996 revenues of US$1.4 million. Canadian publishing's small size relative to the United States was a reflection of the dominance of U.S. publishing rather than meager demand for books. Indeed, in 1997 Canada was the biggest importer of U.S. books worldwide (US$775 million in shipments), accounting for four of every ten U.S. books exported.

The Canadian book publishing industry languished in the 1990s and endured an anemic 1 percent annual growth rate between 1990 and 1995 (one-tenth that of U.S. publishers). Book sales in 2001 reached C$1.13 billion, but the country's lack of a national sales data analysis service made it impossible to determine how sales figures broke down, though analysts felt certain that most purchases were of U.S. titles. In recent years, Canada's largest publishers were Tele-Direct (Publication) Inc., Harlequin Enterprises, Readers Digest Association, Thomson Canada Ltd., and textbook publishers McGraw-Hill Ryerson and Prentice-Hall Canada.

In 2001, the Canadian book industry saw the merger of two giant companies, the struggling Chapters bookstores and more solidly entrenched Indigo enterprises. (Chapters had been previously restructured in 1995 as a merging of Cole's and W.H. Smith books). The mergers branch of the Canadian government Competition Bureau asked Indigo to sell 23 Chapters bookstores but no offer came for the properties. As a result, in 2002 Indigo was given a mandatory code of conduct limiting what it can do and not do with the Chapters chain stores. Indigo was expected to close many of the troubled stores. The limitations were intended to help Canada's independent booksellers and publishers during increasingly hard times as the large chains continue to dominate the book sales industry.

Mexico's book market, centered largely in Mexico City, was the world's largest Spanish-language book market in the late 1990s, with 15,505 titles published in 1997. But while the volume of consumer books increased 6 percent between 2001 and 2002, sales lagged thereafter due to economic recession and declining interest in reading. According to a Euromonitor report, Mexicans read, on average, only one or two books each year, and the country has only 500 bookstores for a population of 100 million. To help stimulate book publishing, the Mexican government provides financial support for publishing and has resisted efforts to impose a tax on books. Most government support, which accounts for 60 percent of publishing production, is for textbooks that are used in basic education programs.

The peso crisis of 1994 had a devastating effect on Mexico's economy, and its book publishing industry was still returning to pre-crisis levels in 1997. Book imports dropped off 50 percent in 1995 following the crisis, while book exports rose to US$98 million. Spurred by the North American Free Trade Agreement (NAFTA), U.S. book exports to Mexico in 1997 rose to US$58.2 million, up from US$40.8 million only four years before. In the early 2000s Mexico remained the fifth largest market for U.S. book exports, worth US$66.1 million in 2004.

By 2001, the peso had rebounded strongly. In 2002 the rising demand for Latin American books also extended to Mexico's relatively prospering book industry. While the 2001 Frankfurt Book Fair was a disappointment, a Mexican book fair exceeded all expectations as worldwide industry representatives flocked to the fifteenth annual Feria Internacional de Libros (International Book Fair) in Guadalajara, Mexico. According to *Publishers Weekly*, the Mexican fair attracted a new high of 386,620 participants (including 13,500 from the book industry and an extremely high librarian attendance). Represented were 1,258 publishing houses from 32 countries.

Europe. Book profits from 2000 to 2005 in Europe were expected to grow, but only at a 2.8 percent rate, according to projections in *The PricewaterhouseCoopers Global Entertainment and Media Outlook*. The European book market is well developed but fragmented and has historically experienced steady, moderate growth. Despite its size and tradition, it is strongly influenced by trends in the United States. Most European publishers are moderate in size, but unlike their U.S. counterparts they handle both the publishing and printing of their titles. More than 90 percent of all printers in Europe are associated with a publishing firm. Most of Europe's publishing companies are diversified beyond book publishing, reflecting the European book industry's evolution from magazine publishing. Moreover, Europe's largest publishing companies are often involved in a range of other media such as television, film, or newspaper publishing.

Although Europe's population is roughly the same as that of the United States, it publishes as much as five times as many titles annually. Between 1982 and 1991 alone, production and sales of books in Europe doubled, with the United Kingdom and Spain enjoying the greatest growth in production between 1976 and 1986 (68 percent and 50 percent, respectively). Germany boasts approximately 2,100 publishers, while the United Kingdom has more than 1,000.

France supports more than 600, and Spain hosts 400. While British, French, and German publishers are the largest in Europe, significant book publishers herald from elsewhere in Europe. These include Austria's Management Trust Holding AG; Belgium's Casterman SA; Italy's RCS Libri, Grandi Opere SpA, and Istituto Geografico de Agostini SpA; Spain's Prensa Espanola; and Norway's "Big Three"—H. Aschehoug and Company, Cappelen, and Glydendal Norsk. Sweden's two largest book publishers in the late 1990s were US$1.23 billion Bonnier Group (Europe's ninth-largest media company) and its oldest publisher P.A. Norstedt & Sner AB (US$22.5 million in sales).

In the 1990s the number of mergers and acquisitions in Europe's book industry intensified, and European publishers continued to pursue opportunities for international expansion, particularly into the United States, where British, Dutch, French, and German publishers have historically established a strong market presence. Norway's book industry enjoyed great growth in the late 1990s, but Sweden's, Finland's, and Denmark's were stable at best. The so-called Retail Price Maintenance systems of France, Netherlands, and Germany—in which discounts on the cover price of books is forbidden—came under pressure in the late 1990s, but the European Commission declared in 2000 that a modified agreement between publishers and booksellers did not violate European Union rules governing competition.

Following the collapse of the Iron Curtain in 1990, a number of Eastern European publishing houses were privatized, demand for German- and English-language books intensified, and book prices skyrocketed (by as much as 300 percent in Hungary, for example). Typical problems affecting the publishing industries of Hungary, the Czech Republic, and Poland in the late 1990s were publishers' inability to afford the cost of purchasing book rights, an inadequate book distribution system, and high book prices. Despite these obstacles, Germany's Bertelsmann AG successfully opened book clubs in Hungary, the Czech Republic, and Poland in the early 1990s.

In 1998 Poland's 1,700 book publishers produced between 12,500 and 20,000 individual titles with shipments valued at less than US$250 million. Thirty imprints commanded roughly 80 percent of all sales. After a flurry of book selling following the collapse of the Soviet empire (in which a Stephen King book could easily sell 300,000 copies) in the late 1990s, the Polish book industry had settled into a much slower but still quite profitable growth phase, reflecting the health of the Polish economy. Despite some inroads by foreign publishers, two communist-era firms hold 40-50 percent of the total book market. Government-run WSIP (School and Pedagogical Publishers) was the largest Polish book publisher in 1998, with sales of US$51.5 million, and privately owned PWN (Polish Scientific Publishers) generated sales of US$50 million with 350 new titles a year.

Russia. Although the fall of the centrally planned Soviet economy in 1990 was expected in the long term to result in a more productive and profitable private book industry for Russia, in the late 1990s and 2000s the Russian book market continued to be dogged by high inflation rates, systemic bribery, a wildly unstructured distribution system, underworld involvement in the book printing industry, and occasionally even murder. The greatest problem afflicting Russian book publishing in the 1990s, however, was illegal printing, a practice that accounted for 90 percent of all foreign books translated into Russian and could be traced in part to a stunted conception of copyright law that dates back only to 1990. Moreover, in the late 1990s Russia still lacked established authors, Western-style bookstores (Moscow claimed only 30 shops in all), and an effective publicity apparatus. For these reasons, in 1994 Germany's Bertelsmann postponed plans to develop schoolbook publishing and printing projects in Russia.

Despite these difficulties, Russian publishers produced at least 440 million books in 1995, and in 1996 Russia boasted one of the world's three highest book-spending rates as a percentage of total leisure and education spending. After the Russian government eliminated the value-added tax and profit tax on books in 1996, production soared to 70,332 new titles in 2001-the highest number in the country's history. The notoriety of success in Russia's publishing had its price, however: in 1997 two executives of a Russian textbook publisher were found murdered. In 2002, there were approximately 54 Russian publishing houses issuing more than 100 new titles each while 43 publishing houses issued more than one million copies each. The top five publishing houses were AST, Eksmo Press, Drofa, Prosveshcheniye, and Olma Press. Only Prosveshchenie was state-owned; the state share of the Russian book market had been reduced to 12.6 percent.

South America. For years South America was just a footnote in the publishing industry, but no longer. *The Outlook* projects that Latin America will be the fastest-growing economic region for book sales in the world, with growth projected "to average 9.1 percent compounded annually, as governments make a concerted effort to promote education and literacy." More than half a million different Spanish-language book titles (including those from Spain and Spanish North America) were printed in 1997. Spanish textbooks, in particular, have found world demand. The growing market for Spanish and bilingual books in the United States, worth US$350 million in 2003, bodes well for Spanish and Latin American publishers. Random House, for example, imports about 120 titles each year from Spain and South America. Knopf's Vintage Espanol imprint announced in 2005 that it would double its output of titles by 2010. Its *Memorias de mis putas tristes* by Colombian Nobel laureate Gabriel Garcia Marquez, which appeared in 2004, sold 120,000 hardcovers and paperbacks.

Brazil, the largest South American book market and eighth in the world in terms of volume in 2004, produced 45,111 new titles in 2000. and generated US$1.87 billion in revenue. Its largest market by far is textbooks, which accounted for 80 percent of volume and value sales in 2002. Major publishers include Editora Atica, Editora Scipione, Ediouro, and Editora Campus. Consumer books fare relatively poorly in Brazil, which has lower readerships levels than other countries in South America. Book sales are also affected by the scarcity of bookstores: 89 percent of municipalities lack even one bookstore.

In the 1980s and early 1990s many South American countries were plagued by unstable currency exchange rates, and the U.S. dollar became the standard currency for the region's book trade. High book prices led to low print runs (rarely exceeding 3,000) for the majority of South American countries, and inadequate copyright protection resulted in book piracy and illegal copying. In the mid-1990s, however, South American economies began to rebound, and the region's book industries enjoyed strong growth. Following a period in which the Spanish book market became increasingly European in focus, the South American book industry began to look to the United States for its book trade. In the 1990s Colombia and Chile joined Argentina and Mexico as major regional producers in the Latin American market. In an effort to promote a cooperative, regional approach for the South American book market, South American book publishing nations formed the Salon Internacional del Libro Latinoamericano.

A cultural industries report noted that during the 2000s, a Brazilian trend saw a larger number of titles being offered. However, the size of print runs for each title was declining.

Asia and the Pacific. The *PricewaterhouseCoopers Global Entertainment and Media Outlook* for the 2001-2005 period said that Asia and the Pacific market will grow at a projected 3.6 percent annual rate. Major checkpoints against growth are a slowing Japanese economy, the threatened lowering of the Japanese yen against the dollar, and an antiquated distribution system that needs to be modernized.

With 60 percent of the world's population and half its total gross national product, Asia constituted an increasingly important force in the global book industry in the late 1990s. Japan, the region's book publishing giant, surpassed all other Asian and Pacific Rim countries with roughly 5,000 book publishers in the mid-1990s, led by three firms: Kodansha Ltd. Publishers, Gakken Company Ltd., and Nihon Keizai Shimbun Inc. China, Australia, New Zealand, South Korea, and other countries in the region have attained significant size as well. Japan and China combined imported US$184 million of U.S. books in 1996 (10 percent of U.S. book exports), and other Asian nations imported another US$129 million from U.S. publishers. These same two groups also exported, respectively, US$358 million and US$130 million worth of books to the United States in 1996.

The Asian book market began to mature in the early 1990s after a period of exceptional growth in which regional book sales doubled annually. With demand abating, the market was expected to be characterized by more competitive products. Pirating, however, continued to be a nagging issue for foreign publishers in the Asian market. The efforts of many Asian countries to invest in education signaled the development of an increasingly important textbook market for international publishers, and in the mid-1990s international textbook producers viewed the local-language educational book market in Asian countries such as South Korea and Taiwan as a source of significant future revenue. The Asian debt and currency crisis of late 1997 and 1998 had a severe effect on book industry sales, however, and some publishers feared that some Asian houses would cancel book contracts and book pirating might increase.

The fastest growing book market in the world in the early 2000s was China, where 190,000 titles were printed in 2003 and sales reached about US$5.6 billion-despite the fact that the average price for a general interest book was only about US$2.40. Textbooks accounted for almost half of all book purchases in China; some 6 percent (about 12,000 in 2003) of books sold were translations, with U.S. titles comprising almost 50 percent of foreign titles. Despite its apparent potential, the Chinese book publishing industry posed significant problems for both domestic and foreign investors. For example, despite the presence of about 30,000 private publishers in the country in 2004, private publishing remained technically illegal; only the country's 568 state-owned presses were operating within the law (printing and distribution, however, have been opened to private and foreign investment). This situation resulted in what *New York Times* writer Mike Meyer described as an "openly illegal" but generally tolerated system by which private publishers can obtain the necessary documentation to put out their titles. Technically, the Chinese government is the sole issuer of International Standard Book Numbers (ISBNs), which a title must have before it can be published. The only choice for private investors, therefore, is to deal with black-market operations known as "culture houses" or "bookseller,s" which will, for fees ranging from US$1,250 to US$2,500, secure the required ISBNs and arrange for some aspects of production and marketing. While some analysts expected state control of publishing to be abolished, it was far from certain that this would soon occur.

Another huge concern for foreign investors was copyright violation. Piracy of intellectual property, according to Meyer, remained rampant in China, but infringement cases were increasingly being pressed and won. Though Chinese publishers have begun to pay authors advances against royalties, piracy makes it difficult to gather reliable sales figures. Publishers in the United States, according to Meyer, say that receive, on average, only US$2,500 per title for Chinese publication rights.

As the Chinese government relaxed some of its control on book content, publishers bought a dizzying array of foreign titles, from religious books to business how-tos. The all-time best-selling work in translation was *Who Moved My Cheese?,* which officially sold 2 million copies. Other top-selling titles included *The Da Vinci Code, Monica's Story,* and the Atkins diet books.

In the 1980s British publishing magnate Robert Maxwell established an ill-fated publishing office in Beijing, and in 1995 Simon & Schuster had opened an office there as well, with plans for offices in Shanghai or Canton in 1998. By the late 1980s, the Chinese publishing group Sino United Publishing (SUP) of Hong Kong began to abandon its traditional focus on propagandistic Communist-flavored books for more profitable fare, including entertainment titles, computers, home decorating, self-help, reference books, and CD-ROMs. Led by China's oldest and largest publisher, Commercial Press, SUP consisted primarily of about 30 Hong Kong publishers left over from the Communist takeover in 1949. By the late 1990s, SUP had even begun teaming up with Taiwan's publishing industry, itself valued at about US$2 billion. They offered marketing services to publishers from the United States, Great Britain, and the Pacific Rim, and in Hong Kong they published titles still officially banned on the mainland. However, with Hong Kong's return to Chinese jurisdiction some of its more liberal policies were reversed. By 1997, SUP was posting revenues of US$205 million.

In January 2003, Annie Wang wrote about the challenges faced by Chinese writers. She noted that "success outside China does not always translate into success on the mainland." China's publishing houses publish approximately 180,000 titles each year, half of which are textbooks. The concern in this country was that of marketability.

In a July 2004 article it did not claim was all-encompassing, *Publishers Weekly* took a closer look at suppliers from Hong Kong/China and Singapore. Asia Pacific Offset experienced tremendous growth in 2003. President Andrew Clarke noted experiencing constant demand for reprints and felt this was evidence of the persistent and ongoing need for just-in-time inventory. Colorcraft found 2003 to be a challenging year impacted by cancellations from American clients fearing SARS. Others made decisions linked to the Iraq conflict. David Kinloch said addressing related issues led the company to become more innovative and customer-oriented to grow. Everbest Managing Director Ken Chung said his company's growth was a by-product of the global economy. He credited strength in European and Australian currency for having a major impact on success. The company's business in the United States, handled mainly through agents, held steady although the currency there was weak.

In another July 2004 article, *Publishers Weekly* announced The Harvard Business School Press signed a three-year, exclusive publishing deal on June 18 with the Beijing-based Commercial Press to publish Harvard Business School Press titles in Chinese. Commercial Press is entitled to publish up to 150 Harvard Business School titles during the course of the deal.

The Middle East. While industry expectations for the Middle East were marginally good, as a 2.8 percent in growth was anticipated through 2005 by *The PricewaterhouseCoopers Global Entertainment and Media Outlook*, there has been a renewed interest in many Middle East topics due to world tensions. This has resulted in higher sales of regional specialty books. Israel led all Middle Eastern countries in the book publishing industry in the early 2000s with roughly 150 book publishers producing about 4,000 titles annually, followed by Egypt and Lebanon (20 each), and Jordan and Saudi Arabia (10 each). Israel exported US$18.8 million in books in 1992 as the region's foremost book exporter, while Saudi Arabia was the Middle East's largest book importing nation, US$82.8 million in value. Among the region's largest book publishers in the mid-1990s were Israel's Steimatzky Ltd. and Yediot Ahronot Ltd., and Saudi Arabia's Modokhil Group.

Africa. Africa's book publishing industry traditionally has been dwarfed by those of other continents. The good news is that there will be some growth, estimated at 2.8 percent through 2005 by *The PricewaterhouseCoopers Global Entertainment and Media Outlook.* While a number of African countries maintained modest book publishing industries, many African states had fewer than five operating publishing houses at the beginning of the 2000s. African countries with the largest number of book publishers included South Africa (100 firms), Nigeria (65), Zimbabwe (50), Ghana (40), and Tanzania (27). In 1992 Africa's leading book-importing countries were South Africa (US$90 million in value), the Ivory Coast (US$40 million), and Morocco (US$27 million). According to a Cape Sector Fact Sheet, more than 60 percent of the South African publishing sector's revenue is generated in the Western Cape. There were believed to be growth opportunities for natural history and tourism-related publishing.

African publishers in the early 2000s were seeking more opportunities to export titles. But as Cynthia Sithole of Zimbabwe Book Publishers Association pointed out, book trade across borders within Africa was stymied by pricing issues, foreign currency problems, and country-specific curriculum requirements in the textbook sector. She called for such measures as the development of an African Book Marketing Trust to stimulate regional trade; utilization of internet marketing; and creation of licensing and co-publishing agreements.

Gordon Graham reported that Book Aid International (BAI) is utilizing book surpluses to make an impact on education in Africa. The company's warehouse does not take special orders by title but does try to fill requests for help on specified levels on subjects from schools and libraries in African countries. BAI initially confronted acceptance problems involving both the British government and publishing industry. Graham pointed out that questions still remain including the following. "How can donated books lead to the idea that books some day have to be purchased?" He contends that while the publishing industry in a developing country is growing, "it is better that surplus books from book-rich countries should be donated instead of being pulped."

BACKGROUND AND DEVELOPMENT

The first important publishing house—begun by Louis Elzevir in Holland—published its first book in 1583. Through the years, publishing houses began to appear in cities across Europe and the United States. As book publishing developed, specialization became commonplace, and a number of publishers concentrated on sheet music or map publishing. In the twentieth century this house specialization took the form of the division of subject matter and content. In the 1930s and 1940s paperbound, pocket-sized books—first introduced by Simon & Schuster—became enormously popular. Public acceptance of paperbacks increased the overall market for books and made it necessary for publishers to adopt high-volume, low-cost production methods.

The 1950s marked a period of tremendous financial and artistic growth for the book publishing industry. In the 1960s, however, a trend developed in the United States wherein firms were bought and consolidated with other companies. Many publishing houses either acquired one another or joined forces with communications conglomerates. As a result, the consolidation of power in the United States pared the number of big publishers controlling the industry down to only a few. By the 1970s and 1980s Europe's book industry had begun to follow the U.S. mass market-driven model and bestseller list began to appear in European papers.

The North American Free Trade Agreement (NAFTA) was expected to lead to significant growth in the U.S. book trade with Mexico and other Latin American markets in the late 1990s and into the 2000s. Similarly, the Uruguay round of the General Agreement on Tariffs and Trade (GATT) produced enhanced protection for international copyrights, which was expected to lead to larger markets for international publishers in Asia, the Middle East, and Eastern Europe. Meanwhile, in Latin America, Africa, and Asia, publishers have reached widely differing degrees of business and technical sophistication. Typical problems facing book publishers in these regions include book piracy, low literacy rates, inflation, censorship, technological limitations, and high production costs.

As publishers worldwide continue to produce more titles than the market demanded, average print runs have declined. Print runs of 5,000 copies for contemporary fiction in Germany, and of 2,000-5,000 in the United States, became the rule. In addition, publishers' shares of book cover prices fell to between 20 and 30 percent in the United States in the mid-1990s.

The acquisition of Random House by German megafirm Bertelsmann in 1998 seemed to single-handedly wrest English-language publishing away from U.S. publishers, and by 1998 only two of the biggest U.S. book publishers—AOL Time Warner and William Morrow—were still domestically owned. But Bertelsmann's willingness to fork over US$1.8 billion for the "Cadillac of publishing" attested to the continuing size and attractiveness of the U.S. market in the global book-buying scene.

CURRENT CONDITIONS

As a result of a softer economy for books and other causes, the book industry was reassessing long-term profit anticipations, noted industry expert James DePonte, a partner in PricewaterhouseCoopers' Entertainment & Media practice. "Books are divided into three market segments: consumer, education, and professional and technical. The consumer segment is the biggest, and the recession is clearly leading some people to reduce their discretionary spending," said DePonte.

The PricewaterhouseCoopers Global Entertainment and Media Outlook (PwC) estimated that global spending on books will grow at a 4.2 percent compound annual rate, rising from US$85.3 billion in 2000 to US$104.6 billion in 2005. Book sales in the United States were projected to increase from about US$34.2 billion in 2004 to US$40.5 billion in 2009, though other analysts predicted much lower growth in keeping with inflation. PwC expected electronic books to perform well, particularly in Asia, with global sales of about US$2.2 billion by 2009.

U.S. book exports reached US$1.69 billion in 2003, according to figures from the U.S. Commerce Department reported by *Publishers Weekly.* Though Canada remained the primary destination for U.S. books, with imports worth US$776.4 million, exports to China increased by 32 percent to reach US$15.5 million. Sales to Japan, Singapore, South Korea, Hong Kong, and India declined. Data from the first half of 2004 showed significant growth in book trade, with U.S. exports growing by 7.8 percent and sales for that six-month period exceeding US$829 million. Predictably, exports to China increased by a substantial margin (17.9 percent), but growth in exports to other markets was welcome news, including the United Kingdom (up 15.9 percent), Japan (12.5 percent), Singapore (40.1 percent), and Mexico (9.6 percent).

A growing trend in 2005 was proprietary publishing, which industry leaders found attractive because proprietary titles are nonreturnable and relatively cheap to produce. Proprietary publishing produces books intended to be sold exclusively by a particular retailer; examples include John Wiley & Sons' 2004 title, *Wi-Fi for Dummies,* produced for communications firm Intel U.K.; and Health Communications Inc.'s *Chicken Soup for the University of Michigan Soul,* produced for the University of Michigan as a fundraiser. Among companies planning to expand into proprietary publishing were HarperCollins, which budgeted US$10 million in 2005 for proprietary titles, and Simon & Schuster. Some insiders, however, treated this trend with skepticism, claiming that it could devalue books and degrade successful brands.

RESEARCH AND TECHNOLOGY

Since the 1980s, the evolution of computer technology has had a significant impact on the international book publishing industry, from book editing and manuscript preparation to book production, distribution, and marketing. By the late 1990s, the Internet and the larger digital revolution were transforming the very nature of the industry, inevitably leading some to predict the demise of the book as a medium.

Technology for digitally ordering, printing, and binding books on demand outside the traditional book shipping process represents one aspect of the publishing technology revolution of the 1980s and 1990s. The use of computerized text editing and word processing software programs by authors and editors for the preparation of book manuscripts also emerged as standard practice in the publishing industries of many developed nations. The use of computers for storing authors' manuscripts and editors' changes, which otherwise would be exchanged via paper, offered publishers increased savings in storage and shipping costs and a more efficient means of creating backup copies of manuscripts. Desktop publishing computer systems for manipulating text and images enabled publishers to reduce typesetting and production costs, streamline book reprinting and inventory control procedures, and shorten book production schedules. By 1998, it had become possible for the development of a book—from writing to final printing—to be conducted all digitally, making it possible for publishers, typesetters, and printers to transmit a book's data files almost instantaneously. PUBNET, a computerized book-ordering network comprising roughly 65 U.S. publishers and 2,400 bookstores, enables publishers to gain detailed book sales summaries direct from booksellers, thereby improving their marketing and distribution decision making.

The emergence of "electronic book" technology in the world's developed nations represented another way in which the global publishing industry was reinventing itself in the 1990s. The trend began in the United States with the conversion to paperless online reference products such as computerized databases on CD-ROM disks (each capable of storing the equivalent of 250,000 pages). Companies then began marketing electronic books on CD-ROMs or computer diskettes that consumers could read using computers or handheld devices. Such electronic books offered a cheaper and less bulky format that would potentially enable readers to have immediate, around-the-clock access to a wide variety of titles as well as increased information searching capabilities. In the early 1990s, 700 U.S. companies providing data packaged in electronic formats formed a national Electronic Publishing Group to advance the interests of that segment of the U.S. publishing industry. And by the end of the decade every major book publisher had an "interactive" book initiative of some kind. John Wiley launched an online service to enable readers to access the journals they subscribed to via the Internet, for example.

With digital technology it also became possible for publishers to offer customers customized books whose precise content they could select from a wide range of choices and then unite in a combination of their choosing. These flexible books could then be printed at book outlets or downloaded from the publisher's Web site. Beginning in 1996 publishers had the ability for the first time to scale print runs to meet exact limited demand. It became no more expensive to print 25 copies than 25,000, offering publishers the hope that they could eliminate one of their most punishing and wasteful costs: the expense of shipping too many books to booksellers and then reclaiming them when, unsold, booksellers returned them.

By the late 1990s scores of large and small book publishers (mostly U.S.) were using the World Wide Web to establish an online presence, initially for book promotion or to offer "reader community" sites. However, Web sites also have been used, in growing numbers, to push direct book sales, create interactive collaborative literary projects, and drum up potential new authors.

In the 2000s, publishers only half-jokingly referred to electronic publishing as "Gutenberg's Revenge," the reference alluding to the high costs and lower-than-anticipated revenues associated with the development that drove a number of e-publishers such as Audiohighway.com, Bookface.com, Booktech, and Contentville.com to join the rash of dot-com closings. Even the highly heralded Netlibrary reported financial problems in 2001, and downsizings led to cut staffs at Questia, Xlibris, iUniverse, ebrary, DigitalOwl, and Intertrust. All told, electronic publishers laid off some 2,000 workers in 2001, according to *Publishers Weekly*. Nonetheless, *Publishers Weekly* explained that the electronic book publishing industry clearly is here to stay, and analysts say the area will become profitable once publishers cut overhead, reduce staff size, and forge ahead with viable business plans. Major cost factors were associated with maintaining a Web presence in 2001. Web losses for Random House were US$790 million, US$444 million of which came from e-commerce. Nonetheless, the creation of so-called "books on demand" promises to continue to pick up momentum in the 2000s, thereby adding revenues to reduce the high costs associated with Web maintenance.

In 2004 and 2005, the internet search engine Google drew controversy with its Google Print for Library program, which creates searchable digital archives of books from participating libraries (four university libraries plus the New York Public Library). Publishers challenged the legality of this program, arguing that it violated copyrights and would potentially cut into publishers' sales. Google officials, however, stated that the company made material viewable only when it had obtained the appropriate permissions to do so. According to a *Publishers Weekly* report, it is likely that more digitization options will emerge in the future, unlocking "scores of titles that [readers] wouldn't necessarily buy. As technology makes book searching easier and more desirable, a clash, many believe, is unavoidable."

INDUSTRY LEADERS

The international book publishing industry boasts a number of giant publishers. The German company Bertelsmann AG, which also owns music and broadcasting operations throughout the world, posted total sales of US$23.2 billion in 2004 and was the largest English- and German-language publisher in the world. Other major German publishers include perhaps the largest paperback publisher, Heyne, the sci-tech house Springer-Verlag, and the US$2 billion Georg von Holtzbrinck Publishing. Between 1985 and 1998 Holtzbrinck channeled US$300 million into the U.S. book industry, acquiring such prominent U.S. publishing houses as Farrar, Straus & Giroux, Henry Holt, and St. Martin's Press.

The French publishing industry was rocked at the turn of the new millenium by the fate of venerable Havas Publications Edition, the country's largest publisher in the 1990s, which was bought by Vivendi in 1998. The deal resulted in the creation of Vivendi Universal Publishing in 2000. The new company pursued an aggressive acquisition strategy, including U.S. publisher Houghton Mifflin for US$2.2 billion in 2001. This made Vivendi Universal the third largest publisher in the world and the second largest education publisher. But massive debt dogged the company, and Vivendi, deciding to concentrate on strengthening its other media divisions, sold its publishing assets to Lagardere Group in 2002. Lagardere received authorization from the European Commission to retain 40 percent of VUP's publishing assets in 2004; the remaining group, taking the name Editis, was bought by Wendel Investissement later that year. Editis reported net revenues of 717.4 million euros (US$865.3 million) in 2004. Among other leading French publishers were Hachette Livre, which produced a broad range of general books, business titles, and reference books; and Gallimard, which publishes about 750 new titles each year. Heavy debt Hachette to merge with French defense industry titan Matra in 1992 to form Matra-Hachette, and in the late 1990s Hachette bought up school publisher Hatier. Hachette Livre reported that it distributed 10,000 new titles annually and sold 140 million reference books each year. In 2003, the company's turnover was 959 million euros (US$1.15 billion).

In Britain, book publishing was dominated by two companies. London-based Pearson plc, which owns the Penguin Group (including the Penguin, Putnam, and Viking imprints), is the world's top education publisher through its Pearson Education unit, which owns the imprints Pearson Scott Foresman, Pearson Addison Wesley, and Pearson Prentice Hall. In 2005, Pearson announced plans to buy AGS Publishing, which produces materials for special needs education, for US$270 million. Sales for the Penguin Group, which publishes such top-selling authors as Tom Clancy and Patricia Cornwell, topped US$1.49 billion in 2003.

Reed Elsevier, a joint venture between the Netherlands' Elsevier N.V. and U.K.-based Reed International PLC, was a leading publisher of educational books through its Harcourt Education division. The company reported total turnover in 2004 of 4.812 billion pounds (about US$8.73 billion). In 1996 the four largest trade publishing groups in the Netherlands accounted for 50-70 percent of the US$480 million Dutch market, which generated 12,000 new titles a year. Among its leading publishers in the late 1990s were Meulenhoff, trade house Veen, and Veen's parent, Wolters Kluwer. A planned merger between Wolters Kluwer and Britain's Reed Elsevier to create an US$8 billion professional and scientific megahouse (challenged only by the Thomson Corporation), was called off in 1998 when the European Commission raised antitrust objections.

In the United States, the largest publisher in the early 2000s was Bertelsmann-owned Random House. Though Random House struggled with declining profits in 2002 and 2003, largely because of the weak dollar against the stronger euro, the company's performance improved considerably in 2004, when operating profits rose 22 percent. Random House posted sales in 2004 of US$2.44 billion. Time Warner Book Group, a subsidiary of Time Warner, enjoyed record sales in 2002 of US$400 million with such best sellers as *The Lovely Bones.* Pearson-owned Penguin Group, which makes about two-thirds of its sales in the United States, saw operating profits drop by 24 percent in 2004, due primarily to the weak dollar. Nevertheless, the firm enjoyed a 40 percent increase in titles that made the *New York Times* bestseller list, including million-copy selling *Eats, Shoots & Leaves.* HarperCollins, a subsidiary of Rupert Murdoch's News Corp., reported annual sales of more than US$1 billion. McGraw-Hill, a leading textbook publisher, posted 2004 revenues of US$5.25 billion.

MAJOR COUNTRIES IN THE INDUSTRY

United States. In the early 2000s the United States' book publishing industry remained the world's largest. However, rising costs since 1997—when the nation's book industry netted US$20 billion—have failed to excite the large conglomerates that dominate the trade.

According to analysts from Veronis Suhler Stevenson, sales of consumer books in the United States reached approximately US$19.53 billion in 2003 and were expected to grow by an annual compound rate of 1.9 percent through 2008, to total US$22.51 billion. Faster growth was expected in the religious books segment, where sales were projected to increase by 2.9 percent annually.

The number of books published in the United States reached a record high in 2004 of 195,000 new titles and editions, according to analysts from R. R. Bowker. Adult fiction grew by 43.1 percent, reversing a three-year stagnation and setting a record high of 25,184 new titles and editions. Adult fiction represented 14 percent of the U.S. market, the highest share since 1961. Output increased 12.3 percent among university presses. These favorable signs prompted Bowker senior director of publisher relations Andrew Grabois to comment that "2004 marked a return to pre-9/11 patterns of publishing." The bad news, though, was that more titles did not translate into more profits. As *Publishers Weekly* reported, U.S. titles rose by more than 30 percent over two years, but sales grew by less than 5 percent. Total sales for Amazon.com rose from US$511,000 in 1995 to US$2.6 billion in 2004, and combined sales for B&N and Borders superstores also increased about five-fold. But mall store sales at Dalton and Waldenbooks shrank during that period from US$1.7 billion to only US$956 million. Interestingly, an eBay search by *Publishers Weekly* in 2005 under the category "book" yielded more than 1.173 billion items.

The Association of American Publishers reported that net sales from its 19 members were down 1 percent in 2004, reaching US$5.46 billion. The biggest disappointment was in children's hardcovers, where sales declined by 15.3 percent despite a 2.7 percent increase in unit volume. Mass market paperback also performed poorly, with sales falling by 8.8 percent. Adult hardcover sales, however, grew by 6 percent. Even better growth was seen in religious books, where sales increased by 9.1 percent.

Three major U.S. publishing houses were sold to non-U.S. conglomerates between 1996 and mid-1998, but U.S. publishers also grabbed a steadily growing share of foreign book markets. In 1998, Bertelsmann shocked the world publishing industry by buying Random House, the world's largest English-language general trade book publisher, from Advance Publications for US$1.4 billion. This made Bertelsmann the largest English-language publisher.

Perhaps no area of publishing had changed quite as much as the publishing houses connected with miscellaneous colleges and universities, particularly in the United States. The major college houses—in terms of sales, longevity, and annual books published—include Cornell University Press, Harvard University Press, and Indiana University Press. These presses must survive on business acumen—not university subsidies. As a result, they continue to put out scholarly titles by academics, but also publish more popular books calculated to reach a wider audience and to earn reviews in major publications. In 2002 these presses also signed publishing deals with ebrary.com, enabling consumers to access and retrieve on-demand, full-text copies of books on their respective lists, including some titles no longer available in print editions.

Harvard University Press, created in 1913, lists more than 2,800 titles in print, including some that have won prestigious awards such as the Pulitzer Prize, National Book Award, Bancroft Prize, and National Book Critics Circle Award. Cornell University Press, established in 1869, is one of the oldest U.S. university presses in continuing existence, and operates with an all-faculty review board. Indiana University Press, although only in existence since 1950, has become the tenth largest university press in the country. It has published the work of first-class scholars and authors such as Umberto Eco, Henry Glassie, Langston Hughes, Alfred Kinsey, and Scott Russell Sanders. In contrast to these successful university presses, the 2000s saw many other university presses in a beleaguered financial state as many university libraries cut their budgets to the bone and acquire fewer titles. In 2001, for example, Northwestern University Press incurred a loss of US$877,000 on revenues of US$1.54 million and is typical of university presses struggling to find a blockbuster best seller to balance traditionally low sales for scholarly books and import books of ideas. By 2004, however, several university presses had succeeded in boosting output by capturing key niche markets, such as Arabic language titles. In 2004, university press output reached a record high of 14,848 new titles and editions; 55 percent of this increase came from history, biography, and law books.

Japan. Reflecting the moribund Japanese economy of the 1990s and 2000s, Japan's book industry suffered throughout the decade, especially in such areas as comic books and paperbacks, but translations of U.S. titles remained profitable. The Japanese book market is dominated by about 10 large family-owned firms that control the country's two large book distributors, and thus 80 percent of the Japanese book distribution market. As in Europe, the Japanese book industry as a whole evolved from the magazine industry, and many of Japan's publishers continue to publish magazines along with books. Dai Nippon Printing Company Ltd. is further diversified in that it also produces promotional materials, direct mail pieces, business forms, CD-ROMs, catalogs, smart cards, and packaging for consumer products. In addition, many of Japan's major book publishers are privately managed, and the top 120 publishers control 50 percent of the nation's book sales volume—a trend toward consolidation that continued through the mid-1990s.

In 2003, Japanese publishers admitted that losses had plagued the nation's industry for the sixth year in a row, according to the Research Institute for Publications and *Publishers Weekly.* Sales for 2001 dropped 3 percent from 2000 in Japan, leading to wide bookstore closings despite publishing successes such as a 10 million Japanese print run of the Harry Potter books. The closings were partially responsible for high book returns said to be around 40 percent. Many in the industry put the blame on consumer preferences for video games and movies.

Despite low sales, though, book consumption was up at libraries, reaching about 500 million books borrowed a year in 2003. Output of new titles was also up, rising 13.3 percent in April 2002. The Japanese government has joined publishers in various efforts to promote reading, including a law passed in 2001 to fund school libraries' purchase of books, and the establishment of multipartisan federation to improve the reading climate for the general public.

Daiki Naito reported on the growing market for electronic books that opened up new opportunities for the industry. He said a Sharp Corporation Web site dedicated to the Zaurus personal digital assistant made it possible for visitors to download pictures and data. More than 50 books could be stored on a data card roughly about the size of a postage stamp.

In June 2004, Suvendrini Kakuchi discussed the phenomenal difference a new novel was making in the conservative Japanese publishing world. Natsuo Kirino's *Out* is about a husband-killer and psychopath gangsters. In 2003, it was nominated for best novel in the prestigious 2004 Edgar Allen Poe Awards. According to Kakuchi, *Yomiuri Shimburn* Book Editor Kenichi Sato pointed out "Kirino's style was a far cry from the past where Japanese writers, like Nobel prize winner Yasunari Kawabata and the country's best post-war novelist Yukio Mishima, gained international limelight for writing hauntingly elegant prose depicting the uniqueness of Japanese culture and portraying women as innocent beauties devoted to men." In New York bookstores, *Out* has become a favorite displayed in the mystery section, rather than Japanese section.

Germany. In 2002, the decision of the massive Bertelsmann-Random House conglomerate to cut costs dramatically at all its publishing houses sent a cry of alarm and another of protest throughout the book industry. Bertelsmann announced worldwide Random House sales of approximately US$1.85 billion for the fiscal year that ended June 30, 2001 (all future fiscal years will end January 1 instead of June 30). The Bertelsmann-Random House deal gave German publishing ownership of 43 percent of the U.S. book market, with U.S. firms claiming only 30 percent. The two largest categories of books in Germany were specialist/scientific books (39 percent of market value) and general literature including fiction (at 53 percent of total market value). The leading categories in terms of volume sales were language and literature (22.3 percent) and the social sciences (21.5 percent). Valued at US$22 billion, Bertelsmann AG of Germany was (with Time Warner and Disney) one of the world's largest media concerns at the beginning of the 2000s, with books generating about 31 percent of its total sales.

United Kingdom. In the 2000s the publishing successes of Harry Potter author J.K. Rowling gained global attention. While the book industry languished elsewhere, during the January-September 2001 reporting period, British book exports were at US$1.25 billion, only slightly less than the US$1.27 billion for the United States—although the British industry is but a fifth of U.S. book operations, according to *Publishers Weekly.* The United Kingdom has traditionally been a major center of operations for the European continent's publishing giants, and in the 1990s through 2000s, it remained an important entry point for U.S. publishers seeking to establish themselves in Europe. Once insulated from U.S. book industry trends, the British book industry increasingly mirrored U.S. publishing practices by the late 1990s. Such U.S. imports as the author book tour, online book ordering, and the book superstore, not to mention the dominance of U.S. titles on British publishers' lists, all attested to the sway of U.S. publishers on Great Britain's market. Britain was the second-largest importer (behind Canada) of books from the United States in 2003, (US$274.6 million in value) and was the largest exporter of books into the U.S. market (US$288 million). But in the first half of 2004, U.K. exports to the U.S. dropped 11.6 percent, placing it third behind China and Canada.

France. During the 2000s, book publishing in France differed from the book industry elsewhere. For example, in 2002 between 50 and 60 percent of all children's book sales stemmed from the sale of comic books such as "Ast rix," considered a classic in France. In 2000, total sales of books in France, including book club sales, were US$2.5 billion, according to an August 2001 report from *Publishers Weekly.* Book and publishing sales grew by 3.2 percent in volume and 2.9 percent in value between 1998 and 2002, according to Euromonitor. Consumer books account for most sales in France, with school and library purchases playing a much smaller role in the market.

FURTHER READING

Asada, Tomiji. "Sales of Books, Mags Down for 5 Straight Years." *Japan Economic Newswire,* 25 February 2002.

Baker, John F. "A Buoyant Mood in London." *Publishers Weekly,* 18 February 2002.

Baker, John F. and Atkinson, Nathalie. "Canada: Reaching Out." *Publishers Weekly,* 13 June 2005.

"Book Consumption Declines in the U.S." *Graphic Arts Monthly,* August 2004.

"Book Exports Up 7.8 percent in Six-Month Period." *Publishers Weekly,* 13 September 2004.

Book Industry Trends. New York: Book Industry Study Group, 2005.

"Books and Publishing in Mexico." April 2003. Available from http://www.euromonitor.com.

"Books Without Buyers." *Publishers Weekly,* 30 May 2005.

"Bowker: Titles up 19 percent in 2003." *Publishers Weekly,* 31 May 2004.

Bowman, Becky. "Northwestern U. Press' Woes Typical of Smaller Publishers." *Daily Northwestern,* 25 February 2002.

"Cultural Industries in the Latin American Economy: Current Status and Outlook in the Context of Globalization," 2005. Available from http://www.oas.org.

Danford, Natalie. "How Do You Say 'Growing Pains' in Spanish?" *Publishers Weekly,* 17 January 2005.

Graham, Gordon. "Promoting Reading in Africa." *The Book & The Computer/Global Exchange,* 15 December 2003. Available from http://www.honco.net.

"Harvard Press Inks Deal with Commercial Press." *Publishers Weekly,* 1 July 2004.

Kakuchi, Suvendrini. "Arts-Japan: A New Novel Gives Women Voice." 8 June 2004. Available from http://www.hoovers.com.

Khanna, Lalitha. "Books Shelved?" *Business Line,* 14 January 2002.

Kirkpatrick, David D. "Random House Cutting Sharply, Stirring Talk In Book Trade." *The New York Times,* 22 January 2002.

Livingston, Gillian. "Indigo Takes Control of 23 Chapters/Indigo Stores After No Buyers Found." *Canadian Press Newswire,* 8 January 2002.

Lottman, Herbert R. "French Sales Top US$2 billion." *Publishers Weekly,* 6 August 2001.

Maysuradze, Yury; and Boris Esenkin. "The Russian Book Market Rebounds." *The Book & The Computer/Global Exchange,* 12 November 2003. Available from http://www.honco.net.

Meyer, Mike. "Letter from Beijing: The World's Biggest Book Market." *New York Times,* 13 March 2005.

Milliot, Jim. "B&N, Borders Report Strong Holiday Gains." *Publishers Weekly,* 14 January, 2002.

———. "Book Exports Inched up in 2003." *Publishers Weekly,* 12 April 2004.

Milliot, Jim. "Pearson: Education on Target, but Penguin Group Slumps." *Publishers Weekly,* 15 November 2004.

———. "Exclusively Yours." *Publishers Weekly,* 20 June 2005.

———. "Google Draws Fire, Creates Book Page." *Publishers Weekly,* 30 May 2005.

———. "Profits Improve at Random." *Publishers Weekly,* 21 March 2005.

———. "Random House Results Skewed by Currency Changes." *Publishers Weekly,* 5 April 2004.

———. "Trends: More Evidence of Softness." *Publishers Weekly,* 30 May 2005.

Milliot, Jim; and Calvin Reid. "Reality Check: Despite Setbacks in 2001, the Groundwork for the Success of E-publishing Has Been Laid." *Publishers Weekly,* 7 January 2002.

Morales, Ed. "Mexico Fair Draws Spanish Publishers from Around the World." *Publishers Weekly,* 10 December 2001.

Naito, Daiki. "Ailing Publishing Industry Turning to e-books for Salvation." *Kyodo News,* 19 March 2002. Available from http://www.japantimes.co.jp.

Paddock, Polly. "The Year in Publishing." *Charlotte (North Carolina) Observer,* 3 January 2002.

Picchi, Aimee. "Viacom Merges Simon & Schuster with Film Group." *Bloomberg News,* 31 January 2002.

Picklyk, Douglas. "By the Book." *Canadian Printer,* December 2001.

PricewaterhouseCoopers Global Entertainment and Media Outlook, 2004. Available from http://www.pwcglobal.com.

Raugust, Karen. "Licensing Watch: Europe." *Publishers Weekly,* 5 May 2001.

Schiffrin, Andre. *The Business of Books: How International Conglomerates Took Over Publishing and Changed the Way We Read.* Verso, 2000.

———. "Independent Publishers: Becoming Their Own Worst Enemy?" *The Book & The Computer/Online Symposium,* 2004. Available from http://www.honco.net.

Sithold, Cynthia. "The Movement of Books across Borders-Current Challengs." *Proceedings of the Indaba 2003.* Zimbabwe International Book Fair. Available from http://www.zibf.org.zw.

"VSS Study Projects Slow Consumer Book Growth." *Publishers Weekly,* 2 August 2004.

"U.S. Book Production Reaches new High of 195,000 Titles in 2004; Fiction Soars." R.R. Bowker, 2005. Available from http://www.bowker.com.

"U.S. Book Sales for 2001 Posted by Association of American Publishers." Available from http://www.publishers.org.

Wang, Annie. "A New Chapter: Chinese Writers Are Discovering That Books Have Become a Tricky Business." *Time Asia Magazine,* 27 January 2003.

Zeitchik, Steven, and Milliot, Jim. "Comeback Kid? Amazon Revival Could Shake up Industry." *Publishers Weekly,* 11 April 2005.

"Zeroing In On Some Savvy Suppliers." *Publishers Weekly,* 1 July 2004.

SIC 4841
NAICS 513210

CABLE AND OTHER PAY-TELEVISION SERVICES

Participants in the global subscription television industry deliver live and recorded programming, most often via cable lines or satellite transmission, to businesses and consumers. Carriers may provide closed circuit television services, direct-broadcast satellite (DBS) or direct-to-home (DTH) satellite services, multi-channel multipoint distribution systems (MMDS) services, and satellite master antenna systems (SMATV) services. Certain firms in the industry also participate heavily in other telecommunications services; see also **Telecommunications Services** later in this chapter for more detailed treatment of those activities. Television networks are not included in this discussion.

INDUSTRY SNAPSHOT

Although the industry's two main segments, cable and satellite, have coexisted for some time, some industry observers foretell the ultimate ascendance of one over the other. Predicting which one might prevail in this struggle depends on the observer: cable companies claim their broadband digital format far exceeds the interactive abilities of satellite, yet satellite proponents have a much easier time implementing mass-audience systems and claim to offer impressive interactive capabilities in their own right. To date, cable is winning the battle in terms of subscriber counts, and cable systems' ongoing technology investments is equipping them to quickly deploy digital services on a large scale in most places. Even Microsoft's Bill Gates has been hedging his bets: while pumping billions into cable, Microsoft also has sizable interests in low-orbit satellite systems that promise to extend the satellite medium into all corners of the global telecommunications field.

In reality, cable television tends to be strongest in parts of the world where satellite is weakest, usually where cable installations were begun in the 1970s and early 1980s, and satellite services lead in markets in which cable infrastructure is lacking. Such an arrangement is unlikely to change anytime soon, even as the respective systems upgrade to digital services. Microwave-based MMDS systems, on the other hand, have thus far only attracted small followings and few expect them to gain a mass viewership on the scale of the other two formats.

The outlook for pay television remains positive. Changes in consumer preferences for video-on-demand and enhanced viewing capabilities have allowed the pay-TV industry to make huge inroads into traditional broadcast markets. Increased disposable income in countries such as China and India with their huge potential markets will also be of benefit to the industry. Countries continue to deregulate industries, allowing companies to pursue foreign investment, although many countries continue to top such investment levels at 49 percent.

In many markets the industry's fastest-growing segments are satellite services and the rapidly increasing digital television market. Indeed, the two formats are increasingly offered in conjunction by leading-edge firms. Satellite service enables operators to establish broad geographic presence rapidly in a relatively non-intrusive way compared to cable or microwave infrastructure, a significant benefit when local laws or terrains restrict the laying of cable. These services also often boast a mix of programming different from that of cable or other alternatives. Aggressive deployment and marketing efforts by such leaders as DIRECTV and some of the Sky Broadcasting ventures have also contributed to the medium's growth. The digital side entices subscribers with higher technical quality in programming and, particularly with digital cable, the potential for interactive services such as Internet browsing and home shopping.

ORGANIZATION AND STRUCTURE

As opposed to terrestrial broadcast methods used by traditional network channels, which may be received essentially by anyone within a certain geographic range, subscription television services employ three methods to transmit controlled-access, high-quality signals: cable, microwave, and satellite. First, coaxial or fiber-optic cables may be directly wired between subscribers and distribution points. Subscriber lines are fed signals by a local "headend," or distribution facility; a network of one or more headends serving a geographic region forms a cable system. All of the world's major cable operators run more than one system, and thus they are sometimes referred to as multiple-system operators (MSOs). Second, services may use a multi-channel, multipoint distribution system (MMDS) to carry signals from a television studio to a microwave transmitter, which then relays them to rooftop receivers. This method is also known as wireless cable. Third, subscription services may offer satellite transmission in which a broadcaster uplinks a signal to a transponder on a satellite, which retransmits either to home dishes (known as DBS or DTH service) or to a satellite master dish (SMATV). Companies offering satellite services may own the satellites used to transmit their signals, but more often they lease space from a third-party satellite vendor.

A separate and increasingly important technological difference is whether services are analog or digital. While both transmit signals via electromagnetic waves, digital services first encode the pictures and sound as binary information, much like computer data, that is then decoded by the receiving television set. Thus, digital signals minimize deterioration during transmission and enable more powerful technical manipulation and embellishment of the programming information. Digital programming may be disseminated through any of the three transmission methods, as well as through terrestrial broadcast, but requires equipment capable of processing digital data at both the sending and receiving ends. Digital technology is in some cases less expensive for operators as well; estimates place the operating cost of digital satellite channels at one-third of that for their analog counterparts. Many analysts say that analog will be history nearly everywhere in the world by 2010.

In addition to their competing technologies, pay-television services differ in pricing and programming options. Most of the world's subscription services involve some form of flat fee, typically monthly, to obtain the most basic level of service. Many operators also offer premium or elective services for additional fees, and some provide programming on a transaction basis known as pay-per-view (PPV) television. Pricing for comparable services in different parts of the world varies widely, as do programming choices. PPV services can be distributed in analog or digital formats via any of the three transmission methods.

Pay-per-view (PPV) services represent a small but expanding world niche. These services typically offer high-profile programming, such as recent movies and live sporting events, on a transaction basis. *Broadcasting & Cable*, a U.S. journal for the trade, reported that at the close of the century viable PPV markets were established only in France, Germany, Hong Kong, Italy, Japan, the Netherlands, and the United States. Test runs were underway in other nations, however.

The industry's structure varies by region and by country. In Western Europe, for instance, several countries possess similar technological infrastructures, but language and regulatory differences make for highly divergent programming. These countries' telephone carriers, many of which until recently were state owned, provide the bulk of cable television services. However, in an era of deregulation and privatization, they are beginning to face challenges from other vendors. The reverse has been true in the United States, where phone companies and cable operators were traditionally separate and only recently have phone services begun to explore cable services. Similarly, parts of Europe and Asia, such as the United Kingdom and Japan, possess limited infrastructure for cable services, and thus satellite and MMDS services predominate. In such places as the United States and Germany, extensive cable networking exists and, as a result, cable is considerably more common than other forms. Meanwhile, cultural norms, socioeconomic conditions, and the quality and breadth of local terrestrial broadcasts help fashion pay-television demand in particular countries and regions; it may not be taken for granted that programming and delivery methods popular in one well-established market will be popular elsewhere.

Subscription television carriers are often different from, although they may be linked to, the enterprises that actually produce television programming. Much of the content originates in various networks, known to the end user as channels, which provide brand names such as CNN or HBO under which to market their programming. The carriers then pay the networks fees based on the number of subscribers to each network's programming. Carriers also may arrange with local broadcast channels and community organizations to deliver local programming to subscribers. However, major operators often hold sizable production facilities as well, and may produce some channels' content. An interesting development in 2002 was the decision of three American baseball teams—the Minneapolis Twins, the Baltimore Orioles, and the New York Yankees—to create their own cable presence. The Yankees have a cable presence on the Yankees Entertainment & Sports Network (YES), and all other major league teams are at least in discussion stages to follow suit.

BACKGROUND AND DEVELOPMENT

Pay television's potential has aroused the attention—and the pocketbooks—of some high-profile investors from outside the industry. Widely seen as a strong vote of confidence in the industry, Microsoft Corporation's 1997 US$1 billion investment in the U.S. cable carrier Comcast signaled that there would be high stakes in the integrated information-entertainment services contest. More dramatically, in 1998 the long-distance telephone powerhouse AT&T Corporation agreed to purchase Tele-Communications Inc. (TCI), the United States' largest cable operator. The move positioned AT&T, which also had a strong Internet service franchise, to provide integrated cable, local phone, long distance, and Internet access services through TCI's infrastructure.

In spite of all the business failures, mergers, and general uncertainties, where even a giant power such as AOL Time Warner has seen its stock plummet 30 percent almost overnight, the cable readiness of developed countries speeds ahead full steam. In 2002, the United States had cable readiness in 97 percent of all TV markets, for example. According to the Cable Center history site, 60 percent of all households, about 64 million, subscribed to cable in 2002.

In Canada, some of the largest providers of cable services have seen their profits sink as a result of intense competition between cable companies. Videotron, both the third largest cable-TV provider in Canada and a Quebecor Inc. company, lost 71,000 of its 1.5 million customers from January 2001 to April 2002; losses amounted to about US$25 million, according to *Bloomberg News*. Videotron's competition comes from direct-to-home satellite services such as Bell ExpressVu (owned by BCE Inc.) and Star Choice (owned by Shaw Communications Inc.).

The rising costs of operating cable have been passed on, in part, to subscribers. Cable television fees jumped 7.5 percent across the United States from 2000 to 2001, according to an April 2002 news release by the Federal Communications Commission.

According to an April 2002 *Hollywood Reporter* article, the stagnant U.S. economy in 2001, mimicked by similar slow economies in other parts of the world in 2002, was expected to keep cable from becoming attractive to investors until 2003 or 2004. In the first three months of 2002, cable stocks lost almost a quarter of their value. Even the giants like Charter Communications and Comcast said growth in digital cable holdings had slowed significantly, according to the *Hollywood Reporter*.

While the times haven't been consistently harsh for all the industry's participants, many have underwhelmed their investors and a few have alienated their customers with rising costs and slow headway toward implementing the radically improved technologies some have promised. As a result of these and other strains on profitability and cash flow, worldwide merger and acquisition activities were brisk in the latter half of the 1990s through the early 2000s.

Part of the upheaval in the subscription television industry is a by-product of international telecommunications trade reforms negotiated under the General Agreement on Trade in

Services (GATS) through the World Trade Organization. These negotiations concluded in 1997, and the telecommunications agreement entered into force beginning in 1998, though individual nations have different compliance schedules. In many leading countries, deregulation initiatives preceded the agreement, which liberalizes trade by reducing entry barriers and reining in monopolies. Television is not covered by the agreement, but in many parts of the world subscription television services have been linked with telephone companies that have needed to undergo myriad changes to prepare for the new competitive environment. These moves were the culmination of more than a decade of telecommunications regulatory changes that sought to demonopolize national industries and spark competition. Despite these advances, however, in many world markets, notably for cable services, de facto monopolies persist and consumers have few alternatives to their regional operator.

From the mid-1990s on, the price of cable TV rose twice as much as the Consumer Price Index, to an average cost of US$50 per month per subscriber in 2004, according to *Forbes*. Considering this, it was no surprise that the top two satellite companies in the country lured nearly 2 million subscribers away from cable in 2003. Even HBO lost subscribers in 2003. According to *Broadcasting & Cable*, networks needed to replace up to 60 percent of their subscribers to stay even.

CURRENT CONDITIONS

By 2004, 54 percent of the money being spent on filmed entertainment worldwide was being spent via pay-TV service rather than through video purchases or in cinemas, which had 33 percent and 13 percent, respectively. According to *Screen Digest*, the amount being spent on pay-TV for this purpose has increased by 4 percent since 1996. Both video and cinema had shown declines during this period.

On a global basis, the market for pay-TV services continues to expand, with markets continuing to grow in countries such as India and China as technology becomes more widely available and governments deregulate the industry. At a corporate level, mergers continue to dominate, and these large companies are positioned to provide the necessary equity for expansion in many underserved areas. But the face of competition is changing as non-traditional players, such as telecommunication companies, enter the market offering bundled packages of video-on-demand, Internet service and telephone services to their customers.

In the United States, after the AT&T coup by Comcast, coupled with the rising star of satellite services, other cable providers began to decline, some up to 28 percent. Still, the cable market was stable, at least for outside advertisers. Upfront advertising revenues hit US$6 billion in 2004, an increase of about 16 percent. Digital cable providers raked in between US$50 billion and US$100 billion of the upfront total.

Many analysts expected that interactive digital capabilities such as video-on-demand (VOD) would play a greater role in future industry growth. Worldwide revenue for VOD alone was valued at US$4.4 billion in 2004, with projections for growth to US$11.5 billion by 2010. History has shown that people are willing to pay for individual preferences and premium services when such items meet an individual need or desire, and one major challenge beyond the mid-2000s was to fill a multitude of niches all at once.

Deloitte Touche Tohmatsu was predicting that digital terrestrial television (DTTV)—whereby broadcast frequencies are used by telecommunications companies to get more bandwith and deliver increased entertainment services—would begin to take market from satellite and particularly cable television suppliers. The technology is seen as an inexpensive method by which consumers could obtain more channels.

INDUSTRY LEADERS

Comcast Cable Communications Inc. The number one company in the United States, Comcast was number three until its acquisition of AT&T Cable in 2002 for US$72 billion. By 2004, Comcast had 21.5 million cable customers and 7 million video customers generating revenues of US$20.3 billion. Of the company's 74,000 employees, 59,000 were involved with its cable operations. In 2004, the company began offering video-on-demand service, allowing customers to select from more than 3,000 programs. The company continues to expand its holdings, owning about 17 percent of Time Warner Cable, with which it joined forces with in January 2005 in order to purchase the cable assets of the U.S.'s fifth largest cable provider, Adelphia Communications.

In 2002, AT&T's cable and broadband digital services were inextricably linked. The company intended to bring broadband to all areas where it had cable during the 2000s. However, in the spring of 2002 AT&T and Comcast were in negotiations for AT&T to sell its cable interests to Comcast, as AT&T president David Dorman dismissed cable as unprofitable to the company's core business. The move was hailed by shareholders, concerned about cash-rich AT&T's plunge in stock values in 2001 and early 2002, who saw the cable sale as a way to unload debt.

The story of AT&T's cable expansion began in 1998 with one of the most important mergers in business history. Despite its stature as the largest U.S. cable company in terms of subscribers, in 1998 Tele-Communications Inc. (TCI) faced debt and costly infrastructure expenses that challenged its profitability. However, significant relief came from AT&T's US$48.3 billion acquisition of TCI. The all-stock purchase integrated TCI into a new AT&T unit named AT&T Consumer Services. Some of TCI's side ventures and affiliates were not folded into AT&T. TCI appealed to AT&T because it had networking in place to potentially access 33 million U.S. households—about a third of all households—compared to AT&T's existing long-distance subscriber base of 66 million.

Still then nominally the United States' largest cable operator with 14.1 million subscribers under its management in 1998, TCI had embarked on a program of fiscal tightening and market focusing that was expected to leave it a close second to Time Warner's combined cable holdings. These moves were prompted in large part by a bitter fiscal 1996 that saw burgeoning debt coinciding with declining subscriber counts and revenues. TCI hoped to improve efficiency and make its vast holdings more manageable through selective downsizing. In 1997 it concluded a couple of agreements with Time Warner that improved each company's customer clustering and placed more subscribers under Time Warner's management.

Time Warner Cable Inc. Time Warner Cable Inc., once the nation's largest cable company, but second after Comcast acquired AT&T, had approximately 10.9 million subscribers in 2004 and revenues of US$8.5 billion. Owned 79 percent by the world's leading media company, Time Warner, with the remainder held by Comcast, this cable company manages an empire that includes a number of distinct corporate entities and joint ventures with other companies. Time Warner also owns a number of high-profile cable networks carried by many pay-television services throughout the world, including Cinemax, CNN, and HBO, the United States' most popular premium channel.

DIRECTV Group. With approximately 13.9 million subscribers and US$11.4 billion in revenue in the Americas in 2004, DIRECTV was a leader among satellite services. Formerly Hughes Electronic, the company changed names in 2004 when it decided to concentrate its efforts on its direct-to-home satellite business. The company is also a leading satellite television provider in Latin America, where its 2004 subscriber based amounted to 1.6 million people. In 2002, the company completed its divestiture of its operations in Japan. In August 2004, DIRECTV also sold its 80.4 percent interest in the satellite operator PanAmSat, one of the world's largest private satellite systems, through which it sold satellite time to other services.

British Sky Broadcasting Group Plc. Launched in 1989, Sky Digital had reached one million homes in the United Kingdom by 1990. That year, the company merged with British Satellite Broadcasting to form British Sky Broadcasting. By 2004, the company was in 7 million homes with offerings of more than 400 channels, and had earnings of more than US$6.6 billion.

The News Corporation Ltd. Few companies are as intricately embroiled in the television industry as Rupert Murdoch's News Corporation of Australia, which has interests in numerous world subscription television services in addition to its vast international holdings of broadcast television, media production, and newspaper concerns. The company, which obtains an estimated 70 percent of its revenues from the United States, owned a 35 percent stake in British Sky Broadcasting Group PLC in 2004, the United Kingdom's largest pay-television service with 14.3 million subscribers. News Corporation also controls Australia's Foxtel cable service and Sky Latin America. Its subsidiary Fox Broadcasting owned 34 percent of DIRECTV in 2004. That year, the company earned approximately US$1.8 billion from its direct broadcast satellite television operations.

The firm was one of the leading backers of a Japan Sky Broadcasting Co. venture slated to come online in 1998, but in early 1998 the resources were merged instead with PerfecTV Corporation, Japan's top digital satellite company, to form Japan Digital Broadcasting Services Inc. With an 11.38 percent stake, News Corporation was one of the venture's five principal shareholders. PerfecTV had 570,000 subscribers entering the merger, and the enhanced offerings of the new service, called SkyPerfecTV, were expected to draw up to a million subscribers by the end of 1998. Also in Asia is News Corporation's Star TV, a free satellite-based service reaching more than 62 million Asian households largely through cable retransmissions. News Corporation planned to phase in subscription-based versions of Star TV in several national markets, including China, India, Indonesia, and Japan. Meanwhile, the company also held a majority interest in American Sky Broadcasting Co., a troubled U.S. start-up that sought to merge with an established satellite partner in 1997; after a fallout with EchoStar, Murdoch's company agreed to merge operations with Primestar in 1998, subject to approval by the U.S. Federal Communications Commission.

In December 2001 News Corp. announced an agreement to bring a cable television with Mandarin-language programming to south China. In 2001 News Corp. posted a loss of US$606 million for the second quarter, compared to a smaller US$23 million loss in 2000. The entire Murdoch empire struggled mightily in 2001, although its sheer size and its entrepreneurial business moves into China showed the company retained considerable vigor in spite of severe setbacks. By 2003, company's revenues stood at US$20.1 billion.

Canal+ Group. In 2004, Canal+ Group remained one of Europe's largest pay-TV providers. It owns 49 percent (the maximum allowed by the French government), of France's Canal Plus, which was ranked as the world's largest PPV service, claiming 4.9 million subscribers scattered across Europe and parts of Africa. In addition, it owned 66 percent of CanalSatellite, a digital pay-TV service with 3 million subscribers in France as of January 2005. In turn, Canal+ Group is owned by media and telecommunications giant, Vivendi.

MAJOR COUNTRIES IN THE INDUSTRY

Europe. In Western Europe, cable was still more prominent in satellite in all but four countries in 2004: Italy, Greece, Spain and the United Kingdom. Approximately US$25 billion was spent on pay television services, with *Screen Digest* predicting the amount would reach almost US$32 billion by 2006, when pay TV market penetration was expected to reach 50 percent. *International Marketing Reports* was predicting that the fastest growing sectors in European pay TV would be in broadband and video-on-demand (VOD). In terms of market size, the United Kingdom was expected to remain the largest, with the U.K., France, Spain, and Scandanavia being the strongest markets by 2008.

United Kingdom. Although in 2003, cable and satellite television serviced reached a combined 9.4 million U.K homes, satellite service dominated the market, accounting for 76 percent of these homes. The market remained highly concentrated, with only four companies accounting for 90 percent of marketshare and with the British Sky Broadcasting Group PLC (BSkyB) servicing 58 percent according to Euromonitor statistics. . Its 7 million subscriptions include pay-per-view and monthly customers. BSkyB and other pay-television services compete with the thoroughly entrenched and popular British Broadcasting Corporation (BBC) for market share, although they do carry BBC programming. The BBC's mostly terrestrial broadcasts are supported by a strong transmission infrastructure that ensures high-quality television reception in the majority of the country, reducing technical performance as a selling point for subscription services in the United Kingdom. However, by 2003 28.7 percent of British homes had a satellite dish and 8.7 percent were cable subscribers. Euromonitor was forecasting the market to grow by 11.4 percent by 2008, with the satellite sector continuing to dominate the pay-TV market.

Germany. Of Germany' 35 million households, 31.9 million of them had cable or satellite television service. Euromonitor expected this number to grow by 11.2 percent by 2008, with cable leading with an expected 60.3 percent market share.

In the 1990s, Deutsche Telekom's far-reaching cable empire dominated the German pay-television market, the largest in Europe. At one time, the company had 17 million subscribers, controlling approximately 90 percent of Germany's pay-television market. The DT monopoly controlled all of the nation's cable television market officially until 1997. In 1999, the subsidiary Kabel Deutschland GmbH was formed to managed DT's cable operations separately, while the market opened up. In 2003, the company was purchased by a consortium of financial investors, including Goldman Sachs. By the end of 2004, Kabel Deutschland had 9.7 million subscribers.

France. Like its German neighbor, the pay-TV industry in France continued to be dominated by cable services in 2003, but the gap was rapidly closing with satellite expected to overtake cable by 2008. In 2003, 52 percent of the 7.3 million houses with pay-TV service had cable. Euromonitor was predicting that satellite would surpass cable reaching a 55 percent market share by 2008. The total number of households with pay-TV service was expected to increase to 9.9 million.

Like other European countries, the market in France remained quite concentrated, with four companies (TF1, Canal+, France Télécom and Suez) controlling 73 percent of the market. Canal+ Group remained the leading provider of both services, covering 30 percent of the households.

Asia. Though less developed than Europe and North America, Asia is home to the world's largest potential regional market for pay-television services. Until the 1997 financial crisis in Asia, pay-television companies had been furiously expanding services in burgeoning Asian economies such as Indonesia, Malaysia, and Thailand, because of their growth potential. Given that Southeast Asia's short-term purchasing power diminished through currency devaluations, however, a number of firms from inside and outside the region began reevaluating their Asian expansion strategies. But by 2004, changes in the competitive environment and regulatory arenas were resulting in extensive improvements in the pay-TV industry in the region. The market was valued at US$18.6 billion that year. The number of multi-channel subscribers had reached more than 192 million, representing a market penetration of 34 percent.

Japan. The regional leader in 2004 in terms of industry-related revenue, Japan's cable and satellite television market was valued at US$5.9 billion by year end. The country expanded the availability of digital cable, but penetration was growing slowly, reaching only 320,000 by 2004. The top two leading pay-TV providers were based in Japan: J-COM Broadband (with 2004 revenues of US$1.49 billion) and Sky Perfect Communications (US$720 million).

China. With its large population base and increasing amounts of disposable income, China had emerged as a significant player in the world's cable and satellite television industry by 2004. Of Asia's 192 million multi-channel subscribers, 105 million were located in China, generating industry-wide revenue of US$3.5 billion.

The pace of growth in terms of digital cable subscriptions slowed due to government regulations, but by 2004 China still remained a leading regional market for this technology. However, during that year, the Chinese government ended the monopoly held by China Digital TV Media, issuing licenses to four other companies. New regulations also allow foreign firms to own up to 49 percent of joint ventures producing programming.

By 2005, the cable industry in China remained highly fragmented, with most provinces and cities operating their own cable system. However, with increased competition and more openness to foreign investment, consolidation of the industry was expected.

Latin America and the Caribbean. In Latin America, as in many places in the world, the pay-television landscape varies widely by locality. Argentina has one of South America's largest market penetration rates, with 47 percent of television households receiving pay services (5 million subscribers), but Brazil is considered a much larger growth market because its infrastructure is comparatively underdeveloped and it has a much larger population—more than four times that of Argentina. Only 5 percent of Brazilian households with televisions are equipped to receive cable (1.5 million subscribers), and television-per-household penetration is relatively low. In response, the Brazilian government has been selling cable and wireless franchises to a number of eager domestic and foreign contenders. Brazil's pay-television market is approaching 12 million subscribers in 2002. By 2005, DIRECTV offered more channels and covered more areas than any other direct-to-home service in the region.

United States. By January 2005, there were almost 110 million television households in the United States, and cable was active in more than 73 million of them. According to Kagan Research, the industry had annual revenue of US$57.6 billion in 2004 provided by 8,875 cable systems and an estimated 390 national cable networks. But competition for viewers continued to be hot; the National Cable & Telecommunications Association (NCTA) was reporting that one out of four subscribers obtained multi-channel programming from a company other than their local cable company. Digital Broadcast Satellite (DBS) was providing the heaviest competition to cable, offering in excess of 150 channels to its customers. The number of DBS subscribers had increased more than 14 percent in the year to reach almost 24 million subscribers by September 2004. The U.S.'s largest satellite provider, DIRECTV, was only second in terms of the number of pay-TV customers to Comcast, the U.S.'s largest cable company. However, Euromonitor was predicting that by 2008, cable would still dominate the pay-TV sector, while industry-wide revenues were forecast to reach US$69.8 billion.

The U.S. industry remains concentrated, with the top five cable and satellite companies (Comcast, Cox Communications, Time Warner, Charter Communications and Adelphia) controlling more than 71 percent of the market in 2003. But the number of industry leaders is due to get smaller. In 2002, Adelphia declared bankruptcy and it 2004 the company's founder, John Rigas and his son, former company CFO Timothy Rigas, were found guilty of fraud. In April 2005, Adelphia agreed to sell its U.S. assets to Time Warner and Comcast.

In its efforts to remain competitive, particularly against satellite providers, the cable industry had spent almost US$95 billion between 1996 and 2005 in order to upgrade its service to fiber optic technology. This technology is necessary for the provision of digital cable and video-on-demand services as well as the Internet and telephone services offered by most cable companies in the United States.

FURTHER READING

"2004 Year-End Industry Overview." National Cable & Telecommunications Association, 2005. Available from http://www.ncta.com.

"AT&T President David Dorman: What's Next for What's Left of AT&T?" *Newhouse News Service,* 12 February 2002.

Atkinson, Claire. "Upfront Wraps." *Advertising Age,* 28 June 2004.

Brister, Kathy. "Cable Fees Increase on Average 7.5 Percent Nationally." *Atlanta Journal and Constitution,* 5 April 2002.

Brown, David. "European Pay-TV Forecasts: Pay-TV data forecasts to 2008." International Marketing Reports Ltd., June 2003. Available from http://www.imr-info.com.

Burgi, Michael. "Fighting to Be Heard." *Brandweek,* 3 May 2004.

"Cable and Satellite TV Services in France, Germany, UK, US." *Euromonitor,* October 2004. Available from http://www.euromonitor.com.

Cassidy, Padraic. "EchoStar Wagers Startups to Close DIRECTV Deal." *Daily Deal,* 4 April 2002.

Draper, Deborah J., ed. *Business Rankings Annual.* Detroit: Thomson Gale, 2004.

EchoStar's Planned $26.8 Billion Merger with DIRECTV." *Business Week Online,* 28 December 2001.

Emling, Shelley. "Vivendi Shakes Up Media Industry: French Company Ready to Battle AOL Time Warner." *Atlanta Journal and Constitution,* 20 January 2002.

Fagan, Mary. "C&W Halves Capital Outlay." *Sunday Telegraph (London),* 24 February 2002.

"France's Biggest Cable TV Groups Up for Sale." *Financial Times (London),* 3 April 2002.

Fritz, Ben. "Report: VOD Demand Is Skyrocketing." *Daily Variety,* 8 June 2004.

Gray, Campbell. "Late Starter? Japan's Pay TV Market." *Media Week,* 1 February 2002.

Higgins, John M. "Premium Networks Take a Hit." *Broadcasting & Cable,* 9 February 2004.

"Hoover's Company Capsules." 2004. Available from http://www.hoovers.com.

Lazich, Robert S., ed. *Market Share Reporter.* Detroit: Thomson Gale, 2004.

Lewis, Katherine Reynolds. "Comast Vows More Fast Web, Digital Video with AT&T Cable Unit." *Bloomberg News,* 29 March 2001.

Luehrs, Bill. "A 'One Size Does Not Fit All' Future." *CED,* 15 December 2003.

Make, Jonathan. "Adelphia Hires Banks to Help Sell Cable-Television Assets." *Bloomberg News,* 5 April 2002.

———. "Hughes' DirectTV to Add More Subscribers Than Forecast." *Bloomberg News,* 21 March 2002.

Mathieson, Clive. "Deutsche Telekom Faces Credit Setback." *Times (London),* 20 March 2002.

Mouawad, Jad. "TV Losses Mount." *Television Digest,* 18 February 2002.

"News Corp.'s Star TV Gets Ready to Shine in China." *Media Week,* 29 March 2002.

Pomerantz, Dorothy. "The Other Cable Guys." *Forbes,* 7 June 2004.

Screen Digest Website, 2005. Available from http://www.screendigest.com.

Szalai, Georg. "Cable Market Picture Darkens: Experts Don't See Recovery on Horizon for Beleaguered Sector." *Hollywood Reporter,* 4 April 2002.

"Tech Innovations, Competition to Drive Pay TV in Asia: MPA." IndianTelevision.com, 20 January 2005. Available from http://www.indiatelevision.com.

Tomesco, Frederic. "Quebecor Cable Unit Losing Subscribers at Faster Pace." *Bloomberg News,* 4 April 2002.

Waters, Richard. "A Media Giant (AOL Time Warner) Finds the Future Less Rosy." *Financial Times (London),* 28 March 2002.

SIC 2771

NAICS 511191

GREETING CARDS

The greeting card industry designs and publishes greeting cards for all occasions. In addition to paper cards, the industry has adapted to Internet demand and makes available many lines of cards intended for electronic transmission. These cards are published for mass sale and exclude hand-painted cards and other one-of-a-kind cards made by crafts people for individual sale.

INDUSTRY SNAPSHOT

Throughout the centuries, people have exchanged messages of goodwill, good wishes, condolence, and love. It was only within the last century, however, that these messages were formalized into "greeting cards," and only in the very recent past that electronic cards became an immensely popular way to communicate. The Greeting Card Association (GCA) reported in 2006 that Americans purchase approximately 7 billion cards annually, generating almost US$7.5 billion in sales. The U.S. Postal Service delivers millions of these communications daily. Christmas is the number one holiday and accounts for about 60 percent of sales of holiday cards. Valentine's Day, which inspired the sale of about 180 million greeting cards in 2006, is second. After that comes sales for Mother's Day, Easter, and Father's Day. Birthday cards account for 60 percent of everyday cards, followed by anniversary, get well, friendship, and sympathy.

The audience for cards is quite clear. Females purchase 80 percent of all cards in general and 85 percent of all Valentines. The industry promotes and endorses special and personal occasions that keep the cards flowing, including "days" for secretaries, bosses, and grandparents. In fact, these personal occasion and "just because" cards hold a majority of the market, even ahead of Christmas. Nearly 87 percent of all card sales fall under the categories of birthday (60 percent of category sales), anniversary, get well, friendship/encouragement, and sympathy. One of the most frequent senders of cards is the United States White House, which sends birthday cards from the current president to citizens over age 80, to newlyweds, and others for approved special occasions.

In short, what was a US$2.9 billion dollar industry in 1988 in the United States grew into an industry with sales of US$5.5 billion in 1997, the last year figures were collected by the U.S. government. This steady, though measured, growth came to a halt at the turn of the century, however. Falling revenues in 2000, 2001, and 2002 for the major players in the card industry, such as Hallmark Inc. and American Greetings, demonstrated that buyers tend to purchase more cards in times of prosperity and economic good news. The volatile dot-com e-card business collapse in 2000 also taught the industry that major losses could be incurred in spite of frequent and repeated customer visits at the "free" card sites. By October of 2001, industry analysts stressed that the September 11 terrorist acts had thrown the greeting card market into further freefall, and though the industry tried to fight back with new lines of patriotic cards, industry-wide losses were expected through 2003. Though unit sales have picked up slightly since then, revenues have remained flat.

According to U.S. government figures, about US$117.8 million worth of U.S. cards were exported in 2004, primarily to Canada, Mexico, Australia, the United Kingdom, and Germany. This was substantially lower than the US$137.2 million exported in 2003 and far below a high of US$152.9 million in 1997. Though the value of U.S. greeting card exports to Canada and Mexico declined from 2003 to 2004, these countries remained the primary destinations for U.S. cards, importing US$90.8 million and US$15.9 million, respectively, in 2004. By contrast, sales to Australia increased in value from only US$1.1 million in 2003 to US$2.0 million in 2004.

Card prices range from US$0.50 to US$10. Though the average price increased from US$2 in 1997 to a range of US$2 to US$4 in 2002, the impact of deep discounting stores helped cut the average price per card to just under US$1 by 2003. In a typical year, a person is likely to receive 20 cards, 8 of them birthday cards. U.S. households purchase about 35 cards annually, and about 90 percent of all households send at least 1 card annually. The GCA publisher member companies account for 90 percent of the industry market share, including independent greeting card publishers, although the top 2 industry giants, Hallmark and American Greetings, dominate with market shares of 50 percent and 35 percent, respectively.

ORGANIZATION AND STRUCTURE

Not that many years ago, one out of every two greeting cards were sold in card shops. In the 1990s that ratio changed to one in three. The change was caused by the growing number of greeting cards sold through mass retailers. Hallmark Cards, Inc. was affected most by this shift, and was forced to close some of its card shops and shift its attention to distribution through third-party retail outlets. American Greetings Corporation and Gibson Greetings Inc. were less affected by this shift as they had traditionally turned to retailers for the distribution of their products. In fact, according to an August 1992 article in *Industry Week,* American Greetings employed the only in-house, full-time sales promotion department in the industry geared to the development of chain-specific promotions and retail traffic.

Industry analysts point to what they call Hallmark's over reliance on its own retail stores for distribution as one reason the company lost market share in the early 1990s. Representing about 42 percent of the market in 1994, Hallmark had claimed 45 percent only five years earlier.

As the marketplace became more diverse, vendors continued to seek new ways of meeting the needs of their customers and increasing sales. Alternative or non-occasion cards were the fastest-growing segment in the greeting card industry. Other significant areas of growth were the senior and Hispanic markets. Environmentalism was another topical issue, the importance of which had not escaped the greeting card industry.

Between 1989 and 1995, employment in the greeting card industry stabilized between 21,000 and 23,000 employees. The industry tends to employ people with creative arts backgrounds, from graphic designers and writers to photographers and printers. Also, the work of many notable writers throughout the years—including Ogden Nash, Charles Dickens, Walt Whitman, Emily Dickinson, Mark Twain, Elizabeth Barrett Browning, and Norman Vincent Peale—has been used in greeting cards. Helen Steiner Rice, who wrote verses for Gibson Greetings (now part of American Greetings), was "discovered" in the 1960s when one of her poems, "The Priceless Gift of Christmas," was read on the Lawrence Welk Show. Greeting cards with her verses were soon in great demand. In 2002, Hallmark started a line of cards under the imprint of famed author and poet Maya Angelou, the Maya Angelou Life Mosaic line. The majority of cards, though, are produced entirely (written, designed, and printed) by employees of the card companies.

According to *VFW Magazine*, Hallmark has successfully reintroduced its Veterans Day card line originally tested in 1985 and 1999. Popularity is accredited to an outpouring of patriotism since September 11 attacks. There were 24 cards in this line available during 2003 including specific cards for Air Force, Army, Coast Guard, Marine Corps, and Navy veterans. Patriotic card lines available throughout the year include congratulations on joining the armed forces, sympathy, and appreciation cards.

BACKGROUND AND DEVELOPMENT

While people have traditionally communicated with each other through permanent or written form, greeting cards as a means of communicating were a relatively new phenomenon, having appeared about a century and a half ago. Historians credit the development of the first Christmas card to Englishman Sir Henry Cole, in 1846. In *The Romance of Greeting Cards*, Ernest Dudley Chase wrote that Cole suggested to Joseph Calcutt Horsley, a Royal Academy artist, that he create a custom Christmas greeting for friends to exchange. Horsley designed such a piece bearing the wish, "A Merry Christmas and a Happy New Year to You," along with a space for the sender to sign. One thousand copies of the card were lithographed, printed, and colored by hand. In the United States, Louis Prang, an exile from the German revolution of 1848, settled in Boston where he started a small lithographic business. In 1866 he perfected a process of multicolor printing and called his printed pieces "Chromos." The expense of this printing process (sometimes involving up to 20 colors) meant that the price of U.S. cards were higher than those produced overseas. Prang began producing Christmas cards in 1874, first placing the cards on the English market and later selling them in the United States. But lower-priced German imports eventually hurt his business and by 1890 he had given it up. While foreign distributors (most notably German) were early players in the greeting card industry, by the early 1900s U.S. producers were poised for market dominance.

The impetus for the development of greeting cards seemed to be the advent of the postage system and the "penny postcard." These early greetings were the forerunner of today's greeting cards and, in fact, Joyce Clyde Hall, the founder of Hallmark, began his career by selling these postcards out of shoe boxes from his room at the YMCA.

By the early 1910s these postcards proliferated. In the United States, Detroit Publishing offered more than 60,000 different cards; in England, the majority were produced by Raphael Tuck and Sons. However, with the onset of World War I, postcard imports from Europe ceased, and the United States soon became the leader in this industry—a position it still held almost a century later in the 1990s.

Early cards focused primarily on Christmas and Valentine's Day. However, the offerings expanded as new holidays were introduced. In 1919, Joyce Clyde Hall recognized the need for cards to commemorate more than holidays and introduced "friendship cards."

In 1921 Hall found himself faced with a legal challenge. He had been provided with a poem which he had used in a Christmas card. Later, the original author asserted that Hall had no right to use the poem. To settle the matter, Hall offered the writer US$500 in cash for the verse. The poem, "A Friend's Greeting," was written by Edgar A. Guest (1881-1959) and turned out to be a best-seller for many years.

By 1939 greeting cards were an US$80 million industry, and by the 1950s the greeting card industry was producing about 5 billion cards annually. The industry grew to US$4 billion in the 1990s. Until 2001, conventional industry belief said that even slow economic times had little impact on the performance of this industry. However, falling sales in the final quarter of 2001 for Hallmark and other brands caused a reevaluation of this truism.

Contributing to the success of the greeting card industry was the continued success of non-occasion cards, with messages such as "sorry you're feeling blue" or "I shouldn't have said what I said." The baby boom generation was credited with the strong sales of these items. Sales of greeting cards in the late 1980s and early 1990s indicated a return to more traditional values according to many greeting card vendors. But as sales of newspapers plunged in the late 1990s and early 2000s, and educators and analysts alike wrung hands over the growing segment of young adult non-readers, the greeting card industry found itself supplementing its traditional cards with warm and fuzzy verses with snappy sight gags and one-line quips, many of them bawdy or even insulting to the reader.

Outside the United States, the greeting card industry has grown more rapidly. Most notable among other countries, India has a burgeoning card market. *The Hindu* reported there have been big changes in the India greeting card market since Archies, now operating online like its western counterparts, came on the scene in 1980. The late 1980s and early 1990s represented a boom time, prompting sales to grow. The ITC Group entered this market with its Expressions brand featuring 784 new designs for Christmas and the New Year available through approximately 12,000 retail outlets in 700 cities. Christmas through New Year is viewed as the most important card season, with nearly 20 percent of sales for the entire year occurring during the period. *The Hindu* also revealed that the greeting card industry contributes significant sums to organizations such as Helpage India and UNICEF. Along with innovative ideas hot in metro areas, industry companies also believe in a "small town market" of customers seeking generic floral patterns and restricted humor.

E-cards were also on the rise. Compared to the way video sales complemented movie theaters, online cards were seen as a positive force in the industry and a driver for printed card sales. Ed Fruchtenbaum, president of American Greeting Cards, said in a 1997 interview with CNN, that the electronic card segment would benefit the traditional sector because of the element of "reciprocity." When a card is received, the person is "likely to respond in e-mail fashion, or you could respond with the traditional greeting cards. So just the way I think videos have prompted people going to movie theaters, I think the whole electronic area will actually prompt more traditional greeting card sending."

Furthermore, GCA reported on a sociological study by Dr. Barry Wellman, professor of sociology at the University of Toronto, and Dr. Keith Hampton, professor of Urban Studies and Planning at the Massachusetts Institute of Technology. The two-year study of a residential Toronto suburb wired with high speed Internet access found the following. "The Internet naturally promotes communication, and of course communication is what relationships are about—and an increased number of relationships is good news for the traditional greeting card market."

Online card centers logged millions of hits per week in the late 1990s. According to Blue Mountain Arts General Manager Bob Gall, the company's site registered more than 10 million hits per day in 1996, and the company estimated 225 million hits per day in 1997. According to Derek Hoffman, who runs Electronic Postcards' site, electronic cards are inexpensive and practical. "Costs involved for postcard sites are in setting the site up, [and] in designing the cards." Not all online offerings were free. Sites such as Hallmark's Connections offer both free cards and cards for purchase by credit card. Americangreetings.com started off as a free site but then initiated a membership fee. In the early 2000s it had more than 2 million subscribers and also generated sales from advertising. Users can send greeting cards via e-mail plus create and print hard copies.

Many free Internet card sites were paid for by revenues generated via advertising banners. While approximately one-third (37 percent) of U.S. households paid for Internet access at the end of 1998 (although that access was higher given school, library, and work access), this figure was estimated to be 58 percent by 2003, according to Inteco. Thus, far more people are likely to purchase a store-bought card than fire off an Internet greeting card. This trend was impacted by fears related to computer viruses. About 100,000 outlets offer consumers cards in the United States, according to the GCA. Nonetheless, Internet family news sites such as Myfamily.com send automatic reminders to friends and family each time a member's birthday rolls around, allowing other members to send a greeting in just a few clicks.

Industry analysts estimate that there were approximately 1,500 greeting card manufacturers in the industry in 1997 and nearly 2,000 in 2002, a far cry from the mere 100 in business in 1941 when the GCA was founded. Through the years, three major companies continued to dominate the market. Known as the "Big Three," Hallmark Cards, American Greetings, and Gibson Greetings (now owned by American Greetings) captured 85 percent of the U.S. market in the mid-1990s and had sizable presence in a number of other countries. Smaller companies had a difficult time competing against these giants and were frequently acquired or merged with another small company. In the 1990s, overall industry growth was a stable but uninspiring 2 percent per year. Between 2000 and 2002, however, the major card companies would have cheered for even slow growth.

TWENTY-FIRST CENTURY TRENDS

Distribution patterns began to expand from card and gift shops to include drugstores, supermarkets, and discount stores. This change was attributed to increasing consumer demand for convenience and one-stop shopping. The demographics of the industry also began to change. While women had traditionally been the primary purchasers of greeting cards, representing about 90 percent of the market, the industry was attempting to reach beyond this market to attract younger customers and male customers. By 2005, mass retail stores were the fastest growing retail distribution channel for U.S. greeting cards, particularly for major companies. Smaller independent card makers, on the other hand, saw better sales growth through specialty stores or the Internet.

By 2001 many Internet card companies instituted an annual charge for unlimited cards, a decision which quickly resulted in a significant drop in access by those who wanted something for nothing. According to Jupiter Media Metrix, visits to sites maintained by American Greetings (the most-accessed Web provider of e-cards with an Internet presence at Americangreetings.com, Bluemountain.com and Egreetings.com) dropped 10 percent in December 2001 to 22.9 million (compared to 25.5 million in November 2001), ordinarily the biggest card-sending period. Furthermore, sites with free greeting cards and no subscription fees saw a good portion of that lost traffic come to them. For example, visits to Yahoo! Greetings and Hallmark.com increased 70 and 74 percent, respectively, from November to December 2001. Some of the smaller online greeting card companies, such as California-based Getacard.com, announced that they were available for sale in the early 2000s.

On the other hand, some small card manufacturers saw the opportunity to capture important niche markets in the early 2000s. Several start-up companies aimed to attract customers from ethnic groups, women, religious denominations, or other markets not well-served by leading card makers. Lyrics2go, for instance, offered greetings influenced by hip-hop culture; it also incorporated new technology that made its cards play 10 seconds of music when they opened. Founder Ron Williams explained in a *USA Today* article that he wanted to create cards that "speak the way that I speak." Still a tiny part of the greeting card market in 2005, small independent companies were selling primarily through the Internet.

While e-cards continued to affect greeting card sales, the growing popularity of text-messaging was seen as a further threat to revenues. As an industry executive told *Asia Times* about the market in India, "The main reason why mobile phone users are adapting to the messaging culture is cost. A simple paper greeting card is 10 times the price of an SMS [short messaging service] message. The cost and speed of the service are turning people away form the plain old greeting cards."

The greeting card industry in the United Kingdom generated about 1 billion pounds (about US$1.7 billion) annually in the early 2000s. More than 2 billion cards are sent there each year, making per capita sales the highest in the world by volume. The average U.K. consumer spends 20 pounds (US$34.75) each year on greeting cards, and in turn receives 55 cards annually.

CURRENT CONDITIONS

Despite the competition from the Internet and other electronic media, the paper greeting card industry was alive and well in the latter mid-2000s. According to the Bureau of Economic Analysis, Americans spent US$11.5 billion on cards in the first three quarters of 2006, a figure that does not include Christmas card sales for the year. The Greeting Card Association reported in 2007 that 90 percent of American households purchase at least one card per year, and on average each family purchases 30 cards a year.

The latter mid-2000s saw the two major American greeting card companies taking steps to remain competitive and innovative. In 2007, Hallmark added two new lines of cards. The New Relationship line, targeted to Valentine's Day buyers, addressed things other than romantic love and included more cards with a humorous message. The Journey line of cards addressed illnesses and situations that had been ignored by greeting card companies in the past, including cancer and eating disorders. Other unique situations for which one could offer thoughts, support, and condolences were quitting smoking, miscarriages, caring for aging parents, loved ones in the military, and traumatic loss. The 176-card line could be purchased only Hallmark Gold Crown stores but may be available for purchase in drug stores in the future, according to a company spokesperson.

The most successful product launch made by Hallmark in 2006 was its line of sound cards. The lines includes 23 cards and cover birthday, anniversary, friendship, and "thinking of you." Each card includes a sound clip that plays 15 to 45 seconds of music when the card is opened. Some examples of songs used in the cards included "Wonderful World" by Louis Armstrong and "All Star" by Smash Mouth.

Marking its 100th anniversary in 2007, American Greetings launched a US$100 million merchandising program called "Winning at Cards," featuring hundreds of new cards that the company hoped were more relevant to their main buyers—women. Three new lines were introduced, known as Share a Laugh (humor), Share your Style (trends), and Lift Your Spirit (inspirational). The company also planned to sell noncard merchandise such as jewelry and envelope seals, placed next to the greeting card sections of stores.

American Greetings' fastest growing segment in 2007 was AG Interactive, which that year had 3.4 million paid subscribers on four Web sites (AmericanGreetings. com, BlueMountain.com, Egreetings.com, and one other site). In addition to electronic greeting cards, the division offered products for instant messaging and mobile platforms. Sales for AG Interactive alone in 2006 totaled $89.6 million.

INDUSTRY LEADERS

HALLMARK CARDS, INC.

Hallmark's slogan, "When you care enough to send the very best," was created in 1954 from the writings of C.E. Goodman, a former Hallmark sales vice president. It had been identified several times through independent research as one of the most believed advertising slogans in the United States. Accompanied by the company's five-point crown logo, the slogan had become a familiar trademark for a well-established company.

By the late 1990s, the privately owned Hallmark held 42 percent of the U.S. greeting card market. This figure remained steady since 1994, as the company outpaced American Greetings' market share. Hallmark published 20,700 cards in more than 30 languages in approximately 100 countries, making it the undisputed leader in the greeting card market. However, the company's market share declined in the early 2000s, owing to what some analysts believe was an overreliance on its own retail stores for distribution, rather than distributing cards through drugstores and other outlets as the other major players do.

Hallmark's lines of cards included the humorous Shoe Box Greetings, its traditional Hallmark Crown, and the newer Windows (recordable greetings). In addition, Hallmark operated a separate division, Ambassador Cards, that was by itself the number three card maker in the United States. Hallmark also was a leading producer of gift wrap, Christmas ornaments, wedding products, and related gift items. Hallmark also owns crayon manufacturer Crayola and offers electronic greeting cards and flowers through its Web site. Hallmark products were showcased by 43,000 retailers across the United States in 2007, 4,000 of which were Hallmark Gold Crown stores. The company is two-thirds owned by the founding Hall family, and the remaining third of the company is owned by the employees themselves. In 2006, the company employed more than 18,000 workers around the world, and controlled more than 50 percent of the U.S. greeting card market. Hallmark Cards had 2006 consolidated revenues of US$4.2 billion.

Hallmark was founded in 1910 by Joyce Clyde Hall, in a room at the Kansas City YMCA where the 18-year-old entrepreneur sold picture postcards from two shoe boxes. Joined by his brother Rollie in 1911, Hall added greeting cards to the line in 1912 and opened Hall Brothers, a store selling postcards, gifts, books, and stationery. The store was destroyed by fire in 1915, but the Halls persevered. Obtaining a loan, they purchased an engraving company and were able to produce their first original greeting cards in time for the Christmas season. A third brother, William, joined the company in 1920. By 1922 the Hall brothers had salespeople in all 48 states and employed 120 people. Prior to 1936 greeting cards had been kept under counters or in drawers. That year, the Hall brothers patented the "Eye-Vision" display case and sold it to retailers across the country.

Hallmark grew rapidly after World War II, opening its first retail store in 1950 and broadcasting the first "Hallmark Hall of Fame" in 1951. The company's name was changed to Hallmark Cards in 1954 and overseas sales were implemented in 1957. Joyce Hall died at the age of 91 in 1982; his son Donald J. Hall became chairman of the company the following year. Joyce Hall played a pivotal role in the company until his death; personally approving every new card produced by Hallmark until he was in his late seventies.

Eventually, Hallmark built a network of card shops, which became its primary means of distribution. Of the 10,000 shops, 216 were company owned; the remainder were owned and run by independent operators. Hallmark's Kansas City headquarters occupied more than 2 million square feet. The facility was adjacent to Crown Center, an 85-acre redevelopment project on the southern edge of downtown Kansas City. Launched in 1968, Crown Center intended to rejuvenate the area surrounding the Hallmark headquarters.

By the late 1990s, Hallmark concentrated its production in three Kansas cities—Lawrence, Leavenworth, and Topeka—and in Kansas City, Missouri. Distribution centers in Connecticut, Missouri, California, and New York handled the shipping of cards to more than 100 countries. Hallmark employees numbered more than 12,000, and in 1996 the company posted sales of US$3.6 billion. Sales sagged in 2001, as the worldwide economy slumped.

Introduced in 1994, the Hallmark Gold Crown Card was the first consumer-reward program in the greeting card industry. It is one of the largest loyalty programs in the United States, with more than 13 million active members.

In the May 29, 2004, issue of *The New Zealand Herald*, journalist Colin Taylor applauded Hallmark for its transformation "from a big industrial ugly duckling into a sleek and downsized corporate swan" by implementing "just in time warehousing." Turnaround for the new system is 24 hours, and the need for massive inventory is eliminated by gathering information, placing orders, and sending out items immediately to customers. This new business model allows for stock stored in Australia to also be sold in New Zealand. As a result, approximately 2,000 more products are available than were previously stored in New Zealand.

AMERICAN GREETINGS

The number two position in the greeting card industry belonged to Cleveland-based American Greetings Corp. In addition to greeting cards, which made up almost 60 percent of its sales in the mid-2000s, American Greetings manufactured and sold gift items, gift wrap, and party supplies. Cards were marketed through drug stores, supermarkets, and large retail stores. In 2006 American Greetings had 29,500 employees and total sales of US$1.8 billion.

In 2000, the company faced widespread criticism and even ridicule in the media after announcing massive layoffs and losses just 30 days after predicting it would achieve massive growth in coming months and years. Instead, American Greetings saw its market value bottom out in a single day, falling from US$1.3 billion to US$746 million. The losses led to layoffs of 1,500, and each share of American Greeting stock fell from US$45 to US$11 at the end of 2001.

More than 125,000 retail outlets worldwide sell American Greetings products. The company also has a major share in mass market and grocery retailers—the fastest growing channels for greeting cards.

American Greetings has wholly owned subsidiaries in the United Kingdom, Canada, Australia, New Zealand, France, and Mexico. It owns 80 percent of S.A. Greeting in South Africa and has licensees in 70 other countries.

One of American Greetings' most successful years was 1995, when it jettisoned the unprofitable Carlton Cards division, its major U.K. brand, and purchased a major card publisher in South Africa. In 1996, American Greetings acquired John Sands, the top card publisher in Australia and New Zealand, and even made an abortive effort to acquire its rival, Gibson, a goal it eventually would reach three years later.

American Greetings traces its beginnings back to 1906, when Jacob Sapirstein (the family later changed its name to Stone) began a card wholesaling business in his Cleveland home, eventually selling postcards from a horse-drawn wagon. His three young sons—Irving, Morrie, and Harry—eventually joined the business and, by 1932, Jacob was producing his own cards.

The company name of American Greetings Publishers was introduced in 1940, and the company went public in 1952. Holly Hobbie was introduced in 1977, Ziggy in 1972, and the Care Bears in 1982—the same year American Greetings first made the *Fortune* 500 list. Jacob died in 1987, and Morry Weiss (Irving's son-in-law) became CEO of the company. Irving was still serving as "founder-chairman" in 1998, at the age of 89. American Greetings had offices and production facilities in Canada, France, Ireland, Mexico, England, and the United States, and controlled about 35 percent of the greeting card industry in 1997.

In 1997 the company set its sights on purchasing the number three greeting cards giant, Gibson Greetings Inc., which posted 1997 sales of US$397.2 million, a 2 percent growth from 1996 figures. Gibson had struggled in the mid-1990s, posting losses of US$28.6 million in 1994 and US$46.5 million in 1995. Initially, the firm fended off American Greetings' takeover attempts, believing it could turn itself around. By late 1999, though, the struggling company had been fully acquired by American Greetings.

In 2001, American Greetings posted US$113.8 million in losses on US$2.5 billion in sales. That year, the firm announced its intent to compete intensely in the Internet greeting card arena, purchasing Bluemountain.com for US$35 million. This was perhaps a bargain, in that Bluemountain.com was sold to Excite@Home for US$1 billion in 1999, the booming days of dot-com profits. By 2005, American Greetings led in the online greetings segment through its AG Interactive division, which operated AmericanGreetings.com, BlueMountain.com, BlueMountainCards.co.uk, Egreetings.com, and MIDIRingTones.com. AG Interactive reported more than 2 million paying subscribers in 2005.

In 2004, Americangreetings.com announced a special campaign offering Mother's Day Cards featuring art by Alzheimer's patients. The artwork was paired with encouraging, inspirational messages. They were sponsored by Janssen Pharmaceutica Products L.P., makers of REMINYL. That medication is prescribed for treatment of mild to moderate Alzheimer's disease. Art was provided by the Alvin A. Dubin Alzheimer's Center.

FURTHER READING

"Can't say it? Post it!" *The Hindu,* 5 June 2004.

Carter, Julie. "Hallmark with Cards." *VFW Magazine,* November 2003.

Desjardins, Doug. "Greeting Cards Get Innovative for 2007." *Drug Store News,* 11 December 2006.

"Everyone's Buying Cards Again." *MMR,* 20 February 2006.

Flynn, Susan Keen. "From the Mailbox to the Inbox." *Inside Business,*February 2007.

Grant, Lorrie. "Little Guys Take on Greeing Card Giants." *USA Today,* 16 June 2005.

"The Facts About Greeting Cards." Greeting Card Association, 2004. Available at http://greetingcard.org.

"Greetings and Sales-utations." *Gifts & Decorative Accessories,* 1 April 2007.

"Hallmark Breaks New Ground." *Chain Drug Review,* 5 March 2007.

Hoover's Company Capsules. Hoover's Inc., 2007. Available from www.hoovers.com.

"Net a Viable Venue for Cards." *MMR,* 20 February 2006.

"New Twists Enliven Greeting Cards Arena." *Chain Drug Review,* 5 February 2007.

Taylor, Colin. "Slimming Works for Card Giant." *The New Zealand Herald,* 29 May 2004.

"Top 25 Export Destinations for Greeting Cards." U.S. Department of Commerce, 2005. Available from http://http://www.ita.doc.gov.

SIC 7375

NAICS 518111

INFORMATION RETRIEVAL SERVICES

Information retrieval services supply textual, numeric, and graphic data, usually in the form of searchable databases, to their customers electronically via CD-ROM and online services. Internet-only access services are discussed separately under the title **Internet Services**, and firms that provide other services related to information technology are covered under **Information Technology Services**.

INDUSTRY SNAPSHOT

Information retrieval services make information easier to access, understand, and use. They allow individuals, with the press of a few keys on a keyboard or the click of a mouse, for example, to quickly explore archives of material that might otherwise take hours or days to search and locate using traditional cataloging systems. Furthermore, information services permit people and organizations to provide and access remote data, update information regularly, efficiently communicate and complete transactions with customers and service providers throughout the world, and reduce consumption of paper, among other benefits.

Commercial information retrieval services emerged in the 1970s and were barely recognized as an industry by the early 1980s. During the mid-1980s, though, the segment realized explosive growth. This growth was the result of technological advances related to personal computers, computer networks, modems, and improved data storage devices. However, due to the growth of the Internet in the mid-1990s, the information retrieval industry experienced a number of changes. News and newspaper and periodical web sites drove a number of small information retrieval services such as NewsNet out of business by the late 1990s. In addition, information retrieval services began to consolidate and change corporate owners. Leading services including Lexis-Nexis and Dialog were sold during this period. Nonetheless, by the mid-2000s demand remained strong and the outlook was positive for information retrieval services with large aggregated databases and strong name recognition such as Dow Jones News/Retrieval and Lexis-Nexis; expanding markets also exist for services that target specific information niches.

By the mid-2000s, the information retrieval industry continued to face the prospect of further consolidation. In addition, industry players competed in an environment characterized by leaner library budgets. However, information providers benefited from the fact that libraries were purchasing greater shares of electronic versus print content.

One trend heading into the second half of the 2000s was the convergence of databases, in that information seekers desired one simple point of access for searching. This was evident in the increased use of federated or meta-searching, in which technology allowed users to search across multiple databases at once for information. In addition, there were signs that popular Internet search engines such as Google would converge with premium databases in some form.

Most information providers were also expanding on their abilities to provide users with data in real time. This was being demanded more, particularly by corporate users. The financial industry, including online brokerages, were also providing an increasing amount of real time data to their clients.

ORGANIZATION AND STRUCTURE

The information retrieval industry encompasses a diverse mosaic of organizations offering a plethora of services. That extreme diversity stems from the fact that the industry, just beginning to mature in the 2000s, is influenced by rapid changes in technology, ease of entry, and an almost infinite array of unfilled market niches. Companies or individuals that can figure out how to fill or create a need in the market using existing technology can profit, often with only a minor capital investment. Creativity, knowledge of a market need, and technological expertise are the greatest limitations. Thus, industry participants range from large online services with millions of customers to individual entrepreneurs who compile and sell information to a small base of customers. Despite this diversity, a handful of large online service providers garner the bulk of industry revenues.

Types of Information. Most information service offerings can be categorized as either business/research or personal. Business/research information retrieval services primarily offer numeric and bibliographic data concerning both technical and topical information. Most companies in this segment compile data from primary sources and reconfigure it for electronic accessibility. Firms that generate proprietary data, such as mutual fund performance or electronic training manuals, are usually classified in their respective industries. Companies may offer abstracts and text from periodicals, books, and journals, or financial and trade data, press releases, news updates, and historical company/industry information. Some companies simply obtain unwieldy, publicly available government data and repackage it into an easily accessible, understandable electronic format.

The largest business/research segments are legal and investment data. Marketing, scientific, and library information services also comprise a large portion of this market. The remainder of the sector serves a variety of niche markets. For instance, services can be tailored specifically to one industry or profession, such as chemical, healthcare, civil engineering, agricultural, banking, insurance, or food service. In addition, many niche services are managed by nonprofit organizations. Major players on the business side of the industry 2005 included North American firms Thomson, Dun & Bradstreet, Bloomberg L.P., ProQuest and Dow Jones. Major players outside of North America included Reuters (United Kingdom), Wolters Kluwer (Netherlands), and Deutsche Presse-Agentur (Germany).

Like business/research information offerings, electronic information services targeting the consumer market may provide current news and financial information. In addition, they typically offer features such as electronic shopping, recreational bulletin boards and other interpersonal communication domains, weather and sports data, encyclopedias, games, travel information, home and garden advice, and thousands of other offerings. In comparison to business information services, most personal systems are inexpensive, primarily because of the number of users in the market. For instance, many consumer-oriented online services allow subscribers unlimited access for less than US$20 per month. In contrast, the effective rate for many business-oriented information databases can exceed several thousand dollars per month.

Market emphasis is reflected by the number of databases offered for each segment. The 2002 edition of the Gale Directory of Databases, which provides a listing of 14,250 databases from around the world, showed that in 2001 some 3,075, or 24 percent, were targeted at business consumers. Some 2,340, or 18 percent, were categorized in the science/technology/engineering sector, which was followed by general information databases at 1,578, or 12 percent. Following general databases, in descending order, were law, health/life sciences, humanities, social sciences, multidisciplinary academic, and finally news. In 2002 Gale alone maintained more than 600 databases, according to the company corporate web site.

Media. The primary means of delivering electronic information services are online systems and CD-ROM. Other media include magnetic diskette, magnetic tape, and audiotext. Consumers access online systems with a modem, a device that allows a computer to send and receive information. Customers usually access a central data bank of information by calling a local telephone number. In addition to the central data bank, most online service providers also supply access to other services and data sources, including communications networks (e.g., bulletin boards where users can communicate with each other). The service provider may charge the customer a flat monthly rate for unlimited access or for the length of time they use the database, the amount of information that they access and print, or the type of information they use. Lexis-Nexis in the 2000s began offering a service to the general public that enabled a potential customer to purchase a single article on demand for a small fee.

One advantage that online systems have is that the medium is especially appropriate for consumers who require up-to-the-minute information. Database managers can continually update information related to stock quotes and other financial data, legal rulings and court proceedings, sporting events, world news, and other variable subjects. Online systems are also advantageous because they allow access to massive amounts of information that would be difficult or impossible for customers to maintain in-house. In fact, the most popular online services offer a conglomeration of individual databases, communication services, and products that can be searched simultaneously. The disadvantage of online services in the late 1990s through 2000s was high cost. Expenses related to collecting timely information, accessing phone lines, and supporting sophisticated data storage and networking equipment can require immense overhead. Customers who access large amounts of tax and legal information, for example, may pay as much as tens of thousands of dollars per month in online charges.

In contrast to online services, CD-ROM products allow customers to store and retrieve information on their own computers using photo-optical technology. Data providers can store hundreds of thousands of pages of data on a single CD, on which customers are able to search and retrieve information. CD-ROM products offer the advantage of relatively low cost in comparison to online systems. The cost of a CD-ROM product can range as low as US$80 or less for the equivalent of an entire set of encyclopedias, for example, or as high as several thousand dollars for an annual subscription to some business CD-ROM services.

CD-ROM also allows users to more easily retrieve photographs and animated images. Additionally, customers may benefit from unlimited access to information at a fixed price; however, some CD vendors incorporate lock systems that limit the amount of information that can be retrieved and, similar to the online model, sell additional increments of information for extra fees. One disadvantage of CD-ROM products is lack of timely data. Because disks are often delivered monthly or quarterly by mail, information is usually less current than that available online.

Floppy disk and magnetic tape systems are similar to CD-ROM retrieval devices but are at a disadvantage in storage capacity, cost, and portability. Audiotext services allow customers to access voice-transmitted information, such as sports scores, via a fee-based telephone number, such as the 900 prefix in the United States. The consumer is charged, often between US$0.50 and US$5 per minute, for his or her call.

BACKGROUND AND DEVELOPMENT

The information retrieval services industry began in the United States during the post-World War II information explosion. The advent of computers during this period allowed the channeling of large amounts of data to scientists, engineers, businesses, and government agencies. U.S. government investments in new information technologies in the

1950s and 1960s were supplemented by increased private sector spending on research and higher education. The net result of research and development efforts was that, for the first time, scientists and researchers could create, store, and quickly access large amounts of data electronically.

The purpose of the earliest retrieval systems was simply to store and print information, mostly for scientific and technical endeavors. As the number and size of the databases grew, systems engineers began to focus on searching capabilities that could filter out unneeded data. Eventually, users were able to type commands into a computer that would search out and display information containing specific keywords or phrases. The first computerized bibliographic database systems stemmed from the U.S. government's need for efficient application of research dollars and the desire to eliminate duplicate analyses. Some of the more popular databases developed in this period included MEDLINE, NASA/RECON, and ERIC. The U.S. government also subsidized nonprofit efforts, such as the American Chemical Society's chemical abstracts database.

In addition to supporting nonprofit services, investments by the United States and later Western European governments in the 1960s and 1970s initiated many of the private information retrieval services that dominated the market in the 1980s and early 1990s. For instance, Dialog, a U.S. online information service, began from a venture between the U.S. National Aeronautics and Space Administration (NASA) and U.S.-based Lockheed Corporation; the venture was called Project RECON. ORBIT Information Technologies, another dominant force in the industry, was developed as a result of U.S.-based System Development Corporation's work with the U.S. National Library of Medicine. As another example, industry giant Mead Data Central (later renamed the Lexis-Nexis Group), also of the United States, got its start from seed money provided by U.S. Air Force projects.

Federal governments in the United States, Western Europe, and Japan also played pivotal roles in developing telecommunications networks that made online services possible. Networks like Tymnet and Telnet, which essentially provide affordable online access for database users through local telephone lines, stemmed from U.S. Department of Defense (DOD) efforts. Called ARPAnet, in 1969 the DOD created a network to connect their many computers across the country. In the early 1980s, ARPAnet was connected to an expanding number of other networks. This resulting network is known today as the Internet, which by 2000 was accessed by 200 million users all over the world. As more efficient telecommunications networks arose and computer technology advanced in the late 1960s and 1970s, a significant commercial market for electronic information services began to emerge. Companies and libraries increasingly relied on technical and electronic legal and scientific information to provide a competitive edge in the marketplace or to make their research efforts more efficient. Furthermore, some users were finding electronic information access to be an important tool for increasing business productivity.

As electronic markets began to grow, many publishing houses began to experiment with electronic publishing as a means of delivering their information. H.W. Wilson and Company of the United States began delivering documents online through WILSONLINE. Likewise, McGraw-Hill and other periodical publishers began offering their publications online. One of the greatest commercial uses of electronic information was for legal research. Lexis, a legal database Mead began offering in 1973, averaged 43 percent annual growth throughout the 1970s and 1980s.

By the end of the 1970s the emerging information retrieval services industry was beginning to establish itself in many sectors of government, academia, and industry. Because of technical limitations, however, the services remained extremely costly. Furthermore, most systems were complicated and required professional research skills for effective use. For example, a database might use a highly structured query language that users had to learn in order to take advantage of its powerful features. As a result, estimated industry revenues were still well under US$500 million by 1980.

Technological breakthroughs in personal computers and data storage devices fueled rapid industry growth beginning in the mid-1980s. At the same time that microcomputers were becoming smaller and faster, users were becoming accustomed to working with modems, computer networks, and other communications technology that allowed large numbers of people to gain access to reservoirs of data. For the first time, information providers were able to expand their services to the end user—the person who actually uses the information—rather than professional researchers.

As end users became the target market for information services, industry participants began to emphasize user-friendly system interfaces that allowed easier data searching and access. Those firms were also quick to take advantage of new data retrieval technologies. For instance, online services were able to gradually increase modem communication speeds from 1,200 bits per second (bps), to 2,400 bps, and finally to 4,800 bps in the late 1980s (modem speeds rose considerably faster in the 1990s and 2000s). As technology advanced, computer equipment prices and online charges began to fall dramatically, a development which began to unlock the massive small business and home information markets. The commercial manufacture and distribution of high-tech storage devices such as CD-ROM drives also strengthened industry revenues. Furthermore, as consumers became comfortable with information services and began to realize their benefit, more users began accessing greater amounts of data.

As new markets emerged, information service companies began to expand their offerings, and huge numbers of new competitors entered the fray. Online information "supermarkets" like Dialog evolved where users could access hundreds of specialized databases covering thousands of publications. Likewise, information "boutiques" that offered simultaneous online access to multiple databases and services for one particular industry or profession emerged. Individual niche services flourished as well. Between 1987 and 1992, the number of electronic databases available internationally leapt from 3,369 to over 9,000. By 1990 worldwide industry revenues had jumped to approximately US$10 billion.

Information retrieval service companies continued to post solid sales gains averaging about 15 percent annually during the early 1990s, despite a worldwide economic slowdown. The number of people subscribing to online services skyrocketed to nearly 8 million in 1993 after falling about 20 percent annually in 1991 and 1992. Business and professional services continued to represent about 95 percent of all sales in the online segment, but consumer services were posting the greatest annual gains—27 percent in 1993. Fast growing online markets during the early 1990s included consumers of medical, legal, and investment information. Online services continued to account for the bulk of industry receipts (about 70 percent) during the early 1990s.

A more notable contribution to worldwide gains than online services was the CD-ROM market. Following their commercial introduction in 1985, CD-ROM services grew relatively slowly. Largely because of the high cost of CD-ROM systems, the technology was utilized primarily in libraries, institutions, and larger corporations during the late 1980s. Between 1985 and 1990 the price of CD-ROM disk drives plummeted 50 percent to around US$1,000 and the average cost of a CD-ROM with information fell from about US$1,000 to US$400. By 1993 the average cost of a CD-ROM drive and disk had declined to a more marketable US$400 and US$75, respectively. Suddenly, the technology was within easy grasp of small businesses and even individual consumers. The result was that the number of CD-ROM drives installed globally ballooned from less than 1 million in the early 1990s to 6 million by 1993. By 1994 more than 20 million CD-ROM drives were in use worldwide.

In the late 1990s the information retrieval service industry underwent changes as it attempted to adapt to the business environment of the period. Companies in the industry began expanding their services and increasing their assets to win over more customers. *Library Journal* predicted that many online information retrieval services would survive after recasting themselves and identifying their place in the information market. Large international companies with massive collections, numerous services, and many customers throughout the world were expected to have the best chances of succeeding, while small companies offering articles from a limited number of newspapers targeting the general consumer would face the most severe challenges.

Because of the changing market for information retrieval services, the industry experienced a consolidation spree at the end of the decade. In December of 1997, Market Analysis and Information Database PLC (M.A.I.D.) bought Knight-Ridder Information, Inc., and laid off 25 percent of its staff. M.A.I.D. renamed the company Dialog Corporation, and it subsequently was sold to The Thomson Corporation. NewsNet and UMI/Data Times also changed hands in 1997. Throughout the decade many of the leading information retrieval services were bought and sold, including Dialog, DataStar, Information Access Company, Lexis-Nexis, Westlaw, ORBIT, and BRS.

The company sales and consolidations stemmed from the increasing competition information retrieval services encountered from the Internet's World Wide Web. The Web allows users to access sources such as the *New York Times* or the *Wall Street Journal* directly without having to go through an intermediary such as Lexis-Nexis and pay information retrieval service fees, although newspapers and magazines may charge fees of their own for searching and retrieving information from their site archives. NewsNet, for example, discontinued its full-text information retrieval service in August 1997 in part because it could no longer generate revenues to sustain itself with competition from Internet news sites.

Small information retrieval services such as NewsNet could not provide a marketable service by simply offering press releases and a limited amount of newspaper and magazine articles, because most newspapers and magazines offered searchable web sites of their own and companies such as the Associated Press made press releases available. Data Times also had the same fate as NewsNet. In 1996, after UMI Company purchased Data Times, an online information retrieval service with full-text regional newspaper articles, to expand its presence in the business and corporate market, the company terminated the Data Times service in late 1997.

Companies such as UMI (now a brand of Proquest), realized the difficulties of entering new markets as they tried to expand their market presence. Instead of developing products for the corporate market segment, UMI reached an agreement with Dow Jones to blend its core product ProQuest, which had an academic, public, and school library focus, with Dow Jones News/Retrieval, with its business and corporate focus. The accord allows both companies to focus on their core businesses and gain access to peripheral markets.

CD-ROM-based information retrieval services grew by the greatest rates in the late 1990s, while the growth of online-based services cooled down in part because of the Internet. By the late 1990s the average cost of a CD-ROM drive fell below US$200 and the average cost of a CD-ROM product had slipped under US$25 (although business databases still ranged into the thousands of dollars). As a result, CD-ROM drives had become standard equipment in most personal computers sold in North America, Japan, and Western Europe by late 1994, fueling a proliferation of CD-ROM information services for both business and consumer markets. CD-ROM growth in relation to online service offerings was reflected by database statistics. General consumers are the world's leading CD-ROM service customers. In 1992, 65 percent of all electronic databases worldwide were provided online, while CD-ROM comprised only 15 percent of the market. By 1997 the figures had changed to 49 percent and 30 percent, respectively. Nevertheless, online information services retained a competitive advantage over CD-ROM versions, namely timeliness.

The information retrieval industry continued to grow at rapid pace in the late 1990s as witnessed in the number and type of databases. Between 1994 and 1997 the number of database products/services rose from 8,778 to 10,338. The number of database vendors rose from 1,691 to 2,115 during the same period. However, the rise in the number of databases fails to show the huge rise in the amount of information supplied by the database segment of the information services industry. Largely because of improved technology related to data storage as well as data transmission and retrieval speed, the total number of electronic database records in the world shot up from 2 billion to 11 billion between 1987 and 1997. However, just before and after the U.S. Supreme Court decided the Tasini case against the *New York Times* in 2001, hundreds of thousands of articles (no accurate count is available) that were written by freelancers or might have been written by freelance writers were pulled from host sites.

North American competitors benefit from immediate access to the largest, most-saturated computer and information technology market in the world. Only a few Western European nations come close to matching U.S. computer use, and the United States continued to bolster its lead. In 1998, for example, computer penetration exceeded 40 percent in the United States, compared to about 35 percent in many Western European nations. However, Western Europe was investing heavily in information technologies and some nations were gaining on the United States. In fact, by late 2002 *Nua Internet Surveys* estimated that the United States ranked third among the world's 605.6 million Internet users, at 182.7 million. Europe was the world leader with 190.9 million users, followed by the Asia/Pacific region (187.2 million users).

CURRENT CONDITIONS

By 2005, the convergence from print to electronic information delivery was continuing. Thomson, for example had witness a 1 to 2 percent growth in its revenues from electronic products, while 98 percent of its financial products were available electronically. This met the growing trend by corporations, particularly those in the financial sector, for data provided in real time.

The shift to providing data electronically was also evident at the world's libraries, large purchases of the information retrieval industries services and products. Some 30 years after the introduction of services like LexisNexis and Dialog, libraries were purchasing greater shares of their holdings in electronic formats. This critical shift was changing the very dynamics of how libraries operated. As George R. Plosker noted in the November-December issue of *Online,* virtually all library services have been affected by technology, from cataloging, circulation, and document delivery to interlibrary loans, the reference desk, and even the training provided to library staff.

According to Plosker, the widespread adoption of the Internet by consumers and businesses alike served to quicken the rate at which technology affected libraries. "Changing user expectations and needs have resulted in new models of library service—use of print and actual visits to the reference desk are down; remote usage of library services is up; and instructional models have gone through major revisions both in approach and curriculum," he explained. "The roles of users, librarians, publishers, and vendors have all been impacted."

The use of popular Internet search engines was a hot topic within the information retrieval industry during the mid-2000s. A wide range of people, from students to learned professionals, relied on the search engines of Google and Yahoo! to meet their research needs. In fact, by 2004 Google was used for some 290 million searches every day. This was a point of concern among some within the information retrieval industry, who noted that premium databases provided results of greater breadth and quality. However, it appeared that some form of convergence might occur. In the January 2004 issue of *Information Today,* Thomson/Gale President Allen Paschal indicated that in 2004, the industry could see search engines "invading the traditional space of the premium and proprietary database providers. They will expand by integrating premium, relevant content in the initial search instead of just linking to Web sites." In 2003, Thomson/Gale formed a partnership with Google in which the search engine's technology could be used within Gale's databases to perform image searches. In addition, functionality was incorporated into Microsoft Office 2003 that provided users with the ability to search for business information from within the software interface, as opposed to requiring the user to perform a separate Web search.

These trends reflected the changing needs of researchers and casual information seekers alike, who desired one simple point of access for searching. This was evident in the increased use of federated or meta-searching, in which technology allowed users to search across multiple databases at once for information. In one respect, this made searching within premium databases similar to searching on the Web. In 2004, MuseGlobal Inc. unveiled MuseSeek, a new consumer-oriented meta-search tool designed for incorporation into other software applications. MuseSeek allowed users to select different information sources via a simple checkbox interface and then perform standard keyword-type searches across those sources.

The advent of meta searching was reflected in the observations of Factiva President and CEO Clare Hart. In the January 2004 issue of *Information Today,* Hart explained that advancements in technology, such as extensible markup language (XML), were removing barriers that separated stores of information and providing users with more valuable results. Hart dubbed such technologies as "the great equalizers of information," and indicated that their benefits included "unlocking content stores, revealing previously unknown information, and linking it to related information stored both within an organization and in other places, such as the Web or commercial information services. Organizations that put these technologies to use as part of their information strategy will gain competitive advantage."

Indeed, to fill a void for news and business information on corporate intranets and help companies gain a competitive advantage, LexisNexis introduced several products during the early 2000s that enabled companies to integrate their proprietary corporate content with relevant outside resources. These included LexisNexis Intranet Publisher and LexisNexis Web Publisher.

In 2005, information retrieval services operated in an industry that was marked by consolidation. While smooth product integration and too much focus on the financial aspect of mergers were of concern to some customers within the library market, others saw consolidation as a positive trend, given that new and better products sometimes resulted. In any case, information retrieval companies were pressed to deliver maximum value to end users, since lean library budgets were a reality. However, some observers indicated that in a climate of reduced resources, providers of e-books and online databases would benefit from increased sales. This would result from increased sales of electronic products, in lieu of comparatively more expensive printed resources.

The Internet. The Internet continued to pose a formidable challenge to the industry in 2005. The growth and mass appeal of the Internet had shaken the industry, rendering obsolete earlier forms of information retrieval services, such as those targeting a general audience with general news. With 200 million people on the Internet worldwide in 2000, publishers realized a strong potential for expanding their readership. As a result, the Internet became a general means of obtaining news and information around the world and especially in the United States, Western Europe, and Japan, the leading information retrieval service countries. As a result, information retrieval vendors increasingly have had to include Internet presence in their business strategies as existing customers preferred the ease of accessing data through Web browsers instead of emulation or proprietary programs, and as potential new customers were steered away by the Internet's allure.

Although the Internet contains a plethora of business, government, and news documents, it lacks the structure of information retrieval services. In contrast to commercial online services with paid subscribers, the Internet is unregulated and uncontrolled. An individual on a personal computer or workstation can tap into the Internet and access tens of thousands of addresses, sites, and services with interactive texts, images, videos, and sounds. However, an individual typically can not simultaneously search a multiplicity of newspapers and periodicals without some kind of information retrieval service fee such as is charged by the Northern Light business library. Consequently, information retrieval services remained competitive by bundling an extensive collection of news and information sources that users could search to suit their needs. Businesses, libraries, and professional researchers require this kind of information technology. Nevertheless, the Internet cut into the usefulness of information retrieval services for general users who may want to search only one or two sources at a time. Thus information retrieval services turned to the Internet for growth themselves. Services such as Dow Jones News/Retrieval, Lexis-Nexis, Dialog, and others offer Internet-based subscriptions to their services; however, as with their non-Internet services, these Web sites are available only by subscription.

The Future. Industry growth will be driven by ongoing technological improvements in data storage, communications, and data processing. Important social changes that will push industry expansion include increased computer literacy, particularly in developed nations with relatively low computer penetration; the trend in the United States and Western Europe toward telecommuting and home businesses; and the development of international data and communication standards. As the cost of technology continues to fall and demand for information grows, the variety of services will increase in response to new market niches. As the volume of available information swells, moreover, demand will increase for value-added service providers that can locate, assess, and organize information in such a way that makes it usable to consumers. There will also be legal challenges by private citizens to the storage of information about private citizens. By 2002 the only apparent changes enacted by large database providers were postings of various legal disclaimers and offers to provide individuals information on their own database particulars at a reduced rate, similar to the way a credit bureau provides individuals with information about particular public records.

RESEARCH AND TECHNOLOGY

Two of the most important technological factors for the information retrieval services industry were storage capacity and retrieval speed. Storage capacity was being enhanced in the form of CD-ROM, which was being designed to absorb increasingly greater reams of data and to deliver that information at greater speeds. At the same time, advances in magnetic storage devices offered the potential of similar storage capacity with much faster information retrieval speeds. Increases in online retrieval speeds were being accomplished through more efficient modems.

Telecommunications services began offering alternative lines for Internet users such as T1 and ISDN lines. T1 lines can transfer data at 1.5 million bps, more than 25 times the speed of state-of-the-art consumer modems via telephone lines at 56,000 bps. T1 connections are used mostly by businesses and organizations with large computer networks or special high-volume requirements. T1s also are used to connect some of the Internet's backbone computers. ISDN (integrated services digital network) lines, another high-end technology, can transfer data at a maximum speed of 128,000 bps. Other potential high-speed transmission technologies include satellite and coaxial cable connections.

Other technologies augmenting industry expansion in the late 1990s and 2000s were related to interactive multimedia, or the integration of audio, video, text, and images into a user-controlled environment. Scanners, for example, were being introduced that could be used to inexpensively convert photographs into high-quality images accessible online or through CD-ROM. Likewise, inexpensive production and editing systems were allowing individuals and companies to generate digital videos at historically low prices, opening entirely new markets for CD-ROM products, for example. Among the most sensational and promising developments was virtual reality. In the future, users will likely be able to access and enter artificial three-dimensional worlds through online services, CD-ROM devices, or other information retrieval systems. Information retrieved by the customer might be combined with touch-sensitive gloves and head-mounted displays to create 3-D environments for a multitude of purposes.

Consumer Services. Among the leading proprietary subscription online services geared for the consumer market in the late 1990s were CompuServe Corporation, Prodigy Services Inc., and America Online, Inc. (AOL). All three were U.S.-based services that catered to individual interests like shopping and hobbies. They originated as closed networks offering a variety of magazines, news services, and member discussion bulletin boards, but as the Internet's popularity surged in the mid-1990s, all three began offering Internet access in addition to their own information content. America Online bought CompuServe in 1997 and kept it in existence as a subsidiary. CompuServe, with its business information focus, brought in US$841.9 million in 1997. Prodigy's 1997 sales totaled only US$225 million and America Online booked US$1.6 billion in revenues. Prodigy had fewer than 1 million subscribers in 1998, while America Online had about 13.5 million, including 2.5 million from CompuServe. America Online has services in Europe as well, as did CompuServe prior to the acquisition. Germany's Bertelsmann AG, which has a partnership with America Online, operates one of Europe's largest consumer online services and took over CompuServe's European service upon America Online's acquisition.

In 2002, Prodigy Communications, a subsidiary of SBC Communications, continued to serve more than 3 million subscribers and 1.3 million DSL Internet customers. In the 2000s AOL experienced highs and lows following a merger with Time Warner in January 2000. In January 2000 the AOL stock price was US$72.62, and on April 12, 2002, it plunged to US$20.10 a share, less than the cost of a month's dial-up service for a customer. In April 2002, AOL's debt level was US$23 billion, according to *Business Week*.

According to a 2003 report from IDC Research, the worldwide volume of Internet traffic was expected to double every year between 2002 and 2007, when users will share a mass of daily information some 64,000 times greater than the contents of the Library of Congress. By 2007, businesses are expected to represent 40 percent of all Internet users, while consumers will account for the majority.

INDUSTRY LEADERS

The Thomson Corporation. In 2005, Canada's The Thomson Corporation was providing information in law, accounting, higher education, tax, healthcare, scientific research, general reference, finance, and corporate e-learning and assessment to customers in approximately 130 countries. The company employed about 40,000 people in 45 countries in 2004. Thomson was organized into four main groups. The Legal & Regulatory division accounted for 42 percent of Thomson's US$8.1 billion in sales, followed by Learning (27 percent), Financial (21 percent), and Scientific & Healthcare (10 percent). Most of the company's revenues came from subscription-based products (65 percent), and most revenues came from North American operations (82 percent). About 66 percent of sales were from electronic products, software and services. By 2004 Thomson had sold most of its print media interests, including some 130 newspapers, as well as its ownership interest in Bell Globemedia, in order to concentrate on electronic resources. Thomson has grown through a series of strategic acquisition. Between 2002 and 2004, the company acquired 114 companies, including Elite Information Group, a provider of practice management software to law firms, and Information Holdings Inc, a provider of intellectual property and regulatory information. The company also sold off some subsidiaries during this period, including Thomson Media group, a provider of mostly print-based information on banking, financial services, and their related technology services.

Dialog Corporation, also owned by The Thomson Corporation, offers online company, industry, business, and international news. Dialog's main platform services include Dialog, Dialog Profound, Dialog DataStar, Dialog NewsEdge and Dialog Intelliscope, which had the power to access some 1.4 billion documents in 2004. Dialog formed a strategic partnership in 2002 with Gale, another professional information source owned by The Thomson Corporation, to build information sources for academe, libraries, and businesses. The first joint ventures were to be targeted toward libraries. Dialog's strength has been in providing information for academic, corporate, business, and scientific markets. Gale's strengths include being an information provider to libraries, academic researchers, and corporate users.

Dialog was started in 1972 by Dr. Roger K. Summit, who envisioned the possibilities of information retrieval in such fields as medicine, law, and business through the use of computers and online technology. By 2002 the North Carolina-based Dialog was accessed by users in more than 100 nations, according to *Internet Wire*. In mid-2004, the company offered more than 900 databases to its subscribers, who performed some 700,000 searches and viewed more than 17 million document pages each month.

The McGraw-Hill Companies Inc. The world's largest producer of textbooks, McGraw-Hill is also an industry leader within the information services industry. In addition to publishing such titles as *Business Week* and *Aviation Week & Space Technology*, owning Standard & Poor's, and publishing more than 9,000 books, McGraw-Hill provides information retrieval services to the government, businesses, schools, and the general public. In 2004, sales reached US$5.25 billion, up almost 9 percent from 2003. That year, the company employed 17,000 people.

Reuters Group plc. Although best known as the world's largest news agency, in 2005 Reuters was earning about 90 percent of its revenue from the supply of information to about 330,000 professionals in the financial services markets of equities, fixed income, foreign exchange, money, commodities, and energy. Founded in London in 1851, by 2005 the company operated in 91 countries with an employee count of 14,500. The company was able to provide real-time data on 5.5 million financial records, maintained data on 35,000 global companies, and provided financial data from more than 300 exchanges and over-the-counter (OTC) markets. The company owned 62 percent of the world's largest electronic securities broker, Instinet through which it also offered access to a wealth of financial information used by traders.

In 1999, a marriage of convenience and mutual profit was arranged between the business information divisions of Reuters and New York-based Dow Jones. The joint-venture company tried to keep both names in its first corporate title after merging—Dow Jones Reuters Business Interactive LLC—but dropped the unwieldy handle in favor of a new brand name: Factiva. By 2004, Factiva was the world's leading supplier of global news and information to corporate end users, and was ranked second in terms of revenue in the archival business news and information marketplace. The company offers exclusive third-party access to Dow Jones and Reuters Newswires, *The Wall Street Journal*, plus an additional 9,000 global sources. By 2003, sales totaled US$245 million, up 1.6 percent from 2002.

Dow Jones & Company, Inc. ranked among the industry leaders for its Dow Jones News/Retrieval Service. This service provided access to more than 3,600 publications from all over the world. With its headquarters in New York, Dow Jones also publishes leading business newspapers such as *The Wall Street Journal* and *Barron's*.

Bloomberg L.P.. Based in New York, privately held Bloomberg posted sales of US$3.5 billion in 2004 as one of the world's top information retrieval services. Bloomberg provides about 170,000 proprietary terminals to investors and universities, which feature up-to-date business news, analysis, and market information. In addition, Bloomberg operates national wire services for the TV, radio, and newspaper industries and publishes magazines. The company had 8,000 employees in 2004 and revenues of about US$3.5 billion. In 2001 company founder Michael Bloomberg was elected the 108th mayor of New York City.

Reed Elsevier Group plc. One of the world's leading medical, legal, education, and business information providers, Reed Elsevier earned about 31 percent of its 2004 revenues from electronic information products. Its subsidiary LexisNexis obtained 61 percent of its revenue electronically, while subsidiary Elsevier earned 43 percent from electronic sources. In 2003, London-based Reed Elsevier plc combined its businesses with Amsterdam-based Reed Elsevier NV to form Reed Elsevier Group as a joint venture. Both parents have retained their separate legal form and trade on separate exchanges although they have combined operations. In February 2005, Reed Elsevier reported total revenues of approximately US$9 billion of which about 55 percent was derived in North America, 18 percent in the United Kingdom, 10 percent in the Netherlands, 11 percent in the rest of Europe, and the remainder from the rest of the world.

Reed Elsevier's division, LexisNexis, provided about 27 percent of its parent's total revenue for fiscal 2005. Several corporate owners swapped Lexis-Nexis throughout its tenure as one of the leading information retrieval services in the world. Reed Elsevier NV became the owner of Lexis-Nexis. Based in Ohio, Lexis-Nexis caters to the legal, news, and business market, providing full-text documents from law journals and selected periodicals. Lexis-Nexis included 16,000 database sources in the year 2004. In 1997, Lexis-Nexis garnered US$715 million in sales from its services and employed 6,700 workers. By 2005, sales totaled about US$2.5 billion, and the company employed 12,900 workers.

Wolters Kluwer nv. Amsterdam-based Wolters Kluwer was the number 1 or number 2 provider of health, tax, accounting, corporate, financial, education, and legal and regulatory information in more than 80 percent of the its markets in 2004. That year, with offices in more than 25 countries, Wolters Kluwer employed 18,393 people in 2004, and earned revenues of about US$4 billion.

ProQuest Company. ProQuest is one of the world's leading providers of information to the academic, automotive, and power equipment markets. Through its ProQuest Information and Learning segment, the company offers an electronic database of periodicals, dissertations, and newspapers under licensing agreements with more than 9,000 publishers worldwide. ProQuest also is a leading archiver of journals and newspapers on microfilm and CD-ROM and produces scanners that aid businesses in converting documents to electronic formats. As of 2004, ProQuest provided access to some 16,000 periodicals, 7,000 newspapers, 150,000 out-of-print books, 550 research collections and more than a 15 million proprietary abstracts. Access to its information is through subscription held by most academic libraries around the world. The company also operates two divisions: UMI (formerly University Microfilms International) and Chadwyck-Healey.

The Proquest Business Solutions segment of the company is the world leader in information products for the automotive products markets, as well as providing information to the power equipment and power sports markets. Automotive dealers can access electronically technical documentation. In addition, Proquest collects and distributes statistics on dealer performance.

The ProQuest Company was formed in 2001 from Bell & Howell Company's two information access businesses, Bell & Howell Information and Learning and Bell & Howell Publishing Services. In 2004, ProQuest sales were US$462.2 million, a decline of 1.5 percent over 2003 levels, although its net income increased more than 34 percent to reach US$67 million. In 2003 and 2004 the company expanded through acquisitions, including the purchase of Copley Publishing Group, Reading A-Z, Axiom Press, Serials Solutions, SIRS Publishing, and Entigo Inc.

MAJOR COUNTRIES IN THE INDUSTRY

United States. The United States initiated the information retrieval industry in the 1970s and continued to lead it in the mid-2000s. The electronic information services market was valued by *Euromonitor* at US$61.4 billion in 2003, up 6 percent over 2002 figures. The five largest companies in the industry in the U.S.—Reed Elsevier, Dun & Bradstreet, Dow Jones, Reuters, and Thomson— controlled just under 40 percent of the market. High growth was expected for the industry, with Euromonitor predicting a rate of 62.5 percent in the five years to 2008.

In 2003, figures from Leichtman Research Group indicated that the United States would continue to be a key information retrieval services market into the early twenty-first century. The research firm estimated that high-speed Internet users, which numbered 14.7 million in 2002, would surpass narrowband subscribers in 2005 and mushroom to 49 million by 2007.

Western Europe. Major roadblocks to success in Western Europe have included language and cultural barriers, as well as a restrictive regulatory environment not present in the United States. Nevertheless, major North American information service providers were joined by several key players in Europe by the late 1990s, including Reuters in England, VNU in the Netherlands, and the French Minitel online service—and both Reuters and VNU garner a large portion of their revenues from sales in the United States. The United Kingdom, France, and Germany were the leading European producers and consumers of electronic information. Telecommunications services in these countries offered ISDN connection, which augmented the demand for not only information retrieval services, but also the Internet.

According to research from Datamonitor, the number of high-speed Internet users in Europe was expected to increase from about 10 million in 2002 to more than 41 million in 2006. By that time, Germany would have the most broadband subscribers, followed by the United Kingdom and France. Along with this increase, consumers in Western Europe were expected to spend more on paid electronic content, with spending reaching US$3.4 billion annually by 2006, or US$76 per user.

United Kingdom: The leader in Europe in terms of use of electronic information services, the U.K. market was valued at US$12.3 billion in 2003, with online-accessed services accounting for 86 percent of this value. Reuters led the market with a 25.5 percent market share, with Thomson, Reed Elsevier, and Bloomberg also being major players there. Financial service companies were the biggest users of the industry.

Germany: Although a much smaller market than its European neighbor, the United Kingdom, Germany's market was growing strongly according to Euromonitor. Valued at approximately US$1.8 billion in 2003, a German company was beating out its rivals in terms of market share; Deutsche Presse-Agentur (dpa) held 9 percent of the market. In fact, of the remaining top four companies that year, only one—Reuters—was foreign. Other industry players were FIZ Karlsruhe GmbH, Verlagsgruppe Georg von Holtzbrinck GmbH, and Verband der Vereine Creditreform eV. The financial industry was the country's biggest user of electronic information.

France: Reuters led the market in France in 2003, where electronic information service sales amounted to about US$3.3 billion. Dun & Bradstreet and France Télécom were other industry leaders.

Japan. As the third-largest market for information retrieval services, Japan lagged well behind the United States and several Western European nations in the amount of information services it provided, but increasing computer literacy in Japan will continue to increase market share. By 2003, 54.5 percent of the Japanese population (80 percent of all Japanese households) was online, along with about 79 percent of Japanese businesses. Nearly 30 percent of Internet users had access to high-speed connections.

In 2003, the electronic information services market was valued at about US$5.6 billion, of which commercial, online-access services made up about 62 percent. Japan was home to a number of high-powered databases of science, engineering, and economic information of interest to U.S. companies and institutions. Japan also enjoyed a leading edge in a few specific emerging information service technologies, such as those related to car navigation systems. Japan's information retrieval industry had suffered a setback during the mid-1990s when corporate users reduced their investments in information technology and services. Furthermore, the Japanese industry lost a share of its customers to open Internet databases. These factors made the industry in Japan much more competitive, though, according to a report from Japan 21st.

Growth Regions. In the late 1990s and 2000s industry growth occurred in Eastern Europe, South America, and particularly the Pacific Rim. Foreign traders throughout the world were seeking information about those markets, and businesses in those regions were expected to demand increasing amounts of business, legal, and financial information about the U.S. and other developed markets. Likely expansion of information services in the Pacific Rim was implied by a high level of investment in communications infrastructure in that region. South Korea and Singapore, for example, were investing in national fiber-optic networks that could eventually permit the rapid transfer of data on computer networks. Although it still trailed more developed nations, South Korea's information services market provided evidence of regional gains.

Further Reading

"AsiaBizTech: Over 50 Percent of Japanese Population Online." *Nua Internet Surveys,* 12 March 2003. Available from http://www.nua.ie/surveys.

"Datamonitor: Broadband Adoption on the Up in Europe." *Nua Internet Surveys,* 20 March 2003. Available from http://www.nua.ie/surveys.

"Dialog And Gale In Alliance To Build New Library Services." *Internet Wire,* 1 April, 2002.

Dialog Home Page. Available from http://www.dialog.com, 2002.

"Dow Jones, Reuters to Combine Interactive Services." *Bloomberg News,* 17 May 1999.

Duffy, Caroline A. "Online Evolution." *PC Week,* 16 January 1995.

Gale Directory of Databases. Detroit: Gale Group, 2004.

"Getting Your Facts Straight." *New Media Age,* 1 November 2001.

Hajime, Kuwata. "Japan's Information Service Industry: Supporting Downsizing & Network Introduction Keys to the Future." *Japan 21st,* March 1996.

"How Many Online?." *Nua Internet Surveys,* September 2002. Available from http://www.nua.ie/surveys.

"IDC Research: Worldwide Net Traffic to Rise." *Nua Internet Surveys,* 3 March 2003. Available from http://www.nua.ie/surveys.

Jarvis, Steve. "Sum of the Parts: Fast-growing Industry Delivers Data to New Markets, Piece by Piece." *Marketing News,* 21 January 2002.

Konieczko, Jill. "The Next Evolutionary Step for Corporate Intranets and Internets: Tools that Integrate Relevant, Continually Updated External Content." *KMWorld,* January 2003.

"Leichtman Research: More High-Speed Net Subscribers in US." *Nua Internet Surveys,* 2 April 2003. Available from http://www.nua.ie/surveys.

"Major Market Profiles: Electronic Information Services in France (Germany, Japan, UK, USA)." *Euromonitor,* October 2004. Available from http://www.euromonitor.com.

Manly, Lorne. "Houdini's Box." *Folio,* February 2002.

"MuseGlobal, Inc. Announced the Release of MuseSeek, a New Consumer-Oriented Version of Its Metasearching Technology." *Online,* January-February 2004.

Picchi, Aimee. "McGraw-Hill Has Fourth Quarter Loss on Expenses for Job Cuts?" *Bloomberg News,* 29 January 2002.

Plosker, George R. "The Information Industry Revolution: Implications for Librarians." *Online,* November-December 2003.

Tenopir, Carol. "E-resources in Tough Times." *Library Journal,* 1 June 2004, 42.

———. "Will Online Vendors Survive?" *Library Journal,* 1 February 1998, 35.

The Thomson Corporation Home Page. Available from http://www.thompson.com, 2002.

"Will AOL and Yahoo Trade Places?" *Business Week Online,* 11 April 2002.

"What's Ahead for 2004?" *Information Today,* January 2004, 1.

SIC 4822, 7375

NAICS 517110, 518111

INTERNET SERVICES

The Internet services industry includes Internet service providers (ISPs), backbone network operators, Web navigation services, Internet security services, and Internet or electronic commerce (e-commerce) providers. Internet service providers may also offer Internet hosting and programming services, e-mail and messaging services, and Web site design services. Companies that use the Internet to promote sales, such as automobile manufacturers allowing customers to price cars online, are not considered part of the industry. For additional information on Internet programming and software, see the entries on **Information Technology Services** and **Packaged Software**.

INDUSTRY SNAPSHOT

The Internet has been the fastest-growing communications technology in history, according to the U.S. Department of Commerce. Radio was available 38 years before gaining 50 million listeners, and television was available 13 years before gaining that many viewers. The Internet reached the 50-million-user mark in four years. By the end of 1997, more than 102 million people were on the Internet. By the end of 2003, there were 700 million Internet users worldwide. According to some estimates, this number was expected to reach 945 million by the end of 2004 and exceed 1 billion by 2007.

The growth in Internet users is occurring in tandem with an increase in the number of Web sites. According to the August 2004 issue of *iStart,* during the first half of 2004, domain name registrations for Web sites carrying the ".com" extension increased by 23 percent over the same time period in 2003. In addition, Web sites carrying the ".net" extensions jumped 20 percent from the first half of 2003.

Businesses have been quick to take advantage of the Internet's potential and are realizing significant business cost savings and competitive advantages. The Internet is a driving force behind communication and collaboration, both within and between companies, globalization, and electronic commerce. In 1997 an estimated US$40 billion in global business was transacted over the Internet. By the end of 2004, global business-to-business ("B2B") was expected to bring in US$2.7 trillion, according to *eMarketer,* with the United States accounting for about US$1 trillion. Although 70 percent of companies had given online purchasing a try by early 2003, some 90 percent of their spending continued to occur offline, according to *eMarketer.* One survey conducted by *Information Strategy* revealed that 98 percent of surveyed businesses had some sort of presence on the Internet and that almost half of those had sites offering interactive communication with customers. About 15 percent of those companies actually conducted business over the Internet, although most marketed services as opposed to physical products.

Figures from Nielsen//NetRatings for March 2005 showed that worldwide, 451.5 million people had access to the Internet from a home computer. Users visited an average of 62 unique domain names that month, viewing about 1,148 total Web pages. Also, people spent approximately 26 hours and 55 minutes on their computers, with average Web surfing sessions of 51 minutes and 11 seconds. On average, individual Web pages were viewed for about 44 seconds.

ORGANIZATION AND STRUCTURE

INTERNET SERVICE PROVIDERS (ISPS)

Service providers allow users, who wish to access the Internet to set up their own networks, to get connected. Companies from several major industries, including local and national telecommunications companies, software developers, and cable television companies, joined in providing both businesses and the general public with access to the Internet. Those who did not offer their own services have often pursued joint ventures with other companies to do so. No longer was simple access the issue—speed was as well.

Access to the Internet is achieved in several ways, including dedicated lines and dial-up telephone line access. Dedicated lines include T1 and T3 lines (fiber optic lines to an ISP) and others, such as digital subscriber lines (DSL). Dial-up lines include Integrated Service Digital Network (ISDN) and phone lines with use of a modem.

A "dedicated line" means that rather than dialing into the Internet each time a user or company wants access, a data transmission line is dedicated to the sole purpose of Internet access, and that line is always open. Dedicated or permanent lines provide much greater speed than dial-up access, and greater bandwidth, the amount of data that can be transmitted at one time over the connection. Dial-up access is available on an individual or network basis and runs more slowly than dedicated lines. However, for individuals and some smaller companies, dial-up access to the Internet is sufficient. Considerations when determining what type of access is appropriate include the number of simultaneous users who need access and the type of tasks they perform. For example, some users may need to send and receive large graphics or data files regularly, and a slow connection would impede their productivity.

Internet service providers (ISPs) provide a network connection that allows users to view the Internet and provide a means for people and corporations to sponsor Web sites. Customers either dial in or use their dedicated line to the ISP, which in turn is linked to other ISP systems known as "national ISPs." Many ISPs purchase their access from network operators or national providers that do not serve the general public.

NETWORK OPERATORS

Some companies made a mark in the industry by selling fiber-optic networks and bandwidth to telecommunications and Internet access providers. One company specializing in this market was Qwest Communications, which provided national fiber-optic services to major telecommunications companies such as WorldCom, Sprint, and GTE.

In order to provide easier access to the Internet for educational and nonprofit institutions, the Federal Communications Commission (FCC) announced in 1997 that it would offer free wireless access at 300 megahertz (MHz) of the radio spectrum for short-distance connections. These connections could bring the Internet to schools, hospitals, libraries, and other institutions for which access costs were prohibitive.

SECURITY

Security is one of the primary concerns for businesses pursuing commercial ventures via the Internet. While all companies are interested in taking advantage of this exploding market, they are understandably concerned about public access to private files and competitive information. Such information has become the number one corporate intelligence target. As a result, security services are a growing market in the Internet services arena. Security services include consulting and security system design services, as well as installation of firewalls (a kind of software security structure) and virtual private networks.

Consulting services can include design and maintenance of corporate security policies, network security design, and site audits. Consultants also provide comprehensive external audit services. These audits include evaluating firewalls, detecting "back doors" on internal networks, and validating security tools. Other consultative services offered are host penetration testing and evaluation of internal compliance with corporate security policies.

Firewalls are installed in computer networks to protect internal hosts from unauthorized outside access. The firewall is placed between a corporation's private network and public access via the Internet. Firewalls monitor access to the corporate network and authorized users. Any activity, whether suspicious or regular, can be monitored and reported to network administrators when necessary. Another tool used to enhance network security is the virtual private network (VPN), which is replacing wide-area networks in many corporations. This type of network offers secure connections over the Internet and can connect branch offices, remote users, business partners, and clients on one network.

A global initiative dedicated to the issue of Web security was launched in 1997 by the Electronic Frontier Foundation and CommerceNet, an Internet commerce industry organization. Termed "TRUSTe," the initiative was created to instill confidence in electronic information exchange by dispensing green "trustmarks," or seals of approval, to Web sites following set privacy guidelines. TRUSTe's initial focus was on the general consumer but later was slated to move into Internet commerce security.

E-COMMERCE

One of the most fundamental shifts in the way companies conducted business during the late 1990s and early 2000s arose from the increased practice of online product ordering. This type of business is referred to as e-business, e-commerce, or I-commerce (for Internet commerce). This shift represented a change in business strategy as much as in technology. IBM was among the first companies seeking to profit from the opportunity to provide corporate customers with e-commerce hardware, software, and services.

Established Internet companies such as browser giant Netscape Communications Corporation also shifted service offerings to take advantage of opportunities in electronic commerce. Netscape was positioning its own Web site as an "Internet tollbooth for each transaction to pass through on its way to accessing services deployed on top of enterprise software from Netscape," according to Dana Gardner in *Info World.*

E-MAIL AND MESSAGING SERVICES

One of the primary lures of the Internet is its e-mail and messaging capabilities. Most companies and services providing Internet access to consumers also offer at least one, if not more, e-mail address for each account opened. This allows subscribers to communicate with anyone who has access to the Internet. In the late 1990s and early 2000s, corporate e-mail and messaging were important software markets, and products were being designed as all-inclusive systems for internal corporate communication as well as outside e-mail. The industry's leading vendors in e-mail and messaging include IBM-owned Lotus Development Corp. (Lotus Notes and cc:Mail), Microsoft (Microsoft Outlook and Entourage), and Novell (GroupWise).

WEB SITE HOSTING, DESIGN, AND PROGRAMMING

Many companies specialize in Web hosting, Web site design, and programming services. Web hosting service provides server or network space to companies or individuals wishing to publish a Web site on the Internet. This type of service is often included among the service offerings of larger Internet service providers, sometimes as part of a package that customers receive when they sign up for Internet access. For example, an access provider might make available a certain quantity of server disk space to each customer who purchases a service contract. Customers can then design and post their own Web site on the Internet using that service provider's network resources.

Additionally, service providers often offer design services, although that segment of the industry is served largely by smaller, specialized firms or independent contractors. Much like the early software industry, start-up costs for Web site design businesses are relatively cheap, and there is great revenue potential. Companies needing Web site design might outsource overall Web site management to a company specializing in site design services, or they may prefer to hire their own "Webmaster," who designs, programs, and maintains the company's site. Since Web sites range from small public relations tools to interactive commercial businesses, companies have to analyze their own needs and resources when deciding which course to take.

Web site designers are often called upon to perform the functions of several professionals, such as graphic artists, software programmers, and network administrators. Web sites need to be aesthetically pleasing so that they appeal to Internet "surfers" and build repeat visitors. If a site is at all complex and requires tasks such as database access and manipulation or electronic commerce, more extensive programming than the Internet's standard publishing language (hypertext markup language, or HTML) is needed. Maintaining the Web site and ensuring that its host network runs smoothly can be additional responsibilities. For these reasons, many companies offering comprehensive Web services hire specialized personnel for each step.

INDUSTRY REGULATION

The Internet consists of several thousand independent networks, each having its own administrative authorities. However, general direction of the Internet is organized by the Internet Society, a voluntary membership organization whose purpose is to "promote global information exchange through Internet technology." Another authority, known as InterNIC (Internet Network Information Center), is responsible for the registration of all computers and networks connected to the Internet as well as providing special consulting services to the member networks. The InterNIC is made up of several commercial organizations and operates under an agreement with the National Science Foundation.

The Internet Society and InterNIC do not, however, regulate ongoing daily functions of the Internet. This is left to each network's administrators. These individual networks can make rules and regulations commanding the proper use of their proprietary data networks and network services. Some networks prohibit commercial data traffic while others prevent insecure local and remote data traffic. Largely, though, the Internet is free of restrictions on its use, despite recurring legislative initiatives in various parts of the world to limit—or tax—its use. Notable exceptions are in countries whose governments frown on the unregulated flow of information. In such places as China, Internet users may not enjoy all the privileges their neighbors in South Korea enjoy.

Continuing regulation was the source of much debate during the late 1990s and early 2000s. Domain name registration, which involves paying a fee to reserve a unique Web address such as "hanknuwer.com," has continued to be a hot issue. Such registration is necessary because e-mail and Web page access is routed through standard Internet-wide name servers that link a textual address, as in "hnuwer@hanknuwer.com," with a coded numeric location of the proper host computer, such as an ISP's server. In other words, domain names are user-friendly names that serve as a front-end alias for the string of numbers and periods that represent an Internet computer's technical address. A given Internet server, in fact, may be host to hundreds of domain names and thousands of e-mail addresses. A site known as the Accredited Registrar Directory keeps listings of domain name registrars that register domain names.

In an effort to regulate domain name registration, the U.S. government has reviewed a proposal to establish a nonprofit agency, run by Internet users and technical experts, that would oversee regulation of domain name assignment and registration. The plan was not fully detailed, however. It allowed for the creation of new domain registries and top-level domains (or TLDs, such as ".com," ".edu," ".gov," and ".org") but attempted to impose U.S. government mandates for standards across countries. In June 1998, the Clinton administration announced that the United States was no longer pursuing control over management of Internet addresses. As reported by Amy Harmon in the *New York Times,* management of the Internet address assignment system was to be transferred to an international nonprofit group with representation from major corporations and individual Web users from around the world. This new group would have authority to establish new top-level domains (such as ".web") and would mediate disputes between companies or individuals seeking the same Web site address. That the U.S. government would relinquish control has been viewed as a move toward allowing continued self-government of the Internet.

Encryption has been another subject of much proposed legislation. Government agencies wanted access to encrypted files for law enforcement purposes but were meeting resistance due to citizens' privacy concerns. Privacy advocates fear that the same technology used by law enforcement officials could serve as a mechanism for rising encroachment on the free exchange of ideas, data, and information over the Internet.

Encryption was also being examined by a European Union commissioner, Martin Bangemann, who proposed the development of an international charter to deal with the issue. In the United States, a Federal Information Processing Standard (FIPS) was adopted for the Advanced Encryption Standard FIPS-197. This standard identifies "a FIPS-approved symmetric encryption algorithm that may be used by U.S. Government organizations (and others) to protect sensitive information," according to the National Institute of Standards and Technology (NIST), an agency of the U.S. Department of Commerce's Technology Administration.

BACKGROUND AND DEVELOPMENT

The Internet is a result of a U.S. government project conducted during the 1970s by the U.S. Department of Defense Advanced Research Projects Agency (ARPA). This project, known as the ARPANET, was designed to be a wide-area network (WAN) service for computer communications. Standard networking protocol, a communications protocol for exchanging data between computers on a network, was developed in 1973 and 1974. This protocol became known as TCP/IP or the "IP suite" of protocols. TCP/IP enabled ARPANET computers to communicate regardless of the operating system or hardware in use. Other such protocols, termed "heterogeneous," include UNIX, an operating system developed during the same period, which became almost synonymous with TCP/IP. Due to its low cost, UNIX soon spread throughout the many educational institutions around the United States. Multi-user systems such as UNIX soon became the most popular method of accessing computer network communications.

Once IP (information processing) protocols were in place, much of the software and services that make up the Internet appeared. The basic services for remote connectivity, file transfer, and electronic mail began appearing in the mid to late 1970s. The Usenet news system appeared in 1981; Gopher made its debut in 1982; and the revolutionary World Wide Web appeared in 1989. By 1990, the ARPANET was connected to many other networks and its role as the Internet network backbone was taken over by the NSFNET (funded by the National Science Foundation). Networking companies and organizations providing data connections to Internet hosts continued providing easy global network access.

In the late 1990s and early 2000s, the Internet consisted of thousands of computer networks that utilized a common set of protocols to establish worldwide communications. Users accessed the Internet through individual networks at educational and commercial institutions, via commercial Internet access providers, and through other organizations. Each individual network was controlled by a different organization, was of a different size, and used a range of network technologies, operating systems, and hardware. However, all were united by common communications protocols and services.

CURRENT CONDITIONS

By 2002, with many "dot-coms" seemingly in full flight or bankrupt, the Internet was being viewed in more realistic terms by analysts. In the fourth quarter of 2001, domain name registrations dropped for the first time, at least partially caused by speculators who chose domain names in hopes of selling them and then opted not to renew their registrations when they failed to find buyers. While online activity per person dropped 10 percent from 2000 to 2002, it still commanded a reasonably high average of 83 minutes each day. By mid-2004, conditions were improving along with the overall U.S. economy. In January 2004, *InternetWeek* reported that online holiday shopping totaled a record US$18.5 billion in 2003, according to combined data from Nielsen//NetRatings, Harris Interactive, and Goldman Sachs. This represented a 35 percent increase from 2002 levels of US$13.7 billion.

According to figures released for March 2005 by Nielsen//NetRatings, there were more than 451 million home-based Internet users around the globe, with 299 million active users visiting an average of 1,148 Web pages each month. Nielsen excludes government, education and pornographic sites from its ratings figures.

In 2005, security continued to be at the forefront of the Internet services industry. IBM's Global Business Security Index Report reported that in 2004, the number of known viruses increased by 25 percent over 2003 levels to reach 112,438. In 2002, 0.5 percent of all e-mails scanned contained a virus, a figure that increased to 6.9 percent by 2004. In addition, IBM found that 73 percent of all e-mail was unsolicited "spam."

Figures from research firm Gartner indicated that "phishing," a tactic in which criminals attempt to trick people into divulging sensitive financial or identity-related data, including credit card numbers, bank account numbers, and social security numbers, by luring them to a fraudulent Web site, resulted in expenses of US$1.2 billion for U.S. banks and credit card companies in 2003 alone. IBM reported that the phishing e-mails increased in number by 5,000 percent in 2004. One example of phishing is an e-mail message that appears to be from a legitimate financial company requesting that the recipient verify their account data. In order to appear legitimate, such e-mails sometimes include actual stolen logos and information from the real company. However, the attacks are often initiated by organized crime groups in faraway locales such as Russia or South Korea.

The research firm Jupiter reported that the number of Internet-connected U.S. households was forecast to reach 89 million by 2007. This represented an increase of 33 percent from 2002 levels. These growing legions of Internet users were fueling the Internet's recovery from the early 2000s dot-com fallout. Indeed, *The Economist* indicated that in the United States alone, some 200 million Americans were expected to spend US$120 billion online in 2004. This was reflected in online holiday sales for 2003, which reached a record US$18.5 billion, up 35 percent from 2002 levels of US$13.7 billion, according to *InternetWeek.*

Of great benefit to Internet service providers during the mid-2000s was the increasing adoption of high-speed or broadband Internet connections, which enabled the transmission of large files and the reception of streaming audio and video feeds. As *The Economist* explained in its May 15, 2004, issue, broadband connections were supporting growth in e-commerce throughout the world, especially in Europe and the United States, and supporting the creation of new jobs. In 2003, Leichtman Research indicated that the United States was home to 14.4 million high-speed Internet subscribers in 2002, up 6.4 million from the previous year. The company predicted that U.S. high- speed subscribers would surpass "narrowband" subscribers in 2005 and reach 49 million as of year-end 2007. Datamonitor predicted that the number of European high-speed subscribers would reach 41 million in 2006, led by Germany and the United Kingdom. DSL was expected to dominate over cable as the leading connection method, except for the Netherlands, where more people would connect to the Internet via cable modems.

In July of 2004, *The New York Times* cited first quarter 2004 data from comScore Networks regarding the U.S. metropolitan areas with the highest and lowest percentages of high-speed Internet connections. Of those households with Internet access, San Diego was the high-speed connection leader, at 55 percent. A close second was Boston (53 percent), followed by New York (51 percent), the Providence, R.I./New Bedford, Massachusetts area (50 percent), Kansas City (49 percent), Detroit (47 percent), the Tampa/St. Petersburg, Florida region (47 percent), the San Francisco/Oakland, California market (46 percent), Los Angeles (46 percent), and Milwaukee (46 percent). By comparison, the lowest percentages of broadband connections ranged from

27 percent in the New Mexico towns of Albuquerque/Santa Fe, New Mexico to 34 percent in Nashville, Tennessee.

Looking forward, some industry observers indicated that the Internet will be increasingly used for communications purposes as opposed to e-commerce. In a June 10, 2003 *Business Week Online* article, David Silver, director of the University of Washington's Resource Center for Cyberculture Studies in Seattle, indicated that this trend had already begun to emerge during the early 2000s. For example, Voice over Internet Protocol (VoIP) technology was furthering this communications revolution, enabling low-cost long distance voice communications and videoconferencing. Oyster Bay, New York-based Allied Business Intelligence indicated that the VoIP market would increase from US$46 million in 2001 to more than US$36 billion by 2008. In the same *Business Week Online* article, Atari founder Nolan Bushnell, described as the "father of computer entertainment," said that "the distinction between talking on the phone and watching movies and playing games will become blurred" amid a Web convergence of different media.

RESEARCH AND TECHNOLOGY

Programming languages have been very important to Internet development, although they are most specifically related to the software development and programming industries. Examples of Internet languages already in high use are the industry standard Hypertext Markup Language (HTML) and more extensive languages such as Java, Perl, and CGI. Although the lines often blur, HTML differs from the latter languages in that it is primarily a system of tags for various document attributes and structures, such as fonts, colors, and image placement, whereas other programming languages offer more powerful development tools to create whole new processes. For example, a developer could write a program that would validate a user's password. The end product of HTML programming is an encoded, tagged document, and the output of the more sophisticated languages is a process-oriented script or program. HTML is the only requisite for producing Web pages, but in all but the most basic Web pages, other programming languages are employed. Still other languages first developed for mainframe or PC applications, such as C++ and Visual Basic, are also used in Web site development.

HTML was the first and best-known Internet language. Its simplicity, however, meant that in order to do complex tasks such as database manipulation on the Internet, new and more complex languages such as Java and Perl had to be developed and used in conjunction with HTML. Proponents of HTML responded by adding technologies such as Dynamic HTML, cascading style sheets, and new tags allowing more functionality. However, many developers were still looking for a new standard that offered some of the same options that higher-level programming languages did, especially in the areas of site automation and interoperability. One such effort was an adaptation of Standard Generalized Markup Language (SGML) called the Extensible Markup Language (XML). HTML is also an application of SGML principles but is much simpler than XML, which was designed to foster the creation of other markup languages and is a subset of SGML. XML defines a document's structure, rather than simply its display format, and allows users to define their own tags.

Another area of research in Web site development was personalization. Personalization options can act as the equivalent of a store's salespeople, sizing up customers and making recommendations. Though the supporting technology could be expensive to design and implement, personalization was proving to be a valuable marketing tool. The necessary software performs tasks such as collaborative filtering, which links user preferences to databases containing user input. Such software is still costly to develop, however, costing between US$15,000 and US$50,000. Some companies were specializing in personalization software development, offering services on a contract basis so site developers could contain costs.

INDUSTRY LEADERS

INTERNET SERVICE PROVIDERS (ISPs)/INFRASTRUCTURE ENTERPRISES

America OnLine, better known as **AOL,** was the world's leading Internet services provider in 2005, with 34 million members in 12 countries. Its parent, Time Warner, was the leading media company in the world. AOL was the first company to offer instant messaging and the first service designed specifically for broadband customers. Founded in 1985, its customers were sending 450 million e-mails and 1.5 billion instant messages everyday by 2005. Its subsidiaries also included the Internet service providers Netscape and CompuServe, MapQuest, and AOL Instant Messenger. The company was also the operator of the dial-up service offered by Wal-Mart Stores Inc.

In 2004, AOL reported revenues of more than US$8.6 million, with US$934 million in net operating income. Its revenues were sourced from subscriber fees and advertising service fees. By this time, the company had experienced several years of decline in terms of number of subscribers, and AOL expected this decline to continue due to the maturation of its market for dial-up service, and the migration of customers to high-speed broadband or lower cost dial-up services.

One of seven product segments of Microsoft, **Microsoft Network (MSN)** provides personal communications services, such as e-mail and instant messaging, and information services, including search products and information and purchasing portals, around the world. The company earns its revenues from providing Internet-related access, software subscriptions, e-mail services, bill payment services and radio from both subscribers and advertisers. According to studies by Nielson Net Ratings and comScore Media Metrix, MSN Web sites are visited by more than 350 million unique users every month. MSN Hotmail is one of the world's largest e-mail services with more than 187 million accounts, and MSN Messenger is one of the world's largest instant messaging services with more than 135 million accounts.

By 2004, MSN was earning more than US$1 billion in revenues from advertising, a 40 percent growth over the previous year. Overall revenue grew by 13 percent to US$2.22

billion. The company was not expecting the same growth trend to continue in 2005 as it felt declines in the number of subscribers to its narrowband service would offset any gains made in advertising and premium Web services.

Founded in 1994 with only 10 modems, **Earthlink** grew into one the largest ISPs in the United States. By 1995, the company had formed an alliance with UUNET Technologies allowing Earthlink to offer dial-up access in 98 cities across the U.S. Its 1999 merger with MindSpring made it the second largest ISP in the country. This followed in 2000 with an alliance with Apple Computers making Earthlink the official ISP (Internet service provider) for its systems. In 2004, the company reported revenues of US$1.38 billion and a positive net income for the first time in several years. In January 2005, Earthlink entered into a joint venture agreement with Korea's leading mobile communications company to market wireless voice and data services in the U.S.

MCI Inc., formerly Worldcom, was a leading player in the Internet industry, operating one of the world's fastest and largest Internet Protocol (IP) networks. In 2004, the company earned US$20.7 billion in revenues, with about 23 percent coming from large global corporate and government customers with complex communication systems, 44 percent from domestic U.S. customers, and the remainder from international and wholesale markets. However, MCI reported net losses in all three sectors, for a total loss of US$3.2 billion in 2004.

MCI's Internet roots stretch back to 1997, when it acquired MFS Communications for US$12 billion. The deal included the Internet infrastructure of UUNET Technologies Inc., which MFS had recently acquired. Once based in Fairfax, Virginia, UUNET was founded in May of 1987. It went public in 1995 and merged in 1996 with MFS Communications. After its acquisition by Worldcom, UUNET became the world's largest Internet service provider. UUNET focused exclusively on providing businesses and online service providers with access to the Internet and its global network backbone. UUNET developed one of the most widely deployed Internet networks in the world. UUNET owned and operated national networks in the United States, Canada, the United Kingdom, Germany, Belgium, the Netherlands, and Luxembourg. It also maintained extensive connections to partners in Europe and the Asia/Pacific region. UUNET's backbone included direct fiber-optic connections between Europe, North America, and Asia, crossing both the Atlantic and Pacific Oceans. Satellite services were also available for remote areas that lacked connections. In addition, UUNET offered products and services such as Internet access, Web site development, wholesale network access, and Internet security. In the early 2000s, UUNET achieved the then-highest Internet backbone access speed level of 10 Gbps OC-192c. In 2002, most of the UUNET services were offered under the WorldCom name.

WorldCom was established in 1983 as Long Distance Discount Services (LDDS). LDDS began by leasing a wide-area telecommunications service (WATS) line and resold time to other businesses. Over the years, LDDS capitalized by acquiring other business, such as Telephone Management Corp. in 1988, National Telecommunications in 1991, and IDB WorldCom in 1994. In 1995, LDDS acquired WilTel Network Services and changed its name to WorldCom. The company also hired Michael Jordan as its spokesperson that year. In 1996, WorldCom acquired UUNET Technologies, MFS, and BLT Technologies, successfully becoming an Internet service provider. In early 1998, WorldCom took control of CompuServe and America Online's network units as part of an agreement by which America Online acquired CompuServe's consumer business. That same year, the company formed its first international partnership, teaming with MCI and Spain's Telefonica to expand the companies' reach in Europe and Latin America.

WorldCom became a telecommunications giant following its 1998 acquisition of MCI Communications Corp., which was hotly contested on antitrust grounds by industry participants. The company provided local and international telecommunications services such as voice, data, and paging services and Internet access. In addition, it provided services over its own network, which included fiber-optic cables around several major cities and between the United States and the United Kingdom, a joint project with Cable & Wireless PLC. The company leased and resold excess network capacity and services to other phone companies, businesses, and government agencies. WorldCom's Internet services focused on offering network access through integrated and dedicated lines.

In 2000, the company reorganized into two divisions: MCI Group and WorldCom Group. The former division concentrated on the consumer market, including dial-up Internet services, while WorldCom managed networking, data, and Internet operations. In 2002, WorldCom filed for Chapter 11 bankruptcy protection amid charges of accounting fraud and an investigation by the U.S. Securities and Exchange Commission (SEC). By April of 2004, the company had installed new executive leadership, reorganized as MCI Inc., relocated its headquarters to Ashburn, Virginia, and paid several billion dollars to settle matters with the SEC.

NAVIGATION SERVICES

Yahoo! Inc. began as one of the first navigation services on the Internet. As opposed to many of its competitors relying on computer programs, Yahoo! used human effort to organize its search engine. In 2005, it was still the most widely used Internet search engine in the world, reaching 345 million unique users in 25 countries and providing service in 13 languages. Revenues in 2004 were approximately US$3.6 billion, with recorded net income of almost US$840 million. Eighty-eight percent of the company's revenue was derived from advertising. The fee paid by advertisers was based on the number of times an image or text appears on a page for a viewer. In addition, fees were being received for consumer and business listings, including those related to job markets, auto sales and real estate sales. In addition, transaction revenue was being received from sales made from Yahoo!'s travel and shopping portals. The remaining 12 percent of revenue was coming from the provision of Internet broadband and dial-up services.

Yahoo! was created in 1994 by David Filo and Jerry Yang, two graduate students at Stanford University. In 1995, Yahoo! and publisher Ziff-Davis launched an online and print magazine titled Yahoo! Internet Life. When Yahoo!

went public in 1996, it was one of the first and most successful initial public offerings in the Internet services industry. Yahoo! expanded further through strategic alliances and partnerships. One such partnership was with Netscape: the two companies created a topic-based navigation service to be used on the Netscape Communicator browser. However, Yahoo! proceeded with far too much confidence in the helter-skelter economy of the late 1990s and early 2000s and for a time stumbled badly with losses, debts, and payroll commitments.

In 2001 and 2002, under new Chief Executive Terry Semel, Yahoo! assured its niche as the most consulted network on the Internet by purchasing the popular employment service HotJobs and slashing its payroll through layoffs. In 2002, Yahoo! made a move toward greater profitability when it offered users not only its free search engine, but also a method to purchase hard-to-locate articles for a fee. In 2005, Yahoo! announced its alliance with Verizon to deliver co-branded broadband service.

The name of the search engine **Google** is derived from "googol," the number 1 followed by 100 zeros, and the company site calls the term symbolic as it tries to organize the seemingly infinite universe called the Internet. Google's origins go back to 1996 when graduate students Larry Page and Sergey Brin at Stanford University created a method to search what they called the "back links" to a given Web site. Their first search engine was called BackRub. In 1998, with investments from friends, family, and Sun Microsystems co-founder Andy Bechtolsheim, Page and Brin began Google. A year later, armed with sufficient venture capital, the founders left their humble leasing space and opened a headquarters in Mountain View, California. Managing to lure AOL/Netscape as a client—the first of many—Google became a seemingly overnight financial success in 1999. In 2000 the company was seeing 18 million user hits a day and was proclaimed by many as the most efficient search engine on the Internet. In 2002 the company made another giant gain when it lured EarthLink, Inc., the number three U.S. Internet service provider, to use the Google search engine instead of its former search engine, Overture.

By mid-2004, Google had become the largest search engine in the world, with nearly 82 million users every month. More than 50 percent of Google's users were located outside of the United States. In fact, the site offered results in 35 different languages, and ranked as the top search engine in Australia, France, Germany, Italy, the Netherlands, Spain, Switzerland, and the United Kingdom. In 2004, the company had sales of almost US$3.2 billion, an increase of more than 117 percent over the previous year, with net income of US$399 million. Although initially the company made its revenue from license fees derived from the use of its search engine on other Web sites, by 2004, the bulk of its revenue came from the sale of advertising. In 2002, their advertising fees became based on the number of times a user clicked on an advertiser's text message when it appeared on a search screen.

In April of 2004, Google announced its initial public offering. In a move that served to generate much publicity, the company said it would offer shares in an auction format. The auction process, which began on 13 August 2004, was met with criticism by some observers. For example, in the August 15, 2004, issue of the *Boston Globe,* columnist Steven Syre called the auction an "unnecessarily complicated, confusing process," marked by "an emphasis on secrecy when transparency should have been the standard." In any case, the IPO stood to raise as much as US$3 billion for Google.

TELECOMMUNICATIONS

Telecommunications companies have been able to establish a strong foothold in the Internet services industry. The two industries are highly interrelated, and telecommunications companies are among those in the best technological position to take advantage of the opportunities available in the Internet marketplace. The company profiled below is an international telecommunications company that has expanded to include significant Internet services offerings. Many local and regional telecommunications companies also offer similar services.

Top-ranked long distance telephone service provider **AT&T** has made its presence known on the Internet. The company accomplished this primarily through its consumer-oriented WorldNet Internet access service but was also looking to gain market share as an Internet service provider for businesses. For that market, they offered AT&T WorldNet Business Services, including Internet dial-up or dedicated access over its backbone network. The company also offered virtual private network and managed network services, data network services, and Web site hosting though its AT&T Easy World Wide Web service. AT&T's 1997 revenues were US$51.3 billion. Revenues reached US$52.6 billion in 2001, but were down to US$30.5 billion in 2004. By that year, the company had divested its cable television services in order to focus on the business services market. In early 2005, the company had agreed to be acquired by SBC Communications.

AT&T was formed in 1899 after changing its name from National Bell Telephone. The company had a virtual monopoly until 1968, when the FCC stripped AT&T of its telephone equipment monopoly and allowed specialized carriers such as MCI access to the phone network, creating room for competition in long distance services. Another government suit led to the 1984 settlement that spun off seven so-called Baby Bells, leaving AT&T with long distance services and Western Electric. In a renewed focus on communications, AT&T divested itself of NCR, Lucent Technologies, and AT&T Capital Corp. during the 1990s. In 1996 the company also began offering Internet access. In promotional efforts, AT&T made deals with Excite, Infoseek, and Lycos to offer WorldNet services on their search engines. A pending deal with Yahoo! would allow users to purchase AT&T services from Yahoo! sites. But by far, AT&T's most substantial transaction was its 1998 acquisition of Tele-Communications, Inc. (TCI), the United States' largest cable television service. In the Internet service industry, TCI had been developing its infrastructure to test Internet access bundled with its cable television service. AT&T, on the other hand, already had a flourishing Internet service but lacked infrastructure for such bundling due to the limited speed and bandwidth over telephone lines.

MAJOR COUNTRIES IN THE INDUSTRY

The Internet has been marked by astounding growth. From 533 million in 2002, the number of worldwide users was expected to reach 945 million in 2004 and exceed one billion by 2007. During the early 2000s, there were nearly 278 million Internet users in the United States and 32 million in Canada. The industry was dominated by the United States, with Europe and the Asia-Pacific region playing lesser roles. According to *Latin Trade,* the investment firm Morgan Stanley indicated that in Japan and North America, Internet users were expected to comprise about 60 percent of the population by 2005. In Europe, penetration was expected to reach 46 percent, while use among Latin Americans was forecast at only 13 percent.

The United States was home to many of the world's leading Web sites in 2004, according to *Business Week.* These sites dominated both domestically and abroad. For example, Google reached 36.7 percent of all European Internet users, followed by MSN (35.7 percent), Microsoft.com (33.3 percent), eBay (20.7 percent) and Yahoo! (19.7 percent). In sixth place was France' Wanadoo (13.2 percent), followed by Italy's Tiscali (10.1 percent) and Spain's Lycos Europe (9.8 percent). Other leaders in the European market included the United States' Amazon.com (9.6 percent), as well as Germany's T-Online (9.3 percent).

In spite of U.S. domination, in the early 2000s there was a great market for international expansion by countries containing lucrative markets. Most were in Latin America, Asia, and Eastern Europe. All were past their first stages of technological advancement and led by government officials who realized the importance of advanced communications to sustain national economies in the information age.

The most sought after market was China, which planned to privatize many state-owned utilities. Although the Chinese government set up many roadblocks for potential ISPs, the potential market still appealed to investors. While there were 12 million Chinese users in 2000, that number reached 80 million by mid-2004. By 2006, *Business Week* cited Piper Jaffray forecasts indicating that 153 million Chinese people would be online, surpassing the United States. Such figures led Yahoo! To introduce a Chinese search engine called Yisou in June of 2004, on the heels of competitor Google, which purchased an interest in a Chinese search engine called Baidu.

FURTHER READING

"Aging Internet Slows Down." *Daily Telegraph, (Sydney)* 30 March 2002.

"Datamonitor: Broadband Adoption on the Up in Europe." *Nua Internet Surveys,* 20 March 2003. Available from http://www.nua.ie/surveys.

"e-Commerce on the Up, but Don't Get Caught Phishing." *iStart,* August 2004. Available from http://www.istart.co.nz.

"E-commerce Takes Off; To Come." *The Economist (US),* 15 May 2004.

"eMarketer: Worldwide B2B Revenues to Pass One Trillion." *Nua Internet Surveys,* 1 April 2003. Available from http://www.nua.ie/surveys.

Fisher, Dennis. "Worms Wreak Havoc on the Net in '03." *eWeek,* 3 April 2003.

Gardner, Dana. "Netscape Pulls It Together." *Info World,* 1 June 1998.

"Global Usage, March 2004." *ClickZ,* 3 May 2004. Available from http://www.clickz.com/stats/big_picture/traffic_patterns/article.php/3348651.

"Global Internet Index: Average Usage." Nielsen//NetRatings, March 2005. Available from http://www.nielsen-netratings.com.

Goldberg, Steven T. "Numbers Do Lie." *Kiplinger's Personal Finance Magazine,* April 2002.

Grech, Herman. "Software Piracy Drops, but Is Still High." *The Times (Malta),* 14 August 2004.

Green, Heather. "China's Great March Online." *Business Week,* 12 July 2004.

Hafner, Katie. "Living the Broadband Life." *The New York Times,* 15 July 2004.

Harmon, Amy. "U.S., in Shift, Drops Its Effort to Manage Internet Addresses." *The New York Times,* 6 June 1998.

"IBM Global Business Security Index Report." IBM, 9 Feb. 2005. Available from http://www-1.ibm.com.

"The Internet Has Enormous Impact on 'Offline' Spending." *The Online Reporter,* 13 September 2003.

Keizer, Gregg. "Online Retailers Tally Record Holiday Sales; Online Holiday Shoppers Spent a Record $18.5 Billion In November and December, a 35 Percent Increase Over Online Sales for the Same Period In 2002, According to the Espending Report." *InternetWeek,* 7 January 2004.

Kharif, Olga. "The Net: Now, Folks Can't Live Without It; Every Year, Millions More People Around the World Use the Internet to Interact In More Ways Than Ever Before, Incorporating It Into All Corners of their Lives." *Business Week Online,* 10 June 2003.

Lardner, James. "Yahoo! Rising." *U.S. News & World Report,* 18 May 1998.

"Leichtman Research: More High-Speed Net Subscribers in U.S." *Nua Internet Surveys,* 2 April 2003. Available from http://www.nua.ie/surveys.

Marsan, Carolyn Duffy. "Domain Name Registrations Drop." *Network World,* 28 January 2002.

"The Nearly World Wide Web." *Latin Trade,* March 2004.

"Net Gains in the Marketspace." *Information Strategy,* June 1997.

Reinhardt, Robert and Robert D. Hof. "Europe Hits the E-Mall. U.S. Companies Dominate as Web Sales Explode Across the Continent." *Business Week,* 12 July 2004.

Roberts, Paul. "Security: The Year Ahead." *InfoWorld,* 5 January 2004.

"TNT Trends: Technology Predictions 2005." Deloitte Touche Tohmatsu, January 2005. Available from http://www.deloitte.com.

SIC 2711
NAICS 511110

NEWSPAPER PUBLISHING

Firms in the newspaper industry develop, publish, and market newspapers, and many, although not all, perform their own printing as well. In the first decade of the twenty-first century some print journalism outlets will merge with other media such as cable television news, Internet news, text television, and telefax newspaper, as part of the trend toward media convergence, say analysts. A few operations globally are noted to have already converged this way or have plans to do so. See also **Periodical Publishing**.

INDUSTRY SNAPSHOT

From the late 1990s through the first years of the twenty-first century, the newspaper industries of most mature markets such as Japan, the United States, and the European Union continued to experience declines in newspaper sales and advertising revenues. These industries all tried to capture younger readers in hopes of keeping them as lifelong newspaper subscribers. Art Valjakka, editor in chief of *Turun Sonomat* in Finland, argues that conservative journalists will have to become multimedia proficient, as newspapers continue to converge with other media such as cable television news, telefax newspaper, and Internet news on demand. In 2001, the World Association of Newspapers argued that all online newspaper access by readers needed to be counted to get a truer picture of the industry's health.

Whatever the arguments, industry analysts worry about the financial health of print journalism, which is particularly threatened in wealthier nations where citizens have diminished reading skills and appreciation. In addition, the industry traditionally is subject to a slump in sales during times of recession. In 2002, newspapers from London to Los Angeles admitted to experiencing the worst overall business slump since the early 1980s, according to *The Guardian* of London, which starkly stated that many citizens have forsaken newspapers to draw their news from the Internet, television, or radio. Some U.K. papers such as *The Mirror* point to 1946 as the last year in memory that sales have been so abysmal.

Newsroom conditions weren't any less gloomy in the United States, particularly after the terrorist attacks on New York City on September 11, 2001 led to a nationwide pulling of ads by the travel industry. In January 2002, the Washington Post Co., publishing home to the *Washington Post,* posted dismal fourth-quarter earnings for 2001 that were about 50 percent of fourth-quarter earnings in 2000. Because of investments and revenue declines of 14 percent in 2001, the *Washington Post*'s 2000 fourth-quarter income was US$37.7 million (worth US$3.98 a share), compared to 2001 fourth-quarter earnings of US$14.5 million and US$1.53 a share. Overall, the picture was rosier for the full 2001 fiscal year as the company listed earnings of US$229.6 million, compared to US $136.5 million in 2000. As reported in the *Washington Post,* the company's revenue was flat at US$2.4 billion and operating revenue was 35 percent lower in 2001 than it had been in 2000. In 2002, the *Post* noted that 2001 ad revenue at the *Wall Street Journal* had slipped 38 percent, and that the *Philadelphia Inquirer* had a 14 percent advertising slump compared to 2000.

As U.S. papers faltered economically, newspapers fast developing Asia and South America saw their circulation and shares of advertising funds rise for the most part. By 2004, Asia published 75 percent of the world's top 100 dailies. The largest newspaper market in the world was China, with a paid circulation of 93.5 million copies daily. India came second, with 78.8 million copies, followed by Japan (70.4 million), the United States (55.6 million), and Germany (22.1 million). Though China led in total circulation, its main paper, *The People's Daily,* ranked eighth in the world in circulation, measured globally at 3.0 million copies.

Despite growth in some Asian markets, the newspaper industry in Korea faced increasing challenges in 2004. According to data from the Korean Society for Journalism and Communication Studies, the country's nine largest newspapers saw a 4.4 percent revenue decrease in 2004, contributing to a 17 percent decline since 2002. Only four papers remained profitable. Aggressive competition from other papers, particularly the free dailies that have sprung up since Metro International launched *Metro* in Seoul in 2002, have cut into circulation, as has competition from online and other news sources.

To the surprise of some business insiders, the global newspaper industry saw a slight circulation gain in 2004, not only among developing markets but in mature markets as well. The World Association of Newspapers (WAN) announced a 2.1 percent rise in global sales and a 5.4 percent increase in advertising revenue. Timothy Balding, WAN director general, described this growth as "extraordinarily positive" and noted that "it has been a very long time since we saw such a revival in so many mature markets." He attributed this success to new products, improved formats, new editorial approaches, and improvements in distribution and marketing. Furthermore, Balding added, advertising revenues had risen substantially: "Despite the competitive challenges in the advertising market, newspapers have more than held their own and their revenues are strongly on the increase again."

Jim Chisolm, a strategist at WAN's 2005 conference, suggested that new digital media will "accelerate the newspaper's renaissance" through such options as text messaging to announce breaking news, participatory activities such as opinion polls and contests, and video feeds. Some of these strategies were used during the tsumani disaster in South Asia in late 2004, when text messaging services were directing information to readers more quickly than print or online services.

Throughout the world, newspapers—particularly those in more developed nations such as the United States and the United Kingdom—are forming partnerships with schools. In the 2000s, virtually all English-speaking publishers realized a need to counteract the long-developing trend toward declining newspaper readership, and reading in general among young adults, according to researchers such as Clark, Martire & Bartolomeo of Englewood Cliffs, New Jersey. Predictions were that readership would continue to decline in future generations unless measures were taken. Elsewhere in the world, the readership of young adults is quite high, as Singapore, for example, counts 92 percent of young adults as readers. While 82 percent of Canadian young adults read, only 40 percent of all young adults in the United States read, according to the World Association of Newspapers.

ORGANIZATION AND STRUCTURE

In the 2000s, the newspaper industry continued to undergo a transition that began in the 1980s. Technological advances and greater competition from other media contributed to the newspaper industry's transformation. Technology both helped and hindered the industry by creating more efficient printing and production equipment, as well as by creating more alternatives such as cable television, satellite television, and the Internet. With the proliferation of alternative media, subscription circulation had peaked throughout much of the world by the 1980s. For example, Australia's newspaper consumption reached its apex in 1956, the United Kingdom's in 1957, the United States' in 1971, and Japan's in 1981. India, China, and other developing countries, on the other hand, constituted some of the world's major growing newspaper markets in the 1990s and 2000s.

Some newspapers in smaller markets are distributed weekly, while larger marketing areas have at least one daily newspaper available, including an especially feature-rich Sunday newspaper. For a time, many cities in the United States had two or more competing newspapers providing news. But, as female readers joined the workplace and so-called white-collar workers wanted their news delivered in the morning, many evening papers, which were sometimes owned by the same company producing the morning edition, folded.

The production of newspapers has always been controversial because editorial writers frequently clamor for environmental reforms, even though the newspaper industry itself is a threat to global forests. Publishers have largely begged off from the environmental consequences of publishing, complaining that the cost of newsprint already threatens the newspaper industry. By 2001, only a small number of companies produced newsprint, and publishers were jittery about the strong possibility of newsprint costs escalating further, according to *Editor & Publisher,* a trade magazine for the newspaper industry. From the 1990s through 2001, newspapers came under fire from environmentalists for hypocrisy and poor environmental practices, when industry lobbyists pleaded with Congress to ease up on restrictions regarding the recycling of newsprint. Other environmentalists have berated the publishing industry for its use of contaminants in inks that are classified as pollutants.

Many newspapers in the United States, Canada, and Europe, and increasingly in other industrialized countries, are owned by large media conglomerates such as Dow Jones & Company Inc., Gannett, CanWest Global Communications Corp., Knight Ridder, News Corp., and Thomson International.

CanWest is an excellent case study example of a modern newspaper company. It is Canada's largest media conglomerate, with coast-to-coast assets including newspapers, television and radio stations, multimedia production facilities, and Internet publishing operations. The company owns all or part of TV stations in Australia, Ireland, and New Zealand. It also owns a film production and distribution company and has plans to launch a book publishing division.

Furthermore, political parties and religious organizations also own and operate newspapers. Because of the costs involved in producing newspapers, many rely on subsidies from other businesses and institutions, which buy newspapers to disseminate and influence information. Nevertheless, many small independent newspapers exist throughout the world.

American City Business Journals (ACBJ), known for its specialized business journals, has become one of the largest publishers of metropolitan business newspapers in the United States. It serves more than 4 million readers in 40 cities.

The World Newspaper Industry notes that newspaper costs fall into five basic categories: newsprint, production, advertising sales, circulation and distribution, and administration. Labor costs are included in these categories and make up 50 percent of all newspapers' costs. Because of the high and escalating costs of newsprint, newspaper publishers implemented more efficient ways of reducing waste of newsprint and also began using lighter paper. Nevertheless, newsprint prices have risen throughout the world since the 1970s and are predicted to skyrocket in the twenty-first century, as consolidations of newsprint manufacturers lead to lessened choice supply and fewer newsprint suppliers.

Technological advances in the 1980s and 1990s, such as the adoption of computers, modems, and more efficient printing systems, reduced some of the industry's production costs during this period. Production costs are divided into prepress, printing, and building. Pre-press costs include news writing expenses, as well as those for page composition, photoengraving, and platemaking. Prepress costs account for nearly 50 percent of all production expenses. Printing costs include production supplies and utilities needed for printing, while building costs include the operation and maintenance of the newspaper facilities.

Circulation expenses account for 75 percent of all circulation revenues for large newspapers and roughly 15 percent of overall newspaper costs. This part of the industry is the most labor intensive because workers must move the time-sensitive newspapers from the factories to the customers on a tight schedule. Distribution costs for large newspapers are higher than those for small papers because large papers must be delivered to a wider geographical area and must negotiate problems such as congested traffic and delivery vehicle maintenance.

Censorship. In certain countries, such as Burma (run by the military junta called the State Peace and Development Council) and Nigeria, governments impose direct censorship of the media including newspapers, according to the U.S. State Department, which views such heavy-handed censoring as a human rights abuse. More commonly, in countries such as Egypt and Saudi Arabia, the censorship is less severe but still a repressive factor for journalists and the public alike. Censoring governments dictate what constitutes acceptable material for publication and often oversee the news content even before it is published. Other countries may censor the media indirectly by establishing instructions and warnings that delineate the boundaries that journalists must respect. The World Association of Newspapers considers the killing of journalists to be the ultimate form of censorship.

The range of censorship varies from highly regulated newspaper industries in countries such as China or Burma to the staunchly defended free press in the United States and Canada. However, even free press nations adhere to forms of voluntary "self-censorship" in times of war, crisis, or other situations, in spite of objections by some journalists who proclaim the public right to know all so that informed decisions can be made. At the request of the government or royal personages, newspapers undergo this form of censorship. For example, during the Afghanistan war in 2001 and 2002, the U.S. military limited press access to certain war zones for journalist and soldier safety and military secrecy; the U.S. press, for the most part, grudgingly obliged. Major Japanese papers also excluded the Prime Minister Tanaka/Lockheed scandal from their pages because of possible negative repercussions. In addition, the press in the United Kingdom omitted coverage of the Falkland War in 1982 at the government's request. In 2001, at least three journalists in Canada writing for CanWest newspapers quit in what they claimed was a protest of the suppression of columns by CanWest's national editorial board.

Newspapers serve two different markets: readers and advertisers. Advertisers exert influence, either small or great, depending upon the publication because the reality is that the industry overall generates far more total revenue from advertising than it does from subscriptions.

Therefore, advertisers can exert a kind of censorship over a newspaper, with this practice occurring around the world. Advertisers increasingly place pressure on newspapers to preview their content prior to publication, as a clause in their contract with publishers, and publishers in the 2000s have tried to exert some control by publishing advertising guidelines and restrictions. Some advertisers ask for preferential placement of ads near favorable news copy, a practice all journalism associations condemn as unethical, although it occasionally occurs. Furthermore, companies have dropped their advertisements from publications over content issues. Tandy Corp., for example, removed its advertisements from the *Arizona Republic* after the paper published a less-than-flattering editorial cartoon about Texas A&M student deaths in a collapsed bonfire in 1999; the ads were pulled at the request of a Texas A&M alumni.

Industry Associations. The World Association of Newspapers (WAN), formerly the International Federation of Newspaper Publishers, began in 1948. Its members, on five continents, number 66 newspaper publisher associations from 93 countries, as well as newspaper executives from 90 countries, 17 global news agencies, and 7 worldwide press organizations. Overall, the WAN has 17,000 newspapers on its membership roster. The association defends freedom of the press, aids the development and expansion of the industry, and encourages cooperation between its members.

The U.S. association, the NAA, represents more than 2,000 Canadian and U.S. member papers and is based in Vienna, Virginia. The NAA mission statement says the organization strives for the advancement of the US$59 billion newspaper industry in the United States and around the world. In 2002, it listed six specific areas of priority: marketing, public policy, diversity, industry development, newspaper operations, and readership.

BACKGROUND AND DEVELOPMENT

China started one of the earliest news collection and dissemination networks in the world during the Han dynasty, which dated from 206 B.C. to 219 A.D. During this period, the imperial court created a message system for garnering news on occurrences and events around the empire. The system was analogous to the postal system of the Middle Ages in Europe, in which the Holy Roman Empire had its agents draft articles on events in the various regions and send them along specified routes. During the Tang dynasty from 618 to 907 A.D., China had a formal publication in place called the *Ti Pao,* translated as "official newspaper," according to *The Newspaper: An International History.* This handwritten publication included information collected along China's message routes. The imperial court itself produced its own newspapers. Later, the *Ti Pao* reached various intellectual groups in China and larger segments of society, around the beginning of the millennium.

China began producing newspapers with some of the standard technology and materials still used centuries later: ink, paper, moving letters, and moveable type. China used these materials well before the appearance of any European newspaper, but it largely did not produce public, scheduled newspapers until Europeans started their own in China during the nineteenth century. Rome also had an early predecessor of the newspaper, the *Acta Diuna* or "daily events," which the government circulated from 131 B.C. to 14 A.D.

The modern newspaper industry grew out of the European invention of the printing press, perfected in the middle of the fifteenth century. With Johan Gutenberg's invention of movable type, European publishers could mass-produce and circulate texts quickly. This technology benefited not only the newspaper industry but also other publishing industries and, moreover, is attributed to the growth of nationalism, industrialism, and widespread literacy. Early publications included the Bible and various encyclopedias.

With the establishment of postal routes and the evolution of greater printing capacities in the early 1600s, Europe's newspaper industry began to grow quickly, bolstered by demand to know developments in the religious wars of the period. Articles from newspapers of the seventeenth century indicate that they covered a wide expanse of Europe on a daily basis and that they had consistent contact with their readers, according to *The Newspaper: An International History.*

By the mid-1660s, forebears of the contemporary industry sprang up in England. The *Oxford Gazette* gained government approval in 1665 and later moved to London, becoming the *London Gazette. The Daily Courant,* the first daily newspaper, reached the market in the early eighteenth century. Benjamin Franklin launched the first paper without government sanction in British colonies in North America during the 1720s. Franklin's *Pennsylvania Gazette* was one of the first commercially successful newspapers, according to The World Newspaper Industry.

The technological developments of the nineteenth century greatly boosted the prosperity of the newspaper industry. The linograph and rotary press increased the speed of newspaper production. In addition, new communications technology such as the telegraph, telephone, and wire services, such as Reuters, aided the collection and dissemination of news worldwide. Typewriters also enhanced the writing of newspaper articles, while wood pulp reduced the cost of producing newspapers. Finally, the railroad in Europe and the United States improved the circulation of newspapers.

In the late nineteenth century and early twentieth century, journalism became more opinionated and press barons such as William Randolph Hearst and Joseph Pulitzer began molding the news to fit their views. A sensational, muckraking style of journalism, called "yellow journalism," became popular in the United States during the late nineteenth century. During this period, competition grew fierce as newspapers fought for readers by relying on sensational stories to win new customers. Given rising literacy and leisure time in the early 1900s, newspaper industries in established markets achieved record revenues and profits, which continued to grow until World War I. After 1918, however, radio began competing with newspapers, capturing a share of their advertising revenues. Later in the century, television emerged as a broadcast medium and reduced advertising in newspapers even further. By the late 1950s, circulation began to decline already in some of the world's largest markets, including the United Kingdom.

The 1980s. By the 1980s, the newspaper industry around much of the world had peaked. Greater competition from television and new technology, such as the Video Cassette Recorder (VCR), captured a larger share of consumers' entertainment spending. During this period, newspapers in the world's major markets began to undergo significant changes to remain a viable news medium. As they struggled to return to profitability, large media conglomerates acquired some of the world's largest newspapers. Newspaper monopolies increased during this period too, as only one paper served a region or a segment of a country's readership.

Lifestyle changes around the world also worked against the newspaper industry in the 1980s. Automobile penetration continued to grow, and so fewer people read newspapers while in transit or bought newspapers from hawkers on the street. In addition, a gradual migration from downtown areas to suburbs during this period, especially in North America, further eroded the circulation of large city papers. Furthermore, the increase of dual income and single-person households in the 1980s meant there seemed to be less time for reading newspapers.

The U.S. newspaper industry led the West in circulation during this period. Because of its expansive geography, the United States housed more daily newspapers serving regional markets than other countries, with 1,688 in the mid-1980s. This was in contrast to 125 in Japan, 93 in the United Kingdom, and 91 in France. U.S. daily circulation stood at 63.08 million and Sunday circulation at 57.6 million in 1985. The *Wall Street Journal* led the country's papers in circulation and profitability during the 1980s with about 2 million subscribers at mid-decade. During the 1980s, Gannett launched what would become the country's second-largest newspaper, *USA Today,* which like the *Wall Street Journal* was a satellite-transmitted paper, meaning that it could be simultaneously printed at regional centers for rapid and efficient national distribution. *USA Today* also eventually developed the circulation tactic of bulk distributions to college populations, hotel guests, and other targeted audiences, substantially elevating its total daily circulation figures. Although U.S. per capita newspaper consumption ranked below that of Scandinavia, the United Kingdom, and Japan, the country's use of newsprint per capita was the highest in the world because U.S. papers were generally larger than their counterparts elsewhere.

The United States also dominated the newspaper industry in terms of influence. U.S. newspapers provided a significant number of the news stories to the United Press International (UPI) and Associated Press (AP) news wires, which disseminated much of the news around the world. U.S. newspapers and wire services generally set the daily news agenda around the world.

Nonetheless, the competition among regional newspapers began to decline in the 1980s, not only in the United States but also around the world. Single newspapers monopolized markets around the country when their leading competitors folded or merged. In many cases advertising demand and advertiser preference for the leading newspaper led to the demise of multi-newspaper markets. In addition, joint-operating agreements (JOAs) became prevalent as newspapers found they could no longer compete with each other. Instead they merged their advertising, circulation, and management personnel, while remaining editorially distinct, under the Newspaper Preservation Act of 1971. In 1984, seven of the top 10 newspapers in the United States were monopolies owned by large newspaper and media conglomerates.

The United Kingdom's newspaper industry ranked among the world leaders in the 1980s. Some of the world's largest newspapers in terms of circulation heralded from the United Kingdom. London's daily newspapers, for example, had a combined circulation of more than 14 million in 1986. By the 1980s, these papers had long served as national newspapers and consequently the country's regional papers remained small. Technology continued to change the U.K. industry during the 1980s. Newspapers had to adapt to commercial radio, television, satellites, and videotext. During this period, landmark U.K. papers such as the *Times* and *Daily Express* lost money, and media conglomerates began to acquire them not for profits but for enhancing their images and increasing their influence.

By the mid-1980s, Germany's newspaper industry took on characteristics of both its U.S. and U.K. counterparts. Germany's geographic size made establishing a national newspaper difficult and expensive, as did its division into 11 states. Hamburg and Frankfurt were the country's largest cities before the reunification, and these cities housed the country's largest newspapers. Hamburg's *Bild Zeitung* was the country's largest daily paper with 5.9 million subscribers, followed by *Anzeiger* with 1.7 million. Axel Springer controlled 29 percent of the market at this time and owned the *Bild Zeitung,* as well as *Die Welt,* a paper created in 1946 by the British government and modeled after the *Times.* The strength of the newspaper industry during this period was due in part to the government's limit on television advertising, which made newspapers the leading source of advertising.

The French newspaper industry, unlike some of its Western counterparts, remained regulated by the government in the mid-1980s. The government controlled France's press agency, Agence France Presse, and guaranteed newsprint to all newspapers at the same price, as well as unbiased, equal distribution. The Parisian daily newspapers faced dwindling circulation in the 1980s. While the 13 Parisian dailies had a combined circulation of 3.8 million in 1980, they had a circulation of only 2.5 million by 1986. Furthermore, the circulation of the country's provincial papers fell to 7.5 million in 1980, down from 9 million in 1946. Hersant led the French newspaper industry with its 22 provincial papers. Like newspaper industries in other industrialized countries, France's became more monopolistic with a trend toward one daily paper per market. By 1985, France had only 10 Parisian newspapers and 75 provincial titles. In addition, per capita consumption continued to fall during the 1980s.

Japan's modern industry began in 1945 during the reconstruction under General Douglas McArthur. In 1947 Japan's newspapers started operating as a free press. By 1985, Japan's largest paper, *Yomiuri Shimbun,* reported a circulation of 5.4 million, followed by *Asahi Shimbun* with 3.8 million. Not only were these papers Japan's largest, they also were the largest in the world. With its dense population and high literacy rate, Japan was the world's second-largest market for newspapers, trailing only the Soviet Union and ahead of the United States. Following the collapse of the Soviet Union, Japan became the global frontrunner.

CURRENT CONDITIONS

Outlook and Trends. Because of shrinking domestic markets since the 1980s in most developed countries, newspaper publishers have expanded their focus to include international markets. For example, the *Wall Street Journal* increased its operations abroad during this period, while the *New York Times* expanded its global presence via joint operations with newspapers in other markets. In May 2004, The Washington Post Co. announced the acquisition of *El Tiempo Latino,* a leading Spanish-language weekly newspaper in the greater Washington area. The publication was eventually named the Best Hispanic Weekly in the United States by The National Association of Hispanic Publications.

With competition from other news media, especially television and the Internet, newspaper circulation declined throughout the 1990s and early 2000s for some of the world's largest newspapers, particularly in the United States. For the six-month period ending March 2005, the circulation for U.S. dailies dropped by an average of 1.9 percent; Sunday edition circulation dropped by 2.5 percent. Declines were highest for large urban newspapers, while circulation for small and medium sized papers remained stable or, in a few cases, even grew. The top-selling paper in the United States remained *USA Today,* with a circulation of 2,281,831 daily, up by .05 percent. Second was the *Wall Street Journal,* with a circulation of 2,070,498, down by 0.8 percent. Most other major papers, however, experienced steep circulation declines. The *Chicago Tribune* daily edition dropped 6.6 percent, while its Sunday edition dropped 4.6 percent. Also reporting significant declines were the *Los Angeles Times* (6.4 percent daily and 7.9 percent Sunday), the *Cleveland Plain Dealer* (5.2 percent daily), the *San Francisco Chronicle* (6 percent daily and 7.7 percent Sunday), the *Washington Post* (2.6 percent daily and 2.4 percent Sunday), the *Houston Chronicle* (3.9 percent), the *Arizona Republic* (3.2 percent), the *Rocky Mountain News* (6.6 percent), the *Denver Post* (6.3 percent), and the *Baltimore Sun* (11.5 percent daily and 8.4 percent Sunday). Both the *New York Times* and the *New York Post* posted slight increases in daily circulation (0.24 percent and 0.01 percent, respectively), though the *Times* saw a 4 percent decline in Sunday sales. Among the few papers reporting significant increases were the *St. Louis Post Dispatch,* up in daily copies by 1.1 percent, though down 2 percent for its Sunday edition; and the *Minneapolis Star Tribune,* up by 0.3 percent daily but down 2.3 percent Sunday.

Lower circulation numbers, analysts predicted, would likely affect advertising revenues. National advertising, which grew by 8.1 percent to US$7.8 billion in 2003, was the fastest-growing newspaper advertising segment, but its continued robust growth looked uncertain as of 2005. Analysts felt that prospects for retail ads, which grew 1.7 percent in 2003 to reach US$21.3 billion, appeared more stable.

The Tabloid Revolution. A significant trend in the early 2000s was the growing popularity of tabloids. In particular, these smaller-sized papers attracted the younger market for which every newspaper was competing. A key player in this segment was Metro International, publishers of 56 *Metro* daily papers in 78 major cities across the world. Aimed specifically at readers in their twenties and thirties, the free tabloid-sized dailies are distributed at college campuses and at busy commuter areas, such as subway stations, and by 2005 they had reached about 15 million readers per day and more than 33 million readers weekly. The company reported in 2005 that advertising revenues have increased by a compound annual rate of 47 percent since the first edition appeared in 1995. According to the company, *Metro* content includes leading local, national, and international stories, produced in a "standardized and accessible format and design, which enables commuters to read the newspaper during a typical journey time of less than twenty minutes. *Metro*'s editorial content is also free from bias and focuses on giving readers the news they need at the time they read, rather than comment or views." The popularity of *Metro* led to the introduction of similar free tabloids, and affected sales of established newspapers in many markets, including Korea.

In response to market research indicating that younger readers prefer a smaller format, several leading papers, including the London *Times* and *Independent,* have converted to tabloid size. Indeed, according to a *Kansas City Star* article by Steve Johnson, newspaper designers believe that many, if not most, major U.S. papers will convert to tabloid by 2010. Though this move would appeal to readers, who have demonstrated a decided preference for smaller-sized papers, the question of advertising revenues could remain tricky. "Advertisers would have to be persuaded that a full-page tabloid ad is worth as much as a full-page broadsheet ad," wrote Johnson, adding that this matter was "proving no easy challenge in the U.K."

In the meantime, several papers in the United States have already experimented with tabloid-sized editions. In 2002, the *Chicago Tribune* launched its *RedEye* edition, aimed at younger commuters; the Chicago *Sun-Times* responded with *Red Streak*. In 2003, the *Washington Post* introduced *Express,* a commuter newspaper of 20 to 24 pages, designed to be read during a 15-minute commute. Tribune Publishing announced that it would produce *amNewYork,* another paper aimed at young urban commuters. In 2004, Meximerica Media announced plans to publish *Rumbo,* a tabloid aimed at Hispanic men and women under age 45.

Uncertain Ad Revenues. Newspapers' share of aggregate advertising spending shrank in many developed countries during the late 1990s and 2000s. In 1995, it stood at only 22.4 percent in the United States. Furthermore, in 1996 television finally surpassed newspapers for the leading share of advertising funds after lagging for 50 years. Even before the disastrous September 11, 2001, terrorist attacks caused advertisers to scale back dollars previously targeted to be spent on newspaper display ads, the non-profit Newspaper Association of America said that advertising expenditures for the second quarter of 2001 dropped 8.4 percent from 2000 figures, totaling US$11.1 billion. The situation began to improve thereafter, with the global newspaper industry reporting a 2 percent increase in advertising revenues in 2003 and a 5.3 percent rise in 2004—the largest increase in five years. Though newspapers' share of the global advertising market continued to decline, falling to 30.5 percent in 2003 and then to 30.1 percent in 2004, newspapers remained the second-largest advertising medium in the world, after television, and analysts expected this position to hold solid for several years.

Developing countries remained the bright spot for the industry as circulation and advertising spending continued to rise. The International Federation of Newspaper Publishers reported that circulation in countries such as Malaysia, Brazil, and India rose dramatically in the mid-1990s, in contrast to declines in Japan, the United States, and the European Union. Furthermore, advertising revenues in developing economies shot up 30 percent during this period.

Global Circulation and Trade. India's newspaper industry is one of the most prominent expanding newspaper industries in the world. India's newspaper count grew from just 300 in 1947, the year the country gained independence from British colonial rule, to 2,000 in the mid-1990s, when India became the world's leader in quantity of daily newspapers. About 70 of India's papers have circulation of more than 100,000, and newspapers reach approximately 22 percent of the country's prodigious population. Newspapers controlled 66 percent of the country's advertising dollars in the mid-1990s, and India's papers ranked among the least expensive in the world, roughly US$0.06 a paper. In 2004, the country's total circulation was measured at 78.8 million, the second largest in the world.

The Germans are among the world's most news-hungry populations. In Europe, the United Kingdom and Germany have about four dailies sold for every ten people. As in the United Kingdom, in Germany the most popular title is a tabloid; Germany's is *Bild Zeitung* with a circulation of 4.4 million. Germany's newspaper circulation grew from the early 1990s to the mid-1990s, largely as a result of the country's reunification. During this same period, Spain reported real growth of 14 percent, Israel of 18 percent, and Turkey of 22 percent. However, circulation expanded from very low levels, according to figures from *Editor & Publisher.* Emerging economies in Asia, South America, and Australia also reported some of the best growth in the industry.

Journalist Safety and Press Freedom. By 2001, journalists experienced more dangerous conditions than they had in the late 1990s. 26 journalists from 14 countries were killed while gathering and reporting news in 1997, down from 46 killed worldwide in 1996. In 1999, that figure jumped to 70 journalists killed. In 2001, some 60 journalists and media workers lost their lives on the job, as Latin America, in particular, became a deadly place to pursue news reporting as a vocation. Other journalists were under siege from arrests and threats of arrest in South Africa, Nigeria, and other countries. In 2002, the abduction and murder of *Wall Street Journal* reporter Daniel Pearl called world attention to the dangers reporters face from zealots, human predators, warlords, and war-zone conditions. 2004 proved the third most deadly year for journalists since 1812, with a total of 78 lives lost; 25 of these occurred as a result of the war in Iraq.

The Internet. The Internet increased competition with newspapers, allowing companies not affiliated with the industry to publish news and information on the Internet. Because of this, newspapers quickly launched online versions of their papers in order to capture media-savvy online consumers and advertisers, who see the attractiveness of Internet consumers. For example, some companies created employment Web sites, which absorbed a share of the employment classified ads newspapers received, while others provided news headlines and information on their sites.

By the mid-1990s, roughly 500 U.S. and European newspapers had already set up online versions of their papers. The U.S. newspapers led the foray into online publishing, ahead of other media in the United States and other newspapers around the world. About 78 South American papers and 28 in Japan also had Internet versions by 1996. In addition to enabling them to compete in their local markets, the Internet also provided newspaper publishers with a means of reaching the entire world, thus increasing their readership and advertising. To compete with non-newspaper news sites online, publishers also formed alliances with various Web sites to provide news and information. Tribune Company, for example, teamed up with America Online to offer *Digital City,* which offers news and entertainment information on six metropolitan areas.

Despite these efforts by newspaper publishers, some industry observers contend that newspapers and broadcast television could still lose a significant share of their audiences to computer-based services. As a result, nearly all major newspapers are studying ways to strengthen and preserve their position in the twenty-first century. In 2002, with media convergence a reality, some industry analysts worried that traditional ethics and standards associated with newspapers during the mid-to-late twentieth century would fall by the wayside as newspapers lost their identity and combined functions with the online press, television cable news, and news-on-demand suppliers.

In 2003, *online publishing news* reported that 20 top news publishing businesses met to discuss their industry's future. Formulating projections to 2005, they concluded that online news publishing was experiencing a period of uncertainty. Although challenged by commercial pressures and lower budgets, underlying growth factors were felt to be strong. Those in attendance included online publishing specialists for *Le Monde, The Wall Street Journal,* and *The Guardian.* They concluded that both medium- and long-term growth looked promising for the market. Speakers believed only 20 to 30 percent of the revenue potential for their companies had been realized in the online environment.

Another 2003 *online publishing news* article claimed that regional dailies were competing more and more on the Web with titles that were not previously seen as competitors. The related prediction was that this trend would lead to continuing investment online for bib-name news titles.

RESEARCH AND TECHNOLOGY

As environmental regulation increased worldwide from the 1980s through the early 2000s, so did the number of regulations impacting print trade in general. Although this included newspapers, the latter lobbied hard for exemptions. The regulation of waste disposal meant that newspapers had to keep closer tabs on what went down the drain, from photography chemicals to printing ink. These regulations meant changing operations, from implementing recycling programs to more drastic changes. More drastic measures included wholesale changes in press technology to shift away from the use of oil-based inks. In the United States, for example, the Resource Conservation and Recovery Act specifies the manner in which items designated as hazardous wastes are to be handled, which covers substances used by the newspaper publishing industry. In the mid-1990s, some industry analysts reported that fines by the U.S. Government had increased five times during this period.

Furthermore, increased environmental concern regarding recycling of newsprint gave rise to proposals mandating the greater use of recycled paper in newsprint. For example, about 16 percent of newsprint used in the United States contains recycled paper. However, environmental groups tried to push for legislation requiring newspapers with circulation greater than 200,000 to use paper products containing no less than 35 percent recycled material. Proponents argued that municipalities could realize savings of US$1.5 billion per year in waste disposal costs. Trade groups, particularly the National Newspaper Association, protested, saying that these types of mandates would lead to much higher capital expenditures for smaller newspapers, even those currently using recycled paper.

Emerging newspaper technology in the late 1990s included the digital press, digital prepress, keyless inking, shaftless presses, and keyless offset presses. The digital press, however, remained unsuitable for newspaper printing in the late 1990s, although publishers could use digital prepress data to preset their conventional presses. Keyless inking technology, on the other hand, alleviated some of the labor from presetting, while shaftless printers increased flexibility and efficiency. Keyless inking systems eliminated manual adjustments by presetting ink levels before the press began, reducing waste from test printing and improving consistency. Sales of keyless offset printers rose throughout the world during this period as one of the leading new printing technologies. The Swiss manufacturer Wifag introduced the shaftless printer in 1995, which features individually motorized moving components and a gearless transmission that reduces waste and labor. The growth of shaftless presses in Europe encouraged their growth in the United States, which began manufacturing and buying them in the late 1990s.

Newspapers also took advantage of on-screen typesetting via computers in the mid-1990s, which enabled publishers to increase the efficiency of the typesetting process. On-screen typesetting eliminated the need for skilled workers to create and design newspaper pages. Instead, workers could now create pages easily with the aid of computer software. The newspaper industry also began adopting digital cameras during this period. These cameras allowed users to capture images on a disk or the camera's hard drive and then transfer them to a computer for adjustment and manipulation. Digital cameras reduced time needed to process photographs and decreased costs spent on newspaper photographs, by eliminating film and dark room expenses.

INDUSTRY LEADERS

News Corp. The News Corporation Limited, owned by contemporary newspaper baron Rupert Murdoch, was one of the leading newspaper conglomerates in the early 2000s and was the top publisher in the world of English-language newspapers. Its publications include the *New York Post, The Times* (London), and the *Australian,* as well as magazines such as *TV Guide* and the book publisher HarperCollins. The company's other media holdings include television stations plus cable and satellite operations in the United States, South America, and Australia, as well as the movie studio Twentieth Century Fox.

As was the case with newspapers across the world, News Corp. suffered a substantial decline in ad revenues in 2001, with second quarter operating revenue dropping by 16 percent. On the whole, only the Australian newspaper holdings seemed able to avoid a battering; it reported an increase in advertising and circulation. While growth remained strongest in Australia through 2004, News Corp. succeeded in boosting its U.K. circulation across all its newspaper titles in 2004, resulting in a 7 percent growth in advertising revenues. Operating income for News Corp.'s newspapers segment rose from US$686 million in 2003 to US$831 million in 2004. More than 75 percent of News Corp.'s sales are from its business in the United States. Murdoch's family controls about 30 percent of the company.

Gannett Company, Inc.. Gannett Company Inc., also a global newspaper and media power, has become the leading newspaper publisher in the United States, in terms of distribution. However, the same is not true of its prestige, as critics condemn its flagship *USA Today* daily with pejorative names such as "McPaper." As of 2004, Gannett's 100 U.S. daily papers claimed a paid circulation of just under 8 million. Since 1997 *USA Today* moved from being the country's second largest newspaper, at 1.6 million circulation, to the number one paper in the early 2000s, with a circulation of about 2.3 million.

Nonetheless, not even the giant Virginia-based chain could completely overcome the advertising woes gripping nearly all U.S. newspapers in the early 2000s. While managing to report a small revenue gain in 2001, Gannett Co. fell prey to a significant advertising revenue loss in the final three months of 2001. The company blamed much of the loss on the September 11 terrorist attacks, as travel ads shrank in all chain dailies. When the bottom line was revealed in 2002, Gannett posted earnings of US$831.2 million on revenue of US$6.3 billion. This was significantly lower than the 2001 Gannett figures of US$1.7 billion on revenue of US$6.2 billion. But earnings improved in 2003, when the company posted operating revenues of US$6.7 billion. The following year, sales rose to US$7.3 billion, resulting in net earnings of US$1.3 billion.

In addition to *USA Today,* Gannett also owns Newsquest. It is one of the United Kingdom's largest newspaper groups with more than 30 titles, including 17 newspapers. Gannett's Internet presence includes more than 60 Web sites.

Asahi Shimbun. Asahi Shimbun Publishing Company produced the world's second-largest newspaper in circulation, *Asahi Shimbun.* In 1996, *Asahi Shimbun's* circulation stood at 12.6 million, but after years of falling ad revenue, intense competition from rival newspapers, and declining readership, its circulation dropped to about 12 million in 2004.

Knight Ridder. Knight Ridder remained a major force in the global newspaper industry and the second most dominant player in the U.S. industry. The company was formed through the merger of Knight Newspapers Inc. and Ridder Publications Inc. in 1974. In the United States, Knight Ridder ranked second as a chain, behind Gannett, with its papers such as the *Detroit Free Press, Miami Herald,* and the *Philadelphia Inquirer.* Overall, the company publishes 31 daily newspapers in 28 markets around the United States with its print and online versions. Knight Ridder reported daily circulation of 9 million and Sunday circulation of 12 million in 2004. The company restructured itself to focus on its core operation, the newspaper business, in the late 1990s by shedding non-newspaper holdings such as its cable interests. Furthermore, Knight Ridder bought a number of new papers during this period, including the Fort Worth Star-Telegram, the Kansas City Star, and the Times Leader of Pennsylvania.

The Miami-based company's sales edged up 3 percent in 1997 to US$2.87 billion. But in 2002, as flagship newspapers in Detroit and Philadelphia continued losing subscribers and revenue, the company posted substantial losses. Non-advertising and non-circulation revenue plunged 41 percent (compared with December 2000 revenues) to US$8.9 million in the final quarter of 2001, according to the company. Meanwhile, non-advertising and non-circulation revenue for 2001 fell by a quarter from 2000 postings to US$133.4 million. By 2004, earnings had begun to improve. In its May 2004 statistical report, Knight Ridder reported total advertising revenue was up 2.9 percent for May and up 2.0 percent year to date. Total sales for 2004 reached US$3.0 billion. As a pioneer in online news, the company operates several Web sites. It also owns stakes in an advertising company and newsprint mill.

Axel Springer. Axel Springer Verlag AG produces *Bild,* Germany's leading newspaper, as well as *Die Welt,* and numerous other papers. As a media conglomerate, Axel Springer also has magazine, book, radio, television, and information holdings. The company owns a stake in 30 publishing companies throughout Europe. Berlin-based Axel Springer's sales totaled US$2.86 billion in 1996, about 7 percent above its 1995 sales. But harder times in the media industry also put Axel Springer under media stress in 2002 as newspaper ad revenues plummeted and its falling stock shares reflected financial losses. In 2002, the media giant informed stockholders it was paying no profits after a year of falling revenues and poor advertising performance. Axel Springer reported a welcome 5 percent revenue increase in 2003, bringing total sales to US$3.0 billion and boosting net income by 155.0 percent over the previous year.

MAJOR COUNTRIES IN THE INDUSTRY

China. In 2004, China led the world in total circulation with 93.5 million copies sold daily. Additionally, China had the largest number of daily papers among the world's top 100. Though its primary newspaper is *The People's Daily,* a national edition that is the official paper of the Communist Party, it was second in circulation to *Shanghai Daily.* As of 2003, China's newspaper industry, which included 2,100 papers, saw revenues from advertising increase by 29 percent in 2004, more than twice the growth for the previous year. Between 2000 and 2004, ad revenues grew by 116 percent.

Japan. Japan, which led the global newspaper industry in the late 1990s and early 2000s, slipped to third place in 2004 in terms of total circulation (70.4 million), but still produced the world's top-selling paper, *Yomiuiri Shimbun,* which sold more than 14 million copies daily. Among the most industrialized countries, Japan remained one of the few to report circulation growth in the late 1990s, as its circulation rose by 1.1 percent from 1993 to 1997, reaching 72.6 million, and several papers reported slight drops by 2000. Japan's newspapers constitute six of the world's highest circulation newspapers, and circulation remained well above its closest competitor, the United States.

United States. The United States ranked fourth globally in 2004, with a still declining circulation of 55.6 million. Circulation figures were 59.9 million in 1999 and 60.1 million in 1998, according to the Newspaper Association of America. The decline in advertising in the industry first began in 1984, according to the Audit Bureau of Circulations. In advertising revenues, the U.S. newspaper industry saw a significant increase during the 1990s, rising from US$53.1 billion in 1997 to US$76.5 billion in 2000, according to the Newspaper Association of America. For more than two decades the industry was particularly dependent upon classified ad sales for revenue. In 1980, classified ads were 28.5 percent of all ad revenue and brought in US$4.2 billion. However, in 2000 the percentage was slightly above 40 percent for a total of US$19.6 billion, according to figures from Merrill Lynch and *Editor & Publisher.*

Consolidation continued to affect the U.S. newspaper industry, with Lee Enterprises' purchase of Pulitzer in 2005 for US$1.46 billion, making Lee the fourth largest owner of dailies in the United States. Lee had previously owned 44 community newspapers, including the *Quad-City Times* of Iowa; Pulitzer increased this number by 14 dailies. The deal added US$440 million to Lee's 2004 revenues.

In 2002, the U.S Department of Labor predicted stagnating employment for news analysts, reporters, and correspondents through 2010, as more evening newspapers close and more cities have only a single local newspaper covering events. Other jobs are expected to be lost due to papers merging and consolidating, according to Department of Labor forecasts. The overall prognosis for reporters is both good and bad. Traditional U.S. papers will see circulation fall, an increase in expenses as computer-assisted reporting and other costs run up, and declines in advertising revenue, unless the industry can stem the loss of advertising to other media. The rosier picture is that employment in other media, and in other venues such as online publications, newsletters, and magazines, will keep the overall employment equal to or only slightly below 2002 levels.

Europe. Europe also had one of the world's strongest markets for newspapers in the late 1990s, although, like other mature markets, most countries in Europe experienced declining circulation in 2001 and 2002. Germany led Europe and was fifth in the world in terms of circulation (22.1 million) in 2004. Nevertheless, this figure represented a 2.11 percent decline over circulation for the previous year. After Germany's early 1990s reunification, its publishers produced 406 newspapers in 1995, up from 356 in 1990. Germany also dominated newspaper and periodical trade in the mid-1990s with exports of US$982.4 million, imports of US$318.5 million, and a trade balance of US$663.9 million, the largest in the world. The U.K. industry was the second largest with circulation of 20 million and 103 papers in 1995. The United Kingdom also was a major newspaper and periodical trader, with exports of US$600.0 million and imports of US$149.2 million. However, the former boom in U.K papers had disappeared by January 2002 as national morning newspaper sales plunged from 13.1 million in December 2000 to 12.9 million in December of 2001. *The Guardian* of London said that newspaper sales were at their lowest levels in two decades, both in the region and countrywide. Perhaps an unwitting comment on national values and character, the United Kingdom's best-selling newspaper is *The Sun,* Rupert Murdoch's racy tabloid with daily sales of 3.5 million.

The U.K. newspaper industry weathered some changes in the early 2000s, as circulation fell by 11.41 percent between 2000 and 2004 and traditional circulation bases shifted. Despite declines among many major dailies, the *Times* and the *Independent* both increased their paid circulation by about 10 percent between 2004 and 2005. Stephen Glover in the *Spectator* attributed this growth to the papers' new tabloid format—a move he considered ldquo;downmarket" but profitable. Other papers saw circulations shrink substantially between the mid-1990s and 2004. The *Sun* dropped from 4 million to 3.25 million, while the *Daily Mirror* declined by almost 33 percent. On the other hand, sales of the *Daily Star* grew by more than 15 percent during this same period. *The Guardian,* which, according to Glover, lost some readers to the *Independent*, planned to adopt a smaller format in 2006. The *Financial Times* lost a substantial number of U.K. subscribers but posted circulation gains overseas. Nevertheless, loss of ad revenues combined with increased production costs eroded the paper's profits.

Though Europe in general rates high as a newspaper market, circulation varies greatly country to country. Italy, for example, has one of the lowest circulation rates in the industrialized world. According to a 2004 AP report, only one in ten Italians, compared to one in three Japanese, buys a newspaper. Out of Italy's total newspaper circulation of 7 million, free tabloids accounted for about 1 million and were growing. Nevertheless, Italy was one of eight E.U. nations reporting a rise in paid circulation (0.19 percent) in 2004. Austria, Belgium, Estonia, Finland, Portugal, and Spain also posted increases, with Poland leading in circulation growth (15.21 percent).

Further Reading

"API Black Newspaper Readership Study Drops Media Bombshell." *The Michigan Front Page,* 2 July 2004.

"Axel Springer Verlag Posts Loss for 2000," *Die Welt,* 21 February 2002.

Baron, Ed. "Lessons from Abroad." *Presstime,* November 2001.

Dobhal, Shailesh et al. "The Great Media Explosion." *Business Today,* 20 January 2002.

Dunnet, Peter J. S. *The World Newspaper Industry,*London: Croom Helm, 1988.

Fine, Jon. "Newspapers" Free-fall: Paid Circ Continues to Shrink." *Advertising Age,* 9 May 2005.

"Gannett Profit Down In 2001; Media Company Blames Ad Slump," *The Washington Post,* 8 February 2002.

Glover, Stephen. "However Bad Things May Seem, the News for Newspapers is Good." *Spectator,* 1 January 2005.

Grant, Tavia. "Media Spat: Profit vs. Free Speech." *The Christian Science Monitor,* 15 February 2002.

Greenslade, Roy. "An Annus Horribilis." *The Guardian,* 17 December 2001.

Hill, Don. "World Journalism Became Even More Deadly, Dangerous in 2001." Available from http://www.rferl.org.

Hovanyetz, Scott. "Knight-Ridder Commercial Revenue Falls." *DM News,* 11 February 2002.

Johnson, Steve. "For U.S. Newspapers, Future May Be in Tabloid Size." *Kansas City Star,* 12 November 2004.

Matthews, Janet. "Republic of Korea Profile." *Asia & Pacific Review World of Information,* 30 August 2001.

Newspaper Association of America (NAA), 2005. Available from http://www.naa.org.

Owen, Richard. "News Corp Feels the Pressure of Worldwide Downturn." *Courier Mail,* 14 February 2002.

"Post Co. Profit Down by Half," *The Washington Post,* 26 January 2002.

Preston, Peter. "On the Press: Papers Feel Pain, but Hope for Gain." *The Observer,* 20 January 2002.

Redmont, Dennis. "Newspapers See Danger in Text Messaging." Associated Press, 7 May 2004. Available from http://www.allheadlinenews.com.

Rosenberg, Jim and Lucia Moses. "The Newsprint Crisis Has Receded for Now." *Editor and Publisher,* 6 August 2001.

Saba, Jennifer. "Text Messaging May Be Way to Reach Young Readers." *Editor & Publisher,* 27 May 2004. Available from http://www.mediainfo.com.

Smith, Anthony. *Goodbye, Gutenberg: The Newspaper Revolution of the 1980's,* New York: Oxford University Press, 1980.

———. *The Newspaper: An International History,* London: Thames and Hudson, 1978.

"Some Papers Lose Big in Today's New Circulation Numbers." *Editor & Publisher,* 2 May 2005. Available from http://www.editorandpublishers.com.

"Ten Top-Selling International Newspapers," *Campaign,* 17 December 2001.

"Twenty Top Publishers Map Out Online Publishing's Future," 2003. Available from http://www.onlinepublishingnews.com.

"U.S. Newspaper Advertising Revenue Shows Signs of Life," 2003. Available from http://www.onlinepublishingnews.com.

"US Newspapers Go Head-to-Head On the Web," 2003. Available from http://www.onlinepublishingnews.com.

Weisbart, Mike. "Circulation Up But Papers Still Hurting." *Korea Times,* 30 May 2005. Available from http://www.times.hankooki.com.

SIC 7372

NAICS 511210

PACKAGED SOFTWARE

The packaged software industry designs, develops, and publishes computer software programs for retail and wholesale distribution. Though some are marketed for specialized or technical end uses—and some may be distributed electronically rather than in literal packages—these products are known as packaged or off-the-shelf software, in contrast to custom programs written for a specific customer. Important industry products include operating system software, system utilities, and application tools and solutions. For a description and analysis of the custom programming business and related computer services, see also **Information Technology Services**.

INDUSTRY SNAPSHOT

Prepackaged software falls into two main categories: system infrastructure software, which includes operating system software, system utilities, and program compilers; and application software. The industry was plagued by a sluggish economy in Europe and Asia in 2002, preceded by an equally woeful U.S. economy and even more woeful software portrait in 2001. However, the situation seemed to have improved for the industry by 2003, with worldwide sales of software exceeding US$200 billion, an amount that also exceeded expectations. Most of the largest firms showed very positive growth rates in 2004, with several showing net incomes after several years of net losses. Analyst and industry participants expected growth to continue, with China pegged for explosive growth.

Three markets—the United States, Western Europe, and Japan—accounted for roughly 90 percent of global sales, but as these markets matured, more-rapid growth was expected to come from emerging markets in Asia, especially China. In general, the volatility of the packaged software industry encourages competition and provides more choices for consumers by forcing software makers to create better products at lower cost. India has emerged as the country where offshoring of software development most often occurs as it provides an educated, English-speaking labor force that is still low cost compared to that in other countries.

A major factor influencing the industry has been the market's continuing trend away from large, expensive, non-standardized (closed or proprietary) mainframes to smaller, cheaper, standardized (open) computer systems. In the mainframe arena, much of the software used was custom developed and often took months from initial planning to final implementation. In some cases, the backlog of software development was so great that by the time the software was installed, it was outdated. This differed greatly from smaller open systems, which provided a means for businesses to use prepackaged software. Prepackaged software was cheaper and took less time to implement because it did not need to be created from ground zero, and as a result worldwide prepackaged software sales increased. However, because copying prepackaged software was easy for the unethical, piracy remained a major issue in the 2000s. Piracy cost software producers billions of dollars in lost revenues from consumers making copies of programs for friends to unscrupulous companies mass-producing illegal copies. The Software Publishers Association estimated that half of all business applications installed in the late 1990s were pirated copies. In mid-2004, software piracy remained a concern to the industry, with 2003 industry losses pegged at US$29 billion, according to research from the Business Software Alliance (BSA) and research firm IDC, cited in *InternetWeek.*

ORGANIZATION AND STRUCTURE

Prepackaged software can be divided into two main categories: system infrastructure software and application software. System software, which manages computer resources and organizes data, can be further divided into three main areas: operating system software, which controls the operations of a computer; system utilities, which manage system resources and data; and program compilers, which act as interpreters of programming languages. Operating systems help the various components of a computer—disk drive, a monitor or monitors, and keyboard—work as a unified whole. The best-known operating system (OS), the Microsoft Disk Operating System (MS-DOS), was produced by U.S. software giant Microsoft Corporation and was ubiquitous on IBM-compatible personal computers (PCs) until the mid-1990s when it was eclipsed by Microsoft's Windows OS. System utilities, while they can be part of an operating system, enhance and increase the performance of computers and monitor resources (e.g., determining how much memory is in use and how much space remains on a disk drive). Program compilers convert programming languages that are readable to users into a form that a computer can process as instructions. The systems software market worldwide generated revenues of US$35.1 billion in 1997, a 13.2 percent increase from 1996. In 2001 Microsoft released a Windows operating system version, Windows XP, that possessed a simpler interface for desktop operations by home and office users. Another popular, and free, operating system is Linux, a Unix-related system created by Linus Torvalds and cohorts. Another powerful Unix-related system with an easier interface than Linux, sold by Apple, is the Mac OS X, a super-modern operating system that combines the power and stability of UNIX with customizable tools for programmers, graphic designers, and other creative occupations.

Application software can be divided into two types: application tools and application solutions. Application tools are software packages that enable access, manipulation, and retrieval of data, and include programming applications that are used to develop other software programs. Application solutions are software packages that perform specific functions, such as word processing and accounting. In 1997 the application tools market worldwide was US$31 billion. The application solutions market that same year was US$56 billion. Growth in application software slowed dramatically in 2001 but was expected to regain momentum in 2003.

In 2003, system-related software accounted for 30 percent of global consumption, while the application sector could be divided into 48 percent consumption of applications and 22 percent for software used in the development and deployment of applications.

One software market to experience particularly rapid growth during the late 1990s was the consumer category, and in 2002, with corporate sales stalled, the industry welcomed individual buyers whose spending helped software sales rebound. In 1997 this segment of the industry grew 15.3 percent to US$5.5 billion. Major purchase areas included educational products ("edutainment"), computer games, and home management software, such as budgeting and tax preparation programs. The edutainment segment of this market was expected to grow rapidly through the late 1990s and 2000s, particularly as universities competed for students choosing distance education options.

Due to the disparities in international copyright and licensing laws and standards in developing, implementing, and maintaining software various international organizations and agreements were made. These organizations and agreements helped to provide some standardization in the industry and to decrease fraud and piracy. In 1987 the Joint Technical Committee 1 (JTC1) was created by the International Organization of Standardization (ISO) and the International Electrotechnical Commission (IEC). It was created to develop standards for information technology. SC7, a subcommittee of JTC1 with 19 countries as voting members, was also created. Its main objective was to develop and adapt standards to improve software engineering processes and commercial transactions, with particular focus on quality assurance standards (internationally accepted practices used in the development of software), life cycle processes (the procurement, creation, operation, and maintenance of software in contracts), and software processes.

One of the main issues addressed by regulatory agencies during the 1990s was software piracy. According to the Business Software Alliance's (BSA) most recent statement, the income from software that pirates take annually is about US$12 billion. The BSA says that 83 percent of the thievery hurts software corporations in North America, Asia, and Western Europe—with the United States the biggest loser of pirated work. A BSA study estimates that Vietnam, China, and Russia have more pirated software in use by corporations than software obtained legally.

As provided for under the 1974 Trade Act of the United States, and amended by the Special 301 provisions of the 1988 Omnibus Trade and Competitiveness Act, United States Trade Representatives (USTR) gained the right to investigate infringements of intellectual property rights worldwide. Countries that did not provide adequate protection of intellectual property rights were placed on a priority list. Countries that had priority status faced possible trade sanctions and restrictions. Countries that did not meet all the requirements to be placed on priority status could instead be placed on the priority watch list or on the lesser watch list. However, to improve the progress of intellectual property rights agreements, "out-of-cycle" reviews and "immediate-action-plans" were implemented to give countries more opportunities to be taken off the priority lists in the mid-1990s. Countries such as Taiwan, Thailand, and Hungary benefited almost immediately from these new measures. Further, the United States eased export restrictions on selected software and cryptographic equipment used for electronic banking and money transactions.

Efforts were made by the United States to control domestic piracy as well. In 1997, at the request of the Federal Bureau of Investigation (FBI), software maker Adobe assisted in a nationwide dismantling of eight bulletin board systems across the country in an FBI operation code-named "Cyber Strike." The bulletin board systems were involved in an organized scheme of trafficking illegal copies of software from Adobe and other vendors.

Other regions also took steps to curb software piracy. In 1993 the European Union developed measures of its own to protect intellectual property rights. One such measure was the Directive on the Legal Protection of Computer Programs. Under this directive, computer programs were protected for the life of the programmer and an additional 50 years, just as with literary works. However, only six European Union member nations and three nonmembers implemented this directive into national law in 1993. In addition, China joined the Berne Convention, an international organization designed to protect the intellectual property right of any of its members, much like the Universal Copyright Convention (UCC), and Taiwan signed a bilateral copyright agreement in 1992.

Another issue that was the subject of much proposed legislation was encryption. Government agencies wanted access to any encrypted files for law enforcement purposes before lifting export restrictions but were meeting resistance due to privacy concerns. As reported in the *New York Times* in May of 1998, proposed U.S. legislation (the E-Privacy act) attempted to balance the reasonable need for law enforcement access with protections from government abuses and the invasion of privacy. While the E-Privacy act was the closest both sides had come to reaching agreement, there was still some dispute over whether it adequately addressed concerns on both sides.

BACKGROUND AND DEVELOPMENT

The prepackaged software industry originated in a 1969 U.S. Justice Department decision that forced IBM to sell software for its mainframe computers separately from the hardware. IBM then included basic software with the computer and additional software was generally developed in-house. With this decision, individual entrepreneurs were finally able to compete with IBM. Small software companies sprang up, usually to offer a single program or utility, while most mainframe software was licensed rather than sold.

For the most part, the rise of the prepackaged software industry was a direct result of the appetite for software for personal computers (PCs). PCs got off the ground late in the 1970s as computer enthusiasts bought computers made by Apple, Tandy, Atari, and Commodore. Software publishers, such as Microsoft, formed to write programming languages for them and soon these languages were sold at retail outlets. By the end of 1979, Microsoft had already sold one million copies of its BASIC programming language. Primitive spreadsheets and other applications began to appear as well, all of them created by relatively unknown companies. At this stage, prepackaged software was something of a cottage industry, with programs written by individuals in their spare time. Because software program creation required virtually no equipment, people who wrote software programs risked only their time but stood to gain US$200,000 to US$1 million if the program was successful, as perhaps 1 percent were. Electronic computer manufacturers, particularly Apple, encouraged these companies because software helped to sell hardware. VisiCalc, the first spreadsheet for microcomputers, was introduced in 1979. Its popularity sold many Apple computers and raised the public awareness level of PCs in general. The Apple FORTRAN programming language was introduced in March 1980 and led to the creation of additional software, especially in the areas of technical and educational applications.

In 1981 IBM introduced its version of the personal computer. Other hardware manufacturers, with the notable exception of fiercely independent Apple, began making hardware compatible with the IBM system, providing standardization for the industry. Because Microsoft won a contract with IBM to supply its MS-DOS as IBM's standard operating system, gradually most IBM-compatible computers came to use Microsoft's product. Such standardization benefited consumers because it meant that application software (which is usually customized to a particular operating system) that ran on one manufacturer's equipment would run on all with a minimum of modification. Standardization also helped software marketing because it created a clearer delineation of which third-party applications were available for a particular system. However, such an arrangement included the disadvantage of propelling the authors of a standard, such as Microsoft, toward monopoly status.

IBM's prestige helped change the image of the PC in the mainframe-dominated business world from that of a toy to that of a valuable tool, and sales of software rose accordingly. In 1980, 300,000 people owned microcomputers; in 1983 nearly 10 times that number did, and all of them were potential software purchasers. By the end of 1983, 500,000 copies of MS-DOS had been sold, carrying Microsoft's annual sales to US$69 million. Other software firms picked up momentum as well. Lotus Development Corporation introduced the 1-2-3 software spreadsheet program in 1983, and it was an immediate success; some businesses even bought computer hardware just so they could utilize the Lotus software.

By 1983, over 21,000 different PC software packages were available. Packaged software generated about US$2.7 billion worth of retail sales a year as early as 1981 and the industry grew at a steady 50 percent a year. Given this record of tremendous growth, the prepackaged software industry and PCs began to attract a great deal of attention from the press and investors, and a number of successful software companies went public. Ninety software firms raised more than US$188 million in venture capital in 1983, and 20 firms went public. With computer hardware no longer as profitable as it had been, many investors transferred investment capital to software companies.

Businesses, even large corporations, found that the cost and time involved in writing custom in-house programs was growing increasingly prohibitive. As a result, corporations turned to prepackaged software, further increasing demand for it. By 1984, packaged software sales reached US$10 billion and software companies that had been tiny entities only a few years earlier were racking up huge sales.

With the sales of software for PCs growing far faster than any other segment, companies that formerly focused on software for mainframe computers bought PC software firms, and firms that had specialized in PC systems also began to sell application software. As competition rapidly intensified and prices for software fell wherever similar programs existed, it became much harder to begin a new software publishing firm without substantial funding resources.

Making it still more difficult for small start-up software firms was the beginning of new marketing tactics and price wars. In the 1990s, large software vendors began giving away certain products either for free or at costs far below market value. For example, in 1993 Computer Associates, the world's third-largest software vendor, released the first million copies of its new accounting package, Simple Money, at no cost. Other companies followed a similar strategy of giving away products to gain market dominance in order to make sales in upgrades and sales in ancillary products. Further, software companies, such as Microsoft, Lotus, and Novell, in conjunction with Borland, began selling various applications together as "suites." These suites usually included a word processing program, a spreadsheet application, and a presentation package at a handsome discount from the individual prices. Further incentives included special introductory prices and low upgrade prices when users owned previous versions or even competitors' packages. However, as software companies dropped prices, profit margins also fell, causing many companies to consolidate and merge. Discount packages from Microsoft, in the 2000s, were firmly in place at college and university bookstores, assuring the company of steady lifelong customers.

In 1997 alone, the worldwide software market was estimated to have grown by 15 percent to US$122 billion. Analysts predicted that the industry would continue to grow through the late 1990s and into the next millennium at an overall rate of 12 to 15 percent. According to IDC, software price pressures were offset by several factors, such as globalization of businesses, year 2000 compliance problems, and the availability of better software solutions. To elevate profits, companies cut costs by sharing research and development costs and integrating businesses. As such alliances increased, more mergers between software publishers were expected to take place.

An ongoing saga, in the 1990s, involved antitrust probes into the business of Microsoft and other computer companies that participated in what were deemed questionable business practices. In 1994 the U.S. Justice Department investigated Microsoft's licensing practices for MS-DOS. Though a lawsuit was avoided, Microsoft agreed to start selling its operating systems to personal computer makers based on the number purchased, rather than on the number of processors sold. Microsoft came into the legal limelight again when in 1995 three online services, CompuServe, America Online, and Prodigy, urged Microsoft not to bundle its own online service with its new Windows 95 and called on Congress to hasten an antitrust probe into the matter. Ultimately, Windows was allowed to release its online service, and the market remained competitive. However, in May of 1998, the U.S. government and 20 states filed suit against the company, accusing Microsoft of "unfairly trying to maintain its monopoly in personal computer software and to extend that monopoly into the new markets of Internet software and commerce," as reported by the *New York Times*. The suit was based on Microsoft's integration and bundling of its Web browser, Internet Explorer, into its latest release of Windows. Though shipment of Windows 98 would not be delayed, the suit did ask that Microsoft loosen contracts with PC makers to facilitate software modification and easier use of competitors' browsers. Interestingly, this trend wasn't limited to the software industry, as in May of 1998 the Federal Trade Commission announced that it was considering a suit against microprocessor giant Intel Corporation for "abusing its position as the monopoly manufacturer of microprocessor chips" and bullying computer manufacturers. The prevalence of Microsoft's Windows OS running on Intel processors gave rise to the term "Wintel" to describe the technological hegemony of the two companies.

In 2001 the government settled its case with Microsoft. In 2002 nine states pursued litigation against the company. Microsoft, in 2001, tried to get a reversal in judgment from the Supreme Court, but the highest federal court refused to hear the plea. An appeals court disagreed with a lower court decision that would have forced mighty Microsoft to divide its operations in two, but it did find that the giant company had violated antitrust laws. The court finding in 2002 has led to lawsuits against Microsoft by AOL Time Warner and its Netscape Communications Corp. that say Microsoft used unfair trade practices to boost its Explorer browser. In March of 2002, Sun Microsystems also pursued a US$1 billion lawsuit against Microsoft, accusing the company owned by Bill Gates of employing anti-competitive practices against Sun's Java platform when the company took out Sun's Java program from the new release of Windows XP.

The Year 2000. One of the biggest concerns in the software industry, which ultimately proved more hype than substance, was the year 2000 (Y2K) issue. During the 1960s and 1970s, memory was costly and programmers saved a good deal by storing dates in systems and software with only the last two digits; for example, 1975 was represented as "75." However, when the date changed to the year 2000, computers across the globe would read 2000 as 1900, causing potentially catastrophic system failures. While the problem was not limited to software, the industry did assume a large portion of the problem. And since all companies worldwide were facing the same deadline, all were competing for the same resources to fix the problem—namely, programmers (to isolate the problems and fix old code) and testing personnel. Some software companies cashed in on the problem by manufacturing and marketing software designed to help companies plan and monitor year 2000 testing projects. The global effect of the year 2000 problem was most fervently expressed by self-professed "Y2K alarmist," Edward Yardeni, a well-known economist.

CURRENT CONDITIONS

The global software industry had revenues of more than US$200 billion in 2003, with the United States dominating the market according to statistics from the United Kingdom's Department of Trade and Industry. That year, the U.S. purchased 53 percent of the world's software, Western Europe 29 percent, and Asia/Pacific 15 percent. However, consumption in emerging countries was expected to outpace that of developed countries. The U.S. was the supplier of more than 80 percent of the world's products. Of the top 20 software suppliers that year, only four were not American.

The software industry suffered through hard times during the early 2000s in the wake of the dot-com bust and an economic recession. In its 2003 Software 500 ranking, *Software Magazine* reported that difficulties continued as the mid-2000s approached. Combined sales of both software and services for the listed companies totaled US$289.7 billion, down from US$301.8 billion the previous year. Some 46 percent of the 500 firms saw their revenues decline, as compared to 34 percent in the publication's 2002 ranking.

While the industry had begun 2004 with a solid start, things cooled off during the second quarter. Amidst project cancellations and delays, analysts revised their estimates for industry growth. For example, Gartner adjusted its projection for 5 percent revenue growth in 2004 to 3 percent. Heading into 2005, analysts were optimistic about the industry's performance. Many forecasts indicated that 2005 would be a strong year, as companies continued hiring more workers and resuming software purchases and IT projects that had been tabled during the recession.

According to the July 15, 2004, issue of *Business Week,* uncertainty about economic recovery within the corporate sector was one factor for the slowdown in activity. However, the software industry faced other challenges as well. One challenge was the sheer number of industry players. As companies scaled back on the number of software vendors from which they purchased applications and services and as the amount of investment capital began to be stretched, mergers and acquisitions became more commonplace. Gartner indicated that up to half of all software companies might disappear by 2006, leaving the most lucrative market for industry giants such as Oracle and Microsoft. Niche market participants were being bought up by such larger companies as these companies tried to increase their offerings to customers. In turn, customers were looking to reduce their contract costs by buying in volume from one supplier.

As the software industry's market has matured, there has also been a tendency toward standardization, particularly of infrastructure technology. As a result, many vendors have merged in order to gain economies of scale.

The application service provider (ASP) model, in which companies buy software as a hosted service instead of buying and installing applications locally, was expected to have a significant impact on the industry through 2010. Companies no longer viewed software as an innovation that they could keep unique to their business to provide them with an advantage over their competition. Technology had become almost "commonplace", another part of the regular operations of any business. *Business Week* reported that by 2010 up to half of all corporate software purchases would be purchased under such a contracted arrangement; software was expected to be "rented" on a per-use, monthly, or annual basis. Companies were also looking at software from the standpoint of how much value it could bring to them. They were not so willing to get rid of existing applications.

Security was at the very forefront of the software industry during the mid-2000s. Companies and home computer users alike were plagued by a host of virus attacks and other security breaches. This prompted some industry players to call 2003 the "Year of the Worm," in reference to a particularly malicious form of computer virus that caused widespread problems and cost companies a great deal of money. Notable worm outbreaks involved the SQL Slammer worm, as well as Code Red.F, Lovgate, and Deloder. In the first quarter of 2003 alone, Internet Security Systems Inc. reported that Internet security attacks and incidents had increased 84 percent from the last quarter of 2002.

As experts prepared for more security threats in 2004 and beyond, efforts were made to bolster security. For example, Microsoft continually worked to identify and patch vulnerabilities in its products. Companies also increased efforts to protect their IT infrastructures—from individual computers to networks—by purchasing security software. Gartner reported that security software sales rose 9.6 percent in 2003, reaching US$5.62 billion. Sales of security applications were expected to rise 10.2 percent in 2004.

In addition to security software, in December 2003 *Software Magazine* noted that systems integration applications were replacing e-business-related programs and services. Indeed, Gartner expected systems integration application market to increase more than 10 percent in 2004, reaching US$9.4 billion. The research firm also forecast strong growth for engineering and design software, which was expected to grow to US$10.7 billion in 2004—up 11.7 percent from 2003.

In mid-2004, software piracy remained a concern to the industry. Citing research from the Business Software Alliance (BSA) and research firm IDC, *InternetWeek* reported that the industry lost almost US$29 billion in 2003 because of piracy, threatening research and development activity as well as employment. Peer-to-peer file sharing networks, used mainly for trading music online, posed a risk for software sharing as more consumers switched to high-speed Internet connections. Piracy was more prevalent in some global markets than in others. For example, the BSA study indicated that while piracy rates were 23 percent in North America, rates were 36 percent in Europe, 53 percent in the Asia/Pacific region, 56 percent in Africa and the Middle East, 63 percent in Latin America, and 71 percent in Eastern Europe. Losses also varied, depending on market value. For example, losses in North America were US$7.2 billion. Losses were much lower in Latin America (US$1.3 billion), even though the region's piracy rate was much higher.

Sending software development offshore was also a trend on the rise in 2004. India—where labor costs are lower and which has a large pool of skilled labor—was the focus of much of this redirection of development. Although the result has been an increase in wages in India, this is not expected to have an effect on the region's cost advantage for another 20 or more years. The largest user of India's offshoring services continues to be the United States, where labor laws allow it. Offshoring is not as easily allowed by many Western European governments.

Research and Technology

Research and development played a major role in the prepackaged software industry, as businesses and computer users turned increasingly to computers and software to make workplaces become more efficient and develop new ways to share information. In response, software makers began developing new tools in emerging markets, such as software agents, middleware, groupware, multimedia software, enterprise resource planning (ERP) software, and Internet software.

Software agents are a form of artificial intelligence that perform definite, reoccurring, and predictable tasks for a computer user or even another software application. They can check appointments stored in an electronic calendar, search for and retrieve information on a particular subject, or monitor network and computer performance and inform the administrator when a problem occurs. As development in this area continued, it was expected that the sophistication and proliferation of software agents would increase. And with the explosion of client/server technology, the promise of open computer systems, and electronic communication, businesses looked for ways to link different types of computer networks, platforms, and software. Such software acts as the mediator and translator for disparate systems and provides information in a common format, making differences between systems nearly invisible to users and program developers. According to International Data Corp. (IDC), "Business enterprises will increasingly deploy large-scale distributed applications, but will depend on an industry that spares business applications developers from the burden of dealing with each network technology's idiosyncrasies." Analysts expected that greater reliance on middleware, or programs that mediate communications between end-use applications and network operating systems, would provide a growing niche in the business software market.

Groupware, another offshoot from the proliferation of client/server technology, was expected to grow to a US$4.2 billion industry in 1999. It allowed groups of people to share information and communicate electronically. The clear leader and one of the first entrants in this area, during the late 1990s, was Lotus Development Corporation's Lotus Notes (Lotus is now a subsidiary of IBM). Companies such as Microsoft and Novell have courted this market with Microsoft Exchange and GroupWise, respectively. Even Internet software giant Netscape entered the picture, offering Netscape Communicator (now owned by AOL Time Warner), a Web browser that also acted as an e-mail package and allowed online conferencing. A similar application to facilitate corporate efficiency is enterprise resource planning (ERP) software. ERP software was customized to help companies manage complete business, manufacturing, and communication functions all within one system. Leaders in the industry included SAP AG, Oracle Corporation, Baan, and PeopleSoft. In 1997 Oracle released Oracle Applications, a suite of 30 software modules for financial, supply chain management, manufacturing, project management, human resources, and sales and marketing, customized for each customer according to its industry.

One of the hottest growth areas for software developers was the Internet and the rush to create Web pages, both personal and corporate. Examples of existing products included Microsoft's FrontPage, bundled with Windows NT and garnering a significant market share. Some products focused on group needs for Web services delivery (NetObjects Fusion by NetObjects) and others targeted those with more creative ideas and Web display needs (such as DreamWeaver and ColdFusion by Macromedia). Some developers integrated Web design tools with Web application-building tools, giving users multiple capabilities within a single product.

Other hot Internet markets were the Internet browser and Internet application-building tools. Netscape held 60 percent of the browser market in 1998, down from 80 percent in 1997. AOL Time Warner and Netscape sued in 2002; the basis being that Microsoft's integration of its Internet Explorer with Windows 98 and later Windows XP was unfair. Internet programming language was also a competitive area with high growth potential. The industry standard was hypertext mark-up language (HTML), but its limited capabilities required the use of additional languages in order for Web sites to perform complex tasks. Sun Microsystems' programming language Java was the target of much controversy in the late 1990s, as reviewers attacked Java's slow loading and running speed on the desktop. As of mid-1998, Sun CEO Scott McNealy allowed other companies to use Java only on his own strict terms, wanting to maintain "100 percent Pure Java" and enforce uniformity. Sun regarded Java as a universal, platform-independent, standard that needed to be protected from alterations which would compromise its system independence. Sun sued Microsoft when the software giant developed a Windows-only version of Java and was rewarded by an injunction from the U.S. District Court in San Jose preventing Microsoft from using the Java logo. However, industry insiders felt Sun needed to make Java more available to other companies and foster growth in the Windows market in order to gain and retain leadership as an Internet programming language provider. Other programming languages popular in 2002 that are used for Internet development included PERL, CGI, C++, VB, ASP, and DHTML.

In 2002, with computer losses mounting, software companies focused on the area of storing networking software in an attempt to return to profitability by grabbing a bigger share of corporate dollars. Nearly all the technology frontrunners and not a few small independents began trying to write software that enables firms, even firms with computers not compatible with other computers, to pull out data from storage providers quickly and efficiently, according to *Investor's Business Daily*. In the rush of data-storing competition, some competitors have been crushed. Exabyte Corp. of Boulder, Colorado, found its shares drop by two-thirds of their value in 2001, as it let go one-third of its workforce, including 110 employees in the United States, reported the *Bloomberg News* in 2002. Another U.S. data storage company, EMC Corp., incurred losses of US$70 million in the fourth quarter of 2001.

WORKFORCE

The need for labor for the software industry was on the rise in 2005, but the trend to send work offshore was raising some flags in several countries. For example, in mid-2005, IBM was proceeding with its plans to lay off 13,000 workers in Europe and the United States. However, globally, it was increasing its employee count, adding 14,000 workers in India. Governments were keeping watch.

According to the U.S. Department of Labor, computer software engineers will have one of the fastest growing occupations into 2012. In the U.S., there were 675,000 software engineers in 2002, of which about 394,000 were application software engineers and the remainder were systems software engineers. Their median annual salary that year was US$70,900.

INDUSTRY LEADERS

Microsoft. The undisputed and often vilified dominator of the software industry, Microsoft earned revenues of US$36.8 billion in 2004, up from US$11.35 billion in 1997. Based on market value, it was the top-ranked global company according to *Forbes* in 2005. However, because of its sales figures and low asset base *Forbes* ranked it at number 47 overall based on a composite of four metrics: sales, profits, assets, and market value. In 2005, its employee base numbered almost 60,000—a number that has shown steady growth. Almost 64 percent work in the United States, but the employees were located in subsidiaries in almost 100 countries. In spite of a global soft economy and a class-action lawsuit against Microsoft by the federal government, recent Microsoft releases of registered trademark products, its Windows operating and server systems, Office suite of products, the Xbox game, and MSN Internet Access services, bolstered Microsoft's revenues. However, the company saw its net income fall more than 18 percent in 2004 to US$8.2 billion.

Bill Gates started the company when he dropped out of Harvard at age 19 and founded "Micro-soft" with friend Paul Allen in a hotel room in Albuquerque, New Mexico, in 1975. In 1979 Microsoft was moved to Gates' hometown of Bellevue, Washington, where he developed software that enabled users to write programs for personal computers. In 1980 Microsoft was chosen to write operating system software for IBM's new PC (over strong competition from Digital Research). Gates and Allen bought the rights to an existing speedy and efficient package, QDOS, which stood for "quick and dirty operating system", from Tim Paterson of Seattle Computer Products for less than US$100,000 and renamed the software MS-DOS. QDOS required just two months to write.

MS-DOS was an instant success and eventually became standard equipment for all IBM and IBM-compatible PCs. Microsoft continued to develop software for other companies, including Apple and Radio Shack. Paul Allen left Microsoft in 1983 but still owns approximately 10 percent of Microsoft stock and sits on the board of directors. Gates continued to take the company in new directions, introducing Windows in the mid-1980s, and by 1986 he took the company public, retaining 45 percent of its shares. In 1993 Microsoft introduced Windows NT, client/server software, keeping pace with increasing use of the network operating system (NOS). In the late 1990s, Windows NT5 (rechristened Windows 2000) and Unix were fighting for position as the dominant corporate system architecture. In 2001 InfoWorld assailed the release of Windows XP, saying it failed to perform as well as the prior edition of Windows 2000. CEO Steve Ballmer promised that the next Windows operating system would be simpler and unified, addressing Windows long-standing deficiencies in its storage system. The next version of Windows was as yet unnamed in 2005, but its nickname became "Longhorn." The company was likely to unveil its new OS sometime in 2006, according to *Business Week.*

Throughout the 1990s and into the early 2000s, Microsoft had trouble with the U.S. Department of Justice as well as several other souces, including the European Commission all claiming antitrust action. In 1995 the company agreed to alter marketing tactics to settle an antitrust investigation. For the same reason, Microsoft called off plans to acquire Intuit, owner of Quicken, a successful financial software package. In 1998 Microsoft was targeted in a lawsuit alleging the company abused its "near monopoly" by bundling its Web browser (Microsoft Explorer) with its Windows operating system. The revised settlement between Microsoft and the federal government, in the spring of 2002, stopped Microsoft from promoting Windows Media Player and the Explorer browser over those of competitors, such as those made by AOL Time Warner. The bottom line is that the government required the Windows operating system to allow its competitors' software to also launch, if that was a customer's preference. In 2004, the European Commission fined the company US$655 million after it found that Microsoft had abused its monopoly position. In addition, the company was told that it must offer a version of Windows that did not include its own media player so that other industry players would have a chance to be competitive.

Security remains an issue with the company's software, but Gates has stated that the company spends between 30 and 35 percent of its research budget on security issues. Its developing operating system was expected to solve almost all of its existing problems in the late 2000s.

International Business Machines Corp. The world's second-largest producer of prepackaged software, IBM reported revenues of US$96.3 billion in 2004, up 8 percent over the previous year. Its net income that year was US$8.43 billion, an 11.2 percent increase from 2003. The world's largest provider of global IT services, the company is also a provider of advanced computing systems as well as personal computing products. Its software division is made up of primarily middleware and operating systems software. Revenues for this division in 2004 were US$15.1 billion, approximately 15.7 percent of the company's total. About 40 percent of the software division's profits come from one-time charges levied on end users for lifetime use of a product.

In 1995, IBM purchased Lotus Development Corporation—formerly the seventh-largest software publisher—for US$3.5 billion. Also, IBM began major restructuring efforts. To make it easier for multinational companies to do business with IBM and break down barriers between countries, a plan was implemented that allowed one contract and one discount to cover multinationals wherever they did business. In addition, in an effort to unify its global operations, the company shifted power from managers who oversaw the operations of an entire country, to managers of 14 industry sectors. IBM has continued to expand it software division through the acquisition of key products. By June 2005, it had acquired SRD (identity resolution software developer), Ascential Software (enterprise data integration software), Gluecode Software (open source application infrastructure software), Meiosys (application relocation software), and Isogon (asset management software).

Charles Flint created Calculating-Tabulating-Recording (CTR) in 1910, by merging his two companies, International Time Recording Company and Computing Scale Company, with a third company called the Tabulation Machine Company, started by Herman Hallerith. In 1914 Flint hired Thomas Watson as the general manager of CTR—he would later become president of the company. Watson created a powerful business sales force that became known for its superior customer service and devoted most of the company's resources to the tabulator division. Under his leadership, the company quickly expanded both in sales and size, moving into Europe, Asia, and Latin America. In 1924 CTR came to be known as International Business Machines, focusing on large tabulations machines. By 1949 it had operations in 58 countries and created IBM World Trade Corporation, which enjoyed the same dominance in foreign markets as it did in the United States.

Fujitsu Ltd. Fujitsu, a Japanese company, was the world's third-largest software provider in 1997, with US$36.37 billion in revenue. But in 2002 the picture darkened for the company. Fujitsu said it planned to let go as many as 4,000 employees after eating a US$2.9 billion loss in the fiscal year ending March 31, 2002, according to *Bloomberg News*. The company made plans to close shops in more than 400 locations around the globe. Besides Japan, operations included Australia, the United States, Mexico, France, Colombia, Indonesia, and Zimbabwe. By 2004, the company reported revenues of US$45.1 billion, up more than 17 percent from 2003. It also recorded net income of US$470.5 after having net losses of US$1.02 billion in 2003 and US$2.88 billion in 2002.

In 1935 Fuji Electric Co., Ltd. created Fujitsu to build telephone equipment. In 1954 it entered the data processing arena by developing Japan's first computer, which was called the FACOM 100. To ensure the success of its new computer industry, Japan's Ministry of International Trade and Industry (MITI) put up trade barriers. In addition, Japan sponsored the development of new computers through a public utility created in the 1950s called National Telephone and Telegraph, which essentially created a guaranteed market for Japanese-made computers. In the 1960s, MITI helped fund and direct Fujitsu's creation of mainframe systems. Despite these efforts, however, Fujitsu computers were still technologically far behind those of IBM. In 1972 Fujitsu invested money into the Amdahl Corporation, which was owned by the primary creator of IBM's extremely successful 360 series computers, and in 1997 they bought the remaining 55 percent of Amdahl to complete its full acquisition. This investment gave Fujitsu the technological knowledge it needed and put Fujitsu on a more level ground with IBM.

Sun Microsystems. Based in Santa Clara, California, Sun Microsystems is a leading software supplier and manufacturer of network computing systems and Unix-based workstations. With 2004 sales of US$11.2 billion, down slightly from 2003, Sun reported a net loss of US$388 million that year. Revenues outside of the United States accounted for about 57 percent of the company's total, with the United Kingdom, German and Japan providing most of the international sales. Sun Microsystems' single-largest customer was the General Electric Company (GE) which accounted for 14 percent of total revenues. The company's software division consists primarily of the development of enterprise infrastructure software, software desktop systems, developer software, and infrastructure management software, with its Solaris operating System and Java technology being most well known.

Sun employed 32,600 people in 2004, making it one of the industry's largest global employers. Sun demonstrated a consistent 15 to 20 percent growth during the late 1990s, before slipping in the 2000s. In February of 2001, Sun shocked even veteran business reporters when management cut the company's revenue expectations by 50 percent. Nonetheless, Sun Microsystems was so adversely hurt by the economy in 2001 that it cut employee performance bonuses and shut down operations for one week, as it required all employees to take days off to cut costs. But the picture in 2002 looked brighter for Sun, and the company reminded one and all, in March 2002, that it continued to be the leading generator of "technical computing revenue." Bounding back, the company announced plans in June 2005 to acquire StorageTek, a manufacturer of tape drives and developer of network management and backup software, for US$4.1 billion. The acquisition will add more than 7,000 employees and more than US$2 billion in sales.

Sun Microsystems was founded in 1982 by four young entrepreneurs, and has since grown into a major multinational company with operations in more than 150 countries. Sun's first product was a high-performance Unix-based system computer, and in 1997 it developed "the world's most powerful single system server." Meanwhile, the company revolutionized the Internet software industry by developing the Java programming language and was subsequently engaged in an ongoing battle with fifth-ranked Microsoft, as a leading Internet software provider.

Oracle. As the world's largest enterprise software company, Oracle grew stronger in January 2005 when it acquired competitor PeopleSoft for US$10.3 billion after a hard-fought takeover battle. It was the largest merger in the software industry to date. Oracle is a provider of Information Architecture; it provides databases designed for large-scale computing; application software, including that designed to aid the management of customer relationships, corporate performance, finances, human capital, procurement, projects, and the supply chain; and it is a provider of middleware products. The merger with PeopleSoft boosted the company's total employee count to more than 50,000 and its application customer count to 23,000.

Oracle reported sales of US$10.2 billion in 2004, up more than 7 percent from 2003. The company's net income rose more than 16 percent that year, reaching US$2.7 billion. This was good news, following difficult years during the early 2000s when poor performance in the financial services and telecommunications industries had an adverse effect on Oracle, according to CEO Jeff Henley.

Oracle's strength was in the ability of its product to run across multi-platform computer environments, share data with other software packages, and use structured query language (SQL). SQL is an industry-standard created by IBM that enables access to various databases and provides information about the data by using a common language. The company's principle business activities include the development and marketing of an integrated suite of computer software products used for database management, computer-aided systems engineering, applications development and decision support, as well as families of software products used for financial, human resource, and manufacturing applications (ERP software). Through its subsidiaries, Oracle markets its products along with related consulting, educational, support, and systems integration services in more than 90 countries.

Programmers Lawrence Ellison and Robert Miner teamed together in 1977 to start a new software firm. Ellison had been a vice president of systems development at Omex Corporation but met Miner at Ampex Corporation where Miner was his supervisor. Both had extensive experience creating customized database programs for government agencies, and they picked up a lapsed US$50,000 contract to build a database for the Central Intelligence Agency (CIA). They pooled their money, rented office space in Belmont, California, and started Oracle. In 1978 it created the Oracle RDBMS (relational database management system), which was the world's first such system to use SQL, and by 1982 the company became profitable with US$2.5 million in revenues.

Computer Associates International Inc. Among the world's largest management software companies, New York-based Computer Associates (CA) was providing software and services that dealt with storage, security, operations, product lifecycle, and service management. With more than 15,000 employees, CA had operations in more than 100 countries in 2005. Market research firm IDC reported that CA was the world leader in asset management software sales, with a global market share of 12.7 percent. By 2004 revenues had reached almost US$3.3 billion.

The company is known for its acquisition (and vigorous downsizing) of struggling software companies. In 2005, it was continuing its acquisition strategy, despite several years of poor financial results. It had announced plans to acquire Concord Communications (a provider of network service management software) and Niku (a provider of information technology management and governance software). Computer Associates acquired ASK Group, a software group that makes database and manufacturing management software, in the mid-1990s, which helped the company penetrate the client/server market. One of CA's ventures was Unicenter, a product released in early 1997 that gives corporations control over entire information technology systems, including software, hardware, and networks. In 2002 the company was offering clients some of the most creative software licensing arrangements in the industry.

Computer Associates International was founded in 1976 as an agreement between Charles Wang and Switzerland's Computer Associates to sell the company's software in the United States. Wang and four employees began by selling CA-SORT, a file organizer for IBM storage systems. By 1980, Wang was successful enough to buy out his Swiss partners. CA continued its success by acquiring existing software products and became the first independent software company to reach US$1 billion in sales in 1989. By the 1990s, CA was marketing software for mainframe utilities, microcomputers, and mainframe databases. Acquired products included spreadsheet software (from Sorcim in 1984), accounting software (from BPI in 1987), and data security software. CA also acquired companies such as Applied Data Research from Ameritech in 1988; Pansophic Systems, a developer of applications for IBM AS/400 machines, in 1991; rival Legent, in 1995; and Cheyenne Software, a network management expert, in 1996.

SAP AG. Founded in 1972, German software giant SAP AG was the world's third-largest independent software supplier in 2005 and was the largest provider of inter-enterprise software products (those that allow businesses to collaborate). It employed more than 32,000 people in more than 50 countries, who served more than 26,000 customers in more than 120 countries. By 2004, sales were about US$10.2 billion, up more than 31 percent over 2003 figures.

The company produces midrange and high-end applications suites and dominates the global client/server arena. SAP gained dominance in the marketplace by offering software modules for business areas, such as accounting, manufacturing, and human resources that were highly integrated with each other. It gave companies a single solution to tracking business operations, instead of having to combine a hodgepodge of disparate systems. Two of SAP's main product lines were R/2 software for mainframes and R/3 software for client/server systems. SAP was also credited as being one of the founders of enterprise resource planning, known in the information technology industry as ERP, and one of the hottest industry trends of the late 1990s. ERP software helps corporate technology professionals automate manufacturing processes, organize accounting books, streamline departments like human resources, and a variety of other functions related to the corporate trend toward reengineering for optimal cost efficiency.

Novell, Inc. Massachusetts-based Novell offered infrastructure software and services in 43 countries in 2005. One of the hardest hit software industries in 2001, Novell, began restructuring in 2002 by cutting one-fifth of its workforce. For 2001 Novell's revenues were US$1.04 billion, down from US$1.16 billion in 2000. Also, in 2001 the company had an unprecedented loss of US$272.9 million, compared to its slim profit margin of US$49.5 million in 2000. By 2003, Novell continued to struggle. That year, revenues fell 2.5 percent to US$1.1 billion, and the company reported a US$161.9 million net loss. The figures were looking better by 2004, when revenues increased slightly to US$1.17 billion, and net income was positive once again at US$57.2 million.

Novell was founded in 1980 and began as a manufacturer of personal computers. The company was on the verge of dissolving when it was rejuvenated by Raymond Noorda, an electronics engineer, who purchased a 33 percent ownership of the company after seeing its software and then propelled the company into the network-computing arena. Novell was the leading network software company (principally through its NetWare product line) and also the industry's tenth-largest software provider in 1996, with software sales of US$1.2 billion. Major competition for Novell came from IBM-owned Lotus Notes, up against Novell's corporate information management and e-mail systems GroupWise and ManageWise, as well as Microsoft's Windows NT network operating system (competition for Novell's NetWare). After an abortive attempt to compete with Microsoft in the desktop suite market by acquiring WordPerfect Corporation, which it soon sold to Canada's Corel Corporation, Novell continued to grasp for new business in the mid- to late 1990s.

MAJOR COUNTRIES IN THE INDUSTRY

China. Barely in the computer software picture in 1990, by 2003 China had emerged as a small, but confident and vigorous, player in the software industry. Valued at about US$7.2 billion in 2000, sales in the industry in China had reached about US$19.3 billion by 2003 according to the China Software Industry Association. That year, China was home to 8,582 software companies that marketed approximately 18,000 products. Of those companies, the top four (IBM, Microsoft, Oracle, and Sybase) received only 19 percent of the total industry's sales. The PC business market for software was expected to grow by 215 percent between 2003 and 2008. China's growth rate in the early to mid-2000s had been hard-to-ignore; it exceeded 30 percent annually. The business software portion of the market was valued at US$2.4 billion in 2003 by *Euromonitor.* Applications software was the largest segment of this sector accounting for more than 50 percent of the market value. The Chinese government has made efforts to eliminate piracy in the industry following China's entrance into the World Trade Organization.

Growth was unfolding at an explosive pace, bolstered by the development of systems integration software. Outsourcing of software production was also helping the industry. China had become the largest external manufacturing base for Japan.

France. According to Syntec informatique, the software industry association of France, the software industry was back on an upward growth track in 2004, with the software package tool sector showing 3 percent growth, while the software application sector showed 1 percent growth. Growth during 2005 was anticipated to be in the range of 4 to 6 percent. France's domestic packaged software market had been valued at US$7.6 billion in 2002 by the U.S. & Foreign Commercial Service, while French companies in the industry posted sales of U.S.$28.5 billion, making it Europe's leading nation in this industry. French developed software is created primarily for the aeronotics, finance, defense, and manufacturing industries, but 70 percent of the packaged software used was being imported primarily from the U.S. More than 30,000 people were employed in the industry.

Three companies were dominant in the market for networking software in 2003—Novell, Microsoft, and Intel—holding a 62 percent share of this US$1.7 billion market sector. Euromonitor predicted growth for this sector at 31 percent for the five years up to 2008. Unix was expected to become the dominant networking software in France.

As experienced in many countries, PC software sales slowed in France in the early 2000s. However, by 2003, the market was picking up again. PC business software sales grew to a value of more than US$2.5 billion, up more than 14 percent over 2002 levels, and the sale of word processing packages made up the largest component of this at more than 34 percent. Industry leader, Microsoft, dominated this market sector taking in over 60 percent of all PC business software-related sales.

Microsoft was also dominant in the multimedia software sector in Francein 2003, controlling almost one third of the market. Other lead players included Apple Computer, Infogrames Entertainment, and IBM. Valued at US$2.3 billion, this sector was expected to grow by 42.7 percent by 2008.

Germany. In 2003, the U.S. Commercial Service found Germany to rank as the second leading software market in the world, although the United Kingdom was considered to be very close in terms of market size. Valued at US$18.75 billion, the software market in Germany had shown slight declines in the early 2000s due to the country's economic slowdown. However, the market was expected to continuing growing in 2004, with anticipated rates of between 3 and 5 percent. Leading this growth trend is an increased demand for security software.

The market remains highly fragmented, with the top 25 companies controlling about 40 percent of the software market. However, the industry was experiencing consolidation. The vast majority of products are imported from the U.S. and sold through German-based subsidiaries. Of the total software market, networking software sales were about US$1.6 billion in 2003, PC business software sales were US$2.2 billion, and multimedia software sales were about US$1.6 billion. Productivity products, such as Internet browsers and e-mail software, were the primary areas of growth in the PC business software sector, while software for commercial used dominated sales in the multimedia sector.

By late 2003, Germany's Federal Ministry of Education and Research had entered into a 30-person venture with China's Ministry of Science to form the Sino-German Joint Software Institute. According to *IPR Strategic Business Information Database,* the inter-governmental venture was created to create high-end software applications, including "operational systems and middleware for a parallel processing next-generation central processing unit, software for mobile communications and multimedia mobile applications, and a common platform for software interface and management."

United Kingdom. Of the top 20 companies supplying the United Kingdom's US$7.3 billion software market in 2003, only four were British. The three leading companies were all American—IBM, Microsoft, and Oracle— and they held a 30 percent market share. The largest U.K. software company was Sage, which develops accounting packages for small- to mid-sized businesses. Sage has increased its presence in the United States through its acquisition of several U.S. software companies.

Japan. In 2003, the PC business software market in Japan was valued at US$7.7 billion. In a period of low economic activity in Japan, this industry had experienced growth of more than 10 percent that year. During 2003, IBM also became the market leader in Japan in this sector. Other sector leaders included Microsoft, Novell and Adobe. Pre-packaged business software was taking an increasing share of the Japanese market as businesses found the costs of customized packages too high. Growth in the pre-packaged market was expected to be almost 45 percent between 2003 and 2008 according to Euromonitor.

In 1996, with a total software market worth of US$14 billion, Japan held 13 percent of the worldwide market. According to *Business Week*, Japan fell behind in the 1980s by "clinging to proprietary systems" when the market was calling for open standards. Overall computer penetration rates in Japan continued to trail U.S. rates in the 1990s. However, the number of personal computers in Japan increased substantially by 8 to 9 million units per year, during the late 1990s, as Japanese companies slowly moved toward the use of PCs and client/server architecture.

United States. In spite of growing competition from around the world, the United States continued to be the world leader in the packaged software industry in the 2004. The Software & Information Industry Association valued the total software market in the U.S. at US$103.1 billion that year. More than 905,000 people were working at 23,311 software establishments in the country, with the largest concentration of companies being in California.

The PC business software market had been valued by Euromonitor as being worth about US$9 billion in 2003, showing a modest increase of 3.6 percent over 2002 figures. In this sector, five companies dominated the market: IBM, Microsoft, Novell, Adobe, and Corel. Industry growth was expected to be good, with market value reaching about US$11.3 billion by 2008.

The media software market in the U.S. is made up primarily of media development tools and software plug-ins, all of which resulted in US$7.1 billion in sales in 2003. This industry sector remained fragmented, with the five industry leaders (Microsoft, Macromedia, Adobe Systems, Avid Technologies, and Real Networks) taking only about one quarter of the market in total. *Euromontor* was expecting this industry to have sales of US$7.2 billion in 2008.

Networking software, comprised of network operating systems and groupware, grew 4 percent between 2002 and 2003, to reach a market value of US$4.1 billion in 2003. In this sector, four companies controlled about 85 percent of the market: Microsoft, Novell, IBM, and Oracle. Growth of about 12 percent was expected in the period up to 2008.

According to the Software Publishers Association, the U.S. software industry would continue to find its largest export market for software application products in Western Europe, which was home to a sizable technology base.

FURTHER READING

"AsiaBizTech: Over 50 Percent of Japanese Population Online." *Nua Internet Surveys,* 12 March 2003. Available from http://www.nua.ie/surveys.

Brinkley, Joel. "FTC Plans Antitrust Suit Against Intel." *New York Times,* 28 May 1998.

"China: Beijing Records Record US$120M in Software Exports." *IPR Strategic Business Information Database,* 4 January 2004.

"China: China and Germany to Jointly Develop Software Industry." *IPR Strategic Business Information Database,* 21 October 2003.

"China: Chinese Sales of Software and System Integration Products to Hit 25.3 Billion." *IPR Strategic Business Information Database,* 1 February 2004.

"China—Software Sector Growing, but Faces Challenges." *Information Week,* 12 February 2002.

Clausing, Jeri. "New Encryption Legislation Billed as a Compromise." *New York Times,* 13 May 1998.

"Computer Software." *Hoovers Online*. Available from http://www.hoovers.com/.

Bureau of Labor Statistics, U.S. Department of Labor. "Computer Software Engineers." *Occupational Outlook Handbook, 2004-05 Edition*, accessed 29 June 2005. Available from http://www.bls.gov.

Deagoni, Brian. "Technology Giants Race to Sell More Storage Software." *Investor's Business Daily,* 5 March 2002.

Defranchi, Charles. "Packaged Software." *U.S. Department of Commerce, International Trade Administration, Office of Computers and Business Equipment,* 1 June 1997.

Desmond, John P. "2004 Software 500: Growth Came in Segments." *Software Magazine,* October 2004. Available from http://www.softwaremag.com.

Desmond, John P. "Infrastructure, Security, Services Sectors Fared Better in a Down Year for the Software 500." *Software Magazine,* December 2003. Available from http://www.softwaremag.com.

"European Stocks May Rise." *Bloomberg News,* 8 March 2002.

Defranchi, Charles. "Market Research: Packaged Software in France." US Department of Commerce, 15 October 2003. Available from http:///www.buyusainfo.net.

Fisher, Dennis. "Worms Wreak Havoc on the Net in '03." *eWeek,* 3 April 2003.

Groot, Doris. "Market Research: Security Software in France." US Department of Commerce, 27 January 2005. Available from http:///www.buyusainfo.net.

Hof, Robert D. "Commentary: Java Can Be a Contender—If Sun Lets It." *Business Week,* 6 April 1998.

Kepos, Paula, ed. *International Directory of Company Histories*. Detroit: St. James Press, ongoing.

Kerstetter, Jim. "Suddenly, a Mushy Software Market; Corporations Aren't Buying Because of Rising Costs or Concerns About the Economy." *Business Week Online,* 15 July 2004.

Kerstetter, Jim. "Finally, Oracle Nails PeopleSoft." *Business Week Online,* 13 December 2004.

Lohr, Steve. "Cutting Here, but Hiring Over There." *New York Times,* 24 June 2005. Available from http:///www.nytimes.net.

Lohr, Steve, and Joel Brinkley. "Antitrust Talks Founder on Microsoft's 'Desktop.'" *New York Times,* 18 May 1998.

"Major Market Profiles: Multimedia Software in USA (France, UK, Germany)." *Euromonitor,* October 2004. Available from http://www.euromonitor.com.

"Major Market Profiles: Networking Software in USA (France, UK, Germany)." *Euromonitor,* October 2004. Available from http://www.euromonitor.com.

"Major Market Profiles: PC Business Software in Japan (China, USA, France, UK, Germany)." *Euromonitor,* October 2004. Available from http://www.euromonitor.com.

Matsutani, Minoru, and Michelle Kessler. "Fujitsu to Cut as Many as 4,000 Jobs." *Bloomberg News,* 8 March 2002.

Moore, Jonathan, Pete Engardio, and Moon Ihlwan. "The Taiwan Touch." *Business Week,* 25 May 1998.

"More Than One-Third of Software is Pirated; Software Piracy Accounted for 36 Percent of the Worldwide Installed Base of

Software, the Business Software Alliance Reported Wednesday. Troubling Signs Developing with use of Peer-to-Peer Techniques Could Worsen the Situation." *InternetWeek,* 7 July 2004.

Roberts, Paul. "Security: The Year Ahead." *InfoWorld,* 5 January 2004.

"Sector Competitiveness Analysis of the Software and Computer Services Industry." U.K. Department of Trade and Industry, 16 June 2004. Available from http://www.dti.gov.uk.

"Software Industry Profile June, 2004." Software & Information Industry Association, 2004. Available from http://www.siia.net.

"Software: Pay-As-You-Go Is Up and Running; 'Selling Software as a Service over the Net Will Help Revive the Sluggish Industry.' 'Security and Design & Engineering Software will Grow at Double-Digit Rates." *Business Week,* 12 January 2004.

Sondag, Jennifer. "SAP Sees Sales Increasing 15 Percent." *Bloomberg News,* 23 January 2002.

Stape, Andrea L. "Data Storage Firm EMC Notes Loss of $70 Million in Fourth Quarter." *Bloomberg News,* 29 January 2002.

Swartz, Jon, and Michelle Kessler. "Microsoft Predicts Tough Year." *Bloomberg News,* 11 March 2002.

"Toys and Games in China (Japan, United States, United Kingdom, Germany, France, Russia): Executive Summaries." *Euromonitor,* August 2004. Available from http://www.euromonitor.com.

SIC 2721

NAICS 511120

PERIODICAL PUBLISHING

Periodical publishers develop, publish, and market all kinds of magazines and journals, and may or may not perform their own printing. Publishers also may or may not have electronic Web versions of the issue currently on the stands. See also **Newspaper Publishing** and **Printing, Commercial.**

INDUSTRY SNAPSHOT

The international periodicals industry is a major source of information and entertainment and serves as a vital advertising medium for other industries. The world's most popular kinds of periodicals are news, sports, lifestyle, outdoor, and computer magazines. From the late 1990s through the early 2000s, the periodical publishing industry grew around the world with modest advances in mature markets, such as Europe and the United States, and more marked growth in developing markets, such as Asia and South America. After the terrorist attacks of September 11, 2001, the industry suffered slower sales, massive returns of single-copy issues, and at some publishing houses, employee layoffs.

Following close after that disaster came the anthrax-related deaths of postal workers, leading consumers to throw away unread direct-mail solicitations they received and causing even industry leaders such as *Reader's Digest* to put direct mailings temporarily on hold. Nevertheless, a handful of magazines, such as *People,* sold well. Moreover, while men's magazines in general dropped dramatically in sales and women's magazines dropped or rose depending on title, some publications actually gained ad pages. These included outdoor magazines, because consumers turned to getaways in print for a vicarious experience while homebound.

A study by the Graphic Arts Marketing Information Service, entitled "Magazines in the 2000-2010 Era," estimated industry growth to be constant at around 5 percent. It concluded that classes of magazines would have different experiences. For example, weekly news magazines and trade publications were expected to see moderate decline due to Web competition.

New launches are always risky, with about 50 percent folding within twelve months, according to University of Mississippi journalism professor Samir Husni, who keeps track of all launches in his annual *Samir Husni's Guide to New Consumer Magazines.* New magazine titles released in late 2001 and 2002 were on particularly shaky ground, given the dry-up in ad sales and loss of direct mail effectiveness in the short run. In recent years, the most stunning magazine launch in terms of public recognition and overall success has been Oprah Winfrey's *O.* In 2002, Winfrey announced plans to launch a South African edition of her magazine.

Because publishers neared saturation levels in mature markets, with all sorts of periodicals covering a plethora of topics, some of them looked to new markets for expansion. They did this by acquisitions or mergers with foreign producers, joint ventures pushing new products, or the licensing of periodical titles to foreign companies for local-language editions. In the early 2000s, the United States was second to Europe in the production of periodicals, putting out more than one third of the number of titles published in Europe. In 2002, the United States distributed approximately 10,493 different periodicals, annually generating advertising revenues in excess of US$17 billion. By 2004, with the economy stabilizing, analysts were predicting over $93 billion in industry revenues by 2008.

ORGANIZATION AND STRUCTURE

The classification "periodicals" encompasses a variety of publications: business news magazines; statistical reports; comic books; fashion, women's, and home magazines; erotic material; religious periodicals; regional or "city" magazines; literary, travel, and general interest magazines; specialized business and professional periodicals; and a host of other periodicals such as newspaper magazines and supplements, and club and association newsletters.

For magazine publishers in developed economies in Europe, Asia, and North and South America, revenues are derived from two primary sources: sales to customers through subscriptions or the newsstand and income from advertising space sold to companies wishing to advertise in the magazine. In purely economic terms, a magazine's editorial content—its stories and images—can be seen simply as a vehicle for matching information or entertainment to an identifiable segment of the population that is willing to pay for it. Once this readership is identified, advertisers seeking to reach that group of consumers supplement the publisher's circulation sales revenues by paying for the opportunity to market their goods through the magazine's ad pages. In the United States, the amount of revenue a typical publisher derives from advertising versus sales (subscriptions and single copies) is roughly equal. In the world's less-developed media markets, however, where the number of potential advertisers is limited, magazine publishers must rely on sales to readers for a greater proportion of their revenue.

The International Federation of the Periodical Press (FIPP) is the only organization of magazine publishers with members from countries around the world. Founded in France in 1925, FIPP serves as a platform for the exchange of ideas and for the freedom, integrity, and development of the world's periodical industry. In 2005, FIPP reported 209 members in 53 countries, representing more than 110,000 magazine titles worldwide with annual advertising expenditure of about US$70 billion. With headquarters in London, FIPP's members include the United Kingdom, the United States, France, the Netherlands, Japan, and South Korea. FIPP itself changed leadership in 2001, as longtime President and Chief Operating Officer Per R. Mortensen departed for another corporate position and was replaced by onetime Magazine Publishers of America CEO Don Kummerfeld.

Global Contrasts. The characteristics of the world's periodical markets vary widely. While magazines in the United States come and go in substantial numbers every year, magazine markets like those of the United Kingdom are comparatively stable, with loyal readerships for specific titles. Similarly, while two-thirds of all new magazines in the United States are quarterly or bimonthly publications, the vast majority of mainland China's magazines are published monthly.

Other aspects of the periodical publishing industry vary widely around the world. The average number of ad pages in a new U.S. consumer magazine rose to 19, while magazines in mainland China carry only one to three ads per issue. Moreover, while subscriptions account for 90 percent of the sales of many consumer magazines in the United States, less than 10 percent of consumer magazine sales are subscription-based in the United Kingdom and even less in Asia. This rate is indicative of the emphasis on newsstand sales throughout Europe. There are several reasons for the meager subscription totals in Asia and Europe. Postage rates in most Asian and European nations are substantially higher than in the United States, making subscriptions sales a much costlier proposition for European and Asian publishers (and for outside publishers looking to enter those markets). In addition, while U.S. publishers maintain exhaustive mailing lists or rent them from other publishers, many other countries in the world have far less-advanced customer lists or have strict privacy laws regarding periodical sales via the mail.

Furthermore, population size also can influence the periodical publishing industry around the world. Given the United Kingdom's small population, for instance, British publishers are generally forced to use much smaller print runs than U.S. publishers. Per-copy production costs for most British magazines are consequently much higher, and British publishers do not have the luxury that U.S. publishers have of accumulating production cost deficits in anticipation of future sales. Similarly, while U.S. publishers in the early 2000s continued to seek ways to reduce the print costs of periodical titles, publishers in Japan continued to produce magazines that required the use of varying paper grades and printing techniques within a single issue. In unstable markets such as Russia, rampant piracy of printed material leads to huge losses through outright theft or illegal duplication, while limited freedom of the press in markets such as China and Singapore places editorial constraints on periodical publishers. Other factors, such as copyright law, postal efficiency, inflation rates, and sophistication of printing technology, all vary from region to region, rendering generalizations about the global periodicals market difficult. Since magazines are judged in far more subtle and subjective ways than other products—with the success of any given magazine resting heavily on matters of style, cultural expectation, and taste—the global periodicals industry in the early 2000s was still far from achieving real homogeneity. For example, Jordan produced only 11 periodical titles in 2002, and Bahrain produced 12. By contrast, Kuwait put out 51 different magazines that year, and Slovenia published 87 titles.

Canada Newswire reported magazine publishers are constantly challenged by postal rate increases and have benefited from unique services such as RR Donnelley's DistributionOptimizer Service. Usage of the service, allowing the company to co-palletize bundled periodicals from different titles onto the same pallet, resulted in improved delivery times, lower postage rates, and more predictable mail costs.

North America. The United States, Canada, and Mexico comprise one of the world's largest periodical markets, with the United States leading the trio as magazine producer with 10,493 titles in 2002. Mexico's magazine publishing sector with about 1,500 titles has come to surpass the approximately 1,400 titles from Canada, in part owing to the implementation of the North American Free Trade Agreement (NAFTA) in the mid-to-late 1990s that stirred greater international activity in Mexico's periodicals market.

Europe. The European magazine market is both saturated and segmented. There is little demand for new magazine titles, and existing titles cannot easily be extended from one market to another. While U.S. magazine publishers continued to make inroads in Europe in the 1990s and early 2000s, European publishers have had a much longer history of aggressive penetration of foreign periodical markets, in particular that of the United States. This imbalance is partly because the U.S. periodicals market is fluid and does not present significant barriers to entry, while the sheer diversity of the European market alone—20 languages in 24 countries—represents a major obstacle to successful foreign entry. Nonetheless, magazines remain a significant medium for advertisers in Europe in contrast to other parts of the world, accounting for about 25 percent of all advertising expenditures. In North America, magazines represent only 14 percent of the total advertising expenditures and in Asia only 7 percent. Much of the international placement of magazines is targeted toward larger airport traffic areas, such as Philadelphia, New York, and Washington, D.C. That also is true of outlet store placements that have the best sales in U.S. communities, with larger ethnic groups represented or larger numbers of international travelers represented.

In 1995 Europe was the largest exporter of periodicals in the world, accounting for no less than 62.8 percent (including books and newspapers) of the total value of global periodical exports and 50.3 percent of global imports. Nonetheless, Europe controls a smaller portion of the world's publishing industry than it did in the mid-1980s when it held 75 percent of the export market. The leading European periodical-producing nations in the mid-1990s through the 2000s were Germany, France, the United Kingdom, Italy, the Netherlands, Belgium, Spain, Austria, and Switzerland. The European Magazine Publishers Federation (Federation Europeenne d'Editeurs de Priodiques or FAEP) is the representative trade association of the European periodical press. It represents 7,000 publishers of 40,000 magazine titles with annual sales in 2001 of US$40 billion. A 2000 survey of publishers in Poland, Hungary, the Czech Republic, Estonia, Latvia, Slovakia, Slovenia, and Lithuania found that nearly 20 percent of all print publishers also put out online editions.

In the mid- to late 1990s U.S. and British magazine imports were also increasingly in demand in Eastern European countries. *Playboy* successfully launched Czech, Polish, and Hungarian editions in the 1990s, while *Business Week* and *Scientific American* introduced local-language editions in Hungary, *Reader's Digest* began a Hungarian-language edition in 1991 and planned a Czech edition, and the magazine *Okay America* was introduced in Poland. As former Soviet-bloc countries joined the European Union in 2004, enjoying improved economic conditions, analysts expected to see increased competition in the region's traditionally fragmented industry, with likelihood of accelerated consolidation.

Russian Federation. In 1995 Russia exported US$61.9 million worth of magazines, periodicals, and books, up more than 300 percent from only US$14.6 million in 1994. *Reader's Digest's* introduction of a Russian-language edition in 1991 illustrated the growing number of international publishers testing the market in the former USSR. In the mid-1990s, however, Russia's publishing industry remained plagued by piracy, inflation, and economic and political uncertainty. By 2002, Russia had made great inroads in the area of copyright and respect for artistic rights of composition. One of the pioneers in the early 1990s in exciting the Russian press about service journalism was Robert Rodale, publisher of *Organic Gardening* and *Prevention* magazines; he was killed in a car accident while visiting Moscow. While Germany and other nations had a financially rough 2001, ad sales in Russia in 2001 were the best since 1997, and the magazine industry's 2001 revenues were 43 percent higher than in 2000. Taking advantage of what its president and COO called the "great growth opportunities" in the Russian market, European media giant SanomaWSOY announced its planned acquisition in 2005 of Independent Media, the Russia's leading magazine publisher.

South America. South America's leading exporters include Colombia, Chile, Argentina, and Brazil. While Colombia and Brazil's international sales fluctuated throughout the 1990s, Chile and Argentina's grew steadily from under US$10 million (including newspapers and magazines) in 1991 to over US$56.6 and US$33.2 million respectively in 1995. Yet dire circumstances developed in the late 1990s, with magazine circulation in Argentina alone dropping by half between 1998 and 2004. In 2001, Argentina had 1,118 international titles and 1,007 domestic titles; in 2002, this number had plummeted to 398 and 692, respectively. Though the number of domestic titles recovered by 2004, international titles were still down far below 2001 levels. Though this climate made South America a risky location for international publishers seeking success in the local magazine market, some international companies made Latin American purchases in 2001, including Thomson Legal & Regulatory, which bought *La Ley,* Argentina's biggest publisher of legal periodicals. Thomson also bought into Brazil publishing by buying *Sintese,* Brazil's highest circulation electronics publication in 2000. Thomson's worldwide revenues in 2000 were self-disclosed at $2.6 billion.

Brazil's largest magazine publishers are sizable companies, such as Grupo Abril (the largest magazine publisher in Latin America), Bloch Editores and Correio Brasiliense. Similarly, leading periodical publishers in Colombia, including Cano Isaza Y Cia and Legislacion Economica Ltda, are often diversified companies with interests in other areas of manufacturing such as stationery and newspapers. Venezuela's magazine publishing industry is anchored in Caracas, where firms primarily focused on magazines, such as Editorial Primavera CA, compete for the magazine market against companies like Editora Noti-Globos CA—primarily a newspaper publisher—and Grabados Nacionales CA—a book publisher and commercial printer. Similarly, Argentina's Editorial Atlantida SA and La Ley SA Editora e Impresora are major magazine publishers involved in their country's book publishing, printing, and (in the case of La Ley) newspaper publishing industries.

Asia and Oceania. In addition to repercussions from the terrorist attacks of September 11, 2001, which quickly and adversely affected ad sales in Asia, the market for Chinese-language magazines became far more competitive as Taiwan and mainland China became associated with the World Trade Organization (WTO). Taiwan had about 6,000 magazines in 2001, but most analysts feel the potential market for readers is untapped as only about 10 percent are found in stores, the others being subscription only. Three thousand of those magazines were launched after 1996 in Taiwan. Magazine publishing in Asia and Oceania consists of several highly individualized markets dominated by Australia, Singapore, China (including Hong Kong), and Japan. In 1995 Australia ranked among the leading 10 importers of periodicals (including newspapers) in the world with imports valued at US$158.1 million. The leading magazine publishers in Australia are Australian Consolidated Press, which publishes both its own titles and magazines licensed by foreign publishers, and Rupert Murdoch's The News Corporation Limited which suffered Australian and global financial reversals in 2001. More than 75 percent of the corporation's sales are from its US businesses. Murdoch's family controls approximately 30 percent of the company.

Mainland China's magazine market has grown substantially in recent years. Advertising in Chinese magazines, while still relative to U.S. magazines, began to increase throughout the 1990s as more Western magazines entered the market. In fact, China ranked eighth for advertising dollars spent on magazines by 1997 with US$6.7 billion. Family, health, and education titles thrive in China's market because many consumers are reported to prefer magazines that promote common good and culture. The number of consumer magazines in China rose from 1,000 in 1978, to about 9,000 titles in 2002. During the 2000s, analysts expect business, computer, and science titles to perform well in China.

Hong Kong returned to Chinese control in 1997, merging one of the world's top ten exporters with one of the world's significant importers. Hong Kong's crowded magazine industry serves a population of only 6 million; an abundance of advertising revenue resulted in an unusually high number of coexisting titles in the mid-1990s. As a result, major U.S. and European magazine publishers—including the U.S. firms AOL Time Warner Inc. and Hearst Corporation and the French publisher Hachette Filipacchi Medias—publish Hong Kong editions of their own titles or magazines that originate in Hong Kong. While Hong Kong is geographically small, it carries disproportionate weight in the global periodicals market.

Singapore's magazine industry is significantly influenced by the censorship imposed by its government. The country's market, therefore, remained small and restricted, and men's lifestyle, business, and fashion magazines, introduced by Western publishers, have not had success. Its leading magazine companies include Singapore National Printers Ltd. and Toppan Printing Co. (Singapore) Pte. Ltd.

South Korea remained a significant trader of periodicals in the late 1990s and early 2000s, where the level of demand for foreign periodicals in the country, reflected in the value of magazines and newspapers imported, exceeded that of Thailand, Malaysia, and even Hong Kong. Licensed magazines from multinational publishers constitute a large segment of the market with strong interest in titles such as *Reader's Digest, GEO, Elle, Marie Claire,* and *Enfants.*

In 2002, Asian magazines continued to struggle. One of the larger corporations, Next Media, with holdings in Hong Kong and Taiwan, cut nearly 200 jobs or 10 percent of its workforce after stock prices fell in 2002. The layoffs saved the company about US$5 million. Even so, analysts expected magazines' fastest growth in the early 2000s to occur in the Asia-Pacific region, with China and India the primary contributors to this increase. For the region as a whole, growth of 2.4 percent annually was predicted between 2004 and 2008, to reach about US$11.9 billion. Advertising revenues for magazines were expected to grow by about 2.7 percent per year. Japan and Australia, the region's leading publishers with 75 percent of total media revenue, were projected to increase advertising revenue by 1.2 percent and 4.4 percent, respectively in 2005. Even larger ad revenue growth (6.6 percent) was expected in India.

BACKGROUND AND DEVELOPMENT

The history of periodicals began with the insertion of book notices in European newsbooks published in the early seventeenth century. By the middle of that century, publishers began to include critical comments in the notices. In the meantime, digests and abstract journals made their first appearances. These periodicals provided information on books, authors, and important scientific and philosophical matters of the day. The *Journal Des Scavans,* first published in Paris on January 5, 1665, is recognized as the parent of the modern periodical manufacturing industry.

Periodicals offering opinion, news, and entertainment proliferated. In the early eighteenth century journals of political thought and a broad range of other interests appeared. The first American periodicals were *American Magazine* and *General Magazine,* both of which started in 1741 and failed less than a year later. While numerous early magazines failed, about 100 magazines and journals had been established in the United States by 1825. By 1850 the total number of magazine titles in circulation rose to 600. During this period *Harper's New Monthly Magazine* was launched. This heavily illustrated periodical paved the way for a new era of magazine publishing. Imitators proliferated, and the industry continued to grow.

In the early twentieth century a number of periodicals that continue to endure were founded around the world. Only in the 1950s did a threat to the industry finally present itself. The medium of television stole both customers and advertisers. The periodical publishing industry proved to be a hardy one, however, and continued to enjoy steady growth around the world from the 1960s through the 1980s.

CURRENT CONDITIONS

In mature markets such as Europe and the United States, magazine publishing grew at a moderate pace from the mid-1990s through 2001, led by heightened interest in specialty magazines, lifestyle magazines, and those with computer and technology themes. In developing markets, the industry expanded at a brisker pace as countries opened their markets to magazine imports, as incomes and leisure time rose, and as wider segments of these populations achieved higher levels of education. A shaky economic period after the September 11, 2001 terrorist attacks in the United States resulted in slow growth for magazine publishing, but stronger economic conditions by 2004 boded well for the industry. Analysts Pricewaterhouse Coopers (PwC) predicted global spending on magazines to rise from US$80.7 billion in 2003 to about US$93.4 billion in 2008.

Magazine publishers around the world continued to grapple with problems associated with the availability and cost of paper. In the face of deforestation worldwide and criticism from governments and environmental organizations, publishers sought new ways to overcome these problems. The Internet offered the most prominent and most successful alternative to traditional print periodicals in the early 2000s. Publishers launched numerous magazines and academic journals, first on proprietary services such as CompuServe and America Online and later on the Internet. Academic journals, in particular, enjoyed the cost efficiency of the Internet for making their articles quickly available to their readership. Besides offering an alternative to paper periodicals, the Internet also blossomed into a popular topic, spawning numerous magazines such as *Wired,* devoted to it.

Many of the established U.S. and European periodical publishers have turned to overseas markets in order to increase their circulation and advertising revenues. As growth in their domestic markets continued to slow down, these publishers tried to take advantage of the burgeoning markets abroad. By forming joint ventures with local publishers and by licensing their periodicals, these publishers made their foray into Asian and South American markets in the mid-to-late 1990s. For example, U.S. Hearst Publications teamed up with local publishers to offer *Harper's Bazaar* in South Korea and Russia, and Italian R.C.S. Rizzoli joined forces with German Burda Verlag GmbH to exploit the Asian magazine market. In order to reap local advertising dollars, some publishers also offer special editions or spin-off titles of their periodicals abroad. *Readers's Digest,* for example, has launched several international projects based on the model of Reiman Publications, which it purchased in 2002. These new magazines are circulation-driven and feature reader-contributed editorial content. Among *Reader's Digest*'s new titles were *Our Canada* in Canada and *Sabor di Casa* (Taste of Home) in Brazil. *Scientific American,* which derives more than 85 percent of its international revenues from circulation, had 18 international editions as of 2004.

Furthermore, companies in the industry continued to consolidate during this period, a trend expected to continue for some time. The United Kingdom's United News & Media PLC merged with MAI PLC, becoming a magazine publishing colossus with an arsenal of 200 magazines. The second-largest U.K. publisher, EMAP, also expanded its empire by acquiring CLT Multi Media, a Luxembourg publisher. Reed Elsevier, the largest U.K. publisher, considered a merger that would have made it the largest periodical publisher in the world. However, the deal with Dutch Wolters Kluwer fell through because of regulatory objections by the European Commission and the United States. Nonetheless, Reed Elsevier acquired Matthew Bender, a publisher of legal books and periodicals, for US$1.6 billion later in 1998, as part of the company's effort to reposition itself as an information and technology publisher. In addition, Japanese Softbank Corporation, a major publisher in the country, acquired U.S. Ziff Davis, known for its business and computer magazines. Finally, Primedia purchased 29 periodicals, including the *Cowles Enthusiast Media* and *Cowles Business Media,* from McClatchy Newspapers Inc. As of 2003, Primedia was the leading publisher of special interest periodicals in the United States.

Research and Technology. The ever-increasing sophistication of the global periodicals industry in the 1990s led to expanded use of cheaper and more advanced means of magazine production (such as the widespread use of desktop publishing software and computer systems for in-house magazine production), an increased focus on the opportunities offered by multimedia and information-distribution technologies for periodical publishers, and the emergence of more specialized periodical niches and submarkets geared to highly specific reader tastes and interests. Periodical publishers worldwide also sought new ways to increase their profits in response to a decline in the growth rate of advertising revenue and heated competition with other periodicals and various media outlets such as television. To improve overall profitability, some U.S. publishers explored staff downsizing, salary freezes, reductions in employee benefits, more efficient mailing procedures, alternative transportation modes, lighter grades of paper, and increased use of subscriber database information. They also increasingly looked to nontraditional revenue sources. Some publishers sold subscriber information to other companies, while others marketed nonprint products and services geared to their readers' interests and lifestyles.

Electronic versions of magazines became increasingly available. By the mid-to-late 1990s, many major U.S. magazines, including *Fortune, Time, People,* and *U.S. News and World Report,* as well as international magazines such as Germany's *Der Spiegel,* were available in electronic editions. These versions enabled readers with a personal computer and Internet access to download articles and images, listen to "sound files," send electronic mail to editors, search back issues, or renew their subscriptions. In the mid-1990s, The Electronic Newsstand Inc. began providing periodical publishers in the United States with an outlet on the Internet, the Global Computer and Information Network. By 1997 more than 90,000 U.S. and Canadian magazines and journals made themselves available on the Internet, with many more in the 2000s. Other nontraditional, "paperless" media, explored by magazine publishers in developed nations, included cable television outlets and interactive multimedia "digital magazines" on CD-ROM.

Industry Leaders

Hachette Filipacchi Medias (HFM). In the magazine shakeout of 2001 and 2002, the media empire that ascended to the top financially, in the wake of AOL Time Warner's mounting economic crises, was the French firm Hachette Filipacchi Medias (HFM), a major figure in international magazine sales. In 2002, Crain Communications announced that Hachette Filipacchi Medias had become the world's largest periodical publisher. With annual sales in excess of 1 billion copies from properties such as *Elle, Premiere, Paris Match,* and *Car and Driver,* the company not only survived the worst year in recent magazines sales, it thrived. Hachette Filipacchi Medias reported annual revenues in 2001 of about US$2.5 billion. In 2004, the company was estimated to produce about 250 magazines and newspapers. Chairman and CEO Gerald de Roquemaurel and Editor-in-Chief Jean-Louis Ginibre ran the company. French media and industrial conglomerate Lagardere bought the remaining one third of HFM in 2000. Roquemaurel actively added to the HFM empire's stable of titles, having added Japanese *Jujingaho,* and in 2001, a 42-percent interest in *Marie Claire,* according to Crain.

Reed Elsevier NV. Like Hachette Filipacchi Medias, the English-Dutch empire of Reed Elsevier not only made it through 2001's general magazine collapse, it actually prospered. In 2001, Reed Elsevier, known for its acclaimed scientific journals, announced a 20 percent increase in its profits for the year. The company benefited from its 2001 acquisition of Harcourt General Inc. for US$5.65 billion. The media group did encounter some losses, most notably the U.S.-based Cahners group, but by cutting staff and other measures Reed Elsevier minimized its damage. Net income for 2004 was US$302 million.

Time Warner. Time Warner Inc., formerly AOL Time Warner, was the largest publishing and entertainment company in the world in 2004. Without question, its four major weekly titles made Time Inc. the global king of news and sports publishing. In 1997 it led all U.S. periodical publishers in share of total ad dollars (21 percent) and with US$24.62 billion in revenues, of which publishing accounted for 17 percent. Formed through the merger of Time Inc. and Warner Communications in 1989, Time Warner published such high circulation periodicals as *Fortune, Money, Entertainment Weekly, Sports Illustrated, People, Life,* and *Time.* The company did not shy away from international markets. Time Warner explored more than 20 joint ventures or other arrangements with European and Asian media companies; among its acquisitions was U.K. giant IPC Group Limited. The merger of AOL with Time Warner in 2001 did not pay off for Time Warner, analysts said in 2002, citing AOL subscription stagnation and other growth barriers.

Nonetheless, in 2004 the AOL Time Warner properties remained among the most competitive in publishing globally. With 64 magazines reaching a self-reported 268 million readers, its Time Inc. brand launched nine major magazines from 1992 to 2002. The company also owns 49 percent of *Essence,* a magazine targeting African American women. In addition, Time manages publication operations of American Express. It owns the United Kingdom's top magazine publisher, IPC Group Limited, with a collection of approximately 80 titles including *Marie Claire.* Total sales in 2004 surpassed US$42 billion, a one-year increase of 10.5 percent.

The Reader's Digest Association, Inc. The world's most popular magazine hearkens back to 1922, when DeWitt and Lila Wallace put out 5,000 copies of their first issue for US 25 cents. In addition to its familiar monthly general interest magazine, Reader's Digest Association Inc. annually publishes several million books in more than 20 countries, and in the 1990s maintained operations in 50 cities around the world. The company's flagship publication, *Reader's Digest,* had a worldwide readership of 85 million in 2004, with sales reaching US$2.38 billion.

In 2001, Reader's Digest Association Inc. disclosed that stalled circulation and fewer ad pages contributed to a lower fiscal second-quarter profit, by 24 percent net income. At the end of 2001, stockholders learned profits had declined to US$78.8 million, or US 78 cents a share, plunging from 2000's US$103.8 million, or US 99 cents, according to *Bloomberg News.* In a January 2002 press release, the Reader's Digest Association reported that 2001 sales fell 4.9 percent to US$784 million, down from 2000 sales of US$824.3 million. The situation did not improve until 2004, after the company implemented a major restructuring plan that included regional consolidations, elimination of some nonprofitable activities, and reduction of staff. In addition, the company focused on improvements in customer services and on investment in new publications. In 2004, Reader's Digest enjoyed successful book launches in three new countries: Romania, Croatia, and Slovenia. The company planned continued expansions in 2005, including new launches in Ukraine, Germany, the United Kingdom, and India.

In recent years, *Reader's Digest* reinvented itself editorially, adding strong health-related coverlines as a way to continue the publication's broad-based appeal in the 2000s. The association also published thriving consumer special interest periodicals and special interest magazines that include *Selecciones, The Family Handyman, American Woodworker, New Choices, Moneywise,* and *Benchmark.*

Axel Springer. Axel Springer Verlag AG, based in Berlin, is one of Germany's leading publishers and a key player in several media. Axel Springer owns newspapers such as *Die Welt* and *Bild.* In addition, the publisher also controls radio, television, and electronic information operations and a share of America Online's German service. The family of the founder owns 55 percent of the firm. In 2002, at the end of February, the Axel Springer enterprise reported reduced revenue, declining ad sales, and losses in other areas of the media empire. That year Axel Springer was struggling to find backers and was refinancing to continue some operations. In addition, it told stock holders that no dividend would be paid, according to the *Los Angeles Times.* Sales improved in 2004, growing by 7.2 percent to reach US$3.2 billion.

Hearst. Although traditionally associated with newspaper publishing, the Hearst Corporation entered the magazine business early in its history, launching *Motor* magazine in 1903 and purchasing *Cosmopolitan* and *Good Housekeeping.* As it gradually sold off some of its newspapers in the 1950s, it continued to expand its magazine empire, adding such titles as *Popular Mechanics, Redbook, Esquire,* and *Cosmopolitan,* between 1950 and 1990. As of 2004, the company owned 81 U.S. consumer magazines. Hearst reported total sales of about US$4.1 billion in 2003. The company expanded its presence internationally by acquiring and forming alliances with local newspapers and magazines. Hearst boasted of 92 international editions distributed in 100 different countries. In 2002, the company disclosed that falling ad revenues had rocked its profit structure. In an attempt to stop the decline, Hearst handed pink skips to 8.5 percent of its workforce.

MAJOR COUNTRIES IN THE INDUSTRY

United States. In 2002, total U.S. business and consumer periodicals amounted to some 10,493 titles, according to FIPP. Of this number, slightly more than half were consumer publications and half were business titles. Revenues from advertising continued to rise through 2001, when the World Trade Center collapse marked a decline in ad spending that contributed to sluggish growth for the magazine industry. In addition, implementation of the National Do Not Call Registry in 2003 restricted a favored marketing strategy for publishers. Nevertheless, advertising revenues for consumer magazines began to improve in 2003, and by 2004 had grown by 11.5 percent over the previous year. Even so, many U.S. magazines continued to confront declining circulations. Five of the top 10 U.S. magazines in 2004 posted a circulation drop compared to the previous year.

Some of the declines in U.S. magazine advertising are voluntary as, under pressure from the *Journal of the American Medical Association,* the tobacco industry agreed to pull ads from youth-oriented magazines such as *Rolling Stone,*

Spin, and *Hot Rod.* The largest markets for U.S. publishers in the early 2000s were women's magazines, news magazines, business magazines, and general audience periodicals. The country's leading periodicals included *TV Guide, Good Housekeeping,, Family Circle,, People, Sports Illustrated, Time,* and *Reader's Digest.*

The U.S. periodical publishing industry has remained a vital one despite increased competition from television, catalogs, and direct mail for the critical advertising dollar; and fierce maneuvering to secure a profitable share of a maturing subscription and newsstand circulation market. In the late 1990s and early 2000s, periodical publishers began to explore new niches in the country's population, giving rise to lavish lifestyle magazines, such as *More,* that targeted affluent baby boomers and ethnic magazines that targeted segments such as Latinos, African Americans, and Asian Americans with titles such as *Latina, Black Enterprise,* and *Inside Asian America.*

In 2001, one of the magazines to suffer massive stock declines and layoffs in its magazine division was the now venerable *Playboy.* Hurt by general 2001 ad declines and its decision to add hard-core, pay-per-view options (although not under the *Playboy* name), it caused some stockholders to unload their holdings. *Playboy* still claims to be the number 1 men's magazine, with more than 3 million readers.

In summer 2003, the San Francisco-based Public Library of Science made an announcement that shook up the academic publishing world. It offered a business model based on charging contributors $1,500 to publish their papers in the journal. The *online publishing news* claimed the library's actions were in response to "steeply rising subscription cost of the most prestigious—and generally highly profitable'research journals."

Germany. Until Germany's periodical industry suffered reversals in the 2000s, it had been Europe's most profitable and, in terms of the number of magazines, biggest player. Magazines are taken far more seriously as a cultural source of ideas in Germany than in many other countries, and only Japan produces a wider range of periodicals. At the start of 2002, the German magazine industry was dominated by the "Big Four": ad sales-beleaguered Axel Springer Verlag, Germany's largest publisher, which back in 1996 boasted sales of US$2.8 billion; Heinrich Bauer Verlag; Gruner + Jahr AG, a subsidiary of the mammoth international publisher Bertelsmann AG; and Burda GmbH, with its 30 magazines and more thanUS$1 billion in revenues.

While Heinrich Bauer Verlag publishes mass circulation periodicals, Gruner + Jahr puts out Germany's largest news-oriented magazine, *Der Spiegel,* and the flashier general interest magazine *Stern.* Axel Springer publishes a highly regarded automobile magazine and shared titles with other major players, such as AOL Time Warner. Burda GmbH is best known as the German version of *Forbes.* Other major German publishers are: Gong-Verlag GmbH, Frankfurter Allgemeiner Zeitung GmbH, Verlag das Beste GmbH, and Weltbild Verlag GmbH.

In 2002, at the end of February, the Axel Springer enterprise was struggling to find backers and was refinancing to continue operations. On February 26, 2002, the *Los Angeles Times* said that its sources reported a $960 million offer—many times over its estimated value—for the Springer media enterprises, by German investors. Nonetheless, as some media stocks appeared to rebound in late February 2002, Germany's Finance Ministry told *Bloomberg News* that the economy in Europe "is on the verge of a new upswing."

France. During the 1980s and early 1990s, the French magazine market was aggressively targeted by foreign publishers, primarily Germany's Big Four. These international investments succeeded because of the country's outmoded distribution procedures and chaotic advertising rates, and because France's periodicals industry had failed to keep its magazines in touch with readers' tastes. As a consequence, German publishers grabbed sizable shares of France's magazine market. France came back strongly in the 2000s, while some German companies faltered due to severe ad sales drops. The dominant player in France's magazine industry during the 2000s was Hachette Filipacchi Medias (HFM), the world's largest periodical publisher. The company boasted annual sales exceeding 1 billion magazines. FIPP claimed Lagardere was eager to buy more magazines throughout the world but had a special interest in doing so in the United States.

In 2004, only *Paris Match,* among weekly magazines in France, posted a circulation gain. Readership grew from 4,332,000 in 2002 to 4,376,000 in 2003 and rose further to reach 4,380,000 in 2004.

United Kingdom. In the 1990s and early 2000s, fashion magazines performed well when advertising volume increased substantially, climbing to its highest level since 1990. Home decorating magazines also became popular during this period. Interest in car and bike magazines also was revived in the late 1990s. The leading British consumer title, *What's On TV,* sold 1.58 million copies a week in 2004, primarily through newsstand sales, which in the United Kingdom accounts for 92 percent of all consumer magazine sales. Thanks to Reed Elsevier's dominance in educational and scientific titles, as well as its U.S. movie trade magazine *Variety,* the United Kingdom managed not only to get through the hard industry times in the 2000s but actually to thrive overall. Nonetheless, to achieve profit totals, Reed Elsevier continued to put out titles with considerably fewer editorial employees than work at U.S. periodical houses. In 2001 and 2002, those lean staffs became even leaner as Reed trimmed 1,000 jobs (2.6 percent of its workforce), according to *Bloomberg News.*

In addition, by February 2002 another U.K. media giant, the business-oriented Pearson Plc., saw its stock price go up a modest 2.8 percent, giving rise to hopes that magazine ad sales could see a return to much higher ad sales of the late 1990s. Rather than panic, some publishers elected to pour money into their magazines to keep quality and readers in anticipation of a return to normal ad sales. Conde Nast, for example, announced that in spite of dwindling ad sales for the British *GQ,* it planned to thicken each issue by 20 pages and to hire celebrities to pen regular columns. In 2002 Conde Nast bought Ideas Publishing Group, which produces publications targeted at Spanish speakers, and renamed it Conde Nast Americas.

Netherlands. Major magazine publishing firms included Verenigde Nederlandse Uitgeversbedrijven BV, Roto Smeets De Boer NV, Hollandse Dagbladcombinatie BV, Sythoff Pers BV, and the English-Dutch partnership of Reed Elsevier PLC, Elsevier NV. Elsevier is the publisher of more than 1,000 scientific and other journals. While Reed Elsevier weathered the 2001 collapse better than most publishers, in late February 2002 it folded its relatively new title, *Electronic Business Asia,* because the monthly publication, devoted to the microchip trade, had about a fifth of 2000 advertising and about one-third the sales income of 2000.

Canada. Canada houses about 1,400 domestic magazines. However, with scarce advertising revenues, only about half of them turn a profit. The Canadian Magazine Publishers Association reported that almost 80 percent of the magazines on newsstands come from outside of Canada, with the majority from the United States.

In the mid-1990s, the Canadian government responded to Canadian magazine publishers' fears by taking steps to protect its domestic periodicals industry from encroaching U.S. publishers (a Canadian edition of *Sports Illustrated,* for example, was introduced in 1993). Although such arrangements had long been in place, new legislation was passed that required that all prospective Canadian editions of foreign magazines first gain the approval of the Canadian government. The law was the latest development in a long-standing battle between Canadian and U.S. magazine publishers for market share. This struggle had previously spurred the abolishment of the tax deduction for businesses that advertised in non-Canadian publications and contributed to legislation that required that periodicals sold in Canada pass strict Canadian ownership and content requirements. Finally, in 1997 the World Trade Organization (WTO) ordered Canada to liberalize its protectionist magazine policy when U.S. complaints persisted. In particular, the WTO objected to Canada's 80 percent excise tax on advertising in Canadian editions or split-run editions of non-Canadian magazines. In 1999, the government greatly softened restrictions on U.S. magazines that wished to allow Canadian advertisers to purchase ad space.

In 2002, as magazine ad sales in general were very soft in Canada, U.S.-based *People* magazine began exploring ways to more aggressively target Canadian advertisers, incurring the displeasure of the Canadian Magazine Publishers Association (CMPA). Hoping to jumpstart Canadian magazine sales, the CMPA joined forces with the Ministry of Tourism, Culture and Recreation to maintain the MagOmania Web site, with a goal of putting all Canadian magazines in easy access of potential readers or advertisers. In 2002 the CMPA continued work on its National Circulation and Promotion Program (NCPP), a US$5.6 million campaign to ignite reader loyalties for Canadian magazines. The battle was hard to win for the industry. As if the industry did not have enough challenges, in 2002 the Canada Post Corporation (CPC) increased magazine postage, on average, 6.5 percent in April 2002, 4 percent in January 2003, and 6 percent in January 2004.

MacLean Hunter Ltd. of Toronto was the largest Canadian periodicals publisher. The newsweekly *MacLean's* remained the company's flagship publication in the 1990s, but MacLean Hunter continued to be primarily a business trade publisher. Other major Canadian periodical publishers included CCH Canadian Limited, Key Publishers Company Ltd., and Hebdos Telemedia. The media corporation Rogers Communications, Canada's largest, publishes 70 consumer and trade magazines and runs cable and wireless services. While it had some losses in 2001, its revenue of US$652 million for the year was 6.7 percent higher than 2000 revenue. The company's total sales for 2004 surpassed US$4.6 billion. Canadian magazine sales were expected to grow by about 2.1 percent between 2004 and 2008, with ad revenues increasing by 4.3 percent annually.

Japan. The Japanese periodicals market remains one of the world's largest. Most of the country's magazine sales come from newsstands because of low subscription levels. Comic book periodicals account for 25 percent of all magazine sales in Japan, and the comic magazine *Weekly Shonen Jump,* which sold more than 7 million copies weekly throughout Japan in the mid-1990s, became "the best-selling product in the history of American comic publishing" when it was introduced to the U.S. market in 2003, according to *Anime Insider* managing editor Robert Bricken, as quoted in a *Time* feature. The launch boosted revenues for publisher Shueisha, which had seen circulation for *Weekly Shonen Jump* decline to only 3.4 million. Because of the crowded field of magazines, there is consequently little room for new foreign entrants without the financial resources to absorb short-term losses. The giant Kodansha Ltd. Publishers leads the Japanese periodical publishing industry. Other firms in Japan's competitive magazine industry include Asahi Shimbun Publishing Co. Ltd., Shueisha Publishing Inc., and Gakken Co. Ltd. Newspaper publisher Nihon Keizai Shimbun Inc. also maintains a significant presence in the industry via its Nikkei Business Publications Inc. subsidiary. In February 2002, all of Japan's business community was given staggering news as continued deflation led to a drop in the value of the yen, leading critics in the business community to fault the Japanese government for launching timely changes in monetary policy. On a hopeful note, Japanese stocks began to rise, albeit modestly, in 2002. Nonetheless, Japanese periodicals in 2001 recorded the fifth consecutive year of diminished sales, although sales actually have been disappointing for eight years, noted Yoshihide Nishitani, president of Mirai-sha Publishers. The decline in sales of magazines was 3 percent in 2001, compared to 2000.

China. China's booming economy in the early 2000s prompted analysts to predict strong growth in consumer and business-to-business magazines, according to BPA Worldwide. While magazines' share of advertising in China has remained relatively small, it has grown by about 33 percent annually since the mid-1980s and was expected to reach US$381 million in 2005. China has reformed its policies on media industry investment to allow greater access to capital, a move that insiders considered likely to spur the development of new publications. As of 2005, China had more than 9,000 magazine licenses. Analysts expected to see increased consolidation in China's magazine publishing industry through the early 2000s. At the same time, increased competition was seen as a factor that would result in the adoption of best business practices. The Chinese magazine industry's readiness to adopt digital technology has allowed it to cut distribution costs significantly.

India. Industry analysts have touted India as a huge market since the country agreed in 2004 to allow foreign investors to obtain full ownership of periodicals there. Magazines on technological subjects show particular potential. International publishing services company IDG established a subsidiary in India in 2004 and introduced a new magazine, *OutSourcing World,* with a circulation of 30,000. In the works in 2005 was IDG's *CIO India,* an Indian version of the global magazine *CIO.* Also in 2005, both *Business Week* and *Forbes* announced plans to develop Indian editions.

FURTHER READING

"Academic Publishers Face New Online Challenge," 2005. Available from http://www.onlinepublishingnews.com.

Asada, Tomiji. "Sales of Books, Mags Down for 5 Straight Years." *Japan Economic Newswire,* 25 February 2002.

Bonisteel, Steven. "At Home's Demise Pushes Losses Higher For Canada's Rogers." *Newsbyter,* 22 February 2002.

"Book Sales." *Bloomberg News,* 24 January 2002.

"CondéNast Announces Major Investment in GQ." *Media Week,* 30 November 2001.

Crawford, Anne-Marie. "A Passion for Magazines." *Ad Age Global,* 1 January 2002.

European Federation of Magazine Publishers, 2005. Available from http://www.faep.org/index.htm.

"Exclusive Analysis of Magazine Circulation, Second-Half-2001." *Min Media Industry Newsletter,* 25 February 2002.

Farrand, Tim. "Reed Elsevier Promises Double Digit Earnings Growth." *AFX European Focus,* 21 February 2002.

Fraher, John. "European Stocks Rise, Led by Media, Auto Shares." *Bloomberg News,* 25 February 2002.

Furman, Phyllis. "Media Companies Post More Losses." *Daily News (New York),* 31 January 2002.

Garger, Ilya. "Look, up in the Sky!" *Time Asia,* 17 February 2003. Available from http://www.time.com.

Grande, Carlos. "Goodbye Boys. The Latest ABCs Show Very Different Fortunes for Men and Women's Titles." *The Financial Times,* 19 February 2002.

Hansen, Glenn. "Magazines: What's Ahead in China and Other World Markets?" BPA Worldwide, 2005. Available from http://www.bpaww.com.

"Industry Trends," 2005. Available from http://www.gain.net.

"Lagardiere Eager to Buy More Magazines," 2005. Available from http://www.fipp.com.

Lin, Lillian. "GIO Chief Encourages Magazine Publishers to Find Winning Formula." *Central News Agency,* 13 November 2001.

Love, Barbara. "International Circ in the Fast Lane." *Circulation Managament,* 5 May 2005. Available from http://www.circman.com.

Mandese, Joe. "Outdoor Is Poster Child for Ad Strength During Recession." *Media Money,* 26 February 2002.

"New GAMIS Study Reveals Future for Magazines," 2005. Available from http://www.gain.net.

Magazine Publishing Statistics, 2002-2004. International Federation of the Periodical Press. Available from http://www.fipp.com.

Patterson, Alan. "Reed Elsevier Closing Hong Kong Magazine on Advertising Slump." *Bloomberg News,* 25 February 2002.

Picchi, Aimee. "Martha Stewart 4th-Quarter Profit Falls As Ads Slip." *Bloomberg News,* 20 February 2002.

———. "Reader's Digest 2nd-Qtr Net Drops on Slower Ad Sales." *Bloomberg News,* 24 January 2002.

"RR Donnelley's DistributionOptimizer Service Reduces Postal Costs for Magazine Publisher," 2005. Available from http://www.hoovers.com.

Stoffman, Judy. "*People Magazine* Eyes Canadian Advertising." *Toronto Star,* 19 February 2002.

Tims, Dana. "Research Earns Spot at Forum." *The Oregonian,* 7 February 2002.

"Tycoon Publisher to Axe 180 Jobs in Latest Blow to Hong Kong." *Deutsche Presse-Agentur,* 16 January 2002.

SIC 2750

NAICS 32311

PRINTING, COMMERCIAL

Printing companies engage in lithographic, gravure, or other commercial printing. The industry likewise performs offset and photo-offset printing and photolithographing.

INDUSTRY SNAPSHOT

The years between 1980 and the mid-2000s were a period of digital revolution for the world's multibillion-dollar printing industry. Forced by nontraditional media, notably CD-ROMs and Internet publishing, to assimilate technology or fold their shops, printers had to find their place in a new era of information delivery. They were hungrier than ever for the benefits of new technology to keep printing competitive by decreasing production costs and improving the quality and timeliness of their services. Other challenges included the industry's habitually fierce competition, the fluctuating cost of paper products, and competition from television and radio for advertiser dollars. In 2002 the latest technology push was for printers to develop so-called remote printing capabilities for documents and photographs through Internet printing, such as the PrintMe Network system. PrintMe Networks allowed professional-level printing to PrintMe printers from wireless and cable-free devices such as personal computers, two-way pagers, and mobile phones, as well as dial-up devices such as fax machines. Other industry-wide developments in the 2000s included plateless press technology and highly evolved computer-integrated manufacturing in the printing process.

Many of the largest commercial printers responded to these marketplace realities through diversification into information services, redefining their role as providing communication solutions rather than just printed products. By the late 1990s, some printers had begun to offer services as diverse as database management and information warehousing. These firms were well placed to do this work for several reasons. Their business had always dealt with the packaging of information; producing CD-ROMs, for instance, could be seen as merely a change in medium. Some, such as R.R. Donnelley, garnered experience with such media through supplying manuals for the computer software industry. Others, such as Cadmus Journal Services, found a niche providing Web publishing for their clients in addition to traditional printing.

As traditional printing companies continued to go out of business, nearly all major companies accepted integrated media as crucial to their existence, realizing that they must offer such services by 2010. In addition to print and video capabilities, large printers as of 2005 had services related to database management, image vending, electronic and technology-related equipment sales, and multimedia sales presentations.

Electronic file transfer forced many printers to become savvy about digital networking requirements, and some even found a profit center in marketing their networking expertise to their clients' in-house needs. The impact of electronic file transfer, direct-to-plate technologies, and digital printing was an ongoing vector of industry change. Due to the high costs of printing and specialized equipment, many newspapers and magazines "outsourced" the printing of publications to printing firms that served as outside contractors.

ORGANIZATION AND STRUCTURE

The three largest commercial printing firms in the Western Hemisphere—R.R. Donnelley & Sons of the United States, Quebecor Printing Inc. of Canada, and Carvajal S.A. of Colombia—accounted for approximately 10 percent of industry sales through the 1990s. At the other end, 58,000 plants competed for 82 percent of the market. A similar structure was found at the national level: 80 percent of U.S. printers had annual sales of less than US$2 million in the early 1990s. Most firms in the industry were small; the 40,000 U.S. commercial printers had an average size of 20 employees. In Japan 80 percent of printing companies employed fewer than 10 workers in the early 1990s. Although average profits were better for larger firms, the profit leaders in the smaller size categories tended to be more profitable than those in the larger categories. Efficiency and marketing penetration were other important factors influencing profitability.

Short-run printing—2- or 3-color and process color printing in runs of fewer than 5,000—accounted for an estimated 26 percent (US$20.1 billion) of the copying and commercial printing market in the United States. Analysts noted that shorter printer runs with smaller signatures and heavy reliance on bindery technology to produce customized publications for narrowly targeted markets was an increasing trend in the U.S. market. Conversely, European printers favored all-at-once printing practices to save time and labor and eliminate the need for special binder operations.

Various regions specialized in certain segments of the printing industry. For example, Brazil emerged as the packaging center of South America, while areas with low production costs, such as Mexico, attracted labor-intensive operations in the areas of bookbinding and other post-press sectors of the printing industry.

Literacy and disposable income were limiting factors in any region's print industry as well. While the United States and Canada produced an average of US$305 worth of printed materials per person in the 1990s, less than US$2.50 per person was produced in Asia outside of Japan. Fifteen percent of the world's population accounted for consumption of more than 80 percent of the world's printed products, according to some industry analysts.

Other factors made it difficult for printers in developing countries to produce high-quality print products and thus compete globally. A consistent supply of materials, such as paper and ink, was vital, but in China, for instance, most printing materials were available only through domestic suppliers (although high-quality paper was sometimes imported for special projects). Careful handling and protection from moisture also was required, necessitating a level of sophistication often lacking in less developed facilities. However, some countries, such as Thailand, succeeded in achieving high printing standards at prices that were a fraction of those in the United States. In a similar manner, the printing industries of other regions, such as the Middle East—which utilized European and Indian equipment and expertise—began to develop businesses that were competitive with long-established printers in the United States and Europe. Investors noted this trend in the industry.

BACKGROUND AND DEVELOPMENT

The commercial printing industry originated with the introduction of handbills and broadsides used to publicize goods for sale or auction, cultural events, and other public notices. Commercial printers were also hired to print currency, stamps, and government documents. Often the same firms became publishers of almanacs, Bibles, and other books. It was not uncommon for publishing firms to diversify into commercial printing, and a single publishing house that supplied newspaper, periodical, book, and commercial printing often dominated developing regions.

Printing in general is one of the world's oldest industries. Woodcuts of illustrations were in use by the ancient Egyptians, Babylonians, and Chinese. However, textual matter was not printed until the eighth century A.D. Approximately 300 years later innovators in China and Korea experimented with moveable type made from various materials including wood, clay, bronze, and iron; however, their efforts were impeded by the complex characters of their written languages.

Aided by the simple Roman phonetic alphabet, Johannes Gutenberg developed a revolutionary method of printing in the mid-fifteenth century, called letterpress. Letterpress and the Bible, traditionally held to be the first book printed by Gutenberg, were responsible for the global spread of printing. In Thailand, for example, the first printers were seventeenth-century missionaries. Letterpress endured for years as the dominant printing process, and it continued to be prized by purists for its clear printing of type. It also offered other advantages, such as the ability to change a line of type without having to create an entirely new plate. Letterpress was eventually displaced by offset lithography for short and medium runs and gravure printing for long runs.

Hand-engraved etchings of illustrations in copper plates, called intaglio, were used to illustrate books. Banknotes were printed using the same practice. Widespread forgery in Great Britain resulted, for in the early nineteenth century there existed thousands of engravers skilled enough to print credible forgeries. Nevertheless, intaglio remained unmatched for security printing due to several unique properties. Since the image areas were engraved into the surface of the plate, the resulting print, made under very high pressure, was three-dimensional. Tonal variation was also unique, created through variations in the width and length of lines. The gravure process that later developed was different, employing millions of minute cells filled to varying depths with ink. Besides hand-etched images, security engravings often included complex, machine-generated patterns whose precision could not be matched by any craftsman. Fluorescent fibers or inks were also used in the quest to make banknotes and stock certificates ever more difficult to duplicate.

With the development of lithography by Aloys Senefelder in 1797, images could be printed from a flat rather than engraved surface. Ira S. Rubel, a U.S. printer, discovered by accident in 1904 that the image from a lithographic plate would still print after being first transferred, or offset, to a rubber cylinder. Plates could last indefinitely in this process. This durability, coupled with the process's economy, print quality, and ability to print on many textures, made lithography tremendously popular.

Joseph Nicéphore Niepce, who four years earlier had made the first permanent photograph, produced the first photogravure plate in 1826. This process, in which an image is transferred onto a plate coated with a light-sensitive material and then etched into it with a solvent, was not practical for commercial printing until the end of the nineteenth century, when Czech artist Karl Klic developed the predecessor to modern rotogravure printing using light to etch an image onto a metal cylinder. In the 1990s, gravure accounted for one-fifth of the commercial printing market, as did flexography, a method of printing with flexible rubber or plastic plates.

Within printing and publishing, the US$20 billion per-year U.S. book segment experienced approximately 3 percent annual growth through the 1990s, although industry profits dropped sharply in 2001, particularly after the September 11, 2001, terrorist attacks. Leading companies continued to fall under the control of such giant conglomerates as Random House, Simon & Schuster, Bantam Doubleday Dell, HarperCollins, and Pearson. As with many other segments of the printing industry, increasing amounts of business was shipped to Asian manufacturers, which became more attractive as they improved quality in four-color printing for the children's book market. U.S. textbook printers, however, were optimistic that new adoptions in 2005 would boost demand. As a result of the No Child Left Behind legislation, state-specific versions of textbooks were needed across the country-creating high overall demand but smaller individual press runs. (For more information on book publishing trends, see also **Book Publishing.**)

In the newspaper segment, annual revenue growth of more than 5 percent seemed to signal an optimistic turnaround for newspapers in the late 1990s, bringing the industry to more than US$50 billion annually. Yet several factors, including loss of advertising revenues in the aftermath of the September 11, 2001, attacks, a decline in paid subscriptions, and increasing competition from television and internet news sources, led to uncertain conditions for the industry through the first decade of the 2000s. Due to the high costs of printing and specialized equipment, many newspapers and magazines "outsourced" the printing of publications to printing firms that served as outside contractors. (See also **Newspaper Publishing.**)

The emergence of newly independent nations of the former Soviet Union created a new market for currency, security printing, directory printing, and other types of commercial printing in the late 1990s and early 2000s. Though export figures to these developing markets had not increased substantially by 2000, analysts predicted a boom in export printing for the United States as these foreign markets stabilized.

One of the challenges shared by printers in the United States and abroad was a shortage of skilled labor. In a 1998 study by the PIA, half of the firms surveyed had a significant problem in finding qualified people to hire. A quarter of those surveyed even had trouble finding entry-level help—an effect of the United States' low 5 percent unemployment rate in the late 1990s as the economy added an average of 3 million new jobs a year. Because all prepress production of publication layout was computerized as the standard practice in North America, Europe, and other high-technology countries (and would be the standard everywhere by 2010), the U.S. Department of Labor reported that the industry expected to add people to the workforce with specialized training or knowledge in electronics, mathematics, and computers.

Graphic Arts Monthly, reported in 2006 that pay increases for workers in the printing industry are not as high as those of general business occupations. The average pay increase for printing industry employees was 2.9 percent in 2005, the same as it was in 2001-2004.

Digital equipment and other technological advances helped the printing industry increase its productivity in the 1990s. Digital image manipulation and graphic design tools were supplemented by color creation, film making, and typesetting programs that placed increased control of the printing process in the hands of clients, graphic designers, and printers.

Economic recession in the early 2000s hit the commercial printing industry hard. In the United States, a sharp drop in print advertising after the September 11, 2001 terrorist attacks contributed to declining revenues for commercial printers, and more than 2,000 printing shops closed between 2001 and 2002—substantially more than the yearly average of 700. Sales revenues for printing companies remained flat through 2002 and 2003 at about US$156.7 billion each year. By the end of 2004, though, analysts were predicting welcome growth of about 4 percent through mid-2006. For the first three quarters of 2004, total print shipments rose 4 percent. Ink on paper shipments grew by 3.5 percent, while digital printing increased by 5.9 percent and value-added products and services grew 4.9 percent. Further growth was projected for 2005, largely due to direct-mail advertising, which was expected to increase by up to 3.5 percent. The labels, wrappers, packaging and related printing segment was poised to grow by 2 percent. The segment likely to sustain slowest growth was periodicals and magazines, expected to increase by only 1 percent.

In the mid-2000s, the United States had between 37,000 and 44,000 commercial printing shops and was the world's largest printing consumer and exporter, with exports valued by the U.S. Department of Commerce at US$1.45 billion. Imports in 2004 reached US$1.43 billion. Canada remained the primary destination for U.S. commercial printing exports (US$430.8 million), followed by Mexico (US$248.7 million), the United Kingdom (US$148.9 million), Netherlands (US$76 million), and Japan (US$59 million). Canada was also the leading source of U.S. imports in 2004 (US$758.7 million), but Mexico slipped to third place behind China, which supplied commercial printing imports to the United States worth US$186.5 million.

Compliance with environmental regulations—which vary dramatically around the world—posed a significant challenge to the printing industry. In the early 2000s, nearly all major companies had one or more environmental experts on the payroll to use for consulting purposes and to field media questions. Due to the potentially hazardous chemicals used or created during the printing processes, the industry had come under scrutiny from environmental agencies and citizen groups. Wastewater discharges from printing establishments, for instance, had long come under sharp criticism. In addition, there were concerns regarding the industry's use of vast amounts of natural resources in the production of newspapers, catalogs, direct mail items, and countless other products. Industry participants hoped that increased use of recycled materials would blunt some of this criticism. Another trend in printing—using digital presses that entirely forego the need for film or plates—lessened the use of harsh chemicals in the industry as a whole as these cutting-edge presses were adopted. (The bulk of dangerous chemicals in the industry were used in the platemaking and film process.) During the early twenty-first century, digital press technology had grown from infancy to adolescence as the number of full color digital presses increased significantly worldwide.

CURRENT CONDITIONS

In the latter mid-2000s, the Internet continued to have a significant impact on the printing industry. According to *Graphic Arts Monthly,* "the Internet is rapidly and dramatically changing the print landscape. . . . New concepts such as Wikipedia, RSS feeds and Web communities (like MySpace and Facebook) are changing how people get information and how they relate to each other, giving consumers more control over when and where they view content—and make purchases." Regardless, the North American print industry showed sustained growth, driven by a healthy economy and expanding advertising and promotion spending. Total U.S. printing shipments in 2006 were US$170.3 billion, up about 3 percent from 2005. The strongest growth was in toner and digital printing, followed by printers' ancillary services.

Print Week agreed that digital printing would be the area of strongest growth in the future. Frank Romano of Rochester Institute of Technology told the journal, "The printing press of the future will be totally digital. Toner and ink-jet technologies are advancing rapidly, and will be poised to replace some gravure, flexo and litho presses by 2015." Another report by *Print Week* claimed that 13.5 percent of all print would be digital by 2008, and subsequent years would show meteoric growth. Demand for digital printing was also growing in Europe, though not as quickly as some expected. *Ink World* estimated Europe's growth rate in digital at 10 percent annually. Part of the reason for the slower than expected growth was printers' reluctance to invest in the equipment needed for full-scale digital operations.

Printing on demand was also a major trend in the latter mid-2000s. With printing on demand, printers can print from one to a few hundred books at time, based on demand, rather than running thousands of copies of a book, with the risk that not all the copies would sell. In 2006, U.S.-based On Demand Books revealed a printer that could produce an entire book in seven minutes; the same year, Hewlett-Packard announced an on-demand partnership with Amazon. Indeed, a report in *Print Week* predicted the on-demand market would quadruple by 2012, and printers were set to capitalize on this rapidly growing market.

Other challenges for the printing industry in the latter mid-2000s included rising costs of materials used in the printing process, such as petroleum, plastic substrates, and adhesive petroleum. As materials costs rose, printers were pressured to not only keep up but to cut production costs. According to a 2006 report published in *Printing World,* the market for printed magazines would shrink to 40 percent of current values by 2016. Thus "printers will have to slash production costs by 50 percent if they are to remain attractive to the publishing industry." This was a challenge for the printing industry, considering the rising costs of materials. Some solutions provided by the report included using recycled paper and becoming more "electronic." *Print Week* presented a similar picture, stating that printers in the United States and United Kingdom will have to reduce production costs by 30 percent by 2011 to remain competitive. Competition from the low-cost labor countries of Eastern Europe, Latin America, and, especially, China, posed a significant threat. China's print sector was expected to grow by 195 percent, from 11.1 billion pounds to almost pounds 33 billion pounds, by 2010.

RESEARCH AND TECHNOLOGY

Evolving technologies were pivotal in the development of the commercial printing industry. Industry observers estimated that printers in the United States alone invested more than US$2 billion in new technology annually to remain competitive. The development of high-quality copying machines spurred printers to adopt more sophisticated printing presses equipped with innovations in color capacity, automation, and press speeds.

Although digital technologies opened up tremendous possibilities for printers, incompatibility among various proprietary systems remained a problem, particularly in the area of data communications since digitized pictures occupied a great deal of computer memory. Realizing that a lack of standards was affecting their own sales, computer manufacturers promoted an international standard for page description, such as the one already in existence for textual data. The page description language PostScript, developed in the mid-1980s by former Xerox programmers, helped meet these needs to a degree. Another format from Adobe Systems Inc., portable document format (PDF), received much attention. Although it was popular on the Web, PDF's prospects looked less promising for the printing trade.

A 2004 GAMIS study revealed that the digital printing process will continue to attract the bulk of R&D. Another finding was that paper grades for conventional printing processes need to be more uniform and consistent.

The flat screen display industry represented a potentially promising new market for printing companies in the early 2000s. Dai Nippon was among major companies developing new organic light-emitting diode (OLED) printing processes.

INDUSTRY LEADERS

Dai Nippon Printing. The world's largest printer, Dai Nippon Printing Co. Ltd. (DNP), was founded in Tokyo in 1876. First known as Shueisha, the company took the name Dai Nippon in 1935. Dai Nippon was Japan's first modern printing company. The company diversified considerably from its original business of printing newspapers and invested heavily in developing new printing technologies. DNP became an innovator in printing such specialized applications as packaging and identification cards. DNP also produces direct mail pieces, books, magazines, business forms, and packaging for consumer products, as well as printing for electronics applications. In 2006 the company's revenues were US$10.9 billion and it had more than 35,000 employees.

In 2003 DNP entered into a partnership with Poet Software, forming a strategic alliance relationship to provide e-catalog content and outsourcing services in Japan. Around this time, DNP had thirty-three Japanese and eight overseas plants. In June 2004 DNP announced that it would implement new technology to create holograms, which will allow viewers to see images from different perspectives by moving the hologram around. Research papers providing such images would be able to clearly share results with readers. In July 2004 DNP announced the transfer of technologies to Taiwan's Sintek and Quanta Display Corp. *Asia Intelligence Wire* also claimed DNP was the world's second largest manufacturer of color filters, and that it was attempting to focus on boosting its presence in Taiwan through cooperative efforts.

Toppan Printing. Ever-expanding Toppan Printing Co. Ltd. was DNP's chief rival since it was formed in 1900 to meet Japan's increased demand for printing. Securities, books, and business forms were originally the core of the company's business, although it was successful in diversifying into electronic circuits, business forms, packaging, and information and marketing services, among other areas. It became the first Japanese printer to establish production facilities in Hong Kong (1962) and the United States (1979). In 2006 Toppan had year-end sales of US$13.1 billion and 35,954 employees. *Asia Intelligence Wire* reported that Toppan saw a smooth run in its fifth-generation color-filter plant in Taiwan and was stepping up construction of its sixth-generation plant. The source also said Sony and Toppan had created a CD-like disk with a 25 GB capacity, consisting mainly of paper. Toppan has operations throughout Asia, Australia, Europe, and North America. In 2005 the company acquired DuPont Photomasks, which manufactures materials used in a variety of electronics applications. Toppan's new hologram printing was introduced in 2005 and targeted at credit card companies and manufacturers of gift cards.

R.R. Donnelley & Sons. Chicago-based R.R. Donnelley & was the leading printer in the United States and the second largest in the world, putting out well-known newspapers and magazines, books, catalogs, and advertising materials. The company traced its origins to the educational, religious, and historical publishing and printing firm of Church, Goodman, and Donnelley, which Richard Robert Donnelley joined in 1864. It was incorporated as the Lakeside Publishing and Printing Company in 1870; after several name changes it became known as R.R. Donnelley & Sons Company in 1882. The company was first publicly traded in 1956. Catalogs (such as the Sears catalog) historically accounted for most of the company's business, though it also was known for printing mass-market books, magazines, telephone directories, computer software documentation, and religious books.

R.R. Donnelley aggressively expanded into digital media and database marketing services in the 1990s. The company had operations in Asia, South America, and Europe and 50,000 employees. In 2004, the company bought printer Moore Wallace, a leader in forms and labels, making it the largest commercial printer in the United States.

The company announced several major initiatives in 2005, including the acquisition of the Astron Group, a provider of document business process outsourcing. In addition, Donnelley entered an agreement with Creative Printing Services, Inc. to create what a Donnelley statement described as a "joint strategy to provide diversity sourcing options to customers in the print industry." Also in 2005, Donnelley's Primedia Technologies division launched Pipeline, an online project-tracking system. The company posted 2006 sales of $9.3 billion.

Quebecor World Inc. Through its subsidiary Quebecor World Inc., Quebecor Inc. of Montreal, Canada, established itself as the fourth largest commercial printer in the world and the second largest in North America in the early 1990s. Pierre Péladeau founded the company in 1965. It was the leading North American producer of retail inserts and circulars in the early 1990s and featured a nationwide network of gravure presses in the United States. Magazine and catalog printing were Quebecor's next largest sources of income. In 2002 the company positioned itself as a leader in the services field for media convergence in addition to printing services, as it offered its *Fortune* 500 clients expertise in additional areas such as Internet services, broadcast media expertise, and print competency from prepress through post press production. The company claimed sales of US$5 million in 2002 from projects related to media convergence and integrated media.

In 2004 Quebecor World Inc. had approximately 37,000 employees working in more than 160 printing and related facilities in the United States, Canada, Brazil, France, the United Kingdom, Belgium, Spain, Austria, Sweden, Switzerland, Finland, Chile, Argentina, Peru, Colombia, Mexico and India. Its printing capabilities include web offset, rotogravure, and sheet fed processes. Finishing and distribution services also are available. The Quebecor Inc. Vidotron ltee subsidiary is one of Canada's largest cable companies. The TVA Group subsidiary owns the dominant TV network in Quebec. In 2006 Quebecor World Inc. posted total sales of US$6.0 billion.

MAJOR COUNTRIES IN THE INDUSTRY

In the 2000s the United States, Japan, and Canada led the world's commercial printing industry, which by sales volume is concentrated in leading industrial countries and in high-population metropolitan areas such as New York, Tokyo, and Montreal. Thus, while a minority of countries account for the lion's share of the printing market, nearly every region of the globe is involved in the industry to some degree. GAIN claimed that printing was America's largest manufacturing industry in terms of establishments. In 2003 there were more than 44,000 printing plants providing 1.1 million jobs and producing approximately US$157 billion in printed products and services. *Strategis* ranked Canada's commercial printing industry as the fourth largest manufacturing employer, with more than 84,000 employees working in 5,834 establishments.

A profile of Hong Kong's printing industry, issued by the Hong Kong Trade Development Council (TDC), characterized it as "famous for quality, quick delivery, competitive pricing, and ability to cope with short-notice printing jobs." The report also noted Hong Kong's industry made substantial advanced machinery investments resulting in production capacity expansion and improved quality standards. In 2002 the United States was Hong Kong's largest market for printed matter, adding up to 39 percent of the total. Filmless printing was considered to be the industry's development trend.

In Mexico, commercial printing grew significantly through the 1990s and early 2000s as manufacturing activities increased, especially among "maquiladoras," shops near the U.S. border where finished goods are assembled for export to the United States. This manufacturing creates demand for printed matter, such as instruction manuals for the products being assembled. In 2000, about 45 percent of Mexico's 11,383 printing shops were formally associated with maquiladoras. This segment exported US$423 million worth of products in 2000, but this figure does not represent the entire value of production, since many items—including price tags and retail inserts for products—do not have a stated export value. In addition, maquiladora plants also print a wide range of books and magazines for U.S. consumption, including *Newsweek, Reader's Digest,* and Scholastic children's books. In the mid-2000s, Mexico was one of the principal trading partners with the United States in commercial printing. It was the second-largest destination for U.S. printed goods, and the third-largest source of U.S. print imports, in 2004.

Brazil, the largest economy in South America, led the way in commercial printing in the early 2000s, with Argentina, Venezuela, and Chile also boasting competitive industries. Printing companies in these countries have benefited from reduced import duties and the machinery leasing policies of U.S. suppliers, for whom the Latin American market is increasingly important. According to *PrintCom Brasil* Publisher Kai Hagenbush, the Brazilian Association of the Printing Industry estimated that the sector invested US $63 billion in modernizing machinery during the past decade. It accounted for 3.3 percent of the country's GNP in 2000. Commercial printing was believed to have accounted for approximately 13 percent of the Brazilian print and media sector's sales. *Ink World* magazine indicated that there is a tremendous move toward globalization due to printers expanding their operations into Mexico through NAFTA. Industry insiders evaluated the market as being one where big companies were swallowing up smaller ones. Overall, Latin America was viewed as being in a "slowdown mode" impacted by the United States' economic status.

Among the Pacific Rim countries, Japan has felt increased pressure from the printing industries of Hong Kong, Singapore, Brunei, Taiwan, and South Korea. Australia and New Zealand also had healthy printing industries. According to the April 2004 issue of *IBISWorld*, from 2002 to 2003 the Australian printing industry had turnover of $5.5 billion, employing 32,926 workers in 2,500 enterprises.

Commercial printing in the United Kingdom was felt to mirror U.S. developments, with a similar level of technological advancement. WGA estimated that that the U.K. sector consisted of approximately 7,870 commercial printers, trade shops, implants, and newspapers. In the early 2000s, about 2,000 jobs were created in the printing industry via major new facilities in northern England. Polestar, Europe's largest independent printing company, opened a 110 million pound (US$193.2 million) gravure plant in Sheffield that started production in March 2005. Prinovis, a joint venture among Bertelsmann-owned Arvato Print, Gruner + Jahr, and Axel Springer, was scheduled to open with 400 employees in Liverpool in mid-2006. In 2005, U.K. newspaper company Associated Newspapers, which had built up one of the largest newspaper printing facilities in the world with KBA, announced a 80 million pound (US$140.4 million) deal with Italian printing company Cerutti to develop a printing plant in Didcot, Oxfordshire, which would begin production in 2008. The company cited Cerutti's new satellite cylinder technology as the primary reason for the deal.

FURTHER READING

"Adding to the Talent Pool." *Dotprint,* 29 June 2005. Available from http://www.dotprint.com.

"A Decade in Print: How Data and Digital Have Changed our Industry Since 1997." *Print Week,* 1 February 2007.

"AnnualReport 2006." Quebec World, 15 April 2007. Available from www.quebecworld.com.

Brown, Andrew. "Internatioal Printing: Going Global." *Print Solutions,* May 2005. Available from http://www.printsolutionsmag.com.

"Digital Printing Technology Report: Digital's Future." *Print Week,* 13 July 2006.

Curwen, Ginger. "Wait Till Next Year: A Lackluster Market in 2004 Has Manufacturers Looking Ahead to the Promise of Better Times in 2005." *Publishers Weekly,* 11 October 2004.

Esler, Bill. "Technology Tremors." *Graphic Arts Monthly,* 1 October 2006.

"Green Scene." *American Printer,* 1 April 2007.

Haughey, James. "Print Prospects Brighten for 2004." *Graphic Marts Monthly,* December 2003.

"Mail Group Stuns Industry to Abandoning KBA for Cerutti." *Dotprint,* 29 June 2005. Available from http://www.dotprint.com.

Makin, Michael, Chuck Miotke, Peter Tobin, and Steve Johnson. "Outlook 07: Ok to Run." *Graphic Arts Monthly,* 1 January 2007.

Mason, Dennis E. "Global Report: Asia: China and Printing." *Printing News,* 25 September 2006.

Milmo, Sean. "Ink and Equipment Manufacturers See Good Opportunities in Digital Market." *Ink World,* July 2006.

James, Bruce. "This Is Truly Print's Future." *Graphic Arts Monthly,* 1 January 2007.

"Technically Speaking: Comment—Competing Globally Takes Productive Technology and a Range of Services." *Print Week,* 31 August 2006.

"Technology Report: Digital Books to your Door." *Print Week,* 18 January 2007.

"Toppan Printing, Tokyo, Expects to Generate First-Year Sales of US$9.2 Million for Its Newly Developed Holograms." *Graphic Arts Monthly,* May 2005.

TrendWatch Graphic Arts Reports. "U.K. Summary," 2004. Available from http://www.trendwatchgraphiccarts.com.

U.S. Commercial Printing Export and Import Statistics, U.S. Department of Commerce, May 2005. Available from http://http://www.ita.doc.gov.

Whitcher, Joann. "Market Outlook: Not Picture Perfect: Key Numbers Are Up, but Print's Performance Is Still a Far Cry from the Pre-2001 Levels." *Graphic Arts Monthly,* December 2004.

SIC 4832

NAICS 515112

RADIO BROADCASTING STATIONS

Radio broadcasters transmit radio programs to the public. Included in the discussion are radio networks and companies that provide pay-radio services.

INDUSTRY SNAPSHOT

Radio broadcasting began as a stable industry controlled in most parts of the world by national and regional governments. Before the collapse of the Soviet Union and other communist nations, those governments exercised complete state control over the airwaves. In Western Europe, state-owned or state-chartered corporations broadcast a limited amount of programming—much of it educational in nature—and commercial channels were almost nonexistent. Japan had a strong radio market, but the rest of Asia remained relatively undeveloped. In the United States, commercial stations dominated the market, but the industry was fragmented due to complex government regulations limiting the number of radio stations that could be owned by one company.

By the mid-1990s, however, rapid technological and political change had completely altered the rules of the global broadcasting industry. In former communist nations, fledgling commercial radio stations challenged state-run corporations, which struggled to change with the times. In Europe, commercial radio stations competed with state-sponsored broadcasters such as the British Broadcasting Corporation (BBC). In the United States, new ownership rules led to a major structural change in the radio industry, and options for mass communications and information technology continued to grow.

By the twenty-first century, technological advances made it possible for music lovers to get commercial-free music anywhere in the world. Online radio programming via the Internet, subscription-based satellite radio, and radio-on-demand services were just a few of the innovations coming to prominence, as traditional radio was seeing an increased slump in listeners. However, radio broadcasting was still strong. According to a study from Arbitron, about 228 million listeners over the age of 11 listened to traditional radio once a week or more.

ORGANIZATION AND STRUCTURE

One of the unifying features of broadcasting around the world is government regulation. Radio broadcasting is less than 100 years old and developed during a century of growing government control over industry. Airwaves are viewed in most countries as a scarce public resource. As such, nearly every radio market in the world has been tightly regulated or directly controlled from its inception by the government.

In Europe, public service broadcasting was the only game in town for many decades, as monolithic state-run institutions provided the programs they thought would educate and entertain. In communist countries, the state was the network, and radio existed to legitimize the government and inform people of its activities.

In the United States, commercial radio had dominated the airwaves for many years, although National Public Radio—a non-profit organization partly funded by the government—provided an alternative in many markets. However, the FCC tightly controlled many aspects of the radio business and was responsible for licensing radio stations and approving their ownership.

Some of those structures crumbled and others changed dramatically in the 1980s and 1990s. As communist governments collapsed in the USSR and Eastern Europe, private ownership of radio stations began to take hold. In Western Europe, more licenses for commercial radio stations were granted, providing competition for traditional state-owned radio stations. In Asia, new stations sprang up, and satellite broadcasts of radio signals became a reality. In the United States, new ownership structures substantially changed the business, as media conglomerates looked for ways to expand the advertising potential of their new holdings.

Large radio networks supplied the content for many radio stations, whether they were government-operated or privately owned. In this arrangement, a network produces programming such as news, music, or commentary, which is then broadcast by a large number of individual stations. The British Broadcasting Corporation is an example of a government-run network, and ABC Radio in the United States is an example of a private network.

Except for certain high-power operations, most AM radio stations regularly reach only a limited geographical area. As a result, there are literally thousands of individual stations in large countries such as the United States. Those AM stations that could reach distant households gave certain "jocks" (such as Tom Shannon of Buffalo, New York; Walter (Salty) Brine of Providence, Rhode Island; and Ed Dickinson of northern California) a semi-celebrity status.

BACKGROUND AND DEVELOPMENT

Before World War I, inventors Guglielmo Marconi, Lee DeForest, Reginald Aubrey Fessenden, and Edwin Armstrong devised the technology needed to broadcast radio signals, but a wartime ban on nonmilitary broadcasting delayed the advent of radio broadcasts until the ban was lifted after the war ended in 1919.

The first AM radio station in the United States, KDKA in Pittsburgh, began operating in 1919. By 1922, there were 570 licensed AM stations in the United States. Commercial networks soon emerged to broadcast programs and advertising on different stations simultaneously. National Broadcasting Company (NBC) was founded in 1926 to operate two networks for its parent company, the Radio Corporation of America (RCA). Columbia Broadcasting Systems (CBS), a major competitor, established a network of 16 stations by 1928.

Radio broadcasting soon caught on in Europe and other regions with the capacity to support commercial or state-sponsored broadcasting. The British Broadcasting Corporation (BBC) was formed in 1922 as a private company and in 1927 was chartered by Parliament as the sole provider of British radio broadcasting. Though it operated under charter from the Crown, it was free of government oversight and functioned as an independent entity. Other European governments set up similar monopolies, though some were subject to more government control.

Frequency modulation (FM) radio, invented by Edwin Howard Armstrong in 1933, developed commercially in the 1940s. In the United States, FM was used as an alternative to AM and featured "highbrow" programs such as in-depth news analysis and classical music. FM receivers were more expensive than AM radios, and because of the higher radio frequencies that FM utilizes, coverage areas were severely limited. As a result, FM was slow to catch on in the 1960s and early 1970s despite its static-free sound quality. Then the cost of FM receivers dropped, and in the mid to late 1970s and 1980s, FM flourished as rock-and-roll stations proliferated in the United States.

In the Soviet Union, radio and television broadcasting was exclusively a propaganda arm of the government until the late 1980s when Communist party and state control over the media eased. In July 1990, Chairman Mikhail Gorbachev ordered major changes in the state-run broadcasting monopoly, allowing radio outlets to operate independently of political organizations and provide objective coverage of news events. The complete collapse of the communist government continued this trend, although restrictions on radio broadcasting remain.

In the 1980s and 1990s many Eastern European radio stations bloomed as governments eased their heavy grip on the airwaves. Major companies such as France's Europe Developpement and CLT Multi-Media of Luxembourg, along with many local firms, invested in commercial radio properties in Eastern Europe. In the 1990s, the Czech Republic, Slovakia, and Poland led the move to open radio licensing for foreign and domestic firms.

At the same time, there was some globalization of the radio industry, as countries loosened ownership rules for broadcast mediums. For example, in 1995 the U.S. Federal Communications Commission (FCC) relaxed its rules on foreign ownership of radio stations, which was expected to bring a number of well-heeled international investors into the U.S. market. Growing satellite transmission of radio programs has made it much easier to distribute programming across national borders.

In 1996, the FCC also eased its restrictions on the number of radio stations one company could own. That led to a frenzied market for radio stations, as major media conglomerates rushed to buy large numbers of stations with the idea of creating vast networks across the country. Radio emerged as perhaps the hottest media market in the United States, and prices paid for stations shot up dramatically. From the beginning of 1996 to early 1998, more than 25 percent of the nation's 10,000 stations changed hands.

Digital production and transmission of radio gained a foothold in the mid-1980s, with some ventures, such as Star Radio in Asia, taking advantage of the new technology by distributing radio via satellite. In the United States, talk radio gained in popularity as personalities like Rush Limbaugh used the medium to rally supporters of a particular political viewpoint, and "shock radio" hosts such as Howard Stern became popular using a format pioneered by still-active and intentionally obnoxious Joey Reynolds, later on the WOR Radio Network. Other formats, such as all-sports, took off as well, and a very few local sports broadcast stars (such as Jack Brickhouse of Chicago, Bob Uecker of Milwaukee, and Phil Rizzuto in New York) garnered a national following for their excellence and/or humor. Listeners with a strong bent for public affairs programming opted for National Public Radio (NPR), becoming fans of morning host Bob Edwards and shows for smart listeners such as *All Things Considered* . However, by 2002, some NPR listeners had begun expressing concern as their beloved "public" radio began welcoming corporate sponsors with increasingly wider arms.

In the 1990s, radio broadcasting stations faced more challenges than ever before, as the options for mass communications and information technology continued to grow. Traditional music and news formats were still popular, but there was also strong growth in "talk radio," which features hosts commenting on issues and taking calls from listeners. This format is particularly popular in the United States. The number of wild and crazy morning duos such as Bob and Tom, stars of an Indianapolis-based syndicated show, seems to ever expand, as stuck-in-traffic commuters look for chuckles with their weather, news, and road reports. In the 2000s, as radio stations in local markets compete for ad dollars and listeners, it is not unusual for a station to alter its format radically, abandoning one audience for another. In 2002 the undisputed ruler of the radio waves, in terms of station ownership, was Clear Channel Communications Inc., of San Antonio, Texas. Nevertheless, even this operation could not turn a profit in 2001 as ad sales slumped. That year, Clear Channel self-reported a net loss of US$1.14 billion on revenue of US$7.97 billion. By comparison, in 2000 Clear Channel recorded a profit of US$248.8 million on US$5.35 billion in revenue, according to the *San Antonio Express-News*.

RADIO EUROPE

In the 1980s and 1990s, mainstream "Top 40" radio stations in the United States fragmented into niche formats that reached more segmented parts of the population. The same process was taking place in Europe early in the twenty-first century as radio stations proliferated in markets that were once tightly regulated. As of 2005, however, European radio was still dominated by either state-run mainstream stations, such as BBC Radio One FM, or Top 40 commercial stations.

CONSOLIDATION

Massive changes in the U.S. radio market were under way in the mid to late 1990s. The most significant change was that the FCC loosened its radio ownership regulations governing duopoly arrangements. Under the revised rules, a single party could own or control both an AM and an FM duopoly in individual markets. A duopoly is defined as two AM and/or two FM radio stations, up to four in total, in the same market. That change led to the consolidation of U.S. radio station ownership by large media groups, which were trying to benefit by reducing promotional costs and boosting the number of total listeners to attract advertisers. As a result, the fragmented U.S. radio industry became highly consolidated over a very short period.

For example, CBS Radio quickly became the nation's largest radio station group with a series of major acquisitions. In April 1997, Chancellor Broadcasting Co., which operated one of the nation's largest radio station groups, merged with Evergreen Media Corp., also a leading station owner. The merger included Evergreen's purchase of 10 Viacom radio stations and the sale of two stations to ABC Radio in order to meet FCC regulations. In March 1998, Jacor Communications Inc., another large radio station group, closed plans to acquire Chancellor Broadcasting and Talk Radio Network Inc.

The hot market for U.S. radio stations continued. In early 1998, the U.S. Justice Department approved two big radio mergers. CBS Corp.'s US$1.6 billion acquisition of American Radio Systems Corp. was okayed on the condition that the companies sell seven radio stations. Capstar Broadcasting Partners, based in Austin, Texas, saw its US$2.1 billion buyout of SFX Broadcasting Inc., based in New York, cleared as well, on condition that the combined companies sell eleven stations.

In March 1998, according to the *Wall Street Journal,* the run-up in radio station prices weeded out all but the biggest and most determined buyers. It also provided "hybrid media companies," publishing businesses with broadcast holdings, the opportunity to cash out their radio side at a substantial profit.

FORMAT CHANGES

As station ownership structures changed, so did program formats. For example, talk radio was fast becoming the dominant format in the United States' AM radio market in the late 1990s. Using this format, large stations reportedly generated profits of 25 to 35 percent. For example, WLS-AM, based in Chicago, was broadcasting Rush Limbaugh and Dr. Laura Schlessinger, the nation's two most popular syndicated talk show hosts, as of early 2002. The lure of radio was great even for established television celebrities. In May 2002, author and political commentator Bill O'Reilly, host of the Fox cable television show *The O'Reilly Factor,*, began taking his views to the radio waves on his show *The Radio Factor With Bill O'Reilly*.

One problem with talk radio, however, was demographics. In 1998, the biggest audience for talk radio—fifty to 60 percent of the estimated 100 million weekly listeners—included people 55 years old and older. However, 99 percent of the audience for U.S. FM album-oriented rock stations was younger than 55, and one-third were between the ages of 12 and 24.

Advertisers, looking for free-spending younger listeners, noted this trend. In 1993, five of the top ten U.S. radio stations based on advertising revenue were AM stations. The top FM station was in fifth place. By 1997, however, only three of the top ten stations were on AM, while FM stations held the number two and three spots.

In 2002, the job market for disc jockeys (DJs) worsened because of station preference for voicetracking, requiring DJs to tape their shows in advance for multiple markets. Corporations that owned a string of radio stations could thus have a single DJ on multiple stations—a half dozen or more at a time. Even the most popular DJs who do voicetracking make a fraction at each station of what the going rate would be for one DJ at one station.

PAY-FOR-PLAY

In 1998, some U.S. radio stations began considering a controversial policy of trading air time for cash payments from record companies, similar to the infomercials shown on some television stations or the advertising inserts in magazines. Under the "pay-for-play" concept, record companies would promote their artists by paying radio stations to broadcast programs such as one-hour country music showcases or even individual songs. The record label would disclose its sponsorship on the air.

In 1997 the CBS Radio network began promoting this idea to country music producers. EMI Group's Capitol Nashville record label, which records Garth Brooks among others, was said to be backing the idea of paying radio station groups as much as US$1 million an hour for prime time programming featuring its artists. Jacor Communications, which had 192 radio outlets including 19 country stations in 1997, reportedly was working on market partnerships and distribution plans with record labels.

However, some critics charged that such commercial arrangements were inherently unethical and might alienate listeners. They also argued that taking programming decisions out of the hands of radio stations would prompt stations to play less popular music just for commercial reasons, leading to drops in their ratings.

The 2000s saw a return of dozens of allegations that some station employees accepted under-the-table money in exchange for preferential playing of newly recorded songs. In 2002 Mary Catherine Sneed, an executive with Radio One Inc., the best known African American music station, alleged that "payola"—the word comes from combining pay and Victrola—practices and kickbacks were about to destroy listener confidence in the industry. Radio rules require stations to disclose if payments were received in exchange for playing an artist's music.

CURRENT CONDITIONS

By the mid-2000s, as traditional radio was seeing an increased and lengthy slump in listeners—14 percent from 1994 to 2004—radio-on-demand, subscription-based satellite radio, and Internet radio programming were just a few of the innovations coming to prominence. Critics of traditional radio complained about incessant advertising and repetitive playlists, among other factors, and this discontent turned their ears, and money, to the newer offerings.

Similar to video-on-demand (VOD) technology for television programming, radio-on-demand was taking off by 2003. Unlike VOD, however, the listener could pick programs on the spur of the moment, rather than being forced to choose programs in advance. The technology allowed the listener to hear programs of his or her choice at any time via the Internet. The BBC Radio Player radio-on-demand service in the United Kingdom logged 1.5 million requests each week.

For listeners who just wanted an alternative to traditional radio, several other new technologies were rising to prominence. For instance, satellite radio, operated on a subscription basis, offered radio channels of digital compact-disc quality music across the United States, primarily to car and truck radios. In addition, the channels were commercial-free. Leaders in this segment were seeing annual valuation ballooning more than 300 percent. There were a reported 2 million subscribers to satellite radio in 2004.

There were approximately 7 million people who tuned in to online radio at the beginning of the century, but by 2004 that number had climbed to 19 million and was continuing to grow by about 43 percent each year.

RESEARCH AND TECHNOLOGY

One technology affecting radio was the World Wide Web, which gave radio stations the opportunity to broadcast on the Internet. U.S. radio companies were taking different approaches to Internet technology in the late 1990s and early 2000s. In November 1997, the CBS Radio network forbade its company-owned radio stations from simultaneously broadcasting on the Internet. CBS Radio wanted to prevent World Wide Web "netcasts" from cannibalizing its broadcast network audience. Non-company-owned radio stations that were part of the CBS Radio network were allowed to continue offering netcasts via the Web.

However, in April of 1998, ABC Radio selected the Real Broadcast Network to broadcast its ABC-owned radio stations and ABC Radio Networks programming in "RealAudio," a hosting and promotional agreement that gave Internet users access to ABC Radio programming. ABC and RealNetworks planned to extend the reach of RealAudio programming to ABC affiliate stations nationwide. RealNetworks Inc., based in Seattle, is a specialist in the "streaming media" market. In the early 2000s, Internet sites were useful for listeners of National Public Radio and nearly all commercial stations as a place where interviews could be accessed easily for downloading and later listening. According to BRS Media, the number of radio webcasters in 2001 was 4,600, about 25 percent of which were webcasting live online.

One of the most important technological changes in broadcasting is digital transmission of radio signals, which has enhanced quality and led to changes in the way programs are produced and distributed. Broadcasters use computers for scheduling radio time via the "radio-in-a-box" method. A Digital Audio System allows radio stations to select programming through use of satellite dishes. Music libraries can be formatted on a computer to play without the presence of a DJ during programming hours.

Satellite radio is yet another new radio concept. The idea is to develop a subscription-based satellite radio system to deliver commercial-absent channels of digital compact-disc quality music across the United States, primarily to car and truck radios. Pay radio programming is designed for broadcast on satellites over a proposed new radio band, the "S-band," with a range of up to 35,000 km.

In 2007, it was estimated that fewer than half a million Americans used HD radio. The technology had earned praises for its digital format resulting in better sound quality on both AM and FM bands. HD radio also lets AM stations offer two audio signals instead of one. FM stations deliver three or four sound streams. Expensive radio sets, however, had impacted extent of usage. Wal-Mart Stores's launch for a 2007 promotion to sell HD-compatible car radios for about US$190 in nearly 2,000 of its stores was expected to dramatically impact HD radio sales and usage.

INDUSTRY LEADERS

XM SATELLITE RADIO HOLDINGS INC.

Of the companies included in *Fortune* magazine's 2005 list of the 2000 largest global companies, only two from the radio industry made the ranking—and both provided satellite radio services in the United Stated. XM Satellite Radio was founded in 1992 and was granted a satellite radio license in the U.S. in 1997. By 2004, it had more than 150 channels serving 3.77 million subscribers. In April 2005, the company announced plans to work with America Online (AOL) to create a new online radio service. The combination was expected to produce the world' largest digital radio network. XM's 2004 revenues of US$244.4 million were a 166 percent increase over 2003 figures; however, the firm continued to show increasing net loss figures year over year.

SIRIUS SATELLITE RADIO INC.

The second radio industry company on *Fortune*'s list was Sirius Satellite Radio. By 2006, Sirius had 135 channels: 70 channels offering commercial-free music and more than 65 channels of sports, talk, news, weather, traffic, and entertainment. It also offered sports content from the National Football League and NASCAR. In 2006, Sirius had more than 6 million subscribers, with an increasing number of subscribers coming from auto dealers offering the radio systems as options in their cars. Subscriptions could also be purchased for Internet-based radio. With an employee base of only 614 people for 2006, the company reported revenue of US$637.2 billion in 2006, an increase of more than 163 percent over the previous year. Sirus established alliances with several carmakers including AUDI, BMW and Ford. Alliances were also established with Best Buy and Sears. The company had entered into a joint venture agreement with the Canadian Broadcasting Corporation to offer satellite radio service in Canada, and was in discussions to offer similar services in Mexico and the Caribbean.

In 2007 Sirus agreed to acquire its rival XM Satellite Radio. That US$13 billion merger would create a satellite radio monopoly. While critics opposed the merger and urged antitrust regulators to reject it, officials of the two companies claimed they would still face tough competition. Sources for that competition were viewed by some as being many different types of rivals including HD-radio stations. Not everyone shared this point of view. Analyst Jimmy Schaeffer of the Carmel Group research firm surmised that HD radio was not major competition for XM and Sirius. HD radio had a half-million listeners while XM and Sirius had about 15 million subscribers.

CLEAR CHANNEL COMMUNICATIONS INC.

Clear Channel was the largest radio company in the United States. In 2006 it owned, operated, programmed or sold airtime for nearly 1,200 radio stations. It also had equity interests in about 240 international radio stations. Countries tuned into its frequencies included Australia, New Zealand and Mexico. With other interests in outdoor advertising and live entertainment, Clear Channel's 2006 sales was US$7.1 billion. Clear Channel owns a 90 percent stake in one of the world's largest outdoor advertising companies, Clear Channel Outdoor Holdings. Clear Channel also owns or manages about 50 TV stations and sell spot advertising for more than 3,300 radio and TV stations through Katz Media. In 2005, the company employed 31,800 people. Clear Channel has agreed to be taken private by an investment group led by Thomas H. Lee Partners and Bain Capital.

Clear Channel was perhaps the biggest winner after the 1996 industry deregulation, having begun with a mere 42 stations. Even though its numbers indicated control of only about 10 percent of the U.S. market, Clear Channel was seen by many as the big, bad corporate behemoth come to run radio into the ground with homogenization of content and incessant advertising. Others hailed the company as a hero, rescuing doomed stations from bankruptcy. After paying a US$1.75 million fine for airing a particularly obscene show of controversial shock-jock Howard Stern, Clear Channel dropped his show completely, citing a lack of desire to promote indecent programming.

In 2006 Clear Channel's Format Lab was unveiled for creative applications. It united a virtual community of more than 200 programmers and production professionals developing fresh and unconventional radio and online content.

In March 2007 Clear Channel announced activation of its plans to add channels music programming from 10 stations to mSpot's radio services. Furthermore, mSpot planned to start distribution in April 2007 of live broadcasts from about 100 Clear Channel stations. Clear Channel agreed to provide Contemporary Hits Radio (CHR) and urban programming from five of its most popular terrestrial stations. Those stations were cited as leaders in these formats for the New York, Los Angeles, Chicago and Miami markets. Innovative programming availability also included Spanish-language content from four Latin channels and a high-energy playlist of Hip-Hop hits that were all created by Clear Channel Radio's Format Lab available commercial-free.

Another March 2007 Clear Channel announcement revealed that *Institutional Investor* had been ranked it the most shareholder-friendly company in the radio and TV broadcasting sector for the second consecutive year. In addition, Clear Channel CFO Randall Mays was included in *Institutional Investor*'s top CFO's list. The surveys appeared in the magazine's February and March 2007 issues.

ABC RADIO NETWORKS INC.

ABC Radio Networks is owned by Walt Disney Corp.'s television and radio broadcasting division. ABC, however, announced plans to sell ABC Radio Network to Citadel Broadcasting. The network distributes programming to approximately 4,600 affiliate radio stations throughout the U.S. ABC Radio Networks' diverse offerings included five full-service line networks, Paul Harvey News & Comment, ESPN Radio Network, long-form programming, ABC News, sports, and daily and weekly features. It also distributed music and entertainment shows including family-friendly pop music from Radio Disney. The company provided sound effects and other production materials used by radio stations to create promotional spots and lead-ins.

CAPITAL RADIO PLC

Capital Radio was the dominant U.K. commercial radio broadcaster in 2005. It held 21 analog and 58 digital licenses.

Its main operations were the two London ILR stations, Capital FM, which was number one in London, and Capital Gold. The FM service was pop and dance music-based; the AM Gold service broadcasts hits from the '50s, '60s, and '70s. Total revenues for 2003 were US$192.2 million.

In 1996, Capital Radio bid for an FM band license in Yorkshire, England as part of its national expansion plans. That initiative continued in 1997 when Capital Radio purchased competitor Virgin Radio for US$106 million. The deal, which was expected to further Capital's digital audio broadcasting plans, also included the transfer of Virgin's US$35.7 million debt to Capital.

In 2001 and 2002, Capital Radio encountered the same setbacks in ad sales that faced other media due to the tepid post-September 11, 2001 business climate. In March of 2002, Capital Radio posted a 7 percent decline in revenue for the six months prior to March 31, 2002. By 2004, sales had increased 12.2 percent over the previous year, reaching more than US$215 million, with net income of US$10.6 million. In September 2004, the company announced its plans to merge with GWR Group, which owned 30 stations and generated US$235 million in revenues in 2004.

CBS Radio Inc.

CBS Radio, formerly known as Infinity Broadcasting, is counted among the U.S.'s leading radio broadcasters. It owned and operated 170 radio stations in the about 40 major markets in the U.S. CBS Radio stations offer a variety of programming from talk and sports to diverse music styles. Its operating strategy called for regional clusters sharing back office functions such as ad sales and marketing. The company also manages radio syndicator Westwood One and produces news, sports, and entertainment shows for more than 5,000 affiliate stations. CBS Radio is a subsidiary of broadcasting giant CBS Corporation.

In 2007, veteran radio host and TV personality Don Ismus was dropped initially by MSNBC and then by CBS. Ismus called the Rutgers University women's basketball team "nappy-headed hos." The National Association of Black Journalists, followed soon by the National Association of Hispanic Journalists, expressed their disgust with Ismus. Civil fights activist Al Sharpton called for Ismus to be taken off the air. Those protests led to a two-week suspension of Ismus' show. Major advertisers started pulling their ads. The companies doing so included industry leaders such as GlaxoSmithKline, General Motors, Proctor & Gamble, Staples and American Express. After that, MSNBC pulled Ismus permanently. Bruce Gordon, a CBS board member and former NAACP president, subsequently publicly called for the dismissal of Ismus. In response, CBS finally let him go. The decisions related to Ismus's actions were considered to be related to economics more than ethics in a time when more minorities and women had taken seats at board room tables. Barron H. Harvey, Howard University School of Business dean summed up the views of many when by saying, "You cannot disrespect the diverse consumer dollar."

Cox Radio Inc.

Cox Radio is one of the U.S.'s largest radio broadcasters with 80 stations in 18 markets. Those markets include Atlanta, San Antonio and Tampa. Through Cox Radio Syndication the company produces programs and distributes them to more than 200 affiliate stations through a partnership with Jones Radio Network. Cox Radio Interactive creates Web sites for its stations and sells advertising on those sites. Cox Enterprises controls 95 percent of the company through its 65 percent equity holding.

Rogers Media

Rogers Media is a division of Rogers Communications, a Toronto, Ontario-based telecommunications conglomerate. Rogers has major interests in cable TV, cellular phones, radio and TV broadcasting, telecommunications, publishing and video stores. In 2005, Rogers Broadcasting held 43 AM and FM radio licenses across Canada, several of which are clustered in major Canadian cities such as Toronto. Rogers reported 2004 revenues of US$4.7 billion.

Major Countries in the Industry

Canada

Coming out of a downturn in the 1980s and early 1990s, the Canadian radio industry entered 2000 on an upswing. By 2003, air time sales by private broadcasters had increased by 8.4 percent to a value of almost US$1 billion and the industry produced the highest profits in its history. FM stations held 75 percent of the market and their market share was expected to increase.

The Canadian Broadcasting Corporation (CBC) through its CBC/Radio Canada segment provides national radio stations operating in English, French and eight aboriginal languages. The stations include CBC Radio One and CBC Radio Two in English, CBC Radio Three, Premiere Chaine and Espace Musique in French. Public funds provide the majority of CBC's operating budget with additional revenue coming in through advertising and subscription fees. CBC has helped to develop Canadian talent in the entertainment business, with its content being more than 90 percent Canadian. Its music, drama, and documentary programs are highly regarded.

Canadian broadcasting is regulated by the Canadian Radio-Television and Telecommunications Corp. (CRTC), which licenses networks and private stations and specifies required percentages of Canadian content in programming.

China

With its large population, it is not surprising that China should have the second largest radio market in the world. In 2004, there were more than 500 local stations in the country, all government controlled. Nearly half of China' population listened to the radio each week, with listeners near the capital tuning in for more than 14 hours per week.

France

In 1989, the Socialist government of France formed the Conseil Superieur de l'Audiovisuel (CSA), or Supreme Audiovisual Council, to supervise radio and television broadcasting. In radio, two government agencies, France Culture and France Musique, produce the bulk of cultural programs. Radio France, a unit of the Conseil, operates six national radio networks: France-Inter, network A (entertainment and news); Network B (educational); France-Culture, network D (culture and public affairs); France-Musique, network E (music); Regional stations, network F; and France Info (24-hour news). Private radio stations also exist. According to Euromonitor, the market was valued at US$1.68 billion in 2003, and was expected to grow to US$2.06 billion by 2008.

GERMANY

Only public corporations were permitted to broadcast in Germany until the mid-1980s, when a new system allowed commercial stations on the air for the first time. However, by 2003, public broadcasters still dominated the industry, holding 57.1 percent of market share, with the top three being Westdeutscher Rundfunk (WDR), Norddeutscher Rundfunk (NDR), and Sudwestrundfunk (SWR). The share held between public and private broadcasters was not expected to change up to 2008. Licensing of broadcasters is handled by the Federal Ministry of Post and Telecommunications, while television and radio owners pay annual fees to support public broadcasting. As in England, German public broadcasters are relatively free to establish their own broadcasting policies, though more so in television than radio. Nine different public corporations offer regional radio and TV programs. In Germany, there were 64.4. million radio listeners each day in 2003.

ITALY

While all broadcasting in Italy was once the province of Radiotelevisione Italiana (RAI), private firms have emerged as major competitors. RAI is still a major player in the radio market, however, providing three radio services on national networks in AM and FM. The first, a national program, offers a balanced output; the second is essentially entertainment; and the third is educational. In addition, there is substantial regional output. RAI devotes 70 percent of its radio output to light entertainment, 16 percent to news and information, 4 percent to cultural programs, and 1 percent to youth and educational programs. RAI's revenues come from a government-determined proportion drawn from the sales of radio and television receiving licenses, and advertising.

JAPAN

The radio market in Japan is more developed than in other Asian countries. Japanese radio broadcasting was begun in 1925 by Japan Broadcasting Corporation (Nippon Hoso Kyokai, or NHK), a public corporation financed by license fees paid by TV and radio users. NHK broadcasts radio and television programs with no commercial interruptions. In 2005, NHK operated three radio networks: two AM and one FM. One of the AM networks was exclusively devoted to educational programs. The FM network service mainly presented cultural and local music programs. NHK had 173 medium wave transmitters for the First Radio network, 141 for the Second, and 474 for the VHF-FM network. NHK also broadcast overseas programs in many different languages on its short wave service, Radio Japan. In the early 2000s, there were about 300 commercial radio stations in Japan.

THE UNITED KINGDOM

British television and radio broadcasting has traditionally been dominated by the British Broadcasting Corporation (BBC), which in 2003 had a 45 percent market share. The BBC gets its operating budget from license fees paid by television users. In 2004, the BBC had ten national radio networks, including five digital stations added in 2002. More than 40 BBC local radio stations serve England and the Channel Islands, and regional and community radio stations cater to Scotland, Wales, and Northern Ireland. A number of private radio stations also have been established, including a new talk radio network. The total market was expected to grow to US$3.2 billion by 2008.

GCap Media was the leading commercial radio operator in the UK with about 120 stations reaching more than 15 million listeners or more than 30 percent of the national audience. That includes 55 analog stations and almost 100 digital stations. GCap also operates several radio networks including Choice FM, Core, The One Network and Xfm. It also owns more than 60 percent of the Digital One commercial digital radio multiplex and it has a 50 percent stake in Wildstar Records. The record company was a joint venture with Telestar Records.

THE UNITED STATES

By 2003, the radio market in the United States was valued at US$22 billion, according to figures by Euromonitor, and was expected to grow to US$29.8 billion by 2008. Local advertising accounted for 78.2 percent of the industry's revenues. At this time, the country's top five radio companies (Viacom, Cumulus Media, Clear Channel, Cox Radio, and Entercom Communications) accounted for 34.2 percent of the market, indicating the highly fragmented nature of the industry in this country. Most U.S. commercial stations specialized in a single type of output, such as popular music, classical music, news, sports, or tourist information. While AM radio stations once specialized in music programs, by the late 1990s, FM stations had taken over most of that market. AM stations in the United States have moved more toward talk and news formats.

Non-commercial radio in the United States is primarily National Public Radio (NPR), which receives funding from the federal government, foundations, and other sources. NPR produces a variety of news, information, and music programs, which are distributed to affiliated stations around the country, most of them on FM. The local stations are owned and operated primarily by non-profit groups and universities. Funding for the local stations comes from grants and listeners' donations.

FURTHER READING

"America Listens to ABC." *ABC Radio Networks,* 2004. Available from http://www.abcradio.com.

Bachman, Katy. "News/Talk Ratings Slump as Iraq Coverage Falls Off Radar." *Mediaweek,* 20 October 2003.

"Clear Channel Communications Lands Premier Spot on Institutional Investor's Top Corporate Rankings." 14 March 2007. Available form http:/www.clearchannel.com.

"Clear Channel Radio Adds Music Channels to mSpot Radio." *Business Wire,* 37 March 2007.

"Does new technology mean the end of old technology?" *Innovation Analysis Bulleting,* Vol. 6. No. 3, October 2004. Available from http://www.statcan.ca.

"dotFM Announces WERZ.FM is the Newest Radio Station to Get a Great-Sounding Web Address." *Business Wire,* 6 February 2001.

Douglas, Torin. "Radio's Hectic Schedule Shows No Sign of Slowing." *Marketing Week,* 18 December 2003.

Draper, Deborah J., ed. *Business Rankings Annual.* Detroit: Thomson Gale, 2004.

Fonda, Daren. "The Revolution in Radio." *Time,* 19 April 2004.

Grillo, Jean Bergantini. "Rebound for Radio in '04." *Broadcasting & Cable,* 5 January 2004.

"HD Radio Pumps Up Volume." *Boston Globe,* 2 April 2007.

Harris, Ron. "A downpour." 15 April 2007. Available from http://www.stltoday.com.

Hellaby, David. "Pay Radio: The Next Big Step." *Gold Coast Bulletin,* 22 January 2002.

"Hoover's Company Capsules." 2007. Available from http://www.hoovers.com.

Lazich, Robert S., ed. *Market Share Reporter.* Detroit: Thomson Gale, 2004.

Lorek, L.A. "Clear Channel CEO Pledges Corporate Changes, Says Company not Radio Monolith." *Knight Ridder/Tribune Business News,* 26 July 2004.

Mullaman, Jeremy. "Weak Signal for Radio." *Crain's Chicago Business,* 31 May 2004.

"Nielsen Media Research." *Mediaweek,* 28 June 2004.

Philips, Chuck. "Radio Exec's Claims of Payola Draw Fire." *Los Angeles Times,* 7 March 2002.

Poling, Travis E. "Clear Channel Tallies $1.14 Billion Loss." *San Antonio Express-News,* 27 February 2002.

"Radio Broadcasting in France, Germany, UK, US." *Euromonitor,* August 2004. Available from http://www.majormarketprofiles.com.

"Radio One Reports Preliminary 4Q Results." *Wireless News,* 22 March 2007.

"Radio Today: How America Listens to Radio, 2005 Edition." Arbitron, December 2004. Available from http://www.arbitron.com.

"Rajar Shows 1 Percent Boost for Commercial." *Campaign,* 14 May 2004.

Roberts, Michael. "Help Not Wanted." *Denver Westword,* 21 March 2002.

SIC 3660

NAICS 517

TELECOMMUNICATIONS EQUIPMENT

Telecommunications hardware manufacturers build myriad components to sustain the world's communications systems. Serving both commercial and residential users, examples of industry products include transmission and switching equipment, telephones, and related devices for facilitating and managing voice and data communications. For information regarding providers of communication services using such equipment, see **Telecommunications Services.**

INDUSTRY SNAPSHOT

The outlook for the telecommunications industry remains vibrant around the world. Demand for telecommunications equipment continues to register healthy gains as enterprise spending on equipment reached $99.7 billion in 2004. Spending was expected to continue rising to $121.8 billion by 2007, according to the Telecommunications Industry Association's (TIA) *2004 Telecommunications Market Review and Forecast.* Global telecommunication revenues reached US$2.1 trillion in 2004, according to the TIA, and were expected to reach $2 trillion worldwide by 2007. The network equipment market was expected to reach $16.4 billion in 2005, followed by 7 percent annual growth through 2007.

In mature markets, manufacturers emphasized emerging technology such as wireless and networking equipment because of the robust demand for the Internet and computer networks, while in developing markets they focused on basic telephone technology such as phones, answering machines, and switching equipment. Consequently, telecommunications equipment companies expect the industry to experience even stronger growth by 2010. The wireless communications segment was the fastest growing in the industry during the mid-2000s. Internet protocol (IP) applications and systems were a major growth area, with 70 percent increases in traffic annually. Revenue for IP applications such as web conferencing also rose quickly, and internetworking equipment was expected to grow more than 7 percent annually through 2007, as reported by the TIA.

The telecommunications industry was headed by a few major companies. The top ten companies in the industry, which controlled just under three-quarters of the global market, were concentrated in North America, Western Europe, and Japan. These regions have historically been the major markets due to extensive telephone communication systems developed to meet the expanding needs of business. Although new technologies and markets were changing the industry, the same companies remained the industry leaders for decades, some for more than a century. Previously, participants in the telecommunications equipment industry were confined to domestic markets. However, international trade in the industry was expanding rapidly. Most leading companies derived at least 30 percent of revenues from foreign sales. The industry was also characterized by high levels of research and development expenditures—high costs are more easily absorbed by huge corporations and conglomerates. By the mid-2000s, the industry was experiencing a high number of mergers and acquisitions, and this trend was expected to continue for the foreseeable future.

ORGANIZATION AND STRUCTURE

The equipment market consists of network equipment, which is used by telephone service operators, and customer premises equipment. Network equipment comprises switching and transmission equipment. Switching equipment includes central office switches, switchboards, packet switches, mobile telephone switching offices, microwave switches, and data communication switches. Unlike other switching equipment, data communication switches are increasingly used on private premises, where they facilitate data transmission within computer networks. Transmission equipment includes multiplexing equipment to make it possible to transmit multiple signals over a single communications line, repeaters to strengthen signals over long distances, and line-conditioning equipment.

Customer premises equipment, also called terminal equipment, is privately owned or leased equipment attached to the telecommunications network. It includes private branch exchange (PBX) equipment to switch multiple lines on private premises; telephones; key telephone systems to handle multiple lines, but fewer lines than PBXs; fax machines; modems to convert between analog and digital signals in order to connect computers to telephone networks; telephone answering machines and voice mail systems; and video communications equipment. Technological innovations enabling switching between wireless fidelity (WiFI) and wireless systems, as well as Internet protocol-based systems, were also emerging during the mid-2000s.

Leading telecom equipment companies manufacture central exchange office switching and PBX equipment and also offer products in most other equipment categories. Many smaller companies manufacture customer premises equipment, but don't produce for the commercial market. Some specialize further in certain types of terminal equipment, such as fax machines or modems. Dozens of new companies also compete in the growing market for data communications equipment, especially in the United States, where it is largely an outgrowth of the country's strong computer industry.

BACKGROUND AND DEVELOPMENT

The precursor to modern telecommunications, the telegraph was based on the invention of the voltaic pile—a device used to convert chemical energy into continuous electric current—in 1880, and the invention of electromagnetic detectors in 1836-37 by William Cooke and Charles Wheatstone in Great Britain and by Samuel Morse in the United States. Telegraph systems involved the interruption of, or change in, the polarity of direct current (DC) signaling to convey coded information over cables. The basic telegraph apparatus was the telegraph key, a switch for making and breaking a circuit to create pulses of information in Morse code. Early manufacturers of telegraph equipment usually manufactured other electric equipment as well. As the industry formed in the latter half of the nineteenth century, specialized manufacturers emerged.

In 1876 Alexander Graham Bell patented the telephone in the United States. He developed both variable resistance and magneto-induction devices. While the former was superior, the latter was more reliable at first and hence was the first commercialized version. Initial outdoor transmissions used telegraph lines. Some early telephone equipment companies had been manufacturing telegraph equipment and branched out, while the rest were entirely new companies, created to satisfy the huge new market. The spread of telephone networks in the twentieth century largely replaced the use of telegraph systems, and telegraph equipment has since become an insignificant part of the industry.

Various advancements in telephone equipment have been made over the years. The first coin-operated telephones were introduced in 1889 and AT&T patented the first automatic dial systems in 1891. In 1912 the vacuum-tube repeater was invented to improve signals carried over long distances. Long distance service was further enhanced with the invention of the diode and the refinement of the triode, audion, and hard valve lamps between 1904 and 1915. By 1960, rotary switching systems began to be replaced by crossbar switching, an electro-mechanical system that used sets of magnets on vertical and horizontal bars. The first electronic switching equipment, as opposed to electro-mechanical, was introduced in the United States in 1965. This equipment accelerated automatic switching and permitted a significant increase in the volume of telephone traffic. Large scale integrated circuits improved in the 1970s to the point of permitting the development of digital switching to replace electronic analog switching in central offices.

Before 1970, the telecommunications equipment industry consisted of a small number of companies—many approaching monopolies—in each country that supplied their respective domestic markets. The market consisted of primarily public telecommunications operators, which, as government monopolies, procured equipment through bids but tended to favor one or two suppliers through close relationships. The objectives were to achieve common equipment specifications and stability of supply. Government telecommunications administrators protected the equipment industry and true free market competition was not fostered. In this sense, the telecommunications industry resembled the structure of the defense industry.

Pockets of international competition did exist, however. Equipment companies from industrialized countries expanded and competed in developing countries where indigenous telecommunications manufacturers were either nonexistent or lacking in needed technology.

Historically, telephones and other customer premises equipment were sold exclusively to telephone operators rather than directly to the customers. Telephone companies in turn leased this equipment to subscribers. Customer premises equipment was considered part of the same network system and compatibility had to be maintained. It also was feared that third-party equipment might somehow damage the network. Regulations in many countries actually prohibited customers from connecting equipment to telephone lines that was not provided or authorized by the telephone company. For example, it was prohibited to use non-AT&T equipment in the United States until 1968, and in Germany, customers were not permitted to purchase telephones privately and connect them to the official telephone network until as late as 1990. The adoption of industry-wide standards for customer premises equipment and deregulation of the telephone equipment industry in various countries allowed customers to choose and buy their own equipment. Consequently, equipment manufacturers began to market directly to customers, selling equipment through retail stores. This also opened up a new market for consumer electronics manufacturers that had not been part of the telecommunications industry.

Customer premises equipment is manufactured both by traditional telecommunications equipment companies, which also continue to produce network equipment, and by numerous consumer electronics manufacturers. Low-end customer premises equipment (i.e., telephones, answering machines, and fax machines) has become more of a commodity and is increasingly manufactured in the emerging economies of Asia, where it can be produced more cheaply due to lower labor costs.

In 1996, the global telecommunications equipment market rose to about US$180 to $195 billion. However, the top manufacturers accounted for US$140 billion or roughly 71 percent of worldwide telecommunications equipment sales, according to figures published by Northern Telecom Ltd. By-product, cable, and wire accounted for 11 percent; transmission devices for 14 percent; consumer equipment for 15 percent; switching equipment for 17 percent; data communication equipment for 20 percent; and wireless technology for 23 percent. Telecommunications equipment imports totaled US$60.7 billion in 1995, according to the International Telecommunication Union. Western Europe accounted for 33 percent of these imports, followed by Asia with 28 percent, and North America with 22 percent.

The industry's collective revenues jumped to about US$1 trillion by 2002. Deregulation, new markets, new technology, and trade liberalization were making the telecommunications equipment industry more competitive, international, and dynamic. Deregulation and privatization of national telephone carrier monopolies throughout the world have been changing the market for telecommunication equipment suppliers. Market forces have compelled telephone companies to purchase high-quality and cost-effective equipment in order to offer competitive services. Existing regulatory restrictions on equipment manufacturers also are being lifted. Global network equipment sales totaled about US$72 billion in 2002. Analysts expected growth of approximately 2 percent for 2004, as the U.S. and world economy rebounded after a dismal period during the early 2000s. Optical networking equipment was seeing growth in the mid-2000s, after multiple years of decline.

Trade accords such as the North American Free Trade Agreement (NAFTA) and the General Agreement on Tariffs and Trade (GATT) led to the Information Technology Agreement (ITA), eliminating tariffs and duties in all participating countries, making foreign markets more accessible to the major telecommunications equipment manufacturers. Under GATT, the 1997 ITA led to further industry expansion because it opened the industry's major markets around the world to international competition. Although the agreement directly affects telecommunications service providers, manufacturers have seen indirect benefits because increased competition spurred telephone companies to purchase equipment for the new telephone networks and to upgrade equipment more often to stay competitive.

After some years of negotiation, many of the world's economically powerful and not-so-powerful countries signed the Information Technology Agreement (ITA), which pledged willingness to eliminate tariffs on specified information technology (IT) products such as computer software, hardware and peripherals, telecommunications equipment, analytical instruments, semiconductor manufacturing equipment, and semiconductors. By 2002, about 95 percent of World Trade Organization member countries had signed the pact. Nations that signed the Information Technology Agreement as of mid-2001 were Albania, Georgia, New Zealand, Australia, Austria, Norway, Bulgaria, Belgium, Iceland, Oman, Canada, Denmark, India, Panama, Costa Rica, Finland, Indonesia, the Philippines, Croatia, France, Israel, Poland, Cyprus, Germany, Japan, Romania, Czech Republic, Greece, Jordan, Singapore, El Salvador, Ireland, Korea, Slovak Republic, Estonia, Italy, Kyrgyz Republic, Slovenia, Taiwan, Luxembourg, Latvia, Switzerland, the Netherlands, Liechtenstein, Portugal, Lithuania, Thailand, Spain, Macau, Turkey, Sweden, Malaysia, the United States, the United Kingdom, and Mauritius.

CUSTOMER PREMISES EQUIPMENT

Because of maturing markets and technological advances, the customer premises equipment (CPE) segment of the industry experienced heightened competition and lower prices in the latter half of the 1990s. Manufacturers outsourced production of lower-end CPE products to low-wage economies such as those in Asia. Much of the new growth in this segment resulted from innovative products, including video-conferencing equipment. In the market for fixed-line telephones, cordless phones were the fastest growing category. The market for fax machines and modems was also booming. However, standard handset phone demand experienced slower growth because of its high penetration level.

Since most customer premises equipment is largely standardized, companies are addressing issues of standardizing public network equipment. These issues include synchronous digital hierarchy/synchronous optical network transmission (SONET) and asynchronous transfer mode (ATM) switching. As equipment conforming to these standards opened new markets, many smaller companies took advantage of the new standards to enter the industry. Public telephone operators, however, were slow to adopt these standards.

Customer premises data communications equipment drove the industry in the 1990s. This segment enjoyed strong growth throughout the decade, and continued growth was expected in the new century. This segment includes modems, fax machines, and computer networking and internetworking equipment, which is used by companies as they establish larger and more complex computer networks. This growing market was being exploited by established telecommunications equipment companies, computer and computer peripheral manufacturers, and new specialized companies, such as Cisco Systems and Bay Networks, which were among the fastest growing companies in the telecommunications equipment industry.

The convergence of telecommunications technology with that of the computer industry contributed to the growth of the customer premises data communications equipment market. This included computer local area network (LAN) adapter cards, switches, routers, and bridges. The introduction of asynchronous transfer mode (ATM) switching to LAN products allowed LAN manufacturers to enter telecommunications companies' markets. LAN equipment manufacturers were taking a growing share of the public network infrastructure market—if not directly, then at least through resellers. Thus, traditional telecommunications equipment companies were beginning to face competition from computer hardware companies. Unaffected by the recession, the LAN market continued to grow rapidly throughout the 1990s. This convergence also spurred growth in the PBX and key system (KTS) markets, where manufacturers have developed equipment to be part of communications networks instead of being independent parts. The U.S. Department of Commerce predicted that the Pacific Rim countries, Eastern Europe, and South America would make up the leading PBX and KTS markets in the early twenty-first century.

Wireless Telecommunications Equipment

Because global wireless penetration stood at only one percent in 1997, this segment of the industry expected explosive growth as new spectrum and digital technologies became more available, more wireless service providers entered the market, prices declined, and mass appeal of wireless telecommunication increased. However, the lack of universal wireless standards may impair the growth of the industry and also may hurt wireless equipment trade in the United States, Europe, and Japan, which have adopted different standards. Excluding the United States, 50 percent of the world's wireless systems used the European GSM/DSC 1800 (Global Systems for Mobile Communications) standard in 1997. Japan also controls a large percentage of the market with its PHS (Personal Handyphone Service) standard, but the United States continues to promote its CDMA (Code Division Multiple Access) standard, which is gaining worldwide popularity.

Worldwide demand for wireless telecommunications equipment increased dramatically as almost every country had at least one cellular telephone service by 2002. The number of cellular telephone subscribers continued to rise throughout the world in the mid-2000s. The United States was the leader, followed by Japan, the United Kingdom, China, and Italy. Analysts expected that companies would continue to license cellular systems, leading to added growth for global wireless equipment makers. Each new license benefited manufacturers because it required building a new cellular system and resulted in greater demand for user handsets.

Current Conditions

As reported by *Euromonitor,* the Chinese market was booming, with an 88 percent growth projected by 2007. Japan was expected to grow 23 percent, followed by South Korea (36 percent) and Australia (68 percent). In Europe, the market in France was set to increase 65 percent, and the U.K. market was set to increase 12 percent. The U.S. market, valued at US$785 billion in 2004, was expected to grow 9.5 percent annually into 2008, to $1.1 trillion. Rapidly growing segments of the industry included voice over internet protocol (VoIP), WiFi (wireless fidelity) and streaming media, fiber optics innovations, dense wavelength division multiplexing (DWDM), and wavelength-division multiplexing (WDM).

According to a Yankee Group study, by 2007 infrastructure equipment costs will have a corresponding decline, to less than 7 percent of revenue. *Euromonitor* forecasts indicate that mobile phones will remain the largest industry sector in China, Japan, South Korea, France, and Germany into 2007. So-called "smart phones," mobile handheld converged devices, saw one of the largest growths in this sector in 2003, posting a remarkable 181 percent growth over 2002, according to *2.5G-3G.*

In addition, by the end of 2004, analysts expected as many as 945 million online users worldwide, compared to 20 million a decade earlier. As a result, Internet service providers and telephone companies realized that they had to invest in more digital switching and new products such as wavelength division multiplexing (WDM) equipment to reduce network congestion.

Because traditional equipment for voice communication has saturated markets in the developed economies of Western Europe, the United States, and Japan, manufacturers anticipate the strongest growth in these regions to come from data communication equipment. With the explosive popularity of the Internet and related activities such as e-mail, e-commerce, and telecommuting, telecom equipment producers plan to focus on this expanding market by providing modems, fax machines, computer networking equipment, and other kinds of data communications equipment.

In developed markets, such as Western Europe and the United States, telephone companies have largely completed digitalization projects begun in the 1970s. Consequently, telecommunications equipment investments have been shifting from switching and transmission equipment toward software and service enhancements. In contrast, developing countries represented a growing market, as the process of industrialization leads them to invest in telecommunications infrastructure, including central office switching and transmission equipment. This enabled leading telecommunications equipment companies to maintain steady growth in sales of switching and transmission equipment through exports, despite maturing domestic markets.

Among the developing markets, Asia represents the fastest growing market, China in particular. South American countries also constitute strong markets for growth in telecommunications production and trade. As South American countries moved toward telephone penetration levels achieved in developed nations, they were becoming one of the most important markets for telecommunication equipment. Internet and wireless technology were expected to grow quickly in Asia and Latin America.

RESEARCH AND TECHNOLOGY

The telecommunications industry invests heavily in research and development (R&D) to devise new equipment and standards that will lead to more reliable, cost-effective services which offer more features. Spending on research and development averages 12 percent of revenues for leading telecommunication equipment companies. On the high end, some companies spend close to 20 percent.

The conversion of central office switches from analog to digital, a worldwide telecommunications industry process that began in the 1970s and continued into the 2000s, allows central switches to be controlled by computers. This creates new possibilities for software development to provide more sophisticated services. In 2005, Infonetics Research reported that Internet Protocol (IP) PBX systems were "growing ferociously," with growth rates of more than 50 percent between 2003 and 2004.

Another process taking place in the telecommunications industry was the gradual replacement of copper wire with fiber-optic cable, which has better transmission quality over long distances, greater transmission capacity (bandwidth), higher security, and greater energy efficiency. To take advantage of the wider bandwidth, equipment was developed to provide concurrent transmission of voice, data, and video signals, based on the synchronous optical network (SONET) standard. SONET, a set of interfaces for fiber-optic transmission devised in 1988, utilizes fiber optic's wider bandwidth, yet is also compatible with copper wire-based systems.

The most recent developments in research and technology have been in data transmission capabilities rather than voice. Higher speeds and greater bandwidth are being demanded for transmitting computer data and are necessary for the transmission of video images for purposes such as video conferencing. New switching technologies developed to address these needs include frame relay, switched multi-megabit data service (SMDS), and asynchronous transfer mode (ATM). SMDS is popular in the United States because it was designed to be compatible with the existing network. Frame relay offers low-cost data-switching capabilities, but has fewer features than SMDS or ATM. ATM had been expected to become the dominant broadband technology by the end of the 1990s, but research and development costs have been high, so it will take longer. Meanwhile, new techniques in data compression are being developed to handle the needs of video transmission.

Manufacturers introduced a promising new piece of telecommunications equipment, the Internet telephone, that immediately resonated with business Internet users and intrigued home Internet users. Internet telephony allows users to place calls via the Internet, bypassing the high costs of long distance voice communication. In terms of equipment, service providers require flexible Internet gateway servers that can accommodate both large and small numbers of users. On the users' side, a special Internet telephone is needed. Voice over Internet Protocol (VOIP) was expected to be a major growth factor in the industry in the mid and late 2000s. Growth was expected to be somewhat limited by quality and reliability issues, as well as less than expected cost savings.

A big improvement over the standard, slow analog modem connection, the Digital Subscriber Line (DSL) enables a customer to tap into the regional telephone network to link a dedicated line with a central office point of presence (POP) account to connect to the Internet. The best DSL modems are up to 125 times faster than a 56.6K analog modem. Broadband connections were starting to outnumber dial-up accounts in many countries in 2005 as costs declined, according to Deloitte's Media and Telecommunications Group.

As of the mid-2000s, mobile phones were no longer getting smaller. Instead, manufacturers were developing converged products that could handle many different capabilities—such as color displays, cameras, and WiFi—without increasing the handset size, by developing converged chips that integrated functions in the architecture itself. Such third-generation (3G) devices were in development by Motorola, Intel, and Texas Instruments, and other companies in 2004. Deloitte projected there would be almost two billion cellular mobile subscriptions worldwide by the end of 2005, and that voice would still account for more than 80 percent of cellular subscription revenues.

INDUSTRY LEADERS

SIEMENS AG

In 1997 Siemens was the world's leading electrical and electronic equipment manufacturer, and telecommunications equipment represented about a third of its business. Siemens' telecommunications products included digital telephone switching systems, communications network software, cellular telephones and base station equipment, broadband network adapter equipment for multimedia transmission, asynchronous transfer mode switches, and telephone handsets. Siemens was the world market leader in PBXs with a 10 percent market share in the mid-1990s. By 2004, the company's total sales from all divisions was US$93.4 billion. Siemens Communications Group, which was responsible for the wire line and wireless equipment, took in US$25.8 billion in revenue in 2003 and employed 95,000 people.

Although Siemens diversified into many areas of electrical, electronic, computer, and semiconductor equipment, the company originated as a telecommunications equipment manufacturer. It was founded in 1847 in Berlin as Siemens and Halske to produce telegraph equipment. Shortly after the invention of the telephone, Siemens patented an improved version and began producing equipment. In the 1920s, Siemens established a joint venture subsidiary in Japan called Fuji Electric, which became the parent company of Fujitsu. The latter firm eventually became Japan's second largest telecommunications company. In 1988, Siemens acquired IBM's Rolm System subsidiary, the third largest supplier of PBX telephone switching equipment in North America.

By 2004, Siemens planned to market its own line of phones based on the Universal Mobile Telecommunications System standard, according to *Bloomberg News.* Previously, in 2002 and 2003, it purchased Motorola-made phones with fast Internet capabilities, as well as Motorola handset chips, and marketed them under the Siemens brand. Siemens also controlled 13 percent of the US$2.3 billion spent in 2001 by global service providers for DSL equipment, according to *Fiber Optics News*.

ALCATEL NV

Alcatel NV was the world's leading manufacturer of telecommunications equipment from 1990 to 1995, until Siemens surpassed it in 1996. However, as spending by global service providers on DSL equipment for 2001 rose to US$2.3 billion, Alcatel was the world leader at 37.8 percent in that area of commerce. In 2004, the company shipped 19.6 million ports, 24 percent more than in 2003. Alcatel also launched its IP-based broadband access platform, the Intelligent Services Access Manager, in 2004 to help service providers offer "100 percent Triple Play" services to all of its customers at the same time, either from the central office or from remote terminals. Alcatel had sales of US$16.6 billion in 2004, with more than 55,000 employees.

A pioneer in telecommunications equipment, Alcatel was founded in France in 1879. In the early 1970s, it was acquired by Compagnie Générale d'Électricité (GCE), a state-owned engineering and electrical equipment conglomerate, which was subsequently privatized in 1986. GCE expanded its telecommunications equipment business with the acquisition of Thomson-Brandt's telecommunications operations in 1983 and the majority stake in the European telephone equipment business of the United States' ITT Corp. in 1986. ITT's operations were merged with Alcatel's to form the new subsidiary of Alcatel NV, which was incorporated in the Netherlands and had headquarters in Belgium. Upon its incorporation, it became the second largest telecommunications equipment company in the world. In 1990, parent company GCE changed its name to Alcatel Alsthom Compagnie Générale d'Électricité, often referred to as Alcatel Alsthom, to reflect its two major subsidiaries.

LUCENT TECHNOLOGIES

AT&T had long been the world's leading manufacturer of telecommunications equipment, but began its descent in 1990 when it lost the top position to Alcatel. In subsequent years, AT&T started to focus more on telecommunications services than on telecommunications equipment, spinning off its telecommunications equipment development operations as Lucent Technologies in April 1996. Lucent was then the United States' second largest and the world's fourth largest producer of telecommunications equipment. In 2004 Lucent reported a 6.8 percent increase in sales to US$9 billion. That year, Lucent acquired 100 percent of Telica, a provider of VoIP switching equipment. Wireless revenues accounted for more than $4 billion of Lucent's revenues, voice networking for $1.3 billion, data and network management for $933 million, optical networking for $715 million, with the remaining revenue derived from other products and services.

MOTOROLA INC.

The Galvin Manufacturing Company, started in 1928, named its first commercially successful car radio under the brand name of Motorola, which is a blend of "motor" and "victrola." The company officially changed its name to Motorola Inc. in 1947, the same year the first Motorola television was introduced. The Motorola TV became so popular that within months of its introduction, the company was the fourth largest television seller in the nation. The company expanded its operations in the 1960s, establishing facilities in Mexico and Japan. The cellular remote telephone system was developed by AT&T's Bell Laboratories in the early 1970s. Motorola aided in the design and testing of the phones and supplied much of the transmission-switching equipment. In 1989 the company introduced the world's smallest portable telephone, and by 1997 had generated annual sales of more than US$29.7 billion as the second largest producer of analog cellular phones and the third largest producer of digital cellular phones.

In the 2000s, however, Motorola appeared to be in freefall. *Forbes* blamed the company's downturn on its failure to recognize quickly that its Iridium satellite phone venture was doomed from the start, and one that saddled the company with bank debts that injured its balance sheet for years to come. In an attempt to contain costs, Motorola conducted wholesale layoffs and firings that shrank the size of losses in 2001 and 2002 but damaged the company's business reputation as a stable place to work. One key hiring in October 2001 was that of new President and Chief Operating Officer Ed Breen, who elevated the mobile phone market share from 12 percent in 2000 to 18 percent in 2002, according to *Forbes*. This restored Motorola to second in the market, behind also-struggling Nokia's 37 percent market share. The company reported US$31.32 billion in total sales in 2004, an increase of 15.8 percent over 2003. *Forbes* noted that Motorola's wireless sales department made inroads into China in the 2000s, "landing $1.4 billion in infrastructure contracts, and has become that country's dominant handset supplier." In 2004, China accounted for 9 percent of Motorola's sales, behind Europe (19 percent) and the United States (47 percent).

NEC CORPORATION

Better known in the fields of computers and semiconductors, NEC is Japan's leading telecommunications equipment manufacturer. Of its total revenues of US$39.9 billion for 1997, communications systems and equipment accounted for US$14.9 billion, or 37 percent. This included digital switching equipment, fiber-optic radio transmission systems, space electronics, mobile communications systems, and customer premises equipment. By 2004, NEC reported US$47.0 billion in sales and 143,000 employees. NEC's largest single client is Nippon Telegraph and Telephone Public Corp. (NTT), one of the largest telephone companies in the world. NEC also exports its telecommunications equipment.

Originally named the Nippon Electric Company, NEC was founded in 1898 as a joint venture between Japanese investors and Bell subsidiary Western Electric Company, then the leading telecommunications equipment company in the United States. Western Electric sold its stake in NEC in 1925 to ITT Corp. of the United States, which held shares in NEC until 1978. NEC started out importing equipment from Western Electric and General Electric, but soon began producing its own telephone sets as the Japanese government expanded the country's telephone systems. Although there were some competitors in Japan, NEC achieved a near monopoly in the telephone equipment market early in the twentieth century.

After NTT was formed in 1952, NEC became one of its four major suppliers, and NTT accounted for more than 50 percent of NEC's sales in the 1950s and 1960s. Communications equipment, with the addition of radio and television broadcasting equipment, remained NEC's major business until the 1960s, when the company diversified into computers and other electronics.

NORTEL NETWORKS

Nortel Networks, formed from the 1998 merger of Canada's Northern Telecom with California-located Bay Networks, is the leading company for which telecommunications equipment accounts for close to all of its revenue, which was US$9.8 billion in 2004. The company's products include network switching equipment, telephone sets, wireless systems, multimedia communication systems, transmission wire and cable, broadband networks, and network applications—in short, every bit of equipment required for Internet use. The United States is its largest market. A pioneer in digital switches, Nortel's predecessor Northern Telecom held close to one third of the U.S. digital switch market at the time of the merger. Nortel Networks Corp. decided to keep its base of operations in Toronto.

Northern Telecom was a partially owned subsidiary of BCE Inc., the holding company of Canada's leading telephone company, Bell Canada. It was established by Bell Canada as its manufacturing arm in 1895 under the name Northern Electric and Manufacturing Company Ltd. In 1914 it merged with Imperial Wire and Cable and assumed the new name of Northern Electric Company Ltd. Since AT&T owned part of Bell Canada, AT&T's manufacturing subsidiary Western Electric owned part of Northern Electric. Northern Electric primarily manufactured products designed by Western Electric until Bell Canada began to buy out Western Electric's shares in Northern Electric in 1957, with the remaining shares going to Bell Canada in 1964. Northern Electric then established its own research and development unit, Northern Electric Laboratories, in 1958, which became the Bell-Northern Research Ltd. subsidiary in 1971. Bell Canada sold shares of Northern Electric to the public in 1973 and retained slightly more than 50 percent. In 1976 the company changed its name to Northern Telecom Ltd. and made the critical, shrewd business decision to make an equipment changeover to digital switches.

OTHER INDUSTRY LEADERS

Other industry leaders included Nokia, the number one supplier of mobile phones, responsible for 33.9 percent of global shipments in the fourth quarter of 2004. Cisco Systems, while not as large as industry leader Siemens, was the "most powerful brand in telecom networking equipment worldwide," as reported in Heavy Reading's "2005 Wireline Telecom Equipment Market Perception Study." The study ranked companies based on name recognition, price, product performance, product quality and reliability, and service and support. Cisco earned $22 billion in revenue in 2004. The five top companies on the survey's list were Cisco, Juniper, Lucent, Nortel, and Alcatel. Chinese vendor Huawai also made a large jump in the rankings, remarkable for the fact that it has yet to establish a significant presence in the North American market.

MAJOR REGIONS IN THE INDUSTRY

THE UNITED STATES AND NORTH AMERICA

As the largest telecommunications equipment market, the United States has led the telecommunications industry in sales and exports, though Japan earns comparable revenues, and both suffered similar losses during the global economic slump of 2001. In 1999 the U.S. market for telecommunications equipment was valued at more than $3.9 billion and continued rising through 2002, when the marked reached $7.6 billion. Following a decline to $5.3 billion in 2003, the future of the U.S. market was dependent on its ability to export into developing countries. This mature and highly competitive industry posed a challenge for the United States telecommunications equipment market. In 2003, the United States exported $112.5 billion of office machines and telecom equipment, as reported by the World Trade Organization (WTO). Imports of the same were valued at $180.5 billion during the same year.

ASIA

Asia led the world in both imports and exports of office machines and telecom equipment in 2003, as reported by World Trade Organization in 2004. The region including Australia, Japan and New Zealand was responsible for 21.6 percent import share, and 19.9 percent export share of manufactures. Other Asian markets imported 30.4 percent and exported 35.7 percent of manufactures.

In the 2000s, analysts were not surprised that even Japanese super companies such as NEC were seeing formerly huge profits erode and recovery as being years away. "It is the fate of developed nations to be caught up with by newly industrialized nations, and, if anything, the true reason for the rapid contraction of Japan's manufacturing base is its failure to change a high cost structure and inflexible industrial and employment systems, and its slowness to foster new industries and to respond to the IT revolution," chided the Japan Research Institute in a November 2001 economic report. In 2002 larger Japanese companies seemed to take the criticism to heart. The *International Herald Tribune* reported that Fujitsu, NEC, and other large industry representatives attempted to turn Japan's poor economic climate around during the 2000s by taking advantage of an abundant resource—its inventors. In 2003, total exports of office machines and telecom equipment for Japan were just over $90 billion and imports totaled $54.5 billion, according to the WTO.

In 2004, it appeared the power in the Asian telecom market was shifting to China. Chinese companies and vendors were winning major contracts, making deals with western partners, and earning new accounts with low pricing. Huawei, a Chinese equipment vendor, earned the rank of fourth in world market share among manufacturers of DSL equipment. The company was close behind industry leaders Alcatel and Siemens, as reported in a survey conducted by Synergy Research Group (SRG). By January 2005, Huawei shocked even its Asian rivals by winning a contract to expand CAT Telecom's CMDA network, besting industry leader Motorola as well as Ericsson and Thailand's Advanced Info Service (AIS). Huawei was also partnering with British Telecom and other European companies during the mid-2000s, earning contracts with its combination of quality equipment and low pricing. ZTE was another company growing quickly in the Chinese market and gaining market share. China imported $96.2 billion of office machines and telecom equipment in 2003, and exports of the same valued $117.9 billion.

GERMANY

As one of the world's largest markets, Germany is also Europe's largest telecom equipment market. Its telecommunications equipment industry grew faster than any other in Europe in the 1990s and early 2000s, and was valued at US$6.62 billion in 2003. Part of the country's growth stemmed from its goal to finish converting remaining analog equipment to digital equipment, which required large expenditures for new equipment. Equipment revenues peaked in 2002 at US$9.6 billion, but like the rest of Europe, the German market decreased significantly between 2002 and 2003. The early 2000s were challenging years for German companies such as Siemens, which were caught in the general downturn that globally affected mobile network businesses. Exports of office machines and telecom equipment for the European Union as a whole totaled $246.4 billion, and imports totaled $302.8 billion, as reported in the WTO's *International Trade Statistics 2004.*

Germany ranked as the world's second largest exporter of telecommunications equipment. In 1997 it exported US$8.5 billion of telecommunications equipment and maintained a positive trade balance. Germany also led in exports of switching equipment. The leading company in the German industry was Siemens. Alcatel NV's German subsidiary Alcatel Sel AG also contributed significantly to the industry.

FRANCE

France was another of the world's largest markets for telecommunications equipment, worth approximately US$5.3 billion in 2003. Revenues peaked in 2002, and like the United Kingdom, saw some decline in the mid-2000s. Still, innovations in wireless and data helped to keep the country's market strong. The leading company was Alcatel Cit, the France-based subsidiary of Alcatel NV.

UNITED KINGDOM

The United Kingdom was Europe's third largest market for telecommunications equipment in 2003, as reported by Euromonitor. In 1997, the U.K. market for telecommunications equipment was valued at more than US$2.6 billion, and continued rising to a high of US$3.68 billion in 2002 before decreasing to $3 billion in 2003. Some recovery of the market was expected due to demand for mobile networks and broadband access, prompting British Telecom and Cable & Wireless to expand and upgrade telephony systems.

FURTHER READING

"2003 Worldwide Mobile Phone Shipments Up 29.7 Percent in Fourth Quarter and 23.3 Percent for the Year, According to IDC." *2.5G-3G,* February 2004.

"2004: A Good Year for Mobile Phone Shipments, Especially in the Fourth Quarter." *Wireless News,* 1 February 2005.

"Alcatel Leads Siemens, Lucent in DSL Market." *Fiber Optics News,* 25 March 2002.

Belson, Ken. "Japan Firms Are Cashing in on Patent Caches." *International Herald Tribune,* 15 March 2002.

"Broadband Equipment Market Grows Over 25 Percent." *The Online Reporter,* 29 May 2004.

Buergin, Rainer. "German Rebound Not Assured." *Bloomberg News,* 10 April 2002.

"Business Telecommunications Equipment in Australia, China, France, Germany, Japan, South Korea, UK, US." *Euromonitor,* August 2004. Available from http://www.majormarketprofiles.com.

"Carriers Say Cisco is Tops in Telecom Equipment Market." *Networks Update,* April 2005.

Davis, Jessica. "Everything but the Kitchen Sink." *Electronic Business,* May 2004.

Donahue, Patrick. "German Stocks Rise." *Bloomberg News,* 17 April 2002.

Harbert, Tam. "A Thaw in Telecom's Nuclear Winter." *Electronic Business,* January 2004.

Hesseldahl, Arik. "Galvin's Semiconductor Slump." *Forbes,* 31 January 2002.

"Japan's NEC to Restructure System Chip Production." *Asia Pulse,* 2 April 2002.

Japan Research Institute, 2002. Available from http://www.jri.co.jp.

Long, Geoff. "Power Shift." *Telecom Asia,* March 2005.

Marsan, Carolyn Duffy. "Domain Name Registrations Drop." *Network World,* 28 January 2002.

"Optical Set for Small Rebound." *Telecom Asia,* October 2003.

"Telecom Recovery?" *Optoelectronics Report,* 15 April 2004.

"Telecom Trends" *Australian Banking & Finance,* 15 February 2005.

"The World's Online Populations," 2002. Available from http://www.cyberatlas.internet.com.

World Trade Organization. "International Trade Statistics." Geneva, Switzerland: 2003. Available from http://www.wto.org.

"Worldwide IP PBX Market Catches Fire." *TelecomWeb News Digest,* 7 March 2005.

"Yankee Group: Wireless Equipment Vendors Face Challenging Market." *Wireless News,* 30 June 2004.

SIC 4810

NAICS 517

TELECOMMUNICATIONS SERVICES

The rapidly changing field of telecommunications services includes local, long distance, and international telephone services, as well as cellular and other mobile phone and paging services. A number of industry firms also transmit cable television services and offer Internet access. See also **Cable and Other Pay-Television Services** and **Internet Services** for further coverage of these activities. Many telecoms also have historical ties to communications equipment manufacturing, which is discussed separately in this chapter under **Telecommunications Equipment**.

INDUSTRY SNAPSHOT

The widespread availability of telephone and other telecommunications services in the United States becomes vivid considering that one-third of the world's population has never made a telephone call, according to the International Telecommunication Union (ITU). In 2003, there were approximately 2.5 billion people served by telephones, an average of 40.32 telephone lines per 100 people, with ranges from 8.65 per 100 to 96.28 per 100, depending on the world region. But one need only glance at KMI Corp.'s cybermaps of existing and planned fiber-optics installation to know that the one-third statistic will become outdated in an astonishingly short time. In particular, many humanitarian groups are raising funds to get cell phones into underserved areas in Africa, Asia, and South America for humanitarian purposes.

As late as 1993, fixed lines outnumbered cell phones 12 to one. However, by 2002 the number of cell phones outnumbered fixed telephone lines, and the margins continued to grow wider. Mobile phone usage is highest in developing counties, especially China and India, according to the ITU. Ironically, mobile calls in the United States and Canada were stalled or decreasing as a result of a fee system charging a cost to both callers and receivers on cell calls.

According to the ITU, investment in telecommunications infrastructure was more than US$200 billion in 2000, and by 2003 it had reached approximately US$215 billion. That year, the global telecommunications services industry generated revenues of an estimated US$1.3 trillion. National telephone service represented 33 percent of the world's telecommunications service revenues, while international service accounted for 5 percent and mobile service for 30 percent.

The leading trends in the telephone services industry included privatization of state-owned monopolies, the opening up of telephone service markets to overseas competition, and deregulation. Other significant trends were the continuing rapid growth of the wireless telephone service segment, the expansion of telephone services in developing countries, and the internationalization of the industry through alliances, joint ventures, and investments. Many of these trends stemmed from the World Trade Organization's 1997 telecommunications agreement between its member countries. The agreement established policies for opening up the world's key markets to international participation and increased competition.

Although many companies struggled to gain market share in the 2000s, while the giant conglomerate Verizon prospered, the industry has been marked by the founding and development of the Competitive Local Exchange Carrier (CLEC). CLECs are telephone companies that compete for customers with the existing Incumbent Local Exchange Carrier (ILEC). ILECs include well-known telecommunications companies such as Sprint. A typical CLEC is US LEC, a voice, data and Internet telecommunications carrier that does business in the southeastern and mid-Atlantic regions of the United States. According to the FCC, CLEC lines grew more than 9 percent over a three-year period in the early 2000s, and were expected to continue growing.

ORGANIZATION AND STRUCTURE

Enterprises that provide telephone communication services to the public through their own communication networks, as opposed to companies that lease these lines, are called public telecommunication operators, telephone carriers, or simply telephone companies. For fixed-line telephone service, users are connected to a switched network of cables through individual mainlines. Radiotelephone service providers also operate communications networks; however, the networks are made of radio broadcast towers and sometimes satellite communications stations instead of telephone cables. Fixed-line telephone services may also use satellites for global transmission.

Telephone communication services were traditionally provided by a single monopoly in each country, often a state-owned enterprise or a government agency. In the latter case, national telephone services are often provided by the same organization that provides postal and telegraph services. This is because telephone communications have historically been considered a public service utility requiring government involvement to ensure widespread distribution and compatibility of service and equipment. Even in countries with more than one telephone company, the industry tends to be heavily regulated and competition may be restricted. The heavy involvement of national governments in the telephone industry has produced a market structure that, until recently, has been very national in character, although the industry does provide international services in the form of international calling. Bilateral treaties govern the sharing of costs for transmitting international phone calls.

Within a given country, different categories of service may be provided by the same company, or the industry may be regulated so that companies may only operate within certain categories of service. These services include local, domestic long distance, international long distance, local mobile telephone communications, national mobile communications, and specialized services such as leased lines. Certain sectors of the industry may be open to competition while others may be handled by a single monopoly. In general, mobile communications tend to be the most open to competition, while local telephone service tends to be the least.

Mobile communication services, which use radio frequencies for transmission, include cellular telephone, paging, personal communications services (PCS), specialized mobile radio, satellite communications, and data services. Paging services, which use cheaper and simpler technology, account for the greatest number of mobile communication subscribers, whereas cellular telephone service is the category that generates the most revenues. Cellular telephone service, developed in the 1960s and introduced in the 1980s, differs from traditional radiotelephone services by using a network of low-power transceivers, each covering its own area, or cell, which ranges from two to 10 miles. Mobile telephone services are provided by both the major public telecommunication operators and by smaller, specialized companies.

In the 1990s, the structure of the worldwide telecommunications industry began to undergo a rapid transformation. In both industrialized and developing countries, various categories of telephone services began to be privatized, deregulated, and opened up for competition. The countries with the most open competition as of 1998 were the United Kingdom, the United States, Japan, Sweden, Finland, and New Zealand. However, despite the easing of restrictions, telephone communication remains one of the most regulated industries.

The International Telecommunication Union (ITU) serves as an international regulatory body for the global telecommunications services industry. The union fosters collaboration among members—governments and private sector companies—for the establishment of consistent rates and service standards and allocates radio frequencies, among other activities. Moreover, as a division of the United Nations, the ITU also strives to bring telecommunications service to developing countries. To this end, the ITU monitors the progress of telephone service penetration in these countries and promotes increased international involvement in resolving this problem.

In February 1997, the World Trade Organization (WTO) announced that its 72 member countries had reached an agreement after several years of negotiations. The participating countries represented about 90 percent of the world's overall telecommunications market. The agreement called for members to open up their markets to foreign competition and to establish regulations to promote and ensure fair telecommunications service trade. The WTO expected this agreement would result in lower prices, better service, more advanced technology, and greater investment, and announced that the agreement would take effect in February 1998 (although member countries had differing implementation schedules). The accord includes provisions for voice telephony, data transmission, facsimile transmission, private leased circuit services, satellite communications, and mobile communications. The agreement came to be known as the Information Technology Agreement (ITA). The ITA, according to the U.S. Department of Commerce, "is a plurilateral trade agreement that requires participants to eliminate their tariffs on a specific list of information technology (IT) products." Examples are analytical instruments; computer software, hardware and peripherals; telecommunications equipment; semiconductor manufacturing equipment; and semiconductors. "The agreement covers approximately 95 percent of world trade in defined information technology products, which is currently estimated to exceed US$1 trillion," according to the U.S. Department of Commerce's International Trade Administration, Office of Information Technologies.

The countries that agreed to the terms of the Information Technology Agreement as of July 2001 were Albania, Georgia, New Zealand, Australia, Austria, Norway, Bulgaria, Belgium, Iceland, Oman, Canada, Denmark, India, Panama, Costa Rica, Finland, Indonesia, Philippines, Croatia, France, Israel, Poland, Cyprus, Germany, Japan, Romania, Czech Republic, Greece, Jordan, Singapore, El Salvador, Ireland, Korea, Slovak Republic, Estonia, Italy, Kyrgyz Republic, Slovenia, Taiwan, Luxembourg, Latvia, Switzerland, the Netherlands, Liechtenstein, Portugal, Lithuania, Thailand, Spain, Macau, Turkey, Sweden, Malaysia, the United States, the United Kingdom, and Mauritius.

BACKGROUND AND DEVELOPMENT

Telephone service was first commercially introduced in the northeast United States in 1877, just one year after Alexander Graham Bell invented the telephone. The first systems were direct lines between pairs of subscribers. In 1878 the first telephone exchanges, for switching calls and lines, were established in towns and cities throughout the United States and permitted multiple subscribers to call each other. Competing private companies, however, provided separate telephone systems that were incompatible.

The technology of telephone service spread rapidly throughout the world shortly after its development. Canada opened its first telephone exchange in the same year as the United States. The first telephone exchange in England was opened in London in 1879. In Switzerland the first private telephone exchange was established in 1880 and telephone exchanges were established in Australia in 1880 and Brazil in 1881. France's first telephone exchange was established in Reims in 1887, and in Japan public telephone service was introduced in 1890.

The development of metallic circuits reduced interference significantly to permit the introduction of long distance service, beginning in 1881, with a connection between Boston, Massachusetts, and Providence, Rhode Island. The introduction in 1884 of hard-drawn copper wire to replace galvanized iron wire resulted in less attenuation of telephone voices and permitted lines to reach between Boston and New York. The first international call was made between the United Kingdom and France in 1891. The invention of the automatic switchgear in 1889 permitted connection without the use of human operators, although the widespread installation of automated switching at central exchanges did not occur until the twentieth century. Long distance service was enhanced with the invention of the diode and the refinements of the triode, audion, and hard-valve lamps between 1904 and 1915.

In the United States, the company founded by Alexander Graham Bell and his financial backers, Bell Telephone Company, was able to dominate the fledgling industry because it held the patents to the technology. When the patents expired and competition emerged, Bell was ahead of the rest with its established telephone networks. Although the industry remained in the private sector for all but one year, 1917-1918, Bell swallowed up smaller competitors, establishing a virtual monopoly. Bell was renamed American Telephone and Telegraph (AT&T) in 1899.

In most of the world, telephone systems were owned by the government. In Britain in 1896, the British Post Office, which had taken over telegraph services in 1869, took over trunk (long distance) service and in 1912 it took over all telephone services. In Germany, the government held a monopoly from the beginning. The German Empire's first postmaster introduced the telephone to Germany and put it under the control of the Bundespost, the state postal authority. In France, telephone service was originally handled by private businesses but was soon taken over by the government. Three private phone companies licensed by the government merged in 1883 to form the Société Générale des Téléphones, which was nationalized in 1889. In 1890 there were 15,432 telephone subscribers in France. The development of the system subsequently lagged behind that of other countries due to bureaucracy. One of the problems was that municipalities wishing to establish a telephone system had to provide funding for the system in advance and were reimbursed by the national telephone systems later, based on the income it received from the local subscribers.

In 1878, the Swiss government announced that telephone systems would come under its control and that telephone network providers must be licensed by the states. The government began installing exchanges in 1881. In 1886 the government bought out the only private system and from then on all telephone services were run by the postal and telegraph authority, the Schweizerische Post-, Telefon- und Telegrafen-Betriebe (PTT), a part of the Switzerland Ministry of Energy, Transportation, and Communications. In Switzerland the government monopoly's service was efficient but not heavily used.

In Japan the government approved a state-run telephone system, which came under the Ministry of Communications in 1899. In 1952, state-owned Nippon Telegraph and Telephone Public Corp. was formed.

Telephone service did not become popular as quickly in other countries as it did in the United States. This was partly due to inferior service and equipment quality resulting from artificially low rates set by the government owners. Outside the United States, only in Scandinavia were early telephone facilities both efficient and relatively widely used. By 1900, one in every 60 people in the United States had a telephone, in Switzerland one in 129, in Sweden one in 155, in Germany one in 397, in France one in 1,216, in Italy one in 2,629, and in Russia one in 6,988.

During most of the twentieth century, telephone service remained under monopolies or government control throughout the world. The breakup of monopolies occurred first in the three biggest telephone markets, the United States, the United Kingdom, and Japan, during the mid-1980s. In the United States, AT&T's monopoly was broken up in 1984 with the spinning off of regional Bell operating companies (RBOCs) and the exclusion of the parent company from offering local telephone services. Also in 1984, British Telecommunications was privatized and the first competitor was issued a license to operate in the United Kingdom. The Japanese state-owned telephone company was privatized and reincorporated as Nippon Telegraph and Telephone Public Corp. (NTT) in 1985. In that same year, three new telephone companies were formed and won approval to compete with NTT. The fact that these former monopolies became more profitable than their state-owned counterparts spurred other countries to follow their example in the 1990s.

TRENDS

A wave of telecommunications service privatization hit the industry in the mid-1990s, following a trend begun in the United States and the United Kingdom in the 1980s. Most of the world's largest companies—NTT, Deutsche Telekom, France Télécom, and others—underwent restructuring to make themselves competitive in the world of publicly traded, diversified global telecoms. These changes allowed telecommunications companies to take advantage of new technology and more efficient operating methods to meet the growing demand for improved quality of service and lower long distance rates. Deregulation also permitted telephone companies to form strategic partnerships with other companies and acquire expertise and innovative technology.

Since competition can lead to both lower rates and better quality, which in turn can stimulate higher volume usage of telephone services and greater revenues, some telecoms have welcomed heightened competition. However, others have feared rapid loss of market share and have stepped up anti-competitive practices, at least unofficially. In 1990, only Japan, the United Kingdom, and the United States permitted competition in basic telecommunications services. By 1995, eight more countries opened up their markets to competition, and by the end of 1998, the International Telecommunication Union expected more than eighteen additional countries to follow this trend. The countries of the European Union were scheduled to open their telecommunications markets to competition in 1998, and some changes took place sooner.

In the local telephone services market, not only will there be competition among local exchange carriers, but new competition is also expected from cellular/personal communication services providers, and from traditional long distance companies entering local markets. Telephone carriers are also entering into competition with other industries, most commonly cable television system operators and Internet service providers. Cable operators are beginning to offer voice and interactive video services through cable networks, and telephone companies are seeking to expand their services to include video.

The volume of telephone traffic rose by approximately 12 percent annually through 2000, according to the International Telecommunication Union (ITU). In 2000 the ITU estimated that telecommunications service users placed 35.8 billion calls. Greater penetration of telecommunications services and greater efficiency were expected to drive increases. Because of more efficient technology and competition, analysts predicted that the price of telecommunications services would drop worldwide.

The trade journal *Telephony* reported that three factors would drive new growth in the telecommunications service industry through the current century: trade liberalization, deregulation, and new technology. First, trade regions such as North America, the European Union, Japan, and East Asian countries such as South Korea, Taiwan, and Malaysia, were likely to spur international expansion by the most competitive firms. Second, analysts expected new technology to fuel greater demand. Telecoms had already begun using optical transmission and switching technology, asynchronous transfer mode (ATM), integrated service digital network (ISDN) and T-1 lines for data communication, and satellite-based communication networks in the mid-1990s.

However, despite the trends of many countries to privatize their telecommunications services and to split them up into smaller companies, the opposite trend occurred in the United States. Although the Bell/AT&T monopoly split up into one large long distance service and a number of regional Bell operations, the various players began to merge back into large-scale companies again. For example, Bell Atlantic merged with NYNEX in 1997, becoming the country's second largest telecom, and then merged with GTE to form the powerhouse Verizon, and by 1998 SBC Communications had acquired Pacific Telesis and Ameritech to form the largest local service carrier. Analysts argue that in order for telecoms to maintain fixed costs for infrastructure, which is important for company survival, they must achieve economies of scale. In 2005, SBC announced plans to acquire AT&T.

INTERNATIONALIZATION AND GLOBAL ALLIANCES

With global deregulation and privatization, the industry also was becoming more international. Well-established privatized telecommunications services, especially those in the United Kingdom and the United States, started to either directly offer telephone services in international markets or form joint ventures with phone companies throughout the world to this end. For example, British Telecommunications and MCI Communications Corporation formed a joint venture called Concert to offer a single worldwide service to multinational corporations. Concert, in turn, has established strategic agreements with Norwegian Telecom, Tele Danmark, and Telecom Finland. MCI also has an alliance with the Canadian long distance company Stentor and a joint venture in Mexico. Mexico's telephone market was scheduled to open to competition in 1998 and other U.S. long distance companies have begun forming alliances with Mexican companies. AT&T, meanwhile, formed the WorldPartners alliance to expand its international influence. AT&T owns 50 percent of the WorldPartners joint venture, Kokusai Denshin Denwa of Japan owns 30 percent, and Singapore Telecom owns 20 percent. AT&T also planned to form a joint venture consortium called Unisource with KPN of the Netherlands, Telia of Sweden, PTT of Switzerland, and Telefonica of Spain.

In addition, Deutsche Telekom, France Télécom, and Sprint teamed up to create Global One, which began in 1996 with sales offices in more than sixty countries. Unisource N.V. came about through the equal partnership of four of the Netherlands' telephone service companies and operates in sixteen European countries with AT&T as a cooperative partner. WorldPartners formed as an association of telecoms from around the world, including Bezeq (Israel), KDD (Japan), Hong Kong Telecom, PT Indosat (Indonesia), and Telecom Malaysia.

TELECOMMUNICATIONS SERVICE IN DEVELOPING ECONOMIES

In March 2002 delegates from 152 countries went to Turkey for a global development telecommunications conference, passing the Istanbul Declaration and Action Plan. The plan was a call to action by private and government sectors to bring telecommunications technology to developing nations between 2003 and 2006. The conference also considered financing and innovative forms of cooperation, according to the ITU.

In early 1998 the world's telecommunications services still could not provide even basic telephone service to meet global demand; as of 1996, 42 million people around the world were registered on waiting lists for telephone service. In Cambodia, for example, the number of telephones per 100 people (teledensity) stood at only 0.07, and 25 percent of the ITU's members—including China and India, the world's most populous countries—had teledensities below 1.0. Even though the telecommunications service industry continues to post higher revenues and profits, it hasn't penetrated areas of Africa and Asia that desperately need telephone service—not only for business and personal use, but also for emergencies. Once telephone service penetrates these areas, teledensity nonetheless will grow slowly, taking about 50 years to climb from one telephone per 100 people to 50 telephone lines per 100 people, according to the ITU. Wireless satellite networks and multinational telecommunications operations hold the potential to accelerate the growth of supply and access to telephone and information services.

Emerging Asian economies such as China, Indonesia, Malaysia, the Philippines, Singapore, and Taiwan continued to achieve significant expansion and continued to invest hundreds of billions in telecommunications infrastructure. Because of the high cost, telephone companies have formed joint ventures and alliances with companies and governments from developed countries.

WIRELESS TELECOMMUNICATIONS SERVICES

The wireless telecommunications segment was one of the fastest-growing segments in the industry, expanding at an accelerated pace throughout the 1990s, but slowing significantly in the early 2000s because of overproduction problems. Cellular phone and paging services were the biggest segments. Cellular services led the way as forerunners in telecommunications service deregulation and liberalization because no universal service requirements existed and because cellular service afforded private companies strong growth potential. In spite of setbacks in the early 2000s, the wireless telecommunications segment expected robust growth through 2005 as a result of customer appreciation of new innovations such as color, camera insertion, and global Internet access for games, business, and personal use.

Via satellite networks, cellular phone service has the technical capacity to provide service to virtually anyone at any location. Consequently, if companies can provide these services at an affordable cost to users in developing countries with low teledensity levels, such as Africa and Asia, they could experience considerable growth quickly and help relieve the dearth of communications and information services that plagues these regions.

Satellite-based wireless services are inherently geared toward international service in that they transcend national boundaries; one network can provide service throughout the world. The two main kinds of satellite networks include fixed satellite services (FSS) and mobile satellite services (MSS). FSS can provide point-to-point and point-to-multipoint service to permanent locations and can transmit telephone, video, and data signals from satellites to terrestrial receivers or earth stations. MSS serves the mobile communications market by connecting users to a base telephone network. Companies such as Qualcomm and American Mobile Satellite Company began providing these services in the United States in the 1980s. In addition, the Iridium consortium planned to begin operating its network of 66 low-earth-orbiting satellites by September of 1998, providing voice, data, fax, and paging service all over the world. To realize the network's potential, Iridium began seeking approval of national governments to operate its services in their countries. Other satellite-based wireless networks included GlobalStar, an international joint project by Loral, QUALCOMM, AirTouch, France Télécom, Alcatel, and Hyundai, among others; and Teledesic, owned by Craig O. McCaw, Microsoft, and AT&T Wireless Services.

CURRENT CONDITIONS

According to the ITU, there were 2.5 billion people with telephone service worldwide in 2003, an average of 40.32 per 100. As would be expected, that figure varied widely depending on world regions. Europe, with 767 million total telephone lines, had the highest average, with 96.28 per 100 people. Africa, on the other hand, had the lowest average, with 71 million total telephone lines representing an average of only 8.65 per 100 people. While Asia had the highest total number of telephone lines, with 1 billion or 40 percent of the worldwide total, it also had the second lowest average, with 28.52 per 100 people. Conversely, Oceania had the fewest total lines, with 30 million, and the second highest average, with 94.85 per 100 people. The combined Americas had 567 million lines, an average of 66.62 per 100 people.

The wireless services segment was experiencing the most growth during the mid-2000s, due in part to the new generation of young people who have grown up preferring digital, online, and wireless technologies of all persuasions. In fact, so-called "wireless substitution" was seen by some industry analysts as the greatest threat to traditional landlines. A 2004 study from TRBI and Research Now! reported that of wireless customers between 16 and 35 years old, 10 percent did not use fixed phone lines. Among respondents from France, 19 percent reported having never used a fixed line phone at all. The Yankee Group reported that 40 percent of the overall market in Europe was wireless.

One of the trends for wireless customers was a preference toward pre-paid calling plans over flat rate subscriptions. According to Baskerville, by 2009 users of pre-paid services would command 59 percent of the total wireless market. Causing the wireless phone segment to grow in the mid-2000s were add-on services and innovations such as color displays, camera insertion, and global Internet access for games, business, and personal use. According to Alexander Resources, so-called infotainment services—SMS (short message service) messaging, data and finance management tools, and news and sports services, among others—were expected to grow from US$1.5 billion in 2004 to US$7.2 billion by 2008. Additionally, the research firm IDC indicated that SMS messaging was set to explode in popularity, from 2.4 billion messages in 2002 to a projected 31.0 billion by 2007. This utilization uptick was expected to push the value of SMS to US$2.0 billion.

Major companies in the industry were seeing greater market growth through service bundling. Bundled offerings might include any combination of local, long-distance, wireless, or Internet services, depending on the company and plan. But with the new trend came a new challenger. Although still in the early stages in 2003, online phone services, in which phone calls take place over the Internet, were overcoming early problems with quality and features and were rising in popularity.

Increased competition between fixed and mobile service providers, a maturation of markets in developed countries, and a large and growing potential market in developing countries such as China and India, was causing many companies to globalize and improve their domestic positions through mergers and acquisitions and through marketing and operational alliances.

RESEARCH AND TECHNOLOGY

Although integrated service/equipment companies persist, despite such notable divestitures as AT&T's spin-off of its equipment arm as Lucent Technologies, most new technology in telephone communications is developed by the industry's supplier, the equipment industry (see **Telecommunications Equipment**). The telephone service industry, in turn, follows through by developing methods of commercializing the innovations in equipment to provide new and better services. Some telephone service operators actually spend nothing on research and development, merely adopting technology developed by others. Whether innovations in equipment technology are translated into new services depends not only on the commercial viability of the technology itself, but also on the adoption of industry-wide standards and a favorable regulatory environment.

The adoption of integrated circuits, computers, and software in the switching operations of telephone service companies has led to greater capacity, lower costs, improved quality, and enhanced features in telephone services. For the full utilization of integrated circuits and computerized capabilities, the telephone central switching facilities and lines must be digital, rather than analog as they have traditionally been. Telephone systems throughout the world are being converted from analog to digital, and customers with providers still using analog are growing increasingly impatient for updates.

Not only do equipment innovations enhance telephone service, but new types of equipment can also take better advantage of the services. More types of equipment are being connected to public switched telecommunications networks, such as fax machines, computers, and mobile telephone base transceivers. The integration of telephone services with computer technology recently led to the introduction of videoconferencing services.

Low-cost laser and fiber-optics have greatly expanded the carrying capacity and bandwidth of information links. Optical fiber is a thin glass filament that transmits information as pulses of light. Light pulses are not affected by random radiation in the environment, as electrical pulses are, and can travel much farther than electrical signals without attenuation, so that higher sound quality is maintained without the use of repeater devices. Also, fiber-optic cable has the advantage of being more secure, because it does not generate electromagnetic radiation that can be detected. Public telecommunication operators throughout the world are in the process of installing fiber-optic cable, often to replace copper wire. Replacement of copper wire by fiber-optic cable is expected for business customers in many countries and for most residential customers in a few countries.

Recent advancements in mobile telephone services have included the ability to transmit at higher frequencies and the splitting of cell areas into smaller areas to increase the level of radio frequency re-use. Cellular services, which at first were only analog, increasingly use digital technology, which provides greater capacity through the more efficient use of the radio-wave spectrum. Digital cellular networks are most pervasive in Europe, whereas in the United States most are still analog. It is becoming possible for subscribers to use cellular phones outside a basic service area because of alliances among cellular service providers. Wireless communications systems based on networks of low earth-orbiting satellites are also being developed.

A new telecommunications technology standard developed in the 1980s, which began replacing standard telephone lines in the 1990s, is integrated service digital network (ISDN). ISDN permits the transmission of voice, video, and data simultaneously over a single digital communications line. It uses out-of-band signaling, which sends control information over a separate channel, and transmits data at 128 kilobits (kbps) per second. However, with its inconsistent costs and with the existence of faster telephones lines, ISDN experienced only mixed success in the mid-1990s. T-1 lines, on the other hand, have much larger bandwidth and can transmit data as fast as 1.54 megabytes per second (Mbps), but high prices hindered their popularity in earlier years. Asymmetric digital subscriber lines (ADSL), another telephone line alternative, reach speeds of 6 to 8 Mbps.

During the 2000s, wireless providers were in various stages of developing improved technology known as third generation (3G) wireless access. Until 3G, wireless Internet access was slow, giving cellular phones limited text-based information, according to the U.S. Department of Labor. Systems with 3G wireless access transmit data at high speeds and speed up Internet access. Connected to a house or business by antenna, 3G wireless becomes the equivalent of line systems. By 2005, 3G wireless access had been launched to great success in Italy and Britain, with Italy having more than 2.5 million subscribers by the end of 2004.

WORKFORCE

Telephone carriers are unusual for companies of their size in that they employ almost their entire workforce in local markets. Although the telephone communications industry remains a significant source of domestic employment in many countries, its share has continued to decline. The falling number of jobs in the industry came as companies sought greater efficiency, more automation, and relied more upon outsourcing. Thus, while employment in the telephone communications industry is declining, employment within a broad range of industries providing telecommunication-related services remains strong. The nature of the workforce is also changing; the adoption of computer technology by telephone service providers requires employees with new skills.

In 2003 there were about 1.08 million wage and salary jobs in the U.S. telecommunications industry, according to the U.S. Department of Labor, with about half employed in wired communications and 20 percent in wireless. The average salary was US$49,420.

INDUSTRY LEADERS

CHINA MOBILE (HONG KONG) LIMITED

Listed on the New York and Hong Kong stock exchanges in 1997, China Mobile was the world's largest mobile phone company on a subscriber basis, serving 214 million customers in March 2005. With 2004 revenues of almost US$25 billion, the company provided employment to more than 88,000 people. The company was formed as the result of the reforming and restructuring of China's telecommunication industry in preparation for entry into the World Trade Organization. Its parent company, China Mobile Communications, remained government owned, but British Telecom giant Vodafone owned just over 2 percent of the shares. The two companies had a strategic alliance, sharing management, technical and operational expertise, research, and new product and service introductions.

VODAFONE GROUP PLC

The number two ranked wireless phone provider in the world was the United Kingdom'Vodafone. At the end of 2004, service was provided to approximately 151.8 million customers in Continental Europe, the United Kingdom, the United States and the Far East. The company employed 60,000 people.

Founded in 1984 as a paging company, the company became independent from its parent, Racal Electronics, in 1991. After merging with AirTouch Communications of the United States in 1999, the resulting company became the largest mobile phone provider at the time. Verizon Wireless in the United States—a joint venture launched in 2000 following the combination of Vodafone's U.S. interests and Bell Atlantic's U.S. cellular, paging and PCS services— is a market leader in the U.S.

VERIZON COMMUNICATIONS

The number one telecommunications firm in the United States in 2004 was Verizon Communications, a company whose growth has seemed all that more spectacular compared to the declining fortunes of its American rivals. The company posted revenues of US$71.3 billion in 2004, and net income of US$7 billion. In addition, the company has a 55 percent interest in the joint venture Verizon Wireless, the number one wireless provider in 2004, which was created in partnership with Vodafone PLC of the United Kingdom. By March 2005, the company employed 214,000 people, had

52.2 million access lines, and had 45.5 million wireless customers.

The Verizon company came into being as a result of the Bell Atlantic Corp. merger with NYNEX Corp., quickly followed with the GTE Corp. merger that ended in the name change to Verizon. Bell was once the leading name in regional phone providing, but Verizon has kept the local providing and has also become a giant provider of long distance, wireless services, and Internet services. In February 2005, the company announced its plans to acquire MCI, the company formed after long distance provider WorldCom filed for the largest bankruptcy in history as a result of accounting fraud. Verizon estimated the acquisition would add US$7 billion in revenue and savings.

NIPPON TELEGRAPH AND TELEPHONE CORP. (NTT)

The world's number one telecommunications service company, NTT posted total 2004 revenues of US$105.67 billion, divided among telephone services including both subscriber lines and cellular telephone services, telecommunications equipment, and other services such as pagers, digital data exchange, integrated service digital network (ISDN) and F-net, leased circuit services, data communication facility services, and telegraph services. NTT also does a small amount of business in selling terminal equipment.

NTT was incorporated as a publicly traded company in 1985 to replace state-owned telecommunications monopoly Nippon Telegraph and Telephone Public Corporation (NTTPC). Although NTT enjoyed a monopoly of Japan's telephone service market, by 1999 the company decided to reorganize and split into separate companies, including two regional services and a long distance service provider. The company also owned 63.5 percent of Japan's leading mobile phone company, NTT DoCoMo. In 2004, NTT employed more than 205,000 people. In 2005, the company announced that it be would end its pager service in 2007, as the number of customers had decreased to 290,000 from a high in 1996 of 6.49 million.

AT&T CORPORATION

One of the U.S.'s leading long distance companies, with more than 30 million customers and 2004 revenues of US$34.5 billion, AT&T was poised to become one of the biggest telecommunications companies in the U.S. with the 2005 announcement of its pending acquisition by SBC Communications.

AT&T originated in 1877 as the Bell Telephone Company, founded by telephone inventor Alexander Graham Bell and his financial sponsors, and changed its name to American Telephone and Telegraph (AT&T)in 1899. AT&T was the parent company of affiliated regional Bell operating companies, and in the early twentieth century AT&T aggressively acquired many smaller competitors. The Graham Act of 1921 exempted telecommunications from the Sherman Antitrust Act, enabling AT&T to maintain a monopoly. In 1982 a Justice Department suit led to a 1984 settlement whereby AT&T had to divest itself of its regional Bell operating companies and stop offering local telephone service. However, U.S. telecom deregulation in the 1990s reinstated AT&T's ability to carry local service. By 1997 the company completed restructuring to focus on three core areas of business: international telephone service, wireless communications service, and Internet access. In 2000, the company further restructured into a group of separate publicly held companies: AT&T, AT&T Wireless, and AT&T Broadband. In 2002, AT&T Broadband merged with Comcast.

DEUTSCHE TELEKOM AG

As the world's third largest and Europe's number one telecommunications service as well as Germany's top fixed phone line provider, Deutsche Telekom (DT) booked more than US$78 billion in total revenues for 2004. More than a third of the company's revenues were generated outside of Germany in the 64 other countries in which it does business, including the United States with its T-Mobile service. With 247,000 employees worldwide, the company had facilities supporting 57.2 million line telephone connections, 77.4 million mobile telephone subscriptions, and 6.1 million DSL customers in 2004. The company also provided paging, interactive videotext, telex, cable television connections, and equipment for television and radio broadcasting and videoconferencing.

Deutsche Telekom was named Deutsche Bundespost Telecom until January 1995 and was established as a state-owned company in 1989 when Germany's posts and telecommunications organization, Deutsche Bundespost, was split into three separate entities for postal, bank postal, and telecommunications services. DT remained under the indirect control of the Ministry of Posts and Telecommunications during the 1990s.

The company struggled to adapt to the industry's new competitive environment of the late 1990s. Some of its practices, which severely penalized customers for leaving its service, drew the ire of EU competition regulators, who considered the German behemoth to be flaunting its anti-competitive tactics. On the other hand, new figures released by Deutsche Telekom in 2001 and 2002 showed a company that apparently won over customers again. In April 2002, Deutsche Telekom's mobile communications companies and shareholdings boasted 66.9 million subscribers. The company's shareholdings reflected a global presence, with DT involvement outside Germany in the United States, the United Kingdom, the Czech Republic, and Croatia.

BT GROUP PLC

The number one telecommunications company in the United Kingdom, BT Group had 29 million lines in 2004, with one million business customers and 19 million consumer customers. Total 2004 revenue was more than US$34 billion and the company employed almost 100,000.

The British Telecommunications Corporation was established in 1981 as a state-owned company, taking telecommunications services out of the post office. The company was privatized and incorporated as British Telecommunications PLC in 1984. The government retained a 48.6 percent stake in the company until 1991. The company further evolved so that in 2002, British Telecommunications PLC (BT) was a wholly owned subsidiary of the BT Group, a holding company. British Telecommunications boasted more than 28 million exchange lines in April 2002 in the United Kingdom. The BT Group's biggest problem in the 2000s was that it lacked the growth potential of rivals France Télécom and Deutsche Telekom, according to an April 2002 *Bloomberg News* article.

FRANCE TÉLÉCOM. SA

France Télécom was established as a state-owned corporation in 1991, replacing the government agency Direction Générale des Postes et des Télécommunications (DGT). The company lost its monopoly in some areas of telecommunications in 1993, with the permission of competing value-added network providers to operate in accordance with the European Union's Open Network Provision. In 2004, the French government owned about 56 percent of the company.

The company garnered 2004 revenues of approximately US$64 billion serving 118.6 million customers in 220 countries and territories. In addition to traditional phone service, France Télécom also provided audiovisual, mobile, cable television, Internet, and terminal telecommunications equipment and software. Its U.K.-based Orange wireless division had 50 million subscribers in 16 countries.

TELEFÓNICA S.A.

With its focus on Spanish and Portuguese-speaking markets, in the mid-2000s Telefónica served over 100 million customers in 13 countries, offering fixed and cellular services. The company had reported sales of more than US$42 billion and employed 173,554 people. In 2004, the company agreed to buy the Latin American assets of U.S. firm BellSouth, making it the leading mobile operator in the region. In March 2005, the company continued acquiring companies, but this time out of its usual domain: a 51 percent stake in Czech phone company, Cesky Telecom, which was being privatized by the Czech government.

MAJOR COUNTRIES IN THE INDUSTRY

THE UNITED STATES

Euromonitor International reported in 2003 that the U.S. market for telephone services was valued at US199.3 billion, a decrease of 1.5 percent from 2002 values. Of this value, the long distance market was estimated to account for 48.8 percent. The cellular and wireless market was valued at US$5.2 billion in 2003.

The telephone communications industry in the United States is unusual in that it is divided into a national and international long distance market as well as a local and regional market. This legal segmentation of the industry stems from the 1984 breakup of the AT&T monopoly. The 22 local Bell operating companies evolved into six regional Bell operating companies, each with its own geographic area of service. These are Bell Atlantic (which acquired NYNEX in 1997) in the Northeast and mid-Atlantic states; Ameritech (acquired by SBC Communications in 1998) in the Midwest; BellSouth in the Southeast; SBC Communications, which operates under Southwestern Bell and Pacific Bell (and acquired Pacific Telesis) in the West and Southwest; and US West in the West. These companies hold monopolies on local telephone service and also tend to dominate local toll and long distance service within their regions.

In 1996 Congress passed the Telecommunications Act of 1996, which promised to open up local markets for competition and permit local telephone companies, national long distance companies, and cable television providers to all compete in the same markets. In addition, the act allows U.S. companies to court international customers and international telecommunications services to penetrate the U.S. market. The immediate result of the act was the bundling of services by telecommunications providers, wherein companies expanded their service arsenals to include local and long distance service as well as wireless, cable, and Internet access services. The legislation gave rise to large-scale mergers.

By 2005, the traditional wireline telephone sector in the U.S. was facing immense competition from cable and wireless companies. Technology known as Voice over Internet Protocol (VoIP) was allowing these companies to provide customers with a bundled package of telecom services, including voice, data and video. However, in 2004, the Federal Communications Commission (FCC) ruled that those companies that had been providing local service at the time of the 1996 Act (known as incumbent local exchange carriers or ILECs), would not have to lease their new fiber lines to competitors. The 2005 announcement of the plans to merge AT&T into SBC Communications, MCI into Verizon, and wireless providers Sprint and Nextel, showed signs that the industry would continue to restructure in the face of increasing competition both domestically and internationally.

CHINA

According to research carried out by DTT, by 2004, China was adding approximately 62 million mobile subscribers per year, much higher than the next highest country, the United States, which was adding 15 million subscribers annually. In terms of active phone lines, China had the second highest number in the world with 22 million, compared to the U.S. with 32 million lines. China was expected to take the lead within the next few years. It was also expected that Chinese companies in the industry would begin to expand beyond their borders. Analysts at The Insight Research Corporation were predicting that with the growth occurring in China, the Asia/Pacific region would overtake North America by 2007 in terms of the amount of revenue received from the telecommunications industry due primarily to the large size of the underserved population. In 2003, the four state-owned telecommunications companies (China Unicom, China Mobile, China Telecom Corp., and China Netcom) had a combined market share of 98.4 percent.

JAPAN

Japan's telephone services are divided between domestic and international. The privatization of Japan's telecommunications services in 1985 resulted in the creation of Nippon Telegraph and Telephone Public Corp. (NTT) for national domestic service and Kokusai Denshin Denwa (KDD) for international service. In that same year three new, independent telephone companies established themselves and won approval to compete with NTT: Daini-Denden, Nippon

Telecom, and Teleway Japan. NTT and KDD nevertheless continue to dominate their respective markets.

In April 2002, the industry was abuzz with the *Mobile Media Japan* report that NTT DoCoMo, NTT's mobile subsidiary, would release a hand-held mobile phone with a speech synthesizer that detects mouth movements. This phone would allow the caller to merely mouth words to be heard by the person on the other end, doing away with an annoyance that has made mobile phone users unpopular in airports and restaurants. The news was welcomed because sales of cell phones had been steadily dropping since January 2001 at the rate of 2.4 percent per year, according to Gartner Japan Ltd., an affiliate of the Gartner Group based in the United States. In 2002, NTT DoCoMo was facing increasing competition from international telecommunications giant KDDI (under the brand of AU Corp.), a company formed in the 1990s by the merger of former rivals DDI, IDO, KDD, and Tu-ka, according to an Ovum report. By 2005, Deloitte Touche Tohmatsu analysts were predicting that consolidation and price wars would continue in Japan.

In 2003, Euromonitor research showed the Japanese market for fixed line telephone services was valued at US$57.8 billion, with the cellular market picking up customers with a market value of US$88.7 billion. Local calls accounted for 51 percent of the value of the fixed line sector. NTT accounted for a substantial share of the market, at 79 percent. By 2008, the market for fixed line services was expected to fall by 22 percent.

GERMANY

Euromonitor data showed that the German market for telecommunications services dropped by 14.1 percent between 2002 and 2003. However, the cellular market grew by 9.8 percent during this period, with 75 percent of the population having some type of mobile phone. Deutsche Telecom was the industry leader with a huge share of the fixed line market (82.4 percent). The cellular market was dominated by four companies: T-Mobil Deutsche Telekom, Mannesmann Mobilfunk, E-Plus Mobilfunk, and the most recent entrant, Viag Interkom.

Deutsche Telekom became the biggest European provider of high speed DSL access in 2002, as the number of customer lines increased from 600,000 in 2000 to 2.2 million in 2001. The company also supplied 55.6 million customer telephone lines. However, in April of 2002, unexpected inflation in Europe had an adverse impact on Deutsche Telekom, which saw its stocks drop 3 percent virtually overnight. The ITU ranked Germany the third largest telephone service market in 1995, representing around US$48 billion in sales. Germany had 53.8 telephone lines per 100 people and 11.6 cellular subscribers per 100 people in 1996, according to the ITU. Deutsche Telekom held a monopoly for years on basic telephone services, including local and international switched networks, but since 1989, mobile telephone service, paging, videotext services, and some satellite communications systems have been open to competition. Moreover, as part of the European Union's telecommunications service agreement, Deutsche Telekom began privatizing its operations as of 1998.

UNITED KINGDOM

Britain was considered the most deregulated telecommunications market in the world for its size, permitting competition on the local, national, and international levels. Following the privatization of BT in 1984, there was a period of a duopoly between BT and Mercury Communications Ltd. until 1991. In the early 1990s, many more small competitors entered the market, including cable television operators and foreign telecommunications companies. The mobile communications market opened up for competition in 1985.

By 2003, BT was still the largest telecommunications company in the country, according to Euromonitor, owning 90 percent of all phone lines. However, its market share had been decreasing, reaching 62.7 percent by 1993. This was due to the increasing use of mobile and data services over those of fixed line. The total market size showed a decline of 7.1 percent over 2002 values, reaching US$46 billion. However, the cellular market grew by 7.7 percent, attaining a subscriber base of 52.6 million users by 2003, a number expected to reach 62.8 million by 2008.

FRANCE

With a telecommunications market valued by Euromonitor at US$35 billion in 2003, France's fixed line services were expected to continue to be eroded by the use of new technologies including cable, mobile, and VoIP. The number of fixed lines decreased by 1.7 percent during 2003, as businesses and other multiple line users moved to mobile phones. The cellular market was expected to grow from 2003 levels of 40.9 million subscribers to 48.4 million by 2008. State-owned France Télécom dominated both the fixed line (63.1 percent market share) and cellular markets (50.2 percent).

In the mid-1990s France Télécom held a monopoly on switched- networked local, trunk, and international telephone service, along with leased lines. A duopoly existed for mobile communications. Data communications were opened to competition in 1993. France Télécom moved to privatize in 1997 to meet its January 1998 deadline to comply with the EU mandate. In 2000, the company purchased the U.K.-based cellular provider Orange. By 2003, the company still held 69.8 percent of the telecommunications market, but it share continued to be hampered by competitors.

FURTHER READING

"The 2005 Telecommunications Industry Review: An Anthology of Market Facts and Forecasts." The Insight Research Corporation, February 2005. Available from http:// www.insight-corp.com/ execsummaries/2005Reviewexecsum.pdf.

Adegoke, Yinka. "10 Percent of European Youth Never Use Fixed Phone Lines." *New Media Age,* 12 February 2004.

———. "Pay-as-You-Go Mobile Users to Outnumber Subscribers." *New Media Age,* 25 February 2004.

"AT&T Looks to Disconnect from Traditional Phone Service Market." *Wireless News,* 22 July 2004.

Baker, Stephen, and Heather Green. "Big Bang!" *Business Week,* 21 June 2004.

"Cablecos Threaten Telcos." *The Online Reporter,* 23 August 2003.

"Cell Phone Revenues May Surpass Land Lines in Europe." *The Online Reporter,* 28 February 2004.

Cellular Telecommunications and Internet Association (CTIA), 2002. Available from http://www.wow-com.com.

Cimilluca, Dana. "SBC Communications to Eliminate 8,000 Jobs This Year." *Bloomberg News,* 18 April 2002.

———. "Telephone-Cell Phones Expected to Exceed Fixed Lines in 2002." *EFE News Service,* 8 February 2002.

Dillon, Nancy. "Dialing for a Deal: AT&T Wireless, Cingular Seen in Merger Talks." *New York Daily News,* 16 April 2002.

Draper, Deborah J., ed. *Business Rankings Annual.* Detroit: Thomson Gale, 2004.

Fuller, Meghan. "CLEC Build Strategy Changes Focus." *Lightwave,* August 2003.

"Hoover's Company Capsules." 2004. Available from http://www.hoovers.com.

International Telecommunication Union, 2004. Available from http://www.itu.int.

"International Trade Statistics." 2003. Available from http://www.wto.org.

KMI Corp., 2002. Available from http://www.kmicorp.com.

Krapf, Eric. "Progress Report." *Business Communications Review,* July 2003.

Lagesse, David. "Who Needs Phone Lines?" *U.S. News & World Report,* 11 August 2003.

Lanman, Scott. "Siemens to Resell Motorola Phones, Buy Motorola Chips." *Bloomberg News,* 15 April 2002.

"Major Market Profiles (short profiles): Executive Summaries." Euromonitor International, 2004. Available from http://www.euromonitor.com.

"Mexico's Mobile Sector Neck and Neck with Fixed-Line Business." *Latin America Telecom,* September 2003.

"Mobile Infotainment Services to Reach $7.2b in '08." *The Online Reporter,* 10 January 2004.

"Mobile Lines Overtakes Fixed in Delhi." *India Telecom,* July 2003.

"Mobile Media Japan," 2002. Available from http://www.discuss.mobilemediajapan.com.

"More Than 11 Million Cellular Lines in Argentina by Year-End." *Latin America Telecom,* June 2004.

Morrison, Diane See. "States of Play." *New Media Age,* 15 April 2004.

Nikkei AsiaBizTech, 2002. Available from http://www.nikkeibp.asiabiztech.com.

Ovum Reports, 2002. Available from http://www.ovum.com.

"Reconnected to growth: Global Telecommunications Industry Index 2005." Deloitte Touche Tohmatsu, 2005. Available from www.deloitte.com.

"Trend of Consumers Switching from Wireline to Wireless-Only Phone Service to Intensify in 2004." *The Mobile Internet (Boston, MA),* December 2003.

"UK Stocks Advance." *Bloomberg News,* 5 April 2002.

Vittore, Vince, and Glenn Bischoff. "Bundling Strategy Provides Soft Landing." *Telephony,* 27 October 2003.

Wearden, Graeme. "NT DoCoMo Hits 20 Million Subscribers." *Net UK News,* 5 March 2001. Available from http://www.news.zdnet.co.uk.

SIC 4833

NAICS 515120

TELEVISION BROADCASTING STATIONS

This industry includes companies that broadcast television programs to the public. Included are commercial, religious, educational, and other television stations, and organizations that primarily provide television broadcasting services and also produce programs. See also **Cable and Other Pay Television Services.**

Industry Snapshot

In the early twenty-first century, television-broadcasting stations faced more challenges than ever as the number of options for mass communications and information technology exploded. Followed by satellite broadcasting and the Internet, cable television had grown as a threat to, and a possible partner with, traditional broadcast stations. While it was unlikely that broadcast networks, with their strong ability to provide mass audiences for advertisers, would soon be eliminated, newer medias were likely to take a growing share of listener and viewer time from broadcast stations.

The world's television market was valued at US$130.7 billion in 2003, a value predicted to increase to US$178 billion by 2008. After three years of a slowdown in growth, the television industry was showing signs of recovery in 2004, with the United States predicted to show the strongest growth at a compound annual growth rate of 7.5 percent. Canada followed, with a growth rate of 6.1 percent, Latin America with 6.1 percent, Asia with 5.5 percent, and the EMEA (Europe, the Middle East, and Africa) with 4.3 percent. As of 2004, more than three-fourths of the revenue spent on advertising was spent on television, and the numbers were still rising.

Organization and Structure

One of the unifying features of broadcasting around the world was government regulation. Television—which did not exist until the mid to late 1940s—developed during a century of growing government control over industry. Also, airwaves were seen in most countries as a scarce public resource. As such, nearly every television market in the world was tightly regulated or directly controlled by the government from its inception. With its high public profile, television broadcasting in many countries was often the focus of controversy over violence, sexual content, and cultural content. In the United States, TV programs were frequently the focus of boycotts by various groups; the U.S. Senate went so far as to pass a bill in 1995 requiring that new televisions contain "violence-blocking" circuitry.

The controversies surrounding television demonstrated that it was a major cultural force in the world economy, one that was undergoing rapid change. New technology and political changes drove major changes in the regulatory and business climate for broadcast stations and networks around the world in the mid to late 1990s. In Europe, public service broadcasting was the only game in town for many decades, as monolithic state-run institutions provided the programs they thought would educate and entertain. In communist countries the state was the network, and television existed to legitimize the government and inform people of its activities. In the United States, three huge commercial networks provided the kind of programs people would watch, based on rating systems. In all cases, viewers' choices were limited. However, by 1995 most of these broadcast monopolies or oligopolies had either disappeared or were in decline.

From the end of World War II to the 1980s, most European countries had two or three state-owned television channels paid for by taxes or license fees. However, in the 1980s and early 1990s, almost every western European country deregulated its broadcast system, adding commercial channels to the mix. Political change spurred this trend, as did the advent of new cable and satellite channels. The change was dramatic. In 1980 there were about 40 television channels in the countries that, as of 2002, made up the European Union (EU). By 1994 there were 150 European channels, with more than 50 of those channels coming by satellite. In 2001, fully 95 percent of homes in the EU had TV and spent 3.5 hours a day watching programming.

The development of digital TV for both terrestrial and satellite transmission, as opposed to traditional analog transmission, helped increase the number of channels even more. For example, Astra 1E, Europe's first dedicated digital satellite, began operating on January 1, 1995. In 1996 Italian pay TV group Telepiu launched three digital channels, and French pay TV operator Canal Plus launched a "bouquet" of 20 digital channels. In the United Kingdom, the government wanted all technical, political, and commercial criteria for digital TV to be worked out by early 1998. The United Kingdom was seen as the world leader in digital terrestrial television broadcasting.

A Unified Future

Some industry observers predicted the ultimate merger of telephone companies, print media, broadcasters, cable stations, and computers into one giant industry. Such media convergence would dramatically change the role of television and shift the balance of power from traditional broadcast, often called "terrestrial" television, to satellite transmission.

However transmitted, television was still clearly a growing industry. From 1980 to 1994, the number of television sets in the world nearly tripled, reaching 1 billion. Ownership of TV sets rose by about 5 percent annually worldwide, 10 percent in Asia, in the early 2000s.

While viewers may have virtually unlimited options in the future, that does not mean they will spend more time viewing, or interacting with, television. According to research by NBC conducted in the early 1990s, when viewers were presented with a choice of up to 100 channels, they actually used only eight regularly.

Background and Development

Early Television

The world's first regular television service was established in England by the British Broadcasting Corporation (BBC) in 1936. The BBC launched its second TV channel, BBC2, in 1964. Over the years, BBC programs were acclaimed for their dramatic quality. The BBC's television monopoly ended in 1954 when the British Parliament established the Independent Television Authority (ITV), which grew into a consortium of 15 regional television companies, each operating a single channel within an assigned area. The organization later became the Independent Broadcast Authority (IBA) when radio was added to its charter. IBA television companies produced many of their own programs and generated revenue through the sale of commercial airtime.

The first television networks in the United States—NBC, CBS, ABC, and DuMont—began life as divisions of major radio networks and television and radio manufacturers. While DuMont's network failed in the 1950s, the big three went on to dominate television broadcasting in the United States, a position they held almost unchallenged until the 1980s, when cable television and a new network, Fox Broadcasting, began to seriously challenge the big three for viewing time. Of programming in the 1950s, then-TV performer Ernie Kovacs used to joke that it was right to call it a medium—TV being neither rare nor well done.

In the Soviet Union, television broadcasting was exclusively a propaganda arm of the government until the late 1980s, when Communist party and state control over the media was relaxed. In July 1990 Chairman Mikhail Gorbachev ordered major changes in the state-run broadcasting monopoly that allowed television outlets to be run independently of political organizations and provide objective coverage of news events. The complete collapse of the communist government continued this trend, although restrictions on television broadcasts remained. In 2002 many journalists and private citizens in Russia were angered as TV6, the last independent television station, owned by outspoken, banished Russian media mogul Boris Berezovsky, found itself under government supervision after being highly critical of President Vladimir Putin and having its plug pulled during a broadcast. Some journalists talked of starting up the controversial station again, but plans in 2002 were vague at best, according to the *Financial Times.*

Financial Difficulties

The financial difficulties of the three big U.S. networks in 2001-2002 reflected those across the entire television broadcasting industry. Instead of ad sales soaring as they had in times of plenty, the ad sales of the "big three" television networks—CBS, NBC, and Capital Cities/ABC Inc.—plummeted in the early 2000s. The Broadcast Cable Financial Management Association, which tracked TV revenues, said the trio combined for a 10 percent loss in revenue, the worst performance by an industry used to making money in spite of poor quality programming. Revenue for the three big networks from ad dollars shrunk from US$11.4 billion in 2000 to US$10.2 billion in 2001, according to the Broadcast Cable Financial Management Association's report. Perhaps in an even more dramatic industry change, the Federal Communications Commission (FCC) regulations that kept conglomerates from swallowing up air space were disappearing fast. In the early twenty-first century, it appeared as if TV was going to join books, periodicals, and other media in the rush to form huge conglomerates—even if doing so was at the expense of TV viewers, noted the *San Francisco Chronicle* in a 2002 article.

Until the mid-1970s, television broadcasting was a fairly stable industry. With few exceptions, broadcasts stayed neatly within national boundaries. The Soviet Union and other communist nations exercised complete state control over the airwaves. In western Europe, state-owned or state-chartered corporations broadcast a limited amount of programming—much of it educational in nature—while commercial channels were almost nonexistent. Japan had a strong television market, but the rest of Asia remained relatively undeveloped. In the United States, the big three television networks reached a mass audience of consumers, all with apparently similar tastes. U.S. television networks, prohibited by law from producing their own prime time shows, mostly acted as distributors of other companies' entertainment products.

In less than three decades, the industry had changed drastically. By the late 1990s and 2000s, rapid technological and political change had completely changed the rules of the global broadcasting industry. In former communist nations, fledgling commercial television stations challenged state-run corporations, which struggled to change with the times. In Europe, commercial television—distributed by broadcast, cable, and satellite—competed with state-sponsored broadcasters such as the British Broadcasting Corporation (BBC). In the United States, the big three networks saw their audience share drop from 90 percent to about 60 percent in 1995, and to 50 percent by early 1998 as cable companies and then direct satellite transmission gradually chipped away at the audience that networks once took for granted.

Also, by the mid-1990s, Fox Broadcasting Co. had emerged as a legitimate fourth network in the United States. Fox's strategy of targeting young viewers soon paid off, garnering the new network a growing share of the network television market. In February 1998, for the first time, Fox finished ahead of one of the big three networks—ABC—in a critical "sweeps" month. TV networks in the United States used the sweeps months to set future advertising rates. ABC had been in a steady decline for three years following its 1995 purchase by the Disney Company. The declines affected ABC's prime time lineups and its other shows, such as news programming. Fox's strength came from its hit series, which then included audience grabbers such as *Ally McBeal* and *Party of Five*. In 2001, as viewers abandoned the series and, even worse, as Fox's backing of NASCAR, pro football, and pro baseball proved disastrous, the fourth network struggled to attract advertisers to keep its flagship station from weakening further.

Another trend saw more and more networks becoming producers of television programming. Beginning in 1994 in the United States, the FCC allowed networks to produce prime time programs for themselves—and competing networks, in some cases. At the same time, companies formerly devoted to programming, such as Time Warner and Paramount Communications, launched new television networks to guarantee outlets for their productions. Also in 2002, a federal appeals court in the District of Columbia ruled that there should be no restrictions on the number of stations a media outlet could own. The ruling also allowed cable and network stations to be owned by one entity in the same market, according to the *San Francisco Chronicle*. The court decision seemed to pave the way for conglomerate ownership of TV stations, putting much of the nation's communications into the hands of a few giant companies like Disney, AOL Time Warner, Viacom, News Corp., and General Electric, noted the *Chronicle*.

The growing globalization of the broadcast TV industry was also evident in the late 1990s through the early 2000s. For example, in 1995 the FCC relaxed its rules on foreign ownership of television stations, which was expected to bring a number of well-heeled foreign investors into the U.S. market. Growing satellite transmission of television programs made it much easier to distribute programming across national borders. Rupert Murdoch's News Corp. made headlines with its satellite broadcasting systems, British Sky Broadcasting Ltd. and Hong Kong-based Star TV, the latter purchased in 1993. While Star was unprofitable as of 1995, it was transmitting to a vast market of 3 billion people in Asia, in different languages and dialects. India opened its market to private broadcasters, largely in response to the success of Star in that country. Star was even responsible for prompting China to ban the use of home satellite receivers, as the aging communist regime feared its "destabilizing" effects.

COMPETITION FROM CABLE

Beginning in the 1980s, cable television companies became major rivals to broadcast television networks. Cable bypassed traditional broadcast networks by beaming TV signals off satellites to local transmission companies, where the signals were received and re-transmitted to area customers via coaxial cable.

The United States was one of the first major industrial nations to be "wired," and as of 1994 about 66 percent of U.S. households with televisions were hooked up to at least basic cable service, meaning that there were 61 million cable subscribers in the United States. In 2001 cable penetration in all U.S. households had reached 81 percent. However, in 2001 the Hispanic population had a relatively low penetration of 63 percent, with 64 million connected to cable or satellite TV, according to Nielsen Media Research and *Broadcasting and Cable*. In other countries, cable penetration varied widely. For example, as of 1994 cable penetration was just 3.8 percent in the United Kingdom, 5.0 percent in Mexico, and 5.6 percent in France. However, by 1994, cable penetration had reached 55.0 percent in Denmark, 42.3 percent in Germany, 34.8 percent in Spain, and 20.3 percent in Japan.

Broadcast television stations the world over continued to see more competition from cable and direct-to-home (DTH) broadcasters, the latter of which used satellite transmission of programming to reach a growing number of subscribers. This competition, and the growing concentration and globalization of the television industry, continued to buffet the broadcast television market, particularly as countries relaxed ownership rules for broadcast media.

The erosion of broadcast television's market share was the most pronounced in the United States. Ratings for the three biggest broadcast TV networks fell steadily throughout the 1990s, to just 50 percent of the total audience in 1998, while cable and DTH viewership continued to grow. In 1998, the major U.S. networks began a negative marketing battle against cable TV, alleging that cable airtime was less valuable than network airtime since cable attracted viewership that had less buying power than network viewership. In general, the networks claimed that U.S. cable viewers were less affluent and less educated than the U.S. population as a whole.

Cable TV executives argued that the networks' attack was based on "desperation." Indeed, advertising spending on cable in the United States climbed steadily in the 1990s, and in 1998 was expected to top US$9 billion, a 15 percent increase over 1997, when spending was US$7.9 billion. U.S. broadcast TV still led the market, with revenue for 1998 expected to reach US$13 billion for commercial time on the big four networks—ABC, CBS, Fox, and NBC. That represented a 5.2 percent increase from 1997. However, the gap between network and cable in the United States was said to be closing. Paul Kagan Associates, a market research firm, predicted that by 2005, advertisers would be spending US$18.9 billion for commercial time on network TV in the United States and US$14.5 billion on cable.

One area in which U.S. cable TV companies were particularly successful in the 1990s and early 2000s was children's television, which was traditionally dominated by the big networks' Saturday morning cartoon lineup. By the late 1990s and 2000s, however, many U.S. networks had scaled back their children's programming, overwhelmed by cable channels such as Nickelodeon and The Cartoon Network. Those cable channels were also very popular exports, with stations in many countries outside the United States licensing the programming.

Fin-Syn Rules Ended

In the mid-1990s and especially in the early 2000s, the growing alternatives to network television in the United States convinced the FCC to relax many of its restrictions on television station content and ownership. One of the most significant moves was the May 1993 repeal of a rule preventing the networks from producing and owning their own prime time programs. Remaining rules preventing the networks from syndicating shows on their prime time schedule expired in November 1995. This change meant the networks could own rerun rights to the prime time shows they carried, a very profitable part of television production. The end of these rules, together known as "fin-syn," allowed the networks to become production companies rather than simply programming outlets.

U.S. station ownership rules also changed in the 1990s. In 1996, the FCC eliminated the 12-station ownership cap, expanded allowable station group audience reach from a 25 percent limit to at least 30 percent of total U.S. households, and allowed ownership of more than one television station in markets with "effective" competition. In 2002 a federal court ruled that even this new ruling was too restrictive, opening the way for conglomerates such as AOL Time Warner to purchase multiple stations and provide cable TV as well.

When those 1996 regulations went into effect, a bidding war broke out for broadcast properties in the United States. Strong bidding by potential acquirers drove prices up to historic levels as large media companies attempted to expand their asset base. In 1998 that hot market continued. For example, in March 1998, Pulitzer Publishing put its TV and radio holdings up for sale. The company's nine network-affiliated TV stations and five radio stations were expected to be sold for more than US$1 billion. Of Pulitzer's nine TV stations, five were affiliated with NBC and two each with CBS and ABC.

These regulatory changes also had the effect of pushing NBC, ABC, and CBS quickly into the production business. All the networks produced some shows for the 1994-1995 season, and Capital Cities/ABC went to the extent of forming its own studio to produce programming in partnership with the new entertainment company DreamWorks SKG, which included Steven Spielberg.

Exporting Television Programming

Prior to the change in syndication rules, the big four U.S. networks' principal source of syndication revenues was in international sales. CBS, for example, covered production deficits on several programs with international sales in the early 1990s. However, the United States was not the only exporter of television programming. Mexico's Televisa and Brazil's TV Globo exported popular soap operas, called telenovelas, to many countries.

In the late 1990s, American action adventure and drama series continued to sell well in international markets. Programs such as *The X-Files* had wide followings in certain international markets. Germany and the United Kingdom were said to be two key markets for U.S. producers. For example, *The X-Files* was one of the top shows in Germany and one of the few U.S. series to broadcast in prime time, appearing on Germany's ProSieben channel.

Non-U.S. broadcasters, particularly in Germany, were also developing co-financing and co-production deals with U.S. studios rather than paying the very high prices the studios were demanding for the right to broadcast their shows. For example, a joint-production deal between MCA and leading German broadcaster RTL gave RTL access to American programming and provided it with additional revenue from licensing the programming in other regions.

New Networks

While the major networks were happy to be producing their own shows, traditional television production houses feared losing outlets for their programs if the networks moved most of their production in-house. This fear was the main reason behind the founding of two additional U.S. television networks: the Warner Brothers Network and the United Paramount Network (UPN). Warner Brothers had 50 affiliates, and UPN had 96 as of early 1995, with each claiming to reach about 80 percent of U.S. viewers. However, 18 percent of Warner's viewers received the network on cable stations. NBC, ABC, and CBS, in turn, were concerned that Warner and Paramount would choose to pull hit shows they produced from the big three networks and put them on their own networks.

When it came to evening news programming, few twenty-first century viewers under the age of 50 can recall when Walter Cronkite and Huntley-Brinkley practically commandeered all Americans to their TV sets for their nightly dose of news. Even in 1982, the three networks found 72 percent of viewers into the big three evening news broadcasts, a figure that dropped to 60 percent in 1994, according to the Pew Center for the People and Press. In 2000 that figure slipped to 30 percent, and after the 2001 terrorist attacks, only 17 percent of viewers preferred the network news to cable outlets such as CNN when it came to getting hard news, noted Pennington. While it was true that even 17 or 30 percent of all households still represented a large viable audience, the over-50 age group that still liked a nightly news fix was not the megabucks-spending audience that advertising agencies wanted for their free-spending clients.

The large U.S. networks managed to hold on to a mass audience even as their share of the market dwindled. However, major changes were underway in traditional U.S. broadcast TV. For one, the "big three" had become the "big four" by the mid-1990s as Fox evolved into a major player in the broadcast market. Also, two of the major U.S. networks were purchased by larger companies. In 1995, the Walt Disney Company agreed to acquire Capital Cities/ABC for US$19 billion in stock and cash and Westinghouse Electric agreed to acquire CBS Inc. for US$81 a share, or US$5.4 billion, in cash. The Disney/Capital Cities deal was a marriage of a top-flight programming producer with a well-managed broadcasting operation, while the new Westinghouse/CBS merger created a broadcasting giant that included 15 television and 39 radio stations. Neither of these deals would have been possible under the old FCC regulations. Further consolidation in the U.S. television broadcasting industry was expected in the late 1990s. The Disney acquisition was expected to have international implications as well. Both Disney and ABC had interests in overseas programming, cable, and broadcast operations and the combined companies were expected to expand non-U.S. operations.

CURRENT CONDITIONS

By 2003, the world's television market was worth US$130.7 billion and, according to analysts at PricewaterhouseCoopers, was expected to increase to US$178 billion by 2008. The industry was experiencing an upswing following three years of slow growth. The United States was predicted to be the beneficiary of most of this growth, with a compound annual growth rate of 7.5 percent. This was followed by Canada, with a growth rate of 6.1 percent, Latin America (6.1 percent), Asia (5.5 percent) and the EMEA (4.3 percent). With their large populations and relatively low market penetration, India and China were expected to be major sources for new growth for the Asian region, as their economic expansion has been the fastest in the world. Non-Chinese television broadcasters were not simply allowed into the market, however. Some, like MTV, were required to syndicate shows to Chinese broadcasters as opposed to having a branded channel. As of 2004, more than three-fourths of the revenue spent on advertising was spent on television, and the numbers were still rising.

By the early 2000s, change was imminent for network television. Networks already were contending with higher production costs than cable, and total audience was down 8 percent among adults up to 49 years old in 2003, according to *Variety*. Most viewership was being lost to cable and satellite, which had double digit gains in the early 2000s, gains that were expected to continue, although more slowly, into 2008.

In the United States, by far the world's largest distributor of television programming, a Nielsen report showed that CBS's show *CSI* was the top-watched program, with a 9.6 rating, but compared to the 16.2 rating of NBC's *Seinfeld* a decade earlier, the ratings were disappointing. In fact, not one of the five most highly rated shows of 2003 even came close to the Nielsen ratings for the top five shows in 1993. By April 2005, this had changed, with CSI having a 16.9 rating and all others in the top five having ratings over 13.0.

By 2004, three-fifths of the top ten shows in the U.S. were reality shows, with 18 programming hours from the networks occupied by reality shows. Such a change was expected to affect other markets down the road, because unlike regular scripted programming, reality shows don't easily lend themselves to future use, and therefore come up with money for the networks only on the front end. In addition, reality shows typically don't last as many years as a hit scripted program can, a large percentage of which are comedies. But only 19 comedies were picked up by the networks in 2004, a decrease from previous years. By 2005, networks were noting the poor economic recovery provided by such shows when they went to syndication.

In addition, revenue from advertising stood to be negatively impacted by, among other issues, the rise in use of digital video recorders (DVR). Networks were forced to look into different streams of income, including video-on-demand (VOD) services, as well as restructuring how advertising could be purchased, away from traditional annual bulk advertising sales in late spring. Programming schedules were rapidly changing, with shows airing multiple times during a week and year-round programming.

RESEARCH AND TECHNOLOGY

As the first decade of the twenty-first century advanced and the technological revolution continued, the competitive climate for traditional broadcasters was expected to become hotter still. For example, in the mid-1990s, telephone companies attempted to become "distributors" of entertainment products via existing phone lines. In the United States, cable companies and phone companies developed plans to supply on-demand movies and other programming, with full "VCR control," allowing customers to select programming from boxes on their TV sets. Another foray, interactive TV, was supposed to take sporting events, game shows, and other traditionally passive TV fare to a new level.

However, by the twenty-first century, many of these bold changes either had yet to materialize or existed only in small pockets of the country. For example, the astronomical costs of installing interactive television systems and the modest customer interest in the systems caused most of the pioneers in this venture to abandon their plans.

One of the most important technological changes in broadcasting in the late 1990s and early 2000s was digital transmission of television signals, which was expected to enhance quality and lead to changes in TV production and distribution. Digital transmission produced a much higher quality television picture and could be used in both terrestrial and satellite TV transmissions. However, the digital broadcasts required separate frequencies from traditional analog broadcasts and also required different equipment on the receiving end.

The plan in most countries was to allow some existing channels to broadcast their programs in both analog and digital format, on different frequencies. The analog signal would eventually be phased out, after a 10 or 15-year period, allowing consumers the time to buy new receivers. As of 1998, those receivers were extremely expensive; but by 2002, that price had dropped somewhat as consumer demand grew.

New digital sets were expected to be quite different than their analog counterparts. For example, in 1988, Mitsubishi Consumer Electronics America Inc. introduced its first digital television, which came in two parts: a projector-screen for viewing and a receiver for picking up and translating the digital signals into images. The receiver contained the electronic hardware of the set, similar to a personal computer. This system would allow consumers to upgrade to new digital TV technology without purchasing a new projector screen.

By 2001 digital television had its admirers for cinema-like screen with outstanding resolution and magnificent Dolby surround sound, and U.S. sales of digital TVs and products jumped to US$2.6 billion. Yet, many cable operators in 2002 still could not bring their customers the service, and the price of digital TVs could be as much as three to fifty times more expensive than the traditional analog set. Still, prices were coming down, and at least 8 million digital TV sets were predicted to be sold by 2005, according to the *Allentown Morning Call.*

The major TV networks and broadcasters proposed a different digital TV standard based solely on high definition television (HDTV). While HDTV did offer extremely sharp pictures, the sets were extremely large and initially priced at about US$10,000.

Some melding of the two formats was expected to take place. For example, in the United States, ABC and Fox adopted digital broadcast formats friendly to Microsoft's digital strategy. The compact operating system was called Windows CE, modified from Microsoft's initial venture into interactive TV with cable companies and telephone companies, a venture that was abandoned due to its high cost. In 2002 Microsoft, Maxi, and Sony hurried toward the final design and release of splashy digital home entertainment hubs.

NEW THREAT TO CABLE TV

Direct broadcast from satellite (DBS) television (also called DTH, or direct-to-home) emerged in the early to mid-1990s, first in Europe and then in the United States. Direct broadcast differed from cable TV in that consumers purchased small satellite dishes to receive the transmission, bypassing the cable companies' coaxial cable systems. Using higher-powered satellites and the latest digital video compression technology, DBS made a successful entry to the U.S. market as DirecTV, a development that posed a major challenge to the traditional cable television industry. DirecTV was said to be one of the factors fueling a mid-1990s trend to merge U.S. cable TV operations. In 2002 a company called DigiVision boasted that it provided direct broadcast services in every ZIP code in the continental United States.

In the DirecTV system, more than 150 CD, audio, and laserdisc video quality digital channels were received by a relatively inexpensive, compact 18-inch satellite dish and receiver/decoder. The capital cost of DirecTV per U.S. television household was about US$7.00, compared to more than US$700 per subscriber capital cost to wire up new households with cable TV. From June to December 1994, DirecTV signed up more than 350,000 subscribers, with millions more projected through the end of the century. The U.S. cable television industry recognized the threat from DBS (some cable companies called it the "Deathstar") and planned to spend aggressively in digital video compression and fiber optic cable to improve reception and increase channel capacity. However, by the late 1990s, DBS growth had plateaued somewhat and cable was successful in holding on to its market share in most areas of the United States.

Outside Europe and the United States, interest in direct broadcast continued in 2004. In India, China, Taiwan, and the Philippines, potential investors—both local and multinational operators—were said to be developing partnerships to set up systems that would reach Asia's newly prosperous middle class viewers.

INDUSTRY LEADERS

VIACOM INC. (CBS INC. AND UPN NETWORKS)

As one of the world's largest media companies, Viacom has interests in a variety of media types, including movie production, television and radio broadcasting, and the Internet. In terms of television broadcasting, in 2004 the company owned the CBC and UPN networks and 39 broadcast stations. In addition, its television segment included television production and syndication services. At year end 2004, the television segment accounted for 38 percent of Viacom's revenues of US$22.5 billion.

In 2004, CBS was the number one network in the United States. Founded in 1927, New York-based CBS operates a national U.S. television network of 20 company-owned stations and more than 200 independent affiliates and a radio network of company-owned stations and affiliates. In 1995,

CBS was purchased by Westinghouse Corp. for US$5.4 billion. The new company was initially named Westinghouse/CBS, but after Westinghouse sold off most of its other assets, the company was re-named CBS Inc. in 1997.

In 1994 and 1995, CBS was battered by the collapse of an agreement to purchase QVC Networks, the loss of NFL football rights to Fox Broadcasting, the defection of several major affiliates to Fox, and low ratings for its prime time schedule, which dropped it to third behind NBC and ABC in the U.S. ratings race. However, CBS made up some ground and in 1998 was number two, ahead of ABC. Also, CBS outbid NBC for rights to broadcast NFL football games and resumed NFL broadcasts in 1998. In 1996 CBS purchased Infinity Broadcasting Co., which had major holdings in TV and radio broadcasting. In 1999 the media story of the year was the Viacom purchase of CBS for nearly US$35 billion in stock, the merger creating what CNN called an US$80 billion giant. In 2002, CBS acquired UPN, both of which remained under Viacom control. In total, Viacom owned 39 broadcast television stations in 2004. It had reached the 39 percent market reach allowed by FCC rules.

General Electric Co. (NBC)

One of the world's largest corporations, Connecticut-based General Electric Co. is the owner of the National Broadcasting Company Inc. (NBC). The number two U.S. network in 2004, NBC owned 29 U.S. television stations (including stations in New York, Chicago, Los Angeles, and Washington, D.C.). Like the other U.S. networks, NBC also had a large stable of 230 affiliate stations. NBC had branched out into other markets, with the acquisition of Superchannel, a general programming channel in Europe, and the development of Asian NBC (a financial channel) and CNBC (a cable channel in the United States specializing in financial news and talk television). In 1998 NBC faced the loss of the top-rated *Seinfeld* show, as well as the loss of its NFL broadcast rights when it was outbid by CBS. In 1997 NBC pledged to invest US$225 million into its MSNBC Internet venture with Microsoft over five years. In 2001 GE's NBC division continued a commitment to reaching the large Hispanic audience worldwide when it paid US$2.7 billion in October 2001 to purchase Telemundo Communications Group Inc., the number two U.S. Spanish-language TV outfit with ten TV stations in metropolitan areas such as New York, Los Angeles, and Chicago.

NBC faltered in ad sales in 2001. Likewise, MSNBC News never really was able to challenge CNN for ad revenue dollars. In January 2002, MSNBC earned only half the audience of CNN and its other competitor, the Fox News Channel, which actually overtook CNN in the ratings in January 2002, though it later lost that edge.

On a brighter note, NBC had much to boast about in 2002. Critics raved about the quality of the Salt Lake City Winter Olympics coverage. After a year of slowed ad sales connected to sports at Murdoch's Fox Network, in particular, NBC was happy to come away with a US$75 million profit that it made after selling US$740 million in ads.

In 2004, NBC Universal Inc. was formed combining NBC and Vivendi Universal Entertainment, which was 80 percent owned by General Electric and 20 percent owned by Vivendi. The company accounted for 8.5 percent of its parents' 2004 revenues of US$151.3 billion.

Walt Disney Company (ABC Television Network)

The primary broadcasting assets of this U.S.-based and second largest media company are the ABC television network, the ABC television station groups, radio station and network operations, and majority ownership of the ESPN cable station. The television station group owned and operated ten television stations reaching 24 percent of all U.S. households, with 226 affiliates in 2004. In 2002, ABC's financial picture looked dismal as its prime-time audience numbers had fallen 23 percent from 2001 levels. Worse, it embarrassed itself and its longtime news commentator Ted Koppel when it tried to shore up ratings in 2002 by publicly dumping Koppel's *Nightline* for David Letterman—a move that blew up when Letterman refused to jump networks to leave CBS. CBS reported US$11.8 billion in revenue in 2004, a 7.7 percent improvement over 2003 figures.

The News Corporation Ltd. (Fox Broadcasting)

This Australia-based company, owned by Rupert Murdoch and one of the world's largest media conglomerates, vastly expanded its TV holdings in the late 1980s and early 1990s. News Corp. made a successful entry into the U.S. market through its Fox Broadcasting Network, and in 1993 the company acquired 63 percent of Star Television.

By 2004, News Corp. was earning more than US$5 billion from its television sector. The company owned 35 U.S. television stations through Fox Television, promoting its strategy of holding duopolies—two stations in one large market— by having such setups in 9 of the 20 major U.S. markets. In Asia, the company's Star Network expanded into Hong Kong and Singapore.

In 2002, controlling chair and chief executive Rupert Murdoch saw his empire quake on unsolid ground after banking on some of the world's formerly lucrative sports events (Major League Baseball, the National Football League, and NASCAR) and losing more than US$1 billion in the last half of 2001. In addition to the slump in sports viewing, viewers grew tired of the shows *Ally McBeal* and *The X-Files* in 2001. On the other hand, Fox News caught and passed its arch rival CNN in the news rating war in early 2002, though it later handed back the coveted ranking. Rupert Murdoch's News Corp. also had been aggressive in the 2000s in acquiring properties, including Chris-Craft Industries Inc., a US$5.4 billion acquisition.

RTL Group S.A.

Bordered by Belgium, France, and Germany, Luxembourg may seem an odd place for Europe's largest television company, Compagnie Luxembourgeoise de Telediffusion SA (CLT). In 2000, the company merged with FreemantleMedia, formerly known as Pearson Television, to form RTL. In 2005, RTL claimed operations of 31 television channels in 10 nations, with 170 million daily viewers. The company employed more than 8,000 people and generated US$6.65 billion in 2004 revenues. RTL was looking to expand in Southern and Central Europe.

MAJOR COUNTRIES IN THE INDUSTRY

AUSTRALIA

The first two commercial TV licenses were awarded in Sydney and Melbourne in 1955, and as of 2002, commercial television stations were well established. By 2005, there were 52 licensed commercial television stations in Australia. Commercial providers were allowed to transmit digitally in 2001. Two public networks receive government funding: the Australian Broadcasting Corporation (ABC), providing Australian content, and the Special Broadcasting Service (SBC), providing multi-cultural programming. The commercial industry was valued at US$2.5 billion in 2002.

CANADA

Canada was the first country in the world to use geostationary satellites for television broadcasting. In 2005, the publicly-owned Canadian Broadcasting Corporation (CBC) continued to provide two national networks for both radio and television, one in English and one in French. A second national network, the privately owned CTV, also operated in the 1990s. Other private television networks served limited areas, such as Global TV in Ontario. Cable and satellite connections also provided Canadians access to U.S. television networks. Canadian broadcasting was regulated by the Canadian Radio-Television and Telecommunications Corp. (CRTC), which licensed networks and private stations and specified percentages of Canadian content in programming.

Two direct-to-home (DTH) satellite services were launched in Canada in 1996: ExpressVu, backed by a Canadian consortium that included telecommunications giant BCE Inc., and Power DirecTV, a joint venture of Montreal-based Power Corp. and U.S.-based DirecTV. Five more Canadian DTH pay-per-view programming services were also licensed. DTH was seen mostly as competition for Canadian cable companies. Not surprisingly, the loss of Canadian television broadcast stations mirrored losses by those in the United States as sales of ads slipped badly.

EUROPE

New digital cable and satellite services were in place in Europe by the end of 1995, bringing even more channels to a marketplace that had had a very small number. According to some observers, it was unlikely that cable television in Europe would ever reach the penetration and usage that it had in the United States since cable operators had to compete with new technology such as direct transmission satellite technology, a much less costly system to install in viewers' homes.

One of the key issues in European television was local content. During their startup phase, many new European stations filled their broadcast time with imported and dubbed American programming, largely because it was about 10 times cheaper than original European production. However, a European Union directive required broadcasters to air European-produced programming at least 50 percent of the time. While considerable controversy surrounded this issue, for well-established European channels it was fast becoming irrelevant in the mid to late 1990s. As their audience and revenues grew, European commercial channels found that viewers preferred local productions, which the stations were better able to afford.

FRANCE

In 1989 the Socialist government of France formed the Conseil Superieur de l'Audiovisuel (CSA), or Supreme Audiovisual Council, to supervise radio and television broadcasting. France had two main public networks, Antenne 2 and France Regions 3, as well as four private stations. The formerly state-run Television Francaise was privatized in 1987. Canal Plus was the country's first private channel, launched in 1984. Cable broadcasting began in 1987 but was very slow to catch on, with Paris being the only area with a significant number of subscribers. The low penetration of cable, affected by slow construction levels and low "sign-on rates," meant that only 1.3 million of France's 21.6 million TV homes subscribed to cable as of 1996. As a result, there was a great deal of interest in satellite digital TV in France in the late 1990s, with two large companies, Canal Plus and TPS, launching digital satellite services. By 2005, the CSA still maintained a tight control over television content.

In 2003, Euromonitor reported that private television represented 52.8 percent of the market in France, with TF1 remaining the dominant channel with a 31.5 percent share. Valued at US$8.6 billion in 2003, the total market was expected to reach US$11.8 billion by 2008. The average consumer spent 3 hours and 33 minutes watching television in 2003.

GERMANY

Only public corporations were permitted to broadcast in Germany until the mid-1980s, when a new system allowed commercial stations to be licensed for the first time. The Federal Ministry of Post and Telecommunications handled licensing of broadcasters, while television and radio owners paid annual fees to support public broadcasting. As in the English system, German public broadcasters were relatively free to establish their own broadcasting policies, though more so in television than radio. Nine different public corporations offered regional radio and TV programs in Germany. In the early 1990s, the regional TV channels combined to produce one evening television program on Channel 1 (Ard). A second national public station was Channel 2 (ZDF). A third channel, ARDIII, broadcast along regional lines. Regionally based state regulatory units, called Medienanstalten, controlled television licenses. Representatives from regional governments, communities, and institutions controlled these 15 units. In addition to public television, as of 1996, Germany had several commercial channels, including ProSieben, RTL, RTL2, and SAT1. There also were several cable and local channels. German broadcasters introduced digital transmission in the late 1990s and 2000s. Public broadcasters ARD and ZDF launched a four-channel digital TV system in 1997. Public broadcasters have faced increasing competition from private, commercial television companies, with RTL Group leading with a market share of 29.8 percent in 2003. However, public broadcaster ARD remained the largest of its kind in Germany, and was, in fact, one of the largest public broadcasters in the world.

In 2001 and 2002, Germany television companies had the same economic woes due to diminished ad sales that had hurt the German publishing industry. In February 2002 ProSieben listed a 27 percent plunge in annual surplus and a drop in pre-tax profit of 50 percent. ProSieben lost additional money in association with other media outlets such as the Kirch media group. However, in 2003, the size of the television market grew 8.4 percent over 2002 figures to a value of US$10.17 billion and was expected to reach US$11.88 billion by 2008.

Italy

While all broadcasting in Italy was once the province of Radiotelevisione Italiana (RAI), private channels emerged as major competitors. RAI broadcast on three channels: RAI 1, 2, and 3. Private channels included Canale 5, Italia 1, and Rete 4. In the mid-1990s, Canale 5 held the highest audience share of the terrestrial networks, at about 20 percent, followed closely by RAI 1 at just below 20 percent. Satellite channels, such as RTL2 and VIVA, were introduced in the mid-1990s. A digital satellite package, DStv, had 40 to 50 channels on the air as of early 1997. However, the service had to compete with dominant terrestrial broadcasters who had a strong lock on the market in the late 1990s. In 2001, while many of the world's television companies were in freefall, Italy's biggest company, MediaSet, and its three commercial channels managed to post "slightly" better ad sales revenues than it earned in 2000.

Spain

Spanish broadcasting was regulated by Radiotelevision Española (RTVE), a governmental organization. Public television was transmitted on two channels, TVE1 and TVE2, with TVE1 reaching the majority of the country's population. A group of regional public stations were also operating. Cable penetration for Spain was relatively high, with well over a third of the country's TV households signed up in the mid-1990s. There were three private networks operating in Spain in 2000: Antena 2, Telecinco, and CanalPlus, a cable channel. In 2000 the government company Telemadrid was privatized by the local Madrid government, according to *Bloomberg News.*

The United Kingdom

The BBC and the Independent Broadcasting Authority (IBA) traditionally dominated British television. However, the Broadcasting Act of 1990 reorganized independent broadcasting by reassigning the TV regulatory responsibilities of the IBA to a new group called the Independent Television Commission (ITC). The ITC was put in charge of licensing and regulating all non-BBC television services, including Channel 4 and Channel 5, as well as cable and satellite services. The BBC continued to expand to operate several channels: BBC One (broad range of programming); BBC Two (comedy and cultural interest); BBC Three (aimed at young adult market); BBC Four (most intellectually and culturally enriched channel); CBBC (children); CBeebies (pre-schoolers); BBC News 24; BBC Parliament; and BBCi (interactive television available to digital television subscribers). The BBC broadcast around the world in 40 languages, and offered a world service in English 24 hours a day. Both the BBC and ITC were public bodies licensed by the government; however, the government rarely interfered with the day-to-day management of the BBC and ITA. The BBC controlled 30 percent of the market in 2003 and 37 percent of the audience share.

As in other European countries, new cable and satellite channels emerged to challenge the dominance of traditional English broadcasters. In 2001, particularly during the fourth quarter, the United Kingdom's ad sales slipped drastically for many television broadcast companies. ITV reported its advertising sales were down 12 percent from 2000. In March 2002 the British giant Granada, a major production studio and one known for its independent investigative features for Bill Kurtis on A&E in conjunction with the *New York Times,* eliminated 1,430 staff jobs. A competitor, Carlton, also let 400 people go. Granada lost US$187 million in revenue for the full year ending September 2001. Ad sales spending for 2002 was already down 2.6 percent early in the year. Total market value grew a nominal 0.3 percent in 2003 to reach US$11.7 billion.

Asia

In 1993 Rupert Murdoch's News Corp. bought control of Star TV. This move helped focus the industry's attention on Asia, clearly one of the world's hot growth markets. Asia was expected to be home to two-thirds of the world's population by 2005, at which time it would be served by 2,000 terrestrial and satellite-delivered channels serving 400 million homes.

Initially, Star TV aired a large proportion of non-Asian produced programming, a strategy that was not expected to be viable in the long term. For example, TVB International Ltd., a successful Hong Kong broadcaster, competed effectively with Star by tailoring its programs for the many different ethnic and linguistic groups in its audience. While there was significant demand for western programming, Asian viewers—like those in other regions of the world—tended to prefer quality programming reflecting their own culture. Also, foreign content was disturbing to many Asian governments, such as those in China and Singapore, who feared that it could destabilize their regimes. However, Star TV was very successful in penetrating Taiwan and India. In response to the success of Star, India's state-owned television network, Doordarshan, launched five satellite channels in 1993 to compete with Star. Unlike India's traditional broadcast channels, time slots on the new satellite channels were sold to independent producers and television companies.

As the Asian market matured—like Europe before it—local producers were expected to have more resources to make higher quality programs, a trend that might hurt U.S. exports of television programming. Still, the vast expansion of channels brought about by cable and satellite services was expected to help U.S. producers maintain a prominent position in overseas markets.

China

China, which as of 1997 still had a minuscule private broadcast industry, was undergoing change in the mid-1990s. Some local Chinese public television stations dramatically changed the content of their broadcasts from propaganda to programs that produced profits for the station. For example, the Shanghai Bureau of Radio and Television had the right to import entertainment shows without central government review and was broadcasting many western programs.

The Chinese market, with its entrepreneur development and huge population, had enormous potential. China was expected to have 263.5 million households with televisions by 2005. Several commercial television stations were developing plans to introduce services to China. The re-acquisition of Hong Kong by China in 1997 already had an impact on the Chinese TV industry, although a clash had not yet occurred between the government and TV program powers-that-be. Hong Kong was the center of Asia's broadcasting industry prior to the takeover, home to two broadcast stations, a major cable operation, and six satellite networks such as News Corp.'s Star TV, NBC Asia, and Turner International Asia Pacific.

In 2001 companies such as Murdoch's entered the Chinese market by avoiding controversy for the most part, giving the government the official right to ban foreign intrusion but not exercising that power. A number of Chinese entrepreneurs and Murdoch's Star TV combined resources to offer Phoenix Television to some 45 million households in 2001, according to the *Los Angeles Times*. However, the general economic slowdown that hit Asia at the end of 2001 and 2002 severely hurt China's television interests as well. In 2002 Television Broadcasts Ltd. carried out a wage freeze on salaries in an attempt to stave off mass firings of employees after 2001 ad sales plunged.

Japan

Radio and television were developed earlier in Japan than in other Asian countries. Japanese radio broadcasting was begun in 1925 by Japan Broadcasting Corporation (Nippon Hoso Kyokai, or NHK), a public corporation financed by license fees paid by television set owners. As of the mid-1990s, NHK broadcast on radio and television with no commercial interruptions. NHK made its first television broadcast in 1952, and since 1953 NHK has broadcast overseas programs such as *Radio Japan* in many different languages. Private commercial broadcasting began in 1952 and gained widespread popularity, with five private networks in operation in the mid-1990s: Nippon TV, Tokyo Broadcasting System, TV Asahi, Fuji TV, and TV Tokyo. Direct satellite and cable television also became common in Japan, with penetration of both these media at 20 percent of Japanese households in the mid-1990s, when Japan had 34.6 million TV homes. As of 1996, Japan still accounted for more than half of all TV ad expenditures in Asia.

In March 2002, as the Japanese economy sagged, it threatened the revenues of four of Japan's biggest TV broadcast groups that had logged record profits one year earlier. However, Nippon Television Network Corp., Tokyo Broadcasting System Inc., Fuji Television Network Inc., and Asahi Broadcasting Corp. all recorded far better than average annual revenue increases in the spring of 2002.

New Zealand

A state-run broadcasting company inaugurated television service in New Zealand in 1960. Beginning in 1988, TV broadcasts were controlled by Television New Zealand Ltd. (TVNZ), a government-owned company. Television deregulation in 1989 removed restrictions on foreign and cross media ownership in New Zealand, allowing for true commercial competition. Television New Zealand operated TV One and TV2, which together dominated the market as of the late 1990s. However, TV3—the only privately owned, national commercial network in New Zealand—was said to be growing in market share. Regional TV stations were licensed to provide selected local program services. Multichannel TV, such as cable and direct broadcast, was not a major factor in New Zealand. TVNZ reported ad sales and revenue were down in 2001, while its market share slipped from 83 percent to 61 percent in the decade ending 2001.

The United States

The United States had about 1,200 commercial television stations, with about half being UHF stations and half being VHF stations. There also were about 370 public TV stations. As of March 2002, 258 TV stations provided customers with digital broadcasting and another 650 informed the FCC they would launch digital service within the next year after overcoming problems with financing, zoning laws, and other miscellaneous complications that kept them from meeting a May 1, 2002, deadline for compliance. At the end of 2003, the total market was valued at US$42.4 billion, and was expected to reach US$56.3 billion by 2008 according to Euromonitor. Network television accounted for the largest share of total revenues with 53.7 percent, with the four leading networks being ABC, CBS, NBC and Fox. NBC was by far the largest network, capturing 35.4 percent of 2003's market.

Jobs in television broadcasting, always competitive, became more difficult even for out-of-work TV veterans to obtain. Network executives began getting overwhelmed with hundreds of resumes and tapes for a single job opening as a result of thousands of positions being lost in the 2000s as a result of cost-cutting and consolidations. On the horizon, anchor and reporter jobs in smaller and mid-sized markets were under scrutiny as network executives increasingly complained that such markets were over-saturated with news coverage. Just as the trend in newspapers since the 1980s has been for a city to have one newspaper, so too was it unlikely that the 2000s would continue to see three or four competing stations offering news programming. In 2002, stations in St. Louis, Missouri, Kingsport, Tennessee, and Bristol, Virginia ordered their news anchors to sign off for the last time and turned to other programming.

Further Reading

Adalian, Josef. "Primetime." *Variety,* 1 December 2003.

Albiniak, Paige. "Networks Adapt to Changing Times." *The Boston Herald,* 24 May 2004.

"Asian Media." *Campaign,* 21 May 2004.

"Australia Now: Broadcasting.' Australian Government, Department of Foreign Affairs and Trade, 2005. Available from http://www.dfat.gov.au.

Bachman, Katy. "Local Sweeps Races Tight." *Mediaweek,* 31 May 2004.

Baker, Jim. "Olympics Golden with Viewers." *The Boston Herald,* 26 February 2002.

Berg, Christian. "Digital TV's Picture-perfect Outlook is Obscured." *The Morning Call (Allentown, PA),* 27 January 2002.

"Broadcast Rights for WWF, Baseball Push Headline Media into Q3 Loss." *Canadian Press Newswire,* 26 July 2001.

Carman, John. "Goliaths of TV Likely to Get Fatter: Ruling Good for Giant Firms—but Viewers May Suffer." *The San Francisco Chronicler,* 21 February 2002.

Chipman, Kim. "Owner of CBS Network Reports 4th-Quarter Loss." *The Record (Bergen County, NJ),* 14 February 2002.

Draper, Deborah J., ed. *Business Rankings Annual.* Detroit: Thomson Gale, 2004.

"Global Entertainment and Media Outlook: 2004 - 2008 (Industry Previews)." PricewaterhouseCoopers, 2004. Available from http://www.pwc.com.

"Fewer Ads, Smaller Crowds Pummel Disney." *The Record (Bergen County, NJ),* 9 November 2001.

Furman, Phyllis. "MSNBC Comes Up Short vs. the Competition." *Daily News (NY),* 31 January 2002.

Hiestand, Jesse. "Scripps Boosts Q1 Forecasts as TV Ad Sales Rise." *The Hollywood Reporter,* 13 March 2002.

Higgins, John M. "Media's Pink Slip Blues." *Broadcasting and Cable,* 28 January 2002.

"Hoover's Company Capsules," 2004. Available from http://www.hoovers.com.

Jack, Andrew. "Last Privately Owned Russian TV Station Taken off Air." *Financial Times (London),* 23 January 2002.

"Japan's 4 Large TV Broadcasters Log Record Group Profits." *Jiji Press Ticker Service,* 28 May 2001.

Kohl, Christian. "European TV Giant Posts US$2 Billion Loss." *Daily Variety,* 5 March 2002.

Laugesen, Ruth. "Broadcast Blues." *The Sunday Star-Times (Auckland),* 24 February 2002.

Lazich, Robert S., ed. *Market Share Reporter.* Detroit: Thomson Gale, 2004.

McConnell, Bill. "Over 650 Stations Want Waivers." *Broadcasting and Cable,* 11 March 2002.

Pennington, Gail. "Is There Room for Network News? And That's The Way It . . . Used To Be." *St. Louis Post-Dispatch,* 27 January 2002.

"ProSieben Suffers Profit Drop." *Financial Times Deutschland,* 28 May 2001.

Romano, Allison. "Checking the Census." *Broadcasting and Cable,* 1 October 2001.

Schmuckler, Eric. "Facing Reality." *Mediaweek,* 31 May 2004.

Tilles, Daniel. "Granada Posts Fiscal Full-Year Loss on Ad Sales Fall." *Bloomberg News,* 28 November 2001.

Trigoboff, Dan. "Live at 11? Maybe Not for Long; As Profit Pressure Mounts, Some Experts Consider Local Newscasts to be Endangered." *Broadcasting and Cable,* 11 February 2002.

"TV Broadcasting in France, Germany, UK, US." *Euromonitor,* August 2004. Available from http://www.majormarketprofiles.com.

Wilkofsky Gruen Associates Inc. "Global Entertainment and Media Outlook: 2002 - 2006." PriceWaterhouseCoopers, May 2002. Available from http://www.pwc.com.

Wong, Kenneth. "TVB to Freeze Wages." *Bloomberg News,* 6 December 2001.

MEDICAL EQUIPMENT AND SERVICES

SIC 8060
NAICS 622

HOSPITALS

This article covers organizations that provide diagnostic services, extensive medical treatment including surgical services, and other hospital services, as well as continuous nursing services. These establishments have an organized medical staff, inpatient beds, and equipment and facilities to provide complete health care. Specialized group industries include the following: general medical and surgical hospitals; psychiatric hospitals; and specialty hospitals such as those for alcoholism rehabilitation, children, cancer, orthopedics, chronic diseases, and drug addiction.

INDUSTRY SNAPSHOT

The global universe of the hospital industry consists of an estimated 100,000 hospitals. While the world's hospitals differ considerably in structure, organization, and services, as well as in purpose and mission, they all strive to fulfill the curative, preventive, and educational health needs of the world's population. Health centers, clinics, and other structures are considered "hospitals." In many parts of the world; however, the hospital industry generally adheres to World Health Organization (WHO) standards distinguishing hospitals as permanent facilities offering inpatient services and/or nursing care and staffed by at least one physician. In the United States, hospitals are operated by government agencies, not-for-profit organizations, and for-profit corporations.

Generally, the quality and extent of hospital care correlates positively with the percentage of a country's gross domestic product (GDP) expended for health care. According to the World Health Organization (WHO), expenditures for health care increased from 3 percent of the global GDP in 1948 to 14 percent in 2004. In less affluent countries, availability of hospital beds varies greatly depending on national factors other than GDP, such as type of government and demographics. Further, a WHO study done in 2000 looked at performance—how much was being done with the available resources. When analyzed this way, the U.S., which had spent the highest percentage of its GDP on health care, only ranked 37th in terms of performance.

In the United States, the overall cost of health care escalated rapidly beginning in the 1970s, rising more than US$1 trillion for the first time in 1996, an average of US$3,759 per person, and at least 10 times the amount spent in the early 1970s. *Modern Healthcare* reported a trend of runaway inflation in the cost of hospital services. The U.S. Department of Labor's Consumer Price Index for medical care showed that prices for health care increased 4.7 percent in 2001, after rising 4.2 percent in 2000. Prices for hospital services rose 7.6 percent in 2001, their biggest increase since 1993. A September 2001 report released by the Center for Studying Health System Change indicated that expenditures for health care increased by 7.2 percent in 2000, the largest increase in 10 years. In its 2004 report, the AHA indicated that healthcare expenditures totaled $1.5 trillion in 2002, with hospitals representing $486.5 billion of this amount. In February 2004, *Health Care Strategic Management* noted that profit margins for U.S. hospitals saw a slight increase in 2002, based on AHA data. That year, hospitals realized an aggregate profit margin of 4.3 percent, up from 4.1 percent the previous year.

ORGANIZATION AND STRUCTURE

The most widely used distinction of hospitals is based on sponsorship or ownership by organizations described as voluntary and non-profit, governmental or public, and for-profit, private or proprietary. In the United States, the total number of hospitals has fallen steadily since 1980; concurrently, the percentage of hospitals operated by for-profit corporations escalated in the 1990s. According to the 1997 *Statistical Abstract of the United States,* there were a total of 6,580 U.S. hospitals, compared to 7,051 in 1980.

The hospital industry, similar to other industries, continued to flex from the recessionary conditions of the early 1990s. Rather than wait for inevitable changes mandated by legislation or more adverse circumstances, most hospitals restructured to implement the most effective cost-cutting mechanisms. According to a survey by the American Hospital Association (AHA), the primary U.S. hospital advocate, a potentially viable restructuring route for nearly 11 percent of the nation's community hospitals involved participation in health networks. Networking was described as a group of hospitals, physicians, insurers, and/or community agencies working together to deliver a broad spectrum of health services designed to eliminate duplication of services and achieve better integration of care among community providers. Networks also operated as proprietary hospitals owned by physicians (individuals or group) or owned and controlled by corporate investors. Hospitals were also teaming up with physicians in various types of integrative arrangements, such as physician-hospital organizations (PHOs), independent practice associations (IPA), management services organizations, medical foundations, and hospital-owned or joint hospital physician-owned group practices. The less formal arrangement offered by physician-hospital networks allowed hospitals and physicians greater flexibility because of less legally binding structures.

In the early 1990s, several territorially controlled hospital services shifted to external organizations arranged through joint venture or other contractual agreements. The AHA's 1993 data listed the most frequently shifted services delivered through these arrangements as hospices, home health, and psychiatric services. Consequently, the precipitous drop in hospital inpatient activity was buffered by an increase in ambulatory outpatient services. Treatments and procedures routinely requiring an inpatient stay in the early 1980s were performed as outpatient procedures at a much lower cost in the early 1990s. Facilities such as Duke University in the United States realized as much as US$60,000 savings per patient costs by shifting more treatment to outpatient clinics. For example, bone marrow transplants, one of several treatments traditionally requiring long-term inpatient care, appeared adaptable to outpatient treatment modality. Medical experts had some doubts as to whether outpatient services adequately filled the gap in health care or created more critical treatment gaps. In cases involving outpatient treatment of chronically ill cancer patients, for example, the issue was whether hospitals would have immediate access to patient information in case of an emergency inpatient admission.

Estimated figures for 1992 indicated 33.2 percent of hospitals' net patient revenue was attributed to outpatient services with 43.5 percent of the hospitals' net surgical revenue produced by outpatient surgery. With the exception of teaching hospitals, practically all U.S. community hospitals, regardless of size or location, provided some type of ambulatory surgical service. Less demand for ambulatory care occurred in teaching hospitals because of their heavy reliance on inpatient, tertiary care. One mid-1990s survey of hospital CEOs predicted that, by the year 2000, outpatient services on the average would account for nearly half of hospitals' net patient revenues.

Community Hospitals. In the United States in 2003, there were 5,764 registered hospitals (7,569 hospitals according to the U.S. Census of 2003) of which 4,895 were community hospitals. Of these, 2,984 were operated by non-government, not-for-profit organizations, 790 were investor owned (for-profit), and 1,121 were run by state or local governments according to American Hospital Association. Community hospitals were open to the public and, in many instances, they bore the brunt of economic defaults primarily because these hospitals more often served as the only "refuge for the poor and ill." From the 1980s through the 1990s, there was an ongoing decline in the number of community hospitals in the United States; in 1980 there had been 3,547 hospitals operated by not-for-profit organizations. In 1993, for example, 34 hospitals closed, approximately 18 merged, and others were absorbed by various structures. More than half of the community hospital closures occurred in larger urban hospitals averaging 200 to 300 beds, which contributed to a 10-year loss of 99,000 hospital beds. New facilities and reopenings possibly offset the void of hospital reductions, but fewer substitutions compensated for the losses of rural hospitals. A relatively small increase in admissions in 1997 failed to balance the chronic admission loss that began in the 1980s.

District Hospitals. Hospitals, particularly in rural areas of developing countries, operated under the umbrella of a district health system. These systems included local health centers that were capable of delivering a variety of curative, preventive, and educational health services. A typical rural health district in Africa served about 160,000 inhabitants with approximately 140 beds, three physicians, and 10 peripheral health units. Each district hospitalized about 4,000 patients annually. Few of these health centers maintained laboratory, X-ray, or surgical facilities. In terms of primary care, health centers or stations were designated as initial referral points for hospital admission. Consequently, direct access to hospitals was limited in favor of service at the local health center. The proximity of local health centers permitted quicker access to health care and also eased the burden on hospital resources. However, the lure of hospital technology frequently led patients to bypass local health centers and go directly to hospitals. A study of one underutilized Vietnamese district health center indicated that 68 percent of hospital referrals were primarily because hospital consultations were given by a doctor without any price differential. Under these circumstances, health centers suffered from the hospital's competition for resources, and hospitals became overloaded with primary care work.

Religious Hospitals. Non-governmental, voluntary, non-profit hospitals included facilities owned or sponsored by religious groups and other nonsecular bodies. In the mid-1990s the Catholic health care ministry in the United States consisted of 594 hospitals and 1,054 long-term facilities. A survey of international health services in the early 1990s documented Catholic hospitals providing services in 58 countries, with the highest number in Latin America, the Commonwealth of Independent States, and Africa. In many countries, religious and governmental organizations shared almost equivalent hospital sponsorship. In Kenya, for example, about 25 percent of the facilities—equivalent to 7,000 hospital beds—were sponsored by religious organizations. Perhaps more than most hospital sponsors, religious organizations had historically maintained an ecumenical presence in providing primary medical care through hospitals, long-term care facilities, or funding of health service networks in the most remote areas of the world. International health intervention by voluntary organizations was probably vastly understated because of meager funding and far less publicity. Other factors contributing to the anonymity of these organizational services were the lack of central service provider registries, and possibly because sponsorship might have been assumed by larger organizations or governments in some instances.

Government Hospitals. Government-sponsored hospitals are characterized as facilities controlled by various levels of national, provincial or state, local county, or municipal governments. A greater proportion of foreign hospitals are government-owned, with hospital utilization determined by governmental structure. For a military-controlled government, a greater number of hospital beds would be reserved for military personnel. Until 1949, China's hospitals were primarily sponsored by missionary organizations. By the mid-1990s, practically all of China's 61,929 hospitals with an excess of 2 million beds were government-sponsored. In the United States in 2003, state and local governments sponsored 1,121 hospitals and the federal government sponsored 239 hospitals according to the American Hospital Association. Government hospital sponsorship included a range of hospitals for illnesses such as psychiatric diseases, tuberculosis and other respiratory diseases, chronic diseases, mental retardation, alcohol and chemical dependency, and other long-term care facilities. Federally sponsored U.S. hospitals provided care for various armed services, veterans, and Native Americans, with the Veterans Administration (VA), the largest federal hospital sponsor, composed of 171 hospitals, 128 nursing homes, and 37 domiciliaries for substance-abuse treatment and postoperative care, providing health care for veterans and their families. In the United States, 1,383 hospitals were operated by some government entity in 2003, as opposed to 2,562 in 1980.

Federal hospitals in the United States have received their share of accusations of management excesses. The VA hospitals' prominence in treating spinal cord injuries, stress disorders, prosthetics, and substance abuse is often tainted by allegations of pork barrel budgets and facility under-utilization. The annual US$28.1 billion budget for VA hospitals in 2004 served about 5 million unique patients per year. That year, about 20 percent of all veterans used VA hospitals. Each year VA receives annual budget increases. Veteran empathy runs high, so ballooning VA budgets meet little, if any, opposition. The least hint of hospital closure or contracting of services to private providers results in loud protest from veterans' groups and from politicians, particularly those representing regions in which VA complexes serve as the major employer for hundreds of community residents. Veterans' groups such as the American Legion believe that the need for enhanced productivity and accountability will ultimately change the structure of VA hospitals.

For-Profit Hospitals. A rapidly growing number of U.S. hospitals were coming under private ownership (1,399 in 2002, compared with 942 in 1980). While there was disagreement about the notion that U.S. hospital care faced excessive commercialization, most analysts concurred with the fact that commercialized health care was a permanent fixture. Quite possibly, according to some reformers, privatization would better provide quality health services, promote hospital productivity, and increase cost containment. The mechanisms for profit-making hospitals included structures such as investor-owned chain hospitals, health maintenance organizations (HMOs), preferred provider organizations (PPOs), exclusive provider organizations (EPOs), or a combination of several structures. Commercial chains would buy out financially strapped hospitals and, in some instances, develop new hospital systems. The most frequent justification for conversion to private markets centered on the potential for augmented financial stability. Another significant reason was greater efficiency and productivity of medical services, although the latter reason, according to some observers, remains to be proven despite the growing evidence supporting commercialization. An analysis by the Congressional Budget Office (CBO) revealed that care provided through insurers or group model HMOs costs 15 percent less than other plans, with a potential of 10 percent overall savings nationally if the entire population enrolled in HMOs. However, in light of the turbulence of U.S. health systems, health analysts expressed some doubt as to whether privatization unequivocally represented the best solution to health reform.

The rise of investor-owned, for-profit hospitals and specialty clinics tended to further dissipate limited community hospital revenue sources. Profit motives accounted for the development of chain-managed resources, largely because available Medicare reimbursements confirmed profits for investors. Several high-tech procedures, such as treatment of end-stage renal disease, formerly administered by hospitals, are now administered by for-profit clinics. The investment appeal of hemodialysis clinics was partially because the service is Medicare-reimbursable.

Psychiatric Hospitals. The psychiatric hospital market reflected some of the strongest growth from the mid-1980s to the mid-1990s. In contrast to other segments of the hospital industry, the number of psychiatric hospitals in the United States increased from 584 in 1986 to 737 in 1993, accompanied by an increase of 191,000 admissions. Higher psychiatric admissions may not have necessarily denoted progress, but the positive elements of these higher admissions became evident in view of shorter hospital stays, which dropped from 106 days in 1983 to 52 days in 1993. From another perspective, these trends also reflected some of the salient refinements of psychiatric treatment, such as improved pharmacological therapy, deinstitutionalization of the chronically mentally ill, and the closure of many large state-run mental hospitals in favor of expanded outpatient treatment services. However, by 2002, the U.S. census was reporting that there were 605 psychiatric and substance-abuse hospitals.

Specialized Hospitals. A growing number of specialized hospitals (30 in 1993 and 532 in 202), sponsored by government, voluntary organizations, and for-profit chains, provided a range of inpatient services for all age groups. In the mid-1990s, services of long-term care and specialized hospitals expanded to include facilities for AIDS patients. A handful of hospitals also specialize in treating patients with tuberculosis or other chronic conditions. Notable research and technological strides offered dramatic improvements in the quality of life for patients with spinal cord, head, and other trauma injuries.

BACKGROUND AND DEVELOPMENT

The medieval Christian period probably reflects the earliest traces of a formal hospital structure. The bishops of the church were instructed by the Council of Nicea in 325 A.D. to found a hospital in every cathedral city in Christendom.

As Europe's Renaissance period spurred scientific and social experimentation, hospital development reaped benefits such as improved hygienic conditions, nursing services, and other patient care refinements. The admission of paying patients, the development of specialty maternity hospitals, and other improvements had permanently integrated hospitals into their communities. The first hospital in the western hemisphere was built in Santo Domingo about 1503.

Under the auspices of religious authority, hospitals were a symbol of refuge for the sick and poor. This image of hospitals continued well into the nineteenth century and even the twentieth, when doctors at Massachusetts General Hospital were not allowed to charge their patients for care as late as 1908. Those who could afford medical care were treated by physicians in their own homes. The burden of patient care costs shifted hospital control and expenses to joint management between religious and civil authorities.

The discovery of ether as an anesthetic was a major turning point in the history of hospitals. W.T.G. Morton, a Georgia dentist, first used ether during a hospital surgical procedure in 1846. Another physician, Crawford Long, claimed to have used ether for surgery as early as 1842, but did not immediately publish his findings. The use of anesthetics greatly decreased the public's fear of hospitals and led to a sharp increase in the number of surgical procedures performed. Likewise, the development of sulfa drugs in the 1930s and penicillin in the 1940s decreased the infection mortality rate associated with surgery and also contributed to a more positive public image for hospitals.

CURRENT CONDITIONS

According to an October 2003 report from The World Bank, the global population reached 6.2 billion people in 2002. That year, global per capita spending on health care totaled US$5,201. However, spending as a portion of GDP varied considerably from region to region, depending on income. The segment of the world's population with the highest income (965 million people) enjoyed per capita health care spending of US$26,942 in 2002. By comparison, per capita spending among those in the middle-income category (2.7 billion people) was US$1,870. For the world's 2.5 billion low-income inhabitants, per capita spending was only $453.

The World Bank's report further revealed that nearly 90 percent of all global health expenditures, which totaled almost $2.4 trillion in the early 2000s, was generated by high-income countries. Those countries in the low- and middle-income categories accounted for a mere 11 percent of expenditures, but endured 85 percent of all diseases.

In its 2005 *Hospital Statistics* report, the American Hospital Association (AHA) indicated that the United States was home to 5,764 registered hospitals in 2003, down 30 from the previous year. In a separate May 2004 report, the AHA revealed that U.S. hospitals treated 556 million outpatients, performed 28 million surgical procedures, saw 110 million patients in their emergency rooms, and delivered 4 million babies in 2002. That year, total admissions numbered 36.3 million.

In 2002, hospitals had a direct impact of $429 billion on the nation's economy. However, when the industry's indirect economic influence on other industries was factored in, this impact amounted to $1.3 trillion. Indeed, during the early 2000s the hospital industry proved to be something of a mainstay during difficult economic times. For example, in 2001 the industry achieved 2.3 annual growth, despite a recession that negatively impacted scores of other U.S. industry sectors.

Patient satisfaction is one key performance indicator within the health care industry. In its March 29, 2004 issue, *Modern Healthcare* reported that U.S. physicians received high marks from most patients during their overnight hospital stays. Citing data from a 2004 Press Ganey Associated survey of 300,000 patients at 1,326 hospitals, the publication indicated that out of 100 possible points, patients' overall satisfaction score was about 91. Most impressive was that the majority of patients gave their physician a top rating of very good (70 percent), followed by a good rating (25 percent). In addition to overall satisfaction, other noteworthy scores included nursing staff courtesy/friendliness (90), physician staff courtesy/friendliness (89), and nursing staff skill (88).

During the mid-2000s, the U.S. hospital industry was poised for a major construction boom. Construction activity began to increase in 2001, as the rest of the nation endured difficult economic times. In 2002, the AHA reported that 19 new acute care hospitals were added in 2002, an increase that had not occurred since 1975. In fact, from 1975 to 2002, acute care hospitals actually decreased by a factor of 16.5 percent, according to *Modern Healthcare.*

Although some industry players were concerned about creating excess capacity, a number of strong trends were supporting the industry's growth initiatives. As writer Michael Romano explained in *Modern Healthcare's* January 12, 2004 issue: "Spurred by the attractive demographics of high-growth suburban areas, changing consumer tastes and the prospect of big business from baby boomers in the coming years, healthcare systems across the country are awakening from a construction slumber attributed in part to the stifling effect of the Balanced Budget Act of 1997." Other supporting elements were attractive interest rates, which remained near record lows during the mid-2000s, as well as improved Medicare reimbursements and the ever-important quest to offer consumers the latest technological advancements.

Summarizing the findings of a February 2004 Turner Construction Co. survey of 200 healthcare industry executives, *Healthcare Financial Management* reported that nearly 70 percent of respondents indicated their organizations would probably pursue a significant capital expansion project by 2007. This percentage was 56 percent in organizations with capital budgets of less than US$5 million, while it was much higher (89 percent) at healthcare systems with capital budgets in excess of US$5 million. Reporting information from Banc of America Securities, *Kiplinger Business Forecasts* indicated that by 2006, 60 percent of non-profit rural hospitals and 85 percent of urban non-profit hospitals had plans to expand or upgrade their facilities.

By the mid-2000s, the issue of medical malpractice liability was reaching crisis levels in certain areas of the United

States. In states where there were no financial limits to malpractice claims, hospitals and physicians shouldered the burden of skyrocketing medical malpractice insurance rates. In some cases, policies were in the six-figure range, making the cost of practicing medicine very high. According to the AHA, in early 2003 crisis conditions existed in Arkansas, Connecticut, Florida, Georgia, Illinois, Kentucky, Mississippi, New Jersey, Nevada, New York, North Carolina, Ohio, Pennsylvania, Texas, Washington, and West Virginia.

These conditions prompted a mass exodus of certain medical specialties from different locales. For example, in Illinois some obstetrician/gynecologists either opted to stop providing obstetric care or left to practice in nearby states like Wisconsin where malpractice insurance was significantly lower because reforms limited liability claims. This same phenomenon affected other "high risk" specialties, such emergency medicine, and neurosurgery. In rural areas where a limited number of specialists served large geographic regions, the resulting physician shortage had dire consequences for area residents. Commenting on this situation in March 2003, AHA Executive Vice President Rick Pollack said: "In some communities, hospitals have been forced to curtail or discontinue services, whether that means shutting down the emergency room for a few hours or permanently closing obstetrics departments. This can leave patients and families hours away from the care they need."

Expenditures. Based on a 2005 AHA report, expenditures for hospital care were more than US$498 billion in 2003. This was an increase of US106 billion over 1999 figures. By 2010, national health expenditures are predicted to total US$2.6 trillion, reaching 15.9 percent of GDP. Factors in this forecasted growth include the accelerating increase in spending for prescription drugs, increases in provider costs, insurers unable to negotiate discounts in prices, and increased income growth.

Revenue Sources. In most countries, hospital revenue was generated primarily from three sources: government assistance or subsidies, third-party payers such as insurers, and self-paying patient fees. The AHA applied the term gross patient revenue to the amount a hospital would receive if all patients paid at full "retail" charges. While this revenue was not an evaluation factor of a hospital's financial position, such revenues reflected the use of services by broad patient categories. For most hospitals, the era of liberal government revenues or subsidies had vanished. Fewer hospitals expected the windfall budgetary increases of former years calculated on cost of living increases or other factors.

To ensure equitable health care for all, several countries such as Canada maintained public health insurance, provincially managed and financed by taxes. The insurance covered all residents and was the sole payer for hospital and physician care. Patients had free choice of doctors and hospitals and faced no out-of-pocket expenses. Many Americans viewed this as an ideal system, although the Health Insurance Association's revelations of behind-the-scene workings of the Canadian system perhaps indicated otherwise. With few exceptions, patients in need of surgery had to endure long waiting periods. Coupled with the lack of private hospitals, many Canadians sought surgery in the United States. Open health care access gave the appearance of equitable health care, but this access potentially contributed to excessive care and waste due to the lack of controls in predetermined treatment efficacy, according to AHA.

Britain and France provided high-quality health care available to all citizens through a national social security system, which in France covered all hospital and maternity expenses and about 80 percent of all other medical, pharmaceutical, and dental bills. In Britain, the National Health Service was supplemented by private medical insurance and hospitals, many of which were smaller (under 100 beds) facilities.

RESEARCH AND TECHNOLOGY

The benefits of advanced medical technology are well documented. However, for most hospitals, state-of-the-art technology also imposed a budget strain in more ways than one. The biggest problem is that maintaining the latest high-tech equipment is nearly impossible because obsolescence invariably follows the latest model. Expanded applications of laser technology accounted for more progressive treatment in areas such as ophthalmology, plastic surgery, and general surgery, However, today's state-of-the-art laser may quickly be superseded by tomorrow's newer, enhanced laser sweeping the market.

A more compelling economic factor for hospitals in emergent countries was the application of more rigid standards in the selection of equipment. Few developing countries developed or manufactured their own technology. Due to their low economic standing, they could not afford to be lured by high-tech equipment that often led to a "technology trap" in which equipment remained unopened because of the unavailability of staff training funds, maintenance parts, or unsuitable environmental conditions. One study estimated overuse and inappropriate use of technology ranging from 30 to 70 percent in some locales. To ease the burden of equipment acquisition and maintenance, many hospitals maintained national and regional inventories for stockpiling equipment and spare parts. Obsolete equipment from hospitals in industrialized countries often became coveted advanced technology for developing countries.

In 2004, the federal budget for medical research in the U.S. was US$28.7 billion, an amount that had doubled since 1998. One study estimated that 5 percent per annum of cost inflation in health care provision is due to developments in medical science and technology. Most notable were advances in genetic research that promoted the cure and control of debilitating and fatal diseases such as cystic fibrosis, multiple sclerosis, and AIDS. In a speech to an international health audience, the Director General of the International Hospital Federation explained that biogenetic research offered potential treatment for 4,000 currently untreatable diseases. Patient and donor selection procedures for utilizing some of these genetic advances introduced several new ethical and practical dilemmas capable of causing hospitals costly litigation.

From the 1990s and into the 2000s, computer technology permeated practically every aspect of hospital management and treatment. Affordable prices and proven advantages have converted most hospital procedures to computerized functions. Computerized records, which were once bulky and frequently illegible can now be retrieved in seconds and in a more comprehensible format.

Although a number of medical centers have implemented electronic medical records systems (EMRS) over the years, most patient records continue to be stored on paper at a single location, according to *The Journal of the American Medical Association*. This can result in rendering crucial patient information such as medical conditions, drug allergies, and electrocardiograms inaccessible in an emergency, and often unavailable even in a routine medical setting. By the beginning of the twenty-first century, the ethical, legal, and technical aspects of EMRS were being debated by physicians and hospital administrators. As of 2004, a growing number of health systems were implementing EMRS technology. It is possible that a new generation of doctors, who have grown up with computer technology, will pave the way to wider adoption of EMRS in the future.

By mid-2004 use of the Internet was resulting in significant savings for hospitals via more efficient materials management operations. By automating and simplifying product selection, order placement, and contract management, employees are able to focus on endeavors that are more meaningful. Automated systems also help to reduce errors, increase the number of transactions per employee, and shorten delivery and receiving times. In July 2004, *Hospital Materials Management* reported that of the 31 hospitals using a materials management system from San Jose, California-based Neoforma, nine realized savings of $500,000 or more by switching to the new system, with the remainder saving $100,000. About 70 percent of the reported savings were expected to recur on an annual basis. In addition to Neoforma, the Global Healthcare Exchange (GHX) of Westminster, Colorado, was a leading player in the healthcare e-commerce arena. The company served 1,684 hospitals and handled nearly 466,000 electronic purchase orders in early 2004. Dallas, Texas-based Broadlink also had a major stake in the industry, serving nearly 700 hospitals and managing some $2 billion in online orders each year.

While many hospitals have perfunctory Web sites that offer little more than basic information about the facility and its services, many now understand the need for a more sophisticated Web site strategy, according to *Health Data Management*. Some have turned their sites into interactive experiences for both patients and doctors. Patients can log on, view and pay their medical bills online, and also access amounts being charged to their insurance providers. Some hospitals allow physicians to view clinical summaries online and even sign their own transcribed reports electronically. They also have online access to a picture archiving and communications system that lets them view diagnostic images.

Another pressing issue for the hospital industry is related to waste disposal. In 2001, the American Hospital Association (AHA) launched the second phase of its Hospitals for a Healthy Environment (H2E) campaign, aiming for the reduction of chemical and hazardous wastes generated by AHA member hospitals. The overall goals of the campaign include the elimination of mercury from facilities' waste streams by 2005, as well as the reduction of hazardous waste (and overall waste) by 33 percent by 2005, and by 50 percent in 2010. The WHO has also taken up the cause and in 1999, released the first worldwide, comprehensive guide on waste disposal called *Safe Management Wastes from Health-Care Activities*. Aimed at hospital management, policy makers, public health professionals, and others, it detailed the importance of waste minimization, recycling, disposal options, handling, and training in regards to chemicals, syringes, vaccine waste, radioactive waste, incineration, and more.

WORKFORCE

According to the Bureau of Labor Statistics, health services was one of the biggest industries in the United States, accounting for more than 12.9 million jobs in 2002. Approximately 16 percent of all positions created between 2002 and 2012 will be in this industry, as are 10 out of the 20 occupations forecasted to likely see the highest rate of growth. About 40.9 percent of the total employed in this industry worked in hospitals, with another 22.1 percent working in nursing and residential care facilities. Registered nurses accounted for 2.3 million jobs, the largest portion of those employed in healthcare. Approximately one in five hospital jobs was in the service sector, including nursing, psychiatric, home health aide, and building cleaning workers. A large number of hospital employees are also in the office and administrative support areas. The predicted rate of employment growth for the hospital industry between 2000 and 2010 is just 10 percent, the slowest within the health services industry. This sluggish rate is attributed to the streamlining of healthcare delivery options; the trend toward more outpatient than inpatient care; consolidation of facilities to control costs; and the likelihood that alternate care sites and clinics will become more widespread. However, the number of job opportunities in the hospital sector is expected to be significant because hospitals tend to employ large numbers of workers.

In 2005, there continued to be an increasing shortage of hospital workers. A number of factors accounted for these shortages. Health care professionals have had a wider range of employment options in recent years, and salaries for some professions are significantly higher outside hospitals. For example, chain drug stores and superstores are able to lure pharmacists with much higher wages than hospitals offer. The labor force shortage itself manifests a vicious cycle of stressors, especially for registered nurses, who often must work under greater pressure to pick up the slack from job vacancies.

By late 2003, some observers were concerned about the extra-long hours nurses and nursing assistants were working in the nation's hospitals. Amid continued staffing shortages, many facilities permitted—and in some cases mandated—that nursing staff work more than 12 hours per day. According to the November 5, 2003 *New York Times*, a report issued by the National Academy of Sciences' Institute of Medicine stated: "Long work hours pose one of the most serious threats to patient safety, because fatigue slows reaction time, decreases energy, diminishes attention to detail, and otherwise contributes to errors." The report recommended that, in the interest of patient safety, staff work no more than

60 hours per week, and no more than 12 hours in any 24-hour time period.

The aging of the labor force is another contributing factor to the shortage. For example, in 2000 the average age for a registered nurse was 43.3 years. By 2010 the majority of nurses will be in their fifties and sixties, and the workforce will continue to decrease as older nurses reach retirement. By 2020, when baby boomers are in their late sixties and seventies and require health care more than ever, the number of working registered nurses is expected to plummet to almost 20 percent below the need required.

Hospitals are trying out a variety of creative strategies to entice new workers to the sector. Incentives include signing bonuses, more comprehensive employee benefits, flexible schedules, and tuition reimbursement. Hospitals have also tried to increase salaries. However, changing the structure of work, improving in the workplace environment, and discovering new pools of potential employees are some of the long-term goals that will continue to challenge the hospital industry.

INDUSTRY LEADERS

HCA Inc. With 190 hospitals and 91 outpatient surgery centers in 2005, HCA was the largest healthcare provider in the U.S. However, it was also part of the global industry having facilities in England and Switzerland. Based in Nashville, Tennessee, HCA responded to increased costs and declines in reimbursement rates with reductions in operations and the paring down of expenses. It also suffered from fraud charges regarding over-billing, investigations, and lawsuits. In 2003, revenues totaled US$21.8 billion, with a one-year sales growth of 10.5 percent, while net income rose almost 60 percent to US$1.3 billion. HCA Inc. employed some 242,000 people in 2003, up from 174,000 in 2001.

Ascension Health. This network of hospitals was established in 1999 by the merger of the Sisters of St. Joseph Health System and the Daughters of Charity National Health System. Headquartered in St. Louis, Ascension is the biggest not-for-profit health care system in the United States. Facilities include approximately 63 Roman Catholic general acute-care hospitals, along with four long-term health care centers, four rehabilitation hospitals, and four psychiatric hospitals. In addition, Ascension operates seven hospitals under joint venture agreements, mostly located in the northeastern, mid-western, and southern parts of the United States. Ascension's governing board has several clergy members, but a non-clergy CEO heads the firm. Operating revenues for 2004 totaled US$10 billion, and the company employed more than 106,000 people.

Catholic Health Initiatives. This not-for-profit health network was formed by the consolidation of four Roman Catholic health care systems: Sisters of Charity of Nazareth Health Care System of Bardstown, Kentucky; Catholic Health Corporation of Omaha, Nebraska; Sisters of Charity Health Care Systems of Cincinnati; and Franciscan Health System of Aston, Pennsylvania. Headquartered in Denver, in 2005 Catholic Health Initiatives' facilities included: 69 hospitals; 43 assisted-living, long-term care, and residential facilities; and five community-based health organizations. In 2004, revenues totaled approximately US$6.7 billion and the organization employed 65,000 workers.

Tenet Healthcare Corp. Although Tenet is one of the United States' largest hospital chains, decreased Medicare funding has caused it to shut down its medical practice management business and sell off some other facilities to reduce costs. In 2005, the chain included 74 acute-care hospitals in 13 states after selling 12 of its hospitals and closing two. In addition, in 2004 the company sold the one foreign hospital it held, which was located in Madrid, Spain. Tenet's subsidiaries have operations in HMOs, clinics, outpatient surgery centers, home health care programs, and more. Due to its reorganization, revenues in 2004 were US$9.9 billion, down from 2003 levels of more than US$13.2 billion. The number of employees dropped from close to 110,000 people in 2003 to 75,743 in 2004.

General Healthcare Group Ltd. The leading private healthcare provider in the United Kingdom, General Healthcare was operating about 50 acute-care hospitals through its BMI Healthcare division. The company was also operating hospitals on behalf of the National Health Service (NHS).

MAJOR COUNTRIES IN THE INDUSTRY

In addition to industry leader the United States, the hospital industry was a lucrative business worldwide, a large part of the $2.4 trillion health care industry.

United Kingdom. The United Kingdom's National Health Service (NHS) is based on a system of healthcare services that are funded by the public and organized through public trusts. All 60 million British citizens and residents have access to health care with some services requiring modest fees. The United Kingdom also has a number of private hospitals not affiliated with the NHS. According to World Health Organization (WHO) data released in 2005, health expenditures in the United Kingdom were 7.7 percent of gross domestic product in 2002. In terms of international dollars"a common currency unit used by the WHO "that takes into account differences in the relative purchasing power of various currencies"—on a per capita basis, expenditures totaled Intl $2,160 that year. Of the total expenditure on health 16.6 was private, an amount that had been decreasing since 1998 when it was 19.6 percent.

In July of 2004, the NHS reported that it had increased the number of doctors and nurses it employed in an effort to reduce waiting times for patients and take a more proactive approach in treating diseases. In 2000, the NHS had established a goal of adding 2,000 general practitioners to its ranks by 2004. However, it exceeded the target by adding 2,660. By adding some 10,000 nurses during late 2003 and early 2004, the NHS also was well on its way of meeting a goal to add 25,000 additional nurses by 2008. In addition to plans to add 1,000 oncologists by 2006, the NHS also reported that previously established targets for both cardiologists and cardiothoracic surgeons had already been surpassed as of early 2004.

Spain. Spain's strong economy, political stability, and low unemployment rate have all contributed to significant improvements in the country's healthcare system, according to *Modern Healthcare International*. Spain's primary care infrastructure is well organized and offers medical care to all 41 million of the population free of charge. Roughly 90 percent of Spain's US$35 billion health care budget is financed by general taxes. This monetary amount funds 750 public hospitals, insures most of the country's 40 million people, and also provides for medical education. Revenues from social security fund the rest of the system. Spain has a large quantity of physicians, with 4.1 per 1,000 patients. By contrast, there are 3.1 physicians per 1,000 patients in the United States and 3 per 1,000 within the European Union. The majority of doctors work 24 hours per week in the public health care system, and earn less than US$50,000 annually. Many supplement their income by also working in private practices.

Spain also has a robust private health care area. Approximately six million residents have private insurance, and another four million purchase supplemental coverage from private insurers. The country had 142 privately owned hospitals. According to WHO data released in 2005, health expenditures in Spain were 7.6 percent of gross domestic product in 2002. On a per capita basis, expenditures totaled Intl $1,640 that year. About 28.7 percent of the total expenditure on health was private.

Canada. In the early 1990s, many hospitals in Canada were merged, downsized, or even shut down due to cutbacks, according to *Modern Healthcare International*. The number of Canadian hospital beds has suffered a significant decline. In 1991 there were 1,128 public hospitals and 175,376 beds; by 1999 there were only 877 public hospitals with 122,006 beds. Hospitals are the most expensive part of Canada's health care system and account for approximately 33 percent of the total health budget. Because hospitals are receiving reduced public funds, Canada is seeing a trend toward privatization, at least in ways that do not violate the country's federal laws governing health care institutions funded by public monies. Some hospitals are turning their lobbies into shopping areas, while others are establishing food franchises on their campuses. Others are looking into e-health services on the Internet whereby patients could have a diagnostic test performed in their own country, but have it read for a fee by a Canadian doctor. According to WHO data, health expenditures in Canada were 9.6 percent of gross domestic product in 2002. On a per capita basis, expenditures totaled Intl $2,931 that year, with the total population being approximately 31 million. About 30.1 percent of the total spent on health was private expenditure.

China. In 2005, the WHO indicated that health expenditures in China were 5.8 percent of gross domestic product in 2002. On a per capita basis, with a total population of 1.3 billion, expenditures totaled only Intl $261 that year, although that figure did represent a 16.7 percent increase over the previous year. About 66.3 percent of the total health expenditure came from private funds. By the end of the twentieth century, China had a total of 311,000 hospitals, clinics, health care centers, disease prevention agencies, research institutes, and medical schools, compared to 314,100 in 1998, according to the country's Ministry of Health. In 1999 the number of workers in the health care system numbered 5.57 million, an increase of approximately 35,000 from 1998. There are 239 hospital beds, 167 physicians, and 102 nurses per 100,000 residents. About 80 percent of the health budget goes to major urban hospitals. However, 69 percent of the total population in China lives in rural areas, and growth of basic health care services for these citizens has been slow due to the lack of investment. Approximately 50 million Chinese citizens were hospitalized in 1999, and clinics and hospitals saw some 2.08 billion patients.

France. The WHO's 2005 analysis of health care systems in the major countries of the world ranked France as having the best, followed by Italy, Spain, Oman, Austria, and Japan. *The Irish Times* reported that France has avoided the problem of waiting lists by building over-capacity into its health care system. The country's number of acute-care beds is above the European average, and rates for bed occupancy are approximately 75 percent. France's social security system, established in the 1940s, funds the health care system. Social insurance is compulsory and covers close to 100 percent of the populace. France's hospitals may be public or private. Hospital physicians' salaries range from FFr295,000 to FFr535,000. Doctors may offer private practice services in public hospitals for up to 20 percent of their work week. The World Health Organization reported in 2005 that health expenditures in France were 9.7 percent of gross domestic product in 2001. On a per capita basis, expenditures totaled Intl $2,736 that year, with a total population of about 60 million. About 24 percent of the total spent on health was from private funds.

The Lancet reported that because the French work week has decreased from 39 to 35 hours beginning in 2002, public hospitals will be creating 45,000 new jobs by 2005. Beginning in June 2000, the French government gave public hospitals over US$4.1 billion to help with job creation and to improve working conditions and salaries for nurses. The country's 1,300 private hospitals and clinics, concerned that a number of nurses will leave to work in public hospitals, call this competition unfair. As a result, they have requested the government aid them with some FFr6 billion in funds.

FURTHER READING

Annual Survey of Hospitals. Chicago: American Hospital Association, 2005.

Boyd, Jade. "Better Late Than Never For Internet Initiatives—Competition and Federal Mandates Drive Health-care Players' Online Strategies." *Internet Week,* 15 October 2001, 31.

Craver, Martha Lynn. "Hospital Construction Boom: Building for the Future." *Kiplinger Business Forecasts,* 9 July 2004.

"Fast Facts on U.S. Hospitals." *Hospital Statistics.* Chicago: American Hospital Association, 2004.

Gillespie, Greg. "Hospital Web Sites Face an Unpredictable Future: Strategies are Evolving as CIOs and Web Site Developers Implement Interactive Applications." *Health Data Management,* May 2001.

Haugh, Richard. "Foreign Profits. Hospitals Seeking a Boost to the Bottom Line Go Overseas, Where All the Patients Pay Up." *H & HN: Hospitals & Health Networks,* July 2001.

"Medical Liability Crisis Affects Communities' Access to Care." Chicago: American Hospital Association. 28 April 2003. Available from http://www.aha.org.

"NHS in England." United Kingdom: National Health Service. 27 July 2004. Available from http://www.nhs.uk.

"Patients Rank Physicians High in Satisfaction Survey." *Modern healthcare,* 29 March 2004.

Pear, Robert. "Report Cites Danger in Overtime for Nurses." *The New York Times,* 5 November 2003.

Romano, Michael. "Back to the Basics; Number of General Hospitals Grows for the First Time in Years Despite Slim Margins, Lagging Reimbursements and a Tight Market." *Modern Healthcare,* 12 January 2004.

Schieber, George. "Increasing Investments in Health Outcomes for the Poor." Washington, D.C.: The World Bank, October 2003.

"Study Documents Savings from E-commerce." *Hospitals Materials Management,* July 2004.

"Study Urges Caution On Expanding Hospital Capacity." *Healthcare Financial Management,* March 2004.

"Surveyed Hospital Execs Say They Plan to Build." *Healthcare Financial Management,* April 2004.

TrendWatch: The Economic Contribution of Hospitals. Chicago: American Hospital Association, May 2004. Available from http://www.aha.org.

TrendWatch: The Hospital Workforce Shortage: Immediate and Future. Chicago: American Hospital Association, 2002. Available from http://www.aha.org.

U.S. Bureau of the Census. *Service Annual Survey.* Washington, 2004. Available from http://www.census.gov.

———. *Statistical Abstract of the United States.* Washington, 2004. Available from http://www.census.gov.

"U.S. Hospital Expenses Hit $462 Billion in 2002, According to Latest AHA Statistical Survey." *Health Care Strategic Management,* February 2004.

The World Health Report 2005. Geneva, Switzerland: The World Health Organization. 10 August 2004. Available from http://www.who.int.

SIC 3851

NAICS 339115

OPHTHALMIC GOODS

Optical goods manufacturers produce a variety of corrective eyewear, implants, and eye-care supplies. Common examples of industry output include eyeglasses, spectacles, contact lenses, sunglasses, and lens cleaning solutions.

INDUSTRY SNAPSHOT

The global optical goods industry was characterized by steady net demand for most of its products and frequent upgrades to the materials and technologies used in production. Vision impairment occured at fairly predictable rates in human populations. Residents of affluent countries were more likely to seek corrective lenses or surgeries when compared to people who lived in developing countries. In the United States, macular degeneration, a condition in which part of the retina becomes scarred, was the number one cause of eyesight loss. The number of macular degeneration cases was expected to double during the next 25 years. Two important factors led industry experts to predict increased demand for ophthalmic goods and services in the future: the continual rise of diagnosed cases of diabetes and the aging of the baby boomer generation.

Demand for particular products within the world's optical goods markets was not always even, however. Both eyeglasses and contacts were subject to fashion trends and enhancements in comfort or other features that rendered older eyewear less appealing to some consumers. For example, in the United States and Western Europe there was a pronounced trend toward disposable contacts, which were considered more comfortable, convenient, and sometimes cheaper than longer-lasting rigid lenses. In most markets, eyeglasses changed substantially so that newer models were lighter weight, thinner, more durable, and more varied in frame styles.

Other industry products were subject to greater fluctuations. Sunglasses, in particular, faced more volatile demand because they are not as essential to vision as corrective lenses. Also, the underlying technology in most sunglasses was much less sophisticated than that of prescription eyewear. Thus, the low-end sunglasses trade was a commodity market.

In order to increase sales for their spectacles and sunglasses, designers sought to make their creations stand out in special ways. Some stuck with innovative applications of their own logo. Others, however, tapped into house motifs to gain new customers from the ranks of people who wanted to show off their brand loyalty. Instead of choosing to wear easily-distingushable Christian Dior glasses, a fashionable consumer might select glasses with Tom Ford's discreet metal T set flush to the temple. The 2007 Coach collection included glasses designed to complement popular handbags. Eyewear designer Alain Mikli reportedly used shapes, colors and distinctive materials to establish brand recognition for his line.

Solutions used to clean contact lenses could be easily interchanged among different brands and, in some cases, different formulations. Coinciding with the rise of disposable lenses, the trend in Europe and the United States was toward multipurpose solutions that perform all necessary sanitizing actions on lenses rather than using separate solutions for each task.

The ophthalmic goods industry was thoroughly internationalized, particularly among the developed nations. World market leaders in various product categories included France, Italy, Switzerland, and the United States. In the mid-2000s, nearly 100 million people wore contact lenses, and an estimated 1.5 billion people wore corrective lenses in 2005. As documented in Ellisor's *2004 Annual Report,* by 2025 almost one-third of the world's total population will be over the age of 45, most of whom will need corrective lenses as a natural result of aging. The best growth was being realized in the markets for plastic, polycarbonate, and high-index lenses.

The spectacles market experienced a short-term increase in sales with an estimated 8.9 million units in 2006. That reflected an increase by 4 percent from March 2005 to March 2006. Prescribed spectacle lenses and frames continued to be the most popular accounting for 90 percent of the total value share of the market.

Eye glass wearers were faced with a sometimes controversial choice other than traditional sales outlets. Several online contact lenses suppliers were prepared to sell the product without checking to see whether consumers had valid prescriptions. This was the major finding when Optician conducted a mystery shopping exercise in 2007. There were 65 calls made to an assortment of online suppliers. The caller expressed an interest in ordering daily disposable lenses based on details read during the conversation. A small number of companies agreed to do this and four orders for contact lenses were made and completed to double check that no valid prescription was required during any phase of the ordering process. Companies willing to do this were located in the U.S. and UK.

ORGANIZATION AND STRUCTURE

The ophthalmic goods industry was a labor-intensive industry populated by numerous smaller, specialized companies churning out everything from sunglasses and safety goggles to shooting glasses and lorgnettes. In 1989, 68 percent of U.S. companies in this industry had fewer than 20 employees. In Canada, the figure was closer to 75 percent. While these smaller companies were engaged exclusively in the production of ophthalmic goods, industry giants such as Bausch & Lomb, typically manufactured a wider array of goods including medicines, dental products, and optical goods.

The labor-intensive nature of the ophthalmic goods industry attracted countries with large pools of low-wage labor such as China and Taiwan. By 1992 East Asia had become a leading supplier of low-end sunglasses and vanity glasses, accounting for 32.8 percent of total ophthalmic goods imported by the United States—just a few points shy of the 35.3 percent share held by the European Union. The EU—besides being a major producer of glasses and contact lenses—dominated the market for designer frames. Japan was another leading producer of ophthalmic goods, and was the world's largest exporter of optical equipment throughout the 1990s. Other leading exporters included, in descending order, the United States, Italy, Germany, France, and China.

Products manufactured by the ophthalmic goods industry ranged from low-cost nonprescription sunglasses to highly sophisticated prescription contact lenses. Some products could be purchased from street vendors; others were only available from qualified optometrists and ophthalmologists. Frames and sunglasses accounted for the bulk of world production of ophthalmic goods. Sunglasses, in particular, attracted a broad spectrum of users and were available in both prescription and nonprescription forms. Technically, sunglasses were supposed to block a portion of sunlight from entering the eyes and protect them from ultraviolet (UV) radiation, which can damage the lens and the retina. The amount of protection sunglasses actually afford depends on the color and the depth of the tint. In practice, however, many sunglasses were little more than fashion accessories, affording little or no protection to the eyes. Growing consumer awareness prompted competition among high-end sunglasses manufacturers to produce more effective UV protection and resulted in the introduction of a new labeling system on some sunglasses telling consumers what percentage of ultraviolet light was blocked. Other types of glasses popular among prescription users included photochromic glasses; these contained tinted lenses that became darker in bright sunlight and lighter in a dark room.

Beginning in the 1980s, manufacturers of ophthalmic goods sought to broaden the market by encouraging consumers to treat eyewear both as medical devices and jewelry. Industry advertising heavily promoted both sunglasses and prescription glasses as fashion accessories. Ads such as Bausch & Lomb's "Take a good look" for its line of Ray-Ban sunglasses and L.A. Eyeworks' "A face is like a work of art. It deserves a great frame." spurred new growth in the market. People who might once have owned only one pair of glasses now needed a different pair for every occasion. Discount vendors sprang up in North America, Japan, and Europe offering consumers a huge variety of frames from which to choose. Growth in this area was substantial throughout the 1980s, with an estimated five out of six vision-impaired Americans still preferring eyeglasses to contact lenses.

In spite of the fact that contact lenses were much less commonly used worldwide than glasses, they were a tremendous source of revenue for the ophthalmic goods industry and a primary source of income for companies such as Bausch & Lomb, Allergan, and CIBA-Vision. Much of the value of contact lenses was derived from the need to replace them more frequently than glasses and from secondary products such as cleaning solutions. The U.S. market for contact lenses was estimated at US$2 billion in 1994 with an estimated 25 million contact lens wearers—76 percent of whom used soft lenses. Though effective in correcting most common vision problems such as myopia (near-sightedness) and hyperopia (far-sightedness), contact lenses had yet to supplant standard eyeglasses. As Ilene Springer pointed out in *Cosmopolitan,* "only about 50 percent of would-be wearers do well the first time lens meets eye. 'Dry eyes,' allergies, unusually shaped corneas, recurring infections, and hypersensitivity can make fittings difficult, sometimes impossible, almost always expensive." Once fitted, contact lenses—even extended-wear lenses—require regular maintenance and periodic replacement. Daily-wear soft lenses—the most popular—could be damaged easily and did not provide as clear vision as glasses or the less popular hard contact lenses. Although providing better vision and capable of correcting even severe astigmatism, hard contacts tended to irritate the eyes and popped out easily. More sophisticated lenses, such as extended-wear rigid gas-permeable lenses, solved many of these problems but were too expensive to attract a large market. Despite their limitations, contact lenses, particularly disposables, remained a high-growth item entering the late 1990s.

Other products manufactured by the ophthalmic goods industry included safety, industrial, and underwater goggles or glasses made of special shatterproof, impact-resistant materials such as polycarbonate and tinted yellow, vermilion, or orange for enhanced visibility.

BACKGROUND AND DEVELOPMENT

Eye problems have been a common cause of human disability since time immemorial. When all secondary causes—such as infectious disease and malnutrition—are removed, the most common eye problems are errors in refraction that are usually caused by defective genes. While humans have attempted to cure these problems for millennia, the development of devices to correct or enhance vision is fairly recent. No one knows exactly when or where eyeglasses were developed, however, Roger Bacon—a thirteenth century English scholastic philosopher—is sometimes credited with their invention. Whatever the case, spectacles had become quite common among the wealthy by the fifteenth century; and by the nineteenth century, advances in optics technology and the introduction of large-scale manufacturing spread them among the general population in Europe and America. Although early spectacles consisted of little more than a pair of crude magnifying lenses in a wire frame, scientific advances in the nineteenth century spurred not only the development of more sophisticated lenses but increasing sophistication in ophthalmologic diagnosis. By the end of the nineteenth century, lenses were being customized to correct the particular problems of individual wearers and the rise of the modern ophthalmic industry had begun. Early innovators included John Jacob Bausch who, together with Henry Lomb, ran a small American company that imported European optical goods. Bausch invented Vulcanite (a hard rubber) eyeglass frames, which were more durable than the wire and metal frames of the day. Fitting the new frames with lenses from Europe, Bausch and Lomb quickly became leaders in the young American ophthalmic goods industry.

More sophisticated testing techniques and rising populations helped assure the industry's continuous growth through the first half of the twentieth century. While eyeglasses were the most important single product, contact lenses were already coming into popular use in the late 1930s. These early contact lenses were known as scleral lenses. Covering almost the entire surface of the eye, they interfered with the movement of tears over the eyeball and had to be used in conjunction with an artificial tear solution. The inconvenience and discomfort of these early lenses proved unattractive to consumers and even as late as the 1960s, companies such as Bausch & Lomb saw no advantage in entering the contact lens market.

In the late 1940s, another type of contact lenses—corneal lenses—was introduced. These covered a smaller portion of the eye surface and floated on the eye's own layer of tears. Originally made of hard plastic, they had to be removed and sterilized daily. By the 1950s, these lenses had been refined enough to make them a genuine alternative to conventional corrective eyewear—despite their high cost and the discomfort they caused. At the same time eye examinations were becoming more common in developed nations, resulting in higher demand for corrective eyewear. These factors led to unprecedented growth in production and sales in the ophthalmic goods industry during the 1960s.

By 1960 annual sales of contact lenses had reached US$60 million in the United States, and hundreds of small companies jumped into the market. At about US$200 a pair, however, they were priced too high for the average consumer. More than half of those who tried them found them uncomfortable and reverted back to conventional corrective eyewear. Nevertheless, the development of this new market created enormous excitement, leading to a flurry of false advertising complaints and acrimonious patent disputes.

Meanwhile, as the contact lens market endured its growing pains, sales of conventional frames and lenses skyrocketed. Much of this growth was attributed to the overall buoyancy of the world economy, rising disposable incomes, and most importantly, to the increasing numbers of people undergoing complete eye examinations—a trend begun in the 1950s and fostered by the postwar introduction of national health plans throughout the industrialized world. In the United States, the number of corrective lens wearers grew by 30 percent between 1955 and 1965. Sales of ophthalmic goods were also facilitated by new product developments such as a new bifocal lens without a visible line separating each half of the lens; and lightweight, shatterproof plastic lenses.

Sunglasses, too, enjoyed record growth in the 1960s with sales nearly tripling between 1960 and 1966. No longer just a practical device to protect the eyes from the summer sun, sunglasses became a year-round fashion accessory—especially in the huge youth market. Dominated by companies such as Bausch & Lomb, whose Ray-Ban sunglasses (first introduced to the public in 1936) were *de riguer* for the truly fashionable, the sunglasses market became one of the most lucrative in the ophthalmic goods industry by the end of the decade.

However, the most notable development of the 1960s—the invention of soft contact lenses— did not make its impact felt until 1972. Made from a thin, soft plastic invented in 1960 by two Czechoslovakian scientists, soft contact lenses were flexible, water absorbent, and highly gas-permeable. Because this permeability allowed sufficient oxygen to reach the cornea soft contact lenses could be worn comfortably for longer periods of time than the hard hydrophobic lenses then in use. In 1966, Bausch & Lomb acquired the exclusive rights to market and manufacture this new lens material and by 1971 had received U.S. Food and Drug Administration (FDA) approval to sell its soft contact lenses. Although expensive, the new lenses were an immediate success, generating enough sales to vault the company into the Fortune 500 and make it the world's leading manufacturer of contact lenses—a position it still held in the 1990s.

Rapid expansion of the ophthalmic goods market continued through the 1970s, encouraged by the introduction of the new soft contact lenses and continuing population growth. At the same time, competition intensified as countries such as Japan entered the market delivering high volumes of low-cost, high-quality frames, lenses, and sunglasses. Sunglasses were such a lucrative business that hundreds of companies around the world jumped into the market attaching the names of well-known fashion designers to products and furthering the establishment of sunglasses as a fashion accessory. So successful was this strategy that conventional frames soon had "designers" as well and the range of styles proliferated. As competition heated up, pricing strategies became of paramount importance and many companies began moving from labor-intensive manufacturing operations to low-cost offshore locations.

In the 1980s, sales in the ophthalmic goods industry continued to climb at a prodigious rate. Despite a disappointing slump in sales of sunglasses in the early part of the decade, they quickly regained their market thanks to the popularity of films like *Top Gun* and *Risky Business* in which well-known actor Tom Cruise was featured wearing sunglasses. Retail sales of sunglasses in the United States increased by 100 percent from 1980 to 1990 and similar increases were seen in other developed countries.

The real story of the 1980s was the rising popularity of contact lenses. Falling prices and advances in soft lens technology fueled explosive growth in this category. While consumer options were limited to hard lenses vs. soft at the beginning of the decade, by 1988 they could select from a wide assortment of standard and specialty contacts, including extended wear lenses, dirt-resistant lenses, more comfortable hard lenses, color-changing lenses, and bifocal lenses. The year 1988 also saw initial test marketing of disposable lenses that eliminated cleaning altogether. The number of wearers—21 million in the United States in 1988—was more than twice what it had been a decade earlier. In the space of only five years, companies such as Bausch & Lomb saw sales more than double from US$584 million in 1984 to more than US$1.2 billion in 1989.

According to Tony Montini, senior vice president of purchasing and merchandising at U.S. pharmaceutical chain Reliable Drug Stores, the ophthalmic goods market was one of the most volatile categories of the 1980s. Quoted in *Chain Drug Review,* he argued that the market had become so overheated that once it reached a certain level it could no longer sustain the kinds of increases it had been enjoying. From 1988 to 1995, increases in the number of contact lens wearers in the United States started to taper off, settling at around 25 million in 1992. At the same time, new product introductions waned and competition within the industry began to focus more on encouraging existing users and wearers of eyeglasses to switch to the new disposable lenses—a category whose steady replacement rate made it look like the product of the future. In addition, medical risks associated with extended-wear lenses were expected to boost demand for disposable lenses.

Stagnant growth in the market and intense competition led to some bizarre strategies. For instance, in 1994 Bausch & Lomb was marketing the exact same contact lens in four different ways—as "daily wear," "planned replacement," extended-wear disposables, and one-day disposables. The lenses were priced at US$70, US$15, US$8, and US$3 respectively. Yet the only difference between the lenses was in cost and use—not material. The company's justification for the price differences was that it hoped to lure people away from eyeglasses by making the more-convenient disposables affordable.

As countries emerged from the recession in 1993, growth in the ophthalmic goods industry showed few signs of picking up where it left off in 1989. From an average annual growth rate of 10 percent through 1989, it had fallen below 2 percent in 1991 and remained between 2 and 3 percent for the next few years. Forecasts for the remainder of the decade put growth at about 3 percent annually. Faced with a glut of sunglasses manufacturers and a mature, low-margin contact lens market, industry leaders diversified into other lines of health products and placed increased emphasis on various contact lens care products. In the contact lens market hopes remained that emerging demand for disposable and colored/tinted contact lenses would provide a new growth area. Also on the horizon was an anticipated increase in the demand for multifocal lenses generated by the rapidly rising number of older people living in developed nations. Perhaps the best news was for U.S. manufacturers, whose dominance of the contact lens market was expected to continue thanks to U.S. advances in contact lenses and polycarbonate and high-index plastic lens materials.

In the eyeglass lens market, increased demand for the new lighter and thinner polycarbonate and high-index plastic lenses was expected to help fuel new growth. Demand for scratch-resistant and ultraviolet-resistant lens coatings—heavily promoted by opticians—was also expected to rise. Additionally, pending FDA requirements that all general-purpose and cosmetic-use sunglasses block 99 percent of certain levels of ultraviolet radiation were expected to have a significant impact on the ophthalmic market—possibly weeding out the current surfeit of manufacturers and stimulating new demand.

CURRENT CONDITIONS

Shipment values for the ophthalmic goods industry totaled US$4.25 billion in 2002. At US$1.89 billion, contact lenses were by far the largest product category, followed by other ophthalmic goods and prescription ground eyeglass lenses (US$1.22 billion), ophthalmic plastics focal lenses (US$576.01 million), ophthalmic glass focal lenses (US$65.8 million), and ophthalmic fronts and temples (US$42.36 million).

The United States was the world's largest market for optical goods and is also a major producer. In 2003, the size of the U.S. market for ophthalmic goods were around $25.6 billion, up more than 2 billion from 2002. The United States exported more than US$1 billion. Exports increased every year since the late 1990s, growing 6.8 percent and 8.5 percent in 2000 and 2001, respectively. With the exception of a 1.1 percent decline in 2001, U.S. imports also have increased every year since the late 1990s. In 2002, imports totaled US$2 billion, up from US$1.9 billion in 2001.

According to U.S. Census Bureau data released in August 2004, the U.S. ophthalmic goods industry consisted of 559 establishments (488 companies) in 2002, down from 573 in 1997. Nearly 31 percent of industry establishments employed 20 people or more. However, small firms were dominant, with nearly 44 percent of establishments employing 1 to 4 employees.

By the end of 2003, *Ophthalmology Times* estimated the number of consumers wearing contacts lenses at 100 million, or around 5 percent of all who use corrective lenses. Due to ongoing improvements in convenience and comfort, significant growth was expected for the contact lens market during the late 2000s. Market share for products such as one-day disposable lenses was growing by double-digit rates during the mid-2000s. Also gaining market share in Asia and Europe were progressive contact lenses, which replaced bifocals and trifocals.

By 2007, glasses were being widely worn as popular fashion accessories. Many people had "wardrobes of glasses" to carry them from day to late night. Instead of small and metal frames, colorful and larger alternatives were in again. Marisa Fox noted that many people were influenced by red glasses worn by the TV hit show title character called Ugly Betty. Others chose plastic frames, glasses with thick temples or some with decorative accents. Costs for a single pair could range from US$49 to US$800 and beyond.

RESEARCH AND TECHNOLOGY

Research and development in ophthalmic goods continued to make strides in the development of new lens materials for both eyeglasses and contact lenses. Plastic lenses—first introduced for eyeglasses in the 1960s—became extraordinarily light, strong, and impact-resistant by the 1990s. New compounds such as high-index plastics and polycarbonate lens materials were developed in the United States that were shatterproof, yet light and affordable. However, because glass and C-39 plastic were easier to work with and less likely to be damaged in manufacturing processes than polycarbonates, the market was limited to sports, industrial applications, and children's eyeglasses. In the early 1990s, development of new computer-controlled molding injection processes overcame these problems and put polycarbonates on equal footing with the more commonly used glass and C-39 plastic. Eventually, polycarbonates were expected to replace existing materials altogether.

One of the most prominent developments in the contact lens field was aspheric lenses. Because they were flatter than conventional spherical lenses, they afforded more comfort and better vision. New polymer blends enabled the development of a lens material that lets oxygen pass through 25 times better than existing contact lenses. Several research groups were also working on producing lenses made of siloxane, a silicone-oxygen compound that produces strong, flexible films. Other developments included lenses to help color-blind people distinguish red from green, cosmetic lenses, ultraviolet-resistant lenses, and lenses chemically treated to darken in the center as light intensifies—basically sunglasses.

Research studies involving young subjects have shown children in elementary school can handle their contacts properly without any increase in complications. In fact, 8- to 11-year olds tended to be more responsible users when compared to most teenagers. Modern advances made contacts more comfortable and easier to keep clean. Consequentially, eye experts were more willing to prescribe contacts for young people.

Clinical research, conducted among contact lens wearers, demonstrated that daily-wear silicone hydrogel contact lenses can improve comfort significantly versus hydrogel lenses in most surroundings. The research also revealed that newer, second-generation silicone hydrogels made from senofilcon A and galyficon A significantly reduced the frequency of commonly reported ocular surface symptoms. Those symptoms included dryness and discomfort in adverse environments and during visually demanding tasks such as night driving and reading. The study population included nearly 500 contact lens wearers between the ages of 18 to 40. The study's primary purpose was to measure the proportion of daily-wear hydrogel contact lens wearers who wear lenses in challenging environments and during visually demanding tasks, and to evaluate their resulting comfort in those situations. Study findings were published in the April 2007 issue of *Optometry and Vision Science.*

University of Washington scientists worked on developing sunglasses that changed color with the touch of a button. They used smart plastics that change when an electric current flows through them. A watch battery activated the protypes that were capable of changing from dark to light blue in seconds. Other scientists reported developments such as lenses to help color-blind people distinguish red from green, cosmetic lenses, ultraviolet-resistant lenses, and lenses chemically treated to darken in the center as light intensifies—basically sunglasses.

Eyecare Trust claimed good photochromic lenses, those capable of darkening upon exposure to sunlight, blocked out 100 percent of the most harmful sun rays 100 percent of the time. The transitions caused adapting to changes from light to dark in a matter of seconds. Researchers at James Robinson, working with University of Leeds scientists, developed a single dye for photochromic lenses. It had two peaks of absorbency allowing the traditional grey or brown of sunglasses to be experienced by wearers.

University of Arizona and Georgia Institute of Technology scientists worked to eliminate traditional bifocals by developing eyeglasses that can automatically refocus. Prototype lenses utilize liquid-crystal material sandwiched between two flat sheets of glass. The transparent coating of indium-tin oxide functions in the manner of an electrode. The lenses' focal length was altered when researchers applied a voltage as low as 1.8V changing orientation of liquid crystals.

Perhaps the most notable development affecting the ophthalmic goods industry during the 1990s and 2000s has been the advances in laser eye surgery, in which surgeons used lasers to sculpt the cornea to focus light more precisely. The procedure was relatively noninvasive, did not require any significant recovery time, and had the potential to eliminate patients' need for glasses or contacts. However, the procedure was not foolproof and was not appropriate for all eye conditions. While this technology received a good deal of publicity during the mid-1990s, by the end of the decade it had failed to make any significant inroads into the vision correction market. This primarily was due to the large number of Americans who wore glasses or contact lenses. For example, there were some 140 million people in the market (as either contact-lens wearers or eyeglass wearers) in 1999, and yet only 1.5 percent were estimated to have had laser correction surgery.

Additional areas on which research focused included cleaning products (developing faster-working products), improved surgical instruments, and improving and creating pharmaceuticals. Researchers also worked diligently on improving drug delivery systems and devices. The reason was that 40 percent of eye diseases originate behind the eye where the retina attaches, but this is an extremely difficult area for medicine administration. In fact, despite the high percentage of diseases in this area, only 5 percent of pharmaceutical sales are for those diseases. Clearly, there is a dual incentive—profit and advances in eye care—to improve drug delivery to the back of the eye. As of 2002 Bausch & Lomb was running trials on a system known as Envision TD, which administers medication by way of a small implant.

Some of the most interesting new research into optical devices focused on so-called electronic glasses, which employed a camera, sensors, and display technology to aid vision. The devices, which were mostly experimental, were intended for people with severe sight loss for whom conventionally styled glasses or contacts are inadequate. As of the late 1990s these systems remained fairly obtrusive compared to conventional glasses because they require electronics to be worn near the forehead, but they represented a substantial improvement over larger, manual telescopic lenses or other existing technology to correct serious vision impairment.

WORKFORCE

According to the U.S. Census Bureau, the ophthalmic goods industry employed 21,086 people in 2002, with a total payroll of US$845.6 million. Of the total number of employees, 67 percent were employed in production, with an average annual salary of US$33,903. Florida employed the most workers (3,038), followed by Colorado (2,827), New York (1,827), and Massachusetts (1,475). Most U.S. industry employees worked for companies with 20 employees or more. A total of 2,922 worked for companies with 20 to 49 employees, followed by firms with 50 to 99 employees (2,438 workers), 100 to 249 employees (3,860 workers), 250 to 499 employees (4,239), and 500 to 999 employees (3,250 workers).

INDUSTRY LEADERS

Bausch & Lomb. The Rochester, New York-based Bausch & Lomb Inc. is one of the world's top ophthalmic goods companies. Its products can be found in more than 100 countries worldwide. Founded in 1853 by German immigrant John Jacob Bausch, the company had revenues of nearly US$2.3 billion in 2007. The company was long known for its premium sunglasses which included the Ray-Ban and Killer Loop brands. Ray-Ban had been sold to Luxottica Group S.p.A. by 2004. The company has a strong line of contact lenses. The company also made personal health care products (contact lens solutions), medical products (contact lenses), and pharmaceuticals (glaucoma treatments and over-the-counter eye drops). Its lens care line, which includes the trade names Boston, ReNu, and Sensitive Eyes.

Demand for surgical tools and instruments (such as for cataract, vitreoretinal, and refractive surgeries) continued to rise. Over the course of its history Bausch & Lomb made significant contributions to the advancement of optical and ophthalmic technology including the creation of Ray-Bans (originally developed in 1929 for the U.S. Army Air Corps), the Cinemascope lens, satellite and missile lens technology, and soft contact lenses. In the late 1990s, however, Bausch & Lomb was accused in the United States with marketing identical products under different brand names and unfairly charging higher prices for some; the dispute resulted in a US$1.7 million settlement. Bausch & has continued to expand its operations through acquisitions and increased its R & D funding.

In 2006, Bausch & Lomb stopped distribution of its ReNu MoistureLoc brand contact lens solution in the U.S. following the diagnosis of eye infections reported by users. The Food and Drug Administration released statistics showing 109 preliminary reports of rare fungal infection that may cause loss of vision had been received by the Centers for Disease Control and Prevention from 17 states.

In May 2007, Bausch & Lomb launched its "Through a Mother's Eyes" program to coincide with Mother's Day. The company partnered its PureVision Multi-Focal contact lenses brand with *MORE* magazine for a special contest. One grand prize winner would receive a year's supply of the product, free eye exam plus beauty makeover from fashion expert and TV show host Finola Hughes. Five lucky winners would receive a gift basket including certificate redeemable for year's supply of PureVision Multi-Focal contact lenses and a free eye exam.

Allergan Inc. Allergan Inc., a leading producer of intraocular lenses and surgical products, lens care items, and pharmaceuticals is also prominent in the ophthalmic goods industry. While Allergan also produces skin care products. Innovative eye care products include medications for cataracts, glaucoma, and pink eye. The company plans to focus future research efforts on developing niche pharmaceuticals, such as those used for glaucoma treatment. Past pharmaceuticals have been successful, most notably Botox, manufactured by Allergan's skin care segment. Botox was initially used for muscle spasms but later became widely used to diminish the appearance of wrinkles.

Established in 1950, the company's first product was an antihistamine eye drop called Allergan. The company adopted the name of the eye drop and in 1960 moved into the nascent contact lens market, specializing at first in contact lens solutions and later manufacturing its own lenses. After watching sales leap from US$100 million in 1980 to over US$700 million in 1989, the company struggled through a difficult transition period in the early 1990s and sales fell off from US$897 million in 1992 to US$857 million in 1993. In 2004 sales were up to US$2.04 billion, a 15 percent increase from 2003. Net income for 2004 was $377 million, compared to a net loss the year before, with 69.1 percent of sales derived domestically in the United States. Eye care pharmaceuticals were responsible for $1.13 billion of net sales. The company spent $345 million on research and development. Allergan earns nearly one-third of its revenues from outside the United States and has operations in Europe,

China, Latin America, and India. The company had 5,055 employees in 2005. For 2006, the company reported revenues of US$3.1 billion.

Essilor. Based in France, Essilor International SA concentrates its research and sales efforts primarily on lenses for eyeglasses. Essilor maintains a presence in more than 100 countries, with 200 prescription laboratories. Worldwide the company employed 26,534 people in 2005 and recorded sales of nearly US$2.9 billion. Among Essilor's products were Varilux progressive lenses and Crizal lenses, which are anti-reflective and smudge-resistant. Essilor was also marketing progressive lenses, which replaced bifocals and trifocals.

Luxottica. Italy's Luxottica Group SpA heads up the world's largest eyewear business. Luxottica Retail is the holding company for eyeglass retailer Lenscrafters and the specialty sunglasses retailer Sunglass Hut International. In addition to carrying designs by top names such as Chanel and Giorgio Armani, Luxottica has in-house designers who created hundreds of new designs every year. Revenues in 2005 were nearly US$5.2 billion, an increase of more than 17.4 percent from 2004.

In April 2007, *India Business Insight* reported that Luxottica had expressed its desire to enter India either directly or via one of its subsidiaries. A related proposal had been sent to Ray-Ban Sun Optics India Ltd. requesting that company issue a no-objection certificate for this purpose. Plans included distributing spectacle frames and sunglasses. In addition, Luxottica planned to establish a wholly owned subsidiary in India for entering into the wholesale cash-and-carry business in luxury and fashion brand eyewear other than the Ray-Ban brand.

Sola International. U.S.-based Sola International Inc. is another major lens maker. It competes directly with Essilor in production of glass and plastic lenses. Plastic lenses account for the majority of Sola's annual sales. That is due in large part to the popularity of its Spectralite brand of lightweight polycarbonate lenses. In 2003, about half of the company's US$650 million sales came from outside North America. That year, the company suffered a US$13.5 million net loss and employed 6,634 people. By 2006, Sola reported having more than 6,800 employees located in 28 countries serving 50 markets worldwide. Sola counted itself among the largest lens makers in the world and had manufactured more than one billion lenses.

Other Leaders. Several large, diversified corporations also play significant roles in the industry. Among them are Johnson & Johnson (J&J), whose Acuvue brand and other disposable contacts make it the world's largest disposable lens producer. The US$47.3 billion-a-year J&J also manufactures numerous personal and medical products that fall outside the scope of the optical goods industry. Switzerland's Novartis AG is another important competitor. Formed through the merger of Ciba-Geigy AG and Sandoz Ltd., Novartis is a US$28.2 billion pharmaceutical, nutrition, and life science conglomerate. Its principal eye products are produced through CIBA Vision and Novartis Ophthalmics.

CIBA Vision led the way with innovative advertising and marketing campaigns. It aggressively went after its goal of creating 500,000 new contact lens wearers in 2007. A study conducted by Opinion Research for CIBA Vision found that contact lens wearers spent three times as more in practice than spectacle wearers. They were also more loyal to a practice and made three times as many visits. CIBA Vision launched a Focus Dailies consumer campaign to raise awareness of 16- to 24-year olds about the benefits of daily disposable contact lenses. The advertorials were designed to spotlight pop singer Rachel Stevens and stress all day comfort of Focus Dailies. CIBA Vision had reportedly achieved success with a London multimedia advertising campaign for its daily disposable contact lens brand Focus Dailies with AquaComfort.

Further Reading

Barr, Joseph T. "The Contact Lens Spectrum Millennium Report." *Contact Lens Spectrum,* January 2000.

"Bausch & Lomb and MORE Magazine Partner to Honor Moms Across the Country." *Business Wire,* 9 May 2007.

"CIBA Targets London with Multimedia Lens Campaign." *Optician,* 27 October 2006.

"Contact Lenses Solution Controversy." *World Entertainment News Network,* 12 April 2006.

"Far-sighted Researchers Envision Autofocus Eyeglasses." *EDN,* 27 April 2006.

Fox, Marisa. "Focus on Frames; Glasses Are No Longer for Vision Correction Alone. Here Are Some Eye-Catching Options." 26 February 2007.

Gaston, Janice. "An Eye for Latest Trends: Fashion in Eyeglasses Always Changing, With Boundless Styles, Colors, Materials." *Winston-Salem Journal,* 23 February 2007.

Hoover's Company Capsules. Austin, TX: Hoover's, Inc., 2007. Available from http://www.hoovers.com.

Kleinman, Rebecca. "Signs of the Times; Sunglasses Branding is Appealing to the Fashion Insider." 24 July 2006.

"New Year, New Focus." *Optician,* 15 December 2006.

"Newer Silcone Hydrogel Contact Lenses Offer Significantly Improved Comfort Over Hydrogel Lenses in Adverse Environments, Clinical Study Shows." 25 April 2007.

"News." *Optician,* 6 April 2007.

"Pop Star Has Eyes for CIBA Campaign." *Optician,* 9 March 2007.

Powell, Cheryl. "First Contact — Lenses Making Advances: More Preteens Wearing Lenses As Advances Make Them More Comfortable and Easier to Clean." *Akron Beacon Journal,* 27 March 2007.

"Ray-Ban Sun Optics Issues NOC to Luxottica." *India Business Insight,* 27 April 2007.

Scerra, Chet. "Contact Lens Martek Sees Growth." *Ophthalmology Times,* 15 December 2003.

Shook, David. "Visions of Blindness Cures." *BusinessWeek Online,* 21 December 2000. Available from http://www.businessweek.com.

"Slipping Through the Net." *Optician,* 10 November 2006.

"Spectacles." *Optician,* 25 August 2006.

United Nations. Statistics Division. *International Trade Statistics Yearbook.* New York, 2004.

U.S. Census Bureau. *2002 Economic Census.* August 2004. Available from http://www.census.gov.

U.S. Department of Commerce, Bureau of the Census, International Trade Administration. *NAICS 339115: Ophthalmic Goods.* 3 September 2004. Available from http://www.ita.doc.gov.

Winder, Rob. "Sunlight Express: Photochromic Lenses Can Turn Prescription Glasses into Sunglasses in a Flash, and Lenses are More Sensitive Than Ever." *Chemistry and Industry,* 19 June 2006.

SIC 3841

NAICS 339112

SURGICAL AND MEDICAL EQUIPMENT

The world's surgical and medical equipment industry manufactures medical, surgical, ophthalmic, and veterinary instruments and apparatus. Representative products include syringes, clamps, hypodermic and suture needles, stethoscopes, laparoscopic devices, catheters and drains, and blood pressure monitoring devices. The industry also includes more high-tech instruments, such as implantable devices, remote monitoring and dosing products, and micro-sized biomonitors and drug-delivery systems.

INDUSTRY SNAPSHOT

In the early years of the twenty-first century, aging populations, the trend toward home healthcare, and a growing interest in delivering products and services over the Internet contributed to a steadily growing market for surgical and medical instruments and apparatus. Growth was expected to rise steadily at around 4.6 percent per year through 2010. Valued at US$57.6 billion in the early 2000s, the U.S. medical and surgical device market alone was expected to grow at a compound annual rate of about 8 percent through 2005, driven largely by devices for non-invasive surgical procedures, especially in the realm of interventional cardiology, according to research from Frost & Sullivan. Giant leaps in technology encouraged the growth of the medical manufacturing market, particularly in the orthopedic segment, which was valued at around $20 billion worldwide, more than half of which was earned in the United States. Growth rates were 13 to 15 percent annually from 2003 to 2005.

Other high growth segments included patient monitoring equipment, retail diagnostics, blood pressure monitoring equipment, and minimally invasive surgical equipment. Laparoscopic handheld instruments alone were expected to generate more than $235 million of revenue by 2009, as reported in *Medical Device Technology* in mid-2004.

Surgical and medical instrument manufacture was fiercely competitive in the mid-2000s. The fact that highly-specialized surgical tools could be invented, produced, and distributed by small high-technology firms allowed manufacturers with relatively small gross sales to have significant impact on certain segments of markets belonging to industry giants. Toward the close of the twentieth century, a way to meet this competition was to grow, amalgamate, and diversify. As high technology assumed a greater place in medicine and various living organisms were incorporated into treatment formats, the concept of biotechnology as an industry segment grew in importance (see also **Biotechnology**).

By the turn of the twenty-first century, fewer major manufacturers concentrated specifically on certain types of equipment, or on pharmaceuticals, or on treatment of a certain disease. Instead they diversified, sometimes through acquisition, to broaden their presence in the biotechnical industry. By embracing biotechnology, companies like Baxter, long dominant as an international supplier of medical and surgical devices, suddenly were in competition with megaliths like Johnson & Johnson and Roche, four times Baxter's size. Medtronic's 2001 acquisition of insulin pump leader MiniMed and Medical Research Group furthered its entry into the chronic disease management market. Tyco International, a conglomerate of high-technology instrumentation businesses, expanded into the healthcare market, swallowing high-profile firms United States Surgical in 1999 and C.R. Bard in late 2001.

The advent of managed care—with attendant pressures to hold down the cost of medical treatment—added further incentive to innovators in the industry, while in some cases limiting their profits. Less invasive surgeries such as laparoscopy, cardiac balloon angioplasty, and laser surgery, while posing manufacturing challenges, permitted less invasive surgical techniques and subsequent cost savings in actual patient care (i.e., shorter hospital stays implying lower labor costs, fewer patient complications, quicker recuperations).

The explosive growth of the Internet, and in particular, e-commerce, found most major medical device manufacturers scrambling to enhance their online presence with streamlined electronic business transactions, supply chain management, and even remote monitoring of implanted devices through dedicated Internet channels.

ORGANIZATION AND STRUCTURE

Inspired in part by increasing emphasis on ISO 9000 standards in all segments of industry, regulatory bodies of several countries set and restructured guidelines for medical manufacture. The use of quality marks, as well as European (CE) certification marks on medical devices continued to be a stumbling block as regulatory officials, device manufacturers, and private certification and testing firms strove to find consensus on what value quality marks add to a product, and whether consumers can be misled by a mark that merely indicates a base requirement for marketing in a particular country, rather than value-added testing. Various government promotion of standardization of safety and quality regulations helped to stabilize the industry, and the same regulations served to ease trade barriers.

The European Community Council formally adopted the Medical Device Directive as a regulatory initiative on

June 14, 1993, with implementation beginning January 1, 1995. The European Free Trade Association (EFTA) followed suit, actively enforcing the directive. Any products imported or manufactured in affected European countries were required to be tested and certified at the direction of European Union-accredited "Notified Bodies." Now it was necessary to meet just a single set of standards. This eliminated the unpleasant marketing/manufacturing decisions of the past, when manufacturers either could limit their exports, manufacture variations on a single product in an attempt to satisfy each member nation, or create equipment that could match twelve separate standards simultaneously.

A variety of trade agreements devised in the last decade of the century had effect, direct and indirect, on the global market for surgical and medical equipment. The North American Free Trade Agreement (NAFTA)—passed in 1994 by the United States, Mexico, and Canada—eliminated tariffs between the three nations. Prior to NAFTA, Canada and Mexico already were the second- and fourth-largest importers of U.S. surgical and medical instruments, and the United States received its third-largest supply of medical and surgical instrument imports from Mexico. With the implementation of NAFTA, the three countries were in ideal positions to increase their respective export market positions with their North American neighbors, especially since imports into North America from other countries were still subject to tariffs that, in some instances, were as high as 50 percent. The effect of NAFTA was still being felt in 2002, as the export market for medical laboratory equipment alone in Canada reached US$2.75 billion and was confidently expected to continue slow, steady growth (5 percent per annum) through the mid-2000s. The U.S. territory of Puerto Rico benefited even more directly from NAFTA, due to the Section 936 preferences of the U.S. Internal Revenue Code. This section of the Code exempted Puerto Rican investments from corporate taxation, and therefore allowed substantial tax breaks for U.S. companies that located operations in Puerto Rico.

The Uruguay Round of the General Agreement on Trade and Tariffs (GATT)—signed in 1994—included an agreement to remove inter-country tariffs on medical equipment and drugs among the world's leading seven market economies, better known as the G-7: Canada, France, Germany, Italy, Japan, the United Kingdom, and the United States. Removal of these tariffs was expected to save manufacturers of medical devices and equipment millions of dollars per year. In late 1994, this initiative was supplemented by the Medical Technologies Agreement, a segment of the overall U.S.-Japan Economic Framework, a structure that facilitated U.S.-Japan bilateral trade negotiations. This agreement was intended to ease U.S. manufacturer penetration of the Japanese public-sector market for medical services and equipment, and it saw fruition almost immediately upon adoption. The agreement called for periodic reviews of related commerce, and the initial review, conducted less than a year after implementation, showed U.S. manufacturers holding 43 percent of foreign market share and 18 percent of the total Japanese market for medical equipment. As promising as these figures were, by the end of the decade the Health Industry Manufactures Association reported that, when all medically related products were included in the assessment, Japan's total expenditure for foreign-produced equipment was approximately 3 percent of its national health care budget.

Lowering of tariffs to speed the acquisition of vital health care products had practical implementation worldwide. In 1998, India expedited the modernization and expansion of national health facilities by instituting government directives permitting state-run hospitals and related public institutions to import approximately US$250 million worth of medical equipment duty free. In spite of the Asian financial crisis of the late 1990s, during the mid-2000s the Indian medical equipment and supplies market was growing at a rate of 10-15 percent annually.

Needs to pool medical knowledge and supplies were addressed by the Global Harmonization Task Force, convened in the 1990s and attended by representatives from Canada, the European Union, Japan, and the United States. The task force's mission was to develop a standard set of quality guidelines for internationally acceptable medical devices. They imposed guidelines for joint reviews of new products and encouraged an information exchange intended to result in a single quality inspection recognized by all major global markets.

The U.S. Food and Drug Administration (FDA) held the sometimes lauded, sometimes deplored distinction of being the world's strictest and most arduous reviewer with the lengthiest approval process for the medical device industry. Certainly FDA approval processes were a source of woe for many U.S. manufacturers of medical and surgical instruments. In the late 1990s, it was not unusual for FDA approved U.S. manufacturers, although holding a competitive edge in certain export markets, to lose that edge when new products were caught in the lengthy FDA application process, and foreign competitors thus were given time to overtake them. There was a certain amount of frustration within the U.S. market, as well, as surgical products readily available in Europe waited on the FDA for acceptance and distribution in the United States.

This lengthy FDA review of medical devices was based on one of two procedures. If the product was not similar to another FDA-approved product already on the market, a manufacturer was required to submit a Premarket Application (PMA) to the FDA. The information included in the PMA was intended to establish product safety as well as therapeutic or diagnostic benefit, all of which had to be demonstrated through intensive animal and human testing. On the other hand, if the new device was generally the same as one already marketed and sold, the manufacturer needed only to file under a procedure known as the FDA 510(k) pre-market notification. Historically, neither procedure was assured of fast approval. Faced by the fact that more and more U.S. companies exported manufacture as they sought more immediately profitable European markets, the FDA in the late 1990s attempted to improve its performance. In 1998 the FDA received 65 PMA submissions, down slightly from 1997, and review time of those submissions increased to 290 days from 207 in 1997. The average time for approval still was problematic—over a year and a half—but the 16.6 month figure in 1997 was down from 25.9 months in 1996, and a number of applications were approved in less than six months. The 510(k) clearance was even more promising, taking only a little over three months (97 days), a 9 percent improvement over performance a year earlier. Even more significant, the FDA could point to two consecutive years (1996 and 1997) completed with zero backlog of 510(k) clearances. The 1997 passage of the FDA Modernization Act sought to streamline the FDA's reviews by allowing reduced filing requirements for relatively simple devices, and allowing third-party review of some others.

The FDA's involvement in medical manufacture was not limited to pre-market situations. In 1990 the U.S. Congress passed the Safe Medical Device Act in an effort to broaden the regulation of safety standards for medical devices. From 1990 onward, all U.S. health care facilities were required to report serious injuries and deaths resulting from the use of medical devices—both to the FDA and to the manufacturer of the product—and to make the information available to the media. The act also provided for civil penalties for violation of the new regulation, more intense post-market surveillance, and required that more data be provided on 510(k) applications. Four years later, the FDA was involved in the revision of the Good Manufacturing Practice Standards. This revision included a design-control process similar to the International Organization for Standardization's quality-control standard ISO 9001. Compliance with the labeling, packaging, and product performance guidelines of this ISO-like standard became critical for U.S. manufacturers trying to market abroad. In the year 2000, the FDA also established guidelines for reprocessing devices labeled "disposable" or "one use only" by the original manufacturer. Reprocessors must follow strict guidelines and seek approval for all devices cleaned, sterilized, or reconditioned.

BACKGROUND AND DEVELOPMENT

The development and rise of the medical equipment industry relied on the emergence of medical science technology. When instruments of a lower technology grade, (e.g., stethoscopes, surgical clamps, hypodermic needles and syringes, and surgical knives) were critical for the general practice of medicine and surgery around the world, there was intense global competition among manufacturers in their production. The competition forced down prices for these products, at the same time engendering a continuous struggle for position within the international marketplace. Then price, which translates into profit, tended to guide further market expansion, and international trade of lower-technology items typically gave way to pressure to permit the manufacture and distribution of their higher-technology counterparts.

Manufacturers with the financial and engineering resources to capitalize on technological innovations grew internationally. Particularly those products that resulted in lowered labor costs (often by reducing patient hospital stays), or that allowed patients to be cared for in environments less costly than full-scale hospital facilities, were the products in greatest demand. As an example, consider the advent of surgical staplers in the mid-1960s. By the 1980s, a full complement of stainless steel and absorbable synthetic staples that dissolve in the body had been designed. Since staplers closed incisions and wounds faster than sutures, they allowed less blood loss and tissue damage and encouraged faster post-operative recovery time. Although four times as expensive as suturing, the speed and convenience of stapling coupled with cost savings during the period of patient recovery to make it an increasingly lucrative product in the industry. Once a product like the stapler was introduced, the door was opened to further innovation. In 1978, United States Surgical Corp. (USSC), one of the world leaders in development and sales of surgical staplers, made several design changes, including a disposable skin stapler that eliminated lengthy cleaning and sterilization procedures necessitated by rival stainless steel staplers. Two years later, this concept was extended, again by USSC, to include a disposable internal stapler.

The balloon, or transluminal, angioplasty catheter—an instrument used to forge through plaque-clogged or narrow arteries as an alternative to heart bypass surgery—became increasingly popular during the 1980s and continued to be used on a widespread basis through the 1990s. This device utilized a balloon guide wire attached to a very thin catheter, and was inserted into a patient's arm or leg. The wire was fed through the arterial system until it reached a clogged area, where the balloon was inflated, widening the arterial passageway by pressing the plaque against the arterial wall. Hundreds of thousands of angioplasties were performed globally on a fairly routine basis. However, because angioplasty did not remove the plaque that caused the blockage, it was not unusual for patients to experience further arterial clogging. In the mid-1990s, manufacturers developed atherectomy instruments that used tiny blades to cut through and remove plaque, but, by the end of the decade, medical focus seemed to be on angioplasty. Instead of performing atherectomy, doctors tended to give angioplasties followed by vascular stenting—the insertion of mechanical dilators designed to hold open areas from which obstructions had been removed. More traditional bypass surgery was beginning to be performed by surgeons manipulating robotic arms and tiny laparoscopes. Although the US FDA still considers such computer-assisted bypass surgery experimental, the potential for less invasive surgery accurate to micrometers continues to drive development and demand for such devices.

The introduction of laparoscopic surgery was an undisputed milestone for surgical and medical instrument manufacturers—and for the entire medical community worldwide. Laparoscopy involved the use of trocars or surgical tubes inserted into tiny slits in the skin as entry points for specialized instruments. The long slender optical instrument called a laparoscope housed a miniature video camera. Directing this camera allowed surgeons to explore within the human body with minimal patient trauma. Laparoscopy changed the practice of surgery, allowing surgeons to perform such high-volume procedures as gall bladder and kidney removals, hysterectomies, appendectomies, hernia removals, and cancer stagings, all with far less invasive methods than had previously been used. Before laparoscopy, performance of these procedures automatically mandated lengthy hospital stays and long recuperation periods for patients. With the advent of laparoscopy, many procedures could be performed in hospital outpatient departments or ambulatory surgery centers. Not only was patient trauma reduced and recovery eased, but costs associated with each procedure and the associated patient stay were dramatically reduced also. It is not an exaggeration to say that laparoscopy changed the face of surgery delivery systems worldwide, although, at the same time, it should be noted that the early implementation of laparoscopy was closely tied to the ability of an institution to train doctors in its use.

The desire to find less invasive means of performing surgery prevailed throughout the 1990s. No particular aspect of surgery was exempt. Moreover, ease of use was equally important. In 1998, a "catarex probe" was introduced by Optex. This device, with a whirling blade and accompanying vacuum, required less surgical expertise in the excision of cataracts. That same year, Sulzer Osypka GmbH (a German component of the Swiss Sulzer Medica, Ltd.) presented a means of repairing certain heart defects with no surgery at all. By introducing two tiny "umbrellas" over a "rail" comprised of a wire catheter, surgeons were able to use the same catheter to screw the umbrellas in place, repairing holes in the atria of the affected heart. To the minimal patient trauma associated with the first use of the device was added the knowledge that a similar catheter could be used to effect unlimited repositioning of the umbrellas, if future adjustment was necessary.

A rising trend in the 1990s was the sale and utilization of used or refurbished medical equipment as a means of containing costs. The United States took over the majority of this market in the mid-1990s, but Canada, China, central Europe, Latin America, and Russia were destinations for reconditioned equipment as well. Especially in those nations where health care budgets were extremely tight, refurbished equipment could more easily be obtained and allowed them to provide current technological advances at a fraction of the original purchase costs. The refurbished medical device market accounts for only a small fraction of the instrument business. Few medical entrepreneurs can afford to weather the high costs of multiple difficult chemical cleaning processes, FDA approval, to say nothing of convincing the surgeon or hospital to purchase used equipment. If being resold or reused in the United States, refurbished devices are subject to U.S. Food and Drug Administration regulations requiring pre-market approval or pre-market clearance before reuse. These rules came following reports of patients harmed by contaminated instruments that had not been sufficiently reprocessed.

The Internet began to revolutionize the medical device market. Late 1999 saw the introduction of the first wireless Internet-based heart monitoring system. The Mayo Clinic and University of California at San Francisco are anticipating clinical trials data from patients on the web. Teleradiology, a new field involving imaging via the internet, allow physicians across the globe to view and mark up medical images in real-time.

CURRENT CONDITIONS

As the world industry leader, the United States consumed 40 percent of global output and accounted for about 50 percent of production of medical devices. After the United States, Western Europe and Japan were the next biggest world markets. During the mid-2000s, the industry was on solid footing, bolstered by continued spending on research and development (R & D) initiatives that ensured success well into the future. Worldwide, the market for medical and surgical devices was valued at approximately US$140 billion in 2002, according to a 2003 report from the research firm Frost & Sullivan. Other estimates valued the industry at US$165 billion, down from US$169 billion in 2001. As reported by Research and Markets, growth was expected to continue at about 5 percent annually through the mid- to late 2000s.

The market for orthopedic equipment specifically was valued at $20 billion worldwide, more than half of which was manufactured in the United States. The market grew 13 to 15 percent annually during the mid-2000s. Rapid growth was expected to continue for the medical device market overall, due to an aging population, longer life spans, higher rates of obesity and injury, growth in emerging markets, and direct-to-consumer marketing, as reported by Jim Lorincz in *Tooling and Production.*

Cardiac surgical devices were another lucrative category during the mid-2000s. In its November 1, 2003 issue, *Venture Capital Journal* revealed that cardiovascular devices represented 7.2 percent of all industry sales in 2002, or US$12 billion. Based on estimates from Standard & Poor's, this sector of the medical device industry was expected to experience 13 percent annual growth through 2005.

A December 2003 report from the Centers for Medicare and Medicaid Services (CMS) revealed that some 80 percent of industry players fell into the category of small or emerging companies during the early 2000s, with annual sales below US$100 million. While contributing only 10 percent of industry sales, these small companies spent 28 percent of all research and development dollars. To fund these efforts, small firms depended heavily on funding from venture capitalists. After peaking at more than US$2.5 billion in 2000, venture capital funding decreased during the early 2000s. However, in its November 1, 2003 issue, *Venture Capital Journal* noted that funding for medical device market increased 54 percent in the second quarter of 2003 alone, signifying a potential comeback. Heading into the mid-2000s, some analysts also predicted an uptick in merger and acquisition activity, as established players sought new technologies and devices for their product lineups.

In an article on the medical device market, *Venture Capital Journal* was optimistic about conditions heading into 2004, noting that because of a population growing older and living longer, in addition to changes in regulations, approval, and cost reimbursement, "demand for innovation remains strong." The journal commented that "the companies that can meet that demand will be rewarded, whether they are established corporations or venture-backed startups."

RESEARCH AND TECHNOLOGY

Most major manufacturers of surgical and medical instruments—and medical products in general—spend more on research and development than other industries. This was especially true of U.S. manufacturers. By the end of the century, in companies that also pursued biotechnical remedies, R&D expenditure often ran as high as US$101,000 per employee.

The global rise in conservative, cost-conscious views about health care sparked criticism of large capital investments in R&D, at least in the United States. Germany and Japan continued to emphasize technology, and with socialized health care in both countries, and this led to speculation that critical resources in those countries possibly were shared more effectively than they were in the United States. At least it could be said that technology and innovation were encouraged in these markets, and that their governments were not left with the economic problem of paying the price of treatment for those without insurance coverage.

In the United Kingdom in the late 1990s, emphasis was placed on research funded in a variety of ways, public, private, charitable, or combinations of these. This research was intended to be "mission-oriented," that is to say, focused on a particular goal that could be identified as being of benefit to the population. This focus may have given rise to the high degree of public support for research in that country. Canada, too, in 1998 anticipated a plan that would double federal funding of university-based medical research. This is not to say that the United States lacked incentive to continue the aggressive medical research begun earlier in the decade—only that the reporting of this research occasionally was received differently by the public it served. In fact, at the beginning of 1998, a glance back at the preceding medical year demonstrated an impressive depth of exploration into a huge variety of surgical and medical issues.

One of the more promising developments in international research and development efforts was the introduction of the Standard for the Exchange of Product (STEP) model data. Initiated in the early 1990s, STEP represented yet another effort to standardize manufacturing procedures and subject product development, from manufacturing to post-marketing surveillance, to state-of-the-art computer-aided manufacturing (CAM) procedures. The improved documentation and communication implied by STEP usage created a single product data exchange standard by which manufacturers were able to select vendors whose tools were compatible with their own computer-aided design (CAD) software.

Nanotechnology is beginning to emerge from the medical research laboratory and see commercial application. Micro-sized devices, commonly known as Microelectromechanical Systems, or MEMS, are currently used in such common applications as ink-jet printer heads and automobile airbag inflation systems. Their use as implantable medical devices promises a new frontier in disease management and treatment. Medical devices that circulate freely in the bloodstream searching out cancerous cells or clogged arteries are currently being developed in Biomedical Engineering Centers in several U.S. universities. Researchers at Ohio State University have manufactured particles in the realm of 1 micron, and foresee their use as drug delivery systems for controlling metastatic cancers.

Telemedicine has also moved toward commercial adoption. In 2000, the FDA approved for marketing a device that allows patients to provide simple medical information such as blood pressure, temperature, and heart rate through a phone or data line. The American Telemedicine Association and providers of home health care services promote the use of telemedicine to patients unable to travel long distances to health facilities. Other applications appearing on the horizon for telemedicine include remote dosing and monitoring of insulin for diabetes patients, and high-risk pregnancy monitoring.

WORKFORCE

The medical and surgical equipment workforce is highly diversified, ranging from mechanical and electrical engineers to high-tech manufacturing technicians, and an increasing number of software developers. With the emergence of Internet-based monitoring devices, the number of Web application programmers and information technology employees is expected to increase. This counters the general downward economic trend in 2002 that forecast information technology careers would remain flat.

INDUSTRY LEADERS

GE Healthcare. With US$14 billion in 2004 sales, GE Healthcare offered a broad range of products and services worldwide. With roots tracing back to 1900, GE Healthcare is a major segment of General Electric and includes subsidiaries GE Healthcare Technologies and GE Healthcare Bio-Sciences. The company's main focus, medical imaging, began with X-ray technology, and continued with products in Computed and Positron Emission Tomography (CAT and PET scanners), Magnetic Resonance Imaging (MRI), and, more recently, full digital scanning. GE also produces a wide variety of clinical information systems, patient monitoring systems, and other medical information technology products. GE Healthcare employed more than 42,500 people in more than 100 countries in the Americas, Europe, and Asia. The company spent approximately $1 billion in research and development in 2004.

Johnson & Johnson. Johnson & Johnson, known the world over for such highly visible brand names as Band-Aid, Tylenol, and Motrin, as well as popular pharmaceuticals such as Hismanal and Ortho-Novum contraceptive products, also was a dominant presence in the field of surgical instruments. In 1941 the number of Johnson-produced surgical products was sufficient for the formation of a separate division, which, in 1949, became known as Ethicon, Incorporated. In 1992, Ethicon subdivided further to form two companies: Ethicon Incorporated and Ethicon Endo-Surgery. The surgical firm produced a variety of endoscopic procedure products and mechanical (non-suture) wound closure implements, including the Palmaz-Schatz Balloon Expandable Stent and the Ultracision Harmonic Scalpel. In 1997 the parent company's purchase of California-based Biopsys Medical added to the Johnson portfolio a surgical device enabling minimally invasive breast cancer diagnostic procedures. Johnson & Johnson's sales reached US$47.3 billion in 2004, up 13.1 percent from the previous year.

In December of 2004, Johnson & Johnson announced it had agreed to purchase fellow industry leader Guidant for $25.4 billion in cash and stock. The merger was the third largest of 2004 and the largest in industry history. By adding

Guidant to its ranks, Johnson & Johnson strengthened its portfolio of medical devices, which would grow to consist of 42 percent pharmaceuticals, 41 percent medical devices and diagnostics, and 17 percent consumer products. The company's best growth was realized in the Asia-Pacific and Africa, where sales increased almost 20 percent. This, and previous acquisitions of Cordis and DePuy, helped solidify Johnson & Johnson's position as a market leader.

With 2004 sales of US$3.7 billion, Guidant was the established leader in the cardiovascular market, producing stents, angioplasty and other balloon catheters, and defibrillator and pacemaker systems. With significant revenues coming from its stent and angioplasty products, Guidant acquired the Intermedics Corporation, a pacemaker manufacturer, in 1999. In mid-2000, Guidant announced the U.S. availability of its first implantable pacemaker/defibrillator. Guidant's history dates from a 1994 spinoff of pharmaceutical giant Eli Lilly. By 2004, the company marketed its products in 100 countries, mainly in the United States, Japan, and Europe.

Baxter International Inc. Of firms dedicated to high technology medical manufacture, Baxter International was clearly a world leader, exporting some 120,000 different products to more than 100 nations. Noted Baxter products included heart surgery equipment, home dialysis systems, various blood and circulatory treatments, heart valves, and a variety of minimally invasive surgical devices. Baxter's research into animal/human organ transplant encouraged addition to its line of surgical devices. Although medical and surgical instruments occupied only a portion of its total sales, all Baxter products were the top or second place sellers in 85 percent of their respective industries. At the close of the century, Baxter, based in Deerfield, Illinois, was aggressively expanding its foreign market, which made up over 50 percent of its total sales. By 1998 Baxter operated 50 manufacturing plants outside of the United States, including facilities in North and South America, Europe, Australia, Asia, and the Pacific Rim. Sales reached US$9.5 billion in 2004, up from US$8.9 billion in 2003. Baxter spent $517 million on research and development in 2004, or 5.4 percent of sales.

Baxter International was founded in 1931 to distribute intravenous solutions manufactured by one of its founders, Dr. Donald Baxter. Another founder, Dr. Ralph Falk took over the company in 1935 and by 1939, introduced a sterilized vacuum-type blood collection device capable of storing blood for three weeks. Expanding rapidly, in 1951 Baxter went public to facilitate its acquisition of other companies. Exponential growth, highlighted by the takeover of five other firms, saw Baxter's sales total US$1 billion in 1978. Less than ten years later (1985) Baxter purchased American Hospital Supply, thereby becoming the largest hospital supply company in the world. Their policy of using acquisition to expand continued as the twenty-first century approached. Early in 1998, Baxter formed an agreement with the prestigious Cleveland Clinic Foundation, granting Baxter exclusive rights to the cardiovascular products developed by the foundation's Lerner Research Institute in return for Baxter's funding of the institute. Later the same year, Baxter acquired a portion of Ohmeda Medical Systems, a pharmaceutical products corporation that had enjoyed recent visibility because its equipment was featured in the popular *E.R.* television series. The company owns facilities in the United States and Canada as well as in Europe, Latin America, and Asia.

Roche Diagnostics. In 1998, Swiss-based Roche merged with Germany's Boehringer Mannheim to form the Roche Group. Internationally dominant in the pharmaceutical industry, the addition of the Boehringer Mannheim family of companies to the Roche affiliation gave the giant conglomerate significant presence in the medical and surgical equipment industry. Boehringer Mannheim, in the years prior to the merger, had ranked fourth in international medical and surgical equipment sales, grossing US$1.4 billion annually. Boehringer Mannheim saw the merger as an opportunity to increase its R&D budget to include many new surgical applications and enhance its existing product offering—and increase its already formidable industry presence. As of the mid-2000s, Roche Diagnostics was the world's foremost provider of in-vitro diagnostics. In addition, the company offered a wide variety of medical testing products and services. With 19,000 employees, the division held 20 percent of the world market for diagnostics, and was responsible for 23.7 percent of the Roche Group's total sales, which totaled US$27.6 billion in 2004. Significant gains in 2004 revenue were reported from Iberia/Latin America (14 percent increase in sales) and the Asia-Pacific region (13 percent), particularly in China, India, Korea, and Taiwan.

Siemens Medical Systems. A division of German multinational Siemens AG, Siemens Medical focuses on four primary device specialty areas: oncology, cardiology, neurology, and molecular diagnostics. With its parent company's history in electronics, its non-invasive surgical products and systems make it a major competitor of GE Medical. Siemens Medical is also know for its groundbreaking Lithostar lithotripsy system for non-surgical treatment of kidney stones and its huge variety of patient monitoring devices—including telemetry devices, pulse oximeters, and other diagnostic tools.

Becton, Dickinson and Company. Becton, Dickinson and Company celebrated its 100th anniversary in 1997. Its B-D logo is ubiquitous in hospitals around the globe. Its three major divisions, BD Biosciences (Clontech, Discovery Labware, Immunocytometry Systems, and Pharmingen); BD Diagnostics (Diagnostic Systems, Healthcare Consulting, and Preanalytical Systems); and BD Medical, fueled the company's US$4.9 billion in 2004 sales, up more 9 percent from 2003. The company's emphasis on global presence and global medical technology had been apparent at its 1897 founding, when Maxwell Becton and Farleigh Dickinson shook hands while on a sales trip and proceeded to import and sell fever thermometers and syringes purchased in England and France. By 1998, Becton, Dickinson operated in more than 40 countries and had expanded its manufacturing operations to include a significant presence in the rapidly growing markets of India and China. Although over 50 percent of its sales were in overseas markets, Becton, Dickinson held over half of the U.S. hypodermic needle and syringe market, and was the nation's leading supplier of intravenous catheters. Spurred by AIDS-related sensitivity to handling of blood and blood products, Becton patented a variety of safety devices in the late 1990s, including Safety-Lock syringes, Hemogard blood tube closure systems and the InterLink needleless injection system.

Medtronic Inc. Minneapolis based Medtronic was established in 1949 as a modest medical equipment repair shop, and quickly specialized in cardiac research. Medtronic is the world's largest maker of implantable biomedical devices. Because of its focus on cardiovascular disease, Medtronic also produced a wide variety of catheters and other minimally invasive instruments used in cardiac surgery. Reaping sales of US$10 billion in 2005, up from US$5.5 billion in 2001, the company has grown markedly since the 1990s. Medtronic sells its products in more than 120 countries, and employs a global workforce of 31,000.

Boston Scientific Corporation. Dr. Joachim Burhenne, who pioneered the field of minimally invasive medical/surgical procedures, was the major inspiring force behind Boston Scientific Corporation, along with co-founder John Abele, who began Medi-tech in the late 1960s. The firm's steerable catheters won it acceptance in surgical circles.

Boston produces a wide variety of catheters, endoscopes, and laparoscopes used in applications ranging from vascular surgery and cardiovascular surgery to urology, gastrointestinal procedures, and pulmonology. Its 1998 acquisition of Schneider from Pfizer Medical Inc. allowed Boston to expand into Schneider's key markets: brachytherapy, aneurysmal disease, and stent products. Boston's flagship products include the NIR coronary stent and the Maverick balloon dilation catheter. A major U.S. exporter, Boston sells its products in approximately 70 countries. The company reported sales of US$5.6 billion in 2004, up a remarkable 68 percent from the previous year.

Stryker Corp. Kalamazoo, Michigan-based Stryker Corporation transformed itself into a top medical device manufacturer with its 1998 acquisition of Howmedica from Pfizer Inc. for US$1.6 billion. Primarily known for its manufacture of surgical instruments, Stryker added Howmedica's line of orthopedic implants and bone and tissue repair devices to its product line. Sales reached US$4.2 billion in 2004, up more than 17 percent from 2003 levels and a significant increase from US$2.2 billion in 2000.

Tyco Healthcare. A recent entrant into the medical device equipment market, Tyco International, under its Healthcare and Specialty Products division was poised to become a worldwide leader at the beginning of the twenty-first century. Numerous large acquisitions, including U.S. Surgical, Mallinkrodt, and in late 2001, C.R. Bard, led Tyco Healthcare to sales of US$7.89 billion in 2004. Parent company Tyco International earned more than $40 billion.

U.S. Surgical (USSC), one of Tyco Healthcare's largest units, was founded by Leon Hirsch, who began his career as a dry-cleaning salesman. USSC grew to into a highly respected, highly technical corporation that became well known for its specially trained sales staff, able to demonstrate surgical staplers right in the operating room. Although sales slipped slightly in the early 1990s, in 1997 USSC posted a 5.3 percent market growth. Dominant in surgical stapler production (responding quickly to competitor Ethicon's introduction of the product), USSC held 75 percent of the world market in surgical staplers by the mid-1990s. The firm assumed leadership of the manufacture of laparoscopes in the late 1980s, and, by 1992, held tightly to 90 percent of that world market. Always aggressive with competitors, in 1993, USSC used a successful patent infringement lawsuit to force Eli Lilly to cease production of a particular laparoscope device. By 1998, USSC's laparoscope innovations led to its marketing of the "MiniSite" 2mm laparoscope, which used fiber-optic technology to enhance visual imagery through the smallest possible surgical access site. Other late 1990s USSC products included the Endo Stitch suturing device, the Versaport trocar system, the VCS Clip Applier (used to join vascular structures without penetration of the lumen), the Surgiview (a disposable laparoscope), and the ABBI Advanced Breast Biopsy Instrumentation System.

MAJOR COUNTRIES IN THE INDUSTRY

United States. In 1998 the emerging biotechnology industry—which embraced a large number of corporations also specializing in medical and surgical device manufacture—was growing at a rate of 11 percent a year. Medical device sales rose at 7 percent a year during the same period. By the end of the twentieth century, U.S. manufacturers controlled between 40 and 50 percent of the US$169 billion medical device world market, although Japan was a strong presence, and both established and emerging Northern European firms were making serious technological gains. The decline of economic recessions in Europe and Japan meant increased spending on U.S. exports such as stethoscopes, needles and syringes, ophthalmic instruments, and sphygmomanometers. Use of laparoscopy, internal stapling, and other less-invasive surgical procedures was on the rise globally. U.S. global dominance in the medical supply industry did decrease slightly as the year 2000 approached, dropping to a 40 percent share of the market by the late 1990s.

The United States held a strong position in the surgical and medical instrument industry throughout the 1990s and into the 2000s, with some areas showing particularly strong growth during the mid-2000s. Sales of patient monitoring equipment were expected to reach $8.7 billion in 2005. Telemetry was the fastest growing segment of that market, with 24.2 percent growth between 2002 and 2005, though a slowdown was expected in the late 2000s. External defibrillators (16.2 percent growth) and glucose self-monitoring equipment (13.1 percent), and sleep apnea monitoring equipment (16.8 percent) were other areas of high growth in the mid-2000s. The retail diagnostic market was expected to surpass $540 million, rising 8.5 percent annually from 2002 to 2009, as reported in *Medical Device Technology,* based on data from Frost & Sullivan.

Driven by devices for non-invasive surgical procedures in general, and interventional cardiac devices in particular, the U.S. medical and surgical device market was expected to grow at a compound annual rate of about 8 percent through 2005. The U.S. market was valued at US$57.6 billion in 2002 by Frost & Sullivan. Other category leaders included reconstructive implants for orthopedic surgery, as well as biologic and spinal devices, and those related to the administration and delivery of medication.

Europe. Europeans saw a 5 percent growth in EU member countries' biomedical markets in the late 1990s. The effect of the Euro currency, rolled out in January 2002 and supplanting all but three European currencies, was yet to be seen. Though mature, Europe's market for medical products still accounted for more than 30 percent of the global medical equipment and supplies market. The market was valued at US$31.1 billion in 2005, and was expected to grow $6.1 billion from 2005 through 2010. Disposable medical supplies were expected to perform well, with the greatest growth rates for high-tech devices expected in angioplasty catheters. Smith & Nephew, a leading medical device company based in the United Kingdom, is expected to compete fiercely with U.S. firms Guidant and Boston Scientific, among others.

China. The Chinese market for medical equipment and supplies was worth $7 billion in 2002, making it the world's third largest. Growing at a faster rate than Western markets, the market increased 10 percent in 2000 alone. *Datamonitor* predicted that the market would more than double by 2007. Most medical device manufacturing in China encompasses low-technology supplies, and no Chinese companies have a major worldwide medical presence. The government cracked down on black markets in China in 2000, primarily affecting sales of pharmaceuticals, but also sales of illegal medical devices.

According to the U.S. Department of Commerce, China imported approximately one-third of its medical devices from the United States by the early 2000s. Excluding Hong Kong, U.S. medical device exports to China increased from US$204 million in 1999 to US$350 million in 2002. Exports reached US$228 million during the first half of 2003. Compared to the same period a year before, this represented a strong increase of 48.6 percent. When U.S. exports to Hong Kong are factored in, the value of the Chinese market is even greater. From 1999 to 2002, U.S. exports to Hong Kong climbed from $215 million to $274 million, with exports for the first six months of 2003 going up 17 percent from the same period in 2002. According to *The Market for Medical Devices & Equipment in Brazil, Russia, India & China,* China's revenues from medical equipment could surpass Germany by 2009, Japan by 2015, and the United States by 2039.

In April 2004, Assistant Secretary of Commerce Linda M. Conlin led a trade mission to Beijing and Chengdu, China, in an effort to promote medical device trade. A document outlining the mission explained that exploding demand boded well for U.S. medical supply exporters, despite the challenges small and medium-sized companies would face to comply with trade rules and establish a viable market presence.

Japan. With the world's third-largest economy, Japan has continually maintained a huge trade surplus. However, its strength in the medical equipment industry was not great enough to completely offset that of either the United States or Germany. In fact, in 2003, Japan held only 13 percent of the worldwide market for general medical equipment. The Japanese government's Ministry of Health and Welfare (MHW) tried to shore up industry revenues through various subsidies, while at the same time positioning regulatory stumbling blocks in the paths of U.S. (and other) firms exporting to Japan. The erosion of the Japanese market by foreign suppliers continued throughout the 1990s, but the nation's pursuit of high technology combined with government support of private business to ensure that, by the end of the 1990s, some 200 Japanese companies had entered the world biotechnical and medical equipment markets. In 2002, the Japanese market for medical and equipment supplies was worth $23.7 billion, 35.5 percent more than five years before. This was expected to rise significantly by 2007 to $37.6 billion, as reported in a 2003 *Datamonitor* report.

FURTHER READING

"2004 Annual Report." Johnson & Johnson, 2005. Available from http://www.jnj.com/2004AnnualReport/index.htm.

"2004 Annual Report." Baxter International, 2005.

Centers for Medicare and Medicaid Services. *Health Care Industry Market Update.* 5 December 2003. Available from http://www.cms.gov/reports/hcimu/hcimu_12052003.pdf.

Ferrari, Mauro, and Jun Liu. "The Engineered Course of Treatment." *Mechanical Engineering*, December 2001, 44-47.

Frost & Sullivan. *Medical Devices.* 24 September 2004. Available from http://www.healthcare.frost.com.

"GE Healthcare Fact Sheet." General Electric Corporation, 2005. Available from http://www.gehealthcare.com.

Herman, William A. "Health Technology is Coming Home." *FDA Consumer*, May 2001, 36.

Hoover's Company Capsules. Austin, TX: Hoover's, Inc., 2004. Available from http://www.hoovers.com.

"How to Invest in Cardiac Surgical Devices." *Venture Capital Journal.* 1 November 2003.

"J&J Cordis/Guidant $25.4 Billion Merger to Control Stent Market." *Caribbean Business.* 23 December 2004.

Lorincz, Jim. "Rx for Healthy Manufacturers." *Tooling and Production.* June 2005. Available from http://www.toolingandproduction.com.

Mraz, Stephen. "MEMS and Medicine." *Machine Design*, 13 September 2001, 61-64.

"Research and Markets: Global Medical Device and Equipment Market Expected to Grow Steadily by Around 4.6 Percent Over Next Five Years." *M2 Presswire.* 24 May 2005.

"Research and Markets: Real Growth Potential in Market for Medical Devices & Equipment in Brazil, Russia, India & China." *Business Wire,* 18 January 2005.

U.S. Department of Commerce. "Mission Statement, Medical Device Trade Mission to China, April 19-23." 2004. Available from http://www.trade.gov/doctm/china_0404.html.

"US Market Update." *Medical Device Technology.* July/August 2004. Available from http://www.medicaldevicesonline.com.

METALS MANUFACTURING

SIC 3423, 3425, 3429

NAICS 332212, 332213, 332510

HAND TOOLS AND HARDWARE

The hand tool industry manufactures tools for metalworking, woodworking, and general maintenance. Among the many tools produced by companies in this category are axes, drill bits, blow torches, c-clamps, hammers, hand clamps, handsaws, glass cutters, chisels, files, spades, can openers, garden hand tools, hay forks, machetes, screwdrivers, hatchets, jewelers' hand tools, mallets, saw blades, wrenches, trowels, and yardsticks.

INDUSTRY SNAPSHOT

Despite its low profile and mature markets, the hand tools and hardware industry has been one of the most consistently successful industries in the world. Less susceptible to recessions and economic fluctuations than many other industries, toolmakers achieved steady growth throughout the 1990s. However, the economic climate of the early 2000s challenged the industry, leading to plant closures and layoffs. By 2003, for example, Snap-on Inc. had closed two of its four manufacturing plants, which had both been in operation for more than 65 years. The outlook for the industry appeared brighter heading into the mid-2000s. As economic conditions improved, so did the demand for hand tools, prompting leaders like The Stanley Works to increase hiring.

Following two successful decades, The Stanley Works remained the industry leader during the early and mid-2000s. This leadership position was built from the mid-1980s to the late 1990s, when the company saw its sales more than double. Other leading tool manufacturers included Snap-on Inc., Cooper Tools Inc., and Blount International Inc. The industry's key customers include carpenters, mechanics, jewelers, farmers, and innumerable do-it-yourselfers. Even when recessions caused slowdowns in the construction or industrial equipment industries, hand tools and hardware manufacturers continued to perform well due to increased demand by consumers who want to save money by making repairs and other tasks themselves.

While many of its products are considered low-tech, the industry itself is highly automated and employs state-of-the-art materials and technologies in its factories. Research has focused on improving the quality, durability, and usability of the many different tools produced. Foreign innovations are eagerly adopted and continual efforts are made to improve the precision of tools and customize them to suit the traditions and preferences of different markets. Beginning midway through the 1990s and continuing into the mid-2000s, technological advances included ergonomic tools designed to prevent injuries from using tools and "smart" tools to perform tasks more precisely than their conventional counterparts.

ORGANIZATION AND STRUCTURE

Hand and Edge Tools. The hand and edge tool industry manufactures basic hand tools and implements for domestic use and for professional mechanics and carpenters. Held in the hand and powered by the person using them, hand tools are distinguished from power tools and machine tools.

The long tradition of hand tool manufacturing in most countries means that different countries or regions have developed tools that often look and work quite differently from those used elsewhere. While European and North American tools are generally very similar, differences do exist. The French, for example, prefer levels shaped liked elongated trapezoids. Central Europeans use pliers to pull out bent nails so they do not need hammers with claws. The differences between Western and Asian tools, however, are much more marked. Japan's well-established tool industry produces tools whose details and overall design are often quite different from anything in use in North America and Europe. While most Japanese tools are produced using sophisticated industrial processes, many traditional forms remain. Many of these tools are well received in other countries, where their quality, versatility, and efficiency attract many professional carpenters and mechanics. U.S. companies such as Stanley Works imported some of these tools and in some cases began manufacturing them themselves.

According to figures compiled by the United Nations, Germany is the world's leading exporter of precision tools (including hand tools, power tools, tools for machine tools, grinding tools, molds, and measuring instruments), followed by Japan, the United States, Italy, the United Kingdom, Switzerland, Sweden, and China. Taiwan is also a leading exporter of low-cost base-metal hand tools such as pliers and wrenches. Other prominent manufacturers of basic tools and implements can be found in Israel, Turkey, Malaysia, and Australia.

As in many other industries, the resources required for investments in automation and other production technologies increasingly have pushed the industry toward greater consolidation. Economies of scale, increased efficiency, and precision are as important in this industry as in any other. The evolution of global trading patterns and increasing competition from low-wage producers has made it essential that production costs be kept to a minimum—something that could only be achieved by increasing automation in factories. Only in Japan, where the tradition of handcrafted tools has been strong, have artisans and small producers been able to hold onto their market niche.

Saw Blades and Handsaws. The products manufactured by saw blade and handsaw manufacturers come in all varieties and styles. What all saws have in common is a serrated edge or a perimeter with a series of sharp, usually V-shaped teeth, each of which removes a small piece from the material being cut. Wood saws are designed to cut with or across the grain of the wood. Ripsaws, also designed to cut with the grain, have teeth that work like chisels, chipping out pieces of wood. Crosscut saws are designed to cut cleanly through wood fibers, while backsaws feature numerous, tiny teeth for use in joinery work. Dovetail saws are similar to backsaws, but are smaller and used for very fine cuts. Other saws such as compass, keyhole, and coping saws are designed to cut curves. The most common metal-cutting handsaw is the hacksaw. Circular saw blades are used in power saws for cutting lumber and boards to size. Chain saws consist of a continuous toothed chain and are used to cut down trees and cut logs. Other types of saw blades include tree-pruning saws and flooring saws.

As with hand tools, the style and design of saw blades and handsaws differs around the world. Asian—particularly Japanese—saws feature some unique innovations. The main difference is that Japanese saws are designed to cut when pulled, allowing them to be very thin and light. Less force is required to use these saws and their harder teeth keep them sharper longer. Their main disadvantage is they can be broken easily if handled carelessly. The double-edged "Ryoba" saw—which combines a ripping-tooth pattern on one side with a cross-cut tooth pattern on the other—proves especially popular because it cuts on both the pull stroke and the push stroke. First imported to the United States by Stanley Works, double-toothed saws grew so popular that the company eventually began making them too.

Japan is also one of the leading exporters of saw blades, shipping about 15 percent of total production to overseas markets. Fifty-five percent of Japanese exports go to Southeast Asia and another 27 percent to North America. Japanese analysts expected to increase their shipments to Southeast Asia as countries in the region developed their own lumber industries.

BACKGROUND AND DEVELOPMENT

Hand tools and saws are as old as humankind itself; their development not only marked the beginning of human technology, but it also launched humanity on a journey that is still unfolding. While wood, bones, and antlers were all shaped into specialized implements, the fundamental element throughout this period was stone. Stone provided the hard edge necessary to shape other materials and to process plants and animals for eating. The three most important properties that stones and minerals required for use as tools were hardness, brittleness, and homogeneity. These properties ensured that the stone was strong enough to be a useful tool, while still being easy to chip or fracture into the desired shape. Humans proved remarkably adept at finding and exploiting stones with these properties—flint, quartz, and obsidian were among the most widely used.

As humans moved from stone to metals, tools became increasingly diverse, efficient, and specialized. Individuals no longer hammered out tools for their own use (although there is evidence that such specialization began before use of metals). Instead, skilled craftsmen and artisans took over the task. Metalworkers hand-forged the cutters and blades, while woodworkers carved and attached the handles. For thousands of years, tool making remained a specialized, cottage industry. Some independent toolmakers sold their wares at markets and fairs, while others produced tools directly for those who could afford to hire them.

With the rise of mass production and advanced metalworking processes during the Industrial Revolution, the modern tool and saw industries began to take shape. In the pre-industrial United States, production was centered in the New England region, as this was where the largest markets and greatest numbers of skilled craftsmen could be found. Later, as the need for skilled craftsmen declined with the onset of industrialization, the industry spread to other areas.

The impact of industrialization turned tool and saw making into a highly sophisticated, assembly-line process that quickly wiped out the traditional art of tool making. Only in countries such as Japan, where ancient traditions remained a powerful force, did individual artisans continue to use the old skills.

Following World War II, the hand tool and saw blade industries enjoyed almost continuous high growth. Expanding economies, growing populations, rising incomes, and intensive construction activity provided these industries with a steady stream of customers. Even the recessions of the early 1980s and 1990s failed to put a significant damper on the prosperity of companies in these industries. Stanley Works, for example, one of the world's oldest and biggest manufacturers of hand tools and handsaws, doubled sales between 1985 and 1990 and continued to increase its sales through the early 1990s. In Japan, growth of these industries was temporarily stalled by slowdowns in construction and manufacturing caused by the rapid rise of the yen in 1985 and 1986. However, the industries quickly recovered and by the end of the decade were posting record sales.

The 1980s and 1990s were also a time of consolidation and increasing integration. Stanley Works, for example, acquired four tool companies in 1986 alone, one of which was based in Taiwan. These acquisitions boosted Stanley's existing position in the hand tools market and also provided it with complementary product lines such as high-end mechanic's tools and industrial implements. Vermont American Corporation, a major manufacturer of hand tools, handsaws, and drill accessories, was bought by a joint venture that included St. Louis-based Emerson Electric Company and an investment bank owned by Sears, Roebuck and Company—whose line of Craftsman tools competed head-to-head with Stanley's products in the consumer tools business.

CURRENT CONDITIONS

Despite an economic downturn, the hand tool industry suffered less damage than other sectors during the early 2000s. However, it did not emerge completely unscathed. The economic slowdown had caused spending cutbacks within the corporate sector and high levels of unemployment, which had a negative impact on hand tool purchases. According to U.S. Census Bureau data released in January 2003, shipment values for hand and edge tool manufacturing fell from US$7.4 billion in 2000 to US$6.9 billion in 2001. Likewise, shipment values also fell for saw blade and handsaw manufacturers, dropping from US$1.6 billion to US$1.5 billion during the same timeframe.

As proof of the industry's difficult times, in 2003 The Stanley Works eliminated 1,000 jobs and shut down two of its plants in an effort to trim costs. From 2001 to mid-2003, Kenosha, Wisconsin-based Snap-on Inc. cut 1,200 jobs throughout the world, amidst heightened competition and depressed industrial economies in both Europe and North America. In July of 2003, the company announced that it would shed another 560 jobs by 2004, in conjunction with tool factory closures in Mount Carmel, Illinois, and Kenosha. In operation since 1937 and 1929, respectively, the two plants represented half of Snap-on's manufacturing facilities.

Heading into the mid-2000s, the hand tool industry also was challenged by pressure from retail behemoths like Wal-Mart, Home Depot, and Lowe's. An article in the October 22, 2003, issue of the *Wall Street Journal,* appropriately entitled "Feeling the Squeeze," explained: "Unlike even just a decade ago, these huge retailers have clout to squeeze suppliers and replace their products with private label in-house brands. As the tool makers respond by rushing to move production to cheaper markets, they risk jeopardizing the quality of the products, the only advantage they have over the private-label offerings."

In March of 2004, *Manufacturing.net* provided a detailed glimpse at conditions within the hand tool industry. Citing data from the Port Angeles, Washington-based research firm Thinking Cap Solutions Inc., it demonstrated that average product prices for hand and edge tools fell almost 0.7 percent from September 2002 to September 2003, while average prices for handsaws and saw blades increased a modest 1.5 percent. At the same time, direct manufacturing costs for these categories were on the rise, increasing 0.2 percent and nearly 0.9 percent, respectively. *Manufacturing.net* also reported that from December 2002 to December 2003, U.S. end markets for these categories were either stagnant or declining. For hand and edge tools, growth amounted 0.1 percent, while growth in the hand saws and saw blades category actually fell 0.1 percent. On the bright side for manufacturers, mechanics' hand tools and hand saws were expected to garner higher prices in 2004, rising between 1.7 and 1.9 percent.

A study by the Freedonia Group published in 2005 found that while the introduction of lighter, more powerful electric tools will aid the U.S. tool market, demand for hand tools would decrease due to increased imports and reduced tool expenditures from the construction industry, resulting in an overall rise in tool demand of 3.8 percent per year through 2009. The report further stated that the trend toward consolidation among retailers would negatively affect prices.

One sign of improving conditions for hand tool manufacturers was an announcement by Stanley Bostitch, a subsidiary of The Stanley Works, that it planned to add 60 to 80 jobs in 2004. These included 45 to 65 sales, engineering, and manufacturing positions at the company's plant in East Greenwich, Rhode Island. As economic conditions improved, Stanley Bostitch was experiencing a strong first quarter, marked by increased demand for the company's tools.

Ergonomic tools remained popular during the mid-2000s. Demand for this hand tool category has been strong because of consumer and company interest in preventing injuries. Ergonomic tools do not cause as much strain and fatigue as conventional tools because they are designed to better fit the human hand. This is a concern of professionals as well as do-it-yourselfers, and it has driven research into improved materials and design.

RESEARCH AND TECHNOLOGY

Hand and Edge Tools. Given the nature of the products it manufactures, a major research issue in the hand and edge tools industry is the development of durable, high-quality, low-cost materials—especially for consumer tools. Items such as garden spades, rakes, and pruning tools need to be lightweight, strong, easy-to-clean, and rustproof. For example, in the 1990s many companies began using plastic materials not only for handles, but also for blades and tines.

Other research has focused on means of maintaining competitive, low-cost production while meeting the requirements of stringent new U.S. anti-pollution laws. Stanley Works, for instance, adapted an advanced chrome-plating process, known as "sputtering," to finish tape-measure cases. The previous system used by the company had produced millions of gallons of contaminated water that the company had been forced to clean up. The new process, on the other hand, used no water, cost the same as the previous method, and provided a stronger, more durable coating.

Automated production technologies were eagerly adopted by hand and edge tool manufacturers. For the big U.S., Japanese, and European companies that could afford them, computer-controlled production lines were the key to competing with the low-cost Southeast Asian producers who invaded their markets during the 1980s and 1990s. Computer-aided design also facilitated the production of more efficient and more precise tools. Reliable precision tools were extremely important to professional mechanics and carpenters, and brand-name manufacturers spared no expense in ensuring that their products were as accurate as possible. Stanley, for example, used sophisticated laser scanners to check the markings on its tape measures to guarantee their accuracy. Ergonomics and ease of use were also important issues in hand and edge tool research.

As part of the industry's ongoing effort to produce more ergonomic tools to prevent wear and tear on users, Bettcher Industries Inc. introduced its Airshirz pneumatic scissors in the late 1990s, specifically created for the poultry industry. Designed to fit comfortably in the palm of a hand, air pressure powers these scissors, not human exertion, which greatly reduces the amount of gripping force and other exertion needed to operate the scissors.

Besides ergonomic tools, manufacturers concentrated on producing other new tool technologies called "smart" tools in the late 1990s. Using laser and computer technology, smart tools perform tasks more quickly and accurately than conventional tools. One such smart tool is the laser level, which has a graphical display and a sensor that can be calibrated electronically. By 2004 laser technology had become very affordable, and was driving sales within the hand tool industry. Indeed, consumers were able to buy laser levels from the likes of Wal-Mart for under US$50. In its December 15, 2003 issue, *DSN Retailing Today* reported that laser-guided tools were "the hottest thing," with strong growth expected for the category in 2004.

Another technological advancement in the hand tool category was the Weight Forward hammer from Rockford, Illinois-based Estwing. By shifting the center of gravity, the tool's design helped to reduce user fatigue, while at the same time maximizing its striking power. The hammer was especially popular in the United Kingdom. In *Contract Flooring Journal,* Estwing distributor the Rollins Group reported that it had sold 10,000 of the hammers from fall 2003 to summer 2004 alone. In 2004, the Weight Forward hammer won an Industrial Design Excellence Award (IDEA) from *Business Week* and the Industrial Designers Society of America.

Saw Blades and Handsaws. According to Naohide Morikawa, managing director of the Japanese Industrial Saw and Knife Association, the quality of saw blades directly affects the productivity and production costs of mechanical processing and woodwork. Consequently, the precision and performance of cutting tools had to match that of other modern precision technologies. Automated, labor-saving, and unmanned operations were equally important in saw blade and handsaw production. With a significant portion of production focused on manufacturing cutting tools for use in modern machining processes, it is essential that saw makers be able to provide cutting tools with long service life, high working and feeding speeds, and extra-high precision.

Advances in materials technology also meant that the number and variety of materials requiring processing was also increasing rapidly. This, in turn, compelled the saw blade and handsaw industry to fund research on the development of new cutting materials suitable for new applications. To compete with advances in laser technology that threatened to reduce the need for industrial saw blades in metal and plastics cutting, Japanese, German, and U.S. manufacturers all concentrated their research and development efforts on advanced design and manufacturing technology.

Even for basic handsaws, investigation of new materials and designs was no less common, particularly for high-end, professional-use products. Accuracy, durability, and flexibility were increasingly important. Demand for cutting tools thin enough and precise enough to minimize material waste is growing as builders and manufacturers seek ways to reduce waste.

INDUSTRY LEADERS

HAND TOOLS

Stanley Works. No hand tool manufacturer is as ubiquitous as Connecticut-based Stanley Works. Stanley Works leads the hand tool industry with 14,100 employees and 2004 sales of US$3.04 billion, up 13.6 percent from the previous year. In 2004, Stanley's net income was US$367 million, up 240 percent from 2003. In July of 2005, the company announced its largest acquisition since its inception in 1843 with its agreement to purchase the Paris-based Facom Tools for $494 million. With roughly 30 percent of the company's sales already originating overseas, the Facom deal would bring that total to 40 percent.

Although Stanley competes with many other much larger companies such as the Black & Decker Corporation, Illinois Tool Works, and Cooper Industries Corporation, none of them comes close to matching Stanley's share of the hand tools market. The company's familiar yellow and black tools dominate the hardware aisles in stores throughout North America and represent the top-selling brand in the United States.

Unlike other companies in the tool industry, Stanley manufactures just about every kind of tool a consumer might want. Its major product lines are consumer tools (carpenter's tools, tool boxes, and masonry tools); industrial tools (hand tools, electronic diagnostic tools, and cabinets); engineered tools (pneumatic nailers, staplers, and office products); hardware (hinges, hasps, brackets, and bolts); and specialty hardware (residential door systems, power-operated gates, and garage door openers).

With manufacturing and distribution centers in more than 30 countries around the world, Stanley is truly a global business. Its plants operate in Germany, Canada, France, Poland, Taiwan, and Thailand. The company's subsidiaries include Best Lock Corp., Blick plc, Frisco Bay Industries Ltd., and ZAG Industries Ltd. Some of the internationally known brand names attached to Stanley's products include Bostitch, Goldblatt, Husky, MAC Tools, and Monarch.

One of the oldest tool-making companies in the world, Stanley Works was born in a converted War of 1812-era armory in New Britain, Connecticut, in 1843. There, Frederick T. Stanley installed New Britain's first steam engine and began producing bolts and house trimmings. In 1852 he and his brother got together with five friends to form Stanley Works.

The business expanded rapidly during the U.S. Civil War and afterwards when westward migration stimulated a growing market for hardware and tools.

By the end of the nineteenth century, Stanley was the leading producer of hand tools in the United States and was poised to expand even more rapidly in the twentieth century. By 1914 the company had established operations in Canada and made numerous domestic acquisitions. In 1926 it set up shop in Germany, and in 1929 formed an electric tool division.

After weathering the Great Depression, Stanley geared up for war production in the 1940s and later launched a massive expansion program that continued into the 1990s. By staying within its product line, Stanley was able to effectively manage its growth and maintain its reputation as a producer of high quality tools. Dozens of companies fell into Stanley's orbit during this period, including Berry Industries (garage doors, 1965), Ackley Manufacturing and Sales (hydraulic tools, 1972), Mac Tools (1980), and National Hand Tool Corporation (1986). During the 1980s, Stanley acquired some 21 companies, which, by 1990, were responsible for about half of the company's total revenues.

In Western Europe, Stanley owns Atro Industriale, an Italian tool-making company. Stanley also has a strong presence in Israel, having purchased ZAG Industries in 1998. In addition, anticipating that future growth would depend on a strong presence in the fast-growing Pacific Rim market, Stanley launched an aggressive bid to capture market share by establishing high-tech plants in Taiwan, Thailand, and Australia. Its acquisitions of Dallas-based National Hand Tool Corporation and Chiro Tool Manufacturing Corporation of Taiwan were motivated in large part by the factories both companies operated in Taiwan.

In the late 1990s, Stanley underwent a significant restructuring process to remain competitive. Former General Electric CEO, John M. Trani, took over the helm at Stanley at the end of 1996 and began making his trademark cost-cutting changes at the company. Stanley consolidated its 123 operations and manufacturing plants into just 70 facilities and laid off 4,500 employees or 25 percent of its workforce. Stanley planned to spend more on research and development and hoped the restructuring would make more funds available for its R&D budget. Stanley also announced it would divest itself of some of its concerns to focus on its core products—tools.

Snap-on Inc. Another leading maker of hand tools is Snap-on Inc. of Kenosha, Wisconsin. Formerly known as Snap-on Tools Corporation, the company changed its name to Snap-on Inc. in the mid-1990s. Specializing in automotive hand and power tools and tool storage products for professional mechanics, Snap-on Inc. posted US$2.4 billion in 2004 revenues. The company's net income of US$81.7 million was up 3.8 percent from 2003 levels. From 2001 to mid-2003, Snap-on eliminated 1,200 jobs worldwide, amid heightened competition and depressed industrial economies in both Europe and North America. In July of 2003, the company announced that it would shed another 560 jobs by 2004, after shutting down two of its four manufacturing facilities.

Snap-on's 11,500 employees—down from 14,000 in 2001—produce a wide range of specialized tools including wrenches, wheel balancing and alignment equipment, sockets, aircraft tools, chisels, punches, pliers, screwdrivers, hammers, pneumatic impact wrenches and chisels, as well as power-assisted equipment and electronic diagnostic equipment.

Incorporated as Snap-on Wrench Company in 1920, Snap-on Inc. was born as the result of an innovative idea that no one else was interested in—interchangeable wrench handles and sockets. Unable to persuade his employer to take the idea seriously, Joe Johnson and co-worker William Seidemann made a sample set of five handles and ten sockets. Two Wisconsin salesmen—Stanton Palmer and Newton Tarble—sold over 500 orders and set up their own distributing business demonstrating tool sets at customer sites. In 1921 they bought out the Snap-on Wrench Company and Palmer became president.

In 1930 the company reincorporated as Snap-on Tools, Incorporated, and in 1931 opened its first foreign subsidiary (Canada). During World War II, Snap-on salesmen began carrying tools in their trucks and vans to meet widespread civilian shortages. The concept has remained Snap-on's trademark. Red and white Snap-on Tools vans loaded with high-quality tools traveled to garages and gas stations throughout North America. High quality, dependability, and, above all, service made Snap-on Tools North America's leading supplier of hand tools to professional mechanics in the 1990s and early 2000s.

Snap-on Inc., like Stanley Works, expanded rapidly during the postwar period. Unlike its competitor, however, Snap-on did not focus on acquiring other manufacturers. Instead, it relied on expanding its dealerships, establishing franchises, and providing mechanics with a reliable source of up-to-date tools, training, and service. Dealers called on customers once a week, demonstrating new products and delivering new tools. In addition, Snap-on offered its customers interest-free credit and eventually built up its own financial services operation.

Snap-on Inc.'s growth closely paralleled that of its rival, Stanley Works. From 1985 to 2001, Snap-on's sales almost quadrupled, climbing from US$540 million to more than US$2 billion. The company earned a reputation for quality when it became the sole supplier of tools to NASA for the space shuttles. In 1992 the company established Snap-on Tools Japan and in 1994 changed its name to Snap-on Inc. to reflect its movement away from its traditional core business of tools. Today, Snap-on tools are available in 150 countries.

Other Leaders. Also prominent in the North American hand tools market is Cooper Tools Inc., a subsidiary of Cooper Industries. Cooper Tools employs 5,477 people worldwide and recorded 2004 sales of US$740.7 million. Elsewhere in the world, leading companies in this category have included Kuang Yuang Industrial Company of Taiwan, Vargus of Israel, and Finetools SDN BHD of Malaysia.

SAW BLADES AND HANDSAWS

Black & Decker. Among the leading companies are those with a strong line of power tools such as Black & Decker

Corporation of the United States and Makita Corporation of Japan. The world's largest power tool maker, Black & Decker is also a leading maker of saw blades. The company's Maryland-based subsidiary Black & Decker Corporation Accessories and Fastenings handles production of saw blades and drill bits for use in the company's tools. Besides the Black & Decker name, the company also owns the DeWalt brand of hand tools. Overall, Black & Decker posted sales of nearly US$5.4 billion in 2004. After eliminating 900 jobs and closing two plants in January 2004, the company reported a 61 percent hike in second quarter earnings. In July 2004, Black & Decker announced that it would acquire Pentair Inc.'s tool unit in a deal worth US$775 million. Pentair manufactured the well-known line of Porter-Cable and Delta power tools. Among Black & Decker's largest customers are Home Depot and Lowe's, two very popular do-it-yourself superstores.

Blount. Another large company operating in this sector is Blount International, Inc., a major manufacturer of saw chains. Blount employed 3,700 people in 2004, down from 5,000 in 2001, and reported sales of US$692.6 million. The company also manufactures timber harvesting equipment and industrial tractors.

Robert Bosch Tool Corp. Based in Mount Prospect, Illinois, the Robert Bosch Tool Corp. was created via the merger of Vermont American Corp. and S-B Power Tool Co. It subsequently acquired the North American tool operations from its parent, Robert Bosch. The company ranks among the leading manufacturers of saw blades and hand saws, and manufactures such well known brands as Bosch, Dremel, Skil, and Vermont American. In addition to power tools, handsaws, and saw blades, the company manufactures Gilmour lawn and garden tools. In 2003, the company employed approximately 4,000 workers and reported sales of US$1 billion.

MAJOR COUNTRIES IN THE INDUSTRY

United States. There were more than 1,000 firms in the hand and power tool market by the mid-2000s, with the top six firms accounting for 55 percent of 2004 sales. With major tool producers such as Stanley Works and Snap-on Inc. based in the country, the United States stands out as the single leading producer and market for hand tools. Still, the country continues to be a net importer of hand tools. Economist James C. Franklin of the Bureau of Labor Statistics, however, projects that employment rates and output volume will decrease by 2006.

U.S. export values for hand and edge tools fell from US$1.1 billion in 2000 to US$988 million in 2001, and remained unchanged in 2002. After falling from about US$1.8 billion in 2000 to slightly more than US$1.7 billion in 2001, imports for this category increased to US$1.9 billion in 2002. For saw blade and handsaw manufacturing, export values increased from US$162 million in 2000 to US$184 million in 2001, and then fell to US$159 million in 2002. Imports in that category fell from US$305 million in 2000 to US$290 million in 2001 before improving to US$330 million in 2002.

European Union. The European Union maintains a strong global presence in the hand tool industry with Germany as a leading exporter of tools. Although Germany is a significant importer, the country exported about twice as much as it imports during the 1990s and early 2000s, controlling roughly 20 percent of the export market.

Asia. In Asia, Taiwan has emerged as a competitor with Japan and China, which have traditionally dominated this industry. Taiwan has become a major exporter of hand tools and hardware. In 2002, its base of mainly small manufacturing firms produced US$295 million worth of power tools alone, mainly on the low end of the quality spectrum. With this in mind, Taiwan relies on imports to satisfy demand for higher-quality power tools among a growing do-it-yourself market, as well as customers in the remodeling and decorating industries. According to a report from *STAT-USA,* Japan supplied 44 percent of Taiwan's imports, followed by Germany (24 percent) and the United States (8 percent). The power tool market in Taiwan was valued at US$41 million in 2002, down 31 percent from the previous year due to weak economic conditions. However, economic growth of 3.3 percent and 3.4 percent was forecast in 2002 and 2003, respectively. This was expected to support 2 to 3 percent annual growth within the power tool sector through 2005.

China was set to make a significant impact on the world economy in 2004 by causing a spike in steel prices. This, in turn, would likely impact the hand tool market. The nation's burgeoning economic growth spurred a flurry of construction projects, in addition to its preparation for the 2008 Olympics. In fact, heading into the mid-2000s China was the world's leading consumer of scrap steel products. Although its industrial production increased 25 percent from March 2003 to March 2004, the nation was relying on its own steel to support domestic growth, instead of exporting to other nations. In the April 2004 issue of *Do-It-Yourself Retailing,* House-Hassen Merchandising Vice President Allen Winn indicated that retailers would likely increase nail prices by 40 percent. Taking a broader view, he said: "Anything that's got steel in it is going to go through the roof."

FURTHER READING

Arditi, Lynn. "Hand-Tool Maker's Subsidiary to Expand." *The Providence Journal (RI),* 19 February 2004.

"Black & Decker Buys Pentair." *Home Channel News,* 9 August 2004.

Content, Thomas. "Kenosha, Wis.-Based Snap-On Tools to Eliminate 560 Jobs by 2004." *The Milwaukee Journal Sentinel,* 22 July 2003.

"Feeling the Squeeze." *The Wall Street Journal,* 22 October 2003.

HardwareB2B. *Taiwan Registers Increase in Hand Tool Exports for 2000.* Asia TradeMart.com, 1 March 2001. Available from http://www.hardwareb2b.com.

Hoover's Company Capsules. Hoover's, Inc., 2005. Available from http://www.hoovers.com.

Howell, Debbie. "Laser-Guided Tools." *DSN Retailing Today,* 15 December 2003.

"Lighter Hammer Reduces Fatigue." *Contract Flooring Journal,* June 2004.

Loftus, Peter. "Black & Decker's Profit Jumps; Deal Is Set for Pentair Tool Unit." *The Wall Street Journal,* 20 July 2004.

Nussbaum, Bruce. "Winners 2004; The Best Product Designs of the Year." *Business Week,* 5 July 2004.

"Power Tools." *STAT-USA Market Research Reports,* 2 June 2003. Available from http://strategis.ic.gc.ca/epic/internet/inimr-ri.nsf/en/gr109699e.html.

"Price Hikes Expected for Some Industries, but Not All." *Manufacturing.Net,* 1 March 2004. Available from http://www.manufacturing.net/.

"Stanley Adds to Tool Box." *Knight-Ridder Tribune Business News,* 19 July 2005.

"Steel Shortage Could Hit Industry Hard." *Do-It-Yourself Retailing,* April 2004.

"Study Gauges Power Tool Demand." *Home Channel News Newsfax,* 23 May 2005.

Taiwan Hardware 2001. *Export Statistics for Taiwan Hardware Products.* Taiwan Customs Statistics, January 2001. Available from http://hardware.cetra.org.tw.

U.S. Census Bureau. *Annual Survey of Manufactures.* Washington, D.C.: U.S. Department of Commerce, Economics and Statistics Administration, U.S. Census Bureau, January 2003. Available from http://www.census.gov.

U.S. Department of Commerce: Bureau of the Census; International Trade Administration. "U.S. Industry Sector Data." 1 August 2004. Available from http://www.census.gov.

SIC 3320

NAICS 331511

IRON AND STEEL FOUNDRIES

Iron and steel foundries manufacture malleable, ductile, investment, and gray iron castings. These establishments generally operate on a job or order basis, manufacturing castings for sale to others or for interplant transfer.

INDUSTRY SNAPSHOT

Foundries are factories that produce metal castings. The foundry industry is a highly fragmented yet essential element of the modern global economy. Metal castings are required in numerous machinery applications, including automobiles, aircraft, and other transportation equipment. Beginning in the late 1990s and continuing into the 2000s, however, castings of iron and steel faced continued competition from aluminum, zinc, various alloys, and plastics. As a result, the more traditional iron and steel castings lost market share and demand for some has been stagnant.

According to *Modern Casting,* the foundry industry was recovering from the manufacturing recession of the early 2000s, and was expected to continue growing through the decade. Imports in particular were projected to see a 5 percent annual increase, with exports also seeing annual growth. Most of the growth was expected to come from manufacturers of light metal castings, such as steel. The hardest hit segment, on the other hand, would be gray iron castings.

Metal casting production remains fragmented due to several influences. In a minority of cases—about 13 percent in the United States—metals are cast directly by manufacturers of end products rather than by specialized foundries. The independent foundries are often highly specialized and serve specific niches, such as automotive brake and powertrain components or turbine equipment for power plants. Ongoing consolidation has greatly reduced the number of ferrous foundries in operation, but it has not given rise to any major producers that can be said to dominate the industry, either on a global level or on a national level in leading countries.

ORGANIZATION AND STRUCTURE

Most of theworld's metal castings are ferrous, which means they ultimately derive from iron ore, as is the case with all types of iron and steel. The casting process involves forming metal shapes or structures by pouring molten metal, in this case iron or steel, into molds or dies. Most molds are made of sand, which is able to withstand high temperatures, but wax and other materials may be used. Wax is used in a form of metal casting known as investment casting. When a die is used, the process is often called die casting. Die casting differs from other methods in that metal shapes are actively pressed in dies using force, whereas other forms of casting allow the metal cast to passively take the shape of a mold. The various production techniques offer different advantages of strength, precision, and cost effectiveness for the casting of different source metals.

The industry is heavily engaged in manufacturing pipes, pipe fittings, and numerous mechanical components. However, other segments of the industry are growing in response to changing market demands. For example, the automotive industry switched most engine components to aluminum in response to consumer demands for lighter, more fuel-efficient cars. While this move has hurt some gray and ductile iron foundries, it has also forced them to find alternative markets.

The automotive and aerospace industries were historically large customers of gray and ductile iron foundries. So large was the demand that each of the Big Three U.S. automakers owned several foundries of this type. In the 1980s and 1990s these industries were beset in some places with production slumps and requirements for new materials. Although the automotive industry and their suppliers enjoyed a brief period of increased demand in the late 1990s and early 2000, by 2001 the industries faced a recession. Consumer demand has changed, decreasing the iron portion of the automotive casting business. Likewise, in the mid- to late 1980s and early 1990s, the poor financial performance of both the U.S. automotive and aerospace industries forced closings of many self-contained foundries. Outsourcing the casting business was a cheaper alternative than underutilizing plant and labor capacities.

In the European Union (EU), most foundries are small businesses employing less than 50 people. However, as more companies automate molding lines, three work shifts are needed to meet required efficiencies, thus creating a change in the European industry toward larger foundries. Due to the need to reduce costs, many foundries have been taken over by large groups, thereby cutting out the middleman and controlling a wide range of casting technologies.

BACKGROUND AND DEVELOPMENT

For at least 5,000 years, humans have been casting metals. Metallurgy began in the Bronze Age, when humans started extracting ores and forming them through melting or hammering. The Iron Age began in Europe around 1100 B.C. Only through contact with Europe did the Americas enter the Iron Age.

Cast iron did not come into commercial use until 1700 when a mechanic named Abraham Darby and some Dutch workmen established a brass foundry in Bristol, England. It was there that he and his men started experimenting with iron as a replacement for brass. This presented technical problems, as brass and iron are completely different pouring mediums in terms of reaction with sand and solidification patterns. Darby received little cooperation from his workers, and the project met with little success. Darby's luck changed when an eager boy working in his shop, John Thomas, said that he thought he "saw where they had missed it." The two worked all through that night and into the next morning before successfully casting a complete iron pot. For proprietary reasons, Darby and Thomas entered into an agreement in which the boy was to remain his servant to keep the secret.

Malleable iron was patented in Europe by Samuel Lucas in 1804. However, he was not the first to develop the alloy. A Frenchman named Reaumur described the process in 1722. In 1630, Englishman David Ramsey was granted a royal patent. In its infancy malleable iron was difficult to attain, due to necessary chemical controls and the lack of equipment to monitor the chemistry. Unfortunately, when a bad batch of malleable iron was made, it was totally useless because it was too brittle and therefore unmachinable. Despite this, its popularity was unparalleled because it offered the fluidity of cast iron and the ductility of steel. In Europe, malleable iron was used for cutlery, pulley blocks, harness hardware, and railroad rails. In 1831, Seth Boyden received a U.S. patent, signed by President Andrew Jackson, after winning a silver medal in 1828 for his castings displayed at the Fourth Annual Exhibition of the Franklin Institute of the State of Pennsylvania.

Ductile iron was not discovered until after World War II. Laboratory metallurgists at International Nickel Company noticed that the addition of a higher content of magnesium than normally required for gray iron produced a structurally different material. Upon observation at a microscopic level, the graphite particles had taken on a spheroidal shape, thus coining the name "nodular iron" in the United States and "spheroidal graphite cast iron" in Great Britain. The recognition of nodular iron's mechanical strength, while providing more ductility than other metals in its class, provided it with its more commonly accepted name, ductile iron. Since its release to the marketplace in 1949, it has gained acceptance as an important engineering material and replaced many of the previous applications formerly reserved for steels and other irons. In the engineering materials community, the discovery of ductile iron is one of the greatest in the twentieth century.

The U.S. metal casting industry was wounded severely in the 1980s.

During the 1970s, the industry was overwhelmed with back orders that exceeded annual capacity. This produced a seller's market, which was reflected in pricing strategies and profit margins. However, shipment volume was the key issue during the 1970s, not quality or price. During the 1980s, foreign competitors emerged who could sell better quality castings at lower prices and provide on-time delivery. When the economy entered recessionary times, consumers turned to overseas suppliers, leaving domestic producers behind. U.S. foundries were operating at no more than 50 percent capacity by the mid-1980s.

By the mid-1990s, U.S. iron foundries had lost nearly 60 percent of the tonnage shipped compared to levels in 1978. Gray iron suffered a huge decline between 1978 and 1982, from approximately 18.5 million tons to 9.5 million tons. Between 1982 and 1990, gray iron shipments continued to decrease. Ductile iron, however, has shown slight growth in shipments since 1982, continuing a trend started in 1966. The growth of ductile iron is largely due to its increasing recognition as a better alternative, economically and structurally, to gray and malleable irons.

The foundry industry experienced largely stagnant demand in the mid- to late 1990s and a recession late in 2000 and 2001. After declines in previous years, some manufacturers viewed the stagnant years as a relatively healthy period. In the United States, annual production of ferrous castings hovered at the 13 million ton level between 1994 and 1997. In 1997 these iron and steel castings were valued at approximately US$18 billion. By 2000 the value of all U.S. castings shipments, including aluminum and other nonferrous metals, was expected to reach US$33 billion on a volume of 16.3 million tons, representing a 10 percent increase in value and a 4 percent rise in volume from 1997 levels.

However, production fell short of projections. In 2000, U.S. Foundries shipped 14 million tons worth of iron and steel castings, the lowest shipping year since 1992, with sales of US$28 million. Projections for 2001 were even more grim, and foundries braced themselves for an economic slowdown, particularly in the automotive industry.

By type of casting, three key production categories dominated U.S. output: gray iron castings (31 percent of 1997 production), ductile iron castings (27 percent), and steel investment castings (26 percent). In 1997 nonferrous castings accounted for nearly 16 percent of all metal castings production in the United States, and of that percentage about two-thirds of nonferrous castings (or about 10 percent of industry output) were made from aluminum. In terms of value, however, nonferrous castings weigh in much more significantly—they claimed more than 40 percent of all U.S. castings revenues in 1996. In 1999, while nonferrous castings made up only 19 percent of all casting shipments, they made up 48 percent of cast metal sales in the United States. Aluminum, which accounted for 13 percent of shipments, claimed 26 percent of the industry's sales.

CURRENT CONDITIONS

Conventional iron and steel castings have encountered rising competition from lighter and more highly engineered materials, particularly aluminum and alloys, as well as from manufacturing alternatives to metal casting. This has been especially true in end markets like the automotive industry, which consumes two-thirds of aluminum castings, in order to decrease vehicle weights to improve fuel efficiency to comply with federal fuel economy regulations. The U.S. government mandated in 1977 that fuel economy for new American cars must average 27.5 miles per gallon. In order to comply, automakers needed to produce lighter cars. The impact on the steel industry was tremendous. In 1980 the average American car contained 600 pounds of cast iron. Two decades later, it contained only 325 pounds, and by 2005 it averaged 220 pounds, according to the American Foundry Society. By 2009, shipments of aluminum castings were expected to grow by 50 percent.

Some of the newer materials are more expensive than steel and iron, and some industry experts believe that by revising specifications for steel and iron castings, they may achieve similar weight reductions that manufacturers seek when using alternative metals. In addition, ferrous metal castings enjoy a strength advantage over aluminum. In very lightweight conditions, aluminum components may require reinforcement, while iron or steel counterparts of similar specification do not. In a few cases, manufacturers have returned to iron castings after disappointing results with aluminum's price and performance. Nonetheless, barring a major technological breakthrough, most observers expect aluminum—along with plastics and engineered materials—to continue to wrest market share from iron and steel castings well into the 2000s.

Much of the cast steel market that remains faces fierce global competition, particularly in the gray iron municipal castings and diesel components markets. In particular, the foundry industry faces growing competition from the booming market in China. Imports of Chinese gray iron castings in the U.S. alone grew by 45 percent in a mere three years, from $85 million in 2000 to $123 million in 2003. In the United Kingdom, however, *Furnaces International* reported that more than 80 percent of foundries were reporting positive outlooks in 2003, particularly in Scotland.

Foundries in the United States use and recycle 100 million tons of sand every year. It is continuously recycled until it loses its properties. Approximately 6 percent of the sand used in the casting process cannot be recycled for foundry use and is then shipped for reuse in brick and concrete production. In 2003, Clayton Thermal Processes Limited unveiled its award-winning system which removed and cleaned sand from casting cores.

Scrap metal is remelted and the residual pollutants create significant problems. While nearly all foundries reuse scrap metals, using 15 to 20 million tons of recycled scrap metal annually, economics force the foundries to use more original materials. Energy costs rose significantly in 2001, impacting both the melting processes and transportation costs. Many foundries purchased more original pig iron for use in production as a result. Furthermore, because foundries require cleaner scrap metal than do steel mills, scrap which is free of paint and other contaminants, the prices for foundry scrap are generally higher than mill scrap.

RESEARCH AND TECHNOLOGY

English automaker Lotus Group and SinterCast of Sweden reported in 1994 to be codeveloping a production process for compacted graphite iron (CGI) for automotive uses. CGI's benefits are that it combines the benefits of gray iron's ease of machining, casting, and thermal characteristics with ductile iron's toughness and strength. SinterCast's process, which calculates the amount of reagent needed in CGI before pouring the iron into the mold, was used earlier in 1993 by Fagor Ederlan of Spain and RH Sheppard of Hanover, Pennsylvania. In another codevelopment during 1993, Tennant Metallurgical of England and Globe Metallurgical of Ohio created Tenbloc, an in-mold inoculation product. Tenbloc represented a new method of pressing and sintering that bonds the inoculating particles. The blocks have proven to be effective in inoculating gray and ductile iron castings.

However, CGI is not the only new material making headlines. Another material, austempered ductile iron (ADI), is gaining acceptance throughout the world due to its lower weight when compared to steel and higher mechanical properties when compared to conventional ductile iron. Previously impossible applications are possible with ADI, and designers around the world are learning how to use it. National standards have been available since 1992 in the United States and Japan. Other countries, such as the United Kingdom, Germany, Canada, and Sweden, submitted standard proposals in 1992.

Electro Steel Castings Ltd. of India is gaining more customers for its ductile iron pipes. The pipes exhibit better mechanical stability than regular cast iron pipe. The lighter weight translates into lower transport costs and greater longevity (150 years), which makes up for the 5 to 10 percent higher cost of ductile iron. The pipes have been accepted by municipalities, corporations, water supply boards, and public health departments and are manufactured in India with local raw materials. Approximately 10,000 metric tons were exported overseas in 1992, and shipments of 30,000 metric tons were expected in the following years. Other countries planning to use ductile iron pipes for water supply systems include Turkey and the Czech Republic. The winner of these contracts, Pont-a-Mousson of France, beat competition from U.S., Japan, German, Czech, Italian, and Austrian firms in 1992.

A relatively new process in the foundry industry, evaporative pattern casting (also known as lost foam) is gaining popularity around the world. Many foundries in the United States, Japan, and Europe embraced the process by the 1990s. In 1992, Indian firm Alexcon Fabricasts established a new operation near Bombay to implement the process. They manufacture high precision aluminum, iron, and steel castings. The technical expertise was supplied by Lost Foam Technologies, a division of Kohler General Corporation.

Favorable activities were taking place in the iron foundry industry, especially with ductile iron. The U.S. government was interested in the replacement of many forged steel components with cast ductile iron. Particularly, the U.S. Navy was researching the increased lethality of ductile iron projectiles over those made from steel. Other contractors were looking for less expensive alternatives to using forged steel components where the mechanical properties of ductile iron can suffice (generally in lower stress applications). However, more research and development is needed for this material because other lighter weight materials are replacing ductile iron in lower stress applications. Ductile iron's low production price tag is enticing and is one of its larger benefits.

Cast thermal analysis, also called numerical modeling/simulation, is a way to improve quality and productivity in the foundry through pattern design optimization. The cost-saving benefits of using numerical modeling are substantial, especially with respect to time and material waste. Computer technology displaces the standard "pour and pray" method of metal casting by helping the engineer optimize the casting design.

For the foundry industry as a whole, the advent of rapid prototyping technology was perhaps one of the most exciting advancements of the 1990s. Rapid prototyping is a computer-integrated method of accelerating the step between the designing and manufacturing of a part. Under normal circumstances, a foundry would take weeks to construct a pattern, and core boxes if necessary, from an original design. With rapid prototyping, this process can take only days, possibly only hours, to create a limited production pattern. The competitive edge this technology offered was substantial, especially considering the accuracy it lent to the price-quoting process.

In 2003, industry leader Intermet produced a new ductile iron called machineable austempered ductile iron (MADI), which was solidly in the middle of available materials in terms of strength. MADI, which was resistant to cracks and subsequent deformation, was designed for easy machineability.

In May 2005, an article in *Foundry Management & Technology* announced Ashland Casting Solution's Exactherm technology provided a solution to the problem of casting thin-walled metal sections. Exactherm, which began development in the late 1990s, would allow metalcasters the ability to custom tailor the thermal properties of a mold or core to meet specific casting section needs and specifically, make possible the casting thin-wall metal sections. "Exactherm is a low-density refractory aggregate that can be used at levels anywhere from 5 percent to 100 percent in sand molds and cores.It's density, thermal conductivity, and specific heat is about 25 percent of silica sand."

WORKFORCE

Casting production requires a large workforce of employees with varying skills and educational levels. There were some 619 foundries in the United States employing more than 65,000 people as of 2002. Most foundries—approximately 80 percent—are small businesses, employing fewer than 100 people. About 14 percent employ between 100 and 250 workers.

Although the workforce is expected to shrink in the 2000s due to decreased product demand and increasing automation, the industry still frequently experiences a shortage of technical, management, and supervisory personnel. Technical personnel are particularly difficult to recruit because engineers are drawn to other technical industries. Disparities between union and non-union shops also played a significant role in wages. Wages in 2000 varied greatly by region and were dependent on skill level and education. On average, employees in casting careers earned upwards of $30,000 with starting wages between $11 per hour for press operators and $16 per hour for journeyman positions and machinists. The industry has continually tried to recruit new employees by offering opportunities to high school graduates and on-the-job training for more skilled positions.

In the UK foundry industry, one-fourth of workers are injured on the job and subsequently kept out of work for three days or more, an average more than double that of the general manufacturing industry average. Accordingly, safety initiatives were begun in 2003 to eliminate one-third of injuries and improve employee health over five years.

INDUSTRY LEADERS

Important trends among foundry companies have been offering integrated services to customers and broadening the revenue base from reliance on individual technologies and single end markets. Sluggish or declining ferrous castings business in a number of segments during parts of the 1980s and early 1990s taught competitive foundries not to depend on one industry, such as the auto or aerospace industries, for all of their sales. Consequently, many leading companies have branched out to offer a wider mix of castings, including both ferrous and nonferrous, to a broader range of customers. Others, capitalizing on the strong trend in the auto industry toward the use of fewer integrated suppliers instead of many small component producers, have sought to expand their offerings to include more assembled components and integrate several steps of the production chain for their clients.

Intermet. Intermet Corporation ranked as one of the world's largest independent foundries. With 2003 sales of US$731 million—low for an industry leader—Intermet's major customers were Ford and Delphi, with 11 percent of sales each, and DaimlerChrysler with 10 percent. More than 80 percent of Intermet's sales are from the North American market. The company produces gray and ductile iron castings, along with aluminum ones, primarily for the automotive industry. Its customers include some 20 top automakers, including the largest in the United States and Germany. In the mid-1990s, Intermet Corporation launched a joint venture with Comalco Limited of Australia to extend its iron making expertise to aluminum. Intermet built a pilot plant in Lewisport, Kentucky, banking on two prevalent trends in the automotive industry: outsourcing and aluminum components. The replacement of iron engine blocks with aluminum was expected to continue to accelerate into the twenty-first century, and the company's development of aluminum castings positioned it to capitalize on the transition.

In 2002 Intermet began production of pressure-counter-pressure process cast (PCCP) aluminum in an attempt to meet demand for lightweight steering knuckles and other chassis and suspension components. The company was anticipated to average between US$22 million and US$25 million in annual PCCP aluminum sales.

Doncasters Group Limited. Doncasters was an important force in the U.K. foundry industry. With GE Aircraft Engines, Rolls-Royce, and Boeing among its major customers, its strength historically was in serving the aerospace industry, which accounted for 60 percent of revenues until its 1998 acquisition of Triplex Lloyd plc, another important U.K. metal caster. Both companies have extensive business with firms in other European countries. Triplex diversified Doncasters' business by adding more automotive and power plant components to the casting mix. The strategic buyout was seen as the method by which Doncasters could insulate itself from downturns in the aerospace sector. But in the mid- to late 1990s, the aerospace business in Europe was recovering, and Doncasters was benefiting. Doncasters demonstrated how the foundry business could be profitable in the 1990s by achieving profit margins consistently in the 10 percent range. The purchase of Triplex Lloyd, which was larger than Doncasters in terms of annual revenues, added some US$328 million (based on 1997 sales) to Doncasters' US$217 million in 1997 revenues. However, the company planned to sell off Triplex's automotive division, which would subtract nearly US$100 million from Triplex's 1997 revenues. The consolidated company generated sales of US$460 million in 2000 and US$ 380.1 in 2001. The company was later acquired by Royal Bank Private Equity.

Precision Castparts Corp. With sales of US$2.2 billion in the fiscal year ending in March 2004, Precision Castparts specializes in investment castings primarily for aerospace customers, notably Pratt & Whitney, Rolls-Royce, and General Electric. However, like Doncasters it has moved toward diversifying its casting and other businesses. The company grew rapidly in the 1990s through a string of acquisitions. In 1997 it acquired seven companies, and as a result its sales nearly doubled between 1996 and 1998. The company reported steadily increasing sales between 1996 and 2001. Precision was hit hard by slowdowns in the aircraft industry during the early 1990s, which saw its sales plummet from US$583 million in 1992 to US$420 million in 1994. In 1993 the company barely turned a profit. The turnaround began in 1995, as both sales and profits, along with its stock price, began an upswing. By 1998 the company recorded a 6.5 percent net profit margin, ahead of its 10 year average of 5.9 percent annually. In 2001 Precision Castparts's sales grew by 39 percent, up to US$2.3 billion, with more than 80 percent of its sales in the United States. The company acquired SPS Technologies in 2003, which produced parts for both aerospace and automotive markets. As of 2004, the aerospace market accounted for approximately US$1.0 billion of PCC's revenue.

FURTHER READING

"Casting a New Vision." *Automotive Industries,* October 2003.

"Company Profiles." *The Industry Standard,* 2001. Available from http://www.thestandard.com.

"Defense Briefs." *Defense Daily,* 19 December 2003.

Die Casting Shaping America's Future. North American Die Casting Association. 2002. Available from http://www.diecasting.org.

"Foundries Exceed Their Expectations." *Furnaces International,* September-October 2003.

"Hoover's Company Capsules." 2005. Available from http://www.hoovers.com.

"Industry Moves to Improve Safety in Foundries." *The Safety & Health Practitioner,* September 2003.

"International Trade Statistics." 2003. Available from http://www.wto.org.

Kirgin, Kenneth H. "A Study of End-Use Markets Shows an Expansion in Casting Shipments for 2004 with Considerable Gains in Aluminum and Steel." *Modern Casting,* 2004. Available from http://www.moderncasting.com.

McClean, Bill. "The Changing Foundry Model." *Solid State Technology,* October 2003.

"Meeting and Beating the Imported Competition." *Foundry Management & Technology.* March 2005.

"Metal Casting Industry Profile." *Department of Energy,* 2002. Available from http://www.oit.doe.gov.

Ogando, Joseph. "Iron Improvements." *Design News,* 7 July 2003.

"Outside the Sand Box." *Foundry Management & Technology,* May 2005.

"PCC Delivers Strong Sales and Income in First Quarter Fiscal 2005." *Modern Casting,* 14 July 2004.

Rauch, A.H., ed. *Source Book on Ductile Iron.* Metals Park, OH: American Society for Metals, 1977.

"Smart Move." *Metallurgia,* February 2003.

Spada, Alfred T. "Northwest Foundries' Survival Tips for the 21st Century." *Modern Casting,* June 2000.

U.S. Bureau of the Census. "Iron and Steel Foundries." *Current Industrial Reports,* 2002.

U.S. Geological Survey. *Mineral Commodity Summaries,* 2001.

SIC 3910

NAICS 33991, 339912

JEWELRY, SILVERWARE, AND PLATED WARE

The jewelry and silverware industry is a prime consumer of precious stones, synthetic stones, and metals, making such goods as rings, necklaces, and earrings, as well as all types of eating utensils made of solid or plated precious metals. Some industry firms also prepare gemstones and settings for use in jewelry and related finished products. For discussion of the industry's raw materials, see also **Mining, Gemstone** and **Mining, Metal**.

INDUSTRY SNAPSHOT

The jewelry manufacturing industry remains highly fragmented, with most production being done by small companies with few, but highly skilled, employees. Several countries dominate the industry, with Italy continuing to be the world leader in terms of gold jewelry design. In the diamond trade, South African company De Beers has major control of the market, although its diamonds are sold to jewelry manufacturers around the world. China has become a major player in the industry, being the leading source of jewelry in the United States. The U.S.-based manufacturing industry continued to be plagued by declines in workforce numbers and market share, claiming the losses were due to cheaper foreign labor markets, and unfair trade practices in other countries.

The World Gold Council reported that 2004 worldwide gold demand was up 30 percent in value and 12 percent in tonnage. Positive growth was reported in the United States, Turkey, Vietnam, India, Egypt, and China. The United States was the largest market in the world, followed by Japan and Saudi Arabia. The Silver Institute also reported increased demand in 2003, with demand for jewelry silver rising more than 10 million ounces over the previous year.

Although created for adornment in North America, Korea, Japan, and Europe, jewelry continues to be purchased as a form of savings in many parts of the world, particularly in China, India and the Middle East.

By 2005, the industry continued to be dogged by problems with dirty gold and the trade of conflict diamonds. The industry was under increased pressure from governments and particularly environmental and human rights groups to better monitor its members in their purchase of precious metals and gemstones from companies and countries that did not have good environmental practices or were using their profits to fund war or terrorist efforts.

In January 2007, both organizations and the diamond industry reported being pleased overall with progress reports at a Kimberley Process meeting. The World Diamond Council, which had endorsed some of Partnership Africa Canada's criticisms of the Kimberley process, said it was "delighted" with the progress. There was cause for concern, however, related to accusations that a Ghana conduit for conflict diamonds smuggled from the Ivory Coast. Amnesty International called for Ghana to be immediately "suspended" from the Kimberley Process.

Jewelry trends have always been linked to what is happening in the fashion world. By 2007, women were moving away from wearing dainty and delicate charms and chains to selecting larger more bold pieces. The move away from minimalism was supported by fashion designs featuring V-necks, scoop necks and cowl necks. Many jewelry designers believed these styles encouraged women to wear chunky chokers. Along those lines, Los Angeles jeweler Cathy Waterman was adding 3 and 4 inch cuffs to her collection.

Predictions in 2007 Financial Forecast proclaimed that high-end jewelers should continue out-performing middle- and low-priced jewelers. Designer jewelry was considered to be closely tied to the luxury sector's success story.

Reflecting back on thoughts related to the production of a major motion picture about the diamond industry, it became clear that hype and buzz made a bigger impression than the movie itself. Although *Blood Diamond* wasn't a big box office sensation, it did spur the media to provide a lot of critical coverage about the conflict diamond issue. The industry reportedly spent US$15 million on a public relations campaign. As a result, industry insiders worked with acclaimed damage control guru Allan Mayer who advised them on strategy and which reporter' to approach with the trade's point of view. A World Diamond Council survey found that two-thirds of jewelers surveyed stated customers had inquired about conflict diamonds since the movie's premiere. Almost all of those jewelers at 97 percent of respondents said that they had trained their staff to handle customer questions about the issue. DiamondFacts.org was cited as giving retailers good background information.

Industry trailblazer Peggy Kirby noted that while many things in the industry had changed, a lot of how business is done hadn't changed at all. "From the sidelines I've watched diamonds around the world, offshore manufacturing, the rise of China and India, battery watches, and in horror, discounts of 70 percent. But I still love this crazy business of jewelry," Kirby admitted.

ORGANIZATION AND STRUCTURE

Both gold and silver are mined from open pits or, more commonly, via shafts. The shafts follow veins of the minerals and can go as deep as 12,000 feet into the earth. Mexico, the United States, Peru, and Canada are primary sources for silver ore. Silverware and hollowware are typically stamped from sheets of silver or stainless steel. Silver plate is then added for plated items. Decorative details and polishing may be done by hand or machine, depending on the quality of the materials used. Primary industry centers for producing diamond and other gem-quality jewelry are the United States, Israel, Russia, Hong Kong, Switzerland, and Belgium.

Refined gold, silver, platinum, and other precious metals are fabricated by manufacturers and made into the basic components of jewelry (e.g., links, hoops, and studs). The final production of fine jewelry is usually done partially by hand, with hand detailing. This increases value to the customer by adding the appeal of uniqueness and rarity to each piece of fine jewelry. The jewelry is often commissioned by and sold through the same store. Tiffany and Co. of New York City, one of the premier retail sellers of fine jewelry in the United States, may order a limited number of designs from a particular jewelry maker or custom design a piece for a customer.

By 2005, seven countries were producing 80 percent of the world's diamonds: Botswana, Russia, South Africa, Angola, Namibia, Australia and Zaire. De Beers and its affiliates were responsible for about 40 percent of the production, and its marketing arm—The Diamond Trading Corporation (DTC)—processed about two thirds of all diamonds by value. Processing diamonds involves sorting and valuing them into one of more than 16,000 categories based on shape, color, size and quality. Ten times per year, the DTC sells its rough diamonds at sales called "sights" to the world's leading *diamantaires,* the industry term for diamond cutters. The world's diamond cutters and traders are primarily found in Antwerp, Mumbai, Tel Aviv, New York and Johannesburg, with Thailand and China making inroads into the industry. Once polished, the diamonds are then sold and traded in one of 24 registered *bourses* (exchanges) around the world. From here the diamonds are sold to jewelry manufacturers and then retailers.

The jewelry manufacturing industry has traditionally been a highly fragmented business made up of small, family-run establishments in which jewelry-making skills are passed down within a family from generation to generation. This tradition is still common, particularly in the diamond-cutting industry. Commodity items such as chains and watch bands are usually mass-produced in factories, while jewelry boutiques make one-of-a-kind pieces to suit the individual tastes of their customers.

The jewelry market is often defined by the primary purpose for the purchase of the piece. 'Adornment jewelry' is, as the name implies, primarily bought to enhance the appearance of the wearer. Demand for this type of jewelry is greatly affected by disposable income, marketing efforts and fashion trends. The cost of this type of jewelry is not always related strictly to the amount of gold or gems in it. The purchase of jewelry for adornment is primarily seen in North America, Japan, Europe and Korea. The type called 'Value jewelry' is jewelry bought as a form of savings, although it is often worn, too. In some countries, this type of purchase is done because of an unreliable banking system, but cultural beliefs may also play a strong role in this viewpoint. India, Thailand, Indonesia, Singapore, Malaysia and the Middle East are the largest purchasers of this type of jewelry.

Most countries involved in the jewelry industry have trade organizations. Most of these organizations in turn belong to The World Jewelery Confederation, also known as CIBJO—Confederation International de la Bijouterie, Joaillerie, OrfSvrerie des Diamantes, Perles et Pierres, which translates to International Confederation of Jewelery, Silverware, Diamonds and Stones. Founded in France in 1926 to promote the European jewelry industry, the organization was restructured in 1961 to be a global one. CIBJO's main mission is to protect consumer confidence in the industry. By 2005, organizations from 40 countries belonged to CIBJO, which was then headquartered in Italy.

Background and Development

Basic types of jewelry—rings, necklaces, bracelets, and earrings—have been evolving since humans began to indulge in self-decoration in prehistoric times. Historic eras are characterized by particular styles of jewelry depending on cultural trends, the availability of precious materials, and the prevailing technology of metalworking at the time. Many elements of jewelry style have become classic techniques that have enjoyed revivals and rediscoveries over the years. For example, filigree (delicate, lace-like jewelry made of intertwined wires of precious metals) was first made in China. Cameos (jewelry having two layers of precious gems, with a figure carved in the top layer) were popularized in Europe during the Renaissance.

Early examples of jewelry were made of animal teeth, shells, and bones. The activity evolved into a fine craft, especially after gold was discovered. Fine gold work was one hallmark of the Etruscan civilization in the fifth century B.C. Their method of creating enameled designs from granulated gold has never been duplicated. Ancient Greeks and Israelites were also skilled goldsmiths, combining gemstones, gold, and silver to make jewelry for kings and nobles. The malleability of gold is one of its most attractive features to jewelers. Gold can be formed into near-transparent sheets, or leaves, thus making it easy to create raised, inset, and other designs with it. It is also rare. Since the fifteenth century, only 80,000 tons of gold have been mined, and estimates are that only 32,000 tons remain to be extracted.

The Romans were highly skilled silversmiths and developed a thriving industry making cups, plates, and dishes. Jewelry was not initially popular in Rome, but as the civilization matured, fairly simple pieces embellished with precious and semiprecious stones came into favor. During Europe's Middle Ages, fine metalworkers worked with both gold and silver. Their main customer was the Catholic Church. Elaborate trappings for priests and altars and accessories used in services were in great demand. Entire altars were clad in gold and silver, set with cloisonné, enamel, sapphire, and rubies. For common people during this time, elaborate rosaries were a form of jewelry.

Until the Renaissance, jewelry served to signal the wearer's social status and wealth. By the fifteenth century, Western cultures began to use jewelry to reflect the sentiments and personal fashion of its owners. In the mid-seventeenth century, Baroque style dictated elaborate, excessive ornamentation in everything from hair decorations to shoe buckles. The discovery in the late seventeenth century of the Golconda and Hyderabad diamond mines in India introduced diamonds to Europe. Reportedly, the first diamond was cut in Venice. From China and Japan came jade, both in its familiar green form as well as stones speckled with different colors. The neoclassic restraint of the early nineteenth century resulted in more simple necklaces and bracelets.

Essentially, diamonds are carbon in its purest form, having been compressed under tremendous heat and pressure over a long period deep inside the earth. Historically, most diamonds have been discovered in Borneo, Brazil, and South Africa. Through the centuries, famous diamonds have been rumored to bring luck—good or bad—to their owners. The history of the Koh-i-noor diamond, for instance, begins with an Indian rajah in the Middle Ages. The diamond was eventually given to Queen Victoria of England. She had it recut and reset. When her jewelers were done, the 191-carat stone weighed 109 carats. It is now one of the famed crown jewels of England. The biggest diamond ever discovered was the Cullinan. In 1905, this 3,106-carat diamond was found in a South African mine. The country's government gave it to England's King Edward VII, who had it cut into 109 smaller stones of varying sizes.

More recently, in 1985, Argyle Diamonds, an Australian firm, began aggressively marketing naturally tinted diamonds that were mined in western Australia. In 1993, the mines yielded more than 40 million carats or about 8 tons of raw diamonds, with an estimated market value of US$380 million. However, only about 6 percent of the diamonds were gem quality, and most of them were only lightly tinted. Bucking the tradition that the only good diamond is a pure, colorless diamond, Argyle Diamonds launched a campaign to persuade consumers that tinted diamonds were also desirable. By marketing the tinted diamonds as "champagne and cognac diamonds," selling for half the price of similarly sized and cut colorless diamonds, the company achieved US$165 million in annual sales in the United States alone. Argyle's extremely rare pink diamonds needed no such marketing strategies. In 1988, a 1.51-carat red Argyle diamond sold for US$740,000 per carat.

Annual worldwide sales of gold jewelry in the early 1990s totaled approximately US$6.4 billion. In fact, 3,106 tons of the metal was used in 1992 to make gold jewelry. Approximately 221.6 million ounces of silver were used to make jewelry and silverware in 1993, which was up 37 percent from the previous year. Led by Japan and the United States, world diamond jewelry sales totaled US$2.72 trillion in 1993. Production of diamonds in the 1990s was dominated by Australia and Africa. Although jewelry sales in most countries were flat in the early 1990s, the emerging middle classes in many Asian countries were expected to boost sales throughout the decade.

In 1994, the United States accounted for 33 percent of worldwide diamond jewelry sales, according to *Jewelers Circular Keystone* magazine. The second largest jewelry market was Japan, which purchased 14 percent of the units and 29 percent of the value. In terms of diamond carats sold, the United States accounted for 40 percent of world sales and Japan accounted for 19 percent. In Europe, Germans bought the most diamonds, but Italians accounted for the largest share of retail value and carats. Europe and South Africa together purchased 24 percent of jewelry units worldwide and 21 percent of the value. The Asia Pacific region purchased 21 percent of the units and 36 percent of the worldwide value.

The Diamond Registry reported that by the end of 2001, the diamond sector was showing resilience despite the turbulence in the world. Rough diamonds were still in demand and most dealers were in decent financial health. However, the Diamond High Council (HRD), the official representative of Belgium's diamond industry, stated that the market was trying to regain its stability in the wake of the terrorist attacks in the United States on September 11, 2001. Antwerp's diamond exports dropped by 18 percent, and the U.S. market took the biggest tumble with imports falling 38 percent.

CURRENT CONDITIONS

At the annual meeting of CIBJO held in March 2005, the main topic of discussion was the maintenance of consumer confidence in the industry. CIBJO president Gaetano Cavalieri indicated that human rights abuses, environmental issues, and poor labor conditions were threatening consumer confidence. The organization itself was facing criticism from external groups over its failure to promote and monitor self-regulation to end the sale of "dirty gold" and "conflict diamonds." Dirty gold issues center around the environmental problems associated with gold mining, while conflict diamonds are so-named because they are diamonds mined after takeover by rebel groups in primarily African countries (Sierra Leone, Liberia, and the Democratic Republic of Congo), the funds of which are used to purchase arms. In March 2005, prominent human rights groups were calling for sanctions on diamonds from Angola, with accusations made that people were no longer allowed to move freely in some areas of the country, and miners were working only for food in unregistered mines.

Online sales were growing tremendously faster than traditional retail channels and offered jewelry stores an opportunity for growth in 2007. According to com.Score Networks, related total online retail sales from November 1 to December 3, 2006 increased 25 percent compared with the same 2005 period. This increase was largely due to a 69 percent increase in jewelry and watch sales.

GOLD

By the end of 2004, according to the World Gold Council, jewelry accounted for about 77 percent of world gold demand, accounting for a value of more than US$35 billion, up from the US$29.6 billion value of 2003. The demand for gold was affected by world events in 2001, but by 2004 demand had increased by 5.2 percent in terms of volume and 18.5 percent in terms of value, despite gold prices reaching their highest point in 16 years. Around the world, the demand for gold jewelry follows very similar seasonal patterns, with most demand being related to gift-giving during special events. The fourth quarter of the year shows the strongest demand, with celebrations such as Christmas, Diwali and New Year festivities occurring in many places. The second best selling period occurs during the first quarter of the year, as this is the time when the Chinese New Year occurs, as does the wedding season in India and Valentine' Day. Turkey, Vietnam and India had the largest increase in tonnage demand for jewelry gold. China, the Middle East, Egypt and the United States also recorded increases in demand.

The price of gold hit US$730.40 per troy ounce on 10 May 2006. That was the highest price in 25 years. This rise made predictions of "$1,000 gold" within a few years seem very realistic. As *Rock & Gem* pointed out, those predictions were based on more than dreams and wishful thinking. They acknowledged a gold market that has changed tremendously in this century.

In 2007, Duvall O'Steen of the World Gold Council claimed that a trend related to increased desire for yellow gold started in about three-and-a-half years ago. This trend was spurred on by positive publicity in major publications such as *USA Today.*

O'Stern also noted that retailers were placing a special type of demand on the supply side. They were striving to come up with lighter-weight pieces and still reflect a "fashion-forward look".

SILVER

The Silver Institute reported that in 2003, world jewelry and silverware fabrication increased by 4.1 percent to 276.7 million ounces. Demand was highest in East Asia, particularly in China, Thailand, and India, the United States, and Europe, particularly in France. According to the Silver Information Center, the bridal market represents approximately one-half of purchases of sterling silver flatware. The typical consumer is an employed female, aged 35 and over, with a high income. Consumers primarily purchase sterling silver flatware for weddings and major holidays such as Thanksgiving and Christmas.

DIAMONDS

In 2004, the world's largest diamond trader, De Beers, reported that world diamond production was valued at an estimated US$11.2 billion. Almost 70 percent of the rough diamond market is controlled by De Beers. The company, which became private in 2001, pays out approximately US$200 million annually to promote diamonds and diamond jewelry. It is famous for its "A diamond is forever" advertising campaign. Its long domination of the industry allows it to control both supply and demand in the market. By the end of 2004, De Beers appeared to be making a comeback from a period of sluggish diamond sales in the late 1990s and early 2000s. Earnings for the company reached US$652 million, up 11 percent from the previous year.

JCK confirmed that Rio Tinto's Argyle Diamond Mine was the world's largest provider of champagne- and cognac-color diamonds. The annual Argyle Tender, held from late August to early October 2006, was conducted under the auspices of Rio Tinto Diamonds for the first time. The tender presented 65 stones. They included eight rounds, 21 emerald cuts, 19 radiant/princess cuts, eight ovals, one pear shape and eight novelty cuts. Experts raved about the superior color saturation making Argyle tender stones among those in high demand as colored diamond market collectibles.

The 2006 Diamond Pipeline analysis from Diamond Intelligence reflected more concern about price than volume. Main rough diamond suppliers were charged with hedging and using the sales mechanism for that purpose. The diamond jewelry retail market grew by approximately 4 - 5 percent in 2006.

Although grading systems of the American Gem Society and the Gemological Institute of America were close, there was heated debate about which one was the best. *JCK* concluded that the American Gem Society's 11 grade scale was "mathematically more discerning". The Gemological Institute of America's five-point scale corresponded to what their research said was actually visible through observation.

After his visit to African diamond mines, hip-hop industry legend Russell Simmons held a press conference announcing creation of a Diamond Empowerment Fund. Simmons shared his belief that diamonds could be good for Africa and that 25 percent of profits for the Fund would be donated to African charities. "I want people to buy a diamond and know that they are part of an empowerment process. The image of diamonds can't always be about successful rich people," Simmons concluded.

PEARLS

Akoya, Black, Freshwater and South Sea are the four main kinds of pearl oysters. World production of pearls is estimated to be US$825 million. As of 2004, white and golden South Sea pearls had the highest demand, particularly in sizes over 14mm. Akoyas from 7mm to 9mm were holding a steady demand. Chinese freshwater pearls were the lowest priced pearls, largely due to proportionally higher production, while Japan continued to be the world leader in saltwater pearl production.

The weak dollar hurts supply of colored stones and pearls to the U.S. market. According to Stuart Robertson, research director for *The Guide* which was published by Gemworld International, the pearl market was emulating colored stone market. That meant top quality, large, colorful and unique pearls were going to Asia first. Robertson also noted that CFWCP rounds, petals and coin shapes were the most popular and dominating the category.

JCK listed clusters as being among the "top trends from the jewelry shows." This look was described as being a welcome alternative to the recent length trend in earrings and necklaces. Clustered pearls were applauded for creating a vintage look without seeming ancient.

PLATINUM

According to research conducted by London-based precious metals consultancy GFMS, platinum was expected to be in surplus supply in 2005, due to overproduction and weakening of demand for jewelry. World demand had decreased approximately 25 percent by the end of 2004, blamed in part on an increase in the purchase of palladium jewelry in China and also on the fact that platinum prices reached a 24-year high.

The United States is the third-largest market in the world for platinum jewelry. In the first three quarters of 2001, demand was adversely affected by increased prices of platinum and a decrease in consumer purchases. By 2003 and 2004, the Platinum Guild International was seeing large success with its "pure, rare, eternal" advertising campaign, promoting platinum as the logical and desirable choice for the wedding market. The ads were also appearing internationally. Reports in *Platinum Today* were indicating that by early 2005, platinum jewelry was proving popular with young American buyers.

Most platinum watches were Swiss-made. According to Jewelers Circular Keystone (JCK), the number of platinum watches exported worldwide from Switzerland was 12,469 in 2006. That marked an increase of 7 percent from the 2005 of 11,651. The United States received 23 percent and continued to be the world's top platinum watch market. Among all watches retailing for US$10,000 and up as part of a US$1 billion market, platinum watches accounted for 8 percent in 2006.

JCK reported some notable trends related to the U.S. platinum watch market. LGI Network, a provider of marketing and sales information on fine watches, said platinum watch sales to women in 2006 increased 34 percent in dollars and 25 percent in units. LGI also noted that sales in the Northeast rose 38 percent in dollars and 31 percent in units for 2006. Furthermore, the West region was the only one experiencing a decline from 2005 in units sold. This fact was true although the West distinguished itself as region with most business in 2006. Platinum Guild International CEO James Courage observed that there was a growing market of young affluent consumers in their early 30s with a growing interest in platinum as a quality metal.

JEWELRY RETAILING

Unity Marketing reported that while jewelry stores still account for almost 60 percent of the total retail market, the market is becoming wider ranging. Purchases of jewelry via discounters and mass merchants such as Wal-Mart is a significant trend, especially among consumers aged 18 to 34. In addition, the luxury market, such as Tiffany's, was strong in the mid-2000s. That left only the middle-range jewelry stores, many of which were shopping mall-based, in trouble. Consumers also purchase jewelry through department stores, television shopping, mail order and the Internet.

By 2003, online purchasing was expected to be about 6 percent of consumer retail spending in the United States. The Department of Commerce estimated that in 2003, Internet sales were approximately US$2.3 trillion. Online shopping for jewelry allows customers to easily compare prices from a variety of vendors, and to potentially purchase jewelry from all over the world. The Manufacturing Jewelers & Suppliers of America (MJSA) notes that jewelry retailers who use the Web to sell their products not only can gain new global customers and increased market accessibility, they can also offer 24-hour ordering and instant product information updates to consumers.

RESEARCH AND TECHNOLOGY

The price of a gemstone depends on its quality. Quality is measured by how clearly light is bent, or refracted, through a cut stone. Diamonds are the standard, with the highest level of refraction. Diamonds are cut along their grain and then carefully faceted. The most popular diamond shape is the brilliant (round) cut, with 58 facets. Amsterdam, Antwerp, and New York City are centers for this highly specialized and exacting trade. Diamonds are weighed in metric carats, with each carat equal to a fifth of a gram.

In 1955 scientists at General Electric created synthetic diamonds made of pressurized graphite. These lab-created gems were originally intended for industrial use. However, the high cost of genuine diamonds has bred an entire industry for synthetic gems. Imitation gems were also fashioned from a particularly hard type of glass. Sometimes a thin piece of a genuine gem is spliced onto a base of an artificial or less precious stone. The Russian Federation was also a leader in the development of synthetic gems. Like the General Electric scientists, they intended only to make the stones for industrial use. However, high-quality lab-created gems are very hard to distinguish from high-quality natural stones.

Recent developments in the industry include a new platinum alloy developed by Steven Kretchmer of the company Steven Kretchmer Design. The new alloy is called Plat/SK and is said to be harder than other alloys and not scratch or dent as easily as the others. It should prove to "produce better jewelry products for the consumer while reducing tooling costs for the manufacturer," as reported in *Benchmark,* the newsletter of the Manufacturing Jewelers and Silversmiths of America Inc.

ENVIRONMENTAL CONSIDERATIONS

Electroplating is a process widely used in the jewelry industry to bond a thin coat of precious metal to a base of common metal. The chemicals used in electroplating and the chemical and metal by-products (such as copper, lead, and ammonia) are toxic. Jewelry manufacturers involved in electroplating are usually required to purify wastewater before releasing it, and the resultant toxic sludge must be handled properly.

Fumes from electroplating and other processes used in jewelry making can be damaging both in the workplace and in the environment. Some manufacturers must remove the fumes before releasing factory air through exhaust systems. To prevent workers from being affected by the fumes, protective hoods and special ventilating systems may be required as well.

MAJOR COUNTRIES IN THE INDUSTRY

THE UNITED STATES

By 2004, jewelry manufacturing done in the United States continued on its 20-year decline in terms of workforce and market share, according to Manufacturing Jewelers and Suppliers of America Inc. In 1977, imports of precious jewelry accounted for only 6 percent of the U.S. market. By 2001, imports accounted for about half of the trade, and by 2003 they were worth US$6.4 billion. The greatest trade deficits in jewelry in 2003 were between the U.S. and China, Italy, India and Thailand.

The United States is the world's second largest market for gold jewelry behind India, purchasing about 350 metric tons with a value of about US$17 billion dollars in 2004. That year, most gold jewelry was being imported, primarily from Turkey, India and Italy, according to the World Gold Council.

The U.S. remained a net importer of polished diamonds during the first quarter of 2005, according to U.S. Census Bureau data. During this period, US$3.5 billion in diamonds were imported, while US$1.9 billion were exported. The price per polished carat imported had increased almost 20 percent over the previous year, with a price of US$843 per carat.

According to research reported in a 2003 issue of *JCK*, the U.S. fine and costume jewelry consumer market totaled US$52.1 billion, with US$26.0 billion from sales at jewelry-only stores. There were about 25,000 jewelry-only companies and 40,000 jewelry-only stores in the United States. Half of sales were diamonds, and one-fourth of sales were during the month of December.

About 39 percent of the U.S. adult population purchases fine jewelry each year. Women make more jewelry purchases than men, but men tend to spend more money on the jewelry they buy. Men also generally purchase jewelry as gifts, while many women make purchases for themselves. Younger consumers from 18 to 24 years of age have the highest incidence of jewelry purchases, with jewelry consumption decreasing as purchasers age. Of those adult consumers who purchase jewelry for themselves, the average amount spent each year is US$500. Chicago was expected to be the largest consumer market by 2007, with a projected US$2.5 billion in combined jewelry and watch revenues.

Italy

The Economist reported that in 1998, Italy produced the most precious metal jewelry in the world, but by 2001 the country's jewelry industry was facing tough challenges and was struggling to remain competitive. While about 80 percent of Italy's jewelry production is exported, competition from Israel, Thailand, India, China, and Turkey has been a strong concern. Italy is also seeing a decrease in its share of the U.S. market, which has represented over one-third of its exports. Federorafi, the trade association for Italy's jewelry producers and goldsmiths, notes that consolidation may be the solution for companies to survive in turbulent times. Those companies suffering the worst produce jewelry in the middle and low price ranges. However, by 2004, Italy remained the world's leading manufacturer of gold jewelry and the leader in jewelry design. However, demand for traditional design was falling while demand for innovative designs was increasing.

Belgium

Considered the world's diamond capital for more than 500 years, Antwerp imports approximately 80 percent of the world's diamonds. Here 1,500 diamond firms and 250 diamond cutters develop the trade.

Germany

Germany trails Italy closely in European jewelry manufacturing. In the mid-1990s, German designers were drawing attention with their contemporary designs. Most of the German jewelry manufacturing industry is located around Pforzheim, a southern German jewelry and watch-making center since 1767. The vast majority of the companies employed no more than 50 people, and the town operated a showroom displaying the wares of all 240 jewelry firms located in the region. Determined to develop their reputation internationally, the manufacturers in the area produced one of the first CD-ROM catalogs of fine jewelry and watches to sell to retailers around the world.

Thailand

Thailand's jewelry industry continues to be a key player in jewelry production and export. Loose diamonds and gold ranked eighth and tenth in terms of imports into the country in 2003. Jewelry and gems ranked seventh in Thailand's list of main exports, and in 1999 the sector boasted sales of US$1.5 billion. The biggest export markets for Thailand's jewelry industry are Japan, Belgium, Israel, and the United States. Strong sales also result when tourists purchase jewelry directly from merchants. Thailand boasts the fifth largest diamond-cutting region in the world. The country imported just under US$700 million of precious stones and diamonds in 1999.

China

Begun only in the 1980s, China's jewelry industry has grown rapidly since then. Following houses and automobiles, jewelry is the third most purchased commodity in the country. It has been estimated that by 2010, the country's domestic purchases will account for 10 percent of the world's sales. Much of the gold jewelry sold is 24-carat (almost pure) and is used for savings or ceremonial purposes.

According to Xinhua News Agency, in 1999 China's jewelry demand continued to be robust, with exported jewelry taking in US$2.14 billion and domestic sales worth US$9.6 billion. Since 2002, the gold jewelry industry has been gradually deregulated, and foreign influence is now allowed. This has brought new designs, which appeal to a more urban market. As part of its proposal for entry into the World Trade Organization, China promised to lower the tariffs on jewelry imports, which had been as high as 50 percent in the past.

The China Jewelry Association notes that jewelry production is increasing, aided by the application of advanced technologies and improved quality techniques. Jewelry production in China involves approximately 24,500 firms that are either private or government owned.

In 2007, *JCK* reported that Gemological Institute of America President Donna Baker predicted China would realize jewelry sales of US$20 billion by the end of decade. Baker had also observed the growth of China's emerging middle-class consumers and predicted they would continue to buy jewelry with gold, diamonds and gemstones at a similar rate in the immediate future.

India

With the world's largest market for gold jewelry, India not only manufactures most of its domestic trade, but had also become a major exporter of gold jewelry. In 2004, demand for gold reached 520 metric tons. Demand for this type of jewelry is largely based on tradition, with gold being seen as a way of saving income as well as defining social position. In addition, it is an important wedding gift in many parts of the country, particularly as it is often the only property a woman is allowed to own. According to *Rock & Gem,* India's huge rural population prefers its Gold in the form of 24-karat investment grade jewelry.

JCK reported that Columbia Gem House and Trigem Designs President Eric Braunwart claimed many Indian manufacturers were investing in local retail chains. This practice was impacting the amount of business they found it necessary to do with the U.S.

The Middle East

Middle Eastern cultures have always had strong ties to the gold and jewelry stones market, but since the mid-1990s, Dubai has come onto the scene as a major trader of gold and jewelry. The country caters to a huge domestic as well as foreign market for its products.

FURTHER READING

Bergenstock, Donna, and James Maskulka. "The De Beers Story: Are Diamonds Forever?" *Business Horizons,* May 2001.

Bres, Glen A. "2007 Forecast: Moderate Growth, Despite Pressures." *Jewelers Circular Keystone,*February 2007.

"Diamonds in Conflict." Global Policy Forum, Accessed May 2005. Available from http://www.globalpolicy.org.

"Dueling Cut Grades." *Jewelers Circular Keystone,*January 2007.

"Fair Trade and the U.S. Jewelry Industry: A Strategy for Manufacturers to Compete Globally in the 21st Century." Manufacturing Jewelers and Suppliers of America (MJSA), 2004. Available from http://www.mjsainc.com.

"Global Platinum Market Faces Surplus in 2005—GFMS." *Creamer Media's Mining Weekly,* April 15, 2005. Available from http://engineeringnews.co.za.

Gomelsky, Victoria. "Pearl Market Buoyed by Upward Pricing Trend." *National Jeweler,* 1 May 2004.

Heebner, Jennifer. "Soft in the Middle." *Jewelers Circular Keystone,* April 2004.

———. "The 2002 Jewelry Industry Fact Sheet." *Jewelers Circular Keystone,* September 2003.

"Jewelry Takes a Turn Toward Big and Bold Looks." *Detroit Free Press,* 23 March 2007.

"Keeping in the Black with Gold." *Lapidary Journal,* January 2007.

"Kimberley Process Meeting Makes Breakthroughs." *Jewelers Circular Keystone,* January 2007.

"Market Intelligence: Jewelry." *World Gold Council,* 2005. Available from http://www.gold.org.

"Platinum Watches." *Jewelers Circular Keystone,* April 2007.

"PGI Reaps Benefits of Ad Campaign." *National Jeweler,* 1 June 2004.

"The Real Impact: The Movie That Everyone in the Jewelry Industry Feared Had Scant Impact on Holiday Sales." *Jewelers Circular Keystone,* April 2007.

Roskin, Gary. "Argyle Tender Offers the Pick of the Pinks." *Jewelers Circular Keystone,*January 2007.

———. "The Rise of Color, Pearls - and Prices." *Jewelers Circular Keystone,* February 2007.

"Saudi Arabia: $1.3 Billion Invested in Gold and Jewelry Sector." *IPR Strategic Business Information Database,* 21 August 2003.

"Saudi Arabia: Increased Activity in Gold and Jewelry Market During Summer 2003." *IPR Strategic Business Information Database,* 21 October 2003.

Schupak, Hedda T. "Jewelry in Her Own Words: Peggy Kirby, One of the Jewelry Industry's First Ladies, Takes Us on a Trip Through the Decades and Shares Almost a Century's Worth of Wisdom." *Jewelers Circular Keystone,* April 2007.

"Top Trends from the Jewelry Shows." *Jewelers Circular Keystone,* April 2007.

"Trade Tells Its Side: The Diamond Industry Was Prepared for a Showdown But the Hype and Buzz Made a Bigger Impression than the Film Itself." *Jewelers Circular Keystone,* April 2007.

"2006 Diamond Pipeline - 2006 Was a Soft Year: Diamond Output by Value Unchanged; Prospects for Rough Shortages up to 2015." 23 April 2007. Available from http://diamondintelligence.com.

Voynick, Steve. "Gold in the 21st Century: How Mining and the Market are Changing." *Rock & Gem,* February 2007.

"World Silver Survey 2004." *Silver Institute,* 2004. Available from http://www.silverinstitute.org.

SIC 3410

NAICS 332431

METAL CANS

This industry consists of companies that manufacture, typically from purchased materials, metal cans, metal shipping barrels, drums, kegs, and pails.

INDUSTRY SNAPSHOT

The world metal can industry—a major component of the US$345.93 billion global packaging industry—represented a growing, multibillion-dollar market in the early and mid-2000s. In 2003, the U.S. market alone was valued at more than US$13 billion. According to the Aluminum Association, Inc., there were 100.5 billion cans produced in the U.S. in 2004. Industry firms produced billions of aluminum cans alone, but intense competition, threats from new packaging technologies, and the enormous costs of metal can manufacture compelled industry firms to develop new can designs and improved manufacturing processes while looking to overseas markets for new sources of revenue.

By far, Americans manufactured the most metal cans for soft drinks, producing more than 57 billion cans in 2004 alone. Production of beer cans was nearly 28.8 billion units. Beverage cans held the highest rate of recycling as well; 51.5 billion cans were recycled in 2004.

The growing popularity of premium beverage packaging solutions by glass and plastic beverage packaging producers was fueled by the explosion of microbreweries and boutique beverage brands, which though more expensive than cans, offered beverage makers a way to differentiate their products with consumers. For instance, the so-called aluminum "bottle can" introduced to the U.S. market in 2004 allowed the containers to be filled on pre-existing bottling lines for glass bottles. Can makers emphasized metal cans' low cost and superior graphics and pressed harder to develop ways to make the "one style fits all" metal can stand out on store shelves. In less developed economies—where beverages sit longer on store shelves and refrigeration is less reliable—can industry firms viewed their prospects for protecting market share more confidently.

By 2004, several new developments stood to help the metal can industry grow, particularly in the area of packaging, which was driven by the market and consumer preferences. Differentiation in packaging's "look" did more to boost the industry than anything else. Pop-top cans have more than half the shelf space in some markets. Unusually shaped (square, barrel, kettle), embossed, and other standout cans have begun appearing on shelves worldwide for some time, and are expected to increase in abundance. Some companies were experimenting with the viability of manufacturing cans that could be resealed. According to *Brand Packaging,* companies were seeing enormous upswings in revenue by offering their products in differentiated cans.

ORGANIZATION AND STRUCTURE

Historically, can making has been a mature, slow-growth, and capital-intensive business that relies on economies of scale and high-volume production efficiencies to squeeze profit from the fraction of revenue not spent on purchasing materials, installing new equipment, product marketing, equipment maintenance, labor, depreciation, and taxes. In contrast to cyclical industries like automobile manufacturing, can making is relatively resistant to boom-and-bust cycles in the economy. In fact, sales of soft drinks, beer, and certain canned food staples often increase during economic downturns as consumers switch from up-market, glass-packaged products to low-cost canned goods.

The metal can industry has been difficult for new entrants to break into because of the enormous capital outlays required to establish high-tech production facilities and distribution networks—in the late 1990s a modern beverage manufacturing line in Europe cost ECU30 million (US$32 million) or more to install. In industrialized nations like the United States, France, and Germany, the can industry has been dominated by a relatively small number of firms. In the European market as a whole, metal can making is relatively concentrated and has traditionally been divided between large firms that manufacture standardized, mass-produced can products such as beverage and food cans and small- to medium-sized firms that specialize in customized cans with irregular shapes or unique label designs.

The price of materials is the controlling factor in the cost of can manufacture. Can makers negotiate supply contracts with metal producers like Alcoa Aluminum, which are heavily reliant on can industry purchases for their sales. To reduce transportation costs, can makers often locate their plants near or in their primary customer's plants. In the United States, the metal can industry has been characterized by periodic flurries of can plant openings and closings as industry firms respond to changing demographics or new conditions in the canned products industry while also attempting to dissuade canners from establishing facilities for the manufacture of their own cans. Historically, major can buyers have not purchased their cans from a single manufacturer but have instead signed contracts with one of the major can makers and divided remaining purchases among the smaller producers. Because canned product firms usually require that their can orders be filled according to uniform specifications, the large can makers have been forced to sell their can line technology to smaller competitors handling the remainder of the customer's order. In the U.S. packaging industry, the ratio of customers to suppliers was seven to one in the mid-1990s.

The expansion of can manufacturing internationally has been affected by the supply of raw materials such as finished metal plate. In less-developed nations can makers may be forced to absorb prohibitive duties and shipping costs to import needed materials and also may be aided by lack of water resources, which prevents packaging competitors in the bottling industry from maintaining essential bottle washing plants. Because shipping costs for metal cans are generally high, direct international trade in the metal can industry has been centered on business between contiguous markets such as the United States and Canada.

Acute price competition, overcapacity in the face of diminishing demand, loss of market share to new packaging methods, and the vagaries of consumer taste in packaged goods are among the perennial hurdles confronted by industry firms. To fortify themselves against such threats, can makers looked to overseas markets in developing countries and to diversification, through mergers and acquisitions or other means, into rival packaging markets or entirely new industries. However, for all the difficulties inherent in can manufacturing, the U.S. metal can industry—the world's largest—has outpaced U.S. manufacturing in general in new product and facilities investment, productivity, and wages.

The products of the larger metal container industry can be divided into two broad categories: metal cans and metal barrels, drums, and pails. The three major product groups are (1) aluminum cans, (2) steel cans and tinware products, and (3) steel shipping barrels and drums larger than 12 gallons. The remaining 5 percent of industry output is divided among miscellaneous metal cans, 1- to 12-gallon steel pails, and other metal barrel types.

BACKGROUND AND DEVELOPMENT

The invention of canning is usually credited to the Frenchman Nicolas Appert, who in 1795 began experimenting with food preservation techniques in response to a call by the French government for the development of a method for preserving food for transport over long distances. Appert discovered that by sealing food tightly in containers covered with wire and sealing wax and then boiling them to destroy contaminating organisms, a wide range of foods could be preserved for extended periods of time. Using the prize money awarded him by Napoleon Bonaparte, Appert established the world's first commercial cannery in Massy, France, in 1812.

Working from Appert's experiments the Englishman Peter Durand was awarded a patent for a cylindrical, tin-coated iron can capable of preserving foods without metal corrosion in 1810, and three years later two Englishmen founded a food processing plant for canned meats, vegetables, and soups for the British navy and army. The first U.S. cannery was established in 1820; and shortly before the U.S. Civil War, it was discovered that the can production process could be shortened by adding calcium chloride to the water in which cans were boiled. Annual production by the emerging U.S. can industry grew from 5 million cans before the Civil War to 30 million in the postwar years and higher still when in 1870 mechanization and factory methods of manufacture were adopted by the nation's can producers.

As scientific understanding of the principles of food preservation improved at the end of the nineteenth century, the quality of the food canned by industry firms greatly increased, just as mass production was transforming canned goods into a common household item. In 1900, so-called sanitary metal food can methods were invented, and can makers were able to market cans with folded airtight double seams, manufactured at greatly improved speeds. A year later, American Can was formed in the United States through the merger of 123 of the nation's 175 can manufacturers, creating a conglomerate that held 90 percent of the industry's market share.

In 1912, a forerunner of can-making giant Toyo Seikan Kaisha began operation in Japan with can line equipment purchased from American Can; and in 1919 the Netherlands' Royal Packaging Industries Van Leer began manufacturing steel drums. Two years later, Britain's metal can leader, Metal Box PLC, was formed through the merger of four British can makers, creating Allied Tin Box Makers Ltd. (renamed Metal Box and Printing Industries a year later). Metal Box's early market dominance was quickly threatened by the adoption by British firms of the U.S. roll form of can manufacture—in which the metal can blank is shaped into a cylindrical form by being fed against a deflecting plate—allowing Metal Box's competitors to turn out more than 200 cans a minute.

Intrigued by the British adoption of the new can making technologies, American Can attempted to acquire Metal Box and Printing Industries in the 1920s, forcing the latter to enter into an agreement with American's competitor, Continental Can (established in 1913), that gave Metal Box exclusive British rights to Continental's technology. Its market position solidified, Metal Box acquired American's British subsidiary British Can, began standardizing can production and business operations at all its plants, and formed subsidiaries and partnerships in France, the Netherlands, South Africa, India, and Belgium. After buying up failing British can makers during the Depression, Metal Box was manufacturing 335 million cans a year by 1937. After World War II, can making speeds catapulted to thousands of cans a minute, and a new aseptic method—in which high temperatures and rapid cooking times are used to separately sterilize the metal can and its contents—allowed products that do not retain their nutrients or flavor well under traditional canning methods to be packaged in metal cans. The enormous growth of the beverage can industry in the 1960s was made possible in part by emphasizing the advantages that cans offered over bottles: they were disposable, required no deposit, were easier to stack, chilled more quickly, did not break, and took up less space in the refrigerator. When the pull-off or "pop top" tab eliminated the need for beverage can openers in 1963, the metal beverage can began to eclipse the bottle as the favored beverage packaging medium.

Aluminum cans—initially introduced in the meat, fish, motor oil, and frozen fruit juice markets—began to make serious inroads into the steel-dominated beverage can market when Reynolds Aluminum developed a method for making aluminum cans that used two pieces rather than three: a top or lid, a single-piece body, and bottom manufactured from can sheet using the single blow of a draw press. It was a manufacturing innovation uniquely suited to the malleable properties of aluminum, and by the mid-1960s the standard 12-ounce aluminum beer and beverage can began to gain a foothold in the U.S. market. Thereafter, the three-piece steel beverage can began a gradual slide in market share, and sales of the two-piece aluminum can rose to 20 billion cans in the late 1970s, 40 billion in the early 1980s, and 100 billion by the late 1990s. Between 1977 and 1997 aluminum can production in North America quintupled.

The collapse of the Soviet Union in the early 1990s drew a number of international can makers to Eastern Europe despite the region's shortage of investment capital, absence of developed solid waste and recycling facilities, weak infrastructure, and severe capital shortages. In the mid-1990s, Continental Can Europe formed Continental Can Polska, and through its German subsidiary Schmalbach-Lubeca constructed a two-piece aluminum can plant for the Polish market. Through its French subsidiary Ferembal, it then acquired Obalex, the Czech Republic's second-largest food can manufacturer. In 1997 Continental Can Europe merged the food can making operations of German can maker Schmalbach-Lubeca and French can maker Pechiney to form Hexacan. The first beverage can plants began to sprout up in Russia in the late 1990s.

In 1996, it was estimated that the global can market would expand by 20 percent by 1999. While the European market grew by an average of 6 percent per year through the 1990s and in 2000, the United States made up the majority of the metal can market. In 2000, out of some 210 billion metal cans, 114 billion were used in North America, more than 100 billion in the United States alone. Asia used 40 billion, and Europe used more than 35 billion, while the South American market consumed 14 billion units and the African market used 7 billion.

In January 2002, the European market promised even further growth when Denmark ended its 20-year ban on the use of steel and aluminum drink cans. The Danish government lifted the ban in conjunction with the establishment of steep recycling rates. The lifting of the ban was expected to result in the consumption of an additional 300-400 million canned beverages annually, adding to the 35 billion units already consumed in the European market each year.

CURRENT CONDITIONS

The worldwide metal can industry became increasingly international in the 2000s. Although business arrangements between foreign can producers go back to at least the 1920s, the global can industry continued to be characterized by a growing trend toward joint ventures, partnerships, licensing agreements, and mergers and acquisitions.

The U.S. metal can industry employed 36,000 workers and generated US$13 billion in shipments in 2003. Slow growth continued in the early 2000s as energy costs associated with producing metal packaging skyrocketed. Price wars among U.S. metal container manufacturers, the ongoing battle between aluminum and steel for market share, new challenges from glass and plastic container products, and the effect of "sin" taxes on beer consumption were among the other factors affecting the health of the U.S. and global can industry. By the mid-2000s, with the enormous rate of change in the consumer packaging industry, metal can production was seeing an upswing.

In the mid-2000s, approximately 37 billion steel cans were manufactured by U.S. firms, and the vast majority of them were used for food canning (99 percent steel) and general packaging (99 percent steel). Steel continued to lose ground to aluminum in its traditional product categories, such as food canning, where aluminum's share of the total food can segment rose from 8 percent to 9 percent. At the same time, steel's roughly US$3 to US$4 per-thousand price advantage over aluminum and new production techniques that neutralize some of the inherent superiority of aluminum as a canning metal, enabled steel to reenter the beverage can market, increasing its share to 8 percent.

The recycling of metal cans continued to be a successful venture for the U.S. packaging industry. Born in the 1960s out of concern for the environment, can recycling evolved into critical factor in the U.S. metal can industry's production process. By using recycled aluminum rather than primary aluminum to make new cans, industry firms were able to save 95 percent on the energy costs of manufacturing cans from raw materials. By 1997, two-thirds of all U.S. beverage cans were recycled. In 2004, 51.3 percent of all U.S. aluminum cans, equaling about 1.51 billion pounds, were recycled.

RESEARCH AND TECHNOLOGY

One major aim of can industry research has been to reduce the amount of metal contained in each can, thus reducing the cost of metal purchases. Between 70 and 80 percent of the cost of a metal can resides in its material content, and a millimeter reduction in the thickness of can walls can result in enormous cumulative cost savings for can manufacturers. Therefore, since 1975 the amount of steel in steel cans has been reduced by about one-third, and by the mid-1990s the walls of steel drink cans had been made 33 percent thinner than aluminum can walls—with a 13 percent reduction in thickness accomplished since 1991 alone.

Industry firms have traditionally looked for material reductions by using thinner gauge feedstock and by reducing the amount of metal wasted in the seams that join the can's parts together. The amount of metal used in the aluminum can end alone, for example, can account for as much as one-third of the can's total weight, and the continued adoption of the so-called 202-type can end in the mid-1990s resulted from the development of "spin flow" machinery capable of making can ends thinner and smaller without any commensurate loss in can stiffness. The development of new methods for can "necking" methods, whereby the upper end of the can is compressed or stretched to fit a smaller can top, enabled industry firms to reduce materials costs and eliminate stages in the can manufacturing process while offering a more "stackable" can.

New can designs in the 1990s included the "composite can," which consisted of a mix of metal and paper and offered a 30 percent reduction in weight with a 10 percent reduction in materials cost over metal cans, as well as greater savings in shipping and handling. Used in Europe primarily for dry foods, the composite can began to be adopted by U.S. can makers for such products as fruit juice, refrigerated dough, and instant coffee. In the mid-1990s, the British steel can industry also began marketing an "ultimate can," which offered 30 percent weight reductions over traditional metal cans and the additional benefit of not requiring new can line equipment during manufacture. Finally, "Ferrolite," a polymer-coated steel-based material developed by CarnaudMetalbox in the 1990s, offered improved corrosion resistance and a novel appearance and texture. In 1993, British Steel Tinplate began marketing baby food containers made from Ferrolite, and in 1995 CarnaudMetalbox began producing Ferrolite-based ends for aerosol cans.

Increasing can thinness went hand in hand with manufacturing processes that strengthened the stiffness of the can metal. These techniques included metallurgical alloying, new hardening processes, physical deformation methods such as fluting, and improved techniques for joining the can's parts. In some processed food cans, for example, a new method of folding the can's base seam underneath, rather than up, the side of the can, offered improved performance. One result of industry research was that the traditional advantages of aluminum over steel in can manufacture began to disappear and lighter, more flexible steel cans were developed that were virtually indistinguishable from aluminum cans while offering steel's strength and impact resistance.

Improved convenience and appearance were other major goals of industry research. Innovations in can "closure" features reflected the industry's attempt to solidify market share by making cans and metal containers less difficult to open and providing greater product differentiation. Such "easy-opening" ends were traditionally centered on aluminum beverage cans, but in the 1990s steel food containers also began to appear with such enhancements, including the ring-pull feature. In the mid-1990s, CarnaudMetalbox began marketing its Quantum can, an easy-opening end for premium food products such as pasta sauce. In the United States, Ball Corporation introduced a large-aperture Touch Top can feature that did away with the traditional "stay-on" tab opener altogether by offering an integrated opening and pouring design. A nondetachable push-button can end known as Ecotop was also marketed in Europe in the 1990s; it required a third less energy to manufacture than traditional "stay-on" tabs, left no sharp edges, and provided a feature that allowed consumers to know when a can had been tampered with. In 1998, Reynolds Metals received a patent for its own Large Opening End, a pouring aperture 37 percent larger that traditional cans that enabled consumers to quaff beverages in greater volume without jeopardizing the structural strength of the can's seal.

The adoption of improved coatings for the interior and exterior of the can also enabled industry firms to, respectively, reduce the reaction of the metal to the can's contents and provide more options for the can's aesthetic appearance. The burnished, highly reflective surface of cans developed in the 1990s allowed canned product manufacturers to create boldly innovative designs rivaling those previously possible only with paper-based labels. By the mid-1990s the amount of coating used in the manufacture of metal cans had been reduced by 25 percent since 1975. These innovations were more than mere window-dressing. Because glass and plastic bottle makers were offering beverage producers greater opportunities to differentiate their products on store shelves, the uniform metal can was hard-pressed to challenge the unique brand identities such alternative packaging afforded. Despite the added cost to consumers to purchase premium beverage packaging products, their sales ate away at metal cans' market share throughout the late 1990s, and Coke's durable plastic contour bottle for Classic Coke was even finding its way into vending machines—once thought the indisputable province of the metal can.

By the late 1990s the U.S. soft drink industry was consuming almost 5 billion 20-ounce plastic bottles a year, and some industry experts were proclaiming the demise of beverage cans in North America. In response, CC&S created a metal can for Heineken beer that was shaped and tinted like a brimming beer glass, and Budweiser worked on an embossed metal can with a "silky" feel to snare choosy, image-conscious beverage drinkers. While contour metal cans required expensive retooling on the assembly line, the embossing process involved much less capital expenditure and seemed to offer can makers a way to way to ward off plastic and glass for the lucrative beverage packaging dollar.

Other innovations under development included new can shapes and sizes, reclosable lids, and flashier graphics. The adoption of continuous casting techniques and computerized manufacturing and quality control methods also greatly improved the productivity of the can making process by reducing scrap and improving the ratio of rejected to acceptable cans. By using 70 different statistical quality control techniques, for example, Reynolds Metals of the United States reduced the number of unacceptable cans sent to customers by 42 percent in 1984 alone. Other industry technology trends included line machines with even faster can-per-minute production rates and the development of can materials that pose less of a threat to the environment. As another example, Japan's Toyo Lightweight Ultimate Can reduced much of the waste associated with metal can manufacture.

WORKFORCE

In the industry's early years, can making was performed by solitary craftsmen who formed each can individually by bending the body piece around a cylindrical mold and soldering the seams and end piece. After food was forced through the open end, the can maker soldered the top end to the can and began the process anew, at an average pace of only 10 finished cans a day. As automation made production rates of 200 cans per minute possible, the artisan was replaced by can line operators responsible for overseeing the production process and maintaining the machinery on the line itself.

In the early twentieth century, wages and labor conditions in the first truly mass production can plants were poor, and in the United Kingdom, for example, the Trade Boards Act forced tin can manufacturers to improve industry pay scales and factory conditions. While automation drastically reduced the number of workers needed to make a can, industry expansion led to higher employment: for example, the largest U.S. producer, American Can, employed 22,000 workers in 1939 (when Fortune magazine observed that "it is almost impossible to be fired from American Can") but more than twice that by the early 1960s.

Employment in the international metal can industry began to decline as a result of increasing international competition, further improvements in can line automation, and loss of market share to other packaging types. Between 1982 and 1990, for example, U.S. employment declined from 50,000 to 35,000, while employment in the United Kingdom was halved from 24,377 in 1981 to 12,384 in 1990. Declines in many of the major U.S. can industry employment categories—from machine forming operators and tenders to executives and managers—were expected to range between 33 and 40 percent between the mid-1990s and 2005.

INDUSTRY LEADERS

Pechiney. Pechiney originated as a chemical and aluminum producer in the nineteenth century, and before its acquisition of American National Can (ANC) in the late 1980s, had no involvement in the packaging industry. Following its nationalization in 1982 (the French government is its majority shareholder), its North American operations were restructured under the name Pechiney Corporation, and the company embarked on a string of mergers and acquisitions that culminated in 1988 with the purchase of ANC, the largest soft drink and beer can maker in the world. The acquisition doubled Pechiney's assets virtually overnight and allowed the company to strike a balance between its consumer-based and raw materials-based interests. By the mid-1990s, Pechiney had become the world's largest packaging company with operations in over 20 countries and diversified interests in aluminum, turbines, international trade, and nuclear fuel and heavy carbon manufacturing. In 2001 earnings fell 26 percent; however, the firm's packaging operations recorded a sharp increase (36 percent) during the same year. By 2002, the company reported revenues of US$12.5 billion.

Packaging accounted for 33 percent of Pechiney's total sales in the early 2000s. Although centered on American National Can with some 35 plants in 10 countries, Pechiney's other can making operations included a European metal food can division (manufacturing lids and cans from aluminum and tinplate among other products) and a North American food plastic division (producing flexible packaging for food, health care, and industrial markets). The European market accounted for 59 percent of Pechiney's packaging sales, while North America made up 33 percent. By relying on the development of new can designs, sale of uncompetitive facilities, strategic partnerships with its international clients, and judicious exploitation of potential markets in developing economies, Pechiney increased its share of the global beverage can market. Its Beverage Cans Americas division was the leading North American manufacturer of aluminum beverage cans and ends in 1995, and Beverage Cans Europe was the leading European manufacturer of aluminum and steel beverage cans and ends. These two beverage divisions alone accounted for 56 percent of Pechiney's packaging sector sales. Earnings in 2001 fell 26 percent; however, the packaging sector recorded a sharp increase (36 percent) during the same year.

Among Pechiney's major can market activities in the 1990s were the formation of a joint venture with a Chinese firm for the operation of an aluminum beer and soft drink can plant in Zhaiqing City, China; a joint venture with a Japanese firm to enter the Asian food can market; and the purchase of a majority stake in Czech company Strojobal, a manufacturer of metal cans and plastic and aluminum products. In 1997 Pechiney's "Food Europe" food can operations were merged with the food can operations of German powerhouse Schmalbach-Lubeca to form a new European food can giant, Hexacan, big enough to challenge Crown/CarnaudMetalbox for leadership of Europe's food can industry. In 1997 Pechiney maintained 300 industrial and sales facilities in 60 countries, with almost two-thirds of its can production occurring outside France.

Pechiney, which also operates aluminum smelting plants, attempted a three-way merger with Alcan and Algroup in 2000. However, the merger was blocked by competition regulators, so the companies subsequently merged more slowly. Alcan acquired Algroup alone that year, and in 2004 Alcan was able to acquire Pechiney for US$4.7 billion.

In 2002, the company announced it would consolidate its shareholdings in smelters in order to boost its position in the fragmented specialist packaging sector, where opportunities were on the rise. Early in 2002, Pechiney was considering the purchase of German metals group VAW, and expanding even further its food packaging sector by strengthening relationships with customers such as Kraft Foods, Nestle, and L'Oreal. The firm also was examining the construction of a large smelter in Australia or South Africa, which would be operational by 2005.

Crown Holdings Inc. Incorporated in 1927, Crown Cork and Seal (CC&S) was one of the first U.S. can makers to explore the international packaging market, forming the Crown Cork International Corporation in 1928 as a holding company for its container and closure subsidiaries in foreign markets. In 1936 it entered the can making business by acquisition, but after suffering financial losses in its domestic operations in the late 1950s, the firm refocused on international markets through overseas container and aerosol can operations. By winning "pioneer rights" from foreign governments seeking to develop their manufacturing sectors, CC&S was granted first crack at new can and closure operations developed in those countries, allowing it to operate profitable can plants with aging machinery that would have rendered it uncompetitive in the free market. Through its policy of establishing its overseas operations only with foreign nationals—and then equipping them with outdated can machinery—CC&S was able to cut startup costs at the same time that it was developing a network of quasi-independent subsidiaries around the world.

In the 1970s and 1980s, its international activities included acquisitions of a British container closure plant, a German aluminum closures facility, and a Swiss packager and new or expanded plants in Canada, Ireland, Scotland, and Brazil. In the 1990s, CC&S teamed up with the Saudi Arabian can firm Ahmad Hamad Algosaibi and Brothers to build beverage can plants in Jordan, Saudi Arabia, and the United Arab Emirates and with a multiparty Asian group to construct a can plant in Vietnam. By the mid-1990s, CC&S's 20-year growth rate exceeded that of all other U.S. can manufacturers.

In 1996 CC&S bought French can making giant CarnaudMetalbox (CMB), making CC&S the world's largest producer of packaging containers. Along with Pechiney, CMB had dominated the European can market, and in addition to its extensive European operations—55 percent of its total sales—CMB had also maintained a strong presence in Asia. In the 1990s, CMB was a prime player in the European can industry's attempts to develop more environmentally friendly manufacturing methods, reducing, for example, the effluent its can plants released during production. In 1991 CMB had established an aerosol can plant on the German-Polish border and purchased Hungary's leading food can and closure producer in 1992. A year later CMB acquired a majority share of GWS Metallipakkus to assume the assets of Finland's GW Sohlberg, positioning it to develop export markets in Eastern Europe, the Baltic States, and Russia. And in 1995 CMB moved into the Chinese market by opening a can making plant in Guangzhou.

In 1996 can production at the newly enlarged CC&S was halted at eight plants by strikes over union contracts. The same year, with its sales topping US$8.3 billion, CC&S sold its paint and oblong can business to B-WAY Corporation and also acquired the Polish packaging firm Fabryka Opakowan Blaszanyck. In 1996 CC&S opened its fourth plant in mainland China, and in 1997 it bought a 96 percent share of Golden Aluminum, the one-time can making operation of Coors Brewery. In 1997 CC&S operated 247 plants in 49 countries. By 2000 CC&S had garnered 20 percent of the world's beverage can market; the firm also produced one-third of the food cans sold in North America and Europe. The company reported revenues of nearly US$7.2 billion in 2004.

Toyo Seikan Kaisha. Founded in 1933 as the successor of a Japanese can company whose canning technology had been acquired from both American Can and Continental Can, Toyo Seikan Kaisha (TSK) survived World War II to become the dominant can manufacturer in Japan during the country's postwar economic renaissance. Restructured, like many Japanese corporations, after World War II, TSK joined an affiliation of other Japanese can makers, known as the Toyo Seikan Group in the 1950s. The group began exploring the international can market, initially through export sales and then through product licensing and joint ventures in Indonesia, South Korea, Singapore, Thailand, and Nigeria.

By the 1990s, the Toyo Seikan Group consisted of 25 subsidiaries and affiliates; maintained technical agreements with such Western firms as Metal Closures, Continental Group, and Owens-Illinois; and had licensing arrangements with 25 companies in 13 countries. Almost three-quarters of the containers it manufactures are sold directly to the Japanese beverage industry, with the remaining container sales devoted to food, household, and general container products.

TSK introduced the Toyo Ultimate Lightweight Can (TULC), an attempt to slow Japan's conversion to aluminum cans by offering a lightweight, nonrusting, two-piece steel can for the beverage market. By 1996 the new TULC already controlled 7 percent of the Japanese market, fueled by Coca-Cola and Lipton's adoption of the can in the Japanese market. Between 1996 and 1997 alone, production of TSK's environmentally friendly TULC can grew 80 percent. With

TULC's domestic success assured, in the late 1990s TSK targeted overseas can markets, primarily the food products sector, but eventually the beer and soft drink markets as well. The company reported 2004 revenues of US$6.3 billion.

Ball Corporation. Until the mid-1940s, the Ball Corporation of Indiana was essentially a manufacturer of bottles and jars, the products it had marketed since its inception in 1880. Forced into diversification by the prohibitive costs of modernizing its glass plants, Ball branched out into the unlikely field of aerospace and electronic components while capitalizing on the enormous changes in the packaging business of the 1960s by perceptively switching to two-piece can manufacture in 1968 (when the three-piece beverage can was still in its heyday). Through can production contracts with such major beverage firms as Anheuser-Busch, Pepsi, and Coca-Cola, Ball carved out a small but profitable niche in the two-piece can market—which it had developed into a solid 11 percent share of the U.S. beverage can market by 1990. In the 1980s and 1990s, Ball turned to the growing overseas can market, and claimed a major piece of the world beverage can market when it acquired Continental Can's European packaging business in 1990. In the 1990s, Ball also expanded operations in Asia, introduced new can designs, and ceased production of the tin-and-aluminum bimetal can.

In 1995 Ball entered the exploding PET/plastic container business and enfolded its glass container business into a newly formed company, Ball-Foster Glass Container. In 1996 it sold 42 percent of the company to its partner, the French materials megacompany Saint-Gobain Group. In 1996 Ball announced plans to build a PET plant in Iowa and a joint venture aluminum plant in Thailand. The same year it sold its aerosol can making business, and in 1997 join the global can industry's march into the newly liberalized Chinese market by acquiring M.C. Packaging of Hong Kong, making it the leading supplier of beverage cans to China. In 2000 the company realized US$3.7 billion in sales, as it did the previous year. Losses totaled US$101.2 million, in the wake of uncertainty in the U.S. stock market and increasing energy costs, affecting production. By 2004, the company reported an increase in revenues, with US$5.44 billion, up 9.3 percent from the previous year.

U.S. Can. With US$844.8 million in 2004 revenues and 2,200 employees, U.S. Can was the top aerosol can manufacturer in the United States and second in Europe. Industrial, automotive, and household products go in its aerosol containers. The company also manufactures general line and paint cans; about 50 percent of one gallon paint cans in the United States were made by U.S. Can in the mid-2000s.

MAJOR COUNTRIES IN THE INDUSTRY

ASIA

The industrializing nations of Asia offered new markets to internationally minded can producers. In 1994, Crown Cork and Seal (CC&S) announced a joint venture to erect an aluminum can plant near Hanoi, Vietnam, with an annual capacity of 400 million cans. France's CarnaudMetalbox began building a similar plant near Saigon, as well as a new plant in Guangzhou, China. China's soft drink consumption reached more than 7 billion liters annually by the year 2000. China's first beverage can plant had opened in 1996, the same year that CC&S had opened its fourth Chinese plant and Ball Corporation had opened a new plant in Thailand. Although Asia's growth potential was promising through the mid-1990s, the continent suffered a financial crisis in 1998, and some beverage manufacturers had to close factories. Can manufacturers were adversely affected by the closures, but Shanghai United Can Manufacturing Co. predicted the market would regain momentum in the early 2000s, due to rapid growth of the Chinese beverage market. In 2000, Japan's largest food and beverage packaging company, Toyo Seikan, reported that it had stabilized and increased its workforce following the financial crisis; profits of just over US$43 million in 1999 increased to more than US$240 million the following year, as the Japanese yen stabilized. In contrast, despite its vast population and the exploratory moves of some world can makers, India continued to remain a largely undeveloped market in the mid-2000s. By 2003, Asia's containers and packaging market reached US$91.69 billion, of which metal accounted for more than 10 percent.

Japan. Japanese can makers have historically relied on the U.S. can industry for industry production trends and technologies. Because of the unique characteristics of the Japanese beverage and food market, however, Japanese can makers have had to adapt Western ideas and equipment to meet the hugely diverse and specialized niches of Japan's food and beverage economy. More than 93 percent of the metal cans produced by the Japanese can industry in the mid-1990s were used for beverages, with 7 percent devoted to food products.

While the Japanese market for beverage and food cans dropped dramatically in the late 1990s, hitting a 20-year low in 1999, it began to grow again by 2000. The Japanese began importing fewer cans in the 1990s, and in 2001 imported only 300 million empty cans, down 25 percent from 2000. The country did, however, import canned foods and beverage, amounting to 390 million units in 2000 and 2001. The food and beverage export business remained stable but flat during the same period, and Japan exported 300 million full cans in 2000 and 2001. By 2003, the mature containers and packaging market in the country reached US$48.58 billion, reflecting a .2 percent compound annual growth rate in the five year period preceding it. Metal packaging represented about 10 percent of that market.

Just as the United States introduced its can technology into the postwar Japanese economy of the 1940s and 1950s, Japan began selling its adaptations and improvements on U.S. can making equipment to Western customers in the 1970s and 1980s. Three of the firms that had most benefited from the postwar transfer of U.S. technology—Toyo Seikan Kaisha, Daiwa Can, and Hokkai Can—emerged as the leaders of the Japanese can industry. By the mid-1980s, Toyo Seikan commanded 55 percent of the domestic can market, Daiwa held 28 percent, and Hokkai claimed 11 percent.

In 1971 the first impact-extruding, two-piece aluminum can lines were introduced in Japan. Later, Daiwa, Japan's leading welded tin plate can maker, began producing the first drawn, wall-ironed steel and aluminum cans. By the mid-1980s, the number of drawing/wall ironing can lines in

Japan had grown to 40 with a total (though underutilized) capacity of 9.5 billion cans per year. By 1973, the three-piece steel can had been introduced for beer but became the standard in the soda vending machine market—where 60 percent of all Japan's beverage can sales occur. As in the United States, however, the two-piece can eventually replaced the three-piece can in Japan's beer and soda markets, reaching 5 billion cans per year in 1983. Aluminum cans began to replace steel cans in the 1970s when Japan's aluminum companies began sponsoring their own aluminum can making plants in order to shift the industry away from steel. The two metals battled for market share until the early 1980s when Japanese demand for canned beverages began to level off.

Japan's depressed economy in the 1990s and early 2000s affected the sales of firms in the larger Japanese packaging industry, and the biggest Japanese packaging firms were hard pressed to grow sales 5 percent a year in the mid-1990s. Roughly 40 billion metal cans were consumed in Japan in 1996. The majority (54%) of steel cans were used for noncarbonated drinks, such as canned coffee and oolong tea. The Japanese can industry produced 34 billion cans in 1993, and in the largest single segment—food and beverage cans—noncarbonated beverage cans (7.8 billion) accounted for 52 percent of the market, carbonated beverage cans (2.9 billion) claimed 18 percent of the market, and food cans (2.7 billion) held 18 percent of the market, with beer cans (1.6 billion) comprising the remaining 11 percent. The market for food cans was declining in the 1990s, with the greatest declines in the marine products segment, such as tuna and sardine cans. Cans for some food products, such as spaghetti meat sauce and soup, were the lone growth sectors.

The Japanese can industry remained one of the world's most innovative, high-quality, and diversified, reflecting the readiness with which Japan's comparatively affluent consumers embrace new product packages and (often expensive) designs. In the beer segment alone, there were more than 147 different formats, ranging from 135 centiliters to 3 liters in size. In keeping with its tradition of looking to the United States for metal can trends, Japanese can manufacturers were importing more aluminum cans from the United States in 1995 than they were producing for themselves.

About 16 billion aluminum cans, one-third of which were produced by Mitsubishi Materials, were consumed in Japan in 1997. Because Japan's metal can industry had the best reputation for quality in the world, metal cans were priced highly, and, accordingly, cheaper imported cans rose to claim 10 percent of total can consumption in 1995. However, their inferior quality led to a consumer backlash against imported cans in the late 1990s.

At the beginning of 1997, Japan's beverage can making industry consisted of 49 aluminum beverage can lines (or plants) and 28 steel can lines. Japanese can industry firms were at the forefront of international can producers capitalizing on mainland China's relaxed trade policies in the late 1990s. In 1997 other representative Japanese can makers included Showa Aluminum Can Corporation and Takeuchi Press Industries Co. Ltd.

EUROPE

Sales growth in the larger European packaging industry (which included nonmetal flexible packaging) recovered from a slump in the early 1990s to run at a brisk 20 percent pace in 1994 and 1995. Total sales for the average European packaging company (including metal cans) were US$9.5 billion in 1995—35 percent higher than 1991. In the late 1980s, the five largest European can makers dominated the production of beverage cans in Europe, and in the 1990s the trend was toward even greater concentration as cooperation agreements, mergers and acquisitions, and joint ventures became common practice in the largest segment of the European metal can market. Conditions in Europe's smaller can making segment (made up of firms with 20 to 200 employees) were more chaotic in the 1990s, however. For these firms, profitability depended on the ability to maintain manufacturing flexibility in order to meet the unique design requirements of their generally low-volume customer.

In the early 1990s, the 3,000 establishments of France's packaging industry—including metal can manufacturers—generated revenues of FFr107 billion (about US$20 billion) and employed 120,000 workers. The recession of the early 1990s led to declines in some metal can segments such as cooked food cans, which declined 6 percent in 1992 and another 5 percent in 1993; but improved conditions in France's food manufacturing sector, which accounted for 78 percent of all metal packaging, resulted in increases in food can production during the mid-1990s. Beverage cans continued to do well, but threats from rival packaging materials and battles to defend market share were expected to result in ongoing overcapacity in the French metal can and overall packaging industries. The lingering effects of the recession were expected to lead to least-cost decision making by industry leaders and consumers too were expected to lean toward low-price canned products.

By the early 2000s, U.S. firms such as U.S. Can; Crown, Cork & Seal (CC&S); and Continental Can were playing a much more aggressive role in Europe's metal can market. In 1996, for example, CC&S bought up CarnaudMetalBox, U.S. Can took over CC&S's aerosol can operations, and Continental Can Europe began eyeing the potentially profitable Russian beverage can market. In 1997, however, Sweden's PLM—the fourth-largest beverage packager in Europe—beat everyone to the punch by undertaking the first beverage can plant in Russia.

In 2002, however, CC&S scaled back on its European and African interests and closed three European plants (one in Belgium, one in Denmark, and a PET bottle plant in Hungary), as well as four U.S. plants, in an effort to streamline its operations. At the same time, the company implemented a salaried workforce reduction in its remaining plants, which cut approximately 100 jobs. CC&S sold its 15 percent shareholding in South Africa's Crown Nampak to Nampak Ltd. for US$275 million early in 2002.

By the mid-2000s, Europe was steadily consuming less non-paper packaging materials and in 2003, the segment accounted for a mere 23.3 percent of the market value share. Can shipments in Europe declined from 40 billion in 2002 to 38 billion in 2003.

United Kingdom. In 1992 the United Kingdom consumed a full 63 percent (7.2 billion tons) of all Europe's beverage can aluminum, with Italy (15 percent) and Sweden (8 percent) distant competitors. Between 1981 and 1990, the number of firms in the United Kingdom canning industry had declined from 52 to 30, reflecting the effects of increased competition, which tended to favor more efficient firms and a greater rationalization of resources industry-wide. By 1997, Britain's total packaging industry (including cans) had sales of more than £10 billion, led by industry leaders like Linpac UK and Specialty Packaging (UK) Plc. In 2003, sales of empty cans increased 2 percent over the previous year to reach 7.7 billion cans.

The emergence of less expensive plastic packaging represented an increased threat to British metal can makers, with the greatest growth occurring in the use of plastics such as PET in beverage, household, and automotive goods. As a result of an ongoing emphasis on recycling and environmental programs such as "Save-a-Can," more than 1 billion cans were recycled annually in the United Kingdom in the mid-1990s, and roughly 70 percent of all metal cans produced by U.K. can makers were eventually recycled.

Germany. Dominated by century-old packaging producer Schmalbach-Lubeca, Germany's metal can industry lost market share to PET bottles throughout the 1990s, with cans' share of cola packaging alone expected to drop from 25 to 15 percent between 1995 and 2006. German conglomerate VIAG, however, enjoyed substantial sales growth, and in 1996 it increased it ownership stake in Schmalbach-Lubeca, the second-largest beverage can producer in Europe, to 61.4 percent. In 1997 Schmalbach-Lubeca and France's Pechiney merged their food can operations to meet the new competition presented by the Crown/CarnaudMetalbox merger. New legislation on non-returnable packs had an extremely negative effect on can volumes in the mid-2000s. This affected the total number of cans shipped in Europe overall in 2003, 38 billion, compared to 40 billion in 2002.

France. France's metal can industry, like much of Europe's, is concentrated among a handful of large firms, the largest of which are Pechiney, CarnaudMetalbox, and Saint-Gobain. European packaging firms as a whole tend to enjoy higher sales and greater international sales than non-European packaging companies. Because France's largest can makers are major international producers, the French market itself represents a comparatively small slice of their total revenues—25 percent of total sales for Saint-Gobain and CarnaudMetalbox, for example, and 10 percent for Pechiney. At the same time, the central role of France's food manufacturing sector in the country's economy has meant that the major French can makers faced little real competition from foreign manufacturers for the food canning market. In the mid-1990s, representative firms in the French can making industry included Application des Gaz, Safet Embamet, and Ferembal, and foreign can makers active in the French market included the Netherlands' Van Leer and the United States' CC&S, and Continental Can. In 1996 U.S. market giant CC&S and France's perennial packaging leader CarnaudMetalbox joined forces to become the world's largest maker of packaging products for consumer goods.

The French packaging industry felt the effects of a national push for environmental waste regulation throughout the 1990s. Legislation enacted in the mid-1990s required that within 10 years 75 percent of all household packaging used in France be recycled. Although the regulations placed the obligation to recycle on firms selling packaged goods, rather than on packaging and canning firms, the latter were expected to emphasize packaging methods that conformed to the new spirit of environmental friendliness.

THE AMERICAS

Latin America. In the late 1990s and into the 2000s, Latin America emerged as a promising new market for world can makers. The region is attractive because of rising consumer incomes and an already high rate of soft drink consumption. In 2000, South Americans consumed some 14 billion canned beverages. Chile's first beverage can plant opened in 1995, and in 1997 CC&S and American National Can announced similar plans for Colombia and Brazil. One industry expert reported that Brazil's aluminum can market in 1997 was growing more rapidly than that of any other nation. In 1996, Grupo FEMSA, the largest producer of two-piece aluminum cans in Mexico, opened a world-class can making "megaplant" in Toluca, Mexico, with an annual capacity of 1.8 billion units.

United States. The top 33 firms in the U.S. metal can industry generated total sales of US$36.1 billion and employed some 80,000 workers in the mid-2000s. The leading 35 firms in the smaller U.S. metal barrel and drum segment of the industry produced roughly US$1 billion in total sales and employed 6,800 workers. A typical U.S. metal can manufacturer in 1994 employed 86 production workers (more than twice the U.S. manufacturing average) and 15 nonproduction employees and generated shipments with an average value of US$38 million (almost four times the U.S. average). Over half of the raw materials traditionally used by industry firms for can manufacture came from blast furnaces, steel mills, and aluminum rolling or drawing plants, and the sectors of the U.S. economy purchasing the highest proportion of cans in the 1980s were malt beverage producers (24 percent), canned soft drink producers (21 percent), canned fruit and vegetable producers (12 percent), and other metal can makers (7 percent). The remaining one-third of the U.S. metal can industry's production was divided among producers of paint, coffee, pet food, frozen fruit juices, drugs, and a variety of other goods.

The largest U.S. producers of metal cans in the mid-2000s were Crown Cork and Seal, American National Can Co. (a subsidiary of Pechiney Packaging of France), Ball Corporation, Reynolds Metals Co. Can Division, and U.S. Can Corporation. The leading U.S. metal barrel and drum producers in 2004 were Imacc Corporation, Hoover Group, and Myers Container Corporation.

Because of its flexibility, light weight, and corrosion-resistant properties, aluminum remained the chosen metal for the majority of the cans produced by U.S. industry firms in the mid-2000s, and aluminum cans thoroughly dominated the beer and carbonated beverage segments (99 percent and 96 percent, respectively). Steel cans, which accounted for 62 percent of the European and U.S. food and beverage packaging market in 1987, made up 45 percent in 2000. Although shipments of aluminum beverage cans were projected to have grown by more than 5 percent between 1993 and 1994, reaching 100 billion cans, they remained at that same level through 1997. Between 1994 and 2000, the European and U.S. can market (including food and beverage, and non-food products such as paint cans) grew by 6 percent annually, but the total food and beverage packaging industry grew by only about 1 percent per year in the same time period. In 2000, the containers and packaging industry used more than 20 percent of the 22 billion pounds of aluminum produced worldwide, ranking only second to the transportation industry. The periodic discounting of soft drink products to boost sales, slower growth in plant capacity as a result of the expense of converting from steel can manufacture to aluminum, and uncertainty over metal prices and the strength of future soft drink demand somewhat dampened the industry's outlook in the mid-2000s.

Aluminum's low distribution costs, high profit-per-packaged-ounce ratio, and adaptability to high-speed can filling lines still made the metal an extremely attractive material for packaging industry firms. By 1997, it was estimated that even the traditionally steel-dominated food can segment was outpaced by aluminum by three to one. However, spurred by the growing popularity of microbrewery beers, glass beer containers began to make a comeback in the mid-1990s in the form of "premium look" bottles, and between 1985 and 1996 glass increased its share of the beer packaging segment from 31 to 37 percent, while aluminum shrank from 56 to 51 percent. In the United States, aluminum beverage cans accounted for almost three-quarters of all package beverage sales in 1996 (64.5 billion soft drink cans alone), with plastic or polyethylene terephthalate (PET) bottles claiming 20 percent. But by June 1997 cans' control of the soft drink packaging segment had slipped to 51 percent, where it remained through 2000. While sales of metal cans were still driven by multipack sales, plastic and glass were beating metal cans in the "single-serve" market.

FURTHER READING

The Aluminum Association Inc. "Aluminum Beverage Can Recycling Rate Rising.' 20 May 2005. Available from http://www.aluminum.org.

"Aluminum 'Bottle Can' Caters to Active Beer Drinkers." *Brand Packaging,* January 2004.

"Asia-Pacific-Containers & Packaging.' *Datamonitor Industry Market Research,* 1 November 2004.

Cancentral.com. Washington: Can Manufacturers Institute, 2005. Available from http://www.cancentral.com.

The Canmaker. West Sussex: Sayers Publishing, 2005. Available from http://www.canmaker.com.

"Can Makers UK Market Report 2004." 2005. Available from http://www.canmakers.co.uk.

"China-Containers & Packaging.' *Datamonitor Industry Market Research,* 1 November 2004.

"Company Profile." *U.S. Can Web Site,* 2005. Available from http://www.uscanco.com.

"Container Demand Spans All Categories." *Beverage Industry,* April 2005.

Furukawa, Tsukasa. "Aluminum Can Demand Expected to Climb Slightly in Japan in 2001." *Industry,* 28 February 2001.

"Global-Containers & Packaging.' *Datamonitor Industry Market Research,* 1 November 2004.

"Global-Metal & Glass Containers.' *Datamonitor Industry Market Research,* 1 November 2004.

"Hoover's Company Capsules." 2005. Available from http://www.hoovers.com.

"International Trade Statistics." 2005. Available from http://www.wto.org.

"Japan-Containers & Packaging.' *Datamonitor Industry Market Research,* 1 November 2004.

Kaplan, Andrew. "Can Happen." *Beverage World,* 15 February 2004.

Makely, William. "It's No Longer Your Mom's Food Can." *Brand Packaging,* February-March 2004.

"Metal Can, Box and Other Metal Container (Light Gauge) Manufacturing." *Valuation Resources,* 2004. Available from http://www.ibisworld.com.

"US Can Recycling Figures Released." *Aluminum International Today,* May-June 2003.

SIC 3441

NAICS 332312

METAL, FABRICATED STRUCTURAL

The structural metal industry manufactures iron and steel structures off-site, for use in buildings, bridges, transmission towers, and ships, among other applications. Although some industry firms are diversified, the bulk of the industry's output is produced from purchased metals.

INDUSTRY SNAPSHOT

For statistical purposes, fabricated structural metal products are divided into four major categories: structural metal for buildings, structural metal for bridges, other fabricated structural metal, and unspecified fabricated structural metal. Accounting for 55-65 percent of industry shipments, fabricated structural metal for buildings is by far the most important product, and the one most susceptible to downturns in the construction industry.

Fabricated structural metal faces increasing competition from other primary construction materials, such as concrete and composites. Moreover, because the industry does little research and development of its own, it is dependent on R&D in other industries for technological advances. Unfortunately, many related technological advances had an adverse effect on the industry, further decreasing the need for fabricated structural metal. Facing similar problems, the steel industry embarked on a number of ambitious research projects aimed at developing higher-quality steels that could compete more effectively. It was expected that successful development and marketing of these products would benefit the fabricated structural metal industry.

Some of the industry's products are carports, bridge sections, greenhouses, silos, utility buildings, and radio towers. In 2003, the U.S. segment of the industry as a whole, including a small segment devoted to metal plate work, generated in excess of US$29.85 billion in revenue and employed nearly 162,000 people. According to *Valuation Resources,* less than five percent of the industry is due to exports or imports. Analysts predict volume growth of about 2 percent per year through 2010, with annual price increases of 2-3 percent.

ORGANIZATION AND STRUCTURE

At first glance, the fabricated structural metal industry in the 1990s resembled an offshoot of the steel industry. And in some cases, it was. Many integrated and nonintegrated steel companies, such as fast-growing Nucor Corporation of Charleston, North Carolina, had sizable fabricated structural metal operations. Construction companies, bridge manufacturers, and heavy industry companies, were also sometimes shareholders or owners of metal fabricating companies. Nevertheless, fabricated structural metal was a distinct industry. Fabricated structural metal companies did not manufacture metal; they constructed structural metal forms from a diverse array of finished metal products such as sheets, bars, and tubes. These products included barge sections, boat sections, expansion joints, floor jacks, floor posts, dam gates, highway bridge sections, radio and television tower sections, and fabricated structural steel. In turn, fabricated structural metal products were assembled to form building frameworks, ships, bridges, transmission towers, and oilrigs.

Like the steel industry, the fabricated structural metal industry represented one of the cornerstones of the industrial era. Massive pieces of iron and steel were hammered, welded, and cut into structural shapes for use in the construction of buildings, bridges, and ships. Workers, clad in safety gear and helmets, forced the metal into the desired forms amid a shower of sparks and metal particles. Huge cranes and forklifts loaded the finished products onto trucks and railcars for delivery. Accidents were frequent and employee turnover was high. Largely bypassed by the technological revolution of the past few decades, the fabricated structural metal industry, like many other traditional industries, was eclipsed by the newer, cleaner, technology-intensive industries of the late twentieth century. Most major steel makers also own some fabricated product facilities, while smaller manufacturers in this section buy from the producer and transform the product through a discrete operation.

The fabricated structural metal industry depends heavily on the construction industry. Commercial and industrial buildings absorbed up to 65 percent of shipments, making the industry highly susceptible to recessions and accompanying declines in new construction. Other important construction markets for fabricated structural metals were public buildings, churches, hospitals, oil drilling rigs, and high-rise apartment buildings. In the United States, federal funding of highway projects was expected to support demand for structural steel, used in bridge and tunnel reconstruction and roadwork, through the mid-2000s. With most major infrastructure already in place in developed nations, there was little room for growth in fabricated metal output. Output remained relatively flat through the 1980s and early 1990s, despite the mid-1980s boom in construction of office buildings and apartment buildings. Capacity utilization rates wavered between 80 and 85 percent, despite efforts at downsizing and capacity reduction.

With most of their output going to the construction industry, fabricated structural metal manufacturers, in effect, served as contractors on construction projects. As a result, the industry was highly dispersed and international trade, in fabricated structural metal products, was relatively low in comparison with other industries. U.S. exports in 2000 reached about US$750 million, with imports valued at only US$475 million. The size and weight of some structural metal, make it an unwieldy and unprofitable export over long distances, particularly when it competes with lower-cost local production.

A major factor in productivity growth has been the use of computer technology in the production process. Computer-assisted design and manufacturing eliminates manual drafting in the design process, thereby reducing labor costs, and resulting in higher product quality and less product rework. In addition, computer numerical control (CNC) machine tools reduce labor requirements, at the same time as they increase the need for skilled labor, while new microprocessor controls, like automatic welding, have enhanced productivity. The use of electronic data interchange (EDI) between producers and customers has increased industry demand for workers with great levels of computer and numerical literacy.

Small establishments (fewer than 20 workers) accounted for more than 90 percent of the fabricated structural metal industry's total plants—although in most countries, they produced only 10-20 percent of total shipments. In the United States, the top 75 companies (out of 677) recorded more than two-thirds of all sales and employed more than half the workforce. In countries such as Japan and South Korea, where giant industrial groups, such as Nippon Steel, Mitsui, Mitsubishi Corp., Sumitomo, and Pohang Iron and Steel Co. Ltd. (POSCO) dominated all areas of private industry, the discrepancy was even greater. Massive industrial conglomerates were also the norm in Europe. In Canada, establishments with fewer than 20 employees represented about two-thirds of all establishments, yet produced only about 15 percent of shipments. Establishments with more than 200 employees made up only 2 percent of the total, but accounted for 20 percent of shipments.

BACKGROUND AND DEVELOPMENT

Fabricated structural metal is a key element of modern industrial civilization. Hidden in the shadow of the mammoth world steel industry, the fabricated structural metal industry plays a central role in modern architecture and shipbuilding. The skyscrapers that house twentieth-century businesses and workers were erected around a framework of fabricated structural metal. The huge suspension bridges that soar across rivers and inland seas are assembled from fabricated structural metal components. And the ships, oil tankers, and aircraft carriers that ply the oceans all depend on fabricated structural metal to keep them afloat. If concrete, glass, and sheet metal, form the skin of modern structures, then fabricated structural metal is the skeleton.

The importance of metal is no accident. The development of the ability to work with metal parallels the development of human society—so much so, that the names of metals are commonly used by historians to label different eras of human civilization. The earliest metal to gain widespread use was copper. Soft and malleable, copper was hammered into simple tools, cooking utensils, jewelry, and other items. Later, when it was discovered that metals could be altered by fire, people began to experiment with different combinations of metals, creating entirely new substances with radically different qualities. Combining tin and copper, for example, produced bronze, a metal much stronger and more durable than that of either of the original metals. Bronze was used for weapons, body armor, tools, utensils, sculptures, and other items. It was also the first metal to be used for structural purposes. Between 292 and 280 B.C., the citizens of the Greek island of Rhodes erected a bronze statue of the sun god Helios beside the city harbor. Too large to be cast in a mold, the statue was built of bronze plates hammered into shape by an army of artisans and assembled on a frame of stone and iron. One of the seven wonders of the ancient world, the statue stood at least 36 meters (120 feet) tall. A raised base of white marble about seven meters (21 feet) high pushed the huge statue even further into the sky. Known as the Colossus of Rhodes, the statue collapsed during an earthquake 60 years later.

By the time the Colossus of Rhodes was built, people had already learned to smelt and forge iron. This powerful new metal quickly began replacing bronze as the preferred metal for weapons and tools. By about 100 B.C., iron was also beginning to see use as a semi-structural material. During the Roman period, advances in smelting technology led to the first appearance of steel, which was stronger, lighter, and more flexible than iron. However, because steel was expensive and difficult to produce, it was used almost solely for swords and similar weapons until the nineteenth century.

Although iron was sometimes used as a building material during ancient Roman times, the most significant developments in the use of metal, for structural purposes, did not take place until the Industrial Revolution. During this period, structural use of iron and steel began in earnest. Railroads were built throughout Europe and North America. Ships began to be assembled from fabricated structural iron and steel. New bridges and highways linked the busy industrial cities. In addition, new buildings were being erected everywhere. The demand for fabricated structural metal seemed inexhaustible and the industry grew rapidly. One of the best-known examples of the use of fabricated structural metal in the nineteenth century is the Eiffel Tower. With no surface covering of concrete, glass, or steel sheet to conceal its framework, the rivets, bolts, and beams that make up this massive structure are clearly visible.

From the late nineteenth century until the years following World War II, the U.S. fabricated structural metal industry was the largest in the world, supplying the insatiable needs of a huge, rapidly growing country. Thousands of buildings, bridges, and ships had to be built. Much of the infrastructure, commonplace in the mid-1990s in the United States, was erected at this time, spurring exponential growth in the iron, steel, and metal fabricating industries. Similar rapid growth was seen in the Soviet Union under Joseph Stalin, as the country focused all its energy on becoming a leading industrial power.

After World War II, both Europe and Japan rebuilt their industries from the ground up, installing newer, more efficient technologies, and often operating their industries with the help of government subsidies and closed markets. Later, other newly industrialized countries such as China, Brazil, and South Korea, built their own industries, and combining efficiency with low wages, not only pushed U.S. fabricated metal out of their national markets, but were even able to compete in the United States itself. Generally, foreign producers entered into joint ventures with local partners or established their own plants to service the local market.

During the 1970s and 1980s, the fabricated structural metal industry struggled to cope with recessions, declining demand, and increased competition. Unlike the steel industry, which faced similar problems, the fabricated structural metal industry showed no signs of reinvigorating itself with new technologies and value-added production. In the United States, annual growth rates during this period averaged less than 2 percent a year and employment fell steadily, declining from 103,500 in 1982 to 67,000 in 1994. The story was much the same in Canada and Europe. Only in the fast-growing, newly industrializing countries of East Asia and South America did the industry experience considerable growth. By the mid-1980s, the U.S. industry was aggressively touting its products in these emerging markets and, by the 1990s, it had begun to achieve significant export gains.

In the mid-1990s, Japanese producers benefited from vast infusions of public funds aimed at jump-starting the faltering economy and replacing Japan's badly outdated public infrastructure. In the 1990s, dozens of massive public construction projects were underway or being planned. For example, a new international airport—the New Kansai International Airport—was built in Osaka Bay. This huge undertaking involved the construction of an artificial island several kilometers out to sea; a multi-part railway, car, and service bridge to connect it to the mainland; and, of course, the airport itself. Another big project completed during this period was a bridge between the main island of Honshu and the island of Shikoku. Other major activities included construction of the world's largest suspension bridge near Kobe, and a tunnel linking Honshu with the northern island of Hokkaido. Although U.S. and other foreign companies competed fiercely for a share of the Japanese largesse, most of the contracts went to Japanese companies. However, as Japan's economy lost footing in the mid-1990s and was battered by the region's 1997 financial crisis, such public spending slowed considerably and wasn't expected to recover before 1999.

China, Taiwan, and other parts of Asia showed steady growth due to their fast-growing economies; cities such as Taipei experienced an explosion of construction activity, which in turn helped fuel growth in the local fabricated structural metal industry. Meanwhile, in the countries hardest hit by the late 1990s financial crisis, including Indonesia, Thailand, and South Korea, growth was expected to subside temporarily as those economies recovered from debt and a shortage of capital.

The recession of the early 1990s hit the fabricated structural metal industry particularly hard in North America. The recession-induced decline in construction of office buildings, commercial structures, manufacturing facilities, and apartment buildings, largely contributed to the slowdown in U.S. fabricated structural metal output. Industry employment dropped by some 6.9 percent, from a high of 1.45 million in 1989 to approximately 1.44 million in 1991. Production capacity was also decreasing as U.S. fabricated metal manufacturers engaged in extensive restructuring and downsizing, or shut down plants altogether. But by the late 1990s, new life was breathed into the fabricated structural metal industry by construction firms who responded to general economic health, in the United States and Western Europe, and increased demand for all types of construction in developing regions since the early 1990s. This surge in building has revitalized the demand for structural metals, which was expected to continue until the notoriously cyclical construction industry began to decline. In addition, residential construction surged in 1998, with housing starts exceeding 1.5 million; analysts expected starts to average 1.40 to 1.45 million starts annually through the early 2000s.

Many of the problems facing the fabricated structural metal industry in the 1990s were not easily remedied. Downsizing and restructuring companies in this sector utilized all diversification, and other strategies, but nothing could be done about the most fundamental problem—the mature, postindustrial societies of Europe, North America, and Japan no longer needed the quantities of fabricated structural metal they once had. As a result, the focus of the industry seemed destined to shift to the developing world, whose growing economies still required vast amounts of steel, structural metal, and other primary products. However, the U.S. fastener sector thrived in the late 1990s, competing globally, improving production efficiency and quality with cutting-edge technology.

Worldwide imports of prefabricated metal materials increased 62 percent between 1997 and 1998. Canada was the largest importer ($181 million with a growth of 57 percent); followed by Mexico ($24 million with a growth of 28 percent); and Japan ($10 million with a growth of over 1,000 percent). During this period, U.S. steel shipments (primarily to Canada, Mexico, and Venezuela, in descending order of volume) fell 17 percent after an increase of 23 percent, from 1996 to 1997. Plant closings and diminishing production line capacity caused the decline in exports from the United States, which is addressing global competition by developing new residential housing products to replace traditional lumber products. Other technological developments of the late 1990s include corrosion-resistant products for autos and appliances.

As it emerged from the recession of the early 1990s, the fabricated structural metal industry began to show signs of fatigue. Dependent on the construction industry for some 95 percent of its output, the industry suffered from both cyclical construction activity and decreasing market share. Advances in technology and the development of new building materials steadily eroded the demand for structural metal products, stifling both output and prices. Despite these factors, however, the continued growth in the construction industry during the mid- to late 1990s helped the fabricated structural metal industry maintain its footing. In 1996, the value of U.S. shipments of fabricated structural metal products was US$11.2 billion. By 1999, that figure had risen to US$18.2 billion.

In both Canada and the United States, capital investments in new and used equipment were well below manufacturing industry averages. Moreover, with prices edging downward in both countries there was little incentive for manufacturers to upgrade existing facilities. Price erosion and sliding demand were even more pronounced in this market, due to increasing competition from concrete for use in bridge construction. On the positive side, industry analysts expected that more than half of the new bridges and bridge repairs, contracted for by the U.S. government, would primarily utilize steel materials, and infrastructure upgrade projects in the United States were expected to rise in the late 1990s and early 2000s.

CURRENT CONDITIONS

Environmental and production cost concerns are one possible source of decreasing revenue, expected for producers of fabricated structural metals in the coming years. The increased use of construction materials that incorporate recyclable waste materials, like engineered wood, flat glass, and concrete, highlights thc lack of significant research and development breakthroughs in this metals industry, and is a trend that is likely to negatively affect the industry's prevalence. Also likely to affect profits in the immediate future is the economic turmoil in Asia. As Asian currencies become more devalued, industry analysts in more developed regions fear a massive influx of cheaper Asian metals into their markets, which would most likely force firms in developed regions to lower their prices to maintain competitiveness, but delimiting profits for the industry as a whole.

In light of these factors, the industry is following the broad trend of globalization which, according to *Valuation Resources,* was at a low level as of 2003. Many major industry players, seeking to maintain profitability in mature markets like Europe and North America, have been buying up their smaller competitors and consolidating their regional markets. Concurrently, many firms are moving production to areas, especially Asia, where labor and materials are far cheaper, environmental and regulatory standards are far less stringent, and where demand for fabricated structural metals promises the greatest future growth.

To protect the U.S. steel industry, the United States imposed steel tariffs of up to 30 percent on foreign imports in 2002, heavily penalizing China, Japan, Germany, Taiwan, and South Korea, while exempting most poor nations, as well as Mexico and Canada. European Commission officials estimate that the tariffs affected some 4 million tons of European steel exported to the United States, diverting an additional 16 million tons of excess steel to Europe from other countries that could no longer trade with the United States. As a result, there was a sharp increase in domestic steel prices during the early 2000s.

There was a major cost to an already suffering U.S. manufacturing sector. Because the tariffs did not cover finished products, but only the steel itself, manufacturers found themselves hit with a double whammy: higher priced steel being the only available option, coupled with cheaper finished products available overseas. Amidst these conditions, many companies went out of business entirely. Although the tariffs were lifted by 2004, the expected lowering of prices did not immediately follow. In addition, the European Union was expected to impose tariffs on U.S. products in 2004, which would hurt manufacturers from the other angle. If the tariffs passed, the estimated US$4 billion in annual duties would effectively end U.S. presence in the European fabricated metals market.

With almost all of the fabricated structural metal industry's major markets, in North America and Europe, expected to remain stagnant or decline in the foreseeable future, leading North American producers sought to diversify their holdings by investing in other industries. Many North American and European companies also looked to Eastern Europe and Asia for new growth opportunities, while Japanese companies increasingly focused their attention on Southeast Asia. Joint ventures, partnerships, and acquisitions of overseas companies were frequently pursued. More concerned with protecting their industry than dominating it, many companies worked together to establish new markets and build new plants.

One way in which the industry was adapting in the mid-2000s was in the increase of firms with design-build capabilities. Dubbed "engineer-to-order" fabricated structural metal manufacturers, such companies were able to remain not only competitive but viable by providing custom manufacturing. The ETO Institute was a new association serving such companies across industry lines.

RESEARCH AND TECHNOLOGY

As an industry primarily devoted to fabricating products, as opposed to creating them, the fabricated structural metal industry traditionally hasn't invested significantly in research and development. Technological advances in this sector were generally spin-offs from advances in related industries (particularly the steel industry), as well as the heavy machinery and equipment industries. Welding techniques, for example, changed regularly as a result of technological developments. Some of the more sophisticated welding techniques in use included: arc welding, achieved by high temperatures generated by an electric arc; and resistance welding, wherein the flow of electricity between two metals creates resistance and fuses them together. In the 1990s, more advanced welding equipment began to be used. Employing lasers, sound waves, or electron beams to cut or fuse metal, these new systems helped increase the precision and speed of fabrication processes.

Early skyscrapers, such as the Empire State Building in New York, contained twice as much steel per square foot as modern skyscrapers. Chicago's Sears Tower, if constructed today, would require 35 percent less steel than it now contains, according to scientists. Because the use of lighter materials such as concrete and composite materials helped reduce construction costs, not to mention the greater strength of modern steel, fabricated structural metal was used less and less frequently over time. To combat this steady erosion of one of its most vital markets, the steel industry began to invest considerable funds in developing new technologies and processes that would increase the usefulness of its products. The steel industry had already begun revamping itself in the 1980s with "minimills" utilizing scrap metal and new high-value-added steels. In the 1990s, an industry trade group, the American Institute of Steel Construction, began funding research expected to help steel increase its share of the apartment building market. One of the main focuses of this research was shallow, vibration-resistant, preassembled, metal-deck framing systems that required no interior beams for spans up to 30 feet.

Other research concentrated on production of high-tensile steel, able to endure a very high working stress while still being suitable for fabrication by flame-cutting and arc welding. Ideal for use in building construction, the successful development and marketing of these steels was likely to directly benefit the fabricated structural metal industry. Steel and fabricated metal manufacturers also encouraged the use of steel in single-family homes. Steel frames were promoted as more durable, more flexible, and easier to replace or upgrade, than conventional wooden frames. In Florida, a developer built log cabins made of hollow tubular steel logs. Sturdy enough to withstand the worst Florida hurricanes, these houses also provided twice the insulation value of conventional building materials. As if to prove the point, some builders even built their own homes entirely from steel. Samuel Tenenbaum, vice-president of Chatham Steel Corporation, erected a home that made use of structural-steel beams and joists; it featured wide-open interior spaces with exposed steel beams, catwalks, railings, and grates. In all, 20 tons of steel were used in the construction of Tenenbaum's unique home.

Bridge manufacturers were also actively working on new systems, targeted at the growing short-span bridge repair and replacement market. Many of these utilized fabricated structural metal components in unique modular and pre-assembled systems, designed to enable rapid replacement of entire bridges or portions of bridges. An "All-Welded Steel Truss Bridge" was developed by the Ohio Bridge Corporation as an economical alternative to concrete beam and slab bridges. Among the advantages of this bridge were fast, easy installation, a much higher load limit, a lighter dead load, and easy replacement and repair of damaged sections. Other systems included modular steel bridge superstructures and customized bridges in prefab form.

WORKFORCE

Employees of the fabricated structural metal industry work in a factory environment where they cut, shape, and join metal parts for use in commercial and industrial buildings, bridges, ship sections, transmission towers, railroad car racks, and offshore drilling platforms. Much of this work requires heavy manual labor and, despite increased factory automation, the fabricated structural metal industry—like other traditional industries—remains relatively labor-intensive. Output per worker is much lower than the manufacturing average. For example, in 2002 the value of shipments produced by the 105,579 U.S. workers employed in this category was only about US$19.2 billion; considerably less per worker than in most other major industries. Employers in this industry required an estimated 62 percent more production worker hours than did all manufacturing to produce an additional US$1 in value-added sales. Average capital expenditures were less than half the manufacturing average—another indication of this industry's high level of labor intensity. The industry that forms heavy metal supports for buildings and other structures has one of the highest rates of occupational injuries and illnesses; welder and cutter are two of its most hazardous occupations.

Workers in this field consist primarily of iron workers, welders, and cutters. Ironworkers assemble the frameworks of bridges, buildings, and other structures. Their work demands a great deal of physical labor as it usually involves lifting and positioning steel beams and other metal items with derricks and cranes. Welders join metals together using various processes such as electric arc welding, gas welding, resistance welding, and laser welding. Cutters use similar techniques to separate or cut pre-formed metal into new shapes or sizes for later assembly.

Workers in this industry face significantly higher health and safety risks than workers in other industries. Workplace accidents and injuries are nearly double the rate for all manufacturing (24.1 per 100 in 1989 versus 13.1 per 100). Overall, accident rates in the fabricated structural metal industry ranked 12th highest among some 370 individual manufacturing industries—an improvement from 1980 when its injury and illness rate ranked fifth highest in manufacturing. More than half of the injuries occurring in the fabricated structural metal industry were the result of overexertion (usually from lifting heavy objects) or of being struck by a falling or moving object. The leading positions affected were welders and cutters, accounting for more than one-fifth of the industry's total injuries. Hard work, high risks, and relatively low wages made the fabricated structural metal industry unattractive to many workers. Average hourly wages in the United States stood at US$19.55 in 2002.

Employment levels in this industry also declined steadily through the 1980s and 1990s, falling sharply during the 1990s recession; modest productivity growth was due to decreasing worker hours, as output per worker grew 13 percent between 1992 and 1999. Between 1989 and 1999, employment in the stampings and forging industry fell 8.1 percent, while declining 9.1 percent in the fasteners segment. Employment of structural and reinforcing iron and metal workers is expected to rise, about as fast as the average, for all occupations from 2000 through the year 2010. The industry also suffered one of the highest rates of accidents and injuries. Despite improved safety standards and regulations, work in the fabricated structural metal industry was almost twice as hazardous as in other manufacturing industries. Moreover, wages were well below manufacturing averages, as was growth in productivity.

INDUSTRY LEADERS

With nearly 700 companies in the United States alone devoting all or part of their operations to the production of fabricated structural metal products, industry market share is widely dispersed. Moreover, many integrated steel manufacturers, such as U.S. Steel Corp. (USX), Bethlehem Steel Corp., and Nucor Corporation, all derived substantial revenues from fabricated structural metal products. Inclusion of fabricated structural metal units within broader corporations was even more common overseas, where mammoth industrial conglomerates, such as Mitsubishi Heavy Industries, Nippon Steel, POSCO, and Friedrich Krupp, operated in a diverse array of industries. Industrial groups such as these manufactured everything from steel and fabricated structural metal to heavy machinery and entire steel production plants.

This depth of integration, so common in Asia, is less prevalent in North America and Europe. While leading U.S. steelmakers often have some interests in the fabricated structural metal industry, none—with the exception of Nucor Corporation—play a significant role. Independent fabricators dominated the industry. In the 1990s, the top 75 companies in this sector generated more than two-thirds of total sales and employed 47,000 of the 70,000 people working in the industry. Because establishments involved in the fabrication of structural metal products were often diversified companies with numerous divisions operating in different industries, their rankings within the industry varied according to the criteria selected.

By the mid-2000s, three notable companies were Commercial Metals Company, L.B. Foster Company, and Butler Manufacturing Company. Commercial Metals Company (CMC) reported 2004 revenues of US$4.76 billion, a 65.8 percent growth over 2003. The company employed 10,604 people. Begun in 1915, CMC operated in well over 100 locations worldwide by the early 2000s, which included thirty steel fabrication plants and four mini-mills. As of 2004, CMC's fabrication capacity was nearly 1 million tons. L.B. Foster Company, which served the railroad, mass transit, and highway industries, reported US$297.9 million in 2004 sales. Butler Manufacturing Company reported 2003 revenues of US$796.2 million, and employed 4,298 people. Begun in 1901, Butler served non-residential markets, primarily in the commercial, industrial, and agricultural sectors. As of 2004, Butler had been acquired by BlueScope Steel Limited of Australia for US$204 million.

The top steel producer in the world in 2005 was Mittal Steel Company N.V. The company was formed in 2004 when Ispat International (70 percent owned by the Mittal family) bought the LNM Holdings (wholly owned by the Mittal family) for $13.3 billion. The combined company produces more than 50 million metric tons per year. The company's 2004 revenue stood at $22.19 billion. Formerly the world's leading steelmaker until the formation of Mittal, is Arcelor SA of Luxembourg. A combination of France's Usinor, Luxembourg's Arbed, and Spain's Aceralia, the company had US$32.54 billion in revenue and 98,000 employees. The third place producer in the world was Japan's Nippon Steel Corporation, with 2004 sales of US$27.7 billion. The company's 46,233 employees worked in fields as diverse as steel production, construction, electronics, and communications.

In South Korea, Pohang Iron and Steel Co. Ltd. (POSCO), the country's largest steelmaker, accounted for virtually all domestic production of iron and steel products, generating US$14.93 million in 2003 revenues.

FURTHER READING

Butler Manufacturing Company Web Site, 2005. Available from http://www.butlermfg.com.

Commercial Metals Company Web Site, 2005. Available from http://www.commercialmetals.com.

Dolor, Felicisimo A. "Manufacturing Indices Post January Increases." *Business World,* 28 March 2003.

"Fabricated Structural Metal Manufacturers and the ETO Institute." *PR Web,* 22 June 2004.

"Hoover's Company Capsules." 2005. Available from http://www.hoovers.com.

"Industry: Fabricated Metal Products." *Iseek,* 2004. Available from http://www.iseek.org.

"Industry Profiles; Fabricated Structural Metal Industry." *Human Resources Development Canada,* 2001.

"International Trade Statistics." 2004. Available from http://www.wto.org.

L.B. Foster Company Web Site, 2004. Available from http://www.lbfoster.com.

Newpoff, Laura. "EU Tariffs Raise Concerns." *Business First of Columbus (Ohio),* 23 February 2004.

"Plate Work and Fabricated Structural Product Manufacturing." *Valuation Resources,* 2004. Available from http://www.ibisworld.com.

Raiford, Dave. "A Heavy Burden Lifted." *Nashville Business Journal,* 12 January 2004.

Sanger, David. "Bush Weighs Raising Steel Tariffs but Exempting Most Poor Nations." *New York Times,* 4 March 2002.

U.S. Census Bureau. *2002 Economic Census.* 2005. Available from http://www.census.gov.

U.S. Department of Labor. *Occupational Outlook Handbook, 2004-05.* 2005. Available from http://www.bls.gov.

SIC 3330

NAICS 331

METALS, PRIMARY NONFERROUS

The nonferrous metals industry fabricates, from crude ores, basic metal products made from materials other than iron or steel. This industry is termed "primary" to distinguish it from so-called secondary producers that remanufacture metals from scrap. Major industry products, in descending order of annual global production by weight, include aluminum, copper, lead, and zinc.

INDUSTRY SNAPSHOT

Primary nonferrous metals, which constitute the vast majority of nonferrous metal production, experience markedly different demand and profitability depending on the type of metal, world production capacity, and the health of specific end-use markets. Thus, while an individual metal smelting and refining company may produce several kinds of nonferrous metals, each may be subject to unique market conditions—a tendency that makes generalizations about all nonferrous metals difficult. Aluminum and copper were the two major segments of this industry.

The market for aluminum, the industry's largest product segment, has continued to experience robust demand in the 2000s. World production of aluminum stood at more than 22.5 million metric tons in 2004. According to the Aluminum Association, the transportation sector is the heaviest consumer of aluminum, with 7.5 billion pounds required each year. Although the automobile and aerospace markets continued to be heavy users of aluminum, those markets were leveling out by the mid-2000s. Instead, the commercial and industrial transportation sectors were rising in the demand for aluminum. North America was by far the largest aluminum-producing region, followed by Europe and Asia. Worldwide aluminum production was increasing rapidly, but demand was increasing more rapidly, creating shortages that were expected to last into at least 2006.

Primary copper, the industry's second-largest product by value, hasn't fared as well as aluminum. Copper prices from the mid-1990s to the mid-2000s have proven particularly volatile because of excess supply due to overproduction. Even though demand increased and production declined, by 2002 supply still exceeded demand, although the gap was closing. These conditions were expected to lead to unpredictable copper prices, despite healthy demand in U.S. and European construction and electrical equipment markets, as well as China's booming economy and subsequent increased copper demand. The world's major copper region was the Americas, followed by Asia. Europe was third in copper production.

ORGANIZATION AND STRUCTURE

Leading nonferrous metals (metals that do not contain iron) are aluminum, copper, zinc, and lead. Aluminum, a lightweight, silvery metal, is the most plentiful metallic element in the earth's crust. The metal is sought after because of its numerous unique physical characteristics. Importantly, aluminum weighs less than one-third an equal volume of steel. Besides its high strength-to-weight ratio, aluminum resists corrosion—it becomes covered with a tough, protective layer of aluminum oxide when exposed to air. Additional properties, such as high conductivity and recyclability, make it useful for a multitude of applications ranging from transportation and long-distance power transmission to construction and food and beverage packaging.

Aluminum. Aluminum, while abundant, is difficult to extract in pure form. It occurs naturally as a silicate (a compound containing silicon, oxygen, and other elements) and is often mixed with other minerals such as sodium and potassium. Aluminum is extracted from an ore called bauxite through the Bayer process, a more expensive procedure in comparison to that used to extract iron, copper, and other common metals. The most common refining technique is the Hall-Heroult process. It entails dissolving alumina (aluminum oxide) in fused cryolite (a naturally occurring fluoride), and then decomposing it through electrolysis to a molten metal.

The United States was the largest manufacturer of aluminum in the late 1990s, accounting for approximately 25.0 percent of global output. Other major aluminum-producing nations in 1999 included: the Russian Federation (15.0 percent of global output); Canada (10.0 percent); Australia (6.3 percent); and Brazil (6.2 percent). Major consumers of aluminum in 1992, in descending order of consumption by weight, were the United States, Japan, the Commonwealth of Independent States (CIS), Germany, and China.

Copper. Copper, a reddish metal, is the 25th most abundant metallic element. Marketable characteristics include high conductivity, malleability, resistance to corrosion, and beauty. Copper, in fact, is second to silver in conductivity, making it useful in the production of electrical wire and cables. It is also commonly used to make money, cooking utensils, pipes, and architectural ornaments, among other goods. Finally, copper is often mixed with zinc to form brass, or with tin to create bronze. Unlike aluminum, copper is relatively easy to extract and is often found in pure form. Ore containing copper is crushed, washed, melted in a furnace, concentrated, purified, and then cast into shapes for milling into finished products.

Most copper is mined in developing nations and processed into intermediate and final products in developed countries. The exception to that rule is the United States, which is both a major producer and consumer of copper. The United States, in fact, is second in mined copper production (by weight) to Chile, but is the largest producer of refined copper. In 1999 aggregate refined copper production worldwide reached 14.1 million metric tons. Major copper-producing nations in 1999 included Chile, the United States, Japan, China, and the Russian Federation. Leading consumers of refined copper, in descending order of consumption by weight, were the United States, Japan, Germany, and China. These four countries accounted for roughly 50 percent of the global copper market.

Zinc. Zinc, the twenty-fourth most common element in the earth's crust and the third-largest nonferrous metal industry product, is a bluish-white metal. Although it is brittle, it becomes malleable at temperatures of 120 to 150 degrees Celsius. When exposed to air, the surface of the metal forms a hard film that resists further oxidation. Zinc is soluble in alcohol, acids, and alkalis. Its properties make it ideal for use as a protective coating for other metals. Its primary end use, in fact, is to make galvanized steel. Zinc is also utilized as an alloying agent, particularly with copper to make brass. Zinc is also put to use in pigments, rubber tires, and wood preservatives, among other goods. Zinc is typically extracted from ore through a distillation process that uses an electric furnace to boil the zinc. Another technique involves leaching the zinc from the ore with sulfuric acid.

Global zinc production in 1999 was approximately 8.3 million metric tons, up 19.7 percent from a worldwide output of 6.9 million metric tons in 1990. Major nations involved in zinc production included China (20.1 percent of global output by weight); Canada (9.4 percent); Spain (4.5 percent); Australia (3.9 percent); and Mexico, Belgium, Finland, and the Russian Federation (each with 2-3 percent). The United States is by far the largest consumer of zinc, accounting for about 15 percent of global consumption in 1992. Other leading zinc users, in descending order, were Japan, Germany, Italy, and France. These five countries together represented approximately 40 percent of the world market. In 1998, zinc import demand was greatest in the United States (1.1 billion metric tons); Germany (531 million metric tons); Belgium (337 million metric tons); and Italy and France (241 million metric tons each).

Lead. Lead, the fourth most commonly processed nonferrous metal, is the thirty-sixth most often-occurring metallic element and is widely distributed throughout the world. It is malleable, dense, and toxic, as well as a poor conductor of electricity. It is also a metal with relatively low tensile strength. Lead is most commonly used to make storage batteries, but is also utilized in applications such as sheathing for electric cables, pipe and tank lining, and X-ray apparatus. It is also used in the manufacture of paints and pigments. Lead is typically extracted from ore through one of two processes similar to those used to make steel or copper. Important by-products of the processes include sliver, gold, and zinc. The purest grades of lead are obtained refining by through electrolysis.

Global production of lead in 1999 reached 5.69 million metric tons. Some of the richest lead deposits in the world were located in the western United States, although those veins had been significantly depleted by the 1990s. Other high-quality, high-volume lead reserves exist in Australia, Canada, Mexico, Peru, and Serbia. By far, the United States has been the world's largest producer of refined lead, accounting for one-fourth of global output in 1999. Other major producers included China, with 16.6 percent of global production, followed by the United Kingdom, Canada, Mexico, Germany, and Italy, each of which produced 4-6 percent of total output. Nations importing the most lead in 1998, in descending order, were the United Kingdom, United States, Germany, Malaysia, and Korea.

Other Nonferrous Metals. Besides aluminum, copper, lead, and zinc, metals produced in smaller amounts in this industry sector include nickel, tin, molybdenum, magnesium, and titanium. About 850,000 metric tons of nickel were manufactured in the early 1990s. Nickel is used mostly as an alloying agent to make stainless and specialty steel. Major producers include the Commonwealth of Independent States, Canada, and Japan. The United States and Japan are the largest consumers of nickel, together accounting for about 30 percent of the world market. In the early 1990s approximately 400 million pounds of tin was produced on an annual basis. Most tin is produced in South America, Asia, and Australia, and about one-fifth of all tin is consumed by the United States. It is used for various industrial processes, including the production of common alloys such as bronze and solder. Molybdenum is used mostly as an alloy in steel because it is strong and withstands high temperatures. It is produced and consumed primarily in the United States and Canada.

The United States is also the largest producer of magnesium. Magnesium is used chiefly as an alloying metal—often with copper and aluminum—for applications that require lightweight and high tensile strength. Titanium is an extremely high-performance metal used primarily for aerospace and defense-related purposes. Major titanium-producing nations include the Russian Federation, Japan, and the United States. This industry also encompasses minor metals such as antimony, bismuth, cadmium, indium, mercury, and cobalt.

BACKGROUND AND DEVELOPMENT

Copper is believed to be the first metal used to make useful articles. It was probably discovered around 8000 B.C. in "the cradle of civilization"—what is now Iraq—near the Tigris and Euphrates rivers. Copper deposits in Egypt are known to have been mined as early as 5000 B.C., and the metal was discovered and used in ancient civilizations in Greece, Asia Minor, China, and southeastern Europe. It was also known to natives in the Americas. Lead and tin were also used by ancient civilizations. Tin has been found in ancient Egyptian tombs, while lead was utilized by the Romans to make pipes for carrying water. For more than 2,000 years white lead (lead carbonate) has been used as a white pigment. Several other nonferrous metals have been known for centuries as well, though they were not produced on a commercial scale.

Indeed, it was the Industrial Revolution, which started in Europe and spread to North America during the nineteenth century, that created massive demand for all types of refined metals. As new methods of mining, refining, and processing metals were developed, production soared. For example, advanced systems that used furnaces and chemicals to extract copper from ore were invented. New lead and tin refining processes were developed as well. White lead, for instance, had long been made using the Dutch process, whereby lead gratings and acetic acid were wrapped in bark and placed in earthenware pots to ferment. That lengthy process was eventually replaced by refining systems that integrated blast furnaces, electrolysis, and other technologies advanced during the eighteenth century.

Unlike copper, tin, and lead, other major nonferrous metals were not discovered until the eighteenth or nineteenth centuries. Furthermore, they were not produced commercially until the Industrial Revolution. Zinc, for example, was not recognized as a separate element until 1746 by German chemist Andreas Sigismund Marggraf, while nickel was identified in 1751 by Swedish chemist Baron Axel Frederic Cronstedt. Subsequent to that discovery, another Swedish chemist, Karl Wilhelm Scheele, identified molybdenum. In 1791 British clergyman William Gregor discovered titanium. Although their existence was known, most of these elements were not isolated or applied commercially until the late nineteenth or early twentieth century.

Representative of the route to commercial success experienced by metals discovered in the eighteenth and nineteenth centuries was aluminum. Aluminum was first isolated in 1825 by Danish chemist Hans Christian Oersted, but another 50 years passed before the first practical method for producing aluminum was developed. Interestingly, two scientists working independently on separate sides of the Atlantic Ocean simultaneously discovered the same process. During the late 1880s, American Charles Martin Hall and France's Paul Heroult initiated the birth of the aluminum industry on their respective continents. Although the aluminum commercialization process mimicked that of other major metals, its success in the marketplace far surpassed that of its nonferrous cousins.

Production of all commercially viable nonferrous metals surged during the early 1900s. Importantly, Japan and the Russian Federation joined the United States and several European countries as industrializing nations. Metal demand for construction, transportation, communication, and consumer industries soared. Both product demand and metal refining technology advanced significantly during World War I and World War II. Although technology and production capacity were significantly advanced during the latter war, by the end of the conflict the metal-producing infrastructure in most regions had been effectively quashed. The exception was the United States, which assumed a dominant role in both ferrous and nonferrous metal categories during the 1950s and 1960s.

Throughout the 1950s and into the early 1970s the United States was the leading producer in major metal categories (with the exception of such categories as zinc and nickel). Although statistics varied by category, the general trend during the period was increased global consumption. In addition, metal industries emerged in other nations that reduced the market share controlled by the United States and a few other leading nations. Japan and western European nations rebounded, becoming strong competitors in aluminum, copper, lead, and other metal categories. Other significant producers emerged during this period as well. The Soviet Union and some East Bloc countries developed vast production capacity, eventually nearing or surpassing U.S. output in important segments such as aluminum and copper. At the same time, several developing countries—Chile, Mexico, Peru, Zambia, South Korea, India, and others—tapped rich natural resources to become major global suppliers of specific metals.

The early 1970s marked the beginning of a shift in the overall metal industry. For a variety of reasons, ranging from energy prices to environmental and labor laws, the competitiveness of the United States, western Europe, and Japan waned. The net effect was that, in general, metal output in those regions stagnated or dropped during the 1970s and 1980s. Meanwhile, the Soviet Union and several other nations boosted production. This trend was evidenced most strikingly by U.S. metal production statistics. U.S. aluminum output, for instance, jumped from 1.46 million metric tons in 1954 to a peak of 4.9 million in 1974. Between 1975 and 1993, however, U.S. shipments fluctuated between about 4 million and 5 million tons as world aluminum output surged from 12 to 19 million tons. Similarly, U.S. copper production grew from 1.1 million tons in 1961 to 1.7 million in 1973. Between 1974 and 1993, however, U.S. output hovered between 900,000 and 1.5 million tons as total global copper production rose by about 25 percent because of the impact of countries such as Chile and Indonesia.

By the 1980s, the global metal industry had become much more geographically diversified. Overall metal demand continued to rise during the 1980s, but much of the growth was attributable to rising consumption in industrializing regions based in the Pacific Rim and Latin America. Long-industrialized nations, faced with slowing economic growth rates since the 1970s, worked to sustain profitability through improved productivity and new products. For example, some market segments, such as specialized zinc coatings and high-performance alloys, offered hefty profit opportunities. Similarly, the demand for aluminum by the beverage and food industry swelled.

An important industry influence in the late 1980s and early 1990s was the decline and collapse of the Soviet Union. Metal output in the Russian Federation and the former East Bloc plunged as a result of the political turmoil in those regions, but these nations dumped stockpiles and excess output of some metals onto the market. Most ceded Soviet market share was indirectly absorbed by rising metal-producing powers like China and India.

Metal industry performance during the early and mid-1990s varied by product segment. Aggregate aluminum output stabilized in the early 1990s after lurching from about 15.4 million metric tons in 1986 to more than 19 million by 1990. Excess production capacity dogged competitors in many regions during the 1990s. The excess was partly the result of economic malaise in some industrialized regions. Augmenting the oversupply problem was the Russian Federation, which maintained more than 80 percent of the aluminum-producing capacity of the former Soviet Union and was still the second largest aluminum manufacturer in the world. As consumption in the Commonwealth of Independent States (CIS) plummeted, the Russian Federation dumped excess supply into world markets, a move that contributed to weak prices and a glut of aluminum and other metals. Supply and demand dynamics, according to some industry analysts, were finally calming again by 1994, though most producers continued to suffer.

Entering the mid-1990s, North America was by far the largest aluminum-producing region—Canada and the United States together made up about 30 percent of global output. Production in that region had been relatively stable for several years, with increases occurring solely in Canada. Areas in which aluminum output was rising most quickly were Australia, South America, and Asia. Most notably, Brazil's aluminum output had careened from about 500,000 metric tons in the mid-1980s to about 1.2 million metric tons by 1992. During the same period, China increased its annual aluminum shipments from 400,000 tons to about 1 million. Both Australia and India, the fourth and tenth biggest suppliers, respectively, achieved similar gains. In the long-term, aluminum consumption and production was forecast to rise at rates of five percent or more annually in developing regions, and more slowly in developed nations.

Copper industry dynamics mirrored those of the aluminum sector during the late 1980s and early 1990s. Aggregate production of refined copper jumped from 9.8 million metric tons to about 10.9 million. Much of the increase in demand came from China and a few other emerging industrial powers. The United States and Canada produced about 25 percent of all copper in the early 1990s, making North America the leading copper-producing region. As with aluminum, the regions achieving the greatest copper production gains were in the Pacific Rim and Latin America. Between 1986 and 1992, production in Chile and China rose 30 percent and 50 percent, respectively, to account for a combined 17 percent of global shipments. Meanwhile, output by the former Soviet Union slipped from 1.3 million tons to 875,000—a drop of more than 30 percent. Long-term demand growth was projected at two to three percent annually during the mid- and late-1990s. Modest growth expectations were attributed in part to a global shift from copper wire to fiber-optic cables.

Zinc output, spurred mostly by growing use as a steel coating in the vehicle and construction industries, grew steadily during the 1980s and early 1990s to about 7.5 million metric tons. Led by Canada, North America was the largest zinc-producing region, accounting for about 30 percent of total output. The Commonwealth of Independent States (CIS) followed closely, although zinc shipments from that region slipped roughly 20 percent between 1990 and 1993 to less than 800,000 tons. Major zinc-producing nations that increased output during the late 1980s and early 1990s included Canada, Mexico, the United States, Italy, China, Australia, and Peru. Zinc prices were suppressed in the early 1990s. However, recovering automotive and construction markets ignited a rally in 1994. The long-term outlook for global zinc appears positive going into the mid-1990s, with small increases in demand expected in both developing and industrialized regions.

Global lead production remained level during the early 1990s—around 5.5 million metric tons—holding steady since the early 1980s. Prices were suppressed by industry overcapacity and generally weak demand. About 30 percent of all lead is manufactured and used in North America. The United States, the largest industry participant, increased its output from about 931,000 tons in 1986 to about 1.18 million tons in 1992. The only other countries achieving notable gains in lead production during that period were Australia, China, and Peru. The biggest industry loser was the CIS. The long-term outlook for the lead industry was regarded by some observers as poor in the mid-1990s, as analysts pointed to likely reductions in the use of lead because of its toxicity and the emergence of increasingly popular lead substitutes.

Other industry trends evident by 2002 included an aerospace manufacturing sector declining from lack of airline passenger consumer confidence after the terrorist events of September 11, 2001. The decreased demand for commercial airplanes—Boeing reporting a 45 percent drop in orders and Airbus Industrie 30 percent for 2001—predicted decreased demand for copper and aluminum. Titanium producers, in general, were battered during the early 1990s by the end of the Cold War and the global economic slump in industrialized nations. As core aerospace markets sagged, the titanium market became glutted, and prices fell. Producers in the CIS, the United States, and Japan—countries that have traditionally dominated the titanium market—suffered as a result. Titanium demand and prices were expected to recover gradually in the wake of improving industrial and civilian aerospace markets and depleted CIS stockpiles, however.

Other nations, including the United Kingdom and China, were also working to boost market share in the mid-1990s.

Although titanium revenue sagged in the early 1990s, molybdenum prices surged 30 to 60 percent depending on region and product type in 1994. The rise was driven by surging international steel production and increased use of molybdenum as an alloying material. The long-term outlook for molybdenum was generally positive going into the mid-1990s, with North American producers expected to benefit most.

While aluminum producers in the 1990s approached adding new capacity with caution, copper production has often veered wildly off track of market demand, and consequently prices remained in a rut. Aluminum producers, although some announced expansion plans in the late 1990s, gained discipline from experiencing depressed prices at times in the 1980s and early 1990s. In 1993 U.S. aluminum manufacturers agreed to limit production to shore up flagging aluminum prices. Their strategy worked, and by the late 1990s leading producers such as Alcoa were idling as much as 450,000 metric tons of their capacity (for a total of over a million metric tons idle industry-wide) to preserve strong prices. By 1998, global aluminum supply exceeded demand by some 600,000 tons, due in part to a fall in demand precipitated by the Asian financial crisis of the mid-1990s. In 2000, the United States led in global aluminum demand, importing 2.2 million metric tons or 7.4 percent of world supply, followed closely by the European Union, with 2.1 million metric tons or 7.2 percent. For the same period, Canada led in world exports, shipping 1.36 million tons, or 4.7 percent of the global total, followed by Russia's exports of 770,000 million metric tons or 2.7 percent of world supply, and Australia's exports of 900,000 metric tons, or 3.1 percent. Industry analysts predict a gradual decline in aluminum market surpluses as U.S. demand was expected to increase while world supply diminishes.

Other metal segments mirrored the performance of the aluminum and copper industries. Producers of nickel, for example, were stymied during the early 1990s by overcapacity, generally weak demand, and low prices. Nickel output in the Western world declined while production in Japan, China, Colombia, and a few other nations climbed slowly. Long-term prospects for nickel were positive going into the mid-1990s, however, with demand expected to rise gradually throughout the late 1990s. By 1997 and 1998 consumption in the West had rebounded by a solid 5-6 percent. While nickel markets such as aerospace were expected to continue to flourish through the end of the century, some observers expected a cyclical decline in steel demand to eat into world nickel demand by 1999.

Similar forecasts were put forth for the tin industry. After surging during the late 1980s, global tin consumption slumped during the early 1990s. Tin continued to lose market share to aluminum and other metals among Western nations, but demand was expected to increase slowly in developing regions throughout the 1990s and early 2000s.

Among other nonferrous segments, lead continued to disappoint producers with its low prices. While in Europe and North America lead use actually exceeds demand, China has exported a large quantity of low-cost lead that has driven prices downward. Added to lead's woes was slack demand in the battery market, one of its largest uses. Lead use in other applications has declined precipitously because of its toxicity to people and the environment.

Zinc, by contrast, was an industry success entering the late 1990s. North America and Europe were expected to consume some 6.5 million metric tons of zinc in 1998, only a slight volume increase from year-earlier demand, but on considerably stronger unit prices. Used in such products as galvanized steel, automotive parts, and construction materials, zinc has enjoyed slow steady demand that has exceeded output.

CURRENT CONDITIONS

In the price-sensitive metals business, supply and demand economics often closely dictate the industry's fortunes. Industry analysts frequently gauge market conditions in terms of global capacity, production, and demand; the ideal condition, from the perspective of a producer, is when capacity barely exceeds production, and production lags somewhat short of demand. Such a combination ensures that unused capacity is not going to waste. Prices will also stay strong because buyers have fewer options and producers are not desperate to rid themselves of excess inventory. From the standpoint of a buyer, of course, oversupply and low prices usually are favored. The commodity nature of most segments of metal production requires that producers be watchful of not expanding production too rapidly so that prices are driven downward.

The market for aluminum, the industry's largest product segment, has continued to experience robust demand in the 2000s. Although worldwide aluminum production increased by 6.1 percent in 2003, with levels expected to increase another 4.1 percent in 2004 and 4.8 percent in 2005, consumption was expected to grow even faster. Anticipated consumption levels were 13.4 percent higher in 2005 than in 2003. Shortages were predicted, as supply was not forecast to keep up with increased demand. China alone was increasing its demand exponentially, and by 2004 it was consuming nearly one-fifth of worldwide aluminum production. There was a projected shortage of 400,000 tons for 2004, and a shortage of 1 million tons in 2005, according to *Aluminum International Today.* Prices were expected to remain high well into the middle of the decade.

Demand for aluminum was expected to continue in many industry sectors. In the automotive industry, Europe's increasing use of aluminum was outstripping American use, with an estimated 25 pounds of aluminum per vehicle in Europe compared to 14 pounds per vehicle in the United States projected by 2010.

Copper prices continued to be unpredictable due to a continuing imbalance in supply and demand. In the early 2000s, the gap was closing somewhat. For example, in 2002 there was a 105,000 ton surplus, as compared to the previous year's 536,000 ton surplus. These conditions were expected to lead to continued low copper prices, despite an increase begun in 2003, largely due to escalating demand for copper in the booming Asian markets. This was particularly the case in China, which increased consumption by 26 percent between 2002 and 2003. Copper demand, especially in China, reached all-time highs in 2004 and 2005, causing copper prices to climb dramatically.

RESEARCH AND TECHNOLOGY

There are three main fronts of research and technology affecting the nonferrous metals industry: new applications for metals that broaden potential markets; new production technologies that improve manufacturing productivity or create better metal products; and advances that reduce environmental hazards related to manufacturing processes. The first aspect directly impacts all metal manufacturing countries, while the latter two are of most interest to developed nations, which routinely compete against less-regulated, low-cost manufacturers in developing regions.

The aluminum segment continued to be impacted by environmental regulations in industrialized nations in the mid-1990s. Increasing pressure to reduce sulfur dioxide emissions in North America and Europe—Japan was a minor presence in the aluminum industry at only 20 million tons produced annually in 1992—boosted operating costs in those areas. Because aluminum production consumes large amounts of energy, companies in many of those nations were building new production facilities in areas with fewer environmental restrictions or greater sources of power from coal alternatives, such as natural gas or hydropower. The net result was that European and North American producers dependent on coal-generated electricity began losing their competitive edge and were forced to either invest heavily in pollution-reduction technologies or expand foreign production. Another factor that hurt developed nations, particularly in North America, was a reduction in demand from the high-profit aerospace industry—a corollary of the demise of the Cold War.

Other technological breakthroughs broadening the aluminum market relate to alloys. Metal matrix composites (MMCs)—alloys that integrate aluminum to achieve a combination of strength and lightness—were being used for a broad range of applications in vehicle industries. Finally, technological advances in recycling technology have made aluminum manufacturing as much as 95 percent more energy efficient than extracting the metal from bauxite.

Like aluminum producers, copper manufacturers were also being impacted by technology, though sometimes negatively. Copper wire, for instance, steadily lost market share to advanced fiber-optic cable for communications applications in the early 1990s. Copper producers, however, have also benefited from the general proliferation of electronic devices, many of which—though often connected by fiber-optic cables—also utilized less-expensive copper wiring. Growing demand for such applications helped industry participants offset losses in piping markets, where plastic was being used as a copper substitute, and losses to aluminum, which was replacing copper in car radiators, for example. Similarly, the zinc segment benefited from growing demand in the automobile and construction industries, which coated an increasingly large portion of steel products with zinc in the 1980s and early 1990s. Integral to that growth market was electrogalvanizing, a relatively new process used to coat and protect steel.

Like manufacturers of aluminum, lead producers in many nations continued to battle environmental regulations designed to curb pollution, as well as increased competition from high-performance lead substitutes in the mid-1990s. In an effort to replace ebbing traditional markets, lead manufacturers were striving to create new ones. Most promising was the growth of the lead battery market. Partly because of pressures to reduce vehicle emissions, the battery market showed solid long-term promise in transportation applications. In addition, a number of countries—Argentina, the United States, Sweden, Belgium, and Canada—were exploring the use of lead as a containment medium for high-level radioactive wastes. Likewise, a new lead compound called diayldithiocarbamate had been developed; proponents of the compound said it could double the life of asphalt while adding only five percent to its cost. New uses for lead were also being pioneered in the field of magneto-hydrodynamics, an advanced electricity-generating technique advanced primarily in Israel.

INDUSTRY LEADERS

Aluminum Company of America. Known to many as Alcoa, the Aluminum Company of America has long topped the nonferrous metals industry through its dominant share of the world's aluminum production. What's more, in 1998 Alcoa bought out the United States' third-largest aluminum firm, Alumax Inc., to further secure its status as the world's preeminent aluminum company. The combined company had a smelting capacity of 3.2 million metric tons—nearly twice that of its nearest competitor. In 1996 and 1997 Alcoa also took over state-run aluminum holdings in Italy and Spain. A few years later, Alcoa formed an alliance with China' Aluminum Corporation. The company operates some 350 facilities in about 38 countries throughout the world.

In 2000, Alcoa acquired Reynolds Metals, then the United States' second-largest aluminum manufacturer and the world's third-largest primary aluminum producer. Best known in the United States for its Reynolds Wrap aluminum foil, Reynolds is highly diversified into all stages of aluminum production and marketing, from bauxite mining to refining to finished goods for the consumer, construction, and automotive sectors. Reynolds began in 1919 as a manufacturer of foil for cigarette packaging, expanding during World War II and with the postwar U.S. economic and population boom. Reynolds emphasized global expansion during the mid-twentieth century, and by 1980 had more than 100 operations in 20 countries. It maintains operations in Europe, Russia, India, and China, among other places.

The U.S.-based Alcoa was founded in 1888 by two Americans—Alfred Hunt and Charles Martin Hall (co-inventor of the Hall-Heroult process used to extract aluminum from bauxite). During the twentieth century Alcoa evolved into a multibillion-dollar corporation and the leader in the aluminum industry, specializing in flat-rolled aluminum sheets used in beverage cans, a market Alcoa still dominates. Entering the mid-1990s, Alcoa was active in three business segments: the production of bauxite, alumina, and alumina-related chemicals; aluminum processing, including the production and sale of basic aluminum-cast, flat-rolled, and engineered products; and the manufacture of nonaluminum metal products, including gold, magnesium, and steel and titanium forgings. The company had 2004 sales of nearly US$23.5 billion. With 119,000 workers that year, Alcoa also was one of the largest employers in the global industry.

Alcan. Alcan Aluminum Limited, the industry leader in Canada, ranked as the world's second-largest primary aluminum maker in 2003. Although Alcan competes with Alcoa for the top position in the global aluminum industry, it originated as a subsidiary of Alcoa. Alcoa spun off Alcan (then called Aluminum Limited) in 1928. The division continued to act as Alcoa's foreign subsidiary for 20 years, branching its operations throughout the world. Alcan eventually became completely independent. By the early 1990s it was operating throughout the world, mining bauxite in seven countries and processing aluminum in nineteen countries. The fully integrated producer was a leading global supplier of fabricated aluminum products, including foil, beverage can sheet aluminum, rod, cable, extruded aluminum, and various construction products in the mid-1990s. Revenue and profit growth was brisk in the late 1980s but slipped during the early 1990s in the wake of global overcapacity and weak prices. Alcan has traditionally been one of Canada's most profitable conglomerates. The year 2004 was no exception, when Alcan earned US$24.8 billion in revenue.

In 2000, Alcan acquired the Swiss firm Alusuisse-Lonza, now renamed Algroup, which was at the time the sixth-largest contender in the international nonferrous industry, as ranked by primary aluminum output. Like Alcoa, Alusuisse was formed in 1888, shortly after the discovery of the Hall-Heroult process. In 2001, the Zurich-based Algroup was one of Switzerland's largest corporations, with 23,000 employees in 18 countries. It consisted of four divisions: Alusuisse primary materials; Alusuisse fabricated products; Lawson Mardon food flexible and tobacco packaging; and Wheaton pharmaceutical and cosmetics packaging. In 2004, Alcan acquired French competitor Pechiney and in early 2005, the company spun off its aluminum-rolled products unit with the newly formed Novelis, a public company.

Pechiney S.A. France's Pechiney is Europe's largest primary aluminum producer. Its 1997 production of primary aluminum stood at 961,000 metric tons, in addition to its output of 480,000 metric tons of flat-rolled aluminum products. Pechiney has particular strength in beverage cans—it shipped an industry-leading 39 billion cans in 1997. The company's nine smelters, six of which are in Europe, contributed to overall 2002 sales of US$12.5 billion, with 320 facilities in 50 countries. The company also produces plastic bottles to complement its metal can business, as well as miscellaneous other packaging concerns. It is the world's largest producer of collapsible tubes. In 2004, Pechiney was acquired by Alcan for US$4.7 billion.

Nippon. Nippon Light Metal Company of Tokyo posted 2004 revenues of nearly US$5.04 billion, a 17.5 percent increase over the previous year. The company's net income skyrocketed, however, to US$109.1 million, an increase of more than 83 percent over 2003. A leading producer of ladders, bridges, fuel tanks, and other fabricated aluminum products, Nippon employed 12,598 people in locations from Asia to North America.

Other Leaders. Numerous other companies hold noteworthy shares of the nonferrous metals markets. Among copper and diversified producers, some of the largest include Asarco Inc., Cyprus Amax, Freeport McMoRan Copper and Gold, Olin Corp., Grupo Mexico SA de CV, Phelps Dodge, Noranda, and Southern Peru Copper.

MAJOR COUNTRIES IN THE INDUSTRY

United States. The United States was the leading global producer of nonferrous metals entering the late 1990s. It supplied roughly 20 percent of total global metal demand and dominated several major industry segments. In 1996 the United States exported more than US$5 billion worth of aluminum and copper alone. It was also the largest importer of aluminum, at US$4.95 billion in 1996, and a major consumer of most other nonferrous metals.

The United States assumed its leadership role following World War II. Before that time, western European nations such as Germany and the United Kingdom led the industry. While countries with metal-producing powers significantly increased production capacity during World War II, by the end of the conflict the United States was the only major industrialized power with its metal-manufacturing infrastructure still intact. U.S. producers benefited from both foreign and domestic demand growth during the 1950s and 1960s; they accounted for more than 30 percent of global production of some metals. Most importantly, shipments of aluminum bulged from less than 1.5 million metric tons in the early 1950s to about 4.5 million by the early 1970s.

The United States' share of world metal production deteriorated rapidly in the early 1970s. Although industry segments differed, the United States generally suffered from a lack of competitiveness and a slowdown in domestic demand. U.S. output of refined copper, for example, actually declined from about 2 million metric tons in 1973 to less than 1.5 million in the late 1980s. Aluminum output stagnated as well, despite a huge rise in new applications in packaging and construction industries, among others. The United States managed to retain its industry lead throughout the 1980s, although its share of world output and consumption continued to decline. By the early 1990s it was producing about 20 percent of the world's output of copper, aluminum, and lead, and about 6 percent of all zinc. The United States also was the largest metal consumer, typically consuming more metal than it produced.

Going into the mid-1990s, U.S. nonferrous producers benefited from a cyclical upswing in demand for most metals. However, prices generally were suppressed by global manufacturing overcapacity. Long-term aluminum demand from the important high-profit aerospace industry had slowed dramatically by 2002. Similarly, the giant packaging segment (28 percent of U.S. aluminum consumption in 1993) had matured and was expected to offer little growth. Industry participants were heartened, though, by the expectation of continued rises in aluminum use in transportation and construction markets. Some industry analysts in the early 1990s indicated the possibility of long-term declines in lead output that could be supplanted by slow but steady growth in copper demand. Entering the mid-1990s, the United States was expected to continue to play a leading role in high-tech, high-profit alloy and specialty metal markets—areas where it enjoys important advantages over low-cost commodity-metal manufacturers in emerging nations.

The U.S. market for aluminum reached 5.5 million metric tons in 2003, a decrease of .2 percent from the previous year. The market was forecast to grow to 6.1 million metric tons in 2008, growing 6.7 percent.

Canada. Canada's nonferrous metal industry, the third largest in the mid-1990s, was intertwined with that of the United States. In fact, Canada is a major exporter of metals to the United States and is heavily influenced by that market. In 1993, for example, Canada exported roughly 30 percent of its aluminum to its southern neighbor. Canada exported much of its metal to other countries as well, particularly the Netherlands. The country also was a major player in the global copper and lead industries, and was second only to the CIS in the manufacture of both slab zinc and refined nickel—much of Canada's nickel and zinc was consumed in the United States, which produces less than 10 percent as much nickel as Canada and about 50 percent as much zinc. In the long-term, some analysts contended, Canadian producers should benefit from healthy reserves of natural resources in major metal categories, as well as access to the giant U.S. metal market.

Commonwealth of Independent States. The business dynamics in the Commonwealth of Independent States were significantly different than those in North America throughout the 1990s. The Soviet Union aggressively expanded its metal-production capacity entering the mid-1980s, a move that established it as the second-largest world manufacturer of aluminum and a key supplier of copper, zinc, lead, and other metals. The country continued to boost capacity through much of the 1980s, largely in an effort to feed its massive military machine. For example, the country produced about 2.4 million metric tons of aluminum on an annual basis during the 1980s, nearly 90 percent of which was consumed for military and aerospace purposes. Aluminum consumption peaked in the late 1980s at around 3 million metric tons, and then plummeted to just 500,000 metric tons by 1997. Likewise, copper shipments fell from more than 1 one billion metric tons in 1987 to less than 900,000 tons in 1990. Output of aluminum, lead, zinc, and other metals mirrored that slump.

The breakdown of the Soviet metal industry was hastened by the disintegration of the country's long-established political establishment in 1991. Production volumes of most metal types plunged as the region spiraled into industrial decay. Metal manufacturers reeled under drastic reductions in demand from core military and aerospace industries at the same time that global metal prices (particularly for aluminum) were turbulent. Indeed, the CIS attempted to raise cash in the early 1990s by dumping both ferrous and nonferrous metals into export markets. European and North American countries, among others, tried to stem the tide with import quotas on CIS-produced metals. Other setbacks for CIS producers included huge jumps in energy prices—a major productivity influence in metal manufacturing—and a deteriorating internal industrial infrastructure. Medium-term prospects for the CIS metal industry were dismal in the late 1990s, and little recovery was expected before the early 2000s.

Other Countries. With the exception of North America and the CIS, the nonferrous metals industry remains relatively fragmented. Specific market segments typically are led by a few countries that may or may not be considered developed nations. National output is primarily determined by available raw materials, and/or the level of domestic consumption. The latter factor accounts for the influence of Japan and western European nations in the industry. Japan's access to locally mined materials is essentially non-existent. However, it was second only to the United States in copper consumption in the early 1990s, and had created the third largest copper-refining industry in the world. Germany, too, was not a leader in the mining of bauxite (for making aluminum) and copper, but it produced about 634 million metric tons of primary aluminum in 1999 and about 696,000 of copper. Despite a dearth of raw materials, Norway was a leading producer of primary aluminum at about 800 million metric tons of output.

Despite their technological and manufacturing prowess, the competitiveness of developed nations—with the exception of the United States and Canada—is generally reduced by dependence on outside sources of raw materials. In addition, producers in developed nations are constrained by labor and environmental restrictions that are significantly stronger than those in developing regions. As a result, several emerging industrial nations have been able to tap large or high-quality natural resources to assume leading roles in specific industry segments. A notable example of this during the 1990s was Chile. Chilean manufacturers accounted for nearly 20 percent of all mined copper in 1999, making it one of the world's 10 leading metal-producing nations. Chile also aggressively expanded output capacity in the mid-1990s through the development of new mines. Similarly, Brazil was the world's fifth largest manufacturer of refined aluminum.

Among the fastest growing of the leading metal-producing nations in the 1990s was China. China's vast supply of natural resources, combined with its rapidly developing industrial infrastructure, made it a potential contender for future global metal industry leadership. China's output of aluminum, for example, surged from about 400,000 metric tons annually in the mid-1980s to approximately 2.8 million tons by 1999. During the 1990s, China's copper production jumped by 116 percent, from 561 million metric tons in 1990 to 1,210 in 1999. China also was the leading global producer of tin. Gross national product (GNP) gains of more than 10 percent annually during the early 1990s boded well for the country's long-term metal industry expansion, although growth slowed to a more moderate 9 percent—three times the U.S. rate of growth—by the late 1990s. By 2003, China was rapidly expanding its presence in the global aluminum market, importing 600,000 tons of aluminum scrap annually and exporting millions of pounds of extrusions. In the three-year period between 1999 and 2002, Chinese exports of aluminum extrusions increased from 9 million pounds annually to 80 million. By 2004, China's aluminum production reached 3.37 million metric tons.

FURTHER READING

"Alcan Sees Europe Outpacing US." *American Metal Market,* 11 August 2003.

"Aluminum Castings." *Aluminum International Today,* May-June 2004.

"Aluminum in France, Germany, UK, US." *Euromonitor,* August 2004. Available from http://www.majormarketprofiles.com.

"Aluminum Prices Strong Until 2005." *Aluminum International Today,* May-June 2004.

"Awaiting Its Surge." *Recycling Today,* November 2003.

Bresnick, Julie. "PD Expects Copper Use to Grow in China, US." *American Metal Market,* 29 April 2004.

Brooks, David. "Still a Waiting Game for Aluminum Extruders." *American Metal Market,* 12 March 2003.

"The Bull May Tire Soon." *Purchasing,* 2 June 2005.

China's Primary Aluminum Production, International Aluminum Institute. 20 June 2005. Available from http://www.world-aluminium.org.

Cole, Kevin. "Metal's Future Remain Murky." *Fabricator,* 29 January 2004. Available from http://www.thefabricator.com.

Dunn, Brian. "New Dawn on Horizon for Nonferrous Metals." *American Metal Market,* 21 January 2002.

"FACE Call for Immediate Abolition of 6 Percent EU Duty." *Aluminum International Today,* May-June 2004.

"Gulf States: Local Aluminum Production to Double by 2010." *IPR Strategic Business Information Database,* 16 December 2003.

"International Trade Statistics." 2003. Available from http://www.wto.org.

"Investors May Depart." *Purchasing,* 2 June 2005.

"Keeping Pace with Demand." *Aluminum International Today,* May-June 2004.

Pisculli, Alysson. "Economic Cooling Has Copper Set to Fly South." *American Metal Market,* 11 June 2003.

———. "Refined Copper Surplus Shrinks as Usage Rises, Output Declines." *American Metal Market,* 12 February 2003.

Primary Aluminum Production, International Aluminum Institute. 20 June 2005. Available from http://www.world-aluminium.org.

Taylor, Brian. "The Right Price." *Recycling Today,* January 2004.

"U.S. Primary Aluminum Production." *American Metal Market Online,* 2004. Available from http://www.amm.com.

SIC 3310

NAICS 331111

STEEL MILLS

Steelmakers operate blast or electric furnaces to create raw iron and steel. From crude steel the same manufacturer may produce any number of intermediate or finished steel products. Examples of industry output include:

- hot-rolled steel products
- cold-rolled steel products
- iron and steel bars
- steel ingots
- stainless steel
- iron and steel forgings
- steel wire and nails
- steel pipes and tubes

Companies that produce steel castings are discussed separately under **Iron and Steel Foundries,** and those that process nonferrous ores into metals are covered under **Metals, Primary Smelting and Refining of Nonferrous Metals.**

INDUSTRY SNAPSHOT

By the mid-2000s, China, Japan, and the United States were the top three steel producers worldwide. In early 2005 the OECD reported that world steel market had grown 8.8 percent in 2004 to reach about 935 million tons of finished products, and that steel demand increased 7.5 percent of 22 million tons over the previous year. World crude steel production passed the 1 billion ton mark for the first time ever in 2004, up 84 million tons over 2003. World trade in steel was up 4.4 percent for the year in 2004, reaching a record 263 million tons. However, steel was seeing a huge increase in both demand and price in the mid-2000s, largely due to market growth in China.

According to the International Iron and Steel Institute, China's steel production reached 270 million metric tons in 2004, an increase of 22.5 percent over 2003 levels. Steel prices were seeing corresponding increases, rising from 30 percent to 50 percent from the end of 2003 to the middle of 2004 alone. The Chinese demand for steel appeared to be growing exponentially for the foreseeable future. There was a 24 percent decline in steel imports by China in 2004 while Chinese steel exports doubled to more than 17 million metric tons.

At the close of 2003, according to *European Report,* Japan was leading the world in steel packaging recycling with 86 percent, followed by South Africa with 63 percent. More steel was being recycled in Europe than ever before, with about 60 percent of total steel packaging recycled. Belgium recycled the most steel packaging with 93 percent, and Portugal recycled the least with 28 percent. Australia's total was 59 percent, and the United States recycled 43 percent.

ORGANIZATION AND STRUCTURE

Steel is manufactured using iron ore, coke, and limestone. Typically, the coke (a high-grade coal distillate) is used as fuel to heat a blast furnace. The coke emits carbon monoxide as it burns, as does the limestone. The ore melts, creating a molten iron and carbon mixture. A basic oxygen furnace (BOF) is used to supply super-heated air, which removes impurities and converts the molten iron into steel. The steel is usually cast into ingots, which are later formed into standard shapes—usually billets, slabs, or blooms. A more advanced production technique, "continuous casting," bypasses ingots. These slabs, billets, and blooms are processed at mills into rails, rolls, plates, tubes, bars, or other more marketable products. Those units are used by automobile companies, for example, to create parts or body panels for vehicles.

The conventional steelmaking technique just described is referred to as integrated manufacturing because it integrates all aspects of the process, including melting the iron ore. In the 1990s, an increasing number of steelmakers, particularly in the United States and other highly developed nations, were utilizing minimills. Minimill producers, or non-integrated steel manufacturers, start with scrap iron or steel, rather than iron ore. They use electric arc furnaces (EAFs), rather than blast and basic-oxygen furnaces (BOFs), to continuously cast blooms and billets. Most minimills produce a limited number of finished products, such as rods and bars used in light construction, but some non-integrated manufacturers also produce plates, sheets, pipes, and other steel goods.

Many integrated steel mills can produce millions of tons of steel annually, while minimills typically churn out between 100,000 and 500,000 tons. However, minimills may generate as much as 10 times more profit per ton of steel produced. A primary advantage of minimills is that they do not have to be located near supplies of iron ore. Instead, they are commonly constructed near primary customers, thus significantly reducing shipping costs. That advantage, when combined with high-tech manufacturing techniques such as use of EAFs, allows non-integrated producers in industrialized nations to compete aggressively with low-cost importers for domestic market share.

Regardless of their production techniques, most steel companies manufacture a category of steel called carbon steel. Carbon steels account for roughly 90 percent of global output. They contain relatively few alloying additives and their high degree of malleability makes them ideal for general purpose uses such as automobile bodies, structural steel for buildings, and shipbuilding. The remainder of industry output is categorized in one of four segments: alloy, stainless, tool, and high-strength low alloy (HSLA). Alloy steels, the second largest industry product segment by output volume, contain various alloying materials such as vanadium, silicon, manganese, and copper. They offer characteristics such as corrosion resistance, high electrical or heat conductivity, and greater strength, qualities that make alloy steel useful for a variety of applications ranging from tools and electrical components to machine parts and armor.

Stainless steel, the third biggest product group, includes chromium/nickel alloy steels that resist corrosion and may be stronger or more heat resistant than lower-grade steels. Large markets include aerospace, medical device, and plumbing-related industries. Tool steels, the fourth industry segment, integrate molybdenum, tungsten, or other elements to produce ultra-hard alloys commonly used in tool and metal-working industries. Similarly, HSLA steels, the most recent family of steel products, use relatively small amounts of alloying materials, but are specially processed for hardness and light weight. Such steels are popular in applications where strength and weight factors are crucial, such as freight cars. In general, newly industrialized nations are more likely to focus solely on the production of low-tech carbon steel, while established western and Japanese manufacturers are more likely to compete in alloy, stainless, tool, and HSLA steel markets.

Competitive Structure. Because of high start-up costs and slow-growth markets, the steel industry is a difficult one to enter. In traditional steel-manufacturing regions—such as western Europe, the Russian Federation, the United States, and Japan—industries are highly consolidated with only a few manufacturers controlling the lion's share of the market in their respective countries. In general, new entrants to the industry are minimill producers, which incur start-up costs about one-quarter as great as those required to open an integrated facility.

Entry barriers are generally lower in emerging nations, where steel demand rose in the 1980s and early 1990s. Still, most newcomers were fully integrated and thus had to secure hefty sources of capital to build steel mills. Other obstacles have varied by country. In some nations, such as South Korea, access to the industry has traditionally been limited by the national government. Likewise, Brazil's steel industry was effectively controlled by the government until the early 1990s, when privatization ensued. In other regions, such as eastern Europe and China, additional hurdles have included the lack of a dependable distribution and supply infrastructure.

On an international level, the steel industry is characterized by fierce competition, not only among individual producers but also among different nations. In fact, the industry has traditionally been heavily influenced by government control for reasons relating primarily to defense and economic stability. In addition, because carbon steel is essentially a commodity, companies compete primarily on price. To help their producers compete internationally, governments in virtually all steelmaking nations support domestic producers through measures such as subsidies or restrictions on imports. By subsidizing steel exported to international markets a government can help its producers establish a presence and boost market share. Likewise, by instituting tariffs or stringent quality controls on imported material, government can help the same companies maintain dominance of their domestic market.

Agreements and Standards. Widespread government support of domestic steel producers has contributed to an environment conducive to trade wars that feature dumping practices (selling steel below cost), sanctions, and retaliatory import restrictions and tariffs. To reduce friction and enhance free markets, several countries have entered agreements with other nations to help ensure free trade and/or regional cooperation. For example, the North American Free Trade Agreement (NAFTA) reduced trade barriers between the United States, Canada, and Mexico. Several European countries have also pursued agreements or acquiesced to regional regulatory bodies in an effort to drop trade barriers and to cooperate against export threats from other regions. The European Commission, for example, works to enhance free steel trade on the continent, among other objectives. Similarly, European Union (EU) members signed bilateral consensus agreements (BCAs) in the late 1980s that eliminated regional tariffs, subsidies, and other government supports.

Several nations in the mid-1990s continued to seek a multilateral steel agreement (MSA) that would effectively put all steelmaking nations on a level playing field. International MSA negotiations failed in 1992, but several nations continued to pursue the effort. The United States was a strong proponent of the MSA because it has battled anticompetitive foreign trade practices for several years in an effort to revive its ailing steel sector. In addition to various tariffs and restraints, the United States, like several other nations, has diminished the effects of other nations' dumping practices by turning to the International Trade Commission (ITC). The ITC has the power to assess dumping penalties and to restrict specific trade initiatives that it deems unfair.

A final major regulatory influence is national environmental law. Japan and other industrialized nations must comply with environmental laws that designate, among other guidelines, the amount and type of pollutants that may be released during the manufacturing process. Steel producers in the United States, for example, invested a combined sum of more than US$100 million annually in pollution control devices for their factories. Environmental legislation was even more costly in certain western European nations. In contrast, manufacturers in less industrialized nations benefited from comparatively weak domestic regulations or slipshod enforcement.

The dominant international steel industry standard in the mid-1990s was ISO 9000, a set of quality standards created for various industries by the International Standardization Organization (ISO). The goal of ISO 9000 is to provide a quality certification program that will ensure that members can meet specific quality standards. Certification was considered a relatively expensive and difficult endeavor in the mid-1990s, but ISO 9000 was gradually being adopted by steel producers throughout the world, particularly in the most industrialized nations. Accreditation or certification was carried out by regional bodies such as the Dutch Council for Certification, the British Studies Intelligeneer (BSI), and Underwriter's Laboratories of the United States.

Background and Development

Steelmaking dates back to fourteenth-century Europe; however, modern mass-production methods were not developed until the mid-nineteenth century in Britain. Simple forges were originally used to heat iron ore and charcoal in a box for several days. Furnaces gradually increased in size, and steelmakers eventually learned to force air over the molten iron to speed the process. Sir Henry Bessemer, a British inventor, is credited with developing the Bessemer Furnace in 1855. It was the first device to refine molten iron with blasts of oxygen. The invention languished until bulk production of oxygen commenced later in the century.

Demand for steel surged with the onset of the Industrial Revolution in Britain. As the Revolution spread to other European nations and the United States in the late nineteenth century, global steel production soared. The open-hearth furnace was developed, an invention that allowed producers to use scrap iron and produce higher-grade steel. Factors spurring industry growth during the early 1900s included new automobile markets, steel-framed construction, and industrialization in Japan and the Russian Federation. Massive demand for steel during World War II spurred giant increases in production capacity and steelmaking technology.

Shortly after World War II, the basic oxygen furnace was developed in Austria. It eventually replaced open-hearth technology, although the latter remained dominant until the 1970s. BOFs forced pure oxygen into the molten iron mixture, allowing furnaces to create a unit of steel in less than one-quarter the time required by open-hearth furnaces. Another pivotal development was the use of electric arc furnaces to manufacture carbon steel—EAFs were originally used only to produce stainless and other types of steel. Other important technological breakthroughs during and after World War II related to the use of alloy additives, a development that initiated a new generation of high-performance steel products.

In 1950, following the giant production surge of the previous decade, global steel producers turned out about 190 million metric tons annually. War-ravaged European, Russian, and Japanese industries were rebuilding during this time, so the United States dominated. In the early 1950s the United States produced nearly 60 percent of global steel output. It led production throughout the 1960s and into the 1970s as well, although other regions achieved steady gains. Japan's steel output soared from 5 million metric tons in 1950 to 23 million in 1960, and then to a whopping 93 million by 1970. Similarly, the European Union produced 32 million tons in 1950, 72 million in 1960, and more than 150 million tons in the early 1970s, although some of that gain was attributable to the integration of Great Britain into the EU.

Perhaps the most impressive postwar recovery occurred in the Soviet Union, where steel output rocketed from 27 million tons in 1950 to a staggering 116 million tons in 1970. In 1974 the Soviet Union overtook the United States as the leading producer of steel. Soviet supremacy in the global steel industry marked the end of the dominance of United States and western European manufacturers. This shift in industry dynamics actually started in the late 1960s when steel demand in western nations leveled off. Factors in the early 1970s—oil availability concerns, and recessionary conditions—exacerbated this trend. At the same time, steel substitutes such as plastics and aluminum rapidly supplanted steel in many applications, including those in the automobile industry. Industry participants also claimed that regulations related to labor practices and pollution control constrained productivity and competitiveness.

Steel output in most industrialized western nations peaked in the 1970s before dwindling, or stagnating, throughout the 1980s. Total global steel output fluctuated around 800 million tons during those two decades, but the share of the market served by the seven largest steel-producing western nations plummeted from 54 percent to just 37 percent. Even Japan's steel output waned after the early 1970s, despite a common perception in western nations that Japan's steel industry was robust. Between the early 1970s and 1990 the total tonnage of steel manufactured by the United States, the European Economic Community (EEC), and Japan slipped from about 420 million tons to about 325 million. Meanwhile, the Soviet Union continued to stretch its lead, increasing output to a peak of 163 million tons in 1988.

More notable than advances in the Soviet Union and some Eastern Bloc countries during the 1970s and 1980s was the rise of steel industries in several third world and newly industrialized countries. Production in Latin America, for instance, shot up from 19 million tons in 1975 to about 30 million tons in 1980. Overall, steel production in emerging countries grew from less than 75 million tons annually in the 1970s to about 175 million tons annually by the late 1980s. The heftiest of these new contenders included South Korea, Brazil, and China. However, numerous countries chipped away at the aggregate global steel market, including nations in the Middle East, Asia, South America, and Africa. Besides labor and regulatory advantages, those producers typically benefited from newer production facilities in comparison to their more industrialized counterparts, as well as better access to regions where steel demand was increasing.

Steelmaking industries in western Europe and the United States staggered as industrializing nations infringed on both the domestic and the ever-growing export markets. The percentage of total steel exported had shot up from 10 percent in 1950 to more than 25 percent by the late 1980s. Battered producers scrambled to sustain profitability and many of them eventually folded or merged with their domestic peers. Throughout the 1980s, many of the world's largest steel companies took drastic actions to reinvent themselves and revive their competitiveness. They automated factories, slashed payrolls by as much as 50 percent or more, integrated new technology, and focused on developing high-performance steels that could compete with proliferating synthetic and aluminum substitutes. By the late 1980s the efforts began to show tangible results.

Critical to the revival of steel industries in the United States, Europe, and even Japan in the late 1980s and early 1990s, were new steel manufacturing technologies, particularly minimills and continuous casting. Minimills sprang up in the United States during the 1960s and by the late 1970s had begun to compete with large steel producers. Their great efficiency and technological superiority were highlighted during periods of industry turbulence such as the latter part of the 1980s. By the early 1990s, minimills accounted for more than 35 percent of all steel output in the United States. Likewise, the share of U.S. steel made with continuous casting jumped from 15 percent to 85 percent by the early 1990s, mimicking Japan's steel sector. European producers eventually followed the lead of their North American and Japanese counterparts.

Despite temporary setbacks brought on by its 1997 fiscal crisis, Asia remains the world's premier steel-producing center, supplying more than 35 percent of the world's crude steel in 2000 alone. China, Japan, and South Korea dominated the industry, and combined they manufactured one-third of global steel. China's booming economy surged on, scarcely affected by the crisis. However, production and consumption dipped sharply in both Japan and South Korea beginning in late 1998. One result of the Asian crisis was to bring home the advantages of consolidation. In October 2000 the region's two main competitors and the largest steel firms in the world, Nippon Steel and POSCO, announced a strategic alliance. NKK Corp and Kawasaki Steel also announced merger plans. Analysts at the Nomura Securities Company forecasted that by 2005 Japan's steel trade would be controlled by two groups, with Nippon Steel on one side and NKK-Kawasaki on the other.

After languishing in the early and mid-1990s, Europe's steel industry—both in the east and the west—began to recover in the latter part of the decade. Demand in places such as Germany, Western Europe's largest producer, rose as key markets such as the auto industry stepped up business. Consolidation of the European Union's steel industry was well underway by mid-2001 when five companies were responsible for some 60 percent of output, up from 23 percent in 1993. Eastern Europe, while showing important gains, continued to perform unevenly as its economies grappled with the free-market transition. Poland's steel production, for example, experienced healthy increases in the mid-1990s, but plunged 11.5 percent between 1998 and 1999. In 2000, with growth from 8.8 to 10.5 million metric tons, the country finally seemed to be heading toward a recovery. Steel production in the leading Eastern European nations—Poland, the Czech Republic, Slovakia and Romania—grew by more than 11.5 percent from 1999 to 2000, reaching 25.2 million metric tons. Among the former Soviet states, Russia performed best in 2000. It finally seemed to emerge from the slump it suffered after the disintegration of the Soviet Union in 1991 and lasted until 1998. In 2000 it surpassed its 1993 levels for the first time, reaching 59.1 million metric tons, an increase of 14.7 percent from 1999. The Ukraine also continued its strong performance. Its 31.4 million metric ton output in 2000 was 14 percent higher than 1999 figures. Despite the apparently strong showing by CIS nations, questions remained concerning the ability of their relatively old facilities to compete in the world market.

North America, on the other hand, remained a strong steel market in 2000, driven by a strong U.S. economy. Overall, North American steel output reached 128.9 million metric tons, three-quarters of which was produced by the United States. That was slightly off the record-setting 130.1 million metric tons produced in North America in 1997. Consumption of steel in North America during 2000 also reached historic highs. In fact, supply fell short of demand during 2000 for some steel products in the United States. The United States led all other nations in steel imports in 1999 with 32.7 million metric tons, which equaled nearly one-third of the steel the country actually produced. Despite general agreement throughout the U.S. industry on the pressing need for widespread consolidation, no companies seemed willing to take the plunge. A joint statement by U.S. Steel and Nucor—the largest integrated producer and the largest minimill producer, respectively—supporting the cut-off of government subsidies to steel facilities unable to compete on the open market in quality or price was seen as a first sign that the industry was embracing consolidation. Still, there was concern that the longer the inevitable was postponed, the more precarious U.S. industry's position would be in the world market. The United States had long produced far less steel than it consumed—estimates of the extra steel needed ranged from 15 to 28 million tons. At least in the beginning, consolidation and plant closings would serve foreign steelmakers, as well as the U.S. industry.

Combining resources was seen not only as a means of giving steelmakers access to the capital needed to invest in new technologies, it was also a way of trimming facilities and firms that were not performing with maximum efficiency, and reducing competition that kept profit margins razor thin. Between 1990 and 1998, the global steel industry witnessed mergers worth about US$66 billion—a pittance compared to industries such as petroleum refining. The trend continued to pick up speed in the 2000s. Significant mergers in both Europe and Asia were planned or already under review by regulatory agencies by late 2001. Determined to rationalize its steel industry, Asia pressed ahead with strategic alliances, mergers, and joint ventures. Although the need for consolidation in the bloated U.S. market was acknowledged almost universally, at the beginning of 2002 no significant steps toward it had been taken.

The rise of e-commerce in the late 1990s ushered a minor revolution into the usually conservative steel business. In the mid-1990s, private, Web-based steel exchanges, such as Metal Suppliers, MetalSite, Metal Network Exchange Services (MNSX), and eSteel, were founded. Each functioned differently. Some allowed producers to auction off their steel to the highest bidder; others acted as online forums where buyers and sellers could hammer out terms; still others gave sellers the ability to post quantities and prices. The sites charged a fee per transaction, but by the early 2000s large steelmakers began taking control of online distribution and foregoing fees. Bethlehem Steel, Bermingham Steel, Nucor Corp., and Weirton made plans to set up private exchanges on their company Web sites. The private exchanges were not left entirely out of the picture. The most enterprising continued to sell their expertise to steel companies as Web consultants.

CURRENT CONDITIONS

Despite rising output and increasing sales, world steel prices fell steadily between 1999 and 2001 at an annual rate of 2.7 percent, according to CRU International, a metals consulting company. It was a trend that could not continue. "Ultimately," a CRU report stated, "prices must bear some relationship to costs." Beginning in 2002, however, steel prices began to rise again. According to *Fortune,* U.S. hot-rolled steel, for example, rose in price from US$260 per ton in June 2003 to US$410 per ton by April 2004. U.S. steel was protected by tariffs in 2002, which were lifted a year and a half later, and in 2003 U.S. steel production was about 101 million metric tons. By 2004, the world steel capacity was nearly 1.2 billion metric tons and expected to increase to more than 1.3 billion per year in 2006.

Demand was also rising in the 2000s, particularly from the booming Chinese market. According to the International Iron and Steel Institute, China's steel demand was up to about 282 million metric tons in 2004, an increase of 11 percent over 2003, and was expected to rise another 10.7 percent in 2005. The cost of steel production was also rising, particularly in the United States, despite the lifting of the 2002 tariffs. According to *Automotive News,* steel prices increased as much as 50 percent from December 2003 to June 2004. Prices of steel were subject to change between the time of agreement and the time of shipment. Scrap steel alone was priced at about US$310 per ton in early 2004. The automotive industry was also a major consumer of hot-rolled steel; General Motors alone required 24,000 tons of steel per day.

Minimills, which produce steel products from recycled materials rather than raw ores, continue to deliver better fiscal results than integrated mills, which create steel from raw minerals. This stems in part from minimills' use of scrap metals. Scrap prices tend to fluctuate favorably with crude steel prices so that when steel prices are down, minimills do not pay high prices for their raw materials.

RESEARCH AND TECHNOLOGY

Research and technology played a heightened role in the global steel industry going into the mid-1990s. Scientific advances were vital to developed nations in their efforts to maintain market share in the face of challenges from low-cost foreign competitors. Improvements in minimill production, for instance, have been essential to producers in western Europe, Japan, and North America. A major drawback of minimills before the late 1980s was their inability to efficiently produce sheet and strip steel. However, SMS Chloemann-Sieman AG (or SMS Concast) of Germany developed a "thin-slab" casting technique that allowed minimills to continuously cast steel in thicknesses of less than two inches. This important development, combined with emerging strip-casting technology, has allowed minimills to compete in the last bastion of the integrated mills, sheet and strip steel, which is preferred by many industries (such as the automobile sector) because it is easier to process.

The first minimill to integrate large-scale, thin-slab casting was Nucor Corp.'s Crawfordsville, Indiana, plant in the United States. The plant began turning out sheet steel in 1989 under the watchful eye of the worldwide steel industry. Other important thin-slab minimill operations commenced shortly thereafter in Germany and Italy. The initial success of those operations resulted in plans for similar thin-slab minimills in the mid-1990s. Nucor, for example, opened a plant in 1992 that was capable of thin-slab casting of about 1 million tons of steel annually. It subsequently announced plans to double that capacity by year-end 1994. Luna ECR (endless roll casting) was a technique introduced at an Italian mill by Danielli in 2000 that could process 500,000 tons of bar. Danielli was working on refining the process to make it economical for specialty steels such as stainless steel.

Related advancements included efforts to develop both thin-slab and thin-strip minimill processes that reduce finished steel contaminants inherent in the production of steel from scrap. Researchers hope that advances in this area will allow minimills to compete with integrated mills in automobile and other major industries that require high-grade flat steel. Notable techniques being developed or implemented in the mid-1990s that promised to increase the quality and efficiency of thin casting included: in-line strip production (ISP), which was being pioneered in Italy; integrated compact mill (ICM) innovations under development by Voest-Alpine of Austria; and the Tippins-Samsung Process (TSP).

Computers promised to bring down costs and pollution and improve the quality of steel produced. In the mid-1990s, Usinor in France introduced SACHEM, a computer system that runs blast furnaces. The system continuously monitors and processes thousands of factors in the furnaces, including temperature, water pressure, and oxygen supply. Not only did SACHEN produce better steel, it also extended the life of by more than a third, decreased the generation of greenhouse gases, and reduced costs by US$1.55 per ton. The European Union was particularly willing to introduce such new, multi-effect processes.

In addition to production-related advancements, research and technology efforts produced better grades of steel in the mid-1990s. Carbon steel still comprised the vast majority of industry output. However, alloy, stainless, tool, and HSLA steels offered higher profit margins and better opportunities for growth, especially for industrialized nations. Steelmakers tried to protect existing markets by offering low-weight, high-strength, malleable, corrosion-resistant steels that were better than existing plastics or aluminum. Other industry observers have pointed to innovations such as high-performance steel coatings made with synthetic materials as keys to future industry growth. Indeed, such steel coating registered marked sales gains in the mid-1990s on the strength of potentially vast markets such as the roofing industry. Proponents contended that coated steel roofing systems installed in the mid-1990s could last 40 years with minimal maintenance.

In the mid-2000s, research in Japan's Steel Research Center was focused on eliminating "creep," which is the natural change in the makeup and structure of metal over time, particularly when it is subjected to pressure or heat. A type of steel was being manufactured that was able to withstand such deformation, making the steel product last considerably longer. The new steel was fortified with carbonitride nanoparticles, which filled in the gaps between steel molecules in order to hold them in place and form stronger bonds. The technology was in the early stages by late 2003, as the new steel still had to prove its flexibility and corrosion resistance.

INDUSTRY LEADERS

Arcelor SA. With annual output of 45 million metric tons and 2003 sales of US$32.5 billion, Arcelor was the undisputed steel champion. Formed by a three-way merger between Arbed of Luxembourg, Usinor or France, and Aceralia of Spain, Arcelor was based in Luxembourg.

The 1997 acquisition of Aristrain, a medium-sized European steelmaker, vaulted Luxembourg's Arbed SA from number seven to the world's third-largest steel company by volume. Its combined holdings manufactured some 24.1 million metric tons of crude steel in 2000. Although it had a diverse product line, the company was heavily involved in supplying Europe's auto industry with steel.

France's Usinor SA was the sixth-ranked steel manufacturer with 2000 output of 21 million metric tons. The company was created in 1988 by the merger of French steel giants Usinor and Sacilor, both of which had been government-owned since the early 1980s when the French industry was in crisis. As a private company, Sacilor dated back to the eighteenth century, and Usinor was formed from a 1948 merger of two French steel companies. By the early 1980s the two were the pillars of the French steel industry in terms of production, but they faced high debt and poor market conditions. The French government intervened and acquired both companies. The subsequent merger, combined with later acquisitions, resulted in a company that produced more than 90 percent of France's steel in the early 1990s. The company produced its steel primarily through integrated mills. Usinor-Sacilor remained government-owned until 1995, when it re-privatized, and it was renamed to Usinor SA in 1997. The company extended its global reach during the early and mid-1990s by investing heavily in both European and overseas steelmaking operations. It also entered into numerous joint ventures with other companies to develop new steelmaking technologies.

Mittal Steel Company N.V. The family-owned and run Netherlands-based Mittal Steel was created in late 2004 with the merger of the public company Ispat International (70 percent owned by the Mittal family) and the Antilles-based LNM Holdings (100 percent owned by the Mittals). The combined company became of the world's largest steel companies, producing 42.8 million metric tons in 2004. Some of the company's leading clients include Ford Motor, General Motors, Maytag and Whirlpool. The company's 2004 sales totaled more than $22 billion while net income stood at $4.7 billion.

With the acquisition of International Steel Group, world steel leader Mittal Steel Company N.V. formed subsidiary Mittal Steel USA and surpassed the United States Steel Corporation in 2004 to become the top U.S. steel mill. Mittal operates 12 manufacturing facilities, primarily in the Midwest. ittal merged ISG's operations with those of its North American subsidiary, Ispat Inland.

Nippon Steel Corporation. Japan's Nippon Steel was third in world steel production in 2004, with about 30 million metric tons produced each year. The company rose to prominence during the post-World War II industrial boom in Japan. By the early 1990s, Nippon was churning out well over US$20 billion worth of steel from eight different iron and steel making plants. Nippon produces its steel primarily through integrated mills. During the late 1980s and early 1990s the company cut costs and overhead in an attempt to remain competitive in the increasingly crowded steel export market. Lackluster performance forced the company to step up those efforts in the early 1990s. The company has likewise attempted to reduce the share of its sales dependent on steel—and it has numerous nonsteel subsidiaries—but as of 2000 steel still accounted for nearly three-quarters of its annual revenues. By the mid-2000s, Nippon was promoting its energy and engineering sectors most heavily. The company posted sales of US$27.7 billion in 2004.

Pohang Iron and Steel Co., Ltd. Producing approximately 31 million tons of crude steel per year in 2003, POSCO of South Korea reported US$14.9 billion in revenues. POSCO enjoyed a rapid ascent to the front ranks of international steel producers. It was formed in 1968 with the help of the South Korean government. In late 2000, under pressure from the United States, POSCO was fully privatized when the Korea Development Bank sold the government's last seven percent share in the company. At the same time, the Korean government announced it was doing away with restrictions on foreign ownership in POSCO. The company's production facilities are among the most technologically advanced and efficient in the world. POSCO has ventures in the United States, China, and other countries. By 2003, in fact, POSCO was exporting approximately 2.5 million tons of steel to China, and was planning to invest well over US$1 billion in China operations by 2006. It formed a strategic venture with Japan's Nippon Steel in 2000.

ThyssenKrupp AG. Another product of a late 1990s merger, ThyssenKrupp was formed through the merger of Thyssen AG and Friedrich Krupp AG, both leaders in Germany's steel industry. Thyssen was founded in 1891. It supplied the German war machine during both world wars, although output was severely curtailed following World War II. The company posted a steady recovery, however, and its steel output peaked in 1974 at about 17 million tons. As the German steel industry slumped during the late 1970s and 1980s, Thyssen diversified into other industries. By 2001, Thyssen was reporting annual sales of US$34.5 billion. ThyssenKrupp AG had 2004 sales of nearly US$48.5 billion.

Corus Group plc. The Corus Group originated from British Steel's acquisition of the Dutch firm Koninklijke Hoogovens. British Steel itself grew out of the 1967 privatization of the British steel industry, which saw the merger of 14 U.K. firms. With nearly US$17.9 billion in 2004 sales, Corus produces a variety of steel products, which it sells in large part to the auto and construction industries. Most of Corus' sales are made to nations of the European Union.

MAJOR COUNTRIES IN THE INDUSTRY

China. Advances by China's steel industry during the 1980s and 1990s catapulted it to the steel industry's forefront. In the early 1950s China produced only 2 million metric tons of steel annually. With help from the Soviet Union, it increased capacity to about 19 million tons by 1960. After the Soviet Union withdrew in 1960, output plummeted and recovery was slow. By the late 1970s, in fact, China's annual production of steel was less than 25 million tons. Output increased to 40 million tons in 1983, however, as China launched a concerted effort to increase capacity. The government-controlled industry produced 60 million tons of steel by 1989. Output surged to 80 million tons in 1992 and then 89 million tons a year later. By 1996, when it reached 101.2 million metric tons, it surpassed both the United States and Japan in annual production. In 2000 it reached 127.2 million metric tons and by 2004, China produced more than 270 million tons, up 22.5 percent from 2003. Production was expected to reach 340 million tons by 2006, representing 30 percent of total world steel production.

China's steel industry is also much less advanced than those of the leading industrial powers. During the 1980s, in fact, much of the steel-making equipment that China purchased was used equipment from Japan, the United States, and western Europe. With easy access to raw materials and cheap labor—but little scrap—much of China's manufacturing capacity in the early 1990s was attributable to large, integrated, and sometimes antiquated plants that relied on huge numbers of workers (China's largest steel plant, Anshan, employed 220,000 workers in 1990; the entire Japanese steel industry employed fewer workers). In the late 1980s and early 1990s, however, the country began to invest in more advanced facilities that incorporated BOF and continuous casting technology. Observers also noted that while China had been a rising star in global steel, most of the growth resulted from internal demand. China exported only 6 percent of its steel output in 1994, but China's steelmakers increased their share of the international market in later years. Although the Chinese industry remains considerably more fragmented than those of other leading countries, in the late-1990s China took the first steps to rationalize its sprawling steel industry. The results were positive. Between 1997 and 2000, China's leading firm, Shanghai Baosteel, jumped from nineteenth place in world rankings to tenth.By 2004, China's steel exports declined 24 percent while Chinese steel exports doubled to more than 17 million tons.

Japan. With approximately 10.6 percent of global production in 2004, Japan was in the number two spot in world steel production. Prior to World War II, Japan's steel industry had been among the world's largest. After the war, however, national steel output plummeted to a puny 5 million metric tons. Japan gradually rebuilt its industrial base, boosting production to 23 million tons by 1960 and then to more than 90 million tons by 1970. Industry output and employment peaked during the early 1970s at about 120 million tons annually and 350,000 workers, respectively. Like other industrialized nations, Japan's steel output gradually shrank—to a low of 97 million tons in 1983—in the wake of dormant market growth and increased competition from industrializing nations. Japan's domestic demand remained flat in 1998 and 1999, only picking up in 2000 when Japanese steel consumption jumped from 68.9 million metric tons to 76.1 million metric tons. In 2004, Japan steel production reached 112.7 million metric tons.

Unlike steel producers in the United States and Europe, Japanese manufacturers benefited from several factors in the 1980s. Massive growth in the domestic production of automobiles and other consumer and industrial goods pushed Japanese steel production upward to around 100 million tons and even surged as high as 110 million tons in 1990. Although Japan fared much better than its industrialized peers during the 1980s, it still suffered from outside competitive pressures and waning domestic demand. By the late 1980s Japanese steelmakers had clearly lost much of their productivity advantage and regional competition proliferated. Steel imports rose but still accounted for only 7 percent of domestic steel consumption by the early 1990s. At the same time, though, a steadily rising yen hurt export demand and the nation's economy slumped into an ugly recession, leaving domestic steelmakers battered.

Japanese steel output hit 101.6 million metric tons in 1995 and 104.5 million metric tons in 1997, just before the Asian financial crisis hit. By 1999 output had decreased to 94.2 million metric tons. Ailing producers continued scrambling to sustain profitability. Since the mid-1980s, in fact, most companies had embarked on streamlining programs that included consolidation of blast-furnace operations, installation of new equipment, and reductions in labor costs—industry employment in Japan fell from 459,000 in 1970 to less than 200,000 in 1999. Cost-cutting efforts continued in the early 1990s as some companies cut into management ranks, reduced production capacity, and stepped up efforts to update mill technology. Looking ahead to the latter part of the 1990s, many Japanese steel producers sought joint ventures or invested in production facilities in China, Thailand, and other countries in the mid-1990s. In the early 2000s, Japanese companies were taking bold steps toward consolidation. Nippon Steel forged a strategic alliance with its erstwhile competitor POSCO. In early 2001 NKK Corp. and Kawasaki Steel Corp., Japan's second and third largest steel makers, respectively, announced a merger—a move that would form the largest steel producer in Japan.

United States. The United States was relegated to third place in terms of industry production following China's mid-1990s ascension. U.S. steel shipments slipped to under 80 million tons in 1991, but a strong manufacturing sector contributed to a rise in output in 1994 and 1995 to roughly 90 million tons. Indeed, the mid-1990s marked a period of tremendous success for U.S. steelmakers, whose shipments peaked in 1997 at 98.5 million metric tons. Production dropped again in 1998 and 1999, going as low as 97.4 million metric tons. The U.S. industry reached 98.9 million metric tons in 2004, up from 93.7 million metric tons in 2003.

The United States dominated global steel production until the early 1970s. Output plummeted, however, from about 120 million tons in 1970 to a discouraging low of 67 million tons in 1982. Inefficient and outdated, U.S. steelmakers embarked on a period of painful restructuring. The workforce was slashed from 521,000 in 1970 to 204,000 in 1990, and 151,000 in 2000. Long-established methodologies and practices were re-examined as well.

While restructuring was an important element of the U.S. steel recovery, the minimill revolution was also vital to the industry's reversal of fortune. By the early 1990s the highly efficient minimills were churning out about 35 percent of all U.S.-made steel. Minimill production continued strongly into the 2000s. TXI Chaparral Steel spent $400 million on a minimill in Petersberg, Virginia, and Ipsco and Steel Dynamics both built new facilities. Nucor completed a plant in Cofield, North Carolina and planned another one in Crawfordsville, Indiana. In fact, Nucor's expansion pushed it past the long-time U.S. industry leader U.S. Steel. The importance of the minimill sector to the U.S. steel resurgence was evidenced by industry statistics. Between 1986 and 1991, for example, U.S. minimills enjoyed sales growth of 66 percent while integrated producers gained only 1 percent. During the same period, employment at minimills jumped 19 percent while employment at integrated facilities dropped 30 percent. Most importantly, U.S. minimills showed an average profit of US$32 per ton during the late 1980s and early 1990s, while integrated producers gleaned a meager US$3 per ton. Armed with such minimill productivity, domestic producers were able to effectively buffet growing threats from low-cost, loosely regulated foreign producers. The U.S. steel industry has hoped to maintain its lead in the conversion to minimill production. It has also expected to focus on the development of high-tech, high-margin steel products intended to open new markets and allow steel to compete with synthetic and metal substitutes.

The Russian Federation. While China's rise during the late 1980s and early 1990s in the international steel industry was a swift one, it was not as dramatic as the decline of the Russian steel industry. Russia remained the fourth largest steel producer in the world in 1997. For most of the 1990s, the country was the world's fourth largest manufacturer of steel, but its annual results were shrinking steadily. In 1999 Germany surpassed Russia in production. By the end of the twentieth century, however, Russia staged a stirring turnaround, putting out 51.5 million metric tons; in 2000 the figure rose again to 59.1 million metric tons. By 2004, Russian production of crude steel stood at 65.6 million metric tons, up from 61.5 million metric tons the previous year.

The downturn in output in the Russian Federation and the other members of the Commonwealth of Independent States (CIS) was the result of a number of factors. A deteriorating industrial infrastructure, skyrocketing energy prices, stifling taxes, weak defense-related demand, and plummeting consumer-related demand all contributed to the country's woes. The Russian government thus turned to privatization and outside financing to update its production facilities, but Russia's steel output had not recovered by the late 1990s. Nonetheless, in 2001 Russia and the Ukraine had a combined 56 million tons of excess production capacity, a discrepancy that resulted in Russia selling steel to developed nations at prices sometimes lower than the cost of production, according to some American firms. Some argued that treaties guaranteeing U.S. purchases of Russian steel should be replaced with aid to develop Russia's domestic steel market.

Germany. Germany slipped from fifth in world steel production in 2004 to sixth, with its 46.4 million metric tons exceeded by South Korea with 47.5 million metric tons. While levels decreased to 40.5 million metric tons in 2002, output was about 44.8 million metric tons by 2003. Germany's steel output peaked in the 1970s at about 60 million tons. Shipments slid to about 40 million tons by the late 1980s. The East German steel sector, stifled for decades by a government-controlled economy, languished. By the late 1980s its steel output had fallen to about 5 million tons annually. In 1991, following reunification, Germany's steel output was about 43 million tons, although the east continued to sag. The German steel industry, although technologically advanced, suffered from extremely high labor costs and chafed under government regulations designed to protect the environment and address other issues. Critics of such regulatory measures contend that the country's competitiveness in relation to other steelmakers declined in the late 1980s and early 1990s as a result of such legislation. Output dwindled going into the mid-1990s, but a surge in prices buoyed profits for many German producers. As in Japan, some German manufacturers were engaged in a period of reorganization in the mid-1990s—eliminating workers, increasing automation, and working to reclaim the former East German steel sector.

FURTHER READING

Bagsarian, Tom. "Beyond Steelmaking." *New Steel,* 1 May 2001.

———. "E-commerce: The Growth of Private Company Exchanges.' *New Steel,* 1 March 2001.

———. "Faster Heats, Fewer Impurities." *New Steel,* 1 April 2001.

———. "Nucor, Ipsco Lead Spending." *New Steel,* 1 September 2000.

———. "The Recovery Accelerates." *Iron Age New Steel,* 1 January 2000.

———. "Strip Casting Gets Serious." *New Steel,* 1 December 2001.

Berry, Bryan. "Restructuring Steel." *New Steel,* 1 August 2001.

Bright Outlook for Steel Industry in 2005-2006 Forecast at OECD/IISI Conference, Organisation for Economic Co-operation and Development. 17 January 2005. Available from http://www.oecd.org.

"Business: Welding Bells: A European Steel Merger." *Economist,* 24 February 2001.

Chang, Peter. "POSCO Doubling Output of Automotive Steel." *Automotive News,* 31 March 2003.

Chappell, Lindsay. "Scrap Steel Prices See Hefty Decline." *Automotive News,* 5 April 2004.

Cheng, Allen T. "Gearing Up for Battle." *Asiaweek,* 22 December 2000.

Cordes, Renee. "Europe's Steelmakers Get Lean and Green." *Business Week,* 19 February 2001.

Draper, Deborah J., ed. *Business Rankings Annual.* Detroit: Thomson Gale, 2004.

"EU/OECD." *European Report,* 6 March 2004.

Furakawa, Tsukasa. "Japanese Steelmakers Map Long-Range Strategies." *American Metal Market International Steel Supplement,* 3 October 2000.

Garvey, Robert A. "Getting Serious About Consolidation." *Iron Age New Steel,* 1 February 2001.

———. "How E-commerce Will Add Value." *New Steel,* 1 November 2000.

Graham-Rowe, Duncan. "How Not to Give Steel the Creeps." *New Scientist,* 19 July 2003.

"Healthy Appetite: As Long as Development Economies Need Steel, the Hunger for Scrap Will Continue." *Recycling Today,* January 2005.

Hogan, William T. S.J. *Minimills and Integrated Mills: A Comparison of Steelmaking in the United States,* Lexington, MA: Lexington Books, 1987.

———. *Steel in the United States: Restructuring to Compete,* Lexington, MA: Lexington Books, 1984.

"Hoover's Company Capsules." 2005. Available from http://www.hoovers.com.

"International Trade Statistics." 2003. Available from http://www.wto.org.

Kosdrosky, Terry. "Suppliers Get Deals to Cushion Rising Steel Prices." *Automotive News,* 28 June 2004.

Marsh, Peter. "Arbed Hopes the World Will Prove Its Oyster." *Financial Times,* 29 March 2000.

"Posco Completes Privatization." *New Steel,* 1 November 2000.

"Posco Looks Beyond the Boom in China to Entrench Position." *Australasian Business Intelligence,* 20 November 2003.

"Prime Time for E-commerce." *New Steel,* 1 August 2000.

Rawson, Randy. "Steel Yourself." *Heating/Piping/Air Conditioning Engineering,* April 2004.

"Recycling." *European Report,* 19 November 2003.

Ritt, Adam. "Endless Casting and Rolling of Bar." *New Steel,* 1 November 2000.

———. "Reversing a Legacy of Poor Returns." *New Steel,* 1 January 2001.

"Semi-Fabricated Steel in France, Germany, UK, US." *Euromonitor,* August 2004. Available from http://www.majormarketprofiles.com.

Serwer, Andy. "This Is Not Your Father's Steel Bubble." *Fortune,* 26 January 2004.

Sherefkin, Robert. "Steel Crisis Drives Supplier to Chapter 11." *Automotive News,* 29 March 2004.

"Specialty Imports Break Record in 2000." *New Steel,* 1 April 2001.

"Stainless: Fewer Players, Faster Growth than Carbon." *New Steel,* 1 December 2001.

"The Table Is Set." *New Steel,* 1 May 2001.

"Usinor, Arbed, Aceralia to Form World's No. 1 Steelmaker." *New Steel,* 1 March 2001.

Wilhelm, Paul J. "Consolidation Will Be Selective and Global." *New Steel,* 1 December 2001.

"Will Euro, Asian Mergers Force U.S. Mills to Act?" *Purchasing,* 3 May 2001.

"World: Steel Output Slows In October 2000." *Metal Bulletin,* 23 November 2000.

"World Steel Production Increases but US Output Slips, IISI Data Shows." *American Metal Market,* 21 June 2005.

World Steel in Figures: 2005. International Iron and Steel Institute. 2005. Available from http://www.worldsteel.org.

Yamaguchi, Yuzo. "Blast Threatens Japan Auto Output." *Automotive News,* 8 September 2003.

MINING

SIC 1220

NAICS 2121

MINING, COAL

Coal mining companies extract lignite, brown coal, Subbituminous coal, bituminous coal, or anthracite from the earth through surface or underground mining techniques. Industry firms may also administer mining operations and off-site preparation plants (also known as cleaning plants and washeries). The industry, particularly in North America, increasingly has touted its reclamation efforts to return soil and landscape to usable condition after all higher grade coal has been mined.

INDUSTRY SNAPSHOT

The global coal industry mines roughly 5 billion tons of material annually. Total recoverable reserves were estimated in the early 2000s at 1.083 trillion tons. Based on the consumption levels of 2004, industry analysts estimated that these reserves might last another 210 years. About 60 percent of recoverable reserves were located in three regions: the United States (25 percent), the Russian Federation (23 percent), and China (12 percent). Another 29 percent was found in Australia, India, Germany, and South Africa.

Despite challenges in some applications and in some areas of the world by other energy sources such as oil and natural gas, coal regained its worldwide reputation as a lower-cost primary fuel at the beginning of the twenty-first century. Global coal consumption through 2025 was expected to grow at a rate of about 1.5 percent a year, according to the U.S. Energy Information Administration (EIA). Areas of growth include Japan, and developing Asian countries where coal has always been regarded as an important source of heat and energy. The United States, where the George W. Bush administration touted coal as an inexpensive answer to the country's costly energy demands, is another growth area. On the other hand, the EIA predicted a drop in use among European and former Soviet Union countries.

Coal fuel supplied 24 percent of global energy needs in 2001, according to the EIA, down significantly from 27 percent in both 1995 and 1985 but slightly higher than 22 percent in 1999. Despite its increasing popularity in India and China, coal's proportion of total energy demand worldwide is expected to fall to 23 percent by 2025. By contrast, in 1950 coal had supplied about 60 percent of the world's energy needs.

India and China were responsible for 36 percent of global coal consumption in 1999, and these two countries alone were expected to account for 67 percent of the increase in demand for coal through 2025. Other countries expected to increase coal consumption markedly by 2020 include South Korea and Taiwan. This anticipated increase in coal consumption led to some optimism on the part of Australian experts who expected that the 2002 estimates of 3.7 billion metric tons annual consumption could substantially increase to 4.2 billion metric tons by 2010, according to *Bloomberg News*.

Most of the coal mined worldwide in 2004 was used to produce electric power, but other major coal applications included those related to iron and steel production and its use in various process industries like cement and textiles. Coal also remained an important source of home heat in many parts of the world.

Early in the twentieth century, North America and Europe were the two leading coal-producing regions. During the mid-twentieth century, though, production volume shifted to Asia, Australia, and South Africa. By the 1990s North American and Western European mining companies represented only an estimated 35 percent of industry output. Though coal deposits are distributed widely across the world, three regions control about 60 percent of coal reserves: the United States, the Russian Federation, and China. Other top coal-producing countries include Australia, India, Germany, and South Africa.

The coal industry near the end of the twentieth century was generally characterized by weak prices, increasing environmental controls, and labor strife; factors especially prevalent in developed nations. Industry success in the most developed regions was also blunted by increasing foreign competition, stagnant demand growth, and taxes on energy consumption. Producers in North America and Western Europe countered by raising productivity, increasing low-cost surface mining, consolidating, and taking advantage of new environmental technologies. Meanwhile, mining companies near economic growth regions like the Pacific Rim enjoyed market expansion and a relatively lenient regulatory climate. Guarded optimism in the industry by 2002 also came from expectations that coal needs by Japan through 2010 could result in more favorable contracts for long-term suppliers.

ORGANIZATION AND STRUCTURE

COAL TYPES

The five grades of mined coal are brown, lignite, sub bituminous, bituminous, and anthracite. Each category differs in moisture content, volatile matter, and amount of fixed carbon. As a result, each is distinguished by factors such as energy produced per unit of weight and the amount of pollutants released during burning.

Brown. Brown coal has an extremely high moisture content, sometimes as great as 60 percent or more. The material is relatively easy to mine and to ignite. However, it only produces around 6 million British thermal units (Btu) per ton, the lowest of all the coal grades. In addition, brown coal is difficult to store because it disintegrates when it is exposed to air and occasionally spontaneously combusts. It also has a high sulfur content, which makes it a major pollutant. Brown coal is most heavily mined in Central and Eastern Europe, although the largest reserves in the world are located in Victoria, Australia.

Lignite. Lignite is similar to brown coal in that it is a brownish-black mineral with a high moisture content, about 30 percent to 40 percent water. It also deteriorates rapidly in air, has a high sulfur content, and is liable to spontaneously combust. Therefore lignite is used mainly to generate electricity in power plants that are located near mines. It was also used in the early 2000s as a substitute for wood in many third-world nations. In contrast to brown coal, lignite may generate 9 to 17 million Btu per ton. The largest lignite deposits in the world are located in the United States and Canada. Lignite is also mined extensively in Europe and the Commonwealth of Independent States (CIS).

Subbituminous. Subbituminous coal is composed of 75 percent to 85 percent carbon and only 15 percent to 25 percent moisture. It produces 16 to 24 million Btu per ton and is used mainly to generate electricity. Its high moisture content and other negative properties make it less desirable than higher coal grades for most applications. Importantly, though, Subbituminous coal contains little sulfur. Furthermore, in some regions of the world, the material is relatively easy to extract through the use of low-cost surface mining techniques. As a result, consumption of this material proliferated in many regions of the world during the late twentieth century.

Bituminous. Bituminous coal, or soft coal, the most common type, is used in a range of applications. It has a deep, dull black appearance. Bituminous coal is composed of 80 percent to 90 percent carbon and about 10 percent to 20 percent moisture, and one ton of bituminous coal typically generates 19 to 30 million Btu. The material has a relatively low sulfur content, which enables it to burn more cleanly than lower grades. Because of its properties, bituminous coal is the principal steam coal used for generating electricity. It is also the primary cooking coal used in the steel-making process. The CIS, the United States, China, South Africa, India, and Australia are the leading producers.

The huge bituminous coal segment can be further categorized as low-, medium-, and high-volatile coal according to its moisture content and heating capacity. Low- and medium-volatility grade bituminous coal typically generates between 18 and 29 million Btu per ton. High-volatile coal, in contrast, usually produces 26 to 30 million Btu per ton. For comparison, a ton of bituminous coal, assuming an average 22 million Btu, produces about the same amount of energy as one cord of hardwood; 22,000 cubic feet of natural gas; or 160 gallons of fuel oil.

Anthracite. Anthracite, the highest grade coal, is mined in only a few countries and in low quantities. In the United States, most of this high-grade coal was has been extracted and exhausted for manufacturing purposes. The material burns with a hot, clean flame and contains only 3 percent moisture when it is mined. It also burns more slowly and uniformly than bituminous coal, which makes it excellent blast furnace material for the steel-making process.

MINING TECHNIQUES

Surface Mining. The two principal coal mining techniques are surface and underground. Surface mining is usually practiced on relatively flat ground in situations where the desired coal is located less than 200 feet from the earth's surface. At mines where the coal is located on steep inclines, though, material may be excavated from open pits that can reach depths of several hundred feet. To get to the coal, miners must first remove the overburden, or strata, that covers the coal bed. Between 1 and 30 cubic yards of strata must be excavated for each ton of coal recovered. Dragline excavators, power shovels, bulldozers, front-end loaders, scrapers, and other heavy pieces of equipment are used to move the strata and extract the coal. Manpower is more likely to be used in less developed nations, while coal mining in developed nations is highly automated.

The two common methods of surface mining are strip and auger. At strip mines, large drills bore holes in the strata. Explosives are then placed and detonated in the holes. Power shovels or draglines operating at surface level move the broken strata, while power shovels dig up the exposed coal and load it into trucks. The strata and coal are removed in long strips. This is done so that the debris from the newest strip can be dumped into an adjacent strip from which the coal has already been recovered. Auger mining, on the other hand, consists of boring a series of holes that are 2 to 5 feet in diameter. These holes are bored parallel to one another and reach depths of 300 or more feet. They are bored in so that they are placed horizontal to a seam of coal that has already been exposed by an outcropping or by strip mining methods. No blasting takes place and the overburden is left intact. The coal is removed and loaded into waiting trucks. Auger mining is frequently used in open-pit mines where the strata is too thick to economically remove via strip methods.

The key advantages of surface mining are low cost and a high extraction rate. Indeed, surface mining is typically much more productive than traditional underground mining and can cost less than half as much per ton of coal produced. Mining companies are typically able to remove about 90 percent of the coal at surface mines, while underground mines permit only 50 percent to 80 percent extraction, depending on the mining methods used.

Underground Mining. Underground mining methods are typically used to extract coal that lies 200 to 1000 feet below the earth's surface, though some mines extend as deep as 2000 feet. Underground mines consist of a series of parallel and interconnecting tunnels from which the coal is cut and removed with special machinery. The process is complex and sometimes dangerous. The mine must be adequately ventilated to protect miners from dust and explosive methane gas that is released by the coal. In addition, careful ground control must be practiced to prevent the roof of the mine from collapsing on workers and equipment.

Three types of coal extraction methods are used in underground operations. Drift mines feature a level tunnel that leads into the mine, while slope mines have an inclined tunnel and shaft mines feature a vertical tunnel. The primary methods of extracting coal from all of these mines are room-and-pillar, longwall, and shortwall. Room-and-pillar mining is often the least efficient method. It typically allows recovery of only about 50 percent of the coal. Some room-and-pillar mines, though, can achieve a much greater recovery percentage. Longwall and shortwall mining practices, in comparison, enable miners to extract up to 80 percent of the usable coal.

In a room-and-pillar operation, coal is mined in a series of rooms cut into the coal bed. Pillars of un-mined coal are left intact to support the mine roof as miners advance through the coal seam. Sometimes the coal in the pillars can be extracted later in the retreat phase of operation. The two basic types of room-and-pillar mining are conventional and continuous. Conventional mining consists of a series of operations that involve cutting and breaking up the coaled, blasting the bed, and then removing the shattered coal. Continuous mining, on the other hand, uses a machine that digs and loads coal in one operation, without blasting. About 90 percent of room-and-pillar coal was extracted using continuous mining in the early 1990s.

Longwall mines use huge machines with cutting heads. The heads are pulled back and forth across a block of coal up to about 600 feet long. Coal is sheared and plowed into slices that are removed by a conveyor. Movable roof supports allow mined-out areas to cave in behind the advancing machine. Shortwall mining is similar to longwall operations, but the continuous mining machine shears smaller blocks of coal that are usually less than 150 feet long.

PROCESSING

Members of the coal mining industry have to secure large quantities of material to be profitable. A relatively small fraction of mined material, often 20 percent of less, contains usable coal. That material is usually hauled from the mine to processing plants, where it is crushed, sized, cleaned, and washed. Refuse, ash, and pyritic sulfur are removed in the cleansing process to make the coal easier to transport and to increase its heating value. In fact, about 28 percent of the raw coal that makes it to the plant is removed as waste. After it is processed, different types of coal are often blended to produce uniform grades of commercial material. Blending may also occur at the point of use.

END USES

Two divisions of coal output are steam and metallurgical. Steam coal, which consumes the large majority of industry output, is most often used to power electric utilities. Metallurgical coal, or cooking coal, is used for industrial applications, particularly iron and steel production. Although they are classified as part of the same industry, steam and metallurgical coal differ in their reserve base, production facilities, distribution channels, and marketing requirements. Other major uses for coal include glass making, cement production, and other industrial uses.

BACKGROUND AND DEVELOPMENT

Coal is not a true mineral, but rather an organic compound formed from the remains of living organic material deposited on the earth's surface 250 to 400 million years ago. The Chinese are believed to be the first to have used coal on a large scale, in about 1000 B.C. The Romans are also believed to have burned the material. The first written history of coal mining dates back to 1200 A.D., when metalworkers in Europe were observed using it. Widespread use of coal did not occur in Europe until the fifteenth and sixteenth centuries, but already by the fourteenth century observers were noting smog conditions where large amounts of coal were burned. Advancements that significantly promoted the use of coal during the eighteenth century included Abraham Darby's use of coal instead of charcoal in blast furnaces and forges and the coal-burning steam engine perfected by James Watt.

The advent of the steam locomotive in the middle and late nineteenth century ignited a huge expansion of the coal industry. The development of this new distribution channel, in conjunction with the start of the Industrial Revolution, resulted in massive industry growth. Between 1865 and 1905 global coal output ballooned from 182 million tons to 928 million tons as the compound displaced wood as the world's primary industrial energy source. The United Kingdom led world coal production throughout the nineteenth century but was surpassed by the United States in 1900. By 1935 world output stood at 1.18 billion tons, about 250 million tons of which was mined in the United States.

Growth in the use of coal as an energy source and as an important part of iron and steel production continued at a moderate pace during much of the middle twentieth century in most industrialized countries. By 1958, for instance, annual demand for coal in the United States stood at about 400 million tons. By the 1950s, however, massive growth in demand in previously undeveloped regions such as the Soviet Union and China pushed annual global consumption past 2.5 billion tons. The Soviet Union, in fact, surpassed the United States as the top coal-producing nation in the late 1950s, although the United States later regained its lead.

Demand for coal continued to increase during the 1960s and 1970s, despite the increasing popularity of alternative energy sources such as petroleum, natural gas, and hydro-power. By the 1980s, though, coal's share of the world energy market had declined from about 60 percent in 1950 to roughly 30 percent. Analysts predicted a resurgence in the popularity of coal during the oil crises of the late 1970s and early 1980. But oil prices eventually dropped and coal demand grew only moderately from 1980 through 2001. Under the administration of George W. Bush, the federal government once again became a proponent of large-scale coal use as a power source, attempting to vehement environmental protests with assurances that it was solidly behind development of cleaner coal-burning technologies.

Proliferation of Surface Mining. Coal was first taken directly from exposed ledges and outcroppings. When this meager supply was consumed, however, miners began to scratch beneath the earth's crust by utilizing surface, or opencut, mining methods. After easily accessible surface coal was extracted and the strata became too thick to remove, companies were forced to mine for coal using costly underground operations. Underground mines, though, could not safely access coal that was close to the earth's surface because the risk of mine collapses was too great. For this reason, much of the coal that lay just beneath the earth's surface, but also under thick strata, remained inaccessible throughout the nineteenth and early twentieth centuries.

In the 1960s and 1970s, improved earth-moving equipment catapulted the surface, or strip mining, industry to center stage in some major coal-producing regions. New tools allowed miners to remove overburden more than 200 feet thick. Massive power shovels, many taller than a 12-story building, were developed that could remove up to 115 cubic yards of debris in a single bite. New earth-hauling trucks sported equivalent capacities. Coal companies found that new surface mining techniques were often less expensive and more efficient than even the best underground mining technology. Surface mining grew in popularity as a result. Surface mining accounted for only 35 percent of total U.S. coal production, for example, in 1965. By the late 1970s, however, auger and strip mining operations accounted for a full 60 percent of industry output in that country.

Industry Development in the 1980s and 1990s. During the 1970s and 1980s industrialized nations reduced their emphasis on coal as an energy source, primarily for reasons related to pollution caused by mining and burning coal. Mining companies throughout Western Europe and the United States were stung by narrow restrictions governing coal mining processes and limits on permissible pollution levels during the burning process. Battles between management and labor unions further disrupted companies in developed countries. In contrast, many developing nations in Asia and South America greatly increased coal output and consumption as producers in those regions took advantage of comparatively lax environmental regulations and low labor costs.

During the 1980s, coal companies in the United States made great strides in productivity by integrating advanced mining technology, slashing workforces, and boosting surface mining. European producers also worked to improve, although their gains were typically meager in comparison to the United States. The end result was a decline in output in many industrialized nations (with the exception of the United States and Canada) and significant global market share gains by producers in developing regions.

Annual world coal production hovered under the 5 billion-ton mark during the late 1980s and early 1990s. Coal output in developed nations stagnated or decreased during the global economic downturn of the early 1990s. During that time, sales of coal to energy producers slumped, as did demand for high-quality cooking coal for steelmaking. Low prices also dogged competitors. Hardest hit were state-run coal producers in the Soviet Union and Eastern Bloc nations. These countries had been suffering production declines since the late 1980s. When the Soviet Union finally dissolved in 1991, the coal industry in the region further deteriorated.

In contrast, coal production in many developing regions continued to surge during the late 1980s and early 1990s. Coal production in India, for example, jumped about 18 percent between 1986 and 1990 to 200 million metric tons and continued to increase into the early 1990s. In fact, several nations positioned near the burgeoning Pacific Rim enjoyed hefty output gains. Australia, for instance, increased coal production 20 percent between 1986 and 1990. By the early 1990s, about half of its 250 million tons of annual production was exported, a level that made Australia the world's largest coal exporter. Developing nations posting solid output gains included China, Venezuela, Colombia, Zimbabwe, and Pakistan.

CURRENT CONDITIONS

The global coal industry was stronger in the late 1990s through 2004 than it had been in the 1980s and early 1990s. Some industry observers believed that it would continue to see robust growth well into the twenty-first century, not in its share of the total energy market, but in terms of actual tonnage of coal mined and consumed. World trade in coal, according to EIA figures, is expected to increase from 656 mmt in 2001 to 919 mmt in 2025.

Much of the optimism reported by *Bloomberg News* and other economic sources was due to expectations that Asian imports of coal suitable for conversion to electricity will reach more than 200 million tons by 2010. Other fuels such as natural gas and oil were projected to continue to replace coal in North America and Europe, but the anticipated expansion of the global economy, especially in Asia and the Pacific Rim, will likely increase the demand for coal in these areas where environmental concerns continued to carry less weight than the need for affordable and plentiful energy. Indeed, the booming economy pushed coal prices from US$40 per metric ton in 2004 to US$53 in 2005, according to Morgan Stanley figures published in *Bloomberg News.* Increased exports from Indonesia and Australia, however, are expected to lower prices in 2006 to an average of US$46 per ton.

Regionally, the conditions through the early 2000s were more varied. In North America production was high, but low prices and excess production capacity made coal mining less attractive to major companies. Some diversified energy companies, such as Atlantic Richfield, sold off their coal mining operations altogether, and even mining companies like Cyprus Amax sold some mines in the attempt to maintain profitability.

In Western Europe production was down. Great Britain's coal industry had shrunk considerably in the mid-1990s, and it passed back into private ownership in 1994. Though the UK coal industry has improved efficiency since then, with total production estimated at between 21 and 29 million tons in 2010 and 15 to 21 million tons in 2016, it faced stiff international price competition. Furthermore, because most UK coal is high-sulfur, emissions control costs are expected to remain a significant factor limiting profitability. Meanwhile, the evolution of the European Union toward a single economy forced member countries such as Germany and Spain to begin cutting back subsidies to their mining industries, stirring up great opposition from powerful unions. A German restructuring plan announced in 2003 called for production drops through 2012.

Coal production in Eastern Europe and the former Soviet Union continued to decline. Poland, Russia, and other countries struggled to create market economies, but their coal industry especially suffered. In Poland, Russia, and the Ukraine, the government closed a number of mines in order to stem its economic losses. Thousands of miners lost their jobs, and in Russia they went for months without pay. In Poland, in particular, environmentalists and world geologists alike became alarmed by the emissions pumped into the atmosphere by coal-burning electric plants. Responding to a continued fall in demand, Poland in 2003 announced that by 2020 it would close 12 of its 35 coal mines. The country persisted with comprehensive restructuring plans after joining the European Union in 2004, announcing a 2 billion euro aid package intended to streamline coal operations and further reduce production capacities.

In Asia and the Pacific Rim, which includes four of the world's leading coal producing countries—China, Indonesia, Australia, and India—prospects were much brighter, despite the financial crisis that struck some countries in the region in the late 1990s.

RESEARCH AND TECHNOLOGY

Technology advanced the coal industry on three primary fronts in the early 2000s: (1) improvements in, and the implementation of, mining techniques that reduce the cost of extracting coal and therefore expand the base of economically recoverable reserves; (2) breakthroughs related to reducing pollutants that result from burning coal; and (3) new uses for coal to broaden markets and potential applications. The latter two were of greatest importance.

Although coal operations became safer and there was far less waste of coal resources, as technology and machinery improve, there was a down side from a labor perspective: the coal industry in the United States and other developed nations continued to reduce the number of workers it employed. In 2000, some 80,000 people were employed in the United States coal industry, nearly 10 times fewer than the number employed 80 years earlier, according to industry figures.

CLEANER BURNING

One breakthrough related to cleaner coal burning was the use of fluidized bed combustors. These mechanisms permit power plants to burn high-sulfur and low-quality coal cleanly and with only minimal sacrifice in efficiency. This technology allowed utility plants in some industrialized nations to continue burning coal in spite of more stringent regulations. Other sulfur-reduction techniques under examination use biotechnology. One system under development, for example, incorporated genetically engineered bacteria that subsists on a diet of sulfur.

NEW APPLICATIONS

Efforts to find new uses for coal in the twenty-first century included research into finely ground coal and oil or coal and water mixtures that were seen as possible substitutes for oil at power plants(some plants in the United States were already using this technique in the late 1990s). Researchers also experimented with mixtures of coal and methanol or natural gas. Other promising technologies centered on the use of synthetic fuels, or synfuels, created through the conversion of coal into other fuels and by-products. The primary advantage of the conversion process was that it eliminates the need for costly rail transportation of base coal material. In addition, several significant by-products can be recovered during the conversion process. The by-product methanol, for example, may become an important source of automobile fuel in the twenty-first century.

The two most popular synfuel processes under development beginning in the 1990s were coal gasification and liquefaction. These techniques were used to convert coal into a variety of clean-burning gases, solids, and liquids. Using these processes, one ton of coal could be converted into the equivalent of 20 to 125 gallons of liquid fuel; 15,000 cubic feet of high-Btu gas; or 75,000 cubic feet of low-Btu gas. Coal liquefaction plants were in operation in South Africa and Spain and under development in other places in the late 1990s. The creation of many other by-products was also possible. Some observers contended that the technology could potentially allow coal producers to reclaim energy market share absorbed by the petroleum industry.

INDUSTRY LEADERS

Many of the world's leading commercial coal mining enterprises—as opposed to state-run operations such as China's—were part of huge diversified mining companies. Moreover, the remaining large state-run coal operations experienced severe production declines in the late 1990s and in most cases were in the process of being privatized.

RIO TINTO

Rio Tinto, a British and Australian company, involved in **gemstone, SIC 1499**, industrial mineral, and **metal mining, SIC 1000** as well as coal, is the world's largest mining company with mine operations in many parts of the world. In 1997 coal was one of its least profitable divisions, accounting for one-seventh of revenue but only 5 percent of profit. Nevertheless, the company announced plans to double its output in the United States, from 41 million tons to 85 million by 2005 and to expand Australian and Indonesian production from 39 million tons to 48 million. The company was also involved in large joint projects with Amcoal and Glencore in Colombian coal fields. A planned open cast coal mine at the Gokwe North energy plant in Zimbabwe, however — which was expected to supply about a third of the country's energy needs — failed to gain adequate government support and was not built. In 2003, Rio Tinto posted net earnings of US$1.5 billion, of which US$157 million was attributed to coal and uranium. Prices for Rio Tinto's coal exports rose sharply in 2004 after China drastically reduced its export levels to divert more coal to domestic consumption. Total revenues in 2004 were US$11.3 billion, with coal accounting for about 20 percent of sales.

PEABODY ENERGY

Peabody Energy Corporation was in 2004 the largest coal producer in the world. In the early 1990s British-owned Hanson PLC had acquired Peabody Holding Company Inc. but later spun it off as part of the Energy Group, which was in turn purchased by Texas Utilities in 1998. Part of that transaction included Lehman Merchant Banking Partners becoming owners of Peabody Energy Corporation and its subsidiary Peabody Coal. Restructuring resulted in significant improvements for the company. By 2004, Peabody Energy reported a doubling of sales by volume and a tripling of productivity and market share. In addition, it claimed a 74 percent improvement in its safety record, as well as a 47 percent reduction in production costs per ton. In 2004, Peabody operated 29 underground and surface mines in the United States and three in Australia; in addition, the company owned a 25.5 percent share in the Paso Diablo Mine in Venezuela. Peabody employed 7,900 people worldwide and controlled 9.5 billion tons of reserves-more than any other company. In 2003 Peabody produced a total of 203.2 million tons of coal, which generated US$2.8 billion in revenues; a record 106.5 million tons came from the Powder River Basin operations in Wyoming, with the top facility—North Antelope Rochelle Mine—producing 80.1 million tons. Total output rose to 227.2 million tons in 2004, resulting in revenues of US$3.6 billion. The company's coal accounts for about 10 percent of the electricity generated in the United States and almost 3 percent worldwide. More than 90 percent of Peabody's sales are to U.S. customers.

ARCH COAL

Arch Coal Inc., created by the 1997 merger of Ashland Coal and Arch Minerals, in 2000 became the second-largest coal producer in the United States and was one of the larger producers in the world. A series of major acquisitions through the late 1990s and early 2000s dramatically boosted the company's output and reserves. In 1998 it acquired the Black Thunder, Coal Creek, and Thundercloud mines in Wyoming's Powder River Basin. In 2004, Arch acquired Triton's North Rochelle mine and combined its operations with those of the neighboring Black Thunder, creating the leading mine in the region. In 2005, according to the company's statistics, the Black Thunder mine produced 5,000 pounds of coal every second of every day, 365 days per year.

In 2004 Arch Coal, which mines only low-sulfur coal, contributed about 13 percent of the U.S. coal supply. It operated 27 mines in the western United States and central Appalachia, which produced more than 125 million tons of coal annually. The company also owned proven reserves of 3.7 billion tons. Arch Coal posted revenues in 2004 of US$1.9 billion, a 32.9 percent increase from the previous year.

MAJOR COUNTRIES IN THE INDUSTRY

CHINA

With plentiful coal reserves, China was the leading producer of coal in the late 1990s. In 1996 it produced a total of 1.376 billion tons of coal. Its coal exports grew substantially in 1996 as well, reaching about 30 million tons, making China the sixth-leading exporter. Those figures dropped substantially in the late 1990s and 2000 as China made strides toward regulation, greater efficiency, and reduced costs; between 1998 and 2001 China reportedly closed 400,000 unproductive mines. China's production, therefore, dropped from 1.05 billion tons in 1999 to only about 950 million tons in 2000. China also became less resistant to overtures from the international business community interested in tapping into the nation's vast coal reserves. In spite of such drops, China continued to be the world leader in both coal production and consumption.

Strong economic growth in China in the early 2000s increased demand for coal, used primarily for the generation of electricity but also in the industrial sector. According to *Petroleum Economist,* China's use of coal for electricity was expected to balloon from 5.9 quadrillion Btu in 1999 to 17 quadrillion Btu in 2020. Production lags in the early 2000s, however, caused concern about China's ability to meet skyrocketing domestic demand. The *Asia Times* reported in 2003 that more than 70 percent of the country's electric power was generated by coal but because of an estimated 3 million ton coal supply shortage power grid zones throughout the country had to impose blackout periods. In late 2003 China ordered producers to boost output to guarantee supplies for power plants. The country also invested in several major energy projects aimed at easing reliance on coal for the production of electricity. The Three Gorges Dam began generating electricity in 2003, and is expected to be able to supply 5 percent of China's total electricity demand by 2010. The West-East Gas Pipeline Project, scheduled to open in 2005, will substantially increase the country's access to natural gas resources. According to EIA figures, demand for coal in China's electricity sector will decline by 44 percent by 2025. Non-electricity sectors, on the other hand, which accounted for 58 percent of demand in 2001, will likely consume a much greater share of China's coal through the early 2000s. The country's first coal liquefaction plant, for example, which will convert coal into petroleum products necessary to meet domestic transportation needs, will start operations in 2007, processing up to 5.5 mmt annually.

In spite of improvements, China's coal industry lagged far behind that of more developed nations in the early 2000s. Safety remained a significant concern, with Chinese mines, particularly the small, illegally run operations, being the most dangerous in the world.

In a ten-month period in 2001, the government closed 11,882 small mines because of alleged safety violations; during that period, China reported 2,378 coal mining-related deaths. Fatalities continued to escalate: in 2003 alone, according to a CNN report, explosions and other mine accidents claimed a shocking 6,702 lives. The BBC reported between 5,000 and 6,000 coal mining fatalities in China in

2004; in 2005, the single worst mine disaster since 1949 claimed 210 lives at the Sunjiawan mine near Fuxin. Indeed, in 2004 China produced only 35 percent of the world's coal, but was responsible for 80 percent of coal mining fatalities. The country's decision in 2003 to boost coal production to meet burgeoning domestic demand caused concern about the potential for even higher casualties in coming years. In 2004, according to the *Asia Times*, China planned to appropriate about US$265 million for safety improvements in its coal mines.

Transportation was also a major problem. The highest quality deposits were in the northern part of the country, far from the major population centers and ports. Coal already used half of the country's railroad capacity and that was insufficient. An estimated 11 percent of the world's coal reserves were buried in China, including some of the highest quality coal reserves in the world. In the long term, easy access to burgeoning Pacific Rim economies bodes well for China's coal industry.

UNITED STATES

The availability of low-cost coal, which in the early 2000s accounted for 50 percent of electric power generated in the United States, significantly reduced energy costs for U.S. businesses. According to the Energy Information Administration, U.S. coal production fell for the second consecutive year in 2003, reaching 1,07 billion short tons. This represented a drop of 2.1 percent from the previous year's output. Demand, however, grew by 2.7 percent in the electricity sector and by 1.6 percent in other sectors. Through the late 1990s and early 2000s production from the Appalachian and interior regions declined, while production in western regions increased. Between 1997 and 2002, U.S. coal exports decreased; the number of U.S. mines dropped by 19 percent and the number of mine workers dropped by 6 percent. According to the National Mining Association, however, the U.S. Energy Information Administration projected a rise in U.S. coal consumption from 1.07 billion tons in 2002 to 1.57 billion tons in 2025. It also projected that the percentage of electricity generated from coal would rise to 52 percent by 2025. A 2001 U.S. National Energy Policy (NEP) report from 2001, however, admitted that the nation was saddled with too many older coal-burning plants that were not fuel-efficient or equipped with scrubbing equipment to reduce health-threatening emissions.

In the mid-1990s, the United States was the second-largest world producer of coal, with about 959 million tons of mined coal of all grades. In 1997 production continued to grow, up 2.3 percent over 1996, despite the decline in prices that had persisted for a decade. Demand for low-sulfur and lower-ash residue coal from the western states, particularly Wyoming Powder River Basin coal, increased due to its low cost and its ability to meet the sulfur emission requirements of the Clean Air Act of 1990. Demand for Appalachian region coal (with the exception of West Virginia coal) lessened because of its higher sulfur content. Some major companies, especially those with interests in the oil industry, began to divest themselves of coal operations in the mid- and late 1990s. Atlantic Richfield was preceded in this trend by Amoco, Exxon, and Shell. By 2002, U.S. production had increased slightly to 975 million tons of coal, mainly bituminous and lignite.

The George W. Bush administration, under fire from environmental groups that object to mounting piles of coal ash residue and air pollution, in 2001 promised tax credits and a US$2 billion commitment over the next decade for cleaner coal technology to reduce sulfur dioxide and nitrogen oxide. But President Bush also pledged to strengthen the industry and preserve jobs. In 2004, the Mine Safety and Health Administration proposed changes to safety and environmental regulations intended to cut industry costs; union officials and health workers, however, argued that such measures would weaken environmental and safety regulations. Also in 2004, federal agencies attempted to streamline the permitting process for new mines, issuing permits for 14 mountaintop-removal mines in West Virginia-up from only three approved in 2002. A federal judge, however, ordered that 11 of these permits be revoked until more information was available about potential environmental damage from this type of strip mining, which uses high explosives to remove the tops of mountains. According to a federal report released in 2003, rubble from mountaintop-removal mining has buried or damaged 1,200 miles of streams in the past 20 years.

RUSSIA

The Russian Federation countries, formerly the Soviet Union, were at one time the world's leading producer of coal. In the years following the breakup of the Soviet Union, however, production declined dramatically, as the newly independent countries adjusted to the new situation and, in some cases, shifted toward market economies. As of the early 2000s coal still made up about a quarter of the federation's energy supply.

Russian coal production in 1997 totaled 244 million tons, slightly more than half the 415 million tons produced before the breakup of the Soviet Union, and 4.8 percent less than 1996 production. At the beginning of 1998 Russian coal miners were owed US$27.5 million in back wages and had not been paid for seven months. In November 1997 the government abolished Rosugol, the corporation set up in 1992 to run the coal industry on a commercial basis, and returned the industry to direct government control. According to a World Bank report quoted by the Sustainable Energy & Economy Network, the Russian coal industry increased productivity by 77 percent between 1994 and 1999.

By 2002, however, state funding amounted to only 10 percent of mining operations, with private owners taking up the slack. By 2003, according to *CoalTrans*, Russian coal mining was dominated by three primary players: Siberian Coal Energetic Company, EurasHolding, and Severstal. With an investment of about US$1 billion for facilities construction and upgrades, private owners increased productivity to a monthly output of 103.4 tons per miner by 2003. Exports also rose, from 14 million tons in 1999 to a record 42 million tons in 2000. In 2004, Russian government sources reported total coal production of about 308.6 million short tons. Russia's coal consumption also rose in the early 2000s; this trend was expected to continue as the country aimed to reduce its use of domestic oil and natural gas in order to maximize exports of these commodities. Russia as of 2005 ranked fifth in the world for coal production.

According to *CoalTrans*, Russia had sufficient coal reserves to enable it to double production through the early 2000s. But transportation remained a problem. The average distance between a coal mine and a seaport in Russia was 4,050 kilometers (km), making freight costs a significant issue. Investment in handling facilities at ports in the Russian Far East was expected to increase export capacities.

GERMANY

Germany's coal industry, which experienced tremendous changes in the late 1990s, provides insight into the overall Western European coal mining environment. Throughout the twentieth century Germany was a leading coal producer. But like many other Western European nations output had fallen since the late 1950s, and other forms of energy had become popular. German coal companies, like those in the United States and throughout Western Europe, had also come under increasing pressure from labor groups and environmental legislation, resulting in a 65 percent drop in output between 1960 and the early 1990s. During the same period, the German coal industry workforce plummeted from more than 450,000 to just over 100,000. Coal industries in other Western European nations similarly suffered. Output in Belgium, for example, fell 40 percent during the 1980s, while production in France declined 20 percent, and the United Kingdom posted a sharp 63 percent drop.

The German government tried to help domestic coal producers in the Ruhr coal basin with hefty subsidies during the mid-1990s. One result of this was that German coal, priced at about four times the average cost of coal on world markets, became some of the most expensive in the world. However, as the European Union continued to work toward becoming a single economy, Germany along with other EU member countries was forced to begin reducing its subsidies. The government's first plan called for a reduction of subsidies from about DM9 billion (about US$5 billion) in 1997 to DM3.8 billion by the year 2005. But strikes and demonstrations by miners and their supporters forced a compromise in which subsidies would be reduced to just DM5.5 billion by 2005. In 2003, a policy arrangement among government, industry, and workers agreed to maintain a long-term core mining industry, which could be ensured by downsizing production from 26 million tons in 2005 to 16 million tons by 2012. The mining workforce would be correspondingly reduced to 20,000 people by 2012. In 2003 Germany announced that between 2006 and 2012, some 17 billion euros in aid would be earmarked for the German coal industry.

To shore up the industry the coal producers merged and created a company called Deutsche Steinkohle, which produced at some 15 coal mines all but 5 percent of Germany's coal. German coal production fell from 540.7 million short tons in 1989 to only 230.9 million short tons in 2002. It was, however, the world's fourth largest consumer of coal, importing 43 million short tons in 2002.

INDIA

Next to China, India was expected by 2020 to be the world's leading consumer of coal as an electricity source, unless the price of coal unexpectedly rises due to favorable contracts given to suppliers by import nations such as Japan. India consumed 359 million short tons in 2000, and was expected to increase demand to 430 million short tons in 2010, according to EIA figures. In 2004, coal supplied more than 50 percent of India's energy needs; 70 percent of coal consumption was used to generate electricity. Since India was a major coal producer, ranked third in the world in 2004, it was able to meet most of its domestic demand without significantly increasing imports.

AUSTRALIA

Australia, due to expectations of profits from growing Asian markets, became the world's leading coal exporter by the early 2000s. Major acquisitions by a small number of multinational coal companies, including Anglo and Glencore, as well as improvements in rail freight service to major coal ports, contributed to record exports exceeding 200 million tons in 2002. Some Australian coal industry experts anticipated that coal exports could increase to 230 million tons by 2010. According to EIA figures, Australia contains about 90.5 billion short tones of coal reserves and is the fourth largest producer in the world. About 60 percent of its total production is exported each year; accounting for 28 percent of the global market in coal.

FURTHER READING

"About Arch Coal." Arch Coal Company, 2005. Available from www.archcoal.com.

Arch Company Profile. Hoover's Online, 2005. Available from www.hoovers.com.

"China Coal Mine Blast Kills 28." CNN, 3 March 2004. Available from edition.cnn.com.

"China Shuts Down 11,882 Small Coal Mines in 10 Months." *People's Daily,* 17 November 2001. Available from www.english.peopledaily.com.

"Coal Prices to Fall 13 Percent in 2006, Morgan Stanley Says." *Bloomberg News,* 5 January 2005. Available form www.bloomberg.com

Drew, Christopher, and Oppel, Richard A., Jr. "Mines to Mountaintops: Rewriting Coal Policy." *New York Times,* 9 August 2004.

Ivanov, Andrei and Judith Perera. "Labor: Unpaid Russian Miners Driven to Desperate Deeds." *Interpress Service,* 6 February 1998.

Nuwer, Hank. "The Coal Truth." *Indianapolis Monthly,* June 2001.

"Over a Third of Polish Mines to Go by 2020." *CoalTrans,* May/June 2003. Available from www.coaltransinternational.com.

Peabody Energy Annual Report, 2004. Available from www.peabodyenergy.com.

"Poland Plans to Grant Two Billion Euros to Coal Industry." *EUBusiness,* 2 June 2004. Available from www.eubusiness.com.

Project Profile: Russia Coal and Forestry Sector Guarantees Project. Sustainable Energy & Economy Network. Avaible from www.seen.org.

Rio Tinto Annual Report, 2004. Available from www.riotinto.com.

"Rio Tinto in Zimbabwe." Mbendi Business Reference, 2004. Available from www.mbendi.co.za.

"Rio Tinto Sees Sharp Rise in Thermal Coal Price." Reuters, 8 March 2004. Available from wwww.biz.yahoo.com.

"Russia Gets Its Act Together." *CoalTrans,* September/October 2003. Available from www.coaltransinternational.com.

UK Coal Production Outlook: 2004-16. Department of Trade and Industry, London, England. March 2004. Available from www.dti.gov.uk.

United Nations Economic and Social Council, Economic Commission for Europe, ad hoc Group of Experts on Coal in Sustainable Development. *Report,* 14 November 2003. Available from www.unece.org.

U.S. Department of Energy, Energy Information Administration. *Country Profiles 2004.* Available from www.eia.doe.gov.

U.S. Department of Energy, Energy Information Administration. *International Energy Outlook 2004.* January 2004. Available from www.eia.doe.gov.

White, Dudley. "World Coal Demand May Rise 14 Percent by 2010." *Bloomberg News,* 22 January 2002.

"World Coal: Sluggish Demand Growth, But It's Still Growth." *Petroleum Economics,* 10 September 2001.

Ye, Miao. "The Human Cost of Coal." *Asia Times,* 15 January 2003. Available from www.atimes.com.

SIC 1499

NAICS 212319

MINING, GEMSTONE

The global gemstone industry is engaged in mining, developing mines, and exploring for gemstones such as diamond, emerald, ruby, sapphire, amethyst, aquamarine, and others.

INDUSTRY SNAPSHOT

The gemstone mining industry comprises two distinct segments: diamond mining and the mining of all other kinds of gemstones, such as ruby and emerald, referred to collectively as colored gemstones. The diamond industry is highly structured and characterized by large corporations and highly mechanized mining operations. Though sub-Saharan Africa dominated diamond mining through the twentieth century, by the early 2000s its total output was surpassed by the combined production of Canada, Australia, Brazil, China, and Russia. The colored gemstone industry is highly fragmented and characterized by small organizations and a great variety of mining operations with little mechanization. Important deposits were being worked on all the continents except Antarctica. According to MBendi Research, the global diamond market increased more than 250 percent since the late 1970s. Global diamond production reached 150 million carats in 2003, of which 80.9 million carats was gem quality. Australia ranked first in total diamond output, while Botswana ranked first in gem diamond production and value.

In terms of dollar value, by far the most important market for gemstones is the manufacture of jewelry. Measured in terms of volume of production, however, the industrial use of diamonds predominates. The demand for gem-quality stones fluctuates with the economy, although in the case of diamonds the price is maintained at a high level by the mechanisms of the diamond cartel led by De Beers. The price for some kinds of colored gemstones, such as rubies, is also affected by the availability of the gems.

One of the major problems facing the industry in the first decade of the twenty-first century was security. Diamond theft and illegal smuggling were practices that particularly plagued emerging countries. Export totals of Pakistani precious and semi-precious stones, for example, fell from US$3.76 million in 1991-1992 to US$2.17 million in 2000-2001, and the *Pakistan Newswire* suggested that smuggling may have contributed to this decline. Mining operations in Colombia and adjacent lands worried about safety issues due to the presence of gang-like drug cartels. And in many diamond-rich areas of Africa, militant groups have seized control of diamond operations and used proceeds to finance armed insurrections.

ORGANIZATION AND STRUCTURE

The gemstone mining industry is both widely dispersed and highly diverse. Gem mining operations are scattered unevenly throughout the world, on all the continents except Antarctica. Many of the most famous and most valuable deposits are found in the poorest and most inaccessible regions. Members of the industry include some of the largest and most powerful corporations in the world as well as individual "treasure hunters," both legitimate and illegitimate.

The products of this industry are also quite diverse. The island country of Sri Lanka, one of the most important centers of the industry, produces 55 different kinds of precious gems, yet there are many varieties that are not found there. In retail trade gems are generally divided into diamonds and colored gemstones, and this division holds throughout the industry. The diamond mining industry is highly developed and tightly structured, while the production of other gemstones is chaotic and in many places quite primitive.

Not including organic substances such as pearl and amber, which are sometimes classified with them, gemstones are defined as natural crystalline minerals that are rare, hard, chemically resistant, and beautiful. For thousands of years, they have been the objects of exploration, speculation, and arduous labor, as well as the subject of myth, legend, story, and song. In modern times some gemstones, particularly diamonds, have proven to be very valuable in industrial applications. The chemical composition of gemstones is in most cases the same as other, non-gemstone minerals. For example, diamond is chemically the same as graphite, and ruby and sapphire are chemically the same as corundum, a mineral that is used as a cutting and polishing material. The difference between gems and other minerals is the size and regularity of the crystal structure. Gems were formed millions of years ago when the necessary conditions of heat and pressure enabled the formation of very large crystals. Growing knowledge of the conditions in which gems were formed has enabled much more scientific exploration for gem deposits in the nineteenth and twentieth centuries than was possible in previous centuries.

DIAMOND

Diamond is the premier gemstone. It is the hardest substance found in nature, 140 times harder than the next hardest gem, and this characteristic has made diamond an indispensable material in many industrial applications. Diamond powder is used to grind and polish other very hard substances in many industries. Fragments of various sizes are embedded in saw blades and drill bits for uses from dentistry to drilling oil wells. Because of its resistance to extremes of heat and cold, thin slices of diamond are used as tiny windows in space probes. Wire is drawn through a hole drilled in a diamond when the diameter of the finished wire must be precise and highly consistent, as in the filaments for light bulbs.

Gem-quality diamond is the most valuable mined substance and the most sought after. The value of an uncut diamond, or "rough," is determined by its size, color, and clarity. Most diamonds are yellowish, but the more nearly colorless stones are more valuable. The rarer colored diamonds—blue, pink, green, purple, brown, yellow, and black, called "fancy"—are often extremely valuable. Frequently diamonds have internal flaws such as enclosed minerals that lower their value. Most diamonds are small, fractions of a carat (a carat equals 0.2 grams), but occasionally very large gems are found and, if they have good quality otherwise, are extremely valuable. The largest ever found, named Cullinan, weighed 3,106 carats, about 1.4 pounds.

Africa was the historic leader in global diamond production through the twentieth century, producing half the world's supply. By 2004, the continent, according to MBendi Research, had produced more than 75 percent of world diamond value to date, worth an estimated US$158 billion. But by 2002, total output (including both industrial and gem-quality diamonds) from five non-African countries (Australia, Russia, Canada, Brazil, and China) exceeded that of Africa. Even so, Africa remained a significant supplier, with 12 of the 19 leading diamond producing countries located on that continent. Botswana ranked first in production of gem-quality diamonds, followed by Australia, Russia, Congo (Kinshasa), Angola, South Africa, Canada, and Namibia. Brazil and China also ranked among the top ten, but the vast majority of their output was industrial quality diamonds.

In 2005, Angola announced that its national mining company Endiama would double its diamond output in 2006. In the 1990s, when the country was engulfed in civil war, Angola produced between 3 and 5 million carats per year. After military conflict ceased, diamond production increased to about 6.5 million carats in the early 2000s. If the country reaches its target of 12 million carats per year, it will become Africa's third largest diamond producer. The Angolan government claimed that adherence to the Kimberly Process has rid the industry of corruption, but some analysts have expressed concern about continued human rights violations and other illegal practices such as smuggling.

COLORED GEMSTONES

There are about 200 varieties of colored gemstones, but only a much smaller number are of great importance in the gemstone mining industry. The others are either very rare or not suitable for making into jewelry. The best-known and most valuable gems are ruby, sapphire, and emerald. Other important varieties are amethyst, aquamarine, zircon, topaz, opal, ametrine, and tourmaline.

Ruby. Ruby is generally the most valuable of the colored gemstones. The name comes from the Latin word for red, and the color varies from a fiery vermilion to a violet red. If the color is very light, the gem is called a pink sapphire. As with most gems, the more even in color and the more transparent the stone is, the more valuable it is. Large rubies, more than five carats, are very rare, and a large ruby that is of top quality may command a higher price than a diamond of the same size and quality. The most important sources for ruby are Myanmar (formerly Burma), Thailand, Sri Lanka, and Tanzania, although it is found in other places as well.

Sapphire. Sapphire is chemically the same as ruby, the difference being simply in the color. There are pink, violet, yellow, green, and colorless varieties of sapphire, but if the stone is simply called sapphire, it is understood to be blue. The most prized color is a pure cornflower blue. When indistinctly colored sapphires are heat-treated at high temperatures, they turn a bright blue permanently. A very desirable characteristic of some sapphires, as well as some rubies and other gems, is the presence of rutile needles within the crystal that reflect light in such a way that it looks like there is a six-pointed star inside the gem. Another arrangement of rutile needles in the crystal make it reflect light like a cat's eye. The most important deposits of sapphires are found in Australia, Myanmar, Sri Lanka, and Thailand. Sapphires have been discovered in Montana, and several mines have been developed there.

Emerald. The word emerald comes from a Greek word meaning green stone, and the color of this gem is so distinctive and characteristic that it is simply called "emerald green." Like large rubies, fine emeralds over two carats in weight are among the most highly valued gems and may bring a higher price even than diamonds. Only the finest emeralds are transparent. Often they are clouded with various inclusions, which are not considered faults but rather a sign of the authenticity of the stone. Unlike rubies, sapphires, and many other gemstones, emeralds are almost always mined directly from the rock in which they were formed, rather than being found in gem gravels created by erosion. This situation exists because they are less durable than these other gems and do not survive the process of erosion and transport. The most important emerald mines as of 2004 were in Colombia, with other sources being Brazil, Zimbabwe, Russia, and Pakistan.

Aquamarine and Beryl. Aquamarine and beryl are gemstones that have the same chemical composition as emerald but different colors. Aquamarine is blue or light greenish blue, the darker blue being considered more desirable. Lower quality stones can be heat-treated to change them to the desired darker color, but too much heat can discolor them. The largest aquamarine of gem quality, found in Brazil, weighed 243 pounds and was cut into many stones with a total weight of over 100,000 carats. Beryl is found in a variety of other colors as well as green and blue. Heliodor is a light yellow-green beryl, morganite is pink, and gosheite is colorless. The most important deposits of aquamarine are found in Brazil, but aquamarine and other forms of beryl are found in

Australia, China, the United States, and a number of other countries.

Amethyst, Citrine, and Ametrine. Amethyst, citrine, and ametrine are three gem varieties of quartz. The color of amethyst ranges from purple through violet to almost pink, sometimes in bands in the same stone. The name means "not drunken" because it was thought that the gem would protect the wearer from getting drunk. Amethyst is the most valuable form of quartz. Citrine varies from a pale yellow to a brownish yellow. Most commercial citrine is actually heat-treated poorer quality amethyst or smoky quartz. Natural citrine is usually pale yellow. Ametrine is a striped quartz variety, half amethyst and half citrine. Sources of these gems include Bolivia, Brazil, Sri Lanka, the United States, Madagascar, Namibia, and a number of other countries.

MINING METHODS

There are two general types of gemstone deposits. When the gems are found in the rock in which they were originally formed, known as the host rock, it is called a primary deposit. Often, however, the host rock eroded away long ago, and the gemstones were carried, usually by water, to a new location. Because gemstones are harder and generally denser than other rock, they survive the erosion forces better and are deposited on the bed of a stream or on a beach, resulting in what is known as a placer deposit. These accumulations of stones are then often buried as a result of subsequent erosion, although not always. In earlier times most finds of gemstones were of placer deposits. Sometimes the original sources were then located.

Mining of placer deposits is generally simpler than mining a primary deposit. If the deposit is at the surface, mining consists of sorting the gravel to find the gemstones. If the gem-bearing gravel is buried, then a pit must be dug, perhaps thirty feet deep or more, and the gravel hauled to the surface for sorting. In Sri Lanka, for example, almost all mining is done in this way in the early 2000s, just as it has been for centuries. Varying degrees of mechanization have been introduced in some places, ranging from gasoline-powered pumps for removing the water from the pits to using bulldozers to uncover the buried gem-bearing gravel. Diamonds, rubies, sapphires, aquamarines, and beryl are a few of the kinds of gems that are mined in this way.

Although placer deposits usually have a higher proportion of gem-quality stones than primary deposits, prospectors always prefer to find the source of the gems, especially in modern times. Usually primary deposits lend themselves to more modern, efficient mining techniques. Modern gemstone mines of primary deposits are in fact similar to other kinds of mines. Depending on the depth at which the gem-bearing rock is found, surface or underground mining methods may be used. Surface mining is usually practiced on relatively flat ground in situations where the desired material is located less than 200 feet from the earth's surface. At mines where the gems are located on steep inclines, though, material may be excavated from open pits that can reach depths of several hundred feet. Dragline excavators, power shovels, bulldozers, front-end loaders, scrapers, and other heavy pieces of equipment are used to move the overburden and then the ore. The ore is then processed to recover the gem material. Primary deposits of diamonds are often mined in this way.

Underground mines consist of a series of parallel and interconnecting tunnels from which the ore is cut and removed with special machinery. The process is complex and sometimes dangerous. The mine must be adequately ventilated to protect miners from dust and provide adequate air underground. In addition, careful ground control must be practiced to prevent the roof of the mine from collapsing on workers and equipment. In some areas where underground methods are used, safety is not highly regarded and accidental deaths are common. Emeralds and diamonds are often mined using underground mining techniques.

Whenever large-scale, mechanized mining is practiced, whether surface mining or underground, large quantities of ore must be processed to recover the relatively small yield of gemstones. Large diamond mines, such as those in southern Africa and Australia, extract huge quantities of ore that must be partially crushed. The crushed material is then sorted by some means to separate the diamonds. One separation method depends on diamond's resistance to water; that is, water will not cling to it. Crushed ore is mixed with water, and then spread on a greased surface. The diamonds settle onto the surface and, because they are not wet, stick to the grease, while the wet ore washes off. A more sophisticated technique relies on diamond's fluorescence, the property of giving off light when bombarded with X-rays. A stream of crushed ore falls down a column past stations that emit X-rays which cause the diamonds to flash. An electric eye records the flash and releases a short blast of air that blows the diamond into a separate chute. In many cases, however, final sorting of the ore is done by hand, under tight security.

The host rock of diamonds is usually a rock called kimberlite, named after the area in South Africa in which it was first recognized. The Argyle deposit in Australia, however, is of lamproite. The diamonds were formed 90 to 190 miles below the surface, in the upper mantle, where temperatures and pressures are extremely high. At some point an eruption occurred, bringing the molten rock carrying the diamonds to the surface and forming a volcano. Over the centuries the volcanic cone eroded, sometimes carrying diamonds downstream to form placer deposits.

BACKGROUND AND DEVELOPMENT

Gems have been valued by humans from the earliest days of recorded history. The earliest written evidence of emeralds being mined comes from Egypt as early as 2000 B.C. These mines, later called Cleopatra's Mines, were rediscovered in 1818. Legend has it that King Solomon sent for gems to impress the Queen of Sheba in biblical times, and the earliest recorded trading of diamonds took place in India and Borneo over two thousand years ago. The Spanish conquerors of the Americas found the indigenous population of Mexico trading emeralds that were mined in the area that later was called Colombia. Eventually the Spanish found the mines and worked them using slave labor.

India was Europe's first source of diamonds, which came via the Middle East and Venice until the Portuguese established a monopoly on the trade by going around Africa in the sixteenth century. In the seventeenth century the Dutch edged out the Portuguese in the Asian trade, and later the British began to exert their influence on India. In the eighteenth century, however, Europe was flooded with diamonds from a new source, Brazil. Prices fell and the trade with India was destroyed. For a century Brazil had an effective monopoly on diamonds, but this situation ended in 1870 when large deposits were discovered in South Africa.

THE MODERN DIAMOND INDUSTRY

Like those in Brazil, the first mines worked in South Africa were of secondary deposits, in the Orange and Vall Rivers. Between 1867 and 1870, thousands of prospectors searched these rivers. Then, in 1870, diamonds were found on the plains between the two rivers. It was soon realized that these new deposits were not placer deposits but were in fact the original source of the diamonds. No matter how deep the miners dug, they still found diamonds. This meant that mechanized methods could be effectively utilized.

The resulting impact on the diamond trade was enormous. While Brazil was producing about a quarter of a million carats per year at that time, by 1871 South African production reached that level, and the following year its output surged to more than a million carats. By 1880 it was 3 million. Actual mechanized methods were not yet established because the mines were located hundreds of miles by oxcart from any port, and because the claims were all very small; each 35 feet square.

In 1879 a railroad to the coast was completed which halved the cost of bringing in machines. The miners also discovered that as they got deeper and deeper the tiny side-by-side mines were not workable.

In the mid-1870s a young man from England named Cecil Rhodes became involved in diamond mining through his brother. He began buying the small claims in one mine, De Beers, and soon had a controlling interest in this mine and within a few years in several others. Soon his company, De Beers Consolidated Mines Ltd., controlled 90 percent of the world's diamond production. In 1887 he entered the Cape Colony Parliament, and in 1890, at the age of 37, he became the colony's prime minister. He died in 1902.

Cecil Rhodes had established the guiding principle of the diamond industry: diamonds are a luxury item, and the supply must be matched with the demand by centrally controlling the entire process from mining to supplying the cutters. In 1914 the first diamond cartel was established. The companies involved were all legally independent but agreed to work together to control the industry. World War I interrupted this experiment, but in 1920 a new cartel was created, including a company whose purpose was to buy up the production of mines outside South Africa.

For more than 70 years, the diamond industry followed Cecil Rhodes's principle, with the result that this industry has been much more stable than other commodity industries such as coal mining. De Beers Consolidated Mines and its sister company De Beers Centenary do not have a monopoly on diamond production, but they do have a huge share, and they do affect the supply when necessary by limiting their own production. The other major component of control is the Diamond Trading Company (DTC; formerly the Central Selling Organization), which is the division of the De Beers organization responsible for selling rough diamonds to cutters.

Through the DTC De Beers enters into contracts with the major producers of diamonds stipulating that it will buy a set amount of their production and limiting what they can do with the rest. The DTC in turn sells the rough diamonds in limited amounts to a limited number of diamond cutters, 160 of them, in batches that the cutter has to accept or reject as a whole. The sales occur ten times a year. If De Beers determines that the supply must be limited to keep the market and the price stable, it will simply not sell all that it bought. It has always had sufficient financial resources to hold back this way. The biggest difficulty for the company is a large independent supplier that will not sell through the CSO.

Through the late 1990s, the global diamond industry experienced an unusual amount of uncertainty. Production was still growing, and prices, at least for the better-quality gems, were still high, but the hold of the diamond cartel led by De Beers was seriously challenged. Argyle Diamond Mines joint venture did not renew its contract with the Central Selling Organization in 1996 and sold its production, primarily low-end and small diamonds, on the open market.

Russia also did not renew its contract when it expired at the end of 1995. After intense and protracted negotiations, President Boris Yeltsin signed a decree late in 1997 authorizing an agreement between De Beers and Almazy Rossii-Sakha (Alrosa), Russia's largest diamond producer and only authorized exporter of uncut diamonds. The agreement stipulated that Russia would sell at least US$550 million worth of diamonds to De Beers per year but not more than 26 percent of its total output. It was also agreed that Alrosa would be allowed to sell some of its high-quality stones within Russia to encourage the development of the local diamond-cutting industry and could sell the rest of its production as it saw fit. The agreement was for only three years instead of the usual five. The challenge from Russia was not limited to this agreement. Alrosa entered into development joint ventures in Angola and Namibia, right in De Beers's backyard. De Beers in turn entered into a joint project with another Russian mining company to develop a diamond mine near Arkhangelsk.

De Beers took the steps it felt necessary to keep the industry stable. It cut down the amount of diamonds it sold to the cutting industry in late 1997 and early 1998. Sales from the CSO in the second half of 1997 were down to 1994 levels, and sales in 1998 fell from US$4.64 billion in 1997 to about US$3.5 billion. The strategy and a prosperous global economy in general brought prices back up in 2000 to a record US$5.67 billion. However, as the economy fell in 2001, De Beers's saw sales plummet to a disappointing US$4.45 billion, severely below expected sales of US$4.8 billion.

CURRENT CONDITIONS

By 2003 the global diamond industry was on a stronger footing. After weak demand through 2002, when SARS and political unrest in the Middle East exerted a negative effect on the world economy, diamond jewelry sales grew in 2003, with especially strong demand in the United States, India, China, Britain, and Japan. The DTC raised its rough diamond prices three times during 2003. Full year sales by the DTC, according to De Beers company data, grew 7 percent in 2003 and reached US$5.52 billion. In response to positive economic projections through 2004, the DTC raised rough diamond prices 3 percent in early 2004.

More than 50 percent of world diamond sales occurred in the United States, according to a BBC report. The U.S. market for unset gem diamonds reached an estimated US$10.5 billion in 2002, according to the U.S. Geological Survey, and the United States is expected to dominate global consumption through the year 2010. In 2004, the United States accounted for more than 35 percent of global demand for gem-quality diamonds, with imports estimated at about US$12.9 billion. Huge growth in Chinese demand, however, is expected to fuel hefty diamond sales in Asia through the early 2000s. According to *Rapaport News*, sales of diamond jewelry in China reached US$1.2 billion in 2003, which made it the largest diamond market in Asia, and demand is expected to double by 2013, with some analysts predicting that by 2010 China will become the world leader in diamond consumption.

On the production side, the industry was strong. Mines in Botswana, already a leader in production, were upping their output, and Russia expected to improve its facilities with the help of foreign investment. Bakwanga Mining (Miba), the largest mining company in Democratic Republic of the Congo, announced in 2004 that it planned to increase production and attract new investors. It expected to produce 8.5 million carats in 2005. The opening of the Ekati mine in Canada in 1998 paved the way for Canada to become a major global supplier. In 2003, the mine produced 5.57 million carats. Canada's Diavik mine, which opened in 2003, produced 3.8 million carats that year and was expected to reach annual production of 6 to 8 million carats. Canada's Snap Lake mine, its first completely underground diamond mine, was scheduled to begin operations in 2006. In 2003, Canada accounted for approximately 15 percent of world diamond mining.

By the early 2000s the "conflict diamonds" problem had become so severe in Africa that the United Nations took action. The term conflict diamonds describes diamonds that come from areas where armed groups fighting against the legitimately established government use diamonds to fund their armed insurgence. Conflict diamonds have financed insurrections in Sierra Leone, Liberia, Democratic Republic of Congo, and Central African Republic, as well as Angola. In 2000 the United Nations unanimously adopted a resolution recognizing the role of conflict diamonds in prolonging brutal conflicts in some African countries. The UN mandated a system of international certification for rough diamond shipments, known as the Kimberly Process, which would prevent conflict diamonds from entering legitimate markets. The Kimberly Process was implemented in 2002. A BBC report from March 2004, however, indicated that the protocol, which relies on voluntary compliance by governments that have signed it, had not been effective in preventing sales of conflict diamonds. In 2004, the U.S. military claimed that Al Qaeda was using conflict diamonds to pay for arms.

Meanwhile, the colored gemstone industry outlook appeared to be improving as governments in developing countries around the world took steps to open their economies to outside investment. New deposits of gemstones were being developed in many locations, notably in Brazil, Myanmar, and Tanzania. Global production of non-diamond gemstones, according to the USGS, exceeded US$2 billion in 2003.

INDUSTRY LEADERS

DE BEERS

Founded in the 1870s by Cecil Rhodes, De Beers remained in 2004 the largest diamond mining company in the world. The De Beers Group owned mines in South Africa and partnered with governments in Botswana, Namibia, and Tanzania to operate mines in those countries. In 2000 it initiated operations in Canada. De Beers production in 2004 accounted for more than 40 percent of the global gem diamond market by value, and its Diamond Trading Company handled about 60 percent of rough diamond sales. De Beers is involved in all aspects of the diamond business, including mining, exploration, sorting, marketing, and advertising and promotion. In 2001, De Beers was acquired by DBI consortium. De Beers corporate headquarters are in Johannesburg, South Africa.

In 2002, De Beers reported that 2001 sales fell from a high of US$5.67 billion in 2000 to US$4.45 billion in 2001. De Beers blamed the U.S. recession and the 2001 terrorist attacks for the bulk of the 2001 slack sales. The company had launched major new initiatives in 1999 and 2000 to address challenges related to market volatility. Its "As is—Plus" campaign was aimed to increase efficiencies throughout its businesses and its "Supplier of Choice" program outlined new marketing and sales strategies to drive consumer demand. Additionally, to strengthen its brand recognition De Beers launched its Central Selling Organization under a new name; the Diamond Trading Company, along with a new logo—the Forevermark—. In 2003 De Beers reported a 7 percent growth in diamond sales through the DTC, worth US$5.52 billion.

In 2004, De Beers Kimberly Mines reached a record production of 2 million carats-almost twice the output for the previous year, and the highest production since 1914. The company's mines in South Africa produced 13.7 million carats in 2004, while operations in Botswana and Namibia contributed 47 million carats.

RIO TINTO

Rio Tinto, the world's largest mining company, was comparatively a newcomer to the diamond business. In the late 1990s it acquired a 60 percent interest in Australia's Argyle Diamond Mine, assuming complete ownership in 2002. Through Argyle, the world's largest diamond mine, Rio Tinto accounted as of 2004 for about 25 percent of world diamond production. Rio Tinto also owns a 60 percent interest in Canada's Diavik mine. In 2002 the company established Rio Tinto Diamonds as the marketing division of its diamond business. Rio Tinto's strategy is to build global demand for smaller gems. In addition to its operations in Australia and Canada, the company includes diamond interests in Zimbabwe and diamond sales offices in Belgium and India.

COLORED-STONE LEADERS

Unlike diamonds, the colored gemstone segment of the industry in the early 2000s continued to be conducted by much smaller enterprises. A significant portion of colored gemstone production is generated by independent individual miners. Nevertheless, some consolidation began to occur in the late 1990s. In 1998, Chivor Emerald, a Canadian company operating in Colombia, was bought by AZCO Mining Inc., which had previously focused on copper mining. Another leading producer was Minerales y Metales del Oriente, which operated the Anahi mine in Bolivia, reportedly the world's leading source of amethyst. GTN Resources Ltd., formerly the Great Northern Mining Corporation NL, owned rights to explore and mine in some of the richest sapphire fields in Australia. A collapse in the sapphire market in 2002, however, caused the company to suspend all mining operations, while drawing revenues from its sapphire reserves. GTN Resources announced plans in 2003 to merge with ZBB Energy Corporation.

MAJOR COUNTRIES IN THE INDUSTRY

DIAMOND MINING

South Africa. Although South Africa ranked only fifth in diamond production in 2004 according to the U.S. Geological Survey (USGS), in many ways it still dominated the industry. De Beers Consolidated Mines, along with its sister company De Beers Centenary, was the largest diamond mining company in the world, with numerous mines in South Africa and large interests in many other companies and mines in other countries. South Africa was also the place where the modern diamond industry began. India and Brazil had each in turn dominated the diamond trade in earlier centuries, but, with the discovery and exploitation of the primary deposits of diamonds in kimberlite pipes and the subsequent introduction of large-scale mechanization, production in South Africa multiplied many times over, and the industry was changed forever.

In 2005, South Africa proposed legislation that would tax exports of rough diamonds. The aim of the bill was to restrict the flow of rough diamonds into foreign cutting and manufacturing facilities, in effect forcing De Beers to sell most of its South African diamonds within the country and thus help to strengthen South Africa's economy.

Australia. Diamonds have been found in Australia since 1851, but it was not until the 1980s that the country positioned itself to be an industry leader. In 2003, Australia ranked first in total production, and second in production of gem and near-gem quality diamonds. The vast majority of Australian diamonds came from one operation, the Argyle Diamond Mines Joint Venture in the Kimberly region of Western Australia. This mine produced 40.9 million carats in 1993, representing 37 percent of global output. Production declined to 30.9 million carats in 2003, about 25 percent of world production. The Argyle deposit, a lamproite pipe rather than a kimberlite pipe, was the richest in the world, yielding nearly seven carats of diamond per ton, but most of the production was "cheap gem" and industrial grade. Although Argyle produced some spectacular pink diamonds, only about 5 percent of its output was considered gem quality.

Botswana. Botswana was the world's leading producer of gem-quality diamonds in 2004, generating 22.5 million carats, according to USGS estimates. Diamonds accounted for three-quarters of Botswana's exports, one-third of its gross domestic product, and one-half of government revenue. Debswana, a company owned jointly by the government of Botswana and De Beers of South Africa, accounted for virtually all of this production and was the world's leading diamond company by value. One of its mines, Jwaneng, is widely believed to be the richest in the world, and another, Orapa, is one of the lowest in cost, making the future promising as the potential for further growth is there.

Russia. According to USGS statistics, Russia was the third largest producer of gem diamonds in the early 2000s, with output reaching 12.0 million carats in 2003 and estimated at 12.5 million carats in 2004. But *Pravda* reported that Russian output in 2003 reached 33 billion [sic] carats, making Russia the world's leading diamond producer. This data, the report explained, were made public after Russia was scheduled to chair the Kimberly Process, which required that the country's diamond statistics be declassified for the first time. Pravda also reported that Russia ranked second in world diamond exports.

Russia's diamond deposits are located in Siberia, where mining conditions are very difficult. Winter temperatures average -40 degrees Fahrenheit and can get as low as -90 degrees Fahrenheit. Even summer brings little relief. The deposits are found in an area of permafrost where the ground thaws to a depth of only a few inches, and the warmer weather brings out hordes of mosquitoes. Nevertheless, the former Soviet Union had invested heavily in developing mines because they were an important source of foreign exchange. Russia continued to exploit this resource, although this industry suffered somewhat, along with the rest of the country, in the transition to a market economy,. Russian diamond mining companies also entered into agreements with Angola and Namibia to develop diamond operations in those countries. In 2002, the U.S. Geological Survey noted that Russia's current mining operations had reached a saturation point and new sources of diamonds needed to be discovered to keep diamond output high.

COLORED GEMSTONE MINING

Sri Lanka. Sri Lanka, formerly called Ceylon, is an island country located off India's southeastern shore, and for centuries has been very important in the colored gemstone trade. As home to the second-highest variety of gemstones in the world after Brazil, Sri Lanka was a major producer in the early 2000s of sapphires and many other gems, including alexandrite, spinel, topaz, garnet, and beryl. It was also developing a competitive diamond-cutting industry. The government continued to resist offers from mining companies to introduce large-scale mechanized mining to its placer deposits, and the sites of many of Sri Lanka's primary deposits were unknown. Production declined somewhat in the mid-1990s, and the government proposed to develop the gem-cutting industry to make up for the decline, seeking in particular to develop relationships with gemstone producers in Tanzania. In 2000, gemstones and jewelry were Sri Lanka's third highest source of export revenues. Gemstone sales remained an important part of Sri Lanka's tourist industry in the early 2000s. Tourists find the gems available for purchase in museums, the best hotels, and even on street corners from hawkers.

Myanmar. Myanmar, once called Burma, for centuries has been the world's leading source for fine rubies and quality jade, but it isolated itself from the gem-trading world when a military-backed socialist government took over in 1963. By the late 1980s upon the resignation of longtime president Ne Win, the military assumed a more dominant position, and the country, renamed Myanmar, grew further isolated from international relations. In 1992, however, a major new deposit was discovered at Mong Hsu, and in 1995 the government decided to open its doors once again to the gem trade. A new gem-trading market was opened in Yangon, the capital, and foreign investors were encouraged to participate in gem-cutting and jewelry-making enterprises. As of 2001, however, only Myanmar citizens were allowed to enter into the actual mining of gems in the tightly controlled nation.

Although by 2001 the government was promoting its fine jade to attract tourism and commerce, the country still had to overcome its long history of bloodshed and enslavement. Myanmar's efforts to increase its gemstone business, however, received a setback in 2003 when U.S. President George W. Bush signed a law banning all imports for one year from Myanmar unless it instituted democratic reforms. Analysts predicted that this action would have a huge impact on the global gemstone business. Nevertheless, Myanmar's promotion of official gem emporiums, which attract private buyers, has helped to boost production and sales. According to government sources, Myanmar increased production of jade tenfold between 1995 and 2003, with an output exceeding 10,000 tons. In 2004, Myanmar reported gemstone exports of about US$60 million.

Colombia. Colombia was by far the leading source for emeralds in the early 2000s. The mining districts of Muzo and Chivor still dominated production, as they had under the Spanish conquistadors. The area was periodically disturbed in recent years by what the local inhabitants called the "emerald wars," which were fought for control of the rich deposits after Colombia privatized land and mining rights in 1973. One of these emerald wars occurred in the 1980s, involving the Medellin drug cartel. In the 1990s the situation became more stabilized, though the 1998 arrest of Victor Carranza Nino, owner of Colombia's largest emerald mining operation, caused the industry to falter. Carranza Nino's release in March 2002 fueled hope that the emerald industry would rebound in the early 2000s. In 2004, the Colombian government was investigating the possibility of using new technology to certify the origin of its emerald exports, thus discouraging trade in smuggled gems.

Colombian emeralds were mined directly from primary deposits in very mountainous country. Both mechanized strip-mining and underground shaft and tunnel methods are used, and thousands of *guaqueros,* or "treasure hunters," sort through the scrap ore seeking emeralds that were overlooked. Others resort to less legal methods such as digging their own tunnels into the soft shale at night, a very dangerous process. In late 2001 Central Colombia's governing body, Boyaca, promised tax breaks and other incentives to mining interests willing to start or increase mining operations for emeralds and other gemstones.

Brazil. Brazil, the country with the greatest variety of gemstones on the planet, was also in the early 2000s the world's leading emerald producer, according to the International Colored Gemstone Association. The southeastern state of Minas Gerais, which means "general mines," was the site of a number of new discoveries in the early and mid-1990s, including emeralds, tourmaline, and sapphire. Good quantities of aquamarine were also being produced in the mid-1990s. A new government took office in 1995 and instituted more liberal economic policies, fostering outside investment in exploration and mine development.

In the 2000s a trend among Brazilian mining companies was to collaborate with international corporations seeking shared gemstone profits. In 2002, for example, the Brazil-based gemstone-cutting firm Stone World contracted with U.S.-based Seahawk Minerals to develop funds for additional mining operations.

FURTHER READING

"Angola to Double Diamond Production in 2006."*Afrol News,* 14 March 2005. Available from http://www.afrol.com.

Australian Department of Mineral Resources. *Mineral Resources, New South Wales,* 2002–03. Available from www.minerals.nsw.gov.au.

Blamey, Chris. "One Company, 50 Million Carats of Sapphire a Year." *World Gem Mining Update,* 2002. Available from www.gemstone.org

"Boyaca Seeks Mining Investment—Boyaca." *Business News Americas,* 5 December 2001.

Canadian Department of Natural Resources. "Canada: A Diamond-Producing Nation." Available from www.nrcan-rncan.gc.ca.

"Commerce: Export of Gems and Jewelry Rose." *Pakistan Newswire,* 9 March 2002.

"Conflict Diamonds 'Still on Sale.'" BBC News, 30 March 2004. Available from newsvote.bbc.co.uk.

"Congo Firm Miba to Increase Diamond Production." *National Jeweler,* 9 March 2004. Available from www.national-jeweler.com.

Coughlin, Donald G. "Sri Lanka: A Gemstone Buyer's Dream." *Gemmology Canada,* 2002. Available from www.cigem.ca.

De Beers Group. Company profile. Available from www.debeersgroup.com.

Debswana Company Profile, 2004. Available from www.debswana.com.

"Diamonds Fuel CAR Conflicts." BBC News, 31 October 2002. Available from news.bbc.co.uk.

Eliezri, I. Z. "The 1995 ICA World Gemstone Mining Report." *International Colored Gemstone Association,* 1996. Available from www.gemstone.org.

"Emerald Czar Released from Jail." *Professional Jeweler,* March 2002. Available from www.professionaljeweler.com.

Federman, David. "The War of the Rubies." *Modern Jeweler,* 2002. Available from gemstone.org.

"The Golden Land of Myanmar," 2002. Available from www.myanmar.com/.

Fu Yingqing. "Israel Interested in Local Diamond Market." *Shanghai Star.* 1 July 2004. Available from http://app1.chinadaily.com.cn.

Gooding, Ken. "Survey—African Mining: Botswana, Diamonds: A Country's Best Friend." *Financial Times,* 15 September 1997.

———. "Survey—African Mining: Namibia as the Deposits Diminish." *Financial Times,* 15 September 1997.

Griffiths, Dylan. "DeBeers Diamond Sales May Rebound after 22 Percent Fall." *Bloomberg News,* 15 February 2002.

Hinde, Chris. "DeBeers Diamond Sales May Rebound after 22 Percent Fall." *Mining Magazine*, March 2002.

ICA World Gemstone Mining Update. Available from www.cigem.ca.

Ivanov, Andrei and Judith Perera. "Commodities: Russian Diamond Giant Challenges De Beers." *Interpress Service,* 12 April 1998.

"Russia: Malyshevskoe Rudoupravlenie Resumed Production of Emeralds." *Inzhenernaya Gazeta,* 1996.

Katz, Sheryl. "China's Jewelry Sales Could Double by 2013." *Diamondnet News,* 4 April 2004. Available from www.diamonds.net.

———. "U.S. Military Official Affirms Al-Qaida/Blood Diamonds Link." *Diamondnet News,* 4 April 2004. Available fromwww.diamonds.net.

Mbendi Research. Africa: Mining—Diamond Mining Overview, 2002. Available from www.mbendi.co.za.

———. World: Mining—Diamond Mining—Overview, 2002. Available from www.mbendi.co.za.

Muller, Emma. "De Beers Between Devil and the Deep Blue Sea." *Business Day* (Johannesburg, South Africa), 18 March 2005. Available from http://allafrica.com.

Reich, Eugenie Samuel. "Tracing Emeralds' Origins Could Foil Smugglers." *New Scientist,* 17 January 2004.

Rio Tinto Company Profile, 2004. Available from www.riotinto.com.

"Russia Conquers the Diamond Market with Striking Export Volumes." *Pravda,* 23 December 2004. Available from http://English.pravda.ru.

Schumann, Walter. *Gemstones of the World.* New York: Sterling Publishing Company Inc., 1997.

"Stone World, Seahawk Sign Sales Pact—Brazil." *Business News Americas,* 30 January 2002.

Thet Khaing. "Emporiums Boost Publicity and Sales of Gems." *Myanmar Times,* May 10-16, 2004. Available from www.myanmar.gov.mm.

United Nations General Assembly. *Resolution on Conflict Diamonds,* 21 March 2001. Available from www.un.org.

"U.S. Bans Products from Myanmar." *Professional Jeweler,* September 2003. Available from www.professionaljeweler.com.

U.S. Geological Survey. *Mineral Commodity Summaries*, January 2004. Available from minerals.usgs.gov.

World Diamond Council. Overview and Statistics. Available from www.worlddiamondcouncil.com.

SIC 1000

NAICS 212

MINING, METAL

Metal mining firms explore the earth for numerous metallic minerals (ores), construct mines, and extract the ores for processing. Notable examples of metal ores mined throughout the world are: aluminum, copper, gold, iron, lead, manganese, nickel, silver, tin, and zinc.

After the materials are extracted from the earth, many industry firms also perform separation or other basic processing on ores, but the manufacture of finished or intermediate metal products, such as through smelting or refining, is not considered part of the mining industry. For discussion of the numerous forms of metal production, see also the chapter entitled **Metals Manufacturing.**

Industry Snapshot

The metal mining industry is truly international in scope with various countries around the world having a prominent presence in one or more metal mining sectors. While the largest countries, including China, Canada, the United States, and Brazil, typically have been able to parlay their vast natural resources into significant economic roles in mining segments, smaller countries have been important players as well.

However, China's role in the industry was particularly notable; its dynamic and growing economy had a huge impact on the industry. By the mid-2000s it had emerged as a world leader in both production and consumption of mined metals. China was the global leader in zinc and iron ore production, as well as a major source of copper, gold, and lead. It also led the world in copper and zinc consumption, while its consumption of iron ore, lead, and gold substantially increased world demand for these metals.

In mid-2000s, mineral ore production continued to serve as a cornerstone of the global economy. According to the U.S. Geological Survey, world total mine copper production was estimated at 15.3 million tons (mmt) in 2006, while production of iron ore was estimated at 1.69 billion mt. Production levels for other industry metals in 2006 included gold (2.5 mmt); nickel (1.50 billion metric tons); silver (19.5 mmt); zinc (10 mmt); and aluminum (33.1 mmt).

Although metal mining is one of the oldest human industries, during the early to mid-2000s it was still characterized by a vigorous search for new sources of unmined ores, new mining technologies, and new markets for ores. By 2000 worldwide exploration for new precious metal mines spent US$2.7 billion. Environmental activists, however, continued to condemn the mining industry because certain mining activities can and do destroy natural habitats and pollute the ground. For example, an accident in 2000 at the Freeport McMoRan Copper and Gold Grasper mine in Indonesia killed several workers and dumped contaminated water into the Wamego River, thus contaminating the surrounding water supply.

ORGANIZATION AND STRUCTURE

Mining methods vary depending on the mineral, its location, and the ratio of extraction costs to the mineral's revenue potential. The three major types of mining methods are surface, alluvial, and underground mining.

Open-pit bench mining and open-pit strip mining involve the extraction of massive deposits that are housed at or near the planet's surface. This method can be used in almost any kind of terrain. Touted by supporters as cost-effective, efficient, and safer than underground mining, critics decry the environmental impact of such methods.

Alluvial mining is employed to find minerals that are mixed with silt, sand, gravel, and other materials commonly found in the vicinity of creeks, rivers, and lakes, while underground mining is used to locate and harvest minerals buried deep beneath the earth's surface. Although underground mining practices reduce the impact on the surface environment and allow operations to proceed in inclement weather, this method is more hazardous to workers, requires more equipment, and is not always ideal for extracting some deposits. Also, production costs of other methods are much higher than those incurred by underground mining operations.

BACKGROUND AND DEVELOPMENT

The modern-style metal mining industry began in the nineteenth century, although metal ores had been mined for several millennia before that time. Iron, copper, tin, and gold had all been mined with varying degrees of success and effectiveness. The Industrial Revolution, however, transformed the economies of developed countries and introduced iron, coal, and limestone as strategically important minerals. Practical steam-powered machinery increased the demand for coal and iron, while breakthroughs in the 1850s enabled inexpensive production of large amounts of steel.

The discovery of gold in California in 1848 proved to be an important factor in the settlement of the western United States. The discovery of significant deposits of silver, gold, and copper made the United States a world leader in metal mining by the beginning of the twentieth century. At the same time that prospectors were fanning out across the United States in search of gold, major discoveries of other metals were made around the world.

Moreover, researchers during the last century found new uses for industrial metals. Advanced economies such as those in Europe and North America increasingly relied on industrial metal mining. While these regions led the world in mining production and the broader metal industry, by the mid-1900s a number of other industrializing nations, notably the Soviet Union, emerged as important metal mining centers.

MINING SAFETY

Mining has long been one of the world's most dangerous industries. While the majority of mining injuries and deaths have historically taken place in coal mines—nearly 3,200 men died in coal mine accidents in the United States in 1907 alone—a significant number of workers have been injured or killed in metal mining operations as well. Even in the mid-1970s, after a number of laws and regulations were enacted, about 8,300 disabling injuries were reported per year in metal and nonmetal mines (not including coal mines) in the United States. In countries with less stringent safety laws, accidents are more common. In 1995, 100 workers were killed in one gold mine accident in South Africa. In 2005, 209 miners were killed in an explosion accident in Liaoning province in China, just three months after an accident in Shaanxi province killed 166 miners. Rock falls, haulage accidents, methane explosions, mishaps with machinery, and suffocation have all caused loss of life.

The first federal mine safety legislation in the United States, which was the principal mining nation in the world at the time, was primarily concerned with coal mining. The Organic Act of 1910, which created the U.S. Bureau of Mines, was passed in reaction to a series of horrible coal mine explosions. Other legislation in the first half of the twentieth century was also passed, but most of these laws had little real power. In 1952, however, the Federal Coal Mine Safety Act was passed. Under this act safety regulations were made mandatory and inspectors were given added powers. Two other bills, the Coal Mine Health and Safety Act of 1969 and the Federal Metal and Nonmetallic Mine Safety Act of 1966, became the primary safety codes for all mining in the United States. In 1973 the Mining Enforcement and Safety Administration (MESA) was created to oversee the U.S. industry.

CURRENT CONDITIONS

The status of the metal mining sectors continued to vary at the start of the new millennium. Factors such as world demand, privatization, environmental concerns and regulations, economic conditions in producer countries, labor relations, and trade agreements all affected the metal mining industry and its various segments. The mining industry was also dependent on the strength and economic trends of many industries including those related to appliances, autos, beverages, and computers. The industry's outlook, however, remained strong due to consumer reliance and demand for many products and services that rely on mining activities. In fact, in the early 2000s, according to the Office of Industrial Technologies, nearly 47,000 pounds of materials had to be mined for each person living in the United States in order to maintain their standard of living.

In response to these trends and factors, the industry began to consolidate during the early years of the 2000s, especially in the precious metals mining sector. Australia-based BHP Ltd. acquired UK mining firm Billiton PLC in 2001, forming BHP Billiton Limited. Newport Mining Corporation secured its leading position among gold mining companies when it purchased Battle Mountain Gold in 2001 and its acquisitions of Normandy Mining of Australia and Canada-based Franco-Nevada Corp. the following year.

IRON ORE

According to the U.S. Geological Survey's Mineral Commodity Summaries, world production of iron ore reached an estimated 1.69 billion tons in 2006. A significant increase in demand from China was the primary factor affecting production and exports and was expected to continue to play a major role in the industry, though at a slightly slower rate of growth. Indeed, iron ore consumption in China was the key factor on which the expansion of the international iron ore industry depended. China led the world in iron ore production in 2006, with an estimated total of 520 mmt. It was followed by Brazil (280 mmt) and Australia (262 mmt). India and Russia also had significant production levels. Iron ore is typically used for manufacturing various types of steel, magnets, auto parts, biochemical and metallurgical applications, paints and inks, cosmetics, and plastics and polishing compounds.

COPPER

World copper production reached an estimated 15.3 million tons in 2006. The top producer by far remained Chile, with an estimated total of 5.4 mmt. The United States produced an estimated 1.2 mmt of copper in 2006, ranking second in world production just ahead of Indonesia, with 1.07 mmt, and Peru, where output reached approximately 1.01 mmt. China was the largest user of copper in 2006, accounting for about 20 percent of world consumption. Copper is used for electrical cables and wiring, plumbing, heating, roofing, building construction, and machinery.

The copper industry began to recover in the early 2000s following a slump in the late 1990s after a major trading scandal caused world copper prices to plunge by more than 30 percent and to remain depressed through 2001. Excess global supplies prompted significant production cutbacks in the United States, Chile, and Peru; at the same time, increased demand from China, where consumption rose by 16 percent in 2003, helped boost world consumption by approximately 275,000 tons. With global inventories reduced as a result of these factors, copper prices rose substantially in 2003. According to figures from the International Copper Study Group cited by the USGS, world copper production rose by 3.7 percent in 2004 while demand grew by 5.7 percent, resulting in an expected production deficit of 700,000 tons. By 2006 copper prices had reached a record high of $4.08 a pound.

SILVER AND GOLD

The vast majority of silver produced is as a by-product of other metal mining, such as copper, lead, and zinc. Silver production increased steadily in the late 1990s and early 2000s, as did consumption, thanks in part to growth in sales of home computers and cellular phones. As mine production neared 18 mmt in 2000, demand reached 29.4 mmt. World production increased to 20 mmt in 2002 but decreased to only 18.8 mmt in 2003 and reached an estimated 19.5 mmt in 2004. It dropped slightly in 2005, to 19.3 mmt, but then rebounded to 19.5 mmt in 2006. With world demand remaining high, the deficit between silver production and supply remained substantial at approximately 700 tons. The use of silver in photographic processing declined significantly between 1999 and 2006 as sales of digital cameras, which do not use film, rose.

The major countries involved in silver mining are Mexico, Peru, and Australia. Silver is used for photographic and chemical applications, jewelry, electronics, currency, alloys, mirrors, and in various medical and scientific applications.

Gold prices, which remained low at the turn of the twenty-first century, rose early in the 2000s in response to the U.S.-led war in Iraq and concerns about global terrorism. The strength of the U.S. dollar in the late 1990s caused demand for gold to weaken and forced many firms to consolidate and pare back operations. South Africa, the largest producer mining nearly 30 percent of the world's gold, reported a 40-year low in production in 1996, and exploration continued to falter into the new millennium. Gold prices were held down through the late 1990s because some central banks sold part of their gold reserves. Holland and Belgium sold in 1996, Australia in 1997, and Switzerland announced plans to dispose of half of its gold reserves in 1999. Consumption of gold, however, grew steadily in the 1990s as the world economy expanded. Increased demand from China, up 12.8 percent from 2003, was a significant factor. While the world jewelry industry is by far the largest consumer of gold, the metal is also used in electronics and dentistry.

By 1998 the price of gold had reached an 18-year low of US$278 per ounce. In 2002 it rebounded slightly to just over US$310. The relatively weak U.S. dollar, however, helped to raise gold prices to an average of about US$400 through most of 2004, with prices reaching an 18-year high of US$455 per ounce late in the year. This record was broken again in 2006, when gold prices reached US$726 per ounce. According to the U.S. Geological Survey, mining companies throughout the world produced an estimated 2.5 mmt of gold in 2006. South Africa remained the primary producer, with 270 mmt. The United States and Australia tied for second, with 260 mmt, followed closely by China with 240 mmt.

LEAD AND ZINC

Lead consumption has declined dramatically since the 1970s, in part because of environmental and health regulations designed to address concerns about some of the metal's properties. However, the abandonment of lead as an anti-knocking additive to gasoline and the development of replacement materials for batteries (which at one time accounted for 80 percent of U.S. lead demand) were regarded as more important factors in lead's fall in popularity. Lead production levels remained fairly unchanged from 1997 to 2000 and were much lower than copper, gold, and iron ore. However, worldwide demand rose by 1 percent in 2003, another 2 to 3 percent in 2004, and yet another 3 to 4 percent in 2006, prompted by increased consumption in China's automotive, telecommunications, and information technology sectors. World production of lead reached 3.27 mmt in 2005 and an estimated 3.26 mmt in 2006, with China the major producer, accounting for about 30 percent of production.

Zinc production, meanwhile, showed continued recovery from fifteen-year lows reached in 1996. Weak prices and high stock levels prompted some restructuring in the industry in the late 1990s, with some smaller and less efficient mines suspending operations or closing permanently while other companies upgraded facilities to enhance efficiency. Improved prices in 2003 and 2004, coupled with strong demand from China. Zinc output reached 10.0 mmt in 2006. Zinc is an important component in the manufacture of galvanized metal, brass, and other zinc-based alloys. In mid-2000s, about 48 percent of zinc was used in construction industries and 23 percent in the automotive industry. China was the largest producer, followed by Australia and Peru.

INDUSTRY LEADERS

U.S. COMPANIES

The United States is the home of many major metal mining companies. Leading gold and silver mining companies located in the United States include Newmont Mining Corporation, which became the leading gold miner in the world with its 2002 purchases of Battle Mountain Gold Co., Normandy Mining, and Franco-Nevada Corp. It posted revenues of US$4.98 billion in 2006 and employed 15,000 people. The company produces approximately 8 million ounces of gold each year, as well as copper, silver, and zinc. Cleveland-Cliffs Inc., which focuses on iron ore, produces approximately 23 million tons of iron ore pellets each year. Its sales in 2004 totaled US$1.73 billion and the company employed 4,085 workers. Phelps Dodge Corp. purchased Cyprus Amax, a highly diversified mining company, in 1999. The deal boosted Phelps's position in the copper industry, making it the second-largest producer in 2004. The company, which also mines gold, silver, and other minerals, posted sales that year of US$11.9 billion in 2006.

ANGLO AMERICAN

The Anglo American Corporation, based in London, is one of the world's largest mining companies, with major operations in gold, platinum, and diamond production. Its 2003 merger between AngloGold and Ashanti Goldfields created the second-largest gold mining company in the world, AngloGold Ashanti, which produced about 7 million ounces annually. Anglo American was also part owner of Anglo American Platinum, the leading platinum producer in the world. Anglo also produced various metals, coal, forest products, and industrial minerals. In 2001 it increased its stake in De Beers, the well-known diamond concern, and in 2002 it acquired the Disputada (Minera Sur Andes) copper operations in Chile, placing Anglo American among the world's top five copper producers. In 2003 the company's revenues from platinum fell 12 percent from the previous year, reaching only US$205 million. Gold earnings fell from US$205 million in 2002 to US$167 million in 2003. Earnings from base metals, however, including copper and zinc, rose from a mere US$69 million in 2002 to US$206 million in 2003. Anglo American's reported a record operating profit of $9.8 billion in 2006.

RIO TINTO GROUP

Rio Tinto was one of the largest metal mining companies in the world in the mid-2000s. Rio Tinto mined primarily for aluminum, iron, and gold; about 20 percent of its sales came from coal. The company had dual headquarters in Australia and the United Kingdom; the Australian side was known as Rio Tinto Limited and the U.K. entity was called Rio Tinto PLC. In 2006 Rio Tinto posted underlying earnings of US$2.2 billion in iron ore, US$746 million in aluminum, US$3.5 billion in copper, US$206 million in diamonds, and US$243 million in industrial minerals. The company's total earnings of US$7.3 billion were 48 percent higher than the previous year.

Rio Tinto employed more than 36,000 people worldwide and increased it capital investment from US$2.5 billion in 2005 to US$3.9 billion in 2006. The company's major mines were located in Australia, North America, New Zealand, and Europe.

BHP BILLITON

BHP Ltd., a steel company, acquired the United Kingdom-based mining concern Billiton PLC in 2001 to form BHP Billiton Ltd. and BHP Billiton Plc. The two firms had separate headquarters in Australia and England, were operated as a single business unit, and together were known as BHP Billiton. The company mined copper, iron, gold, and coal and also had steel and petroleum operations. Total sales in 2006 were US$39.0 billion.

CODELCO

Corporacion Nacional del Cobre de Chile (Codelco), the state-run mining company of Chile, was the world's largest producer of copper. The company's revenues reached an all-time high of US$10.4 billion in 2005. Codelco also owned the world's largest copper reserves, amounting to 17 percent of known copper deposits. The company mined about 1.8 mmt of copper per year. Nearly 17 percent of Chile's exports stemmed from Codelco's mining operations. Its business also accounted for nearly 3 percent of the region's gross domestic product.

TECK COMINCO LIMITED

Cominco was purchased by gold mining company Teck in 2001. The newly merged company mined gold, zinc, metallurgical coal, and copper, and had global exploration ventures. The majority of the firm's operations were held in Canada, the United States, and Peru. Company sales reached US$6.5 billion in 2006, of which most derived from zinc mining and refining. The firm controlled the Red Dog mine in Alaska, one of the largest zinc mines in the world.

MAJOR COUNTRIES IN THE INDUSTRY

UNITED STATES

Some members of the metal mining industry in the United States remained among the largest and most influential in the world. Armed with large reserves of many metal minerals within its own borders, the United States had long been an important player, although at any given time some industry segments had performed better than others. According to the U.S. Department of Energy's Industrial Technologies Program, by the early 2000s mined products contributed almost 5 percent of the U.S. gross domestic product, and mining operations directly employed more than 320,000 people. In 2001, a total of 1.2 billion tons of crude metal ore and 3.3 billion tons of crude industrial ore were extracted from U.S. mines. More than 90 percent of crude metal and industrial ores were taken from surface mines.

In 2006 the United States' total metal mining production industry was worth US$23.5 billion, representing a 51 percent increase from 2005. Of this total, copper was responsible for the most (36 percent), followed by gold (22 percent), iron ore (13 percent), molybdenum (13 percent), zinc (10 percent), and lead (3 percent). The largest increases in value came from zinc (117 percent increase), copper (97 percent), palladium (65 percent), and gold (68 percent). Aluminum, copper, and iron and steel remained the leading imports in terms of value. Total value of imports of metals and industrial minerals equaled $5.9 billion in 2006; imports were worth $6.3 billion.

LATIN AMERICA

The countries of Latin America have deep reserves of metal mineral deposits, and in the 1990s the region was the recipient of much investment by large international mining companies. This influx coincided with reforms of mining and investment laws throughout Latin America and a move toward privatization in some countries. In 2004 the Fraser Institute included four Latin American countries among the top ten in the world for mineral exploration based on their financial attractiveness for investment: Chile (5th), Peru (7th), Mexico (8th), and Brazil (10th).

In the mid-2000s, Mexico remained a leading producer of several mineral commodities, including lead, gypsum, and zinc, and was the world's largest producer of silver. Exploration activity in Mexico focused on gold and silver. However, low prices for nonferrous metals, along with labor issues and high energy prices, caused production difficulties in 2002, resulting in several mine closures as well as termination of new projects. Copper production decreased by 10 percent and gold by 9 percent; though silver production also declined slightly, Mexico's output remained the world's highest. While overall metal production in Mexico decreased in 2002, output grew for lead and zinc. The total value of Mexico's mineral production that year declined from US$4.8 billion to US$4.6 billion. However, gold production was expected to increase in Mexico due to the completion of two new mines there.

As a result of its long-established program of privatization, as well as free-trade agreements with countries in both North and South America, Mexico had many international mining companies involved in exploration and production projects. Argentina, Brazil, Colombia, Bolivia, and Peru also made significant changes in order to attract foreign investment to help develop their metal mining industries.

In Brazil the government set plans in motion to reform its mining companies in order to triple the country's mining revenues by 2010. The country produced significant quantities of aluminum, copper, gold, iron, tin, nickel, and zinc. According to USGS analyses, the country will remain one of the world's most important producers of metals and other minerals through the 2000s. Mining development and exploration related to gold and copper in Peru was expected to reach US$10 billion in the first decade of the new millennium. In 2002, Peru was one of the world's largest producers of copper, lead, silver, and zinc. Mineral production that year (including metals and fuels) was valued at US$4.6 billion. Argentina also signed a cross-border agreement with Chile in order to promote mining activities. Ecuador passed mining laws to bolster exploration and development.

CANADA

In 2003, Canada's mining and mineral processing industry accounted for $40.8 billion—about 4 percent—of the country's gross domestic product and employed 388,898 people. According to the Mining Association of Canada, the mining industry had the highest level of productivity growth compared to the country's other industrial industries. Overall, Canada exported $46.6 billion in minerals and metals in 2003, accounting for more than 13 percent of its total exports and making it the world's largest exporter of metals. Canada is a leading miner of uranium, nickel, titanium and zinc, aluminum, gold, copper, and lead.

AFRICA

Africa has deposits of sixty different metal and mineral products including gold, diamonds, uranium, manganese, chromium, nickel, bauxite, and cobalt. Exploration efforts were strong in gold and diamonds, and countries including Mozambique, Nigeria, and Madagascar were being explored for base metal and industrial mineral deposits. The African mining industry was centered in southern Africa (South Africa, Ghana, Zimbabwe, Tanzania, and Zambia), and exploration and development projects were underway in virtually every part of the continent. According to Mbendi Information Services, nearly 30 percent of the earth's mineral reserves are found in Africa.

One of the world's largest minerals producers, South Africa mined significant amounts of vanadium, titanium, aluminum, copper, chromium, nickel, iron, lead, and zinc. The company's gold mining operations, after a 30-year decline in production from 1970 to 2000, began an upward trend in 2002. Three major new mines opened in 2002 and 2003, increasing production by about 30 tons per year. The mining industry continued to face challenges, however, into the mid-2000s. According to Pricewaterhouse Coopers, the world's largest mining companies throughout the world saw investment increases of about 30 percent and income increases of almost 60 percent in 2005, due to economic growth and increase in demand in China. However, investments in mining in South Africa declined by one third between 2004 and 2005, and profits grew by only 12 percent. Some of the reasons for the problem, according to an article in *The Economist,* include currency fluctuations, congested railways and ports, and red tape and regulatory uncertainty.

EUROPE AND CENTRAL ASIA

Western Europe's mining industry diminished in importance in the late 1990s. Countries increasingly relied on imports from Africa, Australia, North America, and South America. As the European Union finalized its transition to a single economy in the early 2000s, various member countries moved to privatize state-owned mineral enterprises. Exploration was carried on for base metals and gold in Ireland, Spain, Portugal, Sweden, Finland, Romania and Turkey. Germany and Poland were major coal producers.

In Central and Eastern Europe the trend toward the development of a market economy and privatization of state-owned enterprises continued. In Poland, which was the ninth-largest copper producer in 2003, the giant state copper corporation KGHM was publicly traded on the Warsaw stock market. Modernization of mining operations was funded by foreign partners, local and foreign banks, and international financial institutions such as the World Bank and the European Bank for Reconstruction and Development. Foreign investment focused on the exploration and development of gold deposits and industrial minerals.

Mineral production in the former Soviet Union was dominated by Russia, Kazakhstan, and the Ukraine in the early 2000s. Russia was the sixth-largest copper producer in 2004, with 675 million tons, and the fourth-largest producer of iron ore, with 95 million tons; Ukraine came sixth in iron ore production with 66 million tons. In 2004 Kazakhstan was eighth in both copper production and in zinc. Other significant metal mining countries in the region were Tajikistan, Uzbekistan, and Georgia. Russia and other countries of the former Soviet Union (FSU) have struggled to keep their economies afloat. In the face of tight domestic and neighboring markets for their ores, the region's mining firms struggled to become more profitable by controlling costs, restructuring their enterprises, and implementing a variety of other tactics to salvage the flagging industry. They also sought foreign capital to reinvigorate their businesses. Through the early 2000s the mining industry in this region continued to stand on shaky ground.

MIDDLE EAST

Primarily known as a supplier of crude petroleum, the Middle East was far less involved in the world metal mining industry. Turkey and Iran ranked as the region's leading producers of metal minerals, while Israel, Jordan, and Saudi Arabia also had significant stakes in one or more production areas.

ASIA AND PACIFIC RIM

Metal mining and processing establishments in this region, which includes China, Indonesia, India, and Australia among others, were key producers in the international industry. Through the mid-2000s, the region experienced the greatest increase in demand for metals as its economies experienced rapid growth. Australia, besides being home to some of the world's largest mining companies, was among the top producers of copper, gold, iron, silver, and zinc.

In 1997 China announced its decision to accelerate its plans, begun in the early 1990s, to reform state-owned industries. The plans called for converting large- and mid-sized enterprises into independent corporations in order to promote globalization. The government continued this conversion into the new millennium. By early 2000 China was the world's leading producer of iron; in 2004 it was also the top producer of zinc, as well as a major source of copper, gold, and lead. Consumption in China also increased significantly: by 2003 the country led the world in consumption of copper and zinc and had also substantially increased demand for other metals, including iron ore and lead.

Indonesia, the third most populous country in the world, made great strides in the 1990s to develop its minerals industries. In 2004 it was the second leading producer of tin and a major source of copper and gold. Along with a number of other countries in the region, however, in late 1997 and early 1998, it was rocked by a serious financial crisis that diminished foreign investment and strapped local firms for money. The region's economic woes continued into the new millennium. Production of some metals decreased in the early 2000s including copper, which fell from 979 mt in 2003 to an estimated 860 mt in 2004. Gold production also declined during that period from 140 mt to 120 mt.

FURTHER READING

Anglo American Annual Report, 2006. Available from www.angloamerican.co.uk.

BHP Billiton Annual Report, 2006. Available from www.bhpbilliton.com.

"China's Consumer Demand for Gold Rises 12.9 Pct in 2004." 3 March 2005. *AsiaPulse* via COMTEX. Available from http://news.tradingcharts.com/forex.

Cleveland-Cliffs Annual Report, 2004. Available from www.cleveland-cliffs.com.

Codelco 2005 Annual Report. Available from www.codelco.cl.

Department of the Interior, U.S. Geological Survey. *Mineral Commodity Summaries.* 3 April 2007. Available from www.minerals.usgs.gov.

Forrest, Michael. "Exploration: No Expenses Spared?" *Materials World,* December 2005.

Gurmendi, Alfredo C., et al. "The Mineral Industries of Latin America and Canada." *U.S. Geological Survey Minerals Yearbook, 2004.* Available from http://minerals.usgs.gov/minerals.

"Hoover's Company Capsules." *Hoover's Online,* 2007. Available from www.hoovers.com.

"Indonesian Metal Mining Industry Has Revived." *Indonesian Commercial Newsletter,* July 2006.

"Mining Accident Kills 209 in China." *ACN: Asian Chemical News,* 21 February 2005.

"Mining Works for Canada." Mining Association of Canada, 2005. Available from www.miningworks.mining.ca/.

"Phelps Dodge Annual Report 2006." 27 February 2007. Available from http://www.fcx.com/ir/ar.htm.

Rio Tinto Annual Review, 2006. Available from www.riotinto.com.

Teck Cominco Limited Annual Report, 2006. Available from www.teckcominco.com.

"Undermined: Mining in South Africa." *The Economist (US),* 18 November 2006.

U.S. Department of Energy, Office of Industrial Technologies. *Mining Annual Report, Fiscal Year 2004.* Available from www.oit.doe.gov.

White, Lane. "The Challenges of Prosperity." *Engineering & Mining Journal,* October 2006.

World Gold Council. Current Statistics and Prices. 3 April 2007. Available from www.gold.org.

PAPER AND ALLIED PRODUCTS

SIC 2621

NAICS 322121

PAPER MILLS

Paper mills manufacture paper from wood pulp, wastepaper, and other fiber or chemical pulp; many of the same firms also produce converted paper products. Integrated pulping and papermaking operations are considered in this discussion when they have a sizable presence in papermaking. See also **Paperboard Mills, Paperboard Containers and Boxes,** and **Pulp Mills.**

INDUSTRY SNAPSHOT

Papermaking has been a global industry for centuries. After paper was invented in China in the second century, the craft of papermaking slowly spread throughout the world. The mechanization of papermaking in the nineteenth century spurred a near-simultaneous development of paper businesses in all major industrial economies. While paper mills and pulp mills are considered separate industries, the two are, in reality, directly connected. A majority of the world's paper is produced at mills integrated with pulp production at the same site and is used for packaging and printing.

Countries with large forest resources, such as the United States, Canada, and the Scandinavian countries, dominate the paper industry since most virgin paper is produced close to its primary raw material—trees. However, recycled fiber plays an increasingly large role in paper production, and many countries—notably Germany, Japan, and South Korea—base the majority of their paper manufacturing industries on recycled paper.

While growth rates in industrialized countries have not been spectacular, developing nations have made strong gains in the per capita usage of paper. As of the mid-2000s, the United States was by far the world's largest manufacturer and consumer of pulp, paper, and paperboard. As the Forest Products Association of Canada reported in 2005, paper demand has doubled since 1985 and is forecast to double again between 2005 and 2010. Overall annual consumption rates are expected to grow by about 3.2 percent by 2015, with consumption growing by about 2.5 percent annually in developed countries but by 5.5 percent in developing nations.

ORGANIZATION AND STRUCTURE

Most paper machinery, equipment, and chemical suppliers sell their products worldwide. Although some countries possess more sophisticated equipment than others do, the process of industrial papermaking is largely the same throughout the world.

Financial Structure. The paper industry is among the world's most capital-intensive manufacturing industries because it requires nearly continuous investment in plants, equipment, and maintenance. Due to the vast amount of money required to build and maintain paper mills, large companies dominate production of papermaking worldwide. To maximize their returns, these firms purchase enormous, high-speed machines to achieve economies of scale by producing paper at the lowest possible unit cost. Since many grades of paper are widely exported, and thus are subject to international standards, most large paper mills throughout the world must remain technically up-to-date. Technological advances have helped paper mills to simultaneously improve quality while driving down production costs.

The volatility of the pulp and paper business cycle was illustrated by changes in the global price of market pulp from 1994 to 1997. In 1994, the price of pulp increased 75 percent in one year, due to increased demand and limited supply. However, in late 1996 the price of pulp began falling, and in six months the price dropped nearly 50 percent due to reduced purchases by customers and increased capacity by suppliers. In May 2002, after years of depressed prices, the paper industry was optimistic when the Canadian government announced that increased demand and shrinking inventories boded well for the industry in coming years. Nonetheless, that same month International Paper Company furloughed some of its mill workers, saying the demand for coated papers failed to meet inventoried stocks.

Two major factors have affected the financial performance of paper companies worldwide: general economic expansion and the capacity rates in individual countries. As with most commodities, when paper is in oversupply its prices tend to fall, and when demand exceeds supply prices typically rise. For paper manufacturers, higher prices usually signal higher profits. The industry's health can be predicted by the health of magazine and catalog ad sales; declining ad sales translate to fewer printed pages and depressed coated stock prices.

BACKGROUND AND DEVELOPMENT

The invention of paper is generally credited to Ts'ai Lun, a member of the Chinese imperial court, around 105 A.D. Ts'ai Lun's paper was made from mulberry and other barks, fish nets, hemp, and rags. The fibers separated from this pulp were passed through a screen, formed into a web, and dried. This handmade process was used for centuries thereafter. The ancient Egyptians also used a substance made of mashed reeds called papyrus for writing purposes and the word "paper" is derived from papyrus. The Greeks wrote on the dried leather skins of animals.

Papermaking arrived in Japan in the seventh century. The process of making paper began to spread into Europe during the twelfth century, and Araba settlers built paper mills in Spain. These mills used rags almost exclusively to make paper. With the advent of book printing in Europe in the middle of the fifteenth century, the use of paper began to grow rapidly. By 1690 papermaking had spread to the American colonies, when William Rittenhouse established the first U.S. paper mill near Philadelphia.

In 1798, a Frenchman named Louis-Nicolas Robert invented a machine to produce paper in a continuous process, instead of the handmade process that used vats and molds. In the early 1800s, two English papermakers, Henry and Sealy Fourdrinier, purchased patents for the machine. After modification, the Fourdrinier's machine became very popular in England and spread to other countries. This machine had, in effect, turned papermaking from a handmade process into an industry. The name "fourdrinier" is still used to describe certain paper machines.

Another revolutionary event in the manufacture of paper occurred in the middle of the nineteenth century. Recycled rag fibers from clothing were used almost exclusively to make paper until the end of the 1860s, when straw fibers began to be used. Straw was quickly followed by the use of groundwood and chemical pulp, both of which were in use in Europe and North America by the early 1870s. Wood pulp had thus become the preferred method because, at the time, it was in plentiful and inexpensive supply for papermaking.

The size and speed of paper machines increased rapidly between 1850 and the beginning of World War I, and by the late 1880s paper use was booming. After World War I, the global paper industry began producing more paper containers and packaging, increasing its use of corrugated medium and linerboard, to make shipping boxes, and producing a host of new products such as tissues and sanitary napkins. During World War II, paper and paperboard were vital materials for the armed forces of both the Allied and the Axis powers, which used paper packaging to ship and store military supplies. Paper drives became common during the war years and marked one of the earliest efforts to recycle paper.

After World War II, the global paper industry developed more scientific approaches to forestry and papermaking. Europe rapidly re-industrialized after the war, and modern paper mills were built. By 1945, there were as many as 14,000 different paper products produced worldwide, and that number continued to expand as new uses were found for paper—such as in milk cartons and drinking cups. Many industry growth trends were centered on the use of disposable paper products.

For centuries, papermaking had been considered an art practiced by experts who used instinct and intuition in manufacturing. The 1950s saw a shift in papermaking from art to science. In the 1950s and 1960s wider and faster paper machines were invented, which helped to greatly increase the supply of paper and board throughout the world. By the early 1970s the paper industry faced challenges worldwide from environmental groups. In question were their emissions of waste products into the air and water. New rules concerning clean air and water forced paper businesses in most industrialized countries to install expensive new air and water treatment systems.

In the 1970s Europe forged ahead in the production of alkaline paper and recycled paper; however, North American producers did not begin manufacturing these types of paper until the late 1980s. The 1980s and early 1990s saw extensive modernization in paper industries throughout the world as new, high-speed equipment and extensive automation brought papermaking quality and efficiency to new highs.

The forestry practices of Canadian pulp and paper companies—particularly clearcutting—began to be attacked by environmental groups such as Greenpeace, in the early 1990s, and a sophisticated media campaign against Canadian producers continued through much of the 1990s. These efforts also spawned a well-organized European campaign to boycott purchases of Canadian market pulp. The Canadian industry mounted a strong defense of its forestry practices. In Europe, many paper mills converted to totally chlorine-free (TCF) bleaching systems to comply with public pressure to remove all chlorine-based chemicals from the papermaking process.

The global paper industry suffered from a negative public image throughout much of the 1990s. Despite industry participants' contentions that they promoted sustainable forestry by replanting land that had been logged, used a high proportion of recycled fiber, attempted to rapidly phase out the use of elemental chlorine from bleaching sequences, and met stringent wastewater requirements, many environmental groups and citizens considered the industry to be detrimental to the earth. Unaccustomed to such spirited, public debate, paper companies in many nations were slow to present their cases to the public. However, with their continued use of forest resources challenged, many companies eventually responded either individually or through their trade organizations, presenting positive, factual information about forestry and papermaking through the news media, advertising, public relations, and other outlets.

While recycled paper had always been a major source of raw material for the paper industry, public pressure in many countries caused European and North American paper companies to expand their use of recycled paper. With limited supplies of wood, Europe traditionally had a high rate of recycling; many of its countries recycled more than 50 percent of their annual paper production. Japan, also short on virgin fiber, typically recycled more than 50 percent of its paper production. Other Asian countries with strong paper industries, such as Taiwan and South Korea, also depended, to a great extent, on recycled paper for much of their paper and paperboard production.

However, with its abundant supplies of wood, North America historically recycled at a much lower rate than Europe or Japan. For example, the U.S. paper industry's recycling rate hovered just above 25 percent in the late 1980s. In the late 1980s, a perceived landfill crisis developed in the United States. Public pressure to expand recycling increased, and by the early 1990s the Canadian and U.S. paper industries quickly improved their recycling capacities. Canadian mills, many of which produced newsprint for the U.S. market, had to comply with the laws of many U.S. states that mandated certain levels of recycled fiber in newspapers published within their boundaries. U.S. mills had to comply with federal guidelines for the purchase of recycled paper, which quickly became a de facto standard for many other purchasers of paper, both public and private.

Consequently, in 1989 the U.S. paper industry set a goal to recycle 40 percent of the paper it produced by 1995. That goal was reached two years early and the industry reset even loftier goals. Recycling also expanded in Europe. Much of the credit was given to strict German recycling laws that other European countries began to adopt. These laws required manufacturers of industrial and consumer products, such as packaging suppliers, to make provisions for collecting and recycling their products, including setting up recycling centers. Such a system was the reverse of that in the United States and Canada, where collection of wastepaper was handled voluntarily by businesses or by municipalities.

However, while environmental concerns about controlling pulp and paper emissions appeared to be abating, the availability of fiber—primarily raw wood from tree harvesting—emerged as an obstacle for the global paper industry. In the late 1990s, European and North American paper producers were confronted with sustained opposition to tree harvesting from environmental groups and harvesting restrictions imposed by government agencies. In the northwestern United States, tree harvesting on federal lands virtually came to a halt due to legal challenges in the early 1990s. Production resumed by the mid-1990s, but at a greatly reduced rate. The pace of "removals" of trees from federal lands continued at a low level into the early 2000s. Likewise, stricter control of harvesting practices on federal land in western Canada was expected to raise the cost of timber operations in that region.

The electronic display and storage of information presented another major challenge to the global paper industry. As computers became commonplace in homes and offices in the industrialized world of the 1970s, many experts predicted that paper would become obsolete. However, by the 1990s it became apparent that the advent of computers and fax machines would have the opposite effect on the paper industry. These electronic devices encouraged users to print out even more paper than before. Nonetheless, due to the increasing sophistication and decreasing prices of computers, they were being used more often to replace paper for the storage and transfer of certain kinds of information. Some predicted this would eventually curtail the growth of paper usage. Others argued that since computers had vastly expanded the amount of information that could be stored, even the printing of a small percentage of this information would keep paper usage growing, albeit at a moderate pace.

In the 1990s many publishers who had traditionally used only paper-based publishing developed electronic products such as e-books. Eager to preserve their market position as information providers, media giants such as the *Financial Times* of London and the German magazine *Der Spiegel,* moved into television. Many major U.S. newspapers produced online versions of their publications for households and offices with personal computers. Most of these new electronic media were companions to traditional magazines and newspapers, serving to duplicate or extend information already available in print.

In the 1990s, the major development in the paper industry was the rapid growth of paper manufacturing in developing regions such as Asia Pacific and South America. These regions, with extensive timber resources, saw major growth in papermaking capacity in the 1990s. Companies such as APRIL and Asia Pacific Pulp and Paper in Asia, and VCP and Aracruz in South America, installed several large new pulp and paper mills, dramatically expanding papermaking capacity in these regions.

Much of the new capacity was targeted for domestic consumption, since Asian economies in particular were growing at double-digit rates for much of the 1990s. This growth, however, was threatened by the financial crisis affecting much of Asia in 1997 and 1998. Despite the economic difficulties, growth in Asian papermaking capacity in Asia was still expected to outpace growth in established economies, such as North America and Europe, going into the twenty-first century.

However, some of the Asian projects faced delays or cancellation due to the economic crisis that hit the region in 1997. The Asian paper market—the fastest growing in the world for much of the 1990s—faced turmoil as the crisis stalled that region's fast-growing pulp and paper industry in 1998. Several paper companies confronted significant financial challenges. As the currencies of major Asian pulp and paper producers, such as Indonesia, fell dramatically against the U.S. dollar, the financial impact on local companies was severe. Larger mills with modern equipment, recently purchased with U.S. dollars, struggled to recoup their investment. High debt loads by these companies made the financial problems even worse.

As the rate of economic growth slowed in Asia in 1997 and 1998, there was considerable speculation that the ownership structure of the Asian pulp and paper industry would change markedly as companies from outside the region—perhaps from North America and Europe—tried to buy Asian pulp and paper producers at what had quickly become bargain prices. For example, in late 1997 Procter & Gamble Co. obtained a controlling share of Sangyong Paper Co., believed to be the first large takeover of a South Korean company by a foreign firm.

However, in the 1990s consumption of paper increased rapidly in areas such as China and Southeast Asia. Further consumption growth was expected in the region through the early 2000s, as the rapid increase in international trade boosted demand for packaging materials. The European Union (EU) experienced sustained growth, fueling a turnaround in its severely depressed paper industry.

In the United States, pricing and profits greatly improved. In 1995 the average price for all grades of paper and paperboard soared 41 percent, on top of an 8 percent increase in 1994. However, those high price levels did not hold. Much of the increase in prices was attributed to customers stocking paper in inventory in anticipation of further price increases. When customers had sufficient inventories, they cut back severely on new purchases and used paper already in inventory. This caused prices to drop sharply in late 1996 and early 1997, as well as in 2001 and 2002.

In the late 1990s, there was substantial international trade in paper and paperboard, dominated by linerboard and coated paper. Worldwide trade in paper began to expand following the conclusion of the Uruguay Round of the General Agreement on Tariffs and Trade (GATT) in 1994. The revised GATT included a "zero for zero" provision for paper, in which all tariffs on paper in industrialized countries would be phased out over a ten-year period, ending in 2005. Canadian and U.S. negotiators attempted to reduce the phase-out period to five years but were unsuccessful in doing do. Also, the North American Free Trade Agreement (NAFTA) between the United States, Canada, and Mexico expanded trade between Mexico and its northern neighbors. (The United States and Canada had already established free trade in paper.) However, the 40 percent devaluation of the Mexican peso in late 1994 temporarily halted the rapid growth in U.S. shipments of paper to Mexico, though those shipments recovered somewhat in 1997.

The freer economic climate between the United States and Canada also encouraged more investment by Canadian companies in U.S. paper manufacturing facilities. For example, in 1997 Montreal-based St. Laurent Paperboard acquired a West Point, Virginia, mill from Cheseapake Corp. of Richmond, Virginia. In 1997 and 1998 the structure of the Canadian paper industry changed considerably, partly in response to the new economic climate. In 1997, Canada's two largest paper companies, Abitibi-Price and Stone-Consolidated, combined to form the leading newsprint producer in the world, Abitibi-Consolidated. Most of the assets of another large Canadian company, Repap Enterprises, were sold in 1997 after the firm encountered severe financial problems. In early 1998, MacMillan Bloedel Ltd. of Vancouver began a major restructuring that included selling, exiting, or spinning off some businesses, closing unprofitable facilities, and downsizing its workforce of 13,000 by 21 percent. The company was expected to sell or spin off its groundwood paper business and to expand and possibly separate its Montgomery, Alabama-based packaging business.

CURRENT CONDITIONS

While the global paper industry remained strong in the early 2000s, it faced several major challenges, including environmental and recycling concerns, an impending fiber shortage, and competition from alternative media. Advances in pulping and bleaching technologies helped reduce mill emissions of toxic substances, and in the early 2000s it appeared that mills in North America and Europe would be able to comply with new environmental regulations without serious damage to their profitability.

The global paper industry is highly competitive and is sustained by a modern, efficient manufacturing base and strong markets. Growth in established markets is expected to be modest—at or slightly above the growth rate of gross domestic product (GDP)—but some fear it may decline before there is annual growth again.

While North America and Europe were traditionally the leading paper producers in the world, new paper capacity was more likely to be built in Asia than anywhere else in the 2000s. Many top paper companies from around the world invested in expansion projects in China. Finland-based UPM, for example, invested US$470 million in a fine paper production facility in Changshu in the early 2000s upgrading its production capacity to 800,000 tons. In 2005, Singapore-based Asia Pulp & Paper and Daio Paper Corporation of Japan announced a joint venture in China worth US$30.2 million to produce a range of tissue products, industrial paper, packaging materials, and other paper.

Consumption of paper in the early 2000s tended to mirror living standards. Nations with high standards of living were the heaviest consumers of paper. For example, per capita consumption was about 190 kg annually in Western Europe and more than 300 kg in North America. By contrast, average per capita consumption in the developing world reached only 17.5 kg, far below the 30kg to 40 kg per capita considered necessary to meet minimum standards for communications and literacy. According to U.N. data, the average rate of paper consumption in Latin America was about 40 kg per capita; in Asia, this figure was approximately 25 kg while per capita paper use in Africa was less than 10 kg per capita. Even so, total paper and cardboard consumption in Asia surpassed that of Europe, and is projected to increase by 3.5 to 5.5 percent annually by 2010.

In June 2004, *Graphic Arts Monthly* reported that, in April, most paper companies had announced new prices for lightweight coated, machine-finished, and economy No. 3 coated rolls for summer deliveries on all non-contract orders. Prices were expected to rise from US$2 to US$3 per cwt. Variables included weight, finish, and brightness options. It was widely held that paper companies were instituting the increase early so that a shock would not occur later in the year, when buying picks up in July and August. Related factors included mills suffering from increased drying, transport, and benefits costs.

Graphic Arts Monthly also stated that the worldwide demand for graphic papers was strong. During the first quarter of 2004, demand for all grades of printing and writing papers increased 2.3 percent. Mill inventories were dropping while exports soared with production growing more slowly. It was estimated that prices for coated groundwood and SC paper for U.S. papers might rise up to 10 percent by 2005.

Technological advances such as the Internet, electronic documents storage, electronic books, microfilm, and microfiche all have played a part in the reduction of paper documents and their storage. Several major studies of electronic media in the late 1990s concluded that paper risked no imminent danger of being replaced by its electronic competitors.

These studies said that demand for almost all grades of paper would be unaffected by electronic media until about 2010, when some negative impact might be felt. However, some trends, such as continually decreasing newspaper circulation, might affect consumption of certain grades earlier than 2010, according to the studies. The long-term survival of paper media in the twenty-first century appeared to depend on several key questions, such as whether or not advertisers would use electronic versions (which made it easier for readers to avoid advertising messages) and whether or not people would read from a screen for extended periods.

WORKFORCE

The level of employment in technically advanced papermaking countries, such as Canada, Germany, Japan, and the United States, declined slowly but steadily in the late 1990s and early 2000s, despite regular increases in papermaking capacity. Increased automation was the main reason for the declining labor figures.

In most countries, paper industry employees were unionized and received wages that exceeded those of workers in other industries. Strong labor unions in countries such as Germany, Canada, and Sweden exerted a powerful influence on the operation of their paper mills. However, in the United States many nonunion mills opened in the 1970s and 1980s, including mills constructed by companies that had unionized mills in other locations. In general, the wages and benefits provided by nonunion U.S. mills were comparable to unionized mills.

Following World War II, paper mills worldwide were highly labor intensive and employed relatively low-skilled workers in production jobs. However, as paper mill automation became prevalent in every major papermaking country (except China), in the 1970s and 1980s, workers began to need more technical skills to understand and direct the computerized operations of paper machines. In Europe, most paper mill workers earned advanced degrees following high school in order to qualify for production work, while in the United States many paper companies increasingly hired recent graduates who held bachelor's degrees and postgraduate degrees in paper science. About ten U.S. universities had pulp and paper programs.

INDUSTRY LEADERS

International Paper. In 2004, U.S.-based International Paper Company (IP) claimed annual sales of US$25.5 billion. With headquarters in Stamford, Connecticut, IP was the largest global paper company, both in production and sales, except in areas such as newsprint, which put it second to Abitibi-Consolidated. It was the top producer of bleached board for milk and food packaging and uncoated freesheet paper. Other IP products includc stationery, art papers, and many other grades of paper. Paper and packaging products account for more than 50 percent of annual sales. IP operated facilities in 31 countries. In the 1980s and 1990s, IP made many acquisitions worldwide, expanding its presence as a global producer of paper and paper products. Those acquisitions included Hammermill Paper (United States), Aussedat Rey (France), Zanders (Germany), Kwidzynie (Poland), and Carter Holt Harvey in New Zealand.

In 1996, IP acquired Federal Paper Board, which had operations in the United States and the United Kingdom, for US$3.5 billion. In 1998, the company acquired Weston Paper & Manufacturing Co. in Terre Haute, Indiana, for US$232 million. Weston's single corrugating medium mill and 11 corrugated container plants were to be added to IP's roster of 5 containerboard mills and 23 box plants in the United States. Internationally, IP had 2 additional mills and 20 container plants. In 2000, IP acquired Champion International Corporation. In 2003, IP sought approval to use its captive insurer to reinsure its group life benefits. The federal application to fund benefits through its captive would be the third ever and the first of its kind to take advantage of the Labor Department's expedited review process, claimed *BestWire Services*. In July 2004, *PR Newswire* reported that IP would be integrating Box USA's 24 industrial packaging converting facilities and containerboard mill into it industrial packaging business, which comprised 11 paper mills and 77 converting facilities worldwide. IP has operations in more than 40 countries and sells products in more than 120 nations.

Abitibi-Consolidated. Abitibi-Consolidated, according to *Associated Press* reports, slipped past International Paper to become the industry's number one world leading newsprint and uncoated groundwood manufacturing firm, as a result of mergers and acquisitions from 1997 through 2000. Formerly known as Abitibi-Price Inc., the newly minted Abitibi-Consolidated merged with Stone-Consolidated Corp., and then acquired Donohue Inc. in a multi-billion-dollar deal. As often occurs with industrial mergers, the combining of production equipment led to the shutting down of older or redundant equipment, and also led to the layoffs or early retirements of company workers. Abititi-Consolidated owns or partners in 30 paper mills, 20 sawmills, 4 remanufacturing facilities, and 1 engineered wood facility throughout Canada, the United Kingdom, the United States, South Korea, China, and Thailand. According to company self-disclosures, it also is the global leader in recycling newspapers and North America's fifth leading lumber producer. Abititi-Consolidated does business in more than 70 countries. Its Pan-Asia Paper joint venture with Norske Skog (Norway) is the largest newsprint company in Asia. In 2004 the company posted sales of US$4.8 billion, up 30.1 percent from the previous year.

As of 1996, Stone Container Corporation was the world's leading manufacturer of unbleached containerboard and craft paper. In the early to mid-1980s Stone grew quickly through several major acquisitions made at very low prices, when the paper industry had bottomed out. In 1989 Stone acquired the Canadian paper company, Consolidated-Bathurst, forming Stone-Consolidated. This company merged with the Canadian firm Abitibi-Price, in 1997, leaving Stone Container with about 25 percent ownership in the new firm. During 1996, Stone Container Corp. recycled a record 3mmt of paper products into new paper and packaging, and combined its retail bag packaging operations with those of Gaylord Container to form S&G Packaging Co.

Georgia-Pacific. Atlanta-based Georgia-Pacific Corporation (G-P) was as of 2004 the world's largest producer of tissue products and the second largest U.S. producer of forest products. It manufactured containerboard and packaging, communications papers, market pulp, and tissue at 81 facilities in the United States and one in Canada as of 1996. G-P was the second-largest U.S. producer of containerboard. In 2001, G-P reported that it produced and sold more than 300,000 tons of kraft paper bags. The company also produced plywood, oriented strand board and other wood panels, lumber, gypsum wallboard, chemicals, and other products at 153 facilities in the United States and 7 in Canada. It is a well-known producer of quality office supply paper. In 2001 and 2002, stock prices dropped in the middle of a nationwide recession, and rumors that G-P was considering Chapter 11 as a result of threatened and actually filed asbestos lawsuits. CEO Pete Correll went public to discount the rumors and to affirm his belief in the company's future. Nonetheless, faced with plunging stock prices, G-P sold about half of its white paper assets to Domtar in 2000. Correll also told stockholders in January 2001 that 2000 was one of the worst years the industry has ever had due to a weak demand for paper and other pulp products. Total bleached and paper sales in 2000 were US$9 billion. G-P sold 60 percent of its Unisource Worldwide distribution segment in 2002. In 2004, the company sold its building products distribution business and non-integrated pulp operations, which cut its debt by almost US$2 billion. That year, total sales reached US$19.6 billion.

UPM-Kymmene. UPM-Kymmene of Helsinki, Finland, was Europe's biggest forest industry group and one of the world's largest paper manufacturers. In 2004, UPM-Kymmene's forest industry operations (including paper) employed 33,433 people and posted sales of US$13.3 billion. The company was formed in 1996 by the merger of Kymmene Corp. with Repola Ltd., the latter of which operated two subsidiaries, United Paper Mills (UPM) Ltd. and Rauma Oy. UPM-Kymmene's main markets were in Great Britain, Finland, Germany, and France. UPM-Kymmene's forest product business is conducted by seven divisions: magazine papers, newsprint, fine papers, packaging materials, sawmilling, special products, and plywood. In 2002, the company addressed lowered prices for paper and predicted that a turnaround was beginning to occur in certain global economies.

In 1997, UPM-Kymmene announced an agreement with Singapore-based Asia Pacific Resources International (APRIL) to exchange 30 percent of their respective fine paper operations in a non-cash transaction. The deal would involve the creation of two new companies owned by the two parent companies. Also in 1997, UPM-Kymmene purchased the Blandin Paper Co., a coated paper producer in Grand Rapids, Minnesota, from parent company Fletcher Challenge Canada. Further, in 2002 UPM-Kymmene acquired G. Haindische Papierfabriken KGaA, a German paper producer, for US$2.4 million. That acquisition has reportedly made UPM-Kymmene the world's largest producer of magazine papers. In July 2004, the company said it was launching a feasibility study at its Blandin paper mill.

Stora Enso Oyj. With roots dating back to the thirteenth century, Swedish-based Stora Enso Oyj claims to be the world's oldest company. In 1288, according to Stora's company history, Bishop Peter received one-eighth of Kopparberg Mountain in a mining charter.

Stora was one of the world's largest forest-products companies during the late 1990s, a position that was strengthened in 1998 by its merger with Enso Oy of Finland. Enso Oy was formed in 1996 through the merger of Enso-Gutzeit and Veitsiluoto. Previous to this transaction, Stora acquired China's biggest fine coated paper producer, Suzhou Papyrus Paper, in 1998 to tap into its annual capacity of 120,000 tons. In 2001, Stora Enso acquired the minority (26.5 percent) stock of SPB Beteiligungsverwaltung GmbH of Austria, making its Stora Enso Timber Oy Ltd. a wholly owned subsidiary of Stora Enso, according to company financial reports. Stora produces large amounts of pulp, printing paper, packaging paper, and board and fine papers, and operates mostly in Europe. Its pulp and paper operations are split into four divisions: Stora Cell, its pulp manufacturing division; Stora Feldmuhle, which manufactures newsprint, uncoated and coated magazine paper, carbonless paper, and fax paper; Stora Billerud, which produces liquid packaging board, regular packaging board, corrugating materials, kraft paper, bag paper, and plastic sacks; and Stora Papyrus, which manufactures coated and uncoated fine papers, colored papers, security papers, and label papers. Amidst a depressed global sales market for all timber products, company sales equaled approximately US$13.4 billion in 2001, with a net income of US$918 million. Sales rose to US$16.7 billion in 2004, with net income of US1.0 billion.

Svenska Cellulosa Aktiebolaget SCA. Svenska Cellulosa AB (SCA) is a European market leader in tissue products, packaging materials, and forest products. SCA's tissue products include consumer products, such as toilet paper and kitchen rolls, as well as those intended for industrial and institutional users, such as wipes and washroom systems. As of 2004, SCA Hygiene Paper was the largest tissue supplier in Europe. Another division produced fluff pulp for products such as disposable diapers. SCA Packaging was Europe's leading manufacturer of corrugated board packaging in the late 1990s. The division also produced containerboard, including both kraftliner and testliner. SCA's forest and timber division managed and developed SCA's forest product division and supplied the group's Swedish plants with virgin wood fiber for the production of paper, packaging, and hygiene products.

In 2004, approximately half of Svenska Cellulosa's annual sales came from tissue products; packaging accounted for another 30 percent, while publication paper accounted for 8 percent of sales. The company has mills in Sweden, the United Kingdom, and Austria. Between 2001 and 2002, the company acquired significant mill holdings from CartoInvest, Encore Paper Co., and Georgia-Pacific Corp. in an attempt to boost market share, according to *Bloomberg News*. In 2001, Svenska Cellulosa reported that its strategy of increasing tissue-making properties led to profits for five straight years. *Bloomberg News* reported that in 2002, the company's stock had risen a whopping 43 percent. In addition, Svenska Cellulosa's revenue shares in forest products fell from 32 percent to 16 percent. The company posted sales of US$13.6 billion in 2004.

Nippon Paper Group, Inc. Nippon Paper Group, formerly Nippon Unipac Holding, is the largest paper-making company in Japan. The company was formed from the merger of Daishowa Paper Manufacturing Co. and Nippon Paper Industries in 2002. Nippon Paper Group controls about 40 percent of the Japanese paper market and operates 17 mills in Japan. It also has overseas facilities in Australia, Canada, Chile, New Zealand, Finland, Russia, South Africa, and the United States. The company's principal markets include newsprint, non-coated printing paper, slightly coated printing papers, coated printing papers, and communications paper. It also markets a range of specialty printing papers, including 100,000 metric tons of heat-sensitive and electrostatic papers. The company also produced chemicals, processed papers, functional film products, and housing materials. Other Nippon Paper business operations served specialized markets, such as landscape gardening, greenery, and lumber.

Nippon Unipac was seriously hurt by falling advertising prices in the international magazine sector at the end of 2001. Nippon Unipac disclosed that group-operating profit for the six months ending September 30 totaled US$163.5 million, a 48 percent drop from the combined group operating profit for the same time period in 2000. The softened market was blamed on ad sale drops for periodicals, and a drop in technical brochures and booklets ordered by electronics companies.

In 2002, the company participated in its thirteenth international reforestation purchase, purchasing a significant interest in WAPRES, a subsidiary of Australia's Marubeni Corp. In 2004 the company reported sales of US$11.2 billion.

Oji Paper. Oji Paper Co. Ltd., Tokyo, is the second-largest paper company in Japan. It was created through the merger of the Oji Paper Company and Kanzaki Paper Manufacturing Company. The company, called the New Oji Paper Co., merged with Honshu Paper Co. Ltd. in 1996, and was subsequently renamed Oji Paper Co. Its main product areas are printing and writing papers (about 71 percent of sales); tissue, miscellaneous papers, and market pulp (14 percent); converted products (9 percent); packaging paper (5 percent); and real estate and other products (1 percent). Adversely affected by plunging paper sales in 2001, Oji Paper cut production of specialty paper and laid off 150 people in 2002. In July 2004, Oji Paper purchased five of two SmartView Paper Web Inspection Systems and three SmartView Winder Advisor Systems for paper machines at its Yonago, Japan mill from the Cognex Corporation, according to *Business Wire.* Sales in 2004 reached US$11.1 billion.

MAJOR COUNTRIES IN THE INDUSTRY

United States. In 2004, the United States was the largest producer and consumer of paper industry products, according to the Food and Agricultural Organization of the United Nations (FAO). The industry faced stagnating conditions in 2000 through 2002. In 2000, U.S. production figures for paper and paperboard production dropped by 2.9 percent to 85mmt. With additional losses due to the ad sales slump in the magazine industry, and reduced printing runs for brochures and instruction booklets in the electronics industry, 2001 figures dropped an additional 7.9 percent from 2000 as the industry hoped for a rebound in late 2002 or 2003. Perhaps the area most seriously hurt in 2002 was New England, where the bankruptcy of the German-owned American Tissue Inc. of New Hampshire put 860 laborers out of work. In Maine, workers routinely were asked to take furlough time.

By 2004, overall conditions had begun to show improvement. *Paper Age* reported that annual shipments of paper and pulp that year were above 2003 levels in all main grades except newsprint. Demand for newsprint, however, declined more than expected.

Japan. Japan was the third-largest producer of paper and paperboard in the early 2000s, and also one of the world's largest consumers of such products. Japan was the largest wood importer in the world, and nearly all of its paper was made from imported wood or recycled paper. However, the Japanese paper industry struggled throughout much of the 1990s due to the stagnant Japanese economy. With the economy in a slow recovery, paper and board production inched upward during the late 1990s. In the 2000s, very little timber for paper was cut in Japan itself, owing to the costs of recovery and replanting for sustainability, according to the FAO. During the early 2000s, hundreds of antiquated sawmills were being shut down, unable to match the production and efficiency of newer sawmills. According to Japan's Ministry of Economy, Trade and Industry, paper and paperboard production totaled 31.8 mmt in 2000 and 30.6 mmt in 2002. Newsprint production rose slightly, from 3.4 mmt to 3.5 mmt.

Large Japanese producers have expanded their ownership of plantations overseas. Oji Paper invested in Australia, while Nippon Paper Industries Co. Ltd. planted hardwood trees in Chile. In 2001, Japan's paper industry entered an era of harder times as ad sales dropped and orders for electronics instruction manuals were also down. Although the drop from 2000 to 2001 was only 1 percent, a much larger figure was expected in 2002 as Oji Paper Co. and other firms reduced total paper production.

Hokuetsu Paper Mills, a major producer of white boxboard, decided to use chlorine dioxide rather than the traditional chlorine gas to produce bleached pulp, resulting in improved wastewater color.

In an attempt to recover from sluggish sales and low paper prices, Mitsubishi Paper Mills planned to cut its workforce and shut down the Tokyo-based Nakagawa Mill. Mitsubishi Paper Mills also announced that it had formed a joint venture with Kodak to sell photographic products in Japan.

China. China's paper industry grew steadily in the mid-1990s as economic reforms instituted by the Chinese government took effect. However, by 2002 the government-mandated birth control regulations had begun to shrink paper and board demand. In particular, the extremely low female population (female fetuses frequently being aborted by parents for economic, status, and cultural reasons) is resulting in a greatly diminished demand for sanitary napkins paper, as well as baby-related products.

In 2002, much of China's paper industry stagnated. The country closed numerous paper mills and let many workers go, as urban unemployment reached 3.6 percent in December 2001. However, demand for paper and paper goods increased after 2002. In 2003, consumption of paper and paperboard reached 48 mmt, or 16 percent of world consumption. According China Paper Association forecasts reported in *Asia Pacific Bulletin,* demand is expected to increase to 70 mmt by 2010. As of 2004, there were more than 3,500 facilities producing paper and paper products in China, with a total capacity of 43 mmt each year. A net importer of paper products, China imported 17 mmt in 2002. To boost domestic production by 5.5 mmt of wood pulp by 2010, the Chinese government is encouraging private investment and joint ventures with foreign investors.

Canada. With its vast forest area (4.2 million square kilometers), Canada was one of the world's leading producers of forest products, market pulp, and newsprint. Canada exports most of the paper and paperboard it produces. In the late 1990s, the Canadian paper industry underwent a major reorganization, as many firms spun off different units, purchased other companies, and sold off assets. In 2001, Canada suffered a slump in paper production, falling 2.2 percent from 2000 figures. By 2003 conditions had improved, with paper industry profits reaching US$1.2 billion in 2004. But the industry expected a decline in 2005, due to sluggish demand for newsprint in North America and increased costs. The Conference Board of Canada expected 2005 profits to drop by about US$500 million, for a total of about US$700 million. In 2006 the industry expected cost increases to level off, leading to projected profits of about US$1.3 billion.

Germany. The 1990s were difficult for the German paper industry, which struggled both with a recession and the integration of relatively inefficient paper mills in former East Germany. It was financially expedient to simply close many of these mills. Larger Finnish companies bought out some German companies in the mid-1990s. This trend continued in 2001, as Germany's largest paper producer, Haindl'sche Papierfabriken KgaA, was acquired by UPM-Kymmene of Finland and Norske Skog of Norway for US$2.6 billion dollars. Meanwhile, upgrades contributed to improvements in capacity. A joint project between Rhein Paper and Voith, which started up in July 2002, produced 737 mt of paper on one day, achieving record manufacturing speeds. The start-up of the new kraft pulp mill in Stendal in 2004, which will produce 552,000 mt of market pulp a year, is also expected to play a major part in boosting the German paper industry.

Finland. With a relatively small population of 5.1 million, Finland possesses substantial forest resources and has developed a strong export-oriented economy, based largely on forest products, machinery, and engineering. Well over half of Finnish paper and paperboard production was in high-grade printing and writing papers. As of 2005, it exported the vast majority of the paper and paperboard it produced and accounted for as much as 15 percent of world paper and paperboard trade. UPM-Kymmene of Finland became a major market player in 2002 as it completed the buyout of a large German company, Haindl'sche Papierfabriken KgaA, in conjunction with a Norwegian firm.

Industry production in Finland increased almost 5 percent in 2000, according to government statistics. Production in 2000 was higher in most categories than during the 1990s. In 2000, paper and paperboard production ascended to a record 13.5 million tons, up 560,000 tons from 1999, according to the Finnish government's Web site.

A major dispute between union and management in 2005, however, threatened these gains. Paper mill workers were locked out of their factories on May 18 following demands that employers cease using temporary workers, keep factories running during some holiday periods, and abandon proposed limits on benefits. As of mid-June, the strike had lasted four weeks and shut down mills owned by UPM-Kymmene and Stora Enso Oyj. According to an AP report, the strike was costing the Finnish forest products industry about US$49 million per day in lost production.

Sweden. Two-thirds of Sweden is woodlands, contributing to its status as one of the world's leading producers of forest and paper products. In the late 1990s, its total forest resources covered 290,000 square kilometers; 240,000 square kilometers were zoned as commercial forests. Sweden's 8.7 million citizens also consumed a substantial amount of paper and paperboard. Swedish paper and paperboard producers focus on lower grades of paper, such as newsprint, corrugating materials, and paperboard. In 2002, the Swedish community received a jolt due to declining ad pages in periodicals, as industry giant (number two in sales nationally) Stora Enso Oyj reported a drop in earnings of 21 percent for the fourth quarter of 2001. Sweden closed 14 paper mills between 1980 and 2001, but capacity steadily improved, reaching 11.2 mmt manufactured at 48 mills in 2001. Sweden's production that year reached 10.5 mmt, of which 8.7 mmt was exported.

FURTHER READING

"Abitibi—Consolidated Reports Improving Results in the First Quarter—Higher Newsprint Prices and Lower Overall Costs Help Mitigate C$ Strength." *PR Newswire,* 23 April 2004.

Biermann, Christopher J. *Essentials of Pulping and Papermaking.* San Diego: Academic Press, 1993.

"Cognex Receives Record Order from Leading Japanese Paper Maufacturer." *Business Wire,* 2 July 2004.

Doyle, Dara. "SCA to Buy Catoinvest." *Bloomberg News,* 19 February 2002.

"Finnish, Norwegian Paper Companies Complete Acquisition of German Rival." *Agence France Presse,* 30 November 2001.

"Finnish Paper Industry Shutdown in Fourth Week." Associated Press, 6 June 2005. Available from http://news.moneycentral.msn.com.

"From Reeds, Paper Got Its Start." *Chapel Hill Herald,* 10 February 2002.

"The Future of Paper . . . From Cyberspace to Fibrespace." Forest Products Association of Canada, 2004. Available from http://www.cppa.org.

"Haindl Renames." *Printing World,* 4 March 2002.

"International Paper Completes Acquisition of Box USA, A Leading Corrugated Packing Company." *PR Newswire,* 2 July 2004.

Kline, James E. *Paper and Paperboard: Manufacturing and Converting Fundamentals.* San Francisco: Miller Freeman, 1982.

"Labor Department Approves Swedish Company's Employee-Benefits Captive." *BestWire Services,* 7 July 2004.

"Oji Paper Sees FY Net Loss 21 Bln Yen vs 6.5 Bln Profit." *AFX News Limited,* 25 January 2002.

"Oji Paper to Halt Western-Style/Special Paper Output in 3 Facilities." *AFX News Limited,* 12 February 2002.

"Paper Rides the Inflation Wave." *Graphic Arts Monthly,* 21 June 2004.

"Positioning Canada in China's Paper Chase." *Asia Pacific Bulletin,* 27 February 2004. Available from http://www.asiapacificbusiness.ca.

"Production of Paper and Paperboard in Japan." Japan Paper Association, 2005. Available from http://www.jpa.gr.jp.

"Pulp and Paper Europe." *Chemical Business Newsbase,* 15 August 2001.

"Pulp and Paper Markets Showed Improvement in 2004." *Paper Age,* 25 January 2005. Available from http://www.paperage.com.

Smook, Gary A. *Handbook of Pulp and Paper Terminology: A Guide to Industrial and Technological Usage.* Bellingham, WA: Angus Wilde, 1990.

Thesaurus of Pulp and Paper Terminology. Atlanta: Institute of Paper Science and Technology, 1991.

"UPM-Kymmene Corporation Launches Feasibility Study at Paper Mill in the US." *Nordic Business Report,* 1 July 2004.

Yoshizaki, Miho. "Nippon Paper Falls." *Bloomberg News,* 5 June 2000.

SIC 2650

NAICS 32221

PAPERBOARD CONTAINERS AND BOXES

Sometimes known as the converted paperboard industry, these manufacturers produce packaging often from purchased paperboard, the manufacture of which is discussed in greater depth under **Paperboard Mills.** Major segments include folding boxes, set-up (or rigid) boxes, corrugated boxes, fiber cans and tubes, and food containers.

INDUSTRY SNAPSHOT

Paperboard container and box makers provide the global economy with packaging and foodservice products. Used in both commercial and consumer applications, such products serve the needs of every industry. The primary application for paperboard containers and boxes is packaging. Boxes can be bright, visually attractive, and informational if they contain individual products, or they can be useful for their sturdiness—including corrugated containers in which various products get sent to consumers or sellers. The first use might be for folding paperboard box manufacturers that produce cereal boxes. The second might be a corrugated container manufacturer's box, to keep the cereal boxes undamaged en route to supermarket shelves. According to *Paper, Film & Foil Converter* magazine, the challenge for manufacturers in the 2000s will be how they can please their customers' need for "lower costs; quicker turnaround; lower quantity minimums; warehousing of packaging; and faster delivery."

Until the 1970s, and Earth Day awareness programming, paper and paperboard packaging was a largely uncontroversial, almost ignored, aspect of a worldwide product distribution system. Then, as concern over landfills, solid waste, and recycling mounted, packaging was singled out as a major source of waste. Pressure grew in Europe and North America to eliminate or recycle packaging. In Germany, legislation was passed requiring packaging producers to collect and recycle their products. Paperboard packaging has now been banned from landfills in many U.S. states.

To comply with such regulations, packaging producers agreed to use more recycled paper and paperboard in their products. Also, many industrial countries introduced the collection of used packaging for recycling. Packaging producers defended their products, explaining that packaging was vital for the maintenance of public health and economic well-being. Packaging producers maintained that by protecting against damage and spoilage, packaging reduced, rather than added to, the solid waste stream.

Producers claimed that competition with suppliers over packaging materials usually spurred suppliers to find ways of using less packaging, since that reduced the cost of their products to end users. This practice provided an automatic "source reduction" without the need for governmental regulation. (On the average, packaging represented 7 percent of the cost of goods sold.) In food and beverage packaging, the industry's reliance on single-use containers helped to improve public health by virtually eliminating one possible method of disease transmission. According to packaging producers, these benefits meant that packaging could be environmentally compatible and would continue to have a prominent role in the world economy.

Globally, the category of corrugated paperboard boxes has been the largest component of the converted paper and board products industry. By the beginning of the 2000s, corrugated boxes were used to ship 90 percent of the goods manufactured throughout the world. Major industrial users of corrugated products included food and beverages, agricultural products, paper and fiber products, petroleum, petrochemical resins, plastics, and rubber products. In order to reduce costs, some manufacturers began to examine the use of reusable plastic containers for business-to-business shipments (such as automobile components). In general, however, corrugated box manufacturers had relatively little need to consider alternative shipping methods. Corrugated containers, in the form of point-of-sale displays, were increasingly used as an integrated transportation and marketing device.

As of 2003, corrugated and cartonboard materials accounted for 30.2 percent of global paper and paperboard demand. World demand for containerboard grew from 91.8 million tons in 1999 to 102.2 million tons in 2003. Asia was expected to have the greatest growth potential, with demand expected to grow 4 percent per year through 2005. China has been the biggest factor in industry growth, due to the rapid expansion of its manufacturing industries and the consequent need for corrugated boxes for shipment.

Consumption of corrugated products tends to reflect the overall standard of living and economic activity in most countries. Highly developed countries with complex, consumer-oriented economies are typically heavy users of corrugated boxes. *Paper, Film & Foil Converter* magazine also revealed that demand for corrugated and paperboard boxes was projected to climb 2.8 percent per year, reaching more than $35 billion in 2007, with corrugated and solid fiber boxes offering the best prospects during the period.

ORGANIZATION AND STRUCTURE

The primary raw material in making both corrugated boxes and folding paperboard boxes is paperboard. The types of boxes and packages they are used to make classify various grades of paperboard. Cartonboard is usually defined as board of various compositions, used to make folding boxboard and set-up (or rigid) boxes; foodboard is defined as single or multi-ply paperboard, used for food and liquid packaging; and corrugated is typically defined as board for containers, consisting of two or more linerboard grades separated by corrugated medium (fluting) glued to the liners.

Corrugated Paper Boxes. In the early 2000s, a large share of the global corrugated box market was integrated; that is to say, the containerboard (linerboard facing and corrugated fluting) used to make corrugated boxes was never sold on the open market. Instead, product was shipped directly from containerboard mills to corrugated box plants, within the same organization. In the United States, 80 percent of corrugated box production was integrated, with just 20 percent produced by independent box plants. The European market was more fragmented—many small independent boxmakers still operated—but a steady trend of consolidation began in the 1990s, with production expected to be under the control of fewer companies in the twenty-first century.

Shipments of corrugated and solid fiber boxes mirror the demand for products that are shipped to market in box containers. When worldwide industrial activity picks up, so does box shipments. When industrial activity increased in most of the major economies worldwide in the early to mid-1990s, corrugated container producers around the world struggled to keep up demand. For example, there was a 6 percent increase in demand for corrugated and solid fiber boxes in 1994. As the economy in the 2000s showed signs of weakening and then definite areas of collapse, the packaging industry's profits reflected a drying up of commercial opportunities as well.

Since there are thousands of different applications for corrugated boxes, many weights, various degrees of thickness, and combinations of liners and corrugating medium, are used to make different types of corrugated board. The corrugating process begins when flat, corrugating medium board is softened with heat and moisture and sent into a set of corrugating rolls. These rolls form the board into curved "flutes." The flute tips on one side of the medium are then coated with adhesive, and a separate, single face-piece of linerboard is laid onto the fluted medium to produce a "single face" web. This sheet of corrugating material is sent to the "double backer," where adhesive is applied to the other side of the flutes, and then back liner is applied to form "combined corrugated board." This combined corrugated board is cut into individual "blanks" on a trimmer-cutter, which, in turn, are passed to a printer-scorer-slotter that converts them into flat boxes. The flat boxes are shipped—usually by truck—to the end user, who opens and glues the box prior to use. Corrugated containers are generally delivered by truck because of the large number of customers and a (traditionally commonplace) demand for timely service. Shipping costs are a relatively high percentage of total costs due to the dispersion of customers and the fact that boxes are high-bulk, low-density, and low-value products. As a result, box plants tend to be located close to customers to reduce shipping costs.

Corrugating materials can be made from a wide variety of materials. The outside linerboard is usually a mix of virgin softwood pulp, virgin hardwood pulp, and/or recycled paper and board. The inner corrugating medium is typically made of virgin hardwood pulp and/or recycled paper and paperboard. In the pulping process, most pulp used as a corrugating medium is not fully "cooked" in the digesting process, since it is beneficial to keep some of the lignin in the pulp (see **Pulp Mills** for more information). This lignin, which acts as glue, helps give the corrugating medium added stiffness.

Recycling. Corrugated boxes have been recycled for years to make them into new containers. However, events in the latter part of the twentieth century put more emphasis on recycling of OCC, which accounted for the majority of all paper products recycled around the world, from the late 1990s through the early 2000s.

Customers typically expect their suppliers to sell them products made from unbleached kraft linerboard, to meet minimum standards of 80 percent sulfate, or kraft pulp, which is derived from previously unused wood chips. Production cost of unbleached kraft linerboard can be lowered if recycled fibers are used. The total production of recycled linerboard in 2000 was 3.9 million tons, a decline of approximately 5 percent from the 4.1 million tons of recycled linerboard produced in 1999.

In the mid-1980s minute amounts of dioxin were discovered in pulp mill bleach plant effluent, in both Europe and the United States. Until that time, a standard procedure in the industry had been to bleach paper and paperboard. However, once the dioxin discovery caused the procedure to become controversial, manufacturers began to produce a majority of corrugated boxes in their natural brown color, which eliminated the need to bleach them white. Since a majority of boxes were not made from bleached paperboard, this environmental concern confronting paper and paperboard boxes was largely negated. Nonetheless, bleaching remained a controversial topic in the global marketplace in the mid-1990s, as a growing percentage of corrugated boxes were still being shipped with a bleached, white, outside liner of paperboard.

Environmental concern spread to how corrugated boxes were disposed of after use. Once collected, these boxes were found to be easily recycled and were also biodegradable in landfills. Worldwide, between 60 and 80 percent of OCC was recovered for recycling into new boxes or other paperboard products in the late 1990s.

Responsibility for the collection of OCC differs around the world. For example, in Germany, with its strict recycling laws, box producers are responsible for recycling and are required to make arrangements for accepting back from consumers every package they produced. This often involves creating recycling centers funded by the manufacturer. In the United States, the consumer of corrugated containers is responsible for recycling. While there have been few U.S. laws requiring consumers of corrugated products (such as supermarkets) to recycle, most have done so because OCC is a valuable commodity.

Many sources have claimed that more companies are using recycled paperboard for the first time and are being pleasantly surprised by its quality and appearance. *Frozen Food Age* said that a survey of packaged goods manufacturers conducted by the 100 Percent Recycled Paperboard Alliance revealed that "the most positive industry sector overall" for recycled paperboard was the frozen food category. The study incorporated 220 telephone interviews with packaging, technical, and purchasing professionals at 143 U.S. companies in the dry and frozen/refrigerated foods, pharmaceutical, toothpaste, pet supply, soap, and office supply industries.

From the late 1980s through the mid-2000s, the amount of recycled paper and paperboard used to produce linerboard and corrugating medium increased sharply in many countries. A wide variety of recycled materials could be used to make these products. While many paperboard mills preferred to use old corrugated containers (OCC), they could also use newsprint, office waste paper, and other grades. When the price of OCC in many markets reached record highs in 1994—jumping in one year from approximately US$50 per ton to more than US$200 per ton in the United States—many began to use lower-cost recycled paper. However, in 1996, a glut of OCC on the market caused prices to fall, and many producers switched back to their preferred source—OCC. This situation continued in 1997, though the price of OCC did rise nearly 25 percent, ending the year at US$76.50 per ton. As of 1997, OCC accounted for more than 60 percent of all scrap paper recovered in the United States, and was a major portion of recycling efforts in other industrialized countries as well.

Paperboard Packaging magazine estimated that almost 4,800 communities have access to paperboard recycling programs. Such efforts have already resulted in recovering 40 percent of all paper, and that percentage was expected to grow. *Official Board Markets* shared praise for efforts of the 100 percent recycled paperboard industry. The 100 Percent Recycled Paperboard Alliance said the industry made great strides in 2003. Executive Director Lynn Harrelson believed key contributing factors were progress in "generating conversions from other substrates, reaching out and capturing business in various industry segments, entering new market segments, and adding new licenses to the 100 percent recycled paperboard symbol."

With the issue of waste remaining a significant concern, corrugated box manufacturers in the late 1990s looked for efficient ways to recycle wax-coated corrugated boxes that were used for shipping moist products, such as produce and fish. Wax board was not accepted for recycling by paper mills because even a very small quantity would reduce the quality of packaging papers. In 1990, the largest Scandinavian paper recycler, Returpapper, began research on how to recycle wax board. Several other paper companies and wax companies joined the research project and produced a practical solution to the problem that involved modifying waxes (prior to application on the box), with a saturated fatty acid and a stabilizing nonionic surfactant. When the newly treated OCC was recycled, a hot dispersion process added alkali and, with redesigned pulp washing equipment, removed the wax, which could then be incinerated.

In the United States, two developments in 1998 promised to help combat the problem of wax boxes in recycling systems. A new marketing program, developed by several industry associations, promoted voluntary guidelines for identifying waxed corrugated boxes so they could be removed from the recycling process. The boxes would be marked on the top inside label with the word "wax" in three languages. On another front, two companies, Thermo Black Clawson and Inland Paperboard and Packaging, jointly developed a new process that could eliminate wax in the re-pulping process. The new process was called Xtrax and was on the market as of early 1998.

The pulp made from OCC needs little cleaning and doesn't have to be bleached. Unlike many grades of recycled paper, OCC suffers minimal loss in fiber strength and other important physical properties. However, there is a limit to how many times fibers can be recycled. For example, Asian corrugated boxes had been recycled many times due to chronic virgin fiber shortages in those countries. As a result, their products tended to be weaker and less resistant to water than U.S. corrugated boxes. The fiber quality of Asian OCC was so low that many U.S. recycling mills excluded it from their processes.

Since corrugated containers tend to be a commodity, competition in corrugated boxes centers on price. Also, international trade in finished boxes was expected to remain low. However, one of the two main raw materials in corrugated boxes—linerboard—was a major export product for paper- and board-producing countries. Many box producers were fully integrated, meaning that they produced both the raw materials for boxes and the boxes themselves. In addition, many box producers owned operations in other countries or were part of joint ventures in several countries. As a result, leaders in the converted products industry tended to be the same as the leaders in the paperboard industry (see also **Paperboard Mills**).

The majority of corrugated products have been used to package non-durable goods, such as general merchandise and food products. Thus, the percentage of corrugated products used for non-durable goods typically rises during recessions because the sale of expensive durable goods—such as furniture and appliances—goes down as consumers delay discretionary spending. In the 2000s, according to a Graphic Arts Marketing Information Service study, manufacturers of boxes serving the non-endurable foods industries could expect to see their customers battling for shelf space regulated by fewer big chain stores. This would lead to a need for the best attention-grabbing visuals on these products, in order to command greater market performance and sales results. "The trend in graphics is toward more specialty colors, more process color, and more sophisticated design," says *Paper, Film & Foil Converter* magazine.

Fiber Cans, Tubes, and Drums. This has been a medium-sized segment of the converted paper and paperboard industry. An important market in this category includes spiral and convolute wound tubes and cores, which are used in such familiar products as paper-towel rollers, in addition to numerous industrial purposes. The demand for tubes and cores is largely driven by industrial production. The following industries are major users: textile products, synthetic fibers, paper mills, flexible packaging, film, carpeting, and construction. The pulp and paper industry, which used cores to wind its rolls of paper and board, was the single largest user of tubes and cores.

Fiber cans—called composite cans in the United States and board cans in Europe—have a paperboard "body" and a paper, metal, membrane, or plastic end closure. These products may also have a variety of liners. Many composite cans contained a high percentage of recycled fibers. They were used throughout the world to contain such products as prepared food, pastries, frozen concentrate, snacks, nuts, and powdered foods and beverages.

In the early 2000s, the world's largest composite can manufacturer was the U.S. firm Sonoco Products, located in Hartsville, South Carolina. Sonoco (formerly the Southern Novelty Company) had a worldwide network of packaging plants to produce its cans, and had been in business since 1899. As of 2004, the company served customers in more than 85 countries. About 44 percent of Sonoco's business was in consumer packaging, including composite cans, while the remaining 56 percent was in industrial packaging.

Sanitary Food Containers. Another medium-sized segment of the converted paper and board industry, sanitary food containers include a diverse number of paper plates, cups, and other disposable paper food packages. Demand for these grew strongly in several major markets during the 1990s and early 2000s. Despite the public's desire to reduce usage of disposable products for environmental reasons, the convenience of disposable paper products continued to appeal to a growing number of consumers worldwide.

Once known for products that were plain white, or that had minimal border decoration, the paper plates and cups market exploded with color, designs, and licensed characters. For example, in the mid-1990s the venerable Dixie Cup franchise, marketed by Fort James Corporation, broadened its line by marketing "Zoo Friends" and "Dino Friends" cups and plates, to appeal to children; other Dixie lines featured Disney characters.

Aseptic packages—known as drink boxes in the United States—are considered a hybrid product, since they include layers of paperboard, metal, and plastic. They have become widely used around the world, displacing products that competed with this portion of the paperboard market (e.g., glass bottles and metal cans). The aseptic processing system, also known as ultra high temperature (UHT) processing, required a major portion of available food-grade paperboard at the beginning of the 2000s.

Aseptic processing was first used in the milk industry to produce products with long shelf life that did not require refrigeration. This process was particularly well suited to European households, which generally had limited space for refrigeration—unlike their U.S. counterparts. In the late 1990s, aseptically processed milk accounted for more than 75 percent of all milk sales in France. Conversely, aseptic milk sales in the United States were negligible. However, during the 1980s and early 1990s aseptic packaging for fruit juices and other drinks captured a healthy share in the U.S. market. While the only aseptic containers commonly available in the United States in the late 1990s were single-serving juice boxes and milk cartons, by 2004 aseptic packaging had been introduced for numerous food products, including soups and broths; soy, grain, and nut beverages; tomato sauces and purees; puddings and flavored milks; and liquid eggs.

Folding Paperboard Boxes. Traditionally, this very large part of the paper and paperboard market was highly dependent on global consumer spending, in part because a vast array of dry, liquid, and frozen food products were packaged in folding paperboard boxes, such as beverages, dry bakery goods, and cereals. One particularly important user of folding paperboard has been the beverage industry, which packaged many of its bottled and canned products in a secondary package made from high-quality paperboard. Many other consumer products also were packaged in paperboard boxes, including small appliances, detergents, toys, and sporting goods.

The worldwide growth in sales of consumer products has expanded the market for folding paperboard boxes. For example, in the mid-1990s both beer and soft drink bottlers were using more multi-can "cases" to package their products. Since the 1980s, folding paperboard box converters, like corrugated box producers, have responded to demands by consumer products manufacturers for packaging with higher visual appeal. Better graphics were thought to promote impulse purchases by consumers, making the carton a primary sales vehicle in a company's marketing efforts.

One of the major competitors for folding boxboard packages is flexible packaging, usually a combination of layers of plastic and/or metal film configured into pouch-like packages. This type of packaging is prevalent outside the United States, where it has replaced many paperboard applications. Flexible packaging is popular for various reasons, including perceived environmental superiority, smaller amount of packaging waste, as well as cultural and economic reasons. France and India marketed motor oil in pouches, with and without outer cartons. In the United Kingdom, Kellogg Company produced breakfast cereal bags using high-quality graphics without an outer paperboard carton. While the concept did not enjoy the same acceptance in the United States, there have been some applications.

CURRENT CONDITIONS

Until recently, there has been little international or even regional trade in finished packaging products; in most countries, corrugated and folding boxes have been produced domestically. Box-making industries usually consisted of small, independent boxmakers. However, as major paper companies in North America, Europe, and Asia grew in size, they moved to vertically integrate themselves by acquiring more box plants. Some branched out even further by buying or building box plant capacity in foreign markets. U.S. and European firms were particularly interested in markets in Asia and Eastern Europe, since they offered much higher growth potential than the largely mature markets of North America and Western Europe.

Corrugated Paper Boxes. Since the mid-1990s, a growing percentage of corrugated boxes were being made using preprinted linerboard, with the rest of the box made from unbleached brown containerboard. In addition, to reduce costs and compete with alternative packaging, the industry in the early 2000s was gradually shifting to production of lighter weight boxes with increased strength. Improved containerboard quality enabled boxmakers to decrease the overall weight of their boxes, thus reducing shipping costs and cost to the end user as well.

Shippers and packagers of food products, the largest market for corrugated products, were one of the highest growth markets for the corrugated packaging industry in the 2000s. Another potential growth area involved the manufacture of corrugated paperboard shipping pallets. Traditionally, shipping pallets (which held multiple containers during transport) had been made of wood. Since many pallets ended up in landfills, growing pressure to replace them was felt industry-wide. New processing technology not only made possible the manufacture of stronger corrugated pallets, but also proved to be a cheaper way to make recyclable pallets. However, the one disadvantage was that corrugated pallets tended to lose strength when they became wet.

A major trend in corrugated containers that emerged in the 2000s was the need for higher-quality printing surfaces on the outside of boxes. At this time, the growing strength of large European hypermarkets and U.S. discount stores, wholesale clubs, and other mass merchandisers, meant that more shoppers were choosing products with no assistance from salespeople. Frequently, the only method consumers had for getting information about the product was to read what was on the retail box. Producers of consumer products began including more photographic images, detailed instructions, and bright colors on their product packages, to help them compete on the store shelf. This led producers of linerboard to make more "preprint" linerboard. Preprint involved printing the outer liner before it was shipped to box plants and made into corrugated board. Typically, preprint was made with "process printing," a less-expensive process than making the lithographic labels traditionally used for photo reproduction on box exteriors.

In the 2000s, the Graphic Arts Marketing Information Service (GAMIS) study pointed to flexography as the single most used manner of printing in the packaging field. In 2001, flexo printing was an almost US$15 billion business, and the GAMIS study indicated that the total would fall somewhere between US$18 billion and US$22 billion by 2005. The authors of the study predicted that flexo manufacturers would take a higher folding-carton market share away from manufacturers that use older technology methods, such as sheet-fed offset printing and the gravure process. The study looked ahead to see specific flexo technology improvements in specific areas, such as "gearless presses; faster plate processing; and the use of ultraviolet inks," noted *Paper, Film & Foil Converter* magazine. Further down the road, the industry is expected to see more consumer requests for products requiring color digital presses. In the meantime, the study advises the vast majority of companies employing traditional offset-printing methods to stay competitive "by raising press performance; increasing speeds, and adding productivity features," according to *Paper, Film & Foil Converter.*

Several industry publications shared news reflecting the growth opportunities in the food packaging industry. Notable among them was the story of Thung Hua Sinn Printing Network, which grew from printing labels to successfully manufacture corrugated paper boxes and set up a subsidiary for flexible packaging known as TPN Flexpak. Another article in *Food & Drug Packaging* spotlighted Bake 'n Ship containers from Laminating Technologies. They allow bakers to bake, freeze, slice, ship and display in one package. In April 2004, *Purchasing* reported that North America's corrugated box makers wanted higher prices, and that prices were expected to remain volatile. Some box makers had proposed price increases of 8-10 percent.

Fiber Cans, Tubes, and Drums. By the early 2000s, manufacturers of fiber cans, tubes, and drums, like other converted product manufacturers, were being asked by customers and government regulatory agencies to use more recycled paperboard, and less virgin paperboard, in their products. This turned out to be a marketing advantage as well—many competing products were made from plastic, which in the 1990s was being recycled at a much lower rate worldwide than paper and paperboard. The paper industry itself was one of the major users of fiber tubes, since most paper and paperboard mills used high-density fiber cores to wind their paper and paperboard rolls, before it was cut into smaller rolls and shipped to converting operations. Long fiber cores were either cut at the mill, to match roll sizes, or shipped to the mill, precut by the core manufacturer.

As competition in the fiber can, tube, and drum market intensified in the 1990s, manufacturers sought new ways of increasing their competitive advantage. For example, Sonoco Products Co. entered into "single supplier" relationships with some paper companies for roll packaging materials and services, in which they would be the only supplier in exchange for the paper companies receiving enhanced services and lower prices. One such agreement was with Weyerhaeuser Company of Federal Way, Washington. Under the three-year, US$25 million agreement, Sonoco provided a full array of cores, roll heads, plastic and metal end plugs, wax-laminated roll wrap, and services such as core cutting and core reclamation, for Weyerhaeuser paper mills in the United States.

The use of fiber drums, however, was down in many countries where many industrial users were slowly eliminating their use of disposable containers. The chemical industry, once a major user of drums, largely replaced metal and fiber drums with portable chemical feed containers, made mostly of plastic. These returnable containers were delivered to the customer and then returned to the manufacturer when empty.

Sanitary Food Containers. The market for paper cups, plates, and other disposable paper products grew in many countries as more families sought to reduce time spent on housework and home meal preparation. The growth of take-out food operations, which frequently used paper plates to serve food, also helped spur consumption. Still, paper plates faced increased competition from molded plastic plates and cups (which were grease resistant and, in many ways, offered superior strength). Extra-thick premium paper plates and cups, which were treated with a plastic outer layer, comfortably competed with their plastic rivals. Moreover, the perceived negative environmental aspects associated with styrofoam helped paper to recapture some of the hot beverage cup market share that was lost in the early 1980s. For example, coffeehouse operators such as Starbucks served their products in paper cups.

Paperboard milk cartons also faced serious competition from plastic. However, paperboard milk cartons could still compete effectively against plastic in smaller sizes, such as one- and two-liter packages and one- and two-quart packages. European milk producers helped to mitigate some of the paperboard industry's revenue losses when they shifted to aseptic packaging for milk (hence, aseptic paperboard packaging). Milk carton manufacturers aggressively developed additional uses for paperboard cartons, such as for laundry detergents and fruit juices.

Folding Paperboard Boxes. The folding paperboard box industry is expected to continue growing in the 2000s, while trying to improve its position with faster delivery times and other services to counter formidable competition from alternative packaging, such as flexible pouches. Improved strength and lighter-weight folding boxboard were expected to improve the competitive position of folding paperboard boxes in the packaging marketplace. Manufacturers of folding paperboard boxes also expected a vibrant market share, because their product was recyclable and contained recycled fiber.

The cost of raw materials for folding paperboard boxes, which was low in the early 1990s, shot up sharply in the mid-2000s. Much of the price increase was passed on to the consumer. Revenues from box production were squeezed by low linerboard availability, high-priced solid bleached sulfate paperboard (SBS) and recycled paperboard, and customer resistance to skyrocketing prices that had to be passed to their own customer base.

However, toward the end of the decade the prices for all grades of paperboard began falling sharply, as customers began to use up inventory they had built up in anticipation of future price increases. This led paperboard mills to take downtime and lower prices in order to restore balance to the market. However, by mid-1997 the price of standard linerboard was still just US$310 per ton, 41 percent below its 1995 peak of US$525. As a result, the costs of finished boxes dropped as well. While prices remained relatively low through the early 2000s, analysts predicted significant improvement after 2003.

RESEARCH AND TECHNOLOGY

A growing demand for four-color, high-quality, folding paperboard boxes led boxmakers to embrace processes and equipment of the printing industry. Many folding boxmakers installed expensive printing presses to meet this demand. In the mid-to-late 1990s some boxmakers consolidated six-color printing presses and web litho folding carton capability into production operations, a process that typically required separate converting steps. Some boxmakers also installed web flexo printing processes, a new folding carton technology that produced even higher-quality printing. Folding box producers also were developing ways to make shorter production runs, since many customers were moving to just-in-time use of paperboard products.

Since the 1990s technical advances led to the development of paperboard grades that run well on both high-speed printing and converting equipment, and also on high-speed carton erecting, filling, and sealing lines. In corrugated board, mills developed the ability to produce lighter weight liner and corrugating medium. Machinery manufacturers then developed machines that produced smaller, finer grades of flute, which have found a ready market, in many cases serving as a replacement for folding cartonboard.

The development of small flute corrugated packaging could eventually lead to the convergence of the traditionally separate corrugated and folding box industries, according to some observers, since the product could be used in applications in both industries. Folding carton manufacturers in Europe, and the United States in particular, were quick to convert to the new small flute corrugating technology in the late 1990s.

New technology became a competitive advantage to some packaging producers. An approach one box manufacturer used to expand markets was based on a strategic decision to sell packaging machinery that used the manufacturer's paperboard packaging. Riverwood Holding Inc. designed and manufactured proprietary packaging machinery for multiple packaging applications (mostly bottled and canned beverages). One of the primary benefits to Riverwood, of selling the machinery, was that the packaging machines were able to "pull through" Riverwood's paperboard boxes. Riverwood installed and serviced the machines in the bottling and canning plants of its customers. This type of machinery was very sophisticated and was able to insert cans and bottles of different heights and diameters into a variety of packages, styles, and configurations. The packaging machinery also was very fast, operating at a rate of up to 3,000 cans per minute. In the late 1990s, Riverwood was said to control about 50 percent of the U.S. beverage carrier market, and close to 15 percent of the beverage carrier market outside the United States. Moreover, Riverwood had significant investments in multiple container plants in Europe.

A growing trend in the early 2000s was the concept of universal packaging, which aims to produce packages that can be easily used by people of different abilities. Duracell, for example, redesigned its paperboard packages for hearing aid batteries to make them easier for users to pick up. Burgopak USA is planning to introduce a new paperboard package for medications in late 2005 which is designed to both store and dispense the product more safely than plastic containers. Corrugated box manufacturers have made improvements to their designs that allow products to be packed and shipped more efficiently, and also to be opened easily-for example, making sure that the consumer will not have to reach to the bottom of a tall box and lift out a heavy item. As the Baby Boomer population ages by 2030, and inevitably develops physical impairments, analysts expect ease of use to become an increasingly important aspect of paperboard container design. Some analysts also predicted that the aging of the population would spur demand for single-serving packaging, since this demographic shift would result in a larger number of single-person households.

MAJOR REGIONS IN THE INDUSTRY

NORTH AMERICA

According to *Package Printing 2001-2005*, a 2002 study commissioned by the Graphic Arts Marketing Information Service, Canada and the United States together represented a significant consumer region for packaging. The authors of the publication found that the two countries annually ship a total of US$125 billion in packaging paper products.

United States. In the early 2000s, the United States was the leading packaging producing country in the world, as well as an importer of packaging from Canada and other nations. Most U.S. production was highly integrated and many of the large packaging producers were expanding globally. An examination of a typical large producer, such as Wayne, New Jersey-based Union Camp Corporation, is illustrative of standard operating procedures in the U.S. paperboard packaging industry. Union Camp's packaging group was its largest operating unit, accounting for 43 percent of company sales in 1996. As well as being an integrated producer of linerboard, kraft paper, and packaging, Union Camp was a major manufacturer of corrugated containers, heavy-duty shipping sacks, and other packaging.

MeadWestvaco Corporation is another U.S. paper company that actively participated in global markets. In the United States, the company's consumer packaging business diversified its product line in the late 1990s with products such as ovenware cartons, which allow the use of one package to ship and display frozen food, and then be heated in a microwave or conventional oven. That efficiency helped to reduce customer expenses by up to 30 percent and packaging volume by up to 40 percent. The company's unbleached packaging unit operated worldwide, including the Rigesa Ltda. unit in Brazil. In 1996, Rigesa upgraded its mill in Tres Barras to improve production of linerboard for corrugated containers. Other enhancements included opening a new container plant in Pacajus, Brazil, to serve a fast-growing export trade. As of 2005, MeadWestvaco operated 34 consumer packaging plants, 14 packing systems facilities, and 4 corrugated container plants. Packaging, its largest business segment, accounted for US$3.7 billion in sales in 2002.

The United States also was the world's largest producer and exporter of linerboard, the principal component of corrugated boxes. As of 1996, exports represented about 15 percent of U.S. kraft liner production, and yet comprised about half the total kraft linerboard exports from the world's 10 major supplying nations.

U.S. corrugated material producers enjoyed an increase in total number of shipments from 1995 to 1996, as the long-term U.S. economic recovery continued. In 2000, however, total shipments suffered a slight slump from previous years. According to the Fibre Box Association's 1996 annual report, shipments by the corrugated industry were a record 377 billion square feet, a 1.4 percent increase over 1995. 75 percent of U.S. corrugated shipments came from vertically integrated paper companies with containerboard mills. However, while total volume increased in 1996, shipment values dropped 11.1 percent to US$20.8 billion, from the all-time record of US$23.4 billion in 1995. Large fluctuations in the price of linerboard and corrugated medium were largely to blame for the decline in corrugated prices, since prices for those grades began dropping in 1996, and continued to fall in 1997, leading to price declines in finished corrugated products. However, as prices for linerboard and medium stabilized and began increasing in 1997, the value of corrugated shipments was expected to increase steadily after 2002, once the economy righted itself again.

The U.S. folding paperboard box industry grew steadily in the early to mid-1990s, from US$7.4 billion in 1991 to US$8.0 billion in 1993, and US$8.79 billion in 1995, according to the U.S. Department of Commerce. In 1996, the U.S. folding carton industry consisted of 445 companies. However, 37 companies, all with sales of more than US$25 million each, accounted for 68 percent of the industry's shipments.

Continued growth in the food and beverages market was expected to boost U.S. sales of corrugated and paperboard boxes to more than US$35 billion by 2007. Corrugated and solid fiber boxes comprised 72 percent of shipments by value in 2002, with most of the remainder being folding boxes.

In May 2004, *Paperboard Packaging* featured an article by Ken Rohleder with insights about trends related to acceptance in the United States of new business models. The models were designed to eliminate non-value added activities and waste. The result is frequently shorter lead times, more deliveries, and lots of tiny box orders. More North American businesses were emulating the European model of creating a mini-converting plant, or "mini-converting plant," that makes corrugated components in the exact quantity required shortly after request is submitted, and sometimes at the client's site.

In June 2004, *Buyouts* announced that ICV Capital Partners acquired Folding Carton Company, which provided custom packaging to the generic and over-the-counter drug industries. "The primary thesis behind the investment rests with the expectation for a flood of new drugs to come off of their patents in the coming years," the publication concluded.

Canada. The Canadian government's statistics show the corrugated paper box and packaging industry in a pattern of steady growth from 1990 to 1998, averaging about 3.4 percent. Yet significant volatility affected the market in the 1990s, with the general pulp and paper industry posting profits only in 1990, 1995, and 1996. Oversupply remained a problem, leading to a $5.1 million loss in 1998 for Canada's largest paperboard manufacturer, Norampac. By early 2000, though, analysts saw indications of recovery, with shipments of linerboard, corrugated medium, and boxboard in 1999 up substantially from 1998 levels. In 2002, Canadian shipments of value-added paper products, which included paperboard containers, reached $9.2 billion.

Norampac, jointly owned by Cascades Inc. and Domtar Inc., is Canada's largest manufacturer of containerboard and a leading Canadian producer of corrugated products. With annual sales exceeding US$1.1 billion, it operates 26 box plants in Canada, the United States, and France.

Canada's largest folding carton user was the food industry. The next largest market share was accounted for by the tobacco industry, followed by the beverage industry. While competitive materials were said to be growing in Canada, the biggest threat was said to be to the glass and metal industries, rather than the folding carton/set-up box industry.

Europe. In the 2000s, Europe was recognized by the packaging industry as a leader in both industry standards and the amount of packaging created by its industries. For example, the United Kingdom produced around 2mmt of packaging each year, according to the Corrugated Packaging Association (CPA). The area of commercial woods in the United Kingdom amounts to about 24,000 square kilometers, with 88 mills serving the industry and a workforce of more than 18,000 workers. The total paper and board capacity is more than 7mmt. Top companies by production totals are BPB Paperboard Ltd. and Iveresk.

On a global basis, Europe has become the second leading producer of corrugated boxes, after the United States. According to the Finnish Forest Industries Federation, western Europe produced 96 million tons of paper and paperboard in 2004, with Germany accounting for 21 percent, Finland 15 percent, and Sweden third at 12 percent. Like other major industrialized regions, Europe's main end use market for corrugated boxes was the food product sector. Lesser users included the agriculture and beverage industries.

One of the major threats to the European corrugated industry, and corrugated producers in other major regions, was the use of returnable plastic crates. Concerned that once users switched to plastic they would not reconsider using corrugated, European producers mounted a public relations campaign in the mid-1990s to emphasize the recyclability and environmental friendliness of corrugated packaging.

In the mid-1990s, the folding carton industries in some European countries were growing at about a 2 percent rate, while other countries showed no growth in tonnage. European folding carton manufacturers were using improved corrugated materials that, while lighter in weight, still had sufficient strength properties. The end result was that converters could make the same number of boxes from less corrugated material. Folding carton sales in 2003 surpassed those in North America, making Europe the second-ranked market behind Asia. According to a Euromonitor report, growth in folding carton sales in Europe and Asia was attributed primarily to increased demand from the cigarette industry.

Before the global economic slowdown began to affect Germany, in late 2001 and early 2002, the country had one of the industry's best national growth rates—3 percent in 2000. However, unemployment already had started to hedge up in 2000, and the industry expected more layoffs before a turnaround could be reached. In 2000, with board and paper production in excess of 18mmt, Germany was Europe's production giant. In response to increased competition from other packaging materials, the German folding carton industry has invested in new production processes, increased speed and flexibility, and improvements in laminatioin and printing.

Paperboard Packaging shared BHS European Sales Manager J. Y. Bacques' observations about changes in the German market related to the demand for fine flute boards. By total volume, it has risen by a collective 4.9 percent for E-, F-, E/B, and B/C flutes. E-flute was showing the largest demand growth at 2.2 percent—a rate that is nearly twice the growth reported for F-flute.

In another related article, *Paperboard Packaging* gave estimates on industry growth through 2007. Of all liners used, European consumption of lightweight liners was expected to rise to 16.2 percent by volume by the end of 2007. Growth in lightweight fluting was expected to outpace growth of lightweight linerboard. Western Europe consumed almost 20 million metric tons of 31 million square meters of waste-based containerboard in 2002 and consumption was set to grow to some 21.5 million metric tons by 2007.

Russia. During the Soviet era, little attention was given to product packaging. Since the early 1990s, however, the paperboard packaging industry has seen explosive growth. Though production in this sector has accelerated, aided by newly imported manufacturing machinery and technologies, demand for corrugated boxes in Russia has outpaced supply since at least 1995. Russia's largest corrugated box manufacturer, Naberezhnochelninsky KBK Mill in Tatarstan, produced some 220 million square meters of corrugated boxes in 2004. Close behind was ZAO Gotek, the fastest growing corrugated box manufacturer, with annual production of 200 million square meters. According to a *Paperboard Packaging* feature, the food industry has been the biggest factor in the growth of paperboard packaging in Russia. Demand for corrugated board in Russia is expected to grow by about 6.3 percent annually through 2015, but the corrugated box market is expected to be less consistent.

Asia. While the Asia-Pacific corrugated industry grappled with a region-wide economic crisis in 1997 and 1998, and again in 2001, it was still the fastest-growing corrugated industry in the world, in terms of both production and consumption. Japan's 473 paper and board mills have a capacity of almost 35mmt, and the industry employed about 44,000 workers in 2002.

Asia's corrugated production (excluding Japan) increased 9.0 percent from 1995 to 1996, and while that rate slowed in the late 1990s, growth was still much higher than in mature markets like North America and Europe. By 2005, Asia was expected to produce 36 percent of all corrugated materials in the world, according to one estimate, with the bulk of that production taking place in China, Indonesia, Thailand, and India. Asia's share of global corrugated demand increased from 13 percent in 1990 to 18 percent in 1996, with the highest demand growth generated by Indonesia, the Philippines, China, Vietnam, Malaysia, and Thailand. By 2005, the region's share of global demand was expected to reach 25 percent.

In his article "Pulp Friction," Eddie Lee shared analysis about China, indicating that rapid growth led to a dramatic increase in imports of paper and paperboard from 9 percent of total consumption in 1979 to about 20 percent in 2004. Lee predicted that forest-rich countries would be beneficiaries of China's growing appetite for imported fiber. Notable among those countries were Brazil, Canada, and Indonesia. Analysts E.J. Krause & Associates reported that Chinese demand for paper and paperboard products was expected to reach 70 million tons by 2010. Demand for containerboard and corrugated paper in China averaged 13.7 percent annual growth as of 2005.

Asia was a growing market for folding cartons as well. While established regions, such as North America, focused on source reduction, the Asia-Pacific region was using more packaging as living standards rose and more packaging materials became available. One significant contributor to the growth in folding carton consumption in Asia was the proliferation of microwavable and oven-ready foods.

Japan saw consumer packaging increase in volume by nearly 5 percent between 1998 and 2002, making it Asia's largest market in this industry. Japan is known for its design of compact and functional packaging; flexible packaging, primarily for the food industry, represents the most commonly used packaging in the country. Despite robust sales through the 1990s, Japan's packaging industry faced uncertain growth in the early 2000s, due to the country's faltering economy. At the same time, though, increased competition among companies across most manufacturing sectors boosted interest in folding cartons as a promotional tool and as a means of cutting distribution costs. As a result, production of folding cartons grew by 5 percent in 2002 to reach almost 26 billion units.

FURTHER READING

Andel, Tom. "Design for Ability." *Paperboard Packaging,* 1 May 2005. Available from http://www.packaging-online.com.

"China Paper/China Forest 2005." E.J. Krause & Associates, Inc., 2005. Available from http://www.ejkrause.com.

Conn, Peta. "Cartons Weather Competitive Packaging Storm." *Euromonitor International,* 3 November 2004. Available from http://www.euromonitor.com.

"Containerboard Production Improves: PPPC." *Official Board Markets,* 20 March 2004.

Donberg, Deborah. "Corrugated, Boxes Rebound." *Paper, Film & Foil Converter,* 1 June 2004.

———. "The Future of Package Printing." *Paper, Film & Foil Converter,* January 2002.

"Frozen Suppliers Like Recycled Paperboard." *Frozen Food Age,* January 2004.

Grishchenko, Gregory. "Russia Hungry for Corrugated." *Paperboard Packaging,* 1 May 2005. Available from http://www.packaging-online.com.

Higham, Robert. "Trending Toward Lightweight: From Modest Beginnings 20 Years Ago, Otor Has Become a Leading Innovator in Europe's Box Making Business." *Paperboard Packaging,* September 2003.

"ICV Boxes in Packaging Deal." *Buyouts,* 7 June 2004.

Krizner, Tricia. "Shorter...Smaller...Faster: Lead Times, Order Sizes and Turnarounds are Getting the Squeeze and Box Makers Feel the Pressure." *Paperboard Packaging,* June 2003.

Lee, Eddie. "Pulp Friction," 4 May 2004. Available from http://straitstimes.asia1.com.sg.

Murphy, Kate. "Thinking Outside the Can: A Fresh Look at Food in a Box." *New York Times,* 14 March 2004.

Nax, Sanford. "Annual Review." *The Fresno Bee,* 19 March 2002.

"North America's Corrugated Box Makers Want Higher Prices." *Purchasing,* 1 April 2004.

"100 Percent Recycled Paperboard Sleeping Giant or Emerging Tiger?" *100 Percent Recycled Paperboard Alliance,* 2005. Available from http://www.rpa100.com.

Packaging in Japan. Euromonitor, April 2003. Available from http://www.euromonitor.com.

"Paper Industry Statistics." Norcross, Ga: TAPPI, 2005. Available from http://www.tappi.org.

"Paperboard Packaging Holds the Things We Need." *Paperboard Packaging,* November 2003.

"Recycled Paperboard Makes Strides." *Official Board Markets,* 27 September 2003.

Rohleder, Ken. "Boxes in Small Batches: Long Popular in Europe, the Corrugated Focused Factory Is Gaining Recognition in North America." *Paperboard Packaging,* May 2004.

Smook, Gary A. *Handbook of Pulp and Paper Terminology: A Guide to Industrial and Technological Usage.* Bellingham, Wash.: Angus Wilde, 1990.

Testin, Robert F., and Peter Vergano. *Packaging in America in the 1990s.* Herndon, Va.: Institute of Packaging Professionals, 1990.

Thesaurus of Pulp and Paper Terminology. Atlanta: Institute of Paper Science and Technology, 1991.

"Tray Goes from Baker's Ovens to Consumers' Tables: Using a Laminated Paperboard Tray as Both a Baking Tray and a Retail Package Saves Money and Improves Quality." *Food & Drug Packaging,* April 2003.

"Trendsetting Manufacturer: TPN Flexpak Has Added a New Dimension to the Art and Business of Product Packaging by Applying a Complete Range of Systems. This Makes it the First Company in Thailand to Venture into Flexible Packaging on This Scale." *Plastics & Rubber Asia,* April 2003.

2003-2004 Pulp & Paper Global Fact & Price Book. Available from http://www.paperloop.com.

SIC 2631

NAICS 322130

PAPERBOARD MILLS

The world's paperboard mills manufacture paperboard, often known in lay terms as cardboard, for various purposes using wood pulp and other fiber pulp. Certain paperboard mills also manufacture converted paperboard products. For discussion of coverted paperboard as used in containers, see also **Paperboard Containers and Boxes.** A general treatment of paperboard's source material, pulp, is given under **Pulp Mills,** and for information about paper manufacturers, see also **Paper Mills.**

INDUSTRY SNAPSHOT

Paperboard production is usually considered a part of the paper industry. Paperboard is defined as any thick, heavyweight paper product. The distinction between paper and paperboard is based on product thickness. While all sheets above 0.3 mm can be classified as paperboard, enough exceptions are applied in the trade to make that definition hazy. For the most part, paperboard is made in the same manner as paper.

In some countries, such as the United States, total paperboard production is equal to or exceeds paper production. In other areas, such as Europe, paper production still exceeds paperboard production by a wide margin. Statistics for these two areas are frequently combined in reports.

Most paperboard is used to make materials for corrugated boxes, and the growth of the global paperboard industry is directly linked to the use of paperboard boxes (commonly called cardboard boxes). Prior to the acceptance of corrugated containers for shipping, wooden crates and boxes were used.

Worldwide production capacity grew steadily after the mid-1990s, but began slowing in 2000 and continued its decline through 2007. Most paperboard is consumed in its country of origin, but paperboard also is a major export product for many countries.

ORGANIZATION AND STRUCTURE

Two grades of paperboard—corrugating medium and linerboard—are used to make corrugated shipping containers. (Corrugating medium is called "fluting" in Europe and other regions.) Those two grades, together known as containerboard, account for the majority of paperboard produced around the world. A third grade—solid bleached sulfate (SBS), also called solid bleached board (SBB)—is used to make folding cartons, such as those used in retail stores. SBS accounts for a large share of the remaining production.

One major distinction among paperboard grades is their classification as folding or non-folding grades. Folding grades must be flexible enough that the surface will not split or crack when the board is folded to make a box.

Most paperboard can be classified as follows:

- Boxboard: board of various compositions used to make folding boxboard and set-up or rigid boxes;
- Foodboard: single or multi-ply paperboard used for food and liquid packaging; or
- Containerboard: board for containers consisting of two or more linerboard grades separated by corrugating medium glued to the liners.

The classification of paperboard usually depends on how it is used. Folding boxboard, for example, is made to permit folding without breaking the surface, while at the same time providing good surface finish and the ability to be used in a wide variety of carton shapes. The bending property is not as important in set-up boxes, which instead require board that can be easily scored (depressed or partially cut). For foodboard, special surface treatments are usually needed to provide water and/or grease resistance. Similarly, liquid packaging grades usually require an additional conversion process in which plastic and/or foil lamination takes place to make the container impermeable to air and water.

The U.S. Department of Labor's OSHA division classifies the following as primarily shipping paperboard or paperboard products: binders' board; bottle cap board; boxboard; bristols, bogus; cardboard; clipboard (paperboard); clay coated board; container board; folding boxboards; leatherboard; liner board, kraft, and jute; manila lined board; matrix board; milk carton board; newsboard; paperboard mills, except building board mills; paperboard, except building board; patent coated paperboard; pressboard; setup boxboard; shoe board; special food board; stencil board; strawboard, except building board; tagboard; and wet machine board.

Packaging is the single largest application for paperboard in most countries. Some countries, such as the United States, tend to use more virgin materials to manufacture paperboard, while others, such as South Korea, use more recycled fiber in their production process. The use of recycled fiber in paperboard production is growing fast, however, particularly in the United States. Most recycled fiber is used in products in which the reclaimed pulp does not need to be cleaned. Cereal cartons, for example, are typically made from a product called combination boxboard, with two white outside layers suitable for printing covering a gray, recycled inner layer. Kraft softwood (made from coniferous trees such as pine) has been the preferred pulp for making paperboard because of its strength. Most paperboard is unbleached (brown), but bleached (white) grades are used where appearance is important, such as for retail packaging.

Corrugated containers are, by far, the dominant global means of packaging goods for shipment. Converting plants, located in every industrialized country, use corrugating medium and linerboard to make boxes. Typically, these converting plants are located in urban areas, close to container users. While there are a large number of independent box converters (also called boxmakers), many box-converting plants are owned by the same companies that manufacture the linerboard and medium.

The two main raw materials used to make corrugating medium are semichemical hardwood pulp and recycled pulp (typically old corrugated containers that have been used and discarded). Hardwood pulp is made from deciduous trees such as oak and maple. The pulp from these trees has short, inflexible fibers that help make the corrugating medium stiff. This, combined with their lower cost in comparison to softwood fibers (from coniferous trees such as pine), make them the fiber of choice for medium. The term semichemical designates that the pulp used to make medium is only partially "cooked" in the digester and is partially washed, so it retains much of the glue-like lignin that hold the fibers together in the wood. With the lignin and other wood by-products remaining in the corrugating medium, it is easier to form a rigid fluted shape with a corrugating machine.

Use of recycled pulp in boxboard varies by country. For example, Asian countries, which often lack resources for virgin pulp, use a high percentage of recycled pulp to make boxboard. The United States, on the other hand, has traditionally used mostly virgin pulp. However, that equation was changing rapidly. Semichemical medium's share of total U.S. medium production declined to about 59 percent in 1996, from 72 percent in 1992 and 79 percent in 1980. The share of recycled medium production grew to 28 percent in 1992 and to 41 percent in 1996.

Medium, like other grades of paper and paperboard, is categorized by "basis weights." The higher the basis weight, the heavier the paper or board. National standards for medium differ, but typical basis weights are 22-, 26-, 33-, 36-, and 40-pound. The standard U.S. weight is 26-pound, which accounted for the majority of all production in the late 1990s and early 2000s.

Medium production is directly related to worldwide production of corrugated boxes, measured as "shipments." After several weak years in the early 1990s, corrugated box shipments accelerated rapidly in 1994, rising 6-7 percent worldwide. This led to a worldwide shortage of containerboard, pushing prices to historic highs in 1994 and early 1995, and dramatically raising the price of finished boxes for end users. However, prices of containerboard began falling in late 1996 and through most of 1997 due to a glut of containerboard on the market. This occurred even though overall demand for boxes kept rising with the generally favorable world economic climate, leveling off in 1999.

Linerboard is made primarily from softwood fibers. These fibers produce a much stronger sheet of linerboard. Still, linerboard may contain significant percentages of hardwood pulp and recycled fiber. Again, a variety of national standards exist for which fibers may be used in linerboard. For example, Korean and Japanese linerboard contains a large percentage of recycled fiber, making their linerboard significantly weaker than virgin linerboard.

By contrast, U.S. linerboard can contain no more than 20 percent hardwood pulp and/or recycled fiber. The recycled fiber is usually made from recovered corrugated material. If U.S. linerboard contains more than 20 percent recycled material, it must be called "recycled linerboard." In fact, 100 percent recycled linerboard grew very fast in the United States beginning in the late 1980s and throughout the 1990s. For example, recycled linerboard production jumped 80 percent in one year, moving from 1.93 million short tons in 1995 to 3.79 million short tons in 1996. At the same time, production of unbleached virgin kraft linerboard dropped 8.8 percent, from 17.65 million short tons in 1995 to 16.11 million short tons in 1996. By 2001, recycled linerboard represented 17 percent of U.S. linerboard production.

One of the highest-quality linerboard grades is solid bleached sulfate (SBS), made from pulp that has at least 80 percent bleached virgin fiber. It is used in high-quality packaging applications, such as boxes that are displayed in retail stores. A major portion of global SBS production is coated with a clay solution to improve its surface for printing. This is particularly important since consumer products manufacturers often use four-color process printing on their products' packages. SBS is commonly used to make cigarette packages and is also used for many food product applications, such as milk carton stock. SBS is available in basis weights ranging from 40 to 100 pounds. Other significant applications for SBS include disposable cups and plates.

The biggest buyer of SBS in the late 1990s was the tobacco industry, estimated to account for 60 percent of total demand. However, this grade was losing share worldwide to both folding boxboard and unbleached linerboard as product manufacturers downgraded from more expensive SBS to unbleached board for frozen food and liquor cartons. Folding boxboard was the primary beneficiary of this trend.

Bleached bristol is another major grade made from SBS pulp. This comparatively lightweight grade is used for paperback book covers, greeting cards, and the covers of telephone directories.

In the December 3, 2003, issue of *Ahead of the Curve*, Janice Bottiglieri shared some expert papermaking trends. One major trend was for paperboard mills to move operations previously off machine to on-machine operations. These operations include coating and converting. Bulab Holdings Chairman Katherine Buckman Davis explained that the most active sectors involved with this trend were lightweight coated, coated paper, and coated board. Motivating factors for advancing this trend were efforts to "increase manpower efficiencies, decrease the need for extra machinery, eliminate the logistical problems of moving and storing paper and board, and reduce the maintenance involved in conducting the various steps." McDermott Consulting Services' Ted McDermott pointed out that "a negative aspect of going on-line is the need to do the product development and try to match the sheet properties of off-line created processes. For extremely flat-surfaced papers or extremely high gloss coated papers, on-line processes cannot achieve the off-line quality level."

Noel Deking shared the following data. For 2002, total bleached packaging paperboard capacity was approximately 5.2 million tons and bleached bristols accounted for an additional 1.4 million tons. In the packaging segment, folding cartonboard represented about 52 percent of the total; milk carton and foodservice products about 42 percent; linerboard about 3 percent; and other miscellaneous converting about 3 percent."

Deking also claimed the industry was experiencing significant restructuring and consolidation, with the top three producers accounting for 65 percent of industry capacity. Noted business links included Westvaco Corp.'s purchase of Temple-Inland Inc.'s bleached board mill, adding about 670,000 tpy of production capacity. Blue Ridge Paper LLC purchased the former Champion International Corp. bleached board mill and its DairyPak packaging business, plus Westvaco's liquid packaging business. Finally, Georgia-Pacific Corp. purchased Fort James Corp., acquiring the Dixie disposable foodservice line, as well as a 225,000 tpy bleached board mill.

BACKGROUND AND DEVELOPMENT

In the United States, corrugated boxes were declared legal for shipping in 1914. As new methods helped improve the strength and durability of corrugated containers, their use in the global economy increased dramatically. World War II spurred major developments in corrugated shipping containers, which were used to ship military supplies. These innovations usually improved water and temperature resistance.

The use of corrugated paperboard containers in the global economy accelerated after World War II, and in most countries exceeded growth in gross national product (GNP). Other paperboard containers were developed as well, such as disposable containers for food and beverages. The popularity of this type of paperboard packaging stimulated sales of solid bleached sulfate (SBS) board.

The global consumption of paperboard tends to mirror economic conditions in individual countries. For example, in the early 1990s paperboard consumption stalled in North America, which was suffering from the effects of a mild recession. In Europe and Asia, however, paperboard consumption grew significantly until those economies went into recession in 1992-1993. In 1993, all of the major economies were either in recession or very slow recovery. As a result, growth in paperboard production suffered. A unified global economic recovery in 1994 and 1995 pushed up demand for linerboard significantly in nearly all markets. By this time paperboard growth again exceeded the growth rate of gross domestic product (GDP), ranging from 3 to 7 percent in major producing countries in 1994.

That growth continued in 1995, fueling a boom in paperboard production. Worldwide capacity expansions in paperboard averaged 4-5 percent in 1996. However, this expansion proved to be too rapid, and prices for most grades of paperboard plunged in late 1996 and early 1997, recovering slightly toward the end of that year and then dropping in 2000 and 2001 as a result of recession and the post-September 11, 2001 general economic slump.

Paperboard is an internationally traded commodity, and much of the growth in demand in the mid- to late 1990s came from Asia, which except for Japan was experiencing rapid growth. However, the financial crisis that hit the region in early 1997 dampened economic growth. As a result, projections for increased paperboard demand in that region have been scaled down.

One of the best growth prospects in paperboard consumption came from the rapid development of liquid packaging systems in the 1990s, including both cartonboard containers and the larger-sized bag-in-box packs. Originally developed for milk and fruit juices, the packs were being used more for soups, purees, and pastes, particularly in Europe and Asia.

According to FAO data, non-printing paper and paperboard production in the United States reached 54.5 mmt (million metric tons) in 2001 and rose to 55.3 mmt in 2003. Exports that year accounted for 6.4 mmt worth US$4.3 billion, a slight increase from 6.2 mmt exported in 2001 and valued at US$4.2 billion. *Business Week* reported that the operating rate for U.S. containerboard facilities stood at 97.5 percent in May 2004.

According to Japanese government figures, the worldwide paperboard industry had begun to see slow but steady improvement by 2003. Shipments of processed food products, including health drinks and snacks, contributed to the rise in containerboard demand, while growth in folding carton and whiteboard was also boosted by growth in food industry demand.

To satisfy booming demand for paperboard products, particularly corrugated cardboard in which to package goods for its growing export markets, China increased imports of recycled cardboard. Unexpected beneficiaries of this trend were U.S. municipalities that, in 2005, were selling waste cardboard to China for US$90 per ton. Combined imports of paper, paperboard, waste paper, market pulp, and converted products totaled 21.99 mmt in 2003, an increase of 17.3 percent from the previous year. Coated boxboard ranked second only to newsprint in import growth in 2003.

CURRENT CONDITIONS

For the sixth straight year, total paper and paperboard capacity in the United States declined in 2006. Capacity dropped 1.6 percent to 97.7 million tons, the sharpest decline since 2001. Competition from paper imports, growth in the U.S. trade deficit with relation to packaged goods, and electronic substitution were some of the factors that directly or indirectly led to the capacity reductions, according to the American Forest & Paper Association (AF&PA). Nevertheless, the United States remained the largest producer of paper and paperboard in the world.

Recycling was an important issue in the paperboard industry in the later mid-2000s. The AF&PA reported that a record amount of paper consumed in the United States in 2006 was recycled. About 53.5 million tons of paper, or 53.4 percent of the total amount consumed, was recycled. The association announced a goal of reaching a 55 percent recycling rate by 2012, partly by increasing the amount recovered from offices and schools. Canada was also increasing the amount of paper it recycled and used. In 2004, approximately 46 percent of the paper and paperboard used in Canada was recycled, and 4.9 million tons of paper was transformed into other products. About 54 percent of the recycled paper used to make other products came from Canada, with the rest mainly from the United States.

Demand for recycled paper was also on the rise. Thirty-two percent of the paper recycled in the United States in 2006 was exported, with 10 million tons going to China.

According to the AF&PA, growing demand in China for newsprint and packaging material was driving increased demand for imports of recyclable paper in that country. Other growing market segments for recycled paper included Americans who were intent on practicing social responsibility. Many printing companies were responding by incorporating environmentally friendly practices into their production processes and increasing the amount of recycled paper used for printing. For example, in 2007 Scholastic Inc. (New York) announced that all 12 million copies of the U.S. edition of *Harry Potter and the Deathly Hallows* will be printed on 30 percent post-consumer waste (pcw) paper, and 65 percent of the 16,700 tons of paper used in the U.S. first printing will be FSC (Forest Stewardship Council) certified. This marked the largest purchase of FSC paper to be used in the printing of a single book title.

Research and Technology

Since production of paperboard is very similar to that of paper, many research trends in paperboard are similar to those in paper mills. Some differences exist, however. One area of particular interest to paperboard manufacturers is the use of "impulse drying" to make linerboard. Currently under development by the Institute of Paper Science and Technology and Beloit Corp. in the United States, impulse drying involves heating one or more rolls in the press section of the paperboard machine. This dries the paperboard web so that less drying is required later in the dryer stage of the process. Since less steam is needed to heat rolls in the dryer section, this innovation enables paperboard manufacturers to reduce steam costs and speed up production. Theoretically, paperboard manufacturers will be able to improve productivity by 50 to 80 percent.

Another area of interest is the use of "stratification" in making paperboard. Stratification requires a special headbox that can produce three or more layers of paperboard simultaneously from different fiber sources. In this way, a layer of recycled fiber, or some other lesser quality fiber source, could be sandwiched between layers of better quality fiber. With newer model headboxes, these layers can be extremely thin. Several European paperboard manufacturers have adopted this technique.

The construction of containerboard improved considerably in the 1990s, as paperboard mills developed new production processes. Mills were able to produce lighter-weight linerboard and corrugating medium that still performed well in boxmaking plants. As a result, machinery manufacturers developed machines that produced finer grades of fluting at box plants. The boxes produced through these processes were able, in many applications, to replace boxes made from folding cartonboard. In 2002, International Paper introduced a recyclable moisture barrier in its bulk boxes.

Industry Leaders

Since many paper companies produce large quantities of both paper and paperboard, leaders in the paperboard industry tend to include many of the companies profiled under **Paper Mills**.

Of the top 10 global pulp and paper companies, several producers have extensive interests in paperboard production. The U.S.-based International Paper Company (IP) was the world's largest forest products company. Although in the early 2000s it owned 6.3 million acres of forested land in the United States, as well as 1.2 million in Brazil and smaller tracts in New Zealand and Russia, by 2007 it had sold much of its forested land, retaining about 500,000 acres in the United States and harvesting rights for about 1 million acres in Brazil and Russia. In 2006 the company posted total sales of US$21.9 billion, with paper and packaging accounting for about two-thirds of sales. That year the company employed 68,700 people.

Atlanta-based Georgia-Pacific Corporation was the second-largest U.S. producer of containerboard and the world's largest producer of tissue products Its major brands included Brawny, Quilted Northern, and Dixie. Sales in 2004 exceeded US$19.6 billion. UPM-Kymmene, Helsinki, Finland, Europe's largest forest industry group, operated a packaging materials division, though it concentrated more on the publishing papers market. Swedish-based Stora Enso Oyj, another of the world's largest forest products companies, produced paperboard, mostly for the European market. In 2006 the company reported total sales of US$15.7 billion.

U.S.-based Smurfit-Stone Container Enterprises is a leading producer of packing materials, with corrugated containers accounting for more than 50 percent of sales (US$8.2 billion) in 2004. Svenska Cellulosa Aktiebolaget produced paperboard through its SCA Packaging unit, which was Europe's leading manufacturer of corrugated board packaging in the mid-2000s. In 2004 the company realized US$13.6 billion in sales.

Caraustar Industries was ranked as a major manufacturer of recycled paperboard and converted paperboard products. It operates more than 100 facilities in the United States along with plants in Mexico and the United Kingdom. Caraustar manufactured products primarily from recovered fiber derived from recycled paperstock. It produced various grades of uncoated and clay-coated recycled paperboard both for internal consumption and customers in four principal markets.

Based in Washington state, Weyerhaeuser Company is one of the largest U.S. forest products companies and North America's largest softwood lumber producer. Its products include lumber, plywood, containerboard, pulp, and papers. The company owns timberland throughout the South and Pacific Northwest. It also has holdings in Canada, Australia, New Zealand, France, Ireland, and Uruguay. Sales in 2006 topped US$21.8 billion.

Oji Paper Co., Ltd., Tokyo, Japan's second-biggest paper company, produced a large amount of paperboard, though its main focus was on paper grades.

MAJOR COUNTRIES IN THE INDUSTRY

UNITED STATES

U.S. paperboard producers ship the vast majority of paperboard consumed in the United States and have a strong position in the international market. Linerboard is one of the strongest export products for the U.S. pulp and paper industry. U.S. linerboard mills, mostly in the southern part of the country, are considered the low-cost producers throughout the world.

According to the U.S. Department of Labor, in the year 2000 employment in the industry amounted to about 123,000 employees. Due to technology advances, the employment numbers are expected to decline through 2010. Most paperboard jobs are located in Georgia, Virginia, and Alabama.

According to *Converting Magazine*, the drop in sales of non-durable packaging materials—caused by a combination of recession and post-September 11 shrinkage in consumer purchases—seemed to level off by the end of 2001. But by 2002, some mid-sized companies were showing the strain of prolonged economic losses. After a disastrous 2000 loss of US$33 million, Idaho-based Potlatch Corp. saw conditions worsen even more in 2001. Even larger companies, such as International Paper, began mass layoffs in February 2002 as the effects of poor fourth quarter 2001 revenues became clear. The giant Smurfit Corp. of Chicago resorted to shutting machines and increasing downtime in its containerboard mills throughout 2001 and early 2002.

Deking reported that industry capacity declined by 200,000 tpy in June 2001, when International Paper Co. closed its bleached board mill in Moss Point, Mississippi. It was the first permanent shutdown of a bleached board machine in more than 25 years. At that time, no new bleached board machine had been constructed since 1995.

In the mid-2000s, the United States was the world's leading paper and paperboard manufacturer, producing 83.4 million tons, or 23.2 percent of the world total, in 2004. According to the U.S.D.A. Forest Service, production of paper and paperboard will grow slowly through 2050, while per capita consumption will increase at a faster pace.

JAPAN

In the mid-2000s Japan was the world's third-largest paper and paperboard producer. Nevertheless, the industry saw declines as the Japanese economy began slipping in the early 2000s. After showing slight production growth in the paper and paperboard industry of 1.2 percent in 1999, Japanese production dropped 3.5 percent from 2000 to 2001. The production for the year (including paper) equaled 30.73 million tons, as holiday sales and information technology business demonstrated corresponding drop-offs, according to the Japan Paper Association (JPA). About 2.6 percent of the decline was in cardboard used in shipping computers and appliances to home consumers, according to the JPA.

Total paperboard production in 2005 was 12.0 mmt, of which the greatest part (9.3 mmt) was containerboard. Folding carton production reached 1.8 mmt, while production of other paperboard totaled 850,000 mt. Most of Japan's production serves its domestic market. Paperboard exports peaked in 2000 at 448,000 tons, then started a steady decline, totaling only 185,000 tons in 2005. About twenty-one percent of exported paperboard was shipped to China in 2005. Taiwan received 12.2 percent, Hong Kong 11.6 percent, and the United States 10.1 percent, with the remainder going to other countries. Imports rose during this time, hitting a peak of 336,000 tons in 2004 then reaching 315,000 tons in 2005. The majority of imported paperboard (61.7%) came from the United States. Korea and Taiwan held the number two and three spots, respectively.

CHINA

China, the world's second-largest manufacturer of paper and paperboard in the mid-2000s, had significant increases in demand as its economy expanded in the 1980s and 1990s. However, demand fell in 2002 due to demographic changes related to government-mandated regulations regarding the number of children one family could have.

China produced around 49 million tons of paper and paperboard in 2005. In addition, *Asia Pulse* reported that "there are more than 1,200 corrugated paper production lines in China with an annual production capacity of over 200 billion square meters."

GERMANY

Germany, the largest corrugated producer in Europe and fifth largest paper and paperboard producer in the world, manufactured 20.4 million tons of paper (excluding newsprint) and paperboard in 2005, according to Pulp & Paper International. With major operations in Germany and 16 other companies, Kappa Alpha Holdings (Kappa Holdings) is one of the largest producers of packaging paper and board for business purposes, with a workforce numbering 17,000 and annual sales of more than US$2.6 billion. In 2001, the giant Kappa Packaging greatly increased its company size after purchasing Swedish business rival AssiDomaen's corrugated and containerboard operations.

CANADA

Canada's forest products industry focuses primarily on the production and export of pulp, newsprint, and printing and writing papers. In the early 2000s, the country faced diminished export earnings in this sector due to global overproduction, which had lowered prices. In 2005, Canada produced 20.4 million tons of paper and paperboard. More than half of its corrugated and folding boxboard production was exported, but the export value of case materials fell from US$737 million in 2000 to only US$498.3 million in 2003. Increased productivity in Canada's pulp and paper industry led to a reduction of about 13,000 jobs by 2002.

SOUTH KOREA

Since 2000, the industry news from Korea has mainly been bad. Company production capacity was only 73.6 percent in 2001, down 13.3 percentage points from 1995. South Korea imports more than 80 percent of the pulp it uses for making paper and paperboard. Almost 70 percent of the fiber used in South Korea to make paper and board comes from recycled paper and paperboard. This heavy reliance on recycled fiber means that South Korean paperboard tends to be weaker than paperboard made with more virgin fiber. Improvements in papermaking processes and high performance wet-strength agents are being used to improve the strength of South Korean paperboard.

Continuous capacity additions and the collapse of local and export paper markets in the fourth quarter of 1995 prompted significant downtime in South Korea's paperboard industry in 1996. According to one report, downtime ranged from 25 to 30 percent and prices on key grades were discounted by as much as 25 percent. South Korean producers also suffered from the 1997 financial crisis, which severely tightened spending and inflated debt. As of 2002, Korea still faced overcapacity of 30 percent in the paper and paperboard sector. Total production in 2005 was 10.5 million tons.

FURTHER READING

"About the Paper Industry." Japan Paper Association, 2006. Available from http://www.jpa.gr.jp/en/.

"AF&PA Shines Light on Recycling." *Official Board Markets,* 31 March 2007.

Bottiglieri, Janice. "Trends in Papermaking: Ideas from the Experts." *Ahead of the Curve.* 3 December 2003. Available from http://newsmanager.commpartners.com.

"Caraustar Industries Energy Assessment Provides a Company-Wide Model." *Energy Matters Newsletter,* Spring 2003. Available from http://www.oit.doe.gov.

China Paper Industry 2005 Annual Report. China Paper Association, March 2006. Available from http://www.chinapaperonline.com.

China Paper Industry Report Year 2003. China Paper Association, April 2004. Available from http://www.chinapaperonline.com.

Cormier, Christopher J. "Linerboard." *Case Watch,* 25 June 2003.

Decking, Noel. "Bleached Paperboard: SBS Mills Ramp Up Production, Backlogs." *Paperloop,* 2004. Available from http://www.paperloop.com.

Fitzgerald, Jay. "China Need for Trash Insatiable," *Boston Herald,* 26 May 2005.

Food and Agricultural Service of the United Nations. FAOSTAT. 15 April 2007. Available from www.fao.org.

"Frequently Asked Questions." *Paper University,* 2005. Available from http://www.tappi.org.

Grishchenko, Gregory. "Russia Hungry for Corrugated." *Paperboard Packaging,* 1 May 2005. Available from http://www.packaging-online.com.

Hoover's Company Capsules. Hoover's Inc., 2007. Available from www.hoovers.com.

Ince, Peter J. *Long-Range Outlook for U.S. Paper and Paperboard Demand, Technology, and Fiber Supply-Demand Equilibria.* USDA Forest Service, 2005. Available from http://www.fpl.fs.fed.us.

"Linerboard Capacity Rises in 2006." *Official Board Markets,* 17 March 2007.

"Outlook of Demand for Paper and Paperboard in 2006." Japan Paper Association, 2006. Available from http://www.jpa.gr.jp.

"Overview of the Recycling Industry." Paper Recycling Association, 2007. Available from http://www.pppc.org.

"Paper and Pulp Industry in Canada." Wikipedia, 2007. Available from http://en.wikipedia.org/.

"Paperboard Mill Performance." *Official Board Markets,* 24 March 2007.

"Paper Packaging: Ready to Rip." *Business Week,* 18 June 2004. Available from http://www.hoovers.com.

Paper Recycling Association, Canada, 2007. Available from http://www.pppc.org.

"Pulp and Paper Manufacturing." European Commission, May 2006. Available from http://ec.europa.eu/.

"The 2003-2004 World Outlook for Paper and Paperboard Mills." *Mindbranch.* Available from http://www.mindbranch.com.

Warnook, Matt. "Environmental Agency Takes Action Against Timber Smuggling." *Wood & Wood Products,* September 2006.

SIC 2611

NAICS 322110

PULP MILLS

Pulp mills manufacture pulp, the primary ingredient in paper, from wood or wastepaper (recycled fiber), although a small number of establishments use other materials for pulping, such as rags, cotton linters, and straw. Most major pulp operations are integrated with paper or paperboard production facilities. For additional information, see also **Paper Mills** and **Paperboard Mills.**

INDUSTRY SNAPSHOT

Pulp mills around the world produce a wide variety of pulps from wood fiber for making paper and paperboard. While the majority of pulp produced globally is chemical pulp, a substantial amount of pulp also was produced using the groundwood process. A growing number of mills make pulp from recycled paper. According to the Food and Agricultural Organization of the United Nations (FAO), total world production of wood pulp in 2003 exceeded 170.3 million metric tons (mmt).

In 2003, the United States led the world in wood pulp production with 53.1 mmt. Canada was second with 26.1 mmt. Other significant pulp-producing nations included Finland (11.9 mmt), Sweden (11.7 mmt), Japan (10.4 mmt), Brazil (8.8 mmt), Russia (6.6 mmt), China (4.0 mmt).

Market pulp is a truly global commodity characterized by rapid price fluctuations in response to changes in capacity and demand. While market pulp is produced in about 25 countries, in the mid-2000s more than two-thirds of world output came from six northern countries: the United States, Canada, Sweden, Finland, Russia, and Norway. China was regarded as the fastest-growing producer of pulp. In addition, production numbers were rising in South America, most notably in Brazil and Chile. One major advantage South American mills enjoy is access to fast-growing pulpwood trees, such as eucalyptus and radiata pine species. These trees reach pulping maturity within 7 years, compared to 30 years in some northern countries.

ORGANIZATION AND STRUCTURE

In most cases pulp mills need to be located near their raw materials—trees or wastepaper—to minimize transportation costs. Many of the leading world pulp producers—such as the United States, Canada, Sweden, Finland, and Brazil—have extensive forest reserves that are used, in part, for pulp production. Other leading pulp producers, such as Japan, possess limited forest resources but import logs and wood chips for pulp production.

While pulping and papermaking are very energy intensive, pulp and paper companies throughout the world are regarded as efficient energy users. They gained this efficiency through producing their own electricity by burning many of their waste products, such as tree bark and spent chemicals from the pulping process. In some countries, pulp and paper mills generate over half of the energy required to run mills. Newer, large pulp and paper mills using chemical pulp are often completely self-sufficient in energy. Nonetheless, environmental groups frequently criticize companies that supply wood to mills for endangering fish in small creeks by clearcutting practices and the dragging of logs through these waterways. In addition, poor logging practices as far as 80 years in the past have brought attention to overlogging practices in the United States and other countries.

Water is used in large quantities in pulp and paper manufacturing, and thus most mills are sited near lakes, rivers, or oceans. In decades past, waste water from the pulping process, known as effluent, was released directly into receiving waters and caused substantial water pollution. Today, however, many pulp mills in countries whose governments adhere to sounder environmental practices reuse and/or clean process water extensively before it is discharged. After water is reused within pulp and paper mills, it is sent to primary, secondary, and in some cases, tertiary treatment plants.

More often, wood pulp is being replaced by recycled paper in new paper production. The percentage of fiber from trees, called virgin fiber, used in global paper and board production dropped from about 75 percent in 1970 to less than 62 percent in 1992, as more recycled pulp replaced wood fiber. By 1997 that percentage had dropped further to 60 percent.

While the percentage of wood pulp in paper is expected to continue declining, it will likely remain the key ingredient in papermaking for years to come. Cellulose fibers can only be recycled a few times—about seven or eight—before they become so weak and short that they are washed out of the papermaking process. The overall use of wood pulp should grow—at least slightly—as the entire market for paper expands. Worldwide production of wood pulp was expected to rise by an average of 2 percent per year for the foreseeable future.

As of the mid-2000s, chemical pulp clearly remained the pulp of choice throughout the world. In 2003, chemical pulp production reached 124.4 mmt, representing approximately 73 percent of global pulp production. Mechanical pulp, at 34.8 mmt, accounted for about 17 percent of the total, while other pulp production was 18.6 mmt, or 10 percent.

While global consumption of pulp spiked higher and lower from year to year in the 1990s, the general trend has been toward higher consumption, particularly as rising incomes contributed to increased consumption of paper and packaging. In 1996 global pulp consumption was 172.9 mmt. The leading pulp-consuming region was North America, at 72.2 mmt, followed by Asia at 46.3 mmt and Western Europe at 37.8 million. Other significant pulp-consuming regions were Latin America at 7.5 mmt and Eastern Europe (including Russia) at 5.65 mmt. While North America continued to lead in consumption of paper and paperboard, which are the chief end products of woodpulp, consumption in the region declined by 2.4 percent in 2000, with usage dropping by 2.3 percent in the United States and by 3.3 percent in Canada. The market for pulp was rosier in Europe, however, where paper and paperboard consumption rose steadily through the 1990s and into the early 2000s. The FAO projected that woodpulp consumption would also grow in Africa, where usage in 1994 was only 1.2 mmt. Consumption on that continent was expected to be 1.9 mmt in 2005, and 2.079 mmt by 2010.

BACKGROUND AND DEVELOPMENT

Before the mid-nineteenth century, paper was made from rags or used paper. Rag collection for papermaking was an important part of the global economy at the time. However, as the global demand for paper continued to increase, the demand for rags began to outstrip supply.

A major revolution in pulping occurred between 1851 and 1918, when wood pulp was invented, developed, and industrialized. This period saw the development and commercialization of all major wood pulping processes, including groundwood, soda, sulphite, and kraft (sulphate). Soda pulping was invented by Burgess and Watt in England, and was patented in 1854 in the United States. Groundwood became established in the 1860s. Kraft pulping was invented in 1884 by German chemist Carl Dahl using sodium sulfate as the pulping agent. The pulp produced a strong brown paper, dubbed *kraft*, the German word for strong. This became the dominant method of pulp production in the twentieth century.

The science of pulping continued to develop along with the growth of papermaking. There were several quantum technological leaps in pulping, including the invention of the chemical recovery boiler, in which spent pulping chemicals are burned for their fuel value. This process recovers the energy in the chemicals and some of the chemicals themselves, which can then be reused. Another key pulping development was the continuous digester, invented by the Swedish firm Kamyr AB, which replaced the slower batch digesting process at most pulp mills.

While wood pulp remains almost completely dominant in the global production of papermaking fiber, there has been renewed interest in using agricultural fibers—such as kenaf—to produce paper. China and India already produce large amounts of pulp from agricultural fibers. Substances such as kenaf can be grown in areas of the world where trees are less plentiful, and they are viewed as more environmentally sustainable than wood pulp. Small-scale research on kenaf is underway in the United States, and there are currently several pulp mills using agricultural fibers throughout the world.

From a financial perspective, the 1990s and early 2000s were disastrous for most pulp mill operations, which suffered very low profits or substantial losses due to free-falls in prices. This was largely due to a soft economy, further injured by fewer pages printed by media publications in the wake of the September 11, 2001, terrorist attacks in the United States. This collapse was caused by stagnating demand and a huge oversupply of pulp.

In 1994, pulp mills worldwide went from gloom to gloating when the price for benchmark NBSK rose an astonishing 75 percent and was headed even higher in 1995. However, in 1996 prices began falling again, and in 1997 many pulp producers worldwide were facing the prospects of very low profits or losses on their operations. By 1998, many Canadian pulp mills were again taking downtime to try to work off excess inventory and stabilize the price of market pulp.

One certainty was increased worldwide competition in pulp production. In 1996, Indonesia produced a record 2.64 mmt of pulp, and was by far the fastest-growing pulp-producing nation in the world. By 2000 its output had exceeded 3.6 mmt, and in 2003 the country produced just over 5.2 mmt. Virtually all new virgin pulp expansion projects in the late 1990s and early 2000s were in the Southern Hemisphere.

After an unprecedented expansion of pulping capacity in the late 1980s, the early 1990s saw demand falling, capacity rising, and prices plummeting. Market pulp prices reached a low for the 1990s of US$390 per ton for northern bleached softwood kraft pulp (NBSK), considered a benchmark in the global pulp business, in the fourth quarter of 1993. By October 1994—with demand rising and capacity static—the price for NBSK had shot up to US$700 per ton and briefly touched US$1,000 per ton at the end of 1995. However, high prices and boom times in the global pulp industry are almost always followed by a price crash as new start-up operations, attracted by high profits, flood the world market with pulp.

That scenario played out in 1996 as lower demand, high inventories, and growing capacity produced another steep drop in pulp prices. By November 1996, prices for NBSK had dropped to about US$570 per ton. Prices continued to drift downward to about US$510 per ton at the end of March 1997. In the second quarter of 1997, however, prices began a gradual rise, and demand in most areas of the world began to increase. By November, the price of NBSK had reached about US$610 per ton.

World suppliers of chemical paper-grade market pulp delivered 31.7 mmt to their customers in 1997, breaking the previous record, which was set in 1995. Among major market pulp-consuming regions, the United States experienced the largest rise in percentage terms, up 13 percent in 1997, or almost 600,000 tons. In terms of volume, growth in Western Europe was the strongest in the world compared to 1996, up more than 800,000 tons, or 8 percent. Demand in Japan rose 2 percent, but deliveries to Asia and Africa (mostly Southeast Asia) declined 3 percent as new pulp mills in these regions came on stream, replacing market pulp from other countries. To satisfy the increased demand for market pulp in 1997, producers worldwide withdrew about 400,000 tons from inventory, which stood at about 2.9 mmt at the end of the year, enough to supply worldwide demand for 34 days.

Despite this good news, however, from 1998 through 2002, considerable uncertainty about the price trend for pulp plagued the industry worldwide. Asian buyers, who accounted for a large share of the demand for market pulp, contended with diminished purchasing power because of the currency depreciations, while pulp sellers in North America and Europe, concerned about payments, slowed their shipments to Asia. This trend was expected to reduce prices for market pulp, at least in the short run. In the 2000s, the United States and Canada sparred about the price of Canada's pulp exports to the United States, as government aid to the Canadian industry made the price of imported pulp products lower than what U.S. producers charged.

While there were regional variations, bleached softwood kraft pulp was still the biggest grade of market pulp, accounting for about 45 percent of global market pulp production in the late 1990s. By 2004 most of the increase in pulp production was attributed to bleached softwood. According to the Market Pulp Association, bleached softwood capacity rose by 4.9 percent that year, while bleached hardwood capacity grew by only 1.5 percent. Recycled pulp remained a relatively small part of market pulp output (most recycled pulp was consumed by integrated pulp and paper mills). However, the amount of recycled market pulp produced in North America grew rapidly in the mid-1990s. For example, in the United States the capacity to produce chemical grade market wood pulp grew by about 0.5 percent annually from 1998 through 2000, when capacity reached about 10.52 million short tons. Recovered paper market pulp capacity in the United States, starting from a small base of 574,000 short tons in 1993, reached 1.76 million short tons in 1997.

The pulp industry finds itself in a volatile market. Indeed, stability has been hard to find. In a single day, the terrorist attacks of September 11, 2001, devastated many industries, which in turn had an immediate, deleterious effect on pulp prices. The promising rise in newsprint prices in the fourth quarter of 2000, in which global newsprint prices climbed to US$605 a ton, disappeared. This was a direct result of a drop in print ads and media pages, which resulted in newsprint prices falling to US$505 a ton.

Thus, the early 2000s marked continued harsh economic times for the pulp-mill industry. The world's largest producer, International Paper (IP), recorded 2001 fourth-quarter earnings of just US$58 million, not even half of 2000 fourth-quarter earnings. Annual 2001 sales for International Paper also faltered, with net earnings of US$214 million, well below comparable 2000 net earnings of US$969 million, according to *Printing World*. As a result, stable companies such as American Tissue, Kimberly-Clark, Voith Paper, International Paper, and many others found themselves forced to lay off employees in 2001 and 2002. International Paper dismissed more than 2,500 employees in

2000 alone. Not until 2003 did the situation significantly improve; that year, IP posted sales of US$25.2 billion and net earnings of US$302 million.

While North America, Europe, and Scandinavia have traditionally been the leading regions in pulp production, other regions have grown in importance—notably South America and Asia. In South America, Brazil and Chile have greatly expanded their pulp production. In Brazil, eucalyptus trees grow to pulpable size nearly seven times faster than trees in the Nordic countries, giving Brazilian pulp mills a strong cost advantage in this area. Similar growth rates are recorded for Chile's radiata pine plantations, which are used for pulpwood as well as timber products. Several major pulp mills were built in Asia during the 1990s, making that region one of the strongest pulp growth areas. Strong economic growth rates in many Asian countries fueled demand for pulp and paper products, leading to the expansion. While Japan remained the dominant pulp producer in Asia, Indonesia was one of the region's fastest-growing producers of pulp, although much of it was cut illegally with the blessings of corrupt provincial officials. China has had several projects on the drawing board as well.

However, the Asian financial crisis that began in early 1997 and continued into the early 2000s had a major impact on that region's fast-growing pulp and paper industry. Several pulp and paper companies were facing dire financial problems. As the currencies of major Asian pulp and paper producing countries, such as Indonesia, fell dramatically against the U.S. dollar, the financial impact on Asian companies was severe. Larger mills with modern equipment purchased in U.S. dollars faced major problems recouping their investment. High debt loads by these companies compounded their troubles.

While economic growth was expected to continue in Asia, the rate of growth was expected to slow significantly. There was considerable speculation that the ownership structure of the Asian pulp and paper industry would change markedly as companies from outside the region tried to buy Asian pulp and paper producers at what had quickly become bargain prices.

Indonesia—the focus of major pulping developments—was also embroiled in controversy in the late 1990s and 2000s following the toppling of its corrupt but stable military regime. While major new pulp mills were built at a very rapid pace, allegations were raised by various environmental groups of illegal logging by pulp companies. Some observers feared that Indonesia's substantial forest resources would be devastated through aggressive harvesting by lumber producers and pulp manufacturers. According to a report from Friends of the Earth cited in *E/The Environmental Magazine,* the pulp and paper industry in Indonedsia "is destroying rainforest so quickly that it will run out of wood by 2007." In 1997 the country was also ravaged by extensive fires.

The European pulp industry was hit hard by the global recession in the early 1990s, with almost no new pulp mills being constructed. While that trend continued through much of the decade, many existing mills invested in new equipment and processes that helped to incrementally increase production. By the early 2000s the European pulp industry faced better conditions, with consumption growing at about 2.2 percent in western Europe and 7.7 percent in Russia in 2004. This trend was expected to continue through 2005.

In North America, the development of recycling pulp mills dominated the news in the mid-1990s. Development of virgin pulp mills virtually ceased, while more than 20 recycled pulp mill projects proceeded. However, most of these mills were never built, and many of those that were went bankrupt when pulp prices dropped sharply in late 1996 and early 1997. In general, these mills had difficulty competing on quality with virgin pulp while maintaining cost efficiency. Nevertheless, many pulp and paper companies producing virgin fiber added recycled fiber lines to their existing mills in the 1990s in order to develop combinations of virgin and recycled pulp. While this new recycled pulp was not sold on the open market, it still added to pulping capacity in the North American market. North American virgin pulp producers, as in Europe, also pursued a strategy of making capital investments at existing pulp mills to help improve productivity and boost production.

In South America, the 1980s saw several large pulp mills open, including the Aracruz pulp mill with the production of 1 mmt per year. Though expansion was less pronounced in the early to mid-1990s, the pulp industry was expected to grow more rapidly in the early 2000s. Several new pulp mills are expected to begin operations between 2005 and 2007, boosting the region's production capacity by an additional 3.565 mmt of hardwood and 425,000 tons of softwood.

Brazil, the leading South American pulp producer through the 1990s and early 2000s, was expected to attract continued investment in its pulping industry. However, lower prices in 1997 meant that some pulp mills lost money and plans for new mills were put on hold. Despite these challenges, some Brazilian producers continued to invest in new capacity. In 2005, the new Veracel pulp mill in Eunápolis, Bahia was scheduled to begin operations. The joint venture between Stora Enso and Aracruz Celulose will be the world's largest single-line bleached eucalyptus pulp mill with an annual capacity of about 900,000 metric tons. As of 2003, Brazil accounted for 25 percent of world capacity for bleached hardwood market pulp. Aracruz, the largest producer in Brazil, controlled almost 50 percent of Brazilian capacity.

Chile entered the major leagues of pulping in the late 1980s and early 1990s, though controversy about the use of "ancient" Chilean forests has mounted. Many of Chile's pulp mills are financed by foreign companies, and much of the pulp is exported. The main market for Chilean pulp is Asia, which took about half the total in 1996, with the remainder going to Europe and elsewhere in South America. Overall, Chilean pulp production was up about 5 percent in 1997. That increase came after a 25 percent spurt in 1996, when volume jumped from 1.65 mmt to 2.06 mmt. From 1998 through the early 2000s, several major projects were underway that would increase Chilean pulp tonnage still further. In 2003, production exceeded 2.7 mmt; exports that year were 2.1 mmt.

Bleaching Controversy. From the mid-1980s into the 2000s, the most contentious environmental and regulatory issue in the global pulping industry was the use of chlorine and chlorine compounds in the pulp bleaching process. This controversy stemmed from the discovery of minute amounts of dioxin in pulp mill effluent in the mid-1980s. This by-product of the pulping process was not previously discovered because instrumentation was not sensitive enough to detect the minute amounts, which were in the parts-per-billion range.

While there was considerable scientific debate about whether minute amounts of dioxin affect human health, most pulp mills around the world dramatically reduced dioxin levels by either substituting chlorine dioxide for elemental chlorine in the bleaching process or by using no chlorine compounds at all. For example, in the United States pulp mills reduced dioxin discharges by 90 percent from 1985 to 1993, to less than three ounces for the entire U.S. pulp industry. By 1994, most of the world's market pulp mills were producing or planning to produce elemental chlorine-free (ECF) pulp using chlorine dioxide. In early 1998, the U.S. Environmental Protection Agency issued its long-awaited Cluster Rule, which regulates air and water emissions of U.S. pulp and paper mills. As expected, the rule endorsed the use of ECF bleaching by pulp mills to meet strict water emission guidelines.

In Europe, a sustained campaign against the use of chlorine by environmental groups in the early 1990s led several European pulp mills to adopt totally chlorine-free (TCF) bleaching methods. One producer, Sweden's Sodra, aggressively marketed its TCF paper by attacking paper not made from TCF pulp. German pulp mills also converted to TCF. However, the fact that these pulp mills produced sulfite pulp (instead of the more common sulfate process), made it technologically easier for them to convert to TCF. It is much more costly to convert a sulfate pulp mill to TCF processes. Despite the pressure, there were many mills in Europe that continued to produce ECF pulp. For example, Stora Billerud's Gruvon mill in central Sweden was a leader in the production of ECF pulp, but in 2001 the parent company put operations in other than its main enterprise.

In the United States, public pressure failed to materialize around the ECF/TCF issue. Most U.S. pulp mills used the sulfate process and most of those were committed to producing ECF pulp. Indeed, by the late 1990s the battle over ECF/TCF bleaching appeared to be over. In the United States, virtually all chemical pulp mills were expected to use ECF bleaching sequences, and production of ECF pulp was expanding rapidly worldwide. While TCF pulp was still produced by several European mills, due to customer demand for the product TCF's percentage of pulp production around the world was very small. In 2001, TCF pulp production increased by 17 percent, while TCF pulp production shrank somewhat, accounting for only about 5 percent of world bleached pulp. Analysts expected this trend to continue, with new mills in Europe, South America, and Asia planning to incorporate ECF bleaching technology. *Reach for Unbleached* estimated that "with global annual growth forecast at 2.5 percent, the industry and its negative impacts could double by 2025."

After the ups and downs of the late 1990s, the pulp market began to see steadier growth. According to the Market Pulp Association, global demand for pulp rose faster than expected from 2001 to 2004, growing by 5.3 percent in 2004. Global production capacity grew by 2.8 percent that year.

Current Conditions

In 2007, prices in the pulp industry were expected to remain high due to increased exports to China and the declining value of the U.S. dollar. According to *Georgia Trend,* "the South is a high-cost producer of market pulp, as are Western Canada and Western Europe. These regions bear the brunt of any decline in global demand for market pulp and paper and are among the last to benefit from rising prices."

The latter mid-2000s saw developments in biotechnology and engineering that would allow the "black liquor" by-product and residue of pulp mills to be "gasified" and converted to liquid fuels and chemicals. In essence, pulp mills would become biorefineries. The American Forest & Paper Association (AF&PA) predicted that 10 percent of the U.S. diesel fuel demand could be met through black-liquor/forest residue gasification. In addition, gasification is much more environmentally friendly than the traditional Tomlinson boiler used by most pulp mills, reducing emissions by 90 percent. Although more research and development was needed in the field to allow practical application of the idea on a widescale basis, some mills were already putting gasification into practice, including Chemrec in Sweden.

Research and Technology

With increasing regulatory attention focused on pulp mill emissions, research devoted to the "effluent-free" mill—also called the "closed mill"—increased sharply in the mid-to-late 1990s. In theory, the closed mill perfectly balances all of the inputs to and outputs from the pulping and papermaking process, so that the mill reuses, recycles, or cleans all waste materials. Widely regarded as impossible just a decade ago, this prospect appears to be feasible, provided that current technology continues to develop and the cost of implementation decreases. Some pulp mills in Canada that use a combination of chemical and mechanical pulping have already "closed" the mill by producing zero effluent. Research continues on how to apply zero-effluent technology to traditional kraft pulping, a more difficult proposition. However, some have questioned the need for the effluent-free pulp mill, arguing that a mill producing effluent without negative effects on the environment would achieve the same end without undue cost. Advocates of the total effect-free (TEF) mill say this type of mill is much more practical and would be achievable more quickly than the effluent-free mill.

In 2005, Integrated Paper Services, Inc. announced a new automatic fiber analysis system, MorFi, which measures the size and shape of hardwood or softwood fibers in dilute pulp suspensions. A new stabilizer introduced in 2005, Clariant's Cartan RCF, reduces costs and improves whiteness during the pulp bleaching process.

The Center for Paper Business and Industry Studies claimed "significant and unpredictable pulp and paper price movements have led to a number of serious consequences for the pulp and paper industry, including excess capacity, unintended inventory build-up, and financial losses." According to the center, the "economic vitality of the industry" will be threatened by the unanticipated price movements. In addition, it claimed there was a need for literature offering "a clear explanation of market trends using a theoretical framework."

INDUSTRY LEADERS

Since pulp and paper production is largely integrated, the leaders in production of "captive pulp" are usually the same companies that lead in paper production. However, market pulp—even though it represents a minority of global pulp production—is a major international commodity. Some of world's largest pulp and paper companies are also leaders in the production of market pulp. For example, the top four market pulp producers are all among the top global pulp and paper companies. However, some smaller companies specialize in market pulp and rank prominently on the list of top market pulp producers. These include Aracruz Celulose (the number one producer of bleached eucalyptus), Sodra, Celulosa Arauco (major owner of forest plantations), and Rayonier (the premiere supplier of high performance specialty celluose fibers).

MAJOR COUNTRIES IN THE INDUSTRY

UNITED STATES

The United States has a very large growing stock of pulpwood in several areas: the Pacific Northwest, the Upper Midwest, the Northeast, and Southeast. Combined with an efficient manufacturing base, this makes the United States the lowest-cost producer of many grades of pulp.

The United States is the leader in world pulp production, with 53.1 mmt in 2003. It also exports substantial amounts of wood pulp (5.1 mmt in 2003). Despite producing and exporting large volumes of market pulp, the U.S. pulp and paper industry still imports a large amount of the commodity, largely because of its open trade with Canada. In 2003, pulp for paper imports totaled 6.0 mmt.

Consumption slowed in the early 2000s. From 1997 to 2002, the United States lost 72 paper mills and, in the combined paper, lumber, and pulp sectors, some 55,000 jobs over the same time period, according to American Forest and Paper Association figures.

CANADA

From 1994 to 2002, some analysts questioned productivity in Canada's pulp mills, but environmental watchdogs argued that a certain amount of lessened productivity was to be expected as the nation reduced the effects of pulp industry pollution. The push to clean up industry pollution has been a major goal of The Sustainable Forest Management Network, a non-profit research center under Canada's federal Networks of Centres of Excellence Program. Strict forest management controls have been in place since the 1990s. The China Canada Cooperation Project in Cleaner Production was viewed as producing quite favorable results.

Canada produced 26.1 mmt of wood pulp in 2003, compared to about 25.7 mmt the previous year. Wood pulp exports in 2003 were 11.5 mmt. According to the Market Pulp Association, Canada was the largest market pulp supplier in 2004, contributing 18 percent of global capacity. In 2003 and 2004, Canada balanced declining shipments to Western Europe and Japan with increased sales to Asia, Africa, and North America.

Some people in the industry expressed concerns in the mid-2000s as companies shut down mills and moved their manufacturing to South America, where, according to an article in *Northern Ontario Business,* "wages are lower, the trees grow quicker and regulations are more lax."

CHINA

China has more pulp mills than any other nation. However, many are very small, and many use agricultural fiber, such as straw and bamboo, instead of wood fiber. In 2003, the country produced 14.3 mmt of pulp from non-wood fibers, but only 4.0 mmt of wood pulp. Pulp production of all kinds was expected to continue increasing and, at the same time, China has emerged as the most voracious user of pulp. Without high demand in China, for example, the global purchases of marketable pulp would have dropped 5 percent from 2000 to 2001, according to *Lloyd's.* Demand in China is expected to remain high; in addition, the country planned major expansions in domestic capacity, including APP China's bleached hardwood kraft pulp mill on Hainan Island, which is expected to produce 1.0 mmt annually. While analysts predicted that this increase could slow hardwood pulp imports, they noted that softwood pulp imports would continue to rise.

U.S. corporations increasingly looked to China for newsprint supplies during the early 2000s. For example, in 2002 Visonper International Company (USA) Ltd. announced its intent to invest US$125 million in an attempt to reap 500,000 tons of paper pulp in China for export.

JAPAN

Wood pulp production in Japan declined from 11.2 mmt in 1996 to only 10.4 mmt in 2003. From December 2001 to February 2002, the drop in the value of the yen led to higher prices for traditional Japanese imports such as beef and pulp. In turn, this led to fears at U.S. pulp suppliers that the devaluation of the yen could have pass-along adverse consequences for U.S. pulp companies, Weyerhaeuser spokesman Frank Mendizabel told the *New York Times.* Indeed, Japan's total wood pulp imports dropped from 3.0 mmt in 2000 to 2.6 mmt in 2001. This decline slowed therafter, with imports reaching 2.5 mmt in 2002 and 2.4 mmt in 2003.

SWEDEN

Sweden's 46 pulp mills produced 11.7 mmt of wood pulp in 2003, showing a slight improvement over the 11.3 mmt of wood pulp produced the previous year. After a ten-year decline in pulp produced, Sweden's pulp inventory rose in 2001.

Finland. With 45 pulp mills, Finland was the third largest world producer of pulp in 2003, with 11.9 mmt of wood pulp.

This represented a significant jump over the 9.68 mmt of pulp produced in 1996. In 2002, Russian and Finnish interests met to solidify future Finnish exports of Russian raw timber for pulp usage. The international decline in pulp prices in the 2000s hit Finland particularly hard. One of the larger companies, Stora Enso, had net profits of US$798 million in 2001, down 35.4 percent from 2000 profits, and the company elected to dissolve its pulp division. In the face of such challenges, Finland has invested significant resources in education related to the pulp and paper industry. Of 300 engineers who earned masters degrees in pulp and paper studies in Europe in 2002, about 200 of them were in Finland.

BRAZIL

Toward the end of the twentieth century, a major trend in the pulp mill industry has been its restructuring through mergers and consolidations as smaller companies band together to make a collective input, according to *Bloomberg News*. For example, Votorantim Celulose e Papel SA bought a 12 percent stake in Aracruz Celulose SA, one of South America's most prominent producers, for US$370 million. In addition, takeovers worth more than US$1.0 billion occurred in Brazil during the early 2000s.

With 8.8 mmt of pulp production in 2003, Brazil is easily South America's largest pulp producer. Output increased substantially in the early 2000s, as miscellaneous pulp interests invested about US$6.6 billion by 2005 to modernize the industry and upgrade production and export facilities, according to the Brazilian Pulp and Paper Association (Bracelp). Wood pulp production rose from 5.9 mmt in 1995 to 7.4 mmt in 2002.

CHILE

World Rainforest Movement shared findings from TERRAM Foundation researcher and economist Consuelo Espinosa who evaluated the impact of pulp production. She said the number of jobs generated by the industry was declining steadily. Although Chile was viewed as an ideal industry model, in fact it generated wealth for some major economic groups but added to the poverty and destitution for local populations. Even so, plans proceeded in 2005 for expansion in pulp production. The Itata sawmill and woodpulp mill, near the city of Concepcion, was expected to produce 850,000 tons of pulp annually (50 percent pine and 50 percent eucalyptus). This capacity would bring the annual output of its owner, the Arauco company, to about 3.1 metric tons of bleached and unbleached kraft pulp.

RUSSIA

While the pulp industry stagnated or retreated elsewhere during the early 2000s, Russia's pulp tonnage increased, rising 7.4 percent from 2000 to 2001, according to *Food & Agriculture Report* and Russian State Statistics Committee reports. In 2000, according to FAO data, Russia produced 5.8 mmt of wood pulp. This figure rose to 6.1 mmt in 2001 and 6.5 mmt in 2002. Wood pulp production in 2003 was 6.6 mmt. In a special article for *The Russia Journal,* Natalya Pinyagina pointed out that the industry had "a lot of potential and should become a locomotive to pull the whole forestry sector to a level that a great forest power deserves to have." She also said "the weak point" was not having enough processing facilities for low-grade timber throughout most of the country.

FURTHER READING

Boswell, Clay. "Chipping into Success." *ICIS Chemical Business Americas,* 5 March 2007.

"Chile: Tree Plantations and Pulp Production Generate Poverty and Destitution." *World Rainforest Movement Bulletin,* 14 June 2004. Available from www.wrm.org.

"Forest Industry Biorefinery Could Provide Big Benefits, Compete on Cost with Coal-To-Liquids Diesel." *Diesel Fuel News,* 15 January 2007.

Forestry Data: Pulp, Paper, and Paperboard. United Nations, Food and Agricultural Organization. 21 January 2005. Available from http://faostat.fao.org.

Humphreys, Jeffrey M. "2007 Industry Outlook." *Georgia Trend,* April 2007.

Louiseize, Kelly. "Americans Leaving Canada: It's a Bad Thing." *Northern Ontario Business,* July 2006.

"Market Pulp Prices Hit 10-Year High Fueled by Mill Closures, Asian Demand." *Pulp & Paper,* August 2006.

Motavalli, Jim. "The Paper Chase." *E/The Environmental Magazine,* May/June, 2004. Available from www.emagazine.com.

"Overview of the Wood Pulp Industry." Market Pulp Association, 2005. Available from www.pppc.org.

"Pulp and Paper Manufacturing." European Commission, May 2006. Available from http://ec.europa.eu/.

Statement on Forest Products Markets in 2004 and Prospects for 2005. United Nations, UNECE Timber Committee and FAO European Forestry Commission. 8 October 2004. Available from www.unece.org.

Whetton, Cris. "Global Perspectives: Pulp and Paper in Europe." *InTech,* 20 August 2003. Available from www.isa.org.

PETROLEUM PRODUCTS

SIC 2992
NAICS 324191

LUBRICATING OILS AND GREASES

The world's lubricant industry refines, blends, and compounds oils and greases from purchased mineral, animal, and vegetable materials. See also **Petroleum Refining.**

INDUSTRY SNAPSHOT

Within the enormous worldwide oil industry, lubricants constitute a downstream specialty business that generates significant revenues and profits for producers. Most of the major oil companies are key players in the lubricants industry, but independent producers still hold a significant share of lubricant volume in many countries. The highest volume of lubricant consumers includes those in rubber manufacturing, transportation and equipment, passenger cars, chemical manufacturing, and railroads and aviation. Other industrial users of lubricants are those involved in primary metals such as aluminum, steel plants, and mining; the printing industry; fabricated metals; food processors; and pulp and paper manufacturing.

The vast majority of all lubricants are made from petroleum base stocks, but newer synthetic lubricants, which offer unusually long service life and enhance functionality, are becoming a larger presence on the global market. By the mid-2000s, specialty companies such as Pennzoil Quaker State and Burmah Castrol were no longer separate entities but had been acquired by so-called "Big Oil" companies.

Two of the associations serving the lubricants industry were the Independent Lubricant Manufacturers Association (ILMA) and the National Lubricating Grease Institute (NLGI). In 2004, there were 300 member companies of the ILMA, which together accounted for one-fourth of the worldwide lubricant production and the vast majority of specialty industrial lubricants. The organization was reviewing its strategic plan in 2004. The NLGI had member companies in 26 countries.

PRODUCT VARIETY

Lubricant manufacturers produce a wide variety of lubricant products, including consumer automotive products such as motor oil, brake fluid, and transmission oil. Other major product areas include commercial automotive, industrial metalworking fluids, general industrial and specialties, and marine lubricants. Within these categories there are hundreds of individual products, including cutting oils, lubricating greases and oils, hydraulic fluids, and rust-arresting compounds.

The primary ingredients in lubricants are base stock (a refined petroleum product) and additives, which impart special qualities to lubricants. Enhancements to base stocks and additives drive improvements in lubricant performance. Most technological improvements focus on creating lubricants that conserve energy and do a better job of controlling deposits. The largest category of base stocks is paraffinics, followed by napthenics and synthetics. Of these three, only synthetic base stocks are expected to grow rapidly—although they account for less than 10 percent of the global base stock market.

ORGANIZATION AND STRUCTURE

Automotive products were one of the major lubricants markets, accounting for well over 50 percent of the total lubricants market in many countries. Within this category, there were three main types of lubricants: crankcase oils (motor oil); transmission and axle lubricants; and fluids for the hydraulic torque converters and fluid couplings in automatic transmissions. Each category was further subdivided by viscosity, the degree of resistance to molecular flow. Automotive lubricants worked by cushioning adjacent metal pieces, oiling moving parts, and keeping dirt out of combustion chambers.

The motor oil market included two major subcategories—the DIY (do-it-yourself) market, for consumers who changed their own oil, and the DIFM (do-it-for-me) market, which included auto dealers, service stations, and the fast-growing quick oil change shops. One of the motor oil growth markets was in synthetics, which were more expensive and lasted much longer than conventional motor oils. Two major brands in this area were Castrol Syntec and Mobil 1. Globally, the trend by the mid-1990s was toward higher-margin synthetic and semi-synthetic oils, which were recommended by luxury car manufacturers such as Bayerische Motoren Werke AG (BMW) and Mercedes.

CHANGING MARKET

In the 1960s, the motor oil market in most countries was dominated by service stations that were operated by major gasoline marketers such as Shell and Mobil. However, the international oil crisis in the 1970s spurred the development of self-service gasoline outlets in many western countries, and more consumers began changing their own oil. This opened the door for new outlets to sell motor oil.

By the 1990s, motor oil sales had spread to many retail outlets throughout the world, including automotive chains, parts stores, supermarkets and hypermarkets, and general merchandise chains. This helped companies such as Pennzoil, Castrol, and Quaker State market their products directly to the consumer and take market share away from the major oil companies. For example, in the United States, Pennzoil held the largest share of the DIY motor oil market in 1992 at 18.9 percent, followed by Castrol at 14.5 percent; Quaker State at 11.9 percent; and Texaco and Valvoline, both at 14 percent. In the mid-1990s, these companies were leaders in the global market, with Shell, Texaco, Castrol, Pennzoil, and Quaker State being the top five.

In the mid-1990s, motor oil producers were using increasingly sophisticated marketing efforts to bring their products to the attention of customers worldwide. For example, in 1994 Quaker State launched an extensive and expensive marketing program to promote its new synthetic oil, Quaker State 4X4, which was targeted at the growing sport utility vehicle market. Quaker State intended to regain some of the market share it lost in the 1980s and early 1990s in the United States and overseas markets.

While consumers who changed their own oil were a major market for lubricant manufacturers, they also created an environmental hazard. Many disposed of used oil by pouring it down household and storm drains. It was estimated that in the United States alone, the amount of improperly disposed motor oil each year was 10 times greater than the entire amount of oil spilled in the *Exxon Valdez* accident. Some lubricants manufacturers responded to this problem by collecting used oil and other lubricants and re-refining them for use as second-quality lubricants. For example, Quaker State operated a Specialty Environmental Services Unit, which collected and recycled used oil, antifreeze, filters and brake fluid, and other substances.

However, even this activity was controversial. In the United States, the Environmental Protection Agency (EPA) received protests from environmental groups and some oil industry groups in the early 1990s on its decision to classify used motor oil as a non-hazardous substance. The groups contended that since used oil could contain hazardous substances, it should be legally regarded as hazardous. Critics cited the fact that most used motor oil was burned as fuel, releasing toxic substances into the air, although they did acknowledge that burning was still better than consumers pouring used oil into sewer systems. Two manufacturers that marketed re-refined lubricating oils from recycled oil were Safety-Kleen and Evergreen Company, with annual capacities of 45 million and 10 million gallons respectively.

OTHER MARKETS

The industrial lubricants category was large and included a vast array of products, such as machine oils, cutting oils, natural and synthetic metalworking fluids, die-casting lubricants, industrial chemical cleaners, dry cleaning fluids, and deodorants. The purpose of these products was similar to that of automotive lubricants, but most had additional attributes, such as being able to prevent rust from high-temperature steams.

The marine market was small compared to the automotive category but included a wide range of products, from lubricants for supertankers to biodegradable two-stroke outboard motor oils. The United Kingdom-based Castrol, one of the leaders in this area, was particularly strong in Europe where it held the top position with a 17 percent market share.

Many lubricants from major companies were marketed through independent distributors. In Europe, distributors usually handled one brand exclusively, while U.S. distributors carried multiple brands of lubricants. Still, reduced margins and stiffer competition were spurring some European distributors to move into multi-line marketing. Large distributors, with their increased financial resources, generally covered broader geographic areas and handled more brands. They placed emphasis on bulk deliveries to commercial, industrial, and agricultural customers. More distributors were concentrating on selling bulk goods, leaving the "case goods" sales to large retail outlets. Some manufacturers purchased distributors in an attempt to vertically integrate their operations. For example, in 1994 Valvoline Inc. purchased six of its European distributors from the Fuchs Group, thereby greatly expanding its European distribution capabilities.

THE ADDITIVE MARKET

Additives were a very important component in the manufacturing of lubricants since they provided lubricants with the special qualities expected by end users. For example, motor oil typically consisted of 80 percent base stock and 20 percent additives. Popular additives included detergents, dispersants, extreme pressure/anti-wear agents, viscosity index improvers, antioxidants, and corrosion inhibitors. About 80 percent of all additives were used in automotive lubricants, with other key additive-using categories being industrial engine lubricants, general industrial lubricants, and metalworking lubricants. Major additive suppliers included Ethyl Corp., Lubrizol Ltd., Paramins (a unit of Exxon Chemical), Oronite Additives (a unit of Chevron Chemical), and Royal Dutch/Shell's petroleum additives business. In 1996 these five entities controlled more than 80 percent of the US$6 billion worldwide lubricant additives market.

BACKGROUND AND DEVELOPMENT

At their most basic level, lubricants are substances inserted between two moving surfaces to reduce friction, which in turn reduces wear and extends the life of the surfaces. Lubricants also reduce the energy required to keep the surfaces in motion. If some contact occurs between the surfaces even after lubrication, the process is called boundary or thin-film lubrication. If the lubricant is thick enough to completely separate the two surfaces, the process is called fluid-film lubrication. In the latter case, the lubricant is kept under pressure to keep the surfaces separated. In another form of lubrication, hydrostatic lubrication, the pressure in the lubricant film is created by a pump. Other types of lubrication include hydrodynamic lubrication and solid lubricants. Lubricants can also dissipate generated heat, control corrosion, and remove sludge deposits in automobile engines. In some machine-tool operations, cooling is the main purpose of lubrication.

Lubricants made from animals and vegetables have been used for thousands of years, but beginning in the nineteenth century, mineral products began to replace them, particularly liquid and semi-liquid lubricants made from petroleum. There have been many ways of applying lubrication, including by hand, drop-feed, wick-feed, bath or splash, oil-mist, and force-feed (oil pump).

Following the development of oil drilling in the nineteenth century, petroleum products—including lubricants—became widely available. In the United States, production was dominated by the Standard Oil trust until its breakup in 1911. In the twentieth century, oil production and refining came to be dominated by the "Seven Sisters,": five major U.S. oil companies that emerged from the Standard Oil trust, Royal Dutch/Shell (which had developed out of an Indonesian oil field discovery in 1885) and the Anglo-Persian Oil Company, formed after a 1908 oil find in Iran—formerly known as Persia. (Anglo-Persian later became known as British Petroleum.) The domination of the oil business by these giant companies was still evident in the 1990s, although many developing nations with large oil deposits had nationalized their oil industries by the latter half of the twentieth century. While these nationalized oil companies tended to dominate their local markets, in the 1990s many of these markets were opened at least partially to outside competition.

The largest lubricants market, automobile engines, was changing in the 1990s as smaller, more powerful, and more efficient engines were developed. The size and speed of these engines generate very high temperatures, in some cases far higher than those at which conventional lubricating oils could still be effective. This quality encouraged development of more synthetic oils that burn very slowly at high temperatures while not leaving the residues of carbon or metallic ash that are deposited by ordinary oils.

Prices of lubricants depend on several factors, including the base oil stock, additives, and other processing costs. Within the industry the price of the benchmark West Texas Intermediate crude (regarded as an industry indicator of world oil prices) was rather volatile in the late 1990s and early 2000s. The average was US$14.40 in 1998, US$19.25 in 1999, US$30.30 in 2000, and US$25.92 in 2001. These shifts are what make it difficult to create stability in the lubricating oils and grease industry because of its reliance on the price of oil on the global market. Fortunately, the major corporations have substantial reserves of oil that help them through fluctuations in price. This helps account for the fact that in the 1990s, mature lubricants markets such as the United States and the European Union (EU) remained relatively flat.

In the 1990s, some East Asian countries—such as China, India, and Indonesia—were emerging economies, and in many of these countries state-run oil companies controlled the lubricants markets. However, some East Asian countries such as India were opening up their markets. As a result of growing East Asian growth prospects, development activity was brisk in the mid-1990s. Following the outbreak of the Asian financial crisis in the late 1990s, however, economic development slowed in general, and this included the lubricating oil and grease industry.

Meanwhile, major companies in the industry were increasingly turning to mergers and alliances in the 1990s to achieve cost savings and increase efficiencies. In early 1998, Pennzoil Company announced that it planned to spin off its downstream operations—including its lubricants and additives businesses—and merge them with Quaker State Corp. This deal brought together two of the biggest brand names in motor oil, which held a combined 35 percent of the U.S. market. A few years later, the company would be acquired by Royal Dutch/Shell.

One concern of lubricant users is environmental regulation, which in many countries requires users to carefully monitor their use and disposal of lubricants. In the 1990s, many users were shifting the burden of compliance back to their suppliers and asking them to provide additional services, such as in-house protection and waste disposal programs. At the same time, lubricant manufacturers were being asked to develop formulations that could be used in new electronically controlled lubricant systems. These systems actually reduced lubricant usage since they applied lubricants in a more precise manner than traditional hydraulic control systems.

CURRENT CONDITIONS

In the mid-2000s, there was a small but growing global trend toward the use of biodegradable lubricants. Biolubricants began being used in the mid-1990s. That segment was expected to remain small until more regulations were developed that mandated the use of biolubricants. One application of biolubricants is in the forest products industry. To harvest trees, heavy equipment that consumes large quantities of lubricants, such as hydraulic fluid and gear oil, is used. Traditional lubricants spewing from hose breaks or other spills could contaminate the forest and remain in the ground indefinitely, while biolubricants could break down in a short period.

Biolubricants are frequently based on vegetable oils, such as canola (rapeseed), soybean, and sunflower seed. For example, in the mid-1990s, Calgene Chemical was producing a rapeseed oil-based line of lubricants for Mobil Corp. that was nontoxic and biodegradable. Also in the mid-1990s, Henkel Corp. developed an engine oil for use in two-cycle engines, often used in lawn maintenance equipment, that was 80 percent biodegradable. In fact, the increased U.S. use of biolubricants was being legislated in the 2000s. The USDA labels a product as "biobased" if 51 percent or more of the makeup is biomaterial. Executive Order 13134 and the 2002 Farm Bill both provided for increased purchase and use of bio-based materials by the government itself.

The oil and grease industry, like most industries in the modern economy, has come under pressure from environmental groups. According to the National Petrochemical and Refiners Association, between 30 and 40 percent of petroleum-based lubricants sold in the United States were accidentally released into the environment in 2004.

According to a study done by the Freedonia Group, by 2006, total demand for lubricant additives was expected to rise about US$190 million over 2002 levels and increase two percent annually through 2008 due to an increase in motor vehicle use and increased manufacturing levels. Growth, however, would be offset by fluid management programs as well as the development of longer-lasting lubrication products. Deposit control additives were the most in demand, with projected 2006 values at US$556 million, followed by viscosity and index improvers with a value of US$357 million. Other additive segments for which demand was expected to increase were antiwear and EP additives, antioxidants, corrosion inhibitors, defoamers, and pour point depressants.

INDUSTRY LEADERS

The leaders in the global lubricants industry varied by category, but tended to include the same seven or eight very large global companies.

BP

This London-based firm remains one of the United Kingdom's largest companies and the world's largest international oil company. Formed by the merging of Amoco and British Petroleum, BP reported 2004 revenues exceeding US$285 billion. BP employs approximately 102,900 people in 100 countries. With 27,800 service stations worldwide, of which more than half were located in the United States, the company had 18.4 billion barrels of proved reserves.

BP also acquired Atlantic Richfield Company (ARCO), as well as a stake in the Russian company TNK-BP. In 2000, BP acquired Burmah Castrol, one of the oldest oil companies in the United Kingdom. The company acquired the Castrol brand in 1966, and Castrol remained the heart of its lubricants business. Castrol has global sales coverage through operating companies in more than 50 countries. The promotion of the Castrol name had established the brand throughout the world as the leading independent oil, as opposed to major oil companies' own brands. Highly successful sponsorship in auto racing helped maintain Castrol's premium image in the marketplace during the 1990s when Castrol was producing more than 2,000 products, including automotive lubricants, synthetic lubricants, metal working oils, hydraulic fluids, technical white oils, antifreeze, silicon brake fluids, marine lubricants, industrial and aviation gas turbine lubricants, and corrosion preventatives.

EXXONMOBIL CORP.

In 2004, the second largest company, ExxonMobil, operated 42,000 service stations in 118 countries. About 16,000 of those stations were located in the United States. That year, ExxonMobil reported more than US$263.9 billion in revenues, up 23.8 percent from the previous year, and 21.2 billion barrels of proved reserves.

Exxon was a highly diversified petroleum company that had a major lubricants business, among many other businesses. The company was once called Standard Oil of New Jersey and marketed its products under the Esso brand. In 1972 the company changed its name to Exxon. Standard Oil of New Jersey was one of the major companies that emerged from the breakup of the famous Standard Oil Trust in 1911.

Fairfax, Virginia-based Mobil Corp. was a major producer of specialty and synthetic lubricants, marketing its products under such names as Mobil 1 and Mobilgrease. In the mid-1990s, Mobil's new lubricant blending and packaging plants in Paulsboro, New Jersey, and Hong Kong were said to be low-cost producers of high-value lubricants. Mobil also was the largest importer of lubricants to China, and in Europe, Mobil was the second-largest lubricants marketer. Mobil and state-owned Indian Oil Corp. formed a joint venture in 1994 to build a US$15 million lubricants plant in Haryana, India, to produce Mobil-brand lubricants for the Indian market.

In 1994 Mobil also created a new subsidiary, Mobil Lubricants Canada, to market and distribute automotive and industrial lubricants, including Mobil 1 motor oil. Mobil took Canadian distribution away from its previous distributor, Imperial. In early 1996, Mobil and British Petroleum entered into a joint venture that merged the two companies' European refining and marketing operations, including their lubricants businesses.

ROYAL DUTCH/SHELL GROUP

The world's third largest petroleum and natural gas company, Royal Dutch/Shell was a Dutch/English partnership of two parent companies, Royal Dutch Petroleum and Shell Transport and Trading. The companies shared a 60/40 interest in three holding companies: the Shell Petroleum Company (United Kingdom), Shell Petroleum NV (the Netherlands), and Shell Oil Co. (United States). These companies were active in more then 100 countries. Depending on the business involved, group leadership alternated between the two parent companies, which maintained headquarters in The Hague and London. Royal Dutch/Shell and Exxon joined forces in a worldwide petroleum additives joint venture in 1996. The company runs 46,000 gas stations worldwide and has oil reserves in excess of 14.4 million barrels. Revenues totaled US$201.73 billion in 2003.

Royal Dutch/Shell acquired Pennzoil Quaker State in 2002. The following year, Pennzoil Quaker State was renamed SOPUS Products. Formed by the merger between Pennzoil and Quaker State, this company owned the top two motor oils and the top oil-changing service, Jiffy Lube. Pennzoil marketed its motor oil (in addition to Performax motor oils and lubricants, Wolf's Head lubricants, and other Pennzoil-brand lubricants) in more than 60 countries. The company's product line includes other brands of motor oils, Snap fuel additives and chemicals, Snap Fix-A-Flat tire inflator, Outlaw fuel additives, and Gumout cleaners.

Pennzoil products were first marketed by South Penn Oil of Oil City, Pennsylvania. South Penn was acquired by

Zapata Petroleum in 1963, and the combined company was renamed Pennzoil. In 1985 Pennzoil won a US$10 billion judgment against Texaco as a result of its unsuccessful attempt to purchase Getty Oil. Pennzoil eventually settled with Texaco for US$3 billion in 1988. In late 1997 Pennzoil fended off a US$4.2 billion hostile takeover offer from Union Pacific Resources Group Inc. Six months later, Pennzoil announced a plan to spin off its downstream operations, including its lubricants and additives businesses, and merge them with Quaker State Corp., bringing together two of the biggest brand names in motor oil.

FURTHER READING

"About Us." *Independent Lubricant Manufacturers Association Web Site,* 2005. Available from http://www.ilma.org.

"About Us." *National Lubricating Grease Institute Web Site,* 2005. Available from http://www.nlgi.com.

Fields, Scott. "One Slick Trick." *Environmental Health Perspectives,* September 2003.

"Hoover's Company Capsules." 2005. Available from http://www.hoovers.com.

"International Trade Statistics." 2005. Available from http://www.wto.org.

Lazich, Robert S., ed. *Market Share Reporter.* Detroit: Thomson Gale, 2004.

U.S. Census Bureau. "Petroleum Lubricating Oil and Grease Manufacturing." U.S. Department of Commerce, Bureau of the Census, 2005. Available from http://www.census.gov.

SIC 1311

NAICS 211111

PETROLEUM AND NATURAL GAS, CRUDE

Industry companies operate oil and gas field properties for the extraction of crude petroleum and natural gas. Key activities include exploration; drilling, completing, and equipping wells; operation of separators, emulsion breakers, desilting equipment, and field gathering lines for crude petroleum; and related preparation activities up to the point of shipment.

For discussion of petroleum production at the next stage of processing, see **Petroleum Refineries** and for more information on petroleum as an energy source, see **Energy.**

INDUSTRY SNAPSHOT

Crude oil and natural gas combined are the world's leading raw materials for energy. They are used in production of motor vehicle fuel and in industrial power, heat, and electricity generation. According to the International Energy Agency, in 1995 oil accounted for 46.9 percent of the world's energy consumption, while natural gas accounted for 17.8 percent. By 2000, this balance had been reversed: natural gas had increased to 22 percent of world energy consumption, while oil had fallen to 39.8 percent. The Energy Information Administration (EIA) predicted that world energy use would grow by 54 percent from 2001 to 2025, with oil remaining the primary source at about 39 percent. Natural gas, however, was expected to remain the fastest-growing primary energy commodity. Concerns about the stability of future oil supplies—as well as a growing interest in hydrogen power—contributed to this trend away from reliance on oil, as did the popularity of natural gas as a more environmentally friendly source of energy than crude oil. Other benefits of natural gas include traditionally stable pricing and a higher number of known gas reserves that have not yet been tapped.

Often viewed as part of the total petroleum industry, the natural resources of oil and gas are chemically similar (they are both hydrocarbons), are often found in the same underground reservoirs, and are often produced by the same companies. Commercial production of oil and natural gas, however, usually comes from distinct oil or gas fields.

Crude oil is a liquid hydrocarbon mixture that may be characterized as "heavy" or "light" depending on its gravity and as "sour" or "sweet" depending on the presence of sulfur impurities. Crude oil is refined to produce fuel (the activity of the **Petroleum Refining** industry) and lubricants (see **Lubricating Oils and Greases**). In its natural state, natural gas is a gaseous mixture consisting of about 80 percent methane, 7 percent ethane, 6 percent propane, 3 percent pentane, 2.5 percent butane, and 1.5 percent isobutane. Natural gas is processed to produce commercial natural gas, which contains only methane and ethane. Natural gas sometimes condenses when it reaches the earth's surface and is then referred to as condensate. Additionally, natural gas may be liquefied to facilitate transportation. Crude oil, condensate, and natural gas liquids are collectively referred to as petroleum liquids.

Oil and gas are commodities whose world market prices are determined by fluctuations in supply and demand. Some producing countries, however, subsidize prices for domestic consumption. Levels of production are usually determined by market price, although quotas, especially for petroleum production, are used in some cases to prevent prices from falling and to prevent oil fields from becoming too rapidly depleted. The most significant international production quota system is the one voluntarily adopted by member countries of the Organization of Petroleum Exporting Countries (OPEC).

The United States was by far the leading market for oil and gas. Through the early 2000s it consumed more than 25 percent of the petroleum and gas produced each year. Though Japan was the world's second-largest oil consumer until 2003, China surpassed Japan that year with petroleum consumption totaling 5.56 million b/d. According to the EIA, China's continued economic growth will stimulate demand for oil reaching 12.8 million b/d by 2025, accounting for about 40 percent of world growth in demand. With consumption far surpassing demand, China's oil imports are projected to reach 9.4 million b/d by 2025.

ORGANIZATION AND STRUCTURE

The scope of the crude oil and gas industry is difficult to measure, because it is an integral part of the broader "petroleum industry." Many leading oil and gas extraction companies are themselves "vertically integrated" petroleum companies. That is, in addition to exploring for and producing crude petroleum and natural gas from wells, they are also involved in the refining of petroleum and processing of gas, the transportation of oil and gas through pipelines and tankers, and even the retail distribution or marketing of refined oil products—such as gasoline and diesel fuel—at their own gas stations. The terms commonly used to distinguish between the exploration and production side and the refining and marketing side of the petroleum industry are "upstream" and "downstream." Thus, the oil and gas extraction industry is also known as the upstream portion of the entire petroleum industry. While some companies specialize in either upstream or downstream activities, the largest companies in oil and gas extraction are integrated petroleum companies.

In the early 2000s, the largest oil and gas companies in the world were state-owned companies in major petroleum-producing countries of the Middle East, Asia, Africa, and Latin America. These firms tended to be integrated petroleum companies with monopolies on domestic production. In some countries, though, domestic companies invited foreign companies with additional capital and expertise to participate in joint exploration and development of reserves in exchange for a share in the equity of production. State-owned companies of oil- or gas-producing countries, however, often preferred that foreign companies act merely as service contractors in order to retain greater control over their own natural resources.

The best-known companies in the industry were the Western multinationals. These integrated petroleum companies boasted numerous subsidiaries throughout the world, both in production and in refined product distribution. These traditionally dominant companies were referred to as the "majors," both globally and within the U.S. industry, which was home to the largest number of international majors. "Independents" are other, smaller companies that tend to operate at the domestic level and may specialize in areas of exploration and production.

Oil and gas production companies either own or lease the land from which they extract the natural resources. Thus, they own not only the oil or gas that they produce but also the underground reserves. Industry participants sell oil to refiners (unless they are integrated companies owning their own refineries) and gas to gas processors and utility companies. Nevertheless, the actual drilling and maintenance of oil and gas wells is often contracted out to third-party companies belonging to the oil and gas services industry segments. Historically, these companies tended to be small, independent enterprises operating on a local level. By the late 1990s, however, industry consolidation had created a handful of "major" international service companies, most notably Halliburton Company, Schlumberger Limited, and Baker Hughes Incorporated. In fact, Halliburton grew even larger through a US$7.7 billion merger with Dresser Industries, Inc. in 1998; Baker Hughes acquired Western Atlas Inc. for US$5.5 billion in August of that year.

Major natural gas-producing countries are not necessarily the same countries as those that lead the world in oil production. This is due in part to the unique properties of natural gas, which must undergo a costly liquefaction process before it can be shipped by tanker. As a result, natural gas tends to be consumed domestically rather than exported. Otherwise, it can be exported only to neighboring countries via pipelines. In the late-1990s, about 100 countries of the world were commercially producing oil or gas; the vast majority produced both. New exploration constantly was bringing new countries into the industry as well.

Oil-producing countries tend to be categorized by whether they are members of OPEC. Along with Saudi Arabia, the largest producer and exporter of oil in the world, OPEC members in 2004 included Algeria, Indonesia, Iran, Kuwait, Libya, Nigeria, Qatar, United Arab Emirates, Venezuela, and Iraq—which, in the wake of the U.S.-led invasion in 2003, was not operating under OPEC production ceilings. OPEC members adopt voluntary production quotas in order to maintain higher prices. OPEC's crude oil production in 1999 was 26.6 million barrels per day (b/d)—39.4 percent of the world's total—and OPEC countries accounted for about 61 percent of world oil exports. An even higher percentage of the world's known oil reserves were under OPEC control as of 1997: 76.8 percent, or about 797.1 billion barrels, of the world total of 1.04 trillion barrels. But by 2004, according to a *Boston Globe* report, OPEC's share of global oil exports had dropped to about 33 percent, largely because of increased production in Russia. OPEC deals only with oil production and not natural gas.

Outside OPEC, the leading countries in terms of proven crude oil reserves in early 2005 were Canada (178.8 billion barrels; this figure includes reserves in the country's oil sands), Russia (60 billion barrels), the United States (21.89 billion barrels), China (18.25 billion barrels), Mexico (14.6 billion barrels), Norway (8.5 billion barrels), Kazakhstan (9 billion barrels), and Brazil (10.6 billion barrels). The leading countries in terms of proven natural gas reserves in 2005 were Russia (1,680 trillion cubic feet), Iran (940 trillion cubic feet), Qatar (910 trillion cubic feet), Saudi Arabia (235.5 trillion cubic feet), the United Arab Emirates (212.1 trillion cubic feet), the United States (189 trillion cubic feet), Algeria (160.5 trillion cubic feet), and Venezuela (151 trillion cubic feet).

BACKGROUND AND DEVELOPMENT

Crude oil has been known since ancient times in various parts of the world. In the Middle East, where mixtures of asphalt and petroleum known as bitumen oozed to the earth's surface, it was used variously as a sealant in building and road construction, as a medicinal ointment, and occasionally as a fuel for illumination. Natural gas emissions, meanwhile, were sometimes ignited to create eternal flames at temples.

It was not until the nineteenth century, however, when refining methods were developed to produce the relatively clean and safe illuminant kerosene, that oil extraction became a true industry. A secondary use of refined petroleum as an industrial lubricant was also developed at the same time. Just when kerosene began to be replaced by electricity at the turn of the century, the emergence of the internal combustion engine afforded a new market for petroleum products, and demand skyrocketed throughout the twentieth century.

Although natural gas as well as oil had occasionally been used as an illuminant starting in the nineteenth century, for much of the history of the petroleum industry it remained an unwanted by-product of oil drilling. Even in the early 2000s, natural gas from wells drilled for oil was often simply flared off. Only in last decades of the twentieth century, as oil supplies and prices became uncertain, was an emphasis placed on natural gas as a source of energy. It was most commonly used for heat and electric power generation. The expansion in the use of natural gas was predicated in large part on changes in distribution. This was accomplished first in the United States in the late 1940s, when two former transcontinental oil pipelines were converted to natural gas pipelines.

Commercial oil extraction for the purpose of refining illuminants began independently in three parts of the world: first around Baku, Azerbaijan (then a part of czarist Russia), next in Galicia (a part of the Austro-Hungarian Empire), and shortly thereafter in neighboring Romania. The earliest commercial oil extraction ventures in the United States took place in northwestern Pennsylvania. In both Baku and Galicia in the early nineteenth century, oil was extracted in hand-dug pits and hoisted to the surface in buckets. In the United States, on the other hand, commercial oil extraction began with the innovation of drilling for oil, a practice that substantially increased output. The world's first oil well, managed by Edwin L. Drake and based on techniques for salt boring, successfully struck oil in August 1859 in Titusville, Pennsylvania.

Large scale production and some degree of order and efficiency were brought to the worldwide oil industry when a few large companies emerged to dominate production in different parts of the world. In most cases, though, the companies that began to control production had actually begun business in other aspects of the oil industry, such as refining or transportation; vertical integration developed only gradually. In the United States the petroleum industry became monopolized by Standard Oil, originally a refining company. A British shipping company, Shell Transport and Trading, which had entered the oil business by shipping Russian oil in 1891, entered the production field via exploration efforts in Borneo in 1895.

In the early years of the industry, a country with oil and gas reserves that lacked domestic firms capable of harvesting its resources often permitted foreign petroleum companies to come in. These companies gathered the natural resources under lease, fee, royalty, and other monetary arrangements. The first major oil field concession from a foreign government was won by Englishman William Knox D'Arcy in Persia in 1901. His enterprise was incorporated in 1909 as the Anglo-Persian Oil Company, which in 1954 changed its name to British Petroleum (BP), which ranked as one of the world's leading multinational petroleum companies in the late 1990s.

Concerns about growing demand, oil shortages, and the need for oil to maintain national security spurred foreign exploration by the major oil companies. This push produced major oil discoveries in Venezuela in the 1920s. By 1929, Venezuela had become the world's second-largest producer after the United States, producing 137 million barrels annually. Venezuela's leading export market was the United States, accounting for up to 55 percent of its crude and refined oil exports. Protective U.S. tariffs introduced in 1932 caused Venezuela to shift its exports to Europe, where it overtook the United States as Europe's leading oil supplier. Venezuela remained the world's leading exporter of oil until 1970.

Shared production by the leading western oil companies became the model in the Middle East. This method of operation was first seen in Iraq. An oil gusher was struck near Kirkuk in 1927, and production was shared by the major western oil companies based on a pre-World War I agreement that had set up an entity called the Turkish Petroleum Company (later renamed the Iraq Petroleum Company) covering the territory of most of the Arab Middle East. Its owners included Anglo-Persian, Royal Dutch/Shell, and a consortium of American companies.

Standard Oil of California (Socal, later named Chevron) began drilling in Bahrain in 1931. The company struck oil a year later, heralding the potential of the Persian Gulf area. Socal later made major discoveries in Saudi Arabia in 1938. That same year, a joint venture of Gulf Oil and Anglo-Persian discovered oil in Kuwait. Commercial oil production began in Kuwait in 1946, in Qatar in 1949, and in Abu Dhabi (part of the United Arab Emirates) in 1953.

To deal with rising production and falling prices on a world level, the major petroleum companies attempted on various occasions to reach market share agreements among themselves. The Achnacarry Agreement of 1928, which involved Royal Dutch/Shell, Anglo-Persian, Jersey Standard (Exxon), Standard Oil of Indiana, and Gulf, allocated quotas for each company in various world markets; it was later agreed that a company's level of production could not surpass the demand of the market quotas unless the output was sold to another company member. Market factors, however, proved to be significant obstacles to the agreement. Many independent oil producers who were not part of the agreement made significant contributions to the market, and even the cooperating oil companies often got into competition with each other.

In the late 1930s the oil industry became increasingly politicized, in part because of growing nationalistic regulation. Several governments, especially in Europe, tried to set prices, impose import quotas, control trade through bilateral agreements, and force foreign companies to participate in national cartels. Most drastically, the Mexican government expropriated all foreign oil company properties in 1938.

Countries with rich natural resources increasingly demanded a larger share of the profits in the 1940s and early 1950s. The financial relationship between foreign oil companies and the governments of the countries in which they operated changed in fundamental fashion during this time. In 1943 a new government in Venezuela reached an agreement with foreign oil companies operating in the country whereby the profits of oil production would be divided evenly between the Venezuelan government and the oil companies. Unprecedented prices were paid for oil concessions in the Arabian peninsula in the region between Saudi Arabia and

Kuwait. Such developments soon prompted other Middle Eastern governments to alter their existing agreements.

In the late 1950s new discoveries were made in other countries, and new companies became involved in international exploration and production. A joint venture of Royal Dutch/Shell and BP discovered oil in Nigeria in 1956, while a French group of state-owned companies found similar success in Gabon that same year. The year 1956 also marked the discovery of oil in Algeria by another French-owned company, Régie Autonome des Petroles (RAP). The most significant oil discoveries of the period were in Libya, where the government leased out 84 concessions to 17 foreign companies in 1957. By 1969 Libya's petroleum output exceeded that of Saudi Arabia, and it was supplying 30 percent of Europe's oil.

The numerous independent oil companies that operated in Libya or elsewhere on single overseas concessions did not feel as constrained in their production as did the major companies, which had to balance production among the various countries where they held concessions. As a result, production increased faster than demand, and prices and profits declined. In addition, the Soviet Union resumed exports of oil to the West in 1955 in response to sluggish domestic demand and excesses of inventory. The Soviet oil was priced lower than that from other regions, and the major international oil companies were forced to respond. They lowered market prices by reducing the relatively unchanging official or "posted" prices by which the countries in which they operated calculated their royalties. Alarmed by the resulting lower royalties, oil-rich nations were stirred into action.

In 1960, representatives of Saudi Arabia, Kuwait, Iraq, Iran, and Venezuela—which together accounted for 80 percent of the world's crude oil exports—formed OPEC to defend prices and regulate production. An agreement reached between OPEC countries and the major oil companies in 1971, known as the Tehran Agreement, marked a pivotal turning point in the industry's history. Under the Tehran Agreement, the OPEC nations were able to take the initiative in raising prices.

In the 1970s, demand caught up with supply. Excess capacity fell from 3 million b/d in 1970 to 1.5 million in 1973, of which only 500,000 barrels were immediately available. By 1973, Saudi Arabia's share of world exports had risen to 21 percent. When the United States supported Israel in the October 1973 Arab-Israeli war, the Arab members of OPEC, entrenched as the world leaders in oil production, responded with a complete boycott of oil to the United States and selected other countries. OPEC also instituted monthly reductions of 5 percent in total production, a step that dramatically impacted the entire world market. Crude oil prices rose from US$2.90 per barrel to US$11.65. Throughout the 1970s the OPEC cartel instituted higher prices on oil, hikes that punished the economies of countries with significant oil-importing needs. Over time, however, OPEC's power was somewhat diminished.

Major oil discoveries in Alaska and the North Sea in the 1960s and 1970s had a significant impact on world production. A joint venture of Atlantic-Richfield (ARCO) and Exxon's Humble subsidiary made the largest discovery to date in North America on Alaska's North Slope in Prudhoe Bay in 1967. The first major discoveries in the North Sea were made on the Norwegian side in 1969 and the British side in 1970. Physical obstacles to recovering and transporting the oil from these areas, though, were notable. North Sea oil did not reach a refinery until 1975, while Alaskan North Slope oil did not come to market until 1977, after completion of the Trans-Alaska Pipeline.

During the early 1990s, the production of petroleum liquids remained steady. Worldwide demand continued to edge upwards despite the recession in the world's industrialized countries during these years. Iraq's invasion of Kuwait in 1990 and the resulting Gulf War produced a temporary spike in the price of crude oil, after which prices remained relatively stable.

The mid- to late 1990s were a volatile period for the entire oil industry. Until late 1997, demand for oil and natural gas continued to increase. Global oil consumption rose from 59.7 million b/d in 1985 to 69 million b/d in 1995, an increase of 15.6 percent. Demand accelerated further in 1996 and 1997, when consumption increased by 2.3 percent and 2.8 percent, respectively. Fueling this growth in demand were the rapidly industrializing nations of East Asia and other regions. Ten of Asia's burgeoning economies were responsible for more than 40 percent of demand growth from 1986 through 1996. The sudden onset of the financial crisis in East Asia in late 1997, however, threatened to significantly dampen this trend. And the announcement in June 1998 that the Japanese economy was in recession posed a further threat as Japan was the second-largest consumer of oil in the world.

In January of 1997, crude oil was selling for about US$20.50 per barrel. Considerable downward pressure on the price of oil that year resulted from an increase in non-OPEC supplies, overproduction by OPEC members, and the return of Iraq's oil supplies to the world market. The threat of another war with Iraq in late 1997 resulted in only a temporary increase in pricing. Then, during the winter of 1997-1998, a number of factors contributed to a sharp decline in crude oil prices. The financial crisis in Asia was the most obvious factor, which significantly curtailed demand throughout the region. Also of importance was the worldwide weather phenomenon known as El Niño, which resulted in warmer-than-normal winter weather for North America and Europe, cutting energy consumption. Longer term, though, the continuing oil glut threatened to keep prices depressed for some time. By March 1998, the price of crude oil had fallen 55 percent to US$11.27 a barrel. It eventually reached a low of US$10 per barrel.

To cope with the deteriorating market conditions, many firms began to forge alliances to share in the costs of exploration and development. In November 1997, Russian natural gas giant Gazprom and Royal Dutch/Shell announced a worldwide strategic alliance, one month after Gazprom took a 30 percent stake in a US$2 billion project to develop a gas field in Iran, which was led by French giant TOTAL S.A. Another alliance involving a Russian oil concern was announced in November 1997 when British Petroleum PLC agreed to take a 10 percent stake in AO Sidanco for US$571 million, as well as a 45 percent interest in Sidanco's massive eastern Siberian gas fields for an additional US$172 million.

Consolidation continued to play a pivotal role in the oil and natural gas industries in the late 1990s and early 2000s. The 1999 merger that formed Exxon Mobil resulted in US$4.6 billion in cost savings by 2001. Other major deals included the US$57 billion merger of British Petroleum and Amoco Corp. to form BP Amoco in 1998, as well as the US$26.8 billion stock purchase of Atlantic Richfield by BP Amoco, now known simply as BP, in 2000. Not only did this make BP the world's leading private petroleum company, the consolidation also resulted in economies of scale worth an estimated US$6 billion. In 2001, Chevron and Texaco joined forces to create ChevronTexaco Corp., the second-largest oil company in the United States and the fourth-largest in the world. The world's fifth-largest integrated oil player was also the result of consolidation. Total Fina Elf (renamed TOTAL S.A. in 2003) was formed in 2000 when Total Fina, the result of a merger between France-based Total and Belgium's PetroFina in 1999, acquired Elf Aquitaine, also based in France.

Despite the increasing size of the majors, leading oil producers in Saudi Arabia and Russia continued to outpace them in terms of oil production. For example, Exxon Mobil's combined oil and gas production level was 4.3 million barrels of oil equivalent per day in 2000, compared the 8 million barrels per day of oil alone produced by Saudi Arabian Oil Company. Saudi Arabia and Russia also led the world in oil exports with daily exportation rates of 7.6 million barrels and 4.7 million barrels, respectively. The two countries differed significantly, however, in production costs. Saudi Arabia had managed to refine its oil production processes to the extent that production costs per barrel remained under US$5.50 per barrel, while Russian per barrel production costs exceeded US$10.

Current Conditions

Volatility in the oil industry continued into the twenty-first century. Political instability in Venezuela abruptly halted much of the country's oil exports in 2003, driving up prices. Civil unrest in Nigeria also contributed to price fluctuations. In addition, the U.S.-led war in Iraq left that country's oil production capabilities uncertain. OPEC countries responded by adhering to strict production schedules. By 2004, worldwide demand for oil had reached its highest level in seven years, led primarily by the United States and China. After reaching a low of US$10 per gallon in the late 1990s, oil prices surged to US$35 per barrel in 2004. OPEC responded by cutting its quotas by 4 percent. Prices did not immediately rise in response, however, due to doubts about the enforceability of the quota and to the increase in production from non-OPEC sources, especially Russia. Resumption of production in Iraq, which in 2004 was operating outside OPEC's production ceilings, was also expected to help mitigate the effects of the OPEC cuts. The EIA estimated that world oil prices would generally moderate after 2004 and then rise slowly through 2025.

Environmental issues have increasingly dogged the oil industry. Oil transportation practices have been called into question as a result of tanker and pipeline spills that have had devastating environmental consequences. Production, too, is increasingly being restricted by environmental regulations. Oil companies, for instance, have been denied permits for offshore drilling in certain locations for environmental reasons. The late 1990s brought another regulatory threat to industry players in the form of the Kyoto Protocol on Climate Change, adopted in December 1997 in Kyoto, Japan. The Protocol aimed to curb the emission of greenhouse gases, much of which resulted from the use of crude petroleum and natural gas, to levels well below those of 1990 by 2012. The European Union signed the Protocol in 1998, and despite opposition from the U.S. Republican Party, as well as public denouncement by U.S. president George W. Bush, the Protocol was finalized in November of 2001. Many industry experts pointed out, however, that the environmental impact of the Protocol would be somewhat compromised by the lack of U.S. participation.

Another critical issue was the amount of oil left to exploit. A *Christian Science Monitor* article reported that, by 2004, oil production had peaked for more than 50 oil-producing countries and that discovery of new oil sources, which had declined for 40 year, had almost ceased. In 2002, world consumption was four times more than the amount of newly discovered oil. With global demand projected to reach 119 million b/d in 2025, according to the U.S. Energy Department, some analysts believed that world production had already peaked. Others calculated a decline in production by 2010, while more optimistic scenarios predicted that output would flatten by 2036. Improvements in drilling technology and exploitation of unconventional oil sources, such as Canada's oil sands and Rocky Mountain shale, could delay the decline—which, analysts agreed, was inevitable.

Concerned about future supply, major oil importers stepped up competition for petroleum resources in Russia, the Caspian Sea region, West Africa, and Libya. China, where demand was expected to quadruple by 2030, proposed a pipeline from Angarsk, Russia to the inland Chinese industrial city of Daqing. China also invested heavily in Africa, where in 2002 PetroChina signed a US$350 million refining deal with Algeria. The United States, too, increased its oil imports from Africa. In 2003, according to the *New York Times*, West African countries such as Angola, Nigeria, and Equatorial Guinea accounted for about 14 percent of U.S. oil imports and were expected to reach 20 percent within a short time. In late 2003 a US$3.7 billion underground pipeline began carrying crude oil 670 miles from Chad to Cameroon on the Atlantic coast. Chad's first share of royalties from the pipeline were expected to be about US$100 million. Royal Dutch/Shell signed a deal in 2004 with National Oil Corp of Libya giving Shell access to about US$1 billion worth of oil and natural gas in North Africa. According to the Center for Strategic and International Studies, crude oil production in West Africa will increase from 2.6 million b/d in 2002 to 6.3 million b/d by 2008. Angola, Nigeria, Chad, and Equatorial Guinea will account for most of this increased output.

Despite skyrocketing demand for oil, driven largely by China, where oil imports increased from less than 30 million tons in 1998 to nearly 70 million tons in 2000, growth in the energy industry was expected to come increasingly from natural gas, hydrogen, and 'renewables" (such as solar and wind power). The *International Energy Outlook 2004* predicted that natural gas, considered more environmentally friendly that crude oil, would be the fastest-growing sector of the energy industry through 2025. World consumption of natural gas was expected to reach 151 trillion cubic feet in 2025, an increase of 67 over consumption levels in 2001. Natural gas consumption was expected to equal consumption of coal by 2010 and to surpass coal by 12 percent by 2025. With a mature natural gas infrastructure in place, industrialized countries were expected to increase their use of natural gas for generating electricity from 20 percent to 30 percent during this period. Gas's share in the electricity sector in developing countries, on the other hand, was expected to grow only from 14 percent to 17 percent.

RESEARCH AND TECHNOLOGY

Throughout the history of the industry, new technologies aided oil and gas discovery, drilling methods, and production. The seismograph turned out to be one of the most important early innovations of the industry. Originally, only the rare presence of actual oil, gas, or tar seepage to the earth's surface indicated the possible presence of oil deposits. The seismograph, originally developed to record earthquakes, was first put to use in oil exploration in eastern Europe by the Germans during World War I. Acoustic shock waves were sent underground, and the seismograph measured the time it took for the signals to return to the surface, as well as their strength upon return. These data were then analyzed to map out underground structures. In the 1990s, a combination of seismic and computer technology was used to create sophisticated three-dimensional diagrams of underground geology.

NEW INNOVATIONS

The relatively new technology of measurement while drilling, which involved the use of advanced sensors near the drill bit, could provide detailed information on geological formations without interrupting the drilling process to retrieve rock samples. Computers are used to analyze the data.

In the 1980s, the techniques of horizontal drilling and changing direction while drilling were devised. Horizontal drilling aids in discovery, facilitates access to reservoirs under certain conditions, and also increases productivity. The practice has been used to create gas storage wells that yield gas production six times greater than vertical wells. Directional drilling uses a steerable motor behind the drill bit to change the trajectory of drilling according to information obtained from sensors near the drill bit. Coiled tubing that is flexible enough to bend, yet rigid enough to push equipment through a borehole, is used to analyze conditions in non-vertical wells. The coiled tubing technology was also used to rework rather than redrill damaged wells. Other developments in drilling center around improvements in equipment. More powerful drilling motors, improved sensing equipment, and new drilling fluids that are more efficient in lubricating and cooling drilling equipment improved the efficiency of oil exploration efforts. Thanks to these and other techniques, the average cost per barrel of finding and producing oil decreased by about 60 percent in inflation-adjusted terms from 1985 to 1995.

In the production area, the industry made use of various techniques of enhanced oil recovery to boost productivity of reservoirs under weak pressure. Such techniques proved especially valuable in reaching partially depleted oil reservoirs. Common methods used included the injection of air, water, steam, or chemicals into underground reservoirs to put more pressure on the oil, making it easier to pump it to the surface.

Advancements in the design and construction of drilling rigs allowed companies to operate deeper wells both on and offshore. In 1918, the deepest wells were 6,000 feet; in 1930, they were 10,000 feet deep. By the early 1990s, ultra-heavy rigs permitted drilling up to 25,000 feet. Another advance allowed offshore drillers to operate in deeper water than ever before. Tender-assisted drilling, whereby a semi-submersible rig is tethered to the ocean floor by cables, gave greater stability while permitting drilling in waters up to 3,000 feet deep.

INDUSTRY LEADERS

SAUDI ARABIAN OIL COMPANY

In the early 2000s, as the sole producer in the world's leading oil producing country, state-owned Saudi Arabian Oil stood as the world's largest petroleum company. It owned roughly 260 billion barrels worth of oil reserves, which accounted for nearly one-forth of global oil reserves. The firm owned all reserves and handled all oil and gas production in Saudi Arabia, except for shared production of the Saudi portion of the Neutral Zone. The company also expanded into refining and marketing activities, although foreign companies continued to have a share in some Saudi refineries. In 2004 the company produced about 10 million b/d, accounting for more than 10 percent of world demand. Oil exports contributed between 90 and 95 percent of Saudi Arabia's total export earnings and between 70 and 80 percent of government revenues in 2004; about 40 percent of the country's GDP was based on petroleum exports.

Saudi Arabian involvement in the oil industry began modestly. In 1933, Standard Oil of California (Chevron) won the first and only concession to explore for oil in Saudi Arabia. It established the California-Arabian Standard Oil Company (Casoc), with Texaco as a joint partner, to undertake oil production. In 1944, Casoc was renamed the Arabian-American Oil Company (Aramco). To market the expanding Saudi production in the Western Hemisphere, Socal and Texaco invited Jersey Standard (Exxon) and Socony-Vacuum (Mobil) into Aramco as additional partners. By 1948, Socal, Texaco, and Jersey Standard all owned 30 percent of the company, while the remaining 10 percent was held by Socony-Vacuum.

In 1973, the Saudi government acquired a 25 percent share in Aramco, a share that was raised to 60 percent in 1974. In 1980, Saudi Arabia paid the U.S. owners of Aramco for the remaining share of the company, although it was not until 1988 that Aramco was formally nationalized as the Saudi Arabian Oil Co., made retroactive to 1976. The 100 percent Saudi-owned company is often referred to as Saudi Aramco. Saudi Minister of Petroleum and Minerals Hisham Nazar was appointed its chairman, although a Saudi had been president of the company since 1983. Many Americans continued to serve in the technical management of the company in the late 1980s.

In 1993, the Saudi Arabian Marketing and Refining Company (Samarec), formed in 1988 primarily to serve the domestic market, was merged into Saudi Aramco. This move created a single integrated national oil company to serve both domestic and international markets. Prior to the merger, Aramco's payroll was 47,000, while Samarec's was 12,000.

In 1995, Saudi Aramco's president and CEO, Ali Naimi, was appointed to be the new minister of oil for Saudi Arabia. The appointment was seen as an indication of the importance of Aramco to the country's oil industry.

NATIONAL IRANIAN OIL COMPANY

Iranian prime minister Mohammed Mossadegh nationalized the operations of Anglo-Iranian Oil (later BP) in 1951 for nationalistic reasons rather than for the revenues. The National Iranian Oil Company (NIOC) was thus created. NIOC took over ownership of the resources and production facilities, but since it was inexperienced at management and overseas marketing, the state-owned enterprise signed an agreement in 1954 with a consortium of major foreign oil companies. Under the terms of this agreement, the foreign firms provided management services and purchased and distributed the output, with NIOC recognized as the operator. This consortium was forced to cease operations in Iran during the 1979 Iranian Revolution.

NIOC directly controlled all oil production, while natural gas production was handled by its National Iranian Gas Co. affiliate. Both companies were controlled by the Ministry of Oil. National Iranian Drilling Co., a subsidiary of NIOC, conducted exploration for oil and gas.

In the mid-1990s, NIOC began to contract out to foreign companies production of new oil and gas fields in Iran. In 1995, TOTAL S.A. became the first foreign oil company allowed back in Iran since the 1979 revolution when it signed a contract to develop the Sirri offshore oil field. Two years later, NIOC contracted with TOTAL, Petronas of Malaysia, and Russia's Gazprom in a US$2 billion project to develop the massive South Pars natural gas field. As the second largest oil producer of OPEC, NIOC produced roughly 3.8 billion barrels per day in 2004 and controlled 9 percent of the world's oil reserves. NIOC's oil earnings constitute 40 to 50 percent of Iran's government revenues and 80 percent of export earnings.

CHINA PETROLEUM & CHEMICAL CORP.

Immediately after the founding of the People's Republic of China in 1949, the China Petroleum & Chemical Corp. (Sinopec Corp.) was established to exploit the country's oil reserves, which at the time were estimated at only 29 million tons. The company held a monopoly on China's petroleum industry until the formation of the China National Offshore Oil Corp. in 1982, and the China National Petrochemical Corporation in 1983. China Petrochemical restructured in 2000, forming Sinopec Corporation as a vertically integrated energy and chemical company. This step, according to the company, was taken in order "to diversify the ownership structure, abide by the rules of the market economy, and establish a modern enterprise system." With proven reserves of 3.3 billion barrels of crude oil and 2.9 trillion cubic feet of gas, Sinopec posted sales in 2003 of US$51.25 billion, a dramatic increase over the US$6 billion of 1993.

PETRÓLEOS MEXICANOS

Petróleos Mexicanos (Pemex) was formed in 1938 as the result of the first nationalization of foreign oil company properties in a non-communist country. Lacking expertise and capital, the new company could not maintain significant production, and oil had to be imported until major new oil discoveries were made in 1972.

Pemex was essentially a decentralized public agency of the Mexican government. It handled all oil and gas exploration, production, refining, transportation, storage, and sales. It is also involved in the production and sales of petrochemicals. Out of total 1996 revenues of US$29.4 billion, 38 percent came from exploration and production. In the early 2000s, Pemex was responsible for about 7 percent of Mexico's total export profits. Pemex held a 5 percent stake in Repsol S.A., a major oil and gas company in Spain and a leading oil company in Europe. In 2003 Petróleos Mexicanos held proved oil reserves of 17.1 billion barrels and natural gas reserves of 15 tcf. Sales in 2003 reached US$55.92 billion.

BP PLC

BP, formerly known as British Petroleum and then BP Amoco, after its 1998 merger with Amoco, became the world's largest private sector petroleum company when it bought Atlantic Richfield Company in 2000. In 2004 BP had proven reserves of 18.4 billion barrels of oil. Sales in 2004 reached US$285 billion, with net earnings of about US$ 15.7 billion. BP produced 1.9 million barrels of crude oil and 8.6 billion cubic feet of natural gas per day in 2004.

The company began with to activities in Iran. The oil from that country served as BP's primary source of income and held a monopoly on production for decades. The company was gradually squeezed out of Iran due to the nationalization of the oil industry there, but the firm took up production elsewhere. BP made major oil discoveries in Alaska's Prudhoe Bay in 1969 and in the North Sea in 1970, and these two regions remained BP's primary sources of oil and gas. Alaskan oil accounted for more than 50 percent of BP's global crude oil production, while British territory in the North Sea accounts for about one-third. BP also operated or had interests in producing fields in Australia, Colombia, Indonesia, and Venezuela, among other countries. In addition to oil and gas exploration and production, BP was also a major refiner and marketer of petroleum products and manufacturer of chemicals and plastics.

EXXON MOBIL CORPORATION

Prior to its 1999 merger with Mobil, Exxon Corp. was the world's second-largest private sector petroleum company, after Royal Dutch/Shell. Exxon usurped Royal Dutch/Shell as the world leader when the US$83 billion deal with Mobil was completed. By 2003, however, Exxon Mobil slipped to second place, behind BP. In 2004, Exxon Mobil had proven reserves of 21.2 billion barrels of oil equivalent and sales of US$263.9 billion.

Formerly named Standard Oil of New Jersey (Jersey Standard), the company's origin was as the holding company of the Standard Oil firm. Until 1911, it held nearly half of the former monopoly's net value. At that time a Supreme Court ruling broke up the company. The largest of the companies created after the disbandment of the Standard Oil Trust, Jersey Standard rapidly expanded its overseas production and marketing activities. By 1954, it had become the largest oil company in the world. In 1972, the company changed its name to Exxon to end confusion with other companies still using the Standard Oil name.

Exxon's slide from preeminence began in the 1970s as nationalization of oil assets previously held by producing companies reduced the company's access to oil. With its reserves shrinking, Exxon's dependence on crude oil for the bulk of its sales slowed the company's growth, allowing Shell to gradually replace it as the world's leading oil company during the 1980s. A further blow to both the company's reputation and its balance sheet was the notorious *Exxon Valdez* oil spill off the coast of Alaska in 1989. By 1992, the disaster had cost Exxon more than US$6 billion in criminal damages and cleanup costs. In mid-1994, a federal jury ruled that the company and the tanker's captain had caused the disaster through recklessness and fined Exxon US$5 billion. The company formally appealed this judgment in 1997; four years later, a U.S. Circuit Court of Appeals found the fine excessive and mandated that the Alaskan state court lower it.

ROYAL DUTCH/SHELL GROUP OF COMPANIES

Royal Dutch/Shell is the world's third-largest private sector petroleum and natural gas company. Its present form was created in 1907 as a partnership between the Dutch company Royal Dutch Petroleum, with 60 percent participation, and the British company Shell Transport and Trading, with 40 percent. These two companies continued to exist as independent entities based in The Hague, Netherlands, and London, England, respectively.

Royal Dutch/Shell's crude oil production was roughly evenly divided between the regions of Europe, Africa, the Middle East, East Asia, and the Western Hemisphere. The leading sources of Royal Dutch/Shell's global production were its operations in the United States, the United Kingdom and its North Sea fields, Nigeria, Oman, and Malaysia. Royal Dutch/Shell was also a leader in natural gas production due to its active involvement in the Netherlands and the United States, which were large gas producers. As of 2000, gas reserved equaled 56.2 trillion cubic feet. Other leading natural gas-producing countries for Royal Dutch/Shell were Canada, Malaysia, the United Kingdom, and Brunei. Sales in 2004 totaled US$201.7 billion, and the firm employed 119,000 workers.

PETRÓLEOS DE VENEZUELA S.A.

Venezuela nationalized all oil holdings in 1975, paying a total of US$1 billion for the assets. Before that foreign companies produced about 70 percent of Venezuela's oil, although the state had been a 50-percent partner in their operations since 1945. In 1977, Petróleos de Venezuela SA (PDVSA) was created as a holding company of subsidiaries that replaced the former companies. Exxon's operations became the subsidiary Lagoven, Royal Dutch/Shell's became Maraven, and operations of other smaller companies were combined into the subsidiaries Memeven and Corpoven. The oil companies continued to operate their former possessions by contract for fees, and thus PDVSA was able to continue to take advantage of their expertise.

PDVSA launched an exploration campaign in the 1980s that yielded oil reserves that nearly doubled the country's known reserves. In 2004 its proven reserves were estimated at 77.2 billion barrels of oil — the largest amount outside of the Middle East — and 147.1 trillion cubic feet of natural gas. In the late 1980s, after oil prices fell, PDVSA accelerated its diversification. It remained an integrated petroleum company but also became involved in coal and bitumen production, petrochemicals, and fertilizers.

Venezuela's crude oil production, although subject to OPEC quotas, rose throughout the late 1990s, reaching 3.14 million b/d by 2000. PDVSA planned to increase its production to 6.5 million b/d by 2006. In order to achieve this goal, PDVSA needed about US$40 billion in new investment. To this end, the firm began offering foreign oil companies the opportunity to return to Venezuela and help PDVSA improve extraction from existing fields. A late 1997 round of bidding brought US$2 billion in contract payments from international oil firms.

Petroleum production fell by as much as 25,000 b/d in 2003 after protestors threatened the government of President Hugo Chavez and threw the country into civil turmoil; as a result, almost all of Venezuela's exports were temporarily halted. According to company statistics, however, production was normalized by later that year, reaching about 3.25 million b/d of crude oil.

The United States was Venezuela's leading export market, primarily through the U.S.-based CITGO gasoline company, which PDVSA acquired in 1990. During 1997, Venezuela passed Saudi Arabia as the largest oil exporter to the United States, having gained a market share of 18 percent. Sales in 2000 grew 64.4 percent to US$53.6 billion, while earnings soared 156 percent to US$7.21 Revenues dropped in 2002 to US$42.58 billion. The firm's oil reserves, totaling 77.2 billion barrels in 2004, were second only to those held in the Middle East.

TOTAL S.A.

With operations in more than 100 countries and reserves of 11.4 billion barrels, TOTAL, based in France, is one of the world's largest integrated oil companies. Total Fina was formed in 1999 after the merger between France's Total and the Belgian company PetroFina. It then bought French company Elf Aquitaine in 2000. The company was renamed TOTAL S.A. in 2003. Sales in 2004 exceeded US$166.2 billion.

Other major multinational petroleum companies included U.S.-based ChevronTexaco Corp.; Gazprom and Lukoil Holding, both of Russia; and Italy's Agip, a subsidiary of state-owned Ente Nazionale Idrocarburi.

MAJOR COUNTRIES IN THE INDUSTRY

RUSSIA

In the early 2000s Russia owned the world's largest reserves of natural gas and the eighth largest reserves of oil. In addition, Russia was the world's largest exporter of natural gas and the second largest exporter of oil. Production of oil surged during the 1980s when the Soviet Union intensified exploitation of its oilfields in Western Siberia. But output slowed after peaking at 12.5 million barrels per day in 1988, with many analysts blaming unrealistic state-mandated production levels for exhausting the USSR's major oil fields. After the collapse of the Soviet Union in 1991, Russian oil production was thrown into chaos, and by 1996 production fell to about 6 million b/d. However, in 1999 the situation began to change because of a surge in world oil prices and improvements to the Russian economy. By 2004, total production had risen almost 40 percent to about 9.27 million b/d. This made Russia the second-largest producer of crude oil, after Saudi Arabia. Improvements in upstream techniques at older oilfields, as well as other production efficiencies, contributed to higher outputs.

In 2003, about 70 percent of the Russian oil industry was controlled by five companies: Yukos and Sibneft, which merged that year to create YukosSibneft, Russia's largest oil company; LUKoil; Surgutneftegaz; and Tyumen Oil, which merged with British Petroleum that year to create TNK-BP. The rest the industry was shared among about 150 small and medium-sized companies. The picture differed sharply for the natural gas industry, however. One state-controlled company, Gazprom, produced almost 90 percent of Russia's natural gas and held almost a third of the world's reserves. The company was also Russia's biggest earner of hard currency. Strict domestic regulations, however, had a negative impact on the company's profits.

While Russia exported more than 70 percent of its crude oil production in the early 2000s, infrastructure problems prevented producers from meeting their export goals. Much of Russia's oil must be shipped long distances by rail, greatly increasing costs. The opening in December 2001 of the Baltic Pipeline System (BPS), which carried oil from West Siberia to the new port of Primorsk, on the Gulf of Finland just north of St. Petersburg, gave Russia a direct outlet to European markets. The pipeline handled about 1 million b/d in late 2004, and this level was expected to expand to 1.2 million b/d in 2005. In addition, Russia announced in 2004 that it would build a Far Eastern Pipeline from Angarsk in southern Siberia to Nakhodka on the Sea of Japan. The 2,500 mile pipeline would cost between US$15 and US$18 billion, and would have the capacity to carry 1.6 million b/d.

Infrastructure also held back Russia's natural gas industry. Many of the country's oil companies sat on natural gas reserves that were not exploited because Gazprom controls the pipeline network, limiting access to export markets. If third-party access to the pipeline network were achieved, natural gas exports could significantly increase. During the early 2000s Gazprom became more interested in diversifying its exports, shifting trade away from Eastern Europe to the European Union, Turkey, Japan, and other markets in Asia. Construction of a proposed natural gas pipeline from Russia to Finland and Britain via the Baltic Sea was scheduled to begin in 2007, but in 2005 Gazprom announced that the project's start would be delayed to 2010.

SAUDI ARABIA

The discovery of oil on the island nation of Bahrain in 1931 suggested that oil could be found on the Saudi Arabian mainland. The events on Bahrain convinced Saudi King Ibn Saud to offer a concession to the foreign firm Socal (Chevron). Oil in large quantities was not discovered until 1938. By 1940, Saudi oil production reached 20,000 b/d; Saudi Arabia was a significant producer thereafter. It overtook the United States as the world's second-largest oil producer—after the Soviet Union—in 1976. Saudi Arabia's proven oil reserves were 261.9 billion barrels in 2004.

The country reached its highest production levels in 1980 when it registered 9.9 billion b/d of oil. Of that total, it exported 9.2 billion b/d, reaping US$101.8 billion in export sales. OPEC production quotas kept Saudi Arabia's production down after that time. By 1985, production dropped to 3.2 billion b/d. Following the 1990 Iraqi invasion of Kuwait, however, Saudi Arabia boosted its production from 5.3 million b/d to 7.5 million b/d. After reaching 9.12 million b/d in 2000, production fell to 8.2 million b/d, still the largest production level in the world, in 2001. Total oil production (including liquid natural gas) averaged 10 million b/d in early 2003, when Saudi Arabia implemented its spare production capacity to help offset losses from Venezuela, Nigeria, and Iraq, but its OPEC quota was cut later that year to 7.9 b/d. In 2004 Saudi Arabia's capacity was estimated at between 10.5 and 11 million b/d. Saudi officials have stated that they plan to increase production to 12.5 million b/d during the next several years.

Most of Saudi Arabia's oil production took place in the eastern part of the country, along the Persian Gulf coast and offshore. But discoveries were made in the northwest near the Jordanian border and the Red Sea coast as well. Since 1987, Saudi Aramco had rights to explore anywhere in the Kingdom.

Long a major exporter to the United States, Saudi Arabia was also a key supplier to Europe and Japan. By the early 2000s, however, Venezuela, Canada, and Mexico had increased their exports to the U.S. market. As a result, Saudi Arabia stepped up exports to Asia, which by 2004 accounted for about 60 percent of Saudi Arabia's crude oil exports. Despite slipping to second place in the U.S. export market, Saudi Arabia hoped to maintain or expand its position as a key supplier to the United States.

UNITED STATES

The United States was the world's leading oil producer until the 1970s and a major exporter until the 1940s. Beginning in 1948, however, U.S. imports of crude petroleum and refined oil products exceeded exports. U.S. oil production peaked at 9.64 million b/d in 1970 and then declined to 8.77 million b/d in 1974, the year in which the United States was surpassed by the Soviet Union as the world's leading producer. Production remained roughly stable over the next decade, but then began to fall in the late 1980s and early 1990s, with only 8.585 million b/d produced in 1993. By 1997, production had fallen further, to less than 7 million b/d, positioning the United States as the third-leading oil producer, trailing Saudi Arabia and Russia. The United States remained in third place in 2000, with crude oil production of 5.83 million b/d; by 2003 production had lagged to about 5.7 million b/d. The EIA reported that this downward trend was expected to continue, while natural gas output continued to climb. The country's leading oil-producing states were Alaska, Texas, Louisiana, California, and Oklahoma. U.S. crude oil reserves at the beginning of 2005 totaled 21.9 billion barrels.

While U.S. oil production declined significantly from 1985 to 2003, consumption remained high. Most of this demand was attributed to the transportation sector. In the first 10 months of 2004, U.S. oil consumption averaged 20.4 million b/d compared to 20.0 million b/d in 2003. Total petroleum consumption in 2005 was expected to grow by 1.4 percent.

In 1993, the United States produced more natural gas than oil by value for the first time. By 1999, the United States accounted for 23.2 percent of worldwide natural gas production, behind only Russia, which accounted for 23.7 percent of production. U.S. natural gas reserves in 2004 were sixth-largest in the world, and totaled 187 trillion cubic feet. Production of dry natural gas was expected to reach about 19.1 tcf in 2005; demand, however, was expected to grow. Consumption reached about 22.0 tcf in 2004, and was projected to rise another 3.7 percent in 2005. To meet growing demand, the United States relied on imports, primarily from Canada. But Canada's increasing domestic use may reduce its export levels of natural gas in coming years. Seeking additional import sources, the United States has begun expanding liquid natural gas (LNG) facilities that could result in a significant rise in LNG imports by 2007. In the early 2000s, most LNG imports came from Trinidad and Tobago, Algeria, and Quatar.

IRAN

Iran has been a major world producer and exporter of oil since the 1920s. All of Iran's oil and gas production was monopolized by the state-owned National Iranian Oil Co. Iranian oil production reached its peak of 6.02 million b/d in 1974. It stood at 5.24 million b/d on the eve of the 1979 revolution, a period of political and economic upheaval that disrupted production and export efforts. The outbreak of the Iran-Iraq War in 1980 caused severe damage to Iran's oil-producing facilities, and production plummeted to 1.32 million b/d in 1981. Production increased gradually during the 1980s and accelerated after the end of the war in 1988 but remained limited by OPEC quotas. In 2004, Iran reported proven oil reserves of 132 billion barrels. The country's oil production capacity was estimated in early 2005 at about 3.9 million b/d, making it the world's second largest producer. Spurred in large part by a sharp increase in domestic production, Iran hoped—with the help of substantial foreign investment for much-needed modernizations to its facilities—to double national oil production by 2015.

Natural gas production in Iran continued to grow rapidly through the late 1990s and early 2000s. Production surpassed the pre-Iran-Iraq War levels by the end of the war in 1988 and continued to rise during the late 1980s and 1990s. In 2005, Iran was second only to Russia in natural gas reserves, which totaled 940 trillion cubic feet. Although Iran was the leading exporter of natural gas among OPEC countries in the 1970s, it was no longer a significant exporter. With almost half of its total energy needs supplied by natural gas, Iran's domestic demand consumed most of its natural gas production. Because it had enormous undeveloped reserves, however, it had the potential to become a major natural gas exporter. The country has announced that it will spend billions of dollars in the next several years to boost natural gas production.

MEXICO

Mexico, a leading oil producer and exporter in the 1920s, disappeared from the world market for several decades and then reemerged as a dominant producer in the late 1970s. With production estimated at 3.8 million b/d, Mexico ranked as the fourth-leading oil producer in the world in 2003; it dropped to fifth place, however, in 2004. Estimates of Mexico's crude oil reserves were revised downward in late 2002 to about 15.7 billion barrels; this figure fell further in 2005 to an estimated 14.6 billion barrels, but the country's ultimate potential reserves (including liquid natural gas) could be as high as 40.6 billion barrels. In 2004 Mexico had proven natural gas reserves of 15 tfc.

After the nationalization of the country's petroleum industry in 1938, the industry turned towards serving the growing domestic market, where demand grew faster than supply. For a time Mexico even had to import small amounts of oil. A major exploration drive revealed large new reserves beginning in 1972, however, and by 1974 the country resumed exporting oil. Production grew from 500,000 b/d in 1972 to 1.9 million b/d in 1980, as Mexico re-established itself as a major oil-producing country on the strength of reserves located on the southern shore of the Gulf of Mexico. Increase in domestic demand, however, decreased 2003 exports to approximately 1.78 million b/d. The vast majority of Mexico's oil exports are sold to the United States.

All oil and gas exploration and production, both inshore and offshore, was conducted by the state-owned company Petróleos Mexicanos (Pemex). In 2003, about a third of Mexico's federal budget came from Pemex revenues. While no foreign companies had equity in Mexican production, Pemex began in the early 2000s to offer certain contracts to foreign companies. The North American Free Trade Agreement (NAFTA) also permitted greater participation in Mexico's oil industry by U.S. and Canadian firms. In 2004, President Vincent Fox proposed several reforms in the energy sector, including proposals to allow private investment and foreign participation in the oil and natural gas industries. He also proposed changes in how Pemex is taxed. It was uncertain, however, whether such measures would receive sufficient legislative support to be enacted.

CANADA

Before 2002, Canada was not among the top 20 countries with proven reserves; by early 2005, however, it ranked second in the world with 178.8 billion barrels. Of this amount, more than 95 percent was in the Alberta oil sands deposits, previously excluded from estimates of crude reserves. Though exploitation of oil sands greatly boosted Canada's production, it is much more costly to extract oil from sand fields than from conventional deposits; this has led to some controversy about the potential growth of oil sands production. Some analysts have warned that high production costs could limit growth in this industry, but the EIA predicted that oil sands production would increase significantly in the next several years. Canada also has considerable offshore oil reserves, which it plans to develop more extensively through the early 2000s. Production at the Hibernia field off the coast of Newfoundland began in 1997; another Atlantic field, Terra Nova, began operations in 2002 and averaged 134,000 b/d in 2003. Exploitation of offshore fields in the Pacific, however, was held up by a federal ban. If this ban is lifted, offshore drilling could begin there by 2010. In 2004, Canada was the seventh largest oil producer with total oil production of 3.1 million b/d. It was also the world's seventh largest oil consumer, using 2.3 million b/d. More than 99 percent of Canada's crude oil exports are sold to the United States.

Canada ranked as the world's third largest producer of natural gas in 2002. Its proven reserves, however, stood at only 56.1 trillion cubic feet in early 2005. At current rates, according to the EIA, Canada will deplete its natural gas reserves in about 8.6 years. Canada is a major supplies of natural gas to the United States, accounting for about 16 percent of U.S. consumption in 2003.

FURTHER READING

British Petroleum PLC. Company Statistics, 2004. Available from www.bp.com.

Clark, Nicola. "Libya Signs Energy Exploration Deal with Shell." *New York Times,* 26 March 2004.

Dougherty, Carter. "China, Seeking Oil and Foothold, Brings Funds for Africa's Riches." *Boston Globe,* 22 February 2004.

Francis, David R. "Has Global Oil Production Peaked?" *Christian Science Monitor,* 29 January 2004.

Hoover's Online. "Petróleos de Venezuela SA Profile." Available from www.hoovers.com.

———. "Royal Dutch/Shell Profile." Available from www.hoovers.com.

Itano, Nicole. "Proposal to Limit Oil and Coal Projects Draws Fire." *New York Times,* 24 March 2004.

Krueger, Jessica. *U.S. Oil Stakes in West Africa.* Center for Strategic and International Studies, Washington, D.C., 2002. Available from www.csis.org.

Palmeri, Christopher. "Industry Outlook 2001—Energy." *Business Week,* 2 January 2001. Available from www.businessweek.com.

Roberts, Dexter and Mark L. Clifford. "China: Hungry for Energy." *Business Week,* 24 December 2001. Available from www.businessweek.com.

Romero, Simon. "Energy of Africa Draws the Eyes of Houston." *New York Times,* 23 September 2003.

Sengupta, Soomini. "The Making of an African Petrostate." *New York Times,* 18 February 2004.

Sinopec Corp. Company Information and Statistics, 2004. Available from http://english.sinopec.com.

Starobin, Paul. "An Opportunity for Russian Oil?" *Business Week,* 3 December 2001. Available from www.businessweek.com..

U.S. Department of Energy, Energy Information Administration. Country Analyses and Briefs, 2003-2004. Available from www.eia.doe.gov.

———. *International Energy Outlook 2004.* Available from www.eia.doe.gov.

SIC 2911

NAICS 324110

PETROLEUM REFINING

Petroleum refiners transform crude oil into such fuels as gasoline, kerosene, distillate fuel oils, and residual fuel oils. Refined petroleum products are also used in lubricants and a wide number of chemical applications. See also **Petroleum and Natural Gas, Crude.**

INDUSTRY SNAPSHOT

After nearly a century of extraordinary growth, the world petroleum refining industry struggled to adapt to the harsher climate of the 1990s. Global production of refined petroleum products leveled off at about 65 million barrels per day (b/d) in the early 1990s. Growth accelerated again in the mid-1990s to more than 70 million b/d, thanks largely to rapid growth in emerging markets, particularly those of East Asia. The Asian financial crisis that began in late 1997, however, along with the beginning of a recession in Japan around that same time, once again dampened demand for refined products such as gasoline. Global production hovered in the 75 billion b/d range in both 1998 and 1999. Production levels surged again in 2000 due to a stronger economy in Asia, as well as economic prosperity in both North America and Europe. However, worldwide recessionary economic conditions began to once again undercut demand at the start of the twenty-first century. In 2003, worldwide consumption hit 78.1 million b/d, with Asia and the Pacific Rim accounting for the highest growth percentages. In addition, 2003 marked the highest prices since the early 1980s.

Furthermore, 2003 brought slight changes to the industry, with little more than a one percent change up or down in North America and Europe, according to *Euromonitor.* The market in Germany, for instance, declined 1.0 percent to 122.4 mt from 2002 and was expected to decline another 8.0 percent into 2008. The petroleum market in France fell 1.5 percent to 92.8 mt. Transportation was the main consumer of petroleum products, and diesel was the largest market sector, with 41.9 mt. The market was expected to reach 100.0 mt by 2008. In the United Kingdom, the total market had fallen half a percent to 79.1 mt, with diesel dominating at 25.2 mt. Declines were expected into 2008, to a total volume of 74.4 mt. In contrast to the European countries, the U.S. market increased in 2003, but only by 1.4 percent to about 7.05 billion barrels. It was expected to grow slightly the following year, with motor gasoline remaining the biggest market sector. By 2008, the sector was projected to command more than 43.0 percent of the refined petroleum market, for a total value of US$3.4 billion.

By the mid-2000s, industry trends were for further consolidation among companies and higher profits for the biggest companies. In addition, because a major industry hurdle was in overcoming its image as one of the most worst environmental destroyers, the so-called "green" innovations in industry research and offerings were expected to have a major impact on the petroleum industry in the coming years. Industry leader BP, for example, was running its "Beyond Petroleum" campaign, having garnered more than 18 percent of the solar power market share in 2003, among other green research investments. By 2004 and early 2005, global demand greatly outpaced supply, which raised prices to record levels. Unusually, however, record high oil prices did not, in turn, cause the normal decrease in demand. This was mostly due to a spike in economic activity worldwide, especially China, and low interest rates. World oil production grew 3.4 percent in 2004 to 71.7 million barrels per day (b/d).

ORGANIZATION AND STRUCTURE

No industry has better epitomized the term "monopoly capitalism" than the oil industry. For example, the U.S. 1890 Sherman Antitrust Act was in large part inspired by the overwhelming monopolistic power of John D. Rockefeller's Standard Oil trust. Even in the 2000s, roughly a century after the breakup of Standard Oil, the offspring of that early conglomerate—Exxon Mobil and ChevronTexaco—remained among the largest corporations in the world, dominating all aspects of the oil industry. With their massive integrated supply, production, and distribution systems, leading oil companies were involved in a myriad of industry activities, including resource extraction, manufacturing, and distribution.

Petroleum refining itself was considered part of the "downstream" side of the oil business. In addition to refining, downstream operations included transportation (mostly via pipelines) of crude oil to refineries and refined oil products to wholesalers, distributors, and retailers. The "upstream" side of the business involved all aspects of finding and recovering crude oil, including exploration, geological studies, testing, drilling, and extraction. Integrated companies—the so-called "majors" such as Exxon Mobil, Royal Dutch/Shell, BP, and ChevronTexaco—carried out both upstream and downstream operations. Raw materials obtained by the upstream arm of the corporation were transferred to the refiner, which in turn supplied the finished products to company-owned wholesalers and retailers.

Competing with the major companies in the late 1990s were numerous, smaller integrated and nonintegrated companies, or "independents." Some of these independents, such as Atlantic Richfield and Phillips Petroleum, were integrated international corporations in their own right, although their numbers dwindled in the early 2000s due to industry consolidation. For example, BP Amoco, which subsequently shortened its name to BP, acquired Atlantic Richfield in 2000. In addition, a merger of Phillips Petroleum and Conoco was scheduled for 2002. Most of the remaining independents were regional companies specializing in refining. Although prominent independents such as Ashland Oil and Valero Energy Corp. played an important role in the refining industry, none of them was on the same level as the majors.

Petroleum refineries converted crude oil into a variety of products. Most of these products, such as fuel, were distributed in the form in which they were to be used, although some products were used in the manufacture of other products such as plastics. The most common refining technique was distillation (also known as fractionating). Heated crude oil was pumped into the bottom of a distillation tower where the lighter oil portions, or fractions, vaporized. The fractions cooled as they rose and condensed into liquids that flowed downward again and were re-vaporized. This process was repeated until the desired degree of purity was achieved. Heavier fractions, such as fuel and diesel oils, condensed at higher temperatures and were tapped off from the lower part of the tower, while lighter, value-added products such as kerosene, gasoline, and butane condensed at lower temperatures and were taken from the top.

More sophisticated refineries conducted additional processing of distilled products, applying various combinations of pressure, heat, or chemical catalysts to break down heavier molecules into lighter ones. These various processes, termed "cracking," were used to create cleaner, more efficient fuels and oils such as high-octane gasoline and lubricants. Catalytic cracking, for instance, used a powdered chemical catalyst to increase the gasoline yield by converting heavy fractions to lighter ones, while hydrocracking added hydrogen to produce products with lower carbon to hydrogen ratios. Other processes included thermal cracking, hydrofining, reforming, and alkalization.

The chief products emerging from these processes included the so-called "light products," the lightest fractions, such as liquefied petroleum gas (LPG), gasoline, aviation fuel, and petroleum solvents; the middle distillates, including kerosene, heating oil, waxes, and diesel fuel; and the heaviest fractions such as asphalts (bitumens) and residual fuel oil, used in industry and power generation. The type of products a given refinery produced depended more on geographical location, customer demand, and seasonal needs than technical capability.

In addition to fuels and oils, refineries produced "intermediate" products such as ethanol, styrene, ethyl chloride, butadiene, and methanol. These intermediates were mostly used in the manufacture of plastics, but they were also needed for antifreeze, synthetic fibers and rubbers, and detergents.

BACKGROUND AND DEVELOPMENT

Petroleum was, quite literally, the fuel that drove modern industrial society, supplying nearly half of the world's total supply of energy. Automobiles, tractors, trucks, aircraft, and ships were powered by petroleum derivatives such as gasoline, kerosene, and diesel oil. Homes and offices were heated by fuel oil and natural gas or by petroleum-generated electricity. Plastics, paints, fertilizers, insecticides, soaps, and synthetic rubber all used petroleum as a raw material. Even synthetic fibers in clothing were derived from petroleum products.

Petroleum was used since ancient times to waterproof boats and repair roads. It also served as a medicine, an ointment, an incendiary, and an illuminant. Serious exploitation of petroleum did not begin until the 1850s, however, when the rising price of lamp oil (derived from whale blubber) prompted a search for a cheap and convenient substitute.

In 1854, a young New York lawyer named George Bissell and some partners formed the world's first petroleum company—the Pennsylvania Rock Oil Company—and began exploiting oil seeps (underground deposits of oil and gas that escape to the surface) around Titusville, Pennsylvania. In 1859 the Pennsylvania Rock Oil Company drilled the world's first well in Titusville, Pennsylvania. Soon after, numerous small operators sprang up throughout the United States, distilling kerosene from crude oil, distributing it in barrels, and selling it by the gallon in retail stores. Oil production began in Russia at about the same time. For the rest of the century, the United States and Russia dominated world production.

In the United States, the era of independent oil producers was short-lived. Most of the nation's refineries were bought up by John D. Rockefeller, who by the late 1870s exercised almost total control over the industry. The Rockefeller monopoly eventually fell victim to the Sherman Antitrust Act (1890), and in 1911, after years of wrangling, Rockefeller's Standard Oil trust was broken up into 34 separate companies.

The rise of the oil industry was closely tied to the emergence of the automobile. While Rockefeller was consolidating control over the American petroleum industry, a Belgian inventor named Etienne Lenoir was developing the first internal combustion engine. By 1885 the first gasoline-powered vehicles hit the road in Germany, and by 1899, more than 30 different manufacturers were producing and selling motor vehicles in the United States. Gasoline, once a useless by-product of the refining process, suddenly became a valuable commodity. The growing popularity of the automobile and the development of an automated production system by Henry Ford in 1914 ensured a growing market for gasoline—a market which, as late as 1997, accounted for 42.3 percent of total U.S. consumption of refined oil products and 28.4 percent of world consumption.

By the late 1930s, the United States had risen to a dominant position in the international trade of oil and refined petroleum products. Outside the United States, only the Dutch/British conglomerate Royal Dutch Shell and Britain's Anglo-Persian Oil Company (now British Petroleum) could compete with the five major U.S. oil companies (Exxon, Mobil, Chevron, Texaco, and Amoco). Known as the "Seven Sisters," these powerful companies controlled the oil fields, refineries, pipelines, and tankers.

The dynamic growth of the U.S. refining industry in the 1920s and 1930s was fueled by vast reserves of petroleum and natural gas and also by the development of advanced thermal and catalytic oil-cracking processes, which in turn stimulated the growth of the petrochemical industry. With the advent of World War II, demand for fuels of all types—especially aviation gasoline—surged, leading to a concomitant expansion of refinery capacity.

After the war, rapid economic growth and pent-up consumer demand kept the refineries running at full capacity. Cheap oil began pouring out of the Middle East, leading to the rapid replacement by petroleum of fuels such as coal and the proliferation of automobiles in western Europe, North America, and Japan. Demand for gasoline, in particular, soared, and from 1951 to 1970 the oil industry enjoyed annual growth rates of seven percent per year, with world production increasing from 12 to 46 million barrels per day. At the same time, growth in the European and Japanese industries began to narrow the U.S. lead in petroleum refining. By the 1970s, many other oil-producing nations, such as Saudi Arabia, Iran, Canada, and Venezuela, were also refining petroleum on a large scale.

Starting in the late 1970s, growth in world demand for refined petroleum products slowed considerably and even fell in 1979 for the first time since the Great Depression. Initially, this slowdown was precipitated by the 1973 Arab oil embargo, which spurred many oil-consuming nations to seek ways to offset the influence of the Organization of Petroleum Exporting Countries (OPEC) on prices and production. Europe and Japan, in particular, accelerated development of alternative sources of energy and attempted to increase the energy efficiency of automobiles.

By the early 1990s, global production of refined petroleum products was roughly 65 million barrels per day, of which nearly 80 percent was in the form of fuel. Gasoline alone accounted for nearly 27 percent of production worldwide and more than 40 percent of American production. Another 47 percent of world production was taken up by distillate and residual fuel oil. Of the remainder, jet fuel accounted for 6.1 percent, liquefied petroleum gases for 3.6 percent, kerosene for 2.5 percent, and lubricants for 1.1 percent.

The petroleum refining industry—particularly in North America—trod an uncertain path, facing both declining profits and increasing costs. In the United States, profits fell to a five-year low in 1992 while the costs of upgrading and research rose 8.3 percent in the same period. As the decade progressed, prospects did not brighten. Following a five-year average decline of 4.8 percent in sales by integrated international refineries, 1996 sales fell by 6.0 percent. These trends were reflected in most of the industrialized world, pushing many of the major oil companies and larger independents to focus more attention on the rapidly industrializing countries of Southeast Asia and Latin America.

For smaller independents, international expansion was not an option, and many went out of business. The number of refineries in the United States fell from 319 in 1980 to 202 in 1992. Twelve more refineries, all with capacities of less than 50,000 barrels a day, shut down in 1992 as cost pressures on surviving independents continued relentlessly. Although the problems of smaller U.S. refiners were aggravated by the recession of the early 1990s, the most difficult problem facing them was the Clean Air Act (CAA). While the large, integrated companies were able to procure the capital necessary for plant reconfigurations, product reformulation, and research and development, the smaller refineries—faced with greater investments on a per-barrel basis—found it enormously difficult to obtain the funds necessary to compete.

The source of much of the refining industry's misery, the CAA called for the 39 U.S. cities with the highest carbon monoxide levels to begin substituting oxygenated gasoline for winter use in November 1992. In 1995, the nine worst cases—Baltimore, Chicago, Hartford, Houston, Los Angeles, Milwaukee, New York, Philadelphia, and San Diego—were required to begin using gasoline that fully met the CAA's Phase I specifications. This reformulated gasoline was required to have a minimum oxygen content of 2 percent by weight with a maximum aromatics content not to exceed 25 percent (including a maximum of one percent benzene by volume), and no heavy metals. Nitrogen-oxide levels were to remain the same or less than 1990 levels, and tailpipe emissions of volatile organic compounds and toxins were to be reduced by 15 percent.

For refiners, these regulations could not have come at a worse time. Not only were margins shrinking as overall demand fell, the quality of crude oil inputs was declining just as the demand for higher quality outputs increased. This situation created an additional cost pressure as more investments were required to process the low-grade crude. Moreover, the new regulations hampered product interchangeability between seasons, geographical areas, and applications, pushing up costs everywhere. The cost to refiners of implementing the Phase I reformulations alone was expected to run from US$3 billion to US$5 billion. Estimates for upcoming compliance costs were as high as US$20 billion, as U.S. refiners faced four more major amendments of the Clean Air Act slated to go into effect by the early twenty-first century.

The difficulties within the refining industry were not confined to the United States. In Canada, petroleum refiners reeled under the impact of slumping demand, overcapacity, and stricter environmental controls. During the first six months of 1991, Canada's leading oil companies—Imperial Oil, Shell Canada, and Petro-Canada—all posted losses, and by 1992, all had announced plant closures. Outside North America, refiners faced similar difficulties. The onset of the Asian financial crisis in late 1997 dampened demand for petroleum products worldwide, providing additional hurdles for refiners to overcome.

While the CAA affected only the refining industry in the United States, a more global regulatory threat appeared late in 1997. In December, an international climate change conference held in Kyoto, Japan produced the Kyoto Protocol on Climate Change, which aimed to curb the emission of greenhouse gases, much of which resulted from the use of refined petroleum. By May of 1998, the European Union had signed the protocol, but the treaty faced considerable opposition in the United States, especially with the Republican control of the U.S. Congress.

The difficult operating environment for refining companies in the 1990s led to a series of mergers, acquisitions, and alliances that profoundly changed the shape of the entire industry. In February of 1996, British Petroleum and Mobil entered into a joint venture that merged the two companies' European refining and marketing operations, creating an entity in the top three in both gasoline and lubricants in Europe. In 1997 alone, the two companies expected to save US$100 million to US$150 million from eliminating redundant operations and cutting overlapping staff.

Similar cost savings were expected from other combinations. Texaco and Royal Dutch/Shell combined their downstream operations in the western and Midwestern United States in 1997. They then extended the venture into a coast-to-coast refining and marketing enterprise through a 1998 joint venture with Saudi Arabian Oil Company involving downstream operations in the eastern United States and along the Gulf Coast. All told, this three-company combination included 12 refineries and controlled 11.4 percent of overall U.S. refinery capacity. Although no refineries were expected to be closed as a result of this joint venture, pretax savings were expected to run as high as US$800 million.

Consolidation continued into the late 1990s as oil giants remained focused on cutting costs. The 1999 merger that formed Exxon Mobil had resulted in US$4.6 billion in cost savings by 2001. The deal also helped to boost sales in 2000 to US$232.7 billion, making Exxon Mobil the largest company in the United States, as well as the largest oil company in the world, a position previously held by Royal Dutch/Shell. The firm's US$17.7 billion in profits that year were the highest ever recorded in U.S. business history. Other major deals included the US$57 billion merging of British Petroleum and Amoco Corp. to form BP Amoco in 1998, as well as the US$26.8 billion stock purchase of Atlantic Richfield by BP Amoco, subsequently known as BP, in 2000. Along with positioning British Petroleum second among global oil industry leaders, the consolidation also resulted in economies of scale worth an estimated US$6 billion. In 2001, Chevron and Texaco joined forces to create ChevronTexaco Corp., the second largest oil company in the United States and the fourth largest in the world. The world's fifth largest integrated oil player is also the result of consolidation. Total Fina Elf was formed in 2000 when Total Fina, the result of a merger between France-based Total and Belgium's PetroFina in 1999, acquired Elf Aquitaine, also based in France.

The industry was also beset in the 1990s by strict new environmental regulations that required enormous investments in research and facilities. Some of the toughest regulations—the Clean Air Act Amendments of the 1990s, for example—were enacted in the United States, resulting in a spate of refinery closures and the collapse of some smaller independent refining companies. Similar problems faced refiners around the world, and the 1990s saw one of the most dramatic shakeouts in the history of the oil business. Once the tumult subsided, however, the survivors emerged fitter and more prosperous than ever.

The late 1990s brought another regulatory threat to industry players in the form of the Kyoto Protocol on Climate Change adopted in December 1997 in Kyoto, Japan, which aimed to curb the emission of greenhouse gases, much of which resulted from the use of refined petroleum, to levels well below those of 1990 by 2012. Despite opposition from the U.S. Republican Party, as well as public denouncement by U.S. President George W. Bush, the protocol was finalized in November of 2001. Many industry experts point out, however, that the environmental impact of the protocol will be somewhat compromised by the lack of U.S. participation.

In many cases, to gain regulatory approval for their deals, firms like Exxon Mobil had agreed to divest a portion of their refining operations. As a result, independent refining firms like Valero Energy Corp. were able to increase their capacity by purchasing these refineries. In addition, many leading refiners, particularly in the United States, continued to grow larger by following a consolidation trend that mirrored the activities of the largest oil companies. Valero, the largest independent oil refiner in the United States with 2001 sales of nearly US$15 billion and earnings of US$564 million, acquired Ultramar Diamond Shamrock at the end of 2001, increasing its number of refineries from 6 to 12 and upping its combined production capacity to 2 million barrels per day. The US$9.8 billion acquisition of Tosco by Phillips Petroleum was considered the largest downstream deal of 2001. In fact, although the value of total global energy merger and acquisition activity fell from US$264.4 billion in 2000 to US$243.5 billion in 2001, the value of downstream mergers and acquisitions, boosted by the major U.S. deals, grew from US$19.9 billion to US$35.4 billion over the same time period.

Of the 761 refineries in operation in 2000, 158 were located in the United States, 95 in China, 35 in Japan, 33 in Russia, and 17 each in India, Germany, and Italy. North America led the world in refining capacity, followed by Asia and Western Europe. Despite seeing improved profit margins in 2000 and 2001—due to improved economic conditions in Asia, which bolstered demand; prosperous economies in both North America and Asia; and aggressive cost cutting efforts—refiners remained concerned about the costs associated with adhering to increasingly stringent environmental regulations like the Kyoto Protocol and later phases of the Clean Air Act. However, one sector of the petroleum refining industry, the catalyst market, expected to benefit from these regulations. Forecasted to grow at an estimated rate of nearly 4 percent per year through 2005, the catalyst market was worth US$1.1 billion in 2000. According to a June 2001 issue of *The Oil and Gas Journal,* growth in catalysts was largely the result of "increasing demand for reformulated and other, less-polluting gasoline mandated by the Clean Air Act Amendments of 1990, plus new regulations calling for reductions in sulfur content in gasoline and diesel fuel."

CURRENT CONDITIONS

By 2003, despite the highest prices in two decades, worldwide consumption had hit 78.1 million barrels per day (b/d), with Asia and the Pacific Rim accounting for the highest growth percentages. China alone commanded more than 40 percent of the growth in total market demand worldwide. Russia was a leader in production, with more than 40 percent of the growth worldwide since the late 1990s. Global oil reserves were estimated at 1.15 billion barrels. By mid-2004, crude prices reached more than US$40 per barrel and by mid-2005, soared to more than US$50 per barrel, almost doubling since 2001, and hitting a record US$58 per barrel in April of 2005.

Producers in 2005 were under tremendous political pressure from consuming nations to bring down oil prices and were pumping close to capacity so that refiners and other buyers could boost supplies in times of increased demand. Despite an increase in the flow of oil, inadequate capacity at U.S. refineries was a major factor in the gas problem of the mid-2000s and sites for new refineries were proposed while the U.S. increasingly relied on imported gas. Since 1976, demand for gas in the U.S. has grown by about one-third but no new refineries have been constructed. Some 325 refineries existed in the U.S. in 1981 with only about 150 remaining as of the mid-2000s, but due to the expansion of existing plants, capacity has fallen only 11 percent. The International Energy Agency predicted a global demand increase of 1.81 million b/d during 2005, upping earlier forecasts due to increased demand in China and North America.

In the mid-2000s, the industry was taking a proactive role in environmentally friendly manufacturing and production practice. Industry giant BP led the way in 1997, and by 2003 had the image of a paradoxically green refiner, with its wildly successful "Beyond Petroleum" and "BP on the Street" campaigns. Royal Dutch/Shell also had success with its ad campaigns showcasing the company's respect for marine environments. ExxonMobil, on the other hand, was slow to catch on, and by the time the company started running its own green ads in 2004, there were boycotts of Exxon products and services in some countries.

With the worldwide focus growing more and more toward environmentally friendly industry practices, the refiners were anxiously watching the U.S. Environmental Protection Agency's policies for clean diesel, set to go into effect in 2006. Among other concerns was that of the potential lack of available supply of pure diesel, making compliance with new regulations prohibitively difficult.

RESEARCH AND TECHNOLOGY

For many years, the driving force behind innovations in petroleum refining technology was cost reduction. Increasing yields and purity and boosting efficiency were the focus of industry research and development. In the 1990s, however, environmental concerns became increasingly important, promoted both by industry self-interest and government regulation. These two considerations—cutting costs and reducing environmental damage—were not always at odds with one another; in many cases, they overlapped. Operational integrations that improved heat transfer efficiency or reduced energy requirements saved money and were beneficial to the environment.

One aspect of pollution prevention—the search for an efficient means to produce the complex reformulated gasoline mandated by the U.S. Clean Air Act—prompted several technological advances involving four-carbon compounds such as butylene, isobutane, and isobutylene. Less harmful than the six-carbon aromatics such as benzene that were previously used in gasoline, these compounds could be combined with methanol to form oxygenates, which could provide the oxygen needed in the new gasoline standard. Of these possible oxygenates, methyl tertiary butyl ether

(MTBE)—a combination of isobutylene and methanol—was most promising.

Among the technologies developed was a system that integrated the isomerization of n-butene to isobutylene with an MTBE catalytic distillation process. This highly versatile system also allowed ethanol to be substituted for methanol to produce ethyl tertiary butyle ether (ETBE). Substituting the five-carbon compound isoamylene for isobutylene enabled production of tertiary amyl butyl ether (TAME)—a product also expected to be important in future gasoline formulations and which boasted an even higher octane content than MTBE.

As in other industries, the ability of computers to rapidly record, compile, and recall enormous volumes of data prompted rapid improvements in efficiency. Computers could measure, monitor, and control refinery processes with pinpoint precision, while their modeling and diagramming capabilities made it possible to develop new processes more quickly and refine existing ones. With the help of ever-more sophisticated computers, petroleum refiners were expected to be able to develop more efficient, less toxic fuels and create new, high-value-added products.

The ability to develop a safer, more diverse range of products was essential for the survival of the petroleum refining industry. With demand for refined products in the developing world unlikely to offset continued slow growth in industrialized countries and with rapid development of alternative energy sources, the oil industry's dominance of the world energy market was expected to decline by the turn of the century. Only by changing and adapting could the industry expect to enjoy success in the twenty-first century.

WORKFORCE

Petroleum refining has not been a labor-intensive industry. Implementation of most of the processes involved required a complex array of machinery, not personnel. Operations were monitored and controlled by computers that in turn were operated and monitored by skilled technicians. Refinery workers analyzed data, made adjustments to machinery as necessary, repaired equipment, and checked output. Mechanical engineers were employed to improve and develop new machinery. Chemical engineers analyzed and monitored the cracking processes. Scientists worked to develop new techniques and products. The overall level of skill required for refinery workers necessitated that management—at least at the plant level—was frequently drawn from the engineering ranks and thus had a better understanding of, and relationship with, employees.

The increasing automation of refining operations combined with the drastic streamlining measures undertaken in the early 1990s by most refiners and the merging of downstream operations in the later 1990s resulted in a steady reduction in the labor force. Amoco alone dropped 8,500 workers from its payroll in 1992, and dozens of other companies followed suit. Plant closures and downsizing resulted in large numbers of workers being laid off in many countries, with no prospects of rehiring.

Nevertheless, this restructuring had its positive side. In 1993, a trend-setting, three-year arrangement was made in the United States between the major oil refiners and the Union of Oil, Chemical, and Atomic Workers. According to the *Monthly Labor Review,* the deal "struck a new balance between the union's goal of improved wages and benefits, safety concerns, and a national health care program and the companies' desire to contain costs and retain operational flexibility." Meanwhile, in Britain, BP sought to revitalize itself by giving individuals more responsibility and by replacing hierarchically structured departments with smaller, more flexible teams that had open, informal lines of communication. Similar initiatives were launched by Canada's Imperial Oil, which gained a reputation for its support of education and its innovative employee assistance programs. However, as large refining firms continued to consolidate in an effort to cut costs and as the number of refineries continued to dwindle in the early 2000s, employment prospects in petroleum refining were not encouraging.

INDUSTRY LEADERS

BP PLC

While Exxon and Shell jostled for dominance of the oil industry in the mid-1990s, Britain's largest company, British Petroleum (BP), quietly held on to its position as the world's third largest international oil company. By 2004, the company was number one worldwide, with sales of more than US$285 billion and a daily capacity of 3.4 million oil barrels.

Another leading oil refining and marketing company in the mid-1990s was Chicago-based Amoco, the fifth largest U.S. oil company with revenues of US$31.9 billion in 1997. The bulk of Amoco's total sales was derived from its refining, marketing, and transportation operations. Amoco supplied products to approximately 9,300 gasoline retail outlets in the eastern, midwestern, and southeastern United States. In the mid-1990s, Amoco underwent a restructuring that was designed to cut expenses and increase flexibility by making individual business units more autonomous. With about 87 percent of its revenues derived in North America, the company also began placing more emphasis on overseas markets, particularly newly opened markets such as China.

The 1998 merger of British Petroleum and Amoco pushed Shell further down the list among the largest oil companies in the world. BP Amoco found itself in the second place spot, a position it cemented in 2000 with its purchases of Atlantic Richfield and Burmah Castrol. Eventually, the name Amoco was dropped from the BP moniker. Sales in 2001 grew 18.5 percent to US$175.4 billion, while earnings surged 32.5 percent to US$8 billion, US$2.2 billion of which was attributed to U.S. refining and marketing operations. With more than 107,000 employees, BP was the leading producer of oil and gas in the United States, and its refining capacity totaled 2.9 million b/d. Plans in 2002 included boosting its refining operations in Germany by acquiring a controlling stake in Veba Oil. In 2003 the company had an interest in TNK-Russia.

EXXON MOBIL CORPORATION

The offspring of Standard Oil, the Exxon Corporation spent the majority of the 1990s vying with Shell for the number one spot in the industry. By 2004, Exxon was the world's second largest oil company—behind BP, not Shell— posting sales of approximately US$263.99 billion. The company had a daily 6.3 million barrel capacity that year. Unlike Shell, Exxon's control over vast stocks of crude oil meant that its earnings from refining and marketing were barely one-third of what it obtained from the production of crude.

Mobil Corporation, another company born of the breakup of Standard Oil Trust, recorded sales of US$58.4 billion in 1997. The world's fourth largest oil company, Mobil owned more than 20 refineries in 12 countries and operated about 18,400 service stations in more than 90 countries. Refining and marketing operations accounted for US$55.01 billion in sales.

When Exxon and Mobil merged to form Exxon Mobil in 1999, a new industry leader was born. After reaching a peak of US$232.7 billion in 2000, sales declined 6.8 percent to US$212.9 billion the following year. Earnings also declined, after reaching an unprecedented US$17.7 billion in 2000, to US$15.5 billion in 2001. Exxon Mobil's refining capacity is roughly 6 million b/d. Employees total 123,000.

The brainchild of John D. Rockefeller, Exxon began in 1882 as the Standard Oil Company of New Jersey (Jersey Standard), which was part of the mammoth Standard Oil Trust. The largest of the companies created after the disbanding of the Standard Oil Trust in 1911, Jersey Standard rapidly expanded its overseas production and marketing activities. By 1954 it had become the largest oil company in the world. In 1972 the company changed its name to Exxon to end confusion with other companies still using the Standard Oil name.

Exxon's slide from preeminence began in the 1970s as nationalization of oil assets previously held by producing companies reduced the company's access to oil. With its reserves shrinking, Exxon's dependence on crude oil for the bulk of its sales slowed the company's growth, allowing Shell to replace it as the world's leading oil company during the 1980s. A further blow to both the company's reputation and its balance sheet was the notorious *Exxon Valdez* oil spill off the coast of Alaska in 1989. By 1992 the disaster had cost Exxon more than US$6 billion in criminal damages and cleanup costs. In mid-1994, a federal jury found that the company and the tanker's captain had caused the disaster through recklessness and fined Exxon US$5 billion. The company formally appealed this judgment in 1997. Four years later, a U.S. Circuit Court of Appeals found the fine excessive and mandated that the Alaskan state court lower the fine.

In the 1990s, Exxon focused on lowering costs and selling non-strategic assets. Writing off the U.S. market as mature, the company concentrated its refining and marketing investments in the Asia/Pacific region and explored opportunities in the new markets of Eastern Europe. After its merger with Mobil, Exxon Mobil worked to cut costs and continued to expand its presence in emerging markets.

ROYAL DUTCH/SHELL GROUP

After decades of taking second place to Exxon, Shell emerged in the 1990s as the world's largest petroleum and natural gas company with sales of US$128.7 billion in 1997. By 2003, the company had slipped to number three. Operations included 47 refineries. A partnership of Dutch (Royal Dutch Petroleum) and British ("Shell" Transport and Trading) parent companies that shared a 60/40 interest in the group's holding companies, Shell was the leading employer in the industry with 101,000 employees in more than 100 countries worldwide. By 2000, however, the firm's work force had fallen to 90,000. Sales in 2001 fell 9.3 percent to US$135.0 billion, but by 2003 they had risen to US$201.7 billion. Group leadership alternated between the two parent companies, which maintained headquarters in The Hague and London. For the most part, however, Shell's overseas subsidiaries operated almost entirely independently of the parent companies and were giant international corporations in their own right.

In 1997, Shell entered into two joint ventures with Texaco and Saudi Arabian Oil Company that together formed the largest refining and marketing operation in the United States. The new venture ran 12 refineries, handling 11.4 percent of overall U.S. refinery capacity, and almost 26,000 gas stations, commanding a market share of 17.5 percent. Shell's refining, marketing, and transporting activities accounted for about 80 percent of its total business in 1997, with the company deriving 46 percent of its sales from Europe, 22 percent from the United States, 19 percent from Asia, and the remaining 13 percent from other countries in the Western Hemisphere. In the late 1990s, however, downstream activities like refining and marketing, particularly in the United States, were largely overlooked in favor of upstream ventures.

In 2001, only US$500 million of Shell's US$10.8 billion in earnings was attributable to U.S. refining and marketing operations. To bolster its presence in this area, the firm acquired the oil refining operations of Motiva and Equilon from ChevronTexaco in 2002. However, some analysts believed the firm was too late to take advantage of the industry's improved profit margins, which had already begun to decline as recessionary economic conditions in the United States continued.

CHEVRONTEXACO CORP.

Formed by the 2001 merger of California-based Chevron and New York-based Texaco, ChevronTexaco is the fourth largest integrated oil company in the world. To gain regulatory approval for the deal, ChevronTexaco agreed to sell its Motiva and Equilon oil refining operations to Royal Dutch/Shell. The majority of the firm's remaining refining operations are housed in its Caltex subsidiary, formerly a joint venture between Chevron and Texaco. The company reported 2004 sales of US$142.89 billion.

Founded in 1902 by "Buckskin Joe" Cullinan to exploit oil discoveries in Texas, The Texas Company rapidly expanded across the globe. In 1936, it formed Caltex with Standard of California, and the two companies used their combined resources to exploit Standard's discoveries in Saudi Arabia and overseas marketing. Also in the 1930s, The

Texas Company became the first oil company to operate service stations in the United States. Renamed Texaco in 1959, the company lost ground to other oil companies as U.S. wells dried up in the 1960s and 1970s and overseas supplies were lost to third world nationalizations. The company's position was further undermined in 1983 when it purchased Getty Oil for US$8.6 billion only to find out that Getty had already agreed to an acquisition by Pennzoil. Ordered to pay Pennzoil US$10.53 billion in damages, Texaco sought bankruptcy protection in 1987, agreeing to a US$3.0 billion settlement with Pennzoil later that year. By 1989, after selling off its West German subsidiary and Texaco Canada (1988), as well as unloading 2,500 unprofitable gas stations, Texaco had recovered sufficiently to launch a refining and marketing joint venture, Star Enterprise, with Saudi Arabian Oil Company (Saudi Aramco).

In the 1990s Texaco's 50-50 refining and marketing joint venture with Chevron—Caltex Petroleum—began upgrading refineries and improving its marketing network in the Asia-Pacific region. Texaco's U.S. refining and marketing businesses were operated within joint ventures with Royal Dutch/Shell and Saudi Aramco. Texaco also divested its non-core chemical operations in the 1990s in order to focus additional resources on petroleum.

Chevron, another one-time Standard Oil subsidiary, was originally named the Standard Oil Company of California—or Socal—and like many of its other ex-Standard stablemates, quickly established itself as a major international company. In the 1930s, Socal gained drilling concessions to oil fields in Bahrain and Saudi Arabia that proved so vast, the company brought in Texaco to help market the crude. The company they formed—Caltex (California Texas Oil Company)—remained a prime source of revenue for both companies throughout the remainder of the century. Renamed Chevron in 1984, the company engaged in extensive restructuring in the early 1990s, announcing plans in 1993 to sell refineries in Texas and Pennsylvania, while at the same time building a refinery in Thailand and expanding refineries in Singapore and Korea. Further restructuring in 1997 resulted in the sale of a refinery and 450 service stations in the United Kingdom to Royal Dutch/Shell.

TOTAL S.A.

Formerly Total Fina Elf, the largest oil company in France with 1997 revenues of US$42.3 billion and 2004 revenues of US$166.2 billion, Total S.A. derived more than half of its sales from downstream operations. Total has reserves of 11.1 barrels of oil and operates in more than 100 countries, with 28 refineries and more than 16,000 Total, Elf, or Fina brand gas stations, primarily in Europe and Africa. Formerly majority-owned by the French government, Elf was fully privatized by 1996 and was aggressively seeking acquisitions in the mid-1990s—but mainly for its chemicals unit, which is responsible for about 20 percent of overall revenues.

Total operated refineries throughout Europe and ran 4,763 service stations in Europe, 2,345 in Africa, and 771 elsewhere in 1997. The French government also held a substantial stake in Total for a long period of the company's history, but by 1997 the government held an interest of less than one percent. After acquiring Belgium's Petrofina in 1999, Total changed its name to Total Fina. The following year, Total Fina acquired Elf Aquitaine to form Total Fina Elf S.A., the fifth largest oil firm in the world. As a result of the merger, sales grew 153 percent to US$107.89 billion, while earnings soared 324 percent to US$6.5 billion. Employees totaled 45,500.

MAJOR COUNTRIES IN THE INDUSTRY

The petroleum refining industry was one of the first to become truly international in scope. Originally concentrated in or near the oil fields, the industry later shifted to the major consuming nations to avoid the dangers of political instability in producing nations. Cheap oil and larger crude tankers made this move feasible. More recently, erosion of OPEC's ability to sustain high prices for its crude oil led exporting nations to build large refineries in their own countries and to invest in existing refining operations in industrialized countries. Saudi Arabia's Arabian-American Oil Company (Aramco), for example, gained control over 50 percent of Texaco's refining business in Texas, while PEMEX, Mexico's state-owned oil company, entered into a joint venture in 1993 with Shell Oil Company to upgrade Shell's refinery in Deer Park, Texas. Meanwhile, U.S. firms were actively building facilities in Southeast Asia and Africa and Shell was adding capacity in the Pacific Rim and Latin America.

Global production of refined petroleum products in 2004 was 71.72 million barrels per day (b/d). North America led the way in refinery production, followed by the Asia-Pacific region, Europe, the Middle East, Central and South America, the former Soviet Union, and Africa. The largest single producer was the United States, followed by Russia, Japan, and China. Consumption of refined petroleum products followed a similar pattern, although consumption exceeded production in both North America and Asia. Between them, the United States, the former Soviet Union, and Japan accounted for 40 percent of world consumption in the mid-1990s, although China's consumption had increased dramatically by the end of the decade. In fact, China's oil imports, including refined petroleum products, grew from less than 30 million tons in 1998 to nearly 70 million tons in 2000. With energy consumption levels second only to those in the United States and a forecasted consumption growth rate of 4 percent annually throughout the early 2000s, China was considered a key growth market for petroleum refiners.

Although dozens of U.S. refineries were shut down during the 1990s and early 2000s, overall U.S. production and capacity did not drop significantly as expansion and upgrading of surviving facilities picked up the slack. In many cases, refineries sold by U.S. companies were purchased by foreign "upstream" operations seeking to diversify their business. Moreover, because the difficulties of the petroleum industry in the United States were paralleled in other leading producers—notably Canada and western Europe—the U.S. share of the world market remained stable throughout the 1990s. U.S. crude oil distillation capacity totaled 16.5 million b/d in the early 2000s, compared to 6.7 million b/d in Russia, 4.9 million b/d in Japan, and 4.3 million b/d in China. Given the relative saturation of North American and European petroleum markets, leading U.S. refiners focused increasing attention on new markets in eastern Europe and Southeast Asia.

FURTHER READING

"BP Releases 'Statistical Review of World Energy 2004.'" *EERE Network News,* 16 June 2004.

Draper, Deborah J., ed. *Business Rankings Annual.* Detroit: Thomson Gale, 2004.

"Energy Markets Turbulent But Strong in 2003." *BP Web Site,* 15 June 2004. Available from http://www.bp.com.

"Global Output Struggles to Meet Demand." *World Oil,* February 2005.

Greenberg, Karl. "Gas Companies Blend Profits, Messages of Saving Nature." *Brandweek,* 21 June 2004.

———. "More Green than Ever Before (Petrol)." *Brandweek,* 23 June 2003.

"Hoover's Company Capsules." 2005. Available from http://www.hoovers.com.

"IEA Raises Global Demand Forecast." *Global Markets,* 14 March 2005.

"International Trade Statistics." 2003. Available from http://www.wto.org.

Lazich, Robert S., ed. *Market Share Reporter.* Detroit: Thomson Gale, 2004.

Lorenzetti, Maureen. "Lower Expectations." *The Oil and Gas Journal,* 23 September 2002.

"M&A Value Dropped in 2001." *The Oil Daily,* 17 January 2002.

"Oil Giants Face New Competition For Future Supply; Big Players Focus on Returns As Rivals Undercut Them; Limping Away From Libya." *The Wall Street Journal,* 19 April 2005.

"Petroleum Refining in France, Germany, UK, US." *Euromonitor,* August 2004. Available from http://www.majormarketprofiles.com.

Roberts, Dexter, and Mark L. Clifford. "China: Hungry for Energy." *Business Week,* 24 December 2001. Available from http://www.businessweek.com.

Schwartz, Nelson D. "Inside the Head of BP." *Fortune* 26 July 2004.

"Steep Weekly Rises in U.S. Oil Supply Cuts Price 4.8 Percent." *New York Times,* 28 April 2005.

"US Sales." *The Oil and Gas Journal,* 4 June 2001.

PROFESSIONAL SERVICES

SIC 8721
NAICS 541211

ACCOUNTING, AUDITING, AND BOOKKEEPING SERVICES

Industry firms furnish accounting, bookkeeping, and related auditing services to organizations and individuals. Although accounting firms may offer data processing as part of their service, companies that provide strictly financial data processing services, such as for corporate payroll, are treated separately under the heading **Data Processing Services.**

INDUSTRY SNAPSHOT

Accounting, auditing, and bookkeeping are three dimensions of a single broad industry. Together, they provide businesses and individuals with the financial information they need to maintain stability and gauge and interpret fiscal health. Accountants and auditors perform a range of functions such as financial record keeping and analysis, business advising, and auditing for diverse employers or clients such as large corporations, non-profit organizations, government agencies, small companies, and wealthy individuals. In contrast, bookkeepers typically work in smaller firms, performing the financial record keeping for the companies for whom they work. Additional duties of bookkeepers may include producing financial statements and reports, preparing bank deposits and payroll checks, purchasing, and invoicing.

Rapid globalization of the accounting industry has accompanied the general globalization of commerce; major accountancy firms have grown from small national partnerships to multinational enterprises. Around the world, four large, multinational accounting and auditing firms dominated the industry in 2005. The "Big Four," ranked in order by 2004 revenue were Deloitte Touche Tohmatsu with revenues of US$16.4 billion, PricewaterhouseCoopers with US$16.3 billion, Ernst & Young International with US$14.5 billion, and KPMG International with US$13.4 billion.

The biggest change to hit the financial sector in decades was the *Sarbanes-Oxley Act* of 2002. The result of several large corporate scandals involving Enron, Arthur Andersen, and WorldCom, the Act set out criminal and civil penalties for securities violations, required auditors to be independent of their clients and increased the amount of disclosure required regarding financial statements, insider trading and executive compensation. Accounting firms saw themselves forced into a position of having to separate their auditing business from their consulting business in order to comply with the Act's independence requirements. The Act's new rules have also meant an increase in the requirements of firms and its auditors, and this in turn has meant increased costs. These increases have led many companies to move away from the Big Four accounting firms; in 2004 each of the Big Four lost more customers than they gained.

ORGANIZATION AND STRUCTURE

Most accounting firms are structured as partnerships rather than as corporations. In a corporation, the shareholders own the company but are financially liable only for the value of their vested interest. In a partnership, the partners are considered the firm's owners and bear unlimited personal liability for the firm. In most cases, firms are structured as partnerships for tax benefits—partnerships are not required to disclose profits. Accountants and auditors often draw criticism for their firms' structures. Critics argue that accountants—who owe their existence to public laws and are charged with the dissemination of financial information—should disclose more information about their businesses than they are currently required to do.

Most large accounting firms, with many offices across a country or around the world, have structures similar to co-operatives, where each firm is treated as a member of the organization, with each being treated as a separate and independent legal entity.

As defined by the U.S. Department of Labor there are four major fields of accounting: public accounting, management accounting, government accounting and auditing, and internal auditing.

Public accountants work for clients to provide a variety of accounting, tax, auditing and consulting services. While most public accountants specialize in one area, they may work for large accountancies that provide the full spectrum of services. Public accountants may also be involved with forensic accounting. They generally have a strong understanding of law, and are involved in investigating white collar crimes, bankruptcies, and contract disputes. Legislation enacted in 2002 now restricts the advice public accountants can give to clients if they are also involved with auditing their clients' financial statements.

Management accountants are also known by a host of other names: cost accountants, industrial accountants, corporate accountants and private accountants. Generally, they work for a company or organization directly, providing information necessary for internal management to make the decisions necessary to operate their companies, including those decisions relating to costs, performance, budgets and asset management.

Government accountants and auditors are public sector workers who ensure that government agencies, the private sector and individuals meet the requirements of regulations and taxation. Internal auditors are responsible for checking the accuracy of their organizations' financial records. Their work has increasingly involved the auditing and control of information technology systems used within a company.

In the 1990s accounting professionals moved increasingly toward the management side of the industry. However, outsourced consulting services already were being scaled back before the Enron scandal of 2002 hit because of problems in perceived, actual, or potential conflicts of interest between those hired from auditing firms to check the books of corporations and issue financial reports, and those who stood to make lucrative gains by working closely with corporate insiders as management consultants.

Accounting involves all management functions of an organization, including purchasing, manufacturing, wholesaling, retailing, and a variety of marketing and transportation activities. Senior accountants—or controllers armed with financial and accounting knowledge of their business—are often selected as production or marketing executives. Accounting firms rely on two major financial statements—the income statement and the balance sheet—to interpret the financial health of businesses. To obtain these statements, accountants analyze, record, quantify, accumulate, summarize, classify, report, and interpret numerous financial events and their cumulative effect on the organization. Accounting firms help clients make informed business decisions by evaluating an organization's performance and by indicating the possible financial implications of various business plans. Solid accounting practices are thus regarded as essential ingredients in the successful operation of almost all organizations and economies.

Industry Standards and Regulations. Although participation is not always mandatory, each field of accounting has its own certification procedures. In the U.S., public accountants can become licensed by a State Board of Accountancy. The American Institute of Certified Public Accountants (AICPA) provides a certification program for public accountants (CPA) which requires them to meet specific education, experience, and ethical standards. Most states require a CPA designation in order to grant a license. In addition, only CPAs are allowed to perform the audits on public companies, which are mandatory by the Securities Exchange Commission (SEC). Other voluntary certification programs exist that can be used to show that a certain level of competency and experience has been achieved in a specific field of accountancy. In the U.S., there are Certified Management Accountant and Certified Internal Auditor designations, to name two. Almost every country has its own certification organizations, and many such certifications are now recognized around the world.

The accounting industry is supervised by a number of governmental boards in each country, with increasing calls for a set core of international standards and regulations. This is particularly the case after the industry shake-up related to the Enron failure. In the United States, accounting rules and standards are set by the Financial Accounting Standards Board (FASB). In the United Kingdom, oversight of the industry is handled by the Accounting Standards Committee (ASC). Working on a more global scale, The International Accounting Standards Board (IASB) is an independent setter of accounting standards and is based in London, England. Board members come from nine countries around the world, but are often representatives for regions or for several countries. Additionally, the World Trade Organization's Council of Trade in Services, one of the WTO's three main subcouncils, established The Committee on Financial Services which reviews and makes suggestions regarding the global trade of financial services, examining regulatory developments affecting this group. In 2002 the World Trade Organization began a new round of negotiations to examine and improve worldwide accounting standards and practices.

Such committees are responsible for defining the rules and processes that accountants and auditors must follow to present a clear and honest picture of financial situations. Most of these committees also serve as the disciplinary bodies responsible for dealing with abuses or transgressions of acceptable accounting practices.

Off-balance-sheet financing, bizarre acquisition accounting, and numerous other accounting abuses, such as the creation of offshore partnerships to hide losses and debts, were cited by critics as indications of substantial flaws in industry practices. Furthermore, an issue that had long troubled the industry was that of auditors' affiliations with the companies they are auditing. Auditors, while formally appointed by a company's shareholders, typically report their findings back to managers, even in instances where the company's financial records suggest fraudulent practices. Further, when accounting firms also serve clients in a management consulting capacity, the potential for additional conflicts of interest becomes readily apparent. As such, the industry has searched for ways to better guarantee impartiality.

One solution called for tougher enforcement of auditing and accounting procedures. In 1997, in light of costly litigation fees continuously paid out by major accounting firms, the U.S. Securities and Exchange Commission (SEC) initiated new auditing requirements demanding notification if an auditor discovered any uncorrected illegal acts. Steps had been taken already in United Kingdom in the late 1980s and 1990s to address similar issues. The Financial Reporting Review Panel, a sister body to the industry's rule-making organization, was given significant power to deter fraudulent accounting practices. Among other actions, the panel can publicly reprimand companies whose adherence to accepted standards and principles is deemed too liberal.

But the biggest regulatory change to hit the accounting field in many years has been the *Sarbanes-Oxley Act* of 2002.

Brought about to restore faith in the system following several huge financial scandals, the Act has had a huge impact on the accounting industry and corporations. Highlights include:

- Boards of Directors must have five financially literate members, including two that must have been or still are CPAs;
- It is unlawful for an auditing firm to also provide its client with non-audit services, including bookkeeping, the design of financial systems, appraisals or valuations, management functions or human resource services, brokerage or investment advice, or actuarial services;
- Auditing firms conducting more than one hundred audits each year, must be inspected annually, while all other require inspection every three years; and
- The Securities Exchange Commission was given the power to recognize the generally accepted accounting principles to be used as determined by an independent standard-setting body, with the need to keep these standards current and appropriately inline with international standards.

Britain had tightened its accounting standards after scandals in the late 1980s and early 1990s. However, all countries were talking reform in the wake of the U.S. scandals.

BACKGROUND AND DEVELOPMENT

Accounting, auditing, and bookkeeping services developed as a result of several needs. Businesses needed to track economic activity to determine and improve their economic health and to fulfill financial obligations, while stockholders and creditors such as banks desired reliable financial information on companies so that they could make informed business decisions themselves. The public accounting profession arose to serve these twin needs.

The roots of the modern accounting industry can be traced back well over 100 years to the formation of the auditing business and the development of generally accepted accounting practices (GAAP)—rules that became increasingly necessary with the rise of the multinational corporation and the introduction of complicated tax laws. However, as some industry critics pointed out in 2002, the multiple, conflicting ways in which GAAP rules have been interpreted have often produced misleading and incompatible financial statements, heightening the need for more globally accepted and implemented standards.

By the start of the twenty-first century, the leading accounting firms had become high-tech marvels, providing not only auditing services, valuations, and tax-planning strategies to the world's largest corporations but also guidance in such areas as risk management, merger and acquisition activity, corporate financing, and production. This blend was likely to change in 2002. Following the Enron affair, an irate U.S. public and Congress demanded greater transparency in industry practices and better precautions to ensure that the types of conflicts of interest that had seriously jeopardized the financial health of a number of U.S. corporations would no longer be permitted to exist.

The waters of high finance are potentially treacherous ones. Several events in the 1980s began to cast the giants of the accounting industry in an unfavorable light. "On both sides of the Atlantic," wrote the *Economist,* accountants "found it hard to resist accounting wheezes urged on companies by clever advisors keen to boost reported earnings per share. In Britain fiddles of this sort were easier because accounting standards were too flexible. But even in America, with more rigid standards, auditors were buffeted by managers insisting on flattering figures in their accounts." Criticism subsequently erupted when several major corporations went bankrupt, leaving many bewildered and unsuspecting investors with substantial losses. Favorable audit reports frequently have preceded the financial collapse of firms, calling into question the integrity of auditing practices. Over a decade before the Enron scandal, the U.S. savings and loan crisis of the late 1980s—in which many thrifts went bankrupt after receiving economic bills of health—was particularly troubling, not to mention enormously expensive.

The late twentieth and early twenty-first centuries brought additional turmoil as many people suspected that auditors' affiliations with managers have caused them to overlook shady financial records at the expense of the shareholders, to whom auditors are bound to report accurate information. This resulted in record numbers of malpractice lawsuits filed against accounting firms. The accounting profession has responded by reexamining legal and ethical issues, with the pace of these inquiries accelerating significantly in 2002.

Several large multinational accounting firms, known worldwide as the Big Six toward the end of the 1900s, dominated the industry and generated a substantial amount of the total industry revenue into the late 1990s. Although their corporate names and identities varied somewhat depending on the location of where they were headquartered, in the United States the Big Six included Price Waterhouse, Coopers & Lybrand, KPMG, Arthur Andersen, Ernst & Young, and Deloitte & Touche. In the early 1990s, uncontested dominance by the Big Six accounting firms was balanced somewhat by the faster growth of smaller firms. However, by the end of the decade global corporations re-emerged as the fastest-growing corporations in the industry, outpacing their smaller counterparts worldwide and swallowing up smaller firms in record numbers.

Operations of the Big Six firms within the international arena increased faster than their U.S. operations due to the rapid expansion of the world marketplace. The nations of Eastern Europe and the Commonwealth of Independent States moved quickly to privatize their accounting industries and update them to meet international standards, creating a very competitive environment for the large multinational accounting firms. And despite the Asian economic turmoil in 1997 and 1998, major industry players continued their efforts to develop a strong presence in Asia in the late 1990s.

By the close of the twentieth century, mergers and acquisitions had become another trend very much at the forefront of the industry. While the Big Six proceeded to acquire smaller firms, merger proposals among the Big Six themselves remained rampant. A planned merger between Ernst & Young and KPMG was abandoned in 1998, while simultaneously Coopers & Lybrand and Price Waterhouse moved forward with merger plans. However, not all industry players greeted such news with open arms. The *Financial Times* reported that the Coopers & Lybrand/Price Waterhouse deal received chilly reception from EU regulators, who suspected that the merger, which the firms claimed would stimulate competition and benefit clients, in actuality would benefit mainly the firms' partners. The deal nonetheless cleared regulatory hurdles, and by 2001 PricewaterhouseCoopers had become the largest U.S. firm offering auditing and accounting, tax services, and management advisory services (MAS).

According to industry analyst John M. Covaleski, consolidation among the top U.S. industry firms continued to characterize the accounting and auditing industry at the start of the new millennium. As Covaleski noted, "Consolidation reinforced its position as a key issue among the accounting industry's elite. Twenty-six of the Top 100 firms were involved in some type of merger or acquisition during 2000."

As markets opened up in the former communist nations and in developing countries in the late-twentieth century, accounting firms were finding tremendous opportunities for growth by capitalizing on these largely untapped markets. While these countries worked quickly to update their systems of accountancy and financial management to align with international standards, major multinational firms mobilized en masse to set up shop in these emerging markets. However, while growth in these markets accelerated, a great deal of uncertainty remained in the late 1990s as to whether and when these ventures would begin to generate substantial profits.

Lawsuits and Liability. As a competitive business, the members of the accounting industry battle each other on a number of fronts. One growing factor, though, loomed as a concern that united all members of the profession: litigation in the form of fraud lawsuits, which had increasingly threatened accounting firms in the 1980s and into the twenty-first century. Indeed, the major U.S. firm Laventhol and Horwath succumbed to bankruptcy under a barrage of lawsuits, prompting some to speculate that one of the Big Six could follow. By early 2002 Arthur Andersen executives were scrambling to prevent a similar fate from befalling their firm. In recognition of this increased threat, five of the Big Six created limited liability partnerships in the 1990s to shield their partners from mistakes made by their peers.

In addition, many firms began to take steps such as client screening and peer review to ensure greater quality control. During the 1990s this industry sector underwent a readjustment process, wherein some accounting firms dropped clients that fell into high-risk categories. Some accounting firms would no longer accept new clients that posed potential risks, such as fledgling companies preparing for an initial public offering. Nevertheless, lawsuits continued to haunt the industry at the start of the new millennium. To reduce legal costs and avoid the federal court system, accounting firms sometimes also pursued alternative dispute resolution methods, particularly mediation and arbitration.

The intense competition of the 1980s led to permanent changes in the accounting industry. Faced with shrinking profit margins in their core businesses, accounting firms moved into new areas of business by the late 1980s in an effort to pump up revenues, and this trend accelerated through the 1990s. The Big Six shifted more and more of their focus toward information control and assurance, corporate financing, human resources consulting, and entrepreneurial services, wherein firms offer financial advising and operating strategies for international expansion to companies seeking to capitalize on a booming global economy and emerging markets.

Overwhelmingly, the major focus of new revenue in the accounting industry in the late 1990s was in consulting. Major firms restructured to incorporate the lucrative consulting arena and in many cases focused their consulting expertise along industry lines. Arthur Andersen was one of the first of the big firms to move into the consulting arena. The company created Andersen Consulting in the 1970s and broadened its products and services considerably. Andersen Consulting developed a specialty in systems consulting and helped many of the world's corporate leaders create systems within their organizations. While the transition into consulting was successful for Andersen, it was not without controversy.

For example, enormous internal debate arose when Arthur Andersen decided to reorganize in the late 1980s into two autonomous affiliates—Arthur Andersen, the tax and audit division that provides smaller-scale consulting services; and Andersen Consulting, the large-scale systems consulting provider—to comprise Andersen Worldwide. The massive changes took their toll on some older partners who liked the old way of doing things and who watched their clout within the firm diminish. However, by 1997, consulting at Andersen Worldwide outpaced traditional accounting services, at totals of US$6.1 billion in global revenue and annual growth of 25 percent at Andersen Consulting, versus US$5.2 billion in revenue and an annual growth of 13 percent at Arthur Andersen. The divisions between these two entities grew, leading to disputes over the leadership position at Andersen Worldwide. In 1998, these divisions culminated in Andersen Consulting's secession from the parent company to become a completely separate entity, renamed "Accenture" in 2000.

Although the trend toward industry dominance by a few large multinational firms was expected to continue, the top auditing and accounting firms had hardly retained their positions by sticking to established formulae. Indeed, the Big Five rapidly branched out their services in the late 1990s, most notably into the fields of financial planning and consulting, including information technology consulting as corporations sought increasingly high-tech solutions to management and control problems and tasks.

In light of the accounting industry's rapid globalization in the late twentieth and early twenty-first centuries, as well as the numerous accounting scandals that came to light in the early part of the century, one of the predominant issues facing the industry was the need for national and international harmonization of accounting standards, principles, and practices. Furthermore, issues of professional ethics were hotly contested in the opening years of the new millennium. This was especially so as accounting and auditing improprieties and dubious practices increasingly came to light after the collapse of multinational energy giant Enron, which had become the largest energy trading company and the seventh-largest company in the United States by 2001. Enron's downfall arguably was brought on, or at least exacerbated, by devious accounting methods and the highly suspect procedures of the Andersen staff members who performed Enron's audits. According to a *Bloomberg News* article appearing in *The International Herald Tribune* on January 16, 2002, "Enron said in November [2001] that financial statements, certified by Andersen, overstated profit by $586 million since 1997, because of improper booking involving affiliated partnerships the company had used to put debt off the books and out of the sight of investors." The Enron failure, involving a write-off of more than US$1.0 billion in investment losses and a US$1.2 billion drop in equity for shareholders, was the largest bankruptcy case ever in the United States as of 2001.

In addition, the rapidly accelerating pace of bankruptcy filings in the early 2000s by previously profitable corporations, such as retail giant Kmart and telecommunications firm Global Crossing, appeared similarly linked to improper accounting and auditing practices by staff from some of the industry's largest firms. This, too, sparked motivation both within and outside of the industry for a worldwide review of accounting and auditing standards, as well as increasing demands for new industry norms, a more-transparent work ethic, and greater diligence in the oversight functions performed by national and international bodies, including the industry's own professional associations.

A rapid turnaround in this trend toward consulting already was occurring in the United States at least by the time the Enron scandal hit, however. Most large auditing and accounting firms, anxious to distance themselves from perceptions of impropriety, took pains to spin off their consulting arms around the turn of the millennium. As firms began to outgrow the national standards and governing bodies to which they were bound, calls increased for a clear, concise, global accounting language, one easily understood worldwide and applicable across national boundaries. In early 2002 different nations adhered to different accounting principles, making measurements of profits and assets derived from the same set of information disparate across nations, complicating the accurate appraisal and comparison of companies' financial standings. Consequently, efforts were underway in regional and international forums, including the World Trade Organization, to develop common global standards and practices for the industry.

Another recent concern of the accounting industry is the way in which firms, using conventional accounting principles, account for intangible assets such as research and development and employee talent. Given the substantial amounts that companies invest in intangibles such as human resource development, some critics have noted that immediate expensing of these assets does not necessarily present an accurate picture of a company's financial health, because this method of measuring corporate financial status does not take into account the huge returns that may be realized down the road.

CURRENT CONDITIONS

By 2005, the accounting industry continued to be dominated by a small number of major multinational firms, known as the "Big Four"—those same corporations as the earlier "Big Six" and "Big Five" with the exception of Coopers Lybrand, which in 1998 had been joined with PriceWaterhouse, and Arthur Andersen, which crumbled in the widely-publicized accounting scandals of the early 2000s. Together, clients of the Big Four include the vast majority of large corporations in most markets worldwide. However, as reported by Matt Krantz for *USA Today*, by the close of 2004 more companies were leaving the Big Four than were being brought on as new customers. An increase in costs brought on by new regulations was seen as the primary motivator of the moves. Managers were also thought to want better access to the top accountants in the firms handling their financials. Smaller accounting and auditing firms offer lower costs and increased access.

The trend toward mergers and consolidation in many industries in the mid-2000s was expected to continue in the accounting, auditing, and bookkeeping services industry as well. In 2004 there were approximately 45,000 firms in the industry, and according to *The Practical Accountant,* by 2014 there will be fewer than 23,000 still in operation. In addition, traditional accounting practices continued to grow increasingly specialized along industry lines as accounting firms recognized the more varied and focused needs of companies in different industries and began offering niche services in such specialty areas as construction, manufacturing, and real estate.

In addition to the changing needs brought on by the improving economy and new tax laws such as the *Jobs and Growth Tax Relief Reconciliation Act of 2003*, the industry was subject to increased governance and oversight. After the fall of powerhouse Arthur Andersen, for example, Congress established both the Sarbanes-Oxley Act of 2002 as an industry regulator and the Public Company Accounting Oversight Board, which would examine accounting firms either annually or every three years, depending on the size of the company. In the event that the board discovers anything amiss, the company could be given up to a year to correct the problem without disciplinary action or publicity.

WORKFORCE

With the increasing requirements posed by new regulations in the industry, the employment outlook was very positive well into the 2000s. As global commerce flourishes and becomes more complex and as high technology increasingly works its way into the accounting and auditing field, the accounting and auditing industry will invariably experience a drop-off in some service functions and dramatic growth in others. Particularly as corporate mergers and acquisitions continue to take place, as bankruptcies accelerate, and as new software and Internet-based solutions for tax preparation and business management become available, the industry will need to reorient itself to reflect changing workforce needs.

During the 1990s, employees of most auditing and accounting firms were hired based on their knowledge of three traditional departments: audit, tax, and consulting. Considering the industry problems that ensued with the collapse of Enron, including the legal problems of Arthur Andersen, changes in the consulting side of the industry were accelerated. Few large firms were expected to continue their practice of including management consulting as a sideline business, no matter how formidably wealth-producing, as the risks of lawsuits increased with greater public and official oversight of the industry.

According to the U.S. Department of Labor's Bureau of Labor Statistics, in 2002 some 1.1 million accountants and auditors worked in U.S. private industry and government positions. About 20 percent of salaried accountants in the United States worked for companies specializing in accounting, tax, payroll, and bookkeeping services, down from about 25 percent in 2000. About 10 percent of U.S. accountants and auditors were self-employed, down from 12 percent in 2000.

Corporate clients of auditing and accounting firms also tended to hire away staff from their auditing companies, perhaps in hopes of gaining an inside edge on how best to profit from particular methods of accounting. This practice, however, was likely to be stopped or at least greatly dampened as a variety of measures were proposed early in 2002 to require, among other things, a two-year waiting period before an outsourced staff member of an auditing and accounting firm who had performed a corporate audit could be hired directly by the corporation he or she had audited.

In an effort to curb their own costs and help make their clients' services more affordable, in the late 1990s some large and small CPA firms turned to accounting "paraprofessionals" to deal with their staffing needs without adversely affecting their billing rates. Paraprofessionals do not hold the CPA title but have basic accounting skills; some possess a knowledge of bookkeeping, others have associate's degrees in accounting, and many have bachelor's degrees in accounting. Some paraprofessionals continue their education and eventually join the professional accounting ranks. The use of paraprofessionals allows accounting firms to register significant payroll savings. Paid at a lower wage than other accountants in the profession, paraprofessionals are generally part-time workers. As a result, the firms pay much less in fringe-benefit costs and have the luxury of scheduling more work during peak periods, such as prior to tax deadlines, while paying for fewer non-billable hours.

Women in the Accounting Profession. Since the mid-1980s, the number of accounting graduates from colleges in the United States has been fairly evenly divided between men and women. By 2002, almost 57 percent of grads were women, according to the American Institute of Certified Public Accountants. The "Management of an Accounting Practice" survey conducted in 1996 revealed that women accounted for 51.3 percent of new hires in the United States. The survey found that the percentage of women owners of accounting firms had risen to 15.5 percent, but many critics continued to note a substantial disproportion of men to women in the upper ranks of the profession. The dearth of women in the upper echelons of the industry thus was the subject of considerable debate at the close of the twentieth century. Some industry analysts attributed the disproportionately small number of women at the top of the industry to a higher rate of female attrition as women left to raise families, resulting in proportionately fewer women than men available for promotion. Significant numbers of accountants interested in working in more family-friendly jobs have found work in the industrial sector or in other financial-service organizations, where work options may be more flexible and hours more predictable. As accountancy positions in the industry's top-tier firms become increasingly demanding, accountants looking for greater flexibility may seek out smaller firms or open their own private practices. However, some studies indicated that women were not dropping out of accounting in significantly greater numbers than men: the female turnover rate in accounting firms was only slightly higher than the male turnover rate in the late 1990s—19 percent for women, compared to 18 percent for men.

Although the working hours of a typical accounting firm can be difficult for anyone to manage, some analysts viewed the female exodus from the industry as the effect of institutional bias against women. Nonetheless, the number of women entering the accounting field almost tripled between the late 1960s and the close of the twentieth century. By contrast, the proportion of men entering the accounting profession steadily declined from 1977 at least through the late 1990s, despite a mild upturn registered at the start of the 1990s.

INDUSTRY LEADERS

As noted, the massive shift toward consulting posed serious ethical considerations for auditing practices by the early 2000s. As accountancy firms took a more active role in the financial strategies of corporate management, the ability of the same firm to gauge the financial outcome of that strategy objectively and accurately became dubious. Furthermore, with the advancement of information technology and tax-preparation automation—in itself a specialty of some computer outsourcing firms—tax-preparation fees at accounting firms have continued to decline, leading the larger accounting and auditing firms to add in newer business and technology services such as management consulting to their menu of products. As the IASC moves closer toward a complete international model, however, "traditional" accounting practices may well regain their footing. Early in 2002, calls were heard from industry professionals to raise the price of audits or expect higher premiums, for example, in order to offset lost revenues as industry leaders shied away from the consulting services they had been offering. After the passage of the Sarbanes-Oxley Act in July 2002, service fees increased by more than 25 percent. By the close of 2003, at least three of the Big Four had raised premiums or rid themselves of 200-500 clients seen as too risky, a move which cost the companies millions in lost revenues. However, despite the regulatory changes, the Big Four continued to amass by far the largest share of industry receipts through 2004.

DELOITTE TOUCHE TOHMATSU

The global group of member firms that makes up Deloitte Touche Tohmatsu has its foundations in England, Scotland and Japan. In 1845, William Welch Deloitte established an office in London, opening its first U.S. office in 1893. George A. Touche formed his accounting firm in 1898, quickly opening a New York office in 1900. Both companies expanded their enterprises, forming new partnerships along the way. In 1968, Iwao Tomita, founding Partner of Tohmatsu Awoki & Co., later Tohmatsu & Co., started operations within Tokyo, and by 1975 was already part of Touche's international network of partner firms. 1990 saw the merger that created Deloitte & Touche, with the international organization being named Deloitte Touche Tohmatsu in 1993. By 2003, the company had branded itself as simply Deloitte.

For the fiscal year 2004, Deloitte Touche Tohmatsu reported US$16.4 billion in sales. The company employed 115,000 people in 148 countries, and expected its most aggressive growth to come from China and India. Deloitte is the only one of the original Big Six accounting firms that has not divested its consulting operations.

PRICEWATERHOUSECOOPERS

With its foundings firmly entrenched in the United Kingdom in the 1800s, today's PricewaterhouseCoopers came into being in 1998, with the merger of Pricewaterhouse with Coopers & Lybrand. By 2004, PricewaterhouseCoopers was claiming that its member firms were performing services for 83 percent of all Fortune 500 companies. The firm reported 2004 revenues of US$16.3 billion, while employing more than 122,000 people in 144 countries. Approximately 42 percent of the employees work in Europe, 25 percent in North America and the Caribbean, and 16 percent in Asia, with the remaining spread fairly evenly among South America, Australia and Africa. The company acknowledges that less than 11 percent of its partners are women, despite having an evenly balanced distribution between men and women in its service ranks. At the end of 2004, the company stated that it was working to improve these figures, and that 22 percent of its new partners were women in 2004.

ERNST & YOUNG INTERNATIONAL

Although the founders of today's Ernst & Young never met, they founded their companies in the United States in the early 1900s and died within days of each other. Arthur Young & Co. was founded in Chicago in 1906, while A.C Ernst and his brother, Theodore, started Ernst & Ernst in Cleveland in 1903. It took until 1989 before the firms were combined. By the end of 2004, the company was employing 100,000 people in 140 countries and earning revenues of US$14.5 billion.

KPMG INTERNATIONAL

KPMG is the only one of the Big Four that is not headquartered in the United States; its home base is in the Netherlands. Formed in 1997 as the result of the merger between Peat Marwick International and Klynveld Main Goerdeler, the company had 2004 sales of US$12.2 billion and company employed 94,000 in 148 countries around the world.

MAJOR COUNTRIES IN THE INDUSTRY

The United States is the de facto headquarters of the international accounting industry. Although KPMG's head office is in the Netherlands, the Big Four all maintain a strong presence in the United States. However, for most of these firms, non-U.S. operations have emerged as leading sources of income and are the expected sources for the greatest amounts of new growth. By 2004, the International Group of Accounting Firms boasted member firms from 60 countries, which generate a collective $600 trillion in sales each year.

The United Kingdom, the birthplace of many of today's largest accounting firms, is the home of the International Accounting Standards Board (IASB), responsible for establishing most of the regulations followed by companies doing business globally.

According to *Accountancy,* the logistics of the accountancy profession in places such as China make it difficult for firms to operate at the level they are accustomed to in nations with more developed accounting systems. Firms with operations in these areas are spending a large part of their resources on training and recruiting professionals. However, many accounting firms see China and India as the new areas for growth. In other developing countries, the accounting industry suffers from a severe shortage of available resources and adequate training for accounting professionals.

FURTHER READING

Accounting Today. "2001 Top 100 Firms Databank." Accountants Media Group, 2001. Available from http://www.electronicaccountant.com.

"Andersen Fires Auditor for Enron." *Bloomberg News,* 16 January 2002. Available from http://www.iht.com.

Babington, Deepa. "Consultant Spin-off Set by Big Five Accountant," *The Philadelphia Inquirer,* 1 February 2002.

Brewster, Mike. "Burying the Past." *Chief Executive (U.S.),* April 2004.

Cairns, David. "Comment: The IASC Foundation's Non-Disclosure of Contributors Is a Surprising Change from Past Practice." 23 February 2002. Available from http://www.accountingweb.com.

Covaleski, John M. "Consolidation, New Markets Help Steer Revenue Growth." Accountants Media Group—Thomson Corporation, 2001. Available from http://www.electronicaccountant.com.

———. "Top 100s Service and Niche Growth Feeds Itself." Accountants Media Group—Thomson Corporation, 2001. Available from http://www.electronicaccountant.com.

Davenport, Paul. "Andersen Agrees to $US217m Settlement." *The Associated Press,* 3 March 2002. Available from http://finance.news.com.au.

Glater, Jonathan D. "4 Audit Firms Are Set to Alter Some Practices." *The New York Times,* 1 February 2002.

Gordon, Marcy. "Inspections of Big Four Accounting Firms Showed Significant Problems, Official Says." *The America's Intelligence Wire,* 24 June 2004.

Grill, Norman G., Jr. "Public Accounting in 2004: Work, Growth, Opportunities." *Fairfield County Business Journal,* 29 December 2003.

Hill, Miriam. "Accounting Firms Demand Change, Then Resist It." *The Philadelphia Inquirer,* 24 February 2002.

Hilzenrath, David S. and Susan Schmidt. "Andersen Seeking Quick Settlement." *The Washington Post,* 28 February 2002. Available from http://www.washingtonpost.com.

Hindo, Brian. "Audit Clients Get the Heave-Ho." *Business Week,* 1 December 2003.

Holderman, Karen. "Accounting, Auditing, and Bookkeeping," September 1999. In *U.S. Industry & Trade Outlook 2000,* ed. U.S. Department of Commerce/International Trade Administration. The McGraw-Hill Companies, 2000.

"Hoover's Company Capsules." 2004. Available from http://www.hoovers.com.

International Group of Accounting Firms. "About Us." 2004. Available from http://www.igaf.org.

"Investigator Fears 'Dozens of Enrons.'" *BBC News,* 24 February 2002. Available from http://news.bbc.co.uk.

Klein, Melissa. "After Enron, Change Sweeps Profession; PwC, Deloitte to Cut Loose Consulting Practices." *Accounting Today,* 25 February-17 March 2002. Available from http://www.electronicaccountant.com.

Krantz, Matt. "More firms flee Big Four accountants" *USA Today,* 26 September 2004. Available from http://www.usatoday.com.

Lazich, Robert S., ed. *Market Share Reporter.* Detroit: Thomson Gale, 2004.

MacInnes, Alexander. "Survey Says: Diversify in Bearish Economy!" Accountants Media Group—Thomson Corporation, 2000. Available from http://www.electronicaccountant.com.

Norris, Floyd. "Let the Auditors Tell Us What They Know." *The New York Times,* 1 February 2002.

Rudov, Cornell. "Industry Back to Profession." *The Practical Accountant,* June 2004.

"SEC Calls for Oversight." *Bloomberg News,* 18 January 2002. Available from http://www.iht.com.

Schlank, Rosemary. "Critics Want IASB To Disclose its Business Backers." 20 February 2002. Available from http://www.accountingweb.com.

"Survival of the Fittest." *The Practical Accountant,* April 2004.

Bureau of Labor Statistics, U.S. Department of Labor.*Occupational Outlook Handbook, 2004-05 Edition,* Accountants and Auditors. Available from http://www.bls.gov.

"USA Regulations: Sarbanes-Oxley in Brief." *Country ViewsWire,* 19 September 2002.

Yoon, Lisa. "Bolting from the Big Four." *CFO, The Magazine for Senior Financial Executives,* April 2004.

SIC 7311

NAICS 541810

ADVERTISING AGENCIES

Advertising agencies produce promotional campaigns and individual advertisements in all media, including print, broadcast, and the Internet. Besides creative work (written copy, artwork, graphics, and Web design), they have expanded their services to include public relations, marketing strategy, and interactive (Internet-based) advertising and market research.

INDUSTRY SNAPSHOT

After suffering what *ADWEEK* dubbed "one of the worst industry downturns ever" during the early 2000s, the advertising industry began to stabilize in 2003 along with the rest of the U.S. economy. In addition to the aftermath of the September 11 terrorist attacks, the global industry weathered other storms, including the U.S.-led war with Iraq and outbreaks of severe acute respiratory syndrome (SARS), and was looking forward to better times. Revenue results from 2004 showed that the industry was continuing on its upward trend, although few agencies had yet to reach pre-2001 levels. Forecasts for the industry's performance were positive. Growth was expected to be steady and measured, with Asia being the region where most growth was expected, particularly in China.

During the early 2000s, cost-conscious advertisers began focusing on more-targeted advertising approaches, including customer relationship management (CRM), to ensure more of a return on their advertising dollar. CRM is a process that attempts to bring together many fragments of information about customers, sales, marketing effectiveness, responsiveness and market trends to help businesses use technology and human resources to gain insight into the behavior of customers and the value of those customers. Buying decisions have become more influenced by the availability of purchase-related information and major purchases, such as automobiles, can be carried out interactively, over the Web. As a result, the specifics of customer wants and needs became key to the industry. The era of tailored customer engagements had begun.

In an attempt to compensate for a dearth of new accounts and worldwide cutbacks by advertisers during the early 2000s, new technologies and outlets were used. New business models such as program repurposing, the use of multiple media platforms and the emergence of interactive TV began to reshape the focus of advertising. Broad-based mass marketing was replaced by more highly focused campaigns designed to target specific consumers. New technological developments allowed advertisers to use e-mail alerts to market directly to pre-selected audiences. By gathering specific data about the particular interests and buying habits of segments of the consumer population and then directing pitches to them, advertisers began to shift from a shotgun approach to a narrower, and supposedly more efficient, strategy.

More demands were made on advertising agencies with the introduction of digital video recorders that gave viewers the ability to fast-forward through television commercials at will. Unlike VCRs, digital recorders store programs on a hard drive instead of a videotape. Initially, analysts projected that such devices would doom television advertising. In some instances, however, such as the Super Bowl of 2002, TiVo, the leading maker of digital video recorders, found that its viewers used the replay option more often for commercials than for the game itself.

High usage of technology pushed Goodby, Silverstein & Partners into the digital age. The 2006 *ADWEEK* U.S Agency of the Year was representative of award-winners who preferred working with pencil and pen but changed how they do business. The agency successfully met its challenge to prove to former and potential clients that there was a capability for keeping up with changing times. Key to that effort was hiring talent with a wider skills set plus adding digital production and animation studios in house.

In a 2007 interview with *ADWEEK*, ad industry legend Hal Riney observed that roles of computers and MBAs had relegated advertising to middle management. As a result, ads had become retail and lacked continuity. Riney believed that restricting creatives by focusing on bean counter issues and strategic briefs hurt the advertising industry.

According to Scott Goodson, Strawberry Frog founder and CEO plus 2007 Global Future Marketing Summit Chair, there are three key components for the new agency model. They are ideas, value and talent. Uniting these components results in a more significant culture where "great ideas create value" then end up commanding a premium price."

ORGANIZATION AND STRUCTURE

Advertising is one of the basic components of marketing. Advertising agencies promote their clients' products, services, and/or ideas through a variety of media outlets, including newspapers, magazines, television, radio, cinema, and billboards. The use of advertising and advertising agencies has spread from a concentration in consumer goods and retailing to virtually all business sectors. Modern full-service agencies provide a wide variety of services to advertisers, including strategy formulation, copywriting, artwork preparation and acquisition, booking of reproduction services, production of television and radio broadcasts, Internet campaigns and research, media selection and buying, market research, trade merchandising, and public relations. Larger agencies may add market research, sales promotion, direct marketing, and public relations to their services, whereas smaller agencies may employ outside specialists for these tasks.

Media advertising is known in the industry as "above-the-line" marketing. Although activities such as direct marketing and sales promotion are often derisively called "below-the-line" advertising because they often employ no creative element, full-service agencies became increasingly involved in such practices in the latter decades of the twentieth century.

Regulation. The National Advertising Division of the Council of Better Business Bureaus was created by the advertising industry in 1971 to provide a system of voluntary self-regulation and as a pre-emptive measure to minimize government intervention in the industry. In the United States, the Federal Trade Commission is responsible for monitoring and regulating advertising.

This combined voluntary and government imposed regulation restricts or bans advertising of particular products, such as tobacco, alcoholic beverages, medicine, and drugs in some or all mediums. In Europe, an EU Directive banning tobacco advertising throughout the European Union became law on 30 July 1998. The tobacco industry and the German government challenged the legality of the law, arguing that the European Union could not regulate single-market issues, an assertion with which the European Court of Justice agreed. The Court acknowledged that advertising crosses national boundaries, for example, in printed publications. The Commission revised a draft directive to prohibit trans-border tobacco advertising and promotion. Tobacco advertising on television is banned in the European Union by a separate law, the *Television Without Frontiers Directive,* which also prohibits the sponsorship of television programs by tobacco companies. The following eight EU countries ban tobacco advertising: Belgium, Denmark, Finland, France, Ireland, Italy, Portugal, and Sweden. The United Kingdom and the Netherlands have announced plans to introduce national legislation to ban such advertising. In 2000, the United States Supreme Court ruled against further government restrictions on cigarette advertising and upheld a ruling that the Food and Drug Administration lacked explicit authority to regulate tobacco.

Li Fang Wu, assistant secretary general for the Chinese Advertising Association, observed "that Chinese ads have to deal with social and government restrictions. Ads can't make fun of some social problems or the government." Punishment for inappropriate ads may be just to pull them but a fine can also be calculated at five times the cost of media time.

BACKGROUND AND DEVELOPMENT

Several economic and social factors contributed synergistically to the proliferation of advertising agencies in the nineteenth century. As the Industrial Revolution resulted in expanded production, advertising was used to sell the increased output. The idea of people being content with what they needed was slowly and inexorably replaced with the psychological and sociological concept that a need could be created in the minds of the consumer through advertising. Once that need was established, manufacturers could produce a supply of goods to meet the perceived, and yet very real demand, of a consumer society driven to fulfill its wants as well as its needs.

The democratization of the press and the explosion of both the number and circulation of magazines combined with an increase in the educational level in the Western world to further expand the value of agencies. Early ad copy was typically verbose and used typography for emphasis because of technological limitations. Catchy slogans and jingles—often coupled with artwork, including trademarks and logos—proliferated as companies competed to secure customers for their products. The early twentieth century brought an increased emphasis on graphic, as well as conceptual, content.

Until the early nineteenth century, all advertisers arranged their own promotions. Rynell and Son, established in 1812 in London, was one of the earliest advertising agencies. Volney Palmer, a newspaper editor, founded America's first advertising agency in the mid-1800s. Instead of buying space for clients and preparing their ads, however, Palmer's firm represented newspapers and sold space in them to advertisers. N.W. Ayer and Son, another U.S. firm, is considered the first client-based agency. Newspapers soon became the primary advertising vehicle, and in spite of the development of many new media formats over the years, newspapers continued to hold the largest share of the global advertising market through the 1990s, despite the emergence of electronic mass media vehicles like radio and television.

As the consumer society became sated, and markets for mundane items, such as detergents, matured and stagnated, advertising took on the role of repackaging the old into the new. It could drive a mass culture to new wants, new desires to have the "new and improved" versions, at least in perception if not in fact, of products it had come to consider "household names."

The spate of mergers and acquisitions in the late 1990s and early 2000s that transformed the structure of the global advertising industry is similar to consolidation maneuvers that took place in the late 1980s. The trend's roots go back to the 1961 foundation of Interpublic Group, a holding company organized to buy and manage individual advertising agencies. Marketing conglomerates patterned after Interpublic proliferated in the late 1980s, which saw the formation and ascent of such "mega-agencies" as Omnicom Group, WPP Group, and Euro RSCG Worldwide. Although these groups offered their clients comprehensive services, some combinations caused conflicts of interest as mergers brought competing advertisers under the same umbrella organization. Advertising organizations worked hard to assure their clients that their campaigns would be treated with confidentiality, pointing to their operation of each acquired agency as an autonomous agency. Some advertisers still shifted their accounts to other agencies.

More and more, clients have started to initiate another type of consolidation. Related efforts involved consolidating its global media planning and media buying account. In 2006, Mediaedge:cia had three major clients consolidate all of their global business The clients were Campbell Soup, Colgate-Palmolive and Ikea. Such moves can bring in substantial earnings for agencies. It is also noteworthy that Mediaedge:cia won the Campbell Soup account, worth an estimated US$400 million a year, without participating in a review process. The agency responded Campbell's request for them to draft a plan indicating how it would handle the new business. A decision was made to award the account one month after presentation.

Along with consolidation, globalization was changing the face of the industry. The internationalization of advertising agencies in the twentieth century was often dependent on their clients' global expansion. As automakers, oil companies, and consumer goods manufacturers established overseas operations, they often took their domestic agencies with them.

As globalization and consolidation shifted the size, reach, and character of new and existing multinationals, they were forced to reach a balance between overall global consistency in their firm's international strategy and the specifics required by adaptation to local or regional cultures. Most corporations that were traditionally centralized began exploring strategies for local adaptation, and those that were traditionally decentralized moved toward integration and broadened their focus to include regional oversight. To achieve these goals multinationals adopted a multiple-tier system in which overarching international strategy was determined by headquarters, and the regional/local groups determined regional/local tactics.

The top global brands began to influence the makeup of agencies as they demanded that advertising services be localized. This change reflected their realization that local differences be addressed despite the continuing globalization, not just of their specific industry, but of the world economy itself. Budget constraints, brought on by the softening of the global economy, led advertisers to seek more certainty that their message would be presented to an audience more likely to be open to its suggestions. Covering narrower segments of a market, whether determined by geography or demographics, became more important for branding than communications aimed at the masses. Consolidation in the media industry also allowed advertisers to buy diverse marketing packages from one conglomerate.

The World Wide Web, which introduced the world of "dot-com" to the advertising matrix in the mid-1990s, had a tremendous potential for advertising. Yet, because it could not guarantee how many consumers would see an advertisement, it proved quirky and difficult to quantify in its nascent stages. However, by the late 1990s, advances in online tracking technology had helped to elevate online advertisements to a widely accepted, cutting-edge medium.

The years bracketing the turn of the millennium were marked by agency consolidation and globalization in the world's advertising market. Multinational advertising conglomerates that included more than one network controlled 58.6 percent of global agency business in 2000 when the worldwide gross income was US$40.46 billion (including direct marketing and sales promotion). The top three firms, accounting for 42.1 percent of total worldwide advertising industry revenues, were Interpublic, with 15.8 percent (US$6.38 billion); Omnicom, with 13.9 percent (US$5.63 billion); and WPP Group with 12.4 percent (US$5.01 billion). These three firms also accounted for 45 percent of the US$18.94 billion in total revenues the U.S. advertising industry secured in 2001. U.S. sales for Interpublic totaled US$3.64 billion (19.2 percent); Omnicom, US$2.73 billion (14.4 percent); and WPP US$2.25 billion (11.9 percent).

As the twenty-first century dawned, agencies were tending toward centralized media strategy and planning with decentralized media implementation and measurement effectiveness. All major agencies had established independent media-buying companies. In addition, agencies were increasingly unbundling their services, separating media, direct marketing, and specialist support departments. The International Advertising Association research on global best practices in marketing and advertising in 2000 identified some trends it believed would shape global brand management.

- Consolidation will continue across the industry, although agency mergers will reach a point of diminishing returns. A convergence of agency and media resources will result from this consolidation trend.
- The rapid pace and ubiquity of technology will lead to the digitization of all creative work.
- The world will continue to shrink, even though it will be no less diverse; successful brands will have both global and local appeal.

- Wireless communications will enable an "anytime, anywhere" knowledge exchange, and no geographic market will have an exclusive on talent.
- Change will be the only constant.

CURRENT CONDITIONS

In his company's 2004 annual report, the CEO of industry giant WPP, Martin Sorrell, stated that the industry was seeing a rise after the recessionary forces that had affected it until 2003. Sorrell expected growth in Asia, a growing Americanization, the Olympics in Beijing, retail concentration, and a demand for internal communication to aid the industry in its recovery.

In addition to demanding more-competitive fees from agencies during the mid-2000s, corporate marketers began to concentrate more on quantitative results, which some advertising industry players admitted they were hard pressed to provide. Some observers argued that this heightened level of scrutiny, which emphasized testing and analysis, was severely hindering the all-important creative process.

Forecasts for the industry were positive in mid-2004, calling for steady and measured growth; no significant spikes were on the horizon. In addition, predictions from industry leaders varied somewhat. On the more conservative end of the spectrum, *Advertising Age* reported that ZenithOptimedia anticipated a 5.7 percent increase in U.S. industry spending in 2004, followed by a 3.8 percent in 2005. Specifically, newspaper advertising was expected to achieve growth of 4 percent, followed by outdoor advertising (4.8 percent), and magazine spending (6 percent). By comparison, Universal McCann Senior Vice President and Director of Forecasting Robert Coen projected that the U.S. advertising industry would grow 6.5 percent in 2004, followed by 7.3 percent in 2005.

Citing additional forecasts from ZenithOptimedia, *Advertising Age* further indicated that Europe held the potential to surpass the United States in advertising spending during 2005, as the former region finally began to experience a more substantial level of economic recovery. Largely on the strength of Germany and the United Kingdom, ad spending in Europe was forecast to reach 4.2 percent in 2004 and 4 percent in 2005.

One important global market during the mid-2000s was Asia. Asian advertising agencies were on solid footing, despite what some observers considered a difficult 2003. However, estimates regarding growth in the region varied. In its 14 May 2004 issue, *Campaign* discussed a report from Initiative Futures that placed Asia-Pacific (not including Japan) advertising expenditure growth at 7.4 percent for 2003. More optimistic was a report from Paris-based Recma that estimated annual growth at 14.3 percent. The two reports were somewhat different in that Recma included billings for Japan. In addition, the methodology used to compile Recma's report was criticized by a number of industry players as being somewhat subjective. In any case, with its booming economy and increased levels of investment by multinational corporations, China was expected to make the Asian market an attractive one for advertisers for years to come.

Some technological developments were expected to have an affect on the industry. For example, the growth in digital television meant that viewers have more control over content; they can skip television ads. As a result, some companies were creating branded programs. For example, Deloitte Touche Tohmatsu reported that it created a 30-minute music video program that viewers could select; the Coca-Cola brand appeared throughout the show.

Industry experts noted a move to turn away from lengthy reviews starting in 2005. This meant clients were more frequently moving their business from one shop to another without seeking ideas from multiple shops. Contributing factors included hard costs and soft costs. Those costs included travel expenses and lost work hours respectively. Substantially savings resulted occurred because reviews typically cost US$100,000 or more.

Ubiquitous Media chairman Bob Schmidt proclaimed the potential for promoting usage of alternative media. Options included his successful attempts to advertise on airport carrousels. Clients with budgets between 50 and 150 million dollars were ideal. Schmidt utilized his background and experiences as a founding partner in a major advertising firm to enhance interest in supplementing traditional media plans by coming up with creative alternatives.

Clients and prospects applauded R/GA's ability to integrate tech know-how and the creative process. "To come up with the big idea, you need to come up with the applications,"" explained Nick Law, R/GA's North American chief creative officer. They did that with the NikePlus and its design-your-own shoe NikeID application. Furthermore, the agency created the Nike Women Rockstar Workout with pop star Rihanna enabling visitors to craft their own experience. They could also learn dance moves from Rihanna's "S.O.S." music video. Last but certainly not least, visitors could find out where to purchase the Nike Women clothing worn in the video.

By 2007, advances in the digital age were blurring content distribution lines and causing concerns related to intellectual property protection. In the past, marketers frequently paid additional compensation for extending the use of campaigns into new geographical regions. This does not operate the same way for new digital directions. According to Rick Kurnit, a partner at Frankfurt Kurnit & Selz, New York, ldquo;the content an ad agency creates can have all sorts of platforms as clients repurpose it in the new digital world". The announcement that Geico's cavemen, from the auto insurance company's popular ad campaign, are set to appear in a TV sitcom pilot cause Noreen O'Leary to wonder what might happen if writers sent them on a high-speed car chase. Steve McClellan reported that Brent Poer, Senior Vice President, connectivetissue, MediaVest USA, posed the following question for consideration if the pilot is picked up and related show cancelled later. "Is the concept a flop——or the brand?"

O'Leary also pointed out that even before the digital era soared along, the advertising industry was losing out with traditional repurposing of ideas. In its first year of sales, US$4.99 Easy Button novelty items earned the marketer US$7.5 million in unanticipated sales. Although it was adapted from the McCann Erikson Staples ad campaign, the advertising firm did not profit from the unanticipated Easy Button sales. Such cases are cause for concern and debate in an industry where many agencies are locked into traditional work-for-hire agreements.

Mindshare was credited with being a great resource for creating integrated mobile sponsorships. Rather than buying ads on shows where competitors spent more money or had special sponsorships in place, Mindshare came up with innovative approaches. For example, The Nextel Cup series of Nascar races saw integration of broadcast commercials with ancillary content on the Web and mobile As a result, consumers were able to obtain more information about the racing circuit plus see interviews featuring drivers and commentators.

INDUSTRY LEADERS

Omnicom Group. Operating as a strategic holding company for three of the world's leading advertising agency brands, New York-based Omnicom was the number-one ranked advertising company in the world according to *Ad Age*. Operating BBDO Worldwide, DDB Worldwide, and TBWA Worldwide to serve its global advertising clients, Omnicom was also operating seven national agencies to serve its U.S. clients, five media services companies (including an asset bartering company and branded-entertainment television production company), and 160 other diversified marketing services companies (including public relations, customer relationship management, and specialty industry communications). Omnicom was also the highest-ranked advertising-related company on the *Forbes* Top 2000 Global Companies list of 2005, ranking at 380 overall. The company employed 62,000 people at year-end 2005. It had revenues of US$11.4 billion in 2006.

Omnicom was involved in a trademark controversy regarding usage of trademark *Fuse*. Fuse, an award-winning sports marketing agency with approximately 35 employees, demanded Omnicom discontinue usage of its trademark. When Omnicom refused to do so, Fuse proceeded with litigation seeking an order to prohibit usage. Omnicom failed to report why it chose to use the Fuse name. The larger company had attempted to acquire Fuse as far back as 2000 and was aware of its existence.

With global industry giants for clients, such as Pepsi, FedEx and VISA, BBDO Worldwide is Omnicom's largest agency, operating 345 offices in 76 countries by mid 2005. This business unit reported gross income of US$1.24 billion in 2003 (up 16.4 percent from 2002). Founded in 1891, the name BBDO is derived from the name used in 1928: Batten, Barton, Durstine & Osborn.

DDB Worldwide Communications, created as Ned Doyle, Mac Dane, and Bill Bernbach in 1949, had 206 offices in 96 countries by 2005. DDB merged with another independent agency, Needham Harper Worldwide, in 1986, creating a global company under the Omnicom Group's umbrella. In 1997, amid a series of acquisitions, DDB Worldwide launched a joint venture with movie director Spike Lee. In 1998, the agency introduced a new "unified strategic-thinking process" for the agency. The process is based on a framework of "six springboards": brand foundations, communications planning, media selection, integrated communication, creative and evaluation. In 1999, it acquired Hoffman Reiser Schalt (now Reiser Schalt DDB) of Germany and, as it attempted to broaden its global reach, bought a large stake in Brazil's DPZ in 2000. Sales exceeded the US$1 billion mark in 2004, up over the previous two years, but not yet reaching 2001's level of US$1.245 billion. In January 2005, *ADWEEK* named DDB the global advertising agency of the year.

TBWA Worldwide, like its sister agencies, was headquartered in New York City, but operating globally. In 2005, it was present in 75 countries operating 237 offices. Major clients included McDonalds, adidas, Apple, Nissan, and Sony PlayStation. In 2004, sales for this business unit were on the rise over the previous two years, reaching US$837.9 million, but had not yet reached 2001 levels of US$954.6 million.

TBWA account leaders and creatives work side by side with media planners from the OMD Omnicom sister shop. The pilot project reflected how agencies are connecting media planning and creative efforts. It was expected to move on to Asia and become a model for servicing clients by offering numerous media options.

WPP Group plc. WPP Group's 74,631 employees in more than 100 countries provided communications services to more than 300 companies listed on the *Fortune* Global 500 list. Based in London, the group's largest agency brands include Ogilvy & Mather, JWT, Young & Rubicam, and since March 2005, Grey Worldwide. Billings in 2004 for the group were approximately US$35.7 billion, with 39 percent coming from North America, 26 percent from Continental Europe, 17 percent from the U.K., and 18 percent from the rest of the world.

New York-based Ogilvy & Mather (O&M) was founded in 1948 and first hit its stride in 1950 with its eye-patched "Hathaway Man," an advertising tool for dress shirts that ran for the next 25 years. Founder David Ogilvy took on legendary status and his book, *Ogilvy on Advertising*, became an industry textbook. O&M eventually merged with its former parent company, the British group Mather & Crowther. Sales reached an estimated US$706 million in 2003, an increase of nearly 20 percent from 2002. In 2000, Ogilvy Interactive, the interactive division of the advertising firm, and AsiaNet Corp. formed Ogilvy AsiaNet to provide Web development and advertising services in Hong Kong, Korea, Taiwan, and China. The company had changed its strategic focus to emphasize global clients, and by the end of 2004, O&M had a fifty-fifty split of global versus national clients.

JWT (formerly J.Walter Thomson) has had many of its global clients for a long time; Ford has been a client for over 60 years, while Unilever has been a client for more than 100 years. Founded in 1846 as an agency to sell advertising space in religious magazines, the company was purchased by J. Walter Thomson in 1877, who soon realized that he could make money designing ads for his publications. Developing the first Creative Department, he is considered to be the father of modern advertising. At the end of 2004, JWT had revenues of US$1.3 billion.

The Interpublic Group of Companies, Inc. Another New York-based advertising giant, Interpublic had 43,000 employees working in 130 countries in 2005. Formed in 1961, Interpublic was the first advertising holding company, and in 2005 operated under five divisions: McCann Worldgroup (home to global services subsidiaries, including McCann Erickson), the FCB Group (including Foote, Cone & Belding Worldwide), The Partnership (independent agencies), Constituent Management Group (marketing services), and Interpublic Alligned Companies. Total group sales were almost US$6.2 billion in 2006.

McCann WorldGroup, which changed its name from McCann Erickson WorldGroup in 2003, recorded US$1.22 billion in gross income in 2003 (up 3.7 percent from 2002). McCann is the lead agency in the Interpublic Group and is considered to be the first agency to consolidate second-string agencies and diversify into less traditional areas of marketing and public relations. Its partners are The Lowe Group and Foote, Cone & Belding Worldwide. McCann Erickson was founded in 1930 and had major long-term accounts that included Standard Oil (now Exxon) and Coca-Cola. Marion Harper, who led McCann Erickson for more than 30 years, founded Interpublic in 1961 as a holding company for an expanding family of autonomous agencies. The concept was shaky at the start but began to catch on in the 1970s, grew in the 1980s, and was the global standard by the 1990s.

Publicis Groupe S.A. Paris-based Publicis Groupe S.A. was the world's fourth-largest communications group in 2004, the number-one agency in Europe, and the number-three in the U.S. It is an advertising and communications firm that operates three major global networks, Publicis Worldwide, Leo Burnett Worldwide, and Saatchi & Saatchi. The company also has a healthcare communications network, combining Nelson Communications with the healthcare activities of the Publicis and Saatchi & Saatchi networks. In addition, Publicis owns Zenithmedia, a joint venture with Cordiant Communications, and Optimedia, a wholly owned subsidiary. The firm offers a range of services to companies in 100 countries with a particular strength in France, Germany, the United Kingdom, Spain, Italy and North America. In 2005, Publicis employed 38,610 people across 1,000 agencies in 110 countries, and had revenues of approximately US$4.7 billion.

Founded in Chicago in the midst of the Depression with eight employees and three clients, by 2005 Leo Burnett Worldwide was the second-ranked agency in the U.S., but it also had significant global interests; it operated 95 offices in 83 countries. The company is well known for establishing a number of international brand icons, including the Jolly Green Giant and the Marlboro Man. Burnett's parent company, The Leo Group, merged with the MacManus Group in January 2000 to form Bcom3. Dentsu acquired a 20 percent stake in the new company in March 2000. However, when Bcom3 was acquired the Publicis Groupe in 2002, Leo Burnett became a unit of Publicis. The company's sales reached US$826 million in 2004.

Zenith became the first US shop to eliminate its media buying, planning and research departments. This move was viewed as a positive step toward "breaking down silos" forcing specialists in different disciplines to work more closely together to create integrated client strategies. The idea to create restructured groups, called "biospheres", was actually inspired by a client. Verizon approached Zenith with a proposal about creating a team-focused group dedicated exclusively to its business. This approach put more emphasis on clients by placing them at the center.

Dentsu. In 2005, Dentsu remained Japan's leading ad agency, as well as the leading global agency brand. Employee counts were 5,800 employees by March 2005, with 2004 sales of more than US$2.7 billion. During the early 2000s, Dentsu controlled more than 20 percent of the Japanese market and almost half of prime television ad slots. A 15-percent interest in Publicis Groupe, as well as a partnership with U.S.-based Young & Rubicam, has given Dentsu an international presence. In 2004, the agency was strengthening its foothold throughout Asia. It completed an initial public offering on the Tokyo Stock Exchange in 2001.

Havas. France's Havas began as the country's first press agency in 1835. In 1975, the holding company format was adopted, and the company's name changed to Eurocom, later changed to Havas in 1996. Euro RSCG is the company's global brand and has a network of 230 agencies in more than 75 countries. It is composed primarily of two divisions: the main above-the-line network Euro RSCG, and approximately 76 below-the-line agencies, grouped in 1999 as the Sales Machine. Havas employs approximately 14,400 people.

In June 2005, Havas's Chairman and CEO, Alain de Pouzilhac, spent months of battling with corporate raider, Vincent Bolloré, who had increased his share in the company to 20 percent. Industry analysts were also watching for a takeover of Havas.

Havas soared in 2006 to experience actual growth in its revenue for the first time in five years. This achievement was largely attributed to excellent performance in net new business combined with acclaimed award-winning creativity.

MAJOR COUNTRIES IN THE INDUSTRY

United States. The United States remained the largest market for advertising in the mid-2000s. In its "60th Annual Agency Report," *Advertising Age* reported that in 2003, U.S. advertising and media agencies achieved domestic revenues of US$10.66 billion, an increase of 3.7 percent from the previous year. At US$9.15 billion, advertising agencies accounted for the bulk of industry revenues, up 3.4 percent from 2002. This paltry growth was a direct result of the demand for more competitive fees by corporate marketers, which served to reduce agency profits.

Euromonitor reported that the top five agencies in the U.S. accounted for more than 76 percent of the market in 2003. These leading agencies were Interpublic, Omnicom, WPP, Havas, and Publicis. Television advertising was the most prominent sector, taking almost 40 percent of ad spending.

A weak U.S. dollar worked to the advantage of U.S. agencies with global operations, as they were able to earn revenues in comparatively stronger foreign currencies. According to *Advertising Age,* the leading 457 advertising and media agencies in the United States saw revenues from international operations climb more than 6 percent in 2003, reaching US$9.88 billion. In all, U.S. agencies saw total worldwide revenues climb nearly 5 percent in 2003, reaching US$20.54 billion.

Japan. As of 2003, Japan was the world's second-largest market in terms of advertising expenditures. That year, expenditures grew 2 percent. ZenithOptimedia indicated that Japan was poised for 3-percent growth in 2004 and 1.5 percent in 2005, which was substantial after several years of virtually no growth. The Ministry of the Economy reported that revenue grew 1.2 percent in April 2005, with employment in the industry also increasing 1.9 percent providing the second month of increases. The increases were considered the result of increases in consumer spending following a period of economic downturn.

During the early 2000s, advertising expenditures in Japan reached US$46 billion. Television was the largest sector with 34 percent of the total market, and Internet, or interactive, advertising was the smallest sector with 1 percent. The major media outlets in Japan are newspapers, magazines, and television. There is little cable penetration. Japan has the world's highest literacy rate, and 99 percent of Japanese households have newspaper delivery. Japan's newspapers have the world's largest total circulation. Magazines are also widely read in Japan, and more than 200 new magazines are started each year. Many Japanese magazines focus on fashion or consumer life. The Japanese allot more broadcast time for television commercials than Americans do, and 15-second commercials are more common in Japan. Commercials are customarily low-key and employ a soft-sell approach. Beautiful imagery, fantasy elements, and humor are popular techniques. The consumer is sought by indirect messages that appeal to the emotions. The specific benefits of a product are rarely mentioned, and the name of the sponsor is sometimes not even given until the end of the commercial.

China. According to the May 14, 2004, issue of *Campaign,* Initiative Futures reported that China was an increasingly important market heading into the second half of the 2000s. Although the nation was sixth overall in worldwide advertising expenditures in the early 2000s, by 2003 it had climbed to third place, behind the United States and Japan. All of the major international advertising firms are present in China. As *Campaign* noted, "All eyes remain fixed on China, where players say there is no sign of a slowdown in investment by multinationals. Instead, adspend for the market will continue to rise as the country ascends the priority list of aspiring global companies."

Television advertising takes the largest single portion of the Chinese advertising market. China's regular television viewing population is 84 percent of its 1.2 billion people. Major articles sold on television include toiletries, foodstuffs, pharmaceuticals, liquor, and home electronics. Television stations in big markets (Beijing, Guangzhou, Shanghai) require advertisers to book and pay for specific spots two to ten months in advance. A highly charged debate continues between isolationist policy-makers who consider foreign investment a threat to China's economic security and their rivals who see closer ties with the world as the key to financial strength.

For 2007, China's media spending was expected to hit US$14 billion. This soaring expenditure did not reflect everything was ideal for advertising agencies. R3 founder and 20-year multinational agency network veteran said, "China is crucial to every agency network and the toughest job in advertising is being a CEO here." Challenges include labor-intensive requests, speeded up progression from review to production and average agency relationships lasting less than three years.

France. In 2003, global agencies dominated France's advertising industry, although two of the top agencies were headquartered in the country: Havas and Publicis. Havas led the market with a 24-percent marketshare. Euromonitor projected slow growth of only 2 percent up to 2008, with most ad spending remaining with the press.

Havas and Publicis Conseil continued to be the most creative advertising agencies in France during 2003, followed by TBWA\Paris. In terms of billing, Havas Advertising led with EU 434.3 million, followed by Publicis Groupe (EU 313.8 million), and TBWA France (EU 212.5 million). French Art Directors' Club President Remi Babinet indicated that, due to the country's relative reluctance to embrace new or entrepreneurial approaches, it was difficult for small, emerging players to find success in France in comparison to other European countries. To further the concentration of agencies in the country, in 2005, analysts were predicting that a takeover of Havas was inevitable.

United Kingdom. The market growth for advertising services in the United Kingdom has resulted in the growing size and strength of the local advertising industry. Also, British advertising has a reputation as one of the world's most effective and creative. With the United Kingdom's use of innovative techniques, campaigns tend to be memorable. Advertisements in the United Kingdom range from subtle to outrageous in order to grab attention and provoke a response. This comes from the years when all television advertising came at the end of a program; such sustained periods of advertising required them to be highly "watchable." However, most ad spending was done with the press, which accounted for 50 percent of the market's advertising value in 2003.

After a period of consolidation in the 1990s, the U.K. advertising industry experienced increasing cross-ownership, internationalization, and a centralizing of accounts by major clients. Nonetheless, creative strength has been maintained by granting autonomy to groups within the major advertising companies. As brands and products mature from a regional to a national, international, and global focus, U.K. advertising companies have expanded their clientele worldwide. In 2003, France's Publicis Group was the leader in the U.K. market, according to Euromonitor. Along with Germany, the United Kingdom was expected to propel Europe past the United States in advertising expenditures in 2005, as the region finally experienced a period of long-awaited economic recovery.

Germany. Most large German advertising agencies are dominated by their U.S. subsidiaries, branches, or affiliates. BBDO Germany, subsidiary to the U.S. agency, was Germany's largest agency in 2003, according to Euromonitor. To increase their competitiveness, many German full-service agencies have entered into partnership arrangements with other domestic and foreign advertising firms, especially from the United States, Great Britain, France, Italy, and Switzerland.

FURTHER READING

"The ABCs of Customer Relationship Management." February 2002. Available from *U.S. Industry and Trade Outlook*. New York: McGraw-Hill, Department of Commerce, and International Trade Administration, 2000.

"Agency of the Future: Change the Model, Change the World." *ADWEEK*, 5 March 2007.

"Asian Agencies: Asia's Rising Stars." *Campaign*, 16 July 2004.

Baar, Aaron. "Review Fatigue Leads to Rise in Handoffs." *ADWEEK*, 5 February 2007.

Berger, Warren. *Advertising Today.* Phaidon Press, 2001.

"Digital Television Puts the Viewer in Control." *TMT Trends: A Focus on Media and Entertainment.*, July 2004. Available from http://www.deloitte.com.

"France: Who's Big and Who's Clever." *Campaign*, 18 June 2004.

Hatfield, Stefano. "China's the New Gold Rush, But Nothing Is As It Appears." *Advertising Age*, 21 January 2002, 20.

"Major Market Profiles: Advertising in France, Germany, UK, and USA (Executive Summaries)." *Euromonitor*, October 2004. Available from http://www.euromonitor.com.

McClellan, Steve. "Network Trumps Rivals With Big Ideas and Global Wins, Often Sans Pitches." *ADWEEK*, 26 February 2007.

"Zenith Media Realignment Puts Clients in the Center." *ADWEEK*, 12 March 2007.

McMains, Andrew. "Network Pulls Together to Post Impressive Growth, Produce Stellar Creative." *ADWEEK*, 8 January 2007.

Morrissey, Brian. "A Potent Tech-Creative Combo Fuels Its Rise to the Top." *ADWEEK*, 22 January 2007.

O'Leary, Noreen. "The Lay of the Land." *ADWEEK*, 5 February 2007.

—"Your Big Idea, Their Next Big Thing." *ADWEEK*, 12 March 2007.

—"Where Do We Go From Here? The Recession Is Behind Us, but the Ad Industry Now Faces New Worries." *ADWEEK*, 22 December 2003.

Parpis, Eleftheria. "Shop Transformed Itself for the Digital Age Without Skipping a Creative Beat." *ADWEEK*, 8 January 2007.

Remson, Adam. "Bob Schmidt is Everywhere." *ADWEEK*, March 2007.

"60th Annual Agency Report; Revenue for U.S. Ad, Media Agencies Gains 3.7 Percent to $10.7 Billion." *Advertising Age*, 19 April 2004.

Voight, Joan. "Riney Laments the Decline of His Agency, Industry." *ADWEEK*, 8 January 2007.

Wentz, Laurel and Normandy Madden. "Global, 2002 Outlook." *Advertising Age*, 7 January 2002.

Whipp, Lindsay. "Japan's service sector grows as spending rises." *Bloomberg News*, 24 June 2005. Available from http://www.iht.com.

"World: Media Analysis—Asia-Pacific Media Agencies Ride Out the Recession." *Campaign*, 14 May 2004.

"Zenith Spensing Forecast Shows Growth but No Surge; U.S. Up Slightly; Shift Continues to Unmeasured." *Advertising Age*, 19 July 2004.

SIC 8711

NAICS 541330

ENGINEERING SERVICES

Engineering firms provide professional engineering services on a contract or hourly basis. Such services include system and structure analysis, specification, design, and project management. Many engineering services are integrated with construction activities. For discussion of the construction industry, see also the chapter entitled **Construction Materials and Services**.

INDUSTRY SNAPSHOT

Among the many changes taking place in the engineering services industry — such as consolidation and pricing structure shifts— diversification emerged as one of the most important, particularly due to the economic downturn and construction slump of the early 2000s. The number of design-build firms, those which offered both engineering and construction services, grew throughout the late 1990s and early 2000s as clients, including those in the public sector, became increasingly comfortable with the design-build concept. By 2003, many companies in the industry were looking to diversify not only products and services, but also location, expanding their focus to international markets. Globalization had become almost a prerequisite for participation and success in the industry.

The forecast for design-build firms beyond the mid-2000s was for growing demand from sectors as diverse as transportation networks, water treatment plants, and automotive manufacturing. Ranked for 2003 by *Design Build,* the top U.S. companies in the industry were Bechtel, Fluor, Jacobs, Foster Wheeler, CB&I, KBR, and Parsons. *Engineering News Record*'s 2004 list of the top global design firms, ranked by total revenue, put eight U.S. companies in the top ten, and six of those were based in California. The other two countries represented were Canada, in the number two spot with SNC-Lavalin International, and the United Kingdom, in the number seven spot with Atkins. Altogether, the top ten firms collectively posted total 2003 revenue of US$18.5 billion.

The leaders in the construction industry continued to be VINCI and Bouygues of France. Employing engineers in almost every category, the leading engineering firms were involved in major projects around the world. This sector had become truly internationalized.

ORGANIZATION AND STRUCTURE

Engineering encompasses a variety of disciplines concerned with the design of structures, devices, machines, and other elements of modern industrial society. Major sectors of the engineering industry include civil engineering, mechanical engineering, electrical engineering, petroleum engineering, and industrial engineering.

The civil engineering field is primarily concerned with the design and construction of public works such as bridges, dams, and other large facilities, while mechanical engineering tackles the area of machine, system, and tool design, including plumbing and ventilation systems. A somewhat related discipline is industrial engineering, which studies designs, methods, and processes for effective and efficient production. Electrical engineers, on the other hand, study the technology of electricity for the purpose of determining the design and application of electricity in power generation and distribution, machine operation, and communications.

Associations. Major associations developed in the nineteenth century to bring together engineers and engineering firms involved in similar areas of work and study. Principal engineering associations in the United States include the American Society of Civil Engineers (ASCE), the American Society of Mechanical Engineers (ASME), and the Institute of Electrical and Electronics Engineers (IEEE).

Quality Standards and Assessments. Quality certification is an issue of growing importance to many establishments involved in providing engineering services. While some engineering standards have long been in place, customers in various markets have increasingly demanded significant assurances that a suppliers' goods will be of a certain quality. As a result, individual companies using engineering services, in addition to professional organizations, have begun to articulate more exacting quality standards and to require that engineers anywhere along the production chain be versed in such standards. Initiatives to meet these demands include quality certification from the International Organization for Standardization (ISO), which confers certification on companies worldwide that meet various requirements for process regularity and product specifications.

BACKGROUND AND DEVELOPMENT

The engineering industry's various branches of study developed at different periods in the evolution of the world's industrial landscape. Many forms of engineering trace their roots to the Industrial Revolution that began in Europe in the latter eighteenth century and continued in the United States through the mid-nineteenth century. A flurry of new inventions during that period, such as the steam engine, triggered demand for new manufacturing machinery, transportation equipment, roads, bridges, canals, and sanitation systems. Fulfilling this demand were designs by individuals who became the forebears of mechanical, civil, and industrial engineering. Later, when electric lights and other electrical applications were pioneered in the late nineteenth century, the field of electrical engineering was born.

Civil engineers have long been central figures in the construction of bridges and roads. In the eighteenth and nineteenth centuries the major advances in this field of study originated in Europe, especially in France, which boasted the leading schools of engineering education in the world. As Daniel L. Schodek noted in *Landmarks in American Civil Engineering,* "French institutions maintained the leadership in formalizing an approach to engineering education based on scientific principles . . . it was the French system that primarily influenced formal education in civil engineering in America." By the beginning of the twentieth century, a recognizable civil engineering profession was thriving in the United States and elsewhere. The arrival of the automobile accelerated the construction of highways, tunnels, and overpasses, all of which required the talents of civil engineers.

Electrical engineering advanced through the invention of the vacuum tube by Lee De Forest in 1907. This vacuum tube (called a triode) spurred the creation of various devices that could transmit an electrical signal. As telephone and radio developed, electrical engineering grew as well. During the twentieth century, government and wartime spending subsidized many engineering achievements. Advances in computers, space technology, and the development of the integrated circuit all contributed to the explosive growth in the electrical engineering industry in the latter part of the 1900s.

The entire international engineering industry in the late 1990s was buoyed by a sense of optimism brought about by robust market conditions. Engineering firms in the United States led the industry in the late 1990s largely because of their continued success in securing international business through local subsidiaries. In 1997 for instance, U.S. design firms garnered more than US$25.4 billion of the US$32.7 billion in total world billings. This strong market, however, did foster some problems, such as the growing shortage of skilled professionals, a trend which steadily boosted compensation and benefits.

Other firms around the world also took note of international opportunities in the late 1990s. Europe established itself as the top regional design market in 1997, posting US$2.4 billion in billings. In second place, Asia reported US$1.7 billion in billings, while the Middle East (US$610.9 million), Latin America (US$576.5 million), Canada (US$419.4 million), North/Central Africa (US$334.8 million), the Caribbean Islands (US$114.8 million), and Antarctic/Arctic (US$21 million) followed. The billing figure for Asia showed a dramatic jump in 1997, but the Asian currency crisis that began in Thailand and reverberated throughout the region signaled that 1998 wouldn't be nearly as lucrative. In the meantime, once Asia's design market cooled off, other regions, particularly Latin America and the Middle East, picked up the slack.

The engineering industry of the late 1990s underwent fundamental change. Consolidation increased the level of globalization, which created large enterprises with increasingly international operations, as well as some niche players. The industry also began moving away from cost-reimbursable contracts to fixed price, lump sum, and turnkey design-build contracts. Such arrangements benefited firms that contracted engineering services by providing, in effect, a price cap on how much a project cost. These arrangements also gave the engineering firm greater autonomy and incentive to complete projects in timely and affordable ways. Another major industry shift occurred because clients of design firms were increasingly operating on a global scale; as a result, they began wanting design firms to deliver more than mere designs, *Engineering News Record* noted. This trend prompted many firms that were purely engineering in scope to add construction capabilities to their offerings.

A particularly bright spot for the engineering services industry was the long-moribund market for power plants, particularly in Latin America. In some cases, rejuvenated demand for power plant design more than doubled individual firms' revenues from that sector. Also, demand for cogeneration system design by industrial firms, which improves power production efficiency by deriving more energy from the same amount of resources, continued to grow, and many of the world's nuclear plants, which had fallen into disfavor in many developed economies, were in dire need of upgrade.

An issue of concern for U.S. firms in the late 1990s was the professional liability of engineers for tort actions brought against them for alleged flaws in design work. The average firm turned down US$190,000 worth of work in 1996 due to professional liability concerns; according to the Association of Consulting Engineers Council, fewer than 20 percent of the claims made against design professionals in the late 1990s had merit, based on a survey of 866 firms. In 1996 only 9 percent of the firms surveyed did not carry professional liability insurance, which cost, on average, 2.31 percent of gross annual revenues.

Uncertainty about U.S. government funding for engineering research prompted more than 100 scientific, mathematical, and engineering societies to issue a statement in 1997 calling upon the U.S. Congress and the Clinton administration to double federal investments in research over the next decade, beginning in fiscal year 1999, which began 30 September 1998. In the late 1990s, according to the American Society of Mechanical Engineers, the U.S. Department of Defense was funding about 40 percent of all federally funded engineering research. In fiscal year 1998, US$40.7 billion was devoted to mechanical engineering-related programs in the U.S. federal budget; of that amount, the Defense Department funded US$33.5 billion, followed by the National Aeronautical and Space Administration (US$4.1 billion), and the Department of Energy (US$1.3 billion).

Firms in the United States continued to be leaders the international engineering world in 2000. According to *Engineering News Record,* the top 500 U.S. design firms collectively posted US$35.1 billion in U.S. design billings in 2000, an increase of 8.1 percent from the year earlier. However, international market billings for this group fell 3.0 percent to US$7.6 billion. This was partially due to continued uncertainty regarding the instability of many markets in southeast Asia; China, however, was viewed as an increasingly friendly market.

The top 200 global design firms, as ranked by *Engineering News Record,* generated US$16.1 billion in international revenues in 2000. The petroleum market accounted for the largest segment, with US$4.14 billion in revenues, or 25.7 percent of the total. Second was transportation, which generated US$3.17 billion, or 19.7 percent. Third was building, with US$1.63 billion in revenues, or 10.2 percent. Power accounted for US$1.56 billion, while industrial secured US$1.54 billion, and water generated US$1.12 billion. Sewer/wastewater, hazardous waste, manufacturing, and telecommunications all brought in less than US$1.0 billion. In 2000, 168 U.S. firms reported an average profit of 7.1 percent, while 10 firms reported a loss. Internationally, 156 firms reported an average profit of 6.7 percent, while 11 reported losses.

Consolidation throughout the late 1990s and early 2000s created several new industry leaders. The merger of Nedeco and Nethconsult, both comprised of several small Dutch operations, boosted Nedeco to second place on *Engineering News Record*'s list of the leading international design firms. The largest firm in that ranking, AMEC, owes its large size to its late 1990s purchase of AGRA Ltd., located in Canada. France-based engineering and construction behemoth Technip acquired Coflexip, a sub-sea engineering and construction firm also headquartered in France, in 2001. The merger, which joined France's two largest engineering and construction companies, created one of the leading engineering and construction firms in all of Europe and one of the world's top five oil and gas engineering organizations. Annual revenues for Technip-Coflexip were predicted to reach US$4 billion in 2002.

Design-build firms gained increasing prominence in the early 2000s, particularly in the United States. While global revenues for the 100 largest design-build firms grew only 3.7 percent to US$58.24 billion in 2000, design-build revenues in the United States jumped 22.3 percent to US$39.89 billion. According to *Engineering News Record*, although total international design-build sales dropped more than 22 percent to US$18.35 billion in 2000, "the trend is clearly away from project-by-project management and toward management of larger construction programs for clients."

CURRENT CONDITIONS

As the U.S. economic recovery seemed established by 2005, the need for skilled engineers was growing, particularly in the aerospace industry. Although product design engineers were in high demand by many industry sectors by 2004, overall growth was below the average for all other industries, due in part to the internationalization of engineering. Project work was being bid on by companies from all over the world.

Those in the engineering services industry understood that to remain viable and competitive in down markets, there must be diversification—not only of products and services, but also of geography. International growth in the mid-2000s was a factor for the major industry players, no matter the home country. Of the reported US$249.3 billion in revenues of the top 25 global construction firms, US$87.8 billion was earned outside of the home country. The Design-Build Institute of America expected that design-build companies would increase their share of the U.S. nonresidential construction market from 35 percent to 45 percent by 2005, and that most of the commercial work would use design-build services by that time.

A trend in the architectural segment of the design-build industry was in the rehabbing of old, urban buildings. Termed "adaptive reuse," the rethinking and revisioning of older buildings can not only save the structures from demolition, but also build up communities through revitalizing an area. Such buildings generally have the advantage of having major systems already in place, which lowers the costs involved.

By the mid-2000s, PLM was emerging as a new must-have technology for design engineers; according to independent research firm Gartner, PLM will be absolutely necessary by 2007 if a company intends to stay afloat. An acronym for product lifecycle management, PLM is software that offers a way for a company's products and services to be managed from start to finish in an automated, accountable, quality-process-control fashion.

RESEARCH AND TECHNOLOGY

All branches of the engineering industry have been profoundly affected by the rise of computers and technological innovations in the 1980s, 1990s, and 2000s.

Computers. Computers continued to increase in importance to engineers in dramatic fashion in the mid-2000s. As computer hardware and software capabilities have grown, a larger share of complex design problems has been resolved using computers, according to *Design News*. Moreover, software has grown more accessible and easier to use for design engineers. Computer workstations with two or more processors on board were the latest trend in hardware systems by the late 1990s. These systems essentially allowed engineers to run two separate, high-power computing operations at once.

The Internet. Some observers credited the Internet as the most important technical innovation to sweep the industry since computer-aided design (CAD) software became mainstream in the 1980s. Benefits of using the Internet by engineers include improved collaboration among engineers, manufacturers, and vendors; increased access to crucial, up-to-date data; and efficient reuse of information.

Prototyping. Rapid prototyping (RP) increases predictability and improves surface finishing. This technology allows engineers to transform their virtual designs in CAD programs to physical models. It allows for early verification of product designs and quick production of prototypes for testing. According to *New Technology Week*, RP includes a variety of technologies, ranging from numerical-control machining techniques to "computer-aided, design-driven solid free form fabrication that does not require human intervention." The United States led this field in the late 1990s, but Germany and Japan were also planning to bolster the use of RP systems. Europe and Japan used RP more than the United States in medical applications, with surgical planning and the creation of artificial limbs the leading uses.

Virtual Design. According to *Mechanical Engineering*, manufacturing and engineering firms around the globe have begun building products using virtual reality. Early adopters have already found that these techniques can significantly reduce the time involved with the design cycle, decrease the need to build actual prototypes and models, and ultimately increase the product's market acceptance and penetration. What's more, the components of the system—computer-aided design (CAD), computer-aided manufacturing (CAM), computer-aided engineering (CAE), and industrial design geometry—can be shared across computer networks, where they can be analyzed and changed if required.

Solid Modeling. In *Design News,* Paul E. Teague noted that software developers across the globe were touting the potential for solid modeling to revolutionize engineering. Using three-dimensional solid modeling software, engineers can review designs online and change them without affecting production schedules. In other words, engineers can visualize the product at each step along the design route, long before making a physical prototype. Solid modeling allows for early troubleshooting to identify problems while they can still be corrected inexpensively. It also allows engineers to generate drawings quickly, and it allows a change in one part to be reflected automatically in the entire assembly.

Fluid Power. According to *Design News*, in the late 1990s engineers in the fluid-power industry—particularly those in industrial automation, automotive, and mobile equipment design—expected to see increased demand for hydraulic valves and controllers that are compatible with fieldbus technology. According to The Fieldbus Foundation, fieldbus is "an all-digital, serial, two-way communications system that interconnects measurement and control equipment such as sensors, actuators and controllers." But the trend toward increased use of fieldbus technology in hydraulics likely will be quite gradual, primarily because there is no agreement on the protocols or standards those components must meet.

Composites. Some industry observers believe that engineers of the future will have vast new materials options to choose from for designs. Materials scientists have made important advances in the development of composite materials that accentuate the positive aspects and blunt the negative characteristics of materials. Europe, which is at the forefront of composite technology, and other industry participants are expected to continue to investigate new composite materials that will free engineers from previous constraints in design. Before it was acquired by Germany's Daimler Benz in the late 1990s, Chrysler Corporation unveiled a car with a body made entirely of plastic. Also on the horizon was greater use of a new kind of plastic polymer, called thermoplastic elastomers, which has properties similar to rubber and is more oil resistant than other similar products. According to *Design News*, plastics will continue to replace metal in automotive applications.

WORKFORCE

In 2002, there were 1.48 million engineering jobs in the United States, according to the U.S. Bureau of Labor Statistics. These were further broken out by engineering specialty:

- electrical - 292,000;
- civil - 228,000;
- mechanical - 215,000;

- industrial - 194,000;
- aerospace - 78,000;
- computer hardware - 74,000;
- environmental - 47,000;
- chemical - 33,000;
- materials - 24,000;
- nuclear - 16,000;
- petroleum - 14,000;
- biomedical - 7,600;
- mining and geological - 5,200;
- marine - 4,900;
- agricultural - 2,900; and
- all others - 243,000.

Jobs in engineering were expected to grow slower than average for all other occupations in the period up to 2012, although some sectors, such as environmental engineering, are expected to have faster than average growth. Some slowdown was determined to be due to the increased use of engineers in other countries.

Income varied by the type of discipline. For example, at the highest end were petroleum engineers, earning a mean income of US$83,370 in 2002 while the lowest end was held by agricultural engineers who earned a median of US$50,700.

The industry continued to be male dominated, both in the workforce and in academia. According to U.S. Census data, the number of female engineers had been slowly increasing, having risen from 5.8 percent of all engineers in 1983 to 10.6 percent in 1999. In 2000, the largest percentage of women engineers were in the categories of computer engineering (27.5 percent) and environmental engineering (22.2 percent), while the lowest sectors were marine engineering (5.1 percent) and petroleum engineering (6.3 percent). Income figures showed a strong disparity between genders. China had more female engineers than the U.S., claiming about 37 percent of the engineering workforce.

Civil engineering in Africa was faced with challenges impacting how the profession functioned on that continent. Lukong Pius Nyuylime shared insights about those challenges. They included poor knowledge of mission, lack of confidence in local engineers, clash of political and technical interest, no patriotism and no incisive socio-economic environment. According to Nyuylime, participants in an international conference organized in Yaounde "were unanimous on the cornerstone-role the civil engineering profession plays in the continent's development.

INDUSTRY LEADERS

VINCI. Created in 1899 by French engineers, VINCI was the leading global contractor in 2005 according to *Engineering News-Record.* The company was providing engineering services to the following industries: transportation infrastructure, energy infrastructure, manufacturing, and telecommunications. The company was the leading civil engineering firm in France and was a major player globally. In 2005, VINCI's revenues were approximately US$25 billion, and the company employed more than 133,513 people. By 2007, VINCI planned to recruit 12,000 French employees on permanent contracts to address an anticipated dramatic increase in spending through 2013.

VINCI led the Apion Kleos consortium. The Greek government chose this concession as its preferred bidder for its biggest motorway concession project. This project called for the financing, design, construction and repair of toll roadway between Atkens and Tsakona, Greece. The project strengthened VINCI's position in Greece where it already operated the Rion-Antirion Bridge. It was both the biggest construction worksite and concession VINCI ever won outside of France.

Bouygues SA. Founded in Paris in 1952, by 2005, Bouygues was one of the world's largest companies offering construction services, with its civil engineering and public works segment beginning operation in 1965. Bouygues was parent to the world's leading roadworks company, Colas. In 2005, it was working on such projects as the Grand Hotel Intercontinental de Paris, the Groene Hart tunnel in the Netherlands, Tangier harbor in Hong Kong, and the Masan Bay bridge in South Korea. Bouygues employed 115,411 people working in about 80 countries. The company was a major employer in Africa, which accounted for 44.3 percent of its some 52,000 workforce outside of France. Bouygues' revenues in 2005 were nearly US$32 billion.

The company made large investments in research and development. In 2005 it was working on such projects as the use of robots on worksites to increase productivity, acoustics and vibrations, low temperature asphalt, and environmentally friendly warm-mix asphalt.

Halliburton Co. A provider of products and services to the oil and gas industry, Texas-based Halliburton offers engineering and construction services through its KBR (Kellogg, Brown and Root) division. This division provides services to the chemical manufacturing and energy industries, as well as being involved in infrastructure construction. The company provides civil engineering, nuclear engineering, weapons engineering, marine engineering, and petroleum engineering services. In 2005, Halliburton employed more than 100,000 people in over 120 countries. There were 60,000 people in the KBR division working in 43 countries. Total Halliburton revenues in 2004 were US$20.47 billion, with KBR accounting for US$12.47 billion in revenue.

In 2007, Halliburton defended the work of its Halliburton Products & Services, Ltd. subsidiary in Iran. U.S. law prohibits citizens and operations to do business directly with Iran. Foreign subsidiaries are permitted to do work there as long as the subsidiary acts as an independent agent. That means it must function in this regard separately from the parent company. The U.S. Senate Subcommittee on Interstate, Commerce, Trade and Tourism questioned how Halliburton had operated based on evidence including a 2004 report on CBS News' 60 Minutes program. The program suggested that Halliburton shared office space plus telephone and fax line with its subsidiary. Halliburton Vice President and Corporate Secretary Sherry Williams denied the accusations. Furthermore, Williams claimed that Halliburton had sought advice from three outside law firms plus federal regulators about the work the subsidiary might perform in Iran.

A positive 2007 announcement reflected that Halliburton won three Hart's *E'P* meritorious engineering achievement awards. Halliburton won the awards for three outstanding technologies. SuperFill surge reduction system allows wellbore fluids to enter the casing freely and exit the drillpipe during casing running operations, effectively reducing surge pressures. AssetPlanner software helps industry members meet the challenges of numerous production demands; Health, Safety and Environmental mandates; and return-on-investment goals by accelerating and optimizing development plans for new or mature fields. ReFlexRite multilateral system provides a re-entry multilateral solution that allows lateral branches to be added to existing single horizontal wells.

Founded in 1919, Brown and Root, Inc. began operating as a subsidiary of Halliburton in 1962. In 1996 it split into three entities, one of which was named Brown and Root Engineering and Construction (BREC). That year, the Houston, Texas-based company posted revenues of US$4.1 billion, with a payroll of 36,000 employees. With operations in more than 60 countries, about two-thirds of its business was conducted outside of the United States. When Halliburton acquired Dresser Industries in 1998, BREC was merged with Dresser's MW Kellogg division to form Kellogg Brown and Root.

Bechtel Group. Bechtel Group of San Francisco, California, continued to be one of the world's leading engineering, construction, and management companies. The firm of 40,000 employees working in 40 countries posted US$17.4 billion in revenues in 2004. The majority (89 percent) of Bechtel's revenues were due to international contracts. The firm's specialties include roads and rail systems, airports and seaports, power plants, pipelines, and telecommunications. The company was founded in 1898 when it was involved with grading railway beds. By 1931, the company was helping with the building of the Hoover Dam.

Fluor Corp. One of the largest engineering, procurement, construction and maintenance service firms in the world is Fluor Corp., an engineer-contractor based in Irving, Texas. Fluor posted US$9.38 billion in sales in 2004 and had more than 35,000 employees. In 2005, the company had offices in more than 25 countries. Fluor relies most heavily on petroleum and industrial engineering markets, as well as the hazardous waste engineering sector. International projects bring in nearly one-third of revenues. In 2005, Fluor's projects included providing engineering support for the modernization of a KoSa plant; front-end engineering and design for the Ju'Aymah gas plant in Saudi Arabia; and engineering, construction and procurement services on the Trans-Alaska Pipeline. Fluor reported revenues of US$14.1 billion in 2006.

In May 2007, Fluor announced that it was selected to provide engineering, procurement, construction management and precommissioning services to Saudi International Petrochemical Co. Ltd. for an acetyls complex in Jubail, Saudi Arabia. The billion-dollar contract involved a project scope including the main plant, set to manufacture acetic acid and vinyl acetate monomer, a high-end speciality plastic for clients, and a new Utilities plant.

CH2M Hill Companies Ltd. CH2M Hill provides engineering and construction services. In 2007 the company employed more than 19,000 people working in regional offices around the world. It expressed the desire to hire 7,000 professionals. CH2M Hill remained "committed to developing people through challenging projects." As a result of impressive growth in many company areas, CH2M planned to focus recruitment efforts on a variety of industries. They included industries such as water, transportation, environmental and industrial. The firm's Applied Sciences Laboratory does a range of environmental and industrial testing. CH2M Hill was providing such environmental services as ecosystem management, human health and ecological risk assessment, and brownfield and remediation services. The company also managed large nuclear projects. Revenues for 2006 were approximately US$4.5 billion. That reflected an increase of 27 percent from 2005. CH2M earned its rankings of No. 5 and No. 38 on *Engineering News Record*'s list of Top 500 Design Firms and Top 400 Contractors respectively. The company's growth as "a market force in the federal area" especially in the area of nuclear waste services was also noted. On the international scene, CH2M was a leader in a program management joint venture for the estimated US$6-billion 2012 London Olympics.

CH2M Hill was chosen to manage the design of an advanced water purification facility for Oxnard, California. It will provide the city with reclaimed water suitable for using with landscape and agricultural irrigation, industrial process water, and groundwater recharge. This project was part of the City of Oxnard's Groundwater Recovery Enhancement and Treatment program. Plans called for the initial phase to be fully operational by year end 2009.

CH2M Hill received a contract from Fort Hills Energy L.P. to provide engineering and procurement services for the Infrastructure Utilities Work for the Fort Hills Project Mine and Upgrader sites. The sites were located in Alberta's Athabasca oil sands area and Edmonton respectively.

Leaders by Market. The top 25 global design firms earned aggregate revenues in 2003 of almost US$31 billion of which US$12.6 billion was earned outside of their home country, according to data from *Engineering News-Record* (ENR). The top five firms in this market were URS of California, SNC-Lavalin of Montreal, Fluor of California, Jacobs of California, and AECOM of California. U.S. companies dominated the 2004 list of the top 25 design firms as compiled by ENR.

The top global contractors earned aggregate revenues in 2003 of approximately US$249.3 billion of which US$87.8 billion was earned outside of their home country. The market leaders in this area were VINCI of France, Bouygues of France, Skanska of Sweden, Shimizu of Japan, and Bechtel of California. Of the top 25 companies three were based in France, five in Japan, four in the U.S., three in China, two in

Germany, and three in Spain. These statistics show the truly international nature of this industry.

MAJOR COUNTRIES IN THE INDUSTRY

By 2005, the engineering field had become truly international. Large-scale projects were contracted out in various parts to companies from around the world. Of the top 150 design firms, almost all of them did some business internationally. The same was true of the top 250 construction firms.

In the U.S., there were accusations that FEMA awarded U.S.$3.6 billion worth of Hurricane Katrina contracts to companies with poor credit histories and bad paperwork. No-bid contracts cleanup work was issued to firms including Bechtel Group, CH2M Hill Companies and Fluor Corp. Investigators were checking to see if the significant waste to taxpayers had also violated federal law.

France was home to several of the world's largest engineering and construction companies in terms of revenues. The United States continued to lead the way in environmental engineering services and design services.

FURTHER READING

Angelo, William J. "Grabbing the Lucrative Adaptive Reuse Market." *Design Build,* July 2004.

"CH2M Hill Hires Nearly 900 Professionals in Q1 2007." *PR Newswire,* 25 April 2007.

"CH2M Hill Receives Infrastructure Utilities Contract for Fort Hills Oil Sands Project." *PR Newswire,* 30 April 2007.

Daniels, Stephen H. and Rob McManamy. "Finding a Silver Lining on an Uncharted Path." *Design Building Magazine,* December 2001. Available from http://www.designbuildmag.com.

"Engineering and Construction Services in France, Germany, UK, US." *Euromonitor,* October 2004. Available from http://www.euromonitor.com.

Fischbach, Amy Florence. "The Top 40 Electrical Design Firms." *EC&M,* 1 May 2004.

"Fluor Wins $1-Billion Contract for Acetyls Complex in Jubail, Saudi Arabia." *Business Wire,* 9 May 2007.

"Halliburton Defends its Dealings: Subsidiary's Work in Iran Was Not Against Law, Executive Contends." *Houston Chronicle,* 1 May 2007.

Halliburton. "Halliburton Wins Three Engineering Achievement Awards." 30 April 2007. Available from http://www.halliburton.com.

"Hoover's Company Capsules." 2007. Available from http://www.hoovers.com.

"IT Unemployment on the Rise." *eWeek,* 29 April 2003.

Jones, Brad. "CH2M Hill Chosen to Design Advanced Water Purification Facility for the City of Oxnard." 25 April 2007. Available from http://www.ch2m.com.

Kerman, Sophie and Andrew Noel. "Vinci First Quarter Sales Climb 27% on Tolls, Road Building." 2 May 2007. Available from http://www.bloomberg.com.

Kross, Robert. "You Need Desktop PLM." *Design News,* 2 June 2003.

Lazich, Robert S., ed. *Market Share Reporter.* Detroit: Thomson Gale, 2004.

Lemyze, Christine. "PLM's Time Has Come." *Design News,* 2 June 2003.

Nyuylime, Lukong Pius. "Civil Engineering — Real Challenge is Quality." *Africa News Service,* 12 April 2007.

"More than a third [of] Chinese Engineers are female." *People's Daily Online*, 5 November 2004. Available from http://www.english.people.com.

"Product Development MEs, EEs Bask in Sunshine." *Design News,* 14 July 2004.

"Research & Stats." Society of Women Engineers, accessed July 2005. Available from http://www.swe.org.

Reina, Peter and Gary J. Tulacz. "Global Firms Increase Their Local Presence." *Engineering News Record,* 23 July 2001. Available from http://www.enr.com.

Rosta, Paul B. "Total 2003 Revenue Exceeds $53 Billion." *Design Build,* July 2004.

Rubin, Debra K. "CH2M Hill's Formula for Success: Fly High But Stay Grounded." *ENR,* 12 March 2007.

Schodek, Daniel L. *Landmarks in American Civil Engineering.* Cambridge, MA: MIT Press, 1987.

"Top Global Design Firms 2004." *Engineering News Record,* 2004. Available from http://www.enr.com.

"Top Global Contractors 2004." *Engineering News Record,* 2004. Available from http://www.enr.com.

"Top 200 Environmental Firms 2004." *Engineering News Record,* 2004. Available from http://www.enr.com.

Tulacz, Gary J. "Design Firms Break Out of the Mold." *Engineering News Record,* 16 April 2001. Available from http://www.enr.com.

———. "Design-Build Trends Draw a Wealth of Work . . . and Competitors." *Engineering News Record,* 19 June 2000. Available from http://www.enr.com.

———. "The Top 100." *Engineering News Record,* 18 June 2001. Available from http://www.enr.com.

"VINCI, Preferred Bidder for a Second Motorway Concession in Greece." 11 May 2007. Available from http://www.vinci.com.

Yen, Hope. "Probe: Katrina Contracts Given to Companies with Poor Credit Histories, Bad Paperwork." 23 April 2007. Available from http:www.timesrecordnews.com.

SIC 8111
NAICS 541110

LEGAL SERVICES

The legal services industry includes offices of lawyers and other legal advisers and services.

INDUSTRY SNAPSHOT

In the mid-2000s, the legal services industry was growing. The top eight firms listed on the 2004 *American Lawyer*'s "Global 100" list had revenues of more than US$1 billion each in 2003. Four of these firms were based in the United Kingdom, with the other four based in the United States. The top 100 firms around the world had aggregate earnings of almost US$48.2 billion.

Consolidation has created larger, more competitive firms with bigger profits. Midsize firms continued to find themselves squeezed out by mega-firms with dozens of offices housing thousands of fee earners. Law firms also are seeing greater profits from their embrace of high technology resources including software and the Internet. These resources allow attorneys to deliver services more efficiently, and cut down on the number of employees needed for case work, thereby resulting in significant cost savings, as well as increased client satisfaction.

The largest voluntary professional organization representing lawyers in the U.S., the American Bar Association (ABA), was founded in 1878 by a group of 100 lawyers to provide some national uniformity in the profession. At that time, lawyers trained under other lawyers as apprentices, rather than having formal law school training. As of 2005, the ABA had more than 400,000 members.

The hiring of diversity managers was becoming a new law firm trend. Many firms were hiring full-time diversity managers. These experts served in a variety of roles. The roles included advising during the staff hiring process, recruiting, professional development and review processes. An Altman Weil survey found only 15 percent of the diversity managers participating in their research study had been employed by their firms for more than three years. Almost one-third of them had only been on board for less than a year.

Legal services offshoring was another trend gaining in popularity and practice. The soaring costs of legal services in both the United States and Europe were leading many companies to send legal work to countries with lower costs such as India. According to research findings reported by ValueNotes, offshoring for legal services vendors was expected to have growth rates ranging anywhere from 30 to 100 percent in the near future. There were concerns about the legal services that would be provided because some industry experts estimated not more than 15 percent of the approximately 79,000 lawyers graduating from more than 400 colleges in India every year were capable of ensuring the high-quality work clients desired.

ORGANIZATION AND STRUCTURE

United States. In the United States, lawyers (also called attorneys) serve as advocates and advisers in both civil and criminal cases. Lawyers generally are required to have a four-year undergraduate degree plus a three-year graduate degree from an accredited law school, and also must pass a written examination to be admitted to practice in any state. Because of a number of scandals involving lawyers beginning in the 1970s—notably Watergate—by 1997, 48 states required that the examination include a section on professional ethics.

Lawyers who pass the exam may be employed as individual practitioners, as employees of a law firm, as government employees, as employees of businesses, or as legal services attorneys (in civil cases) or public defenders (in criminal cases), representing those who can't afford to hire an attorney. In the early 1960s, the U.S. Supreme Court determined that all defendants in felony cases have the right to an attorney; in 1974, the federal government established the Legal Services Corporation, a private nonprofit corporation that represents the indigent in civil cases, even though such representation is not legally required. Lawyers also can become judges, magistrates, or hearing officers, who hear cases and render decisions. In the United States all licensed lawyers may argue in a courtroom, unlike the system in the United Kingdom.

In addition to lawyers, there are many other paraprofessional personnel who assist in providing legal services. Paralegals, who assist lawyers by doing research, investigating facts, and preparing legal documents, are usually college graduates, but they do not need special licensing or examinations. Law clerks assist judges in research or in writing documents. Title examiners, abstractors, and searchers assist real estate or bank attorneys in determining the legal status of property being bought and sold, by examining public and private records.

Most U.S. law firms are structured as partnerships in which senior attorneys own the company and share in the profits. Some firms may also divide partner status into various ranks, with the highest rank culminating in full partnership. Partner status is typically conferred on lawyers after they've been with a firm for a number of years based on such considerations as seniority, their level of annual billings, and their success rate in trials.

The globalization of the legal services industry has created an increasing demand for firms that can seamlessly take care of all of a client's needs under one single establishment. A growing number of accounting firms have been pushing the American Bar Association (ABA) and state bar associations to allow multidisciplinary partnerships (MDPs). These certified public accountants (CPAs) want to offer legal services in addition to their financial and business service offerings. Accounting firms are the biggest employers of attorneys worldwide. At least three of the Big Four accounting firms were affiliated with or had acquired law practices in many nations, allowing them to offer legal services. However, accounting firms are not allowed to own law firms in the United States, even though this is common in many countries in Latin America, Europe, and other parts of the world.

Many of those in the legal profession have a number of concerns regarding MDPs. They believe that confidentiality, independent judgment and advice, and loyalty to clients could be compromised if firms were allowed to offer both accounting and legal services. They also question whether there really is a demand among clients for seamless access to all professional services. Another concern is that MDPs that provide legal services will pose increased competition to the legal services industry.

According to *Accounting Horizons*, the ABA organized the Commission on Multidisciplinary Practice (MDP Commission) to examine and make recommendations on the issue of enabling lawyers to become partners and share fees with non-lawyers, including accountants, stockbrokers, and financial planners. After the MDP commission heard testimony and conducted open hearings on the matter, it recommended unanimously that the Model Rules of Professional Conduct (MRPC) be amended to permit MDPs. In August 1999, the ABA deferred voting on the recommendation, dependent on further study. The MDP Commission instituted more hearings and again proposed its recommendation, but the ABA voted against it in July 2000. However, the MRPC is strictly advisory, and individual states are free to adopt, change, or ignore it. A number of states have been holding their own debates on MDPs, and it is likely that the ABA will take another look at the MDP issue in the future.

Europe and Canada. England, Wales, Scotland, and Northern Ireland each have distinct court systems and bodies of law. However, all of these countries divide professionals who provide legal services into two categories: (1) barristers, who hold exclusive rights to argue in the higher courts; and (2) solicitors, who meet with clients and provide advice to them. Generally, these two coordinate their efforts for the client. France maintains a similar division, dividing advocates into *avocats* (the equivalent of barristers) and *avouets* (the equivalent of solicitors). English barristers belong to one of four Inns at Court, which are combinations of a school and a professional organization. French law students must decide whether to follow a career path as a judge or a lawyer. Canada combines qualities of numerous legal systems, by requiring that lawyers complete college and law school, pass an examination, and serve an "articling period" of apprenticeship to another lawyer.

Background and Development

Written codes of law date back at least to 1700 B.C., when Babylonian king Hammurabi had his kingdom's laws carved on a huge column of stone. His code contained hundreds of categories of offenses for which punishment was in kind; that is to say, the crime of the transgressor was enacted upon him or her as punishment. For instance, if a builder cut corners and a house collapsed, killing the owner's son, the builder's son would be executed. The Judeo-Christian Ten Commandments, probably dating to around 1300 B.C., drew heavily from Hammurabi's code and served as the basic framework for many modern Western laws. The first law school might have been based in Bologna, Italy, around 1150 A.D. Students would hire a teacher to explain the Roman law; one teacher, Irnenius, was so popular that he had to hire other teachers to assist him, thus setting up the first law faculty. By the time of the reign of Henry II in England (1154-89), a person brought before a court could appoint an advocate to plead a case.

In 1215, King John of England signed the Magna Carta (or "great charter"), which gave his subjects basic legal rights such as freedom of religion and the right to a fair trail. The Magna Carta served as the foundation of the Anglo-American law system. In the United States, the Constitution and its Bill of Rights were influenced by the Magna Carta and embodied one of the first examples of modern law. However, many other countries derive their legal systems from Roman law, such as the Napoleonic Code in France. In countries whose laws are based on the Anglo-American system or Roman law (which includes most of Western Europe), there is also a well-established system of trained specialists who provide legal advice and services. Many other countries have their own unique legal systems, based on indigenous law (some African countries, for example) or religious law (Islamic countries). In these countries, the system of trained lawyers and judges prevalent in Western countries might instead consist of tribal heads or religious leaders. However, in the late twentieth century these systems were increasingly influenced by the Western legal systems.

Current Conditions

United States. In 2003, the market for legal services in the United States was valued by Euromonitor at US$166.8 billion, with services for individuals making up 40.3 percent of the total. The market was expected to grow to US$207 billion by 2008, with individual and commercial law being the two largest segments, valued at US$82.5 billion and US$81 billion, respectively.

The top law practices in the multi-billion dollar U.S. legal services industry have a worldwide presence. Some employ thousands of attorneys, and revenues were increasing at an annual rate of 8-10 percent. Firms with expertise in intellectual property and high technology issues are finding success, as well as those that specialize in mergers and acquisitions. The United States is becoming an increasingly litigious society, and the overabundance of attorneys has led to fierce competition. While there are still high-priced lawyers serving an elite clientele, the average American has no problem attaining legal representation, thanks to the growing number of lawyers, along with the increasing availability of low-cost legal services.

Legal trends identified by *Crain's Detroit Business* included noncompete clause interpretation, mediation, class-action suits, and intellectual property disputes. In addition, there was an upswing of specialized niche firms, dubbed "boutiques" by those in the industry. Another popular trend in the 2000s was prepaid legal service insurance plans. Both business owners and individuals can pay a low monthly fee and can access basic legal services on an as-needed basis. Using this type of service eliminates costly retainer fees for consumers who may have normally done without legal services due to the high cost. Services provided in prepaid legal insurance plans often include home purchases or sales, will preparation, and legal consultation by telephone.

According to *American Lawyer,* Skadden, Arps, Slate, Meagher & Flom was the top grossing U.S. firm in 2003, as well as the second place firm worldwide, with US$1.3 billion in revenue and 1,650 lawyers. Other top-five ranked U.S. firms included Baker & McKenzie, which was in the number five spot worldwide; Jones Day; Latham & Watkins; and Sidley Austin Brown & Wood. Collectively, these five firms pulled in more than US$5.0 billion in 2003 revenues.

Analysis of the 2006 to 2007 NALP Directory of Legal Employers revealed that major law firms employ one associate for every partner and the overall ratio of lawyers to partners was 2.19. It represented more than 132,000 lawyers in more than 1,500 law offices nationwide primarily with more than 100 lawyers. Among cities with the highest representation in the directory, lawyer/partner ratios ranged from a low of 1.6 in Milwaukee to a high of 3.16 in New York.

Although industry experts believed it would not happen for some time, some lawyers expressed concern about implementation of a tax on legal services. This tax would also include services offered by private counsel. It was viewed as a means to align the tax base and the economy.

United Kingdom. Valued at US$32.4 billion in 2003 and expected to reach a value of US$38.5 billion by 2008, the United Kingdom was home to several of the world's leading law firms. *The American Lawyer* reported that in 2003 four of the top ten firms worldwide were based here: Clifford Chance (ranked number one in the world), Freshfields Buckhouse Deringer (ranked third), Linklaters (ranked fourth), and Allen & Overy (ranked sixth). Within the U.K., the industry was highly fragmented, with no one organization controlling more than 4 percent of the market, however many mergers and acquisitions were taking place.

Corporate services made up the largest share of the legal market in the U.K., according to Euromonitor, and was expected to account for 36 percent of the market by 2008. Most law practices for private practice chose to head their organizations in London.

Legal Services Minister Bridget Prentice said that new kinds of business structures would continue to increase the choices of models for delivering legal services. Firms owned and managed by non-lawyers providing legal services would enable this progression. The Legal Services Bill, introduced in Parliament in November 2006, was believed to be a key enabler. The Bill called for an independent oversight regulator, the Legal Services Board, and was expected to get Royal Assent in summer 2007. Implementation was expected to occur from two to three years from Royal Assent.

France. Having grown 14 percent in a year to reach a value of US$18.4 billion in 2003, the market for French legal services was expected to show continued rapid growth, according to Euromonitor, growing another 40 percent by 2008. The Notaires de France association reported that in 2003 there were 8,021 lawyers of whom 6,033 worked as partners in 2,487 civil partnerships or professional corporations, with the remainder having individual practices. In total, the industry in France employed almost 46,000 people.

Based on revenues, about half of all activity dealt with real estate, construction, sales and leases. Family instruments and deeds of succession accounted for 33 percent of revenues.

France's ratio of one lawyer to every 2,000 citizens is significantly lower than that of other European countries. No Franco-French law practices exist that have more than one hundred partners. An expanding number of U.S. and U.K. law firms have set up shop in France since the late 1990s, and many now boast bigger Paris offices than those of the top French law practices. The big players in the French legal services industry are those practices with ties to the Big Four accounting firms, including Fidal with it association with KPMG and HDS Ernst & Young. However, some of these law firms have seen attorneys and clients leave for foreign competition. Specialized, smaller practices still thrive, mainly in the capital and corporate finance sectors. Seeing this trend, domestic firms are reevaluating firm management. The two largest firms in France are Andersen Legal Association d'Avocats and Landwell & Associes/Partners. U.S. legal practices with a strong presence in France include Cleary, Gottlieb, Steen & Hamilton, a presence since the end of World War II, and Coudert Freres.

Italy. A number of London's top law firms have entered into Italy's domestic market, but a downward trend is likely due to slowness in the securities market, as well as continuing debt issues. Italy's top two indigenous practices are Gianni, Origoni, Grippo & Partners and Pavia e Ansaldo.

Spain. Madrid and Barcelona are home to most of Spain's top law practices. The country's legal services market is made up of international firms, independent law practices, and multidisciplinary partnerships. Spain's successful economic expansion since the mid-1980s has resulted in a sophisticated and vibrant market. Despite downturns in the global economy, Spanish law firms are continuing to thrive. Increased activity in the private sector has resulted in stronger demand for attorneys, especially in the fields of international trade, property litigation, and labor.

Russia and the CIS. Russia's 1998 currency crisis caused a number of the country's Western law practices to shut down or significantly cut back on staff. However, *The World Legal Forum* noted that in the early 2000s, the Russian economic climate seemed to be improving. Many international firms in Russia do work in the energy sector. Higher oil prices and increased foreign investment in the energy market have also led to cautious optimism. President Vladimir Putin's reform agenda also has helped, including the introduction of a number of pro-investor bills and the modernization of Russia's tax system. Most indigenous Russian firms have difficulty competing with foreign firms, particularly in international matters as they do not have global practices. However several domestic firms get signicant referral business. These firms include Alrud and Pepeliaev, Goltsblat & Partners. The largest foreign law practices in Russia were: Linklaters CIS; Freshfields Bruckhaus Deringer; LeBoeuf, Lamb, Greene & MacRae LLP; and White & Case LLC.

Hong Kong. The legal services sector in Hong Kong is made up of two types of legal professionals, barristers and solicitors. Barristers are litigation and advocacy specialists, while solicitors undertake general practice. Barristers must receive instruction from solicitors to perform services for clients, the majority of which are related to criminal cases, shipping, intellectual property, construction, personal injuries, and landlord-tenant disputes.

When it comes to allowing foreign attorneys to participate in its legal services industry, Hong Kong is the most favorable jurisdiction in Asia, according to the Hong Kong Trade Development Council. By the end of July 2001, there were approximately 39 foreign firms, and more than 500 foreign solicitors were practicing in Hong Kong. Mainland China is the biggest export market for Hong Kong's legal sector, since most demand comes from both Hong Kong and foreign corporations that are currently investing in or are planning to invest in China.

Legal professionals in Hong Kong will benefit from China's bilateral agreement with the United States over accession to the World Trade Organization (WTO). They offer expert knowledge of Chinese law and their client base in China is strong. These factors, among others, make for a bright outlook for Hong Kong's legal services industry. However, by the mid-2000s the market was considered be "over lawyered," leading to intense competition. In 2004, U.K.-based Denton Wilde Sapte left the market altogether.

China (mainland). *The American Lawyer* reported that, although China's ties to the West had been mainly via Hong Kong, its legal sector was increasingly seen as standing tall on its own. Many Western law firms gave up on establishing offices in mainland China after the government imposed more restrictions on citizens after the Tiananmen Square incidents in 1989. However, the Chinese government's willingness to bring about a more modernized financial infrastructure in the late 1990s brought a number of foreign law practices to the country. By the early twenty-first century, more than one hundred firms had opened offices inside the mainland. China's admission to the World Trade Organization (WTO) is another significant factor in the expansion of foreign firms. However, heavy restrictions still plague Western firms in China. For example, they are prohibited from hiring Chinese attorneys and are forbidden to practice Chinese law.

The industry was valued at US$1.6 billion in 2003, with more than 10,000 firms and 110,000 certified lawyers in the practice, according to Euromonitor. The majority (47 percent) served the commercial sector. The industry remained highly fragmented, with the top five firms having only about 2 percent of the market. The legal services market was expected to grow by 31 percent by 2008, with commercial services accounting for 52 percent of revenues.

In February 2007, MWE China Law Offices announced it had established a strategic alliance with McDermott Will & Emery. McDermott was one of the world's top 25 law firms. MWE China Law Offices agreed to serve as a separate law firm and provide more quality services for its clients with support from its U.S. partner. McDermott operated nine offices in the U.S. and five offices in Europe.

Japan. In the early 1990s, only a small number of Western lawyers worked in Japan, reported *The American Lawyer.* They were mainly employed by Japanese corporations looking to purchase assets in the United States and Europe. The late 1990s burst of Japan's economic bubble reversed the situation, and Western companies began lining up to buy weakened Japanese assets at reduced costs. As a result, British and American firms added lawyers to their Japan-based operations and began to influence Japan's legal services industry with Western legal and cultural practices. However, restrictions still abound for Western firms. Japan prohibits mergers between Japanese and foreign law firms. Although they are allowed to share office space, they must keep the partnership structure and billing separate. Within the industry itself, many mergers had occurred between law firms. The largest firm in the country in 2003 was Nagashima Ohno & Tsunematsu, with Anderson Mori, Asahi Koma, Nishimura, and Mori Hamada & Matsumoto being the industry's other key player.

The market was mainly concerned with corporate issues, primarily those involving mergers and acquisitions (33 percent of the market). The industry was valued at US$1.09 billion in 2003, and was projected to grow a significant 78 percent by 2008, according to *Euromonitor.*

South Korea. Valued at US$1.61 million by 2003, South Korea's legal industry was worth more than China's or Japan's that year. According to Euromonitor, there were 10,300 companies in the industry. The largest company in South Korea was Kim & Chang. Due to the economic ties between the two countries, many lawyers in South Korea are trained in the U.S. However, the qualification process in South Korea remained much more rigorous, with more people unable to pass the bar exam than people able to pass.

RESEARCH AND TECHNOLOGY

Readers of novels by Charles Dickens will recall how long-suffering legal clerks were responsible for preparing court documents by hand, as well as sifting through dusty court files and yellowing books to conduct research on cases. In many ways, this was still the state of legal research until the 1970s. Prior to the development of word processing equipment, legal secretaries had the agonizing task of typing documents on manual, and later electric, typewriters, and were forced to retype entire documents if a lawyer decided to add an extra paragraph. Research was conducted by law students, paralegals, and newly graduated lawyers at firms, using paper indexes to books of court opinions and statutes. With the development of desktop and laptop computers, plus online research services, the field of legal research and document preparation was changed drastically, so that research that would have taken hours or even days to conduct by hand became the work of a few minutes on a computer. Lawyers who had left all of their document preparation and research to their staffs began to do much more of this work on their own computers.

In the late 1960s, the Ohio State Bar Association decided to put state case law onto a computer, allowing users to locate cases by typing in a word or phrase. In 1973, LEXIS-NEXIS, the first commercial, full-text online legal information service, was created by Ohio's Mead Corporation, originally providing case law for only three states (New York, Ohio, and Missouri). Because personal computers were not available to the general public at the time, users of the service had to go to courthouses that had special terminals, or purchase terminals at an extremely high cost. Shortly afterward, the West Publishing Company of Minnesota introduced a similar service, WESTLAW. West had the advantage of already being the publisher of volumes of federal and state laws and court opinions. LEXIS-NEXIS and WESTLAW thus began a rivalry for the lucrative legal research market that continued through the next three decades.

By the late 1990s, both LEXIS-NEXIS and WESTLAW had become key components of multibillion-dollar businesses, and almost every lawyer and law student in the

United States had easy access to the two services via personal computers. In 1994 LEXIS-NEXIS was purchased by London-based publisher Reed Elsevier plc, and in 1996 West Publishing and WESTLAW joined Minnesota's Thomson Corporation (as parts of the new West Group). The two companies vied for the law student market, knowing that these students (who received unlimited free access) were likely to keep their preferred service once they graduated and became paying customers. Both LEXIS-NEXIS and WESTLAW provided access to thousands of full-text databases of state, federal, and international statutes, cases, law and business journals, and news sources. They also had established Internet-based services for attorneys practicing in specialized fields. By 2000, LEXIS-NEXIS had more than three billion documents accessible via books, CD-ROMs, and on the Internet. Subscribers numbered more than two million, and 2000 sales growth was at 29.9 percent. Along with Lexis.com, which offers legal data on the Web, the company's online products include a legal directory, jurisdictional and citation services, legal research information, and a legal filing service, all available under various other brand names.

By the end of the twentieth century, the Internet had made a major impact on both law firms and users of legal services. The average person can now use various Web sites to perform routine legal research, download legal forms, and handle many of their basic legal needs, all without having to consult an attorney. If hiring a lawyer becomes inevitable, free Internet services can help with the selection process. For example, Lawyers.com offers profiles of 420,000 attorneys worldwide to help users find the right legal counsel for their needs.

Law practices are growing increasingly reliant on the Internet. By the mid-2000s, such technologies were becoming increasingly necessary to legal firms. In particular, Web-based technologies such as portals and extranets were seeing exponential growth into 2004, allowing many legal services to be conducted completely electronically, including hearings. Attorneys can perform case research, market their practices, and communicate with clients and their fellow lawyers, all by going online. Transport of documents can be done via encrypted e-mail at speeds surpassing traditional means. Firms in multiple locations can access data in case files and law libraries via password-protected intranets. Digital courtrooms are another popular online trend. This technology allows for virtual meetings of judges, juries, expert witnesses, and the like, resulting in significant cost savings for courthouses. Videoconferencing software and technology is likely to pave the way for trials to be held over the Internet.

The Internet also is being used in law schools to supplement coursework and allow students easier access to their professors. In addition, the American Bar Association is looking at letting law schools offer students credit for distance learning.

WORKFORCE

Demand for lawyers was expected to continue growing through 2012 at about the average rate for all professions. A majority of the lawyers operated in the United States, and about three-quarters of them worked in private or solo practices. Others held jobs in government offices, banks, insurance companies, real estate agencies, and other firms including not-for-profit organizations.

Demand for paralegals was expected to rise beyond the average rate through 2012, as these workers increasingly take on a number of legal tasks previously carried out only by attorneys.

According to the ABA's Commission on Women in the Profession report called "Visible Invisibility: Women of Color in Law Firms", conditions were extremely poor for minority females in U.S. law firms with 25 or more lawyers. Nearly half of the women of color reported experiencing demeaning comments or harassment compared to only 3 percent of white men. Regarding retention, 53 percent of women of color remained at law firms while 72 percent of white males chose to remain.

A National Association of Law Placement study evaluated the female partners at law firms. It found an average of 17.3 female partners at firms throughout the United States. The number of female law school graduates was about 49 percent annually. They still, however, trailed behind their male counterparts in climbs up the corporate ladder to arrive at partner ranks or high-profile management jobs in law firms.

Managing partners at nearly every firm were finding it difficult to decide how to divide their time between managing the firm and practicing law. Partners and associates of diverse firms agreed there was a fundamental necessity for balancing being a lawyer with leadership duties. Some firms opted not to have a managing partner as part of their structure. There were also firms who functioned by relegating a lot of the recommendation- and decision-making responsibilities to committees.

INDUSTRY LEADERS

Clifford Chance LLP. In 2005, London-based Clifford Chance remained the highest-ranked law firm worldwide, with 6,700 people working from 30 offices in 20 countries in the Americas, Asia, Europe, and the Middle East. Boasting approximately US$1.7 billion in revenues for 2003, Clifford Chance offered services around six global practice areas: banking and finance, capital markets, corporate (including mergers and acquisitions),litigation and dispute resolution, real estate, and tax, pensions and employment. The practice came into being by way of a merger in 2000 with Punder Vohard Weber & Axster of Germany, and U.S. firm Rogers & Wells. Clients include Siemens, Pfizer, and Citigroup.

In 2007, Clifford Chance announced that is had signed a contract with offshore vendor Integreon. Integreon was expected to have 300 seats dedicated for Clifford Chance.

Skadden, Arps, Slate, Meagher & Flom LLP. Founded in 1948, New York-based Skadden, Arps was the second-highest ranked law firm in the world on both *The Lawyer* and *The American Lawyer* global 100 lists in 2004. In 2005, the company had approximately 4,400 employees, including about 1,700 lawyers, working in 20 offices throughout the world. The practice has provided legal counsel for almost one-half of the *Fortune* 250 industrial and service companies, and specializes in mergers and acquisitions, bankruptcy, and securities.

Freshfields Bruckhaus Deringer. Freshfields had approximately 2,500 lawyers practicing in 27 centers in Europe, Asia, the Middle East and the United States. The London-based Freshfields was the third-ranked global law firm. In 2005, the firm's lawyers practiced in such areas as antitrust, competition and trade; corporate, mergers and acquisitions, and securities; dispute resolution; employment, pensions and benefits; finance; information technology; real estate; and tax. About 66 percent of the company's lawyers worked outside of the U.K. In 2003, the firm had estimated revenues of approximately US$1.4 billion.

In April 2007, Freshfields announced that it had advised on the largest IPO to date. The retail portion of this global offering involving China CITIC Bank was more than 220 times over-subscribed while the institutional portion was also significantly oversubscribed. Total proceeds from the IPO were US$5.4 billion and will exceed US$6.2 billion if over-allotment option was exercised in full.

Linklaters. Specializing in commercial law, London-based Linklaters had 30 offices in 23 countries, including the world's major financial centers, in 2007. Of the firm's more than 2,000 lawyers, about 55 percent worked outside of the U.S. The company's legal services cover 20 core practice areas such as asset finance, banking, mergers and acquisitions, intellectual property, restructuring and insolvency, and tax. Revenues in 2003 were about US$1.3 billion.

Baker & McKenzie. One of the world's largest law firms, Baker & McKenzie has 3,400 attorneys practicing in approximately 70 offices. The Chicago-based firm had offices throughout Asia, Europe, the Middle East, Latin America, and North America. It continued to be the most global of all U.S. firms. Sales for 2005 were approximately US$1.35 billion. The practice's main areas of expertise include tax and international trade. In 1999, Baker & McKenzie named a woman to its top partner slot, becoming one of the first major law firms to do so. The firm, founded in 1949, had about 8,500 employees by 2005.

Allen & Overy LLP. In 2005, the international legal practice of Allen & Overy employed approximately 4,800 staff in 25 major centers in Asia, Europe, the Middle East, and North America. Clients included BT Group, Equitable Life Assurance Society, Merrill Lynch, Shell Chemicals and Virgin Mobile. Allen & Overy advises private clients on commercial trust, partnership, property and tax issues. Based in London, the firm was founded in 1930, gaining fame when it worked for King Edward VIII during his abdication. Allen & Overy expanded globally beginning in 1978 when it opened offices in Dubai and then Brussels. In 2003, the firm had earnings of about US$1.4 billion.

Jones Day. As one of the largest practices in the world, Jones Day was also one of the oldest. It was founded in 1893 in Cleveland, Ohio. The practice offers legal counsel to more than half of the *Fortune* 500 companies. In 2005, Jones Day employed some 2,200 lawyers in 30 locations in the U.S., Latin America, Europe, Asia/Pacific region and the United States. Major clients included General Motors, IBM and Texas Instruments. Sales for 2005 grew to approximately US$1.3 billion.

In 2007, for the third consecutive year, Jones Day announced that its partner Bernard Amory was named regulatory communications lawyer of the year by the Who's Who Legal Awards. The award selection process reviewed thousands of nominations from clients and private practice professionals in the course of an ongoing research process to identify the pre-eminent lawyer and firm in each of 27 practice areas covered in *The International Who's Who of Business Lawyers of 2007*. The resource was a compendium edition of all the individual Who's Who legal publications released in April.

Further Reading

American Bar Association, 2004. Available from http://www.abanet.org.

The American Lawyer. *The Global 100.* 2004. Available from http://www.law.com.

Ankeny, Robert. "On the Docket." *Crain's Detroit Business,* 2 February 2004.

Barksdale, Titan. "Proposed Tax on Legal Services is Floated: Lawyers Express Opposition; Legislator Says It Won't Happen Anytime Soon." *Winston-Salem Journal,* 28 January 2007.

Draper, Deborah J., ed. *Business Rankings Annual.* Detroit: Thomson Gale, 2004.

Frank, Kimberly E., et al. "CPAs' Perceptions of the Emerging Multidisciplinary Accounting/Legal Practice." *Accounting Horizons,* March 2001.

"Freshfields Advises on the World' Largest IPO This Year to Date." 27 April 2007. Available from http://www.freshfields.com.

Gannon, Joyce. "Firms Teach Women Lawyers Importance of Networking to Climbing Law Firm Ladder." *Pittsburgh Post-Gazette,* 18 October 2006.

Heilman, Dan. "Hiring Diversity Managers - a New Law Firm Trend." *Minnesota Lawyer,* 5 March 2007.

"Hoover's Company Capsules." 2007. Available from http://www.hoovers.com.

Johnson, Glen. "Legal Services Offshoring: Hype Vs. Reality." *The America's Intelligence Wire,* 3 January 2007.

"Jones Day Partner Bernard Amory Named Regulatory Communications Lawyer of the Year for the Third Consecutive Year." April 2007. Available fromhttp:www.jonesday.com.

"Law Firm Leverage Varies With Firm Size and Location." *Daily Record,* 5 February 2007.

"The Lawyer Global 100: The world's elite law firms 2004." *The Lawyer,* November 2004. Available from http://www.thelawyer.com.

Lazich, Robert S., ed. *Market Share Reporter.* Detroit: Thomson Gale, 2004.

"Legal Services in Australia, China, France, Germany, Japan, South Korea, UK, US." *Euromonitor,* October 2004. Available from http://www.Euromonitor.com.

Pribek, Jane. "ABA Reports Women of Color Still Having a Tough Time in Large Law Firm Environment." *Wisconsin Law Journal,* 22 November 2006.

"Recommended Law Firms and Lawyers Worldwide." *The Legal 500*, viewed July 16, 2005. Available from http://www.legal500.com.

"Report Examines Forces Reshaping the Legal Profession." *Fairfield County Business Journal,* 21 July 2003.

Solnik, Claude. "When it Comes to Law Firm Management, It's Whatever Works, Baby." *Long Island Business News,* 12 January 2007.

"UK Government: Make Legal Services More Accessible to Consumer Says Bridget Prentice." *Europe Intelligence Wire,* 26 March 2007.

U.S. Bureau of the Census. *Service Annual Survey.* Washington, 2004. Available from http://www.census.gov.

U.S. Bureau of Labor Statistics. "National Occupational Employment and Wage Data." *Occupational Employment Statistics.* Washington, 2004. Available from http://stats.bls.gov.

U.S. Industry and Trade Outlook. New York: McGraw-Hill, Department of Commerce, and International Trade Administration, 2000.

"US Law Firm Marches Into China." *Alestron,* 1 February 2007.

World Legal Forum. *Country Overview.* 2001. Available from http://www.worldlegalforum.co.uk.

SIC 8742

NAICS 541611

MANAGEMENT CONSULTING SERVICES

Management consultants provide administrative, strategic, and technical advice and training to organizations in the public and private sectors. Examples of these services include financial planning, organizational planning, marketing advice, information technology consulting, human resource planning, and logistics advice. Certain industry firms also provide management accounting and auditing services; see also **Accounting, Auditing, and Bookkeeping Services** for a discussion of these activities. Others specialize in various forms of information technology planning and systems management, which is discussed in greater detail under the heading **Information Technology Services.**

INDUSTRY SNAPSHOT

The management consulting industry is highly fragmented and polarized. Participants vary widely in size, type, and specialization; the majority of firms are either extremely large or extremely small. Management consulting services range from general management advice to technology development to financial advising to strategy implementation. The industry is also characterized by its broad scope and increasingly blurred functional boundaries. Barriers to entry are low, it remains largely unregulated, and there are no certification requirements for becoming a management consultant. However, consultants can obtain a Certified Management Consultant (CMC) designation, which is internationally recognized. Members must adhere to a strict code of professional conduct.

The industry's US$125 billion in revenues are concentrated primarily among large U.S. and Western European consulting and accounting firms. However, while the United States weighs in with the largest presence in the industry, the U.S. market is maturing. Accordingly, opportunities for market growth exist in emerging markets in Eastern Europe, the Commonwealth of Independent States, Latin America, and the Pacific Rim. Most large U.S. and European firms are shifting their revenue bases abroad—thus increasing integration of the world market.

For many years, an attractive feature of the industry was its stability and durability. Consulting was considered largely recession-proof by many analysts because during times of economic decline, businesses tended to look to consultancy firms for restructuring advice and financial planning. When the dot-com bubble burst and recessionary economic conditions took hold in North America and Europe, however, growth in worldwide management consulting revenues began to slow. After several difficult years, the industry appeared to be recovering by mid-2004, but growth rates were expected to remain low. Industry revenues increased 3 percent in 2004, to approximately US$125 billion, according to Kennedy Information Research Group.

ORGANIZATION AND STRUCTURE

In the larger, more mature U.S. and Western European markets, demand is concentrated largely in the private sector. However, the trend for growth in the U.S. has been in the government and healthcare areas of the marketplace. In newer, smaller markets, including central and Eastern Europe, India, and Asia, public sector institutions, including government bodies and international organizations account for larger proportions of the demand. In particular, national governments in these regions are among the most rapidly growing client base because they utilize consultancy firms to increase economic competitiveness. China has accounted for the largest amount of growth in the Asia Pacific region.

The global management consulting industry comprises six major industry sectors:

Information Technology (IT). An increasingly competitive consulting sector, IT includes companies that use computer and telecommunications technologies to solve business problems, create/seize business opportunities, and address business and management issues surrounding the implementation and integration of new technologies such as electronic commerce, technology needs assessment, and change management. Many of these types of consulting companies have found their recent growth to be increasingly coming from outsourcing. Numerous IT consultancies have evolved beyond merely offering consulting services and have become full-service firms, with many traditional IT firms forming their own consulting subsidiaries. Alliances with providers are becoming common. IT consultants may consult with a company to determine its IT needs; purchase, install and integrate the recommended software and hardware; and eventually operate the system for the client.

Human Resources. Firms in this group plan, develop, and implement programs that help managers motivate and compensate employees, as well as develop their ability to achieve corporate objectives. Examples include total quality management, team building, competency modeling, job analysis, benefits packaging, diversity planning, and pension funding. According to Kennedy Information Research, in 2003, this sector of the management consulting industry was responsible for US$13.2 billion in revenues.

Strategy. These establishments help managers and directors develop and implement comprehensive, deliberate, strategic plans for improving an organization's competitive position or furthering its corporate mission. Such services often include growth and Internet strategies, acquisition and divestment advice, restructuring planning, and privatization implementation.

Recent trends have shown clients to be tired of strategy in itself. They have become increasingly sophisticated consumers of strategy consulting services, and are looking for results that can be implemented quickly. Clients have become more results-driven with the result being a greater desire for compensation to consultants being tied to these results.

Operations. Operations consultants help managers improve production methods and business processes to increase efficiency and effectiveness. Activities include materials requirements planning, inventory planning and control, statistical quality control, customer relationship management (CRM), and project scheduling. This sector of the consulting industry is expected to have the largest growth rate in the next few years.

Finance and Accounting. These firms advise managers on matters of financial management, investment, and reporting to help them maximize the value of their organizations and ensure their future viability. Examples include shareholder value studies, treasury management, financial planning and risk management, and financial market review.

Marketing and Sales. These consultants provide managers with information and advice to help them maintain or increase market share. These firms' services include market analysis and segmentation, new market entry/positioning, product research, and new product development.

Traditionally, firms have billed their clients on an hourly basis, charging anywhere from $100 to more than $500 per hour. In the 1990s, however, a growing number of consulting businesses, especially smaller firms, began generating a substantial amount of their charges from performance-based fees for projects with a measurable outcome, often as much as 70 percent. Recognizing the importance of results and accountability, these firms began accepting payment based on the clients' realized results. Some skeptics criticized this practice, suggesting that it could raise ethical concerns; for example, consultants accepting performance-based fees might be tempted to advise clients in such a manner as to encourage greater short-term results, neglecting the long-term stability of the company. To offset this potential danger, many consulting firms included members of the clients' management staff on the consulting team.

During the North American and European economic slowdown of the early 2000s, the industry saw a return to more traditional billing practices. According to a 2001 issue of *Consultants News*, performance-based pricing in the management consulting industry declined 50 percent between 1999 and 2000. This shift was due, in part, to the need for clients concerned about containing costs to obtain specific price quotes before hiring consultants.

Major suppliers of management consulting services are a diverse, competitive, and rapidly consolidating group. Firms differ along a number of dimensions including organization type, organization size, area(s) of expertise, degree of specialization, clients and industries served, geographic presence, and global reach. The five major types of suppliers are:

Consulting Firms. These are organizations for which the sole or primary line of business is the delivery of management advice and assistance. The majority of consulting firms are small, with annual billings of less than US$5 million. High profit potential, growing demand for management consulting services, and low barriers to entry fueled an influx of small firms and individual practitioners during the 1990s. Although fewer in number, large consulting firms, typically defined as those with annual revenues exceeding US$1 billion, account for a significant portion of global industry revenues. Fourteen firms met this criteria in 2001, many of which derived a significant proportion of their revenues outside of their home countries.

A shrinking number of mid-sized firms, generating between US$5 million and US$1 billion in revenues, operated successfully in the early 2000s. Limited global reach coupled with significant overhead costs make it increasingly difficult for mid-sized firms to maintain a foothold in this highly competitive market. Industry sources predicted that these firms would slowly be forced out of the market by larger competitors looking to diversify service lines and expand access to international markets. Mid-sized firms are prime candidates for mergers and takeovers because of ready access to local/regional markets and well-established client bases. The highest proportion of mid-sized firms operate in Europe.

"Big Four" Accounting Firms. This group of U.S. companies is composed of the four largest accounting and audit firms in the world—PricewaterhouseCoopers, Ernst & Young, Deloitte Touche Tohmatsu, and KPMG International. Arthur Andersen was part of this group—then known as the Big Five—until its conviction for obstructing justice in the case against Enron. Prior to its demise, it did manage to spin-off Andersen Consulting, which achieved autonomy from its parent in 2000 and changed its name to Accenture. Accenture is now the world's largest technology and management consulting company.

It was during the 1960s, when markets for traditional accounting services began to mature, that these firms first diversified into management consulting services, primarily focusing on the information technology and financial services segments of the market. Like Andersen, the Big Five firms granted increasing autonomy to consulting divisions throughout the 1990s. In fact, under increasing pressure from U.S. federal regulators unhappy about the potential conflicts of interest inherent in a company offering both auditing and consulting services, Ernst & Young sold its consulting arm to France's Cap Gemini Group in 2000. KPMG spun its consulting activities off as KPMG Consulting the following year.

Computer Software and Hardware Companies. Suppliers from this group are the newest to the management consulting industry. In the early 1990s large information technology firms such as computer vendors, systems integrators, and software developers, began diversifying into management consulting when competition for core services intensified. A handful of these companies developed substantial management consulting practices, including Electronic Data Systems (EDS), International Business Machines (IBM), Digital Equipment Corporation (DEC), Unisys Corporation, and Sema Group. Most of these companies either bought into the market through formal mergers and acquisitions or gained access through informal alliances and loose networks with consulting organizations.

Independent Practitioners. This group is the most internationally diverse. Local independent consultants were among the first suppliers to respond to demand in new markets and they still play a significant role as markets have grown and matured. The lack of regulatory agencies to monitor professional competence and minimal start-up costs allows almost anyone to enter the market. Such businesses consist mainly of entrepreneurs, laid-off business professionals, former large-firm consultants, industry specialists, and, increasingly, university professors.

Consulting Divisions of Large Businesses and Government Organizations. Internal consulting divisions began to spring up within large business and government organizations during the 1970s. For the most part they provided management advice to various divisions within the organization. During the 1980s internal divisions expanded their client bases beyond parent company borders. In the early stages of growth in eastern Europe, Asia, and other markets, internal consultants to national and government organizations were among the first groups to offer management consulting advice.

The global management consulting industry remains virtually unregulated. Unlike most other professional service industries, there are no certification requirements for becoming a management consultant. However, the Institute of Management Consultants, a primary industry association, does offer the Certified Management Consultant (CMC) certification program.

BACKGROUND AND DEVELOPMENT

The origins of the industry can be traced back to "time and motion" studies performed in the United States in the 1880s. Around that time Frank and Lillian Gilbreth improved methods for laying bricks by eliminating unnecessary steps or "motions" in the bricklaying process. Frank W. Taylor similarly increased productivity in the U.S. steel industry by identifying and timing individual elements involved in various processes and then pinpointing sources of inefficiency.

In 1881 the first management consulting firm was established in Cambridge, Massachusetts, by Arthur D. Little. The firm, bearing the same name as the founder, quickly established itself as a viable business and maintained a leadership position in the management consulting industry for over 100 years. That same year saw the establishment of the first U.S. collegiate business school, the Wharton School, also located in Cambridge, Massachusetts. Nearly two decades later, in 1900, the first graduate school of business appeared, Dartmouth Amos Tuck School, followed by the Harvard Business School in 1908. The first European institute, Institute European d'Administration (INSEAD), appeared in Fontainbleau, France, in 1959. Business schools supplied both qualified consultants and business research to the management consulting field.

During the first half of the twentieth century, a contingent of small consulting firms and enterprising individuals began to advise businesses in the United States and Europe, primarily on matters of industrial productivity. These early consultants developed new methods for saving time and other resources and applied them universally across businesses and industries. Some of the better known firms that appeared during this period include: U.S. firm Booz, Allen and Hamilton (1914); Belgian firm Buck Consultants (1917); Italian firm Orga SRL (1925); U.S. firm McKinsey and Company (1926); Swiss firm Gherzi Management Consultants (1929); Dutch firms Van de Bunt Management Consultants (1933) and B.W. Berenschot (1938); British firm PA Consulting (1943); and French firm Bossard (1956).

The 1960s brought a number of significant events that accelerated and influenced the development of the management consulting industry. U.S. accounting firms began diversifying into management consulting around this time. Within 10 years these firms captured significant shares of the U.S. management consulting market and began to expand into international markets. Toward the end of the decade large consulting firms also began to diversify service lines and expanded into international markets. For the most part, global expansion involved establishing highly autonomous foreign offices staffed by local consultants who understood local business environments.

In 1963 Bruce Henderson founded the Boston Consulting Group (BCG) in Cambridge, Massachusetts. The firm operated as the first "pure strategy" consulting firm and developed several new management tools including "the growth share matrix" and "the experience curve." The tools were used in strategic planning to assess a company's competitive position or its individual business units. BCG's success had a number of long-term ramifications for the industry. It catalyzed the development of a long string of strategy "boutiques," many of which were founded by former BCG consultants. It also demonstrated how new management theories and business methodologies could earn a firm competitive advantage. Finally, its aggressive recruiting of MBAs drove up salaries for entry-level management consultants.

The 1980s were a period of tremendous growth, expansion, turbulence, and change. Thousands of business professionals laid off during massive downsizings in the major U.S. industries joined the growing ranks of consultants. U.S. consulting industry revenues doubled between 1980 and 1985, and doubled again within two to three years. Meanwhile the European market was growing at a rate of 50 percent, fueled by demand for information technology consulting and assistance with privatization efforts. New markets began to open up around the world; small local firms and individual consultants began to spring up in these new markets. With U.S. and European markets showing early signs of maturity, large consulting firms rushed to establish an early foothold in the promising new markets. As a result the global market became larger and more integrated.

Eastern Europe and Asia were the fastest-growing new markets in the 1990s. Large Japanese corporations and Asian organizations emerged as major new clients, along with world organizations and governments in eastern and central Europe. The breakup of the Soviet Union led to increased demand for political risk studies, industrial infrastructure analyses, legal system assessments, and investment/market analysis in former Soviet nations. Ongoing development of Poland, Romania, and other transition economies in Eastern Europe fueled the region's demand. As the dominant U.S. market continued to mature, most major firms concentrated resources on acquiring firms in these markets to establish themselves in these potentially lucrative areas without facing the cultural barriers involved in establishing new ventures.

Bolstering explosive industry growth in the mid-to-late 1990s was the Y2K computer problem. Consultants were contracted en masse to help businesses reconfigure their computing environments to be compatible with four-digit dating systems. This massive, global project involved consultants in the fields of information technology, systems implementation, financial planning, and strategy.

The management consulting industry also became increasingly polarized throughout the decade. Large firms continued to grow larger by diversifying service lines to meet industry-specific needs, recruiting heavily to meet skyrocketing demand, and snatching up mid-sized firms and information technology suppliers. These industry leaders evolved into "mega-service providers," or "one-stop-shopping centers," in order to secure lucrative contracts with multinational corporations whose needs were as broad as their geographic bases. On the other hand, small firms and individual practitioners, such as business school professors and business technology experts, began entering the industry in record numbers. These niche practices typically focused on specific business concerns, such as operational strategies, and specific practices, such as electronic commerce.

The late 1990s witnessed the emergence of complex contracts involving larger, more integrated teams of consultants and clients. The consulting activities of large firms shifted from "formulation" to "implementation," as the role of management consultants evolved from "management advisor" to "management tool." With this growing emphasis on implementation, especially in the area of information technology consulting, the management consulting industry became increasingly difficult to define. Services ranging from customized software development to the more traditional strategic planning advice were bought and sold under the management consulting label. Important boundaries between management consulting, accounting, and computer/telecommunications fields began breaking down, and the leading firms in these three fields consolidated rapidly.

Major industry mergers and acquisitions during this time period included the 1998 marriage of Price Waterhouse and Coopers & Lybrand to form PricewaterhouseCoopers, a deal which reduced the Big Six accounting firms to the Big Five. Two years later Paris, France-based Cap Gemini Group bolstered its industry standing from eighth place to third place by acquiring the consulting operations of Ernst & Young for US$11 billion. Also in 2000, United Kingdom-based PA Consulting Group, Ltd. paid US$96 million for Hagler Bailly, a U.S.-based consultancy. In September of that year, Hewlett-Packard attempted to purchase the information technology consulting arm of PricewaterhouseCoopers; however, the US$17 billion stock deal fell through the following month due to unstable information technology market conditions.

An unprecedented level of cutbacks and layoffs dominated the U.S. and U.K. management consulting landscapes early in the twenty-first century. The electronic commerce boom of the late 1990s had fostered an environment in which most leading consultancies were forced to compete with upstart Internet consultancies like Scient and Viant not only for business from clients looking to develop Internet strategies, but also for a rapidly shrinking pool of qualified employees. When the electronic commerce market began to slow and the North American economy softened in 2000, many firms found themselves overloaded with highly paid help. As a result, to offset revenue growth slowdowns caused by the weak economy, many firms cut staff in the interest of profitability. In an effort to remain competitive, however, many companies also started discounting their fees, as well as trimming back their typical annual fee increases.

Demand for management consulting services remained fairly strong in areas such as continental Europe, where the Internet arrived more slowly and where deregulation of certain industries was taking place. In the long term, some industry analysts expected Latin America and Mexico to offer substantial growth opportunities as well.

The absence of mandatory certification requirements and lack of enforceable industry standards have remained prominent concerns. One conflict-of-interest concern involves the increasing number of business relationships between management consultancies and information technology supplies that could bias consultants' recommendations regarding information technology products. Another pressing issue is the conflict between accounting firms' auditing activities, which require absolute objectivity, and their management consulting activities, which increasingly involve long-term, high-contact engagements. "Relationship consulting," in which consulting firms work with clients over a period of several years to monitor and ensure progress on the implementation of ideas, has been a growing trend adding to this dilemma. Dialogue and legislative action related to conflict-of-interest issues throughout the 1990s came to a head in the late 1990s, when the U.S. Securities and Exchange Commission (SEC) took aim at Big Five auditors, in particular KPMG, to ensure independence from consulting clients. Rival firms took notice, and began to spin off or sell divisions.

Like KPMG Consulting and Ernst & Young, Accenture also split from its accounting parent. However, the reason for this break was more closely tied to the perception by Anderson consultants that the slower growth auditing business was eating into the profits garnered by Anderson Consulting, which had operated in a double-digit growth environment throughout the 1990s. Along with newly earned independence, KPMG Consulting and Accenture gained access to additional capital via public offerings, a new phenomenon among the upper echelon of management consultants. Many analysts believed that these firms would use the cash to fund acquisitions, mergers, and other deals that will help them maintain their standing in an industry predicted to continue its trend of rapid consolidation.

Perhaps most indicative of the level of change taking place in the management consulting industry's is the widespread management shuffling undertaken by many leading firms. 6 of the top 14 consultancies replaced their CEOs in either 2000 or 2001. Most of these appointments took place at newly independent consultancies like Accenture, KPMG Consulting, and Cap Gemini.

Current Conditions

Following a period of decline during the weak economy of the early 2000s, the management consulting industry appeared to be recovering by mid-2004. Industry revenues were US$119 billion in 2003, increasing to US$125 billion in 2004. While some leading firms such as Accenture experienced noteworthy growth during 2004, other large players such as Capgemini showed slower sales growth. Overall, pricing for consulting services remained flat during the mid-2000s, although conditions were ripe for improvement.

During the early 2000s, consulting firms that focused heavily on strategy as opposed to technology suffered the most. For example, The Boston Consulting Group saw its revenues stay relatively stable, while McKinsey & Co. saw declines of approximately 12 percent from 2000 to 2003. When the economy fell into a slump, consulting firms suddenly competed for a dwindling number of contracts that were far less lucrative than before. As competition increased, consulting firms also were forced to be more competitive with their fees.

Heading into the mid-2000s, the technology market showed promise for consultants, especially in the areas of wireless technology, project management, and security/reliability. However, leading corporations—especially those that experienced significant losses during the dot-com boom—emerged from the early 2000s with more skepticism of management consultants. Entering the mid-2000s, the corporate sector was more focused on measurable results from investments in consulting services. In its May 2004 issue, *Entrepreneur* shared insight from Norman Eckstein, chairman of Institute of Management Consultants USA Inc., who indicated that large companies were seeking arrangements with consultants that resembled partnerships. In addition, the biggest consulting firms were both reducing the number of projects and employing smaller numbers of consultants on a short-term basis in order to appease corporate clients.

Moving forward into the second half of the 2000s, the management consulting industry was leaner and arguably more efficient than ever before. Although some observers had questioned the viability of some industry leaders during the early 2000s, it appeared that management consultants would always have some role in the corporate sector. As *The Economist* explained, "Independent strategic advice may be in greater demand given the growing calls for good corporate governance and scrutiny of conflicts of interest."

Research and Technology

Research has always been a key aspect of the management consulting industry. Consultants spend a significant portion of their time identifying, understanding, and developing tools to help clients address business and management issues. From the industry's inception in the 1880s until the early 1960s, research and development consisted largely of industrial productivity studies. In 1963 the Boston Consulting Group shifted the industry's research focus to strategic planning when it developed the growth share matrix and the experience curve.

During the 1980s management research and consulting advice concentrated on quality improvement. Tools and techniques including total quality management, continual quality improvement, and quality circles were developed and sold to businesses in the United States and Europe. The hub of research shifted again in the 1990s toward re-engineering and change management. Management consultants during this period largely aimed at developing ways to better integrate business, human, and technological processes. More recently, firms have focused on information technology-based consulting and systems implementation, particularly as they relate to the Internet and electronic commerce. As the corporate climate has become more dependent upon sophisticated and efficient technological and communications systems, the management consulting industry has shifted a substantial portion of its research efforts into this specialized field of knowledge.

Each major shift in the focal point that emerges from the consulting industry's research efforts—productivity, strategy, quality, and integration—creates a surge of growth in the industry. New firms enter the market as specialists in the "hottest" areas, diversifying into other areas as revenues grow and client bases expand. Large firms add new service lines or acquire existing niche companies to capitalize on the increased demand.

Business schools play an important role in the research and development of new consulting approaches. Ongoing research at these institutions and the resulting reports provide a constant flow of information and ideas for consultants to apply to their work. Professors of management and senior partners at large firms market their consulting services by publishing management articles and research results in leading business and industry journals.

Advancements in information technology facilitate expansion and globalization of large consulting practices, enabling firms to build barriers to entry into the top tier of the industry. Extensive telecommunications networks and sophisticated computer technologies permit large firms to mobilize worldwide teams and resources. Moreover, electronic storage and retrieval capabilities empower firms to store, build upon, and readily access massive amounts of knowledge and experience.

WORKFORCE

During the year ended February 2005, the Bureau of Labor Statistics (BLS) indicated that the management consulting industry added 30,300 new jobs. During 2004, Accenture increased its employee count by 17,000; it doubled its staff to 10,000 in India alone.

According to BLS figures, the United States employed approximately 783,300 management and technical consultants on a wage and salary basis in February 2005. During the mid-2000s, the BLS placed the consulting field fifth among the most rapidly growing industries. In fact, positions for wage and salary workers were expected to increase 55 percent. By comparison, the BLS anticipated a combined growth rate of 16 percent for all other industries.

Employers in this diverse, highly communicative, idea-based industry seek out primarily intelligent, creative, presentable employees with a diverse and well-rounded knowledge base. Along with more traditional needs such as financial planning and growth strategies, which require a substantial amount of formal business training, firms look for people with industry-specific knowledge. Consultants are often involved in system installation and development of global networks, for which technical knowledge is a primary asset, and with more basic writing and people skills. As a result, firms have broadened their recruiting efforts from the top tier of business schools to seek out potential employees with training in computers, sciences, and the liberal arts. Firms look primarily for consultants with the most distinguished pedigrees, which enables them to justify higher fees. Most major industry players maintain business units whose sole function is to recruit, hire, and train employees.

The life of a management consultant is notoriously arduous, involving a substantial amount of time away from home. But what consultants lose in free time and effort they make up for in salary. Starting salaries for consultants typically range from US$35,000 to US$125,000. Partners tend to make between US$120,000 and US$500,000. Bonuses comprise increasingly larger portions of the salary as people move up the ranks of a firm. At some firms, those occupying the senior levels account for close to 25 percent of the firms' total salary expense. Among the highest salaries are those for leading management "gurus," many of whom were professors at leading business universities. Consultants working for themselves or for small firms generally earn substantially lower salaries than those working for large firms.

After a period of intense recruitment in the late 1990s, management consulting firms began trimming their employee ranks. Attrition at two of the industry's leading firms, Accenture and McKinsey, fell from 20 percent in 2000 to 12 percent in 2001. Accenture laid off 4 percent of its workforce and asked hundreds of employees in the United States, Asia, and Europe to take a leave of absence that year. PricewaterhouseCoopers also lightened its workforce and reduced pay to all U.S. consulting employees by 7 percent. Similarly, Capgemini cut 4 percent of its workforce in the United States, Britain, and Scandinavia, and KPMG Consulting laid off 7 percent of its staff. As a result of these moves, between October of 2000 and October of 2001 the worldwide consulting industry saw its ranks fall by nearly 5 percent from a total of 600,000 employees to 572,000 employees.

For the most part, the ranks of self-employed consultants and small consulting firms are comprised of laid-off or retired business professionals, former consultants for large firms, and academics. Academics joined the part-time consulting workforce at a rapid rate in the 1990s. Most consultants in these categories are specialists in their industry or practice area.

INDUSTRY LEADERS

McKinsey and Company. McKinsey and Company is considered one of the most prestigious management-consulting firms in the world. As a generalist firm, McKinsey engages a broad range of clients and offers a diversified portfolio of services, though the bulk of its work is concentrated in the areas of strategy and organization. McKinsey is particularly known for its efficient data gathering and its extensive and frequent reporting. With approximately 11,500 professionals working in some 82 offices in 44 countries worldwide, McKinsey's worldwide management consulting revenues have declined in recent years, dropping from an estimate US$3.4 billion in 2000, to US$3 billion in 2003.

McKinsey opened its first office in Chicago, Illinois, in 1926 and its first foreign office in London in 1959. Against the industry trend toward information technology specialty, McKinsey remains primarily a strategy consultancy firm. McKinsey's growth in the late 1990s had been concentrated in Russia, Eastern Europe, China, and India.

McKinsey invests heavily in internal research and development. The firm spends approximately US$50 million annually researching, recording, and communicating business information and theory. Its centralized database of information provides offices around the world with ready access to key corporate and business information. McKinsey's conservative environment is exemplified by their traditional "up or out" worker policy, in which employees who fail to move up in the company are dismissed. This policy is aided by the firm's extensive employee training. McKinsey's conservative but prestigious atmosphere has fostered many well-known international business figures and high-ranking government officials. According to research firm Universum, European MBA students ranked McKinsey as the No. 1 desired employer in 2003, a position it has held for seven years.

Accenture Ltd. The largest worldwide management consulting firm, Accenture (formerly Andersen Consulting) posted revenues of more than US$15.1 billion in 2004, a 12.8 percent growth over 2003. Employees in 2004 totalled about

100,000, growing by more than 17,000 over the previous year as the company expanded its presence in India and increased its employee base in the U.S. It has 110 offices in 48 countries. Operations are highly decentralized with ownership and control of foreign offices vested in local professionals. The company's largest revenue source comes from the communicatons and high tech fields (27 percent), while the manufacturing (22 percent) and financials services fields (20 percent) follow.

Andersen Consulting became a dominant player in the global market in 1989, when it was established as a separate business unit from Arthur Andersen. Andersen Consulting restructured its organization in 1997 into 127 specialized industry units, along with units for outsourcing and knowledge management.

In 1998, Andersen Consulting voted to split completely from Arthur Andersen, by then renamed Andersen Worldwide. Wanting to separate itself from what it viewed as the less lucrative auditing business of its parent, the consultancy earned full autonomy from Andersen Worldwide in 2000, at which time Anderson Consulting changed its name to Accenture. The firm completed its initial public offering the following year.

Deloitte Touche Tohmatsu. Having dropped the word "International" from its name in 1997, Deloitte acknowledged its solid reputation as a global company. The company's member firms employ approximately 170,000 people in 148 countries. Deloitte is the only one of the original Big Five accounting firms that has not divested its consulting operations, although it did attempt to do so, but put down these plans in 2003.

Deloitte Consulting, which focuses on strategic planning, information technology, and financial management consulting, is the largest unit of Deloitte, accounting for about 25 percent of its sales. With more than 21,000 employees operating in 34 countries, Deloitte Consulting posted revenues of US$3.25 billion in 2003, up from US$2.56 billion in 2000.

BearingPoint Inc. As the former consulting division of accounting giant, KPMG International, BearingPoint became a separate subsidiary in 1999. It officially separated from its parent in 2000, and launched its IPO in February 2001. In 2002, the company hired on many of Andersen Consulting's former U.S. employees and acquired Andersen's business consulting businesses in Hong Kong, China, Australia, Sweden, Norway, Finland, Switzerland, Singapore, Korea, Spain, Japan and France. That was also the year the company changed its name from KPMG Consulting to BearingPoint and began trading on the NYSE.

By 2005, the company employed 16,000 people in 200 offices covering 39 countries. It concentrates primarily on business and technology strategy, and technology services including: systems design, architecture, applications implementation, network infrastructure, systems integration, and managed services. It had revenues in 2003 of more than US$3.1 billion. According to Chairman and CEO, Rod McGeary, as stated in the Feb 2005 issue of Consulting Magazine Online, the company is the market leader in China and sees this as an area of future international growth.

IBM Global Services. IBM Global Services is the world leader in technology consulting and services, and is among the largest providers of business consulting and systems integration. This business segment of IBM earned more than US$45 billion in 2004, and employs more than 175,000 people.

In 2002, IBM purchased the consulting arm of the largest accountancy in the world, PricewaterhouseCoopers. The purchase came as the result of the economic slowdown and corporate accounting scandals of the time. PwC Consulting, as PricewaterhouseCoopers' consulting subsidiary was known, was pursued by several suitors, including Hewlett-Packard.

A.T. Kearney. A.T. Kearney was founded in 1926 when McKinsey spun off a segment of its operations. After being acquired by EDS's Management Consulting Services in 1995, A.T. Kearney doubled in size and emerged as one of the world's premier consulting firms, particularly in the automotive industry. The acquisition by EDS substantially enhanced the firm's industry expertise and greatly benefited its information technology consulting, the area from which A.T. Kearney derives the bulk of its revenue. However, integration difficulties took their toll on the firm's performance throughout the late 1990s.

A.T. Kearney employs 4,000 individuals, including 2,500 consultants who operate in 35 different countries. The firm operates in the Americas, Europe, and Asia, and is quickly moving into emerging markets in Argentina, Brazil, Russia, India, and Turkey.

Sales in 2000 reached US$1.3 billion, 65 percent of which stems from international operations. By 2003, the firm's revenues had fallen to US$846 million, down almost 16 percent from the previous year. Revenues fell again in 2004, to US$806 million, with losses of US$10 million. According to *The Financial Times* this has prompted parent EDS to enter into talks for a buyout by partners.

Capgemini. Based in Paris, France, management consultant Capgemini catapulted from eighth place to third place among the largest management consultancies in the world when it paid US$11 billion for the consulting arm of Ernst & Young in 2000, forming Cap Gemini Ernst & Young. On 15 April 2004, the company shortened its name to Capgemini. The purchase, the largest in industry history, boosted Capgemini's North American operations to roughly 33 percent of total sales.

Founded in 1967, today, Capgemini is the largest IT consultant in Europe. With nearly 60,000 employees, sales in 2003 reached US$7.2 billion. The firm offers information technology consulting services, particularly in the areas of systems integration and software development, as well as corporate strategy development and implementation.

Booz Allen Hamilton Inc. More so than its major competitors in the management consulting industry, Booz Allen Hamilton, a management and technology consulting firm, concentrates its business on large international businesses and on government contracts. With a heavy proportion of its operations in U.S. defense and military contracts, along with other local, state, federal, and foreign government consulting, the firm generated US$2.7 billion in revenues in the fiscal year ended 31 March 2004, up 22.7 percent from 2003. The company's more than 16,000 employees span more than 30 countries. Operations are divided into two business niches, one focused on government clients and the other devoted to the commercial sector. The company was founded in 1914.

PA Consulting Group Ltd. PA Consulting was the largest worldwide consulting firm in 1970. The firm's revenues faltered in the 1980s, and the lag was exacerbated by the recession in the early 1990s. Despite its slippage in rank, PA Consulting has remained a formidable competitor in the international management consulting market. Founded in the United Kingdom in 1943, PA Consulting operates with 3,000 professionals in 35 countries. The company has a strong focus in the area of change management. Its worldwide revenues rose steadily through the 1990s, and reached almost US$600 million in 2003.

Roland Berger Strategy Consultants GmbH. Three-quarters owned by Deutsche Bank, Roland Berger Strategy Consultants is the largest management consulting firm of European origin. Since its establishment in 1967 by Roland Berger, the firm has grown to a size of nearly 1,700 consultants in 31 offices in Europe, Asia, and the Americas. In 2003 its worldwide management consulting revenues totaled US$665 million, primarily in its core European markets of Germany, the United Kingdom, and France.

Founded in 1967 as Roland Berger & Partners, the consultancy has grown quickly with an emphasis on innovation and expansion strategy consulting. The firm acquired IPG, a British strategy consultant, in 1999. The following year, Roland Berger & Partners changed its name to Roland Berger-Strategy Consultants to better reflect its specialization.

Major Countries in the Industry

From the industry's inception through the present, the United States has hosted the world's largest management consulting firms. However, along with the business climate in general, the consulting industry was becoming more global in focus during the mid-2000s. Outsourcing and offshoring were two hotly discussed topics throughout the world. The issue was especially of concern in North America, where everything from manufacturing jobs to computer programming and customer service tasks were being sent to countries such as China and India, which had lower labor costs. In order to remain competitive, more companies began to pursue outsourcing. For example, in its April 2004 issue, *Fast Company* indicated that, according to research firm Gartner Inc., 40 percent of all *Fortune* 500 companies were expected to have outsourced work to other nations by the year's end. Management consulting firms large and small provided advisement in this area.

Ernst & Young LLP was one leading global consultancy that helped companies to successfully implement and manage outsourcing initiatives. Ernst & Young accomplished this through its Business Risk Services unit, which helped companies perform risk assessments, engage in strategic planning, manage licensing, improve operational processes, evaluate third-party vendors, and more. Ernst & Young worked with organizations to help them outsource specific functional elements or entire processes. Accenture was another leading global consulting enterprise that assisted companies to use outsourcing as part of a strategy for maximizing performance. During the mid-2000s, the company offered consulting services in three main areas: business process outsourcing, application outsourcing, and technology infrastructure outsourcing. Infosys—a leading Indian outsourcing services provider specializing in IT—formed its own U.S.-based consulting subsidiary in April 2004. The firm was led by a team of business consulting heavyweights, including CEO Stephen Pratt, who in 2003 was dubbed one of the world's top 25 consultants by *Consulting Magazine.* Smaller consulting operations, such as Houston, Texas-based Backes Crocker LLC, also worked with companies to start new outsourcing initiatives or manage existing ones.

In addition to advising clients on the business of offshoring, some consulting firms engaged in one variation of the practice by relocating their headquarters to foreign locations. Critics, including union groups and government officials, argued that this was a tactic to avoid federal and state tax payments. In the 21 June 2004 issue of *Computerworld,* Illinois State Comptroller Dan Hynes took issue with Accenture for moving its headquarters to Bermuda. Although the company insisted that it paid its share of U.S. taxes, Hynes characterized the company an expatriate, and argued that it was "unfair and unpatriotic" to award state contracts to the consulting giant. A bill drafted by Hynes and introduced to the Illinois legislature sought to prevent expatriate firms from receiving state contacts. In addition to states like California and North Carolina, which already had passed similar laws, *Computerworld* noted that Massachusetts, Minnesota, Ohio, Pennsylvania, and Texas were evaluating like measures.

American firms are present in nearly every existing market, and are the undisputed leaders in technology and innovation in the world. In 1997 alone, the Big Five accounting firms combined with the 40 top American strategy firms comprised nearly half of the industry's US$73 billion in worldwide revenues.

The growth rate in the U.S. market hovered around 10 percent in the 1990s as the industry there began to mature. Expansion of leading American providers into Europe, South America, the Asia-Pacific region, and Middle East, Africa, and India fueled growth in those regions and served to integrate the world market into a more unified whole. The largest purchasers of management consulting services, however, are still the United States, the European Union, Canada, and Japan.

The European Union is the other major region in the management consulting industry. According to European Federation of Management Consulting Associations (FEACO), European-based firms generate about US$50 billion of the industries' total revenues, and in 2002 employed 300,000 management consultants. The United Kingdom and Germany account for about 27 percent of the market each, with France representing a further 17 percent. Outsourcing and customer relationship management (CRM) are the two areas showing the most marked increases in importance. Growth in this market is hoped to be encouraged further by the proposed easing of entry restrictions for consulting companies wanting to do business in other member states. Management consulting is now considered the most popular career choice for European engineering and business students.

In the late 1990s many analysts consider China to be one of the most exciting emerging markets, as the consulting market there, particularly the information technology sector, was beginning to ripen. While Hong Kong is clearly the leading center of consulting activity in the region, with more than 100 international and local management consulting companies, many firms are moving into mainland China, particularly Beijing, to take advantage of growing opportunities there. As state control of industry segments continues to diminish, consultancy firms are expected to meet a lucrative market. Major international firms, such as Anderson, McKinsey, PricewaterhouseCoopers, and Accenture, already have established themselves in this region.

FURTHER READING

"Almost 90 Percent of U.S. Industrial Companies Outsource." *Purchasing,* 19 February 2004.

Ante, Spencer E., and Ben Elgin. "Tech Jobs are Sprouting Again." *Business Week,* 10 May 2004.

"Consultant, Heal Thyself." *Economist,* 2 November 2002.

"Consulting's Long-Awaited Bounce; Kennedy Information System's Bradford Smith Explains Why the Resurgence Is Likely to Continue, and Why Accenture Leads the Way." *Business Week Online,* 7 July 2004.

The FEACO Survey of the European Management Consultancy Market in 2003, July 2004.

Klein, Melissa. "Slowdown in Economy, Stock Markets, Squeeze Consultants." *Accounting Today,* 8 October 2001.

Koudsi, Suzanne. "Consulants: Who Are We?" *Fortune,* 3 September 2001.

London, Simon, "EDS in Talks to Sell AT Kearney" *The Financial Times,* 26 February 2005.

Martin, Justin. "Consulting Reincarnation." *Chief Executive,* June 2001.

Michaels, Adrian. "Deloitte Holds Fast on Keeping Its Consultancy." *Financial Times,* 1 July 2001. Available from http://news.ft.com.

"Profitability Elusive for Many Firms." *Consultants News,* 2001.

Reingold, Jennifer. "A Brief (Recent) History of Offshoring." *Fast Company,* April 2004.

"Some Good Advice." *Entrepreneur,* May 2004.

"Top American Consultants Take Own Advice and Join Indian Firm." Bangalore, India: Infosys Technologies Ltd. 8 April 2004. Available from http://www.infosys.com.

U.S. Department of Labor, Bureau of Labor Statistics. "Management, Business, and Financial Occupational Occupations." *Occupational Outlook Handbook, 2004-05 Edition* 21 June 2004. Available from http://www.bls.gov.

U.S. Industry and Trade Outlook, Washington: U.S. Department of Commerce/International Trade Administration, 2000.

Verton, Dan. "Illinois Moves to Blacklist Accenture: State Comptroller Cites Firm's Offshore Status." *Computerworld,* 21 June 2004.

Ward, Hazel. "Public Sector Pushes for Impartial IT Advice." *Computer Weekly,* 18 January 2001.

"Winners' Curse; Management Consultants." *The Economist,* 21 July 2001.

SIC 7360

NAICS 5613

PERSONNEL SERVICES

Personnel services link job seekers with employers under various arrangements. By far the most common form is through temporary staffing, wherein the employee is paid by the personnel service to work temporarily for another firm needing assistance. Other types of personnel services include employment agencies, which seek to place job seekers in permanent positions, and recruitment agencies, which also contract to fill permanent positions, but typically perform more screening—and sometimes searching—to find employment candidates who meet certain criteria.

INDUSTRY SNAPSHOT

In 2006, the worldwide personnel services industry was a valued contributor to building and sustaining a dependable workforce. An outstanding case study of the U.S. featured American Staffing Association (ASA) survey data reporting that U.S. annual sales for temporary and contract staffing totaled U.S.$72.3 billion in 2006. The dominant sector in the industry was temporary staffing. According to the ASA, on an average day in 2006 these firms employed 12.4 million temporary workers and contract workers. That reflected an increase of 300,000 more than the previous year. In the mid-2000s, those employees in "highly skilled" fields such as accounting, law, science, and engineering were the fastest-growing category of temporary workers.

The Manpower Annual Talent Shortage Survey findings claimed 41 percent of employers throughout the world were experiencing difficulty in filling jobs. Openings that were particularly challenging to fill included sales representatives, skilled manual trades people and technicians. Technician areas included technical workers for the areas of production/operations, engineering and maintenance. Manpower surveyed nearly 37,000 employees across 27 countries and territories as a follow-up to a 2006 survey. Sales representatives were listed as the most difficult position to fill in the U.S., Japan, Hong Kong, Taiwan, Singapore, New Zealand, Ireland, and Peru. Other jobs on the 2007 "Hot Jobs" to fill list included engineers, accounting and finance staff, laborers, production operators, drivers, management/executives and machinists/operators.

The industry experienced phenomenal growth during the 1990s, as average daily employment increased steadily from 0.98 million jobs in 1991 to a record 2.54 million in

2000. However, conditions changed in the wake of an economic recession that was exacerbated by the terrorist attacks against the United States on September 11, 2001. Subsequently, daily staffing fell to 2.18 million workers in 2001 and 2.06 million workers in 2002. Overall, the ASA reported that 739,000 contract and temporary staffing jobs were lost as a result of the 2001 economic recession. After peaking in the third quarter of 2000, contract and temporary-staffing levels declined through the first quarter of 2002, falling 28 percent before conditions started to improve.

According to Adecco S.A., the world's largest employment services company, the United States, United Kingdom, Italy, France, Spain, Switzerland, Canada, and Australia were among the world's largest staffing markets, accounting for the majority of global staffing demand. However, Euromonitor was expecting the market for employment services in China to grow by a staggering 160 percent between 2003 and 2008.

Although Manpower found that 14 countries reported improved hiring plans from 2006, the global outlook was mixed for second quarter of 2007. There were optimistic hiring projections worldwide for Singapore, Peru, Argentina, South Africa, India, Australia, New Zealand and Japan. Countries in the Europe, Middle East and Africa region reported job prospects were strongest in South Africa, Ireland, Switzerland, Norway and the UK. Countries in the Asia Pacific region predicted weaker job markets ahead for Taiwan, India and Hong Kong. As far as countries surveyed in the Americas, Argentina and Peru were the most confident of hiring increases.

ORGANIZATION AND STRUCTURE

Origins and Development. The personnel services industry originated in the early to mid-twentieth century from three key developments: (1) government agencies that were created to combat unemployment, grounded on the emergence of unemployment as a social problem in industrial society; (2) demand during and immediately after World War II for temporary clerical work, originally when permanent employees were sick or on vacation; and (3) executive search firms, or so-called headhunters, who were sought to help companies recruit highly qualified personnel. While other kinds of organizations also evolved with and from these developments, in terms of revenues and influence, for-profit temporary staffing agencies have assumed paramount stature.

During the 1990s, temp services grew large enough that their volume of job placements could be measured as a percentage of national labor forces, although, as of the late 1990s, in no country did that percentage exceed 5 out of every 100 workers. In 1997 the Netherlands was estimated to have the highest proportion of temporary staffing in its labor force, with 3 percent of all Dutch workers employed by temporary services. France ranked second with 2 percent, followed by the United States and the United Kingdom, which were even at 1.8 percent. Temporary staffing was estimated to account for 0.5 percent of the working populations in both Germany and Japan.

The personnel services industry has its roots in the clerical staffing business, but the industry has broadened its spectrum of placements to include factory workers on up to top executives. In early 2001, office and clerical positions accounted for slightly more than 20 percent of all temporary and contract positions, according to the ASA. About 35 percent of workers were employed in the industrial sector, followed by professional and management (21 percent), information technology (9.3 percent), health care (7.8 percent), and technical (6.4 percent).

By 2004, highly skilled professionals such as accountants, attorneys, biochemists, and engineers were the fastest-growing category of temporary workers. In fact, at the largest staffing enterprises these workers constituted up to one-third of placements. Marketing professionals were another emerging occupational group within the temp industry.

The biggest development impacting the personnel services industry during the early 2000s was the 2001 economic recession, which led to the loss of 739,000 contract and temporary staffing positions, according to the ASA. Contract and temporary staffing levels reached a high point in the third quarter of 2000, and then declined through the first quarter of 2002, falling 28 percent before any signs of improvement appeared. This mirrored trends in the larger U.S. job market, which lost 2.7 million jobs between March 2001 and August 2003, based on figures from the U.S. Department of Labor's Bureau of Labor Statistics (BLS).

Sales in the temporary help sector continue to make up the biggest share of revenue in the personnel services industry. Sales in this sector increased more than threefold between 1990 and 2000, reaching a record US$63.6 billion. However, the economic recession caused industry sales to decrease US$7.4 billion in 2001, to US$56.2 billion. After declining to US$55.2 billion in 2002, sales improved with the larger economy, reaching US$56.3 billion in 2003.

In July of 2003, a conference was hosted by Adecco at the London Business School to explore temporary staffing in a number of countries. At the conference, Hiroshi Saito, a management professor at Kanto Gakuen University in Tokyo, touched upon a number of important developments that were benefiting the temporary staffing industry in Japan. One major trend was the gradual relaxation of government restrictions on temporary employment agencies, which were first allowed in Japan during 1985.

According to an article in *Japan Press Weekly,* the nation's temporary workforce doubled from 1999 to 2002 as the Japanese government allowed temporary staffing in a growing number of industries. As of April 1, 2004, restrictions on the use of manufacturing workers were lifted. Although many manufacturing firms had already worked around these restrictions by outsourcing assembly lines to so-called external service providers, the development was expected to further industry growth.

At the London Business School conference, Saito explained that Japan was home to approximately 500,000 temporary employees in 2003, 66 percent of whom held clerical jobs, followed by information technology workers holding 12 percent of the jobs, and technical and engineering positions holding 10 percent. The remainder worked in a variety of other fields.

In 2003 approximately 75 percent of Japan's temporary work force consisted of young adults, 70 percent of whom were women. Although staffing companies like Adecco were preparing to capitalize on the growing use of temporary workers in Japan, some observers were critical of this trend. Opponents argued that Japanese firms were maximizing profits at the expense of the nation's youngest workers, who found well paying, permanent full-time positions hard to come by.

Logistics of Personnel Placement. Personnel services conduct their businesses in a variety of ways, but all successful ones must be able to do two things: obtain employer contracts to place employees and recruit qualified workers to fill open slots. Finding employer contracts involves marketing the service via advertisements, direct marketing, and sometimes word of mouth. Effective marketing requires that personnel services be aware of potential clients' needs, which may be very specific, and that the service convey an image of competence and cost-effectiveness to sway an employer to use that particular service.

At least equally important is a personnel service's need to recruit satisfactory workers, since if an agency earns a reputation with a customer for supplying unqualified help, it will in all likelihood lose that account. Most of the world's large agencies perform one or more stages of screening to ensure they hire employees who will meet their clients' expectations. The minimal screening usually involves completion of a conventional job application form to collect such data as work history and educational background, followed by some form of personal interview with the applicant. Most firms also administer a variety of tests, some general and some job-specific, to better ascertain applicants' skills. Examples of such tests include general math and reading quizzes, typing tests, computer software proficiency exams, and job-specific questionnaires. The largest companies have developed proprietary software for evaluating candidates' aptitudes. When applicants lack the necessary skills, some agencies offer training services. In addition, once a worker has been placed in a position, most temp services perform some form of follow-up with the employer to determine whether it was a successful match.

Workers placed through temporary services are employed by the agency rather than the client. In countries without universal health insurance, such as the United States, often this means the temporary worker receives no insurance benefits, although temp services may offer benefits to varying degrees. Employers usually pay for the temp service on an hourly basis, and a portion of this fee becomes the worker's wage, with a share taken by the agency as well. Some agencies may charge additional flat fees for their services.

Because staff placement demands an understanding of the work being contracted, many firms, especially smaller ones, elect to specialize within certain markets. Specialization also allows larger companies to market a more easily identifiable service—for example, experienced computer programmers, rather than generic "temps"—to potential customers. This sort of specialization is probably most extensive in Europe and the United States in the industry's health care segment, which supplies trained workers to serve as nurses' aides and in-home health care assistants. Many other specialties exist, though, including legal staffing, scientific services, or computer specialists.

To the extent a personnel firm offers specialized services, it may operate in either a commodity-like market or a premium-service market. Generalized services in major markets, such as France, the United Kingdom, and the United States, are usually commodity services and operate on relatively tight margins. Specialized, particularly technical, services can charge substantially more for their workers and tend to experience wider profit margins.

The degree of specialization also signifies the barriers that exist to enter a given market. To be credible to their customers, the most specialized firms must have individuals on their recruiting and placement staff who are highly experienced in the targeted field, (e.g., a scientific staffing agency requires in-house scientists who evaluate applicants and work with customers). Building this level of expertise represents a substantial barrier to entry and helps preserve such specialty companies from price competition. At the same time, in the commodity markets for general office and light industrial help, which requires only very broad skills, the entry barriers are low, but the ability to set favorable pricing—and hence, often profitability—is minimal.

CURRENT CONDITIONS

Industry Status. In 2004, Adecco estimated that the industry's revenues were US$400 billion worldwide, with employee leasing and independent contractors (US$200 billion) representing the largest category. At US$140 billion, temporary staffing was the next largest category, followed by the US$30 billion search and placement services segment. These market share figures do not include penetration rates; penetration rates in 2003 in the U.K. were the highest at 3.8 percent, while rates in the Netherlands were 3.3 percent, 2.4 percent in France, 1.7 percent in the United States, and 1.1 percent in Japan and Portugal.

According to the Bureau of Labor Statistics, employment services were expected to grow at an annual average rate of 3.8 percent through 2014, creating nearly1.6 million new jobs. Furthermore, the U.S. staffing industry was expected to grow faster by adding more jobs than any other industry during the next decade. The Remedy Temp Quarterly Labor Forecast showed an expected year-over-year increase of 4 percent in demand for temporary workers during the third quarter of 2006.

In Europe, most agency-placed employment occurs in the manufacturing sector, with most temporary work going to young, mostly low-skilled workers. An interesting anomaly in the personnel industry occurs in Spain. Here more than 30 percent of the country's total employed workforce is under temporary contract, with 76 percent citing an inability to find permanent employment as the reason. In Germany and Switzerland, most temporary work was being undertaken as a means to obtain employment training.

In the United Kingdom, the number of workers supplied via temporary agencies increased 250 percent between 1992 and 2001. By mid-2004, Great Britain was home to more than half of Europe's temporary employees. Around this time, regulatory changes were made to protect the employment rights of U.K. temporary workers. However, *Management Today* indicated that the changes did little to specify the stance of agency employees in such areas as maternity leave and unfair dismissal. Additionally, while the revisions required agencies to sign contracts with their employees, certain exceptions left the nature of agency staff's contractual relationships unclear, in terms of whether they worked for the temporary agency or the client company. Euromonitor valued the employment services market in the U.K. at about US$43 billion in 2003, with the temporary help sector accounting for 93 percent of the total market. In the temporary sector, the IT, computing and telecommunications fields provided the most jobs. The industry remains highly fragmented with the majority of the 10,000 employment services offices being single-office agencies. In France, the market was valued at US$21.9 billion in 2003, with more than 40 percent of the market being attributed to construction-related jobs.

Changes were on the horizon in Europe during the mid-2000s. One major development was the European agency workers directive. Published by the European Commission in 2002, the directive "aims to allow temporary agency workers employment conditions that are equally favourable to those available to a permanent worker in the same job and in the same company," according to a July 2004 *BusinessEurope.com* article. Scheduled to become law in 2006, the directive is only applicable to temporary workers who are provided via an agency and who have worked a minimum of six weeks.

In Asia, employment service market values were growing. In Japan, the industry was valued at US$20.6 billion, with temporary staffing accounting for almost 94 percent of the market. The industry was not quite so big in China, and was valued at about US$1.24 billion in 2003. However, that figure represented a 20.7 percent growth over 2002, and the market was expected to grow by 160 percent in the five years up to 2008. Recruitment services took the lion's share of the market, accounting for 63 percent of the market's value. State-run agencies were still dominant in China, but the number of private agencies was on the rise.

By June 2006, a trend was noted for foreign recruitment firms to use acquisition and other methods to enter the China market. For example, America-based Monster bought shares in China's first online recruitment operator ChinaHR.com. Randstad of Holland invested in a Shanghai human resource firm. Britain's largest recruitment firm, started its China operations in Shanghai after its acquisition of St. George's Harvey Nash human resources service firm.

By May 2007, Taneesha Kulshrestha reported that only 9 percent of Indian employers expressed difficulty in filling positions due to lack of suitable talent compared to 41 percent of employers throughout the world. Other countries where shortages were not so severe included Ireland, Netherlands and China.

Indian companies were starting to hold more recruitment firms accountable for attrition and job hopping of employees. Attrition across some sectors such as retail and banking had jumped by substantial percentages. Changes in payment for recruitment utilizing a "33-33-33 fees model" meant 33 percent was paid when the mandate reached recruitment firm, one-third was given when offer letter was accepted by an employee and remaining amount was paid when employee came on board.

Industry Trends. While most people using personnel services, particularly temporary placement services, are young, the aging population in many countries was affecting the personnel services industry. Many labor markets were expected to shrink due to falling birthrates, with the average age of the workforce expected to rise to 41 years by 2005. However, while the total size of the working population was decreasing in Europe, it was showing small gains in the U.S. These gains were attributed to the trend for Americans to retire later, while Europeans were retiring earlier.

Employers in Japan and Singapore led the way with plans to retain older workers. There were retention strategies for reportedly 83 percent and 53 percent of the employers in those countries. Manpower suggested that laws and incentive programs in these countries that promoted recruiting and retaining workers 50 or older were contributing factors. In the U.S., only 18 percent of employers reported having a recruitment strategy.

With the globalization of economies came the globalization of the world's labor force, and the personnel industry giants provided an increasing amount of service directed at this "internationalization" by giving placed employees a consistency of working conditions and terms as they moved from one country to another. Governments have been increasingly favoring policies that allow for the inflow of temporary, specialized labor, rather than permanent status.

Declines have been seen in the demand for unskilled or low-skilled labor. Rapid changes in technology have been the primary influencer behind this trend. In addition, the growing number of service-oriented jobs has been related to a rise in the need for so-called "social skills." Most personnel agencies were seeing the need to place more-educated people, and many were offering training services to upgrade the skills of the client's employees.

Temporary employment can often be seen as an indication of the health of the economy, since companies are able to quickly adapt to changes in demand by increasing or decreasing their reliance on temporary workers. Since the 1970s, the most significant growth in temporary staffing services has taken place during the early stages of economic recovery, according to the American Staffing Association (ASA).

In its *Annual Economic Analysis of the Staffing Industry,* released in mid-2004, the ASA cited figures from the W.E. Upjohn Institute for Employment Research indicating that the most important reason for hiring temporary help was to assist in times of unanticipated increases in business. Almost one-half of companies said that they use temporary employees to fill the shoes of absent permanent employees, or to fill a job vacancy until a permanent worker is hired. Temporary workers also are used by companies for special projects, just-in-time production practices, and seasonal needs, and are often screened as possible permanent hires.

Heading into the mid-2000s, one major trend that was unfolding in the personnel services industry was the so-called "emergent workforce," a term used by staffing firm Spherion Corp. to describe a segment of workers who value such things as performance-based rewards, a high degree of control over their careers, and growth opportunities. Comprising an estimated 31 percent of the U.S. workforce in 2004, Spherion projected that emergent workers would account for a growing portion of the workforce heading into the late 2000s. By 2007, this group was expected to constitute more than half of all U.S. employees.

Along these lines, during the mid-2000s a growing number of U.S. workers, especially professionals, were opting to forego traditional employment arrangements in lieu of contract or project-based employment, which offered more flexibility and time with family. These desires became more important for many Americans in the wake of the September 11, 2001 terrorist attacks, which forced many people to evaluate the things that mattered most in their lives. While IT and accounting professionals had pursued these types of arrangements for some time, by 2004 lawyers, biochemists, and even marketing professionals were doing so.

By 2006, many companies and recruitment firms were signing "no-poaching." agreements. This prevented parties from stealing away employees from client companies. Some avoided unethical practices by not clients' employees and making those who approached the firms progress through the traditional recruitment process.

Another trend was for companies to use head-hunters to hire "laterals." These placements were defined by Sujata Dutta Sachdeva of *The Economic Times* as being for employees with 18 months or more of experience. Companies tended to prefer them because they required less training than employees new to their fields otherwise known as "freshers."

By March 2007, remuneration packages for temporary workers in the Indian job market were catching up to permanent ones. An exclusive preview from *The Economic Times* revealed the latest TeamLease salary survey showed a 14 percent growth in salaries for temps in 2006. In addition, salary increments for temps in manufacturing sector had increased to 17 percent in 2006 from 14 percent in 2005.

INDUSTRY LEADERS

Adecco SA. The biggest human resource services agency overall worldwide, Adecco ranked in the number one or number two position in 10 of the world's top 13 markets in 2005. It was the world leader in terms of market share, revenue, cash flow and capitalization. Revenues for 2006 were nearly US$27 billion, a growth of more than 24 percent more than in 2005. Its net income for 2006 was approximately US$806 million reflecting one-year net income growth of 50.4 percent. This Zurich-based firm provides both temporary and permanent placement of workers in the industrial, clerical, and technical fields. Staffing services also encompass professional and white-collar employees in fields such as accounting, information technology, and engineering. Adecco manages its services through professional business lines such as Adecco Engineering & Technical; Adecco Finance; Adecco Legal; Adecco Information Technology; Adecco Medical & Science; Adecco Sales, Marketing & Events; and, Adecco Human Capital Solutions. In addition, Adecco's Lee Hecht Harrison Services division was the third-largest outplacement company in the world in 2005. In early 2006, Adecco bought German staffing firm DIS Deutscher Industrie Service. Adecco Group Network reportedly connected more than 700,000 associates with clients each day through a network of more than 33,000 employees and 6,600 offices in more than 70 countries and territories worldwide.

Adecco was established through the merging of Adia of Switzerland and Ecco of France in 1996. The world's largest privately held staffing firm, TAD Resources International, was added to the fold in 1997. Begun in Cambridge, Massachusetts in 1956, TAD had revenues of US$1.2 billion by the time of its acquisition. In 1999, the firm acquired the information technology and staffing firm, Delphi, and also acquired one of the largest personnel services companies in Japan, Career Staff. The year 2000 saw Adecco merge with North American giant, Olsten Temporary Staffing, which operated 1,400 offices in 14 countries by 1999. In 2005, Adecco was continuing its strategy of growth through market development and acquisition; it was in negotiations to purchase Spain's Humangroup, a staffing and outsourcing company.

In 2004, North American group CEO Julio Arrieta and Chief Financial Officer Felix Weber resigned when the company's operations in this region were embroiled in an accounting scandal that prompted investigations by U.S. and Swiss officials, including the U.S. Securities and Exchange Commission. Problems seemed to be related more to poor accounting procedures than to anything more sinister, but the Chairman of the company, John Bowmer, resigned in June 2004.

Manpower Inc. The second biggest staffing firm in the world, Milwaukee, Wisconsin-based Manpower operated 4,300 offices in 68 countries in 2005. The company's sales for 2006 were approximately US$17.6 billion. Most of Manpower's sales come from placing workers in industrial, office, and professional positions. In 2005, the company placed 3 million people in temporary or contract positions with 400,000 client companies. Manpower's subsidiary Right Management offered career transition and organizational consulting services.

Founded in Milwaukee in 1948, Manpower opened its first franchised office location in 1954. In 1955, it began its international growth, opening a Canadian office and then expanding into Europe the next year. By 1965, it was operating in more than 30 countries. Since 2000, the company has shown significant growth through acquisitions, acquiring Elan Group, Jefferson Wells International, and Right Management Consultants in the first four years of the 2000s.

Vedior N.V. Headquartered in Amsterdam, The Netherlands, Vedior was providing long- or short-term work to about 1 million workers annually in 375 countries by 2005. In 2006, its 2,450 offices encompassed service area covering 50 countries spanning much of Europe, North and South America, South Africa, Asia, and Australia. Vedior's 2006 sales was US$7,660 million. France provided the largest market for Vedior, generating more than 44 percent of sales. The average number of employees in 2006 was 14,366. It acquired several companies in 2004 and early 2005 including Amplitude of France (training services), Active Plus of Poland (outplacement), Ma Foi of India and Sri Lanka (HR outsourcing), Platoforma of Portugal (specializing in teleservices placements), and Andrew Farr of the U.K. (specializing in accounting and finance).

Randstad Holding N.V. Headquartered in the Netherlands, Randstad was the temporary employment services market leader in Belgium, Germany, the Netherlands, Poland, and the Southeastern United States in 2005. In 2004, its daily average of staffing employees totaled approximately 224,600. The company was offering a wide range of staffing services via three business segments: Yacht (professional staffing), Capac & Randstad Inhouse Services (in-house services), and group companies such as Tempo-Team and Randstad that provided specialized staffing. Sales for 2004 were nearly US$7 billion, an increase of about 9.6 percent over the previous year.

Randstad announced that it acquired an additional 23 percent of the capital of the Chinese HR services provider, Talent Shanghai. It previously acquired a stake in May 2006. Randstad now owns 47 percent of the capital. Talent Shaghai delivers a complete range of human resource management services including recruitment, executive search, and graduate placement services.

Kelly Services, Inc. Founded in 1946 and headquartered in Troy, Michigan, Kelly Services operated company-owned offices in 32 countries and territories by 2007. By then it was placing 750,000 people into temporary positions annually. These positions were wide-ranging, including accountants, call center workers, substitute teachers, engineers, physicians, information technology specialists, legal professionals, industrial workers, clerical, scientific professionals and more. Sales for 2006 was more than US$5.68 billion.

In April 2007, Kelly Services President and CEO Carl Camden discussed his company's "leadership role among business, labor, and civic organizations committed to making health care reform a reality." Kelly Services was a founding member of the "Better Health Care Together" campaign which issued four "common sense principles for achieving a new American health care system by 2012" in 2007.

Also in 2007, Kelly Services launched the 2007 Virtual Kelly Job Expo. It was cited as being "the first of its kind in Australia." Open from May 18 through 27 it offered a new, high-tech way to conveniently search for jobs. Kelly Services Country Manager James Bowmer described it as combining old methods of expos and fairs with job boards and on line searches. The Job Expo effectively offered alternatives for people who were not available to attend traditional fairs.

FURTHER READING

"Adecco Sees Temp Market Growth in Japan." *Asia Africa Intelligence Wire*, 11 October 2003.

American Staffing Association. "Staffing Growth Moderates in 2006." 26 February 2007. Available from http://www.amaeicanstaffing.net.

Berchem, Steven P. "The Bright Spot. ASA's Annual Economic Analysis of the Staffing Industry." *Staffing Success*, May-June 2004.

Bernstein, James. "CEO of U.S. Unit of Temp Agency Adecco Resigns Amid Accounting Problems." *Newsday*, 17 January 2004.

Berkhout, Ernest E. and Marko J. van Leewen. "International Database on Employment and Adaptable Labour (IDEAL)." May 2004. Available from http://www.randstad.com.

Callahan, Sean. "Temp Staffing Takes Hold in Marketing." *B to B*, 9 February 2004.

Davies, Claire. "Focus On: Employment Law Changes." *BusinessEurope.com*, July 2004.

"Engineering and Industrial Jobs at the Kelly Services Online Job Expo." Available from http://www.ferret.com.au.

"Facing the Challenge: The Lisbon Strategy for Growth and Employment." November 2004. Available from http://europa.ue.int.

"Foreign Recruitment Firms Eye China Market." *Alestron*, 16 June 2006.

"Global Manpower Employment Outlook Survey Reveals German Employers Set to Increase Hiring, as Demands for New Employees in India and the U.S. Are Expected to Ease. 13 March 2007. Available from http://www.manpower.com.

Gurchiek, Kathy. "Employers Not Feeling the Love Toward Older Workers." 21 May 2007. Available from http://www.shrm.org.

Hoover's Company Capsules. Austin, TX: Hoover's, Inc., 2007. Available from http://www.hoovers.com.

Johnson, Joan. "Staffing Services Growing Faster Than Economy." *Colorado Springs Business Journal*, 23 June 2006.

"Kelly Services CEO Urges Reform to Cover Nation's 45 Million Uninsured." 23 April 2007. Available from http://insurancenews.net.com.

Kulshrestha, Taneesha. "India's Talent Resources Better Than Global Peers." 22 May 2007. Available from http://www.financialexpress.com.

Manpower. "Manpower Employment Outlook Survey: Global. 3rd Quarter 2005." 2005. Available from http://www.manpower.com.

Manpower. "Manpower Inc. Annual Talent Shortage Survey Reveals Sales Representatives, Skilled Trades People and Technicians Top Most Wanted List Globally." 29 March 2007. Available from http:/www.manpower.com.

Rajawat, K Yatish & Chhavi Dang. "Now, Cos Look to Fix Attrition Liability on Recruitment Firms." *The Economic Times*, 21 September 2006.

Randstad Holding. "Randstad Increases Ownership in Talent Shanghai to 70 Percent." 23 May 2007. Available form http;//www.ir.randstad.com.

Sachdeva, Sujata Dutta. "Lateral Placements: Head-hunters' Delight." *The Economic Times*, 26 February 2006.

"Secure Rights of Temporary Workers." *Japan Press Weekly*, 25 February 2003. Available from http://www.japan-press.co.jp.

Sinha, Vivek. "Temps Are Now Getting Their Money's Worth." *The Economic Times*, 27 March 2007.

Thottam, Jyoti, Esther Chapman, Avery Holton, Kathleen Johnston, and Constance E. Richards. "When Execs Go Temp." *Time*, 26 April 2004.

"Workplace Rights a Temporary Fix." *Management Today*, May 2004.

RETAIL AND WHOLESALE TRADE

SIC 5511, 5521

NAICS 441110, 441120

AUTOMOBILE DEALERS

The world's car dealerships sell new and used cars and light trucks to the general public. They include manufacturer franchises and independent retailers. New car franchises also often perform repair services, including manufacturer-authorized repairs. For more details on trends affecting the broader automotive industry, see also the topics **Motor Vehicles** and **Motor Vehicle Parts and Accessories.**

INDUSTRY SNAPSHOT

Globally, the retail car industry remains highly fragmented. There are very few big players, with most dealerships being independent used car dealers or franchisers of the the major car brands. The industry is highly dependent on economic trends, with disposable income levels greatly dictating purchasing levels and patterns. Some markets remain virtually untapped. In mature markets, industry participants were continuing to use incentives to lure customers' purchases.

In China, only 3 percent of the population owns cars, and the world's major car manufacturers see this as the major growth area. China's Deputy Minister of Commerce Ma Xiuhong told the *Detroit Free Press* that Chinese automakers did not have the dealer relationships in order to successfully make major plans for moving to the U.S. The newspaper noted, however, that several Chinese automakers planned to export vehicles to the U.S. Chrysler's partner, Chery Automobile, was cited.

According to the *Detroit Free Press,* owners of the oldest GM-affiliated dealership in India expected an increase in sales among first-time buyers with the Chevrolet Spark. The minicar was believed to be well suited to India's roads and developing economy. By May 2007, Mahendra and Mayank Merchant reported having booked 30 orders for the Spark. Their dealership originally focused on selling Oldsmobiles. During India's decades of economic isolation, it sold Hindustan Motors' big Ambassadors. The father and son team owned two dealerships — an original one opened by Mahendra Merchant's father more than 60 years ago in the heart of Mumbai and another one near Mumbai's international airport.

The *Detroit Free Press* also reported that dealers who sell Chrysler, Dodge, and Jeep vehicles were optimistic that resolution of what would happen to the Chrysler Group might improve their sales. These comments followed a DaimlerChrysler announcement that Cerberus Capital Management offered to pay US$7.4 billion for 80 percent stake in Chrysler. Premier Chrysler-Jeep Chicago Dealership Owner Garrett Jioulos predicted, "It's going to be very refreshing. The dealer body will be a lot happier."

Dealerships tried to reach out to customers and their families by linking to special campaigns. One example took place during May 2007 National Military Appreciation Month. California teenager and founder of millionthanks.org Shauna Fleming was featured in a TV commercial celebrating the partnership supporting her efforts as the national spokesperson for the month. GM dealerships throughout the U.S. served as sites where well wishers could drop off letters or sign large cards for Americans serving in the military and on duty in Iraq and Afghanistan. The campaign's goal was to collect at least one million letters during the month to send to troops. "We appreciate our troops being there," stated Taft Chevrolet President Devinder Bains. "My gratitude for the troops comes since I come from a military background. My father and brothers served in the military in India."

ORGANIZATION AND STRUCTURE

While the central function of car dealerships is, of course, selling cars, dealerships often engage in two related business lines: financing and repairs. Small dealerships usually do not have resources to offer financing, but larger chains may grant car loans as a service to their customers and as a source of additional revenue and profit. Many more dealers also furnish maintenance and repair services, typically to customers of the dealership or to owners of cars from the dealership's franchised line.

Pricing. Pricing has long been a debated issue in auto retailing, and it is one that regained attention as the new superstores eschewed negotiable pricing in their outlets. As in many retail trades, new car retailers priced their products based in part on a manufacturer's suggested rates and in part on other factors including current demand and incentive programs which usually resulted in cars selling at less than the manufacturer's suggested level. Sometimes the disparity between a car's list price and its usual selling price could be great. In France, for example, auto dealers routinely sold Renault and Citroen models, which manufacturers marked up at a premium to comparable imported models.

A major determinant in traditional pricing had also been buyer negotiation—more often termed haggling—based on what the buyer might know about the dealer's costs or prices of competitive products. In the 1990s and 2000s consumers increasingly paid attention to, and had greater access to, information about dealers' costs, the value of various option packages, and the average mark-up on car prices to cover dealer costs and profit. This information gave consumers considerable bargaining power and helped keep prices—and consequently, dealer profits—low compared to earlier periods.

Traditional used car pricing usually involved a similar process of negotiation. However, with used cars the cost and market value could be much more ambiguous. Factors such as a used car's age, condition, and relative popularity figured into its valuation, and while published "book" values were available for comparison, the procedure might be cloaked in much greater subjectivity in comparison to new car pricing. The murkiness of used car valuation is, in part, what made the used car side of the business more profitable, as dealers often had flexibility to mark up trade-ins and other acquisitions at much higher rates than new cars. But it also led to some abuses, notably when consumers were unaware of the average market price for a car (or the exact condition of all of its components) and a dealer convinced him or her to pay much more than it was worth.

New Car Franchises. Compared to other retail businesses, car dealerships were unusually dependent on manufacturers in that new cars in Japan, Western Europe, and North America were sold almost exclusively by companies that had been granted one or more dealership franchises by manufacturers. All of the world's leading automakers thus regulated, with increasing scrutiny, the number and type of retailers that sold their products. Some manufacturers watched with discomfort as consolidators purchased the businesses that they had granted franchises to. A notable dispute erupted in 1997 between Republic Industries Inc., parent company of AutoNation, and the automakers Honda and Toyota. The manufacturers attempted to ban Republic from acquiring more than a certain number of their franchise holders within certain markets and over a specific time frame. Toyota, for example, mandated a nine-month waiting period between acquisitions of its franchises and imposed maximum limits of seven separate Toyota franchises and three Lexus franchises per retailer.

New car dealership franchises were usually granted along the lines of the manufacturers' different marketing divisions. This means, for instance, that General Motors Corporation issued separate licenses to market different lines, such as Chevrolet and Pontiac; in other words, a Chevrolet-brand dealer did not automatically have rights to sell Pontiac models.

In the late 1990s, automakers both in the United States and abroad sought to derive a more-efficient cost structure from auto retailing. For example, in the United Kingdom, car manufacturers were redrawing their marketing districts in order to grant a wider geographic market to a fewer number of dealers. Similar moves were underway in the United States by the country's Big Three (Ford, General Motors, and DaimlerChrysler). In particular, Ford and General Motors began to trim the numbers of their franchises. General Motors reduced its 8,000-dealer base in the United States—the world's largest—by 1,000 between 1998 and 2000. Offsetting such moves in part, however, was an increase in the number of import-franchised dealerships, including those from Japan, Europe, and South Korea. In fact, these import dealerships increased by 299 in 2000, while Big Three dealerships declined by only 296.

Used Car Dealers. While new car dealers often marketed used cars as well, including many that were traded in during the purchase of new cars, used car firms exclusively dealt in previously owned vehicles. These cars were obtained from wholesalers, auctions, or private individuals. As a result, used car dealers were considered independent, required no license from manufacturers, and were able to sell any make and any model.

BACKGROUND AND DEVELOPMENT

Automotive retailing throughout the world underwent rapid transformation in the 1990s. In major markets —such as those of Japan, Western Europe, and the United States — the widely fragmented retail structures began to give way to larger, consolidated dealerships. Although new auto demand was relatively flat during the mid-1990s, squeezing already tight profit margins at dealerships and North American dealerships were posting higher levels of sales and earnings than ever before by the end of the decade. Fueled by these sales, the number of dealerships in the United States grew to 22,007 in 2000, compared to 22,004 in 1999. Although the addition of three dealerships may appear insignificant at first glance, the increase was important as it marked the first such upswing in the United States since 1986. Between 1992 and 1997, the total number of car dealers in the United States had declined by about 4 percent.

Drawing the most attention in the decade, perhaps, was the rise of dealership consolidators and so-called superstore chains, which assembled an extensive line of new or, more often, used cars in a customer-friendly sales environment. The superstores, which originated in the United States with such chains as AutoNation USA and CarMax, were based on mass merchandising's category-killer concept, first pioneered in the United States by the likes of Toys "R" Us, and later refined by such chains as Home Depot and Office Depot. The goal of these chains was to combine in one place a wide selection of popular merchandise—theoretically, everything falling under a particular retail category—that might otherwise be sold by several separate traditional retailers. CarMax, launched by the Circuit City electronics category chain, and its counterparts sought to bring economies of scale to the traditionally local and decentralized automotive retail sector. The same was the goal of dealer consolidators, which acquired a large number of dealerships in targeted markets instead of creating a unified brand image for all of their outlets. They then merged back-office administrative operations, including ordering and advertising, while usually keeping the local name and image of the dealerships.

Critics of these chains pointed out that the revenue growth of many consolidators and superstores resulted solely from the rapid accumulation of new sales outlets, such as AutoNation's acquisition of nearly 400 stores in less than 16 years. Because operations like AutoNation had yet to prove their ability to operate any more profitably than their more traditional rivals in the late 1990s, skeptics disagreed over the impact these dealer groups would have on the industry. In fact, despite the publicized frequency of dealer buyouts by consolidators, consolidators controlled less than 5 percent of the market in 1997.

Consolidation did appear to pay off for the largest industry players, however. According to *Automotive News*, the 100 largest dealership groups sold 2.1 million units in 1999, which accounted for 12.3 percent of sales in the United States, and 2.4 million units, or 13.6 percent of sales in 2000. Some analysts predicted that these large dealer groups would control 15.0 percent of the U.S. market by 2004.

Profitability proved to be a key issue for car dealers in the late 1990s. After the value of manufacturing was subtracted, about one-fourth of the average new car's retail price was left to cover dealer costs and profit. In 1998, the average U.S. new car sold for US$22,000, leaving US$5,500 for the dealer. On the slim margins typical of the late 1990s, profits averaged just 1-2 percent of a car's sales price. Between 1999 and 2000, the average price of a new automobile grew only 1.8 percent, the lowest increase since 1991. Many industry watchers, including manufacturers and the emerging consolidators, speculated that room for considerable efficiency gains existed in car distribution that would allow a much higher share of the dealer mark-up to go toward profits. This belief underpinned the business philosophy of the consolidators.

Fueled by low unemployment and high consumer confidence, auto markets in Western Europe and North America reached near record levels in both sales and production in the late 1990s and early 2000s. Although many dealers expected to see a softening of new car sales in 2001 as economic conditions weakened, just the opposite proved to be true. The catalyst for this turnaround was the decision by General Motors to launch a zero-interest financing campaign for new car buyers. The success of the "Keep America Rolling" program, which was put in place to boost sales after the September 11 World Trade Center disaster, prompted other automakers to follow suit. As a result, what had been predicted to be a bleak year for dealers emerged as the second-best sales year in industry history. Dealers found themselves in the unique position of being able to reap the benefits of the expensive marketing campaign, while not having to eat the associated costs, which did undercut earnings for most major car manufacturers in 2001.

By the dawn of the twenty-first century, the Internet had become an important marketing tool for car dealers. According to data compiled by J.D. Power and Associates, a growing number of car dealer Web sites attracted a total of more than 8 million visitors a month in 2001. Research Web sites, such as those operated by Kelley Blue Book, secured roughly 20 million monthly visitors that year. These numbers reflected the fact that although only 5 percent of new vehicle purchasers actually completed transactions online, nearly 60 percent of new car buyers used the Internet to research their purchases before contacting a dealer. Predictions in the late 1990s that the Internet would replace traditional dealers, as businesses like Autobytel.com began to sell directly to consumers via the Internet, proved false. Instead, most of the online players who survived the dot-com meltdown of 2000 worked directly with traditional dealers. For example, in 2001 Autobytel generated roughly 4 percent of all new vehicle sales in the United States, by directing online shoppers either to dealer Web sites or to dealer showrooms.

CURRENT CONDITIONS

Globally, the retail industry for automobiles remained highly fragmented, although consolidation was beginning to occur. Further consolidation was likely due to increased capital requirements of dealerships, the limited options open to dealers to exit the business, and the strategy of some manufacturers to strengthen their brand identity by consolidating their franchised dealerships.

In early 2005, car sales in Europe remained sluggish. Europe's largest market, Germany, continued to experience an economic slowdown, and the market for cars matched this trend. German purchasers, once noted for replacing their cars often and buying only the best, were driving cars that averaged 8 years old. In France, car sales were also down 1.3 percent in 2004.

In the U.S., the automotive industry remained the largest sector of the retail industry in 2004, with total sales of approximately US$1 trillion. This equated to about one-quarter of all U.S. retail sales. According to a 2005 study by the National Automobile Dealers Association, franchised new car dealers sold 16.86 million new vehicles in 2004, worth US$714 billion, and 20 million used vehicles, 11.8 million of which were retailed, and 7.9 million of which were wholesaled. Dealers watched interest rates rise in the middle of 2004. Coupled with rising inventory expenses, dealers expected that profits would subsequently decrease.

Industry consolidation slowed in the U.S. during 2004, but was expected to continue at a moderate pace. The number of dealerships dropped marginally, but continued on its downward trend reaching 21,640 dealerships down from a high of 25,150 in 1987. However, dealerships in 2004 were larger, selling greater volumes; in 2004, 6,490 dealerships sold more than 750 new vehicles each per year, whereas in 1985, there were only 3,850 dealerships with sales that high.

Hybrid model vehicles, which use both gas and electric power, were set to increase in sales each year. While sticker price of hybrids was still a factor in 2004, it was expected that prices would drop as the technology developed. Even so, hybrids were in demand from both environmentally aware consumers and high mileage drivers alike.

By 2007, there was a growth in import dealerships in some of the strongest U.S. domestic markets. According to *The Dallas Morning News,* import dealers were "getting bigger and better" while becoming the largest group of area auto retailers. Many of the import dealerships were striving to improve their service departments and offering heightened levels of customer service including vehicle delivery services and concierges.

In its *2007 Market Data Dealer Data* report, *Automotive News* shared significant financial and census data. In 2006, the average U.S. dealership's net pre-tax profit amounted to 1.5 percent of total sales per the NADA. The number of import-exclusive U.S. dealerships rose by 223 last year to 6,127. There were 21,761 new-vehicle dealerships at the beginning of 2007 which was down from 328 for the same time in 2006.

With only 3 percent of its population owning cars by 2004, China was poised to become a industry growth leader in terms of sales. Major manufacturers were vying for opportunities to establish facilities in the country. Demand for automobiles was expected to reach 5 million before 2010, with China expected to account for 3 million of this.

Research and Technology

AutoCheckMate developed a costs-saving technology that photographs vehicles when they are left for service. Two versions of the system track vehicle information that is available on a Web site. One version utilizes a hand-held camera and digital camera combination to record information that includes vehicle identification numbers. The other version is designed for high-volume dealerships. It uses a hand-held scanner, sensors and up to 16 cameras to obtain vehicle data. The first and second versions cost US$5,900 and US$49,900 respectively. It was estimated that dealerships spent up to US$8,000 a month on lot damage.

Drive Technology Group Inc. offered valuable assistance to dealers via its Drive Way product. Dealerships could buy a license from Reynolds and Reynolds, the largest vendor of dealer management systems, that allowed Drive Technology to link its product in the same manner a new employee would do so. DriveWay functions as a special software designed to extract data from dealership systems, encrypt it and securely submit it to the party that needs to use the data. Rather than using a modem, DriveWay uses dealership's high-speed network and bandwidth. Drive Technology offered valued assistance at a time when Reynolds decided to shut down access to modems that had been used to maintain systems. Its customer roster included dealership groups willing to pay upfront costs of less than US$100 and pay an average monthly license of US$50.

Current Conditions

According to *The Dallas News,* both domestic and import dealership employees received approximately the same levels of pay and benefits. The pay managers received related to dealership size more than brand. Sales increases at import dealerships meant salespersons there had the opportunity to earn more through their commissions. Developments in Dallas were believed to mirror occurrences throughout the U.S.

One of the most successful dealerships owners discovered that investing in employees benefited everyone. Detroit Auto Dealers Association President Joe Serra runs a profitable business, ranked 21st largest dealership group by *Automotive News,* that earned more than US$800 million plus sold 20,715 new and 10,283 used vehicles in 2006. "I have partners in each of the stores. I'm an investor," Serra told the *Detroit Free Press.* Serra believes in helping out employees and even gives their children scholarships. AutoNation Chief Operating Officer Mike Maroone said, "His dad [Al] was one of the first mega-dealers, Joe's just taken it to the next level."

Industry Leaders

AutoNation Inc. Fort Lauderdale, Florida-based AutoNation, which has roots as a waste disposal company dating to the 1980s, rose quickly in the mid-1990s to become the world's largest, flashiest, and most controversial automotive retailer. Under the leadership of H. Wayne Huizenga, also the founder of market-leading Blockbuster Video and Waste Management, AutoNation embarked upon a string of dealership acquisitions. Simultaneously, the firm bought up a number of the largest car rental firms in the United States and Europe.

AutoNation was reputed for buying out franchise dealerships at substantially higher valuations than had ever before been practiced in the industry, particularly during its first years of 1995-1997. Indeed, when Ford Motor Company endeavored a small-scale experiment in buying out a few of its dealers, it found that dealers were unwilling to accept Ford's conventional buyout offer because they apparently wanted sums on par with AutoNation's high-stakes acquisitions. Although AutoNation was by no means the only aggressive consolidator in the United States, it came to symbolize the tumult facing the industry. In early 1998 a leading auto industry trade journal featured an issue with extensive treatment of how smaller dealers were responding to competitors like AutoNation. Most sentiments were against the consolidation trend, although some industry executives expressed the surprising view that nearby superstores were helping their conventional businesses because their heavy advertising and novelty attracted more car shoppers to a central area, many of whom also browsed traditional dealerships along the way.

By the beginning of the twenty-first century, AutoNation had divested its car rental holdings and closed its 23 used car megastores. Believing that it had grown too quickly, the firm also decreased its number of dealerships from 290 in 1999 to 282 in 2000. Franchises also were pared down from 395 to 375 over the same time period, with 358 reported in 2004. During 2004, the company retailed 650,000 new and used cars of 35 different brands. Sales that year increased slightly to reach approximately US$19.4 billion, and net income continued to show signs of improvement. Autonation was ranked 112th in the *Forbes* 500 of 2005.

By 2007, AutoNation reported owning 254 new car franchises in more than 16 states with approximately 25,000 employees. It also offered high-tech sales policies and online sales options through its AutoNation.com and individual dealer Web sites. Additional AutoNation offerings included maintenance and repair services, auto parts plus vehicle financing and insurance. The company reported sales revenue of approximately US$19 million for 2006. It had budgeted US$400 million in 2007 for share repurchases and capital investments for 2007.

AutoNation's first quarter 2007 financial results were impacted by weak sales of new cars in California and Florida. Sales in those states jointly account for 50 percent of AutoNation's new vehicle sales. Profit from continuing operations fell 15.4 percent to US$82.9 million. Revenue was down 3.8 percent from the same quarter in 2006 to approximately US$4.4 billion while operating income fell 7.3 percent to US$187.4 million. The housing market slump was considered to be a major contributing factor for the decline.

AutoNation CEO Mike Jackson shared his views with *Detroit Free Press* about the Cerberus Capital Management decision to buy Chrysler announced in 2007. "This is a new chapter, and they do indeed have the right partner. I think it's a big step forward."

United Auto Group Inc. United Auto Group, headquartered in Bloomfield Hills, Michigan, posted sales of US$9.9 billion in 2004, up 14 percent over 2003 figures. Headed by Marshall Cogan, another key figure in the rise of the consolidation movement, the company was one of the United States' largest consolidators. Focusing primarily on the luxury car market, the company continued its acquisition strategy. In 2002, it acquired Sytner Group, one of the U.K.'s leading luxury car retailers. By March 2005, Synter operated 87 franchises. In January 2005, United also purchased the remaining 50 percent interest in Tulsa Auto Collection, six dealerships originally owned by the Ford Motor Company. By 2007, the firm operated 314 retail automotive franchises, representing 41 different brands and 26 collision repair centers. It employed nearly 16,000 workers at its 169 franchised dealerships in 19 states and Puerto Rico plus 145 international dealerships mainly in the United Kindgom. In May 2007, United Auto announced it had acquired the Classic Automotive Group in Austin, Texas. The acquisition represented four new franchises that were anticipated to add US$300 million in annualized revenue to the company's operations.

Sonic Automotive Inc. One of the fastest growing dealership groups at the turn of the twenty-first century, Sonic Automotive moved from fifth place to third place among the largest car dealers in the United States. Bruton Smith founded the firm in 1997 with five dealerships. By 2007, the company operated 175 new- and used-car dealerships and more than 35 collision repair centers in about 15 states. It posted revenues of approximately US$7.9 billion and employed 11,300 people. Sonic sells more than 35 brands of cars and light trucks plus offers vehicle-financing plans. Strategic plans called for continued focus on growth in metropolitan markets. Sonic owns Don Massey Cadillac, the largest Cadillac dealer in the United States.

Sonic and Rocket City Automotive Group announced plans to partner in the final development and launch of eAutoDrop Franchise concept. The launch was expected to occur by June 2007.

CarMax Inc. A publicly traded spin-off of the United States' Circuit City Stores Inc., CarMax was credited with introducing the no-haggling, wide-selection, customer-friendly superstore concept to the auto retail industry. By 2004, it was the United States' largest dealer of used cars. Founded in 1993, the used car chain grew much more slowly and attracted less media attention than groups such as AutoNation, but during the 1990s it forged a solid position in a number of U.S. regional markets, primarily in the southeast. Among the amenities it offered were fixed pricing, somewhat akin to grocery stores' so-called everyday low pricing, snacks, and recreation areas for children. The group doubled its outlets from 20 in 1998 to more than 40 in 2001 and 63 by March 2005. Some of these units sold new cars, as well as the typical selection of used cars that were less than six years old with fewer than 60,000 miles. For fiscal year 2005, CarMax posted US$5.3 billion in revenue, up more than 14 percent from the previous year. The company maintained a payroll of 11,175 workers.

By 2007, CarMax had earned distinction as being a Fortune 500 company and one of the Fortune 2007 "100 Best Companies to Work For". The company operated 80 used car superstores in 38 markets. During the 12 months ending in 28 February 2007, CarMax retailed 337,021 used vehicles and sold 208,959 wholesale vehicles at its in-store auctions.

On-line shoppers can visit http://www.carmax.com to search a CarMax inventory of more than 25,000 used and new cars. For April 2007, added a customer ratings and reviews feature to the site. In fiscal year 2007, there were more than four million site visits per month.

European Motor Holdings plc. One of the United Kingdom's largest dealer groups, European Motor Holdings operated 37 franchises in 2005, all of European-make cars, at 34 locations throughout the United Kingdom. Its key franchises included Volkswagen, Rover, Volvo, Mercedes-Benz, and BMW. Just over half of European Motor Holdings' unit sales came from used cars. Like its U.S. counterparts, European Motor had not achieved tremendous profitability by the late 1990s, with net margins holding steady at about 1.5 percent. However, when sales in 2001 fell marginally to an estimated US$650 million and earnings increased by 10.2 percent, margins rose to 2.0 percent. By 2004, the company reported more than US$967 million in sales, continuing a trend of record sales and profits. By 2006, European Motor Holdings owned and operated 50 dealerships in the U.K. and continued serving as the sole distributor for Perodua economy cars. The company also operated motor auctions and international automotive imports, a vehicle washing equipment unit, an electrical parts reconditioning unit plus timber/plywood packing business.

European Motor was founded in 1991 when a group of nine motor retail businesses joined forces. The following year, the group purchased Casemount Holdings Ltd., which evolved into its motor services arm. Eight more dealerships were added that year as well. Normand Motor Group Ltd., which included sixteen dealer franchises throughout southeastern and northwestern England, was acquired in 1994. Two years later, European Motor bought Telford Motor Auctions. The firm secured exclusive rights to import and distribute the Perodua, a compact vehicle manufactured in

Malaysia, in 1997. This marked the first import of Malaysian vehicles into the United Kingdom.

Yafun Automobiles Group. China's largest automotive dealer, Yafun, operated more than 800 outlets in 300 cities in China during 2004. In 2003, the company quoted sales of approximately US$30 billion and employed almost 16,000 people. Yafun expected to sell 850,000 vehicles in 2005, including 660 domestic new vehicles, 41,000 imported new vehicles, and 149,000 used vehicles. The company reported having a revenue of US$8 billion.

In December 2005, *China Daily* reported that Yafun had taken GM's joint venture in China to court. The lawsuit named both SGM (Shenyang) Beisheng Automobile Co., the GM venture, and China National Arts & Crafts Corp. The later company was a state-owned trader. Yafun requested compensation of US$6.24 million and that 102 Chevrolet SUV's be returned to the named companies. Charges related to Yafun's difficulty in selling vehicles due to problems obtaining license plates for vehicles.

Group 1 Automotive Group. Group 1 keeps driving ahead as the second-largest Ford Motor Company dealership group in the United States. It owns and operates more than 140 franchises at 105 dealerships. In addition, it is responsible for approximately 30 collision service centers in more than 12 states. These dealerships offer new- and used- cars plus light trucks through about 30 different brands. Group 1 also offers financing plans, maintenance and repair services, and sells replacement parts. Since acquiring about 12 dealerships in 2006, the company has continued to focus on growth strategies.

Major Countries in the Industry

United States. The United States was the world's largest retail auto market, with annual sales of new vehicles valued at more than US$714 billion in 2004, according to the National Automobile Dealers Association. The average car dealer saw a 2.2 percent increase in average sales, with 60.9 coming from new car sales, 27.5 percent from used car sales, and 11.5 percent from the sales of service and parts.

The U.S. industry is highly fragmented, with the large, publicly held retailer accounting for only 7 percent of the market. While most observers were struck by the rapid emergence of consolidators like AutoNation and CarMax, the amount of consolidation slowed in 2004. Smaller, traditional franchised dealerships continued to handle the largest share of the industry's business. Others added that consumers were not inexorably drawn to the superstore notion, either. Certain analysts believed that, stereotypes of bad car-purchasing experiences aside, some consumers enjoyed the power of bargaining for the best price, and many might be overwhelmed by a superstore's size.

Car dealerships remained large employers, showing an 8 percent increase in the number of employees over the five years leading to 2004. Estimates put the employee count at 1,129,600, with about 21 percent being in sales, and 53 percent being in service or parts sales.

In 2005, car dealers continued to use incentives to entice sales. Low financing options, cash rebates and attractive leasing options were used to encourage purchases.

In 2007, National Automotive Dealers Association asked the U.S. Senate to bring more transparency to the used-car buying process by requiring insurance companies to provide consumers more access to data on their vehicles. Information about severely damaged, stolen and flooded vehicles was of particular interest. Related concerns grew out of the fact that many totaled vehicles and flood-damaged Katrina cars were making it back on to roads after being rebuilt. A vehicle with a salvage title could be easily "cleaned" or "washed" in a state with weak title disclosure rules. The association made an appeal for insurance companies to do more to prevent title fraud.

Japan. In Japan, demand at car dealership was particularly bleak, even though exports in 1997 were bolstered by the weak yen. Overall unit demand in Japan dropped by 5 percent in 1997 as the effects of a new tax and general economic austerity weighed heavily on the country's appetite for new cars. As a result, Japanese car dealers were resorting to new methods to entice the price-conscious Japanese public. In all of the major markets, downward pressure on prices, particularly on used cars, was further eroding dealers' narrow profits in 1997 and 1998. German imports found success in the Japanese retail market in 2000. Volkswagen Group Japan sold a record 58,481 units, due mainly to its solid local dealer network, as well as to the popularity of the new Beetle.

In May 2007, *Bloomberg* reported that Japan's domestic vehicle sales fell for a 22nd straight month. Sales of cars, trucks and buses —with the exception of minicars— fell 10 percent to 217,911 vehicles in April from 2006. The Japan Automobile Dealers Association released the sad news. It reflected the second worst for April since the group started tracking sales in 1978.

Further Reading

"Auto Dealers Urge Congress to Make Available Data on Totaled Vehicles." 11 April 2007. Available from http://www.insurancejournal.com.

"Auto Retail Industry Maintains Strength in 2003." McLean, Virginia: National Automobile Dealers Association, 11 May 2004. Available from http://www.nada.org.

"Auto Sales Outlook Favorable for Second Half of 2004." McLean, Virginia: National Automobile Dealers Association, 15 July 2004. Available from http://www.nada.org.

Box, Terry. "Import Dealerships Surge Ahead." *The Dallas Morning News,* 26 April 2007.

"Car Dealers Worried U.S. FTA May Bring Used Autos." *Digital Chosunilbo (English Edition),* 2 May 2007. Available from http://ww.english.chosun.com.

"CarMax Launches Customer Ratings and Reviews on carmax.com." *PR Newswire,* 23 April 2007.

"Car Retailer Down 15.4 Percent As Sales Lag in Kcy Markets." *South Florida Sun—Sentinel,* 27 April 2007.

"Dealerships Total Up Despite Big 3 Loss." *Automotive News,* 26 March 2001.

de Saint-Seine, Sylviane. "EMH Rises to No. 1 on the Chart." *Automotive News Europe,* 28 July 2003.

Draper, Deborah J., ed. *Business Rankings Annual.* Detroit: Thomson Gale, 2004.

Dyer, Leigh. "President of Sonic Automotive Resigns." *Knight Ridder/Tribune News Service,* 28 April 2004.

"GM Venture Sued by Beijing Car Chain." *People's Daily Online,* 9 December 2005. Available from http://english.people.com.

Gaudio, Thomas. "Controlling Damage Costs at Dealerships." 30 April 2007. Available from http://www.njbiz.com.

Gopwani, Jewel. "Small Car is a Big Deal for Dealers." *Detroit Free Press,* 13 May 2007.

Harris, Donna. "Consumers Use Web for Research, Not Sales." *Automotive News,* 21 October 2001.

———. "Most Dealers Expect Lower Profits in '04." *Automotive News,* 21 June 2004.

———. "Public Retailers' Growth Plan." *Automotive News,* 14 June 2004.

Hoover's Company Capsules. 2007. Available from http://www.hoovers.com.

"International Trade Statistics." Geneva, Switzerland: World Trade Organization, 2003. Available from http://www.wto.org.

Keeler, Doug. "Taft Chevrolet Joins Drive to Send Letters to American Servicemen." *Taft Midway Driller,* 23 May 2007. Available from http://www.taftmidwaydriller.com.

Kitamura, Makiko. "Toyota Leads 22nd Monthly Drop in Japan Vehicle Sales." 1 May 2007. Available from http://www.bloomberg.com.

Kisiel, Ralph. "Tech Firm Offers Way to Tap Dealer Data." *Automotive News,* 14 May 2007.

Lazich, Robert S., ed. *Market Share Reporter.* Detroit: Thomson Gale, 2004.

"Leading U.S. Groups." *Automotive News,* 25 June 2001.

Mann, Joseph. "AutoNation Profits Sink on Weaker Sales." *Knight Ridder/Tribune News Service,* 21 July 2004.

Merx, Katie. "China's Cars to Reach U.S. Gradually." *Detroit Free Press,* 17 May 2007.

"NADA Data 2005: Economic Impact of America's New-Car and New-Truck Dealers." *Auto Exec,* May 2005. Available from http://www.nada.org.

Osburn, Chaz. "Dealers Saved by 0 Percent." *Automotive News,* 21 January 2002.

Sawyers, Arlena. "Acquisitions Alter Dealership Ranking." *Automotive News,* 23 April 2001.

———. "CarMax Lowers 1st-Qtr. Forecast." *Automotive News,* 17 May 2004.

"2007 Market Data Dealer Data." *Automotive News,* 14 May 2007.

Tierney, Christine. "Automakers hope Paris auto show revives European sales." *The Detroit News,* 21 September 2004. Available from http://www.aiada.org.

"Top 10 Numbers." *Automotive News,* 14 April 2003.

Webster, Sarah A. "Car Dealer on a Roll." *Detroit Free Press,* 29 May 2007.

———. "Cerberus Deal Pleases Top Dealer." *Detroit Free Press,* 16 May 2007.

———. "Dealers Hope Customers Will Start Coming Back." *Detroit Free Press,* 15 May 2007.

———. "Michigan's United Auto Group Still on a Roll." *Knight Ridder/Tribune Business News,* 28 April 2004.

Welch, David. "AutoNation's Driver Takes a Sharp Turn." *Business Week,* 13 March 2000.

Wilson, Amy. "Only Retailers Shine in 2001." *Automotive News,* 14 January 2002.

SIC 5961

NAICS 454113

CATALOG AND MAIL-ORDER SERVICES

The catalog and mail-order industry, also known as non-store retailing or home shopping, sells products and services through television, catalog, online services, and direct mail. Certain firms have sizable mail-order operations in addition to other activities, such as manufacturing finished goods or store retailing, and may also be discussed under those categories.

INDUSTRY SNAPSHOT

Catalog and mail-order houses encompass companies that market products through all non-store retail channels, including catalogs, mail, radio, computer, and television. The three major non-store retailing markets, in descending order of size, are consumer, business, and charity.

Providing customers with a means to shop directly from their homes and offices, catalog and mail-order services continue to play a role in the retail industry. Although the glory days of the paper-based catalog may have gone, the globalization of the marketplace and decreases in the time consumers have for shopping have breathed new life into the industry. Coupled with the growing acceptance and use of the Internet by consumers, changes are being seen as traditional catalog providers have supplemented their sales channels with the Internet. The growth of television around the world and into new, developing markets has also brought with it the use of this medium as a sales tool. Home shopping television networks are proving highly successful, and are spreading around the globe.

According to the Direct Marketing Association's Multichannel Marketing in the Catalog Industry report, print was still king. Catalog companies' Internet sales were estimated at 39 percent of total direct sales in 2005. That estimate compared to 38 percent in 2004. An impressive survey finding revealed that 74 percent of respondents considered their catalogs to still be their primary sales vehicle.

ORGANIZATION AND STRUCTURE

Although large retailers, such as the United States' J.C. Penney Company, typically maintain an inventory warehouse, most industry participants keep little, if any, inventory on hand. When a customer orders a product the retailer contacts a wholesale supplier that ships the item to the retailer or directly to the customer—an arrangement referred to as just-in-time inventory. Because they refrain from traditional retail purchasing, manufacturing, and inventory management activities, many non-store retailers are essentially marketing companies. Some catalog companies, for instance, simply assemble a group of complimentary products manufactured by other firms and market those items in a catalog. Similarly, many direct-mail and broadcast-media retailers essentially act as middlemen, selling products that are manufactured and stored by wholesalers.

The benefits of non-store retailing are numerous. In the case of catalog and direct-mail marketing, retailers enjoy more efficient access to markets. Indeed, tailored customer lists allow companies to carefully target select segments of the market. Besides advantages associated with segmented marketing, mail-order retailers typically enjoy reduced fixed costs that would otherwise be incurred by operating a retail store or using face-to-face or telemarketing sales techniques. Expenses in the areas of rent, inventory, and payroll, are all reduced in the catalog and mail-order industry. Furthermore, mail-order companies have access to much larger geographic markets than do many retail establishments.

A chief drawback of non-store retailing, however, can be high advertising costs. The expense of producing and delivering catalogs, fulfilling orders, and serving customers, often leaves retailers with slim profit margins (or losses if response to a promotional effort is poor). Retailers often expect only 0.5 percent to 3 percent of recipients of advertising to actually respond to a solicitation by mail. The problem is compounded in many regions, particularly Europe, by high postal rates and restrictions on mail advertisements that increase mailing costs. High shipping expenses are also a drawback, particularly for large or heavy goods like appliances and furniture.

Because of high mail and shipping costs, cross-border sales by catalog and mail-order houses remain limited. Nevertheless, some firms have successfully entered world markets. Sales between the United States and the European Union, for instance, increased throughout the 1990s on the strength of increasingly uniform markets. The 2002 adoption of the single united currency, the euro, was expected to increase sales even more dramatically. The most exportable mail-order products in the 1990s, in order of revenue size, were information, education, and collectible products. Several U.S. firms successfully marketed specialty American products in Asian countries. Overseas mail-order firms also enjoyed increased success in the United States. Firms that instituted successful exporting ventures to the U.S. market in the 1990s included Aer Rianta, Bertelsmann AG, Jelmoli, Moore Ltd., Patrimonium, Quelle, and Otto Versand.

The International Direct Mail Advisory Council, created by the Universal Postal Union, a division of the United Nations, promotes cooperation between the public and private sectors to advance the mail-order industry worldwide. The organization conducts studies on the direct-mailing conditions throughout the world and established an advisory council made up of mail-order companies. The council's immediate goals included standardizing addresses and mailing customs.

BACKGROUND AND DEVELOPMENT

A Venetian book merchant, Aldus Manutius, provided one of the first mail-order services in 1498, selling Greek and Latin books through a catalog. Later, American Benjamin Franklin is credited for starting the modern mail-order industry in 1744 with a direct-mail offer in the United States. He produced a mail-order catalog bearing this promise: "Those persons who live remote, by sending their orders and money to said B. Franklin, may depend on the same justice as if present." Mail-order techniques were well-suited to the fragmented North American population. In 1863, in fact, the U.S. Congress authorized the issuance of a discount stamp for mailers of "printed matter and manuscripts," known as second-class mail. It also issued a third-class stamp for "bulk mailers." Several large U.S. companies pioneered mass mail-order techniques, relying heavily on direct mail to promote their businesses. Sears, Roebuck and Co., which introduced innovative mail-order catalogs in the early 1900s, became one of the most effective practitioners of direct marketing.

Three of the largest mail-order houses that gained prominence in the early 1900s were Sears, Montgomery Ward (founded in 1872), and Spiegel (founded in 1865). Similar but smaller organizations emerged in other parts of the world. In Japan, for example, department stores like Mitsukoshi and Takashimaya began marketing to rural customers through catalogs in the late nineteenth century. These and other industry pioneers usually offered general merchandise at low prices. They often manufactured their own products and counted on large-scale advertising to generate high sales volumes. Such operations continued to experience moderate sales growth throughout the mid-1900s and even started to gain appeal in Germany, the United Kingdom, and a few other nations. Growth in Japan, though, was squelched until 1972 by a government edict that restricted direct advertising. In the 1980s a variety of technological, demographic, and financial developments converged to cause explosive growth in catalog and mail-order sales.

Technological advances that catapulted many competitors to success in the 1980s included computers and software that increased marketing efficiency and improved customer service. Computer systems that became popular during the early 1980s allowed competitors to manage and manipulate large amounts of consumer data. They were also used to track and manage inventory more effectively. When a customer ordered a product, the mail-order house could electronically alert its warehouse, or its supplier, and quickly ship the product. Inexpensive desktop computer systems allowed small, specialty non-store retailers to more easily compete with larger firms on a national scale.

Other factors contributed to the increased profitability of the industry as well. Credit card systems eased payment problems, for instance. Some analysts contend that the non-store retail industry benefited most from pivotal demographic changes that developed over the course of the 1980s. One of the most important shifts was the rise in the percentage of working women, elderly people, and dual-income households in the United States, Japan, and Europe. Those market groups vastly increased their level of mail-order buying during the decade.

Worldwide consumer catalog and mail-order sales alone stood at US$176 billion in 1996, up from US$150 billion in 1993, according to *Direct Marketing*. Germany represented the largest market for catalog shopping, while the United States led in overall mail-order and catalog sales, according to an *Advertising Age* report. Although the growth rates slowed in more mature markets such as the United States, Germany, and Japan, in the mid- to late 1990s they remained steady. Emerging economies, however, experienced far more dramatic increases in mail-order sales growth. Chile's sales shot up by 300 percent in 1996, while India's rose by 20 percent, and the Czech Republic's by 25 percent.

The high-growth consumer products of the mid- to late 1990s included animal care merchandise, books, computer hardware and software, wine and liquor, and gardening products. In the business sector, they included stationery products, computer hardware and software, and medical supplies. Items that experienced lower growth during this period were video cassettes, cosmetics, physical fitness products, and audio recordings.

With a flooded retail store market in mature industrial countries, some industry observers believed that these retailers, some of whom have already invested in powerful customer databases, will turn to the mail-order business to boost their sales and increase store traffic. As a consequence, they forecast possible mergers of retailers and mail-order companies, so that retailers can combine their strong databases with successful mail-order operations.

Moreover, Sigmund Kiener, a member of the managing board of Quelle Group, argued in *Direct Marketing* that for mail-order companies to remain successful in the late twentieth and early twenty-first century they would have to provide more diverse products or services and they would also have to distinguish themselves from other companies. With advanced information networking systems in place, companies can expand their product lines quite easily. Kiener urged that companies must invest in umbrella brands with strong name recognition that span several product or service categories, in order to build their corporate identities. Marketing research will continue to play an important role in mail-order and catalog business, because companies will require catalogs and mail-order literature that target its individual customers. Finally, Kiener identifies developing a multinational customer base as another challenge the industry must face. When approaching international markets, however, companies must target a keenly defined market sector in order to succeed.

Along these lines, mail-order and catalog companies began to switch from general advertisements and solicitations to more specific and individualized ones or market their products to specific niches. Using new technology such as customer databases that track shopping and ordering habits, mail-order houses can produce catalogs geared directly to the individual tastes of customers. As a result, companies maximize the response to their advertisements and reduce expenses for wasted advertisement.

Business Week Online has reported that the catalog retail industry showed relative strength in 2001, in rankings of industries in the top 10 percent of the S&P Super 1500. Although it was predicted consumers would be spending cautiously during the 2001 holiday season, and on into 2002, due to layoffs and low consumer confidence, trends showed purchasers likely to shop via catalogs and the Internet. Time saving and convenience were touted as plusses for the catalog retailers, including Lands' End, which had reported third-quarter earnings much higher than expected. The mail-order and catalog industry, however, had concerns toward the end of 2001 when lethal doses of anthrax were sent through the mail to unsuspecting individuals. As the anthrax was believed to be tainting other letters that it came in contact with, 66 percent of those surveyed said they preferred to receive less unsolicited mail during the time of crisis, and 45 percent were worried about chemicals and viruses being sent through the mail in addition to anthrax, according to research performed by CLT Research. Approximately 38 percent of those surveyed said they would miss receiving catalogs if they were no longer sent in the mail. The industry was looking at different ways to send materials, including the use of transparent envelopes and plastic wrapping for catalogs. Where wrapping was a necessity, it was determined that the sender's address and an endorsement by a group such as the Ad Council would increase the chances that recipients would open the mail.

While analysts expected that television shopping would constitute the direct-marketing distribution channel of the future, by the mid-1990s it proved to have a more modest impact. The television mail-order industry emerged during the 1980s in the United States and spread to Europe and Japan by the early 1990s. The two giants of this segment were QVC and Home Shopping Network (HSN), but their sales remained well below predictions in the early 1990s. For example, these two stations reported around US$3 billion in combined revenues in 1996, in contrast to forecasts that the industry would gross US$10 billion by 1996 and US$100 billion by 2003. By the beginning of the twenty-first century, television shopping continued to make strides. In 2000, HSN had sales of more than US$1.7 billion in jewelry, clothes, and cosmetics, according to *Business Week Online*. Korea-based LG Home Shopping, despite being launched during the 1998 Asian financial crisis, expected 2001 sales of US$779 million, an increase of 68 percent over sales in 2000. Executives at the 24-hour shopping channel predicted sales would increase by 50 percent in 2002, despite a crowded field of competitors.

A study by Jupiter Media Metrix indicated that interactive TV (iTV) technology would soon have home shopping viewers make their purchases via remote control devices, rather than calling in by telephone to order showcased products. By 2005, iTV shopping programs were expected to garner sales of US$3.4 billion and were predicted to demonstrate cost savings for home shopping networks, enabling them to cut down on call centers.

With the popularity of the Internet in the mid- to late-1990s, mail-order houses and general retailers alike set up Web sites to market their products. With millions of Internet users throughout the world, companies saw great potential for sales. Security concerns and tax uncertainties hindered the industry. Some users remained wary of providing their credit card numbers on the Internet, fearing hackers might intercept them, which led to the creation of secure servers that scramble confidential information. Various government agencies also wrangled over how to tax Internet commerce. Nevertheless, Internet commerce continued to grow. Moreover, some online marketers achieved great success, especially Amazon.com, which had its first-ever profitable quarter ending December 31, 2001, with profits of US$5 million. During the same quarter in 2001, the company posted a loss of US$545 million but also garnered a pro-format profit of US$35 million, as well as record fourth-quarter sales of US$1.12 billion. Sales in Japan, France, Germany, and the United Kingdom increased by 81 percent to a total of US$262.4 million.

Online shopping was also expected to increase during the 2001 holiday season, due in part to the reluctance of consumers to travel and deliver gifts in person in the wake of the terrorist attacks on the United States on September 11, 2001, according to *InfoWorld*. *Business Week Online* reported that online sales in the European market were expected to increase by 50 percent during the 2001 holiday season, reaching as much as US$8.6 billion. Germany and the U.K. were likely to lead the pack and account for 65 percent of online holiday shopping. France was expected to demonstrate only 8 percent, and Italy and Spain were projected to weigh in at very low percentages. Internet shopping also gained popularity in Scandinavia but was expected to amount to only 9 percent of holiday sales.

In 2001, the number of Europeans using the Internet grew approximately 40 percent to 140 million. In Europe, 36 percent of households were online, compared to 55 percent in the United States. Online consumers appeared to feel more confident and secure about shopping on the Web, and concerns about credit card theft, privacy issues, and fraud had lessened. This was in part due to the majority of online selling being handled by trusted brick-and-mortar retailers, given that a large number of dot-com companies were no longer in business.

The DMA Vice President of Information and Special Projects Ann Zeller had discussion with *Bottom Line* about the *DMA/Catalog Age State of the Catalog/Interactive Report 2004*. Zeller indicated that, in spite of challenging early years in the first decade of the twenty-first century, forces such as consumer Web and e-mail acceptance and improved minimal cost technology in IT and telephony were laying the groundwork for a much stronger catalog industry. Report findings showed nearly 30 percent of catalogers' online sales were incremental or new customer sales that cataloguers would not have acquired without their Web sites.

While online shopping and e-retailing showed momentum, catalogs were not likely to go away, and direct-mail strategies of catalogers were still solid. *Business Week* reported that Coldwater Creek, a catalog seller of apparel for women, found that the best way to attract users to its Web site was not through banner ads but by using its own catalog and other traditional direct marketing strategies to lure consumers online. E-mail campaigns and banner ads are significantly cheaper than mailing catalogs, which can cost up to US$1.00 a customer, assuming the company is taking advantage of volume discounts. However, according to research compiled by Shop.org, catalog-based e-retailers were consistently more profitable than Internet-only stores or Web sites of brick-and-mortar retailers. The catalog industry sites using direct marketing methods spent only about US$14 to acquire new Web-based customers, while traditional retailers spent US$34 and Web-only e-retailers spent US$55.

Besides online services, other emerging mail-order media in the mid-1990s included CD-ROM systems on personal computers, in-flight ordering systems on commercial jets, and screen-based telephones. Although the future of the industry was unclear, many industry participants envisioned a global retail industry dominated by direct advertising and mail-order media that was made possible by low-cost, interactive, electronic information systems. Pricewaterhouse Coopers estimated that worldwide online and interactive television sales would top US$350 billion by 2010.

The industry also faced the challenge of reducing waste because of its approximately 100 billion advertising pieces mailed annually throughout the world. As a result, company practices were perceived by some as environmentally unsound. With growing consumer environmental awareness in Western Europe, the United States, and Japan, consumers voiced strong concern for the environment, calling for the reduction of advertisement and packaging and patronizing companies that espoused similar environmental sensibilities. Environmental legislation mandating the use of recycled—and often more expensive—paper by advertisers proliferated. Some countries in Europe simply outlawed mail advertisements that were not specifically requested by the recipient. To shed this negative image and to save money, some mail-order companies started to reduce the amount of paper used by viewing on-screen before printing, verifying addresses before mailing advertisements, using recycled paper and recycling paper, and publicizing a commitment to environmental protection.

ForestEthics, a San Francisco-based environmental advocacy organization, threatened to go public with a "blacklist" of cataloguers that it believed were practicing harmful eco practices. Among the names mentioned were Land's End, J.C. Penney, and L.L. Bean. During a March 2004 American Forest Products Association Paper Week conference seminar, ForestEthics accused the companies of not using enough recycled material and instead using too much pulp fiber sourced from endangered forests.

CURRENT CONDITIONS

Although the world's largest retail market is the United States, the largest catalog retailer remained Germany's Otto Group. However, the increased use of the Internet for home shopping as well as suitable distribution channels had made it possible to be successful in this industry on a global basis. The largest catalog companies often provide catalogs and web sites that are directed to specific country or regional markets around the world. The industry continued to experience consolidation, particularly of companies that had experienced difficulty adapting from a pure catalog format to one that included the Internet.

Around the world, traditional catalog providers were seeing increasing competition from other forms of home-shopping providers. Dell Inc. sells its computers directly to consumers, avoiding any middlemen or retailers by using direct-selling methods, including its Internet site. Dell had sales in 2005 of more than US$49 billion. HSN started in the home shopping business in 1977 selling product over the radio. By 2004, the fourth-largest cable network in the U.S. was using television, catalogs and the Internet to create sales of US$2.4 billion. HSN also operated home shopping services in Germany, Japan, and China.

Online auction provider eBay was also providing consumers with a way to shop from home. Although the company itself generates revenues through advertising and listing fees, eBay earned revenues of almost US$3.3 billion on gross merchandise volume of US$34.2 billion in 2004. The company had 135.5 million registered users, of which 56.1 million were considered active. Amazon.com also showed that hard-copy material was not needed at all for direct selling. Started in 1995, the company reached profitability in 2004, although it had incurred significant debt. It had grown into the world's most diverse retailer.

RESEARCH AND TECHNOLOGY

In the mid- to late 1990s, catalog and mail-order companies were increasingly moving their computer systems toward client/server architecture, with relational databases and distributed processing. Information database systems allowed companies to produce highly specific catalogs and marketing materials, tailored to smaller groups and individuals. Companies expected to eventually be able to print a set of catalogs for niche markets, each featuring a different product mix and marketing message. On the distribution end, just-in-time inventory practices assumed a primary role in helping companies to maintain profit margins through lower fixed costs and better customer service.

Industry observers anticipated that new advertising media would drive the evolution of the mail-order industry. Some expected that these new mail-order channels would eclipse sales made through traditional broadcast, print, and telephone media by the early 2000s. The burgeoning multimedia environment, which was expected eventually to integrate video, telecommunications, optical disc technology, and personal computers, would result in consumer-controlled, interactive advertising. Advertisers would be forced to adjust their marketing techniques as consumers gained greater control in choosing which ads and media they internalize. To that end, pilot interactive television systems were already available in some countries. Finally, advancements in recycled paper, printing technology, and ink would help the direct-mail segment move toward reduced waste and lower production costs.

WORKFORCE

The catalog and mail-order industry offers relatively meager employment opportunities in relation to retail businesses with similar sales volumes. While the workforce in this industry was expected to grow at a faster pace than employment in most other retail sectors, throughout the 2000s, advances in automation and information systems, particularly in Europe and the United States, could curtail job growth as companies eliminated labor-intensive positions. The greatest job opportunities in the giant North American mail-order industry were expected to be in the areas of computer programming and information system management, as companies sought to integrate and streamline customer, inventory, and financial information.

The National Retail Federation (NRF) urged U.S. Congress to approve legislation authorizing creation of Association Health Plans to help small business meet the rising cost of employee health insurance. In 2004 NRF was the world's largest retail trade association, with membership including all retail formats and channels of distribution including department, specialty, discount, catalog, Internet, and independent stores, as well as the industry's key trading partners and establishments, more than 23 million employees. In April 2004, NRF applauded the Bush administration's decision to reject a trade case filed by the AFL-CIO against labor conditions in China that called for high tariffs to be imposed on all merchandise imported from China.

INDUSTRY LEADERS

OTTO GMBH & CO. KG

The Otto Group (formerly Otto Versand) entered 2007 retaining its title as the world's largest mail-order group. It was also dubbed as being the world's number two, following Amazon, in B2C online trade. Based in Hamburg, Germany, the company was selling a variety of merchandise including sporting goods, appliances, and clothing by operating in 19 countries in Europe, North America and Asia. It had about 123 subsidiaries. The Otto Group was organized into the four business segments of multichannel retail, financial services, services and wholesale. The company produces more than 600 print catalogs per year, and customers can also purchase goods via the Web and CD-ROM. Otto owns a number of German travel agencies and is a majority stakeholder in the U.S.-based Crate & Barrel retail chain. It also controls Actebis Holding, a major distributor of computers in the European market. Executive board chairman Michael Otto's family owns the majority of Otto and separately controls Spiegel, the U.S. catalog company. Preliminary figures put the company's fiscal 2005 sales at more than US$18 billion, with more than 50 percent coming from sources outside of Germany. However, the mail order segment of the business had experienced the same declines facing the rest of the industry in Germany.

Otto announced plans to launch a new fashion branded catalog in summer 2007. The catalog, called *Oli*, is targeted at an affluent, youthful market. It will offer "high-street fashion" plus lots of fashionable accessories.

In March 2007, Otto launched *Montage* a catalog and online women's wear home-shopping service also targeted at an affluent market. Plans called for publication of nine seasonal catalogs for the brand exceeding a traditional model of two catalog seasons per year.

In keeping with its aspirations to revitalize the UK business, Otto restructured marketing operations. Colin Webb, the former Boots and Norwich Union marketing chief, was named UK group commercial director.

AMAZON.COM

Amazon.com was launched on the Web in 1995. It operates retail Web sites based in the United States, the United Kingdom, Germany, Japan, Canada, France, and China. Having started as an online book seller, these sites had grown to provide consumers with a wide selection of products, including clothing, electronics, entertainment products, toys, gourmet foods, jewelry, and household products. The company also provides an online marketplace for third-party sellers. In 2004, Amazon.com had sales revenues of more than US$6.9 billion of which about 56 percent came from U.S.-based sales. However, international sales showed the highest growth rate for the company, increasing by more than 53 percent over 2003 levels. Amazon.com was turning a net profit at the end of 2004, but it was only its second year of doing so since its inception. In 2005, Amazon announced plans to help Sears Canada recreate its web-based sales offering, and the company also added Macy's Department Store products to its list of offerings.

In 2007, Amazon announced the opening of its Major League Baseball Fan Shop at http://www.amazon.com/mlb. There fans of all ages could find books, jerseys, hats, collectibles, toys and novelties linked to their favorite team. The standard free shipping offers were available.

Amazon also unveiled its plans to employ 450 people at its Irish support center. That staff will focus on helping customers on its British and French Web sites. They will handle orders, e-mails and telephone calls from customers who use http://www.amazon.co.uk and http://www.amazon.fr.

LANDS' END

Founded by Gary Comer, Lands' End was the world's top direct seller of apparel in 2005. Lands' End focused on marketing its clothing primarily through its flagship catalog and specialty catalogs. The company also boasts approximately 16 full price and outlet stores in the United States, 3 outlet stores in the United Kingdom and 1 outlet store in Japan. In addition, Land's End has been developing a growing online presence, with Web sites based in the U.S., the U.K., Japan, Germany, France and Ireland. Owned by Sears, Roebuck (which was purchased by Kmart in 2005), Lands' End products can also be found in approximately 370 Sears stores. Geared mainly toward middle-aged consumers, Lands' End also sells home goods, luggage, accessories, and corporate gift items. The company has reduced production of catalogs in favor of an expanded global Web presence. In both 2002 and 2003, sales totaled almost US$1.6 billion, and total net income was nearly US$67 million. Since having a new owner, Lands's End docs not disclose sales or provide information about its overall Internet sales. The company employs about 5,500 year-round employees and seasonal employees. The most recent total for seasonal employees was 7,000. In 2005, the company cut 375 jobs and closed a call center due to heavier use of the Internet for orders. Top competitors are L.L. Bean, The Gap, and Spiegel.

In a move reflecting high-tech savy, Land's End introduced a new proactive chat feature on it Web site in the summer of 2006. The Lands End site tracks visitor's movements on the site. After shoppers spend a long time on pages or go back and forth between them, the system alerts a pop up to ask if they want to talk with a live person for assistance. By December 2006, seven percent of eligible site visitors had taken advantage of the offer.

Land's End took advantage of its business relationship by adding new merchandise and store-in-store boutiques within 100 Sears stores. It also added baby clothing and women's intimate apparel into its merchandising mix, too.

Land's End made the decision to expand its holiday catalog offerings to include some of Sear's big ticket items including 42-inch plasma TVs for US$2,000. This decision was met with mixed reviews when some critics expressed dissatisfaction with the company's move away from only selling its classic clothing. The move was believed to be evidence of impact mostly new management team since Sear' take over was having on Land's End.

A creative promotion for its Land's End Business Outfitters offered to provide makeovers to three companies in the summer of 2007. Companies were urged to visit http://www.makeover.landsend.com to enter their story and possibly receive a makeover for their employees. Land's End Business Outfitters apparel experts will work with the selected three companies to develop an apparel program especially suited to their needs. Options include uniforms, business suits, polo shirts and khakis.

L.L. BEAN, INC.

Based in Freeport, Maine, L.L. Bean was founded in 1912 by Leon Leonwood Bean and is controlled by its founder's descendants. In the beginning, it started as a one-room operation selling the single product called "the Maine Hunting Shoe". In 1967, L.L.'s grandson, Leon Gorman, took over the company as president. Gorman assumed the role of chairman of the board in 2001 and passed company leadership to Chris McCormick. McCormick became the first non-family member ever to hold the position.

The company specializes in outdoor specialty merchandise. L.L. Bean sells mainly via more than 61 catalogs with special formats delivered to the United States and more than 140 countries. Web-based orders were continuing to rise in numbers rapidly. The company does have a retail store in Freeport, Maine that is open 24 hours, 365 days a year and welcomes more than 3 million visitors a year. In addition, it has factory stores in the United States and Japan. L.L. Bean's merchandise is made up of more than 16,000 items and includes outdoor clothing as well as household furniture. Sales in 2004 were estimated at approximately US$1.4 billion and the company employed 3,900. L.L. Bean made the news in May 2004 when it filed lawsuits against four companies for allegedly using pop-up ads that appeared when customers visited L.L. Bean Web site. According to *Dow Jones Business News*, L.L. Bean vice president for E-commerce Mary Lou Kelley said the only legitimate windows that would pop up on the company's Web site would be one-question customer surveys.

In 2007, L.L. Bean shared many exciting plans for the future while celebrating its 95th anniversary. The company is investing more than U.S.790 million in its Freeport hometown for several projects including developing a retail complex and parking structure in conjunction with partner Berensen Associates scheduled for completion in 2008. L.L Bean also planned to open three new stores in 2007 in Connecticut, New York and Massachusetts. An additional five stores were scheduled to open in 2008. Net sales for 2006 were U.S.$1.54 billion marking 4.6 percent increase exceeding 2005 net sales of U.S.$1.47 billion. The regular workforce in Maine increased by 400 positions for a total of more than 4,350 employees. L.L. Bean's board of directors approved a 7.5 percent bonus for more than 4,900 eligible employees. These employees were listed on both regular and temporary rosters who had worked a minimum of 1,000 hours during the 2006 calendar year and were actively employed through December 2006. Major competition includes Bass Pro Shops, Spiegel, and Land's End.

J.C. Penney Corporation, Inc.

In the early 2000s, J.C. Penney ran one of the top catalog operations in the United States, but its chain of department stores, numbering more than 1,000, were suffering from competition from discount stores such as Wal-Mart and Target. In 2004, J.C. Penney sold its Eckerd drugstore chain with nearly 2,800 stores and formerly constituting 45 percent of the company's sales to The Jean Coutu Group (stores and support facilities in 13 northeastern and mid-Atlantic states) and CVS (southern stores and Eckerd's pharmacy and mail order businesses) for US$4.5 billion. Sales in 2002 totaled approximately US$32 billion while annual net income totaled some US$98 million. Employees in 2002 numbered 229,000. Fiscal 2005 sales were US$18.4 billion, of which US$2.74 billion was from catalog/Internet sales. Internet sales accounted for 30 percent of the total catalog/Internet sales amount, and were the fastest growing segment, having increased by 32 percent over 2004 levels. J.C. Penney posted revenue of U.S.$19.9 billion in 2006. It also reported operating 1,033 department stores throughout the U.S. and Puerto Rico. In addition, it boasted having one of the largest apparel and home furnishing sites on the Internet at http://www.jcpenney.com. It also had the U.S.'s largest general merchandise catalog business. J.C. Penney had approximately 155,000 employees.

Hanover Direct

Based in Edgewater, New Jersey, Hanover Direct sends out approximately 200 million catalogs annually. The firm sells home fashions through its *Domestications* and *The Company Store* catalogs; and men's and women's clothing via its *International Male* and *Silhouettes* catalogs. The company did sell gifts through the *Gump's By Mail* catalog, but it sold this division in early 2005. All catalogs have corresponding Web sites. Hanover Direct has struggled during the last decade including a US$233.3 million loss in 2003. In the fourth quarter of 2003, it did show a quarterly profit of US$364,000 after losing US$16.6 million three months earlier. Thomas Shull resigned in May 2004 as Hanover Direct chairman, chief executive, and president. According to Knight-Ridder/Tribune Business News, the action came after the company revealed, in regulatory filings, that Shull and several other top executives had cashed in on more than $3 million in special bonuses provided in case they lost their jobs through a change in ownership. William Wachtel, a managing partner of Wachtel & Masyr LLP law firm and Hanover board of directors member, took over as chairman. He is also a manager of Chelsey Direct LLC, which gained a controlling interest in Hanover in November 2003. Major competition comes from Federated, Otto Versand, and Williams-Sonoma.

Quebecor World Inc.

Quebecor World is the leading catalog printer in North America and has long-term partnerships with the world's most successful retailers and branded goods companies that utilize catalogs. The market leader also excells in most of its product categories including magazines, inserts and circulars, books, direct mail, directories and other value added services. The company has approximately 29,000 employees working in more than 120 printing and related facilities in the United States, Canada, Argentina, Austria, Belgium, Brazil, Chile, Columbia, Finland, France, India, Mexico, Peru, Spain, Sweden, Switzerland and the U.K.

In November 2006, Quebecor announced a catalog transformation plan which included important investments in new press and bindery technology. It also incorporated relocation plans for existing assets to Quebecor's facilities in Jonesboro, Arkansas; Merced, California and Corinth, Massachusetts. A significant part of the plan calls for transformation of the Corinth plant into a dual-process, premiere rotogravure and offset catalog facility. This plan addressed observations related to catalog customers' demands. Those demands called for shorter cycle times and efficient use of raw materials. The transformation plan would result in closing of a printing facility in Elk Grove Village, Illinois and bindery facility in Bensenville, Illinois. These closures would impact approximately 400 employees. However, Quebecor expected to create an additional 75 employee positions at its other facilities to accommodate additional volume.

Major Countries in the Industry

United States

In 2000, a study by the Direct Marketing Association (DMA) reported that, despite the sluggishness of the economy at the time, catalog sales in the United States were expected to increase at more than two times the rate of overall growth in the retail sector. The study predicted that 2001 would see US$120 billion in catalog sales, an increase of 8.9 percent over the US$110.2 billion generated in 2000. This prediction seems to have come true in the U.S., where many had been predicting the death of catalogs with the growing presence of the Internet. In 2003, Euromonitor valued the mail-order and home shopping market at US$207.5 billion.

In 2005, *Investor's Business Daily* was reporting that rather than being the source of death for the catalog industry, the Internet was actually helping it grow. The catalog industry was supplementing their marketing efforts by providing online catalogs in addition to their hardcopy counterparts. Although catalogs remain the core business of these firms, the Internet allows them to weather the storm of slowdowns in the economy and higher postal rates.

Catalogers have looked to lessen costs and streamline operations by lessening the number of pages in their offerings; reducing the weight or size of the pages; and making changes in catalog style. They have also explored using freestanding inserts in newspapers, alternative delivery methods, telemarketing, and home shopping to keep them in the black. Euromonitor was predicting that year-on-year growth for the mail order and home shopping industry would be between 4 percent and 10.3 percent in the years leading up to 2008. Internet-based sales were expected to be the area showing the highest growth, with sales expected to reach US$161 billion by 2008, an increase of almost 24 percent over 2003 levels. In the U.S., the mail order and home shopping industry remained highly fragmented.

Research and Markets claimed that mail-order prescriptions accounted for nearly US$44billion of total U.S. prescription sales in 2005. Sales for the mail segment increased by 7.6 percent in 2005. This compared with an increase of 16.5 percent in 2004. Mail-order prescriptions accounted for 244 million of the 3.38 billion total prescriptions in 2005.

Europe

According to the European Mail Order and Distance Selling Trade Association (EMOTA), the number of firms in Europe with established mail-order operations exceeds 2,000. As of 2004, the European mail-order industry had sales of just under 50 billion euro and average per capita sales of approximately 130 euro; it employed about 300,000 people. Although the mail-order industry was set up as international in structure, barriers do exist because of differences in European countries regarding taxation, postal service distribution, international payment, and differences in legislation. Sales to purchasers in other European countries were only about 3 percent; however, transition to the euro, although it was expected to take time, was expected to broaden the reach of mail-order companies and avoid the high cost of converting currencies.

According to research group Mintel, of the home shopping industry in Europe, catalog shopping had dropped from a once-high of 53 percent of the market to 25 percent in 2004. Internet-based shopping had overtaken it as the leading form, capturing a 32 percent market share; however, catalog shopping still exceeded it in terms of value. As a percentage of all retail sales, catalog sales were still low at 3 percent, and this was expected to decline to 2 percent by 2009.

United Kingdom. Valued at US$28.6 billion in 2003, the U.K. mail-order and home-shopping market differed from the U.S. market in that in the U.K. general mail order accounted for the largest market share (60 percent), whereas in the U.S., the Internet was the largest source for the industry. Great Universal Stores was the nation's industry leader, taking 22.5 percent of the market, according to Euromonitor. Together with Otto Versand and Littlewoods, these three leading companies controlled 60 percent of the market. The market was expected to experience huge growth in the period up to 2008, with growth rates predicted to exceed 48 percent.

Germany. German consumers showed a preference for using catalogs to do their home shopping. Of the total market, valued at almost US$60 billion in 2003, almost 68 percent came from catalog shopping, with the market expected to be valued at almost US$81 billion by 2008. Market leader, KarstadtQuelle—created as the result of a merger between Germany's leading department store and leading mail-order company— held 13 percent of the market in 2003.

Japan

In Japan the mail-order sector started in the 1950s and achieved double-digit yearly growth during the 1980s. Growth slowed in the early 1990s, but the market continued to expand, while the general retail market remained sluggish. Japanese consumers liked the convenience of home shopping and the fact that mail-order firms often sold goods at lower prices than traditional outlets. The country's parcel delivery system allowed companies to enter the market without the need for proprietary delivery services.

By the end of the twentieth century 8 million out of the total population of 125 million Japanese were online, according to statistics from International Data Corp., and that number was forecasted to reach 32 million by 2003. In Japan Web shopping was expected to rise from US$2 billion in sales in 1998 to US$45 billion by 2003. The recession caused the Japanese to spend less, but they still were actively buying on U.S.-based Web sites to save money on imported merchandise. A study by *Nikkei Weekly* showed that 39 percent of new Web users are female. Japanese purchase many of the same goods via the Internet that Americans do, but the country's e-commerce industry has yet to grow as quickly as that of the United States, due in part to high telephone rates.

In December 2001, Japan's retailer Sumitomo Corp. announced a joint venture with Otto Versand to pool their resources in the online mail-order sector, according to *European Report*. Called Sumisho Hermes General Service Inc., the new company was divided 51 percent and 49 percent between Sumitomo and Otto Versand. The two companies have worked together since the establishment of Otto-Sumisho in 1986, which sells Otto Versand catalog merchandise in Japan and manages Eddie Bauer products there as well.

Further Reading

"Amazon.com Opens Support Base in Ireland for British, French Web Customers." 23 April 2007. Available from http://biz.yahoo.com.

"Amazon.com Pays Tribute to America's Pastime with a New Destination for Baseball Fans." *Business Wire,* 2 April 2007.

"Are Your Employees Dressed for Success?" *PR Newswire,* 20 March 2007.

Borck, James R. "Fighting the Grinch." *InfoWorld,* 26 October 2001. Available from http://www.infoworld.com.

"Chairman Quits Edgewater, N.J.-Based Mail-Order Firm.rdquo; *Knight-Ridder Business Tribune News,* 7 May 2004.

"Coaxing with Catalogs." *Business Week,* 6 August 2001.

"Dead Man Walking: Spiegel Sell-Off Begins." *Catalog Age,* 29 April 2004.

"Eco Group to Launch Catalog 'Blacklist'" *Catalog Age,* 29 April 2004.

"Eddie Bauer,in Need of a New Image, Goes Casual with an Outdoor Twist." *Knight-Ridder/Tribune Business News,* 14 May 2004.

Grover, Ronald and Lowry, Tom. "The New Barry Diller." *BusinessWeek Online,* 10 September 2001. Available from http://www.businessweek.com.

Hajewski, Doris. "Filling a Bigger Wish List: Lands' End Finds New Beginning in Cross-Merchandising with Sears." 10 December 2006.

"Home shopping catalogue sales overtaken by Internet." *Screen Pages*, 2005. Available from http://www.screenpages.com.

Ihlwan, Moon. "A Gold Mine Called Home Shopping." *BusinessWeek Online,* 5 November 2001. Available from http://www.businessweek.com.

Kiener, Sigmund. "The Future of Mail-order." *Direct Marketing,* January 1995.

"L.L. Bean Reports 2006 Net Sales Results." 9 March 2007. Available from http://www.llbean.com.

"L.L. Bean Sues 4 Cos for Pop-Up Ads Linked to Web Site" *Dow Jones Business News,* 17 May 2004.

Magill, Ken. "Catalogers Say Books are Still Primary Sales Drivers: DMA." *Direct,* 12 December 2006.

"Mail Order and Home Shopping in France, Germany, UK and USA." *Major Market Profiles*, 2004. Available from http://www.euromonitor.com.

"Mail Order: Sumitomo-Otto Versand Joint Venture." *European Report,* 12 December 2001.

"Mail Order Survives, Thrives." *Investor's Business Daily,* February 2005. Available from http://www.the-dma.org.

Nolan, Kelly. "Is There No Ending to Lands' Offerings?" 8 January 2007.

"Otto Group and Hagebau Combine Forces in Direct Order DIY Sales." 2 April 2007. Available from http://www.ottogroup.com

"Otto Targets Affluent Youth Fashion Market." *Marketing Week,* 5 April 2007.

Paul, Evan Thomas. "Catalog Industry Targeted for Destroying Endangered Forests at Annual Catalog Conference," 5 May 2004. Available from http://http//www.forestethics.org.

"Powerful Brands. Integrated Shopping Channels. Style and Quality at a Smart Price. Engaging Customer Service. It's What Sets Us Apart!" http:www.jcpenney.net.

"Quebecor World Transforms U.S. Catalog Platform to Further Enhance Customer Value." *Canadian Corporate News,* 8 November 2006.

"Research and Markets: Mail Order Prescriptions Accounted for Nearly $44 Billion of Total U.S. Prescription Sales.

Saliba, Clare. "Study: Interactive TV Shopping Poised for Growth." *E-Commerce Times,* 14 June 2001. Available from http://www.ecommercetimes.com.

Shearman, J. Craig. "Retailers Welcome Bush Rejection of China Trade Sanctions," 28 April 2004. Available from http://www.nrf.com.

———. "Retailers Urge Passage of AHP Legislation," 13 May 2004. Available from http://www.nrf.com.

"SpiegelCatalog Partners with Editorial Dream Team to Give Women What They Want," 22 January 2004. Available from http://www.spiegel.com.

Stovall, Sam. "Can They Deliver?" *BusinessWeek Online,* 27 November 2001. Available from http://www.businessweek.com.

Thompson, Maryann Jones and Yamada, Michiyo. "Web Shopping Booming in Japan." *Industry Standard,* 4 May 1999. Available from http://www.cnn.com.

Yamamoto, Yuri. "Mail-Order Companies Home in on Markets." *Nikkei Weekly,* 7 April 1997.

Zeller, Ann. "Five Questions: On the Current State of the Catalog Industry," 2005.Available from http://www.the-dma.org.

SIC 5411

NAICS 445110

GROCERY STORES

Retail grocers purvey a broad line of fresh, frozen, canned, and other prepackaged foods. Many of these stores also carry a variety of nonfood items such as health and beauty aids, paper goods, and cleaning supplies, but food and beverages make up the majority of their product lines and sales volumes. Excluded from this discussion are convenience stores and specialty food shops, such as butchers and produce markets.

INDUSTRY SNAPSHOT

Within the world's largest economies, the grocery retailing industry, remained fiercely competitive, slimly profitable, and dominated by a few multibillion-dollar companies in each national market. Not only were grocery stores competing with each other, they also were having to stave off restaurants and other prepared-food vendors for a share of consumers' food budgets—a battle grocery stores have been losing gradually in leading world markets. Large-scale retailers responded by offering so-called home meal replacements and other nontraditional services that differentiate them from conventional grocery stores and restaurants. Still other grocery retailers have experimented with home delivery of groceries, marketing the service to busy professionals or senior citizens, although it is not expected to replace traditional shopping. Many larger grocers have also included conveniences such as in-store pharmacies, which are perceived as a customer convenience and also garner higher profit margins than food products.

According to 2005 research from IGD, the top 10 retail grocery markets in terms of value were the United States with US$759 billion, Japan with US$ 451 billion, China with US$277 billion, India with US$194 billion, United Kingdom with US$156 billion, France with US$152 billion, Germany with US$136 billion, Italy with US$133 billion, Russia with US$129 billion, and Spain with US$64 billion. Although U.S.-based giant Wal-Mart continued to dominate the industry on a world scale, the expansion of grocery firms into the global marketplace continued to be done more by European companies, such as France's Carrefour, Ahold of the Netherlands, Germany's Metro Group, and Tesco of the United Kingdom. Carrefour was considered to be more "global' than Wal-Mart as it operated in more countries.

A potential growth trend was in online grocery services. Despite a slow U.S. start and many setbacks, including the well-publicized failure of Webvan.com, Forrester Research reported that the industry generated worldwide market revenues of US$10 billion. This was still a drop in the bucket of worldwide revenues from consumer packaged goods (CPG) that year; US$10 billion represented only 2 percent of CPG revenue worldwide in 2003. Other independent research firms, including Jupiter Research, forecast major growth of online grocery shopping. By the mid-2000s, operations such as NetGrocer in the United States and Tesco in the United Kingdom continued to grow their online businesses.

ORGANIZATION AND STRUCTURE

Business Structure. Three business set-ups describe the world's major food retailing enterprises: corporate chains, affiliated independent stores, and retailer-owned cooperatives. Corporate chains are the simplest because their retail outlets are fully owned or controlled by the corporate parent. Such chains generally show the highest degree of homogeneity across stores and regions; individual outlets may also be franchised to local or regional owners, but they usually follow a rigid formula for operations and marketing, and they procure stock through prescribed corporate channels.

Like corporate chains, independent affiliates and retailer-owned cooperatives may share a common retail identity, but ownership and control vary considerably. Independent affiliates are groups of independently owned stores that purchase at least part of their goods, which may include a common private label, through a central wholesaler. The wholesaler generally provides goods to independent stores at lower prices than small retailers would otherwise be able to obtain in their small-volume purchases. The independents choose whether to include this affiliation in their names and marketing. In the trade, the term "independent" can describe small operations of up to ten stores. Among affiliated independents, then, the corporation of prominence is often not any of the retailers; instead it's the wholesaler with which the independent stores affiliate. (See also **Wholesalers.**)

Retailer-owned cooperatives, also known as buying groups, go one step further than affiliated independents. These independent stores affiliate with a central buying organization and also own shares of it. As with affiliates, the voluntary retail members choose whether to market the common identity in their stores. Because they own the buying group, the retailers also share in any profits or losses the buying groups incur and, depending on their size, may have administrative clout with the buying group's management. In this sense, the buying group is a joint venture among all its members.

In practice, distinctions often blur the various types because of crossover activities. A corporate chain may distribute merchandise on the side to independent stores or affiliates; a wholesaler or buying group might open or acquire retail outlets. These models also do not take into account the simplest form—independent, unaffiliated stores. Although in many places they are numerically prevalent over any other form, few such operations could be considered major participants in the industry.

Store Formats. In leading countries most of the industry's sales occur in supermarkets, which in the trade are defined as having US$2 million or more in annual sales. Supermarkets also are characterized by offering a full line of food, including fresh produce, meats, frozen foods, and dry packaged and canned goods, as well as diverse nonfood items such as cosmetics, toiletries, and cleaning goods. Many also offer in-store food preparation services, especially deli counters and bakeries. Supermarkets range in size from approximately 30,000 to 70,000 square feet.

Hypermarkets are largely a European format of massive, all-in-one stores that include a full department store with a complete grocery line, and often a gas station and other service amenities. The quintessential European hypermarkets, such as those by Carrefour S.A. of France, which is credited with pioneering the concept in the 1970s, may be upwards of 300,000 square feet in size.

Supercenters in the United States, although smaller and more limited in scope, are somewhat analogous to European hypermarkets. Wal-Mart experimented with the hypermarket concept, with a 225,000-square-foot store, but it met a lackluster reception from U.S. consumers; the consensus in U.S. retailing is that the hypermarket format is unlikely to attract much following in the near future, due to already-vibrant retail trade in many of the product groupings such a large store would offer. The super center, ranging from 100,000 to 200,000 square feet, was Wal-Mart's solution. Like hypermarkets, supercenters include extensive food selection comparable to that of the largest supermarkets. These offerings are coupled with a general line of housewares, linens, discount apparel, toys, small electronics, and hardware.

Deep-discount stores, also known as limited assortment stores, offer no-frills merchandise at prices ranging from 5 percent to 25 percent less than that of name-brand merchandise available through conventional stores. Led by such chains as Germany's Aldi Einkauf GmbH, these discounters may sell only private-label and off-brand products and may not stock a full or even consistent line of groceries. The physical store tends to be austere as well. The leading European chains leave their groceries in boxes on wood pallets rather than stocking them on shelves.

General-line grocery stores are numerically predominant in most places of the world, even while in the industrial economies they make up a relatively small percentage (as little as 20 percent) of industry sales. These stores may offer only a limited line of the most common produce items, no fresh meats, and a small selection of the most commonly used canned, frozen, and prepackaged goods. On the smaller end, the distinction may begin to blur with that of convenience stores. General grocery stores are often independent or small regional chains and, in some markets, are highly vulnerable to loss of sales to—or acquisition by—supermarkets and other larger format retailers.

Product Share. By product category, according to *Supermarket Business,* the typical U.S. supermarket obtains 26.35 percent of its sales volume from shelf-stable food items; 14.58 percent from meat, fish, and poultry; 10.89 percent from fresh produce; 9.61 percent from nonfood dry goods; 6.59 percent from deli services; 6.10 percent from dairy products; 5.37 percent from frozen foods; 4.65 percent from health and beauty items; 4.65 percent from general nonfood merchandise such as audio and video supplies, toys, periodicals, and photographic goods; 3.57 percent from in-store bakeries; 3.29 percent from other baked goods; and the remaining 4.35 percent from prescription drugs and other miscellaneous items.

Private-label, or store-brand, goods garner an estimated 3 percent of all grocery sales in Japan. In the United States, individual chains report that private labels generate an average of 20 percent of unit sales; this figure is not fully comparable, however, because that percentage is not based on industry sales as a whole. In Europe, private labels account for up to 50 percent of sales by some chains, most notably in the United Kingdom, although national averages are more in the range of 20 to 40 percent. Despite their low-cost, low-quality connotation in markets such as the United States, private labels in Europe are sometimes used to market premium merchandise. This practice varies widely, however, and more often than not the private label is used to market value-oriented product lines.

Market Forces. A variety of economic and demographic factors influence the industry's fortunes:

- Demand fluctuation. Economists describe the demand for basic grocery staples as inelastic. That is, groceries are consumed at relatively fixed rates regardless of cyclical economic conditions or modest price fluctuations. Demand for premium or luxury foods, conversely, tends to be more susceptible to demand swings, as consumers become more or less willing to part with their money for what is perceived as desirable but unnecessary. In some cases, premium goods are the most profitable for retailers, but private-label or store brand staples may also be quite profitable.
- Disposable income. For obvious reasons, the maintenance and growth of consumers' disposable income is closely tied to the continuing and expanding sales of all but the most basic groceries.
- Consumer confidence. In a broader sense, consumer confidence is also a factor to the extent that consumers may not have more money than before, but they may be more willing to spend from existing incomes or credit lines if they perceive economic health. In practice, of course, consumer confidence usually rises in part due to real income gains.
- Competition. The number, scope, and physical dispersion of stores in a given locality dictate the competitive environment. Stores compete mainly on price, convenience, and the range of products and services they offer. In less saturated markets, such as those of Eastern Europe and parts of Asia, one grocery store may possess a local monopoly for consumers of average or less than average means, while upper-income consumers may have additional choices. Particularly in industrial economies, grocery retailers increasingly compete with food service establishments, such as full-service restaurants (see also **Restaurants**), fast food chains, and eat-in coffee and bakery shops, for consumers' food purchases.
- Local demographics. Although competitive strategies such as aggressive pricing or acquisition can fuel short-term growth, an expanding local population is often a requisite for the long-term sales health of individual grocery stores. In addition, especially in competitive retail climates, stores must be in tune with local buying preferences in order to stock the most saleable product mix.
- Location. Finally, related to both demographics and competition, is a store's physical location relative to residential centers and competing venues. Optimal location is within short driving or walking distance from a large share of the intended customer base, near other retail or entertainment attractions, to benefit from the convenience of cross-purpose shopping patterns. However, grocers must be far enough from direct competitors or other outlets of the same chain, so as not to over saturate the market. Likewise, ease of access, such as ample free parking, also is important and has been a selling point for some recent European suburban store openings.

BACKGROUND AND DEVELOPMENT

In the latter half of the 1990s, Europe's combination of market saturation in the West, market development in the transition economies of the East, and lagging retail sales, had made the continent a hotbed for merger activities. Some European chains, such as those in Germany, actually experienced declining domestic sales. Therefore, acquisitions were a key to survival for many industry players. There was little indication that this consolidation phase would end soon.

In the United States, the Federal Trade Commission in 1999 and 2000 halted several mergers, which would have made supermarket chains anti-competitive. Prior to 1999, the FTC generally examined mergers on a store-by-store basis. However, when in December 1999 royal Ahold N.V. terminated its acquisition of Pathmark stores because of FTC opposition, the grocery merger climate cooled. Only months later, in June 2000, the FTC filed an injunction to block Kroger from buying 74 Winn-Dixie grocery stores in Texas and Oklahoma, claiming the purchase would have given Kroger a 33 percent market share in Fort Worth, Texas.

Saturated domestic markets increasingly portend foreign expansion for the most robust of these chains and acquisition by competitors for the less dynamic players. Perhaps no place has felt the brunt of the industry's appetite for expansion more than Latin America, where European and U.S. interests have gobbled up local chains and built new retail outlets, voraciously, in search of fast sales growth. These foreign chains have descended on Latin America with cookie-cutter success formulas and competitive savvy and, in the process, are stimulating indigenous firms to modernize and compete. For example, Grupo Pao de Acucar SA, Brazil's largest domestic grocery chain and second largest to Carrefour of France, responded to uninvited foreign suitors and competitors by opening that country's first 24-hour hypermarket and implementing sweeping technological upgrades and logistical improvements. But the foreign grocery conquistadors have already been confronted with the downside of such rapid expansion; a Brazilian economic slowdown in 1997 diminished short-term returns and caused more than one European grocery concern to scale down its ambitious growth plans. The competitive climate is similar in Asia.

Further promising to recolor the global supermarket landscape entering the twenty-first century was the foray by U.S. discount giant Wal-Mart Stores Inc. (the world's largest retailer in terms of sales) into the supermarket arena with its supercenter format. A scaled-down version of the European hypermarket, Wal-Mart's supercenters combined a full-service grocery department with an extensive line of housewares, clothing, toys, and other nonfood merchandise, at highly competitive pricing. Wal-Mart's threat is by no means confined to its home country, either; as of 1998 it had outlets in eight countries. By 2001, Wal-Mart had 1,100 locations in nine countries outside the United States. Its 1997 purchase of a 21-store German chain heralded its entrance into the already crowded western European field, although the move was seen by some analysts as a jumping point for penetration of the less saturated eastern European market. The popularity of shopping clubs, such as Sam's Club (a Wal-Mart sister company) and Costco, also grew through the 1990s and into the 2000s, creating more competition for the traditional grocery supermarkets.

As of 2002, perhaps the single greatest market of opportunity for food retailers lay in China, where an immense population, a briskly expanding economy, and a relative dearth of Western-style retail venues attracted growth-oriented merchants. Similar market conditions occurred elsewhere in Asia, notably Indonesia and to a lesser extent India, but these economies were decidedly less robust than China's. Among leading companies, Carrefour, Royal Ahold, and Wal-Mart were best poised for substantial expansion in China, although it was likely that local retail powerhouses would also emerge.

CURRENT CONDITIONS

According to 2005 research from IGD, the top 10 retail grocery markets in terms of value were the United States, Japan, China, India, United Kingdom, France, Germany, Italy, Russia, and Spain. U.S.-based giant Wal-Mart continued to dominate the industry on a world scale, but the expansion of grocery firms into the global marketplace continued to be done more by European companies, such as France's Carrefour, Ahold of the Netherlands, Germany's Metro Group, and Tesco of the United Kingdom.

The presence of a Wal-Mart, according to *Chief Executive,* was a dearth to local grocery stores. In the first five years after the opening of a new Wal-Mart, other area grocery stores lost between 8.0 and 17.0 percent in annual sales. Wal-Mart continued to look for ways to expand internationally, as did most other large grocery chains, with mergers with and acquisitions of exising grocery companies being the most used method for growth. Most future growth was expected to occur in Eastern and Southern Europe and Asia, particularly China and India.

Over the past decade, large-scale retailers, particularly those in the United Kingdom and the United States, have made sizable gains in cost efficiency through technological innovation and tight organizational control. These cost-cutting measures, often motivated by lean economic conditions, caused some U.S. observers to question whether such parsimony is not hurting sales by restricting the product line too tightly or by decreasing the level of customer service. It was likely, though, that because of their close ties to profitability, these practices would persist in firms that had adopted them and would continue spreading to the grocery chains of Asia, central and eastern Europe, and Latin America.

In Europe, moves to liberalize laws restricting merchants' hours in the Netherlands and Germany were expected to boost sales in those nations, enabling consumers to make more convenience trips to stores. While largely unregulated in the United States, longer store hours are a relatively new phenomenon in many parts of Europe. But as the continent seeks to rejuvenate its commercial sector, these and other traditional prohibitions on retail activities were expected to continue to be challenged in the political arena.

A major consumer trend in Europe was a rapidly-growing aged population. It was estimated that by 2010, 45 percent of the population in the European Union would be over the age of 45. The impact of this age demographic on grocers meant stores would likely sell fewer food products and expand space for health and beauty products within an already-growing non-food sales space.

The Economic Research Service branch of the U.S. Department of Agriculture reported that the U.S. population had not only become more ethnically diverse, it was also better educated and wealthier. The aging of the Baby Boomer population makes for an aging market as well. In the mid-2000s, the explosion of different diets, such as low-carb diets—which were expected to grow sales of such branded foods exponentially into 2006—a desire for convenience, and more attention to nutrition labels coupled with a general interest in healthier eating and so-called whole foods prompted U.S. grocery stores to change or expand their product lines. Nearly 34,000 new grocery products were introduced in 2003.

RESEARCH AND TECHNOLOGY

The industry requires advanced technology for a host of logistical concerns, including inventory tracking and ordering systems, frequent-customer discount programs, and transportation management.

Integrated computer systems are the logistical lifeblood of modern supermarket chains. One interlinked system often tallies customers' orders at the register, tracks for inventory movement, and orders new stock from suppliers. Newer systems may also maintain a customer profile database for marketing and promotional uses. These computers are based on a 1980s innovation known as efficient consumer response (ECR); a theory of just-in-time inventory management that employs technology to minimize standing inventories (and, consequently, costs) while ensuring maximal breadth of stock on-hand at any given time. In other words, ECR's goal is to make every item the store carries available at any time yet supplied in tightly controlled quantities based on purchasing patterns, so that the store is never overstocked on any item and has no excess of unmoving inventory. The detailed information on inventory patterns that these systems collect also serves to aid central planners to allocate resources differently, based on store-specific purchase trends.

A growing factor in grocery retailing is the use of the Internet. Some major chains, particularly in Britain, France, and the United States, have made strong offerings of Internet-based services. Some chains simply list online the locations of their outlets and other general information, but the more daring have begun offering ordering services via the Internet or affiliate with Internet vendors to do so. Some observers have speculated wildly that the Internet spelled doom for conventional retailing, as customers could place orders directly from wholesalers or manufacturers at lower prices and remove the retail go-between. However, after failures of Internet grocers in the 1990s, the industry was making a comeback in the mid-2000s. Safeway had reported that its online sales had doubled between 2002 and 2004. According to *Wired* magazine, online grocery sales reached US$2.4 billion in the United States. Safeway was using the Internet grocery technology of Tesco of the United Kingdom. Tesco was a success story in the online grocery shopping business. By 2005, more than 150,000 orders were being placed at its online site each week, with sales reaching more than US$1.3 billion. By 2010, it was expected online grocery shopping in Europe would reach the US$100 billion mark, or 10 percent of all grocery purchases. Based on interviews of 6,000 consumers in six countries, the report stated that Europeans found the produce fresher than when it was bought in grocery stores and liked the convenience of online buying.

Americans were less receptive to online grocery shopping. In October 2000, Priceline.com's Web House Club Inc., which enabled shoppers to collect bids on up to 600 grocery items, failed in the food-manufacturing segment. Although the service had attracted some 2 million members, manufacturers were reluctant to absorb the losses from selling at lower prices. Their reluctance was credited to the unsuitability of the Internet buying concept to the sale of perishable goods, high costs in opening and operating grocery stores, and the expense of grocery stores' major fixed assets, such as trucks, equipment and fixtures, and warehouses. Although the Priceline.com model was less than successful in the grocery industry, some grocers continued to explore online grocery buying possibilities, which could either be individual-store based or rooted in a large supermarket chain.

Nonetheless, Internet grocery services in the twenty-first century were expected to be a growing trend, worth as much as US$85 billion in the United States by 2007, according to an Arthur Andersen study. In a separate 2003 study, Forrester Research reported worldwide market revenues at US$10 billion.

The British chain Safeway Plc., formerly part of U.S. giant Safeway Inc., began to deploy new logistical tracking technology, using a positioning system to monitor its delivery trucks. The system provided detailed information about the location and status of all of its fleet. The chain then used the information to redirect shipments around traffic congestion, determine exactly when stock would arrive at a given location, and even to monitor the performance of its drivers. The chain expected to recoup the US$2.5 million system's annual operating expenses of US$570,000 within the first year of use.

New to the industry in 2002 was a self-service technology that its makers postulated would curtail long supermarket lines. The most commonly-used system was Montreal-based Optimal Robotics' U-Scan Express, which combined a touch-sensitive video display, a bar-code scanner, an ATM-like payment device, scales, and a surveillance camera, to enable customers to check themselves out. The system enabled customers with few items, typically 15 or fewer, to scan their own groceries, compute discounts and coupons, and pay with check, cash, or credit cards. The system entered retail stores in 1998, and by 2002 had become commonplace, particularly among larger retailers. Whether this sort of technology dramatically quickened checkout lines was uncertain, but it clearly offered potential to reduce staff overheads of retailers.

A different kind of self-service technology promised to be perhaps more efficient for shoppers and retailers alike. In Britain, South Africa, and the United States, among other places, experiments were conducted with several types of "scan-as-you-go" technologies. Rather than waiting until the end of a shopping trip to account for all items a customer selects, these systems employed handheld scanners or other monitors to track each item from the moment the customer first picked it up. Depending on the system's sophistication, it might either provide a final sales receipt to be paid at a register or automatically debit the shopper's pre-established account. In either case, these systems also provided special shoplifting deterrents. In fact, they allowed more detailed tracking of merchandise than almost any other transaction method.

WORKFORCE

Grocery stores employed 2.5 million people in the United States in 2002, with approximately 30 percent of them working part time. This high part-time status was reflected in the lower than average earnings of US$335 per week compared to $506 per week for all workers in the private sector.

According to the U.S. Bureau of Labor Statistics employees were often needed in the evenings and on weekends, but employers typically offered flexible hours. The work could be repetitive, marked by long hours of standing. Additionally, the work could be dangerous, and cashiers in particular had a much greater risk of workplace homicides than the total workforce.

Typically, supermarket employees were hired into entry-level positions that required little or no previous experience. In 2002, about 30 percent of the employees were under the age of 24. Although entry-level grocery employees needed no specific skills, many employers preferred to fill cashier positions with high school graduates. Most employees were trained on the job and were advanced to jobs with increasing responsibilities over time.

Employment was expected to grow as fast as average through 2010; however, electronic commerce could slow the demand for grocery and retail employees and cashiers in particular.

Major Countries in the Industry

France

France maintained, by a slim margin, the most consolidated grocery industry in Europe. About 40 percent of all grocery purchases were made in hypermarkets in 2003, with industry giant, Carrefour, having a dominating 23 percent market share. Other major players included Centers Distributeurs E Leclerc, ITM Enterprises, Casino, and the Auchan Group. As in a number of leading markets, France regulated construction of large-scale hypermarkets—usually located outside the city centers—which curtailed growth for some firms. But while such new store openings could drive sales growth of individual chains, by most measures France's grocery market was fairly saturated. As in other European countries, these conditions were a catalyst for international expansion of French-owned grocery companies. As of 2003, the market was valued at US$181.1 billion, and was expected to grow by 15 percent to reach US$212.0 billion by 2008.

Carrefour S.A. Europe's leading retailer, and the second leading retailer in the world, France's Carrefour operated more than 6,000 stores in 30 countries by 2005. As of 2003 sales were approximately US$88.4 billion and the company employed over 400,000 people. In its home country, Carrefour was the largest food retailer, garnering 23 percent of the market in 2003. Carrefour's position was secured in Europe when it merged with food retailer Promodès in 2000. That year, the company's net sales leaped by more than 62 percent of its 1996 sales, with 59.5 percent coming from France, 13.8 percent from Spain, 13.5 percent from Brazil, 5.9 percent from Argentina, 2.9 percent from Taiwan, and the remaining 4.3 percent from elsewhere. After 1996, the company upped its share in other European grocery concerns and, as its sales results showed, aggressively pursued foreign expansion, though subsequent foreign-market uncertainties caused Carrefour to proceed with caution. In 1997 a stall in the Brazilian economy and the broader Asian financial crisis sparked worries among investors and analysts that Carrefour would be adversely affected. Nonetheless, the firm pressed ahead with new store openings in China, Indonesia, South Korea, and Taiwan, but scaled back plans for Thailand and Latin America. Carrefour sold off its stake in the U.S.-based Office Depot in 1997. Considering its home market saturated by 2005, the company was seeking to expand into foreign markets, and attempt to dominate them. It chose to increase its holdings in Brazil, where it held the second spot to fellow French company, Casino. Brazil represented 5 percent of the group's holdings, and the company planned to add between 7 and 10 hypermarkets. Its plan was to increase its market share in Brazil from 12.6 percent to 20 percent by 2008.

ITM Enterprises SA (Intermarche). ITM Enterprises SA, is a group of approximately 3,000 independent grocers in France known as Les Mousquetaires. ITM buys and distributes merchandise for its members, offering them purchasing power and a distribution system they would not otherwise have. ITM is the majority owner of supermarket chain, Intermarche. In 2004, the company reported revenues of US$48 billion and employed 112,000 people. After barely testing the waters of major cross-border expansion in the mid-1990s, in 1997 Intermarche led a Switzerland-based buying group that purchased a 75 percent share in the large German chain Spar Handels AG, which had recently acquired 36 stores from another leading French retailer, Promodes. In addition to giving Intermarche control of Spar Handels' retail operations, the move made the Intermarche group Europe's largest food distributor. In 1998, Spar Handels and Intermarche merged procurement activities to effect the sought-after economies of scale.

Germany

As of 2003 the German grocery remained highly concentrated, with the country's five largest retailers accounting for 77 percent of the market. As with other economies entering the European monetary union in 1999, Germany faced uncertain costs of conversion to the European Currency Unit, or Euro, which some thought might eat into profits in the short term. Added to those woes was a 1998 increase in Germany's value-added tax, which rose 1 percentage point to 16 percent. This was followed by an economic downturn in the 2000s. As a result, German consumers turned their preferences to discount grocery outlets. Discounter ALDI used its philosophy of purchasing cheap site land, selling its own brands, and keeping employee counts limited to bring its market share to 40 percent of the German grocery spend. Valued at US$235 billion in 2003, Euromonitor was predicting the total grocery market would grow by 18 percent by 2008, with discount stores continuing to hold the largest share.

ALDI Group. Begun in Essen, Germany in 1948, by 2005 ALDI had grown to become an international grocery store chain with more than 5,000 stores in 14 countries, including 11 other European nations, the United States, and Australia. The stores were noted for their discounted, ALDI-branded product offerings, and their no-frills approach to product display. Customers must pay for bags and place a deposit for shopping carts, products are displayed on crates and in boxes, and the number of staff is kept to a minimum. The approach has been so favored by German consumers, that by 2004, the company claimed to control 40 percent of the German market. Remaining privately owned, the company's revenues were reported to be approximately US$31 billion in 2003.

Metro AG. Once the second largest retailer in the world behind Wal-Mart, by 2005, Metro AG's global position had fallen, but was still high; ranked the third-largest trading and retail group in Europe and the fifth largest in the world, its 2004 year-end sales figure was US$71 billion. Of this total, 49 percent was from the other 29 countries in which it had a presence. The company provided employment to more than 250,000 people. At the beginning of 2005, the company's management was noting the stagnating demand and heavy competition facing it in Germany and Western Europe. However, the company was experiencing good growth in Eastern Europe and Asia, and the company was planning to continue expansion in these regions.

Tengelmann Warenhandelsgesellschaft KG. In 2004, Tengelmann earned more sales outside of its home country of Germany than it did inside. This was the largely the result of its majority ownership of North America's A&P food chain (Great Atlantic and Pacific Tea Company) as well as its other holdings in many European countries. In 2004, the company reported revenues of almost US$34 billion, with A&P accounting for almost 12 billion of this. As well as food retailing, the company is also involved in textile and non-food discount stores, do-it-yourself supply stores, and pharmacies. At the end of 2004, Tengelmann announced plans to continue expansion into Southern and Eastern Europe.

JAPAN

In 2003, the Japanese market was estimated at US$438.8 billion, and was expected to reach US$402.7 billion by 2008 according to Euromonitor. Japan's prolonged recession and slow recovery was thought to have changed consumer buying patterns from a quality-only orientation to somewhat more of a value-oriented approach—yet one that was still highly brand conscious. Although consumer shopping preference in Japan favored the large-scale options provided by supermarkets and hypermarkets, the percentage of total market sales achieved in these venues dropped slightly in 2003 to 67.8 percent from 68.9 percent in 2002. Although the preference for large store formats mirrored its compatriots in Europe and North America, Japan's grocery industry remained very fragmented with the top five retailers accounting for only 8.4 percent of the market in 2003. Relative to other nations, groceries cost considerably more in Japan than in many other developed nations. Retailers, some unaccustomed to the notion of price competition, struggled to adjust to this new paradigm. They responded by introducing private-label lines, by increasing imports of cheaper, foreign goods, and by reducing operating overheads to finance price slashing. By 2003, almost 15 percent of Japanese consumers' spending was on groceries, and they were showing an increasing preference for discount grocery retailers. Euromonitor was predicting the strong potential influence of foreign retailers on the discount grocery market.

Japanese retailers participated in markedly complex, multi-level distribution arrangements that industry analysts saw as obstacles to improved profitability. Some chains began to streamline procurement and distribution, but efficiency gains in this area would continue to be an issue in the short term.

As with other leading countries, Japan continued to experience consolidation of its grocery chains as less competitive enterprises were acquired by a few leading retail conglomerates, whose financials also had not been consistently robust. A number of Japanese firms continued to make retailing inroads in China, where they had advantages of proximity over European and U.S. competitors.

Ito-Yokado Co. Ltd. A conglomerate of convenience stores, supermarkets, restaurants, department and specialty stores, and manufacturing, Ito-Yokado remained a major player in Japan's retail sector by the end of 2004. In addition to holding more than 10,000 Seven-Eleven stores (as well as being majority owner of the world-wide franchisor of the Seven-Eleven brand), the company operated 159 supermarkets in Japan. Company-wide revenues in 2004 were more than US$63 billion, with approximately US$3.4 billion coming from its supermarket holdings. In 2005, the company was continuing its expansion of supermarkets into the Chinese market.

THE NETHERLANDS

Royal Ahold N.V. At year-end 2004, Ahold was the third-largest grocery retailer in the world with locations primarily in Europe and the United States. The company posted sales of approximately US$70.6 billion, of which 70.7 percent was from U.S. sources, 24.6 percent from Europe, 4 percent from South America and less than 1 percent from Asia. In 2003, the company faced an accounting scandal after it overstated earnings in the United States. At this point, Ahold entered on its self-described "Road to Recovery," restructuring itself around its core food business by selling its Spanish winery stake, and divesting itself of its supermarkets in South America and Asia. In early 2005, Ahold sold it's chain of convenience stores in the U.S. and began selling some of its Bi-Lo, Food City and Bruno's supermarkets.

UNITED KINGDOM

The U.K. grocery market had revenues of US$169.5 billion in 2003, an amount that was expected to increase to US$202.3 billion by 2008. Growth in the sector had been rapid since the late 1990s, experiencing a more than 22 percent growth rate in the five years up to 2003. According to Euromonitor, this growth was not expected to slow, with the large grocery store chains of Tesco and ASDA maintaining their dominant positions in the country.

Tesco Plc. In 2005, Tesco remained the United Kingdom's largest grocery retailer, with sales of US$62 billion for the year ended February 2005 in its 2,365 stores. While the U.K. accounted for 80 percent of Tesco's sales, 11 percent came from other European countries and 9 percent from Asia. The company is also a leader in the promotion of online grocery sales, with the company handling 150,000 such orders each week.

ASDA. Taking over second place from Sainsbury in the U.K., ASDA uses Wal-Mart style pricing, advertising, and display to promote its grocery business, while introducing an increasing line of non-grocery items to its stores. Bought by

Wal-Mart in 1999, ASDA was originally formed by a group of farmers in Yorkshire. In 2005, the company operated 265 stores and 19 depots in the U.K. and employed about 122,000 people. The company was aiming to add 10 to 12 new stores per year.

J Sainsbury Plc. Once second in the U.K. grocery chain, Sainsbury lost its position to Wal-Mart managed ASDA. In anattempt to recover lost profit, the company was focusing its marketing strategy on providing "great quality food at fair prices," offering many of its own private-label products. In 2004, the company sold its U.S. grocery business, Shaw's supermarkets.

UNITED STATES

By sales volume grocery stores were, after motor vehicles, the United States' second largest retail category, accounting for more than US$705 brillion in 2003 according to Euromonitor. However, this value seems subject to variation. According to the Food Marketing Institute in 2004, U.S. grocery sales reached a total of US$634.8 billion. Supermarket retailers (those with sales over US$2 million) had sector-wide sales of US$457.4 billion, of which 84.5 percent was from chain stores and the remainder was from independently owned stores. Smaller grocery stores had 2004 sales of US$17.5 billion, with a further US$32.6 billion coming from wholesale clubs, and US$127.2 billion coming from convenience stores. Of the 246,130 stores selling grocery items, 34,252 of these were supermarket chains, 11,799 were independent supermarkets, 13,182 were grocery stores (under US$2 million in sales), 1,034 were wholesale clubs, and the remainder were convenience stores.

Industry-wide, grocers in the United States had witnessed a decline in their net-profit-after-taxes figures. After reaching their highest levels since 1980 in 2001/2002 at 1.36 percent of sales, this figure had fallen to 0.88 in 2003/2004. Due to this economic decline, there was also a decline in new store openings and major store remodellings. Most new store openings were attributed to the giants in the industry, with most store closings reported by the smaller chains, those operating between 10 and 100 stores.

U.S. grocery chains were comparatively less internationalized than their European counterparts. In a few cases, such as with Safeway in Britain, U.S. chains once held foreign operations and sold them. But other than trade within North America and with the recent exception of Wal-Mart, U.S. food stores were noticeably absent from foreign markets. In addition, the domestic market remained highly fragmented, with the top five retailers (Kroger, Safeway, Albertson's, Royal Ahold, and Publix Super Markets) accounting for only 27.6 percent of the market in 2003 according to Euromonitor. These top-five retailers were facing huge competition from discount general retailers, most notably Wal-Mart and Target.

Wal-Mart Stores Inc. Considered the greatest challenge facing the U.S. grocery industry, Wal-Mart's grocery sales were projected to reach US$70 billion by the end of 2005. Its push to increase its presence in the grocery market had caused a reduction in margins and reduced the market share of many other industry players. For the fiscal year ended January 31, 2005, 28 percent of Wal-Mart's total sales of US$285.2 billion were derived from grocery sales. The company continued its international expansion, purchasing ASDA, the United Kingdom's second largest grocery chain, Supermercados Amigo in Puerto Rico, and Bompreço supermarkets in Brazil.

The Kroger Company. Kroger was once the United States' largest grocer, a position it lost to Wal-Mart, although in 2004, Kroger was still considered the country's largest grocer in terms of primary business. By January 2005, the company operated 2,532 supermarkets and 795 convenience stores. In addition, the company had 436 fine jewelry stores and operated 42 manufacturing plants producing dairy, deli, meat, grocery, and bakery products for its stores. In fiscal 2004 its revenues totaled US$56.4 billion. Founded in 1883, by 2005 Kroger was operating under a variety of names, including Kroger, Ralphs, Fred Meyer, Food 4 Less, King Soopers, Smith's, Fry's, Fry's Marketplace, Dillons, QFC and City Market. In its efforts to thwart competition, Kroger had been reducing prices faster than it was able to reduce cost, and was thus seeing declines in its profit margins. The company's management was expecting growth to come from expansion of its number of stores.

Safeway Inc. Safeway garnered sales of US$35.8 billion in 2004, an increase of less than 1 percent over 2003 figures. As of March 2005, the company operated 1,801 stores, primarily in the Western, Midwestern, and Mid-Atlantic regions of the United States, and in Western Canada. It also held a 49 percent stake in the 115-store Mexican chain, Casa Ley. Safeway operated several regional supermarket companies, including The Vons Companies in Southern California, Dominick's Supermarkets, Alaska's largest retailer Carr-Gottstein Foods, eastern U.S. grocer Genuardi's Family Markets, and Randall's Food Markets. It also owned more than half of e-retailer Groceryworks.

FURTHER READING

Coupe, Kevin. "On-line Grocery." *Chain Store Age,* April 2004.

Draper, Deborah J., ed. *Business Rankings Annual.* Detroit: Thomson Gale, 2004.

Duff, Mike. "Alternative Channels Embrace Emerging Trends." *DSN Retailing Today,* 5 July 2004.

"European Food Retailers: Eat or Be Eaten." *Retail Intelligence,* February 2002.

"Facts and Figures." *Food Marketing Institute,* 2004. Available from http://www.fmi.org.

"Free Factsheets." IGD, 2005. Available from http://www.igd.com.

Gates, Kelly. "Feeding the Future." *Supermarket News,* 19 July 2004.

Gjaga, Marin; Alexander Lintner and Henry M. Vogel. "Dancing with the 800-Pound Gorilla." The Boston Consulting Group, 2002. Available from http://www.bcg.com.

"Grocery Stores, Food Retailers and Supermarkets in China, Australia, France, Germany, Japan, UK, US." *Euromonitor,* 2004. Available from http:// www.euromonitor.com .

"Hoover's Company Capsules." 2004. Available from http://www.hoovers.com.

"In Wal-Mart's Wake." *Chief Executive (US),* January/February 2004.

"Industry Environment," 2001. Available from http://www.active-media.com.

King, Julia. "Online Grocery Buying Booming in Europe." *Commuterworld,* 29 March 2000.

Lazich, Robert S., ed. *Market Share Reporter.* Detroit: Thomson Gale, 2004.

"Top 20 Sales Share." *Supermarket News,* 12 January 2004.

Visseyrias, Mathilde. "Carrefour Aims for 20 Percent Share of Brazilian Market." *Europe Intelligence Wire,* 19 May 2005.

"Verdict on European Grocery Retailing," 26 March 2001. Available from http://www.foodfen.org.uk.

SIC 7514

NAICS 532111

PASSENGER CAR RENTAL

Car rental firms provide short-term use of automobiles and light trucks to consumers and businesses.

INDUSTRY SNAPSHOT

In some respects less traditional in makeup than other industries, the car rental industry nonetheless is a major player in the world market. Its initial development was primarily a U.S. phenomenon, and U.S.-owned companies have continued to dominate the entire industry. Smaller European operations arose, primarily after the Second World War, but the more lucrative of them eventually found themselves affiliated with, or owned by, the U.S. firms.

The terrorist attacks of September 11 and a sluggish economy both contributed to declining revenues and fleet sizes during the early 2000s. For example, in the United States, the nation's rental car fleet fell from a high of 1.83 million vehicles in 2000 to 1.64 million vehicles in 2002. For these same years, revenues fell from US$19.4 billion to a projected $16.43 billion, according to *Fleet Central*. By 2004, the car rental industry was showing improvement. A stronger stock market, improved profits within the corporate sector, an uptick in business travel, and a weak dollar that helped to attract tourists from Latin America and Europe were all factors that increased optimism among industry players. In 2003, U.S. industry revenues increased slightly from 2002 levels, reaching a projected US$16.45 billion. By 2004, this amount had increased to US$17.4 billion.

ORGANIZATION AND STRUCTURE

At the peak of post-World War II industry development, most major car rental corporations were owned by large conglomerates. For a time, Ford Motor Company wholly owned Hertz Corporation and Budget Rent A Car Corp. General Motors controlled 81.5 percent of the National Car Rental System, while Thrifty Rent-A-Car System and Dollar Rent-A-Car System were owned by a Chrysler Corp. holding company. Vendors operating under franchise or license agreements privately owned individual car rental locations, with few exceptions. Adjustments in the industry to keep pace with changes in global economy saw these alignments give way in the last years of the century. By 1997, Hertz, Dollar, and Thrifty traded publicly. Avis continued to be primarily a public corporation, but Cendant Corporation owned 20 percent of the company, and Republic Industries, known for its sprawling auto dealership empire, owned Alamo, National Car Rental, and Spirit Rent-A-Car. Enterprise, sharing industry domination with Hertz, stood alone as a private company.

The focus on the relationship between car rental and air travel was not accidental. The car rental industry blossomed after World War II when commercial air travel began to be commonplace. Car rental entrepreneurs capitalized on the need for convenient ground transportation for business travelers. The late 1970s and early 1980s saw the deregulation of the airline industry—a move that dramatically increased air travel and provided consequent stimulus to the car rental market. As airlines competed for business by lowering fares, air travel suddenly lay within the grasp of innumerable travelers who had been theretofore earth-bound by the need for economy.

However, following the airline crisis in September 2001, many airlines faced bankruptcy despite a US$15 billion federal bailout plan. Some in the car rental industry feared that as airlines approached bankruptcy they could be forced into mergers at the same time the air travel industry was re-regulated. Higher fares for air travel would potentially damage car rental revenues.

In the 1970s and 1980s, car rental companies quickly capitalized on the resulting growth in air travel by increasing the size of rental car fleets and number of rental agency outlets. As more car rental companies entered the field, it became necessary for each to distinguish itself in some way, by price or by service. Many companies specialized in niche markets (corporate, leisure, or insurance replacement). Others emphasized geographic coverage, focusing on local, national, or international operation.

The economic downturn of the 1990s witnessed a shakeout in the industry, particularly among the car rental companies that catered to corporate accounts. The ability to quickly shift supply to meet demand became the single factor that dictated a given company's future. Consumers insisted upon newer cars, cheaper prices, and better service, and, at the same time, the auto industry suddenly was unable to continue supplying car rental companies with large numbers of "program" cars. Those companies that could overcome supply issues through implementation of good management techniques, shrewd pricing schemes, and large distribution systems tended to thrive. Where attrition failed to attack and thin the ranks of smaller firms, increasing competition led to a series of mergers and acquisitions that restructured the industry by the mid-1990s. At the close of the century, several major car rental firms, previously owned by automobile manufacturers, were trading publicly. Ever-increasing emphasis was placed on levels of service and the convenience that could be provided to customers through increased automation, better reservation and delivery systems, and the existence of huge worldwide fleets. Corporate service contracts were negotiated with sharper pencils in hand, and the resulting improvements in cash flow worked to improve the health of the industry as a whole.

By the end of the century, most car rental firms were niche players, some catering primarily (though not exclusively) to corporate accounts, and some addressing the needs of individuals seeking a rental car for personal reasons. Large firms expanded their businesses, becoming ever larger and keeping track of large fleets with the help of sophisticated reservations systems and high-speed computers.

BACKGROUND AND DEVELOPMENT

The car rental business arose out of a prototypically American entrepreneurial spirit. The industry traced its roots to Walter L. Jacobs, who in September 1918, at the age of 22, took wrench and brush in hand and repaired and repainted a dozen Model T Fords—and proceeded to use them to open a car rental operation in Chicago. In five years time, Jacobs had expanded his operation to the point where his annual revenues neared US$1 million. That year, in 1927, Jacobs sold his creation to John Hertz, president of Yellow Cab and Yellow Truck, and Coach Manufacturing Company. Jacobs stayed on as an operating officer, but it was Hertz who gave the business his name and bright yellow trademark. "Hertz Drive-Ur-Self" attracted enough attention that, three short years later, General Motors Corporation purchased the operation at the same time that it acquired John Hertz's Yellow Truck company.

Hertz became the first car rental company to set up rental offices at railroad stations—a logical step, since the train was the predominant mode of travel in the 1920s. Similarly, Hertz was the first to establish advance-reservation capabilities. In 1932 it opened a facility at Chicago's Midway airport, thus becoming the first car rental agency to capitalize on the potential needs of air travelers. By the advent of jet travel, in 1953, two-thirds of Hertz's customers were out-of-towners, 70 percent of those who rented for business reasons. Further analysis of the industry showed that in the 1950s, 60 percent of car rental customers reached their rental locations by air, while only 30 percent were traveling by rail. Hertz and other rental firms altered business strategy accordingly.

The emergence of Avis, Hertz's closest early competitor, was almost entirely a consequence of the postwar establishment of the airline industry as the primary mode of commercial travel. As early as 1946, Warren E. Avis, a World War II Army Air Corps flyer and auto dealer in Detroit, was confident that airlines were about to become the preferred transportation mode throughout the world. Capitalizing on the fact that no car rental agency had an airport operation complete with a fleet of cars (Hertz's pioneer efforts consisted only of an airport office), Avis opened the Avis Airlines Rent-A-Car System, both at Miami Airport and at Metropolitan Detroit's Willow Run Airport. His venture was an immediate success. The fledgling business grew steadily and Avis built a network of local, independent operators, each licensed to do business at airports under the Avis name. New York, Chicago, Dallas, Washington, Los Angeles, and Houston soon joined the Avis System.

In a continued effort to carry his business to his customers, in 1948, Warren Avis opened numerous downtown locations serving major hotels and office buildings. By 1954, the Avis System included 185 locations in the United States, 10 in Canada, and one in Mexico, as well as established working agreements with local rent-a-car companies in England, France, Germany, Ireland, Italy, Scotland, and Switzerland. That same year, Avis was sold to Richard Robie, who expanded the company's corporate-owned locations to 16 additional cities, developed the first nationwide plan for one-way car rentals, and began distribution of the company's own charge card.

Boosts in international travel prompted car rental companies to expand beyond national boundaries. By 1955, Hertz operated in Ireland, Switzerland, Canada, and France, as well as in 227 U.S. airports and more than 20 domestic railroad stations. In 1957, the Hertz facility at Orly airport (Paris) was the first source of on-site car rentals at a European international airport. In quick order, additional Hertz's locations appeared in Spain, Belgium, Denmark, Germany, the Netherlands, New Zealand, Aruba, Australia, the Ivory Coast, Guatemala, Iceland, Japan, Kenya, and Tobago.

Car rental companies dramatically increased their fleets to meet increased domestic and international demand. In 1958, Hertz spent more than US$60 million for nearly 18,000 vehicles, making it, at the time, the single largest purchase of cars in history. Within five years, the Hertz fleet grew to 85,000 vehicles in 386 cities in 73 countries. As the industry grew, the disposition of used cars became a challenge. Typically, rental fleets were renewed on a 9- to 15-month basis, with discarded cars sold from the fleets through the offices of various wholesaling firms. As car rental fleet sizes grew, however, used car wholesale markets became glutted and prices depressed. To remedy this, Avis opened its own retail car sales operation, selling most of the used cars in its fleet to individual buyers. By the 1970s, the buying public considered used cars sold by Avis and other leading car rental companies to be legitimate bargains. As new car prices escalated, late-model used cars became increasingly attractive to buyers. By 1987 Avis was retailing some 50,000 cars annually from over 100 used car sales locations nationwide.

The year 1978 brought the beginning of a phased-in deregulation of the airline industry, and with it came the biggest challenge to date for car rental companies. With airlines allowed to compete more freely, flights became available to nearly any worldwide destination, and new airlines were founded. With the flood of new competition, airlines offered attractive fares to induce more people to fly to more places. As air passenger volumes surged, car rental companies found they had to follow the marketing precedent set by the airlines. To encourage loyalty from their customers, car rental companies offered bonus "points" to stimulate repeat business. In 1972, Hertz introduced the #1 Club Gold. Club members were listed in a data file that included license, address, and credit card information, all available for instant recall—allowing customers the convenience of being able to rent a car without having to wait in line and fill out forms. In 1991,

Hertz expanded the club to include Canadian travelers. In 1992 the club reached Europe, in 1993 Australia, and in 1994 Japan, Singapore, and Hong Kong.

The 1980s brought sharply higher oil prices, the 1981-82 air traffic controllers' strike, and competitive pricing—all of which made it difficult for car rental companies to raise prices to cover inflation-driven cost increases. With more players in a heightened competitive environment, customer service became the primary focus. Customers now routinely demanded no-hassle reservations and easy car drop-off—and were not satisfied if these features were just a perk provided to favored customers. In response, Hertz became the first car rental company to offer express service for car return, as well as instant return and self-service return. Soon thereafter, Avis introduced its Avis Express service at major airports around the country, helping to speed harried customers through airline terminals. The Avis service allowed deplaning customers to bypass the terminal counter and go directly to an Avis shuttle bus, or Avis Express facility, where completed agreements and pre-assigned cars awaited them. In 1983, the system was extended, and Avis was able to produce a printed rental agreement within seconds at any Avis rental counter throughout Europe. Further enhancements, in 1984, gave Avis the first automated self-service return system in the car rental industry, something that was made possible by third-generation "Wizard" computer terminals. Not to be outdone, Hertz introduced computerized driving directions (CDD) and made available car seats for children, hand controls for the physically challenged, and portable cellular phones. To further enhance a customer feeling of security, Hertz established a 24-hour emergency road service, one more example of the emphasis on customer service that characterized end-of-the-century industry development.

The 1990s saw the industry's first major shakeout when a general economic downturn put pressure on pricing which made it difficult for companies to raise rates. At the same time customers were increasingly demanding better service, including easier reservation, pick-up and drop-off procedures, and frequent customer rewards. Economic resurgence proved to be a mixed blessing. As the economy improved, the auto industry experienced a rise in car sales. Manufacturers were able to sell every car being produced, and special program sales to agencies dropped off dramatically. In one example, *Business Travel News* reported that General Motors reduced the number of cars it supplied to car rental companies by nearly 50 percent, between model year 1992 and model year 1994 (from 795,000 to 400,000).

New approaches to success had to be tried. Expansion and consolidation were classic means to stabilize an industry, and the opportunity for expansion was, at the time, dramatic. The economies of the former communist-bloc nations were opening, and political instability throughout the world was relatively low. In the mid-1990s, Hertz opened four locations in the Commonwealth of Independent States (former Soviet Union). When the Channel Tunnel (Chunnel) connecting the United Kingdom and France was opened, Hertz was there to become the first car rental company to service the entire European Union.

Smaller car rental agencies began to reassert themselves. Ranked third in overall fleet size, Alamo Rent-A-Car entered the European market in 1987 when it acquired airport sites in England. In the mid-1990s, Alamo partnered with local firms to acquire additional locations in Germany. Prior to the German acquisition, which more than doubled its European presence, Alamo already operated at 35 locations in six European countries. To make its increased global offering even more attractive to customers, in 1994 Alamo announced a partnership with Hilton Hotel Corporation, enabling its customers to earn Hilton Honors points by renting a car. Expansion was ongoing. In 1994 and 1995, Alamo added airport locations in Prague (Czech Republic); Amsterdam (The Netherlands); Zurich and Geneva (Switzerland); Frankfurt, Munich, and Dusseldorf (Germany); Brussels (Belgium); and Manchester, Norwich, and Southampton (United Kingdom). In 1994, Alamo became one of the last major car rental companies to adopt the policy of examining customers' driving records to determine whether or not to rent them a car. (A customer with three bad driving citations and/or one drunk driving conviction within the previous two years was not eligible to rent a car.) Similar policies had been introduced by Hertz and Avis in 1993, and, like their larger colleagues, Alamo found driver-screening a necessary step in the reduction of liability insurance costs.

At the end of the twentieth century and beginning of the twenty-first century, globalization became even more important to rental car companies, as the travel industry saw sharp increases in global travel, due in part to global industry trends. As traditional car rental customers and business travelers traveled abroad more frequently, rental car companies expanded to meet the needs of global travelers seeking familiar companies and service while away from home. Technological advances, particularly in communications, enabled car rental companies around the globe to more efficiently book rental cars and increase profitability.

In 2000, more than 1.8 million cars and trucks were available for rental in the United States alone. After a decade of little or no increase, at the beginning of the century, car rental rates began to move upward at a rate of 5 to 7 percent annually beginning in the 1990s. Corporate travel rates, negotiated between major firms and car rental suppliers, also became more lucrative. The additional revenue generated was available due to the investment in various revenue/yield management systems by major car rental companies. Hertz, Dollar, Thrifty, Budget, and Avis car rental traded publicly, forcing executive management teams to focus sharply on improving shareholder values. Airline travel increased several percentage points each year, and even conservative estimates saw the car rental industry keeping pace. At the same time, the increasing globalization of the world's economies gave rental firms, catering to business interests, incentive to increase their presence worldwide.

At the turn of the century, large distribution systems, large fleets, and computerized reservation and management systems kept major industry players profitable. Hertz lost its ranking as number one in the industry, despite managing to produce greater revenue—with its smaller fleet—than did first place Enterprise Rent-A-Car. In 2000, although they swapped position depending on whether they were ranked internationally by revenues, fleet size, or personnel totals, the top four car rental firms indisputably were Enterprise, Hertz, ANC Rental Corp., and Avis. They were followed closely by Budget Rent A Car, Dollar Rent A Car, the rapidly growing Thrifty Rent A car, and U-Save Auto Rental.

In 1995, Chrysler reorganized its Thrifty and Dollar units into one autonomous company to make them more attractive for purchase. Thriving as the Dollar Thrifty Automotive Group, Inc. and bolstered by Dollar's affiliation with Eurocar, three years later Dollar/Thrifty ignored their former parent's intent and remained happily independent. Alamo Rent A Car Inc. flirted with the possibility of buying General Motors' National Car Rental System, but, instead, in 1995 National was sold to auto sales giant Republic Industries. Two years later, Alamo also found itself under the Republic Industries umbrella. Hertz and Avis continued to trade publicly, but Avis enjoyed (and exploited) a close relationship with Cendant, which owned 20 percent of Avis' stock. In March 2000, Hertz merged with Ford Motor Co. and became a wholly owned subsidiary of the automaker. Enterprise, the only one of the car rental giants to function as a private company with privately held stock, steadily challenged Hertz for industry dominance, and in 2000 surpassed Hertz's sales by US$500 million, although Enterprise had only 30 more airport locations nationwide than its rival.

After weathering difficult years during the early 2000s, marked by a drop in business travel following the terrorist attacks of September 11, 2001, the car rental industry appeared to be poised for better times heading into the mid-2000s. In its March 1, 2004, issue, *Travel Weekly* reported that "despite the war in Iraq, SARS and travel jitters, the industry's financial situation remained stable in 2003 as car companies maintained tight fleets, controlled costs and generally managed to avoidrate-cutting."

In 2004, *Fleet-Central* reported that, within the U.S. rental car market, the number of vehicles in service continued to decline. From a high of 1.83 million vehicles in 2000, the U.S. fleet fell to 1.74 million vehicles in 2001, 1.64 million in 2002, and 1.62 million in 2003. U.S. industry revenues fell from a high of US$19.4 billion in 2000 to US$18.2 billion in 2001 and a projected US$16.4 billion in 2002. In 2003, a slight improvement was expected, as revenues reached a projected US$16.5 billion.

CURRENT CONDITIONS

The world leader in the industry continues to be the United States. According to *Auto Rental News*, the U.S. industry was worth almost US$17.4 billion in revenues in 2004, up significantly over 2003 levels of US$16.5 billion. In 2004, 17,663 car rental locations provided more than 1,770,000 vehicles. The company leader in the industry, supplying almost 30.5 percent of all cars, was Enterprise. This was followed by Hertz (21 percent), Vanguard (12 percent), Avis (11 percent), and Budget (6 percent), although Avis and Budget were both owned by Cendant Corporation. Euromonitor predicted that the U.S. industry would grow by more than 20 percent between 2004 and 2008, and that the leisure market would remain the largest sector, accounting for about 40 percent of all rentals.

Car rentals have always been closely tied to travel. In 2004, the most visited country in the world remained France, with more than 76 million people traveling there. In France, in 2003, Euromonitor valued the car rental industry at almost US$2 billion, with almost 59 percent of rentals being for leisure purposes. This sector was expected to grow by another 9 percent by 2008. In France, Hertz, Avis Europe, and Europcar dominated the market, with each holding a share of between 20 and 22 percent.

In the United Kingdom, sixth in the world as a tourist destination, the car rental industry was valued at US$1.98 billion in 2003—almost the same figure as that of France. However, more than 54 percent of cars were rented for business purposes. In the U.K., Hertz, Avis Europe, National, and Enterprise dominated the market. The industry was expected to grow by 11.8 percent between 2004 and 2008, with most cars continuing to be rented by domestic corporate customers.

In early 2004, reservations and car rentals in parts of Europe were up over 2003 levels, with leisure rentals doing especially well in the United Kingdom, France, and Italy. However, *Travel Trade Gazette UK & Ireland* reported that rates were declining due to pressure from car rental brokers. This subsequently resulted in losses for industry leaders in 2003. For example, Avis lost EU$47.4 million that year. In 2004, Avis Europe continued to express concerns over the downward pressure being exerted on profit margins. Fierce competition and customers' increasing use of the Internet and brokers to book rentals were the causes.

In July 2004, smaller car rental companies in Finland were experiencing difficulties. Because business travel had not improved in that country, large rental companies were focusing more on the leisure market and stealing market share from smaller players, according to *Nordic Business Report*. In addition, changes in automobile taxation caused car values to fall sharply. This was expected to cause many small Finnish firms to shut their doors following the summer 2004 car rental season.

Measuring confidence levels among rental car agency operators, an Abrams Consulting Benchmark study indicated that 21 percent were very optimistic about the industry in early 2004, followed by 45 percent who were somewhat optimistic. 20 percent of industry players had neutral opinions on the industry, while 7 percent were somewhat pessimistic and another 7 percent were very pessimistic. A number of factors served to bolster the largely positive outlook within the industry. These included a stronger stock market, improved profits within the corporate sector, an uptick in business travel, and a weak dollar that helped to attract tourists from Latin America and Europe. In addition, the National Business Travel Association hinted that car rental rates were poised for a 2 percent increase in 2004.

Although at one time almost all of the major car rental companies had been owned by vehicle manufacturers, this was not true by 2005. Of the major players, only Hertz in the U.S. and Paris-based Europcar International were owned by manufacturers (Ford and Volkswagen, respectively). Originally, manufacturers had used car rental subsidiaries to assist in evening out the sales cycle of new car purchasing, but owners without that need now operate under a different competitive environment. According to Perot Systems, companies are now more focused on profitability, customer service, branding, and globalization. The car rental industry has become more concerned with cost containment and revenue growth, all while trying to provide customers with a wider selection of vehicles with more amenities. The use of the Internet as a means to book rentals has increased rapidly. Companies have also become increasingly focused on establishing brand identity in new markets, and are doing more niche marketing to customer groups defined by their usage (leisure, corporate, replacement, and truck rentals).

RESEARCH AND TECHNOLOGY

Once the increase in air travel had made the rental car industry a classically competitive one, commitment to technology became crucial to industry position for various rental companies. Technology in car rental, generally, was equated with efficient reservation and distribution of vehicles. In 1971, Hertz introduced a centralized reservation and data center to run its global point-of-sales reservation system. The center, based in Oklahoma City, operated on-line 24 hours a day, 365 days a year. By 1993, the center was handling more than 100,000 phone calls and more than 80,000 preprinted messages per day. Hertz's investment in the raw computing power necessary to support the operation was enhanced by the addition of a high-speed data communications network that allowed 33 Hertz claims management offices, in 10 states, to process insurance claims.

One year after Hertz automated car reservations, Avis introduced the Wizard System. Wizard was even more comprehensive than the Hertz system, and in 1972 Avis found itself with the first and largest computer-based, on-line, real-time, global rental, reservation, and management information system, in the industry. Hardware and software enhancements in 1979 and 1984 kept Wizard ahead of its competitors. The third-generation (1984) Wizard computer terminal included Rapid Return—an automated check-in service available to Avis customers at major airports and key downtown locations in the United States. Use of Rapid Return meant that an Avis renter could enter a vehicle number, mileage, and fuel level into a stand-alone computer terminal and receive a completed transaction record, or receipt, in less than one minute.

In 1998, the Wizard System continued to provide Avis with a significant technological advantage over its competitors. In enhanced form, it remained "state of the art" for nearly 30 years after its introduction—in part because of its comprehensive range of applications. The Wizard performed reservation and rental counter functions and vehicle inventory control, as well as flagging cars for preventive maintenance services. It recorded buyers of Avis used cars and transmitted the information to computers of car manufacturers in case of a safety recall. It performed as an excellent worldwide management information system and, on demand, produced reports tailored to corporate customer specifications for accounting and cost control purposes, and delivered them electronically to the client company's own computer. Offices in countries around the world used Wizard to communicate 24 hours a day, every day, via the computer network. Wizard IV, the late 1990s version of the system, was expected to further increase operating efficiency and the quality of customer service.

The largest of the car rental companies have integrated communications technology into their businesses, enabling shorter advance booking time, computerized maps for customers, 24-hour customer service call centers, and improved marketing information. Information technology and satellite tracking systems, at the beginning of the twenty-first century, took car rental service and fleet availability to even higher levels, as companies were able to predict with more accuracy their customers' needs and to estimate the size of available fleet cars. The information technology available to car rental companies was put to the test during the last two weeks of September 2001, when as many as 100,000 cars had been displaced, as air travelers scrambled to rent cars to make it to destinations thousands of miles from their grounded airplanes. By using the Internet to communicate and track the vehicles, rental franchises were able to effectively return the cars to their proper locations.

Global positioning satellites have also become more commonplace in the car rental industry and are used in service to customers and to benefit the car rental company itself. Budget installed NavLynx Telematics in its cars and used the system as a marketing tool, boasting customers would never be lost again. However, in December 2000, the company was also able to locate, within five minutes, a car stolen from its Toronto fleet, after it was driven to Calgary, Alberta, 2,000 miles from its last known location.

In lieu of technology or to supplement a lesser technology, some car rental companies sought to appeal to customers through various customer-friendly product offerings. National introduced the Emerald Club, members of which could bypass the rental counter and select their own cars personally, without the need to process paperwork. "Choice Rental" and "Quick Rent" enhanced the experience of other National customers, and the company's Handheld Return Service gave each customer a human interface to help speed airport car return. Thrifty used a "high-tech" approach, similar to that of Avis and contracted with SABRE Direct Connect and Apollo's Inside Link to provide the necessary communication technology. Enterprise's innovation was a "we'll pick you up" approach, improving customer convenience by literally bringing the rental vehicle to the customer's doorstep.

In a triumph of low technology, a small but very stable company, with the iconoclastic name Rent-a-Wreck of America, Inc., determined that substantial cost-savings could be passed to customers if the rented cars were good quality, mechanically sound, older vehicles. Not precisely "wrecks," these cars nonetheless lacked aesthetic appeal when compared to the brand-new vehicles offered by the competition, yet the ugly ducklings proved very popular. And although tiny (US$3.8 million annual revenue, fleet size 15,000 units) when compared to Hertz and Avis, by the end of the century Rent-a-Wreck boasted over 25 years of successful operation and had expanded into such disparate markets as Norway and the United Arab Emirates. Like industry leader Enterprise, Rent-A-Wreck capitalized on local markets worldwide, with 90 percent of its US$102 million in 2000 revenues coming from local market transactions.

By the mid-2000s, some industry observers were critical of the industry's use of technology to track vehicles, specifically the enforcement of geographic restrictions and the enforcement of maximum speed levels. However, proponents argued that technology such as GPS systems were necessary to monitor corporate assets and ensure driver safety. For example, such technology made it possible for rental car companies to locate stolen vehicles or determine if a renter was driving in a region where auto insurance did not apply. In support of tracking measures, industry players noted that technology was normally used on an exception basis. In other words, instead of monitoring the use of every vehicle, tracking technology produced red flags to notify companies when rental contracts were in violation.

WORKFORCE

Jobs in the automotive rental industry are mainly entry-level positions at which an employee may work up to management or to ownership in a franchise. The Department of Labor predicted the demand for counter and rental clerks would grow through the year 2010 at the same rate as general employment. Although jobs were available throughout the United States and worldwide, the majority of them were located in metropolitan areas and near airports, where the need for car rental sites was the greatest. The median wage for automotive rental clerks in 2002 was US$8.31 per hour.

Although entry-level rental clerks were typically only required to have a high school diploma, they were required to be knowledgeable about the company, its services, and procedures. Most of the larger car rental companies developed training programs for new hires, which included information about the company as well as customer service, although training programs varied greatly in thoroughness and longevity. Some employers trained new employees with a series of videotapes, brochures, books, and pamphlets, while others developed formal classroom programs which ranged in duration from a few days to weeks.

Car rental company employees were typically expected to work evenings, nights, and weekend hours but were also given flexible schedules and might work part- or full-time. Full-time employees usually received benefits such as insurance and paid holidays and vacations.

According to the Bureau of Labor, working conditions in the rental industry were usually pleasant, and most stores and service establishments were clean, well lighted, and temperature-controlled. The job also required long hours of standing and often-stressful constant customer contact.

INDUSTRY LEADERS

ENTERPRISE RENT-A-CAR COMPANY

Still privately owned by its founder and his family in 2005, Enterprise Rent-A-Car Co. was the largest car rental company in theU.S. and the rest of the world in terms of revenue and fleet size. Enterprise was started in 1957 as "Executive Leasing" by Jack Taylor, a World War II Navy fighter pilot and former sales manager at a St. Louis, Missouri Cadillac dealership. Originally the firm provided only executive leasing services. In the early 1960s, Taylor expanded the business to include the rental of cars for short periods and extended his operation into new cities. In 1961, Enterprise's automotive fleet numbered 1,000 lease cars. By 1969, the number was 5,000 lease cars, and by 1973, an additional, 1,000 rental units were in service. At the same time, the company diversified to include non-automotive-related businesses.

In 1976, Enterprise established a special fleet leasing company to handle the vehicle management needs of large commercial accounts. The following year, Enterprise's lease car count was over 10,000. In the 1970s and 1980s, rental and leasing operations grew substantially, with the rental operation directed largely at the "home city" rental market. This market was comprised of two broad segments: the replacement segment—customers needing a car because of an accident, mechanical repair, or theft—and the discretionary segment—customers needing a car for short business and leisure trips and other special occasions. As a service to property and casualty adjusters, Enterprise operated Claims Connection, which allowed adjusters to arrange for rental cars with a single phone call. By the 1990s, Enterprise had become the largest rental car company in the United States, in both fleet size and number of locations. Company officials boasted rates up to 30 percent lower than most airport rental car companies and served customers from more than 2,000 offices located near where people lived and worked. In 1990 Enterprise had 100,000 rental units and 30,000 lease units. By 1998, the company had 300,000 rental units in service, an increment that was even more stunning when the number was compared to the 30,000 units Enterprise had in 1986 or the mere 5,000 available 1980.

By 2004, its fleet had grown to more than 600,000 cars in service, and its sales totaled US$7.4 billion, up from US$4.5 billion in 2000. The company was present in some 6,000 locations in the U.S., Canada, the U.K, Germany, and Ireland, and employed more than 57,000 workers.

THE HERTZ CORPORATION

Owned by the Ford Motor Company, Hertz was a leader among the world's car rental companies in 2004. Scattering a fleet of 525,000 vehicles among 7,200 locations in 150 countries, Hertz had accomplished more "firsts" and led in more categories than any competitor anywhere on the globe. By the late 1990s, the company's Worldwide Reservation Center handled approximately 40 million phone calls and delivered approximately 30 million reservations annually, a total that had increased steadily over the previous decade. Hertz provided customers with a wide variety of current-model cars for short-term rental—daily, weekly, or monthly—at airports, in downtown and suburban business centers, as well as in residential areas and resort locales.

In 2000, Hertz slipped from first in the industry, in terms of revenue and transactions, to a strong second in ranking, with Enterprise Rent-A-Car's sales exceeding Hertz's US$4 billion and fleet of 350,000 cars in service. By 2004, Enterprise continued to outpace Hertz in both revenues and fleet size. Revenue for Hertz was US$6.68 billion.

Considered the founder of the entire industry, Hertz traced its origins to a Chicago car rental operation that Walter L. Jacobs established in 1918. After the entrepreneurial beginning, once it reached the US$1 million mark in revenue, the company was sold to a series of holding companies and partnerships, each of which furthered its overall growth. Jacobs first sold the company to John Hertz, president of Yellow Cab and Yellow Truck and Coach Manufacturing Company. The rental business, then Hertz Drive-Ur-Self System, was acquired in 1926 by General Motors Corporation, at the same time that GM bought Hertz's Yellow Truck operation. This General Motors affiliation continued until 1953, when the Omnibus Corporation purchased the several Hertz properties. Omnibus promptly divested itself of its bus interests in order to concentrate solely on car and truck, renting and leasing. A year later (1954) the company was re-christened, and the Hertz Corporation, per se, was listed for the first time on the New York Stock Exchange.

In 1954, the new corporation bought Metropolitan Distributors, a pioneer in New York truck leasing. Metropolitan Distributors dated back to the First World War and was the largest concern of its kind located in any single city. The resulting expanded Hertz was an attractive property. After 13 years of operation, in 1967, it was purchased by RCA. Although a wholly owned subsidiary of RCA Corporation, Hertz operated as a separate entity, with its own management and board of directors. In 1985 Hertz joined UAL, Inc. Then in 1987, Hertz was sold to Park Ridge Corporation, a company that had been formed by Ford Motor Company and certain members of Hertz senior management, for the exclusive purpose of purchasing Hertz. The next year, Volvo North America Corporation joined Ford and Hertz management as an investor in Park Ridge Corporation, and, in 1993, Park Ridge blended with the Hertz Corporation in a full merger. One year later, Ford purchased the outstanding shares of Hertz and made it an independent, wholly owned subsidiary of Ford.

As a car rental pioneer, Hertz was the first company to make car rental something that was operated in places other than backstreet garages. It was first to market "fly-drive" rentals, pairing the use of a rented car with specific flight plans. As long ago as 1926, Hertz introduced a credit card, calling it a "National Credential" card, and using it to facilitate billing for regular customers. Thirty-odd years later, in 1959, this "National Credential" card became the Hertz International AUTO-matic Charge Card.

Hertz also was first to provide customers with Computerized Driving Directions (CDD), detailed directions to local destinations, complete with distance figures and approximate drive times. This service proved so popular that, by the end of the century, it had been made available in the United States and Canada, all across Europe, and in Australia.

CENDANT CORPORATION

Real estate and travel services conglomerate Cendant Corporation is the world's second-largest hotel franchisor, but also the world leader in the general-use car rental business, operating under the Avis and Budget brands. The company's vehicle services division also includes fleet services and car parking lot subsidiaries, although the company sold its PHH Arval fleet management business and its Wright Express fuel card business in February 2005. The vehicle services division accounted for 31 percent (US$6.13 billion) of Cendant's total revenues of US$19.79 billion, with the rental car section accounting for 22 percent (US$4.35 billion) of total revenues.

Of the approximately 4,900 car rental locations that made up the Avis System worldwide, Cendant owned and operated 1,080 locations and franchised a further 850 locations as of the end of 2004. Avis-branded locations accounted for about 13 percent (US$2.57 billion) of Cendant's revenues. Cendant owned and/or franchised 2,170 Budget-branded car rental locations of the total of 3,070 in the Budget system at the end of 2004. The vast majority of the revenues from both brands occur from airport locations. However, the company was making increasing revenue from the use of its cars as replacements in insurance claims. In 2004, Cendant strengthened its ties with the State Farm Insurance Company, and was working to form similar alliances with other insurance carriers using replacement cars.

Avis Rent A Car System Inc. Ranked by total revenue and volume of rental transactions, Avis Rent A Car was the second largest, general use, car rental business in the world in 2005. Warren E. Avis, who correctly anticipated the need for car rental agencies at airports, founded Avis in 1946. Avis Airlines Rent-A-Car System steadily expanded into major city airports around the country. In 1948, Warren Avis himself pressed for expansion that included downtown locations serving hotels and office buildings. As he began to establish a national reputation for quality service, Avis dropped the 'airlines' from the company name. In 1954, Avis sold the business to Richard Robie, a Boston-based car rental agent, for US$8 million. Over the next two years, Robie expanded the company's corporate-owned locations to 16 cities, developed the first nationwide plan for one-way car rentals, and began distribution of the company's own charge card.

Business expansion caused a severe capital drain, however. In 1956, Robie sold the company to British investors headed by Amoskeag Company, which formed Avis, Inc. to acquire the assets of the Avis System, and created a wholly owned subsidiary—Avis Rent A Car System, Inc.—to conduct business operations.

Steady growth continued into the 1960s as Avis expanded into car leasing, developed various car rental enhancements, and added operations in Austria, Belgium, Norway, Spain, and elsewhere. Using electronic data processing equipment, Avis established the industry's first central billing charge card system for corporate accounts. In 1962, the company was sold to New York-based investment bankers Lazard Freres. That year, Avis adopted the familiar advertising slogan "We're only number two. We try harder"—the first time an advertiser admitted to not being the biggest in the market. It was a ploy that proved to be an enormous motivator for Avis employees.

In 1965, revenues reached US$74.5 million, and ITT Corporation acquired Avis. Over the next several years, Avis moved to strengthen its position in the international market by increasing corporate-owned operations instead of franchised operations, and, by 1973, Avis surpassed all competitors in Europe. Avis began to operate as a public company in 1972, when ITT was ordered to divest itself of certain businesses. It went public through the sale of 48 percent of its total outstanding shares; a court-appointed trustee held the balance of the shares. Having been passed through ownership by several companies for 10 years, Avis finally was sold in 1987 to its 11,500 employees for US$1.75 billion, administered through an employee stock ownership plan (ESOP).

In 1991, Hertz filed a lawsuit against Avis, alleging false advertising claims that was based on a survey Hertz believed used questionable methods. The suit was settled in early 1992 in Hertz's favor, but Avis paid no damages. By 1993, the company had paid off over 82 percent of its ESOP acquisition debt and planned to retire the debt completely in 1995. In 1993 the company had a fleet of rental vehicles operating in 138 countries. Avis Europe was 8.8 percent owned by Avis and was the market leader in Europe.

By 2004, Avis' fleet numbered about 200,000 vehicles, down from 220,000 vehicles in 2001. Revenue totals were US$2.5 billion in 2002, down from more than US$3.4 billion in 2001. Although it boasted more than 1,700 locations in the United States, Canada, Puerto Rico, the U.S. Virgin Islands, Argentina, Australia, and New Zealand, most of Avis' business still came from its U.S. operations. Avis officials saw Cendant's 20 percent ownership of the company as an extremely positive element, and, as the new century approached, Avis looked forward to exploring new ways that Cendant could help the company to increase its market share. In 2001, Cendant purchased all of the outstanding Avis shares, and Avis became a wholly owned subsidiary of Cendant.

Budget Rent A Car System Inc. Acquired by Cendant in 2002, Budget Rent A Car was one of the largest car rental operations in the U.S. in the mid-2000s. While it lacks the market share of Avis, Hertz, or Enterprise, with almost 1,900 locations worldwide in 2005, Budget was one of the best-known brand names in the industry. During the latter years of the last century, Budget displayed huge growth. In 1996, the company purchased Van Pool Services, Inc. (VPSI) from Chrysler Corporation, thus acquiring the U.S. leader in commuter van pooling services. In a later transaction, Budget also obtained Pentagon Express, another van pool service company. The Budget Group, Inc. was formed in 1997, when Budget Rent A Car was acquired by Team Rental Group, Inc., and the new entity was named Budget Group. In 2002, the company's assets in the U.S., Canada, Latin America, the Caribbean, Australia, and New Zealand were sold to Cendant. The remaining worldwide assets were sold to Avis Europe Plc.

AVIS EUROPE PLC.

Europe's largest car rental company in 2005, with operations in Africa, the Middle East, and Asia, Avis Europe operated both the Avis and Budget brands under an exclusive licensing deal from Cendant Corp. Under the Avis brand, Avis Europe had 3,000 locations in 108 countries, while it operated 800 locations in 61 countries under the Budget brand. The company shares marketing and technology initiatives with Cendant, although the two companies are separately owned. Established in 1965 as a division of Avis Inc., Avis Europe was taken private in 1989, but was re-floated on the London Stock Exchange in 1997. That year, the company acquired the license for the Avis brand in Asia, followed in subsequent years by major licensee agreements in Greece, Germany, France, and the Netherlands. In 2003, the company acquired many of the assets of Budget. Sales revenue for Avis Europe were about US$1.5 billion in 2004, with the company employing slightly more than 6,100 people.

VANGUARD CAR RENTAL USA INC.

In October of 2003, Vanguard Car Rental USA acquired ANC (after it had declared bankruptcy), which controlled the Alamo and National car rental chains. Together, the two chains had sales of US$2.4 billion in 2002, down from US$3.5 billion in 2000.

With 15 million annual reservations, 1,000 locations, and a 322,000-car fleet, exceeded in number only by Enterprise and Hertz, Alamo was the rental car industry's success story of the 1990s. Held by Republic Industries since 1995, Alamo was divided into three divisions: Alamo North America, handling all North American operations; Alamo Europe, which performed a similar office for Alamo activity in Europe and the United Kingdom; and Alasys, which existed to handle insurance replacement and local market business.

Alamo was founded in 1974, initially serving primarily Florida locations with a relatively small fleet of 1,000 cars. In slightly over 20 years, Alamo increased its number of locations to 217 domestic outlets and 180 international offices. Although early corporate expansion was conservative, an aggressive growth plan, put into place in 1980, set a pace that continued through the end of the century.

National Car Rental was formed in 1947, resulting from an amalgamation of 24 independent car rental operators. In 1961, National was purchased by LTV Corporation, which, in 1969, in turn sold it to Household International Inc., a Chicago-based conglomerate. In 1974, National was a wholly owned subsidiary of Household, but it was put up for sale 12 years later in 1986. Purchased by an investment group that included General Motors, National eventually became GM property outright when the latter company became the major shareholder in the investment group. GM held National until 1995, when it agreed to sell to yet another group of investors for a reported price between US$1.25 and US$1.5 billion. The sale (to William E. Lobeck and partners) thwarted a bid by Alamo Rent A Car to acquire National (Alamo's attempt to challenge Hertz for the top spot in airport-related car rentals). National went on to acquire Canada's Tilden Rent-A-Car System, Ltd. in the summer of 1996 (National and Tilden had been affiliated since 1959). Early in 1997, National became a wholly owned subsidiary of Republic Industries, but continued to aggressively pursue market expansion. In the spring of 1998, the company took over Australia's DASFLEET Rentals, a company formerly owned by the Australian government. By that year, National served customers in 132 countries from 3,000 locations, and counted over 200,000 vehicles in its automotive fleet, 145,000 of which were in the United States and Canada.

EUROPCAR INTERNATIONAL

Owned by Volkswagen AG, Europcar was operating a fleet of 220,000 vehicles at 2,650 locations in 118 countries in 2005, making it Europe's leading car rental company. Countries in which it had operations included those in Europe, the Middle East, Africa, the Asia-Pacific region, the Caribbean, Mexico, Central America, and South America. The company's revenues were approximately US$1.4 billion in 2004, at which time it employed about 5,000 people.

Europcar was founded in Paris in 1949, and was acquired by Renault in 1970. The company began to expand in Europe, and acquired Budget in Italy in 1974. In 1988, Volkswagen bought half of the company, with the other half being purchased by Wagon-Lits. Accor acquired Wagon-Lits in 1992, and by 1999 had sold its share of Europcar to Volkswagen, making it the sole owner.

DOLLAR THRIFTY AUTOMOTIVE GROUP INC.

Operating under two brands—Dollar Rent A Car and Thrifty Rent A Car—the Dollar Thrifty Automotive Group was operating 1,600 owned and franchised locations in about 70 countries in 2005. About half of its locations were in Canada and the United States. The two brands came under one company umbrella in 1995. As a single entity, the two companies produced US$1.42 billion in revenues in 2004, up from US$950 million in 2000. The company employed 8,300 workers.

Dollar Rent A Car was founded in Los Angeles in 1966. Chrysler purchased the company and incorporated it into its Pentastar Transportation Group in 1990, where it remained until Pentastar was renamed Dollar Thrifty. Thrifty's operation, slightly older than Dollar, was founded in 1958. Thrifty's acquisition by Chrysler in 1989 predated the Chrysler acquisition of Dollar Rent A Car. The Dollar Thrifty Automotive Group (DTAG) first traded publicly in 1997. In December of that year, Dollar's agreement with Europcar International S.A. of France saw the two companies' locations number over 2,800. (Dollar was known in Europe as "Euro-Dollar.") Although the companies remain independent, the two have forged a regional partnership in which Dollar refers customers to Europcar, and Europcar reciprocates, an arrangement that has coincided with Dollar's retreat from Europe. The combined Dollar/Europcar fleet exceeded 185,000 vehicles. To these totals, Thrifty added 52,000 cars and 1,204 locations, giving the group a combined international presence of 237,000 vehicles and 4,004 outlets.

FURTHER READING

About Budget. Daytona Beach, FL: Budget Group, Inc., 2002. Available from http://www.budgetrentacar.com.

Alamo History. Fort Lauderdale, FL: Alamo Rent A Car, Inc., 2002. Available from http://www.ancrental.com.

Avis Corporate Information. Garden City, NY: Avis Rent A Car, Inc., 2002. Available from http://www.avis.com.

"Car Rental Companies Set to Further Rebound in 2004: Weak Dollar, 'Solid' Prices Bolster Confidence in Segment's Recovery." *Travel Weekly,* 1 March 2004.

"Major Market Profiles: Car Rental in US (UK, France, Germany)." *Euromonitor,* October 2004. Available from http://www.euromonitor.com.

"Car Rental Industry Point of View: The New Breed of Car Rental." Perot Systems Corporation, accessed 9 July 2005. Available from http://www.tacsnet.com.

"Coming in 2002: A Nationalized Travel Industry?" 2001. Available from http://www.elliott.org.

"Counter and Rental Clerks." U.S. Department of Labor, Bureau of Labor Statistics, May 20, 2004. Available from http://www.bls.gov.

Elliott, Christopher. "ACTIF Speaks Out for its Members—Recent Attack on Rental Industry for Use of Vehicle Tracking Technology." *Auto Rental News,* 4 February 2004. Available from http://www.fleet-central.com.

Enterprise Rent-a-Car Fact Sheet. 2002. Available from http://www.enterprise.com.

"Finland: Small Car Renting Businesses In Trouble." *Nordic Business Report,* 1 July 2004.

Hertz History. Park Ridge, NJ: Hertz Corporation, 2002. Available from http://www.hertz.com.

Hoover's Online. "Hoover's Company Capsules." Austin, TX: Hoover's, Inc., 2004. Available from http://www.hoovers.com.

Mann, Jennifer. "Car Rental Industry Is Still Untangling Logistcial Knots After Terror Attack." *The Star (Kansas City),* 27 September 2001.

Occupational Outlook Handbook, U.S. Bureau of Labor, 2002.

"Rates Fall While Rentals and Reservations Grow." *Travel Trade Gazette UK & Ireland,* 8 March 2004.

"Rental Cars - Travel Statistics." Car Rental Express (CRX), viewed on 9 July 2005. Available from http://www.carrentalexpress.com.

Thrifty Rent-A-Car System, Inc. *General Information,* Tulsa, OK: Thrifty Rent-A-Car System, Inc., 2002. Available from http://www.dtag.com.

"U.S. Car Rental Market." *Fleet Central,* 25 August 2004. Available from http://www.fleet-central.com.

SIC 5812

NAICS 722110

RESTAURANTS

Restaurants are involved in retail sale of prepared foods and beverages for on-site or immediate consumption, such as fast-food restaurants, diners, refreshment stands, and full-service restaurants. Caterers and institutional food service establishments are also included in this category.

INDUSTRY SNAPSHOT

Large fast-food chains lead the restaurant industry, which by 2005 consisted of approximately 8 million restaurants worldwide in an extremely competitive environment. Most restaurants were single unities, independently owned and operated, while about 300 companies were involved in chain restaurants. McDonald's was the world's leading restaurant chain in terms of sales and the second largest based on number of sites. Yum! Brands, formerly Tricon Global Restaurants Inc., was the world's second largest restaurant company in terms of sales, with 33,000 units in 100 countries, and the largest in terms of restaurant units. Its major brands were also global leaders in their markets: KFC (chicken), Pizza Hut, and Taco Bell (Mexican-themed). In the food service sector, Compass Group PLC ranked as the world's largest company, followed by Sodexho Alliance SA.

Worldwide, the restaurant industry saw considerable growth in 2003 as the economy began to stabilize and consumer confidence increased. According to *Euromonitor*, the industry grew 4.5 percent in the United States, reaching US$189.9 billion. In the United Kingdom, the industry grew 3.0 percent, to US$23.1 billion. China also experienced growth of 9.4 percent to US$110.4 billion. The market in France held steady at US$33.9 billion, but the Japanese market decreased 7.5 percent to US$138.8 billion.

Organization and Structure

Traditionally, the restaurant industry has consisted of two main sectors: full-service restaurants (including family restaurants, casual dining establishments, dinner houses, and grill-buffets) and quick service restaurants (QSR), also known as fast-food restaurants. The QSR sector typically serves hamburgers, chicken, sandwiches, pizza, Mexican dishes, and breakfast and snack items. The National Restaurant Association (NRA) of the United States breaks the industry down further, into restaurants that provide full menus with table service, limited menus with table service, and limited menus without table service. Of establishments with a limited menu and providing table service, most are small, independently owned operations.

The restaurant industry is a mature industry, and in many countries, such as the United States and in Western Europe, competition is very tough as many markets are saturated. In addition, restaurants must compete with expanded supermarket offerings that include a vast array of frozen foods, deli foods, and other fully or partially prepared meals for at-home dining. As a result, many large restaurant companies have turned to acquisition to expand their menu offerings, to increase their number of locations, and to capture market share in a region or niche that previously was unavailable to them.

Franchising. Since the 1970s, the growth of franchising has propelled the growth of the larger restaurant industry. The popularity of franchising stems from the parent company's ability to expand without as much expense, as start-up costs are usually paid by whoever purchases the franchise. In addition to a license fee and equipment and stock purchases, the local owner, or franchisee, pays the franchiser royalties based on sales. For the person buying into a well-known franchise, this is an extremely low-risk investment, when compared with independent eating establishments, which do not have an established clientele to be tapped. However, franchise owners lose flexibility. Independent restaurant owners can plan their own menus, avoid royalty expenses, and run their business as they see fit. Franchises are restricted by terms of the franchise agreement. Ultimately, independent restaurant owners—who rely largely on "word-of-mouth," local newspapers, and radio spots for their advertising—find it nearly impossible to compete against the huge, national marketing budgets of the large chains that advertise heavily on television and through promotional tie-ins with movies and sports.

The degree of franchising offered throughout the restaurant industry varies. Some companies, such as Subway, prefer nearly all their outlets to be operated by franchisees, while Darden does not offer franchising domestically in the United States. Others strive for a combination. For example, 61 percent of McDonald's 2001 revenues were derived from franchisees, 27 percent from company-owned sites, and 12 percent from affiliates. The franchisor may also change the percentage of its company- versus franchisee-operated locations as part of restructuring efforts or to better position its brands. For example, in *Fortune* Brian O'Keefe reported that Tricon Global Restaurants, later known as Yum! Brands, shuttered franchisees in England where sales had slumped and opened company-owned restaurants in France, Holland, and Germany to spur franchisee interest there. As O'Keefe wrote, "part of the trick for any large franchise operator is to allow local flexibility while maintaining quality control and a central marketing message."

Background and Development

Although the restaurant industry consists primarily of small, local, independently owned diners and cafes, the number of well-known, large, mega-chain restaurants has continued to increase. Contributing to this growth was the increased number of single-person households and single-parent families, as well as the increasing numbers of working women throughout the world. Less time was allotted for meal preparation and convenience became more important. Since the early 1970s, franchised eating-places have almost tripled their share of the market, from 15 percent of industry volume to about 43 percent in the mid-1990s.

Several factors contributed to the expansion of the restaurant industry. Restaurants were considered easy business ventures by anyone who could cook; thus, there was a proliferation of new restaurants. However, half of these ventures fail or change management every five years, according to the U.S. Small Business Administration.

Most growth in the restaurant industry, however, is due to the increase in franchised establishments, both fast food and casual dining. In particular, the late twentieth century saw tremendous growth in the global expansion of American brands, such as McDonald's, KFC, Starbucks, and Applebee's. Since its beginnings in 1997, when PepsiCo spun off its fast-food chains—KFC, Pizza Hut, and Taco Bell—to form Tricon Global Restaurants, Tricon opened more than 5,100 restaurants, nearly 63 percent of which were outside the United States. According to an article in *Fortune*, the U.S. mega-chains tailored their menus to reflect local customs and tastes when opening new locations abroad. For example, KFC (formerly Kentucky Fried Chicken) serves tempura crispy strips in Japan, potatoes and gravy in northern England, rice and soy sauce in Thailand, and potato-and-onion croquettes in Holland.

By the late 1990s, competition cooled down in mature markets as some analysts warned that the chain restaurant market was saturated—especially the fast-food segment. As a result, some restaurant chains announced their plans to reduce their expansion, in contrast to the ambitious multinational expansion plans touted by leading chains in the early and mid-1990s. In addition, with the influx of independent and regional dinner house and casual dining restaurants, veteran operations such as T.G.I. Friday's, Bennigan's, and Applebee's started to recast their images and refocus their restaurants to differentiate themselves from the competition. Friday's began as primarily a singles' bar and evolved into a family-oriented casual dining restaurant that still has strong bar sales. Other such restaurants followed this pattern, trying to offer something unique and attempting to strike a balance between their bar and restaurant facets.

Restaurants and their investors gravitated toward themed formats in the late 1980s and early 1990s, as the popularity of these restaurants surged among consumers. However, by the latter part of the 1990s some theme restaurants proved to be largely a fad as the sales of some of the largest operations such as Planet Hollywood began to wilt and investors pulled out.

In the mid-1990s, restaurants and supermarkets introduced prepared foods for carry-out service or what they termed "home meal replacements" (HMR). These allowed customers to enjoy freshly cooked foods in the convenience of their own homes. This trend boded well with the proliferation of VCRs, TVs, computers, and other electronic entertainment devices in homes around the world. HMR sales rose to US$50 billion in 1997, up 13 percent from 1996, and were expected to climb to US$170 billion by 2005. Other product and service trends of the mid to late 1990s were salad bars/dinner buffets, specialized menus (e.g., health food and vegetarian), and home delivery. The continued rise in single-parent families, single-person households, and dual income households fueled the growth of the industry worldwide, especially in mature industrialized countries. Restaurants reported that more than 50 percent of their revenues came from carry-out sales.

However, growth in the United States has slowed considerably. The National Restaurant Association (NRA), which compiles an annual report of the industry in the United States, noted in its 2001 report that the growth in foodservice sales grew almost 4 percent to nearly US$393 billion, capping ten consecutive years of growth. However, the inflation-adjusted growth rate of 0.8 percent was the fifth lowest since 1970. The NRA predicted sales growth for 2002 to be a meager 1.4 percent. Yet *Nation's Restaurant News* reported that some industry analysts remained optimistic, citing that the industry has managed to grow, although narrowly, despite the economic slowdown of 2001; a 1.3 percent decline in the U.S. gross domestic product late in the year; and the sharp downturn in the tourism and hospitality sectors after the terrorist attacks of September 11.

September 11 also had a negative impact on the foodservice industry in the United Kingdom, as reported by Foodservice Intelligence. The United Kingdom and parts of Western Europe also had to deal with outbreaks of foot-and-mouth disease (FMD), a highly contagious disease affecting livestock such as cattle, sheep, and pigs. People rarely contract the disease, but may be carriers. As there is no cure for the disease, infected animals must be quarantined and ultimately destroyed. A February 2001 outbreak of FMD in Great Britain spread into parts of Ireland, France, and the Netherlands, resulting in the destruction of more than 4 million animals. Nearly a year later, in January 2002, officials announced that Britain was rid of the disease. Despite these problems, Foodservice Intelligence believed long-term growth of the British restaurant industry would not be adversely impacted, projecting that foodservice sales would grow to 24.1 billion pounds sterling by 2006. Perhaps a more serious, long-term issue for the U.K. restaurant industry is avoiding a general stagnation of the restaurant dining experience by failing to provide new and innovative concepts to attract customers.

Entirely different from FMD, although often lumped together in the public's mind, were the outbreaks of bovine spongiform encephalopathy (BSE), also known as mad-cow disease, that plagued Britain, parts of Europe, and Japan in the early twenty-first century. BSE, which kills brain cells by creating sponge-like holes, was first identified in Britain in the mid 1980s and by the end of 2000, more than 179,000 cases of BSE were confirmed. In 1996 scientists discovered that the human variant, Creutzfeldt-Jecob disease, was directly linked to BSE. As a result, the European Union banned British beef exports. Viewed largely as a British problem, increases in the number of cases of BSE were reported in France, Portugal, Ireland, and Switzerland in 2000. Both FMD and BSE altered the eating habits of Europeans in the affected countries, and caused a decline in tourism, according to Amanda Mosle Friedman in *Nation's Restaurant News*. One British analyst estimated a 10 percent decline in beef sales in the United Kingdom in 2001 as more people turned to white meat and fish. The U.K. tourism industry, estimated at US$88 billion annually, was expected to drop 60 percent in mid-2001. Nevertheless, the fast-food sector has seen overall growth throughout Europe, outpacing upscale restaurants, steak houses, and other traditional restaurants.

McDonald's was particularly hard hit by BSE, as its European sales faltered so much that by late 2000, worldwide profits were adversely affected, according to *The Wall Street Journal*. Ironically, as consumer confidence gradually reappeared toward beef products in Europe, infected cows were discovered in Japan in the fall of 2001. And although McDonald's uses Australian and New Zealand rather than Japanese-raised beef in its Japanese restaurants, consumers there were avoiding beef; in the fourth quarter of 2001, sales dropped more than 10 percent from the same period the previous year.

CURRENT CONDITIONS

The leading restaurateurs in the global restaurant business are U.S.-based, and the largest restaurant market is also the United States. According to a 2004 industry study by the National Restaurant Association, industry revenues were US$440 billion, an average of US$1.2 billion each day. There were an estimated 878,000 restaurants with 1 million workers. According to MRSI, a marketing research company based in Ohio, by 2005 there were about 8 million restaurants in the world and about 300 restaurant companies. The industry remains highly competitive, with the number of restaurants exceeding consumer demand.

INDUSTRY TRENDS

Industry Growth. Most large food service companies have found growth happens faster through acquisitions than through development of their own sites. However, growth for many was still focused on franchise development and expansion into foreign markets.

Sandwiches. At the onset of the twenty-first century, the sandwich became the fastest growing item in the U.S. restaurant industry—particularly in the fast-food and "fast-casual" dining establishments. Long regarded as a humble food item, companies such as Cosi, Briazz, Corner Bakery Café, and Panera Bread Co., and even traditional fast-food chains such as Arby's, have elevated the sandwich to near-gourmet stature with handmade breads and imaginative combinations of fillings using high quality ingredients. Even burger behemoth McDonald's tried to get into the game by test launching five different deli-style sandwiches under the Oven Selects name. By 2004, the sandwich market was valued at US$17 billion, up 7 percent from the previous year. The rise of the sandwich was attributed to consumers' waning interest in burgers and fries in favor of healthier options, combined with the desire for quick, on-the-go meals. What has made sandwiches so attractive to restaurateurs is the premium price they command: compared to a 99-cent burger, sandwiches can cost four dollars or more. Yet consumers do not seem to mind the higher prices. In fact, *The Wall Street Journal* cites a study by Technomic Inc., a Chicago food-consulting firm, which reported that U.S. sales of custom-made sandwiches are growing 15 percent annually, dramatically outpacing the 3 percent sales growth rate for burgers and steaks.

Go Healthy. The explosion of health-conscious diets, from the low-carb to the low-fat and all points in between, caused restaurants of all types to reinvent their menus. In fast food, restaurants were busily adding salads and special sandwiches to the menu, or retooling classic favorites to suit different dieters. At McDonald's in 2004, children could choose apples over fries or milk over soda pop with a Happy Meal. Vegetarian meal options were also on the rise. However, in many countries with aging populations, it was the older portion of the market that was most influencing product decisions.

Workforce. The aging population was also influencing the available work pool from which restaurants could find staff. Many countries were seeing an increase in the use of senior members of the population.

Multibrand Restaurants. Another trend in the fast food industry is the multibrand restaurant concept, where two to three recognized brands sell food side-by-side under the same roof. This may be done through the use of separate counters, so that the restaurant looks like a mini food court, or one brand may dominate the menu and offer a few favorites of another brand. For example, Yum!—the leading multibranding restaurateur with its three major fast food chains—sells its Personal Pan Pizzas through the drive-thru window of some Taco Bell and KFC stores. Multibranding has proven successful since it provides additional convenience and food choices for customers, while allowing companies a way to introduce multiple brands to an area that they may not otherwise target due to the high cost of property or low population levels. Instead of building and maintaining two or three separate units, the company operates one store. Yum! was looking to expand the multibrand concept beyond its own brands, and acquired A&W All-American and Long John Silver's restaurants.

Fast-Casual Restaurants. Another emerging concept in the early twenty-first century was the "fast-casual" restaurant, which like fast-food chains does not have a dining room wait staff, and therefore, no tipping. However, the fast-casual restaurant offers a higher-quality menu than the fast-food chains.

Contract Food Service. The global food service market relies on institutions, corporations, and organizations that outsource their food operations. The world's largest food service provider is Compass Group PLC of Britain, followed by France's Sodexho Alliance SA. U.S.-based Aramark Worldwide Corp. is a distant third in the industry with operations that are largely focused in the United States. According to data from Merrill Lynch and reported by *The Wall Street Journal*, 37 percent of institutions around the world worked with contract food service companies rather than an in-house food staff. The United States was the largest market for the industry with 55 percent of institutions turning to outsourced food services. Organizations often outsource their cafeteria and catering needs, rather than relying on an in-house staff, because large food service companies such as Compass or Sodexho are usually less expensive solutions. Such companies obtain ingredients more cheaply due to global buying power, and costs are kept lower since food service employees are generally paid less and with fewer benefits than their corporate counterparts. Another benefit in outsourcing to a large, multinational company such as Compass or Sodexho is that many organizations operate in multiple countries and prefer to work with a single, global food service provider for all their locations.

RESEARCH AND TECHNOLOGY

The 1990s saw increased use of computer and telecommunications technology in the restaurant industry, such as vibrating paging systems given to waitstaff and patrons to indicate when food or tables were ready; integrated systems that handle order taking, dining, and accounting functions; and automated scheduling, payroll, accounting, inventory control, and sales analysis devices. The use of sophisticated computer technology has continued into the twenty-first century to provide greater convenience and speed to the customer in the hopes of boosting sales as well as to increase staff efficiency through the use of wireless systems. Many European restaurants use wireless applications, and the concept is growing in the United States. At an Irving, Texas facility of Nokia, a cellular phone manufacturer, foodservice giant Sodexho is introducing a cashless payment system that takes advantage of the fact that most of Nokia's employees carry cell phones. Cafeteria customers use their cell phones as a "speed-pay" device by scanning them in front of a specially designed reader at the cafeteria's entrance. At checkout, the order is rung up and the customer scans his or her phone again at a second reader to process the payment to a pre-authorized credit card account. At some McDonald's locations employees are using "wearable computers" so that when the drive-up window line becomes too long, waitstaff are alerted and can take orders from customers waiting in line, entering the order on a portable device that transmits it to the kitchen. The devices can also be used in full-service restaurants to enter orders and process payment directly at the table. Other types of wireless systems allow managers to keep tabs on a location when they are on the road. Alerts are sounded if building doors are unlocked or if a freezer door remains open, and some devices even offer video feeds of restaurant activity. The Internet was also being used more frequently by customers to select restaurants; MRSI reseach indicated that 45 percent of 25 to 34 year olds had used the Internet to find out about restaurants to which they had never been.

INDUSTRY LEADERS

Compass Group PLC. As the world's largest foodservice company in 2005, UK-based Compass operated in more than 90 countries. The company posted revenues of US$21.5 billion in 2004, an increase of more than 12 percent over 2003. The company employed more than 412,000 people worldwide. Compass Group provides contract foodservice to corporations, hospitals, educational institutions, and retailers, as well as at entertainment venues, airports, and railway stations in the United States, Europe, and in emerging markets in Asia and South America.

Founded in 1941 as Factory Canteens Limited, Compass Group got its start feeding munitions workers. In the 1960s, after a period of acquisition and mergers, Factory Canteens emerged as Grand Metropolitan Catering Services, which became Compass Services in 1984 and then Compass Group in 1987. Throughout the 1990s a number of acquisitions and mergers occurred as Select Service Partner (part of SAS Airlines), Canteen Vending, Eurest International, SHRM, and Restaurant Associates joined Compass Group. In 1998 Compass Group was awarded its first global contract, to provide foodservice operations for Philips. In 2000 Compass Group merged with the hospitality company Granada Group to become Granada:Compass, but a year later it was demerged and re-listed as Compass Group. In 2002 Seiyo Food Systems Inc. of Japan became a wholly owned subsidiary of Compass Group. Compass Group was named the Official Catering Services Supplier for the 2002 Olympic and Paralympic Winter Games in Salt Lake City, Utah. In 2004, Compass became food service provider for the French National Rail Company, as well as becoming the first foreign company to provide passenger food service on trains in China.

Sodexho Alliance. Sodexho Alliance is the world's second largest contract food service provider with 2004 revenues of about US$14 billion, up 9 percent over 2003 levels. Employing 313,000 people, the company had operations in 76 countries in 2005, providing food service functions to businesses, schools, and hospitals. In 2001 Sodexho Alliance purchased Sodexho Marriott Services, a leading food service company in the United States, to be its North American subsidiary and renamed the company Sodexho Inc.

McDonald's Corporation. Serving about 46 million customers a day worldwide, in more than 100 countries, McDonald's ranks as the largest restaurant company in the world. Of its 30,000 restaurants, more than 8,000 are company owned and operated, 18,000 are owned by franchisees, and about 4,000 are owned by affiliated companies. Worldwide sales totaled US$19.1 billion in 2004 of which about 75 percent was sales from company-operated restaurants, and the remainder was from franchise fee revenues. Globally, 35 percent of revenues were derived from the United States and 35 percent from Europe, with France, Germany and the United Kingdom accounting for 65 percent of Europe's total. The company employed 438,000 workers and also operated the Boston Market and Chipotle Mexican Grill restaurant chains. Its brand name is one of the most highly recognized brands, along with Coca-Cola and Marlboro.

McDonald's first opened in San Bernadino, California in 1948. The original owners, Dick and Mac MacDonald, signed a franchise agreement along with machine salesman Ray Kroc. In 1961, Kroc bought out the MacDonald brothers for US$2.7 million. McDonald's golden arches first appeared in 1962; Ronald McDonald also made his first appearance that year. In 1967, McDonald's opened its first restaurants outside the United States, with locations in Canada.

Throughout the 1970s, McDonald's restaurants grew by more than 500 per year. Also during the 1970s, items such as the Egg McMuffin and McDonald's Happy Meals were added. In 1978, McDonald's became the largest single-brand restaurant chain in the United States based on number of locations when it overtook Kentucky Fried Chicken, now known as KFC. At the time, McDonald's had 4,465 restaurants in the United States, 236 more than KFC. Throughout the 1980s, U.S. sales growth slowed to about 5 percent annually due to increased domestic competition. In response, McDonald's added "value menus" and new products to appeal to health-conscious consumers. In the mid- to late 1990s, McDonald's entered into a partnership agreement with Wal-Mart and formed alliances with Amoco and Chevron to place McDonald's retail outlets at selected locations. Through a joint venture with the Food Service Administration of the Moscow City Council, McDonald's opened its first restaurants in Russia during the 1990s. Its first restaurant, the Moscow-McDonald's was "rubles only" and served approximately 50,000 customers per day.

In the late 1990s McDonald's held its position as the world's leading restaurant chain, but its market share declined. In addition to increased competition, the company's rampant expansion in the 1990s eroded its profits. Critics argued that the company failed to introduce any successful new products in the decade to entice new customers and ensure repeat visits; observers also charged that McDonald's supersaturated the market with its chains, especially in the United States.

Starting in the late 1990s, McDonald's began acquiring other chains to diversify its business as a result of the increasingly burger-saturated market in the United States. In 1998

McDonald's bought Chipolte Mexican Grill. In December 1999, it acquired Boston Chicken Inc.'s 751 units for US$173.5 million, when Boston Chicken was in the midst of bankruptcy proceedings. McDonald's initially planned to convert many of Boston Chicken's units to McDonald's or one of its partner brands, but after closing about 100 units decided to see if new life could be breathed into the chain and planned to open 40 units in 2002, including sites in Australia and Canada.

In 2003, McDonald's began a revitalization strategy in an attempt to improve its financial standing and move in line with consumer preferences. New food lines were introduced, including breakfast and salad products, and the company began to modernize many of its store designs, hoping to have system-wide sales increases of 3 percent to 5 percent during 2005.

Burger King Corporation. Ranked as the second-largest fast-food restaurant chain in the world, Burger King had 11,201 restaurants in 61 countries. Of these restaurants, 10,136 were franchises and 1,065 were company owned and operated. System-wide sales in 2004 reached US$11.1 billion for this company, privately held by Texas Pacific Group (TPG), a management investment company.

Until 2002, Burger King was a private subsidiary of London-based Diageo plc, which formed out of a 1997 merger between Grand Metropolitan PLC (GrandMet) and Guinness PLC (brew and alcohol producer and publisher). GrandMet was a food, liquor, and retailing giant begun in London in the early 1920s. Some of GrandMet's most visible brands included Green Giant, Pillsbury, Burger King, and Haagen-Dazs. In 2002 Diageo sold the company to TPG for US$1.5 billion.

James McLamore and David Edgerton founded Burger King in Miami in 1954. In its early years, the company began catering to families in the postwar years, offering a simple menu of moderately priced, broiled burgers. The chain expanded rapidly, and in 1967 the two founders sold the company to Pillsbury, which GrandMet acquired in 1988. Attempting to turn the tide of slower sales, the company renewed focus on Burger King's core menu and cut prices and costs. The company also began new advertising campaigns such as "It Just Tastes Better" in 1998.

Yum! Brands Inc. With more than 33,000 restaurants in more than 100 countries, Louisvill, Kentucky-based Yum! Brands is larger than McDonald's in terms of locations. Sales in foreign countries have been on the rise, with the company reporting that China was the fastest growing and most profitable country for the company after the United States. In 1997, PepsiCo Inc. spun off its popular restaurant division as Tricon Global Restaurants, which owned Pizza Hut, KFC (Kentucky Fried Chicken), and Taco Bell. Tricon later became Yum! In 2004, Yum!, which also owned A & W All-American Food Restaurants and Long John Silver's restaurants, reported US$9 billion in revenue and 256,000 employees. Of its total revenues, 89 percent came from sales from company-operated restaurants, with the remainder coming from franchise fees.

KFC Corporation: In the early twenty-first century, KFC (then known as Kentucky Fried Chicken), founded by Colonel Harland Sanders in 1952, dominated the world fast-food chicken market. In 2004, KFC operated 13,266 restaurants of which about 58 percent were in the 88 countries in which it operated outside of its home base in the U.S. About 23 percent of its restaurants were owned and operated by the company, with the rest being franchised. Although KFC is best known for its Original Recipe and Extra Crispy fried chicken, the company also introduced KFC's Rotisserie Gold chicken and chicken sandwiches in the U.S., which have appealed to increasingly health-conscious consumers. In other countries, the menu is more focused on chicken sandwiches and chicken strips, with overall choice being reflected by local tastes.

Pizza Hut: Pizza Hut originated in 1958 in Wichita, Kansas, and expanded over the following decades with restaurants in Russia, France, the United Kingdom, Australia, and Hong Kong. As of the end of 2004, it was the leading U.S. pizza company, with a 16 percent market share. The company operated 7,500 units in the U.S. and 4,774 in the other 85 countries in which it operated. About 22 percent of the restaurant units were operated by the company, with the remainder being franchised.

Taco Bell: Founded in 1962, Taco Bell was the United States' leading Mexican-themed fast-food restaurant, with a 64-percent share of that market segment in 2004. The company was still primarily based in the United States where it had 5,900 units, 22 percent of which were company operated. However, it had expanded into other markets, having 238 units in 10 other countries. These units were primarily owned by franchisors, with only 5 percent being company operated. At the onset of the twenty-first century, the company launched the "Think Outside the Bun" ad campaign to compete head-on with hamburger-oriented fast food chains. Part of the campaign included offering products with premium ingredients, such as steak, to boost the appeal of its menu to more consumers, while still retaining low prices.

Wendy's International Inc. Founded by Dave Thomas in 1969 in Columbus, Ohio, Wendy's acquired the Canadian Tim Hortons chain in 1995 for about US$400 million. The deal diversified Wendy's mainly hamburger business as Tim Hortons offered items such as coffee, doughnuts and freshly made sandwiches. Wendy's 6,671 restaurants, generating US$3.6 billion in 2004, were mainly located in the United States and Canada, with only a few hundred international units, mostly focused in Latin America. Of its total Wendy$rsquo;s restaurants, about 22 percent were operated by the company, with the remainder being franchised. In addition, the company had 2,721 Tim Hortons restaurants, of which more than 90 percent were located in Canada. This chain was highly franchised, with less than 2 percent of the units being company operated. In addition, the company operated or franchised 295 Baja Fresh restaurants, and 19 Cafe Express restaurants in Texas.

Wendy's did not intend to expand its business much beyond Canada and the United States, but focused on acquisitions and mergers to achieve growth. *The Wall Street Journal's* Shirley Leung reported that "Wendy's core business was still growing and posting healthier profits and sales gains than its two larger hamburger competitors. While McDonald's and Burger King struggled with menu changes and discount pricing, Wendy's stuck with a core menu featuring its hallmark square-shaped burgers and an everyday value pricing strategy." However, the U.S. market may be too saturated to allow expansion through additional Wendy's restaurants. Therefore, Wendy's CEO and Chairman Jack Schuessler told Leung that he expected future growth to come from acquisitions and joint ventures outside of the traditional hamburger business. Leung also reported that Wendy's expects 12 to 15 percent long-term growth.

In January 2002, Wendy's lost its founder and long-time pitchman when Dave Thomas died of liver cancer at the age of 69. Thomas appeared in hundreds of Wendy's commercials since 1989, representing a down-to-earth spokesman to whom many Americans felt they could relate.

Doctor's Associates Inc. (Subway Restaurants). Subway, the world's leading chain of submarine sandwich restaurants, was founded by seventeen-year-old Fred DeLuca and family friend Peter Buck in 1965 as a submarine sandwich counter in Bridgeport, Connecticut. By 1974 there were 16 units throughout the state and Subway started offering franchising opportunities. As of 2005, Subway, owned by Doctor's Associates Inc. of Milford, Connecticut, had 23,453 units in 82 countries, all of which were held by franchisors (except for one which was being used as a testing facility). In 2005, *Entrepreneur* magazine ranked Subway as the number-one franchise opportunity for the thirteenth time in 17 years. Revenues for 2003 were US$468 million, but this was mostly franchise fees; system-wide sales were US$6.8 billion.

In February 2001, Subway opened its 1,000th international location in Australia. Subway became the largest U.S. restaurant chain based on number of units when it took over the top spot from McDonald's at the end of 2001, until Yum! took that spot at the top. In 1999 Subway began a successful ad campaign featuring Jared, a real consumer who claimed to have lost a tremendous amount of weight by eating Subway's low-fat, large-sized sandwiches.

Darden Restaurants Inc. Darden Restaurants recorded sales of US$5 billion in 2004, an increase of 7.5 percent over 2003 levels. Considered the world's largest casual-dining restaurant chain, the company operated all of its 1,325 restaurants in the U.S. and Canada; none were franchised. However, the company did license its Red Lobster brand to a Japanese firm which had 38 such restaurants in Japan. The company was formed from the 1995 spin-off of General Mills' restaurant holdings, and includes the restaurant chains Red Lobster, Olive Garden, Bahama Breeze, and Smokey Bones BBQ. The first restaurant, Red Lobster, was opened in Florida in 1968. Red Lobster dominates the U.S. seafood-restaurant sector, while The Olive Garden leads U.S. casual Italian-themed restaurants.

Brinker International Inc. One of the world's largest casual dining companies was Brinker international Inc., which reported US$3.7 billion in sales in 2004. Based in Dallas, Texas, Brinker operated a system-wide total of more than 975 units that included Chili's Grill & Bar, Romano's Macaroni Grill, On The Border Mexican Grill and Cantina, Maggiano's Little Italy, Corner Bakery Café, Cozymel's Coastal Mexican Grill, Big Bowl, Rockfish Seafood Grill, and eatZi's Market & Bakery.

Applebee's International Inc. Applebee's, headquartered in Overland Park, Kansas, operated 1,671 casual dining restaurants in the United States and in 12 countries by the end of 2004. Applebee's posted 2003 system-wide sales of US$1.1 billion. About 75 percent of Applebee's sites are franchise restaurants, with the remainder company-owned.

Starbucks Corporation. Founded in Seattle, Washington in 1971, Starbucks was operating in 36 countries including the United States by 2005. In the United States, the company operated 6,376 stores and licensed a further 2,573. Internationally, it operated 997 stores and franchised or had joint-venture partnerships at a further 1,576 locations. In addition to its restaurants, the company sells its products through grocery stores through an affiliation with Kraft Foods, and to corporate foodservice suppliers. Approximately 77 percent of its retail sales were beverages, 14 percent was food items, 5 percent whole bean coffees, and 4 percent coffee-making equipment and other merchandise. Starbucks preferred to own and operate its own shops, particularly in the U.S., but did license where it thought others had ownership of an advantageous location or market. Sales for 2004 reached US$5.3 billion. By 2005, the company was opening 3 to 4 stores per day worldwide.

Whitbread Group plc. The United Kingdom's biggest full-service restaurant group, Whitbread is also the U.K.'s largest hospitality provider, operating hotels and health and fitness clubs. Its 1000-unit restaurant segment includes such brands as pub restaurants Brewers Fayre and Beefeater, and it is also the owner of the Costa chain of coffee shops, the largest in the U.K. The company operates about 500 Pizza Hut locations under a joint venture agreement with Yum! Brands, and American restaurant TGI Fridays, under agreement with Carlson. Whitbread had company-wide revenues of approximately US$3.3 billion in 2004.

Autogrill S.p.A. Clothing family Bennetton controls Italy-based food concession operator, Autogrill. In 2005, it was the world's leading operator of food concessions, having more than 4,200 outlets in 890 locations around the world. These concessions are located primarily in airports, railway stations and along highways in 15 countries in Europe, North America and the Pacific region.

The company's sales for 2004 reached more than US$4.1 billion, while it provided employment for more than 48,000 people. With its foundings as a small bar in Milan in 1928, the company grew through expansion and acquisition. In 1999, the company purchased the catering division of Host Marriot Group, which operates Burger King, Sbarro, Pizza Hut and Starbucks franchises in 18 of the 20 busiest airports in the U.S. In 2005, Autogrill was set to purchase Aldeasa of Spain, a retailer at airports in South America, North Africa and Europe. In addition, it was acquiring 49.9 percent of the German company, Steigenberger Gastronomie, which operated at Frankfurt airport.

Major Countries in the Industry

United States. The United States constitutes the world's largest market for restaurants and many of the world's largest restaurant chains hail from here. The National Restaurant Association estimated the industry have sales of US$475.8 billion at the end of 2005, with approximately 900,000 restaurants and foodservice outlets. Providing employment for approximately 12.2 million people, the restaurant industry is the nation's largest employer outside of the public sector. More than 70 percent of all restaurants are single-unit, independently owned enterprises, with most having fewer than 20 employees. *The Washington Post* reported that Americans spend US$110 billion annually on fast food. Each day, roughly 25 percent of the U.S. adult population can be found at a fast-food outlet and 90 percent of children aged three to nine eat at McDonald's at least once a month.

According to statistics published by Darden Restaurants, the casual dining sector accounted for US$47 billion in 2000. Darden Restaurants predicted the casual dining sector will be the fastest growing restaurant segment in the United States with compound annual growth of 6-8 percent throughout the first decade of the twenty-first century. Meanwhile, the fast-food sector will grow 5-6 percent and the mid-scale and fine dining sector will grow less than 3 percent. Demand will continue for restaurants and prepared foods as more and more women work out of the home, the population ages, and people in general are pressed for time and seek convenient and economical alternatives to home meal preparation.

However, in 2000, the number of meals eaten in the home began to increase for the first time in a decade, while restaurant meals declined. *DSN Retailing Today* reported the results of a study conducted by The NPD Group that revealed that, in 2000, in-home meal preparation grew by 0.1 percent after declining 1-2 percent annually since the late 1980s. In 1999 each American ate out an average of 66 times per year and ordered takeout 73 times. By 2000 the average number of restaurant meals per person had dropped to 64, and the number of carry-out orders dropped to 70. But in-home meals are not necessarily made-from-scratch meals. The NPD study showed that the use of a frozen meal dish increased from 9.4 percent in 1997 to 11.5 percent in 2000. According to *DSN,* "The (NPD) study concluded food products that make meal preparation easier and less costly than restaurant meals made an impact with consumers. Other contributing factors include the economic downturn and the 'cocooning' trend spawned by the terrorist attacks" of September 11, 2001.

Further evidence of the increase of in-home meals, and a general move away from fast food—burgers in particular—may also be seen by the fact that in 1996 the top 100 U.S. fast-food restaurants increased their number of locations by 6.1 percent. However, this growth rate has dropped dramatically, so that by 2000 the companies added only 1 percent more locations, according to data collected by Chicago food-consulting firm Technomic Inc. and reported by *The Wall Street Journal.* Although hamburgers are the item of choice for most American fast-food consumers, 2000 sales for fast-food chicken items grew faster than those for burgers or pizza. Chicken sales increased 5 percent to US$11.4 billion, while burger sales grew 4.7 percent to US$46.0 billion, and pizza sales rose 4.4 percent to US$24.5 billion, as reported by *The Wall Street Journal.*

European Union. The European market has shown a shift in consumer preferences toward processed products, convenience foods, and snack foods, as well as concern for nutritional, health, and environmental problems. According to *Nation's Restaurant News,* American fast foods are changing the way Europeans eat, and there is also a greater similarity between French and American meals at the fine-dining level. Overall, McDonald's continued to lead the restaurant industry in Europe, though other domestic and international chains have gnawed away at the company's market share. While nearly all German restaurants are small restaurants and pubs, as opposed to large chains, U.S.-style chain restaurants such as McDonald's are popular, as they were in France.

United Kingdom. The U.K. food service market was valued at US$44.3 billion in 2003. That year, there were approximately 177,600 restaurants according to Euromonitor, with cafe/bars making up the largest share at 42.8 percent. Many cafes and bars had been part of mergers and acquisitions in the early to mid-2000s, with many brewers selling their pubs. Citing a 2001-2002 report from Martin Information, *Leisure & Hospitality Business* reported that the number-one restaurant company in terms of sites in the United Kingdom was Whitbread. McDonald's held the second position, and Six Continents (which demerged its restaurant chain to create Mitchells & Butlers) took third place. Several issues were going to have an effect on the U.K. food service industry. The *Licensing Act* was revised in 2005, allowing pubs to apply for longer opening hours, and a revised smoking charter was in the works which would ban smoking from all restaurants and from pubs that served prepared food.

Japan. The Japanese restaurant market was valued at approximately US$138.8 billion in 2002, and was expected to decline somewhat to US$136.0 billion in 2007, largely due to continued consolidation. Consolidation was occurring as companies sought to remain competitive in an environment characterized by severe price competition, expansion and renovations of restaurants, and expanding menus. Since many Japanese people live far from where they work, and because they live in small apartments, eating out is often a necessity. In addition, Japanese employees of the twenty-first century are no longer guaranteed life-long jobs with a single company. The jobless rate was 5.5 percent in December 2001, compared to 2.0 percent in the early 1990s, according to the *International Herald Tribune.* And young people often postpone marriage in favor of the single life. As a result, the Japanese restaurant industry has continued to grow, particularly the fast-food segment. The Japanese restaurant industry changed dramatically after 1969, when it became possible for foreign companies to invest in Japan. Once the Japanese Foreign Capital Law was revised, restaurants from abroad began investing in the Japanese market. Fast-food restaurants such as McDonald's and KFC are popular, as are casual dining establishments such as Denny's.

Throughout the 1970s family restaurants enjoyed a period of great popularity as places to gather for a variety of social reasons, from business meetings to birthday celebrations. From 1975 to 1985, chains began targeting market needs, spawning take-out businesses such as Hokka Lunch Box, tavern rooms such as Murasaki, and coffee bars. Next came luxurious French restaurants and delivery businesses, including Domino's franchises. Since 1985, the industry has organized itself around specific types of restaurants, including luxury, specialty-oriented, unique, group-oriented, family-oriented, natural food, and entertainment-oriented venues.

At the onset of the twenty-first century, family restaurants sought to reinvigorate their image as places with mediocre service and outdated, overpriced food choices. Japan's popular new franchises target twenty and thirty-something customers and feature contemporary menu formats such as *yakiniku* (Korean barbecued meat and vegetables); *kaiten-sushi* (sushi served via a conveyor belt); *izakaya* (Japanese pub) cuisine; *shabu shabu* (Japanese-style boiled beef); and ramen (Chinese noodles). According to *The Nikkei Weekly*, restaurant companies that operate multiple restaurant formats, particularly those in the mid-range sector, were an emerging trend in the Japanese restaurant industry and were expected to be successful. For example, Tokyo-based Kiwa Corp.'s various restaurant formats include casual Chinese fare, a Peking duck eatery with a theme-park-like setting, and a European-style restaurant. Foreign cuisine is popular in Japan, as an increasing number of Japanese have traveled abroad. Another multi-format restaurant company is Global-Dining Inc., whose concepts include Monsoon Cafe (offering Southeast Asian food), La Boheme (Italian), Zest (Tex-Mex), Tableaux (multinational), and Gonpachi (izakaya cuisine).

China. Unlike other Pacific Rim countries that were experiencing a sluggish or declining growth rate, China's economic growth rate at the beginning of the twenty-first century was expected to be 7.0 to 7.5 percent annually. However, this was significantly down from the mid-1990s when the country experienced double-digit growth, according to *Nation's Restaurant News*. The market was forecast to reach US$193 billion by 2007. An outbreak of Severe Acute Respiratory Syndrome (SARS) hit the restaurant industry hard in 2003, particularly those serving tourist areas. However, domestic growth helped offset some of the negative ramifications brought on by SARS. One chain that made inroads into China was Yum! Brands, which began opening its KFC restaurants there in the late 1980s. Franchising was a relatively new option in China, but took off as businesspeople witnessed the success of McDonald's and KFC in the country.

FURTHER READING

"As Americans Flock to Fast-food Chicken, KFC, Boston Market Heat Up Competition." *The Wall Street Journal Online,* 6 November 2001. Available from http://www.wsj.com.

Brinker International Inc. 2001 Annual Report. Available from http://www.brinker.com.

Carroll, Jill; and Shirley Leung. "U.S. Consumption of French Fries is Sliding as Diners Opt for Healthy." *The Wall Street Journal Online,* 20 February 2002. Available from http://www.wsj.com.

"Carrying Burger King's Flame." *The Star,* 31 December 2001.

"Chains Set Sights on China." *Restaurants & Institutions* 1 August 2001.

Darden Restaurants Inc. Annual Report 2001. Available from http://www.darden.com.

Draper, Deborah J., ed. *Business Rankings Annual.* Detroit: Thomson Gale, 2004.

Foodservice Intelligence. "Foodservice Intelligence News: Industry Needs to Innovate to Serve Adventurous Customers." January 2002. Available from http://www.fsintelligence.com.

"Free-for-All in Food Services Pushes Menu Prices Down." *The Nikkei Weekly,* 3 September 2001.

Friedman, Amanda Mosle. "Monetary Shift Spells Unity in 'Euro-land.'" *Nation's Restaurant News,* 6 August 2001.

Gallinger, Jason. "Independent Restaurants Are Not Ready to Be Swallowed Whole by Chains." *Pittsburgh Business Times,* 27 October 2000. Available from http://www.bizjournals.com.

Gallun, Alby. "McDonald's Sizzling, but Will It Last?" *Crain's Chicago Business,* 26 April 2004.

Gauthier, Roselyne. "Competitive, But Lucrative: France's Food Service Industry." *AgExporter,* October 2000.

Goodman, Ellen. "Burger Nation." *The Washington Post,* 10 February 2001.

"Hoover's Company Capsules." 2004. Available from http://www.hoovers.com.

Hutchcraft, Chuck. "Something in the Air." *Restaurants & Institutions,* 15 August 2001.

Jargon, Julie. "McDonald's Wants Own Piece of Hot Deli Sandwich Market." *Crain's Chicago Business,* 26 July 2004.

"KFC and McDonald's Battle for China's Fast Food Market." *Asia Africa Intelligence Wire,* 8 January 2004.

Lazich, Robert S., ed. *Market Share Reporter.* Detroit: Thomson Gale, 2004.

Leung, Shirley. "Fast-Food Chains Upgrade Menus, and Profits, with Pricey Sandwiches." *The Wall Street Journal Online,* 5 February 2001. Available from http://www.wsj.com.

———. "McDonald's Profit Sinks 40%, Weakened by Global Slump." *The Wall Street Journal Online,* 25 January 2001. Available from http://www.wsj.com.

———. "Tricon Raises 2002 Earnings Outlook On Higher Sales and Multi-Branding." *The Wall Street Journal Online,* 11 February 2002. Available from http://www.wsj.com.

———. "Wendy's Sees Its Future Growth In Acquisitions, Joint Ventures." *The Wall Street Journal Online,* 11 February 2002. Available from http://www.wsj.com.

Liddle, Alan J. "2000 Top 100." *Nation's Restaurant News,* 26 June 2000. Available from http://www.nrn.com.

Lyddon, Chris. "McDonald's Makes Big Move to Healthy Food." *just-food.com,* 26 July 2004.

MacArthur, Kate. "Salad, Prime Sandwiches Stem Fast-Food Woes." *Advertising Age,* 28 July 2004.

Morishita, Kaoru. "Menu Makeover." *The Nikkei Weekly,* 16 July 2001.

———. "New Concepts Trump Old-Style Family Restaurants." *The Nikkei Weekly,* 16 July 2001.

"National Restaurant Association, State Restaurant Associations to Joint Venture on Instill Foodservice Portal Website." *US Newswire,* 14 June 2000.

O'Keefe, Brian. "Global Brands." *Fortune,* 26 November 2001.

Papiernik, Richard L. "Industry Sales for 2002 Projected to Hit $407B." *Nation's Restaurant News,* 7 January 2002.

"Restaurant Industry Forecast." *National Restaurant Association,* 2004. Available from http://www.restaurant.org.

"Restaurants and Cafes in China, France, Germany, Japan, UK, US." *Euromonitor,* 2004. Available from http://www.euromonitor.com.

Spielberg, Susan. "Darden Posts 10.7 Percent Sales Jump." *Nation's Restaurant News,* 5 July 2004.

"Study Shows Home Meals on Rise." *DSN Retailing Today,* 19 November 2001.

Tanikawa, Miki. "Japanese Eateries Offer Ready-Made Investments." *International Herald Tribune,* 12 January 2002.

Thorn, Bret. "Down, But Not Out: Despite Years of Turmoil Asian Foodservice Looks to Recapture Its Former Glory." *Nation's Restaurant News,* 26 November 2001.

"Top 100 Companies Ranked by US Foodservice Revenues." *Nation's Restaurant News,* 28 July 2004.

"Tricon Global Posts 28% Gain in Income in 4th Quarter." *The New York Times,* 12 February 2002. Available from http://www.nytimes.com.

Tricon Global Restaurants. *2000 Annual Report,* 2001. Available from http://www.triconglobal.com.

"Twenty-First Century Foodservice: High-Tech Devices Speed Customer Throughput." *Food Service Director,* 15 October 2001.

"UK: Burger King to Open 25 New Outlets in 2004/05." *just-food.com,* 2 June 2004.

"Whitbread Tops Restaurant Survey." *Leisure & Hospitality Business,* 6 September 2001.

SIC 5300

NAICS 452111, 452112, 452990, 452910

RETAIL DEPARTMENT STORES, VARIETY STORES AND GENERAL MERCHANDISE STORES

Department stores carry a diverse line of nonfood merchandise, including general wearing apparel (suits, coats, and dresses), home furnishings (furniture, floor coverings, curtains, draperies, linens, major household appliances), and housewares (table and kitchen appliances, dishes, and utensils). Many department stores offer their own credit lines and various supplemental services as well. Variety stores carry a diverse line of goods in the low-price range. General merchandise stores carry goods similar to department stores, but normally have fewer than 50 employees. For discussion of food retailing, see **Grocery Stores**.

INDUSTRY SNAPSHOT

The retail industry, the second largest industry in the United States in terms of number of establishments and number of employees, enjoyed unprecedented gains in the late 1990s and through 2000. In part, this was due to strong consumer confidence, low interest rates, and high employment levels. Between 1994 and 2000, the retail industry grew rapidly. By late 2000, however, as the United States and much of Europe and Asia were experiencing recession, retailers began to feel the effects of the sluggish global economy, a slowdown in manufacturing, high consumer debt, and job layoffs. The unstable economic environment following the 2001 terrorist attacks, coupled with the rise of Wal-Mart and other discount retailers, pushed many retailers over the financial edge.

By the mid-2000s, as economic recovery was well under way and the retail landscape had improved, the landscape had changed forever. Consumers around the world were showing a preference for discount shopping and a shopping format that allowed them to buy all their goods under one roof. Major department store chains had merged to gain economies of scale in an effort to compete against discounters such as Wal-Mart, or had divested themselves of some businesses in an effort to focus on their core retail undertakings. By the end of 2004, the leading retailer of any kind in the world was U.S.-based Wal-Mart. France's Carrefour followed, the company credited with giving the world the hypermarket format.

In response to marketing pressures, stores restructured internal organizations and changed marketing patterns. Where they could, stores also took advantage of the same new technology that had changed their marketing environment. Department stores were particularly quick to embrace advanced computer technology. The ability to centralize operations, have a complete and up-to-date status of inventory, and get an accurate reading of items purchased were only a few of the data-related advantages offered by computerized point-of-sale systems. Retailers were able to reduce not only their paperwork but also the lead times necessary to update stock. Particularly in the United States, improved logistics led to a shift from standalone stores offering personalized shopping assistance to mega-chains, which were able to bring identical merchandise into nearly identical mall stores at competitive prices.

BACKGROUND AND DEVELOPMENT

The modern department store has it roots in the U.S. mail-order catalog business that flourished in the nineteenth century. With catalogs offering quality merchandise at competitive prices, the United States pioneered the concept of self-service retailing. The first true "department" stores may have been the general stores and trading posts that sprung up in the small towns of the frontier United States, supplying locals with every necessity from sewing needles to plowshares. In the East, New York City saw the first urban department stores establish themselves as early as 1846. Although their primary business came from the city's elite, early urban merchants wanted to expand operations to people of all classes. While accepted marketing practices of the time consisted of holding goods behind a counter and bringing them forth on request, these new outlets openly displayed merchandise on floor racks to encourage browsing. Parallel retail development had occurred in a number of European countries by the mid-nineteenth century, but the global significance of the U.S. retail industry probably owes its existence to the steady growth and westward settlement—which just happened to come at a time that U.S. families on the East Coast were being introduced to the availability of, heretofore, unimagined luxuries and conveniences.

Richard Sears, who had the innovative concept of expanding mail-order business into catalog sales—and eventually into retail outlets—is credited with the creation of the modern department store. In 1886 Sears, then a railroad station agent, bought a shipment of watches. He proceeded to mail out these watches to purchasers, and the R.W. Sears Watch Company was born. Sears advertised for a watchmaker to help him support the growing business, and in 1887 Sears hired Alvah C. Roebuck. Their early catalogs advertised only watches and jewelry. However, in 1889 the pair sold the watch business in a move that was a precursor to real growth. After two years without an established company identity, in 1891 a new mail-order firm came into being, and, in 1893 that firm formally became Sears, Roebuck and Company. In 1896 the company produced its first general catalog and brought low prices and money-back guarantees to its primary customer base—farmers who had previously been vulnerable to the idiosyncrasies of local general stores.

The success of Sears and other pioneer U.S. department stores caught the attention of the global industry. Similar operations sprung up around the world, often from widely diverse beginnings. In the United Kingdom, a Russian refugee named Michael Marks sold out of an open stall in the market square in Leeds until 1894, when he formed a partnership with cashier Tom Spencer. Marks and Spencer broke new ground for retailers by buying directly from manufacturers, eliminating the middleman and reducing cost of goods and time to market, at the same time. In Japan, Takshimaya had been a clothing retail outlet as early as 1831. In 1922, the company initiated full department store operations. G.J. Coles & Coy, the forerunner to today's Coles Myer, was a variety store that expanded to serve remote areas throughout Australia. As other major department stores followed a similar pattern of expansion, the largest stores in each nation often based development specifically on the U.S. department store concept. Both Coles Myer and Japan's Ito-Yokado blatantly modeled their businesses after U.S.-style stores, and they were not alone.

The concept of large-scale, organized credit service began in 1911, when Sears offered payment plans to farmers for large mail-order purchases. By the 1920s, layaway installment plans were common, and their practicality was emphasized by the lean years of the Depression and wartime shortages. In a time when plastic credit cards were not part of the world's culture, the introduction of department store charge plates not only made purchasing easier for budget-conscious customers, but at the same time these store cards, usable only in the issuing store, were a great incentive to customer loyalty.

In the affluent years following World War II, most department stores turned to upscale clients and merchandise, relegating low-end bargains to "bargain basements" and occasional sales. This created a marketing gap into which discount operations such as Kmart (an outgrowth of S.S. Kresge's "five and dime" stores) quickly moved to fill. In 1962, Wal-Mart came on the scene, with expansion remaining slow (only 15 stores) until the company went public in 1970. By 1980, the company had grown to include 276 stores in 11 states with revenues of US$1 billion. Rapid growth began in the 1980s at the end of which the company had grown to 1,400 stores with revenues of US$26 billion. Once it had such large buying power behind it, the company was able to introduce just-in-time ordering of merchandise. In its efforts to keep prices low, Wal-Mart established a computer-based inventory system that monitored sales of individual products and thus inventory. When inventory levels got low, the computer system would advise suppliers to ship out more product. Wal-Mart cut down on its storage needs and did not find itself faced with product consumers did not want. This was to revolutionize the retail industry and make it increasingly difficult for smaller companies to remain competitive as they did not have the ability to demand just-in-time delivery.

By the 1980s, department stores, per se, were suffering badly from their earlier marketing errors. Beset by newer department stores, specialty stores, discounters, and mail-order houses, the classic firms went through a testing time of leveraged buyouts, mergers, and acquisitions. Surviving stores adjusted in-house operations to reduce cost and broaden their customer bases and in doing so lost portions of their traditional market. This state of flux continued into the 1990s, when yet another new competitor was introduced—technology. By 2000 it became evident the survivors of the retail industry had recognized the potential of e-commerce.

Shifts in market positions during the first half of the 1990s prompted retailers to adopt several competitive countermeasures. They experimented with downsizing and consolidation, merchandise mix changes, more consumer services, and greater use of advanced technologies, such as quick response systems, to control inventory costs and increase productivity. Electronic data interchange (EDI) allowed purchasing departments to institute store warehousing with a minimum of hard copy paper trail. Malls, which surrounded retail department stores with competing specialized retail outlets, also provided the same department stores with a ready supply of shoppers. Foreign markets, particularly those in emerging nations such as China, India, and smaller countries on the Pacific Rim and in Latin America, beckoned. In 1998, the United States' National Retail Federation was salivating at the prospect of a reopened China and urged its membership to lobby the government for retention of China's most-favored-nation (MFN) trade status.

Several demographic changes during the 1990s also contributed to a shift in retail strategies. The typical retail customer of the 1990s was significantly different than the retail customer of the preceding decade. One striking change was the decline in the number of households composed of married couples. In 1980 married households comprised 60.8 percent of the retail market segment. By 1991 this percentage had decreased to 55.3 percent. Not surprisingly, during this same period the number of people living alone increased. This demographic shift influenced buying habits and forced retailers to respond with appropriate marketing and products. The renewed popularity of catalog sales may have been caused, in part, by the busy schedules of individuals living alone or in single-parent households. But these were not the full-line catalogs of the previous century. Approaching 2000, the catalog image had changed. No longer did the price-conscious, commodity-crammed tome represent the direction of the market. In fact, 1992 saw patriarch Sears mail out its last full-line catalog. Instead, catalogs, even those that covered relatively broad product lines, began to have "image." Dime-store-like wares were sold from convenient, pocket-sized booklets, by firms like Fingerhut and Lillian Vernon. In 1998, it was easy for stay-at-home shoppers to glance at exterior catalog format and differentiate immediately between offerings of rugged outerwear that came from Eddie Bauer and L.L. Bean and the seductive lingerie available through Victoria's Secret. Catalogs proved a good way to globalize a retail market as well. Curio shops in Europe used their charm to capitalize on U.S. fascination for travel and things from abroad, even as U.S. companies extended their mailings to include an increasingly broader geographical area.

In the 1990s, the population's increasing familiarity with the Internet combined with an increase in the number of teenagers and young adults, and analysts predicted that the first years of the twenty-first century would represent a boom for "storeless" shopping. Direct retail sales, which included telemarketing and temporary exhibits with door-to-door sales, topped US$22 billion in 1997. Interactive television shopping channels and Internet retail pages both anticipated increased business as the year 2000 approached. By 1997, television-based shopping had hit a plateau at a disappointing US$4.5 billion annually. The relatively poor performance of television shopping networks was tied to the sequential nature of its offerings. It simply took a long time to shop that way. On the Internet, however, a click of the mouse placed the shopper in the store he favored, a second click put the desired product in a "shopping basket," and a final click confirmed the purchase. In the late 1990s, department store Web pages could be both an enticement to investigate a store itself and a convenient place to shop online. In 1997, the fledgling Internet marketing industry stood at US$2.4 billion annually and was growing rapidly, fueled by the popularity of retail pages belonging to specialty bookstores and computer manufacturers.

One reaction to competition of any kind caused the retail industry to seek new ways to advertise product. Critics referred to the marketing tactics of the late 1990s as a "promotion frenzy." Certainly, the number and frequency of in-store sales increased dramatically between 1980 and 2000. Virtually anything that could serve as a differentiator was tried. Newspaper coupons offered discounts. Stores opened at odd hours. Christmas and other holiday sales began months in advance of the festival date. Nordstrom department stores capitalized on its upscale status, advertising almost excessive customer care. Other stores remained regional, marketing to the audience they knew best—and did so with some success. Restricting themselves to the south central United States, Dillard's Inc. and rival Proffitt's Inc. perked along quietly, together taking away US$10 or US$12 billion each year from larger national rivals.

Sometimes the differentiator was something bizarre. Ultimate among upscale promoters, giant retailer Neiman Marcus sold one-of-a-kind collectibles, extravaganza events, and monogrammed jet planes—all available through either store or catalog. Other times, the difference was something understated and conservative. Harrod's in Oxford Street, Knightsbridge, and London, simply displayed the best goods for the best people, insisting on proper attire for shoppers and refusing to sell to those of whom it did not approve. Although Harrod's-sponsored duty-free shops graced airports around the world, sedately presiding at its traditional Knightsbridge address, this paragon of upscale stores bore an unexportable level of prestige.

Until the latter part of the twentieth century, few retailers attempted to expand into foreign markets. However, the easing of investment restrictions in some foreign countries and the emerging trend of establishing affiliated firms in other markets, characterized this new era in retailing. In the mid-1990s, the countries with the largest department stores were the United States, Japan, Great Britain, Australia, and France. Of these stores, those catering to increasingly global markets included Marks & Spencer Plc., Ito-Yokado, J.C. Penney, and Coles Myer. Responding to increasing pressure from rival retail outlets, television and the Internet, industry voices pressed for further global expansion to exploit an untapped world market made up of audiences less vulnerable to high-technology competition.

As the year 2000 approached, it became increasingly apparent that those retail stores and chains that were in good economic health were those that combined increased value for money spent with a newly awakened customer consciousness. Stores that developed their own "store brands"—various private-label lines of goods—also enjoyed greater assurance of repeat customers.

By the early 2000s, consumer trends leaned toward frugality and value. As consumers sought more value, they tended to abandon department stores in favor of discount stores. In the late 1990s and early 2000s, consumers also flocked to warehouse and wholesale clubs, which feature products sold in bulk at much lower prices. By the end of 2001, warehouse clubs claimed a US$70 billion share of an already tight retail industry. Warehouse shopping outlets grew at a rate of 10 percent annually, twice as fast as the rest of the retail industry.

The U.S. economy, in a recession since the first quarter of 2001, resulted in a slowdown of manufacturing, rising energy prices, job layoffs, and rising consumer debt, all of which posed challenges to the retail industry. The industry was plagued with a number of bankruptcies, most notably Montgomery Wards, Ames Department Stores, Casual Male Corp., eToys, Bradlees, Stern's, and Kmart. Not bankrupt, but facing difficulty and closures in 2002, were J.C. Penney, Nordstroms Inc., Saks Inc., Microwarehouse, and Big Lots Inc.

Montgomery Wards filed for bankruptcy in 2001, for the second time in just two years, and closed all 258 locations. The sluggish 2000 holiday shopping season failed to provide enough earnings to keep the company from bankruptcy. Bradlees Corp. closed its 105 retail locations the same year, when the chain could not keep pace with Wal-Mart and Target in the New England states. Kohl's department stores bought 15 of the closed locations and Wal-Mart and Home Depot snatched up 10. Months later, Stern's, owned by Federated Department Stores, closed all locations in February 2001.

Kmart filed for Chapter 11 bankruptcy protection early in 2002, after two lackluster holiday shopping seasons and several years of economic instability. The company had upgraded some 100 stores nationwide to Super Kmarts, adding full service grocery and perishable items. However, the expansion could not address the company's inefficiency and instability. At the same time Kmart announced the bankruptcy filings, it also began examining which underperforming stores would close, and before emerging from Chapter 11 in May 2003, Kmart had closed 600 stores.

CURRENT CONDITIONS

During the years 2003 and 2004, the global economy seemed on an upswing, although some countries were still facing economic downturns. Global retailers as a whole were performing better. According to research by Deloitte Touche Tohmatsu, only 6 percent of retailers had reported a net loss in 2003, while more than twice that amount had reported losses in 2001. This improvement had led to an increase in the number of mergers and acquisitions around the world. Perhaps most striking was Kmart's emergence from bankruptcy and its subsequent merger with Sears. Other prominent acquisitions included the May Department Stores' purchase of Marshall Fields in the U.S. and the purchase by Baroness Retail of Debenhams in the United Kingdom.

Retailers were facing new marketing challenges. Developed countries were finding their populations aging, and as a result were beginning to design programs specifically targeting this segment of the market. Consumers were also becoming more accepting of the Internet as a source for their shopping, a trend seen to even greater degree in Europe than in North America. This trend toward online shopping was considered the result of consumers feeling stretched for time, a condition also being reflected in their preference for retailers that provided them with all their shopping needs under one roof. The lines were continuing to be blurred between the various retail sectors. Department stores had merged with grocery stores to form hypermarkets. Wholesalers were being cut out of the middle through the formation of warehouse clubs. This change in store format was being encouraged further by the increasing preference for discount shopping by consumers around the world, a trend expected to continue.

China was considered by most analysts and retail managers to be the area of the world which held the most growth potential. Having begun to allow foreign ownership and investment, the country was positioned for rapid expansion of its market. In 2004, the government removed restrictions requiring foreign investors to partner with existing Chinese companies; foreigners could open stores independently and were no longer restricted in terms of the number of stores they opened. Having established itself as a major exporter of many of the goods produced for sale in the discount stores of foreign markets, retailers had a ready domestic source of product, and growing amounts of disposable income for the domestic population. While many U.S. companies continued to find growth through expansion domestically, there was a continuing trend of many large retailers to expand globally.

While total U.S. retail industry revenues climbed 6 percent to US$300.1 billion, department stores were down by 1 percent over the previous year. In 2004, the top ten U.S. department stores, according to *WWD,* were Wal-Mart, with sales higher than the combined total of the next nine stores on the list, Target, Sears, Kmart, J.C. Penney, Federated, May, TJX, Kohl's, and Dillard's.

RESEARCH AND TECHNOLOGY

Point-of-sale systems used a variety of computerized features to improve the accuracy and efficiency of store operations, including electronic invoicing from wholesaler to dealer, shelf-stocking by the use of bar-coded stickers, and cycle accounting—which replaced massive annual inventory taking by utilizing portable minicomputers to regularly rotate department counts. The use of "quick-response" systems grew rapidly in the 1990s. A quick-response system usually involved a strategic alliance between a retailer and manufacturer and used electronic data interchange (EDI) to issue invoices and payments. EDI permitted system users to track consumer-purchasing patterns, further enhancing the process of supply and demand. The greatest benefits of all quick-response systems included prompt inventory turnover, with fewer out-of-stock situations, speedy customer response capability, and reduced overall operating costs.

Coles Myer, an Australian store, and Japan's Ito-Yokado led the industry in utilization of electronic scanning, and by the late 1990s optical barcode scanners had become commonplace. May Department Stores upgraded its investment and inventory systems, a move that it believed promoted better communication and greater efficiency in restocking its stores. J.C. Penney implemented a state-of-the-art, automated merchandise replenishment system. Penney's variation on factory materials requirement planning (MRP) triggered orders based on projected sales demand, so that stores were constantly stocked with basic merchandise items.

The technology used every day in other industries was quickly embraced by the retail world. Communication by satellite allowed corporate buyers worldwide to communicate easily with department managers. Point-of-sale computer inquiries facilitated customer check cashing, layaway, and package pickup—and virtually all other cross-store communications once handled by pneumatic tube or manual labor.

WORKFORCE

As of 2004, the retail trade division in the U.S. represented about 12.6 percent of all establishments and employed 11.7 percent of all workers. In April 2005, almost 15 million Americans worked in the retail industry, down from a high of 16 million in December 2000, with the average non-supervisory worker earning US$12.08 per hour. Many stores compensated their salespeople using hourly wages, commissions, or a combination of the two. The majority of employees in retail were clerks or managers. Typically benefits were very limited in smaller retail stores. The larger retailers and department stores typically were comparable to other employers and may have included health insurance, vacation time, and other paid time off.

Industry Leaders

Wal-Mart Stores Inc. Wal-Mart is not only the largest retailer of any sort in the world, it is also one of the world's biggest companies, ranking 12th on *Fortune* magazine's list of the 2000 largest global companies in 2005. Wal-Mart is best known for its operation of large discount stores. Including Wal-Mart, Sam's Clubs, and Wal-Mart Supercenters in the count, the company had more than 5,289 stores around the world in 2004, of which 70 percent were in the United States. Outside the United States, company stores flourished in Argentina (11 stores), Brazil (149), Canada (262), China (43), Germany (91), South Korea (16), Mexico (679), Puerto Rico (54), and the United Kingdom (267). Much of the company's growth in the 2000s was the result of the acquisition of existing companies in each country. The company owned about 37 percent of Japanese retail chain Seiyu by the start of 2005, and had plans to exercise warrants bringing its ownership level to 70 percent by 2007.

Wal-Mart founder Samuel Walton opened the first Wal-Mart in Rogers, Arkansas, in 1962. By the end of that decade, Walton and his brother operated 18 Wal-Mart stores and 15 Ben Franklin franchises in small towns throughout Arkansas, Missouri, Kansas, and Oklahoma. Wal-Mart went public in 1970. Initially trading over the counter, in 1972 the company was listed on the New York Stock Exchange. In 1983, Wal-Mart opened its first three Sam's Wholesale Clubs and began its expansion into bigger-city markets. In 1987, the company introduced a new merchandising concept that Walton called Hypermart USA. Hypermarts combined grocery stores and general merchandise markets with services such as restaurants, banking, and videotape rental. Capitalizing on hypermart success, the company introduced several of its own brands, including Sam's American Choice product line, which included beverages, colas, and fruit drinks, and Great Value, initially used for a line of 350 packaged food items in its superstore centers. In 1970, Wal-Mart sales were US$44 million. By January 2005, they totaled more than US$285.2 billion, of which US$56.3 billion was from international operations.

In 2005, Wal-Mart was planning to open 40 to 45 new discount stores and 240 to 250 new Supercenters, with relocations or expansions accounting for 160 of the new Supercenters. In addition, the company planned to open 30 to 40 Sam's Clubs. Internationally, 155 to 165 new stores were planned in existing markets.

PPR S.A. PPR Group (formerly known as Pinault-Printemps-Redoute) began in the timber industry in 1963, but through its expansion policy, the company found itself focusing on retail and luxury goods in 2003. After buying 44 percent of Gucci in 1999 of which it owned almost 100 percent by 2005, the company began to withdraw from its business-to-business lines and from consumer credit. In 2004, the company posted sales of approximately US$30.6 billion, of which 60 percent was derived from its retail division. With a presence in 65 countries, 56 percent of its revenues are derived from outside of its home base of France.

Target Corp. Target stores anchor the Target Corporation's retail empire. Formerly Dayton-Hudson, Target Corp. was the number two discount retailer in the United States, second only to Wal-Mart, in 2004. With more than 1,300 stores, Target had US$46.8 billion in sales and controlled about 9 percent of the market.

J.L. Hudson's men's clothing store was established in 1881 in Detroit, Michigan, by owner Joseph L. Hudson. In ten years (by 1891) Hudson's had become the largest U.S. retailer of men's clothing. Diversifying to include all sorts of wearing apparel and household furnishings after World War II, both Hudson's and Minnesota's Dayton stores (founded in 1902), realized that the suburbs would soon replace city centers as major shopping areas. In parallel efforts, the two retailers began to build suburban shopping centers in the Detroit and Minneapolis areas. In 1956, Dayton built the world's first, fully enclosed shopping mall, Southdale, in Edina (a suburb of Minneapolis, Minnesota). Two years earlier, in 1954, Hudson's opened Northland Shopping Center in Southfield, Michigan, at that time the largest shopping center in the world. The corporation's low-end and specialty merchandising began in 1962, when Hudson's opened its first Target discount store and, four years later, when B. Dalton Bookstores were created, again by Hudson's.

In 1969, Dayton-Hudson Corporation was formed by the merger of Dayton Department Stores and J.L. Hudson's. Hoping to emulate the success of Target stores, in 1978 the corporation bought California-based Mervyn's, department stores and throughout the next two decades extended Mervyn's locations across the country. In 1990, the next Dayton-Hudson acquisition was the prestigious, century-and-a-half old Marshall Field's department store—one of Chicago's biggest retailers. With the help of Marshall Field's, Dayton-Hudson pioneered retailing's entry into the new world of "infomercials." Its 30-minute program, called "Marshall Field's Presents," aired in 30 national markets—despite serving only six of those markets. After failing to turn around the companies, Target sold both Mervyn's and Marshall Field's in 2004.

Marks and Spencer Group LLC. Tracing its roots back to a Leeds, England market stall in 1884, in 2005 the department store chain, Marks & Spencer, operated 375 stores and served 10 million customers each week. In addition, the company franchised 155 stores in 28 countries in Europe, the Middle East, Asia, and the Far East. The company entered the Canadian market in the 1970s but failed to gain a strong foothold in this market. By 1999, it had closed all its Canadian-based stores. Marks & Spencer continued to struggle financially, and began to sell off some of its non-U.K. based assets, including 220 Brooks Brothers clothing stores in the United States and its stores in France. In 2004, it reported revenues of approximately US$15.2 billion with U.K.-based sales up 3.8 percent. In late May 2005, company executives announced that profits had fallen by almost 20 percent. Industry experts were claiming that this was because the stores were increasingly being seen as having old-fashioned product lines, with women's fashions being particularly hard hit. The company was experiencing mild increases in sales of its food lines, and was planning expansion in this area.

Kmart Corporation and Sears, Roebuck and Co. Sears, Roebuck began in Minnesota in 1886 with Richard W. Sears and his R.W. Sears Watch Company. In two years' time, Sears had published his first mail-order catalog, an 80-page document advertising watches and jewelry. In two more years, the catalog had grown to 322 pages and included some full-line items—clothes, jewelry, and durable goods, such as sewing machines and bicycles. For the next hundred years, Sears catalogs brought modern retail products to every region of the country. By the mid-1960s, Sears posted US$1 billion in monthly sales, but in 1991 a national recession and intense competition caused Sears serious difficulties. Earnings for the entire year of 1991 were just US$200 million. The following year, Sears catalog was no more, and the company began a process of reconstruction and reorganization that was still ongoing in 1998.

In a remarkable turnaround, the company repositioned its automotive services to concentrate on tire and battery replacement, rather than general repairs. It opened new HomeLife furniture stores to provide space in the main stores for clothes, and it introduced a new cosmetic line. In the 1990s, it operated HomeLife, Sears, Parts America, National Tire and Battery, Orchard Supply Hardware, and other retail stores in the United States, in addition to catalog and Sears-stores in Canada, and Sears-stores in Mexico. In 1992, it was estimated that one in thirty Americans had worked for Sears in some capacity at some time. Company sales totaled US$54.83 billion in 1994. However, when profit margins narrowed, Sears looked to restructure again, aiming the new reorganization at methods that would improve dollar returns for corporate shareholders. Employee counts were reduced, and stores were remodeled to increase customer appeal. In the summer of 1998 Sears continued to downsize. The company sold its interest in Britain's prestigious Selfridges Department Store, as well as its British Shoe business, and planned to opt out of the United Kingdom's Freemans mail-order system. Domestically, Sears divested itself of several other successful—but tangential—operations, including Allstate Insurance, Dean Witter financial services, and its Discover credit card.

In 2004, Sears had nearly 2,4000 Sears-branded and affiliated stores in Canada and the United States. That year, the company posted revenues of US$36.1 billion, down 12 percent from the previous year when it had acquired Land's End. Sales continued to decline, even as competitors were bouncing back.

In March 2005, Sears joined with Kmart Corporation, making the combined company the third largest U.S. retailer. Kmart faced stiff competition from Wal-Mart and after attempting to redefine its niche, the company filed for bankruptcy in 2002. In 2003, it emerged from bankruptcy and began a major restructuring plan for its then 2,100 store. In 2004, Kmart's store count had dropped to almost 1,500 stores, 400 of which it was planning to convert to the Sears name.

Kmart operates in the United States, Canada, Puerto Rico, and the Czech Republic. The corporation grew from a Detroit five-and-dime store, opened in 1899 by Sebastian Kresge. Kresge enjoyed quick success, selling jewelry, housewares, and personal goods. By 1912, there were 85 Kresge stores producing annual sales of US$10.3 million. In the late 1950s, food grew into the largest single department at the Kresge stores, and in 1962, the first Kresge discount store was opened and baptized "Kmart." The Kmart stores were an instant success; by 1963, there were 63 facilities, and by 1966 that number had increased to 122.

The late 1970s, however, witnessed the rise of new competitors with more inviting stores and specialty stores that took over Kmart's share of the firm's staples, such as sporting goods, drugs, and personal grooming items. Changes in public taste showed up in lagging profits, which sank 28 percent in 1980. Kmart responded by remodeling existing stores and stocking them with more fashionable merchandise and installing a computer system to monitor inventories, orders, and shipments. In the mid-1980s, Kmart added several celebrity spokespeople to its payroll, including actress Jaclyn Smith, racecar driver Mario Andretti, and caterer Martha Stewart. Despite Martha Stewart's legal troubles in 2004, including a conviction for lying about stock sales, Kmart was committed to the Martha Stewart Everyday brand, a series of products that was instrumental in the rise of Kmart sales in the 1990s. Profits for 1987 rose 19 percent, and by 2001 total sales reached US$37.03 billion, but the discounter continued to struggle for market share. In the 1990s Wal-Mart made decisive inroads on Kmart's customer base, and the firm continued to lose sales to niche stores as well. Kmart management concluded that the chain needed to diversify its product line to offer one-stop shopping across the traditional retail boundaries. Kmart's plan was to convert many of its existing stores to Big Kmart outlets, which featured a limited grocery line in addition to general merchandise, and Super Kmart stores, which offered an extensive line of groceries along with amenities like a bakery, a deli, and in-store banking. The new formats also highlighted trendier merchandise in contrast to the chain's established product line, which was viewed by some as dowdy and unfashionable.

Carrefour S.A. In 2004, the largest retailer outside of the United States was France's Carrefour S.A., which had 6,000 stores worldwide. By size, Carrefour was only behind Wal-Mart. Carrefour's 2003 sales reached more than US$88.47 billion, drawn from overseas operations in Argentina, Brazil, Portugal, Spain, Taiwan, and the United States, as well as its Paris headquarters. Established in 1959, Carrefour was considered the originator of the 100,000-square-foot hypermarket that became its trademark in Europe and other parts of the world. Carrefour hypermarkets offered produce, groceries, clothing, consumer goods, and household appliances in a large, open marketplace environment. Globally, the hypermarkets provided a variety of products and services: minimarkets, gasoline, insurance, home improvements, furniture and electrical appliances, vacation packages, and credit cards. The company also operated a number of discount stores and invested in a variety of products from frozen foods to real estate. Carrefour's interests extended to a number of U.S. retailers, including involvement with Office Depot and PETsMART.

MAJOR COUNTRIES IN THE INDUSTRY

United States. In 2005, the United States continued to hold the dominant position in the retail industry. Eight of the top ten retail companies of all types globally were American.

Wal-Mart was simply the largest retailer of any kind, anywhere, and was the largest retail employer as well, employing 1.7 million people around the world at the start of 2005. The department stores market was valued by Euromonitor to be worth US$118.4 million in 2004, with variety stores adding a further US$412.1 billion. With 32.8 percent of the warehouse and superstore market in 2003, Wal-mart's next four biggest competitors could not match it in terms of sales, even if one was to combine all their sales. However, they were multi-billion dollar companies in their own rights. In fact, Costco was actually bigger than Wal-Mart as a wholesale club operator, beating out Wal-Mart's Sam's Club stores. Target Corporation was the country's second-ranking discount retailer, operating in 47 U.S. states in 2005. In terms of the department store sector of the retail industry, this remained somewhat consolidated in the U.S. in 2003, with the top five players (Sears Roebuck, JCPenney, Federated, The May Department Stores and Dillards) accounting for 64.6 percent of the market. Size seemed to matter to the management of the department store sector, with mergers and acquisitions of smaller stores continuing. However, the market was expected to experience several more years of declining sales. Much of this decline would be the result of the increasing influence of discount stores on the market place. Variety stores, such as Wal-Mart and Target, were expected to remain the largest market sector, with growth projected at 32 percent by 2008.

Japan. Throughout the 1990s, it appeared unlikely that there would be any significant growth in the number of Japanese department stores, although the *Large Store Law* attempted to regulate their development. Under this law, any store with more than 500 but less than 1,000 square meters was permitted to be opened only by notification to the government. Large-scale stores were allowed to stay open until 8:00 p.m. Additionally, such stores could stay open until 9:00 p.m. up to 60 days per year and could close only 24 days per year without reporting to the government. The Japanese department store industry was expected to continue to compete on the basis of differentiation between stores and companies. Thus, the number of department stores was limited, and each was encouraged to retain its own identity. Any significant increase in Japanese domestic competition seemed unlikely. The only danger was to Japanese department stores that limited business, as did Takashimaya, to the top end of the consumer market. These were challenged by leading superstore retailers—notably Ito-Yokado—which were steadily improving retail product quality. The superstores were larger, more diverse, and arguably more efficient than the traditional department store, and lacked only the tradition itself that earmarked the older firms.

But, the 1990s also saw the deregulation of Japan's retail industry. Initially foreign investors entered the market through joint ventures with existing Japanese companies, but by the end of the 1990s, foreign companies were setting up on their own. Membership clubs offered by Costco and hypermarkets introduced by France's Carrefour caught the attention of consumers. In 2002, Wal-Mart bought controlling interest in The Seiyu Ltd. Although Seiyu was a grocery chain, Walmart's variety store format was sure to take effect on the company.

The late 1990s and early 2000s brought much disruption to Japan's retail sector. Like its counterparts in the U.S., department stores faced steep competition from discounters. However, by 2003, both large department stores and discounters faced continuing problems, with sales declines expected to continue through 2008. The department store sector in Japan was highly concentrated, with the top three companies (Daimaru, Takashimaya, and Mitsukoshi) accounting for 71.8 percent of the market. Japanese consumers prefer large hypermarkets, very large commercial enterprises that are a combination of a department store and a supermarket. Euromonitor was predicting that hypermarkets would overtake department stores as the largest sector in the retail industry in Japan, making up 42.8 percent of the market by 2008.

France. The French consumer continued to have a love affair with department stores—two in particular: Rallye and Galeries Lafayette. Together these two companies controlled more than three-quarters of the department store retail market in France in 2002. The Galeries Lafayette store in Paris had the highest sales volume of any retailer in Europe. Valued at US$10.4 billion in 2003, the market was expected to continue on its upward swing, increasing 14 percent by 2008.

The French company Carrefour is attributed with the creation of the hypermarket, where a supermarket is placed under the same roof as a department store. This concept has been copied successfully by many other companies, including Wal-Mart, and has been responsible for turning Carrefour into the second largest retailer in the world.

United Kingdom. As in many other developed countries, the department store sector continued to face intense competition from discount retailers in the mid-2000s. Once the leading retailer in the U.K., Marks & Spencer had been forced to sell off most of its overseas ventures in the late 1990s and early 2000s. The year 2005 found it struggling with declining sales and profits, and a lackluster consumer image.

However, other industry players were showing signs of growth and expansion. Debenhams, noted for its fashion departments, showed sales increases of more than 9 percent in 2003, and was a franchisor of stores in the Middle East, Indonesia, Denmark, Sweden, Iceland, and the Czech Republic. In 2005, it planned to open new stores in Saudi Arabia and Dubai, as well as Cyprus and Indonesia. John Lewis Partnership, so named because its 63,000 permanent staff members are partners in the business, operated 26 high-end department stores in 2005, and owned the high-end grocery store chain Waitrose. Despite their success, the Allders department store chain of 45 stores fell into bankruptcy in early 2005 after it failed to find a buyer for its company. In the following months, other major chains bought up some locations while many others closed their doors.

The British department store market, which was valued by Euromonitor at US$13.6 billion in 2003, was expected to grow by 10.8 percent by 2008. Although Wal-Mart had made major inroads into the market through its purchase of grocery chain ASDA, consumers seemed reluctant to accept the Wal-Mart brand name as it was seen to promote an American lifestyle on the British consumer. However, ASDA was gradually converting its format over to the hypermarket style popular in the U.S., and most of the company's advertising mimicked that presented in America.

China. With its huge population and increasing openness to foreign investment, China was being actively pursued by retailers. Although in 2003 its department store market was worth about half that of the U.S., the market was expected to grow from US$58.2 billion to US$102.5 billion by 2008. The market remained highly fragmented, with the five leading companies being domestic. As a group, Shanghai No.1 Department Store, Dashang, Beijing Hualian, Shanghai Yuyuan, and Beijing Wangfujing held less than 12 percent of the market. Major inroads were being made by foreign companies in the wholesale club market of the retail trade. Wal-Mart entered the Chinese marketplace in 1996 and by 2005 was operating 40 supercenters, three Sam's Clubs and two Neighbourhood Markets. Having already become a source of manufacturing for the goods many foreign retailers sell, China has a ready supply of domestically produced products to feed into its growing retail marketplace.

FURTHER READING

"2005 Global Powers of Retailing." Deloitte Touche Tohmatsu, January 2005. Available from http://www.deloitte.com.

Burrows, Dan. "Carrefour Sales Up, Cuts Forecast." *WWD,* 9 July 2004.

———. "Discounters Don't Disappoint." *WWD,* 20 February 2004.

Desjardins, Doug. "Style Inhabits the Unlikeliest Places." *DSN Retailing Today,* 5 April 2004.

Draper, Deborah J., ed. *Business Rankings Annual.* Detroit: Thomson Gale, 2004.

"Engineering and Construction Services in Australia, China, France, Germany, Japan, South Korea, UK, US." *Euromonitor,* August 2004. Available from http://www.majormarketprofiles.com.

Hogsett, Don. "Penney Sees Profits Soar 173 Percent." *Home Textiles Today,* 24 May 2004.

"Hoover's Company Capsules." 2004. Available from http://www.hoovers.com.

Howell, Debbie. "Kmart's Got Cash, But Then What?" *DSN Retailing Today,* 19 July 2004.

"International Trade Statistics." 2003. Available from http://www.wto.org.

Jacobson, Greg. "Will Sears Grand Be Part of the Solution?" *MMR,* 11 August 2003.

Jones, Sandra. "How Sears Came Down with Seasonal Disorder." *Business 2.0,* July 2004.

Kalish, Ira. "Global Consumer Business: Strategies for a Challenging World." Deloitte Touch Tohmatsu, 2004. Available from http://www.deloitte.com.

"Kmart and Martha Stewart Living Omnimedia Have Agreed to Extend Through 2009 Their Long-Term Distribution Agreement for the Everyday Label." *DSN Retailing Today,* 17 May 2004.

"Kmart: Martha Stewart Still 'Valued Brand Partner.'" *DSN Retail Fax,* 19 July 2004.

Lazich, Robert S., ed. *Market Share Reporter.* Detroit: Thomson Gale, 2004.

Moses, Alexandra R. "Kmart Files for Chapter 11 Bankruptcy Protection After Key Supplier Cuts Off Shipments." *Detroit Free Press,* 22 January 2002.

"A New Era In Japan's Retailing Market: Deregulation Paves the Way for Inroads by Foreign Groups." The Japan Society of Northern California, 2004. Available from http://www.usajapan.org.

"Retail Industry Trends," Plunkett Research, 2002. Available from http://www.plunkettresearch.com.

Sears, Roebuck and Co. "Sears: Historical Chronology." *Sears, Roebuck and Co. Web Page,* 2002. Available from http://www.sears.com.

Vargas, Melody. "U.S. Retail Sales Rise 6.3 Percent Over Last Year," 14 July 2004. Available from http://retailindustry.about.com.

"The WWD List: Broadline Leaders." *WWD,* 6 May 2004.

SIC 5000, 5100

NAICS 42

WHOLESALERS

The broad wholesale industry generally serves as an intermediary between commercial buyers and sellers of commodities and merchandise. A common example is buying a manufacturer's products and selling them to a retailer. The industry consists of three types of firms: wholesale merchants; manufacturers' sales branches or sales offices; and agents or brokers. Wholesale merchants buy merchandise for resale to three types of resellers: retailers, contractors or professional business users, and other wholesalers. The second group of wholesalers, manufacturers' sales offices, includes separate sales subsidiaries or sales offices maintained by manufacturing, refining, or mining enterprises for the purpose of marketing their products. The third group includes firms that act as agents or brokers in buying merchandise for, or selling merchandise to, individuals or companies on a commission basis.

INDUSTRY SNAPSHOT

With the implementation of automated ordering, shipping, and inventory control systems, wholesalers were able to increase their output and revenues without having to increase their workforces. This technology made the industry more efficient and cost effective. To remain competitive, wholesalers offered retailers the convenience of dealing with one supplier by forming consortia that allowed companies offering complementary products to cooperatively supply their array of goods. In addition, wholesalers started to stock and maintain inventories on their customers' sites, which created an extra value to the customers doing business with wholesalers. Such an emphasis on value derived in part from a trend in retailing toward eliminating wholesale agreements and dealing directly with manufacturers. The U.S. wholesale industry remained one of the largest and most advanced in the world, with US$2.9 trillion in 2003 revenues.

Wholesalers not only buy and sell goods, they also provide a wide range of services designed to add value and facilitate smooth functioning of the market. For retail clients, wholesalers anticipate their needs and demands and stock large quantities of goods at locations convenient to the retailer. Wholesalers assemble shipments, deliver merchandise, extend credit, service goods sold, assist with sales promotion and publicity, and provide marketing information and sales assistance. In support of retailers, they also offer billing, collections, and record keeping services. For the manufacturer, wholesalers buy, sell, and store merchandise, finance production by purchasing in advance, and reduce risk by screening customers and providing market information.

Wholesalers are a key link between manufacturers and the marketplace—a position that historically gave them enormous power over both their customers and their suppliers. Their ability to anticipate consumer needs and demands, combined with their purchasing power and wide distribution abilities, made many wholesalers much more than mere "middlemen." Wholesalers could influence retail buying decisions, create new markets, and make or break a new product. They were so powerful that producers often had to adjust manufacturing priorities, product design and development, and marketing strategies in accordance with the wishes of their wholesale customers. However, manufacturers and retailers were not resigned to the power of the wholesalers. By the 1990s major manufacturers and retailers alike were actively seeking ways to bypass wholesalers, a movement facilitated by new advancements in transportation and delivery systems, heightened competition, falling prices, and computerized technologies. Retail giant Wal-Mart started a retail revolution when it demanded just-in-time delivery from suppliers. The rise of electronic commerce in the late 1990s prompted many industry analysts to predict that the Internet would eventually eliminate the need for traditional distributors. However, by the early 2000s most experts had come to view the Internet as a distribution management tool, albeit an unpredictable one.

Under pressure from suppliers and customers, wholesalers saw their market gradually eroded by alternative channels of distribution such as warehouse clubs, mail order, and giant retailers that dealt directly with manufacturers. Costco Wholesale Corporation, for example, buys the majority of its merchandise directly from manufacturers and sells to business and consumer members, earning revenues of more than US$48 billion in 2004. Manufacturers, eager to increase their profit margins, welcomed these new distribution channels, as did price-conscious consumers. This trend was particularly evident in consumer goods, a market that was simultaneously shrinking for wholesalers while also accounting for increased portions of their total sales. These changes were not only apparent in the United States, but also in Europe, Canada, and Japan.

Faced with these challenges, wholesalers were forced to reexamine their competitive strategies, and they began to reorient their services and product mix. Many wholesalers determined that in order to survive they would have to provide value-added services, improve productivity, expand geographically, diversify into new product lines, enlarge existing lines, and develop new markets. Rising competition prompted strategic alliances and consolidation among the largest wholesale and distribution firms. Although the total number of wholesalers continued to fall in the mid-2000s, the market for small niche players that could target specialized needs remained open, and overall employment was expected to rise.

Organization and Structure

Virtually all goods sold in all but the most underdeveloped economies pass through at least one wholesaler. Although under increasing pressure from newly emergent economic and technological forces, the wholesale industry was still one of the largest and most diverse sectors in the economies of most countries.

The trend toward integration of manufacturing, retailing, and wholesaling functions in many industries can make it difficult to develop an accurate overall picture of the wholesale industry. Despite the emergence of some very large global companies, the industry remains extremely fragmented. The wholesale industry sells everything from raw materials such as petroleum, minerals, and forest products, to manufactured goods such as packaged food, automobiles, and consumer electronics. Wholesalers obtain the products they sell from manufacturers, mining operations, agricultural concerns, and other wholesalers. Consequently, the level of wholesale trade activity depends on a wide variety of factors including the health of the economy, international commodity prices, and the rates of growth in employment, income, investment, and trade. Moreover, because wholesalers sell to each other, sales figures generated by the industry are not equivalent to the value of goods it actually handles.

The largest group in the industry is wholesale merchants. This group accounted for roughly 60 percent of all sales and 85 percent of all firms in both the United States and Canada. With the possible exception of Japan, which maintains a rather complicated distribution system compared to most industrial countries, the parallels between wholesale industries in different nations suggest that wholesale merchants accounted for similar shares in other countries.

Wholesale merchants, also known as jobbers, include several subcategories such as industrial distributors, voluntary group wholesalers, exporters, importers, cash-and-carry wholesalers, drop shippers, truck distributors, retailer cooperative warehouses, terminal elevators, cooperative buying associations, assemblers, buyers, and cooperatives engaged in the marketing of farm products. Merchant wholesaling firms are the primary distribution channel for all major products carried by wholesalers, with the exception of motor vehicles and parts.

Merchants are distinguished from brokers because they actually buy and take ownership of the goods they distribute, whereas brokers do not. Agents and commission brokers sell goods on a commission basis and tend to be more specialized than merchant wholesalers. Auction companies, manufacturing agents, food brokers, and import/export agents and brokers all fall into the category of agents and brokers. The types of products most often sold by agents and brokers include farm products, food, petroleum products, apparel, and dry goods.

Manufacturers' sales subsidiaries, on the other hand, are often indistinguishable from merchants in that they also usually "buy" the products they sell from their parent company. Because major international industries such as petroleum refining and automobile manufacturing maintain their own wholesalers, these types of firms, though small in number, account for a sizable portion of total wholesale sales. They are also prominent in the international realm of wholesaling. For example, foreign-owned wholesale establishments in Canada amounted to less than 5 percent of all firms in the late 1990s. However, because these firms were concentrated in the petroleum, automotive, machinery and equipment, hardware, and plumbing and heating products sectors, they accounted for 27 percent of the industry's sales. Of that, about half was generated by U.S.-owned establishments.

The chief function of wholesale merchants is to sell goods to trading establishments; industrial, commercial, institutional, farm, or construction contractors; or professional business users. The chief function of brokers is to bring buyer and seller together. In addition to selling or setting up deals, wholesale establishments often carry out a wide range of other functions including carrying inventory; extending credit; assembling, sorting, and grading goods in large lots; breaking bulk and redistribution into smaller lots; delivery; refrigeration; and various types of promotion such as advertising and label design. Wholesalers may also service, repair, or lease the products they handle.

The number of functions an individual wholesale firm carries out is influenced by several factors, such as the characteristics of the products it sells, the end user, and the structure of the industry in which it sells. Full-service wholesalers such as electrical, pharmaceutical, and hardware wholesalers generally perform all the marketing functions and carry an extensive product line. Limited-function wholesalers carry a more narrow product line and don't include such services as credit or merchandise delivery. Manufacturers' sales subsidiaries usually offer the same mix of functions as full-service wholesale merchants, and are owned by large companies that frequently modify their products and require rapid, accurate information on sales. Sometimes, manufacturers' subsidiaries also sell competitors' products. To be successful, a wholesaler must find the right mix of functions and be able to offer them at a cost lower than its suppliers or customers could achieve on their own.

Specialization in a specific product group such as resources, consumer goods, or industrial goods, is common among all wholesalers whether they are multibillion-dollar nationwide organizations such as the U.S. companies SUPERVALU and C&S Wholesale Grocers, or small rack jobbers which stock and service individual displays or counters at different stores.

Many establishments classified as wholesalers also sell directly to consumers and other businesses. These firms include businesses selling office and store furniture, lumber and building materials, farm supplies, fuel oil, and all types of machinery and equipment. In some cases, the same outlet may conduct what can be considered wholesale and retail activities at the same time by offering different prices depending on the buyer's status. Resellers, for example, may not have to pay sales tax, whereas an end user may. Wholesalers may also own separate retail subsidiaries or divisions that conduct retail trade fed by the company's wholesale operations.

Size is a valued asset in the wholesale industry. The efficiency of both individual companies and the industry as a whole is determined by such factors as economies of scale, links with producers, and the ability to provide customers with the best prices, service, convenience, and quality. Size gives wholesalers buying clout with suppliers and allows them to spread fixed costs over a wider sales base. In the United States and Canada, the industry tends to be more concentrated. The sheer physical size of both nations makes it essential for wholesale firms to be able to capture the economies of scale and resources needed to collect and distribute goods efficiently.

The tendency toward large firms is especially evident in the wholesaling of consumer products, where multibillion-dollar enterprises with strong links to retailers dominate such sectors as food, pharmaceuticals, motor vehicles and parts, hardware supplies, and building products. Major wholesaling firms in this segment often have their own network of corporate stores, franchises, or company-sponsored retail dealerships. In other cases, leading consumer product wholesalers capture markets by forging close links with independent retail chains, franchises, or cooperatives. These structures often prove extremely successful, taking market share away from both the large retailers and the wholesalers with their own retail outlets. For example, 85 percent of retail hardware outlets in Canada are independents associated with a single wholesaler, Home Hardware. To reach these retailers, manufacturers have to sell through Home Hardware. Moreover, by avoiding direct involvement in the retail business, these wholesale firms do not risk offending their clients by directly competing with them. The competitive advantages enjoyed by firms operating in this manner have caused an increasing number of major retailers to convert their own stores into franchises and focus on wholesaling.

Only in the field of industrial products—where the main customers are other businesses and trade contractors—does size play a less prominent role. Because of the diverse range of products they handle and the need for good product knowledge and service, industrial goods wholesalers frequently specialize. Consequently, market share for individual companies is relatively low. Nonetheless, large companies also play a role in this market, particularly in the heavy equipment, farm machinery, electrical, plumbing and heating equipment, and paper products sectors. Vertical integration with manufacturers of these products is also common among some larger firms.

Although the scales are tilted heavily in favor of large firms, many small wholesalers are able to compete successfully by carving out exclusive market niches. High levels of specialization, in-depth product knowledge, and personalized service help smaller wholesalers find and maintain customers. Importing is one area where smaller companies are able to thrive by taking advantage of the rising number of independent boutiques and gift shops that specialize in unique and unusual items from around the world. Major retailers also turn increasingly to wholesalers to handle their import requirements. As global trading patterns evolved and manufacturing became more specialized, wholesalers with knowledge of foreign markets and services were likely to gain an edge on those who relied solely on domestic suppliers.

The implementation of the U.S.-Canadian Free Trade Agreement, and later the North American Free Trade Agreement (NAFTA)—a pact between the United States, Canada, and Mexico—opened up new markets for wholesalers in these countries. American and Canadian wholesalers began to expand into each other's countries and into Mexico. The primary impediment to the establishment of foreign affiliates was investment restrictions in certain countries.

In contrast to the wholesale industries in North America and Europe, which placed a premium on size, efficiency, and economies of scale, Japan's distribution system was extraordinarily complex and inefficient. In 2002 there were 380,000 wholesaler stores in Japan and nearly 1.2 million retailers—both down significantly from the mid-1990s. The Japanese distribution network was diverse and complicated, differing for each product by the size of the producer and end retailer or user. Japan had a greater number of retailers and wholesalers per capita than any other country in the world, and small retail outlets—so-called mom-and-pop shops—accounted for the majority of consumer shopping.

In the early 1980s, in spite of its success in manufacturing and its apparent modernity, much of Japan's cultural and social life remained rooted in its agricultural past. Unlike Western cities with their identifiable core and surrounding suburbs, large Japanese cities resembled an assemblage of small villages, each with their own business districts and close community ties. This village structure was reflected in the distribution system, with numerous small wholesalers supplying numerous small retailers within very narrowly defined geographic regions. Further complicating the Japanese system were the high price of land and restrictive laws that prevented large stores from being opened without approval from neighboring small merchants. With one in five Japanese employed in the distribution system, small merchants were a powerful political force capable of stalling any attempts by the government to give more leeway to large businesses. Moreover, with price coordination pervasive in Japan, consumers had no incentive to favor large stores over small stores, since even "discount prices" were almost identical. As a result, according to Charles J. McMillan in *The Japanese Industrial System*, pricing and retailing strategies largely regulate the relationships in distribution channels. For consumers, this meant that Japanese prices were frequently among the highest in the world because of the many layers in the distribution channel. McMillan argued that alleged dumping by Japanese manufacturers in overseas markets had more to do with the greater efficiency of foreign distribution systems than with any deliberate attempt by Japanese manufacturers to gain market share.

By the 1990s signs of change became evident in the Japanese distribution system. Pressure from foreign exporters and rising consumer dissatisfaction with inflated prices led to increased efforts to modernize the system, particularly on the part of manufacturers, importers, and large department stores. According to a report released by Japan's Economic Planning Agency, the simplification of Japan's distribution system in the late 1990s was considered a key factor in the decrease in consumer prices in both 1998 and 1999. The impetus for reform in the distribution industry was "heated competition among discount businesses in a number of industries," according to a July 2000 article in *Yomiuri Shimbun*.

In many developing countries, the system of wholesale trade is highly fragmented. Small companies deliver a variety of goods to retailers, selection often being depended on availability and bargaining ability. Many distribution systems are still government controlled, with inefficiencies in terms of networks, labor, and product flow.

Background and Development

In its most rudimentary form, wholesaling referred to the buying of goods from the manufacturer or producer and the subsequent selling of those goods to retail stores and other businesses, which in turn sold them to the public. Wholesaling also involved buying goods from other wholesalers and reselling them to yet other wholesalers. It could involve buying goods from one supplier, exchanging those goods for goods from another supplier, and then selling the newly acquired goods. This "middleman" function evolved largely because of the great differences in needs, market size, and product availability in different regions of the world.

Although primitive forms of wholesaling may have existed as far back as the first urban civilizations of the Middle East, the world's first true wholesalers and distributors were probably the ancient Phoenicians. Like the Dutch and the British after them, this seafaring people built a civilization based almost entirely on trade. From ancient Britain to Judea, the Phoenicians transported and traded the goods of the ancient world. By the time of the Romans, trade had become even more geographically extensive. According to M.P. Charlesworth in *Trade-Routes and Commerce of the Roman Empire*, Roman business people had journeyed to Ireland and traveled to the edge of the Baltic Sea, made contact with the Scythians of the Tauric Chersonese, conducted transactions with the Chinese traders beyond the lonely Stone Tower of Tashkurgan, traded in the markets of India, and exchanged goods with the Aethiopians.

Unlike modern wholesalers, these early traders seldom specialized. They left Rome carrying whatever commodity they thought would be in demand elsewhere and traded it in some distant market for another product that could be expected to yield a profit in Rome or could be traded elsewhere for yet another product. Trade continued in much the same fashion for centuries. Slave traders in the eighteenth century operated in a similar way, buying stocks of cheap cloth and jewelry in England, exchanging it for slaves in Africa, reselling those slaves at a substantial profit in the Americas, then buying cotton and other goods for resale in the home market at even greater profits.

Although all contemporary trading professions descended from these early merchants, those that most closely resembled them, according to James E. Vance, Jr. in *The Merchant's World: The Geography of Wholesaling*, were the wholesalers. Wholesaling was the driving force behind the expansion of the mercantile economy, opening up new continents and pushing into frontier areas. Not surprisingly, the art of wholesaling was perfected in the new nations of North America. Faced with scattered, thinly spread populations, yet desiring to achieve a standard of living comparable to that enjoyed by their European brethren, North Americans organized an efficient, large-scale wholesale trading system that Vance ranked among the outstanding accomplishments of the North Americans during the nineteenth century. This system was nonexistent in Europe, where an increased demand for specialized products prior to the Industrial Revolution was largely met by a rise in the numbers of local artisans. North America's different conditions led instead to an expansion of trade. Relatively large middle classes of petty merchants, small manufacturers, and professionals quickly rose to meet the demands of frontiersmen for new products. These merchants shipped goods to the interior and often settled branches of the family close to the frontier to ensure that trade was efficient and profitable.

During the Industrial Revolution, the wholesaling that had risen out of conditions peculiar to North America became an economic necessity for all industrializing nations. Production was highly concentrated and goods were manufactured in quantities far surpassing the levels achieved by the small manufacturers and artisans of the past. Demand, on the other hand, was dispersed throughout the nation, even throughout the world. Inevitably, wholesalers sprang up in England, Germany, and France, as well as in North America, to meet the demands of consumers for the products of the new age. With the proliferation of goods, specialization emerged and modern wholesaling was born.

Wholesaling was an essential component of the industrial economy. Wholesalers linked buyers and sellers, adding economic value through efficient performance of selling and physical distribution. By selling efficiently, wholesalers made it possible for even small manufacturers to reach out to customers and helped all manufacturers to reach more distant markets. As the link between producer and customer, wholesalers were best equipped to perform many crucial marketing functions such as new product introduction, in-store merchandising, sales support, order taking and processing, customer service, training, returns processing, and problem solving. Other valuable services the wholesaler could provide included local stocking, consolidated shipments with the orders of many suppliers, and shorter delivery times. All of these factors placed enormous power in the hands of the wholesaler—power that helped the industry grow rapidly, often at a rate that exceeded overall national economic and population growth rates. They also prompted a growing movement towards integration and consolidation—a movement well underway by the mid-twentieth century as successful regional wholesalers expanded their reach, acquired other wholesalers, and built stronger ties with manufacturers and retail outlets.

Since 1970 the wholesale industry continued to expand more rapidly than the overall economy. Canadian statistics show that annual growth in the wholesale portion of the gross domestic product (GDP) in constant 1986 dollars averaged 4.5 percent per year from 1971 to 1981, compared to 3.8 percent for the Canadian economy as a whole. The first real setback for wholesalers did not come until the 1981-1982 recession when sales, employment, and the number of establishments declined relative to the previous year's levels. To survive the recession, many wholesalers restructured, dropped marginal product lines, reduced staff, and shut down warehouses. Consolidation intensified as larger firms ate up smaller ones.

This restructuring made wholesalers even more competitive during the boom years of the mid-1980s. Growth in wholesale trade accelerated at an annual average of 8.6 percent in Canada as compared to 4.3 percent for the Canadian economy as a whole. By 1988 the Canadian wholesale industry's share of their total GDP had increased to 5.5 percent—a rate of growth matched in most other leading economies. Growth slowed at the end of the decade but continued at better than 2 percent through 1994. During the 1980s the industry also increased capital investments. Real expenditure increases by wholesalers in Canada, for example, were 22 percent in 1983 and 25 percent in 1984. Most of these investments were aimed at improving the efficiency and quality of customer services; they also went into machinery and equipment purchases, such as computer technology. Overall real capital expenditures declined in 1985 but continued to increase through the remainder of the decade.

With the onset of the recession at the end of the 1980s, expenditures again fell while mergers, consolidations, and restructuring once again increased. From 1987 to 1993, the number of U.S. wholesaling firms declined from 364,000 to only 280,000, a 25 percent drop. Wholesale companies suffered not only from reduced overall demand, but also from increasing competition from alternative channels of distribution such as warehouse clubs and discount stores. These additional pressures may have accounted for the industry's accelerated adjustments and restructuring. By 1992 alternative channels of distribution—direct manufacturer-to-retailer sales, warehouse clubs, discount stores, and home center stores—accounted for 24 percent of the wholesale market.

In the mid-1990s the wholesale industry continued to play a vital role in global distribution. The U.S. industry alone posted sales of approximately US$2.3 trillion in 1996, up from US$2.2 trillion in 1995. In real terms, however, wholesalers had gained little ground since 1988, although low inflation rates had benefited the industry's growth. In 1997 the top ten companies in the industry recorded combined sales of about US$136.3 billion.

Wholesalers started to adopt electronic data interchange (EDI) technology during this period. EDI is a standardized electronic transmission system that wholesalers use for orders, reports, and payments. While most large firms used EDI to some degree, the prohibitive cost of installing and operating an EDI system prevented widespread implementation of the technology by the industry's many small wholesalers. However, as new technology became less expensive in the late 1990s, smaller firms found themselves better able to afford the increasingly necessary upgrades.

The wholesale industry grew more customer oriented in the mid- to late 1990s. However, many wholesale companies lacked the selection that customers wanted, so wholesalers providing complementary services began to collaborate, forming consortia to offer customers a wider array of products. Wholesale consortia allow customers the convenience and efficiency of doing business with just one supplier.

Studies in the United States showed that wholesalers, despite their low-tech portrayal at times, were on the vanguard of the technological revolution and grew at a faster rate than all other industries in the country. Between 1989 and 1994, the industry's sales grew by 15 percent, in contrast to the manufacturing and housing industries which expanded by 11.4 and 10.2 percent during the same period, respectively. The industry's implementation of technology for ordering, shipping, and inventory control allowed it to increase its output by 23 percent without expanding its employee ranks, according to *Business Week.*

Furthermore, using EDI the industry successfully reduced its lead times, shipping its products to customers in shorter amounts of time. Wholesalers used methods such as frequent shipment, and just-in-time delivery or continuous replenishment arrangements to bring about these decreased lead times. With the advances in technology, manufacturers could track consumer tastes and preferences directly from the retailer's cash register. Customers could transmit an order directly to the supplier via fax or e-mail and have the goods delivered to their door the next day. At the same time, advances in production technology made it possible for manufacturers to develop short-run, customized production lines tailored specifically to the needs of a single customer. However, while the wholesale industry embraced technology, some of its clients were able to use technology to circumvent wholesalers. Local market knowledge, direct customer contact, and links with suppliers—all once privileges of the wholesaler—could now be achieved by retailers and manufacturers without the wholesaler's intervention.

Despite the industry's growth and its increased efficiency, wholesalers continued to face greater competition from alternative forms of distribution. The trend toward alternative channels of distribution appeared first in the United States but quickly spread to Canada. In Europe and Japan, where markets were more tradition-bound and strictly regulated, these new developments had less impact on the industry. Nevertheless, even in Japan, discount stores and warehouse clubs made rapid gains due to loosening regulations and the growing demand of consumers for prices that better reflected the strength of the yen in the early to mid-1990s. While Japan's prices had always been well above world averages, the rising yen exacerbated these differences—differences that were painfully obvious to the increasing numbers of Japanese traveling overseas.

Direct manufacturer-to-retail arrangements constituted the most formidable challenge to the industry in the mid- to late 1990s. These arrangements usually took the form of strategic alliances between manufacturers and major retail chain stores, warehouse clubs, discount stores, and home center stores. Other alternative channels included mail order, catalog sales, and direct sales from manufacturer to industrial user or from retailer to industrial users.

Product lines sold through alternative distribution channels included consumer durables such as sports equipment, toys, jewelry, furniture, and electrical appliances, as well as nondurables such as clothing. Large retail chains and club stores with direct links to suppliers were another major source of competition for wholesalers, particularly smaller firms. The rapid expansion of superstores such as Wal-Mart, Kmart, and Target drained business from many independent retailers and convenience stores, forcing them to close down and taking away the livelihood of local wholesalers. These superstores had the buying power to negotiate directly with manufacturers and eliminate the need for the wholesale intermediary.

Another factor contributing to the erosion of the wholesaler's position within the supply chain was the deregulation and increased efficiency of the transportation industry. Deregulation reduced costs, while new computer technologies facilitated precise tracking and scheduling, as well as order taking and processing. With shipping companies like United Parcel Service guaranteeing delivery anywhere in the world within 48 hours, suppliers could easily afford to bypass distributors and ship directly to customers. Furthermore, technological advances made it possible for customers to enter orders via electronic data interchange, eliminating the need for the distributor to take orders. Freight-consolidation software and sophisticated new materials handling systems reduced the need for local stocking.

Trade accords such as the North American Free Trade Agreement (NAFTA) and the General Agreement on Tariffs and Trade (GATT) offered wholesalers the possibility of expanding more rapidly into new markets. These agreements called for the gradual reduction and ultimate elimination of tariffs and other trade barriers on a plethora of goods by the early 2000s. Wholesalers, especially large ones, viewed these accords as avenues for compensating for lost market share domestically. For example, Canadian wholesalers looked forward to access to the huge U.S. market, while U.S. wholesalers positioned themselves for expansion into Mexico and Canada.

GATT, by reducing restrictions on trade and business in many countries, including the European Union, the United States, and Japan, facilitated increased efficiency of existing foreign affiliates and made it easier to establish new ones. Competitive wholesalers operating in this new international economic environment were presented with a wide range of opportunities to increase their market share. By investing in newer technologies and opening export markets, successful wholesalers could strengthen their position and institute the additional value-added services needed to fend off the challenge posed by the alternative distribution channels.

Globalization was a key force in wholesale trade during the late 1990s. By 1998 roughly 20 percent of sales reported by U.S. merchant wholesalers were attributed to products manufactured internationally. Some analysts expected international goods to account for nearly 30 percent of U.S. merchant wholesaler sales by 2003. As the industry grew increasingly global, wholesalers began to focus on reducing costs and improving efficiency, turning to new technology to enhance inventory management. Wholesalers implemented warehouse automation, bar code scanning, and other data collection and identification technologies during the late 1990s to achieve these ends. To improve inventory management, many wholesalers relied on integrated supply: they owned and managed inventories at their customers' facilities. The integrated wholesaler/vendor supply market was forecast to reach US$11 billion by the early 2000s, compared to US$700 million in 1994, according to the *U.S. Industry and Trade Outlook*.

U.S. companies began to pursue global expansion via acquisitions and mergers in the late 1990s. In 1998 U.S. wholesalers completed 86 international deals, according to *Mergers & Acquisitions*. Avnet Inc., a leading U.S.-based electronics distributor, made several international acquisitions in the late 1990s, including electronics components distributor Eurotronics B.V. On the domestic front, the firm also purchased Marshall Industries, another leading North American electronics distributor, in October 1999. Bolstered by its new holdings, Avnet usurped Arrow Electronics in 2000 as the largest electronics distributor in North America.

Several noteworthy deals also took place among U.S. pharmaceutical suppliers in the early 2000s. For example, Cardinal Health Inc., the second largest drug wholesaler in the United States, paid US$2.1 billion for Bindley Western Drug Co., the fifth largest industry player, in 2001. A few months after that deal was completed, Bergen Brunswig and AmeriSource merged in a US$7 billion deal to form Amerisource Bergen, then the largest U.S. drug wholesaler with US$35 billion in annual revenues and a 29 percent share of the drug distribution market. When the deals were complete, the firms began reducing their number of distribution centers in an effort to streamline operations and cut expenses.

Wholesalers remained optimistic about doing business in China at the turn of the century. China began to open its market up to wholesale enterprises in the late 1990s with the launching of the country's first distribution center. Not only did this benefit domestic distributors, it also boded well for foreign investors trying to gain access to China's market, according to *Nikkei Weekly*. Japanese companies in particular were optimistic about the wholesale distribution center because they had found it difficult to obtain wholesale licenses in the past. China's entrance into the World Trade Organization in 2001 promised further opportunities to international wholesalers looking to expand into Asia.

CURRENT CONDITIONS

By 2003, the wholesale industry was valued at US$2.9 trillion. The consolidation that began at the end of the century continued into the mid-2000s, largely due to globalization, e-commerce, and cost issues. However, a newer trend was for smaller, more regional companies to merge, in order to claim and serve a particular niche, rather than to compete against the huge corporations. Because of this, overall employment was expected to remain healthy. According to the Bureau of Labor Statistics, employment for the wholesale industry as a whole was projected to rise 11 percent between 2002 and 2012.

Certain segments of the wholesaling industry appeared ripe for consolidation in the early 2000s. For example, the largest 250 industrial distributors in the United States held only a 15 percent share of the industrial distribution market there in 2001, according to *Industrial Distribution*. Many analysts believed this market fragmentation would likely prompt future mergers and acquisitions as the leading players sought to increase their market share. While small firms able to offer specialized services would likely survive, analysts believed mid-sized players would eventually be squeezed out of the market, many via buyouts by industry leaders.

In addition, e-commerce was no longer seen as a threat to the industry. Instead, it was considered to be a useful tool. For example, Pembroke Consulting forecast that by 2008, the wholesale industry would attribute one-third of annual revenues to online orders. On the positive side, customers would more frequently take some of the work on themselves, because they would be able to do more research online. This self-education would better prepare them to buy, which would reduce both cost and hassle for the wholesaler. Prices also would stabilize as a result. On the negative side, an informed consumer can be a demanding and inflexible consumer. Customers in various market segments were expected to use their research to bypass the wholesaler entirely and go straight to the manufacturers.

In 2004, the wholesale trade in Canada had total sales in excess of US$355 billion in 2004, with food accounting for 17 percent of the total, motor vehicles 16 percent, and machinery and equipment 9 percent. In the United States, 2004 merchant wholesale sales were valued at US$3.34 trillion, with food accounting for 12.4 percent, pharmaceuticals and sundries at 9 percent, and professional and commercial equipment at 8.7 percent.

In China, as in many other developing nations, the wholesale distribution system remained extremely fragmented. Despite the country's huge potential consumer base and the increasing amount of foreign investment, wholesale markets are divided up on a regional basis, with about 60 percent of the wholesalers operating in all markets being state-owned. By 2004, these markets were still dominated by the traditional booth method of trading whereby prices were determined over the counter and so did not always reflect supply and demand relationships. The country also continued to use a cash payment method rather than payment through a central banking system as done in developed countries. China's wholesale industry was also plagued by a lack of standardization in terms of product distribution, leading to huge inefficiencies in manpower and waste in product.

RESEARCH AND TECHNOLOGY

Research and development in the wholesale industry focused almost entirely on the development of computer-based systems to improve inventory control, communications, logistics, and overall efficiency. For wholesalers, however, technology was a dual-edged sword. While technology made it possible for wholesalers to streamline their operations, improve efficiency, and increase their overall competitiveness, it also made it possible for suppliers and customers to develop alternative channels of distribution that bypassed the wholesalers. A study co-sponsored by Canada's Ministry of Industry, Science and Technology found that the communications and wholesale industries were more likely than any other service industries to introduce computer-based technologies. Usage in the wholesale industry was above average in 24 of the 29 technologies examined, and wholesalers led the way in implementation of computerized order entry, computerized inventory control, and electronic data interchange.

Some industry analysts predicted that electronic commerce via the Internet would replace EDI, and that it might eventually even eliminate the need for traditional distribution companies. However, by the early 2000s most experts had come to view Internet technology as another distribution tool. According to Richard Trombly in *Industrial Distribution*, "the birth of e-commerce brought with it the threat of disintermediation. Many experts predicted that distributors would be removed from the supply chain. For many reasons, this never came to pass. Like integrated supply, vendor managed inventory, catalog houses and retail competition, e-commerce is now just one of the facts of business for distributors."

Because wholesaling is such an information-intensive business, it is imperative that wholesalers implement the latest computer technology in order to compete successfully. From orders and invoices to stock-keeping units and freight bills, huge volumes of data flow through the industry. By taking advantage of information technology, including electronic commerce tools, wholesalers are better able to manage their operations, operate with lower inventory and fewer warehouse locations, and improve customer services.

Wholesalers who led the way in the implementation of sophisticated computer data processing, communication systems, and other innovations were the large wholesaling firms operating in the industrial and resource sectors, as well as the leading food distributors. With their close links to suppliers, these firms were more easily able to obtain the capital required for investment in leading-edge technology than their smaller rivals. An example of this technology is efficient consumer response (ECR), a just-in-time restocking system keyed to customer buying patterns. ECR required a significant investment in sophisticated scanning technology, and although it threatened to squeeze the wholesaling profits made on inventory stocked in warehouses, it was considered a necessary investment by the suppliers and customers who did business with wholesalers.

Although smaller companies were slower to enter the computer age, by the mid-1990s declining costs and increasing capabilities made it easier for them to benefit from the new distribution technologies. More wholesalers in the United States, Canada, and elsewhere began to mechanize and automate their warehouse operations, use computers to improve inventory control, and coordinate just-in-time systems with manufacturers and customers. In the United States and Europe, some large wholesalers operated fully automated facilities by the late 1990s.

Industry Leaders

In an industry that has more than a million companies operating worldwide, generates sales in excess of US$10 trillion, and handles every known product, leadership is invariably confined within specific product sectors. Within individual sectors, large companies dominate the market, often accounting for 50 percent or more of sales while representing 1 percent or less of the total number of companies active in the sector. The world's largest wholesale companies are primarily U.S. firms, the largest of which deal in groceries, information technology, and pharmaceuticals.

Ingram Micro. The largest wholesaler of information technology products in the world, Santa Ana, California-based Ingram Micro supplies 280,000 products to about 165,000 retailers throughout 100 countries. In the United States, the company was selling to such giants as OfficeMax, Office Depot, CompUSA, and Amazon.com. Products include desktop and laptop computers, monitors, printers, CD-ROM drives, storage devices, and other related merchandise. The firm buys its products from almost 1,400 suppliers, including such leading hardware and software manufacturers as IBM, Hewlett-Packard, Microsoft, Xerox, NEC/Mitsubishi, and Canon. Begun in California in 1979, the company grew to achieve its global position through a series of acquisitions and mergers in North America, Europe, Asia-Pacific and Latin America. In 2004, the company improved its position in the Asia-Pacific region substantially when it acquired Tech Pacific of Singapore, one of the area's largest technology distributors. Ingram reported sales of US$25.5 billion in 2004 and employed 13,600 people.

McKesson. McKesson Corporation, with sales of US$80.5 billion for the year ended March 2005, is the largest wholesale distributor of pharmaceuticals, health and beauty products, and medical supplies in North America. By 2005, the company was distributing approximately one-third of all the pharmaceuticals in the United States, and was ranked fifteenth on the Fortune 500 listing. San Francisco-based McKesson distributes the products of more than 3,000 pharmaceutical manufacturers and medical-surgical supply developers to more than 25,000 pharmacies, and also distributes its products to 50,000 hospitals, health care clinics and physician practices. In 2005 the company's largest customer, Rite Aid Corporation, accounted for 7 percent of its sales, while in total, its top ten customers accounted for 49 percent. The company's Canadian subsidiary is the largest pharmaceutical distributor in Canada, and it also owned 49 percent of Mexico's leading distributor, Nadro.

Franz Haniel (Celesio AG). In 2004, Franz Haniel & Cie. GmbH of Germany owned 60 percent of Europe's largest pharmaceutical distributor, Celesio AG. Celesio (formerly GEHE AG) earned revenues of more than US$26 billion in 2004, employing more than 32,000 people in the 15 European countries it served. In addition to wholesale, the company also owns pharmaceutical retailers in seven countries.

AmerisourceBergen. AmerisourceBergen Corp. was created in August 2001 from the merger of Orange, California-based Bergen Brunswig and Valley Forge, Pennsylvania-based AmeriSource, two leading U.S. pharmaceutical distributors. The deal created an industry giant with sales of US$53.2 billion in 2004. AmerisourceBergen supplies approximately 25,000 health care facilities, pharmacies, and grocery stores with pharmaceuticals and related merchandise.

In the late 1990s, Bergen Brunswig had ranked among the world's top ten wholesalers with sales of US$11.6 billion. In 1998 Bergen Brunswig agreed to be purchased by rival Cardinal Health. However, concerns raised by the U.S. Federal Trade Commission (FTC) prompted Cardinal to rescind its offer. A similar deal between AmeriSource and McKesson was also nixed after the FTC raised regulatory issues.

SUPERVALU. SUPERVALU Inc., the world's largest food wholesaler in 2004, supplied 3,200 grocery retailers in the United States with the products of more than 500 manufacturers through the company's 24 distribution centers. For 2005, Supervalu reported sales of US$19.5 billion, with 46 percent coming from its distribution segment; the company also owned 1,549 retail food stores. In the late 1990s, the Minneapolis-based firm helped its clients compete against chains by providing services in all phases of store operations, from accounting to choosing store locations. Besides distributing national and brand-name products, it also manufactured its own line of products. The biggest threat to SUPERVALU was not that its customers, mainly independent grocers, might set up their own distribution systems, but that they would fall victim to the big price-busting grocery chains. The company responded by expanding into retail to boost sales and generate more volume for its wholesaling business. The move into retail also was an effort to reduce SUPERVALU's reliance on the low-margin food wholesaling industry in which margins averaged 1 percent, compared to 5 percent for the retail food industry, which is also considered low-margin.

FURTHER READING

"Annual Benchmark Report for Wholesale Trade: January 1992 Through January 2005: A Detailed Summary for Wholesale Sales, Inventories, and Purchases." *Current Business Reports,* US Census Bureau, March 2005. Available from http://www.census.gov.

Draper, Deborah J., ed. *Business Rankings Annual.* Detroit: Thomson Gale, 2004.

"EPA's 'High-Price Myth' Losing Believers." *Yomiuri Shimbun,* 5 July 2000.

Eyriey, Nick. "Forbidden Fruit." *Office Products International,* October 2003.

Fein, Adam J. "The Road to Opportunity in Wholesale Distribution," 2004. Available from http://www.naw.org.

Frederick, James. "Revolutionizing an Industry." *Drug Store News,* 17 December 2001.

"Hoover's Company Capsules." 2004. Available from http://www.hoovers.com.

Lazich, Robert S., ed. *Market Share Reporter.* Detroit: Thomson Gale, 2004.

McMillan, Charles J. *The Japanese Industrial System.* Berlin: Walter de Gruyter, 1984.

Parsley, William A. "A Tip of the Hat," 2004. Available from http://www.naw.org.

Robertson, Jack. "Payment Terms Remain Sticky Issue in China." *EBN,* 1 December 2003.

Smock, Douglas A. "Distributors: Times Are Changing." *Purchasing,* 6 May 2004.

Sullivan, Laurie. "Distribution." *EBN,* 7 July 2003.

"The Tenth Five-Year Plan of Retail and Wholesale Industry and its Development." China Daily, 2005. Available from http://bizchina.chinadaily.com.cn.

"There's Still Room for Smaller Wholesalers." *Chain Drug Review,* 5 November 2001.

Trombly, Richard. "A Direct Threat." *Industrial Distribution,* March 2002. Available from http://www.manufacturing.net.

U.S. Department of Labor, Bureau of Labor Statistics. "Wholesale Trade." *Career Guide to Industries,* 27 February 2004.

U.S. Industry and Trade Outlook. New York: McGraw-Hill and U.S. Department of Commerce, 2000.

"Value-added Services Drive Distributor Sales." *Purchasing,* 15 April 2004.

Wholesale Trade. Statistics Canada, January 2002. Available from http://www.statcan.ca.

World Trade Organization. "International Trade Statistics." 2003. Available from http://www.wto.org.

TEXTILES, APPAREL, AND LEATHER

SIC 2300

NAICS 315

APPAREL

Usually from purchased textiles, apparel makers cut and assemble fabrics into all types of finished clothing. Footwear is not discussed here. For discussion of leather apparel, see **Leather Goods and Accessories,** and for more information on textile production, see **Textile Mills.**

INDUSTRY SNAPSHOT

Apparel has long been made in locations around the world, and the global clothing market represents a substantial area of consumer spending, but in the last decades of the twentieth century there was a pronounced migration of its mass production from higher-wage industrial economies to lower cost labor markets in the developing world. Through the mid- to late 1990s and into the 2000s, apparel manufacturers in industrial nations continued to seek countries with low-cost labor for production. Developing economies in Asia and South America received the bulk of these production contracts. Simultaneously, apparel companies in developed economies began reducing their domestic workforces as a direct result of sourcing labor from low-wage countries. Meanwhile, apparel firms that could not compete with low-cost manufacturers either merged with larger companies, diversified, or closed.

In the mid-2000s, the European Union, the United States, Japan, and Canada remained the world's leading import markets for clothing. China (including Hong Kong), the United States, South Korea, Japan, India, the United Kingdom, Italy, and France make up some of the world's key clothing producers, importers, and exporters. World trade in apparel was highly regulated through the late twentieth century, but the movement away from trade barriers in the 1990s and early 2000s profoundly affected the industry, paving the way—in the view of many analysts—for China to become the world's dominant player. In 2002, according to the *Miami Herald,* 70 percent of all growth in apparel imports to the United States came from China and Vietnam. According to the American Textile Manufacturers Institute (ATMI), China's share of the U.S. import market, averaging about 9 percent in the 1990s when quotas were in effect, skyrocketed to 53 percent in 2003 after several categories of clothing were removed from quota requirements. This trend intensified after 2005, when remaining trade quotas expired. Indeed, in January 2005 alone, the value of Chinese apparel exports to the United States increased by more than 41 percent, and the value of its clothing exports to the European Union in the first four months of 2005 grew by 80 percent. The U.S. government reinstated the quotas on two categories of textile imports (body-supporting garments such as bras and synthetic filament fabric) from China in July 2005, after the two countries failed to reach an agreement following four rounds of talks in Beijing. In December 2005, a tentative agreement was reached that placed quotas on 34 different textile products imported from China, effective through 2008.

Due to various anti-sweatshop campaigns, many major apparel retailers and brand name manufacturers became increasingly aware that ensuring decent working conditions in production facilities could affect their reputation in the eyes of consumers as well as the corporate bottom line. Leading categories in the global apparel industry include outerwear; men's shirts; women's blouses and shirts; men's pants; and women's coats, jackets, suits, skirts, and vests. In 2007, a group of U.S. senators proposed a bill to ban the sale in the United States of imported goods made in sweatshop factories.

ORGANIZATION AND STRUCTURE

The international apparel industry has three primary sectors: designers or jobbers, manufacturers, and retailers. Designers or jobbers develop apparel items by purchasing materials, designing concepts, developing prototypes, and hiring manufacturers. Manufacturers mass produce the apparel items based on the samples created by the designers. Finally, retailers market the clothing to the public. A host of different relationships and arrangements may exist among these three sectors. For example, a designer may produce only clothing concepts and prototypes and then contract manufacturers to mass produce them. The designer might sell its products directly to a number of retailers. On the other hand, a designer might not only produce concepts and prototypes but also operate a retail or direct marketing business and therefore outsource only the manufacturing. Major companies may include divisions corresponding to all three of these sectors.

The International Apparel Federation (IAF) is one of the leading clothing associations dedicated to the advancement of the apparel industry worldwide. In addition, leading apparel-producing countries have their own trade associations, many of which are also members of the IAF. Two of the major associations are the American Apparel Manufacturing Association (AAMA), which promotes and enhances the production and marketing of U.S. clothing, and the European Clothing Association (ECA), which works with European apparel producers to improve manufacturing and sales. The ECA also includes the Union Française des Industries de L'Habillement (UFIH), France's apparel industry association.

TRADE AGREEMENTS

To ensure fair trade around the world, the international community, including leading apparel producers, importers, and exporters, has implemented multilateral trade agreements. Two of the most important ones for the global apparel industry are the General Agreement on Tariffs and Trade (GATT) and the North American Free Trade Agreement (NAFTA). GATT, a renegotiation of an existing trade pact by the same name, resulted from the Uruguay Round talks from 1986 to 1994 and took effect in 1994. The agreement mandates the reduction and gradual elimination of tariffs that hinder foreign competition. In particular, GATT required the phasing out of textile and apparel import quotas by 2005. Further, GATT replaced the Multifiber Arrangement (MFA), which permitted quota restraints, with the Agreement on Textiles and Clothing (ATC). The ATC allows countries to select the quota categories they want to phase out. GATT also established the World Trade Organization to serve as a permanent organization for the development of fair, systematic global trade policies.

Founded in 1995 the World Trade Organization (WTO) governs trade between nations participating in the Uruguay Round of Multilateral Trade Negotiations. The organization's objective is to liberalize trade and ensure stable and fair trading conditions for participating members. Based in Geneva, Switzerland, the WTO allows any country to challenge the trade policies of any other country before its tribunal, the Dispute Settlement Body. The WTO consists of 148 members, including countries from all around the world as well as leading apparel producers such as the United States, the European Union, Japan, India, and Singapore. China joined the WTO in December 2001.

Implemented in 1994, NAFTA gradually reduced and ultimately eliminated tariffs among North American countries, making way for substantially freer trade by 2005. NAFTA consists of agreements between the United States and Canada as well as bilateral agreements with Mexico. Besides phasing out tariffs, NAFTA also established temporary trade quotas to protect the participating countries from price dumping and other disruptive practices while the agreement was being implemented.

The African Growth and Opportunity Act (AGOA), which went into effect in 2000, created a special trading agreement between the United States and 37 sub-Saharan African nations that allowed these countries duty-free access to U.S. markets for several categories of consumer goods, including apparel. As a result of AGOA, U.S. imports of clothing from sub-Saharan Africa grew by 43.9 percent in 2003 and another 35 percent in 2004.

CHANGES IN THE INDUSTRY

By the mid-1990s, new factors began to influence the success of clothing manufacturers. Producers contended that worker productivity does not solely determine a company's competitiveness. Instead, according to *WWD,* competitiveness is determined by the overall productivity and efficiency of the company. Therefore, industry observers expected to see significant restructuring in the apparel industry, including the implementation of information technology, in order to achieve this kind of productivity.

Manufacturers in the early 2000s also noted changes in consumer preferences in economically developed regions such as the United States, the European Union, and Japan, where consumers demanded value and quality instead of the lowest price or a particular brand, as they did in previous decades. Even in developing markets, brand loyalty had weakened, as consumers were exposed to an array of competing brands. In addition, apparel makers found that the most stable demand for products around the world was for high-priced luxury and fashion items. Analysts recommended that producers discontinue the practice of manufacturing clothing seasonally and produce it instead by the product category, according to *WWD.*

Moreover, manufacturers in high-wage economies, including France, Germany, the United States, and Japan, continued to outsource production of apparel items from the domestic market to lower-wage economies. France depended on manufacturers in Spain and North Africa, while Germany outsourced to Eastern Europe and Turkey for lower-cost production. In addition to Mexico, the United States relied on countries across the globe, such as India and Singapore, for low-wage manufacturing. Finally, Japan contracted manufacturers in developing Asian countries. Since investment in apparel manufacturing equipment remained small relative to other industries, apparel firms could shift production from country to country with little investment.

Another trend among clothing manufacturers was the formation of alliances among the countries involved in the apparel production process. This trend broke with earlier patterns of going from economy to economy in search of the lowest production costs. Such alliances were intended to create a stronger bond between the apparel firms and the countries that manufacture the clothing.

Besides internationalizing production, apparel firms in industrial countries sought to expand cross-border trade of their goods. This was necessary as the markets matured in many of the major apparel-producing countries, leaving them with few available channels of expansion. Consequently, apparel firms from the United States, France, Germany, Italy, Japan, and other maturing countries started to market their products in places such as South Korea, Russia, and Turkey, as well as South America.

At the start of the twenty-first century, apparel manufacturers and retailers were struggling with a changing global economy and looking at strategies such as licensing, consolidation, and global expansion to stay afloat. Leading U.S. department store chains Bradlees and Montgomery Ward both went out of business in 2000, and U.S. clothing manufacturers C.L. Fashions and Bugle Boy shut down as well. J.C. Penney Company was forced to close a number of its stores due to declining sales, and Marks and Spencer, the biggest apparel seller in the United Kingdom, experienced a significant decrease in profits. Retailers looking to expand included Sweden's H&M (Hennes & Mauritz), which in 2005 had about 1,200 stores in 24 countries. Japan's Fast Retailing, with 582 stores in Japan, was expanding into the United Kingdom and China. Designers hit with the high cost of manufacturing were looking at ways to survive through licensing strategies. Mossimo avoided bankruptcy when it signed a three-year, US$1 billion agreement with Target. Polo Ralph Lauren, Calvin Klein, and Giorgio Armani, along with other designers, cut back on licensing agreements in hopes of attaining higher quality assurance and a faster product turnaround.

The apparel industry continued to face the problem of clothing producers' reliance on sweatshop labor. Sweatshops force employees, including children, to work long hours for low wages and to endure unsafe working conditions. While sweatshop conditions are often thought only to exist in developing countries, they also occur in major industrial nations such as the United States. Developing Asian countries such as the Philippines, Malaysia, Thailand, and Vietnam also contain sweatshops. Some of the operations deceive Western apparel firms by having front businesses and coercing employees to remain silent. In 1998 a number of major apparel firms in the United States and nongovernment organization (NGO) participants in the Apparel Industry Partnership put forth a code of conduct through the Fair Labor Association to monitor and certify companies that meet its standards. The Netherlands' Clean Clothes Campaign, the UK's Ethical Trading Initiative, and Australia's Fair Wear campaign were among other global initiatives established to help bring attention to and end substandard labor practices in the garment industry.

Current Conditions

The textile and apparel industry was becoming more and more global in the mid- to later 2000s. India and China were seeing an exceptional number of fashion designers open new stores in their country.

Some of the countries whose textile and apparel industries were picking up included Egypt and Isreal, where an agreement made with the United States in 2004 allowed finished products manufactured in specific regions in Egypt duty-free access to the U.S. market. According to *WWD,* Israeli exports of apparel-related items to Egypt, including woven and knitted fabric, packing materials, and chemicals for washing and dyeing, increased by more than 300 percent to about US$93 million in 2005, as compared to less than US$30 million in 2004. The textile industry was already an important part of the Egyptian economy, with 1,500 textile manufacturers employing almost half a million people and producing US$3.2 billion in products a year (equal to 3.5 percent of Egypt' gross domestic product), and analysts expected continued growth. Some of Egypt's advantages, according to the Israel Economic Mission, are its size, geographic location, and lower energy and labor costs. Says Ahmed Hosni, Egypt's commercial and economic counselor in New York, only China and India have lower hourly labor costs when it comes to textiles. In the third quarter of 2006 Egyptian textile exports to the United States had grown to more than US$463 million, as compared to US$312 million during the same period in 2004. Top U.S. buyers included Gap, Wal-Mart, Levi Strauss, VF Jeanswear, and Target.

Nicaragua was also an up and coming player in the industry. According to *Logistics Today,* by 2005 it had become the second fastest growing exporter of apparel to the United States (behind China). Nicaragua's apparel and textile exports to the United States grew 22.57 percent in 2004, as compared to China's 25.38 percent. Nicaragua's advantages in the trade include the favorable terms it receives in the Central American Free Trade Agreement (CAFTA), lower labor costs than other Central American countries, and faster shipping times than Asia.

Research and Technology

With government and industry funding, apparel manufacturers and retailers around the world, but especially in the United States, Japan, and the United Kingdom, have researched ways of developing communications and network systems to improve contact between apparel customers and manufacturers. The goals of the research are to track consumer trends more carefully and to offer consumers custom-tailored garments in a short amount of time.

In addition to developing communications networks, designers and manufacturers began to implement computer-aided design software into the production process in order to produce fast, accurate clothing designs. Also, to increase productivity and to avoid relying on sweatshops for low-cost production, manufacturers invested more in plant automation. In the mid-1990s, researchers sought to create sensors to enable automated cutting and sewing as well as machinery to perform intricate weaving and sewing. Moreover, developers also moved to integrate all aspects of the apparel production process into a cohesive and systematic computer-integrated manufacturing program as opposed to separate application for design, manufacturing, and marketing. Laser technology was also being used for finishing work, including appliques, labels, badges, and other types of decoration.

The move toward e-tailing, or selling on the Internet, gave new life to many industries, and the garment industry was no exception. Online apparel sales in the United States were expected to continue to increase. Another technological advance affecting the industry was the virtual dressing room. Clothing buyers can use a virtual model, custom built to their specifications, to try on an outfit and then make their purchase with a touch of a button.

INDUSTRY LEADERS

LEVI STRAUSS & CO.

Based in San Francisco, Levi Strauss was the number one manufacturer of brand name apparel in the world in the mid-2000s. With a market presence in more than 110 countries, the company sold jeans and sportswear under the brand names of Levi's, Slates, and Dockers. Levi Strauss was once the top jean brand for youth, but tough competition from hipper trendsetters slowed sales, forcing the company to issue layoffs of some of its U.S. workforce. The company added more youth-oriented lines including Engineered Jeans and Superlow. Sales, which totaled approximately US$4.26 billion in 2001, fell slightly to US$4billion in 2003 and grew by only 0.4 percent 2004. Sales in 2005 reached US$4.12 billion. Employment, too, declined significantly from 16,700 people in 2001 to 12,300 in 2003 and about 9,635 in 2005. Major competition came from VF, Gap, and Tommy Hilfiger.

VF CORPORATION

With about 27 percent of the U.S. market, VF Corporation was the number one jeans manufacturer in the world. Its jeans brand names include Wrangler, Rider, Lee, and Rustler. Other apparel lines include Jantzen swimwear, Red Kap industrial work clothing, Healthtex infant and children's apparel, and North Face outdoor equipment and clothing, among others. Though most of its sales came from jeans, the company also offered knitwear, outdoor gear, heavy-duty work clothes, children's clothing, and men's and women's clothing (VF sold its lingerie line to Fruit of the Loom in 2006). In 2005, VF bought Reef Holdings Corporation, a producer of surfwear. Sales in 2006 were US$6.21 billion, and the company employed 52,700 people. VF Corp.'s primary competitors were Gap, Levi Strauss, and Sears.

BENETTON GROUP S.P.A.

This Italian company specialized in casual clothing for men, women, and children, which it sold in 120 countries. Benetton, which produced over 1 million apparel items annually, sold its wares through department stores and 5,100 franchised stores with the Benetton name, as well as company-owned and franchised megastores. The company also sold accessory items such as sunglasses, watches, and shoes. Sales for Benetton in 2005 reached US$2.2 billion, and the company employed nearly 8,000 people. Major competition came from Gap, H&M, and Inditex.

HUGO BOSS AG

Based in Germany, Hugo Boss was the early twenty-first-century key maker of designer executive wear. The company designed and licensed its clothing, fragrances, and accessories through its namesake shops and other retail stores all over the world. Hugo Boss also made casual clothes and moved into the women's wear market. The company employed 7,584 workers in 2005. Sales that year totaled US$1.55 billion.

GAP INC.

Based in San Francisco, The Gap ran more than 3,100 stores worldwide in the mid-2000s, primarily in the United States, Japan, Germany, France, and Canada. The company's Gap stores specialized in casual clothes for both men and women. Other chains were Old Navy, Banana Republic, Forth and Town, babyGap, and Gap Kids. The company also added an intimate apparel brand called GapBody. The Gap employed 153,000 people in 2005. Sales for 2006 totaled approximately US$16.02 billion.

H&M

Started in 1947, Sweden-based H&M designs and sells inexpensive but fashionable clothing for men and women in the 18 to 45 age bracket. About 60 percent of its clothing is manufactured in Asia, with the remainder produced in Europe. H&M operated about 1,200 stores in 24 countries. Sales were about US$8 billion in 2005.

MAJOR COUNTRIES IN THE INDUSTRY

CHINA

According to *Xinhua,* apparel production in China totaled 670 million pieces in 1978. By 2000 this figure had risen to 11.6 billion, demonstrating a yearly increase of 14 percent. Exports of garments in 2000 totaled US$36.1 billion, fifty times the rate in 1978. According to the *People's Daily,* by 2002 China had 45,000 garment businesses that produced more than 310 pieces of clothing every second, making a profit of US$60,000 every minute. China's exports of textiles and apparel were valued at US$100 billion a year by early 2005. The top five apparel manufacturers were Guangdong, Zhejiang, Jiangsu, Shandong, and Shanghai.

Textwatch reported that China saw its exports of apparel shrink. Some of the decrease was due to a corresponding rise in the country's machinery and electronics imports. However, the free trade movement, begun in the United States in 1994, had a major impact on China's garment exports. The Caribbean Basin Initiative allowed Caribbean and Central American countries' textile and apparel exports duty-free entry to the United States. This made it possible for cheap apparel made in Honduras to flood the market. By the late 1990s apparel manufacturers in such countries as Sri Lanka, Myanmar, and Bangladesh began to hone in on China's market share by offering less expensive goods to clothing retailers in the United States. Further, the passing of the Trade and Development Act of 2000 by the U.S. Congress allowed for quota-free and duty-free entry of certain apparel products exported from 48 sub-Saharan countries. However, Chinese garment makers were most concerned with competition from Mexico due to the country's increasing exports to the United States.

Although China joined the World Trade Organization, U.S. trade barriers regarding apparel made in China were expected to remain for several years. The WTO accession agreement between Beijing and Washington stipulated that U.S. quotas on garments and textiles originating from China would be eliminated by 2005. However, a safeguard implemented in the accord against the United States being flooded with China-made goods would be enforced until 2008. Nevertheless, concern continued to grow about a sharp rise in Chinese exports to the United States and the European Union. According to a report from the International Textile, Garment, and Leather Workers' Federation, between January 2002 and March 2003, China increased its exports of dressing gowns to the United States by 698 percent and of gloves by 291 percent. Exports of these items from the Philippines, Mexico, Guatemala, Bangladesh, and Sri Lanka fell drastically. Guatemala's exports, for example, dropped 65 percent. In the first ten months of 2002, China's shipments of knitted underwear to the EU grew by 114 percent, while shipments of winter jackets increased by 264 percent, and exports of sweat suits rose 176 percent. From January 2004 to January 2005, when quotas expired, China's total exports of textiles and apparel to the European Union increased 46.5 percent, reaching a value of US$1.43 billion.

This dramatic growth prompted European textile companies to press for a 7.5 percent limit on annual growth of clothing exports from China; the United States also urged China to voluntarily limit export growth. In 2005, the Chinese government announced that it would not impose official limits, but that rising costs for raw materials and labor would slow growth in its textile and apparel exports. In May 2005, citing a surge of as much as 1,500 percent in Chinese clothing exports since January that year, the U.S. government proposed a cap on exports of cotton trousers, underwear, and knit shirts and blouses from China. The proposed restrictions would limit export growth to 7.5 percent more than the corresponding level for the previous year. China announced that it would fight the proposed cap.

UNITED STATES

By the beginning of the twenty-first century, the United States retail industry was undergoing significant changes, with many retailers shutting down their businesses, filing for bankruptcy, closing unprofitable stores, and consolidating, according to *U.S. Business Reporter.* Garment manufacturers were expected to feel a substantial impact from this trend with reduction of sales due to elimination of distributors and decreasing profits as failed retailers reduced inventory with heavy mark-downs.

Consumer spending on clothing and shoes in the United States reached about US$297.5 billion in 2000 and rose to US$311.2 billion in 2003. Spending on women's and girls' apparel accounted for US$160.6 billion in 2002, while men's and boys' apparel accounted for US$94.7 billion. Production of men's and boys' apparel totaled 1.635 billion pieces in 2003, valued at US$10.47 billion. These figures represented a 2.5 percent decline in volume and a 7.4 percent decline in value from the previous year. Women's apparel totaled 3.45 billion pieces, valued at US$23.89 billion, representing an 11.2 percent decline in volume and 11.8 percent decline in value from 2002.

In the mid-2000s, imports comprised the vast majority of the U.S. apparel market, with about 96.6 percent of sales in 2002 and 2003. While imports from China dramatically increased after 2003, most U.S. clothing imports continued to come from Mexico, Central America, and Caribbean countries. In 2003, CAFTA countries supplied 24.7 percent of U.S. apparel imports, with Mexico and China each supplying about 11 percent. However, the end of quotas in 2005 threatened to shift this balance. Some analysts have predicted that China could take up to 70 percent of the U.S. textile and apparel market; others, however, have pointed out that Western Hemisphere countries, which are much closer to the United States and can ship items more quickly, can remain competitive. "Costs remain a driving factor," wrote Fred Abernathy and David Weil in the *Washington Post,* "but the proximity advantage will grow even greater in a post-quota world as retailers raise the bar ever higher on the responsiveness and flexibility required of their suppliers."

U.S. apparel retailers and catalogers increasingly established sales outlets overseas to sell their products. The largest export categories were home furnishings and men's outerwear. Men's and boys' trousers were the dominant products exported to Canada, Japan, and the European Community. Mexico was a major player in the growth of U.S. garment imports, with the United States taking advantage of quota and duty provisions allowed by the North American Free Trade Agreement (NAFTA). Over two-thirds of Mexican imports were made up of components originated in the United States. On the other hand, Asian imports employ virtually no U.S. components.

EUROPEAN UNION

The European Union (EU) includes key industry players such as France, Italy, Germany, and the United Kingdom—major producers and exporters and important importers of apparel items. In 2004, after enlargement to 25 member nations, the EU textile and apparel industry employed about 2.7 million people in about 177,000 enterprises. Textile and clothing turnover in 2002 exceeded 200 billion euros (about US$252.4 billion).

Italy. In terms of employment, production, sales, and consumption, Italy was by far the largest player in the EU apparel industry in the early to mid-2000s, according to a report published by the EU in 2004. Italy employed some 314,568 apparel industry workers in 2001, with a turnover that year of US$39.7 billion. Clothing consumption that year was valued at US$66 billion. Between 1995 and 2001, Italy's clothing exports increased by 89 percent. About 48 percent of Italy's clothing exports were sold outside of the EU. Italy also continued to import substantial quantities of clothing each year from countries such as China and the United States.

By the mid-2000s, the Italian industry sought to cope with increased competition from China by outsourcing a greater proportion of its manufacturing jobs. Though this trend was expected to grow, some firms preferred to keep production domestic in order to ensure high quality standards.

France. France's apparel industry in 2001 employed about 93,600 workers—a significant decrease from approximately 270,000 workers in the late 1990s. In 2001, apparel turnover was valued at US$15.8 billion; consumption that year, however, was about US$36.6 billion. Consequently, France had to import a large amount of clothing items to meet internal demand. France also was a key exporter of apparel products: between 1995 and 2001, France's export market increased 31 percent. In 2001, some 41 percent of France's clothing exports were to non-EU nations. By 2003, however, the French textile and apparel industry faced both increased competition from Asia and a decline in domestic consumer spending. Between 2002 and 2003, clothing and textile consumption in France dropped about 1 percent in value. According to the U.S. Commercial Service, French textile and apparel companies reported sales of US$17.2 billion in 2003. Apparel accounted for about 74 percent of the industry. Women's wear was the largest segment, at 53 percent, followed by men's wear (32 percent), children's wear (12 percent) and infant's wear (3 percent). Total French textile and apparel imports amounted to US$21.0 billion in 2003, with exports reaching US$13.7 billion.

Germany. Germany's apparel industry faced declining sales in the late 1990s. The country's apparel manufacturers convened often to devise a way out of the industry's slump. Critics of the German industry attributed its lackluster performance to the industry's emphasis only on quality, which brought it success in the 1970s and 1980s but failed to win new customers or retain old ones in the 1990s. Failures were also cited at the retail level. Analysts called for greater commitment to customer satisfaction to pull the industry out of its quagmire. In addition, observers recommended more advertising and further foreign market penetration.

In 2001, according to EU statistics, German apparel turnover was valued at US$11.5 billion. According to the Goethe Institute, a slowdown in domestic spending affected the German apparel industry more than the rise in cheap imports. As a result, some German manufacturers turned to niche products, such as specialized socks for individuals suffering from some kinds of skin diseases, like athlete's foot. Designer fashions, too, became better established in the world market, as leading German brands such as Hugo Boss, Willy Bogner, and Strenesse established themselves in the global fashion market. Apparel consumption in 2001 was US$76.2 billion; and between 1995 and 2001, exports rose 33 percent.

United Kingdom. Another important market, the United Kingdom employed about 88,000 workers in the apparel industry in 2001. Turnover that year, according to EU data, was US$9.9 billion, and clothing consumption reached US$62.5 billion. The UK women's wear market declined 2.2 percent from 2001 to 2002, to a value of US$18.8 billion, while men's wear increased 19 percent for that period, reaching about US$9.85 billion. Though Britain has not historically been a major export market for apparel, exports grew 44 percent from 1995 to 2001.

Market analysis company Key Note reported that Marks and Spencer, the UK's biggest single clothing retailer, shocked the industry in September 1999 with its announcement that it would stop sourcing the majority of its apparel from the United Kingdom and would terminate contracts with a number of key suppliers without notice. By the beginning of the twenty-first century, this decision had resulted in the closing of several large factories and job losses in the thousands. The high cost of labor and inability to compete with lower-wage countries contributed to a bleak outlook for the UK apparel industry.

FURTHER READING

Abernathy, Fred and David Weil. "Apparel Apocalypse?" *Washington Post,* 18 November 2004, p. A39.

Adapting to Shifting Trade Winds." *WWD,* 19 September 2006.

American Apparel & Footwear Association Trends, Annual 2004. Available from http://www.apparelandfootwear.org.

"Apparel Spending Dips in 2003." *Display & Design Ideas,* 31 March 2004. Available from http://www.ddimagazine.com.

"As China's Apparel Exports Grow, So Do Nicaragua's." *Logistics Today,* May 2005.

Becker, Elizabeth. "Textile Quotas to End Soon, Punishing Carolina Mill Towns." *New York Times,* 2 November 2004.

Buckley, Chris. "China to Fight U.S. Limit on Textile Imports." *New York Times,* 16 May 2005.

Bussey, Jane. "Asian Countries Gain Larger Share of Global Clothing Business." *Miami Herald,* 28 April 2003.

"Ethiopia: The Next Sourcing Hot-Spot?" *just-style.com,* 1 March 2007.

"European Union: Import of Chinese Apparel Shows Massive Increase Post Quota." *Stitch World,* 2005. Available from http://www.apparelresources.com.

"Hoover's Company Capsules." *Hoover's Online,* 2007. Available from www.hoovers.com.

Ilari, Alessandra. "'Made in Italy' Looks to 'Made in China.'" *Women's Wear Daily,* 19 February 2004.

"Japan Looks to Revival of Exports." *WWD,* 20 March 2007.

Kaiser, Amanda, and Katherine Bowers. "Smaller World." *WWD,*12 December 2006.

Kearney, Neil. "What Future for Textiles and Clothing Trade after 2005?" International Textile, Garment, and Leather Workers' Federation white paper, 9 February 2003. Available from http://www.itglwf.org.

"Secrets, Lies, and Sweatshops." *Business Week,* 27 November 2006.

"Special Report: Clothing—Quota Chaos." *Promotions & Incentives,* 20 October 2005.

Study on the Implications of the 2005 Trade Liberalisation in the Textile and Clothing Sector. European Union, Paris, France, February 2004. Available from http://Europe.eu.int.

"Textile Agreement Reached with China." *ANSOM: Army, Navy, Supplies, Outdoor Merchandise,* 15 December 2005.

"The Textile and Clothing Industry—Not a Victim of Globalisation." Goethe Institute. May 2003. Available from http://www.goethe.de.

Thompson, Ginger. "Fraying of a Latin Textile Industry." *New York Times,* 25 March 2005.

Tucker, Ross. ""Duty Free Zones Spur Growth in Egypt." *WWD,* 12 December 2006.

U.S. Bureau of Census. *Annual Survey of Manufacturers: Statistics for Industry Groups and Industries: 2005.* U.S. Department of Commerce, Economics and Statistics Administration, November 2006. Available from http://blue.census.gov.

U.S. Department of Commerce/International Trade Administration. *U.S. Industry and Trade Outlook 2000.* New York: McGraw-Hill, 2000.

"U.S. Reimposes China Textile Quotas After Talks Fail." *ACN: Asian Chemical News,* 12 September 2005.

U.S.: Senate Bill Bans Imported Sweatshop Goods." *just-style.com,* 24 January 2007.

"World Business Briefing, Asia: China: No Plan to Reduce Textile Exports." *New York Times,* 18 March 2005.

SIC 2386, 3151

NAICS 315292, 315992

LEATHER GOODS AND ACCESSORIES

This segment of the broader global leather industry produces various forms of leather apparel, including gloves, jackets, vests, and hats, and miscellaneous accessories such as belts, purses, and bags.

INDUSTRY SNAPSHOT

The global leather apparel industry produces within two broad categories: light leather and heavy leather. The category of light leather usually refers to the tanned skins that come from smaller animals and reptiles, known simply as skins, while the heavy leather distinction refers to leather that comes from larger species of animals, often called hides. Most apparel and accessories crafted by this industry come in both light and heavy leather styles, with heavy generally being the more valuable form.

ORGANIZATION AND STRUCTURE

TRADE REFORMS

The 1990s saw important developments in the arena of world trade, including renewed emphasis on broadening the scope of liberalized trade. Two key trade agreements that had potential to rejuvenate the leather industry were concluded in the first half of the decade: the General Agreement on Tariffs and Trade (GATT) and the North American Free Trade Agreement (NAFTA). Both agreements eased market access to many of the world's leading economies covering a wide range of merchandise. GATT stipulated a gradual phase-out of all protective tariffs and quotas and their complete elimination by 2005.

In North America, NAFTA was passed in 1994. It also called for a gradual reciprocal phase-out of tariffs placed on leather exports and imports between Mexico and the United States. Concurrently, members of the European Union continued to make strides throughout the decade toward unifying their respective economies. This initiative culminated in the 1999 rollout of monetary union, or the Euro, among a majority of the EU member states. In the long term, Europe's economic unification was expected to make market entry in its numerous distinct nations easier for exporters to the region. In addition, the establishment of the World Trade Organization (WTO) in 1995 provided nations with a cooperative forum for the creation and implementation of trade agreements and policies. Its membership grew to 147 nations in 2004, including many developing countries. The 1995 WTO Agreement on Agriculture promoted reforms centering on fair, market-oriented trading systems, detailing specific commitments to reduce support and protection in the areas of domestic support, export subsidies, and market access, and through the establishment of strengthened and more operationally effective GATT rules and disciplines.

PRODUCTION PROCESS

The process of manufacturing gloves and leather apparel involves more or less the same number of major stages. Dependent upon their unique qualities, however, the number and types of operations performed within each stage can vary widely. The major manufacturing stages are tanning of hides and skins; finishing and dyeing; leather preparation; and garment making, including cutting, closing, stitching, and "laying off."

Types of Gloves and Mittens. Several types of light and heavy leathers enter into the production of gloves and mittens. Certain dress gloves, for instance, are produced from kidskins. Kidskins come from milk-fed baby goats that are raised in a delicate manner to protect against bruises and scratches, guaranteeing smoothness and a resilient quality uncommon to most gloves. Many are brush-dyed to ensure that the inside of the gloves remains white. Traditionally worn on formal and semi-formal evening occasions, kidskin gloves enjoy a reputation as the aristocrats of glovewear.

Mocha leather is used for both men's and women's gloves, and when finished, takes on the appearance of a fine silky velvet. This type of leather comes from black longhair sheep, native to Asia and Africa, whose skin is tanned with alum or formaldehyde. At first, mocha gloves, desired for their thickness and weight, were produced for men only. Later they were shaved, skived (a leather industry term referring to the operation of cutting leather more or less horizontally to reduce its thickness), or friezed (which refers to the process of removing the epidermis or grain layer by scraping with a hand-held knife and, later, by automated machine) to a fine thinness deemed acceptable for both men's and women's wear. Mocha leather is preferred for its durability, and, from a manufacturer's standpoint, for the ease with which it is dip-dyed or brush-dyed.

Suede gloves, of Swedish origin, come from kidskin or milk-fed baby lambs. Most are finished with a nap on the flesh side of their skin. Compared to other leathers, suede is the thinnest and most perishable of all. For glove manufacturers, suede is highly desired for its adaptability to all colors in brush-dyeing.

Capeskin leather, named for its Cape Town, South Africa, port of embarkment, is made from small African sheep. It possesses a sturdy, lightweight quality, with a very fine grain that when finished is soft to the touch and pliable. Buffing provides it with a glossy fashionable finish.

Pigskin leather made from wild Mexican or South American Peccary boars is the finest of all pigskin leathers. Domestic U.S. pigs, in comparison, are raised primarily for meat, and produce a hide fit only for luggage and upholstery. However, unregulated hunting depleted the numbers of Peccary boars, and the Mexican government eventually had to take steps to limit their killing. Peccary leather produces a soft glove, with a distinctive grain pattern owing to the pattern of its hair follicles arranged in detached lines of three.

Goatskin is tanned with sumac to produce a distinctive leather-grain glove. Goatskin gloves come from leather obtained from South America, South Africa, India, and Spain. Possessing strong and durable characteristics, goatskin is used mostly for men's gloves. Cabretta leather is obtained from a species of haired sheep native to certain provinces in Brazil. This type of skin was used mainly for shoe leather until the 1930s when it became available in glove form. Cabretta, close in appearance to Capeskin and very durable, is produced with a smooth, bright, glossy finish. Gloves made from lambskin leather come from young sheep that have grown beyond the milk-fed stage, having eaten grasses and grains that considerably change the character of their skin. Lambskin is not as fine, resilient, and durable as kidskin gloves or suede.

Buckskin, deerskin, reindeer, calfskin, bovine, and horsehide form the major group of heavy leathers used in glove making. As a group they are known for their durability, heaviness, warmth, and pliable nature. Tanned to be washable, they are mostly manufactured as men's work gloves. Heavy hides are also put to use in the production of leather apparel and handbags.

Background and Development

The leather goods and accessories industry is highly dependent on overall economic health and consumer spending. From 1989 to 1999, the major regions of economic growth—the developed economies of the United States, Western Europe, and Japan—still had not resumed earlier levels of demand despite economic recoveries. Demand strengthened somewhat, beginning in 2000 and the first half of 2001, as markets for light leather began to recover. But the global market for leather clothing and accessories was generally disappointing in 2002 and 2003, due to tepid economic growth and the impact of Severe Acute Respiratory Syndrome (SARS), which temporarily disrupted global trade. On the other hand, production of hides and skins increased, particularly in developing countries. Prices for hides and skins, however, declined through this period due primarily to falling demand in developed countries, which are the primary import markets for leather items.

One particular region exerting a significant downward impact on the production of light leather finished products consisted of the former planned economies of Eastern Europe and the new states that emerged from the breakup of the former Soviet Union. Throughout the region, economic conditions in general were in a state of prolonged decline or stagnation in the 1990s. Formerly producing a substantial amount of leather goods and accessories, these nations saw their production plummet 26.2 percent from 428.4 million square meters in 1991 to 316 million square meters in 1999 as government subsidies dried up and as local consumers were unable to sustain demand in the harsh transition to market economies.

Significant changes occurred in the industry after the 1990s. The Asian market as a whole was seen by industry observers as one of the preeminent future markets in the world industry, while African leather production surged in the late 1990s after a dramatic decline in production between 1990 and 1993. In the 1990s, South America also registered significant increases, with leather production growing 2.9 percent between 1990 and 1999, especially in Ecuador. Large regional declines, on the other hand, were recorded in the former planned economies of Eastern Europe and the Commonwealth of Independent States.

A pronounced trend that gained momentum beginning in the late 1950s was the shift in all leather producing activities from developed to developing economic regions. Not without periods of difficulty, much of this shift transpired due to a post-World War II climate of liberalized world trade jointly initiated by political authorities in the developed countries. Indicative of their export orientation, developing regions or countries such as Mexico, China, Korea, and Turkey, with a significant presence in the world leather industry, typically maintained a final leather product manufacturing capacity that exceeded domestic consumption. While many factors are responsible for these changes, environmental regulation was one of the major reasons for the migration of leather processing from the developed countries to developing countries. Between 1977 and 1996, global production of leather increased by 12.7 percent. Production in developing countries, especially of goat and sheep skins, grew 49.3 percent, while in developed countries it dropped by 7.5 percent. During the same period, developing countries' market share increased from 35.6 percent to 47.2 percent. Asia's production jumped some 94 percent during this period, while production in most developed countries declined. For example, North America's production dropped 12.1 percent while Europe's diminished by 16 percent from 1977 to 1996. Although production declined, net exports of bovine raw hides and skins from developed countries nearly tripled during the same period. Even in the area of leather-making machinery production—an activity once dominated solely by developed countries, particularly Italy and Germany—challenges emerged from countries such as China, India, South Korea, Taiwan, and Thailand.

Because developed regions account for a major share of finished leather product consumption met through developing country exports, the state of industry conditions in these markets determines the health of the industry overall. In particular, the direction of macroeconomic variables such as per capita income and consumer expenditure are critical. The uneven economic recoveries of Europe and the United States in the mid- to late 1990s showed signs of improved consumer spending; however, in Japan and parts of Southeast Asia economic downturns quashed consumer purchase levels. For the developing countries involved in the export production of finished leather goods, this translated into an acute period of global competition manifested by increasing overcapacity, frequent exchange rate adjustments to stimulate trade, and worsening unemployment.

From 1999 to 2001, bovines yielded 10.99 billion square feet of light leather, of which 56 percent was used for shoes. Sheep and goat hides yielded 4.5 billion square feet of leather, most of which was used for clothing and accessories. According to the Food and Agricultural Organization of the United Nations (FAO), world production of bovine hides and skins increased by roughly 10 percent from the mid-1980s to 1999, with developing nations accounting for most of this growth. Asian nations, where tanning operations expanded significantly, produced more hides and skins than any other region by the early 2000s. World output of sheepskins rose by 4 percent during this period, while production of goatskins increased by more than 70 percent. In developing countries, goatskin output rose by about 76 percent, and it increased in developed countries by 15 percent.

In 2002, world bovine hide production was estimated by the FAO at a record 5.8 billion tons, an increase of 2 percent from 2001, when production fell by 1.7 percent. Production grew again in 2003, by an estimated 1.5 percent. The increase was considerably higher in developing countries, where higher rates of animal slaughter occurred. According to data from the International Council of Tanners, some 3.3 billion square feet of leather were used to make garments in 2000, which accounted for 18 percent of leather used throughout the world that year.

In general, international leather prices increased by 2 percent in 2000 and in the first part of 2001, reflecting larger exports from European countries that were still insufficient to match import demand. Exports also grew among developing nations, which positioned themselves for increasingly significant roles in international trade as tariffs and other restrictions began to be phased out according to GATT and World Trade Organization agreements. China's growing prominence in the market contributed to substantial export growth in the late 1990s and early 2000s. Between 1992 and 2000, U.S. imports of leather clothing from China increased by almost 300 percent. According to the *New York Times,* Chinese imports accounted for more than 95 percent of the entire American leather clothing market in 2000.

Besides issues of international trade, productivity improvements were foremost in the strategies of developed country firms. The redeployment of manufacturing equipment and workstations into "rink" or horseshoe-shaped production processes gained momentum in firms in developed countries. The rink system was structured around a teamwork concept so that instead of an operator being assigned to a specific task, a worker might become proficient in any number of operations while the team was also responsible for all final inspections. The United Nations Industrial Development Organization (UNIDO) reported "prodigious" per-operator productivity gains that jumped by 20 percent or more, a reduction in the amount of manufacturing floor space devoted to output time, higher quality products, and a marked decline in the product rejection rate.

On the political front, there was also speculation that the anti-cruelty to animals political sympathies championed by animal rights activists, mostly in Western Europe and the United States, might impart a dampening effect on leather consumption, as they had already on fur purchasing.

From the early 1980s through the early 2000s, distinct regional trends in light leathers manufacturing occurred, the bovine light leather trade expanding around 9.4 percent per year sustained by a strong demand for leather and leather products. The most pronounced trend was noted by the progressive emergence of Asia's industry presence, surpassing Latin America as the principal exporting region of light bovine leather while remaining a primary supplier of sheep and goat leather among developing countries. In the same period, precipitous declines in the regions of the former planned economies of Eastern Europe and the Commonwealth of Independent States overshadowed the mild upturn in production levels in traditionally dominant Western Europe. Meanwhile, modest declines in North America were offset by a marked upward trend in South America.

The dramatic regional declines noted in the former planned economies of Eastern Europe and in the new states making up the Commonwealth of Independent States occurred in both the light and heavy leather industries. But of the two, light leather production was hit the hardest. The sharpest declines were recorded in regional leaders Poland, the Czech Republic, and Slovakia. On an annual basis, these three countries accounted for 40 to 50 percent of the region's light leather manufacturing. While their respective market shares remained fairly stable, actual production levels tapered sharply along with those of neighboring transition economies. To secure the confidence of international financial institutions, political authorities in Poland and the Czech Republic pledged to combat inflationary tendencies through fiscal austerity and the pursuit of tight monetary policies that kept interest rates high.

RISE OF DEVELOPING ECONOMIES

A pronounced trend that gained momentum after the late 1950s was the shift in all leather producing activities from developed to developing countries. Though not without periods of difficulty, much of this shift transpired due to a post-World War II climate of liberalized world trade jointly initiated and adhered to by political forces in the developed countries. As the production of light and heavy leather products in the Commonwealth of Independent States and Eastern Europe was expected to progress along a downward course, the continued ascendancy of the developing countries appeared more probable.

The rapid emergence of developing regions in the leather goods and accessories industry had some producers in developed regions nervous. In 1996, the European leather goods industries committee filed a complaint with the European Commission, which regulates trade and competition, about the massive influx of leather goods imported into the region from China, which had by 1999 become the world's largest leather-exporting country. Such complaints were likely to result in some form of anti-dumping legislation designed to protect Europe's manufacturers from the threat of over-importing after remaining trade quotas regulating the global clothing market were removed in 2005.

Indicative of their export orientation, developing countries with a significant presence in the world leather industry typically maintained a final leather product manufacturing capacity that exceeded domestic consumption. The shift of final leather products from developed to developing countries was connected to the labor-intensive nature of leather apparel production. Since both developed and developing countries faced more or less the same material and overhead costs, developing countries were able to produce with a substantial cost advantage because of comparatively low-wage labor. In more than a few instances, firms in developed countries chose to relocate parts or all of their final leather production process to developing nations. During years in which U.S. exports of leather apparel rose steadily, much of those exports included parts shipped to less developed countries, especially Mexico, for final assembly before shipment back into the U.S. for consumption. Similar developing country outward processing arrangements were a common practice undertaken by firms in the EU.

CURRENT CONDITIONS

According to figures from the International Council of Tanners, the world's top leather producers in the mid-2000s were China (4.4 billion square feet), Italy (2.0 billion square feet) and India (1.4 billion square feet), followed by Korea (973 million square feet), the United States (831 million square feet), Russia (782 million square feet), and Brazil (756 million square feet).

The major end use of all leather produced in the world in the mid-2000s was footwear, accounting for 56 percent. Furniture was responsible for 12.5 percent, followed by garments (11.4%), automotive uses (6.3%), gloves (4.4%), and other leather products (9.4%).

RESEARCH AND TECHNOLOGY

Prior to the 1980s, the general trend in the manufacture of leather products centered on incremental refinements in the existing techniques to enhance productivity. Some of these included the strategic redeployment of machinery and workers to significantly reduce an item's output time and the introduction of labor-saving equipment such as automatic stackers and hide hoists. Many other techniques concentrated on research and product development devoted to leather processing with solvent tanning and the use of synthetic materials.

By the 1980s and 1990s, major technological developments swept through the leather products industry, making previous developments seem minor in comparison. In the leather preparation stage, one critical operation centered on a multipurpose machine known as the "drum." Made from wood, it is used for a wide variety of operations such as chemically removing hair from the hide or skin, coloring or dyeing, lubricating, and leather softening. Although in its outward appearance the subsequent drum looked much like its predecessors from the 1890s, it had been transformed at the close of twentieth century to a high-tech, precision-engineered piece of equipment inside. Powered by electromechanical means, the drum is equipped with complex process instrumentation, programmed and controlled by a microprocessor, and some were even linked to personal computers. The late-twentieth-century drum contained systems allowing for the quick discharge and re-circulation of leather processing liquors. Unlike earlier versions, it was constructed with pegs that tended to stretch and draw hides in a manner that positively enhanced the efficiency of chemical treatments. In the early 1990s, UNIDO estimated that more than 90 percent of global hide production was processed using the wooden drum. It also reported that newer alternative systems made from stainless steel and polymer were being used.

By the early 2000s, improvements in the tanning process made it possible to soften low-quality skins sufficiently to use them in high-quality garments. Stamping and printing technologies allowed manufacturers to make inexpensive skins resemble luxury materials such as snakeskin or alligator skin. Since, according to FTC labeling guidelines, any product made of animal hide can be labeled as genuine leather, these new technologies enabled producers to use the hide from any type of animal. Other developments in the tanning and preparations stages were in hide splitting, shaving, and drying operations. In through-feed splitting operations a hide is inserted in one side of a machine and comes out on the opposite side in two layers. The splitting operation acts to cut the grain or top epidermis from the body of the skin producing a porous quality that makes it more flexible for downstream processing. In former times it could take up to four laborers to operate the splitting machine, but by the 1990s, the operation was performed by a continually sharpened band-knife. The introduction of microprocessor controls to this application made it easier to program and monitor for splitting thickness.

Shaving machines are actuated using microprocessor controls to bring about a higher degree of accuracy, instantaneous change of thickness, and greater control over undesirable leather ribbing (once caused by shaving machine vibrations). One of the most critical operations performed in leather processing, leather drying is a balanced operation in which care has to be exercised to dispose of all excess water while still ensuring that the leather remains flexible and soft. Natural air-drying has been traditionally considered the best method; however, from a business standpoint it is very time consuming. Subsequently, factory air-flow drying came to be the standard method. In the mid-1980s, an energy-saving dehumidification drying process was developed in France that incorporated a controlled closed-circuit energy recovery system using heat pumps. Subsequent approaches to drying included the use of infrared radiation or microwave energy. A major advantage of microwave drying is that it evaporates water without raising the temperature of the leather, which may detract from its softness. When drying leathers, it is common to stretch or "toggle" them to prevent area loss. Previously a labor-intensive operation, labor-saving toggle machines were introduced in which hides are stacked horizontally to ensure membrane flexibility.

In the product development stage, advances in microprocessor technology affected leather cutting and stitching operations in developed countries. Traditionally, finished leather materials were cut manually. Swing beam presses were then introduced, later augmented by traveling head presses, through which layers of material were fed by conveyor under a computer-automated cutting head. Computer programs were later developed to determine the nesting of leather components in order to minimize material waste and to detect surface imperfections.

Microcomputer-controlled sewing machines were diffused throughout the developed final leather products industry in the 1980s, which led to significant labor savings. Sewing machines received different stitching instructions from preprogrammed data input devices while the operator's role consisted of simply loading, unloading, and initiating the stitching sequence. Programming was conducted either on a separate digitizing unit or on one attached to the machine to allow for direct input. Because they significantly reduced both the amount of required operator training time and the number of tasks previously performed, these new machines ushered in a period of pronounced skill loss in the labor force. Because of their higher capital intensity and productivity-enhancing impact, it was wondered whether they might stem the process of shifting final leather production processes to developing countries, which tend to rely more heavily on manual labor.

Ecological concerns also affect the world's leather industry. In developed countries, research efforts were directed to finding suitable replacements for chrome in tanning operations, and in leather processing and finishing operations there was a move away from using solvent-based chemicals in favor of water-based alternatives. The passage of stringent environmental legislation in developed countries accelerated the search for environmentally friendly manufacturing processes. However, progress was slow, as escalating tariffs discouraged producers from investing in environmentally sustainable technologies, according to the World Trade Organization. Although no directly comparable data are available, the costs of compliance in developed countries generally were much higher than in developing countries. For instance, the cost of treating solid residues from processing hides and skins in developed countries could be as much as four times higher than in many developing countries because of tighter pollution limits, higher transportation and waste site costs, and higher labor costs. Tanning processes cause environmental problems by producing solid residue and large volumes of toxic effluent. The problem of correcting for environmental pollution has not been resolved as much as it has been displaced to developing countries where authorities—under pressure to attract and maintain foreign investment—have been reluctant to pass or enforce environmental legislation.

MAJOR COUNTRIES IN THE INDUSTRY

CHINA AND KOREA

In 2000, world leather production was boosted by increases in China and the Republic of Korea. When expressed in terms of its regional market share in light leather, Asia's ascending status was clear. China and the Republic of Korea accounted for more than 30 percent of global imports of bovine hides and skins in 2000, resulting from the country's economic turnaround. China ranked first in world production of leather, and Korea was fourth. China's export market also grew dramatically during the early to mid-2000s. Taking advantage of cheap labor and improved production technologies, China's leather industry was able to offer quality clothing at prices low enough to serve even moderate-income consumers. As the *New York Times* reported, about half of China's leather garment exports to the United States in 2000 were made from pigskin, which is much cheaper to produce than most other types of leather but is relatively coarse. With advanced stamping and printing techniques, however, Chinese manufacturers were able to make relatively low-quality skins soft enough to be sewn into fashionable clothing. Indeed, prices became so attractive that, by 2000, leather apparel was increasingly seen by U.S. consumers as a mass-market product instead of a luxury item. That year, the value of China's global exports of leather apparel and accessories exceeded US$2.4 billion. By 2003, this figure had grown to more than US$3.9 billion.

ITALY

Italy was the dominant country in the EU in the leather industry and ranked as the number-two leather producer in the world. In the early 2000s Italy produced 214.8 million square meters, or 66 percent of Europe's leather. It was also the world's largest importer of bovine hides; 68 percent of the hides processed in Italy in 2005 were bovine. Of the leather produced in Italy in the mid-2000s, 46.7 percent was used for footwear, followed distantly by furniture upholstery (24.6%), leather goods (12.8%), garments and gloves (6.7%), car interiors (4.7%), and other uses (4.5%). A majority of the 168 million pounds of leather exported from Italy in 2005 went to Hong Kong. China was the second largest market for Italian leather exports, followed by Romania and Austria.

INDIA

In the mid-2000s, India ranked third in the world in leather production, after China and Italy, and employed some 2.5 million people, about 30 percent of them women. A report by Exim Bank in India projected another 1 million jobs would be added in the industry by 2011. Annual production was valued at about US$4 billion, with exports earning about US$2.4 billion in 2005. Sixty-eight percent of leather exports were shipped to Europe, and 12 percent to the United States. Hong Kong and China were also big markets for Italian leather exports, and Russia was emerging as another important market. The ANCI reported a 54.2 percent growth in exports to Russia in 2006, amounting to US$107.9 million in goods.

Faced with increasing competition from cheaper markets, Indian leather companies hoped to increase their share of the American market by improving the quality of their products. According to the *Daily News Record,* by 2003 India was importing about 20 percent of its finished skins from high-quality producers in Italy, Portugal, and Africa. Producers were also upgrading manufacturing and finishing equipment. The Indian leather industry (including shoes) grew 17 percent in 2004. India expected to double the value of its leather exports by 2010.

According to *WWD,* India has the world's largest cattle population and the second largest livestock population. However, due to the predominance of the Hindu religion, in which cows are considered sacred, strict laws about slaughterhouses exist. In the past, the leather manufacturing industry was dominated by Muslims, although the journal reported this may change as others see the profitability of the business.

UNITED STATES

Within North America, the United States led the region in light leather production by a small margin and was the fifth largest leather producer in the world. Because of expedited U.S. feedlot production, cattle grown in a relatively short time period yield a higher average weight per hide than most other countries. Many U.S. light leather apparel producers and glove and mitten manufacturers did not survive the competitive challenge posed by foreign imports. Many thus decided to relocate production to developing regions where labor costs were considerably lower. Even U.S. light leather tanners met their domestic demand for finished leather products by sourcing them overseas, mostly to South Korea and China.

According to the U.S. Census Bureau, total U.S. shipments of leather and allied products equaled US$3.4 billion in 2004, up from US$3.0 billion in 2001. California was the highest producing state, followed by Missouri and Texas.

According to *Los Angeles Business Journal,* in 2000 the United States imported US$1.7 billion of leather apparel—a whopping 71 percent increase from the previous year. Handbags alone accounted for US$1.2 billion. Since 2000, leather apparel in the United States has been increasingly marketed to middle income consumers. According to the *New York Times,* discount chains such as Target, Kmart, and Wal-Mart offer a range of products including bomber jackets, skirts, jeans, and halter tops priced from US$39.99 to US$109.99.

According to U.S. International Trade Administration statistics, the United States exported US$78.9 million of leather clothing in 2004, an increase of 22.5 percent from the previous year. Top destinations were Japan, the United Kingdom, Italy, Canada, Mexico, and Germany. In addition, the country exported US$124.1 million of miscellaneous leather products, up 43.6 percent from 2003. U.S. imports of leather apparel, which declined by 13.5 percent in value from 2003 to 2004, still far surpassed exports at a total of US$1.197 billion. China was the leading supplier, followed by Italy and India. Imports of other leather products totaled US$390 million.

RUSSIA

The leather industry in Russia experienced a 14 percent growth rate between 2002 and 2005, according to the European Commission. The value of the market in 2005 was reported at 125 million euros and Russian Leathernet reported that output of finished leather at factories in Russia was growing.

BRAZIL

Brazil's light leather production totals accounted for nearly all of South America's market share in the mid-2000s. Because much of its final leather goods output was produced for export to developed countries and its labor costs were on the rise, it remained unclear whether Brazil could maintain its advantage against lower labor cost countries such as China, Indonesia, and Vietnam. In terms of heavy leather global production, South America experienced significant growth. Brazil managed to continue as a major force despite some slippage. Rising demand for automobile upholstery accounted for a significant portion of Brazil's increase in leather output in the 2000s, and shoe manufacture also consumed much of Brazil's leather. Still, the country exported US$3.5 million of leather apparel and accessories in 2003.

FURTHER READING

Current Industrial Reports. Washington, DC: Department of Commerce, 2004.

Dadaglio, Giovanni. "Africa Positions Itself for the Global Leather Market." *International Trade Forum*, February 2003. Available from http://www.tradeforum.org.

Food and Agricultural Organization of the United Nations. *Hides and Skins Commodity Notes,* March 2004. Available from www.fao.org.

Foreman, Katya. "Europe's Hot Category: Leather Goods Brands in Retail Growth Push." *WWD,* 26 March 2007.

International Council of Tanners. "Leather Statistics," 2004. Available from http://www.tannerscouncilict.org.

Mathur, Shobha. "Moving Up the Value Chain." *Industrial Economist,* 2005. Available from http://www.indeconomist.com.

"News." Russian Leathernet, 15 April 2007. Available from www.leathernet.ru/.

"Overview: Leather Industry." European Commission, 2006. Available from http://ec.europa.eu/.

United Nations Statistics Division. *Industrial Commodity Statistics Yearbook,* 2004. Available from http://unstats.un.

Upadhyay, Ritu. "India Leather Industry Eyes $7 Billion in Sales by 2010." *WWD,* 18 July 2006.

U.S. Census Bureau. "Leather and Allied Product Manufacturing." *Annual Survey of Manufacturers,* 2004. Available from www.census.gov.

White, Samantha. "Confidence in the Future." *Leather International,* April 2006.

Zargani, Luisa. "Russian, Japanese Buyers Drive Mipel." *WWD,* 2 April 2007.

SIC 2200

NAICS 313

TEXTILE MILLS

Textile mills produce a vast range of finished and intermediate textile products, but production centers on broadwoven fabrics from cotton, wool, and other natural and man-made fibers. These textiles are used in such diverse applications as clothing, household linens, furniture, and motor vehicle interiors. Certain industry firms also perform textile finishing by applying chemicals and processes to purchased fabrics. See also the article entitled **Apparel.**

INDUSTRY SNAPSHOT

At the dawn of the twenty-first century, the textile industry in the United States and other developed countries faced some severe challenges, requiring significant restructuring of manufacturing priorities and operations. From the 1980s to the late 1990s the international competitiveness of the textile industry in developed countries—where labor costs were steeper than in the developing world—steadily improved with the introduction of more efficient machinery. However, this increased productivity led to accelerating layoffs of textile workers and rapidly increasing mill closures by 2002, as fewer people were needed to produce the same—or even greater—volumes of goods.

In addition, the impact of the Asian financial crisis of 1997 to 1998 on the textile industry in developed countries continued to be substantial. Asian textiles, whose prices fell significantly during the crisis, were being imported to developed countries in ever-increasing volumes, contributing to the adverse state of textile industries in some developed countries, including the United States. In 2001 at least one hundred U.S. textile mills closed and some 60,000 to 75,000 U.S. textile workers were laid off. The situation was even worse in 2003, when a total of 99,400 apparel and textile workers in the United States lost their jobs.

After heavily investing in newer and more efficient but costly technology and equipment, U.S. textile mills found it harder to compete with the lower-priced textile imports from Asia entering U.S. markets in the early 2000s. In consequence, large numbers of U.S. mills shifted production to emphasize non-apparel textiles such as home furnishings and industrial textiles, reduced their workforces, merged with other companies, forged tighter links with apparel and other end-use manufacturers, sought opportunities to shift production to sites in the developing world, or closed their doors entirely. Many formerly flourishing U.S. textile milling centers, particularly in the southern states, were forced to realign their local economies, which some did by welcoming in new types of manufacturing and service industries to employ laid off textile workers and offer new opportunities for growth.

Despite the problems brought on by the Asian financial crisis Asia's textile business at the start of the new millennium was showing renewed strength. Responsible for the vast majority of the world's broadwoven cotton milling, Asia continued to shape the global textile industry. In particular, China remained a towering competitor. The burgeoning Chinese economy was a powerhouse in textile milling and supported thriving industries in textile machinery—the equipment used in textile mills—and in apparel, the biggest end market for milled textiles. China has been the world's largest producer of woven cotton textiles since the 1980s, a position that was strengthened by the Chinese economic boom that began in the 1990s. The Asian financial crisis of the late 1990s mainly dampened China's intra-region trade but did not diminish the volume of its textile exports. When China joined the World Trade Organization in December 2001, its position as the dominant player in the international textile industry was further assured.

Organization and Structure

Global Patterns of Production and Consumption

While China continued to be the world's largest producer of textiles in the early 2000s, by most measures the developed countries of Japan, the United States, and the European Union were the world's largest consumers of textile products. Textile mills around the globe produced fabric from either natural raw material fibers such as cotton, wool, silk, and flax, or two principal types of manufactured fibers: artificial fibers (previously called cellulosic) and synthetic fibers (previously called non-cellulosic). Consumer demand for end-use products containing fabric significantly impacted intermediate levels and types of fabric production.

The textile milling and production process involves a variety of operations including opening and cleaning, carding, spinning, weaving, knitting, and finishing. Textile mills purchase production machinery from textile machinery manufacturers that were historically responsible for introducing advanced machinery. As is true in most other industries, newer equipment in the textile industry tends to save labor and to waste less material, stimulating significant reductions in unit costs.

Firms of all sizes located in developed and developing countries alike produce broadwoven fabrics—that is, fabrics woven on wide looms. In developed nations, the textile industry tends to be dualistic in nature, as a large number of small and medium-sized firms produce a limited range of fabrics and account for a relatively small proportion of output, while a few large firms produce a wider range of fabrics and a disproportionate share of output. Whether a country is developed or developing, the textile industry in a particular country is shaped by diverse factors such as the complexity of products produced; the amount of available capital; the skill level, sophistication, and wages of workers; the degree of vertical integration; industry concentration levels in the country; the overall importance of the industry to the country's entire economy; and the country's degree of participation in the international marketplace.

The Production Process

The production of textile fibers and fabrics is a multistage sequence involving opening and cleaning, carding, weaving, and wet processing. Firms that transform cotton fiber, for example, into broadwoven fabric employ a wide range of machines, equipment, and workers to perform a variety of operations. In addition to broadwoven fabrics, the textile industry produces weft, lace, and warp knit fabrics, mainly in circular form. The textile industry also comprises carpet and rug production as well as yarn-spinning mills and plants producing man-made fibers. Because the production of cotton fabric is integral to the success of the textile industry worldwide and involves many of the same steps as the production of fabric from other fibers, the following is a detailed description of the cotton-textile production process.

First, opening-room machinery loosens up cotton layers taken from bales of cotton and reduces them into smaller pieces, then delivers the fiber to cleaning machines for further processing. If the cotton fibers are not properly selected or are imprecisely fed, production efficiency is reduced and quality suffers. In the second, or carding, stage, a machine called a "card" disentangles and collects the cotton fibers to prepare for the next phase, weaving. In the weaving phase, looms weave the cotton fibers into fabric.

Finally, the fabric is subjected to a multi-step, wet-processing phase that involves preparation, where the fabric is separated from the loom and natural contaminants are removed; dyeing, where color is added; and finishing, where enhancements such as durable press, water repellency, stability, mothproofing, soil resistance, and flame-proofing are incorporated into the fabric. Not all woven-cotton fabrics pass through the entire wet-processing chain. For instance, surgical goods undergo intensive preparation yet require no dyeing or finishing. Only the preparation and finishing steps are necessary for certain yarn-dyed goods. In general, the fabric's fiber content and intended end-use determine which wet-processing procedures the fabric will undergo.

Technological advances such as computer automation introduced from the 1960s through the 1990s in the production of cotton broadwoven fabric significantly improved the efficiency and profitability of textile mills. In the opening and cleaning stage, for example, computers were installed to select the most desirable combination of cotton bales for the specific end product. Bale pluckers and automatic feeds could be programmed to retrieve a set quantity of fiber from the bales, making possible the processing of more than 1,000 pounds of fiber per hour while assuring a homogeneous blend, a performance far superior to any achieved with manual feeding. Automated blending contributed to more evenly distributed variations in fiber characteristics, more uniform processing, improved fabric quality, lower raw material costs, and reduced costs in labor. Automated equipment in the opening department was completely controlled by microprocessors, delivering well-opened stock via chute feeds to the cards and eliminating the need for picker laps and their transportation. Using automated equipment, masses of cotton fiber were gradually opened to progressively smaller tufts without ever being compressed.

Prior to the 1960s, card operations reached a processing range of 4 to 18 pounds per hour depending on the type and quality of cotton fiber used and the desired purity level and nep (one or more entangled fibers) count. In the early 1970s new, modified carding technology was implemented, improving processing speed to an average 50 pounds per hour. By 1980 high-production cards commonly operated at processing speeds of 100 to 250 pounds per hour. The direct feeding of cotton sheets to the card via chutes led to the automation of the cardroom. Compared to the earlier lap-fed cards, chute feeding presented numerous advantages, eliminating run-out problems such as fabric damage caused by lap ends' jerking the feed roll, more constant feed rates, higher operating efficiency, more uniform yard-to-yard weights, reductions in labor costs and error, improved dust and trash removal, lower maintenance and production costs, and reductions in operating space. However, because chute feeding lacked blending capability, manufacturers were compelled to use additional blending machinery. Other carding improvements—including the use of electronic clutches, solid state circuitry, DC motors, microprocessors, and minicomputers—translated into more precise control and higher efficiency.

Regarding improvements in weaving technology, shuttleless looms such as the rapier/projectile, air-jet, and water-jet looms and subsequent refinements began to displace shuttle looms in the 1970s. Textile firms saw the advantages of shuttleless looms in reducing labor costs while producing a higher-quality product. Besides their higher speed and productivity, shuttleless looms are superior to shuttle looms for safety and environmental reasons. Shuttleless looms ended the problem of errant shuttles striking and injuring workers. Furthermore, shuttleless looms operate without the noise-producing checking motion of conventional, shuttle-weaving machines; rapier looms also incorporate insulated covers into their design, further reducing noise levels. In 2000 there were 2,864 shuttle looms in the United States; by the end of 2002 this number had fallen to 1,949. The number of shuttleless looms, which had climbed to 51,556 in 2000, fell to 39,472 by the end of 2002.

The newer looms achieve greater productivity primarily because of their faster, more reliable weft insertion systems and greater machine width. Early shuttleless looms used large weft packages creeled in by the weaver, eliminating the need for support labor such as magazine tenders. Later developments in shuttleless weaving technology incorporated features such as automatic pick finders, which make repairs less time-consuming, and self-lubrication, which reduces parts' wear and maintenance downtime. The precision-wound, flat-cheese type of weft package is a peripheral device developed and used with shuttleless looms. It was invented because weft insertion speeds of shuttleless looms triggered a problem of weft breaks when the weft yarn was unwound from its package. The precision-wound, flat-cheese weft package unwinds a length of yarn from the weft package prior to picking and thus lowers the quality requirements for weft packages and permits the use of weaker, previously unacceptable yarns.

Aside from shuttleless looms and related innovations, another notable characteristic of more recent weaving machines is a greater reliance on electronics. Electronic monitoring systems alert weavers and technicians to operational stoppages. The telemechanique system distinguishes between weft, warp, and mechanical stoppages and identifies the causes of mechanical stoppages. By the 1980s, push-button control and electronic weft-stop motions had become standard features of most weaving looms.

Throughout many developed countries, electronic monitoring systems were implemented first on weaving machines but soon extended to provide efficiency data broken down by department, shift, weaver and fixer sets, style sets, and machine levels. Because of the systems' memory capability, electronic monitoring systems eliminate the need to read pick clocks at the end of each shift. Moreover, system stops are recorded and classified within weft, warp, and mechanical categories, enabling managers and technicians to easily pinpoint and rectify problem areas.

Technological advances in wet processing toward the end of the twentieth century focused on reducing energy consumption and curtailing water usage in response to rising energy costs and to the more stringent government regulation of water pollutants. In most developed countries, the textile industry, compared to other industries, has ranked among the industrial leaders in cutting energy consumption requirements. Since dyeing and finishing together accounted for more than three-fourths of all energy consumed in cotton fabric production, due to the energy needed to evaporate water and solvents from fabric, the wet-processing stage was singled out for energy-saving innovations. Washers were designed with counter-current water flows to curtail both energy consumption and chemical usage. Systems designed to recycle water and recover heat were incorporated into washers. Solvent removal equipment was redesigned to eliminate wetting and drying steps; newer dryers featured heat recovery and reuse designs. Improved dyeing technology required lower liquor ratios and allowed faster dyeing with less energy and fewer chemicals. Finishing machines were built for increased speed and lower "pickup" levels using hard roll pads or foam applications, and tenter frames became more energy efficient through improved air flow.

GLOBAL INSTITUTIONAL FRAMEWORK

In the years immediately following World War II, most textile trade was governed by bilateral agreements that limited the volume of textiles one country could send to another. The United States and Britain repeatedly met challenges from the Asian textile producers in the post-war period with protectionist measures typically involving complicated rules and high tariffs. Over time, bilateral agreements were negotiated that somewhat reduced the tendency to place other non-quota restrictions on trade and offered some promise of advancing a more open trading climate. Nevertheless, many countries were unwilling to live with quotas, especially where cotton textile exports were a principal source of hard currency. In addition, because bilateral agreements were negotiated on a country-by-country basis, they were very time- and energy-consuming to design and implement.

As alternatives to bilateral arrangements, new multilateral frameworks were established to govern world trade in the second half of the twentieth century. The first such agreement was the 1948 General Agreement on Tariffs and Trade (GATT). A series of renegotiated and updated GATTs followed approximately every five years, culminating in the 1986 to 1994 Uruguay Round of GATT negotiations which established the World Trade Organization (WTO) on January 1, 1995. After that, WTO members met regularly in a General Council, three main subcouncils—including the Council for Trade in Goods, or Goods Council, that governed international trade in textiles—and in a number of committees and other groups. As of 23 April 2004, 147 nations were members of the World Trade Organization, which had replaced the GATT as the formal, institutionalized body of international trade practices and policies but was following a revised and significantly expanded set of GATT rules.

From the outset, GATT's overriding aim was to "liberalize world trade and place it on a secure basis." GATT was internally structured with a code of rules for conducting international trade, using an international forum for settling trade disputes. Despite the stated intentions of the GATT, various departures from the rules were commonplace, especially for textiles. In general, a more liberalized trade climate for textiles did emerge among the developed countries in North America and Western Europe in the early post-war years thanks to GATT. However, during the 1950s the textile trade relationship progressively deteriorated between these countries and Japan, the socialist countries of Eastern Europe, and the less industrialized countries of the world.

In 1960 textile trade effectively was separated from GATT's fundamental principle of fostering liberalized trade with the adoption of an "Avoidance of Market Disruption" clause. This provision allowed countries to impose import restrictions: 1) simply if a "potential" increase in imports was expected to have an injurious impact; 2) if a particular country's textile imports were identified as the source of a problem (a practice that under GATT rules would be considered discriminatory); and 3) if a sizable price difference existed between certain cheaper textile imports and comparable goods in a domestic market.

In February of 1962, 19 major trading countries signed on to the Long Term Arrangement Regarding Cotton Textiles (LTA), which, under GATT auspices, remained in effect for several five-year periods, each followed by a new round of negotiations. Under the terms of the LTA, import countries were allowed to return to bilateral agreements and unilateral restraints. By 1973, 82 countries had signed the LTA. One unforeseen consequence was that many exporting countries merely switched over to the quota-free production of manufactured fibers. U.S. textile producers attempted to include manufactured fibers under the LTA but were unsuccessful. Instead, a separate treaty was negotiated in 1974 called the Arrangement Regarding International Trade in Textiles, later referred to as the Multifiber Arrangement (MFA).

Cotton textiles eventually were phased into the MFA during a second round of negotiations (MFA II), when several new provisions were added that had not been part of the LTA. These provisions included the creation of a multilateral textile surveillance board to monitor implementation of the MFA, stricter rules for determining market disruption claims, and an allowance for growth in quota levels at a rate of 6 percent annually instead of 5 percent as permitted under the earlier LTA. MFA II also featured greater flexibility in quota arrangements such as the "swing" provision that permitted the transfer of a quota from one category to another, the "carry forward" clause that allowed an exporting country to borrow against next year's quota, and the "carry over" clause which allowed an exporting country to add unused quota onto the limits for the following year. MFA II was followed by MFA III, in force from 1982 to July 1986.

MFA IV originally was to be in force from August 1986 to July 1991 but was extended to 1994 then superceded by the 1995 Agreement on Textiles and Clothing (ATC) that included a mechanism for phasing out bilateral quotas. As early as 1986, developing countries were pushing to phase out the MFA itself but were rebuffed by the powerful U.S. textile lobby, according to Dr. Sri Ram Khanna, an international consultant on the Asian textile industry. The failure to achieve a phase-out of quotas at that time led the developing countries to set up the Geneva-based International Textiles and Clothing Bureau, one of whose main tasks was to create a coordinated plan to liberalize textile trade.

One of the most significant developments affecting the international textiles industry was the Uruguay Round of the

GATT, a series of multilateral negotiations conducted by GATT member states from 1986 to 1994, which ultimately led to the creation of the World Trade Organization. In its impact on the textiles sector, the Uruguay Round addressed myriad trade disagreements associated with the MFA treaty and reestablished a climate of quota-free liberalized trade. The International Textiles and Clothing Bureau played an instrumental role in influencing the MFA phase-out embodied in the 1994 GATT accord. The 1995 Agreement on Textiles and Clothing (ATC) that resulted from the Uruguay Round replaced the earlier MFA arrangements and was designed to eliminate bilateral quotas completely over a ten-year period.

The ATC represented a marked departure from past similar agreements. The document contained procedural guidelines to resolve longstanding points of contention such as the integration process of MFA quotas and other "gray area" textile measures, the administration of quota phase-outs during the transition period, transition safeguards, the circumvention of quotas, reciprocity between developed and developing countries for all categories of textiles, and the establishment of a Textiles Monitoring Body or Board (TMB) to referee the quota phase-out process.

The TMB, an 11-member committee set up under the WTO's Council for Trade in Goods (Goods Council), was responsible for monitoring the quota phase-out integration process. The TMB also functioned as a standing, textile dispute resolution body for the phase-out transition period. Near the end of each phase-out stage, the TMB had to prepare a comprehensive report on the progress and degree of compliance with the ATC's overall goal of trade liberalization.

The textile trade integration process established by the Uruguay Round, which went into effect on 1 January 2005, entirely eliminated the quota system. The phase-out process was structured in four stages, each of which allowed progressively higher quotas of textile imports up to the point where quotas were completely disbanded. At the start of the phase-out process, small suppliers, who accounted for less than 1.2 percent of all textile quotas in December 1991, were allowed to leap immediately to the higher, second-stage quota rate. Members operating with "gray area" quotas—those that could not be justified under MFA or GATT rules—had to officially notify the TMB, bring their quotas into conformity with GATT rules, and eventually phase out quotas through the self-destruct mechanism built into the transition process.

Despite the objections of the United States, exporting countries continued to administer transition quotas. However, administrative procedures were subjected to mutual consultation between exporter and importer governments, and a circumvention clause—inserted due to pressure from the powerful U.S. textile lobby—targeted specific remedial action against imports that arrived through unlawful channels. The circumvention clause specified the following: for transshipment violations, a penalty of entry denial; for rerouting, quota debits; for declarations of false origin, legal action; and for false declarations of fiber type or quantity shipped or false description of goods, a penalty of new quotas. All remedial action had to follow strict rules of evidence.

The transition safeguards provision of the ATC was intended to protect an importing country's domestic textile industry from rising imports. The action to prevent damage, however, had to be applied against all countries and not against an individual country. During the 10-year transition period MFA-like quotas were permissible on individual countries but were subjcct to close scrutiny. The ATC's reciprocity clause, pushed by the European textile producers, obligated WTO members: 1) to promote improved access to textile markets by undertaking tariff reductions; 2) to agree to limit tariff ceilings; and 3) to eliminate non-tariff barriers by streamlining customs, administrative, and licensing procedures. This clause also ensured the implementation of fair trading policies, forbid dumping and anti-dumping procedures and subsidies, and called for protecting intellectual property rights. Lastly, discrimination against textile imports as a means of retaliating against general trade policy disputes was prohibited.

EMPLOYMENT

The extremely hazardous and undesirable working conditions of the early textile mills in the United States and England, coupled with the long hours—typically, 14-hour workdays—sparked the first labor strikes and efforts to form unions in the United States beginning in the 1830s and in Europe as well during the nineteenth century. Attempts by U.S. mill laborers to unionize were only partially successful, however, despite the large number of strikes and walkouts by textile workers, including young New England women in the mills of Lowell and other rapidly growing, northern industrial towns. As new groups of immigrants arrived in the United States from Ireland and French Canada, ready to work for lower wages than the native-born workers would accept, mill owners profited, replacing the local residents with immigrants when the mills reopened after the Civil War.

Similarly, beginning in the 1880s countless "sweatshops" sprang up in U.S. cities where garment workers, typically Italian, Jewish, and Chinese immigrants, toiled for long hours amid miserable conditions, often with little hope for improving their working conditions and pay due to the waves of new immigrants who were arriving on U.S. shores and could easily replace them. The first successful apparel workers union, the International Ladies' Garment Workers' Union, was founded in New York City in 1900.

Additional groups of immigrants came to take up jobs in the mills in the closing decades of the nineteenth century and the beginning of the twentieth. Lowell, Massachusetts, for example, became home to immigrants representing over 40 ethnic groups, among them Greeks, Poles, Italians, Swedes, Portuguese, Armenians, Lithuanians, Jews, and Syrians, who followed the French Canadians and the Irish into the mills. What had started out as a somewhat paternalistic working environment, where young local women lived in communal boardinghouses located on the mill property, became an increasingly cutthroat operation where workers' needs and interests were neglected by those who owned and ran the mills.

In 1912 general strikes among mill workers in Lowell finally produced results. Led by union organizers from the Industrial Workers of the World (IWW), the Lowell strikes resulted in a 10-cent raise for mill workers, similar to the results of strikes by textile mill workers in other New England cities. However, the strikes also convinced some mill owners to relocate in the South. Organizing effective labor unions in the textile mills of the United States has been a challenging endeavor, because mill owners generally were able to utilize the influxes of immigrants as sources of cheaper labor. Even at the start of the twenty-first century, the percentage of unionized U.S. textile mill workers was very low compared to the percentage of unionized workers in other U.S. industries, a situation reflected in the somewhat lower-than-average wage rates for textile mill workers. In October 2001 the average hourly wage for U.S. textile workers was US$11.36, just 13 cents per hour more than in October 2000, according to the U.S. Bureau of Labor Statistics, as reported in a December 2001 article in *Textiles World.*

Concern among consumers world-wide over poor working conditions and wages in many textile and apparel jobs of multinational corporations situated in developing countries grew through the 1990s and early 2000s. This led to international activism on behalf of workers in developing countries. For example, many activists increased their efforts to curb the use of child labor in the carpeting industries of countries like India and Pakistan and to ensure that working conditions for employees in multinational firms like Nike are monitored and improved. In the late twentieth century, American and European consumers increased their use of selective boycotting to seek improved pay structures and working conditions for foreign laborers in such plants.

Growing attempts to unionize labor in the textile industries of developing countries offer promise that working conditions and wages among the world's poorest industrial laborers will gradually improve. For example, union activity in Nigeria, Africa's largest country, grew in strength over a twenty-year period of industrial restructuring beginning in the late 1970s. There, the National Union of Textile, Garment, and Tailoring Workers of Nigeria (NUTGTWN) helped reorganize an industry that was rapidly expanded and modernized thanks to Nigeria's burgeoning oil industry. However, the very fact that in North America NAFTA itself caused an outflow of textile and apparel jobs to developing countries such as Costa Rica, Honduras, and Mexico in North America, costing many U.S. textile workers their jobs, exemplifies the complexity of situations in the international textile industry which cannot be fully addressed by international boycotts or unionization alone. Since the late twentieth century, multinational corporations increasingly relocated their production to plants in the developing world. This led to growth in the economies of certain developing countries while increasing numbers of workers were laid off from their jobs at some of the former textile-producing giants of the developed world. On the other hand, some of this relocation of production activity benefited U.S. workers. For example, by relocating their apparel production operations to Mexico but requiring that U.S.-produced yarns and fabrics be used in manufacturing apparel, U.S. companies arguably have kept a number of textile-milling jobs in the United States that otherwise might have been lost.

In general, however, employment in the global textile industry paralleled the drop in production growth rates in the ending decades of the twentieth century. The average annual growth rate in textile employment for 1963 to 1973 measured 3.2 percent for developing countries but declined to 1.1 percent for these countries for the period 1973 to 1990. In terms of U.S. employment, by the late 1990s, approximately 608,000 workers were employed in the U.S. textile industry, a figure that fell significantly and steadily over the next several years in response to the greater technological efficiency of milling machinery and to the competitive challenge presented by Asian textile imports. By October 2001 the number of textile workers in the United States had fallen to approximately 456,700, some 383,600 of whom were production workers. The unemployment rate for U.S. textile workers that month was 9.4 percent, a full 4 percentage points higher than the general U.S. unemployment rate of 5.4 percent. In 2003, U.S. textile mills employed only 241,300 workers, eliminating 38,400 jobs. Between 1990 and 2003, employment in U.S. textile mills fell by 49 percent.

Background and Development

Although textiles have been produced since prehistoric times, the modern era of textile production using capitalist methods took root in England with the Industrial Revolution that began in the 1700s. Toward the close of the 1600s, a growing volume of cotton textiles was being imported to England from India, then a British colony, the result of British legislation passed in 1690. Indian fabric appealed to English urban tastes but competed with England's own fledgling textile industry. The British Parliament, whose members reasoned that the British textile industry could develop best if isolated from outside competition, soon banned Indian cottons. This marked the start of a long period of significant growth in the production of British textiles during the eighteenth and nineteenth centuries, first through cottage industries and later through the use of more advanced techniques and equipment located in an expanding number of large industrial plants.

Advancement of the British textile industry was assisted by British manufacturers willing to offer cash rewards to textile machine inventors who created more productive machines. In 1733 John Kay (1704-64) developed the mechanical flying shuttle, which for the first time allowed a single worker to weave cotton fabric in widths that exceeded the length of an adult person's arm. Before this invention, production of broadwoven cotton fabrics required two workers' moving a shuttle back and forth to insert thread. However, Kay's flying shuttle exerted backward pressure on spinners to supply the necessary level of yarn, a difficult if not impossible task. This problem was soon corrected by three inventions: John Hargreaves's spinning jenny, a carding machine that introduced the simultaneous spinning of multiple threads, in 1764; Sir Richard Arkwright's water frame, introduced in 1771, which spun cotton fiber into thread; and especially Samuel Crompton's spinning mule in 1779, which yielded strong, fine-quality yarns able to withstand the rigors of the weaving process. Around the same time, and in a complementary manner, Eli Whitney's 1793 invention of the cotton gin enabled cotton fibers to be separated from cotton plants much faster than by the previous hand method, addressing the industry's need for more raw material to keep up with advanced spinning technologies.

The development of new spinning and weaving techniques profoundly altered how cotton textiles were produced. Unlike the inferior machines and less productive techniques used in the cottage industry, these new technologies required larger industrial structures and a close proximity to water to generate mechanical power. Most importantly, in what constituted the early modern factory system, these technologies enabled industrial textile manufacturers to produce cotton textiles at a lower unit cost and to drive rural cottage industry rivals, and later each other, to ruin. Arkwright was the first industrial capitalist to establish a series of English textile mills, his plants employing from 150 to 600 workers, many of them children. Arkwright's 1795 power-loom invention was initially greeted with hostility and resisted by handloom weavers fearing for their livelihood; its widespread introduction remained blocked until 1810.

Although England continued to maintain a commanding lead in textile technological developments, a similar pattern of factory-based textile production soon spread across the United States and Europe. Two groundbreaking developments that occurred in the United States in 1793 were the invention of Whitney's cotton gin and the opening of Samuel Slater's cotton mill in what would later become Pawtucket, Rhode Island. Slater, who had apprenticed at one of Arkwright's mills in England, emigrated to the United States after memorizing the complete plans for a water-powered machine for spinning yarn, which he quickly constructed in 1790. Together with his partners Almy and Brown, Slater also designed and built new power-driven equipment for carding and spinning cotton. Slater's mill was the first of many mechanized, water-powered mills to appear in the Northeastern United States over the next several decades.

The U.S. textile industry began developing in earnest with the War of 1812 between the United States and Britain. The war placed unprecedented demand on the fledgling U.S. industry to produce cloth and blankets for the American military. Aided by exhaustive embargoes placed on foreign products, the U.S. textile industry registered important growth during the war, culminating in 170 mills by the war's end. Ironically, it was the transfer (or theft) of power-loom technology developed in England that played a critical part in the early success of the U.S. textile industry.

In 1826 Lowell, Massachusetts, became the first planned industrial city, replete with more than a mile of textile mills built along the banks of the Merrimack River to supply water power to the new industrial site. By 1850 six miles of canals had been built in Lowell to power the city's rapidly growing textile plants that included forty mill buildings, 320,000 spindles, and 10,000 looms, whose number equaled the 10,000 textile workers employed there. By 1890 some 15,000 workers ran the looms and machines that produced the ever-growing yards of fabric in this young American city, though by that date Fall River, Massachusetts, had come to surpass Lowell in terms of the number of laborers employed in the textile industry (19,000) and in its status as the city in the United States with the highest production of textiles.

The nineteenth century brought about tremendous economic upheaval in England, the European continent, and the United States. Refinements in existing textile technologies augmented productivity as the cotton textile industry spurred industrial development in a number of countries. Assisted by high tariffs levied on imported textiles in 1816—increased in 1824 and 1828—the United States pursued a protectionist policy of import substitution that shielded its textile industry from external competition. Southern cotton, cultivated and picked by slave laborers trafficked to North America from the Caribbean and Africa, provided the raw material for textile production in the North, much to the chagrin of abolitionists in the North, where the textile industry was concentrated in the ante-bellum years. The growing reliance of the U.S. textile industry on cotton produced by slave labor contributed to the underlying conditions that led to the U.S. Civil War in the 1860s.

By 1860, on the eve of the Civil War, cotton textile production had grown to become one of the leading manufacturing industries in the United States. Besides the protective tariff structure, other factors that aided the industry included rapid population growth, diffusion of the power loom, a burgeoning transportation infrastructure that significantly reduced transportation costs and increased profits, and a sustained increase in per-capita income.

By 1900 Britain and the United States reigned supreme among the developed countries in cotton textile production. Canada and several countries in western Europe also made significant progress in developing their textile industries. In almost every instance, the textile industries were nurtured along through deliberate government intervention. By 1913, the United States and Western Europe produced about 85 percent of the world's cotton textiles.

In the 1920s and 1930s extensive mill closings in U.S. northern cities produced widespread layoffs and the relocation of the textile industry to U.S. southern states. Between 1890 and 1930, the center of textile manufacturing in the United States shifted from the cities of New England to the states of the American South. There, newly built textile mills took over the critical role played for several generations by the New England mills.

During World War I, world cotton textile production grew rapidly as production increased by 90 percent. Between 1918 and 1929, however, developed countries experienced a decline in the relative share of textile output because of increasing competition from Japan. Shortly after World War I, Japan began an impressive drive to develop its cotton textile industry by concentrating on export growth. Indeed, by 1933 Japan had displaced England and the United States as the leading exporter of cotton textile products. The example set by Japan also served as a model for other developing Asian countries, which pursued a similar growth strategy to gain entry into the world cotton textile market.

Japan's success prompted retaliatory moves by the United States and Britain. In 1932 Britain enacted protective measures to limit Japan's access to its textile markets. Other industrialized countries followed suit, and by 1936 Japanese exports of cotton textiles were subject to quota restrictions in 40 of the 106 markets in which Japan's textile producers participated. U.S. textile producers brought their concerns about Japanese export penetration to the U.S. Tariff Commission, which drew up the first-ever, unilateral, voluntary export restraint (VER) agreement. Although the VER proved ineffective in stemming Japan's export tide, Japanese and American textile trade associations managed to negotiate a bilateral pact that limited Japan's exports through 1940.

During World War II, the developed countries responded to competitive textile threats by resorting to protectionist measures. This response set the pattern for the increasingly hostile textile trade climate over the next half century. Left untouched by the destruction of World War II, the U.S. and British cotton textile industries were uniquely positioned to recapture their leadership status in world textile markets after the war. The textile industries in most other developed countries did not survive the war, while Japan's in particular suffered serious damage. However, Japan's textile industry recovered rapidly and by 1953 once again was surpassing the United States and Britain in exports of cotton textiles. During this period, Hong Kong, South Korea, Pakistan, and India became increasingly industrialized and positioned themselves as significant players throughout world markets.

After a vibrant period of steady growth and rising employment from 1953 to 1973, worldwide levels of textile employment and production (broadwoven cotton textiles being no exception) entered a protracted period of worldwide decline from 1973 to 1990. A GATT study pinpointed the erosion of consumer demand in developed countries as a major factor underlying the downturn: this reduced demand created a glut of textile products that in turn resulted in a global trend of textile overcapacity. Developing countries were hit particularly hard since much of their textile output was produced for export to the developed countries. From 1963 to 1973, the average annual growth rate in world textile production had been 4.5 percent, with developing countries registering a 5.5 percent growth rate. However, from 1973 to 1990 the worldwide average annual growth rate plummeted to 1.1 percent, with the growth rate of textile production in developing countries' falling to 2.8 percent for the same period.

In less than a century, from 1900 to 1986, textile mill production of raw cotton fiber underwent a fivefold increase in volume. Cotton remained the predominant world fiber, although its relative share among all fibers fell from 81 percent in 1900 to just 45 percent by 1986. As cotton use declined, consumption of manufactured fibers climbed from 12.3 percent in 1950 to 49.8 percent in 1986. The relative decline in the production of cotton textile fabrics compared to fabrics of manufactured fibers, however, resulted not only from the displacement of cotton in established end uses. Changes in the respective shares of cotton and manufactured fibers also reflected growth in income and population, fluctuations in the relative prices of raw materials and end products, and developments in processing technology. The substitution of manufactured fibers for natural fibers grew fastest in developed countries, initially fueled by manufacturing economics. Among manufactured fibers, by the late 1980s chemical synthetics such as rayon accounted for roughly 85 percent of consumption. In the 1990s, growing attention from the high-fashion world also encouraged the shift to man-made fibers.

By the late 1990s the global textile industry experienced highly divergent conditions and results by region and sometimes even by quarter. The Asian financial crisis of 1997, caused by the currency devaluation and structural adjustment required by the International Monetary Fund, reduced the demand for textiles within affected countries—including Thailand, Indonesia, and South Korea—both for domestic sales and for manufactures as finished export goods. At the same time, the Asian crisis drove prices down and made Asian textiles—which often already enjoyed a cost advantage over textiles produced in Europe and the United States—even more affordable abroad. Consequently, major importers like the United States increased their trade deficits in textiles by snapping up less expensive imports from Asia. A concurrent drop in U.S. textile exports to Asia for finishing and assembly swelled the U.S. trade deficit as well.

The late 1990s recession in Asia prompted an atmosphere of reengineering, with Asian countries usually resolving to update or reorganize their textile industry and aiming to create new markets for themselves among Western European or United States buyers. In the late 1990s, Bangladesh began privatizing its government-owned textile mills. India weighed the benefits and disadvantages of drawing upon increased government support to underpin its textile industry. Sri Lanka fought a fierce battle in textiles as leakage from the foreign-owned textile plants in Sri Lanka's free trade zone created havoc in the country's domestic textile and garment market. Japan's efforts were targeted at updating its textile technology, since many Japanese factories were considerably out of date.

In 1997 the United States and China signed an historic textile-trading agreement that assured U.S. access to Chinese textile markets. In return, China was granted a slightly higher U.S. import quota. The agreement, prompted by a huge trade disparity between the United States and China in the textile arena, was widely hailed and approved by both sides. While Chinese economists predicted that lowering restrictions to U.S. textile goods would force some state-run Chinese textile mills out of business, China in fact flourished under this agreement, becoming a member of the World Trade Organization itself in December 2001.

CURRENT CONDITIONS

In 2005, the international trade in textiles and apparel was valued at approximately US$495 billion. China alone controlled 10.6 percent of the trade in textiles and a whopping 47.1 percent in the apparel market. With international trade quotas on textiles lifted as of January 2005, many analysts predicted that China's share of the global market would soon reach 50 percent, with its share of the U.S. market at 70 percent. China's dominance in the industry, some analysts feared, would push many smaller developing nations out of the market altogether.

Because of lower-priced textile imports from Asia, the future viability and direction of the textile industry in developed countries like the United States has been called into question. Prospects for increased profitability might be closely tied to new regional and cross-regional trade liberalization agreements. For example, the Caribbean Basin Initiative (CBI), the Andean Trade Preference Expansion Act introduced to the U.S. Senate in 2001, and the African Growth and Opportunities Act (AGOA), part of the U.S. Trade and Development Act of 2000, aimed to establish new multilateral frameworks for improved international textile trade between the United States and various partner countries. The Central American Free Trade Agreement, proposed in 2002, would allow that region permanent duty-free access to U.S. markets. Textile workers in the United States, however, oppose this measure, which they consider a further threat to their own survival. European textile and apparel producers have also attempted to create greater trade opportunities through multilateral agreements with Eastern European and North African producers and markets. AGOA has had some success: between 1999 and the beginning of 2005, Africa' share of the U.S. textile and apparel market increased from 0.95 percent to 2.5 percent. Yet China's rapidly growing industry threatened to eradicate this foothold, causing Kenya Apparel Manufacturers and Exports Association chairman Jas Bedi to voice concern that, unchecked, China could "drive the whole world out of business."

Developing countries, too, sought new trade relationships in the textile industry with fellow developing nations as well as with developed states. For instance, in early 2002 India's Synthetic and Rayon Textiles Exports Promotion Council (SRTEPC) announced its intention to increase the number of sub-Saharan countries with which Indian textile manufacturers would be trading in order to increase the volume of Indian exports. Doing so was expected to improve the climate for Indian textile manufacturing and trade and help counteract the negative effects of a worldwide drop in cotton prices in 2001 and the imposition in India of a 10 percent increase in import duties on raw cotton in January 2002 that was expected to make Indian textiles less competitive on the global market. Cross-border joint ventures and partnerships also were used to improve trade opportunities between the textile industries of more developed and less developed countries, both within and across geographical regions.

In terms of textile imports, Western Europe was the world's largest regional consumer in 2000, accounting for over one-third of the world's textile imports. Asia came in a close second, its regional share encompassing over 30 percent of world textile imports. North America followed, accounting for about 13 percent of the world's textile imports in 2000. Latin America, the Central/Eastern Europe/Baltic/CIS region, the Middle East, and Africa each accounted for less than one-tenth of the world's textile imports that year. Analysts predicted that European countries and the United States would remain the primary consumers of textiles and apparel through the early 2000s.

CHINA

The growing dominance of China in the early 2000s profoundly influenced the global textile industry and was expected to play an increasingly significant role after remaining WTO quotas expired in 2005. After some quotas in the U.S. market were abolished in early 2002, China's exports to the United States (including textiles and garments) grew by 300 to 500 percent that year alone. In some categories, U.S. imports of Chinese textiles and finished goods rose 600 percent; in 2004, textiles contributed to a record US$162 billion trade deficit with China, the largest U.S. deficit ever with a single country. China's exports to the European Union rose by 164 percent in 2002, and by more than 500 percent in just the first four months of 2005. At the same time, textile and finished goods exports from other producers plummeted. From January 2002 to March 2003, for example, U.S. imports of textile-made luggage from the Philippines and Thailand fell by 54 percent and 48 percent respectively, while imports from China grew by 664 percent. Facing calls from the European Union and the United States to limit textile and apparel exports, China said in 2005 that it would not reduce global shipments, valued at about US$100 billion, but that higher costs for raw materials and labor would slow growth in this sector.

Since textiles and clothing account for up to 95 percent of industrial exports in some Asian economies, China's growth caused considerable concern about the future viability of the textile industry in poorer countries. It was widely believed that, after 2005, China would capture about 50 percent of the global textile and apparel market, and by 2007 would account for 70 percent of U.S. textile and garment imports. Because of China's dominance in this market, as many as 30 million textile industry jobs in smaller developing countries could be at stake.

In 2000, textiles and garments comprised 95 percent of Bangladesh's exports of industrial goods. For Laos, they comprised 93 percent; for Cambodia, 83 percent; for Pakistan, 73 percent; for Sri Lanka, 71 percent; for Nepal, 61 percent; and for India, 30 percent. The industry employed about 1.8 million workers in Bangladesh, as well as 1.4 million in Pakistan and 250,000 in Sri Lanka. After 2002, however, many textile manufacturing countries were forced to downsize. Indonesia closed 835 factories in 2002 alone and curtailed operations in 767 others. Fifty factories closed in Guatemala and 200 closed in Mexico. According to a working paper from the International Textile, Garment, and Leather Workers Federation, most of the 150 factories planning to open in Mexico in the early 2000s instead chose to locate in China. The El Salvador government reported the loss of 6,000 textile jobs in 2004; in only the first two months after WTO quotas expired in 2005, 18 additional textile and garment factories in Central America closed, eliminating 10,000 jobs. According to a *New York Times* article, only India, Pakistan, and Brazil may have textile industries strong enough to continue competing successfully against China.

While textile producing countries braced for massive changes that could threaten the very survival of their industries, analysts pointed out that consumers in importing countries would enjoy significant savings as of 2005. In the United States, for example, consumers could save about US$6 billion once quotas are lifted on clothing.

THE EUROPEAN UNION

The European Union, the second-largest exporter of textiles in the early 2000s, had about 177,000 textile and clothing companies in 2002 and employed more than 2 million people; textiles alone accounted for 70,000 firms and employed just over 1 million workers. Exports to non-European countries were valued at 25.49 billion euros (approximately US$32.63) in 2000, and grew slightly to 25.59 euros (about US$32.76) in 2003. High labor costs also affected the industry; as a result, some manufacturers relocated from relatively higher wage countries such as Germany to lower-wage countries such as Poland or Romania. Ten of these former Eastern-Bloc nations, however, joined the EU in May 2004.

In 2001, Italy was the major player in the EU textile industry, with 31 percent of the EU market. Next was the United Kingdom with 15 percent, Germany with 14 percent, France with 13 percent, Spain with 9 percent, and Portugal with 6 percent. Turkey, as of 2004 not a negotiating EU membership, was another important European manufacturer. According to a *Textile Industries* report, Turkey produced 893,000 tons of cotton yarn and 1,590 million meters of cotton fabric in 2001. That year, Turkey's textile exports were valued at about US$10.3 billion.

Though high labor costs hurt the European clothing industry, Europe remained more competitive in textiles because that industry, which was less labor-intensive than garment manufacturing, could more effectively use new technologies to increase productivity. At the beginning of the 2000s, Europe had a trade surplus in textiles, mainly because it exported fabrics to Eastern Europe and North Africa to be made into clothing which was then re-imported to Europe. In 2003, the United States remained the EU's single most important export market for textiles, buying about 10 percent of its total textile exports that year compared to 12 percent in 2000.

UNITED STATES

The U.S. textile industry, struggling with plant closings and high labor costs., closed more than 50 textile plants and eliminated 10 percent of jobs in 2003. Among them was Pillotex, which in 2000 had been one of the country's largest textile companies; its closure, which analysts blamed on cheap imports flooding the market, eliminated 6,000 jobs. In 2003, U.S. textile imports increased 6 percent, reaching about US$17 billion. Exports rose by 1 percent. Textile production in 2003 (including yarn, thread, fabric, and finishing) was valued at US$39.8 billion—an 8 percent drop from the previous year. Textile corporate sales, which gained 3 percent in 2002, fell 3 percent in 2003 to US$47 billion. Exports of textile mill products were valued at US$10.5 billion in 2000 and remained relatively stable through 2003. Exports rose in 2004, exceeding US$11.6 billion.

The primary consumers of U.S.-produced textiles and apparel in the early 2000s were Mexico, Canada, Honduras, the Dominican Republic, El Salvador, and Japan. U.S. exports to neighboring countries increased significantly after implementation of the North American Free Trade Agreement (NAFTA) in 1994. In 2000, for example, U.S. exports of textile mill products to Mexico showed an increase of 33.6 percent over the comparable figure for 1999, although U.S. apparel exports to Mexico decreased by 4.4 percent over that year. U.S. textile and apparel exports to Canada showed a similar pattern: U.S. textile exports to Canada in 2000 were 2.5 percent higher than in 1999, while U.S. apparel exports to Canada declined by 0.7 percent in one year. In 2002, according to U.S. Department of Commerce and Bureau of Labor Statistics cited by the American Textile Manufacturers Institute, the value of U.S. textile exports to Mexico grew by 3.5 percent, reaching US$3.2 billion. Exports to Canada during that period rose 3.4 percent and were valued at US$2.6 billion. At the beginning of the 2000s, the fabric produced in American textile mills had the following end uses: apparel, 36 percent; home furnishings, 16 percent; floor coverings, 25 percent; and industrial or other uses, 23 percent.

The increasingly favorable trade climate between the United States and Caribbean nations created by the Caribbean Basin Initiative (CBI) improved U.S. textile and apparel exports to CBI nations dramatically in just one year's time. U.S. textile exports to CBI countries in 2000 were valued at US$947 million—up 35.5 percent from the year before—and apparel exports were valued at US$4.09 billion—up 14 percent. In 2001, CBI nations together were the second-largest market for U.S. textile exports. As of 2005, more than 70 percent of garments manufactured in Central America were produced from U.S. fabric and yarn.

INDUSTRY LEADERS

Coats Holdings Ltd, formerly Coats Viyella , was the largest company in the world producing sewing thread and craft materials at the opening of the twenty-first century. As of 2004, this United Kingdom-based firm had almost finished divesting its Viyella business, which focused on clothing and home furnishings, and was concentrating exclusively on Coats, which manufactures industrial and craft thread. Sales in 2003 exceeded US$1.78 billion.

Unifi Inc. was the world's largest company producing and processing textured yarns, particularly multi-filament nylon and polyester yarns, for use in apparel, home furnishings, upholstery, automotive and industrial materials, hosiery, and sewing threads. In 2004, Unifi, based in Greensboro, North Carolina, posted sales of US$746.5 million.

The largest U.S. textile firms in 2004 were Mohawk Industries, with revenues of US$5.8 billion in 2004; Milliken, a textiles and chemical company with revenues in 2003 estimated at US3.4 billion; and Springs Industries, whose 2003 revenues were an estimated US$2.5 billion. Another leading company, Westpoint Stevens, filed for bankruptcy in 2003 and as of 2005 was expecting to be acquired by an investment group led by W.L. Ross. Westpoint's 2003 revenues were US$1.64 billion. Burlington Industries, with revenues of US$993 million in 2002, also filed for bankruptcy and was purchased by Ross in 2003 for US$614 million. Interface, with 2004 revenues of US$881.7 million, is the world's leading producer of commercial carpet. Top European textile companies include Sara Lee Courtaulds, created in 2000 when the Sara Lee Corporation acquired U.K.-based Courtaulds Textiles.

WORKFORCE

The effects of rapid globalization and the elimination of trade barriers have not been entirely positive for vast numbers of workers and consumers in developing countries or for those workers in developed countries now displaced by foreign labor as multinational corporations continually relocate to places with lower labor costs. Employment figures in the U.S. textile industry continued to fall at the opening of the twenty-first century. According to the American Textile Manufacturers Institute (ATMI), the U.S. textile industry employed 428,000 workers in the year 2003, a significant drop from the 1997 employment level of 607,500 and a 10 percent drop from the previous year. The most serious job losses, however, came in 2001, when textile industry employment fell by 13 percent. Most U.S. textile workers were concentrated in North and South Carolina and Georgia. As of

2001, North Carolina had 97,700 textile workers, South Carolina had 56,400, and Georgia had 39,700. Other states with significant numbers of textile workers were California with 32,300; Alabama, 27,500; Virginia, 15,300; Tennessee, 11,700; and Massachusetts, 10,600.

Working hours in the U.S. textile industry also declined over a short span of years. The average U.S. textile employee worked 41.5 hours per week in 1997 but by October 2001 was working only 39.6 hours. The index of aggregate hours worked in the textile industry was 12 percent less at the close of 2001 than it was in 2000. Employment in developing countries, on the other hand, was more variable in the textile industry.

RESEARCH AND TECHNOLOGY

MAN-MADE FIBERS AND FABRICS

The demand for new fabrics and more functionality is a driving force in research. While flax, a natural fiber, has been woven into linen for at least seven thousand years and cotton has been in use almost as long, the first man-made fiber, rayon, was invented only at the start of the twentieth century. In 1910, the American Viscose Company brought together two different chemicals and methods of manufacturing to create two types of rayon: viscose and cuprammonium. Nearly one hundred years later, the viscose form of rayon was the only type still produced in the United States. The Celanese Corporation started commercial production of acetate, the next man-made fiber, in the United States in 1924. The year 1939 saw the appearance of nylon, the product that made the E. I. du Pont de Nemours & Company Inc. world famous. Even sixty years later, nylon was second only to polyester as the synthetic fiber most commonly used in the United States.

At mid-twentieth century, acrylic was produced commercially by E. I. du Pont de Nemours, the same company responsible for starting commercial production of polyester fiber in the United States in 1953. In 1954 the Celanese Corporation began producing triacetate fiber in the United States, though domestic U.S. production of triacetate stopped in 1985. Spandex, whose filaments can stretch at least 100 percent then spring back to the original, was first produced commercially in the United States by E. I. du Pont de Nemours in 1959. Two years later, Hercules Incorporated began commercial production of polyolefin/polypropylene in the United States. In 1966 polyolefin became the first fiber in the world to win the Nobel Prize; 40 years later, no other fiber had yet managed to do the same.

Micro fibers—fibers with less than one denier per filament—were first produced commercially in the United States in 1989 by E. I. du Pont de Nemours. Micro fibers (or microdenier) are the world's thinnest fibers, finer even than silk. As FabricLink's *Fabric History* explains, "To relate it to something more familiar—A human hair is more than 100 times the size of some micro fibers." Micro fibers have been produced from a wide range of synthetic fibers, including polyester, nylon, and acrylic.

At the turn of the millennium, the world's most popular synthetic fibers were super fabric polyester; rayon, the world's cheapest fabric to produce; viscose, a more expensive type of rayon; Polartec, favored by hikers, campers, and upholstery makers; Lycra and spandex; nylon and Pewlon; Elite, the Italian elastic; and Tencel, a strong, silky fiber made from wood pulp. Tencel is the trade name given to lyocell, a man-made fiber first produced commercially in the United States in 1993 by Courtalds Fibers. Lyocell comes from trees grown expressly for this fiber whose wood is processed in an environmentally friendly way by spinning the solvent and recycling the dissolving agent. Tencel is considered the first "natural" man-made fabric—in other words, it is not a chemical combination like acetate or polyester.

Recent research by such companies as DuPont and the Japanese giant, Toray, is leading the world further into the production of man-made fibers. In mid-1998, DuPont premiered Tactel, a new thread designed with the fashion world in mind—smooth, non-wrinkling, opalescent, and soft. Royal Dutch/Shell and the Korean company SK Chemicals in June 1998 announced production of Corterra, a knittable, stretchy material that can be dyed a wide variety of colors. It was initially used in underwear and athletic wear, replacing the coarser and less breathable spandex/nylon blends. In the late 1990s, the Finnish company Kultratrurve OY used a century-old English patent to become the first to spin fabric from peat. The resulting cloth—static resistant, hypoallergenic, warmer and lighter than wool, and inexpensive to produce—was anticipated to have a healthy future in medical dressings, wound care, and fabrics, fleeces, and felts for clothing and furniture.

In 2001 interesting experimental and commercial fabrics were being created in the United States by the Fosshield Technology Division of the Foss Manufacturing Co. in Hampton, New Hampshire. Company researchers, by meshing synthetic fibers with silver, a natural antimicrobial agent, created a new polyester Fossfibre bicomponent fiber embedded with AgION, an inorganic zeolite based on silver. This fiber offered promising new possibilities for the production of hospitality, medical, travel, and sanitary materials. According to *Textiles World* in the article "Microbes Begone!", Fossfibre with AgION is especially useful because it contains no drugs, and bacteria therefore cannot develop a resistance to it. Furthermore, products created with this new fiber, such as the Fosshield antimicrobial cleansing wipes(a durable, no woven wipe that can be used in the home by consumers to clean any non-fabric surface)can be washed and rewashed many times without losing their antimicrobial properties.

While production of traditional woven textiles has continued to decline in the United States, production of technical textiles—which are used primarily in industries—has grown. In North Carolina alone, the largest textile-producing state, the number of nonwoven fabric mills increased by 30 percent from 1993 to 2003, while employment grew by 9 percent.

FIBER RECYCLING

As consumer consciousness about protecting the environment has grown, increased interest in product recycling has led to research into recycling fibers and fabrics into new materials. Researchers have found new ways to recycle fibers such as wool and to determine how fibers damaged during wear can be beneficially reprocessed. Creative uses have also been found for non-fiber products, recycling them into materials to create apparel and other textiles. For example, a fleecy sweatshirt can be created from 25 large soda bottles by spinning plastic fibers, then pressing, chewing, and spinning them again into Polartec or one of its sibling fabrics.

NEW FABRIC FINISHES, COLORS, AND TREATMENTS

Not only are new fibers under development, but new finishes are being researched to gloss familiar cloths. For example, researchers in the 1990s eagerly experimented with cross-pollinations from carpet, upholstery, and even tire manufacturers to create new apparel textile enhancements. Certain silks now benefit from a Teflon bath, and linen infused with Lycra is more wrinkle resistant and more wearable. By the late 1990s enzymatic dyeing had become one of the most promising new widely used technologies. Traditional chemical or natural dyes may leave fabric stiff with dye or create colors that fade, and certain more vibrant colors such as red and orange have been linked to health problems. However, fabrics washed with certain enzymes are measurably softer and smoother and accept dyes more readily. Enzymatic treatments affect almost all properties of a fabric, including its tensile strength, shearing, bending, compression, and surface.

MASS CUSTOMIZATION

One of the most exciting recent developments in the textile industry was the trend toward mass customization which started in the mid-1990s. Heralded by analysts as a new industry paradigm, mass customization combines the technologies and efficiencies of mass production with the marketing appeal of custom products. Using integrated computer networks, manufacturers can rapidly take and fulfill custom orders for textiles, theoretically without the high costs associated with traditional custom-manufacturing.

The apparel market appeared especially conducive to mass customization. For example, with mass customization a consumer would be able to place an order for a custom-designed pair of jeans from a local store and have the jeans made to order and delivered within days. A 1998 study conducted by Auburn University in collaboration with industry giants such as DuPont saw in the near future the use of 3-D scanners that could record the exact body measurements of apparel customers. More information from the customer would elicit information on design and fabric options, and the order would be submitted to a textile and apparel factory in real time. The study also modeled future possibilities whereby end users would be able to access a textile mill's production capabilities in order to request exact fabrics, clothing styles, upholstery, carpets, with the customer's preferences, including their preferred fit (tight, loose, relaxed, elastic), recorded on a magnetic card. While the demand for mass-customization might not supplant conventional product demand, mass-customized apparel could represent an important new niche market in the twenty-first century.

FURTHER READING

American Textile Manufacturers Institute. "ATMI Urges Congress, Administration to Adopt More Equitable Textile Trade Policies," 7 February 2002. Available from www.atmi.org.

———. "Quick Facts about U.S. Textiles," 2004. Available from www.atmi.org.

———. "Textile Companies," accessed 7 February 2002 at www.atmi.org.

———. "Textile Industry Year-End Trade and Economic Report," 2 January 2002. Available from www.atmi.org.

Becker, Elizabeth, and Barboza, David. "Free of Quota, China Textiles Flood the U.S." *New York Times,* 10 March 2005.

Becker, Elizabeth. "Textile Quotas to End Soon, Punishing Carolina Mill Towns." *New York Times,* 2 November 2004.

Becker, Elizabeth. "U.S. Quiet on China Trade Tax, but Europe Welcomes It." *New York Times,* 14 December 2004.

Bharati, Vivek. "Managing Change: Gaping Holes in Textile Sector." *The Financial Express,* 27 February 2004. Available from fecolumnists.expressindia.com.

Buschle-Diller, Gisela, et al. "Effect of Enzymatic Treatment on Dyeing and Finishing of Cellulosic Fibers." *National Textile Center Annual Report,* 1997.

Canadian Textiles Institute. "The Textile Industry; Fact Sheet," 2000. Available from www.textiles.ca.

De Silva, Dalton. "Sri Lanka: Government Selects Textiles as Priority Industry." *South Asian Business Analyst,* November 1997.

Ellis, Kristi. "Revised Labor Report Hits Industry Harder." *Women's Wear Daily,* 9 February 2004.

European Union Textiles and Clothing Statistics. 2 February 2005. Available from http://europa.eu.int.

Fabric History, accessed 22 January 2002 at www.fabriclink.com.

Goodman, Peter S. and Blustein, Paul. "A New Pattern is Cut for Global Textile Trade." *Washington Post,* 17 November 2004, p. A1.

"Industry Report Underscores Grim Conditions in 2003." *Textile World,* January 2004. Available from www.textileworld.com.

"International Business: European Softens China Stance." *New York Times,* 16 March 2005.

Kearney, Neil. "What Future for Textiles and Clothing Trade after 2005?" International Textile, Garment, and Leather Workers Federation. 2 September 2003. Available from www.itglwf.org.

Lange, Mark. *Economic Outlook for U.S. Cotton.* National Cotton Council of America, 27 September 2001. Available from www.cotton.org.

Lazich, Robert S., ed. *Market Share Reporter, 2002.* Farmington Hills, MI: Gale Group/Thomson Learning, 2002.

Luke, John E. "Will Productivity Save U.S. Textiles?" *Fibre World,* November 2001. Available from www.textileindustries.com.

Mulama, Joyce. "International Labour Day in Kenya: A Murky Future for Textile Workers." *News from Africa,* 5 May 2005. Available from http://www.newsfromafrica.org.

Nelson, Valerie J. "By Design: With The Softness of Silk and the Strength of Polyester, Tencel . . . " *Los Angeles Times* (17 October 1996): 2.

Rodie, Janet Bealer. "Quality Fabric of the Month: Microbes Begone!" *Textiles World,* December 2001. Available from www.textileindustries.com.

Shetty, Aarti. "Prices Rocket Following 10% Import Duty Hike on Raw Cotton." *The Financial Express (New Delhi),* 14 January 2002. Available from new.financialexpress.com.

Soras, Constantine G. "Fed Rates Hit 40-Year Low." *Textiles World,* December 2001. Available from www.textileindustries.com.

Stengg, Werner. *The Clothing and Textile Industry in the EU: A Survey,* June 2001. Available from europa.eu.int.

Textile Federation—The Official Organisation of the South African Textile Industry. "Newsclip—Africa Growth & Opportunity Act," accessed 11 January 2002 at www.texfed.co.za.

Thompson, Ginger. "International Business: Fraying of a Latin Textile Industry." *New York Times,* 25 March 2005.

Trivedi, Vijay. "Synthetic Textile Exporters to Tap Sub-Saharan Regions." *The Financial Express (New Delhi),* 14 January 2002. Available from new.financialexpress.com.

Union of Needletrades, Industrial and Textile Employees (UNITE!). "UNITE: A New Union with a Long History," accessed 7 February 2002 at www.uniteunion.org.

"USA: Textile Chief Blames Asian Imports for Troubles," accessed 13 January 2002 at www.just-style.com.

U.S. Department of Commerce/International Trade Administration. *U.S. Industry & Trade Outlook 2000.* The McGraw-Hill Companies, 2000.

U.S. Department of Commerce, Office of Textiles and Apparel. *Andean Pact; Bolivia; Colombia; Ecuador; Peru; Proposed Legislation: Bill to Renew and Expand Andean Trade Preferences Could Provide Opportunities for U.S. Fabric and Yarn Exports,* 17 December 2001. Available from web.otexa.ita.doc.gov.

———. *China: China's Accession to the WTO,* 14 December 2001. Available from web.otexa.ita.doc.gov.

———. *Sub-Saharan Africa: The African Growth and Opportunity Act Provides New Opportunities for U.S. Yarn and Fabric Sales,* 4 June 2001. Available from web.otexa.ita.doc.gov.

———. *Trade Data: U.S. Imports and Exports of Textiles and Apparel.* Available from otexa.ita.doc.gov.

U.S. Department of Labor, Bureau of Labor Statistics. "Textile, Apparel, and Furnishings Occupations," accessed 15 January 2002 at www.bls.gov.

———. "Textile Mill Products," accessed 15 January 2002 at www.bls.gov.

Valenti, Catherine. "Textile Industry Unraveling: Increased Competition, Economic Woes Plague U.S. Textile Industry." *ABCnews.com*, 30 November 2001. Available from more.abcnew.go.com.

Waldrep, G. C. III. *Southern Workers and the Search for Community: Spartanburg County, South Carolina.* Urbana and Chicago, IL: University of Illinois Press, 2000.

Wang, Peter W. K. "What's Latest with World Textile Significance." TransWorld Information, 2004. Available from www.ttnet.net.

World Trade Organization. "International Trade Statistics 2003." Available from www.wto.org.

———. "Textiles." Available from www.wto.org.

———. "Trading into the Future: The Introduction to the WTO; The Agreements—Textiles: back in the mainstream," accessed 17 January 2002 at www.wto.org.

———. "The WTO," accessed 7 February 2002 at www.wto.org.

TRANSPORTATION AND DEFENSE EQUIPMENT

SIC 3721

NAICS 336411

AIRCRAFT

The global aircraft industry manufactures new and rebuilt aircraft for the commercial and general aviation markets. For discussion of military aircraft, see also **Defense and Armaments**.

INDUSTRY SNAPSHOT

Civil aircraft production is dominated by the commercial market, supplying the jets and turboprops used by the world's passenger and cargo airlines. As of the mid-2000s, just two manufacturers—Boeing in the United States and Airbus S.A.S. in France—have controlled nearly the entire market for commercial aircraft for more than a decade. This lead was secured primarily by manufacturing medium and large jets for 100 or more passengers, the industry's most lucrative and capital-intensive segments. Aircraft manufacturers noted the rising demand for large-capacity, wide-body planes and expected that the average number of seats per plane would increase to 240 by 2015. They expected that Asian countries would help drive this trend with a 356-seat average capacity per plane by 2015. Airbus was set to deliver its 555 passenger A380 in 2008.

The huge costs and risks of aircraft manufacturing encouraged business consolidation and a proliferation of international joint ventures in what has been termed a "borderless industry." Few countries could be considered self-sufficient in production, and even for those that could, most competitors in the industry pursue multiple cross-border ventures in order to keep costs down and draw on the special competencies and efficiencies of firms around the globe.

Globally, the industry experienced continued growth in the early 2000s. Boeing's World Air Cargo Forecast predicted an annual expansion rate of 6.2 percent through 2023, tripling the levels of overall air traffic. Strong growth was reported in international trade, with the most reported in the Asia-Pacific region. Traffic in North America and within Europe was expected to realize below average increases. The U.S. firms Cessna Aircraft Co. and Raytheon led the continuing strong surge in sales in the general aviation segment. The U.S. industry reached US$147 billion in 2003 sales. That year, Boeing, with about 280 units, and Airbus, with about 300 units, produced a combined US$33 billion in aircraft. These had a per-unit value of US$50 million or more, according to *Fortune*. For the first half of 2004, the companies delivered a combined 312 aircraft. According to researchers from the Teal Group, US$421 billion in aircraft will be built by 2012.

ORGANIZATION AND STRUCTURE

Although the field includes all types of aircraft, including large transports, hang gliders, rotary-wing aircraft (such as helicopters), and balloons, a few conglomerates specializing in civil transports and military aircraft dominate the global aircraft industry. Since most modern aircraft are incredibly complex (the Boeing 747, for example, has 6 million parts), a worldwide network of approximately 400 subcontractors supplies major structures and subassemblies, such as wings and fuselages, to manufacturers of finished aircraft. These subcontractors are supplied, in turn, by up to 4,000 firms that manufacture components or raw materials. Parts that differentiate a product, or those strongly identified with a company, are usually produced in-house due to their strategic and competitive importance.

A strong customer base and careful order book management are needed in order to recoup high development costs for airliners or large business jets. Standards for safety, quality, and value, among other things, are obviously crucial. To break even on the design and manufacture of a new airliner, for example, a company like Boeing or Airbus must receive an order for, receive the money for, and provide delivery of hundreds of airliners globally. Because that process can take years, many orders fall through. Thus, the industry gauges not just orders and transactions but completed orders, and otherwise has made an art of order book management. In 2001 alone, Airbus experienced 101 order cancellations (90 percent of which were due to company bankruptcies). Some of these cancellations may yet reenter the Airbus order book and become part of the company's healthy backlog.

The industry is not only cyclical, it relies on a small number of consumers, mostly airlines and governments. Due to long lead times and backlogs, airlines may hastily buy aircraft in advance of their true needs to keep from missing out on model availability in future periods or to avoid availability at much higher prices.

Airline specifications and regulations also affect the design, marketing, and sales of passenger aircraft. Because safety is a highly visible priority in aviation, no civilian operator would readily buy an aircraft that has not been certified by an agency such as the Federal Aviation Administration (FAA) in the United States, the Civil Aviation Authority (CAA) in the United Kingdom, or the Interstate Aviation Committee (IAC) in the Commonwealth of Independent States. In 1993 the Airbus A330 became the first aircraft to be certified simultaneously in the United States and Europe. To enhance the marketability of their aircraft, Airbus and Boeing also sought extended range certification. This extension would allow flights on routes within 180 minutes' flying time of diversion airports, rather than 60 minutes, the standard for most twin-engine aircraft. Boeing and Airbus accomplished this objective for their A330 and 777 models.

For general aviation, the 1990s were a period of consolidation. Companies either streamlined their production (as in the case of Beech Aircraft Corp.), were acquired by large conglomerates (for example, the business jet operations of British Aerospace were acquired by Raytheon Co.), or both (Cessna was acquired by Textron). In 1997 two of the industry's largest producers, Boeing Company and McDonnell Douglas Corporation, merged. Other well-known companies, such as Piper Aircraft Corp. and Fairchild Aircraft in the United States, as well as Fokker N.V. of the Netherlands, filed for bankruptcy during this period.

Ultralight aviation grew out of a hang gliding resurgence in the 1970s. In 1976 a U.S. adventurer attached a golf-cart engine to a hang glider, creating an inexpensive way to go aloft. Like the earliest flying machines, ultralights and homebuilts—sophisticated craft that come in a kit for home assembly—became the province of tinkerers and serious amateurs. These small machines made aviation more affordable and more accessible for its proponents. They are available for a fraction of the cost of factory-built aircraft (typically less than US$5,000) and are governed by a different set of FAA standards (such as a 254 lb. total weight limit and a five-gallon fuel tank limit). In the mid-1990s approximately 10,000-15,000 ultralights were in existence in the United States. Although not as lucrative as other segments, the ultralight/homebuilt industry has been both the source and beneficiary of many innovations. Less-developed countries such as Peru have actually used ultralights as military training craft.

Rotorcraft, helicopters, and similar craft accounted for about 3 percent of the civil aircraft market in the late 1990s. At that time, worldwide drops in military spending negatively affected the civil helicopter market, for the military dumped its surplus rotorcraft into the civil market, reducing sales. In the civil helicopter sector, Bell Helicopter-Textron shared healthy fractions of the market with Eurocopter, MD Helicopters, and Robinson (which eschewed turbines for piston engines in its entire product line). Total civil helicopter deliveries averaged approximately 500 units per year with a value of US$1 billion in the late 1990s. In the early 2000s, analysts expected slightly less favorable results, especially for rotorcraft manufacturers that failed to specialize in niche markets or had not managed to merge with, or been acquired by, other producers.

With an aging fleet and handicapped by older aircraft-manufacturing technology, the Commonwealth of Independent States (CIS) had the potential to become an important market for aircraft. China was expected to surpass Japan as the largest international aircraft market early in the twenty-first century. Eastern Europe, Asia, and the Pacific Rim, along with China, were expected to be growth markets. Similarly, demand in Central and South America rose and aircraft makers expect this region to be a major customer in the early 2000s.

Asian carriers in particular seem promising. Boeing predicted that they would purchase US$232 billion in new aircraft by the year 2010; indeed, the world market was predicted to be worth US$857 billion. The long-term commitment required by aerospace developers seemed philosophically compatible with traditional Asian business strategy. The region has a large market and a large supply of skilled workers—crucial in an industry with high quality standards. Joint ventures have proliferated in the region, as local manufacturers sought experience and American and European firms sought a competitive marketing edge. Singapore, Indonesia, Taiwan, China, and South Korea all have aircraft manufacturing programs. However, the lingering recession in Japan and in other Far East countries in the early 2000s was thought to be an unfavorable factor in the growth of demand for new aircraft.

BACKGROUND AND DEVELOPMENT

Long before aircraft with viable commercial applications were developed, aviation was the province of dreamers and idealists. The quest for flight has been documented as early as the first century in Ovid's tale of Daedalus and Icarus; according to mythology, Icarus made wings of wax and bird feathers, flew too close to the sun, and died. The brothers Joseph Michelle and Jacques Etienne Mongolfier introduced a passenger-carrying hot air balloon in France in 1783. Military tacticians, always searching for the "high ground," employed the balloon as an observation post as early as 1794 during the battle of Maubeuge in France. Not surprisingly, in 1910 a form of balloon called an airship, or dirigible, was the first aircraft to be used for commercial aviation.

Numerous isolated eccentrics tinkered with gliders in the nineteenth century. Before falling to his death in 1896, Otto Lilienthal studied birds and found the secret of flight to be in the curved wing. He and the Scottish engineer Percy Pilcher, who was also killed experimenting with gliders, laid the foundation for the Wright brothers' invention of the airplane at the turn of the twentieth century. Lilienthal also received credit for manufacturing the first aircraft for sale, the Lilienthal Type 11 glider.

Many others had sought to build powered aircraft, too often constructing machines with flapping wings, called "ornithopters." On December 17, 1903, bicycle makers Orville and Wilbur Wright earned credit as the first to produce an aircraft capable of powered, sustained, and controlled flight. Such a lofty honor had been coveted around the world. Thus, the early development of the "flying machine" was hindered by bickering and fierce legal battles. For example, Gabriel Voisin, who along with his brother, Charles, was the first to build aircraft in France on a commercial basis, scoffed at the influence of both the Wright brothers and other aviation pioneers.

A company founded by Glenn Curtiss made the first commercial sale of an aircraft in 1909 to the Aeronautic Society of New York. In the same year, one of the Wright brothers succeeded in meeting U.S. Army specifications for an aircraft and sold it to the government for US$30,000. The Wrights promptly sued Curtiss for patent infringement, virtually freezing the development of the aircraft industry in the United States until World War I. After the war, U.S. Army war surplus Curtiss JN-4 "Jenny" trainers, along with the de Havilland Moth, manufactured in Great Britain, would carry the postwar barnstorming craze across the country. The Piper Cub, introduced in 1937, quickly became the best-selling one-engine plane of all time in general aviation.

Although Leonardo da Vinci had sketched a helicopter design in 1483, the first sustained helicopter flight was not achieved until 1935, with a coaxial model built by Louis Breguet and René Dorand in France. Within the next five years, Igor Sikorsky had perfected a single-rotor type of helicopter in the United States, opening the door for many practical applications.

The early companies formed by the pioneers eventually merged with and were acquired by larger concerns. For example, the Wright Company, formed in 1909 when a group of New York investors bought the Wright brothers' patents for US$100,000 in cash, was sold to another group in 1915. That group then merged with the Glenn L. Martin companies to form the Wright-Martin Aircraft Corporation, which later became the Wright Aeronautical Company, which merged in 1929 with the Curtiss Aeroplane and Motor Company to form the Curtiss-Wright Corporation, controlled by North American Aviation.

Larger conglomerates dependent upon government support continued to dominate the aircraft industry throughout World War II and the postwar period. The First World War had demonstrated the possibilities of aircraft in wartime; by World War II, aircraft had become an integral part of modern warfare. Many of the phenomenal advancements in aircraft design—jet engines, swept-back wings, electronic flight controls, and composite materials—were funded by governments in wartime. Air Force One, a Boeing 747 that serves as both the U.S. president's air transport and mobile command post in the event of a war, illustrates how important aircraft have become to national security. The technological improvements in military aircraft have been accompanied by a proportional increase in their price tags; a typical 1945 fighter plane cost about US$51,000 (or about US$430,000 in 1998 dollars). By the 1990s, the F-16 jet fighter, a staple of the U.S. Air Force, was selling for approximately US$25 million.

Two new airliners developed in the 1960s, the wide-body ("jumbo") jet and the supersonic transport (SST), met with much different degrees of success. The Boeing 747, the first jumbo jet, which started service on February 9, 1969, was warmly welcomed and widely purchased. Meanwhile, economic and environmental concerns caused the United States to cancel its SST program. The Anglo-French SST (the Concorde) and the Soviet SST (the Tu-144) entered service in 1976 and 1977, respectively. Due to high fuel costs and other concerns, the airlines did not embrace the Concorde, and production ceased in 1979. Meanwhile, in the Soviet Union a series of disastrous crashes halted development and production of the Tu-144.

Asian countries such as South Korea, Malaysia, Vietnam, Indonesia, and the Philippines ordered numerous new planes, as their economies grew rapidly in the mid-1990s. But economic problems began to plague East Asian countries in the late 1990s, causing devaluations of their currencies and forcing them to reconsider their aircraft orders and projects. In early 1998 Philippine Airlines canceled its order of four 747-400 planes from Boeing. Latin America also emerged as a thriving market for the aircraft industry, with orders for US$4 billion worth of planes announced in 1997. Because of their growing economies, Asian and South American countries made up the largest new growth markets for such aircraft. But South Korea, Indonesia, Malaysia, and even Japan experienced shrinking economies in the late 1990s, leaving short-term expansion of the East Asian market far from certain.

Though constantly under the threat of quick market erosion, from the mid-1990s through 2001 the industry reported fairly strong sales overall. Results differed considerably by segment. By the end of that period, a cyclical slowdown—evident early in 2001 with apparent airline overcapacity and confirmed in late 2001 with the September 11 terrorist attacks—all but guaranteed contraction in the aircraft industry in 2002. The attacks spurred a heavy round of aircraft order cancellations worldwide in the following months. In 2002 some of the cancellations were rescinded as passenger traffic recovered. This prompted some analysts to quietly call for a modest recovery in many segments in 2003. Passenger bookings subsequently rebounded, and excess plane capacity was absorbed or retired, even as the SARS scare in Asia and the instability of many world regions also contributed to the decline of passenger air travel.

CURRENT CONDITIONS

Taking into account other factors, commercial sales were accurately predicted to rise in the 2000s due to the need to replace older, less fuel-efficient aircraft that did not meet new international noise and emissions standards. During a climate-change conference in Kyoto, Japan, United Nations participants laid the groundwork for much stricter aircraft emission regulations to take effect in the early 2000s, under the Kyoto Protocol. The European Union established its own standards, which mandated a 16 percent reduction of nitrous oxide emissions from all new-model engines beginning in

2000 and from all other models beginning in 2006. In 2003, a bill was proposed in the U.S. Senate that allocated several million dollars to reduce both emissions and noise. As a result of the new standards, aircraft producers expected additional orders for new planes and new engines. Airbus expected a need for 782 new aircraft each year into 2020.

During the early 2000s growth was being driven by the need to replace older aircraft and by fleet expansion in developing countries. As the popular Boeing 747s used by many airlines approached the end of their operational lives, manufacturers started offering replacement models, such as Boeing's 777 and Airbus' A340 and A330. In 2001 the U.S. aerospace industry alone generated US$50 billion in sales of civil aircraft (commercial and general aviation), engines, and parts. This represented a 13.0 percent increase in aircraft shipments and a 4.2 percent growth in civil sector business. In fact, industry analysts predicted that the Asian market would account for about a fifth of sales through 2005. Major manufacturers, such as Boeing and Airbus, received contracts from airlines around the world, so many that in 2003, for example, Boeing had a 1,100 plane order backlog, and Airbus had a 1,500 plane order backlog.

Research and Technology

In the wake of the September 11, 2001, terrorist attacks, the U.S. federal government, on an interim basis, issued orders to the airlines to ensure that existing cockpit doors on commercial aircraft would be locked at all times and secured with extra bars and barriers. It also immediately went a step further, developing a standard redesigned, reinforced cockpit door that the airlines were required to install on all aircraft by 2003.

With an annual research budget exceeding US$1 billion for its aeronautical division, the U.S. National Aeronautics and Space Administration (NASA) contributes substantially to advances in aircraft technology. NASA has assisted the general aviation industry in the United States in such areas as developing new wing and blade designs—including the civil tiltrotor project—and cockpit technology for business and commuter aircraft. NASA plans to develop aircraft that meet the world's new environmental and safety standards.

Boeing is another leading aircraft technology researcher. Each year the company devotes between US$1.5 billion and US$1.8 billion for research and development. In the mid-1990s, the majority of the company's research funds went to developing its 777. In the early 2000s, with the delivery of its 777s, Boeing turned to refining its existing aircraft and designing new planes. In cooperation with NASA and several universities, Boeing began to develop a blended-wing-body (BWB) plane. The BWB's advantages include superior fuel economy, lower production costs, greater capacity, and greater range than the conventional aircraft of the 1990s. The BWB's prodigious capacity comes from the design of the wings, which hold seats for passengers. Researchers estimate that the plane could be ready by 2015. Meanwhile, Boeing plans to meet the fast-approaching requirements for environmentally friendly aircraft with its 717-200, which features reduced emissions and lower noise levels than its rivals. Test flights of the 717-200 began in early 1998.

In the mid-1990s United States and Russian researchers jointly studied the possibility of developing new supersonic civil aircraft. Although supersonic projects had largely ceased in 1978, both countries had renewed their interest. The U.S. component of the research team consisted of NASA, Boeing, Rockwell-Collins, Pratt & Whitney, and General Electric. The Russian component of the team included Tupolev, the developer of the Tu-144 supersonic jet. The collaborators basically went to work rebuilding the plane's engine in order to use the plane to study the ozone layer and sonic-boom problems.

In contrast to the huge government-sponsored research programs of the aerospace conglomerates, the research and development (R&D) efforts of the makers of ultralights and "kit planes," designed to be assembled by the user, were lean but smart. The popular kit designs offered by Burt Rutan and others in the 1970s offered advanced materials such as exotic composites, plastic foams, and fiberglass and epoxy laminates. Also featured in these designs were canards, small wings placed at the nose of the aircraft, and winglets, fins at the end of the main wing, both of which increased efficiency and stability. Computer modeling enabled designers to incorporate the most advanced wing shapes into designs to be built at home. At least one company has adopted these technologies to produce an inexpensive, six-passenger business turboprop (less than US$1 million, compared to US$3 million and up for competitors).

A significant experimental aircraft was the Gossamer Condor. In 1977 it enabled the first human-powered flight. In 1986 came perhaps Rutan's greatest achievement—the Voyager, the first aircraft to circle the world without refueling. By the early 2000s, Rutan's conceptions of lightweight craft with intercontinental range had found a military application in the U.S. armed forces—highly capable drones, used effectively during the hostilities in Afghanistan. High-altitude drones with extended range were also expected to acquire satellite-like global or regional communications roles in the new century. Rutan's designs and principles have found their civil application in the Beech Starship, a small business turboprop, and in a small jet fighter/trainer.

Instrumentation is another area of continuing research. A computerized display of flight information, the Electronic Flight Information System (EFIS), has promised to improve the decision-making abilities of pilots by providing an integrated, improved display of navigational, meteorological, and aircraft performance information in the cockpit. State-of-the-art airliners and business craft such as the Boeing 757 and 767, the Airbus A-310, and the Beech Starship are equipped with this system.

The Global Positioning Satellite (GPS) system, first developed for use by the U.S. military, relies on groupings of satellites to provide extremely precise location information (including altitude) to receiving units within airplanes—some small enough to be handheld and inexpensive enough to be used by the general aviation market. However, the units' small size and accuracy have caused concern about their potential misuse in armaments.

Environmental groups in the United States, Europe, and Australia have focused on noise pollution. At the turn of the century, the U.S. Airport Noise and Capacity Act of 1990 had forced U.S. airlines to make their fleets meet quieter noise specifications. Smaller business jets were exempt from this rule. The International Civil Aviation Organization (ICAO) imposed similar standards.

Heavily congested airports have suggested the need for 600-800 seat, ultra-high-capacity aircraft (UHCA or VLCT, very large commercial transport). Airbus began research on such a project, estimated to cost between US$6 billion and US$8 billion. Boeing also began research for its proposed UHCA, the 747-X. The potential market for these aircraft was projected at between 400 and 500 aircraft by 2010. In the early 2000s, Boeing studied development of smaller capacity, but higher speed, transports than the proposed UHCAs.

A concept for a 300-seat supersonic airliner, dubbed the "Orient Express," has been the subject of a study group comprised of engineers and others from Boeing, Aerospatiale, British Aerospace, Japan Aircraft Development Corp., Tupolev, and Alenia. Traveling at Mach 3, or three times the speed of sound, the aircraft would cut travel time between Tokyo and Los Angeles to 4 hours, from the current 10. Fares were projected to eventually fall to a level just 20 percent higher than those for conventional flight.

Two types of vertical takeoff and landing (VTOL) aircraft also were being developed to serve inner-city airports. Ishida Corp. of Japan (in collaboration with U.K. and U.S. firms) is developing the 14-passenger TW-68. With wings that rotate 90 degrees, the craft would allow vertical takeoff and landing. Due to traffic congestion, Boeing projected a need for thousands of civil tiltrotor aircraft (such as the Bell/Boeing V-22) in the first few decades of the new century.

Workforce

Aircraft companies worldwide employ a vast and skilled labor force, albeit one accustomed to volatility. Aircraft manufacturers strive for stability in employee rosters, although this is seldom possible over the long term in such a cyclical industry. Due to training costs and other investments in labor, such as security clearances, manufacturers had tended to resist dismissing workers, but this pattern has changed as companies like Boeing have been apt to change head counts quickly in order to maintain the bottom line. As manufacturers' fortunes rise and fall, aircraft workers have seen job cuts in the tens of thousands followed by thousands of new hires. The industry likewise has an extensive and active trade union membership and a history of strikes.

Due to the complexity of manufacturing aircraft, the low-unit volumes, and the demand for customization of the finished product, few manufacturers have found labor-saving automation to be cost-effective except in limited applications, such as computer-aided design (or "paperless design"), which was first used extensively in creating the prototype of the B-2 stealth bomber.

Aerospace workers often earn high salaries in relation to other industries, but wages have been under severe pressure as a result of wavering profits and fierce competition. Boeing factory workers in St. Louis, for instance, secured an average wage of US$24.50 an hour as part of their 2001 contract. This amounted to an average gain of 7 percent over the previous rates, which had been in effect since a contentious 1996 pact. But wage gains in some places were offset by heavy layoffs at Boeing in 2001 and 2002 in the midst of the U.S. recession and skittish demand for aircraft following the September 11 terrorist attacks. Boeing, in particular, has been an aggressive negotiator with its workers, and has relocated and outsourced many skilled jobs to lower-wage markets like China and Russia. In an earlier cost-cutting measure, Boeing sold a major machining facility to the British company GKN plc, a move that fueled labor concerns over offshore control.

Workers at Canada's Bombardier plants have been more strident in their bid to raise salaries and benefits. In 2002, Montreal-based members of the International Association of Machinists and Aerospace Workers (IAM) went on strike to demand a 5 percent annual wage increase, a retirement age of 58, and greater security against the outsourcing of jobs. Historically, though, Canadian aerospace workers have earned less than some of their counterparts in the advanced market economies. In 2002, Airbus employees in France also campaigned for a higher wage boost than the 2.5 percent offered by management.

Industry Leaders

Boeing. By many measures Boeing Company is one of the world's largest aircraft producers. Its net earnings in 2004 were US$1.8 million, a one-year increase of 160 percent, on revenues of US$52.4 billion. In 2005, the company announced 193 orders from 16 airlines for its 787, which Boeing claims has 32 percent less associated maintenance costs that its rival, the Airbus A330. Boeing was third in the defense aircraft industry, but in terms of commercial market share it trailed Airbus by a very thin margin. In 2004, Boeing won a key contract to sell its new 787 to Northwest Airlines, Airbus' third-largest customer. The advantages cited as reasons for choosing the 787 were operating economies. The 787 consumed 20 percent less fuel and cost 10 percent less to operate than other liners of similar size.

Boeing had its origins in the Pacific Aero Products Company, incorporated in Seattle in 1916 by William Edward Boeing, who soon renamed it the Boeing Airplane Company. In 1928 Boeing Airplane, Boeing Air Transport (a subsidiary airline formed earlier), and engine manufacturer Pratt & Whitney were merged to form the United Aircraft and Transport Corporation. The Air Mail Act of 1934 disintegrated the large conglomerates of the day, such as United Aircraft and Transport, which by then had merged its airline acquisitions to form United Airlines. The Boeing Airplane Company emerged as an independent entity.

Outside the civil aircraft sector, Boeing established interests in the fields of data communications (Boeing Computer Services, 1970), artificial intelligence (Carnegie Group, 1984), and defense electronics (ARGOSystems, 1987). Throughout its history Boeing has been a large supplier of military planes and remains one of the world's largest defense contractors.

In 1997 Boeing dramatically increased its hold on the aircraft market by acquiring one of its leading competitors, McDonnell Douglas Corporation, formerly the third-largest manufacturer of airplanes. With the merger, Boeing controlled about 50 percent of the aircraft industry. McDonnell Douglas had been formed by the 1967 merger of The McDonnell Company and Douglas Aircraft, makers of such illustrious transports as the DC-3 (named C-47 by the U.S. military). For a time during the 1950s, Douglas had produced over half of the world's airliners.

The Boeing 737, the best-selling aircraft in history, has dominated the medium-size, medium-range category and, in the late 1990s, remained Boeing's top model. The most profitable lines for Boeing have been its jumbo jets, such as the 747, and the smaller, 130- to 150-seat planes, like the 737-300. However, since the 1990s both of these lines have faced formidable competition from Airbus. Boeing was set to introduce its 7E7 Dreamliner in 2008.

Airbus. Airbus S.A.S. is a French company held jointly by manufacturers from four nations. One of the world's two largest makers of planes, it was conceived in the 1960s as Europe's answer to the United States' domination of the large commercial transport market. France and Great Britain had discussed such a venture as early as 1965. But Britain dropped out of the project due to political disputes. In 1969 the West Germans agreed to partner with France to build the A300, a wide-body, twin-engine airliner. The French company Aerospatiale agreed to hold 37.9 percent of the consortium. In 1971 Construcciones Aeronauticas SA (CASA) of Spain joined Aerospatiale, taking on a 4.2 percent share, and Deutsche Airbus (since 1992 wholly owned by Daimler-Benz) assumed another 37.9 percent share. British Aerospace joined in 1979 and held a 20.0 percent share of the consortium. Associate members Fokker (Dutch) and Belairbus (Belgian) also have participated in some projects. As of 2003, the European Aeronautic Defence and Space Company (EADS) owned 80 percent of Airbus, and BAE SYSTEMS owned the remaining 20 percent. The company's main aircraft assembly plant is located in Toulouse, France.

In 2004 Airbus booked 370 orders and sales of US$34.4 billion, triple the company's 1997 earnings of US$11.6 billion. Such gains represented substantial inroads in market share. The company claimed 52.7 percent gross market share by number of aircraft units. Its greatest announcement during the mid-2000s was its assembly of the largest aircraft in aviation history, the double-decker Airbus A380, capable of carrying more than 550 passengers. As of 2004, Airbus had 139 orders and commitments for the new model. Including the launch of the company's new A350, Airbus had twelve models, including the wide-body twin-engine jets A300 and A310; the single-aisle twin-engine jets A319, A320, and A321; and the four-engine jet A340. Airbus also has developed the A3XX, a super-jumbo jet capable of transporting more than 600 passengers, which it expected to be the main driver of its sales in the twenty-first century.

Bombardier Inc. Based in Montreal, Bombardier was the world's third-largest commercial aircraft maker as of 2004 and specialized in regional airplanes. With sales of US$16 billion in 2004, Bombardier controls the largest percentage of the market in this segment. In 2001 it took in 230 new orders and, among the major producers, was probably the least affected by the downturn that year. The company's leading planes include the Canadair Regional Jet (CRJ) and the de Havilland Dash-8.

Embraer. The Brazilian manufacturer Embraer-Empresa Brasileira de Aeronautica, created in 1969, makes small regional jets and turboprop transports, of which it is the second-largest producer after Bombardier. The firm was especially hard hit by cancellations and low order volume in 2001, when orders crashed by 90 percent from the previous year. The year 2000 had been a banner year for orders, though, so some drop-off was expected. Embraer expected to deliver a total of 135 planes in 2002 and only slightly more in 2003. That year, the company reported US$2.1 billion in sales. Like many other smaller manufacturers, the company has performed significant subcontract work, specifically on the McDonnell Douglas MD-11 and the Boeing 777. The company also produces military aircraft in cooperation with Alenia and Aermacchi in the AMX program.

MAJOR COUNTRIES IN THE INDUSTRY

United States. The United States has been a world leader since the dawn of aviation in the early 1900s. In the late 1990s, the United States produced about 60 percent of the world's aircraft, led primarily by the Boeing Corp. but also by companies such as Cessna, Raytheon, and Bell Helicopter. The United States is both the world's largest producer of and the world's largest market for civil aircraft: more than half of all flights originate or terminate within the country. The United States remained the world leader in 2004, with more than 5,200 passenger aircraft delivered, valued at US$412.7 billion. The U.S. aerospace industry started 2005 off well, with most domestic companies showing profit increases. Raytheon's net income rose 30 percent, with aircraft sales showing an 18 percent increase. In 1951 the United States produced 80 percent of the world's airliners, a figure that declined to about 60 percent in the twenty-first century with the ascent of Airbus and regional manufacturers such as Bombardier. The FAA predicted that the U.S. contribution to the worldwide commercial fleet would rise to 7,419 by 2009.

Approximately 80 percent of active civil U.S. aircraft are classified as general aviation aircraft; the United States accounts for 75 percent of the world's estimated 322,630 fixed-wing (as opposed to rotary-wing) general aviation aircraft, excluding the Commonwealth of Independent States and China. The country's greatest difficulties have been in the rotary wing sector, particularly helicopters and piston-engine aircraft, both of which have suffered considerable trade deficits. Despite these deficits, the United States remains the world's top exporter of aircraft, especially to Asia and the European Union.

France. France is a major competitor of the United States in both the commercial and general aviation markets. In 2004, France delivered 482 passenger aircraft with $57.7 billion.

By 2001, the country's industry leader Airbus S.A.S. captured 50.2 percent of the commercial airliner market in terms of numbers and 61.0 percent net market share in terms of value. France also competes strongly in the general aviation market, with its piston-engine planes and helicopters.

State-owned Aerospatiale, which owned a 37 percent share of Airbus, was created in 1970 through the merger of Sud-Aviation, Nord-Aviation, and SEREB. The company is a member of several international joint ventures relating to military and civil transports, and has begun manufacturing planes in the United States. Another notable French company is Dassault-Breguet, which introduced the first of its highly successful line of Mirage fighters in 1955. The company's Falcon series of business jets also is well respected. However, France's insistence on government-owned aircraft companies plagued its industry in the late 1990s. Airbus is now the only major competitor to commercial industry leader Boeing. In the late 1990s, its other shareholders called upon the French government to allow it to become a single corporate entity in order to continue competing as strongly as possible against Boeing.

Germany. In the late 1990s and early 2000s, Germany played a central role in many European joint ventures, such as Airbus and Eurocopter. That helped explain why, in 2004, Germany's sales in aircraft were US$96.6 billion for 989 passenger aircraft delivered. Part of the German aerospace conglomerate Messerschmitt-Bolkow-Blohm GmbH (MBB) can be traced to a company Willy Messerschmitt founded in 1923, which produced sport planes, gliders, and military craft such as the Bf 109 and the world's first operational jet fighter, the Me 262. The company now manufactures helicopters and business aircraft and is a member of various joint ventures. Daimler-Benz AG, Germany's largest manufacturer, which owns MBB as well as Deutsche Aerospace, took over a former Soviet plant in Dresden and has refurbished it to repair existing Soviet-built aircraft and manufacture sections of new Western aircraft such as the Fokker 100. Daimler-Benz also owns a large share of Airbus.

China. China represented an expanding market for aircraft and also was a minor producer, mainly to meet its own domestic demand. According to a Chinese government forecast issued in 2001, the country was expected to buy 400 new aircraft between 2001 and 2005 in order to support a projected passenger load of 100 million a year. As of 2000, China had 67 million passengers on its planes, making it the world's sixth-largest market in terms of volume. In 2004, China delivered 1,790 passenger aircraft woth $241.7 billion, as reported in Airbus' *Global Market Forecast 2004-2023.*

Two state-led manufacturing consortia lead China's production, China Aviation Industry (AVIC) I and II. Both produce civil aircraft, but AVIC II is more heavily involved in defense transport.

China sent mixed signals to potential manufacturing partners and suppliers around the world. It engaged most of the world's leading aircraft makers in partnership talks, but several of these projects were stalled by government policies. The Chinese airlines, for their part, have been eager to order foreign-built planes, but even some of these orders have been delayed by government interventions. One reason may be that the government has been divided over whether to protect the domestic industry or gain access to the resources of the world's largest aircraft manufacturers. Regional jets are expected to be one of the most demanded items in the Chinese market in the first two decades of the twenty-first century.

Japan. Japan is home to a medium-sized contingent of aircraft manufacturers that serve mostly as subcontractors to larger producers like Boeing and Embraer. The result for Japan was passenger aircraft delivered of US$106.4 billion in 2004, placing it fifth among the world's aircraft producing countries. Mitsubishi Heavy Industries, Kawasaki Heavy Industries, and Fuji Heavy Industries have cooperated in the development of the Boeing 777, which may explain that airplane's strong Asian sales. Flight instruments, electronic control components, and carbon fiber for the tail section have all been supplied by Japanese companies.

In the early 2000s Japanese firms sought to take a more central role in building medium-to-large regional craft, jets with 80-110 seats, and had a number of design concepts in early testing. Analysts have estimated that the Japanese industry still lags 10 years behind that of the United States.

Asia Pacific. The Asia Pacific region was expected to show significant growth, and was viewed by the European Aeronautic Defence & Space (EADS) consortium as one of its top three markets in 2005. That same year, Airbus announced that India would be purchasing 570 aircraft over the next 20 years to meet the demand of its expanding market. Boeing also announced in April 2005 that the company would focus marketing efforts on Asian carriers. The country's aviation industry was growing rapidly, and a number of new airlines opened during the early 2000s. In the Airbus *Global Market Forecast 2004-2023,* the report stated that "China and India have the potential to reshape the travel industry."

FURTHER READING

Airbus S.A.S. "2001 Commercial Results Consolidate Airbus' Position as World's Leading Aircraft Manufacturer." Available from http://www.airbus.com.

"Airbus Sees Strong Cargo Market." *The Journal of Commerce Online,* 30 March 2004.

Bernstein, Mark. "Four Years from Launch, What's the Buzz on the A380." *World Trade,* April 2004.

"Boeing: A Comeback in the Air." *Business Week Online,* 13 April 2005.

"Boeing Commercial Airplanes." *Airfinance Journal,* April 2005.

"Bright Outlook in 2004." *Airline Business,* 1 February 2004.

"China to Buy 400 Aircraft in Five Years." *Alestron,* 3 July 2001.

"Component Tracking." *Flight International,* 13 April 2004.

Draper, Deborah J., ed. *Business Rankings Annual.* Detroit: Thomson Gale, 2004.

"EADS Consolidates in Asia Pacific." *Australasian Business Intelligence,* 13 January 2005.

Flores, Jackson. "Forecasts." *Flight International,* 27 April 2004.

Global Market Forecast 2004-2023. Airbus S.A.S., 2004-2005. Available from http://www.airbus.com.

"Hoover's Company Capsules." 2004. Available from http://www.hoovers.com.

"India Will buy 570 Aircraft - Forecast." *Airline Industry Information,* 22 June 2005.

Kingsley-Jones, Max. "Production." *Flight International,* 13 December 2004.

Lazich, Robert S., ed. *Market Share Reporter.* Detroit: Thomson Gale, 2004.

Napier, David H. "2001 Year-End Review and 2002 Forecast: An Analysis." Aerospace Industries Association, 2002. Available from http://www.aia-aerospace.org.

"Senate Bill Would Promote Quiet Aircraft Technology." *Noise Regulation Report,* April 2003.

Sobie, Brendan. "Supersonic Transports." *Flight International,* 6 July 2004.

Taylor, Alex. "Lord of the Air." *Fortune,* 10 November 2003.

"Teal Group Analysts Predict that 6,743 Commercial Aircraft, Valued at $421 Billion, Are to Be Built Between 2003 and 2012." *Airfinance Journal,* September 2003.

"U.S. Firms Start Year Well." *Flight International,* 3 May 2005.

SIC 3480

NAICS 33299

DEFENSE AND ARMAMENTS

The armaments industry designs and manufactures the world's military equipment and accessories, including air, sea, and ground weapons. Examples of industry products range from military handguns and grenade launchers to planes, missiles, and tanks. Nuclear weapons are not discussed in this section. Certain firms in this industry also produce for the commercial aerospace sector; for more information on these activities, see also **Aircraft Manufacturing.**

INDUSTRY SNAPSHOT

In the 1980s, toward the end of the Cold War, global military spending peaked at more than US$1.36 trillion. It leveled off at about US$800 billion in the mid-1990s, due primarily to massive reductions in the post-Cold War era. Boosted by the U.S. war on terror and increased defense budgets in China and India, world military spending rose for a sixth consecutive year to reach $1.04 trillion in 2004 which equaled 2.6 percent of global gross domestic product. The United States remains, by far, the world's principal weapons producer and broker, and it is home to a number of leading manufacturers that arm many nations throughout the world. The country accounted for nearly half of all military expenditures in 2004. Russia also retains its position as the world's second-largest armament manufacturer, followed by the European Union and China.

The three basic arms industry segments are land weapons (ordnance), aircraft, and ships. The military equipment industry was helped in the 1990s by the post-Gulf War rearmament in the Middle East as well as the prolonged peacekeeping mission in the former Yugoslavia for which the United States, France, Germany, the United Kingdom, and other participating countries required defense equipment. Continued confrontation between the United States and Iraq kept defense spending a priority in the United States into the late 1990s. The September 11, 2001, terrorist attacks on the World Trade Center and the Pentagon, subsequent military action in Afghanistan, and the U.S.-led war with Iraq in 2003, resulted in spending increases that lasted well into the 2000s.

ORGANIZATION AND STRUCTURE

In 2004 global military expenditures, excluding nuclear weapons and certain aerospace equipment and systems, totaled some US$1.04 trillion, with the United States accounting for nearly half of that figure at $US455 billion. Global arms sales, however, declined for the third year in a row, to $25.6 billion in 2003. The majority of those arms were purchased by the U.S. federal government to supply its armed forces. These purchases were made by nearly every country in the world, and rebel groups as well. Major arms-consuming regions outside of North America included the European Union, the Middle East, Commonwealth of Independent States, and east and central Asia. Developing nations accounted for a little over two-thirds of the global arms export market. The decline in arms sales in the early to mid-2000s was attributed to the growth of protectionist policies in developed countries and an unstable international economy which had developing nations upgrading existing weapons systems rather than purchasing new ones.

The United States and the Soviet Union dominated the arms industry during the latter half of the twentieth century. The United States made slightly over 50 percent of worldwide arms sales in 2000, about US$18.6 billion in all. Russia retained the vast majority of the Soviet Union's military might after the Soviet state was dismantled in the early 1990s. Into the twenty-first century, the former rivals continued to design the world's leading weapons systems, many of which were produced throughout the world. Certain systems manufactured outside the United States have been under licensing agreements with U.S.-based developers. Significant portions of U.S. weapons, for example, were manufactured under license in Italy and Japan. Many weapons have also been produced in the Commonwealth of Independent States (CIS)—a voluntary economic organization that includes all Soviet states except the three Baltic republics—France, Germany, and a few other nations.

The arms industry in the early 1990s represented the culmination of a century of industry volatility. Indeed, arms industry statistics—which can be difficult to pin down accurately—have historically experienced wild fluctuations within the global political landscape. The entire industry can be depressed one year, and within a few months experience a robust turnaround, the result of a major regional conflict that has boosted sales. Likewise, arms sales vary greatly according to procurement budgets set by political bodies in specific countries.

The 1990s saw a nearly invisible shift in the defense industry structure, at least in the United States, where service industries assumed an increasingly important role. That change was due to the growing importance of information technology to modern weapons design. By the end of the decade, service workers—employees who install, maintain, troubleshoot, operate, and integrate hardware and software systems—accounted for almost three out of four of U.S. Defense Department contract jobs, up 50 percent from 1984 levels. IT companies BDM, SAIC, and Computer Sciences Corporation became major suppliers to the American military.

Weapons Types. The three basic arms industry segments are: (1) ordnance, or land weapons; (2) aircraft; and (3) ships, including destroyers, submarines, carriers, and smaller ships. Land weapons, for the purposes of this discussion, include artillery, land vehicles, and small arms such as rifles and hand grenades. Major categories of artillery, or heavy weapons, include cannon, which typically fire low-velocity, exploding projectiles; mortars, which fire shells at a high, arcing trajectory; howitzers, which fire a variety of shells; and rocket launchers. Land weapons also include anti-aircraft weapons and missiles, which account for a comparatively large proportion of weapons expenditures worldwide.

Types of missiles include: guided, which are directed by remote control or internal mechanisms; surface-to-surface, including small tactical and larger strategic missiles; air-launched; and surface-to-air. Leading U.S. missile systems in the 1990s included the AIM-9M Sidewinder and AIM-7F Sparrow air-to-air missiles; the RGM-84A Harpoon antiship system; the TOW-2 antitank missile; and the Patriot antimissile system. Equivalent Russian missiles included the Aphid, Atoll, and Apex air-to-air missiles; the Styx antiship system; and the Spigot and Spandrel antitank missiles. Italy, the United Kingdom, and France also possessed several similar missile systems.

Land vehicles include tanks, personnel and equipment carriers and transports, and other armed and unarmed vehicles. The dominant armored vehicle in the mid-1990s was the U.S. M1A1 Abrams battle tank. Developed at a cost of US$20.4 billion, each tank cost about US$4.4 million to produce and was designed to absorb direct hits from certain armor-piercing shells. The high-tech M1 was powered by a turbine engine that allowed the massive vehicle to cruise at 60 miles per hour while a damper allowed the operator of the 120 mm cannon to fire laser-aimed projectiles with high accuracy. The tank was also equipped with infrared sights for night vision. The M1's peers included the Russian-designed T-80 and T-72, as well as tanks built in Germany (the Leopard series), the United Kingdom (Challenger, Chieftan, and Vickers), and France (AMX-30B2), among others.

Major weapons in the aircraft segment include the U.S. F-22, F-16 Falcon, F-15 Eagle, and F/A-18 Hornet—all fighter/attack jets. Similar Russian planes were the aging MIG-29 Fulcrum, Su-27 Flanker, and Su-24 Fencer. North Atlantic Treaty Organization (NATO) contributions to the fighter jet segment have included the Mirage (France), and the Tornado (United Kingdom, Germany, and Italy). In addition to these fighters were larger craft such as the U.S. C-17 airlift-type plane and the B-2 (Stealth) Bomber. Also included in the aircraft group are helicopters, among the most respected of which has been the U.S. UH-60 Blackhawk developed in the early 1990s.

Background and Development

Organized warfare was first recorded around 3500 B.C. following the first settlements of Western civilization. As communities expanded to accommodate growing herds and populations, conflicts rose between neighboring villages. Crude weapons, such as catapults and hunting tools, were used throughout the period. It was not until about A.D. 1300, particularly with the invention of gunpowder, that more advanced weaponry evolved. After pikes and longbows were introduced in the fourteenth century, for example, the French invented the cannon in the fifteenth century. The first ship-borne cannon was introduced in the sixteenth century, and breakthrough inventions such as the rifled gun barrel followed in the 17th and 18th centuries. Despite advances, weapons remained crude by modern standards until later in the eighteenth century.

By the eighteenth century artillery had become a staple of every serious war machine. Soldiers were usually armed with guns, and horse-drawn cannon were common. However, up to that time, the arms industry was relatively undeveloped, as most armies expected their soldiers to supply their own weapons and ammunition. The onset of the Industrial Revolution in Europe changed the arms industry during the early 1800s. The ability to effectively make more complex and expensive weapons made it necessary for governments to assume a greater role in purchasing arms. The end result was competition among many nations to design and build the most destructive weapons. That competition culminated in the early twentieth century with the creation of advanced weapons such as tanks, armored personnel carriers, flame throwers, and even military aircraft.

New weapons developed during the late 19th and early 20th centuries radically changed the concept of war and battle. It suddenly became possible, for example, to rapidly transport soldiers over water, land, and through the air, or for ships to do battle without ever coming in sight of their adversary. Similarly, long-range cannon, missiles, bombers, and jets effectively reduced the capacity of ground and sea troops to defend a position. Importantly, the introduction of atomic explosive devices in 1945 had a momentous impact on the concept of warfare, and therefore, on the arms industry. That development contributed to a new phenomenon in the global weapons industry: the world arms trade became dominated by two nuclear superpowers, the United States and the Soviet Union.

The Cold War. Beginning in the 1950s the arms industry was influenced by Cold War politics and the ensuing arms race between the United States and the Soviet Union. Immediately after World War II, the United States came to dominate armament production in the noncommunist sphere. For more than a decade, the United States was effectively the sole supplier of major weapons to the free world. Besides equipping its own forces, the United States outfitted armies throughout Western Europe and much of Latin America, Asia, the Middle East, and parts of Africa. At one point in the early 1950s, in fact, the United States was shipping nearly US$15 billion worth of military equipment and services annually to war-torn Western European nations alone. The United States began to cede its monopoly on the Western military market during the late 1950s. By the early 1960s the United States still controlled about 40 percent of the total global arms export market, while other NATO countries were supplying more than 15 percent—the rest was served primarily by Eastern Bloc nations. Still, the United States continued to be the leading global arms manufacturer, supplying more than 90 percent of all noncommunist arms.

Between the 1950s and the 1980s the two countries became engaged in a heated competition to develop the most deadly and feared conventional and nuclear weapons. Massive investments by both nations in arms technology produced a dazzling array of high-tech weaponry that tested the limits of human ingenuity. By the 1980s, in fact, both countries and their allies had amassed enough firepower to destroy civilization many times over. The acronym MAD (mutually assured destruction) was coined to describe the military stalemate or balance of power that existed between the Eastern and Western blocs.

The Cold War intensified during the 1950s and 1960s as the Soviet Union continued to amass military might along with the United States and its allies. Like the United States, the Soviet Union sustained its dominant lead over other nations of the world through intense research and development expenditures, including those related to aerospace initiatives. The Soviet Union was initially slow to enter the arms export market; between 1968 and 1972, it exported a total of about US$25 billion of arms to foreign countries compared to about US$55 billion exported by the United States. But it significantly increased foreign sales in the 1970s and 1980s, exporting US$175 billion worth of weapons between 1973 and 1982 compared to about US$115 billion shipped by U.S. arms manufacturers. In contrast, all other nations combined exported less than US$100 billion between 1973 and 1982. Meanwhile, the United States and the Soviet Union each budgeted hundreds of billions of dollars annually for their own defense.

The global defense industry boomed during the 1980s as the United States launched its final drive to end the Cold War. In the mid-1980s the U.S. government increased its military procurement budget and began investing aggressively in the research and development of a new generation of nuclear and non-nuclear weapons and defense systems. The result was explosive industry growth as the U.S. arms procurement budget ballooned to a peacetime record of about US$115 billion annually. The Soviet Union had little choice but to try and match the challenge and sustain the balance of power. By the late 1980s, though, the United States was close to winning the arms race as it made plans to begin developing its costly and controversial "Star Wars" missile defense system.

Meanwhile, other nations began to increase their sales and purchases of arms. In 1987 global defense spending reached an all-time high of approximately US$1.15 trillion for defense equipment and armaments. The arms export market (all markets except the United States and the Soviet Union) had grown to about US$70 billion by 1988. American and Soviet arms producers still dominated the overall industry because of demand in their home countries, but the export market outside of those nations was increasingly available to arms suppliers. By the mid-1980s the United States and the Soviet Union were supplying about 20 percent and 30 percent, respectively, of the arms export market. Other NATO countries controlled about 30 percent of the market, and the remaining 20 percent was met by other nations.

With the end of Cold War spending levels after the collapse of the Soviet Union, world weapons production decreased significantly. The declines eventually leveled out, thanks to Middle East rearmament after the Gulf War and the Western intervention in the war in the former Yugoslavia. By the end of the decade, some producing nations were even reporting increases again. A major shift in the 1990s saw the developing world take over the lead in arms imports. The developing world's share of total world arms imports rose 35 percent in 1989 to 57 percent in 1999. Another trend was the consolidation of the industry by a wave of mergers and acquisitions in the latter half of the decade. Consolidation began in the United States and then moved to Western Europe. Similar consolidation was seen as inevitable in the overly large industries of Russia and China as well.

After the Cold War, there was a tendency toward multinational military operations in the 1990s. Global defense spending dropped continuously from its apex in 1987, reaching a post-Cold War nadir in 1998. Expenditures rose again between 1998 and 2000 to approximately US$798 billion, an increase of about 5 percent. Most of the world's military powerhouses slashed their defense budgets drastically in the 1990s and early 2000s, although the administration of President George W. Bush requested significant defense increases for the first half of the 2000s in response to perceived terrorist threats and the war in Afghanistan. The Stockholm International Peace Institute suggested that the plans for military growth of some nations will result in increased global procurement expenditures in the later 2000s.

Although defense has historically been a domestically based industry, more and more governments have begun to expand armament sources to include foreign companies. By 1999, for example, the United States was eighth on the list of the world's top importers, purchasing a not negligible US$800 million in arms from the United Kingdom, Germany, Israel, Australia, and the Netherlands.

The reasons for this trend are varied. For example, the cost of producing modern, high-tech military technology has skyrocketed, and few nations besides the United States or possibly Russia are able to support the costs of a domestic industry that provides for all defense needs. A single 1972 F-16 cost US$30 million in 1996, which was still substantially less than F-22s, which are expected to cost US$100 million each, according to figures released by *The Economist.* If domestic companies cannot afford to produce weapons, a government must purchase them elsewhere. Similarly, if a government cannot purchase all weapons produced by a domestic firm, that firm must seek foreign markets. France has even claimed that arms exports are necessary for maintaining its trade balance.

As an alternative to individual governments producing their own defense equipment, certain countries have organized joint ventures to share development and manufacturing costs. In 2001, France, Germany, Italy, Spain, Sweden, and the United Kingdom launched the European Technology Acquisition Programme (ETAP). ETAP was an unprecedented agreement that joined both governments and specific industries in the development of new aircraft. In 2001 the American defense contractor Raytheon and the French Thales announced that their national regulators had approved a joint venture for the production of new radar systems and command and control centers.

Cross-border cooperation between defense companies brought both advantages and problems. Besides dispersing the prohibitive costs of armament production, multinational defense projects also ensure that participating nations possess uniform, interoperable equipment. This is vital at a time when coalitions of countries such as NATO and United Nations troops cooperate in peacekeeping or other missions. Such operations function more smoothly when all participants have compatible technology and equipment. Indeed, a substantial share of the costs to bring new members into NATO result from technological upgrades of those nations' military equipment to attain compatibility. However, technology exchange can also be a stumbling block to cooperation when different nations view export controls on technology differently. For example, tensions arose between the United States—which works to prevent its state-of-the-art weaponry from reaching unstable regions or so-called rogue states—and its European allies, who are often willing to make such exports to keep home companies commercially viable.

As companies all turned to the world market, there was a ratcheting up of competition for weapons sales. In the ensuing struggle for survival during the mid-1990s, the global defense industry underwent a wave of consolidation. Boeing acquired defense industry leader McDonnell Douglas, and Rolls-Royce purchased the U.S. defense firm Allison. In November 1999, UK giant British Aerospace merged with Marconi Electronic Systems to form BAE Systems. A pan-European merger of Matra BAe Dynamics, Aerospatiale Matra Missiles, and Alenia Marconi Systems' missile division resulted in MBDA, the second largest missile company in the world. Intense consolidation of the European market was expected to continue for three to five years, and to sweep through Russian and Chinese defense firms too.

Current Conditions

According to a report issued by the Congressional Research Service (CRS) in 2005, worldwide military spending reached US$1.04 trillion in 2004. The United States led with spending of US$455 billion, nearly half of the total figure and more than the 32 next most powerful nations combined.

A separate CRS report from August 2004 revealed that the total value of worldwide arms transfer agreements decreased sharply from US$41 billion in 2000 to US$25.6 billion in 2003. A difficult global economy was largely to blame for the reduction. Developing nations, which represent the industry's most lucrative market, opted to upgrade existing weaponry instead of purchasing new supplies. During the early 2000s, developing nations accounted for more than 60 percent of all arms transfer agreements. However, in 2003, levels fell to 53.6 percent.

During the mid-2000s, the defense industry was benefiting from the U.S.-led war with Iraq. The war began with a massive military assault on the city of Baghdad in March 2003, as the Bush administration sought to free Iraq from Dictator Saddam Hussein and uncover weapons of mass destruction. The invasion was followed by a long-term military presence; by September of 2004, the U.S. military had roughly 130,000 troops in Iraq and had suffered more than 1,000 casualties.

Unlike the nation's first war with Iraq during the early 1990s, which was fought largely from the air, soldiers involved in Operation Iraqi Freedom faced significant combat on the ground from opposition forces that were well armed. In its 17 June 2004 issue, the *New York Times* noted: "By the time of the coalition invasion, Iraq had one of the largest conventional arms stockpiles in the world. According to one American military estimate, this included three million tons of bombs and bullets; millions of AK-47's and other rifles, rocket launchers and mortar tubes; and thousands of more sophisticated arms like ground-to-air missiles. Much of the arsenal was stored in vast warehouse complexes, some of which occupied several square miles. As war approached, Iraqi commanders ordered these mountains of munitions to be dispersed across the country in thousands of small caches."

Although the Baghdad invasion called for a significant share of armaments, defense contractors already were benefiting from increased spending on weapons before the assault. For example, in its February 2003 issue, *Aviation Week & Space Technology* reported that the Department of Defense modified an existing contract with leading defense contractor Raytheon calling for the manufacture of 167 additional Tactical Tomahawk missiles. The contract modification was valued at $224.5 million. In addition, the publication revealed that the U.S. military had tentative plans to purchase some 2,200 PAC-3 interceptor missiles from Lockheed Martin, along with 1,400 Patriot PAC-2 GEM+ missiles from Raytheon.

By late 2003, Congress had approved President Bush's request for US$87 billion in funding for operations in Iraq and Afghanistan. Of this total, US$67 billion was earmarked for military spending. Heading into the mid-2000s, U.S. defense contractors and related industries stood to benefit from ever heftier levels of defense spending. From 2001 to 2004, U.S. defense spending increased more than 35 percent as the nation sought to modernize its fighting forces. The U.S.-led war with Iraq in 2003 made defense spending a top priority.

In the February 9, 2004 issue of *Aviation Week & Space Technology,* David A. Fulghum provided information from Pentagon Comptroller Dov Zakheim that revealed some specifics about the United States' planned defense purchases. Of the US$74.9 billion marked for procurement in the Fiscal 2005 defense budget, Fulghum noted that plans were in place to obtain "42 F/A-18E/Fs, 24 F/A-22s, 14 C-17s and 11 V-22s. Another $68.9 billion is tagged for research and development. A total of $2 billion, a 32 percent increase, will go for unmanned aerial vehicle (UAV) production including four Global Hawks (with long-lead funding for six more), nine Predators (among them two of the faster, larger B-models) and 24 Shadow-200s. Another $1.6 billion is earmarked for precision weaponry."

RESEARCH AND TECHNOLOGY

Government spending on research and technology declined during the latter 1990s along with the overall global reduction in defense spending. Nevertheless, a vast amount of new technology developed near the end of the Cold War was introduced during that period. Most notable were new generation aircraft and missile systems developed by the United States and its allies. The U.S. government, in fact, continued to spend heavily on weapons research and development during the early 1990s, although expenditures declined by 50 percent by the mid-1990s. In 1994, for example, the United States was completing development of its new stealth fighter jets, the F-22, the F/A-18E/F fighter, and the Joint Strike Fighter. Other aircraft that were in the works in 2001 were the V-22 Osprey Aircraft and the C-17 Transport Aircraft. Similarly, the United States introduced innovative and costly new stealth aircraft—the B-2 bomber and the F-117A fighter jet, as well as the F-22—in the mid-1990s.

In addition to the most technologically advanced jets and bombers in the world, the United States also introduced the world's most advanced helicopters in the early 1990s. The principal helicopter under development throughout the 1990s was the RAH-66 Comanche, a highly advanced, armored reconnaissance unit that far surpassed any helicopter being developed elsewhere in the world. Of lesser but still impressive technological prowess was the AW-64 Apache Attack Helicopter. This jet-powered machine was capable of cruising through battlefields at high speeds and simultaneously launching a barrage of cannon fire, rockets, and laser-guided missiles in multiple directions. The Apache's fatal Hellfire missile system allowed a pilot to unleash an armor-piercing missile that was aimed and guided by a soldier on the ground, thus allowing the Apache pilot to seek other targets.

In addition to high-tech weaponry developed late in the Cold War, some of the most advanced defense devices included high-flying planes and satellite systems that gathered intelligence and helped ground forces communicate. Advanced military imaging satellites used by both Commonwealth of Independent States and Western forces, for example, were capable of reading a car's license plate from space. Further, early warning satellite systems could quickly detect launched missiles and relay their flight patterns to observers on the ground. Similarly, the U.S.-bred Airborne Warning & Control System (AWACS) could monitor and control air and land combat from a plane in the air.

In the mid-1990s numerous projects under development by companies throughout the world manifested the ongoing trend toward high-tech space age weaponry. One example was work done in the United States on a new breed of non-lethal weapons designed to incapacitate, but not necessarily kill, the enemy. Although they were considered at least a decade away from actual use in the field, the weapons showed great promise, and manufacturers and the U.S. government were investing in their development. Among the many non-lethal technologies under development were optical munitions, which used isotropic and directed radiators to generate a high-powered, multi-dimensional, visible light source that could disrupt enemy sensors, among other applications. Similarly, high-power microwave projectiles could be used to disable enemy information systems. Other non-lethal weapons being created in the mid-1990s included: laser dye rods, which created an intense flash and blinded personnel and optical sensors; pulsed chemical lasers, which created a high-pressure "plasma blast wave" that incapacitated people and destroyed materials; and acoustic bullets that caused blunt-object trauma rather than ripping the skin and vital organs.

In September 2005, the U.S. military planned to mount microwave guns onto armored vehicles in Iraq. Officially called Active Denial Systems, the new weapons would be used for subduing mobs of insurgents that operated in close proximity to civilians. Developed at the Air Force Research Laboratory in New Mexico, the weapons produced a burning sensation beneath the skin when directed at a target, which subsided when the target moved away from the energy beam, and resulted in no physical damage. The military planned to name armored vehicles equipped with the devices as "Sheriffs."

INDUSTRY LEADERS

The Boeing Company. The Boeing Company was the third-largest defense company in the world in 2004 with sales that year of nearly US$52.5 billion. Boeing owes this position largely to acquisitions made in the 1990s: the McDonnell Douglas Corporation of the United States in 1997 and Rockwell's defense and aerospace business in 1996. In 2001 it also acquired the satellite operations of Hughes Electronics. Boeing manufactured the F-15 Eagle fighter bomber, the F/A-18 Hornet strike bomber, and an array of other fighter, bomber, and transport aircraft. About 60 percent of its sales come from commercial aircraft like the 737, the 747, and the 767.

General Dynamics. General Dynamics, also of the United States, was another key arms manufacturer in the mid-2000s. In late 2004, General Dynamics consisted of four principle divisions: Information Systems and Technology (battlespace information networks, data acquisition/processing, advanced electronics, and management systems); Combat Systems (land and amphibious combat machines and systems, including power trains, turrets, armored vehicles, gun systems, and munitions); Aerospace (mid-size, large cabin, and ultra-long-range business aircraft); and Marine Systems (submarines, surface combatants, auxiliary ships, and large commercial vessels). In the mid-1990s General Dynamics started acquiring related businesses including Lockheed Martin's armament unit and Teledyne's vehicle systems division. General Dynamics was a defense industry leader throughout the 1980s and early 1990s. After posting revenues of US$10.17 billion in 1990, however, the company experienced a rapid decline in orders from the military. However, by the mid-1990s General Dynamics' sales began to stabilize. By 2001 sales had reached US$12.2 billion, a 17 percent increase over 2000. Sales rose more than 15 percent in 2004, to US$19.2 billion.

BAE Systems. BAE Systems, formerly British Aerospace, was Europe's largest defense contractor in 2004. The company was formed with the merger of British Aerospace and Marconi Electronic Systems in November 1999. British Aerospace was a long-time leader in global defense markets, distinguished by its products such as the Hawk, Tornado, Gripen, and Harrier fighter jets. Moreover, the company will develop the state-of-the-art Eurofighter. BAE also built missiles, electronic defense systems, naval vessels, commercial aircraft, space systems, and a wide range of ordnance and ammunition. The company was the core of the United Kingdom's defense industry. It garnered revenues of US$14.4 billion in 2000, 0.2 percent over 1999. Sales were US$17.5 billion in 2004, up 17.5 percent from the previous year. BAE agreed to acquire the United Kingdom's Alvis, a manufacturer of armored vehicles, in mid-2004. About 72 percent of BAE's sales are to the military.

Lockheed Martin Corporation. U.S.-based Lockheed Martin Corporation, the largest defense contractor in the world, develops and manufactures aerospace products and systems, submarine-launched ballistic missiles, and defense electronics. Products and services included those related to aircraft, missiles, space, electronics, and aerospace design and support. The company reported that in 2000, about 19 percent of its sales were attributable to its aeronautical segment that builds combat and airlift aircraft, such as the F-22 fighter, the Joint Strike Fighter, and the C-130J transport for the military. Roughly 67 percent came from missiles and space systems. Lockheed assumed a lead in the global defense industry in the mid-1990s as a result of strong demand for several of its technologies. Sales rose from about US$9.8 billion in 1991 to nearly US$24 billion in 2001 because of the company's diversification and penetration of new defense markets such as the Middle East and Asia. In 2000, the company sold its subsidiary Hanford Corporation. During the early 2000s, the U.S. government accounted for about 70 percent of Lockheed's sales, which reached US$35.5 billion in 2004, up 11.6 percent over the previous year.

European Aeronautic Defence and Space Company. The European Aeronautic Defence and Space Company (EADS) is the world's second largest aerospace/defense company, after Boeing. It was formed in July 2000 with the merger of three firms: DaimlerChrysler Aerospace of Germany, Aerospatiale Matra of France, and Construcciones Aeronauticas SA (CASA) of Spain. In addition to commercial aircraft, EADS manufactures military planes, helicopters, missiles, defense satellites, and electronics. Company sales grew 19.5 percent between 1999 and 2000, reaching about US$18.3 billion. In 2001, EADS entered into a joint project with five other European companies to develop new manned and unmanned military aircraft. By 2004, sales were US$43.32 billion, up 14.5 percent from 2003.

MAJOR COUNTRIES IN THE INDUSTRY

United States. The United States' large defense budget and its control of export markets made it the undisputed leader in the arms industry during the mid-2000s. In addition to sales of major weapons systems, such as M1A1 Abrams Main Battle Tank kits and a wide variety of missiles, the United States also exports significant numbers of spare parts, components, and weapons upgrades to other nations, and also provides service and training.

In 2001 alone, about one-third of the United States' US$302 billion defense budget went to defense contractors for procurement, research, or development. That sum also accounted for about 37 percent of world military expenditures in 2000. As a consequence of the September 11, 2001, terrorist attacks on the World Trade Center and the Pentagon, the administration of President George W. Bush requested a defense budget of US$379 billion in 2003.

By the mid-2000s, about 3.5 percent of the U.S. gross domestic product went to defense spending, an increase from 2.9 percent in 2000. The United States' US$401.7 billion defense budget for Fiscal Year 2005 was 7 percent higher than the estimated 2004 levels of US$375.3 billion, and 10 percent higher than actual 2003 levels of US$365.3 billion. In addition to an overall defense spending increase of 35 percent from 2001 to 2004, the Bush Administration doubled spending related to missile defense systems during the same timeframe.

Besides accounting for roughly half of global arms purchases, the United States controlled just over 50 percent of the global arms export market during the early 2000s. Its share, valued at almost US$18.6 billion in 2000, was up by almost US$6 billion from 1999 largely on the strength of a purchase of 80 F-16 aircraft by the United Arab Emirates. Its dominance of the export market stemmed from the marketing savvy of the U.S. government and U.S. arms manufacturers, as well as the technological superiority of its weapons. That technological edge was honed with hundreds of billions of dollars of research and development into new weapons over several decades.

Although the U.S. defense industry stumbled during the global weapons industry downturn of the early and mid-1990s, its future seemed secure entering the new century. By 1999, the U.S. accounted for 64 percent of the world's arms exports, an all-time record. According to the U.S. State Department, U.S. exports went to more than 154 of the world's 190 independent nations in 2000. The United States has sustained criticism abroad for its large defense trade surplus, which persists because the U.S. Congress has at times mandated that defense equipment be domestically produced. In 1999, for example, the United States imported US$2 billion in armaments from the European Union, but exported US$15 billion worth of weapons to the European Union.

The U.S. government, which strictly regulates arms exports by U.S. manufacturers, officially views arms transfers or exports as a legitimate instrument of U.S. foreign policy. The goals of its arms sales decisions were to help U.S. allies defend themselves and remain compatible with U.S. forces, promote regional stability in areas of critical interest to the United States, ensure that U.S. forces would retain their technological superiority over potential adversaries, and enhance the ability of U.S. arms makers to sustain a long-term technology and manufacturing advantage.

According to an August 2004 Congressional Research Service (CRS) report, in 2003 the United States ranked first with US$14.5 billion in global arms transfer agreements, followed by Russia (US$4.3 billion), Germany (US$1.4 billion), France (US$1 billion), Italy (US$600 million), China (US$300 million), and the United Kingdom (US$100 million). All other European countries accounted for US$2.3 billion in arms transfers, and a combination of other countries accounted for US$1.1 billion.

The United States also ranked first in actual worldwide arms deliveries in 2003 (US$13.6 billion). The United Kingdom was ranked second at US$4.7 billion, followed by Russia at US$3.4 billion. France and Germany both recorded deliveries valued at US$1.2 billion, followed by China (US$500 million) and Italy (US$100 million). All other European countries accounted for US$2.4 billion in deliveries, and a combination of other countries accounted for US$1.6 billion.

Russia. With control of 70 percent of the former Soviet Union's weapons industry, Russia remained the second largest national player in the global armament industry during the early 2000s, even though its production, sales, and exports stood well below 1980s figures. In 1995 Russia reported exports of US$2.5 billion —well beneath Cold War levels—but between 1998 and 2000 the Russian defense industry boosted production to about 18.7 percent of 1991 levels, the last year of Soviet production. It had reported sales worth US$4 billion in 2000. Exports accounted for about 60 percent of the industry's business in 1999 to 2000. During the early 2000s, Russia's main arms customers were China and India, which together accounted for 70 percent of Russia's 2000 sales. Agreements with Iran were expected to increase significantly after 2001. Russia's own military spending totaled US$56 billion in 1999.

Russia has specialized in inexpensive, durable weapons; however, it is facing increasing competition, especially from its partners in the Confederation of Independent States such as the Ukraine. Market pressures are expected to eventually result in a wave of mergers, acquisitions, and bankruptcies that will shrink but toughen the Russian industry. Nonetheless, there remained deep skepticism in some quarters about the ability of many Russian firms to survive in the free market. To become competitive, the industry will have to cultivate export markets—in 2001 the Russian government expected to purchase no more than 30 percent of its production capacity. Russian industry will also have to overcome the meagerness of its product lines. During the early 2000s, two-thirds of all sales came from combat aircraft such as the MIG fighter. As of 2004, many developing nations were reluctant to acquire more advanced weapons systems from Russia, due to concerns about the country's inability to provide adequate levels of support and training, as well as quality spare parts.

Citing information from Itar-Tass, *IPR Strategic Business Information Database* reported that Russia's arms exports surpassed the US$5 billion mark for the first time in 2003, reaching US$5.1 billion. This represented an increase from US$4.2 billion in 2002 and US$3.2 billion in 2001, and was attributed to continued overall growth of military product sales. China and India remained Russia's principal trading partners during the mid-2000s, although the country exported military products to 52 countries in all. According to Rosoboroneksport, Russia's export agency, trade was increasing with partners in Southeast Asia, including Vietnam, Malaysia, and Indonesia. One significant deal between Russia and China was the sale of 24 Su-30 MKK multi-fighter aircraft in 2003, which was valued at US$1 billion.

During the mid-2000s, Russia devoted 2.6 to 2.7 percent of its gross domestic product to defense spending. According to the August 24, 2004, issue of Russia's *St. Petersburg Times,* the country's 2005 budget called for a 28 percent increase in defense spending. At 528 billion rubles, this was an increase from 411 billion rubles in 2004 and 93 billion rubles in 1999. Russia's increased spending levels have been devoted largely to improving conditions within the military, as opposed to upgrading weapons systems.

China. China is another important player in the global arms production market. The country established itself as a major player in the arms industry during the 1970s and 1980s when it began producing and later designing its own arms, although many of its designs were simply takeoffs of Soviet-built equipment. In that period China was the leading arms exporter among developing nations, shipping nearly US$15 billion of weapons abroad between 1978 and 1988. In the early 1990s Chinese arms exports shrank by nearly 70 percent between 1990 and 1993 after its biggest customer, Iraq, was defeated in the Persian Gulf War. Between 1997 and 1999, China exported arms worth US$2 billion to a variety of nations in Asia, Africa, and the Middle East. China had a military budget of US$36.5 billion in 1999.

By the late 1990s China maintained the largest defense equipment labor force with 3 million workers in 1,000 factories. However, many of those plants were located in remote rural areas and as a result they were largely unable to engage in international trade. Poor-quality equipment and an uneducated labor force also hurt the industry. The Chinese government began addressing such problems in 1998 when it inaugurated a reorganization of its defense production sector. Ultimately, however, many companies will likely be shut down and the industry streamlined. China has achieved success in building advanced armament such as its multiple-warhead nuclear missiles, as well as its M-9 and M-11 ballistic missiles. However, the bulk of the country's output remained old-model weapons lacking modern technical advances. Unlike other Asian countries, China remained cut off from Western technology from the European Union and the United States. Instead, China's only defense technology trading partner was Russia, but China's low procurement budget and Russia's insistence on not selling the country its most advanced equipment left China still far behind its neighbors in assembling a technologically superior weapons arsenal.

In 2003, the value of China's arms transfers fell to US$300 million, its lowest level since 1996. China mainly supplied light weapons and small arms to countries such as Africa. In addition, the country was more focused on upgrading its own military force than on selling weapons, namely missiles, to other nations.

European Union. The European Union (EU) was a world leader in armament production and exportation, second only to the United States. In 1999, led by France, the United Kingdom, and Germany, the EU controlled 22.5 percent of the global defense equipment exports. In the 1990s, the fragmented European defense industry had to be consolidated to compete on the world market with the U.S. defense juggernaut. A good deal of streamlining occurred in the early 2000s. British Aerospace merged with Marconi Electronic Systems to become BAE Systems in 1999 while Daimler Chrysler Aerospace, Aerospatiale Matra, and CASA merged to form the EADS aerospace powerhouse in 2000. In late 2001, the governments of the United Kingdom, Germany, France, Sweden, Italy, and Spain agreed to form ETAP, a project to coordinate aircraft development led by firms from the six nations. The same year, three European firms merged to form MBDA. Called the first pan-European defense company, MBDA was jointly owned by BAE Systems, EADS, and Finmeccanica. The EU was also the leading arms importing region in 1999 with 29 percent, a 59 percent increase from 1998.

By the early 2000s, some industry observers were concerned about the future of Europe's defense industry. Amidst great global demand for U.S. weapons, and a reduction in arms producers in the Near East, European firms continued to form joint ventures with one another, as in the case of the Eurofighter project. Additionally, the Joint Strike fighter was evidence that European firms also were working collaboratively with the United States on some projects. In order to survive, some analysts insisted that Europe needed to put a greater emphasis on the development of its own cutting-edge weaponry. In the December 23, 2002, issue of *Country ViewsWire,* Daniel Keohane of the Centre for European Reform also saw more multinational defense projects as a solution to the region's woes.

United Kingdom. The United Kingdom, which traditionally vied with France to be the leading weapon maker in the European Union, was also a leading global arms exporter. The United Kingdom ranked second (behind the United States) in actual worldwide arms deliveries in 2003, with US$4.7 billion, based on a Congressional Research Service (CRS) report. Although the country produces some weapons under license from U.S. companies, it was also recognized as a technical innovator, particularly in aerospace-related weaponry. Much of the country's defense industry activity was carried out through BAE Systems, formerly British Aerospace, a large, diversified company primarily engaged in defense-related businesses. With privatization of the industry and expanding global projects, the United Kingdom expects its industry to thrive as U.S. companies have. Between 1997 and 1999 the United Kingdom was Europe's leading arms importer, purchasing about US$6.6 billion worth of military equipment. Its total military budget for 2000 was US$34 billion.

France. France's production, procurement expenditures, and exports made it one of the EU's leaders in the arms industry. According to a Congressional Research Service (CRS) report, in 2003 France ranked fourth in global arms transfer agreements (US$1 billion). Along with Germany, France ranked fourth in actual worldwide arms deliveries that year, with deliveries valued at US$1.2 billion.

During the mid-1990s, France was able to maintain its leadership status despite cutbacks in domestic procurement budgets and falling exports. France's defense-related workforce also plummeted to about 250,000 in the mid-1990s. The French defense industry had revenues totaling about US$11 billion in 2000 and a workforce of 157,000. Between 1997 and 1999, France imported about US$1.3 billion in defense equipment, one of the lowest import rates in Europe. Between 1999 and 2000, French exports plunged by 30 percent to US$2.4 billion, the lowest level since 1994. Its defense production fell by 9 percent during the same period. Between 1991 and 2001, according to the Conseil des industries de defence francaises, France's defense spending dropped by 17 percent. In 2000 France's defense budget stood at US$27.3 billion, down about US$4 billion from 1997.

The French arms industry was long dominated by a dozen large companies, partly government owned, that had benefited since the 1960s from a government emphasis on investments in defense technology. In 2000, however, France ended strict government control of arms production and sales to the country's armed forces when it opened the bidding process for French contracts to other European companies.

Germany. In 2003, Germany ranked third in global arms transfer agreements (US$1.4 billion). Along with France, the country ranked fourth in actual worldwide arms deliveries that year, with deliveries valued at US$1.2 billion.

Germany was the European Union's second-largest arms manufacturer in the late 1990s and its leading exporter. The German arms industry re-emerged during the 1950s and 1960s, and developed a reputation for design innovation. Like their peers, most German arms makers experienced domestic defense cutbacks and reduced arms exports in the mid-1990s. In 2000 Germany's defense budget totaled US$23.3 billion, down from US$35 billion in the late 1990s. Equipment procurement accounted for less than US$4.1 billion of that year's budget. German defense equipment manufacturers announced they would follow U.K. producers in consolidating operations and working more with the United States to remain competitive in the 2000s.

FURTHER READING

Blanche, Ed. "Iran Goes Shopping," *Jane's Defence Weekly,* 21 March 2001.

Chamberlin, Jeffrey. *Comparisons of U.S. and Foreign Military Spending: Data from Selected Public Sources.* Washington, D.C.: Congressional Research Service, Library of Congress, 28 January 2004.

Cook, Nick. "BAE Systems Rocky Ride to Global Status," *Interavia Business & Technology,* June 2001.

———. "Europeans Plan Future Air Programmes," *Janes Defence Weekly,* 28 November 2001.

"Defense Mergers At All-Time High," *CDIs Weekly Defense Monitor,* Volume 3, Issue #26, 8 July 1999. Available at http://www.cdi.org.

"EU Industry: Cooperation on Arms Purchases Needed, Says Study." *Country ViewsWire,* 23 December 2002.

"European Industry Looks Ahead," *Jane's Defence Industry,* 1 January 2001.

Firestone, David. "Lawmakers Back Request by Bush on Funds for Iraq." *The New York Times,* 18 October 2003.

Foss, Christopher F. "Pan-European Defence Company is Ratified," *Janes Defence Weekly,* 2 January 2002.

Freinberg, Tony, and Sean Rayment. "Microwave Gun to be Used by US Troops on Iraq Rioters." *The Telegraph,* 19 September 2004. Available from http://www.telegraph.co.uk.

Galeotti, Mark. "Russia's Arms Bazaar," *Jane's Intelligence Review,* 1 April 2001.

"Global Arms Market Surges," *Periscope Daily Defense News Capsules,* 4 September 2001.

"Global Arms Sales," *Interavia Business & Technology,* 30 September 2004.

"Global Arms Sales Down for the Third Year in a Row," *Federation of American Scientists Press Release,* 1 September 2004. Available from http://www.fas.org.

"Globalized Weaponry," *In Focus,* Interhemispheric Resource Center, and Institute For Policy Studies, Vol. 5, No. 16, June 2000. Available fromhttp://www.foreignpolicy-infocus.org.

Grimmett, Richard F. "Conventional Arms Transfers to Developing Nations, 1993-2000." Washington, D.C.: Congressional Research Service, Library of Congress, 16 August 2001.

———. "Conventional Arms Transfers to Developing Nations, 1996-2003." Congressional Research Service, 26 August 2004.

Holmes, Stanley, "A Call to Arms Awakens Defense," *Business Week,* 1 October 2001, p. 62.

Hoover, Kent. "Bush Boosts Defense, Tech R&D, Reduces Other Areas," *Business First-Columbus,* 30 March 2001.

Keller, William W. *Arm in Arm,* New York: Basic Books, 1995.

Koch, Andrew "Consolidation Will Allow Technology to Spread,", *Jane's Defence Weekly,,* 15 August 2001.

Lewis, J.A.C. "Cash Benefit of France's Export Sales in Doubt," *Jane's Defence Weekly,,* 10 May 2000.

———. "French Arms Exports Drop 30 Percent," *Janes Defence Weekly,* 16 January 2002.

"Long March To Modernisation," *Jane's Defence Weekly,,* 11 September 2001.

Mann, Paul. "NATO's Transatlantic Market Pits Politics Versus Business," *Aviation Week & Space Technology,* 21 May 2001.

Markusen, Ann. "The Case Against Privatizing National Security." Council for Foreign Relations, July 2001.

"Military Spending on Rise," *The Associated Press,* 8 June 2005.

Morocco, John D. "European Nations To Team Up On Next-Generation Technology," *Aviation Week & Space Technology,* 18 June 2001.

Mulholland, David, "Global Arms Sales up in 2000, Russia Moves to Second Place," *Janes Defence Weekly,* 29 August 2001.

———. "New anti-terrorism crusade may bolster industry," *Janes Defence Weekly,* September 19, 2001.

Nicoll, Alexander. "France to Open Door on Defence Contracts," *Financial Times,* 21 May 2001.

Office of Management and Budget. "Overview of the President's 2005 Budget." Washington, D.C.: Executive Office of the President of the United States. 19 September 2004. Available from http://www.whitehouse.gov.

Pronina, Lyuba. "Budget Bolsters Defense." *St. Petersburg Times,* 24 August 2004.

"Raytheon and Thales team up," *Jane's Defence Weekly,,* 1 August 2001.

"Russia: First Time—Arms Exports Reach 5BN Dollars." *IPR Strategic Business Information Database,* 27 January 2004.

Schneider, Greg, "There'll Always Be An Arms Industry," *Washington Post,* 21 May 2001.

SIPRI Yearbook 2001: Armaments Disarmament and International Security, Oxford: Oxford University Press, 2001.

Velocci, Anthony L. Jr. "Consolidation Juggernaut Yet To Run Its Course," *Aviation Week & Space Technology,* December 3, 2001.

———. "U.S. Primes Buoyed by Weapons Purchasing." *Aviation Week & Space Technology,* 3 February 2003.

Wall, Robert, "New Arms Policies Seen Altering Warfare" *Aviation Week & Space Technology,* 3 September 2001.

———. "New Patriot Missiles Ready for Combat." *Aviation Week & Space Technology,* 3 February 2003.

Wall, Robert, David A. Fulghum, and Alexey Komarov. "Russian Defense Industry Struggles With Reform," *Aviation Week & Space Technology,* 20 August 2001.

"World Military Spending Topped $1 Trillion in 2004," *Reuters,* 7 June 2005.

"World Military Expenditures and Arms Transfers 1999-2000," U.S. Department of State, Bureau of Verification and Compliance, October 2001.

Wright, Evan. "How Much Is That Uzi in the Window?" *The New York Times,* 17 June 2004.

SIC 3714

NAICS 336399

MOTOR VEHICLE PARTS AND ACCESSORIES

The automotive parts industry manufactures motor vehicle parts and accessories, rather than motor vehicles or passenger car bodies, which are discussed under **Motor Vehicles.** In addition, automotive tire production is covered separately in the article entitled **Tires and Inner Tubes.**

INDUSTRY SNAPSHOT

The global motor vehicle parts and accessories industry, valued at US$900 billion in 2004, is a relative newcomer to the global marketplace. The industry became international in scope as major car manufacturers turned away from direct manufacture of auto parts in favor of heavy reliance on auto parts suppliers to develop major car components. This happened for the simple reason that many auto parts could be made more cheaply off-site by suppliers than by the large automakers themselves. In 1988, literally no global automotive parts suppliers existed, but within a decade some 50 very large integrators manufactured or assembled various automotive systems for sale to the world's major automotive manufacturers, and by the mid-2000s the industry was quite fragmented. Some analysts who observed the ongoing flux in the industry projected that the number of major systems suppliers would shrink to as few as 16 by 2008.

The performance of the automotive parts industry is tied directly to the performance of the automobile industry. This fact, in addition to rising materials prices and interest rates, combined to make the future of many suppliers uncertain in the mid-2000s. Auto parts suppliers were continually faced with demands by their largest customers, car makers, to lower prices and increase quality. As a result, even with favorable market conditions, auto parts manufacturers struggled to maintain consistent profit margins, despite increased demand. In 2004, while some companies were posting record profit increases, many others were posting the opposite. By 2004, major companies were turning to offshore outsourcing to remain viable and competitive.

ORGANIZATION AND STRUCTURE

At the turn of the twenty-first century, auto parts suppliers dealt in five commodity areas: power-train, chassis, body, interior, and electronic. Some companies specialized in subsets of these commodity areas (e.g., brakes and safety systems), but the major categories remained identifiable. The auto parts industry also had two primary sectors: the original equipment (OE) sector, which included parts for the car manufacturers; and the aftermarket parts sector, which included replacement parts for cars and trucks. The major players in the OE sector were distinguished by product and customer base. Tier One suppliers were those that produced parts sold directly to automakers, while Tier Two suppliers sold parts to Tier One companies, and Tier Three suppliers sold the raw materials used to manufacture parts to Tier Two and Tier One operations.

Sales of original equipment parts were dependent on many factors, such as the size, number, and complexity of any given car or truck market, and the number of parts and accessories that OE car manufacturers produced themselves. Parts were distributed through new car dealers, oil companies, major parts distributors, and smaller jobbers. Common products included wheels, bodies, frames, axles, transmissions, transaxles, bearings, valves, springs, bumpers, brakes, fuel injectors, seats, seat belts, airbags, and cushioning and safety padding materials. In the early 1980s, OE suppliers often signed annual contracts with auto manufacturers covering only the current model year. By the 1990s, multi-year contracts were being written—sometimes for the life of the vehicle. The late 1990s consolidation of the supplier industry was reinforced by the actions of the automakers themselves, who dealt with fewer but more technologically advanced OE suppliers worldwide. Sometimes this limitation of supplier numbers became extreme. In the early 1990s, Chrysler made the decision to reduce its 2,500 suppliers to no more than 750 primary suppliers over the next several years. By 1997, Chrysler had reduced its supplier count to 1,200, and was aiming for an ultimate target of just 150 major suppliers.

The aftermarket parts segment of the auto parts market tended to be more stable and subject to fewer fluctuations than the OE segment, though some OE suppliers also sold to the aftermarket. Aftermarket parts consisted primarily of items that could be described as consumable, subject to the daily wear and tear of vehicle operation (e.g., spark plugs, piston rings, brake pads, rotors, batteries, oil and gas filters, shock absorbers, struts, springs, exhaust systems, wiper blades, and air filters). During periods of economic recession OEM demand usually dropped, but sales in the aftermarket remained level and frequently strengthened during economic downturns—largely because financially-strapped car owners tended to fix and repair cars rather than buy new. The major threat to the aftermarket parts industry was the increasingly high level of quality in original parts. Obviously, if original equipment lasted longer, it had a negative effect on demand for replacement parts. Aftermarket parts traditionally were sold through service stations, general and specialized repair shops, tire stores, department stores, dealers, auto parts stores, and discount stores, but in 1998 electronic home shopping loomed as a plausible alternative. Analysts expected the aftermarket business to maintain moderate long-term growth, but eventual consolidation echoing the consolidation of OE suppliers was likely, especially in the United States.

The OE and aftermarket parts manufacturers shared an ability to make specialized parts that required a high level of technical skill. Because they could spread the costs of research and design, as well as tool and die costs, over many different contracts, "outside" auto parts manufacturers held an important cost advantage over the parts divisions of the automakers—an advantage that frequently was supplemented by the lower cost of non-union labor. These cost factors gave outside firms significant influence in the design and engineering of new parts for upcoming car models, as car manufacturers depended on suppliers to help keep costs low and technological advancements high.

BACKGROUND AND DEVELOPMENT

The early development of the auto parts industry was closely linked to the growth of the automobile early in the twentieth century. As the production of automobiles increased, so did the need for automotive parts. For many decades, the automotive parts industry served a limited number of models, which allowed parts makers to concentrate their efforts on producing mass quantities of a small assortment of components. In the 1970s, however, as Japan began exporting vehicles to the United States, the variety of models began to expand. The following decade, the popularity of small trucks began to surge. As a result, parts makers found themselves having to increase the number of parts they offered, while reducing the quantities of each part manufactured. Although this broadening of the automotive parts market did increase sales for many auto parts makers, it also undercut earnings growth due to the costs associated with manufacturing a more diversc group of parts. The industry growth also prompted many new players to enter the market, increasing competition.

The auto parts industry began to grow in earnest during the late 1980s and early 1990s, when many major car manufacturers began to rely more heavily on auto parts suppliers to develop major car components, mainly because many auto parts could be made more cheaply off-site by suppliers than by the large automakers themselves. These suppliers were often forced by their largest customers, the car manufacturers, to endure price freezes or reductions. The parts makers responded by cutting the costs of their own business operations. In the mid-1990s parts suppliers found that their efforts eliminated many of their extraneous costs, but further cost reductions were needed that could not be accomplished through traditional approaches and strategies. Chrysler and General Motors (GM) helped their parts suppliers with two innovative and cost-effective methods to meet the competitive cost challenges for the latter part of the 1990s.

Chrysler Corporation gave many of its parts suppliers responsibility for complete component system building. These suppliers were asked to build the systems within a target price that was set by Chrysler, while still maintaining high levels of quality and features. If the suppliers reduced costs below target levels, then enhancements had to be added to their systems. If parts supplier costs exceeded target levels set by Chrysler, then savings had to be found elsewhere in the system without cutting back on enhancements or quality. This guaranteed substantial cost savings to Chrysler—savings they shared with the parts suppliers in the form of incentives to pursue additional operational goals that ultimately benefited Chrysler. Although the pressure on parts suppliers was tremendous, the resulting synergistic relationship between parts supplier and auto company worked to enhance the competitive strength of all involved.

Following Chrysler's innovative action, General Motors devised a plan dispatching teams of engineers, designers, and purchasing cost accountants to meet with teams of employees at the parts manufacturers' plants. Under the direction of GM worldwide purchasing director, Dr. J. Ignacio Lopez (who was later discovered and indicted for theft of GM trade secrets), one-week meetings called PICOS (purchased input concept optimization for suppliers) were set up to help suppliers rid their operations of inefficiencies and bottlenecks. These joint GM and parts supplier teams were intended to be close-knit efforts to find solutions to parts supplier production problems. However, some parts suppliers did not welcome the GM efforts to view proprietary cost information, and Lopez's tendency to view cost as a primary criterion forced many suppliers to choose between operating at a loss and dropping out of competition. The "Inquisitor" (a derogatory term used to describe Lopez given his more manipulative policies) made few friends among suppliers—especially among those who had spent many years working with General Motors in joint development of a specific project, only to lose the resulting contract to a competing supplier whose lower bid did not need to include the cost of development. For these and other embittered suppliers, it was particularly ironic that, after Lopez departed, the suppliers' international competitive positions actually had been strengthened by his methodology. The early desperate haste to cut costs and streamline operations ultimately had its reward, and the resultant lean and mean suppliers were well-positioned to bid for new contracts at General Motors and around the world.

As the auto supply industry moved into prominence in the last decade of the twentieth century, auto manufacturers began looking for suppliers to do more than just build parts; they sought sources capable of design, engineering, integration, and global delivery. The motivation for this search was a simple desire to control costs. Because they were not as heavily unionized, many suppliers operated more cheaply than the bigger automakers. In the early 1990s, for example, the Big Three U.S. automotive companies (GM, Ford, and Chrysler) paid upwards of US$42 per hour in labor costs, while supplier Lear Seating paid only US$12 and ITT Automotive only US$14 per hour. It was understandable that Ford found it practical to sell its seat assembly line to Lear in November 1993 for approximately US$600 million. In May 1994 Chrysler turned its seat cover operations over to Johnson Controls and its wiring assembly plants to Yazaki. General Motors divested itself of no fewer than 41 parts operations between 1993 and 1994. Toyota already was manufacturing less than 25 percent of its own parts, compared to GM's 47 percent, and the success of the Japanese model served as further incentive to global auto manufacturers to use the growing parts industry.

Also affecting the auto parts industry during the 1990s was the increase in the number of car features that were standard on many models. Standard air conditioning, tilt steering, stereo radios, power windows, power door locks, and power seats all helped to increase sales for car manufacturers and parts suppliers alike. By the early 1990s, almost 94 percent of all U.S. cars were delivered with air conditioning, up from 76 percent a decade earlier. Automatic transmissions were installed in 89 percent of all cars, a less dramatic rise (from 82 percent) possibly dampened by increased use of standard transmissions on sport-utility vehicles. Power side windows were on 79 percent of all U.S. cars, almost twice as many as were delivered in the early 1980s. Stereo radios were frequently standard, and the year 2000 driver looked for CD players and CD changers to take the place of cassette players in luxury models. As each new feature was developed for an automobile, it entered the parts market as well. Antilock brakes, aluminum wheels, and airbags became familiar options. In spite of controversy surrounding their use, by the end of the century driver and passenger airbags were relatively standard, and side-impact airbags were expected to follow suit. In addition, increased safety consciousness continued to encourage higher demand for anti-lock braking systems (ABSs) on cars and trucks.

By the mid-1990s, "quality" had become a buzzword throughout the global auto parts industry. Notably, with quality as the primary standard of measurement, an international comparative study by Andersen Consulting reported that among the seventy-one auto parts manufacturers sampled, just thirteen had attained a level of world-class production. Of these thirteen, only three were U.S. firms. Charts on defect rates were used to indicate the quality of links in the supply chain. Monitoring the internal defect rate of parts failing their first inspection at a given OEM identified incoming defects in parts provided by smaller auto parts manufacturers. Similar checks followed part development, and the final link in the chain was the customer, who voiced a complaint if faulty parts passed through earlier inspection points. Analysis showed the Japanese to be consistently at the top of the quality supply chain, and the United Kingdom and Italy were consistently at the bottom.

Car manufacturing plants for all countries acted as quality screeners to prevent customers from receiving defective parts, and did so with some success. The number of incoming defects generally was roughly four to five times the number of final customer complaints. U.S. car companies were particularly good at screening the bad parts out of their cars, although as had been suggested, they needed to be. In the United States, although incoming defects were found in 6,100 parts per million, only 262 customer complaints per million parts were recorded.

Automakers traditionally evaluated the quality of auto parts by counting the number of bad parts per million. In turn, the suppliers providing those auto parts were assigned ratings, and the goal of zero-defect ratings was sought by all automakers and suppliers. To attract more business, suppliers eventually began to use the ratings designations and quality awards as marketing tools. In response, automakers began to expect more. For example, BMW reduced its number of annual supplier awards to just three winner categories: most innovative idea, best economic idea, and best environmental idea. No longer was quality considered something deserving of a prize or even comment because highest quality was demanded and assumed therefore to exist. With all suppliers providing product that was absolute top-quality, any contest between them was moot.

Along with general quality issues and industry-mandated efficiency of operation, automotive parts manufacturers in the United States had another, more specific target. ISO 9000 standards of quality and efficient operation were familiar in Europe. To the ISO set of standards, U.S. automobile manufacturers (Chrysler, Ford, General Motors) added a superset: QS 9000. For major suppliers, it was mandatory to be QS 9000 compliant, or in some cases to be working on QS 9000 compliance, to do business with the Big Three. Although return on investment purported to be threefold, since becoming QS compliant frequently carried a price tag of well over US$100,000, only companies able to invest that amount in a gamble on possible future business could continue to operate independently.

Competition, cost cutting, and consolidation characterized the auto parts industry as the year 2000 approached. Automakers long had striven to reduce manufacturing costs, improve efficiencies, and streamline production. In this environment, parts suppliers were pressured to make substantial cost reductions in their operations. The parts suppliers in turn sought to improve their own production techniques and reap greater profit out of their own operations. Cost cutting, new managerial techniques, and production efficiencies were key to survival for many parts manufacturers in an increasingly volatile marketplace. Forced to be cost conscious to be competitive, many auto parts companies followed the automakers in an attempt to adopt successful Japanese production techniques. Just-in-time manufacture, statistical process controls, *kanban* systems, and core competencies were parts issues just as they were car issues. In the mid- to late 1990s, Japanese firms established numerous "transplant" operations in North America and Europe and thus further influenced rival domestic firms. The impact of Asian parts makers was felt in another way, as their increasing presence combined with that of East European parts makers to force Western European suppliers into a more global focus.

Globalization had profound implications for the worldwide auto parts industry. Only those systems integrators capable of responding to a world market could survive. Before consolidation in the global automotive parts industry reached its peak, Japan had approximately 2,100 auto parts suppliers serving nine original equipment manufacturers (OEMs). Europe had about 2,300 suppliers serving eighteen OEMs, and the United States had 10,000 suppliers serving three OEMs and foreign transplants. In the late 1990s, however, those numbers began to shrink as manufacturers struggled to cope with the increasingly global nature of the automotive industry. Smaller suppliers, unable to meet the needs of global systems integrators, began to fall by the wayside. Those that survived did so by focusing on the needs of a higher tier of larger suppliers, rather than attempting to do business directly with the automakers. Estimates suggested that more than 50 percent of Tier One suppliers would be out of business by the year 2000 and that those remaining in business would have been forced to cut their production costs between 18 and 24 percent in order to compete successfully. Approximately 1,400 Tier One suppliers went out of business as the new century approached, and the attrition of global, mega-suppliers was just as severe as that affecting smaller firms. Industry analysts anticipated that no more than twenty-five parts and systems firms would be global players by 2002 and just eighteen would survive by 2005.

The oft-mentioned consolidation that typified the automotive supplier industry in the late 1990s was orchestrated, in part, by a number of highly profitable venture-capital, "buyout" firms that saw opportunity both in "spinoff" auto parts manufacturers (e.g., Visteon and Delphi), and in the independent market. Positioning themselves as middlemen, these firms purchased attractive but struggling parts companies, matched them with other, frequently larger, companies, and then resold them. Often the purchased companies remained in operation for some time, held by a financing firm that oversaw operational streamlining. Whether the target-company was resold or nursed to profitability and held—even for as long as 11 or 15 years—the end result was earnings for the buyout firm. If capital was available, it was an undeniably attractive way to go. In 1998, just one financier was simultaneously exploring five such deals in Europe and several more in the United States.

In addition to economic-based mergers, the various acts of consolidation allowed global auto parts suppliers to position themselves to better serve customers in multiple parts of the world. For instance, the Perkings Group Companies in Britain formed a joint venture with Ishikawajima-Shibaura Machine Company of Japan to manufacture at least 50,000 diesel engines per year by 2000. United Technologies Automotive entered into a joint venture with Dongfeng-Citroen Automobile of China to make harnesses and body wiring. Italy's Magneti Marelli and the U.S.-based TRW Inc. entered into an agreement to produce air-bag sensors for the Italian industry. These and other similar business consolidations served to bring production directly to the consumer. Germany's Mann+Hummel Automotive sought to increase its presence and name recognition in the U.S. market. To do this, it acquired the North American operations of Geiger Technic Inc., based in Kalamazoo, Michigan. Similarly, the Degussa Corporation (Quebec, Canada) opened a million-unit catalyst emissions control plant in Puebla, Mexico, and the United States' CDI Corporation opened a new office in Paris.

It took more than a superficial glance at the auto parts industry to ascertain its health at the turn of the century. Increased demand as automotive manufacturers outsourced the manufacture of more and more car components meant that OEM parts production was proportionately on the rise. Gross sales mounted higher and higher, and casual examination seemed to indicate satisfactory growth in business. Even the almost excessive number of mergers and acquisitions could be described as symptomatic of healthy worldwide expansion on the part of the acquiring companies. Unfortunately, though, even as sales increased, profitability was decreasing. From a mid-1990s peak profit margin of 8.2 percent, by 1998-1999 auto suppliers suddenly found themselves looking at margins that were narrower than they had been since the beginning of the decade. Returns on investment were lower, and ratios of debt to assets increased.

Out of all of this money squeeze, a pattern presented itself which was termed by one analyst as the "Lopez Effect." He referred to the huge gap that had formed between successful "best-in-class" suppliers and the struggling firms at the other end of the spectrum. There seemed to be no middle ground—no modestly successful companies chugging along at comfortable profitability but without a huge global presence. These extremes in levels of supplier success were attributed to the ruthless buying patterns endorsed by the previously mentioned Ignacio Lopez during his tenure with General Motors and to their impact on suppliers who were forced to strip operations to bare-bones essentials in order to meet GM's pricing demands. Suppliers that survived the experience, and companies who emulated them even without having done business with Lopez, were the companies whose profitability appeared stable and whose market presence seemed most assured. Those that continued to operate in a "pre-Lopez" mode, without trimming the fat from their operations, failed with almost predictable regularity.

The Lopez Effect, the need for global presence, carefully orchestrated buyouts, and the demand for high quality product, all combined to make the close of the twentieth century a difficult time indeed for many supplier firms. But the end result, like that of the Lopez Effect alone, seemed to be the evolution of a limited number of stable, profitable, highly efficient, high-quality systems-integrating companies.

Auto manufacturers looked to modular assembly as the wave of the future, a posture that dealt yet another blow to smaller suppliers without the wherewithal to develop whole component systems (steering column assemblies, power trains, entire dash board and electrical systems), instead of individual parts to be used on automaker assembly lines. This trend was reflected in the decision by Ford Motor Company to hand control of its Batavia, Ohio-based transmission plant over to a German transmission supplier in 1999.

Industry consolidation continued in 1999 as Lear Corp., Johnson Controls Inc., TRW Inc., and Dana Corp. all used acquisitions to position themselves among the largest automotive suppliers in the world—those with more than US$10 billion in sales. The largest mergers of the year included the purchase of United Kingdom-based LucasVarity PLC, the industry's nineteenth largest player, by TRW for US$6.5 billion and the purchase of United Technologies Automotive, ranked fifteenth among global auto parts leaders, by Lear Corp. for US$2.3 billion. Among the twenty-five largest auto parts makers in 2000, ten were based in North America; their combined sales reached US$113 billion that year. Sales for the remaining fifteen industry leaders—eleven of which were based in Europe and four of which were based in Japan—totaled US$95 billion. The greater success of the smaller number of North American firms was at least partially the result of heightened consolidations levels there.

The automotive parts industry, particularly in North America and Europe, was characterized by sluggish sales, poor earnings, and layoffs in 2001. As weaker economies took their toll on the automotive industries there, demand for automotive parts began to slacken. Even in times of economic prosperity, however, growth in markets like North America and Europe was forecast at less than 2 percent. As with the automobile industry, most analysts believed that the majority of future growth in the automotive parts industry would take place in emerging markets such as Eastern Europe, Latin America, and Asia-Pacific.

CURRENT CONDITIONS

The U.S. aftermarket segment of the industry was valued at US$250 billion in 2004, according to the Automotive Aftermarket Industry Association. According to Euromonitor, the U.S. aftercare and accessories market was dominated by the replacement parts segment, which in 2003 accounted for US$72.6 billion of the US$123.5 billion total market. Of this amount, the top five companies controlled 46.1 percent, revealing the fragmented nature of the industry and the likelihood of consolidation. In Europe, aftermarket business was profitable, but in decline. Datamonitor expected European revenues to drop gradually during the mid-2000s, realizing a total decline of about 1 percent by 2008. Critical factors for the industry included lower volumes of replacement parts and competitive pricing.

In fact, suppliers were doing business with fewer and fewer smaller supply companies. A contemporary survey suggested that a majority of suppliers made this move based on price and product delivery as well as quality, but the end result was an overall improvement in parts quality. An even more emphatic result was the reduction in total number of Tier Two and Tier Three suppliers, as survival of the fittest became far more than just an expression. In 2004, the companies seeing the most strength were those that were not dependent on the "Big Three" automakers—GM, Ford, and DaimlerChrysler—which collectively reported falling sales.

Further pushing the industry toward consolidation were cost pressures, which for auto companies and suppliers alike continued to increase. By 2004, for example, average steel costs were 29 to 75 cents per pound, an increase of between

11 and 45 percent. Suppliers were no longer able to pass along added costs resulting from rising prices of steel, plastic, and aluminum. OEMs demanded more capacity, designing, and engineering responsibilities from the suppliers but, in keeping with their own need to cut costs, were not prepared to help suppliers pay for the added services and capabilities. In fact, a study from Alix Partners found that the supplier industry was suffering major setbacks, with up to 17 percent of companies in danger of bankruptcy by 2006. While some companies, such as Denso with its huge profit increases, were doing well, combined 2003 losses from other companies were in the multi-billion dollar range. Industry leaders such as Delphi were turning to offshore outsourcing to trim costs and stay afloat, particularly to China, India, and other developing countries in Asia.

RESEARCH AND TECHNOLOGY

High levels of competition, automaker insistence on high quality, and an increasingly sophisticated end-user market, all combined to make auto parts research and development departments very aggressive. In 1997, Robert Bosch GmbH, although firmly established in the industry, invested over US$1.8 billion in research and development and dedicated 14,000 employees to research. Since the mid-1990s, its R&D expenditures increased at a steady rate of well over US$2 million each year, and the company's focus on "smart" restraint systems suggested there would be no slackening of effort in the future. Bosch's Automotive Occupancy Sensing (AOS) system, under development in 1998, used infrared and ultrasonic sensors to check front seat occupancy and prevent unnecessary air-bag deployment. Future enhancements to the system were expected to aid in the use of anti-theft devices, adjustments to seat and headrest positions, mirror dimming, communication, and determining a driver's wakefulness—all in addition to safer and more efficient use of air bags and driver and passenger restraints.

Accidental injury and even death involving air-bag use caused many parts companies to explore ways to improve air-bag deployment. Existing air-bag systems combined optical, ultrasound capacity and weight sensors to trigger air-bag use, but passenger injuries combined to suggest that "smarter" air-bags were a necessity. Atlantic Research Corporation developed Variflow inflators capable of accommodating increasingly advanced sensor information. They and other corporations worked in an environment that added side-impact air bags to the earlier concept of driver- and passenger-seat devices.

As more computer technology was introduced into the automobile, Information, Communications, Entertainment and Safety (ICES) centers were bundled together by parts manufacturers into space-age, driver/passenger friendly units. Visteon demonstrated an ICES installation in 1998 that provided everything from a navigation guide and climate control to in-car Internet access. Driven by Intel's Pentium processor and running on Microsoft software, the unit enhanced the likelihood of driver safety by operating entirely on voice commands—not unlike the computers providing navigation guides and climate control to the fictional Enterprise of Gene Roddenberry's *Star Trek*. Analysts predicted that the use of electronic systems in cars would grow from 15 percent of total vehicle content to 20 percent of total vehicle content by 2010.

Laser taillights, new-formula finishing compounds, and continued focus on ABS braking systems all characterized the car-owner-friendly direction of many new developments. United Technologies Automotive utilized surface acoustic wave technology in its hand-held remote vehicle entry systems—the first time such technology had been used outside the aerospace industry. These convenient sending units allowed drivers to unlock their cars from several feet away without fumbling for keys and represented just a small part of UTC's nearly US$2 billion annual R&D expenditure.

Less showy examples of supplier technological advances abounded. Auto manufacturers and parts suppliers had long been required to consider three basic options for material use in component construction—steel, aluminum, or composites. Steel was a favorite. It was economical to use in high volumes, reasonable in cost, recyclable, and had good crash properties. Unfortunately steel had its share of weaknesses as well, including high tooling costs and material weight, and the need to treat it to prevent rust.

Aluminum and composites lent themselves to many different parts and accessories because of strength and weight characteristics. On the one hand, aluminum could reduce weight by as much as 50 percent, and it employed familiar manufacturing processes, had good surface qualities, and was easy to recycle. On the other hand, aluminum piece cost was high, the metal was difficult to repair, apt to dent and scratch, and it had poor formability. Composites lured manufacturers with low tooling costs, good formability, and reparability, up to 15 percent mass savings, rust resistance, and low-volume vehicle choice, but they were expensive, sensitive to high oven temperatures, could produce surface irregularities, and they were not readily recyclable.

When metals were the material of choice, some form of welding process had to be used to build the part. A few automobile and parts manufacturers were hesitant to implement high-tech lasers for welding. Motoman and Progressive Tool and Industries Company estimated that reluctance to use laser welding was costing them between US$100 and US$200 per vehicle. The advantages of laser welding over spot welding included reduction in vehicle weight by as much as 200 pounds, stronger weld bodies, and rust prevention. Laser welding also was a time-saver. Finishing a wheel well with spot welding could take up to three minutes. Doing the same thing with a laser weld took just 32 seconds and produced a 15 percent stronger bond. The newest laser technology in the mid-1990s was called YAG, an acronym for neodymium yttrium aluminum garnet. General Motors, Toyota, and Honda were quick to embrace the concept, but conservatism on the part of plant managers slowed worldwide implementation of YAG technology.

Advances in computer-aided design (CAD) and computer-aided manufacture (CAM) helped to drive both the automotive and supplier industries in the 1990s. Solid modeling and life-sized graphics gave way to computer designs created entirely at a computer workstation. Corporate investment in computer use and training could be high, but use of computers long had ceased to be news by the early 1990s.

Still, enhancements to computer use occurred. In addition to on-board computing in automobiles themselves (something that made life easier for automobile driver, passenger, and repair department), the role of the designer also was facilitated by new software applications and hardware availability. The Standard for the Exchange for Product Model Data (STEP) was a universal computer language that provided information on specific auto parts to computer design programs such as CATIA and Unigraphics. The language was designed to eliminate the need for suppliers to maintain more than one engineering system, even if they serviced multiple customers. To this end, GM, Ford, Chrysler, BMW, Mercedes-Benz, Porsche, and Opel all endorsed STEP.

The Partnership for a New Generation of Vehicles, formed in 1994 as an arrangement between the U.S. Government and its three largest auto manufacturers, required assistance from the U.S. auto parts industry. The goal of the partnership was the development of a new supercar. The prototype vehicle was expected to get 80 miles to the gallon, seat six, and cost no more than US$15,000. Some 200 suppliers were involved with the project by 1995, channeling resources and brainpower to help to introduce the new car to the world by 2004. It was expected that the new car would be 40 percent lighter than cars of the mid-1990s and would make heavy use of composite materials. The project received a boost in 1998, when U.S. President Clinton's budget increased funding to PNGV by 22 percent, to US$277 million. The U.S. Department of Energy received the largest chunk of the federal windfall (US$164 million), as development costs continued to be shared by the government and the auto industry. In 1998, PNGV research and development was refocused to concentrate on four key automobile systems: hybrid electric vehicle drives, direct injection engines, fuel cells, and increasingly lightweight materials. Spinoff from PNGV research placed the United States in an enviable position when the Kyoto Protocol on Global Warming of 1997 required the United States to make dramatic reductions in carbon dioxide emissions within ten years. Efforts associated with PNGV promised the availability of mass-marketed "clean" electric vehicles well within that timeframe. Also affecting these research efforts was the zero-emission vehicle law passed in California, which would require 10 percent of the vehicles by each automaker sold in that state to be zero-emission vehicles by 2004.

Industry Leaders

Robert Bosch GmbH. Based in Stuttgart, Germany, Bosch, a name long-identified in Germany with the automotive industry, held to its leading place among global automotive suppliers with sales of approximately US$30.0 billion in 2000, a number reflecting 7 percent growth over 1999 revenues. By 2004, Bosch reported US$54.6 billion in sales, a 19.6 percent increase over 2003 levels. Automotive parts accounted for roughly 70 percent of total revenues.

Bosch traditionally dedicated a significant portion of its earnings to research and development. This aggressive approach to new technology and innovation assured Bosch continued presence in the world market, as it brought forth various road handling improvements, voice recognition systems, and even devices for collision avoidance. Major Bosch systems included antilock braking and fuel injection and various auto electronics components, including starters and alternators. In 1998, new Bosch offerings included a high-pressure accumulator injection system for diesel engines and advanced mobile radio telephone technology—even a car radio which could be used to make telephone calls, the first such device in the world.

At the end of the twentieth century, Bosch subsidiaries and business affiliations reached out to 131 countries, and 130 of their production plants were outside Germany. This extensive globalization was hardly accidental, as Bosch had opened its first foreign office in the nineteenth century and had established a factory in the United States that, in the years before World War I, exceeded its domestic plants in capacity. In 2004, Bosch increased automotive production by 5 percent, most of which was attributed to demand in China and elsewhere in Asia.

Delphi Corporation. Based in Troy, Michigan, Delphi Corporation, formerly Delphi Automotive Systems, is the world's largest and most comprehensive automotive parts manufacturer with 190,000 employees working in 31 countries. The firm was formerly known as the General Motors Corporation Automotive Components Group Worldwide (ACGW) and spun off into an autonomous subsidiary in the mid-1990s. In 1999, GM spun Delphi off completely, and sales for the newly independent entity grew 8.3 percent that year to US$22.4 billion. Sales reached record levels in 2000 but tumbled 10.5 percent in 2001 to US$26.1 billion as recessionary economic conditions softened the global auto parts industry. By 2004, Delphi was back up to US$28.6 billion in sales. While General Motors continued to account for 70 percent of Delphi's revenues, the firm also sold its products to a huge portfolio of international automakers including Fiat, Mercedes-Benz, Hyundai, Audi, Volkswagen, Daewoo, Skoda, Rover, Honda, Renault, Mitsubishi, Toyota, DaimlerChrysler, Ford, Isuzu, Suzuki, and SEAT.

In 1997, the transfer of Delco from Hughes Electronics (another General Motors subsidiary) provided Delphi with both a significant increase in total sales and a strong presence in the electronics portion of the supplier industry. When that deal was completed, Delphi's products included steering systems, chassis systems, thermal systems, energy and engine management systems, electric systems, and interior lighting systems. While nearly three-fourths of the company's sales were to North American customers, Europe, the Middle East, and Africa combined to contribute about 20 percent of total sales, and both South America (including Mexico) and the Pacific Rim represented already substantial, growing markets. Delphi manufacturing facility positioning reflected continuing growth outside the United States. The company was in direct operation of 78 plants in North America, but operated 63 in Europe, the Middle East and Africa; 55 in Mexico and South America; and 12 in Asia-Pacific locations.

While the development of Delphi (in its incarnation as General Motors Corporation Automotive Components Group Worldwide) closely followed the development of General Motors Corporation (see **Motor Vehicles**), the growth of its electronic subsidiary, Delco, is worth independent examination. Delco was originally founded in 1912 by C. F. Kettering, the inventor of the electric starter, and the company originally built starters for Cadillac motor cars. General Motors acquired Delco in 1936 and quickly expanded its product line to include radios. Delco's first car radios were built for Chevrolet and were strictly aftermarket items installed as dealer options. Through the rest of the 1930s and 1940s, Delco concentrated its manufacturing efforts on a variety of car radio products to satisfy the expanding automotive and home electronics markets. In 1956 the company developed the high-power transistor, which spawned the development of a variety of experimental products, including an in-dash portable radio and a 45-rpm automobile record player that anticipated the later automobile CD changer (but understandably was never brought to market). Delco's ready market for automotive components and radios grew with GM automobile sales, which provided a stable and profitable source of income. During the 1960s and 1970s, Delco began production of AM/FM stereos and introduced new power and automotive-control systems.

Visteon Corporation. Formerly Ford Automotive Components Group—which comprised Ford Glass Division, Ford Climate Control Division, and divisions producing electronic controls, systems, trim, and engine accessories—Visteon Corporation was spun off from Ford Motor Company in 2000 as the second largest automotive parts supplier in the world, a position it retained in 2003. The group had been operating as an independent division of Ford since the late-1990s. The second largest manufacturer of automobiles and auto parts in the world, Ford had viewed the reorganization of all wholly owned parts suppliers into a single entity as the most logical way to prepare for the increased incorporation of electronics into motor vehicles. Because the company structure already was in place, Visteon began with 79,000 hand-picked employees, all veterans of Ford's international success. In 2004, Visteon employed 70,200 people.

Despite efforts to extend its global reach, less than 30 percent of sales came from operations outside North America in 2004. In addition, Ford Motor Company continued to account for 82 percent of Visteon's revenues, which fell 4 percent to US$18.7 billion that year. Its heavy reliance on Ford, which suffered several setbacks in the early 2000s due to negative publicity surrounding accidents related to the Firestone tires it used on its popular Ford Explorer sport-utility vehicle, contributed to Visteon's decline for the year. The first quarter of 2005 looked promising for the company, however. Visteon announced results of $5 billion for the first quarter, including record non-Ford revenues of $1.7 billion (a 30 percent increase).

Denso Corporation. Formerly known as Nippondenso, the Denso Corporation changed its name into a more international format in the late 1990s. Denso is one of Japan's largest manufacturers of auto parts, although the majority of Denso's plants are located outside Japan. Due to weaker demand in North America and Europe, sales in 2001 fell 10.6 percent to US$15.9 billion as earnings tumbled 18 percent to US$481 million. By 2004, however, sales were up to US$24.3 billion. In part because of its extensive global presence, Denso boasted a worker population that neared 86,000 in 2001 and 96,000 in 2004.

Denso sold a variety of products to manufacturers worldwide, ranging from air conditioners and heating units to anti-lock braking systems and fuel systems. Toyota Motor Corp., its former parent, still owned 24 percent of the firm in 2004.

Johnson Controls Inc. With 2004 sales of US$26.5 billion and earnings of US$817.5 million, Johnson Controls was a leader in the global automotive parts industry. That year, the company's employee base totaled 123,000. Johnson Controls was founded by Professor Warren Johnson in 1885. Initially existing to manufacture and market Johnson's own invention (the thermostat), a hundred years later the company boasted worldwide leadership in two lines of business: building controls and automotive systems. In spite of the emphasis on "controls" suggested by its name, Johnson's automotive division was the dominant corporate revenue-producer. More than 40 percent of Johnson's total sales came from business with the U.S. Big Three, for which the company provided seating, various interior systems, and batteries.

Lear Corporation. The largest supplier of car seats in the world, Lear Corporation also manufactures floor and acoustic systems, instrument panels, and other interior products including headliners and door panels. Employing 111,000 people around the world, Lear marketed to Volvo, BMW, Fiat, Saab, and Volkswagen, in addition to the United States' Big Three. In spite of a growing global presence, in the late 1990s more than half of Lear's sales were to Ford and General Motors. Expanding through acquisitions and mergers since its 1917 founding as American Metal Products, Lear accelerated this growth process in the latter years of the century—securing Empetek, Dunlop-Cox, Keiper Car Seating, and ITT Automotive in 1997 and buying two privately-held Italian firms (Gruppo Pianfe S.r.L and Strapazzini S.r.L.) in 1998. Lear also paid US$2.3 billion in 1999 for United Technologies Automotive. Global sales rose 7.7 percent to US$16.96 billion in 2004, while earnings skyrocketed 11 percent to US$422.2 million. Lear employed more than 110,000 people in 34 countries.

TRW. After its US$7 billion purchase of LucasVarity plc in 1999, one of the largest acquisitions in industry history, Toledo, Ohio-based TRW Inc. found itself competing with the leading firms in the global auto parts industry, those with US$10 billion or more in revenues. LucasVarity was formed in 1996 via a merger between Lucas Industries plc and Varity Corporation. Prior to its takeover by TRW, a lion's share (40 percent) of Lucas's US$6.56 billion in international sales came from braking systems used in Mercedes-Benz and Ford vehicles, as well as Korea's Kia automobiles. As a result, the merger strengthened TRW's international operations by giving it access to the European braking systems sector. In 2004, private investment group Blackstone purchased the company from TRW, renaming it TRW Automotive Holdings Corp.

Product lines for TRW also included restraint systems and controls, steering and suspension systems, electronics, and engine components and engineered fasteners. Automotive parts accounted for roughly 60 percent of sales, which fell to US$12.01 billion in 2004. Net income for 2004 was $29 million. TRW employed approximately 60,000 people worldwide, primarily in Europe and North America.

TRW was founded in 1901 as the Cleveland Cap Screw Company. Within a few years of start-up, the company was producing most of the engine valves supplied to the burgeoning automotive industry. Mass production of engine valves allowed the company to flourish until the Great Depression in the United States forced it to diversify and develop products for the aviation industry. A joint venture with Ramo-Wooldridge Corporation to build the intercontinental ballistic missile led to the merger that formed Thompson Ramo Wooldridge—renamed TRW in 1965.

In the 1980s, TRW returned to its core businesses by landing an exclusive contract with Ford Motor Company to supply airbags. The company expanded its European manufacturing capacity by opening plants in France, the United Kingdom, and Brazil. Further European expansion included acquiring a 92 percent stake in the Czech Republic's largest auto engine valve and steering systems maker and participating in joint ventures with companies such as Italy's Magneti Marelli.

Dana Corporation. Dana Corporation was founded in 1904 in Toledo, Ohio, by Clarence Spicer, whose fascination for mechanical design led him to question the bicycle drive methodology that operated automobiles at the turn of the century. Experimenting with a propeller shaft drive, Spicer designed "universal" joints which allowed the spin of the drive shaft to be governed by the engine and then reverse direction and turn wheels on an axle set at right angles to the shaft. Less than 100 years later, Dana Corporation (named for an early CEO) operated facilities in 30 separate countries, employed 97,300 people, and grossed more than US$12.4 billion in revenues. By 2004, Dana's sales were US$9.1 billion (13 percent more than in 2003), and its workforce had shrunk to 46,000. Continuing to manufacture axles and driveshafts, Dana also sold piston rings, filters, bearings and sealing products, brake and chassis products, and thermal and fluid management systems to automakers around the world.

Valeo SA. One of the largest automotive parts operations in Europe, Paris-based Valeo operates in 26 countries including the United States, Germany, Argentina, the United Kingdom, Brazil, China, South Korea, Spain, India, Japan, Poland, Tunisia, and Turkey. Primarily a manufacturer of engine cooling systems, clutches, and friction material, Valeo reported revenues of US$12.8 billion in 2004, up just over 11 percent from the previous year, and employed more than 62,000 people.

During the acquisition frenzy of the late 1990s, Valeo acquired ITT Electrical Systems for US$1.7 billion. After watching its new electrical systems arm struggle to stay afloat, Valeo placed the U.S.-based unit under Chapter 11 bankruptcy protection in 2001. Shortly thereafter, in response to slowing demand for auto parts, Valeo announced its intent to cut 5,000 jobs worldwide in 2002.

MAJOR COUNTRIES IN THE INDUSTRY

Japan. U.S. trade with Japan was as fraught with controversy as it was key during the latter years of the twentieth century. Toyota Corporation and other Japanese car manufacturers were under considerable scrutiny as they made some effort to purchase a greater number of auto parts from outside their country. The Japanese-U.S. trade agreement of the mid-1990s, known as the U.S.-Japan Auto Framework Agreement, sought to improve the balance of trade between the two countries. In fact, U.S. auto parts exports to Japan increased by 20 percent in 1996, although export to Japan was less than 5 percent of U.S. automotive parts exports. A joint venture (New United Motor Manufacturing Inc., or NUMMI) between Toyota and General Motors, ran by Toyota, provided a mid-1990s boost to as many as 35 auto parts manufacturers. These companies exported approximately US$80 million in auto parts to Japan in 1995, where five years previously the export total had been just US$2 million. An ITT study done in 1997 gave Japanese firms nearly 15 percent of the world auto parts market.

Economic turmoil in Japan undercut auto production there, and as a result auto parts production in Japan declined 5.8 percent in 1998 to US$118.7 billion (12.46 trillion yen). This decline was in line with a mid-1990s report released by the Japan Auto Parts Industries Association (JAPIA), *The Automobile Parts Industry Facing the 21st Century*, which forecast slow growth in auto parts sales to the year 2005. Reasons cited included cyclical economic patterns, exchange rate uncertainty, increased overseas competition, and a fall in exports from Japan as companies moved operations closer to their markets. Market growth was expected to come from expanding foreign markets and increases in the domestic replacement parts market. Suppliers were encouraged to develop strategic alliances with foreign producers to maintain competitiveness, to control the manufacturing and supply cost of auto parts, and to work with companies to develop a standardization system for their vehicle parts. The Japanese government also was given specific responsibility to support an "International Division of Labor," as well as the Japanese small business sector, which, according to JAPIA, embraced 92 percent of the entire auto parts business in the country.

The Japanese government also was given a proactive role in enhancing labor/management relations, particularly in the areas of retaining aging workers and training new employees, including the rising numbers of women in the industry. To encourage company innovation, the government took interest in intellectual property and patent right protection. At the same time, the Japan Ministry of International Trade and Industry (MITI) helped the country's six minicar producers to agree on standardization of engines, electronics, transmissions, braking systems, and heating and air conditioning systems. These manufacturers included Honda, Mitsubishi Motors, Suzuki, Daihatsu, and Fuji Heavy Industries. This was a significant boon to parts manufacturers, since, according to the Ministry of Transportation and the Japan Automobile Manufacturers Association, there were approximately 4 million minicars on Japanese roads, with 75,000 new vehicle registrations annually.

Some analysts suggested that low volume production would prevent Japanese suppliers from being part of the exclusive list of auto parts survivors predicted to emerge in the early 2000s. However, four of the top twenty-five auto parts suppliers in 2000 were based in Japan. In addition, a newly emerging component of the parts market promised to significantly improve the Japanese industry outlook. Increasing use of electronic systems and subsystems in new cars provided a natural market for Japan's traditional high-technology strength.

United States. Although both the original equipment and the auto parts replacement market remained stable in the later half of the 1990s, the economic recession of the early 2000s was expected to undermine original equipment production and possibly favor the auto parts replacement market as increasingly cost conscious individuals would likely keep their vehicles for longer periods of time. Earlier estimates had suggested that 49 percent of total U.S. sales would come from under-car parts, 14 percent from drive train parts, and 13 percent from engine parts and cooling systems, but regardless of the products marketed, the challenge to keep manufacturing lean and maximize profit was the same. According to Euromonitor, the market was expected to grow 18.8 percent by 2008, to a value of US$146.7 billion.

Consolidation, acquisition, and foreign expansion had all underlined efforts of U.S. suppliers to ensure continued success through global presence. The North American Free Trade Agreement (NAFTA) offered additional support to the U.S. aftermarket, since tariffs were reduced on parts exported to Mexico and Canada. Trade agreements with Japan focused particularly on the balance of trade in auto parts and other items related to automobile manufacture. Under pressure to do so, Japan bought more parts from the United States in the late 1990s, but Japan also increased its transplant presence in North America, skewing the balance of trade in another way.

European Union. To counter the increased presence of U.S. and Japanese manufacturers, European parts makers prepared to expand on the European Union's common market by eliminating all barriers to trade by the second decade of the twenty-first century. European manufacturers worked to downsize and streamline processes, occasionally emulating the lean manufacturing processes so popular in Japan. Carrying globalization from the Old to the New World, European companies also increased investments in the U.S. market. According to Euromonitor, the market in France was expected to grow 9 percent by 2008, to a value of 3.4 billion Euro, with engine and transmission being the largest sector. The market in Germany was expected to grow 28 percent by 2008, to a value of 77 billion Euro. Finally, the U.K. market was expected to grow 4.8 percent by 2008, with transmission and braking systems as the largest sector.

FURTHER READING

"Auto Parts Makers Go Global." *AutoTrends,* December 2001. Available from http://www.jama.org.

"Auto Parts Suppliers Must Cut Costs." *United Press International,* 20 November 2003.

"Automotive Aftercare and Accessories in France, Germany, UK, US." *Euromonitor,* August 2004. Available from http://www.majormarketprofiles.com.

Automotive Aftermarket Industry Association. "U.S. Motor Vehicle Aftermarket Increased 3 Percent in 2003." *AAIA 2004/2005 Aftermarket Factbook,* 2004. Available from http://www.apaa.org.

Butter, Jamie. "Ford's Woes Costing Visteon." *Detroit Free Press,* 20 October 2001. Available from http://freep.com.

Chappell, Lindsay. "4 Join the Giants." *Automotive News,* 19 June 2000.

Cole, August. "Delphi Echoes Automakers' Gloom." *CBS MarketWatch,* 10 December 2001. Available from http://www.marketwatch.com.

Content, Thomas. "Auto Parts Suppliers' Share Prices Shift Into High Gear." *Knight Ridder/Tribune Business News,* 1 December 2003.

———. "Industry Analysts Predict Strong 2004 Sales for Auto Parts Suppliers." *Knight Ridder/Tribune Business News,* 6 January 2004.

Dana Corporation Fact Sheet. Dana Corporation, 2005.

Donnelly, Paul. "Logistics Management Is Mission Critical When Parts Manufacturers Go Offshore." *World Trade,* March 2004.

Draper, Deborah J., ed. *Business Rankings Annual.* Detroit: Thomson Gale, 2004.

Fitzgerald, Craig. "Three Point Landing." *Automotive Industries,* May 2004.

"Hoover's Company Capsules." 2004. Available from http://www.hoovers.com.

"India to Become a Hub of Auto Parts." *Asia Africa Intelligence Wire,* 31 August 2003.

"Industry Trends." Automotive Parts & Accessories Association, 2004. Available from http://www.apaa.org.

"International Trade Statistics." 2003. Available from http://www.wto.org.

Lazich, Robert S., ed. *Market Share Reporter.* Detroit: Thomson Gale, 2004.

Sherefkin, Robert. "Euro Doesn't Spur US Supplier Buys." *Automotive News Europe,* 28 June 2004.

———. "Study Sees Tough Time for Suppliers." *Automotive News,* 7 June 2004.

———. "U.S. Share of Auto Parts Business Expected to Fall 18 Percent." *Crain's Detroit Business,* 22 March 2004.

"U.S. Auto Parts Suppliers Face a Hit from NAFTA Next Year." *The Kiplinger Letter,* 8 April 2004.

Valdeo S.A. SWOT Analysis. Datamonitor, April 2005.

"Visteon Announces First Quarter 2005 Results." Visteon Corporation, 27 April 2005.

Wrigley, Al. "Auto Parts Suppliers Looking Offshore to Escape '201' Hike." *American Metal Market,* 29 January 2003.

SIC 3711

NAICS 336111

MOTOR VEHICLES

One of the largest sectors of the global economy, the automobile industry manufactures passenger cars, trucks, commercial cars, and buses. Included in this discussion are firms that build chassis and passenger car bodies. Although some industry companies also manufacture motor vehicle parts, this topic is covered separately under the heading **Motor Vehicle Parts and Accessories.**

INDUSTRY SNAPSHOT

In the mid-2000s, the worldwide leader in the motor vehicle industry was the United States, followed closely by Japan in second place, and Germany in third. The top six companies in the industry secured more than half of global sales, although the rest of the industry's (ROI) companies were steadily gaining market share on GM, Toyota, Ford, DaimlerChrysler, Volkswagen, and Honda. Although the three mature world markets—Japan, North America, and western Europe—continued to account for the majority of global motor vehicle production and sales, nearly all of the industry's future growth was projected to come from emerging markets in the Asia-Pacific region, Latin America, the Middle East, and eastern Europe.

Due to increasing globalization, the saturation of mature markets, and economic decline in North America and Europe, the automobile industry worldwide is characterized by intense competition. As a result, most major manufacturers restructured operations in an effort to speed product development, reduce costs, and improve production efficiency. In addition, many manufacturers shifted production facilities to developing countries to take advantage of less expensive labor, reduce exposure to currency fluctuations, and avoid trade restrictions. Automakers also have been forced to lower prices, trim their ranks, and slow production to deal with waning demand for new vehicles. Adding difficulty for automotive manufacturers was the rise in steel prices, which increased by 30 to 40 percent in 2004. Iron was expected to rise in price by another 20 percent in 2005, according to Datamonitor. Automakers and suppliers were both seeing reductions in profits as a result.

At the same time, the growing worldwide environmental movement has prompted automakers to increase research and development expenditures in an effort to build commercially viable electric and electric-gas hybrid vehicles and to make their cars fully recyclable. In the mid-2000s, Toyota was leading the way with "Prius," its gas/electric hybrid sedan. According to the Alliance of Automobile Manufacturers (AAM), 2004 "Tier 2" vehicle models were almost 100 percent cleaner than those of three decades before. In fact, more than one-third of all new vehicles met the strict, mandatory 2009 standards a full five years early. R.L. Polk & Company reported that registrations for hybrid electric vehicles in the United States were 81 percent higher in 2004, at 83,153 new registered vehicles, than in 2003. The Toyota Prius captured 64 percent of that market, with 53,761 new registrations. The Honda Civic Hybrid took 31 percent of the market with 25,586 registered hybrid cars in 2004.

ORGANIZATION AND STRUCTURE

The global automobile market can be divided into roughly six segments: three mature markets and three relatively new markets that reflect emerging economies. As they had been for decades, Western Europe, North America, and Japan were dominant in the mid-2000s. However, Eastern Europe, the Pacific Rim (excluding Japan), and Latin America presented a rapidly developing secondary consumer market.

THREE MATURE MARKETS

In 2004, the three mature markets taken together controlled more than 85 percent of the world's motor vehicle production and sales. Japan and Europe gained in market share during the early 2000s. The major difference between U.S. and foreign markets was that producers in the United States and Canada sold the majority of vehicles produced within the domestic market, while manufacturers in Japan exported more than 40 percent of total production. Global sales of all vehicles in 2004 were 61,387,595 units, 5.5 percent more than in 2003, as reported by Dale Jewett in *Automotive News.*

North America. Dominated throughout the latter part of the twentieth century by General Motors (GM), Ford Motor Company, and DaimlerChrysler, the U.S. car market was not so much characterized by an industry drive to increase total sales, but rather reflected the Big Three's intense competition with foreign manufacturers for market share. In the 1970s, U.S. automakers held 90 percent of the domestic passenger car market. By 2000, this figure had plunged to a mere 54 percent, due to the growing popularity of transplant cars (foreign cars made in U.S. plants) and imports. The rapid growth in sales of light trucks—which over the 10 years ending in 1992 doubled to reach 5.0 million units and increased by half again to a record 7.9 million units in 2004—helped U.S. manufacturers regain some of their lost market share. In fact, in 2004 more than half of all new vehicle sales were trucks. Truck sales were inflated in part by the extreme popularity of sport-utility vehicles, but standard pickups, compact pickups, and vans added to the total. However, although the Big Three held a dominant 79 percent share of the U.S. light truck market in 2000, that number had fallen from a high of nearly 85 percent. The popularity of sport-utility vehicles (SUVs) manufactured by rivals such as Toyota and Honda had allowed those firms to steal domestic light truck market share from the Big Three. By 2004, GM and Ford still held around 24 percent of the world market for motor vehicles, losing about 1.5 percent market share from 2003. The numbers improved when North American automakers' stakes in foreign automakers were included. GM Daewoo in South Korea sold just over 900,000 units in 2004, and Ford had a 34 percent controlling stake in Mazda.

Japan. Domestic car and truck sales in Japan totaled 3.96 million units in 2004, reflecting a slowdown of 1.6 percent, as reported by Datamonitor. Demand for passenger cars fell by .8 percent, and trucks by 5.8 percent. Sales growth in the Japanese domestic market was limited by a number of factors: a fluctuating economy in the 1990s that included national recessions punctuated by weak recoveries, unfavorable currency exchange rates, and a culture that considered cars a luxury rather than a necessity. However, global sales in Japan accounted for 30.9 percent of the global market, a small gain of almost 1 percent from 2003. The Japanese automotive market was dominated by six large domestic producers: Toyota, Nissan, Honda, Mitsubishi, Mazda, and Suzuki.

Western Europe. The European automobile market, traditionally restricted to include seven major western industrialized nations, expanded in the 1990s with the dissolution of the communist bloc into two major marketing segments. However, traditional leaders such as Germany, which produced more than 9.5 million vehicles in 2004, continued to dominate the market. Germany was the third-largest automobile producer in the world. France, with Renault and PSA Peugeot-Citroen SA, and Italy with Fiat S.p.A., were also major producers in the global automotive market.

Enticed by the rapidly growing markets of eastern and central Europe, the largest automakers in these five nations positioned themselves to deal with continued growth and increased competition, and several companies established joint ventures with or acquired controlling interest in other companies to obtain broader market presence.

THREE EMERGING MARKETS

Asia-Pacific. Perhaps the most volatile emerging market in the 1990s was the Asia-Pacific region, excluding Japan. Although in 1991 sales to this part of the world amounted to only 4 million units, that number climbed to 6 million units by 1996, and 8 million by the year 2000.

China and India, the two most populous nations on earth, underwent economic reforms throughout the 1990s that were expected to increase buying power and open markets to international competition. In China alone, the possible increase of automobiles on the road was staggering, with estimated growth starting at 5 million units and increasing to 40 million by the year 2000. Chinese domestic manufacturers struggled with a possible overcapacity problem in 1997, when receipt of government subsidies was contingent upon meeting generous manufacturing quotas. Still, analysts called for continuing high market growth, though possibly with results somewhat below original expectations. In 2004, Chinese automakers increased global market share to 3.8 percent, but sales slowed to 7.4 percent growth in 2004. The slowdown, in contrast to 36.5 percent growth in 2003, was attributed to credit restrictions imposed by the Chinese government. Exponential growth certainly was possible in India, where in 1998 some 950 million people boasted fewer than 6 million registered automobiles. However, immediate expansion of the Indian market was thwarted in the late 1990s by a combination of economic and trade issues. Not only did India slap a 40 percent tariff on automotive imports, in late 1997 the country began to require potential importers to observe a 50 percent "local content" rule. At the same time, most Indian manufacturers were partnered with Japanese and South Korean automakers that were suffering the throes of their respective domestic economic upheavals. Still India held 1 percent of the global market, and sales passed 600,000 units, led by Tata Motors Ltd. and Mahindra & Mahindra, listed in *Automotive News* as two of the three fastest growing automakers.

Indonesia, Taiwan, and the Philippines similarly struggled with slow economies. However, South Korea, the largest emerging market in the Asia-Pacific region, did recover from a significant drop in 1998 production to become the world's seventh-largest producer of vehicles, with a production level of 2.8 million units in 1999. This was due in large part to the success of Hyundai Motor Company, the largest car maker in South Korea, and the ninth largest automaker in the world with unit sales of more than 3 million. South Korean vehicle exports reached US$31.8 billion by December 2004, 12.6 percent of overall exports for the country, as reported in the *Asia Africa Intelligence Wire.* Thailand's automotive industry was also gaining, and production was expected to exceed 1 million units in 2005. Vehicle exports through September 2004 were more than 236,000, more than all of 2003, as reported by the Thai Automotive Industry Association.

In spite of the small immediate market for new cars, a veritable stampede of foreign manufacturers descended upon the Pacific Rim. Ford and GM from the United States, Korea's Daewoo and Hyundai, Japan's Mitsubishi, and a full European contingent (Fiat, Mercedes, BMW, Peugeot, Volkswagen) all looked for a piece of the pie—even though any success in the Pacific was relative. In one instance, in the 18 months between January 1997 and June 1998, South Korea—arguably among the more Westernized of Pacific Rim nations—purchased fewer imported cars (including all sources) than the number of cars it had sold in the United States in just over two weeks. To bolster the economy, the Asia Pacific Economic Cooperation (APEC) forum sought to achieve free trade throughout the Asia-Pacific region by the year 2010 for industrialized countries. Developing nations were expected to follow suit by 2020. However, in the late 1990s, the Asian automobile economy temporarily appeared to be of greater significance as an exporter than as a consumer.

Eastern Europe. At the fall of communism in eastern Europe, several large markets underwent major economic restructuring. Purchasing power remained low as the recovery took hold, but some areas showed evidence of pent-up demand for Western goods, including automobiles. Analysts predicted that most domestic firms, formerly protected from competition, would either cease to exist or be acquired by established foreign automakers. By 1993, German automakers Bayerische Motoren Werke (BMW) and Volkswagen, as well as U.S. giant General Motors, had established transplants in eastern Europe. The eastern European market for automobiles, supported by 280 million consumers in the Commonwealth of Independent States alone, was anticipated to grow to 6 million units annually by 2010.

Latin America. Competitors in the Latin American market sold 2 million vehicles annually in the early 1990s. Mexico, Argentina, Chile, Venezuela, and Bražil were undergoing economic reforms and provided a combined market of 125 million consumers. By mid-2004, Chile had imported more than 56,000 automobiles valued at US$465 million, showing 15 percent growth compared to the same period during 2003. Primary exporters to Chile included Japan and South Korea. Although some automakers were reluctant to commit major financial resources in Latin America due to lingering concerns about political instability, the Big Three U.S. automakers, as well as Volkswagen and a few other European manufacturers, established production facilities in Mexico and Brazil. The main advantage of Latin American production was an abundance of inexpensive labor, and the North American Free Trade Agreement (NAFTA), which reduced trade barriers between the United States, Canada, and Mexico, and was expected to make Mexico even more attractive to producers from the United States and Canada. Accordingly, Mexico's production levels grew steadily throughout the 1990s, reaching a high of 1.5 million in 1999; it was the tenth-largest producer of motor vehicles in the world.

BACKGROUND AND DEVELOPMENT

The development of the automobile was truly international in scope. Individuals from many countries contributed innovations that led to the technical features and production methods commonly used on modern cars. The first functional self-propelled vehicle (a three-wheeler powered by steam) was invented by Frenchman Nicholas Joseph Cugnot in 1769. Nearly a century later, Belgian inventor Etienne Lenoir created the first internal combustion engine. The first gasoline-powered vehicles were constructed by Germans Karl Benz and Gottlieb Daimler in 1885, and Armand Peugeot offered the first motorized vehicles for public sale in France four years later.

In the United States, brothers Charles and Frank Duryea of Massachusetts worked from Benz's designs to launch their own gasoline-powered automobile in the early 1890s. By 1899, some 30 different manufacturers produced and sold various types of motor vehicles in the U.S. market. In 1914, U.S. inventor Henry Ford, who built his first car in 1896, developed an automated production system that revolutionized the industry. Ford's assembly line with its moving belts allowed his company to produce four times as many Model Ts as the year before and continually reduce prices while adding new features to the product. By 1920, half of all the cars on the road worldwide were Model Ts. Many other well-known U.S. manufacturers came into existence at this time as well, including Buick, Cadillac, Chrysler, Oldsmobile, Packard, and Studebaker.

As the 1930s came to a close, the worldwide automobile industry continued to see many innovations. Automatic transmissions were introduced, and manufacturers began to concentrate more on styling, aerodynamics, and fuel efficiency. Although personal car production came to a virtual halt during World War II as most countries devoted all industrial capacity to national defense, the war brought improvements to the industry in the form of better assembly line production. World War II also introduced women to the factory workplace. Postwar prosperity and pent-up demand meant the industry greeted world peace in 1945 with a booming worldwide automobile market.

The automobile industry followed a typical pattern of globalization, in which the largest producers in each nation first exported products and then gradually moved sales and production operations to lucrative overseas markets. The United States' Ford Motor Company had the very earliest success in reaching the markets of Western Europe. Ford began assembling cars in the United Kingdom in 1911, and became Great Britain's largest producer by 1914. Ford began exporting to Japan in 1925 and, following World War II, built plants in several major European nations. General Motors followed a slightly different route, establishing an export company in 1911 to handle overseas sales, entering the Japanese market in 1927. After World War II, GM expanded its European operations by purchasing existing companies, such as Vauxhall in the United Kingdom and Opel in Germany.

The first imports to the U.S. market included exotic European luxury and sports cars: Rolls Royce, Mercedes, Jaguar (later purchased by Ford Motor Company), and Porsche. Until the 1960s, imports accounted for less than one half of one percent of all U.S. auto sales. Led by Volkswagen and its popular Beetle, imports improved their foothold in the U.S. market, and rose from a 10 percent share in 1968 to 15 percent in 1970. The oil crises of the 1970s increased the price of fuel and led many consumers to seek smaller, more fuel-efficient, foreign cars as the 1980s came and went. Japanese manufacturers were most successful in anticipating the demand for fuel economy, and quickly gained market share at the expense of U.S. producers. Design, quality, price, and economy of operation all combined to see foreign market share continue to increase, and in 1998 nearly 40 percent of cars and 18 percent of trucks in 1998 did not bear U.S. manufacture name plates. Ironically, in the late 1990s the wheel turned full circle, and luxury cars were once again among the most popular of imported vehicles.

Throughout the 1990s, tough competition and minimal growth precipitated a trend toward restructuring throughout the North American market. Automakers struggled to reduce new product development time and improve quality (the latter in order to counter a perceived German and Japanese competitive advantage), while still containing costs. Competitors throughout the U.S.-Canadian market also were affected by passage of NAFTA as North American producers gained access to inexpensive labor and the rapidly growing Mexican market, while domestic content requirements dampened the prospects of car producers from other parts of the world.

That decade also saw the dominance of the United States' Big Three automotive companies fade, while Japanese manufacturers first enjoyed huge success and then were forced to maintain similar market share under the aegis of a volatile and occasionally shaky domestic economy. Recovery following the depressed early 1990s was followed by a more generalized Pacific Rim recession in the late 1990s, although Japanese overseas efforts continued to prosper. The proliferation of transplant auto companies reshaped the industry—but no single event could equal the impact of the merger of automotive giants Chrysler Corporation and Daimler-Benz AG.

The Daimler-Chrysler merger would have been noteworthy in any industry for the complete secrecy in which initial talks and various planning stages took place. The May 1998 merger announcement took the auto world by total surprise and led to immediate speculation that an overall industry restructure was on the horizon. Smaller international automakers looked with interest or concern for possible overtures from major manufacturers who sought to compete with Daimler-Chrysler's unprecedented world presence.

The Daimler-Chrysler association was not a takeover—and it was not a merger, per se, in the sense that the two manufacturers' products did not overlap. In a marriage of near-equals, Daimler contributed production of luxury cars, and Chrysler a variety of smaller passenger cars, trucks, and utility vehicles. Combined sales were expected to reach US$130 billion, placing the company into the economic stratosphere of Ford and GM. In one stroke, the balance of the auto industry was changed, as rivals began pursuing their own form of consolidation in an effort to remain competitive. In 1999, Ford added the car operations of Volvo to its increasingly global mix of holdings; it later bought Land Rover. GM acquired a portion of Suzuki, as well as of Subaru. Renault paid US$5.4 billion for a 37 percent share of Nissan. In addition, Volkswagen bought Italian luxury sports carmaker Automobili Lamborghini SpA and Rolls Royce Cars of Britain. South Korean leader Hyundai Motor Co. bought Kia Motors Corp. and Asia Motors Corp. Not to be outdone, DaimlerChrysler itself also participated in the merger and acquisition activity, purchasing a controlling share of Mitsubishi Motors. The value of automotive mergers and acquisitions reached an industry record of US$71.3 billion in 1999. As the cash reserves of major automakers dwindled, merger and acquisition spending slowed to US$22 billion in 2000.

Less dramatic industry activity included the economic consolidation of the European Union, which reduced some trade restrictions and provided Japanese competitors with new opportunities to establish a presence in the western European market. The resulting increase in competition encouraged European manufacturers—in many cases still lagging behind North American and Japanese automakers in terms of quality and production efficiency—to modernize facilities and restructure operations in order to remain competitive.

The North American automotive industry boomed in 1999 and 2000, bolstered by favorable economic conditions, such the lowest unemployment rate in decades, the growth of personal income levels, and a high level of consumer confidence. Sales in the United States grew 3.6 percent to reach a record 17.5 million units in 2000. However, the Big Three continued to lose ground to rivals like Toyota and Honda, who were largely responsible for the 5 percent global market share loss by the Big Three between 1997 and 2000. This was due at least in part to efforts by Japanese car makers to expand their product lines to more closely resemble those of the Big Three.

Current Conditions

Recessionary economic conditions in North America and Europe began taking a toll on those regions' automotive industries in early 2001. An oversupply problem in North America prompted auto manufacturers to shut down assembly plants for days and, in some cases, weeks, during the first quarter of the year. Immediately following the tragic bombing of the World Trade Center towers in New York City, automotive sales tumbled. When analysts began predicting that U.S. unit sales would fall nearly 6 percent to 16.5 million, General Motors launched a no-interest financing program, dubbed "Keep America Rolling," that proved quite successful in boosting sales. The free financing appealed to increasingly cost conscious consumers, and when sales at General Motors began to rebound, other carmakers began to launch their own special promotions. In 2005, General Motors hit the jackpot again by offering its employee-pricing program to everyone, which resulted in sales increases of 47 percent in June 2005, the company's best year since 1986, as reported in the *Detroit Free Press.* Following in the company's success, Ford and Chrysler offered similar plans in mid-2005. An overall increase in U.S. automotive sales of 15.9 percent was due in large part to the GM program.

In early 2005, overseas automakers continued to gain U.S. market share. Sales of cars and light trucks in April 2005 alone were 1,504,332, an increase of 5.7 percent over the year before. However, GM and Ford still lost market share, as did U.S. automakers overall. While the Chrysler Group showed substantial sales increases, and General Motors and Ford's new cars were selling well, overall the Big 3 U.S. auto companies lost market share, bringing them to about 43 percent of the domestic market. Japanese companies were gaining rapidly. Nissan North America showed a gain of almost 32 percent, Toyota Motor Sales U.S.A. increased sales by almost 26 percent, and American Honda Motor Co. climbed 18 percent.

As of the mid-2000s, some manufacturers in the industry were considering increasing or beginning a build-to-order (BTO) segment. Such vehicles, although they would be fewer in number than traditional vehicles, would command a premium price from buyers who could custom design their own vehicles. In addition, cars would not be built on uncertain forecast but on known demand. Time would tell whether or not the industry as a whole would move in this direction.

Research and Technology

Issues of general ecology and global warming continue to give impetus to development of alternative fuel vehicles. Automakers resisted the demand for many years, citing the high cost of fuel cells and various business and marketing risks involved, but legislative changes worldwide forced investment in the technology. In the United States, under the Alternative Motor Fuels Act of 1988, manufacturers of alternate-fuel vehicles were to be included "favorably" in the Corporate Average Fuel Economy program, and otherwise encouraged to build such vehicles. The State of California passed a law requiring any automaker that sold more than 5,000 vehicles annually in the state to guarantee that a certain percentage of those vehicles would emit no harmful substances into the atmosphere (2 percent Zero Emission Vehicles (ZEV) by 1998; 10 percent by 2003). Electric vehicles presented the most feasible technology for meeting California standards, and manufacturers worldwide began investigating ways to produce a practical electric car. Early models were unpopular because of slow cruising speeds and lack of performance, but by the end of the century electric car production began to be practical.

Nissan's electric R'nessa was able to attain 80 km/h in 12 seconds, and had a maximum speed of 120 km/h. In 1998, an electric racecar actually debuted at Le Mans. Toyota combined an internal combustion engine with an electric motor-driven car to take advantage of reduced pollutants without sacrificing automobile performance. And, that same year, General Motors introduced a number of ecofriendly concept cars at the North American International Auto Show, notably the Parallel Hybrid performance car. By 2001, both Toyota and Honda were selling gas-electric hybrid vehicles at the retail level. The four-door Toyota Prius, priced in the low US$20,000s, got 55 miles-per-gallon (mpg) on city roads, while the two-door Honda Insight, priced in the upper US$teens, boasted 70 mpg on highways.

However, alternative fuel vehicles were not limited to passenger cars. In Germany, the Mercedes Nebus (new electric bus) graced the laboratories of Daimler-Benz, and a dual-fuel conversion system was developed allowing Isuzu trucks to take advantage of clean-burning natural gas. In addition, Daimler-Benz partnered with Ford Motor Company to produce Ballard Power System's proton exchange membrane fuel cell.

With landfill space rapidly depleting worldwide, another research issue of increasing importance to the industry was automobile recycling. By the 1990s, the U.S. automobile industry alone consumed 23 million tons of steel, plastic, and other materials annually, and only 75 percent of these materials were reclaimed. By the mid-2000s, automotive manufacturers had improved significantly. According to the Alliance of Automobile Manufacturers, "Today, 95 percent of cars retired from active use each year are processed for recycling, with about 75 percent of a car's material content (steel, aluminum, copper, etc.) eventually being recycled for raw materials use, including material that goes back into the manufacturing of new parts for new automobiles." The most difficult recycling challenge for automakers was plastic, since an average car might contain 100 different formulations that had to be labeled and sorted in order to be reused. German automaker BMW took a progressive approach toward recycling that anticipated even the most stringent environmental standards in its domestic market. BMW's "design for disassembly" program was expected to result in the first fully recyclable car. In addition, the company formed partnerships with German automobile dismantling firms in order to create its own recycling infrastructure.

In 1992, the Big Three formed the United States Council for Automotive Research (USCAR) in order to cooperatively develop generic, fundamental technologies that would permit them to bring vehicles to market sooner and do so at less cost to customers and less impact on the environment. U.S. government antitrust regulations prevented the automakers from working on specific vehicles or discussing pricing issues, but the initiative enabled the automakers to share the cost and risk associated with the "pre-competitive" development of new technologies. Some USCAR initiatives include:

- new composite materials
- increased emphasis on computer-aided design (CAD) and manufacturing (CAM)
- occupant safety
- advanced batteries
- automobile recycling

The Big Three automakers also joined 250 other companies and government organizations in experimenting with Intelligent Vehicle Highway Systems (IVHS). This term covered a wide range of high-technology devices intended to automate different aspects of automobile operation. IVHS research included equipping cars with radar to prevent collisions, installing transponders to track commercial vehicles, and developing satellite-linked navigation systems for automobiles.

Along with incorporating environmental regulations and new technology into their practices, motor vehicle manufacturers also developed many new production practices during the 1990s. Automakers in the United States and Europe, following the lead of those in Japan, formed partnerships with suppliers in order to ensure product quality and reduce costly parts inventories. They reorganized workflow in their plants into tightly coordinated phases known as "just-in-time" or "lean" production—an adaptation of Japanese manufacturers' *kanban* system. In addition, manufacturing workers were empowered to form teams and to provide input on improving product quality and production efficiency.

By the mid-2000s, computer chips were being incorporated in many new vehicle designs. From regulating safety features to emissions, computers were an indispensable addition for the industry. According to the Alliance of Automobile Manufacturers (AAM), the computer technology in standard motor vehicles in 2004 was an average of 1,000 times more powerful than the computer technology used to guide the Apollo 11 lunar mission.

WORKFORCE

In 2004, the U.S. industry alone directly employed 1.3 million people. According to the Alliance of Automotive Manufacturers, when jobs dependent on the industry are included, that number soars to 13.3 million employees. Workers in the global automobile industry earned vastly different wages depending on the country in which they were employed. Germany, France, the United States, Canada, and Japan routinely paid employees four to nine times as much as workers earned in the developing countries in Latin America and the Pacific Rim. The high cost of health care and other benefits, as well as the influence of labor unions, also contributed to high labor costs in more affluent nations. By the 1990s, global automakers were eager to locate new plants in areas with low wage rates, and older plants in more expensive areas became vulnerable to closure.

The intense global competition of the 1990s produced increased emphasis on productivity and cost reduction. Worldwide, automakers reacted by reducing their labor forces, often outsourcing certain types of work to maintain continued levels of production. Japanese automakers were forced to rethink their traditional policy of lifetime employment, and some began implementing layoffs.

In the United States, nearly all workers at Ford, Chrysler, and GM manufacturing plants were represented by the United Auto Workers (UAW) union.

Reflecting the workforce reductions taking place throughout the automobile industry, UAW membership declined from its 1979 peak of 1.5 million to reach a level of 769,685 in 1998. Responding to changes in the auto industry as a whole, UAW leaders maintained their traditional positions on some issues but also tried to adapt to automakers' emerging needs. Especially, the UAW asked for a greater voice in decisions affecting product quality. Quite simply, the unions saw the need to cooperate with manufacturers to ensure that unionized companies were able to retain market share. The arrival of Japanese transplants in the United States presented a further challenge both to Japanese automakers and to the UAW. Initially, these new plants screened workers carefully and offered self-directed team environments in order to discourage union activity. Despite such efforts, however, most transplant operations were unionized within a few years.

Managerial employees in the automobile industry in North America and Europe faced significant changes in the nature of their jobs. In the 1990s, many automakers reworked product development processes to include representatives from marketing and manufacturing as well as design and engineering. These and other operational changes required coordination and teamwork across functional and geographic boundaries. From quality-oriented shop floor team meetings to full-scale executive retraining, members of the industry redesigned themselves to permit a flow of information from the bottom up.

INDUSTRY LEADERS

General Motors Corporation. General Motors is the world's largest manufacturer of automobiles, in terms of both revenue and unit production. In 2004, GM led the industry in sales of trucks and SUVs, and passed Toyota in car sales. Sales in 2004 were US$193.5 billion, and income was US$2.8 billion. The company realized market share gains in several regions around the world, including Latin America, Africa, the Middle East, and China. The European market saw losses due to intense competition. General Motors' profits were also hit by $5.2 billion in healthcare expenses in 2004, around $1,500 per vehicle sold in 2004.

General Motors was incorporated in 1908 by William C. Durant and initially manufactured cars under the Olds and Buick nameplates. Between 1909 and 1920, GM acquired more than 30 companies, and eventually expanded its nameplates to include Chevrolet, Pontiac, Cadillac, GMC, Saturn, and Buick. The company discontinued the Oldsmobile brand in 2004. GM also purchased stakes in several overseas manufacturers to continue to broaden its reach, and by the mid-1990s owned 50 percent of Swedish importer Saab-Scania and 37.5 percent of the Japanese automaker Isuzu. The firm also held a 12 percent share of the western European market, mostly through sales in Germany and the United Kingdom.

Throughout the 1990s, GM was criticized for maintaining a bloated payroll, failing to outsource its component businesses to lower-cost contractors to the extent other car companies had, and operating seven distinct U.S. marketing divisions, in addition to various international brands. GM also suffered from lower employee productivity and slower production times than those of rivals. All of these issues seemed to come to a head in mid-1998 when the UAW called a strike at a metal stamping plant in Flint, Michigan. Within weeks, the stoppage had idled nearly a third of GM's workforce and caused losses in the billions. At issue was the company's decision not to invest in previously planned upgrades to the unproductive Flint plant. The union claimed the issues involved worker health and safety as well as a threat of subcontracting the plant's work—all issues covered under a 1996 agreement. Eventually, GM settled the strike without gaining many concessions from the union—although it did pledge to improve the plant's productivity and hold off some other disputes until 1999 contract talks. Shortly afterward, GM also announced modest internal reforms, but nothing on the scale many believed necessary. In 2001, the firm announced its intent to lay off 10 percent of its North American workforce the following year.

DaimlerChrysler AG. DaimlerChrysler was the result of a 1998 merger between Daimler-Benz, the fourth-largest automaker in the world, and sixth-largest Chrysler Corporation. The deal created the industry's third-largest player and sparked an unprecedented wave of industry consolidation by rivals looking to complete with the new global giant. The company's brands include Dodge, Jeep, and Mercedes. Daimler-Chrysler's sales grew 12 percent in 2004, reaching US$192.3 billion. At the end of 2004, the company employed 384,723 people worldwide.

Chrysler was founded by Walter P. Chrysler in 1925 and grew rapidly during the early years of the automobile industry. The company went through several cycles of crisis and recovery, with the most notable example coming in the early 1980s when Chrysler president Lee Iacocca convinced the U.S. Congress to pass the US$1.5 billion Chrysler Loan Guarantee Act in order to save the company from bankruptcy. A major factor in Chrysler's recovery was the 1983 introduction of the Caravan/Voyager minivan, a utilitarian vehicle that appealed to families and went unchallenged by competitors for many years. The product eventually accounted for 25 percent of Chrysler's sales and 66 percent of its profits, and its success enabled the company to repay its loans ahead of schedule. Chrysler further improved its position in the growing light truck market by purchasing American Motors Corporation (AMC) and its popular Jeep line in 1987.

In 1998, on the eve of the merger with Daimler-Benz, Chrysler struggled with minor quality problems that became all the more noticeable because of direct competition with quality-conscious Toyota and Honda. The company also appeared to stagnate slightly in terms of productivity, inventory turns, and market share. Just as Daimler took advantage of Chrysler's worldwide presence and broader automobile product line, Chrysler in 1998 was ripe for Daimler's historical attention to detail and aggressive policies of growth. However, it wasn't until late 2000 that a new management team began overhauling the Chrysler operations, which by then were losing millions of dollars each quarter. In 2004, the company employed 384,723 people.

Ford Motor Company. The third largest automotive manufacturer in the world, Ford Motor Company posted US$171.6 billion in sales in 2004, with a net income of US$3.5 billion. Of those revenues, $3.9 billion was generated in the Americas, $2.47 billion in Europe, and $407 million in the Asia Pacific and Africa. Ford was established in 1903 by assembly-line inventor Henry Ford. The company introduced its first product, the Model A, later that year, and in 1908 followed with the Model T, which dominated the industry for the next 18 years. In 1913 Ford pioneered the moving assembly line in production for the 1914 model year. Ford later expanded its nameplates to include Lincoln and Mercury. The company purchased 25 percent of Japanese automaker Mazda (then called Toyo Kogyo) in 1979, and also held 10 percent of Kia Motors in South Korea, 100 percent of British luxury-sport manufacturer Jaguar, and 75 percent of Aston Martin, also of the United Kingdom. The Ford family continued its active participation in the daily operation of the company into the twenty-first century. When CEO Jac Nasser resigned in 2001, William Clay Ford Jr., great grandson of Henry Ford, took the helm.

Troubling the firm at the turn of the century was negative publicity surrounding accidents related to the Firestone tires it used on its Explorer sport-utility vehicle. In addition, the Escape, Ford's new, smaller sport-utility vehicle, was recalled several times after its initial release. Reflecting Ford's reliance on sport-utility vehicles was its 28.9 percent share of the U.S. light truck market, compared to the 19.1 percent of the domestic passenger automobile market it held in 2000. To shore up its position in the global market, Ford also spent a considerable portion of its cash reserves on foreign acquisitions in the late 1990s and early 2000s, paying US$6 billion for the passenger car division of Volvo in 1999 and acquiring Land Rover shortly thereafter. Early in 2002, the firm announced plans to cut 35,000 jobs, shut down five plants, and discontinue four vehicles by 2005. In 2004, Ford employed a total of 324,864 employees, a 1 percent decrease from 2003 attributed by the company to capacity reductions and improvement in manufacturing efficiency.

Toyota Motor Corporation. Japan's largest and the world's fourth largest automaker, Toyota Motor Corporation posted sales of US$172.7 billion in 2005, a 5.6 percent hike over 2004. The company sold 6.7 million units and competed directly with the Big Three for North American market share. Toyota introduced several new trucks and sport-utility vehicles in 2000. That year, its share of the U.S. light truck market reached 7.6 percent, while its share of the U.S. passenger automobile market totaled 11 percent. In 2005, Toyota was close to achieving 15 percent of the global market overall, and gaining on surpassing General Motors as the industry leader. During the mid-2000s, its gas and electric hybrid sedan, "Prius," was sweeping the European and U.S. markets.

Toyota was founded in 1926 by Sakichi Toyoda, whose entrepreneurial experience began with the manufacture of looms. Sakichi's son Kiichiro Toyoda took the family company into the automobile business in 1933, and in 1937 took it public under the name Toyota. The company was forced to retool to make trucks during World War II and suffered financial difficulties for several years afterward. It regained its prosperity during Japan's economic recovery in the 1950s, and successfully entered the U.S. market in 1965. By 1970 Toyota was the fourth-largest automobile manufacturer in the world. The company opened its first production plant in the United States in 1984 through a US$1.5 billion joint venture with General Motors. Although the alliance seemed unlikely to some industry observers, the New United Motor Manufacturing Inc. (NUMMI) plant offered benefits to both companies. The experience allowed Toyota to begin U.S. production cautiously during a time of increasing protectionism and provided the company with a better understanding of U.S. labor relations. It also gave GM insight into high-quality Japanese production methods. Already exporting a number of passenger models (4Runner, Camry, Celica, Corolla, Tercel), Toyota moved into the luxury car line in 1989 with its launch of the Lexus. In the next decade, the continued appeal of the Lexus combined with an across-the-market popularity of luxury vehicles to enhance Toyota's global position.

Like other Japanese producers, Toyota was hurt by the mid-1990s rise in the value of the Japanese yen in relation to the U.S. dollar—something that made Japanese products less affordable in overseas markets—as well as several periods of national recession. In response, Toyota undertook an extensive cost-cutting program and increased its commitment to building transplants around the world; foreign sales grew increasingly key to Toyota's business strategy. In the late 1990s, Toyota held 32 percent of the Japanese market, over 16 points ahead of its nearest competitor, and continued to dominate the U.S. import market. The Toyota Camry was the third best selling car in the United States, trailing the Ford Taurus and Honda Accord. With US$20 billion in cash reserves, Toyota entered the twenty-first century as one of the strongest performers in the automotive industry.

Honda Motor Company Ltd. Honda Motor Company, Japan's third-largest automaker, ranked sixth in global sales with US$80.7 billion for 2005. The company, which in addition to its automotive business is the world's largest producer of motorcycles and small engines, posted a profit of US$4.5 billion that year. Honda is the only major automaker that has not pursued, or at least considered, consolidation with other players.

Honda originated in 1928 as an automobile repair shop in Hamamatsu, Japan. Founder Soichiro Honda saw his facilities destroyed during World War II, but the company recovered by producing motorcycles in the late 1940s. Honda expanded into car and truck production in the 1960s and began exporting to the U.S. market. Since its Civic and Accord models were more fuel-efficient than U.S. cars, Honda's sales boomed during the oil crises of the 1970s. Honda joined the movement into the luxury segment by launching its Acura line in 1986. The company purchased 20 percent of the United Kingdom's Rover in 1990, but was later outbid for controlling interest by German automaker BMW. In 1992, Honda established a presence in China through a joint venture to produce motorcycles there.

In the late 1990s, Honda exported roughly half of the units it produced. Dependence on U.S. sales left Honda particularly vulnerable to currency fluctuations in the early part of the decade, prompting Honda to expand its manufacturing operations in North America. A large number of units were produced by North American transplant operations and, in the United States, the popular Honda Accord was outsold only by the Ford Taurus. Although the company produced commercial vehicles, virtually all exported units were passenger cars—the Accord, Acura, Civic, and Prelude. In 2000, Honda held a 10 percent share of the U.S. passenger car market, ahead of Big Three rival DaimlerChrysler. It began gaining ground in the light trucks sector at the turn of the century with its new CR-V sport utility vehicle and its Odyssey minivan. The firm's Acura luxury division also began to perform well at roughly the same time.

Nissan Motor Co. Ltd. The second largest car maker in Japan, Nissan is continuing the cost cutting measures it launched in 1999 under new CEO Carlos Ghosen, installed that year shortly after France's Renault acquired a controlling 37 percent stake in Nissan, which by 2004 had risen to 45 percent. Ghosen's Nissan Revival Plan called for the reduction of 21,000 jobs by 2003, an unprecedented number of layoffs for a Japanese firm. Part of that plan included the shutdown of three plants, the last of which was bulldozed in 2001. Nissan also is planning to move production of its Maxima sedan from Japan to the United States. Sales in 2004 reached US$70 billion, 23 percent growth from 2003. That year the company employed 123,748.

When it was founded in Tokyo in 1911 by Hashimoto Masujiro, Nissan was known as Kwaishinsha Motor Car Works. In 1925 the name was changed to DAT Motors, which meant "fast rabbit" in Japanese. The company introduced a small car called Datsun in 1931, then organized its small vehicle operations separately as Nissan Motors in 1933. The company entered the U.S. market in 1958 under the name Datsun and gained market share quickly in the 1960s with its high-quality, low-cost products. It undertook a slow and costly name change back to Nissan in the United States in 1981, about the time it began to establish transplants in overseas markets. Like other leading Japanese automakers, Nissan introduced a luxury line, Infiniti, in 1989. In 1990, Nissan took over Fuji Heavy Industries, the Japanese producer of Subaru automobiles. The auto manufacturer was hurt in the mid-1990s by a recession at home and unfavorable currency exchange rates, problems which eventually prompted the firm's decision to partner with Renault.

Regie Nationale des Usines Renault SA. Renault is the second-largest automaker in France, behind Peugeot, which boasted a 13 percent share of Europe's market compared to Renault's 11 percent share in 2000. Sales in 2004 totaled US$55.5 billion, reflecting growth of almost 18 percent; profits grew 55 percent to US$4.8 billion. The firm's decision in 1999 to expand operations outside country borders with the purchase of a controlling share of Nissan proved a wise one, particularly after its European market share began to fall.

Renault was founded in 1898 near Paris by Louis Renault, and the company produced the world's first sedan in 1899. At the close of World War II half a century later—Renault had produced trucks and planes for Germany during the occupation of France—Louis Renault was accused of collaboration with the enemy and died in prison. The French government took over the company in 1945, but reduced its share in the company from 26 percent to 16 percent in 2003. Renault entered the U.S. market by purchasing 46 percent of American Motors Corporation in 1979. When the venture proved unprofitable (producing a net loss of US$1.5 billion by 1984), Renault sold its stake in AMC to Chrysler. In order to regain its corporate health, Renault exited the U.S. market, and in the early 1990s laid off 50,000 workers and modernized several plants. The firm remains focused on small and mid-sized automobiles. Renault also invested in the Asian market, purchasing a 37 percent share in Nissan in 1999 and took over the company's leadership. By the mid-2000s, Renault owned 44 percent of Nissan.

Volkswagen AG. The largest automaker in Europe, Volkswagen AG posted sales of US$121.3 billion in 2004. an increase of almost 11 percent from 2003. Volkswagen is one of the largest employers in the industry with 336,800 workers worldwide. Although its most popular vehicles include the Beetle, Jetta, and Passat, Volkswagen also owns luxury lines like Rolls Royce, Bentley, Audi, and Lamborghini.

Volkswagen originated in 1937, when Ferdinand Porsche received financial backing from Adolf Hitler to produce an affordable "people's car" in Germany. Although production was delayed until after World War II, by the 1950s the company launched its popular microbus and began building plants overseas. In the 1960s the unpretentious Volkswagen Beetle gained popularity as a counterculture symbol in the United States—and eventually became the best selling car in the world. In 1978, Volkswagen opened the first transplant in the United States, though the location closed 10 years later. By the mid-1990s, although its U.S. market share was less than 1 percent, Volkswagen was the sales leader in Europe and controlled 50 percent of the growing Chinese market. In addition, Volkswagen's 1990 investment in the Czechoslovakian automaker Skoda ensured that it could take advantage of the economic recovery in eastern Europe.

Volkswagen dropped a marketing bombshell in 1998, when it introduced an updated version of its beloved Beetle. More luxurious in interior design and slated for a more affluent market than the ubiquitous "Bug" of the postwar years, the new Beetle took its audience by storm. Like its predecessor, it was undeniably cute, but it was slightly larger than the old version, much more expensive, and boasted such amenities as standard air-conditioning.

Fiat S.p.A. In the late 1990s, Fiat controlled 14 percent of the European market, but was highly dependent on the sheltered Italian sector. To extend its reach beyond Western Europe, the firm agreed to divest 20 percent of itself to General Motors, in exchange for a 6 percent stake in the North American giant. Sales in 2005 grew 4.5 percent to $66.1 billion. Sales of Italian commercial vehicles dropped 2.4 percent overall during the year, but Fiat Auto saw a .6 percent increase, selling 17,565 vehicles and raising its market share to 40.1 percent.

Fiat traces its corporate beginnings from articles of association of the "Societa Anonima Fabbrica Italiana Torino," signed in 1899. Giovanni Agnelli was a member of the society's board of directors. The company grew steadily, and during World War I manufactured more than a thousand vehicles for the Italian army. By 1920, Agnelli was chairman of the organization, and he promptly embraced Henry Ford's style of mass production in an effort to keep automobile costs within acceptable consumer range. Fiat continued to manufacture a broad variety of passenger cars and commercial vehicles, including a number of sports and racing models. In 1945 Agnelli died, but the company's momentum carried it forward through the years following Italy's defeat in World War II, and the Agnelli family retained ownership of roughly 30 percent of the corporation through 2002. By the mid-1980s, Fiat was continuing to introduce a large number of new models of affordable passenger cars each year, along with traditional luxury sports models (Alfa Romeo, Maserati, Ferrari). In 1988, Fiat's Termoli 3 plant was opened, billed as the most highly automated car factory in the world.

Major Countries in the Industry

Japan. In response to protectionist sentiments and changing economic conditions, all the major Japanese manufacturers built production facilities in the United States in the 1980s. These remote manufacturing locations became commonly known as "transplants." By 1993 a full 50 percent of the vehicles sold in the U.S. market by Japanese companies were produced in the United States. This mirrored the worldwide trend toward locating production facilities closer to final markets—a trend that helped automakers avoid tariffs and quotas, reduce exposure to currency fluctuations, take advantage of inexpensive labor, and understand local market conditions.

In the mid 1990s, Japan's domestic market was undergoing a period of transition, even while the effect of the nation's manufacturers on the global market was increasing. In 1997 Japanese automakers exported more than 40 percent of total output, or 4.55 million units, although exports had declined steadily for nearly a decade as more production facilities were located overseas. In mid-decade, imports to the Japanese domestic market passed the 10 percent mark for the first time, as successful U.S. sales supplemented those of European cars.

The Japanese domestic market faced a recession in the early 1990s and a second economic downturn at the end of the decade. Complicating matters for Japanese automakers, the value of the yen first rose against the U.S. dollar, making Japanese products relatively more expensive in the U.S. market, and then fell, resulting in instability in the entire Japanese economy and impacting all sorts of worldwide business. By 2004, sales were back up again, with the most popular models being two minivans—the Honda Odysssey and the Toyota Sienna—and the subcompact Nissan Cube. The global market improved slightly over 2003, though Japanese domestic sales were down. Japanese companies held 30.9 percent of the global market based on number of units sold in 2004.

These difficult market conditions combined to place extraordinary pressure on the profitability of Japanese automakers in the 1990s. In response, Japanese producers were forced to raise prices, continue to shift production to overseas markets, and reevaluate some of the basic business philosophies that contributed to past success. The factors that had differentiated the Japanese automobile industry included a high level of worker involvement; cooperative labor-management relations; extremely loyal employees who tended to remain with a single company for the duration of their careers; a strong commitment to quality; and early implementation of just-in-time production processes. In addition, Japanese automakers were closely linked to suppliers through a *keiretsu* (group affiliation) system. But in the face of declining profitability, Japanese automakers increasingly loosened keiretsu ties and purchased parts from outside suppliers, overhauled lean production systems and offered less variety in order to control costs, and reevaluated the nature of their responsibility toward employees.

Actual Japanese motor vehicle exports to the United States declined significantly throughout the 1990s, from 3.4 million units in 1986 to 1.6 million units in 2004. Total exports to North America were 1,726,465, about 3.4 percent less than in 2003. Conversely, production in U.S.-based Japanese automaker plants rose over the same time period, surpassing 4 million units by 2004. The North American plants of Japanese automakers accounted for 63 percent of U.S. automotive sales in 2000, compared to less than 12 percent in 1986. Transplant manufacturing served the dual purpose of reducing manufacturing costs and increasing marketability of product (by reducing the stigma of foreign manufacture).

Japanese exports to Europe, however, rose 10 percent to 1,275,229, a gain attributed in *Automotive News* to the weakening yen against the euro. Thanks to the improved market in Europe, Japanese exports overall increased by 4.2 percent, to 4,957,663. Toyota Motor Corporation alone was responsible for exports of more than 800,000 units, and the company expected an increase of another 12 percent to more than 900,000 during 2005.

United States. The 2000s saw U.S. dominance, or at least Big Three dominance, of the automobile market change its shape. Concentrating more on popular and profitable pickup trucks and sport-utility vehicles, the United States lost 3.0 percent of its domestic passenger car market share—which in 1998 was just 61.1 percent. Domestic car production dropped to 6.9 million units, reflecting lowered sales of all passenger cars except luxury models. On the other hand, sale of new trucks increased to a record 7.1 million units. In the late 1990s, of the top ten vehicles in the United States, six were trucks, sport-utility vehicles, or vans. The Alliance of Automobile Manufacturers reported that in 2004, 58 percent of new vehicles were light trucks, and the number of new trucks sold reached 7.9 million. For the first time, light trucks outsold passenger cars in all fifty states.

The United States was a genuinely open market for automobiles. A total of 31 automobile manufacturers competed in the U.S. market in the early 1990s, and additional manufacturers entered the market as the decade wore on and smaller international companies flexed their wings. In 2000, both Toyota and Honda held more of the U.S. passenger car market than Big Three rival DaimlerChrysler; however, the Big Three continued to dominate the domestic light truck market. In mid-2004, *Ward's Auto World* reported that the ten companies not in the top six—GM, Ford, DaimlerChrysler, Toyota, Honda, and Nissan—had gone from 7.3 percent of the 1996 market to 13.4 percent of the 2002 market. The companies boasting the largest growth were Hyundai, Volkswagen, Kia, Mitsubishi, and BMW.

The proliferation of transplants in the United States, and the resulting confusion about the national origin of automobiles sold in the U.S. market, led to passage of a content labeling law in 1994. All new vehicles sold in the United States were required to bear a label stating the percentage of the car's value contributed by parts of U.S. or Canadian origin, the city and country where the car was assembled, the two countries that contributed the greatest value of parts to the car, and the country of origin for the engine and transmission. Although some Japanese manufacturers felt that the law unfairly linked all vehicles of a certain model together regardless of where they were produced, some German automakers predicted that consumers would be pleased to learn that their new vehicle was 100 percent German. By 1996, transplants (more properly known as the International Auto Sector, or IAS) had generated nearly 1.3 million jobs in the United States. As transplant influence and presence grew, voices rose suggesting that they should be fully integrated into the economy and viewed in the same light as the traditional Big Three of U.S. auto manufacture.

Europe. Taken collectively, European car manufacturers were enjoying a good deal of success in the late 1990s. Porsche held an initial lead in corporate growth with an annual increment exceeding 70 percent, and the merger of Daimler-Benz with Chrysler allowed Daimler, already Germany's largest company, to increase its standing in the global market. Audi and BMW achieved strong market gains, as did Jaguar, operating as a wholly owned subsidiary of Ford Motor Company. Saab held its own, although Volvo struggled in the late 1990s. Volkswagen, already a powerful presence in the car market, introduced the popular "new" Beetle. By the mid-2000s, European automakers were retaining market share of 33.5 percent of global sales. Volkswagen was ranked the fourth largest automaker in the world, selling more than 5 million units in 2004, following closely by DaimlerChrysler AG with 4.7 million units sold.

German luxury automakers had been unprepared for the strong showing the new Japanese luxury lines made in the U.S. market in the early 1990s. BMW responded by purchasing British manufacturer Rover in order to diversify into small cars and sport-utility vehicles, and later added the quintessential luxury car manufacturer Rolls Royce to its portfolio. BMW also began increasing its imports to Japan, as did Audi and Mercedes-Benz; all three of the German imports began to attract younger clients, increasing their sales in Japan by 34 percent between 1991 and 2001.

Since Germany's strong environmental movement led the country to adopt the strictest environmental standards in Europe, the German automobile industry was well positioned as environmental standards rose around the world. German automakers developed the first luxury compacts in response to protests by environmental groups against large cars, and they initiated the most advanced programs in the world for automobile recycling, even as Mercedes (Daimler-Benz) worked to enhance its electric car offering.

South Korea. International focus remained on the emerging industrial economies surrounding the Pacific Rim. China and India offered huge consumer potential, but it was South Korea that emerged as the new auto-producing nation of the late 1990s. Hyundai, Kia, and Daewoo—in particular Hyundai—pursued international markets with increasing success.

In the mid-1990s, Hyundai, the dominant Korean automobile producer, clung to a growth rate of just six-tenths of a percent over previous years and planned to lay off 8,000 workers—approximately 17 percent of its total head count. In 1998, Hyundai's U.S. sales were 28 percent higher than they had been in the preceding year, and Kia doubled its nascent U.S. sales in the same time frame. Daewoo, South Korea's third-largest automaker, viewed late summer of 1998 as a target date to begin export of their product to the United States. These marketing strategies served to counter and even nullify the effects of a sagging domestic economy. Total South Korean automotive exports reached 1.63 million vehicles in 2001.

FURTHER READING

"America's Automobile Industry." Alliance of Automotive Manufacturers, 2004. Available from http://www.autoalliance.org.

"Busines in Asia Today." *Asia Africa Intelligence Wire,* 14 December 2004.

Butters, Jamie. "Ford, Chrysler to Follow GM's Discount Lead." *Detroit Free Press,* 6 July 2005.

Connelly, Mary, and Lindsay Chappell. "Crisis Could Hit Chrysler Revival." *Automotive News Europe,* 3 May 2004.

"Current Statistics." Japan Automobile Manufacturers Association, July 2004. Available from http://www.japanauto.com.

Dawson, Chester. "An Endurance Test for Japanese Carmakers." *Business Week,* 26 April 2004.

———. "Nissan: Saying Sayonara." *Business Week,* 24 September 2001.

Draper, Deborah J., ed. *Business Rankings Annual.* Detroit: Thomson Gale, 2004.

"Fiat Auto Increases Market Share in Commercial Vehicles" *Europe Intelligence Wire,* 8 March 2005.

Flint, Jerry. "Broken Lights." *Forbes Global,* 7 June 2004.

———. "Smug No More." *Forbes,* 10 May 2004.

"Ford Motor Company SWOT Analysis." *Datamonitor,* 2005.

Green, Jeff. "Industry Outlook 2001: Autos." *Business Week,* 8 January 2001.

"Hoover's Company Capsules." 2004. Available from http://www.hoovers.com.

"Industry Report: Automobile Industry." *US Business Reporter,* 2001. Available from http://www.activemedia-guide.com.

"International Trade Statistics." 2003. Available from http://www.wto.org.

"Is BTO the Auto Industry's Answer to Poor Profitability?" *just-auto.com,* 26 July 2004.

Japan Automobile Manufacturers Association. "Gas Prices Climb Gradually in Japan." *Japan Auto Trends,* July 2004.

Jewett, Dale. "Toyota Gains on GM in Global Race." *Automotive News,* 16 May 2005.

Lazich, Robert S., ed. *Market Share Reporter.* Detroit: Thomson Gale, 2004.

"Light Truck Country." *Alliance of Automobile Manufacturers,* 2005.

"Middle East: Seismic Change in Middle East Consumer Patterns." *IPR Strategic Business Information Database,* 25 July 2004.

"New Vehicles Now 99 Percent Cleaner." Alliance of Automotive Manufacturers, 27 May 2004. Available from http://www.autoalliance.org.

"R.L. Polk Says HEV Registrations Increased 81 Percent in 2004." *Electric and Hybrid Vehicles Today,* 27 April 2005.

Stoddard, Haig. "Suddenly Vulnerable." *Ward's Auto World,* 1 May 2004.

Teahen Jr., John K. "April: Japan's Big 3 Were Hot, But the U.S. Big 2 Were Not." *Automotive News,* 9 May 2005.

"Thailand: Government Drives Auto Industry Globalisation." *just-auto.com,* 29 November 2004.

"Today's Automobile: A Computer on Wheels." Alliance of Automotive Manufacturers, 22 March 2004. Available from http://www.autoalliance.org.

"Vehicle Imports Increase 23% in May." *The America's Intelligence Wire,* 23 June 2004.

"Ward's Reports Estimated Production." *PR Newswire Industry News,* 30 July 2004.

Yamaguchi, Yuzo. "Japan Exports to N.A. Fall 3.4% in 2004; Success of Prius Hybrid, Scion Put Toyota Up 3.9%." *Automotive News,* 7 February 2005.

SIC 3731

NAICS 336611

SHIPBUILDING AND REPAIR

The shipbuilding and repair industry is made up of government and privately owned (commercial) shipyards that build and repair various types of ships, lighters, and barges. These vessels may be self-propelled or may require towing by another vessel. For discussion of transportation services via ship, see also **Water Transportation.**

INDUSTRY SNAPSHOT

In the mid-2000s, Asian shipbuilders remained the clear leaders in the shipbuilding and repair industry, with South Korea, Japan, and China holding rank as the top three, respectively. European and U.S. yards lagged considerably behind Asia mainly due to years of Asian government subsidies to the region's shipyards. Contention over worldwide subsidies, rising global labor and construction costs, mergers, joint ventures and other collaborative relationships, and a shrinking pool of qualified workers were key issues.

As of May 2005, orders for oil tankers and bulk carriers fell from the previous year by 35 and 16 percent respectively, but containership contracts rose nearly 70 percent as the result of increased trade in the Asia Pacific region. Demand for large containerships stagnated by the mid-2000s as ship owners waited to see if world trade would make use of all the new ships that would enter service beginning in 2006, as reported by Bruce Barnard in *The Journal of Commerce Online.* However, the market for smaller ships was still performing well, as the need for ships to service large vessels grew.

As of April 2007, most U.S. shipyards were enjoying a booming business while repair yards were struggling to survive. More and more Navy ships were being kept out at sea for longer periods of time. Consequentially, maintenance dollars were being moved to operating accounts. Large steel jobs were being sent overseas.

Additional concerns were apparent when the Metal Trades Department of the AFL-CIO sued the Coast Guard about allowing domestic shipyards to use pre-assembled foreign ship parts and engines. This suit claimed that the Coast Guard ignored Jones Act requirements that ships moving between U.S. ports be built in the U.S.

Momentum was evident for the concept of a "Green Passport" for ships. The passport would contain an inventory of all materials potentially hazardous to human health or the environment used in the construction of a ship. It would be produced by the shipyard during construction stage and passed on to the purchaser of the vessel. The document format would accommodate recording the addition of subsequent changes in equipment and materials. Successive owners of the ship would maintain the accuracy of the passport. The final owner would be responsible for delivering it, along with the vessel, to the recycling yard.

ORGANIZATION AND STRUCTURE

The International Maritime Organization (IMO), a special agency within the United Nations, adopts maritime conventions to improve maritime safety and prevent pollution. The IMO also intervenes in legal issues, such as liability and compensation, and works to promote marine traffic. Members of the IMO comprised most of the world's shipping nations, or about 164 governments, in mid-2004. The IMO's budget for 2004-05 was more than US$84 million. Members contributions are based on the size of the country's merchant fleet. Top contributors to IMO as of 2005 included Panama, Liberia, the Bahamas, Greece, the United Kingdom, and Japan.

Recognizing that technological advances can be a key component to increasing marine safety and reducing pollution, the IMO's Technical Cooperation and Facilitation, Maritime Safety, Legal, and Marine Environment Protection committees devise technical resolutions to address these issues. Resolutions and recommendations are then presented to the assembly, the IMO's governing body, which is made up of representatives from the 164 governments. The assembly typically meets every two years.

CURRENT CONDITIONS

Shipbuilding emphasis has shifted eastward in the past three decades. Western Europe's shipbuilders have lost market share, first to Japan, then to South Korea, and, more recently, to China. Losing the ability to compete on pricing, European yards were forced to specialize and focus on gas and chemical tankers and cruise ships. In 2001, the European Commission, the agency that regulates competition in the European Union (EU), asked for support for European subsidies from the EU's General Affairs Council to bring the EU in line with the Organization for Economic Cooperation and Development (OECD) agreement to end subsidies and other forms of aid to shipbuilders and repairers. The agreement was opposed by the United Kingdom, Denmark, Sweden, the Netherlands, and Finland, and the United States opted not to participate in the agreement.

By 2002, tensions between the EU and South Korea were rising, as the EU accused its Asian competitor of price dumping, which is pricing a vessel at less than fair market rate in order to undercut other shipyards. When negotiations between the two world players broke down, the EU filed a complaint with the World Trade Organization (WTO) in October 2002. According to the EU, by selling ships below production cost, South Korea was destroying Europe's shipbuilding industry, causing layoffs and bankruptcies. Nevertheless, some industry observers argued that the EU's maritime status was improving, and that its claims were somewhat misleading because many European-owned vessels fly so-called "flags of convenience," which hide true national affiliations. In March 2005, the WTO gave South Korea 90 days to end the questioned shipbuilding subsidies.

Fierce competition, government subsidies, overcapacity, high labor and production costs, and an Asian financial crisis all contributed to decreasing revenues among most commercial shipbuilders worldwide. The worldwide practice of government subsidies contributed to an "artificial" pricing market for the industry and led to price dumping. This in turn created a kind of domino effect among shipbuilders and repairers. By May 2005, orders for container ships had declined.

By the mid-2000s, Asian shipyards continued to produce the bulk of the world's large commercial vessels—tankers and bulk carriers. Indeed, three Asian countries—South Korea, Japan, and China—dominate the commercial shipbuilding market. South Korea, the world's shipbuilding leader, received orders for 159 ships from 26 countries during the first quarter of 2004 alone, with compensated gross tons ordered (cgt) reaching a record 5.26 million, up 31 percent from the same period in 2003. South Korea completed nearly US$4.5 billion worth of ships during the first three months of 2004, a number that was expected to reach or exceed US$12 billion by the year's end. South Korea's record-breaking pace continued through the first half of the year, by which time it had received orders for 256 new vessels, contributing to a backlog of 847 vessels.

The government in Malaysia vowed to strengthen the capacity and capability of shipbuilding and ship repair sector in the country under the recently launched Third Industrial Master Plan. This effort was among the five strategic thrusts for long-term growth and viability of the marine transport subsector. Related areas of concentration were set as enhancing domestic capabilities in building and repairing capabilities as well as intensifying and upgrading engineering skills, strengthening infrastructure and support facilities, strengthening institutional support and expanding activities in the fabrication of offshore structures.

European yards remained the largest producers of cruise ships, ferries, and container ships. Lagging far behind in this sector with a paltry share of the world market, U.S. yards continued to focus primarily on military contracts with only a few yards competing for international commercial contracts. In early 1998 the largest private U.S. shipyard, Newport News Shipbuilding Inc., of Virginia, announced that it would stop building commercial ships altogether and would focus instead on Navy contracts. Late in 2001, Newport News was acquired by Northrop Grumman Corp. in a deal valued at US$2.6 billion. Northrop combined the two shipbuilding divisions, forming a US$4 billion shipbuilding enterprise named Northrop Grumman Newport News. As of mid-2004, the unit was one of only two entities capable of designing and building nuclear-powered submarines.

In March 2007, Russian President Vladimir Putin signed the decree "On the open joint-stock company Amalgamated Shipbuilding Corporation". Under the presidential decree, the Centre for Shipbuilding and Ship Repair Technology is established on the basis of the federal state unitary enterprise Central Shipbuilding Technology Research Institute (St Petersburg). Main activities will focus on "development and implementation of new-research-intensive shipbuilding and ship repair technologies; technological support for the design, construction, technical maintenance, repairs and disposal of ships and vessels in Russia and abroad; the design and technical upgrade of the production assets of shipbuilding and ship repair centres; the design and production of ship fittings and shipbuilding engineering output; the development, production and supply of specialized equipment and technological fittings."

The future of Canadian shipbuilding and repair remained uncertain after the new Prime Minister Stephen Harper was sworn into office. Industry insiders were excited about Harper's statement calling for three made-in Canada icebreakers capable of sailing in the North and promoting goals to protect the country's Arctic sovereignty. There was speculation that the icebreakers, whether they are armed or not, would be assigned to the Canadian Coast Guard. With the Canadian Coast Guard in charge of enforcing northern shipping rules, it was believed to throw up less of a red flag than having Navy vessels do it. To implement this plan, the Coast Guard's role would have to change as the Senate had recommended it should do so.

Leading U.S. shipbuilders were primarily engaged in servicing military (i.e., Navy) contracts. As a result, they have not been active participants in the commercial sector until recent years. Most analysts and industry insiders agree that without drastic improvements in labor and production efficiency, increased use of technology, changes in management culture, and the removal of global government subsidies, the U.S. industry is not likely to substantially increase its market position in the foreseeable future.

A clarion call was issued for "lean enterprise" to be practiced by the shipbuilding and repair industry. This involved trimming costs, simplifying production lines and cutting down on inventory with the goal of reducing turnaround time on projects and eliminating waste. Empire, a Norfolk industrial supply house, "started on a lean journey" in 2005 after it was requested to do so. The request came from Empire's largest customer, Norfolk Grumman Newport News. The Navy was also reportedly trying to become "lean" with related methods resulting in a savings of more than US$230 million in the fiscal year 2005.

Ranked third in the world among leading shipbuilding nations, mainland China announced a similar port expansion project as part of its strategy to turn Shanghai into an international shipping center. Included in the US$633 million expansion plan is dredging a major channel to the sea that could accommodate deep-draught container vessels. Dredging of the channel is expected to be completed by 2020. Other waterways would be dredged as well for container traffic into the Jiangsu and Hubei provinces. Construction would also begin on the country's largest and most state-of-the-art shipyard at Waigaoqiao, in the Pudong New Area of Shanghai.

RESEARCH AND TECHNOLOGY

As safety, pollution, and competition became increasingly important issues, improvements in ship design and capacity, yard and port expansion projects, and new government and international programs occurred. Typical vessel capacity expanded rapidly during the closing decades of the twentieth century. For example, in the 1960s typical capacity was 1,000 TEUs (20-foot equivalent units), by the 1970s it was 2,000 TEUs, by the 1980s it had increased to between 3,000 and 4,000 TEUs, and by the late 1990s vessels of 6,000 TEUs with the capacity to carry 8,000 TEUs were common. In 1998, South Korea announced its intention to build 8,000-TEU containerships. The vessels would be constructed by Samsung Heavy Industries, one of the country's leading shipbuilders. Samsung's proposals called for vessels of 345 m in length, 45.3 m in width, draft of 27 m, and a deadweight of 150,000 tons. To increase fuel efficiency and loading capacity, the hull design was to be 5 percent lighter in size-to-weight ratio than the 6,000-TEU vessels of its Japanese competitors. Samsung was working with a German firm to run tests of the structural integrity of the new hull design. The vessels would be powered by a 93,000 hp diesel engine and would be able to reach a speed of 25 knots. Samsung expected the new vessels to be in production by 2000. A U.S. Corps of Engineering study reported that by the end of 1999, some 34 percent of the global box ship fleet would be made up of more than 300 vessels of 4,000 TEUs or more. One German study estimated the cost of the 8,000-TEU vessel to be US$110 million to US$120 million, but some analysts wondered whether that figure might not be overly optimistic.

In response to the need for ports capable of handling ever increasing amounts of cargo and supersized vessels, in early 1998 the port of Hong Kong, China announced its plans to increase the port's capacity. In 1997 Hong Kong handled 14.5 million 20-foot equivalent units (TEUs) of containers and retained its position as the world's busiest container port. Its 1998 capacity was forecast to reach nearly 16 million TEUs of containers, a 7.5 percent increase in container traffic from the year before. The Hong Kong Port Development Board chairman noted that port expansion was necessary to keep up with industry changes, notably increasing vessel sizes and the formation of large shipping consortia.

It is generally agreed that further upsizing of container ships is inevitable. Vessels of 10,000 TEU and above are being designed, and there is no engine power constraint for craft of this size.

WORKFORCE

BAE Systems Ship Repair President Al Krekich expressed his concerns about the graying of his industry's workforce. Remarks were shared during the "Momentum in Shipbuilding and Repair" panel discussion at the Propeller Club of the United States maritime industry advocacy group international convention. One of the industry's biggest emerging challenges was recruiting young people. The average age of the estimated 800 workers at the BAE System's Norfolk shipyard was 50 years old. That was younger than estimates for the Norfolk Naval Shipyard in Portsmouth. Krekich said "an injection of youth" was needed in order for the industry to keep moving ahead in the future.

Another convention panel member, Maritime Industry Consultants principal John Graykowski, said retention of workers was also a major concern. Graykowski strongly advised establishing a "a national shipbuilding university" to produce highly trained workers capable of working with technological advances that offered excellent ways to contain costs.

An additional convention panel member, Shipbuilders Council of America President Alan Walker, noted that many shipyards created apprentice programs for training younger employees. The U.S., however, was not viewed as promoting the kinds of skills needed for shipyard work.

INDUSTRY LEADERS

SOUTH KOREA

During the mid-2000s, South Korea's top shipbuilders were Hyundai Heavy Industries Co. Ltd. and Samsung Heavy Industries Co. Ltd. Daewoo Heavy Industries Co. Ltd., a leader during the early 2000s, was exiting the shipbuilding industry. As reported by *The Journal of Commerce Online,* orders at South Korean shipyards were full until the end of 2007, and some orders were being taken for 2008 delivery.

Hyundai Heavy Industries Co. Ltd. (HHI). As of 2004, Hyundai Heavy Industries (HHI) enjoyed status as the largest shipbuilder in the world. HHI formerly was a subsidiary of the Hyundai Group, a large diversified conglomerate. However, in February 2002 it was spun off from its parent and became an independent enterprise. This involved HHI's takeover of the Hyundai Mipo Dockyard and Hyundai Samho Heavy Industries. In 2004, HHI employed almost

26,000 workers across six business divisions. In addition to the shipbuilding division, these included Construction Equipment, Electro Electric Systems, Engine & Machinery, Industrial Plant & Engineering, and Offshore & Engineering. HHI's 2004 revenue from new orders in 2004 was US$9.35 billion, 4.7 percent less than $9.8 billion in 2003. The company anticipated solid revenue growth in 2005 due to price increases implemented because of dramatic increases in steel costs and increased demand for container ships and tankers. For 2005, HHI reported sales of US$10.144 billion and 25,175 employees. Its shipbuilding division made tankers, bulk carriers, containerships plus high-tech gas and chemical carriers.

Samsung Heavy Industries, Inc. (SHI). South Korea's Samsung Heavy Industries (SHI) was an affiliate of the Samsung Group, a conglomerate with holdings in machinery, electronics, chemicals, finance, and motor engines. SHI focuses mainly on shipbuilding and offshore business, but also competes in the construction equipment market. In addition to ship automation and building automation systems, SHI designs and manufactures large passenger ships, LNG carriers, shuttle tankers, and drill ships. In 2004 SHI reported US$4.46 billion in annual sales and employed 8,572 people. By 2005 annual sales had increased to US$5.47. In January 2006 SHI was ranked as the world's third-largest shipbuilder. It announced plans to establish a joint venture with Malaysia Marine and Heavy Engineering (MMHE) to repair liquefied natural gas (LNG) carriers. The joint venture aims to tap into the LNG ship repair market following an increase in orders to construct the LNG carriers. To be capitalized at US$1 million, the Kuala Lumpur-based firm was established as 30 percent owned by SHI and 70 percent owned by MMHE. SHI has overseas facilities, including a Chinese factory devoted to the production of ship blocks.

Daewoo Heavy Industries, Ltd. (DHI). Daewoo Heavy Industries (DHI) was a leading Korean shipbuilder during the early 2000s. By mid-2004 its parent, the Daewoo Group, was spinning DHI off as an independent company. In addition, DHI had divested its automobile and shipbuilding units, the latter going to Australian interests. From this point forward, DHI operated the following divisions: Construction Equipment, Industrial Vehicles, Machine Tools, Factory Automation Systems, Diesel Engines, and Defense Systems. The company's shipbuilding business unit once produced LNG carriers, submarines, LNG vessels, double-hulled crude-oil tankers, bulk carriers, and containerships. In 2003 DHI reported earnings of 1.9 billion, increasing more than 20 percent from the previous year.

JAPAN

In 2004, the Shipbuilder's Association of Japan (SAJ) included 19 members with combined orders of 8 million tons. Among the members were seven major companies, most of which had broad-ranging non-marine business sectors. The shipbuilding segments alone of these seven companies made up approximately 11 percent of their total corporate sales. The 11 other SAJ members were medium-sized firms that relied on marine-related contracts. For them, the shipbuilding and repair segment comprised 86 percent of their total corporate sales.

MITSUBISHI HEAVY INDUSTRIES LTD. (MHI)

As with many of Japan's leading shipbuilders, MHI is a fully diversified conglomerate. MHI's business units cover aeronautics, industrial plants and equipment, and steel construction and shipbuilding, to name just a few. In 2003, shipbuilding represented about 8 percent of MHI's US$21.6 billion in revenues, behind machinery manufacturing and power systems. MHI's shipbuilding sector includes containerships, liquefied natural gas (LNG) carriers, very large crude carriers (VLCC), and marine pollution and offshore production structures and equipment.

KAWASAKI HEAVY INDUSTRIES LTD. (KHI)

Kawasaki (KHI) was another of Japan's leading shipbuilders, with 2004 sales of US$10.98 billion and more than 29,000 employees. KHI has two shipyards, Sakaide and Kobe, both more than 100 years old. KHI's shipbuilding expertise covers bulk carriers, tankers, LNG carriers, high-speed ferries, research submersibles, containerships, and liquid petroleum gas (LPG) carriers. In addition, KHI supplies a variety of marine equipment and engines. Like Mitsubishi Heavy Industries, KHI is a diversified conglomerate with business units covering environmental products, industrial plants, aeronautics, general purpose engines, construction, and civil engineering, in addition to its shipbuilding and marine engineering business unit.

MAJOR COUNTRIES IN THE INDUSTRY

SOUTH KOREA

In 2002, South Korea edged ahead of Japan to become the world's largest shipbuilder. That year, *The Journal of Commerce Online* reported that South Korea achieved a market share of 31.8 percent, ahead of Japan's 31.7 percent. Although the world leader position has shifted between the two nations, by 2003 South Korea retained its position ahead of other countries with 16 million gross tons in new orders, keeping its lead over Japan. During the first half of 2003, Korea's orders for new ships increased 171 percent from the previous year, and by the end of 2003 Korea held 43 percent of the global market. At 232 vessels, 7.8 million tons, this half-year total surpassed the country's figures for all of 2002. By comparison, Japan received orders totaling 4.99 million tons between January and August of 2003, up 13 percent from the same time frame the previous year. During the first half of 2004, South Korea continued at a record pace, recording orders for 256 new vessels, 9.06 million tons, an increase of more than 16 percent from 2003.

South Korean shipyards expanded capacities in the 1990s. As of early 2001, they were able to exploit a depreciation of the won and boost their business to a point that they reported a three-year backlog. Korean construction includes tankers and bulk carriers, roll-on/roll-off (ro/ro) vessels, car carriers, containerships, chemical carriers, and others. Most of Korea's shipbuilding industry is located in the South Kyongsang province and comprises approximately 80 shipbuilding firms that construct, salvage, or repair a broad variety of vessels. Korean shipbuilders, like most of the Asian shipbuilding nations, rely heavily on computer-aided design (CAD), or computer-aided design/computer-aided manufacturing (CAD/CAM), and automation of facilities.

High-speed ferries, supersized containerships, and liquefied natural gas (LNG) carriers were particular highlights of Korean shipbuilding. Importantly, Korea pioneered the world's first double-hulled tanker, a significant contribution given that international conventions now require that single-hulled oil tankers be replaced by double-hulled vessels. Both the Korean government and the industry itself invested heavily in technology and automation to improve efficiency, contain costs, and meet production schedules. To further spur industry growth, the Korean government plans to expand shipbuilding and repair facilities and to create nearly 30 new ports. By the year 2011, South Korea expects to double its seaport capacity to accommodate 560 million tons of freight per year. Despite such positives, the Asian financial crisis of the late 1990s hit Korean shipbuilders especially hard, causing several to file for bankruptcy protection.

JAPAN

Second-place Japan saw new ship contracts double during the first quarter of 2004, rising from 1.2 million compensated gross tons (cgt) to almost 2.5 million cgt. By the early 2000s, South Korea had pulled ahead of Japan to lead the shipbuilding industry. According to Korea's Ministry of Commerce, Industry and Energy, the nation's research and development technologies have given it an edge over Japan in terms of being able to build more customized vessels for customers, whereas Japan has produced more standardized ships.

Japanese shipbuilders had previously managed to maintain their lead ahead of South Korea, in spite of the Asian financial crisis of the late 1990s. This was partially due to differences in how both nations obtained construction materials. Japanese shipbuilders relied on domestic suppliers for such high-end additions as equipment, whereas Korean companies strongly relied on imports of machinery and steel. Japanese yards also relied heavily on high technology, particularly computer-aided design and drafting, and Japan's largest shipbuilders were broadly diversified conglomerates with subsidiaries in heavy engineering sectors.

Japan, like the other leading shipbuilding nations, witnessed a decline in prices despite an overall increase in the world's shipbuilding orders. By the end of 2000, employment in the shipbuilding industry was 85,000, and further workforce reductions were expected, reflecting a global trend. Japan finished 2003 with 28 percent global market share.

CHINA

Although it trailed its Asian counterparts, China was poised for explosive growth by the mid-2000s. In order to reach its goal of becoming the world's shipbuilding leader by 2015, China was investing billions of dollars to improve its position. After allowing foreign investment in its ports in March of 2002, China benefited from US$2.2 billion in investments that year, followed by an estimated US$3.6 billion in 2003. The nation's efforts were met with significant results. From a paltry share of only 0.8 percent in 1982, China saw its stake in the global shipbuilding market increase to 12.6 percent by the end of 2003. That year, orders for new vessels increased 173 percent, and the nation completed a record 6 million deadweight tons (dwt). This was an increase of 46 percent from 2002, surpassing forecasts of 5 million dwt.

As of May 2005, shipbuilders in the province of Shandong in east China held orders for 120 ships totaling US$566 million, as reported by *Xinhua News Agency.* China's shipbuilding industry is led by the China State Shipbuilding Corp. (CSSC) and the China Shipbuilding Industry Corp. By 2010, CSSC was expected to complete the world's largest shipyard. Located at the mouth of the Yangtze River on the Shanghai coast, the new yard will be capable of producing up to 12 million deadweight tons per year. Although the new shipyard, along with its burgeoning economy, would go far to help China achieve its goal of world shipbuilding dominance, industry analysts revealed a number of significant challenges. These included falling shipping container rates, the competitiveness of Chinese currency in comparison to the U.S. dollar, a possible containership glut, and productivity issues at China's state-operated companies.

EUROPE

In 2003, the European Union (EU) indicated that its shipbuilding world market share fell drastically during the early 2000s, from 19 percent in 2000 to 13 percent in 2001. In 2002, a 50 percent drop in orders caused the EU's market share to decline even more, reaching 7 percent, which rose slightly to 8.7 percent by the end of 2003.

Although the EU attributed a significant amount of its market share decline to alleged price dumping by Koreans, some industry observers argued that conditions were not as bad as the EU claimed. In June 2003 the *The Journal of Commerce Online* said that "Europe is strengthening its position as a maritime power with dominant market positions in almost every sector from tankers and bulk carriers, to cruise liners, containerships and liquefied gas carriers."

In addition to mentioning European-owned vessels flying under the flags of other nations and European interests in such shipping industry leaders as A.P. Moller, the article went on to explain that German banks were "Europe's 'unseen' shipowners," who "have built up a massive fleet of container vessels for charter thanks to investors seeking a tax-efficient home for their savings. This is a big business with charter tonnage now accounting for nearly 50 percent of the fleet of the world's top 30 liner shipping companies."

The late 1990s brought increased consolidation and collaboration among European yards in an effort to remain competitive. Drastic workforce reductions throughout the EU were common. By 1996, European shipyard employment was about 113,000 and further reductions during 1998 were expected. In 1998, Germany, Poland, Spain, and Denmark were expected to experience the greatest additional reductions in labor. The employment picture was more optimistic for Norway, the Netherlands, and Italy. Northern European countries had higher wages on average than their southern counterparts. There were also strong contrasts in work hours ranging from an annual working hour rate of 1,400 to about 2,300 hours. In the 1960s, the Netherlands shipbuilding workforce numbered around 50,000 workers. That figure has dropped to about 10,000 employees in 100 shipyards with only 4,000 being employed in building ocean-going ships.

In 2007, plans were announced to merge the three UK yards still in the business of building surface warships into one operation. Industry insiders predicted that the deal would lead to an even split of ownership between the two companies but BAE would control more than 50 percent of the voting rights. BAE and VT yards are slated to do most of the work on two 65,000-metric ton aircraft carriers for the Royal Navy. According to Nick Chaffey, the global head of defense at PA Consulting, consolidation in naval shipbuilding is not a European phenomenon. It is considered to be a global issue that is even beginning to affect the United States. Chaffey also noted that current actions are helping to prepare for the period somewhere between 2015 and 2020 when orders from the British will likely dive. The industry needs to be restructured by then.

THE UNITED STATES

During the early 2000s, the U.S. shipbuilding industry ranked tenth in the world in terms of tonnage built. Productivity in the maritime industry is quite low compared to other large manufacturing sectors such as the aerospace and automobile industries. Shipbuilding in the United States has historically been considered a strategic industry, supporting both military and commercial interests. As of 2002, the U.S. shipbuilding and repair industry consisted of about 250 private companies and five publicly owned and operated repair yards. U.S. shipbuilding and repair revenues totaled US$10.2 billion 1998. About 10 percent of the companies accounted for 85 percent of these revenues. The shipyards on the Eastern and Gulf Coasts account for more than 80 percent of the revenues for the entire industry.

Lack of technological innovation and automation, upgrading of worker skills, and collaborative partnerships among yards, plus complex management hierarchies all contributed to the United States' low market share. In contrast, Asian yards excelled at using technology, regularly upgrading workers' skills, developing collaborative ventures, and maintaining flatter, less complex management hierarchies. Outside forces, particularly foreign government subsidies, price dumping, and overcapacity, further contributed to the problem. At the turn of the century, efforts were also under way to streamline yard operations and increase efficiency by means of technology and flatter management structures.

In 2003 the U.S. shipbuilding industry, and some 2,000 workers, benefited from a defense appropriations bill that included more than US$1 billion to build two new ships at Northrop Grumman's Avondale shipyard. Despite this good news, the overall outlook for U.S. shipbuilders paled in comparison to those in Asia.

In 2006 industry insiders applauded the Navy's new system of awarding ship repair contracts. The "multiship, multioption" allows shipyards to win contracts to maintain a class of ships. This process replaced the former single-ship awards. The Navy also made it possible to generate more money for shipbuilding with its quest to build a 313-ship fleet. Scaling back in the Navy's fleet size during recent years from approximately 600 ships in the late 1980s to 275 hurt big shipbuilding companies and smaller suppliers. Diversification was considered to be a key strategy for survival. Reduction in the Navy's maintenance budget, however, did create cause for concern.

FURTHER READING

Bangsberg, P.T. "Shipbuilding Boom Cools for S. Korea Yards." *The Journal of Commerce Online,* 6 January 2004.

———. "Record China Shipbuilding in 2003." *The Journal of Commerce Online,* 12 January 2004.

Barnard, Bruce. "Big Box Ship Orders Slow." *The Journal of Commerce Online,* 3 May 2005.

———. "EU: New Report Details Unfair Pricing By Korea Yards." *The Journal of Commerce Online,* 13 May 2003.

———. "Europe View: Shipowners Leave Builders in Dust." *The Journal of Commerce Online,* 4 June 2003.

"Canadian Shipbuilding & Repair: The Most Uncertain of Times." *Canadian Sailings,* 13 March 2006.

"China Breaks Ground for World's Largest Shipyard." *World Trade,* March 2004.

"China to Overtake South Korea, Japan as World's Biggest Shipbuilder." *Channel NewsAsia,* 25 March 2004.

Chuter, Andrew. "And Then There Was One." Available from http://www.defensenews.com. 23 April 2007.

"Container Ship Orders Decline." *The Journal of Commerce,* 9 May 2005.

Dawson, Philip. *Cruise Ships: An Evolution in Design.* Conway Maritime Press, June 2000.

"Flexibility is Key When Work Drops: Hampton Rubber Has Found Ways to Diversify Into New Lines of Work - Helping it Shore Up Declines in the Ship Repair Business." *Daily Press,* 13 March 2007.

"Flying Start to Year for World's Top Builders." *The Journal of Commerce Online,* 13 May 2003.

"Full Steam Ahead?" *Economist,* 21 February 2004.

Glass, Jon W. "Executive Says Recruiting is a Challenge in Ship Repair Industry." *Virginian-Pilot,* 13 October 2006.

Glass, P. "U.S. Repair Yard Hit Hard by Competition." *Workboat,* April 2007.

"Hyundai Heavy Industries Set for Rally as Ship Prices Rise." *The Journal of Commerce Online,* 22 December 2004.

"Korean Shipbuilders Set Record for Foreign Orders." *The Chosun Ilbo,* 18 July 2004. Available from: http://English.chosun.com.

McWilliams, Jeremiah. "Author Urges Ship Repair Industry to Get 'Lean'." *The Virginian-Pilot,* 9 March 2006.

"Move to Strenghten Shipbuilding, Repair Sector." *Business Times,* 8 August 2006.

"Recycling of Ships." Available from http://www.imo.org. 4 April 2007.

"Russia's Putin Signs Decrees on Shipbuilding Corporation, Ship Repair Centre." *BBC Monitoring International Reports,* 22 March 2007.

"Samsung Heavy to Form Ship Repair Joint Venture in Malaysia." *AsiaPulse,* 23 January 2006.

"The 2003 Defense Appropriation Bill Provides a Big Boost for the U.S. Navy Ship Construction Program at Northrop Grumman's

Avondale Shipyard in New Orleans. (Louisiana)." *EconSouth,* Spring 2003.

"WTO Hits Korean Shipbuilding Aid." *The Journal of Commerce Online,* 8 March 2005.

Zoccola, Mary and Dennis Clark. "Assessment of the U.S. Shipbuilding Industry Completed." U.S. Department of Commerce (May 2001).

SIC 3743

NAICS 336510

TRAIN EQUIPMENT

Railroad equipment manufacturers build the world's passenger and freight transit equipment, including subway trains and street cars, locomotives, railcars, and parts and equipment used to run railroad systems.

INDUSTRY SNAPSHOT

In the early 2000s, freight car manufacturing across the globe declined, falling from 75,685 cars in 1998 to 34,247 cars in 2001. Railcar demand from 2001 to 2003 was dismal, the lowest in twenty years. The outlook was improving in the mid-2000s, however, especially as the industry consolidated further. According to the Railway Supply Institute, North America had ordered 20,315 new cars through the third quarter of 2004. This was an increase from 19,770 orders the previous quarter. Tank cars, box cars, non-articulated platform flat cars, and aluminum gondola cars were in the highest demand. At the same time, locomotive production continued its tradition of steady growth, fueled by developments that increased efficiency. Besides new trains and infrastructure, many countries sought safer methods of controlling and monitoring railroads. Therefore, information and technology firms began to develop and market computerized signal and communication systems for the railroad industry.

Railroad companies also invested money in new railroad equipment to lure commercial and freight clients to areas where train use had decreased over the years, such as in the United States. New technologies available to railroads included more durable yet lighter-weight freight trains capable of traveling 80 miles per hour, as well as electronic tracking systems to ensure safety on the railroad. In addition, the industry was focusing on the development of more environmentally friendly cars and locomotives in the mid-2000s.

Emerging economies such as those of China, South Korea, and Indonesia began expanding and improving railway systems and contracting railroad equipment manufacturers to produce advanced machinery to carry their transportation systems into the next century. The United States also started to upgrade its passenger and freight railroad equipment, and South American countries such as Brazil took measures to improve railroad transportation as well. By the mid-2000s, China's booming market also caused increased demand in this sector.

Several industry insiders and analysts, including 65-year industry veteran Norman W. Seip and Thomas D. Simpson of the Railway Supply Institute, felt more good times were in store for railroads and related industries. However, as Simpson pointed out, "the new railroad freight car building industry has been a cyclical one with spectacular highs and industry-sapping lows". Although some suppliers remained anxious about the future, builders were enjoying exploring their opportunities.

The demand for switchers was tremendous. As a result, there were many designs and opportunities for small companies normally linked to rebuilding. A new generation of switchers were distinguished by microprocessor engine controls enabling them to replace more efficient four-axle units in many Class I yards.

Economic Planning Associates (EPA) issued a freight car forecast calling for delivery of 69,000 railcars and intermodal platforms in 2007. The forecast was "based on opening year backlogs and further growth in orders". Furthermore, EPA expectations for 2008 included continued demand for a number of car types, a revival of demand for coal cars, boxcars and intermodal equipment plus an increase in tank car production capacity with support deliveries of 70,500 units.

ORGANIZATION AND STRUCTURE

Although the organization of the railroad industry varied by country, the role of the railroad equipment manufacturer remained largely the same in each context: it sold equipment such as locomotives, signal systems, and railcars to the railroad operators, whether owned and operated by a government or a monopoly and whether for freight or passengers. Railroad leasing companies and other manufacturers and producers who relied on railroads might also purchase train equipment.

In the mid-1990s, railroad operators began working more closely with equipment manufacturers in order to ensure high standards of reliability and performance were met as increasingly complex technology came on-line, according to *International Railway Journal.* Since many train lines crossed national boundaries, notably in Europe, railroad operators realized they had to procure equipment compatible with different national railroad systems. In Germany, for example, Deutsche Bahn (DB) worked closely with Siemens and other manufacturers to develop the InterCity Express 2.2 and the InterCity Express Tilting trains to meet the railroad's standards for smoother, more comfortable, and more efficient travel.

Based in Alexandria, Virginia, the Railway Progress Institute (RPI) represented the global railroad industry and served more than 100 members. Originally called the Railway Business Association, the RPI served both freight and passenger railroads, and the association's key objectives included the following: promoting a free enterprise system of railroads throughout the world, advancing high-speed train penetration and light rail systems in urban cities, and representing its members' interests.

BACKGROUND AND DEVELOPMENT

Inventors developed early railroad equipment in the first part of the nineteenth century. The English engineer Richard Trevithick built the first steam engine in 1802, which did not run on tracks and reached a maximum speed of 6 miles per hour. The following year, Trevithick developed a locomotive designed for tracks, which weighed more than six tons and could reach speeds of only about 2 miles per hour, taking four hours to get to the end of the 8 miles of track Trevithick laid for the train.

In 1814 another engineer, George Stephenson, built a five-ton steam engine that could pull eight cars loaded with 30 tons of cargo. Stephenson designed this train for a mine in England and went on to build a number of other trains, including his 1825 "Locomotion," which became the first passenger train. The Locomotion traveled a 16-mile track from Stockton to Darlington, England.

In the middle part of the century, the rest of Europe and the United States began installing railroads and purchasing steam engines from the British company founded by Stephenson. Countries such as the Netherlands, Germany, France, and the United States imported trains from Britain during the early years of the railroad equipment industry. The United States alone purchased about 100 steam engines from Britain between 1829 and 1841.

In Asia, the United States, and the United Kingdom, railroad equipment manufacturers supplied these countries with their first locomotives at the turn of the century. However, by the 1920s Japan began to produce its own trains, and by 1935 Japan had manufactured 687 locomotives. Later in the century, Japan became a major proponent of the railroad, creating the world's first high-speed railway in 1964 which stretched about 257 miles across the country and reached speeds of 100 miles per hour.

Throughout the 1970s, 1980s, and 1990s, the prosperity and prospects of the railroad equipment manufacturing industry depended on the overall economics of the countries in question. In the stable and even flourishing economies of Europe, the United States, and China, railroad manufacturers experienced heightened demand and solid growth in the 1990s as they received new contracts to produce equipment for the modernization of old railroad systems. Several large railroad companies in the United States, including Amtrak and Union Pacific Corp., as well as city and state transit authorities, ordered high-speed trains and electronic tracking systems. Europe continued to expand its high-speed railway production, including new orders for locomotives from British Rail. In addition, China forged ahead in the creation of the Eurasia Continental railroad system.

However, in the turbulent economies of South Korea and Thailand, which experienced devaluations of currencies and mushrooming debt in the mid-1990s, demand slumped and existing contracts were reevaluated. South Korea's new president, Kim Dae-jung, called for the review of the country's 412-kilometer Supertrain project because of its escalating construction costs. Furthermore, Thailand halted production of its Skytrain project, which would have eased Bangkok's notorious traffic problems, when it terminated its contract with the developer, Hopewell Co. When construction stopped in August of 1997, Hopewell had built only 20 percent of the railroad.

In the global market, Germany, Canada, France, the United States, Japan, and China led the world in railroad equipment manufacturing in the mid-1990s. To remain competitive, companies in the industry had to accommodate railroad operators and restricted budgets and funding. Railroad operators in Europe pressured manufacturers to provide low-cost—low cost to purchase, operate, and maintain—railroad equipment, forcing manufacturers to seek lower prices from their sub-suppliers. *Railway Age* reported that in some cases railcar costs dropped by 30 percent between 1994 and 1997, spurring on production of light-weight, flexible, more durable, and more efficient equipment.

Of the technologies produced to meet these economic pressures, the self-propelled diesel railcar was one of the most successful in the mid-1990s. Leading models included the RegioSprinter from Siemens, Talent from Bombardier and Talbot, Dieseltreibwagen from GEC Alsthom, and RegioShuttle from Daimler-Benz. North American railroad operators began considering adopting this kind of railroad equipment as well in the mid-1990s.

The locomotive sector of the industry experienced significant changes in the mid-1990s with the introduction of new locomotive technologies. During this period, railroads adopted diesel locomotive alternator and electric traction motor technology. In addition, self-propelled railcar technology began replacing its locomotive-hauled counterpart, and electric locomotives continued to supplant diesel trains. In 1995, the world locomotive fleet included 94,000 diesel locomotives—down 12 percent from 1992—and 53,000 electric locomotives—up 5 percent from 1992.

Since a new locomotive ran about US$200,000 in the mid-1990s and yearly maintenance and fuel costs totaled US$300,000, many railroad operators turned to rebuilding and remanufacturing equipment instead of purchasing new trains. As a result, locomotive replacement sales slackened in the early 1990s. However, with the new more powerful and more fuel-efficient locomotives, manufacturers hoped to entice railroad operators once again. In 1995, *International Railway Journal* reported that shipments of locomotives totaled US$9.2 billion.

Enhanced performance of newer diesel-electric locomotives pushed locomotive sales to near record levels in the early 2000s, particularly in North America. Although most major North American railroads had finished replacing aging fleets by 2000, "a wholesale building bust doesn't appear imminent," wrote a *Railway Age* columnist in July of 2000. "Robust domestic railroad traffic driven by a healthy economy and a growing export market should keep builders' order books filled for at least the next few years." However, most major North American railroad companies did plan to reduce locomotive orders in the coming years, particularly as the North American economy weakened.

Light-rail systems without trolley wires made their way to North America in 2001. Bombardier delivered three Talent diesel-electric light-rail vehicles to Ottawa, Ontario; service was scheduled to begin in 2002. In the United States, at roughly the same time, New Jersey Transit began working on converting an unused 32-mile Conrail track into a light-rail line. When construction was completed, the line would make use of 20 Adtranz diesel-electric cars.

Asia remained an important market in the railroad equipment industry in the early 2000s. Foreign competition began to make its way into China as the market for imported goods began to open there. German and Chinese officials continued to work together on plans for a 26-mile magnetic levitation (maglev) train in Shanghai, capable of reaching speeds of 340 mph. If completed, the train was expected to be the first public transit system in the world to make use of maglev technology. China also remained involved in the development of the Eurasia Continental Bridge, which would connect Rotterdam, The Netherlands, to the Jiangsu Province of China, with both roads and railways. In addition, improved economic conditions in Thailand prompted transportation officials to examine ways to resurrect the Hopewell mass transit system, which had been suspended due to a recession.

Current Conditions

Railcar demand was falling in the early 2000s, accompanied by falling prices, which in 2003 were 20 percent lower than those at the beginning of the decade. According to *Railway Age,* from mid-2001 to mid-2003, railcar builders suffered the lowest demand in nearly twenty years, producing only about 30,000 units, less than one-third of the industry's capability. In addition, in order to redesign cars to meet stricter 286 truck technology requirements, railcar manufacturers were set to lose an additional amount per railcar of up to US$2,000. While the future was looking up by the middle of the decade, it was still predicted that this segment would experience consolidation on a large scale. Things looked brighter in 2005, as the freight-car industry saw orders rise steadily. As reported in *Trains Magazine,* more than 20,000 new freight cars were ordered during the third quarter of 2004 alone, up 3 percent from the second quarter and three times the amount from third quarter 2003. Because of high demand, manufacturers showed a backlog of more than 61,000 cars. Demand for covered hoppers, flatcars, and aluminum gondolas was greatest, as carriers worked to meet demand and replace aging equipment. The industry saw strength in North America and Europe, as well as emerging markets.

In Europe, the Paris Transit Authority hired Alstom and Bombardier to build 805 metro cars in a multi-year contract worth roughly US$584 million. By 2005, the new cars would replace roughly 40 percent of the existing fleet operated by Paris Transit. Alstom and Bombardier also agreed to jointly supply 10 tilting trains, worth US$120 million, to Swiss Railways. In addition, Alstom secured a US$118 million contract to build 100 electric railcars for French National Railway, and Bombardier won a US$76 million contract to refurbish 60 three-car trains for Netherlands Railways. Danish State Railways awarded a US$579 million contract to Italy-based Breda for 83 four-car diesel trains.

China and Russia were both considered potential growth markets by several railroad equipment industry analysts. China's extensive railway system was in need of extensive upgrades, as was Russia's. According to the U.S. Foreign and Commercial Service Moscow, more than 33 percent of electric locomotives and 50 percent of diesel locomotives in Russia were in need of replacement in the early 2000s. Competition in these markets was expected to intensify as Japanese, European, and U.S. manufacturers all attempted to gain market share. Iran was emerging as a growth area as well. In 2005, German and Chinese companies were competing to work with the Tail Transportation Industry Company (Rtico) to on a $680 million contract to develop a third metro line in Tehran. The project included electrical work, signaling and utilities, as well as the manufacture of rolling stock, for which Bombardier of Canada was bidding as well.

Research and Technology

The 1990s brought the railroad equipment industry new technology to improve railroad travel efficiency and safety. Some of the most prominent advances included intelligent trains and tracking systems, high-speed trains, and safety equipment. Intelligent trains and tracking systems used computer and digital communications technology, which create a train and track system controlled by computers that have a strong communication link with railroad monitors. Some researchers sought to integrate Global Positioning System (GPS) satellites into railroad communications systems. This technology helped eliminate human error in railroad transportation because the computer system could automatically stop a train if an impending collision was miles away.

New high-speed train technology started to emerge in the mid-1990s that would allow trains to travel up to 150 miles per hour and contain advanced operation and track systems to ensure safety at high speeds. The faster high-speed trains, those that travel more than 110 miles per hour, required non-electric locomotives in order to reach maximum speeds and accelerate quickly. In addition, non-electric locomotives alleviated the need to install expensive electric locomotive infrastructure. In the late 1990s, the California High-Speed Rail Authority launched a US$25 million plan to develop one of the first high-speed railway lines in the United States. In November of 2000, the U.S. Federal Railroad Administration also began conducting research on T-16, a former Amtrak car refitted with technology that allowed it to test performance at speeds as high as 160 mph.

New safety equipment being developed included innovative warning systems, more reliable signal systems, and techniques for making trains more conspicuous. The first kind of safety device consisted of signals using light and sound to alert drivers of approaching trains. Researchers were trying to determine what kinds of signals would provide enough advanced warning for motorists. In order to make locomotives more conspicuous, researchers experimented with alternating lights combined with standard headlights, as well as advanced horn systems and reflectors on train cars to make them more visible.

Though researchers began experimenting with tilting train technology in the mid-1960s, it did not emerge as a viable alternative until the mid-1990s because economic problems plagued major researching countries, such as Germany, leading to slow progress when research terminated between

1975 and 1986. However, in 1987 research resumed and demonstrated that tilting wheels could lead to more efficient regional transportation. Tilting trains required only minimal modification of existing infrastructure and could smoothly handle curves at higher speeds than conventional trains because of the tilting technology. Tilting trains also worked well in large urban areas and on railroad lines shared with slower trains such as freight trains, according to *International Railway Journal*. However, critics pointed out that tilting trains could not travel as quickly as high-speed trains on specially built tracks. In addition, the tilting could cause more wear on the outer part of the rail, requiring more frequent track repair and maintenance, and tilting wheels might cost more to repair than conventional wheels because they contain more parts. Nonetheless, railroad operators, such as Deutsche Bahn (DB), began upgrading with this technology. By the early 2000s, DB wanted to operate 120 tilting trains, which would constitute the largest fleet of tilting trains in Europe. Other countries developing tilting trains in the late 1990s included Italy, Switzerland, Finland, and Spain.

In the freight train sector, DB decided to move its freight car technology into the twenty-first century by having new intelligent freight cars built. DB opted for this technology to remain competitive with other modes of transport and to improve freight train safety and reliability. Intelligent freight cars contain technology to replace antiquated railroad practices and procedures such as shouting messages, transmitting data by hand, loading and unloading cars manually, and performing safety checks without the aid of technology. In the mid-1990s, DB tested 20 intelligent freight cars with hopes of implementing the technology by the beginning of the next decade.

The 2000s brought attention to the polluting effects of railways. With focus on noise pollution reduction, the European Commission was hopeful that computer-aided engineering would prove helpful in designing a quieter train system. In terms of air pollution, at the end of 2003 in North America, in an effort to develop less polluting units, a hybrid switching locomotive was being tested by RailPower Technologies, Railserve, and Chevron. Named the "Green Kid," the 1,000HP hybrid locomotive was intended to reduce air pollution to significantly lower levels than those of traditional units.

INDUSTRY LEADERS

Bombardier. In May of 2001, Adtranz was acquired by Montreal, Quebec-based Bombardier Inc. Prior to its takeover of Adtranz, Bombardier ranked fourth in the world and first in North America for manufacturing subway cars, light-rail vehicles, monorails, and high-speed trains. Upon completion of the merger, Bombardier became the largest rail transportation equipment maker in the world, in addition to the third largest aircraft manufacturer worldwide. Rail transportation equipment accounted for roughly 40 percent of the firm's US$10.7 billion in sales in 2001. By 2004, the company reported US$16 billion in revenue from all divisions.

The Swiss/German joint venture ABB Daimler-Benz Transportation (Adtranz) led the world in railcar production in the late 1990s. Formed in 1996, Adtranz manufactured a complete line of railroad equipment, including railroad control systems, locomotives, high-speed trains, passenger trains, trams, subway trains, and people movers. The company operated in about 50 countries throughout the world with a strong presence in Europe and an expanding presence in Asia and South America. Bombardier competed with the likes of Boeing and Airbus in aircraft manufacturing.

In the fall of 2006, there was news of a Bombardier partnership with March Networks of Canada. The companies united to develop an advanced, onboard mobile security system for passenger railcars. It was set to become part of Bombardier's SEKURFLO product line.

Bombardier was happy to share updates reflecting the popularity of the light rail vehicles and trams of its Flexity family. Several cities ordered the advanced vehicle designs. Frankfurt am Main was notable among them with its order of 146 Flexity Swift vehicles. The transport operator Stockholm SL (AB Storstockholms Lokaltrafik) aimed to increase its Flexity Swift fleet of 22 bi-directional vehicles by another nine such vehicles. Delivery on the order was set for August 2008. The low-floor vehicles, 30 meters in length, carry a maximum of 212 passengers.

Alstom. Alstom was another of the world's leading railroad equipment producers. It was initially a joint venture between France's Alcatel Alsthom and the United Kingdom's Marconi plc. Alstom specialized in the production of high-speed train and power generation equipment including signaling devices. In the 1990s, Alstom continued to thrive, receiving major contracts to manufacture railroad equipment from around the world. Some of the company's key contracts included supplying high-speed trains for a Florida state transportation project and developing new trains for Amtrak in conjunction with Bombardier. Alstom also collaborated with the Korea High-speed Railway Construction Authority in South Korea's Supertrain project. Via a multitude of acquisitions, rail transportation operations at Alstom grew 12 percent annually between 1995 and 2000. In November of 2000, Alstom forged a joint venture with the Electro-Motive Division of General Motors Corp., one of the largest makers of diesel-electric locomotives in the world, to offer locomotive maintenance services on a global scale. Sales for all divisions in 2004 were US$20.5 billion. The firm employed more than 75,000 workers across the globe in 2004. Construction industry leader Bouygues owns approximately one-quarter of Alstom.

In March 2007, Alstom President and CEO Patrick Kron signed two contracts with the Chinese Ministry of Railways. They call for Alstom and Datong Electric Locomotives to supply 500 Co-Co electric freight locos for heavy haul routes. The first 10 Prima locos will be assembled at Belfort and Alstom will supply components for the next 190 to be assembled at Datong where the remaining 300 will be built.

PRO BAHN awarded Alstom its "Rail Passenger Award 2007" for its innovative and passenger-friendly trains. The award acknowledged construction of 42 electric multiple units of type ET 474.3 delivered to S-Bahn Hamburg in a consortium with Bombardier. The dual-current trains can be operated in both a DC network of surburban trains and the AC network of the long-distance trains. They are equipped with a lateral shoe gear as well as with a roof pantograph. The trains can obtain their traction energy either from a lateral third rail or from an overhead line.

Siemens. A diversified industrial company, Siemens AG was also a world leader in railroad equipment production. Based in Berlin, Siemens provided interfaces between the electrical and mechanical parts of a train's drive system, as well as between trains and railroad signal equipment. The company developed technology for freight, local, and long-distance trains. Moreover, Siemens built the world's largest electronic microcomputer interlocking system for the Dutch National Railroad. Siemens strengthened its position in the railroad equipment industry in 1996 with the acquisition of locomotive manufacturer Krupp AG and a joint venture with driverless train producer Lagardere Groupe. In 2004, the company reported overall sales of US$93.4 billion. At the turn of the twenty-first century, Siemens made significant inroads into Brazil, where its orders grew 36 percent between 1999 and 2000, and China, where it secured a US$22 million signaling and operation contract for a new metro line in Guangzhou. The firm also exported 12 light-rail cars from its plant in Sacramento, California, to Venezuela, marking the first export of new light-rail vehicles from the United States in 70 years.

Growth was evident by Siemens decision to expand its main light rail vehicle manufacturing facility. The company subsequently booked orders for propulsion systems on three major carbuilding contracts.

In April 2007, Siemens announced that the Spanish railway company Renfe would run its high-speed Velaro train on a line 650 kilometers. The world's fastest series production train was scheduled to travel from Madrid to Barcelona. Its design featured drive system components and technical modules in the Velaro mounted on the bottom of rail cars. The result was about 20 percent more passenger space than locomotive-hauled trains. Velaro sleeps 404 people in the three classes of Club, Preferente and Turista. A special feature allows seats to be rotated in the direction of train travel. Siemens agreed to deliver 26 Velaro trains to Renfe plus be responsible for maintenance during a 14 year period.

Trinity Industries, Inc. Trinity Industries, based in Dallas, Texas, is an industrial company with operations in five business segments, including railcars. In 2004, Trinity earned almost $2.2 billion in revenues, showing sales growth of more than 50 percent. By the third quarter of 2004 Trinity's order backlog was 19,800 cars, the company's highest since 1999. Trinity was the largest supplier of freight and tank railcars in Europe and in the United States. The company operated manufacturing facilities in Mexico and Romania.

Trinity Industries Chairman, President and CEO Timothy R. Wallace reported receiving orders for 10,012 railcars in North America during the second quarter of 2006. As a result, the company shipped 6,233 cars. On June 30, Trinity's backlog of undelivered cars was 29,320, an increase of more than 3,700 from March 30.

The Greenbrier Companies. Headquartered in Lake Oswego, Oregon, Greenbrier is a supplier of equipment and services to the railroad industry, primarily in North America, and manufactures and refurbishes freight wagons in the European market. The company owns a lease fleet of approximately 10,000 railcars. It also performs management services for approximately 125,000 railcars. In 2004, Greenbrier earned $729.5 million in revenue, an increase of more than 65 percent over 2003. In 2004, Greenbrier's Polish manufacturing company, Wagony Swidnica, was awarded a large order from the Iraqi Coalition Provisional Authority. The Polish company, acquired by Greenbrier in 1998, employed 900 workers in the lower Silesia region or Poland. Greenbrier was also capitalizing on emerging markets in China, entering into two long-term cooperation agreements with Chinese railcar maker Zhuzhou Rolling Stock Works. In April 2007, Greenbrier reported owning approximately 10,000 railcars and performed management services for approximately 135,000 railcars.

MAJOR REGIONS IN THE INDUSTRY

Europe. European railways, while seeing its share of the transportation market shrink over past years, still carries 30 percent of the continent's goods, as reported in the *Economist* in 2005. Railways from Eastern Europe were taking advantage of opportunities from legislation designed to bring new operators and private funding. European companies remained among top industry leaders during the mid-2000s.

German companies produced locomotives and train cars, as well as signal and track systems, making the country an important manufacturer of railroad equipment. The country's level of production sank in the mid-1990s after peaking in 1992. In 1996, German output remained about 28 percent below its 1990 level. Nonetheless, Germany continued to lead the world in exports of railroad equipment with US$1.2 billion of export sales in the mid-1990s. The country's primary customers included the Netherlands, the Russian Federation, Switzerland, China, and Hungary. Germany worked to expand its reach in China in the late 1990s. In the early 2000s, German and Chinese officials continued to work together to create a 26-mile, 340 mph maglev train, the first public transit system in the world to make use of maglev technology, in Shanghai.

Since railroad equipment is essential to French mass transportation and since one of the leading producers is based in France, the country plays an instrumental role in the global railroad equipment industry. Like other leading manufacturers, France's output dropped considerably in the mid-1990s. In 1996, France's output fell 29 percent beneath its 1990 level. Still, France ranked as the world's fourth-largest exporter of railroad equipment and the country recorded US$644.2 million in proceeds from its exports in 1995. The United Kingdom constituted the country's main market for railroad equipment, accounting for 45 percent of France's train exports with US$292.3 million. France also exported railroad products to Germany, Belgium-Luxembourg, Chile, and the United States.

In the early 2000s, France began to invest heavily in its rail-based mass transportation system. For example, the

Paris Transit Authority awarded Alstom and Bombardier a US$584 million contract to build 805 metro cars over several years; by 2005, the new cars will replace roughly 40 percent of the existing fleet operated by Paris Transit. In addition, the French National Railway hired Alstom to build 100 electric railcars for US$118 million.

China. China emerged as an important market in the railroad equipment industry in the early 2000s. Foreign competition began to make its way into the Republic as the market for imported goods began to open there. Along with its work with German officials on a high-speed maglev train in Shanghai, China also remained involved in the development of the Eurasia Continental Bridge, which will use roads and railways to connect Rotterdam, The Netherlands, to the Jiangsu Province of China.

Canada. Canada's role as a railroad equipment exporter increased rapidly in the 1990s, and the value of its exports almost doubled in just five years. Between 1991 and 1995, Canada's exports climbed from US$458 million to US$965 million, propelling Canada into its position as the world's second-largest exporter. By far, the country's leading trading partner in 1995 was the United States, with US$892 million worth of imports, accounting for 92 percent of Canada's exports. Other importers of Canadian railroad equipment included Turkey (US$35 million), the United Kingdom (US$11 million), Saudi Arabia (US$10 million), and Indonesia (US$4 million). The United States remained Canada's largest trading partner in the early 2000s. In 2001, Canada became the first North American nation to makes use of light-rail systems without trolley wires when Bombardier delivered three Talent diesel-electric light-rail vehicles to Ottawa, Ontario; service was scheduled to begin in 2002. Bombardier, the industry's top company, was actively working on contracts with developing areas overseas during the mid-2000s.

United States. Although the U.S. rail system is comparatively underdeveloped compared to those of Western Europe and Japan, railroad equipment production grew substantially in the 1990s. Between 1992 and 1995, the country's production level shot up by 54 percent, and between 1994 and 1995 it increased by 11 percent. Although the U.S. railroad equipment market expanded in the 1990s with the aid of a Congressional mandate to research and implement high speed train networks throughout the country, overall demand remained small. Therefore, U.S. manufacturers turned to other markets to sell products. The country's biggest markets in 1995 were Canada with US$548.7 million in imports and Mexico with US$67.2 million. In other trade, U.S. manufacturers targeted Chile, Romania, Swaziland, and Turkmenistan as strong export markets. In 1998, U.S. producers planned to ship US$30 million worth of railroad equipment to Chile and US$50 million worth to Romania. U.S. manufacturers also sought to supply railroad equipment to Swaziland and Turkmenistan, which were starting to develop railroad systems.

Reflecting a global drop in the number of freight cars manufactured during the late 1990s and early 2000s, the U.S. rail car fleet fell by roughly 19,000 cars between 1999 and 2000. The locomotive fleet experienced a more modest drop of 228 cars over the same time period. In the early 2000s, the nation bought roughly US$20 billion in railway equipment and supplies annually and employed more than 150,000 workers in more than 500 U.S. businesses. By 2005, manufacturing and transportation revenues were improving for the North American rail industry.

The Class I market was credited with driving growth as a result of the California Air Resources Board and Texas Commission on Environmental Quality regulations in urban rail yards. Furthermore, *Railway Age* Executive Editor Marybeth Luczak claimed the U.S. Environmental Protection Agency was another key influence on growth. Luczak believed that Tier 3 proposals, with a 2012 deadline, would be issued in 2007. Those regulations were expected to target the switchers.

Three companies involved in the "Responsible Care" program, the U.S. chemical industry's performance initiative to reduce emissions and improve worker safety, united to reduce emissions and improve worker safety plus work on a joint project team. The team focus centered around creating "next generation tank car" for transportation of highly hazardous chemicals. Dow Chemical, Union Pacific and Union Tank Car formed the trio.

Japan. Japan's railroad equipment industry emerged around 1917 when engine manufacturers such as Hitachi, Kawasaki, Osaka, and Mitsubishi produced the country's first domestically made locomotives. Japan quickly blossomed into Asia's leading manufacturer of locomotives, as well as a major supplier of railroad equipment to Asia and Northern Africa. In 1995, Japan was the world's fifth leading exporter of railroad equipment. Its largest external market was Egypt, which imported equipment valued at US$123.6 million. The United States imported US$70.0 million of railroad equipment, and assorted Asian countries bought about US$20.4 million worth of equipment. Japan has the largest railway system of any of the other leading economies. In the late 1990s, the Japanese government began working with Chinese authorities to establish the Japan-China Railways Council to facilitate the exchange of railway technologies, and to increase trade between the two countries. This work continued into the early 2000s.

FURTHER READING

"Alstom Receives Pro-Bahn Rail Passenger Award 2007." 16 March 2007. Available from http://www.railwaygazette.com.

"Alstom Signs Chinese Contracts." 1 April 2007. Available from http://www.railwaygazette.com.

Briginshaw, David. "Bombardier Addresses Overcapacity." *Railway Age,* June 2004.

"CAE on Track for Quieter Trains." *What's New in Industry,* November 2002.

"Chevron Products Co." *Traffic World,* 20 October 2003.

"China: Eurasia Network Links China with Outside World." *China Daily,* 14 January 2000.

"EPA Forecast: 69,000 New RailCars in 2007." *Railway Age,* March 2007.

"Flexity - Success Story in European Cities." 15 April 2007. Available from http://www.bombardier.com.

"Freight-Car Orders Climb in 2004: Builders Increase Pace of Deliveries, But Backlog at Recent High." *Trains Magazine,* February 2005.

"Germans and Chinese Compete for Metro Work; Rtico to Incorporate Foreign Assistance." *MEED Middle East Economic Digest,* 4 March 2005.

"Greenbrier and Boston Transit Announce Iraqi Freight Car Order for Poland." *PR Newswire,* 17 June 2004.

"Greenbrier in Chinese Freight-Car Deals." *The Journal of Commerce Online,* 15 December 2004.

Harrison, E. Hunter. "CN." *The Journal of Commerce,* 10 January 2005.

"Hoover's Company Capsules," 2007. Available from http://www.hoovers.com.

"Huffing and Puffing." *Economist,* 28 May 2005.

"Industry Outlook: Railroads Demand Limits on Hazmat Liability." *Railway Age,* July 2006.

"Industry Outlook: Tank Cars, the Next Generation." *Railway Age,* September 2006.

Judge, Tom. "Heavy-Haul Hammer Test." *Railway Age,* April 2003.

Kruglinski, Anthony. "A Veteran Railroad Supplier Looks Ahead." *Railway Age,* September 2006.

———. "'Bob the Carbuilder' Speaks Out." *Railway Age,* July 2003.

———. "Railcar Production: Looking for a Sign." *Railway Age,* September 2001.

Lazich, Robert S., ed. *Market Share Reporter.* Detroit: Thomson Gale, 2004.

Luczak, Marybeth. "Cleaner, Greener Locomotives." *Railway Age,* February 2007.

"New Railroad Freight Car Orders in North America Fell in the Third Quarter." *Traffic World,* 3 November 2003.

"Rail Update: Supply Briefs for Trinity Industries" *Railway Age,* September 2006.

"Siemens Grows in Sacramento, Adds Propulsion Orders." *Railway Age,* September 2006.

"Siemens: Innovation News." 5 April 2007. Available from http://www.siemens.com.

Simpson, Thomas D. "Will the Good Times Continue?" *Railway Age,* July 2006.

"2006 Freight Car Orders Soar." *Railway Age,* February 2007.

"Transit Briefs: Canada" *Railway Age,* October 2006.

U.S. & Foreign Commercial Service. "The Russian Railway Sector." June 2000. Available from http://www.bisnis.doc.gov.

Vantuono, William C. "New Power Plays to Watch." *Railway Age,* August 2006.

———. "Power Play." *Railway Age,* July 2000.

Wilkins, Van. "What's New in Rail Equipment." *Mass Transit,* September 2000.

TRANSPORTATION SERVICES

SIC 4500

NAICS 481

AIR TRANSPORTATION

Air transportation providers include commercial airlines that offer scheduled and non-scheduled domestic and international flights, airfreight transportation (air courier), and the operation of airports and terminals. For further discussion of commercial aircraft, see also **Aircraft Manufacturing**.

INDUSTRY SNAPSHOT

According to the International Air Transport Association (IATA), the worldwide air transportation industry served 1.6 billion passengers annually in 2004, a number that was projected to increase to 2.3 billion by the end of the decade. Likewise, employment levels were projected to increase from 28 million workers to 31 million workers during the same time period. In the freight segment, this industry transported two-fifths of the world's goods by value in the mid-2000s.

The industry staggered under post-September 11 declines in traffic and revenue. Many companies restructured, merged, or went bankrupt. The effects of Severe Acute Respiratory Syndrome (SARS) in Asia and the war in Iraq also caused a slowdown in passenger travel. In 2004, the industry was back up to pre-2001 passenger and cargo levels, with an industry profit of US$3.2 billion reported early in the year, despite soaring fuel costs. By mid-year, passenger traffic increased 20 percent and cargo traffic increased 13 percent. China and India were considered the countries expected to have the highest rates of passenger growth between 2004 and 2008.

Analysts were concerned that high and rising fuel costs would cause the industry to become unprofitable. The top three passenger airlines all reported losses for the year 2004. Air cargo services continued to experience growth, with industry leader FedEx showing a one percent growth in net income.

Growth also continued in the expansion of airports and terminals around the world, with many operating companies exploring the option of privatization.

Most major airlines sell tickets via Internet transactions—directly or through special travel Web sites. Many also use e-ticketing, designed to alleviate the risk for passengers of carrying—and potentially misplacing—a conventional paper ticket. According to *Forrester Research,* the vast majority of all airline tickets were issued online by 2003, with revenues for this activity totaling billions of dollars. The industry collectively was aiming to achieve total e-ticketing by 2007.

ORGANIZATION AND STRUCTURE

The global air transportation industry includes carriers of passengers, mail, and freight. Whether with single-engine or multi-engine aircraft, companies in this industry operate scheduled and nonscheduled air service over local, regional, national, and international routes. The industry is divided into three sectors: air passenger services, air cargo services, and general aviation.

Air passenger service includes scheduled passenger transportation, as well as support activities such as maintenance of aircraft; training of pilots, flight attendants, ticket agents, and ground crews; maintenance of computerized reservation and accounting equipment; and food preparation.

Air cargo (freight) services include transportation of mail, business and manufacturing commodities, food, and livestock. On a cost-per-mile basis, air cargo transport costs are higher than truck, water, and rail transport. However, sending freight by air allows shippers to reduce product inventories, handling costs, and warehouse expenses.

General aviation is the third segment of the air transport industry. This segment includes non-airline, nonmilitary aviation concerns such as fixed-base operators, flight schools, tour and recreational operators, and corporate flight departments. About half of all hours flown in general aviation are attributed to commercial activities or business aircraft. Such commercial flight activities include chartered passenger and cargo flights, sky advertising, crop dusting, and mapping for geographic information systems.

Business flying includes corporate and individually owned aircraft. Such aircraft account for about one-third of total flying time in general aviation. A variety of aircraft is used for business flying, including helicopters, single and twin engine planes, and jets, ranging in cruising speed from

150 miles per hour to 500 miles per hour. The flexibility of corporate and private aircraft allows salespeople, executives, and others who travel frequently to avoid inconvenient airline schedules and to access areas that are often difficult to reach by commercial flights.

ECONOMIC INDICATORS

There are three key measures in analyzing an airline's profitability:

- passenger revenues per revenue passenger mile, the total seats that are occupied by paying passengers on all flights flown multiplied by the number of total miles flown
- load factor realized, a measurement of revenue passenger miles divided by available seat miles
- operating costs per available seat mile, all compensation, fuel, and other operating costs divided by the available seat miles

Airline seats are counted among a company's assets. When an airline seat is not filled on a flight, that is unused capacity, and the potential revenue from that seat is lost. The break-even point for an airline is reached when approximately 60 percent of its seats are filled. Airline seats are basically commodity items today, despite companies' attempts to differentiate themselves in terms of on-time service, convenient routes and flight schedules, quality of food, and frequent-flier programs. Thus, price competition can be intense. When it is, airlines are often forced to operate close to, and sometimes below, the break-even point.

Fixed assets are also important to a company's profitability. Large capital investments are made in fixed assets, such as airplanes, computerized reservation systems, and baggage and cargo handling equipment. These investments often account for more than 60 percent of a company's total assets and can be purchased outright with cash, financed with long-term debt, or leased. Because airplanes and equipment are expensive, the importance of leasing for airline companies remained significant through the early 2000s. By leasing, airlines can reduce the cost of obtaining expensive equipment, such as the newest Boeing passenger jets (the 757, 767, and 777). Some leases are operating leases, in which required payments are shown in the notes of a company's financial statements. Others are called capital leases, which appear as both assets and liabilities on a company's balance sheet.

Operating costs per available seat mile also figure into airline profitability. A significant cost to any airline is fuel. A one-cent change in the cost of fuel can increase or decrease consolidated industry operating profits by as much as US$100 million. This is another reason airlines lease newer aircraft: these aircraft are significantly more fuel efficient and thus cheaper to operate. Other costs include salaries (often up to 40 percent of a carrier's costs), property and liability insurance, and swings in the overall economy. When the economy is strong, air traffic usually increases. If an unusually high number of accidents occurs in a year, insurance premiums can go much higher for many airlines.

BACKGROUND AND DEVELOPMENT

AIR PASSENGER SERVICES

Germany was the first country to offer air passenger service—doing so with hydrogen-filled dirigibles in 1910. In 1914 the United States became the first country to offer scheduled passenger service. However, it was difficult for airlines to profit by carrying passengers until 1925, when U.S. government subsidies enacted with the Kelly Air Mail Act helped companies like United, American, and Delta make it through tough times. The companies' aircraft of choice, the Ford Trimotor, was a closed-cabin monoplane that could carry up to 15 passengers.

In the 1920s and 1930s, European governments were able to develop an extensive airline system. While airmail delivery was neither as sophisticated nor as efficient as in the United States, passenger services were actually more sophisticated. Great Britain had a commercial air route to India in place by 1929. What soon followed in Great Britain was a well-developed mail, freight, and passenger service to many foreign countries.

Such improvements were attributable, between 1920 and 1939, to significant advances in operations, navigation, weather forecasting, and aerodynamics that helped the air transportation industry grow by leaps and bounds. Europe, Asia, and North America were within reach upon the introduction of the DC-3, the first large modern passenger aircraft. Its significant features included metal construction, dependable and efficient engines, variable-pitch propellers, and a retractable landing gear.

During and after World War II, international passenger flight further developed. Longer-range, four-engine aircraft were built after the war. Passengers were more comfortable in the new planes' fully pressurized cabins. They were put at ease knowing that the airplanes were equipped with advanced instrumentation that usually allowed safe flight through storms and heavy winds.

By 1958, flight by passenger jet had become the most common form of long-distance travel, superseding passage on ocean liners and railroads. In 1970, wide-body jumbo jets began service. Passenger travel at supersonic speeds became available with the introduction of service on the French Concorde in 1976.

AIR CARGO SERVICES

In the years before World War I, many countries had used aircraft to deliver mail. After the war, air transportation services were developed. In 1918 the U.S. War Department provided the U.S. Post Office with planes and pilots, leading to the country's first scheduled air service. The Kelly Air Mail Act helped motivate private carriers to deliver mail under contract, often in open-cockpit, single-engine planes. The Air Commerce Act of 1926 hastened the development of radio navigation and airports by making government agencies responsible for the management of ground-based radar and terminal facilities.

The 1920s saw the dawn of the shipping of mail and commodities by air. A few firms offered all cargo schedules around the Great Lakes of the United States. In the latter part of the decade, U.S. automobile manufacturer Henry Ford developed a private airline to carry his company's freight. As larger aircraft came into service in the 1930s, the air cargo business expanded, but it provided much less revenue than passenger travel and mail delivery. Before World War II, cut flowers, fashion clothing, machinery parts, pharmaceuticals, jewelry, and live animals were common freight because of their high value, high perishability, or uncommon size. After the war, several all-cargo carriers were formed, mostly due to the worldwide thirst for goods of all kinds and to the advent of larger aircraft. Planes could actually carry tons of goods, from coal to construction equipment. Pressurized cabins enabled longer-range livestock delivery. By 1950, complete automobiles, heavy machinery, and frozen foods were common transport items. Advances in container technology enabled smaller shipments to be packaged in larger containers for easier handling and lower chance of theft. Worldwide delivery of overnight mail became a reality in the 1970s, with air cargo companies competing with national postal services for business.

GENERAL AVIATION

The growth of world economies after World War II led to the development of more formidable business and commercial flying in many countries. In the 1960s, single and twin-engine aircraft were produced with turboprop engines. Fully pressurized business jets allowed faster and more economical flight at high altitudes. Typical business aircraft seat up to 15 passengers and are flown by professional pilots.

REGULATION

The air transportation industry is regulated nationally and internationally. In 1926 the U.S. Air Commerce Act set standards for planes and pilots. That helped the development of commercial and civil aviation. In 1938 the Civil Aeronautics Authority assumed regulatory duties but was divided in 1940 into the Civil Aeronautics Board and the Civil Aeronautics Administration. Together, these agencies were responsible for setting industry regulations, accident investigation, airline development, and the enforcement of safety standards. In 1958 the Federal Aviation Agency took on many of these duties and also developed a standard military and civil air navigation and air traffic control system. The agency was renamed the Federal Aviation Administration (FAA) in 1967, becoming part of the U.S. Department of Transportation.

The National Transportation Safety Board assumed accident investigations from the Civil Aeronautics Board, which was disbanded in 1978. An additional body of the United Nations, the International Civil Aviation Organization (ICAO), was formed in 1947. It continues to be responsible for developing the world's navigation, safety, and dependability standards, as well as being the international body responsible for resolving legal issues.

In the mid-1940s, the U.S. government sought to create a global airline industry. The Chicago Conference brought the nations of the world together to achieve this goal. But the result was just the opposite. Other nations greatly feared U.S. carriers would dominate worldwide airline travel if operating rights and fares were determined purely by market forces. Thereafter, many nations protected their private carriers by instituting extensive controls over entry and pricing in international markets. The Bermuda Agreement between the United States and Great Britain in 1946 granted international operating authority only through bilaterally negotiated treaties. As a result, entry into international markets was greatly restricted: international traffic rights were only granted when full reciprocity between countries had been achieved.

The activities of the International Air Transport Association (IATA) also worked to delay free-market flying and industry deregulation. Members of IATA met periodically to set pricing standards for specified regions, which resulted in regional cartels that looked to IATA to set prices. IATA conferences regularly set tariffs that many international bilateral agreements had to account for. Pooling agreements were also anticompetitive. These agreements divided the revenues of two bilateral nation carriers equally, making sure one carrier didn't profit more than another. Competition was easily dampened in such an international climate.

The U.S. government became increasingly frustrated with the anticompetitive activities of IATA and the international airline industry. It opposed the 1955 IATA tariff schedule and the 1962 IATA proposal, which attempted to increase rates for roundtrip air travel. After many European countries proposed to ban all U.S. carriers from landing in their respective lands, compromises were made. This climate continued throughout the 1960s and into the 1970s. The United States believed a consumer friendly, competitive international market was best for the world. Other countries favored industry-centered, protectionist policies. Until 1978, the global airline industry was basically structured as a worldwide cartel. After 1978, deregulation, privatization, and bilateral treaties had completely transformed this segment of the world economy. Free-trade forces, rather than protectionist policies, ruled the international skies.

During President Carter's administration in the late 1970s, the United States cracked the uncompetitive hammerlock of the international airline industry by instituting three major initiatives: domestic deregulation, the "Open Skies Policy," and the IATA "Show Cause" order. Alfred Kahn, regarded as the father of U.S. airline deregulation policy, was appointed chairman of the Civil Aeronautics Board in 1977. He was a highly influential proponent of freer domestic airline markets. The pro-consumer, highly competitive stance that the United States advocated internationally was instituted at home through the passage of the Airline Deregulation Act of 1978. Route structures and price setting were now to be the decisions of the domestic carriers, not the U.S. government. A "hub and spoke" route system was quickly created, as well as the right to expand internationally. The U.S. carriers fine-tuned their domestic routes, which created a stronger link into their international flights.

The Open Skies Policy, otherwise known as the "Policy for the Conduct of International Air Transportation," resulted in treaties with 20 nations, increasing the number of agreements between U.S. and non-U.S. carriers. The strong, deregulated system in the United States was better able to handle an increase in international traffic. The "Show Cause" order weakened the ability of IATA to set international airline prices. This effectively ended IATA's ability to create and maintain international regional cartels. U.S. carriers increased traffic on the routes subject to the new liberalized agreements. They confidently decreased traffic on those routes that were more regulated. These actions by the U.S. government greatly encouraged other governments to adopt similar free market policies. In this way, the old protectionist order slowly faded away.

The increase in international airline competition was felt in several ways. The creation of more liberalized bilateral trade agreements gave U.S. airlines greater access to many international markets. The number of international gateways increased, as did the level of competition. The location of the gateways also changed. For instance, in the U.S.-European market, the traditional gateway of New York in 1976 gave way to new inland gateways such as Atlanta and Dallas by 1988. These new gateways were also a good way for U.S. airlines to gain competitive advantages over the European carriers. U.S. carriers also established hub systems in certain locations, making them formidable competitors not just to domestic rivals but also to their foreign counterparts. For example, American Airlines is dominant in Dallas, Delta in Atlanta, and United in Newark.

There has been a shift in the competitive struggle among U.S. carriers for international traffic as well. Before U.S. deregulation in 1978, carriers such as Eastern, Pan Am, and TWA were allowed by the U.S. government to establish strong international routes at the expense of weak domestic routes. Conversely, American, Delta, and United were permitted to develop their domestic routes at the expense of weaker international ones. U.S. policy at the time was not to let any carrier have a competitive advantage in both domestic and international routes. After deregulation, the domestic carriers with strong, established routes in the United States made attractive partners to foreign carriers who were eager to sign bilateral route agreements to gain access to the U.S. market. The stronger, larger domestic carriers, specifically American, Delta, and United, retained their domestic hub and spoke systems. Freed to establish domestic systems after 1978, U.S. international carriers now appeared less attractive to potential foreign partners and were a less competitive force internationally. Lacking a strong series of national routes, such as the hub and spoke system developed by the national airlines, the U.S. international carriers were not able to feed their international routes. The result was that the strong U.S. domestic carriers bought the international routes of their more international or regional siblings, such as TWA, Eastern, and Pan Am. Unfortunately, it was not soon enough to avoid the bankruptcies of the latter two carriers. The shifting and reinvestment that took place within the United States for rights to international markets increased the international competitiveness of U.S. carriers as a group.

In response to Carter administration policies, other nations agreed that government ownership and protectionism placed their carriers at an international disadvantage. Chile and New Zealand deregulated domestic airlines soon after U.S. changes. Canada followed in 1988, with Australia, South Korea, and Japan deregulating in 1990. In 1987 Europe implemented a three-year plan to increase international service by developing access routes to regional airports for commuter carriers within the European Community.

In 1995 the International Chamber of Commerce (ICC) reported that of 150 airlines worldwide, 70 had majority government ownership, 60 had no government-held shares, and 20 had minority government ownership. It was clear that privatization of international carriers proceeded apace and was another solution to the problem of inefficient operations. Airlines often became more competitive being relieved of the burdens of state-run management and with new, previously unavailable access to capital markets. The trend in late 1980s and throughout the 1990s was clear: in general, governments increasingly relinquished control over their airlines by selling off all or part of them to private investors, many of them non-nationals.

Complete privatization of British Airways and Japan Air Lines became a reality in 1987, as it had for Mexicana in 1988 and Air Canada in 1989. In 1992 the Netherlands reduced its share of state ownership in KLM from 55 percent in 1986 to 38 percent. Lufthansa's share of state ownership fell from 65 percent to 51 percent in 1989. Brazil trimmed its holdings in VASP, and similar programs have been underway for SAS, Sabena, Alia, Sudan Airways, Air-India, Pakistan International, and Air New Zealand. As of 2001, there was an extensive list of airlines awaiting full or partial privatization, including carriers from Europe, Latin America, the Caribbean, and Africa.

In 1995, the International Chamber of Commerce saw fit to recommend that in all countries, state aid to airlines be absolutely minimized. The ICC asserted that state ownership or assistance had typically distorted the market and was detrimental to airlines and users, that government shareholders were often meddlers in management issues, that state aid now must be strictly limited in time and scope, and that state aid should otherwise be available only in very exceptional circumstances and on a transitional basis.

Still, in the late 1990s, outside the United States, partial or majority state ownership remained the rule, not the exception—certainly in Asia, Africa, the Middle East, and Europe. In 1995 in the European Union, five major carriers had government holdings of between 90 and 100 percent. Several important Asian airlines were owned by the government to the tune of 55 to 100 percent of shares.

Mergers, brought about by deregulation, strongly influenced the international airline industry. In the United States, increased concentration resulted from mergers among the following: USAir and Piedmont, Northwest and Republic, TWA and Ozark, American and AirCal, USAir and PSA, Continental and Frontier and People Express, Texas Air and Eastern, and Delta and Western. U.S. hubs were strengthened by this concentration, which appeared also to be the impetus for a number of mergers outside the United States: British Airways and British Caledonian, Swissair and Crossair, British Airways and Brymon Airlines, Lufthansa and Interflug, KLM and NLM Cityhopper and Netherlines, Transavia and Martinair, and Air France and UTA and AirInter and TAT.

Strategic alliances grew in the international airline industry, as many firms pursued economies of scale and scope while retaining a domestic status. In 1995, 136 airlines worldwide had formed more than 280 alliances, whether involving joint sales and marketing, joint passenger and cargo flights, code-sharing, joint frequent-flier plans, management contracts, catering, or joint ventures to handle maintenance and cargo handling.

British Airways and United created a joint marketing program in which they shared price promotions, gate space, and codes. British Airways also established an alliance with Air Russia, a new carrier that would serve Europe, Moscow, North America, and Asia. Schedules, marketing, and even managers were shared between Lufthansa and Air France to protect their market shares.

Cross-holding arrangements and minority ownership between international airlines had also developed since the U.S. initiatives of the late 1970s. Some of them included Air New Zealand (20 percent owned by Quantas, 7.5 percent by American, 7.5 percent by JAL); America West (20 percent owned by Ansett); Austrian (10 percent owned by Swissair, 10 percent by Lufthansa, 1.5 percent by Air France); Continental (18.4 percent owned by SAS); Delta (5.7 percent owned by Singapore Airlines, 5.7 percent by Swissair), Lan Chile (30 percent owned by SAS), Northwest (11.1 percent owned by KLM); and Sabena (20 percent owned by KLM, 20 percent owned by British Airways).

Computerized reservation systems (CRSs) give significant competitive advantages to their owners. They have been increasingly used as strategic weapons in the war for passengers by restricting access and display of industry information in certain markets. Carriers individually too small to develop their own CRSs have banded together to form them. Five carriers in Asia—Cathay Pacific, China Airlines, Malaysia Airlines, Singapore Airlines, and Philippine Airlines—created the Abacus CRS. Air Canada and Canadian Pacific consolidated their CRSs to create the Gemini system, which interfaces with United's Apollo system. Lufthansa, Air France, SAS, Iberia, and seven other carriers developed Amadeus. British Airways, KLM, Alitalia, Aer Lingus, Swissair, and four other carriers formed Galileo. USAir and four of the Galileo carriers also bought a half interest in United's Apollo, later absorbed by Galileo.

Hubbing was increasing in the international airline industry, and it has roughly followed the experience of the U.S. domestic market. Hubs are like a wheel and spoke system on a bicycle. Each carrier funnels its routes (spokes) into a group of major regional airports (hubs) that are strategically placed within the country. Direct flights between small cities are mostly eliminated in favor of flights to major points, the hubs, that later provide a route to other destinations. Most carriers have kept their hubs unattractive to competitors by operating what could be called near-monopolies; the competition has generally been among hub locations. Carriers that dominate certain hubs have more power over pricing, landing slots, and gate spaces than carriers that merely service the particular location with a few daily flights. Large economies of scope and scale can be generated by having multiple hub locations, and this trend has led to increased globalization of the international airline industry.

Some factors remained to inhibit the competitiveness of the international airline industry. Capacity constraints—caused by not enough landing slots, slow growth of additional airports, and shortages in air traffic control systems—caused barriers to entry that impeded further competition and improved the prospects of monopoly power. International traffic rights that favor some carriers over others were also an anticompetitive factor—carriers with access to tightly restricted markets often gained competitive advantages over carriers without favored access. Increasing antitrust problems generated from large mergers and alliances internationally were leading to more concentration of carrier power. Finally, the history of governments preventing free-market competition in favor of protecting their domestic carriers—or at least their "national" airline—through tariffs, bilateral agreements, landing rights, or price restrictions also threatened to return the industry to its historically anticompetitive status.

In the late 1990s, international airlines continued to move toward smoke-free cabins on both transatlantic and transpacific flights. In 1990 smoking was banned on all U.S. domestic flights except those to Hawaii, Alaska, and flights over six hours long. No-smoking policies were rapidly extending to all manner of commercial airline flights. Air Canada was the first airline to ban smoking on all of its international flights. In the United States, American, Continental, Northwest, TWA, United, and USAir were among the first to ban smoking on transatlantic flights. In 1995, Delta followed Air Canada's lead, banning smoking on all of its international flights and in all its lounges. Northwest banned smoking on its flights to London, Paris, Frankfurt, and Hong Kong. Quantas did likewise on its flights from North America to Australia and New Zealand.

Although some airlines acquired new planes to replace old ones, the industry consistently retained its older fleet. Most older jets wound up in the fleets of smaller, upstart airlines, increasing the industry's overall capacity and eroding profits. To combat unrestrained and imprudent capacity expansions, airlines around the world began to rely more heavily on their alliances. Ironically, no sooner had the prospect of much freer global competition emerged, than such alliances were found to mitigate the need for larger fleets. In 1997 United, Lufthansa, SAS, Air Canada, Thai Airways, and Varig formed the Star Alliance, which worked cooperatively toward their individual objectives. Other alliances included Delta, Swissair, Sabena, Austrian Airlines, American Airlines, and British Airways.

The European Union (EU) implemented airline deregulation, which reached its final stage among the EU countries in April 1997. Government involvement in the airline industry of Europe had bred inferior service, bureaucratic management, high labor costs, and low productivity, according to many critics. Airlines in Germany and the United Kingdom quickly privatized to compete in the newly deregulated market and reaped strong profits quickly. But airlines in countries such as France and Italy continued to be largely state-owned and struggled in the new business climate.

Deregulation reduced the degree of government involvement in the industry and opened up EU markets to competitors from other countries. Though the industry had felt few dramatic effects of deregulation by 1998, new airlines emerged, and established airlines began moving into new markets.

In the late 1990s, because domestic and established airlines held a substantial advantage over newcomers—they had already carved out a market presence—and because of limited capacity at airports, competition was below most analysts' expectations. In addition, predation and a lack of new airplanes impeded the success of new airlines. Predation occurred when airlines intentionally lowered their fares to incur losses, forcing other airlines to lower their fares and incur losses, too. Since the larger, incumbent airlines had more ample capital, they sometimes drove new entrants out of business in this way.

Deregulation projects also began in Asia in the late 1990s. Japan overturned its long-standing policy and permitted new airlines to form and compete in the Japanese market. However, the country's flight slot shortage left newcomer Skymark with few flights to offer. Furthermore, Japan Airlines started a bargain subsidiary, which increased Skymark's competition. Meanwhile, with the sale of 33 percent of its shares in 1997, China Eastern became China's first publicly traded airline. China Airlines then announced it would sell off part of its shares that were owned by the government. However, the financial crisis in Asia during the late 1990s negatively impacted the airline industry and, with it, deregulation. With bad debt and depreciating currency haunting the region in 1997, Asian airlines reported a 24 percent drop in profits. South Korea's Korean Air Lines led the way with US$700 million in losses.

Some of the key concerns the industry grappled with in the early 2000s included safety, security, and competition. Two crashes in the United States, the country with the largest airline industry, thrust the first two issues onto center stage. In 1996 the crash of Valujet flight 592 in the Florida Everglades led to greater scrutiny of less well-known carriers by the Federal Aviation Administration (FAA). ValuJet had to suspend its flights for three months, undermining the low fare and bargain segment of the industry. Moreover, the FAA increased inspection of small airlines, created new regulations for outsourcing maintenance, and ordered the industry to install smoke detectors and fire extinguishers in cargo compartments.

Later that year, the explosion of TWA Flight 800 shortly after takeoff from John F. Kennedy Airport in New York raised suspicions of terrorism and brought about implementation of a number of expensive and time-consuming preventive measures. The airlines were forced to begin running some luggage through costly and sophisticated explosives detectors. The TWA disaster also started them on the road to matching all baggage pieces on domestic flights with their respective ticket holders. After September 11, 2001, these measures were put on the fastest track possible. Ultimately, investigators concluded that a fire in the fuel tank was responsible for the crash of TWA flight 800. In May of 2001, the FAA issued a new rule that required significant changes in how airplane fuel tanks are designed, maintained, and operated in an attempt to prevent another such explosion.

In spite of publicity about crashes, calls for more competition and new entrants rang out steadily in the late 1990s and early 2000s. Members of Congress and the U.S. Department of Transportation suggested that the industry needed more competition from new airlines. However, small U.S. airlines such as ValuJet, Air South, and Vanguard remained unprofitable in the mid to late 1990s. In Europe, on the other hand, new airlines began sprouting up after a wave of deregulation throughout the region. Of these new entrants, Belgium's Virgin Express was one of the most successful.

The airline industry's success strategy has been to increase traffic faster than capacity and to expand unit revenues faster than costs. However, by 2001 a recession had taken hold of the U.S. economy and recession persisted in Japan and certain other Far Eastern countries. World airline profits were in decline well before the terrorist attacks of September 11, 2001, mainly due to shrinking global demand for air travel and the industry's efforts to increase capacity before achieving an increase in traffic. For the 270 airlines belonging to the International Air Transport Association (IATA), 2001 saw the first year-to-year decline in traffic since 1991. With the lower traffic, profits declined.

In the aftermath of the September 11, 2001, terrorist attacks, the U.S. airline industry's security measures were scrutinized, and they were found lacking, especially for domestic flights. Congress reacted by creating the Transportation Security Administration (TSA) in late 2001, primarily to put new security measures into U.S. airports. Former Secret Service Director John Magaw was appointed as the head of this new agency, which took control of U.S. airport security in 2002.

By the middle of 2003, all commercial airplanes were required to have more secure cockpit doors. During the transition time, locks and security bars were added to most cockpit doors and movement to and from the cockpit was restricted. However, a bid by U.S. airline pilots to arm themselves with handguns was rejected by the TSA in May of 2002. According to the TSA head, as quoted in *Airwise News,* "Specially trained air marshals should be the only armed officers on board." Although the number of air marshals flying on U.S. flights is increasing, there will never be a marshal for every flight.

Taking all accident causes into consideration, according to the IATA, by the mid-2000s the rate of airline accidents had been reduced by more than half since the mid-1980s. In addition, new aircraft were 75 percent quieter and 70 percent more fuel-efficient than the first wave of commercial jet aircraft. Some 1.6 billion passengers and 40 percent of the world's freight was carried by the air transportation industry in the mid-2000s.

Initiatives such as the U.S. open skies agreements further strengthened and promoted global airline alliances. The United States negotiated a number of open skies agreements beginning in the mid-1990s. This liberalized air traffic with Asia and Oceania, as well as between the United States and South America and Europe. The United States provided an antitrust exemption and a code-sharing clause in those agreements to make them more palatable to other nations. In August 2004, China's Civil Aviation Administration signed an agreement with the U.S. Department of Transportation, which had the potential to be an open skies agreement in 2006, adding 14 passenger flights each week between the two countries.

CURRENT CONDITIONS

In April 2005, Giovanni Bisignani, Director General and CEO of the International Air Transport Association, announced at the Air Finance Conference in New York that high fuel prices were making the air industry unprofitable. "The fuel bill has risen from US$44 billion in 2003 [to] US$63 billion last year. If oil averages at US$43 per barrel for 2005, the bill will be US$76 billion. And that would leave us with an industry loss of US$5.5 billion for 2005 and over US$40 billion for the period of 2001 to 2005," said Bisignani. He further stated that labor costs accounted for 18 percent of operating costs in Asia and 38 percent in the United States, costs that were very difficult to reduce. He indicated the need for the industry to eliminate complex technical processes that did not add value to the consumer. For example, he estimated that e-ticketing could save the industry US$3 billion per year. Further, Bisignani noted that in the U.S., taxes on tickets had risen from 7 percent in 1972 to 26 percent in 2004, and the industry was being burdened by US$5.6 billion in costs related to security measures. He stated the need for governments to allow the air industry to act in a more global business manner, allowing cross-border capitalization and mergers.

The privatization of airports was expected to continue. In 2004, Toyko's Narita Airport Authority privatized. Hong Kong, Thailand and India were also studying the possibility of privatizing airports.

According to IATA statistics for the year to date ended February 28, 2005, passenger traffic had grown 7.3 percent, with all global regions reporting growth. Much of this growth was attributed to the recovery after the impact of Severe Acute Respiratory Syndrome (SARS) in 2003, economic expansion, and intense competition driving down prices for consumers. Growth in passenger traffic was strongest in Latin American (13.6 percent), Africa (11.2 percent), and the Middle East (11.1 percent). However, China and India were considered the countries expected to have the highest rates of passenger growth between 2004 and 2008. The Asia/Pacific region showed growth during 2004, but at a much slower pace than other regions due in part to the effects of a devastating earthquake and resulting tsunami that took the lives of at least 126,000 people and left 800,000 homeless. Global growth for the period 2004 to 2008 was expected to be 6.0 percent annually.

In 2005, the industry was still dealing with the increased security requirements resulting from the September 11, 2001 terrorist attacks. Having met the requirements for strengthened cockpit doors, and new restrictions to items allowed on-board aircrafts, the industry was still working to balance data privacy issues with the requirements by many nations to supply passenger data and was also working at ways to streamline the requirement for baggage screening.

In terms of air cargo, the IATA reported that this sector had a 6.5 percent annual growth rate by the end of February 2005, with the Middle East showing a 17.6 percent growth rate, while Latin America showed a decline of 2.7 percent. Despite this growth, rising fuel costs were expected to negate any resulting growth in profits. The growth rate for this industry was expected to be 6.0 percent annually between 2004 and 2008, with China and India again expected to be the areas with the most rapid growth.

In all, global air traffic for all purposes increased by 15 percent in 2004, but hull loss (the statistic used to monitor air accidents) declined, making the year the safest on record. The IATA was working to increase this decline to 25 percent by 2006 through the implementation of its IATA Operational Safety Audit, the first global standard for safety audits.

In April 2005, thousands watched as the largest passenger jet, the Airbus A380, took off for its maiden test flight. In December 2004, it was announced that the project was US$1.9 billion over budget. Airbus, owned by European company EADS and the U.K.'s BAE Systems, had secured 154 orders by the time of its test flight, and claimed to need 250 orders in total to break even. Airbus determined that future growth would come from having large planes that could offer passengers cheaper seats on flights to major international cities. Its U.S. rival, Boeing, had determined that the future was in short-haul flights and so decided to concentrate on mid-sized aircraft.

RESEARCH AND TECHNOLOGY

In the late 1990s, Boeing Corporation debuted the world's largest twin-engine jet, able to fly 4,000 miles and to carry upwards of 370 passengers. Called the 777, its engines were as large as the diameter of a 737 jet fuselage. The 777 represented the last new airliner production design of the twentieth century. The jet cost Boeing US$4 billion to develop and was the largest commercial project the company had undertaken since building the 747 twenty-five years earlier.

The 777 was designed with the help of United Airlines, All Nippon Airways, and British Airways and was flexible enough that passenger seating, galleys, and toilets could be moved by airline employees to meet the cabin needs of particular routes. The new aircraft was also the first to be totally designed by a computer. Design engineers, tooling specialists, and production experts used computer-aided design essentially to pre-assemble prototype aircraft online. Using this new technology, expensive reworking of the aircraft was virtually eliminated.

In the early 2000s, Boeing began vying with the European consortium Airbus Industrie to build a super jumbo jet capable of flying more than 500 passengers at a time. The increased demand for international travel in the late 1990s, coupled with the shortage of landing spots at crowded airports, especially in Asia, added to the pressure placed on manufacturers to design bigger planes that, by containing more passengers, would place fewer traffic demands on airports. However, there was less attention paid by Boeing and other manufacturers to building a next-generation supersonic passenger aircraft, especially after the crash of an Air France Concorde in July 2000 outside Paris, which killed 113 people. Officials said they believed a metal strip on the runway ruptured a tire and sent debris hurtling toward the fuel tank, triggering a fire and a fuel leak. The metal strip was believed to have come from another jet. After the crash, all Concordes, including those owned and operated by British Airways, were grounded for more than 15 months in order to be revamped for greater safety.

In November 2001, the Concorde, the world's only supersonic jetliner, returned to the skies. The event was a badly needed morale booster during one of the worst slumps in the history of aviation, due to the September 11 attacks on the United States. The revamped Concordes sported fuel tank liners of bulletproof Kevlar, a flameproof reinforced undercarriage, and newly designed, extra tough radial tires—all added to prevent a recurrence of the earlier catastrophe. But the Concorde never recovered financially, and both British Airways and Air France retired their planes in 2003, citing both technical and economic reasons.

Advances in satellite technology were also making air travel safer, quicker, and more profitable for both transatlantic and transpacific carriers. The global positioning system (GPS) is a receiver technology that the U.S. military began using in the early 1980s. This technology was used to improve commercial air navigation. A new satellite navigation system was designed to increase the capacity of airports in Asia, where, in the late 1990s and early 2000s, air travel was increasing faster than in any other part of the world. Traffic in Asia was expected to double from 1995 to 2005, with growth catalyzed in this region by the retirement of out-of-date air traffic control systems.

Current GPS systems keep aircraft separated by 60 miles over the Pacific—12 times the minimum distance required over land. When air traffic is heavy, many flights have to be diverted, which wastes fuel and time. With GPS, airplanes are seen by groups of satellites in orbit; pilots know the exact location of their own and other aircraft. Utilizing this system, a plane can more safely travel the shortest distance between two points instead of traveling a predetermined flight path that would take it hundreds of miles out of the way. Precision landings will be easier at airports that don't have a full complement of instrumentation or equipment. Flights over China and Russia also became safer and faster.

A GPS network for the United States began full operation in 1997. GPS receivers are already being used by boaters, surveyors, and delivery drivers to pinpoint positions based on satellite radio signals. The U.S. system is expected to enhance the nation's radar system, helping pilots to land more easily in bad weather and to fly straighter routes between cities.

WORKFORCE

In 2002, the air transportation industry employed approximately 559,000 people in the United States. Although the jobs with the highest profile are those of pilots and flight attendants, 34.3 percent of the total number of people working in this industry were in office and administration support functions. Pilots, copilots and flight engineers made up 11.9 percent of the workforce, while flight attendants accounted for 17.4 percent. The remainder filled an array of jobs including mechanics, cargo handlers, and cleaners. The median annual salary for a pilot in 2002 was US$126,840, while a flight attendant earned a median of US$43,200 and a cargo handler earned US$23,890. CollegeGrad.com was predicting that salaries would increase by 12 percent in the period between 2002 and 2012, slightly lower than the 16 percent expected for all industries combined.

In the wake of the terrorist attacks in New York and Washington on September 11, 2001, U.S. military forces, principally National Guard troops, were immediately dispatched to assist existing airport security personnel in their duties. Within several months, however, once new, stricter screening procedures were in place, those forces became far less visible. Meanwhile, Congress took away the responsibility for airport preflight and security screening from the airlines and placed it with a new Transportation Security Agency (TSA). The TSA, with an expected workforce of 35,000 to 40,000 employees, was predicted to be the largest U.S. government agency begun since the 1960s. However, Congress also provided that within three years of the new TSA security inspectors commencement of duties, airlines might be permitted to go back to their previous methods of contracting out screening/security services.

A source of contention in the U.S. airline industry is the FAA's 35-year-old policy requiring pilots of commercial aircraft with 30 or more seats to retire once they reach the age of 60. This policy was justified in part by a 1981 National Institutes of Health study that found pilots had a much higher accident rate after age 60. Airline pilots, including the Professional Pilots Federation, have challenged the findings and counter that they have to pass physical examinations every six months. Pilots in the federation believe this is an age discrimination and civil rights issue, that they shouldn't be the only group of employees in the United States forced to retire upon reaching a certain age. The FAA has been criticized in previous years about the policy, but U.S. courts often defer to the agency to set its own standards. Great Britain and other countries have raised age limits from 60 to 65, the FAA's own pilots are allowed to fly past 60, and small commuter airlines in the United States allow pilots to fly past 60.

On the other hand, the Airline Pilots Association, the United States' largest pilot union, has supported the FAA's rule since 1980. A spokesperson for the union agrees that 60 is an arbitrary cutoff but said that the early to mid-60s is the appropriate range for mandatory retirement because of the demanding career and lifestyle of a pilot.

Salaries remain a hot issue in the industry. Within days after the terrorist attacks of September 11, 2001, travel traffic dipped significantly, and large airline layoffs followed. This put downward pressure on salaries that had already been cut in the previous few years. A major operating cost of any airline, salaries can represent more than 40 percent of total airline costs. Many of the world's major carriers are unionized. Before deregulation, carriers were willing to let the unions bargain for higher salaries and benefits because they could pass on such higher costs to the flying public as higher fares. Since deregulation, however, many airlines have realized that they cannot operate competitively within such higher salary structures, especially when competing against non-unionized regional and discount carriers. The airlines have tried to hire new employees at lower rates; they have granted stock options and other incentives to existing employees in lieu of higher salaries; and they have sometimes filed for bankruptcy in order to renegotiate labor agreements.

In 1994, UAL Corp., parent of United Airlines, sold 55 percent of its stock to company pilots and machinists in exchange for US$4.9 billion in wage and productivity concessions to make it the United States' largest employee-owned corporation and the largest employee-owned airline worldwide. The buyout of UAL was an alternative to cuts in jobs and operations badly needed to enable the airline to compete with regional low-cost carriers.

U.S. government and labor leaders hailed this new level of employee control as evidence of a new spirit of cooperation between management and labor. Employees were given four seats on the company's board of directors. Management was prevented by contract from laying off workers or selling assets that would have a detrimental effect on jobs. In the late 1990s, similar airline/employee agreements were struck around the world. For example, Air France Group planned to sell shares to its employees as part of its privatization efforts.

The airline industry remained heavily unionized in some countries in the late 1990s, especially in North America and Europe. Company executives of airlines trying to restructure in deregulated environments have criticized unions. They argue that the unions' inflexibility interferes with the competitiveness and modernization of airlines. Nonetheless, unions continued to play a strong role in the industry. With the formation of global airline alliances, unions began moving toward global unionization. The Star Solidarity Alliance, representing 210,000 workers, formed after multinational airlines teamed up to create the Star Alliance. The International Transport Workers Federation (ITF) then coordinated the Union Solidarity coalition to benefit airline workers around the world through the sharing of information and strategies.

INDUSTRY LEADERS

FEDEX CORPORATION

FedEx, formerly Federal Express, specializes in overnight delivery of packages, documents, and heavy freight, and is the top express transportation company worldwide. With 2004 sales of US$24.7 billion, the company's 196,000 employees handle 6 million shipments each day to more than 220 countries and territories, using 671 aircraft to serve more than 375 airports around the world. It operates 10 express air hubs. Its delivery divisions include FedEx Express, FedEx Ground, FedEx Freight, and FedEx Custom. This company does not differentiate between revenue earned by air transport verses that earned through truck or other means. Net income increased by one percent in 2004, reaching US$838 million.

Founded in 1971, FedEx was originally conceived in a college term paper. In 1973, the company began service in 25 cities with a fleet of 14 small aircraft. In the mid-1980s, FedEx opened its European hub and generated US$2 billion in one year alone. In early 2000, FDX diversified into customs brokerage with the purchase of Tower Group International, a unit that eventually formed the core of a new subsidiary, FedEx Trade Networks Inc. The trading unit also provided trade consulting and international transportation and logistics services. In April, FDX changed its name to FedEx Corp., and the core express delivery business took on the moniker FedEx Express.

In 2008, FedEx will take delivery of the first Airbus 380 Freighter, with plans to have a further nine by 2011. The plane will be able to carry more than 330,000 pounds (150 metric tons) within 40,000 cubic feet (1,100 cubic meters) and will have a range of 11,100 kilometers (approximately 5,994 nautical miles).

BAA PLC

In 2005, BAA, the world's leading airport company, owned and operated seven of the largest airports in the United Kingdom, including Heathrow, the world's busiest international airport. The company also has stakes in or management contracts with 10 airports outside of the country, and manages the retail operations of two U.S.-based airports, Baltimore/Washington International and Boston Logan International. The company manages airport operations as a whole, including passenger and baggage screening, fire services, runways and lighting, catering, parking, and flight information systems. The company was privatized in 1987. By 2004, its earnings were almost US$3.6 billion and it employed 12,533 people.

After the longest public inquiry in the history of British planning, BAA was given approval to add a fifth terminal at Heathrow Airport. Prior to beginning construction, the company was required to build a railhead and steelbar factory in order to reduce the amount of construction traffic on local roadways. In addition, two rivers had to be diverted. When completed in 2011, the terminal will be able to handle an additional 30 million passengers. In April 2005, the company also created Global Airport Services to develop and operate duty-free retailing at non-BAA airports.

AMR CORPORATION

AMR Corporation is the parent company of American Airlines, the largest scheduled passenger airline in the world. With its regional carrier, American Eagle (the largest regional system in the world), AMR managed a total active fleet of 996 aircraft in 2005. Its 2004 revenues were more than US$18.6 billion, an increase over the previous year's amount of US$17.4 billion. However, employment levels fell 4.5 percent to 92,100 people, and the company reported a net loss of US$761 million.

American Airlines grew from the consolidation of companies owned by the Aviation Corporation (AVCO). AVCO, formed in 1929, acquired enough small transportation companies by 1930 to form a coast-to-coast network, which it called American Airways. In 1934 American Airways developed a more integrated route system and became American Airlines. By the late 1930s, American overtook United to become the leading U.S. airline. In May 1982, a plan for reorganization under the newly established AMR Corporation was approved at the American Airlines annual meeting. In 2001 AMR acquired the assets of TWA.

UAL CORPORATION

United Airlines, a subsidiary of the UAL Corporation, ranked second in the industry, despite its reorganization under bankruptcy protection in 2003. In 2004, the company had sales of US$16.4 billion but reported a net loss of US$1.72 billion. Headquartered in Chicago, United serviced 201 destinations worldwide in 26 countries and two U.S. territories, and employed 61,200 people, down from the 2000 level of 91,700 workers. In 2004, the company carried approximately 70.8 million passengers.

United began operations in 1926 as Varney Airlines, the nation's first scheduled service. Varney, along with Pacific Air Transport and National Air Transport, eventually merged with Boeing Air Transport, including Boeing Airplane Company and Pratt and Whitney. United Airlines was created as a management company for Boeing's airline division, becoming an independent business when Boeing Air Transport was dissolved. On July 12, 1994, stockholders approved the airline's plan to turn over 53 percent of the company's ownership to its employees in exchange for wage concessions. However, one of the major changes in the reorganization of 2003 was the transfer of company ownership away from the employees and the elimination of the employee ownership plan.

DELTA AIR LINES INC.

Ranked as the third largest airline in the world in terms of sales in 2004 was Delta Air Lines. However its US$15 billion in revenue was overshadowed by a net loss of more than US$5.1 billion, the highest ever for an airline in one year. As of April 2005, Delta provided air freight and passenger transportation services in the United States and 36 other countries. The company employed 69,150 and operated 845 aircraft, 500 of which it owned and 345 which were leased. Delta avoided having to seek bankruptcy protection at the end of 2004 after its pilots agreed to US$1 billion in concessions.

Delta was founded in Macon, Georgia in 1924. It was first named Huff-Daland Dusters. The world's first crop-dusting service, Huff-Daland was created to combat a boll weevil infestation of cotton fields. In 1928 C. E. Woolman and two partners bought the company and renamed it Delta Air Service. Their 1952 purchase of Chicago and Southern Airlines made them the fifth largest U.S. airline at the time. Delta began international service to Asia in 1987, and by 1989 international traffic provided 11 percent of their revenues.

JAPAN AIRLINES CORP.

Japan Airlines Corp. (JAL) is the product of a merger between Japan's leading airline, Japan Airlines Co., and its third largest airline, Japan Air Systems, completed at the close of 2004. With 208 destinations in 35 countries, the combined company posted 2004 revenues of approximately US$18.3 billion and employed more than 54,000 people.

Japanese Air Lines was formed in 1951 by a group of bankers led by Seijiro Yanagito. Until well after the end of World War II, the Allies didn't permit JAL to use Japanese flight crews, so the airline leased pilots and equipment from Northwest. In 1953 the airline was reorganized as Japan Air Lines, with ownership split 50/50 between the government and the public. JAL expanded quickly, covering Asia, Europe, and later the United States. In 1987 the government of Japan sold its stake in the airline to the public, ending nationalization of the air transport industry in Japan and opening overseas routes to JAL's main competitor, All Nippon Airways.

BRITISH AIRWAYS PLC

British Airways (BA), the second largest international scheduled airline in the world, earned US$13.9 billion in revenue in 2004 employing almost 52,000 people to fly more than 36 million people and transport 796,000 tons of cargo. At the end of 2004, the company's fleet included 293 aircraft.

British Airways was formed in 1935 as a merger of three private U.K. airlines: Hillman's Airways, Spartan Air Lines, and United Airways. In 1939 the airline was combined with Imperial Airways to form the state-owned British Overseas Airways Corporation (BOAC). In 1972 BOAC was merged with another state airline, British European Airways (BEA), to form British Airways. British Airways, in partnership with Air France, began offering supersonic passenger service on the Concorde in 1976. In 1987 the airline was sold to the public and purchased its chief competitor in the United Kingdom, British Caledonian. In 2003, British Airways retired its fleet of seven Concordes for technical and commercial reasons.

The airline sought and made alliances with airlines in Europe, Asia, and North America to increase traffic while keeping costs down. In the early 2000s, British Airways owned 25 percent of USAir and shared flight codes, frequent-flyer plans, and merged travel lounges, which reduced costs for both companies. By tying bonuses to profit performance, BA retained cost-conscious employees, who helped the airline increase productivity by 65 percent since 1985 and cut costs by almost US$950 million in the years 1994 to 1997.

AIR FRANCE-KLM GROUP

In May 2004, the first international merger of two major European airlines occurred when Air France acquired Dutch airline KLM. The merger was expected to make the company the largest in the world in terms of revenues, and the third largest in terms of passenger traffic. Each airline continued to operate separately and KLM remained in Dutch control with 51 percent of it voting rights held by the state and two foundations. This would enable it to retain its foreign landing rights.

Ranked second in Europe in the global air transportation industry was Air France Group, which resulted from the merger between Air France and Air France Europe, with US$13.7 billion in 2003 revenue. Headquartered in Paris, it had 200 destinations in 90 countries. In 1976 Air France began flying supersonic Concorde aircraft from Paris to Dakar to Rio de Janeiro. In 1977 it began offering Concorde service from Paris to New York. The company was founded in 1933 through the merger of Air Union, Société Générale de Transport Aerien, Compagnie Internationale de Navigation Aerienne, Air Orient, and Compagnie Aeropostale. The company was nationalized in 1945. The French government owned 99 percent of the company's stock until the late 1990s, when the government started selling it. Pilot and employee stock options diminished the government's share to 44 percent by 2003.

DEUTSCHE LUFTHANSA AG

Germany's Lufthansa, with US$22 billion in revenue in 2004, was the number three airline in Europe and the number two cargo airline worldwide. The airline moved 50.9 million passengers and 1.7 million tons of cargo and mail using a fleet of 377 aircraft. In March 2005, Lufthansa acquired Swiss International Airlines adding another 80 aircraft to the total fleet.

Deutsche Lufthansa (DLH) was created by the Weimar Republic in 1926 when it merged Deutscher Aero Lloyd and Junkers Luftverkehr. By 1931 DLH was Europe's most comprehensive air route network. Operations ceased after the war until 1954, when the Allies permitted Deutsche Lufthansa to recapitalize. Lufthansa started small, with only domestic routes. However, by 1958 it was flying nonstop between Germany and New York. Lufthansa gradually expanded its routes to include Cairo, Tokyo, Prague, and other world capitals.

An aggressive privatization and restructuring program helped it rebound from a 1991 loss of US$300 million to achieve profits of more than US$300 million in 1996. In the early 1990s, the airline faced declining yields, strong competition, and overcapacity in many markets. Long vacations, high wages, and short workweeks hampered productivity. However, management was able to consolidate many of its subsidiaries and holdings while also improving its relationship with labor. The government, which in those years spent heavily on reunifying with East Germany, didn't have the resources to prop up a failing airline. It agreed to a privatization program that reduced its holdings from 52 percent to 35 percent. The company reduced its costs by 15 percent and its head count by 17 percent through employee attrition, a new pension plan, responsible labor contracts, new information technology, and organizational changes. By these measures, Lufthansa managed to increase its productivity by 31 percent, modernize its fleet, and reduce its debt.

FURTHER READING

"Air Industry Information." 26 April 2005. Available from http://www.collegegrad.com.

"Airbus A380 Set for Maiden Flight." BBC News, UK Edition, 27 April 2005. Available from http://news.bbc.co.uk.

"Airport Executives Plead for More Time." *Airwise News,* 23 May 2002. Available from http://news.airwise.com.

"Bush Installs Magaw as Head of Transportation Security." *Airwise News,* 8 January 2002. Available from http://news.airwise.com.

"China, US Sign Air Traffic Expansion Plan." *Airwise News,* 2 August 2004. Available from http://news.airwise.com.

Draper, Deborah J., ed. *Business Rankings Annual.* Detroit: Thomson Gale, 2004.

"FAA Issues New Fuel Tank Rules." *Airwise News,* 8 May 2001. Available from http://news.airwise.com.

"Global Air Traffic Up 20 Percent." *Airwise News,* 28 July 2004. Available from http://news.airwise.com.

"Hoover's Company Capsules," 2004. Available from http://www.hoovers.com.

International Air Transport Association. "Industry Statistics," 2004. Available from http://www.iata.org.

———. "Press Releases," 2004, 2005. Available from http://www.iata.org.

"International Trade Statistics," 2003. Available from http://www.wto.org.

"Major Market Profiles (USA, Germany, France, and UK)." Euromonitor International. October 2004. Available from http://www.euromonitor.com.

Osborn, Graeme. "Freedom to Fly." *Flight International,* 11 March 2003.

Tait, Leonie. "US Airlines: Keepin' It Simple." 10 March 2005. Euromonitor International. Available from http://www.euromonitor.com.

"TSA Chief Rules Out Cockpit Guns." *Airwise News,* 21 May 2002. Available from http://news.airwise.com.

"Transportation in Canada 2003: Annual Report," 17 May 2004. Transport Canada. Available from http://www.tc.gc.ca.

Yang, John. "Securing the Skies: Secure Cockpits, Air Marshals Still in Future." *ABC News,* 7 February 2002. Available from http://abcnews.com.

SIC 4311

NAICS 4911

POSTAL SERVICES

The world's postal and package delivery services are performed primarily by government agencies, although increasingly, private sector corporations, sometimes categorized as courier services, perform similar services. See also **Trucking and Courier Services**.

INDUSTRY SNAPSHOT

The global postal services industry is one of the largest international networks in the world. According to the Universal Postal Union (UPU), by 2003, 96 percent of the world had postal service. Organizations with postal services operations—typically governmental bodies, but increasingly, non-public entities—handle billions of mailing items, including letters, packages, bills, and advertising, throughout the world each year. According to the UPU, in 2004 the industry employed five million people worldwide and handled more than 436 billion letters and parcels each day.

The level of mail volume tends to correlate directly with the overall level of economic activity in a country. Accordingly, a surge in growth within the postal services industry, especially in international mailing, has accompanied the increasing globalization of commerce. Many postal organizations have invested heavily to establish global infrastructures. Moreover, the concentration of this market sector has been opening up. While industrialized countries still lead this industry, developing countries such as China, India, and Brazil were increasing substantially in the mid-2000s.

Postal services in advanced nations face substantial challenges from competing technologies. Fax machines, electronic mail and messaging systems, electronic funds transfers, Internet-based services and electronic commerce, which reached a value of US$20 million in 2003, and other communications technologies have sliced into traditional postal business. In many regions, these technologies are in their infancy but guarantee increased competition in the near future. Stamps.com, for example, had more than 314,000 subscribers by the end of 2003, and 80 percent of revenues for the industry segment. Industry analysts and leaders agree that the future of postal services depends greatly on the rapid and efficient implementation of new technologies. Consequently, most of the world's advanced postal businesses are significantly revamping their organizations and expanding their research and development efforts to accommodate electronic correspondence and transactions.

ORGANIZATION AND STRUCTURE

Postal facilities range from enormous processing centers that handle several million items a day and employ thousands of people to small kiosks with one part-time employee. The efficient management of postal operations in countries such as the United States and Germany requires the organization of large transport fleets, extensive property management, the supervision of hundreds of thousands of employees, and the implementation and maintenance of advanced information technologies.

Some governmental postal organizations, like the United States Postal Service (USPS), are required by law to break even financially and thus use their "profits" as an impetus to implement new technologies and improve overall service. Typical measurements used to determine a postal administration's service level include the percentage of on-time deliveries, customer surveys, and the balance sheet. Because labor and transportation expenses constitute the bulk of a postal operation's operating costs, the search for labor-cutting technologies and efficiency management has been among the top priorities of postal service companies and agencies worldwide.

Postal delivery services feature three basic components: letters, parcels, and express. Letters are distinguished from parcels either by weight or by contents (documents versus goods, respectively). Express service includes both letters and parcels and is characterized by speed of delivery. Postal administrators generally have a monopoly on letter services, while parcel and express services are offered in competition with private carriers. The production process for postal services can be divided into five stages: collection, sorting for destinations, transportation, final sorting, and delivery of mail.

Postal administrators also offer financial services, which can be categorized as postal payment, such as money orders and postal orders; girobank ,including mortgage and foreign currency; savings bank; and other payments such as pensions, welfare services, licenses, and taxation. In some cases, postal administrators historically also have had authority over the telecommunications sector in their nations, but many industrialized countries were reorganizing their telecommunications services into separate entities.

UNIVERSAL POSTAL UNION

An enterprise as important and complex as the exchange of international mail requires a broad framework of rules and regulations among nations. In the mid-nineteenth century, most large European countries signed at least a dozen individual treaties for foreign mail. Given different currencies and units of measurement, these agreements required detailed accounts that were extraordinarily elaborate and perplexing. Indeed, at one point there were more than 1,200 different postal rates in effect in Europe.

In 1863 a conference held in Paris to standardize those agreements was attended by 15 European and American postal administrations. However, it became obvious that bilateral treaties between individual countries would not work and that a single treaty governing the international post was needed. In 1874 the representatives of 22 postal administrations met in Switzerland and signed the Treaty of Berne. Initially known as the General Postal Union, this international collaboration was renamed the Universal Postal Union (UPU) in 1878. It has retained this name into the twenty-first century.

In 2005, some 190 nations belonged to the UPU, which on July 1, 1948 became a specialized agency of the newly established United Nations. Any UN member state can belong to the UPU, which is funded through member contributions according to a variegated rate scale. Other sovereign states not belonging to the United Nations can join the UPU if at least two-thirds of the UPU member states assent. The UPU works together with other UN agencies and international organizations in order to carry out its objectives. Governed by the Universal Postal Congress, which performs legislative functions, and by two councils, the Postal Operations Council and the Council of Administration, the UPU set a strategic plan for 2000 to 2004. Approved by the Universal Postal Congress and known as the Beijing Postal Strategy, the plan's main objectives, in summary form, were:

- To ensure customers' global postal access for goods and messages;
- To make delivery services more reliable, secure, and efficient;
- To become more cost effective;
- To respond better to postal customers;
- To integrate technological, regulatory, and economic changes by reforming and developing postal services; and
- To increase collaboration among postal stakeholders.

In 2005 the countries of the UPU had more than 700,000 postal outlets and collectively delivered 430 billion mail items per year.

About two-thirds of national post offices worldwide also offered financial services, with 60 offering savings bank options in 2002. The UPU has a formal agreement to cooperate with the World Savings Bank Institute (WSBI). In situations where natural catastrophes or armed conflict have disrupted normal social life—including regular mail delivery services—the UPU assists by setting up humanitarian services and short-term arrangements to reconnect broken postal links.

In accordance with its mandate, the UPU was to create a single domain for exchanging postal items and for unobstructed freedom of transit within that domain. Each UPU member country has pledged to respect the inviolability of mail in transit and to convey it by the most rapid means of transport used for its own domestic mail delivery. UPU rules govern weight specifications, size limits, and conditions of acceptance for international mail. Historically, the UPU also standardized the basic rates that member countries could charge for delivering postal items within the union's territory. In recent years, however, its stated rates have been used as guidelines rather than fixed rules, and postal administrators have had more freedom to set rates for international mail.

The UPU also provides technical assistance for the modernization of postal administrations, especially those in the least developed nations. Aid includes recruiting and dispatching experts, granting vocational fellowships, and setting up national training schools for postal workers and management. Funding comes from both the UPU budget and the contributions of developed nations. The UPU has also promoted stamp collecting through the promulgation of a code of ethics and various other activities, including philatelic studies and the dispatch of stamp experts to postal administrations.

In 2006, approximately five years after establishing the Quality of Service Fund, UPU tapped into the Fund to underwrite 279 projects. Those projects were focused on improving postal services in developing and least advanced countries. Estimated costs were US$39.6 million. The UPU annual budget was approximately US$29 million with 60 percent of it being earmarked for projects in developing countries. Although most projects focused on one country, the QSF also had financed 13 regional projects allowing countries to pool their resources.

In March 2007, the International Air Transport Association and UPU agreed to collaborate on ways to "harmonize standards and procedures to improve coordination between airlines, postal administrations and third party handlers to pave the way for consistent and accurate reporting of mail movement status." Furthermore, the both bodies agreed to expand their usage of Electronic Data Interchange.

BACKGROUND AND DEVELOPMENT

The ancient Romans developed a highly efficient postal system, known as the *cursus publicus,* that served and connected far-flung possessions. Relay stations were placed at frequent intervals along the empire's roads, and men, chariots, and about 40 horses were kept at each station. According to some accounts, the messengers of these relay systems were so efficient that they could cover more than 170 miles in 24 hours—a speed not achieved again in Europe until the nineteenth century. After the collapse of the Roman Empire in the fifth century, this postal system decayed.

Relay systems with posthouses were first developed in China around 1000 B.C. and were also used extensively in the Americas by the Mayan and Incan civilizations. When Marco Polo visited China in the thirteenth century, he found a postal system far in advance of anything Europe had at the time. According to his account, 10,000 posthouses existed in China, with one placed every 25 to 30 miles. Besides numerous horsemen, foot runners lived in villages three miles apart. They wore girdles hung with bells to alert the relay runner waiting at the next station.

Increases in literacy during the European Renaissance and the invention of Gutenberg's printing press in 1450 gave new impetus for the creation of more widespread and more complex postal services. The trend toward more powerful nation-states, however, resulted in government-run systems that eventually displaced private carriers. In 1477, Louis XI set up a Royal Postal Service in France that employed 230 mounted couriers. In England, Henry VIII created a Master of the Posts position to maintain regular postal service along the main roads from London in 1516. Initially, these state-run services only served the government. Before long, however, the revenue-producing potential of postal services for public use was recognized.

Although states sought to keep their postal monopolies, keen entrepreneurs nevertheless found opportunities to introduce services that governments were not providing. As letter-carrying became profitable, private businesses sprang up to exploit the market. Most postal businesses were purely local, although some, like that of the Parr family in Austria, created nationwide enterprises. Under the patronage of the Habsburg Empire, the Taxis family built up the most famous, most extensive system. Their service grew throughout the sixteenth century until it covered most of Europe and employed nearly 20,000 couriers. The Taxis service lasted until the late nineteenth century in Germany.

In 1680, William Dockwra established a postal service in England that was more efficient than that of many cities today. He opened 450 receiving stations in different parts of London, and messengers called for mail every hour. Letters and packages were carried to sorting offices, and the hour of receipt and initial letter of the sorting office was stamped on each piece of mail. According to one account, as many as twelve deliveries were made each day in business districts, and four to eight daily deliveries were made in residential areas, resulting in huge demand. Two years later, however, the government sued Dockwra for infringing on the state monopoly and closed down his service—only to reopen it later, with no compensation to Dockwra.

The early nineteenth century publication in Great Britain of *Post Office Reform: Its Importance and Practicability* by Rowland Hill was a milestone in postal history. Hill's study demonstrated two crucial points: (1) The intricate rate system in place inflated costs by requiring huge amounts of paperwork and staff, and (2) The collection of money payments on delivery, another enormous cost, could be eliminated. Hill recommended that a uniform postage rate be instituted: a penny for each half-ounce, with a minimum of four pence. Further, rather than have the addressee pay the cost upon delivery, the sender would now be responsible, prepaying the cost by attaching postage stamps. The wisdom of Hill's proposals was quickly seen, and his reforms were introduced into the British postal system in 1840. Hill's ideas quickly spread to other countries, and both Switzerland and Brazil began issuing postage stamps in 1843. Hill was knighted for his efforts.

The advances in transportation technology that took place in the nineteenth and twentieth centuries profoundly impacted postal systems worldwide. As rail services became widespread, specially adapted railway cars became moving post offices for sorting and canceling stamps, thus greatly accelerating mail delivery. Regular airmail flights began in the United States in 1918, and the first regular international service, between Paris and London, was inaugurated a year later.

In many countries, post offices offer financial services to the public, often to the chagrin of private competitors. Until the early 1990s, many commercial banks ignored the threat of post office banks. However, when post offices started promoting financial services more aggressively, creating new customers and luring away bank customers, their attitudes changed. Post office managers invested in financial service operations to make up for lost revenues in mail-handling and telecommunications services, which slowly were being opened to competition, and to replace revenues lost in the worldwide transition to such technological innovations as electronic mail, electronic bill-paying services, electronic funds transfers, and e-commerce. Profitable financial services offered through post offices, however, garnered considerable criticism from the private sector in some parts of the world. Private bankers have protested that in many countries, postal groups are subsidized by governments and thus pose unfair competition, for example.

By the close of the twentieth century, the most crucial issues for national post offices included privatization and growing competition from privately owned postal delivery services such as the United Parcel Service (UPS), Federal Express (FedEx), DHL Worldwide Express, and Airborne Express. Many industry analysts noted that commercial pressures had caused a liberalization of the international mail market. At century's end, many public sector postal organizations were considering or actively shifting segments of their business to the private sector to more easily stave off competition from their private counterparts. However, while the European Union tried to usher its member states toward a more competitive industry, many nations appeared to be succeeding in slowing privatization efforts in order to avoid breaking up their post office monopolies. Nonetheless, given the enormous growth potential identified in this sector, the struggle for dominance among private postal corporations and their governmental counterparts continued to characterize the industry in the early twenty-first century.

The opposition of national post offices to greater competition was evident in actions various government-supported postal services took against private remailers. Remailers' services make economic sense when, for example, cost or quality considerations make posting mail to Holland from France rather than from Germany more cost and/or time-effective. To illustrate, a remailer could ship out mail from Germany to Holland in bulk, thus avoiding German postal charges, and then post all of the mail in France. State post offices tried to use the rules of the UPU to justify turning back incoming mail from remailers. The German Bundespost went further, claiming that a letter with a return address in Germany would have to be posted in Germany. Most governmental postal administrations, however, recognized the increasingly competitive atmosphere as an irreversible trend and took steps to branch out their services, thereby regaining market share previously lost to private competitors and increasing their own competitive standing.

Postal administrations at the start of the twenty-first century continued to face problems of competition from the private sector despite attempts by some government postal services to reorganize and, in some cases, to operate independently of the public treasury. The United States Postal Service (USPS) case exemplifies the constraints post offices may operate under in attempting to separate from national government control and to function more autonomously. In 1970 the U.S. Congress abolished the Post Office Department through the Postal Reorganization Act and simultaneously established the USPS, which began operations on July 1, 1971. However, the Congress left in place a host of regulatory and legislative restrictions. A Postal Rate Commission reviews prices. It retains full power to rule on any postal rate increase. The USPS was subject to vociferous Congressional opposition to post office closures and to the political power of hundreds of thousands of active and retired postal employees. Additionally, under the 1970 legislation, the USPS was required to continue to provide universal service. In other words, it was forbidden to allow any one class of mail or group of customers to subsidize another. On the other hand, subsequent legislation has allowed the USPS to enter into joint ventures, which the organization has taken full advantage of, setting up agreements with postal operations in a wide range of countries including Brazil, Chile, Mexico, Canada, the United Kingdom, China, and Japan.

In a concerted effort to update operations to meet increased competition presented by new technologies, many postal administrations have attempted to gain an edge on the market by engaging in cooperative arrangements with businesses outside the postal industry. The USPS, for example, made a landmark agreement around the turn of the millennium with Federal Express, one of its largest private competitors, by teaming up with FedEx to offer more streamlined express mail services with time-guaranteed deliveries. In 1997 the United Kingdom's Royal Mail, the letter division of the U.K. Post Office, entered into a joint venture with Microsoft Corporation to provide electronic mail service to its customers. The Dutch postal and telecommunications group, Koninklijke PTT Nederland, acquired TNT Express Worldwide, highlighting a trend that industry analysts expect to continue in coming years: the merger of European post offices with logistics companies.

Moreover, in order to combat intense competition, many national post offices have flirted heavily with privatization. The United Kingdom's Post Office, one of the nation's largest employers, was the subject of privatization considerations for several years. After planning to sell off substantial portions of Royal Mail and Parcelforce in the late 1990s, the British government decided that its postal operations would remain in the public sector. Germany, in contrast, went ahead with plans to privatize its postal bank, Deutsche Postbank. Switzerland's postal services implemented a major diversification strategy and heavily branched out its financial services at the close of the twentieth century. In addition, Italy's postal administration, which employed 200,000 at century's end but was viewed as one of Europe's least efficiently run postal services, prepared for a major transformation of its organizational structure by becoming a joint stock company. Industry analysts expect the trend toward privatization will increasingly affect postal services throughout the developed world.

CURRENT CONDITIONS

According to the UPU, in 2003, 96 percent of the world had postal service, with 81 percent receiving their mail at home and 15 percent having to collect their mail from a postal outlet. The remaining 4 percent without service were located primarily in Africa. Domestically, 424.5 billion letters were mailed, while 6 billion letters were sent internationally, although both numbers showed declines over the figures reported the previous year. Similar declines were seen in the number of parcels mailed, which was 4.4 billion domestically and only 47 million internationally. The area showing the most growth was in the delivery of items by express post. The number of items increased 6 percent in 2003 to 34.7 million items, with most of the growth coming from Arab and Asian Pacific countries.

Since the end of the 1980s, most postal services had been decreasing the number of outlets they had, resulting in a 15 percent decline in the total number of outlets during this period. By 2003, there were approximately 660,000 post offices around the world. Following this trend, declines in employment continued into 2003, at an average of about 2.1 percent per year to reach approximately 5 million employees in 2003, according to the UPU. However, the worldwide postal industry was showing increases in revenue, reaching levels of approximately US$265 billion by 2003.

Increasingly, postal operators have been expanding their product offerings to include logistics services; hybrid mail, where e-mail messages are sent to the postal outlet, printed out and then delivered to the recipient; and online services, including e-mail, e-commerce, and e-banking. Competition from new technologies was expected to continue, with the use of e-mail and cellular phone use and its related text messaging capabilities on the increase. Many postal organizations were also offering a variety of government-related services. Italy's Poste Italiane, for example, was using its customer access to offer passport application and immigration application services. Poste Italiane was reportedly the first European postal service to sell postage via the Internet. With approximately 14,000 branches by 2007, USPS announced plans to offer mobile phones and Poste Italiane-branded products plus its own call plans and services while running on the Vodafone network. It was similar to another Vodafone deal in Italy with French retailer Carrefour. In the United Kingdom, customers could pay their utility bills, purchase foreign currency, renew their car licenses, and purchase a variety of gifts and stationary at their local post office. There too, many post offices are also the local shop for newspapers, bread and milk.

Although by 2005 the handling of mail was still predominantly monopolized by governments, regulations were changing to allow competition into the market. For example, member countries of the European Union were scheduled to end the monopolies by 2009, allowing private carriers to enter the market by handling increasingly smaller postal weights. According to the UPU, by 2003, 94 percent of its member countries faced competition from non-public entities. In terms of domestic service, 80 percent had competition with letter mail, while 85 percent had competition with parcel mail. The numbers were higher in terms of international mail, with 85 percent facing competitors in letter mail and 90 percent in parcel mail. Many postal organizations were forming alliances with courier companies. For example, the USPS created an agreement whereby FedEx would handle the air transportation of mail, replacing the services offered by commercial airlines. FedEx's existing market knowledge and infrastructure offered advantages to both parties. FedEx also had shipping agreements with France's La Poste, and the Trinidad and Tobago Postal Corporation.

In the international mail market, industry participants expected most growth into 2008 to occur in Europe and the Commonwealth of Independent States (CIS), countries of the former USSR. Many analysts believed that China represented the greatest potential market for postal administrations. Due primarily to the country's massive population, rapid modernization, emergence as a formidable economic power, and reacquisition of the business center Hong Kong, China offered a lucrative future market to the world's postal organizations. Accordingly, many major international companies were continuing to invest in the Asian-Pacific region. UPS was overhauling its infrastructure in an effort to strengthen its operations, DHL Worldwide Express was expecting service increases of about 30 percent annually, and TNT Express Worldwide was purchasing transportation networks.

RESEARCH AND TECHNOLOGY

Perhaps the best way to understand the role of technology in postal operations is to follow a letter from pickup to final delivery in a highly automated postal system. In the advanced Canadian system, the process included the following steps:

- *Receiving*—mail is picked up from letter boxes and unloaded at the receiving dock of the nearest mail processing plant.
- *Preparing*—bags are opened and unloaded. Any undersized, oversized, or irregular items are segregated from standard letters.
- *Canceling*—at the processing plant, a canceller automatically faces the letter mail and cancels it with a date stamp.

- *Encoding*—a multi-line optical character reader (MLOCR) scans the postal code and compares it with the address to determine whether the code is accurate. An optical character reader (OCR) reads postal codes that are typed or laser printed. The MLOCR or OCR then applies vertical barcodes used to separate letters into sorting bins.

In some plants, if the MLOCR cannot read a postal code, a video encoding system (VES) identifier barcode is printed on the back. The image of the front is sent to a video-coding desk where a coder types in the postal code, which is stored in memory, and the letter is fed once more into the MLOCR. The MLOCR matches the stored postal code with the VES identifier bar, and the correct barcodes are printed on the front.

- *Consolidation*—the mail is consolidated for shipping to the downstream (processing for delivery) plants.
- *Dispatching*—mail going outside an area is transported via trucks, vessels, or airlines to the appropriate mail processing location.
- *Receiving*—mail is received at the downstream plant, primarily in containers inside larger bins from the originating plants.
- *Preparing*—incoming mail from the originating plants is grouped by delivery areas.
- *Sorting*—the letter sorting machine reads the bar codes supplied by the MLOCR and OCR. The machine directs each letter to one of many destination bins.
- *Dispatching*—mail is dispatched to stations and letter carrier deposits.
- *Delivery*—mail is delivered by letter carriers or via community mail centers, postal boxes, rural mail boxes, or general delivery.

Because postal service has traditionally required so many workers, introducing labor-saving technology is key to implementing efficiencies and controlling costs. Since most USPS expenditures go toward labor costs, automating the mailing process has been a major priority for that postal administration. Most emerging technologies are in the electronics field. For example, by the late 1990s, the USPS had developed a postal machine that could read up to 30 percent of handwritten addresses on envelopes, with hopes of increasing the success rate to 100 percent shortly thereafter. This project was the main thrust of a US$4 billion automation program at the time, aimed at eliminating thousands of letter-sorting jobs. The USPS, Canada, and France also participated in a cooperative agreement to test a new global electronic courier service, PostECS, which was anticipated to ensure the security of official documents transmitted over the Internet. To follow and trace mail through every step of its processing and delivery, post offices began using tiny radio transmitters, or tags, affixed to pieces of mail. In addition to these innovations, postal administrations have incorporated electronic certification, authentication, encryption, and even electronic postmarks into their already highly automated systems and procedures.

Even before the anthrax scare struck the United States, as well as Britain and Pakistan, in the closing months of 2001, the U.S. Mailing Industry Task Force, representing both public and private mailing enterprises, including the USPS, advanced several recommendations to improve security in the industry. These included the recommendation to create "intelligent mail," whereby "a unique, digital stamp for each piece of mail would make it possible to track and trace mail," according to the USPS's 2001 annual report.

With the world's major courier companies able to track packages through their systems, customers increasingly demanded a method of tracking and tracing letter mail sent by regular post. The USPS created the CONFIRM system by which mailers include two bar codes on their mail which then allow the customer to track where the mail is in the system.

Centre of Enterprises with Public Participation (CEEP) expressed concern about progress of European countries toward full liberalization. CEEP requested that the European Parliament and the Council guarantee "sustainable funding" along with its postal services directive based on the European Commission's October 2006 proposal. CEEP referenced a 120-page study conducted by Oxford-based consultancy OXERA and funded by nine public postal operators on universal service funding mechanisms in the postal sector. The study pointed to several regulatory policy questions that needed to be addressed before the market was fully liberalised.

WORKFORCE

Having reached its peak at the start of the 1990s, the number of people employed globally by the postal service declined almost 20 percent by 2003, from a high of 6.2 million employees to 5 million employees.

Around the world, labor-management relations have plagued the postal services industry and generated significant negative publicity. In January 2005, French postal workers walked out to protest the opening of the system to outside competition. In November 2004, postal workers in Belgium and Italy took part in a general strike to protest their governments' economic policies. The emphasis on higher productivity and cost saving has not helped labor-management relations in the postal services of many developed countries, including the USPS, which in 2003 employed more than 729,000 persons. The main U.S. postal unions have complained of increasingly poor working conditions. In the late 1990s, some employees reported being overloaded with tasks during their regular working hours but then harassed for putting in overtime hours. By the turn of the millennium, U.S. postal workers had filed more than 100,000 grievances against the USPS. Workers also complained of physical hardships. Letter sorter operators, for example, complained that typing several-digit zip codes at a rate of one per second for 45 minutes without a break led to carpal tunnel syndrome, involving damage to their wrists.

Some critics of the U.S. postal unions, however, maintained that U.S. postal workers were too coddled. Under civil service rules, as many as five years could pass before a worker would be fired, even for just cause. Major mailers, angered with increasingly high postal rates, charged that even where automation had eliminated the need for workers, redundant workers remained on the job, doing very little. Post office supervisors, charged with keeping mail flowing, claimed that some postal workers would call in sick to avoid putting in a day's work.

More seriously, labor-management frictions, combined with the often hectic atmosphere of postal operations, led to the seemingly ubiquitous threat of physical violence in the workplace, which sometimes proved fatal. A rash of shootings at post offices in the United States in the 1990s perpetuated existing fears of workplace violence and generated substantial negative publicity for the U.S. postal industry, including the caricaturing of disgruntled postal workers. This was so despite the fact that, statistically speaking, postal employees were at no greater risk of exhibiting violent behavior—which some referred to as "going postal,"—than employees in other U.S. occupations. Recognizing the harmful effects of such an atmosphere on both a tangible and a financial level, postal administrators have worked hard in recent years to improve labor-management relations.

MAJOR COUNTRIES IN THE INDUSTRY

THE UNITED STATES

The U.S. mailing industry is a significant part of the nation's infrastructure and economy. According to the UPU, the industry employed 826,955 people in 2003. Operating income was about US$70.1 billion. About 647 letters were mailed per person in the U.S. each year. The quasi-independent USPS, successor to the formerly government-run Postal Department, delivered more than 46 percent of the world's mail volume in 2004, employing more than 707,000 people to do so. By 2006, USPS had revenues of US$72.6 billion and 696,138 employees. It delivered more than 210 billion pieces of mail to more than 144 million addresses.

The USPS also faced significant threats and challenges. Shortly after the September 11, 2001, terrorist attacks struck the United States, the USPS was hit by the potentially devastating threat posed by several anthrax-laced or anthrax-containing letters sent through the public mail system. Two postal employees died of anthrax infections and several others were contaminated with the deadly virus. In response, the USPS had to rapidly mount a campaign in which at least nine anthrax-contaminated postal units and branches were temporarily closed, decontaminated, and later reopened; 267 postal hub facilities linked to the Washington, D.C. and Trenton, New Jersey mail-processing facilities where anthrax was discovered were tested and retested; about 16,000 postal employees in New York, New Jersey, Florida, and Washington, D.C., who were potentially exposed to the anthrax virus, were tested for anthrax infection and given prophylactic antibiotics; all postal employees were offered flu injections, since early symptoms of anthrax closely resemble those of the flu; and special security measures were put in place to detect the presence of biochemical contaminants in the mail-processing system and to irradiate and sanitize mail.

The emergency response to the anthrax scare, the USPS's endeavors to prevent future anthrax attacks, and the necessity of rebuilding postal facilities and assets destroyed at or near the World Trade Center site would cost unanticipated millions of dollars, prompting the USPS to request a special allocation from the U.S. Congress in early 2002 to help offset these extraordinary expenses. In addition, the USPS expected that an increase in the cost of first-class postage would be required to help balance its books. In March 2002 the decision was officially made to raise the price of a first-class stamp from 34 cents to 37 cents (US$0.34 to US$0.37), a change that would go into effect a few months later. Even so, the national recession that began around the time of the September 11 terrorist attacks, coupled with a significant drop in mailing volumes after the start of the anthrax attacks (and an associated 6.6 percent decrease in U.S. postal revenues for September and an 8.0 to 10.0 percent decrease for October, according to Union Network International), contributed to a loss in income by the USPS of US$1.7 billion for the fiscal year ending September 30, 2001.

Despite the major challenges it faced, the USPS continued to be one of the world's largest mailing operations in 2004. The organization ran 37,000 postal outlets. The amount of mail processed that year reached 206 billion pieces.

Legislation passed by the U.S. Congress that has significantly impacted postal operations in the United States and around the world included annual allocations from the U.S. federal government to the Postal Service Fund to pay for free and reduced-rate mail. In 2001 this amounted to US$96 million, including US$67 million to cover the costs of free mail for the blind and for U.S. voters living overseas. In 2003, there were 56.8 million pieces of free mail for the blind and handicapped out of a total 424.9 million pieces of mail. In 2004, industry analysts pointed out that substantial rate increases were necessary, because the USPS was legally required to financially break even at worst, which it had not done for the first three years of the decade. Increased competition from the US$20 million Internet postal industry, of which Stamps.com was the clear market leader, was another challenge for the USPS.

In July 2006, USPS announced plans to establish a "Global Business" unit. This move comes at a time when private and public sector leaders are working together more and more to meet postal industry demands. The global business focus brings all international postal efforts into one unit covering operations, transportation, finance, planning, information technology, account management and postal relations. Related predictions called for an increase of its US$1.9 billion annual share of the international shipping market. USPS Vice President of Network Operations Management Patti Vogel was named as the head for new unit. Vogel was already involved with USPS effort to release international and military air mail rates from the Department of Transportation. Claims had been made that international and military air rates were much higher than they would be if USPS could bid out related shipments in the same manner it does for domestic mail.

Northrop Grumman received a US$874.6 million fixed-price contract from USPS to provide 100 Flats Sequencing Systems (FSS). The FSS were designed to advance automating the flats mail stream. That stream included large envelopes, catalogs, and magazines. The first FSS production units at USPS facilities nationwide are expected to begin in 2008. Remaining FSS installations were set for completion by 2010.

USPS also entered into a long-term contract with United Airlines scheduled to begin on April 28, 2007 and continue until September 30, 2011. The contract involved agreement for transporting domestic mail. Among passenger carriers, United Airlines was already ranked as the number-one carrier of international mail among passenger carriers.

In addition, USPS agreed to combine its eight primary international mail offerings into four categories familiar to U.S. customers. As of May 14, 2007, U.S. customers would be able to utilize Priority Mail and Express Mail packaging for items with foreign and domestic destinations. New international product names are Express Mail International, Priority Mail International and First-Class Mail International. The premium international service will continued to be known as Global Express Guaranteed.

USPS officials told its Board of Governors about plans to have one technology capable of continuously tracking mail and providing customers with feedback by 2009. The "Intelligent Mail" system would rely on one standardized intelligent barcode used on each piece or container of mail. The technology would make it possible for business customers to monitor progress of mail as it progressed from arrival at a postal facility to delivery at its destination. Related tasks would be automated for optimal service.

USPS proclaimed that all of its Priority and Express Mail packages were made of 100 percent recyclable paper. This impacted the approximately 500 million packages were used each year with estimated value of US$6 billion. Related changes in processes and practices called for rewriting contracts with approximately 200 suppliers requiring they revise composition of paper provided to USPS. New packages reportedly included 60 separate material components and 1,400 individual ingredients.

As part of its efforts to offer convenient service options for its customers, USPS contracted with private operators offering hours that expanded service opportunities. Controversy arose related to USPS' decision to let Full Gospel Interdenominational Church in Manchester, New Hampshire operate a "Sincerely Yours Inc." outlet as the only post office in the downtown area. U.S. District Court Judge Dominic J. Squatrito ruled that religious displays in area where postal products were sold inappropriately endorsed Christianity and recruited outsiders to join the church in advancing its mission. It was deemed inappropriate for the church to exhibit religious items while conducting duties for the USPS or U.S. government.

A price increases took effect in May 2007 for stamps and other products. A "Forever Stamp" was introduced that could be used forever on First-Class Mail letters even if postage increases occurred in the future. The stamp was priced at 41 cents each.

SELECTED OTHER MAJOR COUNTRIES

The Japanese postal system, Japan Post, was made a public corporation owed wholly by the government in April 2003. The company planned to divide along product and service lines before fully privatizing. In 2004, Japan Post reported about US$12 billion in sales and employed more than 271,000 people. Plans were announced for Japan Post to become privatized on October 1, 2007 into a holding company and four service firms. In January 2006, Japan Post Corp. was established by Japan Post as a preparatory company for the privatization and will transfer to the holding company. Profit estimates were predicted to be in the [yen] 500 billion to [yen] 600 billion range up to fiscal year 2011. The overall workforce was expected to be approximately 241,400.

The postal and telecommunications system in Germany was completely reorganized in the early 1990s, and by the late 1990s the *Postdienst* postal service enterprise was operating as its own public enterprise. *Postdienst* further poised itself for enormous international expansion by acquiring the world's leading express delivery company in terms of cross-border deliveries, DHL Worldwide Express, just before the turn of the millennium. The German postal service Deutsch Post AG, which also was the largest postal service provider in Europe as of 2004, reported US$60.7 billion in revenues that year and employed more than 346,000 people.

The second ranked postal operator in Europe, and fourth worldwide, France's La Poste, is a public enterprise under autonomous management. In 2002, the company handled 25 billion domestic letters and more than one billion international letters in 2002. La Poste reported US$18.2 billion in revenue that year. In 2006, the European Commission sent France a recommendation that it end the unlimited guarantee given to La Poste in its capacity as a public body by the end of 2008. Such a move would be part of its monitoring of existing state aid schemes under the EC Treaty. The unlimited guarantee afforded La Poste the opportunity to have an advantage over its competitors when obtaining financing and distort competition for a market in the process of becoming liberalised.

Royal Mail Holdings of the United Kingdom became a public limited company owned by the British government in 2001, operating under the brand names Royal Mail, Post Office, and ParceForce Worldwide. One of the United Kingdom's leading businesses, Royal Mail employed more than 212,000 workers by 2004 and had sales of approximately US$15.8 billion. By 2005, the organization was processing 82 million items each day. The company owned only 500 of the 14,400 postal branches, with the remainder being owned by the people who ran them. Parcelforce Worldwide was the United Kingdom's leading carrier of time-critical packages. By 2006, it was estimated that Royal Mail delivered more than 2 billion letters on behalf of their competition under deals allowing private companies to collect mail, sort it and hand it to Royal Mail for delivery. The business market was believed to hold most promise for growth where 10 customers accounted for 20 percent of total market and 100 for 40 percent of that market.

In the developing world, India has one of the largest volume mail services, although it was showing dramatic declines in volumes. Domestic letter mail volume dropped from 13.6 billion items in 2001 to 8.7 billion items in 2003. That year, 566,000 people were employed in the postal service.

In 2006, India Post announced plans for incorporating a "one-stop-shop" approach enabling customers to make all of their routine bill payments. These payments included service tax and road tax. After achieving success as a collection point for citizens filing income tax returns, India Post planned to enhance its offerings of information access and other services to customers by making them available through its service centres. These services were expected to added up to nearly 20 to 30 percent of India Post's future profits.

In 2007, India Post announced that it would be making a substantial investment in upgrading technology. The Department of Post also identified three core services for heavy investment in the future as parcels, financial services and logistics. Revenues were expected to increase substantially based on efforts related to logistics. After technology upgrades were completed at all post offices, the Department of Post planned to increase ancillary services such as its "instant money order scheme" and "postal retail."

China established the "China Post Group" which separated regulatory functions of the former State Post Bureau from its business activities. The China Post Group also united the China Postal Air Freight Corporation and the China Postal Savings Bank. China Postal Group had registered capital of US$10 billion. It planned to restructure linked businesses including mail delivery services plus the publication and issuing of stamps.

In the Pacific Rim, national postal administrations have been working to modernize their operations to embrace the international market. The New Zealand Post, a leader in postal reform reported annual sales of US$678.88 billion. After successfully revitalizing its own services, it helped Malaysia restructure its postal unit and has provided advice to the government of South Korea on postal service modernization. The primary emphases of both endeavors have been cutting labor costs and increasing productivity by implementing more efficient management methods and integrating new technologies into postal operations.

In March 2006, *The Economist* reported on the status of Sepomex. It is Mexico's state-owned postal system. Sepomex only had one automated mail sorting-machine. Letters and parcels were still frequently delivered via bicycle. There were only 20,000 employees serving approximately 103 billion people. In spite of all this, Sepomex managed to retain 60 percent of Mexico's postal market sharing the remaining percentage with private companies. Government claims that 95 percent of the mail was delivered within target times ranging from one to ten days were questioned.

FURTHER READING

American Postal Workers Union. "Former USPS Official Decries Bulk Mail Discounts; Stamps Could Be Cheaper Without Giveaway to Big Business," 2002. Available from http://www.apwu.org.

Anderson, Neil. "The Global Fight on Postal Markets, " 2001. Available from http://www.nalc.org.

———. "Union Attacks Postal Giveaway," 9 January 2002. Available from http://www.apwu.org.

Armbruster, William. "USPS May Seek Rate Hike in 2004." *The Journal of Commerce Online,* 8 January 2003.

Associated Press. "Postal Service to Seek Financial Assistance from Congress in Wake of Attacks, Anthrax Scare," 22 October 2001. Available from http://belointeractive.com.

Boyd, John D. "Global Ambitions: USPS Picks Vogel to Lead New Global Business Unit; European Postal Services Seek Complete Deregulation." *Traffic World,* 24 July 2006.

"China Bifurcates Postal Services." *PTI — The Press Trust of India Ltd.,* 1 December 2006.

"Editorial: Partners to a Point: Postal Services, Proselytizing Don't Mix." *Sacramento Bee,* 30 April 2007.

Friedman, Daniel. " USPS Reaches Key Milestone in Green Purchases." 22 May 2007. Available from http://federaltimes.com.

Gallagher, Thomas L. "IATA Gets Technology Help." *Traffic World,* 8 March 2007.

———. "USPS Seeks International Growth." *Traffic World,* 27 March 2007.

Geddes, Rick. "The Structure and Effect of International Postal Reform." 2003. Available from http://www.aei.org.

"Hoover's Company Capsules." 2007. Available from http://www.hoovers.com.

Hudgins, Edward L. "Securing the Postal Front," The Cato Institute, 25 October 2001. Available from http://www.cato.org.

"India Post Plans Diversification." *The Times of India,* 17 November 2006.

"Japan Post Eyes [yen] 587 Bil. FY11 Profit." *Yomiuri Shimbun,* 25 April 2007.

Lazich, Robert S., ed. *Market Share Reporter.* Detroit: Thomson Gale, 2004.

Michaels, Adrian and Andrew Parker. "Mobile Tie-Up Poste Italiane to Lift Slow Growth." *The Financial Times,* 5 April 2007.

Milner, Mark. "Postal Services: Message to Ministers: Future of Royal Mail Requires Judgement of Solomon: A Year of Competition Strenghtened the Business — But the Future is Uncertain." *The Guardian,* 29 December 2006.

Mishra, Ashish Kumar. "India Post Gets Tech Savvy to Take on Competition." *Economic Times,* 18 January 2007.

Montgomery Research. *Pushing the Envelope: Achieving High Performance in a Competitive Postal Environment,* 30 April 2004. Available from http://www.accenture.com.

"New Postal Contract Signed Between United Airlines and USPS." *Airline Industry Information,* 2 April 2007.

"Northrop Grumman Gets Big USPS Contract." *ePostal News,* 12 March 2007.

"On Mexican Time; Mexico's Postal Services." *The Economist,* 25 March 2006.

"Postal Rates, Delivery Delays." *The Kiplinger Letter,* 9 July 2004.

"Postal Services: France Called on to Withdraw La Poste's Unlimited Guarantee." *European Report,* 5 October 2006.

"Postal Services: Public Employees Worried by Prospect of Full Liberalisation." 28 February 2007.

Seth, Yogima. "India Post Plans Diversification." *The Times of India,* 17 November 2006.

Thuresson, Michael. "Stamps.com's Survival May Hinge on Takeover Appeal." *Los Angeles Business Journal,* 10 November 2003.

Union Network International. "Anthrax Attack Update: Postal Unions Lobby U.S. Congress for Funds to Respond to Crisis," 8 November 2001. Available from http://www.union-network.org.

United States Postal Inspection Service. "Annual Report of Investigations, 2001." Washington, D.C.: United States Postal Inspection Service, November 2001. Available from http://www.usps.com.

United States Postal Service. "Annual Report, 2001." Washington, D.C.: United States Postal Service, 2002.

———. "Annual Report, 2003." Washington, D.C.: United States Postal Service, 2004.

Universal Postal Union. "Postal Market 2004." September 2004. Available from http://www.upu.int.

———. "Postal Statistics," 2002. Available from http://www.upu.int.

———. "Worldwide Postal Network in Figures." January 2004. Available from http://www.upu.int.

"UPS Claims QSF Fund a Success." *ePostal News,* 1 May 2006.

"USPS Combines International Mail Services Into Familiar Brands." *Direct,* 25 April 2007.

"USPS: Don't Forget That Stamps Cost More Now." *Sun-News,* 18 May 2007.

"USPS Eyes 2009 for Total Intelligent Mail Adoption." *Direct,* 11 January 2007.

SIC 4000

NAICS 4821

RAIL TRANSPORTATION

Entities in this industry sector are involved with the line-haul transportation of passengers and freight via rail systems (except passenger transportation by rail within or around specific urban centers—see SIC 4100). Industry firms also conduct support activities related to the operation of rail terminals for line-haul passengers and freight, yards, sidings, and switching . Not included in this heading are railway constructions (SIC 1629), and the manufacture of rail equipment (SIC 374).

INDUSTRY SNAPSHOT

Almost every country in the world has a rail system, although the degree to which it is put to use for passenger versus freight use can vary dramatically. How the industry is regulated, even the size of the track used, can often appear as individual as the country. The industry is most often subdivided between freight and passenger operations, and within passenger operations it is subdivided further into local and long distance (high-speed) services. This industry discussion focuses on freight and long-distance passenger services and their complimentary services, including terminals and switching.

By 2003, some 746,000 miles of rail lines were being used to transport freight and people between cities, across countries, and increasingly, across nations. Between 2002 and 2050, the world population was expected to grow to 9.3 billion people. As a result, the need for efficient, economical and environmentally friendly means of transport for this growing population and the products they consume was resulting in technological advancements in the speed of trains, the weight of cargo that could be carried, the efficiency of train fueling systems, and the computerization of the logistics behind moving mass numbers of people and products.

By the mid-2000s, the railway industry was looking up, thanks to the substantial increase in "intermodalism," the seamless combination of various modes of transport—such as trains, boats, and trucks—to ship freight. In intermodal transport, the freight is shipped in trailers or containers that can be directly interchanged between different modes of transportation. In the U.S. alone, intermodal traffic went from a mere 3 million containers in 1980 to nearly 10 million in 2003, and, according to the Association of American Railroads (AAR), intermodal traffic set records in 21 of those 23 years.

ORGANIZATION AND STRUCTURE

According to *Worldwide Rail Market,* published for the German rail equipment manufacturing firm Vossloh AG, there were almost 746,000 miles (1.2 million kilometers)of rail lines around the world by 2003. According to SCI Verkehr GmbH, a German rail consulting company, the longest network could be found in Asia (with approximately 284,000 miles), followed by North America (approximately 194,000 miles of track), Europe (162,000 miles), Latin America (67,000 miles), Africa (56,000 miles), and Australia/Pacific (39,500 miles). However, how these rail lines are used varies significantly by region. For example, the primary use of rail lines in North America is for freight, and as a result, most lines are single-track, with relatively few rail crossings. In Europe, lines are used for both passenger and freight, and travel through large urban centers, requiring more complicated organizational and safety structures for their functioning.

Most countries regulate their rail industries through government-run organizations. For example, in the United States, the Federal Railroad Administration, under the Department of Transportation, is responsibile for safety legislation. The International Union of Railways (known as the UIC), located in Paris, had 162 members in 2005, including all rail transport and infrastructure managers in Europe, and most major railways in the remainder of the world. The organization was working to develop international transport by rail, and prepared standards, regulations and recommendations to this aim.

Trends in the growth of the world's population and the increasing global mobility of that population, as well as increases in the amount of trade between countries, have led to increased cooperation with other transportation industries, regional trade agreements, privatization, railroad mergers, and transportation innovations. In North America, the U.S.-Canadian Free Trade Agreement, signed in 1988, resulted in Class I railroads on both sides of the border accelerating their connections into each other's territories. Both the United States and Canada expanded into Mexico in the early 1990s. For example, in 1991 a joint venture between Burlington Northern (BN) and the Mexican corporation Grupo Protexa S.A. produced Protexa Burlington International (PBI), an innovative rail-barge link between Galveston, Texas, and Mexican Gulf ports. Two years later, Canadian National Railway began connecting with PBI via BN to deliver Canadian grain to Mexico. Territorial expansion was further increased both by a wave of rail mergers in the United States in the mid-1990s and by the North American Free Trade Agreement (NAFTA), which diminished most trade barriers between the United States, Canada, and Mexico.

With trade between the United States and Canada creating a north-south orientation, railroads shifted their east-west systems accordingly. The two nations began sharing track, railbeds, and operations on both sides of the border. U.S. railroads, for example, gained entry to Canada through interline agreements with Canadian railroads, as when the Atchison, Topeka, and Santa Fe Railway Company (Santa Fe) entered into an interline connection with the Canadian National Railway Company's Grand Trunk line at Chicago. In essence, railroads could finally provide complete service from Mexico to Canada.

Under an agreement with Mexico's government, NAFTA allowed Canadian and U.S. railroads to market their services in Mexico, to operate unit trains with their own locomotives, to construct and own terminals, and to finance rail infrastructure. The agreement did not, however, allow full foreign ownership of a Mexican transportation firm. While pre-cleared containers and boxcars could cross the border into Mexico, neither Canada nor the United States was permitted to handle their own shipments into Mexico. Mexican law required foreign railroad operators to turn shipments over to Ferrocarriles Nacionales de Mexico (FNM), Mexico's national railway. Neither Mexico nor the United States allowed locomotives from the other nation to cross the border. Power units, therefore, had to be switched at border terminals such as Laredo or Brownsville, Texas, a policy that helped trucking firms capture about 75 percent of all U.S. southbound trade with Mexico.

Southern Pacific (SP), which would later be acquired by Union Pacific (UP), invested directly in Mexico's infrastructure with Mexican partners Ferropuertos (rail ports). SP developed a network of distribution centers at Mexican rail ports that enabled timely unloading. In 1993, it completed construction on an intermodal facility at Monterey that was operated by Mexican firms.

In Europe, a spirit of cooperation, spurred by the establishment of the European Union in 1993, led to the creation of a pan-European rail network. Prior to the EU, national and state-run railways had traditionally refused to collaborate. Cooperative efforts were initiated in 1991 when European transport ministers, in an effort to improve intermodal links, adopted standard measurements for containers and other units used by rail transport industries. Previously, non-standardized shipping lots and container sizes used throughout Europe had been a major problem for the transport and distribution industries.

Four different rail gauges and seven different types of loading gauges on European railroads had hampered any previous possibility for an interconnecting system. Rail systems had been especially outdated in Spain, Portugal, Greece, and Ireland where truck and loading gauges were not standardized, signaling systems were mismatched, bridge and tunnel dimensions varied, power lines used uneven voltage, and track slope and curve gradients differed.

EU directives called for increased rail use to reduce truck traffic on Europe's overly congested and polluted roadways. In the early 1990s, trucks accounted for 70 percent of all freight movements in the EU. A goal was set to affect an 8 percent increase in cross-border intermodal traffic hauled by a combination of trucks, railways, and barges, no later than 1997. The EU plan called for a pan-European combined transport network involving an investment of US$2.5 billion in new rail, terminals, boxcars, and locomotives to boost multimodal transport across the borders of member nations. A planned 30,000 kilometers of high-speed track, to be built in two phases, was scheduled for completion by 2005. Some US$590 million was earmarked for high-speed rail links that would connect the northern route (Paris-London-Brussels-Amsterdam-Cologne) with the southern route (Seville-Barcelona-Lyon-Turin-Milan-Venice). Further connections would be made with Tarvisio and Trieste, Italy; Madrid, Spain; and Lisbon and Oporto, Portugal.

EU directives also called for approximately US$120 billion to be spent on developing and implementing high-speed passenger rail systems. Eurotunnel, the Anglo-French channel-tunnel consortium, developed "Le Shuttle" service, connecting London with Paris and Brussels through the Channel Tunnel. Often dubbed the "Chunnel." Service, it began in November 1994 and made it possible for passengers to travel between London and Paris in three hours and between London and Brussels in three hours and 15 minutes.

Gauge unification was completed on the United Kingdom-Benelux-Italy and Germany-Spain-Portugal routes in the early 1990s. Completion of a rail link between Munich, Germany and Verona, Italy via a tunnel through the Brenner Pass was targeted for completion in the early 2000s. Other links on the EU's list of priority Trans-European Networks included the Betuwe project, a US$4 billion, 75-mile rail freight corridor expected to carry between 60 and 65 million tons of freight a year on Nederlandse Spoorwegen Cargo. The corridor connected Rotterdam, the world's biggest port, to the German railway network. The Betuwe project remained under construction as of 2002.

Rail operations in many other countries continued to be government owned and operated, most notably in some of the less industrialized Asian nations. Passenger fares were subsidized, making rail travel cheap. Typically, densely populated nations increased funding on railway projects to develop programs to extend and update rail networks. In 1994, South Korea undertook a 432-kilometer high-speed rail project, the first phase of which was to be completed in 2003. The network, designed to link Seoul with the southern port of Pusan, was the largest outside Japan. In Thailand, rail networks were built to connect Bangkok to major regional centers. In Taiwan, plans to construct a 345-kilometer high-speed train between Taipei and Kaohsiung were launched in late 1999 with an expected completion date of October 2005. Indonesia developed viable rail service between Bandung and Jakarta. Given the limitations of truck service, that line was considered by shippers to be the best way to transport goods such as garments and textiles. Plans also called for a mass transit system in Jakarta. In 2002, Vietnam developed a US$10.6 billion modernization plan for its railway system in Hanoi. Scheduled upgrades included a railway line to Ho Chi Minh City.

In China, the need to develop better rail networks became synonymous with continued economic growth. Some 70 percent of China's goods were transported on only 34,000 miles of track. Recognizing that overly subsidized and outmoded railroads had stalled railway development, the Chinese government called for the industry's privatization. China's first railway corporation was formed in 1993 when the Guangzhou railway bureau of the ministry was converted into Guangzhou Railway. Chinese officials examined France's TGV, Germany's ICE, Japan's "bullet train," and Sweden's X2000 rail systems and inadvertently set off a rash of competitive bidding by foreign train manufacturers aspiring to do business with China.

In 1992, China officially inaugurated the Eurasia land bridge, a rail link extending over 6,700 miles from Lianyungang, China to Rotterdam, the Netherlands. The rail connected China with Kazakhstan, Uzbekistan, Kyrgyzstan, Tajikistan, Russia, Belarus, Poland, Germany, and the Netherlands. It was the second transcontinental railway after the Trans-Siberian Express Railway (TSER). By then, China's biggest project was the 2,370-kilometer Beijing-Kowloon line. Extended southward to Canton, the rail freight system line was scheduled to connect Beijing to Hong Kong by 1997 and to extend to more than 4,400 freight stations in China.

Although the Ministry of Railways (MOR) did not privatize the Chinese railway network, it did reorganize the system into two fairly independent entities, North Loric and South Loric, which oversaw a total of 14 regional units. Between 1998 and 2002, the MOR planned to spend roughly US$29.6 billion refurbishing and extending its 50,000 miles of rail.

Efforts in Russia involved upgrading the Trans-Siberian Express Railway (TSER), which had almost 67 varying railroad gauges. A 50-50 joint venture partnership between the Russian Ministry of Railways and the U.S. maritime arm of CSX Corporation (Sea-Land Services) set up a land bridge rail service that utilized the 7,000-mile Trans-Siberian Railroad. A computer system to trace containers moving within the rail system was installed, and more than 3,400 railcars were dedicated to the service. In 1994, Sea-Land began offering two weekly express block train departures between Rotterdam and Moscow. The routing moved through Brest, Poland on the Russian border where it switched from the Western rail gauge to the Russian gauge, then onward to a rail terminal in Moscow. The Moscow terminal was designed to operate on a hub-and-spoke concept to consolidate shipments onto feeder block trains going to Vostochny on Russia's east coast. Service continued from Moscow to Yekaterinburg, Russia; Alma Ata, Kazakhstan; Tashkent, Uzbekistan; and to Vostochny and Vladivostok in eastern Russia.

Sea-Land also established rail service from the Russian port of Novorossiysk on the Black Sea to the region's interior, allowing increases in rail volume and greater demand for container shipment from Japan, India, the United States, and several Mediterranean countries. Plans to privatize Russia's railroad network were launched in the early 2000s, with the first stage completed in October 2003 by way of the formation of the Joint Stock Company (JSC) Russian Railways.

BACKGROUND AND DEVELOPMENT

The earliest railroads, built in Europe in the eighteenth century, employed rail that guided wagons with specially shaped wheels. The big push for railroad development came in 1823 when English inventor George Stephenson introduced steam power for railroad freight service for the Yorkshire-based Stockton & Darlington Railway. Dubbed Locomotion No. 1, the service could haul 35 cars at 12 miles an hour. The first great railway successes occurred in Great Britain. Early in the industry's development, the government insisted on uniform gauges and on laws regarding brakes and safety standards.

France built its first railway line in 1828. Belgium, Germany, Italy, the Netherlands, and Russia all had networks in operation by the 1830s. Most railroads adopted the British standard, with the exception of railways in Spain and Portugal. Although European railroads were primarily state-owned, Russian lines were not nationalized until 1919 during the communist revolution.

Because canal transportation was the most common method of moving freight, rail transportation in the United States did not begin to develop swiftly until the 1830s, when population centers began to increase in the western regions. In July 1862 President Abraham Lincoln signed the Pacific Railroad Act, authorizing the Central Pacific and the Union Pacific railroads to build the first great line from the Atlantic to the Pacific coasts. The project was completed in 1869. By 1900, the U.S. network of rail lines had reached nearly 200,000 miles of track.

The decades following the Civil War saw a host of technical advances that spurred industry development. However this rapid expansion of the U.S. rail industry also resulted in a series of discriminatory rate wars and in abuses and corruption. As a result, the U.S. Government, under the Interstate Commerce Act of 1887, made the railroads the first industry to be regulated by a federal agency. With the passage of the Transportation Act of 1920, the Interstate Commerce Commission gained complete authority over every area of railroading.

In Canada, rail service began in 1836 and expanded to 6,960 miles by 1880. In 1881, as part of an agreement under which British Columbia entered the Canadian Confederation, Canada formed the Canadian Pacific Railway Company and completed its transcontinental railway. The Canadian National Railway Company (CN) was organized in 1922 to take over several railroads bankrupted as a result of years of speculative railway building. In 1987 the government was forced to deregulate its railroads, making it possible for them to bargain for rates with shippers and to successfully compete with deregulated U.S. railroads. Until the early 1990s, however, revenues were pressured, resulting in a weak business outlook. To streamline operations, CN announced it wanted to sell some 20 percent of its eastern and central network by 1995 and another third of the network to short-line operators. Canadian Pacific (CP), which ranked third among North American railroads in miles of track but seventh in revenue-ton miles in 1992, received permission in 1993 to sell or abandon most of its rail operations from Sherbrooke, Quebec to Saint John, New Brunswick. In late 1993, both railroads were allowed to share a 300-mile line between Quebec and Ontario where the carriers previously had been operating parallel tracks a few miles apart. Both railroads outlined terms of a merger that would meld marketing and administrative functions and share tracks and rail yards.

Asian countries with significant railroad systems included India, China, and Japan. India's system was built in the 1850s and patterned after the British model, though it used a different gauge. China began building railroads in the 1870s but had only 7,500 miles in operation by 1920. Under communist rule, the People's Republic of China increased its total track length to 32,600 miles. Japan built its first lines in the 1870s.

The invention of cars, trucks, and airplanes as alternate forms of transportation seriously challenged the railroad industry, and by the early 1970s the industry's share of traffic had dropped to 37 percent. In particular, the increased use of trucking created stiff competition for freight payloads. By the mid-1970s, ten U.S. railroads had declared bankruptcy. The Railroad Revitalization and Regulatory Reform Act of 1976 was passed to revitalize the industry. With the formation of the federally subsidized Consolidated Rail (Conrail), portions of six bankrupt Northeast railroads were successfully restructured as a single viable freight system.

In 1980, under the Stagger Rail Act, the U.S. government began to deregulate and ease restrictions on the rail industry, allowing carriers to abandon unprofitable lines, redirect resources to buy new equipment, and rebuild tracks in profitable corridors. The act also freed railroads to negotiate rates directly with customers. The result was an expansion of the railroad industry and an investment of nearly US$160 billion in track and equipment. Nonetheless, by 1987, after spending billions on modernizing track and rolling stock, the government privatized Conrail.

Privatization and liberalization efforts continued into the 1990s. While the railroad industries in the United States and Japan had been privatized in the 1980s, many European players did not begin to move away from government involvement until the mid-1990s. For example, the United Kingdom's British Rail became a private company in the mid-1990s; other countries such as Germany contemplated implementing similar privatization programs.

In the 1990s, the United States had the largest network of rail mileage, followed by Europe. The total rail mileage in Canada, Mexico, and Central America combined amounted to one-third of that in the United States. The ten leading companies in the railroad transportation industry reported combined sales of more than US$118.9 billion in 1996. That year, the *International Railway Journal* estimated that annual capital investment in the industry exceeded US$50 billion worldwide. Germany led in railroad capital investment with plans of pumping US$10 billion annually into the industry through 2001, while China had the second most ambitious investment program with roughly US$6 billion allocated to the railroad industry in 1996.

Later in the decade, the European Union took steps toward creating a freight rail "freeway." The countries initially involved in the agreement included Germany, the Netherlands, Austria, and Italy. In mid-1997, key organizations for rail transport users and railroads, such as the Community of European Railways and the International Union of Road-Rail Transport Companies, supported the EU's plan to establish these rail freeways. The governments of Europe determined that the corridor between these four countries constituted one of the highest-volume corridors in Europe and that a rail freeway would bring about accelerated transportation to and from Germany and Mediterranean ports by increasing freight speeds to 50 kph (31 mph) and eliminating delays when crossing national boundaries. Similarly, the planned Trans-Asia Railway Project was expected to not only connect Malaysia, Thailand, Cambodia, Laos, Vietnam, and China, but also to expand passenger and cargo traffic.

Intermodalism—planning and coordinating the entire transport trip from ship to train to truck—contributed to industry growth in Europe, the United States, and other world markets as one of the fastest growing segments of the industry in the mid to late 1990s. Because trucking cost nearly twice as much as freight railroad services, new double-stack railcars offered an economic alternative—the more boxes a single carrier could move at one time, the cheaper the cost. Consequently, in some areas distinctions between rail and trucking companies became blurred as trucking firms and railroads began working together, providing complementary services and no longer competing with each other. Trains carried freight over long distances, while trucks worked the profitable short-haul lanes that fed into rail hubs. Leading railroads, such as Deutsche Bahn, UP, and CSX, offered intermodal services.

Intermodalism also gave rise to third-party coordinators who planned the transport of goods through the various modes of transportation needed. Railroads increased their use of these third-party retailers or "middlemen" who dealt directly with importers and exporters in the late 1990s. Intermodal marketing companies (IMCs), which marketed rail services and provided shippers with door-to-door services, became leading sources for intermodal shipments for railroads. France and Germany introduced intermodal freight systems with their Kombiverkehr and Intercontainer services. Under these arrangements, the dispatching customer controlled the entire chain, including delivery and collection at the receiving end.

Global rail freight volume grew 1.8 percent in 2000, according to the International Transport Union, based in Paris, France. Global passenger travel grew less than 1.0 percent, although the popularity of high-speed trains in Europe accounted for 2.3 percent passenger traffic growth there. Rail-based freight traffic in Europe rose 7.0 percent, while intermodal freight traffic increased 8.0 percent. According to the *International Railway Journal,* European freight transported via rail had fallen from 21.0 percent in 1970 to 8.0 percent by the late 1990s. In the middle of the decade, Britain privatized its railway operations, which led to the creation of Railtrack, a private company.

In North America, consolidation stopped when the U.S. Surface Transportation Board (STB) banned railroad mergers for a 15-month period starting in March 2000. Canadian National Railway and Burlington Northern Santa Fe, which had announced their intent to merge into North American Railways Inc. in December of 1999, appealed the mandate. However, the U.S. Court of Appeals found in favor of the STB in July of 2000. Rather than endure a delay that would likely reach a period of two years, the two firms decided to cancel their merger plans.

Privatization and deregulation of the world's railroads continued as European countries, such as the United Kingdom and Germany, and Latin American countries like Mexico worked to reduce government involvement in their transportation industries, including railroads. Even Russia was on the privatization bandwagon, announcing in 2001 its intent to privatize the Russian State Railways via a reform project that would take place over the following decade.

Despite growth in both passenger and freight traffic, the European Commission launched a rail freight revitalization program in 2001 in an effort to increase rail freight traffic throughout the European Union. Also impacting the European rail industry was the collapse of Railtrack. Performance problems, including several fatalities, along with a growing debt load were cited as reasons for the refusal of the British government to continue subsidizing Railtrack in 2001. Many industry analysts believed that Britain would create a non-profit entity, which would likely be overseen by the Strategic Rail Authority, to replace Railtrack. Shortly after Railtrack's demise became public, the Strategic Rail Authority announced its intent to increase its capital investment in the national rail network in an effort to increase passenger traffic by 40 to 50 percent and freight traffic by 80 percent.

France was unique among the largest European players for resisting such privatization efforts, despite the financial hardships of its state railway operator, Société Nationale des Chemins de Fer Français (SNCF). According to the June 2001 issue of *The Economist,* the European Commission pressured France to split its track and rail operations for two reasons: to foster transparency in financial reporting and to allow for competition in the track segment. In 2001, Reseau Ferre de France (RFF), a state-owned firm which paid SNCF to manage the French rail network, struggled with a debt load of euro 22.8 billion, which required interest payments of euro 2.4 billion annually. The European Commission began calling for the French government to reduce support for its national rail network and allow competition on at least some segments of its lines.

The advent of rail "freeways," was marked by the European Commission's creation of a rail freeway connecting German, Austrian, Netherlands, and Italian ports, facilitating smooth transport between those countries. Finally, more countries began adopting high-speed trains—capable of traveling more than 180 kilometers per hour (kph), or 110 miles per hour (mph)—to ease highway traffic congestion and reduce environmental degradation. Germany, France, and Japan led in this movement. In fact, both France and Japan boasted high-speed trains, known as TGVs, capable of traveling at an average speed of 360 kph (190 mph) by 2001.

In North America, despite the ban on outright mergers from the U.S. Surface Transportation Board, strategic alliances between the North American railroad industry leaders, including UP, BNSF, CSX, CN, CP, and Grupo Transportacion Ferroviaria Mexicana (TFM), continued to unfold. For example, CP established an office in Mexico City due to the success of its joint service with UP and three Mexican railways. CN, UP, and TFM began offering intermodal service that connected Montreal, Toronto, and Detroit, with Houston and Laredo, Texas, and Mexico City in 2001. Also that year, UP and Norfolk Southern extended their intermodal service to include Miami and Jacksonville, Florida.

Current Conditions

With the world's population set to grow from its 2002 level of 6.2 billion people to 9.3 billion people by 2050, the need for an increasingly efficient means of transporting these people and the goods they produce and require grows. Deregulation of industries and the dismantling of trade barriers have resulted in huge increases in the amount of international trade. According to Deutsche Bank, since the mid-1970s, the amount of production that was exported rose from 10 percent to 25 percent in 30 years. The ability of existing rail structures to cope with this problem continued to be a concern in 2005. Rail networks were faced with environmental issues as well as decreasing amounts of space for expansion in many countries, particularly in and around major urban centers. According to research conducted for Vossloh AG, the rail transport industry had been undergoing a renaissance since the mid-1990s as railways held two major advantages over other modes of transport in terms of meeting increasing trade and passenger transport demands. First, almost every medium-sized town in the world has a rail station to connect it to other centers. Second, compared to the use of roads and airports, railways remained relatively underused (although problems existed in many major urban centers). Railways remained one of the best methods of mass transportation of people and goods. Advances in technology were also helping to improve the efficiency of systems, with faster trains being developed, and increases in the ability to manage the logistics of transportation.

Safety was also a key concern. After the terrorist attacks of 2001, the industry turned to developing security plans and features. The Railway Alert Network (RAN), linked to the Surface Transportation Information Sharing and Analysis Center, was developed to collect and disseminate security information to the industry. In the mid-2000s, RAN was recognized by the U.S. government as one of the most successful security systems in any private industry.

According to SCE Verkehr of Germany, by 2003, Asia was the leader in the share of freight traffic transported (in tons-km) with 3.1 million tons-km. This was followed by North America (2.4 million), Europe (0.3 million), and the rest of the world (0.3 million). In terms of passenger traffic (in passengers-km), the figures are notable for the absence of North America as a region distinct enough to warrant its own showing. By 2003, Asia was transporting 1.4 million passengers-km, Europe 0.2 million, and the rest of the world (including North America, Africa, Australia and Africa) 0.2 million.

In Asia, with the exception of Japan and South Korea, most of the railways were still simple in their infrastructures by 2005. According to research by Vossloh AG, no other area of the world was expected to have the increase in rail lines as Asia, particularly those devoted to moving freight. However, in Europe the future focus was expected to be on the improvement of existing systems, including the increase of rail speed, in efforts to prepare for the expansion of the European Union of countries and the resulting increase in trade expected.

The nation's freight rail systems made 20.5 percent of their revenue from the transport of coal, which accounted for 43.6 percent of the tonnage shipped, according to the Association of American Railroads (AAR). North America was expected to devote more resources to the addition of high-speed passenger rail lines between major centers. Amtrak began operating the Acela Express between Boston and New York and Washington and New York. Five years later, in 2005, the trains were carrying 9,000 to 10,000 passengers each weekday, and were capable of reaching speeds of up to 150 miles per hour. In 2005, service was expected to begin linking Philadelphia with New York and Washington. The future may be the JetTrain, expected to reach speeds of up to 160 miles per hour, and planned for the busy Toronto-Montreal corridor in Canada.

Other key trends in the industry included the continued growth of intermodalism, the seamless combination of various modes of transport—such as trains, boats, and trucks—to ship freight. In the mid-2000s, intermodal transportation was experiencing the highest growth in the United States, having emerged from the depressed economy of the early 2000s in strong shape. By 2003 there were 9.9 million intermodal trailers in the United States, and industry analysts expected that intermodal service would drive the railroad industry's growth for several years. As of 2004, for the first time, intermodal represented the highest source of the U.S. industry's revenue, at 22 percent. Containers were about three-fourths of the total intermodal volume in the mid-2000s.

By the mid-2000s, North American freight rail capacity was reaching its limit. In the United States, there were 142,000 miles of rail in 2004. Despite the transfer of freight shipping to truck operators, railroads still handled the bulk of freight shipping in the United States—forty-two percent of intercity freight, according to the AAR. To help meet demand, Union Pacific and CSX, as well as other railroad operators, were speeding up production and re-working operating plans to meet the increasing and strained demand. Canada was also beginning to suffer the same system stress in 2004. According to AAR, freight demand was projected to increase nearly 70 percent by 2020.

RESEARCH AND TECHNOLOGY

In 2005, work continued on the development of magnetically levitated (maglev) trains. Such technology would mean increased speeds, safety, reliability and lower maintenance as the drive system would be independent of wheel-and-rail friction. In December 2003, a maglev train reached speeds of 581 kilometers per hour during Japanese testing. Although the technology has been around since the 1960s, little has been done to develop it commercially. However, in 2003, a maglev line did open to connect Shanghai with Pudong airport. By July 2004, one million people had taken the train system, which had reached speeds of 501 kilometers per hour. By December 2004, Germany was still working on developing a maglev system.

France developed the Train a Grande Vitesse (TGV) in 1981, which led to a US$10 billion investment in its TGV-Atlantique 325, a train capable of speeds up to 515.3 kph. By 2001, France and Japan had each developed TGVs with average speeds of 360 kph (190 mph).

In 2003, the World Congress on Railway Research stated that the new technologies in the field of railway research included developments in energy consumption, reducing diesel exhaust, electronic braking, track design and train control systems. With the increase in traffic on rail systems, the advancement of computer monitoring and control systems continued to be of significant importance.

INDUSTRY LEADERS

EAST JAPAN RAILWAY COMPANY

East Japan Railway Company (known as JR East), the largest of the six regional passenger companies resulting from the 1987 break-up of Japan's state-owned Japan National Railway, was a leader in the industry with 2004 revenues of US$24.1 billion, an increase of 12 percent over 2003 levels. With history dating back to 1872, the company served about 59 million people in the Kanto and Tohoku parts of Japan with 16 million daily customers, transporting billions of people a year in the Tokyo area via 4,680 miles of track. Three bullet train networks operated between Tokyo and Nagano, Niigata, and Morioka. Employees totaled approximately 77,000.

DEUTSCHE BAHN GROUP

In 2004, Deutsche Bahn Aktiengesellschaft (DB), Europe's largest railway, was reporting sales of US$36.9 billion, an increase of about 4.1 percent over 2003 levels. In 2003, the company carried approximately 1.7 billion people by rail through 5,665 stations. The firm's cargo division, which merged with the cargo operations of Nederlandse Spoorwegen in 1999, carried 282.3 million tons of freight in 2003. Incorporated in 1951, the company is owned by the German government, although officials have been working to privatize Deutsche Bahn since the mid-1990s. The company had been decreasing its workforce since it reached a peak of 602,000 in 1948. Employees were reduced to 498,000 in 1960; 398,000 in 1970; 288,768 in 1996; and 225,512 in 2004.

Since the beginning of the 1980s, managers from the private sector have been appointed to Deutsche Bahn's board. This discontinuation of adherence to civil service status for the company's management was designed to lead to greater commercial orientation for the company. This objective was only partially attained, since government policy did not allow DB the necessary freedom of action in the early 1990s. Movements to end the bureaucratic status of the railroad were driven by the reunification of Germany, the accompanying takeover of the East's Deutsche Reichsbahn (another large German railroad transportation company), and the development of the European Union transport policy. The unification treaty called for the ultimate technical and organizational merging of the two railways.

SOCIÉTÉ NATIONALE DES CHEMINS DE FER FRANÇAIS

Government-owned Société Nationale des Chemins de Fer Français (SNCF) is France's largest passenger and freight rail network. Its freight service is the second largest in Europe, with a market share in 2002 of 20.5 percent. Aproximately 50 percent of its traffic is international. The company reported sales of US$28.3 billion in 2003. Its well-known TGV trains were able to reach speeds of 250 mph. SNCF employed 243,944 people.

UNION PACIFIC

Union Pacific (UP) was the largest railroad company in the United States in 2004, with 32,615 miles of track, sales of US$12.2 billion, and an employee base of more than 48,000 people. The company's primary role is the transportation of freight. In 2005, UP's largest customer was APL, a steamship company, followed by General Motors. The company was investing heavily to increase its ability to transport coal, its largest growth area.

UP was formed by the passage of the Pacific Railroad Act of 1862. The act called for the creation of a public corporation, Union Pacific Railroad Company, to build a railroad from Nebraska to the California-Nevada border. The railroad's completion supplied a critical impetus to the development of the U.S. West, which quickly developed into a land of pioneers. The company's acquisition of Southern Pacific in 1996 secured its position as the U.S. leader.

CSX CORP.

By 2005, CSX had become the largest operator of rail networks in the eastern United States. In 2004, with its 23,000 miles of rail concentrated in the United States, CSX Corp. provided rail transportation and distribution services in 23 states in the East, Midwest, and South; the District of Columbia; and two Canadian provinces. Revenues were US$8 billion that year, and employees totaled 35,847. Growing intermodal operations were handled by the CSX Intermodal unit.

CSX had its origins in the Baltimore and Ohio Railroad (B&O), which was formed in 1827. After several consolidations and mergers, the CSX Corp. was incorporated in 1978. Since then, the corporation diversified into fiber-optics, natural resources, and water transportation. However, due to low profits and a stagnant stock performance, the company underwent a major restructuring program, selling its telecommunications and oil and gas businesses and putting the money back into its own outstanding common stock. In the late 1990s, the firm acquired a 42 percent stake in Conrail. Rival Norfolk Southern purchased the remaining 58 percent.

MAJOR COUNTRIES IN THE INDUSTRY

UNITED STATES

In the United States, although major passenger routes exist, the rail system is primarily used for freight, accounting for 40 percent of all freight transportation, according to the Association of American Railroads. Rail moves 65 percent of all coal in the country, 70 percent of the cars manufactured, and 30 percent of the grain. In 2005, the U.S. was the world leader in the amount of freight moved by rail. In 2003, freight railroad operators garnered about US$38.3 billion in revenues, using almost 1.3 million freight cars and employing more than 174,000 people. The efforts of U.S. railroads to significantly reduce rates and substantially enhance service quality made the United States freight rail system the most productive in the world. However, National Railroad Passenger Corporation (Amtrak)—federally subsidized to forestall losses since inaugurating service in 1971—encountered significant problems in the late 1990s, including sluggish traffic and revenues, declining federal subsidies, and deteriorating locomotives. Almost totally owned by the U.S. Department of Transportation, in 2005 the company was still facing continuing calls for the organization to lose its subsidization.

RUSSIA

In an interview given to the Euro-Asian Transport Union in September 2004, G.M. Fadeev, Minister of Railways of the Russian Federation, noted that 81 percent of the total cargo turnover and 39.4 percent of the passenger turnover was handled by the country's rail system. In that year, the railways employed 1.5 million people. The minister estimated that by 2010, the amount of cargo transit in Russia could reach 70 to 80 million tons per year, five times the amount being moved in 2004. The 17 regional railways of Russia covered a total of 86,200 kilometers. To improve its rail system, Russia's Ministry of Railways invested in advanced container terminals using computerized management systems. Together with the railway authorities of Germany, Poland, and Belarus, the Commonwealth of Independent States (CIS) railways introduced a fast-track container block train between Moscow and Berlin. Further investment was planned for a Moscow-Smolensk-Brest rail link to enable greater integration with western European railways. Due to a 17.2 percent increase in rail freight traffic in 1999, the Ministry of Railways was able to post a US$1 billion profit. Coal proved to be the most common commodity transported, followed by construction materials, iron and manganese ore, ferrous metals, and timber.

The Trans-Siberian Railroad between Moscow and Vladivostok, begun in 1891 and completed in 1916, became the longest continuous railroad in the world. In the early 1990s, efforts to upgrade the Trans-Siberian Express Railway (TSER), which used 67 different gauges of rail, were begun through a joint venture partnership between the Russian

Ministry of Railways and U.S.-based Sea-Land Services. To make access possible to the 7,000-mile Trans-Siberian Railroad, Sea-Land set up a landbridge rail service. In the mid-1990s, Russia and Finland began constructing a US$68 million railroad connecting the two countries to carry 6 million tons of cargo annually. Extending 600 kilometers (370 miles), the new railroad was to support the transportation of up to 28 million tons a year.

INDIA

India's first railroads were built in the 1850s. Although they were intended to emulate British standards, India's rail network did not equal western standards. Instead, Indian lines were built extensively in broad gauge (1.66 meter) and in meter gauge. Since nationalizing the entire system in 1947, the Indian government substantially increased its investment by working to improve the rail system. As of 2002, some 37,900 miles of railroads were operated in India, making it the third largest system in the world. There were direct rail connections from Bombay to all parts of India. Rail service was also available at India's major seaports. In the late 1990s, Indian Railways continued to operate under traditional management practices and experienced strong demand in excess of capacity for both passengers and freight. The railroad expects to remain competitive for long-distance transit and transport, even though India plans to create a modern highway system.

CHINA

As of 2002, China operated the world's fourth most extensive rail network, with about 37,000 miles of track. By 2004, this network had grown to 45,000 miles. Roughly 60 percent of all freight traffic in China was transported by rail, as was 35 percent of passenger traffic. Though rail was introduced in China as early as the 1870s, only 7,500 miles were in operation by 1920. The network became much more extensive when the communist government took control in 1949. Recognizing that its network was outmoded, the government called for its privatization in 1994. First, however, it formed its first railway corporation, the Guangzhou Railway Corp., in 1993. Recognizing the need for fast and efficient rail systems, Chinese officials began examining high-speed rail networks being developed in France, Germany, Japan, and Sweden. China also began courting international investors, including the World Bank, to fund its railroad projects, despite reports that the country's passenger and cargo traffic declined by 39 percent in 1996. China planned to build 6,000 kilometers of electric railways between 2001 and 2005 as part of the Ministry of Railroad's plan to connect China with Russia, Tibet, Eastern Europe, and Southwest Asia. In addition, China's entrance into the World Trade Organization early in the twenty-first century opened the rail market there to increased competition. As a result, China was considered a key growth market by many analysts. In 2004, rail car demand had reached nearly three times actual capacity.

GERMANY

In the mid-1990s, Germany operated the world's fifth most extensive rail network. Subsequent developments in Germany's rail system made it a leader in rail technology. Most notable was the intercity express (ICE), which traveled at a top speed of 280 kph. In 1993, ICE service was inaugurated between Berlin, Munich, Frankfurt, and Stuttgart. The development of Intercargo Express trains proved that containers up to 32 twent-foot equivalent units (TEUs) could be transported at top speeds of up to 100 mph. ICE trains began traveling between Bremen in the north to Stuttgart in the south, reducing regular transport times by two hours. Through 2001, Germany planned to invest US$10 billion a year to develop and implement ICE train service connecting major cities throughout the country and to introduce additional high-speed railways throughout Germany. These investments were considered necessary to prepare the railroad industry for privatization. Privatization plans were continuing in 2005.

FURTHER READING

"AAR Statement on New York Times Article on Grade Crossing Safety." Association of American Railroads, 11 July 2004. Available from http://www.aar.org.

Bangsberg, P.T. "One-Track Mind." *The Journal of Commerce,* 31 May 2004.

"China: An $8 Billion Market." *Railway Age,* July 2001.

Draper, Deborah J., ed. *Business Rankings Annual.* Detroit: Thomson Gale, 2004.

"Freight Rail Security Plan Emphasizes Timely Intelligence." Association of American Railroads, 5 May 2004. Available from http://www.aar.org.

Gallagher, John. "Running Out of Track." *Traffic World,* 21 June 2004.

"Hoover's Company Capsules." 2004. Available from http://www.hoovers.com.

"International Trade Statistics." 2003. Available from http://www.wto.org.

Kaufman, Lawrence H. "Mexico: Land of Opportunity." *Railway Age,* February 2001.

Leenan, Maria; Mark Doing; Karl Strang and Nicolas Wille. "Worldwide Rail Market." Vossloh AG, October 2003. Available from http://www.vossloh.de.

"Market and Investment Volumes in Railway Technology in Central and Eastern Europe" Vossloh AG, 2004. Available from http://www.vossloh.de.

"Ministers of Transport from European and Asian Countries: A Look into the Future." Euro-Asian Transport Union. Available from http://www.eatu.org.

"North American Freight Railroad Statistics." Association of American Railroads, 2002.

"Rail Freight Traffic Up from Last Year." Association of American Railroads, 22 July 2004. Available from http://www.aar.org.

"Railroads Announce Surge in Intermodal and Carload Freight." Association of American Railroads, 14 May 2004. Available from http://www.aar.org.

"Railroads Say 'You're Hired!'" Association of American Railroads, 28 April 2004. Available from http://www.aar.org.

"Tres Grand Void; French Railways." *The Economist,* 2 June 2001.

U.S. Foreign & Commercial Service. "The Russian Railway Sector." June 2000. Available from http://www.bisnis.doc.gov.

Vantuono, William C. "Betting on a Breakthrough." *Railway Age,* December 2003.

SIC 4210

NAICS 484

TRUCKING AND COURIER SERVICES

The broad category of trucking and courier services includes three distinct subsets: (1) local trucking services, which may include storage facilities; (2) long-distance trucking services; and (3) courier services, except those by air. Many industry firms specialize in just one or two of these areas. A portion of the industry competes with services offered by government-sponsored and private postal delivery services. For more information, see also **Postal Services**.

INDUSTRY SNAPSHOT

Trucking services comprise three broad market sectors: truckload (TL), less-than-truckload (LTL), and small package (courier). In the United States, they also are classified by three general groupings: Interstate Commerce Commission (ICC)-regulated trucking, non-ICC intercity trucking, and non-ICC local trucking. Trucking companies primarily compete amongst themselves, although barge, steamship, railroad, or airline services are regarded as competitors.

After a dismal few years at the turn of the century, the trucking and courier services industry was looking up in 2005, as manufacturers began to produce and ship more freight to meet increasing demand of a growing world marketplace and handle the increasing volume of international trade resulting from improvements in the economies of developing countries and easing of trade barriers. Cost hikes related to the need for higher wages, compliance upgrades, and fuel costs were digging into profits. Consolidation was occurring at a rapid pace, although the industry remained highly fragmented, with the largest players accounting for small percentages of the total market in each country.

Additionally, in order to stay competitive, the trucking industry was evaluating the need to invest in equipment and technology. Intermodal transportation, in which freight is shipped in trailers or containers that can be directly interchanged between trucks, boats, and trains, also was rising as the preferred shipping model across industries. The trucking industry in the mid-2000s was seeing new regulations regarding safety and security, emissions, training, and taxes. By 2005, trucking was still regulated by individual country governments, although in the United States, trucking safety is regulated federally, while licensed and monitored on a state basis.

ORGANIZATION AND STRUCTURE

Truckload (TL) freight is the largest segment in the trucking business in terms of tonnage. These loads, which usually fill an entire truck, primarily are hauled directly from sender to receiver. The freight they haul can range anywhere from raw materials to finished products.

Less-than-truckload (LTL) freight, defined as shipments weighing less than 10,000 pounds, usually goes through a five-step process: local pick-up, sorting at a terminal facility, line haul, sorting at a destination terminal, and local delivery. LTL carrier operations and small package carriers use regional or national networks, sophisticated sorting terminals, and local pick-up and delivery service. Many LTL carriers historically handled packages as a component of their LTL business, but much of this traffic was served by specialized package carriers.

Courier services, also known as small package services, provided by such companies as United Parcel Service (UPS) and Federal Express (FedEx) in the United States, include two- to three-day ground delivery, as well as expedited next-day delivery. Group transportation has played an increasingly important role in small package and express letter services, sometimes termed couriers, thereby blurring the distinction between ground and air services. FedEx, while considered an air carrier for classification purposes, owns and operates an enormous truck fleet, not only for local pick-up and delivery, but also in lieu of aircraft for the line-haul portions of shorter trips. Similarly, UPS utilizes air and rail intermodal services to expedite its traditional ground carrier traffic. Likewise, Roadway Services, a traditional LTL player, operates Roadway Express, which serves both the ground delivery and air express package markets.

The industry is further divided based on driver/ownership: companies that transport goods for payment are for-hire carriers, companies that own its own fleet are private carriers, and individual owner-operators own or lease the tractor (truck) and haul goods using other trailers.

BACKGROUND AND DEVELOPMENT

The trucking industry has its roots in Great Britain where, in the 1870s, vans were hauled by steam engines. In 1885 Karl Benz invented a gasoline-powered internal-combustion automobile that spurred the development of a similarly powered load-carrying vehicle produced in 1896 by Gottlieb Daimler. In 1892, Frenchman Maurice Le Blance introduced a steam-powered cartage vehicle specifically for commercial users. The Automobile Club of America staged a contest in 1903 to test the durability and speed of heavy hauling trucks. The event's success resulted in a flourishing industry. By 1908, 4,000 trucks were on the road in the United States. By 1914, the start of World War I, 300,000 were in service; and by the war's end in 1918, a million were in use.

While early trucks resembled horse-drawn wagons, by 1915 they included roofs, roll-down curtains, windshields, doors, and side windows, and by the 1930s most truck cabs were entirely enclosed. The semi-trailer, in which the truck's front end rests on the rear portion of the hauling truck tractor, became commonplace by the 1920s. The early 1930s saw the introduction of the diesel engine. World War I saw a great boost in the trucking industry, with the U.S. Army adding to its fleet at rapid speeds. Trucks continued to develop rapidly given their prominent role in World War II.

Between the late 1920s and the early 1930s, the trucking industry in the United States became dominated by large numbers of itinerant owner-operators. Customers saw the industry becoming more unstable, unreliable, and chaotic. To correct the problem, in 1933 the National Industrial Recovery Act (NRA) was enforced to bring together two organized groups of trucking officials to agree to a code of fair competition. The groups proposed a code in which trucking firms would be subject to maximum hours of labor and minimum wages for all employees. The resulting Motor Carriage Act of 1934 provided for safety regulations of interstate carriers as well as economic regulation of for-hire carriers under the authority of the Interstate Commerce Commission (ICC), a regulatory agency that was formed in the late nineteenth century.

The ICC required that operators of for-hire trucks wishing to carry freight across state lines had to be licensed by the ICC. Licenses were granted only if the need for additional truck capacity could be provided. Cargo types were also limited, with some commodities, such as food, highly restricted. Only farmer cooperative truckers or truckers operating private carriers were exempt. Rate bureaus were formed to research and analyze costs to establish competitive trucking rates. A U.S. Justice Department antitrust exemption gave regulated trucking firms the right to collectively set rates subject to the ICC's approval.

In 1980, the U.S. Congress passed the Motor Carrier Act, a trucking deregulation bill that increased competition among trucking firms by limiting collective rate making, easing entry restrictions, and all but eliminating the ICC's authority to set rates. The act also stimulated competition by allowing unregulated private trucking firms, formerly forbidden to carry other firms' freight, to transport freight from wholly owned subsidiaries of their parent companies. Elimination or modification of the circuitous routing and empty backhauls characteristic of the regulated environment made the trucking industry much more efficient, lowering trucking rates and benefiting both shippers and consumers.

Passage of the bill signaled a major victory for those who had for decades opposed the cartel behavior of the ICC, the trucking industry, and organized labor. Deregulation was estimated to save shippers US$5 billion annually. This legislative act paved the way for new trucking firms to enter the market and set lower rates. The ICC also loosened its route setting and commodities restrictions. While large trucking firms have since faced tough competition, deregulation has resulted in a competitive industry with thousands of new trucking firms in business.

The deregulation wave of the 1980s, however, left the intricate web of controls on U.S. intrastate trucking almost untouched. In all but eight states, restrictions on truck weight and size on interstate highways, combined with prescribed rates and routes, continued to circumscribe the industry. With deregulation, shippers around the world found they could employ the entire gamut of transportation modes to meet their shipping needs. Many manufacturers found trucking to be the most attractive option when production was behind schedule or if low train tunnels along certain routes made shipping certain products by rail impossible. For shippers needing to meet steamship schedules, trucks offered a faster and more flexible option than rail. Additionally, shippers needing to transport small quantities found LTL services appealing. LTL trucking companies could consolidate small shipments from a number of different companies into a single truckload. Prior to LTL shipping companies, shippers had to persuade truckers to bend their schedules to accommodate their production cycles. Many companies had to rely on their own private fleets for local and regional delivery. Meeting tight delivery schedules was next to impossible.

From a U.S. manufacturer's perspective, the biggest advancement in the trucking industry came when truckers began forming alliances with railroads in 1990. For example, J.B. Hunt Transport Inc. and Schneider National formed alliances with Conrail, Norfolk Southern, Southern Pacific, Union Pacific, and Burlington Northern. Such alliances offered manufacturers the speed and flexibility of trucks and the low cost of rail service. As a result, trucking companies began to utilize equipment that accommodated intermodal containers rather than tractor trailers so that containerized cargo could be easily moved between both transportation modes.

The Intermodal Surface Transportation Efficiency Act (ISTEA) of 1991 set a goal to reduce paperwork by forcing states to adopt uniform measures, such as making fuel tax payments to a single state. In 1994 an International Fuel Tax Agreement and the International Registration Plan were also designed to fit the single-state payment/registration pattern. In total, these various uniformity measures were estimated to save carriers between US$500 million and US$1 billion annually in administrative costs.

Under the Clinton administration, the U.S. government moved to consolidate its bureaucracy, and as a result the 108-year-old ICC was closed in 1994. Some of its former functions were transferred to the jurisdiction of a new agency called the Commerce Board, which operated under the U.S. Department of Transportation.

The U.S. trucking industry achieved record levels in both production and earnings in the late 1990s. According to the U.S. Bureau of Census, motor carrier revenue grew by 7.8 percent in 1998, reaching US$187.4 billion. Local trucking activities, which grew by 12.8 percent, accounted for US$66.9 billion of the total, while long-distance trucking, which grew by 5.2 percent, brought in the remaining US$120.5 billion. Nearly every segment of the trucking and courier services industry in 1998 saw considerable growth. As demand grew, companies found themselves facing driver shortages, which prompted them to offer higher pay and better equipment to drivers.

During this time period, the trucking industry also began to transform itself from a narrowly defined industry into a flexible one, ready to provide a number of services to meet clients' changing cargo-transport needs. Large trucking services with national and international delivery capabilities, as well as small niche services, were in the best position to capitalize on the industry's changes in the late 1990s. Medium-size services struggled to carve out their place in the global trucking market with less potential for growth because of their inability to provide the geographic coverage of the large companies or the specialized services of the small companies. This transformation resulted from deregulation in the European Union and the United States during the early to mid-1990s, which allowed trucking services to concentrate on the needs of shippers. Previously, the industry generally had operated under rigid policies that forced shippers to adapt to trucking services.

Globalization of the trucking industry increased, due in part to trade accords such as NAFTA, as well as the expansion of trading blocs such as the European Union. In addition to providing trucking services to destinations throughout the world, trucking fleets started to expand their operations internationally by forming alliances with trucking companies and freight forwarders in other countries. However, although NAFTA created seamless trade between the United States and Canada, it failed to bring about liberalized trucking between Mexico and the United States, and trucking companies began to pressure the government to remove the restrictions.

The European Union also began implementing policies to create smooth trade among its 15 member countries and to convert its regionalized and fragmented trucking industry into a large complex industry on par with the U.S. industry. Because the European Union's freight rail service was fragmented and costly to use, trucking accounted for about 85 percent of the region's freight transport. Nevertheless, restrictions hampered the trucking industry there. Major trading countries such as France and Spain imposed bans on trucks hauling most kinds of freight on Sundays and holidays, in part to ease road congestion and to appease domestic drivers who wanted Sundays off and feared foreign drivers would deliver on Sundays without such restrictions. Other countries such as Belgium and Luxembourg planned to implement similar measures in the late 1990s. These restrictions affected the United Kingdom the most because about 60 percent of U.K. European exports were transported via truck. With pressure from the various factions involved in the dispute, the European Commission began to consider developing a sweeping policy for all member countries.

Another prominent trend in the industry was the ongoing development of intermodal transportation—the integration of various modes of transportation such as truck, train, and aircraft. Many of the industry's largest players, such as UPS, Nippon Express, and FedEx, had already adopted multiple modes of transportation by the late 1990s, having fleets of planes and trucks. These changes in the structure of the industry reduced the distinction between less-than-truckload and truckload transport services and promised to completely blur the distinction by the early 2000s. In addition, in an effort to remain competitive, trucking companies began offering a full spectrum of logistics operations to customers, including basic transportation (local, regional, truckload, less-than-truckload, and air freight), inventory management and warehousing, light assembly, and state-of-the-art information systems.

Furthermore, some companies that shipped products began to reduce and eliminate their inventories in the late 1990s to cut storage costs, which made transportation even more important. Shippers relied on trucking services to transport their products quickly and to meet strict deadlines in order to enact their inventory reductions. Similar to their air-express counterparts, trucking companies introduced single-rate, one-bill, seamless door-to-port or door-to-door scheduled delivery worldwide.

The trucking industry also began to make use of the Internet in the late 1990s, as companies set up World Wide Web sites to market their services and to allow customers to place orders and check on order status and prices. By 1998 most of the major trucking companies provided their clients with tracking capabilities at their Web sites, so individual and business customers waiting for deliveries could check the status of those deliveries online.

The rise of electronic commerce in the late 1990s had a profound impact on some of the industry's largest players, particularly those in the United States, where the Internet revolution had taken hold. UPS had been allowing clients to track shipments online since the mid-1990s. In the late 1990s rival FedEx determined that UPS had gained an advantage in Internet-based shipping partly because it focused on deliveries to residences, which increased as consumers began buying books, CDs, computers, software, and a multitude of other products on the Web. In January 1999, hoping to compete with UPS—which had a fleet of 13,500 trucks—FedEx established FedEx Home Delivery to handle its new residential ground delivery operations. Online shopping grew to roughly US$4 billion over the holiday season of 1999; at that time, FedEx handled shipping for only 10 percent of all goods sold online, compared to the 55 percent handled by UPS.

The economy was uncertain at the turn of the century. Many smaller players had already crumbled under the combined pressure of slowing demand and higher operating expenses. More than 1,300 small U.S.-based trucking firms shut their doors in 2000. Demand for transportation and shipping services began to tumble, according to *Logistics Management & Distribution Report*, as the multitude of businesses that had upped production for the flourishing economy of the late 1990s found themselves burdened with surplus inventories in 2000. Compounding the problem was a surge in oil costs, reflected in the price of diesel fuel used by trucks. By late 2000, diesel fuel rates in the United States had reached an average of US$1.65 per gallon, reflecting a 73 percent increase over prices in the late 1990s.

Logistics grew increasingly important to the trucking and courier services industry in the early 2000s. In one instance, UPS was able to use its expertise in logistics to oversee the transport and delivery of 4.5 million vehicles to 6,000 North American automobile dealers for Ford Motor Company. By following just-in-time principles, UPS was able to reduce delivery time by 25 percent, and also reduce inventory requirements at Ford, thereby saving the automaker roughly US$240 million. A similar project for National Semiconductor Corp. proved equally successful. According to a May 2001 article in *Business Week*, UPS designed and constructed a National Semiconductor warehouse, based in Singapore, that uses "a delivery process that is efficient and automated, almost to the point of magic." Once new products, such as computer chips, are manufactured and sent to the Singapore warehouse, "it is UPS's computers that speed the box of chips to a loading dock, then to truck, to plane, and to truck once again. In just 12 hours, the chips will reach one of National's customers, a PC maker half a world away in Silicon Valley. Throughout the journey, electronic tags embedded in the chips will let the customer track the order with accuracy down to about three feet." In a two-year period, UPS logistics services cut National Semiconductor's shipping and inventory management expenses by an estimated 15 percent. By 2001, smaller trucking companies were offering similar just-in-time services to their clients.

Despite these technological and operational advances, the industry remained susceptible to economic conditions. When the slowing North American economy entered a full-fledged recession in 2001, trucking and courier services firms like UPS and FedEx began to feel the pinch. The economic downturn that eventually spread to Europe and Asia undercut freight volumes as businesses shipped less inventory. At the same time, diesel fuel costs soared, reaching rates nearly 75 percent higher than those of the late 1990s. By the mid-2000s, industry analysts made clear that shippers were going to have to shoulder much of the rising cost of transportation, as trucking rates were set to increase exponentially to cover rising operating costs, from fuel to equipment to driver salaries.

Tension between Mexican and U.S. road freight officials escalated as U.S. authorities continued denying Mexican freight trucks access to U.S. destinations, despite a previous agreement that borders would be open as of January 1, 2000. In 2001, the NAFTA International Tribunal ruled that the United States was in violation of its NAFTA obligations. Those opposed to allowing Mexican freight trucks into the United States argued that Mexican trucks were unsafe and that U.S. jobs would be lost to foreign competition. Eventually, Mexican trucking association Canacar began calling for the cancellation of all NAFTA policies relating to road freight. Heated negotiations continued into 2002.

Current Conditions

Into the 2000s, private trucking was seeing a surge, due to such factors as strict security regulations in the wake of worldwide instability and threat of terrorism and war, which made greater oversight of the trucking industry necessary. In addition, the higher cost of private trucking was going down. According to the National Private Truck Council, the freight carried by private trucking companies was expected to grow 50 percent by 2020. Of the US$462 billion in revenues for intercity trucking, private trucking accounted for about 60 percent in 2002. As of 2003, there were 33,000 companies with private fleets of at least 10 vehicles.

The start of 2005 showed that tractor capacity for trucked freight remained at historical highs, although it had decreased slightly in the first quarter of the year. According to *Bulk Transporter* magazine, truck capacities were averaging over 95 percent although they were expected to decline to 90.5 percent by the first quarter of 2006.

High diesel prices continued to be a problem, with diesel prices in the United States averaging US$2.17 per gallon at the beginning of March 2005. According to the American Trucking Association, fuel accounts for about 25 percent of a trucking company's operating costs, and therefore increased prices have been cutting into profits. India, Sri Lanka, Malaysia, Thailand and Indonesia had all increased fuel prices in 2005, causing some truckers to hold demonstrations and work slowdowns. In April 2005, Britain's Road Haulage Association (where truckers pay among the world's highest fuel prices) was calling for a reduction of tax levels on fuel prices.

Also around the world, drivers continued to face increased regulation on driving hours. In the United States, the Federal Motor Carrier Safety Administration issued new rules to shorten driving hours and required compliance by January 2004. In April 2005, Britain introduced legislation to decrease the average number of hours a driver could work in a week from 55 to 48. This legislation was coming after the BBC reported the Road Haulage Associations claims that an extra 45,000 drivers were going to be needed in order to meet demand.

Advances in satellite navigation and logistics technologies are increasing efficiencies in the industry.In a further effort to reduce costs and maintain efficiency, the industry was consolidating. The biggest news in 2003 was the merging of Yellow Corp. and Roadway Corp. The US$1.1 billion merger resulted in a new company valued at approximately US$6 billion, with a command of about 60 percent of the LTL market. With the 2002 shutdown of competitor Consolidated Freightways, the only other unionized carrier was ABF Freight System, valued at US$1.3 billion.

In the courier portion of the trucking industry, Transport Canada was considering the several trends to be among the most important facing the industry. First, mergers and acquisitions would continue as companies worked to establish intermodal forms of transport for packages in order to remain competitive. In addition, postal services around the world would continue to partner with courier companies to increase their services in the face of declines in the volume of letter mail.

Increases in sales via the Internet were also having an impact on courier services, as they continued to be the distributor of choice for many sales companies. Also, more international shipping was being seen as trade liberalized around the world and the economies of developing countries improved.

Research and Technology

The escalating importance of transportation and logistics to business in the 1990s placed greater demands on fleet managers than ever before. The greatest impact in the streamlining of business was new information technology. In the early 1990s, satellite systems were introduced to the industry to track vehicles along routes and to determine package status via combinations of barcode scanning and wireless transmission of shipment data. By the late-1990s, this technology was standard for almost all trucking companies.

In 1991 UPS completed the construction of an US$80 million computer and telecommunications center in Mahwah, New Jersey, which served as the cornerstone of its global computer network. The center was part of the company's US$1.5 billion investment in a five-year plan to develop state-of-the-art high technology to drive its delivery network. In 1993 UPS installed a satellite earth station to provide a direct satellite link between the United States and Germany. By having its own earth station, UPS reduced the potential for transmission failures and allowed package tracking data to flow more reliably between the two countries.

UPSnet was a cost-efficient and highly reliable global telecommunications fiber-optic network that linked 1,200 UPS distribution sites in 1992, including 80 international locations. The network was a vital component of UPS' international expansion in the air express delivery business. The system provided immediate access to information for tracking international shipments, expediting customs clearance, billing and delivery confirmation, and electronically capturing and transmitting signatures.

UPS' proprietary International Shipments Processing System (ISPS) was an integrated network designed to process and track parcels moving within the company's international shipping network. It provided electronic shipment information directly to U.S. and Canadian customs bureaus prior to the arrival of shipments, and was able to monitor the precise status and location of packages clearing customs in more than 180 countries and territories. The system had many benefits, including reduced transit time, improved reliability of package and document transport, lowered service costs, simplified import-export shipment process, and replaced manual document preparation and key-entry tasks.

Some trucking companies such as OTR Express employed sophisticated computer systems to track customers and their shipping trends in order to expedite service. One such system developed by Ohio-based Roberts Express involved a two-way satellite network, an automated shipment and control system, and personalized Customer Assistance Teams. The system allowed for rapid customer response by tracking the nearest truck via satellite and an in-house computer system. By utilizing its computer network, the trucking firm was able to make pickup or reach its destinations within 15 minutes of the promised delivery time.

In 1994 the U.S. National Highway Traffic Safety Administration (NHTSA) developed technology called the Autonomous Driver Alertness Monitor (ADAM) to curb fatigue-related accidents. An NHTSA study found that out of 6.5 million crashes in 1990, some 57,000 were caused by drowsiness. When a driver blinks repetitively, ADAM sets off a loud noise or flashing light to jolt the driver. The monitors could either be placed on drivers' eyeglasses or on seatbelts. To help prevent driver fatigue, some trucking firms also used the Princeton Logistics System, a computerized dispatch program that assists long-haul drivers in selecting backhaul loads that will shorten their drive home. Many companies practiced "team driving," in which two drivers split the pay, which is based on mileage, and make the haul together. The advantage was to maximize productivity and time by keeping the truck moving.

Safety and environmental issues have also greatly impacted the industry. Trucks equipped with anti-lock brakes became more commonplace. In the United States, drivers who haul freight long distance are required to take periodic alcohol and drug tests to ensure they are free of judgment-impairing substances when they are behind the wheel. German truck manufacturers Freightliner and Daimler-Benz tested a second generation of truck design that uses an interactive video computer system. Called Vector, the system videotapes the highway as the truck drives along, interprets data such as speed and traffic, and directs the truck to travel at a certain speed. Application of this technology was not expected to reach the marketplace until the twenty-first century. Meanwhile, other designs addressing fuel consumption, emissions standards, and engines were being tested in order to meet tougher standards imposed by the Clear Air Act and to allow trucks to operate more efficiently and profitably.

WORKFORCE

Truck drivers entering the field generally received informal training, although several trucking companies such as C.R. England have truck driver schools. Many learn by riding with and observing experienced drivers. Given the shortages in the industry, job opportunities in trucking are abundant and are expected to increase in both the United States and Europe.

Long hours on the road, weeks away from home, nonunion wages at nonunion trucking companies, and the cramped quarters of the sleeper cab have all been cited as drawbacks of trucking industry employment. Truckers have complained about being forced to load and unload freight themselves or having to pay out of their own pockets for extra help at the dock, a practice termed "lumping." Such complaints have caused many trucking companies to focus on shorter regional markets, typically 250 to 500 miles in length, and forge partnerships with railroads to offer intermodal service.

Employees at some large carriers have been forced to accept wage cuts. In some cases, wage negotiations with trade unions have spurred bitter management-labor showdowns and strikes, with work rules and health, welfare, and pension benefits nominally at issue. Most notable was the 1997 UPS labor strike in which UPS eventually sued the International Brotherhood of Teamsters for US$50 million, claiming the strike had been illegal. The strike was resolved on terms that favored the union, and some analysts predicted that the result would cause labor costs to increase for all unionized LTL companies. In 1998 the Teamsters announced their plans to seek similar employee compensation packages for other major companies: Yellow Freight System, Roadway Express, Consolidated Freightways, and ABF Freight System. Some companies reported losing business to non-unionized competition because of their ability to offer lower rates.

INDUSTRY LEADERS

COURIER SERVICES

United Parcel Service Inc (UPS). With sales of US$36.5 billion and roughly 384,000 employees worlwide, United Parcel Service (UPS) was the largest package shipper in the world in 2004. That year, this Atlanta, Georgia-based company moved 3.6 billion packages to more than 200 countries and territories. The company does not separate out the revenue earned from trucking verses that earned from other forms of transport, including air, as much of its courier services involves a variety of transport forms for each delivery.

In 2003, the company introduced plans to spend US$600 million dollars to improve its pickup and delivery processes. Considered the most technologically savvy of the world's largest shipping firms, UPS uses systems such as UPSnet, with more than 500,000 miles of communications lines, as well as a satellite that tracks hundreds of thousands of packages each day and connects roughly 1,300 UPS distribution plants in 46 different nations.

UPS was founded in August 1907 in Seattle, Washington, as a result of teenagers Jim Casey and Claude Ryan starting a telephone message service called the American Messenger Company. Soon, the boys found themselves making small-parcel deliveries for local department stores. In 1952 the company expanded to include small package delivery within a 150-mile radius of specific metropolitan areas, with Los Angeles becoming the first. Its first international operation occurred in 1975, with service to Ontario, Canada. In 1976 service was initiated within West Germany, and by 1985 service had expanded to six other European countries. An important milestone was reached when, in 1987, UPS became the first package delivery company in history to deliver to every address in the United States and Puerto Rico. That year the company also expanded its international service to Japan and parts of Canada. In 1988, the company acquired Italian service partner Alimondo, providing UPS with 40 facilities throughout Italy. That same year its International Air Service delivery network extended to 41 countries. UPS also announced the acquisition of Asian Courier System (ACS), a Hong Kong-based carrier, and the British company Arkstar Limited and its subsidiaries, including Atlasair Parcel Service Ltd., providing UPS with a network of 19 branches throughout Britain. In 1991, UPS introduced Euro-Expedited Service, a pan-European ground package and freight delivery service, as an economical alternative to air express. By 1992 UPS was the largest package distribution company in the world.

FedEx. Federal Express specializes in overnight delivery of packages, documents, and heavy freight, and is a top express transportation company worldwide. With 2004 sales of US$24.7 billion, the company's 196,000 employees handle 6 million shipments each day to more than 220 countries and territories, using more than 71,000 ground delivery vehicles. Its delivery divisions include FedEx Express, FedEx Ground, FedEx Freight, and FedEx Custom. This company does not differentiate between revenue earned by truck transport and that earned through air or other means.

Founded in 1971, Federal Express was originally conceived in a college term paper. In 1973 the company began service in 25 cities with a fleet of 14 small aircraft. In the mid-1980s, Federal Express opened its European hub and generated US$2 billion in one year alone. Although the company was experiencing losses in the international arena in the 1990s, its total sales were US$11.5 billion and it employed more than 126,000 people. Shortly after Federal Express bought ground shipper Caliber System in the late-1990s, the company consolidated all operations under a new parent company named FDX Corporation.

In early 2000, FDX diversified into customs brokerage with the purchase of Tower Group International, a unit that eventually formed the core of a new subsidiary, FedEx Trade Networks Inc. The trading unit also provided trade consulting and international transportation and logistics services. In April, FDX changed its name to FedEx Corp., and the core express delivery business took on the moniker FedEx Express. Ground delivery operations were renamed FedEx Ground. To expand its less-than-truckload freight operations, the firm paid US$1.2 billion for American Freightways Corporation in December 2000. FedEx merged American Freightways with former Caliber unit Viking Freight into its FedEx Freight arm. As part of the deal, FedEx assumed US$250 million in American Freightways' debt, a fact which concerned some analysts as FedEx was already spending billions of dollars each year maintaining its costly infrastructure.

DHL Worldwide Network. Belgian based, yet owned by the German Deutsche Post, DHL Worldwide is a global leader in international express shipping. Begun in 1969 as an air shipper of paper from California to Hawaii, the company was soon expanding globally. By the end of 2002, Deutsche Post owned the company, and in 2003 the parent merged its other acquisitions into DHL. By 2003, the company's 160,000 employees used 75,000 vehicles to move more than 1 billion shipments to more than 220 countries and territories. DHL's revenues that year were more than US$28 billion.

TNT N.V. Although it is the primary manager of the postal system of the Netherlands, TNT is also a world leader in the express delivery and logistics businesses. What began in Australia in 1946 as a single truck operation, had grown by 1996 to an international firm large enough to acquire the postal service of the Netherlands, a venture that had started the privatization process in 1989. Through a series of joint ventures and acquisitions, by 2004 the firm had grown to employ more than 162,000 people, and had revenues of more than US$17 billion, with 37 percent of that coming from express delivery.

Yamato. Yamato Transport Co. Ltd. was the forerunner of private parcel delivery service in Japan, and in 2004, it had been the market leader in that country for two decades. A strong domestic service includes home moving, delivery of refrigerated goods, and facsimile transmission. Links with UPS in the United States allow Yamato to make deliveries in 200 countries outside Japan. Founded in 1919 by young entrepreneur Koshin Kogura, Yamato was the first courier service in Tokyo. By its fiscal year end in March 2004, Yamato employed nearly 132,000 workers and brought in approximately US$9.4 billion per year.

TRUCKING COMPANIES

Nippon Express. Nippon Express Co. Ltd. was Japan's leading general transportation company in 2004 with a fleet of more than 30,000 trucks, trailers, and other vehicles. Revenues were US$11.7 billion at March 2004, of which 48 percent came from trucking. Founded in the 1930s, Nittsu—as it is familiarly called—assumes full responsibility for the door-to-door, worldwide delivery of all types of goods, including electronic components, oil refinery equipment, and fine arts. As a result of opening markets in the European Union, Nippon Express has been developing its European trucking network and improving its warehousing facilities. In addition to trucking services, Nippon Express offers rail and air transport services through its subsidiaries. In 2004, the firm employed 38,749 people in 1,100 domestic service centers, with an additional 11,900 employees working in 297 service centers in 32 countries and 165 cities around the world.

Schneider National. In 2005, the largest truckload carrier in the United States was privately owned Schneider National. The company also had a strong presence in Canada and Mexico. Founded in 1935, the company grew through a series of acquisitions over the years, and began to acquire the right to transport in various states, and then throughout North America. In 2003, the company employed 20,000 people, including 15,000 drivers and contractors, and earned US$2.9 billion.

J.B. Hunt Transport Services Inc. Begun in 1969 with five trucks and seven refrigerated trailers, by 2004 the company operated 9,900 trucks (tractors) and 45,759 trailers providing trucking services to the United States, Canada and Mexico. Sales in 2004 reached US$2.8 billion, and the company employed almost 16,000 people.

Yellow Roadway Corporation. After a series of acquisitions, Yellow Roadway Corporation continued to work under a series of brand names, including Yellow Transportation, Roadway Express, New Penn, and Reimer Express. The 2003 acquisition of Roadway doubled the size of the company. In 2004, the company reached revenue levels of US$6.8 billion and employed 50,000 people. The company is the leader in less-than-truckload (LTL) transportation in the United States, consolidating freight from various suppliers in order to improve cost efficiencies for customers. In 2005, the company was working to acquire USF Corporation, a large U.S. LTL transportation company with 2004 sales of US$2.4 billion and an employee count of 20,000.

MAJOR COUNTRIES IN THE INDUSTRY

United States. The U.S. trucking industry remained the world's strongest throughout into the mid-2000s. *Euromonitor* indicated that the U.S. trucking market increased from US$468.2 billion in 2002 to US$490 billion in 2003. Of this total, 66.2 percent came from intercity trucking, which was expected to remain the largest sector to 2008, growing to 67.2 percent. In 2001, approximately 70 percent of trade crossing the U.S./Canadian border was transported via truck. *Euromonitor* forecast increases of 14 percent by 2007, from a 2003 value of US$484.6 billion.

European Union. The European Union's trucking industry was strong in the late 1990s; trucks continued to ship more than 80 percent of the region's cargo, because European railroads still were largely regulated during that period. With the European Union's establishment in 1993 came deregulation to Western Europe's trucking industry and a change in rules dictating cabotage. Non-national trucking carriers were now permitted to pick up and backhaul cargo throughout the European Union. Internal spot checks replaced systematic halts at frontier customs posts, thereby quickening traffic flow and preventing long border delays. These new rules were not welcomed by all EU member nations, however. Germany, a main transit route for cargo traveling to and from Turkey, the Netherlands, and Belgium, opposed the rules, saying that increased truck traffic would result in congestion, pollution, and road damage. Nonetheless, the German market was forecast to increase more than 20 percent between 2003 and 2008, according to *Euromonitor.*

Similarly, the U.K. market was expected to increase 12 percent over the same time period. Switzerland was the most vocal against truck traffic. Its central European location—positioned as the main transit route for truck movement to and from Italy, the Balkans, Turkey, and the Middle East—forced laws requiring trucks to only travel its roads during the daytime. The Swiss also passed a referendum to prohibit all through-truck traffic as of the year 2004. After that year, all cargo was required to travel via rail.

Asia. In Asia the trucking industry also fared well in the mid-1990s in leading countries such as Japan and China. Two main companies—Nippon Express and Yamato Transport—dominated Japan's industry. Demand for small package shipments drove the industry during this period, leading to 3.1 percent growth in the first half of 1996, according to the *Journal of Japanese Trade & Industry.* However, competition in the industry accelerated in the late 1990s and shippers faced ongoing pressure to lower their distribution costs.

Trucking started to play a greater role in shipping cargo in China in the 1990s. The country's trucking industry remained small in the 1980s, accounting for about 6 percent of China's freight traffic, but by the early 1990s trucking's share had risen to 13.6 percent. Although trucking services cost more than train services, Chinese companies prefer trucking services because of problems with the country's railroads: train delays, scarce availability, and lost and damaged goods. Truckers provide more reliable service that is less prone to damage. Furthermore, China's highway expansion during this period helped the trucking industry to prosper. Hong Kong, over which China resumed control in 1997, also has a strong trucking industry that accounted for 25 percent of the province's total annual freight volume. Although many analysts considered China a key growth market for international trucking and courier services players, the market remained fairly closed in the early 2000s.

FURTHER READING

"Across the Alps." *The Economist,* 14 April 2001.

Allen, Margaret. "Delivering the Goods." *Journal of Commerce and Commercial,* 7 December 2001.

American Trucking Association. "ATA Advocates Realistic Solution to Freight Transportation Challenges." 22 May 2003. Available from http://www.truckline.com.

———. "ATA Truck Tonnage Index Shows 5.4 Percent Increase in April." 28 May 2003. Available from http://www.truckline.com.

———. "Facts about Trucking." February 2002. Available from http://www.truckline.com.

———. "Trucking Will Dominate Freight Movement." *U.S. Freight Transportation Forecast to 2014,* 7 March 2003.

Arndt, Michael. "Industry Outlook 2001: Transportation." *Business Week,* 2 January 2001.

"Canadian Courier Market Size, Structure and Fleet Analysis Study." Transport Canada, 2003. Available from www.tc.gc.ca.

Draper, Deborah J., ed. *Business Rankings Annual.* Detroit: Thomson Gale, 2004.

Gelinas, Tom. "Competition!" *Fleet Equipment,* May 2004.

Haddad, Charles. "UPS vs. FedEx: Ground Wars." *Business Week,* 21 May 2001.

Harrington, Lisa H. "NAFTA and Trucking." *Transportation & Distribution,* September 2001.

Henry, John. "Trucking Industry Thrives Despite New Regulations." *Arkansas Business,* 12 July 2004.

"Hoover's Company Capsules." 2004. Available from http://www.hoovers.com.

"Intermodal, Truck Freight Seen Weakening." *Bulk Tansporter,* April 2005. Available from http://bulktransporter.com.

"International Trade Statistics." 2003. Available from http://www.wto.org.

"Modern Bulk Transporter's Annual Gross Revenue Report 2003: Operating Ratios Deteriorate Further." *Modern Bulk Tansporter,* May 2004.

Lazich, Robert S., ed. *Market Share Reporter.* Detroit: Thomson Gale, 2004.

Schulz, John D. "Trucking's Good News, Bad News." *The Journal of Commerce,* 31 May 2004.

———. "Trucking's Private Renaissance?" *Traffic World,* 3 May 2004.

"Supply Chain a Key to UPS Growth, Says CEO." *Journal of Commerce Online,* 14 July 2004.

Tanzer, Andrew. "Chinese Walls." *Forbes,* 11 November 2001.

"Truck Recruitment in High Gear." *BBC News: UK Edition,* 26 May, 2004. Available from http://news.bbc.co.uk.

"Truckers Traveling Rough Road." *Logistics Management & Distribution Report,* May 2001.

"Trucking in France, Germany, UK, US." *Euromonitor,* October 2004. Available from http://www.majormarketprofiles.com.

SIC 4400

NAICS 483

WATER TRANSPORTATION

Industry firms transport freight and passengers on the open seas or inland waters. The freight segment is also commonly known as the merchant marine. Maritime transportation companies also furnish such services as lighterage, towing and tugboating, and canal and marina operation. For further information about water transportation vessels, see also the article entitled **Shipbuilding.**

INDUSTRY SNAPSHOT

Merchant fleets of every nation carry merchandise between ports throughout the world in direct competition with each other. Intermodal ships (those involved in goods delivery using two or more transport modes) primarily consist of containerships, roll-on/roll-off (ro/ro) vessels, and container/barge carriers. General cargo ships include breakbulk vessels, partial container ships, and other ships designed to carry non-containerized cargo. Primary U.S. operators include CSX (Sea-Land Service Inc.), American President Lines (APL), and Seabulk International Inc.

According to the United Nations Conference on Trade and Development (UNCTAD), 6.17 billion metric tons of goods were shipped by sea in 2003, an increase of 3.7 percent over 2002. Oil tankers and dry bulk carriers made up 72.9 percent of the world fleet, continuing to increase over previous years. The average age of a ship was 12.5 years, with 27.7 percent of ships being 20 years or older, and general cargo ships having the oldest average age of 17.4 years. Most markets showed increases in the volumes transported during 2003. The volume of crude oil increased by 3.4 percent and bulk products, including iron ore and coal, increased by 9.1 percent.

Using data supplied by Lloyd's Register, UNCTAD reported that of the 30,228 ships registered by January 31, 2003, Greece was the world leader in terms of the number of vessels domiciled there, a term for where the parent is located, accounting for 19.52 percent of the world's shipping vessels. This was followed by Japan with 13.60 percent, Norway with 7.57 percent, China with 5.77 percent, the United States with 5.54 percent, and Germany with 5.31 percent.

According to 2003 U.S. Maritime Administration statistics (MARAD), there were 416 total ships in the U.S. merchant fleet, with 13.3 million combined deadweight tons (DWT). The majority were tanker ships, with a total of 110, followed by 87 container ships and 64 ro/ro ships. By 2004, the total combined fleet of the world's top twenty countries was 28,650 vessels, with a combined DWT of 821.7 million.

Steamship lines worldwide have employed various means to improve their productivity, increase sailing frequencies and port coverage, and reduce costs. Common methods have included vessel sharing agreements, slot and terminal rationalization arrangements, and the introduction of new technologies. Shipping lines also relied on shipping conferences, or groups of carriers that service particular trade routes, to facilitate cooperative arrangements and establish rates, although the importance of such conferences had begun to decline. Conferences lessened the need for individual lines to build new ships when serving new routes. Intra-industry cooperation also enabled steamship lines to overcome the double hurdle of overcapacity and declining world petroleum demand.

ORGANIZATION AND STRUCTURE

Cargo vessels constitute the largest component of water transportation. Depending on their design, they may haul general cargo (finished and unfinished goods), dry bulk, or liquid bulk. These vessels are structured as common carriers—vessels available for public use to provide transportation for passengers or cargo—and operate on regular time tables and port rotations.

Containerized vessels are designed to be highly efficient. Containers used to haul cargo need less labor and time to load and unload than breakbulk (noncontainerized) vessels. The containerized category encompasses intermodal ships, including roll-on/roll-off (ro/ro) vessels, and container/barge carriers. Ro/ros make it possible for cargo stored in containers to be passed over ramps through doors in the ship's sides while cars, trucks, and other vehicles could be driven on and off the vessel's aft (rear) end.

The five trade lanes that account for the vast majority of U.S. international ocean liner shipments are as follows: U.S.-northern Europe, U.S.-Asia, U.S.-Mediterranean, U.S.-South America, and U.S.-Australia. These trade lanes have varied in their characteristics. Containerized shipping was concentrated in three trade lanes: Asia-North America, Asia-Europe, and Europe-North America. The northern Europe and Asia trades have been the largest, in both volume and value.

Some commodities, such as dry bulk like grain, lumber, cement, potash, coal, ore, etc., cannot be containerized and therefore are shipped in vessels specially designed for those cargo types. Many have special hoisting devices that assist in unloading. Liquid bulk such as crude oil and refined petroleum is transported in tankers, which require special features such as cofferdams separating the tanks to prevent leakage, expansion trunks, mechanical venting, and steam heating to reduce oil viscosity in cold weather.

Beyond vessel design, a prominent feature of international liner shipping is the existence of carrier conferences, an affiliation permitted in almost all countries. The characteristics of concerted activity and partial immunity from competition and antitrust laws are common to such conferences worldwide. However, every nation regulates conference activities in different ways, and U.S. regulation of conferences in ocean shipping is, to an extent, unique. Members of a conference enter into an agreement under which they agree to fix and maintain rates to be charged by the members of the conference.

Most nations recognize the conference system but differ in their respective laws and regulations. The European Union gives antitrust immunity to conference carriers alone. In Europe, conferences are free to organize themselves as their members see fit and may limit membership. By limiting membership, closed conferences are better able to control capacity and thereby to exert greater influence over rates. Australia provides partial antitrust immunity and exempts only rate-fixing, pooling or apportioning of business, cargo restrictions, decisions on conference membership, loyalty agreements, and practices essential to the conference service and of overall benefit to exporters. Likewise, Canada grants conference carriers block antitrust immunity. Independent carriers, though, are subject to competition laws. As in Australia, Canadian policy holds that discussion agreements between conferences and independents are illegal. Japan has granted the broadest exemption in that all ocean transporters, liner and non-liner in both domestic and foreign trades, receive blanket antitrust exemption. Although the United States continues to recognize the existence of conferences, since the passage of the Ocean Shipping Reform Act of 1998 (OSRA) conferences operating in the United States have lost much of their commercial power. They can no longer require members to adhere to conference rates and cannot place restrictions on the service agreements members negotiate. In addition, conferences cannot require members to disclose the rates they charge.

The International Maritime Organization (IMO), an agency of the United Nations, began in 1958 when it was determined that there was a need for an international body to regulate safety in the shipping industry. In 1960, the IMO created a new version of the International Convention for the Safety of Life at Sea (SOLAS), and in 1973 created the Convention for the Prevention of Pollution from Ships covering accidental and operational oil pollution, and also pollution by chemicals, goods in packaged form, sewage, garbage and air pollution. However, how these conventions are implemented varies from country to country.

BACKGROUND AND DEVELOPMENT

Transportation of goods over water, as ancient as civilization, did not come to full fruition as an industry until explorers, seeking new trade routes for cargo, opened all-sea routes from Europe to Asia and the Americas. To accommodate increased trade volumes, large merchant ships had to be built. Spanish carracks, which held some 1,600 tons of cargo, and later, galleons, became the forerunners of the full-rigged ships that dominated trade between the seventeenth and nineteenth centuries.

The nineteenth century saw the invention of the clipper ship. Carrying both passengers and cargo, these ships became known for their speed, some traveling as fast as 18 to 20 knots. Even with the introduction of the steamship in the mid-nineteenth century, some clipper ships continued, for a time, to post the fastest speeds. By late century, however, clipper ships began to be replaced with Britain's adaptation of iron-hulled steamships.

The introduction of the steamship in the nineteenth century radically transformed ocean shipping and led to the creation of steam-powered liner systems. By the twentieth century, mechanically propelled vessels had replaced nearly all sail-powered cargo ships. With the exception of wind-driven dowhs and junks in Africa and some Asian nations, by 1960, almost 60 percent of all commercial ships were powered by diesel engines, 30 percent by steam turbine, and the rest by steam-reciprocating engines. Nuclear power, which proved impractical for commercial purposes, came into use in military ships in the 1960s.

The seas remained territory mainly for cargo-carrying lines, however. With increases in global trade in the mid-twentieth century, the seas soon became crowded with cargo vessels operated by both large and small corporate entities. Vessels were redesigned to allow for the transporting of mixed cargo. Other designs accommodated single bulk commodities such as grains, mineral ores, coal, and oil. Until the late 1960s and early 1970s, these general cargo or breakbulk ships were widely used by the liner trades. After a truckload or boxcar load of cargo was delivered to the pier, breakbulk ships were loaded by breaking the truckload (or boxcar load) into small quantities that were lifted onto the ship by a sling and boom and then stowed. This process was fairly labor-intensive, costly, and time consuming.

To become more efficient and accommodate large quantities of payloads, cargo ships underwent major redesigns. In the late 1960s, containerized vessels were introduced, capable of hauling cargo in 20 and 40-foot containers. These large metal boxes could be placed on tractor-trailer chassis, loaded at the exporter's plant, sealed, shipped by truck or train to the port, lifted onto the container ship by a dockside crane, and stacked in specially designed slots. The container itself was then unloaded at the destination. This could be accomplished without directly handling the cargo inside the container. Vessels were specifically designed or adapted to carry these containers. A roll-on/roll-off design made it possible for containers to be passed over ramps through doors in the ships' sides while cars, trucks, and other vehicles could be driven on and off the vessel. Containerized ships, which accommodate containers filled by consolidators or shippers, were designed to receive cargo by cranes or special hoisting equipment.

Containerization had its greatest impact on the cost of labor. In 1960, in-port labor costs accounted for 80 percent of the total cost of a typical voyage. With containerized shipments, average handling time per voyage fell from 157 hours to 31 hours, reducing cargo-handling costs from 80 to 65 percent . With steamship lines introducing containerization on all the major trade routes, many turned to intermodal services in which containers could be lifted on and off trucks, railroad cars, and steamships, allowing for seamless shipping over land and water. Intermodal services minimized bottlenecks in port as cargo was transferred between modes of transportation. Such efficiencies allowed the development of just-in-time production methods that turned transportation into an important part of a coordinated warehousing/production logistical system.

The development of modern tankers hauling crude oil rendered them incomparable to earlier models. Supertankers, carrying 24,900 tons of deadweight, were first built in 1949. After the closing of the Suez Canal during the 1956 crisis, larger and more efficient tankers—many constructed by the Japanese—were built to haul 100,000 tons around the Cape of Good Hope, thus bypassing the canal. Even larger tankers, known as large crude carriers and capable of accommodating 250,000 to 275,000 tons, were also soon built. Eventually, the success of these large vessels led to the development of ultra-large crude carriers boasting capacities up to 400,000 tons. In the 1990s, still larger vessels were in the works, with special consideration given to protect tankers against oil spills in case of collision.

To help large vessels navigate harbors and channels, tugboats (or towboats) were introduced. Utilizing standard engines, they were able to generate enormous towing and pushing power due to a very large, slowly rotating propeller. Refrigerated fishing boats capable of catching, processing, and freezing fish while at sea represent a further development in vessel design. Water taxis, including hovercraft, which make use of air pressure to ride just over the surface of the water, and hydrofoils, which operate at speeds of 50 knots due to the hydrodynamic advantages gained by having the vessel's hull largely out of the water while the hydrofoils alone remain submerged, have also come into use.

SHIPPING CONFERENCES

Shipping conferences, or associations of ocean carriers operating in specific trades, played a major role in freight-carrying steamship lines. After the first conference was formed in 1875 to serve the Calcutta-England trade, their use rapidly spread. Conferences were primarily formed to counter and avoid rate wars, which resulted from rapid increases in tonnage transported between 1860 and 1880. Shipping companies competed for business by building ships of increasing speed and size to realize greater economies of scale. National policies of most large trading nations favored the development of a strong national flag merchant fleet. Every major power in Europe, as well as Japan, Brazil, and some of the British dominions, employed subsidies to expand, protect, and control merchant shipping.

Conferences were formed to promote cooperation among conference members. In general, they:

- agreed upon a common tariff to minimize price competition;
- attempted to control the supply of available shipping space by agreeing on sailing schedules and the amount of tonnage available;
- often employed a revenue or cargo-sharing pool;
- made rebates or loyalty payments to reward shippers who made extensive use of conference ships; and
- attempted to keep new competitors from entering the trade (or convince them to join the conference).

The operation of conferences in the early twentieth century prompted two major investigations of the system. In 1909, the British Royal Commission concluded that the conference system was warranted and a deferred rebate system should be accepted. From 1912 to 1914, the U.S. Congress also conducted a major investigation of conferences. It concluded that conference agreements were used to restrain competition among the conference members, but also found certain advantages in the conference system. Among these benefits were improved service arising from greater stability of rates and greater regularity of sailings that occurred as conference members coordinated their schedules.

By rationalizing sailing dates and ports of call, conference carriers were able to reduce costs. In turn, stable rate levels promoted investment in newer and more efficient ships. Disadvantages included the monopolistic nature of the conference, the possibility of earning excess profits, indifference to cargo delivery, arbitrary policies for settling claims, failure to give adequate notice of rate changes, and retaliation and discrimination against shippers. It was believed that large volume shippers received better rates and service. As a result, the U.S. Congress enacted the Shipping Act of 1916, which offered limited acceptance of the conference system. The Shipping Act provided conferences with antitrust immunity, while maintaining a major regulatory role in seaborne transportation for government agencies. To get around the more onerous portions of the law, but also ensure the stability and effectiveness of its business-friendly aspects, conferences began using a dual-rate contract system that awarded shippers who signed requirements or loyalty contracts with conferences lower tariff rates. By the end of the 1950s, more than 60 conferences and thousands of shippers used some form of dual-rate contract.

In 1959 the U.S. Congress began to draft amendments to the Shipping Act of 1916 after a 1958 Supreme Court ruling found dual-rate contracting illegal. In 1961, an amendment to the act was signed into law that reversed the Supreme Court's decision and authorized dual-rate contracts unless the Federal Maritime Commission (FMC) found, after notice and hearing, that the contract would be detrimental to the commerce of the United States. The 1961 amendment required, however, that all carriers file their tariffs with the FMC. The FMC was also empowered to subpoena information from conferences and carriers to determine whether to approve an agreement.

In the wake of the 1961 amendment, further calls for reform were fueled by carrier complaints about delays in the FMC's approval process for conference agreements, application of vague standards for approval, and loss of predictability in regulatory decision-making. As newcomers crowded into the U.S. trades, many routes became heavily overrun, contributing to a growing instability of rates and service. Moreover, intense competition led several established carriers to offer shippers informal and illegal rebates on published rates.

The Shipping Act of 1984 replaced the foregoing legislation, focusing on unjust discrimination between shippers and attempting to harmonize the objectives of facilitating an efficient ocean transportation system while controlling the potential abuses and disadvantages allegedly inherent in the conference system. After much debate on the effects of allowing discriminatory pricing for ocean shipping services, the 1984 revision specially authorized service contracts as a compromise between carrier and shipper interests. In exchange, however, Congress removed the antitrust immunity for dual-rate contracts that had previously been granted. Now carriers and conferences had to file these contracts confidentially with the FMC, which in turn would make public a summary of these contracts. The idea was to block the conferences' ability to abuse their market position.

While the 1984 legislation was intended to bring competitive enhancements, opponents continued to argue that conferences were legalized cartels and should not be exempt from any antitrust laws. They maintained that competitiveness in the open marketplace should be encouraged to stimulate creative pricing and that subsidies by foreign governments to their own national shipyards should also be abolished, putting U.S. shipyards in a more competitive position. Buyers of steamship services—particularly those transporting large volumes—argued that they had the legal right to negotiate price and service levels based on fair market value, and that foreign companies do not operate under these constraints.

One example of the tremendous power exhibited by the conferences was the operation of the Trans-Atlantic Agreement (TAA), formed in 1992. Nearly 70 percent of the steamship lines carrying freight on the North Atlantic entered into TAA's price-setting pact as a means to increase rates on a route that was losing revenues due to diminished trade between the United States and Europe. The rates agreed upon by TAA members caused an uproar among shippers, who claimed that the conference caused freight rates to rise by 54 percent in one year, and that no alternative means of transportation existed. Similar and ongoing complaints lodged against the TAA by shippers have resulted in nearly continuous investigation of conference practices by the FMC and the European Commission.

The U.S. Congress continued to weigh these issues, facing the dilemma of how to preserve the declining U.S.-flag merchant fleet. The outlook for shipyards also looked grim, particularly given the decline in naval orders due to the government's ongoing downsizing of the military. However, a 1992 congressional study maintained that although the U.S.-flag fleet was losing ground in the relative ranking of the world's fleets, it ranked very high in the number of container ships, ro/ros, and barge carriers. In 1990, the U.S.-flag container ship fleet ranked second in the world in deadweight tons, and third in number of ships. According to the *U.S. Industry and Trade Outlook,* water transportation's contribution to the gross domestic product was expected to increase by 4 percent per year for the period of 1999 to 2004. The position of the U.S.-flag merchant fleet remains in doubt, however, as leading shipping lines, including Sea-Land, APL, and Lykes, consider shifting their registries to other countries with more lenient fiscal and operating regulations.

Other U.S. legislation has impacted the marine industry. The Merchant Marine Act of 1920, commonly known as the Jones Act, required that all waterborne commerce between points in the United States, including its territories and possessions, be carried on vessels built in the United States, owned and staffed by U.S. citizens, and registered under the U.S. flag. In addition, this act and the 1936 Merchant Marine Act sought to preserve the U.S. maritime industry through a system of subsidies. The larger concern was to have an adequate merchant marine the U.S. military could turn to in time of war. This issue was escalated during the Persian Gulf War, and remains a stumbling block to legislative reform in the U.S. maritime transportation industry.

The Ocean Shipping Reform Act of 1998 (OSRA), the long-awaited revision of the Shipping Act of 1984, went into effect in May 1999. Among other provisions, the new law changed the nature of service contracts between carriers and their customers. They were no longer public documents but confidential agreements that were not even open to fellow members of conferences. Hence, carriers would be able to negotiate their rates independent of conference rate structures. Under OSRA, conferences were prohibited from requiring members to disclose their rates. It was felt that by freeing prices from those set by conferences, shippers would have greater flexibility in negotiating favorable rates. With their power to determine the rates for specific routes stripped away—for U.S. trade, at any rate—conferences, and the monopolistic practices they represented to some, were expected to slowly disappear or to evolve into shippers associations or similar marketing organizations.

International shipping was seriously affected by the financial collapse in several Asian nations that accompanied the Asian economic troubles of the late 1990s. By 1999, conditions had apparently improved. International shipping reached a record high of 5.23 billion tons, according to the United Nations Conference on Trade and Development (UNCTAD). That represented a growth rate of only 1.3 percent, however, the lowest in more than a decade.

By 1999, world surplus tonnage had decreased to 23.7 DWT (deadweight tons), or 3 percent of the world fleet, the lowest in the entire decade. By the end of the decade, although demand for maritime transportation of freight was threatening to overtake supply, price competition was driving rates down. In 2000 the industry rallied and rates jumped to their highest levels in 30 years, enabling both container shipping firms and dry bulk carriers to realize profits. Larger firms, like Nippon Yusen Kaisha, had recovered from the 1990s downturn and reported highly profitable years. Consolidation continued, most notably the acquisition of Sea-Land Service Inc. by the A.P. Moller-Maersk Line in 1999. The most profitable shipping concerns became those that were a part of a conglomerate corporation that also operated concerns in related fields including shipbuilding, intermodal transportation, and freight handling. Such shipping lines included Hyundai and Hanjin of Korea, Mitsui OSK and K Line of Japan, P&O Nedlloyd of the United Kingdom, and Hapag-Lloyd of Germany.

The passage of the Ocean Shipping Reform Act of 1998 (OSRA) was a momentous event for commercial shipping. OSRA completely altered how service contracts between carriers and shippers were negotiated and regulated. It freed carriers to negotiate rates without interference from shipping conferences. Its effect was almost instantaneous. During the first year it was in effect, the Federal Marine Commission reported more than 141,000 service contracts. With the international maritime industry in a period of growth and ferment that lasted into the 2000s, government regulatory bodies worldwide continued to attempt to guide its development. OSRA ushered in a new era in regulation and was perhaps the most significant factor, influencing regulators in other countries as well.

Throughout 2000 and 2001 the Canadian parliament tried, unsuccessfully, to hammer out legislation of its own based on the U.S. model. Following OSRA's lead, bodies such as the European Union and the Organization for Economic Cooperation and Development (OECD) came out in favor of doing away with antitrust exemptions for shipping conferences, and replacing those industry agreements with confidential individual service contracts. The U.S. Federal Maritime Commission (FMC) also played a key international role, taking repeated action to end Japanese port regulations that discriminated against non-Japanese carriers. In 1997 it fined Japanese ships entering U.S. harbors, to put pressure on the Japanese government. In 1998 the Japanese agreed to reform their port regulations. However, amid signs that discrimination had not ended, the FMC reopened and expanded its investigation into Japanese port practices in August 2001.

In 2001, the bottom fell out of the industry and rates plummeted. Containership prices plunged by 15 percent. A crude oil tanker that earned US$65,000 a day in March 2001 could earn but US$16,000 a day the following June. The crash sent waves throughout the industry, causing American Eagle Tankers to call off an initial public offering and Overseas Shipholding Group to cancel a US$150 million stock offering.

CURRENT CONDITIONS

A major incident affecting the shipping industry was the loss of the oil tanker 'Prestige' off the Spanish coast in November 2002. Carrying 77,000 tons of heavy fuel, the ship began to list in severe weather and started leaking its load. Spanish authorities would not allow the ship to be brought into shore and after being towed out to sea, the ship sank. The result was 200 kilometers of polluted Spanish coastline and sections of France's southern coast. The Spanish government estimated that US$9.9 billion would be needed to clean up the coast. Besides the environmental effects, the incident raised several serious concerns. First, the Prestige had not been inspected in 12 months, highlighting the low rate of inspection in many countries. France and Spain stated that single-hull ships would not be allowed to sail within their 200-mile economic zone. The European Union set in motion plans to phase out and ban single-hull vessels, while the United States raised a bill to ban them by 2005. At the time of the accident, there were 5,500 single-hull vessels in operation, compared to 2,500 with double hulls. Also at issue was the need for the development of places of refuge for vessels in distress.

Of major concern to shipping companies during 2003 and 2004 was the cost of implementing security measures, predominantly caused by the United States as it cancelled the visa procedure for crew members, citing the need to be able to ensure that the holder of the visa was the person to whom it was issued and that the issuer could be authenticated. A lack of international agreement on the standards to be used for biometric technology delayed resolution of the issue further.

According to Lloyd's Register, in January 2005, the world merchant marine comprised 46,222 registered shipping vessels totaling 597.7 million gross tons. These included 18,150 general cargo ships, 11,356 tankers, 6,139 bulk carriers, 5,679 passenger ships, 3,165 containerships and 1,733 other types of vessels.

The United Nations Conference on Trade and Development (UNCTAD), reported that the leading countries in terms of their percentage share of the world fleet's deadweight tonnage were Japan with 14.2 percent, Germany at 6.3, China at 6.1, United States at 5.9, and Hong Kong at 4.0. However, in terms of beneficial ownership (where the parent company is located), Greece controlled 20.26 percent of the deadweight tonnage, Japan 14.17 percent, Norway 6.6, Germany China 6.3, United States 5.9, and Hong Kong 3.98. Growth in the industry was expected to continue, mainly due to the economic performance of the United States, Japan and China.

WORKFORCE

In its *2000 Manpower Update,* Baltic and International Maritime Council/International Shipping Federation (BIMCO/ISF) reported that, worldwide, there were about

823,000 ratings (sailors) and 404,000 officers available. These figures reflected an ongoing oversupply of ratings—worldwide demand was only 599,000. However, there was an ever-growing demand for officers, estimated at 420,000 worldwide, which the current labor pool was unable to satisfy. The need for officers may increase even more around 2005, as older officers reach retirement age. Recruitment into the sea trades increased throughout the world during much of the late 1990s, until it was dampened by the Far East financial crisis. Although the size of the world fleet increased between 1995 and 2000 by one percent annually, ships' labor needs were offset as older ships were phased out and more modern vessels that needed smaller crews were introduced. There was a steady change in the nationality of the global workforce during the 1990s as well. The number of seafarers from the Organization for Economic Cooperation and Development (OECD) nations, primarily Europe, Japan, and North America, dropped from 31.5 percent of the total workforce in 1995 to 27.5 percent in 2000. By 2004, UNCTAD was reporting that Asia was providing 60 percent of the world's ratings, with the largest supplier being the Philippines, followed by Indonesia, Turkey, China and India.

Employment in the U.S. water transportation sector fell gradually from about 211,000 in 1980 to 175,000 in 1995, according to the Bureau of Labor Statistics. It picked up again in 2000, eventually reaching 201,000. Nonetheless, in 2000, water transportation workers comprised only 4 percent of the total U.S. transportation workforce, as opposed to 7 percent in 1980. The *2002 National Occupational Employment and Wage Estimates* issued by the Bureau of Labor Statistics reported that 25,360 sailors and marine oilers employed in the industry earned a mean annual salary of US$30,550. Captains, mates, and pilots numbered about 22,530 and earned a mean annual salary of US$51,430. There were about 8,020 ship engineers employed in 2002, and they earned US$52,190. These figures were all above the mean annual wage of US$27,220 in transportation and moving occupations as a whole.

In the mid-2000s, recognizing the aging population of merchant marine sailors and the need to hire qualified replacements, some schools were offering career technical training in the field. San Diego, California's Sweetwater School District, for example, offered its high school students a Regional Occupational Program course in Maritime Services, which prepared students to work immediately in full-time maritime positions after graduation.

INDUSTRY LEADERS

A.P. MOLLER-MAERSK GROUP

Ranked the leading container shipping company in the world by the United Nations in 2002, Danish-owned A.P. Moller-Maersk Line was founded in 1904 as A/S Dampkibsselskabet Svendborg but was quickly renamed the A.P. Moller Group, after its founder, Arnold Peter Moller. In 2005 the company's fleet totaled more than 250 vessels, with almost 12 million deadweight tons, including tankers, liners/container vessels (Maersk Sealand), bulk carriers, supply ships, special vessels, and drilling rigs. With offices in more than 100 countries and approximately 62,300 employees worldwide, the company reported 2004 revenues of approximately US$28.9 billion, an increase over 2003 levels of US26.5 billion. The group included various subsidiaries that specialized in various types of shipping including Maersk Sealand (container shipping), Maersk Tankers and Maersk Gas Carriers (tanker shipping), and Maersk Bulk (bulk shipping).

Maersk Line, the company's cargo liner service, has linked the United States with Asia since 1975 with fast, fully containerized ships operating on a fixed weekly schedule. In 1999 it was expanded greatly by Moller's acquisition for US$800 million of the international liner business of Sea-Land Service Inc., a deal that included all of Sea-Land's vessels, containers, container terminals, and some leases. The takeover was the largest deal to date in the consolidation of the shipping industry. Sea-Land's 70 containerships boosted Maersk's fleet to around 180 vessels, and made the new firm, named Maersk Sealand, twice as large as its nearest competitor in the container shipping business. By 2002, Maersk Sealand was providing service between USA/Asia, USA/northern Europe, USA/Middle East/Mediterranean, USA/eastern and western Africa, Europe/Middle East, Europe/Asia, Europe/eastern and western Africa, Asia/Middle East, Asia/eastern and western Africa, and Japan/Indonesia and Thailand.

MEDITERRANEAN SHIPPING COMPANY S.A.

Family owned, MSC of landlocked Geneva, Switzerland was the second largest container ship company in the world in 2003. Founded in 1970 by Gianluigi Aponte, the company had 255 vessels by 2004. The company entered the cruise line business in 1988. Estimates of this private company put the number of employees at 20,000 and revenues at US$3 billion per year.

ROYAL P&O NEDLLOYD N.V.

Founded in 1837, P&O has grown into a major transport company. By 2005, its fastest growing area of business was the operation of ports, with operations in 18 countries. It was the leading provider of ferry service in the United Kingdom, with a fleet of 26 ships. In 2004, it had revenues of more than US$5.8 billion of which one-third each came from its ports and ferries businesses, and 16 percent came from its container shipping business. In 2004, the 50-50 joint venture P&O had with Royal Nedlloyd, P&O Nedlloyd, was turned into a public entity, for which P&O retained 25 percent of the shares. The new company was named Royal P&O Nedlloyd, and was the third largest container company in the world at the time of its creation.

In 2005, P&O Nedlloyd had a fleet of 156 vessels that called at 217 ports in 99 countries. Its 2004 revenues reached US$6.7 billion. The company's history goes back to the era of the steam ship, when its founders started trade links between northern Europe and the Mediterranean/Balkan region. In December 1996, P&O Containers and Nedlloyd Lines merged to form P&O Nedlloyd. In April 2004, the company became publicly traded on the Amsterdam exchange.

MITSUI O.S.K. LINES LTD.

Mitsui O.S.K. Lines (MOL), was founded in 1884 as Osaka Shosen Kaisha, launching an "express" service that traveled between Yokohama and New York in less than 26 days. By 2005, the company was Japan's largest marine transportation company, with the largest merchant fleet in the world. The company operated containerships and car and truck carriers, and dry bulk carriers transported a huge variety of products including electrical goods, iron ore, liquefied natural gas, and crude and refined petroleum products. The MOL Group of companies also operated tugboats, ferries, and cruise ships, and managed ports. MOL's revenues at March 2004 were more than US$9.4 billion and the company employed more than 7,000 people.

NIPPON YUSEN KAISHA LINE

Nippon Yusen Kaisha Line (NYK Line) was originally established in 1885 and headquartered in Tokyo. By 2005, NYK's core businesses were container transport, tramp shipping, and passenger cruise ships, and it boasted the largest liner fleet in Japan and the largest fleet of car and truck carriers in the world. Its 2000 profits of US$290 million were more than double its results for 1999. By 2004, the company's revenues had reached more than US$13.2 billion.

NYK was particularly noted for having led the development of new Pacific trade routes by incorporating the Panama and Suez Canals as short cuts. Its Asia East Coast Express (AEX) service, which used the Suez Canal, connected southeastern Asia to ports of call on the U.S. East Coast within 22 days. Its Singapore California Express connected Singapore to the U.S. West Coast within 16 to 18 days.

The line responded to changing market forces in the mid-1990s by entering into an alliance with NOL of Singapore, Hapag-Lloyd AG of Germany, and P&O Containers of the United Kingdom in 1995. NYK inaugurated a new containership service for the United States and Europe trade in 1998. The same year, it opened a branch in Taipei on Taiwan. Two years later, the firm opened NYK Logistics in the Peoples Republic of China.

HAPAG-LLOYD AG

HAPAG-Lloyd history extends back to the mid-nineteenth century when two companies, the Hamburg-Americanische Packetfahrt Aktien Gessellschaft (the Hamburg-American Steamship Co.), HAPAG for short, and Norddeutscher Lloyd (North German Lloyd) were founded. Originally formed as passenger lines, HAPAG and Lloyd were the leading German ship lines for both passenger and cargo service through the first half of the twentieth century. They merged in 1970 to form Hapag-Lloyd. Shortly after that, the company established the TRIO Group, a global co-operative venture with four other companies, NYK and Mitsui O.S.K. Lines, both of Japan, and Overseas Containers Ltd. and Ben Line of the United Kingdom. The group shared 19 giant containerships and was the largest investment in the history of shipping. The 1980s and 1990s were difficult ones for the company, although its liner shipping branch turned regular profits in the early 1990s. The firm was reorganized in 1994 to streamline operations. By the time it celebrated its 150th anniversary in 1997, it was shipping about 1.1 million 20-foot containers annually with profits of US$48 million—a 23 percent jump from 1996. As of 2002, the company reported US$4 billion in revenue.

HAPAG-Lloyd was acquired in a US$1.5 billion stock buyout by the German tourism giant TIU (then known as Preussag) in 1998. In April 2005, the company christened the biggest containership to that point in the world. The size of three football fields, the vessel can transport 8,750 twenty-foot equivalent units (TEUs) and will be employed in the Asia/Europe trade. By 2008, the company expects to have seven more ships of this size. Owned by German tourism giant TIU, in 2004 the shipping company accounted for 19 percent of its parent's revenues of US$24 billion.

HANJIN SHIPPING COMPANY LTD.

Hanjin Shipping Company Ltd., of South Korea, was established in 1977. It opened its first international lane in 1978, serving the Middle East route with one vessel capable of carrying 750 TEUs. In 1979 Hanjin began its Pacific-Southwest (PSW) service and in 1983 it included all-water service to the U.S. East Coast, as well as between South Korea and Japan. In 1988 the company merged with Korea Shipping Corp. and assumed its present form. By 1991, Hanjin had begun its pendulum service, connecting Europe and PSW routes; entered into a joint all-water service agreement with Yangming Marine Line; and started its Round-the-Asia service with joint operator Dongnama Shipping Co. Trans-Atlantic service was initiated in 1995, and weekly service linking Portland, Oregon with ports in northern China began in 1997. Hanjin also purchased a majority interest in German shipper DSR Senator Lines GmbH, largely through providing DSR with capital to offset its losses in fiscal year 1995. Hanjin, DSR, and Cho Yang Lines USA Inc. consolidated their shipping resources in 1996, creating a combined fleet comprising 70 vessels with a carrying capacity of 194,000 TEUs. In 2001 Hanjin was ranked the second largest firm in the world in containership loading tonnage. The company owned 83 containerships with an average loading tonnage of 3,506 TEUs. In November 2001, Hanjin formed the United Alliance with COSCO Container Lines, Senator Lines, K Line, and Yang Ming Marine. The group was organized to work together in international trade with its combined fleet of more than 300 ships. Hanjin reported 2004 revenues of US$5.9 billion, up significantly from US$4.7 billion in the previous year.

CHINA OCEAN SHIPPING (GROUP) COMPANY

China Ocean Shipping (Group) Company (COSCO), the state shipping company of China, was founded in 1961 and began service between China and the United States in 1982. COSCO's U.S. East Coast and Gulf Coast service utilized a fleet of eight container vessels, five with a carrying capacity of 1,500 TEUs and three with 1,200 TEU capacity. The company served the U.S. West Coast using a fleet of six vessels with a combined carrying capacity of 2,500 TEUs.

Throughout the mid to late 1990s, COSCO played a steadily increasing role in global maritime trade. The company reversed its traditional position as an independent carrier and entered into a space-sharing agreement with K Line and Yang Ming Line on its Asia-Europe routes in 1996. This arrangement was officially renewed in 1998. In 1997, COSCO announced that it was expanding its service to include trans-Atlantic routes, thus offering a new challenge to the dominance of the TAA. COSCO showed its willingness to shed its independent status when circumstances warranted in 1998, joining the Westbound Pacific Stabilization Agreement (WSTA) in what appeared to be a prelude to the company's entering a shipping conference. In 2005, the company was claiming revenues of US$17 billion, although it does not make its financials publicly available, with a merchant fleet of 600 vessels with an annual capacity of 270 million tons.

FURTHER READING

"Analysts Predict Higher Rates." *Journal of Commerce,* 15 March 2004.

Ardizzone, Sally. "Program Preps Students for Career as Merchant Marines." *San Diego Business Journal,* 10 March 2003.

"As Tankers Tank, Shipping Tempts Markets." *Journal of Commerce,* 10 July 2001.

Barnard, Bruce. "Mergers, Acquisitions Roil Industry." *Journal of Commerce,* 25 April 2000.

Berkenkopf, Katren. "Hamburg: Hapag's Aggressive Approach." *Lloyds List,* 28 April 2000.

"BIMCO/ISF 2000 Manpower Update: Summary Report.", April 2000. Available from http://www.marisec.org/resources/2000manpowerupdate.htm.

Bonney, Joseph. "Strength in Numbers." *Journal of Commerce,* 13 August 2001.

Colby, Charles C. *North Atlantic Arena: Water Transport in the World Order,* Carbondale, IL: Southern Illinois University Press, 1966.

Damas, Philip, "Who's Making Money?" *American Shipper,* 1 July 2000.

Damas, Philip; and Chris Gillis. "Inside the Maersk Machine." *American Shipper,* March 2001.

Damas, Philip; Gillis, Chris; and Robert Mottley. "Maritime Flags Unravel." *American Shipper,* 1 March 2000.

De La Pedraja Toman, Rene. *The Rise and Decline of U.S. Merchant Shipping in the Twentieth Century,* New York: Twayne Publishers, 1992.

Draper, Deborah J., ed. *Business Rankings Annual.* Detroit: Thomson Gale, 2004.

Dupin, Chris. "The Bottom Line." *Journal of Commerce,* 28 May 2001.

———. "Compatible Regimes?" *Journal of Commerce,* 6 November 2000.

———. "Mending Fences." *Journal of Commerce,* 5 November 2001.

———. "OECD Rekindles Antitrust Issue." *Journal of Commerce,* 7 January 2002.

Edmonson, R.G. "FMC Renews Japan Port Probe." *Journal of Commerce,* 13 August 2001.

Freudmann, Aviva. "Carrier Shifts Focus Back to Transport." *Journal of Commerce,* 25 February 2000.

———. "Conference, 5 Ship Lines Are Fined US$7 Million." *Journal of Commerce,* 18 May 2000.

———. "Traditional Ro-Ro Ships Becoming Endangered." *Journal of Commerce,* 16 February 2000.

Giovanetti, Geoffrey N. "Is Ocean Freight Becoming a Commodity?" *Journal of Commerce,* 7 June 2004.

"Hoover's Company Capsules." 2004. Available from http://www.hoovers.com.

"International Trade Statistics." 2003. Available from http://www.wto.org.

Koenig, Robert. "Preussag Shuffles the Deck." *Journal of Commerce,* 26 June 2000.

Mitchell, Carlyle L. "Canada's Ocean Industries: Contribution to the Economy 1988 - 2000." September 2003. Available from www.dfo-mpo.gc.ca.

Mongelluzzo, Bill. "A Surfeit of Services." *Journal of Commerce,* 10 May 2004.

Pandya, Nick. "Rise: Cool Companies: No. 39: The Maersk Company Limited." *Guardian (London),* 2 September 2000.

Pei, Jianfeng. "OSRA Credited with Positive Effects on Ocean Shipping." *Purchasing,* 24 August 2000.

Peterkofsky, Roy I. "How to Make It Work." *Journal of Commerce,* 19 April 2004.

"Review of Maritime Transport, 2004." United Nations Conference on Trade and Development (UNCTAD Secretariat), 2004. Available from http://www.unctad.org.

Richardson, Paul. "Who's Next to Be Merged?" *Journal of Commerce,* 29 March 2000.

Tirschwell, Peter M. "FMC Defines Ocean Common Carrier." *Journal of Commerce,* 9 May 2000.

———. "Time Is Money." *Journal of Commerce,* 31 May 2004.

Tower, Courtney. "Canada Readies Maritime Reform." *Journal of Commerce,* 29 March 2000.

———. "Canadian Shippers Demand OSRA-like Law." *Journal of Commerce,* 18 July 2001.

U.S. Department of Transportation Maritime Administration. "Maritime Statistics," 2004. Available from http://www.marad.dot.gov.

UTILITIES AND PUBLIC SERVICES

SIC 8211

NAICS 611110

ELEMENTARY AND SECONDARY SCHOOLS

Elementary and secondary schools furnish academic training for scholars ranging in age from approximately 5 to 17 years. Courses of study usually are offered in age-level divisions (commonly known as grades in the United States), and schools generally subdivide younger and older groups of students into elementary and secondary schools, respectively. Included within this category are both public and private institutions. The industry includes parochial schools and military academies providing academic courses, as well as secondary schools that provide both academic and technical courses.

INDUSTRY SNAPSHOT

Most experts, government officials, and the general public agree that effective education is necessary for a nation's economic health. The world's industrialized nations, including such countries as the United States, France, Germany, Japan, and the United Kingdom, typically invest heavily in public education. By contrast, education in the developing world, while often a recognized priority of governments and families, receives considerably less support from the public treasury, with significant variation by nation and region. Consequently, economic opportunities for young people just out of secondary school are extremely variable around the world. In turn, weak economic growth in a particular part of the world can encourage surges of immigration to more affluent nations, which eventually leads to higher costs for administering, operating, and maintaining schools in the countries whose populations may burgeon from immigration inflows.

To compete in an increasingly global economy, national, regional, and local school officials and administrators in many countries examine educational operations in other economically successful countries. Interest thus has grown in developing international studies of education, and efforts to compile truly comparative educational statistics across nations have increased noticeably. For example, in 2004 the United Nations Educational, Scientific, and Cultural Organization (UNESCO) reported on worldwide education statistics with the "Global Education Digest." The comparative report looked at the educational systems, trends, goals, and standards of many countries around the globe. Among other findings, the study reported a significant correlation between a country's income and its emphasis on education at any level, with average time spent in formal schooling ranging from 4 to 17 years. In addition, the study found that 10 percent of students in 35 countries repeat primary grades, and in 38 countries repeat secondary grades.

Concern over developing a future workforce capable of meeting employer needs has led numerous educational institutions and employers to develop collaborative programs to train students for twenty-first century jobs. Enhanced programs for teaching reading, writing, and mathematics; new emphasis on "managerial" skills such as communication, decision making, and problem solving; and efforts to improve the variety and quality of vocational and technical skills-training programs have been the result. In many nations, school systems increasingly have emphasized training in computer literacy to give elementary and secondary school students the necessary skills and hands-on experience for computer use in college and industry.

Although educators around the world share the need to keep pace with changes in the global economy and even more rapid changes in technology, approaches to educational innovation have varied widely across countries. While the United States has clung to a "single-ladder" approach to education, with essentially one course of elementary and secondary study taken by all students, other nations have seen advantages in offering more specialized education to students beginning at an earlier age. Germany in particular has endorsed early differentiation between vocational and pre-university preparation. In the United Kingdom, the number of comprehensive secondary schools—those that somewhat resemble U.S. public high schools by including students on all academic paths—grew around the turn of the millennium. Additionally, egalitarian, "progressive" education was supplanted by more orthodox schooling in some parts of the United Kingdom in the late 1990s. However, the British continued to emphasize official testing in order to evaluate schools, determine student achievement, and steer students in academic or vocational directions. In France students are assured of carefully legislated curricula designed to provide equal opportunities to all students. Once reserved for the academic elite, the coveted French *baccalauréat* has been subdivided into academic and vocational tracks and is now awarded to all students who successfully complete their secondary studies. With Japanese legislation outlawing educational discrimination based on ability or potential, Japanese students are trained identically throughout elementary school, their achievement seemingly more closely related to parental example and expectation than to any particular government education policy. The Japanese have provided very little specialized vocational education; nonetheless, Japanese schools methodically support a strict work ethic for students.

ORGANIZATION AND STRUCTURE

Internationally, elementary and secondary school systems encompass a wide variety of institutions such as:

- Government-funded elementary and secondary schools (known as "public" schools in the United States);
- Self-standing, publicly or privately funded kindergartens;
- Privately funded day schools, boarding schools, and secondary finishing schools;
- Religiously affiliated schools (some of them known as "parochial," or parish-supported, schools);
- "Charter" schools (publicly subsidized and supervised but independently run schools);
- Vocational high schools;
- Military academies;
- College-preparatory schools;
- Visual and/or performing arts academies;
- Schools for students with special needs such as physical, behavioral, emotional, learning, psychological, and/or other mental handicaps or disabilities;
- Online, Internet-based schools; and
- Home schools.

In many countries governed by parliamentary systems, various national government organs such as ministries of education, youth, and sports set the tone for the writing and implementation of educational policy and/or for evaluating the success of schools. The U.S. Department of Education in many ways operates similarly to a ministry in that educational policy decisions are often made in this executive agency and then supported through specific education laws enacted by the U.S. Congress. As in a parliamentary system, the U.S. national government also features educational initiatives and guidelines presented by the head of government (the U.S. President), which are then elaborated by others within the executive and legislative branches. However, U.S. education policy is often diluted through the influence of state governments, who until the twenty-first century have been allowed wide jurisdiction in educational standard-setting and the detailing and funding of educational programs.

Governments around the world assume responsibility for supporting educational costs to widely varying degrees. In some countries, especially in the developing world, school fees and textbook costs are borne by the parents of students, making schooling often inaccessible to those lower on the socioeconomic scale, even where some government support has been provided for building the physical infrastructure of schools and/or for outfitting schools with basic furnishings. This limits the opportunity of many students to go to school and severely hampers universal access to education.

The United Kingdom features a wide range of both public and private school options to students at the elementary and secondary levels. The United States also provides these options, but on a lesser scale. Most other countries have tended to see smaller proportions of students enrolled in private academies in contrast to government-supported schools. While private schools in the United States frequently are day schools, in Britain and on the European continent many non-government school pupils live in residential houses attached to the schools.

Vocational Training. Many European and emerging Pacific Rim countries provide highly specialized vocational education to high school students through combinations of apprenticeship systems, on-the-job training, and traditional academic learning. Almost all countries outside the United States offer specific vocational paths of study and make these available to students well before graduation from secondary school.

Only gradually has vocational training in the United States become a more sophisticated offering, frequently involving school-to-work partnerships with business and industry. Despite the appeal of U.S. higher education to foreign students, the competitive position of U.S. workers declined in the 1990s in some industry sectors, especially when compared to workers' status in some European and Pacific Rim countries. Critics suggested that this resulted from a lack of support in the United States for vocational training and education programs.

Germany's vocational training system in particular has been highly acclaimed worldwide, and is given much credit for Germany's economic success. What has made the German system unique is the intense interconnection of business and education in ways untried in most other industrialized nations. Although the percentage of students seeking admittance into German vocational training programs fell in the early 1990s, the system has been seen as highly successful overall. Businesses benefit because they receive a supply of well-qualified workers and can fine-tune vocational training to specific future needs. Graduates benefit because on-the-job training provides them with experience in the workplace and their learned skills are marketable. On the other hand, in the late 1990s critics contended that the German vocational training system produced an excess of skilled blue-collar workers when the need for such workers was decreasing. Rapid changes in technology made it difficult to reform the system at a pace that kept up with current needs, but in the new millennium efforts are ongoing to increase the system's flexibility and responsiveness to Germany's changing workforce needs.

BACKGROUND AND DEVELOPMENT

Growth of Education and Literacy Worldwide. The broad and varied nature of schooling throughout the ages makes it impossible to summarize in just a few brief paragraphs the story of how the world's schools developed and evolved into the modern institutions and complex structures they are today. Perhaps a cursory review of the historical development of elementary and secondary education in one of the foremost economies of the world—the United States—can illustrate some of the challenges other countries have also faced over time in their endeavors to educate their children and youth. The basis for this decision to highlight the United States rests on the fact that economic development cannot occur without the development of a nation's human capital; consequently, a look at a portion of the educational history of a country whose economic prowess clearly dominates world attention is certainly worth taking. For a more comprehensive review of the development of educational programs and structures in all parts of the world—developed and developing countries alike—Gale's tri-volume *World Education Encyclopedia,* Second Edition, or other similar works are highly recommended to the reader.

Development of U.S. Public Schooling. Compulsory, "normal," and free public education was developed and expanded in the United States as the country rapidly industrialized during the nineteenth century. Prior to the early 1800s, any schooling that a child received was not regulated and often was home-based. Schooling either consisted of only the rudiments of reading, writing, and mathematics or was directed toward providing a classical education that included the study of Latin and Greek. Very little attention was paid to developing an educational middle ground where the average pupil could be given the basic foundation for a liberal arts education. As the population grew and the United States became more industrialized and urbanized, however, this began to change.

Horace Mann (1796-1859) was a key American social reformer, educator, and statesman who, according to Susan Ritchie, "greatly advanced the cause of universal, free, non-sectarian public schools." Mann believed that while other reforms were "remedial," education was "preventative" of other social ills and education therefore took priority over other arenas for social development and reform. Viewing education, intelligent voting, and religious freedom as the primary supports of American liberties, Mann, who was trained as a lawyer and served for three years in the Massachusetts state senate before becoming Secretary to the Massachusetts Board of Education in 1837, advocated the spread of educational opportunity to the broader population.

While serving as Board Secretary until 1848, Mann provided greater funding for schools in Massachusetts and laid the groundwork for secularizing religious schools, making public schooling more generally available. He also enhanced teacher-training programs and argued for more humane forms of discipline in schools. No matter the social or political arena in which he worked—whether the Massachusetts state senate, the U.S. Congress (where he served as a U.S. Representative for more than one term), or the newly formed Antioch College in Yellow Springs, Ohio, for which Mann served as the college's first president in the 1850s—Mann was forever an educator at heart. As Ritchie noted, Mann regarded the "importance of universal public education as the means for the creation of a just society."

After the concept of free education for all children had been firmly established and public schools had begun to spread across the growing United States by the mid-1800s, educators shifted their attention to enhancing the quality of education. At first American common schools were similar to those in Europe, often consisting of one room and one teacher who taught students ranging in age from 6 to about 13. Older pupils, who generally were needed at home to work on the family farm or business, rarely attended. In fact, in rural and frontier areas older boys occasionally raided and terrorized small schools, priding themselves on "breaking them up" and sometimes running beleaguered instructors out of town. In the minds of some (especially adult male community members), females were expected to be only barely literate and advanced education for girls was deemed unnecessary, undesirable, or even unhealthful. In the early one-room schoolhouses, each child was instructed separately (rather than in a group or grade), progressing through a series of books and moving from one grade to the next as the requisite work was completed. It was not unusual for a student to be in a third reader, for example, while still struggling with a math primer. The predominant method of education was modeled on Johann Pestalozzi's theories that emphasized first-hand observation of actual objects rather than the rote memorization of facts.

By the late 1800s, however, many attitudes concerning the universality of schooling had changed, and growing support for public schools accessible to all was apparent. Moreover, new ideas were introduced regarding the type of education most beneficial to developing a democratic citizenry and an actively growing workforce that could meet the needs of the country's expanding industrial economy and increasingly diverse population.

By the 1880s the United States was experiencing an influx of millions of new immigrants. This immigration wave rapidly expanded the urban population and created new challenges for the common schools, including the key question of how to provide the greatest amount of education to the largest number of children in the shortest amount of time. New schools were developed to accommodate larger classes, higher enrollments, and new teaching practices. To make it possible for one teacher to instruct many students, differences between the students had to be eliminated as much as possible. Children began to be grouped on the basis of their ages, and curricula were developed for specific age groups.

The teaching methods of German philosopher and psychologist Johann Herbart were imported from Europe by educators to help meet this new challenge. Herbart believed that effective education was predicated on instruction and that the building blocks were the materials of instruction, or the subject matter. European and American schools influenced by Herbart's theories thus were teacher- and curriculum-centered rather than child-centered. To many educators, the most attractive component of Herbart's theory was the idea of a lesson plan, whose very existence suggested that instruction could be provided systematically to all students. Herbart's emphasis on the importance of motivating students to learn was a new concept in the 1880s. By the turn of the twentieth century, streamlined teaching methods and broader-based curricula had become standard.

Another educator who substantially transformed American philosophical and educational thought and practice in the late 1800s and early 1900s was John Dewey (1859-1952). Trained as a philosopher and experienced in teaching at the secondary and university levels, Dr. Dewey strongly believed in applying the basic principles of the scientific method to the study of human thinking and progress. As Richard Field wrote, Dewey developed at the end of the nineteenth century an "empirically based theory of knowledge that was in concert with the then developing American school of thought known as pragmatism." This led to Dewey's establishing an experimental laboratory school at the University of Chicago in 1894, where the seminal pragmatist tried out his pedagogical theories and published his first important educational study, *The School and Society,* in 1899. Moving to Columbia University in New York in 1904, Dewey continued his rich career of teaching, philosophical research and writing, and social action, producing many well-regarded studies and treatises that included *How We Think* in 1910 (revised in 1933) and *Democracy and Education* in 1916. Besides making crucial contributions to American educational theory and practice, Dewey worked very actively during his lifetime for other social reforms such as women's suffrage and the unionization of American teachers. Dewey remained at Columbia for the rest of his professional career, living and working to the age of 92.

Field aptly sums up Dewey's educational contributions by remarking, "Dewey, throughout his ethical and social writings, stressed the need for an open-ended, flexible, and experimental approach to problems of practice aimed at the determination of the conditions for the attainment of human goods and a critical examination of the consequences of means adopted to promote them, an approach that he called the 'method of intelligence.'" The "progressive education" movement of the 1920s in the United States, inspired in large measure by Dewey's work and leadership, aimed to make creative and socially useful education available to all. To some degree, Dewey and other adherents of progressive education were reacting to the testing movement that had begun in the 1910s after Alfred Binet's 1905 publication of the first scale for measuring intelligence. By the 1920s children increasingly were being given intelligence quotient (IQ) and achievement tests, and increasing numbers of schools and classrooms grouped students by ability and intelligence, all of which worked against the basic tenets of progressive education, which stipulated that all children were capable of learning and of developing their natural potential, given the right educational environment.

While progressive teaching in the 1920s and 1930s did much to improve scholarship by eliminating the rigid categorization and isolation of subjects, with educators now teaching each subject in relation to others, progressive education was not without its downside. Eventually, practical difficulties associated with child-centered classes and the need for children to learn "at their own pace" (Piaget), along with the tendency to equate "progressive" with "permissive," child-rearing, dampened people's enthusiasm for progressive educational innovation and brought a return to more traditional learning methods and goals. However, discoveries about student learning and creative means to spark student interest continued to influence teaching methods for the remainder of the twentieth century and into the twenty-first. As one writer with the University of Vermont's John Dewey Project in Progressive Education observed, a number of late twentieth century educational developments in the United States were profoundly shaped by Dewey's philosophy and work: "Open classrooms, schools without walls, cooperative learning, multiage approaches, whole language, the social curriculum, experiential education, and numerous forms of alternative schools all have important philosophical roots in progressive education."

Schools in the United States came under heavy criticism in the 1950s and 1960s due to several key political developments. In 1954 a landmark court case, *Brown v. The Board of Education*, went to the U.S. Supreme Court. The court's decision put an end to the concept of "separate but equal" educational opportunities for students of different racial or ethnic backgrounds, striking down the legal basis for segregation in public schools. Resistance to that court decision placed schools in the middle of a bitter and often violent, decades-long debate that included questions of whether busing students from one district to schools in another could be a viable way to encourage more equitable educational outcomes.

With the launching of the first space satellite (Sputnik) by the Soviet Union, U.S. schools, which most of the Western world had expected would help lead the United States to postwar scientific dominance, became a Cold War battleground. The "new math" and "new science" of the 1950s and early 1960s were direct responses to the fear that the United States was losing its technological preeminence to the Soviet Union.

During the 1970s significant educational attention was focused on developing improved educational strategies and programs to accommodate students with special needs. "Mainstreaming" students with handicaps and learning difficulties into regular classroom settings increasingly became the norm once special education classes and resource rooms had been implanted in schools to educate those students with special educational requirements.

By the 1980s, the barometer for measuring a country's educational success was the extent to which a system's graduates contributed to the workforce, and in turn to the economy, of the country. The globalization of industry may have meant that specific companies were functioning in multiple national environments, but ensuring the availability of local human resources continued to be essential to the economic success of each nation.

Since a direct, causal relationship between school spending and academic results is difficult to establish, many U.S. school districts sought new ways to gauge the effectiveness of their educational spending. Site-based reporting, developed at Fordham University and nationally distributed by

Coopers and Lybrand, became available to school districts in the 1990s. This evaluation system helped school districts set benchmarks in order to determine where expenditures were either excessive or falling short of the norm.

As new immigration and the offspring of "baby boomers" born from the mid-1940s to mid-1960s rapidly increased the U.S. school-age population, an end-of-the-century school enrollment boom caught U.S. educators by surprise. By the 1999-2000 school year 92,012 public elementary and secondary schools were operating in the United States. Most of these (84,902) were schools offering regular education programs, while 1,947 offered special education; 1,048 focused on vocational education; and 4,115 were alternative schools. Some 89,599 of these schools reported teaching a total of 46.9 million students, 98 percent of them in regular public schools, which in Mississippi, New Hampshire, and North Dakota were the only kind of public schools that existed. The largest student populations were in the states of California, Florida, Illinois, New York, and Texas, each of which had more than 2 million students in public schools. In contrast, the District of Columbia and Wyoming each reported having fewer than 100,000 public school students.

In the 1990s U.S. public schools employed approximately 6 million people, or about 30 percent of all civilian government employees. Rapidly escalating costs of special education and other services added to schools' financial burdens. Educational allocations had grown to such proportions as to risk being cut when the federal government began to take serious steps to balance the national budget. In the late 1990s federal expenditures for U.S. public elementary and secondary schools reached an annual US$290 billion, or nearly 4 percent of the GDP, making education a major U.S. national budget item. In March 2002, however, the national budget proposed by President George W. Bush included significant cuts in spending on many elementary and secondary school programs, according to the National Priorities Project, a U.S. non-profit, activist group collaborating with local grassroots organizations to clarify national budget issues for ordinary citizens.

In the mid-1990s approximately 28,000 of the 110,000 schools then operating in the United States were nonprofit private institutions, including religiously affiliated schools and tax-exempt, independent schools. Another 7,000 taxpaying, private academic schools and 4,000 private, vocational schools were outside the mainstream of U.S. public school systems. By 1998 these "charter," or PSA schools—privately run institutions subject to state regulation—had increased dramatically in number.

The U.S. Department of Education noted in the early 1990s that 60 percent of preschoolers attended private preschools, while just 7 percent of all secondary-school students were enrolled in private institutions. Because of the extremely high total enrollment in U.S. schools, the overall percentage growth of enrollment in private schools was slow to increase, but by the mid-1990s private-school attendance had risen to nearly 9 percent. Students at all grade levels who came from high-income families were more likely to go to private school, although the increase in the number of charter schools began to affect this pattern in the late 1990s. Nor did the enrollment in church-related schools always follow money. Statistics from the early 1990s indicated that the majority of preschool, kindergarten, elementary, and secondary students attending church-related schools were from low- to middle-income families.

By the fall of 1999, some 27,223 private elementary and secondary schools were operating in the United States. These schools fell into three main categories: Catholic schools (most of them parochial, or parish-based, schools); other religious schools; and non-sectarian schools. Non-Catholic religious schools represented almost half of these private schools, or 49 percent. Catholic schools were second-most numerous, at 30 percent of the total, while nonsectarian schools accounted for 22 percent of the private schools in operation at that time. The southern United States had the largest share of private schools (30 percent), while the West had the smallest share (20 percent). Sixty-one percent of private schools offered elementary grades only, while 30 percent featured a combination of elementary and secondary grades and just 9 percent were secondary-only schools. Of the private schools operating in fall 1999, most (82 percent) were offering regular programming. The remainder specialized in Montessori techniques, special education, vocational and/or technical training, alternative approaches, early childhood programs, or other special emphases. The private schools taught more than 5 million elementary and secondary students in the fall of 1999. All together, students attending private school represented about 10 percent of all elementary and secondary students in the United States.

In the 1990s, U.S. economists worried that a weak school system was hurting the ability of the United States to compete in the global economy. Despite modest improvements in some test scores, U.S. students still ranked behind many of their international peers in science and math. Large financial outlays for education in the United States too often failed to make any significant impact on education quality. In the search for a new direction in education, some observers championed new methods that focused on the importance of competition and pushed schools to be innovative and to discard ineffective rules and regulations.

One model under discussion was a voucher system, allowing parents to receive government money to send their children to the public or private school that could best meet their children's needs. Citing free-market principles, proponents saw the voucher system as a way to create competition in an educational marketplace and exert pressure for educational and financial reform. Another approach tried in the United States to stimulate interest in public schools was represented by magnet schools, whose concept was to draw particularly capable or talented students to public schools through specially designed or unique programming. The hope was that magnet schools would stem the accelerating outflow of students from public school systems to private schools, especially in some of the more financially challenged urban areas.

Yet one more approach to school reform was to allow parents, teachers, and organizations to set up charter schools. Charter schools, an alternative to voucher systems, were seen to encourage at least limited competition. Charter schools remain public schools in that they are required to meet certain publicly developed standards and to not discriminate in admissions. However, charter schools are independent of traditional school systems. Charter schools have been viewed as potentially providing new incentives for school districts to become more dynamic and entrepreneurial; in fact, some have backing from for-profit corporations. Slow to catch on in some areas, by the close of the 1990s charter schools began demonstrating certain advantages and disadvantages. With only one central governing board, charter schools are free to develop unique and optimal curricula. The continued existence of any charter school is based on a performance contract, and performance monitoring ideally allows for the disbanding of any school that does not meet standards. However, charter schools also have the potentially undesirable effect of diverting attention and financial support away from crumbling and under-funded public schools that, in the absence of charter schools, might stand a better chance of receiving very necessary fiscal and community support for repairs and reform.

U.S. strategies for reforming elementary and secondary education programs around the start of the new millennium have included compensatory education programs for disadvantaged students and programs that give students from all socioeconomic categories access to English-language skills, basic literacy and math skills, and other prerequisites to high-level thinking and problem-solving skills. Because very wide discrepancies often exist in U.S. educational offerings and the quality of public schools from one state to another—let alone from one school district to another—the potential is great for public dissatisfaction in the United States, and many U.S. parents and students view private schools as an increasingly desirable alternative. Whether a family chooses a private school for their children depends on a variety of factors, however, including satisfaction with area public schools, family income, private school tuition, and sometimes the mere availability of public schooling for students of certain ages—for example, preschoolers, since publicly funded preschools do not exist in many parts of the United States.

As the twentieth century came to a close, the United States was not alone in critically assessing its school systems. Stimulated by the concern that students would not be prepared to meet future workforce needs, national governments, private industry, and a host of public and private organizations and agencies directed attention toward improving the quality of education in both developed and developing countries.

In the year 2000 a series of cross-national tests of student achievement known as the Program for International Student Assessment (PISA) began. Testing the skills of 15-year-olds in reading, mathematics, and science, PISA is designed to measure general and interdisciplinary skills as well. The first assessment was administered in the year 2000 and focused on measuring reading literacy. In 2003 the second cycle of PISA will be administered to test mathematics literacy in particular, and in 2006 the third cycle will highlight science literacy. All three categories of literacy, however, will be tested during each cycle's round of testing.

Initial results of the first cycle of PISA demonstrated significant differences in learning achievement across countries, even in the developed world. Because PISA is primarily an assessment of students in the Organization for Economic Cooperation and Development (OECD) countries, which for the most part are economically developed nations, less will be known from this series of tests than may be gathered through other international assessments and statistical projects undertaken by more global, education-related organizations and agencies like UNESCO or the World Bank.

In any case, the first cycle of PISA turned up some interesting findings. In all twenty-seven of the OECD countries and the four non-OECD countries whose testing results are comparatively reported by the National Center for Education Statistics in "Highlights from the 2000 Program for International Student Assessment," girls significantly outperformed boys in reading literacy. This was especially so in Finland and Latvia, where the average score difference between girls and boys on the combined reading literacy tests surpassed 50 percent. Other countries with strong gender differences in reading literacy were New Zealand and Norway, where girls did better than boys by a more than a 40 percent average score difference. In fact, in all countries but two (the Republic of Korea and Brazil), the average score difference between girls and boys in reading was at least 20 percent, in the girls' favor. In contrast, fewer significant gender differences were found in the areas of mathematics and science.

In mathematics literacy, boys outperformed girls in thirteen of the twenty-seven OECD countries and also in Brazil (though not in the United States, where no significant gender disparity was found). Average score differences approached 30 percent in Austria, the Republic of Korea, and Brazil, in the boys' favor. In the science literacy test, very few significant gender differences showed up in the testing. Males scored significantly higher than females in science in only three countries: Austria, Denmark, and the Republic of Korea. In New Zealand and Latvia, girls outperformed boys in the science assessment.

In the mid-1990s an OECD study on educational attainment in 21 industrial countries showed the United States leading all countries in the proportion of its population that had earned a college or university degree. This was no mean achievement, since other OECD countries also performed well. In most of the countries under study, more than half of the adult population had completed high school. In four countries, more than 80 percent of the population had secured high school diplomas (Germany, Norway, Switzerland, and the United States). Historical U.S. graduation rates serve to intensify the significance of these figures. In the nineteenth century, less than 3 percent of Americans graduated from high school, and graduation rates remained at less than 50 percent until the middle of the twentieth century. By 1997 approximately 83 percent of American students either held a high school diploma or had completed secondary-school equivalency requirements.

Opinions varied widely as to how the United States was performing in terms of educational quality compared to other industrialized nations just before the century's end. Studies in the early 1990s showed 75 percent of American students scoring below proficiency levels in mathematics, while the average 10- to 11-year-old in Japan and Russia tested out two years ahead of his or her peers in the United States. An OECD study conducted a few years later suggested that while 14-year-old Americans lagged in math, their reading and science levels matched those of children of the same age in France.

According to comparative educational statistics provided by the U.S. Department of Education, U.S. students in the 1990s compared favorably to their counterparts in other large industrialized nations in reading, but unfavorably in mathematics and science. Test scores indicated that U.S. schoolchildren were holding their own in reading and writing, and the Department of Education claimed improvement in scientific and technological skills as well. Other internal evaluations also suggested that U.S. students were bettering some achievement levels. Standard Achievement Tests (SATs) given in the latter part of the twentieth century to high school students in the United States demonstrated a significant upward trend in student performance. Seventy-four percent more students scored above the benchmark level 650 in 1996 than did fifteen years earlier. A large percentage of this improvement was traceable to the influx of Asian-American students, who performed unusually well on the tests. However, even with the testing scores of Asian Americans factored out, a 57 percent improvement was still shown.

International Futures. As industrialized countries continue to struggle to improve educational opportunities for their children and youth, transition and developing economies face yet more strenuous challenges to introduce their students to the skills necessary to succeed in a rapidly globalizing economy. In Russia, for example, students have found themselves far freer in choice of dress and behavior than during the Cold War, and schools are now giving attention even to individual spiritual growth, which would have been anathema under the old Communist regime. However, with the breakdown of the Soviet economic system, government agencies have been severely strapped for the funds needed to outfit and maintain schools and pay teachers' salaries. The result has been that fewer educational opportunities may be found in certain parts of Russia now than were available during the Cold War days. Similarly, in parts of the developing world such as sub-Saharan Africa, where funds from the richer countries of the world were once in rather plentiful supply through international development assistance programs, allocations from certain major international donors for economic and social development programming were substantially redirected to other geographical regions and budgetary purposes after the end of the Cold War. This has placed responsibility for the continued development of educational programs in such places as Africa more squarely on the shoulders of regional and national government leaders, at decided risk to the children and youth of some of the world's most impoverished nations. Additionally, the structural adjustment programs of the International Monetary Fund (IMF) of the late twentieth century have made economic prosperity an even further-off target in many poor countries and in many ways have jeopardized the well-being of students in those lands.

As governments around the world examined ways to improve education in the twenty-first century, many of them were unable or unwilling to provide the necessary funds to develop high-quality school systems that feature access to all. Parents therefore often view private institutions as an educational alternative for their children. In the United States, for example, interest in charter schools and home schooling in the late 1990s and early-2000 years grew as parents sought alternatives to more traditional forms of public and private education. This has prompted U.S. federal, state, and local government officials and school administrators to reconsider how public funds for education may best be allocated and to examine possible viable alternatives to public schooling.

CURRENT CONDITIONS

According to U.S. Census data from 2002, there were more than 53 million school-aged children (between 5 and 17 years old) about 48.1 million of whom were enrolled in public schools. That year, schools received revenues of approximately US$8,552 per student, with the highest revenue per student being in New York State at US$13,230 and the lowest being in Utah at US$6,054. By the 2003-2004 school year, the median revenue figure across the U.S. had risen to US$9,764 per student, with the District of Columbia rising to the highest level at US$13,947. In total, it was estimated that the total revenue figure for public schools during the 2004-2005 school year was more the US$508 billion, while total expenditures were US$495 billion.

As of 2004, there were approximately 75,000 public schools in the United States. According to *Market Share Reporter,* New York City had the largest school district in terms of enrollment, with 1.1 million students. In second place was Los Angeles with 747,000, followed by Chicago with 442,000, Miami-Dade County in Florida with 364,000, Broward County in Florida with 263,000, and Clark County in Nevada with 255,000. Other major districts were located in Houston and Philadelphia. According to the National Center for Education Statistics, enrollment in public schools was expected to increase 5 percent by 2013, while private school enrollment was expected to increase 7 percent. Statistics were unavailable for homeschoolers, but a 2003 study showed approximately 1.1 million homeschool students. Funding for the U.S. public school system was becoming bleak in many states, which were either forced to cut their budgets in the mid-2000s or have funding cut by the state.

The need for education reform of one type or another has been pointed to for decades, whether the call is one of "back to basics," "the need to compete in a global world," or "educating the whole child." One of the more recent examples began in 2002, when President Bush signed the No Child Left Behind Act into law. Intended to ensure the adequate education of every child in public school, the law required annual testing on basic skills in language and math for third through eighth grades. If students did not make the cut on tests and scores did not consistently improve, the schools themselves would be penalized financially, and required to fund outside tutoring for students, or expected to allow students to transfer to other schools, or both.

In 2004, there were 6,000 schools tagged as having achievement problems under the new law, and some analysts projected that the number could swell to one-third of the public schools in the country by 2006. Proponents of the law said that the worth of educating every child was being affirmed and that substandard or underachieving schools would no longer be able to maintain the status quo. Critics of the law pointed to the fallacy that tests and learning are the same, that the cost of the law was excessive, and that the federal government had given itself too much local control.

RESEARCH AND TECHNOLOGY

As knowledge of the world expands and as technology for information processing improves, public schools have come under increasing pressure to more thoroughly prepare students for the information age. Interactive learning arguably began in the latter part of the twentieth century with the introduction of tape recorders in some classrooms and was further developed and enhanced with the installation of computing facilities in the schools of some industrialized countries as early as the late 1960s, the growth of educational software packages, the use of the Internet, and videoconferencing equipment and programs in schools.

Teaching and learning in the information age demand new methods to prepare students to meet new technology. The move into the computer age is an understandably expensive one education-wise. Significant initial costs are associated with acquiring and maintaining computer hardware and the associated software. Wiring, cabling, telephone lines, and technical support, plus necessary continual upgrades of information technology, can far exceed initial investments.

WORKFORCE

According to the National Education Association, the estimated total number of instructional staff employed in the United States during the 2004-2005 school year amounted to almost 3.54 million of which about 25 percent were male. About 1.82 million were elementary school teachers, 1.29 million were secondary school teachers, more than 245,000 were nonsupervisory instructional staff, and there were slightly more than 186,000 principals. The average elementary teacher was earning US$47,487, while a secondary school teacher earned US$48,000.

Elementary and secondary schools provide diverse job opportunities at different skill levels. Overall, the education level of most workers in the field is relatively high. For example, at the turn of the millennium, to be a teacher in an elementary or secondary school in the United States required, at a minimum, a bachelor's degree that included significant coursework in educational theory and psychology, though not necessarily in specific school subject areas, at least not for those preparing to teach at the elementary level. In Germany most teachers at the close of the twentieth century spent five years in college. They were then examined and assigned a mentor for two years of practical training, and examined again before being allowed to seek employment. In Japan teachers underwent a four-year undergraduate program emphasizing academic specialization and then were mentored during their first years of teaching.

The educational services sector was the second-largest industry in the overall U.S. economy in 2002, providing about 12.7 million jobs. Workers in the industry were employed various components of education and its related services, from counseling students to driving school buses to serving cafeteria lunches. However, most occupations were professional, including administrative, managerial, service, and other workers. Teachers accounted for half of all employment in education. By the fall of 1999, some 395,317 full-time equivalent (FTE) teachers were providing instruction to U.S. elementary and secondary students in private schools alone, with 38 percent of those teachers working in Catholic schools, 39 percent employed in other religious schools, and 24 percent working in nonsectarian schools.

Internationally, the average salaries for education-related employees such as school administrators, teachers, counselors, and librarians often are significantly higher than the average salaries for other occupations. In the United States, however, educators' salaries are sometimes markedly lower than salaries for other professionals, such as doctors and lawyers. Teacher earnings increase with higher educational attainment and longer years of service. Educational services employees who worked a traditional school year (September to June) were free to earn additional money during the summer while regular classes were not in session.

Not unionized until the middle of the twentieth century, by the 1990s U.S. elementary and secondary teachers and educational services workers were either union members or covered by union contracts at a rate of almost 41 percent. In contrast, only 18 percent of workers in all other industries combined were unionized or covered by union contracts. The American Federation of Teachers (AFT) and the National Education Association (NEA) were the largest teachers' unions in the United States at the turn of the millennium.

Variations in Teacher Workloads. Compared to school systems in many other industrialized nations, teachers in the United States spend very little structured time sharing information with each other about students, teaching materials, or teaching techniques. Generally, the U.S. teacher's time at school is spent with students, either teaching academic subjects or monitoring playgrounds and lunchrooms.

In a number of Asian countries, the situation is quite different. An early-1990s study of Asian educational practices showed that teachers in Beijing had trouble believing that the teaching workload in U.S. schools was as high as it actually was. The study reported, "'When,' they asked, 'did the teachers prepare their lessons, consult with one another about teaching techniques, grade the students' papers, and work with individual students who were having difficulties?'" Teachers in China, as in other Asian nations, only teach three or four hours each day, spending the rest of their workday managing other aspects of their students' education. A similar focus on time outside of the classroom was permitted teachers in Europe, where teachers averaged just 18 hours of direct classroom instruction per week in the late 1990s. In contrast, U.S. teachers usually spent 25 hours in direct classroom instruction during a given five-day week, and elementary school teachers faced students 30 or more hours each week. On average, U.S. teachers experienced a regular workweek lasting 36.5 hours, to which was added approximately 11 hours a week spent on miscellaneous duties, namely grading papers and preparing lesson plans.

MAJOR COUNTRIES IN THE INDUSTRY

All countries in the world seek to provide education in some form or another to their children. Some countries are much better than others in providing substantial government funding for schools. Whether traditional knowledge is imparted informally through "bush" schools to village youth in Sierra Leone or formal training in advanced computing technology and mathematics is provided through a *Gymnasium* to urban secondary students in Germany, the peoples of the world all believe in teaching their children the values of their society, the principles they believe will contribute to their children's healthy development, and the skills necessary to negotiate the adult world. No country truly can be considered "major" or "minor" in its approach to education, since all countries clearly derive great benefit from educating their children and youth and raising children into adults who can contribute to the future growth of the economy and the benefit of society.

At the same time, a number of countries stand out in dedicating significant public and private financial and human resources to developing, outfitting, and maintaining schools and programs to educate their young. The teaching methods and educational theories of these countries are often imported by other countries around the world. For this reason, a few of the countries whose emphasis on education has been significant and influential over the past century or two are worth examining more closely.

Japan. Japan provides a comprehensive approach to primary education for nearly all of the nation's school-age children. Attendance is compulsory through the lower level of secondary school (six years of elementary school and three years of middle school covering the ages 6 to 15 years.). After that time attendance is not required, although about 97 percent of students who graduate from middle school do attend high school, or *kotogakko*. About 90 percent of all students graduate from high school. The majority of high schools are public, though about 30 percent of Japanese high school students choose to attend private schools.

Children begin elementary school at age 6 and at age 12 begin middle school. Enrollment in high school is a competitive exercise, with admission based on a combination of analysis of student grades and the administration of achievement tests. Achievement test scores are sent to the schools where a student has applied but are never shown to the students themselves. Because exams assume such an important role in student advancement, many students' after-school hours that in other countries would be spent on social or recreational pursuits instead are spent in special tutorial programs called *juku*. Pure vocational education is rare in Japan, although a growing number of students do pursue some kind of vocational training. Japanese schools teach hard work, which leads to high student academic achievement. The education system was being reviewed to allow more independent teaching styles.

United Kingdom. Education in the United Kingdom is characterized by an unusual range of choices. Will schooling be public or private? Which public school should be attended? Which private school? Should the educational focus be vocational or academic? Every British child between the ages of 5 and 16 must attend school of some sort (ages 4 to 16 in Northern Ireland). Many students begin at schools funded and administered by local education authorities (LEAs). The remainder attend schools that U.S. pupils would term "private"—that is, schools funded by private individuals. The U.K. terminology for such institutions usually is "public," since they are owned and administered by the general public rather than by the state. Whether granted a "public" or "private" appellation, these independently operated schools function as a business, with teachers and headmasters in control of the school budget.

A very large proportion of British children (in England, 94 percent of preschool-age children) actually begin their schooling at age 3 or 4, attending nursery schools or "reception classes" in elementary schools that prepare them for primary-school attendance. At age 5 (age 4 in Northern Ireland), children attend a primary school, where they remain until approximately age 11. Most students continue on in secondary schools which accept all students regardless of background and ability and require no particular testing as a prerequisite for entry. On the other hand, those students preferring to complete their education in public schools must first pass stiff entrance examinations at the school of their choice, whether they seek admission to a publicly funded "grammar school" or to even more ancient and prestigious institutions. Though tuition is costly, the price of attending "public" schools rarely deters the generally affluent students who attend them. Even those parents who must scrape and save to enroll their children in the more prestigious academies see the social and academic opportunity afforded by their children's attending these schools as worth the expense. School pride associated with public secondary schools is intense, whether or not the school in question is well-known internationally. The phenomenon of multiple generations of students attending the same private school is not an unusual one, and indeed some private institutions have been preparing young scholars for several centuries.

Whether or not students attend a fee-based public school, U.K. parents have an element of choice in selecting secondary schools. State schools are under close governmental scrutiny. Exams are administered to students at ages 7, 11, 14, and 16, to both establish the performance of the school and to evaluate the individual student. In addition, schools undergo intense school inspections which evaluate schools, teaching staff, and administrative staff on a wide variety of criteria. Exam results, along with school truancy records and school inspection reports are open to public view and routinely are used by parents as a guide to selecting the best state school for their children.

Completion of secondary schooling, whether in state or public schools, is heralded by two stages of examination. Students aged 16 take the main state examination for each subject they have studied. These are the famous "O-level" exams, and performance on them generally dictates whether or not a student will continue vocational training or go on to university. Admission to university is predicated on satisfactory completion of a fixed number of advanced, or "A-level" exams, which are administered after approximately two years of further study. In 1988 the General Certificate of Education (GCE), awarded on completion of O-level testing, was replaced with the General Certificate of Secondary Education (GCSE). Students on a course of advanced study that is considered vocational when compared to the pure academics measured by A-levels (drama, business studies) may use their secondary-school diplomas to enter universities offering comparable areas of study. Regardless of the educational track, practically speaking this means that British students attending university—Oxford, Cambridge, or the less exclusive regional "red-brick" colleges—begin their college learning approximately two years ahead of their U.S. counterparts.

Businesses in the United Kingdom have been encouraged to participate in bettering schools, particularly in vocational education, and the British government has established a national curriculum for use in state schools. The tests that measure how successfully this curriculum is being imparted become part of an aggressive monitoring of the schools in question. It is not impossible for a dissatisfied education inspector to mandate wholesale staff dismissal and replacement, or more commonly, to advise the replacement of an underachieving school's headmaster or headmistress.

France. Public education in France is highly centralized. The country is divided into a number of geographically-based education districts, called "academies." A rector who reports directly to the Minister of National Education, Research, and Technology heads each academy. The French educational system was set up to ensure uniformity, and thereby presumably quality, in education throughout the country, but critics have claimed the system is inflexible and precludes local citizens from voicing their opinions on educational problems.

Ten years of public school attendance are mandated, from ages 6 to 16, but in actual practice most children attend school for at least a dozen years. It is possible for a child to be in school for 16 years prior to enrolling in a university. Public education is free, although about one-sixth of French elementary schoolchildren and one-fifth of secondary students attend private schools, about 95 percent of these schools being Roman Catholic. Primary and elementary training is divided into preschool (pre-elementary) training for toddlers through age 6, primary school (*école primaire*) for students aged 6 through 11, and secondary school (*collège*) attended by students aged 12 to 15. The four-year course of *collège* study culminates in the *brevet de collège* diploma, awarded to students who complete their final two years of coursework with sufficiently high grades and who perform well on the timed, written examination in French, History-Geography, and Mathematics that concludes this level of their secondary studies.

Most French students also take advantage of a second cycle, or *lycée*, of secondary-level education. On entrance to the *lycée*, students either select a three-year course of study leading to the General Baccalaureate (usable as a passport to the university) or to one of two types of technical training programs: the three-year Technological Baccalaureate program that opens the way to post-secondary schools of technology, professional, or arts studies; or the Professional Baccalaureate program that leads directly to a job or to on-the-job training after two years of study.

Germany. In Germany, although a strong national standard of education exists, each German state controls an educational system distinct from that of the other states. A permanent national commission is responsible for providing uniformity in curriculum, requirements, and standards imposed largely through textbook selection, though the implementation of these standards varies from state to state. Private schools exist in Germany, but since public education—even university study—is free and exceedingly high in standard, the number of private schools is quite small.

German students are required to attend school from ages 6 to 18. Kindergartens are available to nurture and support the development of children of preschool age (3 to 5 years old). However, kindergartens are not part of the German state school system, and parents frequently must contribute to their cost of operation. The 12 years of mandatory state school attendance consists of 9 or 10 years of full-time attendance (varying by state) and the remaining years either consisting of full-time studies or divided between school and on-the-job training. Students are asked at a relatively early age to identify their personal academic or vocational goals. Elementary education, or *Grundschule*, lasts six years in Berlin and Brandenburg and four years elsewhere in Germany, followed in many parts of the country by a two-year orientation phase, *Orientierungsstufe*.

Students begin to diverge even further from each other in their courses of study after the elementary-school years. About one-fourth of German secondary students go on to the *Hauptschule*, a secondary general school for grades 5 through 9, or 7 through 9, depending on the length of elementary education a student has had. Successful completion of the *Hauptschule*, which covers basic academic training plus introductory vocational studies, merits the awarding of a school-leaving certificate that qualifies the graduate to enter a vocational apprenticeship program, usually lasting two to three years. Some graduates go on to complete tenth grade, and if they earn especially high grades, they may receive a more prestigious school-leaving certificate. Vocational training schools are chosen by a number of students who complete the *Hauptschule*.

Another two-fifths of German secondary students attend the *Realschule* instead of the *Hauptschule* for grades 5 through 10. The *Realschule* is designed to prepare students for such occupations as mid-level administrators and managers, service workers, civil servants, and the like. One to three years of study in a full-time vocational school known as a *Berufsfachschule* is also possible for students who complete the *Hauptschule* or the *Realschule*. About one-fourth of German secondary students enter the *Gymnasium* directly after their elementary school years. Several kinds of these schools exist, but the emphasis is mainly on academic subjects. After a total educational career of 12 or 13 years of schooling, students in the *Gymnasium* sit for the *Abitur* examinations, which open the door to university studies.

Certain alternatives to the above schooling arrangements also exist in some parts of Germany, including the *Gesamtschule*, a form of post-elementary school that allows students a broader, less-tracked type of education than the traditional split between vocational versus academic studies. About 13 percent of German secondary students attend the *Gesamtschule*. Germany also provides special schools known as *Sonderschulen* to educate disabled students.

FURTHER READING

American Federation of Teachers, 2004. Available from http://www.aft.org.

Boser, Ulrich. "A New Law Is Put to the Test." *U.S. News & World Report,* 22 March 2004.

Broughman, Stephen, and Lenore A. Colaciello. "Private School Universe Survey: 1999-2000," *NCES Statistical Analysis Report,* NCES 2001-330. Washington, DC: National Center for Education Statistics, Office of Educational Research and Improvement, U.S. Department of Education, August 2001. Available from http://nces.ed.gov.

Bureau of Labor Statistics, U.S. Department of Labour. "Educational Services." *Career Guide to Industries, 2004-05 Edition*, viewed July 16, 2005. Available from http://www.bls.gov.

Field, Richard. "John Dewey (1859-1952)." In *The Internet Encyclopedia of Philosophy,* 2001. Available from http://www.utm.edu.

"Global Education Digest 2004: Comparing Education Statistics Across the World." United Nations Educational, Scientific, and Cultural Organization, 2004. Available from http://www.uis.unesco.org.

John Dewey Project on Progressive Education. "A Brief Overview of Progressive Education." College of Education and Social Services, University of Vermont, 2002. Available from http://www.uvm.edu.

Lazich, Robert S., ed. *Market Share Reporter.* Detroit: Thomson Gale, 2004.

Marlowe-Ferguson, Rebecca, and Christopher Lopez, eds. *World Education Encyclopedia, Second Edition.* Farmington Hills, Michigan: The Gale Group-Thomson Learning, 2001.

National Center for Education Statistics. "1.1 Million Homeschooled Students in the United States in 2003." Washington, DC: U.S. Department of Education, 2003. Available from http://nces.ed.gov.

———. "Common Core of Data: Information on Public Schools and School Districts in the United States." Washington, DC: U.S. Department of Education, 2002. Available from http://nces.ed.gov.

———. *Highlights from the 2000 Program for International Student Assessment (PISA),* NCES 2002-116. Washington, DC: Office of Educational Research and Improvement, U.S. Department of Education, 2002. Available from http://nces.ed.gov.

———. "International Comparisons in Education." Washington, DC: Office of Educational Research and Improvement, U.S. Department of Education, 2002. Available from http://nces.ed.gov.

———. *Outcomes of Learning: Results from the 2000 Program for International Student Assessment of 15-Year-Olds in Reading, Mathematics, and Science Literacy,* NCES 2002-115. Washington, DC: U.S. Department of Education, 2002.

———. "Overview of Public Elementary and Secondary Schools and Districts: School Year 1999-2000," *NCES Statistical Analysis Report,* NCES 2001-339R. Washington, DC: U.S. Department of Education, September 2001. Available from http://nces.ed.gov.

———. "Projections of Education Statistics to 2013." Washington, DC: U.S. Department of Education, 2004. Available from http://nces.ed.gov.

National Priorities Project. "Proposed FY2003 Budget and Analysis: States and Local Governments to Lose Funding for Many Programs," 2002. Available from http://www.nationalpriorities.org.

OECD. *Education at a Glance: OECD Indicators 2001 Edition.* Organization for Economic Co-operation and Development, 2001. Available from http://oecdpublications.gfi-nb.com.

"Rankings & Estimates: Rankings of the States 2004 and Estimates of School Statistics 2005." National Education Association, June 2005. Available from http://www.nea.org.

Ritchie, Susan. "Horace Mann." In *Dictionary of Unitarian and Universalist Biography,* 2001. Available from http://www.uua.org.

"Testing, Testing." *Community Care,* 20 May 2004.

UNESCO Institute for Statistics. "Quest 2001, Survey 2001 Electronic Questionnaire and Manuals." United Nations Educational, Scientific, and Cultural Organization, 2001. Available from http://www.uis.unesco.org.

World Bank, The. *World Development Indicators 2001.* Washington, DC: The World Bank, 2001.

SIC 4911, 4920

NAICS 22111

ENERGY

The world's energy industry produces, transmits, and distributes electricity and natural gas. Electric power generation may derive from any number of methods, including the burning of fossil fuels, harnessing of wind or water motion, or energy from nuclear reactions. Often several separate companies or organizations are involved in the production and distribution chain, which spans from initial production to delivery to end users. Various firms and public utilities specialize in certain phases of energy production; others integrate several of the production steps. For example, some firms may generate electricity and sell it to distributors that, in turn, resell to the general public. Similarly, natural gas companies may operate pipelines that feed distribution companies, which then provide natural gas to end users in businesses and private residences.

INDUSTRY SNAPSHOT

Of the total worldwide energy supply in 2002, the International Energy Agency (IEA) noted in its 2004 report that 41.6 percent was coming from non-coal and non-oil sources. These other sources included natural gas, nuclear, hydro, combustible renewables and waste, and others, including wind and solar. This was up from 30 percent in 1973.

On a global basis, 16.1 trillion kilowatt hours of electricity was supplied in 2002, with the largest producing countries being the United States, China and Japan. However, all were also large users, and France exported more electricity than any other country. Most electricity was still being produced using coal, but there was a growing use of natural gas and nuclear in some countries. Alternative renewable forms of electricity generation were continuing to make inroads, with many investments in wind, geothermal and combustible renewable sources.

U.S., German, British and Japanese electric utilities dominated the top rankings, with the European-based companies showing the strongest signs of globalization. Total consumption of electricity worldwide was projected to reach 16.4 trillion kilowatt hours by 2010, 18.5 by 2015, 20.7 by 2020, and 23.1 by 2025. Total consumption of energy generation fuels, on the other hand, was projected to reach 193.6 quadrillion btu by 2010, 213.9 by 2015, 235.5 by 2020, and 258.6 by 2025.

In terms of natural gas production, on a global basis, more than 96 trillion cubic feet was produced in 2003. Since 1976, most growth had occurred in the countries of the former Soviet Union. Russia, Canada and Norway were the world' leading exporters, and although the U.S. was the second largest producer, it was a net importer in order to meet its demand levels.

The leading companies in the natural gas industry are those that hold or formerly held monopolistic control over domestic distribution rights, including those in the United Kingdom, Japan, the Netherlands, France, and Germany, as well as companies from the United States and other countries that were involved in worldwide exploration for or production of natural gas. In 2004, the world had a total 6.1 quadrillion cubic feet in natural gas reserves, of which the top 20 countries controlled nearly 90 percent, more than 5.4 quadrillion cubic feet.

The vast majority of the energy industry's growth is projected to arise from emerging markets in developing nations, which include Asian, Latin American, and Eastern European countries, where large pent-up demand exists for power, or there is a need to retool existing power plants, with China, Latin America, and Africa seeing the biggest annual increases in demand. The energy needs of developing nations, coupled with widespread global initiatives to deregulate the electric and gas industries and privatize state-owned companies, were increasing competition in an industry once viewed as being necessarily monopolistic.

ORGANIZATION AND STRUCTURE

Electric Services. Each nation generally has its own type of electric power industry structure, which in the case of more developed countries was typically solidified in the first half of the twentieth century. While traditional national and regional markets continued to exist in the late 1990s, deregulation and privatization of utilities was rapidly changing the organization of the electric power industry.

By the early 1990s, private capitalization of independent power projects set the stage for a new global business environment. This environment was characterized regionally by a surplus of power in developed countries such as the United States and Britain, which were in the throes of utility deregulation, and power demand from developing countries in Asia-Pacific and Latin American markets. While Western European utilities have joined in some of the consortia providing power in emerging markets, the independent power movement has roots in the United States and Britain, where utilities facing deregulation, competition, and fixed returns have turned to external markets for higher profits.

In the United States, regulation and deregulation began substantially changing the power industry in 1978 when the Public Utility Regulatory Policies Act was adopted to encourage conservation by allowing non-regulated independent producers to generate electricity that could be sold to utilities. This act was the birth of an independent power industry that grew faster than most expected; independent producers were responsible for half of the generating capacity that went on line during the 1980s. The 1992 Energy Policy Act granted the industry wholesale transmission or "wheeling of power" rights, which allowed utilities to buy energy from utilities across state lines in 1993. The act also gave states the power to permit retail wheeling (or transportation) of power to individual businesses and consumers. Between the late 1980s and early 2000s, the U.S. Federal Regulatory Energy Commission (FERC) approved roughly 850 wholesaler power transmission permits.

In the late 1990s, states were moving at various speeds toward deregulating their retail electricity markets. By April 1998, according to Strategic Energy Ltd., California, Rhode Island, Massachusetts, and Pennsylvania had already opened their retail markets to competition, while six other states—Montana, Nevada, Kansas, Illinois, New Hampshire, Maine, and Oklahoma—had passed retail wheeling legislation and were making progress toward completing the transition to competitive markets. By spring 1998, retail wheeling legislation had been proposed in 11 other states, and legislative or regulatory activity had taken place in the remaining 29 states. By early 1998, 11 states had opted to test the deregulated waters first by instituting pilot programs allowing certain customers to participate in limited retail choice experiments, as a prelude to retail competition. In the early 2000s, highly publicized problems with retail deregulation in California, including widespread blackouts, prompted many states to suspend plans to open their energy markets to competition.

Natural Gas. Since the mid-1980s, the natural gas regulatory climate in the United States has changed dramatically as well. In 1985, FERC issued an order requiring pipelines to become open-access carriers for both gas producers and users, making pipeline companies transportation services. In November 1993, FERC order 633, which is aimed at reducing regulation and encouraging competition, took effect, making local utilities responsible for their natural gas supplies from well head to consumer. Additionally, pipeline companies were no longer allowed to sell gas directly to customers, but rather had to utilize a marketing unit. The order resulted in pipeline companies abandoning their sales operations and developing gas market affiliates to serve as intermediaries.

Between 1988 and 1991, Britain largely completed its plan to privatize the electricity industry, with the exception of nuclear power. In the process, the government's public monopoly responsible for generation and transmission of power in England and Wales was separated into two generating companies, PowerGen PLC and National Power, and a transmission company, National Grid Co. Efforts to privatize the natural gas industry moved more slowly, although by 1994 plans had been made to begin phasing in deregulation of the local gas industry starting in 1996, when a portion of British

Gas PLC customers would gain the right to choose their gas supplier.

By 1998, as a result of privatization efforts in the United Kingdom, residential electricity bills in England and Wales had fallen an average of 21 percent. In mid-1998, British ministers announced plans to overhaul the country's electricity industry once again. Writing in the *Financial Times* of London, Andrew Taylor noted that the ruling Labour Party was keen to reform wholesale trading arrangements in the national electricity pool, claiming the structure had unduly favored growth in gas-fired power plants, which contributed to Britain's exceeding its pollution targets. Ministers proposed tighter restrictions for future gas-fired power plants in order to preserve a market for British coal while the new trading arrangements were introduced. In May 1999, the United Kingdom became the first country to grant all of its gas and electricity consumers, both residential and commercial, the right to choose their utilities.

The electric and gas industries can effectively be divided into seven market regions: United States-Canada, Western Europe, Japan, Asia-Pacific excluding Japan, Eastern Europe and the former Soviet Union, Latin America, and the Middle East and Africa. In the more developed regions, power generally exists in surplus, while the underdeveloped regions—particularly Latin America and the Asia-Pacific region, where excess demand for power goes unsatisfied—were expected to hold the vast majority of growth for the electric and gas industries. Between 1995 and 2020, the Energy Information Administration predicted electricity demand in developing countries would grow at more than twice the rate of growth in industrialized countries. Still, *International Energy Outlook 2001* predicted that natural gas would be the fastest growing sector of the energy industry: "Gas use is projected to almost double, to 162 trillion cubic feet in 2020 from 84 trillion cubic feet in 1999. With an average growth rate of 3.2 percent, the share of natural gas in total primary energy consumption is projected to grow to 28 percent from 23 percent. The largest increments in gas use are expected in Central and South American and in developing Asia."

United States-Canada. Portions of the United States' and Canada's power systems are joined via gas transmission lines and electric power networks. Canadian government-owned electric utilities, such as Ontario Hydro, which operated as a private business, have traditionally exported surplus power to northeastern U.S. states. Historically, Canada has also been the major exporter of natural gas to the United States. Between 1986 and 1993, imports of natural gas into the United States rose from 689 billion cubic feet annually to 2.1 trillion cubic feet, largely as a result of the 1992 completion of Canada's Iroquois pipeline system. The three Canada-to-U.S. gas transportation corridors grew dramatically each year between 1989 and 1997. The three corridors experienced more growth in the capacity to deliver gas between 1990 and 1997 than any of the other seven major interregional transportation corridors. In 1998 the Northern Border system was extended into the Midwest from Montana, adding 650 million cubic feet per day in natural gas capacity. As a result, imports from Canada grew by nearly 9 percent in 1999. The Maritimes and Northeast line, completed in December of 1999, added 400 million cubic feet per day in capacity, and the Alliance Pipeline, connecting North Dakota and Chicago in December 2000, boosted capacity by another 1.3 billion cubic feet.

The U.S. electric power industry contains a wide range of entities, although in the late 1990s it continued to be dominated by investor-owned utility monopolies that had historically provided service to large and consolidated markets. As of March 1998, there were 223 investor-owned utilities in the United States, compared with 4,132 independent, or non-utility, power producers. The remainder of power providers included such diverse sources as publicly owned utilities, federal utilities, and cooperatives. There was also a new class of power provider made possible by deregulation: the power marketer, an independent middleman that buys and sells wholesale electricity at market prices but lacks its own generation, transmission, or distribution capacity. U.S.-based Enron Corp., the energy marketing and trading giant that underwent a highly publicized bankruptcy in 2001, is an example of such a firm. As a result of the Enron scandal, which centered around questionable accounting practices utilized by the firm, some analysts began to question the viability of other energy marketers operating without generation, transmission, or distribution capacity.

Western Europe. In contrast to Asian markets, Western European power companies operated in a market with substantial power reserves during the early 1990s. Nonetheless, private power projects—as opposed to government-regulated or owned utilities—began to attract increased interest in Europe, as did private financing of new generating capacity. An increasing number of governments made their national power industries more competitive based on successes they saw. As deregulation spread in the region, competition and the number of private power projects increased. Projects included new power plants, the purchase and refurbishment of existing plants, and cogeneration projects designed to provide heat and power to industrial concerns.

By the late 1990s, Europe's electricity markets had become increasingly integrated, thanks to a 1997 directive adopted by the European Union intended to provide independent power producers greater access to power networks in other countries. Cross-border investments were made in the European electricity market, and regional power pools emerged. For example, in Scandinavia, Sweden, Finland, and Norway operated a joint electricity pool in the late 1990s.

The European Union also agreed in the late 1990s on a timetable for deregulating Western European gas markets, the first phase of which was scheduled for completion in August 2000. The region's principal natural gas producing countries in 1999 included the northwestern European nations of the Netherlands and Norway (which held the area's largest reserves) and the United Kingdom. Leading natural gas consumers included Germany (a major importer), the United Kingdom, Italy, the Netherlands, and France. Its key electric power producers in 1999 included Germany, France, and the United Kingdom, and to a lesser degree Italy and Spain. In the early 2000s, the electricity and natural gas industries of Europe became increasingly intertwined due to deregulation efforts, as well as the increasing use of natural gas in electric power generation.

Japan. This Pacific Rim country boasts some of the world's largest utilities in terms of assets and revenues. A leading consumer and importer of natural gas, Japan lacks substantial mineral resources. As a result, the country had a high demand for new power plant construction, particularly nuclear capacity, throughout the 1990s. In the mid-1990s, Japan was largely a closed market with utilities enjoying monopolies, although discussions were being conducted regarding privatization. In January 1996, in a first move toward decreasing Japanese electricity customers' bills, the Electric Utility Industry law was drastically modified. This threw the electricity sector into turmoil. Independent power producers moved into the market later in 1996 and were able to offer rates lower than the electric monopolies, giving Japan a taste of how low prices can go in a competitive marketplace. As in Europe, electric power and gas companies in Japan also began moving into one another's markets. Deregulation efforts continued into the early 2000s.

Asia-Pacific Outside Japan. According to an analysis published in the *International Energy Outlook 1998*, Asia's large emerging nations, including China, India, Indonesia, and Pakistan, had strong and fast-growing demand for energy that outstripped the rate at which local governments or companies could increase capacity. This afforded excellent opportunities to foreign firms with experience serving large markets efficiently. Between 1979 and 1996 only 10 percent of China's electric power industry investment was foreign. With 1.2 billion people in the late 1990s, China was the world's most populous nation, and electricity consumption there was forecast to grow 5.8 percent per year through 2020. Key power-producing nations of the region include China and India, while Indonesia and Malaysia are the area's leading natural gas producers. In 2000 the largest natural gas field in China, with estimated reserves of more than 7 trillion cubic feet, was discovered in the Tarim Basin.

Latin America. By the late 1990s, there were no Latin American countries where privatization had not been adopted or considered in some form. The region's leading electricity providers in the late 1990s were Brazil and Mexico, while the leading natural gas producer was Venezuela, with known reserves of 147 trillion cubic feet as of the early 2000s. Brazil was far and away the largest economy of the region, and was expected to account for 77 percent of the growth in the region's electricity consumption by 2020. Central and South America led the developing world in privatization of the electricity sector. In 1997 Brazil followed in the footsteps of Chile and Argentina in selling off state-owned utility assets to private investors. As gas use in Latin America was expected to increase by roughly 7.5 percent each year through 2020, many leading utilities began expanding pipeline networks and increasing use of existing lines. In early 2000, for example, Brazil's state-owned Petrobras contracted for increased natural gas deliveries from Bolivia via an existing pipeline.

Eastern Europe. The principal electric power producing country in this region was Russia, which accounted for 5.7 percent of world production in 1999. Russia also was the world's largest producer of natural gas that year, accounting for 23.7 percent of world production, although Uzbekistan was also on the list of top 10 global natural gas producers. This region of the world is rich in natural gas, claiming 37.3 percent of the world's reserves. Of that amount, about a third of the world's natural gas reserves are located in Russia, with an additional 2.0 percent located in Turkmenistan.

In Eastern Europe, substantial expansion plans of the 1980s had, by the 1990s, given way to plans that involved refurbishing existing older plants, which were often inefficient fossil fuel-burning or nuclear plants. The electric industries of Eastern Europe and the former Soviet Union were quite distinct from those in other parts of the world, where electricity capacity strains to keep up with demand. In this region, electricity was an overdeveloped resource, and thus had no capacity shortage, but the industry suffered from outdated technology that made production inefficient and more environmentally harmful. Natural gas consumption, on the other hand, was projected to grow from 28.1 trillion cubic feet in 1999 to 37.5 trillion cubic feet in 2020.

Middle East and Africa. The Middle East and Africa held substantial natural gas reserves in the late 1990s. Algeria was the area's leading natural gas producer, while Iran and Saudi Arabia were the area's largest consumers. In total, four of the top five countries in terms of natural gas reserves were located in the Middle East and Africa in 2001. They included Iran, with 15.4 percent of the world's reserves; Qatar, with 7.5 percent; United Arab Emirates, with 4.0 percent; and Saudi Arabia, with 4.0 percent. Algeria claimed about 3.0 percent of global natural gas reserves, while Nigeria had 2.3 percent and Iraq had 2.1 percent. One trend in the area in the late 1990s was substituting gas for oil in domestic consumption, so more oil could be exported.

In September 1997, three energy companies—France's Total, Russia's Gazprom, and Malaysia's Petronias—had inked an agreement with the Iranian National Petroleum Company to develop 2 billion cubic feet per day in reserves from the South Pars field, which holds about 40 percent of Iran's natural gas reserves. In 2000, Italy's Eni and National Iranian Oil reached a US$3.8 billion deal to further develop South Pars.

BACKGROUND AND DEVELOPMENT

Development of the Electric Power Industry. The technological developments leading to the birth of the electric power industry were international in scope. In 1831 Englishman Michael Faraday and American Joseph Henry independently discovered the induction principle that made possible the development of the electric generator, which in turn made possible the widespread and economical production and distribution of electric power. It took 50 years following their discovery to lay the necessary technological groundwork for the electric power industry, although by the 1850s generators were being manufactured commercially in several countries. In 1870 the first practical generator capable of producing a continuous electric current was built by the Belgian manufacturer, Zenobe Theophile Gramme.

Most historians credit the U.S. inventor and entrepreneur Thomas Alva Edison for fathering the electric power industry. Edison was dedicated to utilizing electricity to provide an improved and less expensive means of lighting than was being accomplished via arc-lighting and manufactured gas. Additionally, according to Milton A. Chase in *Electric Power: An Industry at a Crossroads*, Edison's goal was to compete with the established gas industry, which had a 50-year head start on electricity as an industry. After Edison developed the electric incandescent lamp for commercial use, he pioneered an industry, via a New York power company, in order to sell electricity to those who purchased his incandescent bulbs. As a result, Edison is widely acknowledged as the person who created the first successful system to produce, distribute, and utilize electric power.

In January 1882 the first public power station using an electric generator began operating in London for demonstration purposes. That same year Edison supervised the installation of the world's first permanent, commercial central power system, in New York state. Both of these stations employed direct-current (DC) systems that were ineffective in terms of transmitting power long distances. Edison's New York power station utilized coal-fired boilers that produced steam to run generators, which became a model for franchised Edison Electric Light operations in other U.S. cities.

Initially, Edison's companies sold power to limited areas within close proximity to central power stations, due to the limitations of the DC-system he employed. The first practical alternating-current (AC) generator was built in Germany and began service to Frankfurt in 1891. In 1892 Edison sent his right-hand assistant, Samuel Insull, to oversee what in the next decade would become the electric powerhouse Commonwealth Edison. That same year Edison's firm merged with the AC-proponent Thomson-Houston company, to become General Electric Company. According to Chase, the basic pattern for the power industry stemmed from the work of Insull, who came from England and helped push the adoption of the alternating-current system, which was accepted by the Edison operations by the turn of the century. Additionally, Insull helped pioneer a build-and-grow strategy for utilities, which became cost effective after power producers diversified their customer base to diffuse the peak load of electricity demand. Insull also became a strong proponent of electric utility monopolies, public relations, and advertising.

During the first years of the twentieth century, technological developments led to ever-increasing capacities being generated by turbine motors. With AC established as the accepted system and with technological advances in turbines and high-voltage transmission systems, Insull and others perpetuated the grow-and-build strategy that encouraged electricity use. Utilities were thus able to install new plants and reach out to more customers. The theory was that with growth in usage and evolving improvements in turbine technology, lower costs for consumers and indefinite growth in business could be expected. One other component of Insull's strategy was the use of holding companies to help finance the construction of new power plants. Aside from providing financial backing, the holding company system also provided management and engineering expertise that, as holding companies acquired smaller systems, could be used to employ system interconnections. The number of new holding companies peaked in the United States in 1924, when 20 corporations controlled 61 percent of the U.S. commercial generating capacity. During the 1920s, some of these holding companies exploited trends toward speculative investment and concocted schemes by which utilities could control huge power domains. These domains were controlled by a limited number of shareholders who needed just a few shares of a preferred stock at the highest level of what some called a pyramid ownership system.

Through the 1920s the largest percentage of electric power was produced by hydroelectric power plants. There are two principal sources for power generators—hydro and thermal, with the former deriving power from generators turned by water and the latter using generators powered by steam. The early hydroelectric plants were the most cost effective of their time; however, technological advances by the 1930s began to make thermal generation the system of choice.

By the early 1930s, 10 holding companies controlled about three-quarters of the United States' power industry. The grasp of holding companies on the electric utility industry was pried loose following the Great Depression and federal investigation into the abuse of holding companies, which caused overexpansion and financial problems for establishments such as Insull's pyramid of companies. Three of Insull's largest firms went into receivership in 1932 and he was indicted on federal charges. He fled to Europe, returned in 1934, and was thrice acquitted of embezzlement and fraud before returning to Europe to live out his days in rich seclusion. In 1935 the Holding Company Act of 1935 was passed, abolishing leveraged holding companies and stripping apart monopolies not connected by contiguous service territory. With the passage of New Deal legislation that initiated federal utilities like the Tennessee Valley Authority (TVA) and rural electrical cooperatives, the landscape of the utility industry was settled and remained unquestioned in the United States until the 1960s.

By the time the Holding Company Act was passed, other industrialized countries had also begun to regulate their growing utility industries. In 1935 the Canadian province of Quebec established its Electrical Commission to regulate electric distribution services and rates. As early as 1926, Britain enacted its Electricity (Supply) Act, which restructured the industry and oversaw construction of a national power transmission grid. By 1932, Japan—engaged in war in mainland China—began operating under a revised Electric Utility Industry Law that gave the country's leaders the final word on such matters as mergers and rates. After World War II, economic and political conditions, according to Chase, encouraged the establishment of national power systems in Canada, the United Kingdom, France, and new communist countries, while only a few private or semi-private systems developed in such countries as Japan and West Germany. The United States, meanwhile, had the world's most heterogeneous industry, consisting of numerous private companies and government utilities, as a result of legislation and New Deal reforms.

Build-and-grow strategies went unchallenged in the United States until the 1960s when, late in the decade, utilities faced the dilemma of high operating costs. In the 1970s the proper mix of generating fuel became an ongoing question throughout the world. Through the 1950s, many nations had relied largely on hydroelectric power, but it proved inadequate for growing industrialized needs. Coal had been a long-standing fossil fuel for thermal generation, although the fuel of choice shifted to oil after prices declined in the 1960s, and then to nuclear generation in the early 1970s. During the late 1970s concerns over nuclear energy led a shift back toward coal, and with the falling of oil and natural gas prices in the 1980s, the situation changed again. Nuclear power fell increasingly out of favor after dangerous leaks at Three Mile Island in the United States in 1979 and at the Soviet Union's Chernobyl plant in 1986, although a build-up of nuclear plants in France and a lack of fossil fuels in Japan helped solidify nuclear power's importance in these countries.

One trend in the energy industry in the late 1990s was investments in foreign electricity markets. U.S. utility companies were buying into the United Kingdom because acquisitions could beef up earnings easily and because Britain was the first country to open its electricity market to competition. Writing in the *Wall Street Journal*, Kathryn Kranhold noted that U.S. electric utilities spent more than US$200 billion between 1995 and 1998 purchasing stakes in 8 of Britain's 12 regional utilities. The largest of these acquisitions through mid-1998 included the US$2.2 billion acquisition of East Midlands Electricity by Dominion Resources, followed by the US$2.1 billion acquisition of London Electricity by Entergy, the US$1.6 billion purchase of Seeboard by Central & South West, and the US$1.4 billion acquisition of Midlands Electricity by GPU Corp. Later in the year, Texas Utilities purchased Energy Group in a US$7.4 billion deal. However, these acquisitions were not foolproof; Entergy, for instance, had been counting on London Electricity to increase earnings, but instead the company promptly reported a 48 percent drop in profits after the deal was completed.

Development of the Natural Gas Industry. Between 6000 and 2000 B.C. the first discoveries of natural gas were made in Iran. These gas "seeps" were thought to have been struck by lightning, fueling the "eternal fires" of the ancient Persians who embraced a fire-worshipping religion. Natural gas was discovered in China as early as 900 B.C., and by 200 B.C. the ancient Chinese (the first people known to utilize natural gas for industrial uses) created a system of bamboo poles through which gas was piped. The gas was burned in order to dry rock salt and manufacture salt. Manufactured gas was discovered in 1609 by Belgian chemist and physician Jan Baptista van Helmont who noticed that a "spirit," which he called "gas," escaped from coal when heated. Natural gas was not discovered in Europe until found in England in 1659. During the late eighteenth and early nineteenth centuries, William Murdock, a British engineer who became known as the father of the gas industry, successfully lit his home with gas manufactured (or distilled) from coal, lit the outside of a factory with gaslight, and installed 900 gaslights in cotton mills.

Murdock's work and that of other inventors sparked the interest of German businessman Frederick Albert Winsor, who wanted to manufacture gas on a substantial scale and in 1804 obtained a British patent to do so. Winsor and his business partners were responsible for the first public street lighting with gas, which occurred in London in 1807. They were also responsible for the creation of the first gas company, formed in 1812. Manufactured gas remained the primary fuel for illuminating streets and houses in Europe for much of the next two centuries. In 1812 the first American gas company was formed to provide street lighting services to Baltimore, and in 1836 the first Canadian gas company was created to light Montreal's streets.

Substantial development of the gas industry derived from discoveries of natural gas reserves in the United States; the earliest discovery occurred in West Virginia in 1775. During the 1820s gunsmith William Aaron Hart developed the first natural gas well in the United States (in Fredonia, New York) and subsequently piped gas to nearby buildings, which burned the fuel for lighting. By the close of the Civil War, about 300 U.S. manufactured gas distribution companies had been formed, and in 1865 the first company known to have distributed natural gas was founded in Fredonia.

In the following decade, the first so-called long distance pipeline, carrying gas 25 miles (a very short distance in modern practice) to Rochester, New York, was completed, and the first iron pipeline transporting natural gas about 5 miles to customers in Pennsylvania began operating. Edison's electric light, and the electric power industry he helped develop, nearly wiped out the natural gas industry in the 1880s, however, and although manufactured gas during the remainder of the century was increasingly used for cooking and heating water, the natural gas industry in the United States remained localized around gas fields due to pipeline transmission restraints. In 1890 a technological breakthrough resulted in the invention of a leak-proof pipeline couple, but construction and other restraints kept pipelines from extending more than 100 miles. Even in 1925, all of the 3.5 million natural gas customers in the United States were within a few hundred miles of gas fields.

The U.S. natural gas industry received a much-needed boost during the early twentieth century, when major reserves were discovered in Texas, Oklahoma, and Louisiana. Between 1906 and 1920, natural gas production more than doubled to 800 billion cubic feet per year. The industry grew rapidly after long-distance transmission of gas became practical in the late 1920s following the introduction of seamless, electrically welded steel pipelines that could carry gas under great pressures and in great quantities. In 1927 the largest reserve in the United States was discovered in Kansas, and found to extend into Texas and Oklahoma, and between 1927 and 1931 more than 10 major natural gas pipeline systems were constructed in the country. By the 1930s, natural gas was transmitted from Texas fields to Midwestern cities, and numerous cities began switching from the more expensive manufactured gas to natural gas, which was increasingly used for heating as well as cooking and water heating purposes. Pipelines constructed after World War II were both longer and wider in diameter, and the rapid discovery of new reserves in the United States continued through the 1960s, while production increased at a substantial pace between the mid-1950s and the mid-1970s.

Until well into the 1950s, natural gas was not available in substantial quantities in most European nations, which continued to rely largely on manufactured gas; "associated" natural gas found during oil drilling was often seen as a nuisance and hence flared or burned away. In 1956 a major gas field was discovered in North Africa, and in later years a major engineering project resulted in the development of a pipeline running from Algeria to the Mediterranean Sea and to Sicily, crossing the sea where it is more than 610 meters deep in some places. Today Algeria is the fourth largest natural gas producing nation. The largest European gas field was discovered in 1959 on the Dutch coast. New discoveries in the 1960s led to robust expansion of the European natural gas industry, particularly in the Netherlands and the Soviet Union. During the mid-1960s Great Britain also became a major player in the industry after it discovered and began to produce sizable quantities of natural gas from reserves beneath the North Sea. In 1971 the largest gas field in Asia was discovered in the North Sumatra basin of Indonesia.

The largest known gas field in the world, Urengoy, was discovered in the Soviet Union in 1966 in the West Siberian region of the Arctic Circle; subsequent discoveries of major fields in the Arctic Circle region followed. Urengoy began production in 1978, and since the 1970s, the longest gas transmission lines have been constructed in the Soviet Union. These pipelines include the Northern Lights system linking Eastern Europe with Siberian gas fields on the Arctic Circle and crossing 700 rivers and the Ural Mountains. In 1983 the Soviet Union surpassed the United States in gas production and became the world's leading producer of natural gas.

In the United States during the late 1960s and early 1970s, the rate of consumption exceeded the rate of reserve discovery. During this same period crude oil shortages helped push natural gas as a significant source of world energy, although natural gas fell out of favor during the late 1970s for fear of low reserves. Since the 1980s, natural gas has enjoyed popularity because of its advantages: natural gas is a relatively clean burning fuel that is free of the soot, carbon monoxide, and nitrogen oxides associated with other fossil fuels used to power electric generators. Many plants built in the 1990s were designed to be powered by natural gas. Worldwide, in the early 1990s there existed the greatest known reserves in history, and nations previously reliant upon manufactured gas were turning increasingly to the less-expensive natural gas. Producing countries were exporting greater quantities of the fuel both via pipeline and in liquid natural gas (LNG) form via tanker ship to destination plants where the liquid was again converted to gas form.

In the late 1990s, the electric and gas utilities were still largely a consortium of national utility industries, although conditions were slowly beginning to change as privatization and reform efforts swept the globe. The resultant competition between companies and across national boundaries reinvigorated what had been a stolid and entrenched collection of energy companies. Historically monopolistic, the electric and gas power industries were in a state of global transition in the last decade of the twentieth century.

In the United States, for instance, deregulation in the electric power industry began in 1998. On the other hand, while the United Kingdom had already successfully deregulated its electric power industry by the late 1990s, many other countries in Europe, including Germany, resisted EU mandates to allow competition in the industry. When faced with an EU deadline to begin allowing competition as of February 1999, Germany finally began to open its markets. By the end of the year, German electricity prices, which for years had been among the highest in Europe, had fallen by roughly 50 percent.

CURRENT CONDITIONS

Electricity. According to 2004 IEA data, global electricity supply in 2002 was more than 16.1 trillion kilowatt hours. The largest electricity producing country in the world was the United States, which produced almost a quarter of world production. However, its consumption demands required the country to import additional supply. China followed in terms of production, with 10.2 percent of world production. Japan was third, with 6.8 percent of the total. France remained the country exporting the most electricity, while Italy and Germany remained the largest importers.

Of the worldwide supply totals, coal was used to generate the most electricity at 39 percent of the total. This was followed by natural gas with 19.1 percent, nuclear with 16.6 percent, hydro with 16.1 percent, oil with 7.2 percent and other sources with 1.9 percent, which included geothermal, wind, combustible renewables and waste.

U.S., German, British and Japanese electric utilities dominated the top rankings, with the European-based companies showing the strongest signs of globalization. Total consumption of electricity worldwide was projected to reach 16.4 trillion kilowatt hours by 2010, 18.5 by 2015, 20.7 by 2020, and 23.1 by 2025. Total consumption of energy generation fuels, on the other hand, was projected to reach 193.6 quadrillion btu by 2010, 213.9 by 2015, 235.5 by 2020, and 258.6 by 2025.

The United States, France and Japan remained the world's biggest producers of nuclear electricity, producing 30.3, 16.4 and 11.1 percent of the total in 2003, respectively. However, only 20 percent of the U.S.'s total domestic electricity generation was from nuclear, while in France nuclear accounted for 78 percent, by far the highest in the world. Canada produced 13.1 percent of the world's hydro electric power, followed by China with 10.8 percent and Brazil with 10.7 percent. Almost all of Norway's electric power came from this source.

Natural Gas. According to the IEA, worldwide gross production of natural gas in 2003 was 96.02 trillion cubic feet. OECD countries accounted for 41.5 percent of worldwide production, the countries of the former USSR 28.2 percent, Asia 10.3 percent, the Middle East 9.4 percent, Africa 5.5 percent, Latin America 4.4 percent, and all other non-OECD European countries 0.7 percent. Compared with 1976 levels, all non-OECD regions showed marked increases in their share of the natural gas produced with the greatest increase in share size seen taken by the countries of the former USSR. Although in 2003 the world's second largest producer of natural gas was the United States (behind Russia), it remained a net importer of gas. Russia, Canada and Norway were the largest exporters of natural gas. Total worldwide production of natural gas was projected by the Energy Information Administration to reach 105.5 trillion cubic feet by 2010, 118.5 by 2015, 134.5 by 2020, and 151.0 by 2025.

The leading companies in the natural gas industry are those that hold or formerly held monopolistic control over domestic distribution rights, including those in the United Kingdom, Japan, the Netherlands, France, and Germany, as well as companies from the United States and other countries that were involved in worldwide exploration for or production of natural gas. In 2004, the world had a total 6.1 quadrillion cubic feet in natural gas reserves, of which the top 20 countries controlled nearly 90 percent, more than 5.4 quadrillion cubic feet.

In an effort to deregulate the industry, California became the first U.S. state to allow customers of its three leading electric utilities to choose providers. State legislators also instituted price caps on allowable charges. This effort backfired, however, when gas and oil prices soared. Unable to pass along price increases to consumers, California utilities struggled to buy the resources they needed to fuel power generation. As a result, California's largest utility, Pacific Gas and Electric, filed for bankruptcy protection in 2001, from which it did not emerge until 2004. To make matters worse, stringent guidelines that slowed new power plant construction contributed to a power shortage and subsequent blackouts. These troubles prompted several other U.S. states to delay opening their markets, although almost half had at least started the deregulation process by that time. According to the European Union, all member countries must fully open their electric power markets by 2005. In addition, roughly 20 percent of natural gas markets in each country must be deregulated by then.

According to *International Energy Outlook 2004,* electricity consumption is expected to double by 2025. Of the fuels used for generation, oil and nuclear sources were expected to experience the highest decline, while renewable sources and natural gas were expected to see the most growth. As of 2003, however, nuclear generation was still strong, with 441 reactors worldwide and more than 30 being built. Renewable sources, such as hydropower and wind power, which had experienced the fastest growth into the mid 2000s, were projected to grow 57 percent over the next two decades. As with most energy sources, the majority of the growth in this segment will come from developing countries, such as China and India, which were planning or building renewable energy plants in 2003. Natural gas as an electricity generator was expected to double in consumption.

Natural gas consumption for all uses was projected to jump a staggering 70 percent. In 2004, reserves were approximately 6.1 quadrillion cubic feet, marking the ninth straight year that reserves had increased. In fact, according to *International Energy Outlook,* "outside the United States, the world has produced less than 10 percent of its total estimated natural gas endowment and carries more than 30 percent as remaining reserves." The growing popularity of natural gas, particularly as a source of electric power, fueled consolidation between gas and electric utilities. Beginning at the turn of the century, this trend continued into the mid-2000s. This type of industry convergence also was the result of increased competition, which prompted utilities to seek economies of scale.

RESEARCH AND TECHNOLOGY

Energy research in the 1990s focused on high-efficiency, environmentally friendly technology in the areas of pollution-free vehicles, fuel sources, and power generators. In 1998, U.S. and foreign automakers pledged to begin building cleaner cars, offering them for sale across the United States starting with the 1999 model year. Cleaner cars were scheduled to be available in late 1998 in the Northeast. This was in accordance with air quality standards adopted in 1992 that require a certain percentage of the vehicles made by 1998 to produce extremely low emissions. Work on electric vehicles also continued by all the major automakers, with Ford, General Motors, Honda, Nissan, and Toyota all offering electric vehicles or hybrid electric vehicles for sale in the 1998 model year, according to the Electric Vehicle Association of America. State-sponsored research in Japan in the late 1990s included electric-powered, compressed natural gas-powered, and methane-powered vehicles, as well as research on fuel cell-powered vehicles, which convert chemical energy from fuel directly into electricity onboard.

Japan's Agency of Natural Resources and Energy had also made substantial research investments into a wide range of power generating technologies, including fuel cells; photovoltaic generators, using solar batteries; wind generators; and geothermal power generators, a type of clean and domestically available energy produced by using heat from the earth's interior, such as that causing hot springs, geysers, and heated groundwater. By the late 1990s geothermal plants existed in Japan, the United States, Italy, New Zealand, Iceland, and Mexico, but the 1997 Asian financial crisis prompted Indonesia to postpone construction of at least eight geothermal plants.

Thanks to clean coal technologies that improved generating efficiency and reduced the amount of carbon dioxide produced by coal-fired generators, coal, historically a dominant fuel for thermal generation, was expected to maintain about a 36 percent share of the electricity generation market through 2020. With increased interest in renewable resources—including wind machines, photovoltaic systems, and geothermal technologies—the Edison Electric Institute predicted that early in the twenty-first century an increasing number of electric utilities would begin employing more economically viable methods of power generation from renewable resources.

WORKFORCE

By the early 1990s, U.S. utilities had already been through several rounds of cost reductions, and major U.S. power producers such as Pacific Gas and Electric Company and Southern Company, major Canadian utilities like Ontario Hydro, and leading British utilities like British Gas PLC were engaged in ongoing staff reductions. In 1994, for instance, British Gas PLC announced that it would cut 25,000 jobs over five years in response to tighter profit margins, increased competition, and rate regulation. Also, in late 1999 Duke Energy launched a series of layoffs designed to cut costs. In the early 2000s, industry consolidation among both gas and electric utilities continued providing opportunities to achieve economies of scale through layoffs and other cost reduction measures.

INDUSTRY LEADERS

UNITED STATES

Although traditionally regionally based, since 1999 the energy industry in the United States had witnessed a trend toward large, global energy firms consolidating the market and value chain.

Duke Energy Corporation was created in June 1997 through the merger of Duke Power Company in Charlotte, North Carolina, and PanEnergy Corp. in Houston, Texas. In 2004, Duke Energy provided electric service to 2.2 million customers in the Carolinas. The company also operated 17,500 miles of natural gas pipelines. The company operated in more than 50 countries, including those in South America, and was a major supplier to 1.2 million Canadian customers. In 2004 Duke Energy had revenues of US$22.5 billion and a total of 21,500 employees. In 2005, the company announced plans to merge with Cinergy, a Midwest company in the natural gas and electric business. The 2004 combined revenues of the companies was estimated at US$27 billion.

Exelon Corporation was the largest electricity distributor in the U.S. in terms of revenue in 2004. The company's markets including the Chicago and Philadelphia areas where it served almost 5.7 million customers. The company posted revenues of US$14.5 billion, with 17,500 employees. In 2005, the company was working with regulators to allow its merger with PSEG, a New Jersey energy company serving 2 million electric customers and 1.2 million gas customers, generating revenues of US$10 million.

The country's largest electricity generator, in 2005 American Electric Power Company Inc.(AEP) owned more than 36,000 megawatts (MW) of power and was linked to 5 million customers in 11 U.S. states. Its generating capacity is largely powered by coal. The company is also a leading marketer of natural gas, natural gas liquids, coal and oil. AEP reported US$14.1 billion in 2004 revenues and about 20,000 employees. AEP was founded in New York in 1906 as American Gas & Electric Company.

Pacific Gas and Electric Corporation emerged from bankruptcy protection in 2004, reported sales of US$11.1 billion. With 4.9 million electricity customers and 3.9 million natural gas customers, the firm served northern and cental California. Due to price caps put in place by California legislators when the industry there was deregulated, Pacific Gas and Electric was unable to offset rising energy prices by increasing its rates. As a result, the firm filed for bankruptcy protection in April 2001. In early 2002, the state of California filed suit against PG&E, alleging that the holding company was to blame for the utility's financial ruin.

GERMANY

In 2004, E.ON AG—the result of the 2000 merger of VEBA Group and VIAG Group— remained the largest investor-owned energy services provider in the world. With approximately 70,000 employees and revenues of US$66.5 billion, the company has been focusing its attentions on its electricity and gas holdings. Its E.ON Energie subsidiary supplied 14 million electricity and gas customers in Central Europe. Its acquisition of Ruhrgas in 2003 brought it Germany's market leader in natural gas distribution, and one of Europe's leaders with a 7,000 mile pipeline system throughout Europe. E.ON UK (formerly PowerGen) is the second largest energy supplier in the United Kingdom. E.ON also owns utility operations in Kentucky, as well as having stakes in plants in Texas and Argentina.

RWE AG is another truly global energy company. In addition to electric and gas service, the company is also involved with water and environmental services.

By 2005, the company had more than 120 million customers across Europe and North America, employed almost 98,000 people and reported 2004 year-end revenues of almost US$56 billion.

JAPAN

The Tokyo Electric Power Company (TEPCO)—one of the world's largest energy companies—posted revenues of almost US$46 billion and employed more than 51,000 workers in 2004. The Tokyo-based company had 27.53 million customers, about 34 percent of the country's market, and its total generating capacity exceeded 62,600MW. Nuclear power accounted for 28 percent of total capacity, while thermal sources accounted for almost 59 percent. As Japan has deregulated its electricity industry, TEPCO has faced increasing competition. As a result, the firm has diversified into other industries, such as local and long distance telephone services.

TEPCO traces its roots to the first Japanese electricity utility, Tokyo Electric Lighting Company, which was founded in the 1880s. However, TEPCO wasn't incorporated until 1951, the year the Japanese electric power industry was reprivatized after being held under government monopoly control during World War II. After its incorporation, TEPCO relied largely on hydroelectric generation of power well into the 1960s. Pilot nuclear power plants went on-line in 1966, and after pollution reached critical stages in the late 1960s, the company discontinued coal-fired generators for a period. TEPCO began shifting away from oil-fired generation during the 1970s, and increasingly began to rely on nuclear generation. By 1991 nuclear power accounted for 28 percent of TEPCO's total generation of power.

In 1991 TEPCO was the world's largest user of liquefied natural gas (LNG) and liquefied petroleum gas (LPG) and was buying from suppliers throughout the world. The company was heavily involved in research and development and its technology had allowed TEPCO to achieve the world's lowest levels of sulfur dioxide and carbon dioxide emissions. The company also developed and displayed a prototype electric car in the early 1990s. Because of its wide-ranging activities, the company has increasingly referred to itself as the TEPCO Group. In the late 1980s it became involved in an optical digital fiber network that led to the creation of a TEPCO cable television system in 1989.

In mid-1998 TEPCO became the first Japanese participant in a World Bank prototype carbon fund designed to reduce the amount of greenhouse gases. It was essentially an emissions trading scheme, similar to the one offered to relatively "dirty" U.S. power plants as part of the Clean Air Act Amendments of 1990. Essentially, the World Bank planned to finance costs associated with various types of greenhouse gas reduction strategies from the fund. The amount of greenhouse gases reduced by the projects earned the company "carbon offsets," or credits, that could be used by the utility to offset emissions by their dirtier plants. The utility also could opt to sell these offsets to other companies who needed them to meet regulatory emissions requirements.

UNITED KINGDOM

BG Group, with 2.7 million customers, had 2004 sales of US$7.8 billion and net income of US$1.7 billion. Until February 1997, British Gas PLC was the largest integrated gas supply operation in the world and was among the United Kingdom's 20 largest companies. However, in 1997 the company's shareholders approved the spin-off of British Gas into two companies: BG Group PLC, which concentrated on gas transportation, exploration, and production; and Centrica, which was the local distribution company. The impetus for the split had begun in 1996, with the de-monopolization and separation of transportation and usage operations from the other gas industry businesses in preparation for competitive markets.

Centrica markets gas, electricity and telecommunications services in England, Wales, and Scotland using several brand names: British Gas, Nwy Prydain and Scottish Gas respectively. Its subsidiary, Centrica Energy, handles upstream gas production, electricity generation, and wholesale gas sales. With the European market expected to be open to competition by 2007, Centrica had already established a joint venture energy supply company in Belgium and begun operating Luseo Energia in Spain in 2003 focusing on the small- to medium-sized business market for electricity. In North America, Centrica offers natural gas and electricity services to the de-regulated Canadian market under its Direct Energy brand, while in the United States, its subsidiary, Energy America, supplies these same services to customers in Ohio, Michigan and Pennsylvania. In 2004, Centrica posted revenues of almost US$32 billion, and employed more than 42,000 people.

British Gas PLC was incorporated in 1986 with the privatization of the state-owned British Gas Corporation, which reversed a 1949 action that had nationalized utilities. In the years preceding 1949, most European gas had been manufactured from coal, but during the 1950s and 1960s coal became too costly and processes were created to convert cheaper oil feedstocks to a coal-gas equivalent. In the 1960s, natural gas arrived in substantial quantity in the United Kingdom for the first time. In 1964 the country entered into a 15-year contract to buy gas from Algeria and began receiving liquefied natural gas (LNG) by tanker. In 1966 natural gas was discovered under the North Sea, leading to an enormous conversion program to transform the country's system and appliances from manufactured to natural gas.

After British Gas was privatized in 1986, the company was no longer restricted geographically to the United Kingdom and its offshore waters, and by 1989 the company had made significant investments in foreign oil and gas assets worldwide. By 1990 British Gas had acquired interests in exploration and production companies, including Acre Oil and part of Texas Eastern North Sea; Tenneco international subsidiaries with exploration and production operations in the North Sea, Africa, and Latin America; a 51 percent interest in Canada's Bow Valley Industries; Consumer's Gas Co., Canada's largest natural gas distributor and an experienced developer of natural gas vehicles; and a small stake in a Spanish utility. By then, the company had spent US$2 billion on acquisitions and held nearly 7 trillion cubic feet of natural gas reserves in 18 countries. In 1992 British Gas entered the South American market and formed a consortium to buy Argentina's gas distribution company MetroGas.

Scottish Power provided electricity and gas service to more than 6 million customers in the United Kingdom and the United States, earning the company revenues of US$10.7 billion in 2004. In the U.S., PacifiCorp had capacity of more than 8,300 megawatts generated from coal, hydro, wind, gas-fired combustion turbines and geothermal. The company was operating its regulated business in Oregon, Washington, Wyoming, California, Utah and Idaho. The company operates wind and thermal energy facilities, and provides natural gas marketing and storage in the U.S. through its PPM Energy subsidiary.

CANADA

Hydro-Quebec, Ontario Power Generation, and Hydro One are government-owned companies run as businesses. Hydro-Quebec and its subsidiaries utilize a mix of about two-thirds hydroelectric plants and one-third generation plants. Ontario Power, in contrast, generates most of its electricity from nuclear and fossil fuel-based power plants, while Hydro One distributes power throughout Ontario. Hydro One and Ontario Power Generation were created when Ontario Hydro split itself into two separate entities in 2000. This move came in response to the Ontario government's legislation, the Energy Competition Act, calling for creation of a competitive electricity market by 2000. Hydro-Quebec had 2004 sales of more than US$8.8 billion, with 3.6 million customers, while Hydro One, with 1.2 million customers, posted roughly US$3.1 billion in sales. Revenues at Ontario Power Generation grew 9.8 percent in 2003 to reach US$4.0 billion.

Both Hydro-Quebec and Ontario Hydro trace their roots to the late nineteenth century when Canadian water was first harnessed in order to mass-produce power. Specifically, Ontario Hydro's lineage stems from the first major generating station in Ontario, which was built to use the power of Niagara Falls. In 1914 Ontario Hydro purchased its first generating station and built its first power plant, and by 1922 Ontario Hydro was the largest utility in the world after completing its first major power station, Queenston-Chippawa (renamed Sir Adam Beck-Niagara Generation Station No. 1), which was then the largest generator in the world. During the 1950s the company turned to the St. Lawrence River and harnessed its power in a joint project with the state of New York. Ontario Hydro constructed an experimental nuclear plant in 1962 and completed its first major nuclear power plant in 1971. By that time the company had enough excess generating capacity to supply electricity to the northeastern United States. Ontario Hydro was incorporated as a government corporation in 1974, and since then has faced growing concerns regarding fossil fuel shortages and environmental damage caused by its operations. Faced with a surplus of power, Ontario Hydro lost US$2.8 billion in 1993. In 1994 the company announced it would cut its generating capacity by 8.4 percent and retire one unit at its Bruce nuclear plant by 1995, two years ahead of an earlier schedule.

Hydro-Quebec's beginnings are related to the construction of Quebec's first large dam and the formation of Montreal Light, Heat and Power Company (MLHPC) in 1901. In 1944, the Quebec Hydro-Electric Commission was created and took over the assets of MLHPC, and the ensuing demand for power was fueled largely by the defense industry. During the 1950s the company used its first bond offering to U.S. markets to finance its Bersimis River project. During the 1960s, Hydro-Quebec acquired numerous private electricity distribution companies, including rural cooperatives, municipal systems, and nongovernment companies. During the 1970s, 1980s, and 1990s Hydro-Quebec's power projects ran into increasing opposition from Native American and environmentalist groups. Of major concern was the James Bay project, which began in 1971 and was completed in 1985, after a system of 41 dams and dykes was constructed. In 1987 Hydro-Quebec began James Bay II, or its Great Whale project, which was designed to place a hydroelectric plant on the Great Whale River and sparked international environmentalist opposition.

In December 1992 Maurice F. Strong, who served as secretary general of the United Nations' 1992 Earth Summit, became chairman of Ontario Hydro, which by that time had been labeled by environmentalists as one of Canada's leading polluters. In the mid-1990s, with increasing numbers of North American utilities cutting costs by promoting conservation and buying electricity from independent power producers—and Hydro Quebec's earnings falling as a result of excess generating capacity, declining sales, and a sizable debt—Ontario Hydro cancelled its plans to expand its generating capacity by more than 40 percent in 25 years. In 1994 Hydro-Quebec announced plans to cut back development of hydroelectric plants in lieu of reduced agreements to sell power to U.S. utilities. Additionally, the company pushed back its completion date for the Great Whale project from 2001-2002 to 2002-2004.

Russia. Unified Energy System of Russia (UES) is a publicly traded company, although 53 percent of it was still owned by the government in 2004. By 2005, UES was operating 440 electric power stations with a capacity of more than 197,000 MW, including 21,000 MW at nuclear power plants. Deregulation of the industry was expected to come into full effect in 2006, at which time the company's distribution and power generation assets were to be separated off.

France. The SUEZ Group, with almost 87,000 employees in 2004, was one of the largest employers in the world's energy and services industry. With total company-wide revenues of US$55 billion in 2004, the company was the tenth-largest electricity producer in the world. It was also the sixth-largest gas producer, handling 20 percent of the Atlantic's liquefied natural gas market. Operating in more than 130 countries, SUEZ also provided water and waste management services.

MAJOR COUNTRIES IN THE INDUSTRY

The United States. The largest producing country in the world, as well as the world's largest consumer, the United States consumes more electricity than it produces. The market's size had grown to 3.4 trillion kilowatt hours by 2003, with Euromonitor predicting growth of 7.3 percent by 2008. Consumption varies across the country depending on climate, regulations, and industrial development, but residential use did dominate total market share and was expected to continue to do so. The country' largest electricity distributor in 2004 was Exelon Corporation in the Chicago and Philadelphia areas.

The production of electricity through nuclear, fossil fuel, hydro or other alternate sources remained a highly fragmented component of the energy industry in the U.S. in 2003. Most of the country's renewal electrical energy is produced in the southern and western parts of the nation, where climatic conditions favor such industry.

While residential consumers dominate the electrical market in the United States, industrial users are the largest users of natural gas accounting for 38.1 percent of the total 2003 market volume of 8.1 trillion cubic feet. Demand had grown slowly over 2002 levels as a result of increasing prices. Although by 2003, the top five U.S. gas utility companies still only accounted for 21.4 percent of the total market, there had been a trend since 1999 away from regional utilities, with larger, global companies which managed the gas process along its entire route from source to end user coming on the scene. This trend was reported by Euromonitor to be the answer to managing the risks associated with the energy market. In 2003, Texas and California were the biggest consumers of natural gas, accounting for 280 billion cubic feet (bcf) and 200 bcf respectively. The country' market was expected to grow to a volume of 22.8 trillion cubic feet by 2008.

Russia. In the early 1990s, the United States lost its distinction as the leading natural gas producer to Russia. In 2005, it held the world's largest natural gas reserves, was the leading exporter of gas, and had the third-largest domestic gas market. In 2004 Russia's production was 222.4 trillion cubic feet, with reserves of 1,680 trillion cubic feet. However, growth in the industry has remained modest since the country's independence. This has been attributed to aging gas fields, a lack of pipelines to use for export, and government regulations. The country's energy strategy, released in 2003, predicted only 1.3 percent growth by 2010.

By 2005, Russia had more than 440 thermal and hydroelectric power plants and 31 nuclear reactors, in all capable of generating 205.6 gigawatts of power. Thermal power—oil, natural gas, and coal—were being used to generate approximately 63 percent of Russia's electrical supply. However, the government was stating that it would increase hydro and nuclear production so that its fossil fuels could be redirected to export. More than half of the country's nuclear reactors were of the same design as the one used in the Chernobyl plant in the Ukraine in 1986, home of the world's worst nuclear accident. With the working life of a reactor given to be 30 years, almost half of Russia's reactors were between 21 and 30 years old by 2005.

Japan. While slightly smaller geographically than the state of California, in 2004 Japan was the world's fourth-largest energy market and second-largest importer, after the U.S. The country imported about 97 percent of its natural gas needs, all in liquid natural gas form. Japan's urban areas were not well served by natural gas distribution lines, a reason often given for the country's high energy costs, the highest in the OECD. Three companies dominated the market: Tokyo Gas, Chubu Gas and Osaka Gas. In terms of electricity, in 2002 Japan generated 1.04 trillion kilowatt hours of which 62 percent was produced from thermal means, 28 percent from nuclear, and 8 percent from hydro. Japan was aiming to increase the amount of electricity produced using nuclear power by 30 percent by 2011.

China. In 2004, China remained the second largest user of energy in the world after the U.S. and the world's second largest producer of hydro electricity with 1.1 trillion kilowatt hours, or 10.8 percent of world production, in 2003. Oversupply of electricity caused by the government's closing of inefficient plants led to a slowdown in new electric generation construction until 2003. That year, the economy grew suddenly, and with this growth came increased electrical demand. As a result, the government approved the construction of 30 large electric power plants which would add an additional 22 gigawatts of power to the system. In the late 1990s China broke ground on what could well become the largest hydroelectric station in the world—the Three Gorges Dam project—projected to have a total capacity of 18.2 gigawatts upon completion in 2009. Although work on the dam continued, embezzlement charges related to the multi-billion financing of the project led to court cases and prison sentences for nearly 100 individuals in 2000. Another large project involving the construction of 25 generating stations on the Yellow River was also in the works.

China has not historically been a major user of natural gas; in 2004 it only accounted for 3 percent of the energy used in the country. However, given that is own reserves stood at 53.3 trillion cubic feet, the government was attempting to expand its use, with the hopes of doubling its usage by 2010.

Canada. By 2005, Canada remained one of the United States' most important sources for energy imports. In 2002, the country was the third-largest producer of natural gas behind Russia and the United States. Canada's natural gas pipeline network is very tied into the U.S., and almost all of its exports went there. In terms of electricity, Canada produces the majority of it through hydro generation (it was the world's largest hydro electric producer in 2005. It maintains an integrated trading network with the United States, importing about as much as it exports. The countries's electrical power grids are so intertwined, that in 2003, North America's largest blackout plunged more than 50 million people into darkness, affecting most of Ontario, Ohio, New York and Chicago.

Germany. In 2002, Germany was ranked as the fifth-largest consumer of energy in the world, and the largest consumer of electricity in Europe. With few resources other than coal, the country must import most of its energy needs. However, coal was used to generate more than 50 percent of the country's electricity, with nuclear power accounting for a further 28 percent. The government has been attempting to increase the amount of energy used that is generated from renewable sources. By 2050, the country expects to have half of its demand met by these sources. Germany's electric and natural gas industries have been deregulated, and although open to competition, still remain highly concentrated. In 2003, although there were 900 energy companies operating in Germany's electric market, four companies controlled 73 percent of the electric distribution business in the country: RWE Power, EnBW, E.On, and Vattenfall. Euromonitor expected growth to remain slow to 2008 due to a downturn in the economy, with most electrical consumption being done by industry. In the natural gas industry in Germany, the country continued to import most of its resources from Russia. Ruhrgas, a subsidiary of energy giant E.On, controlled 43 percent of Europe's second-largest gas market in 2003.

Algeria. In 2002 Algeria, the second largest country in Africa, was the fifth leading producer of natural gas in the world, with 2.8 trillion cubic feet. A major gas exporter, most natural gas is sent to Europe and the United States. Two government-owned companies dominate the industry: Sonatrach is responsible for production and wholesale distribution, while Sonelgaz controls distribution to retail markets. The government was planning to open up the retail market to foreign investors, but price liberalizations aimed to occur in 2005 were met by mass protests following a record cold spell in Algeria. Most of the country's electrical production remained gas fired.

The Netherlands. In 1998 the Netherlands produced 2.8 trillion cubic feet of natural gas. Reserves in 2001 were 63 trillion cubic feet, about 1.2 percent of the world total. The public/private company Nederlandse Gasunie (50 percent state-owned) served the 97 percent of Dutch homes heated by natural gas. Esso and Shell each controlled 25 percent of the company, which purchased, transported, and marketed the country's natural gas. The company is significant because natural gas is responsible for meeting half of the country's total energy needs, the highest percentage of natural gas use for any country in the world.

FURTHER READING

"About Us," *American Electric Power Website,* 2004. Available from http://www.aep.com.

"Can Deregulated Energy Markets Provide a Diverse and Secure Energy Supply?" Ernst & Young, January 2005. Available from www.ey.com.

"The Changing Structure of the Electric Power Industry 2000: An Update." *International Energy Outlook 2000.* Energy Information Administration, U.S. Department of Energy, Washington, D.C. Available from http://www.eia.doe.gov.

Chase, Milton A. *Electric Power: An Industry at a Crossroads.* New York: Praeger, 1988.

"Country Analysis Briefs." Energy Information Administration, 2005. Available from http://www.eia.doe.gov.

Energy Information Administration. "International Energy Outlook 2004," April 2004. Available from http://www.eia.doe.gov.

"Energy Statistics from the EIA." Energy Information Administration, Washington, D.C., 2001. Available from http://www.eia.doe.gov.

"Hoover's Company Capsules." 2004. Available from http://www.hoovers.com.

International Energy Agency. "Key World Energy Statistics." 2004. Available from http://www.iea.org.

Lazich, Robert S., ed. *Market Share Reporter.* Detroit: Thomson Gale, 2004.

"Natural Gas." *International Energy Outlook 2001.* Energy Information Administration, Washington, D.C. Available from http://www.eia.doe.gov.

Palmeri, Christopher. "Industry Outlook 2001—Energy." *Business Week,* 2 January 2001.

Roberts, Dexter and Mark L. Clifford. "China: Hungry for Energy." *Business Week,* 24 December 2001.

Schwankhaus, Dieter. "Success of Wind Power: A Question of State and Federal Subsidies?" Ernst & Young, 2004. Available from http://www.ey.com.

NAICS CONVERSION TABLE

The following listing cross-references six-digit 2002 North American Industry Classification System (NAICS) codes with four-digit 1987 Standard Industrial Classification (SIC) codes. Because the systems differ in specificity, some NAICS categories correspond to more than one SIC category.

AGRICULTURE, FORESTRY, FISHING, & HUNTING

111110 Soybean Farming *(SIC 0116)*
111120 Oilseed (except Soybean) Farming *(SIC 0119)*
111130 Dry Pea and Bean Farming *(SIC 0119)*
111140 Wheat Farming *(SIC 0111)*
111150 Corn Farming *(SIC 0115)*; *(SIC 0119)*
111160 Rice Farming *(SIC 0112)*
111191 Oilseed and Grain Combination Farming *(SIC 0119)*
111199 All Other Grain Farming *(SIC 0119)*
111211 Potato Farming *(SIC 0134)*
111219 Other Vegetable (except Potato) and Melon Farming *(SIC 0139)*; *(SIC 0161)*
111310 Orange Groves *(SIC 0174)*
111320 Citrus (except Orange) Groves *(SIC 0174)*
111331 Apple Orchards *(SIC 0175)*
111332 Grape Vineyards *(SIC 0172)*
111333 Strawberry Farming *(SIC 0171)*
111334 Berry (except Strawberry) Farming *(SIC 0171)*
111335 Tree Nut Farming *(SIC 0173)*
111336 Fruit and Tree Nut Combination Farming *(SIC 0179)*
111339 Other Noncitrus Fruit Farming *(SIC 0175)*; *(SIC 0179)*
111411 Mushroom Production *(SIC 0182)*
111419 Other Food Crops Grown Under Cover *(SIC 0182)*
111421 Nursery and Tree Production *(SIC 0181)*; *(SIC 0811)*
111422 Floriculture Production *(SIC 0181)*
111910 Tobacco Farming *(SIC 0132)*
111920 Cotton farming *(SIC 0131)*
111930 Sugarcane Farming *(SIC 0133)*
111940 Hay Farming *(SIC 0139)*
111991 Sugar Beet Farming *(SIC 0133)*
111992 Peanut Farming *(SIC 0139)*
111998 All Other Miscellaneous Crop Farming *(SIC 0139)*; *(SIC 0191)*; *(SIC 0831)*; *(SIC 0919)*; *(SIC 2099)*
112111 Beef Cattle Ranching and Farming *(SIC 0212)*; *(SIC 0241)*
112112 Cattle Feedlots *(SIC 0211)*
112120 Dairy Cattle and Milk Production *(SIC 0241)*
112210 Hog and Pig Farming *(SIC 0213)*
112310 Chicken Egg Production *(SIC 0252)*
112320 Broilers and Other Meat-Type Chicken Production *(SIC 0251)*
112330 Turkey Production *(SIC 0253)*
112340 Poultry Hatcheries *(SIC 0254)*
112390 Other Poultry Production *(SIC 0259)*
112410 Sheep Farming *(SIC 0214)*
112420 Goat Farming *(SIC 0214)*
112511 Finfish Farming and Fish Hatcheries *(SIC 0273)*; *(SIC 0921)*
112512 Shellfish Farming *(SIC 0273)*; *(SIC 0921)*
112519 Other Animal Aquaculture *(SIC 0273)*
112910 Apiculture *(SIC 0279)*
112920 Horse and Other Equine Production *(SIC 0272)*
112930 Fur-bearing Animal and Rabbit Production *(SIC 0271)*
112990 All Other Animal Production *(SIC 0291)*; *(SIC 0219)*; *(SIC 0279)*
113110 Timber Tract Operations *(SIC 0811)*
113210 Forest Nurseries and Gathering of Forest Products *(SIC 0831)*
113310 Logging *(SIC 2411)*
114111 Finfish Fishing *(SIC 0912)*
114112 Shellfish Fishing *(SIC 0913)*
114119 Other Marine Fishing *(SIC 0919)*
114210 Hunting and Trapping *(SIC 0971)*
115111 Cotton Ginning *(SIC 0724)*
115112 Soil Preparation, Planting and Cultivating *(SIC 0711)*; *(SIC 0721)*
115113 Crop Harvesting, Primarily By Machine *(SIC 0722)*
115114 Postharvest Crop Activities (except Cotton Ginning) *(SIC 0723)*
115115 Farm Labor Contractors and Crew Leaders *(SIC 0761)*
115116 Farm Management Services *(SIC 0762)*
115210 Support Activities for Animal Production *(SIC 0751)*; *(SIC 0752)*; *(SIC 7699)*
115310 Support Activities for Forestry *(SIC 0851)*

MINING

211111 Crude Petroleum and Natural Gas Extraction *(SIC 1311)*
211112 Natural Gas Liquid Extraction *(SIC 1321)*
212111 Bituminous Coal and Lignite Surface Mining *(SIC 1221)*
212112 Bituminous Coal Underground Mining *(SIC 1222)*
212113 Anthracite Mining *(SIC 1231)*
212210 Iron Ore Mining *(SIC 1011)*
212221 Gold Ore Mining *(SIC 1041)*
212222 Silver Ore Mining *(SIC 1044)*
212231 Lead Ore and Zinc Ore Mining *(SIC 1031)*
212234 Copper Ore and Nickel Ore Mining *(SIC 1021)*; *(SIC 1061)*
212291 Uranium-Radium-Vanadium Ore Mining *(SIC 1094)*
212299 Other Metal Ore Mining *(SIC 1099)*; *(SIC 1061)*
212311 Dimension Stone Mining and Quarry *(SIC 1411)*
212312 Crushed and Broken Limestone Mining and Quarrying *(SIC 1422)*
212313 Crushed and Broken Granite Mining and Quarrying *(SIC 1423)*
212319 Other Crushed and Broken Stone Mining and Quarrying *(SIC 1429)*; *(SIC 1499)*

212321 Construction Sand and Gravel Mining *(SIC 1442)*
212322 Industrial Sand Mining *(SIC 1446)*
212324 Kaolin and Ball Clay Mining *(SIC 1455)*
212325 Clay and Ceramic and Refractory Minerals Mining *(SIC 1459)*
212391 Potash, Soda, and Borate Mineral Mining *(SIC 1474)*
212392 Phosphate Rock Mining *(SIC 1475)*
212393 Other Chemical and Fertilizer Mineral Mining *(SIC 1479)*
212399 All Other Non-Metallic Mineral Mining *(SIC 1499)*
213111 Drilling Oil and Gas Wells *(SIC 1381)*
213112 Support Activities for Oil and Gas Field Exploration *(SIC 1382)*; *(SIC 1389)*
213113 Support Activities for Coal Mining *(SIC 1241)*
213114 Support Activities for Metal Mining *(SIC 1081)*
213115 Support Activities for Non-metallic Minerals, (except Fuels) *(SIC 1481)*

Utilities

221111 Hydroelectric Power Generation *(SIC 4931)*; *(SIC 4939)*; *(SIC 4911)*
221112 Fossil Fuel Electric Power Generation *(SIC 4931)*; *(SIC 4939)*; *(SIC 4911)*
221113 Nuclear Electric Power Generation *(SIC 4939)*; *(SIC 4911)*; *(SIC 4931)*
221119 Other Electric Power Generation *(SIC 4939)*; *(SIC 4931)*; *(SIC 4911)*
221121 Electric Bulk Power Transmission and Control *(SIC 4911)*; *(SIC 4931)*; *(SIC 4939)*
221122 Electric Power Distribution *(SIC 4911)*; *(SIC 4931)*; *(SIC 4939)*
221210 Natural Gas Distribution *(SIC 4939)*; *(SIC 4923)*; *(SIC 4924)*; *(SIC 4925)*; *(SIC 4931)*; *(SIC 4932)*
221310 Water Supply and Irrigation Systems *(SIC 4941)*; *(SIC 4971)*
221320 Sewage Treatment Facilities *(SIC 4952)*
221330 Steam and Air-Conditioning Supply *(SIC 4961)*

Construction

236115 New Single-Family Housing Construction (except Operative Builders) *(SIC 8741)*; *(SIC 1521)*
236116 New Multi-Family Housing Construction (except Operative Builders) *(SIC 8741)*; *(SIC 1522)*
236117 New Housing Operative Builders *(SIC 1531)*
236118 Residential Remodelers *(SIC 1521)*; *(SIC 1522)*; *(SIC 1531)*; *(SIC 8741)*
236210 Industrial Building Construction *(SIC 8741)*; *(SIC 1629)*; *(SIC 1541)*; *(SIC 1531)*
236220 Commercial and Institutional Building Consstruction *(SIC 1531)*; *(SIC 1541)*; *(SIC 1542)*; *(SIC 1799)*; *(SIC 8741)*; *(SIC 1522)*
237110 Water and Sewer Line and Related Structures Construction *(SIC 1623)*; *(SIC 1629)*; *(SIC 1781)*; *(SIC 8741)*
237120 Oil and Gas Pipeline and Related Structures Construction *(SIC 1629)*; *(SIC 8741)*; *(SIC 1623)*; *(SIC 1389)*
237130 Power and Communication Line and Related Structures Construction *(SIC 1629)*; *(SIC 8741)*; *(SIC 1623)*
237210 Land Subdivision *(SIC 6552)*
237310 Highway, Strret, and Bridge Construction *(SIC 1622)*; *(SIC 1721)*; *(SIC 1611)*; *(SIC 8741)*
237990 Other Heavy and Civil Engineering Construction *(SIC 1622)*; *(SIC 1629)*; *(SIC 1799)*; *(SIC 8741)*
238110 Poured Concrete Foundation and Structure Contractors *(SIC 1771)*
238120 Structural Steel and Precast Concrete Contractors *(SIC 1791)*
238130 Framing Contractors *(SIC 1751)*
238140 Masonry Contractors *(SIC 1741)*; *(SIC 1771)*
238150 Glass and Glazing Contractors *(SIC 1793)*; *(SIC 1799)*
238160 Roofing Contractors *(SIC 1761)*
238170 Siding Contractors *(SIC 1761)*
238190 Other Foundation, Structure, and building Exterior Contractors *(SIC 1791)*; *(SIC 1799)*
238210 Electrical Contractors *(SIC 1711)*; *(SIC 1731)*
238220 Plumbing, Heating, and Air-Conditioning Contractors *(SIC 1711)*; *(SIC 1791)*; *(SIC 1796)*; *(SIC 7699)*
238290 Other Building Equipment Contractors *(SIC 1796)*; *(SIC 7622)*; *(SIC 1799)*
238310 Drywall and Insulation Contractors *(SIC 1742)*; *(SIC 1743)*
238320 Paint and Wall Covering Contractors *(SIC 1721)*; *(SIC 1799)*
238330 Flooring Contractors *(SIC 1752)*
238340 Tile and Terrazzo Contractors *(SIC 1743)*
238350 Finish Carpentry Contractors *(SIC 1751)*
238390 Other Building Finishing Contractors *(SIC 1799)*; *(SIC 1761)*
238910 Other Specialty Trade Contractors *(SIC 1481)*; *(SIC 1799)*; *(SIC 1795)*; *(SIC 1794)*; *(SIC 7353)*; *(SIC 1389)*; *(SIC 1241)*; *(SIC 1081)*; *(SIC 1711)*; *(SIC 1629)*
238990 All Other Specialty Trade Contractors *(SIC 1771)*; *(SIC 1799)*

Food Manufacturing

311111 Dog and Cat Food Manufacturing *(SIC 2047)*
311119 Other Animal Food Manufacturing *(SIC 2048)*
311211 Flour Milling *(SIC 2034)*; *(SIC 2041)*
311212 Rice Milling *(SIC 2044)*
311213 Malt Manufacturing *(SIC 2083)*
311221 Wet Corn Milling *(SIC 2046)*
311222 Soybean Processing *(SIC 2075)*; *(SIC 2079)*
311223 Other Oilseed Processing *(SIC 2074)*; *(SIC 2076)*; *(SIC 2079)*
311225 Fats and Oils Refining and Blending *(SIC 2074)*; *(SIC 2075)*; *(SIC 2076)*; *(SIC 2077)*; *(SIC 2079)*
311230 Breakfast Cereal Manufacturing *(SIC 2043)*
311311 Sugarcane Mills *(SIC 2061)*
311312 Cane Sugar Refining *(SIC 2062)*
311313 Beet Sugar Manufacturing *(SIC 2063)*
311320 Chocolate and Confectionery Manufacturing from Cacao Beans *(SIC 2066)*
311330 Confectionery Manufacturing from Purchased Chocolate *(SIC 2064)*
311340 Non-Chocolate Confectionery Manufacturing *(SIC 2064)*; *(SIC 2067)*; *(SIC 2099)*
311411 Frozen Fruit, Juice, and Vegetable Processing *(SIC 2037)*
311412 Frozen Specialty Food Manufacturing *(SIC 2038)*
311421 Fruit and Vegetable Canning *(SIC 2033)*; *(SIC 2035)*
311422 Specialty Canning *(SIC 2032)*
311423 Dried and Dehydrated Food Manufacturing *(SIC 2034)*; *(SIC 2099)*
311511 Fluid Milk Manufacturing *(SIC 2026)*
311512 Creamery Butter Manufacturing *(SIC 2021)*
311513 Cheese Manufacturing *(SIC 2022)*
311514 Dry, Condensed, and Evaporated Dairy Product Manufacturing *(SIC 2023)*
311520 Ice Cream and Frozen Dessert Manufacturing *(SIC 2024)*
311611 Animal (except Poultry) Slaughtering *(SIC 0751)*; *(SIC 2011)*; *(SIC 2048)*

311612 Meat Processed From Carcasses *(SIC 2013)*; *(SIC 5147)*
311613 Rendering and Meat By-product Processing *(SIC 2077)*
311615 Poultry Processing *(SIC 2015)*
311711 Seafood Canning *(SIC 2077)*; *(SIC 2091)*
311712 Fresh and Frozen Seafood Processing *(SIC 2077)*; *(SIC 2092)*
311811 Retail Bakeries *(SIC 5461)*
311812 Commercial Bakeries *(SIC 2051)*; *(SIC 2052)*
311813 Frozen Bakery Product Manufacturing *(SIC 2053)*
311821 Cookie and Cracker Manufacturing *(SIC 2052)*
311822 Flour Mixes and Dough Manufacturing from Purchased Flour *(SIC 2045)*
311823 Pasta Manufacturing *(SIC 2098)*
311830 Tortilla Manufacturing *(SIC 2099)*
311911 Roasted Nuts and Peanut Butter Manufacturing *(SIC 2068)*; *(SIC 2099)*
311919 Other Snack Food Manufacturing *(SIC 2096)*; *(SIC 2052)*
311920 Coffee and Tea Manufacturing *(SIC 2099)*; *(SIC 2043)*; *(SIC 2095)*
311930 Flavoring Syrup and Concentrate Manufacturing *(SIC 2087)*
311941 Mayonnaise, Dressing, and Other Prepared Sauce Manufacturing *(SIC 2035)*; *(SIC 2099)*
311942 Spice and Extract Manufacturing *(SIC 2095)*; *(SIC 2099)*; *(SIC 2899)*; *(SIC 2087)*
311991 Perishable Prepared Food Manufacturing *(SIC 2099)*
311999 All Other Miscellaneous Food Manufacturing *(SIC 2015)*; *(SIC 2032)*; *(SIC 2087)*; *(SIC 2099)*

Beverage & Tobacco Product Manufacturing

312111 Soft Drink Manufacturing *(SIC 2086)*
312112 Bottled Water Manufacturing *(SIC 2086)*
312113 Ice Manufacturing *(SIC 2097)*
312120 Breweries *(SIC 2082)*
312130 Wineries *(SIC 2084)*
312140 Distilleries *(SIC 2085)*
312210 Tobacco Stemming and Redrying *(SIC 2141)*
312221 Cigarette Manufacturing *(SIC 2111)*
312229 Other Tobacco Product Manufacturing *(SIC 2141)*; *(SIC 2121)*; *(SIC 2131)*

Textile Mills

313111 Yarn Spinning Mills *(SIC 2281)*; *(SIC 2299)*
313112 Yarn Texturing, Throwing and Twisting Mills *(SIC 2282)*
313113 Thread Mills *(SIC 2284)*; *(SIC 2299)*
313210 Broadwoven Fabric Mills *(SIC 2211)*; *(SIC 2221)*; *(SIC 2231)*; *(SIC 2299)*
313221 Narrow Fabric Mills *(SIC 2241)*; *(SIC 2299)*
313222 Schiffli Machine Embroidery *(SIC 2397)*
313230 Nonwoven Fabric Mills *(SIC 2297)*; *(SIC 2299)*
313241 Weft Knit Fabric Mills *(SIC 2257)*; *(SIC 2259)*
313249 Other Knit Fabric and Lace Mills *(SIC 2258)*; *(SIC 2259)*
313311 Broadwoven Fabric Finishing Mills *(SIC 2231)*; *(SIC 2261)*; *(SIC 2262)*; *(SIC 2269)*; *(SIC 5131)*
313312 Textile and Fabric Finishing (except Broadwoven Fabric) Mills *(SIC 2282)*; *(SIC 2284)*; *(SIC 2299)*; *(SIC 2258)*; *(SIC 2269)*; *(SIC 2257)*; *(SIC 2231)*; *(SIC 5131)*
313320 Fabric Coating Mills *(SIC 2295)*; *(SIC 3069)*

Textile Product Mills

314110 Carpet and Rug Mills *(SIC 2273)*
314121 Curtain and Drapery Mills *(SIC 2391)*; *(SIC 5714)*
314129 Other Household Textile Product Mills *(SIC 2392)*
314911 Textile Bag Mills *(SIC 2392)*; *(SIC 2393)*
314912 Canvas and Related Product Mills *(SIC 2394)*
314991 Rope, Cordage and Twine Mills *(SIC 2298)*
314992 Tire Cord and Tire Fabric Mills *(SIC 2296)*
314999 All Other Miscellaneous Textile Product Mills *(SIC 2299)*; *(SIC 2399)*; *(SIC 2396)*; *(SIC 2395)*

Apparel Manufacturing

315111 Sheer Hosiery Mills *(SIC 2251)*; *(SIC 2252)*
315119 Other Hosiery and Sock Mills *(SIC 2252)*
315191 Outerwear Knitting Mills *(SIC 2253)*; *(SIC 2259)*
315192 Underwear and Nightwear Knitting Mills *(SIC 2254)*; *(SIC 2259)*
315211 Men's and Boys' Cut and Sew Apparel Contractors *(SIC 2361)*; *(SIC 2385)*; *(SIC 2322)*; *(SIC 2384)*; *(SIC 2395)*; *(SIC 2369)*; *(SIC 2389)*; *(SIC 2329)*; *(SIC 2325)*; *(SIC 2321)*; *(SIC 2311)*; *(SIC 2326)*; *(SIC 2341)*
315212 Women's and Girls' Cut and Sew Apparel Contractors *(SIC 2369)*; *(SIC 2395)*; *(SIC 2389)*; *(SIC 2384)*; *(SIC 2361)*; *(SIC 2341)*; *(SIC 2385)*; *(SIC 2339)*; *(SIC 2337)*; *(SIC 2335)*; *(SIC 2331)*; *(SIC 2342)*
315221 Men's and Boys' Cut and Sew Underwear and Nightwear Manufacturing *(SIC 2341)*; *(SIC 2369)*; *(SIC 2322)*; *(SIC 2384)*
315222 Men's and Boys' Cut and Sew Suit, Coat, and Overcoat Manufacturing *(SIC 2311)*; *(SIC 2369)*; *(SIC 2385)*
315223 Men's and Boys' Cut and Sew Shirt, (except Work Shirt) Manufacturing *(SIC 2321)*; *(SIC 2361)*
315224 Men's and Boys' Cut and Sew Trouser, Slack, and Jean Manufacturing *(SIC 2369)*; *(SIC 2325)*
315225 Men's and Boys' Cut and Sew Work Clothing Manufacturing *(SIC 2326)*
315228 Men's and Boys' Cut and Sew Other Outerwear Manufacturing *(SIC 2329)*; *(SIC 2369)*; *(SIC 2385)*
315231 Women's and Girls' Cut and Sew Lingerie, Loungewear, and Nightwear Manufacturing *(SIC 2341)*; *(SIC 2342)*; *(SIC 2369)*; *(SIC 2384)*; *(SIC 2389)*
315232 Women's and Girls' Cut and Sew Blouse and Shirt Manufacturing *(SIC 2331)*; *(SIC 2361)*
315233 Women's and Girls' Cut and Sew Dress Manufacturing *(SIC 2335)*; *(SIC 2361)*
315234 Women's and Girls' Cut and Sew Suit, Coat, Tailored Jacket, and Skirt Manufacturing *(SIC 2369)*; *(SIC 2385)*; *(SIC 2337)*
315239 Women's and Girls' Cut and Sew Other Outerwear Manufacturing *(SIC 2369)*; *(SIC 2385)*; *(SIC 2339)*
315291 Infants' Cut and Sew Apparel Manufacturing *(SIC 2341)*; *(SIC 2361)*; *(SIC 2369)*; *(SIC 2385)*
315292 Fur and Leather Apparel Manufacturing *(SIC 2371)*; *(SIC 2386)*
315299 All Other Cut and Sew Apparel Manufacturing *(SIC 2329)*; *(SIC 2339)*; *(SIC 2389)*
315991 Hat, Cap, and Millinery Manufacturing *(SIC 2353)*
315992 Glove and Mitten Manufacturing *(SIC 2381)*; *(SIC 3151)*
315993 Men's and Boys' Neckwear Manufacturing *(SIC 2323)*
315999 Other Apparel Accessories and Other Apparel Manufacturing *(SIC 2339)*; *(SIC 2385)*; *(SIC 2387)*; *(SIC 2389)*; *(SIC 2396)*; *(SIC 2399)*

Leather & Allied Product Manufacturing

316110 Leather and Hide Tanning and Finishing *(SIC 3111)*; *(SIC 3999)*

316211 Rubber and Plastics Footwear Manufacturing *(SIC 3021)*
316212 House Slipper Manufacturing *(SIC 3142)*
316213 Men's Footwear (except Athletic) Manufacturing *(SIC 3143)*
316214 Women's Footwear (except Athletic) Manufacturing *(SIC 3144)*
316219 Other Footwear Manufacturing *(SIC 3149)*
316991 Luggage Manufacturing *(SIC 3161)*
316992 Women's Handbag and Purse Manufacturing *(SIC 3171)*
316993 Personal Leather Good (except Women's Handbag and Purse) Manufacturing *(SIC 3172)*
316999 All Other Leather Good Manufacturing *(SIC 3131); (SIC 3199)*

WOOD PRODUCT MANUFACTURING

321113 Sawmills *(SIC 2421); (SIC 2429)*
321114 Wood Preservation *(SIC 2491)*
321211 Hardwood Veneer and Plywood Manufacturing *(SIC 2435)*
321212 Softwood Veneer and Plywood Manufacturing *(SIC 2436)*
321213 Engineered Wood Member (except Truss) Manufacturing *(SIC 2439)*
321214 Truss Manufacturing *(SIC 2439)*
321219 Reconstituted Wood Product Manufacturing *(SIC 2493)*
321911 Wood Window and Door Manufacturing *(SIC 2431)*
321912 Cut Stock, Resawing Lumber, and Planing *(SIC 2439); (SIC 2429); (SIC 2426); (SIC 2421)*
321918 Other Millwork (including Flooring) *(SIC 2421); (SIC 2426); (SIC 2431)*
321920 Wood Container and Pallet Manufacturing *(SIC 2441); (SIC 2448); (SIC 2449); (SIC 2499)*
321991 Manufactured Home (Mobile Home) Manufacturing *(SIC 2451)*
321992 Prefabricated Wood Building Manufacturing *(SIC 2452)*
321999 All Other Miscellaneous Wood Product Manufacturing *(SIC 2429); (SIC 3999); (SIC 2499); (SIC 2426); (SIC 2421); (SIC 3131)*

PAPER MANUFACTURING

322110 Pulp Mills *(SIC 2611)*
322121 Paper (except Newsprint) Mills *(SIC 2611); (SIC 2621)*
322122 Newsprint Mills *(SIC 2621)*
322130 Paperboard Mills *(SIC 2611); (SIC 2631)*
322211 Corrugated and Solid Fiber Box Manufacturing *(SIC 2653)*
322212 Folding Paperboard Box Manufacturing *(SIC 2657)*
322213 Setup Paperboard Box Manufacturing *(SIC 2652)*
322214 Fiber Can, Tube, Drum, and Similar Products Manufacturing *(SIC 2655)*
322215 Non-Folding Sanitary Food Container Manufacturing *(SIC 2656); (SIC 2679)*
322221 Coated and Laminated Packaging Paper and Plastics Film Manufacturing *(SIC 2671)*
322222 Coated and Laminated Paper Manufacturing *(SIC 2672); (SIC 2679)*
322223 Plastics, Foil, and Coated Paper Bag Manufacturing *(SIC 2673)*
322224 Uncoated Paper and Multiwall Bag Manufacturing *(SIC 2674)*
322225 Laminated Aluminum Foil Manufacturing for Flexible Packaging Uses *(SIC 3497)*
322226 Surface-Coated Paperboard Manufacturing *(SIC 2675)*
322231 Die-Cut Paper and Paperboard Office Supplies Manufacturing *(SIC 2675); (SIC 2679)*
322232 Envelope Manufacturing *(SIC 2677)*
322233 Stationery, Tablet, and Related Product Manufacturing *(SIC 2678)*
322291 Sanitary Paper Product Manufacturing *(SIC 2676)*
322299 All Other Converted Paper Product Manufacturing *(SIC 2675); (SIC 2679)*

PRINTING & RELATED SUPPORT ACTIVITIES

323110 Commercial Lithographic Printing *(SIC 2771); (SIC 2782); (SIC 3999); (SIC 2752)*
323111 Commercial Gravure Printing *(SIC 2754); (SIC 2771); (SIC 2782); (SIC 3999)*
323112 Commercial Flexographic Printing *(SIC 2759); (SIC 2771); (SIC 2782); (SIC 3999)*
323113 Commercial Screen Printing *(SIC 2782); (SIC 2771); (SIC 2759); (SIC 2396); (SIC 3999)*
323114 Quick Printing *(SIC 2752); (SIC 2759)*
323115 Digital Printing *(SIC 2759)*
323116 Manifold Business Form Printing *(SIC 2761)*
323117 Book Printing *(SIC 2732)*
323118 Blankbook, Loose-leaf Binder and Device Manufacturing *(SIC 2782)*
323119 Other Commercial Printing *(SIC 2759); (SIC 2771); (SIC 2782); (SIC 3999)*
323121 Tradebinding and Related Work *(SIC 2789)*
323122 Prepress Services *(SIC 2791); (SIC 2796)*

PETROLEUM & COAL PRODUCTS MANUFACTURING

324110 Petroleum Refineries *(SIC 2911)*
324121 Asphalt Paving Mixture and Block Manufacturing *(SIC 2951)*
324122 Asphalt Shingle and Coating Materials Manufacturing *(SIC 2952)*
324191 Petroleum Lubricating Oil and Grease Manufacturing *(SIC 2992)*
324199 All Other Petroleum and Coal Products Manufacturing *(SIC 2999); (SIC 3312)*

CHEMICAL MANUFACTURING

325110 Petrochemical Manufacturing *(SIC 2865); (SIC 2869)*
325120 Industrial Gas Manufacturing *(SIC 2869); (SIC 2813)*
325131 Inorganic Dye and Pigment Manufacturing *(SIC 2816); (SIC 2819)*
325132 Organic Dye and Pigment Manufacturing *(SIC 2865)*
325181 Alkalies and Chlorine Manufacturing *(SIC 2812)*
325182 Carbon Black Manufacturing *(SIC 2816); (SIC 2895)*
325188 All Other Inorganic Chemical Manufacturing *(SIC 2819); (SIC 2869)*
325191 Gum and Wood Chemical Manufacturing *(SIC 2861)*
325192 Cyclic Crude and Intermediate Manufacturing *(SIC 2865)*
325193 Ethyl Alcohol Manufacturing *(SIC 2869)*
325199 All Other Basic Organic Chemical Manufacturing *(SIC 2869); (SIC 2899)*
325211 Plastics Material and Resin Manufacturing *(SIC 2821)*
325212 Synthetic Rubber Manufacturing *(SIC 2822)*
325221 Cellulosic Manmade Fiber Manufacturing *(SIC 2823)*
325222 Noncellulosic Organic Fiber Manufacturing *(SIC 2824)*
325311 Nitrogenous Fertilizer Manufacturing *(SIC 2873)*
325312 Phosphatic Fertilizer Manufacturing *(SIC 2874)*
325314 Fertilizer (Mixing Only) Manufacturing *(SIC 2875)*
325320 Pesticide and Other Agricultural Chemical Manufacturing *(SIC 2879)*

325411 Medicinal and Botanical Manufacturing *(SIC 2833)*
325412 Pharmaceutical Preparation Manufacturing *(SIC 2834)*; *(SIC 2835)*
325413 In-Vitro Diagnostic Substance Manufacturing *(SIC 2835)*
325414 Biological Product (except Diagnostic) Manufacturing *(SIC 2836)*
325510 Paint and Coating Manufacturing *(SIC 2851)*; *(SIC 2899)*
325520 Adhesive and Sealant Manufacturing *(SIC 2891)*
325611 Soap and Other Detergent Manufacturing *(SIC 2841)*; *(SIC 2844)*
325612 Polish and Other Sanitation Good Manufacturing *(SIC 2842)*
325613 Surface Active Agent Manufacturing *(SIC 2843)*
325620 Toilet Preparation Manufacturing *(SIC 2844)*
325910 Printing Ink Manufacturing *(SIC 2893)*
325920 Explosives Manufacturing *(SIC 2892)*
325991 Custom Compounding of Purchased Resin *(SIC 3087)*
325992 Photographic Film, Paper, Plate and Chemical Manufacturing *(SIC 3861)*
325998 All Other Miscellaneous Chemical Product Manufacturing *(SIC 2819)*; *(SIC 2899)*; *(SIC 3952)*; *(SIC 3999)*

Plastics & Rubber Products Manufacturing

326111 Unsupported Plastics Bag Manufacturing *(SIC 2673)*
326112 Unsupported Plastics Packaging Film and Sheet Manufacturing *(SIC 2671)*
326113 Unsupported Plastics Film and Sheet (except Packaging) Manufacturing *(SIC 3081)*
326121 Unsupported Plastics Profile Shape Manufacturing *(SIC 3082)*; *(SIC 3089)*
326122 Plastics Pipe and Pipe Fitting Manufacturing *(SIC 3084)*; *(SIC 3089)*
326130 Laminated Plastics Plate, Sheet, and Shape Manufacturing *(SIC 3083)*
326140 Polystyrene Foam Product Manufacturing *(SIC 3086)*
326150 Urethane and Other Foam Product (except Polystyrene) Manufacturing *(SIC 3086)*
326160 Plastics Bottle Manufacturing *(SIC 3085)*
326191 Plastics Plumbing Fixtures Manufacturing *(SIC 3088)*
326192 Resilient Floor Covering Manufacturing *(SIC 3069)*; *(SIC 3996)*
326199 All Other Plastics Product Manufacturing *(SIC 3999)*; *(SIC 3089)*
326211 Tire Manufacturing (except Retreading) *(SIC 3011)*
326212 Tire Retreading *(SIC 7534)*
326220 Rubber and Plastics Hoses and Belting Manufacturing *(SIC 3052)*
326291 Rubber Product Manufacturing for Mechanical Use *(SIC 3061)*
326299 All Other Rubber Product Manufacturing *(SIC 3069)*

Nonmetallic Mineral Product Manufacturing

327111 Vitreous China Plumbing Fixture and China and Earthenware Fitting and Bathroom Accessories Manufacturing *(SIC 3261)*
327112 Vitreous China, Fine Earthenware, and Other Pottery Product Manufacturing *(SIC 3269)*; *(SIC 3263)*; *(SIC 3262)*
327113 Porcelain Electrical Supply Manufacturing *(SIC 3264)*
327121 Brick and Structural Clay Tile Manufacturing *(SIC 3251)*
327122 Ceramic Wall and Floor Tile Manufacturing *(SIC 3253)*
327123 Other Structural Clay Product Manufacturing *(SIC 3259)*
327124 Clay Refractory Manufacturing *(SIC 3255)*
327125 Nonclay Refractory Manufacturing *(SIC 3297)*
327211 Flat Glass Manufacturing *(SIC 3211)*
327212 Other Pressed and Blown Glass and Glassware Manufacturing *(SIC 3229)*
327213 Glass Container Manufacturing *(SIC 3221)*
327215 Glass Product Manufacturing Made of Purchased Glass *(SIC 3231)*
327310 Cement Manufacturing *(SIC 3241)*
327320 Ready-Mix Concrete Manufacturing *(SIC 3273)*
327331 Concrete Block and Brick Manufacturing *(SIC 3271)*
327332 Concrete Pipe Manufacturing *(SIC 3272)*
327390 Other Concrete Product Manufacturing *(SIC 3272)*
327410 Lime Manufacturing *(SIC 3274)*
327420 Gypsum and Gypsum Product Manufacturing *(SIC 3275)*; *(SIC 3299)*
327910 Abrasive Product Manufacturing *(SIC 3291)*
327991 Cut Stone and Stone Product Manufacturing *(SIC 3281)*
327992 Ground or Treated Mineral and Earth Manufacturing *(SIC 3295)*
327993 Mineral Wool Manufacturing *(SIC 3296)*
327999 All Other Miscellaneous Nonmetallic Mineral Product Manufacturing *(SIC 3272)*; *(SIC 3292)*; *(SIC 3299)*

Primary Metal Manufacturing

331111 Iron and Steel Mills *(SIC 3312)*; *(SIC 3399)*
331112 Electrometallurgical Ferroalloy Product Manufacturing *(SIC 3313)*
331210 Iron and Steel Pipes and Tubes Manufacturing from Purchased Steel *(SIC 3317)*
331221 Cold-Rolled Steel Shape Manufacturing *(SIC 3316)*
331222 Steel Wire Drawing *(SIC 3315)*
331311 Alumina Refining *(SIC 2819)*
331312 Primary Aluminum Production *(SIC 3334)*
331314 Secondary Smelting and Alloying of Aluminum *(SIC 3341)*; *(SIC 3399)*
331315 Aluminum Sheet, Plate, and Foil Manufacturing *(SIC 3353)*
331316 Aluminum Extruded Product Manufacturing *(SIC 3354)*
331319 Other Aluminum Rolling and Drawing, *(SIC 3355)*; *(SIC 3357)*
331411 Primary Smelting and Refining of Copper *(SIC 3331)*
331419 Primary Smelting and Refining of Nonferrous Metals (except Copper and Aluminum) *(SIC 3339)*
331421 Copper (except Wire) Rolling, Drawing, and Extruding *(SIC 3351)*
331422 Copper Wire Drawing *(SIC 3357)*
331423 Secondary Smelting, Refining, and Alloying of Copper *(SIC 3341)*; *(SIC 3399)*
331491 Nonferrous Metal (except Copper and Aluminum) Rolling. Drawing, and Extruding *(SIC 3356)*; *(SIC 3357)*
331492 Secondary Smelting, Refining, and Alloying of Nonferrous Metals (except Copper and Aluminum) *(SIC 3313)*; *(SIC 3341)*; *(SIC 3399)*
331511 Iron Foundries *(SIC 3322)*; *(SIC 3321)*
331512 Steel Investment Foundries *(SIC 3324)*
331513 Steel Foundries (except Investment) *(SIC 3325)*
331521 Aluminum Die-Castings *(SIC 3363)*
331522 Nonferrous (except Aluminum) Die-Castings *(SIC 3364)*
331524 Aluminum Foundries *(SIC 3365)*
331525 Copper Foundries *(SIC 3366)*
331528 Other Nonferrous Foundries *(SIC 3369)*

Fabricated Metal Product Manufacturing

332111 Iron and Steel Forging *(SIC 3462)*
332112 Nonferrous Forging *(SIC 3463)*
332114 Custom Roll Forming *(SIC 3449)*
332115 Crown and Closure Manufacturing *(SIC 3466)*
332116 Metal Stamping *(SIC 3469)*
332117 Powder Metallurgy Part Manufacturing *(SIC 3499)*
332211 Cutlery and Flatware (except Precious) Manufacturing *(SIC 3421)*; *(SIC 3914)*
332212 Hand and Edge Tool Manufacturing *(SIC 3423)*; *(SIC 3523)*; *(SIC 3524)*; *(SIC 3545)*; *(SIC 3799)*; *(SIC 3999)*
332213 Saw Blade and Handsaw Manufacturing *(SIC 3425)*
332214 Kitchen Utensil, Pot and Pan Manufacturing *(SIC 3469)*
332311 Prefabricated Metal Building and Component Manufacturing *(SIC 3448)*
332312 Fabricated Structural Metal Manufacturing *(SIC 3449)*; *(SIC 3441)*
332313 Plate Work Manufacturing *(SIC 3443)*
332321 Metal Window and Door Manufacturing *(SIC 3442)*; *(SIC 3449)*
332322 Sheet Metal Work Manufacturing *(SIC 3444)*
332323 Ornamental and Architectural Metal Work Manufacturing *(SIC 3446)*; *(SIC 3449)*; *(SIC 3523)*
332410 Power Boiler and Heat Exchanger Manufacturing *(SIC 3443)*
332420 Metal Tank (Heavy Gauge) Manufacturing *(SIC 3443)*
332431 Metal Can Manufacturing *(SIC 3411)*
332439 Other Metal Container Manufacturing *(SIC 3429)*; *(SIC 3537)*; *(SIC 3412)*; *(SIC 3499)*; *(SIC 3444)*
332510 Hardware Manufacturing *(SIC 3429)*; *(SIC 3499)*
332611 Steel Spring (except Wire) Manufacturing *(SIC 3493)*
332612 Wire Spring Manufacturing *(SIC 3495)*
332618 Other Fabricated Wire Product Manufacturing *(SIC 3315)*; *(SIC 3399)*; *(SIC 3496)*
332710 Machine Shops *(SIC 3599)*
332721 Precision Turned Product Manufacturing *(SIC 3451)*
332722 Bolt, Nut, Screw, Rivet, and Washer Manufacturing *(SIC 3452)*
332811 Metal Heat Treating *(SIC 3398)*
332812 Metal Coating, Engraving, and Allied Services (except Jewelry and Silverware) to Manufacturing *(SIC 3479)*
332813 Electroplating, Plating, Polishing, Anodizing, and Coloring *(SIC 3471)*; *(SIC 3399)*
332911 Industrial Valve Manufacturing *(SIC 3491)*
332912 Fluid Power Valve and Hose Fitting Manufacturing *(SIC 3492)*; *(SIC 3728)*
332913 Plumbing Fixture Fitting and Trim Manufacturing *(SIC 3432)*
332919 Other Metal Valve and Pipe Fitting Manufacturing *(SIC 3494)*; *(SIC 3499)*; *(SIC 3429)*
332991 Ball and Roller Bearing Manufacturing *(SIC 3562)*
332992 Small Arms Ammunition Manufacturing *(SIC 3482)*
332993 Ammunition (except Small Arms) Manufacturing *(SIC 3483)*
332994 Small Arms Manufacturing *(SIC 3484)*
332995 Other Ordnance and Accessories Manufacturing *(SIC 3489)*
332996 Fabricated Pipe and Pipe Fitting Manufacturing *(SIC 3498)*
332997 Industrial Pattern Manufacturing *(SIC 3543)*
332998 Enameled Iron and Metal Sanitary Ware Manufacturing *(SIC 3431)*
332999 All Other Miscellaneous Fabricated Metal Product Manufacturing *(SIC 3291)*; *(SIC 3432)*; *(SIC 3494)*; *(SIC 3497)*; *(SIC 3499)*; *(SIC 3537)*; *(SIC 3599)*; *(SIC 3999)*

Machinery Manufacturing

333111 Farm Machinery and Equipment Manufacturing *(SIC 3523)*
333112 Lawn and Garden Tractor and Home Lawn and Garden Equipment Manufacturing *(SIC 3524)*
333120 Construction Machinery Manufacturing *(SIC 3531)*
333131 Mining Machinery and Equipment Manufacturing *(SIC 3532)*
333132 Oil and Gas Field Machinery and Equipment Manufacturing *(SIC 3533)*
333210 Sawmill and Woodworking Machinery Manufacturing *(SIC 3553)*
333220 Rubber and Plastics Industry Machinery Manufacturing *(SIC 3559)*
333291 Paper Industry Machinery Manufacturing *(SIC 3554)*
333292 Textile Machinery Manufacturing *(SIC 3552)*
333293 Printing Machinery and Equipment Manufacturing *(SIC 3555)*
333294 Food Product Machinery Manufacturing *(SIC 3556)*
333295 Semiconductor Manufacturing Machinery *(SIC 3559)*
333298 All Other Industrial Machinery Manufacturing *(SIC 3639)*; *(SIC 3559)*
333311 Automatic Vending Machine Manufacturing *(SIC 3581)*
333312 Commercial Laundry, Drycleaning, and Pressing Machine Manufacturing *(SIC 3582)*
333313 Office Machinery Manufacturing *(SIC 3578)*; *(SIC 3579)*
333314 Optical Instrument and Lens Manufacturing *(SIC 3827)*
333315 Photographic and Photocopying Equipment Manufacturing *(SIC 3861)*
333319 Other Commercial and Service Industry Machinery Manufacturing *(SIC 3559)*; *(SIC 3699)*; *(SIC 3599)*; *(SIC 3589)*
333411 Air Purification Equipment Manufacturing *(SIC 3564)*
333412 Industrial and Commercial Fan and Blower Manufacturing *(SIC 3564)*
333414 Heating Equipment (except Electric and Warm Air Furnaces) Manufacturing *(SIC 3433)*; *(SIC 3634)*
333415 Air-Conditioning and Warm Air Heating Equipment and Commercial and Industrial Refrigeration Equipment Manufacturing *(SIC 3443)*; *(SIC 3585)*
333511 Industrial Mold Manufacturing *(SIC 3544)*
333512 Machine Tool (Metal Cutting Types) Manufacturing *(SIC 3541)*
333513 Machine Tool (Metal Forming Types) Manufacturing *(SIC 3542)*
333514 Special Die and Tool, Die Set, Jig, and Fixture Manufacturing *(SIC 3544)*
333515 Cutting Tool and Machine Tool Accessory Manufacturing *(SIC 3545)*
333516 Rolling Mill Machinery and Equipment Manufacturing *(SIC 3547)*
333518 Other Metalworking Machinery Manufacturing *(SIC 3549)*
333611 Turbine and Turbine Generator Set Unit Manufacturing *(SIC 3511)*
333612 Speed Changer, Industrial High-Speed Drive, and Gear Manufacturing *(SIC 3566)*
333613 Mechanical Power Transmission Equipment Manufacturing *(SIC 3568)*
333618 Other Engine Equipment Manufacturing *(SIC 3519)*; *(SIC 3699)*
333911 Pump and Pumping Equipment Manufacturing *(SIC 3561)*; *(SIC 3743)*
333912 Air and Gas Compressor Manufacturing *(SIC 3563)*
333913 Measuring and Dispensing Pump Manufacturing *(SIC 3586)*

333921 Elevator and Moving Stairway Manufacturing *(SIC 3534)*
333922 Conveyor and Conveying Equipment Manufacturing *(SIC 3523)*; *(SIC 3535)*
333923 Overhead Traveling Crane, Hoist and Monorail System Manufacturing *(SIC 3536)*; *(SIC 3531)*
333924 Industrial Truck, Tractor, Trailer, and Stacker Machinery Manufacturing *(SIC 3537)*
333991 Power-Driven Hand Tool Manufacturing *(SIC 3546)*
333992 Welding and Soldering Equipment Manufacturing *(SIC 3548)*
333993 Packaging Machinery Manufacturing *(SIC 3565)*
333994 Industrial Process Furnace and Oven Manufacturing *(SIC 3567)*
333995 Fluid Power Cylinder and Actuator Manufacturing *(SIC 3593)*
333996 Fluid Power Pump and Motor Manufacturing *(SIC 3594)*
333997 Scale and Balance (except Laboratory) Manufacturing *(SIC 3596)*
333999 All Other General Purpose Machinery Manufacturing *(SIC 3569)*; *(SIC 3599)*

Computer & Electronic Product Manufacturing

334111 Electronic Computer Manufacturing *(SIC 3571)*
334112 Computer Storage Device Manufacturing *(SIC 3572)*
334113 Computer Terminal Manufacturing *(SIC 3575)*
334119 Other Computer Peripheral Equipment Manufacturing *(SIC 3578)*; *(SIC 3699)*; *(SIC 3577)*
334210 Telephone Apparatus Manufacturing *(SIC 3661)*
334220 Radio and Television Broadcasting and Wireless Communications Equipment Manufacturing *(SIC 3663)*; *(SIC 3679)*
334290 Other Communication Equipment Manufacturing *(SIC 3669)*
334310 Audio and Video Equipment Manufacturing *(SIC 3651)*
334411 Electron Tube Manufacturing *(SIC 3671)*
334412 Printed Circuit Board Manufacturing *(SIC 3672)*
334413 Semiconductor and Related Device Manufacturing *(SIC 3674)*
334414 Electronic Capacitor Manufacturing *(SIC 3675)*
334415 Electronic Resistor Manufacturing *(SIC 3676)*
334416 Electronic Coil, Transformer, and Other Inductor Manufacturing *(SIC 3661)*; *(SIC 3677)*; *(SIC 3825)*
334417 Electronic Connector Manufacturing *(SIC 3678)*
334418 Printed Circuit/Electronics Assembly Manufacturing *(SIC 3679)*; *(SIC 3661)*
334419 Other Electronic Component Manufacturing *(SIC 3679)*
334510 Electromedical and Electrotherapeutic Apparatus Manufacturing *(SIC 3842)*; *(SIC 3845)*
334511 Search, Detection, Navigation, Guidance, Aeronautical, and Nautical System and Instrument Manufacturing *(SIC 3812)*
334512 Automatic Environmental Control Manufacturing for Regulating Residential, Commercial, and Appliance Use *(SIC 3822)*
334513 Instruments and Related Product Manufacturing for Measuring Displaying, and Controlling Industrial Process Variables *(SIC 3823)*
334514 Totalizing Fluid Meter and Counting Device Manufacturing *(SIC 3824)*
334515 Instrument Manufacturing for Measuring and Testing Electricity and Electrical Signals *(SIC 3825)*
334516 Analytical Laboratory Instrument Manufacturing *(SIC 3826)*
334517 Irradiation Apparatus Manufacturing *(SIC 3844)*; *(SIC 3845)*
334518 Watch, Clock, and Part Manufacturing *(SIC 3579)*; *(SIC 3873)*; *(SIC 3495)*
334519 Other Measuring and Controlling Device Manufacturing *(SIC 3829)*
334611 Software Reproducing *(SIC 7372)*
334612 Prerecorded Compact Disc (Except Software), Tape and Record Reproducing *(SIC 3652)*; *(SIC 7819)*
334613 Magnetic and Optical Recording Media Manufacturing *(SIC 3695)*

Electrical Equipment, Appliance, & Component Manufacturing

335110 Electric Lamp Bulb and Part Manufacturing *(SIC 3641)*
335121 Residential Electric Lighting Fixture Manufacturing *(SIC 3645)*; *(SIC 3999)*
335122 Commercial, Industrial, and Institutional Electric Lighting Fixture Manufacturing *(SIC 3646)*
335129 Other Lighting Equipment Manufacturing *(SIC 3648)*; *(SIC 3699)*
335211 Electric Houseware and Fan Manufacturing *(SIC 3634)*
335212 Household Vacuum Cleaner Manufacturing *(SIC 3635)*; *(SIC 3639)*
335221 Household Cooking Appliance Manufacturing *(SIC 3631)*
335222 Household Refrigerator and Home and Farm Freezer Manufacturing *(SIC 3632)*
335224 Household Laundry Equipment Manufacturing *(SIC 3633)*
335228 Other Household Appliance Manufacturing *(SIC 3639)*
335311 Power, Distribution, and Specialty Transformer Manufacturing *(SIC 3548)*; *(SIC 3612)*
335312 Motor and Generator Manufacturing *(SIC 3621)*; *(SIC 7694)*
335313 Switchgear and Switchboard Apparatus Manufacturing *(SIC 3613)*
335314 Relay and Industrial Control Manufacturing *(SIC 3625)*
335911 Storage Battery Manufacturing *(SIC 3691)*
335912 Dry and Wet Primary Battery Manufacturing *(SIC 3692)*
335921 Fiber Optic Cable Manufacturing *(SIC 3357)*
335929 Other Communication and Energy Wire Manufacturing *(SIC 3357)*
335931 Current-Carrying Wiring Device Manufacturing *(SIC 3643)*
335932 Noncurrent-Carrying Wiring Device Manufacturing *(SIC 3644)*
335991 Carbon and Graphite Product Manufacturing *(SIC 3624)*
335999 All Other Miscellaneous Electrical Equipment and Component Manufacturing *(SIC 3699)*; *(SIC 3629)*

Transportation Equipment Manufacturing

336111 Automobile Manufacturing *(SIC 3711)*
336112 Light Truck and Utility Vehicle Manufacturing *(SIC 3711)*
336120 Heavy Duty Truck Manufacturing *(SIC 3711)*
336211 Motor Vehicle Body Manufacturing *(SIC 3714)*; *(SIC 3711)*; *(SIC 3713)*
336212 Truck Trailer Manufacturing *(SIC 3715)*
336213 Motor Home Manufacturing *(SIC 3716)*
336214 Travel Trailer and Camper Manufacturing *(SIC 3792)*; *(SIC 3799)*
336311 Carburetor, Piston, Piston Ring and Valve Manufacturing *(SIC 3592)*

336312 Gasoline Engine and Engine Parts Manufacturing *(SIC 3714)*
336321 Vehicular Lighting Equipment Manufacturing *(SIC 3647)*
336322 Other Motor Vehicle Electrical and Electronic Equipment Manufacturing *(SIC 3714)*; *(SIC 3694)*; *(SIC 3679)*
336330 Motor Vehicle Steering and Suspension Components (except Spring) Manufacturing *(SIC 3714)*
336340 Motor Vehicle Brake System Manufacturing *(SIC 3292)*; *(SIC 3714)*
336350 Motor Vehicle Transmission and Power Train Part Manufacturing *(SIC 3714)*
336360 Motor Vehicle Fabric Accessories and Seat Manufacturing *(SIC 2396)*; *(SIC 2399)*; *(SIC 2531)*
336370 Motor Vehicle Metal Stamping *(SIC 3465)*
336391 Motor Vehicle Air Conditioning Manufacturing *(SIC 3585)*
336399 All Other Motor Vehicle Parts Manufacturing *(SIC 3519)*; *(SIC 3599)*; *(SIC 3714)*
336411 Aircraft Manufacturing *(SIC 3721)*
336412 Aircraft Engine and Engine Parts Manufacturing *(SIC 3724)*
336413 Other Aircraft Part and Auxiliary Equipment Manufacturing *(SIC 3728)*
336414 Guided Missile and Space Vehicle Manufacturing *(SIC 3761)*
336415 Guided Missile and Space Vehicle Propulsion Unit and Propulsion Unit Parts Manufacturing *(SIC 3764)*
336419 Other Guided Missile and Space Vehicle Parts and Auxiliary Equipment Manufacturing *(SIC 3769)*
336510 Railroad Rolling Stock Manufacturing *(SIC 3531)*; *(SIC 3743)*
336611 Ship Building and Repairing *(SIC 3731)*
336612 Boat Building *(SIC 3732)*
336991 Motorcycle, Bicycle, and Parts Manufacturing *(SIC 3751)*; *(SIC 3944)*
336992 Military Armored Vehicle, Tank, and Tank Component Manufacturing *(SIC 3711)*; *(SIC 3795)*
336999 All Other Transportation Equipment Manufacturing *(SIC 3799)*

FURNITURE & RELATED PRODUCT MANUFACTURING

337110 Wood Kitchen Cabinet and Counter Top Manufacturing *(SIC 5712)*; *(SIC 2541)*; *(SIC 2434)*
337121 Upholstered Wood Household Furniture Manufacturing *(SIC 2512)*; *(SIC 2515)*; *(SIC 5712)*
337122 Nonupholstered Wood Household Furniture Manufacturing *(SIC 2511)*; *(SIC 5712)*
337124 Metal Household Furniture Manufacturing *(SIC 2514)*
337125 Household Furniture (except Wood and Metal) Manufacturing *(SIC 2519)*
337127 Institutional Furniture Manufacturing *(SIC 2531)*; *(SIC 2599)*; *(SIC 3952)*; *(SIC 3999)*
337129 Wood Television, Radio, and Sewing Machine Cabinet Manufacturing *(SIC 2517)*
337211 Wood Office Furniture Manufacturing *(SIC 2521)*
337212 Custom Architectural Woodwork, Millwork, and Fixtures *(SIC 2541)*
337214 Nonwood Office Furniture Manufacturing *(SIC 2522)*
337215 Showcase, Partition, Shelving, and Locker Manufacturing *(SIC 2426)*; *(SIC 2541)*; *(SIC 2542)*; *(SIC 3499)*
337910 Mattress Manufacturing *(SIC 2515)*
337920 Blind and Shade Manufacturing *(SIC 2591)*

MISCELLANEOUS MANUFACTURING

339111 Laboratory Apparatus and Furniture Manufacturing *(SIC 3821)*
339112 Surgical and Medical Instrument Manufacturing *(SIC 3829)*; *(SIC 3841)*
339113 Surgical Appliance and Supplies Manufacturing *(SIC 2599)*; *(SIC 3842)*
339114 Dental Equipment and Supplies Manufacturing *(SIC 3843)*
339115 Ophthalmic Goods Manufacturing *(SIC 3851)*; *(SIC 5995)*
339116 Dental Laboratories *(SIC 8072)*
339911 Jewelry (including Precious Metal) Manufacturing, *(SIC 3469)*; *(SIC 3479)*; *(SIC 3911)*
339912 Silverware and Plated Ware Manufacturing *(SIC 3479)*; *(SIC 3914)*
339913 Jewelers' Material and Lapidary Work Manufacturing *(SIC 3915)*
339914 Costume Jewelry and Novelty Manufacturing *(SIC 3961)*; *(SIC 3479)*; *(SIC 3499)*
339920 Sporting and Athletic Good Manufacturing *(SIC 3949)*
339931 Doll and Stuffed Toy Manufacturing *(SIC 3942)*
339932 Game, Toy, and Children's Vehicle Manufacturing *(SIC 3944)*
339941 Pen and Mechanical Pencil Manufacturing *(SIC 3951)*
339942 Lead Pencil and Art Good Manufacturing *(SIC 3952)*; *(SIC 2531)*; *(SIC 3579)*
339943 Marking Device Manufacturing *(SIC 3953)*
339944 Carbon Paper and Inked Ribbon Manufacturing *(SIC 3955)*
339950 Sign Manufacturing *(SIC 3993)*
339991 Gasket, Packing, and Sealing Device Manufacturing *(SIC 3053)*
339992 Musical Instrument Manufacturing *(SIC 3931)*
339993 Fastener, Button, Needle, and Pin Manufacturing *(SIC 3131)*; *(SIC 3965)*
339994 Broom, Brush and Mop Manufacturing *(SIC 2392)*; *(SIC 3991)*
339995 Burial Casket Manufacturing *(SIC 3995)*
339999 All Other Miscellaneous Manufacturing *(SIC 3999)*; *(SIC 2499)*

WHOLESALE TRADE

423110 Automobile and Other Motor Vehicle Merchant Wholesalers *(SIC 5012)*
423120 Motor Vehicle Supplies and New Parts Merchant Wholesalers *(SIC 5013)*
423130 Tire and Tube Merchant Wholesalers *(SIC 5014)*
423140 Motor Vehicle Part (Used) Merchant Wholesalers *(SIC 5015)*
423210 Furniture Merchant Wholesalers *(SIC 5021)*
423220 Home Furnishing Merchant Wholesalers *(SIC 5023)*
423310 Lumber, Plywood, Millwork, and Wood Panel Merchant Wholesalers *(SIC 5031)*; *(SIC 5039)*
423320 Brick, Stone and Related Construction Material Merchant Wholesalers *(SIC 5032)*
423330 Roofing, Siding, and Insulation Material Merchant Wholesalers *(SIC 5033)*
423390 Other Construction Material Merchant Wholesalers *(SIC 5039)*
423410 Photographic Equipment and Supplies Merchant Wholesalers *(SIC 5043)*
423420 Office Equipment Merchant Wholesalers *(SIC 5044)*
423430 Computer and Computer Peripheral Equipment and Software Merchant Wholesalers *(SIC 5045)*

423440 Other Commercial Equipment Merchant Wholesalers *(SIC 5046)*
423450 Medical, Dental and Hospital Equipment and Supplies Merchant Wholesalers *(SIC 5047)*
423460 Ophthalmic Goods Merchant Wholesalers *(SIC 5048)*
423490 Other Professional Equipment and Supplies Merchant Wholesalers *(SIC 5049)*
423510 Metals Service Centers and Other Metal Merchant Wholesalers *(SIC 5051)*
423520 Coal and Other Mineral and Ore Merchant Wholesalers *(SIC 5052)*
423610 Electrical Apparatus and Equipment, Wiring Supplies, and Related Equipment Merchant Wholesalers *(SIC 5063)*
423620 Electrical and Electronic Appliance, Television, and Radio Set Merchant Wholesalers *(SIC 5064)*
423690 Other Electronic Parts and Equipment Merchant Wholesalers *(SIC 5065)*
423710 Hardware Merchant Wholesalers *(SIC 5072)*
423720 Plumbing and Heating Equipment and Supplies (Hydronics) Merchant Wholesalers *(SIC 5074)*
423730 Warm Air Heating and Air-Conditioning Equipment and Supplies Merchant Wholesalers *(SIC 5075)*
423740 Refrigeration Equipment and Supplies Merchant Wholesalers *(SIC 5078)*
423810 Construction and Mining (except Petroleum) Machinery and Equipment Merchant Wholesalers *(SIC 5082)*
423820 Farm and Garden Machinery and Equipment Merchant Wholesalers *(SIC 5083)*
423830 Industrial Machinery and Equipment Merchant Wholesalers *(SIC 5084)*; *(SIC 5085)*
423840 Industrial Supplies Merchant Wholesalers *(SIC 5085)*
423850 Service Establishment Equipment and Supplies Merchant Wholesalers *(SIC 5087)*
423860 Transportation Equipment and Supplies (except Motor Vehicles) Merchant Wholesalers *(SIC 5088)*
423910 Sporting and Recreational Goods and Supplies Merchant Wholesalers *(SIC 5091)*; *(SIC 5136)*; *(SIC 5137)*
423920 Toy and Hobby Goods and Supplies Merchant Wholesalers *(SIC 5092)*
423930 Recyclable Material Merchant Wholesalers *(SIC 5093)*
423940 Jewelry, Watch , Precious Stone, and Precious Metal Merchant Wholesalers *(SIC 5094)*
423990 Other Miscellaneous Durable Goods Merchant Wholesalers *(SIC 5099)*; *(SIC 7822)*
424110 Printing and Writing Paper Merchant Wholesalers *(SIC 5111)*
424120 Stationery and Office Supplies Merchant Wholesalers *(SIC 5112)*
424130 Industrial and Personal Service Paper Merchant Wholesalers *(SIC 5113)*
424210 Drugs and Druggists' Sundries Merchant Wholesalers *(SIC 5122)*
424310 Piece Goods, Notions, and Other Dry Goods Merchant Wholesalers *(SIC 5131)*
424320 Men's and Boys' Clothing and Furnishings Merchant Wholesalers *(SIC 5136)*
424330 Women's, Children's, and Infants' Clothing and Accessories Merchant Wholesalers *(SIC 5137)*
424340 Footwear Merchant Wholesalers *(SIC 5139)*; *(SIC 5199)*
424410 General Line Grocery Merchant Wholesalers *(SIC 5141)*
424420 Packaged Frozen Food Merchant Wholesalers *(SIC 5142)*
424430 Dairy Products (except Dried or Canned) Merchant Wholesalers *(SIC 5143)*
424440 Poultry and Poultry Product Merchant Wholesalers *(SIC 5144)*
424450 Confectionery Merchant Wholesalers *(SIC 5145)*
424460 Fish and Seafood Merchant Wholesalers *(SIC 5146)*
424470 Meat and Meat Product Merchant Wholesalers *(SIC 5147)*
424480 Fresh Fruit and Vegetable Merchant Wholesalers *(SIC 5148)*
424490 Other Grocery and Related Product Merchant Wholesalers *(SIC 5149)*
424510 Grain and Field Bean Merchant Wholesalers *(SIC 5153)*
424520 Livestock Merchant Wholesalers *(SIC 5154)*
424590 Other Farm Product Raw Material Merchant Wholesalers *(SIC 5159)*
424610 Plastics Materials and Basic Forms and Shapes Merchant Wholesalers *(SIC 5162)*; *(SIC 5199)*
424690 Other Chemical and Allied Products Merchant Wholesalers *(SIC 5169)*
424710 Petroleum Bulk Stations and Terminals *(SIC 5171)*
424720 Petroleum and Petroleum Products Merchant Wholesalers (except Bulk Stations and Terminals) *(SIC 5172)*
424810 Beer and Ale Merchant Wholesalers *(SIC 5181)*
424820 Wine and Distilled Alcoholic Beverage Merchant Wholesalers *(SIC 5182)*
424910 Farm Supplies Merchant Wholesalers *(SIC 5191)*
424920 Book, Periodical and Newspaper Merchant Wholesalers *(SIC 5192)*
424930 Flower, Nursery Stock and Florists' Supplies Merchant Wholesalers *(SIC 5193)*
424940 Tobacco and Tobacco Product Merchant Wholesalers *(SIC 5194)*
424950 Paint, Varnish and Supplies Merchant Wholesalers *(SIC 5198)*
424990 Other Miscellaneous Nondurable Goods Merchant Wholesalers *(SIC 5199)*
425110 Business to Business Electronic Markets *(SIC 5122)*; *(SIC 5145)*; *(SIC 5144)*; *(SIC 5143)*; *(SIC 5139)*; *(SIC 5141)*; *(SIC 5137)*; *(SIC 5136)*; *(SIC 5094)*; *(SIC 5192)*; *(SIC 5113)*; *(SIC 5112)*; *(SIC 5111)*; *(SIC 5099)*; *(SIC 5146)*; *(SIC 5131)*; *(SIC 5169)*; *(SIC 5093)*; *(SIC 5199)*; *(SIC 5195)*; *(SIC 5194)*; *(SIC 5193)*; *(SIC 5191)*; *(SIC 5182)*; *(SIC 5172)*; *(SIC 5147)*; *(SIC 5162)*; *(SIC 5159)*; *(SIC 5154)*; *(SIC 5153)*; *(SIC 5149)*; *(SIC 5148)*; *(SIC 5181)*; *(SIC 5031)*; *(SIC 5048)*; *(SIC 5047)*; *(SIC 5046)*; *(SIC 5045)*; *(SIC 5044)*; *(SIC 5012)*; *(SIC 5049)*; *(SIC 5032)*; *(SIC 5043)*; *(SIC 5023)*; *(SIC 5021)*; *(SIC 5015)*; *(SIC 5014)*; *(SIC 5013)*; *(SIC 5092)*; *(SIC 5039)*; *(SIC 5088)*; *(SIC 5033)*; *(SIC 5091)*; *(SIC 5051)*; *(SIC 5087)*; *(SIC 5085)*; *(SIC 5084)*; *(SIC 5083)*; *(SIC 5082)*; *(SIC 5078)*; *(SIC 5063)*; *(SIC 5052)*; *(SIC 5064)*; *(SIC 5065)*; *(SIC 5072)*; *(SIC 5142)*; *(SIC 5074)*; *(SIC 5075)*
425120 Wholesale Trade Agents and Brokers *(SIC 5113)*; *(SIC 5139)*; *(SIC 5145)*; *(SIC 5144)*; *(SIC 5143)*; *(SIC 5142)*; *(SIC 5141)*; *(SIC 5146)*; *(SIC 5137)*; *(SIC 5136)*; *(SIC 5099)*; *(SIC 5122)*; *(SIC 5147)*; *(SIC 5112)*; *(SIC 5111)*; *(SIC 5131)*; *(SIC 5181)*; *(SIC 7389)*; *(SIC 5088)*; *(SIC 5199)*; *(SIC 5094)*; *(SIC 5194)*; *(SIC 5193)*; *(SIC 5192)*; *(SIC 5195)*; *(SIC 5182)*; *(SIC 5148)*; *(SIC 5172)*; *(SIC 5169)*; *(SIC 5162)*; *(SIC 5159)*; *(SIC 5154)*; *(SIC 5153)*; *(SIC 5149)*; *(SIC 5191)*; *(SIC 5023)*; *(SIC 5046)*; *(SIC 5045)*; *(SIC 5044)*; *(SIC 5043)*; *(SIC 5039)*; *(SIC 5033)*; *(SIC 5047)*; *(SIC 5031)*; *(SIC 5013)*; *(SIC 5021)*; *(SIC 5015)*; *(SIC 5014)*; *(SIC 5093)*; *(SIC 5012)*; *(SIC 5092)*; *(SIC 5032)*; *(SIC 5082)*; *(SIC 5048)*; *(SIC 5091)*; *(SIC 5087)*; *(SIC 5085)*; *(SIC 5083)*; *(SIC 5078)*; *(SIC 5075)*; *(SIC 5052)*; *(SIC 5049)*; *(SIC 5084)*; *(SIC 5051)*; *(SIC 5074)*; *(SIC 5063)*; *(SIC 5064)*; *(SIC 5065)*; *(SIC 5072)*

RETAIL TRADE

441110 New Car Dealers *(SIC 5511)*
441120 Used Car Dealers *(SIC 5521)*
441210 Recreational Vehicle Dealers *(SIC 5561)*
441221 Motorcycle Dealers *(SIC 5571)*
441222 Boat Dealers *(SIC 5551)*
441229 All Other Motor Vehicle Dealers *(SIC 5599)*
441310 Automotive Parts and Accessories Stores *(SIC 5731)*; *(SIC 5013)*; *(SIC 5531)*
441320 Tire Dealers *(SIC 5014)*; *(SIC 5531)*
442110 Furniture Stores *(SIC 5021)*; *(SIC 5712)*
442210 Floor Covering Stores *(SIC 5023)*; *(SIC 5713)*
442291 Window Treatment Stores *(SIC 5714)*; *(SIC 5719)*
442299 All Other Home Furnishings Stores *(SIC 5719)*
443111 Household Appliance Stores *(SIC 7629)*; *(SIC 7623)*; *(SIC 5722)*; *(SIC 5999)*
443112 Radio, Television, and Other Electronics Stores *(SIC 5731)*; *(SIC 5999)*; *(SIC 7622)*
443120 Computer and Software Stores *(SIC 5045)*; *(SIC 5734)*; *(SIC 7378)*
443130 Camera and Photographic Supplies Stores *(SIC 5946)*
444110 Home Centers *(SIC 5211)*
444120 Paint and Wallpaper Stores *(SIC 5231)*; *(SIC 5198)*
444130 Hardware Stores *(SIC 5251)*
444190 Other Building Material Dealers *(SIC 5031)*; *(SIC 5032)*; *(SIC 5039)*; *(SIC 5063)*; *(SIC 5074)*; *(SIC 5211)*; *(SIC 5231)*
444210 Outdoor Power Equipment Stores *(SIC 5083)*; *(SIC 5261)*
444220 Nursery and Garden Centers *(SIC 5261)*; *(SIC 5191)*; *(SIC 5193)*
445110 Supermarkets and Other Grocery (except Convenience) Stores *(SIC 5411)*
445120 Convenience Stores *(SIC 5411)*
445210 Meat Markets *(SIC 5421)*; *(SIC 5499)*
445220 Fish and Seafood Markets *(SIC 5421)*
445230 Fruit and Vegetable Markets *(SIC 5431)*
445291 Baked Goods Stores *(SIC 5461)*
445292 Confectionary and Nut Stores *(SIC 5441)*
445299 All Other Specialty Food Stores *(SIC 5451)*; *(SIC 5499)*
445310 Beer, Wine and Liquor Stores *(SIC 5921)*
446110 Pharmacies and Drug Stores *(SIC 5912)*
446120 Cosmetics, Beauty Supplies, and Perfume Stores *(SIC 5087)*; *(SIC 5999)*
446130 Optical Goods Stores *(SIC 5995)*
446191 Food (Health) Supplement Stores *(SIC 5499)*
446199 All Other Health and Personal Care Stores *(SIC 5047)*; *(SIC 5999)*
447110 Gasoline Stations with Convenience Stores *(SIC 5411)*; *(SIC 5541)*
447190 Other Gasoline Stations *(SIC 5541)*
448110 Men's Clothing Stores *(SIC 5611)*
448120 Women's Clothing Stores *(SIC 5621)*
448130 Children's and Infants' Clothing Stores *(SIC 5641)*
448140 Family Clothing Stores *(SIC 5651)*
448150 Clothing Accessories Stores *(SIC 5611)*; *(SIC 5632)*; *(SIC 5699)*
448190 Other Clothing Stores *(SIC 5699)*; *(SIC 5632)*
448210 Shoe Stores *(SIC 5661)*
448310 Jewelry Stores *(SIC 5999)*; *(SIC 5944)*
448320 Luggage and Leather Goods Stores *(SIC 5948)*
451110 Sporting Goods Stores *(SIC 5941)*; *(SIC 7699)*
451120 Hobby, Toy and Game Stores *(SIC 5945)*
451130 Sewing, Needlework and Piece Goods Stores *(SIC 5714)*; *(SIC 5949)*
451140 Musical Instrument and Supplies Stores *(SIC 5736)*
451211 Book Stores *(SIC 5942)*
451212 News Dealers and Newsstands *(SIC 5994)*
451220 Prerecorded Tape, Compact Disc and Record Stores *(SIC 5735)*
452111 Department Stores (except Discount Department Stores) *(SIC 5311)*
452112 Discount Department Stores *(SIC 5311)*
452910 Warehouse Clubs and Superstores *(SIC 5411)*; *(SIC 5399)*
452990 All Other General Merchandise Stores *(SIC 5331)*; *(SIC 5399)*
453110 Florists *(SIC 5992)*
453210 Office Supplies and Stationery Stores *(SIC 5049)*; *(SIC 5112)*; *(SIC 5943)*
453220 Gift, Novelty and Souvenir Stores *(SIC 5947)*
453310 Used Merchandise Stores *(SIC 5932)*
453910 Pet and Pet Supplies Stores *(SIC 5999)*
453920 Art Dealers *(SIC 5999)*
453930 Manufactured (Mobile) Home Dealers *(SIC 5271)*
453991 Tobacco Stores *(SIC 5993)*
453998 All Other Miscellaneous Store Retailers (except Tobacco Stores) *(SIC 5261)*; *(SIC 5999)*
454111 Electronic Shopping *(SIC 5961)*
454112 Electronic Auctions *(SIC 5961)*
454113 Mail-Order Houses *(SIC 5961)*
454210 Vending Machine Operators *(SIC 5962)*
454311 Heating Oil Dealers *(SIC 5171)*; *(SIC 5983)*
454312 Liquefied Petroleum Gas (Bottled Gas) Dealers *(SIC 5171)*; *(SIC 5984)*
454319 Other Fuel Dealers *(SIC 5989)*
454390 Other Direct Selling Establishments *(SIC 5421)*; *(SIC 5963)*

TRANSPORTATION & WAREHOUSING

481111 Scheduled Passenger Air Transportation *(SIC 4512)*
481112 Scheduled Freight Air Transportation *(SIC 4512)*
481211 Nonscheduled Chartered Passenger Air Transportation *(SIC 4522)*
481212 Nonscheduled Chartered Freight Air Transportation *(SIC 4522)*
481219 Other Nonscheduled Air Transportation *(SIC 0721)*; *(SIC 7319)*; *(SIC 7335)*
482111 Line-Haul Railroads *(SIC 4011)*
482112 Short Line Railroads *(SIC 4013)*
483111 Deep Sea Freight Transportation *(SIC 4412)*
483112 Deep Sea Passenger Transportation *(SIC 4481)*
483113 Coastal and Great Lakes Freight Transportation *(SIC 4424)*; *(SIC 4432)*; *(SIC 4492)*
483114 Coastal and Great Lakes Passenger Transportation *(SIC 4481)*; *(SIC 4482)*
483211 Inland Water Freight Transportation *(SIC 4492)*; *(SIC 4449)*
483212 Inland Water Passenger Transportation *(SIC 4489)*; *(SIC 4482)*
484110 General Freight Trucking, Local *(SIC 4212)*; *(SIC 4214)*
484121 General Freight Trucking, Long-Distance, Truckload *(SIC 4213)*
484122 General Freight Trucking, Long-Distance, Less Than Truckload *(SIC 4213)*
484210 Used Household and Office Goods Moving *(SIC 4213)*; *(SIC 4214)*; *(SIC 4212)*
484220 Specialized Freight (except Used Goods) Trucking, Local *(SIC 4214)*; *(SIC 4212)*
484230 Specialized Freight (except Used Goods) Trucking, Long-Distance *(SIC 4213)*
485111 Mixed Mode Transit Systems *(SIC 4111)*
485112 Commuter Rail Systems *(SIC 4111)*

485113 Bus and Motor Vehicle Transit Systems *(SIC 4111)*
485119 Other Urban Transit Systems *(SIC 4111)*
485210 Interurban and Rural Bus Lines *(SIC 4131)*
485310 Taxi Service *(SIC 4121)*
485320 Limousine Service *(SIC 4119)*
485410 School and Employee Bus Industry *(SIC 4119)*; *(SIC 4151)*
485510 Charter Bus Industry *(SIC 4141)*; *(SIC 4142)*
485991 Special Needs Transportation *(SIC 4119)*
485999 All Other Transit and Ground Passenger Transportation *(SIC 4111)*; *(SIC 4119)*
486110 Pipeline Transportation of Crude Oil *(SIC 4612)*
486210 Pipeline Transportation of Natural Gas *(SIC 4922)*; *(SIC 4923)*
486910 Pipeline Transportation of Refined Petroleum Products *(SIC 4613)*
486990 All Other Pipeline Transportation *(SIC 4619)*
487110 Scenic and Sightseeing Transportation, Land *(SIC 7999)*; *(SIC 4119)*; *(SIC 4789)*
487210 Scenic and Sightseeing Transportation, Water *(SIC 4489)*; *(SIC 7999)*
487990 Scenic and Sightseeing Transportation , Other *(SIC 4522)*; *(SIC 7999)*
488111 Air Traffic Control *(SIC 4581)*; *(SIC 9621)*
488119 Other Airport Operations *(SIC 4581)*; *(SIC 4959)*
488190 Other Support Activities for Air Transportation *(SIC 4581)*
488210 Support Activities for Rail Transportation *(SIC 4789)*; *(SIC 4013)*; *(SIC 4741)*
488310 Port and Harbor Operations *(SIC 4499)*; *(SIC 4491)*
488320 Marine Cargo Handling *(SIC 4491)*
488330 Navigational Services to Shipping *(SIC 4492)*; *(SIC 4499)*
488390 Other Support Activities for Water Transportation *(SIC 4499)*; *(SIC 4785)*; *(SIC 7699)*
488410 Motor Vehicle Towing *(SIC 7549)*
488490 Other Support Activities for Road Transportation *(SIC 4173)*; *(SIC 4231)*; *(SIC 4785)*
488510 Freight Transportation Arrangement *(SIC 4731)*
488991 Packing and Crating *(SIC 4783)*
488999 All Other Support Activities for Transportation *(SIC 4729)*; *(SIC 4789)*
491110 Postal Service *(SIC 4311)*
492110 Couriers *(SIC 4215)*; *(SIC 4513)*
492210 Local Messengers and Local Delivery *(SIC 4215)*
493110 General Warehousing and Storage Facilities *(SIC 4225)*; *(SIC 4226)*
493120 Refrigerated Storage Facilities *(SIC 4222)*; *(SIC 4226)*
493130 Farm Product Storage Facilities *(SIC 4221)*
493190 All Other Warehousing and Storage Facilities *(SIC 4226)*

Information

511110 Newspaper Publishers *(SIC 2711)*
511120 Periodical Publishers *(SIC 2721)*; *(SIC 2741)*
511130 Book Publishers *(SIC 2741)*; *(SIC 2731)*
511140 Database and Directory Publishers *(SIC 7331)*; *(SIC 2741)*
511191 Greeting Card Publishers *(SIC 2771)*
511199 All Other Publishers *(SIC 2741)*
511210 Software Publishers *(SIC 7372)*
512110 Motion Picture and Video Production *(SIC 7812)*
512120 Motion Picture and Video Distribution *(SIC 7822)*; *(SIC 7829)*
512131 Motion Picture Theaters, Except Drive-In *(SIC 7832)*
512132 Drive-In Motion Picture Theaters *(SIC 7833)*
512191 Teleproduction and Other Postproduction Services *(SIC 7819)*
512199 Other Motion Picture and Video Industries *(SIC 7819)*
512210 Record Production *(SIC 8999)*
512220 Integrated Record Production/Distribution *(SIC 3652)*
512230 Music Publishers *(SIC 2731)*; *(SIC 2741)*; *(SIC 8999)*
512240 Sound Recording Studios *(SIC 7389)*
512290 Other Sound Recording Industries *(SIC 7389)*; *(SIC 7922)*
515111 Radio Networks *(SIC 4832)*
515112 Radio Stations *(SIC 4832)*
515120 Television Broadcasting *(SIC 4833)*
515210 Cable and Other Subscription Programming *(SIC 4841)*
516110 Internet Publishing and Broadcasting *(SIC 8999)*; *(SIC 2711)*; *(SIC 2721)*; *(SIC 2731)*; *(SIC 2741)*; *(SIC 2771)*
517110 Wired Telecommunications Carriers *(SIC 4822)*; *(SIC 4813)*
517211 Paging *(SIC 4812)*
517212 Cellular and Other Wireless Telecommunications *(SIC 4812)*; *(SIC 4899)*
517310 Telecommunications Resellers *(SIC 4812)*; *(SIC 4813)*
517410 Satellite Telecommunications *(SIC 4899)*
517510 Cable and Other Program Distribution *(SIC 4841)*
517910 Other Telecommunications *(SIC 4899)*
518111 Internet Service Providers *(SIC 7375)*
518112 Web Search Portals *(SIC 8999)*
518210 Data Processing, Hosting, and Related Services *(SIC 7389)*; *(SIC 7374)*; *(SIC 7379)*
519110 New Syndicates *(SIC 7383)*
519120 Libraries and Archives *(SIC 7829)*; *(SIC 8231)*
519190 All Other Information Services *(SIC 7389)*

Finance & Insurance

521110 Monetary Authorities-Central Banks *(SIC 6011)*
522110 Commercial Banking *(SIC 6029)*; *(SIC 6081)*; *(SIC 6022)*; *(SIC 6021)*
522120 Savings Institutions *(SIC 6036)*; *(SIC 6035)*
522130 Credit Unions *(SIC 6061)*; *(SIC 6062)*
522190 Other Depository Intermediation *(SIC 6022)*
522210 Credit Card Issuing *(SIC 6022)*; *(SIC 6141)*; *(SIC 6021)*
522220 Sales Financing *(SIC 6141)*; *(SIC 6153)*; *(SIC 6159)*
522291 Consumer Lending *(SIC 6141)*
522292 Real Estate Credit *(SIC 6162)*
522293 International Trade Financing *(SIC 6081)*; *(SIC 6082)*; *(SIC 6111)*; *(SIC 6159)*
522294 Secondary Market Financing *(SIC 6111)*
522298 All Other Non-Depository Credit Intermediation *(SIC 6111)*; *(SIC 6153)*; *(SIC 6081)*; *(SIC 5932)*; *(SIC 6159)*
522310 Mortgage and Other Loan Brokers *(SIC 6163)*
522320 Financial Transactions, Processing, Reserve and Clearing House Activities *(SIC 7389)*; *(SIC 6019)*; *(SIC 6099)*; *(SIC 6153)*
522390 Other Activities Related to Credit Intermediation *(SIC 6099)*; *(SIC 6162)*
523110 Investment Banking and Securities Dealing *(SIC 6211)*
523120 Securities Brokerage *(SIC 6211)*
523130 Commodity Contracts Dealing *(SIC 6099)*; *(SIC 6221)*; *(SIC 6799)*
523140 Commodity Brokerage *(SIC 6221)*
523210 Securities and Commodity Exchanges *(SIC 6231)*
523910 Miscellaneous Intermediation *(SIC 6799)*; *(SIC 6211)*
523920 Portfolio Management *(SIC 6282)*; *(SIC 6371)*; *(SIC 6733)*; *(SIC 6799)*
523930 Investment Advice *(SIC 6282)*
523991 Trust, Fiduciary, and Custody Activities *(SIC 6289)*; *(SIC 6099)*; *(SIC 6091)*; *(SIC 6021)*; *(SIC 6733)*; *(SIC 6022)*

523999 Miscellaneous Financial Investment Activities *(SIC 6799)*; *(SIC 6792)*; *(SIC 6289)*; *(SIC 6099)*; *(SIC 6211)*
524113 Direct Life Insurance Carriers *(SIC 6311)*
524114 Direct Health and Medical Insurance Carriers *(SIC 6321)*; *(SIC 6324)*
524126 Direct Property and Casualty Insurance Carriers *(SIC 6331)*; *(SIC 6351)*
524127 Direct Title Insurance Carriers *(SIC 6361)*
524128 Other Direct Insurance Carriers (except Life, Health, and Medical) *(SIC 6399)*
524130 Reinsurance Carriers *(SIC 6331)*; *(SIC 6351)*; *(SIC 6361)*; *(SIC 6321)*; *(SIC 6311)*; *(SIC 6324)*
524210 Insurance Agencies and Brokerages *(SIC 6411)*
524291 Claims Adjusters *(SIC 6411)*
524292 Third Party Administration for Insurance and Pension Funds *(SIC 6371)*; *(SIC 6411)*
524298 All Other Insurance Related Activities *(SIC 6411)*
525110 Pension Funds *(SIC 6371)*
525120 Health and Welfare Funds *(SIC 6371)*
525190 Other Insurance and Employee Benefit Funds *(SIC 6321)*; *(SIC 6324)*; *(SIC 6331)*; *(SIC 6733)*
525910 Open-End Investment Funds *(SIC 6722)*
525920 Trusts, Estates, and Agency Accounts *(SIC 6733)*
525930 Real Estate Investment Trusts *(SIC 6798)*
525990 Other Financial Vehicles *(SIC 6726)*

Real Estate & Rental & Leasing

531110 Lessors of Residential Buildings and Dwellings *(SIC 6513)*; *(SIC 6514)*
531120 Lessors of Nonresidential Buildings (except Miniwarehouses) *(SIC 6512)*
531130 Lessors of Miniwarehouses and Self Storage Units *(SIC 4225)*
531190 Lessors of Other Real Estate Property *(SIC 6515)*; *(SIC 6517)*; *(SIC 6519)*
531210 Offices of Real Estate Agents and Brokers *(SIC 6531)*
531311 Residential Property Managers *(SIC 6531)*
531312 Nonresidential Property Managers *(SIC 6531)*
531320 Offices of Real Estate Appraisers *(SIC 6531)*
531390 Other Activities Related to Real Estate *(SIC 6531)*
532111 Passenger Cars Rental *(SIC 7514)*
532112 Passenger Cars Leasing *(SIC 7515)*
532120 Truck, Utility Trailer and RV (Recreational Vehicle) Rental and Leasing *(SIC 7513)*; *(SIC 7519)*
532210 Consumer Electronics and Appliances Rental *(SIC 7359)*
532220 Formal Wear and Costumes Rental *(SIC 7299)*; *(SIC 7819)*
532230 Video Tapes and Disc Rental *(SIC 7841)*
532291 Home Health Equipment Rental *(SIC 7352)*
532292 Recreational Goods Rental *(SIC 7999)*
532299 All Other Consumer Goods Rental *(SIC 7359)*
532310 General Rental Centers *(SIC 7359)*
532411 Commercial Air, Rail, and Water Transportation Equipment Rental and Leasing *(SIC 4499)*; *(SIC 4741)*; *(SIC 7359)*
532412 Construction, Mining and Forestry Machinery and Equipment Rental and Leasing *(SIC 7359)*; *(SIC 7353)*
532420 Office Machinery and Equipment Rental and Leasing *(SIC 7377)*; *(SIC 7359)*
532490 Other Commercial and Industrial Machinery and Equipment Rental and Leasing *(SIC 7352)*; *(SIC 7359)*; *(SIC 7819)*; *(SIC 7922)*
533110 Owners and Lessors of Other Non-Financial Assets *(SIC 6794)*; *(SIC 6792)*

Professional, Scientific, & Technical Services

541110 Offices of Lawyers *(SIC 8111)*
541191 Title Abstract and Settlement Offices *(SIC 6541)*
541199 Other Legal Services *(SIC 7389)*
541211 Offices of Certified Public Accountants *(SIC 8721)*
541213 Tax Preparation Services *(SIC 7291)*
541214 Payroll Services *(SIC 7819)*; *(SIC 8721)*
541219 Other Accounting Services *(SIC 8721)*
541310 Architectural Services *(SIC 8712)*
541320 Landscape Architectural Services *(SIC 0781)*
541330 Engineering Services *(SIC 8711)*
541340 Drafting Services *(SIC 7389)*
541350 Building Inspection Services *(SIC 7389)*
541360 Geophysical Surveying and Mapping Services *(SIC 1081)*; *(SIC 1382)*; *(SIC 1481)*; *(SIC 8713)*
541370 Surveying and Mapping (except Geophysical) Services *(SIC 7389)*; *(SIC 8713)*
541380 Testing Laboratories *(SIC 8734)*
541410 Interior Design Services *(SIC 7389)*
541420 Industrial Design Services *(SIC 7389)*
541430 Graphic Design Services *(SIC 7336)*; *(SIC 8099)*
541490 Other Specialized Design Services *(SIC 7389)*
541511 Custom Computer Programming Services *(SIC 7371)*
541512 Computer Systems Design Services *(SIC 7373)*; *(SIC 7379)*
541513 Computer Facilities Management Services *(SIC 7376)*
541519 Other Computer Related Services *(SIC 7379)*
541611 Administrative Management and General Management Consulting Services *(SIC 8742)*
541612 Human Resources and Executive Search Consulting Services *(SIC 7361)*; *(SIC 8742)*; *(SIC 8999)*
541613 Marketing Consulting Services *(SIC 8742)*
541614 Process, Physical, Distribution and Logistics Consulting *(SIC 8742)*
541618 Other Management Consulting Services *(SIC 8748)*; *(SIC 4731)*
541620 Environmental Consulting Services *(SIC 8999)*
541690 Other Scientific and Technical Consulting Services *(SIC 0781)*; *(SIC 8748)*; *(SIC 8999)*
541710 Research and Development in the Physical Sciences and Engineering Sciences *(SIC 8731)*; *(SIC 8733)*
541720 Research and Development in the Life Sciences *(SIC 8731)*; *(SIC 8733)*
541730 Research and Development in the Social Sciences and Humanities *(SIC 8732)*; *(SIC 8733)*
541810 Advertising Agencies *(SIC 7311)*
541820 Public Relations Services *(SIC 8743)*
541830 Media Buying Agencies *(SIC 7319)*
541840 Media Representatives *(SIC 7313)*
541850 Display Advertising *(SIC 7312)*; *(SIC 7319)*
541860 Direct Mail Advertising *(SIC 7331)*
541870 Advertising Material Distribution Services *(SIC 7319)*
541890 Other Services Related to Advertising *(SIC 5199)*; *(SIC 7319)*; *(SIC 7389)*
541910 Marketing Research and Public Opinion Polling *(SIC 8732)*
541921 Photographic Studios, Portrait *(SIC 7221)*
541922 Commercial Photography *(SIC 7335)*; *(SIC 8099)*
541930 Translation and Interpretation Services *(SIC 7389)*
541940 Veterinary Services *(SIC 0741)*; *(SIC 0742)*; *(SIC 8734)*
541990 All Other Professional, Scientific and Technical Services *(SIC 7389)*

Management of Companies & Enterprises

551111 Offices of Bank Holding Companies *(SIC 6712)*
551112 Offices of Other Holding Companies *(SIC 6719)*

Administrative & Support, Waste Management & Remediation Services

561110 Office Administrative Services *(SIC 8741)*
561210 Facilities Support Services *(SIC 8744)*
561310 Employment Placement Agencies *(SIC 7361)*; *(SIC 7819)*; *(SIC 7922)*
561320 Temporary Help Services *(SIC 7363)*
561330 Employee Leasing Services *(SIC 7363)*
561410 Document Preparation Services *(SIC 7338)*
561421 Telephone Answering Services *(SIC 7389)*
561422 Telemarketing Bureaus *(SIC 7389)*
561431 Other Business Service Centers (including Copy Shops) *(SIC 7389)*; *(SIC 7334)*
561439 Private Mail Centers *(SIC 7389)*
561440 Collection Agencies *(SIC 7322)*
561450 Credit Bureaus *(SIC 7323)*
561491 Repossession Services *(SIC 7389)*; *(SIC 7322)*
561492 Court Reporting and Stenotype Services *(SIC 7338)*
561499 All Other Business Support Services *(SIC 7389)*
561510 Travel Agencies *(SIC 4724)*
561520 Tour Operators *(SIC 4725)*
561591 Convention and Visitors Bureaus *(SIC 7389)*
561599 All Other Travel Arrangement and Reservation Services *(SIC 4729)*; *(SIC 7389)*; *(SIC 7999)*; *(SIC 8699)*
561611 Investigation Services *(SIC 7381)*
561612 Security Guards and Patrol Services *(SIC 7381)*
561613 Armored Car Services *(SIC 7381)*
561621 Security Systems Services (except Locksmiths) *(SIC 7382)*; *(SIC 1731)*
561622 Locksmiths *(SIC 7699)*
561710 Exterminating and Pest Control Services *(SIC 4959)*; *(SIC 7342)*
561720 Janitorial Services *(SIC 4581)*; *(SIC 7342)*; *(SIC 7349)*
561730 Landscaping Services *(SIC 0782)*; *(SIC 0783)*
561740 Carpet and Upholstery Cleaning Services *(SIC 7217)*
561790 Other Services to Buildings and Dwellings *(SIC 7389)*; *(SIC 7699)*
561910 Packaging and Labeling Services *(SIC 7389)*
561920 Convention and Trade Show Organizers *(SIC 7389)*
561990 All Other Support Services *(SIC 7389)*
562111 Solid Waste Collection *(SIC 4212)*; *(SIC 4953)*
562112 Hazardous Waste Collection *(SIC 4212)*; *(SIC 4953)*
562119 Other Waste Collection *(SIC 4212)*; *(SIC 4953)*
562211 Hazardous Waste Treatment and Disposal *(SIC 4953)*
562212 Solid Waste Landfills *(SIC 4953)*
562213 Solid Waste Combustors and Incinerators *(SIC 4953)*
562219 Other Nonhazardous Waste Treatment and Disposal *(SIC 4953)*
562910 Remediation Services *(SIC 1799)*; *(SIC 4959)*
562920 Materials Recovery Facilities *(SIC 4953)*
562991 Septic Tank and Related Services *(SIC 7699)*; *(SIC 7359)*
562998 All Other Miscellaneous Waste Management *(SIC 4959)*

Educational Services

611110 Elementary and Secondary Schools *(SIC 8211)*
611210 Junior Colleges *(SIC 8222)*
611310 Colleges, Universities and Professional Schools *(SIC 8221)*
611410 Business and Secretarial Schools *(SIC 8244)*
611420 Computer Training *(SIC 8243)*
611430 Professional and Management Development Training Schools *(SIC 8299)*
611511 Cosmetology and Barber Schools *(SIC 7231)*; *(SIC 7241)*
611512 Flight Training *(SIC 8249)*; *(SIC 8299)*
611513 Apprenticeship Training *(SIC 8249)*
611519 Other Technical and Trade Schools *(SIC 8243)*; *(SIC 8249)*
611610 Fine Arts Schools *(SIC 7911)*; *(SIC 8299)*
611620 Sports and Recreation Instruction *(SIC 7999)*
611630 Language Schools *(SIC 8299)*
611691 Exam Preparation and Tutoring *(SIC 8299)*
611692 Automobile Driving Schools *(SIC 8299)*
611699 All Other Miscellaneous Schools and Instruction *(SIC 8299)*
611710 Educational Support Services *(SIC 8299)*; *(SIC 8748)*

Health Care & Social Assistance

621111 Offices of Physicians (except Mental Health Specialists) *(SIC 8011)*; *(SIC 8031)*
621112 Offices of Physicians, Mental Health Specialists *(SIC 8011)*; *(SIC 8031)*
621210 Offices of Dentists *(SIC 8021)*
621310 Offices of Chiropractors *(SIC 8041)*
621320 Offices of Optometrists *(SIC 8042)*
621330 Offices of Mental Health Practitioners (except Physicians) *(SIC 8049)*
621340 Offices of Physical, Occupational, and Speech Therapists and Audiologists *(SIC 8049)*
621391 Offices of Podiatrists *(SIC 8043)*
621399 Offices of All Other Miscellaneous Health Practitioners *(SIC 8049)*
621410 Family Planning Centers *(SIC 8093)*; *(SIC 8099)*
621420 Outpatient Mental Health and Substance Abuse Centers *(SIC 8093)*
621491 HMO Medical Centers *(SIC 8011)*
621492 Kidney Dialysis Centers *(SIC 8092)*
621493 Freestanding Ambulatory Surgical and Emergency Centers *(SIC 8011)*
621498 All Other Outpatient Care Facilities *(SIC 8093)*
621511 Medical Laboratories *(SIC 8071)*
621512 Diagnostic Imaging Centers *(SIC 8071)*
621610 Home Health Care Services *(SIC 8082)*
621910 Ambulance Service *(SIC 4119)*; *(SIC 4522)*
621991 Blood and Organ Banks *(SIC 8099)*
621999 All Other Miscellaneous Ambulatory Health Care Services *(SIC 8099)*
622110 General Medical and Surgical Hospitals *(SIC 8062)*; *(SIC 8069)*
622210 Psychiatric and Substance Abuse Hospitals *(SIC 8063)*; *(SIC 8069)*
622310 Specialty (except Psychiatric and Substance Abuse) Hospitals *(SIC 8069)*
623110 Nursing Care Facilities *(SIC 8051)*; *(SIC 8052)*; *(SIC 8059)*
623210 Residential Mental Retardation Facilities *(SIC 8052)*
623220 Residential Mental Health and Substance Abuse Facilities *(SIC 8361)*
623311 Continuing Care Retirement Communities *(SIC 8059)*; *(SIC 8052)*; *(SIC 8051)*
623312 Homes for the Elderly *(SIC 8361)*
623990 Other Residential Care Facilities *(SIC 8361)*
624110 Child and Youth Services *(SIC 8322)*; *(SIC 8641)*

624120 Services for the Elderly and Persons with Disabilities *(SIC 8322)*
624190 Other Individual and Family Services *(SIC 8322)*
624210 Community Food Services *(SIC 8322)*
624221 Temporary Shelter *(SIC 8322)*
624229 Other Community Housing Services *(SIC 8322)*
624230 Emergency and Other Relief Services *(SIC 8322)*
624310 Vocational Rehabilitation Services *(SIC 8331)*
624410 Child Day Care Services *(SIC 7299)*; *(SIC 8351)*

ARTS, ENTERTAINMENT, & RECREATION

711110 Theater Companies and Dinner Theaters *(SIC 5812)*; *(SIC 7922)*
711120 Dance Companies *(SIC 7922)*
711130 Musical Groups and Artists *(SIC 7929)*
711190 Other Performing Arts Companies *(SIC 7929)*; *(SIC 7999)*
711211 Sports Teams and Clubs *(SIC 7941)*
711212 Race Tracks *(SIC 7948)*
711219 Other Spectator Sports *(SIC 7941)*; *(SIC 7948)*; *(SIC 7999)*
711310 Promoters of Performing Arts, Sports, and Similar Events with Facilities *(SIC 6512)*; *(SIC 7922)*; *(SIC 7941)*
711320 Promoters of Performing Arts, Sports, and Similar Events without Facilities *(SIC 7941)*; *(SIC 7922)*
711410 Agents and Managers for Artists, Athletes, Entertainers , and Other Public Figures *(SIC 7941)*; *(SIC 7922)*; *(SIC 7389)*
711510 Independent Artists, Writers, and Performers *(SIC 7819)*; *(SIC 7929)*; *(SIC 8999)*
712110 Museums *(SIC 8412)*
712120 Historical Sites *(SIC 8412)*
712130 Zoos and Botanical Gardens *(SIC 8422)*
712190 Nature Parks and Other Similar Institutions *(SIC 7999)*; *(SIC 8422)*
713110 Amusement and Theme Parks *(SIC 7996)*
713120 Amusement Arcades *(SIC 7993)*
713210 Casinos (except Casino Hotels) *(SIC 7999)*
713290 Other Gambling Industries *(SIC 7999)*; *(SIC 7993)*
713910 Golf Courses and Country Clubs *(SIC 7992)*; *(SIC 7997)*
713920 Skiing Facilities *(SIC 7999)*
713930 Marinas *(SIC 4493)*
713940 Fitness and Recreational Sports Centers *(SIC 7991)*; *(SIC 7997)*; *(SIC 7999)*
713950 Bowling Centers *(SIC 7933)*
713990 All Other Amusement and Recreation Industries *(SIC 7911)*; *(SIC 7993)*; *(SIC 7997)*; *(SIC 7999)*

ACCOMMODATION & FOODSERVICES

721110 Hotels (except Casino Hotels) and Motels *(SIC 7011)*; *(SIC 7041)*
721120 Casino Hotels *(SIC 7011)*
721191 Bed and Breakfast Inns *(SIC 7011)*
721199 All Other Traveler Accommodations *(SIC 7011)*
721211 RV (Recreational Vehicle) Parks and Campgrounds *(SIC 7033)*
721214 Recreational and Vacation Camps *(SIC 7032)*
721310 Rooming and Boarding Houses *(SIC 7021)*; *(SIC 7041)*
722110 Full-Service Restaurants *(SIC 5812)*
722211 Limited-Service Restaurants *(SIC 5499)*; *(SIC 5812)*
722212 Cafeterias *(SIC 5812)*
722213 Snack and Nonalcoholic Beverage Bars *(SIC 5461)*; *(SIC 5812)*
722310 Foodservice Contractors *(SIC 5812)*
722320 Caterers *(SIC 5812)*
722330 Mobile Caterers *(SIC 5963)*
722410 Drinking Places (Alcoholic Beverages) *(SIC 5813)*

OTHER SERVICES

811111 General Automotive Repair *(SIC 7538)*
811112 Automotive Exhaust System Repair *(SIC 7533)*
811113 Automotive Transmission Repair *(SIC 7537)*
811118 Other Automotive Mechanical and Electrical Repair and Maintenance *(SIC 7539)*
811121 Automotive Body, Paint, and Upholstery Repair and Maintenance *(SIC 7532)*
811122 Automotive Glass Replacement Shops *(SIC 7536)*
811191 Automotive Oil Change and Lubrication Shops *(SIC 7549)*
811192 Car Washes *(SIC 7542)*
811198 All Other Automotive Repair and Maintenance *(SIC 7549)*; *(SIC 7534)*
811211 Consumer Electronics Repair and Maintenance *(SIC 7622)*; *(SIC 7629)*
811212 Computer and Office Machine Repair and Maintenance *(SIC 7699)*; *(SIC 7378)*; *(SIC 7629)*
811213 Communication Equipment Repair and Maintenance *(SIC 7629)*; *(SIC 7622)*
811219 Other Electronic and Precision Equipment Repair and Maintenance *(SIC 7629)*; *(SIC 7699)*
811310 Commercial and Industrial Machinery and Equipment (except Automotive and Electronic) Repair and Maintenance *(SIC 7623)*; *(SIC 7694)*; *(SIC 7699)*
811411 Home and Garden Equipment Repair and Maintenance *(SIC 7699)*
811412 Appliance Repair and Maintenance *(SIC 7699)*; *(SIC 7623)*; *(SIC 7629)*
811420 Reupholstery and Furniture Repair *(SIC 7641)*
811430 Footwear and Leather Goods Repair *(SIC 7251)*; *(SIC 7699)*
811490 Other Personal and Household Goods Repair and Maintenance *(SIC 7219)*; *(SIC 7699)*; *(SIC 3732)*; *(SIC 7692)*; *(SIC 7631)*
812111 Barber Shops *(SIC 7241)*
812112 Beauty Salons *(SIC 7231)*
812113 Nail Salons *(SIC 7231)*
812191 Diet and Weight Reducing Centers *(SIC 7299)*
812199 Other Personal Care Services *(SIC 7299)*
812210 Funeral Homes *(SIC 7261)*
812220 Cemeteries and Crematories *(SIC 6553)*; *(SIC 7261)*; *(SIC 6531)*
812310 Coin-Operated Laundries and Drycleaners *(SIC 7215)*
812320 Drycleaning and Laundry Services (except Coin-Operated) *(SIC 7211)*; *(SIC 7219)*; *(SIC 7212)*; *(SIC 7216)*
812331 Linen Supply *(SIC 7213)*; *(SIC 7219)*
812332 Industrial Launderers *(SIC 7218)*
812910 Pet Care (except Veterinary) Services *(SIC 0752)*
812921 Photo Finishing Laboratories (except One-Hour) *(SIC 7384)*
812922 One-Hour Photo Finishing *(SIC 7384)*
812930 Parking Lots and Garages *(SIC 7521)*
812990 All Other Personal Services *(SIC 7299)*; *(SIC 7389)*
813110 Religious Organizations *(SIC 8661)*
813211 Grantmaking Foundations *(SIC 6732)*
813212 Voluntary Health Organizations *(SIC 8399)*
813219 Other Grantmaking and Giving Services *(SIC 8399)*
813311 Human Rights Organizations *(SIC 8399)*

813312 Environment, Conservation, and Wildlife Organizations *(SIC 8699)*; *(SIC 8399)*
813319 Other Social Advocacy Organizations *(SIC 8399)*
813410 Civic and Social Organizations *(SIC 8641)*; *(SIC 8699)*
813910 Business Associations *(SIC 8611)*; *(SIC 8699)*
813920 Professional Organizations *(SIC 8621)*
813930 Labor Unions and Similar Labor Organizations *(SIC 8631)*
813940 Political Organizations *(SIC 8651)*
813990 Other Similar Organizations *(SIC 6531)*; *(SIC 8641)*; *(SIC 8699)*
814110 Private Households *(SIC 8811)*

Public Administration

921110 Executive Offices *(SIC 9111)*
921120 Legislative Bodies *(SIC 9121)*
921130 Public Finance *(SIC 9311)*
921140 Executive and Legislative Offices, Combined *(SIC 9131)*
921150 American Indian and Alaska Native Tribal Governments *(SIC 8641)*
921190 All Other General Government *(SIC 9199)*
922110 Courts *(SIC 9211)*
922120 Police Protection *(SIC 9221)*
922130 Legal Counsel and Prosecution *(SIC 9222)*
922140 Correctional Institutions *(SIC 9223)*
922150 Parole Offices and Probation Offices *(SIC 8322)*
922160 Fire Protection *(SIC 9224)*
922190 All Other Justice, Public Order, and Safety *(SIC 9229)*
923110 Administration of Education Programs *(SIC 9411)*
923120 Administration of Public Health Programs *(SIC 9431)*
923130 Administration of Social, Human Resource and Income Maintenance Programs *(SIC 9441)*
923140 Administration of Veteran's Affairs *(SIC 9451)*
924110 Air and Water Resource and Solid Waste Management *(SIC 9511)*
924120 Land, Mineral, Wildlife, and Forest Conservation *(SIC 9512)*
925110 Administration of Housing Programs *(SIC 9531)*
925120 Administration of Urban Planning and Community and Rural Development *(SIC 9532)*
926110 Administration of General Economic Programs *(SIC 9611)*
926120 Regulation and Administration of Transportation Programs *(SIC 9621)*
926130 Regulation and Administration of Communications, Electric, Gas, and Other Utilities *(SIC 9631)*
926140 Regulation of Agricultural Marketing and Commodities *(SIC 9641)*
926150 Regulation, Licensing, and Inspection of Miscellaneous Commercial Sectors *(SIC 9651)*
927110 Space Research and Technology *(SIC 9661)*
928110 National Security *(SIC 9711)*
928120 International Affairs *(SIC 9721)*
999990 Unclassified Establishments *(SIC 9999)*

SIC Index

This index lists four-digit U.S. Standard Industrial Classification (SIC) codes in numerical order with the name of the corresponding topics and page numbers in this volume. Not all topics fully match the scope of the associated SIC's.

0001-0999

1000-1499

1500-1699

2000-2999

3000-3999

4000-4999

5000-5999

6000-6999

7000-7999

8000-8999

Geographic Index

This index contains references to regions, continents, countries, and other major geographic divisions cited in the text. Citations for each region are sorted by the entries in which the area is discussed.

F

G

H

J

K

L

M

N

O

P

Q

R

S

T

GEOGRAPHIC INDEX

W

Y

Z

General Index

This index contains references to companies, significant persons, government agencies, legislation, and keywords cited in the text. Citations for main topics are in boldface.

GENERAL INDEX

B

D

E

G

H

J

K

L

N

O

P

Q

R

S

T

U

W

X

Y

Z

Grey House Publishing
Business Directories

he Encyclopedia of Emerging Industries

ıe fifth edition of the Encyclopedia of Emerging Industries details the inception, emergence, and current status of nearly 120 ›urishing U.S. industries and industry segments. These focused essays unearth for users a wealth of relevant, current, factual data eviously accessible only through a diverse variety of sources. This volume provides broad-based, highly-readable, industry formation under such headings as Industry Snapshot, Organization & Structure, Background & Development, Industry Leaders, ırrent Conditions, America and the World, Pioneers, and Research & Technology. Essays in this new edition, arranged alphabetically r easy use, have been completely revised, with updated statistics and the most current information on industry trends and velopments. In addition, there are new essays on some of the most interesting and influential new business fields, including pplication Service Providers, Concierge Services, Entrepreneurial Training, Fuel Cells, Logistics Outsourcing Services, ıarmacogenomics, and Tissue Engineering. Two indexes, General and Industry, provide immediate access to this wealth of formation. Plus, two conversion tables for SIC and NAICS codes, along with Suggested Further Readings, are provided to aid the er. The Encyclopedia of Emerging Industries pinpoints emerging industries while they are still in the spotlight. This important source will be an important acquisition to any business reference collection.

This well-designed source...should become another standard business source, nicely complementing Standard & Poor's Industry Surveys. It contains nore information on each industry than Hoover's Handbook of Emerging Companies, is broader in scope than The Almanac of American Employers 1998-1999, but is less expansive than the Encyclopedia of Careers & Vocational Guidance. Highly recommended for all academic libraries and specialized business collections." –Library Journal

ourth Edition/ 1,400 pages / Hardcover ISBN 978-1-59237-242-3/ $325.00

ncyclopedia of American Industries

he Encyclopedia of American Industries is a major business reference tool that provides detailed, comprehensive information on a ide range of industries in every realm of American business. A two volume set, Volume I provides separate coverage of nearly 500 anufacturing industries, while Volume II presents nearly 600 essays covering the vast array of services and other non-manufacturing dustries in the United States. Combined, these two volumes provide individual essays on every industry recognized by the U.S. tandard Industrial Classification (SIC) system. Both volumes are arranged numerically by SIC code, for easy use. Additionally, each ıtry includes the corresponding NAICS code(s). The Encyclopedia's business coverage includes information on historical events of ›nsequence, as well as current trends and statistics. Essays include an Industry Snapshot, Organization & Structure, Background & evelopment, Current Conditions, Industry Leaders, Workforce, America and the World, Research & Technology along with uggested Further Readings. Both SIC and NAICS code conversion tables and an all-encompassing Subject Index, with cross-ferences, complete the text. With its detailed, comprehensive information on a wide range of industries, this resource will be an nportant tool for both the industry newcomer and the seasoned professional.

"Encyclopedia of American Industries contains detailed, signed essays on virtually every industry in contemporary society. ... Highly recommended for all but the smallest libraries." -American Reference Books Annual

ifth Edition; 3,000 pages / Two Volumes / Hardcover ISBN 978-1-59237-244-7/ $650.00

he Directory of Business Information Resources, 2007

Vith 100% verification, over 1,000 new listings and more than 12,000 updates, this 2007 edition of *The Directory of Business Information esources* is the most up-to-date source for contacts in over 98 business areas – from advertising and agriculture to utilities and holesalers. This carefully researched volume details: the Associations representing each industry; the Newsletters that keep members urrent; the Magazines and Journals - with their "Special Issues" - that are important to the trade, the Conventions that are "must ttends," Databases, Directories and Industry Web Sites that provide access to must-have marketing resources. Includes contact ames, phone & fax numbers, web sites and e-mail addresses. This one-volume resource is a gold mine of information and would be a velcome addition to any reference collection.

"This is a most useful and easy-to-use addition to any researcher's library." –The Information Professionals Institute

,500 pages; Softcover ISBN 1-59237-146-9, $195.00 ◆ Online Database $495.00

Nations of the World, 2007/08 A Political, Economic and Business Handbook

This completely revised edition covers all the nations of the world in an easy-to-use, single volume. Each nation is profiled in a single chapter that includes Key Facts, Political & Economic Issues, a Country Profile and Business Information. In this fast-changing world it is extremely important to make sure that the most up-to-date information is included in your reference collection. This edition is ju the answer. Each of the 200+ country chapters have been carefully reviewed by a political expert to make sure that the text reflects th most current information on Politics, Travel Advisories, Economics and more. You'll find such vital information as a Country Map, Population Characteristics, Inflation, Agricultural Production, Foreign Debt, Political History, Foreign Policy, Regional Insecurity, Economics, Trade & Tourism, Historical Profile, Political Systems, Ethnicity, Languages, Media, Climate, Hotels, Chambers of Commerce, Banking, Travel Information and more. Five Regional Chapters follow the main text and include a Regional Map, an Introductory Article, Key Indicators and Currencies for the Region. As an added bonus, an all-inclusive CD-ROM is available as a companion to the printed text. Noted for its sophisticated, up-to-date and reliable compilation of political, economic and business information, this brand new edition will be an important acquisition to any public, academic or special library reference collection.

"A useful addition to both general reference collections and business collections." –RUS

1,700 pages; Print Version Only Softcover ISBN 1-59237-177-9, $155.00

The Directory of Venture Capital & Private Equity Firms, 2007

This edition has been extensively updated and broadly expanded to offer direct access to over 2,800 Domestic and International Venture Capital Firms, including address, phone & fax numbers, e-mail addresses and web sites for both primary and branch locations. Entries include details on the firm's Mission Statement, Industry Group Preferences, Geographic Preferences, Average and Minimum Investments and Investment Criteria. You'll also find details that are available nowhere else, including the Firm's Portfolio Companie and extensive information on each of the firm's Managing Partners, such as Education, Professional Background and Directorships held, along with the Partner's E-mail Address. *The Directory of Venture Capital & Private Equity Firms* offers five important indexes: Geographic Index, Executive Name Index, Portfolio Company Index, Industry Preference Index and College & University Index. With its comprehensive coverage and detailed, extensive information on each company, *The Directory of Venture Capital & Private Equi Firms* is an important addition to any finance collection.

"The sheer number of listings, the descriptive information provided and the outstanding indexing make this directory a better value than its princip competitor, Pratt's Guide to Venture Capital Sources. Recommended for business collections in large public, academic and business libraries." –Cho

1,300 pages; Softcover ISBN 1-59237-176-0, $565.00/$450.00 Library ◆ Online Database (includes a free copy of the directory) $889.C

The Directory of Mail Order Catalogs, 2007

Published since 1981, the *Directory of Mail Order Catalogs* is the premier source of information on the mail order catalog industry. It is the source that business professionals and librarians have come to rely on for the thousands of catalog companies in the US. New for 2007, The Directory of Mail Order Catalogs has been combined with its companion volume, *The Directory of Business to Business Catalog* to offer all 13,000 catalog companies in one easy-to-use volume. Section I: Consumer Catalogs, covers over 9,000 consumer catalog companies in 44 different product chapters from Animals to Toys & Games. Section II: Business to Business Catalogs, details 5,000 business catalogs, everything from computers to laboratory supplies, building construction and much more. Listings contain detailed contact information including mailing address, phone & fax numbers, web sites, e-mail addresses and key contacts along with importan business details such as product descriptions, employee size, years in business, sales volume, catalog size, number of catalogs mailed an more. Three indexes are included for easy access to information: Catalog & Company Name Index, Geographic Index and Product Index. *The Directory of Mail Order Catalogs*, now with its expanded business to business catalogs, is the largest and most comprehensiv resource covering this billion-dollar industry. It is the standard in its field. This important resource is a useful tool for entrepreneurs searching for catalogs to pick up their product, vendors looking to expand their customer base in the catalog industry, market researchers, small businesses investigating new supply vendors, along with the library patron who is exploring the available catalogs i their areas of interest.

"This is a godsend for those looking for information." –Reference Book Revie

1,700 pages; Softcover ISBN 1-59237-156-6 $350.00/$250.00 Library ◆ Online Database (includes a free copy of the directory) $495.0

ports Market Place Directory, 2007

r over 20 years, this comprehensive, up-to-date directory has offered direct access to the Who, What, When & Where of the Sports dustry. With over 20,000 updates and enhancements, the *Sports Market Place Directory* is the most detailed, comprehensive and rrent sports business reference source available. In 1,800 information-packed pages, *Sports Market Place Directory* profiles contact formation and key executives for: Single Sport Organizations, Professional Leagues, Multi-Sport Organizations, Disabled Sports, gh School & Youth Sports, Military Sports, Olympic Organizations, Media, Sponsors, Sponsorship & Marketing Event Agencies, ent & Meeting Calendars, Professional Services, College Sports, Manufacturers & Retailers, Facilities and much more. *The Sports arket Place Directory* provides organization's contact information with detailed descriptions including: Key Contacts, physical, mailing, ail and web addresses plus phone and fax numbers. Plus, nine important indexes make sure that you can find the information you're oking for quickly and easily: Entry Index, Single Sport Index, Media Index, Sponsor Index, Agency Index, Manufacturers Index, and Name Index, Facilities Index and Executive/Geographic Index. For over twenty years, *The Sports Market Place Directory* has sisted thousands of individuals in their pursuit of a career in the sports industry. Why not use "THE SOURCE" that top recruiters, adhunters and career placement centers use to find information on or about sports organizations and key hiring contacts.

300 pages; Softcover ISBN 1-59237-189-2, $225.00 ◆ Online Database $479.00

ood and Beverage Market Place, 2007

od and Beverage Market Place is bigger and better than ever with thousands of new companies, thousands of updates to existing mpanies and two revised and enhanced product category indexes. This comprehensive directory profiles over 18,000 Food & verage Manufacturers, 12,000 Equipment & Supply Companies, 2,200 Transportation & Warehouse Companies, 2,000 Brokers & holesalers, 8,000 Importers & Exporters, 900 Industry Resources and hundreds of Mail Order Catalogs. Listings include detailed ntact Information, Sales Volumes, Key Contacts, Brand & Product Information, Packaging Details and much more. *Thomas Food and verage Market Place* is available as a three-volume printed set, a subscription-based Online Database via the Internet, on CD-ROM, as ell as mailing lists and a licensable database.

"An essential purchase for those in the food industry but will also be useful in public libraries where needed. Much of the information will be difficult and time consuming to locate without this handy three-volume ready-reference source." –ARBA

500 pages, 3 Volume Set; Softcover ISBN 1-59237-152-3, $595.00 ◆ Online Database $795.00 ◆ Online Database & 3 Volume Set ombo, $995.00

he Grey House Homeland Security Directory, 2007

his updated edition features the latest contact information for government and private organizations involved with Homeland curity along with the latest product information and provides detailed profiles of nearly 1,000 Federal & State Organizations & gencies and over 3,000 Officials and Key Executives involved with Homeland Security. These listings are incredibly detailed and clude Mailing Address, Phone & Fax Numbers, Email Addresses & Web Sites, a complete Description of the Agency and a complete st of the Officials and Key Executives associated with the Agency. Next, *The Grey House Homeland Security Directory* provides the go-to urce for Homeland Security Products & Services. This section features over 2,000 Companies that provide Consulting, Products or rvices. With this Buyer's Guide at their fingertips, users can locate suppliers of everything from Training Materials to Access ontrols, from Perimeter Security to BioTerrorism Countermeasures and everything in between – complete with contact information nd product descriptions. A handy Product Locator Index is provided to quickly and easily locate suppliers of a particular product. astly, an Information Resources Section provides immediate access to contact information for hundreds of Associations, Newsletters, agazines, Trade Shows, Databases and Directories that focus on Homeland Security. This comprehensive, information-packed source will be a welcome tool for any company or agency that is in need of Homeland Security information and will be a necessary quisition for the reference collection of all public libraries and large school districts.

"Compiles this information in one place and is discerning in content. A useful purchase for public and academic libraries." –Booklist

00 pages; Softcover ISBN 1-59237-151-5, $195.00 ◆ Online Database (includes a free copy of the directory) $385.00

he Grey House Transportation Security Directory & Handbook

his brand new title is the only reference of its kind that brings together current data on Transportation Security. With information n everything from Regulatory Authorities to Security Equipment, this top-flight database brings together the relevant information ecessary for creating and maintaining a security plan for a wide range of transportation facilities. With this current, comprehensive irectory at the ready you'll have immediate access to: Regulatory Authorities & Legislation; Information Resources; Sample Security lans & Checklists; Contact Data for Major Airports, Seaports, Railroads, Trucking Companies and Oil Pipelines; Security Service roviders; Recommended Equipment & Product Information and more. Using the *Grey House Transportation Security Directory & Handbook*, managers will be able to quickly and easily assess their current security plans; develop contacts to create and maintain new ecurity procedures; and source the products and services necessary to adequately maintain a secure environment. This valuable esource is a must for all Security Managers at Airports, Seaports, Railroads, Trucking Companies and Oil Pipelines.

00 pages; Softcover ISBN 1-59237-075-6, $195

The Grey House Safety & Security Directory, 2007

The Grey House Safety & Security Directory is the most comprehensive reference tool and buyer's guide for the safety and security industry. Arranged by safety topic, each chapter begins with OSHA regulations for the topic, followed by Training Articles written b top professionals in the field and Self-Inspection Checklists. Next, each topic contains Buyer's Guide sections that feature related products and services. Topics include Administration, Insurance, Loss Control & Consulting, Protective Equipment & Apparel, Noise Vibration, Facilities Monitoring & Maintenance, Employee Health Maintenance & Ergonomics, Retail Food Services, Machine Guard Process Guidelines & Tool Handling, Ordinary Materials Handling, Hazardous Materials Handling, Workplace Preparation & Maintenance, Electrical Lighting & Safety, Fire & Rescue and Security. The Buyer's Guide sections are carefully indexed within each topic area to ensure that you can find the supplies needed to meet OSHA's regulations. Six important indexes make finding informati and product manufacturers quick and easy: Geographical Index of Manufacturers and Distributors, Company Profile Index, Brand Name Index, Product Index, Index of Web Sites and Index of Advertisers. This comprehensive, up-to-date reference will provide every tool necessary to make sure a business is in compliance with OSHA regulations and locate the products and services needed to meet those regulations.

"Presents industrial safety information for engineers, plant managers, risk managers, and construction site supervisors..." –Cho

1,500 pages, 2 Volume Set; Softcover ISBN 1-59237-160-4, $225.00

The Grey House Biometric Information Directory

The Biometric Information Directory is the only comprehensive source for current biometric industry information. This 2006 edition is t first published by Grey House. With 100% updated information, this latest edition offers a complete, current look, in both print and online form, of biometric companies and products – one of the fastest growing industries in today's economy. Detailed profiles of manufacturers of the latest biometric technology, including Finger, Voice, Face, Hand, Signature, Iris, Vein and Palm Identification systems. Data on the companies include key executives, company size and a detailed, indexed description of their product line. Plus, the Directory also includes valuable business resources, and current editorial make this edition the easiest way for the business community and consumers alike to access the largest, most current compilation of biometric industry information available on the market today. The new edition boasts increased numbers of companies, contact names and company data, with over 700 manufacturer and service providers. Information in the directory includes: Editorial on Advancements in Biometrics; Profiles of 700+ companies listed with contact information; Organizations, Trade & Educational Associations, Publications, Conferences, Trade Shows and Expositions Worldwide; Web Site Index; Biometric & Vendors Services Index by Types of Biometrics; and a Glossary of Biometric Terms. This resource will be an important source for anyone who is considering the use of a biometric product, investing in the development of biometric technology, support existing marketing and sales efforts and will be an important acquisition for the busines reference collection for large public and business libraries.

800 pages; Softcover ISBN 1-59237-121-3, $225

The Grey House Performing Arts Directory, 2007

The Grey House Performing Arts Directory is the most comprehensive resource covering the Performing Arts. This important directory provides current information on over 8,500 Dance Companies, Instrumental Music Programs, Opera Companies, Choral Groups, Theater Companies, Performing Arts Series and Performing Arts Facilities. Plus, this edition now contains a brand new section on Artist Management Groups. In addition to mailing address, phone & fax numbers, e-mail addresses and web sites, dozens of other fields of available information include mission statement, key contacts, facilities, seating capacity, season, attendance and more. This directory also provides an important Information Resources section that covers hundreds of Performing Arts Associations, Magazines Newsletters, Trade Shows, Directories, Databases and Industry Web Sites. Five indexes provide immediate access to this wealth of information: Entry Name, Executive Name, Performance Facilities, Geographic and Information Resources. *The Grey House Performin Arts Directory* pulls together thousands of Performing Arts Organizations, Facilities and Information Resources into an easy-to-use source – this kind of comprehensiveness and extensive detail is not available in any resource on the market place today.

"Immensely useful and user-friendly ... recommended for public, academic and certain special library reference collections." –Bookl

1,500 pages; Softcover ISBN 1-59237-138-8, $185.00 ◆ Online Database $335.00

he Rauch Guide to the US Adhesives & Sealants, Cosmetics & Toiletries, Ink, Paint, lastics, Pulp & Paper and Rubber Industries

he Rauch Guides are known worldwide for their comprehensive marketing information. Acquired by Grey House Publishing in 2005, w updated and revised editions will be published throughout 2005 and 2006. Each Guide provides market facts and figures in a ghly organized format, ideal for today's busy personnel, serving as ready-references for top executives as well as the industry wcomer. *The Rauch Guides* save time and money by organizing widely scattered information and providing estimates for important isiness decisions, some of which are available nowhere else. Each Guide is organized into several information-packed chapters. fter a brief introduction, the ECONOMICS section provides data on industry shipments; long-term growth and forecasts; prices; mpany performance; employment, expenditures, and productivity; transportation and geographical patterns; packaging; foreign trade; d government regulations. Next, TECHNOLOGY & RAW MATERIALS provide market, technical, and raw material information r chemicals, equipment and related materials, including market size and leading suppliers, prices, end uses, and trends. PRODUCTS MARKETS provide information for each major industry product, including market size and historical trends, leading suppliers, five-ar forecasts, industry structure, and major end uses. For easy access, each *Guide* contains a chapter on INDUSTRY ACTIVITIES, RGANIZATIONS & SOURCES OF INFORMATION with detailed information on meetings, exhibits, and trade shows, sources of atistical information, trade associations, technical and professional societies, and trade and technical periodicals. Next, the OMPANY DIRECTORY profiles major industry companies, both public and private. Generally several hundred companies are alyzed. Information includes complete contact information, web address, estimated total and domestic sales, product description, and cent mergers and acquisitions. Each Guide also contains several APPENDICES that provide a cross-reference of suppliers, bsidiaries and divisions. The Rauch Guides will prove to be an invaluable source of market information, company data, trends and recasts that anyone in these fast-paced industries.

he Rauch Guide to the U.S. Paint Industry Softcover ISBN 1-59237-127-2 $595 ♦ The Rauch Guide to the U.S. Plastics Industry oftcover ISBN 1-59237-128-0 $595 ♦ The Rauch Guide to the U.S. Adhesives and Sealants Industry Softcover ISBN 1-59237-129-9 595 ♦ The Rauch Guide to the U.S. Ink Industry Softcover ISBN 1-59237-126-4 $595 ♦ The Rauch Guide to the U.S. Rubber Industry oftcover ISBN 1-59237-130-2 $595 ♦ The Rauch Guide to the U.S. Pulp and Paper Industry Softcover ISBN 1-59237-131-0 $595 ♦ he Rauch Guide to the U.S. Cosmetic and Toiletries Industry Softcover ISBN 1-59237-132-9 $895

ew York State Directory, 2007/08

he New York State Directory, published annually since 1983, is a comprehensive and easy-to-use guide to accessing public officials and rivate sector organizations and individuals who influence public policy in the state of New York. *The New York State Directory* includes nportant information on all New York state legislators and congressional representatives, including biographies and key committee ssignments. It also includes staff rosters for all branches of New York state government and for federal agencies and departments that npact the state policy process. Following the state government section are 25 chapters covering policy areas from agriculture through eterans' affairs. Each chapter identifies the state, local and federal agencies and officials that formulate or implement policy. In ddition, each chapter contains a roster of private sector experts and advocates who influence the policy process. The directory also ffers appendices that include statewide party officials; chambers of commerce; lobbying organizations; public and private universities nd colleges; television, radio and print media; and local government agencies and officials.

ew York State Directory - 800 pages; Softcover ISBN 1-59237-190-6; $145.00
ew York State Directory with Profiles of New York – 2 volumes; 1,600 pages; Softcover ISBN 1-59237-191-4; $225

Profiles of New York ♦ Profiles of Florida ♦ Profiles of Texas ♦ Profiles of Illinois ♦ Profiles of Michigan ♦ Profiles of Ohio ♦ Profiles of New Jersey ♦ Profiles of Massachusetts ♦ Profiles of Pennsylvania ♦ Profiles of Wisconsin ♦ Profiles of Connecticut ♦ Profiles of Indiana ♦ Profiles of North Carolina ♦ Profiles of Virginia ♦ Profiles of California

Packed with over 50 pieces of data that make up a complete, user-friendly profile of each state, these directories go even further by the pulling selected data and providing it in ranking list form for even easier comparisons between the 100 largest towns and cities! The careful layout gives the user an easy-to-read snapshot of every single place and county in the state, from the biggest metropolis to the smallest unincorporated hamlet. The richness of each place or county profile is astounding in its depth, from history to weather, all packed in an easy-to-navigate, compact format. No need for piles of multiple sources with this volume on your desk. Here is a look at just a few of the data sets you'll find in each profile: History, Geography, Climate, Population, Vital Statistics, Economy, Income, Taxe Education, Housing, Health & Environment, Public Safety, Newspapers, Transportation, Presidential Election Results, Information Contacts and Chambers of Commerce. As an added bonus, there is a section on Selected Statistics, where data from the 100 largest towns and cities is arranged into easy-to-use charts. Each of 22 different data points has its own two-page spread with the cities listed in alpha order so researchers can easily compare and rank cities. A remarkable compilation that offers overviews and insights into each corner of the state, *Profiles of New York*, *Profiles of Florida* and *Profiles of Texas* go beyond Census statistics, beyond metro area coverage, beyond the 100 best places to live. Drawn from official census information, other government statistics and original research you will have at your fingertips data that's available nowhere else in one single source. Data will be published on additional states in 2006 and 2007.

Each Profiles of… title ranges from 400-800 pages, priced at $149.00 each

Research Services Directory: Commercial & Corporate Research Centers

This Ninth Edition provides access to well over 8,000 independent Commercial Research Firms, Corporate Research Centers and Laboratories offering contract services for hands-on, basic or applied research. *Research Services Directory* covers the thousands of types of research companies, including Biotechnology & Pharmaceutical Developers, Consumer Product Research, Defense Contractors, Electronics & Software Engineers, Think Tanks, Forensic Investigators, Independent Commercial Laboratories, Information Brokers, Market & Survey Research Companies, Medical Diagnostic Facilities, Product Research & Development Firms and more. Each entry provides the company's name, mailing address, phone & fax numbers, key contacts, web site, e-mail address, as well as a company description and research and technical fields served. Four indexes provide immediate access to this wealth of information: Research Firms Index, Geographic Index, Personnel Name Index and Subject Index.

"An important source for organizations in need of information about laboratories, individuals and other facilities." –ARI

1,400 pages; Softcover ISBN 1-59237-003-9, $395.00 ♦ Online Database (includes a free copy of the directory) $850.00

International Business and Trade Directories

Completely updated, the Third Edition of *International Business and Trade Directories* now contains more than 10,000 entries, over 2,00 more than the last edition, making this directory the most comprehensive resource of the worlds business and trade directories. Entrie include content descriptions, price, publisher's name and address, web site and e-mail addresses, phone and fax numbers and editorial staff. Organized by industry group, and then by region, this resource puts over 10,000 industry-specific business and trade directories at the reader's fingertips. Three indexes are included for quick access to information: Geographic Index, Publisher Index and Title Index. Public, college and corporate libraries, as well as individuals and corporations seeking critical market information will want to add this directory to their marketing collection.

"Reasonably priced for a work of this type, this directory should appeal to larger academi public and corporate libraries with an international focus." –Library Journ

1,800 pages; Softcover ISBN 1-930956-63-0, $225.00 ♦ Online Database (includes a free copy of the directory) $450.00

To preview any of our Directories Risk-Free for 30 days, call (800) 562-2139 or fax to (518) 789-0556

Grey House Publishing Canada
Canadian Information Resources

anadian Almanac & Directory, 2007

he Canadian Almanac & Directory contains ten directories in one – giving you all the facts and figures you will ever need about anada. No other single source provides users with the quality and depth of up-to-date information for all types of research. This tional directory and guide gives you access to statistics, images and over 45,000 names and addresses for everything from Airlines to oos - updated every year. It's Ten Directories in One! Each section is a directory in itself, providing robust information on business d finance, communications, government, associations, arts and culture (museums, zoos, libraries, etc.), health, transportation, law, ucation, and more. Government information includes federal, provincial and territorial - and includes an easy-to-use quick index to d key information. A separate municipal government section includes every municipality in Canada, with full profiles of Canada's rgest urban centers. A complete legal directory lists judges and judicial officials, court locations and law firms across the country. A ealth of general information, the Canadian Almanac & Directory also includes national statistics on population, employment, imports d exports, and more. National awards and honors are presented, along with forms of address, Commonwealth information and full lor photos of Canadian symbols. Postal information, weights, measures, distances and other useful charts are also incorporated. omplete almanac information includes perpetual calendars, five-year holiday planners and astronomical information. Published ntinuously for 160 years, The Canadian Almanac & Directory is the best single reference source for business executives, managers d assistants; government and public affairs executives; lawyers; marketing, sales and advertising executives; researchers, editors and urnalists.

ardcover ISBN 978-1-89502-149-3; 1,600 pages; $315.00

ssociations Canada, 2007

he Most Powerful Fact-Finder to Business, Trade, Professional and Consumer Organizations

ssociations Canada covers Canadian organizations and international groups including industry, commercial and professional sociations, registered charities, special interest and common interest organizations. This annually revised compendium provides etailed listings and abstracts for nearly 20,000 regional, national and international organizations. This popular volume provides the ost comprehensive picture of Canada's non-profit sector. Detailed listings enable users to identify an organization's budget, founding ate, scope of activity, licensing body, sources of funding, executive information, full address and complete contact information, just to ame a few. Powerful indexes help researchers find information quickly and easily. The following indexes are included: subject, cronym, geographic, budget, executive name, conferences & conventions, mailing list, defunct and unreachable associations and gistered charitable organizations. In addition to annual spending of over $1 billion on transportation and conventions alone, Canadian ssociations account for many millions more in pursuit of membership interests. Associations Canada provides complete access to this ghly lucrative market. Associations Canada is a strong source of prospects for sales and marketing executives, tourism and onvention officials, researchers, government officials - anyone who wants to locate non-profit interest groups and trade associations.

ardcover ISBN 978-1-59237-219-5; 1,600 pages; $315.00

inancial Services Canada, 2007/08

inancial Services Canada is the only master file of current contacts and information that serves the needs of the entire financial ervices industry in Canada. With over 18,000 organizations and hard-to-find business information, Financial Services Canada is the ost up-to-date source for names and contact numbers of industry professionals, senior executives, portfolio managers, financial dvisors, agency bureaucrats and elected representatives. Financial Services Canada incorporates the latest changes in the industry to rovide you with the most current details on each company, including: name, title, organization, telephone and fax numbers, e-mail and eb addresses. Financial Services Canada also includes private company listings never before compiled, government agencies, ssociation and consultant services - to ensure that you'll never miss a client or a contact. Current listings include: banks and branches, on-depository institutions, stock exchanges and brokers, investment management firms, insurance companies, major accounting and w firms, government agencies and financial associations. Powerful indexes assist researchers with locating the vital financial nformation they need. The following indexes are included: alphabetic, geographic, executive name, corporate web site/e-mail, overnment quick reference and subject. Financial Services Canada is a valuable resource for financial executives, bankers, financial lanners, sales and marketing professionals, lawyers and chartered accountants, government officials, investment dealers, journalists, brarians and reference specialists.

00 pages; Hardcover ISBN 978-1-59237-221-8 $315.00

To preview any of our Directories Risk-Free for 30 days, call (800) 562-2139 or fax to (518) 789-0556

Directory of Libraries in Canada, 2007/08

The Directory of Libraries in Canada brings together almost 7,000 listings including libraries and their branches, information resourc centers, archives and library associations and learning centers. The directory offers complete and comprehensive information on Canadian libraries, resource centers, business information centers, professional associations, regional library systems, archives, library schools and library technical programs. The Directory of Libraries in Canada includes important features of each library and service, including library information; personnel details, including contact names and e-mail addresses; collection information; services availab to users; acquisitions budgets; and computers and automated systems. Useful information on each library's electronic access is also included, such as Internet browser, connectivity and public Internet/CD-ROM/subscription database access. The directory also provides powerful indexes for subject, location, personal name and Web site/e-mail to assist researchers with locating the crucial information they need. The Directory of Libraries in Canada is a vital reference tool for publishers, advocacy groups, students, researc institutions, computer hardware suppliers, and other diverse groups that provide products and services to this unique market.

850 pages; Hardcover ISBN 978-1-59237-222-5; $315.00

Canadian Environmental Directory, 2007/08

The Canadian Environmental Directory is Canada's most complete and only national listing of environmental associations and organizations, government regulators and purchasing groups, product and service companies, special libraries, and more! The extensiv Products and Services section provides detailed listings enabling users to identify the company name, address, phone, fax, e-mail, Web address, firm type, contact names (and titles), product and service information, affiliations, trade information, branch and affiliate data. The Government section gives you all the contact information you need at every government level – federal, provincial and municipal. We also include descriptions of current environmental initiatives, programs and agreements, names of environment-related acts administered by each ministry or department PLUS information and tips on who to contact and how to sell to governments in Canada The Associations section provides complete contact information and a brief description of activities. Included are Canadian environmental organizations and international groups including industry, commercial and professional associations, registered charities, special interest and common interest organizations. All the Information you need about the Canadian environmental industry directory of products and services, special libraries and resource, conferences, seminars and tradeshows, chronology of environmental events, law firms and major Canadian companies, The Canadian Environmental Directory is ideal for business, government, engineers and anyone conducting research on the environment.

Hardcover ISBN 978-1-59237-218-8; 900 pages; $315.00

Grey House Publishing
General Reference Titles

ıe Value of a Dollar 1600-1859, The Colonial Era to The Civil War

llowing the format of the widely acclaimed, T*he Value of a Dollar, 1860-2004, The Value of a Dollar 1600-1859, The Colonial Era to The vil War* records the actual prices of thousands of items that consumers purchased from the Colonial Era to the Civil War. Our itorial department had been flooded with requests from users of our Value of a Dollar for the same type of information, just from an rlier time period. This new volume is just the answer – with pricing data from 1600 to 1859. Arranged into five-year chapters, each year chapter includes a Historical Snapshot, Consumer Expenditures, Investments, Selected Income, Income/Standard Jobs, Food sket, Standard Prices and Miscellany. There is also a section on Trends. This informative section charts the change in price over ne and provides added detail on the reasons prices changed within the time period, including industry developments, changes in nsumer attitudes and important historical facts. This fascinating survey will serve a wide range of research needs and will be useful in high school, public and academic library reference collections.

0 pages; Hardcover ISBN 1-59237-094-2, $135.00

he Value of a Dollar 1860-2004, Third Edition

guide to practical economy, *The Value of a Dollar* records the actual prices of thousands of items that consumers purchased from the vil War to the present, along with facts about investment options and income opportunities. This brand new Third Edition boasts a and new addition to each five-year chapter, a section on Trends. This informative section charts the change in price over time and ovides added detail on the reasons prices changed within the time period, including industry developments, changes in consumer titudes and important historical facts. Plus, a brand new chapter for 2000-2004 has been added. Each 5-year chapter includes a storical Snapshot, Consumer Expenditures, Investments, Selected Income, Income/Standard Jobs, Food Basket, Standard Prices and iscellany. This interesting and useful publication will be widely used in any reference collection.

"Recommended for high school, college and public libraries." –ARBA

0 pages; Hardcover ISBN 1-59237-074-8, $135.00

Vorking Americans 1880-1999
olume I: The Working Class, Volume II: The Middle Class, Volume III: The Upper Class

ıch of the volumes in the *Working Americans 1880-1999* series focuses on a particular class of Americans, The Working Class, The iddle Class and The Upper Class over the last 120 years. Chapters in each volume focus on one decade and profile three to five milies. Family Profiles include real data on Income & Job Descriptions, Selected Prices of the Times, Annual Income, Annual ıdgets, Family Finances, Life at Work, Life at Home, Life in the Community, Working Conditions, Cost of Living, Amusements and uch more. Each chapter also contains an Economic Profile with Average Wages of other Professions, a selection of Typical Pricing, ey Events & Inventions, News Profiles, Articles from Local Media and Illustrations. The *Working Americans* series captures the estyles of each of the classes from the last twelve decades, covers a vast array of occupations and ethnic backgrounds and travels the ıtire nation. These interesting and useful compilations of portraits of the American Working, Middle and Upper Classes during the st 120 years will be an important addition to any high school, public or academic library reference collection.

"These interesting, unique compilations of economic and social facts, figures and graphs will support multiple research needs. They will engage and enlighten patrons in high school, public and academic library collections." –Booklist

olume I: The Working Class ◆ 558 pages; Hardcover ISBN 1-891482-81-5, $145.00 ◆ Volume II: The Middle Class ◆ 591 pages; ardcover ISBN 1-891482-72-6; $145.00 ◆ Volume III: The Upper Class ◆ 567 pages; Hardcover ISBN 1-930956-38-X, $145.00

Vorking Americans 1880-1999 Volume IV: Their Children

his Fourth Volume in the highly successful *Working Americans 1880-1999* series focuses on American children, decade by decade from 380 to 1999. This interesting and useful volume introduces the reader to three children in each decade, one from each of the Working, Iiddle and Upper classes. Like the first three volumes in the series, the individual profiles are created from interviews, diaries, atistical studies, biographies and news reports. Profiles cover a broad range of ethnic backgrounds, geographic area and lifestyles – verything from an orphan in Memphis in 1882, following the Yellow Fever epidemic of 1878 to an eleven-year-old nephew of a beer aron and owner of the New York Yankees in New York City in 1921. Chapters also contain important supplementary materials ıcluding News Features as well as information on everything from Schools to Parks, Infectious Diseases to Childhood Fears along ith Entertainment, Family Life and much more to provide an informative overview of the lifestyles of children from each decade. 'his interesting account of what life was like for Children in the Working, Middle and Upper Classes will be a welcome addition to the eference collection of any high school, public or academic library.

00 pages; Hardcover ISBN 1-930956-35-5, $145.00

Working Americans 1880-2003 Volume V: Americans At War

Working Americans 1880-2003 Volume V: Americans At War is divided into 11 chapters, each covering a decade from 1880-2003 and examines the lives of Americans during the time of war, including declared conflicts, one-time military actions, protests, and preparations for war. Each decade includes several personal profiles, whether on the battlefield or on the homefront, that tell the stor of civilians, soldiers, and officers during the decade. The profiles examine: Life at Home; Life at Work; and Life in the Community. Each decade also includes an Economic Profile with statistical comparisons, a Historical Snapshot, News Profiles, local News Articles and Illustrations that provide a solid historical background to the decade being examined. Profiles range widely not only geographically, but also emotionally, from that of a girl whose leg was torn off in a blast during WWI, to the boredom of being stationed in the Dakotas as the Indian Wars were drawing to a close. As in previous volumes of the *Working Americans* series, information is presented in narrative form, but hard facts and real-life situations back up each story. The basis of the profiles come fr diaries, private print books, personal interviews, family histories, estate documents and magazine articles. For easy reference, *Workin Americans 1880-2003 Volume V: Americans At War* includes an in-depth Subject Index. The *Working Americans* series has become an important reference for public libraries, academic libraries and high school libraries. This fifth volume will be a welcome addition to a of these types of reference collections.

600 pages; Hardcover ISBN 1-59237-024-1; $145.00
Five Volume Set (Volumes I-V), Hardcover ISBN 1-59237-034-9, $675.00

Working Americans 1880-2005 Volume VI: Women at Work

Unlike any other volume in the *Working Americans* series, this Sixth Volume, is the first to focus on a particular gender of Americans. *Volume VI: Women at Work*, traces what life was like for working women from the 1860's to the present time. Beginning with the life of a maid in 1890 and a store clerk in 1900 and ending with the life and times of the modern working women, this text captures the struggle, strengths and changing perception of the American woman at work. Each chapter focuses on one decade and profiles three to five women with real data on Income & Job Descriptions, Selected Prices of the Times, Annual Income, Annual Budgets, Family Finances, Life at Work, Life at Home, Life in the Community, Working Conditions, Cost of Living, Amusements and much more. For even broader access to the events, economics and attitude towards women throughout the past 130 years, each chapter is supplemented with News Profiles, Articles from Local Media, Illustrations, Economic Profiles, Typical Pricing, Key Events, Inventions and more. This important volume illustrates what life was like for working women over time and allows the reader to develop an understanding of the changing role of women at work. These interesting and useful compilations of portraits of women at work will be an important addition to any high schoo public or academic library reference collection.

600 pages; Hardcover ISBN 1-59237-063-2; $145.00

Working Americans 1880-2005 Volume VII: Social Movements

The newest addition to the widely-successful *Working Americans* series, *Volume VII: Social Movements* explores how Americans sought and fought for change from the 1880s to the present time. Following the format of previous volumes in the Working Americans series, the te examines the lives of 34 individuals who have worked – often behind the scenes — to bring about change. Issues include topics as diverse as the Anti-smoking movement of 1901 to efforts by Native Americans to reassert their long lost rights. Along the way, the book will profile individuals brave enough to demand suffrage for Kansas women in 1912 or demand an end to lynching during a March on Washington in 1923. Each profile is enriched with real data on Income & Job Descriptions, Selected Prices of the Times, Annual Incomes & Budgets, Life at Work, Life at Home, Life in the Community, along with News Features, Key Events, and Illustrations. The depth of information contained in each profile allow the user to explore the private, financial and public lives of these subjects, deepening our understanding of how calls for change took place in our society. A must-purchase for the reference collections of high school libraries, public libraries and academic libraries.

600 pages; Hardcover ISBN 1-59237-101-9; $145.00
Seven Volume Set (Volumes I-VII), Hardcover ISBN 1-59237-133-7, $945.00

The Encyclopedia of Warrior Peoples & Fighting Groups

Many military groups throughout the world have excelled in their craft either by fortuitous circumstances, outstanding leadership, or intense training. This new second edition of The Encyclopedia of Warrior Peoples and Fighting Groups explores the origins and leadership of these outstanding combat forces, chronicles their conquests and accomplishments, examines the circumstances surrounding their decline or disbanding, and assesses their influence on the groups and methods of warfare that followed. This edition has been completely updated with information through 2005 and contains over 20 new entries. Readers will encounter ferocious tribes charismatic leaders, and daring militias, from ancient times to the present, including Amazons, Buffalo Soldiers, Green Berets, Iron Brigade, Kamikazes, Peoples of the Sea, Polish Winged Hussars, Sacred Band of Thebes, Teutonic Knights, and Texas Rangers. With over 100 alphabetical entries, numerous cross-references and illustrations, a comprehensive bibliography, and index, the Encyclopedia of Warrior Peoples and Fighting Groups is a valuable resource for readers seeking insight into the bold history of distinguished fighting forces.

"This work is especially useful for high school students, undergraduates, and gener readers with an interest in military history." –Library Journ

Pub. Date: May 2006; Hardcover ISBN 1-59237-116-7; $135.00

To preview any of our Directories Risk-Free for 30 days, call (800) 562-2139 or fax to (518) 789-0556

e Encyclopedia of Invasions & Conquests, From the Ancient Times to the Present

ıroughout history, invasions and conquests have played a remarkable role in shaping our world and defining our boundaries, both ysically and culturally. This second edition of the popular Encyclopedia of Invasions & Conquests, a comprehensive guide to over 0 invasions, conquests, battles and occupations from ancient times to the present, takes readers on a journey that includes the Roman nquest of Britain, the Portuguese colonization of Brazil, and the Iraqi invasion of Kuwait, to name a few. New articles will explore e late 20th and 21st centuries, with a specific focus on recent conflicts in Afghanistan, Kuwait, Iraq, Yugoslavia, Grenada and ıechnya. Categories of entries include countries, invasions and conquests, and individuals. In addition to covering the military pects of invasions and conquests, entries cover some of the political, economic, and cultural aspects, for example, the effects of a nquest on the invade country's political and monetary system and in its language and religion. The entries on leaders – among them rgon, Alexander the Great, William the Conqueror, and Adolf Hitler – deal with the people who sought to gain control, expand wer, or exert religious or political influence over others through military means. Revised and updated for this second edition, entries e arranged alphabetically within historical periods. Each chapter provides a map to help readers locate key areas and geographical ıtures, and bibliographical references appear at the end of each entry. Other useful features include cross-references, a cumulative bliography and a comprehensive subject index. This authoritative, well-organized, lucidly written volume will prove invaluable for a riety of readers, including high school students, military historians, members of the armed forces, history buffs and hobbyists.

"Engaging writing, sensible organization, nice illustrations, interesting and obscure facts, and useful maps make this book a pleasure to read." –ARBA

ıb. Date: March 2006; Hardcover ISBN 1-59237-114-0; $135.00

ncyclopedia of Prisoners of War & Internment

his authoritative second edition provides a valuable overview of the history of prisoners of war and interned civilians, from earliest nes to the present. Written by an international team of experts in the field of POW studies, this fascinating and thought-provoking ılume includes entries on a wide range of subjects including the Crusades, Plains Indian Warfare, concentration camps, the two world ars, and famous POWs throughout history, as well as atrocities, escapes, and much more. Written in a clear and easily ıderstandable style, this informative reference details over 350 entries, 30% larger than the first edition, that survey the history of isoners of war and interned civilians from the earliest times to the present, with emphasis on the 19th and 20th centuries. Medical nditions, international law, exchanges of prisoners, organizations working on behalf of POWs, and trials associated with the eatment of captives are just some of the themes explored. Entries range from the Ardeatine Caves Massacre to Kurt Vonnegut. ntries are arranged alphabetically, plus illustrations and maps are provided for easy reference. The text also includes an introduction, bliography, appendix of selected documents, and end-of-entry reading suggestions. This one-of-a-kind reference will be a helpful ldition to the reference collections of all public libraries, high schools, and university libraries and will prove invaluable to historians ıd military enthusiasts.

"Thorough and detailed yet accessible to the lay reader. Of special interest to subject specialists and historians; recommended for public and academic libraries." - Library Journal

ub. Date: March 2006; Hardcover ISBN 1-59237-120-5; $135.00

he Religious Right, A Reference Handbook

imely and unbiased, this third edition updates and expands its examination of the religious right and its influence on our government, tizens, society, and politics. From the fight to outlaw the teaching of Darwin's theory of evolution to the struggle to outlaw abortion, ıe religious right is continually exerting an influence on public policy. This text explores the influence of religion on legislation and ciety, while examining the alignment of the religious right with the political right. A historical survey of the movement highlights ıe shift to "hands-on" approach to politics and the struggle to present a unified front. The coverage offers a critical historical survey of ıe religious right movement, focusing on its increased involvement in the political arena, attempts to forge coalitions, and notable ıccesses and failures. The text offers complete coverage of biographies of the men and women who have advanced the cause and an up date chronology illuminate the movement's goals, including their accomplishments and failures. This edition offers an extensive pdate to all sections along with several brand new entries. Two new sections complement this third edition, a chapter on legal issues nd court decisions and a chapter on demographic statistics and electoral patterns. To aid in further research, The Religious Right, ffers an entire section of annotated listings of print and non-print resources, as well as of organizations affiliated with the religious ght, and those opposing it. Comprehensive in its scope, this work offers easy-to-read, pertinent information for those seeking to nderstand the religious right and its evolving role in American society. A must for libraries of all sizes, university religion epartments, activists, high schools and for those interested in the evolving role of the religious right.

" Recommended for all public and academic libraries." - Library Journal

ub. Date: November 2006; Hardcover ISBN 1-59237-113-2; $135.00

From Suffrage to the Senate, America's Political Women

From Suffrage to the Senate is a comprehensive and valuable compendium of biographies of leading women in U.S. politics, past and present, and an examination of the wide range of women's movements. Up to date through 2006, this dynamically illustrated referenc work explores American women's path to political power and social equality from the struggle for the right to vote and the abolition c slavery to the first African American woman in the U.S. Senate and beyond. This new edition includes over 150 new entries and a bra new section on trends and demographics of women in politics. The in-depth coverage also traces the political heritage of the abolition, labor, suffrage, temperance, and reproductive rights movements. The alphabetically arranged entries include biographies of every woman from across the political spectrum who has served in the U.S. House and Senate, along with women in the Judiciary and the U Cabinet and, new to this edition, biographies of activists and political consultants. Bibliographical references follow each entry. For ea reference, a handy chronology is provided detailing 150 years of women's history. This up-to-date reference will be a must-purchase fc women's studies departments, high schools and public libraries and will be a handy resource for those researching the key players in women's politics, past and present.

"An engaging tool that would be useful in high school, public, and academic librar looking for an overview of the political history of women in the US." –Book

Pub. Date: October 2006; Two Volume Set; Hardcover ISBN 1-59237-117-5; $195.00

An African Biographical Dictionary

This landmark second edition is the only biographical dictionary to bring together, in one volume, cultural, social and political leaders both historical and contemporary – of the sub-Saharan region. Over 800 biographical sketches of prominent Africans, as well as foreigners who have affected the continent's history, are featured, 150 more than the previous edition. The wide spectrum of leaders includes religious figures, writers, politicians, scientists, entertainers, sports personalities and more. Access to these fascinating individuals is provided in a user-friendly format. The biographies are arranged alphabetically, cross-referenced and indexed. Entries include the country or countries in which the person was significant and the commonly accepted dates of birth and death. Each biographical sketch is chronologically written; entries for cultural personalities add an evaluation of their work. This information is followed by a selection of references often found in university and public libraries, including autobiographies and principal biographica works. Appendixes list each individual by country and by field of accomplishment – rulers, musicians, explorers, missionaries, businessmen, physicists – nearly thirty categories in all. Another convenient appendix lists heads of state since independence by country. Up-to-date and representative of African societies as a whole, An African Biographical Dictionary provides a wealth of vital information for students of African culture and is an indispensable reference guide for anyone interested in African affairs.

"An unquestionable convenience to have these concise, informative biographies gathered in one source, indexed, and analyzed by appendixes listing entrants by nation and occupational field." –Wilson Library Bullet

Pub. Date: July 2006; Hardcover ISBN 1-59237-112-4; $125.00

American Environmental Leaders, From Colonial Times to the Present

A comprehensive and diverse award winning collection of biographies of the most important figures in American environmentalism. Few subjects arouse the passions the way the environment does. How will we feed an ever-increasing population and how can that foo be made safe for consumption? Who decides how land is developed? How can environmental policies be made fair for everyone, including multiethnic groups, women, children, and the poor? American Environmental Leaders presents more than 350 biographies o men and women who have devoted their lives to studying, debating, and organizing these and other controversial issues over the last 200 years. In addition to the scientists who have analyzed how human actions affect nature, we are introduced to poets, landscape architects, presidents, painters, activists, even sanitation engineers, and others who have forever altered how we think about the environment. The easy to use A–Z format provides instant access to these fascinating individuals, and frequent cross references indicat others with whom individuals worked (and sometimes clashed). End of entry references provide users with a starting point for further research.

"Highly recommended for high school, academic, and public libraries needing environment biographical information." –Library Journal/Starred Revie

Two Volume Set; Hardcover ISBN 1-57607-385-8 $175.00

World Cultural Leaders of the Twentieth Century

An expansive two volume set that covers 450 worldwide cultural icons, World Cultural Leaders of the Twentieth Century includes eac person's works, achievements, and professional careers in a thorough essay. Who was the originator of the term "documentary"? Whic poet married the daughter of the famed novelist Thomas Mann in order to help her escape Nazi Germany? Which British writer serve as an agent in Russia against the Bolsheviks before the 1917 revolution? These and many more questions are answered in this illuminating text. A handy two volume set that makes it easy to look up 450 worldwide cultural icons: novelists, poets, playwrights, painters, sculptors, architects, dancers, choreographers, actors, directors, filmmakers, singers, composers, and musicians. World Cultural Leaders of the Twentieth Century provides entries (many of them illustrated) covering the person's works, achievements, and professional career in a thorough essay and offers interesting facts and statistics. Entries are fully cross-referenced so that readers can learn how various individuals influenced others. A thorough general index completes the coverage.

"Fills a need for handy, concise information on a wide array of international cultural figures."-ARB

Two Volume Set; Hardcover ISBN 1-57607-038-7 $175.00

To preview any of our Directories Risk-Free for 30 days, call (800) 562-2139 or fax to (518) 789-0556

Universal Reference Publications
Statistical & Demographic Reference Books

merica's Top-Rated Cities, 2007

nerica's Top-Rated Cities provides current, comprehensive statistical information and other essential data in one easy-to-use source on e 100 "top" cities that have been cited as the best for business and living in the U.S. This handbook allows readers to see, at a glance, oncise social, business, economic, demographic and environmental profile of each city, including brief evaluative comments. In dition to detailed data on Cost of Living, Finances, Real Estate, Education, Major Employers, Media, Crime and Climate, city reports w include Housing Vacancies, Tax Audits, Bankruptcy, Presidential Election Results and more. This outstanding source of formation will be widely used in any reference collection.

"The only source of its kind that brings together all of this information into one easy-to-use source. It will be beneficial to many business and public libraries." –ARBA

500 pages, 4 Volume Set; Softcover ISBN 1-59237-184-1, $195.00

merica's Top-Rated Smaller Cities, 2006/07

perfect companion to *America's Top-Rated Cities, America's Top-Rated Smaller Cities* provides current, comprehensive business and ing profiles of smaller cities (population 25,000-99,999) that have been cited as the best for business and living in the United States. xty cities make up this 2004 edition of *America's Top-Rated Smaller Cities*, all are top-ranked by Population Growth, Median Income, nemployment Rate and Crime Rate. City reports reflect the most current data available on a wide-range of statistics, including nployment & Earnings, Household Income, Unemployment Rate, Population Characteristics, Taxes, Cost of Living, Education, ealth Care, Public Safety, Recreation, Media, Air & Water Quality and much more. Plus, each city report contains a Background of e City, and an Overview of the State Finances. *America's Top-Rated Smaller Cities* offers a reliable, one-stop source for statistical data at, before now, could only be found scattered in hundreds of sources. This volume is designed for a wide range of readers: individuals nsidering relocating a residence or business; professionals considering expanding their business or changing careers; general and arket researchers; real estate consultants; human resource personnel; urban planners and investors.

"Provides current, comprehensive statistical information in one easy-to-use source... Recommended for public and academic libraries and specialized collections." –Library Journal

100 pages; Softcover ISBN 1-59237-135-3, $160.00

rofiles of America: Facts, Figures & Statistics for Every Populated Place in the United States

rofiles of America is the only source that pulls together, in one place, statistical, historical and descriptive information about every place the United States in an easy-to-use format. This award winning reference set, now in its second edition, compiles statistics and data om over 20 different sources – the latest census information has been included along with more than nine brand new statistical topics. his Four-Volume Set details over 40,000 places, from the biggest metropolis to the smallest unincorporated hamlet, and provides atistical details and information on over 50 different topics including Geography, Climate, Population, Vital Statistics, Economy, come, Taxes, Education, Housing, Health & Environment, Public Safety, Newspapers, Transportation, Presidential Election Results d Information Contacts or Chambers of Commerce. Profiles are arranged, for ease-of-use, by state and then by county. Each county egins with a County-Wide Overview and is followed by information for each Community in that particular county. The Community rofiles within the county are arranged alphabetically. *Profiles of America* is a virtual snapshot of America at your fingertips and a nique compilation of information that will be widely used in any reference collection.

A Library Journal Best Reference Book "An outstanding compilation." –Library Journal

0,000 pages; Four Volume Set; Softcover ISBN 1-891482-80-7, $595.00

he Comparative Guide to American Suburbs, 2007

he Comparative Guide to American Suburbs is a one-stop source for Statistics on the 2,000+ suburban communities surrounding the 50 rgest metropolitan areas – their population characteristics, income levels, economy, school system and important data on how they ompare to one another. Organized into 50 Metropolitan Area chapters, each chapter contains an overview of the Metropolitan Area, a etailed Map followed by a comprehensive Statistical Profile of each Suburban Community, including Contact Information, Physical haracteristics, Population Characteristics, Income, Economy, Unemployment Rate, Cost of Living, Education, Chambers of Commerce nd more. Next, statistical data is sorted into Ranking Tables that rank the suburbs by twenty different criteria, including Population, er Capita Income, Unemployment Rate, Crime Rate, Cost of Living and more. *The Comparative Guide to American Suburbs* is the best ource for locating data on suburbs. Those looking to relocate, as well as those doing preliminary market research, will find this an ivaluable timesaving resource.

"Public and academic libraries will find this compilation useful... The work draws together figures from many sources and will be especially helpful for job relocation decisions." – Booklist

,700 pages; Softcover ISBN 1-59237-180-9, $130.00

To preview any of our Directories Risk-Free for 30 days, call (800) 562-2139 or fax to (518) 789-0556

The Asian Databook: Statistics for all US Counties & Cities with Over 10,000 Population

This is the first-ever resource that compiles statistics and rankings on the US Asian population. *The Asian Databook* presents over 20 statistical data points for each city and county, arranged alphabetically by state, then alphabetically by place name. Data reported for each place includes Population, Languages Spoken at Home, Foreign-Born, Educational Attainment, Income Figures, Poverty Status, Homeownership, Home Values & Rent, and more. Next, in the Rankings Section, the top 75 places are listed for each data element. These easy-to-access ranking tables allow the user to quickly determine trends and population characteristics. This kind of comparati data can not be found elsewhere, in print or on the web, in a format that's as easy-to-use or more concise. A useful resource for those searching for demographics data, career search and relocation information and also for market research. With data ranging from Ancestry to Education, *The Asian Databook* presents a useful compilation of information that will be a much-needed resource in the reference collection of any public or academic library along with the marketing collection of any company whose primary focus in on the Asian population.

1,000 pages; Softcover ISBN 1-59237-044-6 $150.00

The Hispanic Databook: Statistics for all US Counties & Cities with Over 10,000 Population

Previously published by Toucan Valley Publications, this second edition has been completely updated with figures from the latest census and has been broadly expanded to include dozens of new data elements and a brand new Rankings section. The Hispanic population in the United States has increased over 42% in the last 10 years and accounts for 12.5% of the total US population. For eas of-use, *The Hispanic Databook* presents over 20 statistical data points for each city and county, arranged alphabetically by state, then alphabetically by place name. Data reported for each place includes Population, Languages Spoken at Home, Foreign-Born, Education Attainment, Income Figures, Poverty Status, Homeownership, Home Values & Rent, and more. Next, in the Rankings Section, the top 75 places are listed for each data element. These easy-to-access ranking tables allow the user to quickly determine trends and population characteristics. This kind of comparative data can not be found elsewhere, in print or on the web, in a format that's as easy-to-use or more concise. A useful resource for those searching for demographics data, career search and relocation information and also for market research. With data ranging from Ancestry to Education, *The Hispanic Databook* presents a useful compilation of informatic that will be a much-needed resource in the reference collection of any public or academic library along with the marketing collection o any company whose primary focus in on the Hispanic population.

"This accurate, clearly presented volume of selected Hispanic demographics recommended for large public libraries and research collections."-Library Journ

1,000 pages; Softcover ISBN 1-59237-008-X, $150.00

Ancestry in America: A Comparative Guide to Over 200 Ethnic Backgrounds

This brand new reference work pulls together thousands of comparative statistics on the Ethnic Backgrounds of all populated places i the United States with populations over 10,000. Never before has this kind of information been reported in a single volume. Section One, Statistics by Place, is made up of a list of over 200 ancestry and race categories arranged alphabetically by each of the 5,000 different places with populations over 10,000. The population number of the ancestry group in that city or town is provided along wit the percent that group represents of the total population. This informative city-by-city section allows the user to quickly and easily explore the ethnic makeup of all major population bases in the United States. Section Two, Comparative Rankings, contains three tabl for each ethnicity and race. In the first table, the top 150 populated places are ranked by population number for that particular ancestr group, regardless of population. In the second table, the top 150 populated places are ranked by the percent of the total population for that ancestry group. In the third table, those top 150 populated places with 10,000 population are ranked by population number for eac ancestry group. These easy-to-navigate tables allow users to see ancestry population patterns and make city-by-city comparisons as well. Plus, as an added bonus with the purchase of *Ancestry in America*, a free companion CD-ROM is available that lists statistics and rankings for all of the 35,000 populated places in the United States. This brand new, information-packed resource will serve a wide-range or research requests for demographics, population characteristics, relocation information and much more. *Ancestry in America: A Comparative Guide to Over 200 Ethnic Backgrounds* will be an important acquisition to all reference collections.

"This compilation will serve a wide range of research requests for population characterist ... it offers much more detail than other sources." –Bookl

1,500 pages; Softcover ISBN 1-59237-029-2, $225.00

ıe American Tally: Statistics & Comparative Rankings for U.S. Cities with Populations over 10,000

is important statistical handbook compiles, all in one place, comparative statistics on all U.S. cities and towns with a 10,000+ ›ulation. *The American Tally* provides statistical details on over 4,000 cities and towns and profiles how they compare with one ›ther in Population Characteristics, Education, Language & Immigration, Income & Employment and Housing. Each section begins :h an alphabetical listing of cities by state, allowing for quick access to both the statistics and relative rankings of any city. Next, the ;hest and lowest cities are listed in each statistic. These important, informative lists provide quick reference to which cities are at :h extremes of the spectrum for each statistic. Unlike any other reference, *The American Tally* provides quick, easy access to nparative statistics – a must-have for any reference collection.

"A solid library reference." -Bookwatch

) pages; Softcover ISBN 1-930956-29-0, $125.00

ıe Environmental Resource Handbook, 2007/08

e Environmental Resource Handbook is the most up-to-date and comprehensive source for Environmental Resources and Statistics. :tion I: Resources provides detailed contact information for thousands of information sources, including Associations & ganizations, Awards & Honors, Conferences, Foundations & Grants, Environmental Health, Government Agencies, National Parks Wildlife Refuges, Publications, Research Centers, Educational Programs, Green Product Catalogs, Consultants and much more. :tion II: Statistics, provides statistics and rankings on hundreds of important topics, including Children's Environmental Index, ınicipal Finances, Toxic Chemicals, Recycling, Climate, Air & Water Quality and more. This kind of up-to-date environmental data, in one place, is not available anywhere else on the market place today. This vast compilation of resources and statistics is a must- ve for all public and academic libraries as well as any organization with a primary focus on the environment.

"...the intrinsic value of the information make it worth consideration by libraries with environmental collections and environmentally concerned users." –Booklist

›00 pages; Softcover ISBN 1-59237-195-7, $155.00 ◆ Online Database $300.00

'eather America, A Thirty-Year Summary of Statistical Weather Data and Rankings

ıis valuable resource provides extensive climatological data for over 4,000 National and Cooperative Weather Stations throughout : United States. *Weather America* begins with a new Major Storms section that details major storm events of the nation and a ıtional Rankings section that details rankings for several data elements, such as Maximum Temperature and Precipitation. The main dy of *Weather America* is organized into 50 state sections. Each section provides a Data Table on each Weather Station, organized ›habetically, that provides statistics on Maximum and Minimum Temperatures, Precipitation, Snowfall, Extreme Temperatures, ggy Days, Humidity and more. State sections contain two brand new features in this edition – a City Index and a narrative :scription of the climatic conditions of the state. Each section also includes a revised Map of the State that includes not only weather ıtions, but cities and towns.

"Best Reference Book of the Year." –Library Journal

)13 pages; Softcover ISBN 1-891482-29-7, $175.00

rime in America's Top-Rated Cities

ıis volume includes over 20 years of crime statistics in all major crime categories: violent crimes, property crimes and total crime. *'ime in America's Top-Rated Cities* is conveniently arranged by city and covers 76 top-rated cities. *Crime in America's Top-Rated Cities* fers details that compare the number of crimes and crime rates for the city, suburbs and metro area along with national crime trends r violent, property and total crimes. Also, this handbook contains important information and statistics on Anti-Crime Programs, 'ime Risk, Hate Crimes, Illegal Drugs, Law Enforcement, Correctional Facilities, Death Penalty Laws and much more. A much- :eded resource for people who are relocating, business professionals, general researchers, the press, law enforcement officials and ıdents of criminal justice.

"Data is easy to access and will save hours of searching." –Global Enforcement Review

32 pages; Softcover ISBN 1-891482-84-X, $155.00

Sedgwick Press
Health Directories

The Complete Directory for People with Disabilities, 2007

A wealth of information, now in one comprehensive sourcebook. Completely updated, this edition contains more information than eve before, including thousands of new entries and enhancements to existing entries and thousands of additional web sites and e-mail addresses. This up-to-date directory is the most comprehensive resource available for people with disabilities, detailing Independent Living Centers, Rehabilitation Facilities, State & Federal Agencies, Associations, Support Groups, Periodicals & Books, Assistive Devices, Employment & Education Programs, Camps and Travel Groups. Each year, more libraries, schools, colleges, hospitals, rehabilitation centers and individuals add *The Complete Directory for People with Disabilities* to their collections, making sure that this information is readily available to the families, individuals and professionals who can benefit most from the amazing wealth of resourc cataloged here.

"No other reference tool exists to meet the special needs of the disabled in one convenient resource for information." –Library Jour

1,200 pages; Softcover ISBN 1-59237-147-7, $165.00 ◆ Online Database $215.00 ◆ Online Database & Directory Combo $300.00

The Complete Directory for People with Chronic Illness, 2007/08

Thousands of hours of research have gone into this completely updated 2005/06 edition – several new chapters have been added alon with thousands of new entries and enhancements to existing entries. Plus, each chronic illness chapter has been reviewed by an medi expert in the field. This widely-hailed directory is structured around the 90 most prevalent chronic illnesses – from Asthma to Cance to Wilson's Disease – and provides a comprehensive overview of the support services and information resources available for people diagnosed with a chronic illness. Each chronic illness has its own chapter and contains a brief description in layman's language, followed by important resources for National & Local Organizations, State Agencies, Newsletters, Books & Periodicals, Libraries & Research Centers, Support Groups & Hotlines, Web Sites and much more. This directory is an important resource for health care professionals, the collections of hospital and health care libraries, as well as an invaluable tool for people with a chronic illness and the support network.

"A must purchase for all hospital and health care libraries and is strongly recommended for all public library reference departments." –AR

1,200 pages; Softcover ISBN 1-59237-183-3, $165.00 ◆ Online Database $215.00 ◆ Online Database & Directory Combo $300.00

The Complete Learning Disabilities Directory, 2007

The Complete Learning Disabilities Directory is the most comprehensive database of Programs, Services, Curriculum Materials, Professional Meetings & Resources, Camps, Newsletters and Support Groups for teachers, students and families concerned with learning disabilities. This information-packed directory includes information about Associations & Organizations, Schools, Colleges & Testing Materials, Government Agencies, Legal Resources and much more. For quick, easy access to information, this directory contains four indexes: Entry Name Index, Subject Index and Geographic Index. With every passing year, the field of learning disabilities attracts more attention and the network of caring, committed and knowledgeable professionals grows every day. This directory is an invaluable research tool for these parents, students and professionals.

"Due to its wealth and depth of coverage, parents, teachers and others… should find this an invaluable resource." -Book

900 pages; Softcover ISBN 1-59237-122-1, $145.00 ◆ Online Database $195.00 ◆ Online Database & Directory Combo $280.00

The Complete Mental Health Directory, 2006/07

This is the most comprehensive resource covering the field of behavioral health, with critical information for both the layman and the mental health professional. For the layman, this directory offers understandable descriptions of 25 Mental Health Disorders as well as detailed information on Associations, Media, Support Groups and Mental Health Facilities. For the professional, *The Complete Mental Health Directory* offers critical and comprehensive information on Managed Care Organizations, Information Systems, Government Agencies and Provider Organizations. This comprehensive volume of needed information will be widely used in any reference collection.

"… the strength of this directory is that it consolidates widely dispersed information into a single volume." –Book

800 pages; Softcover ISBN 1-59237-124-8, $165.00 ◆ Online Database $215.00 ◆ Online & Directory Combo $300.00

lder Americans Information Directory, 2006/07

mpletely updated for 2006/07, this sixth edition has been completely revised and now contains 1,000 new listings, over 8,000 dates to existing listings and over 3,000 brand new e-mail addresses and web sites. You'll find important resources for Older nericans including National, Regional, State & Local Organizations, Government Agencies, Research Centers, Libraries & ormation Centers, Legal Resources, Discount Travel Information, Continuing Education Programs, Disability Aids & Assistive vices, Health, Print Media and Electronic Media. Three indexes: Entry Index, Subject Index and Geographic Index make it easy to d just the right source of information. This comprehensive guide to resources for Older Americans will be a welcome addition to any erence collection.

"Highly recommended for academic, public, health science and consumer libraries…" –Choice

00 pages; Softcover ISBN 1-59237-136-1, $165.00 ◆ Online Database $215.00 ◆ Online Database & Directory Combo $300.00

ne Complete Directory for Pediatric Disorders, 2007

iis important directory provides parents and caregivers with information about Pediatric Conditions, Disorders, Diseases and sabilities, including Blood Disorders, Bone & Spinal Disorders, Brain Defects & Abnormalities, Chromosomal Disorders, Congenital art Defects, Movement Disorders, Neuromuscular Disorders and Pediatric Tumors & Cancers. This carefully written directory ers: understandable Descriptions of 15 major bodily systems; Descriptions of more than 200 Disorders and a Resources Section, tailing National Agencies & Associations, State Associations, Online Services, Libraries & Resource Centers, Research Centers, pport Groups & Hotlines, Camps, Books and Periodicals. This resource will provide immediate access to information crucial to nilies and caregivers when coping with children's illnesses.

"Recommended for public and consumer health libraries." –Library Journal

200 pages; Softcover ISBN 1-59237-150-7 $165.00 ◆ Online Database $215.00 ◆ Online Database & Directory Combo $300.00

he Directory of Drug & Alcohol Residential Rehabilitation Facilities

iis brand new directory is the first-ever resource to bring together, all in one place, data on the thousands of drug and alcohol sidential rehabilitation facilities in the United States. *The Directory of Drug & Alcohol Residential Rehabilitation Facilities* covers over 000 facilities, with detailed contact information for each one, including mailing address, phone and fax numbers, email addresses and eb sites, mission statement, type of treatment programs, cost, average length of stay, numbers of residents and counselors, creditation, insurance plans accepted, type of environment, religious affiliation, education components and much more. It also ntains a helpful chapter on General Resources that provides contact information for Associations, Print & Electronic Media, Support roups and Conferences. Multiple indexes allow the user to pinpoint the facilities that meet very specific criteria. This time-saving ol is what so many counselors, parents and medical professionals have been asking for. *The Directory of Drug & Alcohol Residential ehabilitation Facilities* will be a helpful tool in locating the right source for treatment for a wide range of individuals. This mprehensive directory will be an important acquisition for all reference collections: public and academic libraries, case managers, cial workers, state agencies and many more.

"This is an excellent, much needed directory that fills an important gap…" –Booklist

00 pages; Softcover ISBN 1-59237-031-4, $135.00

Sedgwick Press
Education Directories

The Comparative Guide to American Elementary & Secondary Schools, 2007

The only guide of its kind, this award winning compilation offers a snapshot profile of every public school district in the United States serving 1,500 or more students – more than 5,900 districts are covered. Organized alphabetically by district within state, each chapter begins with a Statistical Overview of the state. Each district listing includes contact information (name, address, phone number and web site) plus Grades Served, the Numbers of Students and Teachers and the Number of Regular, Special Education, Alternative and Vocational Schools in the district along with statistics on Student/Classroom Teacher Ratios, Drop Out Rates, Ethnicity, the Number of Librarians and Guidance Counselors and District Expenditures per student. As an added bonus, *The Comparative Guide to American Elementary and Secondary Schools* provides important ranking tables, both by state and nationally, for each data element. For easy navigation through this wealth of information, this handbook contains a useful City Index that lists all districts that operate schools within a city. These important comparative statistics are necessary for anyone considering relocation or doing comparative research on their own district and would be a perfect acquisition for any public library or school district library.

"This straightforward guide is an easy way to find general information. Valuable for academic and large public library collections." –ARBA

2,400 pages; Softcover ISBN 1-59237-223-6, $125.00

Educators Resource Directory, 2007/08

Educators Resource Directory is a comprehensive resource that provides the educational professional with thousands of resources and statistical data for professional development. This directory saves hours of research time by providing immediate access to Associations & Organizations, Conferences & Trade Shows, Educational Research Centers, Employment Opportunities & Teaching Abroad, School Library Services, Scholarships, Financial Resources, Professional Consultants, Computer Software & Testing Resources and much more. Plus, this comprehensive directory also includes a section on Statistics and Rankings with over 100 tables, including statistics on Average Teacher Salaries, SAT/ACT scores, Revenues & Expenditures and more. These important statistics will allow the user to see how their school rates among others, make relocation decisions and so much more. For quick access to information, this directory contains four indexes: Entry & Publisher Index, Geographic Index, a Subject & Grade Index and Web Sites Index. *Educators Resource Directory* will be a well-used addition to the reference collection of any school district, education department or public library.

"Recommended for all collections that serve elementary and secondary school professionals." –Choice

1,000 pages; Softcover ISBN 1-59237-179-5, $145.00 ◆ Online Database $195.00 ◆ Online Database & Directory Combo $280.00

Sedgwick Press
Hospital & Health Plan Directories

1e Comparative Guide to American Hospitals, 2007

is is the first ever resource to compare all of the nation's hospitals by 17 measures of quality in the treatment of heart attack, heart ure and pneumonia. This data is based on the Hospital Compare study, produced by Medicare, and is available in print and in a ique and user-friendly format from Grey House Publishing, along with extra contact information from Grey House's *Directory of spital Personnel. The Comparative Guide to American Hospitals* provides a snapshot profile of each of the nations 6,000 hospitals. These ormative profiles illustrate how the hospital rates in 17 important areas: Heart Attack Care (% who receive Aspirin at Arrival, pirin at Discharge, ACE Inhibitor for LVSD, Beta Blocker at Arrival, Beta Blocker at Discharge, Thrombolytic Agent Received, CA Received and Adult Smoking Cessation Advice); Heart Failure (% who receive LVF Assessment, ACE Inhibitor for LVSD, scharge Instructions, Adult Smoking Cessation Advice); and Pneumonia (% who receive Initial Antibiotic Timing, Pneumococcal ccination, Oxygenation Assessment, Blood Culture Performed and Adult Smoking Cessation Advice). Each profile includes the raw rcentage for that hospital, the state average, the US average and data on the top hospital. For easy access to contact information, h profile includes the hospitals address, phone and fax numbers, email and web addresses, type and accreditation along with 5 top y administrations. These profiles will allow the user to quickly identify the quality of the hospital and have the necessary information their fingertips to make contact with that hospital. Most importantly, *The Comparative Guide to American Hospitals* provides an easy- -use Ranking Table for each of the data elements to allow the user to quickly locate the hospitals with the best level of service. This and new title will be a must for the reference collection at all public, medical and academic libraries.

500 pages; Softcover ISBN 1-59237-182-5; $225.00

he Directory of Hospital Personnel, 2007

he Directory of Hospital Personnel is the best resource you can have at your fingertips when researching or marketing a product or rvice to the hospital market. A "Who's Who" of the hospital universe, this directory puts you in touch with over 150,000 key cision-makers. With 100% verification of data you can rest assured that you will reach the right person with just one call. Every spital in the U.S. is profiled, listed alphabetically by city within state. Plus, three easy-to-use, cross-referenced indexes put the facts your fingertips faster and more easily than any other directory: Hospital Name Index, Bed Size Index and Personnel Index. *The irectory of Hospital Personnel* is the only complete source for key hospital decision-makers by name. Whether you want to define or structure sales territories... locate hospitals with the purchasing power to accept your proposals... keep track of important contacts colleagues... or find information on which insurance plans are accepted, *The Directory of Hospital Personnel* gives you the information u need – easily, efficiently, effectively and accurately.

"Recommended for college, university and medical libraries." -ARBA

500 pages; Softcover ISBN 1-59237-178-7 $325.00 ◆ Online Database $545.00 ◆ Online Database & Directory Combo, $650.00

he Directory of Health Care Group Purchasing Organizations, 2006

his comprehensive directory provides the important data you need to get in touch with over 800 Group Purchasing Organizations. y providing in-depth information on this growing market and its members, *The Directory of Health Care Group Purchasing Organizations* ls a major need for the most accurate and comprehensive information on over 800 GPOs – Mailing Address, Phone & Fax Numbers, -mail Addresses, Key Contacts, Purchasing Agents, Group Descriptions, Membership Categorization, Standard Vendor Proposal equirements, Membership Fees & Terms, Expanded Services, Total Member Beds & Outpatient Visits represented and more. Five ndexes provide a number of ways to locate the right GPO: Alphabetical Index, Expanded Services Index, Organization Type Index, eographic Index and Member Institution Index. With its comprehensive and detailed information on each purchasing organization, *he Directory of Health Care Group Purchasing Organizations* is the go-to source for anyone looking to target this market.

"The information is clearly arranged and easy to access...recommended for those needing this very specialized information." –ARBA

,000 pages; Softcover ISBN 1-59237-0091-8, $325.00 ◆ Online Database, $650.00 ◆ Online Database & Directory Combo, $750.00

To preview any of our Directories Risk-Free for 30 days, call (800) 562-2139 or fax to (518) 789-0556

The HMO/PPO Directory, 2007

The HMO/PPO Directory is a comprehensive source that provides detailed information about Health Maintenance Organizations and Preferred Provider Organizations nationwide. This comprehensive directory details more information about more managed health ca organizations than ever before. Over 1,100 HMOs, PPOs, Medicare Advantage Plans and affiliated companies are listed, arranged alphabetically by state. Detailed listings include Key Contact Information, Prescription Drug Benefits, Enrollment, Geographical Ar served, Affiliated Physicians & Hospitals, Federal Qualifications, Status, Year Founded, Managed Care Partners, Employer Reference Fees & Payment Information and more. Plus, five years of historical information is included related to Revenues, Net Income, Medica Loss Ratios, Membership Enrollment and Number of Patient Complaints. Five easy-to-use, cross-referenced indexes will put this vas array of information at your fingertips immediately: HMO Index, PPO Index, Other Providers Index, Personnel Index and Enrollme Index. *The HMO/PPO Directory* provides the most comprehensive data on the most companies available on the market place today.

"Helpful to individuals requesting certain HMO/PPO issues such as co-payment costs, subscription costs and patient complain Individuals concerned (or those with questions) about their insurance may find this text to be of use to them." -AR

600 pages; Softcover ISBN 1-59237-158-2, $325.00 ◆ Online Database, $495.00 ◆ Online Database & Directory Combo, $600.00

Medical Device Register, 2007

The only one-stop resource of every medical supplier licensed to sell products in the US. This award-winning directory offers immediate access to over 13,000 companies - and more than 65,000 products – in two information-packed volumes. This comprehensi resource saves hours of time and trouble when searching for medical equipment and supplies and the manufacturers who provide then Volume I: The Product Directory, provides essential information for purchasing or specifying medical supplies for every medical devi supply, and diagnostic available in the US. Listings provide FDA codes & Federal Procurement Eligibility, Contact information for every manufacturer of the product along with Prices and Product Specifications. Volume 2 - Supplier Profiles, offers the most comple and important data about Suppliers, Manufacturers and Distributors. Company Profiles detail the number of employees, ownership, method of distribution, sales volume, net income, key executives detailed contact information medical products the company supplies, plus the medical specialties they cover. Four indexes provide immediate access to this wealth of information: Keyword Index, Trade Name Index, Supplier Geographical Index and OEM (Original Equipment Manufacturer) Index. Medical Device Register, 2007 is th only one-stop source for locating suppliers and products; looking for new manufacturers or hard-to-find medical devices; comparing products and companies; know who's selling what and who to buy from cost effectively. This directory has become the standard in its field and will be a welcome addition to the reference collection of any medical library, large public library, university library along wit the collections that serve the medical community.

"A wealth of information on medical devices, medical device companies... and key personnel in the industry is provide in this comprehensive refere work... A valuable reference work, one of the best hardcopy compilations available." -Doody Publishi

3,000 pages Two Volumes; Hardcover ISBN 1-59237-181-7; $325.00

The Directory of Independent Ambulatory Care Centers

This first edition of *The Directory of Independent Ambulatory Care Centers* provides access to detailed information that, before now, could only be found scattered in hundreds of different sources. This comprehensive and up-to-date directory pulls together a vast array of contact information for over 7,200 Ambulatory Surgery Centers, Ambulatory General and Urgent Care Clinics, and Diagnostic Imaging Centers that are not affiliated with a hospital or major medical center. Detailed listings include Mailing Address, Phone & Fa Numbers, E-mail and Web Site addresses, Contact Name and Phone Numbers of the Medical Director and other Key Executives and Purchasing Agents, Specialties & Services Offered, Year Founded, Numbers of Employees and Surgeons, Number of Operating Rooms Number of Cases seen per year, Overnight Options, Contracted Services and much more. Listings are arranged by State, by Center Category and then alphabetically by Organization Name. Two indexes provide quick and easy access to this wealth of information: Entry Name Index and Specialty/Service Index. *The Directory of Independent Ambulatory Care Centers* is a must-have resource for anyon marketing a product or service to this important industry and will be an invaluable tool for those searching for a local care center that will meet their specific needs.

"Among the numerous hospital directories, no other provides information on independent ambulatory centers A handy, well-organized resource that would be useful in medical center libraries and public libraries." –Cho

986 pages; Softcover ISBN 1-930956-90-8, $185.00 ◆ Online Database, $365.00 ◆ Online Database & Directory Combo, $450.00